The Hornbook

Dr. Johnson described the hornbook as "the first book of children, covered with horn to keep it unsoiled." Pardon's New General English Dictionary (1758) defined it as "A leaf of written or printed paper pasted on a board, and covered with horn, for children to learn their letters by, and to prevent their being torn and daubed."

It was used throughout Europe and America between the late 1400s and the middle 1700s.

Shaped like an old-fashioned butter paddle, the first hornbooks were made of wood. The paper lesson the child was to learn was fastened to the wooden paddle and covered with a piece of horn. The transparent strip of horn was made by soaking a cow's horn in hot water and peeling it away at the thickness of a piece of celluloid. The horn was necessary to protect the lesson from the damp and perhaps grubby hands of the child. Hornbooks commonly contained the alphabet, the vowels, and the Lord's Prayer. Later hornbooks were made of various materials: brass, copper, silver, ivory, bronze, leather, and stone.

As the art of printing advanced, the hornbook was supplanted by the primer in the book form we know today. Subsequently West Publishing Company developed its "Hornbook Series", a series of scholarly and well-respected one volume treatises on particular areas of law. Today they are widely used by law students, lawyers and judges.

THE LAW OF SECURITIES REGULATION

Third Edition

By

Thomas Lee Hazen

*Cary C. Boshamer Distinguished Professor of Law,
School of Law, The University of
North Carolina at Chapel Hill*

HORNBOOK SERIES®

WEST
GROUP

ST. PAUL, MINN., 1996

 *TEXT IS PRINTED ON 10% POST CONSUMER RECYCLED PAPER*

2nd Reprint—2000

To LSH, Margret, and Elliott

*

Introduction

Securities law, especially at the federal level, was once considered a specialty that only the large Wall Street law firms had to worry about. That is certainly no longer the case. Lawyers all over the country are finding themselves in contact with the registration provisions of the Securities Act of 1933. There is hardly a lawyer who himself or herself does not have either directly or indirectly some investment in the stock or bond markets. Furthermore, clients are likely to have similar investments. There is also an ever-increasing number of participants in the options and futures markets.

Because of the widespread possibility of federal remedies that exist for investors who are injured in the securities markets, every lawyer should have at least a passing familiarity with the federal securities laws. Conscientious lawyers should keep abreast of developments due to the ever-increasing alternative investment opportunities including options, index futures and the like. Also, since the definition of securities is an expansive one, a large number of investment opportunities that are not in the traditional forms of stock or bonds may still be subject to the regulatory and protective provisions of both federal and state securities law. It follows that securities law has become relevant to general practitioners as well as specialists.

Additionally there are large numbers of lawyers who have a general corporate and commercial practice which touches upon both state and federal securities laws. No matter how small the business, if it is in corporate (or limited partnership) form the antifraud provisions and attendant potential civil liabilities loom in the background as something for the corporate planner to keep in mind. Also the exemptions from federal and state registration are not as straightforward as they may seem and thus any corporate planner should be aware of the necessary precautions to secure the desired exemption.

This treatise is designed both for attorneys needing an introduction to the securities laws as well as for specialists dealing with these issues on a daily basis.

RESEARCH AIDS[1]

Researching the law in the area of securities regulation is not an easy task since a vast body of law is contained in administrative rules, inter-

---

1. For a helpful guide to these and other available sources, *see* Sargent & Senter, Research in Securities Regulation Revisited, 79 Law Libr.J. 255 (1987); Sargent & Greenberg, Research in Securities Regulation: Access to the Sources of the Law, 75 Law Libr.J. 98 (1982).

pretations and no-action letters that are not officially reported. In addition to the database of Westlaw which contains all of the pertinent information, The Federal Securities Law Reporter, a multiple volume looseleaf reporter published by Commerce Clearing House is the most comprehensive source; a companion source is the Blue Sky Law Reporter which treats the various state securities regulation statutes and administrative law. The Bureau of National Affairs' Securities Regulation and Law Reporter can be very helpful in keeping lawyers up-to-date with the rapidly changing law of securities regulation. Prentice–Hall also publishes a looseleaf service. Looseleaf services in related fields include the Commodity Futures Law Reporter and the Federal Banking Law Reporter, both of which are published by Commerce Clearing House.

THOMAS LEE HAZEN

Preface to the Third Edition

The five years between the Second Edition and this one have witnessed continued metamorphosis of the securities laws. Throughout this period, derivative investments have continued to impact the financial markets. The SEC has continued its small business initiatives in order to simplify and facilitate the reporting and registration requirements and has adopted an entire new series of disclosure guides for small business issuers (Regulation S–B). The Management Discussion and Analysis portions of registration under the Securities Act of 1933 and reports under the Securities Exchange Act of 1934 have continued to increase in significance. In addition, we have moved into the electronic age for SEC filings with the permanent implementation of Commission's Electronic Data Gathering, Analysis, and Retrieval ("EDGAR") system. The Supreme Court has continued to narrow the scope of many private remedies, thereby changing many of the rules for securities litigation. Also, the arbitration programs have come of age. Broker-dealer and customer disputes are now more likely to be resolved by arbitrators than by courts. These are just some of the new developments discussed in the Third Edition.

As was the case with the first two editions, the coverage of this treatise is selective. There is considerable detail to the treatment of the Securities Act of 1933, including its registration requirements as well as exemptions therefrom. Also, there is detailed treatment of the consequences of violations of the Act including treatment of SEC sanctions and private remedies. With regard to the Securities Exchange Act of 1934, the focus is on the rules relating to issuers of securities (the Act's registration and reporting requirements). Special emphasis is given to the proxy rules, the Act's takeover provisions, and to private remedies. There is also extensive discussion of broker-dealers' customer obligations and liabilities, as well as an overview of the self regulatory system. In addition, in the Practitioner's Edition, there is expanded coverage of the arbitration rules. The Practitioner's Edition also contains extended coverage of SEC procedures and the workings of the Commission.

In-depth treatment of the Investment Company and Investment Advisers Acts of 1940 remains selective, providing a general overview and then focusing primarily on those Acts' regulatory and civil liability provisions. An overview is also given of the Public Utility Holding Company Act of 1935 and the Trust Indenture Act of 1939. There is an overview of the coverage of state securities laws, with special emphasis on the role of state takeover legislation. The Practitioner's Edition includes a discussion of selected other laws relevant to the securities markets. In particular, there is discussion of the Racketeer Influenced and Corrupt Organizations ("RICO") Act, the Federal Mail Fraud Act, the Securities Investor Protection Act (relating to broker-dealer insolvencies), and an overview of the parallel regulation of the commodities futures and options markets.

The Practitioner's Edition contains four appendixes. Appendix A consists of the SEC release adopting the Management Discussion and Analysis requirements, which, as mentioned above, are continuing to increase in importance. Appendix B consists of the Commission's electronic filing rules. Appendix C is devoted to the arbitration programs: first giving the SEC's implementation of the arbitration rules and, secondly, the current version of the rules of the three major arbitral forums (the New York Stock Exchange, the American Stock Exchange, and the National Association of Securities Dealers). The federal securities statutes, along with current rules and forms, including the disclosure guides of Regulations S–K and S–B are found in a separate statutory supplement which is published annually.

The Third Edition contains a number of new sections, designed to better organize and expand the treatment of civil liabilities. Also, by interlineating the new sections, this edition adheres to the same numbering system for sections as previous editions, with one exception.[1]

The Third Edition contains reported developments through February 1995. As was the case with the previous editions, there will be annual supplementation of the Practitioner's Edition. The one-volume Student Edition is considerably abridged but contains references to the Practitioner's Edition in order to facilitate further study.

Acknowledgments for the Third Edition

As with previous editions, I am deeply grateful to the support provided by the University of North Carolina School of Law. I am particularly appreciative to Eric Hardin and the many other students and support staff who have helped me with this project.

THOMAS LEE HAZEN

Chapel Hill, North Carolina
May, 1995

---

1. Section 13.2.1 from the Second Edition (dealing with the particularity requirement for pleading fraud) has been renumbered as § 13.8.1. This was done to move that material to a more logical location (along with the statute of limitations) and further to permit expanded treatment of the basic elements of the Rule 10b–5 remedy at the beginning of the chapter.

Preface to the Second Edition

Securities Regulation has remained a fast-changing area of the law. In the five years since the First Edition was published, there have been a number of significant developments which are incorporated into the Second Edition.

For example, there has been continued proliferation of the ways in which investors can participate in the financial markets. This proliferation has occurred not only through the creation of new investment vehicles but also through expansion of the options and futures markets. Some commentators point to increased speculation in the options and futures markets as a contributing factor to the crash of October, 1987. Some controls have been put into place, such as "circuit breakers" which trigger a temporary trading halt. As this treatise went to press, Congress and regulators were considering various controls designed to help prevent a repeat of the events of the fall of 1987.

Another significant development has been the increased remedies for illegal trading on nonpublic information. A major shift in the resolution of customer disputes with broker-dealers has taken place in that many of those disputes are now arbitrable while formerly they were not.

There have also been several significant developments in the case law affecting the scope of private remedies available under the federal securities laws. For example, many changes have occurred in the law relating to statutes of limitations and secondary liability of collateral participants in securities law violations. New sections have been added in the Second Edition to provide for more in-depth discussion on these topics for claims according to whether the claims relate to causes of action under the Securities Act of 1933 or the Securities Exchange Act of 1934.

The foregoing new developments are just a few of the significant developments that have led to this Second Edition. These developments and the ever-increasing expansion of the nature of securities practice has led to the evolution of the one-volume First Edition into a two-volume Practitioner's Second Edition of this treatise.

As was pointed out in the Preface to the First Edition, the coverage in this treatise is selective. There is considerable treatment of the Securities Act of 1933's registration requirements for securities distributions. There is extensive coverage of the exemptions from registration as well as for the consequences of failure to comply with the registration requirements. With regard to the Securities Exchange Act of 1934, the disclosure and reporting requirements for issuers of publicly traded securities are considered with an emphasis on the proxy regulations and the regulations governing takeovers. Considerable discussion is devoted to the regulation of insider trading. Although the materials relating to market regulation remain selective, they have been expanded from the

First Edition. Because of the increasing importance of arbitrations, a number of sections have been added that deal with the arbitration of disputes involving customers and broker-dealers. The Practitioner's Edition also contains an expanded discussion of the workings of the Securities and Exchange Commission.

The treatment of the Investment Company and Investment Advisers Acts of 1940 is selective and is designed to present an overview of those acts' operation. The same is true for the Public Utility Holding Company Act of 1935 and the Trust Indenture Act of 1939. As was the case with the First Edition, the Second Edition gives but only the briefest overview of the operation of state securities laws; except that more extensive coverage is given to the role of state takeover legislation. The Practitioner's Edition contains expanded material on other laws including RICO (the Racketeer Influenced and Corrupt Organizations Act), the federal Mail Fraud Act, and the laws affecting the commodities markets. There also is a new section on the federal Mail and Wire Fraud Act.

The Practitioner's Edition contains three appendixes. Appendix A contains the SEC guidelines for disclosures relating to management discussion and analysis of financial condition. Appendix B contains an overview of the new rules governing broker-dealer arbitration procedures. Appendix C consists of a WESTLAW Guide for securities research. The selected SEC forms and Regulation S–K which appeared in the appendix to the First Edition are now contained in a statutory supplement.

The Second Edition contains many new sections. Rather than changing the section numbers that appeared in the First Edition, the new sections are interlineated. The Second Edition contains developments through June 1, 1989. As was the case with the First Edition, there will be annual supplementation. The one-volume Student Edition contains references to the Practitioner's Edition in order to facilitate a more in-depth study.

Acknowledgments for Second Edition

In addition to the many individuals who helped me with the First Edition (see the Preface to the First Edition, *infra*), I would like to acknowledge the many hours of fruitful discussion with my colleagues at the School of Law of the University of North Carolina at Chapel Hill. In particular, I would like to thank Professor N. Ferebee Taylor for the hours spent parsing the intricacies of SEC Rule 10b–5 and Professor Robert G. Byrd for his insights on the law of fraud and on remedies. I would also like to thank the many student assistants who helped in the preparation of this edition and, in particular, Sandra Goddard, and Molly Farrell, UNC Law School class of 1988 and Brian Zeurcher, UNC Law School class of 1989.

THOMAS LEE HAZEN

Chapel Hill, North Carolina
October, 1989

Preface to the First Edition

This book is designed to give an overview of the securities laws with the understanding that the space limitations presented by a single volume do not permit an in-depth treatment of all aspects of federal and state law. This book is not merely a primer. The hope is to provide a firm understanding of the basics of securities law and adequate guidance as to further sources for the more esoteric aspects of the law of securities regulation.

Many areas of federal regulation preclude a surface treatment. The coverage of this book represents an attempt to strike a balance between the need for sufficient depth and the space limitations. In many instances choices have been made to allow in-depth treatment of some of the more common areas and to limit the details of the more specialized areas.

Towards these ends, a large portion of the book is devoted to discussion of the federal Securities Act of 1933 and the Securities Exchange Act of 1934. Primary emphasis is placed upon the regulation of the securities markets as it applies to issuers of securities and to most investors. Lawyers who do not specialize in securities law are likely to come into contact with a number of areas covered by the Securities Act of 1933 and the Securities Exchange Act of 1934. These include the registration requirements for securities distributions and the various exemptions from registration. Both the 1933 and 1934 Acts provide a wide range of remedies for investors injured by fraudulent practices and material misstatements and omissions. Shareholder suffrage is a major thrust of the Exchange Act's proxy regulations. The Exchange Act also includes the Williams Act Amendments that contain the federal regulation of tender offers—a topic in the forefront of today's financial news. Another topic of current concern is the sanctions against insider trading based on non-public information. A major developing area has been the creation of mechanisms for a national market system in order to help eliminate many of the inefficiencies of the traditional exchange and over-the-counter markets.

Although regulation of the broker-dealer industry is a very important aspect of securities law, the treatment in this book is selective. There is only brief treatment of the state securities laws, in part because of the ever-increasing importance of the federal laws and also because of the high degree of jurisdictional variation and the need to consult the law of each applicable state. The book also examines the other federal acts administered by the SEC: the Public Utility Holding Company Act of 1935, the Trust Indenture Act of 1939, the Investment Company Act of 1940, and the Investment Advisers Act of 1940. The treatise also contains some materials on related laws including the Securities Investor

Protection Act that governs broker-dealer insolvency, Article 8 of the Uniform Commercial Code which governs securities transactions, the Foreign Corrupt Practices Act, the Racketeering Influenced and Corrupt Organizations Act, and the ever-increasing blurring of the lines of demarcation between investment banking and commercial banking. There is also a brief overview of federal regulation of the commodities markets.

Perhaps the most important thing to keep in mind is that federal securities law is a rapidly changing area of the law; not only because of statutory amendments and new SEC rules but also because of the wide variety of judicial developments. Accordingly this book will be updated with pocket parts.

As with any work of this size there are a number of people whose hard work and support made this endeavor possible. In addition to my family, which has endured the long nights and short weekends, this book would never have been produced without the support from the University of North Carolina School of Law. In particular I would like to thank Dean Kenneth S. Broun for his support and encouragement. My colleague Marianne K. Smythe has been most patient with my ignorance and has provided me with much insight into the workings of the Securities and Exchange Commission. The diligent work of Jackie Creech, Vickie Bass, Lisa Gammon, Cindy Sanderson, Joyce Raby, Shelby Mann, and Paul Sherer was an important ingredient of this book. I would also like to acknowledge the invaluable research assistance of the following students and graduates of the School of Law: Chari Anhouse, Brenda Boykin, Robert Jay Fortin, Catherine Hinkle, Cecilia Rauth, and Nancy Short.

THOMAS LEE HAZEN

Chapel Hill, North Carolina
December, 1984

WESTLAW® Overview

Hazen's *Securities Regulation* offers a detailed and comprehensive treatment of basic rules, principles and issues in securities regulation law. Some readers may desire to use only the information supplied within the printed pages of this hornbook. Others, however, will encounter issues in securities regulation law that require further research. Those who opt for additional material can rapidly and easily gain access to WESTLAW. WESTLAW is West's computer-assisted legal research service.

WESTLAW contains extensive securities-related databases. To assist with comprehensive research of the law of securities regulation, a WEST-LAW appendix is included in this edition. The WESTLAW appendix provides information on databases, search techniques and sample research problems for readers who wish to do additional research on WESTLAW. It provides concise, step-by-step instruction on how to coordinate WEST-LAW research with this book. By using this text with the WESTLAW appendix, the reader is able to move from the hornbook to WESTLAW with great speed and convenience.

THE PUBLISHER

*

Summary of Contents

*

Table of Contents

THE LAW OF SECURITIES REGULATION

Third Edition

*

Chapter 1

THE BASIC COVERAGE OF
THE SECURITIES ACT

Table of Sections

§ 1.1 Overview of the Securities Markets and Their Operation

Publicly held securities in the United States are traded both on formally centrally organized securities exchanges, which are operated as auction markets, and in the more loosely organized "over-the-counter" markets.[1] The largest and most prestigious national securities exchange

---

§ 1.1

1. The over-the-counter markets are operated under the aegis of the National Association of Securities Dealers (NASD). *See* §§ 10.2–10.3 *infra*. A parallel over-the-counter market exists for municipal securities; municipal securities dealers are regulated by the Municipal Securities Rulemaking Board (MSRB). *See* § 10.4 *infra*. Both the NASD and MSRB, like the national securities exchanges, are self-regulatory organizations (SRO's) which are operated under the oversight of the Securities and Exchange Commission. *See* 15 U.S.C.A. § 78o.

For general discussions of the securities industry and the securities markets *see, e.g.,* Sidney M. Robbins, The Securities Markets: Operations and Issues (1966); SEC, Special Study of the Securities Markets, H.R.Doc. No. 95, 88th Cong. 1st Sess. (1963); Robert Sobel, N.Y.S.E.: A History of the New York Stock Exchange (1975); Robert Sobel, Amex: A History of the American Stock Exchange, 1921–1971 (1972); James E. Walter, The Role of the Regional Securities Exchanges (1957); Peter Wyckoff, Wall Street and The Stock Markets (1972); Sheldon Zerden, Best Books on the Stock Market: An Analytical Bibliography (1972); Jeffrey W. Gordon & Lewis A. Kornhauser, Efficient Markets, Costly Information, and Securities Research, 60 N.Y.U.L.Rev. 761 (1985); Dennis S. Karjala, Federalism, Full Disclosure and the National Markets in the Interpretation of Federal Securities Law, 80 Nw.U.L.Rev. 1473 (1986); William K.S. Wang, Some Arguments That

is the New York Stock Exchange which is followed both in size and in prestige by the American Stock Exchange.[2] Both of these national exchanges are recognized and regulated pursuant to section 6 of the Securities Exchange Act of 1934[3] and thus are subject to supervision and oversight by the Securities and Exchange Commission.[4] The exchanges, which are modelled on an auction system, provide investor protection through the minimum standards for securities as imposed by their listing requirements and also through their requirements for broker-dealer membership. Beyond the two national exchanges, there are seven other exchanges, many of them referred to as regional exchanges: the Boston Stock Exchange, the Chicago Board Options Exchange, the Cincinnati Stock Exchange, the Inter–Mountain Exchange, the Midwest Stock Exchange, the Pacific Stock Exchange, and the Philadelphia Stock Exchange.[5] A number of the stocks traded on some regional exchanges are also traded on the New York Stock Exchange. Commencing in the 1970s, some of the regional exchanges began to focus more on options than on equity securities.[6] The American Stock Exchange has also become active in the options market. More recently, the New York Stock Exchange began listing options as well.

The largest number of issuers have their securities traded on the over-the-counter markets although exchange listed securities generally have greater trading volume or turnover. In the 1980s and 90s, the over-the-counter markets, especially through the National Association of Securities Dealers' National Market System, have become a much more serious factor in United States capital markets. Unlike the national exchanges, the over-the-counter markets merely provide a forum for

---

the Stock Market is not Efficient, 19 U.C.Davis L.Rev. 341 (1986). For articles suggesting that basing regulation on the assumptions of the efficient market hypothesis may be questionable, *see, e.g.,* Thomas L. Hazen, Rational Investments, Speculation, or Gambling—Derivative Securities and Financial Futures and Their Effect on the Underlying Capital Markets, 86 Nw.U.L.Rev. 987 (1992); Donald C. Langevoort, Theories, Assumptions, and Securities Regulation: Market Efficiency Revisited, 140 U.Pa.L.Rev. 151 (1992). *See also, e.g.,* Lawrence A. Cunningham, From Random Walks to Chaotic Crashes: The Linear Genealogy of the Efficient Capital Market Hypothesis, 62 Geo. Wash. L. Rev. 546 (1994).

2. Although the generally considered the second most prestigious exchange, the overall prestige of the American Stock Exchange has yielded to the over the counter markets and, in particular, the National Market System and the National Association of Securities Dealers' Automated Quotation system (NASDAQ). In fact, a number of companies, particularly in technology related industries, which could qualify for listing on the New York Stock Exchange have elected to remain in the over the counter markets. Notwithstanding its apparently waning prestige in some circles, the American Stock Exchange continues to list the securities of a number of well known companies, particularly those in energy-related industry.

3. 15 U.S.C.A. § 78f.

4. *Id. See* §§ 10.2-10.4 *infra* for a discussion of the markets' structure and regulation.

5. Prior to 1991, there was a tenth registered exchange; however, the Spokane Stock Exchange became a casualty of the SEC's increased enforcement efforts with regard to penny stocks. The SEC's penny stock rules are discussed in § 10.7 *infra.*

6. For discussion of the options markets *see* SEC, Report of the Special Study of the Options Markets, 96th Cong. 1st Sess. (1978). *See also* §§ 1.4.1, 1.5.1 (Practitioner's Edition only) for discussion of the explosion of stock options and other derivative investments.

brokers and dealers to arrange their own securities trades. Much of the trading on over-the-counter markets has been facilitated by the National Association of Securities Dealers Automated Quotation System (NAS-DAQ). In addition to the automated quotation system, the most frequently traded over-the-counter stocks are listed in the national market system which has many attributes of a securities exchange.[7] As is the case with the NASDAQ, the national market system is operated under the supervision of the National Association of Securities Dealers. A number of smaller over-the-counter companies listed in NASDAQ which do not qualify for the national market system have their securities listed in the NASDAQ small capitalization system.[8] Less frequently traded and many low priced over-the-counter securities used to be relegated to the "pink sheets" which were lists of quotations that were circulated daily. Today, technological advancements have led to listing these securities on an electronic bulletin board.

The National Association of Securities Dealers (NASD) is a self-regulatory organization which is organized and governed under the oversight of the Securities and Exchange Commission pursuant to section 15 of the Securities Exchange Act of 1934.[9] In recent years there has been a concerted movement towards a consolidated, national market system which would replace the current exchange system.[10] Although there have been proposals, there has not been a consolidation of the national exchanges with the over-the-counter markets. There has been some limited movement in this direction as there is now off-exchange trading in many listed securities. In light of the power and prestige of the leading national exchanges, it is unlikely that they will disappear. On the other hand, it is clear that the expansion of the NASD's national market system has become an increasingly important factor in the American securities markets. These markets have become the home of many of the more glamorous "go-go" high technology stock issues. In fact, in many newspapers today, the over-the-counter stock listings are given more prominence than the previously more prestigious American Stock Exchange.

The operation of the market place, whether through a centralized national exchange or the over-the-counter markets, is dependent on the broker-dealer industry. The stock exchanges limit access to their trading floor to members who have purchased "seats" on the exchange. The

7. The NASD's national market system is discussed in § 10.13, infra.

8. In an attempt to remain competitive with NASDAQ, the American Stock Exchange created a two-tiered market by relaxing some of its listing requirements for qualifying smaller capitalization companies. This second tier is known as AMEX emerging issues. Under the new listing criteria, the AMEX provided an exchange-based auction marketplace for smaller companies that were not able to meet the exchange's more rigorous first-tier listing criteria. See Creation of New AMEX Marketplace for Smaller Companies Approved by SEC, 24 Sec.Reg. & L.Rep. (BNA) 295 (March 6, 1992); William Power & Herb Block, AMEX's New Home for "Start–Ups" Wins SEC Nod, Wall.St.J. p. C1 (March 6, 1992). The AMEX is discontinuing this second tier. See Wall St.J. p. C11 (May 12, 1995).

9. 15 U.S.C.A. § 78o.

10. See § 10.13 infra.

exchanges have rules and regulations covering the conduct of member brokers and dealers, including minimum capital requirements. These rules are designed to increase public trust and strengthen the integrity of the market place. Similarly, the National Association of Securities Dealers has membership requirements and regulatory rules of conduct. The Securities and Exchange Commission directly regulates broker dealers as well as indirectly through its oversight responsibilities for the exchange rules and National Association of Securities Dealers. This oversight responsibility extends to the self-policing activities of the securities exchanges and the NASD. Securities regulation thus consists not only of direct SEC involvement but also a massive self regulatory system operating under SEC oversight.

As noted above, since the early 1970s, there has been increasing movement toward a national market system. The development of a true national market system would avoid variations among the national and various regional exchanges in the quotation of securities. Also, it was believed that the national market system would greatly save on the "paper crunch" and will provide a more efficient exchange mechanism. Technological advancements generally, and increased computer capability in particular, have paved the way for more efficient markets both on the exchanges and through the NASD's over-the-counter facilities. Regulation of the securities markets and the broker dealers operating in these markets is discussed in a subsequent chapter.[11]

In addition to market regulation, the federal securities laws regulate issuers, purchasers and sellers of securities. Securities trading activities can be divided into two basic subgroups. Most of the day-to-day trading on both the securities exchanges and over-the-counter markets consists of "secondary" transactions between investors and involve securities that have previously been issued by the corporation or other issuer. All of the proceeds from these sales, after commissions to the brokers, go to the investors who are parting with their securities; none of these proceeds from the secondary trading markets flow back to the companies issuing the securities. This aspect of the secondary securities markets is frequently referred to as "trading" and is regulated primarily by the provisions of the Securities and Exchange Act of 1934.[12] The process by which securities are first offered to the public, frequently referred to as primary offerings or distributions, is governed primarily by the Securities Act of 1933.[13] This is the way in which corporate capital is raised in the public equity markets. Also covered by the Securities Act of 1933 and included within the concept of securities distributions are so-called secondary distributions which occur, for example, when a large block of securities has been placed in the hands of a private investor, institution, or group of investors and is subsequently offered to the public. As is the case with secondary transactions generally, the proceeds from secondary

11. *See* chapter 10 *infra.*

12. 15 U.S.C.A. §§ 78a *et seq.*

13. 15 U.S.C.A. §§ 77a *et seq.*

distributions inure to the benefit of the selling shareholder(s).[14]   In the case of both primary and secondary distributions, unless an appropriate exemption is applicable, registration of the securities will be required under the Securities Act of 1933.[15]   This, then, is the focus of the 1933 Act—initial, primary, and secondary distributions of securities; although some selected provisions of the Act apply to more private, non-open-market transactions.   Whereas the distribution process triggers the registration provisions of the 1933 Act, for the most part the extent to which securities are widely held and actively traded triggers the jurisdictional requirements of the Securities Exchange Act of 1934.[16]   Registration and periodic reporting by issuers under the 1934 Exchange Act depend generally upon the degree to which the securities are widely held.[17]

In addition to the securities markets, investors may look to the various commodities markets and the trading of commodity futures. At one time the commodities markets were limited to agricultural and other tangible commodities such as precious metals and fossil fuels. Today more than seventy percent of all commodity futures transactions involve financial futures. There thus have developed a wide range of overlapping or hybrid investments that have attributes of both commodities and securities. Although there have been a number of jurisdictional disputes,[18] the commodities futures markets generally are regulated by the Commodity Futures Trading Commission pursuant to the Commodity Exchange Act.[19] Beginning in the 1970s and carrying through the 1980s and 90s, the futures and commodity options markets regulated by the CFTC and the options markets regulated by the SEC have become increasingly competitive with the increased trading in derivative financial instruments, including treasury bill, foreign currency and stock index futures (as compared, for example, with the trading of stock index and foreign currency options).[20] The options are regulated by the SEC but futures and commodity options (including options on futures) are

---

14. It is not uncommon for an offering to be a combination of a primary and secondary distribution.

15. *See* chapters 2, 3 *infra.*

16. An important exception is found in the general antifraud Rule 10b–5, 17 C.F.R. § 240.10b–5, the reach of which extends to purchases or sales of any securities where the facilities of interstate commerce are implicated. Rule 10b–5 and the implied private right of action thereunder are discussed in chapter 13 *infra.* In addition to Rule 10b–5, the general antifraud proscription in connection with tender offers, section 14(e), is not limited to companies subject to the 1934 Act's registration and periodic reporting requirements. 15 U.S.C.A. § 78n(e), which is discussed in § 11.15 *infra.*

17. *See* §§ 9.2–9.3 *infra.*

18. For example, one area of current dispute is whether managed commodities accounts are securities. *See* § 1.5 *infra.*

19. 7 U.S.C.A. §§ 1–24. *See generally* Philip M. Johnson & Thomas L. Hazen, Commodities Regulation (2d ed. 1989); Commodities Futures L.Rep. (CCH).

20. Although the form of a futures contract may differ from a listed option, their operational effect and investment strategies are very similar, if not identical, when dealing with financial options and futures.

not.[21]

§ 1.2 Scope and Coverage of Federal and State Securities Regulatory Schemes

Beginning in the late nineteenth century, industrialists located primarily in the the eastern part of the United States found fertile ground for securities in the developing American frontier. There were many questionable promotional practices and, as a consequence, pressures arose to regulate the marketing of fraudulently valued securities. Accordingly, in 1911 Kansas passed the first state security statutory regulation. This, like subsequent securities legislation in other states, has come to be known as a "blue sky law." There are a number of explanations for the derivation of the "blue sky" appellation, the most common of which was because of the Kansas statute's purpose to protect the Kansas farmers against the industrialists selling them a piece of the blue sky. A number of states followed suit and blue sky laws began to spring up throughout the country. Today, all states have blue sky legislation.[1] The state blue sky laws not only focused on providing investors with full disclosure of relevant facts, but also required that all securities registered thereunder "qualify" on a merit basis, evaluating the substantive terms of the securities to be offered. Blue sky laws continue to retain this dual regulatory focus. In order to rule on the merits of such investments, the state securities commissioner or administrator typically was given the power to determine whether the securities were suitable for sale. Notwithstanding the broad regulatory potential of the merit approach, the blue sky laws proved to be relatively ineffective in stamping out securities frauds, especially on a national level.[2] Following enactment of the early state securities laws, federal legislation was successfully resisted for a while. However, the stock market crash of 1929 can be viewed as the straw that broke the camel's back.

Although the general economic conditions went a long way toward causing the Wall Street crash of 1929, the number of fraudulently floated securities that contributed to the great crash should not be underestimated. In fact, the congressional hearings which led up to the fist federal securities legislation are replete with examples of outrageous conduct by securities promoters that most certainly had a disastrous impact on our nation's economy. In relatively short order, Congress

---

21. In a controversial ruling, the SEC granted securities exchanges' applications to list index participation units which have some characteristics of futures but were found to be securities. Sec. Exch. Act Rel. No. 34–26709 (April 11, 1989). *See* §§ 1.4.1, 1.5, 1.5.1.

§ 1.2

1. *See generally* Louis Loss, Commentary on the Uniform Securities Act (1976); Hugh Sowards & N. Hirsch, Blue Sky Legislation (1977 ed.); Conrad G. Goodkind, Blue Sky Law: Is There Merit in the Merit Requirements?, 1976 Wis.L.Rev. 79; Richard W. Jennings, The Role of the States in Corporate Regulation and Investor Protection, 23 Law & Contemp.Prob. 193 (1958). Blue sky laws are discussed in Chapter 8 *infra*.

2. Although such a merit analysis exists in many states in limited form, it has not had a significant impact in eliminating unduly speculative securities from the public markets.

entered into the regulatory arena with the Securities Act of 1933, which became known as the "Truth in Securities" Act.[3] The federal legislation, which can be characterized as the first true consumer protection law,[4] contained many of the features of state blue sky laws, except that it did not (and, as amended, still does not) establish a system of merit regulation. Instead, under the guidance of a federal agency, the Act focuses on disclosure. At the time of enactment, the 1933 Act was administered by the Federal Trade Commission. The FTC's securities law jurisdiction was replaced in 1934 with the creation of the Securities and Exchange Commission.

The Securities Act of 1933, as noted in the preceding section, is directed primarily at the distribution of securities. Subject to certain enumerated exemptions, the 1933 Act generally requires the registration of all securities being placed in the hands of the public for the first time regardless of whether this is accomplished through a primary or secondary offering.[5] After considerable debate, Congress decided not to follow the pattern of the state acts and eschewed the idea of a merit approach, opting instead for a system of full disclosure. The theory behind the federal regulatory framework is that investors are adequately protected if all relevant aspects of the securities being marketed are fully and fairly disclosed. The reasoning is that full disclosure provides investors with sufficient opportunity to evaluate the merits of an investment and fend for themselves. It a basic tenet of federal securities regulation that investors' ability to make their own evaluations of available investments obviates any need that some observers may perceive for the more costly and time-consuming governmental merit analysis of the securities being offered.

The Securities Act of 1933 contains a number of private remedies for investors who are injured due to violations of the Act.[6] There are also general antifraud provisions which bar material omissions and misrepresentations in connection with the offer or sale of securities.[7] The scope of the Securities Act of 1933 is limited; first, insofar as its registration and disclosure provisions cover only distributions of securi-

---

3.　15 U.S.C.A. §§ 77a–77aa; Milton H. Cohen, "Truth in Securities" Revisited, 79 Harv.L.Rev. 1340 (1966). *See generally* Francis Pecora, Wall Street Under Oath (1939); William O. Douglas & George E. Bates, The Federal Securities Act of 1933, 43 Yale L.J. 171 (1933); James M. Landis, The Legislative History of the Securities Act of 1933, 28 Geo.Wash.L.Rev. 29 (1959).

4.　In fact, when he signed the bill into law, President Franklin Roosevelt observed that we were moving from a period of *caveat emptor* into one of *caveat vendor*.

5.　*See* chapters 2, 3 *infra.* This includes not only primary distributions (sold by the issuer), but also secondary distributions wherein the securities are sold by individuals or institutions who did not acquire the securities in a public offering. *See* § 4.24 *infra.*

6.　These are: section 11, 15 U.S.C.A. § 77k, for material misstatements and omissions in registration statements; section 12(1), 15 U.S.C.A. § 77*l* (1), for securities sold in violation of the registration requirements, and section 12(2), 15 U.S.C.A. § 77*l* (1), creating an action by purchasers against their sellers for material misstatements or omissions. *See* chapter 7 *infra.*

7.　Section 17(a), 15 U.S.C.A. § 77q(a). *See* § 7.6 *infra.*

ties and second, as its investor protection reach extends only to purchasers (and not sellers) of securities.

In 1934, Congress enacted the Securities Exchange Act of 1934 which is a more omnibus regulation. The extent of the regulation was so vast that Congress felt it was not possible to continue overburdening the Federal Trade Commission with this new administrative responsibility and thus established the Securities and Exchange Commission which is now one of the most influential and well respected federal agencies, although it is relatively modest in size.[8] The Exchange Act of 1934 is directed at regulating all aspects of public trading of securities. The Act does not focus only on securities, their issuers, purchasers, and sellers; it also regulates the marketplace, including the exchanges, the over-the-counter markets, and broker dealers generally.

In terms of its investor-protection thrust, the Exchange Act of 1934 has a much broader reach than the Securities Act of 1933. To begin with, the 1934 Act's protections extend to sellers as well as purchasers of securities. There are two distinct jurisdictional triggers for the 1934 Act's investor-protection provisions. First, the 1934 Act contains a general provision that bars fraud and material misstatements or omissions of material facts in connection with any purchase or sale of security.[9] The only jurisdictional limitation on this provision is that there must be the use of an instrumentality of interstate commerce.[10] Although these general antifraud proscriptions have a broad reach, the vast majority of the 1934 Act's regulation of securities issuers derives from the Act's periodic reporting and disclosure requirements which emanate primarily from the fact that securities traded on a national exchange (and now most of those traded in the over-the-counter markets) must be registered with the Securities and Exchange Commission.[11] Registration of issuers' securities under the Exchange Act involves full disclosure of the issuer's business, financial position and management as well as numerous periodic reporting requirements.[12] The Exchange Act also includes special provisions dealing with stock manipulation,[13] im-

---

8. *See generally* SEC, A Twenty–Five Year Summary of the Activities of the Securities and Exchange Commission 1934–1959 (1961); Joel Seligman, The Transformation of Wall Street—A History of the Securities and Exchange Commission and Modern Corporate Finance (1982); Edward N. Gadsby, Historical Development of the SEC—The Governmental View, 38 Geo.Wash.L.Rev. 29 (1959); Bevis Longstreth, Book Review, 83 Colum.L.Rev. 1593 (1983). As is discussed more fully in chapter 9 *infra*, the SEC has every power that can be given to an administrative agency, save one: the Commission does not have the authority to resolve disputes between private parties.

9. Section 10(b), 15 U.S.C.A. § 78j(b). Most notable is Rule 10b–5 promulgated thereunder. 17 C.F.R. § 240.10b–5. *See* § 13.2 *infra*.

10. The interstate commerce requirement has been broadly construed so as to make it highly doubtful that a case will ever be dismissed on the absence of this jurisdictional basis. *See* § 14.1.1 *infra* (Practitioner's Edition only).

11. For purposes of the Act, the regional exchanges are regulated as national exchanges. *See* chapter 9 *infra*. There is a class of securities which although not registered under the 1934 Act, are subject to the periodic reporting requirements. *See* § 9.3 *infra*.

12. *See* §§ 9.2, 9.3 *infra*.

13. Section 9, 15 U.S.C.A. § 78i; § 12.1 *infra*.

proper trading while in possession of non-public material information,[14] insider short swing profits,[15] and misstatements in documents filed with the Securities and Exchange Commission.[16] Further, because of the importance of shareholder suffrage in public issue corporations, Congress included regulation of the proxy machinery of all publicly traded corporations that are subject to the Act's reporting requirements.[17] Most of the foregoing provisions have been part of the regulatory scheme since the Act's inception in 1934. More recently, in 1968, Congress added the Williams Act Amendments which impose candid disclosure and reporting requirements on tender offers and on other attempts to purchase control of publicly traded corporations.[18] Each of these provisions of the Exchange Act is taken up in more detail in subsequent sections of this book.

Following the Securities Exchange Act of 1934, Congress enacted a number of additional securities laws that form part of the federal regulatory scheme. This legislation includes: the Public Utility Holding Company Act of 1935 which deals with the special problems raised by financing public issue utilities;[19] the Trust Indenture Act of 1939 which addresses debt financing of public issue companies;[20] as well as the Investment Company[21] and Investment Advisers Acts of 1940,[22] which regulate mutual funds and those professional investment analysts in the business of generating and providing financial advice to investors. In 1970, Congress added the Securities Investor Protection Act[23] which was enacted to address the increasing concern over the then increasing number of insolvent brokerage firms and broker dealer firm failures.

Since its inception, the Securities and Exchange Commission has played an important role in maintaining the efficiency and integrity of the American securities markets. However, the system is far from perfect. As the market crash of October 1987 and the market "break" of 1989 demonstrated, wild market gyrations can seriously harm investors who get caught in the squeeze. Just as the market crash of 1929 triggered the current regulatory frameworks, the 1987 crash has led to some regulatory changes and the continued aftershocks are likely to lead to some more. The SEC, Congress, and others undertook numerous studies and investigated various ways to regulate market mechanisms in a manner that will preserve the market's efficiency and help prevent a repeat of the events of October 1987. It is likely that in the future,

---

14. In addition to Rules 10b–5 and 14e–3, 17 C.F.R. §§ 240.10b–5, 240.14e–3, *see, e.g.,* sections 20A and 21(d)(2)(A), 15 U.S.C.A. §§ 78t–1, 78u(d)(2)(A). *See generally* § 13.9, *infra.*

15. Section 16(b), 15 U.S.C.A. § 78p(b); §§ 12.4–12.7 *infra.*

16. Section 18(a), 15 U.S.C.A. § 78r(a); § 12.8 *infra.*

17. Sections 14(a)–(c), 15 U.S.C.A. §§ 78n(a)–(c); chapter 11 *infra.*

18. Sections 13(d), (e), 14(d), (f), 15 U.S.C.A. §§ 78m(d)(e), n(d)(f); chapter 11 *infra.*

19. *See* chapter 15 *infra.*

20. *See* chapter 16 *infra.*

21. *See* chapter 17 *infra.*

22. *See* chapter 18 *infra.*

23. 15 U.S.C.A. §§ 78aaa–78*lll*. *See* § 19.4 *infra.*

regulatory reforms will reflect the results of the current reexamination of market mechanisms.

While no system is perfect, the SEC has had significant beneficial impact on the American securities markets and our regulatory framework has become a model for other countries. Needless to say, however, the SEC has not been without its critics.[24]

American Law Institute's Proposed Federal Securities Code

In 1968 the Council of the American Law Institute began work on the Proposed Federal Securities Code project. Professor Louis Loss was named as the Code's chief reporter. After six tentative drafts and various revisions, in 1980, the American Law Institute endorsed the final draft of its Proposed Federal Securities Code.[25] The Proposed Securities Code certainly was not without its critics.[26] Although at one time the Code was endorsed by the SEC,[27] it was not even formally introduced into Congress; with the passage of time, it has become evident that the proposed Code will not become law.[28] Nevertheless, the Proposed Code has proven to have been a worthy project for a number of reasons.

---

24. *E.g.,* William J. Baumol, The Stock Market and Economic Efficiency (1965); Homer Kripke, The S.E.C. and Corporate Disclosure: Regulation in Search of a Purpose (1979); James H. Lorie & Mary T. Hamilton, The Stock Market, Theories and Evidence (1973); George J. Benston, Required Disclosure and the Stock Market: An Evaluation of the Securities Exchange Act of 1934, 63 Am.Econ.Rev. 132 (1973); David J. Schulte, The Debatable Case for Securities Disclosure Regulation, 13 J. Corp. L. 535 (1988); George J. Stigler, Public Regulation of the Securities Markets, 37 J. Bus. 117 (1964), Symposium, 70 Va.L.Rev. 755 (1984); Symposium, 20 Conn.L.Rev. 261 (1988); Note, The Efficient Capital Market Hypothesis, Economic Theory and the Regulation of the Securities Industry, 29 Stanford L.Rev. 1031 (1977). *See also, e.g.,* William L. Cary, Politics and the Regulatory Agencies (1967); Manuel F. Cohen & George Stigler, Can Regulatory Agencies Protect the Consumer? (1971); William L. Cary, Administrative Agencies and The SEC, 29 Law & Contemp. Prob. 653 (1964); Edward N. Gadsby, The Securities and Exchange Commission, 11 B.C.Ind. & Comm.L.Rev. 833 (1970).

In the 1980s, the SEC based much of its regulatory philosophy on the Efficient Market Hypothesis which has come under attack in recent years. *See, e.g.,* Thomas L. Hazen, Rational Investments, Speculation, or Gambling—Derivative Securities and Financial Futures and Their Effect on the Underlying Capital Markets, 86 Nw.U.L.Rev. 987 (1992); Donald C. Langevoort, Theories, Assumptions, and Securities Regulation: Market Efficiency Revisited, 140 U.Pa.L.Rev. 151 (1992). *See also, e.g.,* Lawrence A. Cunningham, From Random Walks to Chaotic Crashes: The Linear Genealogy of the Efficient Capital Market Hypothesis, 62 Geo. Wash. L. Rev. 546 (1994).

25. A.L.I., Proposed Federal Securities Code (1980). *See generally* William H. Painter, The Federal Securities Code and Corporate Disclosure (1979); Program, ALI Proposed Federal Securities Code, 34 Bus.Law. 345 (1978); Symposium, The American Law Institute Federal Securities Code, 33 U. Miami L.Rev. 1425 (1979); Symposium, American Law Institute's Proposed Federal Securities Code, 32 Van.L.Rev. 455 (1979); Symposium, Proposed Securities Code, 1 Pace L.Rev. 279 (1981).

26. *See* Lewis D. Lowenfels, The Case Against the Proposed Federal Securities Code, 65 Va.L.Rev. 615 (1979); BNA Interview: Pollack Questions the Advisability of Passing Federal Securities Code at the Time, 484 Sec.Reg. & L.Rep. (BNA) AA–1 (Jan. 3, 1979).

27. Sec. Exch. Act Rel. No. 34–17153 (Sept. 18, 1980). A year and a half later the Commission reaffirmed its endorsement. Sec. Act Rel. No. 33–6377 (Jan. 21, 1982).

28. *See* Richard W. Jennings & Harold Marsh, Jr. Securities Regulation: Cases and Materials xvii (5th ed. 1982); C. Edward Fletcher, Rise Phoenix—A Guide to the Defunct Federal Securities Code, 11 Am.J. Trial Ad. 103 (1987); Plan to Revise Securities Laws Lies Dormant, Wall St. Journal p. 31 (Oct. 8, 1981).

First, many of its suggestions have since become embodied in the existing regulatory scheme. Second, the drafter's comments provide an excellent analysis of the state of the law. In deciding cases under the current law, courts have looked for guidance both to the body of the Proposed Code and to its comments.

The Proposed Code established three principal goals: "(1) simplification of an inevitably complex body of law in the light of almost a half-century of administration and litigation; (2) elimination (so far as possible) of duplicate regulation; and (3) reexamination of the entire scheme of investor protection with a view towards increasing its efficiency. * * *"[29] Although presented in a unitary statute, the Proposed Code was divided into twenty parts[30] which would have retained the same basic regulation that is currently embodied in the six different federal securities acts. The Proposed Code's major innovations as identified by the chief reporter[31] were: (1) a functional arrangement of the law with clear cross-references; (2) issuer registration with continuous disclosure as a substitute for multiple registration of securities and distributions; (3) codification and simplification of many of the SEC's "most abstruse rules;" (4) reform with regard to extraterritorial jurisdiction of the federal securities laws;[32] (5) significant preemption of state securities laws;[33] and (6) substantial although not total codification of civil liability.[34] Over time, there have been significant strides towards the accomplishment of most, if not all, of these goals.

§ 1.3   The Securities and Exchange Commission; Structure of the SEC

The Securities and Exchange Commission is a highly departmentalized federal agency, which is reflected in its wide range of authority and

---

29. ALI Proposed Federal Securities Code xix (1980). The second principle—avoidance of needless duplicate filings—has to a large extent been implemented by the SEC's integrated disclosure system. *See* § 3.3 *infra.*

30. I. Legislative Findings and Declarations; II. Definitions; III. Exemptions; IV. Issuer Registration; V. Distributions; VI. Post Registration Provisions; VII. Broker, Dealer, and Investment Adviser Registration and Qualifications; VIII. Self–Regulatory Organizations; IX. Market Regulation; X. National Market and Clearance–Settlement Systems; XI. Municipal Securities; XII. Broker–Dealer Insolvency; XIII. Trust Indentures; XIV. Investment Companies; XV. Utility Holding Companies; XVI. Fraud, Misrepresentation, and Manipulation; XVII. Civil Liability; XVIII. Administration and Enforcement; XIX. Scope of the Code; XX. General.

31. Louis Loss, Codification of the Federal Securities Law in the United States: A Case Study in Legislative Reform, as reprinted in Louis Loss, Fundamentals of Securities Regulation 38, 51–52 (Student Ed.1983).

32. Extraterritorial jurisdiction under the current law is discussed in § 14.2 *infra.*

33. State securities laws are discussed in chapter 8 *infra.* Preemption of state tender offer laws is considered in § 11.22 *infra.*

34. "This last category does not completely codify the law of 'insider trading'—some of which must be allowed to continue to evolve ad hoc in the common law tradition—but nevertheless gives fairly precise answers to some twenty-five questions." L. Loss *supra* footnote 31 at 52. The answers provided by the code are not as precise as one might want; furthermore, recent developments in Rule 10b–5 jurisprudence have changed the law that the Code would have codified. Rule 10b–5, 17 C.F.R. § 240.10b–5 is discussed in §§ 13.2– 13.12 *infra.*

various types of administrative responsibilities.[1] The Commission is a true "super agency," notwithstanding its relatively small size as compared with other federal regulatory agencies. In spite of the SEC's broad range of authority and the general criticism of governmental overregulation, the Commission has been recognized as one of the more efficient federal agencies.

The Commission consists of five commissioners serving five-year terms.[2] They are appointed by the President subject to the normal confirmatory action by Congress. One of the five commissioners is designated as Commission Chairman. Of the five commissioners, no more than three can be from the same political party.

The five commissioners comprise what is sometimes referred to as the full commission, as compared with division heads and SEC staff members. The full Commission, in addition to exercising its supervisory power over all of its divisions, has direct review power of rulings and hearings before an administrative judge as well as the final authority on the promulgation of all SEC rules. The commissioners as a group necessarily fulfill the function of the final arbiter of overall SEC policy. The adjudicatory responsibilities of the Commission are carried out through the administrative law judges, while the rest of the Commission's administrative powers are handled through its four divisions and five regional offices.

The Division of Enforcement is responsible for the investigation of all suspected securities laws violations.[3] Once it is believed that a violation has been committed, the result may be SEC judicial enforcement actions, reference to the Justice Department for criminal prosecution, or administrative sanctions imposed after a hearing. These actions may be taken against registered issuers, their officers and employees, registered broker-dealers, and members of exchanges or self-regulatory associations, such as the NASD. The Division of Corporation Finance[4] has primary responsibility for examining all registration documents for compliance with the securities laws' disclosure requirements. The Division of Corporation Finance, or "corp fin," also prepares various disclosure guides that are promulgated by the Commission. The Division of

---

§ 1.3

1. The SEC, its Rules of Practice, and its structure are discussed more fully in §§ 9.6–9.63, *infra* (Practitioner's Edition only). Descriptions of current SEC activities and structure can be found in the Commission's annual reports. *See generally* Homer Kripke, The S.E.C. and Corporate Disclosure; Regulation in Search of a Purpose (1979); SEC, A Twenty–Five Year Summary of the Activities of the Securities and Exchange Commission, 1934–1959 (1961); Joel Seligman, The Transformation of Wall Street—A History of the Securities and Exchange Commission and Modern Corporate Finance (1982); Edward N. Gadsby, The Securities and Exchange Commission, 11 B.C.Ind. & Comm.L.Rev. 833 (1970); David L. Ratner, The SEC; Portrait of the Agency as a Thirty–Seven Year Old, 45 St. John's L.Rev. 583 (1971); Walter Werner, The SEC as a Market Regulator, 70 Va.L.Rev. 755 (1984).

2. *See* § 9.44 *infra* (Practitioner's Edition only).

3. SEC enforcement is discussed in § 9.5 *infra*. The Division of Enforcement is discussed in § 9.47 *infra* (Practitioner's Edition only).

4. *See* § 9.45, *infra* (Practitioner's Edition only).

Corporation Finance is also extremely helpful in aiding the preparation of first-time or difficult disclosure documents, especially through the Commission's regional and district offices.   The Division of Market Regulation[5] is devoted to regulatory practices and policies relating to the exchanges, the over-the-counter markets, and broker-dealers.   There is some overlap with the Division of Investment Management[6] which is concerned with the regulation under the two 1940 acts of the investment company industry and investment advisors.   Finally, the Division of Investment Management is charged with handling the Commission's responsibilities under the Public Utility Holding Company Act of 1935. The former Division of Corporate Regulation, which at one time had responsibility for the Public Utility Holding Company Act, had been charged with supervising bankruptcy organizations under the Federal Bankruptcy Act.   The responsibilities under the Federal Bankruptcy Act have since been transferred to the Commission's regional offices.[7]

In the Commission's hierarchy, there are various offices below the four divisions.   The Office of the General Counsel[8] is charged with the responsibility of advising both the Commission and all of its divisions on questions of law.   The General Counsel also represents the Commission in litigation, both at the trial and appellate court levels, and is instrumental in preparing Commission sponsored legislation.   In 1989, the Commission consolidated the functions of the Office of Opinions and Review into the Office of the General Counsel.   The Office of the Accountant[9] generates Commission policy on various accounting practices; it also represents the Commission when dealing with self-regulatory organizations, such as the Financial Accounting Standards Board (FASB).   The Chief Economist and Directorate of Economic and Policy Analysis[10] as their names imply, are in charge of generating various economic studies used by the Commission and its divisions.   The Office of Policy Planning formerly had the task of coordinating the Commission's long term goals; this function has been transferred to the Directorate of Economic and Policy Analysis.

The next level of Commission hierarchy contains the offices that handle the day-to-day operation of the Commission's activities: administrative services, controller, data processing, personnel, public information, records, and registrations and reports.   Under the direct supervision of the Executive Director,[11] the five regional offices (and their

---

5. *See* § 9.46, *infra* (Practitioner's Edition only).

6. *See* § 9.48, *infra* (Practitioner's Edition only).

7. The regional offices and regional administrators are discussed in § 9.50, *infra* (Practitioner's Edition only).

In 1984, the Commission adopted a new policy of publicly announcing the position it takes on issues involving Chapter 11 reorganizations under the Federal Bankruptcy Act. *See* Corp. Reorg. Rel. No. 232, [1984–85 Transfer Binder] Fed.Sec.L.Rep. (CCH) ¶ 83,703 (Oct. 24, 1984).

8. *See* § 9.54, *infra* (Practitioner's Edition only).

9. *See* § 9.54, *infra* (Practitioner's Edition only).

10. *See* § 9.56, *infra* (Practitioner's Edition only).

11. *See* § 9.62, *infra* (Practitioner's Edition only).

respective district offices), along with the district offices that exist in the four busier regions, carry out the work of the Commission on a regional level and work closely with attorneys preparing disclosure documents that are to be filed with the Commission.[12]

Each Division and Office in the Washington, D.C. office of the Commission has responsibility for the development, direction, and policy guidance for all operating programs under his jurisdiction.[13] Each of the Regional Directors (formerly called regional administrators), is responsible for the implementation of all programs and for supervision of all employees in his or her region.[14] Prior to 1993, the Regional Administrators were located in New York, Boston, Atlanta, Chicago, Fort Worth, Denver, Los Angeles, Seattle, and Philadelphia.[15] Some of the larger regional offices have branch offices.[16] As a result of the reorganization, Chicago, Denver, Los Angeles, and New York remain regional offices; their regional administrators are redesignated as regional directors. The Seattle office became a district of the Los Angeles regional office which continues to oversee the San Francisco district; the Salt Lake City office became a district office under the Denver regional office, as did the Fort Worth office; while the Philadelphia and Boston offices were made district offices of the New York regional office. In the second stage of the plan, the Atlanta office became a district office and Miami was designated the regional office that will oversee the Atlanta district.[17]

The following chart depicts the SEC's organizational structure.[18]

---

12. *See* § 9.50, *infra* (Practitioner's Edition only).

13. 17 C.F.R. § 200.11(a)(1). The Headquarters Office is located at 450 Fifth Street, N.W., Washington, DC 20549. *Id.*

14. 17 C.F.R. § 200.11(a)(2).

15. 17 C.F.R. § 200.11(b). *See id.* for complete addresses of each of the Regional Administrators.

16. The Chicago Regional Office has a branch office in Detroit, the Fort Worth Regional Office has a branch office in Houston, the Denver Regional Office has a branch office in Salt Lake City, and the Los Angeles Regional Office has a branch office in San Francisco.

17. For more detailed description of the regional and district offices, *see* § 9.50, *infra* (Practitioner's Edition only).

18. *See* §§ 9.44–9.63, *infra* (Practitioner's Edition only) for discussion of SEC personnel and their functions.

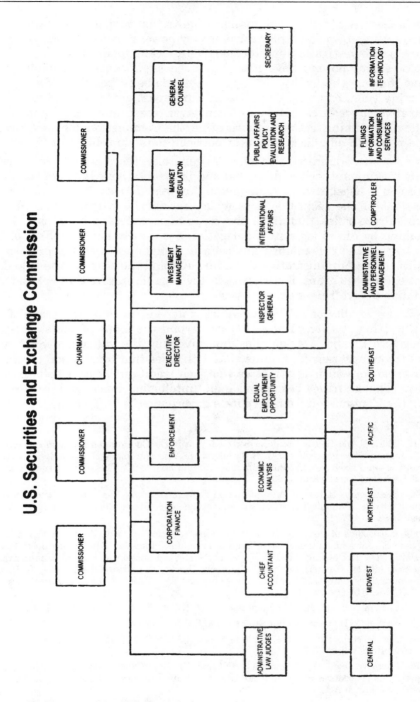

§ 1.4   The Work of the SEC

Congress has given the the Securities and Exchange Commission the responsibility of administering the regulation provided by all six of the securities laws.[1] The Commission acquits that responsibility with each of the three basic administrative agency powers: rule-making, adjudicatory, and investigatory-enforcement.[2] In recent years, the Commission's enforcement powers have been expanded significantly. In addition to now having the ability to seek treble damage penalties for insider trading violations,[3] the Commission can impose civil penalties in administrative procedures,[4] and has been given cease and desist authority.[5] The only administrative authority that the Commission does not have is the power to adjudicate disputes between individual litigants.[6]

As with administrative agencies generally, there are two varieties of rule-making authority: delegated and interpretative. Much of the Commission's legislative or rule-making power derives from the certain sections of the securities laws which specifically empower the SEC to promulgate rules that have the force of statutory provisions.[7] Rule-making by direct legislative delegation necessarily has the effect of law so long as the rule-making has been in compliance with the process set forth in the Administrative Procedure Act and the scope of the rule does not exceed the grant of authority in the organic statute that created this administrative rule-making power.

The validity of SEC rulemaking is dependent upon the scope of the authorizing statute. Rules that go beyond the scope of the statute are therefore invalid. Major questions involving the validity of SEC rules are frequently raised in connection with rules that touch upon corporate governance, which is a matter that has traditionally been left to state law. The securities laws provide an "intelligible conceptual line excluding the Commission from corporate governance."[8] Accordingly, the D.C.

---

§ 1.4

1. The SEC's activities are described each year in the Commission's annual report. *See* § 1.2 *supra. See generally* SEC, A Twenty Five Year Summary of the Activities of the Securities and Exchange Commission 1934–1959 (1961); SEC, The Work of the Securities and Exchange Commission (1974).

2. *See* Thomas L. Hazen, Administrative Enforcement: An Evaluation of the Securities and Exchange Commission's Use of Injunctions and Other Enforcement Methods, 31 Hastings L.J. 427 (1979).

For discussions of the roles for administrative agencies, *see, e.g.,* Frederick F. Blachly & Miriam E. Oatman, Administrative Legislation and Adjudication (1934); Joseph P. Chamberlain, Noel T. Dowling, Paul R. Hays, The Judicial Function in Federal Administrative Agencies (1942); Kenneth C. Davis, Administrative Law Treatise (2d ed. 1978); R. Pound, Administrative Law (1942); Felix Frankfurter, The Task of Administrative Law, 75 U.Pa.L.Rev. 614 (1927).

3. Section 21A of the Exchange Act, 15 U.S.C.A. § 78u–1. *See* §§ 9.5, 13.9 *infra.*

4. Section 21B of the Exchange Act, 15 U.S.C.A. § 78u–2.

5. *E.g.,* section 21C of the Exchange Act, 15 U.S.C.A. § 78u–3. *See* § 9.5.1 *infra* (Practitioner's edition only).

6. *Compare, e.g.,* the Commodity Futures Trading Commission which through its reparations procedures can adjudicate customer/broker disputes. Section 14 of the Commodity Exchange Act, 7 U.S.C.A. § 18.

7. *See e.g.,* section 3(b) of the 1933 Act giving the Commission power to promulgate exemptions from registration, 15 U.S.C.A. § 77c(b); and section 10(b) of the 1934 Act which delegates to the Commission the responsibility to promulgate rules determining the scope of anti-fraud liability, 15 U.S.C.A. § 78j(b).

8. Business Roundtable v. SEC, 905 F.2d 406 (D.C.Cir.1990).

Circuit Court of Appeals invalidated the Commission's attempt to regulate substantive voting rights of shareholders.[9]

Commission rule-making is not limited to legislatively delegated rules. The SEC has also promulgated a number of interpretive rules which are designed to aid corporate planners and attorneys in complying with the statutes' requirements.[10] Unlike the rules promulgated pursuant to specific statutory delegation, interpretative rules do not carry with them the force of law; they simply reflect the Commission's interpretation of the law created by the statute. Nevertheless, interpretative rules are extremely important in guiding practitioners through the regulatory maze. Equally important is that fact that when interpreting the scope of a statute, federal courts traditionally give deference to administrative interpretation.[11] The reasoning underpinning this deference is the reliability of the agency's expertise as compared to the court's general knowledge and authority.

The SEC issues interpretative rules in a number of situations. A special variety of interpretative rule are the so-called safe harbor rules.[12]

Beyond its expressly delegated and interpretative rule-making activities, the Commission disseminates unsolicited advisory opinions in the form of SEC releases[13] which may include guidelines or suggest interpretation of statutory provisions and rules. In addition to periodic interpretative releases, each time the Commission proposes a new rule or rule amendment, the proposal is accompanied by a release. Similarly, when new rules or amendments are adopted, the SEC's formal adoption is accompanied by an interpretative release. The SEC positions announced in interpretative releases necessarily provide less precedential and predictive value than do rules that are promulgated as a result of the more formal interpretive rule-making process.

One step below interpretative releases, in terms of precedential hierarchy, are the Commission's "no action" letters. These no action

---

9. *Id. See* discussion in § 11.1 *infra.* Another example of the SEC's clash with corporate governance issues arose in the context of the regulation of "going private" transactions. *See* § 11.17 *infra.*

10. The current versions of the rules are compiled annually in volume 17 of the Code of Federal Regulations (hereinafter cited as "17 C.F.R. § ___"). Since the Commission has many rule changes each year, looseleaf services should also be consulted. *See, e.g.,* Fed.Sec.L.Rep. (CCH). A WESTLAW check will help reveal the most current versions of the SEC's rules.

All of the Commission's activities are reported in the SEC Digest and SEC Docket which are published weekly and daily by the Commission. This information also is available on WESTLAW.

11. Chevron U.S.A. v. Natural Resources Defense Council, 467 U.S. 837, 104 S.Ct. 2778, 81 L.Ed.2d 694 (1984).

12. For examples of safe harbor rules, see Rule 144 (exemption for secondary transactions), Rule 147 (exemption for intrastate offerings), Rule 175 (forward looking statements), and 506 (exemption for offerings by an issuer not involving a public offering) of the 1933 Act, 17 C.F.R. §§ 230.144, 230.147, 230.175, 230.506.

13. The Commission's releases are published in the Federal register and also appear in the various looseleaf services. This information also is available on WESTLAW.

letters are analogous to IRS private letter rulings. No action letters are SEC staff responses to private requests for indication of whether certain contemplated conduct is in compliance with the appropriate statutory provisions and rules. Most requests for a "no action" letter are compliance oriented and thus are handled by the Division of Corporation Finance, although on occasion the other divisions may render similar assistance in their areas of expertise. No action letters can be very helpful to practitioners.[14] However, it must be kept in mind that the SEC's responses are staff interpretations rather than formal Commission action and thus have extremely limited, if any, precedential weight.[15] The SEC staff position in a no action letter has been described as a statement to the effect that

> This is my view based on the facts as you describe them. You may not rely on it as if it were a Commission decision. If you don't like it, you are at liberty to disregard it and follow your own construction, subject to the risk that I may recommend appropriate action to the Commission and the Commission may institute proceedings or take other steps if the Commission agrees with my view.[16]

A no action letter is purely a matter between the SEC staff and the party requesting it. The request for a no action letter does not bind the party requesting it to act in a certain way so as to create any protectable expectations in third parties. Accordingly, it has been held that a corporation's shareholders cannot force management to frame a transac-

---

14. *See, e.g.,* Thomas P. Lemke, The SEC No–Action Letter Process, 42 Bus.Law. 1019 (1987).

15. *See, e.g.,* Roosevelt v. E.I. Du Pont de Nemours & Co., 958 F.2d 416, 427 n. 19 (D.C.Cir.1992) (principle of deference to agency views does not apply to no action letters as they are not formal agency positions); Amalgamated Clothing & Textile Workers Union v. Wal–Mart Stores, Inc., 821 F.Supp. 877 (S.D.N.Y.1993) (court refused to follow position in no action letter since SEC had since taken a different view in the context of formal rulemaking); New York City Employees' Retirement System v. Dole Food Co., 795 F.Supp. 95, 100–101 (S.D.N.Y.1992), *vacated as moot* 969 F.2d 1430 (2d Cir.1992) (courts are not bound by no action responses). *See* footnotes 18–20 *infra* and accompanying text.

No action letters are not final agency decisions and thus are not subject to judicial review. Amalgamated Clothing & Textile Workers Union v. SEC, 15 F.3d 254 (2d Cir.1994) (shareholder could not obtain judicial review of SEC no action letter permitting management to exclude shareholder proposal as the SEC letter did not represent a "final order"). *See also, e.g.,* Board of Trade of City of Chicago v. SEC, 883 F.2d 525 (7th Cir.1989), *appeal after remand* 923 F.2d 1270 (1991) (SEC no action letter permitting proprietary trading system to deal in options without registering as an exchange was not reviewable); Kixmiller v. SEC, 492 F.2d 641 (D.C.Cir.1974).

Similarly, SEC staff letters of comment in response to filings with the Commission are not judicially reviewable. *See* Koss v. SEC, 364 F.Supp. 1321 (S.D.N.Y.1973).

The informality of the no action letter process has implications beyond the question of judicial review. No action responses as an informal statement of the SEC's views do not have legal consequences for any of the the the parties. Also, since the responses are interpretative rather than legislative, they do not require notice and opportunity for comment such as is required, under the Administrative Procedure Act, for SEC rulemaking. *E.g.,* New York City Employees' Retirement System v. SEC, 45 F.3d 7 (2d Cir.1995).

16. Professional Care Services, Inc., [1973–74 Transfer Binder] Fed.Sec.L.Rep. (CCH) ¶ 79,770 at p. 84,080 (SEC No Action Letter March 15, 1974) (quoting 3 Louis Loss, Securities Regulation 1895 (2d ed. 1961)).

tion according to the terms of its no action request.[17] Conversely, when the Commission has responded favorably to a request for a no action letter, the SEC's interpretation will not preclude a third party from challenging the transaction. The no action position may, of course, have some persuasive effect insofar as it represents the Commission's interpretation and exhibits the SEC's current thinking on particular matters. The limited precedential effect of no action letters was reinforced with the Commission's recent initiation of administrative proceedings to address conduct that had previously been the subject of favorable no action responses.[18] In conjunction with the initiation of the administrative proceeding, Commissioner Fleischman issued a written statement emphasizing that since no action responses are limited to the particular facts in the requesting letter, it is risky to make general conclusions from specific responses.[19] It is clear that a court will not give the same deference to a no action response as it would to formal rulemaking or interpretative pronouncements.[20]

A number of commentators have criticized the "no action" letter as an inefficient method of law making.[21] The no action letter as an ad hoc method of advising admittedly is time-consuming and cumbersome. Further, it fails to provide practitioners with significant precedential or predictive aid. The value of no action letters is even further diminished, as described more fully below in a discussion of the registration process under the Securities Act of 1933, by the availability of comment letters and less formal telephone conferences provided by the Division of Corporation Finance and various regional offices as guides for revision of documents filed with the Commission. Nevertheless, given all of its shortcomings, the no action letter process has been an influential one in forming securities law. No action letters can be of great help in shedding light on the SEC's current view of many significant issues.

---

17. Beaumont v. American Can Co., 797 F.2d 79 (2d Cir.1986), *affirming* 621 F.Supp. 484 (S.D.N.Y.1985).

18. Morgan Stanley & Co., Sec.Exch.Act Rel. No. 34–28,990, Admin.Proc.File No. 3–7473 (March 20, 1991) (charging violations of limits on sale of control person stock in connection with stock sale to satisfy margin requirements).

19. As stated by Commissioner Fleischman, "since the particular letter under discussion states that it's limited to the facts of its own case and that only the addressee is protected by it, others claiming to be similarly situated can't be allowed to reason from the letter to derive general propositions on which the addressee itself could not rely." *Id.* (written statement of Commissioner Fleischman).

20. Amalgamated Clothing & Textile Workers Union v. Wal–Mart Stores, Inc., 821 F.Supp. 877 (S.D.N.Y.1993) (no action responses do not represent official agency positions), *relying on* Roosevelt v. E.I. DuPont de Nemours & Co., 958 F.2d 416, 427 n. 19 (D.C.Cir.1992) (principle of deference to agency views does not apply to no action letters as they are not formal agency positions); New York City Employees' Retirement System v. Dole Food Co., 795 F.Supp. 95, 100–101 (S.D.N.Y.1992), *vacated as moot* 969 F.2d 1430 (2d Cir.1992) (courts are not bound by no action responses).

21. Louis Loss, Summary Remarks (ABA National Institute—Advisors to Management), 30 Bus.Law. 163, 164–65 (Special Issue 1975); Lewis D. Lowenfels, SEC No action Letters: Conflicts with the Existing Statutes, Cases and Commission Releases, 59 Va. L.Rev. 303 (1973).

Aside from the foregoing quasi-legislative responsibilities, the Commission also has regulatory oversight and quasi-judicial power over brokers, dealers, and exchanges that it licenses under the Exchange Act of 1934.[22] Correlative to this power is the agency's ability to impose administrative disciplinary sanctions upon those subject to the licensing authority—this includes broker-dealers, investment advisors, investment companies, as well as professionals such as attorneys or accountants who practice before the SEC. The Commission also can impose administrative sanctions against other persons who violate the securities laws. In addition to direct enforcement authority the Commission may in its discretion publish the results of its investigations.[23] Perhaps the most expansive use of this authority has been exerted under Rule 2(e) of the Commission's rules of practice which allows the SEC to discipline professionals who appear before the Commission.[24]

The third major administrative function carried out by the SEC is that of enforcement. Through the Division of Enforcement, the Commission investigates all potential violations of each act that it administers. Where appropriate, such violation will be addressed through the SEC's administrative sanctions referred to above, or forwarded to the Department of Justice for criminal prosecution.[25] The Commission also performs a direct prosecutorial function by virtue of its authority to seek injunctions against alleged violators, as well as appropriate ancillary relief in the federal district courts. Originally, the ability to secure ancillary relief was implied from the court's inherent equity authority.[26] The Commission has since been given express statutory authority to seek disgorgement of ill-gotten gains,[27] imposition of civil penalties,[28] and

---

22. 15 U.S.C.A. § 78o. *See* chapter 10 *infra.*

23. 15 U.S.C.A. § 78u(a). *See* Sec.Exch.Act Rel. No. 34–15664 (March 21, 1979). For criticism of the publication of investigations *see* In re Spartek, Inc., 491 Sec.Reg. 8 L.Rep. (BNA) E–1 (SEC Feb. 21, 1979) (Karmel, dissenting).

24. 17 C.F.R. § 201.2(e). *See generally* Kenneth J. Bialkin, Sanctions Against Accountants, 8 Rev.Sec.Reg. 823 (1975); Norman S. Johnson, The Expanding Responsibilities of Attorneys in Practice Before the SEC: Disciplinary Proceedings Under Rule 2(e) of the Commission's Rules of Practice, 25 Mercer L.Rev. 637 (1974); Richard L. Miller, The Distortion and Misuse of Rule 2(e), 7 Sec.Reg.L.J. 54 (1979).

25. The Commission's administrative sanctions now include the imposition of civil penalties as well as cease and desist power. For discussion of the development of the Commission's enforcement authority, *see generally* Arthur F. Mathews, Criminal Prosecutions Under the Federal Securities Laws of SEC Criminal Cases, 39 Geo.Wash.L.Rev. 901 (1971); Note, Penal and Injunctive Provisions of the Securities Act, 23 Wash.U.L.Q. 251 (1938). *See also* § 9.5, *infra.*

26. *See generally* Thomas L. Hazen, Administrative Enforcement: An Evaluation of the Securities and Exchange Commission's Use of Injunctions and Other Enforcement Methods, 31 Hastings L.J. 427 (1979); Arthur F. Mathews, Effective Defense of SEC Investigations: Laying the Foundation for Successful Disposition of Subsequent Civil, Administrative and Criminal Proceedings, 24 Emory L.J. 567 (1975); Arthur F. Mathews, SEC Civil Injunctive Actions, 5 Rev.Sec.Reg. 969 (1972); Note, Injunctive Relief in SEC Civil Actions: The Scope of Judicial Discretion, 10 Colum.J.L. & Soc.Prob. 328 (1974).

27. Section 21A of the Exchange Act, 15 U.S.C.A. § 78u–1.

28. *Id.*

bar orders[29] as part of its judicial enforcement arsenal.

Congress enacted legislation in 1990 that expanded significantly the role of the Commission in enforcement matters. As part of the Securities Enforcement and Penny Stock Reform Act of 1990,[30] the Commission was given cease and desist power.[31] The new law further empowers the Commission to impose civil penalties in administrative proceedings.[32] The new legislation also increases civil penalties for violations of the securities laws generally,[33] and empowers the SEC to go to court to secure an order barring officers and directors from associating with issuers under the Commission's jurisdiction.[34]

§ 1.4.1 The SEC's Subject–Matter Jurisdiction; The CFTC–SEC Jurisdictional Accord

Jurisdictional Concerns

As discussed directly above, the Securities and Exchange Commission has wide-ranging responsibility with regard to the securities markets. The expanded sophistication of the securities markets has led to sweeping changes in the regulatory role of the Commission. As discussed in the preceding sections, the heart of the Securities and Exchange Commission's jurisdiction is the regulation of securities markets and securities trading. Beginning in the 1970s, the development and diversification of derivative investment products has created overlapping jurisdiction between the SEC and the Commodity Futures Trading Commission (CFTC).

Traditionally, the futures markets were devoted to agricultural and other tangible commodities. However, those markets began to trade financial futures and other derivative instruments wherein the underlying commodities were instruments more commonly associated with the securities markets, including treasury bonds or stock index futures. When combined with foreign currency contracts and other related futures and options, it is estimated that more than seventy percent of the

---

29. Under appropriate circumstances, a court may order that a violator of the securities law be barred from association with a company subject to the SEC's registration and reporting requirements. Section 21(d)(2) of the Exchange Act, 15 U.S.C.A. § 78u(d)(2).

30. Pub.L. No. 101–429.

31. Securities Act of 1933 § 8A, 15 U.S.C.A. § 77h–1; Securities Exchange Act of 1934 §§ 21C, 23(d), 15 U.S.C.A. §§ 78u–3, 78w(d); Investment Company Act of 1940 § 9(f), 15 U.S.C.A. § 80a–9(f); Investment Advisers Act of 1940 § 203(k), 15 U.S.C.A. § 80b–3(k). *See* discussion in §§ 9.5, 9.71 *infra*.

32. Securities Exchange Act of 1934 § 21B, 15 U.S.C.A. § 78u–2; Investment Company Act § 9(d), (e), 15 U.S.C.A. § 80a–9(d), (e); Investment Advisers Act § 203(i), 15 U.S.C.A. § 80b–3(i). *See* discussion in § 9.5 *infra*.

33. Securities Act of 1933 § 20(d), 15 U.S.C.A. § 77t(d); Securities Exchange Act of 1934 § 21(d)(3), 15 U.S.C.A. § 78u(d)(3); Investment Company Act § 42(e); 15 U.S.C.A. § 80a–41(e); Investment Advisers Act § 209(e); 15 U.S.C.A. § 80b–9(e). *See* discussion in § 9.5 *infra*.

34. Securities Exchange Act of 1934 § 21(d)(2), 15 U.S.C.A. § 78u(d)(2). *See* discussion in § 9.5 *infra*.

volume on the commodities exchanges is attributable to financial instruments as opposed to tangible commodities.

The expansion of the public trading of options on securities[1] has met with competition from the public trading of futures contracts on securities. The Commodity Exchange Act vests the CFTC with exclusive jurisdiction over futures contracts.[2] The Commodity Exchange Act further requires, however, that except as otherwise expressly provided, the CFTC's jurisdiction will not interfere with the area mapped out for the SEC.[3] The increasing competition between options on securities and futures thus set the stage for jurisdictional clashes between the SEC and CFTC.[4]

The SEC initially took the position that futures contracts on securities were subject to its jurisdiction since such a derivative instrument clearly fell within the statutory definition of "security."[5] The battle was first fought over futures on GNMA certificates.[6] After several years, the SEC and CFTC entered into a jurisdictional accord which formed the basis for legislative reform.

The Jurisdictional Accord

In 1981, representatives of the SEC and CFTC met with the purpose of eliminating the confusion concerning the jurisdictions of the two agencies. The resulting Johnson–Shad accord[7] was incorporated into section 2(a)(1)(B) of the Commodity Exchange Act,[8] section 2 of the Securities Act of 1933,[9] and section 3 of the Securities Exchange Act of 1934.[10] Under the terms of the accord and resulting legislation, the SEC retains jurisdiction over options on securities while the CFTC is granted

---

§ 1.4.1

1. *See* § 1.5.1 *infra.*

2. This is found in section 2(a)(1) of the Commodity Exchange Act, 7 U.S.C.A. § 2. *See generally* Philip M. Johnson & Thomas L. Hazen, Commodities Regulation (2d ed. 1989).

3. "[N]othing contained in this section shall (i) supersede or limit the jurisdiction at any time conferred on the Securities and Exchange Commission or other regulatory authorities under the laws of the United States or of any State, or (ii) restrict the Securities and Exchange Commission and such other authorities from carrying out their duties and responsibilities in accordance with such laws." 7 U.S.C.A. § 2.

4. *See, e.g.,* Christopher L. Culp, Stock Index Futures and Financial Market Reform: Regulatory Failure or Regulatory Imperialism, 13 Geo.Mason U.L.Rev. 517–605 (1991); Thomas L. Hazen, Rational Investments, Speculation, or Gambling—Derivative Securities and Financial Futures and Their Effect on the Underlying Capital Markets, 86 Nw. U.L.Rev. 987 (1992); Thomas A. Russo & Marlisa Vinciguerra, Financial Innovation and Uncertain Regulation: Selected Issues Regarding New Product Development, 69 Tex. L.Rev. 1431 (1991); Comment, Ending the Turf Wars: Support for a CFTC–SEC Consolidation, 36 Vill.L.Rev. 1175 (1991).

5. 15 U.S.C.A. §§ 77b(1), 78c(10). *See* § 1.5, *infra.*

6. For a more detailed description of the jurisdictional battle *see* P. Johnson & T. Hazen, *supra* footnote 2, § 4.37.

7. *See* [1980–82 Transfer Binder] Comm.Fut.L.Rep. (CCH) ¶ 21,332.

8. 7 U.S.C.A. § 2a.

9. 15 U.S.C.A. § 77b(1).

10. 15 U.S.C.A. § 78c.

exclusive jurisdiction over futures contracts and options on futures contracts where the underlying commodity is a security or a group of securities. Thus, the CFTC now has jurisdiction over futures contracts on individual government securities,[11] on indices of stocks and municipal bonds, and over options on such futures contracts. Futures and commodity option contracts on individual nonexempt securities are prohibited. The SEC has jurisdiction over stock index *options* while the CFTC presides over stock index *futures*.[12] Although conceptually they are commodities instruments, the SEC has jurisdiction over options on foreign currencies if they are traded on a national securities exchange[13] while the CFTC regulates foreign currency futures and options that are not traded on a national securities exchange.

The respective roles of the CFTC and SEC are depicted in the following diagram from the House Report[14] which depicts the Congressional allocation of jurisdiction:

CFTC	SEC	PROHIBITED
Options, futures and options on futures in nonsecurities (e.g., agricultural products, metals, forest products, energy)	Direct trading in all securities	Futures, and options on futures, in now-registrable securities (except exempted securities)
	All options directly on securities and indices	
Futures, and options on futures in securities exempted	1933 and 1934 registration of public sale of pool securities	
Futures, and options on futures in "qualified" stock indices		
	Options directly on foreign currencies if traded on a stock exchange	
Options directly on foreign currencies		

The rationale behind this allocation was explained by the House Committee Report as follows:

> With respect to commodity futures trading, the agreement reaffirms Congress' designation of the CFTC as the sole regulator in its

---

11. *See, e.g.,* Messer v. E.F. Hutton & Co., 847 F.2d 673 (11th Cir.1988) (neither federal nor state securities laws applied to United States Treasury Bill futures contracts; the CFTC has exclusive jurisdiction).

12. *See, e.g.,* Richard E. Nathan, The CFTC's Limited Authority Over Hybrid Instruments, 7 Commod. Law Letter 2 (April/May 1988). In a move that has rekindled the jurisdictional dispute, the SEC approved index participation units as securities for trading on securities exchanges. *See* footnotes 22–29 *infra* and accompanying text.

13. *See* Exch. Act Rel. No. 34–22853, 51 Fed.Reg. 5129 (Feb. 3, 1986). *Cf.* Robert B. Hiden, Jr. & Donald R. Crawshaw, New Instruments, Foreign Currency Warrants and Section 4c(f) of the Commodity Exchange Act, 7 Commod. Law Letter 11 (April/May 1988).

14. H.R.Rep. No. 565(I), 97th Cong., 2d Sess. 39 (May 17, 1982).

field. It does not affect in any way the CFTC's jurisdiction over agricultural futures or over futures in other nonsecurities instruments or products. The CFTC also retains its exclusive jurisdiction over the trading on boards of trade of futures contracts (or options on futures contracts) on securities issued or guaranteed by the United States Government or other securities which are exempt from the registration requirements of the Federal securities laws, other than municipal securities.

The agreement recognizes the SEC as the sole Federal regulator of the securities options markets. Thus, the agreement states that the CFTC will have no authority to regulate or oversee regulation of the trading of options directly on any security.

In recognition of the SEC's unique responsibilities over the trading markets for corporate equity and municipal securities, the agreement specifies certain criteria to govern approval by the CFTC of futures trading in a group or index of such securities. Such group or index (1) must be a widely published and accurate measure of a broad segment of the corporate or municipal securities markets, (2) must not be susceptible to manipulation nor to use in the manipulation of the underlying securities market or securities options market and (3) must be settled by cash or by other means not involving the delivery of municipal securities or securities subject to the registration requirements of the Federal securities laws. Any securities index futures contract that does not meet the three tests will not be permitted to trade.

Should the SEC object to CFTC designation of any particular securities group or index future, the SEC will be afforded an opportunity for an oral hearing before the CFTC to present the bases for its objection. In the event that the CFTC nonetheless approves the trading of such futures contract, the SEC may petition for review in a Federal court of appeals.

The agreement recognizes that futures trading on individual corporate or municipal securities raises particularly difficult issues. Accordingly, it would not permit the trading of futures on individual corporate and municipal securities. Both agencies, however, intend to devote further study to issues in this area with a view toward a recommendation to lift this restriction. * * *

In accepting this joint proposal the Committee hopes to put to rest the tension previously existing between the two agencies which hampered both the futures and the securities industries.

It is the hope that the jurisdictional accord will turn the focus of debate from the issue of which agency has or should have jurisdiction [over] the merits of the proposals made to the agencies. This resolution should serve the public interest, in general, and business, commerce and investment, in particular, by removing impediments to useful new instruments so that in meritorious cases their benefits could be made available without undue delay.

The committee has long recognized and accepted the inherent differences between the futures industry and the securities industry and endorses the concept of separate regulation. Basically, the CFTC will retain its traditional rule of regulating markets and instruments that serve a hedging and price discovery function while the SEC will regulate markets and instruments with an underlying investment purpose.[15]

Investment Companies and Commodities Pools

In addition to the question of whether a particular investment instrument is a security or, alternatively, a commodity futures or option contract, the SEC's and CFTC's jurisdictional clash also arose in the context of professional investment managers and advisors. A pooled investment in securities is frequently marketed in the form of a mutual fund. Such pooling of securities investments qualifies the issuer (or operator of the pool) as an investment company.[16] Investment companies are regulated by the Investment Company Act of 1940,[17] which is administered by the SEC. In contrast, a pooled investment in commodities futures and options, commonly known as a commodity pool, falls within the jurisdiction of the CFTC which requires the registration of commodity pool operators (CPOs).[18] While the CFTC regulates the operation of commodities pools, commodities pools' raising of capital through the issuance of securities is subject to the federal securities laws.

The CFTC has decided not to require commodity pool operator registration for registered investment companies. When an investment company subject to SEC regulation invests in commodity instruments as part of its securities portfolio management, such companies have been excluded from CFTC regulation as commodities pool operators.[19]

Investment Advisers and Commodity Trading Advisors

The overlap between the SEC and CFTC also arises in the context of professional investment advisors. Investment advisors rendering advice with regard to securities investments are subject to the SEC's jurisdiction under the Investment Advisers Act of 1940.[20] Professionals who render advice with regard to commodities related investments are known as Commodity Trading Advisors (CTAs) and are subject to the CFTC's jurisdiction.[21]

---

15. *Id.* at 39–40.

16. *See, e.g.,* In the Matter of ABC Portfolio Development Group, Inc., [1994–1995 Transfer Binder] Fed. Sec. L. Rep. (CCH) ¶ 85,422 (SEC 1994) (sales of investment pool interests were sales of interests in an investment company subject to the Investment company Act of 1940 and also were securities subject to the 1933 and 1934 Acts).

17. 15 U.S.C.A. §§ 80a–1–80a–54. *See* chapter 17 *infra.*

18. *See* section 4m(2) of the Commodity Exchange Act, 7 U.S.C.A. § 6m(2).

19. CFTC Regulation § 4.5(a)(1), 17 C.F.R. § 4.5(a)(1).

20. 15 U.S.C.A. § 80b–1 *et seq. See* chapter 18 *infra.*

21. *See* section 4m(2) of the Commodity Exchange Act, 7 U.S.C.A. § 6m(2).

The Impact of Recent Events

The legislation which resulted from the CFTC–SEC jurisdictional accord has proven to be a workable solution. However, the market crash of October 1987, raised concern as to whether there should be more coordination between the securities markets and the futures markets which are based on derivative instruments. Following the stock market crash of October 19, 1987, a number of commentators and legislators called for increased coordination of the SEC and CFTC in regulating the securities markets and derivative instruments. While it seems likely that such coordination will occur, at this time it appears doubtful that jurisdiction over all derivative and financial instruments will be transferred to one agency.

Index Participations and Other Hybrids as Securities or Commodities

In 1988, three securities exchanges filed applications to permit trading of stock index participation instruments (also known as stock baskets). A stock basket (like an index futures or option contract) allows investors to participate in gains (or losses) derived from an index based on the collective price of the underlying securities. In March 1989, the SEC granted the applications and approved trading of three types of stock baskets on the applicant securities exchanges.[22] Stock index futures have been trading on the commodities exchanges for a number of years. The SEC's recognition of these new index participation units as securities has opened another round of the SEC/CFTC jurisdictional struggle.[23] The Chicago Mercantile Exchange challenged the SEC action, claiming that the new instruments are futures contracts and as such are subject to the exclusive jurisdiction of the CFTC.[24] The Seventh Circuit ruled that index participations were subject to the exclusive jurisdiction of the CFTC.[25]

In holding that the CFTC had exclusive jurisdiction over these index participation units, Judge Easterbrook explained that the basic premise underlying the 1982 jurisdictional accord was that if an instrument could be classified as both a security and a futures contract, exclusive jurisdiction of its trading lies with the CFTC.[26] In the wake of the decision, the Bush administration introduced legislation that would transfer jurisdiction over all stock index futures to the SEC.[27] Other proposals for regulatory reform that have been suggested include giving the SEC oversight responsibility with regard to the CFTC's financial and stock index jurisdiction.[28] It is thus fair to say that Congress is currently

---

22. Sec. Exch. Act. Rel. No. 34–26709 (SEC March 14, 1989).

23. *See* Ricks, Stock Basket Approval Stirs Court Action, Wall St. J. p. C1 (Wednesday, March 15, 1989).

24. *Id.*

25. Chicago Mercantile Exchange v. SEC, 883 F.2d 537 (7th Cir.1989), *cert. denied* 496 U.S. 936, 110 S.Ct. 3214, 110 L.Ed.2d 662 (1990).

26. *See also* the discussion in § 1.5.1 *infra.*

27. *See* 22 Sec.Reg. & L.Rep. (BNA) 731 (May 11, 1990).

28. *E.g.,* Report of the Presidential Task Force on Market Practices (Jan. 8, 1988).

reexamining the 1982 accord. It seems doubtful, however, that any adjustments to the jurisdiction of the SEC and CFTC will be the result of another accord between the two agencies.[29]

At the same time that the CFTC was contesting the applicability of the securities laws to index participations, it exempted a number of hybrid instruments (having characteristics of both securities and commodities-related investments) from the coverage of the Commodity Exchange Act.[30] Hybrid investments qualifying for the exemption include instruments that combine commodity option or futures characteristics with debt instruments, preferred equity instruments, and depositary transactions.[31]

Registration of Exchanges

Another aspect of the jurisdictional dispute arose in connection with two commodities exchanges' challenge to SEC registration of a clearing agent for an electronic trading system for options on government securities.[32] The Seventh Circuit reversed the SEC order granting clearing agent registration for an agent of an electronic system for trading options on government securities.[33] However, the victory was short-

---

29. *See* Brady Rules Out any Compromise on SEC–CFTC Jurisdictional Dispute, 22 Sec.Reg. & L.Rep. (BNA) 1031 (July 13, 1990). *See also, e.g.*, Thomas A. Russo & Marlisa Vinciguerra, Financial Innovation and Uncertain Regulation: Selected Issues Regarding New Product Development, 69 Tex.L.Rev. 1431 (1991) (calling for unified regulation). In 1990, the President recommended transferring jurisdiction over stock index futures from the CFTC to the SEC. *See* 22 Sec. Reg. & L.Rep. (BNA) 731 (May 11, 1990). Proposals to coordinate CFTC and SEC regulation was contained in the Market Reform Act of 1990 (*see* S.Rep. on S. 648, Sen. Comm. on Banking, Housing & Urban Affairs, S.Rep. No. 101–300, 101st Cong., 2d Sess. (May 22, 1990)) but were not enacted. The Futures Trading Practices Act of 1991 as adopted by the Senate would take a functional approach in allocating jurisdiction between the CFTC and the SEC over hybrid investment vehicles. The bill would allocate jurisdiction to the CFTC if more than 50% of the overall value or expected change in value of the instrument is attributable to the commodity component. *See* Report on S. 207, Sen.Comm. on Agriculture, Nutrition and Forestry, Rep. No. 102–22, 102d Cong., 1st Sess. (March 12, 1991).

30. CFTC Regulations §§ 34.1–34.3, 17 C.F.R. §§ 34.1–34.3. *See* Statutory Interpretation Concerning Certain Hybrid Instruments, [1990–1992 Transfer Binder] Comm.Fut. L.Rep. (CCH) ¶ 24,805 (CFTC April 11, 1990).

The SEC has granted a temporary exemption from the broker-dealer registration requirements for persons acting as brokers or dealers with regard to certain over-the-counter derivative instruments. Order Exempting Certain Brokers and Dealers From Broker–Dealer Registration, Exch. Act Rel. No. 34–35135, [1994–1995 Transfer Binder] Fed.Sec.L.Rep. (CCH) ¶ 85,476 (SEC 1994). The qualifying derivatives are cash-settled debt options, swaps, and other related instruments. *See also, e.g.*, In the Matter of BT Securities Corporation, [1994–1995 Transfer Binder] Fed.Sec.L.Rep. (CCH) ¶ 85,477 (SEC 1994) (consent order) (treasury-linked swap contracts are options on securities and this subject to the securities laws but could qualify as an exempt government security under §§ 3(a)(12), 3(a)(42) of the Exchange Act).

31. *Id. See also, e.g.*, Interpretive Letter No. 90–2, [1987–1990 Transfer Binder] Comm.Fut.L.Rep. (CCH) ¶ 24,625 (CFTC March 2, 1990) (exempting hybrid instruments of foreign banks subject to regulatory supervision by the New York Banking Department).

32. The SEC has the responsibility for registering clearing agencies for exchanges. 15 U.S.C.A. § 78q–1. *See* § 10.13 *infra*.

33. Board of Trade of City of Chicago v. SEC, 883 F.2d 525 (7th Cir.1989), *appeal after remand* 923 F.2d 1270 (1991). It was contended that the registration as a clearing agent was improper since this in essence involved the SEC's recognition of an unregistered

lived. On remand, the SEC ruled that the agent did not have to register as a securities exchange and reaffirmed its earlier position that it could be registered as a clearing agent.[34] The Seventh Circuit upheld the Commission's ruling.[35]

§ 1.5   Definition of "Security"

What do the following have in common: scotch whiskey,[1] self-improvement courses,[2] cosmetics,[3] earthworms,[4] beavers,[5] muskrats,[6] rabbits,[7] chinchillas,[8] fishing boats,[9] vacuum cleaners,[10] cemetery lots,[11] cattle embryos,[12] master recording contracts,[13] animal feeding programs,[14]

---

securities exchange. The court agreed with the plaintiff's contention that the SEC first had to make a formal determination of whether the activity in question in fact involved operating as a securities exchange.

34. *See* 22 Sec.Reg. & L.Rep. (BNA) 56 (Jan. 12, 1990).

35. Board of Trade of City of Chicago v. SEC, 923 F.2d 1270 (7th Cir.1991).

§ 1.5

1. SEC v. Glen–Arden Commodities, Inc. [1973 Transfer Binder] Fed.Sec.L.Rep. (CCH) ¶ 94,142 (E.D.N.Y.1973); SEC v. M.A. Lundy Associates, 362 F.Supp. 226 (D.R.I.1973); SEC v. Haffenden–Rimar International, Inc., 362 F.Supp. 323 (E.D.Va.1973), *affirmed* 496 F.2d 1192 (4th Cir.1974).

2. SEC v. Glenn W. Turner Enterprises, Inc., 474 F.2d 476 (9th Cir.1973), *cert. denied* 414 U.S. 821, 94 S.Ct. 117, 38 L.Ed.2d 53 (1973).

3. SEC v. Koscot Interplanetary, Inc., 497 F.2d 473 (5th Cir.1974).

4. In re Worm World, Inc., 3 Blue Sky L.Rep. (CCH) ¶ 71,414 (S.D. Dept. of Commerce & Consumer Affairs 1978).

5. Continental Marketing Corp. v. SEC, 387 F.2d 466 (10th Cir.1967).

6. State v. Robbins, 185 Minn. 202, 240 N.W. 456 (1932).

7. Stevens v. Liberty Packing Corp., 111 N.J.Eq. 61, 161 A. 193 (1932).

8. SEC v. Chinchilla, Inc., Fed.Sec.L.Rep. (CCH) ¶ 90,618 (N.D.Ill.1953); Hollywood State Bank v. Wilde, 70 Cal.App.2d 103, 160 P.2d 846 (1945).

9. SEC v. Pyne, 33 F.Supp. 988 (D.Mass.1940). *But cf.* Deckebach v. La Vida Charters, Inc., 867 F.2d 278 (6th Cir.1989) (yacht purchase and management agreement lacked a horizontal common enterprise and thus was not a security).

10. Bell v. Health–Mor, Inc., 549 F.2d 342 (5th Cir.1977).

11. Holloway v. Thompson, 112 Ind.App. 229, 42 N.E.2d 421 (1942); In re Waldstein, 160 Misc. 763, 291 N.Y.S. 697 (1936). *But cf.* Memorial Gardens of the Valley v. Love, 5 Utah 2d 270, 300 P.2d 628 (1956) (burial lots not securities in absence of purchase for speculative investment).

12. *E.g.,* Eberhardt v. Waters, 901 F.2d 1578 (11th Cir.1990) (sale of cattle embryos was a security under Georgia blue sky law).

13. *E.g.,* Kolibash v. Sagittarius Recording Co., 626 F.Supp. 1173 (S.D.Ohio 1986). *But cf.* Faircloth v. Jackie Fine Arts, Inc., 682 F.Supp. 837 (D.S.C.1988), *affirmed in part, reversed in part on other grounds* 938 F.2d 513 (4th Cir.1991) (art master reproduction plates held not to be securities because of lack of dependence on the efforts of others); Routh v. Philatelic Leasing, Ltd., 1988 WL 161240, [1987–88 Transfer Binder] Fed.Sec. L.Rep. (CCH) ¶ 93,672 (E.D.Wash.1988) (lease of stamp masters held not to be a security because there was no common enterprise). *See also* the authorities cited in footnotes, 37–40, *infra.*

14. *E.g.,* Bailey v. J.W.K. Properties, Inc., 904 F.2d 918 (4th Cir.1990) (cattle breeding program was an investment contract and hence a security; investors had little or no control over breeding operations or success of investment).

pooled litigation funds,[15] and fruit trees?[16] The answer is that they have all been held to be securities within the meaning of federal or state securities statutes. The vast range of such unconventional investments that have fallen within the ambit of the securities laws' coverage is due to the broad statutory definition of a "security;" section 2(1) of the Securities Act of 1933 is representative:

> The term "security" means any note, stock, treasury stock, bond, debenture, evidence of indebtedness, certificate of interest or participation in any profit-sharing agreement, collateral-trust certificate, preorganization certificate or subscription, transferable share, investment contract, voting-trust certificate, certificate of deposit for a security, fractional undivided interest in oil, gas, or other mineral rights, any put, call, straddle, option, or privilege on any security, certificate of deposit, or group or index of securities (including any interest therein or based on the value thereof), or any put, call, straddle, option, or privilege entered into on a national securities exchange relating to foreign currency, or, in general, any interest or instrument commonly known as a "security", or any certificate of interest or participation in, temporary or interim certificate for, receipt for, guarantee of, or warrant or right to subscribe to or purchase, any of the foregoing.[17]

In determining the basic coverage of the securities laws, the slightly different definitions of a security in the 1933 and 1934 Acts[18] are to be treated as "virtually identical," according to the Supreme Court.[19] The statutory language is expansive and has been interpreted accordingly. The broadly drafted statutory definition has continued to give the courts problems in providing predictable guidelines.[20] Nevertheless, an attor-

---

15. B.J. Tannenbaum, Jr., 18 Sec.Reg. & L.Rep. (BNA) 1826 (SEC No Action Letter Dec. 4, 1986). *Cf.* Driscoll v. Schuttler, 697 F.Supp. 1195 (N.D.Ga.1988) (release of investors' securities fraud claims was not a security). *But cf.* Fibreboard Corp., 20 Sec.Reg.L.Rep. (BNA) 1426 (SEC No Action Letter avail. Aug. 31, 1988) (settlement agreement was not a security).

16. *E.g.,* SEC v. W.J. Howey Co., 328 U.S. 293, 66 S.Ct. 1100, 90 L.Ed. 1244 (1946); SEC v. Tung Corp. of America, 32 F.Supp. 371 (N.D.Ill.1940).

17. 15 U.S.C.A. § 77b(1). *See also, e.g.,* 15 U.S.C.A. § 78c(a)(10) (1976); Unif.Sec.Act § 401(e). The 1982 amendments to the federal act adding stock options are not retroactive. LTV Federal Credit Union v. UMIC Government Securities, Inc., 704 F.2d 199 (5th Cir.1983).

18. For example, the 1934 Act excludes short term commercial paper from the definition. Section 3(a)(10), 15 U.S.C.A. § 78c(a)(10). In contrast, although included in the 1933 Act's definition of security, short term commercial paper is exempt from that Act's registration requirements. Sections 2(1), 3(a)(3), 15 U.S.C.A. §§ 77a(1), 77c(a)(3).

19. Tcherepnin v. Knight, 389 U.S. 332, 335, 88 S.Ct. 548, 552, 19 L.Ed.2d 564 (1967).

20. *See generally* Thomas Arnold, "When is a Car a Bicycle?" and Other Riddles: The Definition of a Security Under the Federal Securities Laws, 33 Clev.St.L.Rev. 449 (1984); William J. Carney, Defining a Security: The Addition of a Market–Oriented Contextual Approach to Investment Contract Analysis, 33 Emory L.J. 311 (1984); Williamson B.C. Chang, Meaning, Reference and Reification in the Definition of a Security, 19 U.C.D.L.Rev. 403 (1986); Corgill, Securities as Investments at Risk, 67 Tul.L.Rev. 861 (1993); Arnold S. Jacobs, The Meaning of "Security" Under Rule 10b–5, 29 N.Y.L. Sch.L.Rev. 211 (1984); Lewis D Lowenfels & Alan R. Bromberg, What is a Security Under the Federal Securities Laws?, 56 Alb.L.Rev. 473 (1993); Lawrence F. Orbe III, A Security: The Quest for a

ney's failure to advise a client of the possibility of an investment offering being classified as a security can constitute legal malpractice.[21]   Notwithstanding the broad statutory definition, not every fraud based on the payment of money is a security.[22]

In deciding whether a particular investment vehicle is a security, a number of generalizations can be made.   The investors' perceptions and expectations will be a significant factor.[23]   Thus, if the investment is marketed by a securities broker, it is more likely to fall under the securities laws.[24]   In a close case, the existence of a parallel regulatory scheme may lead to the court to find that the securities laws are not necessary for investor protection.[25]   It must be remembered, however, that the existence of a parallel regulatory scheme will not preclude a finding of a security; it simply may tip the balance in a case that is very close to the margins.   The courts have used various tests for determining whether a security exists.

This section will begin by discussing the evolution of the judicial approach to defining a security.   This is followed by specific application of the definition to various activities: leasing programs, benefit plans and annuities, real estate, stock, notes, commodities, managed accounts, and partnerships.   The section concludes with a discussion of the "risk capital" test of what constitutes a security.

Judicial Interpretation of "Investment Contract"

The judicial definition of security has developed primarily from interpretation of the statutory phrase "investment contract."   With the lead of the Supreme Court, federal and state courts have strived to arrive at a workable definition and have formulated various tests and approaches.   Throughout the history of struggling for an appropriate definition, courts have been mindful of the fact that the bottom-line question is whether the particular investment or instrument involved is

---

Definition, 12 Sec.Reg.L.J. 220 (1984); Marc I. Steinberg & William E. Kaulbach, The Supreme Court and the Definition of "Security": The "Context" Clause, "Investment Contract" Analysis, and Their Ramifications, 40 Vand.L.Rev. 489 (1987).

21.   Popham, Haik, Schnobrich, Kaufman & Doty, Ltd. v. Newcomb Securities Co., 751 F.2d 1262 (D.C.Cir.1985).

22.   *E.g.* Deckebach v. La Vida Charters, Inc. of Florida, 867 F.2d 278 (6th Cir.1989) (purchase of yacht for charter was not a security); Morgan v. Financial Planning Advisors, Inc., 701 F.Supp. 923 (D.Mass.1988) (rare coins were not securities); United States v. Jones, 648 F.Supp. 225 (S.D.N.Y.1986) ("pigeon drop" scheme not a security).

23.   *E.g.,* Reves v. Ernst & Young, 494 U.S. 56, 110 S.Ct. 945, 108 L.Ed.2d 47 (1990) (short-term notes were securities); *see* discussion *infra* at footnotes 94–118.

24.   *E.g.,* Pollack v. Laidlaw Holdings, Inc., 27 F.3d 808 (2d Cir.1994) (mortgage participations sold by securities broker were securities).

25.   Reves v. Ernst & Young, 494 U.S. 56, 110 S.Ct. 945, 108 L.Ed.2d 47 (1990) (explicitly identifying this as a factor in determining whether a note can be excluded as short-term commercial paper); Marine Bank v. Weaver, 455 U.S. 551, 102 S.Ct. 1220, 71 L.Ed.2d 409 (1982) (bank-issued certificate of deposit not a security subject to federal securities laws since it is already federally insured and purchasers therefore do not need that extra layer of protection the laws afford).

one that needs or demands the investor protection of the federal (or state) securities laws.[26]

In its first pronouncement on this issue, the United States Supreme Court focused on the general character of the investment vehicle in question.[27] Specifically, the Court looked to (1) the terms of the offer, (2) the plan of distribution, and (3) the economic inducements that were held out to the prospective purchaser. Just three years later, the Court in SEC v. W.J. Howey Co.[28] announced: "An investment contract for purposes of the Securities Act means a contract, transaction or scheme whereby a person [1] invests his money [2] in a common enterprise and [3] is led to expect profits [4] solely from the efforts of the promoter or a third party." This case arose from the promotion of small lots of fruit trees when the offeror also offered a "management" contract by which an affiliate of the issuer would pick and market the fruit with the profit inuring to the investor. In finding the promotional scheme to be a security, the Court pointed out that not only are formal stock certificates not required, but a nominal interest in the physical assets of the enterprise, such as actually owning fruit trees, does not preclude the determination that a security in fact exists. The Court did not present any single determinative factor but rather looked to the investment package as a whole including the ways in which the investment was marketed. This aspect of the decision is most significant since a reading of all of the relevant cases leads to the conclusion that what is being offered may not be as important as how it is being presented.

From the Efforts of Others. Under recent refinements to what has come to be known as the *Howey* test, the requirement that the profits be secured "solely" from the efforts of others has been diluted to one that the profits come "primarily" or "substantially" from the efforts of others.[29] However, where the investor's efforts are significant in the success of the enterprise, an investment contract (and hence a security) will not be found to exist.[30] Nevertheless, the fact that *some* efforts of

---

26. Marine Bank v. Weaver, 455 U.S. 551, 102 S.Ct. 1220, 71 L.Ed.2d 409 (1982) (bank-issued certificate of deposit not a security subject to federal securities laws since it is already federally insured and purchasers therefore do not need that extra layer of protection the laws afford). *But cf.* Pollack v. Laidlaw Holdings, Inc., 27 F.3d 808 (2d Cir.1994) (state mortgage regulation was not adequate parallel).

27. SEC v. C.M. Joiner Leasing Corp., 320 U.S. 344, 64 S.Ct. 120, 88 L.Ed. 88 (1943).

28. 328 U.S. 293, 298–99, 66 S.Ct. 1100, 1102–03, 90 L.Ed. 1244 (1946).

29. *See, e.g.,* SEC v. Glenn W. Turner Enterprises, Inc., 474 F.2d 476 (9th Cir.1973), *cert. denied* 414 U.S. 821, 94 S.Ct. 117, 38 L.Ed.2d 53 (1973); SEC v. Koscot Interplanetary, Inc., 497 F.2d 473 (5th Cir.1974). *See also, e.g.,* SEC v. International Loan Network, Inc., 968 F.2d 1304 (D.C.Cir.1992) (memberships entitling members to receive fees upon recruitment of new members were securities).

30. *E.g.,* Stewart v. Ragland, 934 F.2d 1033 (9th Cir.1991) (interest in oil and gas wells was not a security where knowledgeable and sophisticated investors had several opportunities to control operation of drilling operations); In re Tucker Freight Lines, Inc., 789 F.Supp. 884 (W.D.Mich.1991) (wage deferral contracts were not securities).

the investor are necessary for the success of the operation, such as with pyramid sales arrangements,[31] licensing agreements,[32] founder-membership contracts and customer referral agreements,[33] including those denominated, at least in form, as franchise contracts,[34] does not change the scheme's character from that of an investment contract. It is clear, however, that a bona fide franchise agreement is not a security.[35] Similarly, a contract to provide bona fide services is not the sale of a security.[36] However, a security exists when a so-called service involves a common enterprise in addition to a significant investment risk and the promoter's efforts are necessary to make the investment a success.[37]

Common Enterprise. Another factor under the *Howey* test that has undergone subsequent scrutiny is the requirement that there be a common enterprise. The common enterprise requirement focuses on the question of the extent to which the success of the investor's interest rises and falls with others involved in the enterprise.[38] Courts have developed the concept of "horizontal commonality" to describe the pooling of like interests among investors in contrast to "vertical commonality" where

31. *E.g.,* SEC v. Glenn W. Turner Enterprises, Inc., 474 F.2d 476 (9th Cir.1973), *cert. denied* 414 U.S. 821, 94 S.Ct. 117, 38 L.Ed.2d 53 (1973); SEC v. Koscot Interplanetary, Inc., 497 F.2d 473 (5th Cir.1974). *See also, e.g.,* SEC v. International Loan Network, Inc., 968 F.2d 1304 (D.C.Cir.1992) (interests in investment club were part of pyramid scheme and thus were securities).

32. SEC v. Aqua–Sonic Products Corp., 524 F.Supp. 866 (S.D.N.Y.1981).

33. *See, e.g.,* Florida Discount Centers, Inc. v. Antinori, 232 So.2d 17 (Fla.1970); Hawaii v. Hawaii Market Center, Inc., 52 Hawaii 642, 485 P.2d 105 (1971). *But see, e.g.,* Gallion v. Alabama Market Centers, Inc., 282 Ala. 679, 213 So.2d 841 (1968); Georgia Market Centers, Inc. v. Fortson, 225 Ga. 854, 171 S.E.2d 620 (1969).

34. *See* Mitzner v. Cardet International, Inc., 358 F.Supp. 1262 (N.D.Ill.1973).

35. *E.g.,* Martin v. T.V. Tempo, Inc., 628 F.2d 887 (5th Cir.1980); Nash & Associates, Inc. v. Lum's of Ohio, Inc., 484 F.2d 392 (6th Cir.1973); Gotham Print, Inc. v. American Speedy Printing Centers, Inc., 863 F.Supp. 447 (E.D.Mich.1994) (franchise agreement was not an "investment contract"). *But cf.* SEC v. Aqua–Sonic Products Corp., 687 F.2d 577 (2d Cir.1982) (licenses to sell dental devices held to be securities).

36. Broadview Financial, Inc. v. Entech Management Services Corp., 859 F.Supp. 444, 450–51 (D.Colo.1994) (agreement under which investment banker would render services to facilitate a merger was not a security); Ripplemeyer v. National Grape Cooperative Association, 807 F.Supp. 1439 (W.D.Ark.1992) (marketing agreements were not securities); GBJ Corp. v. Sequa Corp., 804 F.Supp. 564 (S.D.N.Y.1992) (consulting agreement is not a security).

37. *E.g.,* SEC v. Comcoa, Ltd., 855 F.Supp. 1258 (S.D.Fla.1994). In *Comcoa,* the promoter was offering an application service designed to aid clients in obtaining FCC license. The client invested $7,000 per license and had to act within eight months of issuance or forfeit the investment. The court found it significant that the clients solicited by the promoter generally did not have the technical skills necessary to assure the success of the license and thus would be dependent upon the promoter's efforts. Further, the court found that vertical commonality was sufficient to satisfy the common enterprise requirement.

38. *See, e.g.,* SEC v. Eurobond Exchange, Ltd., 13 F.3d 1334 (9th Cir.1994) (finding common enterprise sufficient to make Eurobond investment program a security); In the Matter of ABC Portfolio Development Group, Inc., [1994–1995 Transfer Binder] Fed. Sec. L. Rep. (CCH) ¶ 85,422 (SEC 1994) (sales of investment pool interests were sales of interests in an investment company subject to the Investment company Act of 1940 and also were securities subject to the 1933 and 1934 Acts).

the promoter shares risk with the investor.[39] Horizontal commonality clearly satisfies the *Howey* common enterprise requirement but the courts are divided as to whether vertical commonality will suffice.[40] However, it is equally clear that when there is no common enterprise, the *Howey* test will not be satisfied.[41]

The cases examining whether vertical commonality will suffice have taken varying approaches. The Fifth Circuit has adopted a broad test of vertical commonality that is satisfied by a showing that the fortunes of the investor are inextricably tied to the promoter's efforts.[42] The broad approach to vertical commonality merely requires that the success of the investment be linked to the *efforts* of the promoter.[43] In contrast, the narrower test of vertical commonality requires that the investor's fortunes be tied to the *fortunes* of the promoter.[44] A number of courts have utilized the narrow view to find that managed commodities accounts are not securities.[45] The Ninth Circuit similarly has adopted a narrow test

---

39. Many of the cases involving horizontal and vertical commonality arose in the context of deciding whether a managed brokerage account is a security. *See* text accompanying footnotes 123–42 *infra*.

40. *Ibid.* Vale Natural Gas America Corp. v. Carrollton Resources 1990, Ltd., 795 F.Supp. 795 (E.D.La.1992).

Investment program that contemplated a pooling of investors' funds satisfied the horizontal commonality requirement, even though there ended up being only one investor. SEC v. Lauer, 52 F.3d 667 (7th Cir.1995), affirming 864 F.Supp. 784 (N.D.Ill.1994).

41. *See, e.g.*, V.F. Associates, Inc. v. Reissman, 1991 WL 49733, [1990–1991 Transfer Binder] Fed.Sec.L.Rep. (CCH) ¶ 95,917 (E.D.Pa.1991), *appeal dismissed* 958 F.2d 366 (3d Cir.1992) (agreement concerning compensation of agent selling life insurance policies to financial planning clients was not a security since it was not an agreement made between a number of passive investors but rather was negotiated by each of the parties individually).

42. This broad test has been rejected by other courts. Schofield v. First Commodity Corp., 638 F.Supp. 4 (D.Mass.1985), *judgment affirmed* 793 F.2d 28 (1st Cir.1986); Mechigian v. Art Capital Corp., 612 F.Supp. 1421, 1427 (S.D.N.Y.1985). *Accord* Silverstein v. Merrill Lynch, Pierce, Fenner & Smith, Inc., 618 F.Supp. 436 (S.D.N.Y.1985). *See also, e.g.*, Vale Natural Gas America Corp. v. Carrollton Resources 1990, Ltd., 795 F.Supp. 795 (E.D.La.1992) (finding sufficient vertical commonality between promoter of oil and gas leases and sole investor).

See also McGill v. American Land & Exploration Co., 776 F.2d 923, 924–25 (10th Cir.1985) (finding vertical commonality sufficient with regard to joint venture and that lack of horizontal commonality with other investors did not preclude a finding of a security).

43. Revak v. SEC Realty Corp., 18 F.3d 81, 87–88 (2d Cir.1994), *relying on* Long v. Shultz Cattle Co., 881 F.2d 129, 140–41 (5th Cir.1989); SEC v. Comcoa, Ltd., 855 F.Supp. 1258 (S.D.Fla.1994) (finding vertical commonality with regard to service to assist application and development of FCC licenses; *see* footnote 37 *supra*).

44. Revak v. SEC Realty Corp., 18 F.3d 81, 88 (2d Cir.1994) (holding that interests in a condominium were not securities); Mechigian v. Art Capital Corp., 612 F.Supp. 1421, 1427 (S.D.N.Y.1985) ("the investment manager's fortunes rise and fall with those of the investor" and finding this test of vertical commonality not to be satisfied in connection with the sale of original artworks).

45. Mordaunt v. Incomco, 686 F.2d 815 (9th Cir.1982), *cert. denied* 469 U.S. 1115, 105 S.Ct. 801, 83 L.Ed.2d 793 (1985); Brodt v. Bache & Co., Inc., 595 F.2d 459 (9th Cir.1978); Milnarik v. M–S Commodities, Inc., 457 F.2d 274 (7th Cir.1972), *cert. denied* 409 U.S. 887, 93 S.Ct. 113, 34 L.Ed.2d 144 (1972); Pophan, Haik, Schnobrich, Kaufman & Dory, Ltd. v. Price, 1984 WL 2395, [1983–1984 Transfer Binder] Fed.Sec.L.Rep. (CCH) ¶ 99,682 (D.D.C. 1984); Wasnowic v. Chicago Board of Trade, 352 F.Supp. 1066 (M.D.Pa.1972), *affirmed mem.* 491 F.2d 752 (3d Cir.1973), *cert. denied* 416 U.S. 994, 94 S.Ct. 2407, 40 L.Ed.2d 773

of vertical commonality to find no security in the case of a coal purchase program the success of which was dependent upon the defendant's unique ore processing technique.[46] In addition, the Second Circuit has held that the absence of strict vertical commonality precluded a condominium interest from being a security.[47]

The general principles of the *Howey* investment contract analysis set forth broad guidelines as to when a security will be found to exist. Many of the cases are best understood not only in terms of the general principles but in the context of the particular type of investment involved. Accordingly, the discussion that follows addresses various types of investment vehicles which have been held to be securities.

Leasing Programs as Securities

A number of decisions have found that interests in leases of master video and audio recordings are investment contracts and thus have held that they are securities under both federal and state law.[48] Similarly, a video production program has been held to be a security.[49] However, when the leasing program lacks a common enterprise[50] or is dependent upon the investor's managerial efforts,[51] a security will not be found to exist. A similar arrangement which may have securities law implications is an equipment leasing program wherein the investor purchases

(1974). Managed commodities account are discussed in the text accompanying footnotes 23–42 *infra*.

46. SEC v. Goldfield Deep Mines Co., 758 F.2d 459 (9th Cir.1985).

47. Revak v. SEC Realty Corp., 18 F.3d 81 (2d Cir.1994). *See also, e.g.,* Secon Service System, Inc. v. St. Joseph Bank & Trust Co., 855 F.2d 406 (7th Cir.1988) (payments in exchange for operating authority lacked a common enterprise and thus were not securities). *Cf.* Deckebach v. La Vida Charters, Inc., 867 F.2d 278 (6th Cir.1989) (yacht purchase and management agreement was not a security due to absence of horizontal commonality).

48. Kolibash v. Sagittarius Recording Co., 626 F.Supp. 1173 (S.D.Ohio 1986) (holding that promised tax benefits satisfied the requirement that there be an expectation of a profit); Hirt v. UM Leasing Corp., 614 F.Supp. 1066 (D.Neb.1985); Sullivan v. Metro Productions, Inc., 150 Ariz. 573, 724 P.2d 1242 (App.1986), *cert. denied* 479 U.S. 1102, 107 S.Ct. 1334, 94 L.Ed.2d 185 (1987) (applying Arizona blue sky law); Freeman v. Campbell, 17 Sec.Reg. & L.Rep. (BNA) 1406 (S.C.Ct.Comm.Pl. July 6, 1985).

49. Nottingham v. General American Communications Corp., 811 F.2d 873 (5th Cir. 1987). *See also, e.g.,* Davis v. Metro Productions, Inc., 885 F.2d 515 (9th Cir.1989) (sale of master videotapes held to be the sale of a security under Arizona blue sky law). *But see* Mace Neufeld Productions, Inc. v. Orion Pictures Corp., 860 F.2d 944 (9th Cir.1988).

50. *See* Routh v. Philatelic Leasing, Ltd., 1988 WL 161240, [1987–88 Transfer Binder] Fed.Sec.L.Rep. (CCH) ¶ 93,672 (E.D.Wash.1988) (lease of stamp masters held not to be a security because there was no common enterprise). *See also, e.g.,* Nakagawa v. Ellis & Ellis Assoc., 1986 WL 36294, [1986–87 Transfer Binder] Fed.Sec.L.Rep. (CCH) ¶ 93,028 (D.Haw.1986) (lease not a security because of absence of a common enterprise); Cahill v. Contemporary Perspectives, Inc., 1986 WL 4696, [1986 Transfer Binder] Fed.Sec.L.Rep. (CCH) ¶ 92,720 (S.D.N.Y.1986) (tax shelter based on sale of films and title for children's books held not a security). *See also, e.g.,* Newmyer v. Philatelic Leasing, Ltd., 888 F.2d 385 (6th Cir.1989), *cert. denied* 495 U.S. 930, 110 S.Ct. 2169, 109 L.Ed.2d 499 (1990) (material questions of fact existed as to whether leases of master stamp plates were securities).

51. *See* Faircloth v. Jackie Fine Arts, Inc., 682 F.Supp. 837 (D.S.C.1988), *affirmed in part, reversed in part* 938 F.2d 513 (4th Cir.1991) (art master reproduction plates held not to be securities because of lack of dependence on the efforts of others).

equipment for lease to someone else.[52]   Many of these programs have
been marketed as tax shelters.[53]   A related issue which has arisen in
connection with tax shelters (as well as other types of investments) is
whether a call for additional payment by a limited partner constitutes an
offer of a new security.   The cases generally hold that when the investor
has an option not to make the additional investment, he or she is making
an investment decision and thus there is a sale of a security.[54]   However,
when the subsequent payments are not a result of a separate investment
decision, there is no sale.[55]

Benefit Plans and Annuities as Securities

The *Howey* test has been refined to require that there be a significant investment of money (or other valuable consideration) with the
expectation of a profit in order to find an investment scheme subject to
federal securities laws.   In International Brotherhood of Teamsters v.
Daniel,[56] the Supreme Court ruled that a compulsory noncontributory
defined benefit employee pension plan is not a security under the 1933
Act's definition.   The Court made note of not only the involuntary
nature of the plan, but also the fact that there was no employee
contribution (*i.e.*, no investment of money); these factors strongly negated any inference that a security was involved.   The Court also noted that
insofar as it was faced with a defined benefit plan, the pay-out to the
employee upon retirement bore no relation to the employee's contribution in terms of time in service.   Another factor considered by the *Daniel*
Court was that there was no substantial expectation of a profit.   Since a
large part of the eventual retirement benefits were to be derived from
the employer's contribution, rather than from the reinvestment income
derived from the efforts of pension plan managers, the profit aspects of
the plan were too insubstantial to fall within the concept of an investment contract.   Moreover, the Court focused on a number of contingencies to the plan's vesting which in turn rendered any "profit" too
speculative to justify a reasonable expectation.   Because of the multiplic-

52.   *See, e.g.,* Albanese v. Florida National Bank of Orlando, 823 F.2d 408 (11th
Cir.1987) (investor control over transactions was "illusory", hence equipment lease was a
security).

53.   *See, e.g.,* Kolibash v. Sagittarius Recording Co., 626 F.Supp. 1173 (S.D.Ohio 1986)
(holding that promised tax benefits satisfied the requirement that there be an expectation
of a profit).   *But see* Meade v. Weber, 647 F.Supp. 954 (E.D.La.1986) (a decision which
seems to be incorrect but may be based on the plaintiff's failure to plead fraud with
sufficient specificity).

54.   *E.g.,* Hill v. Equitable Bank, N.A., Ass'n, 599 F.Supp. 1062 (D.Del.1984) (additional
contribution was a sale of a security since investor had the option of dissolution).   *See*
§ 5.4 *infra.*

55.   *E.g.,* Stewart v. Germany, 631 F.Supp. 236 (S.D.Miss.1986) (cash contributions
after initial investment did not constitute separate sales of securities); Bourdages v. Metals
Refining Ltd., 1984 WL 1209, [1984 Transfer Binder] Fed.Sec.L.Rep. (CCH) ¶ 91,828
(S.D.N.Y.1984) (capital call was not the purchase of a new security since investor had no
choice and thus was not asked to make an investment decision).

56.   439 U.S. 551, 99 S.Ct. 790, 58 L.Ed.2d 808 (1979).   *Accord* Coward v. Colgate–
Palmolive Co., 686 F.2d 1230 (7th Cir.1982).   *See also* Childers v. Northwest Airlines, Inc.,
688 F.Supp. 1357, 20 Sec.Reg. & L.Rep. (BNA) 1166 (D.Minn.1988) (ESOP was not a
security).

ity of factors involved in the *Daniel* decision, it cannot be safely said that no pension plan will ever be characterized as security.[57] In fact, benefit plans that have the investment characteristics of securities will fall under the Act. For example, a voluntary contributory plan with a variable annuity might well be found to be subject to the securities laws.[58] Similarly, interests in a voluntary employee stock option plan clearly are securities.[59]

While variable annuity contracts come within the ambit of the securities laws,[60] fixed annuities, as is the case with insurance policies, generally do not.[61] However, the Seventh Circuit held an annuity with a

57. *See* Ronald C. Stansbury & Joel K. Bedol, Interests in Employee Benefit Plans as Securities: *Daniel* and Beyond, 8 Sec.Reg.L.J. 226 (1980); *See also, e.g.,* Timothy Tomlinson, Securities Regulation of Employee Stock Ownership Plans: A Comparison of SEC Policy and Congressional Intent, 31 Stan.L.Rev. 121 (1978). *See also* Foltz v. U.S. News & World Report, Inc., 627 F.Supp. 1143 (D.D.C.1986) (where a security was found to exist with regard to a stock bonus plan pursuant to which voting trust certificates were convertible into stock if at termination of employment issuer refused to repurchase the stock represented by the voting trust certificate). *Compare* Childers v. Northwest Airlines, Inc., 688 F.Supp. 1357 (D.Minn.1988) (compulsory, noncontributory employee stock ownership plan was an incident of employment and hence not a security).

58. *Cf.* SEC v. Variable Annuity Life Insurance Co., 359 U.S. 65, 79 S.Ct. 618, 3 L.Ed.2d 640 (1959) (variable annuity held to be a non-exempt security). *See also,* SEC v. United Benefit Life Insurance Co., 387 U.S. 202, 87 S.Ct. 1557, 18 L.Ed.2d 673 (1967) (flexible fund annuity held not an exempt annuity); § 4.9 *infra.*

59. *E.g.,* Uselton v. Commercial Lovelace Motor Freight, Inc., 940 F.2d 564 (10th Cir.1991), *cert. denied* 502 U.S. 983, 112 S.Ct. 589, 116 L.Ed.2d 614 (1991) (contributory voluntary employee stock ownership plan was a security; ERISA did not provide sufficient protection to displace the application of federal securities laws); Hood v. Smith's Transfer Corp., 762 F.Supp. 1274, 1290–1291 (W.D.Ky.1991).

60. *See, e.g.,* SEC v. Variable Annuity Life Insurance Co., 359 U.S. 65, 79 S.Ct. 618, 3 L.Ed.2d 640 (1959) (variable annuity held to be a non-exempt security). *See also,* SEC v. United Benefit Life Insurance Co., 387 U.S. 202, 87 S.Ct. 1557, 18 L.Ed.2d 673 (1967) (flexible fund annuity held not an exempt annuity); Associates in Adolescent Psychiatry, S.C. v. Home Life Insurance Co., 941 F.2d 561 (7th Cir.1991), *cert. denied* 502 U.S. 1099, 112 S.Ct. 1182, 117 L.Ed.2d 426 (1992) (categorizing a mutual fund an "annuity" will take it out of the ambit of the securities laws). *Cf.* Equitable Variable Life Insurance Co., 21 Sec.Reg. & L.Rep. (BNA) 1426 (SEC No Action Letter available Aug. 9, 1989) (refusing no action relief with regard to Investment Company Act Rules 6c–3 and 6e–3 for variable life insurance policies); Legal Opinion Letter No. 331, 17 Sec.Reg. & L.Rep. (BNA) 893 (Comptroller of the Currency Legal Opinion Letter 1985) (variable annuity contract is a security).

Although a variable annuity is a security, they may, under appropriate circumstances be offered by banks. According to the Comptroller of the Currency, brokering and offering variable annuities to banking customers is an incidental power needed to carry on the business of banking. Nationsbank of North Carolina, N.A. v. Variable Annuity Life Insurance Co., ___ U.S. ___, 115 S.Ct. 810, 130 L.Ed.2d 740 (1995). *See* § 19.5 *infra* for a discussion of the jurisdictional issues relating to banks and securities.

61. Associates in Adolescent Psychiatry, S.C. v. Home Life Insurance Co. of New York, 729 F.Supp. 1162 (N.D.Ill.1989), *affirmed* 941 F.2d 561 (7th Cir.1991), *cert. denied* ___ U.S. ___, 112 S.Ct. 1182, 117 L.Ed.2d 426 (1992) (insurance contracts used to fund defined benefit, defined contribution employee plan held not to be securities); Dryden v. Sun Life Assurance Co. of Canada, 737 F.Supp. 1058 (S.D.Ind.1989), *affirmed without opinion* 909 F.2d 1486 (7th Cir.1990) (insurer's whole life policies were not securities); Otto v. Variable Annuity Life Insurance Co., 611 F.Supp. 83 (N.D.Ill.1985), *reversed* 814 F.2d 1127 (7th Cir.1986). The *Otto* decision was distinguished in Associates in Adolescent Psychiatry, S.C. v. Home Life Insurance Co. of New York, 729 F.Supp. 1162 (N.D.Ill.1989), *affirmed* 941 F.2d 561 (7th Cir.1991), *cert. denied* ___ U.S. ___, 112 S.Ct. 1182, 117 L.Ed.2d 426 (1992),

minimum guarantee to be a security.[62] The Commission has adopted a safe harbor rule under which qualifying annuities with guaranteed purchase benefits based on the purchase price and interest credited thereto, provided further that the annuity contracts are not marketed as investments need not be registered as securities.[63] The safe harbor thus depends on the investment risk falling on the insurer rather than the insured.

Real Estate Interests as Securities

In a decision that predated *Daniel*, the Supreme Court, in United Housing Foundation, Inc. v. Forman, ruled that shares of stock in a cooperative residential housing project did not fall within the Securities Act's definition.[64] Although "stock" is expressly included in the Act's definition of security, the fact that the shares were denominated as stock by the corporation was not considered dispositive of the matter since the shares had none of the traditional characteristics which stocks generally possess.[65] The Court upheld substance over form and focused upon the economic reality of the investment venture. The Court distinguished resort condominium cases in which someone might well be induced to purchase the property primarily for investment,[66] since the buildings in question were used as bona fide primary residences. Although the other criteria of the four-factor *Howey* test may have been met, there was no expectation of a profit, despite promised rent deductions through profits rebated from commercial leasing. The Court found that this "return" on the commercial properties was, at best, tangential to the stock and

which held that insurance contracts used to fund defined benefit, defined contribution employee plan were not securities.

Even if a fixed annuity were found to satisfy the investment contract test so as to constitute a security, it would qualify for an exemption from the 1933 Act's registration requirements. 15 U.S.C.A. § 77c(a)(8) which is discussed in § 4.9 *infra*. *See* SKJ Commodities Corp., [1987–88 Transfer Binder] Fed.Sec.L.Rep. (CCH) ¶ 78,675 (SEC No Action Letter November 3, 1987).

62. Otto v. Variable Annuity Life Ins. Co., 814 F.2d 1127 (7th Cir.1986) (the court noted that the minimum was low and there was an expectation of a higher payout).

63. 17 C.F.R. § 230.151. *See* § 4.9 *infra*.

64. 421 U.S. 837, 95 S.Ct. 2051, 44 L.Ed.2d 621 (1975). *Accord* Hackford v. First Security Bank of Utah, 464 U.S. 827, 104 S.Ct. 100, 78 L.Ed.2d 105 (1983) (shares of "stock" in range land entitling owners to grazing privileges held not a security since there was no profit expectation).

65. "Despite their name, they lack what the court in Tcherepnin deemed the most common feature of stock: the right to receive 'dividends contingent upon an apportionment of profits'. 389 U.S. at 339. Nor do they possess the other characteristics traditionally associated with stock: they are not negotiable; they cannot be pledged or hypothecated; they confer no voting rights in proportion to the number of shares owned; and they cannot appreciate in value." 421 U.S. at 851, 95 S.Ct. at 2060.

66. *See, e.g.*, Aldrich v. McCulloch Properties, Inc., 627 F.2d 1036 (10th Cir.1980); Robert D. Rosenbaum, The Resort Condominium and The Federal Securities Laws—A Case Study in Governmental Inflexibility, 60 Va.L.Rev. 785 (1974); Annot., What Interests in Real Estate are "Securities" Within Meaning of § 3(a)(10) of Securities Exchange Act of 1934, 52 A.L.R.Fed. 146 (1981). *See also, e.g.*, Williamson v. Tucker, 645 F.2d 404 (5th Cir.1981) (real estate joint venture).

thus the residential lease agreements were properly characterized as residential housing contracts rather than as investment contracts.[67]

Generally, a conveyance of real estate will not be subject to the securities laws.[68] Thus, for example, a condominium interest will not ordinarily be a security.[69] However, when a transaction has the investment type indicia normally associated with investment contracts a security may be found to exist.[70] Thus, for example, a security will exist where condominium interests are marketed with collateral agreements giving rise to a profit expectation.[71] Similarly, the currently fashionable marketing of real estate interests through time-share or shared equity programs raises securities law issues because of the possibility of finding

67. 421 U.S. at 855–58, 95 S.Ct. at 2061–63. *See* Hackford v. First Security Bank of Utah, [1983–1984 Transfer Binder] Fed.Sec.L.Rep. (CCH) ¶ 99,402 (10th Cir.1983) (shares of stock entitling owners to grazing privileges held not a security). *See* C.N.S. Enterprises, Inc. v. G. & G. Enterprises, Inc., 508 F.2d 1354 (7th Cir.1975), *cert. denied* 423 U.S. 825, 96 S.Ct. 38, 46 L.Ed.2d 40 (1975) (discussing the commercial investment distinction governing the characterization of short term notes as securities); People v. Syde, 37 Cal.2d 765, 235 P.2d 601 (1951) (discussing the service contract/investment contract distinction). *But see* Exchange National Bank of Chicago v. Touche Ross & Co., 544 F.2d 1126 (2d Cir.1976) (favoring a literalist approach over the commercial investment distinction). *See also, e.g.,* Kaye v. Pawnee Construction Co., 680 F.2d 1360, 1366 (11th Cir.1982) (short term note held not a security).

68. *E.g.,* Wals v. Fox Hills Development Corp., 24 F.3d 1016 (7th Cir.1994) (sale of time share unit was not sale of a security).

See generally David M. Fields, Real Estate Interests as Investment Contracts: An Update and a New Application—The Shared Equity Program, 12 Real Est. L.J. 307 (1984). *See also, e.g.* Robert C. Art, Sell a Condominium, Buy a Securities Law Suit: Unwarranted Liabilities in The Secondary Market, 53 Ohio St.L.J. 413 (1992).

Cf. In re National Mortgage Equity Corp. Mortgage Pool Certificates Securities Litigation, 723 F.Supp. 497 (C.D.Cal.1989) (pooled mortgage agreements were not securities); In re EPIC Mortgage Insurance Litigation, 701 F.Supp. 1192 (E.D.Va.1988), *affirmed without opinion* 910 F.2d 118 (4th Cir.1990) (pass through mortgage certificate was not a security). *But see, e.g.,* Zolfaghari v. Sheikholeslami, 943 F.2d 451 (4th Cir.1991) (although individual mortgage is not a security, mortgage pools can be securities; whether the pool is a security is a question of fact).

69. Revak v. SEC Realty Corp., 18 F.3d 81 (2d Cir.1994) (condominium interest was not an investment contract and hence not a security); Pliskin v. Bruno, 838 F.Supp. 658 (D.Me.1993) (same). *See also, e.g.,* Rolo v. City Investing Co. Liquidating Trust, 845 F.Supp. 182 (D.N.J.1993) (contracts to purchase lot and house were not securities; accompanying mortgage notes were not securities). *Compare, e.g.,* Adams v. Hyannis Harborview, Inc., 838 F.Supp. 676 (D.Mass.1993) (condominium unit sold as managed investment rather than a residence was a security).

70. Hocking v. Dubois, 885 F.2d 1449 (9th Cir.1989), *cert. denied* 494 U.S. 1078, 110 S.Ct. 1805, 108 L.Ed.2d 936 (1990) (question of fact as to whether rental pool arrangement was a security), noted in 58 Ford L.Rev. 1121 (1990); Reeves v. Teuscher, 881 F.2d 1495 (9th Cir.1989) (upholding finding that undivided interest in real estate development was a security); Adams v. Cavanaugh Communities Corp., 1994 WL 100749, [1994–1995 Transfer Binder] Fed.Sec.L.Rep. (CCH) ¶ 98,396 (N.D.Ill.1994) (lots that were not suitable for individual development were the subject of investment contracts which constituted securities).

71. *See* Hocking v. Dubois, 839 F.2d 560 (9th Cir.1988); Adams v. Hyannis Harborview, Inc., 838 F.Supp. 676 (D.Mass.1993); Hodges v. H & R Investments, Ltd., 668 F.Supp. 545 (N.D.Miss.1987). However, the existence of a rental pool does not automatically make a leasehold interest a security. Allison v. Ticor Title Insurance Co., 907 F.2d 645 (7th Cir.1990), *appeal after remand* 979 F.2d 1187 (7th Cir.1992); Owners of "SW 8" Real Estate v. McQuaid, 513 F.2d 558, 562 (9th Cir.1975).

an investment contract.[72]   However, properly marketed as a vacation residence, time share interests will not be securities.[73]   However, when the time share interest is offered more as an investment, the securities laws are more likely to be implicated.[74]

Country club interests may be classified as securities under some state laws,[75] but ordinarily will not be subject to federal law because of the absence of a profit expectation.[76]   However, if there is a profit potential, then the federal definition may be invoked.[77]

Fractional undivided interests in oil and mineral rights are expressly covered by the statutory definition of security.[78]   However, a leasehold interest has been held to be an interest in realty and thus not a security.[79]

Outside of the real estate context, it has been held that a syndication agreement will not be subject to the securities laws where "the agreement is designed to allow the investor to *use* or *consume* the item

72.   *See* Fields, *supra* footnote 68.

73.   So long as there is no pooling of profits, the fact that there is a pooling of weeks with regard to residential occupancy does not create a security. *See* Wals v. Fox Hills Development Corp., 24 F.3d 1016 (7th Cir.1994), *affirming* 828 F.Supp. 623 (E.D.Wis.1993) (the court pointed out that each time share owner's interest was a separate slice of an interest in realty).

74.   *Cf.* Teague v. Bakker, 931 F.2d 259 (4th Cir.1991) (jury question as to whether securities laws were implicated by lifetime partnership interests entitling partners to a short stay at resort).

75.   *E.g.* Silver Hills Country Club v. Sobieski, 55 Cal.2d 811, 13 Cal.Rptr. 186, 361 P.2d 906 (1961).

76.   Rice v. Branigar Organization, Inc., 922 F.2d 788 (11th Cir.1991) (sale of membership and undeveloped lots in beach club development was not the sale of a security); Ivy Hills Country Club, Inc., 23 Sec.Reg. & L.Rep. (BNA) 858 (SEC No Action Letter available May 23, 1991) (nonequity membership in undeveloped country club are not securities); Greystone Golf Club, Inc., 23 Sec.Reg. & L.Rep. (BNA) 611 (SEC No Action Letter available April 17, 1991) (country club memberships are not securities where members will not share in income and the only dividend would be on liquidation); U.S. Home Corp. [1990 Transfer Binder] Fed.Sec.L.Rep. ¶ 79,431 (SEC No Action Letter avail. Jan. 19, 1990) (country club memberships were not securities; memberships could only be resold to residents of the community and sales literature did not emphasize the possibility of a profit on resale).

77.   Club at Pelican Bay, Inc., 26 Sec. Reg. & L. Rep. (BNA) 104 (SEC no action letter available Jan. 7, 1994) (refusing to issue a no action response for transferable country club interests).

78.   *See* Cascade Energy & Metals Corp. v. Banks, 896 F.2d 1557 (10th Cir.1990), *cert. denied* 498 U.S. 849, 111 S.Ct. 138, 112 L.Ed.2d 105 (1990).   *See* Peter K. Reilly & Christopher S. Heroux, When Should Interests in Oil and Gas be Considered Securities? A Case for the Industry Deal, 34 S.Tex.L.Rev. 37 (1993).

79.   Deutsch Energy Co. v. Mazur, 813 F.2d 1567 (9th Cir.1987); Coal Resources, Inc. v. Gulf & Western Indus., Inc., 756 F.2d 443 (6th Cir.1985), *on remand* 645 F.Supp. 1028 (S.D.Ohio 1986); Norden v. Friedman, 19 Sec.Reg. & L.Rep. (BNA) 1665 (Mo.App.1987). *See also, e.g.,* Sparks v. Baxter, 854 F.2d 110 (5th Cir.1988) (joint venture in oil and gas leases was not a security).   *Cf.* Ratner v. Sioux Natural Gas Corp., 770 F.2d 512 (5th Cir.1985) (finding no purchase and thus not reaching the question of whether oil and gas leases were securities).

purchased." [80]   However, the result should be otherwise if the shares are marketed as an investment rather than simply a consumable.

Stock as a Security

Stock is expressly included in the statutory definition of security. Nevertheless, utilizing the economic reality test of earlier cases, it was held that the sale of stock in a closely held corporation may not be a "security" especially if it is, in essence, a transfer of the ownership and management of the corporation's assets.[81]   The circuits were in conflict as to the validity of this "sale of business" exception for including stock as a security.[82]   One court went so far as to hold that the sale of fifty percent of the outstanding shares is not a sale of securities subject to either state or federal securities regulation.[83]   The Tenth Circuit has held that transfer of eighty-one percent of the stock to a purchaser who was to manage the business was a sale of the business and thus not subject to the securities laws.[84]   The Seventh Circuit, in an even more questionable decision, imposed a rebuttable presumption that no security is involved when more than fifty percent of the stock is purchased.[85]   It is significant that like some of the more recent Supreme Court pronouncements, many lower court decisions have utilized the economic reality test to restrict coverage of the securities laws as compared with the earlier decisions which used this test to expand the Act's scope with regard to regulating unconventional investments.   In these later cases the courts have reasoned that since full ownership of a closely held corporation involves neither a pooling of interests nor a common enterprise, the economic reality test requires a finding of no security.[86]   These cases ignored the fact that in the Supreme Court's decision in *Forman* the "stock" had none of the usual indicia of corporate shares.

In companion decisions the Supreme Court rejected outright the sale of business doctrine, reasoning that when a business enterprise elects the corporate form and offers shares with the traditional indicia of ownership, the statutory definition is satisfied.[87]   The Court's recent

---

80.   Wabash Valley Power Association v. Public Service Co. of Indiana, 678 F.Supp. 757 (S.D.Ind.1988) (contract for construction of nuclear power plant held not a security since investor planned to use resulting power); Kefalas v. Bonnie Brae Farms, Inc., 630 F.Supp. 6, 8 (E.D.Ky.1985) (thoroughbred breeding syndication was not a security even though purchaser did not own mares and hoped for price appreciation in breeding rights).

81.   *E.g.,* Landreth Timber Co. v. Landreth, 731 F.2d 1348 (9th Cir.1984) *reversed* 471 U.S. 681, 105 S.Ct. 2297, 85 L.Ed.2d 692 (1985).

82.   Rejections of the sale of business doctrine include Ruefenacht v. O'Halloran, 737 F.2d 320 (3d Cir.1984) *affirmed* 471 U.S. 701, 105 S.Ct. 2308, 85 L.Ed.2d 708 (1985); Daily v. Morgan, 701 F.2d 496 (5th Cir.1983); Seagrave Corp. v. Vista Resources, Inc., 696 F.2d 227 (2d Cir.1982).

83.   Oakhill Cemetery of Hammond, Inc. v. Tri–State Bank, 513 F.Supp. 885 (N.D.Ill. 1981).

84.   Christy v. Cambron, 710 F.2d 669 (10th Cir.1983).

85.   Sutter v. Groen, 687 F.2d 197 (7th Cir.1982).

86.   Anchor–Darling, Industries, Inc. v. Suozzo, 510 F.Supp. 659 (E.D.Pa.1981).

87.   Landreth Timber Co. v. Landreth, 471 U.S. 681, 105 S.Ct. 2297, 85 L.Ed.2d 692 (1985); Gould v. Ruefenacht, 471 U.S. 701, 105 S.Ct. 2308, 85 L.Ed.2d 708 (1985). *Accord*

holding confirms that it will not aggressively utilize the economic reality test to limit applicability of the securities acts to transactions falling within a literal reading of the statute. It therefore appears that the Court's earlier restrictive ruling in *Forman* relating to stock in a government subsidized residential housing cooperative may well be *sui generis* (or close to it) and thus entitled to relatively little precedential effect except on facts very similar to those in *Forman*.[88] Notwithstanding the rejection of the sale of business doctrine, a corporate acquisition that is not structured in terms of a stock transaction will not implicate the securities laws.[89] The form of a corporate acquisition will generally determine the extent to which the securities laws are implicated.

The more recent Supreme Court rulings rejecting the sale of business doctrine have impact beyond the sale of closely held businesses. The decisions soundly reject the application of *Howey* as the exclusive test of what is a security. Specifically, the *Howey* test is still good law with regard to "investment contracts," but other investment instruments such as stock and notes which are expressly included in the statute will be analyzed differently. For example, it may fairly be said that stock, notes, and other specifically included investment vehicles are presumptively considered to be securities.

It should be observed that the mere fact that stock certificates are transferred does not make the transferee a purchaser of securities where the shares are cancelled as part of the merger transaction. For example, the First Circuit has held that stock in a disappearing corporation acquired during the course of a statutory merger is not a security

---

One–O–One Enterprises, Inc. v. Caruso, 848 F.2d 1283 (D.C.Cir.1988) (option to purchase stock is a security; four-part *Howey* test did not apply in light of *Landreth Timber*). *See also, e.g.,* St. Philip Towing & Transp. Co. v. Pavers, Inc., 768 F.2d 1233 (11th Cir.1985); Mercer v. Jaffe, Snider, Raitt & Heuer, P.C., 736 F.Supp. 764 (W.D.Mich.1990) (common stock had stock-like characteristics and was a security); Walsh v. Emerson, 1990 WL 47319, [1989–1990 Transfer Binder] Fed.Sec.L.Rep. ¶ 94,962 (D.Or.1990) (retirement plan in the form of stock was a security); Cohen v. William Goldberg & Co., 262 Ga. 606, 423 S.E.2d 231 (1992), *on remand* 207 Ga.App. 174, 428 S.E.2d 117 (1993) (stock in a closely held corporation subject to transfer restrictions was a security). *See generally* John A. O'Brien & John E. Moye, The Sale of Business Doctrine: *Landreth* Adds New Life to the Anti–Fraud Provisions of the Securities Acts, 11 Vt.L.Rev. 1 (1986). *Cf.* Note, Close Corporation Stock as a "Security" Under Uniform Commercial Code Article 8: North Carolina Embraces the Statute of Frauds in Stancil v. Stancil, 69 N.C.L.Rev. 1432 (1991) (analyzing cases rejecting the sale of business doctrine under the UCC and holding that transfers of closely held stock are covered by the Code).

There is still some question as to whether the sale of business doctrine can be used under state securities laws to find the absence of a security. *Compare* Jabend, Inc. by Aebig v. Four–Phase Systems, Inc., 631 F.Supp. 1339, 1345 (W.D.Wash.1986) (indicating that the doctrine may be applicable under California law) *with* Specialized Tours, Inc. v. Hagen, 392 N.W.2d 520 (Minn.1986) (rejecting the sale of business doctrine).

88. *See* Seger v. Federal Intermediate Credit Bank of Omaha, 850 F.2d 468 (8th Cir.1988) (Class B stock in production credit association was held not to be a security). In *Seger,* borrowers had to purchase stock in order to obtain a loan. The stock was transferable only to other borrowers; the stock was not voted in accordance with the number of shares; and although theoretically possible, dividends were not expected.

89. Coal Resources, Inc. v. Gulf & Western Industries, Inc., 756 F.2d 443 (6th Cir.1985), *on remand* 645 F.Supp. 1028 (S.D.Ohio 1986), *reversed* 865 F.2d 761 (6th Cir.1989).

purchase from the perspective of the acquiring corporation.[90] The decision is not likely to have significant impact unless it is too broadly construed.[91] The share certificates that could be traced back to the premerger stock issuance were delivered and subsequently cancelled as part of the merger in conjunction with the disappearing corporation's cessation of existence. The court concluded that the share certificates so acquired during the course of the merger were not securities since the disappearing corporation which had issued the securities no longer existed. The court explained that the most that could be said of the stock certificates is that they were evidence that the surrendering shareholders had owned stock in the disappearing corporation and were entitled to shares in the survivor;[92] the certificates did not represent stock in terms of the rights transferred to the acquiring corporation. Since the acquiring corporation was the plaintiff, it could not establish that it had acquired a security.[93]

Notes as Securities

A number of recent cases have addressed the issue of whether a loan agreement constitutes a security. Section 3(a)(3) of the Securities Act exempts any "note * * * aris[ing] out of a current transaction" with a maturity not exceeding nine months.[94] In contrast section 3(a)(10) of the Securities Exchange Act of 1934 excludes such short term notes from the definition of a security. The courts by and large have employed the economic reality test by asking whether the transaction under scrutiny is an investment vehicle which would trigger the securities acts' coverage or whether it is more properly characterized as a commercial venture which should not be subjected to the securities laws.[95] Then, in 1990, the Supreme Court employed a similar "family resemblance test" in

90. Versyss Inc. v. Coopers & Lybrand, 982 F.2d 653 (1st Cir.1992), *cert. denied* ___ U.S. ___, 113 S.Ct. 2965, 125 L.Ed.2d 665 (1993).

91. The suit in question was brought by the acquiring corporation which was claiming damages for a premerger violation of section 11 of the 1933 Act in connection with the registration of securities. The 1933 Act registration had not been prepared in connection with the merger but the section 11 action is not limited to plaintiffs who acquired the shares in the public offering so long as the shares can be traced back to the offering. Section 11 is considered in § 7.2 *infra*.

92. The court observed that "at worst the share certificates were wallpaper." 982 F.2d at 656.

93. However, since the registration in question was not issued in connection with the merger, that would have been a difficult case to establish. The "in connection with" requirement is discussed in §13.2.3 *infra*. Additionally, the acquiring corporation as an issuer of its own securities could maintain a suit as a seller of those securities, provided that it could show a material misstatement or omission in connection with the "sale" of its securities pursuant to the merger.

94. Mishkin v. Peat, Marwick, Mitchell & Co., 744 F.Supp. 531 (S.D.N.Y.1990) (banker's acceptance with maturity of less than nine months is not a security under section 3(a)(10) of the Exchange Act); 15 U.S.C.A. § 77c(a)(3). The Act further exempts all renewals thereof which are "likewise limited."

95. *See, e.g.,* Arthur Young & Co. v. Reves, 856 F.2d 52 (8th Cir.1988), *reversed* 494 U.S. 56, 110 S.Ct. 945, 108 L.Ed.2d 47 (1990) (demand note was not a security); Smith International, Inc. v. Texas Commerce Bank, N.A., 844 F.2d 1193 (5th Cir.1988) (promissory note was commercial and thus not a security).

holding that a variable rate demand note issued by a farmers' cooperative was a security.[96] Even in the face of the family resemblance test or the commercial-investment dichotomy, the fact that the issuer of a short-term note is a bank does not preclude the finding that a security exists.[97] Thus, when notes or loan agreements have investment attributes, the courts have found securities to exist.[98] However, the courts have seemed increasingly willing to find a commercial rather than investment context, especially when bank financing is involved. The statutory definition of security has been held not to be implicated when the loan agreement is purely commercial, is relatively short term, and has a rate of interest comparable to the applicable prevailing commercial rate which is not varied with the profitability of the lender.[99] Further, the fact that there is a profit expectation will not be sufficient to warrant the finding of a security when the transaction is purely commercial.[100]

The "Family Resemblance" Test for Notes

In Reves v. Ernst & Young,[101] the Supreme Court attempted to resolve some of the issues relating to the question of when a note will be a security. *Reves* involved variable rate demand notes that were issued by a farmer's cooperative. The Court rejected application of the *Howey* four-factor test, reasoning that this test is limited to the definition of investment contract. The investment contract analysis is inapplicable to the other items specifically enumerated in the Act's definition of security. The Court in *Reves* applied the "family resemblance" test in holding that certain demand notes were securities. The family resemblance test

---

96. Reves v. Ernst & Young, 494 U.S. 56, 110 S.Ct. 945, 108 L.Ed.2d 47 (1990).

97. Exchange National Bank of Chicago v. Touche Ross & Co., 544 F.2d 1126 (2d Cir.1976). *See also,* Bachmeier v. Bank of Ravenswood, 663 F.Supp. 1207 (N.D.Ill.1987); Securities Industry Association v. Federal Reserve Board, 468 U.S. 137, 104 S.Ct. 2979, 82 L.Ed.2d 107 (1984) (commercial paper is a "security" under the Glass–Steagall Act). For a good discussion of considerations courts use in determining whether or not a security is present, *see* American Bank & Trust Co. v. Wallace, 529 F.Supp. 258 (E.D.Ky.1981), *judgment affirmed* 702 F.2d 93 (6th Cir.1983). *Cf.* Willamette Savings & Loan v. Blake & Neal Finance Co., 577 F.Supp. 1415 (D.Or.1984) (retail installment contract is not a security).

98. *E.g.,* SEC v. Eurobond Exchange, Ltd., 13 F.3d 1334 (9th Cir.1994) (Eurobond investment program held to be a security); McGill v. American Land & Exploration Co., 776 F.2d 923, 925 (10th Cir.1985) (note issued in connection with joint venture held to be a security); Underhill v. Royal, 769 F.2d 1426 (9th Cir.1985) (notes for "loan agreement program" maturing in three years held to be securities).

99. Union National Bank of Little Rock v. Farmers Bank, 786 F.2d 881 (8th Cir.1986) (bank's purchase of 100–interest in an unsecured note was not a security); James v. Meinke, 778 F.2d 200 (5th Cir.1985) (guarantee of commercial loan held not to be a security); Futura Development Corp. v. Centex Corp., 761 F.2d 33 (1st Cir.1985), *cert. denied* 474 U.S. 850, 106 S.Ct. 147, 88 L.Ed.2d 121 (1985) (seller of property issuing secured promissory note in connection with sale of property to corporation that was not personally liable on the note held not to be a security).

100. James v. Meinke, 778 F.2d 200, 204–205 (5th Cir.1985); Moy v. Warren, 1994 WL 2453, [1984 Transfer Binder] Fed.Sec.L.Rep. (CCH) ¶ 91,601 (D.Or.1984). *See also, e.g.* Arthur Young & Co. v. Reves, 856 F.2d 52 (8th Cir.1988) (Farmers' Cooperative's demand notes were not securities), *reversed* 494 U.S. 56, 110 S.Ct. 945, 108 L.Ed.2d 47 (1990).

101. 494 U.S. 56, 110 S.Ct. 945, 108 L.Ed.2d 47 (1990), *rehearing denied* 494 U.S. 1092, 110 S.Ct. 1840, 108 L.Ed.2d 968 (1990). *See, e.g.,* Steinberg, Notes as Securities: *Reves* and its Implications, 51 Ohio St.L.J. 675 (1990).

that was adopted in *Reves* to a large extent is a different way of articulating the investment–commercial dichotomy that has been employed by the circuit and district courts. In applying the family resemblance test, the Court identified four types of "notes" that do not fit within the definition of security: (1) notes delivered in connection with consumer financing, [102](2) a note secured by a home mortgage,[103] (3) short-term notes to a small business secured by the business' assets, and (4) bank character loans.[104] The more closely any particular note resembles any of these four categories, the more likely it is that the securities laws are not to be invoked.

The Court in *Reves* held that since "note" is one of the items enumerated in the Act's definition, there is a presumption that a note is a security.[105] However, the presumption may be rebutted by evaluation of the following four factors:

(1) an examination of the transaction in order to assess the motivations that would prompt a reasonable lender (buyer) and creditor (seller) to enter into it—for example, was the transaction in question an investment transaction or a commercial or consumer transaction?

(2) the plan of distribution used in offering and selling the instrument—for example, is the instrument commonly traded for investment or speculation?

(3) the reasonable expectations of the investing public—are the notes generally perceived as investment opportunities? [106] and

(4) whether some factor such as the applicability of a parallel regulatory scheme significantly reduces the risk[107] and thereby ren-

---

102. Thus, for example, Consumer automobile loans purchased by a savings and loan association from a car dealer were not securities. Resolution Trust Corp. v. Stone, 998 F.2d 1534 (10th Cir.1993). The finding of no security was made even though the transactions involved a package of loan with enhancements, known as EARs (Enhanced Automobile Receivables); the enhancements included a buyback provision for delinquent loans. The court reasoned that the motivation of the buyer and the seller was commercial and further pointed out that the notes were sold in a highly specialized and sophisticated institutional secondary market.

103. *See, e.g.,* Rolo v. City Investing Co. Liquidating Trust, 845 F.Supp. 182 (D.N.J. 1993) (home mortgage notes were not securities).

104. The Court was relying on the Second Circuit's analysis in Exchange National Bank of Chicago v. Touche Ross & Co., 544 F.2d 1126, 1138 (2d Cir.1976).

105. 494 U.S. at 64–66, 110 S.Ct. at 951–52, 108 L.Ed.2d at 60–61. *See also, e.g.,* Holloway v. Peat, Marwick, Mitchell & Co., 900 F.2d 1485 (10th Cir.1990), *cert. denied* 498 U.S. 958, 111 S.Ct. 386, 112 L.Ed.2d 396 (1990); National Bank of Yugoslavia v. Drexel Burnham Lambert, Inc., 768 F.Supp. 1010 (S.D.N.Y.1991) (there is a presumption that a note of more than nine months is not subject to 1934 Act exclusion from definition of security; holding "time deposits" to be securities); Varnberg v. Minnick, 760 F.Supp. 315 (S.D.N.Y.1991) (open account demand notes were not securities; secondary market was not contemplated).

106. *Cf.* General Electric Corp., 26 Sec. Reg. & L. Rep. (BNA) 1076 (SEC No Action Letter available July 13, 1994) (limited advertisements for commercial paper were not likely to mislead public into believing that notes were securities).

107. *See, e.g,* Marine Bank v. Weaver, 455 U.S. 551, 102 S.Ct. 1220, 71 L.Ed.2d 409 (1982), *on remand* 683 F.2d 744 (3d Cir.1982) (federally insured certificate of deposit was

ders the protection of the federal securities laws unnecessary.[108]

In applying these factors, the *Reves* Court was unanimous in finding that the uncollateralized, uninsured, unregulated notes at issue were securities. However, there was a split as to whether they fell within the exemption for notes with maturities of less than nine months from the date of issuance. The majority held that although the notes were payable on demand, the demand might not come for "years or decades" in the future and accordingly, the short-term exemption should not apply. The four dissenters took the position that the demand feature meant that the notes reached their maturity at issuance.[109]

The family resemblance test that was applied in *Reves* does not provide as much of a bright line as one might have hoped. Yet it does establish that since there is a presumption that a note is a security, the burden of persuasion falls on the party seeking to exclude the note from the Act's coverage.[110] The Court has thus announced a rule that will exclude only those instruments which, because of their terms and the way in which they are issued, do not have the basic characteristics of investment securities.[111] The test thus necessarily becomes highly individualized to the facts of the particular case. As the presumption indicates, issuers and sellers of notes must be aware of the potential securities law ramifications.[112] In addition to the question of whether the issuance of a note constitutes a security, it has been held that a substantial modification of an existing note will constitute a new security.[113]

As a result of the *Reves* test, securities that most closely resemble purely commercial or banking transactions will not be classified as

not a security). *But cf.* Pollack v. Laidlaw Holdings, Inc., 27 F.3d 808 (2d Cir.1994) (lower court was in error when it concluded that state regulation concerning mortgages was adequate protection so as to preclude mortgage participations from being considered securities).

108. 494 U.S. at 67, 110 S.Ct. at 952.

109. 494 U.S. at 76, 110 S.Ct. at 957, 108 L.Ed.2d at 67 (Rehnquist dissenting in part; Justice Rehnquist was joined by Justices White, O'Connor & Scalia).

110. *See, e.g.,* Arthur Children's Trust v. Keim, 994 F.2d 1390 (9th Cir.1993) (notes were securities); Schwartz v. Oberweis, 826 F.Supp. 280 (N.D.Ind.1993) (defendant failed to rebut presumption that notes were securities; decided under Indiana blue sky law). Placing the burden here is consistent with treatment of exemptions. As discussed more fully in chapter 4 *infra,* anyone claiming an exemption from the 1933 Act's registration provisions has the burden of proof.

111. *See, e.g.,* Pollack v. Laidlaw Holdings, Inc., 27 F.3d 808 (2d Cir.1994) (mortgage participations sold by securities brokers were properly characterized as investment rather than commercial and thus were securities).

112. *Cf.* Caucus Distributors, Inc. v. Alaska, 793 P.2d 1048 (Alaska 1990) (promissory notes issued by a Lyndon LaRouche fundraising group held to be securities under blue sky law). *Accord* Caucus Distributors, Inc. v. Maryland Securities Commissioner, 320 Md. 313, 577 A.2d 783 (1990).

113. Diaz Vicente v. Obenauer, 736 F.Supp. 679, 692–94 (E.D.Va.1990), relying in part on Smith v. Cooper/T. Smith Corp., 846 F.2d 325, 327 (5th Cir.1988), *remanded* 883 F.2d 357 (1989) (modification of stock purchase agreement was subject to securities laws); Keys v. Wolfe, 709 F.2d 413, 417 (5th Cir.1983) (semble); Ahern v. Gaussoin, 611 F.Supp. 1465, 1478–79 (D.Or.1985).

securities.[114] The Second Circuit, applying the *Reves* analysis, has ruled that under the family resemblance test, participation interests in short-term commercial loans were not securities.[115] The presumption that a security exists may be rebutted,[116] but the burden is on the party seeking to be excluded from the securities laws' purview. Thus, absent evidence that the note does not contain any of the benchmarks of a security as identified by the Court in *Reves*, the securities laws will apply. This presumption carries forward to commercial paper as well as to notes issued by savings and loan institutions.[117] Thus, for example, in the ordinary case commercial paper issued by a corporation will be a security.[118]

Certificates of Deposit as Securities

Related to the issue of when a note is subject to the securities laws, is the applicability of those laws to bank certificates of deposit. The Supreme Court has ruled that a federally insured certificate of deposit issued by a bank is not subject to the securities laws.[119] When, however, an investment firm markets certificates of deposit as liquid investments and maintains a secondary market for the certificates of deposit, their sale has been held to be subject to the securities acts.[120] Some subse-

---

114. *Compare, e.g.,* Prochaska & Associates v. Merrill Lynch Pierce Fenner & Smith, Inc., 798 F.Supp. 1427 (D.Neb.1992) (promissory notes that were payable in three months and were secured by business inventory were not securities; the court noted that the notes were not to be publicly traded and there was no public perception that they were securities) *with* Deal v. Asset Management Group, 1992 WL 212482, [1992–1993 Transfer Binder] Fed.Sec.L.Rep. (CCH) ¶ 97,244 (N.D.Ill.1992) (notes secured by residence to finance remodeling were securities; there was an offering to at least six persons and a promised 18 to 20% return; thus, the notes were reasonably perceived as securities). *See also, e.g.,* Comment, Bank Loans as Securities: A Legal and Financial Economic Analysis of the Treatment of Marketable Bank Assets Under the Securities Acts, 40 U.C.L.A.L.Rev. 799 (1993). *Cf.* Resolution Trust Corp. v. Stone, 998 F.2d 1534 (10th Cir.1993) (resales of enhanced consumer automobile loans were not securities; the court stressed that the sophisticated institutional purchasers and the seller viewed the loans as commercial).

115. Banco Espanol De Credito v. Security Pacific National Bank, 973 F.2d 51 (2d Cir.1992), *cert. denied* ___ U.S. ___, 113 S.Ct. 2992, 125 L.Ed.2d 687 (1993). *Cf.* Resolution Trust Corp. v. Stone, 998 F.2d 1534 (10th Cir.1993) (enhanced automobile receivables ("EARs") were not securities).

116. *E.g.,* Deal v. Asset Management Group, 1992 WL 212482, [1992–1993 Transfer Binder] Fed.Sec.L.Rep. (CCH) ¶ 97,244 (N.D.Ill.1992) (discussed in footnote 114 *supra*).

117. Bradford v. Moench, 809 F.Supp. 1473 (D.Utah 1992) (thrift certificates issued by a savings and loan association were securities).

118. In re NBW Commercial Paper Litigation, 813 F.Supp. 7 (D.D.C.1992), relying on Securities Industry Association v. Board of Governors, 468 U.S. 137, 104 S.Ct. 2979, 82 L.Ed.2d 107 (1984) and the *Reves* decision. *Compare, e.g.,* General Electric Corp., 26 Sec. Reg. & L. Rep. (BNA) 1076 (SEC No Action Letter available July 13, 1994) (limited advertisements for commercial paper were not likely to mislead public into believing that notes were securities).

119. Marine Bank v. Weaver, 455 U.S. 551, 102 S.Ct. 1220, 71 L.Ed.2d 409 (1982), *on remand* 683 F.2d 744 (3d Cir.1982). *Accord, e.g.,* Brockton Savings Bank v. Peat, Marwick, Mitchell & Co., 577 F.Supp. 1281 (D.Mass.1983). *See also* Tafflin v. Levitt, 865 F.2d 595 (4th Cir.1989) (certificate of deposit issued by savings and loan association was not a security); Tab Partnership v. Grantland Financial Corp., 866 F.Supp. 807 (S.D.N.Y.1994) (CD rollover program was not a security).

120. Gary Plastic Packaging Corp. v. Merrill Lynch, Pierce, Fenner & Smith, Inc., 756 F.2d 230 (2d Cir.1985).

quent and prior lower court decisions have held that certificates of deposit issued by foreign banks are deemed to be securities.[121] The reasoning is that United States government-regulated banks and federally insured commitments do not require the protection of the securities laws whereas foreign instruments may.[122]

Commodities and Managed Accounts as Securities

Another fertile area of litigation has been with regard to the classification of commodities. Based upon the extent of managerial and market-making activities offered by the seller, a gold investment has been held to be a security.[123] However, when all that is offered is the underlying commodity combined with storage and marketing services there is no security as the investor is relying upon the market price of the commodity rather than the seller's marketing or managerial efforts.[124] In contrast, when the object underlying the futures contract is itself a security, the futures contract may also be classified as a security.[125] This type of arrangement is in economic reality more like a securities option contract which is clearly a security. However, where the subject of the futures contract is not a security but merely an index based on securities prices, a security has been held not to exist.[126]

121. Meason v. Bank of Miami, 652 F.2d 542 (5th Cir.1981), *rehearing denied* 659 F.2d 1079 (5th Cir.1981) (Grand Cayman bank); R.J. Wolf v. Banco Nacional De Mexico, 549 F.Supp. 841 (N.D.Cal.1982), appeal dismissed 721 F.2d 660 (9th Cir.1983), *reversed on appeal after remand* 739 F.2d 1458 (9th Cir.1984), *cert. denied* 469 U.S. 1108, 105 S.Ct. 784, 83 L.Ed.2d 778 (1985) (time deposit in Mexican bank is a security, the court reasoning that there was adequate protection for the certificate holders under the Mexican government's bank regulatory framework).

122. The Court in *Marine Bank* looked to the preamble to section 2's definitions ("unless the context otherwise requires") as justifying excluding a certificate of deposit which otherwise would fall within section 2(3)'s definition of security. However, the existence of state regulation alone will not be sufficient to preclude application of the federal securities laws. *See* Bradford v. Moench, 809 F.Supp. 1473 (D.Utah 1992) (thrift certificates issued by a savings and loan association were securities; state regulation of savings and loan association was not sufficient risk reducing factor under the family resemblance test).

123. SEC v. International Mining Exchange, Inc., 515 F.Supp. 1062 (D.Colo.1981). *See also* Connors v. Lexington Insurance Co., 666 F.Supp. 434 (E.D.N.Y.1987) (precious metal investment with repurchase plan held to be a security); In re Leonesio, Exch.Act Rel. No. 34–23524, [1986–87 Transfer Binder] Fed.Sec.L.Rep. (CCH) ¶ 84,020 (Aug. 11, 1986) (gold program held to involve the sale of securities). *Cf.* Gary Plastic Packaging Corp. v. Merrill Lynch, Pierce, Fenner & Smith, Inc., 756 F.2d 230 (2d Cir.1985) (market-making for certificates of deposits led to finding of a security).

124. *See, e.g.,* Noa v. Key Futures, Inc., 638 F.2d 77 (9th Cir.1980). *Cf.* Dahl v. English, 578 F.Supp. 17 (N.D.Ill.1983) (artwork held not to be a security). Similarly, although a futures contract is not a security, GNMA forward contracts implicate the securities law as well as federal commodities regulation. Abrams v. Oppenheimer Government Securities, Inc., 737 F.2d 582 (7th Cir.1984).

125. Abrams v. Oppenheimer Government Securities, Inc., 737 F.2d 582 (7th Cir.1984). *Cf.* Levine v. Merrill Lynch, Pierce, Fenner & Smith, Inc., 639 F.Supp. 1391, [1986–87 Transfer Binder] Fed.Sec.L.Rep. (CCH) ¶ 92,841 (S.D.N.Y.1986) (discretionary options account).

126. Mallen v. Merrill Lynch, Pierce, Fenner & Smith, Inc., 605 F.Supp. 1105 (N.D.Ga. 1985). *See generally* David J. Gilberg, Regulation of New Financial Instruments Under the Federal Securities and Commodities Laws, 39 Vand.L.Rev. 1599 (1986). *See* § 1.5.1 *infra.*

A more sensitive question has arisen regarding managed accounts where the claim is made that there is no common enterprise and that the brokers or account managers are providing a service rather than offering an investment contract. These accounts generally vest the broker-manager or investment adviser with the authority to execute trades for the customer's account. The courts are in conflict as to whether a stock brokerage or commodities brokerage trading account is a security so as to trigger both the registration and anti-fraud provisions of the federal securities laws. Most of the cases to date have arisen with regard to the anti-fraud provisions.

The Fifth[127] and Eighth[128] Circuits have held that a managed broker-age account is a security. The pivotal issue is the existence of a common enterprise. The courts have analyzed this in terms of vertical or horizontal commonality. The Fifth Circuit has adopted a broad test of vertical commonality that is satisfied by a showing that the fortunes of the investor are inextricably tied to the promoter's efforts.[129] The Second Circuit has rejected the broad view of vertical commonality in favor of a stricter view.[130] The broad test of vertical commonality simply requires that the success of the investment be linked to the *efforts* of the promoter.[131] In contrast, the narrower test of vertical commonality requires that the investor's fortunes be tied to the *fortunes* of the promoter.[132] Utilizing this test, the Seventh,[133] Third[134] and Ninth Cir-

---

127. SEC v. Continental Commodities Corp., 497 F.2d 516 (5th Cir.1974). *See also e.g.,* Taylor v. Bear Stearns & Co., 572 F.Supp. 667 (N.D.Ga.1983); Westlake v. Abrams, 565 F.Supp. 1330 (N.D.Ga.1983).

128. Booth v. Peavey Co. Commodity Services, 430 F.2d 132, 133 (8th Cir.1970) (indicating the presence of a remedy under the securities acts for churning in a discretionary commodities account). *Cf.* SEC v. Professional Associates, 731 F.2d 349 (6th Cir.1984) (trust agreements held to be securities).

129. This broad test has been rejected by other courts. Schofield v. First Commodity Corp., 638 F.Supp. 4 (D.Mass.1985), *judgment affirmed* 793 F.2d 28 (1st Cir.1986); Mechigian v. Art Capital Corp., 612 F.Supp. 1421, 1427 (S.D.N.Y.1985). *Accord* Silverstein v. Merrill Lynch, Pierce, Fenner & Smith, Inc., 618 F.Supp. 436 (S.D.N.Y.1985). *See also, e.g.,* Vale Natural Gas America Corp. v. Carrollton Resources 1990, Ltd., 795 F.Supp. 795 (E.D.La.1992) (finding sufficient vertical commonality between promoter of oil and gas leases and sole investor).

See also McGill v. American Land & Exploration Co., 776 F.2d 923, 924–25 (10th Cir.1985) (finding vertical commonality sufficient with regard to joint venture and that lack of horizontal commonality with other investors did not preclude a finding of a security).

130. Revak v. SEC Realty Corp., 18 F.3d 81 (2d Cir.1994).

131. *Id.* at 87–88, *relying on* Long v. Shultz Cattle Co., 881 F.2d 129, 140–41 (5th Cir.1989).

132. Revak v. SEC Realty Corp., 18 F.3d 81, 88 (2d Cir.1994) (holding that interests in a condominium were not securities); Mechigian v. Art Capital Corp., 612 F.Supp. 1421, 1427 (S.D.N.Y.1985) ("the investment manager's fortunes rise and fall with those of the investor" and finding this test of vertical commonality not to be satisfied in connection with the sale of original artworks).

133. Milnarik v. M–S Commodities, Inc., 457 F.2d 274 (7th Cir.1972), *cert. denied* 409 U.S. 887, 93 S.Ct. 113, 34 L.Ed.2d 144 (1972).

134. Wasnowic v. Chicago Board of Trade, 352 F.Supp. 1066 (M.D.Pa.1972), *affirmed mem.* 491 F.2d 752 (3d Cir.1973), *cert. denied* 416 U.S. 994, 94 S.Ct. 2407, 40 L.Ed.2d 773 (1974).

cuits[135] have held that managed commodities accounts are not securities.

Those cases holding that a commodities account is not a security generally point to the absence of a common enterprise; the fact that the investor's funds are not pooled with those of anyone else, as is the case with a mutual fund or investment club, precludes the finding of horizontal commonality where the investor shares his or her risk with other investors.[136] These courts have thus viewed a trading account as a pure service rather than an investment contract.

Those courts holding a discretionary trading account to be a security have found sufficient common enterprise in "vertical commonality," whether narrow or broad, which is the common enterprise that exists between the investor and the broker making the investment decisions. These courts point out that the broker's commission is usually tied to the profits and/or the asset value of the account and therefore, he is sharing the risk with the investor. Although the Second Circuit has not yet acted, the New York district courts favor the result that an individual discretionary commodities account is not a security.[137] A critical factor in these cases is often that the dealer is compensated on a fixed commission basis rather than a percentage of the profits. Notwithstanding the conflict of authority, the Supreme Court, although it had the opportunity, decided not to consider the question of whether vertical commonality is sufficient to characterize a discretionary trading account as a security.[138] It seems clear, however, that where there is a pooling of investors' funds there is sufficient horizontal commonality to warrant the finding of a security.[139]

Common enterprise aside, it is evident that when dealing with a managed account, all other components of the definition of a security have been met, as there is certainly an investment of money with the expectation of a profit to be derived from the expertise and efforts of the broker or investment advisor who is handling the account. It has been suggested that under the risk capital test the common enterprise re-

---

135. Mordaunt v. Incomco, 686 F.2d 815 (9th Cir.1982), *cert. denied* 469 U.S. 1115, 105 S.Ct. 801, 83 L.Ed.2d 793 (1985); Brodt v. Bache & Co., Inc., 595 F.2d 459 (9th Cir.1978). *Accord* Pophan, Haik, Schnobrich, Kaufman & Dory, Ltd. v. Price, 1984 WL 2395, [1983– 1984 Transfer Binder] Fed.Sec.L.Rep. (CCH) ¶ 99,682 (D.D.C.1984).

136. *See* United States v. Faulhaber, 929 F.2d 16 (1st Cir.1991) ("Without a doubt" mutual fund shares have the significant characteristics that make them securities). *See also, e.g.,* U.S. SEC v. Lauer, 864 F.Supp. 784 (N.D.Ill.1994) (actual pooling of investor funds in connection with international investment program satisfied horizontal commonality).

137. *E.g.* Cohen v. Merrill Lynch, Pierce, Fenner & Smith, Inc., 722 F.Supp. 24 (S.D.N.Y.1989); Lowenbraun v. L.F. Rothschild, Unterberg, Towbin, 685 F.Supp. 336 (S.D.N.Y.1988).

138. Omni Capital Int'l, Inc. v. Rudolf Wolff & Co., 484 U.S. 97, 108 S.Ct. 404, 98 L.Ed.2d 415 (1987), *affirming* 479 U.S. 1063, 107 S.Ct. 946, 93 L.Ed.2d 995 (1987). *See also* Mordaunt v. Incomco, 469 U.S. 1115, 105 S.Ct. 801, 83 L.Ed.2d 793 (1985) (White, J. dissenting from a denial of certiorari).

139. Wagman v. FSC Securities Corp., 1985 WL 2139, [1984–85 Transfer Binder] Fed.Sec.L.Rep. (CCH) ¶ 92,445 (N.D.Ill.1985). *Cf.* SEC v. American Board of Trade, Inc., 593 F.Supp. 335 (S.D.N.Y.1984), *grant of preliminary injunction reversed* 751 F.2d 529 (2d Cir.1984) (pooling of funds for investments in U.S. Treasury Bills).

quirement is not an element of whether a security exists.[140]　Another way to frame the issue in the brokerage account cases is to ask whether the contract in question represents a bona fide service agreement[141] or whether the nature of the arrangement is more in line with the traditional investment concept that has led courts to find a security to exist in analogous arrangements.

As discussed above, the extent to which vertical commonality will justify the finding of a security also has arisen outside of the commodity account context.[142]

Partnership Interests as Securities

Another type of arrangement that clearly falls into the reach of the securities law is the limited partnership; [143] in some instances joint ventures and general partnerships might also fall under the acts' coverage.　In the case of a limited partnership interest, the Uniform Limited Partnership Act requires that, at least to some extent, the investment be a passive one.　Any significant degree of control or management in the enterprise may transform the limited partner into a general partner.[144] Accordingly, any time there is a bona fide limited partnership interest, by definition, the investor puts his or her funds at risk depending primarily upon the efforts of others—*i.e.,* the managing partners.　Since virtually all limited partnership interests involve the investment of money or some other property and further are geared to the expectation of a profit (sometimes in the form of a tax shelter), the traditional definition of a security is clearly fulfilled.[145]　However, it has been held

---

140.　Unif. Limited Partnership Act § 7.　*See* Abrams, Imposing Liability for "Control" Under Section 7 of the Uniform Limited Partnership Act, 28 Case W.Res.L.Rev. 785 (1978); Feld, The "Control" Test for Limited Partnerships, 82 Harv.L.Rev. 1471 (1969).

141.　*See, e.g.,* Lowenbraun v. L.F. Rothschild, Unterberg, Towbin, 685 F.Supp. 336 (S.D.N.Y.1988) (investment portfolio is not a security since it lacks vertical commonality; mere allegation that defendant promised plaintiff would realize a ten percent return was insufficient to establish a Rule 10b–5 claim);　Cruse v. Equitable Securities of New York, Inc., 678 F.Supp. 1023 (S.D.N.Y.1987) (brokerage account is not a security).

142.　The Ninth Circuit has adopted a narrow test of vertical commonality with regard to a coal purchase program dependent upon the defendant's unique ore processing technique.　SEC v. Goldfield Deep Mines Co., 758 F.2d 459 (9th Cir.1985).

The Second Circuit has held that the absence of strict vertical commonality precluded a condominium interest from being a security. Revak v. SEC Realty Corp., 18 F.3d 81 (2d Cir.1994).

See also, e.g., Secon Service System, Inc. v. St. Joseph Bank & Trust Co., 855 F.2d 406 (7th Cir.1988) (payments in exchange for operating authority lacked a common enterprise and thus were not securities).　*Cf.* Deckebach v. La Vida Charters, Inc., 867 F.2d 278 (6th Cir.1989) (yacht purchase and management agreement was not a security due to absence of horizontal commonality).

143.　*See* the authorities in footnote 145 *infra.*

144.　*See, e.g.,* Weil v. Diversified Properties, 319 F.Supp. 778 (D.D.C.1970);　Grainger v. Antoyan, 48 Cal.2d 805, 313 P.2d 848 (1957);　Silvola v. Rowlett, 129 Colo. 522, 272 P.2d 287 (1954);　Rathke v. Griffith, 36 Wn.2d 394, 218 P.2d 757 (1950);　Trans–Am Builders, Inc. v. Woods Mill, Ltd., 133 Ga.App. 411, 210 S.E.2d 866 (1974), *see also, e.g.,* Martin v. Peyton, 246 N.Y. 213, 158 N.E. 77 (1927).

145.　*See, e.g.,* Reeves v. Teuscher, 881 F.2d 1495 (9th Cir.1989); SEC v. Interlink Data Network of Los Angeles, 1993 WL 603274, [1993–1994 Transfer Binder] Fed. Sec. L. Rep.

that when the limited partner is also expected to manage and operate the business, a security will not exist.[146]   Some state securities acts expressly include limited partnership interests in the definition of security.[147]

Since a general partnership interest and most joint ventures will ordinarily carry with them a substantial say in the management of the enterprise, they will not fall under the securities laws' purview unless there is substantial reliance on the efforts of others.[148]   However, where a joint venturer or general partner does not exercise control and in essence is a passive investor, a security will be found to exist.[149]   A sale-leaseback arrangement has similarly been held to be a security where the lessors were in fact passive investors.[150]

Limited Liability Companies

A relatively new form of doing business is the limited liability company.[151]   Limited liability companies are designed to give investors the benefit of pass-through tax treatment that applies to limited partnerships without imposing the limitation that limited partners may not exert too much control in the day-to-day management lest they be declared general partners and thereby lose their limited liability shield. A limited liability company (and hence shares in those companies) has corporate attributes, including possibly the centralization of management.   Nevertheless, limited liability companies can be set up without

(CCH) ¶ 98,049 (C.D.Cal.1993); Miltland Raleigh–Durham v. Myers, 807 F.Supp. 1025 (S.D.N.Y.1992).

146.   Pamaco Partnership Management Corp. v. Enning, 27 F.3d 563 (4th Cir.1994); Darrah v. Garrett, [1984 Transfer Binder] Fed.Sec.L.Rep. (CCH) ¶ 91,472 (N.D.Ohio 1984) (limited partner who exercised substantial control did not purchase a security).

147.   See Rivlin v. Levine, 195 Cal.App.2d 13, 15 Cal.Rptr. 587 (1961) (California statute at that time excluded limited partnerships from security laws except if the partnership interest was offered to the public, West's Ann.Cal.Corp. Code § 25100(e)).

148.   Holden v. Hagopian, 978 F.2d 1115 (9th Cir.1992) (failure to adequately allege that general partnership interest was a security); Klaers v. St. Peter, 942 F.2d 535 (8th Cir.1991), *appeal after remand* 8 F.3d 650 (1993) (real estate partnership interests were not securities; amendment to partnership agreement involving additional infusion of capital did not implicate the securities laws).

See generally Joseph C. Long, Partnership, Limited Partnership, and Joint Venture Interests as Securities, 37 Mo.L.Rev. 581 (1972); Larry E. Ribstein, Private Ordering and the Securities Laws: The Case of General Partnerships, 42 Case W.Rec.L.Rev. 1 (1992); Note, General Partnership Interests as Securities Under the Federal Securities Laws: Substance over Form, 54 Fordham L.Rev. 303 (1985).

149.   Stone v. Kirk, 8 F.3d 1079 (6th Cir.1993) (joint venture interests were securities where the investors relied substantially on the expertise and managerial skills of the promoter); McGill v. American Land & Exploration Co., 776 F.2d 923 (10th Cir.1985); Kline Hotel Partners v. Aircoa Equity Interests, Inc., 725 F.Supp. 479 (D.Colo.1989) (material questions of fact existed as to whether general partnership interest was a security).

150.   *See* the discussion in the text accompanying footnotes 48–55 *supra.*

151.   More than thirty states have adopted limited liability statutes. *See e.g.,* Ala. Code §§ 10–12 *et seq.*; Colo. Rev. Stat. §§ 7–80 *et seq.*; Del. Code Ann. tit. 6 §§ 18–101 *et seq.*; Fla. Stat. Ann. §§ 608.401 *et seq.*; Mich. Comp. Laws Ann. §§ 450.4101 *et seq.*; N.C. Gen. Stat. chap. 57C.

centralized management and in such cases should be treated like a general partnership which ordinarily is not a security.[152] However, if the limited liability company agreement provides a centralized management, for the same reasons that a limited partnership interest ordinarily will be a security, interests in limited liability companies may implicate the securities laws.[153] A number of states have dealt with this new form of doing business by expressly treating limited liability companies as securities.[154] Some states have provided exemptions from registration for closely held limited liability companies and/or for professional limited liability companies.[155] There have yet to be any federal cases on point but it is virtually certain that, at least when the company structure is based on a centralized management distinct from all or some of the owners, limited liability company shares will be viewed as satisfying the elements of the *Howey* test so as to classify them as securities. The structure of a limited liability company may be so similar to that of a corporation or limited partnership, that in those instances a security should be found to exist. However, unlike "stock," interests in a limited liability company are not expressly included in the list of securities under the statutory definition and thus would be included under the more generic "investment contract" terminology. When the owners of a limited liability company are not expected to exercise control over the day-to-day business operations, much as is the case with a limited partnership,[156] interests in limited liability companies should be classified as investment contracts, except in those instances in which the investor will be playing a substantial role in the management of the business. Such would be the case for example, in a professional limited liability company, or limited liability partnership, comprised of lawyers, accountants, or some other profession.

---

152. Since neither partnership interests nor shares in limited liability companies are expressly listed in the Act's definition of "security," unlike corporate stock, they qualify as securities only if they fall within the definition of an "investment contract." *See* text accompanying footnotes 143–150 *supra* for discussion of general partnership interests as securities and the text accompanying footnotes 81–93 *supra* for discussion of the treatment of stock.

See generally Carol R. Goforth, Why Limited Liability Company Membership Interests Should Not be Treated as Securities and Possible Steps to Encourage that Result, 45 Hastings L.J. 1223 (1994).

153. For a discussion of limited liability companies and the securities laws, *see* Mark A. Sargent, Blue Sky Law: Will Limited Liability Companies Punch a Hole in the Blue Sky?, 21 Sec. Reg. L.J. 429 (1994).

154. *See, e.g.,* N.H. Rev. Stat. Ann. § 421–B:13 (requiring limited liability companies to indicate whether they are registering their interests as securities or are relying on an exemption); Indiana Code § 23–2–2–1 (including limited liability company within the definition of security).

155. *E.g.* Kans. Sec. Act § 17–1262(k)(1); La. Rev. Stat. § 51:709(12); No. Dak. Cent. Code § 10–04–06(4), (6); Wis. Stats. Ch.551 § 551.02(13)(b); N. Mex. Securities Rules 86–6.02(k)(5).

156. *See* discussion *supra. See also* the discussion of stock as a security in the text accompanying footnotes 81–93 *supra.*

Risk Capital Analysis

Supplementing the *Howey* test, many state courts and a few federal courts have followed the so-called risk capital test. In a California case the court observed:

> It bears noting that the act extends even to transactions where capital is placed without expectation of any material benefits. Thus from its exemption of securities of certain nonprofit companies the act specifically excepts "notes, bonds, debentures, or other evidence of indebtedness whether interest-bearing or not." * * * Since the act does not make profit to the supplier of capital the test of what is a security, it seems all the more clear that its objective is to afford those who risk their capital at least a fair chance of realizing their objectives in legitimate ventures whether or not they expect a return on their capital in one form or another. Hence the act is as clearly applicable to the sale of promotional memberships in the present case as it would be had the purchasers expected their return in some such familiar form as dividends. Properly so, for otherwise it could too easily be vitiated by inventive substitutes for conventional means of raising risk capital.[157]

Although couched in different terminology, the risk capital analysis is aimed at the same criteria as the *Howey* test, although, as noted above, it may not be necessary to find a common enterprise. The key is the dependency upon others for the success of the enterprise and the promotion of the activity as an investment vehicle. One federal court has observed that it is unsettled whether the risk capital test applies to "only original 'start up' capitalization or whether it also extends to transactions connected with subsequent capitalization."[158] Finally, the investment of money or property is a primary factor. The only element expressly lacking from the risk-capital test, at least to the extent of requiring a pooling of interests, is the requirement of a common enterprise. Thus, for example, the risk-capital test, if accepted, can be used to find a security in the absence of either horizontal or vertical commonality, as would be the case with managed brokerage accounts. There seems to be an increasing basis for applying the risk capital test for determining whether a particular investment vehicle is a security under the federal securities laws.[159]

---

157. Silver Hills Country Club v. Sobieski, 55 Cal.2d 811, 13 Cal.Rptr. 186, 361 P.2d 906 (1961). *See also, e.g.,* Crocker National Bank v. Rockwell International Corp., 555 F.Supp. 47 (N.D.Cal.1982). The risk capital analysis was invoked in Tanenbaum v. Agri-Capital, Inc., 885 F.2d 464 (8th Cir.1989) (whether cattle embryo contract was the sale of a security was a question of fact; applying Arkansas law). For a case rejecting the risk capital test *see* Wieboldt v. Metz, 355 F.Supp. 255 (S.D.N.Y.1973).

158. Securities Administrator v. College Assistance Plan, 533 F.Supp. 118, 123 (D.Guam 1981), *judgment affirmed* 700 F.2d 548 (9th Cir.1983), commenting on Jet Set Travel Club v. Commissioner, 21 Or.App. 362, 535 P.2d 109, 112 (1975).

159. Simon Oil Co., Ltd. v. Norman, 789 F.2d 780, 781–82 (9th Cir.1986); Home Guaranty Insurance Corp. v. Third Financial Services, Inc., 667 F.Supp. 577 (M.D.Tenn. 1987) (mortgage guarantees are not securities under risk capital test). Deauville Sav. & Loan Assoc. v. Westwood Sav. & Loan Assoc., 648 F.Supp. 513 (C.D.Cal.1986) (loan participation not a security under risk capital test); Ahern v. Gaussoin, 611 F.Supp. 1465

Alternative Remedies

Fraudulent transactions involving investment schemes may be attacked outside of the securities laws. Because of recent expansion of remedies under the Racketeer Influenced and Corrupt Organizations Act[160]—more commonly known as RICO—, in a case involving a borderline instrument or investment scheme, it was found that allegations of mail fraud and/or wire fraud may support the RICO treble damage penalty without the plaintiff having to show that a security was involved.[161]

§ 1.5.1 Derivative Investments: Stock Options, Index Options, and Futures

Derivative Instruments—An Overview

Over the past three decades, the securities markets have been infused with options trading in order to provide an alternative way to participate in short term investments in securities. Put and call options on individual securities allow investors to hedge their positions and thereby limit risk. While reducing risk may be the motivation for some investors, much options trading has been on a speculative basis. Since its inception, public trading of options on securities exchanges has been an active financial market. The success of the options markets for individual securities paved the way for expansion into markets for index options which are subject to Securities and Exchange Commission regulation and markets for futures based on stock indexes, which are subject to the jurisdiction of the Commodity Futures Trading Commission.[1] The index markets permit investors to diversify their holdings by not tying their investments to the stock of a particular issuer. Index options and futures are broadly-based indexes the value of which is dependent upon the current per share price of the stocks comprising the index. By utilizing the index markets investors can take positions in groups of stocks tied to a publicly traded index option or futures contract. The index markets also have provided additional opportunities for the new

(D.Or.1985) (finding notes to be securities under the risk capital test); Annot., "Risk Capital" Test for Determination of Whether Transaction Involves Security, within Meaning of Federal Securities Act of 1933, 68 A.L.R.Fed. 89 (1984).

160. 18 U.S.C.A. §§ 1961–1968. *See* Sedima, S.P.R.L. v. Imrex, Co., 473 U.S. 479, 105 S.Ct. 3275, 87 L.Ed.2d 346 (1985).

RICO provides a treble damage remedy for persons injured in their business or property as a result of a pattern of racketeering activity. Securities fraud is expressly included as one of the predicate acts that can form the basis of a RICO violation. RICO is discussed in § 19.3, *infra* (Lawyer's Edition only).

161. *E.g.* Carpenter v. United States, 484 U.S. 19, 108 S.Ct. 316, 98 L.Ed.2d 275 (1987) (upholding insider trading convictions under mail fraud act). *But cf.* McNally v. United States, 483 U.S. 350, 107 S.Ct. 2875, 97 L.Ed.2d 292 (1987) (rejecting intangible rights theory of mail fraud; requiring actual or anticipated receipt of money by defendant). Mail and wire fraud are discussed in § 19.3.1 *infra* (Practitioner's Edition only).

§ 1.5.1

1. *See* § 1.4.1 *supra.*

breed of arbitrageurs known as risk arbitrageurs.[2]

Options provide an important way to hedge long positions in securities. A long position exists when an investor owns securities, as opposed to a short position when an investor has sold options or securities thereby obligating him or her to purchase them at a later date. For example,[3] an investor owning 1000 shares of ABC Co. stock which is currently trading at $12 per share may want to limit the risk of a price decline. In such a case, an appropriate hedge strategy would be to buy put options with a strike price of $10 per share. This would guaranty that at any time until the expiration date the investor could sell the stock for $10 per share. Buying the puts will cause the investor to incur the cost of the premium that the market has placed on the put and thereby the investor increases his or her total cost but limits the risk of loss.

Another example of an option strategy occurs when the investor believes that the market is likely to decline and therefore he or she maintains a large cash balance. In order to hedge against the possibility that their negative market outlook is wrong, investors may want to purchase call options, in selected stocks or broader-based index options, which would allow participation in a market rise. The purchase of call options involves less cash than investing in the underlying stocks but also is much more speculative as the investor stands to lose his or her entire investment if the option expires when the stock price is below the option exercise price.

Index Options and Futures

Beyond options on individual stocks, both options and futures are now available based on indexes comprised of a "basket" of securities. There are options based on indexes comprised of certain stocks. There are broad-based market indexes such as the Value Line index and one based on the Standard & Poor Five Hundred Index. There are narrower composite indexes such as those paralleling the Standard & Poor One Hundred Index and the Dow Industrial Average. Furthermore, there are industry-based indexes such as the technology index or indexes based on investments in a particular locale. A parallel development has occurred in the futures markets with the advent of financial futures.

In addition to futures contracts based on government securities,[4] there are now publicly traded futures contracts based upon the same types of indexes that underlie options which are traded on securities

2. *See* Thomas L. Hazen, Volatility and Market Inefficiency: A Commentary on the Effects of Options, Futures, and Risk Arbitrage on the Stock Market, 44 Wash. & Lee L.Rev. 789 (1987); Janet E. Kerr & John C. Maguire, Program Trading—A Critical Analysis, 45 Wash. & Lee L.Rev. 991 (1988).

3. For additional examples of option strategies and a more detailed analysis of the risks involved, *see, e.g.,* Understanding the Risks and Uses of Listed Options (Oct.1982) (jointly prepared by the American Stock Exchange, Chicago Board Options Exchange, Pacific Stock Exchange, Philadelphia Stock Exchange, and the Options Clearing Corporation).

4. *See, e.g.,* Messer v. E.F. Hutton & Co., 847 F.2d 673 (11th Cir.1988) (United States Treasury Bill futures are subject to CFTC, not SEC, jurisdiction).

rather than commodities exchanges. The overlap, however, is not complete. Commodity options and futures on individual nonexempt securities are not permitted;[5] thus derivative instruments based on such securities must be traded in the securities markets.

Over and beyond straight-forward futures contracts, there is now a public market for options on futures. It is argued that all of these financial instruments make the market more efficient as they provide alternative investments that help keep the markets on a more even keel.[6] Money managers have taken advantage of these new investment vehicles. Many mutual funds and other pooled investment vehicles[7] have arisen in connection with the options markets. Additionally the options and financial futures markets provide new ways for money managers to diversify and hedge their portfolios.

Widely followed options and futures indexes have also provided a new mechanism for traders who base their investments on the markets' technical factors rather than the fundamentals of the underlying securities or commodities. The computer age has aided such technical investors since simultaneous investments across several markets are now much more accessible.

Index Participations as Securities

In 1988, three securities exchanges[8] filed applications to permit exchange trading of stock index participation instruments (also known as stock baskets). In March 1989, the SEC granted the applications and approved trading of stock baskets on these securities exchanges.[9] Stock index futures have been trading on the commodities exchanges for a number of years.[10] The SEC's recognition of these new index participation units as securities reopened the SEC/CFTC jurisdictional struggle.[11] The Chicago Mercantile Exchange has challenged the SEC action, claiming that the new instruments are futures contracts and as such are subject to the exclusive jurisdiction of the CFTC.[12]

The Seventh Circuit ruled that index participations were subject to

---

5. *See,* § 1.4.1 *supra.*

6. *See, e.g.,* Joseph M. Burns, A Treatise on Markets, Spot, Futures, and Options (1979); Hazen *supra* footnote 2.

7. Sales of interests in investment pools will be treated as securities transactions. *See* In the Matter of ABC Portfolio Development Group, Inc., [1994–1995 Transfer Binder] Fed. Sec. L. Rep. (CCH) ¶ 85,422 (SEC 1994) (sales of investment pool interests were sales of interests in an investment company subject to the Investment Company Act of 1940 and also were securities subject to the 1933 and 1934 Acts).

8. The American Stock Exchange, the Philadelphia Stock Exchange, and the Chicago Board Options Exchange.

9. Sec. Exch. Act Rel. No. 34–26709 (SEC March 14, 1989).

10. *See* § 1.4.1 *supra* and § 19.6 *infra* (Practitioner's Edition only).

11. *See* Thomas E. Ricks, Stock Basket Approval Stirs Court Action, Wall St.J. p. C1 (Wednesday, March 15, 1989). *See also* § 1.4.1 *supra.*

12. *See* Ricks *supra* footnote 11.

the exclusive jurisdiction of the CFTC.[13] The court, per Judge Easterbrook, looked to the 1982 jurisdictional accord between the SEC and
CFTC under which investments that could be classified both as securities and commodities were placed under the CFTC's jurisdiction.[14]
Judge Easterbrook explained that the basic premise underlying the
accord was that if an instrument could be classified as both a security
and a futures contract, exclusive jurisdiction of its trading lies with the
CFTC. Since the index participations were held to be futures contracts,
it was not necessary to decide whether the index participations were
securities. In the wake of the decision, the Bush administration introduced legislation that would transfer jurisdiction over all stock index
futures to the SEC.[15] The Market Reform Act of 1990 contained
proposals to coordinate CFTC and SEC regulation but this legislation
was not enacted.[16] The Futures Trading Practices Act of 1991 as
adopted by the Senate[17] would have taken a functional approach in
allocating jurisdiction between the CFTC and the SEC over hybrid
investment vehicles. The 1991 bill would have allocated jurisdiction to
the CFTC if more than 50 percent of the overall value or expected
change in value of the instrument is attributable to the commodity
component. Another feature of the 1991 bill is that it would have
allocated to the SEC jurisdiction over all index participation units that
were adopted or proposed to the Commission before the end of 1990.
The parallel 1991 House legislation was silent on jurisdictional issues,
thus leaving the matter to be resolved in legislative conference. As
enacted, the Futures Trading Practices Act of 1992 deleted the Senate
provisions but called for further study on hybrid investments.

At the same time that the CFTC was contesting the applicability of
the securities laws to index participations, it exempted a number of
hybrid instruments from the coverage of the Commodity Exchange Act.[18]
Hybrid investments qualifying for the exemption include instruments
that combine commodity option or futures characteristics with debt
instruments, preferred equity instruments, and depositary transactions.
The exemption is available to qualifying hybrid instruments only when
the qualifying hybrid instrument: (1) is indexed to a commodity on a

13. Chicago Mercantile Exchange v. SEC, 883 F.2d 537 (7th Cir.1989), *cert. denied* 496
U.S. 936, 110 S.Ct. 3214, 110 L.Ed.2d 662 (1990).

14. The jurisdictional accord is discussed in § 1.4.1. *Compare, e.g.,* SEC Grants
Unprecedented Relief to Allow Novel Mutual Fund to Proceed, 22 Sec.Reg. & L.Rep. (BNA)
1090 (July 27, 1990) (permitting investment company to market nonredeemable shares of
unit investment trust holding a portfolio of securities comprising the Standard & Poor 500
Index; these funds were viewed as distinguishable from the IPs that were considered in the
Chicago Mercantile Exchange decision).

15. *See* 22 Sec.Reg. & L.Rep. (BNA) 731 (May 11, 1990).

16. *See* S.Rep. on S. 648, Sen.Comm. on Banking, Housing & Urban Affairs, S.Rep. No.
101–300, 101st Cong., 2d Sess. (May 22, 1990).

17. *See* Report on S. 207, Sen.Comm. on Agriculture, Nutrition and Forestry, Rep. No.
102–22, 102d Cong., 1st Sess. (March 12, 1991).

18. CFTC Regulations §§ 34.1–34.3, 17 C.F.R. §§ 34.1–34.3. *See* Statutory Interpretation Concerning Certain Hybrid Instruments, [1990–1992 Transfer Binder] Comm.Fut.
L.Rep. (CCH) ¶ 24,805 (CFTC April 11, 1990).

basis no greater than one-to-one; (2) has a loss limitation; (3) has a commodity-independent yield of at least 50 percent but no more than one hundred and fifty percent of the estimated yield at the time of issuance of a comparable nonhybrid instrument; (4) does not have a commodity component which is severable from the debt, preferred equity, or depository instrument; (5) does not call for settlement or delivery by means of a delivery instrument specified in the rules of a designated contract market; and (6) is not marketed as a futures contract or commodity option or as having the characteristics of a futures contract or commodity option, except to the extent that such a description is necessary to accurately describe the investment or to comply with applicable disclosure requirements.[19]

New Strategies; Program Trading

Program trading involves the use of computers by large investors to track price discrepancies between index futures contracts, index options, and the cash value of the stocks underlying the indexes. The computer driven program permits the large investor to monitor the relative prices of index futures, options and the cash value of the index. When it appears that there is a discrepancy between the option or futures premium and the cash value, the trader will lock in a profit by arbitraging one against the other. For example, if the futures price is discounted below the cash value of the index then the trader who is long in the stocks will begin a "sell program" in which he or she will sell the stock and buy the discounted futures contract. When the futures are trading at a premium above the cash value, the trader will begin a "buy program" which consists of selling the futures contract and buying the stocks that comprise the index.

The newly developed index funds have further magnified the effects of program trading. Successful program trading, as is the case with any type of arbitrage, requires large volume transactions with low individual transaction costs. Furthermore, it would take an investment of approximately twenty-five million dollars to invest in the stocks underlying the Standard & Poor Five Hundred, which is one of the popular indexes and thus forms the basis for index futures and options arbitrage. Thus, program trading is not a viable route for most individual investors. The index funds, set up as mutual funds, permit individual investors to participate in program trading by pooling their investments into a fund managed by an investment adviser who invests in indexed stocks, futures and options in accordance with the program trading guidelines discussed above. The events leading up to and following the market crash of October, 1987 have resulted in numerous studies concerning the effects of index arbitrage and computerized trading on the stock mar-

---

19. *Id. See also, e.g.,* Interpretive Letter No. 90–2, [1987–1990 Transfer Binder] Comm.Fut.L.Rep. (CCH) ¶ 24,625 (CFTC March 2, 1990) (exempting hybrid instruments of foreign banks subject to regulatory supervision by the New York Banking Department).

ket.[20]

In addition to the foregoing program trading methods, other systems have been developed to help balance stock market movements. One result has been that when analysts' technical systems issue a buy or sell signal, the markets react in a very volatile manner. Also, on the third Friday of each month when options are set to expire, there have been some truly exceptional market responses. This is especially true on triple witching days when the options, index options, and index futures all expire. It is ironic that financial instruments whose justification is the increase of market efficiency have been accused of having quite the opposite effect in terms of increasing volatility and wide swings in both market averages and individual securities. As a result, there have been a number of proposals for dealing with the volatility created by program trading. These proposals include requiring arbitrageurs to disclose all long and short positions in order to help the market anticipate the reaction as the options and futures expire or become due.

The Market Reform Act of 1990[21] gives the Securities and Exchange Commission the authority to promulgate rules designed to limit program trading. The Commission is further given the power to promulgate rules aimed at preventing manipulation of the price levels of the equity securities markets or substantial segments of the securities markets. [22] This provision is designed to allow the Commission to focus on manipulation of stock indexes which represent all, or a portion, of the market. The Commission is given the authority to prohibit or limit trading practices during periods of "extraordinary volatility."[23] The power to prohibit or limit trading practices is given when those trading practices have in the past contributed "significantly" to extraordinary levels of

---

20. *See, e.g.,* Report of the Presidential Task Force on Market Practices (Jan. 8, 1988) (frequently referred to as the Brady report); CFTC Division of Economic Analysis and Division of Trading and Markets, Final Report on Stock Index Futures and Cash Market Activity During October 1987, (Jan. 6, 1988); CFTC Division of Economic Analysis and Division of Trading and Markets, Interim Report on Stock Index Futures and Cash Market Activity During October 1987 (Nov. 9, 1987); SEC Report by the Division on Market Regulation: The October 1987 Market Break (Feb.1988); U.S. General Accounting Office, Report to Congressional Requesters, Financial Markets Preliminary Observations on the October 1987 crash (Jan. 1988); Miller, Hawke, Malkiel & Scholes, Preliminary Report of the Committee of Inquiry Appointed by the Chicago Mercantile Exchange to Examine Events Surrounding October 19, 1987 (Dec. 22, 1987). *See generally* Eric A. Chiappinelli, Red October: Its Origins, Consequences, and the Need to Revive the National Market System, 18 Sec.Reg.L.J. 144 (1990); C. Edward Fletcher III, Of Crashes, Corrections, and the Culture of Financial Information—What They Tell Us About the Need For Federal Securities Regulation, 54 Mo.L.Rev. 515 (1989); Hazen, *supra* footnote 1; Roberta S. Karmel, The Rashomon Effect in the After-the-Crash Studies, 21 Rev.Sec. & Commod. Reg. 101 (1988); Jerry W. Markham & Rita M. Stephanz, The Stock Market Crash of 1987–The United States Looks at New Recommendations, 76 Geo.L.J. 1993 (1988); Lewis D. Solomon & Howard B. Dicker, The Crash of 1987: A Legal and Public Policy Analysis, 57 Fordham L.Rev. 191 (1988); Symposium on the Regulation of Secondary Trading Markets: Program Trading, Volatility, Portfolio Insurance, and the Role of Specialists and Market Makers, 74 Cornell L.Rev. 799 (1989). *See also, e.g.,* Richard A. Booth, The Uncertain Case for Regulating Program Trading, 1994 Colum. Bus. L. Rev. 1.

21. *See* the discussion in § 10.1 *infra.*

22. 15 U.S.C.A. § 78i(h)(1).

23. 15 U.S.C.A. § 78i(h)(2).

volatility and thus threatened the maintenance of fair and orderly markets.[24] The new legislation also gives the Commission emergency powers in times of market disruptions as well as rulemaking power with regard to large trader reporting.[25]

§ 1.6 The Decision to Go Public

Unless it is structured to fall within one of the 1933 Act's exemptions,[1] any time a company plans for financing other than through a bank loan, the financing will implicate the Act's registration provisions.[2] Of course, many capital raising plans are accomplished through exempt offerings. However, when an exemption is not available, or when a company decides to go public for other reasons, it is necessary to register the offering under the Securities Act of 1933.

The registration statement that is to be filed with the SEC[3] is the result of a joint effort by, among others, the issuer, the issuer's attorneys—(both inside house counsel and outside general counsel), the underwriter, the underwriter's attorneys, and the accountants who serve as auditors for the financial statements. In many cases there will also be special securities counsel whose responsibilities are to help draft and supervise the preparation of the registration statement and to be watchful for SEC disclosure problems. The registration statement generally will be printed professionally and in many instances technical experts will need to be retained to prepare reports about the issuer's business. The substantial expense involved in this process means that issuers will frequently prefer alternative means of financing. In addition to the substantial expense, a registered offering requires strict compliance with the applicable disclosure provisions lest there be substantial liability exposure of the key participants in the registration and offering process.[4] Additionally, particular aspects of the issuer's business or past operations may create especially problematic disclosure issues.[5]

The initial step in the registration process is the decision to embark upon public financing. Thus, the first question to be answered is whether or not the needed capital should be procured by way of a registered public offering or, alternatively, through a private placement[6] or some other exempt method of financing. As a general matter, exempt

---

24. *Id.*

25. *See* § 10.1 *infra. Cf.* Timpinaro v. SEC, 2 F.3d 453 (D.C.Cir.1993) (SEC professional trader rule remanded for further administrative proceedings to demonstrate that the rule was proper; the rule was not struck down and was thus retained pending SEC remand).

§ **1.6**

1. 15 U.S.C.A. §§ 77c, d. *See* chapter 4 *infra.*

2. 15 U.S.C.A. §§ 77f, g.

3. There are various alternative forms for the registration statement. *See* § 3.3 *infra.*

4. *See* chapter 7 *infra.*

5. *See, e.g.,* Daniel I. Winnike & Christopher E. Nordquist, Federal Securities Law Issues for the Sticky Offering, 48 Bus.Law. 869 (1993).

6. 15 U.S.C.A. § 77d(2); 17 C.F.R. § 240.506. *See* §§ 4.19–4.21 *infra.*

offerings entail less cost, both in terms of the actual marketing expenses as well as professional fees, printing and other indirect costs of preparing the registration statement. Exempt offerings may also involve less exposure under the Act's civil liability provisions[7] than registered public offerings.[8]

In deciding whether or not to embark upon a registered offering, there are a number of advantages and disadvantages that need to be considered.[9] The potential advantages and disadvantages must be weighed carefully in order to determine whether a public offering is the most appropriate means of financing.

Advantages of going public

The advantages include creating a public market that will allow for future public financing to provide for company expansion, diversification, increase in working capital or retirement of preexisting debt. In many instances the company may be in need of large capital infusions and such substantial sums may not feasibly be available through bank loans or other means of private financing. The issuer may want the potential for additional equity rather than debt financing. Furthermore, the presence of a favorable climate in the public market may make a registered public offering the most efficient fundraising device. The creation of a public market for an issuer's securities will result in increased liquidity of the holdings of the principal owners, as well as the holdings of the minority shareholders.

Frequently, an issuer's offering of its securities will be accompanied or followed by a secondary offering. In a secondary offering insiders or others who have received the issuer's securities (generally as part of a previous nonpublic transaction) decide to sell their shares to the public.[10] In such a situation, the selling shareholders may be able to ride "piggy back" on a registered primary offering. Even in the absence of a registered secondary offering, with the public market created by the

---

7. Nevertheless, an unsuccessful attempt to secure an exemption can result in substantial civil and criminal liability. *See* sections 5 and 12(1) of the 1933 Act, 15 U.S.C.A. §§ 77e, 77l(1) which are discussed in §§ 2.2–2.5, 7.2. In addition, there may be liability under the various antifraud provisions for materially misleading statements in connection with exempt offerings. *See* section 12(2) of the 1933 Act and Rule 10b–5 of the 1934 Act. 15 U.S.C.A. § 77l(2); 17 C.F.R. § 240.10b–5, which are discussed in § 7.5, 13.2–13.11 *infra.* There is an overview of 1933 Act civil liabilities in § 1.7 *infra.*

8. In addition to the provisions imposing liability for violation of the registration requirements and the general antifraud provisions (*see* footnote 6 *supra*), there is express liability for material misstatements or omissions in the registration statement. *See* section 11 of the 1933 Act, 15 U.S.C.A. § 77k, which is discussed in §§ 7.3–7.4.1 *infra.*

9. *See generally* William M. Prifti, Securities: Public and Private Offerings §§ 2–7 (1974); Gerard J. Robinson & Klaus Eppler, Going Public (1978 rev.); Victor H. Boyajian, Early Planning for Your Initial Public Offering, 22 Sec. Reg. 67 (1994); Carl W. Schneider & Joseph M. Manko, Going Public–Practice, Procedure and Consequences, 15 Vill.L.Rev. 283 (1970); Russell B. Stevenson, Jr., Preparing a Company for an Initial Public Offering, 27 Rev. Sec. & Commod. Reg. 203 (1994); Winneke & Nordquist, *supra* footnote 5; Note, Considerations Involved in a First Public Offering of Stock, 8 Wake Forest L.Rev. 423 (1972).

10. *See* §§ 4.24, 4.25 *infra.*

primary offering, existing shareholders may be able to sell their shares in the aftermarket.[11] An issuer's public financing thus may help selling shareholders who may want to liquidate their holdings in whole or in part and thereby take advantage of the liquidity and favorable market conditions created by the primary offering of the issuer.[12]

Another frequent beneficial by-product of going public is that the process gives the company increasing prestige and publicity among the general public thus providing the issuer with a more favorable image and putting it in a better competitive position for its products or services. Additionally, the fact that a corporation has a public market for its securities may create an air of financial success. In some cases, a public offering will improve the company's net worth and enhance its ability to raise additional funds in the future. There are also collateral benefits of going public such as the company's ability to adopt attractive employee stock option and/or stock purchase plans in order to attract good key employees. A further advantage to going public is that the company whose stock is publicly traded may be in a better position to acquire other companies through the means of an exchange offer using the shares acquiring company as consideration for the share of the target company.[13]

Disadvantages of going public

There are a variety of potential disadvantages to public financing, however. Thus, it is necessary for the issuer to carefully consider all aspects of the alternative means of financing. Along with the foregoing favorable aspects of public financing, it must be kept in mind that economic and market conditions may not be ripe for taking advantage of this method. A number of other potential pitfalls can be identified. For example, in addition to the substantial cost of a registered offering, there is the high expense of maintaining a public company, not the least of which is the increased expense and potential liability exposure created by the registration and periodic reporting provisions of the Securities Exchange Act of 1934.[14] Public ownership, especially when it involves common stock, frequently results in loss of control over many management matters. Dividend policy is very likely to be affected, since in order to maintain a marketable security, depending upon the industry and the practices of competing companies, the directors frequently have

---

11. Such shares may remain restricted after the public offering. That is, the preexisting shareholders may not be able to sell their securities without registration or an applicable exemption. *See* §§ 4.23–4.26.1. SEC Rule 144 sets forth a safe harbor for selling these shares without registration. 17 C.F.R. § 230.144 which is discussed in § 4.26 *infra*.

12. Tag-along, or piggy-back, secondary distributions frequently create disclosure problems concerning dilution of the public's investment and use of the proceeds. *See, e.g.,* In the Matter of Universal Camera Corp., 19 S.E.C. 648 (1945); §§ 3.7, 4.25 *infra*.

13. The converse may also be true. A public company with diluted ownership may be an easier target, albeit an expensive one for takeover by others than a company with a closely-knit ownership.

14. 15 U.S.C.A. §§ 78 *l*, 78m. *See* chapter 9 *infra*. *See generally*, Carl W. Schneider & Jason M. Schergel, "Now That You Are Publicly Owned," 36 Bus.Law. 1631 (1981).

to be willing to declare dividends—so as to make the security marketable in competition with other securities of a similar type as well as with the higher yielding bond market. In operating the enterprise, management of a publicly held company has to pay heed to the day–to–day market activity in the stock, and thus may focus more closely on the short term as opposed to the long term goals of the business. Just as a publicly traded company may be in a better position to acquire other companies, the fact that a company is publicly held may make it an easier target as a take-over candidate.[15]

Perhaps the most serious potential economic disadvantage of going public, from a financial point of view, is that contrary to the best plans and intentions of the underwriter and financial analyst, the securities might not find a receptive market. When a public offering falls upon an unreceptive market, the result is that the stock will sell at a discount substantially below the anticipated price that was probably based on past earnings (if any) and the company's book value.[16] This will in turn decrease public and investor confidence in the issuer's business. Whenever the market provides such a soft reception, the issuer and selling shareholders may find themselves with less capital than had been anticipated.

Another factor which frequently is determinative in selecting the form and method of corporate financing is the actual cost of the registration statement itself. A public offering can easily cost more than several hundred thousand dollars when one includes the printing costs, underwriters commissions, directly resulting legal fees and auditing fees, as well as indirect costs that may be necessary to put the company in a position to withstand the public disclosures required in the registration statement. Finally, as mentioned above, the potential liabilities that may result from a problematic public offering may mitigate in favor of an exempt offering.[17]

It has been asserted that increasingly onerous SEC disclosure requirements have made public financing so expensive that a number of businesses are in fact deprived of access to the public market. One response has been simplification of the disclosure requirements, especially with regard to relatively small issues.[18] These developments in disclosure may well ease a number of the negative aspects of public financing for many comparatively small issuers.

---

15. Takeovers and the tender offer provisions are discussed in §§ 11.10–11.22 *infra.*

16. One way to account for some of the hazards of an unreceptive offering is to embark on a contingent offering, if the circumstances so warrant. *See* footnotes 19–24 *infra* and accompanying text.

17. *See* footnotes 6–7 *supra.*

18. The SEC has adopted two 1933 Act registration forms (Forms SB–1 and SB–2) which are available to small business issuers. *See* § 3.3 *infra.* Additionally, there are simplified 1934 Act disclosures for these issuers as well. *See* § 9.3 *infra.* In fact, the Commission has adopted a simplified set of disclosure instructions generally applicable to small business issues. Reg. S–B.

Contingent public offerings

Issuers who frequently embark on public offerings do so in response to general financing needs, including, for example, expansion of the business. It is not uncommon for an issuer to envision a project that requires a minimum capitalization from the offering. This type of specifically targeted financing does not cause a problem where the issuer has an established track record or there are other reasons to believe that the securities will be sold at the offering price. However, sometimes an issuer will want to take precautions when a minimum amount of funds is needed. In such a case the securities may be offered on an "all or none" basis.[19] In an "all or none" offering, if within a specified period there is not a full subscription to all shares being offered, the offering is cancelled. A variation on the "all or none" offering is a "part or none" offering in which a refund offer will be made if less than a specified portion of the offering has been subscribed to. In both "all or none" and "part or none" offerings, the subscribers' funds typically will be placed in an escrow account and are not made available to the issuer unless the terms of the offering have been fulfilled.[20]

The issuer's financing needs may not be the only cause of "all or none" or "part or none" clauses in the terms of the offering. The "part or none" offering, like "all or none" offerings, can have the effect of assuring potential investors that there is sufficient investment interest to make the offering worthwhile. Both "all or none" and "part or none" offerings put a great deal of pressure on those marketing the securities[21] and thus these offerings may be susceptible to manipulation.[22] Issuers embarking on all or none and part or none offerings must be specific as to the offering price, the duration of the offering, and the amount of securities that must be sold to make the offering effec-

19. *See* Robert B. Robbins, All-or-None Offerings: An Update, 19 Rev.Sec. & Commod. Reg. 181 (1986); Robert B. Robbins, All-or-None Offerings, 19 Rev.Sec. & Commod. Reg. 59 (1986).

20. *See* Richard W. Jennings & Harold Marsh, Jr., Securities Regulation: Cases and Materials 30 (6th ed. 1987).

21. SEC v. Blinder, Robinson & Co., 542 F.Supp. 468, 476 (D.Colo.1982), *affirmed* 1983 WL 20181, [1984–85 Transfer Binder] Fed.Sec.L.Rep. (CCH) ¶ 99,491 (10th Cir.1983), *cert. denied* 469 U.S. 1108, 105 S.Ct. 783, 83 L.Ed.2d 777 (1985) ("in an 'all or none' offering of securities by a new company, whether all the securities have been sold to the public in bona fide market transactions is of particular importance because the 'all or none' contingency is the investors' principal protection. Each investor is comforted by the knowledge that unless his judgment to take the risk is shared by enough others to sell out the issue, his money will be returned"). It has been suggested, however, that the applicable SEC regulations were not imposed in response to this concern. Robert B. Robbins, All-or-None Offerings, 19 Rev.Sec. & Commod. Reg. 59, 62 (1986).

22. *See, e.g.,* C.E. Carlson, Inc. v. SEC, 859 F.2d 1429 (10th Cir.1988) (underwriter held liable for falsely creating the impression that a "part or none" offering was successful). Other examples of fraudulent representations regarding the satisfaction of the "all or none" contingency include A.J. White & Co. v. SEC, 556 F.2d 619 (1st Cir.1977), *cert. denied* 434 U.S. 969, 98 S.Ct. 516, 54 L.Ed.2d 457 (1977); SEC. v. Blinder, Robinson & Co., 542 F.Supp. 468 (D.Colo.1982), *affirmed* 1983 WL 20181, [1984–85 Transfer Binder] Fed.Sec.L.Rep. (CCH) ¶ 99,491 (10th Cir.1983), *cert. denied* 469 U.S. 1108, 105 S.Ct. 783, 83 L.Ed.2d 777 (1985); SEC. v. Manor Nursing Centers, 340 F.Supp. 913, 918 (S.D.N.Y. 1971), *modified* 458 F.2d 1082 (2d Cir.1972).

tive.[23]	Also, the possibility of a refund in an offering that is not fully subscribed to cannot be offered on a selective basis but must be offered to all would-be purchasers.[24]

§ 1.7 Overview of Private Remedies Under the Securities Act of 1933 and the Securities Exchange Act of 1934

Violations of the federal securities laws can give rise to criminal penalties. Violations can also result in civil enforcement actions by the SEC.[1] In appropriate cases, transgressions of the securities laws may result in SEC administrative proceedings[2] or disciplinary actions by securities exchanges or national securities associations.[3] Enforcement of the federal securities laws is not limited to governmental action nor to proceedings by self regulatory organizations. The securities laws provide various private rights of action which are summarized below and discussed in more detail throughout this treatise.

There are a number of private remedies that can be invoked to redress violations of the securities laws. Thus, for example, there are broad antifraud remedies applicable generally to securities transactions.[4] There are more specific provisions relating to such matters as well as those provisions specifically tailored to certain types of transactions such as public offerings,[5] tender offers,[6] and proxy solicitations.[7] There is an express right of action[8] for material misrepresentations in securities offerings that are registered under the Securities Act of 1933.[9] Also, an action for rescission may be brought by a purchaser against a seller who has sold securities in violation of the Securities Act's registration re-

---

23. 17 C.F.R. § 240.10b–9. Manipulation in connection with offerings is discussed in chapter 6 *infra.* *See* in particular § 6.3 *infra.*

24. SEC Rule 10b–9 declares it to be a manipulative or deceptive act or contrivance to offer a refund unless all the securities are offered pursuant to an "all or none" or "part or none" offering. 17 C.F.R. § 240.10b–9(a). *See* §§ 6.3, 12.1 *infra.*

§ 1.7

1. *See* § 9.5 *infra.*

2. *See id.*

3. *See* § 10.2 *infra.*

4. *See,* for example, section 10(b) and Rule 10b–5 of the Securities Exchange Act of 1934 and section 17(a) of the Securities Act of 1933. 15 U.S.C.A. §§ 77q(a), 78j(b); 17 C.F.R. § 240.10b–5. *See* chapter 13 *infra.* *See also* section 12(2) of the Securities Act which provides a remedy for injured purchasers against sellers of the securities. 15 U.S.C.A. § 77l(2) which is discussed in § 7.5 *infra.* In addition the Exchange Act provides a remedy against persons responsible for materially misleading filings with the SEC. 15 U.S.C.A. § 78r(a). *See* § 12.8 *infra.*

5. *See* footnotes 9–10 *infra.*

6. Sections 13(d), (e) and 14(d), (e) of the Exchange Act, 15 U.S.C.A. §§ 78m(d), (e), 78n(d), (e). *See* §§ 11.10–11.19 *infra.*

7. Section 14(a) and Rule 14a–9 of the Exchange Act, 15 U.S.C.A. § 78n(a), 17 C.F.R. § 240.14a–9. *See* §§ 11.1–11.9 *infra.*

8. Section 11 of the Securities Act, 15 U.S.C.A. § 77k. *See* §§ 7.3–7.4.2 *infra.*

9. *See* chapter 2 *infra.*

quirements.[10] The Securities Exchange Act contains remedies against manipulation of exchange-listed securities[11] and against illegal insider trading.[12] Investors may also have remedies against broker-dealers who have violated the securities laws.[13]

Many of the foregoing private remedies overlap in their coverage and are generally viewed as cumulative.[14] As pointed out above (and discussed more fully in subsequent sections of this treatise), the private remedies are complemented by SEC administrative and enforcement actions[15] as well as by the potential for criminal prosecution. In addition, the 1933 Securities Act and 1934 Exchange Act remedies are supplemented by remedies under the other securities laws.[16] Even beyond the remedies that are available under the federal securities laws, it may be possible to bring an action for treble damages under RICO (Racketeer Influenced and Corrupt Organization Act).[17] Federal remedies are also supplemented by state law remedies.[18]

Most of the private remedies under the federal securities laws are found in the express provisions of the statute. There are circumstances under which federal courts have been willing to imply private remedies from federal statutes. In recent years, the Supreme Court has been much more restrictive in its approach to implied remedies generally and also to those specifically under the securities laws.[19] Nevertheless, implied remedies play an important role in enforcement of the securities laws' antifraud rules. Most notably, there is the implied remedy under SEC Rule 10b–5 [20] for fraud in connection with the purchase or sale of securities [21] and the remedy for fraud in connection with the solicitation

---

10. Section 12(1) of the Securities Act of 1933, 15 U.S.C.A. § 77*l*(1). *See* § 7.2 *infra*. The 1933 Act registration requirements are discussed in chapter 2 *infra*. Exemptions from 1933 Act registration are discussed in chapter 4 *infra*.

11. Section 9(e), 15 U.S.C.A. § 78i(e). *See* § 12.1 *infra*.

12. Sections 10(b), 16(b), and 20A, 15 U.S.C.A. §§ 78j(b), 78p(b), 78t–1. *See* §§ 12.2– 12.7, 13.9 *infra*.

13. *See* § 10.14 *infra*. *See also* § 10.2.1 *infra*.

14. *See* Herman & MacLean v. Huddleston, 459 U.S. 375, 103 S.Ct. 683, 74 L.Ed.2d 548 (1983), *on remand* 705 F.2d 775 (5th Cir.1983).

15. *See* § 9.5 *infra*.

16. *See, e.g.,* § 17.10 *infra* (civil remedies under the Investment Company Act); § 18.4 *infra* (sanctions for violations of the Investment Advisers Act).

17. 18 U.S.C.A. §§ 1961–1968. *See* § 19.3 *infra* (Practitioner's Edition only).

18. State law remedies may be found both in common law rights of action and under the state securities laws. State securities laws are discussed in chapter 8.

19. *E.g.,* Thompson v. Thompson, 484 U.S. 174, 108 S.Ct. 513, 98 L.Ed.2d 512 (1988); California v. Sierra Club, 451 U.S. 287, 101 S.Ct. 1775, 68 L.Ed.2d 101 (1981); Middlesex County Sewerage Authority v. National Sea Clammers Association, 453 U.S. 1, 101 S.Ct. 2615, 69 L.Ed.2d 435 (1981); Transamerica Mortgage Advisors, Inc. v. Lewis, 444 U.S. 11, 100 S.Ct. 242, 62 L.Ed.2d 146 (1979); Cort v. Ash, 422 U.S. 66, 95 S.Ct. 2080, 45 L.Ed.2d 26 (1975). See 13.1 infra.

20. 17 C.F.R. § 240.10b–5.

21. 17 C.F.R. § 240.10b–5. *E.g.,* Herman & MacLean v. Huddleston, 459 U.S. 375, 103 S.Ct. 683, 74 L.Ed.2d 548 (1983); Affiliated Ute Citizens v. United States, 406 U.S. 128, 92 S.Ct. 1456, 31 L.Ed.2d 741 (1972), *rehearing denied* 407 U.S. 916, 92 S.Ct. 2430, 32 L.Ed.2d 692 (1972); Superintendent of Insurance of New York v. Bankers Life & Cas. Co.,

of shareholder votes.[22]   These two remedies have been so firmly entrenched in the federal jurisprudence that they have survived the general cutback in the recognition of private remedies.

Unfortunately, the trend towards restricting the rights of private
plaintiffs has continued in the realm of implied remedies as well as in
the context of defining the scope of express remedies.   Thus, in 1994, the
Supreme Court ruled, disagreeing with the virtually unanimous view of
the circuit and district courts to the contrary, that there is no implied
action against aiders and abettors under for violations of the federal
securities laws.[23]   Then, in 1995, the Court imposed a limit on the
express remedy under section 12(2) of the act that is not found in the
express language of the statute.[24]

The table that follows compares the private remedies that may be
available under the Securities Act of 1933 and the Securities Exchange
Act of 1934:

---

404 U.S. 6, 92 S.Ct. 165, 30 L.Ed.2d 128 (1971), *on remand* 401 F.Supp. 640 (S.D.N.Y.
1975).   *See* §§ 13.2–13.12 *infra.*

22.   Rule 14a–9, 17 C.F.R. § 240.14a–9.   *E.g.,* J.I. Case Co. v. Borak, 377 U.S. 426, 84
S.Ct. 1555, 12 L.Ed.2d 423 (1964).   *See* §§ 11.3–11.5 *infra.*

23.   Central Bank of Denver v. First Interstate Bank of Denver, __ U.S. __, 114 S.Ct.
1439, 128 L.Ed.2d 119 (1994); *see* § 13.16 *infra.*

24.   Gustafson v. Alloyd Co. __ U.S. __, 115 S.Ct. 1061, 131 L.Ed.2d 1 (1995); *see*
§ 7.5 *infra.*

Section	Scope	Standing to sue	Permissible defendants	Standard of care	Reliance required	Causation required	Statute of limitations
1933 Act section 11 (see §§ 7.3–7.4.1 infra)	misleading registration materials; express liability	purchaser of securities in registered offering	issuer, its directors, signers of the registration statement, underwriters auditors, and experts	strict liability of issuer; others have defense of reasonable investigation or reliance on experts	no	yes (negative causation defense)	one year from discovery, not more than three years after bona fide offered to the public (1933 Act § 13)
1933 Act section 12(1) (see §§ 7.2, 7.5.1–7.5.4 infra)	violation of section 5's registration and prospectus requirements, express liability	purchaser of securities sold in violation of section 5	seller who sold to plaintiff (see Pinter v. Dahl, 108 S.Ct. 2063 (1988)	strict liability	no	no	one year from discovery, not more than three years after bona fide offered to the public (1933 Act § 13)
1933 Act section 12(2) (see §§ 7.5–7.5.4 infra)	material misstatement or omission; limited to public offerings express liability	purchaser	seller who sold to plaintiff (see Pinter v. Dahl, 108 S.Ct. 2063 (1988)	defense that seller did not know and with reasonable care would not have known	no (but plaintiff must not have known of the error)	probably	one year after discovery, not more than three years after sale (1933 Act § 13)
1933 Act section 17(a) (not recognized by most courts)(see § 13.13 infra)	antifraud; implied by some courts, not by others	purchaser	any person responsible for or aiding and abetting the material misstatement, omission, or fraud	negligence (see Aaron v. SEC, 446 U.S. 680 (1980))	yes	yes	one year after discovery not more than three years after sale (1933 Act § 13) (see §§ 13.8, 13.13 infra)

Section	Scope	Standing to sue	Permissible defendants	Standard of care	Reliance required	Causation required	Statute of limitations
1934 Act section 6 (see § 10.2.1 infra)	action against exchange for failure to enforce rules; implied by some courts	injured investor	exchange	bad faith required (cf. Commodity Exchange Act § 22(b) (7 U.S.C. § 25(b))	N/A	N/A	unresolved
1934 Act section 9(e) (see § 12.1 infra)	manipulation of exchange listed securities; express liability	purchaser or seller of the manipulated security	any person responsible for the manipulative conduct; aiders and abettors	willful conduct required	N/A	yes	one year after discovery but no more than three years after the violation
1934 Act section 10(b), rule 10b-5 (see §§ 13.2-13.14 infra)	material misrepresentations; deception required; implied remedy	purchaser or seller	any person responsible for the material misrepresentations; aiders and abettors	scienter (see Aaron v. SEC, 446 U.S. 680 (1980); Blue Chip Stamps v. Manor Drug Stores, 421 U.S. 723 (1975)	yes, may be presumed	yes	one year after discovery but no more than three years after the violation or sale (see § 13.8 infra)
1934 Act sections 13(d), 14(d) (see §§ 11.11, 11.14, 11.18 infra)	Williams Act filings, implied by some courts	unresolved; may be limited to target company and its shareholders. Cf. Piper v. Chris-Craft Indus., 430 U.S. 1 (1977)	any person responsible for late or materially misleading filings; aiders and abettors	unresolved	unresolved	unresolved	unresolved

Section	Scope	Standing to sue	Permissible defendants	Standard of care	Reliance required	Causation required	Statute of limitations
1934 Act section 14(a), rule 14a-9 see §§ 11.2-11.5 infra	misleading proxy solicitation, implied remedy	shareholders	any person responsible for materially misleading proxy materials; aiders and abettors	probably negligence (see § 11.3 infra)	probably	yes	one year after discovery but no more than three years after sale (see § 13.8 infra)
1934 Act section 14(e) (see §§ 11.15, 11.19 infra)	misrepresentations in tender offers; deception required; implied by some courts	target company and its shareholders. Cf. Piper v. Chris-Craft Indus., 430 U.S. 1 (1977)	any person responsible for misrepresentations or omissions; aiders and abettors	scienter is probably required	probably	yes	one year after discovery but no more than three years after sale (see § 13.8 infra)
1934 Act section 15 (see § 10.14 infra)	misconduct by broker-dealers; not recognized by most courts	injured investors	broker-dealers	unresolved	unresolved	unresolved	unresolved
1934 Act section 16(b) (see §§ 12.3-12.7 infra)	disgorgement of short-swing insider profits; express liability	issuer, issuer's shareholders	officers, directors, and 10% beneficial owners	strict liability	no	no	no more than two years after profit was realized
1934 Act section 18(a) (see § 12.8 infra)	misleading statements in documents filed with the SEC; express liability	purchaser or seller	any person responsible for the misleading filing	defense for those acting in good faith, without knowledge of the misrepresentations	yes; plaintiff must have read the document	yes	one year after discovery but not more than three years after cause of action accrued

Section	Scope	Standing to sue	Permissible defendants	Standard of care	Reliance required	Causation required	Statute of limitations
1934 Act section 20A (see § 13.9 infra)	disgorgement of illegal insider profits	contemporaneous traders	any person trading while in possession of material non-public information in violation of law	scienter	no	no	five years after violation
1934 Act section 29(b) (see § 13.14 infra)	rescission of contracts violating the Act; implied remedy	party to contract	other party to contract	unresolved	unresolved	unresolved	unresolved

Chapter 2

REGISTRATION REQUIREMENTS OF THE SECURITIES ACT OF 1933

Table of Sections

Sec.

§ 2.1   The Underwriting Process

Underwriters form an essential link in the process of offering securities for public consumption. Underwriting practices have varied over time. There is no single universally accepted underwriting mechanism; instead, there are a variety of underwriting arrangements. The particular underwriting arrangement for any offering will generally be a reflection of the financial exigencies of the situation. This section discusses the basic types of underwriting arrangements. In contrast, a later section of this treatise examines the 1933 Act definition of underwriter[1] which may bring within its reach individuals and entities who are not underwriters in the generic sense of the word. Classification as a statutory underwriter can result in the imposition of civil liability.[2] Additionally, the presence of underwriter status may preclude an exemption from the Act's registration requirements.[3] Those issues are discussed in subsequent sections of this treatise.[4] The discussion that follows addresses formal underwriting arrangements that are commonly found in public offerings (and in some cases in private offerings).

There are a number of methods by which an issuer can raise capital, both for starting out its business and for expansion and/or continuation

---

§ 2.1

1. Section 2(11), 15 U.S.C.A. § 77b(11). *See* § 4.24 *infra.*

2. Section 11 of the 1933 Act imposes liability on underwriters for material misstatements and omissions in a public offering's registration statement. 15 U.S.C.A. § 77k. *See* § 7.3 *infra.*

3. Section 4(1) of the 1933 Act sets forth an exemption for transactions not involving an issuer, underwriter or a dealer. 15 U.S.C.A. § 77d(1). *See* §§ 4.23–4.24 *infra.*

4. *See* §§ 4.23, 4.24, 7.3 *infra.*

of an existing concern. Financing can be carried out by the issuer directly or through an intermediary or underwriter. Perhaps the simplest method is direct financing—that is, without an investment banker, underwriter, promoter or other intermediary.[5] Although direct financing may be simpler, the vast majority of public offerings are underwritten.

Direct Offerings

While it is relatively rare, direct financing does have its place, albeit a small one. There are generally said to be five basic methods of direct financing, although variations may exist. There can be a direct public offering by the issuer; this is especially rare because most issuers do not have the wherewithal or expertise in the financial industry to handle a public offering. A full scale public offering generally requires a broker-dealer network and sales persons registered with the SEC and National Association of Securities Dealers (NASD).[6] Accordingly, public offerings generally are not suitable as direct offerings. It should be noted that at the state level, under the Uniform Securities Act,[7] anyone who participates in the distribution of a security as a broker or agent of the issuer must register with the appropriate state agency. A second and slightly more common version of the direct offering by an issuer is one to existing security holders where it is contemplated that all existing shareholders will purchase the securities, thus eliminating the necessity for a promotional or retailing sales effort.

The third and perhaps most common type of direct financing utilizing traditional debt and equity securities is the direct private placement whereby the issuer turns to a bank, financial institution or significant private investor to raise all desired capital. For many endeavors, especially established concerns with good track records, such qualified willing investors are readily available and the issuer need not avail itself of an underwriter or promoter in order to stimulate investor interest. The fourth, relatively rarely used technique is the distribution of securities through public sealed bidding. The fifth and final type of direct financ-

---

5. *See generally* Samuel N. Allen, A Lawyer's Guide to the Operation of Underwriting Syndicates, 26 New Eng.L.Rev. 319 (1991); Stephen P. Ferris, Janine S. Hiller, Glen A. Wolfe & Elizabeth S. Cooperman, An Analysis and Recommendation for Prestigious Underwriter Participation in IPOs, 17 J.Corp.L. 539 (1992); Symposium, Current Problems of Securities Underwriters and Dealers, 18 Bus.Law. 27 (1962); Stephen J. Weiss, The Underwriting Agreement–Form and Commentary, 26 Bus.Law. 647 (1971); John A. Wing, Guidelines for Underwriter Activity, 25 Bus.Law. 397 (1970).

The Glass–Steagall Act requires that investment banking functions be distinct from commercial banking. 12 U.S.C.A. § 227. In practice this dichotomy is becoming increasingly blurred. *See generally* Harvey L. Pitt & Julie L. Williams, The Glass–Steagall Act: Key Issues for the Financial Services Industry, 11 Sec.Reg.L.J. 234 (1983). For a general history of investment banking *see, e.g.,* United States v. Morgan, 118 F.Supp. 621, 635–55 (S.D.N.Y.1953) (Medina, J.).

The Glass–Steagall Act and its decreasing efficacy in separating investment banking and commercial banking are discussed in § 19.5 *infra* (Practitioner's Edition only).

6. The regulatory framework for broker-dealers is taken up in chapter 10 *infra*.

7. Uniform Securities Act § 201. The state "blue sky" laws are discussed in chapter 8 *infra*.

ing is generally associated with commercial lenders and consists of directly secured bank loans, mortgage loans, equipment loans, and lease-back arrangements.[8]

Nature and Varieties of Underwriting Arrangements

As noted above, most financing that involves any significant selling effort will be conducted through promoters, investment bankers or underwriters. Although generally associated with public offerings, underwriting arrangements are also common with relatively wide-spread unregistered exempt offerings.[9] There are various ways in which an investment banker's expertise and services may be used in connection with the raising of capital. First, and most common with regard to public offerings of securities in this country, is the negotiated underwriting agreement with an investment banker, or group of investment bankers, to handle a public offering, which is usually conducted pursuant to full-fledged federal registration. The negotiated underwriting agreement is also common in connection with a limited or qualified public offering that may take place in reliance upon one of the qualified exemptions from the registration requirements of the 1933 Act.[10] Another less frequently used method of securing an underwriter for public offering is the use of sealed bids. A currently popular variation on the competitive bidding is the "Dutch auction" wherein prospective underwriters bid for a portion of an upcoming offering.[11]

The term "underwriter" derives its meaning from former British insurance practices. When insuring their cargo shippers would seek out investors to insure their property. The insurers would add their signatures and would write their names under those of the shippers; hence the term "underwriters." Both in terms of the insurance industry and the securities markets, the concept of underwriting has expanded significantly since its inception. In many instances, underwriting no longer reflects pure insurance but may be in the form of various types of either best efforts or firm commitment agreements.

There are three basic varieties of negotiated underwriting arrangements in the securities industry.[12] Those three are: strict underwriting, firm commitment underwriting, and best efforts underwriting.

---

8. As discussed in a previous section, a number of recent decisions have held that equipment leases are "investment contracts" and thus are securities. *E.g.,* Albanese v. Florida National Bank of Orlando, 823 F.2d 408 (11th Cir.1987). *See* § 1.5 *supra.*

9. *See* Sec. Act Rel. No. 33–1256 (1937). *See generally* chapter 4 *infra.*

10. *See* sections 3 and 4 of the Act, 15 U.S.C.A. §§ 77c, 77d.

11. Since each underwriter individually is responsible for a portion of the offering, there is no need for the traditional structure of a managing underwriter to coordinate the offering. Also, under a Dutch auction, it is possible for different underwriters to be offering the security at divergent prices. For a more detailed description *see* Exxon Corp., [1977–78 Transfer Binder] Fed.Sec.L.Rep. (CCH) ¶ 81,198 at p. 88, 159 (SEC No Action Letter, Div.Corp.Fin. April 7, 1977).

12. *See generally* 1 Louis Loss & Joel Seligman, Securities Regulation 317–372 (3d ed. 1989) (listing 5 types of underwriting arrangements: (1) strict or "old fashioned" under-

Strict Underwriting

Strict underwriting, also known as "old-fashioned" or "stand-by" underwriting is insurance in its strictest sense. In lieu of utilizing an investment banker as an agent to resell the securities to the public, the issuer turns to an "insuring house" which will advertise and receive subscriptions and applications for shares from the public. When the subscription lists are closed, the issuer in turn allots the securities to the applicants secured by the insuring house. The underwriters guarantee to purchase the unsold portion of the allotment. This strict method is relatively rare and is generally found only in connection with offerings to existing security holders.

Firm Commitment Underwriting

The second type and most common arrangement is firm commitment underwriting. Under a typical firm commitment agreement the issuer sells the entire allotment outright to a group of securities firms represented by one or more managers, managing underwriters or principal underwriters. In a firm commitment underwriting agreement, the underwriting group, headed by the managing or principal underwriters, agrees to purchase the securities from the issuer. The term "firm commitment" is somewhat misleading since it is common practice to have a "market out" clause which excuses the underwriters from the obligation to purchase in the event of a substantial change in the issuer's financial condition.[13] Typically, the principal underwriters will sign the firm commitment underwriting agreement. These managers or principal underwriters in turn contact other underwriters who are to act as wholesalers of the securities to be offered. In many instances the distribution network will include the use of a selling group of other investment bankers or brokerage houses. Members of the selling group generally do not share the underwriters' risk and are thus retailers who

---

writing, (2) firm-commitment underwriting, (3) best efforts underwriting, (4) competitive bidding, and (5) shelf registrations (see § 3.8 *infra*)).

For example in 1980 of all public offerings 65 were firm commitment (or "stand-by"), 21 were best efforts and 14 were handled directly by the issuer. *See* Harry G. Henn & John R. Alexander, Laws of Corporations 786–91 (3d ed. 1983); Louis Loss, Fundamentals of Securities Regulation 81–91 (1983).

For examples of underwriting agreements *see* 1B. Fletcher Corporation Forms Annotated § 1552 (4th rev. ed. 1980) ("stand-by" agreement); *id.* § 1551.2 ("firm commitment" agreement); 9A Clark A. Nichols, Cyclopedia of Legal Forms Annotated §§ 9.700, 9.701 (rev. ed. 1971) ("stand-by" agreement); 7A Jacob Rabkin & Mark H. Johnson, Current Legal Forms With Tax Analysis, Form 19.65 (1981) ("best efforts" agreement); *id.* Form 19.64 ("firm commitment" agreement); David L. Ratner & Thomas L. Hazen, Securities Regulation: Materials for a Basic Course 1968 (4th ed. 1991. documentary supplement) ("firm commitment" agreement); Weiss *supra* footnote 5 ("firm commitment" agreement).

13. A typical "market out" clause provides that the underwriters are excused from their firm commitment should there be "a material adverse event affecting the issuer that materially impairs the investment quality of the offered securities." *See, e.g.,* First Boston Corp., [1985–86 Transfer Binder] Fed.Sec.L.Rep. (CCH) ¶ 78,152 (SEC No Action Letter Sept. 2, 1985). *Compare* Walk–In Medical Centers, Inc. v. Breuer, 818 F.2d 260 (2d Cir.1987) (affirming $33 million judgment against an underwriter who claimed that "adverse market conditions" excused performance of underwriting agreement).

are compensated with agents' or brokers' commissions rather than by sharing in the underwriting fee.

Section 2(3) of the 1933 Act[14] excludes from its definition of "offer to sell" preliminary negotiations and agreements between the underwriter and the issuer and among underwriters in privity with the issuer. However, absent an exemption, prior to the filing of the registration statement no offers can be made to members of the investing public; nor can there be sales or contracts for sale prior to the effective date. Although section 2(3)'s exclusion probably includes the final contract between the underwriter and the issuer, it may be wise not to have more than an understanding and to reserve formal execution of the final contract until immediately after the filing of the registration statement. In fact, the typical practice is to follow such a course.

There is no definitive ruling on how "preliminary" the negotiations and agreements must be in order to qualify for exclusion.[15] In many cases such questions are merely academic as it is common that the final underwriting agreement is not signed until the eve of the offering. Prior to that time the issuer and underwriter operate under a nonbinding letter of intent.[16]

Underwriting arrangements may contain an escape clause which permits the underwriting group to terminate the underwriting agreement if there has been a substantial change in the issuer's operation or, for example, if there has been a change in "operating political or marketing conditions." While this is broader than the traditional force majeure clause found in other industries, it is not generally abused. The underwriter is protected even beyond such escape clauses. For example, where the issuer's prospectus is misleading, the underwriting contract has been held unenforceable, thus entitling the underwriter to withdraw from the distribution.[17]

Best Efforts Underwriting

The third basic type of underwriting arrangement is known as "best

---

14. 15 U.S.C.A. § 77b(3). *See* § 5.3 *infra*.

15. The legislative history explains that "the sole purpose * * * is to make clear that the usual agreement among underwriters as well as the agreement between the underwriters and the issuer (or controlling person, as the case may be) may be made before the registration statement has been filed." S.Rep. No. 1036, 83 Cong., 2d Sess. 11 (1954).

Cf. Dunhill Securities Corp. v. Microthermal Applications, Inc., 308 F.Supp. 195 (S.D.N.Y.1969) (no action in quantum meruit based on letter of intent).

16. A letter of intent containing an agreement to underwrite an offering is not a binding contract for the sale of securities. Southwest Realty, Ltd. v. Daseke, 1990 WL 85921, [1990 Transfer Binder] Fed.Sec.L.Rep. (CCH) ¶ 95,256 (N.D.Tex.1990) (the court noted that at best the letter of intent represented the parties' agreement to use their best efforts to complete the deal and did not bind either party to the deal).

17. Kaiser–Frazer Corp. v. Otis & Co., 195 F.2d 838 (2d Cir.1952), *cert. denied* 344 U.S. 856, 73 S.Ct. 89, 97 L.Ed. 664 (1952). *But see* Walk–In Medical Centers, Inc. v. Breuer Capital Corp., 818 F.2d 260 (2d Cir.1987), *affirming* 651 F.Supp. 1009 (S.D.N.Y.1986) (holding the underwriter liable for unjustifiably terminating the underwriting agreement).

efforts" and does not put the underwriter at risk.[18] Best efforts underwriting is generally used by less established issuers that cannot find an investment banker who is willing to make a firm commitment because of the speculative nature of the distribution. In some instances, well established companies may try to avail themselves of best efforts underwriting arrangements in order to save on the cost of distribution since the underwriter's fee will often be lower where the underwriter is not taking the risk of an unsold allotment. With a best efforts underwriting agreement the investment banker or brokerage firm, rather than buying the securities from the issuer for resale to the public, sells them for the issuer merely as an agent. Under such best efforts arrangements, the underwriter is generally paid in the form of an agent's commission rather than from a dealer's profit or based on a percentage of the overall proceeds of the offering.

Underwriting by Auction

There are numerous variations on the foregoing three basic types of underwriting arrangements.[19] For example, competitive bidding by potential underwriters is the most common method for offerings involving financing by municipalities, other state governmental agencies, and public utilities.[20] A variation of this in the private sector is the relatively infrequently used "Dutch auction".[21] Investment bankers are continuing to develop variations on the foregoing methods.[22]

Additional factors

Most, if not all, underwriters of any securities offering will generally be members of the National Association of Securities Dealers (NASD).[23] Underwriting agreements are subject to the NASD's Rules of Fair Practice which deal *inter alia* with the distribution of shares, overallotment options, and "compensation factors." [24] Underwriting agreements and registration materials must be filed with the NASD's Corporate

---

18. *See* Harold I. Freilich & Ralph S. Janvey, Understanding "Best Efforts" Offerings, 17 Sec.Reg.L.J. 151 (1989).

19. Delayed registered offerings (shelf registrations) have been a relatively new development and are examples of new practices generated by the investment banking industry. *See* 1 Louis Loss & Joel Seligman *supra* footnote 12 at 353–372. *See also* § 3.8 *infra.*

20. *See* 1 Louis Loss & Joel Seligman *supra* footnote 12 at 343–352. *See* § 10.5 *infra* for a discussion of municipal securities dealers.

21. *See* footnote 11 *supra;* 1 Louis Loss & Joel Seligman *supra* footnote 12 at 370–372.

22. *See* 1 Louis Loss & Joel Seligman *supra* footnote 12 at 372–380.

23. *See* § 10.2 *infra* for discussion of broker-dealer regulation and the NASD. Also, as noted above, the Uniform Securities Act requires registration at the state level of anyone participating in a distribution as a broker or agent of the issuer. *See* footnote 7 *supra* and accompanying text.

24. *See* NASD Rules of Fair Practice Art. III, Sec. 1; NASD Manual (CCH) ¶ 2151 and the NASD interpretations thereunder. *See also, e.g.,* In re Lowell H. Listrom & Co., Exch.Act Rel. No. 34-22689, [1985–86 Transfer Binder] Fed.Sec.L.Rep. (CCH) ¶ 83,946 (SEC Dec. 5, 1985) (upholding NASD censure for delay in transmitting funds and improper extensions of credit in connection with "all or none" best efforts underwriting).

Financing Department in Washington, D.C.[25] Upon filing, the NASD may respond with a letter of comment.[26]

§ 2.2 The Operation of Section 5 of the Securities Act of 1933—An Overview

Absent an exemption,[1] section 5 of the 1933 Act[2] strictly prohibits all selling efforts prior to the filing of a registration statement.[3] It also restricts selling efforts and absolutely prohibits sales until the registration statement has become effective. Section 5 thus divides the registration process into three time periods: the pre-filing, waiting, and post-effective periods. Once the public offering is contemplated, the time prior to the completion of the initial registration statement and filing is known as the *pre-filing period*.[4] After the registration statement has been filed with the SEC there is a statutory *waiting period*[5] prior to the effective date, although the actual waiting period rarely is the twenty-day period specified in the statute.[6] Section 5's requirements continue through the *post-effective* period until the distribution has been completed.[7] Section 5's prohibitions are implemented by regulating the scope of all offers as well as sales of securities so long as there is sufficient use of interstate commerce unless there is an applicable exemption.

The basic purpose of the 1933 Act's registration requirement, as well as section 5's prohibitions and limitations on permissible offers to sell securities, is to assure that the investor has adequate information upon which to base his or her investment decision. It is generally conceded to be a fiction that each investor or potential investor reads the prospectus from cover to cover; and thus it has been suggested by some observers that most required disclosure is not in fact relevant to the

---

25. *See* the CCH analysis of NASD Rules of Fair Practice Art. III, Sec. 1; NASD Manual ¶¶ 2151, *et seq.* For a registered offering the filing requirements include a copy of the 1933 Act registration statement, seven copies of the preliminary prospectus and seven copies of the underwriting agreement. The filing must be accompanied by a filing fee of $100 plus .01% of the gross dollar amount of the offering up to a gross dollar amount of $50,000,000. NASD By–Laws Schedule A, Sec. 6; NASD Manual (CCH) ¶ 1301A.

26. In addition to the NASD Manual and the authorities in footnote 5 *supra, see* William M. Prifti, Securities: Public and Private Offerings ch. 6 (1974).

§ 2.2

1. Exempt securities and transactions are discussed in chapter 4 *infra.*

2. 15 U.S.C.A. § 77e. *See* Eric A. Chiapinelli, Gun Jumping: The Problem of Extraneous Offers of Securities, 50 U.Pitt.L.Rev. 399 (1989).

3. The Act does not expressly require an intent to violate the registration requirement. Nevertheless, a criminal conviction would appear to require at least a minimal amount of *mens rea. See, e.g.,* United States v. Lindo, 18 F.3d 353 (6th Cir.1994) (upholding conviction for sale of unregistered securities where defendant had reason to know that he was involved in an illegal transaction).

4. *See* § 2.3 *infra.*

5. Section 8(a) of the 1933 Act, 15 U.S.C.A. § 77h(a).

6. *See* § 2.4 *infra.* An exception is found for issuers who use Form S–8 for employee compensation plans. Rule 462 provides that an S–8 registration is effective when filed. 17 C.F.R. § 230.462. In addition, issuers using other registration forms may apply to the Commission for acceleration of the effective date. 17 C.F.R. § 230.461. *See* § 3.5 *infra.*

7. *See* § 2.5 *infra.*

majority of purchasers.[8] However, investment professionals, such as research analysts, investment advisers and broker-dealers, when viewed as a group, read all publicly disseminated information in addition to other information which is otherwise available. The opinions of these market professionals, frequently reflected in terms of buy or sell recommendations, create an informed and supposedly efficient market which, in turn, prices the securities at an appropriate level. Accordingly, it is asserted that notwithstanding the absence of lay investor interest in the bulk of the SEC disclosure documents, the relevant information nonetheless is filtered into the market and is reflected by the price established by an informed market.[9] Another justification for requiring disclosure even though many investors may not ever read the information in question is that the market participants' knowledge that full disclosure has been made instills investor confidence and hence stability which would otherwise be lacking, as has been the case with many foreign securities markets. To this end it is noteworthy that lack of investor confidence was a major factor in the great Wall Street crash of 1929.[10] All of section 5's prohibitions must be viewed and understood in the context of the informational goals of the Securities Act of 1933.

Anyone reading section 5 in a vacuum would justifiably conclude that each and every security sale and all offers for sale require registration under the 1933 Act. However, the reader must look beyond section 5's basic prohibitions, first to section 3 of the Act[11] which provides numerous exemptions for specified types of securities, and also to section 4 of the Act[12] which exempts a large number of securities transactions. Most important in terms of the aggregate number of excluded transactions in the public markets is section 4(3)'s exemption[13] for the majority of transactions involving a dealer (even when acting on a customer's behalf) and section 4(4)'s exemption[14] for unsolicited brokers transac-

---

8. *See, e.g.,* Homer Kripke, A Search for a Meaningful Securities Disclosure Policy, 31 Bus.Law. 293 (1975); Symposium, New Approaches to Disclosure in Registered Securities Offerings—A Panel Discussion, 28 Bus.Law. 505 (1973).

9. However, in one influential decision it was held that there are three audiences to whom the registration statement is directed, and that the disclosures must be understandable for each of the following audiences: (1) the amateur investor who reads only for the broadest types of information, (2) the professional advisor and/or manager who makes a close study of the prospectus and bases his or her decisions on the conclusions drawn from this study, and (3) the analyst who relies on the prospectus as one of several sources in forming an opinion. *See* Feit v. Leasco Data Processing Equipment Corp., 332 F.Supp. 544, 565–66 (E.D.N.Y.1971). *But cf.* Wielgos v. Commonwealth Edison Co., 892 F.2d 509 (7th Cir.1989) (indicating that at least with a well seasoned, actively followed issuer, the more important audience for the registration disclosures is the sophisticated analyst and that disclosures may be tailored accordingly).

10. Full disclosure is not a cure-all. Thus, this author has suggested that the inefficiency of the securities, options, and futures markets were a major factor behind the crash of October, 1987. *See, e.g.,* Thomas L. Hazen, Volatility and Market Inefficiency A Commentary on the Effects of Options, Futures, and Risk Arbitrage on the Stock Market, 44 Wash. & Lee L.Rev. 789 (1987). *See also* § 1.5.1 *supra.*

11. 15 U.S.C.A. § 77c. *See* §§ 4.2–4.14 *infra.*

12. 15 U.S.C.A. § 77d. *See* §§ 4.15–4.28 *infra.*

13. 15 U.S.C.A. § 77d(3). *See* §§ 2.5, 4.23 *infra.*

14. 15 U.S.C.A. § 77d(4).

tions. When read together these two sections exempt from registration the overwhelming majority of day-to-day securities transactions. Section 4(1) (which exempts transactions not involving an issuer, underwriter, or dealer) and section 4(4) (unsolicited brokers transactions) operate to limit the scope of the Act's coverage to distributions as compared with day-to-day trading activities.[15] Further, section 4(2) of the Act[16] exempts non-public offerings by issuers. There are yet additional exemptions for purely intrastate offerings[17] as well as qualified exemptions for "small issues" which can be as large as five million dollars.[18] Accordingly, as a practical matter, section 5 primarily applies to public distributions of securities that are offered on a relatively large scale. Nevertheless, since the burden of proving any of the foregoing exemptions falls upon the person exerting the exemption, inattention or carelessness can easily lead to inadvertent violations of the prohibitions of section 5.[19]

As noted above, section 5 divides the registration process into three parts: the pre-filing period, the waiting period, and the post-effective period. Section 5(a)(2) [20] prohibits the delivery of any security for sale unless a registration statement is in effect. Section 5(b)[21] imposes prospectus requirements for both offers and sales and applies to both the waiting and post-effective periods. Section 5(c),[22] which is the broadest in prohibitions, applies only to the pre-filing period. The following diagram[23] depicts the operation of section 5:

---

15. Day to day trading is addressed by the Securities Exchange Act of 1934. *See* chapters 9–13 *infra.*

16. 15 U.S.C.A. § 77d(2). *See* §§ 4.15–4.22 *infra.*

17. 15 U.S.C.A. § 77c(a)(11). *See* § 4.12 *infra.*

18. 15 U.S.C.A. § 77c(b). *See* § 4.14 *infra.*

19. The potential for inadvertent violations is heightened by the fact that scienter is not required to establish a violation of section 5. *E.g.,* SEC v. Thomas D. Kienlen Corp., 755 F.Supp. 936 (D.Or.1991). Violation of section 5 can lead to strict liability to the purchaser of the securities. 15 U.S.C.A. § 77*l*(1) which is discussed in §§ 7.2, 7.5.1–7.5.4 *infra.* For a synopsis of the various publicity limitations throughout the prefiling, waiting, and post-effective periods, *see* Joseph P. Richardson & Joseph E. Reece, Gun Jumping, 26 Rev.Sec. & Commod. Reg. 1 (1993).

20. 15 U.S.C.A. § 77e(a)(2). *See* § 2.5 *infra.*

21. 15 U.S.C.A. § 77e(b). *See* §§ 2.4–2.5 *infra.*

22. 15 U.S.C.A. § 77e(c). *See* § 2.3 *infra.*

23. *See* David L. Ratner, Securities Regulation in a Nutshell 45–46 (3d ed. 1988). *See also* David L. Ratner & Thomas L. Hazen , Securities Regulation: Cases and Materials 25–26, 47 (3th ed. 1991).

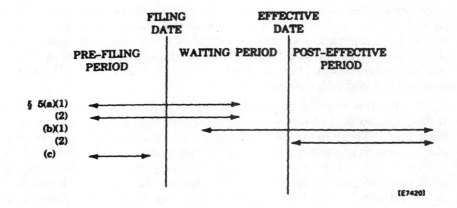

Section 5(c) prohibits all offers to sell as well as all offers to buy prior to the filing of a registration statement. This necessarily includes oral as well as written offers. This is the only restriction on oral offers and is also the only restriction on offers to buy. Section 5(c) on its face would seem to be applicable to negotiations between issuers and underwriters. However, section 2(3)[24] of the Act expressly excludes from the definition of offer to sell preliminary negotiations between an issuer and an underwriter or among underwriters in privity with the issuer. Without such an exclusion, it would be impossible to negotiate a public offering as the issuer would have to file the registration statement prior to even establishing either the terms of the offering or the underwriting agreement. The exclusion of preliminary underwriter negotiations and agreements is a major exception to the pre-filing prohibitions; although, as will be seen in subsequent sections, limited pre-filing publicity is permissible.[25] Section 5(c)'s prohibition[26] on all offers and sales operates during the pre-filing period and any violations thereof have come to be known as illegal "gun jumping."

By virtue of section 5(b) of the Act,[27] all written offers or prospectuses must conform with the statutory prospectus requirement. Section 2(10) of the Act[28] defines prospectus to include any written offer[29] in

---

24. 15 U.S.C.A. § 77b(2).

25. *See, e.g.,* 17 C.F.R. § 230.135 which is discussed in § 2.3 *infra.*

26. 15 U.S.C.A. § 77e(c).

27. 15 U.S.C.A. § 77e(b).

28. 15 U.S.C.A. § 77b(10). *See, e.g.,* SEC v. Thomas D. Kienlen Corp., 755 F.Supp. 936 (D.Or.1991) (brochure describing "safety", "improved performance", and "lower costs" of mutual fund was a prospectus and thus violated section 5(b)(1) when used during the waiting period).

29. Although not expressly covered by the statute, computer email, computer disks, and other digitally encoded communications would appear to and certainly should fall within the definition of prospectus. Such an interpretation is bolstered by the fact that radio and television communications are expressly included. The SEC has not addressed the issue directly but has indicated that electronically transmitted messages would qualify as prospectuses. Sec. Act Rel. No. 33–6982; 57 FR 16141 (March 19, 1993) ("Some electronic

addition to offers made over radio or television. Accordingly, oral offers to sell are not covered nor are offers to buy, both of which are thus unregulated during the waiting period; they are also unregulated during the post-effective period. Sections 10(a) and 10(b) of the 1933 Act[30] set out the requirements for permissible written offers during both the waiting and post-effective periods.[31]

Under the express terms of section 8 of the Act,[32] a registration statement becomes effective twenty days after the last amendment has been filed. This twenty day waiting period is subject to the Commission's authority to issue a stop order which postpones the effective date until removal of the stop order and also is subject to the Commission's willingness to grant acceleration of the effective date upon application by the registrant.[33] The drafters of section 8 may have contemplated that ordinarily a registration statement will become effective within twenty days of its filing and that in rare cases this period would be extended by amendment to the registration statement or by the issuance of a stop order or a refusal order. However, this apparent statutory pattern is not reflective of actual SEC practice. The registration review process generally consists of correspondence between the Commission staff and the registrant.[34] Typically, the Commission staff will respond to an initial filing with a detailed letter of comments. Especially in the case of first-time registrants, this informal give and take will generally go beyond the twenty day statutory period. It is common for issuers to file delaying amendments in order to give adequate time to respond to the SEC staff's suggestions.[35] When the informal discussions between the

---

media, such as computer bulletin boards, may provide the capacity to read the disclosure for a sufficient period of time and to reproduce the disclosure and order form in print").

30. 15 U.S.C.A. § 77j(a), (b).

31. *See* §§ 2.4–2.5 *infra.*

32. 15 U.S.C.A. § 77h. The procedure for amendments is set out in 17 C.F.R. §§ 230.470–479. These rules apply to both pre-effective and post-effective amendments.

Section 8 is described more fully in § 3.5.1 *infra* (Practitioner's Edition only).

33. *See also* the more detailed discussion of acceleration procedures and requirements in § 3.5.1 *infra.*

34. *E.g.,* Universal Camera Corp., 19 S.E.C. 648, 658 (1945); Sec. Act Rel. No. 33–5231, 1 Fed.Sec.L.Rep. (CCH) ¶ 3057 (Feb. 3, 1972). *See* § 3.5 *infra.* Although this is the way in which the SEC normally proceeds, it may depart from the informal review process and initiate formal section 8 proceedings. *See, e.g.,* Doman Helicopters, Inc., 41 S.E.C. 431 (SEC 1963) (rejecting the registrant's argument that the SEC must first resort to the informal review process before instituting formal proceedings). In *Doman Helicopters* it was claimed that a stop order was not warranted since the initial filing was only a "preliminary filing" and the SEC never initiated its informal review. Once the section 8 hearings began, the registrant filed an amendment to delay the effective date which was claimed to have avoided the necessity of stop order proceedings. The Commission ruled that in light of the serious deficiencies in the registration statement as originally filed, section 8 proceedings were warranted. The seriousness of the deficiencies in *Doman Helicopters* was exacerbated by the fact that there were already more than 8,000 public investors.

The SEC thus is not required to resort first to the more usual informal methods of review.

35. SEC Rule 473 formally recognizes the propriety of delaying amendments. 17 C.F.R. § 230.473. However, not all forms are eligible for delaying amendments. Forms F–

registrant's counsel and the Commission staff result in a registration statement that the SEC will find acceptable, it is not uncommon for the registrant to seek acceleration of the effective date.[36]

Frequently, the pricing of an offering will not take place until just before the effective date. Although the participants planning a public offering will generally have at least a "ball park" figure for the planned offering price, general market fluctuations often require leaving the determination of a precise figure until the effective date. In these cases it is necessary to file an amendment to the registration statement which relates to the price. Under the terms of section 8 of the Act, the filing of an amendment would ordinarily trigger an additional twenty-day waiting period before the effective date. However, when such price amendments are filed, the Commission will consent to immediate effectiveness thus precluding the statutory twenty day period from running anew.[37]

The filing of a registration statement is not a step to be taken lightly. Once a registration statement has been filed, it cannot be withdrawn without Commission approval.[38] It is stated Commission policy to permit withdrawal of the registration statement if "consistent with the public interest and protection of investors." [39] It would therefore appear that in the normal course of events the Commission would ordinarily approve a request for withdrawal. However, when it is believed that the registration process warrants imposing sanctions against the participants, the Commission might elect to refuse permission for withdrawal and go ahead with formal proceedings under section 8.[40]

The sections that follow describe the effects of SEC regulation during the pre-filing, waiting, and post-effective periods.

§ 2.3 The Pre-Filing Period

Section 5(c)[1] sets forth the basic prohibitions for the pre-filing period. There can be neither legal offers to buy nor offers to sell securities until a registration statement has been filed. Section 5(c) is the broadest proscription as it covers all offers—whether written or oral

---

7, F–8, F–9, and F–10 for use by private foreign issuers are not eligible for delaying amendments. Delaying amendments are not expressly authorized for Forms S–3, S–4, F–4, and S–8. The various registration forms are described briefly in § 3.3 *infra*.

36. SEC Rule 461 sets out the requirements for acceleration. 17 C.F.R. § 230.461. *See* § 3.5 and § 3.5.1 (Practitioner's Edition only) *infra*.

37. 15 U.S.C.A. § 77h(a); 17 C.F.R. § 230.475.

38. 17 C.F.R. § 230.477.

39. *Id.*

40. *See* the discussion of section 8 proceedings in § 3.5.1 *infra*.

The imposition of a stop order or refusal order may disable the participants from participating in certain exempt offerings over the next five years. *See, e.g.,* Rules 262 (Regulation A) and 505 (part of Regulation D), 17 C.F.R. §§ 230.262; 230.505(b)(2)(iii), which are discussed in §§ 4.15, 4.18 *infra*.

§ 2.3

1. 15 U.S.C.A. § 77e(c).

and whether to buy or to sell. In contrast, the prohibitions for both the waiting and post-effective periods apply only to written, radio or television offers to sell as defined by section 2(10) of the Act[2] and not to oral offers to sell nor to any offers to buy. In addition to the prohibition against offers during the pre-filing period, section 5(a)[3] bars all sales during both the pre-filing and waiting periods.

Preliminary negotiations and agreements between an issuer and underwriters (and among underwriters which are to be in privity with the issuer) are excluded from section 2(3)'s definition of sell or offer to sell[4] and thus do not violate the gun jumping prohibitions contained in section 5(c); nor do they implicate the prospectus requirements of section 5(b) or the sale prohibition of section 5(a).

Therefore, absent an exemption, or the exclusion for underwriters' preliminary negotiations and agreements, offers to buy, offers to sell (whether written or oral), and sales are all prohibited during the pre-filing period. Accordingly, the 1933 Act's broadest prohibitions take effect prior to filing of the registration statement. This broad reach makes sense to the extent that at this time there is absolutely no public information about the offering, except for information which may have been disclosed if the issuer is already a public company and therefore subject to the 1934 Act's periodic reporting requirements.[5] In light of the absence of reliable up to date information about the issuer and/or the terms of the upcoming offering, any premature sales-related activity or "gun jumping" would circumvent the purpose of the 1933 Act's registration and prospectus requirements. Such a circumvention would thus amount to a violation of section 5.

What is an Offer to Sell?—Solicitations of a Buying Interest

Section 2(3) of the Act[6] defines offer to sell in terms of any activity that is reasonably calculated to solicit or generate a buying interest. The determination of whether there is an offer is not a matter of state contract law but rather is a question of federal law depending upon

---

2. 15 U.S.C.A. § 77b(10). *See* § 2.1 *supra.* Although not expressly included in the section 2(10)'s definition of prospectus, it would appear that e mail messages, computer disks, and other offers to sell embodied in digital form with some degree of permanency would qualify as a prospectus. *Cf.* Sec. Act Rel. No. 33–6982; 57 FR 16141 (March 19, 1993) ("Some electronic media, such as computer bulletin boards, may provide the capacity to read the disclosure sufficient period of time and to reproduce the disclosure and order form in print").

3. 15 U.S.C.A. § 77e(a).

4. 15 U.S.C.A. § 77b(3). A letter of intent to underwrite an offering is not a binding contract for the sale of securities. Southwest Realty, Ltd. v. Daseke, 1990 WL 85921, [1990 Transfer Binder] Fed.Sec.L.Rep. (CCH) ¶ 95,256 (N.D.Tex.1990) (the court noted that at best the letter of intent represented the parties' agreement to use their best efforts to complete the deal and did not bind either party to the deal).

5. In the case of an issuer with outstanding securities, information about the company may be available due to the 1934 Exchange Act's registration and periodic reporting requirements. *See* chapter 9 *infra.* The Commission's relatively new integrated disclosure policy is an attempt to eliminate unnecessary duplication without sacrificing investors' informational rights. *See* § 3.3 *infra.*

6. 15 U.S.C.A. § 77b(3).

whether the challenged conduct has conditioned the public's mind by generating a buying interest.[7] Definitional problems frequently arise in connection with inadvertent "gun-jumping" publicity that may violate section 5(c) of the Act. The initial leading authority on this point is the SEC decision, In the Matter of Carl M. Loeb, Rhoades & Co., and Dominick & Dominick.[8] In that case, the underwriter prepared and disseminated a press release six weeks prior to the filing of the registration statement. The press release announced that a hitherto one-person real estate venture owning over one hundred thousand acres "in the area of the gold coast" in Florida was about to go public. The press release went on to identify the investment banker that would be handling the underwriting arrangements and further named the issuer's principal officers. The press release generated a buying interest, as evidenced by the fact that over one hundred securities dealers contacted the named managing underwriter asking that they be included in the underwriting syndicate.[9] The SEC examined the press release and held that although in the form of a news item, the release disclosed much more information than was necessary to simply alert the public of a newsworthy event and thus constituted an offer to sell within section 2(3)'s definition. The key to the Commission's decision seemed to be not only the fact that more than one hundred securities firms had shown a buying interest but further that the press release identified the name of the principal underwriter, hence directing potential buyers to the selling source.

Following the *Loeb, Rhoades* decision, there was concern that the line of demarcation between legitimate prefiling publicity and an illegal offer to sell was a murky one. Accordingly, the the SEC tried to clarify the issue when it amended rule 135.[10] The current version of the rule enumerates the types of pre-filing publicity that will not be considered in violation of section 5(c)'s gun jumping prohibitions. Rule 135 is silent on the extent of its reach—that is, whether it is a safe harbor or an exclusive harbor. Nevertheless, one court[11] has indicated it to be the exclusive method for disseminating permissible pre-filing information. Presumably, this view of exclusivity is limited to press releases and other announcements geared solely to the impending public offering. The SEC has explained, for example, that the issuer should continue to make full disclosure in its 1934 Act periodic reports as well as to continue the

---

7. *E.g.,* SEC v. Thomas D. Kienlen Corp., 755 F.Supp. 936, 940 (D.Or.1991) (letter to customers describing mutual fund as safest in the country violated § 5(c)). *See, also, e.g.,* SEC v. Graystone Nash, Inc., 820 F.Supp. 863 (D.N.J.1993) (magazine article was reasonably calculated to generate a buying interest and thus was an offer and prospectus under the securities laws).

8. 38 S.E.C. 843 (SEC 1959), noted in 1959 Duke L.J. 460; 54 Nw.L.Rev. 131 (1959). For a more recent summary of the gun jumping prohibitions, *see* Joseph P. Richardson & Joseph E. Reece, Gun Jumping, 26 Rev.Sec. & Commod.Reg. 1 (1993).

9. The press release also announced the issuer's intent to embark upon a "comprehensive statement of orderly development."

10. 17 C.F.R. § 230.135.

11. Chris–Craft Industries, Inc. v. Bangor Punta Corp., 426 F.2d 569 (2d Cir.1970).

types of publicity that the issuer undertakes as a matter of its ordinary course of business.[12]

Rule 135

Rule 135 provides that, solely for the purpose of section 5 of the Act, a notice given by an *issuer* to the effect that it proposes to make a public offering is not an offer for sale if the notice contains only the specified information and states that an offer can be made only through the use of a prospectus. It is noteworthy that the rule does not address itself to press releases by promoters or underwriters. It is quite possible that the omission of underwriters and promoters from Rule 135 reflects a view that any publicity by such persons is likely to be viewed as sales efforts.[13] It would certainly seem to make sense to limit prefiling publicity to the information sent out by the issuer whose interest in disseminating the information may be other than initiating the sales effort. Furthermore, limiting prefiling publicity to the issuer is consistent with Rule 135's goal of balancing the right to disseminate newsworthy information against the risks of generating a buying interest in the security which will be registered, before adequate information is available. Notwithstanding this reading of Rule 135, it should be remembered that the prohibition is limited to participants in the offering and securities professionals in light of the exemption for transactions by persons other than issuers, underwriters, and dealers.[14]

Rule 135 publicity can legitimately contain (1) the name of the issuer; (2) the title, amount, and basic terms of the offering; (3) in the case of a rights offering to existing security holders, the subscription ratio, record date and approximate date of the proposed rights offering as well as the subscription price; (4) where securities are exchanged for securities of another issuer, the nature and "basis" of the exchange;[15] (5) in the case of an offering to employees of the issuer or any affiliate, the class of employees and the amount proposed to be offered, including the offering price; and (6) any statement required by state law or administrative authority.

Rule 135 does not expressly permit mention of the offering price in the prefiling publicity for most public offerings. Only Rule 135 subsections 3 and 5, which deal with rights offerings to existing securities holders and offerings to employees, expressly permit mention of price. There is authority supporting the exclusivity of these provisions permitting reference to price. For example, within the tender offer context, in

---

12. *See, e.g.,* Sec.Act Rel. No. 33–5180 1 Fed.Sec.L.Rep. (CCH) ¶ 3056 (Aug. 16, 1971), discussed in the text following footnote 29 *infra.*

13. The naming of the underwriting in prefiling publicity has in fact been held to be a significant factor in finding an illegal selling effort. *See* In the Matter of Carl M. Loeb, Rhoades & Co., 38 S.E.C. 843 (SEC 1959). *See also, e.g.,* Chris–Craft Industries, Inc. v. Bangor Punta Corp., 426 F.2d 569 (2d Cir.1970).

14. Section 4(1), 15 U.S.C.A. § 77d(1), which is discussed in § 4.23 *infra.*

15. Rule 135(4) in allowing the basis of the exchange is in contrast to subsections (3) and (5) which permit mentioning the offering price.

the announcement of a proposed exchange offer for which no registration statement had been filed, a valuation of securities not yet issued that were to be distributed as part of the exchange package went beyond the terms of Rule 135 and was thus held to render the press release an offer to sell the securities in violation of section 5(c).[16]

SEC Rule 135, as noted above, refers only to pre-filing publicity by issuers and says nothing about information provided by others. By virtue of section 4(1)'s exemption,[17] persons who are not issuers, underwriters or dealers may issue any pre-filing information. This exemption, of course, is subject to the caveat that anyone acting on behalf of the issuer, its affiliates, or other participants in the offering will be considered one of the underwriters[18] or their agents according to common law agency principles.[19] If Rule 135 is in fact exclusive,[20] then neither underwriters nor dealers can issue any pre-filing publicity without an exemption such as those found in Rules 137, 138 and 139,[21] which are discussed directly below.[22] It is arguable that any other publicity would be a selling effort or at least reasonably calculated to stimulate a buying interest and thus within section 2(3)'s definition. Even if Rule 135 is deemed not to be exclusive, any non-exempt underwriter or dealer generating pre-filing publicity would be subject to careful factual scrutiny along the lines of the *Loeb, Rhoades* analysis as to whether an illegal selling effort has taken place. In any event, the safest course is to adhere strictly to Rule 135 and thus make no disclosures beyond its terms as well as limit the dissemination of such information to the issuer.[23]

The Impact of 1934 Act Reporting Requirements on the Pre-filing Quiet Period

The pressure for affirmative disclosure that may result from the 1934 Act reporting requirements including the proxy rules and the tender offer provisions,[24] or in the case of non-reporting companies from Exchange Act Rule 10b–5,[25] may be at odds with section 5(c)'s limitations on publicity. In such a case "[t]he Commission * * * emphasizes that

16. Chris–Craft Industries, Inc. v. Bangor Punta Corp., 426 F.2d 569 (2d Cir.1970). The SEC has since indicated that mentioning price in the context of a takeover will not always be an offer to sell. Sec.Act Rel.No. 33–5927, 3 Fed.Sec.L.Rep. (CCH) ¶ 24,284(H) (April 24, 1978).

17. 15 U.S.C.A. § 77d(1). *See* § 4.23 *infra.*

18. *See* section 2(11); 15 U.S.C.A. § 77b(11).

19. *See also* section 15's liability of controlling persons. 15 U.S.C.A. § 77o discussed in § 7.7 *infra.*

20. *See* footnote 10 *supra.*

21. 17 C.F.R. §§ 230.137–230.139.

22. *See* text accompanying footnotes 32–43 *infra.*

23. Even where the offering is purely a secondary one, a literal reading of the rule would limit the press release to the issuer as opposed to the actual registrants. Secondary distributions are discussed in §§ 4.23–4.26 *infra.*

24. *See* Chris–Craft Industries, Inc. v. Bangor Punta Corp., 426 F.2d 569 (2d Cir.1970).

25. 17 C.F.R. § 240.10b–5. *See* §§ 13.2–13.11 *infra.*

there is no basis in the securities acts or in any policy of the Commission which would justify the practice of non-disclosure on the grounds that it has the securities in registration under the Securities Act of 1933." [26] This balance is to be applied during the pre-filing period[27] but it has been held that too much disclosure will nevertheless violate section 5(c),[28] thus frequently placing the issuer between a rock and a hard place. Close questions necessarily require careful examination of the gun jumping prohibitions in conjunction with the materiality requirements of the applicable affirmative disclosure requirements. For example, the shareholders who are asked in a proxy statement to approve authorization of shares for future distribution must be given more pre-filing information than would otherwise be permissible under Rule 135.

Even beyond the conflicting pulls of the 1933 Act's gun jumping prohibitions and the Exchange Act's call for full disclosure, gun jumping tensions can arise in other areas in which the issuer is engaged in the public dissemination of information. The SEC suggests that issuers establish internal controls to protect against improvident release of information while securities are in registration.[29] Specifically, the Commission has admonished:

Issuers in this regard should:

1. Continue to advertise products and services.

2. Continue to send out customary quarterly, annual and other periodic reports to stockholders.

3. Continue to publish proxy statements and send out dividend notices.

4. Continue to make announcements to the press with respect to factual business and financial developments; *i.e.,* receipt of a contract, the settlement of a strike, the opening of a plant, or similar events of interest to the community in which the business operates.

5. Answer unsolicited telephone inquiries from stockholders, financial analysts, the press and others concerning factual information.

6. Observe an "open door" policy in responding to unsolicited inquiries concerning factual matters from securities analysts, financial analysts, security holders, and participants in the communications field who have a legitimate interest in the corporation's affairs.

7. Continue to hold stockholder meetings as scheduled and to answer shareholders' inquiries at stockholder meetings relating to factual matters.

---

26. Sec.Act Rel. No. 33–5180, Fed.Sec.L.Rep. (CCH) ¶ 3056 (Aug. 16, 1971).

27. By "in registration" the SEC means "at least from the time an issuer reaches an understanding with the broker-dealer which is to act as managing underwriter prior to the filing of a registration statement and the period of 40 to 90 days during which dealers must deliver a prospectus." Id. *fn. 1.*

28. Chris–Craft Indus., Inc. v. Bangor Punta Corp., 426 F.2d 569 (2d Cir.1970).

29. Sec.Act Rel. No. 33–5180, 1 Fed.Sec.L.Rep. (CCH) ¶ 3056 (Aug. 16, 1971).

In order to curtail problems in this area, issuers in this regard should avoid:

    1.   Issuance of forecasts, projections, or predictions relating but not limited to revenues, income, or earnings per share.

    2.   Publishing opinions concerning values.[30]

These guidelines are intended to permit necessary informational flow but no more. For example, a significant increase in product advertising that coincides with a public offering might well be viewed as an improper selling effort. On the other hand, notwithstanding section 5(c)'s gun jumping prohibitions, generalized discussions about the issuer's prospects may be sufficiently vague so as to militate against a finding that an illegal offer to sell has taken place.[31]

Broker–Dealer Recommendations

The securities markets thrive on the dissemination of information relating to publicly traded companies. A large body of public information concerning securities is generated by broker-dealers, investment advisers, and other financial analysts. The gun jumping rules address this type of publicity. Over and beyond the basic securities exemptions found in section 3 and transaction exemptions located in section 4 of the Act, which are discussed in a subsequent chapter,[32] there are a number of exclusions from section 5(c)'s gun jumping prohibitions for the prefiling period. Many of these exclusions apply with equal force to the waiting and post-effective periods.

Persons who are neither members of the underwriting syndicate nor part of the selling group may, under Rule 137,[33] make recommendations concerning the securities of an issuer that is subject to the reporting requirements of the Securities Exchange Act of 1934.[34] Rule 137, which was promulgated pursuant to section 2(11)'s definition of "underwriter,"

---

30. *Id.* Additional SEC guidance as to what constitutes permissible activity during the waiting period can be found in Sec. Act Rel. No. 33–5009, 1 Fed.Sec.L.Rep. (CCH) ¶ 1465 (Oct. 7, 1969) (publication of information prior to or after the filing and effective date of a registration statement); Sec.Act Rel. No. 33–3844, 1 Fed.Sec.L.Rep. (CCH) ¶¶ 3250–3256 (Oct. 8, 1957) (publication of information prior to or after the effective date of a registration statement). *See, also, e.g.,* Sec.Act Rel. No. 33–4697, 1 Fed.Sec.L.Rep. (CCH) ¶¶ 3257–3260 (May 28, 1964) (offers and sales of securities by underwriters and dealers).

See also, e.g., Joseph R. Lovejoy, Initial Public Offerings: Prefiling and Preeffective Publicity, 13 Ann.Inst.Sec.Reg. 359 (PLI 1982); Bruce A. Mann, Initial Offerings: Problems in the Course of Distribution, 13 Ann.Inst.Sec.Reg. 351 (PLI 1982); Morton A. Pierce, Current and Recurrent Section 5 Gun Jumping Problems, 26 Case W.Res.L.Rev. 731 (1976).

31. *See* American Nursing Care of Toledo, Inc. v. Leisure, 609 F.Supp. 419, 429 (N.D.Ohio 1984).

32. *See* Chapter 4 *infra.*

33. 17 C.F.R. § 230.137. *See also* rule 142 which defines participation in a distribution for purposes of section 2(11). 17 C.F.R. § 230.142.

34. Sections 13 and 15(d) of the 1934 Act provide for periodic reporting of issuers whose securities are traded on a national exchange, have been subject to a 1933 Act registration or where there are more than 500 holders of a class of equity securities and the issuer has more than $3 million in assets. 15 U.S.C.A. §§ 78m, 78o(d). *See* 15 U.S.C.A. § 78(g); 17 C.F.R. § 240.12g–1 and the discussion in § 9.2 *supra.*

permits a dealer which is not participating in the distribution to publish information, opinions, and recommendations that are distributed in the regular course of its business, provided that the dealer will not be receiving any remuneration directly or indirectly from the issuer with regard to such recommendation or with regard to the upcoming securities distribution. Since Rule 137 was promulgated pursuant to the statutory definition of "underwriter," [35] its scope is not limited to the pre-filing period, and it therefore exempts all permissible information, opinions, and recommendations disseminated during the waiting and post-effective periods as well.

Rule 138[36] provides additional exemptions from illegal gun jumping by excluding certain recommendations and opinions of participating dealers from the scope of section 2(3)'s definitions of "offer for sale" and "offer to sell" as used in section 2(10)'s definition of prospectus as well as in section 5(c).[37] Unlike Rule 137, which is discussed directly above, rule 138 applies to participants in the offering process. Where an issuer is qualified to use the short-form registration statement as provided in Form S–2[38] or Form F–2 (for foreign issuers) and has filed a registration statement for a non-convertible senior security, a dealer, although a member of the underwriting syndicate or selling group, may issue recommendations concerning the common stock or *convertible* senior securities of the same issuer. Rule 138 further provides that where the registration statement covers solely common stock or senior securities that are convertible into common stock and the issuer qualifies for Form S–2 or Form F–2, a dealer, although a member of the underwriting syndicate or selling group, may publish recommendations with regard to non-convertible senior securities of the same issuer. Since Rule 138 was promulgated pursuant to section 2(10), its exclusion carries over to the prospectus requirements of section 5(b) during both the waiting and post-effective periods.[39]

Rule 139[40] was promulgated pursuant to the definition of "offer for sale" and "offer to sell" as used in both sections 2(10) and 5(c).[41] Rule 139 applies to an issuer subject to the 1934 Act's periodic reporting requirements contained in section 13 or 15(d) of that Act.[42] The rule exempts certain communications of dealers participating in the under-

---

35. 15 U.S.C.A. § 77b(11). *See* § 4.24 *infra.*

36. 17 C.F.R. § 230.138.

37. *See* 15 U.S.C.A. §§ 77b(10), 77e(c).

38. Form S–2 is available only to issuers registered under section 12(g) of the 1934 Act or subject to section 15(d)'s periodic reporting requirements. *See* §§ 3.3, 3.4, 9.2 *infra.* Many such issuers may also qualify for the shorter Form S–3. In 1994, the Commission amended the Rule to make it clear that it applied to domestic issuers qualifying for Form S–3, foreign issuers qualifying for Form F–3, and for qualifying first-time registration for large foreign issuers. *See* SEC Adopts Rules to Reduce Paperwork for U.S., Foreign Registrants, 26 Sec. Reg. & L. Rep. (BNA) 1679 (Dec. 12, 1994).

39. 15 U.S.C.A. §§ 77b(10), 77e(b). *See* §§ 2.4–2.5 *infra.*

40. 17 C.F.R. § 230.139.

41. 15 U.S.C.A. §§ 77b(10), 77e(c).

42. *See* footnote 34 *supra,* § 3.3 *infra.*

writing syndicate or selling group, only if all of the following conditions are met: (a) the information, opinions, or recommendations are found in a publication that has been regularly published over the past two years on an annual or more frequent basis and when each issue of said publication contains a comprehensive list of that dealer's currently recommended securities; (b) the information in regard to the securities in registration or proposed to be in registration is not given any greater space or prominence than other securities and does not contain projections of future performance beyond the current fiscal year; and (c) except for issuers meeting the requirements for registration on Form S–3 or F–3, an opinion at least as favorable was published by the dealer in either the last publication of the same character or in a subsequent publication of a different character which was previously distributed by such dealer.

Under Rule 139(a), recommendations for securities where the issuer meets the requirements for filing registration Form S–3 or F–3 are not offers to sell provided that the recommendations are contained in a publication distributed with reasonable regularity in the broker's or dealer's regular course of business, without the additional requirement, still applicable for securities not so qualifying for the shortened form of registration, that the recommendations follow a prior equally favorable or more favorable recommendation in the last such publication.[43] In other words, when the issuer qualifies for one of the short forms, a broker or dealer can initiate coverage of the security or upgrade an existing recommendation and now qualify for Rule 139's safe harbor.

SEC Rules 137, 138, and 139, all of which apply only to 1934 Act reporting companies, are not limited to the prefiling period and apply throughout the registration process. These rules recognize the fact that many investment bankers have research analysts who are separate from the underwriting department.[44] Accordingly, the rules permit the research department to continue with its business without violating the prohibitions of section 5 of the 1933 Act. These exclusions are conditioned upon certain protections, including the fact that the issuer be sufficiently large and that it is subject to the reporting requirements which further insure that there is sufficient public information already available. It would appear to be beyond question that any broker's or dealer's recommendation of a security that does not fall within the

---

43. 17 C.F.R. § 230.139(a). *Compare id.* § 230.139(b)(3). *See* Sec.Act Rel. No. 33–6550, 49 Fed.Reg. 37569, 3 Fed.Sec.L.Rep. (CCH) ¶ 22,766 (Sept. 19, 1984). Form S–3 and Form F–3 (for foreign issuers) are available to issuers who qualify for use of Form S–2 or Form F–3 but have a sufficiently large market following to justify an even shorter registration form. *See* § 3.3 *infra.*

In 1994, the SEC amended Rule 139 to clarify that it is available for qualifying first-time registration for large foreign issuers. *See* SEC Adopts Rules to Reduce Paperwork for U.S., Foreign Registrants, 26 Sec. Reg. & L. Rep. (BNA) 1679 (Dec. 12, 1994).

44. Investment bankers must establish a system of internal controls to assure that the two departments are in fact separated. This is colloquially referred to as the "Chinese Wall" requirement. *See generally,* Martin Lipton & Robert B. Mazur, Chinese Wall Solution to the Conflict Problems of Securities Firms, 50 N.Y.U.L.Rev. 459 (1975). *See* § 10.2.4 *infra.*

foregoing exemptions would clearly violate section 5 unless, of course, some other exemption could be found.

§ 2.4 The Waiting Period

Applicable regulatory provisions

Once the registration statement has been filed, the waiting period begins. Since section 5(c) is no longer in effect after filing, anyone is free to make an offer to buy the security in registration, as well as to make oral offers to sell, provided that no sale is consummated lest there be a violation of section 5(a).[1] In addition to section 5(a)'s ban on sales prior to the effective date, the key to both the waiting and post-effective periods is found in the prospectus requirements of the 1933 Act. Section 5(b)(1)[2] makes it unlawful to utilize the mails or any instrumentality of transportation in interstate commerce to transmit any prospectus with regard to a security for which a registration statement has been filed, unless the prospectus meets the requirements of section 10 of the Act.[3] Section 5(b)(2)[4] prohibits the delivery of a security for sale unless accompanied or preceded by a prospectus meeting the requirements of section 10(a).[5]

The broad definition of prospectus gives significant impact to section 5(b)(1)'s requirements. Section 2(10)[6] defines "prospectus" to include all written offers to sell the security, in addition to any offer to sell transmitted by means of radio or television. Although section 2(10) does not address the issue directly, it would appear that an offer to sell transmitted through electronic mail, delivered on computer disk or other digitally encoded manner would qualify as a prospectus. The SEC has not taken a definitive position on the status of electronically transmitted offers to sell but has indicated that there is a strong argument that they should be treated the same as written, television, and radio communications (as opposed to oral or telephone communications).[7]

In line with the expansive definition applicable to offers to sell generally,[8] the definition of prospectus is far-reaching.[9] For example, a

---

§ 2.4

1. 15 U.S.C.A. §§ 77e(a), 77e(c). *See* § 2.3 *supra.*

2. 15 U.S.C.A. § 77e(b)(1).

3. 15 U.S.C.A. § 77j.

4. 15 U.S.C.A. § 77e(b)(2). Since section 5(a) prohibits sales during the waiting period, the practical impact of section 5(b)(2) is during the post-effective period.

5. The section 10(a) prospectus is discussed in §§ 2.5, 3.2 *infra.*

6. 15 U.S.C.A. § 77b(10).

7. The Commission alluded to this problem in the course of proposed rule amendments regarding mutual fund advertising. In Sec. Act Rel. No. 33–6982; 57 FR 16141 (March 19, 1993) the SEC published a proposed rule change to allow certain advertisements for mutual funds to include an order form if the "off-the-page prospectuses" contain specified information.

8. *But see, e.g.,* Eckstein v. Balcor Film Investors, 8 F.3d 1121 (7th Cir.1993) (failure to include important information in supplemental sales literature was not a material omission when the information was fully disclosed in the prospectus). *See* section 2(3), 15 U.S.C.A.

---

9. See note 9 on page 93.

contract for sale falls within the definition.[10]   Section 2(10)'s definition
not only includes advertisement circulars and notices which offer the
securities for sale but also expressly covers communications confirming
sales of securities in registration.   This is an especially significant aspect
of the definition of prospectus since, by virtue of Rule 10b–10 of the 1934
Act,[11] all transactions by a broker for a customer's account must be
preceded by a written confirmation, which pursuant to section 5(b)(1)
must conform to section 10's disclosure requirements unless an applicable exemption can be established.   Section 2(10) further sets forth an
important exclusion from the definition of prospectus which permits use
of "identifying statements" and "tombstone ads" which are considered
directly below.[12]

Section 10 of the 1933 Act sets out the requirements of a statutory
prospectus–i.e. one that is sufficient to avoid violation of section 5(b)'s
prohibitions.   Section 10(a) requires the prospectus to include all relevant information about the issuer.[13]   Section 10(a)(3) further provides
that whenever the prospectus is used more than nine months after the
registration statement's effective date, the information must be updated
so as to be accurate within a time frame of not more than sixteen
months prior to use of the prospectus.[14]

In addition to section 10(a)'s statutory prospectus, section 10(b) [15]
permits the Commission to promulgate rules that allow the use of a
"summary prospectus" so as to satisfy section 5(b)(1)'s prospectus
requirement.   Although most section 10(b) summary prospectuses can
be used during both the waiting and post-effective periods, they are valid
only for section 5(b)(1)'s offer requirements and do not extend to section
5(b)(2)'s delivery for sale proscriptions.   The Commission has exercised
its rulemaking power under section 10(b) to authorize summary prospectuses under Rule 430 (the preliminary or "red herring" prospectus); [16]
and Rule 431[17] which permits a summary prospectus prepared by the

§ 77b(3), which is discussed in § 2.3, supra.   E.g., SEC v. Thomas D. Kienlen Corp., 755
F.Supp. 936 (D.Or.1991) (brochure describing "safety", "improved performance", and
"lower costs" of mutual fund was a prospectus and thus violated section 5(b)(1) when used
during the waiting period).

9.   See, e.g., SEC v. Graystone Nash, Inc., 820 F.Supp. 863 (D.N.J.1993) (magazine
article was reasonably calculated to generate a buying interest and thus was an offer and
prospectus that violated section 5(b)).   Compare The Supreme Court's treatment in
Gustafson v. Alloyd Co., ___ U.S. ___, 115 S.Ct. 1061, 131 L.Ed.2d 1 (1995) which is
discussed in § 7.5 infra.

10.   See Pacific Dunlop Holdings Inc. v. Allen & Co., 993 F.2d 578 (7th Cir.1993), cert.
granted ___ U.S. ___, 114 S.Ct. 907, 127 L.Ed.2d 98 (1994).   See also, e.g., SEC v. Thomas
D. Kienlen Corp., 755 F.Supp. 936 (D.Or.1991) (letter to customers stating that new
mutual fund would be safest in the country was a prospectus).

11.   17 C.F.R. § 240.10b–10.

12.   See text accompanying footnotes 20–24 infra.

13.   15 U.S.C.A. § 77aa.   See chapter 3 infra.

14.   15 U.S.C.A. § 77j(a)(3).

15.   15 U.S.C.A. § 77j(b).

16.   17 C.F.R. § 230.430.

17.   17 C.F.R. § 230.431.

issuer and filed with the registration statement. The preliminary or "red herring" prospectus which is permitted pursuant to Rule 430[18] is not explicitly grounded upon section 10(b)[19] but obviously is based upon that statutory grant of rulemaking authority.

Permissible Offers During the Waiting Period

In essence, there are four types of permissible offers to sell that may be made during the waiting period:

1. *Oral communications.* Section 5(b) applies only to prospectuses as defined in section 2(10) which, as noted above, is limited to written, radio and television offers to sell and thus does not include oral communications. Since section 5(c)'s prohibition on all offers to sell expressly expires upon the filing of the registration statement, there are no prohibitions on oral offers after the filing. The waiting period thus permits selling efforts with regard to securities in registration. For example, brokers, and even dealers who are members of the underwriting group, may make all offers to sell either on a face-to-face basis or over the telephone, so long as there is no final contract to purchase the security prior to the effective date. Notwithstanding the absence of section 5 implications, oral offers to sell during the waiting and post-effective periods are, of course, subject to the securities acts' general antifraud provisions.

2. *The "tombstone advertisement"* (also known as the identifying statement). Section 2(10)(b) expressly excludes from the definition of "prospectus" a communication if it "does no more than identify the security, state the price thereof, state by whom orders will be executed, and contains such other information as [may be required by Commission rules and regulations]" and if it specifies from whom a statutory prospectus may be obtained.[20] The Commission promulgated rule 134[21] which specifies twelve categories of information that may be included in the tombstone ad (or other identifying statement) without running afoul of the 1933 Act's prospectus requirements. The twelve items permitted by Rule 134 are as follows: (1) the issuer's name, (2) the "full title" of the security and the amount being offered for sale, (3) a "brief indication of the general type of business of the issuer," (4) the price, or method of its determination or probable price range—recall that for most offerings the mention of price is not permitted prior to the filing of the registration statement by virtue of Rule 135,[22] (5) if applicable, the yield or estimated yield of a fixed interest debt security, (6) the name and address of the sender or person placing the tombstone ad or identifying

---

18. 17 C.F.R. § 230.430.

19. *See* 1 Louis Loss, Securities Regulation 232–34 (2d ed. 1961).

20. 15 U.S.C.A. § 77j(b)(10).

21. 17 C.F.R. § 230.134. *See also* Rule 142 which defines the meaning of participating in a distribution. 17 C.F.R. § 230.142.

22. 17 C.F.R. § 230.135. Rule 135(3), (5) permit price to be mentioned in prefiling publicity concerning rights offering to existing security holders and offering to employees. *See* § 2.3 *supra.*

statement and the fact that he or she is participating or plans to participate in the distribution of the security; (7) similarly, the name of the managing underwriters may be listed in the tombstone ad or other identifying statement—it is significant to note that this subsection of Rule 134 permits the naming of the underwriter which is expressly prohibited during the prefiling period by virtue of Rule 135,[23] (8) the approximate date of the proposed public sale; (9) if applicable, whether in the opinion of counsel, the security is a legal investment for fiduciaries; (10) if applicable, whether in the opinion of counsel, the security is tax exempt or the extent to which issuer has agreed to pay taxes based on income; (11) whether the security is being offered by virtue of a rights offering to existing security holders, and if so, a brief description of the terms of the rights offering; and (12) any statement that is required by state law or administrative bodies, presumably both state and federal.

Inclusion of any information not specifically permitted by Rule 134 renders the rule unavailable and thus can result in a prospectus that fails to comply with section 10's requirements.[24] This, in turn, will result in a violation of section 5 of the Act.

3. *Preliminary prospectus.* The preliminary prospectus or so-called "red herring" is authorized by Rule 430.[25] The preliminary or "red herring" prospectus may contain substantially the same information as a full-blown section 10(a) statutory prospectus "except for the omission of information with respect to the offering price, underwriting discounts or commissions, discounts or commissions to dealers, amount of proceeds, conversion rates, call prices or other matters dependent upon the offering price." [26] Rule 430 thus permits but does not require the mention of price which may also be included in the tombstone ad used during the waiting period. In addition to the possible price exclusion, the preliminary prospectus must include a legend in red ink—to the effect that a registration statement has not yet become effective and that a formal offer to sell can only be made subsequent to the effective date.[27]

---

23. 17 C.F.R. § 230.135. The prefiling period and rule 135 are discussed in the preceding section. *See* § 2.3 *supra.*

24. *See* Charles Schwab & Co., 18 Sec.Reg. & L.Rep. (BNA) 1286 (Aug. 11, 1986) (description of mutual fund's past performance in fund's advertising material exceeds the limitations on information that may be disseminated pursuant to rules 134 and 135a).

25. 17 C.F.R. § 230.430. Unlike the summary prospectuses discussed below, rule 430 was not promulgated pursuant to section 10(b). *See* 1 Louis Loss footnote 19 *supra* at 232–34. The SEC requires a legend printed in red on the cover page of the preliminary prospectus, explaining that the prospectus is preliminary and that sales cannot be made until the post-effective period. Reg. S–K, Item 501(b)(8). The SEC, however, has been permitting use of colors other than red. In fact, the counterpart requirement for small issuers does not require the caption to be in red. Reg. S–B, Item 501(b)(8); Reg. S–B, Item 501(b)(6).

26. 17 C.F.R. § 230.430(a). In the case of an offering by an issuer which is not subject to the 1934 Act periodic reporting requirements, the preliminary prospectus must contain a good faith estimate of the range of the offering price and the number of shares to be offered. Reg. S–K, Item 501(b)(6).

27. The full legend must read as follows:

A registration statement relating to these securities has been filed with the Securities and Exchange Commission, but has not yet become effective. Information contained

4. *Summary prospectus filed as part of the registration statement.*
SEC Rule 431[28] permits an additional type of summary prospectus which
operates solely for the purpose of section 5(b)(1) and thus not for the
delivery for sale requirements of section 5(b)(2).[29]   Communications
complying with Rule 431 may be used during the post-effective period for
section 5(b)(1) purposes.[30]   The Rule 431 prospectus must be filed with
the registration statement and can be used only if the issuer is a 1934
Act registered reporting company.[31]   In addition, the Exchange Act
reports must be current.[32]   The Rule 431 summary prospectus must
contain all of the information that is specified in the official SEC form
accompanying the applicable registration statement form and further
may not include any information which is not permitted in the tombstone ad as spelled out in Rule 134(a).[33]   The rule 431 summary
prospectus must also contain a caption similar to that required for the
preliminary prospectus as well as a statement setting forth that copies of
a more complete prospectus may be obtained from designated brokerage
firms.   Eight copies of the Rule 431 summary prospectus must be filed
with the commission at least five working days prior to the use thereof.
Issuers which qualify for use of the Rule 431 summary prospectus may
use a *preliminary* summary prospectus during the waiting period.

Broker-Dealer Recommendations

Rules 137, 138 and 139 which are discussed in the preceding section,
permit publication of certain recommendations by dealers, provided that
each of the appropriate rule's conditions are met.[34]   Aside from the
foregoing exceptions or pursuant to an exemption in sections 3 or 4 of

herein is subject to completion or amendment. These securities may not be sold nor may
offers to buy be accepted prior to the time the registration statement becomes effective.
This prospectus shall not constitute an offer to sell or the solicitation of an offer to buy
nor shall there be any sales of these securities in any State in which such offer,
solicitation or sale would be unlawful prior to registration or qualification under the
securities laws of any such State.

17 C.F.R. § 230.430(b); Reg. S–K, item 501(c)(8).

28.   17 C.F.R. § 230.431. The Commission has proposed expanding the category of
issuers who can use the summary prospectus. *See* 22 Sec.Reg. & L.Rep. (BNA) 899 (June
15, 1990).

29.   15 U.S.C.A. §§ 77e(b)(1), (2).

30.   15 U.S.C.A. § 77e(b)(1). However the rule 431 summary prospectus may not be
used to satisfy section 5(b)(2). 15 U.S.C.A. § 77e(b)(2). *See* § 2.5 *infra.*

31.   17 C.F.R. § 230.431(b).

32.   In order to be eligible for use of the Rule 431 summary prospectus, the issuer must:
(1) either (a) be organized under the laws of the United States, any state, territory or the
District of Columbia or (b) be a foreign private issuer which qualifies for use of 1933 Act
registration Form F–2; (2) be a registered reporting company pursuant to section 12 of the
Securities Exchange Act of 1934; (3) have been subject to the Exchange Act's registration
and periodic reporting requirements for thirty-six months prior to the filing of the 1933 Act
registration statement; and (4) has not failed to pay any dividend or sinking fund
installment on preferred stock and has not defaulted on any debt or long-term lease
payments (unless the aggregate of such defaults are not material to the issuer's financial
position) since the end of its last fiscal year. 17 C.F.R. § 230.431(b).

33.   17 C.F.R. § 230.134(a). *See* text accompanying footnotes 21–23 *supra.*

34.   17 C.F.R. §§ 230.137–139. *See* § 2.3 *supra.*

the 1933 Act, only the above-mentioned four types of offers may be made during the waiting period.[35]

Suspension of Prospectus Delivery Requirements for Certain Transactions by Dealers

SEC Rule 174 suspends the prospectus delivery requirements for certain securities transactions with regard to transactions by dealers not participating in the distribution.[36] Rule 174, as is the case with rules 137 through 139 which are discussed in the preceding section, applies to 1934 Act reporting companies.[37] Rule 174 dispenses with the prospectus delivery requirements for offers and sales by nonparticipating dealers after the effective date.[38]

Broker-Dealer Standard of Conduct with Regard to Prospectus Delivery Requirements

Exchange Act Rule 15c2–8[39] sets forth standards of conduct for broker-dealers with regard to the 1933 Act's prospectus delivery requirements. The rule makes it a deceptive act or practice for a broker or dealer to participate in a distribution covered by a 1933 Act registration statement and not to make available to each associated person sufficient copies of the preliminary prospectus prior to any customer solicitation.[40] The rule also provides that the managing underwriter must take "reasonable steps" to assure that all participating brokers and dealers are furnished with sufficient copies of the preliminary prospectus, each amended preliminary prospectus and the final prospectus.[41] The rule further requires a participating broker or dealer to take reasonable steps

---

35. Former Rule 434, which was rescinded in 1982 permitted the use of a document that summarizes the statistical and financial information contained in a preliminary prospectus pursuant to Rule 433 (*i.e.*, a summary of the information required by section 10(a)'s statutory prospectus). To be valid the former Rule 434 summary prospectus had to be filed as part of the registration statement and the issuer must have been a 1934 Act reporting company. The former rule 434 summary prospectus was expressly limited in use to the waiting period and section 5(b)(1). However, the independently prepared "buff card" prospectus could be used as supplemental sales literature during the post-effective period provided that a section 10(a) prospectus had already been given to the recipient.

36. 17 C.F.R. § 230.174. Rule 174 is discussed in more detail in the next section; § 2.5 *infra.*

37. *See* § 2.3 *supra.*

38. Section 4(3) of the Act exempts the prospectus delivery requirements for dealers after the expiration of a forty or ninety day period following the effective date. *See* § 4.27 *infra.* Rule 174 dispenses with the prospectus delivery requirements prior to the expiration of the forty or ninety day period so long as the dealer is not participating in the distribution and where the issuer is subject to the 1934 Act's periodic reporting requirements. 17 C.F.R. § 230.174. The rule also reduces the so-called "quiet period" to twenty-five days for issuers whose securities are traded on a national exchange or through the NASD's Automated Quotation system (NASDAQ). 17 C.F.R. § 230.174(d). *See* § 2.5 *infra.*

39. 17 C.F.R. § 240.15c2–8.

40. 17 C.F.R. § 240.15c2–8(d). The rule further provides that all such persons shall immediately be sent copies of any amended preliminary prospectus.

41. 17 C.F.R. § 240.15c2–8(f).

to comply with written requests for a copy of the latest preliminary prospectus.[42]

§ 2.5 The Post–Effective Period

Section 5(a) of the 1933 Act[1] prohibits all sales of securities facilitated by the use of the mail or other instrumentalities of interstate commerce to effect a sale prior to the effective date of the registration statement. Once the registration statement becomes effective, section 5(a)'s prohibitions cease to apply and the only limitation on securities sales, aside from the disclosure and anti-fraud provisions, are those contained in the prospectus requirements of section 5(b) of the Act.[2] Section 5(b)(1) requires that all prospectuses (*i.e.*, written, radio or television offers to sell) must comply with the statutory prospectus requirements of section 10.[3] The operation and effect of section 5(b)(1) are much the same as for the waiting period[4] except that some of the methods of permissible offers during the waiting period are not allowed during the post-effective period. The summary prospectus that has been filed as part of the registration statement as defined in Rule 431[5] may be used during both the waiting and post-effective periods, but solely for the purpose of satisfying section 5(b)(1)'s requirements and not for the delivery before sale requirement contained in section 5(b)(2). However, the preliminary prospectus or "red herring" that is permitted by Rule 430 during the waiting period is expressly limited "for use prior to the effective date."[6] Accordingly, the "red herring" may not be used during the post-effective period either for subsection (b)(1) or (b)(2).

Section 2(10)(a) of the 1933 Act permits the use of supplementary sales literature after the effective date even if such literature is neither in conformance to nor contained in the statutory prospectus.[7] However, a significant limitation upon use of supplementary sales literature is that it must be proven by the registrant, or other person relying on the permissible use of such literature, that prior to or at the same time as receiving it a section 10(a) statutory prospectus had been sent or given to a person receiving the supplementary sales literature. There are no

---

42. 17 C.F.R. § 240.15c2–8(b).

§ 2.5

1. 15 U.S.C.A. § 77e(a).

2. 15 U.S.C.A. § 77e(b). For a depiction of the operation of section 5 *see* the chart in the text accompanying footnote 23 in § 2.2 *supra*.

3. 15 U.S.C.A. § 77j. *See also, e.g.,* SEC v. Graystone Nash, Inc., 820 F.Supp. 863 (D.N.J.1993) (magazine article was reasonably calculated to generate a buying interest and thus was an offer and prospectus that violated section 5(b)).

4. *See* § 2.4 *supra.* Thus, for example, during the waiting and post effective periods, oral offers to sell and all offers to buy are unregulated by section 5. Although, oral communications are subject to the antifraud provisions of the 1933 and 1934 Acts.

5. 17 C.F.R. § 230.431. *See* § 2.4 *supra.*

The Commission proposed expanding the category of issuers who can use the summary prospectus. *See* 22 Sec.Reg. & L.Rep. (BNA) 899 (June 15, 1990).

6. 17 C.F.R. § 230.430.

7. 15 U.S.C.A. § 77b(10). This is sometimes referred to as "free writing".

explicit statutory restrictions on the types of information that may be included in the supplementary sales literature. It must not be forgotten, however, that unduly optimistic promotional sales talk will render the supplementary sales literature in violation of the anti-fraud provisions of both the 1933 and 1934 Acts.[8]

Another aspect of the post-effective period is that although the registration statement need not be updated for most developments subsequent to the effective date,[9] the prospectus must continue to be accurate.[10] For example, where there has been a change of events, a change in earnings, or a revaluation of projected performance, the prospectus must be updated lest it be in violation of section 10(a).[11] This is so even if there is no need to update the registration statement.[12]

Frequently, changes in the prospectus will be made by affixing stickers that contain the updated or corrected information.[13] Rule 424(c) explicitly allows for prospectus supplements, commonly referred to as "stickers," to be filed with the Commission when it becomes necessary to update the prospectus.[14] In the usual case,[15] it is not necessary to attach them to a full prospectus before filing, although a full prospectus will usually be required to be given to investors. Stickering saves the registrant the expense of reprinting the entire prospectus. When a prospectus has been updated by post-effective amendments, before it can be used ten copies of the updated prospectus must be filed with the Commission.[16]

Although the SEC provides for the use of stickers as an alternative to the filing of a post-effective amendment, there is no clear guide

---

8. *See* § 1.7 *supra* and §§ 7.5, 7.6, 13.2–13.13 *infra*.

9. *See* Funeral Directors Mfg. & Supply Co., 39 S.E.C. 33, 34 (SEC 1954).

10. *See* SEC v. Manor Nursing Centers, Inc., 458 F.2d 1082 (2d Cir.1972); Note, Prospectus Liability for Failure to Disclose Post–Effective Developments: A New Duty and Its Implications, 48 Ind.L.J. 464 (1973).

11. SEC v. Manor Nursing Centers, Inc., 458 F.2d 1082 (2d Cir.1972). *See also, e.g.,* SEC v. Melchior, 1993 WL 89141, [1992–1993 Transfer Binder] Fed.Sec.L.Rep. (CCH) ¶ 97,356 (D.Utah 1993) (material omissions from prospectus rendered it in violation of section 5(b)). *But cf.* SEC v. Southwest Coal & Energy, 624 F.2d 1312 (5th Cir.1980) (decided under Regulation B's exemption for certain undivided oil or gas rights); SEC v. Blazon Corp., 609 F.2d 960, 968–69 (9th Cir.1979) (defective offering circular is not *per se* fatal to a Regulation A exemption). Regulation A is discussed in § 4.15 *infra*. Regulation B is contained in 17 C.F.R. §§ 230.300–230.336.

12. SEC v. Manor Nursing Centers, Inc., 458 F.2d 1082, 1099 (2d Cir.1972).

13. *See, e.g.,* Investment Company Institute, [1987–88 Transfer Binder] Fed.Sec.L.Rep. (CCH) ¶ 78,683 (Feb. 25, 1988) (disclosure changes required by rule 485(a) may be made through use of stickers); Preferred Equities Group, Inc., [1987 Transfer Binder] Fed.Sec. L.Rep. (CCH) ¶ 78,462 (SEC No Action Letter April 7, 1987) (stickering prospectus and post effective amendments to registration statement to reflect changes in the underwriting group); University Real Estate Fund–12 [1982–83 Transfer Binder] Fed.Sec.L.Rep. (CCH) ¶ 77,380 (SEC No Action Letter Dec. 23, 1982) (stickering prospectus to reflect changes in interest rates on promissory notes during the offering).

14. 17 C.F.R. § 230.424(c).

15. There is an exception in some employee benefit plan contexts. Sec. Act Rel. No. 33–6714, 1987 WL 113872 (May 27, 1987), p. 41.

16. 17 C.F.R. § 230.424(c).

concerning the point at which information becomes so significant that stickering alone will not be sufficient. Most reported discussions of stickering do not clearly distinguish between the types of updating that require a post-effective amendment as opposed to just a sticker. Materiality is the point at which either will be required.[17] Some information is important enough to require an amendment.[18] For example, in the shelf-offering context, one release suggested that changes qualifying as "fundamental" in the meaning of Item 512(a)(1)(ii) of Regulation S–K seem to require an amendment as opposed to a sticker.[19]

Failure to make timely amendments to the prospectus will not only implicate the securities laws' antifraud provisions but may also necessitate the making of a rescission offer to all purchasers who received the defective prospectus.[20] Furthermore, although there is authority to the contrary, the Second Circuit has held that once a prospectus is found to be materially misleading, not only does it no longer comply with section 10(a) since there is not a valid statutory prospectus, but also the use of this document will not comply with section 5(b) thus putting the sender in violation of the Act and accordingly making any sale based on the use of such prospectus subject to the strict rescission remedy set out by section 12(1) of the Act.[21] Section 12(1) liability exists even if the seller attempts to "cure" the illegal offer by a legal sale effectuated by use of a valid section 10 prospectus.[22] Section 12(1) is remedial and promotes

---

17. *See, e.g.,* In the Matter of Blinder, Robinson & Co., Inc., Admin. Proc. File No. 3–6380, 1990 WL 321585 (SEC Initial Dec. April 27, 1990) ("whether . . . purchase . . . was a material development which should be disclosed by a . . . 'sticker.' ").

18. Except for scattered references, it would appear that materiality is the only threshold of importance. A 1993 release suggests, or implies, that the distinction between information meriting a sticker and that requiring an amendment is one of kind, not degree. Sec. Act Rel. No. 33–7015, 1993 WL 370960 (Sept. 21, 1993) ("Stickers . . . are used to update certain types of information (but not year-end financial statements)."). There is no comprehensive list of what other types of information fall in each class.

19. Examples given of "fundamental" updates include changes in interest rates, redemption prices, maturities, final method of distribution, or underwriters. Multijurisdictional Disclosure, Sec. Act Rel. No. 33–6841, 1989 WL 257670 (July 24, 1989).

20. *See, e.g.,* Alan R. Bromberg, Curing Securities Violations: Rescission and Other Techniques, 1 J.Corp.L. 1 (1975); Michelle Rowe, Rescission Offers Under Federal and State Securities Law, 12 J.Corp.L. 383 (1987).

21. SEC v. Manor Nursing Centers, Inc., 458 F.2d 1082 (2d Cir.1972). *See also* SEC v. Melchior, 1993 WL 89141, [1992–1993 Transfer Binder] Fed.Sec.L.Rep. (CCH) ¶ 97,356 (D.Utah 1993) (material omissions from prospectus rendered it in violation of section 5(b)). *But see* SEC v. Southwest Coal & Energy, 624 F.2d 1312 (5th Cir.1980) (decided under Regulation B); SEC v. Blazon, 609 F.2d 960 (9th Cir.1979) (decided under Regulation A). As discussed more fully in § 7.2 *infra,* section 12(1) provides a right of rescission for purchasers of securities sold in violation of section 5 of the Act. 15 U.S.C.A. § 77l (1); Diskin v. Lomasney & Co., 452 F.2d 871 (2d Cir.1971); Jefferies & Co. v. Arkus–Duntov, 357 F.Supp. 1206, 1214–15 (S.D.N.Y.1973).

22. Diskin v. Lomasney & Co., 452 F.2d 871 (2d Cir.1971); 3 Louis Loss, Securities Regulation 1695–96 (1961).

In *Diskin,* a broker wrote a letter to a customer during the waiting period offering to commit to sell 5,000 shares "at the public offering price when, as and if issued" but failed to enclose a waiting period prospectus for that security. A statutory prospectus was subsequently received by the customer prior to his agreement to purchase the security. In a private suit under section 12(1) of the 1933 Act, by a purchaser claiming that the securities had been sold in violation of section 5, the court ruled that an illegal offer is not cured by a subsequent legal sale. The court reasoned:

compliance with the Act. It has been applied even where the claimant is not at an informational disadvantage.[23] Of course, this strict rescission liability is in addition to other private remedies under the anti-fraud provisions of the Act. First, liability exists expressly under section 11 of the Act for the misleading statements in the prospectus.[24] Secondly, section 12(2) of the 1933 Act provides express liability for the seller's fraud.[25] These are all in addition to any implied liabilities that may exist under section 17(a) of the 1933 Act,[26] or under SEC Rule 10b–5,[27] of the 1934 Act.

Sections 5(b)(1) and 5(b)(2) operate together to assure that absent an exemption, any purchaser of a security in registration will receive a complete section 10(a) statutory prospectus at some point during the transaction. During the waiting period for any given offering there may be a number of offerees who receive only limited summary prospectuses, or no prospectus at all if their interest is solicited orally or over the telephone.[28] Ordinarily, these offerees will have to receive a section 10(a) prospectus prior to any sale to them. In addition, Rule 10b–10 of the Exchange Act[29] requires that all transactions for a customer's ac-

---

The result here reached may appear to be harsh since [the purchaser] had an opportunity to read the final prospectus before he paid for the shares. But the 1954 Congress quite obviously meant to allow rescission or damages in the case of illegal offers as well as of illegal sales. Very likely Congress thought that, when it had done so much to broaden the methods for making legal offers during the "waiting period" between the filing and the taking effect of the registration statement, it should make sure that still other methods were not attempted. Here all [the seller] needed to have done was to accompany the September 17, 1968 letter with any one of the three [types of written offers that are permitted during the waiting period] ... Very likely Congress thought a better time for meaningful prospectus reading was at the time of the offer rather than in the context of confirmation and demand for payment. In any event, it made altogether clear that an offeror of a security who had failed to follow one of the allowed paths could not achieve absolution simply by returning to the road of virtue before receiving payment.

452 F.2d at 876.

23. For example, in Byrnes v. Faulkner, Dawkins & Sullivan, 550 F.2d 1303 (2d Cir.1977) section 12(1) was held to apply in an action by a market maker for the stock in registration.

24. 15 U.S.C.A. § 77k. *See* § 7.3 *infra.*

25. 15 U.S.C.A. § 77l(2). *See* § 7.5 *infra.*

26. 15 U.S.C.A. § 77q(a). As is discussed more fully elsewhere, while earlier decisions tended to recognize an implied right of action, the current trend is to the contrary. *See* § 13.13 *infra;* Thomas L. Hazen, A Look Beyond The Pruning of Rule 10b–5: Implied Remedies and Section 17(a) of the Securities Act of 1933, 64 Va.L.Rev. 641 (1978).

27. 17 C.F.R. § 240.10b–5; §§ 13.2–13.12 *infra.*

28. *See* § 2.4 *supra.*

29. 17 C.F.R. § 240.10b–10. Rule 10b–10 which requires disclosure of the broker's role in the transaction and mark-up, mark-down or similar remuneration received by the dealer has been amended to also require disclosure by nonmarket-makers of any variation between the price charged to the customer and the trade price reported in accordance with an effective transaction reporting plan. 17 C.F.R. § 240.10b–10(8)(i) (1986). *See* § 10.3 *infra.*

Rule 15c2–8(b) provides that unless the issuer was previously subject to the Exchange Act's reporting requirements (or exempted from such reports under section 12(h)), a broker-dealer must deliver a preliminary prospectus to any person expected to receive a confirmation of sale at least forty-eight hours prior to the mailing of the confirmation. 17 C.F.R. § 240.15c2–8(b).

count be confirmed in writing. Since section 2(10) of the 1933 Act includes such a written confirmation in the definition of prospectus, if sent through the mails it must be accompanied by a section 10 prospectus to avoid a violation of section 5(b)(1). Secondly, before a security in registration can be delivered for sale under section 5(b)(2) it must be accompanied or preceded by a section 10(a) prospectus.[30] Thus, absent an exemption, sections 5(b)(1) and 5(b)(2) will provide a prospectus to most offerees and virtually all purchasers.

The prospectus delivery requirements discussed above are supplemented by state law requirements that certain contracts be in writing. For example, the Uniform Commercial Code provides that an oral contract of sale involving a security is unenforceable if the customer makes a prompt objection after having received the broker's written confirmation.[31] Since, as discussed above, a confirmation is a prospectus, a purchaser of securities in a public offering who receives a confirmation without a statutory prospectus may be able to claim that the confirmation is ineffective for statute of frauds purposes. Even when the statute of frauds has been satisfied, a customer seeing the prospectus for the first time when the confirmation or securities are received may still be able to disaffirm the sale as a matter of contract law, especially if the prospectus contains unexpected or surprising information.[32]

The seller of a security, delivering a security for sale, who does not himself or herself send the prospectus bears the burden of proving that one has been received by the purchaser.[33] It has been held, however, that under appropriate circumstances the seller may justifiably assume that a statutory prospectus has been received.[34] Although the seller can rely on a prospectus having been sent by someone else,[35] the risks are great since failure to meet the burden of proving that one was in fact received will result in strict liability under section 12(1)[36] as well as possible exposure to SEC, civil or criminal sanctions.[37]

---

30. 15 U.S.C.A. § 77e(b)(2). *See* Annot. What Constitutes Violation of § 5(b)(2) of Securities Act of 1933 (15 USCS § 77e(b)(2)), Requiring Security to be Accompanied or Preceded by Prospectus, 28 A.L.R.Fed. 811 (1976).

31. Unif.Comm.Code § 8–319. *See, e.g.,* Leason v. Rosart, 811 F.2d 1322 (9th Cir.1987) (customer objecting to oral contract promptly after receipt of confirmation held not bound due to statute of frauds). *Compare* Merrill Lynch, Pierce, Fenner & Smith, Inc. v. Cole, 189 Conn. 518, 457 A.2d 656 (1983) (seller failed to object within ten days of confirmation; statute of frauds defense was thus not available); Shpilberg v. Merrill Lynch, Pierce, Fenner & Smith, Inc., 535 S.W.2d 227 (Ky.1976) (failure to object within ten days precluded statute of frauds defense).

32. *Cf.* Russell v. Dean Witter Reynolds, Inc., 200 Conn. 172, 510 A.2d 972 (1986).

33. *See* In re Jaffe & Co., [1969–70 Transfer Binder] Fed.Sec.L.Rep. (CCH) ¶ 77,805 (SEC, April 20, 1970).

34. Competitive Associates, Inc. v. Advest Co., 1975 WL 419, [1975–76 Transfer Binder] Fed.Sec.L.Rep. (CCH) ¶ 95,302 (S.D.N.Y.1975) (purchaser was mutual fund represented by an agent of its portfolio manager who is under a fiduciary duty with regard to its investment decisions).

35. *See* Sec. Act Rel. No. 33–2623 (SEC Gen'l Counsel July 25, 1941); Sec. Act Rel. No. 33–628 (SEC Gen'l Counsel, June 4, 1936).

36. 15 U.S.C.A. § 77l (1).

37. *See* chapter 7 *infra*.

It is to be noted further that use of a section 10(b) prospectus for section 5(b)(1) purposes will not satisfy the prior receipt requirement of section 5(b)(2). Accordingly, prudent practice would dictate delivery of a prospectus with the security even where the seller himself has previously sent a section 10(a) prospectus.

The prospectus requirements do not apply if an appropriate exemption from 1933 Act registration can be established. In addition to the more general securities exemptions contained in section 3 and transaction exemptions contained in section 4 of the 1933 Act,[38] there are certain circumstances under which section 5(b)'s prospectus delivery requirements do not apply. Thus, for example, section 4(3) of the Act[39] exempts transactions by a dealer, including an underwriter no longer acting as such, for securities not constituting part of an unsold allotment provided that the transaction has not taken place prior to the expiration of forty days after the registration statement's effective date or the first date that the security was "bona fide offered" to the public, whichever is later. The statutory forty day period for registered offerings is extended to ninety days if the issuer has not previously sold securities pursuant to an effective registration statement, unless a shorter period has been specified by the SEC.[40] This forty or ninety day period sometimes has been referred to as the quiet period.

As pointed out above, section 4(3) expressly authorizes the SEC to shorten this quiet period. The Commission has exercised this authority in Rule 174 which dispenses with the prospectus requirements prior to the expiration of the forty or ninety day period for dealers who are neither underwriters nor members of the selling group.[41] Rule 174

---

38. 15 U.S.C.A. §§ 77c, 77d. *See* chapter 4 *infra.*

39. 15 U.S.C.A. § 77d(3). Section 4(3)(A) provides that dealers need not deliver a prospectus more than forty days after the securities were first "bona fide offered to the public". This was intended to cover unregistered offerings and to protect nonparticipating dealers with regard to subsequent transactions. *See, e.g.,* Kubik v. Goldfield, 479 F.2d 472 (3d Cir.1973) (a bona fide offering may occur despite the fact that the offering was not registered and therefore in violation of the 1933 Act); David Ratner, Securities Regulation—Materials For a Basic Course 64 (3d ed. 1986). In *Kubik, supra,* the court held that appearance of the stock in the over-the-counter "pink sheets" may be sufficient to establish that the stock was bona fide offered to the public via an illegal offering.

In comparison to section 4(3)(A), the period established by section 4(3)(B) applies to offerings for which a registration statement has been filed and runs from the date the securities were first bona fide offered to the public or the effective date, whichever is later. This forty day period is extended to ninety days in the case of first-time issuers. As noted *infra,* rule 174(b) dispenses with the prospectus requirement during the forty or ninety day period for issuers which were subject to the Exchange Act's periodic reporting requirements prior to the offering in question. 17 C.F.R. § 230.174(b). In addition, for other issuers, Rule 174(d) reduces the prospectus delivery period to twenty-five days if the security is listed on a national securities exchange or authorized for inclusion in an interdealer quotation system such as NASDAQ. 17 C.F.R. § 230.174(d).

By virtue of section 4(3)(C), any sales of securities that were part of an unsold allotment are subject to the prospectus delivery requirements even if the statutory period has expired. 15 U.S.C.A. § 77d(4)(C).

See also § 4.27 *infra.*

40. *Id.*

41. 17 C.F.R. § 230.174.

dispenses with the prospectus delivery requirements if immediately prior to the filing of the registration statement the issuer was subject to the 1934 Act periodic reporting requirements,[42] or if the registration statement of a private foreign issuer using American Depositary Receipts is on Form F–6 provided that the deposited securities need not be registered under the 1933 Act.[43] Rule 174(c)[44] further dispenses with the delivery requirements where the registration statement relates to offerings to be made from time to time[45] and the forty or ninety day period specified in section 4(3) has expired.

As described above, Rule 174's exemption for nonparticipating dealers from the post-effective prospectus delivery period is limited to securities of issuers which, immediately prior to the filing of the registration statement, were subject to the 1934 Act's periodic reporting requirements.[46] Thus, the exemption does not apply to first-time issuers or issuers whose securities were not widely held prior to the filing of the registration statement.[47] In 1988, Rule 174 was amended to provide more limited relief for many of those registrants who have not previously been subject to the 1934 Act's reporting requirements.[48] Under Rule 174(d), the prospectus delivery period for nonparticipating dealers is shortened to twenty five days for dealers (including underwriters no longer acting as such) with regard to securities which, as of the offering date, are listed on a national securities exchange or authorized for inclusion in an automated quotation system sponsored by a registered securities association (*i.e.*, NASDAQ).[49] As in the case for the statutory post–effective delivery requirement period for registered offerings, Rule 174's twenty-five day period begins to run from the later of (1) the registration statement's effective date or (2) the first date upon which the security was "bona fide offered to the public." [50] In light of Rule 174(d), the full statutory prospectus delivery period for nonparticipating dealers applies primarily to securities which are traded through the NASD's bulletin board system or in the pink sheets.[51] It must be remembered, that, as is the case with the other exemptions provided by Rule 174, the shorter twenty-five day prospectus delivery period does not apply to a dealer who is acting as an underwriter.[52]

---

42. 17 C.F.R. § 230.174(b).

43. 17 C.F.R. § 230.174(a).

44. 17 C.F.R. § 230.174(c).

45. *See* 17 C.F.R. § 230.415 which is discussed in § 3.8 *infra.*

46. 17 C.F.R. § 230.174(b). *See* text accompanying footnotes 42–43 *supra.*

47. The 1934 Act period reporting requirements are discussed in § 9.2 *infra.*

48. *See* Sec. Act Rel. No. 33–6763, [1987–88 Transfer Binder] Fed.Sec.L.Rep. (CCH) ¶ 84,226 (SEC April 4, 1986).

49. 17 C.F.R. § 230.174(d). *See* §§ 10.3, 10.13 *infra* for a description of NASDAQ.

50. 17 C.F.R. § 230.174(d).

51. Quotations for securities not listed on a national exchange or traded through NASDAQ are available from pink sheets which are circulated by the market maker. *See* § 10.3 *infra.*

52. 17 C.F.R. § 230.174(f).

Once an underwriter has completed his underwriting commitment and the public offering is complete, the underwriter is under no duty to make continuing disclosures about the issuer.[53] Rule 174 also imposes an additional requirement for penny stock offerings.[54] In the case of a blank check penny stock offering, the ninety day period does not begin to run until the securities are released from escrow pursuant to Rule 419.[55]

Another exemption from the prospectus delivery requirements is found in Rule 153 which deals with sales to be "preceded by a prospectus" as used in section 5(b)(2); this does not apply to the delivery requirements of section 5(b)(1).[56] Where a transaction involving a security in registration has been carried out on a national securities exchange,[57] Rule 153 provides that a sale is preceded by a prospectus to a member of the exchange where section 10(a) prospectuses have been delivered to the exchange for redelivery to its members upon request. Rule 153 applies to sales to members of a national exchange occurring prior to forty days after the effective date or the first date upon which the security was "bona fide offered to the public," whichever is later, provided that (a) the exchange has requested sufficient copies of the prospectus appearing reasonably necessary to comply with its members' requests and (b) the issuer or an underwriter has complied with all such requests.[58] Additionally, under Rule 153a,[59] when securities are issued pursuant to a reclassification, merger, consolidation or acquisition of assets in a transaction subject to Rule 145,[60] section 5(b)(2)'s prospectus delivery requirement is satisfied by delivery of a qualifying proxy statement to shareholders entitled to vote or whose consent is required for the transaction.

Beyond the prospectus delivery requirements and exemptions that are discussed above, the Commission has established standards of conduct for brokers or dealers participating in the distribution of securities covered by a 1933 Act registration statement. SEC Rule 15c2–8[61] requires that each participating broker or dealer take reasonable steps to comply with all written requests for a final section 10(a) prospectus after

---

53. In re Chaus Securities Litigation, 1990 WL 188921 (S.D.N.Y.1990).

54. The SEC's penny stock rules are discussed in § 10.7 *infra*

55. 17 C.F.R. § 230.174(g). *See* 17 C.F.R. § 230.419.

56. 17 C.F.R. § 230.153.

57. *See* section 6 of the Exchange Act, 15 U.S.C.A. § 78f which is discussed in § 10.2 *infra*.

58. 17 C.F.R. § 230.153(a)(1). Where the member of the exchange is to receive a prospectus as agent for a customer, the member as agent should forward a prospectus to the customer who is the principal in the transaction. It has been observed that the purchaser's broker does not have to pass the prospectus on to the customer where the sale takes place subsequent to the forty or ninety day period specified in section 4(3) of the Act. 1 Louis Loss Securities Regulation 251–254 (2d ed. 1961). *But see* section 4(4)'s exemption for unsolicited brokers' transactions. 15 U.S.C.A. § 77d(4) which is discussed in § 4.23 *infra*.

59. 17 C.F.R. § 230.153a.

60. 17 C.F.R. § 230.145. *See* § 5.2 *infra*.

61. 17 C.F.R. § 240.15c2–8(c). The rule has similar proscriptions with regard to the waiting period. *See* § 2.4 *supra*.

the effective date and until the termination of the distribution or expiration of the forty or ninety day period provided in section 4(3). Participating brokers and dealers must also take reasonable steps to assure that all associated persons who are expected to solicit customers after the effective date shall have sufficient copies of the final section 10(a) prospectus.[62] Additionally, managing underwriters must take reasonable steps to assure that all participating brokers and dealers have, pursuant to their requests, sufficient copies of the final prospectus.[63]

As discussed in a previous section,[64] broker-dealer buy recommendations might well ordinarily qualify as offers to sell and thus would be subject to the prospectus requirements if disseminated in writing during the waiting or post-effective periods.[65] SEC Rules 137, 138, and 139 exclude certain broker-dealer recommendations from the prospectus requirements.[66]

---

62. 17 C.F.R. § 240.15c2–8(e).

63. 17 C.F.R. § 240.15c2–8(g).

64. *See* discussion in § 2.3 *supra.*

65. *Id.*

66. 17 C.F.R. §§ 230.137, 230.138, 230.139. *See* discussion in § 2.3 *supra.*

Chapter 3

THE REGISTRATION PROCESS

Table of Sections

§ 3.1 Preparation of the Registration Statement

Once an issuer has elected to embark upon a public offering and has decided upon the type of security (*i.e.* debt or preferred or common stock) to be offered, the issuer in consultation with its financial advisers will fix the relative rights and preferences. The next step frequently is to meet with financial advisers, potential underwriters and counsel in order to hammer out the basic terms of the offering including the anticipated price and, if applicable, yield. After this has been accomplished, each of the participants in the registration statement—*i.e.*, the issuer, counsel, auditors, and the underwriter—will embark on its respective role in the joint preparation process.[1] The underwriters will not only be engaged in the preliminary steps in forming the underwriting syndicate but will also be enmeshed in substantial factual investigation of the issuer's condition; this investigation is to assure that the offering

---

* Deleted section 3.5.1 can be found in the Practitioner's Edition.

§ 3.1

1. In addition to the authorities in footnote 2 *infra, see* Harold S. Bloomenthal, Cannon Y. Harvey & Samuel E. Wing, 1985 Going Public Handbook (1985); Practicing Law Institute, How to Prepare an Initial Public Offering (1987); Practicing Law Institute, How to Prepare an Initial Public Offering (1986).

Factors relating to the decision of whether to go public are discussed in § 1.6 *supra.*

will be marketable and also to make certain that all disclosures are accurate. Taking reasonable steps to assure the accuracy of the registration statement is necessary to protect the underwriter from potential liability under the 1933 Act.[2]

Each of the participants in the preparation of the registration statement has a duty of reasonable investigation.[3] The highly factual nature of the due diligence standard precludes a one-size-fits-all template for formulating a due diligence program so as to guarantee success in establishing that the requisite reasonable investigation has been made. Risks that may be peculiar to the issuer's business may trigger more specific duties of reasonable investigation. Notwithstanding the variable nature of the reasonable investigation requirement, a number of generalizations may be made. The following activities[4] are examples of the steps to be taken by the lawyers involved in the registration process.

2. *See* Candace K. Beinecke, Stephen Luger & Thomas W. Mitchell, Sample Time and Responsibility Schedule for an Initial Public Offering of Common Stock, in Practicing Law Institute, How to Prepare an Initial Public Offering 37 (1987); Robert A. Spanner, Limiting Exposure in the Offering Process, 20 Rev.Sec. & Commod.Reg. 59 (1987); Carlos L. Israels, Checklist for Underwriters' Investigation, 18 Bus.Law. 90 (1962). *See also, e.g.,* Escott v. BarChris Construction Corp., 283 F.Supp. 643 (S.D.N.Y.1968); Merritt B. Fox, Shelf Registration, Integrated Disclosure, and Underwriter Due Diligence: An Economic Analysis, 70 Va.L.Rev. 1005 (1985). *See generally* Carl W. Schneider, Joseph M. Manko & Robert S. Kant, Going Public—Practice, Procedure and Consequences, 27 Villanova L.Rev. 1 (1981); John A. Wing, Guidelines for Underwriter Activity, 25 Bus.Law. 397 (1970). *See also* Howard D. Sterling, Legal Audit Upon Going Public: Non–Securities Law Aspects, 22 Bus.Law. 765 (1967).

3. The SEC has now codified the appropriate standard of care for participants in a registered public offering:

In determining whether or not the conduct of a person constitutes a reasonable investigation or a reasonable ground for belief meeting the standard set forth in section 11(c), relevant circumstances include, with respect to a person other than the issuer:

(a) The type of issuer;

(b) The type of security;

(c) The type of person;

(d) The office held when the person is an officer;

(e) The presence or absence of another relationship to the issuer when the person is a director or proposed director;

(f) Reasonable reliance on officers, employees, and others whose duties should have given them knowledge of the particular facts (in light of the functions and responsibilities of the particular person with respect to the issuer and the filing);

(g) When the person is an underwriter, the type of underwriting arrangement, the role of the particular person as an underwriter and the availability of information with respect to the registrant; and

(h) Whether, with respect to a fact or document incorporated by reference, the particular person had any responsibility for the fact or document at the time of the filing from which it was incorporated.

17 C.F.R. § 230.176. *See* footnote 2 *supra* and § 7.4 *infra*.

4. *See generally* William M. Prifti, Securities: Public and Private Offerings 301–06 (West Handbook 1974). *See also e.g.,* Carlos L. Israels & George M. Duff, Jr., When Corporates Go Public (1962); Gerard T. Robinson & Klaus Eppler, Going Public: Successful Underwriting (2d ed. 1978); Schneider, Manko & Kant *supra* note 2; Wing *supra* note 1; Report by Special Committee of Lawyers' Role in Securities Transactions of the Association of the Bar of the City of New York, 32 Bus.Law. 1879 (1977). *See also, e.g.,* Sterling *supra* footnote 2 and the authorities in footnote 1 *supra*.

First, it is necessary to amass information concerning the issuer's operations. This entails a thorough factual investigation of all aspects of the business including an examination of the past dealings of insiders and affiliated companies. This complete factual investigation should include both personal interviews of the issuer's key personnel and careful document reviews of the issuer's files. The inquiry should extend to conferences with the head of each division of the issuer as well as the company's principal officers and managers.

The document reviews should be used to establish a complete history of the company. Corporate minute books frequently provide a good starting point for historical investigation. There should be a comprehensive review of the shareholder and director minutes of the company as well as those of all subsidiaries and affiliates. The review of past minutes not only will help uncover factual information but it also serves as a "legal check-up"; any past illegalities or significant improprieties will most likely have to be disclosed in the registration statement. The initial document review will help establish a precise view of the issuer's capitalization. Accounting expertise will be necessary at this stage. A review of the charter and bylaws as well as all loans and guarantees and other financing agreements (including long-term leases) will shed light upon any applicable limitations and restrictions on current and future financing.[5] In addition a complete review of the company's dividend policy may reveal restrictions on financing.

The registration statement's detailed disclosure requirements[6] mandate a thorough analysis of the company's business including a detailed description of all divisions, departments and lines of business and accounting practices. There should thus be inquiry into all major customers and suppliers including a determination of the issuer's dependency on one or more of them, as well as of the existence of alternative major customers and suppliers. The investigation should involve a complete examination of the issuer's marketing, merchandising and pricing methods and policies, and a description of past practices. There should be a survey of the physical plant including an examination of all leases (copies may be necessary for the registration statement) as well as title searches where applicable. The survey should also encompass equipment including its condition as well as anticipated maintenance and replacement requirements.

Counsel will have to obtain copies of all significant labor agreements. Are any due to expire? Are strikes or substantially higher labor expenses likely to result? If so, these are issues that may have to be discussed in the registration statement.

The registration statement must identify and describe security arrangements including pledges, assignments and accounts receivable. If

5. It is to be noted that loans through the Small Business Association may contain restrictions with regard to both the company and its principal officers. *See* 15 U.S.C.A. §§ 631–649.

6. *See* §§ 3.2–3.4 *infra*.

the issuer has a parent, subsidiary or other affiliated corporations, careful attention must be given to intra-corporate, inter-subsidiary, and parent-subsidiary transactions. Counsel has to keep a watchful eye for potential conflicts of interest that may appear in mark-ups, supply and requirements contracts, loans, salaries and stock ownership.

There must be a thorough investigation with regard to the issuer's management structure. It is necessary to obtain detailed resumes of each officer and director encompassing the past five years. Corporate minutes may be helpful in gathering information about management. In many cases personal interviews will be advisable. There should be a detailed description of all direct and indirect management compensation as well as any insider transactions which have occurred within the past two years.[7] Relevant insider transactions include borrowings, loans, transactions in the issuer's shares as well as contracts between the issuer and companies controlled by the insiders. Counsel should compile a list of the issuer's securities held by its officers and directors, including all shares beneficially owned such as those held by family members, trusts, or corporations. There should be close scrutiny of all fringe benefits. Restricted and qualified stock option plans and stock or cash bonus incentive plans should be scrutinized closely. A careful review should be made of all employment and employment-related agreements.

The preregistration review should also encompass a study of the issuer's research and development activities—both in the past and whatever may be contemplated for the immediate future. This should include an explanation of the accounting methods, percentage and completion method, and the stage of development.

In preparing for the registration statement the issuer should compile its operating statistics including relevant trends and ratios. There should be a description of production backlog with respect to all firm orders. There must be a complete inventory, including a breakdown by lines of business and product lines. Counsel should review past tax returns to determine whether all taxes have been paid and whether future taxes have been properly estimated and withheld. Counsel should be fully aware of all competitors' activities including industry trends, reports (if available) and the price range and relative strength of comparable products. Counsel should also inquire as to whether the issuer has been in compliance with all applicable state and federal regulatory, environmental,[8] health and safety, and labor laws.

The team preparing the registration statement must thoroughly understand all of the issuer's financial relationships. Banking relation-

---

7. *See* item 404 of Regulation S–K which sets forth the types of transactions and relationships with management. Transactions with officers, directors, and affiliates draw particular attention in the registration materials. *See* § 3.7 *infra.*

8. *Cf.* Levine v. NL Industries, Inc., 926 F.2d 199 (2d Cir.1991) (disclosure of environmental compliance costs; action under Exchange Act Rule 10b–5). *See also, e.g.,* Note, "Shh! Maybe in My Backyard!" An Equity and Efficiency–Based Critique of SEC Environmental Disclosure Rules and Extraterritorial Environmental Matters, 78 Minn. L. Rev. 1045 (1994).

ships must be fully examined and described in detail (including lines of credit, and revolving credit agreements). A comprehensive review of the issuer's cash flow, including the source of funds, should be undertaken. Counsel with the aid of accountants should determine all contingent liabilities, including an evaluation of all pending litigation—at a minimum all pleadings should be reviewed. Current financial statements must be prepared. Most registration forms require a balance sheet at least as current as ninety days prior to filing and audited profit and loss statements for three years (or two years unaudited for an offering pursuant to Regulation A's qualified exemption for small issues).[9]

Counsel should examine all significant contracts to which the issuer is a party; this includes insurance coverage. There should also be a review of all patents and trademarks. All special risk factors with regard to the issuer generally, industry-wide conditions, and the particular securities to be offered must be analyzed and described in detail in the registration statement. There should be a review of all prior offerings, both private and public. Copies of all prior registration statements and underwriting agreements should be obtained and analyzed, as should be the case with 1934 Act filings such as Forms 8–K, 10–K, 10–Q and proxy statements.[10]

It is important that the pre-filing investigation focus not only on the issuer's business generally, but also on the specific disclosure issues that may arise from the terms of the securities to be covered by the registration statement. Counsel must assure proper documentation of resolutions and corporate minutes authorizing the offering. It may be necessary to increase capitalization and in some cases a formal shareholder vote may be required. All undesired stock transfer and issuing restrictions should be eliminated from the charter and/or bylaws. It may be necessary to secure the consent of creditors or other third parties before issuing the shares in question.

There must be compliance with all corporate law requirements of the state of incorporation as well as any state in which the issuer is qualified to do business as a foreign corporation. There must also be compliance with the blue sky laws of all states in which securities are to be offered.[11] Finally, depending upon the nature of issuer's business, there may be state or federal administrative approval that must be obtained prior to the offering.

After the foregoing factual inquiries and document preparation have taken place, there are a number of legal tasks that must be attended to as part of the underwriting process. These will generally be performed by issuer's counsel or in some cases by underwriters' counsel. It is often necessary to hire special securities counsel to coordinate the offering and

---

9. 17 C.F.R. § 240.251 *et seq. See* § 4.15 *infra.*

10. *See* chapters, 9, 11 *infra.* If the issuer is using Form S–2 or S–3, which integrate 1933 Act and 1934 Exchange Act disclosures, due diligence requirements may be affected. *See* §§ 3.3, 3.4, 7.4 *infra.*

11. Blue sky laws are considered in chapter 8 *infra.*

supervise preparation of the registration statement. Such special counsel should then be present at preliminary discussions between the issuer and underwriters concerning the terms of the offering. Both issuer's and underwriters' counsel will be involved in the preparation of a letter of intent between the company and managing underwriter. The letter of intent generally will set forth the number of shares to be offered, the offering price, and basic underwriting terms and will provide for pre-clearance with the National Association of Securities Dealers (NASD).[12]

Counsel will then meet with the accountants to review the financial information required for SEC filing; a timetable should be established. The issuer must select a stock transfer agent and a financial printer. It will be necessary to estimate the number of copies of both the registration statement and prospectus needed for the SEC, blue sky law compliance, broker-dealers, securities exchanges and customers. At this point counsel should be making the factual inquiries outlined above as well as gathering all of the information necessary for the registration statement.

Underwriters' counsel will be preparing the underwriters' agreement with the issuer, agreement among underwriters and agreements for the selling group. They must also prepare a questionnaire for underwriters to establish, among other things, sufficient financial responsibility to bear the underwriting risk. Counsel should also assist in drafting a letter inviting participation in the underwriting group. Both issuer's and underwriters' counsel should make a survey of all applicable blue sky laws prepare a blue sky list, and draft a tentative timetable.

When ready, proofs of the registration materials should be distributed to all counsel, the issuer's principal officers, the accountants and the managing underwriters, all of whom should conduct a thorough review. The issuer's directors should also receive and review copies of the registration materials. Sometime prior to sending the mock-ups to the printer, a first stage of the "due diligence" meeting[13] should be held and may need to be reconvened after thorough review and receipt of all comments. The next step is to file the registration statement along with the payment of applicable fees.[14] If certain summary or preliminary prospectuses are to be used,[15] additional SEC filings may be necessary. At this time, blue sky filings may also be necessary as will filings with the NASD.[16] In the event that the securities are to be listed on an exchange, listing applications must be prepared and filed.[17]

Counsel's job does not end with the filing of the registration statement. There are a number of post-filing activities that must be completed, in addition to work on any amendments that must be filed. The

---

12. *See* NASD Manual (CCH) ¶ 2151.02. The NASD is discussed in § 10.2 *infra*.

13. The due diligence requirement is discussed directly below and in § 7.4 *infra*.

14. *See* § 3.4 *infra*.

15. Summary and preliminary prospectuses are discussed in § 2.4 *supra*.

16. *See* NASD Manual (CCH).

17. *See* American Stock Exchange Manual (CCH); New York Stock Exchange Manual (CCH).

issuer may want to prepare and distribute press releases; this may also take place prior to filing provided there are no gun jumping violations as spelled out by SEC Rule 135.[18] Provisions will have to be made for stock certificates including obtaining CUSIP (Committee on Uniform Security Identification Procedures) numbers (unless the shares will be uncertificated). Special securities counsel along with the issuer's and underwriters' counsel will have to review the accountant's cold comfort letter. Underwriters' counsel will have to prepare a distribution list and transmit letters to other underwriters and members of the selling group.

Once the registration materials are filed, the relevant administrative agencies (including the SEC and applicable state securities administrators) may respond with letters of comment.[19] All counsel must review SEC, NASD, and blue sky letters of comment. Counsel will then prepare replies and applicable amendments to be filed with the SEC, NASD and state securities administrators. It will often be necessary to file "delaying" amendments in order to give the registrant sufficient time to respond to the letters of comment.[20] At this point it is time to arrange for the due diligence meeting of counsel, management, and underwriters where all of the filings as amended will be scrutinized. All initial prospectuses must be updated, a process which includes sending of amendments to all who received initial prospectuses. If applicable, underwriters' counsel will have to supervise preparation for newspaper and NASD quotations. It is at this stage that tombstone ads[21] will generally be prepared. It is also necessary to prepare for NASD and SEC clearance and draft notifying telegrams to blue sky commissioners. The final underwriting agreement will not generally be signed until coordination of SEC clearance time and date and all last-minute amendments such as the price amendment have been filed.

Frequently, the final step in the registration process is the pricing of the issue. In most instances, the price will be determined jointly by the underwriters and issuer. Because of their firm commitment obligations, underwriters will generally be conservative in pricing an issue. In the case of additional offerings of securities that are already publicly traded, the price ordinarily will be determined by the closing price on the day before the offering. As an alternative to a fixed price for an offering, securities may be offered "at the market" which means that the pro-

---

18. 17 C.F.R. § 230.135. *See* § 2.3 *supra.*

19. As is explained more fully in § 3.5 *infra*, the SEC employs an informal review process through letters of comment rather than resorting to formal refusal order proceedings under section 8 of the Act. 15 U.S.C.A. § 77h.

20. The delay may be necessary since it takes time for the SEC staff (or other regulator) to review the registration statement and prepare the letter of comment. Absent such a delaying amendment, the registration would become effective twenty days after it was filed. 15 U.S.C.A. § 77h. Delaying amendments, which are expressly permitted by SEC Rule 473 (17 C.F.R. § 230.473) are typically accomplished by placing code words on the face of the registration statement. *See* Charles C. Cohen, Book Review, 7 J.L. & Comm. 119, 120 n. 4 (1987).

21. 17 C.F.R. § 230.134. *See* section 2(10) of the 1933 Act; 15 U.S.C.A. § 77b(10) and § 2.4 *supra.*

ceeds will be based on a fluctuating market price.[22] While an "at market" offering may find a warmer reception in a thin market, a primary drawback is that the issuer (or selling shareholders in a secondary distribution) cannot predict exactly how much money will be raised until the distribution has been completed. "At market" offerings are particularly susceptible to manipulation.[23] Accordingly, the SEC does not permit stabilizing activity during "at market" offerings.[24] When a minimum amount of capital is needed by the issuer and there is some concern that the offering may not be fully subscribed, the shares can be offered on an "all or none" or "part or none" basis.[25] In such a case, the terms of the offering will specify the minimum number of shares that must taken by investors in order for the sale to proceed. If within a specified period there is not a full subscription to all shares being offered, the offering is canceled and any monies refunded. Alternatively, the offering may take place, provided the subscribers will be offered a refund. This latter option cannot be offered selectively but must be offered to all would-be purchasers.[26] Issuers embarking on "all or none" and "part or none" offerings must be specific as to the offering price, the duration of the offering, and the amount of securities that must be sold to make the offering effective.[27]

After filing the final amendments and the application for acceleration with the SEC, counsel should prepare a closing memorandum. A number of tasks remain. Notification telegrams and copies of the final prospectus must be sent to appropriate blue sky authorities. Transfer agent instructions must be distributed as must payment instructions.

There should then be one final review of all documents and the current status of the issuer. Generally there will be a cold comfort letter prior to closing. The stock certificates must be checked and counted. All payments must be made in accordance with the prospectus's description. It may be necessary to coordinate market making activities or even stabilizing activities[28] which can be carried out only if in full compliance with SEC Rule 10b–7.[29] Circumstances may require post effective amendments to registration statements and the prospectus. For first time registrants it will be necessary to file with the SEC a "Report of Sales."[30]

---

22. "At market" offerings are discussed in § 6.3 *infra*.

23. *See, e.g.,* In re Hazel Bishop, Inc., 40 S.E.C. 718 (SEC 1961).

24. 17 C.F.R. § 240.10b–7. *See* § 6.2 *infra*.

25. *See* § 6.3 *infra*.

26. 17 C.F.R. § 240.10b–9. For an analogous equal opportunity Rule, *see* Rule 14d–10, 17 C.F.R. § 240.14d–10 which mandates equal treatment for all holders of shares subject to a tender offer, which is discussed in § 11.14 *infra*.

27. 17 C.F.R. § 240.10b–9.

28. Market makers are discussed in § 10.3 *infra*.

29. Where an issue faces a soft market the SEC permits stabilizing bids under certain circumstances. 17 C.F.R. § 240.10b–7. Unless Rule 10b–7 is fully complied with such activity will constitute illegal stock manipulation. *See* Rule 10b–6 and section 9 of the 1934 Act. 15 U.S.C.A. § 78i; 17 C.F.R. § 240.10b–6. *See also* §§ 6.1, 12.1 *infra*.

30. 17 C.F.R. § 230.463.

The foregoing steps are merely illustrative of a typical registration and may vary according to the nature of the issuer and the offering.[31] Variations may also result from use of one of the alternative registration forms that are described briefly in the next section. Many of the steps described above will also be necessary in a registration pursuant to Regulation A's qualified exemption for small offerings[32] or in preparing offering circulars for other exempt offerings.[33] Also, much of the attorney's factual investigation will have to be made for private placements, especially those in reliance upon SEC Regulation D.[34]

Compilation of a checklist of the necessary steps can be helpful in fulfilling due diligence obligations while preparing registration materials.[35] It has also been suggested that selecting one person as a "due diligence officer" to oversee the registration process will help assure compliance.[36]

The sections that follow provide an overview of the disclosure process. The discussion is not intended to provide a step-by-step "how to" guide. The most helpful source for framing disclosures are the Commission's Regulation S–K[37] (or Regulation S–B, for small business issuers[38]) for descriptive disclosure items and Regulation S–X[39] for accounting matters.

§ 3.2 Information Required in the Registration Statement and the Statutory Prospectus; Schedule A

The registration statement is the basic disclosure document that must be filed with the SEC for 1933 Act registration.[1] There are a number of alternative disclosure forms which may be available to issuers

---

31. *See* the authorities cited in footnotes 1–4 *supra.*

32. *See* section 3(b) of the 1933 Act; 15 U.S.C.A. § 77c(b) and § 4.15 *infra.*

33. *See, e.g.,* the informational requirements for offerings under Regulation D. 17 C.F.R. § 230.502(b). Regulation D is discussed in §§ 4.16–4.19, 4.22, *infra.*

34. 17 C.F.R. §§ 230.501–230.508, discussed in §§ 4.16–4.22 *infra.*

35. *See, e.g.,* Carlos L. Israels, Checklist for Underwriters' Investigations, 18 Bus. Law. 90 (1962), as updated in ABA, Selected Articles in Securities Law 71 (1968); Robert A. Spanner, Limiting Exposure in the Offering Process, 20 Rev. Sec. & Commod. Reg. 59 (1987).

36. Spanner *supra* footnote 35.

37. 17 C.F.R. § 229.10 *et seq.,* 7 Fed. Sec. L. Rep. (CCH) ¶¶ 71,001 *et seq.* Violations of Regulation S–K or S–B disclosure requirements are not *per se* actionable but can be used to support a claim based on one of the express or implied liability provisions. *See* Feldman v. Motorola, Inc., 1994 WL 160115, [1993–1994 Transfer Binder] Fed. Sec. L. Rep. (CCH) ¶ 98,133 (N.D.Ill.1994) (Rule 10b–5).

38. 17 C.F.R. § 228.10 *et seq.,* 7 Fed. Sec. L. Rep. (CCH) ¶¶ 70,701 *et seq.* A small business issuer is a United States or Canadian company with annual revenues of less than $25,000,000. If the company is a majority owned subsidiary then the parent must also be a small business issuer in order to qualify. Investment companies do not qualify as small business issuers. Reg. S–B, Item 10(a)(1).

39. 17 C.F.R. § 210.1–01 *et seq.,* 6 Fed. Sec. L. Rep. (CCH) ¶¶ 69,101 *et seq.*

§ 3.2

1. *See* 15 U.S.C.A. §§ 77f, 77g.

for registration.[2] The availability of the various forms depends upon the nature of the issuer and/or the circumstances surrounding the offering, as well as the types of securities offered. Regardless of the registration form to be filed, it is a document that is divided into two principal sections. The information contained in the first portion of the registration statement is the same as that which will be found in the prospectus as required by section 10(a) of the 1933 Act and Schedule A.[3] The Schedule A or statutory prospectus must be delivered before the consummation of any sale pursuant to a registered offering.[4] Schedule A provides only a bare-bones outline of the types of disclosures which are required. Detailed disclosure requirements are found in the SEC's registration forms and in Regulation S–K (and Regulation S–B, for small business issuers).

Schedule A contains 27 items that must be included in the prospectus:

1. The issuer's name

2. The issuer's state of incorporation or organization

3. The location of the principal place of business, and if foreign issuer, the name of its authorized agent in the United States

4. The names and addresses of directors or persons performing similar functions, as well as the executive, financial and accounting officers; also, if a partnership, the name of all partners and, if applicable, the name of all promoters

5. The names and addresses of all underwriters

6. The names and addresses of all persons beneficially owning more than 10 percent of any class of the issuer's stock or more than 10 percent of the aggregate amount of the outstanding stock

7. The amounts of securities held by persons described in item 6, including whether or not these persons have indicated an intention to subscribe to the securities in registration

8. The general character of the issuer's business

9. The statement of the issuer's capitalization, including a description of all classes of stock and relative rights or preferences

10. If applicable, a statement of the securities in registration that are covered by outstanding options, or options to be created in connection with the offering; and the names of all persons to be allotted more than 10 percent of such options

11. The amount of capital stock of each class of securities issued that were included in the shares of stock to be offered

12. The amount of outstanding funded debts, as well as any debt created by the securities to be offered, including a brief descrip-

---

2. The various forms for registration are discussed in § 3.3 *infra*.

3. *See* 15 U.S.C.A. §§ 77g, 77j(a), 77aa.

4. 15 U.S.C.A. § 77e(b)(2).

tion of the maturity date, interest rate, and character of amortization provisions

13. The "specific purposes in detail and the approximate amounts to be devoted to such purposes, so far as determinable, for which the security to be offered is to supply funds, and if the funds are to be raised in part from other sources, the amounts thereof and the sources thereof, shall be stated"

14. All compensation paid or estimated to be paid by the issuer or its predecessor, directly or indirectly, during the past and ensuing years to directors, officers, and other persons performing similar functions, who shall be named whenever this compensation exceeds $25,000 per year

15. The estimated net proceeds to be derived from the offering

16. The price at which the proposed security will be offered to the public or other method by which the price will be computed, including any variation with regard to discounts to be offered to any classes of persons including underwriters and insiders of the issuer

17. All underwriters' commissions or discounts paid both directly or indirectly by the issuer, including "all cash, securities, contracts, or anything else of value, paid, to be set aside, disposed of, or understandings with or for the benefit of any other persons in which any underwriter is interested, made, in connection with the sale of such security"

18. A reasonably detailed itemized account of the actual or estimated expenses, exclusive of commissions, incurred by the issuer in connection with the sale of the security to be offered

19. The net proceeds to be derived from any security sold by the issuer in the two years preceding the registration statement's filing, including the offering price of said security and the principal underwriters

20. Any promotional fees paid during the two years preceding the registration statement's filing

21. The names and addresses of the sellers of any property, including goodwill, to be acquired other than in the ordinary course of business in whole or in part with the proceeds of the offering covered in the registration statement

22. The interest, if any, of directors, principal executive officers, and 10 percent stockholders in any property acquired other than in the ordinary course of business within two years prior to the filing of the registration statement or proposed to be acquired at such date

23. The names and addresses of counsel who have passed on the legality of the offering

24. Dates of and parties to, and the general effect concisely stated of every material contract made, "not in the ordinary course of business, which contract is to be executed in whole or in part at or after the filing of the registration statement, or which contract has been made not more than two years before such filing." Management contracts, special bonus or profit sharing arrangements are expressly deemed to be material contracts

25. A balance sheet accurate as of a date not more than 90 days prior to the registration statement's filing. The balance sheet must show all assets, "the nature and cost thereof, whenever determinable, in such detail and in such form as the commission shall prescribe (with intangible items segregated), including any loan in excess of $20,000 to any officer, director, stockholder or person directly or indirectly controlling or controlled by the issuer, or person under direct or indirect common control with the issuer. All the liabilities of the issuer in such detail and such form as the commissioner shall prescribe, including surplus of the issuer showing how and from what sources such surplus was created * * *. If such statement be not certified by an independent public or certified accountant, in addition to the balance sheet required to be submitted under this schedule, a similar detailed balance sheet of the assets and liabilities of the issuer, certified by an independent public or certified accountant, of a date not more than one year prior to the filing of the registration statement, shall be submitted"

26. Detailed profit and loss statements of the issuer in such form as the commission shall prescribe for the most recent fiscal year and the two preceding fiscal years, year-by-year

27. If all or part of the proceeds of the offering are to be applied directly or indirectly to the purchase of any business, a certified profit and loss sheet of such business must be included[5]

In addition to the foregoing information, the front page of the prospectus must highlight the salient points of the offering. This summary must contain, among other things, the identity of the issuer and the underwriter, description of the securities offered, whether any part of the offering is secondary (not by the issuer), the use of the proceeds, and any special risks presented by the offering that warrant prominent attention.[6] Schedule A merely provides a skeletal description of the types of information that must be disclosed. Additional guidance can be gained from the instructions on the applicable SEC registration form.[7] More detailed guidance for disclosure is contained in Regulation

---

5. 15 U.S.C.A. § 77aa. During the waiting period a shorter form may be used to generate a buying interest but a statutory prospectus must nevertheless be delivered prior to delivery of the security. Also, during the post-effective period, the short form waiting period prospectuses can no longer be used. *See* §§ 2.4, 2.5 *supra.*

6. Regulation S–K, Items 501–502, 17 C.F.R. §§ 229.501–229.502; Regulation S–B Items 501–502, 17 C.F.R. §§ 228.501–228.502. *See* §§ 3.6–3.7 *infra.*

7. *See* § 3.3 *infra* for a description of the various registration forms.

S–K,[8] and for small business issuers in Regulation S–B.[9] Guidelines for disclosures relating to accounting matters are found in Regulation S–X.[10]

Schedule A further requires the filing of the following materials with the SEC: all agreements with underwriters; all opinions of counsel relating to the offering; all material contracts described in item 24 above unless the SEC determines that disclosure would impair the contract and is not necessary to protect investors; copies of the articles of partnership or association, or trust agreement, as the case may be; and copies of all underlying agreements or indentures affecting the securities to be offered.

The second part of the registration statement consists of additional information which is not sent out in the prospectus but which is available in the SEC files for public inspection. As noted at the outset of this section, Schedule A is only the starting point. It is necessary to look to the applicable registration form which will supply the bare-bones description of what has to be disclosed. It is then necessary to turn to Regulation S–K or, in the case of small business issuers, to Regulation S–B for a detailed description of the ways in which the information must be presented. In addition, Regulation S–X sets forth the disclosure guide and presentation requirements for financial information.

§ 3.3 Registration Forms and Integrated Disclosure

For more than fifty-five years, the SEC has administered two parallel disclosure systems: one for the registration of public offerings under the Securities Act of 1933 and the other for the periodic reporting requirements of the Securities Exchange Act of 1934.[1] The parallel systems resulted in a great deal of duplicative filings and unnecessary paperwork. In 1982, the Securities and Exchange Commission adopted an integrated disclosure system for registration of securities under the 1933 Act.[2] While some duplication remains, the institution of integrated

---

8.   17 C.F.R. § 229.10 *et seq.*, 7 Fed. Sec. L. Rep. (CCH) ¶¶ 71,001 *et seq.*

9.   17 C.F.R. § 228.10 *et seq.*, 7 Fed. Sec. L. Rep. (CCH) ¶¶ 70,701 *et seq.* A small business issuer is a United States or Canadian company with annual revenues of less than $25,000,000. If the company is a majority owned subsidiary then the parent must also be a small business issuer in order to qualify. Investment companies do not qualify as small business issuers. Reg. S–B, Item 10(a)(1).

10.   17 C.F.R. § 210.10–1 *et seq.*, 6 Fed. Sec. L. Rep. (CCH) ¶¶ 69,101 *et seq.*

§ 3.3

1.   *See* § 9.2 *infra* for a discussion of the Exchange Act's periodic reporting requirements.

2.   *See* Sec.Act Rel. No. 33–6383, Acc.Rel. No. 306, [1937–82 Acc't'g Rel. Transfer Binder] Fed.Sec.L.Rep. (CCH) ¶ 72,328 (March 3, 1982). The concept of integrated disclosure is based in large part on the American Law Institute's Proposed Federal Securities Code.

Over the years there has been a great deal of discussion concerning the appropriate focus for 1933 Act disclosure requirements. *See generally* Homer Kripke, The SEC and Corporate Disclosure–Regulation in Search of a Purpose (1979); Bruce A. Mann, Prospectuses: Unreadable or Just Unread?—A Proposal to Reexamine Policies Against Permitting Projections, 40 Geo.Wash.L.Rev. 222 (1971); Panel Discussion, New Approaches to Disclosure in Registered Security Offerings—A Panel Discussion, 28 Bus.Law. 505 (1973); Carl W.

disclosure has made great strides in easing the disclosure burden. The current system integrates and simplifies the disclosure requirements under the 1933 and 1934 securities acts.[3] The Commission has explained that its goal in adopting the new system was "to revise or eliminate overlapping or unnecessary disclosure and dissemination requirements wherever possible, thereby reducing burdens on registrants while at the same time ensuring that security holders, investors and the marketplace have been provided with meaningful, nonduplicative information upon which to base investment decisions."[4] As discussed in the preceding section, Schedule A provides a skeletal outline of the types of information to be made available in connection with a registered offering of securities. Each of the registration forms provided by the SEC go into slightly more detail in describing the types of disclosures that must be made. The applicable forms frequently refer to Regulation S–K, or Regulation S–B, for small issuers, which set forth in detail the ways in which the relevant information should be set forth. Regulation S–K addresses the presentation of disclosure items generally. A particularly important part of Regulations S–K and S–B is the Management Discussion and Analysis (MD&A) of financial condition and results of operations. The MD&A is not limited to discussion of the existing business; it also extends to a discussion and analysis of planned operations. Regulation S–X addresses accounting matters in significant detail. Thus, in preparing for a registered offering, it is necessary to consult not only the applicable registration form, but also to become conversant with the relevant disclosure items in Regulations S–K and S–X (and, if applicable Regulation S–B).

As part of its small business initiatives of 1992, the SEC adopted Regulation S–B which qualifies and with respect to many items replaces Regulation S–K as the applicable disclosure guide for small business issuers.[5] Domestic issuers having revenues of less than 25 million dollars for their most recent fiscal year qualify for use of Regulation S–B's simplified disclosures that are applicable for both 1933 and 1934 Act

---

Schneider, Nits, Grits and Soft Information in SEC Filings, 121 U.Pa.L.Rev. 254 (1972); Note, Mandatory Projections and the Goals of Securities Regulation, 81 Colum.L.Rev. 1525 (1981).

This is a microcosm of the continuing debate concerning the proper role for disclosure generally. *See, e.g.,* James H. Lorie and Mary T. Hamilton, The Stock Market—Theories and Evidence (1973); George I. Benston, Required Disclosure and the Stock Market: An Evaluation of the Securities Exchange Act of 1934, 63 Am.Econ.Rev. 132 (1973); Friend & Westerfield, Required Disclosure in the Stock Market: A Comment, 65 Am.Econ.Rev. 467 (1975); George J. Stigler, Public Regulation of the Securities Markets, 19 Bus.Law. 721 (1964). Special Report, 1982 Integrated Disclosure Adoptions, Fed.Sec.L.Rep. (CCH) No. 956 (March 11, 1982).

3. Unlike the 1933 Act which is directed towards securities distributions, the 1934 Exchange Act deals with day-to-day trading and the securities markets in general. *See* § 1.2 *supra,* chapters 9, 10 *infra.*

4. Special Report, Integrated Disclosure Adoptions *supra* footnote 2 at 15.

5. *See* Sec. Act Rel. No. 33–6949, 6 Fed.Sec.L.Rep. (CCH) ¶ 72,439 (SEC July 30, 1992); Sec. Act Rel. No. 33–6924, [1991–1992 Transfer Binder] Fed.Sec.L.Rep. (CCH) ¶ 84,931 (March 11, 1992).

filings.[6]   A company having more than 25 million dollars worth of its voting stock held by nonaffiliates does not qualify as a small business issuer.

Integrated Disclosure

In addition to its specialized registration forms and small business initiatives, the Commission has established a three-tiered system of registration and prospectus disclosure of registrant-oriented information based upon the registrant's reporting history and market following. The integrated disclosure system recognizes that transaction-specific information, that is, information specific to the securities issuance, should always be disclosed in the registration statement and prospectus. The more general registrant-oriented information, however, may already be available in reports by the registrant under the Exchange Act and need not be duplicated unnecessarily. Exchange Act reporting companies include all issuers whose securities are traded on a national exchange and those with three million dollars in assets and having a class of equity securities held by more than five hundred persons.[7] The framework for this relatively new three level system is provided by three new registration forms: S–1; S–2; and S–3. Form S–1 remains the basic, long-form registration statement that is generally available to issuers unless they qualify for one of the other forms. It requires complete registrant and transaction information to be provided in the prospectus.[8] As a practical matter, Form S–1 is to be used primarily by first-time issuers and companies with publicly held securities but only a limited number of shareholders.

Form S–2 requires a lesser degree of detail in disclosure. It may be used by all registrants which have reported for three years or more under the Exchange Act.[9] Information which the issuer has provided on Form 10–K of the Exchange Act is incorporated by reference into the prospectus. Along with the description of the offering in the prospectus, the registrant must provide either an annual report or comparable information in the prospectus itself.[10] The more common practice to date has been to use a unitary prospectus rather than to attach the glossy annual report.[11]

6. "Small business issuer" is defined in 1933 Act Rule 405 and 1934 Act Rule 12b–2. 17 C.F.R. §§ 230.405, 240.12b–2. *See also, e.g.,* Continental Waste Industries, Inc., 26 Sec. Reg. & L. Rep. (BNA) 1189 (SEC No Action Letter available Aug. 12, 1994) (Registration of securities issued in a merger permitted under Regulation S–B even though the combined company would exceed $25 million in revenues; permission was conditioned on at least one of the constituent companies being subject to S–B reporting prior to the transaction and the other not being subject to Regulation S–K reporting, in addition to other eligibility requirements).

7. 15 U.S.C.A. § 78*l*; 17 C.F.R. § 240.12g–1. *See* § 9.2 *infra.*

8. *See* Special Report, Integrated Disclosure Adoptions *supra* footnote 2 at 19–20. *See* the description of Schedule A in § 3.2 *supra.*

9. The Exchange Act reporting requirements are discussed in chapter 9 *infra.*

10. *See* Special Report, Integrated Disclosure *supra* footnote 2 at 20–23.

11. This has been explained as due to the high cost of annual reports.

Form S–3[12] requires the least detailed level of disclosure to investors by allowing for the fullest possible incorporation by reference from Exchange Act reporting. Unless there has been a material change in the issuer's affairs, no registrant-oriented information will be required to be disclosed to investors. Only the transaction-specific description of the offering need be specified in the prospectus. When promulgated, in order to use Form S–3, the registrant was required to meet the three year reporting requirement of Form S–2 in addition to a "market following" test. In 1992, the SEC reduced the thirty-six month reporting requirement to a twelve month reporting requirement. As originally adopted the "market following" test contained alternative standards of one hundred and fifty million dollar minimum value of voting stock held by non-affiliates ("the float"); or a one hundred million dollar float and an annual trading volume of at least three million shares.[13] In 1992, the Commission reduced this market float requirement to an aggregate market value of seventy-five million dollars regardless of the annual trading volume.[14] The theory behind the market following test is that such widely-held securities have a sufficiently large informed market following so that more detailed disclosure is not necessary. In addition, in 1992, Form S–3 was expanded to permit registration of investment-grade asset-backed securities irrespective of any previous reporting history.

The applicability and use of an appropriate registration statement form may be significant in determining the appropriate level of disclosure. When a company has a wide market following, professional analysts will be following news about the company and will be keeping track of developments involving the issuer and its industry. The Seventh Circuit has indicated that as a result, when such a wide market following is present, the disclosure need only be geared to the professional analyst.[15] In the course of the opinion, it is asserted that it is sufficient that the disclosure in such a case be geared to professional investors since small investors rely on market price rather than the information in the registration statement.[16] The unfortunate implica-

12. Form S–3 is among those for which delaying amendments are not expressly authorized for postponing the effective date.

13. *See* Special Report, Integrated Disclosure, *supra* footnote 2 at 23–30. Another requirement for the use of Form S–3 is that neither the issuer nor a subsidiary be in default on any bank loans. *See, e.g.,* Fidelity Medical, Inc. [1991–1992 Transfer Binder] Fed.Sec.L.Rep. (CCH) ¶ 76,012 (SEC No Action letter June 5, 1991).

Issuers that qualify for Form S–3 can also take advantage of increased integration with disclosures made in connection with proxy solicitations. *See* Exch.Act Rel. No. 34–23788, [1986–87 Transfer Binder] Fed.Sec.L.Rep. (CCH) ¶ 84,043 (Nov. 10, 1986). Proxy-related disclosures for Exchange Act reporting companies are discussed in §§ 11.1–11.9 *infra.*

14. As part of its 1993 amendments, the Commission relaxed the requirements for shelf registration of S–3 offerings. For example, it is now possible to register multiple classes of securities for a shelf offering without specifying the amount of each class to be offered.

15. Wielgos v. Commonwealth Edison Co., 892 F.2d 509, 518 (7th Cir.1989).

16. *Id.*:

No investor absorbs sheafs of dense type, which Commonwealth Edison printed or incorporated in connection with this shelf offering. Descriptions in Forms 10–K and

tion of Judge Easterbrook's opinion is that small investors may be denied the information they need in the name of market efficiency.

In addition to the basic framework for registration established by Forms S–1; S–2; and S–3, there are some additional and more specialized forms which have been promulgated by the Commission. These forms, which are discussed below, are geared to special situations. Except for Forms SB–1 and SB–2, all registration statements are to be filed with the SEC's central office in Washington, D.C. Form SB–1 and Form SB–2 filings may be made either in the central Commission office or in the regional office closest to the issuer.[17]

Specialized Registration Forms

Offerings to Employees

Form S–8 is available to 1934 Act reporting companies with regard to securities offered to employees, including the employees of subsidiaries who are offered the parent's securities, pursuant to any benefit plan.[18]

Securities Issued in Connection with a Merger or Other Corporate Reorganization

Form S–4 (and Form F–4 for foreign issuers)[19] may be used for registration of securities issued in mergers, combinations, consolidations, acquisitions of assets, recapitalizations, and other transactions governed

---

registration statements are almost useless to individual investors. They require absorption by professional traders and investors. What these professionals need is new information specific to the issuer. Telling them over and again how the NRC works, or that costs are rising in the nuclear power industry, or even that Commonwealth Edison had run into trouble with its welds (which became known a few months before this stock was sold), has nothing to do with the accuracy of prices in the market. Investors who buy 500 shares of stock rely on the market price; Wielgos concedes that he did not read Commonwealth Edison's disclosures. Everything we can see demonstrates that the market had in its possession all significant information about Commonwealth Edison. That firm lived up to the technical requirements of Item 103.

The *Wielgos* decision is discussed in § 3.7 *infra*.

17. Regional filing of Forms SB–1 and SB–2 are permitted only for small business issuers which are not already 1934 Act reporting companies. 1934 Act reporting companies using either of these forms must make their filings in the Washington, D.C. office. Although the instructions permit regional filings, the instructions further point out that although every effort will be made to process the filing at the initial location, the Commission may reassign the registration form to a different office for processing.

18. *See, e.g.*, BI, Inc., 22 Sec.Reg. & L.Rep. (BNA) 1117 (SEC No Action Letter available July 11, 1990) (Form S–8 can be used to register one-time offering to non-employee director). *Cf.* MB Communications, Inc., 26 Sec. Reg. & L. Rep. (BNA) 821 (SEC No Action Letter available May 23, 1994) (permitting use of Form S–8 for registration of transactions following a spin-off).

Unlike other registrations generally, there is no waiting period for issuers using Form S–8. 17 C.F.R. § 230.462.

19. Forms S–4 and F–4 are among those forms which do not have express authorization for use of delaying amendments to postpone the effective date.

by SEC Rule 145.[20] Form S–15 formerly was available, subject to compliance with the specified conditions, in certain mergers in which a vote of the acquired corporation's securities holders is not required; and in an exchange offer for securities of another issuer which would result in ownership of more than fifty percent of that class of the other issuer's securities. However, Form S–15 was rescinded, leaving Form S–4 as the appropriate form for mergers and other business combinations.

Small Business Issuers

Beginning in the mid 1970s, the SEC has made great strides to facilitate small issues and offerings by small issuers.[21] The Commission created Form S–18 as a short form registration statement to be used for small issues and could be used for offerings when the aggregate offering price did not exceed seven and one half million dollars and the securities are to be sold for cash; Form S–18 was a major step in the continuing effort to make public offerings more economically feasible for small businesses and other less established enterprises. In many instances registration under Form S–18 was preferable to qualifying for an exemption from registration since there were no restrictions on resales of the securities;[22] the same is true of the successor forms SB–1 and SB–2 which are discussed below. Form S–18 was available only if the issuer was not subject to 1934 Act reporting requirements; nor was it available to a majority-owned subsidiary of a 1934 Act reporting company. Thus, as a practical matter Form S–18 was available essentially only for a first-time public offering.

In 1992, the SEC proposed and adopted a new registration form, Form SB–2, which replaced Form S–18.[23] Unlike its predecessor, Form S–18, the availability of Form SB–2 is premised upon the size of the issuer rather than on the dollar amount of securities to be offered.

---

20. 17 C.F.R. § 230.145. *See* § 5.2 *infra.* Form S–4 is coordinated with disclosures in connection with shareholder votes, which are governed by the proxy regulation under the 1934 Act. 15 U.S.C.A. § 78n. *See* chapter 11 *infra.*

Form S–4 replaced former Form S–14. For other SEC steps towards increased integration of the 1933 Act disclosures and those mandated by the Exchange Act's proxy Rules, *see* Exch.Act Rel. No. 34–23788, [1986–87 Transfer Binder] Fed.Sec.L.Rep. (CCH) ¶ 84,043 (Nov. 10, 1986).

The SEC has proposed a streamlined Form S–4 to replace Forms S–14 and S–15. Sec. Act Rel.No. 33–6534 (May 9, 1984). The Commission also proposed Form F–4 to be used by foreign issuers in similar transactions. Sec. Act Rel.No. 33–6535 (May 9, 1984). Form F–4 has since been adopted.

21. Regulation D is the prime example. *See* §§ 4.17–4.22 *infra. See also, e.g.,* Sections 3(b) and 4 of the 1933 Act (15 U.S.C.A. §§ 77c(b), (d)) as well as Regulations A and D, 17 C.F.R. Pts. 251 *et seq.,* 501 *et seq.,* which are discussed in chapter 4 *infra.*

22. For example, SEC Rule 144 limits resales of securities purchased in transactions governed by Regulation D. 17 C.F.R. § 230.144. Rule 144 is discussed in § 4.26 *infra. See also* Jerry L. Arnold & Merle W. Hopkins, Small Firm Registration in the S–18 Era: Perceptions of Professionals, 8 Corp.L.Rev. 135 (1985).

23. Adopted in Sec. Act Rel. No. 33–6949, [1991–1992 Transfer Binder] Fed.Sec.L.Rep. (CCH) ¶ 84,931 (SEC July 30, 1992); proposed in Sec. Act Rel. No. 33–6924, [1991–1992 Transfer Binder] Fed.Sec.L.Rep. (CCH) ¶ 84,931 (March 11, 1992). Form SB–2 was not a complete substitute for the former Form S–18. However, subsequent adoption of Form SB–1 made the replacement complete.

Form SB–2 thus is made available to small business issuers for an unlimited amount of securities. The new form is available to a "small business issuer" which is defined as an issuer with revenues of less than $25 million dollars for its most recent fiscal year provided that the issuer is not a foreign private issuer, a foreign government, an investment company, or a majority-owned subsidiary of a non "small business issuer." As noted above, the simplified disclosure requirements for Form SB–2 appear in Regulation S–B which sets forth small business issuer disclosure requirements under both the 1933 and 1934 Acts; formerly small business issuers were governed by Regulation S–K. The new disclosure provisions for small business issuers were adopted in conjunction with an expansion of some of the exemptions from registration.[24] In 1993, the Commission continued its small business initiatives by adopting Form SB–1 for use by small business issuers.[25] Form SB–1 is available to small business issuers for up to ten million dollars worth of securities in any twelve month period. However, offerings to employees made under Form S–8 are not included in the ten million dollar ceiling. Furthermore, a small business issuer may use Form SB–1 until the dollar ceiling has been reached, at which time the issuer must look to another form; in such a case Form SB–2 would usually be the most appropriate (unless, of course, the issuer no longer qualifies as a small business issuer). Form SB–1 is a streamlined disclosure document, designed to facilitate the registration process. In adopting the new form, the Commission gives the registrant the alternative of using the question and answer format that is permitted for Regulation A offerings.

Penny Stock and Blank Check Offerings

Although they are not contained in a separate registration form, there are special disclosure rules applicable to certain penny stock offerings. In adopting its new penny stock rules,[26] the Commission promulgated Rule 419 which applies to "blank check" offerings.[27] A "blank check" company is a company in its development stage, offering penny stock either (1) where the company has no specific business plan or purpose, or (2) where the company has indicated that its business purpose is to merge with an unidentified company (or companies) issuing penny stock as defined in 1934 Act Rule 3a51–1.[28] The "blank check"

---

24. In particular, the Commission raised the dollar ceiling for Regulation A offerings from $1.5 million to $5 million, and deleted some of the limitations in Rule 504 of Regulation D. Sec. Act Rel. No. 33–6949, [1991–1992 Transfer Binder] Fed.Sec.L.Rep. (CCH) ¶ 84,931 (SEC July 30, 1992). *See* §§ 4.15, 4.19 *infra*. For discussion of the Commission's Small Business Initiatives, *see generally* Ralph S. Janvey, The SEC's Small Business Initiatives: Regulatory Reform or Shabby Conduct?, 21 Sec.Reg.L.J. 4 (1993); Leslie T. Levinson & Anthony De Toro, A Guide to the SEC's Small Business Initiative, 17 Seton Hall Legis.J. 75 (1993).

25. *See* Sec.Act Rel. No. 33–6996, [1992–1993 Transfer Binder] Fed.Sec.L.Rep. (CCH) ¶ 85,134 (SEC April 29, 1993).

26. The penny stock Rules are discussed in § 10.7 *infra.*

27. *See* Sec. Act Rel. No. 33–6932, [1991–1992 Transfer Binder] Fed.Sec.L.Rep. (CCH) ¶ 84,937 (April 13, 1992).

28. 17 C.F.R. § 240.3a51–1. *See* § 10.7 *infra.*

registration rules apply only to offerings by blank check companies.[29] Rule 419[30] requires that proceeds received and securities in a blank check offering must be deposited into an escrow account and held for the sole benefit of purchasers during the offering. Upon the consummation of a business acquisition in which the fair value of the acquired business represents at least eighty percent of the maximum offering proceeds, the blank check company must file a post-effective amendment to its registration statement. The post-effective amendment must disclose information concerning the acquisition. When purchasers of the blank check company receive the post-acquisition information in a prospectus, the purchasers must be given the opportunity to withdraw their deposit funds. Funds from the offering will not be released from the escrow account until the acquisition has been consummated. Furthermore, if the acquisition does not occur within eighteen months subsequent to the effective date of the initial registration statement, the proceeds from the offering must be returned to the purchasers.

In connection with its adoption of the blank check company offering rule, the Commission adopted Rule 15g–8 under the 1934 Act[31] which prohibits trading of all "blank check securities" held in the escrow account. With a blank check company offering, the prospectus delivery requirements for all dealers apply until ninety days following release of the shares from escrow.[32]

Securities Issued by Investment Companies and Investment Trusts

Forms N–1, N–1A, and N–2 are for 1933 Act registration of securities issued by registered investment companies.[33] Form S–6 is available for registration of the securities or units in investment trusts that are registered on Form N–8B–2 of the Investment Company Act of 1940.[34] Form N–5 is for use by small business investment companies.

Offerings by Certain Real Estate Investment Trusts

Form S–11 is available for securities issued by certain real estate investment companies, as well as those considered real estate investment

---

29. Thus, for example, the Rules do not apply to investments in limited partnerships (or other direct participation programs) involving a detailed plan of business development, even though specific investment properties are not identified.

30. 17 C.F.R. § 230.419.

31. 17 C.F.R. § 240.15g–8.

32. 17 C.F.R. § 230.174(g). *See* § 2.5 *supra* and § 4.27 *infra*.

33. Forms N–1 and N–1A are for open-end investment companies while Form N–2 is for closed-end companies. *See* 15 U.S.C.A. §§ 80a–8 *et seq.*, which is discussed in chapter 17 *infra*. In 1989, the SEC proposed amendments to closed-end fund registration form N–2. *See* Sec. Act Rel. 33–6842; Inv. Co. Act Rel. No. 34–17091, [1989 Transfer Binder] Fed.Sec.L.Rep. ¶ 84,433 (July 28, 1989). Among other things, the amendments would permit the types of simplified prospectuses available to other classes of investment companies.

34. In 1985, the SEC proposed Form N–7 which would replace Forms N–6 and N–8B–2. *See* Sec.Act.Rel. No. 33–6580, [1984–85 Transfer Binder] Fed.Sec.L.Rep. (CCH) ¶ 83,774 (May 14, 1985). Proposed Form N–7 has not been adopted but is retained as a proposal. If adopted, Form N–7 would integrate the reporting requirements imposed by the 1933 Act and those prompted by the Investment Company Act of 1940.

trusts, as defined in section 856 of the Internal Revenue Code.[35]

Securities of Foreign Private Issuers

Form F–6 is available for the registration of American Depositary Receipts (ADRs) with respect to depositories holding securities of foreign issuers;[36] Forms F–1, F–2, and F–3 are to be used by foreign issuers.[37] The differences between Forms F–1, F–2, and F–3 are analogous to those for domestic issuers under Forms S–1, S–2, and S–3, which are discussed above. Forms F–7, F–8, F–9, and F–10 were adopted in 1991 in connection with the multijurisdictional disclosure system.[38] These forms can be used in connection with offerings of certain securities by Canadian issuers. Form F–7 may be used for rights offerings by Canadian issuers which have a class of securities listed on the Toronto Stock Exchange, the Montreal Exchange, or the Senior Board of the Vancouver Stock Exchange. Form F–8 may be used for business combinations involving Canadian issuers listed on any of the foregoing exchanges. Form F–9 may be used for investment grade debt and preferred stock offerings by substantial issuers. Form F–10 is available for registration of any securities of "substantial" Canadian issuers. The qualification requirements for these forms are relatively complex.[39]

Multijurisdictional Disclosure System

As noted above, in 1991, the Commission adopted a multijurisdictional disclosure system (MJDS) to facilitate registration and reporting of qualifying securities of Canadian issuers.[40] In adopting the MJDS, four new registration Forms were added. Form F–7 is available to an issuer organized in Canada, which is either a foreign private issuer or a Crown corporation, and has had a class of securities listed on either the Toronto Stock Exchange, Montreal Exchange, or Senior Board of the Vancouver Stock Exchange for the thirty-six months preceding SEC registration and is presently in compliance with such exchange's listing obligations. Form F–7 may be used for securities issued for cash upon

35. I.R.C. § 856.

36. Rather than having the markets trade the securities themselves, many private foreign issuers have their securities placed in a central depositary with investors receiving depositary receipts for their share of the securities. These receipts are then traded much in the same manner.

37. Forms F–1, F–2, and F–3, as is the case with other forms for private foreign issuers (Forms F–4, F–7, F–8, and F–9), are among those for which there is no express authorization for using delaying amendments to postpone the effective date.

The SEC has eliminated 1934 Act exemptions for most private foreign issuers, although existing publicly traded companies are still exempt by virtue of a grandfather clause. 17 C.F.R. § 240.12g–3(b). *See* § 14.2 *infra.*

38. *See* Sec. Act Rel. No. 33–6902, [1991 Transfer Binder] Fed.Sec.L.Rep. (CCH) ¶ 84,812 (SEC June 21, 1991).

39. *See id.* and the instructions for the applicable form. The multijurisdictional disclosure system (MJDS) is discussed *infra.*

40. Sec. Act Rel. No. 33–6902, [1991 Transfer Binder] Fed.Sec.L.Rep. (CCH) ¶ 84,812 (SEC June 21, 1991). *See also* the proposing releases. Sec.Act Rel. No. 33–6897 [1990–1991 Transfer Binder] Fed.Sec.L.Rep. (CCH) ¶ 84,701 (SEC Oct. 16, 1990); Sec.Act Rel. No. 33–6841 (July 26, 1989).

the exercise of rights issued to existing securities holders. The required disclosures under Form F–7 consist of those disclosures which are required by the home jurisdiction to be delivered to shareholders.

Form F–8, like Form F–7 is available to issuers organized in Canada, which are either foreign private issuers or Crown corporations, and have had a class of securities listed on either the Toronto Stock Exchange, Montreal Exchange, or Senior Board of the Vancouver Stock Exchange for the thirty-six months preceding SEC registration and are presently in compliance with such exchange's listing obligations. However, Form F–8, which is designed for use in mergers, combinations or other corporate reorganizations requiring a vote of the shareholders, has the additional requirement that the issuer have an aggregate market value of its public float of outstanding equity shares of at least (Can.) $75 million. Form F–9, is designed for investment grade debt or preferred securities which are issued for cash or in an exchange offer and are either non-convertible or not convertible for a period of at least one year from the date of issuance (and then may be convertible only into a security of another class of the issuer).

As is the case with Forms F–7 and F–8, Form F–9 may be used for certain offerings by an issuer organized in Canada, which is either a foreign private issuer or a Crown corporation, and has had a class of securities listed on either the Toronto Stock Exchange, Montreal Exchange, or Senior Board of the Vancouver Stock Exchange for the thirty-six months preceding SEC registration and is presently in compliance with such exchange's listing obligations. If the securities are to be convertible after one year, the issuer must have an aggregate market value of outstanding equity shares of at least (Can.) $180 million and an aggregate market value of its public float of outstanding equity shares of at least (Can.) $75 million and the securities are issued either for cash or in connection with an exchange offer. The outstanding share and public float requirements do not apply if the securities do not carry any conversion rights. Form F–10 is available to qualifying issuers for registration of any securities. Issuers must satisfy five conditions in order to qualify for use of Form F–10. Form F–10 may be used by (1) issuers organized in Canada, (2) which are either foreign private users or Crown corporations, and (3) have had a class of securities listed on either the Toronto Stock Exchange, Montreal Exchange, or Senior Board of the Vancouver Stock Exchange for the thirty-six months preceding SEC registration and are presently in compliance with such exchange's listing obligations.[41] Fourth, in order to qualify for Form F–10, the issuer must have an aggregate market value of outstanding equity shares of at least (Can.) $360 million.[42] Fifth, the issuer must have an aggregate market

---

41. If the offering is in connection with a merger or other business combination each participant company must meet the 36 month listing requirement except that the listing requirements do not apply to participating companies which contribute less than 20% of the registrant's total assets.

42. If the offering is part of a business combination, the aggregate market value of each participating company must be (Can.) $360 million except that the aggregate share value

value of its public float of outstanding equity shares of at least (Can.) $75 million.[43]

The original thought behind MJDS was that agreements such as the one with Canada would be negotiated with other countries as well. However, the Commission has apparently decided to abandon the MJDS approach for other countries in favor of working out a more generalized series of international disclosure standards.[44]

Registration of Standardized Options on Securities

Another specialized form—Form S–20—may be used to register certain standardized options on securities.[45]

Other Implications of Integrated Disclosure

While adopting the integrated disclosure system, the SEC also made a number of other amendments to simplify or to improve the disclosure system. One of these changes, which is important in relation to disclosure documents, is that registrants now need only to attest that they have reasonable grounds to believe that they fulfill the requirements for the use of a particular form.[46] With the many changes made in disclosure documents, future registrants should find securities disclosure much simpler, less expensive and easier to comply with.

Disclosure Guides and Procedures

In order to facilitate understanding of the registration process, the SEC has divided the applicable disclosure rules into three categories. Regulations S–K and S–B[47] spell out in detail what must be disclosed and the manner in which it is to be presented. Regulation C[48] sets forth the relevant procedures. Regulation S–X[49] provides accounting rules and

---

requirement does not apply to participating companies which contribute less than 20% of the registrant's total assets.

43. If the offering is in connection with a business combination, the public float requirement applies to each participating company except for those contributing less than 20% of the registrant's total assets.

44. *See* Remarks of Commissioner Roberts as reported in CCH Fed. Sec. L. Rep. Rep. Bulletin No. 1602, p.8 (March 30, 1994).

45. Options and other derivative investments are discussed in §§ 1.4.1, 1.5.1 *supra*.

46. Sec. Act Rel.No. 33–6389 (March 8, 1982); Special Report, Integrated Disclosure Adoptions, *supra* footnote 2 at 32.

47. Regulation S–K is the generic, long-form version of the disclosure guides. 17 C.F.R. § 229.10 *et seq.*, 7 Fed. Sec. L. Rep. (CCH) ¶¶ 71,001 *et seq.* Regulation S–B is a simplified version which is available to small business issuers. 17 C.F.R. § 228.10 *et seq.*, 7 Fed. Sec. L. Rep. (CCH) ¶¶ 70,701 *et seq.* A small business issuer is a United States or Canadian company with annual revenues of less than $25,000,000. If the company is a majority owned subsidiary then the parent must also be a small business issuer in order to qualify. Investment companies do not qualify as small business issuers. Reg. S–B, Item 10(a)(1). 17 C.F.R. §§ 229.10–229.802.

48. 17 C.F.R. §§ 230.400–230.494.

49. 17 C.F.R. §§ 210.1–01–210.12–17, 6 Fed. Sec. L. Rep. (CCH) ¶¶ 69,101 *et seq.* Both Regulation S–X and the SEC policy generally follow the basic accounting policies set forth by the Financial Accounting Standards Board (FASB) which for SEC purposes take precedence over "GAAP" (generally accepted accounting principles). *See generally* Louis

requirements for the form and contents of financial statements. Regulation S–X applies to financial statements required by any of the securities acts.

Due Diligence and Integrated Disclosure

A collateral issue related to integrated disclosure is the extent to which it affects the due diligence of participants in the registration process. As is discussed elsewhere,[50] the issuers, officers and directors, signers of the registration statement, underwriters, accountants, and certain experts each have due diligence obligations with regard to the accuracy of the registration materials. In many instances, the due diligence obligation includes a duty to investigate the accuracy of statements made in the registration materials. When a registration statement incorporates by reference information from other filings made with the SEC, the extent of this due diligence obligation may be effected. For example, does the auditing CPA or underwriter have equal responsibility for the information that is derived from other SEC filings? The efficiency to be achieved by integrated disclosure would appear to be undercut by requiring due diligence examination of all previous 1934 Act filings that become a part of the registration materials by virtue of Forms S–2 and S–3.

EDGAR

The SEC has entered the electronic age through the use of its computerized system known as "EDGAR" (Electronic Data Gathering And Retrieval Project); under the program the SEC can receive electronically transmitted computerized filings.[51] The computerized filings can be transmitted by telephone or can be sent to the Commission on diskette or magnetic tape. To date, EDGAR has been used for 1933 and 1934 Act registration statements as well as selected 1934 Act filings and for some filings under the Investment Company Act of 1940.[52] Since its inception as a pilot program, the Commission has been expanding the EDGAR program and eventually plans rules that, subject to exceptions, would *require* electronic filings.[53]

The first Pilot EDGAR program began in 1984 with 262 volunteers. In 1989, development of Operational EDGAR began. In 1991, Pilot EDGAR users began to make test filings on the Operational EDGAR system, and on July 15, 1992, they were able to make "live" filings on

---

T. Rappaport, SEC Accounting Practice and Procedure (3d ed.1972); Symposium on Accounting and the Federal Securities Laws, 28 Vand.L.Rev. 1 (1975).

50. *See* § 3.1 *supra* and § 7.4 *infra.*

51. The relevant EDGAR rules are found in Appendix B, *infra* (Practitioner's edition only). For a description of a trial program known as "Pilot Edgar" *see* Sec.Act Rel. No. 33–6604, [1985–86 Transfer Binder] Fed.Sec.L.Rep. (CCH) ¶ 83,918 (SEC Sept. 23, 1985). *See generally* Amy L. Goodman & Patricia M. Jayne, Edgar, The SEC's Disclosure System, 19 Rev.Sec. & Commodities Reg. 161 (1986); Donald C. Langevoort, Information Technology and the Structure of Securities Regulation, 98 Harv.L.Rev. 747 (1985).

52. *See* Survey, Federal Securities Regulation, 41 Bus.Law. 925, 966–67 (1986).

53. Sec.Act Rel.No. 33–6651 (June 26, 1986).

EDGAR. In the same month, Regulation S–T was first published, proposing rules and a phase-in schedule. Regulation S–T was adopted and became effective in the spring of 1993.

As discussed below, eventually, absent the registrant being able to establish a hardship, electronic filing will be required in most cases. EDGAR filing requirements apply equally to third-party filers, including beneficial owners of securities who are required to file reports, tender offerors under the Williams Act, as well as to persons making proxy solicitations under section 14 of the 1934 Act.[54]

With the adoption of Regulation S–T, the SEC began a gradual phase-in in order to bring the EDGAR system to its full use. The filers were divided into groups, each with a different phase-in date. Until its phase-in date, a filer may not make live filings on EDGAR, although it is encouraged to make test filings to become familiar with the routine. After the phase-in date, the filer is required to file electronically the documents specified in Rule 101(a) of Regulation S–T.[55] The phase-in schedule as determined in April, 1993 was as follows. Most of the original Pilot group was immediately phased in on April 26, 1993, when Regulation S–T became effective. Additional groups of seven hundred to nine hundred filers were admitted on July 19, October 4, and December 6, 1993. The filers phased in to this point were considered a "test group," and a six-month period to observe EDGAR in operation was established. At the end of that period, the SEC expects to make whatever final adjustments to the system it deems to be necessary and declare EDGAR fully operational. It appears that the test period ended on June 6, 1994. After that date, an additional fifteen hundred filers were scheduled to be phased in each calendar quarter (except for the first quarter of each year).[56] This phase-in stage is scheduled to continue until May, 1996, at which point a blanket phase-in will bring every

---

54. EDGAR Rule 101, 17 C.F.R. § 232.101. If these filers are not regular filers with the SEC (such as individual 5% owners filing Schedule 13D), they must submit Form ID to receive an authorization code to use EDGAR.

The Williams Act and the Proxy Rules are discussed in chapter 11 *infra.*

55. 17 C.F.R. § 232.101(a).

Rule 101 identifies three types of filings: those that must be electronic, those that may be electronic, and those that must be on paper. 17 C.F.R. § 232.101. The first group includes 1933 Act registration statements and delaying amendments, proxy materials, corporate reporting, and Williams Act forms under the 1934 Act, a variety of forms under the 1935, 1939, and 1940 Acts, and most amendments to the above. The second group consists primarily of annual reports to shareholders (except as incorporated by reference into documents of the first group, in which case the incorporated portion must be filed electronically as an exhibit to the referring document. Rule 303(b), 17 C.F.R. § 232.303(b)). The third group includes 1934 Act filings submitted to the Division of Market Regulation; EDGAR does not appear to be for broker-dealers. Also not accepted by EDGAR are no-action letters, filings relating to 1933 Act exemptions from registration (including Form 1–A), filings made with regional offices, and sales literature. This classification system is a permanent feature, not a scheduling convenience like the phase-in arrangement.

56. For an updated version of the EDGAR requirements, *see* Sec. Act Rel. No. 33–7073 (SEC July 8, 1994).

remaining filer into the EDGAR filing system. Requests to accelerate or delay a filer's phase-in date will be considered by the Commission.[57] For up to one year after their phase-in date, filers will be required to submit both electronic and paper versions of the EDGAR filings. The mandatory nature of the EDGAR filing system is subject to hardship exemptions.[58]

The technology of electronic filing has necessitated some changes and clarifications[59] of SEC procedures.[60] Additionally, there are some technological limitations. For example, EDGAR cannot receive graphics and images, unless they can be converted into normal characters. Graphics and images must be described in a narrative appendix. If the appendix makes a good-faith attempt to accurately describe the graphic material, it will not be subject to the applicable anti-fraud provisions.[61]

§ 3.4 Filing the Registration Statement

After the registrant has completed all of the necessary investigations[1] and has prepared the registration statement according to the applicable registration form,[2] disclosing all of the required items, as discussed in the preceding sections, it is time for filing with the Commission.[3] Sections 6[4] and 7[5] of the 1933 Act spell out the statutory filing requirements. Regulation C[6] sets forth the applicable procedural rules

---

57. Edgar Rules 901(a)(2), 902(d), 17 C.F.R. § 232.901(a)(2), 902(d).

58. Two types of hardship exemptions from Rule 101(a) are provided by Rules 201–02. Rule 201 allows for temporary exemptions when unexpected technical problems prevent electronic filing. All the filer must do to avail itself of this exemption is to submit the document on paper with Form TH (Notification of Reliance on the Temporary Hardship Exemption). Rule 202 creates an ongoing exemption for continuing hardship. This exemption must be pre-approved by the SEC.

59. Thus, for example, for the purposes of determining when a document has been "signed" (e.g., for section 11 liability under the 1933 Act), electronically transmitted names intended to be signatures are included. EDGAR Rule 302(a), 17 C.F.R. § 232.302(a). In addition, the filer must, at the time of filing, produce a traditional signature page and keep it on file for five years. EDGAR Rule 302(b), 17 C.F.R. § 232.302(b).

60. There is a host of technical requirements for complying with the EDGAR format. These are described in the *EDGAR Filer Manual: User's Guide for Electronic Filing with the U.S. Securities and Exchange Commission*, which is made available and periodically updated by Rule 301. EDGAR can either be used with a modem or by physically submitting diskettes or magnetic tape, but the latter methods are no better from the standpoint of cost and convenience to the filer than paper filings (except that they satisfy Rule 101(a)). There is also an EDGARLink software program.

The EDGAR rules are reproduced in Appendix B *infra* (Practitioner's Edition only).

61. EDGAR Rule 304, 17 C.F.R. § 232.304.

§ 3.4

1. *See* § 3.1 *supra*.

2. *See* §§ 3.2, 3.3 *supra*.

3. *See* § 9.35 *infra* (Practitioner's Edition only) for additional discussion of SEC filing procedures.

4. 15 U.S.C.A. § 77f.

5. 15 U.S.C.A. § 77g.

6. 17 C.F.R. §§ 230.400–.494.

while Regulation S–K[7] and Regulation S–B[8] spell out the substantive disclosure requirements.

Section 6(a) requires filing in triplicate with at least one copy of the registration statement signed by "each issuer, its principal executive officer or officers, its principal financial officer, its comptroller or principal accounting officer, and the majority of its board of directors or persons performing similar functions (or, if there is no board of directors or persons performing similar functions, by the majority of the persons or board having the power of management of the issuer) * * *."[9] In addition to the three copies required to satisfy the statutory filing requirements, SEC Rule 402[10] mandates filing of ten additional copies "for use in the examination of the registration statement, public inspection, copying and other purposes." The ten copies required by Rule 402(a)(2) need not be filed with any of the required exhibits that must be attached to the original or ribbon copy, except that copies of the following must be attached to each copy of the registration statement: underwriting agreements, the indenture, if any, and any other documents that relate to the distribution of the securities in registration. Rule 402 also requires that the specified signatures appear on the ribbon copy and that the signature lines on all other copies are at least conformed thereto. All registration forms, except for Forms SB–1 and SB–2 are to be filed with the Washington, D.C. office of the Commission. Form SB–1 and Form SB–2 may be filed either in the Washington, D.C. office or in the nearest regional office.

The Commission further specifies in Rule 403[11] that all hard copy filings must be "on good quality, unglazed, white paper, approximately 8½ by 11 inches or approximately 8½ by 13 inches in size, insofar as practicable." Rule 403 permits tables, charts, maps, and financial statements to be presented on larger paper if folded to the specified size. The rule also provides that the prospectus may, as is usually the case, be on smaller paper. It further requires that, "insofar as practicable," all documents must be printed, lithographed, mimeographed, or typewritten. All filed material must be in English or, if in a foreign language, accompanied by an English translation. All filings must be sequentially numbered with the total number of pages being set forth on the first page of the original or the ribbon copy. The original or ribbon copy of

---

7. 17 C.F.R. §§ 229.10 *et seq.*, 7 Fed. Sec. L. Rep. (CCH) ¶¶ 71,001 *et seq. See generally* Carl W. Schneider, Joseph M. Manko & Robert S. Kant, Going Public–Practice, Procedure and Consequences, 27 Vill.L.Rev. 1 (1981).

8. 17 C.F.R. § 228.10 *et seq.*, 7 Fed. Sec. L. Rep. (CCH) ¶¶ 70,701 *et seq.* A small business issuer is a United States or Canadian company with annual revenues of less than $25,000,000. If the company is a majority owned subsidiary then the parent must also be a small business issuer in order to qualify. Investment companies do not qualify as small business issuers. Reg. S–B, Item 10(a)(1). 17 C.F.R. §§ 229.10–229.802.

9. 15 U.S.C. § 77f(a).

10. 17 C.F.R. § 230.402.

11. 17 C.F.R. § 230.403.

the registration statement must also contain an index of all exhibits, identifying each exhibit and listing the page upon which it appears.

Under a pilot program, registrants had the option of making their filings on electronic media.[12] However, as discussed in the preceding section, under a phase-in program, electronic filing will eventually be required for most issuers. Under the Commission's Electronic Data Gathering And Retrieval Project ("EDGAR") filings can be made over the telephone lines or can be delivered to the commission on diskettes or magnetic tape.[13]

SEC Rule 404[14] sets forth additional requirements regarding the proper form of the registration statement. At the registrant's option, rather than following the question-and-answer format for each item as required by the applicable SEC filing form, it is permissible to file a copy of the prospectus provided, of course, that it contains all information that would appear in direct response to each item. For disclosure items in the registration statement that are not called for in the prospectus[15] it is necessary to disclose according to the itemized format, that is, by providing as part of the registration statement the text of these items together with the answers. In addition, every registration statement must have a cross-reference sheet that shows where in the prospectus required information is to be found. There also is a requirement that the facing page of the registration statement contain the approximate date for the proposed offering. In addition to the information that must be in the prospectus and registration statement as spelled out by the applicable registration form, Schedule A requires the inclusion of a number of exhibits that must be attached to the formal SEC filing.[16] Beyond the signature requirements of section 6,[17] section 7 of the 1933 Act requires the filing of the written consent of "any accountant, engineer, or appraiser, or any person whose profession gives authority to a statement made by him" who is named as having prepared or certified a portion of the registration statement or as having prepared or certified a report or a valuation for use in connection therewith.[18] It is also necessary to secure the written consent of persons who are about to become directors and are identified as such in the registration statement but are not signers.[19]

After all the required copies and exhibits have been prepared in conformity to requirements of the SEC rules, it is time for filing. The

---

12. *See* Sec. Act Rel. No. 33–6604, [1985–86 Transfer Binder] Fed.Sec.L.Rep. (CCH) ¶ 83,918 (SEC Sept. 23, 1985).

13. *Id.* In addition to the discussion in § 3.3 *supra, see* the EDGAR rules in Appendix B, *infra* (Practitioner's edition only).

14. 17 C.F.R. § 230.404.

15. The prospectus requirements are discussed in § 3.2 *supra.*

16. Schedule A §§ (28)-(32) are discussed in § 3.2 *supra.*

17. 15 U.S.C.A. § 77f. *See* text accompanying footnote 9 *supra.*

18. 15 U.S.C.A. § 77(g); 17 C.F.R. §§ 230.435, 230.436.

19. 17 C.F.R. § 230.438.

Commission imposes a minimum filing fee of one hundred dollars, with a higher figure computed as .0002 times the maximum aggregated price at which the securities are proposed to be offered.[20]

§ 3.5 Processing the Registration Statement After Filing

Under the terms of section 8(a) of the Act, once the registration statement has been filed, it becomes effective on the twentieth day after filing, with the twenty day period beginning to run anew on the date that each amendment is filed.[1] As is explained more fully below, the formal statutory time periods and procedures are rarely invoked. Section 8(b) of the 1933 Act[2] empowers the SEC to issue a refusal order for deficiencies that are apparent on the face of the registration statement, provided that the Commission acts within ten days after the filing. Section 8(d)[3] permits the SEC to issue a stop order to prevent the effective date of a registration statement and section 8(e)[4] permits the Commission to institute investigations as to whether a stop order should be issued.

The procedures spelled out in section 8 of the Act do not provide an accurate picture of the SEC registration review process as it generally proceeds. Although Congress may have contemplated that the Commission would initiate formal section 8 proceedings whenever defective registration statements are filed, such formal proceedings are the exception rather than the rule. Instead, registration review is accomplished through the less formal means of written correspondence and telephone

---

20. 15 U.S.C.A. § 77f(b).

§ 3.5

1. Section 8(a); 15 U.S.C.A. § 77h(a). The waiting period is discussed in § 2.4 *supra*. An exception to the twenty-day waiting period is found for issuers who use Form S–8 for employee compensation plans. Rule 462 provides that an S–8 registration is effective when filed. 17 C.F.R. § 230.462. In addition, issuers using other registration forms may apply to the Commission for acceleration of the effective date. 17 C.F.R. § 230.461.

2. 15 U.S.C.A. § 77h(b). For discussion of the other SEC enforcement powers *see* § 9.5 *infra*.

3. 15 U.S.C.A. § 77h(d). *See* William R. McLucas, Stop Order Proceedings Under The Securities Act of 1933: A Current Assessment, 40 Bus.Law. 515 (1985)

4. 15 U.S.C.A. § 77h(e). For a discussion on the scope of the section 8(e) investigation process *see* Las Vegas Hawaiian Development Co. v. SEC, 466 F.Supp. 928, 932 (D.Hawaii 1979). In the *Las Vegas Hawaiian Development Co.*, the SEC responded to the initial filing (which was accompanied by a delaying amendment) with a sixteen-page letter of comment. After two corrective amendments and the passage of more than a year following the initial filing, the Commission issued an order under section 8(e) authorizing a staff investigation to determine whether section 8(d) proceedings were necessary. The registrant then filed suit seeking an order compelling the Commission to act. The investigation continued through the date of the decision (nearly eight months after the SEC authorized the section 8(e) investigation) without the SEC taking any action. The registrant alleged exhaustion of administrative remedies (the court noted that "it is the remedy that must be exhausted, not the petitioner," 466 F.Supp. at 933). The court held that it had the power to order the Commission to decide whether to initiate section 8(d) proceedings but that petitioner had failed to allege sufficient facts to support such relief. *See also, e.g.,* Boruski v. Division of Corporation Finance, 321 F.Supp. 1273 (S.D.N.Y.1971) (refusing to require SEC to expedite processing of the registration statement).

conversations between the SEC staff and the registrant's counsel.[5]

The Commission's reliance on the informal review process dates back to its earliest years.[6] As previously explained, the formal procedures set out in section 8 are used infrequently. For example, in 1970, only 28 such examinations were initiated out of 4,314 registration statements filed, while only six resulted in the initiation of stop order proceedings.[7] There has been no significant increase in the use of section 8 proceedings. Although the scarcity of formal review proceedings has been described as "a tribute to the administrative flexibility of the Commission,"[8] some might also attribute it to undue pressures exerted by the Commission during its informal discussions and negotiations with registrants.[9] Another, more plausible explanation for the lack of more detailed review is the fact that the SEC is both understaffed and overworked.[10]

Rather than relying on the stop order and the refusal order proceedings, the Commission staff generally responds to the initial filing with a detailed "letter of comment" or "deficiency letter," advising the issuer of changes that the Commission would like to see in the registration

5. Although not a formal process, the SEC Rules do provide a basis for the giving of informal advice. *See* 17 C.F.R. § 202.2 (prefiling assistance and interpretive advice) and 17 C.F.R. § 202.3 (processing of filings). *See also* § 9.34 *infra* (Practitioner's Edition only).

6. *See, e.g.* In the Matter of Universal Camera Corp., 19 S.E.C. 648, 659, [1945–1947 Transfer Binder] Fed. Sec. L. Rep. (CCH) ¶ 75,560 (SEC 1945) wherein the Commission explained the informal process of commenting on initial filings and the efficiency of this process:

It has been our practice to use sparingly the statutory authority to delay or suspend the effectiveness of deficient registration statements. Many necessary adjustments are worked out through prefiling conferences. Beyond that we have adopted the practice of informing registrants, informally, by letter, of material questions that arise during examination of the statement once it is filed. The registrant is thereby afforded opportunity to file corrective amendments without the necessity of formal proceedings.

These practices usually have resulted in prompt correction or clarification of the statement. With relatively few exceptions, amendments worked out through such informal procedures have been found to satisfy the statutory requirements and to justify acceleration of the effective date.

7. 36 S.E.C. Ann.Rep. 29, 34, 35 (1970). *See also, e.g.,* 46 S.E.C.Ann.Rep. 141 (1980).

Although the SEC normally relies on the informal review procedures that are discussed below, the Commission is not precluded from bypassing the informal review process and initiating formal section 8 proceedings. *See, e.g.,* Doman Helicopters, Inc., 41 S.E.C. 431 (SEC 1963) (rejecting the registrant's argument that the SEC must first resort to the informal review process before instituting formal proceedings). In *Doman Helicopters* it was claimed that a stop order was not warranted since the initial filing was only a "preliminary filing" and the SEC never initiated its informal review. Once the section 8 hearings began, the registrant filed an amendment to delay the effective date which was claimed to have avoided the necessity of stop order proceedings. The Commission Ruled that in light of the serious deficiencies in the registration statement as originally filed, section 8 proceedings were warranted. The seriousness of the deficiencies in *Doman Helicopters* was exacerbated by the fact that there were already more than 8,000 public investors.

8. Richard W. Jennings & Harold Marsh, Jr., Securities Regulation 183 (5th ed.1982).

9. *See, e.g.* Orel Sebring, Log Jam on the Potomac—The Current Delay Problem of the SEC, 15 Bus.Law. 921 (1960).

10. *Cf.* John Mulford, "Acceleration" Under the Securities Act of 1933–A Reply to the Securities and Exchange Commission, 14 Bus.Law. 156 (1958).

statement. These comments are not limited to specific disclosure items but also refer to readability and the ease with which the disclosures can be understood.[11] As a practical matter, virtually all registration statements filed with the Commission require at least one amendment.[12] Failure to respond to the letter of comment (or deficiency letter), in and of itself, has no legal consequences, except that it carries with it the implied threat of the Commission's initiating a formal stop order proceeding. Accordingly, rather than risk public disclosure and adverse publicity of the deficiencies that would result from formal SEC action, most registrants will readily comply with the Commission's requests. In the event that the registration statement is about to become effective as a result of the expiration of the twenty day period, the SEC will generally suggest that the issuer file a "delaying amendment" in order to avoid the more drastic initiation of formal administrative proceedings. Since an amendment starts a new twenty day waiting period, even the most trivial change will operate as a delaying amendment.

Sometimes either the Commission or the need for last minute additions will require minor amendments to the registration statement after all other deficiencies have been corrected. A common procedure to prevent delaying the effectiveness of the registration due amendment is to apply to the Commission for acceleration of the effective date pursuant to section 8(a).[13] For example, it is frequently very difficult to arrive at a firm price for a new issue prior to the eve of the offering. Accordingly, it is common practice for the issuer or registrant to omit the offering price from the preliminary SEC filing. After the correction of all other deficiencies the issuer or other registrant will then file a "price amendment" followed by a request for acceleration to allow the offering to proceed as contemplated.[14]

In addition to the requirements of full disclosure and accuracy that can prevent a registration statement from becoming effective, the statute and rules provide that the prospectus must constantly be kept current even after the effective date. A prospectus containing misleading information, even though it becomes misleading after the effective date, is not in compliance with section 10 of the Act.[15] This is true even if it would not be necessary to the registration statement and prospectus to update the full registration statement.[16] Post effective amendments are frequently made by affixing stickers that contain the updated or corrected information.[17] Stickering saves the registrant the expense of reprinting

11. 17 C.F.R. § 230.421.

12. *See, e.g.,* R. Jennings & H. Marsh *supra* footnote 8 at 174–75. *See also* Louis Loss, Fundamentals of Securities Regulation 128–30 (1983).

13. 15 U.S.C.A. § 77h(a). *See* text accompanying footnotes 23–34 *infra.*

14. *See* L. Loss *supra* footnote 12 at 130–31.

15. SEC v. Manor Nursing Centers, 458 F.2d 1082 (2d Cir.1972). *See* § 2.5 *supra.*

16. SEC v. Manor Nursing Centers, 458 F.2d 1082 (2d Cir.1972).

17. *See, e.g.,* Preferred Equities Group, Inc., [1987 Transfer Binder] Fed.Sec.L.Rep. (CCH) ¶ 78,462 (SEC No Action Letter April 7, 1987) (stickering prospectus and post

the entire prospectus. There may be some instances, however, when the changes are so significant that stickering will not be sufficient.[18] Before a prospectus containing post-effective amendments can be used, ten copies of the updated prospectus must be filed with the Commission.[19]

SEC Review Procedures

The SEC has various types of review procedures for 1933 Act registration statements. There were formerly four primary types of review.[20] In 1980, the Commission initiated a new system known as "selective review." [21] Under this new procedure, while all first time issuers continue to receive a thorough review, repeat offerings by reporting companies will be reviewed only on a selective basis. This additional process was motivated by the fact that by 1980, the Division of Corporation Finance was faced with review of fifty-five thousand SEC filings to be reviewed by one-hundred staff members, reflecting an increased workload but a smaller reviewing staff.[22] It therefore became impractical to maintain the more comprehensive review policies that formerly existed. Nevertheless, the former varieties of review may be indicative of what an issuer may encounter under the current process of selective review.

SEC Policies on Acceleration Requests

In the event that the issuer desires an effective date prior to the expiration of twenty days after the filing of the last amendment to the registration statement, it can file with the Commission a request for an acceleration of the effective date pursuant to Rule 461.[23] The rule provides that the issuer should advise the Commission of the request for acceleration not later than the second business day before the desired effective date. The Commission has a wide range of discretion in deciding whether or not to grant the request for acceleration. There are no express statutory guidelines for acceleration and the few guides that

---

effective amendments to registration statement to reflect changes in the underwriting group).

18. *See* § 2.5 *supra*. In the usual case, it is not necessary to attach them to a full prospectus before filing, although a full prospectus will usually be required to be given to investors (with an exception in some employee benefit plan contexts). Sec. Act Rel. No. 33–6714(May 27, 1987), p. 41.

The question arises, what types of updating require a post-effective amendment as opposed to just a sticker? Most reported references treat the two as interchangeable. Materiality is the point at which one updating, whether by way of stickering or otherwise, is required. In the Matter of Blinder, Robinson & Co., Inc., 1990 WL 321585 (April 27, 1990).

19. 17 C.F.R. § 230.424(c).

20. Deferred review, cursory review, summary review and customary review. *See generally* Sec.Act. Rel. No. 33–5231 (Feb. 3, 1972, rescinded Nov. 17, 1980).

21. SEC News Digest, Nov. 17, 1980. *See also,* Edward F. Greene, The SEC and Corporate Disclosure, 36 Bus.Law. 119, 126–27 (1980).

22. This was a significant increase in the filings as reported in Sec.Act Rel. No. 33–5231 (Feb. 3, 1972).

23. 17 C.F.R. § 230.461. *See also* the discussion in § 3.5.1 *infra* (Practitioner's edition only).

have been prepared by the Commission are exceedingly vague. When the SEC denies a request for acceleration of the registration statement, the denial is usually based upon incomplete or inadequate disclosure.[24] The Commission in one of its seminal decisions,[25] relied on the statutory criteria that were added to the Act in 1940[26] and which set forth four basic but quite generalized criteria that it will consider in deciding whether or not to grant a request for acceleration:

(1) the adequacy of the information about the issuer that was available to the public before the registration,

(2) the ease with which the nature of the securities can be understood,

(3) the ease with which the relationship of the securities to the capital structure of the issuer can be understood, and,

(4) the ease with which the rights of holders of the securities can be understood.[27]

The lack of definite guidelines is but one of the criticisms that has led to objections to the Commission's use of acceleration.[28]

As explained by the Commission, the acceleration procedure was enacted by Congress in order to give added flexibility to the SEC and at the same time reduce the harshness that otherwise resulted from a rigid twenty day waiting period:

This provision for acceleration was added to the Act in 1940 to relax the rigidity of the previous requirements. Its terms make plainly evident the persistent concern of Congress for the protection of investors and emphasize the intention of Congress to require that before permitting a registration to become effective the Commission must be satisfied that the information in the statement itself, together with any information previously available to the public about the issuer, will enable prospective investors to understand clearly what it is they are asked to buy.

---

24. *See* 17 C.F.R. § 230.460.

25. In the Matter of Universal Camera Corp., 19 S.E.C. 648, 658, [1945–1947 Transfer Binder] Fed. Sec. L. Rep. (CCH) ¶ 75,560 (SEC 1945).

26. The Act was amended to as to provide for more discretion than the prior, more rigid language permitted. In the Matter of Universal Camera, 19 S.E.C. 648, 658, [1945–1947 Transfer Binder] Fed. Sec. L. Rep. (CCH) ¶ 75,560 (SEC 1945). *See also, e.g.,* In the Matter of Thomascolor, Inc., 27 S.E.C. 151, [1945–1947 Transfer Binder] Fed. Sec. L. Rep. (CCH) ¶ 75,837 (SEC 1947).

27. In the Matter of Universal Camera Corp., 19 S.E.C. 648, 657–58, [1945–1947 Transfer Binder] Fed. Sec. L. Rep. (CCH) ¶ 75,560 (SEC 1945). The Commission also noted that Congress did not draft the Act so that the SEC would grant acceleration "casually" or "as a matter of course." *Id.* At 657. Rather, the SEC is directed to exercise its discretion only if the public interest will thus be served. *Id. See* § 3.5.1 *infra.*

28. *See, e.g.,* Edward N. Gadsby & Ray Garrett, Jr., Acceleration Under the Securities Act of 1933–A Comment on the A.B.A.'s Legislative Proposal, 13 Bus.Law. 718 (1958); John Mulford, "Acceleration" Under the Securities Act of 1933—A Reply to the Securities and Exchange Commission, 14 Bus.Law. 156 (1958).

Consistently with these provisions the Act authorizes the Commission to take steps that may be necessary to defer the public sale of any security subject to registration until the statement is cleared of material inaccuracies or omissions and contains a complete and correct statement of the information requisite to a clear understanding of the security's character and quality.[29]

In addition to the four criteria discussed above, the Commission has set forth a number of factors that it will weigh in considering the request for acceleration. The SEC has announced that it may refuse to grant acceleration in the following situations: (a) when the issuer has an indemnification agreements with its officers, directors or underwriters that transcends or is inconsistent with SEC policy on indemnification agreement unless there is a waiver or a compliance with SEC policies; (b) when there is a pending SEC investigation under any provision of the acts administered by the SEC of the issuer, a person controlling the issuer, or one of the underwriters; (c) when one or more of the underwriters due to the underwriting commitment may put at risk its financial responsibility as established by Rule 15c3–1[30] of the Exchange Act; or (d) when there is or has been market manipulation by any person "connected" with the offering.[31] These are just some of the grounds for denial of acceleration that are listed in Rule 461.[32]

On occasion, the SEC has been harshly criticized for using denial of acceleration as an ad hoc sanction for these events which, standing alone, would not provide a sufficient basis for the issuance of either a refusal order or a stop order.[33]

Indemnification agreements are not the only issue that has led the Commission to deny requests for acceleration of the effective date. In 1989, the Commission staff refused to grant acceleration as not in the public interest because of a clause in the issuer's charter requiring shareholders to submit to arbitration any claim asserted against or on behalf of the issuer.[34]

Due to the wide latitude that the Commission allows itself for the denial of acceleration, requests for acceleration should not be made lightly. This is especially so where the registrant is concerned about the marketability of the securities being offered. News of SEC denial of an acceleration request may alert the investment community to potential problems (both real and unreal) with the securities. Except with price amendments or relatively minor amendments which start the twenty day

---

29. Universal Camera, 19 S.E.C. 648, 658 (SEC 1946).

30. 17 C.F.R. § 240.15c3–1.

31. Rule 461(b), 17 C.F.R. § 230.461(b).

32. *See* the discussion in § 3.5.1 *infra* (Practitioner's Edition only).

33. *See* Mulford *supra* footnote 28.

34. When issuer's counsel objected, he was informed that the Commission had informally approved the staff's position. A FOIA request for the staff's submission to the Commission was denied. *See* Carl W. Schneider, Arbitration in Corporate Governance Documents: An Idea the SEC Refuses to Accelerate, 4 Insights, no. 5 at p. 21 (May 1990).

period running anew, because of the customary review procedures for new issuers and the more speculative ventures, acceleration may as a practical matter be limited to more established companies.

Withdrawal of Registration Statement

Once a registration statement has been filed, the Commission's approval is required before it can be withdrawn.[35] Ordinarily, the Commission will accede to requests to withdraw the registration statement. It is the Commission's stated policy to permit withdrawal of the registration statement if "consistent with the public interest and protection of investors." [36] However, when it is believed that the registration process warrants imposing sanctions against the participants, the Commission might refuse to permit withdrawal in order that it may institute formal proceedings under section 8.[37] Formal proceedings under section 8 can have significant consequences. For example, the imposition of a stop order or refusal order may disable the participants from participating in certain exempt offerings over the next five years.[38]

Deleted section 3.5.1 can be found
in the Practitioner's Edition.

§ 3.6 Frequent Deficiencies in Registration Statements

Registration statement disclosures cover a wide range of topics, including the company's business generally, the terms of the offering, as well as identification and discussion of significant risk factors. There are a number of areas that are particularly susceptible to inadequate or misleading disclosures.[1] First, the registration statement may fail to

---

35. 17 C.F.R. § 230.477; Peoples Securities Co. v. SEC, 289 F.2d 268 (5th Cir.1961) (registrant does not have an absolute right to withdraw registration statement); Columbia General Investment Corp. v. SEC, 265 F.2d 559 (5th Cir.1959) (same). *See, e.g.,* Resource Corp. International v. SEC, 103 F.2d 929 (D.C.Cir.1939), *affirming* 24 F.Supp. 580 (D.D.C.1938) (voluntary abandonment of registration statement does not force SEC to terminate stop order proceedings before an order is issued); SEC v. Hoover, 25 F.Supp. 484 (D. Ill.1938) (registrant could not withdraw registration statement once stop order proceedings were commenced).

36. 17 C.F.R. § 230.477.

37. *See, e.g.,* Resource Corp. International v. SEC, 103 F.2d 929 (D.C.Cir.1939), *affirming* 24 F.Supp. 580 (D.D.C.1938) (SEC's finding that withdrawal of the registration statement would not be in the public interest was not diminished by the registrant's abandonment of the registration statement); SEC v. Hoover, 25 F.Supp. 484 (N.D.Ill.1937) (registrant did not have an unqualified right to withdraw abandoned registration statement). *Cf.* In the Matter of Columbia Baking Co., 38 S.E.C. 213, [1957–1961 Transfer Binder] Fed. Sec. L. Rep. (CCH) ¶ 76,569 (SEC 1958) (material deficiencies found but since the offering had been abandoned, no stop order was issued). *But cf.* Jones v. Kennedy, 121 F.2d 40 (D.C.Cir.1941) (SEC wrongfully refused withdrawal of stop order; but Commission was not liable to the registrant). *Compare* Columbia General Investment Corp. v. SEC, 265 F.2d 559 (5th Cir.1959) (*Jones* decision, *supra,* denying the SEC's right to refuse withdrawal is limited to instances in which investor interests are not involved).

38. *See e.g.,* 17 C.F.R. §§ 230.252; 230.505(b)(2)(iii). *See* §§ 4.15, 4.18, *infra.*

§ 3.6

1. *See* Regulation S–K. 17 C.F.R. §§ 229.10–229.802. *See generally* Gerard J. Robinson & Klaus Eppler, Going Public (rev.ed.1978); Carl W. Schneider, Joseph M. Manko &

adequately explain the issuer's prior adverse trends in sales and in income. For example, the Commission has taken the position that it is not sufficient merely to state that the issuer's income declined due to increased expenses. The 1933 Act demands, and the SEC requires, full disclosure as to precisely which expenses were increased and the reasons for their increase. Further, the issuer should explain whether such increased costs are reasonably expected to continue and, if so, whether past performance is a reasonable guide to the future.[2] A second common deficiency in registration statements is the failure to include information concerning the relative contribution to sales and/or income of the issuer's various products, product lines, lines of business, divisions, and subsidiaries. The Commission requires identification of the sources of income and/or losses according to division and lines of business. The allocation according to lines of business does not depend upon whether or not the issuer operates its divisions on a parent-subsidiary basis. A third frequently occurring problem is the registration statement's failure to give a full, fair, and detailed description of the use of the proceeds to be raised by the offering. The Commission requires specific identification of the use of the proceeds from the offering. A fourth common disclosure problem arises out of the registration statement's treatment of transactions between the issuer and management or principal shareholders. Because of the obvious sensitivity of insider transactions, especially when there is an actual or potential conflict of interest situation, disclosure problems frequently arise.[3] Similar disclosure problems can arise under the Exchange Act.[4]

A fifth common deficiency in 1933 Act disclosure documents is the registrant's failure to make the prospectus readable and understandable by the general investing public. The SEC has stated its belief that these problems are exacerbated by the failure to use simple language, tables, charts and other pictorial visual devices.[5] A sixth common deficiency is that the 1933 Act prospectus may have either an insufficient or overly verbose introductory statement. According to the Commission, an introductory statement, when required, should include identification of all of

---

Robert S. Kant, Going Public–Practice Procedure and Consequences, 27 Vill.L.Rev. 1 (1981); Daniel J. Winnike & Christopher E. Nordquist, Federal Securities Law Issues for the Sticky Offering, 48 Bus.Law. 869 (1993). *See also* § 3.7 *infra* and the authorities cited in footnote 13 *infra*.

2. After a long history to the contrary, the SEC now permits disclosure of projections of economic performance, although it is not required except in very limited circumstances. Sec.Act Rel. No. 33–5992 (Nov. 7, 1982). *See generally* Bruce A. Mann, Prospectuses: Unreadable or Just Unread?—A Proposal to Reexamine Policies Against Permitting Projections, 40 Geo.Wash.L.Rev. 222 (1971); Note, Mandatory Disclosure of Corporate Projections and the Goals of Securities Regulation, 81 Colum.L.Rev. 1525 (1981); Note, The SEC Safe Harbor for Forecasts—A Step in the Right Direction?, 1980 Duke L.J. 607; Note, Disclosure of Future–Oriented Information Under Securities Laws, 88 Yale L.J. 338 (1978).

3. *E.g.,* In the Matter of Franchard Corp., 42 S.E.C. 163 (SEC 1964). *See* § 3.7 *infra.*

4. *See, e.g.,* Kidwell v. Meikle, 597 F.2d 1273 (9th Cir.1979); Wright v. Heizer Corp., 560 F.2d 236 (7th Cir.1977), *cert. denied* 434 U.S. 1066, 98 S.Ct. 1243, 55 L.Ed.2d 767 (1978). *See* § 13.11 *infra.*

5. *See* Sec.Act Rel. No. 33–6276 (Dec. 23, 1980); Sec.Act Rel. No. 33–6235 (Sept. 2, 1980).

the factors that make the particular offering speculative and also of those aspects that are unique to that offering as opposed to the industry or type of offering in general.[6] It is the SEC's position that overly verbose statements are obscure and therefore contrary to full disclosure requirements. Lack of readability can be just as harmful as a failure to disclose enough since the material information may well get lost in the issuer's verbosity, thus negating the intended impact of the cautionary introductory statement.

A recent Seventh Circuit decision raises significant questions concerning the appropriate audience for registration statements. Whereas the SEC has taken the position that the registration statement should be written with the ordinary investor in mind, Judge Easterbrook in Wielgos v. Commonwealth Edison Co.[7] took the position that, at least in the case of widely-followed securities, the adequacy of disclosures should be judged by the needs of sophisticated analysts. In *Wielgos*, the registrant had a sufficiently wide market following that it used registration form S–3. The court held that disclosure should therefore be geared to the professional investors who in effect set the price for the stock. Thus, according to Judge Easterbrook:

> Descriptions in Forms 10–K and registration statements are almost useless to individual investors. They require absorption by professional traders and investors. What these professionals need is new information specific to the issuer. Telling them over and again how the NRC works, or that costs are rising in the nuclear power industry, or even that Commonwealth Edison had run into trouble with its welds (which became known a few months before this stock was sold), has nothing to do with the accuracy of prices in the market. Investors who buy 500 shares of stock rely on the market price ... [8]

Judge Easterbrook is most certainly correct in his assertion that registration statements should not be cluttered with useless detail.[9] In fact, the SEC has long taken this position. On the other hand, Judge Easterbrook's elitist description of the market and the inefficiency of catering to the small investor ignores the basic disclosure thrust of the securities laws and portends unfortunately narrow tests of materiality.

Another relatively recent disclosure problem that has emerged, both with regard to 1933 Act registration statements and to SEC filings in general, is the issuer's failure to disclose improper transactions involving domestic political activity, including campaign contributions, or foreign

---

6. *See e.g.,* In the Matter of Universal Camera Corp., 19 S.E.C. 648 (1945); Regulation S–K, items 502–503, 17 C.F.R. §§ 229.501–502.

7. 892 F.2d 509 (7th Cir.1989). *See also* the discussion in § 3.3 *supra.*

8. 892 F.2d at 518.

9. Thus, for example, it was not actionable to fail to explain in detail the elementary economic principle that increased competition could have an adverse effect on the company's profits. O'Sullivan v. Trident Microsystems, Inc., 1994 WL 124453, [1993–1994 Transfer Binder] Fed. Sec. L. Rep. (CCH) ¶ 98,116 (N.D.Cal.1994).

involvement.[10] A number of problems have also arisen in the context of the so-called "new disclosure" concerning social issues with which the issuer has a controversial relationship. Similarly, ethical investors may want to know where their invested funds are going. The courts and the Commission have dealt with these problems in the context of an expanding definition of the concept of "materiality." [11] Since the hallmark of disclosure for both the 1933 Act registration statement and all 1934 Act filings is embodied in the concept of "materiality," the problems relating to disclosure in registration statements and other required filings are quite similar. Because the primary purpose of 1933 Act registration statements is to provide full and adequate information regarding the distribution of securities, certain types of disclosures may be more sensitive and thus of more concern with regard to public offerings than to other required filings.[12]

The above-mentioned primary deficiencies in registration statements that have been identified by the SEC are merely examples of problems that may occur. The discussion above and the sections that follow are intended to highlight some of the most problematical 1933 Act disclosure issues, but they are by no means all-inclusive. A complete discussion of the 1933 Act disclosure problems is too lengthy to be included in a text of this scope and, accordingly, other sources must be consulted.[13]

Over the years, the Commission has developed various guides to help with disclosures. The SEC has consolidated its disclosure policies into Regulation S–K[14] (and Regulation S–B for small issuers). The applicable registration form lists the items that must be disclosed and then refers to Regulation S–K or Regulation S–B for further guidance. Regulation S–K and Regulation S–B are comprised of item-by-item explanations of the ways in which various information should be presented in SEC disclosure documents. Thus, in drafting registration materials and other disclosure documents, Regulation S–K (or Regulation S–B) must be consulted. Over recent years, Management Discussion and Analysis (MD&A) of financial condition and results of operations has become increasingly important.[15] And, of course, careful attention must be paid to Regulation S–X and the financial disclosures generally.

10. *See, e.g.,* SEC v. Jos. Schlitz Brewing Co., 452 F.Supp. 824 (E.D.Wis.1978).

11. *See,* James O. Hewitt, Developing Concepts of Materiality and Disclosure, 32 Bus.Law. 887 (1977); Lewis D. Lowenfels, Questionable Corporate Payments and the Federal Securities Laws, 51 N.Y.U.L.Rev. 1 (1976); A.A. Sommer, Jr. Therapeutic Disclosure, 4 Sec.Reg.L.J. 263 (1976). *See also* §§ 11.14, 13.5 *infra.*

12. For a good discussion of materiality in the 1933 Act offering process *see* Feit v. Leasco Data Processing Equipment Corp., 332 F.Supp. 544 (E.D.N.Y.1971).

13. *See generally* 3A Harold S. Bloomenthal, Securities and Federal Corporate Law §§ 7.08, 7.09 (1981 rev. ed.); I, IV Louis Loss, Securities Regulation, 316–351, 2360–2390 (2d ed.1961, 1969 Supp.); Thomas Gilroy, Disclosure in Connection with Securities Act Registration, in Avery S. Cohen and Stanley I. Friedman, eds., Introduction to Securities Laws Disclosure, (1976).

14. 17 C.F.R. §§ 229.10–229.802.

15. Regulation S–K, item 303; Regulation S–B, item 303. See § 3.7 and Appendix A (Practitioner's Edition only) *infra.*

§ 3.7   Problems Relating to Disclosure of the Dilution of the Public's Investment, Business Risks, Transactions With Controlling Persons, and Projections

Because of both the potential for self-dealing and the access to inside information, transactions by the issuer's insiders frequently require detailed disclosure in the 1933 Act registration statement. The Commission shows particular concern where a significant portion of the proceeds will not be going into the issuer's business. Whenever an investment is a speculative one, the prospectus must provide the potential investor with notice and give detailed disclosures as to the reasons therefor. The prospectus must also contain an explanation of risks peculiar to the issuer or the issuer's industry.

The discussion that follows addresses the ensuing topics that raise particularly difficult and sensitive disclosure issues: dilution of the public's investment; business risks, transactions of controlling persons, projections (and other soft information), and management discussion and analysis of financial condition and results of operations (MD & A). This is followed by a discussion of the proper approach to framing disclosures and statements relating to projections. Also discussed is the emerging "bespeaks caution doctrine" which provides that adequate cautionary language may limit or eliminate potential liability for overly optimistic predictions and projections.

Dilution of the Public's Investment, Business Risks

A vintage case which, nevertheless, still accurately reflects the Commission's disclosure policy is In the Matter of Universal Camera Corp.[1] In that case, the issuer embarked upon an offering of securities that would have resulted in the rearrangement of control in an existing corporation. The issuer was to receive just under twenty percent of the aggregate offering proceeds,[2] a figure which could possibly have increased to just under forty percent upon exercise of certain warrants.[3] The registration statement that was filed came under sharp criticism in the administrative stop order proceedings initiated by the Commission. To begin with, the SEC objected that the issuer's registration statement was deficient due to an inadequate introductory statement. Although the registrant included the required legend on the first page to the effect

---

§ 3.7

1. 19 S.E.C. 648 (SEC 1945).

2. The registration statement covered a public offering of 663,500 shares of class A stock, of which 530,500 shares were being sold by existing shareholders as a secondary distribution. The selling shareholders had acquired the shares covered in the secondary offering for a total of $30,000 but they were to receive $2,100,865 from reselling them through the registered offering. The remaining 133,000 Class A shares represented a primary offering by the issuer which was to receive $524,985 in net proceeds.

3. The registration statement also covered warrants which if fully exercised would cause the issuer to receive an additional $863,500.

that the investment was a speculative one, it failed to clearly "describe the speculative aspects" so as to be "plainly evident to the ordinary investor."[4] It is certain that today the Commission would require an equally explicit introductory statement explaining the speculative nature of such an investment. Under current law any prospectus covering a speculative offering must explain why the issue is speculative by giving all pertinent details without obscuring any of the key facts or burying them in a lengthy narrative.[5]

Perhaps the most serious disclosure problem in Universal Camera's registration statement was the failure to adequately to describe the intended use of the proceeds from the offering. This was a particularly sensitive issue on the facts before the Commission since the bulk of the securities in registration represented a secondary offering and, thus, none of the proceeds from these sales was to flow to the issuer. Specifically, the Commission pointed to the registration statement's failure to explain to the investor the significance of the low percentage of proceeds the issuer was to receive, and its failure to reveal that the shareholders, who were to make a huge profit on their secondary sales, would nonetheless have retained both voting control in the corporation and a forty-three percent participation in earnings by virtue of the Class B stock which they would continue to hold.[6] Thirdly, the registration statement failed to contrast plainly the offering price with the book value of the securities offered. Finally, the registration materials discussed inadequately the potential impact of the warrants and their eventual exercise.

As is discussed more fully in a subsequent section,[7] particularly difficult disclosure problems can arise in connection with an initial public offering of a company with substantial preexisting shareholders even where those shares are not to be offered in connection with the registered offering. By virtue of Rule 144,[8] it is possible that there will be a substantial influx of these shares into the market upon the expiration of ninety days following the public offering.[9] In such a case,

---

4. 19 S.E.C. at 652.

5. *See* Regulation S–K items 502–503, 17 C.F.R. §§ 224.502–503. *See generally* 17 C.F.R. § 231.4936 (1982) (rescinded March 3, 1982). In Sec.Act Rel. No. 33–6332 (August 6, 1981) the SEC proposed to eliminate the Guides for the Preparation and Filing of Registration Statements and Reports, with limited exceptions. These guides have been replaced by Regulation S–K. Sec.Act Rel. No. 33–6384 (March 3, 1982).

6. 19 S.E.C. at 653.

7. *See* § 4.25 *infra.*

8. 17 C.F.R. § 230.144. *See* § 4.26 *infra.*

9. After there has been a registered public offering, the issuer becomes subject to the 1934 Act periodic reporting requirements. Section 15(d) of the 1934 Act, 15 U.S.C.A. § 78o(d). *See* § 9.3 *infra.* Once this information has been available for ninety days unregistered securities may be sold. Rule 144(e) permits, within a three month period, public sales of unregistered securities of up to the greater of one percent of the outstanding securities or the average weekly reported trading volume. Rule 144(c) contains the informational requirements.

the 1933 Act registration statement must adequately disclose the possibility of these sales and the downward price pressure that could result.[10]

In the course of the *Universal Camera* opinion, the Commission explicitly called for plainly phrased statements as opposed to elaborate and hence more technical prose. This 1948 opinion marked the beginning of an SEC impetus for readable prospectuses in order to make them understandable to less sophisticated investors.[11] The Commission is not alone in this concern as courts have also recognized the necessity to use simple language.[12]

In addition to the misstatements and omissions relating to the issuer's financial structure and the impact of the offering upon the issuer's capital structure, Universal Camera's registration statement was further woefully deficient with regard to the description of the corporation's business. In the period immediately preceding the filing of Universal Camera's registration statement, the issuer had received the bulk of its profits from government war-related contracts for the sale of binoculars. Clearly this enterprise was not likely to continue after the war and the registration statement did not sufficiently disclose the company's pre-war activities nor its post-war plans. The registration statement simply talked in terms of "designing and preparing improved and additional photographic products which would find a ready sale" without discussing or describing in detail the nature of such products. The Commission held that this was a significant deficiency in the registration statement, especially in light of the express requirements of the registration form that was used for the filing and which called for detailed disclosure.[13] In the course of the proceedings the issuer agreed to amend the registration statement so as to cure its deficiencies, and accordingly the SEC in the exercise of its power to award relief in the public interest, dismissed the Commission proceedings.

The *Universal Camera* decision is instructive on a number of sensitive disclosure problems. It highlights the importance of describing the specific use to be made of the proceeds, especially with regard to a

---

10. Furthermore, it is conceivable that if there is a substantial volume of these unregistered secondary sales, they might be integrated into the initial offering even though they fall within Rule 144(e)'s volume limitations. The integration doctrine is discussed in § 4.29 *infra*.

11. *See generally* Regulation S–K, 17 C.F.R. §§ 229.01 *et seq.*

12. *See, e.g.,* Feit v. Leasco Data Processing Equipment Corp., 332 F.Supp. 544, 549 (E.D.N.Y.1971) ("Using a statement to obscure, rather than reveal, in plain English, the critical elements of a proposed business deal cannot be countenanced under the securities regulation acts * * *. The prospective purchaser of a new issue of securities is entitled to know what the deal is all about. Given an honest and open statement, adequately warning of the possibilities of error and miscalculation and not designed for puffing, an outsider and the insider are placed on more equal grounds for arms length dealing. Such equalization of bargaining power through sharing of knowledge in the securities market is a basic national policy underlying the federal securities laws.") *But c.f.* Wielgos v. Commonwealth Edison Co., 892 F.2d 509 (7th Cir.1989) (focusing on sophisticated analysts as the audience for a Form S–3 prospectus) which is discussed in § 3.6 *supra*.

13. 19 S.E.C. at 655.

secondary offering that accompanies a primary one. The opinion further stresses the necessity to use identifying statements such as the legend required for speculative issues to alert the reader to risky aspects of the offering. Finally, the issuer must clearly disclose the nature of its business, both in terms of the past and also with regard to future plans. The registration materials must be especially descriptive where the issuer's business is cyclical or unusually dependent upon external events. Similarly, effects of costs of compliance with regulatory requirements of environmental protection laws must also be adequately disclosed.[14]

One further noteworthy aspect of the *Universal Camera* decision is the fact that, in the course of its opinion, the SEC emphasized that "it is not this Commission's function under the Securities Act to approve or disapprove securities * * *. The Act leaves it to the investor, on the basis of the facts disclosed, to weigh the earning prospects of a registered security against the risks involved and to judge for himself whether he wishes to invest his money in it." [15] This accurately sets forth the direct impact of the 1933 Act. However, the indirect effects of full disclosure cannot be ignored. Detailed disclosures may make a particular offering so unsalable as to have the effect of precluding a public sale. This type of merit scrutiny can be achieved directly under the state securities laws that permit a merit analysis of the securities in registration.[16]

Transactions of Controlling Persons

A second instructive opinion is found in the 1964 SEC decision of In the Matter of Franchard Corp.[17] The issuer was a real estate development syndication managed by Mr. Glickman who was the principal owner and manager of the development project. The issuer undertook a series of public offerings. All prospectuses properly showed that Glickman owned most of the Class B and a major portion of the Class A stock. However, they failed to disclose that during the period of these offerings all of his Class B and most of his Class A stock had been pledged to banks for loans totaling four and one-quarter million dollars at interest rates up to twenty-four percent. Notwithstanding the pledges, Glickman retained his voting rights in the stock. The issue before the Commission was whether these loans to the major shareholder and manager of the enterprise ought to have been disclosed. The applicable forms for filing of the registration statement expressly provide for the disclosure of all material transactions between the issuer, its affiliates and management.[18] It was at least arguable that the pledges of stock in question were not subject to such provisions since these were not

---

14. *See, e.g.,* Levine v. NL Industries, Inc., 926 F.2d 199 (2d Cir.1991) (disclosure of environmental compliance costs; action under Exchange Act Rule 10b–5).

15. *Id.* at 656, 657.

16. *See, e.g.,* Uniform Securities Act § 304; chapter 8 *infra*.

17. 42 S.E.C. 163 (SEC 1964).

18. *See* Schedule A item (14); Form S–1 item 17; Form S–2 item 12.

transactions between Glickman and the issuer but rather were between Glickman and a bank that was not affiliated with the issuer.[19] However, the Commission pointed out that an investor's evaluation of management is an important part of any investment decision, especially in a business such as real estate syndication in which the management's know-how is the primary asset of the enterprise. Thus, any facts which would be likely to indicate a possible change of management would be material to the reasonable investor. The Commission concluded that disclosure of the secured loans was necessary because it would put the investor on notice that Glickman's interest in the company might be foreclosed upon, and that the corporation's management would change as a result. In the course of its opinion in *Franchard*, the Commission also highlighted the importance of adequately disclosing questionable activities by management. Questionable dealings by management can bear upon the issue of management integrity generally, which, of course, may be a valid investor concern.

The precise limits of the *Franchard* decision's rationale are not self-evident. The decision raises questions as to the materiality of disclosures relating to the personal aspects of the lives and dealings of key personnel. It is relatively evident that Glickman's crucial position in running the enterprise made his high risk personal financial transactions material to prospective investors. On the other hand, there are many companies which are dependent upon one or a few key executives who may be undergoing changes or pressures in their personal lives that might bear upon their management ability. At what point do these factors become material? For example, must it be disclosed that a corporate chief executive officer is in ill health? Is it a material fact that a major corporate executive is under psychiatric care and potentially suicidal?[20] Is it relevant that a corporate executive is in the midst of a harrowing divorce and suffering severe depression which might interfere with his or her management ability? Clearly, at some point such information becomes more personal to the executive than useful to the investing public. But it is equally clear that an attorney preparing a registration statement has no bright line tests regarding which aspects of a key executive's personal life will be deemed material for disclosure purposes. When an executive's personal dealings affect the issuer's business or at least present a strong potential for doing so, the materiality threshold may be reached and therefore disclosure will probably be necessary.

---

19. Glickman, who was president of the company, had also taken personal loans from the issuer and its affiliates. These loans clearly should have been disclosed as transactions with the issuer. *Id.*

20. Over the years corporate related suicides have, unfortunately, been in the news. For example the suicide of United Brands' president triggered an SEC investigation which unveiled substantial violations of the Foreign Corrupt Practices Act. Also, an airline C.E.O. shot himself in the head upon learning that his defensive tactics had been thwarted and his company was about to be taken over. *See* "Airline Tragedy: Continental Loses its Chief," 104 Fortune 7 (September 7, 1981).

There are two other decisions that deserve mention in this discussion of transactions by controlling persons. In one case[21] the registration statement was claimed to have been materially misleading because it failed to disclose that two major shareholders intended to dispose of their holdings shortly after the public offering. These transactions amounted to twenty-five percent of the number of shares covered by the registration statement but only four percent of the total stock that was outstanding after the offering. The federal district court held that there was a triable issue of fact as to the materiality of the alleged omission and accordingly refused to dismiss the complaint. In another case[22] the registration statement disclosed the sale of one hundred and twenty thousand shares in a private placement that had taken place two years earlier. It was further stated that those private placement purchasers had agreed not to dispose of their shares in a transaction that would constitute a public distribution unless a registration statement covering such sales had become effective. Shortly after an unrelated registered offering, these private placement purchasers sold a total of seven thousand shares without filing a registration statement and in reliance upon the exemption provided in SEC Rule 144.[23] The plaintiff alleged that these sales were contrary to the disclosures in the registration statement, and, since they had been intended all along, rendered the registration statement materially misleading. The plaintiff further claimed that although the unregistered sales may have been in compliance with Rule 144, they depressed the market price of the plaintiff's stock that had been purchased during the primary offering and thus that failure to have described this predictable impact was a material omission. The court, agreeing with the plaintiff, held that the registration statement was misleading in failing to adequately describe Rule 144 and its exemption from the registration requirements of section 5. A fair description of the effects under Rule 144 would have put the investor on notice of the possibility of insider sales that would not need to be registered and might also have an adverse effect on the market price.

The foregoing cases are illustrative of sensitive disclosure problems that may arise in connection with a registered offering. Counsel must be particularly mindful of these problems in making the pre-filing investigation into the issuer and the circumstances surrounding the offering.[24]

---

21. Birdman v. Electro–Catheter Corp., 352 F.Supp. 1271 (E.D.Pa.1973).

22. Langert v. Q–1 Corp., 1974 WL 377, [1973–1974 Transfer Binder] Fed.Sec.L.Rep. ¶ 94,445 (S.D.N.Y.1974).

23. 17 C.F.R. § 230.144. *See* § 4.26 *infra.*

24. Preparation of the registration statement is discussed in § 3.1 *supra.*

An example of the SEC's expansive view is the expansion of disclosures relating to legal proceedings against officers and directors so that they now apply equally to control persons and promoters. Sec. Act Rel. No. 33–6530, [1984 Transfer Binder] Fed.Sec.L.Rep. (CCH) ¶ 83,615 (May 2, 1984) (proposed amendments to Regulation S–K, item 401). These changes were adopted essentially as proposed. Sec. Act Rel. No. 33–6545 [1984 Transfer Binder] Fed.Sec.L.Rep. ¶ 83,652 (Aug. 19, 1984).

In Regulations S–K and S–B[25] the Commission gives specific guidelines on how to disclose various types of information; these guides apply to both 1933 Act and 1934 Act disclosures. In addition, the SEC will, on occasion, identify specific problem areas. Consistent with the Commission's effort to identify potential trouble spots in the disclosure process, the SEC has adopted guidelines for disclosure of special risks associated with an issuer's repurchase (REPO) and reverse repurchase (reverse REPO) agreements covering securities or other assets.[26] Special disclosures regarding REPO and reverse REPO agreements are required when the market value of the securities or assets in question exceeds ten percent of the value of the issuer's total assets.[27]

Projections and Soft Information

At one time the SEC objected to the use of favorable projections and other "soft" information in disclosure documents on the ground that investors would likely be misled.[28] This policy came under much criticism.[29] The Commission reconsidered its policies[30] and now not only permits but encourages, and in some cases mandates the use of non-misleading projections by certain issuers.[31] SEC Rule 175[32] (applicable to

25. Regulation S–K is the generic, long-form version of the disclosure guides. 17 C.F.R. § 229.10 *et seq.*, 7 Fed. Sec. L. Rep. (CCH) ¶¶ 71,001 *et seq.* Regulation S–B is a simplified version which is available to small business issuers. 17 C.F.R. § 228.10 *et seq.*, 7 Fed. Sec. L. Rep. (CCH) ¶¶ 70,701 *et seq.* A small business issuer is a United States or Canadian company with annual revenues of less than $25,000,000. If the company is a majority owned subsidiary then the parent must also be a small business issuer in order to qualify. Investment companies do not qualify as small business issuers. Reg. S–B, Item 10(a)(1). 17 C.F.R. §§ 229.10–229.802.

26. Reg. S–X, item 501.07, adopted in Sec. Act Rel. 33–6621, Fin.Rep.Rel. No. 24, 6 Fed.Sec.L.Rep. (CCH) ¶ 72,424 (Jan. 22, 1986).

27. Reg. S–X, item 501.07.

28. *See* Carl W. Schneider, Nits, Grits, and Soft Information in SEC Filings, 121 U.Pa.L.Rev. 254 (1972). *Cf.* Goldman v. Belden, 580 F.Supp. 1373 (W.D.N.Y.1984), *judgment vacated* 754 F.2d 1059 (2d Cir.1985) ("faulty economic prognostication" did not violate antifraud provisions).

The Commission took the view that material unfavorable projections need be disclosed while favorable projections should not be contained in disclosure documents. This asymmetrical view was changed in Rule 175. 17 C.F.R. § 230.175.

29. *E.g.*, Bruce A. Mann, Prospectuses: Unreadable or Just Unread?—A Proposal to Reexamine Policies Against Permitting Projections, 40 Geo.Wash.L.Rev. 222 (1971).

30. *See* Sec.Act Rel. No. 33–5992 (Nov. 7, 1978; rescinded in Sec.Act Rel. No. 33–6384 (March 3, 1982)). (Guides for disclosure of future economic performance). *See also* Note, Disclosure of Future–Oriented Information Under Securities Laws, 88 Yale L.J. 338 (1978).

31. Victor Brudney, A Note on Materiality and Soft Information Under the Federal Securities Laws, 75 Va.L.Rev. 723 (1989); Carl W. Schneider, Soft Disclosure; Thrusts and Parries When Bad News Follows Optimistic Statements, 26 Rev.Sec. & Commod.Reg. 33 (1993). *See also, e.g.*, Joseph W. Bartlett & J. David Waldman, Select Problems in Late–Round Private Financings: Soft Information; Integration; Debt vs. Equity, 17 Sec.Reg.L.J. 227 (1989). *See also, e.g.*, Note, The SEC Safe Harbor Forecasts—A Step in the Right Direction?, 1980 Duke L.J. 607. *See also* Note, Mandatory Disclosure of Corporate Projections and The Goals of Securities Regulation, 81 Colum.L.Rev. 1525 (1981).

Current Commission policy goes beyond merely encouraging projections. Thus, for example, in Management Discussion and Analysis of Financial Condition, 1934 Act reporting issuers are told to disclose on a quarterly basis, "known trends" that are reasonably likely to affect earnings, revenues, liquidity, and other matters relating to the issuer's financial condition. *See* 17 C.F.R. § 229.303(a).

32. 17 C.F.R. § 230.175.

1933 Act disclosures) and Rule 3b–6[33] (applicable to 1934 Act disclosures) provide a safe harbor for projections by 1934 Act reporting companies[34] and for similar disclosures made in the 1933 Act registration statements.[35] These rules provide that there is no liability for "forward-looking statements"[36] unless the issuer made or reaffirmed such a statement without a reasonable basis or unless the disclosure was not made in good faith.[37] Thus, a good faith statement of present intent does not become actionable simply because of a change of intent;[38] however, the change of intent which makes the previous statement no longer accurate will give rise to an obligation to give timely notice of that change by making a corrective disclosure.[39]

The fact that a projection turns out not to be realized does not,

---

33. *See, e.g.,* Peregrine Options, Inc. v. Farley, Inc., 1993 WL 489739, [1994–1995 Transfer Binder] Fed. Sec. L. Rep. (CCH) ¶ 98,313 (N.D.Ill.1993) (statement by tender offeror that second-step merger would occur "as soon as practicable" would be outside of safe harbor if not reasonable when made).

34. *See* 15 U.S.C.A. §§ 78g, 78m(a), 78o(d) which are discussed in § 9.2 *infra.*

The SEC is considering revising its safe harbor for forward-looking statements. Accordingly, the Commission has issued a comment release and has sought public comment. *See* SEC Concept Release on Safe Harbor for Forward–Looking Statements, Sec. Act Rel. No. 33–7101, [1994–1995 Transfer Binder] Fed. Sec. L. Rep. (CCH) ¶ 85,436, 26 Sec. Reg. & L. Rep. (BNA) 1405 (Oct. 13, 1994).

35. In the Spring of 1994, the SEC announced its intention to consider fleshing out the safe harbor provided in these rules. The decision to consider amending the rules presumably was in response to concerns that the safe harbors did not provide as much of a bright-line test as filers and securities lawyers would like.

36. Forward-looking statements are defined as:

(1) A statement containing a projection of revenues, income (loss), earnings (loss) per share, capital expenditures, dividends, capital structure or other financial items;

(2) A statement of management's plans and objectives for future operations;

(3) A statement of future economic performance contained in management's discussion and analysis of financial condition and results of operations included pursuant to Item 303 of Regulation S–K; or

(4) Disclosed statements of the assumptions underlying or relating to any of the statements described in paragraphs (c)(1), (2), or (3) above. 17 C.F.R. § 230.175(c).

The Rule does not require projections of future performance. *See* Rubin v. Long Island Lighting Co., 576 F.Supp. 608 (E.D.N.Y.1984); Caspary v. Louisiana Land & Exploration Co., 579 F.Supp. 1105 (S.D.N.Y.1983), *judgment affirmed* 725 F.2d 189 (2d Cir.1984) (decided in connection with proxy solicitation). *See also* footnotes 48–49 *infra* for the distinction accountants make between projections and forecasts.

37. 17 C.F.R. § 230.175(a). *See, e.g.,* Wielgos v. Commonwealth Edison Co., 892 F.2d 509 (7th Cir.1989), *affirming* 688 F.Supp. 331 (N.D.Ill.1988); *See also, e.g.,* Roots Partnership v. Lands' End, Inc., 965 F.2d 1411 (7th Cir.1992).

38. In re Phillips Petroleum Securities Litigation, 881 F.2d 1236, 1245 (3d Cir.1989), *on remand* 738 F.Supp. 825 (D.Del.1990).

39. *Id. See also, e.g.,* 5A Arnold Jacobs, Litigation and Practice Under Rule 10b–5 § 61.01[c][iii] at 3–68—3–70 (2d ed. 1988). *Cf.* Backman v. Polaroid Corp., 893 F.2d 1405 (1st Cir.1990) (although not initially misleading, subsequent developments triggered a duty to correct overly optimistic predictions); Kirby v. Cullinet Software, Inc., 721 F.Supp. 1444 (D.Mass.1989) (duty to correct first quarter projection). *See generally* Carl W. Schneider, Update on the Duty to Update: Did Polaroid Produce the Instant Movie After All?, 23 Rev.Sec. & Commod.Reg. 83 (1990).

without more, give rise to an action under the securities laws.[40]   Many courts have indicated that they will tolerate a certain amount of sales puffery to the extent that reliance on such statements would not be reasonable.[41]   However, nondisclosure that in the past there had been a repeated failure to meet projected performance may be actionable.[42] Similarly, a projection that is inconsistent with undisclosed facts will be actionable.[43]   However, when the forecast is consistent with past performance, no action will lie.[44]   Nor will a projection turn out to be actionable when the alleged undisclosed facts were not material.[45]

Overly optimistic projections can, of course, form the basis of a private civil action by purchasers injured by materially misleading statements.[46]   Similarly, forward looking statements which fail to include projected losses may be materially misleading.[47]   Nevertheless, following the rules established under the common law of fraud, a mere projection,[48] forecast,[49] or prediction of future events is not actionable.[50]   How-

---

40.   *See, e.g.,* Hillson Partners Limited Partnership v. Adage, Inc., 42 F.3d 204 (4th Cir. 1994) (allegations were not sufficient; the complaint must set forth with specificity the reason why the discrepancy between the projections and the actual performance constituted fraud); Kowal v. MCI Communications Corp., 16 F.3d 1271 (D.C.Cir.1994) (failure to adequately allege that projections which turned out to be overly optimistic had not been made in good faith).

41.   *E.g.,* Marion Merrell Dow, Inc., 1994 WL 396187, [1994–1995 Transfer Binder] Fed. Sec. L. Rep. (CCH) ¶ 98,357 (W.D.Mo.1994) (projection that company was looking forward to growth in earnings per share were "vague soft puffing statements" that could not have been reasonably relied upon as a guarantee).   *See* the discussion of materiality in § 13.5A *infra.*

42.   *See* Schwartz v. Michaels, 1992 WL 38294, [1992–1993 Transfer Binder] Fed.Sec. L.Rep. (CCH) ¶ 97,259 (S.D.N.Y.1992).

43.   *E.g.,* Malone v. Microdyne Corp., 26 F.3d 471 (4th Cir.1994); In re Applied Magnetics Corp. Securities Litigation, 1994 WL 486550 [1994–1995 Transfer Binder] Fed. Sec. L. Rep. (CCH) ¶ 98,345 (C.D.Cal.1994) (optimistic statements were actionable in light of allegations that management knew company's technology was obsolete).

44.   *E.g.,* Bentley v. Legent Corp., 849 F.Supp. 429 (E.D.Va.1994) (statements that operations were "on plan" or "on target" were not actionable).

45.   *E.g.,* Marion Merrell Dow, Inc., 1994 WL 396187, [1994–1995 Transfer Binder] Fed. Sec. L. Rep. (CCH) ¶ 98,357 (W.D.Mo.1994) (undisclosed facts relating to currency fluctuations, increased competition, and government regulation were in the public domain and were not the type of firm–specific information that need be disclosed in connection with growth projections).

46.   Goldman v. Belden, 754 F.2d 1059 (2d Cir.1985); Eisenberg v. Gagnon, 766 F.2d 770 (3d Cir.1985), *cert. denied* 474 U.S. 946, 106 S.Ct. 342, 88 L.Ed.2d 290 (1985); In re Washington Public Power Supply System Securities Litigation, 650 F.Supp. 1346 (W.D.Wash.1986).

47.   C.E. Carlson, Inc. v. SEC, 859 F.2d 1429 (10th Cir.1988) (affirming denial of summary judgment for defendant); Froid v. Berner, 649 F.Supp. 1418 (D.N.J.1986) (insider trading case).   *But see* Walker v. Action Indus., Inc., 802 F.2d 703 (4th Cir.1986), *cert. denied* 479 U.S. 1065, 107 S.Ct. 952, 93 L.Ed.2d 1000 (1987), *rehearing denied* 480 U.S. 926, 107 S.Ct. 1389, 94 L.Ed.2d 703 (1987) (no duty to disclose financial projections in tender offer statements or press release).

48.   According to the American Institute of Certified Public Accountants, financial projections deal with financial position, results of operations, and changes in financial position that are based on "knowledge and belief, given one or more hypothetical assumptions."   AICPA Financial Forecasts and Projections Task Force, Guide For Prospective Financial Statements 12.   Projections, thus, set forth one or more possible scenarios of future performance.

---

49.   See notes 49 and 50 on page 154.

ever, when the incorrect prediction implies the presence of facts which do not exist, then an action will lie for misrepresentation.[51]

Absent a specific line item disclosure requirement or the impetus of the Management Discussion and Analysis,[52] there is no requirement that management make projections or predictions.[53] The fact that management has made internal projections and even has made confidential projections to entities outside the corporation does not in itself trigger a duty of public disclosure.[54] A company is thus not subject to a public disclosure requirement simply because it made some private projections.[55] The court went on to point out, that the nondisclosure to the public of projections might have been actionable had the projections been "based upon existing negative factors that were known only to the company." [56] A fiduciary duty based on state law may create a duty to disclose internal projections but only if they can be deemed material.[57] The rule thus remains that in many instances the decision to make public projections is a voluntary one.

Management Discussion and Analysis

In addition to these voluntary projections, an issuer must disclose in the registration statement material changes in financial condition and

---

49. In contrast to financial projections, financial forecasts are based on actual expectations rather than upon hypothetical assumptions but reflect "to the best of the responsible party's knowledge and belief, an entity's expected financial position, results of operations, and changes in financial position" based on "assumptions reflecting conditions it expects to exist and the course of action it expects to take." *Id.* at 11.

50. *E.g.,* Hillson Partners L.P. v. Adage, Inc., 42 F.3d 204 (4th Cir.1994) (Chief executive officer's statements in press release that the year would produce "excellent" results were merely predictions and thus not actionable misrepresentations of fact); In re Crystal Brands Securities Litigation, 862 F.Supp. 745 (D.Conn.1994) (disclosure of liquidity crisis did not create inference that earlier optimistic predictions were fraudulent).

51. *E.g.* Hanon v. Dataproducts Corp., 976 F.2d 497 (9th Cir.1992) (summary judgment was inappropriate since a factual issue existed as to whether company's optimistic statements about new product were made at a time when it was known that the product could not be made reliably).

52. Item 303 of Regulation S–K requires management to give certain projections with regard to known material adverse or favorable trends in operations and financial condition. *See, e.g.,* Mark S. Croft, MD & A: The Tightrope of disclosure, 45 S.C. L. Rev. 477 (1994). *See also* Appendix A (Practitioner's Edition only).

53. *See, e.g.,* Proxima Corp. Securities Litigation, 1994 WL 374306, [1993–1994 Transfer Binder] Fed. Sec. L. Rep. (CCH) ¶ 98,236 (S.D.Cal.1994).

54. Levit v. Lyondell Petrochemical Co., 984 F.2d 1050 (9th Cir.1993). *See also, e.g.,* In re Convergent Technologies Securities Litigation, 948 F.2d 507 (9th Cir.1991) (failure to give detailed internal projections about new product line was not actionable); In re Compaq Securities Litigation, 848 F.Supp. 1307 (S.D.Tex.1993) (no duty to disclose management's internal consideration of effects of general economic conditions).

55. Levit v. Lyondell Petrochemical Co., 984 F.2d 1050 (9th Cir.1993). *Accord* Walter v. Holiday Inns, Inc., 985 F.2d 1232 (3d Cir.1993). *But cf.* Schwartz v. System Software Associates, Inc., 813 F.Supp. 1364 (N.D.Ill.1993) (undisclosed internal written forecasts could demonstrate that public disclosures were materially misleading).

56. 984 F.2d at 1053.

57. Walter v. Holiday Inns, Inc., 985 F.2d 1232 (3d Cir.1993) (partnership's failure to make internal projections known was not a breach of fiduciary duty since the projections were not actionable).

operations that are expected to take place as a result of the financing to be raised by the offering covered by the 1933 Act registration.[58] Similarly, soft information relating to asset valuations may be mandated material disclosures under the Securities Exchange Act of 1934.[59] Even more striking is the soft information required by item 303 of Regulation S–K in the course of its Management Discussion and Analysis (MD & A) of financial condition and report of operations, requiring management to disclose and discuss both adverse and favorable trends and uncertainties.[60] The MD & A disclosures focus not only on current operations but also on management's plans for the future. The SEC has taken a vigorous stance on these MD & A disclosures.[61] On appropriate facts, inadequate MD & A disclosures will give rise to liability.[62] Although item 303 requires disclosure of "known trends or uncertainties," it does not alter the basic rule that projections are not required. Thus, a failure to make a projection is not actionable unless there is a nondisclosure of facts or known trends that were "known only to the company." [63] Similarly, in contrast to the MD & A mandate that management make timely disclosure of known trends, it is clear that standing alone there is no duty to disclose internal projections of future performance.[64] On the other hand, disclosure would be required if the internal projections were sufficiently convincing to rise to the level of a trend.

---

58. Regulation S–K, item 303, 17 C.F.R. § 229.303. In general, projection of future earnings and/or dividends is not mandatory. *See also, e.g.,* Alfus v. Pyramid Technology Corp., 745 F.Supp. 1511 (N.D.Cal.1990) (the cases "clearly" state that Rule 10b–5 does not require financial projections; item 303 of Reg. S–K applies to annual reports and not to other methods of disclosure such as a press release).

59. Flynn v. Bass Brothers Enterprises, Inc., 744 F.2d 978 (3d Cir.1984) (section 14(e) of the Williams Act requires disclosure of material asset valuations given in the course of a tender offer; fact that valuations were not prepared by experts precluded a finding of materiality). *Contra* Starkman v. Marathon Oil Co., 772 F.2d 231 (6th Cir.1985), *cert. denied* 475 U.S. 1015, 106 S.Ct. 1195, 89 L.Ed.2d 310 (1986) (valuations based on highly speculative assumptions need not be disclosed); Rice v. Hamilton Oil Corp., 658 F.Supp. 446 (D.Colo.1987) (forecasts need not be disclosed when not based on proven oil and gas reserves). *See* §§ 11.15, 13.5 *infra. See also, e.g.,* Arazie v. Mullane, 2 F.3d 1456 (7th Cir.1993) (optimistic statements about future performance were protected by Rule 3b–6's safe harbor and thus were not actionable). *Compare* Walker v. Action Industries, Inc., 802 F.2d 703 (4th Cir.1986), *cert. denied* 479 U.S. 1065, 107 S.Ct. 952, 93 L.Ed.2d 1000 (1987) (financial projections need not be disclosed in press release); Howing Co. v. Nationwide Corp., 625 F.Supp. 146 (S.D.Ohio 1985), *judgment reversed* 826 F.2d 1470 (6th Cir.1987) (disclosure of earnings projections was soft information and thus disclosure was not required under the proxy Rules of the Exchange Act). *See* §§ 11.4, 13.5 *infra.*

60. *E.g.,* Form S–1, Item 11(h); Form SB–2, Item 17. *See* Management Discussion and Analysis of Financial Condition, Sec. Act Rel. No. 33–6835 (SEC May 18, 1989) which appears in Appendix A to the main volume (Vol. 2).

61. *See* In re Caterpillar, Inc. Exch. Act Rel. No. 34–30532, 6 Fed.Sec.L.Rep. (CCH) ¶ 73,829 (SEC March 31, 1992) (settlement order involving MD & A analysis and failure to adequately discuss the possible risk of lower earnings in the future).

62. *Compare Caterpillar,* footnote 61 *supra with* Ferber v. Travelers Corp., 802 F.Supp. 698 (D.Conn.1992) (finding adequate discussion in MD & A of "known trends" and "uncertainties" relating to problems with issuer's real estate portfolios).

63. Levit v. Lyondell Petrochemical Co., 984 F.2d 1050, 1053 (9th Cir.1993), relying in part on In re Convergent Technologies Securities Litigation, 948 F.2d 507, 516 (9th Cir.1991).

64. In re VeriFone Securities Litigation, 11 F.3d 865 (9th Cir.1993).

The line between those disclosures which are required and those which may be avoided is far from a clear one. It has been suggested that some learning may be drawn from the distinction that accountants draw between a projection[65] (defined as extrapolation from existing data) and a forecast[66] (an appraisal of what is reasonably likely to occur in the future).[67]

When an issuer of securities elects to make forward looking statements containing predictions and/or projections, the door has at least been opened for potential liability resulting from materially misleading statements. It has thus been held that neither section 11 of the Securities Act of 1933[68] nor Exchange Act Rule 10b–5[69] exempts predictions from its reach.[70]

What Constitutes Adequate Disclosure?

In framing disclosure documents, it is not necessary to attempt to predict the future.[71] Accordingly, it was not actionable to fail to speculate that investigations which had been disclosed would likely lead to indictments of the corporation and its chief officer.[72] In what may prove to be a very influential opinion, the Seventh Circuit in Wielgos v. Commonwealth Edison Co.[73] found that erroneous statements concerning cost estimates and start-up times for nuclear power plants were within Rule 175(a)'s safe harbor for forward looking statements.[74] The decision makes it clear that the rule protects erroneous projections so long as they are made in good faith and can be said to have been made upon a reasonable basis.[75] In other words, the fact that a prediction of the future turns out to be wrong does not mean that it was untrue at the

---

65. *See* footnote 48 *supra.*

66. *See* footnote 49 *supra.*

67. Remarks of Professor Ted J. Fiflis at Securities Law for NonSecurities Lawyers (Charleston, S.C. June 3, 1994).

68. 15 U.S.C.A. § 77k. *See* §§ 7.3–7.4 *infra.*

69. 17 C.F.R. § 240.10b–5. *See* §§ 13.2–13.6 *infra.*

70. Isquith v. Middle South Utilities, Inc., 847 F.2d 186 (5th Cir.1988), *cert. denied* 488 U.S. 926, 109 S.Ct. 310, 102 L.Ed.2d 329 (1988).

71. *E.g.,* In re Quarterdeck Office Systems, Inc. Securities Litigation, 1992 WL 515347, [1992–1993 Transfer Binder] Fed.Sec.L.Rep. (CCH) ¶ 97,646 (C.D.Cal.1992) (nondisclosure of adverse sales trends was not actionable absent allegation that issuer had knowledge of those trends prior to press release).

72. Ballan v. Wilfred American Educational Corp., 720 F.Supp. 241, 248 (E.D.N.Y. 1989). *Accord,* In re Par Pharmaceutical, Inc. Securities Litigation, 733 F.Supp. 668 (S.D.N.Y.1990). *See also, e.g.,* Levit v. Lyondell Petrochemical Co., 984 F.2d 1050 (9th Cir.1993); In re Convergent Technologies Securities Litigation, 948 F.2d 507 (9th Cir.1991) (failure to give detailed internal projections about new product line was not actionable).

73. 892 F.2d 509 (7th Cir.1989).

74. The 1934 Act has a counterpart safe harbor for projections in Rule 3b–6. *See, e.g.,* Arazie v. Mullane, 2 F.3d 1456 (7th Cir.1993) (holding that optimistic statements about future performance were protected by the safe harbor and thus were not actionable); Warshaw v. Xoma Corp., 856 F.Supp. 561 (N.D.Cal.1994) (general optimism regarding FDA approval of new drug was not actionable).

75. 892 F.2d at 511–12. *Accord* Krim v. BancTexas Group, Inc., 989 F.2d 1435, 1446 (5th Cir.1993).

time it was made.[76] For example, optimistic statements of management's ability to deal with competitive factors will not in themselves be actionable.[77] Along the same lines, the mere fact that a prediction was confusing does not render it materially misleading.[78]

The court in *Wielgos* pointed out that it is not necessary to disclose the underlying assumptions and further that the assumptions may have been "poor" in that they assumed nothing would go wrong. Nevertheless, since the assumptions were based on past experience, the good faith requirement had been satisfied. The court further pointed out that the investing public must have been on notice of the precarious nature of projections when dealing with nuclear power plants and the risks of failing to secure necessary regulatory clearance.

The Bespeaks Caution Doctrine

As discussed above, the essence of liability for materially misleading projections is not that the prediction did not prove accurate but rather that the investor has been misled as to the reliability of the projections. Thus, it is beyond question that under appropriate circumstances, warnings and disclaimers can limit investors' ability to reasonably rely on projections of future earnings.[79] A number of courts have adopted what is sometimes referred to as the "bespeaks caution" doctrine.[80] The doctrine holds that sufficient cautionary language may preclude misstatements from being actionable.[81] The doctrine, which may only be applicable in cases involving projections or other estimates,[82] relates to

---

76. Daisy Systems Corp. v. Finegold, 1988 WL 166235, [1989 Transfer Binder] Fed.Sec. L.Rep. ¶ 94,520 (N.D.Cal.1988). *See, e.g.,* VT Investors v. R & D Funding Corp., 733 F.Supp. 823 (D.N.J.1990) (opinion and prediction about the likelihood of finding an acquirer for the business was not unreasonable, had a sound basis, and thus was not actionable). *See also* the authorities in footnote 40 *supra.*

77. In re Software Publishing Securities Litigation, 1994 WL 261365, [1993–1994 Transfer Binder] Fed. Sec. L. Rep. (CCH) ¶ 98,094 (N.D.Cal.1994). *Cf.* O'Sullivan v. Trident Microsystems, Inc., 1994 WL 124453 [1993–1994 Transfer Binder] Fed. Sec. L. Rep. (CCH) ¶ 98,116 (N.D.Cal.1994) (not actionable to fail to explain in detail the elementary economic principle that increased competition could have an adverse effect on the company's profits).

78. *See, e.g.,* Rand v. M/A–Com, Inc., 824 F.Supp. 242 (D.Mass.1993).

79. Friedman v. Arizona World Nurseries Ltd. Partnership, 730 F.Supp. 521 (S.D.N.Y. 1990).

80. For a discussion of the evolution of the doctrine, *see* In re Donald Trump Casino Securities Litigation, 793 F.Supp. 543 (D.N.J.1992), *affirmed* 7 F.3d 357 (3d Cir.1993).

See generally Donald C. Langevoort, Disclosures that "Bespeak Caution," 49 Bus. Law. 481 (1994). *See also* the discussion in §§ 13.5A, 13.5B *infra.*

81. *See, e.g.,* In re Donald J. Trump Casino Securities Litigation, 7 F.3d 357, 371 (3d Cir.1993):

when an offering document's forecasts, opinions or projections are accompanied by meaningful cautionary statements, the forward-looking statements will not form the basis for a securities fraud claim if those statements did not affect the "total mix" of information the document provided investors. In other words, cautionary language, if sufficient, renders the alleged omissions or misrepresentations immaterial as a matter of law.

82. *See, e.g.,* Anderson v. Clow, 1993 WL 497212, [1993 Transfer Binder] Fed. Sec. L. Rep. (CCH) ¶ 97,807 (S.D.Cal.1993). *See also, e.g.,* Kline v. First Western Government

materiality since it addresses the question of whether the misstatements are materially misleading when judged in light of the total mix of information available to the investor.[83] The bespeaks caution doctrine, which applies both to material misstatements and omissions in connection with projections and predictions,[84] should not be applied too quickly.[85] Cautionary language will not always be adequate to prevent an antifraud claim,[86] especially if it is generalized and boiler-plate.[87] Nor should the doctrine be applied if the falsity of the statements was known to the defendants at the time of the cautionary warnings.[88] In order for the bespeaks caution doctrine to justify the dismissal of fraud claims, the cautionary language must be sufficient to negate any reasonable reliance on predictions that may appear optimistic.[89]

Duty to Update and Correct

As discussed in a later section,[90] although there is no duty to disclose material information absent a line-item disclosure requirement, after there has been a disclosure, there is likely to be a duty to update or correct the information[91] should it become stale or inaccurate. Accordingly, once a company has made earnings (or other) projections, it has an obligation to make corrective disclosures when it becomes evident that

Securities, Inc., 24 F.3d 480 (3d Cir.1994) (refusing to apply bespeaks caution doctrine to claim based on affirmative misrepresentations in tax opinion).

83. *See, e.g.,* In re Donald J. Trump Casino Securities Litigation, 7 F.3d 357, 371 (3d Cir.1993); Sable v. Southmark/Envicon Capital Corp., 819 F.Supp. 324 (S.D.N.Y.1993) (bespeaks caution rationale applied).

84. *See, e.g.,* In re Donald J. Trump Casino Securities Litigation, 7 F.3d 357, 371 (3d Cir.1993).

85. *See, e.g.,* Langevoort *supra* footnote 80 at 503.

86. *E.g.,* Rubinstein v. Collins, 20 F.3d 160 (5th Cir.1994); Wade v. Industrial Funding Corp., 1993 WL 650837, [1993–1994 Transfer Binder] Fed. Sec. L. Rep. (CCH) ¶ 98,144 (N.D.Cal.1993); In re First American Center Securities Litigation, 807 F.Supp. 326 (S.D.N.Y.1992).

87. Rubinstein v. Collins, 20 F.3d 160 (5th Cir.1994); Wade v. Industrial Funding Corp., 1993 WL 650837, [1993–1994 Transfer Binder] Fed. Sec. L. Rep. (CCH) ¶ 98,144 (N.D.Cal.1993) (minimal boilerplate language did not provide a sufficient warning); In re Phar–Mor, Inc. Securities Litigation, 1993 WL 623308 [1993–1994 Transfer Binder] Fed. Sec. L. Rep. (CCH) ¶ 98,100 (W.D.Pa.1993) (generalized disclaimer language in offering materials did not sufficiently negate alleged misinformation in private placement memorandum).

88. *See* In re ZZZZ Best Securities Litigation, 864 F.Supp. 960 (C.D.Cal.1994).

89. *See, e.g.,* In re Phar–Mor, Inc. Litigation, 848 F.Supp. 46 (W.D.Pa.1993) (generalized disclaimer language in offering materials did not sufficiently negate alleged misinformation in private placement memorandum); In re Marion Merrell Dow, Inc. Securities Litigation, 1993 WL 393810, [1993 Transfer Binder] Fed. Sec. L. Rep. (CCH) ¶ 97,776 (W.D.Mo.1993) (the allegedly misleading statements did not contain warnings of specific risk factors).

90. *See* § 13.10 *infra.*

91. For a recent decision involving the duty to update, *see* In re Time Warner, Inc. Securities Litigation, 9 F.3d 259 (2d Cir.1993). The duty to correct misinformation does not apply, however, when the information came from a third party unrelated to the issuer. *See, e.g.,* Raab v. General Physics Corp., 4 F.3d 286, 288 (4th Cir.1993); Warshaw v. Xoma Corp., 856 F.Supp. 561 (N.D.Cal.1994).

the projections are inadequate.[92]

§ 3.8   Delayed and Continuous Offerings—Shelf Registrations

It is generally contemplated that the entire allotment of securities covered by a registered offering will be made available for purchase on the effective date. This is not always the case, however. For example, insiders, promoters or underwriters might receive securities directly from the issuer with an intent to resell at a later date.[1] Delayed offerings may also arise in connection with corporate acquisitions.[2] Also, in light of recent fluctuating interest rates, it may be desirable to get a debt offering all ready to go by filing the applicable registration statement but then wait for a propitious moment to finalize it and offer the securities for sale. These and other delayed offerings have led to what is known as shelf registration.[3] In a shelf registration the registration statement is filed but the securities are put on the shelf until the manner and date of the offering are determined.

For a long time the SEC took a dim view of shelf registrations, primarily because of the potential for misleading the investing public. Section 6(a) of the 1933 Act provides that a registration statement's effectiveness is limited to securities to be offered.[4] The Commission formerly adhered to the position that "it is misleading to include in a registration statement 'more securities than are presently intended to be offered, and thus give securities offered at some remote future date at least the appearance of a registered status.' "[5] Furthermore, there was concern that permitting delayed offerings would conflict with the thrust of the Securities Act; it, thus, had been observed that "[t]he fact that the time and manner of distribution is not presently determinable clashes with the theory that the registration statement must speak as of the date of its effectiveness."[6]

---

92. Kirby v. Cullinet Software, Inc., 721 F.Supp. 1444 (D.Mass.1989) (claim survived motion for summary judgment). *Accord* Backman v. Polaroid Corp., 893 F.2d 1405 (1st Cir.1990) (although not initially misleading, subsequent developments triggered a duty to correct overly optimistic predictions).

§ 3.8

1. *See generally* Symposium, Current Problems of Securities Underwriters and Dealers, 18 Bus.Law. 27, 44–55 (1962).

2. This may arise in a transaction when controlling persons of the acquired company receive securities of the acquiring corporation. Rule 145 governs such transactions and Form S–14 allows for delayed offerings under limited circumstances. *See* 17 C.F.R. § 230.145 which is discussed in § 5.2 *infra.*

3. *See generally* 1 Louis Loss, Securities Regulation 290–96 (2d Ed.1961); Scott Hodes, Shelf Registration: The Dilemma of the Securities and Exchange Commission, 49 Va. L.Rev. 1106 (1963); Shelf Registrations, 8 Rev.Sec. & Comm. Reg. 882 (1975).

4. 15 U.S.C.A. § 77f(a) ("A registration statement shall be deemed effective only as to the securities specified therein as proposed to be offered.").

5. Shawnee Chiles Syndicate, 10 S.E.C. 109, 113 (SEC 1941).

6. Richard W. Jennings & Harold Marsh, Jr., Securities Regulation: Cases and Materials 390 (5th ed. 1982).

Over time, much of the weight behind the foregoing objections has yielded to market realities coming from various constituents of the financial community; there was an increased call for the additional flexibility in financing that would result from allowing more shelf registrations. One reason that has been advanced is that shelf registrations will promote more competitive rates among underwriters as shelf registrations give issuers more negotiating room.[7] Additionally, shelf registrations have proved very helpful with debt offerings during periods of fluctuating interest rates.[8]

Through the early 1980s the Commission allowed shelf registrations only in a limited number of cases in which the offering plan was relatively definite and part of a larger offering.[9] In 1982, the Commission promulgated a shelf registration rule which was effective on an experimental basis until December, 1983.[10] In November 1983, the Commission decided that the experiment had been a success and adopted Rule 415, with some modification, on a permanent basis.[11] Except in certain circumstances (such as dividend reinvestment plans), shelf registration is not available to issuers which must use the long-form registration Form S–1 or even the abbreviated Form S–2 as opposed to the registration forms available for the most seasoned issuers.[12] Additional circumstances under which the less seasoned issuers may take advantage of shelf registration are set forth below. Shelf registration is available, without restriction on the circumstances surrounding the offering, to those more established issuers which qualify for short form registration

---

7. For a detailed discussion of the pros and cons, *see* Sec.Act Rel. No. 33–6423 (Sept. 2, 1982).

8. Issuers of debt securities who file shelf registrations are in a position to take advantage of favorable interest shifts in deciding the timing for their offerings.

Until 1992, when filing a shelf registration, issuers had to declare whether the offering would be debt or equity. This may have dissuaded many companies from taking advantage of the rule because of the effect that such an announcement might have on existing security prices. Now, however, it is no longer necessary to make such a declaration. Issuers using Form S–3 can file for the shelf and make the determination of the type of offering at the time it is decided to take the registration off the shelf and proceed. *See* Sec. Act Rel. No. 33–6964 (SEC Oct. 22, 1992) which amended Form S–3 to permit "unallocated shelf registration." In 1994, unallocated registration privileges were extended to foreign issuers using Form F–3. *See* Sec. Act Rel. No. 33–7053 (April 19, 1994).

9. Sec.Act Rel. No. 33–4936, Guides 4, 10, 36, 53 (Dec. 9, 1968) (rescinded). *See also* Form S–14.

10. 17 C.F.R. § 230.415 (1982). *See* Sec.Act Rel. No. 33–6423 (Sept. 2, 1982); Sec.Act Rels. Nos. 33–6332, 33–6334 (Aug. 6, 1981). *See generally* Ralph C. Ferrara & John P. Sweeney, Shelf Registration Under Temporary Rule 415, 5 Corp.L.Rev. 308 (1982); Comment, Professional Responsibility, Due Diligence and Rule 415: Another Dilemma, 10 Fla.State U.L.Rev. 619 (1983).

11. Sec.Act Rel. No. 33–6499 (Nov. 17, 1983).

For discussion of the Rule *see* Barbara A. Banoff, Regulatory Subsidies, Efficient Markets, and Shelf Registration: An Analysis of Rule 415, 70 Va.L.Rev. 135 (1984); Therese A. Maynard, Blue Sky Regulation of Rule 415 Shelf Registered Primary Offerings: The Need for a Limited Form of Federal Preemption, 22 Ariz.St.L.J. 89 (1990); Note, Due Diligence Under Rule 415: Is the Insurance Worth the Premium?, 38 Emory L.J. 793 (1989); Note, The Impact of the SEC's Shelf Registration Rule on Underwriters' Due–Diligence Investigations, 51 Geo.Wash.L.Rev. 767 (1983).

12. *See* § 3.3 *supra* for discussion of the various 1933 Act registration forms.

on Form S–3 or F–3 (for foreign issuers).[13]   Additionally, in order to qualify for any shelf registration, it must reasonably be expected that the securities so offered will be sold within two years of the effective date.

---

13. Forms S–3 and F–3 are available only to the most widely-traded issuers. Forms S–2 and S–3 are part of the integrated disclosure system and are available only to issuers subject to the 1934 Act reporting requirements. *See* § 3.3 *supra* for a discussion of alternative forms for 1933 Act registration. *See* §§ 9.2, 9.3 *infra* for discussion of the 1934 registration and reporting requirements.

Chapter 4

EXEMPTIONS FROM 1933 ACT REGISTRATION

Table of Sections

---

§ 4.1   Securities and Transactions Exempt From the 1933 Act's Registration Requirements—Sections 3 and 4 of the 1933 Act

Section 3 of the Securities Act of 1933[1] exempts various types of securities, most of which are dependent upon the nature of the issuer and/or terms of the security. Section 3(b)[2] empowers the SEC to exempt securities which in the Commission's discretion and by virtue of either the "small amount involved" or limited character of the public offering do not need the registration protection of the Act. The subsection (b) exemptions which are limited to five million dollars for any one issue of securities are found in Regulation A (up to $5 million dollars),[3] SEC Rule 505 (up to $5,000,000)[4] and Rule 504 (up to $1,000,000).[5] The Commission has also exercised its exemptive power under section 3(b) to exempt from registration employee stock compensation plans (ranging from $500,000 to $5,000,000 annually) provided that the issuer is not subject to the Securities Exchange Act's periodic reporting requirements.[6] Section 3(c) of the Act[7] gives the Commission similar exemptive power with regard to investment companies that are registered under the Small Business Investment Act of 1958; the Commission has exercised this power in Regulation E[8] which covers offerings up to $5,000,000.

---

§ 4.1

1. 15 U.S.C.A. § 77c. *See generally* J. William Hicks, Exempted Transactions Under the Securities Act of 1933 (1980); I, IV Louis Loss, Securities Regulation 559–715, 2586–2682 (2d ed. 1961, 1969 Supp.).

2. 15 U.S.C.A. § 77c(b). *See* § 4.14 *infra*. Although not couched in terms of an exemption, registration Form S–18 is a short form for use in offerings of no more than 7.5 million dollars. Thus, for example, although they are subject to the antifraud provisions of both the 1933 and 1934 Acts, Treasury securities are exempt from 1933 Act registration. *See, e.g.,* Kahn v. Salomon Brothers Inc., 813 F.Supp. 191 (E.D.N.Y.1993).

3. 17 C.F.R. §§ 230.251–.264. *See* § 4.15 *infra*.

4. 17 C.F.R. § 230.505. *See* § 4.17 *infra*.

5. 17 C.F.R. § 230.504. *See* § 4.18 *infra*.

6. 17 C.F.R. § 230.701, adopted in Sec. Act Rel. No. 33–6768, [1987–88 Transfer Binder] Fed.Sec.L.Rep. (CCH) ¶ 84,231 (April 14, 1988). *See* § 4.15.1 *infra*.

7. 15 U.S.C.A. § 77c(c).

8. 17 C.F.R. §§ 230.601–.610a.

In contrast to the section 3 exemptions which are expressly designated as exempt securities, section 4 of the Act contains a number of exemptions that apply to specific transactions. These include the exemption for nonpublic offerings by issuers,[9] transactions by persons other than issuers, underwriters and dealers,[10] unsolicited brokers' transactions,[11] certain dealer transactions occurring after the effective date,[12] transactions involving certain mortgage notes secured by real property,[13] and transactions up to five million dollars that are offered and sold only to "accredited investors."[14]

In addition to the foregoing exemptions that are aptly denominated as transaction exemptions, a number of the so-called exempt securities are in essence transaction exemptions. This is the case with the exemption for exchanges between an issuer and its security holders,[15] the intrastate exemption for purely local offerings,[16] and the exemptions provided by SEC rules promulgated under sections 3(b) and (c).[17] These exemptions expire at the termination of the qualifying transaction. Most of the security exemptions in section 3 are couched in terms of the nature of the security and/or its issuer, and will attach so long as the security maintains the required attributes, rights and obligations.

Both the section 3 and section 4 exemptions dispense with the Act's registration requirements but they do not prevent potential liability under the antifraud provisions contained in sections 12(2)[18] and 17(a).[19]

---

9. Section 4(2), 15 U.S.C.A. § 77d(2). *See* § 4.20 *infra.*

10. Section 4(1), 15 U.S.C.A. § 77d(1). *See* § 4.23 *infra.*

Transaction exemptions cover the entire transaction, not individuals. Thus, an individual who is neither an underwriter nor a dealer but participates in a transaction with an underwriter or dealer cannot hide behind section 4(1)'s transaction exemption. SEC v. Netelkos, 592 F.Supp. 906, 915 (S.D.N.Y.1984). *See also* United States v. Wolfson, 405 F.2d 779 (2d Cir.1968), *cert. denied* 394 U.S. 946, 89 S.Ct. 1275, 22 L.Ed.2d 479 (1969); §§ 4.23, 4.24 *infra.*

11. Section 4(4), 15 U.S.C.A. § 77d(4). *See* § 4.23 *infra.*

12. Section 4(3), 15 U.S.C.A. § 77d(3). *See* § 4.27 *infra.*

13. Section 4(5), 15 U.S.C.A. § 77d(5). *See* § 4.28 *infra.*

14. Section 4(6), 15 U.S.C.A. § 77d(6). *See* § 4.17 *infra. See also* 15 U.S.C.A. § 77b(15) (definition of accredited investor).

15. Section 3(a)(9), 15 U.S.C.A. § 77c(a)(9). *See* Thompson Ross Securities, 6 S.E.C. 1111 (SEC 1940); § 4.10 *infra.*

16. Section 3(a)(11), 15 U.S.C.A. § 77c(a)(11). *See* § 4.12 *infra.*

17. 15 U.S.C.A. §§ 77(b), (c). *See* § 4.4 *infra.*

18. 15 U.S.C.A. § 77*l* (2) (1976). *See* § 7.5 *infra.*

Although, on its face, section 12(2) would appear to be available for any misstatement or omission made by a seller of securities, the Supreme Court has held otherwise. In Gustafson v. Alloyd Co., ___ U.S. ___, 115 S.Ct. 1061, 131 L.Ed.2d 1 (1995), the Court held that the section 12(2) remedy is available only with regard to sales made via the use of a prospectus as that term is used in the 1933 Act.

19. 15 U.S.C.A. § 77q(a) (1976). *See* § 7.6 *infra.* However, it is extremely unlikely that a private remedy exists under section 17(a). *See* § 13.13 *infra.* Nevertheless an exemption from registration will not affect liability for material misrepresentations under Exchange Act Rule 10b–5, 17 C.F.R. § 240.10b–5. *See* §§ 13.2–13.11 *infra. See, e.g.,* Leoni v. Rogers, 719 F.Supp. 555 (E.D.Mich.1989) (§ 3(a)(11) provides an exemption from registration but not from Rule 10b–5).

Similarly, an exemption from registration under the 1933 Act does not affect possible liability for fraud under the 1934 Act,[20] except for short-term commercial paper which is excluded from the 1934 Act's definition of security.[21]

The burden of proof for establishing any of the exemptions lies with the person claiming an exemption. A corollary to the burdens of proof and persuasion resting with the person seeking to establish the availability of the exemption is the fact that exemptions are to be strictly construed.[22] Because of the strict construction and burden of proof, transactions must be carefully structured and documented in order to be sure of securing an exemption.[23]

The sections that follow discuss all of the 1933 Act exemptions in more detail.

§ 4.2 Securities Issued Prior to 1933—Former Section 3(a)(1)

Section 3(a)(1), which was repealed in 1987,[1] exempted securities issued prior to or within sixty days after the effective date of the 1933 Act. Since the exemption was expressly limited to "new offerings," any additional issue or secondary distribution of securities, although originally issued prior to the effective date of the Act, were nevertheless subject to section 5's prohibitions and the Act's registration requirements.[2] Accordingly, over time, it became increasingly unlikely that this exemption would have any practical applicability. Because of its apparent obsolescence, section 3(a)(1) was repealed in 1987.

20. *See, e.g.,* Kahn v. Salomon Brothers Inc., 813 F.Supp. 191 (E.D.N.Y.1993) (plaintiff stated claim under SEC Rule 10b–5 for alleged fraud in connection with United States Treasury securities).

21. *See* section 3(a)(10) of the 1934 Act, 15 U.S.C.A. § 78c(a)(10). *Compare* the exemption in section 3(a)(3) of the 1933 Act, 15 U.S.C.A. § 77c(a)(3), which is discussed in § 4.4 *infra.*

22. *See, e.g.,* SEC v. Murphy, 626 F.2d 633 (9th Cir.1980) (nonpublic offering exemption); Doran v. Petroleum Management Corp., 545 F.2d 893 (5th Cir.1977) (nonpublic offering exemption); Sec v. McDonald Investment Co., 343 F.Supp. 343 (D.Minn.1972) (intrastate exemption).

23. *But cf.* Dennis v. General Imaging, Inc., 918 F.2d 496 (5th Cir.1990).

§ 4.2

1. 15 U.S.C.A. § 77c(a)(1) (1982). *See* Pub.Law 100–181, 101 Stat. 1252 (1987).

2. SEC v. North American Research & Development Corp., 424 F.2d 63 (2d Cir.1970); SEC v. A.G. Bellin Securities Corp., 171 F.Supp. 233 (S.D.N.Y.1959); SEC v. Saphier, 1 S.E.C. Jud.Dec. 291 (S.D.N.Y.1936); In the Matter of Ira Haupt & Co., 23 S.E.C. 589 (SEC 1946); Sec.Act Rel. No. 33–358 (SEC Oct. 26, 1935). *See also,* SEC v. A.G. Bellin Securities Corp., 171 F.Supp. 233 (S.D.N.Y.1959).

§ 4.3 Securities of Governments, Banks, Insurance Companies, and Qualified Pension Plans—Section 3(a)(2)

Section 3(a)(2) of the 1933 Act[1] exempts qualified securities which are either issued or guaranteed by governmental organizations or federal reserve banks. Section 3(a)(2) also provides an exemption for securities of certain insurance companies. The exemption applies to securities issued by state, local and federal governments, including their subdivisions and administrative bodies.[2]

Government and Municipal Securities

Section 3(a)(2) exempts securities issued by the federal government, federal agencies, states, and qualifying state government agencies (including municipalities). In addition to straight-forward direct government financing, the section 3(a)(2) exemption also covers qualifying joint efforts of government and industry. Accordingly, the exemption covers government-guaranteed obligations. The Commission, in Rule 131, takes the position that a security which is issued by a governmental unit but is payable from payments to be made by a private party under a lease, sale, or loan arrangement is deemed a "separate 'security' " issued by the lessee or obligor under the loan arrangement[3] and would not appear to be exempt. Rule 131(a) is thus addressed to the types of arrangements that are generally covered by industrial development bonds, which are also known as IDB's or IDA bonds. Industrial development bonds may, however, qualify for exemption. Subsection (b) of Rule 131 states that such securities are not separate and therefore not required to be registered under the Act if the obligation is payable from the general revenues of the governmental unit or if the obligation relates to a public project or facility owned and operated by or on behalf of a unit under governmental control.[4] Also, if the obligation relates to a

---

§ 4.3

1. 15 U.S.C.A. § 77c(a). *See, e.g.,* Peoples National Bank of Washington v. Nichols, 619 F.Supp. 287 (D.Or.1985) (section 3(a)(2) exemption applied to bank guaranteed loans). *Cf.* Marine Bank v. Weaver, 455 U.S. 551, 102 S.Ct. 1220, 71 L.Ed.2d 409 (1982) (federally insured certificate of deposit is not subject to the securities laws); Wolf v. Banco Nacional De Mexico, 739 F.2d 1458 (9th Cir.1984), *cert. denied* 469 U.S. 1108, 105 S.Ct. 784, 83 L.Ed.2d 778 (1985) (Mexican bank's certificate of deposit was held not to be a security subject to federal regulation).

2. Most of the governmental securities issued under section 3(a)(2) are not traded on exchanges or through the National Association of Securities Dealers. In order to fill this regulatory gap, Congress created The Municipal Securities Rule–Making Board to cover broker-dealers who are not registered under the 1934 Exchange Act. *See* 15 U.S.C.A. §§ 78*o*, 78*o*–4. Municipal securities regulation is discussed in § 10.5 *infra.*

The major default on public power bonds in the State of Washington and two close calls with New York City bonds may have jeopardized the current breadth of the section 3(a)(2) exemption for governmental issues. For a discussion of the regulation that does exist *see* § 10.5 *infra. See generally* Note, Industrial Development Bonds, A Proposal For Reform, 65 Minn.L.Rev. 961 (1981); Note, Municipal Bonds and the Federal Securities Laws: The Results of Forty Years of Indirect Regulations, 28 Vand.L.Rev. 561 (1975).

3. Rule 131(a), 17 C.F.R. § 230.131(a).

4. Rule 131(b), 17 C.F.R. § 230.131(b).

facility leased to and under the control of a private party but is part of a public project, it is exempt from registration under the 1933 Act.[5] Accordingly, for an industrial development bond to qualify for the Act's exemption, its payout provisions must be drafted so as to comply with SEC Rule 131(b).[6]

Just as state and local government guarantees can qualify a security for exemption, so can a federal guarantee. However, the fact that there is a federal guarantee will not assure the exemption when the investment involves risks not ordinarily associated with instruments issued or guaranteed by the government.[7]

Municipal Securities Dealers

Notwithstanding the exemption from the registration requirements, the Commission has established disclosure requirements in connection with its regulation of municipal securities dealers. In 1990, the Commission adopted Rule 15c2–12[8] which requires that a municipal securities underwriter must receive from the issuer a "final official statement" of the terms and conditions of the offering.[9] The rule also provides that the final official statement be delivered to potential customers upon request.[10] Paralleling the 1933 Act's preliminary prospectus requirement, the Rule makes a provision for a preliminary official statement which may be used prior to the final statement. The Commission has established three exemptions, one paralleling the private placement exemption and the others based on short-term maturity. Each of the three exemptions from Rule 15c2–12 applies only to securities offered in denominations of $100,000 or more. The first exemption applies to securities offered in denominations of $100,000 or more if they are sold to no more than 35 sophisticated purchasers each of whom is not purchasing for more than one account and is not taking the securities with a view to distribution.[11] Second, securities offered in denominations of $100,000 or more and having a maturity of nine months or less are exempt from the rule.[12] Third, securities offered in denominations of $100,000 or more are exempt if at the holder's option they may be tendered for redemption for at par value and such option may be exercised at least every nine months.[13]

---

5. *Id.*

6. *See* Sec.Act Rel. No. 33–5103 (Nov. 6, 1970).

7. *See, e.g.,* J.P. Morgan Structures Obligations Corp., [1994–1995 Transfer Binder] Fed. Sec. L. Rep. (CCH) ¶ 76,906 (SEC No Action Letter July 27, 1994) (interests in swap transactions involved different risks).

8. 17 C.F.R. § 240.15c2–12. *See* James R. Doty, The Regulation of State and Local Government Securities, 24 Rev.Sec. & Commod.Reg. 59 (1991).

9. 17 C.F.R. § 240.15c2–12(b).

10. 17 C.F.R. § 240.15c2–12(b).

11. 17 C.F.R. § 240.15c2–12(c)(1).

12. 17 C.F.R. § 240.15c2–12(c)(2).

13. 17 C.F.R. § 240.15c2–12(c)(3).

Pension Plans

In addition to government securities, section 3(a)(2) further exempts certain qualifying employee pension plans which are set up in the form of a trust or a collective trust maintained by a bank or an insurance company.[14] In order to qualify for the exemption under the terms of the statute, the plan must be a qualified plan under section 401 or 402(a)(2) of the Internal Revenue Code.[15] The section 3(a)(2) exemption applies to all such employee plans, regardless of whether they are pension, profit sharing, or stock plans.[16] Although the statute further empowers the Commission to exempt plans for self-employed individuals (Keogh plans),[17] the Commission has exempted only a limited class of such plans. SEC Rule 180[18] exempts Keogh plans of certain partnerships but the exemption is available only for certain types of businesses. The Keogh plan exemption for partnerships is available only to law firms, accounting firms, investment banking firms, and pension consulting or investment advisory firms "furnishing services of a type that involve such knowledge and experience in financial and business matters that the employer is able to represent adequately its interests and those of its employees."[19] Furthermore, in order to qualify for the Rule 180 exemption, the partnership must enlist the aid of independent investment advice in establishing the plan.[20] Presumably the rationale for not granting an across-the-board exemption for Keogh plans is that in selecting one's long term retirement strategy, a self-employed individual is in effect making an investment decision. In contrast, a qualified employee plan is not selected by an employee/investor. Furthermore, the employee who participates in a "qualified" plan may have the protections of the Employee Retirement Income Security Act (ERISA).[21] Section 3(a)(2) does not give the SEC exemptive power with regard to individual retirement accounts (IRA's)[22] which thus must be registered unless covered by some other exemption.[23]

14. *See* Rule 132, 17 C.F.R. § 230.132. *Cf.* Rule 701's exemption for certain compensation plans of issuers not subject to Exchange Act reporting requirements. 17 C.F.R. § 230.701. *See* § 4.15.1 *infra*.

15. I.R.C. §§ 401, 402(a)(2). Also exempted are plans of governmental employers qualifying under I.R.C. § 414(d).

16. There are parallel exemptions from the 1934 Exchange Act. 15 U.S.C.A. §§ 78c(A)(12), 78*l* (g)(2)(H). It is to be noted that not all pension plans qualify as securities. For example, a compulsory defined benefit plan is not a security within the meaning of section 2(1) of the Act. International Brotherhood of Teamsters v. Daniel, 439 U.S. 551, 99 S.Ct. 790, 58 L.Ed.2d 808 (1979); 15 U.S.C.A. § 77b(1). *See* § 1.5 *supra*.

17. *See* I.R.C. § 401(c).

18. 17 C.F.R. § 230.180.

19. 17 C.F.R. § 230.180(a)(3)(i).

20. 17 C.F.R. § 230.180(a)(3)(ii).

21. Polaroid Corp., [1972–73 Transfer Binder] Fed.Sec.L.Rep. (CCH) ¶ 79,204 (SEC 1973).

22. *See* I.R.C. § 408.

23. Bank sponsored IRAs are exempt as bank securities under section 3(a)(2). *See also* section 3(a)(5)'s exemptions for savings and loan associations. 15 U.S.C.A. § 77c(a)(5) which is discussed in § 4.6 *infra*.

There are additional limitations on section 3(a)(2)'s employee plan exemption. Where a pension plan gave the trustee the discretion to invest in companies controlled by the employers, it was held that no exemption would attach.[24] Similarly, where the trust was administered by a bank that was acting merely as a custodian and therefore did not exercise substantial investment responsibility, the section 3(a)(2) exemption was denied.[25]

As the foregoing discussion indicates, the section 3(a)(2) exemption is limited to plans administered by others. Thus, for example, stock purchase and stock option plans do not fall under the exemption. However, the Commission has exempted from registration employee stock compensation plans (ranging from $500,000 to $5,000,000 annually) provided that the issuer is not subject to the Securities and Exchange Act's periodic reporting requirements.[26]

Bank Securities

Section 3(a)(2) also exempts securities issued by Federal Reserve Banks, including certificates of deposit.[27] Section 3(a)(2) does not cover securities issued by industrial loan companies or their subsidiaries as those are dealt with under section 3(a)(5).[28] However, Federal Land Bank stock is covered by section 3(a)(2)'s exemption.[29]

§ 4.4　Short Term Commercial Paper—Section 3(a)(3)

Section 3(a)(3) of the Securities Act of 1933[1] exempts notes, drafts, notes of exchange, or bankers' acceptances arising "out of a current

24. Corpus Christi Bank & Trust, [1973–74 Transfer Binder] Fed.Sec.L.Rep. (CCH) ¶ 79,676 (SEC 1973).

25. Capital Funds, Inc. v. SEC, 348 F.2d 582 (8th Cir.1965), *affirming* [1964–66 Transfer Binder] Fed.Sec.L.Rep. (CCH) ¶ 77,131 (SEC 1964); Commercial Credit Co., [1971–72 Transfer Binder] Fed.Sec.L.Rep. (CCH) ¶ 78,554 (SEC 1971).

26. 17 C.F.R. § 230.701, adopted in Sec. Act Rel. No. 33–6768, [1987–88 Transfer Binder] Fed.Sec.L.Rep. (CCH) ¶ 84,231 (April 14, 1988). *See* § 4.15.1 *infra*. The exemption is based on section 3(b) which permits the Commission to exempt offerings not exceeding $5,000,000. 15 U.S.C.A. § 77c(b). *See* § 4.14 *infra*.

27. 15 U.S.C.A. § 77c(a)(2). Sears v. Likens, 912 F.2d 889 (7th Cir.1990) (securities issued or guaranteed by state bank are exempt from 1933 Act registration requirements). *Cf.* Levine v. Diamanthuset, Inc., 722 F.Supp. 579 (N.D.Cal.1989) (bank deposit confirmation sent by bank in connection with diamond investments was not a security).

28. 15 U.S.C.A. § 77c(a)(5) (1976). *See* § 4.6 *infra. See also, e.g.,* Bradford v. Moench, 809 F.Supp. 1473 (D.Utah 1992) (industrial loan corporations are not "banks" within the meaning of § 3(a)(2)'s exemption).

29. Dau v. Federal Land Bank of Omaha, 627 F.Supp. 346 (N.D.Iowa 1985). *Accord,* Creech v. Federal Land Bank of Wichita, 647 F.Supp. 1097 (D.Colo.1986) (relying on Schlake v. Beatrice Production Credit Ass'n, 596 F.2d 278, 281 (8th Cir.1979) which held that banks in the Farm Credit System have governmental status); Wiley v. Federal Land Bank of Louisville, 657 F.Supp. 964 (S.D.Ind.1987); Kolb v. Naylor, 658 F.Supp. 520 (N.D.Iowa 1987).

§ 4.4

1. 15 U.S.C.A. § 77c(a)(3). *Cf., e.g.,* Mishkin v. Peat, Marwick, Mitchell & Co., 744 F.Supp. 531 (S.D.N.Y.1990) (banker's acceptance with maturity of less than nine months is not a security under section 3(a)(10) of the Exchange Act). *See generally* Paul Lowenstein, The Commercial Paper Market and the Federal Securities Law, 4 Corp.L.Rev. 128 (1981).

transaction" with a maturity at the time of issue of not more than nine months. The nine month limitation does not include grace periods or any renewal of the security which is limited in the same manner as the original obligation. Short term commercial paper is thus granted an exemption from 1933 Act registration although it is, nevertheless, subject to the Act's antifraud provisions. In contrast, short term commercial paper is expressly excluded from the definition of "security" under the Securities Exchange Act of 1934[2] and thus is not subject to that Act's antifraud provisions.[3] As discussed more fully in an earlier section of this treatise,[4] in Reves v. Ernst & Young,[5] the Supreme Court applied the "family resemblance" test in holding that certain demand notes were securities. Since "note" is one of the items enumerated in the Act's definition, there is a rebuttable presumption that a note is a security.[6] Simply identifying an instrument as "commercial" will not exclude it from the ambit of the securities law.[7] Accordingly, commercial paper issued by a corporation carries the same presumption of being a security.[8]

If a short term note which otherwise would be exempt under the 1933 Act (or excluded from the Exchange Act) is part of a package and tied to some other investment contract, the exemption does not apply. Thus, for example, where a money market fund consists wholly of short term commercial paper, the participation interests in the fund itself are still subject to registration.[9] Similarly, there is a line of cases holding

---

2. 15 U.S.C.A. § 78c(a)(10).

3. *Id.* The 1933 and 1934 Act exemptions will frequently depend upon the terms of the instrument in question. *See, e.g.,* § 1.5 *supra.*

4. *See* § 1.5 *supra.*

5. 494 U.S. 56, 110 S.Ct. 945, 108 L.Ed.2d 47 (1990), *rehearing denied* 494 U.S. 1092, 110 S.Ct. 1840, 108 L.Ed.2d 968 (1990).

6. 494 U.S. at 64–66, 110 S.Ct. at 951–52, 108 L.Ed.2d at 60–61. *See also, e.g.,* Holloway v. Peat, Marwick, Mitchell & Co., 900 F.2d 1485 (10th Cir.1990), *cert. denied* 498 U.S. 958, 111 S.Ct. 386, 112 L.Ed.2d 396 (1990). The following four factors are relevant in deciding whether to rebut the presumption:

(1) an examination of the transaction in order to assess the motivations that would prompt a reasonable lender (buyer) and creditor (seller) to enter into it—for example, was the transaction in question an investment transaction or a commercial or consumer transaction?

(2) the plan of distribution used in offering and selling the instrument—for example, is the instrument commonly traded for investment or speculation?

(3) the reasonable expectations of the investing public—are the notes generally perceived as investment opportunities? and

(4) whether some factor such as the applicability of a parallel regulatory scheme significantly reduces the risk and thereby renders the protection of the federal securities laws unnecessary.

7. In re NBW Commercial Paper Litigation, 813 F.Supp. 7 (1992), relying on Securities Industry Association v. Board of Governors, 468 U.S. 137, 104 S.Ct. 2979, 82 L.Ed.2d 107 (1984) and the *Reves* decision.

8. *Id.*

9. *See* SEC v. American Board of Trade, Inc., 593 F.Supp. 335 (S.D.N.Y.1984), *grant of preliminary injunction reversed* 751 F.2d 529 (2d Cir.1984) (pooling of funds for investment in United States Government Treasury Bills); SEC v. M.A. Lundy Associates, 362 F.Supp. 226 (D.R.I.1973). *See also* Wagman v. FLS Securities Corp., 1985 WL 2139, [1984–85 Transfer Binder] Fed.Sec.L.Rep. (CCH) ¶ 92,445 (N.D.Ill.1985).

that if the transaction seems to comply in form with the requirements of the exemption but the short term note is in essence an investment contract, as opposed to a commercial transaction, the securities acts will apply absent another exemption.[10]

In deciding whether a particular instrument is a note or investment contract, many courts have looked to the economic realities in terms of a commercial/investment dichotomy[11] while others have adhered to a more literal approach based on the terms of the instrument.[12]

The Commission has pointed out that the section 3(a)(3) exemption "applies only to prime quality negotiable commercial paper of a type not ordinarily purchased by the general public." [13] The case law is in accord with the view of the Commission.[14] An appropriate test for the note's quality is whether the paper would be eligible for discounting by Federal Reserve Banks.[15] A leading case[16] has stated that in order to qualify for the comparable 1934 Act exemption, short term commercial paper must be "(1) prime quality negotiable commercial paper (2) of a type not ordinarily purchased by the general public, that is, (3) paper issued to facilitate well recognized types of current operational business requirements and (4) of a type eligible for discounting by Federal Reserve banks."

In addition to bank notes, the section 3(a)(3) exemption applies to short term paper issued by finance companies to cover their installment loans. The fact that a loan is extended beyond the original ninety day period will not destroy the exemption.[17] However, the exemption will not apply to short-term loan agreements containing automatic "roll-

---

10. "Investment contract" as distinct from a "note" is an alternative form of "security" as defined in section 2(1) of the Act. 15 U.S.C.A. § 77b(1). *See* § 1.5 *supra.*

11. According to this view if an instrument is an investment contract it falls under section 2(1)'s definition of security and is not exempt under section 3(a)(3). *E.g.* Great Western Bank & Trust v. Kotz, 532 F.2d 1252 (9th Cir.1976); C.N.S. Enterprises, Inc. v. G. & G. Enterprises, Inc., 508 F.2d 1354 (7th Cir.1975), *cert. denied* 423 U.S. 825, 96 S.Ct. 38, 46 L.Ed.2d 40 (1975); Lino v. City Investing Co., 487 F.2d 689 (3d Cir.1973); SEC v. Diversified Industries, Inc., 465 F.Supp. 104 (D.D.C.1979). *See* § 1.5 *supra.*

12. *E.g.* The Exchange National Bank of Chicago v. Touche Ross & Co., 544 F.2d 1126 (2d Cir.1976).

13. Sec. Act Rel. No. 33–4412 (Sept. 20, 1961). *Accord, e.g.,* General Electric Corp., 26 Sec. Re.g & L. Rep. (BNA) 1076 (SEC No Action Letter available July 13, 1994) (limited advertisements for commercial paper were not likely to mislead public into believing that notes were securities). *See generally* Sonnenschein, *supra* note 3.

14. *See e.g.,* Zeller v. Bogue Electric Mfg. Corp., 476 F.2d 795 (2d Cir.1973), *cert. denied* 414 U.S. 908, 94 S.Ct. 217, 38 L.Ed.2d 146 (1973); Sanders v. John Nuveen & Co., 463 F.2d 1075 (7th Cir.1972), *cert. denied* 409 U.S. 1009, 93 S.Ct. 443, 34 L.Ed.2d 302 (1972).

15. Sec. Act Rel. No. 33–4412 (Sept. 20, 1961).

16. Sanders v. John Nuveen & Co., 463 F.2d 1075, 1079 (7th Cir.1972), *cert. denied* 409 U.S. 1009, 93 S.Ct. 443, 34 L.Ed.2d 302 (1972) (quoting from Sec. Act Rel. No. 33–4412, 17 C.F.R. § 231.4412 (1961)). *Accord* Zeller v. Bogue Electric Mfg. Corp., 476 F.2d 795, 800 (2d Cir.1973), *cert. denied* 414 U.S. 908, 94 S.Ct. 217, 38 L.Ed.2d 146 (1973) ("the mere fact that a note has a maturity of less than nine months does not take the case out of Rule 10b–5, unless the note fits the general notion of 'commercial paper' reflected in the SEC release.").

17. Sec. Act Rels. Nos. 33–4412, 33–401 (Sept. 20, 1961; June 18, 1935).

over" provisions.[18] It has been held that interim construction loans may properly be subject to the exemption,[19] but where a real estate investment trust issued short term notes in large denominations, the seventy-five thousand dollar minimum investment was said to run afoul of the Commission's policy with regard to interim mortgage financing.[20]

§ 4.5 Securities of Eleemosynary Organizations—Section 3(a)(4)

Section 3(a)(4) of the Act[1] exempts from registration all securities issued by a not-for-profit issuer that is organized and operated exclusively for religious, educational, benevolent, fraternal, charitable, or reformatory purposes. In order to qualify for the exemption, no part of the issuer's net earnings may inure to the benefit of "any person, private stockholder, or individual."[2] With regard to nonprofit organizations, the availability of this exemption has generally been treated as coextensive with the issuer's federal tax status. Accordingly, if the issuer is tax-exempt it will qualify for the section 3(a)(4) exemption. It is the SEC's position that in the absence of a favorable IRS ruling, the Commission will not give its opinion as to the availability of the exemption.[3] On the other hand, the fact that the issuer is a tax-exempt entity does not necessarily create a section 3(a)(4) registration exemption.[4] The Commission has pointed out that a favorable I.R.S. ruling does not assure the securities exemption.[5] Thus, any profit or implication of a profit to the organizers, members, or anyone else—including a promised gift to investors—will render the exemption unavailable.[6] Similarly, when a corporation had social and recreational purposes as well as charitable, the Commission has refused no action relief.[7]

---

18. Sec. Act Rel. No. 33–4412 (Sept. 20, 1961).

19. First Chicago Corp., [1970–71 Transfer Binder] Fed.Sec.L.Rep. (CCH) ¶ 78,010 (SEC 1971).

20. First Union Real Estate Equity and Mortgage Investments, [1972–73 Transfer Binder] Fed.Sec.L.Rep. (CCH) ¶ 78,837 (SEC 1972).

§ 4.5

1. 15 U.S.C.A. § 77c(a)(4).

2. 15 U.S.C.A. § 77c(a)(4).

3. Haverford Hospital Association, [1977–78 Transfer Binder] Fed.Sec.L.Rep. (CCH) ¶ 1,152 (SEC 1977); Sec.Act Rel. No. 33–6253, 1 Fed.Sec.L.Rep. (CCH) ¶ 373 (SEC Oct. 28, 1980).

4. See Jewish Community Federation, [1973 Transfer Binder] Fed.Sec.L.Rep. (CCH) ¶ 79,419 (SEC 1973).

5. Westminster Foundation, 1978 WL 12368 (SEC No Action Letter March 9, 1978).

6. E.g., SEC v. Universal Service Association, 106 F.2d 232 (7th Cir.1939), cert. denied 308 U.S. 622, 60 S.Ct. 378, 84 L.Ed. 519 (1940) (no exemption available where "contributors" were to receive profits); SEC v. Children's Hospital, 214 F.Supp. 883 (D.Ariz.1963) (3(a)(4) exemption was not available to hospital bond offering where substantial purpose of the organization of the hospital was to enrich the promoters).

7. National Skeet Shooting Association, [1979 Transfer Binder] Fed.Sec.L.Rep. (CCH) ¶ 82,393 (SEC No Action Letter July 5, 1979); Westminster Foundation, 1978 WL 12368 (SEC No Action Letter March 9, 1978).

Section 501 of the Internal Revenue Code[8] contains more than twenty-five different tax exemptions for organizations. The language of the section 3(a)(4) exemption from 1933 Act registration tracks most closely section 501(c)(3) in its application to religious, benevolent, fraternal, or reformatory purposes.[9] A question might thus be raised as to whether any of the other tax exemptions would qualify equally for the securities registration exemption. In its interpretative release analyzing the procedures for securing a favorable no action letter on the section 3(a)(4) exemption,[10] the Commission did not expressly limit the securities exemption to section 501(c)(3) organizations. Although most of the no action requests receiving a favorable response do in fact involve section 501(c)(3) organizations,[11] there are a few involving other tax exempt organizations.[12]

The availability of the section 3(a)(4) exemption does not insulate the securities from the securities laws' antifraud provisions.[13] As is generally true under the Act, the exemption provided by section 3 is merely an exemption from registration.[14]

§ 4.6 Securities of Building and Loan Associations, Farmers Cooperatives and the Like—Section 3(a)(5)

Section 3(a)(5) of the 1933 Act[1] provides an exemption from registration for securities issued by savings and loan associations, building and loan associations, cooperative banks, homestead associations, and similar institutions, provided that the issuer is subject to supervision by state or federal governmental authorities. The exemption does not apply, however, where the issuer takes for itself more than three percent of the offering's face value in the form of a fee or other remuneration, either at the time of investment or termination.[2] Section 3(a)(5) further exempts

---

8. I.R.C. § 501(c).

9. *See, e.g.,* St. Alban's Congregational Church (SEC No Action Letter May 17, 1976).

10. Sec.Act Rel. No. 33–6253, 1 Fed.Sec.L.Rep. (CCH) ¶ 373 (SEC Oct. 28, 1980).

11. *See, e.g.,* Kaiser Foundation Hospitals, [1980 Transfer Binder] Fed.Sec.L.Rep. (CCH) ¶ 76,409 (SEC No Action Letter May 12, 1980) (no action response for securities issued by section 501(c)(3) hospital and guaranteed by section 501(c)(4) health maintenance organization); Willmar Student Housing Building Corp. (SEC No Action Letter July 2, 1973) (section 501(c)(4) organization received favorable no action response).

12. National Skeet Shooting Association, [1979 Transfer Binder] Fed.Sec.L.Rep. (CCH) ¶ 82,393 (SEC No Action Letter July 5, 1979) (refusing no action relief for section 501(c)(4) organization organized for social and recreational purposes); Topeka Chamber Industrial Development Corp. [1979 Transfer Binder] Fed.Sec.L.Rep. (CCH) ¶ 82,181 (SEC No Action Letter June 25, 1979).

13. *E.g.,* SEC v. World Radio Mission, Inc., 544 F.2d 535 (1st Cir.1976); *cf.* United States v. Lilly, 37 F.3d 1222 (7th Cir.1994) (Church pastor selling certificates of deposit to finance church expansion could not hide behind the First Amendment right to free exercise of religion).

14. 15 U.S.C.A. §§ 77c, 77d. *See* § 4.1 *supra.*

§ 4.6

1. 15 U.S.C.A. § 77c(a)(5).

2. *Id.*

securities issued by farmer cooperatives and certain corporations that qualify for the federal taxation exemption.[3]

There are limits on the section 3(a)(5) exemption that are not evident from the statute on its face. There is an administrative interpretation to the effect that stock of mortgage loan companies is exempt only if the issuer sells its stock and other securities to residents of the state in which it is organized, or if issued only to borrowers.[4] Furthermore, the section 3(a)(5) exemption is unavailable if substantially all of the savings or building and loan institution's business is not limited to making loans to members.[5] The availability of the exemption is relatively straightforward so long as there are bona fide qualified securities as opposed to a scheme to avoid registration.

§ 4.7   Certain Securities Issued by Federally Regulated Common Carriers—Section 3(a)(6)

Section 3(a)(6) of the 1933 Act[1] exempts participation interests in railroad equipment trusts. Under the statutory language, an " 'interest in a railroad equipment trust' means any interest in an equipment trust, lease, conditional sales contract, or other similar arrangement entered into, issued, assumed, guaranteed by, or for the benefit of, a common carrier to finance the acquisition of rolling stock, including motive power.' "[2]

As is the case with the other section 3 exemptions, the inapplicability of the registration provisions does not have any effect upon the potential liability for material misstatements under the Act's antifraud sections.[3]

§ 4.8   Certificates Issued Under the Bankruptcy Act by Receivers and Trustees—Section 3(a)(7)

Section 3(a)(7) exempts from registration certificates issued by trustees, receivers, or debtors in possession under the Federal Bankruptcy Act provided that the certificates are issued pursuant to court approval.[1] Even though the exemption may apply to securities sold as part of the original issue, it does not extend to downstream sales in which case the person selling to secondary recipients of the certificates

---

3. *See* I.R.C. §§ 501(a), 501(c)(2), (16), 521.

4. Sec. Act Rel. No. 33–86 (FTC Dec. 13, 1933).

5. SEC v. American International Savings & Loan Association, 199 F.Supp. 341 (D.Md.1961).

§ 4.7

1. 15 U.S.C.A. § 77c(a)(6).

2. *Id.*

3. *See* Welch Foods, Inc. v. Goldman, Sachs & Co., 398 F.Supp. 1393 (S.D.N.Y.1974).

§ 4.8

1. 15 U.S.C.A. § 77c(a)(7).

must register unless some other independent exemption is available.[2] The statute expressly requires court approval of the issue in order to render the exemption available.

The section 3(a)(7) exemption supplements the exemptions for bankruptcy reorganizations which are found in section 3(a)(10).[3] The section 3(a)(7) exemption which applies to trustee certificates has its counterpart in the Bankruptcy Act[4] which not only provides an exemption from section 5 of the 1933 Act but also from the Trust Indenture Act of 1939,[5] as well as from state and local laws. Section 1145(a) of the Bankruptcy Act[6] exempts from 1933 Act registration, as well as provides an exemption from state securities laws, securities of the bankrupt if they are (1) offered under a reorganization plan and are (2) exchanged for claims or interests in the debtor.

§ 4.9   Insurance Policies and Annuity Contracts—Section 3(a)(8)

Section 3(a)(8)[1] exempts from 1933 Act registration insurance policies and annuity contracts issued by corporations that are subject to the supervision of a state insurance commissioner, bank commissioner, or agency or officer performing a similar regulatory function. The Commission has pointed out that if the insurance or annuity contract does not place upon the issuer a "meaningful mortality risk" the policy cannot be regarded as "life insurance" or an exempt "annuity."[2] Furthermore, simply taking on a "meaningful mortality risk" does not assure the issuer an exemption from registration under the securities laws where the annuity or other insurance contract is in essence an investment contract.[3] For example, the Supreme Court has held that

---

2. *Cf.* Sequential Information Systems, Inc., [1972–73 Transfer Binder] Fed.Sec.L.Rep. (CCH) ¶ 79,139 (SEC 1972) (a certificate holder who exchanges certificates for stock cannot use the section 3(a)(7) exemption when reselling the stock to the public).

3. 15 U.S.C.A. § 77c(a)(10). *See* § 4.11 *infra.*

4. 11 U.S.C.A. § 364(f). These certificates can be issued by either a trustee or a debtor in possession (*see* 11 U.S.C.A. §§ 1107(a), 1108) while section 3(a)(7) also exempts certificates issued by a receiver. The exemption provided by section 364(f) of the Bankruptcy Act does not apply to downstream sales or to sales by certain underwriters. *See* 11 U.S.C.A. § 1145(b)(1).

5. 15 U.S.C.A. § 77aaa–77bbbb. *See* chapter 16 *infra.*

6. 11 U.S.C.A. § 1145(a). Section, 1145(a)(2), allows the "offer" or "sale" of securities via warrants, options, rights, and conversion privileges, if two general requirements are met. Section 1145(a)(1) allows the exchange to include partial cash payment. Section 1145(a)(3) governs sale of a debtor's portfolio securities (limited exemption). *See also* SEC Rule 148, 17 C.F.R. § 230.148 which was made obsolete by the new bankruptcy act. (resale of securities issued originally under a Title II exemption). Section 1145(a)(4) provides a broker's exemption similar to section 4(3) of the 1933 Act. *See* 15 U.S.C.A. § 77d(3). Section 4(3) is considered in § 4.27 *infra.*

§ 4.9

1. 15 U.S.C.A. § 77c(a)(8).

2. Sec. Act Rel. No. 33–6051 (April 5, 1979). *See* SEC v. United Benefit Life Insurance Co., 387 U.S. 202, 211, 87 S.Ct. 1557, 1562, 18 L.Ed.2d 673 (1967).

3. Sec. Act Rel. No. 33–6051 (April 5, 1979).

when analyzing a variable annuity under which the entire investment risk rests with the purchaser, the section 3(a)(8) exemption does not apply.[4] As is the case with any question of whether an investment contract exists,[5] the expectations of the policyholder must be viewed in light of an "economic reality" test and the court's inquiry thus is not limited to the policy on its face.[6] Ordinarily a fixed annuity will qualify for section 3(a)(8)'s exemption.[7]

The exemption may apply even if a bona fide life insurance policy or annuity has collateral provisions giving the policyholder additional benefits. For example, the SEC takes the position that although premium deposit funds on bona fide life insurance policies remain on deposit with the insurer and provide an alternative to a bank account, unless there is a substantial transfer of the investment risk to the policyholder, there will still be a section 3(a)(8) exemption.[8]

In 1984 the SEC proposed Rule 151 as a safe harbor to codify the existing state of the law under section 3(a)(8).[9] Rule 151 was adopted in March, 1986. Under this rule, an annuity contract qualifies for an exemption if (1) the contract is issued by a company subject to state insurance regulation, (2) the insurer assumes the investment risk under the contract, and (3) the contract is not marketed primarily as an investment.[10]

---

4. SEC v. Variable Annuity Life Insurance Co., 359 U.S. 65, 79 S.Ct. 618, 3 L.Ed.2d 640 (1959). *See* Robert P. Blank, Gordon L. Keen, Jr., Glen A. Payne & Kenneth H. Miller, Variable Life Insurance and the Federal Securities Laws, 60 Va.L.Rev. 71 (1974). *See also* Legal Opinion Letter No. 331, 17 Sec.Reg. & L.Rep. (BNA) 893 (Comptroller of the Currency 1985).

5. *See* § 1.5 *supra.*

6. *See* Associates in Adolescent Psychiatry, S.C. v. Home Life Insurance Co., 941 F.2d 561 (7th Cir.1991), *cert. denied* 502 U.S. 1099, 112 S.Ct. 1182, 117 L.Ed.2d 426 (1992) (merely labelling a mutual fund an "annuity" will not take it out of the ambit of the securities laws; however, a bona fide defined benefit annuity is not a security); Grainger v. State Security Life Insurance Co., 547 F.2d 303 (5th Cir.1977), *cert. denied* 436 U.S. 932, 98 S.Ct. 2832, 56 L.Ed.2d 777 (1978), *rehearing denied* 439 U.S. 883, 99 S.Ct. 227, 58 L.Ed.2d 198 (1978).

7. *E.g.,* Otto v. Variable Annuity Life Insurance Co., 611 F.Supp. 83 (N.D.Ill.1985). *See also, e.g.,* SKJ Commodities Corp. [1987–88 Transfer Binder] Fed.Sec.L.Rep. (CCH) ¶ 78,-675 (SEC No Action Letter Nov. 13, 1987) (annuity contract offered by a registered commodity trading advisor did not involve the sale of a security).

8. Sec. Act Rel. No. 33–6051 (April 25, 1979). *See* In re Baldwin–United Corp., 55 B.R. 885 (Bkrtcy.S.D.Ohio 1985) (single premium deferred annuity was exempt where underwriting company took both significant investment risk and significant mortality risk). *See also, e.g.,* Dryden v. Sun Life Assurance Co. of Canada, 737 F.Supp. 1058 (S.D.Ind.1989), *affirmed* 909 F.2d 1486 (7th Cir.1990) (insurer's whole life policies were not securities).

9. Proposed in Sec.Act Rel. No. 33–6558, [1984–85 Transfer Binder] Fed.Sec.L.Rep. (CCH) ¶ 83,710 (Nov. 21, 1984).

10. 17 C.F.R. § 230.151, adopted in Sec. Act Rel. No. 33–6645, [1986–87 Transfer Binder] Fed.Sec.L.Rep. (CCH) ¶ 84,004 (May 29, 1986). Rule 151 was held not to have been satisfied in Otto v. Variable Annuity Life Ins. Co., 814 F.2d 1127 (7th Cir.1986), *cert. denied* 486 U.S. 1026, 108 S.Ct. 2004, 100 L.Ed.2d 235 (1988). *Accord* Berent v. Kemper Corp., 780 F.Supp. 431 (E.D.Mich.1991), *judgment affirmed* 973 F.2d 1291 (6th Cir.1992). *Compare* Associates in Adolescent Psychiatry, S.C. v. Home Life Insurance Co. of New York, 729 F.Supp. 1162 (N.D.Ill.1989), *affirmed* 941 F.2d 561 (7th Cir.1991), *cert. denied* 502 U.S. 1099, 112 S.Ct. 1182, 117 L.Ed.2d 426 (1992) (distinguishing *Otto*).

§ 4.10   Securities Exchanged Exclusively With Existing Security Holders—Section 3(a)(9)

Section 3(a)(9) provides an exemption from 1933 Act registration for securities exchanged by the issuer exclusively with its existing security holders, so long as no commission or other remuneration is paid for promotional activities in soliciting the exchange.[1] The exemption is not available for securities exchanged in the course of Bankruptcy Act proceedings that would be governed by 11 U.S.C.A. § 1145.[2]

The section 3(a)(9) exemption is limited to an exchange of securities of a single issuer.[3] As noted above, another requirement of the exemption is that the exchange be exclusively with the issuer's existing securities holders. An issuer cannot use the exemption by creating a class of securities that is substantially the same as the class of securities being issued to persons who are not existing holders of the issuer's securities.[4] But where there are distinct classes of securities or a single class is distributed in two separate distributions, based on timing and circumstances, the section 3(a)(9) exemption will apply.[5]

As noted above, the integration doctrine applies so as to put in jeopardy any exchange with security holders in which the same class of securities is offered to the general public for cash or other consideration.[6] The section 3(a)(9) exemption is not available for an exchange of shares involving securities of more than one company.[7]

Integration problems are especially sensitive in light of section 3(a)(9)'s requirement that the securities be issued *"exclusively"* in connection with an exchange between the issuer and existing securities holders. However, stand-by purchase agreements made by persons other than existing security holders will not in and of themselves

---

§ 4.10

1. 15 U.S.C.A. § 77c(a)(9). *See, e.g.,* International Controls Corp., [1990–1991 Transfer Binder] Fed.Sec.L.Rep. (CCH) ¶ 79,604 (SEC No Action Letter Aug. 6, 1990) (no action would be recommended for issuer's exchange offer to registered debenture holders).

2. 11 U.S.C.A. § 1145. *See generally,* J. *William* Hicks, Recapitalizations Under Section 3(a)(9) of the Securities Act of 1933, 61 Va. L.Rev. 1057 (1975). *See also* § 4.8 *supra*; 4.11 *infra*.

3. *See* Reserve Life Insurance Co. v. Provident Life Insurance Co., 499 F.2d 715, 722 (8th Cir.1974), *cert. denied* 419 U.S. 1107, 95 S.Ct. 778, 42 L.Ed.2d 803 (1975) (securities issued by successor trust are not exempt).

4. *See* Sec. Act Rel. No. 33–6274 (Dec. 23, 1980) interpreting Sec. Act Rel. No. 33–4552 (Nov. 6, 1962).

5. *See* SEC v. Murphy, 626 F.2d 633, 645 (9th Cir.1980); Hillsborough Investment Corp. v. SEC, 276 F.2d 665 (1st Cir.1960); Sec. Act Rel. No. 33–2029 (Opinion of General Counsel, Aug. 8, 1939). *See* Louis Loss, Fundamentals of Securities Regulation 303–06 (1983). *See* §§ 4.12, 4.20–4.21 *infra* for a discussion of the SEC's integration doctrine.

6. Sec. Act Rel. No. 33–2029 (Opinion of General Counsel Aug. 8, 1939) (differences in class of securities issued constitute separate "issues"; integration doctrine not applied). Integration is discussed in §§ 4.12, 4.20–4.21, and 4.29 *infra*.

7. In re UDS, Inc., 16 Sec.Reg. & L.Rep. (BNA) 1981 (SEC No Action Letter Nov. 30, 1984).

invalidate the section 3(a)(9) exemption.[8]

The section 3(a)(9) exemption is available for an otherwise qualifying exchange even if, in addition to the surrender of securities, security holders participating in the exchange must include a cash payment in order to make necessary equitable adjustments respecting dividends or interest paid or payable as compared to other securities holders of the same class.[9] The statutory exemption expressly requires that there be no promotional or underwriting fees, lest the exemption be unavailable. SEC Rule 150[10] excludes from the statutory phrase "commissions or other remuneration" payments by the issuer to its security holders in connection with the exchange provided that such payments are part of the terms of the offer of exchange.

The prohibition on fees is limited to underwriters' and promoters' compensation. The exemption is not lost because of reasonable expenses that may be incurred in connection with the transaction, including printing costs, clerical costs, and payments to third parties providing services in connection with the exchange. The point to be kept in mind is that these expenses may not include payment for promotional activity.

Although the section 3(a)(9) exemption is denominated as a security exemption, it is in fact limited to a specific exchange transaction rather than being dependent upon factors intrinsic to the securities so issued.[11] Thus, once the exchange is completed, an independent exemption must be found for any resales. For example, any subsequent resales of the securities by a controlling person could, by virtue of section 2(11),[12] characterize the seller as an "underwriter" and therefore he or she would not be able to avail himself or herself of a section 4(1) transaction exemption.[13] It has long been the Commission's view that when resales would place the seller in the position of being a statutory underwriter, the section 3(a)(9) exemption is lost.[14]

As noted above, section 3(a)(9), although denominated as an exempt security, functions as a transaction exemption. Since section 3(a)(9) operates in much the same way as a transaction exemption does, an exchange of securities with the issuer's shareholders is subject to being integrated with other transactions taking place at or around the same time.[15] Accordingly, planners of section 3(a)(9) transactions should take

---

8. Squibb Corp., [1970–71 Transfer Binder] Fed.Sec.L.Rep. (CCH) ¶ 78,190 (SEC 1971). *But see* Salomon Bros., [1972–73 Transfer Binder] Fed.Sec.L.Rep. (CCH) ¶ 79,038 (SEC 1972).

9. 17 C.F.R. § 230.149.

10. 17 C.F.R. § 230.150.

11. *See* In the Matter of Thompson Ross Securities Co., 6 S.E.C. 1111, 1118 (SEC 1940).

12. 15 U.S.C.A. § 77b(11). *See* § 4.24 *infra*.

13. 15 U.S.C.A. § 77d(1). *See* §§ 4.23, 4.25 *infra*.

14. Sec. Act Rel. No. 33–646 (Feb. 3, 1936).

15. *E.g.,* Sec. Act Rel. No. 33–2029 (Aug. 8, 1939). *See* Richard W. Jennings & Harold Marsh, Jr., Securities Regulation: Case and Materials 442 (6th ed. 1987):

Accordingly, an exchange of securities with existing security holders cannot be combined with a § 4(2) private offering of the same class of securities to institutional

care to assure that if other offerings are contemplated or have recently taken place, they are sufficiently distinct to avoid the possibility of integration.[16]

The section 3(a)(9) exemption is conditioned on the issuer's good faith and thus is not available if the exchange is part of a plan to evade the securities laws' registration requirements.[17] A number of factors will be considered by the SEC in evaluating the extent of the issuer's good faith. These factors include: the length of time that the securities surrendered to the issuer were outstanding prior to the exchange, the number of security holders originally outstanding, the marketability of the securities exchanged, and whether the exchange was motivated by the issuer's financial considerations rather than in order to facilitate a secondary distribution by a few existing security holders.[18]

§ 4.11 Securities Issued in Judicially or Administratively Approved Reorganizations—Section 3(a)(10)

Section 3(a)(10)[1] of the 1933 Act exempts from registration securities issued in exchange for other securities, where the issuance has been approved by a court or an appropriate administrative body. In order for the exemption to apply, the administrative or judicial approval must be after a "hearing * * * at which all persons to whom it is proposed to issue securities * * * shall have the right to appear."[2] Absent another exemption, all down-stream public sales of securities acquired under the exemption must be registered under the 1933 Act.[3] The section 3(a)(10) exemption is a relatively narrow one as not all approved reorganizations are covered. This is because several other requirements must be met. There must be express statutory authority for the approval by a state or

---

investors. Indeed, if the exchange with shareholders is itself a public offering, the private exemption will also be lost. If, however, the offerings entail different "issues" of securities, the exemption is not destroyed.

The integration doctrine is discussed in § 4.29 *infra*.

16. *See* § 4.29 *infra*.

17. Sec. Act Rel. No. 33–646 (Feb. 3, 1936).

18. *Id.*

§ 4.11

1. 15 U.S.C.A. § 77c(a)(10). *See generally* Barbara A. Ash, Reorganizations and Other Exchanges Under Section 3(a)(10) of the Securities Act of 1933, 75 Nw.U.L.Rev. 1 (1980); Seymour Glanzer, Howard Schiffman & Mark Packman, Settlement of Securities Litigation Through the Issuance of Securities Without Registration: The Use of Section 3(a)(10) in SEC Enforcement Proceedings, 50 Fordham L.Rev. 533 (1982).

Section 3(a)(10) should not be confused with section 3(a)(7)'s exemptions for certificates issued by a trustee under the federal Bankruptcy Act, 15 U.S.C.A. § 77c(a)(7), or the exemptions provided in the Bankruptcy Act, 11 U.S.C.A. § 1145. *See* § 4.8 *supra*.

2. 15 U.S.C.A. § 77c(a)(10).

3. The Commission has indicated that stock acquired in a merger in which the fairness has been passed upon by a state agency is exempt under section 3(a)(10) and the stock received by the shareholders is not restricted stock under Rule 144. Borland Finance Co., 19 Sec.Reg. & L.Rep. (BNA) 1769 (SEC No Action Letter Oct. 10, 1987). The shareholders' holding period is to be determined by Rule 145(d)(2) and they are not permitted to tack on the Rule 144 holding period of the disappearing corporation's stock. *Id*. *See* §§ 4.24–4.25, 5.2–5.3 *infra*.

federal governmental authority.[4] There must also be a formal hearing.[5] The approval must be after consideration of the fairness of the exchange. The courts have yet to give a clear test for the type of examination that satisfies the requirement of a fairness inquiry.[6]

A recent SEC no action response agreed with the assertion that shares issued in settlement of a class action could qualify for the section 3(a)(10) exemption.[7] Court approval of the class action settlement included a determination as to the fairness of the terms. The no action response went on to state that since the company was subject to the 1934 Act reporting requirements, nonaffiliates could resell their shares without regard to Rule 144's restriction but affiliates could resell only in compliance with Rule 144(e)'s volume limitations.[8]

Where all the terms of an exchange are finalized prior to the formal governmental hearing, the exemption will not be available.[9] Additionally, collateral administrative approval of an exchange will not support the exemption. Unless the agency is expressly authorized by law to approve the fairness of an exchange from the standpoint of investors, and in fact holds a fairness hearing after public notice, the exemption will not apply. An example of such a nonqualifying order is found when the Federal Reserve Board approves an exchange offer by a corporation organized to become a bank holding company.[10] However, where a state insurance commissioner is charged with considering fairness in approving an exchange, such a reorganization exchange will be protected by the section 3(a)(10) exemption from registration.[11] Many states have enacted banking[12] and insurance[13] legislation under which any recapitalization will have a fairness hearing that will render the section 3(a)(10) exemption available. Applicable federal statutes include the federal banking acts,[14] the Public Utility Holding Company Act,[15] and the Investment Company Act of 1940.[16]

4. Sec. Act Rel. No. 33–312 (March 15, 1935).

5. *Id.*

6. *See* the authorities cited in footnote 1 *supra.*

7. Bank of Boston Corp., 25 Sec.Reg. & L.Rep. (BNA) 327 (SEC No Action Letter avail. Feb. 23, 1993).

8. *Id.* Since the stock did not fall within the category of "restricted securities," Rule 144(d)'s two-year holding period did not apply. Rule 144 is discussed in § 4.24 *infra.*

9. Fidelity Financial Corp., [1972–73 Transfer Binder] Fed.Sec.L.Rep. (CCH) ¶ 78,840 (SEC 1972).

10. Peoples Mid–Illinois Corp., [1971–72 Transfer Binder] Fed.Sec.L.Rep. (CCH) ¶ 78,-397 (SEC 1971).

11. American Defender Life Ins. Co. [1975–76 Transfer Binder] Fed.Sec.L.Rep. (CCH) ¶ 80,248 (SEC 1975).

12. N.H.Rev.Stat.Ann. 388:1–388:15; Vernon's Ann. Tex.Civ.Stat. art. 852a.

13. *E.g.,* Conn.Gen.Stat.Ann. ch. 38; N.C.Gen.Stat. §§ 58–86.3–86.9.

14. 12 U.S.C.A. §§ 1828(c), 1841–50.

15. 15 U.S.C.A. § 79kkk(e); Sec. Act Rel. No. 33–3000 (June 7, 1944). *See* chapter 15 *infra.*

16. 15 U.S.C.A. §§ 80a *et seq. See* chapter 17 *infra.* For other examples *see* the authorities cited in footnote 1 *supra.*

The section 3(a)(10) exemption from registration has been used in connection with court approved settlements of private litigation.[17] It has recently been held that the exemption's requirement of a fairness hearing was satisfied in a judicially approved settlement of an SEC enforcement action.[18]

§ 4.12 The Exemption for Purely Intrastate Offerings— Section 3(a)(11); SEC Rule 147

An issuer may embark upon a public offering of its securities and avoid the federal registration requirements under the intrastate exemption provided that all aspects of the offering are within the confines of a single state and are purely local in nature.[1] The intrastate exemption from 1933 Act registration is found in section 3(a)(11) which exempts "[a]ny security which is part of an issue offered and sold only to persons resident within a single State or Territory, where the issuer of such security is a person resident and doing business within, or, if a corporation, incorporated by and doing business within, such State or Territory."[2] Both the courts and the SEC have narrowly interpreted the scope of the intrastate offering exemption, thus making it a feasible alternative only in a relatively few situations. The statutory exemption speaks in terms of "part of an issue" which seems to imply that the exemption may be available only for primary offerings. There is authority supporting the interpretation that the intrastate exemption does not apply to secondary offerings.[3] However, other exemptions which utilize the "part of an issue" concept may apply to secondary offerings.[4] To the extent that an exempt intrastate offering is a public one, it will be subject to the state's blue sky registration requirements.[5]

---

17. See generally Ash, supra footnote 1 at 30–31, 38–39. See also Glanzer, Schiffman & Packman supra footnote 1.

18. SEC v. Blinder & Robinson, 511 F.Supp. 799 (D.Colo.1981).

§ 4.12

1. 15 U.S.C.A. § 77c(a)(11).

2. Id. See generally J. William Hicks, Exempted Transactions Under the Securities Act of 1933, ch. 4 (rev. ed. 1980); I, IV Louis Loss, Securities Regulation 591–604, 2600–06 (2d ed. 1961, 1969 supp.); Harold S. Bloomenthal, The Federal Securities Act Intrastate Exemption—Fact or Fiction? 15 Wyo.L.J. 121 (1961); J. Richard Emens & John R. Thomas, The Intrastate Exemption of the Securities Act of 1933 in 1971, 40 U.Cin.L.Rev. 779 (1971); Daniel J. McCauley, Jr., Intrastate Securities Transactions Under the Federal Securities Act, 107 U.Pa.L.Rev. 927 (1959); Hugh L. Sowards, The Twilight of the Intrastate Exemption, 25 Mercer L.Rev. 437 (1974).

Where a seller seeks summary judgment, it is sufficient to show that the securities were sold only to residents; it is then up to the plaintiff to show noncompliance with the exemption's requirements. Busch v. Carpenter, 827 F.2d 653 (10th Cir.1987).

3. E.g., SEC v. Tuchinsky, 1992 WL 226302, [1992 Transfer Binder] Fed.Sec.L.Rep. (CCH) ¶ 96,917 (S.D.Fla.1992), relying on III Louis Loss & Joel Seligman, Securities Regulation 1142–44 & fns. 5–6 (3d ed. 1989) and cases cited therein.

4. See Regulation A, a section 3(b) exemption, which utilizes the "part of the issue" language, but is expressly applicable to secondary offerings. 17 C.F.R. § 230.251(b).

5. Smaller offerings may find an exemption under state law as well. State securities laws are considered in chapter 8 infra.

Although contained in section 3 of the Act, and thus couched in terms of exempt securities as compared with the language of section 4's transaction exemptions,[6] in actuality the intrastate exemption is tied to the particular transaction in question and therefore is not limited to the security itself in regard to the nature of the issuer's rights and obligations thereunder. Unlike the other section 3(a) exemptions for certain types of securities, such as those for securities issued or guaranteed by a governmental subdivision, bank deposits, short term commercial paper, and securities of non profit, charitable organizations, the section 3(a)(11) intrastate exemption will attach only as long as the transaction meets certain transactional requirements although there is no change in the terms of the underlying security. While the exemption is dependent upon the premise that all securities which form a part of the offering will come to rest in the hands of local residents, an out of state resale seven months after the primary offering to residents may not void the intrastate exemption for the original offering.[7] The SEC has opined that offers made outside of the United States to persons not citizens of the United States will not destroy the intrastate exemption.[8]

The title "intrastate" exemption is technically a misnomer to the extent that it may indicate a lack of sufficient interstate contact so as to deprive the SEC of jurisdiction. The exemption is aimed at offerings which are local in character and for which all interested parties including the issuer and all offerees reside in that locality. The exemption is not in any way dependent upon the absence of the 1933 Act's jurisdictional requirement that the sale of a security be through a means or instrumentality of interstate commerce.[9] The choice of a state's boundaries is a somewhat arbitrary line for the limits of the locality considering the exemption's purpose. However, it is one of convenience as it eliminates what otherwise might be difficult factual questions in determining the scope of the local offering exemption. Despite the purpose of the exemption as evidenced by the legislative history, a corporation located in the heart of New York City may not rely on the local "intrastate" exemption for issuance of stock to a New Jersey resident directly across the river, while an issuer in Amarillo, Texas may rely on the exemption for sale to a resident of the southernmost tip of Texas.

Section 3(a)(11) is not a detailed statutory provision. Persons deciding to rely on the exemption have to draw from the relatively scant judicial precedent and SEC interpretive releases and rules available.

---

6. *See* § 4.1 *supra.*

7. Busch v. Carpenter, 598 F.Supp. 519 (D.Utah 1984), judgment affirmed in part, reversed in part 827 F.2d 653 (10th Cir.1987).

8. Commonwealth Equity Trust, 19 Sec.Reg. & L.Rep. (BNA) 355 (SEC No Action Letter Feb. 20, 1987). *See also* First Nat'l Bank & Trust Co. (SEC No Action letter Dec. 19, 1985); Scientific Mfg., Inc. (SEC No Action Letter June 13, 1983); Rule 147(e), (f).

9. If the tests were purely jurisdictional, no exemption would be necessary since by definition the transaction would be beyond the reach of the federal securities laws.

Prior to SEC Rule 147[10] most precedential guidance was found in SEC no action letters. Because of the close factual questions involved, it became common practice for issuers deciding to rely on the intrastate exemption to request a no action letter from the Commission before proceeding. However, the no action letter is a most inefficient method of administrative law making. Furthermore, reliance upon no action letters, which by their very nature are expressly confined to the facts as given, provides little precedential value and thus little comfort to the corporate planner trying to tailor the transaction to the exemption. In response to the uncertainty surrounding the scope of the exemption, the SEC promulgated Rule 147 as a "safe harbor rule." Full compliance with the rule will give the issuer and anyone else relying on it safety from claims that the transaction in question has gone beyond the bounds of section 3(a)(11). However, like the other safe harbor rules,[11] Rule 147 is not exclusive and failure to comply with the rule does not even raise a presumption that the statutory exemption is not available. Accordingly, the pre-Rule 147 case law and SEC interpretations continue to be relevant today.

From the face of the statute it is apparent that in order to qualify for a section 3(a)(11) exemption, not only all purchasers but also all offerees of the securities in question must be residents within a single state. Furthermore, the issuer must be a resident of the same state and be doing business there. In the case of a corporation, in addition to the requirement that its principal place of business be within the state, it is necessary that the state be the corporation's place of incorporation. This last requirement necessarily eliminates the vast number of corporations which, while doing business in one state, select some other jurisdiction such as Delaware to be the state of incorporation in order to take advantage of that state's more attractive corporation laws.

Even where the above-mentioned statutory requirements have been satisfied, the issuer still is not perfectly safe under the intrastate exemption. For example, it has been held that where an offering was made only to Minnesota residents and the issuer, a Minnesota corporation, had its only office in Minnesota, the fact that the proceeds would be used outside of the state was sufficient in and of itself to make the intrastate exemption unavailable.[12] The decision raises significant questions about the exemption's application to any issuer with out-of-state operations and if the offering proceeds may be even indirectly attributed

---

10. 17 C.F.R. § 230.147. *See generally* Eric L. Cummings, Intrastate Exemption and the Shallow Harbor of Rule 147, 69 Nw.U.L.Rev. 167 (1974); Donald B. Gardiner, Intrastate Offering Exemption: Rule 147—Progress or Stalemate?, 35 Ohio S.L.J. 340 (1974); J. William Hicks, Intrastate Offerings Under Rule 147, 72 Mich.L.Rev. 463 (1974); Robert S. Kant, SEC Rule 147—A Further Narrowing of the Intrastate Offering Exemption, 30 Bus.Law. 73 (1974); Note, Securities Regulation: SEC Rule 147: Ten Years of SEC Interpretations, 38 Okla.L.Rev. 507 (1985).

11. *E.g.,* Rules 506 and 144 which are discussed in §§ 4.22, 4.26 *infra. See e.g.,* Tom A. Alberg & Martin E. Lybecker, New SEC Rules 146 and 147: The Nonpublic and Intrastate Offering Exemptions from Registration for Sale of Securities, 74 Colum.L.Rev. 622 (1974).

12. SEC v. McDonald Investment Co., 343 F.Supp. 343 (D.Minn.1972). Compare Rule 147 which imposes an eighty percent minimum on the proceeds to be used within the state. 17 C.F.R. § 230.147(c)(2)(iii).

to that portion of the business.[13] This use of the proceeds requirement is not as troubling if it is viewed in terms of the overall business operations,[14] but it seems to be overreaching if it will void the exemption for securities of an issuer who derives substantial income from in-state operations. For example, an issuer using the proceeds of the offering to purchase wine outside the state for resale within the state can still satisfy the in-state business requirement.[15]

Similarly, a local issuer that planned to use eighty-five percent of the proceeds from an intrastate offering to pay off a loan to an out of state bank that was used to finance purchase of an in-state bank dealing primarily with in-state customers was allowed to rely on the exemption.[16] In contrast, it is clear that where the issuer's income producing operations are located outside of the state, the intrastate exemption will not be available.[17]

As is the case with SEC policy and court decisions on issuer residence, in order to qualify for the safe harbor of Rule 147, both the issuer's place of incorporation or organization and its "principal office" must be located within the same state; and if an individual, his or her principal residence must be located within that state.[18] Rule 147 further requires that in order for an issuer to be deemed doing business within the state, it must have derived at least eighty percent of its gross revenues per annum as well as eighty percent of its assets (including those of its subsidiary on a consolidated basis) from activities and/or real property located within the state over the past fiscal year.[19] This eighty percent requirement is not included within the statute but indicates the Commission's position that the statutory concept of "doing business" means that something more than having the state as its principal office and the place of incorporation or organization is necessary.

Following the lead of the court decisions discussed above, Rule 147 imposes a condition that eighty percent of the net proceeds of the

---

13. The issuer planned to use the proceeds for loans secured by real property outside of the state. Although the loan contracts were to be governed by Minnesota law and despite the fact that the issuer had in-state income as well, the court denied the exemption. In its broadest reading, the decision can be seen as adding to the statutory doing business requirement a rule that the proceeds from the particular offering be used in the state.

14. *See* SEC v. Truckee Showboat, Inc., 157 F.Supp. 824 (S.D.Cal.1957); 17 C.F.R. § 230.147(c)(2). *See also* footnotes 15–17, *infra*.

15. Adventures in Wine, [1976–77 Transfer Binder] Fed.Sec.L.Rep. (CCH) ¶ 80,952 (SEC 1977). *See also* Midwest Management Corp. v. Stephens, 291 N.W.2d 896 (Iowa 1980) (Rule 147 is not exclusive; the key factor is the location of the income producing activity, not whether the revenues come from outside the state); Fina Bancorp., Inc., 19 Sec.Reg. & L.Rep. (BNA) 961 (SEC No Action Letter June 15, 1987) (semble).

16. Fina Bancorp., Inc., 19 Sec.Reg. & L.Rep. (BNA) 961 (SEC No Action Letter June 15, 1987). The SEC staff reasoned that since the issuer's business was primarily instate, paying off the existing loan to an out of state lender was not inconsistent with Rule 147(2)(iii)'s doing business requirement. *See* 17 C.F.R. § 230.147(c)(2)(iii).

17. *See, e.g.,* Busch v. Carpenter, 827 F.2d 653, 658 (10th Cir.1987); Chapman v. Dunn, 414 F.2d 153, 158–59 (6th Cir.1969); SEC v. Truckee Showboat, Inc., 157 F.Supp. 824 (S.D.Cal.1957).

18. 17 C.F.R. § 230.147(c)(1).

19. 17 C.F.R. § 230.147(c)(2)(i), (ii).

offering be used in the state.[20] When taking a look at the face of the statute there is at least a question as to whether either of the rule's eighty percent requirements is an overreaching interpretation. Nevertheless, they are interpretations which have to date not met successful challenges either at the administrative or judicial level. Since Rule 147 is a safe harbor rule, such challenges are unlikely. The eighty percent test nevertheless is evidence of the SEC's position that something more than the principal office requirement is necessary. Thus, it is fair to assume that issuers falling significantly below the eighty percent threshold may have difficulty establishing the statutory exemption.

Both under the statutory exemption and pursuant to Rule 147, downstream sales of part of an intrastate issue to nonresidents can destroy the availability of the intrastate exemption. Obviously, an issuer cannot select an in-state resident to operate as a conduit or underwriter[21] and thereby avoid the limitations of the exemption. However, even inadvertent downstream sales to nonresidents, at least those taking place within a reasonably short period after the distribution for which the exemption is claimed, will destroy the exemption for all sales made pursuant to the exemption. The safe harbor guidelines for limitation on resales is found in Rule 147(e)[22] which prohibits all resales to nonresident purchasers within nine months "from the date of the last sale by the issuer of such securities." Even outside of the safe harbor rule, it is clear that a limited number of nonresident resales will render the exemption inapplicable to the entire offering.[23] In such a case, even the resident purchasers will be placed in a position of being able to claim that the securities they purchased were sold in violation of section 5, thus giving them a right of rescission under section 12(1).[24] It has long been the Commission's position, however, that once securities sold pursuant to the intrastate exemption have finally come to rest in the hands of residents, subsequent isolated resales to nonresidents will not destroy the prior exemptions.[25] In terms of planning such transactions, the nine month safe harbor guidelines of Rule 147 provide a good rule of thumb.

Notwithstanding Rule 147's detail as to the requirements of residency so far as the issuer is concerned, the rule is much more open with regard to purchasers' and offerees' residence. The test applicable to an

---

20. 17 C.F.R. § 230.147(c)(2)(iii).

21. Underwriter is defined in section 2(11), 15 U.S.C.A. § 77b(11). *See* § 4.24 *infra.*

22. 17 C.F.R. § 230.147(e). A shorter period might still be permitted under the case law interpreting the scope of the statutory exemption. *See* footnote 7 *supra.*

23. *See* Hillsborough Investment Corp. v. SEC, 276 F.2d 665 (1st Cir.1960), *s.c.* 173 F.Supp. 86 (D.N.H.1958).

24. Sec. Act Rel. No. 33–4434 (Dec. 6, 1961). *See* 15 U.S.C.A. § 77*l* (1) which is discussed in § 7.2 *infra.*

25. Sec. Act Rel. No. 33–4434 (Dec. 6, 1961). *See also* Busch v. Carpenter, 827 F.2d 653 (10th Cir.1987), *affirming in part* 598 F.Supp. 519 (D.Utah 1984); Commonwealth Equity Trust, 19 Sec.Reg. & L.Rep. (BNA) 355 (SEC No Action Letter Feb. 20, 1987); First National Bank & Trust Co. (SEC No Action Letter Dec. 19, 1985); Scientific Manufacturing, Inc. (SEC No Action Letter June 13, 1983).

individual is "his principal residence"[26] which seems to limit each individual to one state, thus eliminating vacation homes and the like. A similar test has been adopted under the statute.[27] Business entities including corporations, trusts, and partnerships qualify as resident offerees and purchasers if they have their principal office in the state.[28] There is no requirement that the offeree be organized under the laws of that state although it would have to be so organized in order to qualify as an issuer. Furthermore, the rule's eighty percent revenue and asset tests do not apply to offerees and purchasers as they apply only to issuers. The rule also provides that where a corporation, partnership, or trust is formed *for the purpose* of purchasing the securities in question, *all* of its beneficial owners must be residents.[29] It thus appears that a bona fide preexisting entity may qualify as a purchaser although it has nonresident owners. As to such entities the SEC has opined that a nonresident trustee of a resident's individual retirement account will not disqualify the trust as a resident purchaser.[30] Similarly, with regard to partnerships, it has been held that the fact that one partner resided in another state was not in itself sufficient to prevent the partnership from being a resident for purposes of section 3(a)(11).[31] The SEC has indicated that Rule 147 would be available for limited partnership interests to be offered solely to residents of the partnership's state of organization even though the general partner was wholly owned by an out-of-state corporation.[32]

Another key factor in an intrastate offering and in deciding whether or not reliance is to be placed upon Rule 147 is the integration doctrine which operates to telescope two or more transactions into one and also applies to other exemptions under the Act.[33] The integration doctrine is the Commission's counterpart of the IRS' step-transaction analysis under which transactions which appear to be separate in form will be scrutinized closely as to substance in order to determine whether or not in fact they should be treated as two distinct transactions. Specifically, with regard to the intrastate exemption contained in section 3(a)(11), the question of the exemption's availability arises in the context of determining whether a given security transaction is "part of an issue" within the

---

26. 17 C.F.R. § 230.147(d)(2).

27. *See generally* J. William Hicks, Exempted Transactions Under the Securities Act of 1933 ch. 4 (1980 rev. ed.).

28. 17 C.F.R. § 230.147(d)(3).

29. 17 C.F.R. § 230.147(d)(3).

30. Fair Valley Properties No. 2, [1981–82 Transfer Binder] Fed.Sec.L.Rep. (CCH) ¶ 77,003 (SEC No Action Letter 1981).

31. Grenader v. Spitz, 390 F.Supp. 1112 (S.D.N.Y.1975), *reversed on other grounds* 537 F.2d 612 (2d Cir.1976), *cert. denied* 429 U.S. 1009, 97 S.Ct. 541, 50 L.Ed.2d 619 (1976).

32. GHM/Massachusetts Health Care Partners–I Limited Partnership, 20 Sec.Reg. & L.Rep. (BNA) 936 (SEC No Action Letter available May 31, 1988).

33. *See, e.g.,* Sidney Sosin, The Intrastate Exemptions, Public Offering and the Issue Concept, 16 W.Res.L.Rev. 110 (1974). The integration doctrine has particular impact with regard to Regulation A offerings (*see* § 4.15 *infra*) and Regulation D's exemptions (*see* §§ 4.16–4.22 *infra*).

meaning of the statute. The determination of which transactions constitute an "issue" or "part of an issue" is a matter of federal rather than state law.[34] In determining whether the integration doctrine will apply and whether the transaction is to be considered part of a certain issue, the Commission will consider a number of factors: "(1) are the offerings part of a single plan of financing; (2) do the offerings involve issuance of the same class of security; (3) are the offerings made at or about the same time; (4) is the same type of consideration to be received, and (5) are the offerings made for the same general purpose."[35] Rule 147 in its preliminary notes expressly adopts this five factor test and points out that "any one or more of the * * * factors may be determinative."[36] The rule establishes a six month safe harbor for avoiding integration with out of state sales.[37]

§ 4.13   The Small Issue Exemptions

The expense of 1933 Act registration makes it uneconomical to look to the public capital markets for many smaller-scale financing needs. This pressure was eased to some extent by the adoption of simplified Form S–18 for offerings under seven and one-half million dollars.[1]

In 1992, the SEC proposed a new registration form, Form SB–2 to replace Form S–18.[2] Form SB–2 was adopted, as was its companion Form SB–1.[3] While the availability of Form S–18 was based on the dollar amount of the offering, Form SB–2 depends upon the size of the issuer regardless of the size of the offering.[4] The new form was part of the SEC's comprehensive small business initiatives that were designed to facilitate smaller offerings and offerings by small businesses.[5] Form SB–

---

34. Sec. Act Rel. No. 33–4434 (Dec. 6, 1961).

35. *Id.*

36. Preliminary note to Rule 147; 17 C.F.R. § 230.147.

37. 17 C.F.R. § 230.147(b)(2). *See* the nine-month limit on resales in Rule 147(e) which is discussed in the text accompanying footnote 22 *supra. See also* Busch v. Carpenter, 598 F.Supp. 519 (D.Utah 1984), *affirmed in part and reversed in part* 827 F.2d 653 (10th Cir.1987) (out of state resale occurring seven months after intrastate offering did not destroy the exemption for the intrastate sales).

§ 4.13

1. *See* § 3.3 *supra. See generally* Jerry L. Arnold & Merle W. Hopkins, Small Firm Securities Registration in the S–18 Era: Perceptions of Professionals, 8 Corp.L.Rev. 135 (1985).

2. *See* Sec. Act Rel. No. 33–6949, 6 Fed.Sec.L.Rep. (CCH) ¶ 72,439 (SEC July 30, 1992); Sec. Act Rel. No. 33–6924, [1991–1992 Transfer Binder] Fed.Sec.L.Rep. (CCH) ¶ 84,931 (March 11, 1992).

3. *See* § 3.3 *supra.*

4. Form SB–2 is available to a "small business issuer" which would be an issuer with revenues of less than $25 million for its most recent fiscal year provided that the issuer is not a foreign private issuer or foreign government, an investment company, or a majority-owned subsidiary of a non "small business issuer." *See* §§ 3.3, 3.4 *supra.* "Small business issuer" is defined in 1933 Act Rule 405 and 1934 Act Rule 12b–2. 17 C.F.R. §§ 230.405, 240.12b–2.

5. These initiatives included the raising of the dollar ceiling on Regulation A, relaxation of the requirements under Rule 504, and the adoption of Reg. S–B, containing disclosure guidelines for small businesses, providing simpler disclosure than Regulation S–K. *See*

1, which also was an outgrowth of the small business initiatives, is available for small business offerings of up to ten million dollars.

In addition to the streamlined registration forms for small business issuers, since 1933, the Congress and the Commission have developed a number of exemptions for small issues.[6] The small issue exemptions were adopted in recognition of the economics involved and more importantly because of the SEC's view that due to their size or scope, or the nature of the purchasers, certain transactions do not call for the expansive disclosure required by a full-fledged 1933 Act registration.

The applicable rules, which are discussed in the succeeding sections, are based upon section 4(2)'s exemption for transactions not involving a public offering,[7] section 3(b)'s exemptions for certain offerings not in excess of five million dollars,[8] or section 4(6)'s exemption for sales exclusively to accredited investors.[9] Small issues that are *purely* local in nature may qualify for section 3(a)(11)'s intrastate exemption[10] which is not dependent on the size of the offering.

In 1982 the Commission adopted Regulation D[11] in an effort to simplify the overlapping rough edges of the most frequently relied upon small issue exemptions. Regulation A[12] is another exemption for offerings by an issuer of up to $5 million per year of which no more than $1.5 million can be attributed to a secondary offering.[13]

The succeeding sections will discuss all of the available small issue exemptions. The chart on pages 212–214 summarizes some of the most

---

generally Janvey, The SEC's Small Business Initiatives: Regulatory Reform or Shabby Conduct?, 21 Sec.Reg.L.J. 4 (1993); Levinson & De Toro, A Guide to the SEC's Small Business Initiative, 17 Seton Hall Legis.J. 75 (1993).

6. *See generally* 3A Harold S. Bloomenthal, Securities and Federal Corporate Law ch. 5 (1981 rev.); J. William Hicks, Exempted Transactions Under the Securities Act of 1933 (1979); Roy L. Brooks, Small Business Financing Alternatives Under the Securities Act of 1933, 13 U.C. Davis L.Rev. 543 (1980); Stuart R. Cohn, Securities Markets for Small Issuers: The Barrier of Federal Solicitation and Advertising Prohibitions, 38 U.Fla.L.Rev. 1 (1986); Julian M. Meer, The Private Offering Exemption Under the Federal Securities Act—A Study in Administrative and Judicial Contraction, 20 Sw.L.J. 503 (1966).

7. 15 U.S.C.A. § 77d(2). *See* § 4.21 *infra*. The section 4(2) exemption is not limited to small issues. It can be used, and frequently is used for large nonpublic offerings. *Id.*

8. 15 U.S.C.A. § 77c(b). *See* §§ 4.14–4.15, 4.18–4.19 *infra*.

9. 15 U.S.C.A. § 77d(6). *See* § 4.20 *infra*.

10. 15 U.S.C.A. § 77c(a)(11). *See* § 4.12 *supra*.

11. 17 C.F.R. §§ 230.501–506. *See* §§ 4.16–4.22 *infra*. *See generally* Marvin H. Mahoney, Regulation D: Coherent Exemptions for Small Business Under the Securities Act of 1933, 24 Wm. & Mary L.Rev. 121 (1982); Theodore Parnall, Bruce R. Kohle & Curtis W. Huff, Private and Limited Offerings After a Decade of Experimentation: The Evolution of Regulation D, 12 N.M.L.Rev. 633 (1982).

12. 17 C.F.R. §§ 230.251–252. *See* § 4.15 *infra*. *See generally* Harvey Frank, The Processing of Small Issues Under Regulation A, 1962 Duke L.J. 507 (1962).

13. *See* Sec. Act Rel. No. 33–6949, 6 Fed.Sec.L.Rep. (CCH) ¶ 72,439 (SEC July 30, 1992); Sec. Act Rel. No. 33–6924, [1991–1992 Transfer Binder] Fed.Sec.L.Rep. (CCH) ¶ 84,931 (March 11, 1992). The exemption was limited to issues up to $1.5 million prior to the 1992 amendment.

frequently used exemptions.[14] The chart does not include section 3(a)(11)'s intrastate exemption.[15]

14. This chart is derived from Sec. Act Rel. No. 33–6389 (March 8, 1982).

15. 15 U.S.C.A. § 77c(a)(11). *See* § 4.12 *infra*.

Comparison Item	Reg. A	Rule 504	Rule 505	4(2) Rule 506	Sec. 4(6)
Aggregate Offering Price Limitation	$5 million by issuer (every 12 months) ($1.5 million/person other than the issuer).	$1.0 million (every 12 months).	$5.0 million (every 12 months).	Unlimited.	$5.0 million.
Number of Investors	Unlimited.	Unlimited.	35 + unlimited accredited investors.	35 + unlimited accredited investors	Unlimited accredited. ONLY Accredited.
Investor Qualification	None.	None.	Accredited or none required.	All purchasers must be sophisticated and wealthy (alone or with purchaser representative). "Accredited" purchaser is presumed to be qualified. [Query whether § 4(2)'s offeree qualification must also be read into rule 506].	
Limitations on Manner of Offering	Offering Circular. Some limited advertising or announcement.	None	General solicitation not permitted.	General solicitation not permitted.	General solicitation not permitted.
Limits on Resale Issuer Qualifications	None. Only U.S. and Canadian issuers. No investment companies or "development stage" companies. No in-	None. No investment companies. Not available to 1934 Act reporting companies. No blank check companies. But see rule 504a.	Restricted. No investment companies or issuers which are disqualified under Reg. A's underlying rule.	Restricted. None.	Restricted. None.

Comparison Item	Reg. A	Rule 504	Rule 505	Rule 506	Sec. 4(6)
Notice of Sales to SEC	Issuer or underwriters which are disqualified by Reg. A wrongdoing rule. Form 1-A: 7 copies to National or Regional Office. Sales material—7 copies to Regional Office 5 days before use. Form 2-A to report sales.	Form D: 6 copies filed within 15 days of first sale, every 6 months after first sale and 30 days after last sale.	Form D: 6 copies filed within 15 days of first sale, every 6 months after 1st sale, and 30 days after last sale.	Form D: 6 copies filed within 15 days of first sale, every 6 months after 1st sale and 30 days after last sale.	Form D (Form 4(6) was rescinded 4/15/82).

Information Requirements	Offering Circular—See rule 253.	No information.	1. If purchased solely by accredited, no information specified.
			2. If purchased by non-accredited:
			  a. Non-reporting companies must furnish:
			    i. Offerings up to $2.0 million: the same kind of information required in a Regulation A offering.
			    ii. Offerings up to $7.5 million: information in part 1 of Form S-18 or available registration, 2 year financials, 1 year audited—if undue effort or expense, issuer other than limited partnership only balance sheet as of 120 days before offering must be audited. If limited partnership and undue effort or expense, financials may be tax basis.
				1. If purchased solely by accredited, no information specified.
				2. If purchased by non-accredited:
				  a. Non-reporting companies must furnish:
				    i. Offerings up to $2.0 million: the same kind of information required in a Regulation A offering.
				    ii. Offerings up to $7.5 million: information in part 1 of Form S-18 or available registration, 2 year financials, 1 year audited—if undue effort or expense, issuer other than limited partnership only balance sheet as of 120 days before offering must be audited. If limited partnership and undue effort or expense, financials may be tax basis.
					No information specified.

Comparison Item	Reg. A	Rule 504	Rule 505	Rule 506	Sec. 4(6)

			iii. Offerings over $7.5 million (not applicable to rule 505).
			
			b. *Reporting Companies:*
			  i. Rule 14a-3 annual report to shareholders, definitive proxy statement and 10-K, if requested, plus subsequent reports and other updating information or
			  ii. Information in most recent Form S-1 or Form 10 or Form 10-K plus subsequent reports and other updating information.
			c. *Issuers must make available prior to sale:*
			  i. Exhibits
			  ii. Written information given to accredited investors
			  iii. Opportunity to ask questions & receive answers
				iii. Offerings over $7.5 million: information—if available in part 1 of registration—of undue efforts or expense, issuers other than limited partnerships only balance sheet as of 120 days before offering must be offering—if limited partnership and undue effort or expense, financials may be unaudible.
				
				b. *Reporting Companies:*
				  i. Rule 14a-3 annual report to shareholders, definitive proxy statement and 10-K, if requested, plus subsequent reports and other updating information or
				  ii. Information in most recent Form S-1 or Form 10 or Form 10-K plus other updating information.
				c. *Issuers must make available prior to sale:*
				  i. Exhibits
				  ii. Written information given to accredited investors
				  iii. Opportunity to ask questions & receive answers	

§ 4.14 Qualified Exemptions for Small Issues; Sections 3(b), 4(6) and 3(c)

Section 3(b)

Section 3(b) of the 1933 Act[1] empowers the SEC to promulgate rules and regulations exempting issues of securities where the aggregate per issue offering price to the public does not exceed five million dollars.[2] The only statutory limitation on the creation of the exemption is that the Commission must find "that the enforcement of [the Act] with respect to such securities is not necessary in the public interest and for the protection of investors by reason of the small amount involved or the limited character of public offering."[3] Over the years, section 3(b), which when enacted in 1933 had a $100,000 cap, has to some extent kept up with inflation.[4] Most recently, the statutory limit was increased in 1980 to the current five million dollars. In the 1990's the SEC has been engaged in a number of small issues initiatives which are designed to make offerings of small issues and by small issuers more efficient without sacrificing the goal of investor protection. With this in mind, in 1992, the Commission recommended that Congress increase section 3(b)'s ceiling to ten million dollars.

Section 3(b) is significantly different from the other major exemptions from registration as it is not self executing. It is dependent upon SEC rules for implementation. It is not simply the size of the offering that leads to the exemption, it is compliance with the guidelines established by the applicable SEC rules.

The section 3(b) exemptions include the qualified exemptions for offerings up to five million dollars sanctioned by Regulation A,[5] and Rule 504's exemption for offerings not exceeding one million dollars.[6] Section 3(b) also empowers Rule 505's exemption for certain offerings up to five million dollars, sold to no more than thirty-five "unaccredited investors" but which may also include an unlimited number of "accredited investors."[7] Additionally, the section 3(b) exemptions for small issues should be read in conjunction with Rule 506's non-exclusive safe harbor for exempt transactions that do not involve a public offering.[8] The Commis-

---

§ 4.14

1. 15 U.S.C.A. § 77c(b).

2. In 1992, the SEC recommended to Congress that the section 3(b) limit be increased from $5 million to $10 million.

3. 15 U.S.C.A. § 77c(b).

4. The maximum amount was increased from $100,000 in 1933 to $300,000 in 1945, and to $500,000 in 1970. Notwithstanding the increases there was a clamoring for additional exemptions from federal registration for small issues. Accordingly, in recent years, the upward limits of the exemption have been significantly expanded: from $500,000 to 1.5 million dollars in 1978 and then again to two million dollars within the same year.

5. 17 C.F.R. §§ 230.251–263. *See* § 4.15 *infra*.

6. 17 C.F.R. § 230.504. *See* § 4.18 *infra*.

7. 17 C.F.R. § 230.505. *See* § 4.17 *infra*.

8. 17 C.F.R. § 230.506. *See* § 4.17 *infra*.

sion has also exercised its exemptive power under section 3(b) to exempt from registration employee and consultant stock compensation plans (ranging from $500,000 to $5,000,000 annually) provided that the issuer is not subject to the Securities and Exchange Act's periodic reporting requirements.[9]

Section 4(6) and Accredited Investors

In conjunction with the 1980 amendments that increased the dollar amount in section 3(b), Congress enacted section 4(6)[10] to further expand the exemptions available for small issues. Section 4(6) exempts all security sales made to "accredited investors" where the aggregate amount sold does not exceed the dollar limit of section 3(b) (*i.e.*, five million dollars). The only conditions to a section 4(6) exemption are that there be no public advertising or solicitation for the offering, and that an appropriate notice of reliance on the exemption be filed with the SEC. SEC Form 4(6) which was the appropriate document for filing a section 4(6) notice was rescinded in 1982 and has been replaced by Form D.

The section 4(6) exemption is available only for sales of securities that have been offered only to "accredited investors" as defined in section 2(15) of the Act.[11] The statutory definition of this term expressly includes a number of institutional investors, including banks, insurance companies, and investment companies that are registered under the Investment Company Act of 1940, small business investment companies licensed by the Small Business Administration, and employee benefit plans that are subject to ERISA. Additionally, the definition of an accredited investor states that "any person who, on the basis of such factors as financial sophistication, net worth, knowledge, and experience in financial matters, or amount of assets under management qualifies as an accredited investor under rules and regulations which the Commission shall prescribe." [12]

The Commission has exercised this rulemaking power by promulgating Rule 215.[13] Rule 215 includes within the definition of "accredited investor" banks, savings and loan associations, and broker-dealers.[14] Rule 215 further includes an issuer's officers, directors and general

---

9. 17 C.F.R. § 230.701, adopted in Sec.Act Rel. No. 33–6768, [1987–88 Transfer Binder] Fed.Sec.L.Rep. (CCH) ¶ 84,231 (April 14, 1988). *See* § 4.15.1 *infra.*

10. 15 U.S.C.A. § 77(d)(6). *See generally* Frederich H. Thomforde, Jr., Relief for Small Businesses: Two New Exemptions from SEC Registration, 48 Tenn.L.Rev. 323 (1981). Section 4(6) is discussed further in § 4.20 *infra.*

11. 15 U.S.C.A. § 77b(15).

12. 15 U.S.C.A. § 77b(15)(ii). *See* 17 C.F.R. § 230.215.

13. 17 C.F.R. § 230.215. *See also* 17 C.F.R. § 230.501(a) which provides a parallel definition that is applicable to transactions falling within the exemptions set forth in Regulation D. Regulation D is discussed in §§ 4.16–4.19, 4.22 *infra.*

14. 17 C.F.R. § 230.215(a). *See also* 17 C.F.R. § 230.501(a)(1). Also included are entities qualifying as private business development companies under the Investment Company Act. 17 C.F.R. § 230.215(b). *See also* 17 C.F.R. § 230.501(a)(2).

partners in the definition of accredited investor.[15] The foregoing are presumably included in the definition because of their sophistication and/or access to information concerning the issuer. The rule goes on, however, to qualify additional individuals and entities solely on the basis of wealth. Thus, the concept of accredited investor includes individuals having a net worth (or joint net worth with their spouse) exceeding one million dollars at the time of the transaction.[16] Also included are individuals having an annual income in excess of two hundred thousand dollars (or joint annual income of three hundred thousand dollars) in each of the two most recent years.[17] Corporations, partnerships, business trusts, and nonprofit organizations having total assets in excess of five million dollars are classified as accredited investors provided that the entities were not formed for the specific purpose of acquiring the securities to be offered.[18] In addition, any entity in which all the equity owners are accredited investors, itself, qualifies as an accredited investor.[19]

Section 2(15)'s concept of an accredited investor is incorporated into Regulation D's small issue exemptions.[20] Section 4(6) was designed as a companion to the exemptions available under section 3(b). This has been accomplished through the Commission's inclusion of the accredited investor concept into Regulation D.

Section 3(c)

In addition to the foregoing exemptions available under section 3(b), section 3(c) of the Act[21] authorizes the Commission by its rules and regulations to exempt securities issued by small business investment companies organized under the Small Business Investment Act of 1958,[22] provided that enforcement of the 1933 Act "with respect to such securities is not necessary in the public interest and for the protection of investors."[23] The Commission has exercised this power by promulgating Regulation E[24] which exempts securities issued by Small Business Investment Companies that are also registered under the Investment Company Act of 1940.[25] Under Regulation E the aggregate offering price of all of the exempt securities cannot exceed five million dollars.[26] The SEC has expanded the scope of Regulation E by raising the aggregate offering

---

15. 17 C.F.R. § 230.215(d). *See also* 17 C.F.R. § 230.501(a)(4).

16. 17 C.F.R. § 230.215(e). *See also* 17 C.F.R. § 230.501(a)(5).

17. 17 C.F.R. § 230.215(f). *See also* 17 C.F.R. § 230.501(a)(6).

18. 17 C.F.R. § 230.215(c), (g). *See also* 17 C.F.R. § 230.501(a)(3), (7).

19. 17 C.F.R. § 230.215(h). *See also* 17 C.F.R. § 230.501(a)(8).

20. Regulation D is discussed in §§ 4.16–4.22 *infra*.

21. 15 U.S.C.A. § 77c(c).

22. Small Business Investment Act of 1958, 72 Stat. 689 (codified in scattered sections of 5, 12 of 15 U.S.C.A.).

23. 15 U.S.C.A. § 77c(c).

24. 17 C.F.R. §§ 230.601–230.610(a)(2).

25. 15 U.S.C.A. §§ 80a–1–80a–64. *See* chapter 17 *infra*.

26. *See* 17 C.F.R. §§ 230.601–.610(a).

price for all securities that may be sold within a twelve month period from five hundred thousand to five million dollars.[27] The aggregate offering price of securities that may be issued without a Regulation E offering circular was raised from fifty thousand to one hundred thousand dollars. The regulation as amended also allows the use of a preliminary offering circular between the time that the notice of the offering is filed and the date on which the securities may be sold. By definition, the section 3(c) exemption is not available to the vast majority of public issuers of securities.

§ 4.15 Regulation A—Qualified Exemption for Offerings Up to $5,000,000 Per Year

The oldest and at one time most widely used of the section 3(b) exemptions for small issues is the qualified exemption from registration established pursuant to Regulation A which is embodied in SEC Rules 251 through 263.[1] The exemption provided in Regulation A is dependent upon the securities being offered through the use of an offering circular, in a manner similar to the use of a prospectus in a registered offering. In order to use the Regulation A exemption, an issuer may not offer securities that exceed an aggregate amount of five million dollars in any one year.[2] As has been the case with section 3(b),[3] the dollar ceiling for a Regulation A offering has increased over time. As will be seen below, this ceiling includes all securities sold under any section 3(b) exemption.

In order to qualify for the Regulation A exemption the issuer (and selling shareholders in the case of a secondary distribution) must comply with the Regulation's notification and disclosure requirements, including the offering circular delivery requirements that, in essence, have the same effect as a "mini registration." The Regulation A disclosure statements contain much of the information that would be included in a full-blown registration statement, and Rule 253's provisions for an

---

27. 17 C.F.R. § 230.603, adopted in Sec.Act Rel. No. 33–6546 [1984 Transfer Binder] Fed.Sec.L.Rep. (CCH) ¶ 83,653 (Aug. 30, 1984).

§ 4.15

1. 17 C.F.R. §§ 230.251 thru 230.263. *See generally* Harvey Frank, The Processing of Small Issues of Securities Under Regulation A, 1962 Duke L.J. 507; Robert R. Burge, Regulation A: A Review and a Look at Recent Developments, 46 Los Angeles Bar Bull. 290 (1971).

2. 17 C.F.R. § 230.254. The exemption did not take full advantage of section 3(b)'s $5,000,000 ceiling until 1992 when it was amended. *See* Sec. Act Rel. No. 33–6949, 6 Fed.Sec.L.Rep. (CCH) ¶ 72,439 (SEC July 30, 1992); Sec. Act Rel. No. 33–6924, [1991–1992 Transfer Binder] Fed.Sec.L.Rep. (CCH) ¶ 84,931 (March 11, 1992). Prior to the 1992 amendments, Regulation A was relatively little used in light of the alternative of registration under the abbreviated former Form S–18 for offerings of up to $7.5 million.

3. The maximum amount was increased from $100,000 in 1933 to $300,000 in 1945, and to $500,000 in 1970. Notwithstanding the increases there was a clamoring for additional exemptions from federal registration for small issues. Accordingly, in recent years, the upward limits of the exemption have been significantly expanded: from $500,000 to 1.5 million dollars in 1978 and then again to two million dollars within the same year. In 1980, the ceiling was raised to the current $5 million and in 1992 the SEC proposed that Congress raise it again to $10 million.

offering circular are analogous to the section 5(b) prospectus delivery requirements.[4] Similarly, Rule 255 provides for the use of a preliminary offering circular prior to the date on which the offering becomes qualified for Regulation A sales.[5] As compared with a registered offering, Regulation A has broader provisions for prefiling gun jumping sales solicitations. In particular, Rule 254 permits a solicitation of investor interest prior to the use of an offering statement.[6] This procedure is colloquially referred to as testing the waters. It is to be recalled that any comparable testing in the context of a registered offering would constitute an illegal offer to sell in violation of section 5 of the Act.[7]

Regulation A thus bears many similarities to a registered offering. However, it must be remembered that Regulation A provides an *exemption* from registration and is not a different form of registration. As a result, any misstatements in the Regulation A notification form and offering circular violate the 1933 Act's antifraud provisions[8] but there is no liability under section 11[9] which concerns only material misstatements and omissions in a *bona fide* registration statement. Liability for misstatements and omissions thus must be based upon the questionable remedy under sections 12(2) or 17(a) of the 1933 Act or upon the implied remedy under SEC Rule 10b–5.[10] Similarly, since a Regulation A offering is not the equivalent of a registered offering, it will not provide the basis for registration by coordination under state blue sky laws.[11]

---

4. 17 C.F.R. § 230.253. The prospectus requirements are discussed in §§ 2.4, 2.5, 3.2 *supra.*

Another similarity between a Regulation A offering and a registered offering is the impact on the market. Thus, for example, the Commission treats public offerings and Regulation A offerings alike with regard to the prohibition against short sellers covering the short sale with securities sold pursuant to an offering. 17 C.F.R. § 240.10b–21(T). *See* § 10.12 *infra.*

5. 17 C.F.R. § 230.255.

6. 17 C.F.R. § 230.254.

7. 15 U.S.C.A. § 77e. *See* § 2.3 *supra.*

8. Sections 12(2) and 17(a), 15 U.S.C.A. §§ 77*l*(2), 77q(a) are discussed in §§ 7.5–7.6 *infra.* Rule 10b–5, 17 C.F.R. § 240.10b–5, is discussed in §§ 13.2–13.12 *infra.*

9. 15 U.S.C.A. § 77k. *See* §§ 7.3–7.4 *infra.*

10. *See* footnote 8 *supra.*

The likelihood of an implied remedy under section 17(a) may at best be only a theoretical possibility in light of the overwhelming majority of recent cases rejecting such a remedy. *See* § 13.13, *infra.*

Although, on its face, section 12(2) would appear to be available for any misstatement or omission made by a seller of securities, the Supreme Court has held otherwise. In Gustafson v. Alloyd Co., ___ U.S. ___, 115 S.Ct. 1061, 131 L.Ed.2d 1 (1995), the Court held that the section 12(2) remedy is available only with regard to sales made via the use of a prospectus as that term is used in the 1933 Act. It is likely that section 12(2) might still apply to those exempt transactions in which there nevertheless is a public offering. The language of the Court in *Gustafson* could be used to support the construction that an offering circular required by Regulation A also would fall within the statutory definition of prospectus. *See* the discussion in § 7.5 *infra.*

11. Most state blue sky laws provide for a simplified registration procedure in coordination with federal registration. *See, e.g.,* Uniform Securities Act § 303. Under these provisions the state registrant merely attaches a copy of the federal form for filing with the state securities official. When a federal exemption from registration is obtained, such as

As outlined above, and discussed more fully below, in order to comply with Regulation A, the qualifying issuer must follow steps similar to those required in a full-fledged registration.[12] Nevertheless, the Regulation A offering will prove to be significantly less expensive than registration, especially in terms of legal, printing, underwriting and accounting fees.

Issuers Eligible for Regulation A

The Regulation A exemption is not available to every issuer. Regulation A may be used only by an issuer which is organized under the laws of the United States or Canada and which has its principal place of business in the United States or Canada.[13] Furthermore, the issuer must not have been subject to the 1934 Act's periodic reporting requirements immediately before the Regulation A offering.[14] The issuer's business may also be a disqualification from the Regulation exemption. The exemption is unavailable for the offer or sale of: (1) fractional undivided interests in oil, gas, or mineral rights,[15] or (2) for securities issued by registered investment companies.[16] Additionally, Regulation A may not be used by "development stage" companies, which are those issuers that have no specific business plan.[17] It is further provided that a plan to merge with unidentified companies does not qualify as a specific business plan.[18] The rationale behind the business plan requirement is to make Regulation A unavailable for "blank check" companies and other common vehicles for initial offerings in the penny stock markets.[19]

Regulation A contains so-called "bad boy" provisions which denies the availability of the exemption where the issuer, its predecessors or any affiliated issuer has been subject to proceedings stemming from violations of the federal securities laws.[20]

by reliance on Regulation A, state registration by coordination is unavailable and the issuer must look to either registration by qualification (the long-form) or registration by notification (the short-form). Uniform Securities Act §§ 302, 304. The state blue sky laws are discussed in chapter 8 *infra*.

12. *See* chapter 3 *supra*.

13. Rule 251(a)(1), 17 C.F.R. § 230.251(a)(1).

14. Rule 251(a)(2), 17 C.F.R. § 230.251(a)(2).

15. Rule 251(a)(5), 17 C.F.R. § 230.251(a)(5). There is a separate exemption for these interests. *See* Regulation B and SEC Rule 300, 17 C.F.R. § 230.300.

16. Rule 251(a)(4), 17 C.F.R. § 230.252(a)(4). The Investment Company Act is discussed in chapter 17 *infra*.

17. Rule 251(a)(3), 17 C.F.R. § 230.251(a)(3).

18. *Id.*

19. Penny stocks and the SEC's initiatives to regulate this market is discussed in § 10.7 *infra*.

20. Rule 262, 17 C.F.R. § 230.262, which is discussed *infra* in this section. These bad boy provisions are also incorporated into Rule 505's section 3(b) exemption. Rule 505, 17 C.F.R. § 230.505; *see* § 4.18 *infra*.

Disqualification Provisions

By virtue of Rule 262,[21] Regulation A is not available where there have been disclosure or other SEC related problems in the past. Specifically, the exemption presumptively is inapplicable where the issuer, its predecessors or affiliated issuers: (1) have filed a registration statement which is currently subject to examination pursuant to section 8 of the 1933 Act,[22] (2) were subject to a refusal order or stop order within the past five years,[23] or (3) were subject to any proceeding pursuant to Rule 258 (which empowers the SEC to issue sanctions similar to those under section 8 with regard to Regulation A)[24] within five years prior to the filing of the Regulation A notification.[25] The rule also disqualifies an issuer from using Regulation A where any of the issuer's predecessors or affiliated issuers have been convicted within the previous five years of any felony or misdemeanor in connection with any security transaction.[26] Thus, for example, an issuer will be disqualified from using Regulation A if its predecessors or any affiliated issuer has been convicted within five years of any crime involving the making of any false filing with the SEC. Similarly, court orders entered within the previous five years, permanently or temporarily restraining or enjoining the issuer from violating the securities laws or from engaging in any act in connection with the purchase or sale of any security involving false filings with the Commission will disqualify the issuer from using Regulation A. Rule 262's issuer disqualification is not limited to violations of the federal securities laws and thus applies if state blue sky laws or other relevant statutes such as the Federal Mail Fraud Act[27] have been violated. Rule 262 will will also disqualify an issuer subject to any order issued by the United States Postal Service against the issuer for false representation.[28]

The disqualifications are not limited to the issuer and its affiliated entities. Similar "bad boy" prohibitions are supplied by Rule 262(b)[29] if the issuer's officers, directors, general partners, or ten percent beneficial owners have been subject to similar SEC sanctions or court orders. Rule 262(c)[30] creates a comparable disability if the Regulation A issuer uses an underwriter who has been subject to similar proceedings within the past five years. The prohibition relating to underwriters also will render the

---

21. 17 C.F.R. § 230.262.

22. Rule 262(a)(1), 17 C.F.R. § 230.262(a)(1). Section 8 is the provision that empowers the Commission to prevent the effectiveness of a 1933 Act registration. 15 U.S.C.A. § 77h. *See* § 7.1 *infra;* § 3.5 *supra.*

23. Rule 262(a)(1), 17 C.F.R. § 230.262(a)(1).

24. 17 C.F.R. § 230.258.

25. Rule 262(a)(2), 17 C.F.R. § 230.262(a)(2).

26. Rule 262(a)(3), 17 C.F.R. § 230.262(a)(3).

27. Mail and wire fraud are discussed in § 19.3.1 *infra.*

28. Rule 262(a)(5), 17 C.F.R. § 230.262(b).

29. 17 C.F.R. § 230.262(b).

30. 17 C.F.R. § 230.262(c).

exemption unavailable if the SEC finds that the issuer used a disqualified *de facto* underwriter.[31]

Rule 262's disqualifications are not absolute. Application may be made to the Commission to waive the bad boy disqualification provisions. The Commission may lift any of the foregoing "bad boy" disqualifications "upon a showing of a good cause, that it is not necessary under the circumstances that the exemption be denied." [32]

Limitations on Size of the Offering

An issuer which is not subject to any of the taints listed in Rule 262 may then qualify for Regulation A provided that the aggregate offering price of all securities so offered, including any other securities sold under Regulation A,[33] does not exceed five million dollars. In addition, there is a further limit with regard to secondary offerings; no more than one and one half million dollars may be attributable to the offering price of securities offered by all selling shareholders. However, there can be no resales by affiliates if the issuer has not had a net income from continuing operations in at least one of its last two fiscal years.[34]

Integration with Other Offerings[35]

Formerly, the Regulation A dollar ceiling would be decreased by any other section 3(b) securities sold within the past year, as well as any securities sold in violation of section 5(a). This was of particular importance because any Regulation A offering which occurs within a year of an offering made in reliance upon another exemption is subject to being overturned if the exemption relied upon for the earlier offering is somehow destroyed or otherwise unavailable. In such a case all securities sold in reliance on Regulation A would also have been sold in violation of section 5(a) since the sales will not have been exempt from registration. Although this method of calculation continues under two other section 3(b) exemptions—Rules 504 and 505[36]—, it is no longer the case under Regulation A. As of the 1992 amendments, Regulation A's five million dollar ceiling includes other securities offered within the past twelve months under Regulation A but there is no aggregation for

---

31. In the Matter of Shearson, Hammill & Co., Sec.Act Rel. No. 7743 (Nov. 12, 1965).

32. 17 C.F.R. § 230.262. *See, e.g.,* Michigan National Corp., 26 Sec. Reg. & L. Rep. (BNA) 37 (SEC no action letter available Dec. 17, 1993) (indicating Regulation A could be used notwithstanding subsidiary being subject to disqualifying injunctive order); ITC Integrated Systems, Inc., 20 Sec.Reg. & L.Rep. (BNA) 1043 (SEC No Action Letter avail. June 16, 1988). *See also, e.g.* E.F. Hutton & Co., 20 Sec.Reg. & L.Rep. (BNA) 1189 (SEC No Action Letter avail. July 10, 1988).

33. For purposes of the rule the distribution is not completed until each of the securities offered "ultimately comes to rest in the hands of the investing public." R.A. Holman & Co., Inc. v. SEC, 366 F.2d 446, 449–50 (2d Cir.1966), *amended on rehearing,* 377 F.2d 665 (2d Cir.1967), *cert. denied* 389 U.S. 991, 88 S.Ct. 473, 19 L.Ed.2d 482 (1967), *rehearing denied* 389 U.S. 1060, 88 S.Ct. 767, 19 L.Ed.2d 867 (1968).

34. Rule 251(b), 17 C.F.R. §§ 230.251(b).

35. *See, e.g.,* C. Stephen Bradford, Regulation A and the Integration Doctrine: The New Safe Harbor, 55 Ohio St. L.J. 255 (1994).

36. 17 C.F.R. §§ 230.504, 505. *See* §§ 4.18, 4.19 *infra.*

securities sold under the other section 3(b) exemptions or in violation of section 5. Beyond, the computation question, Regulation A provides a safe harbor from integration for prior offers and sales of securities and for subsequent offers or sales where the subsequent transactions involve: (1) securities sold under a registration statement,[37] (2) securities offered as part of an incentive plan pursuant to the exemption provided in Rule 701,[38] (3) securities sold pursuant to an employee benefit plan,[39] (4) sales of securities outside the United States that are exempt under Regulation S,[40] or (5) any sales made more than six months after the Regulation A offering is completed.[41] Even if transactions do not qualify for the safe harbor from integration, integration may be avoided if the transactions satisfy the test for integration generally.[42]

Filing and Notification Requirements

Rules 252, 256 and 257[43] contain Regulation A's filing and notification requirements. Seven copies of notification, now known as an offering statement, must be filed on Form 1-A either at the Commission's national office in Washington, DC or with the SEC Regional Office. The Commission has provided two alternative formats for Form 1-A. First, there is a narrative format that parallels the traditional registration form under the Act. In an attempt to make the process easier for may issuers, the Commission has also established an alternative form in question and answer format. Regardless of which format is used, the offering statement must be signed by the issuer, its chief executive and financial officers, a majority of its board of directors,[44] and all persons for whose account any of the securities are to be offered.[45] There is a nonrefundable five hundred dollar initial filing fee, with no subsequent fees for amendments.[46] All amendments to the initial notification must be filed together with three additional copies and must be signed in the same manner as the original filing. Parallelling the procedure for 1933 Act registrations, absent a delaying notation, the offering statement becomes effective on the twentieth calendar day following its filing.[47] Filing of amendments begins the twenty day period anew.[48]

---

37. Rule 251(c)(2)(i), 17 C.F.R. § 230.251(c)(2)(i).

38. Rule 251(c)(2)(ii), 17 C.F.R. § 230.251(c)(2)(ii). The Rule 701 exemption is discussed in § 4.15.1 *infra*.

39. Rule 251(c)(2)(iii), 17 C.F.R. § 230.251(c)(2)(iii).

40. Rule 251(c)(2)(iv), 17 C.F.R. § 230.251(c)(2)(iv). Regulation S (Rules 901 *et seq.*) is discussed in § 14.2 *infra*.

41. Rule 251(c)(2)(v), 17 C.F.R. § 230.251(c)(2)(v).

42. *See* Sec. Act Rel. No. 33–4552 (Nov. 6, 1962). Integration is discussed in § 4.29 *infra*.

43. 17 C.F.R. §§ 230.252, 256, 257.

44. This parallels the requirements for a registration statement. *See* chapter 3 *supra*.

45. Rule 252(d), 17 C.F.R. §§ 230.252(d).

46. Rule 252(f), 17 C.F.R. § 230.252(f).

47. Rule 252(g)(1), 17 C.F.R. § 230.252(g)(1).

48. Rules 252(g)(3), 252(h)(1), 17 C.F.R. §§ 230.252(g)(3), (h)(1).

Rule 259[49] permits the issuer to withdraw the Regulation A notification upon application unless the notification is subject to a suspension order pursuant to Rule 258,[50] or it becomes subject to such an order within fifteen days of the application to withdraw. Rule 261 gives the Commission power similar to that which exists with regard to full fledged registration statements under section 8 of the Act.[51] A Rule 258 suspension of the Regulation A exemption may be issued if the notification or offering circular or any sales literature contains material misstatements or omissions, if the offering would be in violation of section 17 of the 1933 Act,[52] if any of the events subsequent to the filing of the notification render the exemption unavailable, if the issuer fails to file reports of all sales pursuant to Regulation A as required by Rule 257,[53] or if wrongdoings sufficient to invoke Rule 252 occur. Where Rule 258 suspension proceedings have been formally initiated, the Commission will refuse to allow a withdrawal of the notification and will therefore issue a formal suspension in the event that the notification is significantly deficient.[54]

Testing the Waters

Rule 254 expressly permits the issuer, prior to the filing of the offering statement, to test the waters in order to obtain indications of interest from potential investors.[55] Solicitations which would otherwise be illegal offers to sell may be made prior to the filing of the offering circular so long as the solicitation does no more than solicit indications of investor interest and makes clear that offers and sales can only be made after filing of the offering statement pursuant to an offering circular. Although it is not a condition of the exemption, Rule 254(b) provides that such solicitations of investor interest be on file with the SEC on or before its use. The rule further sets forth specific warnings and disclaimers that should be in the prefiling solicitation. Specifically, it must be explained that no money is being solicited or will be accepted, and that sales will be made only by use of an offering circular.[56] The solicitation of interest must also make it clear that an indication of interest does not result in an obligation of any kind.[57] The solicitation

49. 17 C.F.R. § 230.259.

50. 17 C.F.R. § 230.258.

51. 15 U.S.C.A. § 77h. *See* §§ 3.5, 3.5.1 *supra.*

52. 15 U.S.C.A. § 77q(a). *See* §§ 7.6, 13.3 *infra.*

53. 17 C.F.R. § 230.257. Rule 257 requires that within 30 days of each six month period after the date of the initial Regulation A offering, the issuer must notify the SEC of all sales by filing four copies of Form 2–A with the appropriate Regional Office.

54. *See* In the Matter of Mutual Employees Trademart, Inc., 40 S.E.C. 1092 (SEC 1962) (decided under former version of Regulation A).

The filing of defective notification materials does not automatically nullify the Regulation A exemption. SEC v. Blazon Corp., 609 F.2d 960, 968–69 (9th Cir.1979). *See also, e.g.* SEC v. Southwest Coal Energy Co., 624 F.2d 1312 (5th Cir.1980) (decided under Regulation B).

55. 17 C.F.R. § 230.254.

56. Rule 254(b)(2)(iii), 17 C.F.R. §§ 230, 254(b)(2)(iii).

57. Rule 254(b)(2)(i), (ii), 17 C.F.R. §§ 230, 254(b)(2)(i), (ii).

should also identify the issuer's business and also must name its chief executive officer.[58]

As noted above, these solicitations can take place only prior to the filing of the offering statement. Accordingly, no sales can take place for at least twenty days from the last such testing the waters. Presumably, this minimum twenty calendar day cooling-off period, which generally will be longer, will give investors sufficient opportunity to receive, read, and evaluate the materials in the Regulation A disclosure documents which are discussed below.

Use of the Offering Circular

In addition to the notification requirements of Form 1–A, which, as described above, are a condition of the Regulation A exemption is the requirement that offers and sales be made only through the use of a qualifying offering circular, subject to the use of prefiling testing the waters solicitations permitted by Rule 254 prior to the filing of the offering statement.[59] Parallelling the requirements for filing of a registration statement under the Act generally, Rule 253[60] imposes requirements of an offering circular that parallel the prospectus requirements contained in section 5(b) of the Act.[61] Similarly, Rule 255 provides for the use of preliminary offering circulars prior to the effective date of the Regulation A qualification statement.[62] Rule 251(d) prohibits written offers of securities to be issued under Regulation A unless an offering circular, or preliminary offering circular, if used before the effective date, containing the information specified in Schedule I of Form 1–A is provided or has previously been provided to the offeree.[63] Rule 251(d)(2)(i)(B) prohibits sales of securities under Regulation A unless a qualifying preliminary or final offering circular is furnished to the purchaser at least forty-eight hours prior to the mailing of the sales confirmation.[64] Rule 251(d)(1)(ii)(C) permits written advertisements and radio or television communication announcing the offering, stating from whom an offering circular may be obtained and which state no more than the name of the issuer, title of the security and the amount to be offered, including the per-unit offering price, the identity of the issuer's general business and a brief statement of the issuer's character and location;[65] this is the counterpart of the identifying statement, or tombstone ad, for a full fledged registered offering.[66]

---

58. Rule 254(b)(2)(iv), 17 C.F.R. §§ 230, 254(b)(2)(iv).

59. 17 C.F.R. § 230.254.

60. 17 C.F.R. § 230.253.

61. 15 U.S.C.A. § 77e(b). *See* § 2.4 *supra*.

62. Rule 255, 17 C.F.R. § 230.255.

63. Rule 251(d), 17 C.F.R. § 230.251(d).

64. 17 C.F.R. § 230.251(d)(2)(i)(B).

65. 17 C.F.R. § 230.251(d)(1)(ii)(C).

66. *See* section 2(10)(b), 15 U.S.C. § 77b(10)(b); Rule 134, 17 C.F.R. § 230.134 which are discussed in §§ 2.3, 2.4 *supra*.

Regulation A is more than a safe harbor, it is an exclusive harbor as there is no self-executing statutory exemption. Accordingly, deviations from the rules' requirements will result in loss of the exemption. The SEC has provided, however, that trivial deviations do not necessarily result in loss of the Regulation A exemption. As is also the case with Regulation D,[67] insignificant deviations from Regulation A will not result in a loss of the exemption provided that there has been a good faith attempt to comply and the deviation does not involve "a condition or requirement directly intended to protect the individual or entity" challenging the transaction.[68] The exception for insignificant deviations does not apply in an SEC administrative proceeding under Rule 258 to suspend the Regulation A qualification.[69]

Many issuers who might otherwise rely on a Regulation A exemption may avail themselves of the streamlined registration for issuers qualifying to use Form SB–1.[70] Form SB–1 is available for offerings not in excess of seven and one-half million dollars. Form SB–2 provides another alternative registration form for small business issuers.[71]

§ 4.15.1 Rule 701—Exemption for Employee Compensation Plans of Issuers Not Subject to Exchange Act Periodic Reporting Requirements

In 1988, the Commission exercised its exemptive power under section 3(b) to exempt from registration employee stock compensation plans (ranging from five hundred thousand dollars to five million dollars annually) provided that the issuer is neither subject to the Securities Exchange Act's periodic reporting requirements nor an investment company which is (or is required to be) registered under the Investment Company Act of 1940.[1] Issuers relying on Rule 701's exemption are not precluded from also relying on other exemptions.[2]

Issuer Qualification

Since the Rule 701 exemption is limited to non-reporting companies, it is not available to issuers whose securities are traded on a national exchange or on the more active over-the-counter markets.[3] The exemp-

---

67. *See* Rule 508, 17 C.F.R. § 230.508.

68. Rule 260, 17 C.F.R. § 230.260.

69. Rule 260(c), 17 C.F.R. § 230.260(c). *See* 17 C.F.R. § 230.258.

70. *See* § 3.3 *supra.*

71. *See* § 3.3 *supra.*

§ 4.15.1

1. 17 C.F.R. § 230.701, adopted in Sec.Act Rel. No. 33–6768, [1987–88 Transfer Binder] Fed.Sec.L.Rep. (CCH) ¶ 84,231 (April 14, 1988). The Investment Company Act is discussed in chapter 17 *infra.*

2. "Attempted compliance with the rule does not act as an exclusive election; the issuer can also claim the availability of any other applicable exemption." 17 C.F.R. § 230.701, preliminary note 3.

3. The Exchange Act's periodic reporting requirements are discussed in § 9.2, *infra.*

tion is available only to the issuer and thus cannot be used by affiliates or anyone else reselling the securities on the issuer's behalf.[4]

Qualified Plans

The exemption set out in Rule 701 applies to a wide variety of compensation plans. It applies to purchase plans, option plans, bonus plans, stock appreciation rights, profitsharing, thrift, incentive, or similar plans.[5] Rule 701 permits an issuer to offer securities pursuant to a written contract or written compensation plan to its employees, directors, general partners, trustees, officers, consultants, or advisers.[6] The securities can be issued only in return for bona fide services but not in return for services rendered in connection with a capital raising transaction involving securities.[7] Thus, the exemption is not available for compensation of underwriters or most promoters.

In its preliminary notes to Rule 701, the Commission observes that "[t]he exemption provided by the rule is not available to any issuer for any transaction which, while in technical compliance with such rule, is part of a plan or scheme to evade the registration requirements of the Act."[8] Thus, issuers must be careful to document the bona fide nature of any compensation plan which they seek to bring within the exemption.

Limitation on Amount

The maximum amount of securities that can be offered within a twelve month period pursuant to a compensation plan varies from five hundred thousand dollars to five million dollars, depending upon the size of the company and number of shares already outstanding. Rule 701(b)(5) establishes a five hundred thousand dollar limit[9] with two alternative means of raising that limit up to section 3(b)'s five million dollar ceiling.[10] The issuer may go above the five hundred thousand dollars annual limit provided that the value of the securities sold does not exceed the lesser of five million dollars or fifteen percent of the issuer's net assets as computed at the end of its last fiscal year.[11] Alternatively, the issuer may go beyond the five hundred thousand dollar

---

4. 17 C.F.R. § 230.701 preliminary note 4.

5. 17 C.F.R. § 230.701(b)(2).

6. 17 C.F.R. § 230.701(b)(1).

7. *Id.* As further explained in preliminary note 5: "[i]n view of the primary purpose of the rule, which is to provide an exemption from the registration requirements of the Act for securities issued in compensatory circumstances, the rule is not available for plans or schemes to circumvent this purpose, such as to raise capital."

8. 17 C.F.R. § 230.701, preliminary note 6. In such a case registration would be required. *Id.*

9. An issuer relying on the $500,000 limit must assure that sales within a twelve month period do not exceed the limit otherwise all offers and sales during the period may lose their exempt status. Jackson, Tufts, Cole & Black, [1988–89 Transfer Binder] Fed.Sec. L.Rep. (CCH) ¶ 78,807 (SEC No Action Letter May 5, 1988).

10. 17 C.F.R. § 230.701(b)(5).

11. 17 C.F.R. § 230.701(b)(5)(i).

limit provided that the value of the securities sold does not exceed the lesser of five million dollars or fifteen percent of the outstanding securities of the same class.[12]

Notification Requirements

Rule 702(T) required that the issuer give notice of all sales pursuant to a Rule 701 exemption.[13] The notice must be filed within thirty days of any sale that places the aggregate sales made within a twelve month period above one hundred thousand dollars. The date of the filing is determined by reference to when it is received at the Commission's office in Washington, D.C.[14] The notice is to be filed on Form 701;[15] five copies must be filed, one of which is to be signed by an authorized representative of the issuer.[16] The notification requirements are contained in a temporary rule which expired by its terms on May 20, 1993.[17] Rule 703(T), another temporary rule which similarly expired on May 20, 1993, provides that the exemption is not available to an issuer where it, its predecessors, or its affiliates are subject to a court order enjoining violations of Rule 702's notification requirements.[18] However, this disqualification could be waived by the Commission upon a showing of good cause.[19]

Integration Doctrine not Applicable

When successive offerings are part of a single plan of financing, ordinarily the Commission may invoke the integration doctrine in order to integrate the multiple transactions into one.[20] Unlike the other exemptions, there is an express exclusion[21] from the integration doctrine. Additionally, unlike the other section 3(b) exemptions,[22] securities sold pursuant to other section 3(b) exemptions need not be counted in the five million dollar ceiling.

Restrictions on Resale

Securities acquired pursuant to a Rule 701 offering are deemed to be restricted securities within the meaning of Rule 144.[23] The securities

---

12. 17 C.F.R. § 230.701(b)(5)(ii).

13. 17 C.F.R. § 230.702(T).

14. 17 C.F.R. § 230.702(T)(d).

15. 17 C.F.R. § 230.701.

16. 17 C.F.R. § 230.702(T).

17. 17 C.F.R. § 230.702(T)(e).

18. 17 C.F.R. § 230.703(T)(a).

19. 17 C.F.R. § 230.703(T)(b).

20. Integration is discussed in § 4.29 *infra*.

21. "Offers and sales exempt pursuant to this § 230.701 are deemed to be part of a single, discrete offering and are not subject to integration with any other offering or sale whether registered under the Act or otherwise exempt from the registration requirements of the Act." 17 C.F.R. § 230.701(b)(6).

22. Regulation A, which is discussed in § 4.15 *supra;* Rule 504, which is discussed in § 4.19 *infra;* and Rule 505, which is discussed in § 4.18 *infra*.

23. 17 C.F.R. § 230.701(c)(1).

may not be resold unless in compliance with the Act's registration requirements or pursuant to an exemption.[24]   In the event that the issuer becomes an Exchange Act reporting company, after ninety days of reporting company status, nonaffiliates of the issuer are permitted to resell the securities acquired in a Rule 701 offering by following the guidelines set forth in Rule 144 but without having to comply with Rule 144's informational requirements, two-year holding period, limitations on amount of securities to be sold, or notification requirements.[25]   In such a case affiliates may also resell their stock under Rule 144 but must comply with all of the rule's limitations except for the holding period.

Applicability of Antifraud Provisions and State Law

In its preliminary notes to the Rule 701 exemption, the Commission points out that the exemption from registration does not in any way limit the issuer's disclosure obligations under the antifraud provisions.[26] Nor does the exemption affect the need to comply with state law registration requirements.[27]

§ 4.16   Coordination of the Small Issue and Limited Offering Exemptions: Regulation D—An Overview

In promulgating Regulation D,[1] the SEC adopted a comprehensive scheme for exemptions relating to small issues and small issuers. Regulation D is "designed to simplify and clarify existing exemptions, to expand their availability, and to achieve uniformity between federal and state exemptions."[2]   The exemptions of Regulation D combine many of the elements of section 3(b)'s qualified exemptions for small issues,[3] section 4(6)'s exemption for offerings to "accredited investors,"[4] and section 4(2)'s exemption for issuer transactions not involving a public

---

24.   17 C.F.R. § 230.701(c)(2).

25.   17 C.F.R. § 230.701(c)(3). Rule 144 is discussed in § 4.26 *infra*. The more relaxed resale restrictions of Rule 701(c)(3) (90 days after the issuer has become subject to 1934 Act reporting requirements) apply to resales of restricted securities by donees of recipients of benefit plans issued under Rule 701. Brobeck, Phlegler & Harrison, 24 Sec.Reg. & L.Rep. (BNA) 1464 (SEC No Action Letter avail. Aug. 27, 1992).

26.   17 C.F.R. § 230.701 preliminary note 1.

27.   17 C.F.R. § 230.701 preliminary note 2. State securities laws are considered in chapter 8 *infra*.

§ 4.16

1.   17 C.F.R. §§ 230.501–230.506. *See* Theodore Parnall, Bruce R. Kohl & Curtis W. Huff, Private and Limited Offerings After a Decade of Experimentation: The Evolution of Regulation D, 12 N.M.L.Rev. 633 (1982); Mark A. Sargent, The New Regulation D: Deregulation, Federalism and the Dynamics of Regulatory Reform, 68 Wash.U.L.Q. 225 (1990).

2.   Sec. Act Rel. No. 33–6389, [1981–82 Transfer Binder] Fed.Sec.L.Rep. (CCH) ¶ 83,106 (March 8, 1982).

3.   15 U.S.C.A. § 77c(b). *See* § 4.14 *supra*.

4.   15 U.S.C.A. § 77d(6). *See* § 4.19 *infra*.

offering.[5] The Regulation consists of three separate but interrelated exemptions.[6] Rule 504, promulgated under section 3(b) provides an exemption for certain offerings not exceeding one million dollars within a twelve month period.[7] Rule 505, which also is a section 3(b) exemption exempts certain offerings not exceeding five million dollars within a twelve month period.[8] The third exemption, Rule 506, permits nonpublic offerings to qualified purchasers without any limitation on dollar amount and is promulgated under section 4(2).[9] In order to encourage coordination with the state blue sky laws, section 19(c) of the 1933 Act empowers the SEC to work with state administrators in establishing uniform exemptions for small businesses.[10] Toward this end the SEC and many states have agreed upon a Uniform Limited Offering Exemption that tracks the requirements of Regulation D.[11] The slowness of the legislative process means that any substantial uniformity is likely to be several years away, although an increasing number of states have either adopted the Uniform Limited Offering Exemption or have at least moved in the direction of coordination with Regulation D.

As noted above, one of the goals of Regulation D is to coordinate federal and state exemptions for nonpublic offerings. Consequently, Title V of the Small Business Investment Incentive Act of 1980 added section 19(c) to the Securities Act of 1933.[12] This Section authorized the Commission to work with state securities administrators in effectuating uniformity between federal and state securities laws. Following the statutory mandate, the SEC worked with the North American Securities Administrators Association (NASAA) to develop a state law Uniform Limited Offering Exemption (U.L.O.E.) which is coordinated with Regu-

---

5. 15 U.S.C.A. § 77d(2). *See* § 4.20 *infra.* Rule 506 provides a safe harbor for the section 4(2) exemption. 17 C.F.R. § 230.506. For a chart depicting the basic coverage of Regulation D *see* § 4.13 *supra.*

6. Regulation D consists of three basic exemptions as set out in Rules 504, 505 and 506. 17 C.F.R. §§ 230.504–230.506. *See* §§ 4.17–4.22 *infra.*

7. 17 C.F.R. § 230.504. In a rule 504 offering, no more than $500,000 of the aggregate offering price may be attributable to securities sold without registration under state law. 17 C.F.R. § 230.504(b)(2)(i). *See* § 4.19 *infra.*

8. 17 C.F.R. § 230.505. *See* § 4.18 *infra.*

9. 17 C.F.R. § 230.506. *See* § 4.22 *infra.*

10. 15 U.S.C.A. § 77s(c). The state blue sky laws are discussed in chapter 8 *infra.*

The Commission has adopted amendments to Form D in order to facilitate coordination with state law. Sec. Act Rel. No. 33–6650, 18 Sec.Reg. & L.Rep. (BNA) 679 (June 5, 1986); *See* SEC Proposes Amendments to Form D to Encourage Wider Adoption by States, 18 Sec.Reg. & L.Rep. (BNA) 799 (June 6, 1986).

11. *See* Ronald L. Fein, Hugh H. Makens & Richard D. Cahalan, Survey—ULOE: Comprehending the Confusion, 43 Bus.Law. 737 (1988); A. Michael Hainsfurther, Summary of Blue Sky Exemptions Corresponding to Regulation D, 38 Sw.L.J. 989 (1984); Therese H. Maynard, The Uniform Limited Offering Exemption: How Uniform is Uniform?, 36 Emory L.J. 649 (1987); Comment, Florida's Response to the Need for Uniformity in Federal and State Securities Registration Exemption Requirements, 12 Fla.St.L.Rev. 309 (1984). *See also, e.g.,* Gregory S. Crespi, The Uniform Limited Offering Exemption: The Need for Amendment of its Disqualification Provisions, 16 Sec.Reg.L.J. 370 (1989).

12. 15 U.S.C.A. § 77s(c).

lation D. In 1983, NASAA adopted the U.L.O.E., integrated with and largely based upon Regulation D, for enactment at the state level.

§ 4.17 Regulation D: Definitions, Conditions, and Filing Requirements—SEC Rules 501, 502, and 503

Regulation D is a series of six rules establishing three small issue or limited offering exemptions from the registration requirements of the 1933 Securities Act.[1] Rules 501 through 503 set forth the definitions, terms, and conditions that apply to the three exemptions provided in Rules 504, 505, and 506.[2] The rules provide exemptions for offerings that are limited in the type and number of offerees as well as for those limited in dollar amount. The definitions in Rules 501 through 503 consolidate, clarify, and expand terms that had been used in former SEC Rules 146, 240, and 242, all of which were rescinded effective June 30, 1982.[3]

Definitions

Rule 501 sets forth eight definitions applicable throughout Regulation D. Briefly, they are as follows.

(1) An "accredited investor,"[4] a term which is also defined in section 2(15) of the Act,[5] is any person who in fact comes within, or whom the issuer reasonably believes comes within, any of eight categories of investors at the time securities are sold to him or her. Generally these categories include wealthy and/or financially sophisticated investors such as banks, insurance companies, tax-exempt organizations, directors and executive officers of the issuer, and natural persons who have considerable net worth or large annual incomes. The Regulation D exemptions either limit or exclude offerings made to any nonaccredited persons. The concept of accredited investor is also relevant to the amount and type of information the issuer must furnish to purchasers during a Regulation D offering.[6] Additionally, section 4(6) of the Act[7] exempts offerings of up to five million dollars where all offerees and purchasers are accredited investors. Failure to take adequate precautions to screen accredited investors is likely to result in the loss of an exemption.[8]

---

§ 4.17

1. 17 C.F.R. §§ 230.501–230.506. *See* Sec. Act Rel. No. 33–6389 (March 8, 1982). *See also*, Theodore Parnall, Bruce R. Kohl & Curtis W. Huff, Private and Limited Offerings After a Decade of Experimentation: The Evolution of Regulation D, 12 N.M.L.Rev. 633 (1982).

2. These exemptions are discussed in §§ 4.18, 4.19, 4.22 *infra.*

3. *See* Sec. Act Rel. No. 33–6389 (March 8, 1982).

4. 17 C.F.R. § 230.501(a).

5. 15 U.S.C.A. § 77b(15); 17 C.F.R. § 230.215. *See* § 4.20 *infra.*

6. *See* 17 C.F.R. § 230.502(b).

7. 15 U.S.C.A. § 77d(6). *See* § 4.20 *infra.*

8. *See, e.g.,* SEC v. Interlink Data Network of Los Angeles, Inc., 1993 WL 603274, [1993–1994 Transfer Binder] Fed. Sec. L. Rep. (CCH) ¶ 98,049 (C.D.Cal.1993).

(2) An "affiliate"[9] is a person who controls, is controlled by, or is under common control with the person with whom he is affiliated.[10]

(3) "Aggregate offering price"[11] is defined to include all consideration, including non-cash items, received by an issuer for the issuance of its securities. The definition includes a comment regarding how to determine the price of securities sold in whole or in part for non-cash consideration. Determination of the aggregate offering price is important for Rules 504 and 505[12] which have dollar ceilings of one million and five million dollars, respectively.

(4) Rule 501 defines "business combination"[13] as any transaction defined in Rule 145[14] of the 1933 Act. This includes mergers and consolidations of more than one organization.

(5) The rule goes on to provide a method for calculating the number of purchasers involved in an exempt offering.[15] This is relevant to the exemptions provided by Rules 505 and 506[16] which are limited to thirty-five purchasers.

(6) Rule 501(f)[17] defines "executive officer" to include the president, and certain vice presidents as well as other policy makers of the issuer.

(7) "Issuer" under Regulation D[18] follows the definition in section 2(4) of the 1933 Act[19] with the exception that in certain offerings during reorganizations under the Bankruptcy Act, the trustee or debtor in possession may be considered an issuer under Rule 501(g).

(8) A "purchaser representative"[20] is defined, broadly, to be a person unaffiliated with the issuer who has such knowledge and experience in financial and business matters that he is capable of evaluating the risks and merits of a proposed offering. A purchaser representative can be used to qualify purchasers for Rule 506's safe harbor for private placements.[21]

---

9. 17 C.F.R. § 230.501(b). Rule 405 defines control as "The possession, direct or indirect, of the power to direct or cause the direction of management and policies * * * whether through the ownership of voting securities, by contract or otherwise." 17 C.F.R. § 230.405.

10. 17 C.F.R. § 230.501(c).

11. 17 C.F.R. § 230.501(c). As explained more fully elsewhere, the aggregate offering price includes all securities sold within the preceding twelve months under section 3(b) or in violation of section 5. *See* § 4.15 *supra* and §§ 4.18, 4.19 *infra.*

12. 17 C.F.R. §§ 230.504, 230.505. *See* §§ 4.18, 4.19 *infra.*

13. 17 C.F.R. § 230.501(d).

14. 17 C.F.R. § 230.145. *See* § 5.2 *infra.*

15. 17 C.F.R. § 230.501(e).

16. 17 C.F.R. §§ 230.505(b), 230.506(b). *See* §§ 4.18, 4.22 *infra.*

17. 17 C.F.R. § 230.501(f).

18. 17 C.F.R. § 230.501(g).

19. 15 U.S.C.A. § 77b(4).

20. 17 C.F.R. § 230.501(h).

21. 17 C.F.R. § 230.502.

Conditions

Rule 502[22] establishes four conditions that are applicable to all Regulation D offerings. Those conditions relate to: (1) the integration doctrine, (2) the information to be supplied to offerees, (3) the manner of soliciting purchasers, and (4) limitations on resales.

Integration

The first condition sets forth a safe harbor to avoid the integration of more than one exempt offering; it also provides a five factor test to be considered for offerings that may not be protected by the safe harbor.[23] In short, there is a window that will last for at least twelve months during which the question of whether to integrate transactions will be answered according to the highly factual five-factor test.[24] There is a safe harbor from integration for transactions taking place outside of that period. As discussed more fully in a subsequent section, Rule 502(a) provides that offers and sales taking place more than six months before the beginning for the Regulation D offering and those taking place more than six months after the completion of the offering will not be integrated into the Regulation D offering.[25] Transactions that are not integrated under either the safe harbor or the five-factor test will not destroy the exemption.

Information to be supplied

The second condition establishes the type of information that an issuer is required to supply to purchasers for an offering exempted by Regulation D.[26] If all of the purchasers are accredited investors as defined in Rule 501, then Rule 502 does not require that any specific information be furnished to them by the issuer. Formerly, the SEC required that if there was at least one unaccredited purchaser, all purchasers (including those who are accredited) had to be provided with the specified information. The SEC deleted this requirement and has replaced it with a *recommendation* that all purchasers be given this information. The amount and format of information required will depend on the size of the offering and whether the issuer is a reporting

---

22. 17 C.F.R. § 230.506. *See* § 4.22 *infra.*

23. 17 C.F.R. § 230.502(a).

24. *See* § 4.29 *infra.*

25. 17 C.F.R. § 230.502(a):

Integration. All sales that are part of the same Regulation D offering must meet all of the terms and conditions of Regulation D. Offers and sales that are made more than six months before the start of a Regulation D offering or are made more than six months after completion of a Regulation D offering will not be considered part of that Regulation D offering, so long as during those six month periods there are no offers or sales of securities by or for the issuer that are of the same or a similar class as those offered or sold under Regulation D, other than those offers or sales of securities under an employee benefit plan as defined in Rule 405 under the Act.

26. 17 C.F.R. § 230.502(b).

company under the Securities Exchange Act of 1934.[27]

Issuers that are subject to the 1934 Act's periodic reporting requirements are required to make available information contained in the most recent annual and quarterly reports as well as any disclosures made pursuant to the proxy rules.[28] With regard to issuers that are not subject to the 1934 Act reporting requirements, the mandated disclosures depend on the size of the offering. With regard to nonfinancial information, Rule 502(b)(2)(i)(A)[29] calls for disclosures that are comparable to the information that would be required in part I of a registration statement that the issuer would be required to file in a public offering,[30] or, if the issuer is eligible to use Regulation A,[31] the types of information that would be required on Part II of Form 1-A. With regard to information relating to the financial statement, the degree of disclosure varies with the size of the offering. For offerings of up to two million dollars, the financial disclosures should generally conform to the requirements of Item 310 of Regulation S-B.[32] Financial disclosures in offerings up to seven and one half million dollars must contain the same type of information that would be required in Part I of Registration Form SB-2, whether or not the issuer would qualify for use of that form; except that only the issuer's balance sheet (which must be dated within one hundred and twenty days of the offering) need be certified.[33] For offerings up to seven and one half million dollars, if the issuer is not a limited partnership and is unable to obtain audited financial statements without unreasonable effort or expense, then only the issuer's balance sheet must be audited and dated within 120 days of the offering.[34] In the case of a limited partnership that cannot obtain audited statements without an undue burden, it is sufficient to furnish financial statements prepared in accordance with federal income tax standards and generally accepted accounting principles.[35]

For offerings over seven and one half million dollars, the issuer must make disclosures as would be required by the applicable 1933 Act registration form. Where the issuer is not a 1934 Act reporting compa-

---

27. The 1934 Act registration and reporting requirements are discussed in §§ 9.2, 9.3 *infra.*

28. 17 C.F.R. § 230.502(b)(2)(ii).

29. 17 C.F.R. § 230.502(b)(2)(i)(A). The disclosures must contain the types of information required by Part II of Form 1-A.

30. The degree of disclosure may vary with the size of the issuer and the size of the offering. The alternative registration forms are discussed in § 3.3 *supra.*

31. Regulation A is available to issuers not subject to the 1934 Act's reporting requirements and may be used for offerings of up to five million dollars. Regulation A is discussed in § 4.15 *supra.*

32. 17 C.F.R. § 230.502(b)(2)(i)(B)(2). However, only the issuer's balance sheet need be audited; that balance sheet must be dated within 120 days of the offering. Regulation S-B is the disclosure guide for small business issuers. *See* § 3.3 *supra.*

33. 17 C.F.R. § 230.502(b)(2)(i)(B)(2). Form SB-2 and its eligibility requirements are discussed in § 3.3 *supra.*

34. 17 C.F.R. § 230.502(b)(2)(i)(2)(B)(2).

35. *Id.*

ny and cannot obtain audited financial statements without unreasonable delay and expense, it may elect to provide an audited balance sheet dated within one hundred and twenty days of the beginning of the offering.[36] With regard to limited partnership offerings by nonreporting companies, if an audited financial statement cannot be obtained without unreasonable effort or expense, then the issuer may provide a balance sheet, dated within one hundred and twenty days of the start of the offering, provided that the balance sheet has been prepared in accordance with federal income tax requirements and the balance sheet has been examined and reported on by an independent or certified public accountant.[37] Failure to comply with any applicable informational requirements will generally be fatal to a Regulation D offering.[38]

Rule 502(b)(1) provides that the foregoing informational requirements do not apply to offerings of up to one million dollars that are made pursuant to Rule 504. As pointed out above, the information requirements do not apply to Rule 505 or Rule 506 offerings in which all purchasers are accredited investors. However, if there are any nonaccredited investors, then each nonaccredited purchaser must receive the required information. Formerly the Commission required that the offering circular go to *all* investors if there were any unaccredited investors. Although the SEC no longer imposes the affirmative disclosure requirements for all investors, it recommends that even accredited investors be supplied with the offering circular.

Prohibition on General Solicitation

The third condition of Rule 502 prohibits the offer or sale of securities by a general solicitation or general advertising.[39] This prohibition applies in both Rule 505 and Rule 506 offerings[40] but not to Rule 504 transactions. As discussed more fully in a later section, the existence of unqualified offerees in a Rule 505 or Rule 506 offering may be sufficient to establish that a general solicitation has occurred.[41] The existence of a general solicitation will be a significant factor in finding the exemption unavailable.[42] While there is no prohibition on general solicitations in Rule 504 transactions,[43] a general solicitation generally will implicate state securities law registration requirements.

---

36. 17 C.F.R. § 230.502(b)(2)(i)(B)(3).

37. *Id.*

38. *See, e.g.,* SEC v. Interlink Data Network of Los Angeles, Inc., 1993 WL 603274, [1993–1994 Transfer Binder] Fed. Sec. L. Rep. (CCH) ¶ 98,049 (C.D.Cal.1993).

39. 17 C.F.R. § 230.502(c). *Cf.* Texas Capital Network, Inc., [1993–1994 Transfer Binder] Fed. Sec. L. Rep. (CCH) ¶ 76,857 (SEC No Action Letter Feb. 23, 1994) (non-profit corporation's matching of business ventures with potential investors did not constitute a general solicitation). For a thoughtful critique of the general solicitation ban, *see* Patrick Daugherty, Rethinking the Ban on General Solicitation, 38 Emory L.J. 67 (1989).

40. *See* §§ 4.18, 4.22 *infra.*

41. *See* § 4.26 *infra.*

42. *See, e.g.,* SEC v. Interlink Data Network of Los Angeles, Inc., 1993 WL 603274, [1993–1994 Transfer Binder] Fed. Sec. L. Rep. (CCH) ¶ 98,049 (C.D.Cal.1993).

43. *See* § 4.19 *infra.*

Limitation on Resales

Finally, Rule 502(d)[44] sets forth limits on the resale of securities acquired in a Regulation D transaction; but these limitations do not apply to Rule 504 offerings. Because the Regulation D exemptions are only "transaction exemptions," any securities acquired pursuant to Regulation D cannot be resold unless the resale is registered or has an independent exemption. As a safeguard against illegal resales, the issuer relying upon a Regulation D exemption, based on either a Rule 505 or Rule 506 offering is required to exercise reasonable care to assure that purchasers are not underwriters as defined by section 2(11) of the 1933 Act.[45] It is common for issuers to require all purchasers in a nonpublic offering to sign letters of investment intent.[46] Rule 502(d) requires the issuer to take precautions against resales including issuing appropriate transfer instructions to the transfer agent and placing a legend indicating the transfer restriction on the share certificate. Section 8–204 of the Uniform Commercial Code provides that any such restrictions must appear in a prominent restrictive legend on the share certificates.[47] Failure to comply with the UCC's provisions can result in liability to transferees who acquire the securities without knowledge of the restrictions.[48]

Notice of Exempt Sales

Rule 503[49] sets forth requirements for filing notice of exempt sales with the SEC. The notice must initially be filed within fifteen days after the first sale of securities in a Regulation D offering. Subsequent notices of all sales are due every six months after the first sale and thirty days after the last sale.

Scope of Regulation D

In addition to the provisions of Rules 501 through 503, the SEC's preliminary notes to Regulation D further explain the exemptions' scope. First, transactions exempt from registration are not exempt from the antifraud or civil liability sections of the federal securities laws.[50] Is-

---

44. 17 C.F.R. § 230.502(d).

45. 15 U.S.C.A. § 77b(11). *See* §§ 4.25–4.26 *infra.* There are no restrictions on resale in a Rule 504 transaction. 17 C.F.R. § 230.504(b)(1). Since any security acquired in a Rule 504 transaction, absent an exemption for that resale, cannot be resold without registration, the purchaser may well be subject to resale limitations. *See* § 4.24 *infra.* Accordingly, although not required by Rule 504, the issuer may nevertheless want to take precautions against such resales taking place. *See* § 4.19 *infra.*

46. *See* § 4.21 *infra.*

47. *See* § 20.5 *infra* (Practitioner's Edition).

48. *See, e.g.,* Dean Witter Reynolds, Inc. v. Selectronics, Inc., 188 A.D.2d 117, 594 N.Y.S.2d 174 (1993) (company was liable to a transferee who acquired shares that had been issued in a private placement and thus were subject to resale restrictions which were not revealed in a restrictive legend as required by UCC § 8–204; the transferee who took thus acquired the stock without notice or knowledge of the restrictions and was entitled to recover damages associated with its attempts to sell the stock).

49. 17 C.F.R. § 230.503.

50. Regulation D, preliminary note 1, 17 C.F.R. § 230.501.

suers relying on Regulation D are under a continuing obligation to supplement the information requirements by updating all disclosures where there have been material changes.[51] Regulation D is intended to be part of a unified system of federal/state limited offering exemptions; nothing in the Regulation excuses compliance with state securities laws.[52]

Regulation D's exemptions are not the exclusive means to getting an exemption under the 1933 Act. Therefore, if an offering fails to qualify under Rule 504, 505, or 506, another exemption under its enabling section 3(b), 4(2), or 4(6) may still be available.[53] The preliminary notes emphasize that exemptions provided in Regulation D are transaction exemptions only, and thus a security acquired in an exempt offering cannot be resold unless its offering is covered by a registration statement or independently falls within an exemption.[54] Regulation D exemptions are available only to the issuer of securities and therefore are not available for use by either affiliates or purchasers of securities that were initially acquired under Regulation D offerings.[55] The fifth preliminary note emphasizes that the exemptions may be available for issues during mergers, consolidations, reclassifications of securities, or other business combinations.[56]

The sixth preliminary note explains that Regulation D is not available to any issuer for any transaction that, although in technical compliance with Rules 501 through 506, is part of a plan or scheme to evade the registration requirements of the 1933 Act.[57] This proviso allows the SEC to look beyond the form of a particular transaction. As such, there is a qualification to the degree of safety provided by the Regulation's safe harbors. Presumably the question here will be whether the issuer and other participants have acted in good faith.

The Commission has also addressed the applicability of Regulation D to transactions occurring outside the United States. First, the Commission notes that as a general proposition registration is not required for sales to non resident purchasers where the sales are made outside of the United States and are effected in a manner that should result in the securities coming to rest outside the United States.[58] The Commission explains that this rule may be relied upon even if Regulation D sales are contemporaneously being made in the United States.[59] Thus, for example, such foreign purchasers are not counted in either Rule 505 or 506's

---

51. *Id.*

52. Regulation D, preliminary note 2, 17 C.F.R. § 230.501.

53. Regulation D, preliminary note 3, 17 C.F.R. § 230.501.

54. Regulation D, preliminary note 4, 17 C.F.R. § 230.501.

55. *Id.*

56. Regulation D, preliminary note 5, 17 C.F.R. § 230.501.

57. Regulation D, preliminary note 6, 17 C.F.R. § 230.501.

58. Regulation D, Preliminary Note 7, 17 C.F.R. § 230.501, relying on Sec.Act Rel.No. 33–4708 (July 9, 1964). *See also* § 14.3 *infra.*

59. Regulation D, Preliminary Note 7, 17 C.F.R. § 230.501.

thirty-five purchaser limit.[60] However, if the issuer is relying solely on Regulation D for the sales to foreigners, then the foreign transactions are considered along with the domestic Regulation D sales.[61]

The 1989 Amendments to Regulation D

In 1989, the SEC proposed and adopted numerous amendments to Regulation D.[62] Under Rule 507, the filing of Form D is required but is no longer a condition of the exemption.[63] On the other hand, Regulation D exemptions are not available to issuers who have been subject to a judicial injunction issued as a result of violations of the filing obligation.[64] Rule 508 provides a savings clause for de minimis departures from Regulation D's requirements. Under Rule 508 where there has been a good faith attempt to comply with Regulation D's requirements, insignificant departures from the requirements of the exemption will not result in loss of the exemption so long as the requirements not complied with were not designed to protect the complaining person.[65] Rule 508 goes on to describe the types of noncompliance that will be deemed significant to any Regulation D offering.[66] Another amendment to Regulation D was a provision that Rules 505 and 506's requirements are met regardless of whether there was a good faith belief held by the issuer that there were not an excessive number of nonaccredited investors so

---

60. *Id.*

61. *Id.*

62. *See* Sec.Act Rel.No. 33–6825, [1989 Transfer Binder] Fed.Sec.L.Rep. (CCH) ¶ 84,404 (March 14, 1989); Sec.Act Rel.No. 33–6812, [1988–89 Transfer Binder] Fed.Sec.L.Rep. (CCH) ¶ 84,346 (Dec. 20, 1988).

63. *Id.* 17 C.F.R. § 230.507. *See* the SEC releases in footnote 62 *supra*. The filing obligation is found in Rule 503. 17 C.F.R. § 230.503.

64. *See* Sec.Act. Rel.No. 33–6812, [1988–89 Transfer Binder] Fed.Sec.L.Rep. (CCH) ¶ 84,346 (Dec. 20, 1988).

65. 17 C.F.R. § 230.508.

66. Rule 508 provides:

(a) A failure to comply with a term, condition or requirement of § 230.504, § 230.505 or § 230.506 will not result in the loss of the exemption from the requirements of section 5 of the Act for any offer or sale to a particular individual or entity, if the person relying on the exemption shows:

(1) the failure to comply did not pertain to a term, condition or requirement directly intended to protect that particular individual or entity; and

(2) the failure to comply was insignificant with respect to the offering as a whole, provided that any failure to comply with paragraph (c) of § 230.502, paragraph (b)(2)(i) of § 230.504, paragraphs (b)(2)(i) and (ii) of § 230.505 and paragraph (b)(2)(i) of § 230.506 shall be deemed to be significant to the offering as a whole; and

(3) a good faith and reasonable attempt was made to comply with all applicable terms, conditions and requirements of § 230.504, § 230.505 or § 230.506.

(b) A transaction made in reliance on § 230.504, § 230.505 or § 230.506 shall comply with all applicable terms, conditions and requirements of Regulation D. Where an exemption is established only through reliance upon paragraph (a) of this section, the failure to comply shall nonetheless be actionable by the Commission under section 20 of the Act.

The adopting release points out that noncompliance with Regulation D's prohibition against a general solicitation is not covered by rule 508's savings provision. Sec. Act Rel. No. 33–6825, [1989 Transfer Binder] Fed.Sec.L.Rep. (CCH) ¶ 84,404 (March 14, 1989).

long as in fact the thirty-five nonaccredited purchaser limitation was complied with.[67]

§ 4.18 Exemption for Limited Offerings Not Exceeding $5,000,000—SEC Rule 505

SEC Rule 505[1] combines elements of the private placement exemption under section 4(2),[2] the safe harbor of Rule 506[3] and section 4(6)'s[4] exemption for offerings to "accredited investors" not exceeding five million dollars. Whereas Rule 506 has no limit on the dollar amount of an offering, Rule 505 exempts offerings only where the aggregate offering price of an issue, together with all securities previously offered pursuant to a section 3(b) exemption or in violation of section 5(a), does not exceed five million dollars within a twelve month period.[5] A Rule 505 offering may be made to an unlimited number of "accredited investors" and no more than thirty-five other "purchasers."[6] "Accredited investor" is defined in Rule 501 as any person who in fact comes within or whom the issuer reasonably believes comes within any of eight categories of investors at the time securities are sold to him or her.[7] Generally, these categories include wealthy and/or financially sophisticated investors such as banks, insurance companies, tax-exempt organizations, directors and executive officers of the issuer, and natural persons who have a large net worth or very sizeable annual incomes.[8] When calculating the number of purchasers for purposes of Rule 505, one must exclude all accredited investors and certain relatives of a purchaser, and trusts, estates and corporations in which a purchaser has more than a fifty percent beneficial ownership.[9] In other instances, a corporation or other business entity will generally be counted as one purchaser,[10] as is each client of an investment adviser or broker.[11]

67. 17 C.F.R. §§ 230.505(b)(2)(ii), 230.506(b)(2)(ii).

§ 4.18

1. 17 C.F.R. § 230.505. For a case holding that rule 501 was satisfied by an offering of less than $5,000,000 to an accredited investor, *see* Wright v. National Warranty Co., 953 F.2d 256, 259–60 (6th Cir.1992).

2. 15 U.S.C.A. § 77d(2). *See* § 4.21 *infra*.

3. 17 C.F.R. § 230.506. *See* § 4.22 *infra*.

4. 15 U.S.C.A. § 77d(6). *See* § 4.20 *infra*.

5. 17 C.F.R. § 230.505(a), (b)(2)(i).

In 1992, the Commission amended Regulation A so that other section 3(b) offerings are not included in Regulation A's $5 million ceiling. Nevertheless, any Regulation A offerings within the preceding 12 months must be counted for the purpose of calculating rule 505's $5 million ceiling and rule 504's $1 million ceiling.

6. 17 C.F.R. § 230.505(b)(2)(ii). In 1989 the Commission amended Rule 505 to provide that the issuer must "reasonably believe" that the purchaser limitations are met. *Id.*

7. 17 C.F.R. § 230.501(a). *See* §§ 4.17 *supra* and 4.20 *infra*. *See also* section 2(15) and rule 215; 15 U.S.C.A. § 77b(15); 17 C.F.R. § 230.215 (1982) which are discussed in § 4.20 *infra*.

8. *See* § 4.20 *infra*.

9. 17 C.F.R. § 230.501(e)(1).

10. 17 C.F.R. § 230.501(e)(2).

11. 17 C.F.R. § 230.501(e) note.

In order to be eligible to take advantage of the Rule 505 exemption the issuer must be neither an investment company nor be subject to any of the "bad boy" disqualification provisions contained in Rule 262(b) and(c) of Regulation A.[12] Further, all offers and sales made under Rule 505 must satisfy the terms and conditions of Rules 501 through 503 of Regulation D.[13]

In addition to defining "accredited investor," Rule 501 defines other terms used in Regulation D.[14] Rule 502 prohibits the use of general advertising or soliciting during an offering exempt under Rule 505; however, it also requires the disclosure of certain information to purchasers who do not qualify as "accredited purchasers" as defined in Rule 501.[15] The SEC recommends, however, that if there are any nonaccredited investors, that all purchasers, including those who are accredited, receive the private placement memorandum. If all purchasers are accredited investors then neither Rule 502 nor Rule 505 requires specific information to be disclosed to any purchasers. Rule 502 also provides a six-month safe harbor for the integration of Regulation D offerings and a five-factor test for determining whether offerings that fall outside the safe harbors will be integrated.[16] In addition, the SEC places limits on resales of securities acquired in a transaction under Regulation D, and, as a preventive measure, requires that issuers exercise reasonable care to determine that they are not selling to section 2(11) underwriters.[17] Finally, Rule 503 requires the issuer to file periodically with the Securities and Exchange Commission notices of sales made under Regulation D.[18]

In 1989, the Commission amended Regulation D to provide that minor variations from an exemption's requirements will not destroy the availability of the exemption. New Rule 508 provides a savings clause for an insignificant failure to comply with a condition of the exemption

---

12. 17 C.F.R. § 230.505(a). *See* 17 C.F.R. § 230.262; § 4.15 *supra*. The Commission reserves the right to waive the disqualification. *Id.;* 17 C.F.R. § 230.505(b)(2)(iii). *See, e.g.,* Michigan National Corp., 26 Sec. Reg. & L. Rep. (BNA) 37 (SEC no action letter available Dec. 17, 1993) (indicating Regulations A and D could be used notwithstanding subsidiary being subject to disqualifying injunctive order).

In 1987, the Commission considered but then, in 1988, rejected extending these "bad boy" disqualifications to rule 506's safe harbor for nonpublic offerings. Sec.Act Rel.No. 33–6758, [1987–88 Transfer Binder] Fed.Sec.L.Rep. (CCH) ¶ 84,221 (March 3, 1988); Sec.Act Rel.No. 33.6683, [1986–87 Transfer Binder] Fed.Sec.L.Rep. (CCH) ¶ 84,054 (Jan. 16, 1987). Rule 506 is discussed in § 4.22 *infra*.

13. 17 C.F.R. § 230.505(b)(1). *See* 17 C.F.R. §§ 230.501–.503; § 4.17 *supra*.

14. *See* § 4.16 *supra*.

15. 17 C.F.R. § 230.502(b), (c). Formerly, the SEC required that if there were any unaccredited purchasers that that all purchasers had to receive this information. While the Commission now suggests that all purchasers receive the same information, it is no longer a condition of the safe harbor exemption.

16. 17 C.F.R. § 230.502(a). *See* § 4.17 *supra*. Integration is discussed in § 4.29 *infra*.

17. 17 C.F.R. § 230.502(d). *See* §§ 4.24, 4.26 *infra*.

18. 17 C.F.R. § 230.503.

that is not "directly intended to protect" the investor, provided that the issuer made a good faith and reasonable attempt to comply.[19] Additionally, with regard to the purchaser qualifications, all that is required is that the issuer reasonably believe that the purchaser qualifications and limitations have been met.[20]

§ 4.19   The Exemption for Small Issues of $1,000,000 or Less—SEC Rule 504

Rule 504[1] provides an exemption from registration for offerings by small issuers not to exceed one million dollars in any twelve month period.[2] It was formerly the rule that no more than five hundred thousand dollars of the aggregate offering price in a Rule 504 offering could be attributable to securities that are sold without registration under state law.[3] The SEC has amended Rule 504 so as to eliminate many of the limitations that formerly existed. Thus, Rule 504 now permits offerings of up to $1 million worth of securities regardless of registration under state law.[4] However, state registration as a precondition to the $1 million ceiling was retained under new Rule 504a for

---

19. 17 C.F.R. § 230.508. The adopting release points out that a failure to comply with the prohibition against a general solicitation does not fall within rule 508's exemptive reach. Sec. Act Rel. No. 33–6825, [1989 Transfer Binder] Fed.Sec.L.Rep. (CCH) ¶ 84,404 (March 14, 1989).

20. 17 C.F.R. § 230.506(b)(2)(ii).

§ 4.19

1. 17 C.F.R. § 230.504. Prior to 1988, rule 504 exempted offerings not exceeding $500,000. *See* Sec.Act Rel.No. 33–6758, [1987–88 Transfer Binder] Fed.Sec.L.Rep. (CCH) ¶ 84,221 (March 3, 1988).

2. 17 C.F.R. § 230.504(b)(2)(i). A note to the rule provides the following illustrations of how the aggregate offering price is calculated under Rule 504:

Note 1: The calculation of the aggregate offering price is illustrated as follows:

Example 1. If an issuer sells $500,000 worth of its securities pursuant to state registration on January 1, 1988 under this § 230.504, it would be able to sell an additional $500,000 worth of securities either pursuant to state registration or without state registration during the ensuing twelve-month period, pursuant to this § 230.504.

Example 2. If an issuer sold $900,000 pursuant to state registration on June 1, 1987 under this § 230.504 and an additional $4,100,000 on December 1, 1987 under § 230.505, the issuer could not sell any of its securities under this § 230.504 until December 1, 1988. Until then the issuer must count the December 1, 1987 sale towards the $1,000,000 limit within the preceding twelve months.

Note 2: If a transaction under this § 230.504 fails to meet the limitation on the aggregate offering price, it does not affect the availability of this § 230.504 for the other transactions considered in applying such limitation. For example, if an issuer sold $1,000,000 worth of its securities pursuant to state registration on January 1, 1988 under this § 230.504 and an additional $500,000 worth on July 1, 1988, this § 230.504 would not be available for the later sale, but would still be applicable to the January 1, 1988 sale.

Id.

3. 17 C.F.R. § 230.504 (1990).

4. 17 C.F.R. § 230.504, as amended in Sec.Act Rel. No. 33–6949, 6 Fed.Sec.L.Rep. (CCH) ¶ 72,439 (SEC July 30, 1992). *See* Sec.Act Rel. No. 33–6924, [1991–1992 Transfer Binder] Fed.Sec.L.Rep. (CCH) ¶ 84,931 (March 11, 1992).

offerings involving blank check companies through November 16, 1992.[5] Similarly, the ban on general solicitations and the requirement that the securities be restricted that were formerly applicable in all Rule 504 offerings have been eliminated.[6] Accordingly, there are no longer restrictions on resale of securities purchased in a Rule 504 offering. In addition to the dollar limit, the exemption is available only to an issuer that is neither an investment company nor subject to the reporting requirements of the Securities Exchange Act of 1934.[7] In order to take advantage of the rule, offers and sales must conform to the terms and conditions set out in Rules 501 through 503. As discussed earlier,[8] these general conditions include a prohibition on general solicitations of purchasers[9] and restrictions on resales of the securities by purchasers in the exempt offering. Rule 504 does not expressly preclude a general solicitation of purchasers and the resale restrictions applicable to other Regulation D offerings are not imposed on Rule 504 transactions.[10] Furthermore, Rule 502(b)(1) expressly excludes Rule 504 offerings from Regulations D's informational requirements; however, to the extent that a Rule 504 offering involves a general solicitation of purchasers, registration will presumably be required under applicable state blue sky laws.[11]

As mentioned above, Rule 504 does not impose restrictions on resale as a precondition to securing the Rule 504 exemption. However, purchasers in a Rule 504 transaction who subsequently decide to sell their shares will need to secure their own exemption from registration. Accordingly, at least in those instances in which the Rule 504 offering is not registered under a state blue sky law, the securities so acquired may be de facto restricted. Moreover, since Rule 504 is a transaction exemption and securities acquired under it cannot be resold without registration or an independent exemption, the issuer using Regulation D may want to take reasonable care to assure that purchasers do not intend to dispose of securities they buy in such a way as to make those purchasers statutory underwriters.[12] Specifically, the issuer must at least (1) make reasonable inquiry to determine whether the purchaser is acquiring the securities for himself or for other persons, (2) disclose in writing before the sale to each purchaser that the securities have not been registered and therefore cannot be resold unless they are registered under the Act or unless an exemption from registration is available, and (3) place a

---

5. 17 C.F.R. § 230.504a (repealed). Although Rule 504a was available for blank check companies, the SEC repealed the rule effective November 16, 1992. Sec.Act Rel. No. 33–6961 (SEC Oct. 16, 1992).

6. 17 C.F.R. Pt. 502, as amended in Sec.Act Rel. No. 33–6949, 6 Fed.Sec.L.Rep. (CCH) ¶ 72,439 (SEC July 30, 1992).

7. Securities Exchange Act of 1934, Pub.L. 291, 48 Stat. 881 (codified in 15 U.S.C.A. §§ 78a *et seq.*). *See* §§ 9.2–9.3 *infra*.

8. *See* § 4.17 *supra*.

9. 17 C.F.R. § 230.502(c).

10. Rule 504(b)(1), 17 C.F.R. § 230.504(b)(1).

11. Rule 502(b)(1), 17 C.F.R. § 230.502(b)(1). State securities laws are considered in chapter 8 *infra*.

12. 17 C.F.R. § 230.502(d).

legend on the securities stating that they have not been registered and reciting restrictions on their transferability and sale.[13] As noted above, these restrictions on resale are not expressly imposed by Rule 504 and, further, do not apply if the securities are registered in states requiring delivery of a disclosure document.

There is no mandatory disclosure as a precondition to the Rule 504 exemption. This is in contrast to the informational requirements of Regulation A's qualified exemption for small issues,[14] Rule 506's safe harbor for private placements,[15] as well as Rule 505's exemption for offerings of up to five million dollars.[16]

Rule 502 establishes a six month safe harbor for the integration of Regulation D offerings and a five factor test for determining whether offerings that fall outside the safe harbor will be integrated.[17] As noted above, Rule 502 expressly provides that if the issuer sells securities pursuant to Rule 504 no specific information is required to be furnished to purchasers.[18]

Rule 501[19] provides definitions of certain terms used in Rules 502–506, and Rule 503 sets forth requirements for filing notice with the Securities and Exchange Commission of sales made under Regulation D.[20] As is discussed elsewhere in this treatise,[21] insignificant departures from Rule 504's requirements will not destroy the availability of the exemption.

§ 4.20 Sales to "Accredited Investors"—Section 4(6)

Section 4(6)[1] exempts from the 1933 Act's registration requirements transactions in which the aggregate sales price does not exceed the maximum amount permitted by section 3(b)[2]—currently five million dollars—provided that all offers and sales are made only to "accredited investors."[3] The section 4(6) exemption is preconditioned upon the absence of general advertising or public solicitation in the offering process. The statute also requires that appropriate notice of sales made

---

13. *Id.* Former Rule 504(b)(ii) required that unless there are no restrictions on resale because of registration under state law, the restrictions must be disclosed. 17 C.F.R. § 230.504(b)(ii) (1988).

14. 17 C.F.R. §§ 230.251–.260. *See* § 4.15 *supra.*

15. 17 C.F.R. § 230.506. *See* § 4.22 *infra.*

16. Rule 505 requires that information be furnished to investors unless all investors are accredited. 17 C.F.R. §§ 230.502(b), 230.505. *See* § 4.18 *supra.*

17. 17 C.F.R. § 230.502(a). *See* § 4.16 *supra.*

18. 17 C.F.R. § 230.502(b)(1)(i).

19. 17 C.F.R. § 230.501. *See* § 4.17 *supra.*

20. 17 C.F.R. § 230.503. *See* § 4.17 *supra. See also* Rule 507, 17 C.F.R. § 230.507.

21. 17 C.F.R. § 230.508. *See* §§ 4.17, 4.18 *supra* and § 4.22 *infra.*

§ 4.20

1. 15 U.S.C.A. § 77(d)(6).

2. 15 U.S.C.A. § 77c(b). *See* § 4.14 *supra.*

3. *See* 15 U.S.C.A. § 77b(15). *See also* 17 C.F.R. § 230.215.

in reliance on section 4(6) be filed with the SEC. Form 4(6) was repealed in 1982 and replaced by Form D.

The term "accredited investor" is defined in section 2(15)(i)[4] to include institutional investors such as banks, registered investment companies, employee benefit plans subject to ERISA, and insurance companies. An alternative method for falling within the category of accredited investor under section 2(15)(ii) is to be someone who on the basis of factors such as financial sophistication, net worth, and knowledge and experience in financial matters, qualifies as an "accredited investor" as defined by the Commission's rules.[5] Specifically, SEC Rule 215[6] defines "accredited investor" as used in section 2(15)(ii) to include eight categories of offerees and purchasers. Rule 215 includes:

(a) Any savings and loan association or other institution specified in section 3(a)(5)(A) of the Act whether acting in its individual or fiduciary capacity; any broker or dealer registered pursuant to section 15 of the Securities Exchange Act of 1934; an employee benefit plan within the meaning of Title I of the Employee Retirement Income Security Act of 1974, if the investment decision is made by a plan fiduciary, as defined in section 3(21) of such Act, which is a savings and loan association, or if the employee benefit plan has total assets in excess of $5,000,000 or, if a self-directed plan, with investment decisions made solely by persons that are accredited investors;

(b) Any private business development company as defined in section 202(a)(22) of the Investment Advisers Act of 1940;[7]

(c) Any organization described in section 501(c)(3) of the Internal Revenue Code, corporation, Massachusetts or similar business trust, or partnership, not formed for the specific purpose of acquiring the securities offered, with total assets in excess of $5,000,000;

(d) Any director, executive officer, or general partner of the issuer of the securities being offered or sold, or any director, executive officer, or general partner of a general partner of that issuer;

(e) Any natural person whose individual net worth, or joint net worth with that person's spouse at the time of his purchase exceeds $1,000,000;

(f) Any natural person who had an individual income in excess of $200,000 in each of the two most recent years or joint income with that person's spouse in excess of $300,000 in each of those

---

4. 15 U.S.C.A. § 77b(15)(i).

5. 15 U.S.C.A. § 77b(15)(ii). *See* 17 C.F.R. § 230.215.

6. 17 C.F.R. § 230.215. The definition appears to be an expanding one. In 1988 the Commission enlarged the definition of accredited investor and also proposed still additional expansion. *See* Sec.Act Rel. No. 33–6758, [1987–88 Transfer Binder] Fed.Sec.L.Rep. (CCH) ¶ 84,221 (March 3, 1988) (adopting new definition); Sec.Act Rel.No. 33–6759, [1987–88 Transfer Binder] Fed.Sec.L.Rep. (CCH) ¶ 84,221 (March 3, 1988) (proposing additional expansion). *See also* § 4.17 *supra*.

7. The Investment Advisers Act is discussed in chapter 18 *infra*.

years and has a reasonable expectation of reaching the same income level in the current year;

(g) Any trust, with total assets in excess of $5,000,000, not formed for the specific purpose of acquiring the securities offered, whose purchase is directed by a sophisticated person as described in § 230.506(b)(2)(ii); and

(h) Any entity in which all of the equity owners are accredited investors.

The significance of the concept of accredited investor is not limited to the section 4(6) exemption. As discussed elsewhere,[8] accredited investors are not counted when computing Rule 505's or Rule 506's thirty-five purchaser limitation.[9] Additionally, offerings made solely to accredited investors are not subject to the offering circular requirements of Rules 505 and 506.[10]

The full effect of the section 4(6) exemption for sales to accredited investors is that it combines many of the features of a private placement[11] and that of the qualified exemption available under section 3(b).[12] The exemption also complements the private placement exemption provided by section 4(2) and Rule 506.[13]

Section 4(6) and the Other Small Issue Exemptions Compared[14]

Under section 3(b), an issuer may make an unregistered public offering pursuant to Regulation A[15] of up to five million dollars in any one year. Regulation A is preconditioned on disclosure of specified information and the use of a qualifying offering circular[16] but, unlike section 4(6), there is no limitation on the nature or number of offerees or purchasers. Both section 4(2) and Rule 506, although not requiring a "mini registration" like Regulation A, impose severe restrictions upon both the nature and number of offerees and/or purchasers. The case law under section 4(2) has also established rather high sophistication and solvency thresholds for qualified purchasers.[17] Further, like section 4(6), but unlike Regulation A, the private placement exemption is premised on the absence of general advertising and solicitation of offers to buy. Section 4(6), although restricting the nature of offerees, puts no limits on the number of purchasers or offerees, except for its ban on general solicitation.

---

8. *See* §§ 4.17, 4.18 *supra* and 4.22 *infra*.

9. 17 C.F.R. § 501(e)(1)(iv).

10. 17 C.F.R. § 502(b)(1)(i).

11. 15 U.S.C.A. § 77d(2); 17 C.F.R. § 230.506. *See* § 4.22 *infra*.

12. 15 U.S.C.A. § 77c(b). *See* § 4.14 *supra*. The same combination is found in Rule 505, 17 C.F.R. § 230.505 which is discussed in § 4.18 *supra*.

13. 15 U.S.C.A. § 77d(2); 17 C.F.R. § 230.506.

14. *See* the table comparing various small issue exemptions in § 4.13 *supra*.

15. 17 C.F.R. §§ 230.251–230.264. *See* § 4.15 *supra*.

16. 17 C.F.R. § 230.256.

17. *See* § 4.21 *infra*.

SEC Rule 505[18], which was promulgated pursuant to section 3(b), provides yet another variation. Rule 505 exempts transactions up to five million dollars and permits sales to an unlimited number of accredited investors but to no more than thirty-five non-accredited investor purchasers. Thus, like section 4(6), Rule 505 is limited to offerings of up to five million dollars. However, unlike section 4(6), Rule 505 permits a limited number of sales to non-accredited purchasers.

Section 4(2) and Rule 506's private placement exemptions impose no dollar limit on the offering and thus are available to a wider range of capital raising ventures. Furthermore, unsophisticated investors may participate in private placements under Rule 506 provided that they are represented by purchaser representatives.[19]

§ 4.21   The Private Placement Exemption—Section 4(2)

Section 4(2) of the 1933 Act[1] exempts "transactions not involving any public offering." The exemption for transactions not involving a public offering is limited to issuers and thus cannot be relied upon by persons other than the issuer. However, non-issuers may be able to take advantage of the so-called section 4(1½) exemption, which is discussed in a later section of this treatise.[2] The section 4(2) exemption, which is also commonly referred to as the private placement exemption, can be useful for both closely held and public issue corporations.[3]

The exemption for non-public offerings applies to offerings to institutional investors that are sufficiently sophisticated and have sufficiently strong bargaining positions that they do not need the protections of federal registration. Secondly, the exemption also applies to an offering that is made to a limited number of qualified private individuals who, like institutional investors, are sufficiently sophisticated and are able to bear the investment's risk so as not to need the Act's registration protections.[4] In addition to the administrative and judicial interpreta-

---

18.   17 C.F.R. § 230.505. *See* § 4.18 *supra.*

19.   17 C.F.R. § 230.506(b)(2)(ii). *See* § 4.22 *infra.*

§ 4.21

1.   15 U.S.C.A. § 77d(2).

2.   *See* § 4.26.1 *infra.*

3.   *See generally,* Stuart C. Goldberg, Private Placements and Restricted Securities (1978); I, VI Louis Loss, Securities Regulation 653–96, 2630–66 (2d ed. 1961; 1969 supp.); Eli Shapiro & Charles R. Wolf, The Role of Private Placements in Corporate Finance (1972); Harold Marsh, Jr., Who Killed the Private Offering Exemption?, A Legal Whodunit, 71 Nw.U.L.Rev. 470 (1976); Marc H. Morgenstern, Private Placement Guidelines—A Lawyer's Letter to a First–Time Issuer, 48 Bus.Law. 257 (1992); Carl W. Schneider, The Statutory Law of Private Placements, 14 Rev.Sec.Reg. 869 (1981); Section 4(2) and Statutory Law—A Position Paper of the Federal Regulation of Securities Committee, 31 Bus.Law 483 (1975); Comment, Private Placements Outside Rule 146, 25 Emory L.J. 899 (1976). For an analysis of private placement exemptions in the international arena, *see* Symposium, Exemptions for Institutional Investors or Concepts of Non–Public Offerings: A Comparative Study, 13 U.Pa.Int'l Bus.L. 473 (1993).

4.   In evaluating an investor's sophistication, generalized financial sophistication is not always sufficient; it is important to look at the context of the particular transaction. *Cf., e.g.,* Marion Merrell Dow Inc. Securities Litigation, 1994 WL 396190, [1994–1995 Transfer

tions relating to the scope of this broadly drafted statutory exemption, SEC Rule 506[5] provides a safe harbor for any issuer who is able to meet the rule's requirements.

The nonpublic offering exemption was enacted for a number of reasons.[6] Congress was concerned with avoiding the cumbersome registration requirements when the benefits to the public were too remote and thus when there was no practical need for the Act's application.[7] The section 4(2) exemption was designed to apply to specific or isolated sales as well as offerings to a very small number of securities holders so that the public interest is not involved. As will be seen from the discussion of the case law that has developed as well as from the parameters of the safe-harbor rule, even today very small offerings to a limited number of purchasers will not be exempt if the offerees and purchasers do not qualify as sufficiently sophisticated (and/or wealthy) investors.[8]

In order to provide more certainty in planning the SEC adopted the safe harbor rule contained in Rule 506. Compliance with the rule will provide an exemption but according to the SEC, noncompliance does not raise even an inference that the exemption is unavailable.[9] Since Rule 506 is only a safe harbor rule, the pre-existing judicial and administrative interpretations remain an important part of the law today as they are still available to issuers who do not choose or are not able to comply with each and every provision of Rule 506.[10]

In SEC v. Ralston Purina Co.[11] the Supreme Court rejected the defendant's contention that an offering of stock that was limited to its own employees was necessarily exempt as not involving a public offering. The defendant, relying on a literal reading of the statute, maintained that an offering to a limited group could not properly be characterized as a public offering. The Court ruled that since the stock being offered was made available to all employees regardless of connection with the issuer and knowledge of the business, the offerees and purchasers represented

Binder] Fed. Sec. L. Rep. (CCH) ¶ 98,356 (W.D.Mo.1994) (generalized financial sophistication of plaintiff did not disqualify him as a class representative where alleged misrepresentations related to matters specific to the pharmaceutical industry).

5. 17 C.F.R. § 230.506 (1982). *See* § 4.22 *infra*.

6. H.R.Rep. No. 85, 73 Cong., 1st Sess. 5–7, 15–16 (1933). *See also* H.R.Rep. No. 152, 73d Cong. 1st Sess. 1–29 (1933).

7. *See, e.g.,* Wright v. National Warranty Co., 953 F.2d 256, 259–60 (6th Cir.1992) (alternative holding, finding a nonpublic offering based on a sale to an accredited investor).

8. *See, e.g.,* Lawler v. Gilliam, 569 F.2d 1283 (4th Cir.1978); G. Eugene England Foundation v. First Federal Corp., 663 F.2d 988 (10th Cir.1973).

9. Rule 506 (17 C.F.R. § 230.506) is discussed in § 4.22 *infra*. As a result of 1989 amendments to Regulation D, de minimus departures from the exemption's requirements will not render the exemption unavailable. 17 C.F.R. § 230.508. *See* § 4.17 *supra* and § 4.22 *infra*.

10. *See* the authorities cited in footnote 3, *supra*. *See also, e.g.,* Leiter v. Kuntz, 655 F.Supp. 725 (D.Utah 1987) (discovery allowed to proceed on question of section 4(2) exemption); Akers v. Bonifasi, 629 F.Supp. 1212 (M.D.Tenn.1984) (section 4(2) exemption upheld); Joachim v. Magids, 737 S.W.2d 852 (Tex.App.1987) (semble).

11. 346 U.S. 119, 73 S.Ct. 981, 97 L.Ed. 1494 (1953).

a sufficiently large and representative slice of the investing public so as to render the exemption unavailable. In discussing the scope of the exemption the Court announced the guidelines that have continued to form the basis for all private placement exemptions. In the first instance, all offerees must have access to the types of information that would be contained in a full-fledged 1933 Act registration statement. Secondly, the offerees must be capable of fending for themselves; in more recent cases this has been interpreted to mean that the offerees must be sufficiently sophisticated to demand and understand the information that is available to them. The ability to fend for oneself is thus dependent upon access to information. It has therefore been held that the exemption will not be available even though the offerees are sufficiently sophisticated where they did not have access to the types of information that would otherwise have to be disclosed in the registration statement.[12] Conversely, the Commission has made it clear that a brochure containing desired information by itself is not sufficient since the nature and/or sophistication of the offerees is an equally important factor.[13] In addition, the offering brochure, even if disseminated only to qualified purchasers, may be deemed insufficient unless the offerees have an opportunity to meet with representatives of the issuer and to inspect relevant corporate books and records.[14]

The Supreme Court in *Ralston Purina* pointed out that even though the number of purchasers involved will not necessarily be the determinative factor, it is a significant one in considering the scope of the exemption.[15] Accordingly, the fact that there were as many as five hundred employee offerees in the *Ralston Purina* case helped tip the balance against a section 4(2) exemption from registration. In addition to (1) the number of offerees, (2) the offerees' need for information and (3) the offerees' access to information, the courts will consider a fourth factor: the size of the offering, both in terms of the number of securities offered and the aggregate offering price.[16] The number of offerees and

---

12. Gilligan, Will & Co. v. SEC, 267 F.2d 461 (2d Cir.1959), *cert. denied* 361 U.S. 896, 80 S.Ct. 200, 4 L.Ed.2d 152 (1959). *See also, e.g.,* Van Dyke v. Coburn Enterprises, Inc., 873 F.2d 1094 (8th Cir.1989).

13. Sec.Act Rel. No. 33–5487 (Jan. 23, 1974).

14. *Cf.* Rule 502(b)(2)(v), 17 C.F.R. § 230.502(b)(2)(v).

15. Other courts have picked up on this, *see, e.g.,* Johnston v. Bumba, 764 F.Supp. 1263 (N.D.Ill.1991); as has the safe harbor rule of Rule 506. 17 C.F.R. § 230.506, which is discussed in § 4.22 *infra*.

Although the number of investors is a significant factor it is not, by itself, determinative. *See, e.g.,* Weprin v. Peterson, 736 F.Supp. 1124 (N.D.Ga.1988) (offering to more than 400 offerees was exempt where all offerees had preexisting relationship with broker-dealers conducting the offering, each offeree received an offering circular specifically addressed to the offeree, and there was no general distribution of the offering circulars).

16. These factors were originally incorporated into an SEC interpretative release. Sec.Act Rel. No. 33–285, 1 Fed.Sec.L.Rep. (CCH) ¶ 2740, 2741–44 (SEC Jan. 24, 1935). *See, e.g.,* SEC v. Murphy, 626 F.2d 633, 644–47 (9th Cir.1980); McDaniel v. Compania Minera Mar de Cortes, Sociedad Anonimo, Inc., 528 F.Supp. 152, 164 (D.Ariz.1981); Barett v. Triangle Mining Corp., 1976 WL 760, [1975–77 Transfer Binder] Fed.Sec.L.Rep. (CCH) ¶ 95,438 at p. 99,210 (S.D.N.Y.1976). *Compare* Van Dyke v. Coburn Enterprises, 873 F.2d 1094 (8th Cir.1989) (exemption upheld) *with* Mark v. FSC Securities Corp., 870 F.2d 331 (6th Cir.1989) (exemption denied due in part to wide-ranging sales efforts).

size of the offering, as measured by the number of units offered, are significant because the larger the numbers of each the more difficult it is to control downstream sales that would eventually filter the securities into the hands of the general investing public. As it becomes more likely that the securities sold pursuant to the private placement exemption will filter down to the investing public without a subsequent 1933 Act registration, the less likely it is that the section 4(2) exemption will be available.

In addition to the foregoing factors, the SEC has indicated that any "public advertising is inconsistent with a claim of private offering."[17] In light of the ban on public advertising, issuers frequently have to turn to investment bankers and other promoters in order to find an existing pool of potential customers. It is clearly permissible for a brokerage firm that is handling the private placement to contact its customers provided they meet the offering's suitability standard.[18] This is a common method of promoting tax shelters and other ventures that require a substantial investment. In such a case it is necessary to determine from the terms and risks of the offering the minimum offeree suitability standards. Where a private placement is not handled by a conduit with a ready list of potential offerees, all activities directed toward contacting the offerees will be closely scrutinized lest the issuer run afoul of the general solicitation prohibition. The use of investment seminars and other promotional meetings has been a significant factor in denying the availability of the exemption for non-public offerings.[19] Investment seminars that are limited to qualified offerees who have been prescreened presumably would not violate the prohibition on a general solicitation. In general, where the issuer is unable to prove that there were a limited number of offerees, the uncertainty concerning the

17. Sec.Act Rel. No. 33–4552 (Nov. 6, 1962). *Accord, e.g.,* Waterman v. Alta Verde Indus., Inc., 643 F.Supp. 797, 807 (E.D.N.C.1986). *Cf.* Texas Capital Network, Inc., [1993–1994 Transfer Binder] Fed. Sec. L. Rep. (CCH) ¶ 76,857 (SEC No Action Letter Feb. 23, 1994) (non-profit corporation's matching of business ventures with potential investors did not constitute a general solicitation).

See generally Stuart R. Cohn, Securities Markets for Small Issuers: The Barrier of Federal Solicitation and Advertising Prohibitions, 38 U.Fla.L.Rev. 1 (1986); Patrick Daugherty, Rethinking The Ban on General Solicitation, 38 Emory L.J. 67 (1989); Gary D. Lipson & B. Leslie Scharfman, General Solicitations in Exempt Offerings, 20 Rev.Sec. & Commod.Reg. 8 (Jan. 14, 1987). *But see* Madison Plaza Ass'n (SEC No Action Letter avail. Jan. 8, 1988) (public advertising for foreclosure sale of limited partnership interests did not preclude availability of section 4(2) exemption).

18. Mary S. Krech Trust v. Lakes Apartments, 642 F.2d 98 (5th Cir.1981), *rehearing denied* 645 F.2d 72 (5th Cir.1981). The court there noted that the burden is on the issuer to establish the identity of all offerees and purchasers and to prove their suitability. *Accord* Weprin v. Peterson, 736 F.Supp. 1124 (N.D.Ga.1988) (offering to persons having a previous relationship with broker-dealers was held to be exempt under section 4(2) where each offeree received an offering circular). *See also, e.g.,* E.F. Hutton & Co., 18 Sec.Reg. & L.Rep. (BNA) 171 (SEC No Action Letter Dec. 3, 1985). *But see* Mark v. FSC Securities Corp., 870 F.2d 331 (6th Cir.1989) (failure to sustain burden of establishing the exemption); Johnston v. Bumba, 764 F.Supp. 1263 (N.D.Ill.1991) (brokers mailed 2500 offering circulars, many recipients had no prior relationship with brokerage firm; defendants failed to establish § 4(2) exemption).

19. *See* Koehler v. Pulvers, 614 F.Supp. 829 (S.D.Cal.1985).

number of offerees can preclude reliance on the section 4(2) exemption.[20]

A common practice of private placement issuers has been to require all purchasers to sign an "investment letter" attesting to their lack of intent to resell the securities to the public. Although this may still be a necessary precaution, and is required under Rule 506,[21] the fact that the issuer requires such investment letters is self-serving and thus will not in and of itself have any probative value as to the existence of the exemption or the issuer's reasonable efforts to assure that no downstream sales would occur without registration.[22]

The burden of proof for establishing the availability of the exemption falls on the person claiming the protection of the exemption.[23] This has led one court to deny the exemption because of the issuer's failure to demonstrate that all offerees "received both written and oral information concerning [the issuer], that all offerees of its securities had access to any additional information which they might have required or requested and that all offerees of its securities had personal contacts with the officers of [the issuer]." [24] Although offerees need not have personal contact with the issuers in all cases, following the lead of the Fifth Circuit, there have been a number of judicial decisions that have given the section 4(2) exemption a limited scope at least with regard to offerees who do not qualify as institutional investors.[25] It is fair to say that in light of all factors the courts have developed, the ultimate question in proving a section 4(2) exemption boils down to one of fact.[26]

20. Western Federal Corp. v. Erickson, 739 F.2d 1439 (9th Cir.1984); Koehler v. Pulvers, 614 F.Supp. 829 (S.D.Cal.1985). *See also, e.g.,* Mary S. Krech Trust v. Lakes Apartments, 642 F.2d 98 (5th Cir.1981).

21. *See* 17 C.F.R. § 230.502(d).

22. SEC v. Continental Tobacco Co., 463 F.2d 137 (5th Cir.1972).

23. *See, e.g.,* Mary S. Krech Trust v. Lakes Apartments, 642 F.2d 98 (5th Cir.1981) (plaintiff carries the burden of proof on each element of the exemption). *See also, e.g.,* Kane v. U.S. SEC, 842 F.2d 194 (8th Cir.1988) (broker must make appropriate inquiries before distributing unregistered securities).

24. SEC v. Continental Tobacco Co., 463 F.2d 137, 160 (5th Cir.1972). *See also, e.g.,* Woolf v. S.D. Cohn & Co., 515 F.2d 591 (5th Cir.1975), *cert. denied* 434 U.S. 831, 98 S.Ct. 115, 54 L.Ed.2d 91 (1977).

25. Van Dyke v. Coburn Enterprises, 873 F.2d 1094 (8th Cir.1989) (section 4(2) exemption upheld; inside offerees had full access to information, outside offerees had the economic bargaining power to obtain any information); *See* Lawler v. Gilliam, 569 F.2d 1283 (4th Cir.1978); Doran v. Petroleum Management Corp., 545 F.2d 893 (5th Cir.1977), *appeal after remand* 576 F.2d 91 (5th Cir.1978); SEC v. Continental Tobacco Co., 463 F.2d 137 (5th Cir.1972); Hill York Corp. v. American International Franchises, Inc., 448 F.2d 680 (5th Cir.1971). *See also, e.g.,* SEC v. Murphy, 626 F.2d 633 (9th Cir.1980); Bowers v. Columbia General Corp., 336 F.Supp. 609 (D.Del.1971).

It is noteworthy that institutional investors will qualify as accredited investors under section 2(15), 15 U.S.C.A. § 77b(15). Offerings limited to accredited investors can be exempt under section 4(6), 15 U.S.C.A. § 77d(6), and Rules 505 and 506, 17 C.F.R. §§ 230.505–.506. *See* 17 C.F.R. § 230.501(e); § 4.18 *supra,* § 4.22 *infra.*

26. *See, e.g.,* Mary S. Krech Trust v. Lakes Apartments, 642 F.2d 98 (5th Cir. Unit B 1981), *rehearing denied* 645 F.2d 72 (5th Cir.1981) Goodman v. DeAzoulay, 554 F.Supp. 1029 (E.D.Pa.1983).

A literal reading of the more recent cases[27] would lead to the following requirements for private placements not involving institutional investor purchasers, arguably regardless of reliance on the safe harbor provided by Rule 506. Each offeree must have access to the types of information which would be disclosed should the issuer be required to undertake a full-fledged registration under the Act.[28] This requirement has been held not to have been satisfied if access was not given to each offeree even though such an offeree without access did not become an eventual purchaser. As one court put it, "[e]ven the offeree-plaintiff's 20–20 vision with respect to the facts underlying the security would not save the exemption if any one of his fellow offerees was blind."[29] It has quite properly been suggested, however, that the statute does not justify denying the exemption to an issuer who although taking reasonable precautions makes an isolated offer or offers to nonqualifying offerees.[30] The cases further require that offerees must also be sophisticated with respect to business and financial matters generally. Additionally, an offeree's knowledge of the particular business may be a factor. Knowledgeable investors with generalized investment experience will qualify as purchasers in a non-public offering when the nature of the enterprise does not require that there be a special level of sophistication.[31] Often, the nature of the investment will require more specific experience on the part of the purchasers.[32]

---

27. *See* footnotes 22–23 *supra.* *See also, e.g.,* Western Federal Corp. v. Erickson, 739 F.2d 1439 (9th Cir.1984).

28. The Fifth Circuit has indicated that disclosure by the issuer and access by the offeree are to be interpreted as disjunctive requirements. Doran v. Petroleum Management Corp., 545 F.2d 893 (5th Cir.1977), *appeal after remand* 576 F.2d 91 (5th Cir.1978).

29. *Id.* at 902.

30. The issuer has the burden of making a *reasonable* inquiry into each purchaser's background. Anastasi v. American Petroleum, Inc., 579 F.Supp. 273, 275 (D.Colo.1984) ("The private offering exemption turns on the issuer's reasonable beliefs rather than the actual condition of the buyer;" decided under former Rule 146 which if anything is more restrictive than the current safe harbor of Rule 506). *See* the authorities in footnote 23 *supra.* *Accord* Platsis v. E.F. Hutton & Co., Inc., 642 F.Supp. 1277, 1303–04 (W.D.Mich. 1986) (the issue "is not an investor's actual suitability, but the issuer's and the seller's reasonable grounds in believing that the plaintiff was suitable.") *Accord* 17 C.F.R. § 230.506(2)(b)(ii). *See* § 4.22 *infra.*

See also Position Paper of the Federal Regulation of Securities Committee, Section of Corporation, Banking & Business Law, 31 Bus.Law 485 (1975). Rule 506 does not contain express offeree qualification requirements but the nature and number of offerees are relevant in determining whether there has been a general solicitation so as to render the exemption unavailable. *See* Sec.Act Rel. No. 33–6455 1 Fed.Sec.L.Rep. (CCH) ¶ 2380 (March 3, 1983) (answer to question 73).

In fact the SEC has provided a savings clause for insignificant departures from Regulation D's requirements. 17 C.F.R. § 230.508. *See* §§ 4.17, 4.18 *supra* and § 4.22 *infra.*

31. Cowles v. Dow Keith Oil & Gas, Inc., 752 F.2d 508, 512 (10th Cir.1985), *cert. denied* 479 U.S. 816, 107 S.Ct. 74, 93 L.Ed.2d 30 (1986).

32. *See, e.g.,* Parker v. Broom, 820 F.2d 966 (8th Cir.1987) (purchaser was familiar with seller and the history of the investment). *Cf.* Marion Merrell Dow Inc. Securities Litigation, 1994 WL 396190, [1994–1995 Transfer Binder] Fed. Sec. L. Rep. (CCH) ¶ 98,356 (W.D.Mo.1994) (generalized financial sophistication of plaintiff did not disqualify him as a class representative where alleged misrepresentations related to matters specific to the pharmaceutical industry); Stoppelman v. Owens, 1984 WL 609, [1984 Transfer Binder] Fed.Sec.L.Rep. (CCH) ¶ 91,511 (D.D.C.1984) (sister company of the issuer qualified as a private placement purchaser).

Questions can be raised as to the propriety of a sophistication requirement as a precondition to a section 4(2) exemption.[33] It is evident that the Supreme Court's primary concern in the *Ralston Purina* case was that offerees in a nonpublic offering have access to the types of information that would be available with a registered public offering.[34] However, as discussed directly above, the courts have since required that the offerees possess a certain degree of sophistication. It has been suggested by some observers that these cases took their lead from Rule 506's predecessor and that investor sophistication may not properly be an element of the section 4(2) nonpublic offering exemption.[35] While offeree access to information is a necessary element of any transaction exempted under section 4(2), it clearly cannot be sufficient. The offerees as a class must somehow represent something other than a slice of the investing public.[36] As the Supreme Court observed in *Ralston Purina*:

> Since exempt transactions are those to which "there is no practical need for [the bill's] application," the applicability of section 4[(2)] should turn on whether the particular class of persons affected needs the protection of the Act. An offering to those who are shown to be able to fend for themselves is a transaction "not involving any public offering." [37]

In discussing the offerees' ability to fend for themselves, the Court was addressing something beyond access to information. The more recent

---

33. *See, e.g.,* Carl W. Schneider, Section 4(1½)—Private Resales of Restricted or Control Securities, 49 Ohio St. L.J. 501, 509 (1988); Carl W. Schneider, The Statutory Law of Private Placements, 14 Rev.Sec.Reg. 869, 874–75 (1981); ABA Committee on Federal Regulation of Securities, Section 4(2) and Statutory Law, 31 Bus.Law. 485, 491 (1975). A number of commentators have taken the opposite view. *See* footnote 35 *infra.*

34. SEC v. Ralston Purina Co., 346 U.S. 119, 73 S.Ct. 981, 97 L.Ed. 1494 (1953). *See* the discussion in the text accompanying footnotes 11–16 *supra.*

35. As one commentator has explained:

There is fairly compelling support for the view that there are no purchaser qualification requirements (apart from access to information) under the self-implementing § 4(2) exemption. Rather these requirements were introduced by the SEC in the safe harbors of Regulation D and its predecessor Rule 146, as part of a trade-off for relaxing other § 4(2) limitations. *See* Swenson v. Engelstad, 626 F.2d 421, 425–26 (5th Cir.1980); Doran v. Petroleum Management Corp., 545 F.2d 893, 904 (5th Cir.1977); Woolf v. S.D. Cohn & Co., 515 F.2d 591 (5th Cir.1975), *vacated and remanded on other grounds* 426 U.S. 944, 96 S.Ct. 3161, 49 L.Ed.2d 1181 (1976). These precedents are analyzed in Schneider, The Statutory Law of Private Placements, 14 Rev.Sec.Reg. 869, 874–75 (1981). After all, the basic protection of the Security [sic] Act's registration provisions lies in disclosure, and not in protecting inappropriate purchasers from their own analytic or economic incapacity.

Carl W. Schneider Section 4(1½)—Private Resales of Restricted or Control Securities, 49 Ohio St. L.J. 501, 509, n. 41 (1988). *See also, e.g.,* Patrick Daugherty, Rethinking the Ban on General Solicitation, 38 Emory L.J. 67 (1989).

36. To take an extreme example, consider an offering of securities to 10 individuals with red hair, when all offerees were given information comparable to that which would appear in a registration statement. Even assuming that all purchasers would be purchasing for investment rather than for resale, the section 4(2) exemption should not be available. *Cf.* SEC v. Sunbeam Gold Mines Co., 95 F.2d 699, 701 (9th Cir.1938).

37. SEC v. Ralston Purina Co., 346 U.S. 119, 125, 73 S.Ct. 981, 984, 97 L.Ed. 1494, 1498–99 (1953). *Accord* Van Dyke v. Coburn Enterprises, 873 F.2d 1094 (8th Cir.1989) (upholding transaction as exempt under section 4(2); the inside offerees had full access while the outside offerees had the economic bargaining power to demand access).

court of appeals decisions, following the lead of the SEC, have identified offeree (or purchaser) sophistication as a relevant factor in determining whether the targets of the offering can in fact fend for themselves. It thus appears that some degree of sophistication is necessary to assure that the transaction is not a public offering.[38]

As noted above, it is clear that access to information is a precondition to any section 4(2) exemption. As the foregoing discussion points out, informational access alone may not be sufficient if the investors are not able to fend for themselves. As a safety precaution, each offeree should receive an offering circular containing full disclosure. Although the offering circular is not expressly required by the cases,[39] it is a device that is frequently used by planners in private placement transactions to assure that the initial access to information requirements are satisfied.

In addition to the data supplied pursuant to initial access to information requirements, each offeree must be provided with an opportunity to ask questions of the issuer and verify information through access to the issuer's books and face-to-face meetings. Beyond the foregoing limitations on the offerees and the prohibition against general solicitation of buying interest, there are added requirements that the cases and SEC releases have established with regard to restrictions on resales. As pointed out above, although it is not sufficient to assure the exemption, investment letters from all purchasers may well be a necessary precondition to the offering. The issuer should place appropriate legends of the restrictions on stock transfer on the stock certificates or other evidence of the security and similar instructions should be given to the stock transfer agent who should be told to issue a stop transfer order for any transfers in violation of the restrictions.[40] These general guidelines that have developed from the case law closely parallel Rule 506's safe harbor requirements.[41] However, since each case is highly factual, the prece-

---

38. *See* Rutherford B. Campbell, Jr., The Plight of Small Issuers Under the Securities Act of 1933: Practical Foreclosure from the Capital Market, 1977 Duke L.J. 1139, 1160 (1970); Robert H. Kinderman, Jr., The Private Offering Exemption: An Examination of its Availability Under and Outside Rule 146, 30 Bus.Law. 921, 941 (1975) (pointing to sophistication as the "most important factor" under *Ralston Purina*); Marvin Schwartz, Rule 146: The Private Offering Exemption—Historical Perspective and Analysis, 35 Ohio St. L.J. 738, 761 (1974).

39. Van Dyke v. Coburn Enterprises, Inc., 873 F.2d 1094, 1098 (8th Cir.1989) (the exemption was available even though "[w]hile reasonable minds may disagree as to whether the appellants had been furnished the necessary information to make an informed investment decision, it is without dispute that they had access to the necessary information").

40. Uniform Commercial Code § 8–204 provides that any such restrictions must appear in a prominent restrictive legend on the share certificates. *See* § 20.5 *infra* (Practitioner's Edition). Failure to comply with the UCC's provisions can result in liability to transferees who acquire the securities without knowledge of the restrictions. *See, e.g.,* Dean Witter Reynolds, Inc. v. Selectronics, Inc., 188 A.D.2d 117, 594 N.Y.S.2d 174 (1993) (company was liable to a transferee who acquired shares that had been issued in a private placement and thus were subject to resale restrictions which were not revealed in a restrictive legend as required by UCC § 8–204; the transferee who thus acquired the stock without notice or knowledge of the restrictions was entitled to recover damages associated with its attempts to sell the stock).

41. *See* 17 C.F.R. § 230.502(b) (1982); § 4.22 *infra*.

dents do not provide the type of certainty that corporate planners would like to have. By way of example, the Fourth Circuit has gone so far as to hold that where the offerees lack sufficient sophistication and access to information, an offering involving one unqualified purchaser may fail to meet the exemption and thus trigger the registration requirements of the Act.[42]

In addition to the above-mentioned limitations on the structure of the offering, the section 4(2) exemption must be read in light of the exemptions provided by section 4(1)[43] (exempting transactions not involving an issuer, underwriter, or dealer), section 4(4)[44] (exempting unsolicited brokers' transactions), section 4(6)[45] (exempting offerings up to five million dollars to accredited investors), and Rule 144[46] (dealing with downstream resales of securities issued under one of the aforementioned exemptions). Even if a qualified offeree purchases a security offered pursuant to a private placement, his or her subsequent downstream sale may well destroy the exemption. For example, someone reselling the security within a short period of time may be deemed an underwriter within the statutory definition provided by section 2(11)[47] and thus the downstream sale would be beyond the scope of the section 4(1) exemption.[48] Further, through the doctrine of integration, downstream sales may relate back and destroy the original section 4(2) exemption.[49] The reasoning would be that since the securities originally offered pursuant to the private placement exemption within an unreasonably short time reached purchasers who would not qualify as private placement purchasers, the original exemption should not be granted.[50]

---

42. Lawler v. Gilliam, 569 F.2d 1283 (4th Cir.1978). *Accord* G. Eugene England Foundation v. First Federal Corp., 663 F.2d 988 (10th Cir.1973). *See also* Leiter v. Kuntz, 655 F.Supp. 725 (D.Utah 1987) (discovery allowed to proceed when defendant claimed that plaintiff was the only offeree). *Cf.* People v. Landes, 84 N.Y.2d 655, 621 N.Y.S.2d 283, 645 N.E.2d 716 (1994) (offering to twelve investors although relatively small was a public offering under state law).

As the Supreme Court observed in the *Ralston Purina* decision, "the statute would seem to apply to a 'public offering' whether to few or many." 346 U.S. at 125, 73 S.Ct. at 984, 97 L.Ed. at 1499. *Compare id.* n. 11:

"The 'public' * * * is of course a general word. No particular numbers are prescribed. Anything from two to infinity may serve: perhaps even one, if he is intended to be the first of a series of subscribers, but makes further proceedings needless by himself subscribing to the whole."

(quoting Nash v. Lynde, [1929] A.C. 158, 169).

43. 15 U.S.C.A. § 77d(1). *See* § 4.23 *infra.*

44. 15 U.S.C.A. § 77d(4). *See* § 4.23 *infra.*

45. 15 U.S.C.A. § 77d(6). *See* § 4.20 *supra.*

46. 17 C.F.R. § 230.144. *See* § 4.26 *infra.*

47. 15 U.S.C.A. § 77b(11). *See* § 4.24 *infra.*

48. *See, e.g.,* Gilligan, Will & Co. v. SEC, 267 F.2d 461 (2d Cir.1959), *cert. denied* 361 U.S. 896, 80 S.Ct. 200, 4 L.Ed.2d 152 (1959); United States v. Sherwood, 175 F.Supp. 480 (S.D.N.Y.1959). *See* § 4.23 *infra.*

49. *See, e.g.,* 17 C.F.R. § 230.502(a).

50. *See* Hill York Corp. v. American International Franchises, Inc., 448 F.2d 680, 688–89 (5th Cir.1971).

In summary, recent cases reveal that an issuer relying on the statutory section 4(2) exemption, rather than upon Rule 506's safe-harbor provisions, may be subjecting itself to a great deal of uncertainty. In addition to the guidelines that appear from the recent judicial decisions, the planner must not lose sight of the original factors established by the *Ralston Purina* decision.[51] In evaluating the availability of the exemption, the courts and the SEC will look not only to the number and nature of the offerees and their access to the types of information that would be contained in the registration statement but also to the relationship of the offerees to the issuer, the relationship of the offerees to each other, the manner of the offering, and the number of shares to be offered.

Integration with Other Offerings

When the integration doctrine is invoked, transactions that are not in form part of a single offering will be treated as one.[52] Difficult integration problems can arise in connection with successive private offerings involving the same or related sponsors.[53] There has been an increasing movement to get the SEC to adopt guidelines relating to the integration of separate investment partnership offerings with common sponsors.[54] Integration problems also arise in connection with non public offerings and related public offerings.[55] A private offering that precedes a public offering may avoid integration by virtue of the narrow safe harbor provided by Rule 152.[56]

Offshore Offerings

The registration requirements of the 1933 Act are applicable only to the extent that there are offers or sales taking place within the United States.[57] Thus, a public offering taking place outside the United States will not implicate the registration requirements. In 1990, the SEC

---

51. *See* text accompanying footnotes 11–16 *supra.*

52. *See* § 4.29 *infra* for discussion of the integration doctrine.

53. *E.g.* In re LaserFax, Inc., [1985–86 Transfer Binder] Fed.Sec.L.Rep. (CCH) ¶ 78,136 (SEC No Action Letter Aug. 15, 1985) (Regulation D offering of convertible debentures would be integrated with prior Regulation D offering of the underlying common stock; the Regulation D offering was to raise seed money for an upcoming public offering). *See* Russell B. Stevenson, Jr., Integration and Private Placements, 19 Rev.Sec. & Commodities Reg. 49 (March 5, 1986). Integration is discussed in § 4.29 *infra.*

54. *See* ABA Bus.L.Memo 7 (Jan.–Feb.1985); Integration of Securities Offerings: Report on Task Force on Integration, 41 Bus.Law. 595 (1986). This proposal has been followed by the state administrators in Oregon and Louisiana.

55. *See* § 4.29 *infra.*

56. 17 C.F.R. § 230.152 which is discussed in § 4.29 *infra. See also, e.g.* Verticom, Inc., 1986 WL 65214 (SEC No Action Letter Feb. 12, 1986) (subsequent public offering, although planned at the time of a section 4(2) nonpublic offering would not be integrated in light of Rule 152). The safe harbor will not apply, however, when the public offering comes first. *See, e.g.,* Circle Creek Aquaculture V, L.P., 1993 WL 93583 (SEC No Action Letter March 26, 1993) (Regulation D offering following an abandoned public offering would be subject to integration).

57. *See* § 14.2 *infra.*

adopted Regulation S which provides a safe harbor exemption for off-shore offerings.[58]

§ 4.22 Safe Harbor for Private Placements Under Section 4(2)—SEC Rule 506

SEC Rule 506[1] provides an exemption for the offer and sale of securities to no more than thirty-five purchasers; as is the case under the Rule 505[2] exemption, "accredited investors"[3] are not counted towards that limit.[4] The rule further places qualifications on permissible purchasers. Each purchaser who is not an accredited investor himself, herself, or through a purchaser representative, must have such knowledge and experience in financial and business matters so that the purchaser or qualifying representative is capable of evaluating the merits and risks of the prospective investment.[5] As was the case with its predecessor Rule 146, Rule 506 is a "safe harbor" rule.[6] If an offering of securities fails to meet the requirements of Rule 506, the issuer may still qualify for a 4(2) exemption if it conforms to requirements developed through cases and SEC releases.[7]

Rule 506 is available to any issuer, whether or not it is an investment company, a non-reporting company, or subject to any of the disqualification provisions contained in Rule 252(c), (d), (e), or (f) of Regulation A.[8] However, all offers and sales made under Rule 506 must

---

58. 17 C.F.R. § 230.901 *et seq.* Regulation S is discussed in § 14.2 *infra.*

§ 4.22

1. 17 C.F.R. § 230.506(b)(2)(i); 17 C.F.R. § 230.501(a), (e).

2. 17 C.F.R. § 230.505. *See* § 4.18 *supra.*

3. Accredited investor is defined in 17 C.F.R. § 230.501(a). *See* § 4.17 *supra. See also* 15 U.S.C.A. § 77b(15).

4. 17 C.F.R. § 230.501(e)(1)(iv).

5. 17 C.F.R. § 230.506(b)(2)(ii). *Cf.* Anastasi v. American Petroleum, Inc., 579 F.Supp. 273 (D.Colo.1984) (under former Rule 146, the exemption depended upon the issuer's reasonable belief not the purchaser's actual condition; thus misrepresentations by the purchaser did not void the exemption). Rule 506(b)(2)(ii) requires that the issuer "reasonably believe" that the purchaser limitations and qualifications have been satisfied. 17 C.F.R. § 230.506(b)(2)(ii).

6. For discussion of former Rule 146, much of which is still applicable under current Rule 506, *see e.g.,* Tom A. Alberg & Martin E. Lybecker, New SEC Rules 146 and 147: The Nonpublic and Intrastate Offering Exemptions From Registration for the Sale of Securities, 74 Colum.L.Rev. 622 (1974); Robert A. Kessler, Private Placement Rules 146 and 240–Safe Harbor?, 44 Fordham L.Rev. 37 (1975); Marvin Schwartz, Rule 146: The Private Offering Exemption—Historical Perspective and Analysis, 35 Ohio St.L.J. 738 (1974).

7. *E.g.,* Weprin v. Peterson, 736 F.Supp. 1124 (N.D.Ga.1988). *Cf.* SEC v. Interlink Data Network of Los Angeles, Inc., 1993 WL 603274, [1993–1994 Transfer Binder] Fed. Sec. L. Rep. (CCH) ¶ 98,049 (C.D.Cal.1993) (exemption was not available where issuer failed to screen for accredited investors, engaged in a general solicitation, and failed to comply with the informational requirements).

8. 17 C.F.R. § 230.506(a). *See* 17 C.F.R. §§ 230.251–62, 230.504(a), 230.505(a); § 4.15 *supra.* In 1987, the Commission considered but then, in 1988, rejected extending the "bad boy" disqualifications to Rule 506's safe harbor. Sec.Act Rel. No. 33–6758, [1987–88 Transfer Binder] Fed.Sec.L.Rep. (CCH) ¶ 84,221 (March 3, 1988); Sec.Act Rel. No. 33–6683, [1986–87 Transfer Binder] Fed.Sec.L.Rep. (CCH) ¶ 84,054 (Jan. 16, 1987).

satisfy the terms and conditions of Rules 501, 502, and 503 of Regulation D.[9]

An unsophisticated purchaser may still qualify as a Rule 506 investor through the use of an appropriate purchaser representative. "Purchaser representative" is defined by Rule 501 to be any person who satisfies or whom the issuer reasonably believes satisfies the following four conditions: (1) is not an insider of the issuer (*i.e.*, affiliate, director, officer or beneficial owner of ten percent of a class of the issuer's equity securities), (2) has such knowledge and experience in financial and business matters that he is capable of evaluating, alone, or together with other purchaser representatives or with the purchaser, the merits and risks of the prospective investment, (3) is acknowledged by the purchaser in writing to be his purchaser representative with reference to each prospective investment considered, and (4) discloses to the purchaser before the purchaser's acknowledgment just mentioned any material relationship between the purchaser representative or his affiliates and the issuer or its affiliates that exists, is contemplated, or has existed within the previous two years, including any compensation received or to be received as a result.[10] Insiders of the issuer, however, are allowed to serve as purchaser representatives for certain relatives, trusts, and estates, as well as for corporations in which they have fifty percent beneficial interest.[11] The concept of purchaser representative allows the issuer to reach unsophisticated wealthy investors who do not satisfy the "nature of purchaser requirements" of Rule 506.[12]

Rule 501[13] also provides the method for calculating the number of purchasers under Rule 506. The following individuals and entities are not to be counted in the thirty-five purchaser ceiling: (1) any relative, spouse, or relative of the spouse of a purchaser who has the same principal residence as the purchaser, (2) any trust or estate in which a purchaser and any of the relatives just mentioned collectively have more than fifty percent of the beneficial interest, (3) any corporation or other organization which a purchaser together with his relatives and trusts and estates owns more than fifty percent of the equity securities or equity interests and (4) any accredited investor.[14]

---

9.   17 C.F.R. § 230.506(b)(1). *See* 17 C.F.R. §§ 230.501–.503; § 4.17 *supra*.

10.   17 C.F.R. § 230.501(h).

11.   17 C.F.R. § 230.501(h)(1)(i), (ii), (iii).

12.   Rule 506(b)(2)(ii) provides:

(ii) *Nature of purchasers.* Each purchaser who is not an accredited investor either alone or with his purchaser representative(s) has such knowledge and experience in financial and business matters that he is capable of evaluating the merits and risks of the prospective investment, or the issuer reasonably believes immediately prior to making such sale that such purchaser comes within this description.

17 C.F.R. § 230.506(b)(2)(ii).

13.   Rule 501 is the general definitional provision for Regulation D. 17 C.F.R. § 230.501. *See* § 4.17 *supra*.

14.   17 C.F.R. § 230.501(e).

Regulation D places limits on the manner of the offering and solicitation methods. Rule 502 prohibits the use of general advertising or soliciting during an offering exempt under Rule 506.[15] Rule 502 also recommends the disclosure of certain information to all purchasers if any one purchaser is not an "accredited investor" as defined in Rule 501.[16] If all purchasers are accredited investors, then neither Rule 502 nor Rule 506 requires specific information to be disclosed to any purchaser.[17]

Rule 502 sets forth a six-month safe harbor for the integration of Regulation D offerings and a five-factor test for determining whether offerings that fall outside the safe harbor will be integrated.[18] Rule 502

---

15. 17 C.F.R. § 230.502(c). A suitability questionnaire sent to customers along with customer account applications, which if sufficiently detailed may create a "substantive relationship" between the customer and the broker so that if sufficient sophistication is established, there will not be a general solicitation in violation of Rule 502. In re E.F. Hutton & Co., 18 Sec.Reg. & L.Rep. (BNA) 171 (SEC No Action Letter Dec. 3, 1985). *Cf.* Platsis v. E.F. Hutton & Co., Inc., 642 F.Supp. 1277, 1303–04 (W.D.Mich.1986) (the issue is the reasonable belief in the purchaser's suitability, not his or her actual suitability).

16. 17 C.F.R. § 230.502(b)(1). The information requirements are set forth in § 4.17 *supra.*

Rule 506 offerings requiring the use of an offering circular or private placement memorandum specified in Rule 502(b) may have implications with regard to possible antifraud liability. In addition to potential liability under SEC Rule 10b–5 (17 C.F.R. § 240.10b–5; *see* §§ 13.2–13.12 *infra*) for material misstatements and omissions, there is the potential for liability of sellers of such securities under section 12(2) of the 1933 Act. 15 U.S.C.A. § 77*l*(2); *see* § 7.5 *infra.* Section 12(2) action can only be used only against sellers of securities. Pinter v. Dahl, 486 U.S. 622, 108 S.Ct. 2063, 100 L.Ed.2d 658 (1988); *see* §§ 7.5, 7.5.1 *infra.* It is not necessary to establish that the defendant acted with scienter in order to make a claim under section 12(2). *See* § 7.5 *infra.*

The section 12(2) remedy is not available for all sales of securities. In Gustafson v. Alloyd Co., ___ U.S. ___, 115 S.Ct. 1061, 131 L.Ed.2d 1 (1995), the Supreme Court held that the section 12(2) remedy is available only to offerings made via the use of a prospectus as that term is used in the 1933 Act. However, it is likely that section 12(2) might still apply at least to those exempt transactions in which there nevertheless is a public offering. *See* the discussion in § 7.5 *infra.* The Court in *Gustafson* focused on the meaning of prospectus as that term is used in section 10 which sets forth the requirements for prospectuses in connection with a public offering. 15 U.S.C.A. § 77j. As the Court explained: "the word 'prospectus' is a term of art referring to a document that describes a public offering of securities by an issuer or controlling shareholder." (___ U.S. at ___, 115 S.Ct. at 1073–74, 131 L.Ed.2d at 21). The offering circular or private placement memorandum required by Rule 502(b) contains the same types of information required in the section 10 statutory prospectus. However, Rule 506 offerings may not be based on a general solicitation of purchasers and thus arguably would not seem to qualify as a public offering. On the other hand, the presence of unsophisticated purchasers may mean that there is a public offering as the Supreme Court defined that concept in SEC v. Ralston Purina Co., 346 U.S. 119, 73 S.Ct. 981, 97 L.Ed. 1494 (1953); *see* § 4.21 *supra.*

The express language of section 12(2) would seem to support the remedy even in those instances in which there is use of a prospectus although a public offering is not involved. Section 12(2) on its face provides that it applies to sales of exempt securities, other than those securities which are exempt under section 3(a)(2). 15 U.S.C.A. § 77*l*(2).

17. 17 C.F.R. §§ 230.502(b)(1)(i), 230.506(b)(1).

18. 17 C.F.R. § 230.502(a). *See* § 4.21 *supra. See* SEC v. Melchior, 1993 WL 89141, [1992–1993 Transfer Binder] Fed.Sec.L.Rep. (CCH) ¶ 97,356 (D.Utah 1993) (finding that multiple limited partnership offerings were subject to Rule 502's integration requirement and thus required registration under the 1933 Act); Circle Creek Aquaculture V, L.P., 1993 WL 93583 (SEC No Action Letter March 26, 1993) (Regulation D offering following an abandoned public offering would be subject to integration). *Compare, e.g.,* Donohoe v. Consolidated Operating & Production Corp., 982 F.2d 1130 (7th Cir.1992), *on remand* 833

also places limits on resales of securities acquired in a transaction under Regulation D and, as a preventive measure, requires that issuers exercise reasonable care to determine that they are not selling exempt securities to section 2(11) underwriters.[19] Finally, Rule 503 requires the issuer to file periodically with the Securities and Exchange Commission certain notices of sales made in reliance upon Regulation D.[20]

As is the case with the section 4(2) exemption,[21] Rule 506 is limited to transactions by an issuer. Therefore, persons other than the issuer who seek an exemption from registration for their sales must look elsewhere.[22] The Commission has tried to present the issuer seeking a private placement exemption with a reasonable safe harbor rule. However, the Commission's efforts under Rule 506's predecessor have not gone without strong criticism on the grounds that the requirements are very difficult to comply with and hence the rule does not provide a sufficiently safe predictor for planners of securities transactions.[23] Also, as was seen in the preceding section,[24] a number of courts have borrowed heavily from Rule 506's predecessor in formulating the scope of the statutory section 4(2) exemption, thus adding a qualification to the Commission's statement that the rule is not exclusive.[25]

Rule 506 does not include any offeree qualification requirements such as those found in its predecessor or the cases interpreting the section 4(2) nonpublic offering exemption.[26] To the extent that Rule 506 is based on section 4(2), rather than section 3(b) or 4(6)—both of which have a five million dollar ceiling—,[27] it is arguable that the statute requires the offeree qualifications to be read into the rule. The SEC in

F.Supp. 719 (N.D.Ill.1993) (applying the SEC's five-factor test and refusing to integrate partnership offerings).

A Regulation D offering of convertible debentures, prior to a planned public offering and following a Regulation D offering for the underlying common stock, presented a good case for integration where the Regulation D offering was to be used as seed money for the upcoming public offering. In re LaserFax, Inc., [1985–86 Transfer Binder] Fed.Sec.L.Rep. (CCH) ¶ 78,136 (SEC No Action Letter Aug. 15, 1985). *Compare* BBI Associates, 19 Sec.Reg. & L.Rep. (BNA) 76 (SEC No Action Letter Dec. 19, 1986) (sale of securities in connection with liquidation not integrated with subsequent initial public offering).

Integration is discussed in § 4.29 *infra*.

19. 17 C.F.R. § 230.502(d). *See* 15 U.S.C.A. § 776(11); § 4.24 *infra*.

20. 17 C.F.R. § 230.503. The SEC has proposed amendments to the notification requirements. *See* Sec. Act Rel. No. 33–6812, [1988–89 Transfer Binder] Fed.Sec.L.Rep. (CCH) ¶ 84,346 (Dec. 20, 1988).

21. *See* § 4.21 *supra*.

22. *See* § 4.26.1 *infra* for discussion of the so-called "4(1½)" exemption.

23. *See, e.g.*, Robert A. Kessler, Private Placement Rules 146 and 240–Safe Harbor?, 44 Fordham L.Rev. 37 (1975).

24. *See* § 4.21 *supra*.

25. *See e.g.*, Doran v. Petroleum Management Corp., 545 F.2d 893 (5th Cir.1977), *appeal after remand* 576 F.2d 91 (5th Cir.1978); SEC v. Continental Tobacco Co., 463 F.2d 137 (5th Cir.1972); Hill York Corp. v. American International Franchises, Inc., 448 F.2d 680 (5th Cir.1971).

26. *E.g.* SEC v. Ralston Purina Co., 346 U.S. 119, 73 S.Ct. 981, 97 L.Ed. 1494 (1953). *See* § 4.21 *supra* and cases cited in footnote 25 *supra*.

27. 15 U.S.C.A. §§ 77c(b), 77(d)(6). *See* § 4.14 *supra*.

adopting Rule 506 wanted to ease the problems associated with offeree qualification under its predecessor—former Rule 146–but there is no indication of the SEC's statutory basis for ignoring the judicially imposed offeree requirements. In fact, the SEC has indicated that the nature and number of offerees remain relevant in determining whether there has been a general solicitation so as to render Rule 506 and section 4(2) unavailable.[28] The safe harbor protection, thus, is no longer dependent upon the issuer being able to prove that *each* offeree was qualified.[29] On the other hand, if the issuer cannot show that it took adequate precautions against the solicitation of nonqualified offerees, it may lose the section 4(2) exemption because of the inability to show that a general solicitation did not take place.[30] Accordingly, the effect of the deletion of the offeree qualification requirement in Rule 506 is that when an issuer takes reasonable precautions but somehow an unqualified offeree is given an offer the safe harbor may still be available. It is important to recall that not all preliminary contacts with prospective offerees will constitute an offer. Thus, it is permissible to make preliminary inquiries to determine if prospective offerees are in fact qualified so long as these preliminary contacts do not give detail as to the nature and terms of the planned offering.[31]

As pointed out above, Rule 506(b)(2)(ii) provides that a purchaser must either be knowledgeable, act through a purchaser representative, or be qualified as an accredited investor.[32] In addition to institutional investors, the definition of accredited investor includes individuals with a net worth of more than one million dollars or an annual income in excess of two hundred thousand dollars as well as married couples with a combined net worth of one million dollars or a combined annual income of more than three hundred thousand dollars.[33] In so defining qualified purchasers, Rule 506 substitutes wealth as a criterion in lieu of investor knowledge and sophistication. Rule 502(b)(1)[34] provides that where all Rule 506 purchasers are accredited, the issuer is not under the affirmative disclosure obligations set forth in Rule 502(b)(2).[35] Formerly the rule required that if there was one unaccredited purchaser, *all* purchasers had to receive a private placement memorandum containing the

28. Sec. Act Rel. No. 33–6455, 1 Fed.Sec.L.Rep. (CCH) ¶ 2380 (March 3, 1983) (answer to question 73).

29. Compare former Rule 146.

30. Since the person claiming the exemption carries the burden of proof, the issuer must show the absence of a general solicitation.

31. The prohibition against a general solicitation does not preclude contacting prospective offerees to determine if they are in fact qualified, so long as the preliminary contacts do not generate a specific buying interest so as to classify the contact as an offer to sell. Offer to sell is defined in section 2(3) of the Act. 15 U.S.C.A. § 77b(3). *See* the discussion of prefiling gun jumping in § 2.3 *supra*.

32. 17 C.F.R. § 230.506(b)(2)(ii). The definition of accredited investor is found in Rule 501(a) (17 C.F.R. § 230.501(a)) and is discussed in § 4.20 and § 4.17 *supra*.

33. 17 C.F.R. § 230.501(a).

34. 17 C.F.R. § 230.502(b)(1).

35. 17 C.F.R. § 230.502(b)(2). *See* the discussion in § 4.17 *supra*. The same affirmative disclosure obligations apply to Rule 505 offerings. *See* § 4.18 *supra*.

specified. Under the current version of the rule there is no such mandate as the informational requirement applies only to unaccredited investors. However, the SEC recommends that in light of antifraud considerations *all purchasers* receive this information.[36] Accordingly, the failure to deliver an offering memorandum to accredited investors will not destroy the safe harbor exemption. Nevertheless, there seems little reason not to follow the Commission's advice and supply the offering circular to accredited investors if one has been prepared for unaccredited investors.

Rules 502 and 506 on their face give the reader the impression that for a private placement made solely to accredited investors there are no informational requirements. Rule 502 only addresses the issuer's need to provide a disclosure statement and does not address the additional requirement (derived from the courts' interpretation of the statute) that all purchasers in a non-public offering have access to current information about the issuer. In the *Ralston Purina* decision[37] the Supreme Court announced *two* prerequisites for the section 4(2) non public offering exemption. First, the offerees must have access to the same type of current information about the issuer that would be required in a registered offering. Second, the purchasers must be sufficiently sophisticated and knowledgeable to evaluate the information. Rule 506(b) permits the offeree qualification to be established if the purchaser is an accredited investor.[38] This goes to only the first part of the *Ralston Purina* test. As a section 4(2) exemption, Rule 506 cannot go beyond the parameters of the statute. Since the statute, as interpreted by the Supreme Court, requires access to current issuer information, such a requirement should be read into Rule 506.[39] Accordingly, Rule 502 should not be read as dispensing with the access to information requirement; its sole purpose is to relieve the issuer of the burden of preparing a disclosure memorandum in offerings where all purchasers are accredited.

In 1989, the Commission amended Regulation D to provide that minor variations from an exemption's requirements will not destroy the availability of the exemption. Specifically, Rule 508 provides that an insignificant failure to comply with a condition that is not "directly intended to protect" the investor will not destroy the exemption, provided that the issuer made a good faith and reasonable attempt to comply.[40]

---

36. *Ibid.*

37. 346 U.S. 119, 73 S.Ct. 981, 97 L.Ed. 1494 (1953). *See* § 4.21 *supra.*

38. 17 C.F.R. § 230.506(b)(2)(ii). Alternatively, an unsophisticated unaccredited investor may qualify through the use of a purchaser representative. *Id.*

39. In contrast, since Rule 505 is a section 3(b) exemption, a Rule 505 offering which is sold only to accredited investors does not have the same access to information requirement. The trade-off is that, unlike Rule 506, Rule 505 is limited to offerings of no more than $5,000,000.

40. 17 C.F.R. § 230.508. The adopting release points out that a failure to comply with the prohibition against a general solicitation does not fall within Rule 508's exemptive reach. Sec. Act Rel. No. 33–6825, [1989 Transfer Binder] Fed.Sec.L.Rep. (CCH) ¶ 84,404 (March 14, 1989).

§ 4.23 An Overview of Transactions by Persons Other Than Issuers, Underwriters and Dealers: Section 4(1); Unsolicited Brokers' Transactions— Section 4(4)

Section 4(1) of the 1933 Act[1] provides a registration exemption for "transactions by any person other than an issuer, underwriter or dealer." Section 4(1), especially when read in connection with the dealers' and unsolicited brokers' transaction exemptions in sections 4(3) and 4(4),[2] exempts most day-to-day transactions that are effected on an exchange or in the over-the-counter markets.[3] Since section 4(2)'s private placement exemption[4] is limited to issuer transactions, it has no application to the millions of shares that are traded daily on the national exchanges and NASDAQ where, although not involving a public offering, the transactions are not effected by issuers. The section 4(1) exemption helps fill this void. Section 4(1), which is also known as the exemption for nonprofessionals, exempts transactions rather than people and thus may not be available to someone who is not an issuer, underwriter or dealer but is involved in a transaction with one.[5] However, the mere involvement by a broker in a secondary transaction will not render the exemption unavailable.[6] Furthermore, unsolicited brokers' transactions are exempt under section 4(4).

Section 4(1)—The Exemption for Nonprofessionals

Issuers. By its terms, section 4(1) exempts all transactions by persons who are not issuers, underwriters or dealers. Section 2(4) of the Act[7] defines "issuer" to include every person who issues or proposes to issue a security. In addition, in the case of a voting trust or other trust certificates, "issuer" refers to the person or persons performing the acts and assuming the duties of depositor or manager under the provisions of the trust or other agreement.[8] The definition of issuer is not limited to

---

§ 4.23

1. 15 U.S.C.A. § 77d(1). *See* Report, The Section "4(1½)" Phenomenon: Private Resales of "Restricted" Securities, 34 Bus.Law. 1961 (1979).

2. 15 U.S.C.A. §§ 77d(3), 77d(4).

3. Section 4(3) exempts transactions by nonparticipating dealers and underwriters no longer acting as underwriters after more than forty or ninety days after the registration statement's effective date. 15 U.S.C.A. § 77d(3).

4. 15 U.S.C.A. § 77d(2). *See* § 4.21 *supra.*

5. SEC v. Holschuh, 694 F.2d 130, 137–38 (7th Cir.1982); United States v. Wolfson, 405 F.2d 779 (2d Cir.1968), *cert. denied* 394 U.S. 946, 89 S.Ct. 1275, 22 L.Ed.2d 479 (1969); SEC v. Culpepper, 270 F.2d 241, 247 (2d Cir.1959); SEC v. Netelkos, 592 F.Supp. 906, 915 (S.D.N.Y.1984). *See also, e.g.* SEC v. Murphy, 626 F.2d 633 (9th Cir.1980).

As explained by the SEC, section 4(1) "was intended to exempt only trading transactions between individual investors with respect to securities already issued and not to exempt distributions by issuers or acts of other individuals who engage in steps necessary to such distributions." Sec. Act Rel. No. 33–5223 (SEC, Jan. 11, 1972).

6. Ackerberg v. Johnson, 892 F.2d 1328, 1334 n. 4 (8th Cir.1989).

7. 15 U.S.C.A. § 77b(4).

8. *Id.*

initial distributions. For example, it has been held that a transaction is not exempt and the issuer concept applies to reissue of stock that had previously been reacquired by the issuing corporation.[9] It has also been held that the concept of issuer applies to a corporation acting as a promoter by setting up a number of limited partnerships for syndication.[10] The statutory definition of issuer does not generally raise any significant problem of judicial interpretation since it is usually easy to identify the issuer for a particular security.

Underwriters. The question of who is an underwriter, which is taken up in more detail in the succeeding section,[11] is not nearly as simple as defining "issuer." Section 2(11)[12] provides that an "underwriter" is anyone who purchases a security from the issuer with a view toward distribution of the security, as well as anyone who offers to sell or offers for sale for an issuer in connection with a distribution, including anyone involved in any indirect participation in such undertaking or the underwriting of the distribution. The most troubling problems of the definition in operation arise in the context of persons who, although not denominated as underwriters in the generic sense of the term, act as conduits for placing the securities in the hands of members of the investing public. In addition to the general definition of underwriter, section 2(11) further provides that anyone who sells securities on behalf of a controlling person of the issuer is deemed an underwriter.[13] There are thus three ways to qualify for underwriter status: (1) purchasing from the issuer with a view towards distribution, (2) direct or indirect participation in an underwriting effort, and (3) selling securities on behalf of a control person. Underwriter status not only renders the section 4(1) exemption unavailable, but it also provides the basis for liability for misstatements in connection with a registered offering.[14]

Dealers. Section 2(12) of the Act[15] defines "dealer" to include any person who for all or part of his or her time is in the business of offering, buying, selling, or otherwise dealing or trading in securities issued by others. It does not matter whether such sales activity is direct or indirect and the statutory definition of dealer further applies whether one is acting as agent, broker, or principal with regard to the securities transactions in question.[16] Since virtually all day-to-day transactions are

9. SEC v. Stanwood Oil Corp., 516 F.Supp. 1181, 1184 (W.D.Pa.1981).

10. SEC v. Holschuh, 694 F.2d 130, 138–39 (7th Cir.1982); SEC v. Murphy, 626 F.2d 633, 644 (9th Cir.1980).

11. *See* § 4.24 *infra.*

12. 15 U.S.C.A. § 77b(11).

13. *See, e.g.,* United States v. Wolfson, 405 F.2d 779 (2d Cir.1968), *cert. denied* 394 U.S. 946, 89 S.Ct. 1275, 22 L.Ed.2d 479 (1969); SEC v. Netelkos, 592 F.Supp. 906 (S.D.N.Y. 1984); § 4.24 *infra.*

14. Section 11(a) imposes civil liability upon underwriters for damages resulting from reliance on material misstatements or omissions in the registration statement. 15 U.S.C.A. § 77k(a). *See* § 7.4 *infra.*

15. 15 U.S.C.A. § 77b(12).

16. In contrast to the 1933 Act's broad definition of dealer, the Securities Exchange Act of 1934 defines dealer in section 3(a)(5) in such a way as to exclude brokers: "The term

effected through the means of a registered broker-dealer, the section 4(1) exemption standing alone would not exclude the transactions from coverage of the Act's registration provisions. However, as noted above, section 4(1) must be read in tandem with section 4(3)'s exemption for most dealers' transactions and section 4(4)'s exemption for unsolicited brokers' transactions.

Section 4(4)—Unsolicited Brokers' Transactions

One of the key provisions for dealing with many day-to-day securities transactions is found in section 4(4)'s exemption for unsolicited brokers' transactions.[17] Section 4(4) exempts "brokers' transactions executed upon customers' orders on any exchange or in the over-the-counter market but not the solicitation of such orders." Neither the 1933 Act nor the SEC rules promulgated thereunder contain a definition of "broker" but it is clear that the concept cannot be coextensive with that of a "dealer" under section 2(12). Additional learning can be gathered by reference to the Securities Exchange Act of 1934. Section 3(a)(4) of the 1934 Act[18] defines "broker" as anyone, other than a bank, engaged in the business of effecting securities transactions for the account of others. The 1934 Act definition of broker comports with the generic meaning of the term and thus would seem to be equally applicable to the 1933 Act. As such, brokers form a subclass of dealers and include anyone who is in the business of effecting securities transactions as agent for others. Accordingly, persons who only execute transactions on their own behalf or as principals may still be categorized as "dealers" but do not fall within the concept of "broker" within the statutory exemption from registration provided in section 4(4). The section 4(4) exemption only applies to transactions in which the broker acts as the purchaser's agent, rather than as an agent for someone else such as the issuer or underwriter.

Another significant aspect of the section 4(4) exemption is that it extends to "brokers' *transactions*." Both the courts and SEC have pointed out the distinction in terminology between "transactions" and the concept of a "distribution."[19] It has accordingly been held that

'dealer' means any person engaged in the business of buying and selling securities *for his own account,* through a broker or otherwise, but does not include a bank, or any person insofar as he sells securities for his own account, either individually or in some fiduciary capacity but not as part of his regular business." 15 U.S.C.A. § 78c(a)(5); *see* § 10.2.1 *infra.* The Exchange Act in turn, in section 3(a)(4), defines broker as someone in the business of trading securities for the accounts of others.

It is clear that the 1933 Act's broader definition of dealer is relevant in deciding the availability of the section 4(1) exemption. Thus, for example, it would appear that a bank can be a dealer under the 1933 Act definition. The intertwining of commercial and investment banking is discussed in § 19.5 *infra* (Practitioner's Edition only).

17. 15 U.S.C.A. § 77d(4). *See also* section 4(3) of the Act, 15 U.S.C.A. § 77d(3) which is discussed in § 4.27 *infra.*

18. 15 U.S.C.A. § 77c(a)(4).

19. *E.g.,* Gilligan & Will Co. v. SEC, 267 F.2d 461, 466 (2d Cir.1959), *cert. denied* 361 U.S. 896, 80 S.Ct. 200, 4 L.Ed.2d 152 (1959), citing H.R.Rep. No. 1838, 73d Cong.2d Sess.

writing of any such undertaking; but such term shall not include a person whose interest is limited to a commission from an underwriter or dealer not in excess of the usual and customary distributors' or sellers' commission. As used in this paragraph the term "issuer" shall include, in addition to an issuer, any person directly or indirectly controlling or controlled by the issuer, or any person under direct or indirect common control with the issuer.[4]

As is discussed more fully below, underwriter status requires the existence of a "distribution," which is generally interpreted to involve a large amount of securities.[5]

A key aspect of the statutory definition is that in order to be classified as a statutory underwriter, the participant must have been acting on behalf of or purchasing from an issuer. In this context, however, the statute provides that a control person is considered to be an issuer. Accordingly, when a substantial amount of securities are sold on behalf of an issuer (or control person) or are purchased from an issuer (or control person) and subsequently resold within a short period of time, underwriter status may attach. On the other hand, the mere fact that a dealer sells a large amount of securities will not necessarily create underwriter status.[6]

The legislative history of section 2(11) reveals that the congressional intent was to include as underwriters all persons who might operate as conduits for securities being placed into the hands of the investing public. So long as the ultimate purchasers are members of the general public, as opposed to qualified private placement purchasers,[7] the transaction calls for the protection of the Securities Act's registration provisions.[8]

The statute excludes members of the selling group from the definition of underwriter. Although certainly involved in the distribution process, those dealers who receive nothing more than their ordinary sales commissions are not classified as section 2(11) underwriters. The exclusion of transactions in which the only remuneration is "the usual and customary distributors' or sellers' commission"[9] is designed to protect members of the selling group and nonparticipating brokers from being included in the concept of underwriter. SEC Rule 141[10] provides that a dealer's commission includes the normal spread between the

---

4. 15 U.S.C.A. § 77b(11).

5. *See* text accompanying footnotes 60–75 *infra*.

6. *Cf.* In re Scattered Corp. Securities Litigation, 844 F.Supp. 416 (N.D.Ill.1994) (brokerage firm involved in short selling of approximately 170 million shares of securities of a single issuer was not an underwriter).

7. *See* 15 U.S.C.A. § 77d(2); 17 C.F.R. § 230.506; §§ 4.21, 4.22 *supra*.

8. H.R.Rep. No. 85, 73d Cong., 1st Sess. 13–14 (1933). The Commission in looking at downstream sales has borrowed heavily from the doctrinal underpinnings of section 4(2)'s non-public offering exemption. Report, The Section "4(1½)" Phenomenon: Private Resales of Restricted Securities, 34 Bus.Law. 1961 (1979).

9. 15 U.S.C.A. § 77b(11).

10. 17 C.F.R. § 230.141.

offering price and the dealer's cost, whether the dealer was purchasing the security prior to reselling it or acting merely as a broker executing a customer's order.[11]

Rule 142[12] excludes from the definition of underwriter persons who are not affiliated with either the underwriter or the issuer and who purchase or make a commitment to purchase all or part of any unsold allotment, so long as the securities are acquired for "investment" rather than for "distribution." The purpose of Rule 142 has been explained as recognition of "the value of secondary capital in facilitating the flow of investment funds into industry, and of the fact that the owners of such secondary capital cannot practicably perform the duty of thorough investigation and analysis imposed by the Act on the underwriter proper."[13] Accordingly, "a person who does no more than agree with an underwriter to take over some or all of the undistributed portion of the issue, and who purchases for investment any securities which his commitment thus obliges him to take up, does not thereby subject himself to liability as an underwriter of the securities of the issue actually distributed to the public."[14]

In contrast to Rules 141 and 142's exclusions of certain transactions from the concept of underwriter, SEC Rule 140[15] expressly includes within the definition one type of indirect participation in the distribution process. Rule 140 confers underwriter status on any entity whose chief business is the purchase of securities of one issuer (or of two or more affiliated issuers) and where that entity utilizes the sale of its own securities to finance the purchases. Under Rule 140, where such holding company or investment company acquires the issuer's securities, those securities will be deemed to have been acquired by an underwriter within the meaning of section 2(11).[16] Beyond the above-mentioned Commission rules, the task of defining "underwriter" has for the most part been left to judicial interpretation and SEC decision-making. For example, just as ordinary brokerage transactions will not classify a broker-dealer as an underwriter, engaging in routine market-making activities, by simply acting as a conduit between broker-dealers, will not result in underwriter status.[17]

It is very common for institutional investors, as well as wealthy individuals, to purchase large blocks of both registered and unregistered offerings. When these investors subsequently sell their securities there frequently may be a question as to the necessity for registration under

11. *Id.*

12. 17 C.F.R. § 230.142.

13. Opinion of SEC General Counsel, Sec. Act Rel. No. 1862 (Dec. 14, 1938).

14. *Id.*

15. 17 C.F.R. § 230.140.

16. *See id.*

17. In re Laser Arms Corp. Securities Litigation, 794 F.Supp. 475 (S.D.N.Y.1989), *affirmed* 969 F.2d 15 (2d Cir.1992).

the Act.[18]   The problem is most likely to arise where the initial offering was not registered under the Act.   Downstream sales are dealt with in Rule 144, which is not the exclusive method of compliance for either affiliates or nonaffiliates of the issuer.[19]   Rule 144 requires a two-year holding period before the securities can be resold under the safe harbor.[20] The rule further imposes limitations on the volume of sales after the two-year period has expired.[21]   The Commission has recognized that the inherent dangers of such large block purchases filtering down to the investing public (even when in connection with a public offering) may call for additional protection under the Act.   Accordingly, the SEC formulated the "presumptive underwriter doctrine" under which anyone who purchased at least ten percent of a registered offering could be considered an underwriter unless the purchaser was able to prove that he or she had sufficient investment intent.[22]   The ten percent threshold is not a hard and fast rule but certainly remains a significant factor in determining underwriting status under the Act.   The presumptive underwriter rule has continued vitality in a "modified form" as it will still be considered in addition to other factors.[23]

Case Law Developments—Inadvertent Underwriters

In one of the earliest judicial pronouncements on point, the Second Circuit made it clear that any substantial involvement in the distribution process would confer underwriter status, thus rendering unavailable the section 4(1) exemption from 1933 Act registration.   In SEC v. Chinese Consolidated Benevolent Association,[24] a not-for-profit association helped solicit investment in foreign government bonds.[25]   The defendants main-

---

18.   *See, e.g.,* United States v. Wolfson, 405 F.2d 779 (2d Cir.1968), *cert. denied* 394 U.S. 946, 89 S.Ct. 1275, 22 L.Ed.2d 479 (1969);   Report, *supra* note 8.

19.   17 C.F.R. § 230.144.   *See also* 17 C.F.R. § 230.144(d)(1).   *See id.* at § 230.144(a)(1) ("An 'affiliate' of an issuer is a person that directly, or indirectly through one or more intermediaries controls, or is controlled by, or is under common control with, such issuer.") Rule 144 is discussed in more detail in § 4.26 *infra.*

20.   Rule 144(e), 17 C.F.R. § 230.144(e).   Although the rule is only a safe harbor, it may be difficult to secure the statutory exemption for sales made substantially in advance of the expiration of the two-year period.   *See* text accompanying footnotes 42–54 *infra.*

21.   17 C.F.R. § 230.144(e).

22.   *See* Robert J. Ahrenholz & William E. Van Valkenberg, The Presumptive Underwriter Doctrine: Statutory Underwriter Status for Investors Purchasing a Specified Portion of a Registered Offering, 1973 Utah L.Rev. 773;   Nathan, Presumptive Underwriters, 8 Rev.Sec.Reg. 882 (1975).   *See also, e.g.,* Wheaten v. Matthews Holmquist & Associates, Inc., 858 F.Supp. 753 (N.D.Ill.1994) (question of fact as to whether seller was a statutory underwriter).

23.   Ahrenholz & Van Valkenberg, *supra* note 22 at 775.   *Cf.* Hedden v. Marinelli, 796 F.Supp. 432 (N.D.Cal.1992) (establishing that someone is a control person is not sufficient to establish underwriter status;   it must also be shown that he or she participated in a distribution).

24.   120 F.2d 738 (2d Cir.1941), *cert. denied* 314 U.S. 618, 62 S.Ct. 106, 86 L.Ed. 497 (1941).   *See also, e.g.,* In the Matter of State Bank of Pakistan, [1991–1992 Transfer Binder] Fed.Sec.L.Rep. (CCH) ¶ 89,946 (SEC 1992).

25.   The Republic of China authorized the issuance of bonds in the aggregate of fifty million dollars.   The defendant, a voluntary association organized in New York, created a committee to solicit funds for China through the sale of these bonds.   The committee acted

tained that they were not acting as securities promoters in the traditional sense, and that in promoting a worthy cause they should be exempt from the Act's coverage. Although their arguments swayed Judge Swan who wrote a vigorous dissent, the court held that the voluntary association's sales efforts were sufficient participation in the distribution and underwriting process so as to render the defendants "underwriters" within the meaning of section 2(11).[26] In his dissent, Judge Swan maintained that a logical extension of the court's opinion would make a newspaper an underwriter if a column or editorial recommends a bond in order to help a struggling government, or merely announces an impending offering.[27] The short answer to Judge Swan's contention is that it is a matter of degree. It is most certainly correct that incidental or collateral selling efforts or recommendations should not be sufficient to render someone potentially liable for violations of the Securities Act. Absent some other exemption, however, when an organization acts as a conduit for the sale of securities, such activity should be sufficient not only to confer jurisdiction but also to trigger the registration requirements, whether or not remuneration is received.[28] This method of analysis makes each decision extremely factual and relatively little firm footing is provided for counselors and corporate planners in relying on the available precedent.[29]

The problems created by the "inadvertent underwriter" cases can create a nightmare for the corporate planner. The difficulty in planning was highlighted by the celebrated decision in SEC v. Guild Films Co.[30] which involved the foreclosure sale of pledged securities.

Foreclosure of Pledged Securities

In *Guild Films,* the inadvertent underwriter was a bank engaging in a foreclosure sale of a substantial block of securities in Guild Films Company; the securities had been held as collateral for loans to a major

merely as a conduit, receiving no remuneration either directly or indirectly as it was participating in what it viewed to be a worthy cause. The only activity of the association was to forward the $600,000 it received to China and to distribute the bonds to the individual purchasers here in the United States.

26. *See* 120 F.2d at 741.

27. *Id.* at 742 (Swan, J., dissenting): "Hence, a single newspaper editorial, published without instigation by the Chinese Government and merely urging the purchase of the bonds in the name of patriotism, would make the newspaper an 'underwriter.' I cannot believe the statute should be so interpreted."

28. *See, e.g.,* In the Matter of State Bank of Pakistan, [1991–1992 Transfer Binder] Fed.Sec.L.Rep. (CCH) ¶ 89,946 (SEC 1992) (foreign bank was a statutory underwriter and violated section 5(c) by advertising foreign government bonds in the United States).

29. The outcome of the ruling in *Consolidated Benevolent Association* was the issuance of an injunction against proceeding with further selling efforts without registration or reliance upon an exemption. The procedural context may be significant as it is possible that the court would give a narrower reading to the definition in a criminal case or in an action for damages. *See also* Leiter v. Kuntz, 655 F.Supp. 725 (D.Utah 1987) (whether sellers were underwriters is a factual determination, precluding motion to dismiss).

30. 279 F.2d 485 (2d Cir.1960), *cert. denied* 364 U.S. 819, 81 S.Ct. 52, 5 L.Ed.2d 49 (1960), noted in 48 Calif.L.Rev. 841 (1960); 60 Colum.L.Rev. 1179 (1960); 74 Harv.L.Rev. 1241 (1961); 36 N.Y.U.L.Rev. 901 (1961); 13 Stan.L.Rev. 652 (1961); 8 U.C.L.A.L.Rev. 663 (1961).

shareholder.[31] The Second Circuit accepted the Commission's argument that the banks were underwriters under section 2(11) even though they may have accepted the stock as collateral in good faith and had not dealt directly with the issuer.[32] The court reasoned that "the banks knew that they had been given unregistered stock and that the issuer had specifically forbidden that the stock be sold. * * * "[33] In the court's view, this was sufficient to put the bank in a position in which it must have either held on to the stock, found some other independent exemption, or registered its sales upon foreclosure. The issue was not the bank's culpability in facilitating downstream sales, but rather whether the sales were made in such a manner as to trigger the need for the protection provided by registration.[34] In contrast when a bona fide pledge is made and there is no substantial likelihood that the pledgee will have to foreclose, it is unlikely that the pledgee will be found to be a statutory underwriter in the event that there is a foreclosure and the securities are sold. This is especially true when there is no public market for the stock in question and thus it is unlikely that a "distribution" will occur.[35]

The Commission has adhered to the rule that sales of pledged securities can, under certain circumstances, create underwriter status. Specifically, under Rule 144(d)(4)(D)[36] all securities sold by a bona fide pledgee are deemed to be acquired when they were acquired by the pledgor, and are aggregated with any sales by the pledgor for the purpose of calculating the rule's ceiling on resales. The rule further

---

31. The shareholder was Hollywood personality Hal Roach. The shares that were used as collateral had been issued pursuant to a private placement, with the purchaser signing the necessary investment letter. The lower court found that notwithstanding the investment letter, Roach's intent was to resell the security at a later date. The bank had obtained the stock as collateral after negotiations to renew Roach's note. When it became necessary for the bank to foreclose on the note, the stock transfer agent refused to enter the sale and suit was brought to compel the transfer. At the same time the SEC brought suit to enjoin the sale on the ground that it would violate the Act's registration provisions.

32. 279 F.2d at 489–90. *See generally* Mark A. Sargent, The "Guild Films" case: The Effect of "Good Faith" in Foreclosure Sales of Unregistered Securities Pledged as Collateral, 46 Va.L.Rev. 1573 (1960).

33. 279 F.2d at 490. *Compare* Seattle—First National Bank v. Carlstedt, 1984 WL 2430, [1984] Fed.Sec.L.Rep. (CCH) ¶ 91,499 (W.D.Okl.1984) (bank purchasing participation in loans made to investors held not to be an underwriter).

34. For a more recent decision requiring registration for sale of pledged securities, *see* United States v. Lindo, 18 F.3d 353 (6th Cir.1994).

See generally Dennis T. Rice, Effects of Registration Requirements on the Disposition of Pledged Securities, 21 Stan.L.Rev. 1607 (1969); Mark A. Sargent, Pledges and Foreclosure Rights Under the Securities Act of 1933, 45 Va.L.Rev. 885 (1959). *See also* Sargent *supra* note 28. A related question is whether the pledge itself is a "sale" under Section 2(3), 15 U.S.C.A. § 77b(3). *See* § 5.1 *infra*.

35. *See, e.g.,* One Fine Corp., 25 Sec.Reg. & L.Rep. (BNA) 567 (SEC No Action Letter avail. April 1, 1993). *See also, e.g.,* Bank of America National Trust & Savings Ass'n, 25 Sec. Reg. & L. Rep. (BNA) 1702 (SEC No Action Letter Dec. 2, 1993); NationsBank of Virginia, N.A., [1993 Transfer Binder] Fed. Sec. L. Rep. (CCH) ¶ 76,699 (SEC No Action Letter June 11, 1993).

36. 17 C.F.R. § 230.144(d)(4)(D). *See* Gary L. Heuter, The Plight of the Pledgee Under Rule 144, 3 Sec.Reg.L.J. 111 (1975). *See also* In re Sovran Financial Corp., [1984–85 Transfer Binder] Fed.Sec.L.Rep. (CCH) ¶ 77,850 (SEC No Action Letter Nov. 5, 1984).

provides that where there is a pledge without any recourse against the pledgor, the acquisition date of the security for purposes of creating downstream selling liability is the date of the pledge rather than the date of acquisition by the pledgor.[37] In 1991, the Commission instituted enforcement proceedings in connection with a broker's sale of control securities to satisfy a margin account.[38] The broker knew that the customer was a control person and apparently ignored the volume limitations applicable to such sales. The initiation of proceedings was especially significant in that the broker in question had relied on no action letters that had been given to others in the past. These proceedings highlight the precarious nature of trying to distill general principles from specific no action responses.[39]

In addition to making it clear that the selling activities of banks and other entities can create inadvertent underwriter status, the courts and the SEC have addressed themselves to the question of the magnitude of the distribution necessary to trigger the Act's registration requirements.[40] These rulings in turn formed the basis for Rule 144 but nevertheless remain important precedent in their own right since the rule is not exclusive.[41]

Investment Intent—The Two–Year Holding Period

In determining whether or not a person is a statutory underwriter, one of the key questions is whether the would-be underwriter had sufficient investment intent at the time of purchase. The issue is raised in the context of whether the securities were purchased with a view towards distribution. One of the primary questions then becomes: how does one determine the seller's original intent at the time the securities were acquired? A sale closely following the acquisition of the securities is strong circumstantial evidence that an investment intent did not exist.[42] It has been held within the context of a criminal prosecution that "[t]he passage of two years before the commencement of distribution of any of these shares is an insuperable obstacle to my finding that [defendant] took these shares with a view to distribution thereof, in the

---

37. *Id.* Cf. Shearson Lehman Hutton Holdings Inc. v. Coated Sales, Inc., 697 F.Supp. 639 (S.D.N.Y.1988) (stock transfer agent had no lawful basis to refuse to transfer stock to pledgee on default).

38. Morgan Stanley & Co., Sec.Exch.Act Rel. No. 34–28,990, Admin.Proc. File No. 3–7473 (March 20, 1991).

39. *See* § 1.4 *supra.*

40. *See, e.g., See also, e.g.,* Bank of America National Trust & Savings Ass'n, 25 Sec. Reg. & L. Rep. (BNA) 1702 (SEC No Action Letter Dec. 2, 1993); NationsBank of Virginia, N.A., [1993 Transfer Binder] Fed. Sec. L. Rep. (CCH) ¶ 76,699 (SEC No Action Letter June 11, 1993). *Cf.* Oak Park Bank, 24 Sec.Reg. & L.Rep. (BNA) 544 (SEC No Action Letter available April 3, 1992) (stock held as collateral could be foreclosed upon and sold without registration). *But see* United States v. Lindo, 18 F.3d 353 (6th Cir.1994) (bank's sales of pledged securities were not exempt).

41. *See* 17 C.F.R. § 230.144(j).

42. *See, e.g.,* In the Matter of DG Bank (Schweiz) AG [1991–1992 Transfer Binder] Fed.Sec.L.Rep. (CCH) ¶ 84,945 (SEC March 5, 1992) (a bank selling restricted securities within two months of their acquisition from the issuer could not establish the availability of the section 4(1) exemption).

absence of any relevant evidence from which I could conclude that he did not take the shares for investment." [43] The Second Circuit's decision has formed the basis of a two-year rule of thumb for the holding period. Since this arose in a criminal prosecution, which carries with it a higher standard of proof, a longer holding period might arguably apply in a civil or SEC enforcement proceeding.

The Commission has adopted this two year holding period as a general rule of thumb and it has also been incorporated into Rule 144 which presents a safe harbor for persons selling restricted securities that have been acquired in a private placement or pursuant to a Regulation D exemption.[44] As noted above, the two-year period arose in the context of a criminal prosecution and the higher standard of proof attendant with it. Therefore, planners should not place undue reliance on the passage of time. Courts and the Commission will also look to the circumstances surrounding the down-stream sale as well as the initial purchase. For example, Rule 144 places limitations on the amount that may be sold even after the two year holding period has expired.[45] It is clear that when properly viewed, the two year period is merely a very rough guideline and not the be-all and end-all of the "underwriter" issue. It has been expressly held that in the last analysis, whether or not the purchaser had an intent to distribute is a question of fact to be answered by looking to all of the particular circumstances.[46]

The "Change in Circumstances" Exception

In the pre-Rule 144 case law, sales made prior to the expiration of the two year holding period from the date of acquisition were permitted if the seller was able to demonstrate that he or she had the sufficient investment intent.[47] As a result, it became common for sellers to claim that although they had the requisite investment intent at the time of purchase, subsequent changes in their personal situations necessitated

---

43. United States v. Sherwood, 175 F.Supp. 480, 483 (S.D.N.Y.1959) (defendant had purchased 8—of the issuer's stock in a private placement and held it for two years). *Compare, e.g.,* Gilligan, Will & Co. v. SEC, 267 F.2d 461 (2d Cir.1959), *cert. denied* 361 U.S. 896, 80 S.Ct. 200, 4 L.Ed.2d 152 (1959) (ten month holding period held insufficient).

44. *See* Sec.Act Rel. No. 33–5223 (Jan. 11, 1972). In 1990, the Commission amended Rule 144 to provide that the two-year holding period runs from the time the securities were purchased from the issuer or an affiliate of the issuer. Accordingly, there is a tacking of holding periods for nonaffiliates who purchase securities from a nonaffiliate. 17 C.F.R. § 230.144(g). *See* § 4.26 *infra.*

Restricted securities can include those acquired by underwriters as compensation for their participation in an offering. *See, e.g.,* Precision Optics Corp., [1993 Transfer Binder] Fed. Sec. L. Rep. (CCH) ¶ 76,627 (SEC No Action Letter Jan. 14, 1993).

45. 17 C.F.R. § 230.144(e).

46. Gilligan, Will & Co. v. SEC, 267 F.2d 461 (2d Cir.1959), *cert. denied* 361 U.S. 896, 80 S.Ct. 200, 4 L.Ed.2d 152 (1959), noted 72 Harv.L.Rev. 789 (1959); 45 Va.L.Rev. 1053 (1959).

47. *See* Gilligan, Will & Co. v. SEC, 267 F.2d 461 (2d Cir.1959), *cert. denied* 361 U.S. 896, 80 S.Ct. 200, 4 L.Ed.2d 152 (1959) (in which the defendant unsuccessfully maintained that a ten month holding period was sufficient).

the resale of the securities.[48] Sellers of securities often took the position that since they had not purchased the securities with a view toward distribution, they should be relieved from the Act's registration requirements. Although the Commission consistently refused to issue no-action letters based on this "change of circumstances" defense, it was frequently relied upon by planners in permitting transactions without registration.[49]

The change in circumstances defense was not available where the changed circumstances were reasonably foreseeable at the time of purchase nor where the only change was that the issuer failed to meet the investor's expectations of success.[50] Additionally, the availability of the change in circumstances defense was directly related to the period of time for which the securities had been held; the shorter the holding period the more compelling the evidence required.[51] The change in circumstances defense only added to the uncertainty in structuring transactions and resulted in "troublesome inconsistency." [52] Accordingly, in adopting Rule 144 the Commission purported to rescind the change in circumstances defense.[53] There is however, a question as to the Commission's authority to make such a pronouncement beyond the context of a safe harbor rule. To the extent that the change in circumstances defense is a valid interpretation in terms of the section 2(11) statutory definition of one who purchases with an intent to redistribute, the SEC cannot by administrative fiat change the meaning of the statute. However, if the change in circumstances defense was merely an administrative interpretation rather than a part of the statutory definition, the SEC can effectively eliminate the defense by changing its interpretation. Also, since Rule 144 is non-exclusive, the change in circumstances defense arguably survives in these cases even if it is abolished for those relying upon the rule. Nevertheless, the SEC has taken the position that it has been abolished in all cases.[54]

Sales on Behalf of Controlling Persons

The last sentence of section 2(11)'s statutory definition of underwriter provides that anyone who sells a security on behalf of a control-

---

48. *See* SEC, "Disclosure to Investors"—Report and Recommendations to The Securities and Exchange Commission From the Disclosure Policy Study, "The Wheat Report," 160–77 (1969).

49. *See generally, e.g.,* 1 Louis Loss Securities Regulation 665–73 (2d ed. 1961); Malcom Fooshee & Edward F. McCabe, Private Placements—Resale of Securities: The Crowell–Collier Case, 15 Bus.Law. 72 (1959); Note, The Investment—Intent Dilemma in Secondary Transactions, 39 N.Y.U.L.Rev. 1043 (1964).

50. *See* Gilligan, Will & Co. v. SEC, 267 F.2d 461, 462–68 (2d Cir.1959), *cert. denied* 361 U.S. 896, 80 S.Ct. 200, 4 L.Ed.2d 152 (1959); "The Wheat Report" *supra* footnote 48 at 166–67.

51. *Id.* at 167.

52. *Id.* at 176.

53. Sec. Act Rel. No. 33–5223 (Jan. 11, 1972).

54. *Id.*

ling person is an underwriter.[55] Although there is no statutory definition of "control" in Rule 405[56] the Commission defines control as "the possession, direct or indirect, of the power to direct or cause the direction of the management and policies of a person, whether through the ownership of voting securities, by contract, or otherwise."[57] Accordingly, the question of who is a control person is highly factual and is not dependent upon ownership of any specific percentage. For example, it has been held that someone owning eight percent of a company's stock was not a control person; if he had been a control person this would have rendered anyone handling sales on his behalf an automatic statutory underwriter.[58] Control can be found to exist where it is exercised other than through stock ownership.[59] Presumably any policy-making officer falls within Rule 405's scope.

The two-year holding period would seem to be equally relevant for purposes of classifying someone as an underwriter for having sold on behalf of a control person. This is the case because the issue is whether the seller had purchased the securities from an "issuer" (*i.e.,* control person) with a view to distribute.

Where a series of coordinated secondary offerings resulted in a corporation's publicly held shares shifting from nine percent of those outstanding to forty-six percent of those outstanding, the broker/dealer handling such sales on behalf of controlling persons was held to have been a statutory underwriter.[60] The Commission rejected the contention that since the transactions were executed upon the selling customer's orders they should be exempt under section 4(4)[61] as unsolicited broker's

---

55. 15 U.S.C.A. § 77b(11). *See generally* Rutherford B. Campbell, Jr., Defining Control in Secondary Distributions, 18 B.C.Inc.Comm.L.Rev. 37 (1976); Thomas Linden, The Resale of Restricted and Control Securities Under SEC Rule 144: The First Five Years, 8 Seton Hall L.Rev. 157 (1977).

56. 17 C.F.R. § 230.405. United States v. Sprecher, 783 F.Supp. 133, 159 (S.D.N.Y. 1992) (the question of control depends on the circumstances of the particular case and the ability to affect management and corporate policy; it is not dependent on stock ownership), *relying on* United States v. Corr, 543 F.2d 1042, 1050 (2d Cir.1976).

Establishing that someone is a control person is only one step in establishing that an underwriter transaction has taken place, it must also be shown that the transaction was part of a distribution. Hedden v. Marinelli, 796 F.Supp. 432 (N.D.Cal.1992). *See also* § 4.23 *supra.*

57. 17 C.F.R. § 230.405(f). *See generally* A.A. Sommer, Jr., Who's "In Control"?—S.E.C., 21 Bus.Law. 559 (1966). *See also* Note, The Controlling Persons Provisions: Conduits of Secondary Liability Under Federal Securities Laws, 19 Vill.L.Rev. 621 (1974).

58. United States v. Sherwood, 175 F.Supp. 480 (S.D.N.Y.1959). This particular ruling arguably should not be entitled to too much precedential effect as these decisions are highly factual within the context of a particular case.

59. 17 C.F.R. § 230.405(f).

60. In the Matter of Ira Haupt & Co., 23 S.E.C. 589 (SEC 1946), noted 14 U.Chi.L.Rev. 307 (1947).

61. 15 U.S.C.A. § 77d(4). The SEC decision in *Ira Haupt* was based on section 4(4)'s predecessor, an earlier version of section 4(2).

transactions.[62] The Commission reasoned that such a large infusion of privately held stock into the public market constituted a "distribution" as opposed to the type of day-to-day transaction or "trading" that section 4(4) was designed to exempt.[63] Thus, it is clear that any large block sales of securities by insiders (*i.e.*, control persons or affiliates) that have not been registered will be subject to the Act's registration requirements, absent some independent exemption.

An interesting question arises as to whether insiders or control persons must register securities purchased on the open market when, after a significant period of time, they decide to sell. In a somewhat analogous situation, the Commission held that even though securities issued prior to 1933 were exempt under section 3(a)(1)[64] a subsequent sale by controlling persons was a new distribution which went beyond the scope of the former section 3(a)(1) exemption.[65] The rationale for requiring registration of such large sales is that a large volume of sales will cause a disruption of an otherwise orderly public market and thus the disclosure protections of the registration requirements are needed. Disclosure informs the market of who is selling and why they are selling. Also, registration will inform the market of the issuer's current condition. This rationale for disclosure through registration can be extended to certain large block transactions by controlling persons. Furthermore, although once public, if the securities have been privately held for a sufficiently long period of time, the impact on the market is the same as if they had never been publicly issued. Unless dealing with restricted stock, large block transactions by institutional investors are not generally registered, but in these instances the sellers presumably do not qualify as control persons and thus are not "issuers" for the purposes of section 2(11)'s definition of underwriter. It arguably does not make sense to require registration solely because such a large block of unrestricted stock had been sold by a control person of the issuer. However, the insider's access to nonpublic information, which would have to be disclosed in a registration statement, can be used to distinguish insider large-block sales from other large transactions.

62. In the Matter of Ira Haupt & Co., 23 S.E.C. 589, 600–06 (SEC 1946). *See* § 4.23 *supra.* *Accord* United States v. Wolfson, 405 F.2d 779 (2d Cir.1968), *cert. denied* 394 U.S. 946, 89 S.Ct. 1275, 22 L.Ed.2d 479 (1969).

63. 23 S.E.C. at 600–06. *Accord* Gilligan, Will & Co. v. SEC, 267 F.2d 461, 466 (2d Cir.1959), *cert. denied* 361 U.S. 896, 80 S.Ct. 200, 4 L.Ed.2d 152 (1959), citing H.R.Rep. No. 1838, 73d Cong. 2d Sess. 41 (1934). Ackerberg v. Johnson, 892 F.2d 1328, 1335 n. 6 (8th Cir.1989) ("the definition of underwriter found in § 2(11), depends on the existence of a distribution, which in turn is the equivalent of a public offering. Section 4(2) contains the exemption for transactions not involving a public offering. Any analysis of whether a party is an underwriter for purposes of § 4(1) necessarily entails an inquiry into whether the transaction involves a public offering"). *Cf.* Leiter v. Kuntz, 655 F.Supp. 725, 727–29 (D. Utah 1987) (factual issue as to whether control person was engaged in a distribution).

64. 15 U.S.C.A. § 77c(a)(1). *See* § 4.2 *supra.*

65. 23 S.E.C. at 599–600.

In United States v. Wolfson,[66] the Second Circuit alarmed the brokerage industry when it noted that brokers were potentially liable as underwriters for selling a controlling person's securities.[67]   The court held that defendant Wolfson, the control person who had siphoned his securities to the public by making sales through a number of brokers, was not exempt since such transactions were through an underwriter as defined in section 2(11).[68]   The court noted that section 4(1) exempts "transactions" and not classes of people.   Citing the section 2(11) definition of underwriter, the court pointed out that the brokers had supplied outlets for the stock of appellants who were "issuers" within the section 2(11) definition of that term even if they were not "issuers" as defined by section 2(4) for purposes of the Act in general.[69]   Thus, the brokers were "underwriters" within the meaning of section 2(11), and according to the court, "the stock was sold in 'transactions by underwriters' which are not within the exception of section 4(1). * * * "[70]   There has been more recent confirmation of the *Wolfson* court's ruling that section 4 exemptions exempt transactions and not persons so that a person who is neither an issuer, underwriter, nor a dealer but participates in a transaction with one, may not be able to rely on the exemption.[71]

The section 4(1) exemption, and hence the definition of underwriter, was not the only issue involved in the *Wolfson* case.   The appellants in *Wolfson* also argued that the brokers could not be underwriters because the sales in question fell within the section 4(4) exemption for brokers' orders executed upon customers' orders on any exchange or in the over-the-counter market.   The court agreed that section 4(4) exempted the brokers for their parts in the transaction, since the brokers had not solicited the orders, and were unaware at the time that the transactions were part of a distribution of securities by appellants.[72]   Wolfson and his associates, on the other hand, were "control persons [who] must find their own exemptions." [73]   Otherwise, the court reasoned, appellants would gain from having kept the true facts from the brokers.[74]   In a situation in which the broker is not an unwitting participant, the size of

---

66.   405 F.2d 779 (2d Cir.1968), *cert. denied* 394 U.S. 946, 89 S.Ct. 1275, 22 L.Ed.2d 479 (1969).

67.   *Id.* at 782–83.

68.   *Id.* Wolfson, together with members of his immediate family and his right-hand man, owned 1,149,775 shares, or over forty percent of the outstanding stock of Continental Enterprises, Inc.; the remainder being spread among some 5,000 outside shareholders. In the eighteen month period between August 1, 1960 and January 31, 1962, 633,825 unregistered shares of the forty percent block were sold through a variety of brokerage houses.

69.   *Id.* at 782.

70.   *Id.*

71.   SEC v. Netelkos, 592 F.Supp. 906, 915 (S.D.N.Y.1984).

72.   405 F.2d at 782–83.

73.   *Id.* at 782.

74.   *Id.*

the total secondary distribution may well preclude the application of section 4(4) to shield the brokers.[75]

Summary

The one clear lesson of the cases and SEC decisions is that section 2(11)'s definition of underwriter is a trap for the careless and unwary.[76] In an attempt to provide additional guidance, the Commission promulgated Rule 144,[77] which is discussed below. Rule 144 does not cover the entire field and although helpful in many situations, it has not eliminated all of the uncertainty discussed herein.

The section 4(1) exemption has been held to include transactions that do not fall within the fact patterns discussed above. In Ackerberg v. Johnson,[78] the Eighth Circuit applied the section 4(1) exemption to sales by control persons made to a sophisticated investor who had access to current information about the issuer. The fact pattern was typical of the type of downstream sale that fits within the so-called section "4(1½)" exemption.[79] However, in holding that the sales by control persons were exempt, the court explained that the section 4(1½) exemption is in fact part of section 4(1).[80]

§ 4.25 Some Additional Problems of Secondary Distributions—Disclosure and Maintaining an Orderly Market

Disclosure Issues

The preceding discussion is addressed to the necessity of filing a 1933 Act registration statement for secondary distributions. Even where a secondary distribution is registered, however, significant pitfalls remain. The very nature of the secondary transaction can raise problems that are not present and disclosure concerns that are even more acute as those associated with primary offerings. For example, when a secondary distribution involving sales by insiders is piggy-backed along with a primary offering, with both being covered by the same registration statement, there can be particularly sensitive disclosure problems. Specifically, where all or a portion of the proceeds of the offering inures to the selling shareholders, the drafters of the disclosure documents

---

75. *See* In the Matter of Ira Haupt & Co., 23 S.E.C. 589 (SEC 1946), discussed in the text accompanying footnotes 60–65 *supra*. *See also, e.g.,* In re Robert G. Leigh, [1990 Transfer Binder] Fed.Sec.L.Rep. (CCH) ¶ 84,700 (SEC Feb. 1, 1990) (customer delivered to broker a large block of restricted stock in a little known company after telling broker that he received the stock as a finder's fee and that he intended to sell most of the shares; sections 4(1) and 4(4) exemptions were thus unavailable because broker had reason to know that customer had acquired the shares from the issuer with a view to selling them).

76. *See, e.g.,* Wheaten v. Matthews Holmquist & Associates, Inc., 858 F.Supp. 753 (N.D.Ill.1994) (question of fact as to whether seller was a statutory underwriter).

77. 17 C.F.R. § 230.144. *See* § 4.26 *infra.*

78. 892 F.2d 1328 (8th Cir.1989).

79. *See* § 4.26.1 *infra.*

80. 892 F.2d at 1335 n. 6, which is quoted in § 4.26.1 *infra.*

must take great pains to explain this.[1] There must be detailed disclosure lest the investing public be deceived into believing that the proceeds are going to the issuer.[2]

Particularly sensitive problems can arise in connection with an initial public offering where there are substantial shareholdings remaining in the hands of investors owning the shares before the company went public. Rule 144,[3] which is discussed in the next section of this treatise, provides a safe harbor for resales of restricted securities and securities held by control persons. By virtue of the safe harbor embodied in Rule 144, once an issuer has been subject to the 1934 Act's periodic reporting requirements for ninety days, a substantial amount of unregistered securities may be sold publicly.[4] Once there is a registered public offering, the issuer becomes subject to the 1934 Act's periodic reporting requirements.[5] Accordingly, unless restricted by contract, there can be the likelihood of secondary sales at the end of the ninety days following the public offering. In such a case, the 1933 Act registration statement must adequately disclose the possibility of these sales and the downward price pressure that could result.[6]

Potential for Manipulation

Another problem that arises in connection with secondary distributions is the maintenance of an orderly market. While similar difficulties may also arise in connection with primary offerings, the existence of a large number of selling shareholders can cause problems for registered secondary offerings. The classic case on this point is In the Matter of Hazel Bishop, Inc.[7] which involved a secondary "at-market" offering.[8] The one hundred and twelve selling shareholders had no central underwriter and there was no attempt to coordinate their sales activities. The Commission issued a stop order, ruling that the temptation to withhold shares in order to stabilize the market and maintain a high price for the selling shareholders was so great that the absence of a coordinated

§ 4.25

1. *See* Regulation S–K, item 507, 17 C.F.R. § 229.507; Regulation S–B, item 507.

2. *E.g.,* In the Matter of Universal Camera Corp., 19 S.E.C. 648 (SEC 1945). *See* § 3.7 *supra.*

3. 17 C.F.R. § 230.144.

4. Rule 144(e) permits, within a three month period, public sales of unregistered securities of up to the greater of one percent of the outstanding securities or the average weekly reported trading volume. Rule 144(c) contains the informational requirements.

5. Section 15(d) of the 1934 Act, 15 U.S.C.A. § 78o(d). *See* § 9.3 *infra.*

6. Furthermore, it is conceivable that if there is a substantial volume of these unregistered secondary sales, they might be integrated into the initial offering even though they fall within Rule 144(e)'s volume limitations. Integration is discussed in § 4.29 *infra.*

7. 40 S.E.C. 718 (SEC 1961). *See also* Jaffe & Co., 44 S.E.C. 285 (SEC 1970). *But see* Collins Securities Corp., [1975 Transfer Binder] Fed.Sec.L.Rep. ¶ 80,327 (SEC 1975), *reversed on other grounds* 562 F.2d 820 (D.C.Cir.1977).

8. The registration statement covered 1.2 million shares which constituted a secondary offering by 112 selling stockholders. Shares of the same class were traded on the American Stock Exchange and the shares covered by the registration statement were to be offered "at market."

marketing plan for the at-market offering violated the Act.[9] Specifically, the SEC pointed out that Rule 10b–6[10] prohibits all manipulative activity including the making of stabilizing bids that do not comply with Rule 10b–7 or 10b–8.[11] Since there was no adequate check against violation of these rules, the Commission issued a stop order for the registration statement covering the shares of the selling shareholders. The situation is especially sensitive where, as here, the existing public market for securities will be conducive to sales made without full compliance with the prospectus delivery requirements.

§ 4.26 SEC Rule 144

As noted in preceding sections,[1] the case law and SEC interpretations of section 2(11)[2] underwriter status and the scope of the exemptions under sections 4(1)[3] and 4(4)[4] have not provided much firm practical guidance to the planner of corporate or other transactions involving the sale of restricted securities as well as the sale of any securities held by control persons. Since many of the questions concerned with the need to register downstream securities sales essentially depend upon the resolution of factual issues, the decisions on point are frequently confusing and often may even appear to be inconsistent with one another.[5] The resulting uncertainty was widely perceived by the practicing bar and documented by the "Wheat Report" recommendations which were transmitted in 1969 to the SEC.[6] In response to this and other issues identified in the Wheat Report, the Commission promulgated a number of new regulations including Rule 144.[7] The Commission thus recognized the need for more helpful guidelines for the securities bar in planning unregistered secondary transactions. Rule 144 was adopted to

9. The SEC also found violations in connection with a previously attempted private placement. Since the prior offering was found to have violated section 5, nondisclosure of this fact was a material omission from the prospectus for the secondary offering. Additionally, the Commission found material misstatements concerning the previous high bid for the stock, in failing to explain that the price had been reached on one day and may have been due to insider buying activity.

10. 17 C.F.R. § 240.10b–6. *See* § 6.1 *infra. See generally* William W. Foshay, Market Activities of Participants in Securities Distributions, 45 Va.L.Rev. 907 (1959). Ezra Weiss & Lawrence W. Leibowitz, Rule 10b–6 Revised, 39 Geo. Wash.L.Rev. 474 (1974).

11. 17 C.F.R. § 240.10b–7 (permitting limited stabilizing activity during qualifying distributions); 17 C.F.R. § 240.10b–8 (permitting limited stabilizing activity in conjunction with certain rights offerings). *See* § 6.1 *infra.*

§ 4.26

1. *See* §§ 4.23–4.24 *supra.*

2. 15 U.S.C.A. § 77b(11).

3. 15 U.S.C.A. § 77d(1).

4. 15 U.S.C.A. § 77d(4).

5. *See* "Disclosure to Investors"—Report and Recommendation to the Securities and Exchange Commission from the Disclosure Policy Study, "The Wheat Report," 160–77 (1969).

6. *Id.*

7. 17 C.F.R. § 230.144. *See* Sec.Act Rel.No. 33–5223 (Jan. 11, 1972). For a more recent interpretive release *see* Sec.Act Rel.No. 33–6099 (Aug. 2, 1979).

provide more guidance to the planner and other participants by clarifying the answers to the question of who is an underwriter and thereby
defining the scope of the statutory exemptions under sections 4(1) and
4(4).[8]

The Commission explained that section 4(1) "was intended to exempt only trading transactions between individual investors with respect
to securities already issued and not to exempt distributions by issuers or
acts of other individuals who engage in steps necessary to such distributions."[9] The SEC further pointed out that the language of section
2(11)'s definition of underwriter[10] is disjunctive, and thus the mere
absence of a view toward subsequent distribution when making the
initial purchase from the issuer would not preclude a finding that the
purchaser had underwriter status.[11] The Commission therefore reaffirmed the absence of any strict intent requirement as an element of
inadvertent underwriter status.[12]

Rule 144 operates as a safe harbor and as such is not the exclusive
method by which an affiliate of the issuer may sell restricted securities
in reliance upon an exemption.[13] The rule also applies to both sales of
restricted securities by all persons and to sales of any securities by
affiliates of the issuer.[14] The rule is thus a safe harbor[15] for both
affiliates and nonaffiliates. However, reliance on non-Rule 144 precedent will impose "a strong burden" on the person claiming the exemption.[16]

"Restricted securities" are defined in Rule 144 as those acquired
directly or indirectly from an issuer in a non-public offering,[17] in a Rule

---

8. *See generally* Dan L. Goldwasser, A Guide to Rule 144 (2d ed. 1978); William J.
Casey, SEC Rule 144 Revisited, 43 Brooklyn L.Rev. 571 (1977); James H. Fogelson, Rule
144—A Summary Review, 37 Bus.Law. 1519 (1982); Robert S. Green, Selling Restricted
Securities Under Rule 144—A Practical Guide, Prac.Law. p. 13 (May 1972); Thomas
Linden, The Resale of Restricted and Control Securities Under SEC Rule 144: The First
Five Years, 8 Seton Hall L.Rev. 157 (1977); Martin Lipton, James H. Fogelson & Wayne L.
Warnken, Rule 144—A Summary Review After Two Years, 29 Bus.Law. 1183 (1974); Marc
I. Steinberg, The Application and Effectiveness of SEC Rule 144, 49 Ohio St.L.J. 473
(1988); Symposium—A Guide to Securities and Exchange Commission Rule 144, 67
Nw.U.L.Rev. 1 (Nov. 1972 Supp.).

9. Sec.Act Rel.No. 33–5223 (SEC Jan. 11, 1972) (citing SEC v. Chinese Consolidated
Benevolent Association, 120 F.2d 738 (2d Cir.1941), *cert. denied* 314 U.S. 618, 62 S.Ct. 106,
86 L.Ed. 497 (1941)).

10. 15 U.S.C.A. § 77b(11).

11. Sec.Act Rel.No. 33–5223 (Jan. 11, 1972).

12. The problems of the inadvertent underwriter are discussed in § 4.24 *supra.*

13. 17 C.F.R. § 230.144(j). It used to be exclusive for affiliates. Sec.Act Rel.No. 33–
5306 (Sept. 26, 1972). *See also* Sec.Act Rel.No. 33–6099 (SEC Aug. 1979).

14. As discussed in footnote 22 *infra,* formerly the Commission treated restricted and
unrestricted securities as fungible.

15. As is the case with other safe harbor rules, presumably Rule 144 will not insulate a
transaction which technically complies with the rule but nevertheless is viewed as a scheme
to evade registration.

16. Sec.Act Rel.No. 33–5223 (Jan. 11, 1972).

17. *See* §§ 4.20, 4.22 *supra.* This includes securities sold in reliance upon Rule 506's
safe harbor. 17 C.F.R. § 230.506. *See also, e.g.,* MCA, Inc., [1992 Transfer Binder]

504[18] transaction, or in any other transaction, with the resale limitations imposed by Regulation D.[19] Due to the safe harbor nature of the rule, there is the alternative of relying upon the pre-Rule 144 case law and SEC interpretations when selling restricted stock.[20] The Commission has emphasized, however, that persons who offer or sell restricted securities without relying on Rule 144 will have a "substantial burden of proof in establishing that an exemption * * * is available," and that "brokers * * * who participate in the transactions do so at their risk."[21]

A significant exception to the vitality of pre-Rule 144 case law and interpretations is the Commission's position that the "change of circumstances" defense no longer applies to downstream sales by persons purchasing from an issuer that had not registered the securities.[22] Furthermore, although the downstream seller's holding period prior to sale is a significant factor, in the Commission's view, "the fact that securities have been held for a particular period of time does not by itself establish the availability of an exemption from registration."[23] Thus, Rule 144's two year provision is not determinative under the case law when deciding what the holding period should be;[24] it may, nevertheless, be useful by analogy. The 1933 Act does not expressly delegate to the Commission the authority to set the parameters of the section 4(1) and section 4(4) exemptions. Rule 144 thus represents the Commission's interpretation of the statute. It is beyond question that the rule purports to go significantly further than the pre-existing case law in limiting the scope of the exemption.

Since Rule 144 applies differently to affiliates and non-affiliates, it is imperative to know who is an affiliate. Under the terms of the rule,

---

Fed.Sec.L.Rep. (CCH) ¶ 76,251 (SEC No Action Letter May 26, 1992) (issuance of shares under incentive plan would not result in restricted securities where the issuer is a reporting company and the number of shares to be issued was small in comparison with the public float of the securities).

18. 17 C.F.R. § 230.504. Rule 504 exempts certain offerings of up to $1,000,000. *See* § 4.19 *supra*.

19. 17 C.F.R. § 230.144(a)(3). Rule 505 exempts certain offerings of up to $5,000,000; Rule 506 provides a safe harbor for section 4(2)'s non-public offering exemption, 17 C.F.R. §§ 230.505, 230.506. Regulation D is discussed in §§ 4.16–4.19, 4.22 *supra*.

20. *See* §§ 4.23–4.25 *supra*.

21. Sec.Act Rel.No. 33–5223 (Jan. 11, 1972).

22. "[T]he 'change in circumstances' concept * * * fails to meet the objectives of the Act, since the circumstances of the seller are unrelated to the need of investors for the protections afforded by the registration and other provisions of the Act." *Id. See* the discussion in § 4.24 *supra*.

Another significant change was the elimination of the fungibility doctrine. Formerly, the SEC took the position that all securities of the same class were fungible so that someone owning both restricted and unrestricted securities could not sell the unrestricted securities without complying with the requirements that would have applied to sale of the restricted securities. With its adoption of Rule 144, the Commission abolished the fungibility doctrine so that restricted and unrestricted securities are treated distinctly.

23. Sec.Act Rel.No. 33–5223 (Jan. 11, 1972).

24. Martin Lipton, James H. Fogelson & Wayne L. Warnken, *Rule 144—A Summary Review After Two Years*, 29 Bus.Law. 1183, 1197 (1974), citing Sec.Act Rel.No. 33–5223 (Jan. 11, 1972). *See* § 4.24 *supra*.

affiliate status attaches to persons who directly or indirectly control, are similarly controlled by, or are under common control with the issuer.[25] Rule 405 defines "control" as the ability to influence directly or indirectly, management decisions.[26] It follows that affiliate status is not limited to those who own stock but would certainly seem to apply to high level executives who are making management's decisions.[27] Although questions relating to affiliate status are highly factual, the SEC's policy is not to issue no-action letters in this area.[28]

Compliance with Rule 144 requires dissemination of sufficient current public information concerning the issuer. There are only two ways to satisfy the rule's information requirements. A company that is subject to the reporting requirements of the 1934 Exchange Act satisfies the rule, provided of course, that all reports are accurate and up to date.[29] For companies that are not subject to the 1934 Act, the issuers must make similar information publicly available in order to qualify for Rule 144 — specifically most of the information required by paragraph (a)(4) of SEC Rule 15c2–11 relating to the publication of quotations by broker-dealers must be disclosed.[30] It is to be noted that unlike the Rule 506 safe harbor exemption for nonpublic offerings by an issuer,[31] Rule 144's information requirements concern information that is publicly available, and does not mandate that this (or any other) information be made specifically available to offerees and purchasers of the restricted securities.

In addition to Rule 144's public information requirement, the rule imposes a two year holding period on all affiliates (as well as nonaffiliates) who have purchased restricted securities from the issuer and who choose to resell them without filing a registration statement.[32] The two-year holding period is borrowed from the rule of thumb established in the *Sherwood* case[33] and is designed to help determine whether the person purchasing the security from the issuer had an investment intent as opposed to having purchased the securities with a view towards

---

25.   17 C.F.R. § 230.144(a)(1).

26.   17 C.F.R. § 230.405(f). *See generally* A.A. Sommer, Jr., Who's "In Control"?—SEC, 21 Bus.Law. 559 (1966).

27.   *See, e.g.,* United States v. Sprecher, 783 F.Supp. 133, 159 (S.D.N.Y.1992):

Stock ownership is but one aspect of control, which can rest with more than one person at the same time or from time to time. *United States v. Corr,* 543 F.2d 1042, 1050 (2d Cir.1976). Thus whether someone is an affiliate for the purposes of Rule 144(k) depends upon "the totality of the circumstances including an appraisal of the influence upon management and policies of a corporation by the person involved." *Id.*

28.   *See* Sec.Act Rel.No. 33–5223 (Jan. 11, 1972).

29.   17 C.F.R. § 230.144(c)(1). The 1934 Act registration and periodic reporting requirements are discussed in §§ 9.2–9.3 *infra.*

30.   17 C.F.R. § 230.144(c)(2). *See* 17 C.F.R. § 240.15c2–11. Insurance companies that do not file periodic reports under the 1934 Act must make publicly available all of the information required by 15 U.S.C.A. § 78*l*(g)(2)(G)(i). 17 C.F.R. § 230.144(c)(2).

31.   17 C.F.R. § 230.506. *See* § 4.22 *supra.*

32.   *See* 17 C.F.R. § 230.144(d)(1).

33.   United States v. Sherwood, 175 F.Supp. 480 (S.D.N.Y.1959). *See* § 4.24 *supra.*

distribution. In determining the two year holding period, any securities obtained by way of stock dividends, splits, recapitalization, or conversions are deemed to have been acquired when the original security was purchased from the issuer.[34] Similarly, securities which have been deposited with a pledgee in the course of a bona fide pledge are deemed to have been acquired by the pledgee on the date that they were originally acquired by the pledgor unless there is no recourse against the pledgor, in which case the pledgee's date of acquisition starts the two year period running anew.[35] When the securities in question have been purchased with a promissory note or pursuant to an installment contract, the two-year holding period does not begin to run until full payment has been made.[36] Full payment for the securities will be found to have taken place when either there is full recourse against the securities' purchaser or the obligation is secured by collateral, other than the securities purchased, having a value at least equal to that of the securities purchased.[37] The rule further provides that securities acquired by gift (from persons other than the issuer) are treated as having been acquired by the donee on the date that the donor acquired them.[38] Once the donor ceases to be an affiliate, however, so do the non-affiliate donees.[39] Additionally, securities acquired from the settlor of a trust or

34. 17 C.F.R. § 230.144(d)(4)(A), (B). *See also, e.g.,* National Securities Network, Inc. [1990 Transfer Binder] Fed.Sec.L.Rep. ¶ 79,437 (SEC No Action Letter available Jan. 5, 1990) (holding period for shares acquired in a merger begins to run from date that the old shares were surrendered). *Cf.* Jay E. Bothwick, Esq., [1991–1992 Transfer Binder] Fed.Sec.L.Rep. (CCH) ¶ 76,010 (SEC No Action Letter June 12, 1991) (pro rata transfers of restricted securities from limited partnership to limited partners does not trigger a new holding period).

35. 17 C.F.R. § 230.144(d)(4)(D). *Compare* SEC v. Guild Films Co., 279 F.2d 485 (2d Cir.1960), *cert. denied* 364 U.S. 819, 81 S.Ct. 52, 5 L.Ed.2d 49 (1960) which is discussed in § 4.24 *supra*. *See* Heuter, The Plight of the Pledgee Under Rule 144, 3 Sec.Reg.L.J. 111 (1975). *See* In re Sovran Financial Corp., [1984–85 Transfer Binder] Fed.Sec.L.Rep. (CCH) ¶ 77,850 (SEC No Action Letter Nov. 5, 1984) (applying the two-year holding period from the date the pledgor acquired the securities). *See also, e.g.,* One Fine Corp., 25 Sec.Reg. & L.Rep. (BNA) 567 (SEC No Action Letter avail. April 1, 1993) (a bona fide pledge did not expose a pledgee to underwriter status where there is no public market for the stock in question and thus it is unlikely that a "distribution" would occur); Charles Schwab Corp. [1991 Transfer Binder] Fed.Sec.L.Rep. (CCH) ¶ 96,011 (SEC No Action Letter June 7, 1991).

36. 17 C.F.R. § 230.144(d)(2).

37. *Id.* The SEC has opined that a pledge of borrowed property and an unconditional bank guarantee satisfy the collateral requirements of Rule 144(d)(2)(B). In re DH Technology Corp., 16 Sec.Reg. & L.Rep. (BNA) 1849 (SEC No Action Letter Nov. 8, 1984).

38. 17 C.F.R. § 230.144(d)(4)(E). *See, e.g.,* Michael P. Coleman and Coleman Charitable Foundation, Inc., 26 Sec. Reg. & L.Rep. (BNA) 110 (SEC No Action Letter available Dec. 29, 1994) (foundation was able to take advantage of tacking where issuer's C.E.O. donated 3.6% of the issuer's stock to a charitable foundation that he had set up). Rule 144's donor-donee tacking provisions have been said to apply to an employee's receipt of a stock bonus. First Central Financial Corp., 19 Sec.Reg. & L.Rep. (BNA) 464 (SEC No Action Letter March 12, 1987).

Ordinarily a gift will not be considered a sale within the definition of section 2(3); 15 U.S.C.A. § 77b(3). *See* § 5.1 *infra*. However, when there is a benefit to the issuer, such as the creation of a public market, a sale might be found to exist. *See, e.g.,* In the Matter of Capital General Corp., Sec. Act Rel. No. 33–7008, [1993 Transfer Binder] Fed. Sec. L. Rep. (CCH) ¶ 85,223 (SEC July 23, 1993).

39. *See* Sec.Act Rel.No. 33–6099, Item 12 (Aug. 2, 1979).

held by a deceased's estate are considered to have been acquired by the trust or estate on the date that they were first acquired by the settlor or the deceased.[40]

In 1990, the Commission made a significant change in the computation of the two-year holding period. Under Rule 144(g)[41] there is a tacking of holding periods for successive holders who are not affiliates of the issuer. This change does not provide a new exemption to the nonaffiliate who sells his or her shares,[42] but it does shorten the holding period for the nonaffiliated downstream purchaser. An additional consequence of the 1990 amendments to the holding period computation is that a put option or short position in the securities of the same class will not toll the holding period since unless there has been an intervening resale starting the period running anew, the holding period is defined in terms of two years from the date of the original issuance or private purchase.[43]

Questions concerning Rule 144's two-year holding period have arisen in the context of corporate reorganizations. When a corporate reorganization results in the exchange of Rule 144 stock for other stock, the holding period can be tacked provided that the exchange is with existing securities holders who retain their proportional ownership interest.[44] Presumably, the same would be true when a corporation holding Rule 144 stock in another entity distributes that stock to its shareholders as a stock dividend or in dissolution. The Commission has indicated that stock acquired in a merger where the fairness has been passed upon by a state agency is exempt under section 3(a)(10)[45] and the stock received by the shareholders is not restricted stock under Rule 144.[46] The shareholders' holding period in a merger exempt under section 3 (as opposed to section 4(2)) is to be determined by Rule 145(d)(2),[47] and the

40. 17 C.F.R. § 230.144(d)(4)(F), (G).

41. 17 C.F.R. § 230.144(g).

42. The sale by the nonaffiliate may, however, be exempt under Rule 144A or the so-called section "4(1½)" exemption. *See* § 4.26.1 *infra*.

43. Jesse Brill, 22 Sec.Reg. & L.Rep. (BNA) 1054 (SEC No Action Letter available June 8, 1990).

44. *See, e.g.*, Morgan, Olmstead, Kennedy & Gardner Capital Corp., [1987–88 Transfer Binder] Fed.Sec.L.Rep. (CCH) ¶ 78,672 (SEC No Action Letter Dec. 8, 1987). *See also, e.g.*, The Presley Companies, [1992 Transfer Binder] Fed.Sec.L.Rep. (CCH) ¶ 76,2444 (SEC No Action Letter March 30, 1992) (shareholders receiving stock in connection with reorganization of existing holding company could use the acquisition date of the former shares for purposes of computing the holding period). In the event that a merger does not qualify for tacking of the Rule 144 holding period, the two year period for the newly acquired shares begins to run from full payment on those shares which occurs with the surrender of the shares that were given in exchange. National Securities Network, Inc. [1990 Transfer Binder] Fed.Sec.L.Rep. ¶ 79,437 (SEC No Action Letter available Jan. 5, 1990). *But see* Homeowners Marketing Services, Inc., 20 Sec.Reg. & L.Rep. (BNA) 1227 (SEC No Action Letter avail. July 14, 1988) (refusing to issue no action response).

45. 15 U.S.C.A. § 77c(a)(10). *See* § 4.11 *supra*.

46. Borland Finance Co., 19 Sec.Reg. & L.Rep. (BNA) 1769 (SEC No Action Letter Oct. 10, 1987).

47. 17 C.F.R. § 230.145. *See* § 5.2 *infra*.

shareholders are not permitted to tack on the Rule 144 holding period of the disappearing corporation's stock.[48]

Option writing strategies can also have implications for the Rule 144 two-year holding period. For example, the SEC has indicated that although option writing strategies will not toll the holding period, the writing of call options may constitute a sale.[49] In determining when the holding period begins to run when an option is exercised, the Commission will, among other things, look to the question of whether the investor has in fact had an investment risk with regard to the options in question.[50]

Similarly, questions have arisen in the context of employee plans with delayed vesting. The Commission staff has taken the position, for example, that if stock is allocated to an employee pursuant to an employment compensation plan, the two-year period begins to run upon the allocation even if the plan does not vest until the employee continues in employment for a specified period of time.[51]

Even beyond the expiration of the two year holding period, Rule 144 places restrictions on all sales made by affiliates in reliance on the rule. Rule 144(e)(1) permits sales by affiliates provided that the aggregate amount sold, combined with all sales of other securities of the same class (whether restricted or not) sold by the affiliate within the preceding three months, does not exceed the specified volume limit. The rule places a limit of (i) one percent of the shares of that class outstanding as shown by the most recent report of the issuer, or (ii) the average weekly reported volume of trading in such securities on national exchanges and/or reported through the consolidated transaction reporting system, or any automated quotation system of a registered securities association such as NASDAQ.[52] As a result of this provision, a substantial amount of secondary sales may take place following ninety days after an initial public offering.[53] As is discussed more fully in the preceding section,[54]

48. Borland Finance Co., 19 Sec.Reg. & L.Rep. (BNA) 1769 (SEC No Action Letter Oct. 10, 1987).

49. Forstmann–Leff Associates, Inc., 21 Sec.Reg. & L.Rep. (BNA) 367 (SEC No Action Letter available Feb. 16, 1989). The holder of Rule 144 stock wrote call options while simultaneously purchasing put options (this option strategy is sometimes referred to as purchasing synthetic stock). The request for no action relief indicated that on the expiration date the shareholder could either settle the put option or settle the call option by purchasing stock in the public market but that he would not be selling his restricted stock (which was expressly excluded from the call option).

50. *See, e.g.,* Bell Sports Holding Co., [1992 Transfer Binder] Fed.Sec.L.Rep. (CCH) ¶ 76,250 (SEC No Action Letter May 19, 1992) (permitting tacking of the holding period upon the exercise of one class of options where there was a cashless exercise but not for two other classes because the grant of an employee stock option did not create an investment risk).

51. Technology Solutions Co., [1993–1994 Transfer Binder] Fed. Sec. L. Rep. (CCH)¶ 76,856 (SEC No Action Letter Jan. 7, 1994).

52. 17 C.F.R. § 230.144(e)(1). NASDAQ (the National Association of Securities Dealers' Automated Quotation system) is discussed in ¶ 10.2 *infra.*

53. Once it has completed a registered public offering, the issuer becomes subject to the 1934 Act periodic reporting requirements. Section 15(d) of the 1934 Act, 15 U.S.C.A. § 78o(d). *See* § 9.3 *infra.*

54. *See* § 4.25 *supra.*

the likelihood of a large amount of such secondary sales can lead to disclosure issues in connection with the registered offering and conceivably even an integration problem, unless there are contractual restrictions against such secondary sales.[55]

Once the two-year holding period has expired, the same volume limitations on sales within a three month period apply to nonaffiliates. However, Rule 144(k) eliminates the resale restrictions when the securities have been beneficially owned by the nonaffiliate for at least three years prior to their sale.[56] Furthermore, under subsection (f),[57] all transactions by either affiliates or nonaffiliates made in reliance upon the rule must be made in "brokers' transactions" as defined in section 4(4) of the Act,[58] or in transactions directly with a "market maker." [59] The person selling the security under Rule 144 may not solicit or arrange for solicitations of offers to buy securities in anticipation of the transaction, nor may he or she make any payment in connection with the offer or sale to any person other than the broker executing the transaction.[60]

Rule 144(g)[61] further defines the scope of section 4(4)'s brokers' transaction exemption for the purposes of the rule. The broker's activity must be limited to the execution of the order or orders to sell as agent for the person selling. In order for Rule 144 to apply, the broker may receive no more than the usual and customary broker's commission, and may neither solicit nor arrange for customers' orders to buy the securities that would be sold in a transaction.[62] There are three exceptions to Rule 144(g)'s ban on solicitation: (1) the broker may contact other dealers who have indicated interest in the securities within the past sixty days, (2) he or she may make inquiries to other customers who have shown an "unsolicited bona fide interest" in the securities within the past ten business days, and (3) the broker may publish bid and asked quotations in an inter-dealer quotation system "provided that such quotations are incident to the maintenance of a bona fide inter-dealer market for the security for the broker's own account. * * * "[63] The final prerequisite under subsection (g) is that the broker must make a reasonable inquiry as to whether the person for whose account the

55. If there is a substantial volume of these unregistered secondary sales, they might be integrated into the initial offering even though they fall within Rule 144(e)'s volume limitations. The integration doctrine is discussed in § 4.29 *infra*.

56. 17 C.F.R. § 230.144(k).

57. 17 C.F.R. § 230.144(f).

58. 15 U.S.C.A. § 77d(4). *See* § 4.23 *supra*.

59. Market makers are dealers who qualify to maintain a trading market for over-the-counter securities. They will frequently be placing orders for their own account. *See* § 10.3 *infra*. The term is defined in section 3(a)(38) of the 1934 Exchange Act, 15 U.S.C.A. § 78c(a)(38).

60. 17 C.F.R. § 230.144(f).

61. 17 C.F.R. § 230.144(g).

62. *Id.*

63. *Id.*

securities are being sold is an underwriter or whether the transaction is part of a distribution.[64] Although subsection (g) was adopted solely pursuant to Rule 144, its terms are certainly helpful by way of analogy to anyone planning a transaction in reliance upon a section 4(4) exemption.[65]

In addition to compliance with all of the foregoing requirements of the rule, subsection (h)[66] requires filing of notice of most Rule 144 sales. Form 144 must be completed whenever the amount of securities sold in reliance on the rule within any three month period is more than five hundred shares, or the aggregate sales price is more than ten thousand dollars. Three copies of the form must be filed at the Commission's principal office in Washington, D.C., and if the securities are traded on any national exchange a copy of the notice must also be given to the principal exchange. Form 144 must be signed by the person for whose account the securities are sold, and must be sent for filing concurrently with the placing of an order to make the sale. Rule 144(h)'s notice and filing requirements do not apply to non-affiliate transactions made more than three years after the non-affiliate acquired the shares, provided the conditions of subsection (k) are satisfied.[67]

It is, of course, possible for an issuer to restrict resales beyond the time periods set out in Rule 144. The enforceability of such a provision, like any other contractual limitations, will be determined by the applicable state law of contracts and stock transfers.[68]

As discussed more fully in the next section, in 1990 the SEC adopted a new exemption for downstream sales to qualified institutional investors. As is the case with Rule 144, Rule 144A[69] classifies certain offers and sales as not involving a distribution, so that persons participating in such offers and sales are not considered "underwriters."

§ 4.26.1   The Section "4(1½)" Exemption for Downstream Sales; Rule 144A

As discussed in previous sections of this treatise,[1] section 4(1)'s exemption for transactions not involving an issuer, underwriter, or a

---

64. A similar duty of investigation is imposed under the statutory exemption. Accordingly, a broker must take reasonable steps to assure that the transaction does not involve a control person and-or restricted stock. *See, e.g.,* In the Matter of Transactions in Securities of Laser Arms Corporation by Certain Broker–Dealers, Sec.Exch.Act Rel. No. 34–28878 (SEC Feb. 14, 1991); In re Robert G. Leigh, [1990 Transfer Binder] Fed.Sec.L.Rep. (CCH) ¶ 84,700 (Feb. 1, 1990), and § 4.25 *supra.*

65. 15 U.S.C.A. § 77d(4). The section 4(4) exemption is discussed in § 4.23 *supra.*

66. 17 C.F.R. § 230.144(h).

67. *Id.*

68. *See* Catherines v. Copytele, Inc. 602 F.Supp. 1019 (E.D.N.Y.1985).

69. 17 C.F.R. § 230.144A. *See, e.g.,* Jeffrey B. Tevis, Asset–Backed Securities: Secondary Market Implications of SEC Rule 144A and Regulation S, 23 Pac.L.J. 135 (1991).

§ 4.26.1

1. *See* §§ 4.23–4.26 *supra.*

dealer[2] and section 4(4)'s exemption for unsolicited brokers' transactions[3] both provide avenues to exempt transactions made by persons other than an issuer. In contrast, section 4(2)'s nonpublic offering exemption[4] is limited by its terms to "transactions by an issuer"[5] and thus is not available to downstream sales.[6] The rationale underlying the section 4(2) exemption seems to support a comparable exemption for downstream sales by nonissuers.

As explained previously, two primary elements of the section 4(2) exemption are: (1) the purchaser's access to current information about the issuer and (2) the purchaser's ability to evaluate that information.[7] In addition, in order to qualify for the section 4(2) exemption, the issuer is not permitted to engage in a general solicitation, but rather must target the offers to a discrete group of offerees.[8]

Basis for the Section 4(1½) Exemption

As observed above, the rationale underlying the nonpublic offering exemption for issues would appear to apply equally to secondary transactions. Conceptually, a sale by a person other than the issuer that meets the informational, purchaser qualification and other requirements of section 4(2) should similarly be exempt.[9]

Consider, for example, a private placement by Issuer Co. where S

---

2.   15 U.S.C.A. § 77d(1).

3.   15 U.S.C.A. § 77d(4).

4.   15 U.S.C.A. § 77d(2). *See* § 4.21 *supra.*

5.   15 U.S.C.A. § 77d(2). *See also* section 4(6) (15 U.S.C.A. § 77d(6)) which exempts issuer transactions not exceeding $5,000,000, provided that the offering is made only to accredited investors. *See* 4.20 *supra.*

6.   The SEC has recognized this statutory limitation on the scope of section 4(2)'s nonpublic offering exemption. *See* Preliminary Notes to Regulation D, 17 C.F.R. §§ 230.500–230.506; Karl Ehmer, Inc. (SEC No Action Letter, available May 9, 1975). In some of its no action letters predating Regulation D, the Commission's staff indicated that the section 4(2) exemption could be used for downstream resales by persons not affiliated with the issuer. *See* Mary Elizabeth Sealander (SEC No Action Letter available Sept. 19, 1977); Colorado & Western Properties, Inc. (SEC No Action Letter available July 14, 1977); Gralla Publications, Inc. (SEC No Action Letter available Feb. 18, 1977); Whitaker Corp. (SEC No Action Letter available April 30, 1976); *see also* ABA Committee on Federal Regulation of Securities, The Section "4(1½)" Phenomenon: Private Resales of Restricted Securities, 34 Bus.Law.1961, 1971 n. 47 (1979) (hereinafter ABA Report).

7.   *See, e.g.,* SEC v. Ralston Purina Co., 346 U.S. 119, 73 S.Ct. 981, 97 L.Ed. 1494 (1953).

8.   The *Ralston Purina* decision (footnote 7 *supra*) talks in terms of offeree access to information and offeree ability to evaluate the investment. *See* the authorities discussed in § 4.21 *supra. Cf.* SEC Rule 506's safe harbor which requires that there not have been a general solicitation of purchasers. 17 C.F.R. § 230.506. *See* 17 C.F.R. § 230.502(c) and the discussion in §§ 4.17, 4.22 *supra.*

9.   As explained by the Commission, the section 4(1½) exemption, is a hybrid exemption not specifically provided for in the 1933 Act but clearly within its intended purpose. The exemption basically would permit affiliates to make private sales of securities held by them so long as some of the established criteria for sales under both section 4(1) and section 4(2) are satisfied. Sec.Act Rel. No. 33–6188 n. 178, 1 Fed.Sec.L.Rep. (CCH) ¶ 1051 (Feb. 1, 1980).

and B both would qualify as purchasers for a section 4(2)[10] offering. Assume further that at the time of the offering S had adequate funds but B did not and S purchased stock pursuant to the section 4(2) exemption. One year later, S decides to sell her stock and learns that B now has sufficient cash on hand. Since the presumptive two-year holding period has not yet passed, S cannot take advantage of section 4(1)'s safe harbor—Rule 144.[11] Similarly, she cannot be certain that she has satisfied the requirements of the section 4(1) exemption. Assuming that the issuer is willing to make current information available to B, there would seem no reason to require registration of S's sale to B as the only alternative to waiting until Rule 144's two-year holding period has elapsed.[12]

Since, in the foregoing example, the issuer could validly issue shares directly to B as a qualified private placement purchaser, why should S not be able to take advantage of a similar exemption? The answer to this question is that, as discussed above, the statutory language of section 4(2) is limited to transactions by an issuer. It can be argued, however, that section 4(1) would support such an exemption. In the above example, S clearly is not an issuer or a dealer, so in order to qualify for the exemption, she must be able to demonstrate that she is not an underwriter. As discussed in an earlier section, an underwriter is someone who assists an issuer during a distribution or someone who has purchased securities from an issuer with a view towards distribution.[13] It would appear that a downstream sale which complies with the requirements of section 4(2) is not properly classified as a distribution[14] and as such the seller is not properly qualified as an underwriter under section 2(11)'s definition. Accordingly, the proper basis of any exemption for the downstream seller in the foregoing example is section 4(1); while the requirements that must be satisfied may be derived from the parameters of the section 4(2) exemption for issuers.[15] Unfortunately,

10. *See, e.g.,* SEC v. Ralston Purina Co., 346 U.S. 119, 73 S.Ct. 981, 97 L.Ed. 1494 (1953) and the other authorities discussed in § 4.21 *supra.*

11. 17 C.F.R. § 230.144. *See* § 4.26 *supra.*

12. Even after the expiration of the two-year holding period, there may be volume limitations on S's resales. Thus, for example Rule 144(e) limits resales to a certain percentage of the outstanding shares or average trading volume. 17 C.F.R. § 230.144(e). *See* § 4.26 *supra.* These resale restrictions do not apply to nonaffiliates of the issuer who have held their shares for at least three years. 17 C.F.R. § 230.144(k). However, the volume limitations on resales remain applicable so long as the seller is an affiliate.

13. 15 U.S.C.A. § 77b(11). *See* § 4.24 *supra.*

14. As the SEC explained long ago, " 'Distribution', although not expressly defined in the Act, comprises the entire process by which in the course of a public offering a block of securities is dispersed and ultimately comes to rest in the hands of the investing public." In re Oklahoma–Texas Trust, 2 S.E.C. 764, 769 (1937), *affirmed* 100 F.2d 888 (10th Cir.1939). The concept of what is a distribution is discussed in § 4.23 *supra.* The concept of distribution is also considered in the context of Rule 10b-6's prohibition on participants' purchases during a distribution. 17 C.F.R. § 240.10b-6; *see* § 6.1 *infra.*

15. *See* ABA Report, *supra* footnote 6 at 1970–71; Carl W. Schneider, Section 4(1½)— Private Resales of Restricted or Control Securities, 49 Ohio St.L.J. 501 (1988); Christopher D. Olander & Margaret S. Jacks, The Section 4(1½) Exemption—Reading Between the Lines of the Securities Act of 1933, 15 Sec.Reg.L.J. 339 (1988).

the SEC no action letters that have been cited as the basis for the section 4(1½) exemption do not provide a consistent statement of what is necessary to satisfy the exemption.[16]

In the situation presented by the example above, there is considerable support for what has become known as the section 4(1½) exemption. Although not expressly contained in the statute nor formally adopted by the Commission,[17] support for the so-called section 4(1½) exemption can be found in SEC no action letters,[18] SEC interpretative releases,[19] the courts' decisions,[20] and the commentators' writings.[21] The absence of a formal SEC rule or interpretative release explaining the exemption means that it is difficult to ascertain the precise scope of the exemption. To a large extent, the parameters of exemption have developed through no action letters and commentators' analysis.[22]

The SEC has recognized that the section 4(1½) exemption is available to affiliates of the issuer[23] and should equally apply to nonaffiliates.[24] There are, of course, some limitations on the use of the exemption. Thus, for example, too many sales in reliance on the exemption within a short period of time might well result in the finding of a distribution.[25] Although the section 4(1½) exemption does not appear to be as restrictive as Rule 144's volume limitations on resales of restricted securities,[26] the magnitude of the transaction and the number of downstream purchasers are factors in considering the availability of the section 4(1½) exemp-

---

16. ABA Report, *supra* footnote 6; Olander & Jacks, *supra* footnote 15 at 353.

17. It has been suggested that the Commission issue an interpretative release that would better define the parameters of the section 4(1½) exemption. Olander & Jacks, *supra* footnote 15.

18. *E.g.*, Sidney Stahl (SEC No Action Letter available April 23, 1981); Illinois Capital Investment Corp. (SEC No Action Letter available May 17, 1976); Elwill Development, Ltd. (SEC No Action Letter available Jan. 18, 1975).

19. Sec.Act Rel.No. 33–6188 n. 178, 1 Fed.Sec.L.Rep. (CCH) 1051 (SEC Feb. 1, 1980); Sec.Act Rel.No. 33–5452, [1973–74 Transfer Binder] Fed.Sec.L.Rep. (CCH) ¶ 79,633 at p. 83,698 (SEC Feb. 1, 1974).

20. *E.g.*, Stoppelman v. Owens, 1984 WL 609, Fed.Sec.L.Rep. ¶ 91,511 (D.D.C.1984) (Unpublished Case); Neuwirth Investment Fund Ltd. v. Swanton, 422 F.Supp. 1187 (S.D.N.Y.1975); Value Line Income Fund, Inc. v. Marcus, [1964–66 Transfer Binder] Fed.Sec.L.Rep. (CCH) ¶ 91,523 (S.D.N.Y.1965). *Cf.* Acme Propane, Inc. v. Tenexco, Inc., 844 F.2d 1317 (7th Cir.1988) (indicating in passing that the section 4(1½) exemption might be available).

21. *See* ABA Report, *supra* footnote 6; Olander & Jacks, *supra* footnote 15; Carl W. Schneider, Section 4(1½)—Private Resales of Restricted or Control Securities, 49 Ohio St.L.J. 501 (1988); Robert B. Titus, Secondary Trading—Stepchild of the Securities Laws, 20 Conn.L.Rev. 595 (1988); Comment,—Reinterpreting the "Section 4(1½)" Exemption From Securities Registration: The Investor Protection Requirement, 6 U.S.F.L.Rev. 681 (1982).

22. *See, e.g.*, ABA Report, *supra* footnote 6; Olander & Jacks, *supra* footnote 15.

23. Sec.Act Rel.No. 33–6188 n. 178, 1 Fed.Sec.L.Rep. (CCH) 1051 (SEC Feb. 1, 1980); Sidney Stahl (SEC No Action Letter available April 23, 1981).

24. *See* Olander & Jacks, *supra* footnote 15 at 361–63.

25. *See* ABA Report, *supra* footnote 6 at 1972. *See also* § 4.23, *supra*.

26. 17 C.F.R. § 230.144(e); *see* footnote 12 *supra* and § 4.26 *supra*.

tion.[27] As discussed more fully below, a general solicitation of purchasers that is not permitted under section 4(2)[28] will render the section 4(1½) exemption unavailable. Similarly, the absence of qualified purchasers or available adequate current information about the issuer would preclude application of the exemption.[29]

In a recent decision, the Eighth Circuit explained that the section 4(1½) exemption is merely an application of the section 4(1) exemption for transactions not involving an issuer, underwriter, or dealer.[30] The court explained that the section 4(1) exemption for private resales depends upon a finding that distribution has taken place and that the definition of distribution is coextensive with section 4(2)'s non-public offering exemption.[31]

Elements of the Section 4(1½) Exemption

The section 4(1½) exemption is most useful for purchasers of securities sold in a private placement who cannot rely on section 4(1)[32] or SEC Rule 144.[33] There are a number of reasons that these exemptions may not be available. The most likely reason for not being able to rely on these exemptions is that the seller has not held the securities for a sufficiently long period so as to preclude a finding that he or she purchased the securities with a view towards distribution. Another possibility is that the seller is a control person who cannot meet Rule 144 volume limitations on resale.[34]

What, then, are the elements of the section 4(1½) exemption? The elements of the section 4(1½) exemption are as follows. First, the purchaser must have access to the current information about the issuer

---

27. It has been pointed out that "a relatively large amount of securities to be sold may be a factor that influences the SEC's Staff to deny a no action position." Carl W. Schneider, Section 4(1½)—Private Resales of Restricted or Control Securities, 49 Ohio St.L.J. 501, 506, 511 (1988). Mr. Schneider also suggests that the number of permissible purchasers may be less than that allowed by Rule 506. *Id.* at 506.

28. *See* text accompanying footnotes 43–44 *infra* and § 4.21 *supra*.

29. *See* text accompanying footnotes 35–42 *infra* and § 4.21 *supra*.

30. Ackerberg v. Johnson, 892 F.2d 1328 (8th Cir.1989).

31. 892 F.2d at 1335 n. 6:

While the term "§ 4(1½) exemption" has been used in the secondary literature . . ., the term does not properly refer to an exemption other than § 4(1). Rather, the term merely expresses the statutory relationship between § 4(1) and § 4(2). That is, the definition of underwriter, found in § 2(11) depends on the existence of a distribution, which in turn is considered the equivalent of a public offering. Section 4(2) contains the exemption for transactions not involving a public offering. Any analysis of whether a party is an underwriter for purposes of § 4(1) necessarily entails an inquiry into whether the transaction involves a public offering. While the term "4(1½) exemption" adequately expresses this relationship, it is clear that the exemption for private resales of restricted securities is § 4(1). We need not go beyond the statute to reach this conclusion.

Cf. Leiter v. Kuntz, 655 F.Supp. 725, 727–29 (D.Utah 1987) (factual issue as to whether control person was engaged in a distribution).

32. 15 U.S.C.A. § 77d(1). *See* § 4.23 *supra*.

33. 17 C.F.R. § 230.144. *See* footnotes 11, 12 *supra* and accompanying text.

34. *See* footnote 27 *supra* and accompanying text.

similar to the types of information that would be made available through a registration statement.[35] This requirement emanates from section 4(2), and, in fact has been characterized as the most important of the section 4(2) requirements.[36] As discussed in an earlier section, while accredited investor status may eliminate the need for offeree and purchaser qualification, it does not eliminate the access to information requirement.[37] Thus, although the issuer is not involved in the transaction directly, the issuer's willingness to make current information available is of the utmost importance in a section 4(1½) transaction.

Second, in addition to the requirement that a purchaser have access to current information about the issuer, the purchaser must meet section 4(2) qualifications. Hence, the purchaser must be sufficiently sophisticated to qualify for the section 4(2) exemption.[38] The applicable case law under section 4(2) has described the purchaser's qualifications in terms of sophistication, ability to understand the risks of the investment, and the suitability of the investment for that particular investor.[39] This definition would include institutional investors as well as experienced individuals.[40] Additionally, Regulation D provides that an unsophisticated investor can qualify as a section 4(2) purchaser through a purchaser representative having the requisite sophistication and expertise.[41] Rule 506 further provides that where the purchasers are accredited investors, the knowledge and sophistication requirements need not be satisfied.[42] It would appear that the same tests should carry over to the section 4(1½) exemption.

Third, any general solicitation of purchasers will destroy the section

---

35. *See, e.g.,* SEC v. Ralston Purina Co., 346 U.S. 119, 73 S.Ct. 981, 97 L.Ed. 1494 (1953); Doran v. Petroleum Management Corp., 545 F.2d 893 (5th Cir.1977), *appeal after remand* 576 F.2d 91 (5th Cir.1978).

36. *See* Schneider *supra* footnote 27.

37. *See* the discussion in § 4.22 *infra.*

38. This requirement has been questioned as a matter of policy. *See* Schneider *supra* footnote 27 at 514, n. 54. However, to the extent that section 4(2) has purchaser qualification requirements, those requirements would seem equally applicable to a section 4(1½) transaction.

39. *E.g.,* SEC v. Ralston Purina Co., 346 U.S. 119, 73 S.Ct. 981, 97 L.Ed. 1494 (1953) and the other authorities discussed in § 4.21 *supra.* It has been suggested that there is support for the proposition that purchaser qualification is not necessary. *See* Schneider *supra* footnote 27 at 509, n. 41. However, this view is based on circuit court dictum and disregards the language of the Supreme Court in *Ralston Purina* as well as the Commission's general position. *See* § 4.21 *supra.*

40. Presumably, section 2(15)'s concept of an accredited investor (15 U.S.C.A. § 77b(15)) which is incorporated into Regulation D as well, would operate as an alternative basis for purchaser qualification for the section 4(1½) exemption.

41. Rule 506 recognizes that the sophistication requirement can be satisfied through a purchaser representative. 17 C.F.R. § 230.506(b)(ii). *See also* 17 C.F.R. § 230.501(h) (definition of purchaser representative).

42. 17 C.F.R. § 230.506(b)(2)(ii). Accredited investor is defined in Rule 501(a) to include institutional investors as well as individuals having a net worth of over $1,000,000 or annual income in excess of $200,000 as well as married couples having a combined net worth over $1,000,000 or combined annual income over $300,000. 17 C.F.R. § 230.501(a). *See* §§ 4.17, 4.20, 4.22 *supra.*

4(2) exemption[43] and thus would be equally fatal to the section 4(1½) exemption.[44] Fourth, if too many section 4(1½) sales take place within a given time frame, there is the possibility that a distribution will be found to exist.[45] In such a case, the seller could be said to have been participating in a distribution, thus rendering the exemption unavailable.[46]

One other aspect of the section 4(1½) exemption deserves mention. While a transaction made in reliance on the section 4(1½) exemption must bear all the indicia of a section 4(2) offering by an issuer, a significant difference is the fact that the proceeds from a section 4(1½) transaction do not go to the issuer but rather to the selling shareholder(s). As discussed in an earlier section,[47] when engaging in registered secondary distributions, drafters of applicable disclosures must make it clear that the proceeds do not inure to the issuer's benefit. Accordingly, it follows that in any transaction based upon the section 4(1½) exemption, it should be clearly explained that the proceeds go to the selling shareholders. It has also been suggested that a selling shareholder who is an insider or control person may have certain additional disclosure obligations.[48]

There is a general consensus that the above-mentioned criteria are relevant in determining the availability of the section 4(1½) exemption. Since the exemption is not based on either a specific statutory provision or SEC rule, it does not provide the degree of certainty generally sought when planning an exempt transaction. However, in absence of authority denying the existence of the exemption, it seems safe to rely on its existence in light of the consensus among the commentators, practicing bar, and the Commission.

---

43. *See* the discussion in § 4.22 *infra.* For this purpose a general solicitation is to be equated with a public offering and may be permitted if the securities are eventually sold to a single purchaser or a very limited group. *See* Schneider *supra* footnote 27 at 507, relying on Madison Plaza Ass'n (SEC No Action Letter avail. Jan. 8, 1988). For a critique of the ban on general solicitation, *see* Patrick Daugherty, Rethinking the Ban on General Solicitation, 38 Emory L.J. 67 (1989).

44. It has been pointed out that while the SEC has issued favorable no action letters in sales of large amounts of stock, involving "a large number of offerees, including public auctions or advertising, so long as the entire block of securities is to be sold to a single purchaser or very limited group." *See* Schneider *supra* footnote 27 at 507, relying on Republic Bank of Oklahoma City (SEC No Action Letter avail. Dec. 1, 1986); Lapeer County Bank & Trust Co. (SEC No Action Letter avail. Oct. 27, 1986); United Properties of America, [1978 Transfer Binder] Fed.Sec.L.Rep. (CCH) ¶ 81,627 (SEC No Action Letter June 9, 1978); David E. Wise, [1976–77 Transfer Binder] Fed.Sec.L.Rep. (CCH) ¶ 80,738 (SEC No Action Letter Sept. 17, 1976); American Telecommunications Corp. (SEC No Action Letter avail. June 25, 1976); New York Terrace Lessee Venture (SEC No Action Letter Dec. 11, 1975); Banner Publishers, Inc. (SEC No Action Letter Nov. 14, 1975); Illinois Capital Investment Corp. (SEC No Action Letter avail. April 14, 1975); Adventure Campers, Inc. (SEC No Action Letter avail. Jan. 10, 1974).

45. *See* footnotes 14, 27 *supra* and accompanying text.

46. *See* § 4.23 *supra.*

47. *See* § 3.7 *supra.*

48. The extent of the seller's disclosure obligations "should depend upon [his] status as an insider and also upon his access to information that is unavailable to the purchaser." Schneider *supra* footnote 27 at 507.

The Section 4(1½) Exemption and the Integration Doctrine

One final point that deserves mention is the problem of integration with other transactions. As discussed more fully in another section,[49] a transaction which in form meets the requirements of an exemption may be integrated with other related transactions for the purpose of rendering the exemption unavailable. Thus when planning a section 4(1½) transaction, the planner should be sure that it is not part of a plan of financing in which other parts of that plan will limit or deny the availability of the exemption. Integration may be particularly worrisome in cases involving issuer private placement sales or registered offerings around the time of the private resales.

Rule 144A

In the fall of 1988, the SEC proposed Rule 144A to permit downstream resales of restricted securities to institutional investors.[50] Proposed Rule 144A, as is the case with Rule 144,[51] classified certain transactions as not involving a distribution, so that sellers of such restricted securities would thus not qualify as "underwriters". As originally proposed, the rule would have defined three types of institutional investors. Tier one consisted of those institutions having assets in excess of one hundred million dollars; tiers two and three consisted of accredited investors,[52] except for individuals and trusts. These tiers would have made the rule broader than it is today; however, the Commission elected to begin with a narrower version of the rule, leaving open the possibility of future expansion. After the comment period, when Rule 144A was reproposed the three tiers were dropped. It was adopted as reproposed.

In April 1990, the SEC adopted Rule 144A in revised form.[53] The rule was conceived in response to the need to better define the scope of

---

49. *See* § 4.29 *infra.*

50. Sec.Act Rel.No. 33–6806, [1988–89 Transfer Binder] Fed.Sec.L.Rep. (CCH) ¶ 84,335 (SEC Oct. 25, 1988). *See* SEC Proposes Rule 144A, Would Ease Resales to Institutional Investors, 20 Sec.Reg. & L.Rep. (BNA) 1624 (Oct. 28, 1988).

51. 17 C.F.R. § 230.144. *See* § 4.26 *supra.*

52. The proposed rule speaks in terms of accredited investors as defined by Regulation D. *See* 17 C.F.R. § 230.501(a) which is discussed in §§ 4.17, 4.20 *supra.* Tier two consisted of resales of "nonfungible" securities; that is, those which are not in a class which is publicly traded. Tier three consisted of securities that are in a class which is publicly traded.

53. 17 C.F.R. § 230.144A. *See* Sec. Act Rel. No. 33–6862, [1989–1990 Transfer Binder] Fed.Sec.L.Rep. ¶ 84,523 (Apr. 23, 1990). *See, e.g.,* Lawrence R. Seidman, SEC Rule 144A: The Rule Heard Around the Globe—Or the Sounds of Silence?, 47 Bus.Law. 333 (1991); Jeffrey B. Tevis, Asset–Backed Securities: Secondary Market Implications of SEC Rule 144A and Regulation S, 23 Pac.L.J. 135 (1991); Note, Increasing United States Investment in Foreign Securities: An Evaluation of SEC Rule 144A, 60 Fordham L.Rev. S179 (1992).

In the summer of 1992, the Commission decided to propose amendments to Rule 144A which would lower the standards for qualified institutional buyers and would thus increase the number of market participants. *See* SEC Agrees to Propose Rule Changes Expanding Shelf Registration, Rule 144A, 24 Sec.Reg. & L.Rep. (BNA) 1059 (July 17, 1992).

The SEC has apparently been satisfied with the operation of Rule 144A and the extent to which it has attracted foreign securities to United States markets. *See* SEC Staff Report

the section 4(1½) exemption—a resale by an individual purchaser to another individual who would have qualified as a purchaser in the original offering. As adopted, however, Rule 144A only deals with resales to qualified institutional investors. What the rule does is to permit unlimited resales of securities that have never been registered under the 1933 Act, so long as all such sales are made to a specific class of large institutional investors.

Rule 144A, like Rule 144, classifies certain offers and sales as not involving a distribution, so that persons participating in such offers and sales are not considered "underwriters" under section 2(11). Essentially, the exemption covers any sale to a "qualified institutional buyer," which is defined as any institution (including insurance companies, investment companies, employee benefit plans, banks, and savings and loan associations) that owns more than $100 million worth of securities of unaffiliated issuers and, in the case of banks and savings and loans, has a net worth of at least $25 million.[54]

In addition to direct transactions among these classes of institutions, the rule also permits securities dealers to participate in transactions, either as purchasers for their own account, provided they themselves own at least $10 million worth of securities of unaffiliated issuers, or as agents for qualified institutions. Indeed, the rule contemplates the formation of an active trading market in Rule 144A securities, in which qualified institutions and dealers can enter bids and offers.

Rule 144A only applies to sales of securities of a class that is *not* listed on a national securities exchange nor traded in the NASDAQ system. In order to avoid minimizing or diluting this requirement, the rule specifies that convertible securities do not constitute a separate class of securities unless they are issued with at least a ten percent conversion premium.[55]

With respect to securities issued by companies subject to the 1934 Act reporting requirements, or by foreign issuers, use of the rule is not conditioned on the availability of any additional information about the issuer. With respect to securities of other issuers, however, the rule is only available if the prospective purchaser has received from the issuer a brief statement of the nature of the issuer's business and certain

---

on Rule 144A, [1993 Transfer Binder] Fed. Sec. L. Rep. (CCH) ¶ 85,208 (SEC Jan. 27, 1993).

54. The SEC thus dropped the three-tiered approach in the original proposal but indicated that, over time, it may decide to expand the scope of qualified purchasers for a Rule 144A exemption.

In deciding whether a purchaser falls within the definition of a qualified institutional buyer, the seller is entitled to rely in good faith on a list of profiles of institutional investors found in a "recognized securities manual." Standard & Poor's Corporation, [1991–1992 Transfer Binder] Fed.Sec.L.Rep. (CCH) ¶ 76,021 (SEC No Action Letter July 8, 1991).

55. 17 C.F.R. § 230.144A(d)(3)(i).

specified financial statements.[56]

Simultaneously with the adoption of Rule 144A, the SEC approved the establishment by the National Association of Securities Dealers (NASD) of a screen-based computer and communication system called PORTAL (Private Offerings, Resales and Trading through Automated Linkages) to facilitate secondary trading of Rule 144A securities. The adoption of Rule 144A and the establishment of the PORTAL system create the potential for an active trading market in foreign securities and in unregistered debt and equity issues of domestic issuers, limited to a designated class of large institutions and dealers. Qualifying offerings of foreign securities to institutional investors may now take advantage of a conditional exemption from Rules 10b–6, 10b–7, and 10b–8 which limit sales by participants during a distribution.[57]

§ 4.27 The Exemption for Certain Dealers' Transactions—Section 4(3)

As noted above,[1] although dealers' transactions are not exempt from registration by virtue of section 4(1),[2] many will be exempt as unsolicited

---

56. 17 C.F.R. § 230.144A(d)(4)(i). The rule further provides that the requirement of reasonably current information will be presumed to be satisfied if there is a balance sheet as of no more than 16 months prior to the date of resale and the balance sheet depicts profit, loss, and retained earnings for the twelve months preceding the date of the balance sheet. To qualify for the presumption, the balance sheet must either be of a date not more than six months prior to the date of resale or, alternatively, be accompanied by a statement of profit, loss, and retained earnings for the period ending no more than six months prior to the resale date. 17 C.F.R. § 230.144A(d)(4)(ii)(A).

This information requirement for non-reporting domestic companies drew a sharp dissent from Commissioner Fleischman. He complained that these requirements would make the rule unavailable to many "emerging growth companies" for whose benefit the rule was supposedly adopted. He also argued that, since sales under the rule can only be made to qualified institutional buyers who are presumed to be able to fend for themselves, the information requirement is unnecessary, noting that under Regulation D, governing initial offerings by issuers, there is no information requirement so long as all sales are made to institutional buyers.

57. Securities Industry Association, [1990–1991 Transfer Binder] Fed.Sec.L.Rep. (CCH) ¶ 79,669 (SEC No Action Letter April 25, 1991). *See also,* SEC Okays Conditional Exemptive Relief for Non–U.S. Offerings, Rights Offers, 23 Sec.Reg. & L.Rep. (BNA) 589 (April 26, 1991). There are six conditions to the exemption. First, in order to qualify for the exemption, the foreign issuer's securities must be currently traded on at least one of five foreign exchanges (International Stock Exchange of the United Kingdom (on the Stock Exchange Automated Quotation System ("SEAQ") or SEAQ International), Montreal Stock Exchange, Paris Stock Exchange, Tokyo Stock Exchange, and the Toronto Stock Exchange). Second, the distribution in question must be one taking place outside the United States. Third, the foreign issuer must have at least one hundred and fifty dollars worth of voting shares held by non-affiliates. Fourth, anyone relying on the exemption must notify the Commission of the transactions. Fifth, the transactions may not involve affiliates of the issuer. Sixth, the foreign issuer must have at least a three year operating history. *See also §§* 6.1, 14.2 *infra.*

§ 4.27

1. § 4.23 *infra.*

2. 15 U.S.C.A § 77d(1). Section 2(12) defines "dealer" very broadly to cover anyone in the business of making securities transactions. 15 U.S.C.A. § 77b(12) ("The term 'dealer' means any person who engaged for all or part of his time, directly or indirectly, as agent, broker, or principal, in the business of offering, buying, selling, or otherwise dealing or trading in securities issued by another person").

brokers' transactions within the meaning of section 4(4).[3] Section 4(3) of the Act[4] exempts still additional dealer transactions from the Act's registration and prospectus delivery requirements. In terms of the number of transactions covered, section 4(3) is probably the most significant of the transaction exemptions. Section 4(3) dispenses with the registration and delivery requirements for all dealers' transactions taking place more than forty days, or in some cases ninety days, after the first date on which the security was offered to the public or after the effective date of the registration statement, whichever is later.[5] This forty or ninety day period is known as the "quiet period". Section 4(3)'s exemption applies both to dealers and to underwriters[6] who are no longer acting as underwriters.

The forty (or ninety) day time period during which a dealer's transactions are *not* exempt under section 4(3)(B) is tolled for any time during which a stop order pursuant to section 8 of the Act[7] is in effect with regard to the registration statement. The forty day period does not apply to first-time issuers who have not previously sold securities pursuant to an effective registration statement; for them the applicable period is ninety rather than forty days after the first sale or effective date of the registration statement. The section also provides that a shorter time period may be established by the Commission as it "may specify by rules and regulations or order."[8]

Since section 4(3)'s dealers' transaction exemption is limited to the prospectus delivery requirements and comes into existence only after the effective date (or bona fide offering date), it has no bearing on prefiling gun-jumping violations of section 5(c)[9] nor upon section 5(a)'s prohibitions against sales prior to the effective date.[10] Similarly, section 4(3) has no bearing upon section 5(b)(1)'s prospectus delivery requirements during the waiting period after filing of the registration statement but

---

3. 15 U.S.C.A. § 77d(4). *See* § 4.23 *supra*. *See also, e.g.,* SEC v. Great Lakes Equities Co., 1990 WL 260587, [1990–1991 Transfer Binder] Fed.Sec.L.Rep. (CCH) ¶ 95,685 (E.D.Mich.1990) (a person who qualified as a "dealer" under section 2(12) was entitled to rely on the section 4(3) exemption).

4. 15 U.S.C.A. § 77d(3).

5. 15 U.S.C.A. § 77d(3)(A), (B). Section 4(3)(A) provides that dealers need not deliver a prospectus more than forty days after the securities were first "bona fide offered to the public". This was intended to cover unregistered offerings and to protect nonparticipating dealers with regard to subsequent transactions. *See, e.g.,* Kubik v. Goldfield, 479 F.2d 472 (3d Cir.1973) (a bona fide offering may occur despite the fact that the offering was not registered and therefore in violation of the 1933 Act); D. Ratner, Securities Regulation—Materials For a Basic Course 64 (3d ed. 1986). In *Kubik, supra,* the court held that appearance of the stock in the over-the-counter "pink sheets" may be sufficient to establish that the stock was "bona fide offered to the public" via an illegal offering.

6. The definition of underwriter is discussed in § 4.24 *supra*. *See* 15 U.S.C.A. § 77b(11).

7. 15 U.S.C.A. § 77h. *See* §§ 2.5 *supra*, 7.1 *infra*.

8. 15 U.S.C.A. § 77d(3)(B). Rule 174 is such a rule. 17 C.F.R. § 230.174; *see* text accompanying footnotes 14–29 *infra*.

9. 15 U.S.C.A. § 77e(c). *See* § 2.3 *supra*.

10. 15 U.S.C.A. § 77e(a). *See* Rule 174, 17 C.F.R. § 230.174, which is discussed below in the text accompanying notes 14–18 *infra*.

prior to the effective date.[11] Accordingly, the dealer's exemption operates only to excuse compliance with section 5(b)(1) and 5(b)(2)'s prospectus delivery requirements[12] during the post-effective period upon expiration of the forty or ninety day period. The vast majority of day-to-day transactions occur more than forty (or ninety) days after the securities were offered to the public. Hence, section 4(3) covers most transactions taking place in the U.S. securities markets.

Section 4(3)(C)[13] further provides that the exemption for dealer transactions does not apply to sales of securities that are either part or all of an unsold allotment to that dealer. This means that regardless of the amount of time that has elapsed since the beginning of the offering, any underwriting activity by a dealer will implicate the prospectus delivery requirements. It is to be noted, however, that once the forty or ninety day period has expired, a dealer, including an underwriter no longer acting as such, can take advantage of the exemption even if another dealer has an unsold allotment.

SEC Rule 174[14] provides an additional exclusion from the prospectus delivery requirements for certain dealer transactions. The rule dispenses with the delivery requirements during the forty day period following the effective date, and during the ninety day period for first time issuers. Rule 174 applies to securities of issuers which prior to the offering are subject to the 1934 Act reporting requirements,[15] as well as to foreign issuers whose securities are traded using American Depositary Receipts that have been registered on Form F–6.[16] Additionally, under Rule 174 the prospectus requirements do not apply to dealers' transactions for all registered offerings that are to be made from "time to time."[17]

As described above, Rule 174's exemption for nonparticipating dealers from the post-effective prospectus delivery period is limited to securities of issuers which, immediately prior to the filing of the registration statement were subject to the 1934 Act's periodic reporting requirements.[18] Thus, the exemption does not apply to first-time issuers or issuers whose securities were not widely held prior to the filing of the registration statement.[19] In 1988, Rule 174 was amended to provide

---

11. 15 U.S.C.A. § 77b(i). *See* § 2.4 *supra.*

12. Section 5(b)(1) requires that any prospectus comply with section 10's statutory prospectus requirements while section 5(b)(2) requires delivery of a section 10(a) prospectus when the securities are delivered for sale. 15 U.S.C.A. § 77e(b)(1), (2), 77j. *See* §§ 2.5, 3.2 *supra.*

13. 15 U.S.C.A. § 77d(3)(C).

14. 17 C.F.R. § 230.174.

15. The 1934 Act registration and reporting requirements are discussed in §§ 9.2, 9.3 *infra.*

16. Private foreign issuers are discussed in § 14.2 *infra.*

17. 17 C.F.R. § 230.174(c). *See* § 3.8 *supra* for a discussion of shelf registration.

18. 17 C.F.R. § 230.174(b).

19. The 1934 Act period reporting requirements are discussed in § 9.2 *infra.*

relief for many of these registrants who have not previously been subject to the 1934 Act's reporting requirements.[20] Under Rule 174(d), the prospectus delivery period for nonparticipating dealers is shortened to twenty five days for dealers (including underwriters no longer acting as such) with regard to securities which, as of the offering date are listed on a national securities exchange or authorized for inclusion in an automated quotation system sponsored by a registered securities association (*i.e.*, NASDAQ).[21] As in the case for the statutory prospectus delivery period for registered offerings,[22] Rule 174's twenty-five day period begins to run from the later of (1) the registration statement's effective date or (2) the first date upon which the security was "bona fide offered to the public."[23] In light of Rule 174(d), the full statutory prospectus delivery period for nonparticipating dealers applies only to securities which are traded through listings in the pink sheets or the NASD electronic bulletin board.[24] It must be remembered, that, as is the case with the other exemptions provided by Rule 174, the shorter twenty-five day prospectus delivery period does not apply to a dealer who is acting as an underwriter.[25]

Rule 174(e) provides that none of its exemptions from the prospectus delivery requirements apply if the registration statement was subject to a section 8 stop order,[26] nor is an exemption available if so ordered by the SEC upon application or its own motion in a particular case.[27] The rule, as is the case with the section 4(3) exemption, explicitly does not affect the obligation of an underwriter to deliver the prospectus although it applies to dealers who though underwriters for the offering have sold or otherwise disposed of their allotment and thus are no longer acting as underwriters.

Rule 174(g) imposes an additional requirement for penny stock offerings.[28] In the case of a blank check penny stock offering, the ninety day period does not begin to run until the securities are released from escrow pursuant to Rule 419.[29]

---

20. *See* Sec.Act Rel.No. 33–6763, [1987–88 Transfer Binder] Fed.Sec.L.Rep. (CCH) ¶ 84,226 (SEC April 4, 1986).

21. 17 C.F.R. § 230.174(d). *See* §§ 10.3, 10.13 *infra* for a description of NASDAQ.

22. 15 U.S.C.A. § 77d(3)(B).

23. 17 C.F.R. § 230.174(d).

24. Quotations for securities not listed on a national exchange or traded through NASDAQ are available from pink sheets which are circulated by the market maker. *See* § 10.3 *infra*.

25. 17 C.F.R. § 230.174(f).

26. 15 U.S.C.A. § 77h. *See* § 7.1 *infra*

27. 17 C.F.R. § 230.174(e)

28. The penny stock rules are discussed in § 10.7 *infra*.

29. 17 C.F.R. § 230.174(g). *See* 17 C.F.R. § 230.419.

§ 4.28 Exemption for Certain Real Estate Mortgage Notes—Section 4(5)

Section 4(5) of the 1933 Act[1] provides an exemption from registration for certain mortgage notes that are secured by specified real property. The section exempts transactions involving one or more promissory notes that are directly secured by a first lien on a single parcel of real estate consisting of land and either a residential or commercial structure.

The section 4(5) exemption also applies to participation interests in qualifying notes. The section 4(5) mortgage note exemption is available only if the notes are offered by a savings and loan association, commercial bank, savings bank or similar banking institution subject to the supervision of and examination by federal or state authority. In order to qualify for the exemption, the minimum aggregate amount purchased by each purchaser may not be less than two hundred and fifty thousand dollars.[2] Furthermore, each purchaser must pay cash within sixty days of the purchase, and each purchase must be made for the purchaser's own account.[3]

The section 4(5) exemption is also available where the notes are generated by a mortgage approved by the Secretary of Housing and Urban Development and are sold with the above mentioned preconditions.[4] Such sales qualify for the exemption only if made to designated institutional purchasers.[5] Section 4(5) further exempts from the 1933 Act registration requirements transactions between the same types of institutional purchasers that involve non-assignable contracts to buy or sell qualifying mortgage notes provided that the purchasers are to be completed within two years.[6] The section 4(5) exemption expressly does not apply to resales of the mortgage notes that do not themselves comply with the exemption.[7]

§ 4.28

1. 15 U.S.C.A. § 77d(5).
2. 15 U.S.C.A. § 77d(5)(A)(i).
3. 15 U.S.C.A. § 77d(5)(A)(iii).
4. 15 U.S.C.A. § 77d(5)(A)(ii). The following purchasers qualify under section 4(5)(A)(ii): "any insurance company subject to the supervision of the insurance commission, or any agency or officer performing like function, of any State or territory of the United States or the District of Columbia, or the Federal Home Loan Mortgage Corporation, the Federal National Mortgage Association, or the Government National Mortgage Association." *Id.* For an interpretation of "similar" institutions that are also covered *see* Institutional Securities Corp., [1976–1977 Transfer Binder] Fed.Sec.L.Rep. (CCH) ¶ 81,639 (May 11, 1977). *See also* Mason–McDuffie Inv. Co., [1977–1978 Transfer Binder] Fed.Sec. L.Rep. (CCH) ¶ 81,336 (Aug. 22, 1977).
5. 15 U.S.C.A. § 77d(5)(A)(ii). *See* footnote 4 *supra.*
6. 15 U.S.C.A. § 77d(5)(B).
7. 15 U.S.C.A. § 77d(5)(C).

§ 4.28.1. Exemption for Certain Offshore Transactions in Securities of United States Issuers

With the growing globalization of the securities markets, there have been an increasing number of questions concerning the applicability of the United States securities laws to transactions taking place outside of the United States.[1] To the extent that a United States issuer offers securities exclusively to non United States citizens in offshore transactions, there is substantial question as to the propriety of requiring registration under the 1933 Act even though there would be jurisdiction to do so. Regulation S provides a safe harbor exemption for certain offshore offerings.[2]

§ 4.29 Integration of Transactions

As discussed throughout this chapter, it is necessary to structure transactions carefully in order to assure that they qualify for exemption from the 1933 Act's registration requirements. It is imperative to consider not only each step in a particular offering, but also to be mindful of past and possible future transactions. Whenever there is a series of securities transactions, it may not be sufficient to assure the exemption that each transaction can stand on its own. In addition to each transaction being able to qualify for an exemption, it must also be clear that when viewed as a whole, the series of transactions does not run afoul of the Act's registration provisions and prospectus requirements,

Under the "integration" doctrine, the SEC will examine multiple offerings to determine whether they should be treated as a single, unitary transaction. Frequently, an issuer will embark on two (or more) separate exempt transactions within a relatively short period. In such a case the Commission may give close scrutiny in order to determine whether all offers and sales from the two (or more) securities offerings should be telescoped and integrated into one transaction.[1] When the

---

§ 4.28.1

1. *See* § 14.3 *infra* for discussion of the jurisdictional issues; including a discussion of the treatment of foreign securities traded in the United States.

2. 17 C.F.R. § 230.901 et seq. A detailed discussion is found in the Practitioner's Edition.

§ 4.29

1. *See generally* ABA Committee on Federal Regulation of Securities, Integration of Offerings: Report of Task Force on Integration of Securities Offerings, 41 Bus.Law. 595 (1986) [hereinafter cited as ABA Task Force Report]; Bartlett & Waldman, Select Problems in Late—Round Private Financings: Soft Information; Integration; Debt vs. Equity, 17 Sec.Reg.L.J. 227 (1989); Darryl B. Deaktor, Integration of Securities Offerings, 31 U.Fla.L.Rev. 465 (1979); Ronald L. Fein & Jacobs, Integration of Securities Transactions, 15 Rev.Sec.Reg. 785 (1982);

Russell B. Stevenson, Jr., Integration and Private Placements, 19 Rev.Sec. & Commod.Reg. 49 (March 5, 1986); Perry E. Wallace, Jr., Integration of Securities Offerings: Obstacles to Capital Formation Remain for Small Businesses, 45 Wash. & Lee L. Review 935 (1988). *See also, e.g.,* ABA Subcommittee on Partnerships, Trusts and Unincorporated Associations, Committee on Federal Regulation of Securities, Integration of Partnership Offerings: A Proposal for Identifying a Discrete Offering, 37 Bus.Law. 1591 (1982). For

integration doctrine is employed it is possible that the two (or more) offerings combined will lose the attributes that entitled them to protection.[2] The integration doctrine is not limited to multiple exempt transactions; it can also be used to integrate a would-be exempt offering with a registered offering where some of the offers or sales in the registered offering would destroy the availability of the exemption.[3] Integration issues also arise in connection with domestic transactions and those taking place abroad. Also, integration may play a role in determining statute of limitations issues. This section will discuss the various applications of the integration doctrine.

Illustrative Examples

A few examples will help illustrate the ways in which the integration doctrine can operate. Consider an intrastate offering made by a local issuer offered only to residents of the state of incorporation and principal place of business. Assume further that some of the purchasers in the intrastate offering are relatively unsophisticated; the offering would nevertheless qualify for the intrastate exemption.[4] Two weeks later, the issuer offers the same class of stock to several wealthy and sophisticated out-of-state investors in a manner that would satisfy section 4(2)'s nonpublic offering exemption.[5] If the integration doctrine were applied to these transactions no exemption would be available because the sophisticated out-of-state purchasers would destroy the intrastate exemption while the unsophisticated in-state purchasers would render the nonpublic offering exemption unavailable.

Similarly, assume that a private placement is followed within two weeks by a registered public offering. If the two transactions are integrated, the private placement sales would be considered part of the registered offering and in violation of section 5.[6] Although the integration doctrine will not be applied every time two offerings take place within close proximity, the possibility must be taken into account. By taking the possibility of integration into account, the transactions can be structured in such a way to minimize or even eliminate the possibility of the doctrine being applied.

---

an excellent overview of the development of the integration doctrine, *see* Richard W. Jennings & Harold Marsh, Jr., Securities Regulation: Cases and Materials 440–47 (6th Ed. 1987).

See also, e.g., Cheryl L. Wade, The Integration of Securities Offerings: A Proposed Formula that Fosters the Policies of Securities Regulation, 25 Loy. U. Chi. L.J. 199 (1994).

2. *But see, e.g.,* Caviness v. Derand Resources Corp., 983 F.2d 1295 (4th Cir.1993) (refusing to apply integrated offering approach to § 13's statute of limitations, holding that the 3 year statute of repose applies to each sale separately).

3. *But see* 17 C.F.R. § 230.152 which provides a safe harbor from integration and which is discussed *infra* in the text accompanying footnotes 54–72.

4. 15 U.S.C.A. § 77c(a)(11). *See* § 4.12 *supra.*

5. 15 U.S.C.A. § 77d(2). *See* §§ 4.21–4.22 *supra.*

6. This assumes that the would-be private placement sales took place prior to the registered offering's effective date or that there was noncompliance with the prospectus delivery requirements. *See* §§ 2.4, 2.5 *supra.*

Outside the context of the safe harbor rules, the integration doctrine is based on a multifaceted subjective test and depends on the facts of the particular transactions in question.[7] Accordingly, the precise parameters of the integration doctrine are uncertain. This lack of certainty is problematic for the planner of exempt transactions who must plan cautiously in order to guard against the risk of integration. This lack of certainty is still one more reason to try to stay within the confines of the SEC's safe harbor rules.[8] In contrast and as explained more fully below, the safe harbor rules provide some safe harbors from integration.

The Integration Doctrine Explained

The integration doctrine first emerged with regard to the intrastate offering exemption[9] in the context of determining which transactions constitute "part of an *issue*" which is offered in accordance with the intrastate limitations.[10] The "part of an issue" concept (and hence integration) applies to section 3(b) exemptions such as Regulation A.[11] Similarly, the issue concept has been carried over to section 3(a)(9)'s exemption[12] for exchanges of securities exclusively with existing securities holders.[13] The integration doctrine has also been applied to section 3(a)(10)'s exemption for administratively approved reorganizations.[14] The SEC has made it clear that integration applies equally to the transaction exemptions under section 4 and, in particular, section 4(2)'s exemption for transactions not involving a public offering.[15] Unless specifically excluded by the exemption,[16] integration could potentially be applied to several other exemptions. Although the potential for integration would otherwise exist, the Commission staff has tended not to integrate contemporaneous issuance of short-term commercial paper under section 3(a)(3)'s exemption[17] with private placements of promisso-

---

7. *See* Sec. Act Rel. No. 33–4552, 1 Fed.Sec.L. Rep. (CCH) ¶¶ 2770–2783 (Nov. 6, 1962); Sec. Act Rel. No. 33–4434, 1 Fed.Sec.L.Rep. (CCH) ¶¶ 2270–2277 (Dec. 6, 1961); 17 C.F.R. § 230.502 NOTE; 17 C.F.R. § 230.147, preliminary note 3.

8. *E.g.,* 17 C.F.R. § 230.506 (nonpublic offerings); 17 C.F.R. § 230.147 (intrastate exemption). *See also* 17 C.F.R. §§ 230.504, 230.505, 230.701.

9. 15 U.S.C.A. § 77c(a)(11). *See* § 4.12 *infra.*

10. *See* Sec. Act Rel. No. 33–4552, 1 Fed.Sec.L.Rep. (CCH) ¶¶ 2770–2783 (Nov. 6, 1962); Sec. Act Rel. No. 33–97, 11 Fed.Reg. 10,949 (Dec. 28, 1933).

11. 15 U.S.C.A. § 77c(b); 17 C.F.R. §§ 230.251 *et seq. See* §§ 4.14, 4.15 *supra. See generally See, e.g.,* C. Stephen Bradford, Regulation A and the Integration Doctrine: The New Safe Harbor, 55 Ohio St. L.J. 255 (1994).

See also Rules 504 and 505 (17 C.F.R. §§ 230.504, 230.505) which are discussed in §§ 4.17–4.18 *supra. But see* 17 C.F.R. § 230.701 (exemption for certain stock compensation plans) which provides that the integration doctrine does not apply. *See* § 4.15.1 *supra.*

12. 15 U.S.C.A. § 77c(a)(9). *See* § 4.10 *supra.*

13. *See* R. Jennings & H. Marsh, *supra* footnote 1 at 442 ("This is accomplished by reading the word 'exclusively' as modifying both 'exchanged' and 'security holders.' ").

14. *See* ABA Task Force Report *supra* footnote 1 at 600–02.

15. *See* Sec. Act Rel. No. 33–4552, 1 Fed.Sec.L.Rep. (CCH) ¶¶ 2770–2783 (Nov. 6, 1962).

16. *See, e.g.,* 17 C.F.R. § 230.701(b)(6).

17. 15 U.S.C.A. § 77c(a)(3). *See* § 4.4 *supra.*

ry notes.[18]

The SEC has developed a five factor test to determine whether the integration doctrine should be applied to two or more transactions:

1. whether the sales are part of a single plan of financing;

2. whether the sales involve issuance of the same class of securities;

3. whether the sales have been made at or about the same time;

4. whether the same type of consideration is received; and

5. whether the sales are made for the same general purpose.[19]

The Commission has not given any guidance on how these factors should be weighted. Accordingly, it would appear that in a particular case any one or more of the five factors could be determinative.[20] Thus, for example, the absence of a prearranged single plan of financing has been held to preclude integration.[21]

The Highly Factual Nature of Integration Questions

The integration doctrine had its genesis in the context of the intrastate exemption.[22] However, because its availability is essentially dependent upon questions of fact[23] depending on the nuances of each

18. *See, e.g.,* First & Merchants Corp. (SEC No Action Letter available July 27, 1978); Pittsburgh National Corp. (SEC No Action Letter available Aug. 15, 1977); Alabama Bancorporation (SEC No Action Letter available July 8, 1977); Security Pacific Corp., (SEC No Action Letter available Oct. 14, 1976); Liberty National Corp. (SEC No Action Letter available May 21, 1976). *See* the excellent discussion in ABA Task Force Report *supra* footnote 1 at 619–20.

19. *See* Sec. Act Rel. No. 33–4552, 1 Fed.Sec.L. Rep. (CCH) ¶¶ 2770–2783 (Nov. 6, 1962); Sec. Act Rel. No. 33–4434, 1 Fed.Sec.L.Rep. (CCH) ¶¶ 2270–2277 (Dec. 6, 1961); 17 C.F.R. § 230.502 NOTE; 17 C.F.R. § 230.147, preliminary note 3. *See also, e.g.,* Donohoe v. Consolidated Operating & Production Corp., 982 F.2d 1130 (7th Cir.1992), *affirming* 736 F.Supp. 845 (N.D.Ill.1990) (refusing to integrate four offerings made within twelve months where each offering was for separate, identifiable groups of oil wells).

20. In its application of the integration doctrine to the intrastate exemption, the Commission explained that "any of the above factors may be determinative." Sec. Act Rel. No. 33–4434, 1 Fed.Sec.L. Rep. (CCH) ¶ 2272 (Dec. 6, 1961). In contrast with regard to section 4(2) the Commission stated that the five factors "should be considered." Sec. Act Rel. No. 33–4552, 1 Fed.Sec.L. Rep. (CCH) ¶ 2781 (Nov. 6, 1962). It seems highly doubtful that this was intended to be a significant difference. *But cf.* R. Jennings & H. Marsh, *supra* footnote 1 at 441 (suggesting a possible difference).

Compare, e.g., Donohoe v. Consolidated Operating & Production Corp., 982 F.2d 1130 (7th Cir.1992) (applying the SEC's five-factor test and refusing to integrate partnership offerings) *with* SEC v. Melchior, 1993 WL 89141, [1992–1993 Transfer Binder] Fed.Sec. L.Rep. (CCH) ¶ 97,356 (D.Utah 1993) (finding that multiple limited partnership offerings were subject to Rule 502's integration requirement and thus required registration under the 1933 Act).

21. *E.g.,* Barrett v. Triangle Mining Corp., 1976 WL 760, [1975–76 Transfer Binder] Fed.Sec.L. Rep. (CCH) ¶ 95,438 (S.D.N.Y.1976); Livens v. William D. Witter, Inc., 374 F.Supp. 1104 (D.Mass.1974).

22. *See* Sec. Act Rel. No. 33–97, 11 Fed.Reg. 10,949 (Dec. 28, 1933) (explaining that the intrastate exemption depends upon the entire issue being offered and sold within the state).

23. *See, e.g.,* Sec. Act Rel. No. 33–4552, 1 Fed.Sec.L.Rep. (CCH) ¶ 2781 (Nov. 6, 1962) (the integration doctrine "depends on the particular facts or circumstances").

situation, it is often difficult to glean any learning from the sparse precedent that exists.[24] Much of the relevant precedent is based on no action letters, which by their nature are of limited precedential value.[25] Interestingly, in 1979 the Commission suspended its practice of rendering no action advice on integration questions but reinstituted its former practice in 1985.[26]

Although the integration doctrine is subjective and, as discussed above, the precedent is not very helpful, a few generalizations can be made. It would seem unlikely that a bona fide employee compensation plan would be integrated with a capital raising offering.[27] Similarly, there would not be any reason to integrate stock issued in connection with a merger or other share exchange and stock issued for cash.

Issuer Integration

The integration doctrine is not limited to successive offerings by the same issuer—sometimes referred to as "offering integration." [28] Successive offerings by issuers having separate forms but economic interdependence may also be integrated; [29] this has been referred to as "issuer integration."[30] Additionally, offerings of different issuers are integrated

---

24. *See, e.g.,* SEC v. Holschuh, 694 F.2d 130 (7th Cir.1982) (integrating offerings by separate coal exploration limited partnerships which acquired their leasehold rights from the same company); SEC v. Murphy, 626 F.2d 633 (9th Cir.1980) (integrating separate offerings by two closely related issuers and the same promoter); General Life of Missouri Investment Co. v. Shamburger, 546 F.2d 774 (8th Cir.1976) (integration of two private placements resulted in forty-two purchasers which exceeded former Rule 146's 35 purchaser limitation that is now found in Rule 506's safe harbor); Bowers v. Columbia General Corp., 336 F.Supp. 609 (D.Del.1971) (refusing to grant preliminary relief, applying the Commission's five factor test); SEC v. Dunfee, [1966–67 Transfer Binder] Fed.Sec.L.Rep. (CCH) ¶ 91,970 (W.D.Mo.1966) (refusing to integrate intrastate offering of notes with an offering of similar notes; nine months separated the two offerings); The Value Line Fund, Inc. v. Marcus, [1964–65 Transfer Binder] Fed.Sec.L.Rep. (CCH) ¶ 91,523 (S.D.N.Y.1965) (applying the Commission's five factor test in refusing to integrate separate private placements).

See also, e.g., Walker v. Montclaire Housing Partners, 736 F.Supp. 1358, 1364–65 (M.D.N.C.1990) (integrated six sales of limited partnership interests so as to trigger North Carolina blue sky law notification requirement for offerings to more than five residents).

25. The questionable reliability of no action letters' precedential value is discussed in § 9.5 *infra.*

26. *See* R. Jennings & H. Marsh, *supra* footnote 1 at 441 n. 2.

27. *E.g.* Pacific Physician Services, Inc. (SEC No Action Letter available August 20, 1985) ("the primary purpose of the offering to key employees [is] to provide such persons with an opportunity to acquire proprietary interests in the Company and to encourage them to remain in its service while the primary purpose of the public offering [is] to raise capital for the Company's business operations, this Division is of the view that the offerings would not be integrated since they are not intended for the same purpose and are not part of a single plan of financing"). *See also, e.g.,* The Immune Response Corp. (SEC No Action Letter Nov. 2, 1987); Royal LePage Ltd. (SEC No Action Letter available June 16, 1986); *Cf.* 17 C.F.R. § 230.701(b)(6) (expressly providing that integration does not apply to employee compensation plans exempt under the rule).

28. *See* ABA Task Force Report *supra* footnote 1 at 617–20.

29. *See, e.g.,* SEC v. Holschuh, 694 F.2d 130 (7th Cir.1982) (integrating offerings by separate coal exploration limited partnerships which acquired their leasehold rights from the same company); *see also* SEC v. Murphy, 626 F.2d 633 (9th Cir.1980).

30. *See* ABA Task Force Report *supra* footnote 1 at 621–23.

because they are part of a single enterprise—this has been dubbed "venture integration."[31]

Safe Harbors for Avoiding Integration

As noted earlier in this section, the Commission has provided safe harbors for avoiding integration. Thus, for example, Rule 502(a)[32] of Regulation D provides that offers and sales made more than six months before the start or six months after the completion of the Regulation D offering will not be integrated.[33] The six month safe harbor is dependent upon there not being any non Regulation D offers or sales of the same class of securities within both six month periods, except that sales pursuant to an employee benefit plan are permitted.[34] This safe harbor applies to Rule 504's exemption for offerings of up to one million dollars,[35] Rule 505's exemption for offerings of up to five million dollars,[36] and Rule 506's safe harbor for nonpublic offerings.[37] In some Regulation D offerings the issuer may not be able to rely on the safe harbor from integration because of other offers or sales within either of the six month periods. In such situations, the Commission's normal integration rules, including the five factor integration test, are applicable for determining whether the Regulation D exemption is available.[38] Thus, for example, where following a private placement complying with Regulation D, the issuer decides to embark on a public offering, the issuer may still rely on Rule 152[39] to avoid integration.[40]

As is the case with Regulation D, Rule 147's safe harbor for intrastate offerings provides a safe harbor from integration provided there are no non Rule 147 offers or sales within six months before the beginning of the offering or six months after its completion.[41] However,

---

31. *Id.* at 620–21.

32. 17 C.F.R. § 230.502(a).

33. *Id.*

34. *Id.:*

Offers and sales that are made more than six months before the start of a Regulation D offering or more than six months after completion of a Regulation D offering will not be considered part of that Regulation D offering, so long as during those six month periods there are no offers or sales of securities by or for the issuer that are of the same or a similar class as those offered or sold under Regulation D, other than offers or sales of securities under an employee benefit plan as defined in Rule 405 under the Act.

35. 17 C.F.R. § 230.504. *See* § 4.19 *supra.*

36. 17 C.F.R. § 230.505. *See* § 4.18 *supra.*

37. 17 C.F.R. § 230.506. *See* § 4.22 *supra.*

38. 17 C.F.R. § 230.502(a) NOTE.

39. 17 C.F.R. § 230.152 which is discussed in the text accompanying footnotes 54–72 *infra.*

40. Vintage Group, Incorporated (SEC No Action Letter April 11, 1988); The Immune Response Corporation (SEC No Action Letter Nov. 2, 1987); Vulture Petroleum Corp. (SEC No Action Letter Dec. 31, 1986). Rule 152 is limited to private offerings and thus arguably would not apply to a Rule 505, as opposed to a Rule 506 offering. Nevertheless, where a Rule 505 offering also meets the requirements of Rule 506, Rule 152 will be available. The Immune Response Corporation (SEC No Action Letter Nov. 2, 1987).

41. 17 C.F.R. § 147(b)(2):

the Rule 147 safe harbor does not exclude from the integration doctrine sales within those six month periods made in connection with employee benefit plans, unless those plans are exempt under section 3 or 4 of the Act.[42] Following the same pattern as Regulation D, where a transaction fails to meet the safe harbor requirements, the Commission's subjective five-factor test will apply.[43] In contrast to the safe harbors described above, Rule 701, a section 3(b) exemption, which provides an exemption for certain employee compensation plans,[44] states that the integration doctrine does not apply to transactions covered by the rule.[45]

For purposes of this rule, an issue shall be deemed not to include offers, offers to sell, offers for sale or sales of securities of the issuer pursuant to the exemptions provided by Section 3 or Section 4(2) of the Act or pursuant to a registration statement under the Act, that take place prior to the six month period immediately preceding or after the six month period immediately following any offers, offers for sale or sales pursuant to this rule, *provided that,* there are during either of said six month periods no offers, offers for sale or sales of securities by or for the issuer of the same or similar class as those offered for sale or sold pursuant to the rule.

42. *Id.* Compare 17 C.F.R. § 230.502(a).

43. 17 C.F.R. § 230.147(b)(2) NOTE.

44. 17 C.F.R. § 230.701. *See* § 4.15.1 *supra.*

45. 17 C.F.R. § 230.701(b)(6) ("Offers and sales exempt pursuant to this § 230.701 are deemed to be part of a single, discrete offering and are not subject to integration with any other offering or sale whether registered under the Act or otherwise exempt from the registration requirements of the Act").

Chapter 5

THE THEORY OF SALE—
CORPORATE RECAPITALIZATIONS,
REORGANIZATIONS AND
MERGERS UNDER THE 1933 ACT

Table of Sections

§ 5.1 1933 Act Application to Unconventional Transactions—Section 2(3)'s Definition of Sale; Gifts, Bonus Plans, and Pledges; Effect of State Law

Section 2(3) of the 1933 Act[1] defines "sale" as including "every contract of sale or disposition of a security or interest in a security, for value." This definition obviously encompasses cash transactions, but what about less conventional transactions such as exercise of options, mergers, exercise of conversion rights, pledges, and the like? Such transactions have given rise to various definitional problems.[2] For many years, the SEC took the view that shares issued in connection with mergers and other qualifying corporate reorganizations did not constitute sales which would trigger the 1933 Act's registration requirements.[3] The Commission has since abandoned its former "no sale" approach to

---

* Deleted section 5.4 can be found in the Practitioner's Edition.

§ 5.1

1. 15 U.S.C.A. § 77b(3).

2. Similar problems have arisen under the 1934 Act's provision regarding the reporting of insider transactions and the disgorgement of insider short-swing profits. Section 16 of the 1934 Act, 15 U.S.C.A. § 78p. *See* §§ 12.2–12.5 *infra*.

3. Former rule 133, 17 C.F.R. § 230.133 (1971) (rescinded by Sec.Act Rel.No. 33–5316 (Oct. 6, 1972)).

mergers and other forms of combinations in favor of 1933 Act coverage.[4] Other definitional issues have arisen when attempting to decide whether stock dividends and corporate spin-offs constitute purchases and sales of securities.[5] These topics, which are discussed in the succeeding sections, have not been the only ones relating to the definition of sale. Thus, questions may arise as to whether various other types of dispositions qualify for sales. In particular, courts and/or the SEC have been called upon to decide the applicability of the definition of sale to gifts, bonus plans, other employee compensation plans, and pledges of securities. Those topics are considered directly below.

Gifts and Bonus Plans

There are yet other definitional issues with regard to what constitutes a "sale." For example, when a charitable donor receives a tax deduction for his or her gift of securities, has there been a disposition for value? Presumably there is no sale in such a situation[6] although the donor receives a tax benefit as a result of the gift.[7] Furthermore, the donee's sale will require registration or an exemption before the securities can fall into the hands of the investing public.[8] The fact that a gift ordinarily is not a sale will not protect someone who is trying to evade the 1933 Act's registration provisions. Accordingly, in those instances when the donor's "gifts" are followed by wide-spread downstream sales, these would-be gifts may be characterized as a subterfuge to evade registration[9] and thus be viewed as sales.[10] The SEC has thus taken the position that "value" for the disposition may be deemed received when the gift results in the creation of a public market for the issuer's

---

4. *See* § 5.2 *infra.*

5. *See* § 5.3 *infra.*

6. According to Professor Loss, it "seems clear * * * that a *bona fide* gift or loan of a security does not normally involve an offer or sale." 1 Louis Loss, Securities Regulation 576 (2d ed. 1961), relying in part on Shaw v. Dreyfus, 172 F.2d 140 (2d Cir.1949), *cert. denied* 337 U.S. 907, 69 S.Ct. 1048, 93 L.Ed. 1719 (1949) which was decided under the short-swing profit provisions of section 16(b), 15 U.S.C.A. § 78p(b) which is discussed in § 12.5 *infra.*

7. To begin with, the value of the benefit received will be far less than had the donor sold the securities. Additionally since the donee, unlike a purchaser of securities, is not giving anything in return, there is no need to protect the donee in the same manner as the law would protect a purchaser. To the extent that the gift is at an inflated value, the resulting problem is one of tax fraud not securities fraud.

8. This is the treatment that the SEC deems appropriate in the context of the transfer of restricted securities. *See* rule 144(d)(4)(E) ("Securities acquired from any person, other than the issuer, by gift shall be deemed to have been acquired by the donee when they were acquired by the donor"), 17 C.F.R. § 230.144(d)(4)(E). Rule 144 is discussed in § 4.26 *supra.*

9. *See* In re H & B Carriers, Inc., 20 Sec.Reg. & L.Rep. (BNA) 742 (Utah Sec.Div. April 26, 1988).

10. This reasoning is analogous to that used in connection with corporate spin-off transactions. *See, e.g.,* SEC v. Datronics Engineers, Inc., 490 F.2d 250 (4th Cir.1973), *cert. denied* 416 U.S. 937, 94 S.Ct. 1936, 40 L.Ed.2d 287 (1974); SEC v. Harwyn Industries Corp., 326 F.Supp. 943 (S.D.N.Y.1971), both of which are discussed in § 5.3 *infra.*

securities.[11] In such a case, registration of the would-be gift will be required unless, of course, an appropriate exemption can be found.[12]

A few state securities laws have addressed the problem directly. At least two states expressly provide an exclusion from the definition of sale for good faith gifts.[13] However, no implication should be drawn that the rule is otherwise under the federal law. An explicit exemption or exclusion for good faith gifts is unnecessary in light of the fact that a bona fide gift clearly does not fall within the statutory definition of sale.

Employee Compensation Plans

A variation on the rule that a bona fide gift is not a sale arises in the context of bonus compensation plans. Following the rationale applicable to gifts, an employee bonus plan which is a true bonus—that is, over and above the employee's bargained-for consideration—is a gift and hence not a sale. On the other hand when a so-called bonus plan is in fact a type of compensation for services, then there has been a disposition for value and a "sale" will have taken place. Along these lines, the SEC has opined that the giving of shares to employees upon their retirement in exchange for "extraordinary services" was in fact a gift rather than a sale and thus did not require registration under the 1933 Act.[14] Thus, a stock bonus that is not bargained for and is given in appreciation of past services can be said to be without consideration and hence not a sale.[15] However, when a so-called bonus or bonus plan is in fact part of an employee's expected compensation, the stock is issued in exchange for value and thus, the "bonus" will be viewed as a sale.[16] Other forms of employee compensation plans will clearly be sales as the shares are

---

11. *See, e.g.,* In the Matter of Capital General Corp., Sec. Act Rel. No. 33–7008, [1993 Transfer Binder] Fed. Sec. L. Rep. (CCH) ¶ 85,223 (SEC July 23, 1993).

12. *See* In re H & B Carriers, Inc., 20 Sec.Reg. & L.Rep. (BNA) 742 (Utah Sec.Div. April 26, 1988) (applying Utah blue sky law). A gift of assessable stock may properly be characterized as a sale. *See* footnote 10 *supra.*

13. *See* Tenn.Code Ann. § 48–2–102(11)(f)(i); Utah Stat. § 61–1–13(15)(d)(i).

A number of states expressly include a gift of assessable stock in the definition of sale. *E.g.,* West's Ann.Cal.Corp.Code § 27017; Mich.Comp.Laws Ann. § 451.801; N.C.Gen.Stat. § 78A–2(8)(a); Pa.Cons.Stat.Ann. Ch. 70 § 1–102(r)(v); Tex.Corps. & Assns.Code Ann. § 581–4(e). Such an inclusion presumably is based on the rationale that the holder of assessable stock may simply by holding the stock incur an obligation to invest additional funds and the acceptance of the gift may therefore involve an investment decision.

14. New Jersey Resources Corp., 17 Sec.Reg. & L.Rep. (BNA) 282 (SEC No Action Letter Jan. 28, 1985) (the Commission response noted that since (1) this was a publicly traded company, (2) the bonus was involuntary from the employees' perspective, and (3) the employees did not part with value there was no need to invoke the protections of the Act's registration requirements).

15. Knoll Int'l, Inc., 18 Sec.Reg. & L.Rep. (BNA) 1763 (SEC No Action Letter Oct. 20, 1986). *See also, e.g.,* Ocean Express Seafood Restaurants, Inc., 19 Sec.Reg. & L.Rep. (BNA) 537 (SEC No Action Letter March 26, 1987).

16. *See, e.g.,* Harris v. Republic Airlines, Inc., 1988 WL 56256, [1987–88 Transfer Binder] Fed.Sec.L.Rep. (CCH) ¶ 93,772 (D.D.C.1988). *See* § 5.3 *infra* for a discussion of employee stock plans. *See also* § 4.15.1 *supra* for a discussion of the exemption for certain compensation plans of issuers which are not subject to the Exchange Act's periodic reporting requirements. *Cf.* SEC v. Ralston Purina Co., 346 U.S. 119, 73 S.Ct. 981, 97 L.Ed. 1494 (1953) (offering to employees was not exempt from registration).

issued in exchange for the employee's services. The SEC has created an exemption for many such plans.[17] And, for those employee stock and option plans that are not exempt, there is a specially tailored registration form.[18]

Pledges

The Supreme Court, in Rubin v. United States, held that a pledge of securities is a sale for purposes of the 1933 Act's antifraud provisions.[19] Although there might seem to be no reason to expect a different result under the 1934 Act, the courts are sharply divided. The Second and Sixth Circuits have ruled that a pledge is a sale for purposes of SEC Rule 10b–5.[20] However, prior to the Supreme Court's decision in *Rubin,* the Fifth and Seventh Circuits ruled that a pledge is not a sale under the 1934 Act.[21] These cases arose out of transactions that were viewed as commercial loans not involving traditional investment risks and thus were held not to be within the purview of the securities laws.[22]

---

17. Rule 701, 17 C.F.R. § 230.701. *See* § 4.15.1 *supra*. Stock and option plans that are limited to key employees may be exempt as transactions not involving a public offering. Section 4(2), 15 U.S.C.A. § 77d(2), which is discussed in § 4.21 *infra*.

18. 1933 Act Form S–8.

19. 449 U.S. 424, 101 S.Ct. 698, 66 L.Ed.2d 633 (1981), decided under section 17(a), 15 U.S.C.A. § 77q(a) which is discussed in §§ 7.6, 13.13 *infra*.

See also Denis T. Rice, the Effect of Registration Requirements on the Disposition of Pledged Securities, 21 Stan.L.Rev. 1607 (1969); James C. Sargent, Pledges and Foreclosure Rights Under the Securities Act of 1933, 45 Va.L.Rev. 885 (1959); § 4.24 *supra*. *Cf.* TCF Banking & Savings, F.A. v. Arthur Young & Co., 706 F.Supp. 1408 (D.Minn.1988) (foreclosure on pledged stock was not a sale under Minnesota blue sky law).

20. Chemical Bank v. Arthur Andersen & Co., 726 F.2d 930, 939–45 (2d Cir.1984), *cert. denied* 469 U.S. 884, 105 S.Ct. 253, 83 L.Ed.2d 190 (1984), relying in part on dictum from Marine Bank v. Weaver, 455 U.S. 551, 554 n. 2, 102 S.Ct. 1220, 1222 n. 2, 71 L.Ed.2d 409, 414 n. 2 (1982), *on remand* 683 F.2d 744 (3d Cir.1982). *See also* Mansbach v. Prescott, Ball & Turben, 598 F.2d 1017 (6th Cir.1979); Mallis v. FDIC, 568 F.2d 824 (2d Cir.1977), *cert. granted* 431 U.S. 928, 97 S.Ct. 2630, 53 L.Ed.2d 243 (1977), *cert. dismissed as improvidently granted* 435 U.S. 381, 98 S.Ct. 1117, 55 L.Ed.2d 357 (1978), *rehearing denied* 436 U.S. 915, 98 S.Ct. 2259, 56 L.Ed.2d 416 (1978); United States v. Gentile, 530 F.2d 461 (2d Cir.1976), *cert. denied* 426 U.S. 936, 96 S.Ct. 2651, 49 L.Ed.2d 388 (1976). The plaintiffs in both *Mallis* and *Gentile* stated parallel claims under section 17(a) of the 1933 Act and Section 10(b) of the 1934 Act. Rule 10b–5 is discussed in §§ 13.2–13.12 *infra*.

21. Alley v. Miramon, 614 F.2d 1372 (5th Cir.1980); Lincoln National Bank v. Herber, 604 F.2d 1038 (7th Cir.1979); National Bank of Commerce of Dallas v. All American Assurance Co., 583 F.2d 1295 (5th Cir.1978).

22. As the Fifth Circuit explained:

[The Second and Sixth Circuit] decisions were grounded upon the rationale that the pledgee assumes a very real investment risk that the pledged securities will have continuing value, a risk that is identical in nature to the risk taken by investors * * *. United States v. Gentile, 530 F.2d 461, 467.

This rationale might be a persuasive argument that federal securities ought to encompass pledges, as well as purchases and sales. It does little to support a decision that they do in fact cover pledges. Congress can be presumed to know the difference between a collateral pledge transaction and a sale and purchase. If it had intended to cover both, it could have easily done so by words traditionally used to differentiate between the two.

National Bank of Commerce of Dallas v. All American Assurance Co., 583 F.2d 1295, 1299–1300 (5th Cir.1978). For a discussion of the commercial/investment dichotomy in deciding what is a "security," *see* § 1.5 *supra*.

At least one post-*Rubin* decision has held that a pledge of bonds to a bank is essentially commercial and thus not a sale of securities.[23] Minimal support for this ruling can be found in the Supreme Court's decision in Marine Bank v. Weaver.[24] The Court in *Weaver* held that a pledge of a federally insured certificate of deposit to a bank in order to guarantee a loan to a third party[25] was not a sale of a security. The *Weaver* case is distinguishable, however, from the pledge of stock in a commercial setting since the Court's ruling was based in large part upon the federal insurance behind the certificate of deposit. The existence of federal insurance was a significant factor which in turn led the Court to find that no security was involved.[26] It is highly questionable, especially in light of the Court's earlier decision in *Rubin*,[27] whether the "no sale" rationale should be extended to the pledge of securities. Certainly, when the pledge of securities carries investment risks, a sale should be found to exist. Furthermore, if the pledgee is a bank or other financial institution, the pledge would be exempt from registration[28] but nevertheless subject to the antifraud provisions. In contrast, a foreclosure sale by the pledgee will require registration unless an exemption can be identified.[29]

Relevance of State Contract Law in Defining Sale

The growing federal law defining what constitutes a sale under the securities laws may on occasion be supplemented by reference to analogous common law principles. In deciding whether an offer or sale has taken place, it is appropriate for the federal courts to look to the applicable state contract law.[30] Thus, state law may be determinative in ascertaining whether preliminary discussions and negotiations are sufficiently far advanced to constitute an offer to sell[31] or even a sale.[32] It is generally held that a sale takes place once the parties to the transaction

---

23. *See* Shelter Mutual Insurance Co. v. Public Water Supply District No. 7, 569 F.Supp. 310 (E.D.Mo.1983).

24. 455 U.S. 551, 102 S.Ct. 1220, 71 L.Ed.2d 409 (1982), *on remand* 683 F.2d 744 (3d Cir.1982).

25. In return for the guarantee, the third party had agreed to pay the plaintiff fifty percent of its profits from its meatpacking operations for the duration of the guarantee. The third party defaulted and the bank foreclosed; the plaintiff's antifraud claims were based on the alleged failure to disclose material adverse facts about the third party borrower's business. *Id.* at 553–554.

26. Chemical Bank v. Arthur Andersen & Co., 726 F.2d 930, 940 (2d Cir.1984), *cert. denied* 469 U.S. 884, 105 S.Ct. 253, 83 L.Ed.2d 190 (1984). *See* § 1.5 *supra*.

27. *See* footnote 19 *supra*.

28. *See, e.g.*, Rule 144(d)(4)(D), 17 C.F.R. § 230.144(d)(4)(D).

29. *See, e.g.*, SEC v. Guild Films Co., 279 F.2d 485 (2d Cir.1960), *cert. denied* 364 U.S. 819, 81 S.Ct. 52, 5 L.Ed.2d 49 (1960), which is discussed in § 4.24 *infra*.

30. *See, e.g.*, Conkling v. Turner, 18 F.3d 1285 (5th Cir.1994) (preliminary negotiations were too vague to establish a contract for sale under applicable state law; there was no way to establish an agreed upon price for the securities in question).

31. *See, e.g.*, American Nursing Care of Toledo, Inc. v. Leisure, 609 F.Supp. 419 (N.D.Ohio 1984) (preliminary oral discussions between the parties did not qualify as an "offer to sell").

32. *See, e.g.*, Lewis v. Bradley, 599 F.Supp. 327 (S.D.N.Y.1984).

are committed to each other.[33] For example, a binding contract to issue shares will generally qualify as a "sale" under the securities acts even though the contract is never fully performed.[34] As discussed more fully in subsequent sections of this treatise,[35] the definition of sale is important for determining not only whether a sale has occurred, but if so, when it took place.

Convertible Securities

Questions concerning other transactions such as conversion of a convertible security[36] may also bring section 2(3)'s definition of sale into play. These questions are considered in a subsequent section of this treatise.[37]

§ 5.2 Corporate Recapitalizations, Reorganizations and Mergers Under the 1933 Act—Rule 145

As pointed out earlier, section 3(a)(9) of the 1933 Act provides an exemption from registration for securities that are exchanged by the issuer exclusively with its existing security holders, provided that no sales commission or other remuneration is paid in connection with solicitation for the exchange.[1] The section 3(a)(9) exemption does not extend to downstream sales by the securities holders or in a case in which the exchange was made to persons who were likely to act as statutory underwriters.[2] The exemption further is limited to 1933 Act registration and thus does not address itself to the 1934 Securities Exchange Act's applicability to solicitation of shareholders' votes needed to approve certain exchanges.[3] Also, section 3(a)(9) is limited to ex-

---

33. *E.g.*, Radiation Dynamics, Inc. v. Goldmuntz, 464 F.2d 876, 891 (2d Cir.1972); Department of Economic Development v. Arthur Andersen & Co., 683 F.Supp. 1463, 1475 (S.D.N.Y.1988); Lewis v. Bradley, 599 F.Supp. 327 (S.D.N.Y.1984); Bolton v. Gramlich, 540 F.Supp. 822, 839–40 (S.D.N.Y.1982); Eriksson v. Galvin, 484 F.Supp. 1108, 1119 (S.D.N.Y.1980); Rochambeau v. Brent Exploration, Inc., 79 F.R.D. 381, 384 (D.Colo.1978).

34. Yoder v. Orthomolecular Nutrition Institute, Inc., 751 F.2d 555 (2d Cir.1985). *Compare, e.g.*, Lewis v. Bradley, 599 F.Supp. 327 (S.D.N.Y.1984) (preliminary discussions between director and company concerning sale of his shares did not constitute a sale because he did not enter into an irrevocable agreement nor were his rights and obligations fixed by the discussions).

35. *See* §§ 5.4, 7.5.4, 13.8 *infra*.

36. For example, in Gilligan, Will & Co. v. SEC, 267 F.2d 461 (2d Cir.1959), *cert. denied* 361 U.S. 896, 80 S.Ct. 200, 4 L.Ed.2d 152 (1959), the court did not question the conversion as a sale although sale of the underlying common stock after conversion was held to require registration. *Accord* Rule 144(d)(4). 17 C.F.R. § 230.144(d)(4) which is discussed in § 4.26 *supra*.

37. *See* § 5.3 *infra*. Similar problems arise with regard to the definitions of purchase and sale with regard to the 1934 Act's prohibitions against insiders' short-swing profits. 15 U.S.C.A. § 78p(b). *See* § 12.5 *infra*.

§ 5.2

1. 15 U.S.C.A. § 77c(a)(9). *See* § 4.10 *supra*. *See generally* J. William Hicks, Recapitalizations under Section 3(a)(9) of the Securities Act of 1933, 61 Va.L.Rev. 1057 (1975).

2. *See* Sec.Act Rels. Nos. 33–646, 33–2029 (Feb. 3, 1937; Aug. 8, 1939).

3. In such a case the exchange is not exclusively with existing security holders of the issuer.

changes of securities of the same issuer and therefore has no application to mergers or other reorganizations in which the security holders receive securities of another issuer.[4]

Section 3(a)(9) is not the only 1933 Act exemption applicable to corporate reorganizations. Section 3(a)(7)[5] exempts certain certificates of interest issued in connection with bankruptcy reorganizations. Further, section 3(a)(10)[6] exempts judicially or administratively approved reorganizations where the approval is issued after a public hearing and considers the fairness of the transaction.[7] In addition, under appropriate circumstances, issuers involved in corporate reorganizations may also be able to avoid registration because the transaction qualifies for an exemption, such as the exemptions for intrastate,[8] nonpublic,[9] Regulation A,[10] or Regulation D[11] offerings. Absent an available exemption, securities issued in connection with corporate reorganizations will have to be registered under the 1933 Act.

The Demise of the "No Sale" Rule and the Rise of Rule 145

A corporation's shareholders' participation in a plan of reorganization or a merger will generally result in the corporation's exchange or issuance of new securities.[12] To the extent that such a reorganization or merger would involve the disposition of shares for value, the solicitation of shareholder consent would seem to fall within section 2(3)'s definition of "offer to sell"[13] with regard to the securities to be issued in the recapitalization, merger, or plan of exchange. Nevertheless, for a long time the Commission took the position that whenever securities were issued as part of an exchange pursuant to a statutory merger, consolidation, or sale of corporate assets, their issuance did not involve a sale of securities within the meaning of section 2(3) of the Act.[14] The "no sale"

---

4. Where the issuer is a 1934 Act reporting company, the federal proxy rules would govern such solicitations. 15 U.S.C.A. § 78n(a). *See* chapter 11 *infra*.

5. 15 U.S.C.A. § 77c(a)(7). *See* § 4.8 *supra*.

6. 15 U.S.C.A. § 77c(a)(10). *See* § 4.11 *supra*.

7. Stock required in a merger where the fairness has been passed upon by a state agency is exempt under section 3(a)(10) and the stock received by the shareholders is not restricted stock under Rule 144. Borland Finance Co., 19 Sec.Reg. & L.Rep. (BNA) 1769 (SEC No Action Letter Oct. 10, 1987). The shareholders' holding period is to be determined by Rule 145(d)(2) and they are not permitted to tack on the Rule 144 holding period of the disappearing corporation's stock. *Id.*

8. 15 U.S.C.A. § 77c(a)(11); 17 C.F.R. § 230.147. *See* § 4.12 *supra*.

9. 15 U.S.C.A. § 77d(2). *See* § 4.21 *supra*.

10. 17 C.F.R. §§ 230.251 *et seq. See* § 4.15 *supra*.

11. 17 C.F.R. §§ 230.501 *et seq. See* §§ 4.16–4.19, 4.20 *supra*.

12. The prominent exception is where the shareholders are cashed out. Redeemable preferred shares issued in a cash-out merger need not be registered so long as they are redeemed immediately. Cambior, Inc., 19 Sec.Reg. & L.Rep. (BNA) 240 (SEC No Action Letter Jan. 22, 1987).

13. 15 U.S.C.A. § 77b(3). *See* § 5.1 *supra*.

14. 17 C.F.R. § 230.133 (1971) (rescinded by Sec.Act Rel.No. 33–5316 (Oct. 6, 1972)).

doctrine had become the focus of frequent and severe criticism[15] and was discarded in 1972 with the Commission's adoption of Rule 145 which treats exchanges pursuant to mergers and reorganizations as sales.[16]

In adopting Rule 145, the Commission declared these share exchanges to involve sales of securities and thus in need of registration under the 1933 Act absent an exemption. The new rule therefore imposed registration requirements on all otherwise non-exempt business combinations involving a shareholder vote and the issuance of shares to the voting shareholders.[17] Rule 145 transactions may be registered on Form S–4 which is designed specifically for corporate combinations. The SEC was mindful of the overlapping Exchange Act coverage and thus further provided for coordination between the 1933 Act prospectus requirements and the proxy rules of the 1934 Act.[18] This type of coordination between the 1933 and 1934 Act is consistent with the 1970s initiative to implement an integrated disclosure system.[19]

Rule 145(a)[20] provides that there is an "offer," "offer to sell," "offer for sale" or "sale" within the meaning of section 2(3) of the 1933 Act when a plan for reclassification, merger, consolidation, or transfer of corporate assets in exchange for securities of another issuer is submitted to securities holders for a vote or otherwise for their consent. An exception to Rule 145 involves a reorganization when the sole effect of the reorganization is a change of the issuer's domicile or state of incorporation. In such a case, 1933 Act registration is not required.[21] However, any additional corporate restructuring beyond the change of domicile will call Rule 145 and, absent an exemption, the registration requirements into play.[22]

Rule 145 thus includes in section 2(3)'s definition of sale and offer for sale most corporate combinations. Accordingly, unless an exemption can be found, any communication, written or oral, designed to influence

---

15. Rule 133 and its "no sale" theory was attacked not only on the basis of being "unforgiveably formalistic" but also because it excluded from the Act's registration requirements transactions which created the need for the type of public disclosures required to be contained in 1933 Act registration statements. 1 L. Loss, Securities Regulation 552 (2d ed. 1961).

16. 17 C.F.R. § 230.145. *See* Sec.Act Rels. Nos. 33–5136, 33–5463 (Oct. 6, 1972, Feb. 28, 1974). *See also, e.g.,* 7547 Corp. v. Parker & Parsley Development Partners, 38 F.3d 211 (5th Cir.1994) (roll-up of limited partnership into corporate form would involve a sale under both the 1933 and 1934 Acts). *See generally* Rutherford B. Campbell, Jr., Rule 145: Mergers, Acquisitions and Recapitalizations Under The Securities Act of 1933, 56 Fordham L.Rev. 277 (1987); William H. Heyman, Implications of Rule 145 Under the Securities Act of 1933, 53 B.U.L.Rev. 785 (1973).

17. *See* footnote 16 *supra.* The rule thus covers mergers, consolidations, sales of corporate assets, and share exchanges involving shareholder votes and to which the corporations are parties.

18. 15 U.S.C.A. § 78n(a). *See* chapter 11 *infra.*

19. *See* § 3.3 *supra.*

20. Sec.Act Rel.No. 33–5316 (Oct. 6, 1972). *See* 17 C.F.R. §§ 240.14a–2, 14a–6, 14c–5.

21. 17 C.F.R. § 230.145(a)(2). *See, e.g.,* C. Brewer Homes, Inc., 26 Sec. Reg. & L. Rep. (BNA)1268 (SEC No Action Letter avail. Aug. 26, 1994).

22. *See, e.g.,* In the Matter of Carolina Pipeline, Inc., 419 Sec.Reg.L.Rep. (BNA) C–1 (SEC Sept. 2, 1977).

the shareholder's vote or consent will necessarily run afoul of the 1933 Act's gun jumping prohibitions unless a registration statement has been filed.[23] The only types of pre-filing publicity that are permitted are those that would comply with Rule 135.[24] The prospectus requirements[25] apply to solicitations regarding the shareholder's vote or consent for Rule 145 transactions.

In addition to the general exceptions or exemptions from the prospectus requirements under the 1933 Act, Rule 145(b) states that certain communications do not constitute a "prospectus" as defined in section 2(10)[26] of the Act; nor do they come within the concept of the "offer to sell" within the meaning of section 5 of the Act.[27]

Rule 145(b) excludes from the definition of prospectus communications which contain no more than (1) the issuer's name, (2) the name of the persons whose assets are to be sold or whose securities are to be exchanged or who are otherwise parties to the transaction, (3) a brief description of the business of parties to the transaction, (4) the date, time and place of the meeting at which the security holders will be voting or giving their consent to the transaction, (5) a brief description of the transaction, (6) the basis upon which the transaction will be made, (7) and any legend or other statement required by state or federal laws or administrative body.[28] Rule 145(b)(1) thus provides an exemption from the gun jumping prohibitions by permitting dissemination of the foregoing information prior to the filing of a registration statement. In addition to the foregoing limited communications which may be sent out during the pre-filing and waiting periods, any written communication that meets the requirements of the 1934 Act's proxy disclosure and filing requirements is not deemed either a "prospectus" or "offer to sell" so as to require a statutory prospectus or filing of the registration statement prior to its dissemination.[29] The rule thus coordinates the 1934 Act's proxy rules with the 1933 Act's registration requirements.

Rule 145 and downstream sales

Rule 145 addresses the problem of downstream sales after the corporate combination has been approved and consummated and the

23. 15 U.S.C.A. § 77e(c). *See* § 2.3 *supra.*

24. 17 C.F.R. § 230.135. *See also, e.g.,* Chris–Craft Industries, Inc. v. Bangor Punta Corp., 426 F.2d 569 (2d Cir.1970); In the Matter of Carl M. Loeb, Rhoades & Co., 38 S.E.C. 843 (SEC 1959). Compare the types of pre-filing publicity permitted under Rule 145(b), discussed in the text accompanying footnotes 28–29 *infra.*

25. 15 U.S.C.A. § 77e(b). *See* 15 U.S.C.A. § 77b(10). A 1934 Act proxy statement will not violate the Act. *See* footnote 29 *infra.* The prospectus requirements are discussed in § 2.4, *supra.*

26. 15 U.S.C.A. § 77b(10).

27. 15 U.S.C.A. § 77e.

28. 17 C.F.R. § 230.145(b)(1). *See* footnote 24 *supra.*

29. 17 C.F.R. § 230.145(b)(2). *See* 17 C.F.R. § 240.14a–12(a), (b). For the applicable filing fees for preliminary proxy materials *see* 15 U.S.C.A. § 78n(g). The proxy rules apply to all votes of holders of securities that are subject to the 1934 Act's reporting requirements. *See* chapter 11 *infra.* The 1934 registration and reporting requirements are discussed in §§ 9.2, 9.3 *infra.*

new securities have been issued. Rule 145(c)[30] imposes 1933 Act obligations upon any party to a transaction covered by Rule 145(a), other than the issuer, including any person who is an affiliate of such a party, at the time it is submitted for the security holders' vote or consent. Parties to a Rule 145 transaction, including affiliates of the issuer, who offer for sale or sell the securities issued in the Rule 145 transaction are deemed to be engaged in a distribution and therefore are underwriters under section 2(11) of the Act.[31]

Rule 145(d)[32] excludes certain downstream sales from those which create underwriters status under subsection (c) of the rule. Any person selling securities acquired in a Rule 145 transaction who would otherwise be deemed an underwriter under Rule 145(c) is excluded from the definition provided that the sales are in compliance with Rule 144(d)'s volume limitations[33] and are executed in unsolicited brokers transactions.[34] In order to take advantage of this exclusion, it is further required that the issuer be a 1934 Act reporting company which has made all current reports publicly available or, alternatively, has made publicly available similar information.[35] Rule 145 was amended in 1984 to expand the scope of permissible downstream sales of securities acquired in a business combination. Nonaffiliates receiving securities in a registered business combination may sell the securities if they have been owners thereof for at least three years or after two years if the issuer meets Rule 144's informational requirements. Stock acquired in a Rule 145 transaction that is not registered but was issued in reliance on section 3(a)(10)'s exemption for administratively approved mergers is not restricted stock under Rule 144.[36]

With regard to computing the holding period generally, the shareholders' holding period is to be determined by Rule 145(d)(2) and they are not permitted to tack on the Rule 144 holding period of the disappearing corporation's stock.[37] The Rule 144 tacking would presumably have been permissible if the merger had been exempt under section 4(2)'s nonpublic offering exemption.[38]

When securities issued in a corporate combination are not registered under the 1933 Act because of reliance on an exemption, downstream sales may trigger the Act's registration requirements, unless the downstream sales are themselves exempt.[39] By virtue of Rule 144(d)(1)'s two-

---

30. 17 C.F.R. § 230.145(c).

31. *Id. See* 15 U.S.C.A. § 77b(11).

32. 17 C.F.R. § 230.145(d).

33. 17 C.F.R. § 230.144(e). *See* § 4.26 *supra.*

34. 17 C.F.R. § 230.144(f), (g). *See* 15 U.S.C.A. § 77d(4); § 4.23 *supra.*

35. 17 C.F.R. § 230.144(c).

36. Borland Finance Co., 19 Sec.Reg. & L.Rep. (BNA) 1769 (SEC No Action Letter Oct. 10, 1987).

37. *Id.*

38. Rule 144 is discussed in § 4.26 *supra.*

39. 15 U.S.C.A. § 77d(1), (4). *See* § 4.23 *supra.*

year holding period for securities held by affiliates,[40] any Rule 145 transaction must be registered on S–4 or on a more general registration form where the securities so issued are to be traded by the recipients in such a large amount as to constitute a distribution.[41] Otherwise, a merger or other form of business combination would be a convenient device for avoiding the Act's registration requirements and getting securities into the hands of the general investing public without a full-fledged registration statement.[42]

§ 5.3　Section 2(3)'s Definition of Sale—Warrants, Employee Stock Plans, Stock Dividends and Spin-Offs Under the 1933 Act

As pointed out earlier,[1] Section 2(3) of the 1933 Act provides that "sale" includes "every contract of sale or disposition of a security or interest in a security, for value."[2] This definition of sale ordinarily includes the requirement that before there has been a sale, there must have been an investment decision by the purchaser.[3] As noted in the two preceding sections, this broad-based definition has led to several questions regarding what constitutes a sale.[4]

Warrants, Conversion Rights and Options

Section 2(1)'s definition of security[5] makes it clear that options, warrants, and conversion rights themselves constitute securities separate and distinct from the underlying common stock or other security, and thus must be registered for sale, absent an applicable exemption.

Section 2(3)'s definition of sale requires that there be a disposition for "value" in order for a sale to take place. When options or warrants are issued to security holders without consideration or in conjunction with the sale of some other security, there is no sale of the options or

---

40. 17 C.F.R. § 230.144(d)(1). *See* § 4.26 *supra.*

41. Form S–4.

42. *See* SEC v. Datronics Engineers, Inc., 490 F.2d 250 (4th Cir.1973), *cert. denied* 416 U.S. 937, 94 S.Ct. 1936, 40 L.Ed.2d 287 (1974); Sec.Act Rel.No. 33–4982 (SEC July 2, 1979); § 5.3 *infra.*

§ 5.3

1. *See* § 5.1 *supra.*

2. 15 U.S.C.A. § 77b(3). *See* § 5.1 *supra.*

3. Thus, for example, stock awarded to a group of employees for "extraordinary service" has been viewed as not involving a sale because the employees were not asked to make a voluntary investment decision. New Jersey Resources Corp., 17 Sec.Reg. & L.Rep. (BNA) 282 (SEC No Action Letter Jan. 28, 1985). *See also* § 5.4 *infra* for a discussion of the investment decision doctrine.

4. For example, as discussed in the previous section, it was formerly the Commission's position that submission of a business combination for a shareholder vote did not constitute a sale even though the transaction contemplated the issuance of securities. *See* 17 C.F.R. § 230.133 (1971) (rescinded); § 5.2 *supra.*

5. 15 U.S.C.A. § 77b(1). *See* Sec.Act Rel.No. 33–3210 (April 9, 1947).

warrants unless they are immediately exercisable.[6] However, options, warrants, or conversion rights that are immediately exercisable will be viewed as the issuer's "offer to sell" the underlying security which in turn will have to be registered unless an exemption can be found.[7] Additionally, options or warrants, although not immediately exercisable, if transferred for consideration, will constitute a sale since they have been disposed of for value.[8] Furthermore, even after the option has been acquired, the exercise of the option may constitute a distinct purchase. Thus, for example, an optionholder who is induced, by allegedly materially misleading statements, to exercise an option can maintain a securities fraud claim as a defrauded purchaser.[9]

Beyond the foregoing guidelines for the treatment of options, warrants, and conversion rights, the Commission has also taken the view that there is no value and hence no sale with regard to certain employee stock purchase plans even though the underlying stock purchase will of course be a sale.[10] In order for an employee stock plan not to qualify as a sale or a solicitation of an offer to buy, a number of requirements must be met:

　　1.　The employer company or an affiliate announces the existence of the plan.

　　2.　The employer company makes payroll deductions at the request of employees for the purpose of participating in the plan.

　　3.　The names and addresses of employees are made available to the broker or other agent for direct communications by it to such employees regarding the plan. This may take the form of addressing the communication to be sent by the broker or other agent, the

---

6. The last sentence of section 2(3) provides the same rule for conversion rights. 15 U.S.C.A. § 77b(3). *See* H.R.Rep. No. 85, 73d Cong. 1st Sess. 11 (1933). *See also* R. Jennings & H. Marsh, Securities Regulation 301 (5th ed. 1982) ("Thus, in the ordinary rights offering in which transferrable warrants are issued to shareholders without any consideration, the warrants themselves need not be registered [so long as they are not currently exercisable]").

7. *See* Sec.Act Rel.No. 33–97 (Dec. 28, 1933); R. Jennings & H. Marsh *supra* footnote 6; 1 Louis Loss, Securities Regulation 579 (2d ed. 1961); Allen E. Throop & Chester T. Lane, Some Problems of Exemption under the Securities Act of 1933, 4 Law & Contemp.Prob. 89 (1937).

8. "Warrant" generally refers to an option to purchase the issuer's stock. Other stock options which are contracts between the prospective purchaser and seller can also require registration. There are several national exchanges which trade options in publicly traded stock. These exchanges are supervised by the SEC. *See* § 10.2 *infra*. There are stringent exchange listing requirements relating to the underlying securities. Since the underlying stock is publicly traded and subject to the 1934 Act's periodic reporting requirements (*see* §§ 9.2, 9.3 *infra*), separate registration of each option series would seem unnecessary. Accordingly the registration requirements are satisfied by a registration statement and prospectus issued by the Options Clearing Corporation relating to the option exchanges in general, explaining the mechanics of and inherent risks in options trading.

In a somewhat related context there can be a question as to whether a stock option constitutes a "sale" for purposes of section 16(b) of the Exchange Act dealing with short-swing insider profits. 15 U.S.C.A. § 78p(b). *See* § 12.5 *infra*.

9. *E.g.,* Campbell v. National Media Corp., 1994 WL 612807, [1994–1995 Transfer Binder] Fed. Sec. L. Rep. (CCH) ¶ 98,449 (E.D.Pa.1994).

10. Sec.Act Rel.No. 33–4790 (July 13, 1965).

inclusion of the broker's communication with the announcement by the employer company, or the holding of an initial meeting of employees at the company's premises.

     4.   The employer company or an affiliate pays no more than its expense of payroll deductions and the reasonable fees and charges of the broker or other agent for brokerage commissions and bookkeeping and custodial expenses.

     Any deviation from these standards may require registration.[11] Unregistered employee stock compensation programs thus must be carefully planned. In 1988, the Commission adopted, in Rule 701, a new exemption for stock compensation plans of issuers that are not subject to the Exchange Act's periodic reporting requirements.[12] This exemption was designed to facilitate offerings which do not implicate the need for the protections of the 1933 Act's registration requirements.

Stock Dividends

     The original House version of the 1933 Act exempted stock dividends paid in the company's own shares (or shares of another company[13]) from the registration requirements. The conference committee deleted the exemption as unnecessary, reasoning that stock dividends "are exempt without expressed provision as they do not constitute a sale, not being given for value."[14] It follows that the declaration and issuance of stock dividends where the shareholders do not have an election to obtain cash in lieu of the stock do not constitute sales of securities. Similarly, stock splits do not constitute sales under the 1933 Act.[15] This does not mean, however, that downstream sales following a stock dividend or stock split may be made with impunity, since these resales of shares received as a stock dividend or stock split will raise potential statutory underwriter questions, especially if there are so many shares sold as to constitute a "distribution."[16]

     The SEC has taken the position that when, as the result of director action, the shareholders have no election to receive the dividend in cash, or when the stock is issued in lieu of a cash dividend pursuant to an

---

     11.   *Id.* (emphasis added).

     12.   The exemption has an annual dollar limit which may vary between $500,000 and $5,000,000, depending upon the issuer's net assets and existing outstanding stock. 17 C.F.R. § 230.701. *See* § 4.15.1 *supra.*

     13.   This frequently is referred to as a spin-off. *See* text accompanying footnotes 24–41 *infra.*

     14.   H.R.Rep. No. 152, 73d Cong. 1st Sess. 25 (1933). *See,* Sec.Act Rel.No. 33–929 (July 29, 1936). *See also, e.g.* Hafner v. Forest Laboratories, Inc. [1964–1966 Transfer Binder] Fed.Sec.L.Rep. (CCH) ¶ 91,443 at p. 94,741 (S.D.N.Y.1964), *affirmed* 345 F.2d 167 (2d Cir.1965) ("a stock dividend does not distribute property but simply dilutes the shares as they existed before.")

     15.   *See* Gurvitz v. Bregman & Co., 379 F.Supp. 1283 (S.D.N.Y.1974).

     16.   *See* Hafner v. Forest Laboratories, Inc., 345 F.2d 167, 168 (2d Cir.1965). *Cf.* SEC v. Datronics Engineers, Inc., 490 F.2d 250 (4th Cir.1973), *cert. denied* 416 U.S. 937, 94 S.Ct. 1936, 40 L.Ed.2d 287 (1974); SEC v. Harwyn Industries Corp., 326 F.Supp. 943 (S.D.N.Y.1971).

election, prior to declaration of the dividend, there is no value and hence no sale.[17] This latter situation rarely arises; however, the use of a no-sale approach here is highly debatable since the shareholder is making an investment decision when the election is made.[18] In the more common situation, when a cash dividend is declared and the shareholder purchases additional shares, as is the case with a dividend reinvestment plan ("DRIP"), the shareholder is clearly parting with value in exchange for receiving the stock and such distributions of shares will be considered sales and thus subject to the 1933 Act registration requirements absent an applicable exemption.[19]

Exchanges of Securities

As noted earlier, there are exemptions from registration for certain exchanges of securities such as those exchanges exclusively with existing security holders,[20] or exchanges which are pursuant to certain judicial or administratively approved transactions.[21] But these exemptions, although denominated as "security exemptions" under section 3 of the 1933 Act, are nevertheless treated as transaction exemptions and thus will not apply to down-stream sales of the securities so issued.[22] With non-exempt exchanges of securities, any change in the rights and obligations of the issuer or securities holders or amendment to the security constitutes both a sale and a new issue, regardless of whether such amendatory action is permissible under state corporation law.[23]

Spin–Offs

Just as a corporation's dividends in its own shares do not constitute sales under the Securities Act,[24] the same rule applies to dividends paid in shares of other corporations, such as in the case of a split-up or spin-off transaction, since the corporation is not receiving value in return. It has been held, for example, that a shareholder who receives stock of another issuer as a dividend may not sue under the antifraud provisions since no sale has taken place where there is no aftermarket for the

---

17. Sec.Act Rel.No. 33–924 (July 29, 1936).

18. In order for the predeclaration election not to lead to a sale, the dividend must be declared in stock rather than cash by the directors. In making such an election, the corporation can still be seen as receiving value—the savings of the cash dividend. Nevertheless the SEC's position has been that no sale occurs presumably because it is only when the dividend is declared that it assumes the status of a debt. *Id.*

19. *Id. But cf.* Sec.Act Rel.No. 33–5515 (SEC Aug. 8, 1974). Dividend reinvestment plans frequently are registered for sale under the SEC's shelf registration rule. Rule 415, 17 C.F.R. § 230.415; *see* § 3.8 *supra.*

20. 15 U.S.C.A. § 77c(a)(9). *See* § 4.10 *supra.*

21. 15 U.S.C.A. §§ 77c(a)(6), (a)(7), (a)(10). *See* §§ 4.7–4.8, 4.11 *supra.*

22. *See, e.g.,* In the Matter of Thompson Ross Securities Co., 6 S.E.C. 1111 (SEC 1940).

23. *See, e.g.,* United States v. New York, New Haven & Hartford Railroad Co., 276 F.2d 525 (2d Cir.1960), *cert. denied* 362 U.S. 961, 80 S.Ct. 877, 4 L.Ed.2d 876 (1960); SEC v. Associated Gas & Electric Co., 99 F.2d 795 (2d Cir.1938).

24. *See* footnote 14 *supra.*

securities so distributed.[25] However, the Commission has made it clear that a spin-off may not be used as a scheme to avoid registration[26] and that in such a case "value" may be found. As discussed below, registration is likely to be required when the shares will be distributed by resales after the spin-off.[27] However, when the spun-off shares are properly restricted against resale, registration will not be required.[28]

On occasion corporations with a large number of shareholders have made use of their existing shareholders to effectuate distributions of shares in private corporations. For example, in SEC v. Harwyn Industries Corp.[29] a company with a large number of shareholders actively sought privately-held companies desiring to go public. After acquiring the shares of these privately-held companies for valid consideration, these shares would be distributed to the public company's shareholders as a stock dividend or spin-off, with the conduit company retaining some of the privately held company's shares. It was then a matter of time before the shares of the once privately held company became traded publicly. The Commission successfully sought an injunction against such transactions without registration or an exemption notwithstanding the defendants' argument that no value was received by the corporation and that hence there was no sale. The court found that not only did the transactions violate the spirit of the Act,[30] but since the transactions created a public market for the securities of the once privately-held corporation, value could be said to have accrued to that corporation.[31] Additionally, when reselling the shares so received via the stock dividend, the spun-off company's shareholders' distribution of shares consti-

25. Rathborne v. Rathborne, 508 F.Supp. 515 (E.D.La.1980), *judgment affirmed* 683 F.2d 914 (5th Cir.1982). *Cf.* Robinson v. T.I.M.E.–DC, Inc., 566 F.Supp. 1077 (N.D.Tex. 1983) (finding no violation but not reaching the sale issue). A spin-off requiring a shareholder vote may be subject to scrutiny under the 1934 Act proxy rules. *See* Rubinstein v. IU International Corp., 506 F.Supp. 311 (E.D.Pa.1980) (finding no material misstatements). The proxy rules are discussed in chapter 11 *infra*.

26. *See* Sec.Act Rel.No. 33–4982 (July 2, 1969).

27. *Cf.* Chronimid, Inc., 26 Sec. Reg. & L. Rep. (BNA)1646 (SEC No Action Letter available Nov. 17, 1994) (registration not required where securities issued in spin-off would be subject to resale restrictions of SEC Rule 144); MB Communications, Inc., 26 Sec. Reg. & L. Rep. (BNA) 821 (SEC No Action Letter available May 23, 1994) (permitting use of Form S–8 for registration of transactions following a spin-off).

28. *E.g.,* Chronimid, Inc., 26 Sec. Reg. & L. Rep. (BNA)1646 (SEC No Action Letter available Nov. 17, 1994) (registration not required where securities issued in spin-off would be subject to resale restrictions of SEC Rule 144).

29. 326 F.Supp. 943 (S.D.N.Y.1971).

30. *Id.* at 953.

31. *Id. See also, e.g.,* In the Matter of Capital General Corp., Sec. 85,223 (SEC July 23, 1993) (finding a gift to be a sale when there is a benefit to the issuer, such as the creation of a public market).

This rationale and similar opinions generated a great deal of commentary on the spin-off question and interpretation of section 2(3)'s value requirement. *See, e.g.,* Joseph C. Long, Control of the Spin-off Device Under the Securities Act of 1933, 25 Okla.L.Rev. 317 (1972); Simon M. Lorne, The Portfolio Spin-off and Securities Registration, 52 Tex.L.Rev. 918 (1974); Leib Orlanski, Going Public Through the Backdoor and The Shell Game, 58 Va.L.Rev. 1451 (1972); Ronald M. Shapiro & Laurence M. Katz, "Going Public Through the Backdoor" Phenomenon—An Assessment, 29 Md.L.Rev. 320 (1969); Note, Registration of Stock Spin–Offs Under the Securities Act of 1933, 1980 Duke L.J. 965.

tuted a disposition for value. The court further noted that the defendants in *Harwyn* acted in good faith, believing that they had a valid basis for not registering.[32] The spin-off has also been used as an intentional evasion tactic especially where the shares spun off and then traded to the public are shares of inactive or shell corporations. In such a case the violation is even clearer.[33]

The foregoing decisions dealing with spin-off and shell corporations arose in the limited context of transactions in which there was no other bona fide business purpose; in other words, the spun-off corporation was acquired solely for the purpose of spinning it off.[34] However, the impact of these rulings is broad as they also have bearing on more legitimate spin-off transactions.[35] Consider, for example, a publicly held company that decides to spin-off a portion of its business—either because it is no longer desired, as a result of an antitrust decree, or as a final step in acquisition of a company with some undesired assets—the transaction although not the result of a scheme to evade registration will nevertheless require 1933 Act registration or an applicable exemption. The rationale underlying the registration requirement is that the transaction places in the hands of the investing public shares that previously were privately held. Although the transaction by which the securities are transferred from the spinning-off corporation to its shareholders may not include value even in the sense of *Harwyn* and its progeny, the transaction is clearly part of a distribution. Since it is anticipated that the securities so distributed to the shareholders may be sold, unless restricted subject to Rule 144 and related law,[36] the spin-off transaction may place the corporation in a position of participating in a distribution within the meaning of section 2(11)'s definition of underwriter.[37] The value requirement of the sale definition is satisfied since the publicly held corporation's shareholders clearly receive value when they sell their spun-off shares. When such downstream sales are of sufficiently substantial magnitude so as to constitute a "distribution," the spin-off transaction would constitute a type of indirect participation in the distribution that in turn would trigger section 2(11)'s definition.[38] However, when it is not reasonably anticipated that there will be downstream resales following the spin-off transaction, registration will not be required.[39]

---

32. 326 F.Supp. at 954.

33. SEC v. Datronics Engineers, Inc., 490 F.2d 250 (4th Cir.1973), *cert. denied* 416 U.S. 937, 94 S.Ct. 1936, 40 L.Ed.2d 287 (1974).

34. *See* the authorities cited in footnote 31 *supra*.

35. *See generally*, Simon M. Lorne, The Portfolio Spin-off and Securities Registration, 52 Tex.L.Rev. 918 (1974).

36. 17 C.F.R. § 230.144. *Cf.* 17 C.F.R. § 230.145(d) (1982). *See* §§ 4.26, 5.2 *supra*.

37. 15 U.S.C.A. § 77b(11) which is discussed in § 4.24 *supra*.

38. *Cf.* SEC v. Chinese Consolidated Benevolent Association, 120 F.2d 738 (2d Cir. 1941), *cert. denied* 314 U.S. 618, 62 S.Ct. 106, 86 L.Ed. 497 (1941).

39. *See* Consolidated Silver Standard Mines Ltd., 17 Sec.Reg. & L.Rep. (BNA) 2034 (SEC No Action Letter Oct. 30, 1985) (spin-off by Canadian corporation with only 3.2 percent of its shares held by 148 shareholders in the United States).

The SEC has indicated that under appropriate circumstances, a bona fide spin-off may be accomplished without 1933 Act registration, provided that adequate public information will be made available. Specifically, the Commission has stated that a 1933 Act registration may not be necessary when prior to the spin-off the subsidiary registered under section 12 of the 1934 Act.[40] In the transactions in question, the shareholders of the parent corporation (the soon-to-be shareholders of the subsidiary) were to receive a financial statement and other information that would be comparable to that which would have been required on the applicable 1933 Act registration form.[41]

Another limitation on unregistered spin-offs is found in Rule 15c2–11 which makes it illegal for a broker to either initiate or continue giving price quotes for a security in the absence of adequate publicly available information.[42] This rule has the effect of preventing the creation of an uninformed public market with regard to any security.[43]

As the foregoing discussion makes clear, the problem created by unregistered spin-off transactions is the ability to effectuate a public distribution without adequate information being made available. Where adequate information is available, registration may not be required. Thus, the SEC staff has taken the position that registration of a spin-off is not necessary when the spin-off is accompanied by an information statement meeting the requirements of Regulation 14C of the Exchange Act,[44] provided that the spun off shares are registered under section 12 of the Exchange Act.[45] Exchange Act registration satisfies the public information requirement as it subjects the issuer to that Act's periodic reporting requirements.[46]

Deleted section 5.4 can be found in the Practitioner's Edition.

---

40. Evans & Sutherland Computer Corp., 26 Sec. Reg. & L. Rep. (BNA) 822 (SEC No Action Letter available May 23, 1994). *Accord* Pacific Telsis Group, 26 Sec. Reg. & L. Rep. (BNA) 267 (SEC No Action Letter available Feb. 14, 1994); ITT Corp., 26 Sec. Reg. & L. Rep. (BNA) 241 (SEC No Action Letter available February 3, 1994). *Cf.* Pacific Telesis Group, 26 Sec. Reg. & L. Rep. (BNA) 570 (SEC No Action Letter available April 1, 1994) (no action request granted as to odd lot purchase programs in connection with spin-off).

41. *E.g.,* Evans & Sutherland Computer Corp., 26 Sec. Reg. & L. Rep. (BNA) 822 (SEC No Action Letter available May 23, 1994); Ralston Purina Corp., 26 Sec. Reg. & L. Rep. (BNA) 527 (SEC No Action Letter available March 25, 1994).

42. 17 C.F.R. § 240.15c2–11.

43. Regulation of broker-dealers is discussed in chapter 10 *infra*.

44. Regulation 14C is discussed in § 11.8 *infra*.

45. *See* Crane Co., 20 Sec.Reg. & L.Rep. (BNA) 1429 (SEC No Action Letter avail. Aug. 31 1988); Lydall, Inc., 20 Sec.Reg. & L.Rep. (BNA) 1427 (SEC No Action Letter avail. Aug. 25, 1988).

46. *See* §§ 9.2, 9.3 *infra*.

Chapter 6

MANIPULATION, STABILIZATION
AND HOT ISSUES

Table of Sections

Deleted section 6.0.1 can be found in the Practitioner's Edition.

§ 6.1 Manipulation and Price Stabilization Involving Public Offerings

Both during and immediately after a public offering, the market is trying to digest the new issue. At this time, price fluctuations are common and there is the potential for price manipulation. As will be discussed in this section, under limited circumstances the issuer may artificially stabilize the price of the security. All other stabilizing activities fall within the category of illegal manipulation.

Section 9 of the Securities Exchange Act of 1934[1] prohibits manipulative conduct relating to the trading of securities listed on a national exchange; also, section 9(e) provides an express remedy in the hands of any investor who is injured as a result of said manipulation.[2] Furthermore, section 10(b) of the 1934 Act[3] specifically empowers the Commission to promulgate rules defining the scope of prohibited manipulative conduct with regard to any security. Problems of secondary distributions[4] as well as primary offerings with a soft or unreceptive market[5]

---

*Deleted section 6.0.1 can be found in the Practitioner's Edition.

§ 6.1

1. 15 U.S.C.A. § 78i.

2. 15 U.S.C.A. § 78i(e). *See* § 12.1 *infra.*

3. 15 U.S.C.A. § 78j(b). Section 10(b) also relates to antifraud protections and is the governing section for Rule 10b–5. *See* §§ 13.2–13.12 *infra.*

4. *See, e.g.,* In the Matter of Hazel Bishop, Inc., 40 S.E.C. 718 (SEC 1961) which is discussed in § 4.25 *supra.*

5. *See generally,* III, VI Louis Loss, Securities Regulation 1529–1615, 3752–78 (2d ed. 1961, 1969 supp.); William W. Foshay, Market Activities of Participants in Securities

create a climate conducive to manipulative activity aimed at keeping the security's price at an artificially high level. Frequently a new issue will arrive and will be welcomed with a significantly higher demand than supply. This is known as a "hot issue;" hot issues present an environment conducive to manipulation.[6] Sometimes manipulation results in giving the appearance of a hot issue.[7]

Section 9(a)(6) of the Exchange Act[8] specifically prohibits any transaction that is entered into for the purpose of "pegging, fixing, or stabilizing" the price of securities unless said transactions are in accordance with the procedures set out by applicable SEC rules.[9] In 1940 the Commission issued a Securities Act Release[10] discussing the possible approaches to the stabilization problem. The SEC saw three choices: (1) it could outlaw all stabilization activities by insiders; (2) it could permit stabilizing transactions without any limitations; or (3) it could issue piecemeal regulation that would have the effect of prohibiting only detrimental stabilizing activity. The Commission opted for the third alternative and has continued to operate under a system of piecemeal regulation ever since.

Frequently issuers decide to raise new capital by selling additional securities of a class that is already publicly traded. The Commission has recognized that the natural effect of the influx of new stock on the market unless a comparable demand is created, would necessarily be to deflate the market price, at least in the short term. Stabilizing activity arguably is necessary for some offerings in order to make the offering a viable one and to assure a greater degree of certainty in the amount of money that an issuer can expect to raise as a result of such a distribution. The Commission thus allows limited stabilizing activity in this type of situation. The stabilizing rules are highly complex in their attempt to permit only necessary activity without providing an avenue for otherwise illegal artificial price manipulation; a brief description follows.

Distributions, 45 Va.L.Rev. 907 (1959); Martin A. Rogoff, Legal Regulation of Over-the-Counter Market Manipulation, 28 Me.L.Rev. 149 (1976). *See, also, e.g.,* Pagel, Inc. v. SEC, 803 F.2d 942 (8th Cir.1986) (upholding finding of price manipulation during a distribution).

6. Hot issues are discussed in § 6.2 *infra.*

7. *See, e.g.,* SEC v. Schlien, 1991 WL 115770, [1990–1991 Transfer Binder] Fed.Sec. L.Rep. (CCH) ¶ 95,904 (S.D.Fla.1991) (upholding sufficiency of allegations that broker-dealer involved in an initial public offering manipulated market by repurchasing securities at a price above the offering price prior to the completion of the offering).

8. 15 U.S.C.A. § 78k(a)(6).

9. For such a rule *see* Rule 10b–7, 17 C.F.R. § 240.10b–7 which is discussed directly below.

10. Sec. Act Rel. No. 33–2446 (March 18, 1940).

In 1994, the Commission decided to undertake a review of the trading practices rules that are described below.[11] The Commission has thus solicited comments on what type of antimanipulative trading rules are appropriate in the current state of the markets. The reexamination was prompted by recognition of differences in market structures and trading practices that have developed since the current regulatory scheme was adopted. Another issue under consideration is the extent to which different treatment might be appropriate for securities of foreign issuers.[12]

Scope of Rule 10b–6

SEC Rule 10b–6[13] prohibits the issuer, underwriters, prospective underwriters, dealers and other persons who are participating in a distribution from bidding for or purchasing any security which is the subject of the distribution as well as any security of the same class which is already traded unless such stabilizing activity complies with Rules 10b–7 and 10b–8.[14] Rule 10b–6 applies to a broad range of persons having a direct or indirect connection with any of the participants of the distribution. In addition to the issuer, underwriters, and prospective underwriters,[15] Rule 10b–6's prohibitions apply to brokers, dealers, and others participating (or who have agreed to participate) in the distribution,[16] affiliated purchasers,[17] as well as to any other person who is acting

---

11. Review of Antimanipulation Regulation of Securities Offerings, Sec. Exch. Act Rel. No. 34–33924, 59 Fed. Reg. 21681, [1993–1994 Transfer Binder] Fed. Sec. L. Rep. (CCH) ¶ 85,335 (SEC April 26, 1994).

12. *See, e.g.,* Modification of Class Exemption Letter Regarding Application of Cooling–Off Periods Under Rule 10b–6 to Distributions of Foreign Securities, Sec. Exch. Act Rel. No. 34–33862, 59 Fed. Reg. 17125 (SEC April 11, 1994); Application of Rules 10b–6, 10b–7, and 10b–8 During Distributions of Securities of Certain Foreign Issuers, Sec.Exch. Act Rel. No. 34–33137, 58 Fed. Reg. 60324, [1993 Transfer Binder] Fed. Sec. L. Rep. (CCH) ¶ 85,248 (SEC Nov. 15, 1993); Exceptions to Rules 10b–6, 10b–7, and 10b–8 Under the Securities Exchange Act for Distributions of Foreign Securities to Qualified Institutional Buyers, Sec.Exch. Act Rel. No. 34–33138, 58 Fed. Reg. 60326, [1993 Transfer Binder] Fed. Sec. L. Rep. (CCH) ¶ 85,249 (SEC Nov. 15, 1993); Exemption Letter Regarding Application of Cooling–Off Periods Under Rule 10b–6 to Distributions of Foreign Securities, Sec. Exch. Act. Rel. No. 34–31943, 58 Fed. Reg. 13288, [1992–1993 Transfer Binder] Fed. Sec. L. Rep. (CCH) ¶ 85,117 (SEC March 4, 1993).

13. 17 C.F.R. § 240.10b–6.

14. 17 C.F.R. §§ 240.10b–7, 240.10b–8.

15. 17 C.F.R. § 240.10b–6(a)(1), (2). *Cf.* SEC v. Graystone Nash, Inc., 820 F.Supp. 863 (D.N.J.1993) (repurchase agreement violated Rule 10b–6); SEC v. Thomas James Associates, Inc., 738 F.Supp. 88 (W.D.N.Y.1990) (underwriters ordered to disgorge profits resulting from manipulation in connection with public offering).

16. 17 C.F.R. § 240.10b–6(a)(3).

17. 17 C.F.R. § 240.10b–6(a)(4). Affiliated purchaser is defined as (a) any person acting directly or indirectly in concert with a participant in the distribution; (b) an affiliate who directly or indirectly controls, or controlled by, or is in common control with the purchases by a distribution participant, (c) an affiliate who is broker or dealer (except for brokers and dealers trading solely in exempted securities as defined in section 3(a)(12) of the Exchange Act), or an affiliate who regularly purchases securities for itself or others or renders investment advice. 17 C.F.R. § 240.10b–6(c)(6). Rule 405 defines affiliate:

An "affiliate" of, or person affiliated with a specified person, is a person that directly, or indirectly, through one or more intermediaries, controls or is controlled by, or is under common control with, the person specified.

17 C.F.R. § 230.405.

on whose behalf the distribution is being made.[18]   Because of the rule's broad application, persons connected with an issue engaging in a distribution must take care lest they run afoul of Rule 10b–6's prohibitions. It is clear, for example, that the issuer's officers are subject to the rule.[19]

At one time, the Commission took the view that the concept of "distribution" under the 1933 Act was coextensive with Rule 10b–6's view of what constitutes a distribution.[20]   However, more recently, the SEC has reversed that position by explaining that the primary thrust of Rule 10b–6 is to prevent manipulation and not to outlaw all trading activities that might otherwise be legitimate during a distribution.[21] Recent amendments to Rule 10b–6 provide the following definition:

> For purposes of this section only, the term "distribution" means an offering of securities, whether or not subject to registration under the Securities Act of 1933, that is distinguished from ordinary trading transactions by the magnitude of the offering and the presence of special selling efforts and selling methods.[22]

The rule thus is not limited to the types of distributions generally covered by the 1933 Act registration requirements.   The rule provides a special exemption for nonconvertible investment grade debt and preferred securities since price manipulation is "very difficult." [23]   Additionally, the prohibitions of Rule 10b–6 terminate with regard to its application to a dealer or underwriter after completion of his or her participation in the offering as well as upon the termination of all stabilization

---

18.   17 C.F.R. § 240.10b–6(a)(4).

19.   *See, e.g.,* SEC v. Burns, 816 F.2d 471 (9th Cir.1987).

20.   In the Matter of Jaffe & Co., 44 S.E.C. 285 (SEC 1970).

21.   In the Matter of Collins Securities Corp., [1975–1976 Transfer Binder] Fed.Sec. L.Rep. (CCH) ¶ 80,327 (SEC 1975), *reversed on other grounds* 562 F.2d 820 (D.C.Cir.1977). In the SEC's words:

> If the term distribution in Rule 10b–6 were to be equated with the concept of public offering or distribution in the Securities Act, this would not only extend the restrictions of Rule 10b–6 beyond their intended purpose but could result in unnecessary disruption of the trading markets, particularly where an exchange specialist or other market maker acquires registered stock in the performance of his normal functions. It would obviously make no sense to conclude that a specialist, who happens to acquire some registered stock in the course of his normal activities, has to get out of the market until after he has disposed of that stock. No one has ever thought that such a result was required, even though specialists might well purchase registered stock being sold under a so called "shelf registration."
>
> We accordingly decline to hold that any offering of securities pursuant to a registration statement automatically constitutes a distribution within the meaning of Rule 10b–6, and the Jaffe decision, insofar as it is to the contrary, is overruled.

Id. at p. 85,800.

Notwithstanding the SEC's narrowing of the definition of distribution it is not limited to the traditional concept of a public offering. *See, e.g.,* SEC v. Graystone Nash, Inc., 820 F.Supp. 863 (D.N.J.1993) (finding violations of 10b–6 in connection with unregistered offering).

22.   17 C.F.R. § 240.10b–6(c)(5). *See* John B. Manning, Jr. & Eric E. Miller, The SEC's Revisions to Rule 10b–6, 11 Sec.Reg.L.J. 195 (1983).

23.   Sec. Act Rel. No. 33–6456 (SEC March 4, 1983); 17 C.F.R. § 240.10b–6(a)(3)(xiii).

arrangements and trading restrictions with respect to the distribution.[24] However, the Rule 10b–6 disability continues even if a particular dealer or underwriter's participation is over if the transactions are entered into at the instigation of an underwriter continuing to act as such.[25]

As described above, Rule 10b–6 applies to a broad range of individuals and entities.[26] There is thus a significant risk of inadvertent Rule 10b–6 violations. This places a significant burden on counsel associated with the distributions to assure that the antimanipulation rules are adequately explained to the participants in the distribution.[27] This is an important role for counsel since inadvertent purchases during a distribution can result in a finding of manipulative conduct. However, in terms of dealing with inadvertent purchases during a distribution, one mitigating factor is that a violation of Rule 10b–6 requires that the defendant have acted with scienter.[28] Thus, it is clear that negligence cannot form the basis of a Rule 10b–6 violation but reckless conduct may.[29]

Exemptions From Rule 10b–6's Prohibitions

In addition to allowing permissible stabilizing activity, which is discussed below,[30] Rule 10b–6 provides a list of a number of transactions to which the rule's prohibitions do not apply, provided that the transactions are "not engaged in for the purpose of creating actual, or apparent, active trading in or raising the price of such security."[31] Any transactions in connection with the distribution between participants in the distribution and that are not executed on a securities exchange are not subject to Rule 10b–6's prohibitions.[32] Otherwise, for example, a sale from the issuer to an underwriter, or from one underwriter to another, would run afoul of the rule. Unsolicited privately negotiated purchases, not effected through a broker or dealer, involving at least a block[33] of the securities in distribution are not covered by Rule 10b–6's prohibitions.[34]

---

24.   17 C.F.R. §§ 240.10b–6(a), 240.10b–6(c)(3).

25.   SEC v. Resch–Cassin & Co., 362 F.Supp. 964 (S.D.N.Y.1973).

26.   *See* text accompanying footnotes 13–18 *supra.*

27.   *Cf.* In the Matter of Hazel Bishop, Inc., 40 S.E.C. 718 (SEC 1961) (wherein the Commission refused to let a distribution go forward because the participants had not taken adequate precautions against Rule 10b–6 violations); Bio–Medical Sciences, Inc. 180 Sec. Reg. & L. Rep. (BNA) C–1 (SEC No Action Letter available Nov. 29, 1972) (not permitting purchase of securities in open market within 30 days of sale of restricted securities due to fear of manipulation).

28.   *E.g.,* SEC v. Burns, 816 F.2d 471, 474 (9th Cir.1987). Scienter is discussed in § 13.4 *infra.*

29.   *E.g.,* SEC v. Burns, 816 F.2d 471, 474 (9th Cir.1987). In other contexts, the vast majority of decisions have held that a showing of recklessness satisfies the scienter requirement. *See* § 13.4 *infra.*

30.   17 C.F.R. § 240.10b–6(a)(4)(viii), (ix). *See* text accompanying footnotes 73–77 *infra.*

31.   17 C.F.R. § 240.10b–6(a)(4).

32.   17 C.F.R. § 240.10b–6(a)(4)(i).

33.   A block of securities is the number of units or shares traded other than in an odd-lot transaction. Ordinarily a block is one hundred shares.

34.   17 C.F.R. § 240.10b–6(a)(4)(ii).

Similarly, an exemption is available for purchases by an issuer which take place more than forty days after the registration statement's effective date or, in the case of unregistered distributions, more than forty days after the commencement of the distribution provided that such purchases are in fulfillment of sinking fund or similar obligations which become due within twelve months of the purchase.[35]

In addition, certain odd-lot and off-setting round lot transactions by odd-lot dealers are not covered by Rule 10b–6's prohibitions.[36] As is the case with many of the other exclusions from the rule, this one is necessary to enable bona fide day-to-day trading to continue without running afoul of the antimanipulation rules.

Various brokerage transactions are excluded from Rule 10b–6's coverage. For example, Rule 10b–6 does not apply to unsolicited broker-age transactions.[37] Also excluded are solicited brokers' transactions which occurred two or nine business days (depending on the price and public float of the securities) prior to the later of the commencement of the distribution or the broker-dealer's participation in the distribution.[38]

Offers to sell and solicitation of offers to buy are excluded from Rule 10b–6's coverage.[39] Similarly, exercise of conversion rights that were acquired prior to the holder's having become a participant in the distribution are excluded from Rule 10b–6's prohibitions.[40]

Certain transactions by underwriters, prospective underwriters, dealers, and affiliated purchasers are also excluded from Rule 10b–6. Bids and purchases occurring prior to the later of (a) two days prior to the distribution or (b) before the purchaser or bidder became a partici-pant in the distribution are permitted for securities having a price of at least five dollars per share and having a public float of at least four hundred thousand shares.[41] A similar exclusion is extended to the exercise of standardized call options for such securities.[42] With regard to lower priced securities, or those which have a public float of less than

---

35. 17 C.F.R. § 240.10b–6(a)(4)(iii).

36. 17 C.F.R. § 240.10b–6(a)(4)(iv) (excluded are "odd-lot transactions and round-lot transactions that offset odd-lot transactions previously or simultaneously executed or reasonably anticipated in the usual course of business by a person who acts in the capacity of an odd-lot dealer").

37. 17 C.F.R. § 240.10b–6(a)(4)(v)(A).

38. 17 C.F.R. § 240.10b–6(a)(4)(v)(B). Excluded are brokerage transactions for stock having a price of at least $5 per share and a minimum public float of 400,000 shares, provided that the transactions take place at least two days prior to the commencement of the distribution. For other securities, brokerage transactions occurring at least nine days before the distribution or the date of that broker's participation in the offering are excluded from Rule 10b–6.

39. 17 C.F.R. § 240.10b–6(a)(4)(vi).

40. 17 C.F.R. § 240.10b–6(a)(4)(vii).

41. 17 C.F.R. §§ 240.10b–6(a)(4)(xi)(A), (xii)(A).

42. 17 C.F.R. § 240.10b–6(a)(4)(xi)(B) (Rule 10b–6 does not prohibit "the exercise of standardized call options of securities qualified under paragraph (a)(4)(xi)(A) of this section, which call options were acquired after the time such person becomes a participant in the distribution, prior to five business days before the commencement of offers or sales of the securities to be distributed"). *See also* 17 C.F.R. § 240.10b–6(a)(4)(xii)(B).

four hundred thousand shares, Rule 10b–6 does not apply to transactions by underwriters, prospective underwriters, dealers, or affiliated purchasers and occurring no later than at least nine business days before the commencement of the distribution or that person's participation in the distribution.[43] Also excluded are unsolicited purchases by such persons prior to the later of the commencement of the distribution or the commencement of their participation in the distribution.[44]

As noted above, transactions in investment grade nonconvertible debt and nonconvertible preferred securities are excluded from Rule 10b–6's operation.[45] In contrast, a distribution of a security which is convertible or exchangeable into another security is considered to be a distribution of such other security as well.[46]

The advent of Rule 144A[47] has paved the way for an increasing number of unregistered offerings of foreign securities to qualifying institutional investors in the United States. One consequence has been a number of requests to the SEC for an exemption from the operation of Rules 10b–6, 10b–7, and 10b–8. The SEC has granted a conditional exemption from these rules for qualifying offerings of foreign securities.[48] There are six conditions to the exemption. First, in order to qualify for the exemption, the foreign issuer's securities must be currently traded on at least one of five foreign exchanges.[49] Second, the distribution in question must be one taking place outside the United States. Third, the foreign issuer must have at least one hundred and fifty dollars worth of voting shares held by non-affiliates. Fourth, anyone relying on the exemption must notify the Commission of the transactions. Fifth, the transactions may not involve affiliates of the issuer. Sixth, the foreign issuer must have at least a three year operating history.

Scope of Permissible Stabilizing Activity

Rule 10b–7[50] sets out the parameters of permissible stabilizing activity during a distribution. To begin with, both the possibility and existence of stabilizing activity must be disclosed to any purchaser prior to completion of each transaction.[51] Issuers frequently satisfy the notice to the purchaser requirement by placing a legend on the inside front

---

43. 17 C.F.R. §§ 240.10b–6(a)(4)(xi)(C), (xii)(C).

44. 17 C.F.R. §§ 240.10b–6(a)(4)(xi)(D), (xii)(D).

45. 17 C.F.R. §§ 240.10b–6(a)(4)(xiii).

46. 17 C.F.R. §§ 240.10b–6(b).

47. 17 C.F.R. § 230.144A. *See* § 4.26.1 *supra.*

48. Securities Industry Association, [1990–1991 Transfer Binder] Fed.Sec.L.Rep. (CCH) ¶ 79,669 (SEC No Action Letter April 25, 1991). *See also,* SEC Okays Conditional Exemptive Relief for Non–U.S. Offerings, Rights Offers, 23 Sec.Reg. & L.Rep. (BNA) 589 (April 26, 1991).

49. The no action letter listed the following qualifying exchanges: International Stock Exchange of the United Kingdom (on the Stock Exchange Automated Quotation System ("SEAQ") or SEAQ International), Montreal Stock Exchange, Paris Stock Exchange, Tokyo Stock Exchange, and the Toronto Stock Exchange.

50. 17 C.F.R. § 240.10b–7.

51. 17 C.F.R. § 240.10b–7(k).

cover of the prospectus.[52] Additionally, stabilizing bids or quotations and related transactions must be reported to the manager of the stabilizing group; formerly these reports had to be filed with the SEC[53] and these reports were open to public view.[54]

In addition to implementing the above-mentioned disclosure and reporting requirements, the SEC regulates the mechanics of all legitimate stabilizing activity. Stabilizing activity may be engaged in only to the extent that it complies with the extremely complex provisions of Rule 10b–7. The typical pattern of permitted stabilization is for a qualified stabilizer to place a bid on the market to purchase all shares at a specified price. The effect of this bid is to retard the market's downward drift. Under the rule, no stabilizing bid may be "higher than the highest current independent bid price [i.e., the result of a non-stabilized bid.]"[55] Furthermore, in no event may a stabilizing bid be placed "above the price at which such security is currently being distributed."[56] Once a stabilizing bid has been placed, the stabilizer may not raise the price of such bid.[57] The net effect of all the foregoing limitations on stabilizing bids is to allow the stabilizer to "follow the market down, but not up."[58]

In adopting its antimanipulation rules, the Commission was aware of the additional risks of price manipulation involved with "at market" offerings.[59] In an at market offering, rather than the issuer setting a predetermined offering price, the securities are offered in accordance with the market price for securities of the same class that are already traded. Rule 10b–7 expressly prohibits all stabilizing activities with regard to any offering at the market.[60] Rule 10b–8[61] operates much the same way as Rule 10b–7 in permitting stabilizing activities with regard to distributions involving rights offerings. As is the case with Rule 10b–7, the details of Rule 10b–8's requirements are highly complex and thus go beyond the scope of this book.

---

52. *See* 17 C.F.R. § 230.426.

53. Formerly all persons involved in stabilizing activities had to file reports. In 1983 the rule was amended to require reporting only to the manager of the stabilizing group who must retain the information for at least one year. 17 C.F.R. § 240.17a–2.

54. 17 C.F.R. § 240.17a–2(f) (rescinded by Sec.Exch.Act.Rel. No. 34–20155 (Sept. 7, 1983)).

55. 17 C.F.R. § 240.10b–7(j)(1)(i).

56. 17 C.F.R. § 240.10b–7(j)(5).

57. 17 C.F.R. § 240.10b–7(j)(1).

58. Richard W. Jennings & Harold Marsh, Jr., Securities Regulation Cases and Materials 530 (5th ed. 1982), citing 17 C.F.R. § 240.10b–7(j)(4). *See also* 17 C.F.R. § 240.10b–7 ("No stabilizing bid or purchase shall be made except for the purpose of preventing or retarding a decline in the open-market price of security").

59. *See, e.g.,* In the Matter of Hazel Bishop, Inc., 40 S.E.C. 718 (SEC 1961).

60. 17 C.F.R. § 240.10b–7(g). *See also* 17 C.F.R. § 240.10b–7(b)(1) ("The term 'offering at the market' shall mean an offering in which it is contemplated that any offering price set in any calendar day will be increased").

61. 17 C.F.R. § 240.10b–8.

Even beyond Rules 10b–7 and 10b–8, there are some limited exceptions to 10b–6's prohibitions against trading during a distribution. For example, Rule 10b–6 does not apply to "exempted securities" under the 1934 Act.[62] "Exempted securities" as defined by section 3(a)(12) of the Act,[63] which parallels many of the 1933 Act exemptions,[64] include bank and government obligations. It is also established that Rule 10b–6 does not apply, *inter alia*, to redeemable securities of open-end investment companies.[65] Further, Rule 10b–6(e)[66] excludes from its coverage qualified employee stock option plans[67] as well as certain employee savings, investment and stock purchase plans.

Rule 10b–6(j) empowers the Commission to exempt by administrative order any transaction.[68] The 10b–6(j) exemption may be granted by the SEC on its own motion or in response to a written request. The exemption from Rule 10b–6's prohibitions may be either unconditional or qualified by such conditions imposed by the Commission.

§ 6.2 The "Hot Issue," Withholding, and Workout Markets

Just as stabilization can become a problem in issues that appear in a soft market, there are manipulation temptations that can arise in a bull market for the securities in distribution. When the offering is oversubscribed, there is frequently little doubt that once the stock begins to trade publicly in the after-market it will exceed the original offering price. In the case of such a "hot issue" there is great potential for abuse. There may also be the temptation to create the appearance of a hot issue in order to create additional buying demand and upward price pressure.

"Workout" Markets

The Commission has held it to be unlawful for a participating dealer or underwriter to turn away subscribers to a new issue while at the same

---

62. 17 C.F.R. § 240.10b–6(d).

63. 15 U.S.C.A. § 78c(a)(12).

64. 15 U.S.C.A. § 77c. *See* §§ 4.1–4.11 *supra*.

65. 17 C.F.R. § 240.10b–6(d).

66. 17 C.F.R. § 240.10b–6(e). *See also* proposed Rule 10b–6(g), Sec.Exch.Act Rel. No. 34–10539 (Dec. 6, 1973).

67. Under appropriate circumstances, many of these plans will not be subject to the 1933 Act's registration requirements. *See* Sec.Act Rel. No. 33–4790 (July 13, 1965).

68. 17 C.F.R. § 240.10b–6(j). *See, e.g.,* In the Matter of Anderson, Clayton & Co., [1977–1978 Transfer Binder] Fed.Sec.L.Rep. (CCH) ¶ 81,112 (SEC March 14, 1977) (exemption granted for purchases by control persons up to 30 days before and beginning 100 days after a shareholder vote on a merger); In the Matter of Kidder, Peabody & Co., [1975–1976 Transfer Binder] Fed.Sec.L.Rep. (CCH) ¶ 80,453 (SEC Feb. 27, 1976) (permitting stabilizing bids conditioned upon compliance with Rules 10b–7 and 10b–8).

time soliciting purchasers for the unsold allotment.[1] This practice of turning away bona fide offers to purchase gives the appearance of a receptive market or even a "hot issue" since it leads the investor to believe that the offering is oversubscribed when, in fact, securities that represented part of the original allotment are still being peddled. This improper withholding of securities to be offered is known as a "workout" market in which the underwriter and/or the issuer as a result of manipulative transactions are giving the appearance of a market that does not conform to reality. Workout tactics involve not only violation of the anti-manipulation provisions[2] but also give rise to violations of the antifraud provisions.[3] Further, these types of tactics are not necessarily limited to distributions finding a soft market but are equally damaging with regard to securities finding a ready market.[4] In such a situation, the withholding raises the price above the offering price. This in turn allows persons purchasing in the distribution to resell for a quick profit.

All or None and Part or None Offerings

All or none offerings present an environment that is particularly conducive to manipulative activity.[5] For example, it is improper for a broker participating in an "all or none" or "part or none" offering to accept customer funds unless it promptly transmits those funds to an escrow agent or other entity.[6] The prompt transmission requirement is designed to safeguard the customer's right to a quick refund in the event that the offering contingency is not met.

Hot Issues

In 1959, the Commission reported a study dealing with price increases that were found to have occurred immediately following certain public registered offerings.[7] The Commission's study found that a

---

§ 6.2

1. In the Matter of Shearson, Hammill & Co., 42 S.E.C. 811 (SEC 1965). *Cf.* Eichler v. SEC, 757 F.2d 1066 (9th Cir.1985) (sanctioning brokers for failing to fill orders from aftermarket in issue that broker had underwritten).

2. Sections 9, 10(b) and 15(c), 15 U.S.C.A. §§ 78i, 78j(b), 78o(c). *See* § 12.1 *infra.*

3. Specifically sections 10(b) and Rule 10b–5, 15 U.S.C.A. § 78j(b); 17 C.F.R. § 240.10b–5; §§ 13.1–13.12 *infra. See also* section 17(a) of the 1933 Act, 15 U.S.C.A. § 77q(a); §§ 7.6, 13.13 *infra.*

4. *See, e.g.,* SEC v. Schlien, 1991 WL 115770, [1990–1991 Transfer Binder] Fed.Sec. L.Rep. (CCH) ¶ 95,904 (S.D.Fla.1991) (upholding sufficiency of allegations that broker-dealer involved in an initial public offering manipulated market by repurchasing securities at a price above the offering price prior to the completion of the offering).

5. *See* Rule 10b–9, 17 C.F.R. § 240.10b–9; Rooney Pace, Sec. Exch.Act.Rel. No. 34–23763 (Admin.Proc.File No. 3–6332 Oct. 31, 1986), [1986–87 Transfer Binder] Fed.Sec. L.Rep. (CCH) ¶ 84,048. *See generally* Robert B. Robbins, All-or-None Offerings, 19 Rev.Sec. & Commodities Reg. 59 (1986); §§ 6.3, 12.1 *infra.*

6. 17 C.F.R. § 240.15c2–4. *See* In re Lowell H. Listrom & Co., Exch.Act. Rel. No. 34–22689, [1985–86 Transfer Binder] Fed.Sec.L.Rep. (CCH) ¶ 83,946 (SEC Dec. 5, 1985).

7. Sec. Act. Rel. No. 33–4150 (Oct. 23, 1959). *See also* the NASD release on Free-Riding and Withholding, NASD Manual (CCH) ¶ 2151.02. The hot issue problem is once again in the forefront. The SEC has studied the hot issues market for small new issues. *See* 15 Sec.Reg.L.Rep. (BNA) 1995 (Oct. 28, 1983). The study led the Commission to conclude that no changes were needed. *See* footnote 15 *infra.*

number of undesirable practices were taking place. In many cases, the underwriter would allot a portion of the registered offering to active trading firms which were not members of the selling group. These firms would in turn make a market for the securities contemporaneously with the public offering. In one case cited by the SEC study, a security that was initially offered at three dollars per share was selling for as much as five to seven dollars by the end of the first day following the offer.

Not all abusive activities during a hot issue are based on price manipulation. For example, another practice identified by the Commission was for underwriters to allot portions of the securities in registration to their partners, officers, employees, and relatives in anticipation of a "hot issue" and quick profit in the stock.

The Commission went on to point out a number of the legal consequences of such activities. In the first instance, any arrangements regarding workouts, special allotments of securities or the creation of trading firms to be used as market makers must be disclosed in detail on the registration statement. Second, any trading firms would clearly fall within the category of "underwriter" within the meaning of section 2(11).[8] Third, also involved would be violations of the Act's antifraud provisions. Specifically, Rule 10b–5 of the Exchange Act[9] and section 17(a) of the 1933 Act[10] would be violated in that the activities would be giving the public the impression that the entire offering has been subscribed to by the public when, in fact, a substantial portion has gone either to insiders or to trading firms.[11] Fourth, these types of workout activities would also violate Rule 10b–6's prohibitions on manipulation[12] which expressly forbid an underwriter or participant in a distribution from bidding for or purchasing securities being distributed. Fifth, the SEC has pointed out that a broker/dealer acting as a trading firm would in all likelihood be in violation of Rule 15c1–8[13] which prohibits sales on the market of securities in distribution. A sixth consequence is that any participating broker/dealer would be subject to possible sanctions imposed by the Commission, stock exchange, or National Association of Securities Dealers.[14] The SEC has expressed the opinion that current regulation is adequate to curb abuses in connection with hot issues.[15]

Another problem associated with hot issues is the practice of "free riding" whereby a subscriber to the offering hopes to resell at a premium

8. 15 U.S.C.A. § 77b(11). *See* § 4.24 *supra.*

9. 17 C.F.R. § 240.10b–5. *See* §§ 13.2–13.12 *infra.*

10. 15 U.S.C.A. § 77(a). *See* §§ 7.6, 13.13 *infra.*

11. Sec. Act Rel. No. 33–4150 (Oct. 23, 1959).

12. 17 C.F.R. § 240.10b–6. *See* § 6.1 *supra.*

13. 17 C.F.R. § 240.15c1–8. Regulation of broker-dealers is discussed in chapter 10 *infra.*

14. *See* NASD Interpretation with Respect to "Free–Riding and Withholding," NASD Manual (CCH) ¶ 2151.06. *See also, e.g.,* SEC Approves Proposed Changes to NASD Rule Relating to "Hot Issues," 26 Sec. Reg. & L. Rep. (BNA) 1709 (Dec. 23, 1994).

15. No Need for Hot Issues Market Rules, SEC Tells Congress, 16 Sec.Reg. & L.Rep. (BNA) 1446 (Aug. 28, 1984).

but plans to withdraw the order if the "temperature seems to go down before allotment." [16]   Free riding clearly falls within the purview of manipulative conduct.[17]   Free riding as manipulative conduct is not limited to new offerings.   For example, investors who open accounts and misrepresent their net worth to a number of brokerage firms and then purchase securities without sufficient funds for payment have engaged in illegal free riding.[18]

Although the Commission prohibits withholding securities from the market as well as channeling securities to relatives of the issuer, underwriters and participating dealers, there is no express limitation on dealers' showing favoritism towards certain customers.   For example, although a brokerage firm's method of allocating securities during a hot issue might be "unfair" in terms of parity among its customers, so long as the stock does not go to a select group of insiders, there is no violation of the securities laws' hot issue prohibitions.[19]

§ 6.3   All-or-None and Part-or-None Offerings; At Market Offerings

All-or-None and Part-or-None Offerings

Frequently issuers will embark on a financing plan with regard to a project that requires a minimum capitalization from the offering.   This type of specifically targeted financing does not cause a problem where the issuer has an established track record or there are other reasons to believe that the securities will readily be sold at the offering price. However, sometimes an issuer will want to take precautions when a minimum amount of funds is needed.   In such a case the securities may

---

16. I Louis Loss, Securities Regulation 435 (2d ed. 1961).

17. *See, e.g.,* SEC v. Ronald Margolin, Brown & Mueller Investments, Ltd., 1992 WL 279735 (S.D.N.Y.1992) (imposing asset freeze against defendants who allegedly entered into transactions planning to use proceeds from matching trades to pay purchase price, there were thus no funds available to pay for losses on the trades); SEC v. Sendo, 1991 WL 208515, [1991 Transfer Binder] Fed.Sec.L.Rep. (CCH) ¶ 96,117 (S.D.N.Y.1991); SEC v. Hansen, 726 F.Supp. 74 (S.D.N.Y.1989) (illegal day trading where customer purchased securities from one broker and sold them the same day through another to pay for the purchase, disavowing purchases if stock price dropped); In the Matter of Bailey & Co., 41 SEC 747 (1964); V L. Loss footnote 16 at 3456–57 (1969 supp.).   Failure to comply with the interpretations designed to prevent free riding can result in sanctions against offending broker-dealers. *See, e.g.,* United States v. Tager, 788 F.2d 349 (6th Cir.1986) (conviction of trader for free riding); In re James J. Duane & Co., Exch. Act Rel. No. 34–21261, [1984 Transfer Binder] Fed.Sec.L.Rep. (CCH) ¶ 83,657 (SEC Aug. 22, 1984) (censure).

18. SEC v. Teyibo, 1993 WL 144859, [1992–1993 Transfer Binder] Fed.Sec.L.Rep. (CCH) ¶ 97,405 (D.Md.1993) (illegal free-riding in U.S. Treasury bonds); SEC v. Margolin, 1992 WL 279735, [1992–1993 Transfer Binder] Fed.Sec.L.Rep. (CCH) ¶ 97,025 (S.D.N.Y. 1992); SEC v. Sendo, 1991 WL 208515, [1991 Transfer Binder] Fed.Sec.L.Rep. (CCH) ¶ 96,117 (S.D.N.Y.1991).

19. *See, e.g.,* In the Matter of Institutional Securities of Colorado, SEC Admin.Proc. File No. 3–5104 (Aug. 14, 1978).

be offered on an "all or none" basis.[1] According to the terms of an "all or none" offering, if within a specified period there is not a full subscription to all shares being offered, the offering is cancelled. A variation on the "all or none" offering is a "part or none" offering where a refund offer will be made to subscribers if less than a specified portion of the offering has been subscribed to. In both "all or none" and "part or none" offerings, the subscribers' funds typically will be placed in an escrow account and are not made available to the issuer unless the terms of the offering have been fulfilled.[2] On occasion, an "all or none" or "part or none" offering will have the effect not only of satisfying the issuer's financing needs but also of assuring potential investors that there will be a sufficient interest in the investment.[3]

Both "all or none" and "part or none" offerings put a great deal of pressure on underwriters and others involved in marketing the securities[4] and thus these offerings may be susceptible to manipulation.[5] In order to help assure that manipulation will not take place in conjunction with such offerings, the Commission promulgated Rule 10b–9[6] which defines certain practices which constitute a "manipulative or deceptive device or contrivance" in violation of section 10(b) of the Exchange Act.[7] Issuers embarking on "all or none" and "part or none" offerings must

---

§ 6.3

1. *See* Robert B. Robbins, All-or-None Offerings: An Update, 19 Rev.Sec. & Commod.Reg. 181 (1986); Robert B. Robbins, All-or-None Offerings, 19 Rev.Sec. & Commod.Reg. 59 (1986).

2. *See, e.g.,* Richard W. Jennings & Harold Marsh, Jr., Securities Regulation: Cases and Materials 30 (6th ed. 1987).

3. SEC v. Blinder, Robinson & Co., 542 F.Supp. 468, 476 (D.Colo.1982), *affirmed* 1983 WL 20181, [1984–85 Transfer Binder] Fed.Sec.L.Rep. (CCH) ¶ 99,491 (10th Cir.1983), *cert. denied* 469 U.S. 1108, 105 S.Ct. 783, 83 L.Ed.2d 777 (1985) ("in an 'all or none' offering of securities by a new company, whether all the securities have been sold to the public in bona fide market transactions is of particular importance because the 'all or none' contingency is the investors' principal protection. Each investor is comforted by the knowledge that unless his judgment to take the risk is shared by enough others to sell out the issue, his money will be returned"). It has been suggested, however, that this corroboration theory "gives Rule 10b–9 far more content than ever appeared in its adopting and interpretative releases." Robert B. Robbins, All-or-None Offerings, 19 Rev.Sec. & Commod.Reg. 59, 62 (1986).

4. *See, e.g.,* C.E. Carlson, Inc. v. SEC, 859 F.2d 1429 (10th Cir.1988) (underwriter held liable for falsely creating the impression that a "part or none" offering was successful).

5. Examples of fraudulent representations of a full subscription include: C.E. Carlson, Inc. v. SEC, 859 F.2d 1429 (10th Cir.1988) (underwriter held liable); A.J. White & Co. v. SEC, 556 F.2d 619 (1st Cir.1977), *cert. denied* 434 U.S. 969, 98 S.Ct. 516, 54 L.Ed.2d 457 (1977) (part or none offering; issuer guaranteed certain purchasers they would not be required to pay for their shares and arranged loans for certain purchasers, violating sections 7(c) and 11(d)(1) of the Exchange Act); SEC v. Blinder, Robinson & Co., 542 F.Supp. 468 (D.Colo.1982), *affirmed* 1983 WL 20181, [1984–85 Transfer Binder] Fed.Sec. L.Rep. (CCH) ¶ 99,491 (10th Cir.1983), *cert. denied* 469 U.S. 1108, 105 S.Ct. 783, 83 L.Ed.2d 777 (1985) (all or none offering; prior to the closing of the offering the underwriter obtained a bank loan to finance certain purchases; the underwriter also used escrow funds prior to the closing date); SEC v. Manor Nursing Centers, 340 F.Supp. 913, 918 (S.D.N.Y.1971), *modified* 458 F.2d 1082 (2d Cir.1972) (secondary offering wherein some selling shareholders reinvested the proceeds from the sale to purchase unsold shares).

6. 17 C.F.R. § 240.10b–9.

7. 15 U.S.C.A. § 78j(b). The other section 10(b) rules are discussed in § 12.1 *infra.*

be specific as to the offering price, the duration of the offering, and the amount of securities that must be sold to make the offering effective.[8] Also, the possibility of a refund in an offering that is not fully subscribed cannot be offered on a selective basis but must be offered to all would-be purchasers.[9]

Paralleling Rule 10b–9 is Rule 15c2–4[10] which provides that it is unlawful for a broker, dealer or municipal securities dealer to engage in an "all or none", "part or none," or other contingent offering unless all investors funds are promptly transmitted to a bank that has agreed to act as an escrow agent.

One purpose of Rules 10b–9 and 15c2–4 is to assure that there is no investment risk incurred by the subscriber until the contingency provided for in the offering has occurred.[11] Another purpose that has been identified by the Commission is to prevent "all or none" and "part or none" offerings when investors are asked merely to give an indication of interest rather than being required to make full payment subject to a refund at a later date.[12]

It is clear that the law is violated by fraudulent representations that a contingency in connection with an offering has occurred when in fact it has not.[13] However, it is not always clear what offerings are subject to and in violation of the requirements of Rule 10b–9 or 15c2–4.[14]

At Market Offerings

In the case of additional offerings of securities that are already traded, the price will generally be determined by the closing price on the day before the offering.[32] Alternatively, securities may be offered "at the

---

8. 17 C.F.R. § 240.10b–9.

9. SEC Rule 10b–9 declares it to be a manipulative or deceptive act or contrivance to offer a refund unless all the securities are offered pursuant to an "all or none" or "part or none" offering. 17 C.F.R. § 240.10b–9(a). *See* SEC v. Electronics Warehouse, Inc., 689 F.Supp. 53 (D.Conn.1988), *affirmed* 891 F.2d 457 (2d Cir.1989), *cert. denied* 496 U.S. 942, 110 S.Ct. 3228, 110 L.Ed.2d 674 (1990) (extending "minimum-maximum" part-or-none offering two weeks beyond the expiration date and authorizing release of the escrow violated Rule 10b–9).

10. 17 C.F.R. § 240.15c2–4. The rule further requires that the escrow agreement be in writing. *See also, e.g.,* NASD Notice to Members 84–64 (Nov. 26, 1984).

11. *See* Sec.Exch. Act Rel. No. 34–6864, [1961–64 Transfer Binder] Fed.Sec.L.Rep. (CCH) ¶ 76,855 (July 30, 1962) ("It is the purpose of the proposed rule to prohibit any person from making any representations to the effect that the security is being offered on an 'all-or-none' basis unless it is clear that the amount due to the purchaser is to be refunded to him unless all of the securities being offered are sold and the seller receives the total amount due to him in connection with the distribution"). *See also, e.g.,* Svalberg v. SEC, 876 F.2d 181 (D.C.Cir.1989) (failure to inform purchasers in all-or-none offering that underwriters could purchase the stock for themselves was a material omission); Sec.Exch. Act Rel. No. 34–6737, [1961–64 Transfer Binder] Fed.Sec.L.Rep. (CCH) ¶ 76,825 (Feb. 21, 1962); Sec.Exch. Act Rel. No. 34–6905, [1961–64 Transfer Binder] Fed.Sec.L.Rep. (CCH) ¶ 76,869 (Oct. 3, 1962). *See generally* Robbins *supra* footnote 3 at 60.

12. Sec.Exch.Act Rel.No. 34–11532, 3 Fed.Sec.L.Rep. (CCH) ¶ 22,730 (July 11, 1975).

13. *See* the cases cited in footnotes 3, 4 *supra.*

14. *See* Robbins *supra* footnotes 1, 3.

Deleted footnotes 15–31 can be found in the Practitioner's Edition.

32. *See* § 3.1 *supra.*

market" which means that the proceeds will be based on a fluctuating market price. While an at market offering will find a warmer reception in a thin market, the drawback is that the issuer (or selling shareholders in a secondary distribution) cannot predict exactly how much money will be raised. At market offerings are particularly susceptible to manipulation; thus registrants must take care to safeguard against opportunities for manipulation.[33] In addition, the SEC does not permit stabilizing activity during at market offerings.[34]

---

33. *See, e.g.,* In re Hazel Bishop, Inc., 40 S.E.C. 718 (1961) which is discussed in § 4.25 *supra.*

34. 17 C.F.R. § 240.10b–7. *See* § 6.2 *supra.*

Chapter 7

LIABILITY UNDER THE SECURITIES ACT OF 1933

Table of Sections

---

§ 7.1 Consequences of Deficient Registration Statements—Administrative Action, Criminal Sanctions, SEC Injunctive Relief and Private Remedies

Deficiencies in the registration materials can result in administrative reaction by the SEC, criminal sanctions and injunctive relief. This

---

* Deleted sections 7.4.1, 7.4.2, 7.5.1–7.5.4 can be found in the Practitioner's Edition.

is in addition to any private remedies that may exist.[1] In order to prevent a deficient registration statement from becoming effective, the SEC can institute formal proceedings for the purpose of issuing a refusal order.[2] Refusal order proceedings must be instituted within ten days of the registration statement's filing.[3] The refusal order can be issued only after the registrant has been given notice and has had an opportunity for a hearing.[4] Alternatively, when faced with material deficiencies in the registration statement, the Commission may commence formal stop order proceedings at any time.[5] But again, the order can be issued only after formal notice and opportunity for a hearing.[6] As is pointed out in an earlier section,[7] most such deficiencies are dealt with informally through the use of deficiency letters and delaying amendments. Accordingly, the formal proceedings established by section 8 do not reflect the normal process for dealing with deficient registration materials.

Any material deficiencies in the registration statement that carry over to the prospectus will result in violations of section 5(b)'s prospectus delivery requirements[8] which call for an accurate and up-to-date prospectus.[9] Any violation of section 5 gives rise to possible criminal sanctions[10] as well as to judicially secured SEC equitable sanctions.[11] Purchasers of securities sold in violation of section 5 have an express civil remedy under section 12(1) against a violator who is also a seller in privity with the purchaser.[12] Section 11 of Act imposes express civil liability upon persons preparing and signing materially misleading registration statements.[13]

In addition to the foregoing remedies for violation of the prospectus and registration requirements, the 1933 Act imposes sanctions for fraud-

§ 7.1

1. *See* §§ 7.2–7.9 *infra.*

2. Section 8(b), 15 U.S.C.A. § 77h(b). *See* §§ 3.5, 3.5.1 *supra.*

3. *Id.*

4. *Id.*

5. Section 8(d), 15 U.S.C.A. § 77h(d). *See* William R. McLucas, Stop Order Proceedings Under the Securities Act of 1933: A Current Assessment, 40 Bus.Law. 515 (1985).

6. Section 8(d), 15 U.S.C.A. § 77h(d).

7. *See* § 3.5 *supra.*

8. 15 U.S.C.A. § 77e(b). *See* Sections 2(10), 10, 15 U.S.C.A. §§ 77b(10), 77j.

9. *E.g.,* SEC v. Manor Nursing Centers, Inc., 458 F.2d 1082 (2d Cir.1972). *See* §§ 2.4, 2.6 *supra.*

10. 15 U.S.C.A. §§ 77e, 77x. *See generally* Arthur F. Mathews, Criminal Prosecutions Under the Federal Securities Law and Related Statutes: The Nature and Development of SEC Criminal Cases, 39 Geo.Wash.L.Rev. 901 (1971). *See* § 1.4 *supra.*

11. 15 U.S.C.A. § 77t. *See generally,* Arthur F. Mathews, Effective Defense of SEC Investigations: Laying the Foundation for Successful Disposition of Subsequent Civil, Administrative and Criminal Proceedings, 24 Emory L.J. 567 (1975); Mathews, Litigation and Settlement of SEC Administrative Enforcement Proceedings, 29 Catholic U.L.Rev. 215 (1980); *See* § 7.2 *infra.*

12. 15 U.S.C.A. § 77l(1). *See* § 7.2 *infra. See* § 1.7 *supra* for an overview of the private remedies available under the Securities Act of 1933 and the Securities Exchange Act of 1934.

13. 15 U.S.C.A. § 77k. *See* §§ 7.3–7.4 *infra.*

ulent conduct in connection with securities sales. Under the general antifraud provision contained in section 17(a)[14] material misstatements and omissions may result in both criminal sanctions and an SEC civil suit. Additionally, there is substantial but divided authority in support of an implied private remedy for violations of section 17(a).[15] In addition to any such implied remedy, section 12(2) of the Act[16] creates an express right of action in the hands of defrauded purchasers. There is recent authority[17] to support the proposition that all of these remedies are cumulative and do not preclude a parallel implied remedy under Rule 10b–5 of the Exchange Act.[18]

Section 13 of the Act[19] sets out the applicable statute of limitations for private remedies under the Securities Act of 1933. Actions under sections 11 and 12(2) must be brought within one year of the date of the misstatement or omission whereas an action under section 12(1) must be brought within one year of the date of the registration violation. Notwithstanding a longer delay in discovery, actions under sections 11 and 12(1) must in all instances be brought within three years after the security was first offered to the public. All section 12(2) actions must be brought within three years of the sale. Section 14[20] renders invalid purported waivers of 1933 Act claims, except in connection with settlement of threatened or pending litigation.[21] The Exchange Act contains a similar provision.[22]

§ 7.2 Civil Liability for Failure to Comply With Section 5's Requirements—Section 12(1)

Section 12(1) of the 1933 Act[1] provides that anyone who offers or

---

14. 15 U.S.C.A. § 77q(a). *See* § 7.6 *infra.*

15. *See* § 13.13 *infra.*

16. 15 U.S.C.A. § 77*l*(2). *See* § 7.5 *infra.*

Although section 12 on its face would seem to apply to any sale, the Supreme Court held that section 12(2) actions cannot be brought to complain of material misstatements or omissions in isolated transactions. In Gustafson v. Alloyd Co., ___ U.S. ___, 115 S.Ct. 1061, 131 L.Ed.2d 1 (1995), the Court held that the section 12(2) remedy for material misstatements and omissions by a seller of securities is available only with regard to sales made via the use of a prospectus as that term is used in the 1933 Act. As discussed in § 7.5 *infra,* in all likelihood, the section 12(2) remedy will still apply to certain exempt transactions—at least those involving a public offering, and possibly any involving the use of an offering circular that is comparable to a prospectus.

17. Herman & MacLean v. Huddleston, 459 U.S. 375, 103 S.Ct. 683, 74 L.Ed.2d 548 (1983), *on remand* 705 F.2d 775 (5th Cir.1983). *See* chapters 12, 13 *infra.*

18. 17 C.F.R. § 240.10b–5. *See* §§ 13.2–13.12 *infra.*

19. 15 U.S.C.A. § 77m. *See* § 7.5.4 *infra* (Practitioner's Edition only). The statute of limitations for implied remedies is discussed in § 13.8 *infra.*

20. 15 U.S.C.A. § 77n.

21. Meyers v. C & M Petroleum Producers, Inc., 476 F.2d 427 (5th Cir.1973), *cert. denied* 414 U.S. 829, 94 S.Ct. 56, 38 L.Ed.2d 64 (1973). *See* § 13.14 *infra.*

22. 15 U.S.C.A. § 78cc(a). *See* Jones v. Miles, 656 F.2d 103 (5th Cir.1981). *See also* § 13.14 *infra.*

§ 7.2

1. 15 U.S.C.A. § 77*l*(1).

sells a security in violation of section 5[2] is liable in a civil action to the person purchasing such security from him. Agency principles apply in determining who is a purchaser for purposes of section 12. Accordingly, someone who purchases securities on behalf of another qualifies as a purchaser under section 12 and thus can bring suit thereunder.[3] A violation of section 5 gives the purchaser a right of rescission (or rescissory damages) under section 12(1) but the violation does not interfere with the passage of title to the securities in question.[4]

An action under section 12(1) may be brought either in law or equity. As is the case with the other express civil actions under the 1933 Act, a section 12(1) action may be brought either in state or federal court, but there is no right of removal to federal court for actions initiated in a state tribunal.[5] Damages under section 12(1) are limited to the return of purchase price of the security with interest, upon tender of the security. If the securities are no longer owned by the purchaser, the defendant is liable for damages based on the loss comprising the difference between the plaintiff's purchase price and sale price.[6] By virtue of section 13,[7] the section 12(1) action must be brought within one year of the violation upon which it is based but in no event may suit be commenced more than three years after the security was *bona fide* offered to the public. For statute of limitations purposes, the sale occurs, and the statute generally begins to run, on the date the parties entered into a binding contract of sale.[8] It has been held that a showing of due diligence by plaintiff and reliance on defendant's representations will be sufficient to extend the limitations period up to the three year limit at least where the basis of the action sounds in fraud.[9] The

2.   15 U.S.C.A. § 77e. *See* §§ 2.2–2.5 *supra.* Since there is no implied remedy for violations of section 5, section 12(1) is the exclusive basis for seeking damages as a result of section 5 violations. *See* Babst v. Morgan Keegan & Co., 687 F.Supp. 255 (E.D.La.1988).

3.   *See* Monetary Management Group v. Kidder, Peabody & Co., 604 F.Supp. 764, 767 (E.D.Mo.1985).

4.   Allison v. Ticor Title Insurance Co., 907 F.2d 645, 648 (7th Cir.1990), *appeal after remand* 979 F.2d 1187 (7th Cir.1992):

   Section 5 (the registration requirement) applies to transactions; each sale must be registered or exempt. A violation does not stick to the instruments like tar. It is a personal offense by the seller, leaving the validity of the securities as contracts between issuer and purchaser unaffected. Future sales may proceed if an exemption is available.

(citing this Treatise). *See also, e.g.,* Resolution Trust Corp. v. Miller, 1994 WL 276354, [1994–1995 Transfer Binder] Fed. Sec. L. Rep. (CCH) ¶ 98,380 (E.D.Pa.1994) (action for rescission could not be brought under section 29 of the 1934 Act against savings and loan association which was not a seller of the securities).

5.   Section 22(a), 15 U.S.C.A. § 77v(a). *See* § 14.1 *infra.*

6.   15 U.S.C.A. § 77*l. See* Kilmartin v. H.C. Wainwright & Co., 580 F.Supp. 604, 607–08 (D.Mass.1984) for discussion of the tender requirement of section 12.

7.   15 U.S.C.A. § 77m. The statute of limitations for actions under section 12(1) is discussed in § 7.5.4 *infra* (Practitioner's Edition only).

8.   *E.g.* Amoroso v. Southwestern Drilling Multi–Rig, 646 F.Supp. 141 (N.D.Cal.1986). *See* § 7.5.4 *infra* (Practitioner's Edition only). *See also* § 5.4 *supra.*

9.   *E.g.,* Finne v. Dain Bosworth, Inc., 648 F.Supp. 337 (D.Minn.1986); Prawer v. Dean Witter Reynolds, Inc., 626 F.Supp. 642 (D.Mass.1985) (section 12(2) claim); Boyd v. Merrill Lynch, Pierce, Fenner & Smith, Inc., 611 F.Supp. 218 (S.D.Fla.1985), *on rehearing* 614

doctrine of equitable tolling does not apply to actions governed by section 13 and thus will not extend the three year period.[10]

Section 14 of the Act provides that "[a]ny condition, stipulation, or provision binding any person acquiring any security to waive compliance with any provision of this subchapter or of the rules and regulations of the Commission shall be void."[11] This anti-waiver provision has been held to invalidate all releases of potential claims under section 12(1),[12] unless the release is executed in connection with a settlement of threatened or pending litigation. Section 14's invalidation of waivers expressly extends to any civil liability imposed by the 1933 Act.[13] Since the Securities Exchange Act of 1934 has a similar anti-waiver provision,[14] the same result would ensue with respect to any Exchange Act claim.[15]

The thrust of section 12(1) is prophylactic rather than merely compensatory. It has thus been held that since the action is designed to enforce registration requirements, the defense of estoppel will not bar a rescission action for a violation of section 5.[16] The Fifth Circuit thus held that only if plaintiff had refused an unconditional tender of a refund would the defendant have been able to raise the defense of estoppel.[17] However, not all courts have agreed.[18] The better view is that estoppel,

---

F.Supp. 940 (S.D.Fla.1985) (action under section 12(2)). *See* Intre Sport, Ltd. v. Kidder, Peabody & Co., 625 F.Supp. 1303 (S.D.N.Y.1985), *modified* 1986 WL 4906, Fed.Sec.L.Rep. (CCH) ¶ 92,714 (1986) (plaintiff failed to meet burden of proving due diligence; lapse of one year period barred section 12 and section 11 claims). *But see* LeCroy v. Dean Witter Reynolds, Inc., 585 F.Supp. 753 (E.D.Ark.1984) (tolling does not apply where section 12(1) violation is based on failure to comply with prospectus delivery requirements and does not sound in fraud). *See* § 7.5.4 *infra* (Practitioner's Edition only).

The burden of establishing due diligence rests with plaintiff. *E.g.* Krome v. Merrill Lynch & Co., 637 F.Supp. 910 (S.D.N.Y.1986) (decided under section 12(2)).

10. *E.g.* Gutfreund v. Christoph, 658 F.Supp. 1378 (N.D.Ill.1987); Bull v. American Bank & Trust Co., 641 F.Supp. 62 (E.D.Pa.1986); Erickson v. Kiddie, 1986 WL 544, [1986 Transfer Binder] Fed.Sec.L.Rep. (CCH) ¶ 92,889 (N.D.Cal.1986); McCullough v. Leede Oil & Gas, Inc., 617 F.Supp. 384 (W.D.Okl.1985); Platsis v. E.F. Hutton & Co., 1985 WL 447, [1984–85 Transfer Binder] Fed.Sec.L.Rep. (CCH) ¶ 91,963 (W.D.Mich.1985); Morley v. Cohen, 610 F.Supp. 798, 816–817 (D.Md.1985); Gale v. Great Southwestern Exploration, 599 F.Supp. 55 (N.D.Okl.1984); Engl v. Berg, 511 F.Supp. 1146 (E.D.Pa.1981); Benoay v. Decker, 517 F.Supp. 490 (E.D.Mich.1981), *affirmed* 735 F.2d 1363 (6th Cir.1984); Shonts v. Hirliman, 28 F.Supp. 478 (S.D.Cal.1939). *See also* Stone v. Fossil Oil & Gas, 657 F.Supp. 1449 (D.N.M.1987) (no tolling for section 12(1) claim but applying tolling doctrine to section 12(2) claim). *See* § 7.5.4 *infra* (Practitioner's Edition only).

11. 15 U.S.C.A. § 77n.

12. Meyers v. C & M Petroleum Producers, Inc., 476 F.2d 427 (5th Cir.1973) *cert. denied* 414 U.S. 829, 94 S.Ct. 56, 38 L.Ed.2d 64 (1973).

13. *Id.*

14. Section 29(a), 15 U.S.C.A. § 78cc(a). *See* § 13.4 *infra.*

15. *See* Jones v. Miles, 656 F.2d 103 (5th Cir.1981). *Cf.* Pawgan v. Silverstein, 265 F.Supp. 898 (S.D.N.Y.1967) (non–waiver provisions of federal securities laws are not read into state law).

16. *See* Henderson v. Hayden, Stone, Inc., 461 F.2d 1069 (5th Cir.1972).

17. 476 F.2d at 429–430. The fact that the defendant imposed a ten day limit on the refund offer was sufficient to eliminate any such defense to the section 12(1) action.

18. *See* Murken v. Barrow, 1989 WL 168062, [1989–1990 Transfer Binder] Fed.Sec. L.Rep. ¶ 94,815 at p. 94,413 (C.D.Cal.1989) ("If [plaintiff] did not receive a prospectus with the confirmation, he could have asserted his right when the value of 1,500 shares had only

as that term is ordinarily understood, is not a defense to a section 12(1) action.[19] Similarly, the fact that the plaintiff is a sophisticated investor who can fend for himself or herself will not preclude recovery under section 12(1).[20] However, the Supreme Court in Pinter v. Dahl[21] ruled that on appropriate facts, although they may be rare, the *in pari delicto* (or equal fault) defense will be available in an action under section 12(1). The Court held that the law applicable in Rule 10b–5 cases[22] carried over to section 12(1) cases as well. Specifically, the *in pari delicto* defense will bar a claim under section 12(1) only when the plaintiff's fault in causing the section 5 violation can be said to be equal to the defendant's. The Court further noted that this test of relative responsibility of the plaintiff and defendant is dependent on a factual inquiry and thus its application may vary from case to case.[23] The Court additionally observed that in order for a section 12(1) plaintiff's claim to be defeated by the equal fault defense, the plaintiff's role in the transaction must have been one of a promoter rather than simply of an investor.[24] As such, the *in pari delicto* defense is quite narrow and will not be applicable in most section 12(1) actions.

Section 12(1) on its face imposes a strict privity requirement since the violator of section 5 is liable only to the person purchasing the security from him. It has been suggested by one observer that if there are no violations with respect to a purchaser, but there are innocent violations which render an attempted exemption inapplicable, no action should lie in the hands of the unaffected purchaser.[25] However, this view has not gained acceptance in the courts. The fact that section 12(1) does not require a causal connection between the violation and any

declined by $4,500. By his failure to assert his statutory right for nearly one year, [defendant] suffered a detriment since the value of the shares declined more than $21,000. [Plaintiff] is estopped to assert any statutory right").

19. The court in *Murken v. Barrow* relied on Royal Air Properties, Inc. v. Smith, 312 F.2d 210 (9th Cir.1962), *appeal after remand* 333 F.2d 568 (1964) which was a suit brought under 10b–5 applying the defenses of estoppel and waiver. The court in *Royal Air* in turn relied on Straley v. Universal Uranium & Milling Corp., 289 F.2d 370 (9th Cir.1961) (invalidating defense of laches but stating that waiver and estoppel are defenses since they are defenses to contracts declared voidable at common law). The court in *Murken v. Barrow* also relied on Belhumeur v. Dawson, 229 F.Supp. 78 (D.Mont.1964) wherein the court considered the defense of estoppel but then concluded that it was inapplicable because "[i]t is the duty of the seller—not of the buyer—to avoid violating the Act". 229 F.Supp. at 87.

20. Byrnes v. Faulkner, Dawkins & Sullivan, 550 F.2d 1303 (2d Cir.1977) (Market maker may claim the protection of section 12(1)).

21. 486 U.S. 622, 108 S.Ct. 2063, 100 L.Ed.2d 658 (1988). *See* Mark S. Klock, Promoter Liability and In Pari Delicto Under Section 12(1), 17 Sec.Reg.L.J. 53 (1989).

22. *See* Bateman Eichler, Hill Richards, Inc. v. Berner, 472 U.S. 299, 105 S.Ct. 2622, 86 L.Ed.2d 215 (1985). *See* § 13.12 *infra*.

23. 486 U.S. at 639, 108 S.Ct. at 2074, 100 L.Ed.2d at 677.

24. *Id.* at 638–39, 108 S.Ct. at 2074, 100 L.Ed.2d at 677.

25. *See* Carl W. Schneider & Charles C. Zall, Section 12(1) and the Imperfect Exempt Transaction: The Proposed I and I Defense, 28 Bus.Law. 1011, 1013 (1973). In 1989, the SEC adopted amendments to Regulation D which provide that minor violations which do not interfere with investor protection will not destroy a Regulation D exemption. Rule 508, 17 C.F.R § 230.508. *See* §§ 4.17–4.19, 4.22 *supra*.

drop in price resulting in injury to the purchaser is further evidence of the prophylactic intent of Congress.[26] Accordingly, a purchaser will be granted rescission when the price of the security drops due to a change in the issuer's circumstances or market factors wholly unrelated to the section 5 action. Also, it has been held that where there has been a violation of the section 5(b)(1) prospectus delivery requirement followed by the purchaser's receipt of a complete statutory prospectus prior to the delivery of the security, the legal sale does not cure the illegal offer and the purchaser is entitled to maintain an action under section 12(1).[27]

Who is Liable Under Section 12?[28]

One problem that arises with respect to both section 12(1) as well as with section 12(2), which imposes liability on the seller for the material misstatements or omissions in connection with any sale of securities whether or not registered under the 1933 Act,[29] is that of identifying permissible defendants. The question is defined in terms of who is a "seller" within the meaning of section 12. The courts have applied common law principles to identify persons other than the actual seller/violator. It has been held that absent some special relationship between the issuer and the seller, a purchaser not in privity with the issuer has no claim under section 12(1) or 12(2).[30] However, it is clear that traditional agency principles that would give rise to a finding of privity in a normal contract situation apply with equal force in the securities context.[31] In applying this general agency rationale in the securities context the courts require *active* participation in the negotiations leading to the sale in question.[32] It has been held that a broker who actively touts a particular stock to a customer may be found to have been a

26. *See, e.g.,* Diskin v. Lomasney & Co., 452 F.2d 871 (2d Cir.1971); In re NBW Commercial Paper Litigation, 813 F.Supp. 7, 20 (D.D.C.1992) (section 12(1) does not have a causation requirement).

27. Diskin v. Lomasney & Co., 452 F.2d 871 (2d Cir.1971). *See also, e.g.,* 3 Louis Loss, Securities Regulation 1695–96 (2d ed. 1961).

28. For a more detailed discussion of who is a seller under section 12, see § 7.5.1 *infra* (Practitioner's Edition only).

29. 15 U.S.C.A. § 77*l*(2) which is discussed in § 7.5 *infra*. Section 12(2) expressly applies to most exempted securities. However, the Supreme Court has limited the section 12(2) remedy to sales that are part of an offering by prospectus. Gustafson v. Alloyd Co., ___ U.S. ___, 115 S.Ct. 1061, 131 L.Ed.2d 1 (1995). See § 7.5 *infra*.

30. Pinter v. Dahl, 486 U.S. 622, 108 S.Ct. 2063, 100 L.Ed.2d 658 (1988), *on remand* 857 F.2d 262 (5th Cir.1988); Collins v. Signetics Corp., 443 F.Supp. 552 (E.D.Pa.1977), *affirmed* 605 F.2d 110 (3d Cir.1979); Unicorn Field, Inc. v. Cannon Group, Inc., 60 F.R.D. 217 (S.D.N.Y.1973). *See also* Swenson v. Engelstad, 626 F.2d 421, 427 (5th Cir.1980). While there has been some suggestion that the *Pinter* decision may dispense with the privity requirement the better view is that it does not. *E.g.,* In re Craftmatic Securities Litigation, 703 F.Supp. 1175, 1183 (E.D.Pa.1989), *affirmed in part, reversed in part* 890 F.2d 628 (3d Cir.1989). *But see* Scotch v. Moseley, Hallgarten, Estabrook & Weeden, Inc., 709 F.Supp. 95 (M.D.Pa.1988) (privity not required under section 12(2) with regard to open-market transaction). *See generally* Robert N. Rapp, Expanded Liability Under Section 12 of the Securities Act: When is a Seller Not a Seller?, 27 Case Wes.L.Rev. 445 (1977).

31. *See* Buchholtz v. Renard, 188 F.Supp. 888 (S.D.N.Y.1960).

32. *See* Wasson v. SEC, 558 F.2d 879 (8th Cir.1977); Lennerth v. Mendenhall, 234 F.Supp. 59 (N.D.Ohio 1964).

"substantial factor" and therefore subject to section 12(2) liability as a seller although he may not have been the actual person transacting the final sale.[33] The continued validity of this holding is in doubt in light of the Supreme Court's decision in *Pinter*. The Court in *Pinter* indicated that a section 12 defendant must have been both an immediate and direct seller of the securities to the plaintiff.[34] The Court stressed that section 12 liability depends on the defendant having been more than a remote participant in the sale.[35] Thus, merely participating in the preparation of the registration statement does not satisfy the active participation requirement so as to render such participants in privity with a purchaser.[36] Even substantial involvement in the preparation of registration and offering materials will not create liability unless there is also active involvement in the negotiations leading to the sale in question. Similarly, an indirect connection with the selling process will not be sufficient to render the defendant liable in an action under section 12.[37]

Many courts have indicated that although couched in terms of the common law concepts of privity and agency, the real test of whether the defendant is a seller in a section 12 action was one of causation.[38] This

33. Hill York Corp. v. American International Franchises, Inc., 448 F.2d 680 (5th Cir.1971).

34. 486 U.S. at 650, 108 S.Ct. at 2080, 100 L.Ed.2d at 684. *See* § 7.5.1 *infra* (Practitioner's Edition only).

35. 486 U.S. at 654, 108 S.Ct. at 2082, 100 L.Ed.2d at 686.

36. Collins v. Signetics Corp., 443 F.Supp. 552 (E.D.Pa.1977), *affirmed* 605 F.2d 110 (3d Cir.1979). *See also, e.g.* Foster v. Jesup & Lamont Securities Co., 759 F.2d 838 (11th Cir.1985) (underwriter not a seller; lack of direct communication between defendant and purchaser), *question certified* 482 So.2d 1201 (Ala.1986), *certified questioned conformed to* 782 F.2d 901 (11th Cir.1986) (Alabama law of aiding and abetting requires less than a showing of "substantial factor"); Ackerman v. Clinical Data, Inc., 1986 WL 53401, [1986 Transfer Binder] Fed.Sec.L.Rep. (CCH) ¶ 92,803 (D.Mass.1986) (issuer held not liable under section 12(2)); Fine v. Rubin, 623 F.Supp. 171 (N.D.Cal.1985) (issuer's officers and directors and nonselling underwriter were not sellers); In re Activision Securities Litigation, 621 F.Supp. 415 (N.D.Cal.1985) (insufficient allegations of personal participation by defendants); Moran v. Kidder, Peabody & Co., 609 F.Supp. 661 (S.D.N.Y.1985), *affirmed* 788 F.2d 3 (2d Cir.1986); In re Diasonics Securities Litigation, 599 F.Supp. 447 (N.D.Cal. 1984) (plaintiffs must be able to identify the seller in order to state a claim under section 12(2)); Anders v. Dakota Land & Development Co., 380 N.W.2d 862 (Minn.App.1986).

37. *E.g.*, Stokes v. Lokken, 644 F.2d 779 (8th Cir.1981) (lawyer not liable under section 12); Wright v. Schock, 571 F.Supp. 642, 657–659 (N.D.Cal.1983), *affirmed* 742 F.2d 541 (9th Cir.1984) (bank and title company not liable). *See also, e.g.*, Pharo v. Smith, 621 F.2d 656, 667 (5th Cir.1980), *cause remanded rehearing granted in part* 625 F.2d 1226 (5th Cir.1980). *See also, e.g.* In re Fortune Systems Securities Litigation, 604 F.Supp. 150 (N.D.Cal.1984) ("substantial participation" test not satisfied by routine activities by issuer's officers and directors in preparation of public offering). *See also, e.g.*, Ackerman v. Clinical Data, Inc., 1986 WL 53401, [1986 Transfer Binder] Fed.Sec.L.Rep. (CCH) ¶ 92,803 (D.Mass.1986) (active participation in preparation of registration statement is not sufficient to establish liability under section 12(2)).

38. Davis v. Avco Financial Services, Inc., 739 F.2d 1057 (6th Cir.1984), *cert. denied* 470 U.S. 1005, 105 S.Ct. 1359, 84 L.Ed.2d 381 (1985); Junker v. Crory, 650 F.2d 1349, 1360 (5th Cir.1981); Croy v. Campbell, 624 F.2d 709, 713 n. 5 (5th Cir.1980); McFarland v. Memorex Corp., 581 F.Supp. 878, 879 (N.D.Cal.1984), relying on Admiralty Fund v. Jones, 677 F.2d 1289, 1294 (9th Cir.1982). *See* In re North American Acceptance Corp. Securities Cases, 513 F.Supp. 608, 632 (N.D.Ga.1981).

more liberalized view of section 12 liability based on a causation analysis has been rejected by the Supreme Court in *Pinter*.[39]

Aiding and abetting liability applies to the securities acts generally for purposes of criminal prosecutions and at least certain SEC enforcement actions.[40] However, it is clear that aiding and abetting liability will not attach in actions under section 12.[41] As a result of a 1994 Supreme Court decision, it is now clear that aiding and abetting cannot support recovery in any private right of action under the securities laws.[42] Although principles applicable to aiding and abetting liability, to a very limited extent, may be relevant for finding liability under section 12, aiding and abetting activity will not result in section 12 liability where the defendant is not a seller of the securities who can be said to have been in privity with the plaintiff purchaser.[43]

Vicarious liability principles carry over to section 12 actions.[44] Also, section 15 of the 1933 Act[45] calls for joint and several liability of controlling persons with regard to violations of either section 11 or section 12 of the Act.[46] Along these lines it has been held that section 15

39. 486 U.S. 622, 108 S.Ct. 2063, 100 L.Ed.2d 658. *See* § 7.5.1 *infra* (Practitioner's Edition only).

40. Notwithstanding a long line of circuit and district court cases to the contrary, in 1994, the Supreme Court ruled that there is no implied right of action for aiding and abetting violations of the Securities Exchange Act's general antifraud provisions. Central Bank of Denver, N.A. v. First Interstate Bank of Denver, ___ U.S. ___, 114 S.Ct. 1439, 128 L.Ed.2d 119 (1994). *See* §§ 7.8, 13.16 *infra*.

41. Craftmatic Securities Litigation v. Kraftsow, 890 F.2d 628, 636 (3d Cir.1989) (no aider and abettor liability for violations of section 12(2)); Royal American Managers, Inc. v. IRC Holding Corp., 885 F.2d 1011, 1017 (2d Cir.1989) (same); Schlifke v. Seafirst Corp., 866 F.2d 935, 942 (7th Cir.1989) (same); Ackerman v. Schwartz, 733 F.Supp. 1231 (N.D.Ind.1989), *appeal dismissed* 922 F.2d 843 (7th Cir.1991); In re Crazy Eddie Securities Litigation, 714 F.Supp. 1285 (E.D.N.Y.1989); In re ZZZZ Best Securities Litigation, 1989 WL 90284, [1989 Transfer Binder] Fed.Sec.L.Rep. ¶ 94,485 (C.Cal.1989); Lambergs v. Total Health Systems, Inc., 1989 WL 63243, [1989–1990 Transfer Binder] Fed.Sec.L.Rep. ¶ 94,831 (D.Mass.1989); In re Thortec Securities Litigation, 1989 WL 67429, [1989 Transfer Binder] Fed.Sec.L.Rep. (CCH) ¶ 94,330 (N.D.Cal.1989). *See* §§ 7.8, 13.16 *infra*. *Contra* Drexel Burnham Lambert, Inc. v. American Bankers Insurance Co., 1989 WL 168012, [1989–1990 Transfer Binder] Fed.Sec.L.Rep. ¶ 94,835 (E.D.N.C.1989) (aiding and abetting liability does exist under section 12(2)).

42. Central Bank of Denver, N.A. v. First Interstate Bank of Denver, ___ U.S. ___, 114 S.Ct. 1439, 128 L.Ed.2d 119 (1994).

43. *See, e.g.*, Klein v. Computer Devices, Inc., 602 F.Supp. 837 (S.D.N.Y.1985); Lazar v. Sadlier, 622 F.Supp. 1248 (C.D.Cal.1985); In re Seagate Technology Securities Litigation, 1984 WL 5832, [1985–86 Transfer Binder] Fed.Sec.L.Rep. (CCH) ¶ 92,435 (N.D.Cal.1985). *Cf.* Hackett v. Village Court Associates, 602 F.Supp. 856 (E.D.Wis.1985) (strongly questioning aiding and abetting theory in section 12(2) action). *Accord* In re Activision Securities Litigation, 621 F.Supp. 415, 421 (N.D.Cal.1985). *See also* Ahern v. Gaussoin, 611 F.Supp. 1465, 1484 (D.Or.1985) (aiding and abetting theory will not support liability under section 11 of the 1933 Act); § 7.8 *infra*. *But see* Ackerman v. Clinical Data, Inc., 1985 WL 1884, [1985–86 Transfer Binder] Fed.Sec.L.Rep. (CCH) ¶ 92,207 (S.D.N.Y.1985). *See generally* Comment, The Recognition of Aiding and Abetting in the Federal Securities Laws, 23 Houst.L.Rev. 821 (1986). *But cf.* Kilmartin v. H.C. Wainwright & Co., 637 F.Supp. 938 (D.Mass.1986) (recognizing aider and abettor liability under section 12(2) in light of liberalized definition of "seller").

44. *See, e.g.* Underhill v. Royal, 769 F.2d 1426 (9th Cir.1985).

45. 15 U.S.C.A. § 77o.

46. The statute provides:

creates merely secondary rather than primary liability for someone who is not a seller under section 12.[47]

§ 7.3 Liability for Misstatements and Omissions in the Registration Statement—Section 11 of the 1933 Act

The prospectus and registration statement can provide the basis of liability to purchasers of the securities covered by the registration statement. Section 11(a) of the Securities Act of 1933[1] creates an express right of action for securities purchasers when a registration statement contains untrue statements of material fact or omissions of material fact.[2]

Material Misstatements and Omissions; Bespeaks Caution Doctrine

Materiality under section 11, as is the case with the securities laws generally, is a question of fact.[3] Thus, in determining whether misstatements or omissions in the registration statement are material, it is appropriate to make reference to the materiality cases under other disclosure provisions.[4] Materiality is to be determined as of the date of the offering, not by using hindsight that may be gained from subsequent

---

Every person who, by or through stock ownership, agency, or otherwise, or who, pursuant to or in connection with an agreement or understanding with one or more other persons by or through stock ownership, agency, or otherwise, controls any person liable under sections 77k or 77l of this title, shall also be liable jointly and severally with and to the same extent as such controlled person to any person to whom such controlled person is liable, unless the controlling person had no knowledge of or reasonable ground to believe in the existence of the facts by which the liability of the controlled person is alleged to exist.

15 U.S.C.A. § 77o. The Exchange Act has a comparable provision. 15 U.S.C.A. § 78t. *See* §§ 7.7, 13.15 *infra*.

47. *See* Herm v. Stafford, 663 F.2d 669, 685 (6th Cir.1981) (a director is not automatically liable as a controlling person; there must be a showing of actual control); G.A. Thompson & Co. v. Partridge, 636 F.2d 945, 957 (5th Cir.1981) (controlling person doctrine explained); McDaniel v. Compania Minera Mar de Cortes, 528 F.Supp. 152 (D.Ariz.1981); Hagert v. Glickman, Lurie, Eiger & Co., 520 F.Supp. 1028 (D.Minn.1981).

§ 7.3

1. 15 U.S.C.A. § 77k.

2. Normal concepts of materiality apply in section 11 actions. Materiality is discussed in § 13.5A *infra*. Thus, for example, the bespeaks caution doctrine, relating to soft information and projections is' applicable in actions under section 11. In re Worlds of Wonder Securities Litigation, 35 F.3d 1407 (9th Cir.1994). Soft information is discussed in § 3.7 *supra*.

The section 11 remedy is limited to damages; injunctive relief is not available. K/A & Co. v. Hallwood Energy Partners, L.P., 1990 WL 37866, [1990–1991 Transfer Binder] Fed.Sec.L.Rep. (CCH) ¶ 95,758 (S.D.N.Y.1990).

3. *See* Kaplan v. Rose, 49 F.3d 1363, (9th Cir.1994); McMahan & Co. v. Wherehouse Entertainment, Inc., 900 F.2d 576 (2d Cir.1990), *cert. denied* 501 U.S. 1249, 111 S.Ct. 2887, 115 L.Ed.2d 1052 (1991) (triable issue of fact concerning whether description of conditional right to redemption of debentures was materially misleading); Kronfeld v. Trans World Airlines, Inc., 832 F.2d 726, 731–32 (2d Cir.1987).

4. *See* §§ 11.4 (materiality under the proxy rules), 13.5A (materiality under Rule 10b–5) *infra*.

events.[5] A corollary of the materiality doctrine has been developed in cases involving projections in offering materials. Under the "bespeaks caution" doctrine,[6] cautionary language in the prospectus may preclude misstatements from being actionable.[7] The doctrine relates to the materiality of the statements under attack since it addresses the question of whether the misstatements are materially misleading when judged in light of the total mix of information available to the investor.[8] The bespeaks caution doctrine, which applies both to material misstatements and omissions,[9] should not be applied too quickly.[10] Cautionary language will not always be adequate to prevent an antifraud claim; it must be sufficient to negate any reasonable reliance on predictions that may appear optimistic.[11]

Who Can Sue; Nature of Suit

An action under section 11 may be brought by "any person acquiring such security" unless it can be shown that at the time of purchase the purchaser knew of the misstatement or omission. Section 11 permits the plaintiff to bring suit either in law or equity in any court of competent jurisdiction. By virtue of section 22(a) of the Act[12] the plaintiff has an absolute choice of forum since actions under the 1933 Act may be brought either in federal or state court and there is no right of removal from a state tribunal to a federal one.[13] The plaintiff suing under section 11 has a further advantage in that by framing the complaint in terms of an action in equity he or she may be able to deny

---

5. *See, e.g.,* Anderson v. Clow, 1993 WL 497212, [1993 Transfer Binder] Fed. Sec. L. Rep. (CCH) ¶ 97,807 (S.D.Cal.1993).

6. In re Worlds of Wonder Securities Litigation, 35 F.3d 1407 (9th Cir.1994) (bespeaks caution applies in section 11 actions). *See* § 3.7 *supra* and § 13.5A *infra*.

See generally Donald C. Langevoort, Disclosures that "Bespeak Caution," 49 Bus. Law. 481 (1994). *See also* the discussion in §§ 13.5A, 13.5B *infra*.

7. *See, e.g.,* In re Donald Trump Casino Securities Litigation, 7 F.3d 357, 371 (3d Cir.1993):

when an offering document's forecasts, opinions or projections are accompanied by meaningful cautionary statements, the forward–looking statements will not form the basis for a securities fraud claim if those statements did not affect the "total mix" of information the document provided investors. In other words, cautionary language, if sufficient, renders the alleged omissions or misrepresentations immaterial as a matter of law.

8. *See, e.g.,* In re Donald Trump Casino Securities Litigation, 7 F.3d 357, 371 (3d Cir.1993); Sable v. Southmark/Envicon Capital Corp., 819 F.Supp. 324 (S.D.N.Y.1993) (bespeaks caution rationale applied).

9. *See, e.g.,* In re Donald Trump Casino Securities Litigation, 7 F.3d 357, 371 (3d Cir.1993).

10. *See, e.g.,* Langevoort *supra* footnote 6 at 503.

11. *E.g.,* Rubinstein v. Collins, 20 F.3d 160 (5th Cir.1994); Wade v. Industrial Funding Corp., 1993 WL 650837, [1993–1994 Transfer Binder] Fed. Sec. L. Rep. (CCH) ¶ 98,144 (N.D.Cal.1993); In re First American Center Securities Litigation, 807 F.Supp. 326 (S.D.N.Y.1992).

12. 15 U.S.C.A. § 77v(a).

13. *See generally* Thomas L. Hazen, Allocation of Jurisdiction Between the State and Federal Courts for Private Remedies Under the Federal Securities Laws, 60 N.C.L.Rev. 707 (1982). *See* § 14.1 *infra*.

the defendant a choice of jury trial that would otherwise exist in an action at law. Section 11(b), which is discussed below,[14] sets forth the defenses and renders the issuer strictly liable for all such material misstatements or omissions while all other defendants are liable subject to a defense of due diligence or reasonable investigation.[15]

Defendants in Section 11 Actions

Section 11(a) lists the categories of persons and entities in addition to the issuer which may be liable for misstatements or omissions in the registration statement: [16] (1) all signers of the registration statement; [17] (2) every director, person performing a similar function, or partner at the time of the filing of the registration statement; (3) all persons named with their consent in the registration statement as about to become a director, person performing similar functions, or partner; (4) every accountant, engineer, or appraiser, or any person whose profession gives authority to statements made by him or her, who has with consent been named in the registration statement as having prepared or certified any part of the filing, or any report or evaluation used in connection with the registration statement; and (5) every underwriter with respect to the security in registration.[18] Although not expressly included in the statute, it seems clear that the attorneys are to be treated as professionals when rendering expert opinions.

Reliance not Necessary

When a section 11(a) plaintiff has acquired the securities more than twelve months after the effective date of the registration statement and

---

14. 15 U.S.C.A. § 77k(b). *See* § 7.4 *infra*.

15. The issuer is responsible for disclosure of all material information but it cannot be held accountable for information that it did not know and had no way of knowing. In re Ultimate Corp. Securities Litigation, 1989 WL 86961, [1989 Transfer Binder] Fed.Sec. L.Rep. (CCH) ¶ 94,523 (S.D.N.Y.1989) (unpublished case) (no liability for failure to disclose "arguably material" information that two officers were planning to leave; evidence indicated that the issuer disclosed their departure as soon as that information became available to the issuer).

16. *See* Hagert v. Glickman, Lurie, Eiger & Co., 520 F.Supp. 1028, 1033 (D.Minn.1981) (no recovery on an aiding and abetting theory under section 11; liability cannot be extended to those who do not fall into the specific categories of section 11). *See also* Feit v. Leasco Data Processing Equipment Corp., 332 F.Supp. 544 (E.D.N.Y.1971); Escott v. BarChris Construction Corp., 283 F.Supp. 643 (S.D.N.Y.1968).

17. Section 6 sets forth who must sign. 15 U.S.C.A. § 77f(a) (1976). The required signers include the issuer, the issuer's principal executive, financial and accounting officers and a majority of the issuer's board of directors or persons performing similar functions. *See* §§ 3.3–3.4 *supra*.

18. 15 U.S.C.A. § 77k(a).

As discussed in an earlier section of this treatise, section 2(11) of the 1933 Act sets forth a broad definition of underwriter which includes, *inter alia*, some who purchases securities from an issuer with a view to distribute. 15 U.S.C.A. § 77b(11); *see* § 4.24 *supra*. However, at least one court has held the concept of "underwriter" as that term is used in section 11 of the act is to be interpreted more in accordance with the generic definition of the terms. In re Jenny Craig Securities Litigation, 1994 WL 750662 [1994–1995 Transfer Binder] Fed.Sec.L.Rep. (CCH) ¶ 98,499 (S.D.Cal.1994) (the fact that institutional investors who sold shares through an underwriter who in turn sold the shares to the public was not in itself sufficient to subject the institutional investor to section 11 liability).

if the issuer has distributed an "earnings statement" for that period, the plaintiff must prove reliance on the material misstatement or omission.[19] However, the purchaser need not prove that he or she actually read the registration statement in order to establish such reliance.[20] Without proof of plaintiff's actual knowledge of the misstatement or omission at time of purchase, there is a conclusive presumption of reliance for any person purchasing the security prior to the expiration of twelve months.[21]

Tracing Securities to the Registration Statement

In order for a purchaser of the security to succeed in an action under section 11 he or she must prove that the shares purchased are traceable to the offering covered by the registration statement.[22] In light of the statutory language, the courts have rigidly enforced the tracing requirement.[23]

Although not limited to plaintiffs who purchased securities during the public offering, section 11 does require that the plaintiff be a purchaser of the securities. Similarly, section 11 standing is limited to persons and entities who have made an investment with respect to securities. Thus, for example, it has been held that the acquiring corporation which receives share certificates of the disappearing corporation in the course of a merger is not a proper section 11 plaintiff.[24] Although a public offering with an allegedly materially misleading registration statement had occurred prior to the merger, the court explained that the acquiring corporation was not purchasing securities but rather according to the state law of mergers was acquiring the assets and liabilities of the disappeared corporation.[25] Although in such a situation,

---

19. 15 U.S.C.A. § 77k(a), last paragraph. The Commission has defined the types of earning statements that will suffice. Simply put, the earnings statement must be made generally available to securities holders and contain the type of financial information that would be found in current 1934 reports. *See* 17 C.F.R. § 230.158.

20. 15 U.S.C.A. § 77k(a).

21. *See, e.g.,* Barnes v. Osofsky, 373 F.2d 269 (2d Cir.1967); McFarland v. Memorex Corp., 493 F.Supp. 631, 641 (N.D.Cal.1980), *reconsideration granted* 581 F.Supp. 878 (N.D.Cal.1984).

22. *E.g.,* In re AES Corp. Securities Litigation, 825 F.Supp. 578, 593 (S.D.N.Y.1993) (refusing to dismiss section 11 claim where plaintiff was able to trace the securities to the offering).

23. For example, in In re Quarterdeck Office Systems, Inc. Securities Litigation, 1993 WL 623310, [1993–1994 Transfer Binder] Fed. Sec. L. Rep. (CCH) ¶ 98,092 (C.D.Cal.1993), the plaintiffs admitted that they had not purchased their shares in the initial public offering but claimed section 11 standing since at that time 97% of the outstanding shares had been issued under the registration statement that was being attacked. The court refused to allow the section 11 claim to proceed since although the probabilities favored a conclusion that the plaintiff's shares had been issued in the registered offering, that conclusion was nevertheless too speculative to support plaintiff as a class representative in a section 11 class action.

24. Versyss Inc. v. Coopers & Lybrand, 982 F.2d 653 (1st Cir.1992), *cert. denied* ___ U.S. ___, 113 S.Ct. 2965, 125 L.Ed.2d 665 (1993).

25. The court explained that the most that could be said of the stock certificates is that they were evidence that the surrendering shareholders had owned stock in the disappearing corporation and were entitled to shares in the survivor. 982 F.2d at 656. The court went on to observe that "at worst the share certificates were wallpaper." *Id.*

a claim might be grounded upon other provisions of the securities laws, it could not be grounded upon section 11 of the 1933 Act.[26]

Additional Requirements; Comparison With Other Remedies

The tracing requirement of section 11 does not carry over to the other provisions of the 1933 Act. Section 12(1)[27] creates liability for securities sold in violation of the requirements of section 5 and section 12(2)[28] liability is based on material misstatements by the seller or offeror whether or not made in a registration statement or in connection with a registered offering. In actions under section 12 the plaintiff need not trace the securities purchased back to the registered offering in question; nor is tracing required in a Rule 10b–5 action[29] based on misstatements in the registration statement or prospectus.[30] Additionally, it has been held that particularized allegations of fraud are not required under section 11 of the 1933 Act.[31] In contrast, claims under section 12(2) of the 1933 Act[32] and claims under Exchange Act Rule 10b–5[33] must be pleaded with particularity.[34] While it is arguable that section 11 claims should be subject to the same type of particularity requirement, the absence of scienter and reliance requirements in section 11 indicate that something less than fraud will amount to a violation. Although the same degree of specificity may not be required in a section 11 claim as in a fraud claim, the plaintiff must be able to tie the misrepresentations into the registration statement; allegations relating to oral representations will not suffice.[35]

---

26. For example, the acquiring corporation as an issuer of its own securities could maintain a suit as a seller of those securities, provided that it could show a material misstatement or omission in connection with the "sale" of its securities pursuant to the merger. SEC Rule 10b–5 is discussed in chapter 13 *infra*.

27. 15 U.S.C.A. § 77*l*(1). *See* § 8.2 *supra*.

28. 15 U.S.C.A. § 77*l*(2). *See* § 8.5 *infra*.

29. 17 C.F.R. § 240.10b–5.

30. Herman & MacLean v. Huddleston, 459 U.S. 375, 103 S.Ct. 683, 74 L.Ed.2d 548 (1983), *on remand* 705 F.2d 775 (5th Cir.1983) (section 11 and Rule 10b–5 are cumulative remedies); *See* Lanza v. Drexel, 479 F.2d 1277 (2d Cir.1973) (purchasers of stock can maintain 10b–5 action based on misleading prospectus covering debenture offering); Stewart v. Bennett, 359 F.Supp. 878 (D.Mass.1973). *See generally* Marc I. Steinberg, The Propriety and Scope of Cumulative Remedies Under the Federal Securities Laws, 67 Cornell L.Rev. 557 (1982).

31. In re Thortec Securities Litigation, 1989 WL 67429, [1989 Transfer Binder] Fed.Sec.L.Rep. (CCH) ¶ 94,330 (N.D.Cal.1989) (pleading upheld); Bernstein v. Crazy Eddie, Inc., 702 F.Supp. 962, 973 (E.D.N.Y.1988) (upholding section 11 claim); Quantum Overseas, N.V. v. Touche Ross & Co., 663 F.Supp. 658 (S.D.N.Y.1987) (upholding section 11 claim but dismissing Exchange Act claim for failing to plead with sufficient particularity); In re Lilco Securities Litigation, 625 F.Supp. 1500 (E.D.N.Y.1986). *See also, e.g.,* In re Jiffy Lube Securities Litigation, 772 F.Supp. 258, 260–61 (D.Md.1991); Steiner v. Southmark Corp., 734 F.Supp. 269 (N.D.Tex.1990).

32. 15 U.S.C.A. § 77*l* (2). *See* § 7.5 *infra*.

33. 17 C.F.R. § 240.10b–5. *See* §§ 13.2–13.12 *infra*.

34. *E.g.,* Kilmartin v. H.C. Wainwright & Co., 637 F.Supp. 938 (D.Mass.1986). *See* § 13.2 *infra*.

35. Platsis v. E.F. Hutton & Co., 642 F.Supp. 1277, 1301 (W.D.Mich.1986). *See also* In re Union Carbide Class Action Securities Litigation, 648 F.Supp. 1322 (S.D.N.Y.1986)

Measure of Damages

Another key difference between section 11 and the express remedies provided by section 12 is the measure of damages. With regard to both actions authorized by section 12 the appropriate measure of damages is rescission and the return of the purchase price paid by the plaintiff.[36] Section 11(e)[37] sets forth three alternative methods of computing the damages in an action under section 11 for material misrepresentations or omissions in a registration statement. Under section 11(e) a plaintiff is entitled to recover the difference between the amount paid for the securities (not to exceed the public offering price) and (1) the value as of time of suit, (2) the price at which plaintiff sold the securities prior to suit, or (3) the price at which the security was sold after suit was brought but before judgment so long as the damages so computed under this third alternative would be less than those based on the difference between the price paid for the security (not to exceed the offering price) and the value at the time suit was brought. As these damage formulations present something other than a bright line approach, problems of proof abound in damage cases under section 11.[38] Proof problems are further exacerbated by the express provision in section 11(e) that the statutory damages shall be reduced to the extent that the defendant is able to prove that any portion of (or all of) said damages "represents other than the depreciation in value of each security resulting from" the misstatement or omission. Since the burden of proving the absence of a causal connection falls on the defendant, loss causation need not be shown in order for plaintiff to establish a prima facie case under section 11.[39] However, to the extent that the defendant is able to establish this negative causation defense, damages will not be recoverable under section 11.

Thus, when the entire decline in the price of the stock is attributable to external market forces, there will be no damages under section 11.[40] It has been held by one court that upon a showing that the

---

(claim dismissed where plaintiff failed to identify the misleading statements in the registration statement).

36. 15 U.S.C.A. § 77*l*.

37. 15 U.S.C.A. § 77k(e).

38. *See* Beecher v. Able, 435 F.Supp. 397 (S.D.N.Y.1975), *affirmed* 575 F.2d 1010 (2d Cir.1978); Note, Causation of Damages Under Section 11 of the Securities Act of 1933, 51 N.Y.U.L.Rev. 217 (1976). *See also* LeMaster v. Bull, 581 F.Supp. 1170 (E.D.Pa.1984) (award of attorney fees to successful plaintiff). *See also, e.g.,* Akerman v. Oryx Communications, Inc., 810 F.2d 336 (2d Cir.1987) (successful defense of negative causation; misrepresentations were "barely material" and there was insufficient proof of an adverse reaction by the market).

Section 11 damages are discussed more fully in § 7.4.1 *infra* (Practitioner's Edition only).

39. *See, e.g.,* Endo v. Albertine, 863 F.Supp. 708 (N.D.Ill.1994); Lyne v. Arthur Andersen & Co., 772 F.Supp. 1064 (N.D.Ill.1991). In contrast, in order to state a claim under SEC Rule 10b–5, plaintiff must show both transaction causation and loss causation. *See* § 13.6 *infra*.

40. Akerman v. Oryx Communications, Inc., 609 F.Supp. 363 (S.D.N.Y.1984), *affirmed and remanded* 810 F.2d 336 (2d Cir.1987). *Cf.* Grossman v. Waste Management, Inc., 589

misrepresentation was material, there is a presumption that the market decline was related to the nondisclosure or misstatement.[41] Accordingly, to the extent that the defendant is able to prove the price decrease was due to external market forces or intervening events relating to the issuer's fundamental position, section 11 damages will be reduced. In contrast section 12 provides for a return of the purchase price regardless of the cause of the decline in market value. In addition to the statutory measure of damages under section 11(e), a court may in its discretion award costs and attorneys fees to the successful party.[42]

Statute of Limitations

Section 13 of the 1933 Act[43] provides for a statutory limitations period of one year after discovery of the misstatement or omission, or after discovery should have been made by the exercise of reasonable diligence, but in no event can a section 11 action be brought more than three years after the security was "bona fide offered to the public." The statute of limitations is the same for actions brought under section 11 or section 12(2). In contrast, the one year statute begins to run from the date of violation for suits based on section 12(1) of the Act to redress violations of section 5. Also, the three year maximum limit for an action for fraud under section 12(2) begins to run from the sale rather than offering date.

Cumulative Nature of Remedies

The fact that the remedy provided by section 11 is an express one does not make it exclusive. For example, it has been held that an implied action under Rule 10b–5 may arise out of the same facts.[44] It

---

F.Supp. 395 (N.D.Ill.1984) (where market price at time of suit was higher than the price plaintiff paid there could be no claim under section 11 absent a showing that defendants had artificially inflated the price of the stock).

41. Akerman v. Oryx Communications, Inc., 609 F.Supp. 363 (S.D.N.Y.1984), *affirmed and remanded* 810 F.2d 336 (2d Cir.1987).

42. 15 U.S.C.A. § 77k(e). *See, e.g.,* Zissu v. Bear, Stearns & Co., 805 F.2d 75 (2d Cir.1986); McWhorter v. Long Royalty Co., 598 F.Supp. 418 (W.D.Okl.1983). *See also, e.g.,* Friedman v. Ganassi, 674 F.Supp. 1165 (W.D.Pa.1987), *judgment reversed* 853 F.2d 207 (3d Cir.1988) (Fed.R.Civ.P. 54 sets forth the appropriate standard for awarding costs in a section 11 case; defendant held not entitled to costs because plaintiff's suit was not entirely without merit). Awards of costs and attorneys fees under section 11(e) are discussed in § 7.4.2 *infra* (Practitioner's Edition only). Costs, attorneys fees and Rule 11 sanctions are also discussed in § 13.7.1 *infra* (Practitioner's Edition only).

43. 15 U.S.C.A. § 77m. *See* In re Activision Securities Litigation, 1986 WL 15339, [1986–87 Transfer Binder] Fed.Sec.L.Rep. (CCH) ¶ 92,998 (N.D.Cal.1986) (Filing of a class action against underwriters as a class tolled the statute of limitations.)

The statute of limitations in actions under section 11 is discussed further in § 7.5.4 *infra* (Practitioner's Edition only).

44. *See* cases in footnote 30 *supra*. *Cf.* SEC v. National Securities, Inc., 393 U.S. 453, 89 S.Ct. 564, 21 L.Ed.2d 668 (1969) (implied remedies under Rule 10b–5 and the proxy rules, 17 C.F.R. § 240.14a–9, are cumulative); Ross v. A.H. Robins Co., 607 F.2d 545 (2d Cir.1979), *cert. denied* 446 U.S. 946, 100 S.Ct. 2175, 64 L.Ed.2d 802 (1980), *rehearing denied* 448 U.S. 911, 100 S.Ct. 3057, 65 L.Ed.2d 1140 (1980) (express liability under § 18(a) of the Exchange Act, 15 U.S.C.A. § 78r(a) is not exclusive and a 10b–5 action may lie).

follows that a plaintiff with a section 11 claim could also bring suit under the express liability provisions of section 12 as well as enforce any implied rights existing under section 17(a) of the 1933 Act.[45]

Defendants and Defenses

The statutory list of all potential section 11 defendants is exclusive.[46] There is generally no problem in identifying at least the potential defendants for any particular section 11 action. Room for interpretation is to be found, however, in connection with the reference to "every underwriter" in section 11(a)(5). Section 2(11) of the 1933 Act[47] gives a broad statutory definition to the term underwriter which goes far beyond the generic meaning of the term as used in connection with registered public offerings. This statutory definition of underwriter includes persons purchasing the securities from an issuer with a view to distribution, all those who offer or sell securities on behalf of an issuer in connection with a distribution in addition to anyone who "participates or has a direct or indirect participation in any such undertaking."[48] Although it has been indicated that "underwriter" under section 11 tracks the full scope of the statutory definition under section 2(11), in order to prevail the plaintiff must still prove the defendant's actual participation in the distribution.[49] An underwriter's liability under section 11 is limited to the extent of the aggregate price of the securities underwritten by him or her. This limitation on damages does not apply, however, if the underwriter received from the issuer some benefit that was not available to similarly situated underwriters.

As mentioned above, section 11(a)(4) creates liability for professionals who lend their services to deficient registration statements. It has been held that an accountant may not be held liable unless the misleading information is expressly attributable to that accountant.[50] Further, it has been held that "as a matter of law" an independent accountant's liability under section 11 is limited to those figures which he or she

---

45. 15 U.S.C.A. § 77q(a). *See* §§ 7.6, 13.13 *infra*.

46. *E.g.,* In re ZZZZ Best Securities Litigation, 1989 WL 90284, [1989 Transfer Binder] Fed.Sec.L.Rep. ¶ 94,485 (C.D.Cal.1989). *See* Hagert v. Glickman, Lurie, Eiger & Co., 520 F.Supp. 1028, 1033 (D.Minn.1981). *See also, e.g.,* Ahern v. Gaussoin, 611 F.Supp. 1465, 1484 (D.Or.1985) (aiding and abetting theory will not establish liability under section 11).

47. 15 U.S.C.A. § 77b(11).

48. *Id.* The section explicitly excludes from the definition of underwriter members of the selling group whose only remuneration is equivalent to a regular broker's commission.

49. *Id. See* § 4.23 *supra*.

Underwriter liability may also be found under SEC Rule 10b–5. In an action under Rule 10b–5, the fact that the defendant nonmanaging underwriters' names appeared in the prospectus meant that the statements made therein could be attributed to the defendants even though they did not actively participate in the preparation of the prospectus. In re ZZZZ Best Securities Litigation, 1994 WL 746649, [1994–1995 Transfer Binder] Fed.Sec. L.Rep. 98,485 (C.D.Cal.1994).

50. McFarland v. Memorex Corp., 493 F.Supp. 631, 644–47 (N.D.Cal.1980), *reconsideration granted* 581 F.Supp. 878 (N.D.Cal.1984). *See also, e.g.,* Steiner v. Southmark Corp., 734 F.Supp. 269 (N.D.Tex.1990) (sufficiently alleging liability of accountants).

certifies.[51] Thus, unless the accountant is an auditor or otherwise lends his or her name to a statement, there is no section 11 liability. Similarly, an attorney who prepares the registration statement is not a proper section 11 defendant unless he or she is also a director or signer of the registration statement.[52] Aside from such cases the attorney will only be liable under section 11 pursuant to a subsection (a)(4) expert opinion.[53] An attorney's activities in preparing and reviewing the registration statement do not mean that the entire registration statement has been "expertised" so as to render the attorney liable under section 11.[54] However, an attorney, whether representing the issuer or underwriter, may be liable under section 17(a) which provides the basis for SEC injunctive relief and may, according to some decisions, even give rise to civil liability based on negligence.[55] Similarly, attorneys have been held liable as "sellers" under section 12.[56] After identifying the proper defendants, the key issue under section 11 is the appropriate standard of care and the defenses that may be asserted under section 11(b) by all defendants other than the issuer, who is strictly liable. This topic is taken up in the succeeding section.

Section 11(f)[57] provides that all persons who are covered by subsection (a) shall be jointly and severally liable unless one or more defendants are guilty of fraudulent misrepresentation and others are not; in such a case only the more culpable defendants are jointly and severally liable. The section further expressly provides for a right of contribution against joint defendants as would be the case in an action on a contract. Such joint and several liability may not exceed the amount that the individual would be held accountable for were he or she sued separately, which would seem to require a showing of fault on the part of each non-

51. McFarland v. Memorex Corp., 493 F.Supp. 631, 643 (N.D.Cal.1980), *reconsideration granted* 581 F.Supp. 878 (N.D.Cal.1984), citing Grimm v. Whitney–Fidalgo Seafoods, Inc., 1973 WL 495, [1977–1978 Transfer Binder], Fed.Sec.L.Rep. (CCH) ¶ 96,029 (S.D.N.Y.1973). *See* Jiffy Lube Securities Litigation, 772 F.Supp. 258 (D.Md.1991) (stating section 11 claim against alleged misstatements attributable to the auditor). *See also, e.g.,* In re Worlds of Wonder Securities Litigation, 694 F.Supp. 1427 (N.D.Cal.1988), *affirmed in part and reversed in part,* 35 F.3d 1407 (9th Cir.1994).

52. *E.g.* Kitchens v. United States Shelter, 1988 WL 108598, [1988–89 Transfer Binder] Fed.Sec.L.Rep. (CCH) ¶ 93,920 (D.S.C.1988). On occasion, attorneys have been proper defendants in a section 11 case. For examples of such cases *see* Feit v. Leasco Data Processing Equipment Corp., 332 F.Supp. 544 (E.D.N.Y.1971); Escott v. BarChris Construction Corp., 283 F.Supp. 643 (S.D.N.Y.1968).

53. *See* Austin v. Baer, Marks & Upham, 1986 WL 10098, [1986–87 Transfer Binder] Fed.Sec.L.Rep. (CCH) ¶ 92,881 (D.Or.1986). McFarland v. Memorex Corp., 493 F.Supp. 631, 644–47 (N.D.Cal.1980), *reconsideration granted* 581 F.Supp. 878 (N.D.Cal.1984).

54. *See* Ahern v. Gaussoin, 611 F.Supp. 1465, 1482 (D.Or.1985); In re Flight Transportation Corp. Securities Litigation, 593 F.Supp. 612, 616 (D.Minn.1984), relying on Escott v. BarChris Constr. Corp., 283 F.Supp. 643, 683 (S.D.N.Y.1968). *Compare* Austin v. Baer, Marks & Upham, 1986 WL 10098, [1986–87 Transfer Binder] Fed.Sec.L.Rep. (CCH) ¶ 92,881 (D.Or.1986) (upholding section 11 claim against law firm consenting to use of its name in registration statement with regard to opinion letter).

55. *See* §§ 7.6, 13.13 *infra.*

56. Junker v. Crory, 650 F.2d 1349, 1360 (5th Cir.1981). *See* § 7.2 *supra.*

57. 15 U.S.C.A. § 77k(f).

issuer defendant.[58]

Section 11 by its terms applies to material misstatements and omissions in the registration statement "when such part became effective." [59] Accordingly, when subsequent events make an effective registration statement misleading, section 11 does not apply. However, section 11 liability will apply to post-effective amendments to the registration materials.

The remedy provided by section 11 is in addition to the general antifraud remedy under section 10(b) of the Exchange Act and Rule 10b–5 promulgated thereunder.[60] Although fraud is an element of any Rule 10b–5 claim and may be present in a section 11 claim, it is not a necessary element of a section 11 claim.[61]

As discussed above, it is generally recognized that there is a right to a jury trial under section 11.[62] However, in a highly complex case involving issues that the jury could not comprehend, the jury trial demand may be quashed.[63]

58. *Id. See* Tucker v. Arthur Andersen & Co., 646 F.2d 721, 727 (2d Cir.1981); Stowell v. Ted S. Finkel Investment Services, Inc., 641 F.2d 323 (5th Cir.1981), *rehearing denied* 647 F.2d 1123 (5th Cir.1981) (contribution allowed for defendants in violation of securities laws only if both parties are at fault and under common liability).   Note, Allocation of Damages Under the Federal Securities Laws, 60 Wash.U.L.Q. 211 (1982). *See* § 7.7 *infra.*

For a more recent case discussing accountant's liability under section 11 and holding that it is limited to expertised portions of the registration statement *see* Ahern v. Gaussoin, 611 F.Supp. 1465, 1482–84 (D.Or.1985).

59. 15 U.S.C.A. § 77k(a). *Cf.* Hartford Fire Insurance Co. v. Federated Department Stores, Inc., 723 F.Supp. 976 (S.D.N.Y.1989) (failure to disclose possible effects corporate restructuring would have on debentures was not material in light of the slight possibility of such an event, when viewed at the time of the offering).

60. *See* Herman & MacLean v. Huddleston, 459 U.S. 375, 103 S.Ct. 683, 74 L.Ed.2d 548 (1983), *on remand* 705 F.2d 775 (5th Cir.1983); In re Lilco Securities Litigation, 625 F.Supp. 1500 (E.D.N.Y.1986). *See* footnote 30 *supra* and § 13.2 *infra.*

61. In re Lilco Securities Litigation, 625 F.Supp. 1500 (E.D.N.Y.1986); In re Consumers Power Co. Securities Litigation, 105 F.R.D. 583 (E.D.Mich.1985) (Fed.R.Civ.P. 9(b) particularity requirement is not applicable to a section 11 claim since fraud is not a necessary element). *Accord* Schneider v. Traweek, 1990 WL 169856, [1990 Transfer Binder] Fed.Sec.L.Rep. (CCH) ¶ 95,507 (C.D.Cal.1990) (section 11 claim need not comply with Rule 9(b)'s particularity requirements). *But see* Haft v. Eastland Financial Corp., 755 F.Supp. 1123 (D.R.I.1991) (although scienter is not required under section 11, Rule 9(b) of the Federal Rules of Civil Procedure requires that the claim be plead with particularity). *Cf.* Wright v. Masters, 1990 WL 251025, [1990–1991 Transfer Binder] Fed.Sec.L.Rep. (CCH) ¶ 95,645 (S.D.Cal.1990) (section 11 claim pleaded with sufficient particularity). *See* text accompanying footnotes 31–35 *supra.*

62. *See, e.g.,* Hohmann v. Packard Instrument Co., Inc., 471 F.2d 815, 819 (7th Cir.1973); Jones v. Orenstein, 73 F.R.D. 604 (S.D.N.Y.1977). *See also* § 7.5.2 *infra* (Practitioner's Edition only) for discussion of the right to jury trial in actions under section 12 of the 1933 Act.

63. *See, e.g.,* Jones v. Orenstein, 73 F.R.D. 604 (S.D.N.Y.1977).

§ 7.4 Defenses Under § 11(b)—Due Diligence, Reliance on Experts and Reasonable Investigation

Statutory Defenses

Section 11(b)[1] contains three types of defenses, for persons other than the issuer, to an action under section 11(a)[2] for material misstatements or omissions in the registration statement. The issuer is strictly liable and no degree of prudence will absolve the issuer of a section 11 claim for damages. The only defenses available to the issuer are the purchaser's knowledge of the inaccuracies, lack of materiality, or expiration of the statute of limitations.

"Whistle–Blowing" Defense

The first two defenses contained in section 11(b) relate to one who discovers the material misstatement or omission and takes appropriate steps to prevent the violation. A person other than the issuer who would otherwise be liable under section 11 is relieved of liability if, prior to the effective date, he or she resigns from the position that connects him or her with the registration statement (or takes all legal steps towards resignation, or ceases to act in that capacity) *and* if he or she has given written notice to the issuer and the SEC of such action and further disclaims all responsibility for the applicable parts of the registration statement.[3] If the registration statement becomes effective without the knowledge of a potential section 11 defendant, he or she may avoid liability by taking appropriate steps toward resignation and advising the SEC, in addition to giving "reasonable public notice that such part of the registration statement had become effective without his knowledge." [4] All the parties to a registration statement are thus put in a position where self-policing is required.

These whistle blowing requirements present particularly sensitive problems for the attorney who becomes aware of potential violations. Anyone would agree that the attorney in such a position should advise the client (who will generally be the issuer) not to proceed with the offering, and also he or she should resign from the representation if the issuer refuses the advice. The statute on its face, however, goes even further and requires that the attorney who would otherwise be liable under section 11 (as a signer, director or section 11(a)(4) expert) blow the whistle on his or her client. This puts an enormous amount of pressure on any attorney involved with an SEC registration in more than an advisory capacity.[5]

----

§ 7.4

1. 15 U.S.C.A. § 77k(b).
2. 15 U.S.C.A. § 77k(a). *See* § 7.3 *supra*.
3. 15 U.S.C.A. § 77k(b)(1).
4. 15 U.S.C.A. § 77k(b)(2).

5. *See* Model Code of Professional Responsibility DR4–101(B); Ted Fiflis, Choice of Federal or State Law for Attorney's Professional Responsibility in Securities Matters, 56 N.Y.U.L.Rev. 1236 (1981); Junius Hoffman, On Learning of a Corporate Client's Crime or

Due Diligence Defense

Section 11(b)(3) contains the most frequently used defense. It provides that any person other than the issuer who is a potential section 11(a) defendant is absolved of liability with regard to any part of the registration statement not made under the authority of an expert provided that the defendant "had, after reasonable investigation, reasonable ground to believe and did believe, at the time such part of the registration statement became effective, that the statements therein were true and that there was no omission to state a material fact * * *."[6] A person who is named in the registration statement as an expert is not liable under section 11(a) for misstatements as an expert if after reasonable investigation there was reasonable ground to believe, combined with an actual belief, that there was no material misstatement or omission.[7] Furthermore, the expert is not liable if the statement in the registration materials "did not fairly represent his statements as an expert or was not a fair copy of or extract" of his or her report or valuation as an expert.[8] As for persons who would otherwise be liable for statements made in reliance upon experts, there is no liability if there was reasonable ground to believe plus an actual belief that the statement did not contain any material misstatements or omissions. Finally, as for any part of the registration statement that purports to be made by a public official or "a copy of or extract from a public official document" there is no liability for anyone who had reasonable grounds to believe and did actually believe that there were no material misstatements or omissions.[9]

Section 11(c) expressly establishes the appropriate standard of care: "the standard of reasonableness shall be that required of a prudent man in the management of his own property."[10] This is a significant departure from the traditional state law standard that applies to officers and directors, which is generally articulated in terms of that conduct which would be befitting of a reasonable officer or director or person

---

Fraud—The Lawyer's Dilemma, 33 Bus.L. 1389 (1978); Simon M. Lorne, The Corporate and Securities Advisor, The Public Interest and Professional Ethics, 76 Mich.L.Rev. 423 (1978).

6. 15 U.S.C.A. § 77k(b)(3)(A). *See generally* ABA Committee of Federal Regulation of Securities, Report of the Task Force on Sellers' Due Diligence and Similar Defenses Under the Federal Securities Laws, 48 Bus.Law. 1185 (1993). For helpful checklists to aid in compliance with section 11's due diligence requirements *see* Carlos L. Israels, Checklist for Underwriters' Investigations, 18 Bus.Law. 90 (1962), as updated in ABA, Selected Articles in Securities Law 71 (1968); Robert A. Spanner, Limiting Exposure in the Offering Process, 20 Rev.Sec. & Commod.Reg. 59 (1987).

See also, e.g., Lucia v. Prospect Street High Income Portfolio, Inc., 36 F.3d 170 (1st Cir.1994) (failure to allege facts showing that defendant knew or should have known of the inaccuracies).

7. 15 U.S.C.A. § 77k(b)(3)(B).

8. *Id.*

9. 15 U.S.C.A. § 77k(b)(3)(D).

10. 15 U.S.C.A. § 77k(c). *See* 17 C.F.R. § 230.176.

under like circumstances.[11] By speaking in terms of the degree of care that one would use in handling one's own affairs, the 1933 Act apparently provides for a higher standard[12] at least to the extent that it does not seem to include the shield of the business judgment rule. The due diligence defense involves mixed questions of law and fact. When the facts are not disputed, summary judgment will be appropriate since leaving such decisions to judges rather than juries will result in more predictability and uniformity of result.[13] However, where there is a material dispute as to the facts, summary judgment will not be appropriate.[14]

What Constitutes Due Diligence ("reasonable investigation" and/or reliance on experts) and The BarChris Decision

Reasonable investigation

To date, the most definitive word on the scope of section 11(b)(3) defenses of due diligence and reasonable investigation has emanated from the New York federal district court decision in Escott v. BarChris Construction Corp.[15] The registration statement in *BarChris* contained a number of misstatements. In the first instance, there were overstatements regarding the comparison of the fiscal year 1960 to past performance, but the court found that such misstatements were not material since the correct figures would have shown a growth potential which was virtually equivalent to that presented in the registration

---

11. *See, e.g.,* Revised Model Business Corp. Act § 8.30(a)(2)(1984); Model Business Corp. Act § 35 par. 2 (1977 Supp.).

12. *See* James D. Cox, Thomas L. Hazen & F. Hodge O'Neal, Corporations ch. 10 (1995); Henry W. Ballantine, Corporations § 63 (rev. ed. 1946). Harry G. Henn & John R. Alexander, Laws of Corporation § 234 (3d ed. 1983).

13. *See* In re Software Toolworks, Inc. Securities Litigation, 789 F.Supp. 1489 (N.D.Cal. 1992), *affirmed in part and reversed in part,* 38 F.3d 1078 (9th Cir.1994).

14. *See, e.g.,* In re Software Toolworks, Inc. Securities Litigation, 50 F.3d 615 (9th Cir.1994) (but holding that underwriter had sufficiently established due diligence defense).

15. 283 F.Supp. 643 (S.D.N.Y.1968). The issuer, BarChris, was in the business of building bowling alleys for contracted customers on a highly leveraged basis. The company had two methods of financing. The primary method involved entering into a contract with a customer for construction and equipment of a bowling alley with the customer making a comparatively small down payment. Upon completion of the facility, the customer would pay the balance of the contract price in notes payable which BarChris would discount. The alternative method of financing consisted of a sale and leaseback arrangement. After completing the interior of the bowling alley, the facility would then be sold to a factor for the full construction price. The factor would then lease the interior to a customer or to a BarChris subsidiary which in turn would lease the facility to the customer.

Under either method of financing BarChris received very little up-front money for construction. It was thus necessary for the company to seek public financing on a number of occasions to provide the necessary cash to cover its operations. The prospectus and registration statement in question were filed in connection with a public offering of debentures.

See generally Ernest L. Folk III, Civil Liabilities Under the Federal Securities Acts: The BarChris Case (pts. 1 & 2) 55 Va.L.Rev. 1, 199 (1969); Harry Heller, Stephen J. Weiss, Carlos L. Israel & Donald E. Schwartz, BarChris: A Dialogue on a Bad Case Making Hard Law, 57 Geo.L.J. 221 (1968); Note, Escott v. BarChris: "Reasonable Investigation" and Prospectus Liability Under Section 11 of the Securities Act of 1933, 82 Harv.L.Rev. 908 (1969).

statement. These misstatements thus failed to cross the materiality threshold as they were not of the magnitude likely to be significant to the reasonable investor.[16] The most substantial misstatements concerned failure to accurately disclose the increases in customer defaults in payment of the notes held by BarChris and the possibility that the issuer would have to repossess certain leased assets which would necessarily injure its cash position.[17] There were additional omissions regarding loans to certain officers of the corporation. The section 11(b) defenses also focused on the registration statement's signers' and participants' failure to ascertain and disclose the inaccuracies regarding the likelihood that the issuer would be foreclosing on several of its notes, as well as their failure to disclose that BarChris was already engaged and about to be further engaged in the actual operation of bowling alleys.

In the course of its opinion, the court in *BarChris* treated each of the classes of defendants separately, thus creating a sliding scale of liability. The decision makes it clear that the highest standard of care attaches to an insider who signed the registration statement, especially if the insider is one of the designated principal officers who must sign prior to SEC filing.[18] Similarly, as to directors, the majority of whom must also sign, the court was careful to draw a distinction between insiders and outsiders. The court further made clear that any expertise brought by a signer, such as a legal or accounting background, will be factored into the formula of the standard of care under the circumstances. This sliding scale of liability as elevated by expert knowledge is arguably contrary to what would appear on the face of section 11(c) to be a unitary standard of conduct, that of the "prudent man" with no mention of any special knowledge that he may possess.[19] Nevertheless, there has been neither judicial nor SEC authority that has questioned the *BarChris* sliding scale of liability.

Reliance on experts

Beyond the appropriate standard of care, the court in *BarChris* also looked at the defense of reliance upon experts and specifically disclaimed any reading of the statute that would entitle signers to point to reliance on an attorney who had read the entire registration statement, even if the attorney is a securities expert reading the papers as a check against possible disclosure problems. Specifically, the court held that the only *expertised* portion of the prospectus and registration statement were audited figures prepared by the independent accountant. It was reasoned that section 11(b)(3) is explicit in its requirement that the portion

---

16. Materiality is considered in §§ 11.4, 13.5A *infra*.

17. The failure to disclose customer delinquencies standing alone was a 1.35 million dollar inflation of the balance sheet. *See* 283 F.Supp. at 680.

18. Section 6 requires that the registration statement be signed by the issuer's principal executive officers, principal financial officer, comptroller or principal accounting officer and the majority of the board of directors or persons performing similar functions. 15 U.S.C.A. § 77f(a). *See* §§ 3.1, 3.4 *supra*.

19. "The standard of reasonableness shall be that required of a prudent man in the management of his own property." 15 U.S.C.A. § 77k(c).

provided by an expert giving rise to justifiable reliance is limited to statements that were "parts of the registration statement which purported to be made upon the authority of an expert." [20]   In so ruling, the court held that even as to other financial data that the accountants may have looked at, the prospectus and registration statement were not expertised.   The same rule was applied to portions of the registration statement that were prepared by attorneys.   Thus, registration materials are not expertised merely because they are examined or even prepared by attorneys, accountants, or other experts.[21]

Although the decision imposed liability on attorneys and accountants, it was based on their role as signers or as experts named in the registration materials.   The *BarChris* court thus did not impose liability upon a professional who renders advice in connection with portions of the registration statement, but does not provide a statement which purports to be made upon his or her expertise.   There does not seem to be any basis for holding professionals not named as experts to be liable for any misstatement under section 11 unless they were signers, directors, or underwriters, as required by section 11(a).   It is clear, however, that any participant in the registration statement's preparation is subject to other potential liabilities.   Negligence will clearly be grounds for a SEC injunction under section 17(a) and may create civil liability.[22]   Conduct approaching fraud will create liability under SEC Rule 10b–5.[23]   Additionally, active participation in any sale as a "seller" creates the potential for liability under sections 12(1) and 12(2).[24]   Another significant aspect of the *BarChris* ruling is that neither attorneys nor accountants who are covered by section 11(a) are justified in relying upon the client; they must make their own independent "due diligence" investigation.

Even in a situation where a defendant may attempt to avail himself or herself on the reliance on experts defense, the courts are not satisfied by blind reliance.   Borrowing from the standard in criminal cases generally, the appropriate requirements for a reliance on experts defense are as follows: (1) *full disclosure* of pertinent facts known by the person claiming reliance, and (2) *good faith* reliance on the opinion given.[25]   With regard to portions of the registration statement that have been prepared by experts, the those who can reasonably rely are relieved of

---

20.   283 F.Supp. at 683.

21.   *E.g.,* In re Flight Transportation Corporation Securities Litigation, 593 F.Supp. 612, 616 (D.Minn.1984) (relying on *Escott v. BarChris Constr. Co*).   *See also, e.g.,* Draney v. Wilson, Morton, Assaf & McElligott, 592 F.Supp. 9 (D.Ariz.1984) (defense of reliance on counsel limited to legal advice).

22.   *See* Aaron v. SEC, 446 U.S. 680, 100 S.Ct. 1945, 64 L.Ed.2d 611 (1980), *on remand* 666 F.2d 5 (2d Cir.1981); §§ 7.6, 13.13 *infra*.

23.   17 C.F.R. § 240.10b–5.   *See* §§ 13.2–13.12 *infra*.

24.   15 U.S.C.A. §§ 77*l* (1), (2).   *See* §§ 7.2 *supra*, 7.5 *infra*.

25.   *See, e.g.,* United States v. Lindo, 18 F.3d 353, 356 (6th Cir.1994);   United States v. Duncan, 850 F.2d 1104, 1117 (6th Cir.1988);   United States v. Phillips, 217 F.2d 435, 442 (7th Cir.1954).

their reasonable investigation and due diligence obligations for the expertised portions.[26]

Although there have been a number of decisions since *BarChris*, that decision remains the leading authority on the appropriate standard of conduct under section 11. The best way to appreciate the full thrust of the *BarChris* opinion (and its progeny) is to examine the court's treatment of each defendant.

Officers' and Directors' Liability

Although not having the title of president, the functional chief executive officer, who was also a member of the corporation's executive committee, was a signer of the registration statement. The court noted that this chief executive officer and member of the executive committee was totally familiar with all aspects of the issuer's business and was "personally in charge" of all dealing with the factors, as well as handling negotiations that included discussion of customer delinquencies. The court found that he "knew all the relevant facts" and "could not have believed that there were no untrue statements" and thus could not assert a valid due diligence defense.[27] The two founders of the business, its titular president and vice-president, had less actual involvement than the chief executive officer and were "men of limited education." The court conceded that "it is not hard to believe that for them the prospectus was difficult reading, if indeed they read it at all."[28] However, the court viewed their limited expertise as irrelevant since a signing officer's liability is dependent upon neither whether he or she has read the registration statement nor if having read it, he or she understood it at all. The test is whether the signing officer acted with due diligence under the circumstances. The court found a lack of due diligence in signing without having read or understood the registration statement. People who do not possess the minimum necessary knowledge should not be serving as officers or directors. In addition, the two signing founding officers had been beneficiaries of loans from the corporation that were not disclosed in the prospectus. On the basis of all of the foregoing facts, the court held that these two signers had failed to meet their defenses of due diligence.

The treasurer and chief financial officer, "a certified public accountant and an intelligent man," was, as his job required, "thoroughly familiar" with the company's finances, including the problem of customer delinquency.[29] He was also a member of the executive committee which gave him access to information as to operations of the business that he might otherwise not be informed of by virtue of his corporate office. In addition, the treasurer worked on the actual preparation of

---

26. *E.g.,* In re Software Toolworks, Inc. Securities Litigation, 50 F.3d 615 (9th Cir. 1994).

27. 283 F.Supp. at 684.

28. *Id.* at 684.

29. *Id.* at 685.

the registration statement, including having met with the company's attorneys. The essence of his defense was that since all the facts and figures appeared in the company's books, the treasurer was justified in relying upon the auditor's expertise. After noting that this created "an issue of credibility" the court ruled that in any event he failed to prove his defense.[30]

Outside Directors' Liability

Another controversial aspect of the *BarChris* court's decision arose with respect to an outside director who was neither an officer nor employee but signed the registration statement. The outside director testified the he did not know that he was signing a registration statement but he vaguely understood that it was something "for the SEC." The court further conceded that the outside director believed all representations as to the company's business made by the insiders. Although he became a director "on the eve of the financing" and "had little opportunity to familiarize himself with the company's affairs" the court nonetheless held him liable for failing to make any investigation whatsoever before having signed the registration statement.[31] This might seem to be an extremely high burden to put upon a newly elected outside director; however, he did sign the registration statement. The court would have been much harder pressed to find liability under section 11(a)(2) of an outside director who had not signed the registration statement.[32] The *BarChris* decision thus provides a good lesson for unwary outside directors who are asked to sign the registration statement.

Attorneys' Liabilities

One of the most controversial aspects of the *BarChris* ruling arose out of court's holding liable a young attorney who was only four years out of law school at the time of the registration statement. He had previously been house counsel and assistant secretary and was then secretary to the corporation and a member of the board of directors. Although he was not a director at the time of the initial filing, he was fully liable under section 11. The court was willing to agree that as corporate secretary and house counsel he was not a principal officer, however, by being keeper of corporate minutes, he certainly had access to inside information.[33] Furthermore, he had examined the contracts in question and had advised the issuer that certain contracts may not have been legally enforceable, a fact not recorded in the registration statement. The court conceded that this young attorney "did not know of many inaccuracies in the prospectus" but that he had sufficient knowl-

---

30. *Id.* at 685.

31. *Id.* at 688. *Compare, e.g.,* Weinberger v. Jackson, 1990 WL 260676, [1990–1991 Transfer Binder] Fed.Sec.L.Rep. (CCH) ¶ 95,693 (N.D.Cal.1990) (outside director met his standard of due diligence and reasonable inquiry).

32. *See* the authorities cited in footnote 15 *supra.*

33. 283 F.Supp. at 687.

edge of the business that he was at least put on inquiry notice of potential problems, and thus should have investigated "the truth of all the statements in the un-expertised portion of the document, which he signed." [34] Since the young attorney made no independent investigation whatsoever, he was held not to have met the burden of proving his due diligence defense. The court did not indicate how much investigation would have been sufficient to let him off the hook.

Another attorney who was hit with liability in the course of the *BarChris* decision was outside counsel who sat on the board of directors. He not only signed this and other registration statements for the issuer, but also took primary responsibility for preparing the initial drafts of one of the registration statements that formed the basis of the suit. Section 11 does not provide any bases for suing someone who simply prepares or drafts a registration statement,[35] yet since this attorney was both a director of the issuer and a signer of the registration statement, he was properly viewed as a section 11 defendant. The court made note of the fact that this was not a legal malpractice action, but "in considering Grant's due diligence defenses, the unique position he occupied cannot be disregarded." [36] This defendant as outside counsel, director and signer, claimed that he was justified in relying upon the statements of his clients, but the court held that under the statute he had a duty to make an independent investigation. The obvious lesson of this aspect of the ruling is that counsel should be hesitant to sign any registration statement since their expertise and access to inside information by virtue of their attorney-client relationship may impose an especially high standard of conduct. Furthermore, since section 11(a)(2) renders all directors liable, an attorney who sits as a director but does not sign the registration statement is equally open for potential liability, especially if he or she worked on the registration statement in any capacity. However, an attorney who helps prepare the registration statement cannot be held liable under section 11 unless he or she is an officer, director, signer of the registration statement, or expert within the meaning of section 11.[37]

Underwriters' Liabilities

Much of the court's opinion in *BarChris* is devoted to the liability of the underwriters and the accountants who performed the 1960 audit. As for the underwriters, the facts were extremely damaging and thus

---

34. *Id.* at 687.

35. Nevertheless, liability may exist under other sections. *See* text accompanying footnotes 22–24 *supra*. *See also* § 7.10 *infra*.

36. 283 F.Supp. at 690. *See* Donald B. Hilliker, Target Defendants for the 1980's— Securities Lawyers—Malpractice Insurance, 1980 Ins.L.J. 563 (1980); Symposium, Responsibilities and Liabilities of Lawyers and Accountants, 30 Bus.Law. 227 (1975); Comment, Due Diligence and the Expert in Corporate Securities Registration, 42 S.Cal.L.Rev. 293 (1969).

37. *E.g.,* In re Flight Transportation Corporation Securities Litigation, 593 F.Supp. 612, 613 (D.Minn.1984) (fact that attorney worked on registration statement did not make the registration expertised by him). *Compare* Austin v. Baer, Marks & Upham, 1986 WL 10098, [1986–87 Transfer Binder] Fed.Sec.L.Rep. (CCH) ¶ 92,881 (D.Or.1986).

justified a finding of liability. The partner in the underwriting firm who had primary responsibility for investigating the issuer was also a director of the issuer. Not only does this position with the issuer create a potential conflict of interest, it also gives access to certain types of inside information that might otherwise not be available to an underwriter as the issuer and underwriter can no longer be viewed as dealing on a purely arms length basis. Furthermore, the court noted that the only investigation made by the underwriter about the issuer was directed towards the decision whether or not to participate in the offering and was *not* directed towards compliance with the requirements of the statute's registration provisions. The court acknowledged that after the underwriter's partner was made a director of the issuer, he did make an independent investigation of the prospectus' accuracy, but as was the case with the other defendants, he failed to follow up on a number of questionable disclosures. The court further pointed out that although there was a "due diligence meeting" one week before the offering date, the underwriters failed to make any independent investigation after the meeting. The court thus held the managing underwriter liable because of its failure to meet the defense of due diligence. In contrast, where underwriters make a reasonable investigation, the defense will be available.[38]

In the course of its opinion in *BarChris* the court chided the underwriters for failing to have looked beyond the contracts represented by the backlog figures.[39] It has been suggested by one commentator that this should not be taken to mean that underwriters always have to make an independent check of inventory backlogs.[40] In an even more troubling aspect of the *BarChris* opinion, the court pointed out that "the other underwriters, who did nothing and relied solely on directors and on the lawyers" did not establish a due diligence defense except as to the

---

38. *See, e.g.,* In re Software Toolworks Inc. Securities Litigation, 50 F.3d 615 (9th Cir.1994). In the *Software Toolworks* litigation, the offering involved securities issued by a computer software company. The underwriters made an independent investigation of video game manufacturers using the issuer's software and also contacted retailers to confirm the strength of the product market. This was held to be a sufficient investigation in the face of financial magazine's allegations of slumping sales. Underwriter was not held liable for failing to discover that the issuer permitted returns of their product notwithstanding contrary indications in the prospectus and registration statement; the prospectus noted that market conditions might necessitate a change in the no–return policy.

39. 283 F.Supp. at 697.

40. Carlos L. Israels Checklist for Underwriters Investigation, 18 Bus.Law, 90 (1962), as updated in ABA, Selected Articles in Securities Law 71 (1968): "It seems reasonably clear that Judge McLean's strictures as to backlog were directed to the specific facts of BarChris. They cannot seriously be construed to require that underwriters attempt an independent check of the backlog of a manufacturing company which might well consist of hundreds, even thousands of purchase orders. At most they indicate that where, as here, the figure could be adequately tested by reference to less than a dozen contracts (each of relatively large amount and thus in that sense 'major' whether or not required to be filed as exhibits) a follow-up on the effectiveness of a prior specific warning is called for."

See also, e.g., Herb Frerichs, Jr., Underwriter Due Diligence Within the Integrated Disclosure System—If It Isn't Broken, Don't Fix It, 16 Sec.Reg.L.J. 386 (1989); Note, Due Diligence Under Rule 415: Is the Insurance Worth the Premium?, 38 Emory L.J. 793 (1989).

1960 audit.[41] The court also went on to question whether the other underwriters can ever rely upon due diligence of the managing underwriter.[42] In analyzing the significance of the *BarChris* decision with regard to the underwriters, it must be remembered that the underwriter's investigation there was supervised by a partner who also was a director of the issuer. As such, the underwriter's investigation was not a truly independent one.[43]

The *BarChris* decision raises questions as to the underwriter's outside counsel's standard of responsibility. In the course of its ruling that the managing underwriter failed to meet the due diligence standard, the court rejected the underwriter's reliance on counsel. The underwriter's outside counsel sent a young associate to check *BarChris'* corporate records. The associate did not check the issuer's contracts nor did he locate several executive committee minutes. The court held that this was an insufficient investigation and thus precluded reliance by the underwriter. Underwriter's counsel did not fit within section 11 and thus were not held liable. The court did not inquire, however, into the law firm's potential liability to its client for malpractice or any common law right of indemnity by a principal against its agent.

Accountants' Liabilities

Finally, as to the accountants,[44] as with all other defendants, the court stressed that the burden of proof of the defense lies with the person asserting it. The field survey for the audit was performed by an individual who was not yet a CPA and had no prior knowledge of the bowling alley industry. This was his first major assignment as a senior accountant. The court conceded that although the investigator may have asked the right questions and received what he considered satisfac-

41. 283 F.Supp. at 697.

42. *Id.* n. 26.

For discussion of the effect of the recently expanded shelf registration rule upon underwriters' due diligence, *see* Note, The Impact of the SEC's Shelf Registration Rule on Underwriters' Due Diligence, 51 Geo.Wash.L.Rev. 767 (1983). Shelf Registration is discussed in § 3.8 *supra*.

43. *Compare* Feit v. Leasco Data Processing Equipment Corp., 332 F.Supp. 544 (E.D.N.Y.1971) (underwriters barely met their burden under section 11; unlike in *BarChris*, the underwriter's investigation was conducted by someone truly independent of the issuer). *See also, e.g.,* In re Software Toolworks, Inc. Securities Litigation, 50 F.3d 615 (9th Cir.1994) (underwriters' investigation was sufficient); Weinberger v. Jackson, 1990 WL 260676, [1990–1991 Transfer Binder] Fed.Sec.L.Rep. (CCH) ¶ 95,693 (N.D.Cal.1990) (section 11 claim against underwriters could not be maintained since they reasonably believed the information to be accurate).

44. *See* Samuel H. Gruenbaum & Marc I. Steinberg, Accountants' Liability and Responsibility: Securities, Criminal and Common Law, 13 Loy. (L.A.) U.L.Rev. 247 (1980); Stephen R. Miller & John T. Subak, Impact of Federal Securities Laws: Liabilities of Officers, Directors and Accountants, 30 Bus.Law. 387 (1975); Symposium on Accounting and the Federal Securities Laws, 28 Vand.L.Rev. 1 (1975). *See also* Anthony M. Vernava & Gerald W. Hepp, Responsibility of the Accountant Under the Federal Securities Exchange Act of 1934, 6 J.Corp.L. 317 (1981).

For a more recent case discussing accountant's liability under section 11 and holding that it is limited to expertised portions of the registration statement *see* Ahern v. Gaussoin, 611 F.Supp. 1465, 1482–84 (D.Or.1985).

tory answers, he failed to verify them. Further, it was apparent that there had been an increase in notes payable but nonetheless the auditor's investigator had "no conception how tight the cash position was." [45] Since the auditor's investigator had met with only one officer and had various other bases of inquiry notice, the court found that the burden of establishing due diligence had not been met and that the auditors were liable for all mistakes in the 1960 audited figures.

Aftermath of BarChris; SEC Rule 176

The *BarChris* decision raises many questions concerning the extent of independent investigation that must be made. Specifically, how much of a factual inquiry must be made? Must attorneys, accountants, and underwriters make trips all over the country to inspect the physical plant of the issuer? Must there be at least a spot-check of company inventories? Must there be title searches of property claimed to be owned by the issuer? Must there be an eyeball review of all substantial contracts of the issuer? Must there be a complete opening of the company's files to outsiders such as the underwriters? These are just some of the questions that arise from the decision. The safe answer to each of these questions is clearly "yes." One effective way to help assure compliance with section 11's due diligence requirement is to appoint a due diligence officer to supervise the preparation of the registration statement.[46]

A second instructive decision on the scope of section 11(b) defenses arose in the context of an exchange offer in Feit v. Leasco Data Processing Equipment Corp.[47] Unlike the underwriters in the *BarChris* case, there was no interlocking directorate or relationship between the issuer and the underwriter. Accordingly, the underwriters were truly outsiders who were dealing at arms length with the issuer. Thus, the court noted that "dealer-managers cannot, of course, be expected to possess the intimate knowledge of corporate affairs of inside directors, and their duty to investigate should be considered in light of their more limited access." [48] The same clearly could not have been said of the underwriters in *BarChris* because of their interlocking management. The court noted that the underwriters in *Feit* did comply with industry standards and made somewhat of an independent investigation. The court concluded that they "have just barely established * * * that they had reasonable ground to believe that the omission of a specific figure was justified."[49] In so ruling the court found that unlike the underwrit-

---

45. 283 F.Supp. at 702.

46. *See* Robert A. Spanner, Limiting Exposure in the Offering Process, 20 Rev.Sec. & Commod.Reg. 59 (1987) (also containing a helpful checklist of due diligence steps).

47. 332 F.Supp. 544 (E.D.N.Y.1971). *See* Note, Section 11 in the Exchange Offer Setting: An Analysis of Feit v. Leasco Data Processing Equipment Corp., 1972 Duke L.J. 1023.

48. 332 F.Supp. at 582. Compare Kitchens v. U.S. Shelter, 1988 WL 108598, [1988–89 Transfer Binder] Fed.Sec.L.Rep. (CCH) ¶ 93,920 (D.S.C.1988) (appraisal firm satisfied burden of proving due diligence).

49. Id. at 582.

ers in *BarChris,* Leasco's underwriters were justified in relying on the client's representations.

It is evident from the foregoing discussion that the courts have not been able to articulate a bright-line test as to the requisite standard of care under section 11. What has emerged, however, is the fact that courts will impose a sliding scale depending upon the defendant's knowledge, expertise, status with regard to the issuer, its affiliates or underwriters, and the degree of the defendant's actual participation in the registration process and in preparing the registration materials.

In an effort to clarify its position, the SEC promulgated Rule 176 which adopts the guidelines set out in the proposed federal securities code.[50] SEC Rule 176 provides:

> In determining whether or not the conduct of a person constitutes a reasonable investigation or a reasonable ground for belief meeting the standard set forth in section 11(c), relevant circumstances include, with respect to a person other than the issuer:
>
> (a) The type of issuer;
>
> (b) The type of security;
>
> (c) The type of person;
>
> (d) The office held when the person is an officer;
>
> (e) The presence or absence of another relationship to the issuer when the person is a director or proposed director;
>
> (f) Reasonable reliance on officers, employees, and others whose duties should have given them knowledge of the particular facts (in the light of the functions and responsibilities of the particular person with respect to the issuer and the filing);
>
> (g) When the person is an underwriter, the type of underwriting arrangement, the role of the particular person as an underwriter and the availability of information with respect to the registration; and
>
> (h) Whether, with respect to a fact or document incorporated by reference, the particular person had any responsibility for the fact or document at the time of the filing from which it was incorporated.[51]

The Commission's rule reinforces the judicial sliding scale of culpability and further provides for the necessity of a case-by-case, highly factual analysis, as is done with common law negligence.

---

50. A.L.I., Proposed Federal Securities Code § 1704(g).

51. 17 C.F.R. § 230.176.

*Deleted sections 7.4.1 and 7.4.2 can be found
in the Practitioner's Edition.*

§ 7.5 Section 12(2)—Liability for Material Misstatements or Omissions by Sellers of Securities

Section 12(2) of the 1933 Act[1] creates an express private remedy for material misstatements or omissions in connection with the sale or offer for sale of a security; the offeror or seller of the security is liable to the purchaser of the security.[2] This section supplements liability under section 11 and 12(1) as it is not dependent upon the Act's registration requirements.[3] The remedies under the securities laws are cumulative.[4] Section 12(2) applies to both written and oral communications.[5] The use of prospectus and oral communications are stated in the alternative. Accordingly, it is inappropriate to give undue weight to the prospectus and thereby give short shrift to the impact of the oral representations.[6] On the other hand, oral statements will not be actionable if they do not materially affect the total mix of information available to the investor.[7]

As is the case with section 12(1), section 12(2) is limited to liability of sellers and thus imposes a strict privity requirement.[8] In a rather

---

§ 7.5

1. 15 U.S.C.A. § 77*l*(2). *See* Martin I. Kaminsky, An Analysis of Securities Litigation Under Section 12(2) and How It Compares with Rule 10b–5, 13 Houston L.Rev. 231 (1976); Edward A. Peterson, Recent Developments in Civil Liability Under Section 12(2) of the Securities Act of 1933, 5 Houston L.Rev. 274 (1967); Robert N. Rapp, Expanded Liability Under Section 12 of the Securities Act: When is a Seller Not a Seller?, 27 Case Wes.Res.L.Rev. 445 (1977); Comment, "Reasonable Care" in Section 12(2) of the Securities Act of 1933, 48 U.Chi.L.Rev. 372 (1981).

2. The section 12(2) remedy is limited to damages; injunctive relief is not available. K/A & Co. v. Hallwood Energy Partners, L.P., 1990 WL 37866, [1990–1991 Transfer Binder] Fed.Sec.L.Rep. (CCH) ¶ 95,758 (S.D.N.Y.1990).

3. 15 U.S.C.A. §§ 77k, 77*l* (1). *See* §§ 7.2, 7.3–7.4 *supra.*

4. *See* footnote 12 *infra.* Thus, for example, restrictive decisions under other provisions of the securities laws do not mandate a restrictive reading of section 12(2). Pacific Dunlop Holdings Inc. v. Allen & Co., 993 F.2d 578, 592–94 (7th Cir.1993), *cert. granted* __ U.S. __, 114 S.Ct. 907, 127 L.Ed.2d 98 (1994).

5. *See, e.g.,* McMahan & Co. v. Wherehouse Entertainment, Inc., 900 F.2d 576, 581 (2d Cir.1990), (phone conversation); Casella v. Webb, 883 F.2d 805, 808 (9th Cir.1989) ("Statements made in the course of an oral presentation 'cannot be considered in isolation,' but must be viewed 'in the context of the total presentation' "). *Cf.* Bruschi v. Brown, 876 F.2d 1526 (11th Cir.1989) (fact that purchaser did not read disclosure documents did not preclude a finding of reliance on alleged oral misstatements; decided under Rule 10b–5).

However, as discussed more fully later in this section, the § 12(2) action applies only to sales of securities offered by prospectus. Gustafson v. Alloyd Co., __ U.S. __, 115 S.Ct. 1061, 131 L.Ed.2d 1 (1995).

6. MidAmerica Federal Savings & Loan Association v. Shearson/American Express, Inc., 886 F.2d 1249 (10th Cir.1989). *But see* Ambrosino v. Rodman & Renshaw, Inc., 972 F.2d 776 (7th Cir.1992) (oral statements were not actionable because written statements were accurate and their accuracy precluded a claim on varying oral statements).

7. *See, e.g.,* Wamser v. J.E. Liss, Inc., 838 F.Supp. 393 (E.D.Wis.1993). As discussed elsewhere in more detail, in order for a particular misstatement or omission to be material, the misstatement in question must have a significant impact on the total mix of information. *See* § 13.5A *infra.*

8. Qualifications for a section 12 seller are discussed in § 7.2 *supra.* *See also* § 7.5.1 (Practitioner's Edition only). *Cf.* Resolution Trust Corp. v. Miller, 1994 WL 276354,

surprising and highly questionable decision, one court has indicated that an offeree who did not actually purchase the stock may bring an action under section 12(2).[9] Nevertheless it seems clear that the plaintiff must be a purchaser since section 12(2) in stating its privity requirement speaks in terms of securities *purchased* from the defendant.[10] The privity requirement has been strictly construed. It has thus been held that limited partners did not have standing under section 12(2) to assert claims that allegedly arose in connection with their partnership's purchases of securities.[11] Accordingly, purchaser status must be established as a result of a direct rather than derivative relationship to the purchase of securities covered by the registration statement. The court indicated, however, that the result might have been different had the limited partners brought a derivative action rather than suing in their individual capacities.

The section 12(2) action may be brought in either law or equity. Additionally, like section 12(1) but unlike section 11 or the implied remedy under Rule 10b–5 of the Exchange Act,[12] damages are limited to either rescission and return of the purchase price or damages based on that amount if the purchaser no longer owns the security.[13] Borrowing from general principles from the law of equity, it has been held that in order to qualify for relief under section 12(2), the plaintiff must make a

---

[1994–1995 Transfer Binder] Fed. Sec. L. Rep. (CCH) ¶ 98,380 (E.D.Pa.1994) (action for rescission could not be brought under section 29 of the 1934 Act against savings and loan which was not a seller of the securities).

9.   Doll v. James Martin Associates (Holdings) Ltd., 600 F.Supp. 510 (E.D.Mich.1984).

10.   *See, e.g.,* Soderberg v. Gens, 652 F.Supp. 560 (N.D.Ill.1987); Steinberg v. Illinois Co., 659 F.Supp. 58 (N.D.Ill.1987). The privity requirement is discussed in § 7.2 *supra.* *See also* the discussion in § 7.5.1 *infra* (Practitioner's Edition only).

11.   Davis v. Coopers & Lybrand, 787 F.Supp. 787 (N.D.Ill.1992).

12.   17 C.F.R. § 240.10b–5. Most cases hold that Rule 10b–5 and section 12(2) are not mutually exclusive remedies. *E.g.* Austin v. Loftsgaarden, 675 F.2d 168 (8th Cir.1982), *appeal after remand* 768 F.2d 949 (8th Cir.1985), *reversed* 478 U.S. 647, 106 S.Ct. 3143, 92 L.Ed.2d 525 (1986); Ellis v. Carter, 291 F.2d 270 (9th Cir.1961); Matheson v. Armbrust, 284 F.2d 670 (9th Cir.1960), *cert. denied* 365 U.S. 870, 81 S.Ct. 904, 5 L.Ed.2d 860 (1961). *Cf.* Herman & MacLean v. Huddleston, 459 U.S. 375, 103 S.Ct. 683, 74 L.Ed.2d 548 (1983) *on remand* 705 F.2d 775 (5th Cir.1983) (section 11 and Rule 10b–5 are cumulative). *But see* Berger v. Bishop Investment Corp., 528 F.Supp. 346 (E.D.Mo.1981), *order reversed* 695 F.2d 302 (8th Cir.1982) (purchasers who have an express civil remedy under § 12(2) may not use the implied right of action under § 10(b)); Rosenberg v. Globe Aircraft Corp., 80 F.Supp. 123 (E.D.Pa.1948); Montague v. Electronic Corp., 76 F.Supp. 933 (S.D.N.Y.1948). *See generally* Marc I. Steinberg, The Propriety and Scope of Cumulative Remedies Under the Federal Securities Laws, 67 Cornell L.Rev. 557 (1982). *See also,* Kaminsky, *supra* footnote 1.

For discussion of section 12(2)'s requirement that a plaintiff still owning the securities tender them to the seller, *see* Wigand v. Flo–Tek, 609 F.2d 1028, 1034–35 (2d Cir.1979); Kilmartin v. H.C. Wainwright & Co., 580 F.Supp. 604, 607 (D.Mass.1984).

13.   For a fuller discussion of damages under section 12, *see* § 7.5.3 *infra* (Practitioner's Edition only).

demand for rescission promptly upon learning of the misrepresentation.[14]

The Supreme Court has held that in computing damages under section 12 tax benefits are not to be considered as income received by the plaintiff and therefore are not to be deducted from the damage award.[15] Thus, the fact that the plaintiffs received tax benefits does not affect their rescissory damages. Unlike an action under section 11,[16] there is no provision in section 12 for the award of costs or attorneys fees. However, where the claim or defense is without merit costs and fees may be awarded as a sanction under Rule 11 of the Federal Rules of Civil Procedure.[17] Additionally, where the section 12 claims are brought with pendent state claims, state law may permit the award of costs and attorneys fees.[18] By virtue of section 13 of the 1933 Act[19] the purchaser must bring suit within one year after discovery of the misstatement or omission, or within one year after the date upon which such discovery should have been made through the exercise of reasonable diligence, but in no event may an action be brought more than three years after the sale.

Section 12(2) liability is narrower than section 11 insofar as privity is required for the former. However, section 12(2) is also broader than section 11 since it applies to all sellers and is not limited to the types of persons specified in section 11(a).[20] Section 12(2) is not limited to written statements and, unlike section 11, applies to oral misrepresenta-

---

14. Westinghouse Electric Corp. v. "21" International Holdings, Inc., 821 F.Supp. 212 (S.D.N.Y.1993), relying on Gannett Co. v. Register Publishing Co., 428 F.Supp. 818, 827–28 (D.Conn.1977) (the necessity of a prompt demand for rescission in an action under Rule 10b–5 also applies to section 12(2) actions).

15. Randall v. Loftsgaarden, 478 U.S. 647, 106 S.Ct. 3143, 92 L.Ed.2d 525 (1986).

16. 15 U.S.C.A. § 77k(e). Section 11 costs and attorneys fees are discussed in § 7.4.2 *supra* (Practitioner's Edition only).

17. Fed.R.Civ.P. 11. Rule 11 sanctions are discussed in § 13.7.1 *infra* (Practitioner's Edition only).

18. Austin v. Loftsgaarden, 768 F.2d 949 (8th Cir.1985), *reversed on other grounds* 478 U.S. 647, 106 S.Ct. 3143, 92 L.Ed.2d 525 (1986); Monetary Management Group v. Kidder, Peabody & Co., 615 F.Supp. 1217 (E.D.Mo.1985).

19. 15 U.S.C.A. § 77m. *See* § 7.5.4 *infra* (Practitioner's Edition only) for a fuller discussion of the statute of limitations. *See also* § 7.2 *supra*.

Plaintiff has the burden of proving the three-year period should apply. Kennedy v. Josephthal & Co., Inc., 814 F.2d 798 (1st Cir.1987), Baden v. Craig–Hallum, Inc., 646 F.Supp. 483 (D.Minn.1986).

Equitable tolling will not extend beyond the three-year period. Finne v. Dain Bosworth, Inc., 648 F.Supp. 337, 341 (D.Minn.1986). *See also* Stone v. Fossil Oil & Gas, 657 F.Supp. 1449 (D.N.M.1987) (limitations period tolled for section 12(2) claim but not for section 12(1)).

For statute of limitations purposes, the sale does not occur until the parties enter into a binding contract. Amoroso v. Southwestern Drilling Multi–Rig Partnership No. 1, 646 F.Supp. 141 (N.D.Cal.1986). *Cf.* Ambling v. Blackstone Cattle Co., Inc., 658 F.Supp. 1459 (N.D.Ill.1987) (sale occurs when investors acquired legal title even though they paid in advance).

20. *See* § 7.5.1 *infra* (Practitioner's Edition only) for a fuller discussion of who is a section 12 seller. *See also* § 7.2 *supra*.

tions.[21] Furthermore, as compared with Rule 10b–5 which would give the injured purchaser an implied right of action under the 1934 Act,[22] section 12(2) liability does not require scienter.

Section 12(2) renders the seller liable if he or she "shall not sustain the burden of proof that he did not know, and in the exercise of reasonable care could not have known, of such untruth or omission." [23] The imposition of a "reasonable care" standard is different language than the "due diligence" rubric of section 11.[24] It is clear that section 12(2)'s requirement of "reasonable care" imparts some sort of negligence standard and that it is not necessary for the purchaser to show any type of scienter on the seller's part.[25] Although there is not a *per se* affirmative investigation requirement, it has been held that the section 12(2) standard of reasonable care may impose a duty to investigate depending upon the circumstances.[26] Reasonable care imparts a sliding scale of standards of conduct and has been held to impose a duty of *continuing investigation* in the case of the exclusive dealer of the security in question.[27] On the other hand, two justices of the Supreme Court have taken the position that any imposition of an affirmative investigation requirement is a misapplication of the "reasonable care" standard since the "investigation" language of section 11 is said to call for a greater undertaking than the "care" requirement of section 12(2).[28] In any event, the reasonable care standard of section 12(2) would seem to put less of a burden on the plaintiff than would a negligence standard in an implied action under section 17(a) of the 1933 Act (should one exist)[29]

---

21. *E.g.,* Metromedia Co. v. Fugazy, 983 F.2d 350, 361–62 (2d Cir.1992), *affirming* 753 F.Supp. 93 (S.D.N.Y.1990). Section 12(2) on its face expressly includes reference to oral communications. *But see* Ambrosino v. Rodman & Renshaw, Inc., 972 F.2d 776 (7th Cir.1992) (oral statements were not actionable because written statements were accurate and their accuracy precluded a claim on varying oral statements).

However, section 12(2) is limited to offerings by prospectus. Gustafson v. Alloyd Co., ___ U.S. ___, 115 S.Ct. 1061, 131 L.Ed.2d 1 (1995).

22. *See* chapter 13 *infra.*

23. 15 U.S.C.A. § 77*l* (2). *See* Mayer v. Oil Field Systems Corp., 803 F.2d 749, 756 (2d Cir.1986) (section 12(2) claim dismissed for failure to show defendant should have known of the misrepresentation; also requiring scienter for aider and abettor liability). *See* ABA Committee of Federal Regulation of Securities, Report of the Task Force on Sellers' Due Diligence and Similar Defenses Under the Federal Securities Laws, 48 Bus.Law. 1185 (1993); Therese H. Maynard, The Affirmative Defense of Reasonable Care Under Section 12(2) of the Securities Act of 1933, 69 Notre Dame L. Rev. 57 (1993).

See also, e.g., Lucia v. Prospect Street High Income Portfolio, Inc., 36 F.3d 170 (1st Cir.1994) (failure to allege facts showing that defendant knew or should have known of the inaccuracies).

24. *See* § 7.4 *supra.*

25. *See, e.g.,* Wigand v. Flo–Tek, Inc., 609 F.2d 1028 (2d Cir.1979).

26. Sanders v. John Nuveen & Co., 619 F.2d 1222, 1228 (7th Cir.1980), *cert. denied* 450 U.S. 1005, 101 S.Ct. 1719, 68 L.Ed.2d 210 (1981).

27. *See* Franklin Savings Bank v. Levy, 551 F.2d 521, 527 (2d Cir.1977) (commercial paper).

28. John Nuveen & Co. v. Sanders, 450 U.S. 1005, 101 S.Ct. 1719, 68 L.Ed.2d 210 (1981) (Powell, J., joined by Rehnquist, J.; dissenting from a denial of certiorari).

29. The courts are sharply divided on whether such a remedy exists. *See* § 13.13 *infra;* Thomas L. Hazen, A Look Beyond the Pruning of Rule 10b–5: Implied Remedies and

or Rule 10b–5's scienter requirement.[30]

Section 12(2) claims must be pleaded with sufficient particularity[31] so as to indicate that the defendant should have known of the misrepresentations or omissions which form the basis of the claim.[32] A defendant can successfully defend against a section 12(2) claim if it can be shown that he or she made reasonable inquiries into the possibility of fraud by the issuer, and discovered nothing wrong;[33] or that nothing could have been discovered even with the exercise of reasonable care.[34] Certain factors may be used to determine whether the defendant did exercise ordinary care: 1) the quantum of decisional and facilitative participation, such as designing the deal and contacting and attempting to persuade potential purchasers; 2) access to source material against which the truth of representations can be tested; 3) relative skill in "ferreting out the truth"; 4) pecuniary interest in the transaction's completion; and 5) the existence of a relationship of trust between the investor and the alleged "seller".[35]

Broadly generalized opinions may not be actionable under section 12(2) to the extent that a certain amount of puffery is permissible.[36] Section 12(2) liability depends upon the misrepresentation or omission being material. Materiality consists of that information which a reasonable investor would find significant in making an investment decision.[37] The question of whether particular misrepresentations or omissions are material is a highly factual determination based on the total mix of

Section 17(a) of the Securities Act of 1933, 64 Va.L.Rev. 641, 654–57 (1978); Paul Horton, Section 17(a) of the 1933 Securities Act—The Wrong Place for a Private Right, 68 Nw.U.L.Rev. 44 (1973); Marc I. Steinberg, Section 17(a) of the Securities Act of 1933 After Naftalin and Reddington, 68 Geo.L.J. 163 (1979).

Implied remedies in general are on the decline. *See* § 13.1 *infra.*

30. *See* § 13.4 *infra. But see* Bozsi Ltd. Partnership v. Lynott, 676 F.Supp. 505 (S.D.N.Y.1987) (applying a recklessness standard under section 12); Center Savings & Loan Association v. Prudential–Bache Securities, Inc., 679 F.Supp. 274 (S.D.N.Y.1987) (semble).

31. The particularity requirement is based on Fed.R.Civ.P. 9(b). For cases articulating the particularity requirement in section 12(2) claims *see, e.g.,* Maywalt v. Parker & Parsley Petroleum Co., 808 F.Supp. 1037 (S.D.N.Y.1992); Roebuck v. Guttman, 678 F.Supp. 68 (S.D.N.Y.1988); Farlow v. Peat Marwick Mitchell & Co., 666 F.Supp. 1500 (W.D.Okl.1987). *See also* the discussion of the particularity requirement in § 13.8.1 *infra.*

32. *See, e.g.,* Bozsi Ltd. Partnership v. Lynott, 676 F.Supp. 505 (S.D.N.Y.1987); Center Savings & Loan Association v. Prudential–Bache Securities, Inc., 679 F.Supp. 274 (S.D.N.Y. 1987).

33. Sanders v. John Nuveen & Co., 619 F.2d 1222 (7th Cir.1980).

34. Junker v. Crory, 650 F.2d 1349 (5th Cir.1981) (seller-attorney could not show that he would not have discovered material omission with reasonable care).

35. Davis v. Avco Financial Services, Inc., 739 F.2d 1057 (6th Cir.1984).

36. Malkani v. Blinder, Robinson & Co., 1986 WL 2961, [1985–86 Transfer Binder] Fed.Sec.L.Rep. (CCH) ¶ 92,496 (S.D.N.Y.1986).

37. *E.g.,* Kaufman & Enzer Joint Venture v. Dedman, 680 F.Supp. 805 (W.D.La.1987) (failure to disclose sales commission was a material omission justifying liability under section 12(2)). *See* TSC Indus., Inc. v. Northway, Inc., 426 U.S. 438, 449, 96 S.Ct. 2126, 2132, 48 L.Ed.2d 757 (1976).

information available.[38]

Reliance is generally an element of a fraud claim.[39] However, it is generally held that once the plaintiff has proved a material omission, it is not necessary for plaintiff to establish reliance in a section 12(2) action.[40] A plaintiff with knowledge of the fraud cannot claim reliance and thus in such a case the section 12(2) claim should be dismissed.[41]

As discussed directly above, a section 12(2) action is dependent upon a showing of or presumption of reliance. Similarly, there is authority requiring the plaintiff to establish transaction causation—namely, that there was some causal nexus between the misstatement or omission and the plaintiff's purchase of the securities.[42] On the other hand, there is recent authority to the effect that an affirmative showing of transaction causation is not required in a section 12(2) action.[43] The courts are in agreement, however, that it is not necessary to prove loss causation in an action under section 12(2).[44]

As is the case with section 12(1), difficult questions arise under section 12(2) as to what degree of active participation in the transaction is necessary to classify someone as a section 12 "seller." [45] Generally,

38. *See* TSC Indus., Inc. v. Northway, Inc., 426 U.S. 438, 449, 96 S.Ct. 2126, 2132, 48 L.Ed.2d 757 (1976). *See* §§ 11.4, 13.5A *infra* for a discussion of materiality.

39. *See, e.g.,* Pell v. Weinstein, 759 F.Supp. 1107 (M.D.Pa.1991), *judgment affirmed* 961 F.2d 1568 (3d Cir.1992) (no section 12(2) claim where plaintiff committed to transaction in question prior to seeing allegedly misleading statements).

40. Wright v. National Warranty Co., 953 F.2d 256 (6th Cir.1992) (reliance is not an element of a section 12(2) claim; the fact that plaintiff was an insider did not by itself bar a section 12(2) action); MidAmerica Federal Savings & Loan v. Shearson/American Express, Inc., 886 F.2d 1249, 1256 (10th Cir.1989) (section 12(2) does not require reliance; plaintiff's sophistication is therefore irrelevant); Currie v. Cayman Resources Corp., 835 F.2d 780 (11th Cir.1988); Austin v. Loftsgaarden, 675 F.2d 168, 177 (8th Cir.1982); In re Conner Bonds Litigation, 1988 WL 110054, [1988–89 Transfer Binder] Fed.Sec.L.Rep. (CCH) ¶ 93,969 (E.D.N.C.1988); Acme Propane, Inc. v. Tenexco, Inc., 666 F.Supp. 143 (N.D.Ill.1987), *reversed* 844 F.2d 1317 (7th Cir.1988); In re Olympia Brewing Co. Securities Litigation, 612 F.Supp. 1367 (N.D.Ill.1985).

41. *E.g.,* Mayer v. Oil Field Systems, Corp., 803 F.2d 749 (2d Cir.1986). *See also, e.g.,* Jankovich v. Bowen, 844 F.Supp. 743 (S.D.Fla.1994) (circumstances surrounding transfer of securities put transferee on notice of possible fraud; accordingly, section 12(2) action failed due to inability to show reasonable reliance on alleged misrepresentations). *Cf.* Pinter v. Dahl, 486 U.S. 622, 108 S.Ct. 2063, 100 L.Ed.2d 658 (1988) (holding that the equal fault defense can be invoked in an action under section 12(1) but only if the parties truly are equally at fault).

42. *See, e.g.,* Sanders v. John Nuveen & Co., 619 F.2d 1222 (7th Cir.1980), *cert. denied,* 450 U.S. 1005, 101 S.Ct. 1719, 68 L.Ed.2d 210 (1981); Nielsen v. Greenwood, 849 F.Supp. 1233. 1251–52 (N.D.Ill.1994). Transaction causation is discussed in § 13.6 *infra.*

43. Caviness v. Derand Resources Corp., 983 F.2d 1295, 1305 (4th Cir.1993).

44. Caviness v. Derand Resources Corp., 983 F.2d 1295, 1305 (4th Cir.1993); Wilson v. Saintine Exploration & Drilling Corp., 872 F.2d 1124, 1126 (2d Cir.1989); Nielsen v. Greenwood, 849 F.Supp. 1233. 1251–52 (N.D.Ill.1994); Polycast Technology Corp. v. Uniroyal, Inc., 792 F.Supp. 244, 259 (S.D.N.Y.1992). Loss causation is discussed in § 13.6 *infra.*

45. *See, e.g.,* Junker v. Crory, 650 F.2d 1349 (5th Cir.1981); Croy v. Campbell, 624 F.2d 709 (5th Cir.1980); Alton Box Board Co. v. Goldman, Sachs & Co., 560 F.2d 916 (8th Cir.1977); Johns Hopkins University v. Hutton, 422 F.2d 1124 (4th Cir.1970), *cert. denied* 416 U.S. 916, 94 S.Ct. 1622, 40 L.Ed.2d 118 (1974); Hagert v. Glickman, 520 F.Supp. 1028 (D.Minn.1981); In re North American Acceptance Corp. Securities Cases, 513 F.Supp. 608

issuers and underwriters are not sellers within the meaning of section 12 unless they actively participate in the negotiations with the plaintiff/purchaser.[46] Similarly, an attorney's having worked on the offering circular will not make him or her a seller.[47] On the other hand, a broker who deals directly with the plaintiff is a section 12 seller.[48] In order to be a seller under section 12, the defendant must not only have a direct relationship with the plaintiff, he or she must also have been directly involved in the sale.[49]

Section 12(2) has no express limits on its application except for those discussed earlier in this section. However, recent decisions have held that section 12(2) applies only to distributions of securities and not to isolated after-market transactions that are not part of a "batch

(N.D.Ga.1981). The "seller" requirement is discussed in § 7.2 *supra*. *See* Rapp *supra* note 1.

See also, e.g., Craftmatic Securities Litigation v. Kraftsow, 890 F.2d 628, 636 (3d Cir.1989) (no aider and abettor liability for violations of section 12(2)); Royal American Managers, Inc. v. IRC Holding Corp., 885 F.2d 1011, 1017 (2d Cir.1989); Schlifke v. Seafirst Corp., 866 F.2d 935, 942 (7th Cir.1989); Ackerman v. Schwartz, 733 F.Supp. 1231 (N.D.Ind.1989); In re Crazy Eddie Securities Litigation, 714 F.Supp. 1285 (E.D.N.Y.1989); In re ZZZZ Best Securities Litigation, 1989 WL 90284, [1989 Transfer Binder] Fed.Sec. L.Rep. ¶ 94,485 (C.D.Cal.1989); In re Worlds of Wonder Securities Litigation, 721 F.Supp. 1140 (N.D.Cal.1989); Lambergs v. Total Health Systems, Inc., 1989 WL 63243, [1989–1990 Transfer Binder] Fed.Sec.L.Rep. ¶ 94,831 (D.Mass.1989). *Contra* Drexel Burnham Lambert, Inc. v. American Bankers Insurance Co., 1989 WL 168012, [1989–1990 Transfer Binder] Fed.Sec.L.Rep. ¶ 94,835 (E.D.N.C.1989) (aiding and abetting liability does exist under section 12(2)).

For a discussion of an attorney's liability under section 12(2) *see* SEC v. Seaboard Corp., 677 F.2d 1289 (9th Cir.1982). *See also, e.g.,*Comment, Section 12(2) of the Securities Act of 1933, 78 Nw.U.L.Rev. 832 (1983).

46. *See* Foster v. Jesup & Lamont Securities Co., 759 F.2d 838 (11th Cir.1985). *See also* Pinter v. Dahl, 486 U.S. 622, 108 S.Ct. 2063, 100 L.Ed.2d 658 (1988) (holding that to be a seller in an action under section 12(1) the defendant must have been both an immediate and direct seller; substantial participation alone will not suffice). *See* § 7.5.1 *infra* (Practitioner's Edition only) for more detailed discussion of who is a seller. *See also* the discussion in § 7.2 *supra*.

47. *E.g.,* Moore v. Kayport Package Express, Inc., 885 F.2d 531 (9th Cir.1989); Royal American Managers, Inc. v. IRC Holding Corp., 885 F.2d 1011, 1017 (2d Cir.1989); Wilson v. Saintine Exploration and Drilling Corp., 872 F.2d 1124 (2d Cir.1989); Abell v. Potomac Insurance Co., 20 Sec.Reg. & L.Rep. (BNA) 1963 (5th Cir.1988); Sellin v. Rx Plus, Inc., 730 F.Supp. 1289 (S.D.N.Y.1990); Ackerman v. Schwartz, 733 F.Supp. 1231 (N.D.Ind.1989) (attorneys could not be liable under section 12(2) since they did not solicit investors or otherwise participate in the selling process); Marshall v. Quinn–L Equities, Inc., 704 F.Supp. 1384 (N.D.Tex.1988); Parquitex Partners v. Registered Financial Planning Services, Inc., 1987 WL 15459, [1987 Transfer Binder] Fed.Sec.L.Rep. (CCH) ¶ 93,255 (D.Or.1987). *But see, e.g.,* Mercer v. Jaffe, Snider, Raitt & Heuer, P.C., 713 F.Supp. 1019 (W.D.Mich.1989) (dismissing section 12(2) claim but upholding aiding and abetting claim under Rule 10b–5 against attorneys who participated in preparing the offering materials), s.c. 730 F.Supp. 74 (W.D.Mich.1990), 736 F.Supp. 764 (W.D.Mich.1990) (insufficient allegations of lawyers' scienter); Stokes v. Lokken, 644 F.2d 779 (8th Cir.1981).

48. *E.g.,* Quincy Co–Operative Bank v. A.G. Edwards & Sons, Inc., 655 F.Supp. 78 (D.Mass.1986).

49. Pinter v. Dahl, 486 U.S. 622, 108 S.Ct. 2063, 100 L.Ed.2d 658 (1988). *See also, e.g.,* PPM America, Inc. v. Marriott Corp., 853 F.Supp. 860 (D.Md.1994) (issuer was not a "seller").

offering." [50]   Although not all courts have concurred, the Supreme Court in a five-to-four decision has imposed a similar limitation on the section 12(2) remedy.[51]   Those courts reaching this unfortunate and erroneous conclusion that section 12(2) should be interpreted as limited to offerings, as opposed to secondary transactions, have relied on the statutory language of section 12(2) which refers to misstatements and omissions made by "*prospectus* or oral communication."[52]   Accordingly, it has been said that the use of the term "prospectus" shows a legislative intent to limit the section's operation to the offering process.   However, the definition of prospectus[53] does not have any such restriction and thus, on its face, applies to all written, television, or radio offers to sell securities.[54]

Such a limiting view of section 12(2) is not only unwise as a matter of policy; it does not comport with the Act's legislative history.[55]   The cases which limit the scope of section 12(2) are inconsistent with the Supreme Court's earlier pronouncement that overlap between multiple remedies under the securities laws "is neither unusual nor unfortu-

---

50.   Ballay v. Legg Mason Wood Walker, Inc., 925 F.2d 682 (3d Cir.1991), *cert. denied* 502 U.S. 820, 112 S.Ct. 79, 116 L.Ed.2d 52 (1991); Comeau v. Rupp, 810 F.Supp. 1127 (D.Kan.1992); Budget Rent A Car Systems, Inc. v. Hirsch, 810 F.Supp. 1253 (S.D.Fla. 1992); Knapp v. Patel [1992–1993 Transfer Binder] Fed.Sec.L.Rep. (CCH) ¶ 97,219 (W.D.Mich.1992); Bennett v. Bally Mfg. Corp., 785 F.Supp. 559 (D.S.C.1992); Bank of Denver v. Southeastern Capital Group, Inc., 763 F.Supp. 1552 (D.Colo.1991); Cox v. Eichler, 765 F.Supp. 601 (N.D.Cal.1990); T. Rowe Price New Horizons Fund, Inc. v. Preletz, 749 F.Supp. 705 (D.Md.1990); Leonard v. Stuart–James Co., Inc., 742 F.Supp. 653 (N.D.Ga.1990); Grinsell v. Kidder, Peabody & Co., 744 F.Supp. 931 (N.D.Cal.1990); First Union Brokerage v. Milos, 717 F.Supp. 1519 (S.D.Fla.1989); Panek v. Bogucz, 718 F.Supp. 1228 (D.N.J.1989). *See also, e.g.,* Scotch v. Moseley, Hallgarten, Estabrook & Weeden, Inc., 709 F.Supp. 95 (M.D.Pa.1988). *Cf.* McMahan & Co. v. Wherehouse Entertainment, Inc., 859 F.Supp. 743 (S.D.N.Y.1994) (sales in aftermarket shortly after public offering bore close enough relationship to initial offering).

See Robert A. Prentice, Section 12(2): A Remedy for Wrongs in the Secondary Market?, 55 Alb.L.Rev. 97 (1991); Elliot J. Weiss, The Courts Have it Right: Securities Act § 12(2) Applies only to Public Offerings, 48 Bus. Law. 1 (1992); Note, Applying Section 12(2) of the 1933 Securities Act to the Aftermarket, 57 U.Chi.L.Rev. 955 (1990).

51.   Gustafson v. Alloyd Co., ___ U.S. ___, 115 S.Ct. 1061, 131 L.Ed.2d 1 (1995).   Pacific Dunlop Holdings Inc. v. Allen & Co., 993 F.2d 578 (7th Cir.1993), *cert. granted* ___ U.S. ___, 114 S.Ct. 907, 127 L.Ed.2d 98 (1994); Hedden v. Marinelli, 796 F.Supp. 432 (N.D.Cal. 1992); McCowan v. Dean Witter Reynolds, Inc., 1989 WL 38354, [1989 Transfer Binder] Fed.Sec.L.Rep. (CCH) ¶ 94,423 (S.D.N.Y.1989) (section 12(2) claim could not be maintained for post-distribution acts); Ralph v. Prudential–Bache Securities, Inc., 692 F.Supp. 1322 (S.D.Fla.1988) (section 12(2) is limited to communications relating to batch offerings of securities and not to subsequent trading); SSH Co. v. Shearson Lehman Brothers Inc., 678 F.Supp. 1055 (S.D.N.Y.1987). *See also* Strong v. Paine Webber, Inc., 700 F.Supp. 4 (S.D.N.Y.1988).

For additional cases refusing to limit section 12(2) *see* the authorities in footnotes 59–61, 68 *infra.*

52.   15 U.S.C.A. § 77*l*(2).

53.   15 U.S.C.A. § 77b(10).

54.   *See* § 2.5 *supra.*

55.   *See, e.g.,* Louis Loss, Securities Act Section 12(2): A Rebuttal, 48 Bus. Law. 47 (1992). *But see* Weiss *supra* footnote 50.

nate." [56] Furthermore, Congress took great care in drafting the provisions of the 1933 Act and it is difficult to imagine that they would have intended a severe limitation on the scope of section 12(2) and not make it an explicit one.[57] It has aptly been observed that "it is almost inconceivable that [the 1933 and 1934 Acts]—which repeatedly have been treated as *in pari materia*—were meant to afford no civil remedy whatsoever to the great bulk of investors who do not participate in distributions."[58] It thus should be clear that section 12(2) has application to private transactions as well as to public offerings. Therefore, for example, although not dealing directly with the specific issue involved in the batch offering cases, the Second Circuit has stated unequivocally that section 12(2) "consistently has been applied to private as well as to public offerings of securities."[59] There seems to be a mounting opposition to the narrower view of section 12(2). For example, the Seventh Circuit rejected the cases to the contrary and has held that section 12(2) does apply to secondary transactions that are not part of a "batch offering."[60] Other courts have concurred in the view that section 12(2) is not so limited.[61] On the other hand, the Supreme Court adopted this unfortunate limitation on section 12(2).[62]

Further reason for rejecting the batch offering limitation can be found in other provisions of the 1933 Act. There is evidence in other provisions that Congress did not intend this limitation that some courts have imposed on section 12(2) actions. In setting forth the applicable statute of limitations, section 13 provides that in a section 12(2) action, the three year repose period begins to run from the date of the "sale." [63]

56. Herman & MacLean v. Huddleston, 459 U.S. 375, 383, 103 S.Ct. 683, 688, 74 L.Ed.2d 548, 556 (1983), *on remand* 705 F.2d 775 (5th Cir.1983); United States v. Naftalin, 441 U.S. 768, 778, 99 S.Ct. 2077, 2084, 60 L.Ed.2d 624, 632 (1979), *on remand* 606 F.2d 809 (8th Cir.1979); SEC v. National Securities, Inc., 393 U.S. 453, 468, 89 S.Ct. 564, 572, 21 L.Ed.2d 668 (1969).

57. *See* Louis Loss, The Assault on Securities Act Section 12(2), 105 Harv.L.Rev. 908, 916–17 (1992); Therese Maynard, The Future of Securities Act Section 12(2), 45 Ala. L. Rev. 817 (1994). *See also* footnote 51 *supra*.

58. Loss *supra* footnote 57 at 916 (footnote omitted).

59. Metromedia Co. v. Fugazy, 983 F.2d 350, 361 (2d Cir.1992), *cert. denied* __ U.S. __, 113 S.Ct. 2445, 124 L.Ed.2d 662 (1993); Cewnick Fund v. Castle, 1993 WL 88243, [1992–1993 Transfer Binder] Fed.Sec.L.Rep. (CCH) ¶ 97,392 (S.D.N.Y.1993).

60. Pacific Dunlop Holdings Inc. v. Allen & Co., 993 F.2d 578 (7th Cir.1993), *cert. granted* __ U.S. __, 114 S.Ct. 907, 127 L.Ed.2d 98 (1994). In so ruling, the court noted that the fact that the Supreme Court has restricted remedies under other sections of the securities laws does not indicate that a restrictive reading of section 12(2) is warranted. *Id.* at 592–94.

61. In addition to the cases collected in footnotes 50–51 *supra* and 68 *infra, see* PPM America, Inc. v. Marriott Corp., 820 F.Supp. 970 (D.Md.1993); Hedden v. Marinelli, 796 F.Supp. 432 (N.D.Cal.1992).

62. *See* text accompanying footnotes 69–87 *infra. See also, e.g.,* First Union Discount Brokerage Services, Inc. v. Milos, 997 F.2d 835 (11th Cir.1993); Tregenza v. Great American Communications Co., 823 F.Supp. 1409 (N.D.Ill.1993).

63. 15 U.S.C.A. § 77n. *See* § 7.5.4 *infra. Cf.* Caviness v. Derand Resources Corp., 983 F.2d 1295 (4th Cir.1993) (refusing to apply integration doctrine in computing the three year repose period applicable to a section 12(2) action; the court explained that each sale is considered separately).

In contrast, in actions under section 12(1), the three year period runs from the time the security was bona fide offered to the public. The decision to base the limitations period in section 12(2) actions on the *sale* rather than public offering date can be taken as an indication that Congress did not believe that the section 12(2) action was dependent upon a public offering. Otherwise, why would Congress have chosen different computation periods for actions under section 12? The wording of the statute of limitations thus supports a congressional intent to permit section 12(2) actions in secondary transactions.

Consider further section 17(b) of the 1933 Act which prohibits disseminating information about a security without disclosing any consideration received or to be received, directly or indirectly, in connection with sales of the security.[64] It has been held that section 17(b) is not limited to securities distributions but applies both to new and already outstanding securities.[65] It makes no sense to impose such a limitation on section 12(2) but not on section 17(b).

Even among those courts that accept the batch offering limitation, there have been signs of caution. Some courts that have recognized the trend of many courts to impose a batch offering limitation on section 12(2) actions have begun to generate exceptions so as to avoid unduly restricting the remedy so provided. Thus, for example, an exception has been recognized for redistributions by a controlling person.[66]

There is no evidence that such a limitation on section 12(2)'s scope is warranted by the legislative intent. Section 2(10) of the Act[67] defines prospectus as a written offer to sell without any indication that it is limited to offers in a distribution. Thus, the better view would be that section 12(2) applies regardless of the context of the sale, provided there has been use of the jurisdictional means.[68] Even if these courts are correct in limiting the significance of "prospectus" to the offering process, it is difficult, if not impossible, to justify ignoring the "or otherwise" clause of section 12(2).

Notwithstanding the above-described difficulties in arriving at a limiting interpretation of section 12(2), in a sharply divided five-to-four

---

64. 15 U.S.C.A. § 77q(b). *See* § 7.6 *infra.*

65. SEC v. Wall Street Publishing Institute, Inc., 851 F.2d 365 (D.C.Cir.1988), *cert. denied* 489 U.S. 1066, 109 S.Ct. 1342, 103 L.Ed.2d 811 (1989), relying on S.Rep.No. 47, 73d Cong.1st Sess. 4 (1933) and H.R.Rep. No. 85, 73d Cong.1st Sess. 6 (1933).

66. Fujisawa Pharmaceutical Co. v. Kapoor, 814 F.Supp. 720 (N.D.Ill.1993) (permitting § 12(2) action against corporate insider who exercised control over the company); Budget Rent A Car Systems, Inc. v. Hirsch, 810 F.Supp. 1253 (S.D.Fla.1992) (but holding the exception inapplicable and dismissing the section 12(2) claim).

67. 15 U.S.C.A. § 77b(10). *See* chapter 2 *supra.*

68. *See, e.g.,* Farley v. Baird, Patrick & Co., 750 F.Supp. 1209 (S.D.N.Y.1990); Mix v. E.F. Hutton & Co., 720 F.Supp. 8 (D.D.C.1989); Elysian Federal Savings Bank v. First Interregional Equity Corp., 713 F.Supp. 737 (D.N.J.1989); Scotch v. Moseley, Hallgarten, Estabrook & Weeden, Inc., 709 F.Supp. 95 (M.D.Pa.1988). *Cf.* Haralson v. E.F. Hutton Group, Inc., 919 F.2d 1014 (5th Cir.1990) (section 12(2) applies to both private and public offerings).

decision in Gustafson v. Alloyd Co.,[69] the Supreme Court reached just such a result. As had been the case in the previous lower court decisions, the Supreme Court focused on the use of the term "prospectus" in section 12(2). Unlike what the lower courts had done in many instances, the Supreme Court did not base its decision on the concept of a "batch offering." Nevertheless, the Court did seem to equate the use of a prospectus with a public offering. As is discussed more fully below, in all likelihood, however, section 12(2) will remain applicable to some exempt offerings.

The Court in *Gustafson* acknowledged that section 2(10) broadly defines prospectus to include any written offer to sell.[70] The Court then looked to section 10 of the Act [71] which sets forth the statutory prospectus requirements; the Court concluded that the term, as it is used in section 12(2), should be read as coextensive with the concept of prospectus in section 10.[72] Accordingly, the Court rejected the plaintiff's contention that the contract for sale qualified as a "prospectus" under section 12(2) [73] and thereby limited section 12 to offerings by prospectus. The Court concluded, "the word 'prospectus' is a term of art referring to a document that describes a public offering of securities by an issuer or controlling shareholder." [74] The majority opinion in *Gustafson* explained: "[t]he contract of sale, and its recitations, were not held out to the public and were not a prospectus as the term is used in the 1933 Act." [75] This decision is not likely to put the matter completely to rest. A number of questions survive the Court's rather strained reading of the 1933 Act.

---

69. ___ U.S. ___, 115 S.Ct. 1061, 131 L.Ed.2d 1 (1995).

70. 15 U.S.C.A. § 77b(10). *See* § 2.4 *supra*. This is supplemented by a broadly interpreted definition of "offer to sell" in section 2(3), 15 U.S.C.A. § 77b(3). *See* § 2.3 *supra*.

71. 15 U.S.C.A. § 77j. *See* § 2.4 *supra*.

72. The Court described section 10's use of "prospectus" as follows:

An examination of § 10 reveals that, whatever else, "prospectus" may mean, the term is confined to a document that, absent an overriding exemption, must include the "information contained in the registration statement." By and large, only public offerings by an issuer of a security, or by controlling shareholders of an issuer, require the preparation and filing of registration statements. See 15 U.S.C. §§ 77d, 77e, 77b(11). It follows, we conclude, that a prospectus under § 10 is confined to documents related to public offerings by an issuer or its controlling shareholders.

___ U.S. at ___, 115 S.Ct. at 1067.

73. Although it probably would under section 2(3). 15 U.S.C.A. § 77b(3); *see* § 2.3 *supra*.

74. ___ U.S. at ___, 115 S.Ct. at 1073–74.

75. *Id.* The Court acknowledged that the definition of prospectus in section 2(3) includes any written communication or circular but concluded that those terms should be read within the context of an advertisement or some other communication disseminated to the public generally. Id. at ___, 115 S.Ct. at ___. The Court in this regard missed the very important point that prospectus also includes any written communication that "confirms the security for sale." 15 U.S.C.A. § 77b(10). It goes without saying that sale confirmations are not publicly disseminated. Furthermore, the treatment of a sales confirmation as a prospectus is an important part of section 5's prospectus delivery requirements. 15 U.S.C.A. § 77e; *see* §§ 2.4, 2.5 *supra*.

First, is the section 12(2) remedy now limited only to statements made in the prospectus? This answer would seem to be "no." To begin with, section 12(2) does speak in terms of offering by prospectus "or otherwise." Even under the strictest reading of the statute it would be difficult to limit the action to statements contained in the prospectus. Furthermore, section 11 of the 1933 Act [76] contains an express remedy for material misstatements and omissions in the registration statement (and, hence, in the prospectus). The only effect of adding section 12 liability, if limited to statements in the prospectus, would be to add "sellers" to the list of permissible defendants in a section 11 action.[77] It thus seems clear that the section 12(2) action must apply to all statements made by the seller to the purchaser whether in the prospectus "or otherwise."

A second question is whether the *Gustafson* limitation is geared to public offerings, as much of the Court's language might seem to indicate; or whether it extends to certain other offerings as well. Section 12(2) on its face creates the action with regard to securities, "whether or not exempted by the provisions of section 3 * * *."[78] Congress, thus clearly contemplated that the section 12(2) remedy could be invoked in an offering of exempt securities. There are, of course, some exemptions that may involve a public offering. For example, a purely intrastate offering is exempt from federal registration [79] but may nevertheless be a public offering under state law and thereby involve the use of a prospectus.[80] Similarly, an offering under SEC Regulation A,[81] authorized by section 3(b) of the Act,[82] will generally involve a public offering. Furthermore, the Regulation A exemption is conditioned upon the use of an offering circular that is comparable to a 1933 Act statutory prospectus.[83] Accordingly, the section 12(2) remedy should be available for material misstatements and omissions by sellers of securities in such offerings.

Even beyond the intrastate exemption and Regulation A, there are other exemptions that may involve the use of an offering circular. For example, Rule 505 requires the use of an offering circular (or private

---

76.   15 U.S.C.A. § 77k; *see* § 7.3 *supra.*

77.   Section 11 liability attaches to the issuer, all signers of the registration statement, the auditor, the underwriters, and any experts making certifications or giving opinions in the registration statement (*ibid.*) and thus does not extend to individuals or entities merely because they are acting as "sellers."

78.   15 U.S.C.A. § 77*l* (2). There is an exception to this for securities exempted by section 3(a)(2). Therefore certain securities that are issued by governments, banks, insurance companies, and qualified pension plans (*see* § 4.3 *supra*) cannot form the basis of a section 12(2) action.

79.   Section 3(a)(11), 15 U.S.C.A. § 77c(a)(11); *see* § 4.12 *supra.* The same would be true of a Rule 504 offering under Regulation D that would have to be registered under state law.   17 C.F.R. § 230.504 Rule 504 is discussed in § 4.19 *supra.*

80.   For discussion of the state "blue sky" registration requirements, *see* § 8.2 *infra.*

81.   Rules 251 *et seq.,* 17 C.F.R. § 230.251 *et seq.; see* § 4.15 *supra.*

82.   15 U.S.C.A. § 77c(b).

83.   Rule 253, 17 C.F.R. § 230.253. *See* § 4.15 *supra.*

placement memorandum) if there are any unaccredited investors; and, that offering circular must contain information comparable to a 1933 Act prospectus.[84] However, a Rule 505 offering will not be a public offering as that term is generally understood because the securities cannot be offered on the basis of a general solicitation to the public.[85] Nonetheless, since Rule 505 is a section 3(b) exemption made by use of a prospectus, the section 12(2) remedy should apply because of its express reference to exempt securities. Additionally, consistent with the language of the statute and the Court's basis for its interpretation, it can be said that section 12(2) would also apply to a nonpublic offering utilizing Rule 506's safe harbor which requires the use of a private placement memorandum containing similar information. Once again, it would appear that the section 12(2) remedy should be available if the private placement memorandum is required as a precondition to the exemption. This construction seems mandated by the express language of the statute. Although the majority opinion in *Gustafson* makes many references to prospectuses used in connection with a public offering, the Court itself acknowledged that this is not always the case.[86] Accordingly, the language of the statute, as well as the opinion of the Court, call for extending the section 12(2) remedy to those exemptions that involve or are conditioned upon the use of an offering document that is comparable to a prospectus.

As pointed out above, the *Gustafson* ruling is not a death knell for section 12(2) actions for unregistered offerings. It is the end for the use of section 12(2) against brokers with regard to day-to-day trading. However, in those instances where plaintiffs formerly were successful in section 12(2) actions not involving an offering by prospectus, there is still the potential for a Rule 10b–5 action, provided the plaintiff can establish that the defendant acted with scienter in making the material misstatements or omissions.[87]

---

84. 17 C.F.R. § 230.505. The informational requirements are set forth in Rule 502(b). 17 C.F.R. § 230.502(b); *see* §§ 4.17, 4.18 *supra.*

85. Furthermore, there is a thirty-five purchaser ceiling; although accredited purchasers are not counted in computing the ceiling. 17 C.F.R. § 230.505. However, since a Rule 505 offering may contain offerees and purchasers that would disqualify the nonpublic offering exemption, it may in fact involve a public offering even without a general solicitation. *See* the discussion of the nonpublic offering exemption in § 4.21 *supra.*

86. *"By and large,* only public offerings by an issuer of a security, or by controlling shareholders of an issuer, require the preparation and filing of registration statements." ___ U.S. at ___, 115 S.Ct. at 1067 (emphasis supplied).

87. 17 C.F.R. § 240.10b–5. The Rule 10b–5 remedy is discussed in §§ 13.2–13.12 *infra;* scienter is discussed in § 13.4 *infra.*

*Deleted sections 7.5.1–7.5.4 can be found
in the Practitioner's Edition.*

§ 7.6   The Securities Act's General Antifraud Provision—Section 17

Section 17 of the 1933 Act,[1] which is drafted in terms of defining a violation of the Act, contains general antifraud proscriptions that supplement section 5[2] and the express civil liability provisions.[3] Section 17(a) prohibits fraud, material misstatements and omissions of fact in connection with the sale of securities.[4] Section 17(a) applies regardless of whether the securities are registered or whether they are exempt from registration under section 3.[5] Unlike its 1934 Act counterpart—SEC Rule 10b–5[6]—section 17(a) applies only to *sales* of and *offers to sell* securities and thus to activities of the offeror or seller but not to fraud by the purchaser. Section 17(a) covers negligent material misstatements and omissions. The Supreme Court has held that while scienter is required to prove a claim under section 17(a)(1) it is not an element of subsections (2) or (3).[7] Despite the fact that a section 17(a) violation can be based on negligence, the courts have indicated that it may be difficult for the SEC to secure an injunction absent a showing of scienter.[8] As

---

§ 7.6

1. 15 U.S.C.A. § 77q. One of the major contributions of section 17(a) of the 1933 Act is that it was the model for Rule 10b–5 of the 1934 Act which has become the broadest of the antifraud proscriptions under the securities laws. *See* § 13.2 *infra.*

2. 15 U.S.C.A. § 77e. *See* §§ 2.1–2.5 *supra.*

3. Sections 11 and 12 are discussed in §§ 7.2–7.5 *supra.*

4. 15 U.S.C.A. § 77q(a):

(a) It shall be unlawful for any person in the offer or sale of any securities by the use of any means or instruments of transportation or communication in interstate commerce or by the use of the mails, directly or indirectly—

(1) to employ any device, scheme, or artifice to defraud, or

(2) to obtain money or property by means of any untrue statement of a material fact or any omission to state a material fact necessary in order to make the statements made, in the light of the circumstances under which they were made, not misleading, or

(3) to engage in any transaction, practice, or course of business which operates or would operate as a fraud or deceit upon the purchaser.

5. 15 U.S.C.A. § 77q(c). Section 3's exemptions are discussed in chapter 4 *supra.*

Section 17(a) thus is available anytime there is fraud in connection with the offer or sale. It has been used for example for an investment program representing that there would be a pooling of interests even though no such pooling ever took place. SEC v. Lauer, 864 F.Supp. 784 (N.D.Ill.1994) (the defendant had claimed that in fact no security existed but the court held that the offering of the investment program and ensuing investment contract was the sale of a security).

6. 17 C.F.R. § 240.10b–5. *See* chapter 13 *infra.*

7. Aaron v. SEC, 446 U.S. 680, 100 S.Ct. 1945, 64 L.Ed.2d 611 (1980), *on remand* 666 F.2d 5 (2d Cir.1981). Scienter is a required element of any Rule 10b–5 violation. *Id. See* § 13.4 *infra.*

8. *See* SEC v. Pros International, Inc., 994 F.2d 767 (10th Cir.1993) (court of appeals affirmed the denial of an injunction in light of the SEC's failure to prove that the defendant's conduct was more than negligent; the court also relied on the fact that the defendant did not profit from the transaction in question).

discussed more fully below,[9] the courts have been divided on the question of whether section 17(a) will support an implied private remedy. The overwhelming majority of recent decisions have not been receptive to the private right of action.[10] The trend against implying a remedy has been so strong that the Eighth Circuit affirmed the imposition of Rule 11 sanctions against counsel signing a complaint alleging a remedy under section 17(a).[11] Accordingly, prior to filing a section 17 claim, counsel should make a careful investigation and be confident that the issue has not been resolved clearly to the contrary in that circuit. Notwithstanding the growing support for the absence of an implied private remedy, violations of section 17 can lead to SEC actions resulting in disgorgement of improper profits.[12]

In addition to section 17(a)'s antifraud prohibitions, section 17(b)[13] prohibits disseminating information about a security without disclosing any consideration received or to be received, directly or indirectly, in connection with sales of the security. Section 17(b) is not limited to formal offers to sell.[14] Also, like section 17(a), 17(b) applies to securities whether or not in registration or exempt under section 3.[15] Section 17(b) was designed to prevent the misleading impression of impartiality in certain recommendations. As explained in the House Report, section 17(b)'s prohibitions were "particularly designed to meet the evils of the 'tipster sheet,' as well as articles in newspapers or periodicals that purport to give an unbiased opinion but which in reality are bought and paid for."[16] Section 17(b) has been held applicable to periodicals receiving compensation for favorable recommendations notwithstanding a challenge that such regulation violates First Amendment rights of free speech.[17] It was also held that section 17(b) is not limited to securities

---

9. *See* § 13.13 *infra.*

10. *E.g.,* Bath v. Bushkin, Gaims, Gaines & Jonas, 913 F.2d 817 (10th Cir.1990). *See also* the authorities in § 13.13 *infra.*

11. Crookham v. Crookham, 914 F.2d 1027 (8th Cir.1990) ($10,000 sanction).

12. SEC v. Mesa Limited Partnership, [1990 Transfer Binder] Fed.Sec.L.Rep. (CCH) ¶ 95,492 (N.D.Tex.1990). SEC remedies are discussed in § 9.5 *infra.*

13. 15 U.S.C.A. § 77q(b):

It shall be unlawful for any person by the use of any means or instruments of transportation or communication in interstate commerce or by the use of the mails, to publish, give publicity to, or circulate any notice, circular, advertisement, newspaper, article, letter, investment service, or communication which, though not purporting to offer a security for sale, describes such security for a consideration received or to be received, directly or indirectly, from an issuer, underwriter, or dealer, without fully disclosing the receipt, whether past or prospective, of such consideration and the amount thereof.

14. *Id.*

15. 15 U.S.C.A. § 77q(c).

16. H.R.Rep. No. 85, 73d Cong., 1st Sess. 24 (1933). *See* SEC v. Wall Street Publishing Institute, Inc., 851 F.2d 365 (D.C.Cir.1988); United States v. Amick, 439 F.2d 351, 365 (7th Cir.1971).

17. SEC v. Wall Street Publishing Institute, Inc., 851 F.2d 365 (D.C.Cir.1988). The First Amendment argument was based on the Supreme Court's decision in Lowe v. SEC, 472 U.S. 181, 105 S.Ct. 2557, 86 L.Ed.2d 130 (1985) which held that the Investment Advisers Act does not require registration of newsletters rendering investment advice.

distributions but applies both to new and already outstanding securities.[18]

§ 7.7 Multiple Defendants—Joint and Several Liability; Liability of Controlling Persons

Contribution Among Multiple Defendants

Section 11(f) of the 1933 Act[1] provides that multiple defendants in section 11 actions are jointly and severally liable for the damages awarded. Consistent with the trend in common law negligence cases, the federal courts have recognized a right of contribution among joint tortfeasors.[2] The extent of this right to contribution is a matter of federal law.[3] In addition to section 11(f), section 18(b) of the 1934 Act[4] also provides for contribution among defendants in an action for false filings under section 18(a).[5] But what about liabilities arising under other sections of the securities acts? Although both the 1933 and 1934 Acts recognize joint and several liability of controlling persons,[6] there is silence on whether this liability is coupled with a right of contribution. Similarly, the Acts are silent as to the existence of a right to contribution in the event of joint and several liability arising out of joint activity.[7]

At one time the universal common law rule was that there was no

---

Although not decided directly on constitutional grounds, the Court's decision in *Lowe* was premised on finding an interpretation of the Investment Advisers Act that would not be unconstitutional. The *Lowe* decision and the Investment Advisers Act are discussed in chapter 18 *infra*.

18. SEC v. Wall Street Publishing Institute, Inc., 851 F.2d 365 (D.C.Cir.1988), relying on S.Rep. No. 47, 73d Cong., 1st Sess. 4 (1933) and H.R.Rep. No. 85, 73d Cong., 1st Sess. 6 (1933).

§ 7.7

1. 15 U.S.C.A. § 77k(f).

2. Globus, Inc. v. Law Research Service, Inc., 318 F.Supp. 955 (S.D.N.Y.1970), *judgment affirmed* 442 F.2d 1346 (2d Cir.1971), *cert. denied* 404 U.S. 941, 92 S.Ct. 286, 30 L.Ed.2d 254 (1971). *See also, e.g.,* Heizer Corp. v. Ross, 601 F.2d 330, 334 (7th Cir.1979); deHaas v. Empire Petroleum Co., 286 F.Supp. 809, 815–16 (D.Colo.1968), *judgment affirmed* 435 F.2d 1223 (10th Cir.1970); Ill. L. Loss, Securities Regulation 1739–40, n. 178 (1961).

3. Globus, Inc. v. Law Research Serv. Inc., 318 F.Supp. 955 (S.D.N.Y.1970); deHaas v. Empire Petroleum Co., 286 F.Supp. 809, 815–16 (D.Colo.1968), *judgment affirmed* 435 F.2d 1223 (10th Cir.1970). *See* Seymour v. Summa Vista Cinema, Inc., 809 F.2d 1385 (9th Cir.1987), *opinion amended on other grounds* 817 F.2d 609 (9th Cir.1987) (in apportioning damage the court may consider the value of plaintiff's settlement with joint-tortfeasor). *See also, e.g.,* Philip M. Nichols, Symmetry and Consistency and the Plaintiff's Risk: Partial Settlement and the Right to Contribution in Federal Securities Actions, 19 Del. J. Corp. L. 1 (1994).

4. 15 U.S.C.A. § 78r(b).

5. 15 U.S.C.A. § 78r(a). *See* § 12.8 *infra*.

6. 15 U.S.C.A. §§ 77o, 78r.

7. According to general principles of common law, when two or more defendants' joint acts combine to form a single, indivisible injury, they are jointly and severally liable. *See* William L. Prosser, Law of Torts § 46 (4th ed. 1971); Roy D. Jackson, Joint Torts and Several Liability, 17 Tex.L.Rev. 339 (1939); Prosser, Joint Torts and Several Liability, 25 Calif.L.Rev. 413 (1937).

right to contribution among joint tortfeasors.[8] The reason for this rule
was the law's reluctance to aid wrongdoers. Many states have modified
the rule to allow contribution in negligence actions but many still do not
allow contribution among intentional tortfeasors.[9] Some state corporate
statutes provide a right of contribution for directors who are liable for
mismanagement.[10] The general rule that has been developing in federal
securities cases is that there is a right of contribution.[11] In the absence
of a statutory provision requiring contribution under the federal securities laws, some courts look to the law of the forum state.[12] Where one
party is considerably more culpable than others, there may not be a
claim for equal contribution.[13] One leading commentator[14] has expressed
doubt as to whether these contribution cases will survive two Supreme
Court rulings denying contribution under other federal statutes.[15] A
number of courts held that there is no implied right of contribution or
indemnity under the securities laws.[16] The Supreme Court has recently
held, however, that there is an implied right of contribution in actions
under SEC Rule 10b–5 of the 1934 Act.[17] In so ruling, the Court
distinguished cases decided under other federal statutes containing an
express right of action but no right of contribution. The case against an
implied right of contribution is stronger where Congress created a right
of action but said nothing about a right to contribution. Although a
number of recent decisions caution against the implication of additional

8. *E.g.* Merryweather v. Nixan, 1799, 8 Term.Rep. 186, 101 Eng.Rep. 1337. *See
generally* W. Prosser *supra* note 7 § 50. This no contribution rule has been the subject of
much debate and is continually being eroded by the courts.

9. *E.g.* Uniform Contribution Among Joint Tortfeasor Act. The trend both in the
courts and legislatures had been to expand the situations in which contribution applies.
See W. Prosser *supra* note 7 § 50.

10. *See* 8 Del.Code § 174(b). Although there are some older cases recognizing a right
to contribution in the absence of statute, "their continued authority is uncertain." W.
Cary & M. Eisenberg, Corporations: Cases and Materials 1402 (5th unab. ed. 1980).

11. In Pinter v. Dahl, 486 U.S. 622, n. 9, 108 S.Ct. 2063, 100 L.Ed.2d 658 (1988), *on
remand* 857 F.2d 262 (5th Cir.1988) the Supreme Court noted that the availability of
contribution under section 12(1) remains to be decided.

12. First Federal Savings & Loan Assoc. v. Oppenheim, Appel, Dixon & Co., 631
F.Supp. 1029 (S.D.N.Y.1986).

13. Smith v. Mulvaney, 1985 WL 29953, [1984–85 Transfer Binder] Fed.Sec.L.Rep.
(CCH) ¶ 92,084 (S.D.Cal.1985); Adalman v. Baker, Watts & Co., 599 F.Supp. 752 (D.Md.
1984).

14. Louis Loss, Fundamentals of Securities Regulations 1205 (1983).

15. Texas Industries, Inc. v. Radcliff Materials, Inc., 451 U.S. 630, 101 S.Ct. 2061, 68
L.Ed.2d 500 (1981) (decided under section 4 of the Clayton Antitrust Act, 15 U.S.C.A.
§ 15); Northwest Airlines, Inc. v. Transport Workers Union, 451 U.S. 77, 101 S.Ct. 1571,
67 L.Ed.2d 750 (1981) (decided under The Equal Pay Act and Title XII of the 1964 Civil
Rights Act, 29 U.S.C.A. § 206(d), 42 U.S.C.A. § 2000e–2).

16. Chutich v. Touche Ross & Co., 960 F.2d 721 (8th Cir.1992) (no implied right to
contribution under Rule 10b–5). Baker, Watts & Co. v. Miles & Stockbridge, 876 F.2d
1101 (4th Cir.1989); First Financial Savings Bank, Inc. v. American Bankers Ins. Co., 1989
WL 168016, [1989–1990 Transfer Binder] Fed.Sec.L.Rep. ¶ 94,827 (E.D.N.C.1989) s.c., 1990
WL 260541, [1990–1991 Transfer Binder] Fed.Sec.L.Rep. (CCH) ¶ 95,696 (E.D.N.C.1990)
(unpublished case).

17. Musick, Peeler & Garrett v. Employers Insurance of Wausau, ___ U.S. ___, 113
S.Ct. 2085, 124 L.Ed.2d 194 (1993).

federal remedies,[18] once the courts have recognized an implied right of action, then it is appropriate to flesh it out so as to render it a reasonable remedy.[19] Implying a right of contribution is consistent with this goal. The Court pointed out that sections 9(e) and 18(a) of the 1934 Act,[20] both of which contain an express right of action provide for a right of contribution. The Court concluded that the similarities between sections 9(e), 18(a), and 10(b) justify the recognition of an implied right of contribution under Rule 10b–5.

The *Musick, Peeler* decision is limited by its facts to Rule 10b–5 of the 1934 Act but has a bearing on 1933 Act suits as well. Section 11 of the 1933 Act contains a right of contribution.[21] In contrast, section 12 of the 1933 Act[22] does not contain an express right of contribution and, especially in light of the Court's reasoning, it remains unclear whether an implied right of contribution would exist there. A right of contribution under section 12 may be less significant, however, since secondary liability is based on controlling person liability or vicarious liability, in which cases principles of indemnity should apply.

The right to contribution is distinct from any contractual agreement for indemnification. Indemnification agreements are considered in a later section.[23]

A number of courts have held that nonsettling defendants may not pursue their right of contribution against settling defendants.[24] However, not all courts have agreed that the policy favoring settlements overrides the right of contribution. For example, in 1994, the Tenth Circuit ruled that the policy underlying the securities laws and the statutory implied right of contribution recognized by the Supreme Court preclude a rule barring the right to contribution by non–settling defen-

---

18. *See* § 13.1 *infra.*

19. *See* ___ U.S. at ___, 113 S.Ct. at 2088–89, relying on Virginia Bankshares, Inc. v. Sandberg, 501 U.S. 1083, 111 S.Ct. 2749, 115 L.Ed.2d 929 (1991) and Blue Chip Stamps v. Manor Drug Stores, 421 U.S. 723, 95 S.Ct. 1917, 44 L.Ed.2d 539 (1975).

20. 15 U.S.C.A. §§ 78i(e), 78r(a). *See* §§ 12.1, 12.8 *infra.*

21. 15 U.S.C.A. § 77k(e). *See* §§ 7.3, 7.4.1 *supra.*

22. 15 U.S.C.A. § 77l. Section 12(1) and section 12(2) actions are discussed in §§ 7.2, 7.5–7.5.4 *supra.*

23. § 7.9 *infra. See, e.g.* Altman v. Josephthal & Co., [1983–1984 Transfer Binder] Fed.Sec.L.Rep. (CCH) ¶ 96,414 (D.Mass.1983) (contribution allowed; indemnification denied). *See* Helen J. Scott, Resurrecting Indemnification: Contribution Clauses in Underwriting Agreements, 61 N.Y.U.L.Rev. 223 (1986).

24. Nelson v. Bennett, 662 F.Supp. 1324, 1332 (E.D.Cal.1987) (quoting In re Nucorp Energy Securities Litigation, 661 F.Supp. 1403, 1408 (S.D.Cal.1987)). *See also* In re National Student Marketing Litigation, 517 F.Supp. 1345 (D.D.C.1981) (nonsettling defendant can claim contribution from settling defendant); McLean v. Alexander, 449 F.Supp. 1251 (D.Del.1978), *reversed on other grounds* 599 F.2d 1190 (3d Cir.1979) (settlement does not bar contribution claim by nonsettling defendant). *See also* § 13.15 *infra.*

Compare, e.g., In re Del–Val Corp. Securities Litigation, 868 F.Supp. 547 (S.D.N.Y.1994) (settling defendants could sue nonsettling defendants for contribution under federal securities claims but could not seek contribution for common law claims under New York law).

dants.[25] The court reasoned that although recognized by way of implication, the right to contribution under the federal securities laws is a statutory right and cannot be taken away by a court relying on considerations of equity.

Liability of Controlling Persons

Section 15 of the Act[26] imposes joint and several liability upon controlling persons for the acts of persons under their control. Section 20 of the 1934 Act has a comparable provision.[27] Notwithstanding a slight difference in language, these two provisions have been interpreted similarly.[28]

Controlling person liability, which is highly factual,[29] will not be imposed if "the controlling person had no knowledge of or reasonable grounds to believe in the existence of the facts by reason of which the liability of the controlled person is alleged to exist." [30] This defense would not be available under common law principles of vicarious liability under the doctrine of respondeat superior. The "lack of knowledge" defense to controlling person liability has been held to relate to the basic facts underlying the course of business; therefore, standing alone, lack of knowledge of the particular transaction does not preclude controlling person liability.[31] The burden of establishing the lack of knowledge defense falls on those persons charged with controlling person liability.[32]

25. TBG, Inc. v. Bendis, 36 F.3d 916 (10th Cir.1994). *But see, e.g.,* In re Consolidated Pinnacle West Securities Litigation, 51 F.3d 194 (9th Cir.1995) (upholding settlement bar order); Eichenholtz v. Brennan, 52 F.3d 478 (3d Cir.1995) (upholding settlement bar order based on finding of proportional fault).

26. *See* Note, Controlling Persons Provisions; Conduits of Secondary Liability Under Federal Securities Laws, 19 Vill.L.Rev. 621 (1974).

27. 15 U.S.C.A. § 78t(a). *See* Note, Rule 10b–5 and Vicarious Liability Based on Respondeat Superior, 69 Calif.L.Rev. 1514 (1981): Note, The Burden of Control: Derivative Liability Under Section 20(a) of The Securities Exchange Act of 1934, 48 N.Y.U.L.Rev. 1019 (1973). *See* § 13.15 *infra.*

28. *E.g.,* Farley v. Henson, 11 F.3d 827 (8th Cir.1993); Hollinger v. Titan Capital Corp., 914 F.2d 1564, 1578 (9th Cir.1990), *cert. denied* 499 U.S. 976, 111 S.Ct. 1621, 113 L.Ed.2d 719 (1991).

29. Due to the highly factual nature of the inquiry, disposition on the pleadings will rarely be appropriate. *See, e.g.,* Hilgeman v. National Insurance Co., 547 F.2d 298, 302 (5th Cir.1977); Hill York Corp. v. American International Franchises, Inc., 448 F.2d 680, 694 n.20 (5th Cir.1971); In re Chambers Development Securities Litigation, 848 F.Supp. 602, 618 (W.D.Pa.1994); In re world of Wonders Securities Litigation, 694 F.Supp. 1427, 1435 (N.D.Cal.1988); Klapmeier v. Telecheck International, Inc., 315 F.Supp. 1360, 1361 (D.Minn.1970).

30. 15 U.S.C.A. § 77o. Controlling person liability does not require the controlling person's participation in the wrongful conduct. *E.g.* G.A. Thompson & Co. v. Partridge, 636 F.2d 945, 957–958 (5th Cir.1981); Metge v. Baehler, 577 F.Supp. 810 (S.D.Iowa 1984), *affirmed in part, reversed in part* 762 F.2d 621 (8th Cir.1985), *cert. denied* 474 U.S. 1057, 106 S.Ct. 798, 88 L.Ed.2d 774 (1986).

31. San Francisco–Oklahoma Petroleum Exploration Corp. v. Carstan Oil Co., 765 F.2d 962 (10th Cir.1985). *But see* Durham v. Kelly, 810 F.2d 1500 (9th Cir.1987) (corporate president's wife exercised some control but not held liable since she did not induce the misstatements in question).

32. *See, e.g.,* Mecca v. Gibraltar Corp., 746 F.Supp. 338 (S.D.N.Y.1990).

Some courts have held that the broader common law rules of respondeat superior do not apply in light of the statutory provisions dealing with controlling person liability.[33] However, an apparent majority of courts have ruled to the contrary in holding controlling person liability and common law principles to be cumulative.[34] More recently, the First and Eighth Circuits joined the majority of the federal courts of appeals in holding that statutorily imposed controlling person liability does not preclude application of common law principles of respondeat superior and agency concepts of actual or apparent authority.[35] Most recently the Ninth Circuit, reversing its previous position, decided *en banc* that controlling person liability does not preempt common law vicarious liability.[36] Accordingly, the court was willing to consider the claim that an employer could be liable under principles of *respondeat superior*.

With this major shift in position, outside of the Third and Fourth Circuits, there remains little authority for the view that controlling person liability is exclusive.[37] However, a recent Supreme Court decision[38] holding that there is no implied right of action against aiders and

---

33. *E.g.* Hatrock v. Edward D. Jones & Co., 750 F.2d 767 (9th Cir.1984). Marbury Management, Inc. v. Kohn, 629 F.2d 705 (2d Cir.1980), *cert. denied* 449 U.S. 1011, 101 S.Ct. 566, 66 L.Ed.2d 469 (1980); Carpenter v. Harris, Upham & Co., 594 F.2d 388 (4th Cir.1979), *cert. denied* 444 U.S. 868, 100 S.Ct. 143, 62 L.Ed.2d 93 (1979); Rochez Brothers, Inc. v. Rhoades, 527 F.2d 880 (3d Cir.1975); Kamen & Co. v. Paul H. Aschkar & Co., 382 F.2d 689 (9th Cir.1967), *cert. denied* 393 U.S. 801, 89 S.Ct. 40, 21 L.Ed.2d 85 (1968).

34. Commerford v. Olson, 794 F.2d 1319 (8th Cir.1986); Henricksen v. Henricksen, 640 F.2d 880 (7th Cir.1981), *cert. denied* 454 U.S. 1097, 102 S.Ct. 669, 70 L.Ed.2d 637 (1981); Paul F. Newton & Co. v. Texas Commerce Bank, 630 F.2d 1111 (5th Cir.1980), *rehearing denied* 634 F.2d 1355 (5th Cir.1980); Marbury Management, Inc. v. Kohn, 629 F.2d 705 (2d Cir.1980), *cert. denied* 449 U.S. 1011, 101 S.Ct. 566, 66 L.Ed.2d 469 (1980); Holloway v. Howerdd, 536 F.2d 690 (6th Cir.1976); Fey v. Walston & Co., 493 F.2d 1036 (7th Cir.1974). *See generally* Daniel R. Fischel, Secondary Liability Under Section 10(b) of the Securities Act of 1934, 69 Calif.L.Rev. 80 (1981); William J. Fitzpatrick & Ronald T. Carman, Respondeat Superior and the Federal Securities Laws: A Round Peg in a Square Hole, 12 Hofstra L.Rev. 1 (1983); Stephen R. Reininger, Exclusive or Concurrent—The Role of Control and Respondeat Superior in the Imposition of Vicarious Civil Liability on Broker–Dealers, 9 Sec.Reg.L.J. 226 (1981); Note, Vicarious Liability for Securities Law Violations: Respondeat Superior and the Controlling Person Sections, 15 W. & M.L.Rev. 713 (1974).

35. Commerford v. Olson, 794 F.2d 1319 (8th Cir.1986) (decided under 1934 Act § 20); In re Atlantic Financial Management, Inc. Securities Litigation, 784 F.2d 29 (1st Cir.1986) (decided under Exchange Act § 20(a)); Hill v. Equitable Bank, 655 F.Supp. 631 (D.Del. 1987); Quincy Co–Operative Bank v. A.G. Edwards & Sons, Inc., 655 F.Supp. 78 (D.Mass. 1986); Xaphes v. Merrill Lynch, Pierce, Fenner & Smith, Inc., 600 F.Supp. 692 (D.Me. 1985).

36. Hollinger v. Titan Capital Corp., 914 F.2d 1564 (9th Cir.1990), *cert. denied* 499 U.S. 976, 111 S.Ct. 1621, 113 L.Ed.2d 719 (1991). Respondeat superior liability is not limited to broker-dealer cases. In re Network Equipment Technologies, Inc., 762 F.Supp. 1359 (N.D.Cal.1991).

37. In addition to the authorities in the Third Circuit, *see* Carpenter v. Harris, Upham & Co., 594 F.2d 388 (4th Cir.1979), *cert. denied* 444 U.S. 868, 100 S.Ct. 143, 62 L.Ed.2d 93 (1979) (denying liability of employer due to failure to satisfy controlling person requirements; the court did not discuss *respondeat superior*).

38. Central Bank of Denver v. First Interstate Bank of Denver, ___ U.S. ___, 114 S.Ct. 1439, 128 L.Ed.2d 119 (1994).

abettors[39] may lead to a new round of challenges to the availability of respondeat superior.[40] The Court ruled that there is no aider and abettor liability absent express statutory authorization. There is no express authorization for application of respondeat superior. Accordingly, a parallel result would be to find that respondeat superior is not available in actions under the securities laws. One arguably distinguishing factor, however, is that aiding and abetting liability under the federal law generally is statutorily imposed and is not ordinarily found simply as a matter of common law principles. It is one thing simply to import accepted common law principles into a federal action, it is quite another to imply a right that would one would ordinarily expect to find in a statute. It is thus reasonable to expect that courts will impose principles of respondeat superior much in the same way that the Rule 10b–5 action generally borrows from common law fraud.[41]

As discussed in the section that follows, when someone knowingly renders substantial assistance to a violator of the securities laws, there is the potential for defendants being held criminally accountable as an aider and abettor.[42] Such liability generally has generally arisen in the context of violations of SEC Rule 10b–5 or section 17(a) of the 1933 Act.[43]

§ 7.8 Multiple Defendants—Aiding and Abetting
The Demise of Aiding and Abetting Generally

As discussed in the preceding section, when multiple defendants have violated the securities laws, their activities will frequently result in joint and several liability.[1] Similarly, the federal securities laws impose liability upon persons in control of the actual violators.[2] However, neither the Securities Act of 1933 nor the Securities Exchange Act of 1934 expressly imposes liability on secondary participants in securities

---

39. Aiding and abetting liability is considered in §§ 7.8, 13.16 *infra*.

40. In the course of its *Central Bank* decision, the Court pointed to the text of the statute as the basis for any remedy. Just as the absence of aiding and abetting language led the Court to deny a remedy, it is arguable that a similar silence could result in the denial of common law principles of vicarious liability. For further discussion of this issue, *see* § 13.15 *infra*.

41. For example, common law principles of scienter, materiality, and reliance have been read into Rule 10b–5. *See* §§ 13.2, 13.2.1, 13.5A, 13.5B, 13.6 *supra*.

42. There also is the possibility that at least as to some defendants, aiding and abetting liability may be imposed in civil actions. Notwithstanding the *Central Bank* decision, aiding and abetting liability may still be imposed against broker–dealers. *See* §§ 7.8, 13,16 *infra*. Prior to the *Central Bank* decision, aiding and abetting liability had a much broader reach. *See, e.g.,* Woodward v. Metro Bank of Dallas, 522 F.2d 84 (5th Cir.1975); SEC v. Coffey, 493 F.2d 1304 (6th Cir.1974), *cert. denied* 420 U.S. 908, 95 S.Ct. 826, 42 L.Ed.2d 837 (1975); David S. Ruder, Multiple Defendants in Securities Law Fraud Cases: Aiding and Abetting, Conspiracy, In Pari Delicto, Indemnification, and Contribution, 120 U.Pa. L.Rev. 597 (1972). *See* §§ 7.8, 13.16 *infra*.

43. 15 U.S.C.A. § 77q(a); 17 C.F.R. § 240.10b–5. *See* chapter 13 *infra*.

§ 7.8

1. *See* § 7.7 *supra*.

2. *See id.*

violations. The district and circuit courts, nevertheless, applied common law principles of aiding and abetting to reach such offenders. However, in 1994, the Supreme Court held that there is no private right of action for aiding and abetting violations of the Securities Exchange Act's general antifraud provisions.[3] The Court reasoned that in the absence of express statutory authority there could be no private right of action for aiding and abetting. In so ruling the Court refused to imply such a remedy from the general criminal statute that makes it a crime to aid and abet any primary federal crime.[4] The Court pointed to the absence of aiding and abetting language in Rule 10b–5 or in any of the securities laws' general remedial provisions.[5] As discussed more fully below, although there is some early authority to the contrary, the majority of the cases held that aiding and abetting principles do not apply to broaden the range of defendants in actions under section 11 or 12 of the 1933 Act. The recent Supreme Court decision under the Exchange Act confirms this result. However, aiding and abetting liability remains appropriate in at least some SEC enforcement actions[6] as well as in criminal prosecutions.[7] In addition to refusing to imply a remedy on the basis of the general criminal law of aiding and abetting, the Court refused to imply aiding and abetting liability from section 10(b)'s and Rule 10b–5's prohibition against anyone who "directly or *indirectly*" violates the rule's antifraud proscriptions.

Aiding and Abetting in SEC Enforcement Actions and in Criminal Prosecutions

The foregoing discussion has focused on collateral participant liability for damages. This is a distinct issue from being held accountable in enforcement proceedings or criminal prosecutions. Sections 11 and 12 of the 1933 Act provide a private right of action with statutorily defined limitations. In contrast section 5 of the Act[59] makes it illegal to sell a

---

3. Central Bank of Denver, N.A. v. First Interstate Bank of Denver, ___ U.S. ___, 114 S.Ct. 1439, 128 L.Ed.2d 119 (1994). *See* § 13.16 *infra*.

4. 18 U.S.C.A. § 2.

5. ___ U.S. at ___, 114 S.Ct. at 1441–42.

6. In the course of its opinion, the Court observed that "Congress has not enacted a general aiding and abetting statute either for suits by the Government (when the Government sues for civil penalties or injunctive relief) or for suits by private parties." ___ U.S. at ___, 114 S.Ct. at ___. The clear implication of this is that the SEC's ability to pursue collateral participants for aiding and abetting violations may be limited to those instances in which there is a specific statutory grant of authority. Thus, for example, the SEC has the authority to proceed against broker-dealers as aiders and abettors. 1934 Act § 15(b)(4)(E), 15 U.S.C.A. § 78o(b)(4)(E) (authorizing the SEC to proceed against broker-dealers as aiders and abettors); *id.* § 21B, 15 U.S.C.A. § 78u–2 (permitting the SEC to impose civil penalties against broker-dealers who are guilty of aiding and abetting). *See* footnote 16 *infra*.

7. *But cf.* The dissent in Central Bank of Denver, N.A. v. First Interstate Bank of Denver, ___ U.S. ___, 114 S.Ct. 1439, 128 L.Ed.2d 119 (1994), indicating that the Court's refusal to imply a private right of action may well lead to the unfortunate result of denying aiding and abetting liability generally under the securities laws.

Deleted footnotes 8–58 can be found in the Practitioner's Edition.

59. 15 U.S.C.A. § 77e. *See* chapter 2 *supra*.

security without complying with the Act's registration and prospectus requirements unless an appropriate exemption can be found.[60]   Similarly, section 17(a) of the 1933 Act and Rule 10b–5 of the Exchange Act make certain material misrepresentations and omissions unlawful. When the government pursues claims under any of the foregoing sections, traditional aiding and abetting principles should apply.   Thus, a collateral participant who, with knowledge, substantially assists a violation of the registration requirements, cannot be held liable under section 12(1) but may be sued by the SEC or the Justice Department for aiding and abetting the section 5 violations.[61]   Similarly, a collateral participant who knowingly and substantially assists a primary violation of section 12(2) or section 11 will not be held liable for damages but may be held accountable as an aider and abettor under section 17(a) of the 1933 Act (or Rule 10b–5 of the 1934 Act).

Controlling Person Liability Distinguished

As discussed in the preceding section of this treatise,[62] controlling persons of primary violators can be held accountable in damages in actions under both sections 11 and 12 of the 1933 Act.[63]   Although requiring proof significantly different from that required for aiding and abetting, controlling person liability does provide an alternative for expanding the scope of permissible defendants in section 11 and section 12 actions.[64]

§ 7.9   Multiple Defendants—Indemnification Agreements

Virtually all state corporation statutes have provisions that authorize the corporation to indemnify officers and directors against liabilities incurred by them in the scope of carrying out the business of their office.[1]   Under these statutes, officers or directors who have been suc-

---

60. Exemptions are discussed in chapter 4 *supra.*

61. The elements of aiding and abetting are discussed further in § 13.16 *infra.*

62. *See* § 7.7 *supra.   See also* § 13.15 *infra.*

63. Section 15 of the Act is the basis for such controlling person liability.   15 U.S.C.A. § 77o.

64. *E.g.,* Ambling v. Blackstone Cattle Co., Inc., 658 F.Supp. 1459, 1467 (N.D.Ill.1987) (denying aider and abettor liability but recognizing controlling person liability).

§ 7.9

1. *See, e.g.,* 8 Del.Code § 145; Revised Model Bus.Corp. Act §§ 8.50–8.58; Model Bus.Corp. Act § 5.   *See generally* Joseph W. Bishop, The Law of Corporate Officers and Directors: Indemnification and Insurance (1981); Harry G. Henn & John R. Alexander, Laws of Corporations § 380 (3d ed. 1983); Bishop, Sitting Ducks and Decoy Ducks: New Trends in the Indemnification of Corporate Directors and Officers, 77 Yale L.J. 1078 (1968); Joseph F. Johnston, Jr., Corporate Indemnification and Liability Insurance for Directors and Officers, 33 Bus.Law. 1993 (1978).

State indemnification provisions are generally limited to actions taken while in a representative capacity.   Accordingly, a director acting in his or her individual capacity will not qualify for indemnification.   However, when the director's position with the company puts him in a position to violate the antifraud provisions, defense of such an action could be subject to indemnification, Heffernan v. Pacific Dunlop, GNB Corp., 965 F.2d 369 (7th Cir.1992), *reversing* 767 F.Supp. 913 (N.D.Ill.1991) (which held that the director was not permitted to seek indemnification for expenses incurred in an action under section 12(2) arising out of a sale of his securities).

cessful in any action against them in their corporate capacity have an absolute right to indemnification for all expenses in defending the suit, including their attorneys fees.[2] Where an action is brought by a third party, a defendant although unsuccessful on the merits of the suit may nevertheless be reimbursed by the corporation acting through a resolution of the board of directors for any judgment and settlement payments in addition to all expenses that were "actually and reasonably incurred" in the litigation, provided that in committing the acts resulting in liability, the defendant "acted in good faith and in a manner he reasonably believed to be in or not opposed to the best interest of the corporation."[3] Many of these state statutes further provide that their indemnification provisions are not exclusive of any other rights that may be conferred by corporate by-law, charter, agreement, or other stockholder or director action.[4] It would seem to follow that expenses that would not be indemnifiable under the terms of the statute, may be indemnifiable pursuant to such a preexisting arrangement.

While the foregoing indemnification rules provide a great deal of controversy in general, they are of particular interest with regard to liabilities incurred for violations of the federal securities law.[5] Because of their federal impact, indemnification agreements have been subjected to scrutiny and limited under the securities laws.

In 1944 the Securities and Exchange Commission molded its initial policy on indemnification agreements, in connection with a registered offering by Johnson & Johnson Company. This has since become known as the "*Johnson and Johnson* formula", and has been followed consistently by the Commission. Under the formula, in order to qualify for acceleration of the effective date unless all of officers', directors', or controlling persons' rights of indemnification arising out of the offering are waived, the registrant must state in the registration statement that the Commission adheres to the position that such indemnification arrangements are against the public policy embodied in the Securities Act and are therefore unenforceable.[6] In order to qualify for acceleration when the indemnification agreements are not waived, the issuer must make the additional undertaking that unless any lawsuit arising out of the offering is settled by controlling precedent, all claims for indemnification arising out of securities liabilities will be submitted for court

---

2. *See, e.g.,* 8 Del.Code § 145(c).

3. *See, e.g.,* 8 Del.Code §§ 145(a), (b).

4. *See, e.g.,* 8 Del.Code § 145(f).

5. *See* Milton P. Kroll, Reflections on Indemnification Provisions and SEC Liability Insurance in the Light of BarChris and Globus, 24 Bus.Law. 681 (1969); Note, Indemnification of Directors: The Problems Posed by Federal Securities and Antitrust Legislation, 76 Harv.L.Rev. 1403 (1963). *See also, e.g.,* Helen S. Scott, Resurrecting Indemnification: Contribution clauses in Underwriting Agreements, 61 N.Y.U.L.Rev. 223 (1986); Note, Contractual Shifting of Defense Costs in Private Offering Securities Litigation, 136 U.Pa.L.Rev. 971 (1988).

6. *See* Regulation S–K, Items 510, 512, 17 C.F.R. §§ 229.510, 229.512. This was formerly contained in Note to SEC Rule 460. 17 C.F.R. § 230.460 (1982). Acceleration of the effective date is discussed in § 2.2 *supra.* *See* 17 C.F.R. § 230.461.

approval.[7] The requirement of court approval does not apply, however, to expenses of a successful defense to such an action. The *Johnson and Johnson* formula has been criticized on several grounds, including its limitation to indemnification agreements and the fact that it does not extend to company-paid insurance policies.[8]

The Commission's policy on indemnification is bolstered by the several court decisions in the case of Globus v. Law Research Service, Inc.[9] In that case it was held that regardless of whether the individual involved is an officer, director, or an underwriter, the policy underlying the Securities Act renders void an indemnification agreement to the extent that as applied it would cover fraudulent misconduct. The court's rationale was that invalidating all such indemnification agreements would "encourage diligence, investigation and compliance with the requirements of the statute by exposing issuers and underwriters to the substantial hazard of liability for compensatory damages."[10] The obvious concern was that permitting any participant in the registration process to contract away his or her potential liabilities would necessarily result in a less wholehearted fulfilling of one's obligations. Although the same rationale would arguably apply to issuer paid liability insurance policies, the *Globus* decision has not been so extended.[11] One court has upheld an indemnification agreement between an investor and the limited partnership which he sued where the litigation that triggered the agreement was frivolous.[12]

Some underwriters have been trying to avoid the *Globus* ruling by entering into contribution agreements which do not purport to give across-the-board indemnity.[13] It is questionable whether the *Globus* rule can (or should) be so easily circumvented. Courts have continued to show their dislike for indemnification agreements in the securities context. Strict construction of the extent of any contractual right to

---

7. *See* Sec. Act Rel. No. 33–4936 guide 46 (Dec. 9, 1968) (rescinded and replaced by 17 C.F.R. § 290.702.)

8. *See generally* Kroll *supra* footnote 5 at 689. *See also, e.g.,* Raychem Corp. v. Federal Insurance Co., 1994 WL 236557, [1993–1994 Transfer Binder] Fed. Sec. L. Rep. (CCH) ¶ 98,223 (N.D.Cal.1994) (permitting insurance to cover indemnification of Rule 10b–5 settlement).

9. 418 F.2d 1276 (2d Cir.1969), *cert. denied* 397 U.S. 913, 90 S.Ct. 913, 25 L.Ed.2d 93 (1970); Globus v. Law Research Service, 318 F.Supp. 955 (S.D.N.Y.1970), *affirmed per curiam* 442 F.2d 1346 (2d Cir.1971), *cert. denied* 404 U.S. 941, 92 S.Ct. 286, 30 L.Ed.2d 254 (1971). *See also, e.g.,* Goldberg v. Touche Ross & Co., 531 F.Supp. 86 (S.D.N.Y.1982) (no indemnity allowed for section 11 violation); Kennedy v. Josephthal & Co., 1983 WL 1314, [1983 Transfer Binder] Fed.Sec.L.Rep. (CCH) ¶ 99,204 (D.Mass.1983) (broker-dealer cannot seek indemnification from issuer and accountants but could seek contribution); Altman v. Josephthal & Co., 1983 WL 1342, Fed.Sec.L.Rep. (CCH) ¶ 99,421 (D.Mass.1983) (indemnification denied but contribution allowed in an action under section 17(a) of the 1933 Act).

10. 418 F.2d at 1289.

11. *See* authorities cited in footnote 1 *supra.*

12. Zissu v. Bear, Stearns & Co., 627 F.Supp. 687 (S.D.N.Y.1986), *affirmed* 805 F.2d 75 (2d Cir.1986).

13. *See* Helen S. Scott, Resurrecting Indemnification: Contribution Clauses in Underwriting Agreements, 61 N.Y.U.L.Rev. 223 (1986). *See also,* Note, Contractual Shifting of Defense Costs in Private Offering Securities Litigation, 136 U.Pa.L.Rev. 971 (1988).

indemnification may prevent a court from having to reach the public policy issue. Thus, for example, an indemnification clause between an underwriter and broker-dealer was held to apply only to representations by the issuer in the offering materials and not to oral misrepresentations made by the brokerage firm seeking indemnification.[14]

Another aspect of the *Globus* opinions is that they do not go so far as to expressly or even impliedly approve of the broader SEC policy as stated in the acceleration requirements. *Globus* is limited to agreements as applied to indemnify individuals and entities for fraudulent misconduct, whereas the Commission's policy apparently is directed toward all indemnification agreements, including those that would cover liability for merely negligent conduct such as where the defendant fails to meet his burden of proof of due diligence and reasonable investigation. Arguably the *Globus* rationale is not limited to liabilities arising out of 1933 Act registration, and therefore, may carry over to all potential liability under the securities acts including those arising under the 1934 Exchange Act and implied liabilities thereunder for fraudulent misconduct. Since actions under Rule 10b–5 now require a showing of scienter,[15] it would appear that according to the court's analysis, any such liability would not be susceptible to coverage by an indemnification agreement.[16] However, a defendant may nevertheless seek contribution from others who are jointly and severally liable.[17]

The Commission has extended its policy against indemnification agreements. The Commission has advised three mutual funds that they cannot lawfully indemnify their investment advisers for legal expenses incurred in SEC administrative proceedings wherein the investment advisers were found to have violated the securities laws.[18] The Commission reasoned that the indemnification agreements were not only in violation of the acts' policies but also contravened the fiduciary duties imposed on investment company directors.[19]

In a related development, the Tenth Circuit has extended the public policy doctrine to dismiss a claim for indemnification of a director against liability for disgorgement of insider short swing profits under

14. McCoy v. Goldberg, 1992 WL 237327, [1992–1993 Transfer Binder] Fed.Sec.L.Rep. (CCH) ¶ 97,009 (S.D.N.Y.1992).

15. Ernst & Ernst v. Hochfelder, 425 U.S. 185, 96 S.Ct. 1375, 47 L.Ed.2d 668 (1976), *rehearing denied* 425 U.S. 986, 96 S.Ct. 2194, 48 L.Ed.2d 811 (1976). *See* § 13.4 *supra*.

16. *E.g.* Globus v. Law Research Service, Inc., 442 F.2d 1346 (2d Cir.1971), *cert. denied* 404 U.S. 941, 92 S.Ct. 286, 30 L.Ed.2d 254 (1971); Kennedy v. Josephthal & Co., 1983 WL 1314, [1983 Transfer Binder] Fed.Sec.L.Rep. (CCH) ¶ 99,204 (D.Mass.1983).

17. *See* notes 9, 13 *supra*. Joint and several liability is discussed in § 7.7 *supra*. *But cf.* In re Nucorp Energy Securities Litigation, 661 F.Supp. 1403 (S.D.Cal.1987) (no implied right of indemnity); Kilmartin v. H.C. Wainwright & Co., 637 F.Supp. 938 (D.Mass.1986) (indemnity is not available in an action under section 12(2)); In re Baldwin–United Corp., [1985–86 Transfer Binder] Fed.Sec.L.Rep. (CCH) ¶ 92,570 (Bkrtcy.S.D.Ohio 1985) (indemnity is not available under section 11 or 12 of the 1933 Act or Rule 10b–5).

18. Sec. Act Rel. No. 33–6463 (April 21, 1983).

19. *Id. See* 15 U.S.C.A. §§ 80a–17(h), (i), 36(a). The Investment Company Act is discussed in chapter 17 *infra*.

section 16(b) of the Securities Exchange Act of 1934.[20] The court reasoned that to permit indemnification for section 16(b) liability would undermine the policy of deterrence of insider trading abuses that is the basis for imposing such liability. The deterrent rather than compensatory focus of section 16(b) is well documented.[21] To the extent that section 11 of the 1933 Act has a similar deterrent focus, the public policy argument has equal force here.

Not all indemnification agreements will be void as against public policy.[22] For example, there is a developing conflict of authority as to whether private agreements concerning payment of attorneys fees by unsuccessful plaintiffs may take precedence over the statutory language.[23] However, an agreement between a buyer and seller will be void to the extent it waives rights under the federal securities laws.[24]

§ 7.10   Special Problems of Attorneys (and Other Professionals)

As noted elsewhere, attorneys play an essential and sensitive role in the preparation of 1933 Act registration materials[1] and with regard to helping prepare a transaction that will qualify for an exemption from registration.[2] The disclosure thrust of the securities laws will frequently put the attorney in the position of suggesting disclosure while the client is adamantly opposed. This tension plus the attorney's potential criminal liability as an aider or abettor[3] of the client's securities law violations

---

20. First Golden Bancorporation v. Weiszmann, 942 F.2d 726 (10th Cir.1991). *See also, e.g.,* In re U.S. Oil & Gas Litigation, 967 F.2d 489 (11th Cir.1992) (indicating indemnification claims are not cognizable under either the 1933 or 1934 Act). Section 16(b) of the Exchange Act is discussed in §§ 12.3–12.5 *infra.*

21. *See* § 12.3 *infra.*

22. *E.g.,* National Union Fire Insurance Co. v. Dahl, 1990 WL 48074, [1989–1990 Transfer Binder] Fed.Sec.L.Rep. ¶ 95,015 (S.D.N.Y.1990) (unpublished case) (the antiwaiver provision contained in section 29(b) of 1934 Act did not preclude enforcement of indemnity agreement in favor of surety who guaranteed investor's promissory note). *See also, e.g.,* In re Integrated Resources Real Estate Limited Partnerships Securities Litigation, 815 F.Supp. 620, 677–78 (S.D.N.Y.1993) (third-party beneficiaries of indemnification agreement in connection with partnership offering may enforce the agreement).

23. Thus, a subscription agreement which provided that plaintiff would pay seller's attorneys' fees was not enforced. Stratmore v. Combs, 723 F.Supp. 458 (N.D.Cal.1989) *affirmed sub nom.* Layman v. Combs, 981 F.2d 1093 (9th Cir.1992) (the agreement also provided that buyers were not waiving any rights under the federal securities laws). *Cf.* Fulco v. Continental Cablevision, Inc., 1990 WL 120689, [1990 Transfer Binder] Fed.Sec. L.Rep. ¶ 95,345 (D.Mass.1990) (indicating that *in terrorem* effect of indemnification agreement covering the costs of unsuccessful securities litigation contravened the policy of the federal securities laws). However, other courts have held that such fee shifting indemnification agreements are not void as against public policy. Barnebey v. E.F. Hutton & Co., 715 F.Supp. 1512 (M.D.Fla.1989).

24. Vince Hagen Co. v. Eighty–Eighty Central Partners, Ltd., 1989 WL 136870, [1989–1990 Transfer Binder] Fed.Sec.L.Rep. ¶ 94,879 (N.D.Tex.1989). The anti-waiver provisions are discussed in § 13.14 *infra.*

§ 7.10

1. *See* § 3.1 *supra.*

2. *See* chapter 4 *supra.*

3. *See* § 7.8 *supra.* *See also* § 13.16 *infra.*

can create devastating problems.[4] There can be especially ticklish problems where an attorney is also a director of the issuer, underwriter or
other participant in the securities transactions.[5] Liability insurance is
at best a partial answer for potential securities law liabilities of attorneys.[6]

The Supreme Court has held that there is no private right of action
for aiding and abetting a violation of Rule 10b–5.[7] However, aiding and
abetting liability presumably remains available in at least certain SEC
enforcement actions and in criminal prosecutions.[8] Additionally, there is
a remote possibility that Congress will reinstate aiding and abetting
liability in private actions. Finally, many professionals, such as attor-

---

4. *See generally* William L. Cary, Edward W. Aranow, Homer Kripke, Alan B. Levenson
and Sidney J. Silberman, Lawyers' Responsibilities and Liabilities Under the Securities
Laws, 11 Colum. J.L. & Soc.Prob. 99(1974); Joseph C. Daley & Robert S. Karmel,
Attorneys' Responsibilities: Adversaries at the Bar of the SEC, 24 Emory L.J. 747 (1975);
Edward F. Donohue, Attorney Liability in the Preparation of Disclosure Documents:
Limiting Liability in the Face of Expanded Duties, 18 Sec.Reg.L.J. 115 (1990); Ralph C.
Ferrara & Marc I. Steinberg, The Role of Inside Counsel in the Corporate Accountability
Process, 4 Corp.L.Rev. 3 (1981); John P. Freeman, Opinion Letters and Professionalism,
1973 Duke L.J. 371; Samuel H. Gruenbaum, Corporate Securities Lawyers' Disclosure
Responsibility, Liability to Investors and National Student Marketing Corp., 54 Notre
Dame Law. 795 (1979); Mendes Hershman, Special Problems of Inside Counsel for
Financial Institutions, 33 Bus.Law. 1435 (1978); Roberta S. Karmel, Attorney's Securities
Laws Liabilities, 27 Bus.Law. 1153 (1972); Mitchell L. Lathrop & William F. Rinehart,
Legal Malpractice and Rule 10b–5 Liability, 5 Loyola (L.A.) U.L.Rev. 449 (1972); Simon
Lorne, The Corporate and Securities Adviser, The Public Interest, and Professional Ethics,
76 Mich.L.Rev. 423 (1978); Lewis D. Lowenfels, Expanding Public Responsibilities of
Securities Lawyers: An Analysis of The New Trend in Standard of Care and Priorities of
Duties, 74 Colum.L.Rev. 412 (1974); Ray L. Patterson, Limits of the Lawyer's Discretion
and the Law of Legal Ethics: National Student Marketing Revisited, 1979 Duke L.J. 1251
(1979); Phillips, Insider Trading Controls for Law Firms, 23 Rev.Sec. & Commod.Reg. 113
(1990); Rice & Steinberg, *supra* footnote 3; Morgan Shipman, The Need for SEC Rules to
Govern the Duties and Civil Liabilities of Attorneys Under Federal Securities Statutes, 34
Ohio St.L.J. 231 (1973); Theodore Sonde, The Responsibility of Professionals Under the
Federal Securities Laws—Some Observations, 68 Nw.U.L.Rev. 1 (1973); Theodore Sonde,
Professional Responsibility—New Religion or the Old Gospel? 24 Emory L.J. 827 (1975);
Marc I. Steinberg, Corporate/Securities Counsel Conflicts of Interest, 8 J.Corp.L. 577
(1983); Symposium, Advisors to Management: Responsibilities and Liabilities of Lawyers
and Accountants, 30 Bus.Law. 227 (Special Issue 1975); Francis M. Wheat, The Impact of
SEC Professional Responsibility Standards, 34 Bus.Law. 969 (1979).

See also, e.g., Steven P. Marino & Renee D. Marino, An Empirical Study of Recent
Securities Class Action Settlements Involving Accountants, Attorneys, or Underwriters, 22
Sec. Reg. L.J. 115 (1994).

5. *See, e.g.*, Escott v. BarChris Construction Corp., 283 F.Supp. 643 (S.D.N.Y.1968)
which is discussed in § 7.4 *supra*. *See also, e.g.*, Martin Riger, The Lawyer—Director—"A
Vexing Problem," 33 Bus.Law. 2381 (1978); Sec.Exch. Act Rel.No. 34–15384 (Dec. 6, 1978)
(there are "inherent conflicts faced by lawyers who serve both as directors and counsel to
corporations").

6. *See* David M. Call, Attorneys' Malpractice Insurance—Does Your Policy Cover Rule
10b–5 Liability?, 30 Bus.Law. 1095 (1975); Hilliker, Target Defendants for the 1980s—
Securities Lawyers—Malpractice Insurance, 1980 Ins.L.J. 563 (1980).

7. Central Bank of Denver, N.A. v. First Interstate Bank of Denver, ___ U.S. ___, 114
S.Ct. 1439, 128 L.Ed.2d 119 (1994). *See* § 13.16 *infra*.

8. In the course of its opinion the Court pointed out that the Commission may pursue
broker-dealers as aiders and abettors. *See* § 9.5, 13.16 *infra*.

neys and accountants my be sued as primary violators.[9]

Under the terms of SEC Rule of Practice 2(e), the SEC in considering an attorney's fitness may consider conduct that would also satisfy the requirements of aiding and abetting. The *Central Bank* decision may raise questions as to the continued viability of this authority.

Secondary Liability

Even in the event that a narrow construction of aiding and abetting liability continues, conduct of attorneys and other professionals may be attacked as primary as opposed to secondary violations.[10] In bringing such actions, more emphasis may be placed on prohibitions of the Act for persons who directly or *indirectly* violate the Act as a basis for establishing an *indirect* primary violation. Additionally, the degree of involvement in the securities transaction may provide the basis for charging primary rather than secondary liability. For example, when an accountant renders an opinion in connection with a securities transaction and something in that opinion implicates the securities laws, the accountant's involvement may be said to be primary. Similarly, when an attorney renders an opinion, under appropriate circumstances that opinion may provide the basis for primary liability[11] and thus eliminate the need to pursue the attorney as an aider and abettor. There may also be an increase in the use of controlling person liability.[12]

Some courts have drawn the distinction between mere silence and actual misstatements. For example, in *Schatz v. Rosenberg*,[13] it was alleged that the seller's attorneys sat by silently and failed to disclose to the purchaser that the seller had made material misrepresentations to the plaintiffs. The Fourth Circuit ruled that even if the attorneys knew of the misstatement, they did not owe a duty to speak to the purchaser.[14] The Court distinguished cases in which the attorney had prepared an opinion letter in connection with the transaction.[15] The court thus reasoned that there is a distinction between alleged liability for failure to

---

9. *E.g.* In re ZZZZ Best Securities Litigation, 864 F.Supp. 960 (C.D.Cal.1994) (accounting firm could be liable as primary violator).

10. *Ibid*.

11. *See, e.g.,* Kline v. First Western Government Securities, Inc., 24 F.3d 480 (3d Cir.1994) (holding attorney's tax opinion actionable under Rule 10b–5).

12. Controlling person liability is considered in § 7.7 *supra* and § 13.15 *infra*.

13. 943 F.2d 485 (4th Cir.1991), *cert. denied* 503 U.S. 936, 112 S.Ct. 1475, 117 L.Ed.2d 619 (1992).

14. *Id.* at 491. *See also, e.g.,* Fortson v. Winstead McGuire, Sechrest & Minick, 961 F.2d 469 (4th Cir.1992) (attorneys did not owe a duty of disclosure to non-client investors); Kline v. First Western Government Securities, 794 F.Supp. 542, 551 (E.D.Pa.1992), *judgment affirmed in part, reversed in part* 24 F.3d 480 (3d Cir.1994) (in order to establish liability for failing to speak it must be shown that the attorney had a fiduciary duty to disclose).

15. 943 F.2d at 491. *Compare, e.g.,* Ackerman v. Schwartz, 947 F.2d 841 (7th Cir.1991) (attorney allowing opinion letter to be sent to investors could be liable as an aider and abettor).

For a recent decision upholding a claim based on an attorney's tax opinion letter, *see* Kline v. First Western Government Securities, Inc., 24 F.3d 480 (3d Cir.1994).

blow the whistle and liability for an affirmative misstatement.[16] The Fourth Circuit denied liability on the basis of state law as well as under the federal securities laws. The court stated that when an attorney does not render a legal opinion but "merely acts as a scrivener" there can be no aiding and abetting liability to the purchaser absent a "conscious intent to violate the securities laws."[17] The court similarly denied any liability under state law to the party on the other side of the transaction based on the attorney's professional obligations. Even for courts that may adopt a broader view of attorney liability than the *Schatz* decision, attorney client privilege may preclude an attorney from coming forward.[18]

The court in *Shatz v. Rosenberg* went too far in protecting the attorneys in question while at the same time sacrificing appropriate limits on client representation. The SEC has indicated that an attorney's failure to blow the whistle and thereby prevent a securities fraud puts the attorney in breach of his or her professional responsibility and also may establish an aiding and abetting claim.[19]

Direct involvement in securities fraud can result in liability. For example, a lawyer who prepared proxy materials filed with the SEC, who knows of material misstatements therein, and then fails to delay the shareholder vote may be held accountable as an aider and abettor[20] (at least in criminal cases).[21] Therefore, even if the Fourth Circuit's analysis in *Schatz* is correct in denying attorney accountability to a party on the other side of the transaction, an attorney who prepares documents and then, with knowledge, sits by while a fraud is perpetrated cannot (and should not) reasonably expect to be free from being held accountable. Similarly, the presentation of legal opinions may form the basis of a primary Rule 10b–5 violation.[22] This is true even though the opinion is explicitly stated to be based on facts provided by the client.[23]

The *Schatz* decision raises a number of serious questions about the attorney's proper representational stance. The Model Code of Professional Responsibility formerly permitted a lawyer to disclose information

---

16. *See also, e.g.,* Riedel v. Acutote of Colorado, 773 F.Supp. 1055 (S.D.Ohio 1991), *appeal dismissed* 947 F.2d 945 (6th Cir.1991), indicating that preparation of prospectus is sufficient to trigger Rule 10b–5 liability and that knowledge of the misstatement of omission would satisfy the scienter requirement. However, mere silence of attorney in the face of client's misstatements does not establish scienter. 773 F.Supp. at 1067.

17. 943 F.2d at 497.

18. *See* Austin v. Bradley, Barry & Tarlow, P.C., 836 F.Supp. 36 (D.Mass.1993) (claim that attorney's failure to disclose client's insolvency was actionable could not be maintained in light of obligation of confidentiality to client).

19. In re Carter & Johnson, [1981 Transfer Binder] Fed.Sec.L.Rep. (CCH) ¶ 82,847 (SEC 1981).

20. SEC v. National Student Marketing Corp., 457 F.Supp. 682 (D.D.C.1978).

21. The Court's decision in the *Central Bank* case precludes aider and abettor liability in private damage actions and probably in SEC enforcement actions. *See* § 13.16 *infra*.

22. Kline v. First Western Government Securities, Inc., 24 F.3d 480 (3d Cir.1994) (holding attorney's tax opinion actionable under Rule 10b–5). Liability for legal opinions was acknowledged in Schatz v. Rosenberg *supra*.

23. Kline v. First Western Government Securities, Inc., 24 F.3d 480 (3d Cir.1994).

to prevent a client from committing a future crime. This version is still in force in a number of states. However, under the current version of the Model Rules for Professional Conduct, the attorney may disclose information only with regard to future crimes involving the danger of severe personal injury.[24] Thus, under the current version of the Model Rules, although an attorney may withdraw[25] from representation in the face of a pending or future economic crime, he or she may not reveal the information. Accordingly, in those states that have adopted the newest version of the Model Rules, there is additional support for the unfortunate result reached in the *Schatz* case. The incorrectness of the *Schatz* result is due to the fact that when an attorney is present during a transaction, his or her silent participation may well be viewed as an implied representation that the transaction is not unlawful. It would seem wholly appropriate to hold the attorney liable to the parties on the other side of the transaction if they reasonably rely on such an implied representation. This would appear to be the type of substantial assistance that is necessary to establish aiding and abetting liability. Unfortunately, however, the *Schatz* ruling is indicative of some courts' reluctance to hold attorneys liable for conduct that arguably can broadly be described as lawyering.

There is authority to the effect that mere inaction when a client fails to take the attorney's advice with regard to disclosure will not result in aider and abettor liability[26] but more substantial involvement may.[27] Similarly, active participation in a transaction can result in primary

---

24. ABA Model Rule of Professional Conduct 1.6. (the lawyer *may* but is not required to disclose information "to prevent the client from committing a criminal act that the lawyer 'believes' is likely to result in imminent death or bodily harm.").

25. ABA, Model Rules of Professional Conduct 1.6.

26. Schatz v. Rosenberg, 943 F.2d 485 (4th Cir.1991), *cert. denied* ___ U.S. ___, 112 S.Ct. 1475, 117 L.Ed.2d 619 (1992) (failure to blow the whistle on a client did not give rise to aider and abettor liability); Schenk v. Continental Coal Reserves, Ltd., 1990 WL 153970, [1990–1991 Transfer Binder] Fed.Sec.L.Rep. (CCH) ¶ 95,711 (N.D.N.Y.1990) (attorneys acting as exchange agents issuing bills of sale were not aiders and abettors); Hayden v. Feldman, 753 F.Supp. 116 (S.D.N.Y.1990) (failure to establish that attorneys working on offering circular should have been aware of alleged fraud); Morin v. Trupin, 747 F.Supp. 1051 (S.D.N.Y.1990) (failure to establish that law firm that prepared private placement memorandum was liable either as a primary violator or as an aider and abettor). In the Matter of Carter & Johnson, Sec.Exch. Act Rel. No. 34–17597 (Feb. 28, 1981). *See* Bush v. Rewald, 619 F.Supp. 585, 590–91 (D.Hawaii 1985) (performance of legal services for corporation does not itself create a duty of disclosure, even when the attorney is a director); Riley v. Brazeau, 612 F.Supp. 674 (D.Or.1985). Aiding and abetting is discussed in § 7.8 *supra* and § 13.16 *infra*.

27. *E.g.* SEC v. National Student Marketing Corp., 457 F.Supp. 682 (D.D.C.1978). *See also, e.g.*, Molecular Technology Corp. v. Valentine, 925 F.2d 910 (6th Cir.1991) (summary judgment reversed due to questions of fact as to whether attorney knew of misrepresentations in amended offering circular which he helped revise); Gilmore v. Berg, 761 F.Supp. 358 (D.N.J.1991) (question of fact as to whether attorney and accountant were guilty of scienter in making allegedly materially misleading statements); In re Rospatch Securities Litigation, 760 F.Supp. 1239 (W.D.Mich.1991) (stating claim against attorney and law firm for allegedly minimizing or concealing company's problems in order to induce purchases of its securities); Levine v. Diamanthuset, 722 F.Supp. 579 (N.D.Cal.1989) (stating primary Rule 10b–5 claim against lawyer who actively made misrepresentations inducing the plaintiff's purchase; adequately pleading aiding and abetting by other attorney and his law firm); SEC v. Electronics Warehouse, Inc., 689 F.Supp. 53 (D.Conn.1988) (stating claim against attorney who permitted the improper closing of escrow in connection with a part-

liability of attorneys; also, attorneys who are directors, experts or signers of the 1933 Act registration statement will be held to a standard of "due diligence."[28] Also, an attorney who actively negotiates a sale may be liable as a seller under section 12(1)[29] dealing with failure to comply with the 1933 Act's registration requirements and section 12(2)'s prohibitions[30] against material misstatements or omissions regardless of whether the securities are subject to 1933 Act registration.

The fact that an attorney did not participate in the preparation of the offering materials does not preclude a finding of liability under section 12.[31] Conversely, the fact that an attorney has worked on a registration statement does not make him or her an expert so as to be liable for misstatements contained therein.[32]

A significant development involving the role of attorneys in preparing disclosure documents arose in connection with the Commission's

or-none offering); Stevens v. Equidyne Extractive Industries, 1980, 694 F.Supp. 1057 (S.D.N.Y.1988) (attorney liability for issuing tax opinion without a warning that the opinion letter was speculative); Renovitch v. Stewardship Concepts, Inc., 654 F.Supp. 353 (N.D.Ill.1987). *See* Daniel R. Fischel, Secondary Liability Under Section 10(b) of the Securities Act of 1934, 69 Calif.L.Rev. 80 (1981); David S. Ruder, Multiple Defendants in Securities Law Fraud Cases: Aiding and Abetting, Conspiracy, In Pari Delicto, Indemnification and Contribution, 120 U.Pa.L.Rev. 597 (1972).

28. Section 11, 15 U.S.C.A. § 78k. *See* footnote 5 *supra*. *See also, e.g.*, Comment, Whose Representations are These Anyway? Attorney Prospectus Liability After *Central Bank*, 42 U.C.L.A.L.Rev. 885 (1995).

29. 15 U.S.C.A. § 77*l* (1). *See* § 7.2 *supra* and § 7.5.1 *supra* (Practitioner's Edition only).

30. 15 U.S.C.A. § 77*l* (2). *See* Junker v. Crory, 650 F.2d 1349 (5th Cir.1981); § 7.5 *supra*. *See also, e.g.*, Kilmartin v. H.C. Wainwright & Co., 580 F.Supp. 604 (D.Mass.1984) ("substantial assistance" by attorney includes preparation of documents with knowledge of misleading statements; aiding and abetting claim upheld).

31. Koehler v. Pulvers, 606 F.Supp. 164 (S.D.Cal.1985) (material issue of fact as to whether attorney's participation rendered him liable as a section 12 "seller"). *Cf.* Sheinkopf v. Stone, 927 F.2d 1259 (1st Cir.1991) (law firm not liable for real estate venture organized by one of its partners where there was no evidence that investor was a client of either the lawyer or the firm).

32. Ahern v. Gaussoin, 611 F.Supp. 1465, 1482 (D.Or.1985); In re Flight Transportation Corp. Securities Litigation, 593 F.Supp. 612, 616 (D.Minn.1984) (relying on Escott v. BarChris Constr. Corp., 283 F.Supp. 643, 683 (S.D.N.Y.1968)). *Compare* Austin v. Baer, Marks & Upham, 1986 WL 10098, [1986 Transfer Binder] Fed.Sec.L.Rep. (CCH) ¶ 92,881 (D.Or.1986) (liability of law firm named as experts). *See also* Moore v. Fenex, Inc., 809 F.2d 297 (6th Cir.1987), *cert. denied* 483 U.S. 1006, 107 S.Ct. 3231, 97 L.Ed.2d 737 (1987) (attorney who worked on offering circular not liable as aider and abettor since he had no knowledge of misstatements). As pointed out in a previous section, the fact that an attorney prepares the registration statement is not sufficient to make him or her a "seller" under section 12(2) of the Act. *E.g.*, Ackerman v. Schwartz, 947 F.2d 841 (7th Cir.1991) (attorney who signed opinion letter but did not solicit investors or otherwise participate in the selling process was not a "seller"); Abell v. Potomac Ins. Co., 858 F.2d 1104 (5th Cir.1988) (bond counsel that helped draft offering materials was not a section 12 seller since none of the investors purchased bonds from those defendants; similarly a real estate developer was not liable under section 12 in the absence of privity); Stokes v. Lokken, 644 F.2d 779 (8th Cir.1981) (attorney neither in privity nor a "substantial factor" with regard to the transaction); Croy v. Campbell, 624 F.2d 709 (5th Cir.1980) (attorney who reviewed tax implications of a sale was not liable as a seller since his participation was not a substantial factor in causing the sale). *Cf.* CFT Seaside Investment Limited Partnership v. Hammet, 868 F.Supp. 836 (D.S.C.1994) (attorneys were not "sellers" under comparable provision of South Carolina blue sky law). *See* § 7.5.1 *supra* (Practitioner's Edition only).

initiation of administrative proceedings against an attorney for allegedly having "caused" the issuer's violation.[33] The proceeding arose in connection with a bidder's violations of the Act based on the filing of misleading tender offer documents. The Administrative Law Judge found that a lawyer who had worked closely with his client, the issuer, was a cause of the violations sufficient to warrant the imposition of an administrative bar order.[34] The ALJ also indicated that a lawyer's negligence could be sufficient to support a finding that he or she was a cause of the violation. This dictum emphasizes the importance of lawyers' exercising due care when involved with disclosure matters. The controversial use of the administrative sanctions against an attorney was appealed to the Commission but the substantive issues were rendered moot. The proceedings were subsequently discontinued because the ALJ held he lacked authority to proceed once the respondent was no longer associated with the company and thus was not in a position to prevent future violations. On appeal, the full Commission affirmed the ALJ's decision solely on the basis of the ruling that he lacked authority to proceed once the respondent's affiliation with the issuer ceased.[35]

In addition to the use of such administrative sanctions, the Commission can invoke its cease and desist authority.[36] For example, the SEC has used its cease and desist authority against an attorney whose allegedly faulty advice constituted aiding and abetting a section 5 violation.[37]

Securities that are offered in connection with shelters can raise particularly sensitive problems. For example, an attorney or an accountant who renders tax advice pursuant to an offering may be held liable for reckless misstatements.[38] Although negligent conduct by an attorney will not give rise to a claim under Rule 10b–5,[39] it may be the basis of a

33. In the Matter of George Kern, [1991 Transfer Binder] Fed.Sec.L.Rep. (CCH) ¶ 84,815 (SEC 1991), *affirming* [1988–1989 Transfer Binder] Fed.Sec.L.Rep. (CCH) ¶ 84,-342 (SEC Initial Decision 1987).

34. Section 15(c)(4) of the Exchange Act gives the Commission the power to bar a person who has caused a violation of the Act from continued association with the issuer. 15 U.S.C.A. § 78o(c)(4). *See* § 9.5 *infra.*

35. In the Matter of George Kern, [1991 Transfer Binder] Fed.Sec.L.Rep. (CCH) ¶ 84,815 (SEC 1991), *affirming* [1988–1989 Transfer Binder] Fed.Sec.L.Rep. (CCH) ¶ 84,-342 (SEC Initial Decision 1987).

36. The Commission's cease and desist authority is discussed in § 9.5 *infra* and § 9.7.1 *infra* (Practitioner's Edition only).

37. In the Matter of Jeffry L. Feldman, Admin. File No. 3–8063 (SEC May 27, 1993).

38. Eisenberg v. Gagnon, 766 F.2d 770 (3d Cir.1985), *cert. denied* 474 U.S. 946, 106 S.Ct. 342, 88 L.Ed.2d 290 (1985) (accountant); Kline v. First Western Government Securities, 794 F.Supp. 542 (E.D.Pa.1992), *affirmed in part, reversed in part* 24 F.3d 480 (3d Cir.1994) (triable issue as to attorney's liability for aiding and abetting); Bush v. Rewald, 619 F.Supp. 585, 597 (D.Hawaii 1985) (attorney). *Compare* Bender v. Rocky Mountain Drilling Assocs., 648 F.Supp. 330 (D.D.C.1986) (attorney writing tax opinion was not required to withdraw opinion upon subsequent knowledge of conflicting facts).

39. Ahmed v. Trupin, 809 F.Supp. 1100 (S.D.N.Y.1993) (insufficient allegation of scienter); Beltram v. Shackleford, Farrior, Stallings & Evans, 725 F.Supp. 499 (M.D.Fla. 1989) (failure to establish even a factual dispute showing that attorneys acted with scienter in failing to predict loss in pending litigation). *See also, e.g.,* Abrash v. Fox, 805 F.Supp.

state law claim for negligent misrepresentation.[40]

What is the lawyer to do when he or she finds a securities law violation or when the client refuses to take the lawyer's advice as to required disclosure? If the lawyer is a signer of the 1933 Act registration materials or is a director or expert named therein, a clear violation will require the attorney to resign if the client refuses to correct the deficiencies; resignation is not sufficient without disclosure to the SEC.[41] This rule necessarily raises conflicts with attorney-client confidentiality, but statements as to a future crime are not privileged.[42] The section 11 obligation relates only to the attorney's civil liability and can easily be

---

206 (S.D.N.Y.1992) (alleged misstatements by an attorney about his qualifications to act as legal advisor in business transactions were not in connection with the purchase or sale of security and thus did not state a claim under SEC Rule 10b–5). *Cf.* Draney v. Wilson, Morton, Assaf & McElligott, 1984 WL 1355, [1984–85 Transfer Binder] Fed.Sec.L.Rep. (CCH) ¶ 91,863 (D.Ariz.1984) (since essence of Exchange Act claim is fraud expert testimony concerning the standard of conduct expected of bond counsel was not admissible, although it might be relevant in the context of an action for legal malpractice). *See also* First Interstate Bank v. Chapman & Cutler, 1986 WL 7346, [1986 Transfer Binder] Fed.Sec.L.Rep. (CCH) ¶ 92,873 (N.D.Ill.1986).

40. Eisenberg v. Gagnon, 766 F.2d 770, 778–80 (3d Cir.1985), *cert. denied* 474 U.S. 946, 106 S.Ct. 342, 88 L.Ed.2d 290 (1985). *Cf.* Quintel Corp. v. Citibank, N.A., 606 F.Supp. 898, 911–14 (S.D.N.Y.1985) (attorney held liable for malpractice in connection with advising client on real estate investment). *See, e.g.,* Popham, Haik, Schnobrich, Kaufman & Doty, Ltd. v. Newcomb Securities Co., 751 F.2d 1262 (D.C.Cir.1985) (advice given to client that investment scheme was not a security can form the basis of a legal malpractice action). *See also* Leslie E. Davis, Donald W. Glazer, Gail S. Mann, & Federic I. Marx, Securities Law Opinions in Exempt Offerings, 20 Rev.Sec. & Commod.Reg. 31 (1987). *But see* Mirotznick v. Sensney, Davis & McCormick, 658 F.Supp. 932 (W.D.Wash.1986) (allegations insufficient under fraud, misrepresentation and state securities laws against attorney who wrote opinion letter).

41. Anyone otherwise liable under section 11 is excused from liability if the defendant can prove:

(1) that before the effective date of the part of the registration statement with respect to which his liability is asserted (A) he had resigned from or had taken such steps as are permitted by law to resign from, or ceased or refused to act in, every office, capacity, or relationship in which he was described in the registration statement as acting or agreeing to act, and (B) he had advised the Commission and the issuer in writing that he had taken such action and that he would not be responsible for such part of the registration statement; or

(2) that if such part of the registration statement became effective without his knowledge, upon becoming aware of such fact he forthwith acted and advised the Commission, in accordance with paragraph (1), and, in addition, gave reasonable public notice that such part of the registration statement had become effective without his knowledge. * * *

15 U.S.C.A. § 78k(b)(1), (2).

42. *See, e.g.,* United States v. United Shoe Machinery Corp., 89 F.Supp. 357, 358 (D.Mass.1950). *See generally* Maureen H. Burke, The Duty of Confidentiality and Disclosing Corporate Misconduct, 36 Bus.Law. 239 (1981); Samuel A. Derieux, Public Accountability Under Securities Laws, 35 Ohio St.L.J. 255 (1974); Samuel H. Gruenbaum, Clients' Frauds and Their Lawyers' Obligations, 68 Geo.L.J. 191 (1979); Junius Hoffman, On Learning of Corporate Client's Crime or Fraud—The Lawyer's Dilemma, 33 Bus.Law. 1389 (1978); Marshall L. Small, An Attorney's Responsibilities Under Federal and State Securities Laws: Private Counselor or Public Servant?, 61 Calif.L.Rev. 1189 (1973). *See also* Kent Gross, Attorneys and Their Corporate Clients: SEC Rule 2(e) and The Georgetown Whistle Blowing Proposal, 3 Corp.L.Rev. 197 (1980); Note, Disclosure Under the Federal Securities Laws: Implications for the Attorney–Client Privilege, 90 Colum.L.Rev. 456 (1990) and the authorities in footnote 4 *supra.*

avoided by not acting as a director of the client or signer of the registration materials.

With regard to the lawyer's obligation generally there remains a tension between the securities laws disclosure requirements and the obligation to one's client.[43] Although it may be necessary for the lawyer to resign in the "egregious" case, this situation will be "rare." [44] In the words of the Commission:

> Some have argued that resignation is the only permissible course when a client chooses not to comply with disclosure advice. We do not agree. Premature resignation serves neither the end of an effective lawyer-client relationship nor, in most cases, the effective administration of the securities laws. The lawyer's continued interaction with his client will ordinarily hold the greatest promise of corrective action. So long as a lawyer is acting in good faith and exerting reasonable efforts to prevent violations of the law by his client, his professional obligations have been met. In general, the best result is that which promotes the continued, strong-minded and independent participation by the lawyer.[45]

These problems will thus have to be viewed on a case-by-case basis.

Beyond the potential for civil liabilities and possible sanctions by the state bar, the SEC can discipline attorneys under SEC Rule of Practice 2(e) which provides that the Commission may suspend, limit or bar "any person" from practicing before it "in any way." [46] It has been suggested that professional misconduct, although not violating the securities laws, can be grounds for a Rule 2(e) suspension from practice before the SEC.[47]

---

43. *See, e.g.,* ABA, Statement of Policy Adopted by American Bar Association Regarding Responsibilities and Liabilities of Lawyers in Advising with Respect to the Compliance by Clients With Laws Administered by the Securities and Exchange Commission, 31 Bus.Law. 543, 546–547 (1975) ("Whenever a proposal is made that a lawyer go beyond his fundamental role of advising his client and assume a function that could require him publicly to contradict his client or disclose possible deficiencies, on the basis of information gained in the course of his professional engagement, there is cause for concern on the part of the public as well as the Bar, since the attorney-client relationship is of fundamental importance to our legal system * * * We do not believe that the policy of disclosure as embodied in the SEC laws warrants an exception to the confidentiality of the attorney-client relationship"). *See also* the authorities in footnotes 4, 42 *supra.*

44. In the Matter of Carter & Johnson, Sec.Exch. Act Rel. No. 34–17597 (Feb. 28, 1981).

45. *Id.*

46. 17 C.F.R. § 201.2(e)(3)(i). *See* Juda H. Best, In Opposition to Rule 2(e) Proceedings, 36 Bus.Law. 815 (1981); Kenneth J. Bialkin, Sanctions Against Accountants, 8 Rev.Sec.Reg. 823 (1975); Robert W. Dockery, Attorney Liability Under SEC Rule 2(e): A New Standard, 11 Tex.Tech.L.Rev. 83 (1979); Ralph C. Ferrara, Administrative Disciplinary Proceedings Under Rule 2(e), 36 Bus.Law. 1807 (1981); Thomas L. Hazen, Administrative Enforcement: An Evaluation of the Securities and Exchange Commission's Use of Injunctions and Other Enforcement Methods, 31 Hastings L.J. 427, 439–442 (1979); Norman S. Johnson, The Expanding Responsibilities of Attorneys in Practice Before the SEC: Disciplinary Proceedings Under Rule 2(e) of the Commission's Rules of Practice, 25 Mercer L.Rev. 637 (1974); Harold Marsh, Jr., Rule 2(e) Proceedings, 35 Bus.Law. 987 (1980); Richard L. Miller, The Distortion and Misuse of Rule 2(e), 7 Sec.Reg.L.J. 54 (1979).

47. W. Loeber Landau, Legal Opinions Rendered in Securities Transactions, 9 Inst.Sec. Reg. 3, 37 (1977) (remarks of Theodore Sonde, Associate Director of Enforcement, SEC).

The Commission has reaffirmed its view that a lawyer's failure to act professionally in connection with 1933 and 1934 Act filings and securities transactions generally can result in Rule 2(e) sanctions.[48]

In addition to the problems discussed above, questions can arise with regard to the scope of the attorney-client privilege. The Supreme Court has recently held that the privilege extends to statements made by lower-level corporate employees as well as by the client's management.[49] The privilege can, of course, be waived by the client. The attorney's publication or distribution of an opinion letter with the client's consent had been held to constitute a waiver of the attorney-client privilege[50] as has the client's consent to an attorney's testimony during an SEC investigation.[51] A company's participation in the SEC's voluntary disclosure program has been held to waive the attorney-client privilege.[52] Also, disclosures of facts by the issuer to accountants and to underwriters' counsel has been held to be a waiver of the privilege.[53]

Attorney–Client Privilege

The attorney-client privilege can be raised only to protect the client's interest and thus will not help an attorney seeking to exclude conversations with former associates concerning possible securities laws violations.[54] The attorney-client privilege can have other impact in securities litigation. For example, the attorney-client privilege has prevented an attorney in a securities case from deposing a former client.[55] Former representation can also result in attorney disqualification.[56]

It is quite common for attorneys to be retained to prepare an internal investigatory report on a client's behalf. In such instances, questions can arise as to whether the attorney client privilege will attach to such a report. At issue is whether the attorneys are performing legal or business services. In Spectrum Systems International Corp. v. Chemical Bank,[57] the New York Court of Appeals ruled that so long as the

---

48. In the Matter of Carter & Johnson, Sec.Exch. Act Rel. No. 34–17597 (Feb. 28, 1981). *See also* § 9.5 *infra* and § 9.7 *infra* (Practitioner's Edition only).

49. Upjohn v. United States, 449 U.S. 383, 101 S.Ct. 677, 66 L.Ed.2d 584 (1981), noted in 95 Harv.L.Rev. 270 (1981), 35 Sw.L.J. 935 (1981), 48 Tenn.L.Rev. 1024 (1981). *See also, e.g.*, Diversified Industries, Inc. v. Meredith, 572 F.2d 596 (8th Cir.1977); State ex rel. Union Oil Co. of California v. District Court, 160 Mont. 229, 503 P.2d 1008 (1972) (house counsel). *See generally* Dennis J. Block & Nancy E. Barton, Internal Corporate Investigation: Maintaining the Confidentiality of a Corporate Client's Communications with Investigative Counsel, 35 Bus.Law. 5 (1979); Glen Weissenberger, Toward Precision in the Application of the Attorney–Client Privilege for Corporations, 65 Iowa L.Rev. 899 (1980).

50. Garfinkle v. Arcata National Corp., 64 F.R.D. 688 (S.D.N.Y.1974).

51. In re Penn Central Commercial Paper Litigation, 61 F.R.D. 453 (S.D.N.Y.1973).

52. In re Subpoenas Duces Tecum, 738 F.2d 1367 (D.C.Cir.1984).

53. In re John Doe Corp., 675 F.2d 482 (2d Cir.1982); In re Micropro Securities Litigation (N.D.Cal.1988) (Unpublished Case) (preliminary drafts of offering documents were not privileged).

54. Hirschfeld v. SEC, 617 F.Supp. 262 (D.D.C.1985).

55. Lund v. Chemical Bank, 107 F.R.D. 374 (S.D.N.Y.1985).

56. Jack Eckerd Corp. v. Dart Group Corp., 621 F.Supp. 725 (D.Del.1985).

57. 78 N.Y.2d 371, 575 N.Y.S.2d 809, 581 N.E.2d 1055 (1991).

investigation and report were commissioned in connection with the rendering of legal advice the attorney-client privilege applied. Although the report contained extensive factual narrative, it still was covered by the privilege. The court noted the strong policy favoring internal investigations of suspected wrongdoing and that such policy would be frustrated by making such reports conducted by attorneys freely discoverable in subsequent litigation. In the course of its opinion, however, the court indicated that had the report focused on business recommendations (such as ways in which to prevent wrongdoing in the future) rather than on whether in fact actionable conduct had occurred, then the document might be viewed as business related rather than connected to the rendering of legal services, and as such might not be covered by the privilege. Nevertheless, so long as the attorneys conducting the investigation and preparing the report were acting as lawyers, it would appear the privilege should apply.

When there is no privilege, or the privilege has been waived, attorneys' memoranda not prepared in connection with a litigation will be freely discoverable.[58] Even where the attorney work-product doctrine applies to materials prepared for litigation, the lawyer's files may be discoverable upon a showing of good cause.[59]

The work product doctrine has been held applicable to attorneys memoranda, notes, mental impressions, and advice regarding matters in litigation or in anticipation of litigation even when provided to auditors in response to the auditor's inquiry in the course of an audit.[60]

As is the case with attorneys, accountants can face extensive liabilities under the securities laws.[61]

---

58. Garfinkle v. Arcata National Corp., 64 F.R.D. 688 (S.D.N.Y.1974); SEC v. National Student Marketing Corp., 1974 WL 415, [1974–1975 Transfer Binder] Fed.Sec.L.Rep. (CCH) ¶ 94,610 (D.D.C.1974). *Cf.* In re Diasonics Securities Litigation, 1986 WL 53402, [1986 Transfer Binder] Fed.Sec.L.Rep. (CCH) ¶ 92,817 (N.D.Cal.1986) (acquisition documents prepared by or disclosed to accountants were not protected by attorney client privilege or work product doctrine since they were prepared for accounting purposes and not in connection with the rendering of legal advice).

59. *See, e.g.,* Hickman v. Taylor, 329 U.S. 495, 67 S.Ct. 385, 91 L.Ed. 451 (1947); Fed.R.Civ.P. 26(b)(3). *Compare* Ward v. Succession of Freeman, 854 F.2d 780 (5th Cir.1988), *rehearing denied* 863 F.2d 882 (5th Cir.1988) (failure to show good cause) *with* In re John Doe Corp., 675 F.2d 482 (2d Cir.1982) (good cause requirement satisfied). *But cf.* United States v. Arthur Young & Co., 465 U.S. 805, 104 S.Ct. 1495, 79 L.Ed.2d 826 (1984) (accountants' workpapers generated in the course of a financial audit are not protected by the work product doctrine; the Court thus refused to extend the attorney work product doctrine). *See* FDIC v. Eagle Properties, 105 F.R.D. 12 (D.D.C.1984) (SEC successfully raised the work product doctrine in response to discovery relating to memoranda prepared in connection with SEC prosecution).

60. United States v. Arthur Young & Co., 84–C–606–B (W.D.Okl.1984). This ruling is interesting in juxtaposition with United States v. Arthur Young & Co., 465 U.S. 805, 104 S.Ct. 1495, 79 L.Ed.2d 826 (1984) which denied work product protection to accountants' work papers. *See* footnotes 58–59 *supra.*

61. *See, e.g.,* Samuel H. Gruenbaum & Marc I. Steinberg, Accountants' Liability and Responsibility, 13 Loyola (L.A.) U.L.Rev. 247 (1980); David B. Isbell, An Overview of Accountants' Duties and Liabilities Under the Federal Securities Laws and a Closer Look at Whistle–Blowing, 35 Ohio St.L.J. 261 (1974); Craig M. Walker, Accountants' Liability, 63 Marq.L.Rev. 243 (1979); Symposium, Advisors to Management: Responsibilities and Liabilities of Lawyers and Accountants, 30 Bus.Law. 227 (1975); Symposium, Accounting and Federal Securities Laws, 28 Vand.L.Rev. 1 (1975); Anthony M. Vernava, Responsibility of the Accountant Under the Federal Securities Exchange Act of 1934, 6 J.Corp.L. 317 (1981). *See* the discussion in § 7.4 *supra*.

Chapter 8

STATE BLUE SKY LAWS

Table of Sections

§ 8.1 State Blue Sky Laws—Their Origins, Purpose and Basic Coverage

This treatise is addressed primarily to the federal law of securities regulation. The emphasis herein should not be taken to indicate, however, that the states do not play a significant role in regulating securities transactions. Each state has its own statutory law governing securities offerings. These state statutes are often referred to as "blue sky" laws. The state securities laws regulate securities distributions as well as broker-dealer activities. Many states also regulate tender offers. A large number of states regulate the activities of investment advisers. The various state laws differ significantly from one another. The discussion that follows is designed to give an overview of state securities regulation.

The state legislatures entered the arena of securities regulation more than twenty years before Congress. In 1911, Kansas enacted the first American legislation regulating the distribution and sale of securities.[1] A number of states followed suit and today every state has enacted a securities act.[2] As noted above, the statutes, which vary widely in

---

§ 8.1

1. Kans.Laws 1911, c. 133. Selective regulation predated the Kansas enactment. In 1852 Massachusetts was regulating securities issued by common carriers. *See* Harry G. Henn & John R. Alexander, Laws of Corporations 843 (3d ed. 1983).

Blue sky laws had been challenged but were subsequently held to be constitutional as a valid use of police power of the states to protect the public against "speculative schemes." Hall v. Geiger–Jones Co., 242 U.S. 539, 550, 37 S.Ct. 217, 220, 61 L.Ed. 480 (1917).

2. A detailed discussion of the state laws and their variations is beyond the scope of this book.

their terms and scope,[3] are commonly referred to as "blue sky" laws, an appellation with several suggested origins. It has been said, for example, that the Kansas legislature was spurred by the fear of fast-talking eastern industrialists selling everything including the blue sky.[4] The discussion that follows is limited to a general overview of the widely varying state blue sky regimes. Most states have adopted wither the Uniform Securities Act or the Revised Uniform Securities Act.[5]

Unlike the federal regulation, the state securities acts generally permit a merit analysis of the investment before certain securities can be offered for sale within that state's borders. This type of substantive scrutiny goes further than the full disclosure approach of the federal laws; registration by qualification permits the state securities administrator to look into the merits of the investment being offered.[6] The state acts also generally provide for a short form registration for securities of more established issuers[7] and for an even simpler registration by coordination where the issue is being registered at the federal level with the SEC.[8] As is the case with the federal registration provisions, the state securities acts provide numerous exemptions.[9] Although many of the state acts do not cover broker-dealers in detail, most of them at least

---

3. Most statutes are based in whole or in part upon the American Law Institute's Uniform Securities Act. *See* 7B Uniform Laws Annotated 509–687 (1985, 1988 Supp.). *See generally* Louis Loss, Commentary on The Uniform Securities Act (1976); Louis Loss & Edward M. Cowett, Blue Sky Law (1958); James S. Mofsky, Blue Sky Restrictions on New Business Promotions (1971); Hugh L. Sowards & Neil H. Hirsch, Blue Sky Regulation (1977 ed.).

4. *See, e.g.,* Hall v. Geiger–Jones, 242 U.S. 539, 550, 37 S.Ct. 217, 220, 61 L.Ed. 480 (1917) (the statute was aimed at "speculative schemes that have no more basis than so many feet of 'blue sky' * * * ").

For a discussion of the origins of the term "blue sky law," *see* 1 Louis Loss & Joel Seligman, Securities Regulation 34 (1989); Jonathan R. Macey & Geoffrey P. Miller, Origin of the Blue Sky Laws, 70 Tex. L. Rev. 347, 359 n.59 (1991).

5. In 1985, the National Conference of Commissioners on Uniform State Laws adopted the Revised Uniform Securities Act (RUSA). *See* Revised Uniform Securities Act Adopted by National Conference, Sec. Reg. & Law. Rep. (BNA) No. 17, at 1481 (Aug. 16, 1985). The revised uniform act, however, has been widely criticized with its fiercest opponent being the National Association of American Securities Administrators (NASAA). *See* NASAA President Endorses Merit Review, Rejects Coercion to Achieve Uniformity, Sec. Reg. & Law Rep. (BNA) No. 17, at 1801–02 (Oct. 11, 1985). NASAA asserted that the revised uniform act: (i) diminishes investor protection; (ii) limits administrative flexibility; and (iii) subordinates state regulation to that of the federal branch. *See* NASAA Committee to Consider Comments on Proposed Investment Adviser Changes, Sec. Reg. & Law Rep. (BNA) No. 18, at 1310 (Sept. 12, 1986); *see also* NASAA Committee Issues Report on Exemptions From Registration, Sec. Reg. & Law. Rep. (BNA) No. 18, at 189 (Feb. 7, 1986) (hereinafter NASAA Committee to Consider Comments). Dissatisfied with the revisions to the Uniform Act, NASAA has gone so far as to propose its own set of amendments to the Act. *See* NASAA Committee to Consider Comments, *supra*, at 1310.

6. Uniform State Securities Act § 304 (hereinafter cited as "Uniform Act"). Revised Uniform State Securities Act § 304 (hereinafter cited as "Revised Act"). *See* § 8.2 *infra*. For a criticism of the merit approach *see, e.g.,* Note, At What Cost Paternalism? A Call to State Legislatures, 22 Ariz.St.L.J. 963 (1990).

7. This is known as registration by notification. *See* Uniform Act § 302.

8. Uniform Act § 303; Revised Act § 303.

9. Uniform Act § 402, discussed in §§ 8.3–8.5 *infra*. Revised Act §§ 401–402. The federal exemptions from registration are discussed in chapter 4 *supra*.

require registration and prohibit fraudulent practices in connection with distributions and other securities transactions.[10]

In recent years, state securities administrators in most states have increased their enforcement of broker-dealer registration. In order to increase efficiency by eliminating duplicative efforts, most states have required broker-dealer registration that parallels that of federal Form B–D.[11] Currently, renewal of federal broker-dealer registration is transmitted electronically by the SEC to the states; before long, initial applications will be similarly transmitted.

In addition to broker-dealer registration, as of 1994, at least forty-three states regulated investment adviser activities[12] while five states and the District of Columbia did not.[13] State securities administrators are supporting increased activity in this area.[14] One reason for the increased concern is the growing financial planning industry.[15] The fact that many financial planners do not qualify as investment advisers under federal law has spurred many state administrators to consider the need for regulation.

Under most blue sky laws, there is a designated state official or administrator who performs functions parallel to those performed by the SEC at the federal level.[16] The administrator may deny a registration and thus prohibit offerings until a proper registration statement has been filed and has become effective.[17] Again, as is the case with the

---

10. Uniform Act §§ 201–204. *See id.* § 409 (criminal penalties); *id.* § 410 (civil liabilities). Many states also regulate investment advisers. *See* Bruce H. Saul, Registration of Investment Advisers Under State Law, 25 Rev.Sec. & Commod.Reg. 41 (1992); footnote 11 *infra* and ch. 18 *infra*.

11. *See* §§ 10.2, 10.2.1 *infra*.

12. Alabama, Alaska, Arizona, Arkansas, California, Connecticut, Delaware, Florida, Georgia, Hawaii, Idaho, Illinois, Indiana, Kansas, Kentucky, Louisiana, Maine, Maryland, Michigan, Minnesota, Mississippi, Missouri, Montana, Nebraska, Nevada, New Hampshire, New Jersey, New Mexico, New York, North Carolina, North Dakota, Oklahoma, Oregon, Pennsylvania, Rhode Island, South Carolina, South Dakota, Tennessee, Texas, Utah, Virginia, Washington, West Virginia, and Wisconsin. Guam and Puerto Rico also regulate investment advisors. Additionally, Massachusetts invoked its emergency rule-making power to permit applicants to become licensed as investment advisers and investment adviser representatives. These rules were effective April 14, 1994 through July 14, 1994. *See* Mass. Regs. § 12.205.

See Garretto v. Elite Advisory Services, Inc., 793 F.Supp. 796 (N.D.Ill.1992) (unregistered investment adviser was strictly liable under Wisconsin Securities Act); Kinsela v. Idaho, 117 Idaho 632, 790 P.2d 1388 (1990) (upholding state regulation of investment advisors).

13. Colorado, Iowa, Ohio, Vermont, and Wyoming.

14. Proposed Uniform Rules for Advisers Circulated for Comment by NASAA Group, 19 Sec.Reg. & L.Rep. (BNA) 645 (May 1, 1987); *See* NASAA Proposed Investment Adviser Amendments to the 1956 Uniform Securities Act, 18 Sec.Reg. & L.Rep. (BNA) 919 (June 6, 1986).

15. The SEC has been considering an investment adviser self regulatory organization, under which there would be coordination with state regulation. The North American Securities Administrators' Association has endorsed the investment advisor self regulatory proposal. In contrast, the financial planners' trade association has proposed a separate s.r.o. for financial planners.

16. *See* §§ 1.3–1.4 *supra*.

17. Uniform Act § 306; Revised Act § 306.

SEC, the state administrator is vested with rulemaking authority.[18]

There is relatively little case law under the state acts, thus leaving the attorney to rely upon whatever administrative rules a state may adopt. There has been a major effort toward uniformity, promoted by the American Law Institute's Uniform Securities Act, from which there are significant departures in many states.[19] In addition, there is a national association of state administrators (The North American Securities Administrators Associations—NASAA) as well as several regional associations. Periodically these groups issue proposed rules, position papers, and draft legislation or policy statements that can aid the lawyer in attempting to comply with the state securities regulations. A major push for uniformity is currently underway in connection with a Uniform Limited Offering Exemption for small issues to be coordinated with Regulation D under the 1933 Act.[20]

A major question under the blue sky laws of most states involves their jurisdictional provisions. The statutes generally are directed at the locus where the securities are offered for sale[21] regardless of the issuer's state of incorporation, state of organization, or principal place of business. It has been suggested that either the situs of the offer or acceptance is sufficient to trigger a state's jurisdiction over the sale and that an offer to sell within a state even though not accepted is also sufficient.[22] So long as there have been offers within the state's borders, there is sufficient in-state contact to justify the use of long-arm statutes to obtain jurisdiction over non-resident sellers.[23]

What is the proper relationship between the federal securities laws and state blue sky laws? The federal securities acts expressly allow for concurrent state regulation under the blue sky laws.[24] The state securi-

---

18. Uniform Act § 412; Revised Act § 705.

19. Notable variations are found in California and in New York's Martin Act. West's Ann.Cal. Corporations Code §§ 25000–25804; N.Y.—McKinney's Gen.Bus.Law §§ 352–359–h. *See* the authorities cited in footnotes 2, 3 *supra*.

20. 17 C.F.R. §§ 230.501–230.506. *See, e.g.,* A. Michael Hainsfurther, Summary of Blue Sky Exemptions Corresponding to Regulation D, 38 Sw.L.J. 989 (1984); Comment, Florida's Response to the Need For Uniformity in Federal and State Securities Registration Exemption Requirements, 12 Fla.St.L.Rev. 309 (1984). Regulation D is discussed in §§ 4.17–4.19, 4.22 *supra*.

21. Uniform Act § 301; Revised Act § 301.

22. *See, e.g.,* Kreis v. Mates Investment Fund, Inc., 473 F.2d 1308 (8th Cir.1973). *See generally* Richard W. Jennings & Harold Marsh, Jr., Securities Regulation 1284 (4th ed. 1977).

23. *See* Travelers Health Association v. Commonwealth, 339 U.S. 643, 70 S.Ct. 927, 94 L.Ed. 1154 (1950); Black & Co. v. Nova–Tech, Inc., 333 F.Supp. 468, 473 (D.Or.1971). In re Activision Securities Litigation, 621 F.Supp. 415 (N.D.Cal.1985). *See* Lintz v. Carey Manor Ltd., 613 F.Supp. 543 (W.D.Va.1985) (discussing conflict of law principles in determining the applicable state blue sky law; there is no problem with overlapping jurisdiction provided that there is not a double recovery). *See also* Ansbro v. Southeast Energy Group, Ltd., 658 F.Supp. 566 (N.D.Ill.1987) (Illinois act could be invoked by Indiana plaintiff against Illinois seller). For discussion of the jurisdictional aspects of blue sky laws *see* R. Jennings & H. Marsh *supra* note 22 at 1284; Cowett, Problems in Jurisdiction of State Securities Laws, 1961 U.Ill.L.F. 300.

24. 15 U.S.C.A. §§ 77r, 78bb.

ties acts have traditionally been limited to disclosure and qualification with regard to securities distributions. Typically the state securities acts have general antifraud provisions to further these ends. In recent years many states have become involved in the regulation of tender offers. These states' tender offer statutes, many of which have been federally preempted, are taken up in another section of this treatise.[25] Even aside from the tender offer context, state blue sky laws can come into conflict with the federal securities laws.[26]

State securities laws typically provide private remedies for investors injured as a result of blue sky violations.[27] Some states have been reluctant to imply remedies under their blue sky laws.[28] Consistent with

25. *See* §§ 11.21–11.22 *infra.* Preemption can arise in other contexts as well. *See, e.g.,* Johnson–Bowles Co. v. Division of Securities, [1992 Transfer Binder] Fed.Sec.L.Rep. (CCH) ¶ 96,894 (Utah App.1992) (suspension of registration was not preempted by NASD obligation to execute customer orders); Comment, State Blue Sky Laws: A Stronger Case for Federal Preemption Due to Increasing Internationalization of the Securities Markets, 86 Nw.U.L.Rev. 753 (1992).

26. *See, e.g.,* Edward M. Cowett, Problems in the Jurisdiction of State Securities Laws, 1961, U.Ill.L.F. 300; Edward M. Cowett, Federal–State Relationships in Securities Regulation, 28 Geo.Wash.L.Rev. 287 (1959); Hayes, State "Blue Sky" and Federal Securities Law, 11 Vand.L.Rev. 659 (1958); Millonzi, Concurrent Regulation of Interstate Securities Issues: The Need For Congressional Reappraisal, 49 Va.L.Rev. 1483 (1963).

27. *E.g.,* West's Ann.Cal.Corp.Code § 2550; 6 Del.Code Ann. § 7323; West's Fla.Stat. Ann. § 517.211; Ill.–S.H.A. ch. 121½ ¶ 137.13; Kan.Stat.Ann. 17–1268; Vernon's Ann.Mo. Stat. § 409.411; Minn.Stat.Ann. § 80A.23; N.J.Stat.Ann. 421–B:25; N.M.Stat.Ann.1978, § 58–138–40; N.C.Gen.Stat. § 78A–56.

See, e.g., Hall v. Johnston, 758 F.2d 421 (9th Cir.1985) (violation of Oregon blue sky law). *But cf., e.g.,* Cors v. Langham, 683 F.Supp. 1056 (E.D.Va.1988) (no remedy under Maryland blue sky law where sales occurred in another state).

Frequently these remedies parallel the federal remedy. Thus, for example, in 1986 the state of Washington amended its statute to impose a scienter requirement in antifraud claims. *See* 18 Sec.Reg. & L.Rep. (BNA) 567 (1986).

See generally Christopher Robbins, Michael E. Stevenson & Scott S. Wakefield, Blue Sky Litigation, 47 Bus.Law 295 (1991). *See also, e.g.,* Ainsworth v. Skurnick, 960 F.2d 939 (11th Cir.1992), *cert. denied* ___ U.S. ___, 113 S.Ct. 1269, 122 L.Ed.2d 665 (1993), *rehearing denied* ___ U.S. ___, 113 S.Ct. 1883, 123 L.Ed.2d 501 (1993) (reversing arbitrators' decision not to award mandatory damages for broker-dealer's securities law violation).

28. *See, e.g.,* The Limited, Inc. v. McCrory Corp., 683 F.Supp. 387, 397 (S.D.N.Y.1988) (no implied remedy under New York law); Baker v. Wheat First Securities, 643 F.Supp. 1420, 1429–30 (S.D.W.Va.1986) (no implied remedy against broker-dealer); In re Catanella & E.F. Hutton & Co. Securities Litigation, 583 F.Supp. 1388, 1439 (E.D.Pa.1984) (no implied remedy under either New Jersey or Pennsylvania blue sky laws); Kirkland v. E.F. Hutton & Co., 564 F.Supp. 427, 443–44 (E.D.Mich.1983) (no implied remedy for failure to comply with broker-dealer registration requirements); Kaufman v. Magid, 539 F.Supp. 1088, 1099 (D.Mass.1982) (Massachusetts blue sky law does not provide an implied remedy for advisory activities); Shofstall v. Allied Van Lines, Inc., 455 F.Supp. 351, 358 (N.D.Ill. 1978) (private rights of action under Illinois blue sky law is wholly statutory and differs from federal law in failing to provide implied remedy for damages; only civil recovery provided for is rescission); Kroungold v. Triester, 407 F.Supp. 414, 419 (E.D.Pa.1975) (no implied remedy under Pennsylvania blue sky law); Tobey v. N.X. Corp., 25 Ill.App.3d 205, 211, 323 N.E.2d 30, 37 (1974) (no implied action for damages under Illinois statute); CPC International, Inc. v. McKesson Corp., 70 N.Y.2d 268, 519 N.Y.S.2d 804, 806, 514 N.E.2d 116, 117–18 (1987) (no private right of action under N.Y.—McKinney's Gen.Bus.Law § 352–C); Green v. Santa Fe Industries, Inc., 70 N.Y.2d 244, 256, 519 N.Y.S.2d 793, 798, 514 N.E.2d 105, 110 (1987) (semble); Loengard v. Santa Fe Industries, Inc., 70 N.Y.2d 262, 266, 519 N.Y.S.2d 801, 803, 514 N.E.2d 113, 114–15 (1987) (semble). *See also, e.g.,*

the federal pattern,[29] many states provide for rescission of securities transactions in violation of their blue sky laws.[30] Another frequent remedy for violations of state blue sky law registration requirements is a rescission offer to all purchasers.[31] The documentation for a rescission offer must adequately explain the violations that were involved in the initial offering.

Issues can arise concerning the proper reach and scope of state securities regulation. Thus, for example, extending blue sky coverage beyond the state's borders may, unless the state has a significant interest, be invalid as an unconstitutional burden on interstate commerce.[32] Many state antitakeover statutes have run into similar problems.[33] Although the prohibition against an undue burden on interstate commerce has been a barrier to some state antitakeover legislation, it has not been a bar to other types of blue sky regulation. Thus, the recognition of a cause of action for fraud has been held not to be a barrier to interstate commerce since the statute create the cause of action was remedial rather than preventive in nature.[34] Blue sky laws have also been held to have a preemptive effect on other state statutes. Thus, for example, although there is some division of authority, the majority of decisions hold that securities transactions are governed by extensive regulation under state securities laws which in turn precludes suit under state unfair or deceptive trade practices acts.[35]

Mirotznick v. Sensney, Davis & McCormick, 658 F.Supp. 932, 943–44 (W.D.Wash.1986) (refusing to expand scope of express right of action under Washington blue sky law).

However, some courts have been more receptive to implied remedies under blue sky laws. *E.g.,* Carothers v. Rice, 633 F.2d 7, 9 (6th Cir.1980), *cert. denied* 450 U.S. 998, 101 S.Ct. 1702, 68 L.Ed.2d 199 (1981) (implied remedy for defrauded sellers under Kentucky blue sky law). *Cf.* Riley v. Brazeau, 612 F.Supp. 674, 679 (D.Or.1985) (drawing analogy to Oregon's express right of action).

29. 15 U.S.C.A. § 77l(1). *See* § 7.2 *supra.*

30. *See, e.g.,* McConnell v. Surak, 774 F.2d 746 (7th Cir.1985) (Illinois blue sky law); Roger v. Lehman Brothers Kuhn Loeb, Inc., 621 F.Supp. 114 (S.D.Ohio 1985) (Ohio blue sky law).

31. *See, e.g.,* In re Van Dyke, 731 F.2d 431 (7th Cir.1984) (Illinois blue sky law). *Cf.* In re LA–MAN Corp., [1985–86 Transfer Binder] Fed.Sec.L.Rep. (CCH) ¶ 78,102 (SEC No Action Letter June 25, 1985) (rescission offer to correct state law violations given exemption from SEC Rule 10b–6).

32. *See, e.g.,* Arizona Corp. Commission v. Media Products, Inc., 158 Ariz. 463, 763 P.2d 527 (App.1988) (over extension of registration requirements). *See also* the authorities cited in footnote 22 *supra.*

33. *E.g.,* Edgar v. MITE Corp., 457 U.S. 624, 102 S.Ct. 2629, 73 L.Ed.2d 269 (1982). *Compare, e.g.,* CTS Corp. v. Dynamics Corp. of America, 481 U.S. 69, 107 S.Ct. 1637, 95 L.Ed.2d 67 (1987) (upholding the Indiana Control Share Act). *See* § 11.22 *infra.*

34. Chrysler Capital Corp. v. Century Power Corp., 800 F.Supp. 1189 (S.D.N.Y.1992).

35. Lindner v. Durham Hosiery Mills, Inc., 761 F.2d 162 (4th Cir.1985) (North Carolina Unfair Trade Practices Act does not apply to securities fraud); Cabot Corp. v. Baddour, 394 Mass. 720, 477 N.E.2d 399 (1985) (Massachusetts Deceptive Trade Practices Act does not apply to securities transactions); Skinner v. E.F. Hutton & Co., 314 N.C. 267, 333 S.E.2d 236 (1985) (North Carolina Deceptive Trade Practices Act does not apply to securities transactions); State v. Piedmont Funding Corp., 119 R.I. 695, 382 A.2d 819 (1978) (Rhode Island Unfair Trade Practices Act does not apply to securities transactions); State ex rel. McLeod v. Rhoades, 275 S.C. 104, 267 S.E.2d 539 (1980) (South Carolina Unfair Trade Practices Act does not apply to securities transactions); E.F. Hutton & Co. v. Youngblood,

§ 8.2 Registration of Securities Under State Securities Acts

The provisions of the original Uniform Securities Act[1] are typical of the three types of securities registration provided by the state blue sky laws. The Revised Uniform Securities Act contains comparable provisions. These three alternatives are known as registration by qualification,[2] the shorter form registration by notification,[3] and registration by coordination[4] with federal registration. The primary difference between the state and federal registration is the power of the state securities administrator to review the merits of the investment represented by the securities sought to be licensed for sale under the long-form registration by qualification. The states vary as to the rigor with which this merit analysis is used. A number of states such as California and Florida have a tradition of aggressive enforcement; an increasing number of states have been moving in this direction. Many of the state securities administrators are particularly aggressive in enforcing limitations on underwriters' compensation and "cheap stock" issued in connection with securities offerings.[5]

741 S.W.2d 363 (Tex.1987) (securities fraud cannot be challenged under Texas Deceptive Trade Practices Act); Kittilson v. Ford, 23 Wn.App. 402, 595 P.2d 944 (1979), *affirmed* 93 Wn.2d 223, 608 P.2d 264 (1980) (Washington Unfair Trade Practices Act does not apply to securities transactions). *Cf.* Bache Halsey Stuart, Inc. v. Hunsucker, 38 N.C.App. 414, 248 S.E.2d 567 (1978), *cert. denied* 296 N.C. 583, 254 S.E.2d 32 (1979) (North Carolina Unfair Trade Practices Act does not apply to commodities transactions in light of pervasive federal regulation). *But see, e.g.,* M Bank Fortworth, N.A. v. Trans Meridian, Inc., [1987–88 Transfer Binder] Blue Sky L.Rep. (CCH) 72,652 (N.D.Tex.1987) (permitting action against Texas Deceptive Trade Practices Act for transactions involving oil and gas drilling venture).

A number of state unfair trade practices acts provide that the remedies provided therein are in addition to those provided elsewhere. *E.g.,* Ariz.Rev.Stat. § 44–1533(A); *see* State ex rel. Corbin v. Pickrell, 136 Ariz. 589, 667 P.2d 1304 (1983).

§ 8.2

1. A.L.I. Uniform Securities Act (hereinafter cited as "Uniform Act"). *See* 7B Uniform Laws Annotated 509–687 (1985, 1988 supp.). The National Conference on Uniform Laws has adopted a revised version of the Uniform Act. *See* Revised Uniform Securities Act Adopted by National Conference, 17 Sec.Reg. & L.Rep. (BNA) 65 (Jan. 9, 1987).

Many statutes contain variations on the Uniform Act but their consideration is beyond the scope of this book. *See* the authorities cited in § 8.1 *supra,* footnotes 2–3.

2. Uniform Act § 304; Revised Act § 304.

3. Uniform Act § 302; Revised Act § 302. For an explanation of section 302 of the Revised Act as compared with the original act, *see* footnote 6 in § 8.1 *supra.*

4. Uniform Act § 303; Revised Act § 303. The North American Securities Administrators Association proposed that the Uniform Act be amended to replace registration by coordination with "registration by filing". Under the proposal, there would be more regulation of offerings that currently qualify for registration by coordination. *See* NASAA Memorandum, 18 Sec.Reg. & L.Rep. (BNA) 430 (March 17, 1986); Robert B. Titus, Uniform Securities Act (1985), 19 Rev.Sec. & Commodities Reg. 81 (April 16, 1986). Included in the proposed amendments was a limit on underwriters' compensation to ten percent of the aggregate offering price.

5. *See, e.g.,* Proposed Revisions to Policy on Cheap Stock Proposed by NASAA, 16 Sec.Reg. & L.Rep. (BNA) 1292 (1984); NASAA Memorandum *supra* footnote 4.

Registration by Qualification

Registration by qualification may be used for any security not covered by one of the blue sky laws' exemptions.[6] Under the Uniform Act, the following disclosures must be made in the registration statement:

(1) The amount of the securities to be offered in the state of registration;

(2) Other states in which the securities have been or will be registered for sale;

(3) Any adverse judgment or decree of a court or administrative agency, at the federal or state level, involving the offering covered by the registration statement;[7]

(4) The name and detailed description of the issuer "and any significant subsidiary";[8]

(5) The name, address and principal occupation of the issuer's officers and directors.[9] This includes disclosure of ownership of the issuer's securities and of material transactions with the issuer or its subsidiaries within the past three years. All remuneration to the persons identified above paid within the past year or to be paid within the next year must also be disclosed.[10]

(6) The registration statement must identify all persons beneficially owning ten percent or more of the outstanding shares of any class of equity security.[11]

(7) Every person who acted as a promoter for the past three years must be identified, together with his or her remuneration.[12]

(8) If the transaction includes a secondary distribution, there must be full disclosure concerning the identity and interest of all non-issuer sellers.[13]

(9) There must be a complete description of the issuer's capitalization in addition to a description of all securities offerings made within the past three years.[14]

(10) There must be full disclosure of all underwriting agreements and commissions.[15]

---

6. Exemptions from the state registration requirements are considered in §§ 8.3–8.5 *infra*.

7. The first three items are required by Uniform Act § 305(c). Revised Act § 305(d). *See* Uniform Act § 304(b).

8. Uniform Act § 304(b)(1); Revised Act § 304(b)(1).

9. Uniform Act § 304(b)(2); Revised Act § 304(b)(2).

10. Uniform Act § 304(b)(3); Revised Act § 304(b)(3).

11. Uniform Act § 304(b)(4); Revised Act § 304(b)(4).

12. Uniform Act § 304(b)(5); Revised Act § 304(b)(5).

13. Uniform Act § 304(b)(6); Revised Act § 304(b)(6).

14. Uniform Act § 304(b)(7); Revised Act § 304(b)(7).

15. Uniform Act § 304(b)(8); Revised Act § 304(b)(8).

(11) The registration statement must describe in detail the intended use of the proceeds from the offering.[16]

(12) There must be a description of all outstanding security options and the holders thereof[17] as well as all options to be created in connection with the offering.

(13) There must be a "concise" but detailed description of all management contracts as well as of any other material contracts not made in the ordinary course of business and within two years of the registration statement.[18]

(14) The registration statement must describe any material litigation, pending or known to be contemplated, to which the issuer is a party.[19]

(15) All sales literature must be dated and filed with the registration statement.[20] The state administrator may require the filing of sales literature in exempted offerings.[21]

(16) The registration statement as filed must include a specimen of the security being registered.[22]

(17) There must be an opinion of counsel as to the legality of the security being issued.[23]

(18) If any accountant, engineer, appraiser or other expert furnishes an opinion, there must be a signed consent for the use of his or her name.[24]

(19) The registration must also contain a balance sheet for the issuer's last three years of operation.[25] Unlike federal registration, there is no requirement that the financial statement be audited.

In addition to the foregoing specified items, the state securities administrator may by rule require additional disclosures.[26] The administrator is further given a wide range of authority to deny the effectiveness

16. Uniform Act § 304(b)(9); Revised Act § 304(b)(9).

17. Uniform Act § 304(b)(10) requires disclosure of the names of all persons identified elsewhere in the registration statement who hold options as well as any persons holding ten percent or more of such options. Revised Act § 304(b)(10).

18. Uniform Act § 304(b)(11); Revised Act § 304(b)(11).

19. *Id.;* Revised Act § 304(b)(12).

20. Uniform Act § 304(b)(12); Revised Act § 304(b)(13).

21. Uniform Act § 403; Revised Act § 405. Unlike the original Uniform Act, Revised Act § 405 does apply to sales literature and advertising sent to both actual and prospective clients of investment advisers.

22. Uniform Act § 304(b)(13); Revised Act § 304(b)(14).

23. Uniform Act § 304(b)(14). In equity offerings the opinion must relate to the nonassessability of the shares. In a debt offering counsel must opine as to the binding obligation of the issuer. Revised Act § 304(b)(15).

24. Uniform Act § 304(b)(15); Revised Act § 304(b)(16).

25. Uniform Act § 304(b)(16); Revised Act § 304(b)(17).

26. Uniform Act § 304(b)(17); Revised Act § 304(b)(18).

of a registration statement.[27]

Registration by qualification frequently includes merit review of the securities being offered and there is movement by some administrators to expand the scope of this power.[28] There has also been the suggestion that the scope of exemptions from merit regulation should be expanded.[29]

The Ninth Circuit has rejected an argument that the merit review authority of a state administrator is void because of the preemptive effect of federal securities regulation.[30] The preemption argument has met with much greater success in invalidating state takeover statutes.[31]

Registration by Notification

A short form registration statement is available for certain issuers. Where an issuer has had an established business for five years, it may avail itself of registration by notification.[32] The Revised Act refers to this process as "registration by filing." The Act's antifraud and civil liability provisions apply with equal force to registration by notification (or filing).

Registration by Coordination

The simplest form of registration under the state acts is in coordination with a federal registration. Registration by coordination is accomplished by filing three copies of the current federal prospectus in addition to any other information as may be required by the state securities administrator.[33] The state registration is effective concurrently with the federal. It is important to note that coordination is only available for a 1933 Act registration and thus, for example, will not apply to offerings

---

27. *See* Uniform Act § 306; Revised Act § 306. *Compare* the authority of the SEC with regard to federal registration. *See* §§ 2.5, 7.1 *supra*.

28. *See* New Jersey Assemblyman to Introduce Merit Review Bill, 17 Rec.Reg.L.Rep. (BNA) 410 (1985). *See also* NASAA Memorandum *supra* note 4; Revised Uniform Securities Act Adopted by National Conference, 17 Sec.Reg. & L.Rep. (BNA) 1481 (1985). *See generally* Report on State Merit Regulation of Securities Offerings, 41 Bus.Law. 785 (1986). *See also* Roberta S. Karmel, Blue Sky Merit Regulation: Benefit to Investors or Burden on Commerce?, 53 Brooklyn L.Rev. 105 (1987); Manning G. Warren III, Legitimacy in the Securities Industry: The Role of Merit Regulation, 53 Brooklyn L.Rev. 129 (1987).

29. *See* Wisconsin Merit Review Study Group Suggests Broader, Simplified Exemptions, 19 Sec.Reg. & L.Rep. (BNA) 65 (Jan. 9, 1987).

30. North Star International v. Arizona Corporation Commission, 720 F.2d 578 (9th Cir.1983). *See also* Carney v. Hanson Oil Co., 690 S.W.2d 404 (Mo.1985). *See generally* Manning G. Warren III, Reflections on Dual Regulation of Securities: A Case Against Preemption, 25 B.C.L.Rev. 495 (1984).

31. *E.g.*, Edgar v. MITE Corp., 457 U.S. 624, 102 S.Ct. 2629, 73 L.Ed.2d 269 (1982). *See* § 11.22 *infra*. *See generally, e.g.*, Robert A. Profusek & Henry L. Gompf, State Tender Offer Laws After *MITE*: Standing Pat, Blue Sky, or Corporation Law, 7 Corp.L.Rev. 3 (1984).

32. Uniform Act § 302.

33. Uniform Act § 303; Revised Act § 303; Revised Act § 303(b)(1) requires the filing of only two copies of the latest form of prospectus filed under the Securities Act of 1933.

subject to the qualified federal exemption under Regulation A.[34]

§ 8.3 Exemptions From Registration Under State Securities Acts

As is the case with the federal Securities Act of 1933,[1] the state blue sky laws set forth numerous exemptions from their registration provisions. Section 402 of the original Uniform Securities Act is typical of state statutory schemes. However, due to the wide variation among states, it is imperative to consult the particular statute at issue.[2]

An exemption under section 402 of the Uniform Act does not provide across-the-board immunity. Exempt securities are still subject to the Act's antifraud provisions[3] but need not comply with either the registration[4] or filing requirements[5] of the Act. This parallels the approach taken under federal exemptions.[6] As is also true with the federal scheme, the state statutes provide for both exempt securities[7] and transaction exemptions.[8] Under the state acts, the person claiming the exemption has the burden of proving its applicability.[9] The state administrator after a hearing may deny or revoke an exemption.[10] Both securities and transaction exemptions are taken up in the sections that follow.

§ 8.4 Securities Exempt From Registration Under State Securities Acts

Most of the securities that are exempt under state law will find a comparable exemption from registration under the federal Securities Act of 1933.[1] The original Uniform Securities Act contains twelve types of exempt securities.[2]

---

34. 17 C.F.R. §§ 230.251–230.256. Regulation A is discussed in § 4.15 *supra*. In addition, registration by coordination is not available for issuers seeking to avail themselves of Regulation D's provisions. *See* 17 C.F.R. §§ 230.501–230.508. Regulation D is discussed in §§ 4.16–4.22 *supra*.

§ 8.3

1. 15 U.S.C.A. §§ 77a *et seq.*

2. *See generally* the authorities cited in § 8.1 *supra*, footnotes 2–3.

3. *See* Uniform Act § 410(a)(2) (civil liability for misleading statements). Revised Act § 605.

4. Uniform Act §§ 301–04; Revised Act §§ 301–06. *See* § 8.2 *supra*.

5. Uniform Act § 403; Revised Act § 405.

6. 15 U.S.C.A. §§ 77c, 77d. *See* chapter 4 *supra*.

7. Uniform Act § 402(a); Revised Act § 401. *See* § 8.4 *infra*.

8. Uniform Act § 402(b); Revised Act § 402. *See* § 8.5 *infra*.

9. Uniform Act § 402(d). The same is true under the federal act.

10. Uniform Act § 402(c).

§ 8.4

1. Federally exempt securities are considered in §§ 4.2–4.12 *supra*.

2. Uniform Act § 402(a); Revised Act § 401. The Revised Act adds two additional exemptions for securities. Section 401(b)(13) of the Revised Act sets forth an exemption for securities issued by cooperatives. Revised Act § 401(b)(14) contains a "blue chip"

Securities issued or guaranteed by governmental subdivisions at the federal, state and local level are exempt; the exemption includes revenue obligations and certificates of deposits for governmental obligations.[3] Also exempt are securities issued or guaranteed by Canadian governmental bodies including provincial and local political subdivisions as are securities issued or guaranteed by any foreign government with which the United States maintains diplomatic relations.[4] The federal legislation contains no such exemption for foreign governmental issuers.[5]

The state securities acts, as is the case with the federal statute,[6] exempt securities issued by and representing an interest in or guaranteed by any bank organized under federal or state law,[7] savings and loan or trust company organized under the laws of any state,[8] and federal savings and loan, building and loan, or similar associations.[9] Also exempt are securities issued or guaranteed by credit unions, industrial loan associations and similar organizations.[10] Unlike the federal acts, the Uniform Act exempts securities issued by and representing an interest in or guaranteed by insurance companies that are qualified to do business in the state.[11] The state exemption does not, however, extend

---

exemption for established investment companies or companies sponsored or serviced by an established investment advisor. Since there are significant variations in many states, the particular state act should be consulted. *See generally* the authorities cited in § 8.1 *supra,* footnotes 2–3.

Also, it should be noted that the burden of proof for establishing entitlement to the exemption is placed on the person claiming it. *See* Uniform Act § 402(d).

3. Uniform Act § 402(a)(1); Revised Act § 401(b)(1). *See* Dau v. Storm Lake Production Credit Association, 626 F.Supp. 862 (N.D.Iowa 1985) (Iowa blue sky law). Section 3(a)(2) of the 1933 Act is in accord. 15 U.S.C.A. § 77(a)(2). *See* § 4.3 *supra.*

This exemption also extends to government agencies as well as instrumentalities of the United States, its states, *etc.* *(e.g.,* Small Business Administration, Tennessee Valley Authority).

4. Uniform Act § 402(a)(2); Revised Act § 401(b)(2). The Uniform Act talks in terms of foreign governments with which the United States "*currently* maintains diplomatic relations" (emphasis supplied). This raises difficult questions with regard to countries where diplomatic ties have been severed. Presumably the statutory exemption applies as of the time of the registration or filing requirement in question; although a contrary interpretation is also possible so that the exemption would not have grandfather clause protection. The Revised Act deletes the word "currently".

5. Under the federal act, foreign governmental issuers who fall within the Act's jurisdictional provisions are treated no differently from private foreign issuers. *See* § 14.2 *infra* for a discussion of the federal securities laws' extraterritorial reach.

6. 15 U.S.C.A. § 77c(a)(5). *See* § 4.6 *supra.*

7. Uniform Act § 402(a)(3); Revised Act § 401(b)(3). A number of states, however, in adopting this non-profit charitable securities exemption, have limited the coverage of the exemption to equity or membership type securities in order to exclude church bonds from the exempt status. *See, e.g.,* Cal. Corp. Code § 25100(j). The Uniform Securities Act has not adopted this approach and extends coverage to all securities. *See* Uniform Act § 402(a)(9).

8. Uniform Act § 402(a)(3); Revised Act § 401(b)(3).

9. Uniform Act § 402(a)(4); Revised Act § 401(b)(3).

10. Uniform Act § 402(a)(6); Revised Act § 401(b)(3).

11. Uniform Act § 402(a)(5); Revised Act § 401(b)(4). At one time insurance companies were exempt from certain provisions of the Securities Exchange Act of 1934. *See* SEC v. National Securities, Inc., 393 U.S. 453, 89 S.Ct. 564, 21 L.Ed.2d 668 (1969), *reversing*

to annuities and similar investment contracts issued by insurance companies.[12] Typically, the state acts also exempt securities issued or guaranteed by federally or state regulated railroads, common carriers and public utilities, as well as where the security is issued or guaranteed by a United States or Canadian governmental body.[13]

The state securities acts generally exempt securities listed on a national or qualifying regional stock exchange.[14] Other securities of an issuer with listed securities generally are exempt from registration so long as the securities to be exempted are either senior or substantially equal to the listed securities.[15] Also exempt from state registration are exchange-listed warrants or options as well as warrants or options to purchase listed equivalent or senior securities.[16]

Securities issued by not-for-profit charitable, educational, religious, social, fraternal or athletic organizations, and trade associations are generally exempt from registration under the state acts.[17] There is a comparable federal exemption.[18] The state acts further exempt short-term commercial paper which is payable within nine months of issuance, not including extensions, renewals and so on.[19] This is virtually identical to the federal exemption.[20]

The Uniform Act provides an exemption for securities issued in connection with employee pension and profit-sharing plans provided that the State Administrator is notified thirty days in advance of the plan's inception.[21] In contrast to the state law approach to employee compensation plans, the issue under federal law has been whether such plans constitute a security.[22] The Uniform Act also contains an optional provision for cooperative associations[23] which has not been adopted in all

---

387 F.2d 25 (9th Cir.1967). However, in 1964 these statutory exemptions were deleted. The federal act continues to exempt insurance policies from registration. 15 U.S.C.A. § 77c(a)(8). *See* § 4.9 *supra.*

12. Uniform Act § 402(a)(5); Revised Act § 401(b)(4).

13. Uniform Act § 402(a)(7); Revised Act § 401(b)(5). The comparable federal exemption is found in section 3(a)(6) of the 1933 Act, 15 U.S.C.A. § 77c(a)(6). *See* § 4.7 *supra.*

14. Uniform Act § 402(a)(8); Revised Act § 401(b)(7).

15. Uniform Act § 402(a)(8); Revised Act § 401(b)(7).

16. Uniform Act § 402(a)(8); Revised Act § 401(b)(7).

17. Uniform Act § 402(a)(9); Revised Act § 401(b)(10).

18. 15 U.S.C.A. § 77c(a)(4). *See* § 4.5 *supra.*

19. Uniform Act § 402(a)(10); Revised Act § 401(b)(11). *See* Manning G. Warren III, The Treatment of *Reves* "Notes" and Other "Securities" Under State Blue Sky Laws, 47 Bus.Law. 321 (1992).

20. 15 U.S.C.A. § 77c(a)(3) (1976). *See* § 4.4 *supra.* *See also* 15 U.S.C.A. § 78(a)(10) (1976).

21. Uniform Act § 402(a)(11); Revised Act § 401(b)(12). Revised Act § 401(b)(12) has dropped the pre-sale notice provision.

22. In International Brotherhood of Teamsters v. Daniel, 439 U.S. 551, 99 S.Ct. 790, 58 L.Ed.2d 808 (1979), the Supreme Court held that a compulsory, noncontributory, defined-benefit employee pension plan is not a security. *See* § 1.5 *supra.* *See also* section 3(a)(2) of the 1933 Act which exempts "qualified" employee pension plans. 15 U.S.C.A. § 77c(a)(2); § 4.3 *supra.*

23. Uniform Act § 402(a)(12).

states. A few states exempt certain oil and gas interests that would otherwise require registration.[24]

A survey of the blue sky laws of the several states reveals that there are several instances of variations from the Uniform Act. It is important to check the applicable state statute before relying on the Uniform Act or any other generalizations.

§ 8.5 Transactions Exempt From Registration Under State Securities Acts

The original Uniform Securities Act sets out twelve types of transactions that are exempt from the Act's registration and filing requirements.[1] The exemptions under particular state acts may contain significant variations and thus the statutes of all states involved in the offering should be consulted.[2]

The original Uniform Act contains two types of private placement exemptions. There is a general exemption for "any isolated non-issuer transaction."[3] As for issuer transactions, there is an exemption for transactions pursuant to an offer directed to not more than ten persons[4] within the state in any twelve month period.[5] The exemption is further qualified in that the purchasers must be buying for investment rather than resale and there can be no promoter's fees for soliciting potential purchasers, subject to waiver of these limitations by the state adminis-

---

24. *See, e.g.,* Wilson v. Al McCord Inc., 611 F.Supp. 621 (W.D.Okl.1985), *judgment affirmed in part, reversed in part* 858 F.2d 1469 (10th Cir.1988) (Oklahoma blue sky law). Note, however, that Revised Act § 401(b)(13) provides an exemption for such securities so long as they are not traded by the public generally.

§ 8.5

1. Uniform Act § 402(b); Revised Act § 402. *See also* Joseph C. Long, Blue Sky Law §§ 5.01–5.02[1] (1993):

> The transactional exemptions are four basic types: (1) There are those that can only be used by the issuer, *see* Uniform Act § 402(b)(4). (2) There are those exemptions that can only be used by nonissuers in secondary transactions, *see, e.g.,* Uniform Act I 402(b)(1), (2), and (3). (3) There are those exemptions which can be used by both an issuer in a primary transaction and nonissuers in secondary transactions, *see* Uniform Act §§ 402(b)(5), (8), and (9). And (4), there are those exemptions that are only available to certain types of individuals, *see* Uniform Act §§ 402(b)(6) and (7).

> However, it is important to note that these exemptions are merely exemptions from the registration provision of the Uniform Securities Act, and do not constitute exemptions from the coverage of the Act itself. *See* Official Comment to § 402(a):

> > The distinction between *exemptions* and *exemptions from definitions* is important in view of the fact that exemptions enumerated in § 402 are not exemptions from the antifraud provisions * * * *

(emphasis in the original).

2. *See generally* the authorities cited in § 8.1 *supra*, footnotes 2–3.

3. Uniform Act § 402(b)(1); Revised Act § 402(1).

4. Section 402(b)(8) excludes certain offerees from the 10 person limit. Revised Act § 402(10) excludes certain offerees from the 25 person limit. *See* text accompanying footnote 7 *infra*.

5. Uniform Act § 402(b)(9); Revised Act § 402(11).

trator.[6] It is important to note that the statute counts only offers to persons within the state. In computing the ten person limit certain categories of offerees are excluded, to wit:

> Any offer or sale to a bank, savings institution, trust company, insurance company, investment company as defined in the Investment Company Act of 1940, pension or profit-sharing trust, or other financial institution or institutional buyer, or to a broker-dealer, whether the purchaser is acting for itself or in some fiduciary capacity.[7]

The ten offeree limit embodied in the limited offering exemption from blue sky registration is thus not as restrictive as would otherwise appear. In the face of objections that the original Uniform Act is too narrow, some states have expanded the number and some have placed a limit on the number of purchasers as opposed to offerees.[8] The limitation on purchasers is more in line with the federal safe harbor exemption under Rule 506.[9] The Revised Uniform Act and a number of states are following the SEC's suggestion that the state exemption be coordinated with Regulation D.[10] It will most likely take at least several years before there is substantial acceptance of the uniform limited offering exemption ("ULOE"). Some state securities laws also provide an exemption for transactions not involving a public offering, much like the exemption provided by section 4(2) of the 1933 Act.[11]

---

6. *Id.;* Revised Act § 402(11). Compare the private placement exemption from federal registration. 15 U.S.C.A. § 77d(2). *See* § 4.21 *supra.*

7. Uniform Act § 402(b)(8); Revised Act § 402(10). In computing the 25 person limit certain categories of offerees are excluded to wit: an offer to sell or sale of a security to a financial or institutional investor or to a broker-dealer.

As explained in the official commentary:

Since the term "financial or institutional investor" is now defined in [Revised Act § 101(5)] the exemption is briefer. The substance, however, remains unchanged.

The term "institutional buyer" in the definition is broad enough to include, among others, a college endowment fund or other comparable investor. The Administrator is, of course, free to add to the scope of the term "financial or institutional investor" through ad hoc interpretations or declaratory rulings under Section 706.

8. *E.g.* West's Ann.Cal. Corporations Code § 25102(f) (35 purchasers provided certain conditions are met); West's Fla.Stats.Ann. § 517.061(12)(a)(1) (35 in-state purchasers provided certain other conditions are met); N.Y.–McKinney's Gen.Bus.Law. § 359–f(2)(d) (40 purchasers, attorney general has discretion to exempt larger offerings).

9. 17 C.F.R. § 230.506. *See* § 4.22 *supra.*

10. *See* Joseph C. Long, Blue Sky Law § 1.04[2][b] (1993) ("An increasing number of states are adding a new exemption that is not found in the Uniform Act in order to coordinate with Regulation D exemption at the federal level.").

E.g. West's Ann.Cal. Corporations Code § 25102(f). This effort is being made through the Uniform Limited Offering Exemption. *See* text accompanying footnotes 10–14 in § 4.16 *supra.* *See also, e.g.,* Gregory S. Crespi, The Uniform Limited Offering Exemption: The Need For Amendment of its Disqualification Provisions, 16 Sec.Reg.L.J. 370 (1989). Regulation D is discussed in §§ 4.16–4.22 *supra.*

11. *See, e.g.,* People v. Landes, 84 N.Y.2d 655, 621 N.Y.S.2d 283, 645 N.E.2d 716 (1994) (offering to twelve investors although relatively small was a public offering under state law). The section 4(2) exemption for transactions by an issuer not involving a public offering (15 U.S.C.A. § 77d(2)) is discussed in § 4.21 *supra.*

In addition to providing for the limited offering exemption, the Uniform Act exempts non-issuer distributions of outstanding securities provided that there is a currently available balance sheet and list of the issuer's officers and directors.[12] There is also an exemption for non-issuer transactions which are effected through a registered broker pursuant to an unsolicited order.[13] This is similar to the federal exemption for unsolicited brokers' transactions.[14] Again, following the federal scheme, the Uniform Act exempts transactions between an issuer or its agent and an underwriter, or among underwriters.[15] This exemption is necessary lest negotiations with and among underwriters violate the Act's gun-jumping prohibitions against sales and offers to sell prior to registration.[16]

The Uniform Act exempts transactions involving debt securities that are secured by a real estate or chattel mortgage.[17] The exemption is not available, however, for the syndication of such an interest. A similar federal exemption is provided by section 4(5) of the 1933 Act.[18]

The state acts typically exempt transactions "by an executor, administrator, sheriff, marshal, receiver, trustee in bankruptcy, guardian, or conservator." [19] There are comparable federal exemptions for many such transactions.[20] The state acts also exempt from registration transactions by bona fide pledgees provided that there is no intent to evade the registration or filing requirements.[21] These transactions have not

---

12. Uniform Act § 402(b)(2); Revised Act § 402(3), (4). As explained in the official commentary, The Revised "Act carries over the prior exemptions for securities listed in nationally recognized securities manuals or for certain fixed maturity or interest or dividend securities, which exemptions have been followed in a large majority of the states. § 402(3) adds a 90–day waiting period, which, as in the preceding paragraph, is intended to bar immediate secondary trading of nonregistered IPO securities."

13. Uniform Act § 402(b)(3); Revised Act § 402(5). The official comments point out that Revised Act § 402(5) follows Uniform Act § 402(b)(3) "except that the language authorizing the Administrator to require specific forms of acknowledgement has been deleted. Current practice in the industry is that each confirmation slip delivered to a customer notes whether or not the transaction was unsolicited."

The justification for this exemption rests upon two points: (1) It is limited to transactions by or through a registered broker-dealer, and (2) the offers to buy are unsolicited. Drafter's Commentary to § 402(b)(3) at 121.

14. 15 U.S.C.A. § 77d(4). *See* § 4.23 *supra*.

15. Uniform Act § 402(b)(4); Revised Act § 402(6). *See* 15 U.S.C.A. § 77b(3).

16. *See* §§ 2.2–2.3 *supra*.

17. Uniform Act § 402(b)(5) which expressly includes deeds of trust; Revised Act § 402(7), which also expressly includes deeds of trust. *Compare* section 4(5) of the 1933 Act, 15 U.S.C.A. § 77d(5) which is discussed in § 4.28 *supra* and applies only to certain real estate mortgages.

18. *Id.*

19. Uniform Act § 402(b)(6); Revised Act § 402(8).

20. 15 U.S.C.A. §§ 77c(a)(7), 77c(a)(10). *See* §§ 4.8, 4.11 *supra*. *See also* section 4(a)'s exemption for transactions not involving an issuer, underwriter or dealer, 15 U.S.C.A. § 77d(1); § 4.23 *supra*.

21. Uniform Act § 402(b)(7); Revised Act § 402(9). The Revised Act talks in terms of a "bona fide secured party" as compared with the original Act's reference to a "bona fide pledgee."

been dealt with as explicitly or clearly under federal law.[22]

The Uniform Act provides an exemption for a transaction involving preorganization certificates or subscription agreements provided there is no sales commission, the number of subscribers does not exceed ten, and no payments are made by any subscriber.[23] The Uniform Act, as is the case with the federal 1933 Act, exempts transactions pursuant to an offer to existing securities holders, provided there is no sales or solicitation commission.[24] The Uniform Act also exempts transactions pursuant to offerings having valid and effective registration statements under both the federal and state acts.[25]

22. *See* SEC v. Guild Films Co., 279 F.2d 485 (2d Cir.1960), *cert. denied* 364 U.S. 819, 81 S.Ct. 52, 5 L.Ed.2d 49 (1960); 17 C.F.R. § 230.144(d)(3)(D). *See* §§ 4.24–4.25 *supra.*

23. Uniform Act § 402(b)(10); Revised Act § 402(12). The drafters explain that Revised Act § 402(12) "basically postpones registration rather than exempting securities from registration. The purpose is to enable a new enterprise to obtain the minimum number of subscriptions required by the applicable corporation law. Thus, there may be a publicly advertised offering of preorganization certificates. But no payment is allowed until the securities are registered unless some other exemption is available."

24. Uniform Act § 402(b)(11); Revised Act § 402(14). The official comments note that "substantially all states have had some comparable provision in their securities acts for many years":

"The 'standby commission' referred to Revised Act § 402(14) permits payment to an underwriter for agreeing to purchase any portion of the securities offered to existing shareholders which are not taken down by the shareholders."

"If any other commission or remuneration is to be paid, the issuer must use the alternative notice procedure in order to claim the exemption. The Administrator ordinarily would disallow the exemption only if the commissions or other compensation appeared unreasonable in light of the risks and obligations being undertaken." *See* 15 U.S.C.A. § 77c(a)(9) which is discussed in § 4.10 *supra.*

25. Uniform Act § 402(b)(12); Revised Act § 402(15) and (16). The official commentary notes that since the 1956 Act was proposed, there has been an easing of some of the restrictions on the nature of preliminary offers which can be made, typically with a red herring prospectus or preliminary official statement. Revised Act § 402(15) and (16) allow pre-effective offers, but not sales, to be made.

Chapter 9

SECURITIES EXCHANGE ACT OF 1934—REGISTRATION AND REPORTING REQUIREMENTS; ROLE AND OPERATION OF THE SECURITIES AND EXCHANGE COMMISSION

Table of Sections

* Deleted sections 9.5.1–9.63 can be found in the Practitioner's Edition.

§ 9.1   The Securities Exchange Act of 1934—Overview

The Securities Exchange Act of 1934[1] is addressed to all aspects of securities transactions and the securities markets generally, as compared with the 1933 Act's focus on distributions of securities. The Exchange Act imposes registration and reporting requirements upon issuers of certain securities;[2] it also regulates securities dealers and other market professionals,[3] national securities exchanges,[4] self regulatory organizations such as the NASD,[5] as well as municipal securities, municipal securities dealers,[6] and government securities dealers.[7]

The Securities Exchange Act's registration and reporting provisions with regard to securities and issuers in turn trigger other reporting and remedial provisions of the Act. For example, the Exchange Act regulates the proxy machinery of reporting companies,[8] tender offers for securities of publicly traded companies,[9] insider short-swing profits,[10] manipulative practices regarding publicly traded securities[11] and prohibitions against fraud in connection with the purchase or sale of a security.[12] In addition, the Act imposes annual and periodic reporting requirements upon securities required to be registered.[13]

The Exchange Act also focuses on the securities markets' structure. This encompasses regulation of the markets themselves as well as of the broker-dealers who participate in those markets. With regard to the market system and the broker-dealer industry, the Act requires registration of all national exchanges as well as all traders, dealers and brokerage firms that are members of these exchanges.[14] Pursuant to the SEC's oversight responsibilities for exchanges and self regulatory organizations,[15] the Commission operates as a licensing authority for broker-dealers and is empowered to prohibit unprofessional conduct.[16] It also sets minimum capital requirements for licensed brokers and dealers.[17]

---

§ 9.1

1. 15 U.S.C.A. §§ 78a *et seq.*

2. 15 U.S.C.A. § 78*l*(g)(1). *See* 15 U.S.C.A. §§ 78n, 78o(d). *See* §§ 9.2–9.3 *infra*.

3. 15 U.S.C.A. §§ 78o, 78o–1. *See* § 10.2 *infra*.

4. 15 U.S.C.A. §§ 78f, 78q, 78s. *See* § 10.2 *infra*.

5. 15 U.S.C.A. § 78o–3. *See* § 10.2 *infra*. The NASD is currently the only non-exchange self-regulatory organization. From time to time consideration has been given to the formation of a municipal securities dealers' association.

6. 15 U.S.C.A. § 78o–4. *See* § 10.5 *infra*.

7. 15 U.S.C.A. § 78o–5. *See* § 10.5.1 *infra*.

8. 15 U.S.C.A. § 78n. *See* §§ 11.1–11.9 *infra*.

9. 15 U.S.C.A. §§ 78m(d), (e), 78n(d), (e), (f). *See* §§ 11.10–11.22 *infra*.

10. 15 U.S.C.A. § 78p. *See* §§ 12.2–12.7 *infra*.

11. 15 U.S.C.A. §§ 78k, 78j. *See* chapter 5 *supra* and § 12.1 *infra*.

12. 15 U.S.C.A. § 78j(b); 17 C.F.R. § 240.10b–5. *See* §§ 13.1–13.12 *infra*.

13. 15 U.S.C.A. §§ 78n, 78o. *See* § 9.3 *infra*.

14. *See* footnote 4 *supra*.

15. *See* footnote 5 *supra*.

16. *See* chapter 10 *infra*.

17. 17 C.F.R. § 240.15c3–1.

The SEC's rulemaking power is, however, limited to the those areas set out in the statute. The securities laws provide an "intelligible conceptual line excluding the Commission from corporate governance." [18] Accordingly, the D.C. Circuit Court of Appeals invalidated the Commission's attempt to regulate substantive voting rights of shareholders.[19] Such regulation goes beyond full disclosure and encroaches upon the traditional province of state corporate law.

SEC rulemaking is limited not only by the statutory mandate of the organic legislation that grants the rulemaking power; it is also limited by the requirement that the rulemaking bear a reasonable relationship to the statutory mandate's purpose.[20]

§ 9.2 Registration of Securities Under the Securities Exchange Act of 1934

Section 12(a) of the Exchange Act[1] makes it unlawful for any broker or dealer to effect any transaction in a security on a national exchange unless a 1934 Act registration has been effected for the security. Accordingly, all securities traded on a national exchange must be registered with the Commission. Registration under the 1934 Act in turn triggers the Act's periodic reporting requirements,[2] proxy regulation,[3] insider trading[4] and antimanipulation[5] prohibitions, as well as the regulation of tender offers.[6]

A registration statement under the Exchange Act[7] must disclose the following information: (1) the organization, capitalization and nature of

---

18. Business Roundtable v. SEC, 905 F.2d 406 (D.C.Cir.1990).

19. *Id. See* discussion in § 11.1 *infra.*

20. *See, e.g.,* Timpinaro v. SEC, 2 F.3d 453 (D.C.Cir.1993) (remanding SEC rule regarding large traders utilization of the Small Order Execution System since the Commission failed to establish that the assertions underlying the rule's prohibition were supported in fact). Although the court remanded for further agency proceedings, it let the rule stand pending remand.

§ 9.2

1. 15 U.S.C.A. § 78*l*(a) (1976). The registration requirement is set forth in section 12(g). 15 U.S.C.A. § 78*l*(g). *See* Checklist for Registration of Securities Under Section 12(g) of the Securities Exchange Act of 1934, 25 Bus.Law. 1631 (1970).

2. *See* § 9.3 *infra. See generally* Carl W. Schneider & Jason M. Shargel, "Now That You Are Publicly Owned * * * ", 36 Bus.Law. 1631 (1981).

3. 15 U.S.C.A. §§ 78n(a)–(c). *See* §§ 11.1–11.10 *infra.*

4. 15 U.S.C.A. § 78p. *See* §§ 12.2–12.7 *infra.*

5. 15 U.S.C.A. § 78i. Section 9 applies only to those securities listed on a national exchange. *Id. See also* section 10 and section 18's express antifraud remedies for false SEC filings. 15 U.S.C.A. §§ 78j, 78r. *See* §§ 12.1, 12.8 *infra.*

6. 15 U.S.C.A. §§ 78m(d)–(e), 78n(d)–(f).

7. The 1934 Act requirements defer to the disclosure called for in Regulation S–K, 17 C.F.R. §§ 229.101 *et seq. See* Regulation S–K, Item 402, dealing with management compensation, which was recently amended in the Exch. Act Rel. No. 34–20220 (Sec. Act Rel. No. 33–6486 (Sept. 23, 1983)).

For example, although section 12(b)(6) calls for reports of compensation in excess of $20,000 per year, new Item 402 speaks in terms of cash compensation in excess of $60,000 per year. 15 U.S.C.A. § 78*l*(b)(6); 17 C.F.R. § 229.402. *See also* SEC Form 10.

the business; (2) the terms, rights and privileges of all classes of outstanding securities; (3) the terms of any securities offered by the issuer within the preceding three years; (4) the names of all of the issuer's officers, directors, underwriters and holders of more than ten percent of any class of equity security of the issuer; (5) compensation of employees other than officers and directors that exceeds sixty thousand dollars per year in cash; (6) description of employee bonus and profit sharing plans; (7) description of management and service contracts; (8) description of options that exist or are to be created with regard to the issuer's securities; (9) all material[8] contracts made by the issuer in the past two years or which are to be executed in whole or in part after the filing and that are outside of the ordinary course of the issuer's business; (10) balance sheets for not more than the three preceding years to be certified as required by the Commission;[9] (11) profit and loss statements for the same period; (12) such further financial statements as the SEC deems necessary for investor protection; and (13) copies of the articles of incorporation or other organizing documents as well as any material contracts to which the issuer is a party as the Commission may require.[10] The Exchange Act provides that the SEC may suspend trading in any securities not complying with the registration reporting provisions unless an exemption is available.[11]

In addition to the above mentioned registration and disclosure requirements for exchange listed securities, the Securities Exchange Act of 1934 also imposes registration requirements on certain over-the-counter securities. By virtue of section 12(g)(1) of the Exchange Act and Rule 12g–1, registration statements must be filed by issuers which have both a class of equity securities having more than five hundred shareholders, and more than five million dollars in total assets.[12]

---

8. Rule 12b–2 defines materiality as follows: "The term 'material,' when used to qualify a requirement for the furnishing of information as to any subject, limits the information required to those matters to which there is a substantial likelihood that a reasonable investor would attach importance in determining whether to buy or sell the securities registered." 17 C.F.R. § 240.12b–2. Materiality is discussed in §§ 11.4, 13.5A *infra*. *See generally* Alison G. Anderson, The Disclosure Process in Federal Securities Regulation, 25 Hastings L.J. 311 (1974); James O. Hewitt, Developing Concepts of Materiality and Disclosure, 32 Bus.Law. 887 (1977).

9. Proper form, procedures, and practices for the accounting statements are found in SEC Regulation S–X. *See also* the financial reporting releases compiled in 5 Fed.Sec. L.Rep. (CCH) ¶¶ 72, 401 *et seq.*

10. 15 U.S.C.A. § 78*l*(b).

11. 15 U.S.C.A. § 78*l*(f). Exemptions from 1934 Act registration are discussed *infra*.

12. The statute requires registration for companies with assets of more than one million dollars but Rule 12g–1 exempts issuers with assets under three million. 15 U.S.C.A. § 78*l*(g)(1); 17 C.F.R. § 240.12g–1. The 1934 Act registration requirements for over-the-counter securities were added in 1964. Securities Acts Amendments of 1964, Pub.L. 88–467, 78 Stat. 565. *See generally* Thomas G. Meeker, Extending Disclosure to Nonlisted Companies, 20 Bus.Law. 265 (1965); Richard M. Phillips & Morgan Shipman, An Analysis of the Securities Acts Amendments of 1964, 1964 Duke L.J. 706; Hugh L. Sowards, The Securities Acts Amendments of 1964: New Registration and Reporting Requirements, 19 U.Miami L.Rev. 33 (1964); Comment, The Securities Acts Amendments of 1964: Effect on the Over-the-Counter Market, 39 St. John's L.Rev. 111 (1964). *See also* Alexander H. Frey, Federal Regulation of the Over-the-Counter Securities Market, 106 U.Pa.L.Rev. 1 (1957).

Section 12(g)(2)[13] sets forth exemptions from the over-the-counter equity security registration requirements. Section 12(g)(1) does not apply to: (a) securities listed and registered on national securities exchanges as those securities must be registered under section 12(a); (b) securities of issuers that are registered under the Investment Company Act of 1940;[14] (c) securities of savings and loans, building and loans associations and similar institutions subject to state or federal authority that represent other than non-withdrawable capital issued; (d) securities of not-for-profit, charitable issuers; (e) securities issued by "cooperative associations" as defined in the Agricultural Marketing Act;[15] (f) securities issued by certain other mutual or cooperative associations; (g) certain insurance company securities; and (h) certain employee stock-bonus, pension or profit-sharing plans.[16] There is an exemption from 1934 Act registration for securities of foreign issuers, over-the-counter American Depositary Shares ("ADS's"), and American Depositary Receipts ("ADR's") representing such securities.[17] This exemption was modified in 1983 and is no longer available for NASDAQ listed securities except that securities qualifying prior to that time retain their exempt status.[18] The Commission has also given certain limited exemptions by administrative rules.[19]

The issuer's disclosure and reporting obligations do not end with the filing of the Exchange Act registration statements. Exchange-listed securities as well as those subject to section 12(g)(1)'s requirements for over-the-counter equity securities incur periodic reporting obligations as

---

Section 12 registration requirements cease when the registered securities have fewer than three hundred shareholders or when there are fewer than five hundred shareholders on the last day of each of the past three years. 17 C.F.R. § 240.12g–4(a).

13. 15 U.S.C.A. § 78*l*(g)(2).

14. *See* section 8 of the Investment Company Act of 1940, 15 U.S.C.A. § 80a–8; chapter 17 *infra*.

15. 12 U.S.C.A. §§ 1141 *et seq.*

16. 15 U.S.C.A. § 78*l*(g)(2).

17. 15 U.S.C.A. § 78*l*(g)(3); 17 C.F.R. § 240.12g3–2. *See* Sec.Act Rel. No. 33–6493 (Oct. 6, 1983). The exemption depends on annually furnishing the Commission with all information that must be disclosed according to the laws of the issuer's domicile.

18. *Ibid.* NASDAQ is the National Association of Securities Dealers' Automated Quotation System. *See* § 14.2 *infra*.

19. These exemptions are:

1. A very limited *temporary* exemption for certain banks. 17 C.F.R. § 240.12a–1.

2. A *temporary* exemption for securities secured by property owned by persons other than the issuer. 17 C.F.R. § 240.12a–2.

3. A *temporary* exemption for certain securities of issuers in bankruptcy, receivership, or reorganization proceedings. 17 C.F.R. § 240.12a–3.

4. An exemption for warrants with no more than a ninety day expiration period that have been issued under a 1933 Act registration statement that also covers the underlying security. 17 C.F.R. § 240.12a–4.

5. A *temporary* exemption for securities substituted for other securities. 17 C.F.R. § 240.12a–5.

6. Options not written by the issuer where the underlying security is registered and traded on a national exchange. 17 C.F.R. § 240.12a–6.

established by section 13(a).[20] These periodic reports include the 10–K annual report and the 10–Q quarterly report. Also required on Form 8–K are filings of certain specified material changes in the issuer's condition or operations.[21]

Beyond setting forth the periodic reporting requirements, 1934 Act registration triggers other disclosure provisions. By virtue of section 14(a),[22] all proxy material for registered securities must be filed with the Commission. Section 14(d) requires SEC filings of almost all tender offers to purchase equity securities subject to the reporting requirements.[23] Anyone who purchases five percent of any class of any 1934 Act registered equity security must file a full disclosure as to the purpose of such acquisition pursuant to section 13(d).[24] This filing requirement applies to transactions that put the purchaser beyond the five percent threshold. Additionally, all purchases or sales of equity securities by officers, directors, and beneficial owners of ten percent of any class of equity security must be recorded in filed reports of such transactions pursuant to section 16(a).[25] In addition to any implied remedies that may exist,[26] investors who are injured in reliance upon materially misleading statements in filed documents may bring suit under section 18(a).[27] Liability also exists for those engaging in manipulative conduct[28] and for ill-gotten insider short-swing profits.[29]

Section 12(a) requires 1934 Act registration of all securities, whether debt or equity if they are registered or traded on a national securities exchange. In contrast, section 12(g)(1)'s registration requirement for over-the-counter securities applies only to equity securities. There is no *per se* registration requirement for over-the-counter debt securities. Part of the gap for non-exchange-traded debt securities is filled by section 15(d) of the Exchange Act.[30] Section 15(d) requires that all persons who issue securities pursuant to a 1933 Act registration statement[31] must file all of the periodic reports required by section 13 of the Exchange Act. Section 15(d)'s periodic reporting requirements are sus-

---

20. 15 U.S.C.A. § 78m(a). *See* § 9.3 *infra.*

21. *See* 17 C.F.R. § 240.13a–11. *See also, e.g.,* MTD Service Corp. v. Weldotron, 1994 WL 455154, [1994–1995 Transfer Binder] Fed. Sec. L. Rep. (CCH) ¶ 98,395 (S.D.N.Y.1994) (8–K filing was not materially misleading for alleged failure to disclose that the company needed to raise cash in order to cure a breach of its loan covenant).

22. 15 U.S.C.A. § 78n(a). *See* Rule 14a–6, 17 C.F.R. § 240.14a–6(j). §§ 11.1–11.9 *infra.*

23. 15 U.S.C.A. § 78n(d). Issuer tender offers for its own shares are covered by section 13(e). 15 U.S.C.A. § 78m(e). *See* §§ 11.10–11.22 *infra.*

24. 15 U.S.C.A. § 78m(d). *See* §§ 11.11, 11.18 *infra.*

25. 15 U.S.C.A. § 78p(a). *See* § 12.2 *infra.*

26. *See* chapter 13 *infra.*

27. 15 U.S.C.A. § 78r(a). *See* § 12.8 *infra.* This may be true more in theory than in practice as liability is generally promised under Rule 10b–5 rather than section 18(a).

28. 15 U.S.C.A. § 78i(e). *See* § 12.1 *infra.*

29. 15 U.S.C.A. § 78p(b). *See* §§ 12.2–12.7 *infra.*

30. 15 U.S.C.A. § 78*o*(d).

31. *See* chapters 2–4 *supra.*

pended in any subsequent year in which the securities issued pursuant to the 1933 Act registration statement are held by less than three hundred shareholders of record.[32] Most of the 1934 Act regulation of the proxy machinery,[33] tender offers,[34] and short-swing insider trading,[35] is limited to issuers whose securities are registered under section 12 and not to those whose periodic reporting obligations arise solely under section 15(d). However, section 18(a)'s provision for express liability[36] to purchasers and sellers of securities relying on materially misleading documents filed with the Commission applies to section 15(d) reporting companies as well. In addition, section 15(d) reporting company status can help an issuer in taking advantage of exemptions from 1933 Act registration.[37] As discussed in chapter 4 of this treatise, a number of the 1933 Act exemptions are available only to 1934 Act reporting companies.

In addition to the information provided by section 12 registration and the periodic reporting under sections 13(a) and 15(d),[38] there may be common law rights to information. For example, state corporate statutes and the common law both establish that a corporate stockholder who states a proper purpose therefor has a right to inspect relevant corporate books and records.[39] These common law and statutory rights of inspection under appropriate circumstances allow shareholders to look beyond the federal filings.

Exemption for Securities of Certain Foreign Private Issuers

As discussed more fully in a subsequent section,[40] foreign private issuers whose securities are publicly traded in the United States fre-

---

32. Transactions that result in the cessation of reporting obligations may be subject to the "going private" rules, 15 U.S.C.A. § 78m(e); 17 C.F.R. § 240.13e–3. *See* § 11.17 *infra*.

When reporting requirements cease, it is prospectively only. Accordingly, the fact that an issuer is no longer required to file reports in the future does not affect its obligations for past reports. *See, e.g.,* Chester County Bancshares, Inc., 26 Sec. Reg. & L. Rep. (BNA) 568 (SEC No Action Letter Available April 1, 1994) (dissolution of bank holding company at the end of 1993 did not alleviate issuer of its need to file a Form 10K annual report for 1993).

33. 15 U.S.C.A. § 78n(a), (b), (c); 17 C.F.R. §§ 240.14a–1 *et seq.* *See* §§ 11.1–11.9 *infra.* *Cf.* In re AM International, Inc. Securities Litigation, 606 F.Supp. 600 (S.D.N.Y. 1985) (outside directors who sit on the audit committee occupy a special position and, as such, are much closer to being treated as inside directors for purposes of liability for misinformation in the 10–K annual filing).

34. 15 U.S.C.A. §§ 78m(d), (e), (f), 78n(d), (f). *See* §§ 11.10–11.19 *infra.*

35. 15 U.S.C.A. § 78p. *See* §§ 12.2–12.7 *infra.*

36. 15 U.S.C.A. § 78r(a). *See* § 12.1 *infra.* The section covers all required filings but does not generally apply to the annual report distributed to shareholders. 17 C.F.R. § 240.14a–3(b). *See* § 11.2 *infra.*

37. *E.g.* Regulation D and Rule 144. 17 C.F.R. §§ 230.144, 230.501–506. *See* §§ 4.17–4.26 *supra.* *See also* Rules 137–139 which permit dissemination of certain recommendations regarding securities of issuers in 1933 Act registration where the issuer is subject to either registration under section 12 of the Exchange Act or 15(d)'s periodic reporting requirements, 17 C.F.R. §§ 230.137–139. *See* §§ 2.4, 2.5 *supra.*

38. *See* § 9.3 *infra.*

39. *See generally,* 2 James D. Cox, Thomas L. Hazen & F. Hodge O'Neal, Corporations ch. 13 (1995); Harry G. Henn & John R. Alexander, Law of Corporations § 199 (3d ed.1983). *See also* § 11.7 *infra.*

40. *See* § 14.2 *infra.*

quently utilize American Depositary Shares (ADS's) and American Depositary Receipts (ADR's) in order to establish the United States public market. In such a case, absent an exemption, registration would ordinarily be required under the Exchange Act.[41] SEC Rule 12g3–2,[42] provides such an exemption. The exemption is conditioned upon an annual filing of information with the SEC that is generally far less complete than would otherwise be required by the Exchange Act.[43] Except for securities that were exempt prior to amendment of the rule in 1983, the exemption is limited to securities traded and ADR's traded on a national exchange as opposed to being traded through the NASD's automated quotation system.[44] In addition, the exemption is not available for private foreign issuers if either (1) more than fifty percent voting control is directly or indirectly vested in citizens of the United States or (2) more than fifty percent of the directors are United States residents.[45] Additionally, in order to qualify for the exemption, the private foreign issuer may not have had registration or reporting obligations under the Exchange Act during the past eighteen months.[46]

Exemption for Securities of Certain Insurance Companies

Section 12(g)(2)(G) of the Act[47] provides an exemption from most of the Exchange Act registration, reporting, and other requirements for securities issued by certain insurance companies. In order to qualify for the exemption, there are three conditions that must be met. In essence, the three conditions are designed to assure that investors receive protections similar to many of those which would be available if the company were registered under the 1934 Act. First, in order to qualify for the exemption, the insurance company must be a domiciliary of a state which requires the filing of an annual statement which satisfies or substantially conforms to the standards established by the National Association of Insurance Commissioners;[48] additionally, the insurance company must be in compliance with its domiciliary state's annual report requirement.[49] Second, the domiciliary state must require that the insurance company comply with proxy solicitation and shareholder consent requirements that conform to the standards established by the

---

41. Similarly, the initial and secondary distributions of such securities will have to be registered under the 1933 Act absent an applicable exemption.

42. 17 C.F.R. § 240.12g3–2. *See* the discussion in § 14.2 *infra*.

43. Rule 12g3–2(b), 17 C.F.R. § 240.12g3–2(b).

44. Rule 12g3–2(d)(3), 17 C.F.R. § 240.12g3–2(d)(3)

45. Rule 3b4(c), 17 C.F.R. § 240.3b–4(c) ("definition of foreign private issuer").

46. Rule 12g3–2(c)(1), 17 C.F.R. § 240.12g3–2(c)(1). This disqualification does not apply, however, to Canadian securities that were registered under the 1933 Act under one of the MJDS disclosure forms (F–7, F–8, F–9, F–10, or F–80). Additionally, the exemption is not available for securities issued in a merger or other exchange of securities that were registered under section 12 or subject to section 15(d)'s reporting requirements. Rule 12g3–2(c)(2), 17 C.F.R. § 240.12g3–2(c)(2).

47. 15 U.S.C.A. § 78*l*(2)(G).

48. Section 12g(2)(G)(i), 15 U.S.C.A. § 78*l*(2)(G)(i).

49. *Id.*

National Association of Insurance Commissioners.[50] Third, in addition to the annual statement and proxy solicitation requirements, the domiciliary state must subject the insurance companies beneficial owners, officers, and directors to the requirements of section 16 of the Exchange Act,[51] including the reporting requirements applicable to share acquisitions and dispositions[52] as well as disgorgement of short-swing profits.[53]

§ 9.3 Annual, Periodic, and Continuous Reporting Requirements for Issuers

Section 13(a)(2) of the Exchange Act[1] requires all issuers of equity securities subject to section 12's registration requirements[2] to file annual and quarterly reports and copies thereof as provided by the applicable SEC rules. When dealing with section 12(a) registrations (for securities traded on a national securities exchange), duplicate originals of the annual and quarterly reports must be filed with the securities exchanges on which the securities are listed. For all section 12 registrations, the issuer's first annual report must be filed for the fiscal year following the last full fiscal year reported in the section 12 registration statement.[3] Most issuers must pay a two hundred and fifty dollar nonrefundable fee upon filing of the annual report.[4]

The general form for annual reports of issuers subject to the Exchange Act's registration and reporting requirements is Form 10–K.[5] The Commission provides alternative forms for special situation issuers. Employee stock purchase, savings and similar plans must use Form 11–K.[6] Form 18–K[7] is for securities issued by foreign governments and political subdivisions. Registered management investment companies use Form N–1R,[8] while small business investment companies are to file

---

50. Section 12g(2)(G)(ii), 15 U.S.C.A. § 78*l*(2)(G)(ii).

51. 15 U.S.C.A. § 78p.

52. 15 U.S.C.A. § 78p(a). *See* § 12.2 *infra.*

53. 15 U.S.C.A. § 78p(b). *See* §§ 12.2–12.5 *infra.* Also included would be the prohibitions against short sales and sales against the box. *See* § section 16(c), 15 U.S.C.A. § 78p(c); § 12.6 *infra.*

§ 9.3

1. 15 U.S.C.A. § 78m(a). Additional affirmative disclosure requirements are discussed in § 13.10 *infra.* *See generally* J. Robert Brown, Jr., Corporate Communications and the Federal Securities Laws, 53 Geo.Wash.L.Rev. 741 (1985). Richard H. Rowe, Administration and Enforcement of the Periodic Reporting Provision of the Securities Exchange Act of 1934, 25 Okla.L.Rev. 157 (1972); Carl W. Schneider & Jason M. Shargel, "Now That You Are Publicly Owned * * * ", 36 Bus.Law. 1631 (1981). *See also, e.g.,* Scott Hodes, Some Pros and Cons of Listing on a Securities Exchange, 10 The Prac.Law. 41 (Apr.1964).

2. 15 U.S.C.A. § 78d(a), (g)(1). *See* § 9.2 *supra.*

3. 17 C.F.R. § 240.13a–1.

4. *Id.* The filing fee does not apply to annual reports for issuers registered under the Public Utility Holding Company Act of 1935 or the Investment Company Act of 1940. These two acts are discussed in chapters 15, 17 *infra.*

5. *See* 4 Fed.Sec.Law Rep. (CCH) ¶ 31,101.

6. *See id.* ¶ 31,151.

7. *See id.* ¶¶ 32,001–32,004.

8. *See* 5 Fed.Sec. Law Rep. (CCH) ¶ 52,301.

their annual reports on Form N–5R.[9]

SEC Rule 13a–13[10] sets out the Exchange Act's quarterly reporting requirements for issuers of registered securities which are generally to be filed on Form 10–Q.[11] By virtue of Rules 13a–13(b) and (c)[12] the quarterly reporting requirements do not apply to either (1) investment companies filing quarterly reports under Rule 13a–12[13] or (2) foreign private issuers filing reports under Rule 13a–16[14] on Form 6K. Furthermore, certain life insurance companies need not complete Part I of Form 10–Q.[15]

In 1992, the SEC introduced a number of small business initiatives that were designed to facilitate registration and reporting from small business issuers.[16] A small business issuer is defined as a company with revenues of less than $25 million, provided that the aggregate market value of the issuer's voting stock held by non-affiliates does not exceed $25 million.[17] Regulation S–B which replaces Regulation S–K as the basic disclosure guide for small business issuers. In addition, simplified forms 10–SB (registration of securities), 10–KSB (annual report), and 10–QSB (quarterly report) are now available for 1934 Act periodic filings by small business issuers.

In recent years the SEC has been experimenting with an electronic data gathering analysis and retrieval project known as EDGAR under which the SEC accepts selected filings such as 10–Ks, 10–Qs, and 8–Ks. These filings can be made through telephone transmission of data, magnetic tape, or diskettes.[18] The Commission has continued to expand the scope of the EDGAR program[19] and has adopted rules that will

---

9. *See id.* ¶ 51,481.

10. 17 C.F.R. § 240.13a–13.

11. 4 Fed.Sec.Law Rep. (CCH) ¶ 31,031.

12. 17 C.F.R. § 240.13a–13(b), (c).

13. 17 C.F.R. § 240.13a–12.

14. 17 C.F.R. § 240.13a–16.

15. 17 C.F.R. § 240.13a–13(c).

16. *See* Sec. Act Rel. No. 33–6949, 6 Fed.Sec.L.Rep. (CCH) ¶ 72,439 (SEC July 30, 1992).

17. 17 C.F.R. § 240.12b–2. At the time of the adoption of the definition, the SEC estimated that there were 3,000 public reporting companies that would qualify as small business issuers. Sec.Act Rel. No. 33–6949, 6 Fed.Sec.L.Rep. (CCH) ¶ 72,439 at p. 62,171 (SEC July 30, 1992).

18. *See* Survey, Federal Securities Regulation, 41 Bus.Law. 925, 966–67 (1986). *See generally* Amy C. Goodman & Patricia M. Jayne, EDGAR, The SEC's Disclosure System, 19 Rev.Sec. & Commodities Reg. 161 (1986); Donald C. Langevoort, Information Technology and the Structure of Securities Regulation, 98 Harv.L.Rev. 747 (1985). The SEC has proposed mandatory electronic filings, subject to exceptions. Sec.Act Rel.No. 33–6651 (June 26, 1986).

19. *See* Sec. Act Rel. No. 33–7123, [1994–1995 Transfer Binder] Fed. Sec. L. Rep. (CCH) ¶85,473 (Dec. 19, 1994) (analyzing the commission's interim EDGAR rules); Sec.Act Rel. No. 33–6933, [1991–1992 Transfer Binder] Fed.Sec.L.Rep. (CCH) ¶84,942 (SEC April 20, 1992) (temporary rules applicable to filings with the Division of Corporation Finance); Sec.Act Rel. No. 33–6934, [1991–1992 Transfer Binder] Fed.Sec.L.Rep. (CCH) ¶84,943 (SEC April 20, 1992) (investment company and investment manager filings submitted to the Division of Investment Management); Pub.Util.Holding Co. Act Rel. No. 35–25,520,

implement the operational phase.[20] Under the new rules, mandated electronic filing for pilot program participants and certain volunteers began in April 1993; all registrants should be phased in by mid–1996.[21]

Beyond the quarterly reports, Rule 13a–10[22] requires issuers of registered securities to file interim reports in certain situations. Under the rule whenever an issuer changes the term of its fiscal year, an interim report must be filed not more than one hundred and twenty days following the close of the interim period. Also, Rule 13a–2[23] defines the reporting requirements for issuers who are successors to issuers of section 12 registered securities.

In addition to the foregoing periodic reporting requirements, section 13(a)(1) of the Exchange Act[24] provides that all issuers of registered securities shall file such additional current information as the Commission shall require to keep reasonably current all statements filed pursuant to section 12 of the Act. The periodic reporting requirements assure that public information is updated every quarter but that may not be sufficient in all cases. SEC Rule 13a–11[25] requires the filing of current reports within 15 days of specified material changes in the issuer's financial condition or method of operations. Form 8–K is the appropriate form for these reports. The SEC has cautioned that in addition, other material developments are subject to "prompt" disclosure by way of press release or otherwise.[26] The Commission has not made it clear whether there is an affirmative duty to disclose in the absence of insider trading or a timely required SEC filing.[27] The statutory language does not appear to impose a disclosure duty absent a line-item disclosure required by the statute or SEC rule. However, both the New York and American Stock Exchanges expressly impose a prompt affirmative disclosure obligation;[28] whether a similar requirement can be implied from the

---

[1991–1992 Transfer Binder] Fed.Sec.L.Rep. (CCH) ¶ 84,941 (SEC April 20, 1992) (applicable to public utility holding company filings).

20. Sec.Act Rels. 33–6944, 33–6947 [1992 Transfer Binder] Fed.Sec.L.Rep. (CCH) ¶¶ 85,016, 85,019 (July 23, 1992).

21. *See* the discussion of EDGAR in § 3.3 *supra*. *See also* Appendix B—*infra*.

22. 17 C.F.R. § 240.13a–10.

23. 17 C.F.R. § 240.13a–2.

24. 15 U.S.C.A. § 78m(a)(1).

25. 17 C.F.R. § 240.13a–11. The time for filing varies depending upon the type of disclosure which trigger the filing obligation. The material developments that must be reported in timely fashion on Form 8–K include: (1) changes in control of the issuer, (2) significant acquisitions or dispositions of assets by the issuer or majority owned subsidiaries, (3) the institution of bankruptcy or receivership proceedings, (4) changes in the registrant's certifying accountant, and (5) director resignations. The form also provides: "The registrant may, at its option, report under this item any events, with respect to which information is not otherwise called for by this form, that the registrant deems of importance to security holders." Form 8–K, item 5.

26. Exch.Act Rel.No. 34–8995 (Oct. 15, 1970).

27. *Id. See* § 13.10 *infra*. Insider trading is discussed in § 13.9 *infra*.

28. NYSE Company Manual, 2 Fed.Sec.L.Rep. (CCH) ¶ 23,121; American Stock Exch. Guide (CCH) ¶¶ 401–406.

Exchange Act and Rule 10b–5 is highly doubtful.[29]

An issuer whose securities are not registered nevertheless will have to file the same periodic reports pursuant to section 15(d)[30] if it issued the securities under a 1933 Act registration. Section 15(d) reporting requirements are suspended when the number of securities holders falls below three hundred.[31] Successor corporations must continue the periodic reporting obligations of their predecessors.[32]

In addition to section 13's periodic reporting requirements, further disclosures are required by the Foreign Corrupt Practices Act amendments[33] which have a very broad reach. The amendments were so broadly drafted as to require neither foreign involvement nor corrupt practices.[34] Section 13(b)(2)[35] requires all issuers subject to section 12 or section 15(d) to:

(A) make and keep books, records, and accounts, which, in reasonable detail, accurately and fairly reflect the transactions and dispositions of the assets of the issuer; and

(B) devise and maintain a system of internal accounting controls sufficient to provide reasonable assurances that:

(i) transactions are executed in accordance with management's general or specific authorization;

(ii) transactions are recorded as necessary (I) to permit preparation of financial statements in conformity with generally accepted accounting principles or any other criteria applicable to such statement, and (II) to maintain accountability for assets;

(iii) access to assets is permitted only in accordance with management's general or specific authorization; and

(iv) the recorded accountability for assets is compared with the existing assets at reasonable intervals and appropriate action is taken with respect to any difference.

When initially adopted these internal controls requirements were the

---

29. 17 C.F.R. § 240.10b–5. *See* § 13.10 *infra*. It can be argued that an affirmative disclosure obligation can be found in Rule 10b–5(3)'s prohibition of conduct that operates as a fraud.

30. 15 U.S.C.A. § 78*o*(d).

31. *Id.*

32. *See* SEC v. Research Resources, Inc., 1986 WL 11446, (S.D.N.Y.1986) (Unpublished Case).

33. Pub.L. No. 95–213, 91 Stat. 1494 (Dec. 19, 1977). *See* § 19.2 *infra* (Practitioner's Edition only).

34. *See generally* Program, Practical Implications of the Foreign Corrupt Practices Act of 1977, and Recent Developments, 35 Bus.Law. 1713 (1980). *See also* authorities in note 35 *infra*.

35. 15 U.S.C.A. § 78m(b)(2). *See, e.g.,* In re Robert S. Harrison, Exch.Act Rel. No. 34–22466 (Sept. 26, 1985). An issuer must institute controls to monitor the activities of its chief financial officer. In re Tonka Corp., Exch.Act Rel. No. 34–22448 (Sept. 24, 1985).

subject of considerable controversy.[36] There have been several proposals for repeal or sharp reduction in scope.

There are a number of especially sensitive disclosure problems under the 1934 Act. These include disclosure of executive compensation,[37] projections of future performance,[38] and disclosures related to corporate takeovers.[39]

Issuers subject to the periodic reporting requirements may take advantage of the relatively new integrated disclosure program. Reporting companies now qualify for short-form registration of public offerings under the 1933 Act.[40]

§ 9.4 Accounting Requirements

In addition to its disclosure requirements, the Exchange Act imposes numerous financial reporting and accounting requirements.[1] Regulation S–X[2] sets forth the SEC's accounting rules for the preparation of SEC filings and the audited financial statements required by the 1933 and 1934 Acts. The Commission's general approach to financial reporting has been to rely upon generally accepted accounting principles (GAAP)

---

36. *See, e.g.,* Mehren, Introduction to the Foreign Corrupt Practices Act of 1970—Law Procedures and Practices, 10 Inst.Sec.Reg. 65 (1979); Program, *supra* footnote 34; Note, Effective Enforcement of the Foreign Corrupt Practices Act, 32 Stan.L.Rev. 561 (1980); Note, Accounting for Corporate Misconduct Abroad: The Foreign Corrupt Practices Act of 1977, 12 Corn.Int'l L.J. 293 (1979).

37. *See* § 11.6 *infra.*

38. *See* § 3.7 *supra.*

39. *See* §§ 11.11–11.22 *infra.*

40. 1933 Act Forms S–2, S–3 and integrated disclosure are discussed in § 3.3 *supra.*

§ 9.4

1. *See generally* James D. Cox, Financial Information, Accounting and the Law: Cases and Materials (1980); Louis H. Rappaport, SEC Accounting Practice and Procedure (3rd ed. 1972); Stanley Siegel and David A. Siegel, Accounting and Financial Disclosure—A Guide to Basic Concepts (1983); Geoffrey T. Chalmers, Overaccountable Accountants? A Proposal for Clarification of the Legal Responsibilities Stemming from the Audit Function, 16 Wm. and Mary L.Rev. 71 (1974); Samuel H. Gruenbaum & Marc I. Steinberg, Accountants' Liability and Responsibility, 13 Loyola (L.A.) U.L.Rev. 247 (1980); Werner F. Ebke, In Search of Alternatives; Comparative Reflections on Corporate Governance and the Independent Auditor's Responsibilities, 79 Nw.U.L.Rev. 663 (1984); David B. Isbell, An Overview of Accountants' Duties and Liabilities Under the Federal Securities Laws and a Closer Look at Whistle–Blowing, 35 Ohio St.L. 5.261 (1974); Stephen R. Miller and John T. Subak, Impact of Federal Securities Laws: Liabilities of Officers, Directors and Accountants, 30 Bus.Law. 387 (1975); Symposium, Advisors to Management: Responsibilities and Liabilities of Lawyers and Accountants, 30 Bus.Law. 227 (1975); Symposium, Accounting and the Federal Securities Laws, 28 Vand.L.Rev. 1 (1975); Craig M. Walker, Accountants' Liability, 63 Marq.L.Rev. 243 (1979); Anthony M. Vernava & Gerard W. Hepp, Responsibility of the Accountant Under the Federal Securities Exchange Act of 1934, 6 J.Corp.L. 317 (1981).

For a recent analysis of problems involving financial reporting, *see* Report of the National Commission on Fraudulent Financial Reporting (October 1987); Roberta S. Karmel, Treadway Commission and the Auditors, N.Y.L.J. p. 3 (Aug. 18, 1988).

2. 17 C.F.R. §§ 210.1–01–210.12–29. *See also* 17 C.F.R. §§ 256.00–1–256a.37 (Uniform System of Accounts for Mutual Service Companies and Subsidiary Service Companies under the Public Utility Holding Company Act of 1935). The Public Utility Holding Company Act is discussed in chapter 15 *infra.*

and generally accepted auditing standards (GAAS).[3] On occasion the SEC will adopt different standards for use in its disclosure documents.[4]

In addition to the financial reports required in connection with 1933 Act registration[5] of securities offerings and those called for by the 1934 Act periodic reporting requirements,[6] section 13(b)(2) of the 1934 Act requires the maintenance of certain corporate accounts.[7] Although adopted as part of the Foreign Corrupt Practices Act of 1977,[8] section 13(b)(2) is not limited to corrupt practices nor does it require foreign conduct.

Section 13(b)(2)(A) requires accounts reflecting "in reasonable detail" the issuer's transactions and dispositions of assets.[9] Section 13(b)(2)(B) requires that the issuer establish a system of internal accounting controls in order to provide "reasonable assurances" that (1) management has either specifically or generally authorized all transactions, (2) all transactions are accounted for in accordance with generally accepted accounting principles or other appropriate standard, (3) management has authorized, either generally or specifically, all access to the issuer's assets, and (4) "the recorded accountability for assets is compared with existing assets at reasonable intervals and appropriate action is taken with respect to any differences."[10] These requirements have sparked a great deal of controversy.[11] It has been held that inaccurate

---

3. *See* J. Cox *supra* footnote 1 at 160 ("The SEC has deferred to the private sector as the primary standard setter but continues to guide the form and substance of disclosure of financial information in important ways. Examples include the issuance of Regulation S–X, an extensive, detailed description of the form and content of financial statements required to be filed; the issuance of its Accounting Series Releases (ASR's) dealing with accounting matters not specifically dealt with by any of the private sector's bulletins, opinions, or statements; and beginning in 1975, the issuance of Staff Accounting Bulletins, which do not have the official sanction of the SEC, but represent the accounting approach, interpretation, and practices of the staff in administering the disclosure requirements. Occasionally, however, the SEC has prescribed in its ASRs a different accounting method than that established by the private sector") (footnotes omitted); Marshall S. Armstrong, The Work and Workings of the Financial Accounting Standards Board, 29 Bus.Law. 145 (1974); James F. Strother, The Establishment of Generally Accepted Accounting Principles and Generally Accepted Auditing Standards, 28 Vand.L.Rev. 201 (1975).

Generally Accepted Accounting Principles are adopted by the Federal Accounting Standards Board (FASB). Generally Accepted Auditing Standards are adopted by the American Institute of Certified Public Accountants (AICPA).

4. *Cf.* Checkosky v. SEC, 23 F.3d 452 (D.C.Cir.1994) (the SEC appeared to give its own interpretation of GAAS and GAAP but the court remanded for further explanation).

5. For discussion of 1933 Act disclosure requirements, *see* §§ 3.3–3.4 *supra*.

6. *See* § 9.3 *supra*.

7. 15 U.S.C.A. § 78m(b)(2).

8. Pub.L. 95–213, 95th Cong. 1st Sess., 91 Stat. 1491 (1977). The Foreign Corrupt Practices Act is discussed in § 19.2 *infra* (Practitioner's Edition only).

9. 15 U.S.C.A. § 78m(b)(2)(A).

10. 15 U.S.C.A. § 78m(b)(2)(B).

11. Timothy Atkeson, Kenneth J. Bialkin, Philip Chenok, Ralph C. Ferrara, Harvey L. Pitt, Mark M. Richard & John R. Stevenson, Foreign Corrupt Practices Act of 1977 and the Regulation of Questionable Payments—A Program by Committee on Federal Regulation of Securities, 34 Bus.Law. 623 (1979); Ebke *supra* footnote 1; ABA Committee on Corporate Law and Accounting, A Guide to the New Section 13(b)(2) Accounting Requirements of Securities Exchange Act of 1934, 34 Bus. Law. 307 (1978); Mehren, Introduction to the

books will not avoid being in violation of the Act merely because the inaccuracies are "small in dollar amount."[12]

The weight of authority supports the view that there is no implied private remedy for failure to maintain corporate books in accordance with section 13(b)(2) and generally accepted accounting principles.[13]

On a related point, the Supreme Court has held that accountants' workpapers generated in the course of an audit and review of an issuer's financial records are subject to IRS subpoena and are not entitled to the protection under the work-product doctrine which would require a showing of good cause prior to compelling production.[14] The Court pointed out that independent auditors perform a "public watchdog function" and thus public obligation acts against application of the work-product immunity from document production.[15]

The SEC has shown a special concern for the practice of opinion shopping whereby issuers seek out auditors who will consent to questionable accounting practices.[16] Another area of SEC concern with regard to accounting has been vigorous enforcement efforts with regard to "cooked books."[17] The SEC has proposed mandatory peer review of independent accountants who certify filings with the Commission.[18]

§ 9.5 Civil and Criminal Enforcement: SEC Injunctions, Investigations, Parallel Proceedings; Administrative Hearings and Disciplinary Sanctions

In fact, the Commission has all administrative powers save one. The SEC does not adjudicate disputes between private parties. The Securities and Exchange Commission has a wide variety of enforcement

---

Foreign Corrupt Practices Act of 1977–Law, Procedures, and Practices, 10 Inst.Sec.Reg. 65 (1979); Note, Effective Enforcement of the Foreign Corrupt Practices Act, 32 Stan.L.Rev. 561 (1980); Note, Accounting for Corporate Misconduct Abroad: The Foreign Corrupt Practices Act of 1977, 12 Cornell Int'l L.J. 2193 (1979); Note, Corruption and the Foreign Corrupt Practices Act of 1977, 13 U.Mich.J.L.Ref. 158 (1979).

12. SEC v. World–Wide Coin Investments, Ltd., 567 F.Supp. 724, 749 (N.D.Ga.1983).

13. *E.g.* McLean v. International Harvester Co., 817 F.2d 1214 (5th Cir.1987); Eisenberger v. Spectex Industries, Inc., 644 F.Supp. 48 (E.D.N.Y.1986).

14. United States v. Arthur Young & Co., 465 U.S. 805, 104 S.Ct. 1495, 79 L.Ed.2d 826 (1984).

15. *Id.* The work product doctrine has generally been limited to attorneys acting in the course of private representation. *Id. See also, e.g.*, Hickman v. Taylor, 329 U.S. 495, 67 S.Ct. 385, 91 L.Ed. 451 (1947); Fed.R.Civ.P. 26(b)(3).

16. *See* In re Broadview Financial Corp., Exch. Act Rel. No. 34–949 (April 17, 1985) (section 15(c)(4) order); In re Wade, Exch. Act Rel. No. 34–21095 (June 24, 1984); Interview With Robert Sacks, Chief Accountant, SEC Division of Enforcement, 17 Sec.Reg. & L.Rep. (BNA) 596 (April 7, 1985). *See generally* Daniel C. Goelzer, The SEC and Opinion Shopping: A Case Study in the Changing Regulation of the Accounting Profession, 52 Brooklyn L. Rev. 1057 (1987); Note, The Opinion Shopping Phenomenon: Corporate America's Search for the Perfect Auditor, 52 Brooklyn L.Rev. 1077 (1987).

17. *See, e.g.*, SEC Authority, Enforcement Issues Head Topics at San Diego Conference, 18 Sec.Reg. & L.Rep. (BNA) 153, 154 (Jan. 31, 1986).

18. SEC Act Rel. No. 33–6695 (April 1, 1987).

roles under the various securities acts.[1] With regard to registration statements under the Securities Act of 1933, the Commission has the power to issue stop orders and refusal orders with regard to defective registration statements.[2] In addition the Commission can impose disciplinary sanctions against broker-dealers registered under section 15 of the Exchange Act,[3] against municipal securities dealers pursuant to section 15B,[4] and against government securities dealers under section 15C.[5] Beyond these administrative enforcement powers, its oversight of regulatory and self-regulatory organizations,[6] and its rulemaking responsibilities,[7] the Commission is given broad investigatory and enforcement powers in the courts.[8]

SEC Injunctions

Under each of the securities acts the SEC has the authority to seek either temporary or permanent injunctive relief in the courts "whenever it shall appear to the Commission that any person is engaged or about to engage in any acts or practices which constitute or will constitute a violation." [9] Courts have observed that the injunctive power should not be used without "positive proof of a reasonable likelihood that past

------

§ 9.5

1. The work of the SEC is discussed in § 1.4 *supra*. The commission is also discussed in §§ 9.6–9.63 *infra* (Practitioner' Edition only).

2. 15 U.S.C.A. § 77h. *See* §§ 3.5, 7.1 *supra*.

3. 15 U.S.C.A. § 78*o*–1. *See* § 10.2 *infra*.

4. 15 U.S.C.A. § 78*o*–4. *See* § 10.5 *infra*.

5. 15 U.S.C.A. § 78*o*–5. *See* § 10.5.1 *infra*.

6. *See* § 10.2 *infra*.

7. *See* §§ 1.3, 1.4 *supra*.

8. *See generally* Thomas L. Hazen, Administrative Enforcement: An Evaluation of the Securities and Exchange Commission's Use of Injunctions and Other Enforcement Techniques, 31 Hastings L.J. 427 (1979); Paul G. Mahoney, Securities Regulation by Enforcement: An International Perspective, 7 Yale J.Reg. 305 (1990); Arthur F. Mathews, Litigation and Settlement of SEC Administrative Enforcement Proceedings, 29 Cath. U.L.Rev. 215 (1980); Harvey L. Pitt & Karen L. Shapiro, Securities Regulation by Enforcement: A Look Ahead at the Next Decade, 7 Yale J.Reg. 149 (1990); Marc I. Steinberg, SEC and Other Permanent Injunctions—Standards for Their Imposition, Modification, and Dissolution, 66 Cornell L.Rev. 27 (1980). *See also, e.g.,* Jonathan Eisenberg, Enforcement Issues and Litigation: Litigating with the SEC—A Reasonable Alternative to Settlement, 21 Sec. Re. L.J. 421 (1994).

9. 1933 Act section 20(b), 15 U.S.C.A. § 77t(b). Similar provisions are found in the 1934 Exchange Act, the 1935 Public Utility Holding Company Act, the Trust Indenture Act of 1939 and the Investment Company and Investment Advisers Acts of 1940. 15 U.S.C.A. §§ 78u(d), 79r(f), 80b–9(e). Preliminary injunctive relief is available upon a showing of a prima facie case of violation and a serious likelihood that the violations would continue. *E.g.,* SEC v. Netelkos, 597 F.Supp. 724 (S.D.N.Y.1984). *See also, e.g.,* SEC v. Bilzerian, 29 F.3d 689 (D.C.Cir.1994) (permanent injunction was appropriate).

Commission enforcement actions that lack merit can result in an award of counsel fees to the defendant. SEC v. Kluesner, 834 F.2d 1438 (8th Cir.1987). *See also* § 9.25 *infra* (Practitioner's Edition only).

In SEC enforcement actions it may not be necessary to establish all of the elements that would be necessary in an action by a private party. Thus, for example, in a Rule 10b–5 action, the SEC does not have to carry the burden of showing justifiable reliance. *See* SEC v. Hasho, 784 F.Supp. 1059, 1106 (S.D.N.Y.1992).

wrongdoing will occur" and proof that there is "something more than the mere possibility which keeps the case alive."[10] Accordingly, even in the face of proof of past violations, failure to prove a reasonable likelihood of future violations is likely to may mean that no injunction will be granted.[11] In light of the severe consequences that can flow from a SEC injunction, the Tenth Circuit has indicated that a violation based merely on negligence and not resulting in a profit or other undue benefit to the defendant may not be sufficient to support an injunction.[12]

In deciding whether to issue an injunction courts will look to the seriousness of the securities law violations[13] and the requested injunction's impact on the defendant.[14] Other factors include the degree of the defendant's culpability[15] and the length of time between the acts com-

---

10. SEC v. Bausch & Lomb, Inc., 565 F.2d 8, 18 (2d Cir.1977) (quoting United States v. W.T. Grant Co., 345 U.S. 629, 633, 73 S.Ct. 894, 897, 97 L.Ed. 1303 (1953)).

11. *See e.g.,* SEC v. Cayman Islands Reinsurance Corp., 734 F.2d 118 (2d Cir.1984); SEC v. Koracorp Industries, Inc., 575 F.2d 692 (9th Cir.1978), *cert. denied* 439 U.S. 953, 99 S.Ct. 348, 58 L.Ed.2d 343 (1978); SEC v. Bausch & Lomb, Inc., 565 F.2d 8 (2d Cir.1977); SEC v. Parklane Hosiery Co., 558 F.2d 1083 (2d Cir.1977); SEC v. Management Dynamics, Inc., 515 F.2d 801 (2d Cir.1975); SEC v. National Student Marketing Corp., 457 F.Supp. 682 (D.D.C.1978); SEC v. Cenco, Inc., 436 F.Supp. 193 (N.D.Ill.1977); SEC v. Geotek, 426 F.Supp. 715 (N.D.Cal.1976), *judgment affirmed* 590 F.2d 785 (9th Cir.1979). *See also, e.g.,* SEC v. First City Financial Corp., 890 F.2d 1215 (D.C.Cir.1989); SEC v. Foundation Hai, 736 F.Supp. 465 (S.D.N.Y.1990) (preliminary injunction issued where SEC established prima facie case of securities law violations and a likelihood of repetition). *Compare, e.g.,* SEC v. Ingoldsby, 1990 WL 120731, [1990 Transfer Binder] Fed.Sec.L.Rep. ¶ 95,351 (D.Mass.1990) (injunction denied where court determined there was no reasonable likelihood of future violations).

See also, e.g., SEC v. Bilzerian, 29 F.3d 689 (D.C.Cir.1994) (permanent injunction was appropriate).

See generally Donald R. Hakerload, Requirement for Injunctive Actions Under the Federal Securities Laws, 2 J.Corp.L. 481 (1977); Steinberg, footnote 8. *But see* SEC v. Benson, 657 F.Supp. 1122 (S.D.N.Y.1987) (injunction issued against chief executive officer notwithstanding his resignation).

12. SEC v. Pros International, Inc., 994 F.2d 767 (10th Cir.1993) (affirming district court's denial of injunctive relief for negligent violations of section 17(a) of the 1933 Act).

13. SEC v. Advance Growth Capital Corp., 470 F.2d 40, 53–54 (7th Cir.1972); SEC v. Manor Nursing Centers, Inc., 458 F.2d 1082, 1102 (2d Cir.1972).

In deciding whether to issue an injunction under the securities laws, it is appropriate for a court to consider equitable factors in determining whether to exercise its discretion in favor of issuing an injunction. SEC v. Management Dynamics, Inc., 515 F.2d 801, 808 (2d Cir.1975); SEC v. Manor Nursing Centers, 458 F.2d 1082, 1102 (2d Cir.1972); SEC v. Electronics Warehouse, Inc., 689 F.Supp. 53, 70 (D.Conn.1988).

In deciding whether to vacate an injunction, the court should examine whether the factors calling for the injunction are still present. SEC v. Blinder, Robinson & Co., 855 F.2d 677 (10th Cir.1988), *cert. denied* 489 U.S. 1033, 109 S.Ct. 1172, 103 L.Ed.2d 230 (1989). *See also, e.g.,* United States v. Swift & Co., 286 U.S. 106, 52 S.Ct. 460, 76 L.Ed. 999 (1932).

14. *E.g.* SEC v. Manor Nursing Centers, Inc., 458 F.2d 1082, 1102 (2d Cir.1972).

15. *See* SEC v. Spence & Green Chemical Co., 612 F.2d 896, 903 (5th Cir.1980), *cert. denied* 449 U.S. 1082, 101 S.Ct. 866, 66 L.Ed.2d 806 (1981); SEC v. Bonastia, 614 F.2d 908 (3d Cir.1980); SEC v. Commonwealth Chemical Securities, Inc., 574 F.2d 90, 100 (2d Cir.1978); SEC v. Universal Major Industries Corp., 546 F.2d 1044, 1048 (2d Cir.1976), *cert. denied* 434 U.S. 834, 98 S.Ct. 120, 54 L.Ed.2d 95 (1977). *See also, e.g.,* SEC v. Lum's, Inc., 365 F.Supp. 1046, 1066 (S.D.N.Y.1973) (reliance on counsel is a relevant factor). *See generally* Steinberg *supra* footnote 8 at 33–41.

plained of and time of suit.[16]　In SEC v. Unifund Sal,[17] the Second Circuit reconsidered the appropriate standard for a court in deciding whether to issue preliminary relief.　The court began by rejecting a requirement that the Commission establish a "strong prima facie case" [18] as a precondition to issuing a preliminary injunction.　The court also rejected the SEC's contention that the test applicable to private litigants—a substantial likelihood of success on the merits in addition to a showing of irreparable harm that would result in the absence of an injunction[19] should be utilized.　Instead, the court required not only a likelihood of success on the merits, but also a showing that there is a risk of future violations and that the seriousness of the violation warrants the preliminary relief.　The court made it clear that the more burdensome the relief requested, the more substantial must be the showing of violation and risk of recurrence.[20]

Although the power is rarely exercised, the injunction once issued may be modified or dissolved on motion by the defendant or the SEC.[21] An SEC injunction has been characterized as "a drastic remedy" and should not be granted lightly, especially when the conduct has ceased. However, laches is not a defense to an SEC injunction action nor will ordinary estoppel bar the SEC from bringing suit.　Similarly, the statute of limitations that is applicable to private suits under the antifraud does not apply to SEC enforcement actions nor to SEC disgorgement actions.[22] In contrast, actions brought to enforce a civil fine, penalty or forfeiture,

---

16.　*See* Steinberg *supra* footnote 8 at 33–41.

17.　910 F.2d 1028 (2d Cir.1990), *rehearing denied* 917 F.2d 98 (1990).

18.　This standard had been enunciated in prior decisions. *See, e.g.,* SEC v. Management Dynamics, Inc., 515 F.2d 801, 807 (2d Cir.1975); SEC v. Boren, 283 F.2d 312, 313 (2d Cir.1960).

19.　The standard applicable for private preliminary relief is discussed in §§ 11.18, 11.19 *infra*.

20.　The court thus vacated a preliminary injunction against future insider trading violations in light of the gaps in the SEC's showing of a prima facie case.　On the other hand, the court upheld the lower court's asset freeze that had been issued in order to protect possible disgorgement and penalties.　The court thus viewed the freeze order as less burdensome than an injunction against future violations.

21.　The SEC's Director of Enforcement has suggested that courts should be willing to modify injunctions on appropriate facts.　This would represent a reversal of the commission's longstanding policy to the contrary.　15 Sec.Reg. & L.Rep. (BNA) 2143 (interview with John Fedders, Nov. 25, 1983).

22.　SEC v. Rind, 991 F.2d 1486 (9th Cir.1993), *cert. denied* __ U.S. __, 114 S.Ct. 439, 126 L.Ed.2d 372 (1993) (disgorgement action); SEC v. Lorin, 869 F.Supp. 1117 (S.D.N.Y. 1994) (SEC enforcement action); SEC v. Downe, 1994 WL 67826, [1993–1994 Transfer Binder] Fed. Sec. L. Rep. (CCH) ¶ 98,140 (S.D.N.Y.1994) (disgorgement action also seeking penalties); SEC v. Lorin, 1991 WL 576895, Fed. Sec. L. Rep. (CCH) ¶ 98,188 (S.D.N.Y. 1991); SEC v. O'Hagan, 793 F.Supp. 218 (D.Minn.1992) (enforcement action), relying on SEC v. Rind, 1991 WL 283840, [1991 Transfer Binder] Fed.Sec.L.Rep. (CCH) ¶ 96,168 (C.D.Cal.1991), *affirmed* 991 F.2d 1486 (9th Cir.1993); SEC v. Willis, 777 F.Supp. 1165 (S.D.N.Y.1991); SEC v. Penn Central Co., 425 F.Supp. 593, 1992 WL 207918, (E.D.Pa. 1976).　*See also* SEC v. Keating [1992 Transfer Binder] Fed.Sec.L.Rep. (CCH) ¶ 96,906 (C.D.Cal.1992) (finding statute of limitations defense to be frivolous and imposing sanctions for having raised it).

appear to be covered by a five-year statute of limitations.[23] Thus, in an SEC enforcement action, in order to determine whether there is a statute of limitations, the court must first decide if the action is one for injunctive relief (including any ancillary remedies) or is one to impose a civil fine. It has been held, for example that a disgorgement action is *not* a proceeding to enforce a civil fine.[24] As an analogy to the rule that there is no statute of limitations in SEC injunctive actions generally, the fact that the SEC may have engaged in some wrongdoing in connection with its investigation and prosecution of a claim, will not disable the Commission from bringing suit.[25] Accordingly, unclean hands is not a defense in an SEC action unless the misconduct rises to the level of a constitutional violation.[26]

Even though third parties may have an interest in SEC investigations, intervention occasionally may be appropriate but generally will not be so after the entry of a consent decree.[27] On a related note, the SEC may not intervene in an action in which it has no direct interest.[28] Even though intervention may not be appropriate, the Commission may nevertheless seek permission to file a friend of the court brief.

The SEC power to seek injunctive and other civil relief for criminal violations has been challenged as in violation of the separation of powers. This attack is essentially based on the same argument that was used in the unsuccessful challenge to special federal prosecutors who are not operating under the attorney general's control.[29] Although one court has noted the "substantial" nature of such a challenge to the SEC's authority,[30] the Commission's authority has been upheld on a number of occasions.[31] More recently, the Fifth Circuit ruled that it was a violation

23. 28 U.S.C.A. § 2462. *See, e.g.,* 3M Co. v. Browner, 17 F.3d 1453 (D.C.Cir.1994) holding that this applies to administrative proceedings as well.

24. SEC v. Rind, 991 F.2d 1486 (9th Cir.1993), *cert. denied* ___ U.S. ___, 114 S.Ct. 439, 126 L.Ed.2d 372 (1993).

25. *See, e.g.,* SEC v. Lorin, 1991 WL 576895, [1993–1994 Transfer Binder] Fed. Sec. L. Rep. (CCH) ¶ 98,188 (S.D.N.Y.1991); SEC v. Gulf & Western Industries, Inc., 502 F.Supp. 343 (D.D.C.1980). *See also, e.g.,* Hunter v. SEC, 1994 WL 477726, [1994–1995 Transfer Binder] Fed. Sec. L. Rep. (CCH) ¶ 98,402 (E.D.Pa.1994) (refusing to grant temporary restraining order against SEC investigation).

26. "Government misconduct requires the dismissal of adverse civil proceedings only where the misconduct was egregious, and the resulting prejudice to the defendant rises to a constitutional level." SEC v. Lorin, 1991 WL 576895, [1993–1994 Transfer Binder] Fed. Sec. L. Rep. (CCH) ¶ 98,188 at p. 99,306 (S.D.N.Y.1991) (quoting from SEC v. Museklla 38 Fed. R. Serv. (Callaghan) 426, 428).

27. SEC v. Byers, 109 F.R.D. 299 (W.D.Pa.1985).

28. *See* In re Bilzerian, 164 B.R. 688 (M.D.Fla.1994) (since it was not a creditor, the SEC lacked standing to intervene in action to determine whether debtor was entitled to a general discharge under the bankruptcy laws).

29. The federal special prosecutor was upheld in Morrison v. Olson, 487 U.S. 654, 108 S.Ct. 2597, 101 L.Ed.2d 569 (1988), *on remand* 857 F.2d 801 (D.C.Cir.1988).

30. Meyer Blinder v. SEC, 87 Civ. 1086 (D.D.C. March 26, 1987) (stay order).

31. *E.g.,* SEC v. Blinder, Robinson & Co., 855 F.2d 677 (10th Cir.1988), *cert. denied* 489 U.S. 1033, 109 S.Ct. 1172, 103 L.Ed.2d 230 (1989); SEC v. Bilzerian, 750 F.Supp. 14 (D.D.C.1990); SEC v. Davis, 689 F.Supp. 767 (S.D.Ohio 1988); SEC v. Warner, 652 F.Supp. 647 (S.D.Fla.1987). *Cf., e.g.,* Interstate Commerce Commission v. Chatsworth

of due process for the district court to have appointed the SEC to prosecute a criminal contempt action against defendants who allegedly violated the terms of civil injunction.[32]

Injunctive and other Relief Against Aiders and Abettors

The Supreme Court in Central Bank of Denver v. First Interstate Bank of Denver, in a five-to-four decision held that there is no implied right of action to redress aiding and abetting a Rule 10b–5 violation.[33] The Court's holding is limited by the facts of the case to private rights of action. Accordingly, at least in theory, aiding and abetting may still be charged at least in certain SEC injunctive and other enforcement actions with regard to criminal prosecutions, there is express statutory authority for pursuing aiders and abettors. The reasoning in the *Central Bank* case casts serious doubts the Commission's ability to go after aiders and abettors in many instances.

The Court recognized that the general federal aiding and abetting statute[34] makes it a criminal offense to aid and abet any substantive criminal violation. This, of course, gives the government the authority to criminally prosecute collateral participants who aid and abet any of the criminal prohibitions of the securities laws. The Court further pointed to the absence of a generalized securities statute creating aiding and abetting liability in SEC actions generally while at the same time pointing to the express authority to pursue broker-dealers as aiders and abettors.[35]

The Court's reasoning thus strongly suggests that, as is the case in a suit brought by a private plaintiff, the SEC lacks the generalized authority to pursue aiders and abettors in the absence of a specific statutory grant. A more receptive court might consider the argument that a refusal to imply a remedy in a private suit is something different from extending the SEC's grant of authority to pursue criminal violations. Since the SEC is charged with enforcing the securities laws generally,[36] it is conceivable that a court might be willing to find the authority to pursue aiders and abettors. However, such an approach would go against both the spirit and tenor of the Court's *Central Bank* decision. It is somewhat anomalous, however, to deny the SEC the general authority to go after aiders and abettors. First, under a strict reading of the *Central Bank* decision the Commission may be forced to

Cooperative Marketing Ass'n, 347 F.2d 821 (7th Cir.1965), *cert. denied* 382 U.S. 938, 86 S.Ct. 390, 15 L.Ed.2d 349 (1965) (ICC enforcement of Interstate Commerce Act held not to violate the executive power of the President).

    32. United States ex rel. SEC v. Carter, 907 F.2d 484 (5th Cir.1990). In *Carter,* the defendant had not challenged the SEC's authority but the court of appeals raised the issue on its own and held that the lower court's appointment was plain error.

    33. Central Bank of Denver, N.A. v. First Interstate Bank of Denver, ___ U.S. ___, 114 S.Ct. 1439, 128 L.Ed.2d 119 (1994).

    34. 18 U.S.C.A. § 2.

    35. Sections 15(b) and 21B of the Exchange Act, 15 U.S.C.A. §§ 78*o*(b), 78u–2.

    36. *See* § 9.5 *supra.*

forgo civil enforcement against an aider and abettor and turn the matter over for criminal prosecution. This would lead to the unusual result that secondary liability can result in the more severe criminal penalties but could not be the basis of less onerous civil enforcement. Additionally, as is the case with enforcement powers generally, the SEC's investigatory powers focus on persons who violate the "Act." Under the Court's reasoning, the Commission might have the power to investigate primary violations but not aiders and abettors. Accordingly, under this interpretation, while the Commission could investigate primary violators, investigation of aiders and abettors who might be criminally prosecuted would have to be relegated to some other investigatory body and this would be a terribly cumbersome result.

It is quite natural to expect that although the SEC may continue to pursue aiders and abettors generally, it will charge primary violations in many cases that formerly may have been dealt with as aiding and abetting situations. In bringing such actions, more emphasis may be placed on prohibitions of the Act for persons who directly or indirectly violate the Act as a basis for establishing an indirect primary violation. Additionally, the degree of involvement in the securities transaction may provide the basis for charging primary rather than secondary liability. For example, when an accountant renders an opinion in connection with a securities transaction and something in that opinion implicates the securities laws, the accountant's involvement may be said to be primary. Similarly, when an attorney renders an opinion, under appropriate circumstances that opinion may provide the basis for primary liability[37] and thus eliminate any need to pursue the attorney as an aider and abettor. There may also be an increase in the use of controlling person liability.[38]

Ancillary Relief in SEC Injunction Actions[39]

The statutory enabling provisions speak solely in terms of the SEC's power to enjoin violations.[40] However, the SEC and the courts have fashioned remedies ancillary to the traditional injunctive decree relying on "the general equitable powers of the federal courts." [41] Ancillary

---

37. *See, e.g.,* Kline v. First Western Government Securities, Inc., 24 F.3d 480 (3d Cir.1994) (holding attorney's tax opinion actionable under Rule 10b–5).

38. The SEC can bring suit based on controlling person liability. SEC v. First Jersey Securities, Inc., 1994 WL 163711, [1993–1994 Transfer Binder] Fed. Sec. L. Rep. (CCH) ¶ 98,189 (S.D.N.Y.1994). *See also, e.g.,* Hateley v. SEC, 8 F.3d 653 (9th Cir.1993) (upholding controlling person liability as basis for NASD disgorgement order). Controlling person liability is considered in § 7.7 *supra* and § 13.15 *infra*.

39. The following discussion is an updated adaptation from Hazen *supra* footnote 8 at 446–48.

40. *See* footnote 9 *supra. But see* the discussion of the Insider Trading Sanctions Act of 1984 in § 13.9 *infra*.

41. James R. Farrand, Ancillary Remedies in SEC Civil Enforcement Suits, 89 Harv. L.Rev. 1779, 1781 (1976); George W. Dent, Jr., Ancillary Relief in Federal Securities Law: A Study in Federal Remedies, 67 Minn.L.Rev. 865 (1983); John D. Ellsworth, Disgorgement in Securities Fraud Actions Brought by the SEC, 1977 Duke L.J. 641; Arnold S. Jacobs, Judicial and Administrative Remedies Available to the SEC for Breaches of Rule

relief has taken many forms, ranging from disgorgement of ill-gotten profits[42] to more imaginative corrective or remedial action. Among such imaginative remedies are the appointment of an independent majority on the board of directors,[43] the appointment of a receiver,[44] prohibitions against exercising voting control in a proxy battle,[45] the appointment of "special professionals" to assure compliance with securities laws,[46] the

10b–5, 53 St. John's L.Rev. 397 (1979); Robert I. Malley, Far–Reaching Equitable Remedies Under the Securities Acts and the Growth of Federal Corporate Law, 17 Wm. & Mary L.Rev. 47 (1975); Arthur F. Mathews, Recent Trends in SEC Requested Ancillary Relief in SEC Level Injunctive Actions, 31 Bus.Law. 1323 (1976); Stanley Sporkin, SEC Developments in Litigation and the Molding of Remedies, 29 Bus.Law. (Special Issue) 121 (1974); Comment, Court–Appointed Directors: Ancillary Relief in Federal Securities Law Enforcement Actions, 64 Geo.L.J. 737 (1976); Note, Ancillary Relief in SEC Injunction Suits for Violation of Rule 10b–5, 79 Harv.L.Rev. 656 (1966); Note, SEC Injunctive and Ancillary Relief Under Rule 10b–5: A Scienter Requirement?, 1977 U.Ill.L.F. 872; Comment, Equitable Remedies in SEC Enforcement Actions, 123 U.Pa.L.Rev. 1188 (1975).

42. Disgorgement of ill-gotten gain is common in insider trading cases. *E.g.*, SEC v. Musella, 1992 WL 420902, [1992–1993 Transfer Binder] Fed.Sec.L.Rep. (CCH) ¶ 97,205 (S.D.N.Y.1992) (holding defendant in civil contempt for violation of disgorgement order). *See* § 13.9 *infra.*

The disgorgement remedy has been utilized in the context of other violations as well. *See, e.g.*, SEC v. Bilzerian, 29 F.3d 689 (D.C.Cir.1994), *affirming* 814 F.Supp. 116 (D.D.C.1993) (disgorgement of profits made in connection with Williams Act violations; also holding that prior criminal fine did not present a double jeopardy bar to disgorgement which is remedial in nature); SEC v. UNIOIL, 951 F.2d 1304 (D.C.Cir.1991) (upholding disgorgement order based on violations in connection with fraudulent publicity campaign); Bilzerian v. SEC, 146 B.R. 871 (Bkrtcy.M.D.Fla.1992) (disgorgement of profits from illegalities in connection with takeover attempts; disgorgement order did not interfere with bankruptcy proceedings involving the defendant); SEC v. Kimmes, 799 F.Supp. 852 (N.D.Ill.1992) (disgorgement of profits obtained from fraud in connection with public offerings).

But Cf. Hateley v. SEC, 8 F.3d 653 (9th Cir.1993) (disgorgement order was abuse of discretion since the ill-gotten profits had already been returned).

43. *See* SEC v. Vesco, 571 F.2d 129 (2d Cir.1978). *See also* SEC v. Mattel, Inc., 1974 WL 449, [1974–1975 Transfer Binder] Fed.Sec.L.Rep. (CCH) ¶ 94,807 (D.D.C.1974) (consent to sanctions). *See generally* Robert I. Malley, Far–Reaching Equitable Remedies Under the Securities Acts and the Growth of Federal Corporate Law, 17 Wm. & Mary L.Rev. 47 (1975).

44. *E.g.*, SEC. v. Elliott, 953 F.2d 1560 (11th Cir.1992) (appointment of receiver did not violate due process); SEC v. United Financial Group, Inc., 474 F.2d 354 (9th Cir.1973); SEC. v. Current Financial Services, Inc., 783 F.Supp. 1441 (D.D.C.1992) (appointment of receiver to collect account receivables during an asset freeze); SEC v. Florida Bank Fund, 1978 WL 1131, [1978] Fed.Sec.L.Rep. (CCH) ¶ 96,707 (M.D.Fla.1978); SEC v. R.J. Allen & Associates, 386 F.Supp. 866 (S.D.Fla.1974).

This power is expressly given to the commission by section 42(e) of the Investment Company Act for violators of the Act's registration requirements. 15 U.S.C.A. § 80a–41(e). However, the remedy has been applied as a matter of the courts' general equity power. *See generally* Farrand, *supra* footnote 41 at 1784–89.

The Investment Company Act is discussed in chapter 17 *infra.*

45. *E.g.* SEC v. Westgate California Corp., SEC Litigation Release No. 6142, 3 SEC Docket 30 (S.D.Cal. Nov. 9, 1978) (settlement order). *Cf.* Chris–Craft Industries v. Piper Aircraft Corp., 480 F.2d 341 (2d Cir.1973), *cert. denied* 414 U.S. 910, 94 S.Ct. 231, 38 L.Ed.2d 148 (1973) (defendant barred from voting for five years on shares obtained illegally). *See generally* Farrand, *supra* note 41 at 1792 n. 74.

46. *E.g.*, SEC v. Beisinger Industries Corp., 552 F.2d 15, 18–19 (1st Cir.1977), *affirming* 421 F.Supp. 691 (D.Mass.1976); SEC v. Joseph Schlitz Brewing Co., 452 F.Supp. 824 (E.D.Wis.1978) (consent decree). *See also* SEC v. First Boston Corp., 86 Civ. 3524 (S.D.N.Y.1986) (consent order that brokerage firm review its "restricted list" and its Chinese Wall procedures); SEC v. First Jersey Securities, Inc., 1985 WL 29946, [1984–1985

imposition of additional reporting requirements,[47] fashioning of orders designed to protect remaining assets,[48] and prohibitions against continued participation as an officer or director of any public company.[49] The Commission has also secured judicial appointment of a "special independent officer" to assure compliance with the terms of the decree.[50]

Although the appointment of a receiver, an award of restitution, and orders designed for the protection of assets (such as through a freeze order) can be viewed as supplemental investor protection, the less drastic remedies are more directly related to assuring future compliance with the securities laws. These less drastic forms of relief would appear to fit more closely within the preventive focus of the acts' injunctive provisions than the more remedial forms of relief, which tend to place the Commission in a position of consumer—or investor—advocate.[51] The SEC had been using ancillary relief as a method for instituting corporate governance reforms[52] but this policy has since been reversed.[53]

Transfer Binder] Fed.Sec.L.Rep. (CCH) ¶ 91,923 (S.D.N.Y.1985) (appointment of consultant to review broker-dealer's practices, pursuant to permanent injunction entered by the parties' consent).

47. *See generally* Farrand, *supra* footnote 41 at 1792–93.

48. *E.g.,* SEC v. Quinn, 997 F.2d 287 (7th Cir.1993) (failure to appeal asset freeze in a timely manner precluded appeal of freeze prior to disposition of case on the merits except for certain issues such as whether defendant may use some of the frozen assets to mount a defense); SEC v. Manor Nursing Centers, Inc., 458 F.2d 1082, 1105–06 (2d Cir.1972); SEC v. College Bound, Inc., 849 F.Supp. 65 (D.D.C.1994) (modifying asset freeze).

49. SEC v. Cosmopolitan Inv. Funding Co., SEC Litigation Release No. 7366 (April 23, 1976); 42 SEC Ann.Rep. 119 (1976).

50. SEC v. Western Geothermal & Power Corp., 1979 WL 1228, [1979 Transfer Binder] Fed.Sec.L.Rep. (CCH) ¶ 96,920 (D.Ariz.1979). *See also, e.g.* In re Kidder, Peabody & Co., Exch.Act Rel. No. 34–24543 (June 4, 1987) (consent order requiring compliance review).

51. An overzealous approach to the SEC's pursuit of ancillary remedies would lead to an undue incursion upon corporate governance issues that are more properly left to corporate chartering statutes. While there is no question that reform is needed in this area, it should not be accomplished by the SEC under the guise of investor protection. Rather, the task of considering corporate governance should be undertaken on its own merits. Lengthy debate over the direction of the modern corporation recently has accelerated. *See generally* Symposium—Corporate Social Responsibility, 30 Hastings L.J. 1247 (1979); Symposium—Reweaving the Corporate Veil, 41 Law & Contemp.Prob. 1 (Summer 1977). *See also* Thomas L. Hazen, Corporate Chartering and the Securities Markets: Shareholder Suffrage, Corporate Responsibility and Managerial Accountability, 1978 Wis.L.Rev. 391.

52. Since 1976, the Commission has favored requiring independent audit committees. In fact, such a rule was adopted in 1977 for issuers whose securities are listed on the New York Stock Exchange. New York Stock Exchange, Inc., Exch.Act Rel. No. 34–13346 (March 9, 1977). In 1978, the SEC's general counsel stated that the Commission had the power to promulgate its own rules requiring independent audit committees for all issuers subject to the reporting requirements of the 1934 Exchange Act and the registration provisions of the 1933 Securities Act. Memorandum of General Counsel Harvey L. Pitt to Chairman Williams (June 10, 1977), reprinted in [1978 Transfer Binder] Fed.Sec.L.Rep. (CCH) ¶ 81,535 (1978). Even though no such rule has been adopted to date, the SEC has been able to accomplish this goal indirectly by entering into consent decrees in settlement of enforcement actions that have incorporated the independent audit committee requirement. *E.g.* Woods Corp., Exch.Act Rel. No. 34–15337 (Nov. 16, 1978); Hycel, Inc., Exch.Act Rel. No. 34–14981 (July 20, 1978); Gambling Corporation Settles Antifraud Action, Agrees to Establish Audit Committee, 515 Sec.Reg. & L.Rep. (BNA) A–12 (July 23, 1979). *But see* SEC v. Falstaff Brewing Corp., 1978 WL 1120, [1978 Transfer Binder] Fed.Sec.L.Rep. (CCH) ¶ 96,583, at 94,473–74 (D.D.C.1978). *See generally* Dennis J. Block

53. See note 53 on page 429.

Disgorgement of ill-gotten profits has become an increasingly popular remedy which is available in SEC judicial enforcement actions generally,[54] as well as for insider trading.[55] Questions have arisen as to the purpose of the disgorgement remedy. Some courts have spoken of disgorgement in terms of a method of seeking restitution for injured investors.[56] While this goal of compensation might be a valuable by-product of the disgorgement remedy, it is not its primary purpose. Disgorgement serves to assure that the wrongdoer will not profit from violating the securities laws. As one court has explained, "[i]t is an equitable remedy meant to prevent the wrongdoer from enriching himself by his wrongs."[57] Accordingly disgorgement may be appropriate even if the amount of the profit disgorged is in excess of what is needed to make the victims whole.[58] Disgorgement has thus been described as more akin to "an injunction in the public interest" than it is to an ordinary compensatory money judgment.[59] It has further been held that a constructive trust may be imposed against such ill-gotten gains even when passed on by the violator to his or her family.[60]

& Neal Schwarzfeld, Corporate Mismanagement and Breach of Fiduciary Duty after Santa Fe v. Green, 2 Corp.L.Rev. 91, 113–14 (1979); George W. Dent, Jr., Ancillary Relief in Federal Securities Law: A Study in Federal Remedies, 67 Minn.L.Rev. 865, 921–922 (1983). Such a requirement forces changes in operating procedures that undoubtedly will alter the substance of corporate transactions and governance. The potential for direct impact of ancillary relief upon corporate governance in similar instances should not be underestimated. Accordingly, in fashioning ancillary remedies the Commission and the courts should be mindful of overstepping the appropriate boundaries of disclosure and other forms of investor protection.

The SEC has indirectly encouraged audit committees through its rulemaking power as well. For example, the internal controls requirement of section 13(b)(2) goes far in that direction. 15 U.S.C.A. § 77m(b). *See* § 9.3 *supra.*

53. *See* George W. Dent, Jr., Ancillary Relief in Federal Securities Law: A Study in Federal Remedies, 67 Minn.L.Rev. 865, 913–922 (1983). A potentially greater incursion into the realm of corporate autonomy may result from the passage of the Foreign Corrupt Practices Act of 1977, Pub.L. No. 95–213, §§ 202, 203, 91 Stat. 1494, 1498–99 (1977). The Act amended the Securities Exchange Act to require increased disclosure of acquisition and ownership information to the SEC, securities exchanges, and to the company itself.

54. *See* section 21(d)(3)(B), 15 U.S.C.A. § 78u(d)(3)(B).

55. *See* section 21A, 15 U.S.C.A. § 78u–1. *See also, e.g.,* SEC v. Chapnick, 1994 WL 113040, [1993–1994 Transfer Binder] Fed. Sec. L. Rep. (CCH) ¶ 98,076 (S.D.Fla.1994) (adequately pleading case for disgorgement).

The SEC's ability to seek disgorgement for insider trading violations which is discussed *infra* this section. The substantive law of insider trading is discussed in § 13.9 *infra.*

56. *E.g.,* SEC v. Blatt, 583 F.2d 1325, 1335 (5th Cir.1978).

57. SEC v. Huffman, 996 F.2d 800, 802 (5th Cir.1993), relying on SEC v. Commonwealth Chemical Securities, Inc., 574 F.2d 90, 102 (2d Cir.1978).

58. SEC v. Huffman, 996 F.2d 800, 802 (5th Cir.1993). *Compare, e.g.,* United States v. Arutunoff, 1 F.3d 1112 (10th Cir.1993), *cert. denied* __ U.S. __, 114 S.Ct. 616, 126 L.Ed.2d 580 (1993) (lowering restitution ordered in connection with criminal prosecution to the extent that the award exceeded the injury to investors).

59. Pierce v. Vision Investments, Inc., 779 F.2d 302, 307 (5th Cir.1986). This sentiment was quoted with approval in SEC v. Huffman, 996 F.2d 800, 802 (5th Cir.1993) (holding that a disgorgement order was not a "debt" under the Federal Debt collection Procedures Act). Defendant may be excused from a disgorgement order to the extent that he or she is able to prove, by a preponderance of evidence, inability to pay. *Id.*

60. *See* SEC v. Antar, 831 F.Supp. 380 (D.N.J.1993) (disgorgement enforced against violator's former wife and children).

Insider Trading Sanctions Act of 1984 (ITSA)

In 1984 Congress gave the Commission additional enforcement power in terms of the ability in a case of insider trading to seek a civil penalty of up to three times the amount of the insider's ill-gotten profits.[61] This relatively new remedy, which, to some extent, has been further clarified and supplemented by the Insider Trading and Securities Fraud Sanctions Act of 1988, raises a number of interesting questions.[62] For example, is the treble penalty, the proceeds of which go to the United States Treasury, a criminal proceeding so as to preclude an ITSA action following or followed by a criminal prosecution? More specifically, can the treble damage penalty be invoked in addition to imprisonment and/or the statutory criminal fine[63] (or both)? Even putting the constitutional issues aside, it would certainly seem to be a case of overkill to allow the Justice Department and the SEC in successive actions to exact cumulative penalties. The statutory remedy raises other questions as well. For example, does the new treble damage penalty have any effect on the SEC's ability to obtain ancillary relief in an injunction action, such as ordering a disgorgement of profits to a private party? The SEC practice in most cases has been to bring an action for disgorgement, combined with its request for a penalty. Combining disgorgement with the penalty has been reflected in SEC settlements. As discussed more fully below, as a result of 1990 legislation, the Commission can order disgorgement in its own administrative proceedings and thus can bypass judicial relief.

An important Supreme Court ruling that was decided outside the context of the securities laws sheds light on the double jeopardy issues that may arise in connection with ITSA and other SEC remedies. In United States v. Halper,[64] the defendant was convicted of having violated the criminal false claims statute and the Mail Fraud Act and then was subsequently sued by the government under the Civil False Claims Act. The district court imposed civil fines totaling one hundred and thirty thousand dollars. On review, the Supreme Court found that a civil penalty may be so unrelated to the remedial goals of the statute that it

---

61. 15 U.S.C.A. § 78u(d)(2)(A). *Cf.* SEC v. Levine, 881 F.2d 1165 (2d Cir.1989) (tax assessment by IRS given priority over funds disgorged pursuant to SEC consent decree); SEC v. Stephenson, 732 F.Supp. 438 (S.D.N.Y.1990) (prejudgment interest was appropriate in an SEC action for disgorgement); SEC v. Musella, 748 F.Supp. 1028 [1989 Transfer Binder] Fed.Sec.L.Rep. ¶ 94,536 (S.D.N.Y.1989) (semble). *See also* § 13.9 *infra.*

ITSA was supplemented in 1988 by the Insider Trading and Securities Fraud Enforcement Act. 15 U.S.C.A. §§ 78t–1, 78u–1 which is discussed in § 13.9 *infra.*

62. *See generally* Howard M. Friedman, The Insider Trading and Securities Fraud Enforcement Act of 1988, 68 N.C.L.Rev. 465 (1990); Comment, Implications of the 1984 Insider Trading Sanction Act: Collateral Estoppel and Double Jeopardy, 64 N.C.L.Rev. 117 (1985). The 1988 legislation is discussed in § 13.9 *infra.*

63. The Insider Trading Sanctions Act also increased the criminal penalty from $10,000 to $100,000 per violation. Recent settlements have combined disgorgement with civil penalties. *See, e.g.,* SEC v. Kidder, Peabody & Co., 1987 WL 16280 (S.D.N.Y.1987) (settlement of more than $25 million); SEC v. Pomerantz (S.D.N.Y.1986) ($79,850 penalty); SEC v. Boesky, 1986 WL 15283 (S.D.N.Y.1986) ($50 million disgorgement, $50 million penalty).

64. 490 U.S. 435, 109 S.Ct. 1892, 104 L.Ed.2d 487 (1989).

constitutes punishment within the meaning of the Double Jeopardy Clause of the Constitution. The *Halper* decision thus makes it clear that double jeopardy issues can arise when a criminal prosecution is followed by a government suit seeking to impose civil penalties.

The fact that a criminal prosecution comes first in time does not necessarily mean that double jeopardy will be a bar to a subsequent action for disgorgement.[65] It has been pointed out that a criminal fine is a different matter from the remedial considerations underlying a disgorgement action.[66] Thus, although it might be preferable to bring the criminal action first, it is not necessary.

The Court in *Halper* took care to point out that its holding does not apply to situations in which there has been no prior criminal prosecution. The Court did not address the situation in which the criminal prosecution is brought after the imposition of a civil penalty. However, following the Court's rationale, it would appear that if the civil penalty is large and further is unrelated to remedial purposes, characterizing it as a punishment should invoke the Double Jeopardy Clause for any subsequent criminal prosecution.

The Court in *Halper* pointed out that the double jeopardy problem does not arise when the civil and criminal penalties are brought in a single proceeding. The *Halper* decision also observed that there are no double jeopardy problems associated with a criminal prosecution followed by a civil suit brought by a private party.

What then, are the implications of the *Halper* decision with regard to ITSA? There is legislative history which supports the view that the ITSA treble damage penalty was designed as a deterrent rather than remedial provision. This would indicate that an ITSA civil proceeding which has been preceded by a criminal prosecution might well run afoul of the Double Jeopardy Clause. If nothing else, the *Halper* decision might spur the SEC to consider seeking civil and criminal sanctions in a single proceeding rather than continue its current policy of going after the defendant in a piecemeal fashion. On the other hand, there are other problems—both tactical and procedural—that can arise from trying to consolidate criminal and civil proceedings.

Another issue raised by the Insider Trading Sanctions Act is the defendant's right to a jury trial. The Supreme Court has held that there is a constitutional right to a jury trial in governmental action for liability under the Clean Water Act but any penalties are to be fixed by the Court.[67] Thus, by analogy, there is no constitutional right to a jury trial for ITSA civil penalties.[68] Additionally, since an SEC disgorgement

---

65. SEC v. Bilzerian, 29 F.3d 689 (D.C.Cir.1994), *affirming* 814 F.Supp. 116 (D.D.C. 1993).

66. *Id.*

67. Tull v. United States, 481 U.S. 412, 107 S.Ct. 1831, 95 L.Ed.2d 365 (1987).

68. *But see* United States v. Marcus Schloss & Co., Inc., 724 F.Supp. 1123 (S.D.N.Y. 1989) ($20,000 penalty in civil ITSA proceeding did not amount to punishment and thus the criminal prosecution was permitted to proceed).

action is equitable in nature, it would appear that there is no right to a jury trial in the SEC action.[69]

Civil Penalties in Other SEC Enforcement Actions

In 1990, Congress expanded the scope and amount of civil penalties that can be ordered in judicial proceedings brought by the SEC.[70] As discussed more fully below, at the same time, the SEC was given the power to impose civil penalties in administrative proceedings.[71] While those administrative proceedings are limited to market professionals registered with or otherwise regulated under the supervision of the SEC,[72] the Commission can institute a civil action in federal court against anyone who is in violation of the securities laws or rules promulgated thereunder.

If it appears to the Commission that a person has violated an SEC rule or regulation, or a cease and desist order, other than a violation which is subject to a penalty under the Insider Trading Sanctions Act of 1984, the SEC may bring a civil action seeking a civil penalty against the violator, by virtue of its general enforcement authority.[73] The amount of the penalty is discretionary so long as it fits within the three-tiered system established by the statute.[74] The second and third tiers permit larger penalties in the case of more culpable conduct. The general rule (first tier) is that the penalty is not to exceed the greater of (i) five

69. The *Tull* decision involved a government claim for liability, injunctive relief, and civil penalty. The court characterized the liability claim as in law rather than equity. Such a characterization of SEC disgorgement actions would apparently give a right to a jury trial. However, this seems unlikely as disgorgement has been viewed as equitable in nature. Furthermore, disgorgement in insider trading cases may be based on a constructive trust or accounting of profits, both of which are equitable claims. *See infra* § 13.19.

See also, e.g., SEC v. Rind 991 F.2d 1486 (9th Cir.1993), *affirming* 1991 WL 21467, [1991 Transfer Binder] Fed.Sec.L.Rep. (CCH) ¶ 96,167 (C.D.Cal.1991); Comment, The Seventh Amendment Right to Jury Trial in Civil Penalties Actions: A Post–*Tull* Examination of the Insider Trading Sanctions Act of 1984, 43 U.Miami L.Rev. 361 (1988).

70. Pub.L. No. 101–429. *See generally* Ralph C. Ferrara, Thomas A. Ferrigno & David S. Darland, Hardball! The SEC's New Arsenal of Enforcement Weapons, 47 Bus.Law. 33 (1991); Arthur B. Laby & W. Hardy Callcott, Patterns of SEC Enforcement Under the 1990 Remedies Act: Civil Money Penalties, 58 Alb. L. Rev. 5 (1994).

28 U.S.C.A. § 2462 contains a general statute of limitations applicable to government proceedings to enforce any civil fine, penalty or forfeiture.

71. The Commission was also given cease and desist authority. *See* § 9.5.1 *infra* (Practitioner's Edition only).

72. The power to impose civil penalties applies to proceedings against a broker-dealer, associated person, municipal securities dealer, government securities dealer, or registered clearing agent, as well as to persons registered under the Investment Company or Investment Advisers Acts of 1940. 15 U.S.C.A. §§ 78u–2, 80a–9(d), (e), § 80b–3(i). *See* 15 U.S.C.A. §§ 78*o*(b)(4), 78*o*(b)(6), 70*o*–4, 78*o*–5, 78q–1.

73. 15 U.S.C.A. §§ 77t(d)(1), 78u(d)(3)(A), 80a–12(e)(1), 80b–9(e)(1). The SEC further has the power to impose civil penalties in the course of administrative proceedings. Section 21B, 15 U.S.C.A. § 78u–2. *See* footnotes 157–168 *infra* and accompanying text.

74. *See, e.g.,* SEC v. Interlink Data Network of Los Angeles, Inc., 1993 WL 603274, [1993–1994 Transfer Binder] Fed. Sec. L. Rep. (CCH) ¶ 98,049 (C.D.Cal.1993) (penalty of more than $12 million, representing the aggregate amount raised in the fraudulent offering under attack was an appropriate penalty).

Section 21B's three tiers are set forth in footnote 165 *infra.*

thousand dollars for a natural person or fifty thousand dollars for any other person, or (ii) the gross amount of pecuniary gain to the defendant as a result of the violation. Second tier penalties may be imposed against more culpable defendants. If the violation involved fraud, deceit, manipulation, or deliberate or reckless disregard of a regulatory requirement, the penalty amount may not exceed the greater of (i) fifty thousand dollars for a natural person or two hundred and fifty thousand dollars for any other person, or (ii) the gross amount of pecuniary gain to the defendant as a result of the violation. Third tier penalties may be imposed against such culpable conduct if it has a significant impact on other persons. If the violation (1) involved fraud, deceit, manipulation, or deliberate or reckless disregard of a regulatory requirement; and (2) directly or indirectly resulted in substantial losses or created a significant risk of substantial losses to other persons, the maximum amount of the penalty is increased to the greater of (i) one hundred thousand dollars for a natural person or five hundred thousand dollars for any other person, or (ii) the gross amount of pecuniary gain to the defendant as a result of the violation.[75]

The foregoing civil penalties are payable to the United States Treasury. If a defendant fails to pay a penalty within the time prescribed, the SEC may refer the matter to the Attorney General, who is directed to file an action in the United States district court for the payment of such penalty.

There are special penalties applicable to judicial actions to enforce cease and desist orders. In an action to enforce a cease and desist order, each separate violation of such order shall be a separate offense, and in the case of violation through a continuing failure to comply with such an order, each day of noncompliance is deemed a separate offense.[76]

Bar Orders

The penalty provisions were only part of the expansion of the SEC's enforcement authority. The 1990 legislation also empowers the SEC to seek judicial orders prohibiting certain violators from serving as officers and directors of 1934 Act reporting companies.[77] In any action by the SEC for an injunction or criminal prosecution under section 20(b) of the 1933 Act,[78] or section 21(d)(1) of the 1934 Act,[79] the court may prohibit, conditionally or unconditionally, permanently or temporarily, any person

---

75. 15 U.S.C.A. §§ 77t(d)(2), 78u(d)(3)(B), 80a–12(e)(2), 80b–9(e)(2).

76. 15 U.S.C.A. §§ 77t(d)(4), 78u(d)(3)(D), 80a–12(e)(4), 80b–9(e)(4).

77. *See* Note, An Historical Perspective to the Corporate Bar Provisions of the Securities Enforcement Remedies and Penny Stock Reform Act of 1990, 49 Wash. & Lee L. Rev. 507 (1992).

The SEC's power to seek bar orders against officers and directors is supplemented by the Commission's authority to impose bar orders administratively against securities professionals. *See, e.g.,* Elliott v. SEC, 36 F.3d 86 (11th Cir.1994) (barring individual convicted of 37 counts of mail fraud from associating with any broker-dealer).

78. 15 U.S.C.A. § 77t(b).

79. 15 U.S.C.A. § 78u(d)(1).

who has violated section 17(a)(1) of the 1933 Act[80] or section 10(b) of the 1934 Act,[81] from acting as an officer or director of any issuer that has a class of securities registered under the Securities Exchange Act of 1934[82] or that is required to file periodic reports under that Act.[83] The bar order may be issued if the violator's conduct demonstrates substantial unfitness to serve as an officer or director of any such issuer.[84]

Section 15(c)(4) Orders

As part of the Insider Trading Sanctions Act of 1984, Congress significantly expanded the SEC's administrative powers with regard to an individual or entity who was a "cause" of a failure to comply with the act's reporting requirements. Prior to the amendment, the section 15(c)(4) power was limited to coverage of violators. The new legislation thus expanded the SEC's power, after notice and opportunity for a hearing, to issue an order calling for compliance or steps towards compliance with any SEC Rule or Regulation.[85] The section 15(c)(4) order extends the SEC's administrative power beyond broker-dealers and thus gives the Commission power to issue administrative sanctions against issuers subject to the 1934 Act, as well as officers, directors and employees of such issuer, or anyone else responsible for, or who could have prevented, the violation.[86] Further, since the section 15(c)(4) order

---

80. 15 U.S.C.A. § 77q(a). Section 17(a) which prohibits any person in the offer or sale of securities, by any means of transportation or communication in interstate commerce or by mail, from employing any device or scheme to defraud. *See* § 7.6 *supra.*

81. 15 U.S.C.A. § 78j(b). Section 10(b) prohibits manipulative or deceptive acts or practices in connection with a purchase or sale of a security. *See* §§ 12.1, 13.2–13.12 *infra.*

82. 15 U.S.C.A. § 78g. *See* § 9.2 *supra.*

83. 15 U.S.C.A. §§ 77t(e), 78u(d)(2). *See* 15 U.S.C.A. § 78o(d), which is discussed in § 9.3 *supra.*

84. 15 U.S.C.A. §§ 77t(e), 78u(d)(2). *See, e.g.,* SEC v. Posner, 16 F.3d 520 (2d Cir.1994) (upholding SEC bar order and disgorgement of profits); SEC v. Patel, 1994 WL 364089, [1994–1995 Transfer Binder] Fed. Sec. L. Rep. (CCH) ¶ 98,340 (S.D.N.Y.1994) (officer and director who admitted insider trading and other fraud violations was barred from serving as an officer or director of a public company); SEC v. Delta Rental Systems, Inc., A.A.E.R.Rel. No. 338, 6 Fed.Sec.L.Rep. (CCH) ¶ 73,805 (S.D.Fla.1991) (permanent bar order). *See generally* Jayne W. Barnard, When is a Corporate Executive "Substantially Unfit to Serve"?, 70 N.C.L.Rev. 1489 (1992).

85. 15 U.S.C.A. § 78o(c)(4):

If the Commission finds, after notice and opportunity for a hearing, that any person subject to the provisions of sections 12, 13, 14 or subsection (d) of section 15 of this title or any rule or regulation thereunder has failed to comply with any such provision, rule or regulation in any material respect, the Commission may publish its findings and issue an order requiring such person, and any person who was a cause of the failure to comply due to an act or omission the person knew or should have known would contribute to the failure to comply, or take steps to effect compliance, with such provision or such rule or regulation thereunder upon such terms and conditions and within such time as the Commission may specify in such order.

See generally, Task Force of ABA Section on Business Law, Report SEC Section 15(c)(4) Proceedings, 46 Bus.Law. 253 (1990).

86. *See* In re Runge, Exch.Act Rel. No. 34–23066 (March 26, 1986) (consent order finding that Senior Vice President should have alerted the audit committee to certain problems in connection with proxy materials); In re Maury, Exch.Act Rel. No. 34–23067 (March 26, 1986) (section 15(c)(4) consent order against Vice President and Comptroller who owed a duty to the issuer and its shareholders "not to assist or even acquiesce in" the

applies to anyone subject to the provisions of section 12, 13, 14 or 15(d) of the Act, it also extends to persons and entities required to make Williams Act filings in connection with the acquisition of reporting company shares.[87] The broad terms of section 15(c)(4) do not place any limits on the types of orders that the Commission may issue. Thus, for example, the SEC could rely on section 15(c)(4) to issue an order barring an individual from being associated with a 1934 Act reporting company.[88] The bar order is but one example of the potential of this new power. The SEC has been using section 15(c)(4) proceedings to deal with a wide variety of violations.[89]

A significant exercise of the Commission's authority under section 15(c)(4) occurred in In the Matter of George Kern,[90] wherein the administrative law judge indicated that an attorney whose negligence resulted in the filing of a false document might be found to have been a cause of a violation of the Act. The ALJ held that he was without power to issue any bar order because at the time of the decision, the respondent was no longer associated with the company in question. The full Commission has affirmed the ALJ's decision solely on the grounds that it was beyond the ALJ's authority once the respondent was no longer in a position to control the company's future compliance. The *Kern* proceeding nevertheless stands as an example of the expansive potential of the section 15(c)(4) remedy.

SEC Investigations[91]

Prior to instigating formal action, the SEC generally investigates possible securities law violations that have been brought to its attention.[92] There are generally two stages of any SEC investigation. First

---

use of false financial statements). *See also, e.g.,* Arthur F. Mathews & Theodore Levine, First Amendment Problems Complicate SEC Enforcement, N.Y.L.J. p. 33 (December 10, 1984).

87. 15 U.S.C.A. §§ 78m(d), (e), 78n(d), (e), (f). The Williams Act is discussed in §§ 11.10–11.22 *infra.*

88. *Cf.* In re Blinder, Robinson & Co., Admin.Proc.File No. 3–6380, [1985–86 Transfer Binder] Fed.Sec.L.Rep. (CCH) ¶ 83,911 (SEC 1985). This, of course, is supplemented by the Commission's authority to seek bar orders in judicial proceedings. *See* footnotes 77–84 and accompanying text.

89. In addition to the authorities in footnotes 86, 88 *supra, see, e.g.,* In re Burroughs Corp., Exch.Act Rel. No. 34–21872 (March 20, 1985) (failure to comply with Foreign Corrupt Practices Act; order to comply with undertaking to restate financial statements and have auditors review internal controls); In re Broadview Financial Corp., 17 Sec.Reg. & L.Rep. (BNA) 665 (1985) (condemning the practice of opinion shopping among auditors).

90. [1991 Transfer Binder] Fed.Sec.L.Rep. (CCH) ¶ 84,815 (SEC 1991), *affirming* [1988–1989 Transfer Binder] Fed.Sec.L.Rep. (CCH) ¶ 84,342 (SEC Initial Decision 1987).

91. *See* §§ 9.30–9.33 *infra* (Practitioner's Edition only).

92. *See generally* Richard H. Rowe, Handling an SEC Investigation (1980); Arthur F. Mathews, Effective Defense of SEC Investigations: Laying the Foundation for Successful Disposition of Subsequent Civil, Administrative and Criminal Proceedings, 24 Emory L.J. 567 (1975); Arthur F. Mathews, Witnesses in SEC Investigations: A Primer for Witnesses and Their Counsel on the Scope of the SEC's Investigatory Powers, 3 Rev.Sec.Reg. 923 (1970); Lewis B. Merrifield III, SEC Investigations, 34 Bus.Law. 1583 (1977); Jeffrey A. Tew & David Freedman, Practice in Securities and Exchange Commission Investigatory and Quasi–Judicial Proceedings, 27 U.Miami L.Rev. 1 (1973).

the SEC staff conducts an informal investigation[93] which may lead to the second stage—a SEC order instituting a formal investigation.

Formal investigations are authorized when the Commission believes that there is a "likelihood" of a violation.[94] The issuance of an order authorizing a formal investigation gives the SEC staff subpoena power.[95] It has been held that the appropriate procedure for challenging an investigative subpoena is to refuse to comply and then raise the issue in the ensuing SEC enforcement action.[96] Courts will generally enforce any such subpoena unless it is shown that the Commission was not acting in good faith and thus enforcement would constitute an abuse of the court's process.[97] As stated by the Ninth Circuit, a subpoena directed to the target of a formal investigation will be upheld upon the SEC's showing: "(1) the agency has a legitimate purpose for the investigation; (2) the inquiry is relevant to that purpose; (3) the agency does not possess the information sought; and (4) the agency has adhered to administrative steps required by law."[98] In a more controversial part of the same opinion, the court also held that targets of SEC investigations have a right to notice of subpoenas served on third parties but that aspect of the ruling has been overturned.[99] The target's ability to intervene in third party proceedings is within the court's discretion where the third party does not voluntarily comply. Under the Ninth Circuit's ruling the target

93. *See* Richard W. Jennings & Harold Marsh, Jr., Securities Regulation: Cases and Materials 1231 (5th ed. 1982) ("The staff investigators may interview prospective witnesses or even prospective defendants [but] no compulsory process is available, and no one is required to talk to the investigators").

94. *Id.*

95. 15 U.S.C.A. § 78u(b).

96. 15 U.S.C.A. § 78u(c); Sprecher v. Graber, 716 F.2d 968, 975 (2d Cir.1983); Fleet/Norstar Financial Group, Inc. v. SEC., 769 F.Supp. 19 (D.Me.1991). Accordingly, a court lacks subject matter jurisdiction over a motion to quash an investigative subpoena.

97. *See* SEC v. Wheeling–Pittsburgh Steel Corp., 648 F.2d 118 (3d Cir.1981) (defendant has the burden of proving improper influence and "abdication of the agency's objective responsibilities"). *See also, e.g.,* Johnson v. SEC, [1993–1994 Transfer Binder] Fed. Sec. L. Rep. (CCH) ¶ 98,124 (S.D.N.Y.1994) (enforcing subpoena); (Garvin v. SEC), 1994 WL 724432, [1993–1994 Transfer Binder] Fed. Sec. L. Rep. (CCH) ¶ 98,126 (D.D.C.1994) (Financial Privacy Act of 1978 did not provide grounds for quashing SEC subpoena).

See also Seymour Glanzer, Howard Schiffman & Mark Packman, The Use of the Fifth Amendment in SEC Investigations, 41 Wash. & L.L.Rev. 895 (1984); Marc I. Steinberg, SEC Subpoena Enforcement Practice, 11 J.Corp.L. 1 (1985).

98. Jerry T. O'Brien, Inc. v. SEC, 704 F.2d 1065, 1067 (9th Cir.1983), *reversed on other grounds* 467 U.S. 735, 104 S.Ct. 2720, 81 L.Ed.2d 615 (1984), *on remand* 773 F.2d 1070 (9th Cir.1985) relying on United States v. Powell, 379 U.S. 48, 57–58, 85 S.Ct. 248, 254–55, 13 L.Ed.2d 112 (1964).

99. Jerry T. O'Brien, Inc. v. SEC, 704 F.2d 1065 (9th Cir.1983), *reversed* 467 U.S. 735, 104 S.Ct. 2720, 81 L.Ed.2d 615 (1984), *on remand* 773 F.2d 1070 (9th Cir.1985). *See also* SEC v. Murphy, 1983 WL 1417, [1983–1984 Transfer Binder] Fed.Sec.L.Rep. (CCH) ¶ 99,688 (C.D.Cal.1983) (the *O'Brien* notice requirement is to be applied prospectively only).

The only express statutory right to notice of an investigatory subpoena served upon a third party is in connection with bank records. Under the Right to Financial Privacy Act an administrative subpoena to a financial institution (banks, savings and loan associations, and similar institutions) is valid only if a copy of the subpoena is served upon the customer ten days in advance of the records being provided. 12 U.S.C.A. § 3405.

could seek to enjoin compliance with third party subpoenas.[100] A major problem with the Ninth Circuit's ruling was that the SEC frequently does not focus on specific targets until the decision has been made to name suspected violators as defendants. However, such notice is not required. The Supreme Court reversed the Ninth Circuit in holding that the SEC frequently does not have to give notice of third-party subpoenas.[101]

Courts on occasion will refuse to issue subpoenas if they are unusually broad in describing the information sought. An interesting variation of this issue has arisen in the context of computer files. A federal district court quashed a subpoena seeking information contained on a computer's hard disk drive where the information was not specified.[102] The court reasoned that just as a subpoena must specify documents (or categories) rather than an entire file cabinet, the same is true for information stored on or in a computer.[103]

A formal investigation is started once the Commission has found a likelihood of wrongdoing. It is only after completion of the investigation that a determination is made as to whether the securities laws were violated and if so by whom. At that time the target generally will be informed of the SEC staff's recommendation to the Commission that there be a formal authorization to bring suit.[104] This gives the target an opportunity to contest the investigation before charges are formally filed.

---

100. 704 F.2d at 1067, relying on United States v. Genser, 582 F.2d 292, 300 (3d Cir.1978), *appeal after remand* 602 F.2d 69 (3d Cir.1979), *cert. denied* 444 U.S. 928, 100 S.Ct. 269, 62 L.Ed.2d 185 (1979). In contrast, the target cannot seek an injunction against a subpoena directed to it since the appropriate remedy is to refuse to comply and contest the subpoena in an enforcement proceeding brought by the SEC. 704 F.2d at 1066–1067.

101. SEC v. Jerry T. O'Brien, Inc., 467 U.S. 735, 104 S.Ct. 2720, 81 L.Ed.2d 615 (1984), *on remand* 773 F.2d 1070 (9th Cir.1985).

102. In re Grand Jury Subpoena Duces Tecum, 26 Sec. Reg. & L. Rep. (BNA) 220 (S.D.N.Y.1994).

103. *Id.*

104. Although the Commission has rejected formal notice requirements, it has consistently informed targets of the intention to proceed with an enforcement action in order to give the potential defendants an opportunity to be heard before the enforcement action is initiated. Exch.Act Rel. No. 34–9796 (Sept. 27, 1972) ("The Commission desires not only to be informed of the findings made by its staff but also, where practicable and appropriate, to have before it the position of persons under investigation at the time it is asked to consider enforcement action * * * The Commission * * * wishes to give public notice of a practice, which it has heretofore followed on request, of permitting persons involved in an investigation to present a statement to it setting forth their interests and position. But the Commission cannot delay taking action which it believes is required pending the receipt of such a submission, and accordingly, it will be necessary, if the material is to be considered, that it be timely submitted. In determining what course of action to pursue, interested persons may find it helpful to discuss the matter with the staff members conducting the investigation. The staff, in its discretion, may advise prospective defendants or respondents of the general nature of its investigation, including the indicated violations as they pertain to them, and the amount of time that may be available for preparing a submission. The staff must, however, have discretion in this regard in order to protect the public interest and to avoid not only delay, but possible untoward consequences which would obstruct or delay necessary enforcement action").

This notice is referred to as a "Wells submission." The advisory committee's recommendations of more formal notice requirements are found in Report of the Advisory Committee on Enforcement Policies and Practices (June 1, 1972).

During investigatory proceedings, witnesses and persons under investigation are allowed to have their attorneys present.[105] Furthermore, nonlawyers such as accountants may also be present.[106] There is a split of authority as to whether SEC investigations are "adversary proceedings" within the meaning of the Equal Access to Justice Act so as to warrant the award of attorneys fees following termination of investigation without prosecution; although most courts appear to take the view that an award is proper under appropriate circumstances.[107] It has also been held that allegedly abusive SEC investigations do not give rise to a claim against the SEC and further the doctrines of sovereign and official immunity preclude suit against the Commission and individuals.[108]

Criminal Sanctions; Parallel Proceedings

SEC investigations that reveal wrongdoing may result in SEC injunction actions brought in federal district court.[109] Alternatively, the SEC can refer the case to the Department of Justice to determine if criminal sanctions are appropriate.[110] The Commission and the Department of Justice may cooperate in their parallel proceedings.[111] In

---

105. SEC v. Whitman, 613 F.Supp. 48 (D.D.C.1985), *reconsideration denied* 625 F.Supp. 96 (D.D.C.1985).

106. SEC v. Whitman, 613 F.Supp. 48 (D.D.C.1985), *reconsideration denied* 625 F.Supp. 96 (D.D.C.1985) (permitting accountant to accompany lawyer notwithstanding possible contrary interpretation of SEC Rule of Practice where absence of nonlawyer would interfere with lawyer's ability to adequately represent client).

107. *Compare* SEC v. Kluesner, 834 F.2d 1438 (8th Cir.1987) (upholding award of attorneys fees under Equal Access to Justice Act); SEC v. Kaufman, 835 F.Supp. 157 (S.D.N.Y.1993) (awarding costs and expenses following dismissal of injunctive action); Wall Street West, (SEC Jan. 12, 1984) (awarding attorneys fees) *with* Family Television, Inc. v. SEC, 608 F.Supp. 882 (D.D.C.1985) (denying attorneys fees).

108. Sprecher v. Von Stein, 772 F.2d 16 (2d Cir.1985). *Accord* Austin Municipal Securities, Inc. v. National Association of Securities Dealers, 757 F.2d 676 (5th Cir.1985) (the NASD and its disciplinary officials enjoy absolute immunity in connection from civil liability for their disciplinary activities). *See also* Kendrick v. Zanides, 609 F.Supp. 1162 (N.D.Cal.1985) (imposing sanctions under Fed.R.Civ.P. 11 for expenses and attorneys fees in frivolous suit brought against SEC staff members).

109. *See* text accompanying footnotes 9–31 *supra.* There is no requirement that the SEC turn the matter over to the Attorney General; the Commission is free to pursue civil proceedings. SEC v. Paradyne Corp., 1985 WL 5839, [1985–1986 Transfer Binder] Fed. Sec.L.Rep. (CCH) ¶ 92,464 (M.D.Fla.1985).

110. 15 U.S.C.A. § 78u(d). *See* United States v. DeVeau, 734 F.2d 1023 (5th Cir.1984), *cert. denied* 469 U.S. 1158, 105 S.Ct. 906, 83 L.Ed.2d 921 (1985) (dismissal of conspiracy count did not preclude finding of sufficient criminal intent for primary violation). *See also, e.g.,* United States v. Groover, 957 F.2d 796 (10th Cir.1992) (indictment charging violations of Rule 10b–5 and general conspiracy statute was not multiplicity); United States v. Benskin, 926 F.2d 562 (6th Cir.1991) (discussing federal sentencing guidelines and upholding upward departure from the guidelines).

See generally Arthur F. Mathews, SEC Enforcement and White Collar Crimes (1979); Arthur F. Mathews, Criminal Prosecutions Under the Federal Securities Laws and Related Statutes: The Nature and Development of SEC Criminal Cases, 39 Geo.Wash.L.Rev. 901 (1971).

111. SEC v. Dresser Industries, Inc., 628 F.2d 1368 (D.C.Cir.1980), *cert. denied* 449 U.S. 993, 101 S.Ct. 529, 66 L.Ed.2d 289 (1980); United States v. Fields, 592 F.2d 638, 646 (2d Cir.1978), *cert. denied* 442 U.S. 917, 99 S.Ct. 2838, 61 L.Ed.2d 284 (1979). *Cf.* Comptroller of the Currency v. Lance, 632 F.Supp. 437 (N.D.Ga.1986) (refusing to stay action by Comptroller of the Currency to enforce Exchange Act reporting requirements with regard to national bank).

contrast, the Supreme Court has refused to endorse parallel proceedings of the IRS and Department of Justice.[112] Also, as pointed out earlier in this section, double jeopardy problems can arise in connection with parallel civil and criminal proceedings when the civil action seeks a civil penalty.

On occasion, there have been claims that parallel proceedings can prejudice the defendant.[113] However, the courts have not been receptive to such claims. Thus, for example, courts have refused to stay the civil action pending the outcome of the criminal case notwithstanding claims of possible adverse publicity resulting from the civil case[114] or feared abuse of the civil discovery procedures to aid in the criminal prosecution.[115] There have also been claims that the SEC's control of civil proceedings violates the constitutional separation of powers but such claims have been rejected.[116]

Section 21(a) Reports

Investigations do not always culminate in enforcement actions, even when the Commission concludes that the securities laws have been violated. The SEC can publicize the results of its investigations. Section 21(a) of the 1934 Act expressly authorizes such public reports.[117] The institution of civil litigation in a matter does not limit the Commission's ability to continue with a section 21(a) investigation parallel to the law suit.[118] To date, however, this power to issue public reports has not

See also Blinder Robinson & Co. v. SEC, 837 F.2d 1099, 1104–05 (D.C.Cir.1988), *cert. denied* 488 U.S. 869, 109 S.Ct. 177, 102 L.Ed.2d 146 (1988) (upholding SEC's power to institute administrative proceedings after successfully obtaining relief in a judicial SEC enforcement action).

112. The Supreme Court has enjoined continuation of IRS investigations after criminal prosecution had been recommended. United States v. LaSalle National Bank, 437 U.S. 298, 98 S.Ct. 2357, 57 L.Ed.2d 221 (1978); Donaldson v. United States, 400 U.S. 517, 91 S.Ct. 534, 27 L.Ed.2d 580 (1971). *See also* Note, Concurrent Civil and Criminal Proceedings, 67 Colum.L.Rev. 1277 (1967).

113. *Cf.* United States v. Elliott, 714 F.Supp. 380 (N.D.Ill.1989) (securities trader who disgorged profits as part of SEC settlement, would not be asked to pay the money again under RICO forfeiture provisions) *See also* discussion in the text accompanying footnotes 54–56 *supra.*

114. SEC v. Grossman, 121 F.R.D. 207 (S.D.N.Y.1987). *See, e.g.,* SEC v. Mersky, 1994 WL 22305, [1993–1994 Transfer Binder] Fed. Sec. L. Rep. (CCH) ¶ 98,077 (E.D.Pa.1994) (issuing a stay of SEC proceedings pending conclusion of criminal proceedings).

115. United States SEC v. First Jersey Securities, Inc. (S.D.N.Y.1987) (Unpublished Case). *But cf.* SEC v. Chestman, 861 F.2d 49 (2d Cir.1988) (staying discovery in SEC civil enforcement action pending completion of criminal action).

116. *See* SEC v. Davis, 689 F.Supp. 767 (S.D.Ohio 1988); SEC v. Warner, 652 F.Supp. 647 (S.D.Fla.1987) (rejecting the constitutional challenge). *But see* Meyer Blinder v. SEC, 87 Civ. 1086 (D.D.C. March 26, 1987) (staying sanction pending determination of the "very substantial constitutional issues").

117. 15 U.S.C.A. § 78u(a). *See* Dennis L. Block & Nancy E. Barton, Securities Litigation—Section 21(a): A New Enforcement Tool, 7 Sec.Reg.L.J. 265 (1979).

118. *See* SEC v. F.N. Wolf & Co., [1993–1994 Transfer Binder] Fed. Sec. L. Rep. (CCH) ¶ 98,015 (S.D.N.Y.1993).

been utilized to its optimal extent.[119]   In fact, section 21(a) has formed
the basis of much recent controversy.   In In re Spartek, Inc.,[120] the
Commission issued a section 21(a) report of a staff investigation including the acceptance of the registrant's offer of settlement.   Commissioner
Karmel vigorously dissented, considering the report to be in excess of the
SEC's jurisdiction.[121]   She reasoned that the publicity function could not
properly be used as an alternative to SEC enforcement actions.[122]   The
SEC has since used the publicity function in this manner.[123]   Additionally, the SEC has issued a statement of practice supporting the use of
section 21(a) reports and asserting that "where it appears to be in the
public interest," settlement statements given to the Commission should
be submitted "with the expectation that the Commission may make the
statements public." [124]   Once again, Commissioner Karmel voiced her
dissent, pointing, *inter alia,* to possible due process objections.[125]

SEC Administrative Proceedings

   The SEC is empowered to hold administrative hearings in the course
of exercising its supervisory authority over broker-dealers,[126] national
exchanges,[127] investment companies and advisers,[128] municipal securities
dealers,[129] government securities dealers,[130] and public utility holding
companies.[131]   These are generally disciplinary proceedings.

   In 1990, the Commission requested that it be given cease and desist
power.[132]   Both houses of Congress passed separate versions of the
legislation that would give the Commission this power.   As anticipated,

---

   119.   *See* BNA Interview: Pollack Questions Advisability of Passing Federal Securities
Code at This Time. 484 Sec.Reg. & L.Rep. (BNA) AA–1 (Jan. 3, 1979).

   120.   Exch.Act Rel. No. 34–15567, 491 Sec.Reg. & L.Rep. (BNA) E–1 (February 21,
1979).

   121.   *Id.* at E–4.

   122.   *Id.* at E–5.

   123.   *E.g.* In re Howard Bronson & Co., Exch.Act Rel. No. 34–21138 (July 12, 1984);
Compass Investment Group, Exch.Act Rel. No. 34–16343 (Nov. 15, 1979); Vance, Sanders
& Co., Exch.Act Rel. No. 34–15746 (April 18, 1979); Marine Protein Corp. Industrial
Development Revenue Bonds, Exch.Act Rel. No. 34–15719, 499 Sec.Reg. & L.Rep. (BNA)
E–1 (April 18, 1979).   *See also, e.g.,* Exch.Act Rel. No. 34–15665 (March 21, 1979).

   For a recent use of the section 21(a) investigatory and reporting power, *see* In the Matter
of Transactions in Securities of Laser Arms Corporation by Certain Broker Dealers,
Exch.Act Rel. No. 34–28878 (SEC Feb. 14, 1991).   The investigation arose out of "pink
sheet" trading of a fictitious company with no assets; the report highlights the role that
broker-dealers can play in preventing fraud in the trading of over the counter securities.

   124.   Exch.Act Rel. No. 34–15664 [1979 Transfer Binder] Fed.Sec.L.Rep. (CCH) ¶ 82,014
at pp. 81,557–558 (March 21, 1979).

   125.   *Id.* at ¶ 81,558.

   126.   15 U.S.C.A. § 78o–1.   *See* § 10.2 *infra.*

   127.   15 U.S.C.A. §§ 78l, 78s.   *See* §§ 10.1, 10.2 *infra.*

   128.   *See* 15 U.S.C.A. § 80a–1 *et seq.,* 80b–1 *et seq.*   *See* chapters 17, 18 *infra.*

   129.   15 U.S.C.A. § 78o–4.   *See* § 10.5 *infra.*

   130.   15 U.S.C.A. § 78o–5.   *See* § 10.5.1 *infra.*

   131.   15 U.S.C.A. § 79a *et seq.*   *See* chapter 15 *infra.*

   132.   *See* 22 Sec.Reg. & L.Rep. (BNA) 155 (Feb. 2, 1990).

the House and Senate legislation were reconciled and the Commission's cease and desist power became law.[133] In addition in 1990, the Commission was given the authority to impose civil penalties in administrative proceedings.[134]

Pursuant to section 6 of the 1934 Act, the Commission is charged with overseeing national securities exchanges.[135] Although the power has been exercised only once,[136] the SEC may suspend or revoke registration of an exchange.[137] The SEC also has the power to expel individual broker-dealers from a national exchange.[138] The 1934 Act additionally charges the SEC with overseeing registered securities associations and other broker-dealer self-regulatory organizations.[139] The Commission can suspend or revoke an association's registration[140] as well as suspend or expel a member of the association.[141] Also, by virtue of its registration of broker-dealers,[142] the Commission has the power to suspend or revoke such registration.[143] The Commission can bar any person from

133. *See* § 9.5.1 *infra* (Practitioner's Edition only).

134. Securities Exchange Act of 1934 § 21B, 15 U.S.C.A. § 78u–2; Investment Company Act § 9(d), (e), 15 U.S.C.A. § 80a–9(d), (e); Investment Advisers Act § 203(i), 15 U.S.C.A. § 80b–3(i).

135. 15 U.S.C.A. § 78f.

136. San Francisco Mining Exchange v. SEC, 378 F.2d 162 (9th Cir.1967).

137. 15 U.S.C.A. § 78s(h)(1).

138. 15 U.S.C.A. § 78s(h)(2). *See, e.g.,* Archer v. SEC, 133 F.2d 795 (8th Cir.1943).

139. 15 U.S.C.A. §§ 78*o* –3, 78q–1, 78s, 78c(a)(26), 78c(a)(34). The Commission is the reviewing authority for sanctions imposed by the exchanges, the National Association of Securities Dealers (NASD), and other self-regulatory organizations pursuant to §§ 6(d), 15A(h), 17A(b)(5), and 19(d)–(f) of the Exchange Act, 15 U.S.C.A. §§ 78f(d), 78*o*–3h, 78*l*–1(b)(5), 78o(d)–(f) (1976). *See generally* Lewis D. Lowenfels, A Lack of Fair Procedures in the Administrative Process: Disciplinary Proceedings at the Stock Exchanges and the NASD, 64 Cornell L.Rev. 375 (1979); Norman S. Poser, Reply to Lowenfels, 74 Cornell L.Rev. 402 (1979); Note, Governmental Action and the National Association of Securities Dealers, 47 Fordham L.Rev. 585 (1979). For a recent case discussing the SEC's standard of review of NASD disciplinary sanctions, *see* Sartain v. SEC, 601 F.2d 1366 (9th Cir.1979). *See also* Bradford National Clearing Corp. v. SEC, 590 F.2d 1085 (D.C.Cir.1978) (discussing the commission's oversight responsibilities).

140. 15 U.S.C.A. § 78s(h)(1).

141. 15 U.S.C.A. § 78s(h)(2). *See, e.g.,* Mister Discount Stockbrokers, Inc. v. SEC, 768 F.2d 875 (7th Cir.1985) (expelling brokerage firm from NASD); Austin Municipal Securities v. NASD, 757 F.2d 676 (5th Cir.1985) (rejecting an antitrust challenge to the NASD's disciplinary power). Don D. Anderson & Co. v. SEC, 423 F.2d 813 (10th Cir.1970) (suspension for violation of 1934 Act); Tager v. SEC, 344 F.2d 5 (2d Cir.1965) (expulsion for violation of 1933 Act); Financial Counsellors, Inc. v. SEC, 339 F.2d 196 (2d Cir.1964) (expulsion for violation of 1934 Act); Gilligan, Will & Co. v. SEC, 267 F.2d 461 (2d Cir.1959), *cert. denied* 361 U.S. 896, 80 S.Ct. 200, 4 L.Ed.2d 152 (1959) (suspension for violation of 1933 Act).

142. 15 U.S.C.A. § 78*o*.

143. 15 U.S.C.A. § 78*o*(b)(5). *See, e.g.,* Svalberg v. SEC, 876 F.2d 181 (D.C.Cir.1989) (permanently barring brokers from serving as principals in any NASD member firm). *Cf.* Antoniu v. SEC, 877 F.2d 721 (8th Cir.1989), *cert. denied* 494 U.S. 1004, 110 S.Ct. 1296, 108 L.Ed.2d 473 (1990) (nullifying Commission order permanently barring association with a broker-dealer because of public statements made by a Commissioner prior to the proceedings which indicated that he had prejudged the matter); Dlugash v. SEC, 373 F.2d 107 (2d Cir.1967) (revocation); Peoples Securities Co. v. SEC, 289 F.2d 268 (5th Cir.1961) (denial of registration); Gilligan, Will & Co. v. SEC, 267 F.2d 461 (2d Cir.1959), *cert. denied* 361 U.S. 896, 80 S.Ct. 200, 4 L.Ed.2d 152 (1959) (suspension). The Commission

associating with a broker-dealer,[144] a member of a registered securities association,[145] or an investment adviser,[146] or bar that person from serving in various capacities with a registered investment company.[147] With respect to all of the powers discussed above, the Commission can impose the less drastic sanction of censure.[148]

The Supreme Court has held that in reviewing SEC sanctions, the courts of appeals should affirm the Commission's findings if they are supported by a preponderance of the evidence.[149] For the purpose of determining the timeliness of an appeal, the period begins to run from the caption date on the SEC final order.[150] Also in judging the severity of sanctions imposed by an administrative law judge, the SEC has refused to base a reduction on lighter sanctions in allegedly comparable cases.[151] The SEC pointed out that the lighter sanctions in other proceedings that were settled may reflect the expediency of settlement rather than the severity of the challenged conduct. Thus, the reviewing body properly gives deference to the decisionmaker below.

Direct appeal to the SEC is the proper method of review for NASD disciplinary sanctions and the sanctions are not reviewable by way of collateral attack in a subsequent SEC judicial enforcement action.[152] The normal review process is from the NASD to the SEC and then to a federal court of appeals.[153] The same procedure applies in the case of sanctions imposed by a securities exchange.

has parallel authority over investment advisers under the 1940 Advisers Act. 15 U.S.C.A. § 80b–3(e).

144. 15 U.S.C.A. § 78o(b)(6). *See, e.g.,* Elliott v. SEC, 36 F.3d 86 (11th Cir.1994) (barring individual convicted of 37 counts of mail fraud from associating with any broker-dealer). Berdahl v. SEC, 572 F.2d 643 (8th Cir.1978); Chatham v. SEC, 604 F.2d 1368 (D.C.Cir.1978); Collins Securities Corp. v. SEC, 562 F.2d 820 (D.C.Cir.1977); Stead v. SEC, 444 F.2d 713 (10th Cir.1971), *cert. denied* 404 U.S. 1059, 92 S.Ct. 739, 30 L.Ed.2d 746 (1972); Exch.Act Rel. No. 34–14668 (April 17, 1978); Exch.Act Rel. No. 34–14918 (July 3, 1976).

145. 15 U.S.C.A. § 78s(h)(3). *See, e.g.,* Mister Discount Stockbrokers, Inc. v. SEC, 768 F.2d 875 (7th Cir.1985). O'Leary v. SEC, 424 F.2d 908 (D.C.Cir.1970); Exch.Act Rel. No. 34–14759 (May 15, 1978).

146. 15 U.S.C.A. § 80b–3(f).

147. 15 U.S.C.A. § 78a–9(b).

148. *See* Exch.Act Rel. No. 34–14761 (May 15, 1978).

149. Steadman v. SEC, 450 U.S. 91, 101 S.Ct. 999, 67 L.Ed.2d 69 (1981), *rehearing denied* 451 U.S. 933, 101 S.Ct. 2008, 68 L.Ed.2d 318 (1981). *See* Note, Scope of Review or Standard of Proof—Judicial Control of SEC Sanctions, 93 Harv.L.Rev. 1845 (1980). *See also, e.g.,* Erdos v. SEC, 742 F.2d 507 (9th Cir.1984).

150. Newell v. SEC, 812 F.2d 1259 (9th Cir.1987).

151. Butcher & Singer, Exch.Act Rel. No. 34–23990 (Jan. 13, 1987).

152. SEC v. Waco Financial, Inc., 751 F.2d 831 (6th Cir.1985), *cert. denied* 474 U.S. 818, 106 S.Ct. 65, 88 L.Ed.2d 53 (1985).

153. *See, e.g.,* Maschler v. National Association of Securities Dealers, 827 F.Supp. 131 (E.D.N.Y.1993). Since judicial review is vested in the courts of appeals, federal district courts cannot assert jurisdiction. *Id.*

Administrative Proceedings and Double Jeopardy

As discussed above, the Supreme Court in *Halper* held that the imposition of a civil penalty in proceedings following a criminal prosecution may violate the Double Jeopardy Clause.[154] What, if any, are the implications of the Double Jeopardy Clause and *Halper* on SEC administrative proceedings that follow a criminal prosecution? It seems clear that administrative proceedings imposing disciplinary sanctions against market professionals, such as suspension of registration, are not criminal in nature and thus do not implicate double jeopardy prohibitions. Similarly, double jeopardy should not interfere with cease and desist powers or other nonmonetary administrative sanctions.[155] On the other hand, if the goal of the administrative proceeding is to impose a civil fine or penalty, then *Halper* would appear to be implicated.

Civil Penalties in Administrative Actions

The Securities Enforcement Remedies and Penny Stock Reform Act of 1990[156] empowers the Commission to impose civil penalties in administrative proceedings.[157] The power to impose civil penalties applies to proceedings against a broker-dealer,[158] associated person,[159] municipal securities dealer,[160] government securities dealer,[161] or registered clearing agent.[162] The SEC has similar authority over persons registered under the Investment Company or Investment Advisers Act of 1940.[163] If, after

---

154. United States v. Halper, 490 U.S. 435, 109 S.Ct. 1892, 104 L.Ed.2d 487 (1989), which is discussed in the text accompanying footnotes 64–66.

155. In the Matter of Incomco, Inc., [1991 Transfer Binder] Comm.Fut.L.Rep. (CCH) ¶ 25,198 (CFTC 1991) (ruling that CFTC could impose trading ban and impose other nonmonetary penalties). *Accord, e.g.,* In the Matter of Fetchenhier, [1991 Transfer Binder] Comm.Fut.L.Rep. (CCH) ¶ 25,173 (CFTC 1991). *See also, e.g.,* United States v. Furlett, 781 F.Supp. 536 (N.D.Ill.1991) (prior imposition of administrative sanctions did not bar criminal action).

156. Pub.L. No. 101–429. *See* Comment, The Securities Enforcement Remedies and Penny Stock Reform Act of 1990: By Keeping up with the Joneses, the SEC's Enforcement Arsenal is Modernized, 7 Admin. L.J. Am. U. 151 (1993) The provisions relating to penny stock are discussed in § 10.7 *infra.*

157. Securities Exchange Act of 1934 § 21B, 15 U.S.C.A. § 78u–2; Investment Company Act § 9(d), (e), 15 U.S.C.A. § 80a–9(d), (e); Investment Advisers Act § 203(i), 15 U.S.C.A. § 80b–3(i).

Following the rule that there is no statute of limitations applicable to SEC judicial injunctive actions (*see* text accompanying footnotes 22–23 *supra*), the SEC took the position that there is no statute of limitations applicable to the Commissions institution of administrative proceedings to enforce the Act. In the Matter of Patricia A. Johnson, Exch. Act Rel. No. 34–33664, [1993–1994 Transfer Binder] Fed. Sec. L. Rep. (CCH) ¶ 85,323 (SEC 1994). However, a court of appeals decision casts some doubt on this position. In 3M Corp. v. Browner, 17 F.3d 1453 (D.C.Cir.1994), the court ruled that 28 U.S.C.A. 2462 which imposes a five-year limitations period to actions seeking enforcement of any civil fine, penalty or forfeiture, applies to both judicial and administrative proceedings.

158. *See* section 15(b)(4), 15 U.S.C.A. § 78o(b)(4).

159. *See* section 15(b)(6), 15 U.S.C.A. § 78o(b)(6).

160. *See* section 15B, 15 U.S.C.A. § 78o–4.

161. *See* section 15C, 15 U.S.C.A. § 78o–5.

162. *See* section 17A, 15 U.S.C.A. § 78q–1.

163. 15 U.S.C.A. §§ 80a–9(d), (e), 80b–3(i).

notice and opportunity to be heard, the Commission finds: (1) a willful violation of the securities laws, (2) a willful violation of the rules of an applicable self regulatory organization, (3) that the respondent has willfully made material misstatements or omissions in required reports, or (4) has willfully failed to adequately supervise persons,[164] then it may impose a civil penalty according to a three-tiered maximum, depending upon the degree of the respondent's culpability and the impact of the violations.[165] In considering whether the imposition of a penalty is warranted, and if so the appropriate amount of the penalty, the Commission is directed to consider a number of factors. The Commission must consider the degree of culpability, the harm to others, the extent to which the violator was unjustly enriched, whether the violator has previously run afoul of the securities laws (or similar laws), the need to deter such conduct, "and other matters as justice may require."[166] In considering whether to impose such a penalty, the Commission must consider any evidence the respondent chooses to introduce that relates to his or her ability to pay.[167] In addition to a penalty, the Commission is empowered to order a disgorgement or accounting of profits.[168]

Cease and Desist Authority

A major part of the 1990 enforcement legislation was the granting to the Commission of its cease and desist power.[169] If the SEC finds, after notice and opportunity to be heard, that a regulated securities professional is violating, has violated, or is about to violate any rule or regulation, the SEC may issue a cease and desist order against that person for any current or future violations, and against any other person

---

164. *See* section 15(b)(4)(E), 15 U.S.C.A. § 78*o*(b)(4)(E).

165. As set forth in section 21B of the Exchange Act:

(b)(1) FIRST TIER. The maximum amount of penalty for each act or omission described in subsection (a) shall be $5,000 for a natural person or $50,000 for any other person.

(2) SECOND TIER. Notwithstanding paragraph (1), the maximum penalty for each act or omission shall be $50,000 for a natural person or $250,000 for any other person if the act or omission described in subsection (a) involved fraud, deceit, manipulation, or deliberate or reckless disregard of a regulatory requirement.

(3) THIRD TIER. Notwithstanding paragraphs (1) and (2) the maximum amount of penalty for each such act or omission shall be $100,000 for a natural person or $500,000 for any other person if—

(A) the act or omission described in subsection (a) involved fraud, deceit, manipulation, or deliberate or reckless disregard of a regulatory requirement; and

(B) such act or omission directly or indirectly resulted in substantial losses or created a significant risk of substantial losses to other persons or resulted in substantial pecuniary gain to the person who committed the act or omission.

15 U.S.C.A. § 78u–3.

166. Section 21C, 15 U.S.C.A. § 78u–3(c).

167. Section 21(C)(d). 15 U.S.C.A. § 78u–3(d).

168. Section 21C(e), 15 U.S.C.A. § 78u–3(e).

169. Securities Act of 1933 § 8A, 15 U.S.C.A. § 77h–1; Securities Exchange Act of 1934 §§ 21C, 23(d), 15 U.S.C.A. §§ 78u–3, 78w(d); Investment Company Act of 1940 § 9(f), 15 U.S.C.A. § 80a–9(f); Investment Advisers Act of 1940 § 203(k), 15 U.S.C.A. § 80b–3(k). *See* John F. X. Peloso & Elizabeth A. Corley, The SEC's Cease and Desist Powers, 26 Rev.Sec. & Commod.Reg. 11 (1993).

who causes the violation due to an act or omission that the person knew or should have known would contribute to such violation.[170] The authority to issue a cease and desist order may be invoked against any person who violates the Act. In addition, the Commission may order an asset freeze if the proceeding is against a respondent who acts, or during the alleged misconduct acted, as a broker, dealer, investment advisor, investment company, municipal securities dealer, government securities broker, government securities dealer, transfer agent, or associate of any of the foregoing.[171]

In any cease and desist proceeding, the SEC may order an accounting and disgorgement, including reasonable interest. In furtherance of this remedy, the SEC may adopt rules and orders concerning payments to investors, rates of interest, periods of accrual, and other matters it deems appropriate to implement this subsection. In addition, by October 1991, the SEC is directed to establish regulations providing for the expeditious conduct of hearings and rendering of decisions for cease and desist proceedings.

When instituting cease and desist proceedings, the notice of proceedings must fix a hearing date between thirty and sixty days after service of the notice, unless an earlier or later date is established by the SEC with respondent's consent.[172] The Commission may enter a temporary order if it determines that the violation is likely to result in: (i) significant dissipation—conversion of assets, (ii) significant harm to investors, or (iii) substantial harm to the public interest.[173] If the SEC determines that notice of the temporary order is impracticable, or contrary to public interest, the order becomes effective upon service. It remains effective pending completion of the proceedings unless the SEC or a competent court limits it or sets it aside.[174]

A respondent who has been made the subject of a temporary cease and desist order may apply to the Commission to have the order set aside or limited. This application to set the order aside may be made at any time after being served with such an order.[175]

170. *See, e.g.,* In the Matter of Haeglin, Acc. & Audit. Enforcement Rel. No. 461, Fed.Sec.L.Rep. (CCH)¶ 73,920 (SEC 1993) (cease and desist order against CFO and President in connection with misleading financial filings). For an example of the SEC's use of its cease and desist authority against an attorney, *see* In the Matter of Jeffry L. Feldman, Admin. File No. 3–8063 (SEC May 27, 1993) (claiming attorney's allegedly faulty advice constituted aiding and abetting a section 5 violation). The cease and desist power has also been invoked against accountants. *E.g.,* In the Matter of Hassebroek, Acc. & Audit. Enforcement Rel. No. 454, Fed.Sec.L.Rep. (CCH) ¶ 73,913 (SEC 1993).

171. 15 U.S.C.A. § 77h–1(c)(2); 15 U.S.C.A. § 78u–2; 15 U.S.C.A. § 80a–9(f)(3)(B); 15 U.S.C.A. § 80b–3(k)(3)(B).

172. 15 U.S.C.A. § 77h–1(b); 15 U.S.C.A. § 78u–3(c); 15 U.S.C.A. § 80a–9(f)(2); 15 U.S.C.A. § 80b–3(k)(2).

173. 15 U.S.C.A. § 77h–1(c)(1); 15 U.S.C.A. § 78u–3(c)(1); 15 U.S.C.A. § 80a–9(f)(3)(A); 15 U.S.C.A. § 80b–3(k)(3)(A).

174. 15 U.S.C.A. § 77h–1(c)(1); 15 U.S.C.A. § 78u–3(c)(1); 15 U.S.C.A. § 80a–9(f)(3)(A); 15 U.S.C.A. § 80b–3(k)(3)(A).

175. 15 U.S.C.A. § 77h–1(d)(1); 15 U.S.C.A. § 78u–2(d)(1); 15 U.S.C.A. § 80a–9(f)(4)(A); 15 U.S.C.A. § 80b–3(k)(4)(A).

In addition to Commission review, the subject of a cease and desist order may seek judicial review. Within 10 days after being served with a cease and desist order entered with a prior SEC hearing (or within 10 days after the SEC renders a decision on an application, pursuant to the SEC review procedure, regarding any cease and desist order entered without a prior SEC hearing), a respondent may apply to the United States District Court in his or her residential district, business district, or the District of Columbia, for an order setting aside, suspending or limiting the cease and desist order.[176] The initiation of judicial review proceedings does not operate as a stay of the SEC's order, unless specifically ordered by the court.[177]

Suspension of the Right to Practice Before the Commission[178]

Under SEC Rule of Practice 2(e) the Commission may suspend, limit, or bar *"any* person" from practicing before it "in *any* way." [179] Rule 2(e) has been used by the SEC to discipline professionals.[180] The Rule 2(e) power has been used against both accountants[181] and lawyers.[182]

If the respondent has been served with an order entered without a prior SEC hearing, he may, within 10 days after the order was served, request a hearing on his application. In such a case, the Commission is directed to hold a hearing and render a decision at the earliest possible time.

176. 15 U.S.C.A. § 77h–1(d)(2); 15 U.S.C.A. § 78u–2(d)(2); 15 U.S.C.A. § 80a–9(f)(4)(B); 15 U.S.C.A. § 80b–3(k)(4)(B).

A respondent served with a temporary cease and desist order entered without a prior SEC hearing may not apply to the court except after hearing and decision by the SEC.

177. 15 U.S.C.A. § 77h–1(d)(3); 15 U.S.C.A. § 78u–2(d)(3); 15 U.S.C.A. § 80a–9(f)(4)(C); 15 U.S.C.A. § 80b–3(k)(4)(C).

178. The following discussion is adapted from Hazen, *supra* footnote 8 at 439–440.

179. 17 C.F.R. § 201.2(e)(3). *See* § 9.7 *infra* (Practitioner's Edition only).

180. *See generally* Ralph C. Ferarra, Administratively Disciplinary Proceedings Under Rule 2(e), 36 Bus.Law. 1807 (1981); Daniel L. Goelzer & Susan F. Wyderko, Rule 2(e): Securities and Exchange Commission Discipline of Professionals, 85 Nw.U.L.Rev. 652 (1991); Harold Marsh, Jr., Rule 2(e) Proceedings, 35 Bus.Law. 987 (1980). *See also, e.g.,* In re Bernstein, AAER–391, 6 Fed.Sec.L.Rep. (CCH) ¶ 73,850 (SEC 1992) (barring controller from SEC practice).

181. *E.g.* Checkosky v. SEC, 23 F.3d 452 (D.C.Cir.1994) (remanding Rule 2(e) sanction of accountants for more adequate explanation of how the rule applied to the improper professional conduct that the ALJ identified); Davy v. SEC, 792 F.2d 1418 (9th Cir.1986) (upholding that SEC's power to discipline accountants under Rule 2(e); also holding that SEC authority under section 23(a) of the Exchange Act is not limited to the regulation of persons enumerated therein). Touche Ross & Co. v. SEC, 609 F.2d 570 (2d Cir.1979); Kenneth J. Bialkin, Sanctions Against Accountants, 8 Rev.Sec.Reg. 823 (1975); John C. Burton, SEC Enforcement and Accountants: Philosophy, Objectives and Approach, 28 Vand.L.Rev. 19 (1975); Jay R. Troger, Reassessing the Validity of SEC Rule 2(3) Discipline of Accountants, 59 Bost.U.L.Rev. 968 (1979). Note, Disciplinary Proceedings Against Accountants: The Need for a More Ascertainable Improper Professional Conduct Standard in the SEC's Rule 2(e), 53 Fordham L.Rev. 351 (1984).

182. *E.g.* In the Matter of Carter & Johnson, Exch.Act Rel. No. 34–17597, [1981 Transfer Binder] Fed.Sec.L.Rep. (CCH) ¶ 82,847 (Feb. 28, 1981)(dismissing case because of lack of scienter); In the Matter of Kearing, Muething & Klekamp, Exch.Act Rel. No. 34–15982 (July 2, 1979); In the Matter of Emmanuel Fields, Sec.Act Rel. No. 33–5404 (June 18, 1973), *affirmed without opinion* 495 F.2d 1075 (D.C.Cir.1974). *See, e.g.,* Dennis J. Block & Charles I. Ferris, SEC Rule 2(e)—A New Standard for Ethical Conduct or Unauthorized Web of Ambiguity?, 11 Cap.U.L.Rev. 501 (1982); Robert W. Dockery, Attorney Liability Under SEC Rule 2(e): A New Standard, 11 Tex.Tech.L.Rev. 83 (1979);

Although use of Rule 2(e)'s sanctions has been questioned in light of the absence of express statutory authority, the Second Circuit has upheld the rule as consistent with the Commission's overall statutory mandate:

> We reject appellants' argument for several reasons. First, it is clear that the SEC is not attempting to usurp the jurisdiction of the federal courts to deal with "violations" of the securities laws. The Commission, through its Rule 2(e) proceeding, is merely attempting to preserve the integrity of its own procedures, by assuring the fitness of those professionals who represent others before the Commission. Indeed, the Commission has made it clear that its intent in promulgating Rule 2(e) was not to utilize the rule as an additional weapon in its enforcement arsenal, but rather to determine whether a person's professional qualifications, including his character and integrity, are such that he is fit to appear and practice before the Commission. * * *
>
> Moreover, an examination of the policies underlying the securities laws indicates that, contrary to appellants' assertions, the Rule is not inconsistent with the Commission's statutory authority.[183]

The court's reasoning emphasizes that Rule 2(e) has a valid role, not as a remedy for violations of the securities acts, but as a tool to maintain the integrity of practice before the Commission.[184] The Ninth and D.C. Circuits have similarly upheld Rule 2(e) as a valid exercise of the SEC's rulemaking authority.[185]

In 1988, the Commission amended Rule 2(e) so that unless the SEC orders otherwise, Rule 2(e) proceedings shall be public. Prior to the controversial amendments, Rule 2(e) proceedings were presumed to be nonpublic unless the SEC ordered that they be public. The SEC has also indicated that scienter must be shown in order to discipline attorneys for violations of the antifraud rules.[186]

Robert A. Downing & Richard L. Miller, Jr., The Distortion and Misuse of Rule 2(3), 54 Notre Dame Law. 774 (1979); Paul Gonson, Disciplinary Proceedings and Other Remedies Available to the SEC, 30 Bus.Law. 191 (1975); Marsh *supra* footnote 180.

183. Touche Ross & Co. v. SEC, 609 F.2d 570, 579 (2d Cir.1979).

Perhaps as a result of the criticism of the potential abuse of Rule 2(e) orders, the SEC has on occasion been willing to consent to narrow orders that will have a minimal effect in proceedings by other parties. *See, e.g.,* In re Coopers & Lybrand, Exch.Act Rel. No. 31–21520 (Nov. 27, 1984).

184. Rule 2(e) sanctions may be imposed for misconduct although not constituting violations of the securities laws. *See* W. Loeber Landau, Legal Opinions Rendered in Securities Transactions, 9 Inst.Sec.Reg. 3, 37 (1977) (remarks of Theodore Sonde, Associate Director of Enforcement, SEC).

185. Checkosky v. SEC, 23 F.3d 452 (D.C.Cir.1994); Davy v. SEC, 792 F.2d 1418, 1421–22 (9th Cir.1986).

186. In re Carter & Johnson, 47 S.E.C. 471, [1981 Transfer Binder] Fed.Sec.L.Rep. (CCH) ¶ 82,847 (1981). *See also, e.g.,* Checkosky v. SEC, 23 F.3d 452 (D.C.Cir.1994) (remanding SEC suspension of accountants for failing to distinguish the *Carter & Johnson* scienter requirement). Curiously, in *Checkosky,* the SEC had indicated that the accountants' GAAP and GAAS violations warranted Rule 2(e) sanctions even if they had not acted with scienter. The Commission found, however, that they had acted recklessly. On appeal, the D.C. Circuit remanded for further explanation of the scienter issue. *See* § 13.4 *infra* for a discussion of scienter generally.

Collateral Estoppel Effect of SEC Proceedings

Frequently private litigation will coincide with or follow either SEC injunctive relief or administrative proceedings, whether these proceedings involve the SEC or one of the self regulatory organizations. In such cases, the question may arise as to the preclusive effect to be given to the prior determination. In general, the federal district courts have a wide range of discretion in deciding whether to apply collateral estoppel.[187] Thus, collateral estoppel effect may be given in a private suit to a prior SEC injunctive action notwithstanding the absence of a jury trial in the first action.[188] When there is an identity of issues, collateral estoppel will be applied to preclude relitigation in an SEC civil action of facts that had been determined in a prior criminal prosecution.[189] Although nonjudicial determination such as agency decisions are less formal than judicial proceedings, courts have given a preclusive effect to such decisions when it is shown that there was the opportunity to fully and fairly litigate the issue.[190]

Since collateral estoppel can only be applied against litigants that were parties in the first proceeding, it will not bar a private suit following settlement of an SEC action, even when the settlement included a disgorgement of profits.[191] However, when the second action is brought under the Insider Trading and Securities Fraud Enforcement Act of 1988,[192] damages in such action are reduced by the amount required to be disgorged pursuant to a court order in an action brought by the Commission.[193] Since settlements are generally embodied in consent orders, this set-off requirement would apply there as well.

Deleted sections 9.5.1–9.63 can be found in the Practitioner's Edition.

---

187. *E.g.* Parklane Hosiery Co. v. Shore, 439 U.S. 322, 99 S.Ct. 645, 58 L.Ed.2d 552 (1979). *See* Thomas L. Hazen, Administrative Enforcement: An Evaluation of the Securities and Exchange Commission's Use of Injunctions and Other Enforcement Methods, 31 Hastings L.J. 427, 451–60 (1979); Note, The Collateral Estoppel Effect of Administrative Agency Actions in Federal Civil Litigation, 46 Geo.Wash.L.Rev. 65 (1977).

188. *Parklane Hosiery, supra* footnote 187. *Cf.* Tull v. United States, 481 U.S. 412, 107 S.Ct. 1831, 95 L.Ed.2d 365 (1987) (no right to jury trial on amount of civil penalty under Clean Water Act); In re Ivan F. Boesky Securities Litigation, 848 F.Supp. 1119 (S.D.N.Y. 1994) (applying *Parklane Hosiery* and permitting the offensive use of collateral estoppel against defendant).

189. SEC v. Gruenberg, 989 F.2d 977 (8th Cir.1993).

190. *E.g.* Bowen v. United States, 570 F.2d 1311, 1322 (7th Cir.1978); Campbell v. Superior Court, 18 Ariz.App. 287, 501 P.2d 463 (1972); Hazen, *supra* footnote 187.

191. Nathanson v. Simpson, 1989 WL 76470, [1989–1990 Transfer Binder] Fed.Sec. L.Rep. ¶ 94,818 (N.D.Ill.1989) (investors suing for violations relating to illegal "Ponzi" scheme).

192. Section 20A of the 1934 Act, 15 U.S.C.A. § 78t–1. The substantive law of insider trading is discussed in § 13.9 *infra*.

193. *Id.* The Commission action for disgorgement is expressly authorized in section 21A, 15 U.S.C.A. § 78u–1. *See also, e.g.,* Litton Industries, Inc. v. Lehman Brothers Kuhn Loeb Inc., 734 F.Supp. 1071 (S.D.N.Y.1990) (once profits have been disgorged in SEC action, private plaintiff cannot seek disgorgement under federal law but may include claim for punitive damages under state law).

Chapter 10

MARKET REGULATION

Table of Sections

§ 10.1   Market Regulation—An Overview

While the Securities Act of 1933 regulates the distribution of securi-

---

* Deleted sections 10.2.1–10.2.3, 10.16–10.22 can be found in the Practitioner's Edition.

ties,[1] the Securities Exchange Act of 1934 charges the SEC with the authority to supervise daily market activity. In addition to imposing disclosure requirements upon issuers of publicly traded securities,[2] the Exchange Act of 1934 regulates the market place. Although the SEC has direct authority, a great deal of market regulation is carried out through its oversight of national exchanges and self regulatory organizations.[3]

Market regulation includes the establishment of fair market practices and minimum capital requirements for broker-dealers in order to minimize the risk of insolvency.[4] A major goal of this regulation is to assure orderly markets.[5] There are also severe prohibitions against fraudulent and manipulative broker-dealer conduct.[6] Additionally, the SEC and the Federal Reserve Board work together in regulating the extension of credit for securities transactions.[7]

Over the past several years, the securities markets have been inundated with a proliferation of new investment vehicles. Trading in derivative instruments such as options on individual securities, index options and index futures,[8] has created a host of new regulatory problems. For example, Congress had to draw an artificial line between the SEC's and the Commodity Futures Trading Commission's sphere of influence with regard to financial instruments. Briefly put, currency options can be traded on a national securities exchange; although, strictly speaking, at least from an analytical standpoint, they would seem to qualify as commodity options. Stock index options trade on the basis of an index based on the price of a preselected group (or "basket") of securities. Index options are traded as securities but index futures

---

§ 10.1

1. *See* chapters 2–3 *supra.*

2. *See* chapter 9 *supra.*

3. *See* § 10.2 *infra.* For a detailed history of broker–dealer operations and regulation generally, *see* Jerry W. Markham & Thomas L. Hazen, Broker–Dealer Operations Under Securities and Commodities Law: Financial Responsibilities, Credit Regulation, and Customer Protection, chs. 1, 2 (1995). *See also* § 10.5 *infra* dealing with municipal securities dealers and § 10.5.1 *infra* dealing with government securities dealers. *See generally* Stuart C. Goldberg, Fraudulent Broker–Dealer Practices (1978 ed.); II, V Louis Loss Securities Regulation chs. 7–8 (2d ed.1961; 1969 Supp.); Nicholas Wolfson, Richard M. Phillips & Thomas A. Russo, Regulation of Brokers, Dealers and the Securities Markets (1977; annual supplements); Walter Werner, The SEC as Market Regulator, 70 Va.L.Rev. 755 (1984).

The SEC oversight responsibilities include the review of SRO rulemaking. *See, e.g.,* General Bond & Share Co. v. SEC, 39 F.3d 1451 (10th Cir.1994) (NASD interpretation of its Rules of Fair Practice amounted to such a major shift in policy as to amount to rulemaking and thus could only be accomplished through the formal rulemaking procedures).

4. *See* § 10.2 *infra.*

5. *See* §§ 10.3–10.4 *infra.*

6. *See* §§ 10.6–10.10 *infra.*

7. *See* § 10.11 *infra.*

8. *See, e.g.,* David J. Gilberg, Regulation of New Financial Instruments Under the Federal Securities and Commodities Laws, 39 Vand. L. Rev. 1599 (1986); Richard E. Nathan, The CFTC's Limited Authority Over Hybrid Instruments, 7 Commod. Law Letter 2 (April/May 1988); § 1.5.1 *supra.*

contracts are traded on commodity exchanges and are regulated by the CFTC.[9] There is considerable concern that the proliferation of publicly traded derivative investments has contributed to increased market volatility.[10] Following the market crash of October, 1987, there has been increased concern over instituting market mechanisms to help curb volatility. There has been some movement in this direction as exchanges have adopted rules which, among other things, require trading halts in the face of wild market swings.[11] In addition the exchanges are now giving priority to individual orders (as opposed to institutional orders) on days with major price movements.[12] As noted below, there is also increased controversy concerning the largely unregulated over-the-counter derivatives market that is open to institutional and other "sophisticated" investors.

Market regulation involves a number of complex requirements which transcend the scope of this book.[13] The sections that follow provide analysis of the more important regulatory aspects.

How The Markets Operate—An Overview

SEC regulation is supplemented by its oversight of the self-regulatory organizations (SROs). The two major stock exchanges—The New York Stock Exchange[14] and the American Stock Exchange[15]—handle the trading of most "prestige" securities, with the New York Exchange, or "big board" generally carrying the highest prestige. One reason for the

---

9. 7 U.S.C.A. § 2a; 15 U.S.C.A. § 77b(1). *See* § 1.4.1 *supra*. For a more detailed description of the jurisdictional battle *see* 2 Philip M. Johnson & Thomas L. Hazen, Commodities Regulation § 4.37 (2d ed. 1989).

10. *See, e.g.,* Report of the Presidential Task Force on Market Mechanisms (Jan. 8, 1988) (frequently referred to as the "Brady report"); CFTC Division of Economic Analysis and Division of Trading and Markets, Final Report on Stock Index Futures and Cash Market Activity During October 1987, (Jan. 6, 1988); CFTC Division of Economic Analysis and Division of Trading and Markets, Interim Report on Stock Index Futures and Cash Market Activity During October 1987 (Nov. 9, 1987); SEC Report by the Division of Market Regulation: The October 1987 Market Break (Feb. 1988); U.S. General Accounting Office, Report to Congressional Requesters, Financial Markets: Preliminary Observations on the October 1987 Crash (Jan. 1988); Miller, Hawke, Malkiel & Scholes, Preliminary Report of the Committee of Inquiry Appointed by the Chicago Mercantile Exchange to Examine Events Surrounding October 19, 1987 (Dec. 22, 1987). *See also, e. g.,* Thomas L. Hazen, Volatility and Market Inefficiency: A Commentary on the Effects of Options, Futures, and Risk Arbitrage on the Stock Market, 44 Wash. & Lee L. Rev. 789 (1987); Roberta S. Karmel, The Rashomon Effect in the After-the-Crash Studies, 21 Rev. Sec. & Commod. Reg. 101 (1988).

In addition, there currently is increasing concern over the unregulated derivative instruments traded among institutional investors.

11. *See* Kurt Eichenwald, Two Exchanges Back a Plan for Halts in Their Trading, N.Y. Times, July 8, 1988 at A1, col. 4.

12. *See id.* at D5.

13. *See* the authorities in footnote 3 *supra.*

14. *See* Birl E. Schultz, The Securities Market—and How It Works (rev. ed. 1963); Robert Sobel, N.Y.S.E: A History of the New York Stock Exchange (1975); New York Stock Exch. Guide (CCH). *See also, e.g.,* Peter Wyckoff, Wall Street and the Stock Markets (1972).

15. *See* Robert Sobel, Amex: A History of the American Stock Exchange 1921–1971 (1972).

prestige of these exchanges is their listing requirements, with the New York's being more difficult for an issuer to satisfy.[16]   There are also seven regional exchanges which at one time only traded secondary stocks and provided regional trading for New York and American Exchange listed securities.[17]   Today some of the regional exchanges such as the Chicago, Pacific, and Philadelphia exchanges are major centers for options trading.[18]   An exchange, as the name implies, provides a central clearing house for the trading of its listed securities. Originally all transactions took place physically on the floor of the exchange. While this in large part is still true today, there has been movement towards more of a national market system with automated quotations and a consolidated tape reflecting all transactions and volume whether or not the transactions are made on the exchange floor.[19]   Trading on the exchange floor is carried out by "specialists" in each listed security, whose job it is to help maintain an orderly market.[20]

Securities not traded on one or more of the national exchanges[21] are traded in the over-the-counter markets[22] which are coordinated by the NASD. There is no central exchange floor but merely a matching of bid and asked quotes for each security. The matching of these offers to buy and offers to sell securities is carried out by market-makers with respect to each security.[23]   With its national market quotation system, the NASD has moved toward a national market system.[24]   This national market system have been successful in keeping many companies that in the past would have moved to the New York Stock Exchange.

16. *See e.g.,* New York Stock Exchange Manual.

In recent years, an increasing number of companies have remained content to stay in the NASD's national market system rather than migrate to the "big board."

17. *See* J. Walter, The Role of the Regional Security Exchanges (1958). The seven regional exchanges are the: Boston Stock Exchange, Chicago Board Options Exchange, Cincinnati Stock Exchange, InterMountain Stock Exchange, Midwest Stock Exchange, Pacific Stock Exchange, and Philadelphia Stock Exchange.

18. Options on publicly traded securities are traded on national exchanges under SEC oversight. *See* § 1.5.1 *supra* and § 10.2 *infra*. The Options Clearing Corporation helps coordinate options trading. Options trading and regulation of the options markets are beyond the scope of this book. *See generally* SEC Report of the Special Study of the Option Market, 96th Cong., 1st Sess. (1978).

19. For a more detailed analysis of the markets, *see* Securities Industry Study, Report of Subcommittee on Securities, Sen.Comm. on Banking, Housing and Urban Affairs, 93d Cong. 1st Sess. 89 (1973); SEC Special Study of the Securities Markets, H.R.Doc. No. 95, 88th Cong., 1st Sess. (1963); SEC Statement on the Future Structure of the Securities Markets (1972).

20. *See* § 10.4 *infra*. Specialists, who are also known as downstairs or floor brokers, do not have a retail business. Compare market makers in the over-the-counter markets who typically are also retail brokers. *See* § 10.3 *infra*.

21. Frequently there are dual or multiple listings on regional exchanges for New York and American Stock Exchange listed securities. Dual listing between the New York and American Exchanges has happened on occasion but is exceedingly rare.

22. *See* Irwin Friend, G. Wright Hoffman, Willis J. Winn, Morris Hamberg & Stanley Schor, The Over-the-Counter Securities Markets (1958).

23. *See* § 10.3 *infra*.

24. *See* 17 C.F.R. §§ 240.11Aa–1–11Ac–2; §§ 10.2, 10.13 *infra*.

Prior to 1976, the exchanges prohibited "off-board" trading of listed securities. This prohibition has now been abolished as part of the movement towards coordinated national markets, thereby permitting off–exchange transactions in exchange–listed securities. The SEC has initiated proposals for a national market system.[25] There is not yet a single, unified national market system, and there may never be. However, strides have been made in this direction through the consolidated reports of transactions in exchange-listed securities provided by the automated Intermarket Trading System (ITS), a communications network that helps centralize activity among the exchanges.[26] The NASD now lists several hundred of its most frequently traded securities in its national market.[27] Although a completely unified national market system might arguably benefit investors and promote market efficiency,[28] old institutions die hard and thus the exchange system and over-the-counter markets are likely to remain the bulwarks of the securities markets for quite a long period of time. Furthermore, there are some indications that the centralized exchanges perform a function, including policing of their members and listed companies, that is not accomplished through an automated quotation system.

One development in the move toward a world-wide market has been the move by a number of exchanges for twenty-four hour trading of securities. The SEC currently prohibits off-hours trades except in connection with foreign markets.[29] As a first step in this direction, the major exchanges have expanded the length of their trading day. However, despite recommendations by its staff, the SEC has refused relaxation of its prohibitions against after hours trading.[30] The SEC has been relaxing its off-exchange trading limitations for exchange members[31] and now allows exchange trading of selected active over-the-counter stocks.[32]

Technological advancements have now created an environment in

25. *See* SEC Statement on the Future Structure of the Securities Markets (1972); Sec.Exch. Act Rel. No. 34–15671 (March 22, 1979); Sec.Exch. Act Rel. No. 34–13662 (June 23, 1977); 15 U.S.C.A. § 78k–1; § 10.12 *infra*. On the national market system generally, *see* Donald C. Calvin, The National Market System: A Successful Adventure in Industry Self–Improvement, 70 Va.L.Rev. 785 (1984). Another example of the development toward a more unified trading system has been electronically linked trading for six stocks listed on both the American and Toronto stock exchanges.

26. *See* Sec.Exch. Act Rel. No. 34–15671 (March 22, 1979); SEC, A Monitoring Report on the Operation of the Intermarket Trading System 5–9 (1981).

27. *See* §§ 10.3, 10.13 *infra*.

28. The national market system is discussed in § 10.13 *infra*.

29. N.Y.S.E. Rule 390, which like all exchange rulemaking is subject to SEC approval.

30. *See* SEC Turns Down Staff Suggestion to Urge NYSE to Lift After–Hours Curbs, 18 Sec.Reg. & L.Rep. (BNA) 767 (May 30, 1985); SEC Staff Likely to Recommend After–Hour Trading in NYSE Stocks, Securities Week P. 1 (May 5, 1986).

31. *See* N.Y.S.E. Rule 390.

32. One reason for such an expansion of trading is to allow the exchange to engage in side-by-side trading of options and their underlying securities for certain over-the-counter stocks. *See* SEC Authorizes Exchanges to Begin Limited Trading in Unlisted OTC Stocks, 17 Sec.Reg. & L.Rep. (BNA) 1593 (Sept. 13, 1985).

which electronic trading systems[33] can facilitate off-exchange trading.[34] Another outgrowth of this technology has been the approval, on a one-year pilot basis, of an NASD electronic bulletin board for computerized quotations for stocks not listed on a national exchange or in the NASDAQ system.[35] Also, in conjunction with its adoption of Rule 144A,[36] the SEC approved the NASD's screen-based computer and communication system called PORTAL (Private Offerings, Resales and Trading through Automated Linkages) to facilitate secondary trading of Rule 144A securities.

Options Trading and Other Derivatives

In addition to the stock and bond markets, the SEC regulates the options markets wherein there is public trading of put and call options for securities and indexes. The options themselves qualify as securities which are separate and distinct from the underlying securities.[37] Accordingly the public trading of options contracts on stock, stock indexes, and other securities is subject to SEC regulation. Options on securities and certain indexes are publicly traded on the American Stock Exchange as well as many of the regional exchanges—primarily the Midwest, Pacific, and Philadelphia Exchanges. Rather than have the exchanges separately register each option that is publicly traded, the Options Clearing Corporation files applicable disclosure documents governing the generic options—*i.e.*, puts and calls. These disclosure documents not only reveal the mechanics of options trading but also the risks peculiarly associated with options trading.[38] These options-related disclosures are also designed to help inform investors as to the various option investment strategies.[39] In 1986, the Commission, finding its options disclosure program to be a success, simplified the disclosure process.[40]

As noted earlier in this section, the CFTC regulates financial futures.[41] Options and index futures have been cited as the cause of

---

33. *Cf.,* the discussion of registration of an electronic system as a clearing agent in the text *infra.*

34. Off-exchange trading permits large institutions to bypass the exchange. By passing the exchange can decrease transaction costs for large investors. It has been predicted that before long about twenty of the nations largest investment funds will bypass the exchanges and trade between themselves.

35. Sec.Exch.Act Rel. No. 34–27975 (May 1, 1990). *See* SEC Approves One–Year Pilot Program for NASD's OTC Electronic Bulletin Board, 22 Sec.Reg. & L.Rep. (BNA) 672 (May 4, 1990).

36. 17 C.F.R. § 230.144A, which is discussed in §§ 4.26, 4.26.1.

37. 15 U.S.C.A. § 77b(1). *See* § 1.5 *supra.*

38. 17 C.F.R. § 240.9b–1 (options disclosure document). *See also* NASD Manual (CCH) ¶¶ 2183–84.

39. *See, e.g.,* Larry L. Varn, The Multi–Service Securities Firm and the Chinese Wall: A New Look in the Light of the Federal Securities Code, 63 Neb.L.Rev. 197 (1984). *See also, e.g.,* Cardle B. Silver, Penalizing Insider Trading, A Critical Assessment of the Insider Trading Sanctions Act of 1984, 1985 Duke L.J. 960, 978 (1985).

40. Exch. Act Rel. No. 34–23115, [1985–86 Transfer Binder] Fed.Sec.L.Rep. (CCH) ¶ 83,977 (April 10, 1986).

41. *See* text accompanying footnotes 8–12 *supra.*

increased volatility.[42] As a result various proposals have been considered, including earlier options and futures expiration and the disclosure of open orders.[43]

As this book went to press, a number of developments were brewing with regard to unregulated derivative instruments. This consists of securities options, swap transactions, and various other hybrid investments that are traded among institutional and other so-called sophisticated investors. These instruments are highly technical and are designed to manage various types of risk. However, during this period, a number of these highly leveraged transactions led to disaster. There were a number of celebrated instances in which major corporations, institutional investors, for example, and even governmental entities lost considerable sums due to the largely unregulated over-the-counter derivative markets. By the mid-1990s, Congress began looking into unregulated derivatives. Since these instruments are highly specialized, considerable doubt exists as to whether anyone other than the maker of the instrument truly understands the risks involved. Recently, major brokerage firms announced a voluntary policy of disclosure relating to their exposure in derivative investments. Congress has also shown an interest in learning more about the unregulated derivatives market. Only time will tell what type of regulation will ensue from the financial disasters linked to unregulated derivatives.

Scope of Regulation

The SEC's rulemaking power with regard to market regulation has its limits. It cannot be used as a ruse for regulating substantive shareholder rights. For example, the scope of the SEC's rulemaking authority was brought into question in Business Roundtable v. SEC,[44] wherein the SEC's authority to regulate substantive voting rights was challenged. The SEC's one-share—one-vote rule (Rule 19c–4)[45] was held invalid. The SEC had argued that section 19(c),[46] which sets forth SEC rulemaking and oversight responsibilities with regard to self regulatory organizations, provided an adequate statutory basis for the rule. Section

---

42. Franklin R. Edwards, Stock Index Futures and Stock Market Volatility: Evidence and Implications, 6 Commod.L. Letter 3 (Nov.-Dec. 1986); Ronald B. Hobson & Paula A. Tosini, Regulatory Issues Relating to Stock Index Futures and Option Markets, 6 Commod.L. Letter 1 (Nov.-Dec.1986). *See also, e.g.,* Jeffrey N. Laderman & John M. Frank, How Chicago Zaps Wall Street, Bus. Week p. 95 (Sept. 16, 1986); Pamela Sebastian, How Program Trading Works and Why it Causes Controversy in the Stock Market, Wall St. J. p. 19 (Jan. 10, 1986). *Cf.* H. Patrick Faust & Ted Doukas, Taking the Bite out of Stock Index Futures Arbitrage Volatility, Futures p. 50 (Dec., 1985).

43. *See* Jeffrey M. Laderman & Vicky Cahan, The Triple Witching Hour: Trying to Make it Less Spooky, Business Week p. 32 (Sept. 22, 1986); SEC Asks Big Board to Test Proposal Aimed at Curbing Sharp Price Swings, Wall Street J. p. 45 (Sept. 11, 1986); SEC Staff Seeks Big Board Test in Price Swings p. 3 (Sept. 9, 1986); Exchanges Lean Towards Friday Afternoon Solutions to Program Trading, Securities Week p. 1 (August 4, 1986). *See* the discussion in §§ 1.4.1, 1.5.1 *supra* for discussion of other recent proposals and developments.

44. 905 F.2d 406 (D.C.Cir.1990).

45. *See* § 11.1 *infra*.

46. 15 U.S.C.A. § 78s(c).

19(c) sets forth three bases for regulation: (1) assurance of fair administration of self regulatory organizations, (2) conformity to the requirements of the Exchange Act, and (3) promulgation of rules "otherwise in furtherance of the" Act's purpose. The SEC relied on the third basis. The court concluded that there was no support for a "special and anomalous exception to the Act's otherwise intelligible conceptual line excluding the Commission from corporate governance."[47] The court similarly held inapplicable sections 6(b)(5)[48] (Commission regulatory authority over exchanges) and 15A(b)(6) (regulatory authority over broker-dealer associations),[49] both of which empower the Commission to promulgate rules to "in general, ... protect investors and the public interest." The court pointed out that this power is limited to regulation "by virtue of any authority conferred by the [Exchange Act]," thereby requiring a more specific basis of authority. Otherwise, there would be no limit to the Commission's rulemaking authority. Finally, section 11A's rulemaking authority to "facilitate the establishment of a national market system for securities"[50] was not a sufficient basis for the regulation of shareholder voting rights. At the end of its opinion, the court pointed out that it was limited to the bases for authority argued by the Commission so the court did not decide whether other statutory provisions could support such a rule.

The demise of Rule 19c–4 does not necessarily call for the invalidity of exchange rules which deal with voting rights. Thus, the New York Stock Exchange rule that was adopted in January of 1990 was not affected by the *Business Roundtable* decision. On the heels of the D.C. Circuit's decision, the NASD proposed a one-share—one-vote rule.[51] The proposed rule would apply to the more actively traded over the counter stocks that are listed on the NASDAQ National Market System. Subsequently the American Stock Exchange, the NASD, and the New York Stock Exchange have agreed upon a uniform voting rights rule. It is to be anticipated that such rules may be challenged as exceeding the Exchange Act's statutory authority. However, as noted above, these SRO rules may not suffer the same demise as the SEC's earlier effort.

The Market Reform Act of 1990

On October 16, 1990, Congress enacted market reform legislation in response to concerns over various market disruptions that have occurred over the past several years. The focus of the new legislation is to provide oversight of major market participants, thereby enhancing the financial integrity of the securities markets.[52] The Market Reform Act

---

47. 905 F.2d at 413.

48. 15 U.S.C.A. § 78f(b)(5).

49. 15 U.S.C.A. § 78o–1.

50. 15 U.S.C.A. § 78k–1. *See* § 10.13 *infra.*

51. NASD Proposes One-Share—One-Vote Rule for Stocks Listed on NASDAQ–NMS System, 22 Sec.Reg. & L.Rep. (BNA) 1127 (Aug. 3, 1990).

52. *See* Fed.Sec.L.Rep. (CCH) Bulletin no. 1418 (Oct. 23, 1990) (remarks of SEC Chairman Richard Breeden).

gives the SEC additional powers in times of market disruptions. For example, the Commission is given the emergency power to close a securities exchange for a period of up to ninety days.[53] The Commission is also given the power to summarily suspend trading in any security for a period up to ten business days.[54] The Act also gives the SEC the emergency power to suspend, alter, or impose rules on a self regulatory organization[55] for a maximum of ten business days.[56] These emergency orders are subject to presidential approval.

Large Trader Reports

In addition to the foregoing emergency powers given to the SEC, the Market Reform Act also imposes identification and reporting requirements for major market participants. Section 13(h) of the Exchange Act[57] imposes these requirements on "large traders." The large trader reporting requirements are a result of concerns that arose following the market break of 1987 and increasing volatility generally which many observers viewed as due to the impact of large traders and their participation in the derivatives and underlying securities markets. Accordingly, under this legislation, the SEC is empowered to promulgate rules "[f]or the purpose of monitoring the impact on the securities markets of securities transactions involving a substantial volume or a large fair market value or exercise value."[58] These reporting requirements, which are to be implemented by SEC rulemaking are modeled on the large trader reporting system that is administered with respect to the commodities markets by the Commodity Futures Trading Commission.[59] Under the Act, the SEC is empowered to impose reporting requirements on broker-dealers maintaining accounts for large traders.[60] The Act gives the Commission broad discretion in defining who is a large trader and in framing the reporting requirements to be imposed, subject to, among other things, the cost of creating and implementing the system.[61] The Commission is given additional authority with regard to examination of broker-dealer records.[62] The SEC is also given broad power to promulgate rules requiring disclosures relating to the financial condition of broker-dealer affiliates and holding companies.[63]

In 1991, the SEC proposed Rule 13h–1[64] but after extensive comments, the Commission made a number of adjustments and reproposed

---

53. 15 U.S.C.A. § 78*l*(k)(1)(B).

54. 15 U.S.C.A. § 78*l*(k)(1)(A).

55. *See* § 10.2 *infra* for discussion of self regulation under the securities laws.

56. 15 U.S.C.A. § 78*l*(k)(2).

57. 15 U.S.C.A. § 78m(h).

58. *Id.*

59. 17 C.F.R. Part 15. *See* 2 Philip M. Johnson & Thomas L. Hazen, Commodities Regulation § 3.118 (2d ed. 1989).

60. 15 U.S.C.A. § 78m(h)(2).

61. 15 U.S.C.A. § 78m(h)(5).

62. 15 U.S.C.A. § 78m(h)(4).

63. *See* 15 U.S.C.A. § 78q(h).

64. *See* Exch. Act Rel. No. 34–29593 (Aug. 22, 1991).

the rule.[65] These reporting requirements are designed to provide the Commission with information that will provide the basis of effective regulation of any adverse consequences of large trader activity.[66]

Regulation of Computerized ("Program") Trading

The Commission is further given the authority by virtue of section 9(h) of the Exchange Act[67] to promulgate rules designed to limit program trading. First, the Commission is given the authority to promulgate rules designed to prevent manipulation of the price levels of the equity securities markets or substantial segments of the securities markets.[68] This statutory provision is designed to allow the Commission to focus on manipulation of stock indexes which represent all, or a portion, of the market. Second, the Commission is given the authority to prohibit or limit trading practices during periods of "extraordinary market volatility."[69] The power to prohibit or limit trading practices is given when those trading practices have in the past contributed "significantly" to extraordinary levels of volatility and thus threatened the maintenance of fair and orderly markets.[70]

§ 10.2   Regulation of Broker–Dealers—The SEC, Self Regulatory Organizations, National Exchanges, and the NASD

While the SEC has some direct jurisdiction over broker-dealers, the overwhelming bulk of broker-dealer regulation is attributable to the Commission's oversight of the activities of self regulatory organizations ("SRO"s) and of national securities exchanges. Section 15(a) of the Exchange Act requires registration with the Commission of all broker-dealers who are engaged in interstate business involving securities transactions.[1] The only complete exemption from the registration re-

---

65. *See* Exch. Act Rel. No. 34–33608 (Feb. 9, 1994).

66. The Commission explained that the reproposed Rule 13h–1 is designed to "provid[e] the Commission with the information necessary to reconstruct trading activity in periods of market stress and for enforcement or other regulatory purposes, without imposing undue burdens on market participants." *Id.*

67. 15 U.S.C.A. § 78i(h).

68. 15 U.S.C.A. § 78i(h)(1).

69. 15 U.S.C.A. § 78i(h)(2).

70. *Id.*

§ 10.2

1. 15 U.S.C.A. § 78*o*(a). Registration involves disclosure of the broker-dealer's business and principal officers on Form BD. There are also extensive disclosure requirements relating to financial condition (17 C.F.R. § 240.15b1–2) and consent to service of process (17 C.F.R. § 240.15b1–5). *See, e.g.,* Exchange Services, Inc. v. SEC, 797 F.2d 188 (4th Cir.1986) (order takers for discount brokers must register as general securities representatives).

Before long all B–D filings will be electronically transmitted to state securities and administrators to facilitate coordinated filings.

See generally Nicholas Wolfson, Richard M. Phillips & Thomas A. Russo, Regulation of Brokers, Dealers & Securities Markets (1977); Gregory S. Crespi, The Reach of the Federal Registration Requirements for Broker–Dealers and Investment Advisors, 17 Sec.Reg.L.J.

quirements is for a broker-dealer "whose business is exclusively intra-state and who does not make use of any facility of a national exchange."[2] An individual who is a registered associated person with a registered broker–dealer may himself or herself be exempt from registration.[3] However, the exemption will not be available when the registered representative is conducting business on his or her own.[4]

SEC Responsibilities—Oversight and Disciplinary Sanctions

Section 15(b)(4)[5] of the Exchange Act empowers the Commission to hold a hearing and impose disciplinary sanctions ranging from censure to revocation of the registration of broker-dealers engaging in certain types of proscribed conduct.[6] The Act lists the following situations in which the SEC may impose sanctions after an administrative hearing: (1) when a broker-dealer makes false filings with the Commission;[7] (2) when the broker-dealer within the past ten years has been convicted of certain crimes or misdemeanors involving moral turpitude or breaches of

339 (1990); David A. Lipton, A Primer on Broker–Dealer Registration, 36 Cath.U.L.Rev. 899 (1987); Randall W. Quinn, Deja vu All Over Again: The SEC's Return to Agency Theory in Regulating Broker–Dealers, 1990 Colum.Bus.L.Rev. 61; Dennis T. Rice, The Expanding Requirement for Registration as "Broker–Dealer" Under the Securities Exchange Act of 1934, 50 Notre Dame Law. 201 (1974).

2. 15 U.S.C.A. § 78o(a). The intrastate exemption is as restrictive as its counterpart under the 1933 Act. See § 4.12 supra.

National exchanges are discussed in the text accompanying note 38 infra. Broker-dealers who deal exclusively in municipal securities are not covered by the general registration provisions. They are regulated through the Municipal Securities Rule–Making Board. 15 U.S.C.A. § 78o–4. See § 10.5 infra.

In 1984 the SEC proposed a safe harbor rule excluding from the definition of broker-dealer persons associated with an issuer and participating in the sale of the issuer's securities. Under the proposed rule, such an associated person is not a broker-dealer if he or she (1) is not subject to statutory disqualification, (2) does not receive a sales commission, and (3) is not associated with a broker-dealer. Sec.Exch.Act Rel. No. 34–20943 (May 9, 1984).

3. Section 15(a)(1), 15 U.S.C.A. § 78o(a)(1). Associated person is a broad concept and is not limited to natural persons. Cf., e.g., McMahon Securities Co. LP v. Forum Capital Markets L.P., 35 F.3d 82 (2d Cir.1994) (entity that was a partner of the member firm was an associated person under NASD bylaws).

4. Roth v. SEC, 22 F.3d 1108 (D.C.Cir.1994).

5. 15 U.S.C.A. § 78o(b)(4). Cf. Antoniu v. SEC, 877 F.2d 721 (8th Cir.1989), cert. denied 494 U.S. 1004, 110 S.Ct. 1296, 108 L.Ed.2d 473 (1990) (nullifying Commission order permanently barring association with a broker-dealer because of public statements made by a Commissioner prior to the proceedings which indicated that he had prejudged the matter).

6. The statute requires the Commission to:

censure, place limitations on the activities, functions, or operations of, suspend for a period not exceeding twelve months, or revoke the registration of any broker or dealer if it finds, on the record after notice and opportunity for hearing, that such censure, placing of limitations, suspension, or revocation is in the public interest and that such broker or dealer, whether prior or subsequent to becoming such, or any person associated with such broker or dealer, whether prior or subsequent to becoming so associated [has violated the act] * * *

Id. SEC hearing procedures are discussed in §§ 9.7–9.23 supra (Practitioner's Edition only).

7. 15 U.S.C.A. § 78o(b)(4)(A).

fiduciary duty;[8] (3) when the person involved has been enjoined from being a broker-dealer or investment adviser or from engaging in or continuing to engage in any conduct or practice in connection with such activity or in connection with the purchase or sale of any security;[9] (4) when a broker-dealer has willfully violated any provision of the Securities Act of 1933, the Exchange Act of 1934, the Investment Company Act of 1940, or the Investment Advisers Act of 1940, or any rules promulgated thereunder;[10] (5) when the broker-dealer has willfully aided, abetted, counseled, commanded, induced, or procured any violation of any of the foregoing statutes or rules;[11] (6) when the broker-dealer is subject to an SEC order barring or suspending his right to be associated with a broker or dealer;[12] and (7) when the broker–dealer has violated any foreign securities law or regulation.[13] Section 15(b)(6)[14] empowers the Commission to impose similar sanctions for the same types of conduct with regard to persons who, although not themselves broker-dealers, are associated or seek to become associated with broker-dealers. Brokerage firms have a duty to supervise their personnel and can be held liable and subject to SEC or self regulatory organization sanctions for breach of the duty to supervise.[15]

---

8. 15 U.S.C.A. § 78o(b)(4)(B). *See, e.g.,* In re Kuznetz, Exch.Act Rel. No. 34–23525, [1986–87 Transfer Binder] Fed.Sec.L.Rep. (CCH) ¶ 84,021 (SEC Aug. 12, 1986) (permanent exclusion from securities industry of brokerage vice president who engaged in egregious conduct including touting stock as "guaranteed" based on purported inside information); In re Paul, Exch.Act Rel. No. 34–21789, [1984–85 Transfer Binder] Fed.Sec.L.Rep. (CCH) ¶ 83,748 (SEC Feb. 25, 1985) (barring from industry for two years a broker-dealer who pled guilty to knowingly filing false tax returns).

9. 15 U.S.C.A. § 78o(b)(4)(C).

10. 15 U.S.C.A. § 78o(b)(4)(D). This subsection also covers conduct in violation of rules of the Municipal Securities Rule–Making Board. *See* § 10.5 *infra.*

11. 15 U.S.C.A. § 78o(b)(4)(E). The express statutory authority to sanction broker-dealers who have aided and abetted violations of the securities laws is extremely important in light of a recent Supreme Court ruling. In Central Bank of Denver v. First Interstate Bank of Denver, ___ U.S. ___, 114 S.Ct. 1439, 128 L.Ed.2d 119 (1994), the Court held that the securities laws do not support an implied private right of action against aiders and abettors. As discussed more fully in a later section (§ 13.16 *infra*), although not directly addressing the issue, the Court's reasoning would seem to call for the same result with regard to SEC actions against aiders and abettors. Aiding and abetting liability has been significant in actions against broker-dealers. *See* § 10.14 *infra.* Section (b)(4) expressly recognizes the SEC's ability to pursue broker-dealers as aiders and abettors. Additionally, although somewhat doubtful in light of the Court's rationale in the *Central Bank* decision, there is at least a possibility that private rights of action may be premised on this section as well. *See* the discussion in §§ 10.14, 13.16 *infra.*

12. 15 U.S.C.A. § 78o(b)(5)(F). *See* 15 U.S.C.A. 78o(b)(6).

13. 15 U.S.C.A. § 78o(b)(4)(G).

14. 15 U.S.C.A. § 78o(b)(6).

15. *E.g.,* Kersh v. General Council of the Assemblies of God, 804 F.2d 546 (9th Cir.1986); Leavey v. Blinder, Robinson & Co., 1986 WL 10556, [1986–87 Transfer Binder] Fed.Sec.L.Rep. (CCH) ¶ 92,996 (E.D.Pa.1986) (imposing controlling person liability under section 12 of the Exchange Act; noting failure to adequately supervise). *Cf.* SEC v. Stratton Oakmont, Inc., 1995 WL 46559, [1994–1995 Transfer Binder] Fed. Sec. L. Rep. (CCH) ¶ 98,503 (D.D.C.1995) (preliminary injunction requiring retention of independent consultant to review firm's sales practices). *But cf.* Buhler v. Audio, 807 F.2d 833 (9th Cir.1987) (no breach of duty to supervise with regard to account executive's off-book transactions). Controlling person liability generally is discussed in § 13.15 *infra.* *See also* § 7.7 *supra* and § 10.14 *infra.*

In addition to direct SEC enforcement, the self regulatory organizations—the exchanges and the NASD—can discipline their members for violations of their rules. Self regulatory organization disciplinary actions are subject to SEC review and, in turn, to review by a federal court of appeals.[16]

In addition to imposing sanctions arising out of the SEC's direct broker-dealer regulation, the Commission is charged with the supervision of a firm's structure and taking measures to assure the broker-dealer's solvency. Section 15(b)(7) requires broker-dealers to meet such operational and financial competence standards as the Commission may establish.[17] Perhaps the most significant of these requirements is the Commission's net capital rule which sets out the minimum standards of broker-dealer solvency based on the balance sheet. The net capital rule, Rule 15c3–1, is among the longest and most complex of the Commission's rules.[18] In short, the rule requires that a broker-dealer's balance sheet reflect a sufficient asset base as well as mandating the applicable accounting standards for determining that asset base.[19] The net capital rule is complicated not only because of its formulas but also because of the rules regarding "haircuts"—the discounted value of the securities before the computation is made. The competence requirements imposed by the Act include provisions for maintenance of adequate records[20] and imposition of standards for supervisory and associated personnel,[21] as

---

SRO rules are also subject to SEC oversight. *See, e.g.,* General Bond & Share Co. v. SEC, 39 F.3d 1451 (10th Cir.1994).

16. Since the statute vests judicial review in the courts of appeals, federal district courts have no jurisdiction to hear such an appeal. *See* Maschler v. National Association of Securities Dealers, 827 F.Supp. 131 (E.D.N.Y.1993).

Courts will not generally permit collateral attack on disciplinary proceedings, at least until appropriate avenues for direct review have been pursued. *See, e.g.,* Alton v. NASD, 1994 WL 443460, [1994–1995 Transfer Binder] Fed. Sec. L. Rep. (CCH) ¶ 98,369 (N.D.Cal. 1994) (dismissing suit against NASD due to broker's failure to exhaust his administrative remedies by challenging disputed disciplinary action against him).

17. 15 U.S.C.A. § 78*o*(b)(7).

18. 17 C.F.R. § 240.15c–3.

19. For a more detailed analysis *see* Jerry W. Markham & Thomas L. Hazen, Broker Dealer Operations Under Securities and Commodities Law: Financial Responsibilities, Credit Regulation, and Customer Protection, ch. 5 (1995). II, V L. Loss, Securities Regulation 1350–56, 3419–32 (2d ed. 1961, 1969 Supp.); Nicholas Wolfson, Richard M. Phillips & Thomas A. Russo, Regulation of Brokers, Dealers and Securities Markets, Ch. 6 (1977). *See* SEC Study on the Financing and Regulatory Capital Needs of the Securities Industry (January 23, 1985). *Cf.* Whiteside and Co., Inc. v. SEC, 883 F.2d 7 (5th Cir.1989) (affirming disciplinary sanctions against brokerage firm and president for "parking" bonds in president's account in order to avoid "haircuts" that would otherwise have to have been taken and would have adversely affected the firm's net capital calculations).

20. *See* the recordkeeping requirements of section 17(h), 15 U.S.C.A. § 78q(h). For a detailed analysis, see Jerry W. Markham & Thomas L. Hazen, *supra* footnote 19, ch. 6.

21. *See, e.g.,* In re White, [1991–1992 Transfer Binder] Fed.Sec.L.Rep. (CCH) ¶ 84,949 (SEC 1992) (censuring broker-dealer for failure to supervise one of its registered representatives). The SEC has recently taken the position that a brokerage firm's compliance officer may qualify as a supervisor and thus be subject to the duty to supervise registered representatives. In re First Albany Corp., Exch.Act Rel. No. 34–30515 (SEC March 25, 1992).

In addition to administrative sanctions for failure to adequately supervise personnel, the securities acts impose controlling person liability upon employers of account executives who

well as a number of related requirements that go into more detail than is appropriate here.[22]

Section 15(c)(1)[23] prohibits securities broker-dealers from engaging in fraudulent practices and conduct. Section 15(c)(1) applies to all registered broker–dealers.[24] It is also specifically declared illegal to misuse customers' funds and securities.[25]

There are a number of Exchange Act requirements that apply to all broker-dealers regardless of membership in a self regulatory organization. As pointed out above, section 15 of the Act expressly empowers the Commission to set financial responsibility requirements for broker-dealers.[26] Section 17(a) of the Exchange Act requires broker-dealers to keep and furnish accurate records of their transactions.[27] The series of SEC rules adopted under section 17(a) was promulgated to provide the Commission with early warning of danger signs so as to telegraph notice of violations of the net capital rule or appropriate standards of broker-dealer conduct.[28] The Supreme Court has held that there is no private damage remedy for violations of 17(a)'s record keeping requirements.[29] Section 17(b) of the Act[30] authorizes the SEC to conduct, from time to time, such "reasonable periodic, special or other examinations" as the

engage in violative conduct. *See, e.g.,* Leavey v. Blinder, Robinson & Co., 1986 WL 10556, [1986–87 Transfer Binder] Fed.Sec.L.Rep. (CCH) ¶ 92,996 (E.D.Pa.1986); Bradshaw v. Van Houten, 601 F.Supp. 983 (D.Ariz.1985) (finding controlling person liability inapplicable where account executive was acting on his own rather than for his employer brokerage firm). Controlling person liability is discussed in § 7.7 *supra* and § 13.15 *infra.*

22. *See generally* Jerry W. Markham & Thomas L. Hazen, *supra* footnote 19. Nicholas Wolfson, Richard M. Phillips, Thomas A. Russo, *supra* note 1 (updated with annual supplements). *See also, e.g.,* Stuart C. Goldberg, Fraudulent Broker–Dealer Practices (1978 ed.).

23. 15 U.S.C.A. § 78o(c)(1). The applicable SEC rules are discussed in § 12.1 *infra. See* Eichler v. SEC, 757 F.2d 1066 (9th Cir.1985) (imposing sanctions for failure to execute transactions and for failure to make prompt transmission of customers' funds).

Although the SEC can impose administrative sanctions, most courts hold that there is no implied private remedy for violations of section 15(c) nor NASD rules. *E.g.* Shahmirzadi v. Smith Barney, Harris, Upham & Co., 636 F.Supp. 49 (D.D.C.1985); Corbey v. Grace, 605 F.Supp. 247 (D.Minn.1985); Binkley v. Sheaffer, 609 F.Supp. 601 (E.D.Pa.1985); Nunes v. Merrill Lynch, Pierce, Fenner & Smith, Inc., 609 F.Supp. 1055 (D.Md.1985).

For a discussion of recent broker-dealer violations *see* Lewis D. Lowenfels & Alan R. Bromberg, Securities Market Manipulations: An Examination of Domination and Control, Frontrunning, and Parking, 55 Alb.L.Rev. 293 (1991).

24. SEC v. Lorin, 1991 WL 576895, [1993–1994 Transfer Binder] Fed. Sec. L. Rep. (CCH) ¶ 98,188 (S.D.N.Y.1991) (rejecting contention that 15(c)(1) applies only to exchange members; the language of the statute clearly provides otherwise).

25. 15 U.S.C.A. § 78o(c)(3).

26. 15 U.S.C.A. § 78o(b)(7). *See* the net capital rule embodied in 17 C.F.R. § 240.15c3–1.

27. 15 U.S.C.A. § 78q(a). For detailed discussion of the record-keeping requirements, *see* Jerry W. Markham & Thomas L. Hazen, *supra* footnote 19.

28. *See* 17 C.F.R. §§ 240.17a–1 *et seq.*

29. Touche Ross & Co. v. Redington, 442 U.S. 560, 99 S.Ct. 2479, 61 L.Ed.2d 82 (1979). *See* § 13.1 *infra.*

30. 15 U.S.C.A. § 78q(b).

Commission deems necessary to enforce the broker-dealer standards of operation and conduct.

Although the fixing of brokerage commission rates has been abolished,[31] the Commission and self regulatory organizations seek to prevent the charging of excessive commissions. For example, the SEC not only determines the types of entities that can receive remuneration from securities trades,[32] it also imposes disclosure requirements regarding the basis of customer charges.[33] The SEC also has an interest in assuring that the competitive rate system works smoothly.[34] Additionally, the NASD through its mark-up policy provides guidelines as to what would constitute an excessive brokerage commission.[35]

---

31. *See* the text at footnote 88 *infra.*

32. *See, e.g.,* In re Financial Charters & Acquisitions, Inc., 17 Sec.Reg. & L.Rep. (BNA) 27 (SEC No–Action Letter Nov. 25, 1984) (unregistered firms may get commissions for referrals to registered broker-dealers).

33. 17 C.F.R. § 240.10b–10(a)(7), (8). *Cf.* 15 U.S.C.A. § 78bb(e)(1); Exch.Act Rel. No. 34–23170 (April 23, 1986) (guidelines to qualify for safe harbor for charges that can be imposed by a money manager in performance of its investment decision-making responsibilities).

Rule 10b–10's safe harbor will not preclude liability under section 10(b)(5) or section 12(2) of the 1933 Act. Krome v. Merrill Lynch & Co., 637 F.Supp. 910 (S.D.N.Y.1986).

For a more complete discussion of Rule 10b–10 *see* Jerry W. Markham & Thomas L. Hazen, Broker–Dealer Regulation § 6.07 (1995).

34. The SEC has rescinded the reporting program requiring broker-dealers to report quarterly on revenue and expenses to monitor commission rates. Exch.Act Rel. No. 34–21422, [1984–85 Transfer Binder] Fed.Sec.L.Rep. (CCH) ¶ 83,702 (Oct. 23, 1984).

35. NASD Rules of Fair Practice, Art. III, sec. 4, NASD Manual (CCH) ¶ 2154. The NASD has established a "five percent" policy as a guide for determining the fairness of the mark-up. The NASD stresses that this is a guide, not a rule and is to be considered in conjunction with other factors. Some of the factors considered in determining the fairness of a mark-up are the type, availability, and price of the security, the amount of money involved in the transaction, the disclosures made to the customer, the broker-dealer's general pattern of mark-ups, and the nature of the broker-dealer's business. *Id.*

The NASD has issued a release which summarizes its current position on the calculation of mark-ups. *See* NASD, Notice to Members 92–16. Difficult questions can arise in calculating and identifying permissible mark-ups. For example, in In re Wade, [1991–1992 Transfer Binder] Fed.Sec.L.Rep. (CCH) ¶ 84, (939 SEC 1992), the Commission reversed the NASD's imposition of sanctions in light of the unclear state of the law as to what constitutes an excessive mark-up in the context of a riskless principal transaction. The Commission announced that prospectively the law would be that in riskless transactions, mark-ups should be based on the cost of acquisition rather than the prevailing market price.

See also, e.g., First Independence Group, Inc. v. SEC, 37 F.3d 30 (2d Cir.1994) (upholding sanctions for excessive mark ups); Orkin v. SEC, 31 F.3d 1056 (11th Cir.1994) (upholding finding that evidence showed broker violated the 5% mark–up rule with regard to over 200 solicited sales transactions); Amato v. SEC, 18 F.3d 1281(5th Cir.1994) (upholding finding that retail broker violated excessive mark–up prohibitions); In re U.S. Securities Clearing Corp., Admin. Proc. File No. 3–8164, 27 Sec. Reg. & L. Rep. (BNA) 17 (SEC 1995) (sustaining sanctions against firm and its president/compliance officer); In re Partnership Exchange Securities Co., Admin. Proc. File No. 3–8030, 26 Sec. Reg. & L. Rep. (BNA) 1179 (SEC 1994) (overturning finding of markup violations since at the time of the transactions in question, the SEC had not clearly explained its policy with regard to the types of transactions in question); In the Matter of First Independence Group, Inc., Exch. Act Rel. No. 34–32817, [1993 Transfer Binder] Fed. Sec. L. Rep. (CCH) ¶ 85,230 (SEC 1993), *affirmed* 37 F.3d 30 (2d Cir.1994) (finding excessive mark–ups in riskless customer transactions); In the Matter of W.N. Whelen & Co., [1991 Transfer Binder] Fed.Sec.L.Rep. (CCH) ¶ 84,620 (SEC 1990) (mark-ups of 14%, 15%, and 9% based on broker's contempora-

In addition to the foregoing substantive requirements attaching to broker-dealer regulation, section 15(b)(8) requires that all broker-dealers be members of a qualifying self regulatory organization (either a national exchange or registered securities association).[36] As part of its move towards reducing paperwork and simplifying disclosures, the SEC has revised Form BD, the registration form for broker-dealers.[37]

There are nine active national exchanges registered under section 6 of the Act.[38] There is only one securities association registered under section 15A[39]—the National Association of Securities Dealers (NASD). Prior to statutory amendment in 1983, broker-dealers who elected not to become members of a national exchange or the NASD could qualify as SECO broker-dealers ("SEC Only"). Today, all broker-dealers doing any substantial interstate retail business will be registered with the

---

neous cost were excessive and in violation of NASD rules); Joseph I. Goldstein & L. Delane Cox, Penny Stock Markups and Markdowns, 85 Nw.U.L.Rev. 676 (1991). *Compare, e.g.,* Bank of Lexington & Trust Co. v. Vining–Sparks Securities, Inc., 959 F.2d 606, 613–14 (6th Cir.1992) (mark-ups for municipal bonds which generally were below 5% were not excessive and were consistent with industry standards); Platsis v. E.F. Hutton & Co., 946 F.2d 38 (6th Cir.1991), *cert. denied* ___ U.S. ___, 112 S.Ct.1669, 118 L.Ed.2d 389 (1992) (brokerage firm did not act with scienter in failing to disclose production credits and mark-ups earned on inventory bond transactions).

36. 15 U.S.C.A. § 78o(b)(8). Up until 1983, broker-dealers could submit themselves to direct SEC control, but the Act was amended to abolish SECO ("SEC Only") regulation.

There has been much discussion concerning self regulation under SEC oversight. *See, e.g.,* William L. Cary, Self Regulation in the Securities Industry, 49 A.B.A.J. 244 (1963); High I. Crossland & Robert J. Sehr, Jr., Gods of the Marketplace: An Examination of the Regulation of the Securities Business, 48 B.U.L.Rev. 515 (1968); Alexander H. Frey, Federal Regulation of the Over-the-Counter Securities Markets, 106 U.Pa.L.Rev. 1 (1957); Richard W. Jennings, Self Regulation in the Securities Industry: The Role of the Securities Exchange Commission, 29 Law & Contemp.Prob. 663 (1964); Sam S. Miller, Self–Regulatory Organizations and the Securities Industry: Does Membership Have its Privileges?, 19 Sec.Reg.L.J. 3 (1991); John E. Pinto, Jr., The NASD's Enforcement Agenda, 85 Nw. U.L.Rev. 739 (1991); Howard C. Westwood & Edward G. Howard, Self Government in the Securities Business, 17 Law & Contemp.Prob. 518 (1952); Marc A. White, National Association of Securities Dealers, Inc., 28 Geo.Wash.L.Rev. 250 (1959); Note, The NASD– An Unique Experiment in Cooperative Regulation, 46 Va.L.Rev. 1586 (1960). There are exemptions from broker-dealer registration. For example, there is a newly-adopted safe harbor from registration for persons associated with the issuer who participate in the distribution of the issuer's securities. 17 C.F.R. § 240.3a4–1. *See* § 10.2.2 *infra* (Practitioner's Edition only).

37. *See* Exch.Act Rel. No. 34–22468, [1985–86 Transfer Binder] Fed.Sec.L.Rep. ¶ 83,919 (Sept. 26, 1985). The new form uses plain English and will track more closely the form used by state regulators. *See* SEC Issues Release on Revisions to Broker–Dealer Registration Form, Sec.Reg. & L.Rep. (BNA) 1753 (Oct. 4, 1985).

38. 15 U.S.C.A. § 78f. Through 1990 there were 10 registered exchanges but the Spokane Exchange has since closed its doors. No doubt, the Spokane Exchange was a casualty of the SEC's increased policing of the penny stock markets. In another recent development, the SEC has approved a two-tiered market for the American Stock Exchange. Under the new listing criteria, the AMEX will provide an exchange-based auction marketplace for smaller companies that were not able to meet the exchange's general listing criteria. *See* Creation of New AMEX Marketplace for Smaller Companies Approved by SEC, 24 Sec.Reg. & L.Rep. (BNA) 295 (March 6, 1992).

39. 15 U.S.C.A. § 78o–3.

NASD.[40] Many NASD members are also members of one or more national exchanges.

There have been a number of significant developments in the operation of the markets. The New York Stock Exchange has departed from precedent in permitting after-hours trading. Perhaps even more significant than the extension of the trading day into two after hours sessions is the fact that these sessions are operated through a screen-based execution system instead of taking place on the floor of the exchange. The New York Stock Exchange's screen-based after hours system is open to all investors for forty-five minutes beginning fifteen minutes after the close of trading.[41] A second screen-based system is open to large program traders dealing in baskets of stocks and lasts for one hour and fifteen minutes after the close of exchange trading. The significance of the screen-based system is that it bypasses the specialist system that has been the heart of the exchange mechanics for so many years.[42]

The fact that exchange operations could be conducted through a screen-based trading system [43] does not mean that every screen-based

---

40. Section 15(b)(9) empowers the SEC to exempt broker-dealers from the SRO membership requirement. The exemption can be by rule or administrative order. 15 U.S.C.A. § 78o(b)(9). *See* Exchange Services, Inc. v. SEC, 797 F.2d 188 (4th Cir.1986) (order takers for discount brokerage firm perform more than clerical tasks and thus must register with the NASD as general securities representatives).

41. *See* Wall St.J. p. C1 (May 22, 1991).

42. Specialists are discussed in § 10.4 *infra*.

43. The International Organization of Securities Commissions has adopted ten principles which are intended to serve as a guide for developers of screen-based systems as well as for regulators, and address financial integrity, surveillance, and disclosure and operational issues including access to the system, system vulnerability and security. First, the sponsor of the screen-based trading system should be able to demonstrate to the applicable regulatory agency that the system meets applicable legal standards, regulatory policies, and/or relevant market customs and practices. Second, the system should "ensure the equitable availability of accurate and timely trade and quotation information" to all participants in the system. The processing, prioritization, and display of quotations within the system should be described to the applicable regulatory agency. Third, the sponsor of the screen-based trading system should describe to the relevant regulatory authorities the order execution algorithm which is the system's rule structure for processing, prioritizing, and executing orders. Fourth, the system should be technically designed so as to operate "in a manner equitable to all market participants" and the system sponsor should describe any differences in treatment between categories of participants. Fifth, prior to implementation and then periodically, the system should undergo an objective risk assessment as to the systems vulnerability to unauthorized access, internal failures, human errors, attacks, and natural catastrophes. Sixth, the system should develop procedures to monitor the competence, integrity, and authority of system users; system users should be supervised and should not arbitrarily or discriminatorily be denied access to the system. Seventh, the system sponsor and appropriate regulatory authorities should consider risk management exposures including those stemming from interfacing with related financial systems. Eighth, there should be mechanisms in place for adequate surveillance of the system for both supervisory and enforcement purposes. The surveillance mechanisms should be available to the appropriate regulatory authorities as well as to the system sponsor. Ninth, the system sponsor and appropriate regulatory authorities should see to it that there is adequate risk disclosure to system users resulting from use of the system. In addition to disclosure of the significant risks of system use, there should be a description of the system sponsor's and providers' liability to system subscribers and users. Tenth, there should be procedures to ensure that the system sponsor, system providers, and system users be made aware of and be responsive to the directives and concerns of the appropriate regulatory

system will be classified as an exchange.[44] As noted above, an automated quotation system which does not involve the actual execution of trades is clearly not an exchange. A screen-based system for trading options on government securities was held not to be an exchange.[45] Judge Posner of the Seventh Circuit reasoned that since the screen-based system involved only three firms each of whom was actively and comprehensively regulated by the SEC, additional regulation was unnecessary. Thus, although the system differed "only in degree and detail from an exchange," the regulation of the three participants and the absence of regulatory gaps led the majority to hold that this was not an exchange under the Act.[46] It was further noted that requiring the extra level of regulation that would ensue from classifying the system as an exchange would "destroy" it.[47] Judge Flaum, dissenting, pointed out that the size of an operation should not affect whether it is classified as an exchange.[48] Judge Flaum's functional approach seems preferable not only in light of the statutory language but also in terms of the ramifications of permitting the SEC to establish an appropriate regulatory policy. Classifying screen-based systems as exchanges would simply give the SEC the task of determining which, if any, should be granted exemptions from registration.[49] Leaving the matter to the development of general principles seems preferable to the courts deciding the matter on a case by case basis. As screen-based trading expands, it is to be anticipated that this issue will be revisited.

Self–Regulation: The National Association of Securities Dealers and the National Exchanges

By virtue of section 15A,[50] the NASD operates as the largest of the self regulatory organizations subject to SEC oversight. Although the Commission has, pursuant to Section 15 of the Act, the direct authority

---

authorities. *See* CFTC Policy Statement Concerning the Oversight of Screen–Based Trading Systems, [1990–1992 Transfer Binder] Comm.Fut.L.Rep. (CCH) ¶ 24,953 CFTC (Nov. 21, 1991). *See also, e.g.,* Comm.Fut.L.Rep. (CCH) Report Letter No. 393 (Nov. 1990). The International Organization of Securities Commissions (IOSCO) consists of securities and commodities administrators from more than fifty nations. *Id.*

44. Cantor Fitzgerald G.P., [1993–1994 Transfer Binder] Fed. Sec. L. Rep. (CCH) ¶ 76,837 (SEC No Action Letter Oct. 1, 1993). The SEC had proposed Rule 15c2–10 would have required SEC approval of certain proprietary trading systems but the proposal was rescinded. Exch. Act. Rel. No. 34–33621, [1993–1994 Transfer Binder] Fed. Sec. L. Rep. (CCH) ¶ 85,322 (SEC Feb. 14, 1994).

45. Board of Trade v. SEC, 923 F.2d 1270 (7th Cir.1991).

46. 923 F.2d at 1273.

47. *Id.*

48. 923 F.2d at 1274–75. Judge Flaum pointed out that the Commission exempts certain low volume exchanges from regulation and the exemption would be unnecessary if the size of the operation went directly to the definitional issue.

49. Leaving the matter to the Commission does not mean that every screen-based system will be regulated. *See, e.g.,* Farmland Industries, Inc., 23 Sec.Reg. & L.Rep. (BNA) 305 (SEC Division of Market Reg. No Action Letter available January 23,1991) (agricultural cooperative's information system for aiding members in purchasing and selling stock among themselves would not have to be registered as a securities exchange).

50. 15 U.S.C.A. § 78*o* –3. There recently has been some movement toward establishing a self-regulatory organization for dealers in municipal securities.

to regulate broker-dealers who are members of the NASD, as a practical matter the bulk of the day-to-day regulation is generally delegated to the self regulatory organization. The NASD is a nationwide organization with fourteen district offices.[51] The NASD has extensive rules governing its members and employees which relate both to organizational structure and standards of conduct.[52]

In 1990, the SEC paved the way for a formalized secondary trading market for sales of unregistered securities to qualified institutional investors. In conjunction with its adoption of Rule 144A,[53] the SEC approved the NASD's screen-based computer and communication system called PORTAL (Private Offerings, Resales and Trading through Automated Linkages) to facilitate secondary trading of Rule 144A securities. Thus, for example, PORTAL opens up to secondary traders securities of foreign issuers that previously were not readily available in the United States.

In addition to the NASD, as observed earlier, there are nine self regulatory organizations that qualify and are registered as national exchanges under section 6 of the Act.[54] The most prestigious national exchange is the New York Stock Exchange, followed by the American Stock Exchange. The New York Stock Exchange lists only stock and bonds while the American Exchange lists stocks, bonds and put and call options. In addition there is the Pacific Exchange which lists stock, bonds and options and the Boston Exchange and the Midwest Stock Exchange which do not list options, the Philadelphia Exchange which lists both corporate securities and options, the Cincinnati Stock Exchange, and the Chicago Board Options Exchange which lists only options. There is, in addition, one relatively little-known exchange: the InterMountain Stock Exchange, headquartered in Salt Lake City, Utah.

Each self regulatory organization has the obligation of policing its members to assure compliance with its rules and regulations. However, many of the smaller and least well-equipped exchanges found it impossible to carry out with any degree of competence their investigatory and regulatory operations. Accordingly, the Exchange Act was amended by

---

51. The district offices were reorganized in 1993 and 1994. *See* § 1.3 *supra* and § 9.50 *supra* (Practitioner's Edition only).

52. The NASD constitution and rules are compiled in NASD Manual (CCH). As is the case with national exchanges, NASD rules are subject to SEC veto. 15 U.S.C.A. § 78s. *See* text accompanying footnotes 57–79 *infra*. *Cf.* McLaughlin, Piven, Vogel, Inc. v. NASD, 733 F.Supp. 694 (S.D.N.Y.1990) (NASD member must exhaust his or her administrative remedies before seeking judicial relief from NASD's refusal to permit inspection of records pertaining to NASD investigation of member). *See generally* T. Grant Callery & Anne H. Wright, NASD Disciplinary Proceedings—Recent Developments, 48 Bus.Law. 791 (1993).

53. 17 C.F.R. § 230.144A, which is discussed in §§ 4.26, 4.26.1 *supra*.

54. 15 U.S.C.A. § 78f. For a discussion of market structure *see* § 10.1 *supra*. *See also, e.g.,* James w. Walker, Jr., Self Regulation and Due Process at the American Stock Exchange, 35 Ohio S.L.J. 290 (1974); Nicholas Wolfson, Kenneth I. Rosenblum & Thomas A. Russo, The Securities Markets: An Overview, 16 How.L.Rev. 791 (1971).

Prior to 1991 there were ten registered exchanges but in 1991 the Spokane exchange closed its doors. The relatively unknown Spokane exchange was a casualty of the SEC's crackdown on the penny stock markets.

additions to section 17(d)[55] which authorize the SEC to allocate among the self regulatory organizations the responsibility for being the designated examining authority for broker-dealers who are members of more than one association or exchange. The statute further allows the self regulatory organizations by contract to agree among themselves to allocate this investigatory and inspections responsibility. Many of the lesser exchanges have availed themselves of this opportunity by contracting away their investigatory and regulatory responsibilities to the NASD. Notwithstanding the self regulatory organization's responsibility, it has been held that a brokerage customer cannot maintain a negligence action against the NASD for failure to adequately supervise its members.[56]

By virtue of section 19 of the Act,[57] the Commission has oversight responsibility with respect to all rule making activity of national exchanges. Similar authority exists with regard to the NASD.[58] Section 19(b)(1) requires that all self regulatory associations file proposed rule changes with the Commission.[59] If the SEC does not institute disapproval proceedings within thirty-five days of the proposed rules' publication (unless extended by the SEC to ninety days), the proposed rules become effective.[60] Section 19(c)[61] empowers the SEC to "abrogate, add to, and delete from" the rules of self regulatory organizations. However, this power is exercised only on a very infrequent basis.

Section 19(a)(1) gives the Commission the authority to register national exchanges.[62] Under section 19(h) the Commission has the

---

55. 15 U.S.C.A. § 78q(d). The statute provides in part that "[i]n making any such rule or entering any such order, the Commission shall take into consideration the regulatory capabilities and procedures of the self-regulatory organizations, availability of staff, convenience of location, unnecessary regulatory duplication * * *."

56. FDIC v. National Association of Securities Dealers, 747 F.2d 498 (8th Cir.1984). *Cf.* Brawer v. Options Clearing Corp., 633 F.Supp. 1254 (S.D.N.Y.1986), *affirmed* 807 F.2d 297 (2d Cir.1986) (no private remedy under sections 6(b), 17A(b)(3), or 19(g)(1) for options clearing agency's failure to comply with its own rules regarding adjustment of option strike price); Cardoza v. Commodity Futures Trading Commission, 768 F.2d 1542 (7th Cir.1985) (no private remedy against commodities exchange for failure to enforce eligibility rules). *But cf.* Sam Wong & Son, Inc. v. New York Mercantile Exchange, 735 F.2d 653 (2d Cir.1984) (upholding complaint against commodities exchange alleging that ulterior motives affected its regulatory stance).

Actions against the NASD and securities exchanges are discussed in § 10.2.1 *infra* (Practitioner's Edition only).

57. 15 U.S.C.A. § 78s.

58. *See* 15 U.S.C.A. § 78o–3. *See, e.g.,* General Bond & Share Co. v. SEC, 39 F.3d 1451 (10th Cir.1994) (NASD interpretation of its Rules of Fair Practice amounted to such a major shift in policy as to amount to rulemaking and thus could only be accomplished through the formal rulemaking procedures).

59. 15 U.S.C.A. § 78s(b)(1).

60. 15 U.S.C.A. § 78s(b)(2). *Cf.* Higgins v. SEC, 866 F.2d 47 (2d Cir.1989) (upholding SEC approval of New York Stock Exchange rule change).

61. 15 U.S.C.A. § 78s(c).

62. 15 U.S.C.A. § 78s(a)(1). The SEC also has the responsibility for registering clearing agencies for exchanges. 15 U.S.C.A. § 78q–1. *See* § 10.13 *infra. Cf.* Board of Trade of City of Chicago v. SEC, 883 F.2d 525 (7th Cir.1989), *appeal after remand* 923 F.2d 1270 (1991) (reversing SEC order granting clearing agent registration for agent for

authority to discipline national exchanges for violating the securities Acts' provisions.[63] There is also the express authority of exchanges to discipline persons associated with an exchange, including power to remove from office or censure its officers or directors for willful violations of the Act.[64] The Commission has exercised its statutory authority[65] to expel a national exchange on only one occasion.[66] But the Commission has with more frequency exercised its authority under subsection (h) to uphold expulsion of members from the exchange.[67] The power to discipline and sanction members is given directly to the exchange with a right of appeal to the SEC which may in its discretion review the record de novo.[68] The SEC decision is then subject to review by a federal court of appeals.[69] The NASD has similar status and authority. The Commission can suspend or revoke the securities association's registration.[70] The NASD has the power to hold hearings or expel its members from the association for conduct in violation of the Act or the NASD's rules.[71]

In addition to the sanctions imposed by the SROs, the Commission can institute its own proceedings. The Commission is empowered to suspend or revoke broker-dealer registration for violations of the securi-

---

electronic system for trading options on government securities). Commodities exchanges had complained that the registration as a clearing agent was improper since this in essence involved the SEC's recognition of an unregistered securities exchange. The Seventh Circuit agreed that the SEC first had to make a formal determination of whether the activity in question in fact constituted operating as a securities exchange. On remand, the Commission ruled that it did not and reissued the registration as a clearing agent. *See* 22 Sec.Reg. & L.Rep. (BNA) 56 (Jan. 12, 1990), *judgment affirmed* 923 F.2d 1270 (7th Cir.1991).

63. 15 U.S.C.A. § 78s(h).

64. 15 U.S.C.A. § 78f(d).

65. 15 U.S.C.A. § 78s(h)(1).

66. San Francisco Mining Exchange v. SEC, 378 F.2d 162 (9th Cir.1967).

67. *See, e.g.,* Archer v. SEC, 133 F.2d 795 (8th Cir.1943), *cert. denied* 319 U.S. 767, 63 S.Ct. 1330, 87 L.Ed. 1717 (1943).

68. 15 U.S.C.A. § 78f; *see* 15 U.S.C.A. § 78s(h).

69. *See* Lewis D. Lowenfels, A Lack of Fair Procedures in Administrative Process: Disciplinary Proceedings at the Stock Exchanges and the NASD, 64 Cornell L.Rev. 375 (1979); Norman S. Poser, A Reply to Lowenfels, 64 Cornell L.Rev. 402 (1979).

70. 15 U.S.C.A. § 78o–1(h). *See, e.g.,* Mister Discount Stockbrokers v. SEC, 768 F.2d 875 (7th Cir.1985) (upholding dismissal of firm from NASD membership and order barring individual from associating with an NASD member firm); Austin Municipal Securities v. NASD, 757 F.2d 676 (5th Cir.1985).

71. 15 U.S.C.A. § 78s(h)(2). *See, e.g.,* Don D. Anderson & Co. v. SEC, 423 F.2d 813 (10th Cir.1970) (suspension for violation of 1933 Act); Tager v. SEC, 344 F.2d 5 (2d Cir.1965) (expulsion for violation of 1933 Act); Financial Counsellors, Inc. v. SEC, 339 F.2d 196 (2d Cir.1964) (expulsion for violation of 1934 Act); Gilligan, Will & Co. v. SEC, 267 F.2d 461 (2d Cir.1959) (suspension for violation of 1933 Act).

See, e.g., Prevatte v. NASD, 682 F.Supp. 913 (W.D.Mich.1988) (administrative remedies must be exhausted prior to judicial challenge of NASD sanctions). *See generally* T. Grant Callery & Ann H. Wright, NASD Disciplinary Proceedings—Recent Developments, 48 Bus.Law. 791 (1993). *Cf.* Whiteside and Co., Inc. v. SEC, 883 F.2d 7 (5th Cir.1989) (finding that SEC affirmance of NASD sanction was not an abuse of discretion).

ties laws.[72] The Commission can also bar any person from associating with a broker-dealer,[73] a member of a registered securities association (*i.e.* the NASD),[74] or an investment adviser[75] as well as barring that person from serving in various capacities with a registered investment company.[76] Additionally, with respect to all of the powers outlined above, the Commission can, of course, impose less severe sanctions, including suspension for a definite period of not more than twelve months or merely censuring persons involved.[77] Section 19(d) sets out the SEC's authority with regard to disciplinary actions by self regulatory organizations.[78] Sections 19(e) and 19(f) set out the standards for commission review of disciplinary proceedings and sanctions imposed by self-regulatory organizations.[79]

In addition to the possibility of a self regulatory organization for municipal securities dealers,[80] the SEC has had under consideration a self regulatory organization for investment advisers.[81] Similarly, the NASD board of governors has adopted a resolution endorsing a pilot project under which it would act as a self regulatory organization for investment advisers and associated persons.[82]

Over and beyond the regulatory structure outlined above, agreements between members of self regulatory agencies that their disputes be arbitrated are generally enforceable.[83] This supplements the general

72. 15 U.S.C.A. § 78o(b)(5). *See, e.g.,* Dlugash v. SEC, 373 F.2d 107 (2d Cir.1967) (revocation); Peoples Securities Co. v. SEC, 289 F.2d 268 (5th Cir.1961) (denial of registration); Gilligan, Will & Co. v. SEC, 267 F.2d 461 (2d Cir.1959), *cert. denied* 361 U.S. 896, 80 S.Ct. 200, 4 L.Ed.2d 152 (1959) (suspension).

See also, e.g., Amato v. SEC, 18 F.3d 1281 (5th Cir.1994) (upholding suspension and fine, respondent failed to establish that he was victim of improper selective prosecution).

The Commission has parallel authority over investment advisers under the 1940 Advisers Act. 15 U.S.C.A. § 80b–3(c). *See* chapter 18 *infra.*

73. 15 U.S.C.A. § 78o(b)(6). *See, e.g.,* Elliott v. SEC, 36 F.3d 86 (11th Cir.1994) (upholding bar notwithstanding respondent's contention that prior conviction of 37 counts of mail and securities fraud was invalid); Berdahl v. SEC, 572 F.2d 643 (8th Cir.1978); Chatham v. SEC, 604 F.2d 1368 (D.C.Cir.1978); Stead v. SEC, 444 F.2d 713 (10th Cir.1971); Sec.Exch.Act Rel. No. 34–14668 (April 17, 1978); Sec.Exch.Act Rel. No. 34–14918 (July 3, 1976).

74. 15 U.S.C.A. § 78s(h)(3). *See, e.g.,* O'Leary v. SEC, 424 F.2d 908 (D.C.Cir.1970); Sec.Exch.Act Rel. No. 34–14759 (May 15, 1978).

75. 15 U.S.C.A. § 80b–3(f).

76. 15 U.S.C.A. § 80a–9(b).

77. *See* Sec.Exch.Act Rel. No. 34–14761 (May 15, 1978).

78. 15. U.S.C.A. § 78s(d). *See* 17 C.F.R. §§ 240.19d–1, .19d–2, .19d–3.

79. 15 U.S.C.A. §§ 78s(e), s(f).

80. *See* § 10.5 *infra.*

81. The North American Securities Administrators' Association has endorsed such an S.R.O. Under the proposal there would be significant coordination with state regulation.

82. In what may be viewed as a competing proposal, the financial planners' trade association has recommended the establishment of a self regulatory organization for financial planners.

83. 15 U.S.C.A. § 78bb(b). *See, e.g.,* French v. Merrill Lynch, Pierce, Fenner & Smith, Inc., 784 F.2d 902 (9th Cir.1986) (affirming arbitration award in dispute between broker-dealer and market maker); N. Donald & Co. v. American United Energy Corp., 746 F.2d

rule that federal securities claims are arbitrable.[84]

Although the federal securities laws do not regulate commodities transactions directly, since stock brokers frequently trade in commodities, improper conduct can run afoul of both the federal securities and commodities regulatory framework.[85] In some instances commodities transactions may be directly regulated by the securities laws, such as is the case with pooled managed commodities accounts.[86]

Potential Conflicts of Interest and The Chinese Wall Requirement

In recent years there has been an increased concern about the potential conflicts of interest resulting from the varied activities of multiservice brokerage firms. For example, when a firm acts as an underwriter or investment adviser for publicly traded issuers it will have access to nonpublic information that would be of interest to its retail customers who may be purchasing or selling the securities in question. The traditional response has been to establish a Chinese Wall (or "firewall") between the firm's various departments and thus to eliminate the potential conflict within each department.[87] Another response to potential conflicts of interest has been for firms to place securities on a "restricted list" when the investment banking or underwriting department becomes involved in a proposed public offering or acquisition.

Increased Competition and the Move Toward a National Market

A relatively recent development in the broker-dealer industry has been increased competition. In 1975, the SEC invalidated fixed commission rates as violative of the antitrust laws.[88] One consequence of the

---

666 (10th Cir.1984); Morgan, Olmstead, Kennedy & Gardner, Inc. v. United States Trust Co., 608 F.Supp. 1561 (S.D.N.Y.1985). *See* §§ 10.15–10.22 *infra* (Practitioner's Edition only).

84. *See* § 14.4 *infra.*

85. *See, e.g.,* Smoky Greenhaw Cotton Co. v. Merrill Lynch, Pierce, Fenner & Smith, Inc., 785 F.2d 1274 (5th Cir.1986), *on remand* 650 F.Supp. 220 (W.D.Tex.1986).

86. *See* § 1.5 *supra.* The courts are split as to whether an individual managed commodities account falls within the definition of "security" so as to subject it to regulation under the securities laws. *Id.*

87. SEC v. First Boston Corp., 86 Civ. 3524 (S.D.N.Y.1986) (consent order disgorging $132,238 in profits plus civil penalty of $264,276; defendant also agreed to review its restricted list and Chinese Wall procedures). *Cf.* In re Smith Barney, Harris, Upham & Co., Exch.Act. Rel. No. 34–21242 (Aug. 15, 1984) (brokerage firm should give its customers time to digest research recommendations reflecting a material change in the firm's position before the firm trades in the securities for its own account). *See also* Caravan Mobile Home Sales, Inc. v. Lehman Brothers Kuhn Loeb, Inc., 769 F.2d 561 (9th Cir.1985) (rejecting plaintiff's suggested per se rule requiring disclosure by multiservice banking firms acting as investment advisors to publicly traded issuers and in a fiduciary capacity with retail brokerage clients). *See generally* Larry L. Varn, The Multi–Service Securities Firm and the Chinese Wall: A New Look in the Light of the Federal Securities Code, 63 Neb.L.Rev. 197 (1984). *See* § 10.2.4 *infra* (Practitioner's Edition only) for additional discussion of Chinese Walls.

88. *See* Gordon v. New York Stock Exchange, Inc., 422 U.S. 659, 95 S.Ct. 2598, 45 L.Ed.2d 463 (1975). *See, also, e.g.,* William F. Baxter, The New York Stock Exchange Fixed Commission Rates: A Private Cartel Goes Public, 22 Stan.L.Rev. 675 (1970); George Bittlingmayer, The Stock Market and Early Antitrust Enforcement, 36 J.L. & Econ. 1

lifting of price restraints has been the advent of discount brokerage houses. Discount brokers charge lower commissions than the full-service firms but do not offer research services or investment advice.

Banking and the Securities Laws

Another development in securities regulation has been the integration of various financial services. Although the Glass–Steagall Act prohibits national banks from dealing in investment securities,[89] this legislation has been severely eroded. For example, bank holding companies have acquired discount brokerage services. Full service brokerage firms have purchased regional banks. There is ever-increasing competition between banks and broker-dealers with money market funds and interest-bearing checking accounts. A related development has been the acquisition of brokerage firms by companies offering other financial services.[90] This is a fast moving area and legislative reform is likely, including possible repeal of the Glass–Steagall Act.

In a very controversial move, the SEC promulgated Rule 3b–9[91] which provided that banks engaged in certain securities transactions normally associated with broker-dealers must register as broker-dealers under the Exchange Act. The rule, which became effective in January, 1986, was severely questioned, including by the American Bankers Association.[92] Although the Commission had implemented the rule it had been granting liberal time extensions to banks which could show they were making a good faith effort to register.[93] The DC Circuit Court

---

(1993); Richard W. Jennings, The New York Stock Exchange and the Commission Rate Struggle, 53 Calif.L.Rev. 1119 (1965).

Other antitrust issues pervade the securities industry. *See generally* Thomas Linden, A Reconciliation of Antitrust Law with Securities Regulation: The Judicial Approach, 57 Geo.Wash.L.Rev. 179 (1977); Richard W. McLaren, Antitrust and the Securities Industry, 11 B.C.Ind. & Comm.L.Rev. 187 (1970); Robert Pozen, Competition and Regulation in the Stock Markets, 73 Mich.L.Rev. 317 (1974); Marianne K. Smythe, Self Regulation and the Antitrust Laws: Suggestions for An Accommodation, 62 N.C.L.Rev. 475 (1984).

89. 12 U.S.C.A. § 24. *See,* Harvey L. Pitt & Julie L. Williams, The Glass–Steagall Act: Key Issues for the Financial Services Industry, 11 Sec.Reg.L.J. 234 (1983). The SEC formerly considered a proposal to require registration of banks that solicit securities business. 15 Sec.Reg. & L.Rep. (BNA) 1995 (Oct. 28, 1983). *See* § 19.5 *infra* (Practitioner's Edition only).

90. Prominent examples include American Express' purchase of Shearson, Prudential Insurance's acquisition of Bache & Co., Sears' purchase of Dean Witter & Co. (Sears already owned Allstate Insurance), and Bankamerica's acquisition of Charles Schwab, a leading discount broker.

91. 17 C.F.R. § 240.3b–9. However, incidental activities will not trigger the registration requirements. *See* In re Federated Securities Corp., [1986 Transfer Binder] Fed.Sec. L.Rep. (CCH) ¶ 78,315 (SEC No Action Letter Jan. 6, 1986).

92. *See* ABA Sues to Block Commission Rule to Require Broker–Dealer Registration, 17 Sec.Reg. & L.Rep. (BNA) 1445 (Aug. 9, 1985), Note, The Validity of SEC Rule 3b–9, Which Requires Banks to Register as Broker–Dealers, 43 Wash. & Lee L.Rev. 989 (1986). *See* § 19.5 *infra.*

93. *See* In re National Association of Securities Dealers, [1986 Transfer Binder] Fed.Sec.L.Rep. (CCH) ¶ 78,309 (SEC No Action Letter Feb. 19, 1986).

of Appeals struck down Rule 3b–9 as beyond the SEC's authority.[94] The
Commission subsequently sought legislation to grant such authority.[95]

In another significant development, the Supreme Court upheld the
Comptroller of the Currency's permitting a national bank to operate a
discount brokerage subsidiary.[96] Similarly, insured state banks that are
not members of the Federal Reserve System have been allowed to engage
in the securities business through subsidiaries and affiliates.[97] It has
also been held that subsidiaries of Federal Reserve banks can provide
brokerage services and give investment advice.[98]

Another developing area has been the move toward a national
market system. In 1975, Congress mandated steps to be taken toward
increased use of technology in furnishing consolidated price quotations
for securities traded on more than one exchange and for the over-the-
counter markets.[99] These developments are discussed in a subsequent
section of this chapter.[100]

The Market Reform Act of 1990

The Market Reform Act of 1990[101] was enacted in response to
concerns over various market disruptions that have occurred over the
past several years. The Act sets forth additional SEC powers in times of
market disruptions. The Commission is given the emergency power to
close a securities exchange for a period of up to ninety days,[102] as well as
the power to summarily suspend trading in any security for a period up
to ten business days.[103] The Act also gives the SEC the emergency power
to suspend, alter, or impose rules on a self regulatory organization for a
maximum of ten business days.[104]

Large Trader Reporting

In addition to the foregoing emergency powers given to the SEC, the
1990 amendments to the Exchange Act also impose identification and
reporting requirements for major market participants. Section 13(h) of

94. American Bankers Ass'n v. SEC, 804 F.2d 739 (D.C.Cir.1986). *See* Note, The Demise of Rule 13b–9, 13 Del.J.Corp.L. 77 (1988).

95. *See* SEC to Ask Congress to Require Banks to Register Securities Affiliates, 19 Sec.Reg. & L.Rep. (BNA) 626 (May 1, 1987).

96. Clarke v. Securities Industry Ass'n, 479 U.S. 388, 107 S.Ct. 750, 93 L.Ed.2d 757 (1987).

97. Investment Company Institute v. FDIC, 815 F.2d 1540 (D.C.Cir.1987).

98. Securities Industry Association v. Board of Governors of the Federal Reserve System, 821 F.2d 810 (D.C.Cir.1987), *cert. denied* 484 U.S. 1005, 108 S.Ct. 697, 98 L.Ed.2d 649 (1988).

99. 15 U.S.C.A. § 78k–1.

100. *See* § 10.13 *infra.*

101. *See* § 10.1 *supra.*

102. 15 U.S.C.A. § 78l(k)(1)(B).

103. 15 U.S.C.A. § 78*l*(k)(1)(A).

104. 15 U.S.C.A. § 78*l*(k)(2). These emergency orders are subject to presidential disapproval.

the Exchange Act[105] grants the SEC the authority to impose these reporting requirements on "large traders." The large trader reporting requirements are a result of concerns that arose following the market break of 1987. Specifically, Congress was concerned that market swings and increasing volatility generally could be attributed, at least in part, to the impact of large traders and their participation in the derivatives and underlying securities markets. Accordingly, the Exchange Act now empowers the SEC to promulgate rules "[f]or the purpose of monitoring the impact on the securities markets of securities transactions involving a substantial volume or large fair market value or exercise value."[106] These large trader reporting requirements, which are to be implemented by SEC rulemaking, are modeled upon and parallel the large trader reporting system that is administered with respect to the commodities markets by the Commodity Futures Trading Commission.[107] Under the Exchange Act, the SEC is granted the authority to impose reporting requirements on broker-dealers that maintain and carry accounts for large traders.[108] The Act gives the Commission broad discretion in defining who is a large trader and in framing the reporting requirements to be imposed, subject to, among other things, the cost of creating and implementing the system.[109] The Commission is given additional authority with regard to examination of broker-dealer records.[110] The SEC is further given broad power to promulgate rules requiring disclosures relating to the financial condition of broker-dealer affiliates and holding companies.[111]

In 1991, the SEC proposed Rule 13h–1[112] but after extensive comments, the Commission made a number of adjustments and reproposed the rule.[113] The Commission explained that the reproposed Rule 13h–1 is designed to "provid[e] the Commission with the information necessary to reconstruct trading activity in periods of market stress and for enforcement or other regulatory purposes, without imposing undue burdens on market participants."[114]

The reproposed rule identifies large traders by first requiring an aggregation[115] of all trades entered and then identifying specific levels of

105. 15 U.S.C.A. § 78m(h).

106. *Id.*

107. 17 C.F.R. Part 15. *See* 2 Philip M. Johnson & Thomas L. Hazen, Commodities Regulation § 3.118 (2d ed. 1989).

108. 15 U.S.C.A. § 78m(h)(2).

109. 15 U.S.C.A. § 78m(h)(5).

110. 15 U.S.C.A. § 78m(h)(4).

111. *See* 15 U.S.C.A. § 78q(h).

112. *See* Exch. Act Rel. No. 34–29593 (Aug. 22, 1991).

113. *See* Exch. Act Rel. No. 34–33608 (Feb. 9, 1994).

114. *Id.*

115. The basic requirement for aggregation is that all accounts owned or controlled by a person or under common ownership or control must be aggregated if the account would not by itself qualify as a large trader account.

activity.[116]   Once a person qualifies as a large trader, he or she would be required to file a Form 13H which would identify the filer as a large trader and also identify its affiliates.   In turn the large trader would receive a large trader identification number (LTID).   The large trader would have to inform each of its broker–dealers of its LTID and all other securities accounts to which it applies.   The LTID is subject to annual updating.   In addition to this filing and identification requirement, Rule 13h–1 would impose substantial record–keeping requirements.   Broker–dealers would be required to maintain complete records of each trade executed for large traders.   These records are to include execution time, date and place of transaction, price, security, quantity, and type of transaction.   The records must thus include the information that would be necessary to enable the SEC to reconstruct trading patterns of large traders.   The rule further gives the SEC and applicable self regulatory organizations the authority to require reporting of large trader transactions of 2,000 shares or $10,000 in fair market value.   The rule contains an exemption from the foregoing requirements for specialists who do not carry accounts for themselves.

Government and Municipal Securities Dealers

None of the regulation discussed above relates to the increasingly large markets for federal, state, and local government securities.   Persons who deal solely in those securities are not covered by section 15's regulatory structure as described above.   In 1975, Congress created the Municipal Securities Rulemaking Board to regulate dealers of municipal securities.[117]   Recently, Congress created a regulatory structure for dealers in federal government securities such as Treasury bonds, bills and notes.[118]

The rule further provides that the person named in the account is an owner as is any other person who owns more than a ten percent interest in an account.   Control is defined as either ownership or full or limited discretionary investment authority.

116.   Large trader activity is triggered by trading, in a single calendar day, of securities having an aggregate market value of $10 million or trading of 200,000 shares (if the shares have an aggregate market value of $2 million).   Additionally, market participants engaged in program trading qualify as large traders.

117.   *See* § 10.5 *infra*.

118.   Government Securities Act of 1986, Public Law 99–571, 100 Stat. 3208.   *See* Senate Panel Approves Bill to Require Government Securities Dealers to Register, 18 Sec.Reg. & L.Rep. (BNA) 1201 (Aug. 15, 1986); SEC Request for Comment, Oversight of the U.S. Government and Agency Securities Markets, Exch.Act.Rel. No. 34–21959 (April 19, 1985).   *See also* Treasury Tells Congress Government Securities Dealers Should be Regulated, 17 Sec.Reg. & L.Rep. (BNA) 2145 (Dec. 13, 1985); Self Regulation Urged for Dealers of U.S. Securities, Wall St.J. p. 18 (March 28, 1985).   *See also* 15 C.F.R. §§ 240.15Ca1–1 to .15Cc1–1; Government Securities Brokers and Dealers Temporary Treasury Regulations and Forms, Fed.Sec.L.Rep. (CCH) No. 1234 part II (June 3, 1987).

Government securities dealers are discussed in § 10.5.1 *infra*.

*Deleted sections 10.2.1–10.2.3 can be found
in the Practitioner's Edition.*

§ 10.2.4 Multiservice Brokerage Firms; The Chinese Wall

At the time that the federal securities laws were originally enacted, the functions of the various professionals in the securities industry were relatively distinct. However, recent years have witnessed not only the elimination of clear distinctions between the permissible activities of banks and securities firms,[1] but also the proliferation of multiservice firms providing a wide variety of financial services. Thus, for example, today, a multiservice securities firm combines the functions of investment banking and corporate counseling with investment advisory, investment management and retail broker-dealer services.[2]

A typical multiservice firm performs numerous functions. These functions typically include: (1) investment banking (including underwriting and rendering advice to corporate issuers); (2) research (which services all of the firm's departments); (3) sales, which includes both retail sales and investment management; and (4) generally firms will have their own trading desk which operates in the over-the-counter markets and also performs arbitrage for their own account. The following simplified graphic depicts a prototypical multiservice securities brokerage firm:

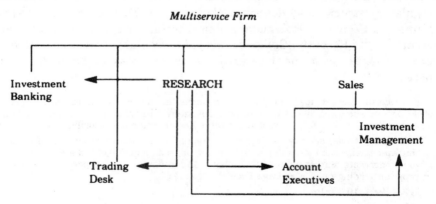

These varied functions give rise to conflicts of interest as the firm has a duty to guard the confidentiality of any non-public information it receives from a corporate client. A major problem is that while the research department is supplying information to each of the other

------

§ 10.2.4

1. *See* § 19.5 *infra.*

2. Commercial banks are subject to the same conflicts. *See generally* Stephen I. Greenberg, William C. Mack, and Jeffrey L. Schulte, The Obligations of Banks in the Public Securities Markets, 1980 Duke L.J. 1063, Edward G. Herman & Carl F. Safanda, The Commercial Bank Trust Dept. and the "Wall", 14 B.C.Indus. & Com.L.Rev. 21 (1972).

departments, the research department should be basing its evaluation on independent research not from confidential information acquired from the firm's other departments. The anti-fraud provisions of the security laws require the firm to disclose all material non-public information it has or abstain from using it in trading or recommending the security in question.[3] This "disclose or abstain" rule further obligates firms to refrain from executing or recommending transactions unless justified in light of all information known to the firm.[4] In response to these conflicting duties, multiservice financial institutions have established internal policies and procedures to restrict the flow of material nonpublic information from the department in which it originates. These procedures are colloquially referred to as "Chinese Walls" or "fire walls."[5]

The Chinese Wall concept in securities law originated in the settlement of a Securities and Exchange Commission proceeding against Merrill Lynch in a case involving the misuse of inside information.[6] Merrill Lynch, while serving as the managing underwriter for an offering of Douglas Aircraft securities, passed on non-public information concerning an expected drop in earnings to favored Merrill Lynch customers who in turn sold their Douglas Aircraft holdings. After having initiated proceedings against Merrill Lynch and certain of its employees, the SEC and Merrill Lynch entered into a settlement order. In accepting Merrill Lynch's offer of settlement, the SEC highlighted Merrill Lynch's new procedures for preventing dissemination of confidential non-public information by the underwriting department to other branches of the firm.[7] While the SEC endorsed Merrill Lynch's new procedures, the SEC did not give blanket approval to the use of Chinese Walls. The SEC stated, "As a matter of Commission policy, we do not, and indeed cannot, determine in advance that the Statement of Policy will prove adequate in all circumstances that may arise."[8] The procedures implemented by Merrill Lynch, though not expressly named, have come to be known as Chinese Walls.

Since the *Merrill Lynch* case, although the Commission continues to

---

3. *See, e.g.*, SEC v. Texas Gulf Sulphur, 401 F.2d 833 (2d Cir.1968) (en banc), *cert. denied* 394 U.S. 976, 89 S.Ct. 1454, 22 L.Ed.2d 756 (1969); In re Cady, Roberts & Co., 40 S.E.C. 907 (1961) and the other authorities discussed in § 13.9, *infra*. *See also, e.g.*, Dirks v. SEC, 463 U.S. 646, 103 S.Ct. 3255, 77 L.Ed.2d 911 (1983).

4. *See* § 10.6 *infra*.

5. *See generally* David A. Lipton & Robert B. Mazur, The Chinese Wall Solution to the Conflict Problems of Securities Firms, 50 N.Y.U.L.Rev. 459 (1975); Larry L. Varn, The Multiservice Securities Firm and the Chinese Wall: A New Look in the Light of the Federal Securities Code, 63 Neb.L.Rev. 197 (1984). *See also, e.g.*, Marianne M. Jennings & Carl D. Hudson, The Ultimate Inside Information: Financial Institutions and Auditors as a Control of Market Response to Clients' Securities Offerings, 42 Ark.L.Rev. 467 (1989); Norman S. Poser, Chinese Walls in the U.S. and U.K., 21 Rev.Sec. & Commodities Reg. 207 (1988).

6. In the Matter of Merrill Lynch, Pierce, Fenner and Smith, Inc., Sec. Exchange Act Release No. 8459, [1967–69 Transfer Binder] Fed.Sec.L.Rep. (CCH) ¶ 77,629 (1968).

7. *Id.*

8. *Id.*

rely on the Chinese Wall in settling administrative proceedings,[9] the development of case law in this area has been sparse.[10] In Slade v. Shearson, Hammill & Co.,[11] the Second Circuit, while not taking a position on the Chinese Wall, discussed its implications.[12] Shearson, Hammill argued that the federal securities laws precluded it from using inside information to the benefit of its customers, and therefore recommended placing a Chinese Wall between its departments to prevent the passage of confidential information.[13] The plaintiffs did not attack the concept of the Chinese Wall but found fault with the assertion that the securities laws prevent a broker from ending a selling campaign once it has received adverse inside information concerning the issuer. The SEC, in an attempt to reconcile the principles that inside information should not lead to market profits and that brokers should deal fairly with their customers, advocated a reinforced Chinese Wall composed of a ban on transmission of inside information between departments, strengthened by a list of companies whose securities the firm could not recommend because of an existing bank relationship.[14]

The SEC again indicated approval of the Chinese Wall in Rule 14e–3 of the Exchange Act, adopted in 1980 to prohibit insider trading by those in possession of material nonpublic information in connection with tender offers.[15] Paragraph (b) of the rule provides a safe harbor exclusion for firms adopting a Chinese Wall if the firm is able to show that (1) the individual making the investment decision had no knowledge of the non-public material information[16] and (2) the firm had implemented "one or a combination of policies and procedures, reasonable under the

---

9. *See, e.g.,* In the Matter of Kidder, Peabody & Co., Sec.Exch.Act Rel. No. 34–24,543 (June 4, 1987) (placing burden of monitoring the Chinese Wall on the firm's legal and compliance departments).

10. There have, however, been numerous law review articles on the subject as well as Chinese Wall defense availability in attorney-client privilege cases and banking cases. *See* footnotes 2 and 5 *supra.*

11. 517 F.2d 398 (2d Cir.1974).

12. The case was remanded to the district court to develop a more complete record. *Id.* at 399.

13. *Id.* at 402.

14. *Id.* at 403. It should be noted that there are many variations on the Chinese Wall: the solid or impermeable wall, the permeable wall, the reinforced wall, and the administered wall. For a complete discussion of these categories *see,* Stephen J. Greenberg, William C. Mack & Jeffrey L. Schulte, The Obligations of Banks in the Public Securities Markets, 1980 Duke L.J. 1063.

15. 17 C.F.R. § 240.14e–3. *See* SEC Exchange Act Rel. No. 34–17120 [1980 Transfer Binder] Fed.Sec.L.Rep. (CCH) ¶ 82,646 (Sept. 4, 1980). The scope of Rule 14e–3 has been significantly limited by the Second Circuit's ruling in United States v. Chestman, 903 F.2d 75 (2d Cir.1990). Rule 14e–3 was held invalid to the extent that it would have applied to conduct not involving scienter. One member of the three judge panel would have invalidated the rule as beyond the statutory authority of section 14(e). The other two judges took the position that Rule 14e–3 is a valid exercise of the Commission's rulemaking authority, although one imposed a scienter requirement. *See* §§ 11.15, 13.9 *infra.*

16. In the release adopting Rule 14e–3 the SEC stated that the individual making the investment decision referred to in Rule 14e–3(b) would not include a person or group of persons supervising such individual. *See* SEC Exchange Act Rel. No. 34–17120, [1980 Transfer Binder] Fed.Sec.L.Rep. (CCH) ¶ 82,646 (Sept. 4, 1980).

circumstances" to ensure that those making investment decisions for the firm do not violate 14e–3.[17] Rule 14e–3 thus is the SEC's formalization of the propriety of the Chinese Wall as a way of avoiding liability for misuse of information.[18] The financial services firm carries the burden of proof to demonstrate its satisfaction of both elements of the safe harbor. The SEC specified two procedures in the rule–restricted lists and Chinese Walls. Although the SEC emphasizes that it does not require these procedures,[19] in light of the serious potential for liability under 14e–3, the prudent course of action would be to satisfy the safe harbor in 14e–3(b). It is important to note that the SEC, in its release adopting the rule, stated that a broker-dealer may not continue to trade for its own account when the broker-dealer possesses material, non-public information relating to the tender offer.[20] The SEC also stated that when a broker-dealer or other financial services institution uses a Chinese Wall "it may be appropriate to advise customers of its use of such procedure * * * because the institution would not be using all information it had received to the benefit of a particular customer."[21] Another use of the Chinese wall (or fire wall) is to permit retail brokers to acquire exchange specialists without running afoul of the restrictions of specialist activity.[22]

The Chinese Wall procedures are not limited to brokerage firms but also apply to investment companies. Thus, for example, the SEC adopted Rule 17j–1 under the Investment Company Act of 1940 which addresses certain insider trading type problems impacting upon investment companies.[23] The rule requires registered investment companies to adopt a written code of ethics containing provisions reasonably

---

17. *Id.*

18. *See* Letter of SEC General Counsel to Judge Cohill in Koppers Co. v. American Express Co., 689 F.Supp. 1371 (W.D.Pa.1988). The SEC has indicated that in order for a firm to meet the burden of proving that its Chinese wall procedures are adequate, the procedures must include significant efforts in training and surveillance. *See* SEC Division of Market Regulation, Report on Broker–Dealer Policies and Procedures Designed to Segment the Flow and Prevent the Misuse of Material Nonpublic Information (March 1990).

19. The Commission noted that the rule's standard of reasonable care under the circumstances takes into consideration the nature of the person's business. A financial services institution may tailor its monitoring system and practices to fit its own situation. The SEC refused to impose a specified industry standard. In rejecting a rigid, bright–line test, the Commission observed that the policies and procedures which may prove to be reasonable for one institution may not be applicable for another institution, even though the two firms may be involved in the same industry. *See* SEC Division of Market Regulation, Report on Broker–Dealer Policies and Procedures Designed to Segment the Flow and Prevent the Misuse of Material Nonpublic Information (March 1990); *See* SEC Exchange Act Rel. No. 34–17120 [1980 Transfer Binder] Fed.Sec.L.Rep. (CCH) ¶ 82,646 (Sept. 4, 1980).

20. *See* SEC Exchange Act Rel. No. 34–17120 [1980 Transfer Binder] Fed.Sec.L.Rep. (CCH) ¶ 82,646 (Sept. 4, 1980).

21. *Id.* at p. 83,461.

22. *See* Sec.Exch.Act Rel. No. 34–23768, 51 Fed.Reg. 41,183 (Nov. 13, 1986) (approving New York and American stock exchange rule changes). Specialists are discussed in § 10.4 *infra.*

23. 17 C.F.R. § 270.17j–1. *See* Investment Company Act Rel. No. 40–11421 [1980 Transfer Binder] Fed.Sec.L.Rep. (CCH) ¶ 82,679 (October 31, 1980).

necessary to prevent its access persons from engaging in any activity prohibited by the securities acts' general anti-fraud provisions.[24] Further, the rule requires that investment companies use reasonable diligence and institute procedures reasonably necessary to prevent violations of the code. Any director, officer, general partner or advisory person who acquires direct or indirect beneficial ownership of any security as defined in the rule is required to report such transaction to their investment company adviser or underwriter. In the release accompanying the rule, the SEC stated that it expected that certain abusive activities would be specifically considered in codes of ethics.[25]

Further SEC approval of the Chinese Wall concept can be found in SEC Rules 137, 138, and 139[26] which have been promulgated under the Securities Act of 1933.[27] Recognizing the fact that multiservice firms have research analysts separate from the underwriting department, Rules 137, 138, and 139 permit the research department to operate without violating section 5 of the 1933 Act as long as internal controls are implemented to insure that the two departments are separate.

In 1984, the Insider Trading Sanctions Act (ITSA) was enacted.[28] ITSA provides for treble damages for civil liability in SEC insider trading enforcement cases.[29] In considering ITSA, both Houses of Congress had occasion to consider the Chinese Wall concept. The House Committee Report in recognizing the 14e–3 endorsement of the Chinese Wall states, "In this context, it is also important to recognize that, under both existing law and the bill, a multiservice firm with an effective Chinese Wall would not be liable for trades effected on one side of the wall, notwithstanding inside information possessed by firm employees on the other side." [30] This statement by Congress adds credibility to the use of Chinese Walls in multiservice securities firms.[31] The 1984 legislation accordingly gave further impetus to the establishment of Chinese Wall procedures. In 1988 Congress adopted the Insider Trading and Securities Fraud Enforcement Act,[32] which, among other things, amended section 15 of the Exchange Act to expressly require broker-dealers to set

---

24. 17 C.F.R. § 270.17j–1.

25. Examples provided included prohibiting an individual with nonpublic information from purchasing or selling any security (1) when he or she knows the investment company is also purchasing or selling, or considering the purchase or sale of that security, or, (2) when he or she knows that security is being recommended for purchase or sale by the investment company. Investment Company Act Rel. No. 40–11421 [1980 Transfer Binder] Fed.Sec.L.Rep. (CCH) ¶ 82,679 (October 31, 1980).

26. 17 C.F.R. §§ 230.137, 230.138, 230.139.

27. *See* the discussion in §§ 2.4, 2.5 *supra*.

28. 15 U.S.C.A. § 78u(d). *See* § 13.9 *infra*.

29. 15 U.S.C.A. § 78u(d).

30. House Committee Report (on ITSA) No. 98–355; 98th Congress 1st Session; H.R. 559, fn. 52.

31. *See* Carol B. Silver, Penalizing Insider Trading: A Critical Assessment of the Insider Trading Sanctions Act of 1984, 1985 Duke L.J. 960.

32. Pub.L. No. 100–704, 100th Cong.2d Sess. *See* H.R.Rep. No. 100–910, 100th Cong.2d Sess. (1988).

up a system of internal procedures to prevent improper misuse of nonpublic information by its employees.[33] The 1988 legislation thus provides an express statutory mandate for the establishment of Chinese Wall procedures.[34]

As noted above, the Commission continues to require Chinese Walls in connection with settlements of actions charging securities law violations. For example, in, SEC v. First Boston Corp.,[35] First Boston had in place a Chinese Wall and a restricted list, yet inside information passed through the wall and the restricted list was not checked. As part of the settlement, First Boston was required to review its Chinese Wall procedures and restricted lists procedures and to report on proposed changes to the SEC. This sanction lends further legitimacy to the Chinese Wall concept.[36]

During the past decade, various stock exchanges have implemented regulations to permit specialists units to be acquired by retail-brokers.[37] The new regulations, approved by the SEC, significantly reduce the restrictions placed on firms with corporate finance, retail sales and research departments from operating research firms.[38] Under the new rules of the exchanges, brokerage firms are allowed to have specialists units as long as a Chinese Wall is maintained. This is probably the greatest endorsement of the Chinese Wall concept and while the future of Chinese Walls is unclear, this method of safeguarding information appears to be stable at present.

---

33.   15 U.S.C.A. § 78o(f):

Every registered broker or dealer shall establish, maintain, and enforce written policies and procedures reasonably designed, taking into consideration the nature of such broker's or dealer's business, to prevent the misuse in violation of this title, or the rules or regulations thereunder, of material, nonpublic information by such broker or dealer or any person associated with such broker or dealer. The Commission, as it deems necessary or appropriate in the public interest or for the protection of investors, shall adopt rules or regulations to require specific policies or procedures reasonably designed to prevent misuse in violation of this title (or the rules or regulations thereunder) of material, nonpublic information.

34.   Section 21A(b)(1) of the 1934 Act, 15 U.S.C.A. § 78u–1(b)(1). *See also, e.g.,* In re Gabelli & Co., SEC Admin. Proc. File No. 3–8564, 26 Sec. Reg. & L. Rep. (BNA) 1683 (SEC consent order 1994) (broker–dealer and affiliated investment advisor failed to establish adequate Chinese wall procedures).

The 1934 Act also directs broker-dealers to establish, maintain, and enforce written policies designed to prevent insider trading violations by their employees. 15 U.S.C.A. § 78o(f). A similar provision exists for Investment advisers. 15 U.S.C.A. § 80b–204A.

35.   SEC v. First Boston Corp., 86 Civ. 3524 (S.D.N.Y. May 5, 1986).

36.   *Id. See also, e.g.,* In the Matter of Kidder, Peabody & Co., S.E.C. Exch.Act Rel. No. 34–24,543 (June 4, 1987) (placing burden of monitoring the Chinese Wall on the firm's legal and compliance departments).

37.   Sec.Exch.Act Rel. No. 34–23768, 36 SEC Docket 1639 (November 3, 1986) (New York Stock Exchange and American Stock Exchange); Sec.Exch.Act Rel. No. 34–24117, 37 SEC Docket 1225 (February 19, 1987) (Philadelphia Stock Exchange).

38.   The exchanges proposed the relaxed rules to encourage larger brokerage firms to purchase specialist units and fund them with increased capital. With greater capital, specialists, who are supposed to maintain orderly markets for listed securities, should be better positioned to absorb market volatility.

In 1987 a regulatory review task force of the National Association of Securities Dealers made various recommendations with regard to Chinese Walls. The task force recommended NASD rules that would require multiservice firms to have written Chinese Wall procedures and to routinely review the operations of such procedures.

§ 10.3 Market Makers in the Over-the-Counter Markets

Since the over-the-counter markets by definition do not have a central exchange for the entering of buy and sell orders, it is necessary to have some sort of central clearing house to perform a comparable function. The National Association of Securities Dealers Automated Quotation System (NASDAQ) is merely an electronic means of publicizing the latest quotes but is not a vehicle for effecting transactions. NASDAQ generally gives both "bid" and "asked" quotes for over-the-counter securities. Several hundred of the more actively traded over-the-counter securities are listed on a "national market" with only one quoted price. The NASD national market is a step toward a national market system[1] that some commentators have predicted will eventually replace the national exchanges.[2]

Traditionally, quotations for securities not traded through the national market system or automated quotation system were found in the "pink sheets." The SEC approved, originally on a one-year pilot basis, a NASD electronic bulletin board for computerized quotations for stocks not listed on a national exchange or in the NASDAQ system.[3] It is to be anticipated that the electronic bulletin boards will replace the pink sheets. Also in conjunction with its adoption of Rule 144A,[4] the SEC approved the NASD's screen-based computer and communication system called PORTAL (Private Offerings, Resales and Trading through Automated Linkages) to facilitate secondary trading of Rule 144A securities. PORTAL promises to become a significant avenue for secondary trading in unregistered securities of both domestic and foreign issuers.

The national securities exchanges, modelled on an auction paradigm, operate in such a way as to match customers seeking to sell securities

---

§ 10.3

1. In 1975 Congress amended the Exchange Act in order to facilitate the move away from regional markets to a national market system. *See* 15 U.S.C.A. § 78k–1. Prior to these amendments there was minimal central coordination. For example, securities could be traded on several exchanges with price variations for a single security on different exchanges. The 1975 amendments establish a means for coordination through market centers. *See* Sec.Exch.Act Rel. No. 34–13662 (June 23, 1977).

The National market system has higher listing criteria than NASDAQ stocks generally. *Cf., e.g.,* Belfort v. National Association of Securities Dealers, 1994 WL 97021, [1993–1994 Transfer Binder] Fed. Sec. L. Rep. (CCH) ¶ 98,162 (S.D.N.Y.1994) (court lacked jurisdiction to review NASD's denial of application to list company in national market system since there was a failure to exhaust administrative remedies).

2. *See* § 10.13 *infra.*

3. Sec.Exch.Act Rel. No. 34–27975 (May 1, 1990). *See* SEC Approves One–Year Pilot Program for NASD's OTC Electronic Bulletin Board, 22 Sec.Reg. & L.Rep. (BNA) 672 (May 4, 1990).

4. 17 C.F.R. § 230.144A, which is discussed in §§ 4.26, 4.26.1 *supra.*

with those seeking to buy.[5]   The over-the-counter market does not operate as an exchange as it is not a centralized organization.[6]   In order to maintain a market for securities without a central exchange, designated broker-dealers operate as "market makers" in the over-the-counter markets, buying and selling as principals for their own account rather than as agents for customers.

The concept of market maker is defined broadly to include dealers who hold themselves out as willing to purchase and sell a particular security for their own account "on a regular or continuous basis." [7]   It is not necessary that the dealer so hold itself out in any particular manner,[8] thus raising the possibility of inadvertent market maker status. Attainment of market maker status will exempt the dealer from some provisions of the securities laws that otherwise would apply such as section 16(b)'s prohibitions against short-swing profits.[9]   Additionally, market making activities are closely scrutinized by the SEC and NASD.

The NASD Rules of Fair Practice establish standards of conduct for market makers to assure that they carry out their operations in an appropriate manner.   Thus, for example, a broker-dealer who accepts payment for its decision to act as a market maker has compromised its position of neutrality and therefore will be subject to SEC sanctions.[10] The acceptance of compensation interfered with the normal factors a broker-dealer should consider in deciding whether to act as market maker; such factors include factors that affect the security's liquidity and intrinsic value.   The market maker's obligation is to maintain an orderly market.   However, when the market maker is executing custom-

---

5.   *See generally* Birl E. Schultz, The Securities Market—and How It Works (rev.ed. 1963); Robert Sobel, N.Y.S.E. History of the New York Stock Exchange (1975); Amex: A History of the American Stock Exchange, 1921–1971 (1972); Peter Wyckoff, Wall Street and the Stock Markets (1972).

6.   The over-the-counter markets consist of publication of bid and asked prices. Automation has played a significant role in making the markets more efficient. *Cf.* NASD v. SEC, 801 F.2d 1415 (D.C.Cir.1986) (NASD charges for securities data must be on a cost-based subscription fee). *See generally* Irwin Friend, G. Wright Hoffman, Willis J. Winn, Morris Hamburg & Stanley Schor, The Over-the-Counter Securities Markets (1958); Marc A. White, National Association of Securities Markets, Inc., 28 Geo.Wash.L.Rev. 250 (1959). For a comprehensive survey *see* Securities Industry Study, Report of Subcommittee on Securities, Sen.Comm. on Banking, Housing and Urban Affairs, 93d Cong. 1st Sess. 89 (1973); SEC, Special Study of the Securities Markets, H.R.Doc. No. 95, 88th Cong., 1st Sess. (1963). *See also, e.g.,* SEC, Statement on the Future Structure of the Securities Markets (1972).

7.   15 U.S.C.A. § 78c(a)(38) ("any dealer, who, with respect to a security, holds himself out (by entering quotations in an inter-dealer communications system or otherwise) as being willing to buy and sell such security for his own account on a regular or continuous basis.").

8.   *See* C.R.A. Realty Corp. v. Tri–South Investments, 568 F.Supp. 1190 (S.D.N.Y.1983).

9.   *Id.;* 15 U.S.C.A. § 78p(b).   *See* §§ 12.2–12.7 *infra.*

10.   In re General Bond & Share Co., Admin.Proc.File No. 3–7666, 25 Sec.Reg. & L.Rep. (BNA) 761 (SEC May 11, 1993), *reversed* 39 F.3d 1451 (10th Cir.1994) (the 10th Circuit held that the NASD's interpretation of its Rules of Fair Practice was such a major shift as to amount to rulemaking which could only be accomplished through formal rulemaking procedures).

er orders, its primary obligation is to those customers.[11]

A broker-dealer acts as a market maker for a particular security or securities. Many securities have more than one market maker. A market maker for a particular security not traded on a national exchange must enter "bid" and "asked" quotes either in the "pink sheets"[12] or over the automated quotation system (NASDAQ). The NASD rules provide that a market maker can qualify as a Primary NASDAQ Market Maker ("PNMM").[13]

A market maker is responsible for making "two-way" bids on the securities for which it makes a market. In other words, the market maker has the responsibility of quoting both a bid price (the price which someone is willing to pay for the security) or an offer wanted (OW) as well as an asked price (the price at which someone is willing to sell the security) or a bid wanted (BW). As such, the market maker must be willing to stand behind these quotations and advertisements for offers and bids wanted. He or she thus must be willing and prepared to both buy the stock or sell it as principal depending upon the demands of the market. Accordingly, the market maker is frequently in the position of holding long and short positions in the securities in which he or she makes the market. The SEC rules require that the market maker is financially able to fulfill these obligations.[14] The SEC rules also give the NASD supervisory power which includes the ability to withdraw a broker-dealer's market making authority.[15]

In addition to conducting market making transactions in which the broker-dealer acts as principal, he or she may also enter into riskless transactions upon a customer's order or upon orders of other broker-dealers. The individual risk that attaches to his or her transactions as a principal puts the market maker in a potential conflict of interest situation vis-à-vis his or her responsibilities as an agent for retail customers. It has been held that a broker-dealer who recommends a security without disclosing that he or she is a market maker has made a material misrepresentation so as to give rise to a private right of action

11. Eichler v. SEC, 757 F.2d 1066 (9th Cir.1985) (market maker's duty to execute customer orders meant that it could not base pricing and order execution on an orderly market without making full disclosure to its customers).

12. "Pink sheets" carry the daily quotes and reports of transactions for securities not listed on the automated NASDAQ System. Prior to NASDAQ all quotes were found in printed sheets issued at the end of the trading day. See, e.g., Arnold I. Burns, Over-the-Counter Market Quotations: Pink, Yellow, Green and White Sheets—A Gray Area in the Law of Evidence, 52 Cornell L.Q. 262 (1967).

13. For example, there are the following thresholds for being designated as a Primary Nasdaq Market Maker: (I) it must be at the best bid or best offer as shown in the NASDAQ quotation system at least thirty–five percent of the time, (II) it must maintain a spread no greater than one hundred and two percent of the average dealer spread, and (III) no more than fifty percent of the market maker's quotation updates may occur without being accompanied by at least one unit of trading.

14. 17 C.F.R. § 240.15c3–1(a)(4). They must maintain net capital in an amount not less than $2,500 for each security in which they make a market, and an aggregate net capital not less than $25,000 though not required to be more than $100,000.

15. See 15 U.S.C.A. § 78o–3(b)(7), following procedures set out in 15 U.S.C.A. § 78o–3(h)(i).

for violation of Rule 10b–5.[16] In order to prevail in such an action, plaintiff must prove all the elements normally required to state a Rule 10b–5 claim.[17] Thus, for example, nondisclosure of the market maker's acting as principal did not result in liability in the absence of proof that the price of the stock was affected.[18] It has been held, however, that a market maker who purchases stock from a customer at a price below the market will be liable for fraud in the transaction.[19]

In addition to imposing civil liability for material omissions in connection with recommendations, the SEC rules require disclosure of market maker status. SEC Rule 10b–10[20] makes it unlawful for a broker or dealer to effect a transaction for any customer or to induce any purchase or sale of a security without disclosing whether the broker is acting as the agent for the customer or as agent for someone else, including whether or not the broker is acting as a market maker or principal. It has been held that disclosure in the transaction confirmation slip will be insufficient to preclude a violation if the customer does not understand the significance of the disclosure.[21]

A broker-dealer is subject to disciplinary sanctions for failure to disclose his or her market maker status in violation of Rule 10b–10. It is one thing to show a failure to disclose market maker or principal status in a given transaction; however, it is quite another thing for the customer to show materiality, reliance, and scienter so as to give rise to a Rule 10b–5 cause of action.[22] In a Second Circuit decision, a 10b–5 claim was recognized for nondisclosure of market maker status in connection with a broker-dealer's recommendation since the market

---

16. Chasins v. Smith, Barney & Co., 438 F.2d 1167 (2d Cir.1970). Liability was imposed even though the sales confirmation disclosed the broker's market making activity. *See also,* Magnum Corp. v. Lehman Brothers Kuhn Loeb, Inc., 794 F.2d 198 (5th Cir.1986); Bischoff v. G.K. Scott & Co., 687 F.Supp. 746 (E.D.N.Y.1986).

17. *See* §§ 13.2–13.12 *infra.*

18. Shivangi v. Dean Witter Reynolds, Inc., 825 F.2d 885 (5th Cir.1987). *But see* Chasins v. Smith, Barney & Co., 438 F.2d 1167 (2d Cir.1970) (where the court permitted rescission without a specific showing of loss causation).

19. Weiner v. Rooney Pace, Inc., [1987 Transfer Binder] Fed.Sec.L.Rep. (CCH) ¶ 93,174 (S.D.N.Y.1987). *See also* Ettinger v. Merrill Lynch, Pierce, Fenner & Smith, Inc., 835 F.2d 1031 (3d Cir.1987) (denying broker's motion for summary judgment on claim that market maker failed to disclose allegedly excessive mark-ups on bonds).

20. 17 C.F.R. § 240.10b–10. For a detailed analysis of Rule 10b–10, *see* Jerry W. Markham & Thomas L. Hazen, Broker–Dealer Operations Under Securities and Commodities Law: Financial Responsibilities, Credit Regulation, and Customer Protection § 6.07 (1995).

21. *Cf.* Cant v. A.G. Becker & Co., 374 F.Supp. 36 (N.D.Ill.1974), *opinion supplemented* 379 F.Supp. 972 (N.D.Ill.1974).

Rule 10b–5 is discussed in §§ 13.2–13.12 *infra.*

22. *See* Cant v. A.G. Becker & Co., 374 F.Supp. 36 (N.D.Ill.1974), *opinion supplemented* 379 F.Supp. 972 (N.D.Ill.1974) (decided under Rule 15c1–4c which was rescinded in 1978 but is to the same effect as Rule 10b–10). *See also* Shivangi v. Dean Witter Reynolds, Inc., 825 F.2d 885 (5th Cir.1987); Shamsi v. Dean Witter Reynolds, Inc., 743 F.Supp. 87 (D.Mass.1989), *reconsideration denied* 1990 WL 120734, Fed.Sec.L.Rep. ¶ 95,356 (1990) (nondisclosure of market maker status may be a Rule 10b–5 violation).

maker status was a material factor in the customer's decision to invest.[23] As noted above, some courts have required proof of actual loss causation in terms of a differential in market price.[24] In the context of an unsolicited transaction, it is not as significant for the investor to know that the broker-dealer effecting the customer's offer is a market maker, except perhaps for the purpose of determining the commission. When a broker's firm acts as a market maker it may be possible for the customer to get a slight break on the commission.[25]

Although Rule 10b–10 establishes disclosure obligations in connection with confirmation of securities transactions, compliance with its requirements does not preclude liability for fraud.[26] It has thus been held that compliance with Rule 10b–10 did not preclude a market maker's liability for failing to disclose allegedly excessive mark-ups.[27] In addition to the federal regulatory structure, market makers can run afoul of state blue sky laws. Thus, for example brokers can be suspended from practice within a state for inadequate disclosures about market maker activity.[28]

In general, market makers are subject to significant regulation by both the NASD and SEC, including inspection of records in order to assure that they are not abusing their market making positions.[29] Furthermore, the NASD watches closely to assure that the market maker in fact maintains an orderly market lest the market maker will be subject to losing approval to act as market maker.[30]

In an attempt to promote the more efficient execution of customer orders and more accurate pricing, as well as to eliminate potential

---

23. Chasins v. Smith, Barney & Co., 438 F.2d 1167 (2d Cir.1970). *But see* Shivangi v. Dean Witter Reynolds, Inc., 825 F.2d 885 (5th Cir.1987).

24. Shivangi v. Dean Witter Reynolds, Inc., 825 F.2d 885 (5th Cir.1987). *See* text accompanying footnote 18 *supra*. *See also, e.g.,* Eichler v. SEC, 757 F.2d 1066 (9th Cir.1985) (affirming disciplinary sanctions against underwriter and market maker which failed to obtain the best executions for its retail customers).

25. When a broker goes through a third party market maker they split the commission. Although a brokerage firm's market making and retail operations are distinct, acting through a broker which is also a market maker does eliminate a middleman.

26. *E.g.,* Ettinger v. Merrill Lynch, Pierce, Fenner & Smith, Inc., 835 F.2d 1031 (3d Cir.1987).

27. *Id.* (Rule 10b–10 requires disclosure of mark-ups for many transactions but not for others). *See also, e.g.,* Hoxworth v. Blinder, Robinson & Co., Inc., 903 F.2d 186 (3d Cir.1990) (upholding preliminary class-wide relief in class action claiming materiality of undisclosed mark-ups); Elysian Federal Savings Bank v. First Interregional Equity Corp., 713 F.Supp. 737 (D.N.J.1989) (allegations of repeated excessive mark-ups stated RICO claim); Joseph I. Goldstein & L. Delane Cox, Penny Stock Markups and Markdowns, 85 Nw.U.L.Rev. 676 (1991).

28. *See* Hibbard Brown & Co. v. Hubbard, 1992 WL 389927, [1992–1993 Transfer Binder] Fed.Sec.L.Rep. (CCH) ¶ 97,293 (Del.Ch.1992), *affirmed in part, reversed in part* 633 A.2d 345 (Del.1993) (one-line oral statement of market maker status was not sufficient disclosure to unsophisticated investors).

29. 17 C.F.R. § 240.17a–5(a); NASD Code for Procedure for Handling Trade Practice Complaints § 26 NASD Manual (CCH) ¶ 3024; NASD Rules of Fair Practice, Art. IV § 5, NASD Manual (CCH) ¶ 2205.

30. For a more detailed analysis, *see, e.g.,* SEC Special Study *supra* footnote 6; Securities Industry Study *supra* footnote 6.

conflicts of interest, the SEC approved the NASD's prohibition against market makers trading ahead of certain customer orders.[31] The interpretation of NASD Rules of Fair Practice[32] applies to all NASDAQ securities and prohibits broker–dealers acting in their market making capacity from trading ahead of their customers' limit orders.[33] This interpretation represented a change of policy which permitted market makers not to give priority to customers' limit orders so long as appropriate disclosures were made.

Even though the NASD interpretation is framed in terms of market making activity, it also applies to all member broker–dealers who consistent with their best execution obligation may not trade ahead of customer limit orders. The new interpretation does not require broker–dealers to accept limit orders from their customers but prohibits giving priority to their own trades if limit orders are accepted. Accordingly, once a broker–dealer accepts a limit order it should cease trading for its own account until the limit order is executed. The NASD has taken the position that the prohibition against trading ahead of customers' limit orders will not apply to member–to–member trades when customer limit orders are routed to an unaffiliated market maker.[34] It is expected that the NASD will be considering whether to extend the trading ahead of customer prohibition to member–to–member trades.

§ 10.4 Specialists and the Stock Exchanges

A specialist is a floor trader who does not have a retail securities business, but instead purchases for his or her own account or executes orders for other brokers, specializing in the securities of particular companies or issues. Unlike the case with the over-the-counter markets, exchange traded securities do not require a market maker to provide a central clearing house for all bid and asked quotations. However, the securities industry has come to recognize that even within the context of an exchange, it is necessary to maintain an "orderly market"—free in the short run from erratic and unreasonable fluctuations in prices of particular securities to the extent possible—and to help match the bid and asked prices between which there is usually a spread.[1] Section 11(b)

31. Exch. Act Rel. No. 34–34279, 59 Fed. Reg. 34,883 (SEC July 7, 1994).

32. Interpretation of Rules of Fair Practice, Article III, Section 1.

33. A limit order is one in which a customer specifies a minimum price that he or she will accept in payment for securities being sold or a maximum price that he or she will pay for securities being purchased. The limit order is an alternative to an "at market" order which simply instructs a broker to purchase or sell a security at the market price.

34. *See* NASD, Sepcial Notice to Members 94–58 (July 15, 1994).

§ 10.4

1. As explained by the SEC,

By trading for their own accounts in both favorable and unfavorable markets, the specialists of the mid-thirties offset temporary disparities between buy and sell interests, thus enhancing the continuity and orderliness of the market. Specialists offered two-sided markets in the securities assigned to them, committing their firm's capital in order to provide the "sell" side of a transaction in a rising market, and the "buy" side of a transaction in a falling one. In a study of the NYSE the Commission, after observing the

of the Securities Exchange Act of 1934 empowers the exchanges to register specialists provided that their rules require compliance with certain conditions established by the SEC.[2] The applicable SEC standards are set forth in Rule 11b–1[3] which requires, *inter alia,* that the exchange set minimum net capital requirements for specialists. The rule also requires the exchange to condition specialist status upon "the maintenance, so far as practicable, of a fair and orderly market."[4] A specialist's continued failure to satisfy the exchange standards subjects him or her to suspension or cancellation of his registration with the exchange.[5] Additionally, SEC Rule 11b–1(a)(2)(v) requires the exchange to provide for "effective and systematic surveillance" of specialists.[6]

Following the direction of the SEC, the New York Stock Exchange and other exchanges have developed a system of specialists for each security traded, with rules enforceable by the exchange itself.[7]

For a long time, the exchanges took the view that by barring retail brokers from the specialist function, they were preventing possible conflicts of interest. However, pressure from the brokerage industry and the exchanges' desire to remain competitive with the over-the-counter markets where there are no such limitations on market makers, has made inroads on the long-time separation of functions. The ground rules are changing. The Pacific and Boston stock exchanges now allow diversified firms to act as specialists. The American Exchange's Board of Governors has approved a similar measure, and the New York Stock Exchange has also adopted a proposal that would allow diversified firms to act as specialists.[8] Retail brokers are now permitted to acquire

---

conduct of specialists during a 19–week period from June 24 to November 2, 1935, concluded that specialists trading for their own accounts "traded against the daily trend" more often than with it, and thus, on the whole, did not tend to accentuate price trends but contributed to the continuity and orderliness of the market.

Securities Exchange Act Release No. 34–27611, (Jan. 12, 1990) (footnotes omitted).

2. 15 U.S.C.A. § 78k(b). There have been criticisms of the specialist system. *See* Dale A. Oesterle, Donald A. Winslow & Seth C. Anderson, The New York Stock Exchange and Its Outmoded Specialist System: Can the Exchange Innovate to Survive?, 17 J.Corp.L. 223 (1992). For a cogent response to this critique, *see* James L. Cochrane, Brian C. McNamara, James E. Shapiro & Michael J. Simon, The Structure and Regulation of the New York Stock Exchange, 18 J. Corp. L. 57 (1992).

3. 17 C.F.R. § 240.11b–1.

4. 17 C.F.R. § 240.11b–1(a)(2)(ii).

5. *Id.* The specialist is also responsible for "odd lot" transactions—where shares are traded other than in even lots of 100. 17 C.F.R. § 240.11b–1(a)(2)(iii).

6. 17 C.F.R. § 240.11b–1(a)(2)(v). The exchanges' responsibilities with regard to specialists parallel the general powers and duties of the self regulatory organizations in policing their members. *See* § 10.2 *infra.*

7. His or her obligations are to assure continuity (that the price of each transaction in a given stock bears some reasonable relation to the preceding transaction) and depth (that the price of a particular stock does not change unreasonably unless a reasonable volume is traded). In the short run, his or her job is not to manipulate the market but to stabilize it. NYSE Rule 104.10, 2 NYSE Guide (CCH) ¶ 2104. The specialist must, therefore, buy against the flow of the market. NYSE Rule 104, ASE Rule 170.

8. *See* Securities Week p. 5 (Jan. 28, 1985); Exchange in Boston Will Allow Brokers to Have Specialists, Wall St. J. p. 23 (Sept. 27, 1984). *See also* Merrill, Paine Webber Eye Amex Specialist Biz in Wake of Rule Change, Securities Week 3 (Nov. 17, 1986).

specialist firms and avoid certain specialist restrictions by imposing a Chinese Wall (or fire wall).[9] Those restrictions include: (1) trading specialty securities, (2) trading options on specialty securities (other than for hedging purposes), (3) accepting orders for specialty securities from institutions, the issuer and its insiders, performing research and advisory services with respect to specialty securities, and (4) transacting business with a company in whose stock the specialist is registered.[10] By 1990, a few brokerage firms had purchased specialist firms and there is the possibility that more such diversified companies will develop.[11]

The specialist's function is to maintain an orderly market. This is best seen in operation by way of an example provided by the New York Stock Exchange:

> To maintain the market a Specialist usually purchases stock at a higher price than anyone else is willing to pay. For example, let's assume that a stock has just sold at 55. The highest price anyone is willing to pay is 54¼ (the best bid), and the lowest price at which anyone is willing to sell is 55 (the best offer). The Specialist, acting as a dealer for his own account, may now decide to bid 54¾ for 100 shares, making the quotation 54¾–55¼, which narrows the spread between the bid and offer prices to ½ point. Now, if a prospective seller wishes to sell 100 shares at the price of the best bid, the Specialist will purchase his stock at 54¾. By doing this, the Specialist not only provides the seller with a better price, but also maintains better price continuity, since the variation from the last sale is only ¼ of a point.
>
> Here, on the other hand, is an example of how the Specialist may sell stock for his own account to maintain a market. Let's assume that with the last sale in a stock at 62¼ the best bid is 62 and the best offer 63. The Specialist offers 500 shares at 62½ for his own account, changing the quotation to 62–62½. A buyer enters the market and buys the stock from the Specialist. Thus the buyer purchased the stock ½ point cheaper than would have been the case without the Specialist's offer, and again, better price continuity and depth have been maintained.[12]

To the extent that the specialist does not operate at the retail level, there is no possibility of a conflict of interest such as that which can arise with a market maker in the over-the-counter markets.[13] However,

---

9. *See* Sec.Exch.Act Rel. No. 34–23768, 51 Fed.Reg. 41,183 (Nov. 13, 1986) (approving New York and American stock exchange rule changes). Chinese walls and fire walls are discussed in § 10.2.4 *supra* (Practitioner's Edition only).

10. *Id.*

11. In fact, the president of the New York Stock Exchange had been attempting to encourage additional acquisitions of specialist firms as a way "to beef up trading capital on the exchange floor." Wall St.J. A40 (April 17, 1990).

12. New York Stock Exchange, Inc., The Specialist: Key Man in the Exchange Market 3 (March, 1975). *See generally* Heide S. Fiske, Can the Specialist System Cope with the Age of Block Trading? 1970 Sec.L.Rev. 559; Nicholas Wolfson & Thomas A. Russo, Stock Exchange Specialist: An Economic and Legal Analysis, 1970 Duke L.J. 707.

13. *See* § 10.3 *supra.*

a higher standard of conduct is imposed on the specialist than the mere avoidance of fraud; he or she must act so as not to cause investors concern over his honesty. Furthermore, the specialist is subject to very strict surveillance. Approximately eight times each year there are random, detailed one-week inspections of each specialist's activities by the exchange. This is in addition to requiring each specialist to make his books available to the exchange inspection which will reveal each transaction. Specialists are subject to special capital requirements imposed by their respective exchanges,[14] and are limited in their dealings with the issuers of the particular stocks,[15] large institutional investors, other broker-dealers (for public customers),[16] and in the purchase and sale of large blocks either individually or as members of a pool.

One of the byproducts of the market break of 1987 and other major disruptions has been the recognition that specialists were not always able to maintain the necessary liquidity on days of high volatility. In fact a number of specialist firms suffered cash crunches as a result of the wide price swings.[17] Another development involving specialists is a new New York Stock Exchange Rule requiring specialists to consult at least four times each year with a senior executive of each of the specialist's listed companies.[18]

The courts have not recognized a private right of action for nonenforcement of the rules relating to specialists.[19]

Technological advancements have led to questions concerning the continued viability of the specialist system. Under a system of screen-based trading, market professionals can execute transactions without the aid of an intermediary such as a specialist or a market maker. Screen based trading differs from an automated quotation system such as NASDAQ in that the quotation system merely delivers the current quotes while a screen-based trading system permits actual "real time" execution of orders. In its recent adoption of a limited after hours trading program, the New York Stock Exchange has ventured into screen-based trading on a limited basis.[20] Some foreign exchanges have

---

14. *See, e.g.,* NYSE Rule 104.20, 2 N.Y.S.E. Guide (CCH) ¶ 2104.

15. *See, e.g.,* NYSE Rule 113, 2 N.Y.S.E. Guide (CCH) ¶ 2113.

16. *See, e.g.,* NYSE Rule 104, 2 N.Y.S.E. Guide (CCH) ¶ 2104 and NYSE Rule 91, 2 N.Y.S.E. Guide (CCH) ¶ 2091.

17. This is one of the reasons that the New York Stock Exchange has become increasingly concerned about specialist solvency. *See* footnote 10 *supra* and accompanying text.

18. NYSE Rule 106. *See* 21 Sec.Reg. & L.Rep. (BNA) 1535 (Oct. 13, 1989). The rule also requires specialists to have semi-annual contacts with the 15 largest NYSE member organizations and any other member organizations that are significant customers of the specialist.

19. 15 U.S.C.A. § 78k(b). *See* Cutner v. Fried, 373 F.Supp. 4 (S.D.N.Y.1974). Implied remedies are discussed in chapter 13 *infra.*

20. The New York Stock Exchange's screen-based after hours system is open to all investors for forty-five minutes beginning fifteen minutes after the close of trading. A second screen-based system is open to large program traders dealing in baskets of stocks and lasts for one hour and fifteen minutes after the close of exchange trading. *See* Wall St. J. p. C1 (May 22, 1991).

made the shift away from floor trading on an across-the-board basis.[21] But it seems unlikely that this will occur in the United States for quite some time.

The International Organization of Securities Commissions has adopted a set of general principles governing the operation of screen-based systems.[22] The ten principles, which are intended to serve as a guide for developers of screen-based systems and regulators, address financial integrity, surveillance, and disclosure, as well as operational issues including access to the system, system vulnerability and security.

First, the sponsor of the screen-based trading system should be able to demonstrate to the applicable regulatory agency that the system meets applicable legal standards, regulatory policies, and/or relevant market customs and practices. Second, the system should "ensure the equitable availability of accurate and timely trade and quotation information" to all participants in the system. The processing, prioritization, and display of quotations within the system should be described to the applicable regulatory agency. Third, the sponsor of the screen-based trading system should describe to the relevant regulatory authorities the order execution algorithm which is the system's rule structure for processing, prioritizing, and executing orders. Fourth, the system should be technically designed so as to operate "in a manner equitable to all market participants" and the system sponsor should describe any differences in treatment between categories of participants. Fifth, prior to implementation and then periodically, the system should undergo an objective risk assessment as to the system's vulnerability to unauthorized access, internal failures, human errors, attacks, and natural catastrophes. Sixth, the system should develop procedures to monitor the competence, integrity, and authority of system users; system users should be supervised and should not arbitrarily or discriminatorily be denied access to the system. Seventh, the system sponsor and appropriate regulatory authorities should consider risk management exposures including those stemming from interfacing with related financial systems. Eighth, there should be mechanisms in place for adequate surveillance of the system for both supervisory and enforcement purposes. The surveillance mechanisms should be available to the appropriate regulatory authorities as well as to the system sponsor. Ninth, the system sponsor and appropriate regulatory authorities should see to it that there is adequate risk disclosure to system users resulting from use of the system. In addition to disclosure of the significant risks of system use, there should be a description of the system sponsor's and providers' liability to system subscribers and users. Tenth, there should be proce-

---

21. This, for example, is the case with the Vancouver Stock Exchange.

22. *See* CFTC Policy Statement Concerning the Oversight of Screen–Based Trading Systems, [1991 Transfer Binder] Comm.Fut.L.Rep. (CCH) ¶ 24,953 CFTC (Nov. 21, 1991). *See also, e.g.,* Comm.Fut.L.Rep. (CCH) Report Letter No. 393 (Nov. 1990). The International Organization of Securities Commissions (IOSCO) consists of securities and commodities administrators from more than fifty nations. *Id.* *Cf.*, Michael B. Sundel & Lystra G. Blake, Good Concept, Bad Executions: The Regulation and Self–Regulation of Automated Trading Systems in the United States Futures Markets, 85 Nw.U.L.Rev. 748 (1991).

dures to ensure that the system sponsor, system providers, and system users be made aware of and be responsive to the directives and concerns of the appropriate regulatory authorities.

§ 10.5 Municipal Securities Dealers

Background

Municipal securities, as referred to in the Securities Exchange Act of 1934, comprise a wide variety of obligations, primarily bonds issued by state, local or other political subdivisions or their agencies, including industrial development bonds.[1] Because of their governmental issue or guarantee, municipal securities are generally exempt from the registration and reporting provisions of both the 1933 and 1934 Acts.[2] Transactions in municipal securities generally take place in more specialized markets by brokers and dealers dealing exclusively with municipal securities and who are, therefore, exempt from the general broker-dealer regulation and rules of the Securities and Exchange Commission. There is no organized exchange subject to SEC oversight nor is there NASD coverage regarding persons dealing only in municipal securities. Furthermore, prior to 1975, the Securities and Exchange Commission had no jurisdiction over these transactions except in circumstances involving fraud. Even with the regulation that was added to the Exchange Act in 1975, the 1933 Securities Act's exemptions and the lack of an organized exchange leave investors with substantially less protection than with the regular securities market for private issuers.[3]

§ 10.5

1. 15 U.S.C.A. § 78c(a)(29):

The term "municipal securities" means securities which are direct obligations of, or obligations guaranteed as to principal or interest by, a State or any political subdivision thereof, or any agency or instrumentality of a State or any political subdivision thereof, or any municipal corporate instrumentality of one or more States, or any security which is an industrial development bond (as defined in section 103(c)(2) of the Internal Revenue Code of 1954) the interest on which is excludable from gross income under section 103(a)(1) of such Code if, by reason of the application of paragraph (4) or (6) of section 103(c) of such Code (determined as if paragraphs (4)(A), (5), and (7) were not included in such section 103(c)) paragraph (a) of such section 103(c) does not apply to such security.

For articles on federal regulation of municipal securities, *See generally* Robert W. Doty & John E. Petersen, The Federal Securities Laws and Transactions in Municipal Securities, 71 Nw.U.L.Rev. 283 (1976); Ann J. Gellis, Mandatory Disclosure for Municipal Securities: A Reevaluation, 36 Buff.L.Rev. 15 (1987); Note, Federal Regulation of Municipal Securities, 60 Minn.L.Rev. 567 (1976); Marc I. Steinberg, Municipal Issuer Liability Under Federal Securities Law, 6 J.Corp.L. 277 (1981); Note, Liability of Issuers of Municipal Securities, 31 Baylor L.Rev. 551 (1979); Comment, Liability of Municipal Officials and Misrepresentations Concerning Municipal Securities, Should the Corporate Standard be Applied?, 73 Nw.U.L.Rev. 137 (1978); Note, Disclosure by Issuers of Municipal Securities: An Analysis of Recent Proposals and a Suggested Approach, 29 Vand.L.Rev. 1017 (1976). *See also* authorities in footnote 3 *infra*.

2. 15 U.S.C.A. §§ 77c(a)(2), 78c(a)(12). *See* § 4.3 *supra*.

3. For evaluations of the limited regulation of the municipal securities markets *see* Eric M. Hellige, Industrial Development Bonds: The Disclosure Dilemma, 6 J.Corp.L. 291 (1981); Note, Municipal Bonds: Is There a Need for Mandatory Disclosure?, 58 U.Det. J.U.L. 255 (1981); Comment, Federal Regulation of Municipal Securities: A Constitutional and Statutory Analysis, 1976 Duke L.J. 1261; Note, Municipal Bonds, and the Federal

The early 1970s witnessed a lack of investor confidence in the municipal securities markets.[4] At the same time the SEC instituted several fraud actions involving municipal securities dealers which were unregulated but nevertheless subject to the Exchange Act's antifraud proscriptions.[5] These and other factors led Congress to conclude in 1975 that "[e]xpanding the protections generally available under the federal securities laws to investors in municipal securities is * * * appropriate."[6]

In 1990, the Commission adopted Rule 15c2–12 which imposes offering information requirements similar to those applicable to private issuers under the Act.[7] Under the rule, the underwriter of a municipal securities offering must receive from the issuer a "final official statement" of the terms and conditions of the offering.[8] The rule requires that the final official statement be delivered to any potential customer requesting it.[9] Paralleling the preliminary prospectus under the 1933 Act, the rule makes provision for a preliminary official statement which may be used prior to the final statement.[10] These disclosure requirements do not apply to all offerings as the Commission has established

---

Securities Laws: The Results of Forty Years of Indirect Regulation, 28 Vand.L.Rev. 561 (1975). *See generally* Nicholas Wolfson, Richard M. Phillips, Thomas A. Russo, Regulation of Brokers, Dealers and Securities Markets § 1.14 (1977).

The major default on bonds issued in the state of Washington ("WPPS") and near default of the city of New York demonstrate the degree to which municipal securities investors are at risk. It is likely that stricter regulation will follow as a result. *Cf.* Note, The SEC Staff Report: Will Alleged Misconduct Finally Lead To Federal Regulation of Municipal Securities?, 12 Suffolk L.Rev. 930 (1978).

4. *See, e.g.,* Sen.Rep. No. 94–75 pp. 3–4 (Banking, Housing and Urban Affairs Committee April 25, 1975).

5. *See* Municipal Securities Rulemaking Board Manual (CCH) ¶ 101.

6. Sen.Rep. No. 94–75 p. 3 (Banking, Housing and Urban Affairs Committee April 25, 1975). *But cf.* Mercer v. Jaffe, Snider, Raitt & Heuer, P.C., 730 F.Supp. 74 (W.D.Mich. 1990), *affirmed* 933 F.2d 1008 (6th Cir.1991) (1975 amendments to Exchange Act to include governmental entities as "persons" did not disturb states' sovereign immunity to suit under Rule 10b–5), s.c., 736 F.Supp. 764 (W.D.Mich.1990).

7. 17 C.F.R. § 240.15c2–12. *See* Robert W. Doty, The Regulation of State and Local Government Securities, 24 Rev.Sec. & Commod.Reg. 59 (1991).

The SEC has also issued new disclosure guidelines relating to secondary market activities and politcal contributions by underwriters. *See* Sec. Act Rel. No. 33–7049 (SEC 1994); Mark Thoman & Amy B. Serper, New Disclosure Requirements for Municipal Securities, 27 Rev. Sec. & Commod. Reg. 111 (1994).

8. 17 C.F.R. § 240.15c2–12(b).

9. 17 C.F.R. § 240.15c2–12(b). However, prior to dissemination, the underwriter must have a reasonable basis for belief in the truthfulness and completeness of the key representations made in any disclosure documents used in the offerings. *See* 53 Fed.Reg. 37,787. Thus, regardless of the statement classification (*i.e.*, as preliminary, near-final, or final), the municipal underwriter must review the disclosure and have a "reasonable belief" as to its accuracy and completeness.

10. It should be noted that the preliminary official statement referred to here need not be the same as the "near-final official statement," that must be reviewed by the underwriters prior to submitting a bid or beginning sales of the bonds. The term preliminary official statement is defined solely by reference to the issuer's intention that it be distributed to potential investors. If an underwriter determines that the preliminary official statement "is inaccurate or contains misleading omissions regarding the issuer," it is not expected to disseminate the document under this requirement. *See* 54 Fed. Reg. 28805 n.41.

three exemptions[11]—one paralleling a private placement exemption and the others based on short-term maturity. First, an exemption is available for securities offered in denominations of $100,000 or more if they are sold to no more than thirty-five sophisticated purchasers, each of whom is not purchasing for more than one account and who is not taking the securities with a view to distribution.[12] Second, securities offered in denominations of $100,000 or more and having a maturity of nine months or less are exempt from the Rule.[13] Third, securities offered in denominations of $100,000 or more are exempt if at the holder's option they may be tendered for redemption at par value and such option may be exercised at least every nine months.[14]

The Municipal Securities Dealer Industry

There are three principal participants in the municipal securities industry.[15] Securities firms, or "dealers," trade in municipal securities for their own account.[16] "Dealer-banks," as is the case with securities firms acting as "dealers" trade for their own account.[17] Thirdly, bond brokers act as agents for sellers and purchasers of municipal securities. The underwriting and syndication of municipal securities are governed by state law. General obligation bonds are generally issued only after competitive bidding while revenue bonds are generally sold on the basis of terms negotiated by the issuing governmental entity.[18] A notable exception to the Glass–Steagall Act's[19] prohibition on commercial bank underwriting of securities is the underwriting of general obligation

---

11. Exemptions to the rule were promulgated at the behest of many commentators who argued that without exceptions the rule would have impeded certain efficient practices.

In addition to the express exemptions contained in the rule, paragraph (d) provides that the Commission may, upon written request, or upon its own motion, exempt any participating underwriter from rule 15c2–12's provisions. 17 C.F.R. § 240.15c2–12(d).

12. 17 C.F.R. § 240.15c2–12(c)(1). In addition, the "[p]articipating [u]nderwriter [must] reasonably believe [the purchaser] has such knowledge and experience in financial and business matters that it is capable of evaluating the merits and risks of the prospective investment * * * ". *Id.*

The Commission stated that the purpose of this exemption was that regulating a limited placement did not further the intent of the Proposed Rule, which was focused primarily on those offerings that involved the general public and where likely to be actively traded in the secondary market. 54 Fed.Reg. 28,799, at 28,809.

13. 17 C.F.R. § 240.15c2–12(c)(2). This exemption, in the view of the Commission, is consistent with the philosophy underpinning section 3(a)(3) of the Securities Act. *See* 54 Fed.Reg. 28,799, at 28,810. *See also*, Securities Act Release No. 33–4412, 26 Fed.Reg. 9158 (Sept. 20, 1961) (discussing short-term corporate debt).

14. 17 C.F.R. § 240.15c2–12(c)(3).

15. Sen.Rep. No. 94–75 pp. 38–39 (Banking, Housing and Urban Affairs Committee April 25, 1975).

16. *Id.*

17. *Id.*

18. *Id.* at 40.

19. The Banking Act of 1933, Ch. 89, 48 Stat. 184 (1933), codified in various sections of 12 U.S.C.A. The Glass–Steagall Act is discussed in § 19.5 *infra* (Practitioner's Edition only).

bonds issued by state and local issuers.[20]

Overview of Municipal Securities Dealer Regulation

Since 1975, brokers and dealers, including most banks or "separately identifiable departments" thereof, not already registered under Section 15,[21] must register pursuant to section 15B(a)(1) of the Securities Exchange Act if they use the United States mails, telephones, or other instrumentality of interstate commerce to trade municipal securities, even if they transact only intrastate business.[22] Issuers and the securities themselves, however, are still exempt from 1934 Act registration.[23]

Federal law does not require issuers of municipal securities to make any disclosures in offering securities,[24] though issuers often release "official statements" before issuance of the securities in order to promote a market for them. Despite the absence of disclosure requirements, the SEC does have authority under section 21(a) to make preliminary investigations of the financial affairs of any city.[25] This investigation is declared not to constitute an impermissible intrusion into the state's sovereignty.[26]

In contrast to the securities' issuers themselves, brokers and dealers of municipal securities may be required by the Municipal Securities Rulemaking Board (MSRB) to disclose "information generally available from other sources" than the issuer itself.[27] Generally, this requirement simply means the broker or dealer must believe that the securities are "bona fide." [28] In contrast to the MSRB approach, the SEC favors a "due diligence" investigation requirement in all securities transactions.[29]

---

20. As of 1975, dealer banks were handling approximately half of all general obligation bond underwriting. Sen.Rep. No. 94–75 p. 40 (Banking, Housing and Urban Affairs Committee April 25, 1975).

21. 15 U.S.C.A. § 78*o. See* § 10.2 *supra.* "Municipal securities dealer" is defined in section 3(a)(30) to include both broker-dealers and banks that act as dealers. 15 U.S.C.A. § 78c(a)(30).

22. 15 U.S.C.A. § 78*o*–4(a)(1). Sec.Exch.Act Rel. No. 34–111585 (August 11, 1975). However, these brokers and dealers are not required to be members of the Securities Investors Protection Corporation.

23. 15 U.S.C.A. § 78*o*–4(d)(1). *See* footnote 2 *supra.*

24. 15 U.S.C.A. § 78*o*–4(d)(1).

25. 15 U.S.C.A. § 78u(a).

26. *See, e.g.,* City of Philadelphia v. SEC, 434 F.Supp. 281 (E.D.Pa.1977), *appeal denied* 434 U.S. 1003, 98 S.Ct. 707, 54 L.Ed.2d 746 (1978).

27. 15 U.S.C.A. § 78*o*–4(d)(2). The MSRB is a self regulatory organization which operates under SEC oversight. Developments in municipal securities regulation are compiled in M.S.R.B. Rep. which is published periodically by the Municipal Securities Rulemaking Board. *See, e.g.,* Robert A. Flippinger & Edward L. Pittman, Disclosure Obligations of Underwriters of Municipal Securities, 47 Bus.Law. 127 (1991); William J. Kiernan, Jr., Disclosure Responsibilities in Municipal Securities Offerings—Some Problems Under SEC Rule 15c2–12, 20 Stetson L.Rev. 701 (1991).

28. *See* MSRB Rule G–14.

29. *See* Walston & Co., Inc., Ad.Proc.File No. 3–722, Rel. No. 34–8165 (1967); In re Luebbe (Benchmark Securities, Inc.), Ad.Proc.File No. 3–5175 (1975); In the Matter of Bache Halsey Stuart, Inc., Exch.Act Rel. No. 12847 (October 1, 1976).

With regard to statements made by either issuers, brokers or dealers, the SEC has jurisdiction to prosecute and impose any sanctions upon them which would be imposed upon any other securities brokers, dealers, or issuers under the antifraud Rules of 10b–5, 10b–3, 10b–16, 10b–9, 15c–1, of the Exchange Act[30] or section 17(a) of the Securities Act of 1933,[31] as the definition of "person" in Section 3(a)(9) includes any "government, political subdivision, agency or instrumentality of government."[32] There does not seem to be an adequate basis for implying a private remedy under the MSRB enabling legislation contained in section 15B.[33]

The MSRB

The governing body of municipal securities brokers and dealers, analogous to the NASD and national securities exchanges for other brokers and dealers, is the Municipal Securities Rulemaking Board, created by the 1975 amendments to the Securities Exchange Act.[34] The primary difference between the self regulatory organizations (SROs) and the MSRB is that covered brokers are members of the SROs. The MSRB is a regulatory, nonmembership organization with primary rulemaking authority over municipal securities brokers and dealers.[35] The

30. 17 C.F.R. §§ 240.10b–3, 10b–5, 10b–9, 10b–16, 15c–1. *See* § 10.2 *supra;* § 12.9 *infra;* chapter 13 *infra.* Gorsey V.I.M. Simon & Co., Inc., 1987 WL 7749, [1987 Transfer Binder] Fed.Sec.L.Rep. (CCH) ¶ 93,173 (D.Mass.1987) (upholding 10b–5 claim). *Compare* Brown v. Covington, 805 F.2d 1266 (6th Cir.1986) (dismissing 10b–5 claim for transactions prior to effective date of 1975 Exchange Act amendments).

It has been held that municipal authorities cannot avoid liability by claiming sovereign immunity. *See, e.g.,* Durning v. Citibank, N.A., 950 F.2d 1419 (9th Cir.1991). *But see* Margaret V. Sachs, Are Local Governments Liable Under Rule 10b–5? Textualism and its Limits, 70 Wash.U.L.Q. 19 (1992) (in 1934 Congress excluded local governments from the definition of person and thus intended that they not be subject to Rule 10b–5 liability; the article maintains that the 1975 amendments, including local governments within the definition of person, were designed to regulate securities professionals, not to impose liability upon local governments).

See also SEC Statement Regarding Disclosure Obligations of Municipal Securities Issuers and Others, SEC Release No. 33–7049, 59 Fed.Reg. 12,748 (1994) ("intend[ing] to assist municipal securities issuers, brokers, dealers, and municipal securities dealers in meeting their obligations under the antifraud provision").

31. 15 U.S.C.A. § 77q(a). *See* § 7.6 *supra,* § 13.13 *infra.* In re Washington Public Power Supply System Securities Litigation, 623 F.Supp. 1466 (W.D.Wash.1985), *reversed on other grounds* 823 F.2d 1349 (9th Cir.1987) (the Ninth Circuit held that there is no private remedy under section 17(a)). *See* Zerman v. Ball, 735 F.2d 15 (2d Cir.1984) (section 12(2) of the 1933 Act can be used for material misstatements in connection with the sale of municipal securities).

32. 15 U.S.C.A. § 78c(a)(9).

33. *See* § 13.1 *infra.* However, private remedies would exist under the established rights of action under the general antifraud provisions. *See, e.g.,* In re New York City Municipal Securities Litigation, 507 F.Supp. 169 (S.D.N.Y.1980) (10b–5 claim by purchasers of municipal securities). *See generally* §§ 7.6, *supra,* 13.2–13.13 *infra.*

34. 15 U.S.C.A. § 78o–4(b)(1).

35. 15 U.S.C.A. § 78o–4(b)(2). "Specifically enumerated areas in which the MSRB must adopt rules include: (1) standards of training, experience, and competence, as well as such other qualifications as the MSRB finds necessary or appropriate in the public interest or for the protection of investors; (2) the prevention of fraudulent and manipulative acts and practices; (3) the promotion of just and equitable principles of trade; (4) providing for

Board consists of fifteen members. The membership of the MSRB "shall at all times be equally divided among public representatives, broker-dealer representatives and bank representatives." [36] The board members are elected in accordance with procedures established in the MSRB rules.[37] The selection of public representatives is subject to SEC approval in order to assure their independence from the broker-dealer and banking industries.[38] As is the case with the self-regulatory organizations under the Exchange Act, the SEC has oversight responsibilities. The SEC has statutory power to force the MSRB to adopt, abrogate or modify any MSRB rules[39] and to sanction or remove board members.[40]

The MSRB has no enforcement power, but must instead seek the aid of the SEC, NASD, or "appropriate regulatory agency" [41] to apply sanctions against municipal securities brokers and dealers. These sanctions can include any that may be ordinarily imposed against other brokers and dealers.[42] Section 15B(c)(7)[43] requires that before such investigation or proceeding is taken against a particular broker or dealer, the SEC and the appropriate regulatory agency must consult and cooperate with each other; however, neither the SEC nor the agency is bound by the other's decision or recommendations.[44] If a broker or dealer is sanctioned or expelled for a municipal securities violation, the sanction applies during the period of suspension to any securities dealings he might undertake.

the periodic examination of municipal securities brokers and municipal securities dealers to determine compliance with the provisions of the Act, the rules and regulations thereunder, and the rules of the MSRB; (5) the form and context of quotations relating to municipal securities, including rules designed to produce fair and informative quotations, and to prevent fictitious or misleading quotations; and (6) the prescription of records to be made and kept by municipal securities dealers and the periods for which such records shall be preserved." Sec.Exch. Act Rel. No. 34–11876 (Nov. 26, 1975).

36. 15 U.S.C.A. § 78o–4(b)(2)(B). For a description of bank dealings in municipal securities that will subject the bank to registration *see* Sec.Exch. Act Rel. No. 34–11585 (Aug. 11, 1975).

37. 15 U.S.C.A. § 78o–4(b)(1). The initial board consisted of fifteen members appointed by the SEC. Five representatives could not be associated with municipal securities dealers or banks dealing in municipal securities and at least one of these "public representatives" had to represent municipal securities issuers. *Id.* § 78o–4(b)(1)(A). Five members were representatives of non-bank municipal securities dealers, and the remaining five were representatives of banks or bank subsidiaries dealing in municipal securities. *Id.* §§ 78o–4(b)(1)(B), (C).

For more complete treatment of the MSRB's rules and regulations, *see* Municipal Securities Rule Making Manual (CCH).

38. 15 U.S.C.A. § 78o–4(b)(2)(B).

39. 15 U.S.C.A. § 78s(c).

40. 15 U.S.C.A. § 78o–4(c)(8).

41. 15 U.S.C.A. § 78o–4(c)(5). The "appropriate regulatory agency" would be the Comptroller of Currency for national banks, the Federal Reserve Board for state member banks, the Federal Deposit Insurance Corporation for insured nonmember banks, and the SEC for any others.

42. 15 U.S.C.A. § 78o–4(c)(2). *See* §§ 10.2–10.4 *supra.*

43. 15 U.S.C.A. § 78o–4(c)(7).

44. 15 U.S.C.A. § 78o–4(c)(6)(A).

In addition, the MSRB has authority to set requirements for examination[45] and qualification[46] for municipal securities brokers and dealers, with such examinations being administered by the appropriate regulatory agency for its members, and by the SEC for other brokers and dealers.

Though the MSRB has authority to set record-keeping requirements for municipal securities brokers and dealers, compliance with SEC Rules 17a–3 and 17a–4 is a satisfactory substitute.[47] The MSRB also has jurisdiction over disputes between municipal securities dealers. In carrying out this authority the MSRB can refer such inter-dealer disputes to binding arbitration.[48]

[For further discussion, *see* the Practitioner's Edition]

§ 10.5.1   Government Securities Dealers

As discussed earlier, brokers and dealers who deal solely in exempted securities need not register under section 15 of the Exchange Act.[1] Municipal securities dealers, who are also exempt from broker-dealer registration, are regulated through the Municipal Securities Rulemaking Board,[2] but there was no comparable regulation for government securities dealers until 1986. Following the insolvency of a number of government securities dealers,[3] Congress enacted legislation to require the regulation of government securities dealers. The government securities dealer registration requirements more closely parallel that of broker-dealers generally than of municipal securities dealers.

Definition of Government Securities

Government securities are those securities which are issued or guaranteed by the federal government or a federal agency.[4] Treasury

---

45.   15 U.S.C.A. § 78o–4(c)(7).

46.   15 U.S.C.A. § 78o–4(b)(2)(A).

47.   Sec.Exch. Act Rel. No. 34–13295 (Feb. 24, 1977). Rules 17a–3 and 17a–4, 17 C.F.R. §§ 240.17a–3, 17a–4, apply to broker-dealers generally. *See* § 10.2 *supra.* For a detailed analysis of the record-keeping requirements, *see* Jerry W. Markham & Thomas L. Hazen, Broker–Dealer Operations Under Securities and Commodities Law: Financial Responsibilities, Credit Regulation, and Customer Protection, ch. 6 (1995).

48.   *See* Swink & Co. v. Hereth, 784 F.2d 866 (8th Cir.1986) (Congress intended that the MSRB rather than the federal courts resolve inter-dealer disputes).

§ 10.5.1

1.   15 U.S.C.A. § 78o(c). *See* § 10.2 *supra* and § 10.2.2 *supra* (Practitioner's Edition only).

2.   *See* 15 U.S.C.A. § 78o–4. The regulation of municipal securities dealers is discussed in § 10.5 *supra.*

3.   *See* footnote 10 *infra.*

4.   The term "government securities" means—

(a) securities which are direct obligations of, or obligations guaranteed by the United States;

(b) securities which are issued or guaranteed by corporations in which the United States has a direct or indirect interest and which are designated by the Secretary of the Treasury;

securities, such as savings bonds, "T–Bills," and "Treasury Notes" are familiar government securities. Lesser-known government-guaranteed securities are those issued by federally-owned agencies, for example Government National Mortgage Obligations or "Ginnie Maes." Finally, there are money market instruments such as "federal funds," and "repurchase agreements." Federal funds are cash reserves which the Federal Reserve Board requires banks to maintain for liquidity purposes and which are manipulated by the Federal Reserve Board to effectuate monetary policy.[5] "Repurchase agreements" or "repos" are investment schemes by which institutional investors and government securities dealers exchange cash for government securities.[6]

[For further discussion *see* the Practitioner's Edition]

§ 10.6 Broker–Dealers and the Shingle Theory

Before exploring the range of duties that comprise broker-dealers' obligations to their customers, it is important to understand one effect that the current trend favoring arbitration of customer disputes has had on the law. Since most disputes between brokers and their customers are now subject to arbitration, much of the law relating to broker-dealer

---

(c) securities issued or guaranteed by any corporation the securities of which are designated by statute as exempt; and

(d) any put, call, straddle, option or privilege on a security described in (a), (b), or (c) other than a put, call, straddle, option, or privilege—

(i) traded on one or more national securities exchanges; or

(ii) for which quotations are disseminated through an automated quotation system operated by a registered securities association.

15 U.S.C.A. § 78c(a)(42).

5. *See, e.g.,* Note, The Government Securities Market: In the Wake of ESM, 27 Santa Clara L.Rev. 587, 589–91 (1987).

6. In a repurchase transaction, a broker or dealer acts as middleman between a lending institution and a borrowing institution. The lending institution has idle cash on which it wishes to earn interest. The broker borrows this idle cash in exchange for government securities as collateral, and agrees to pay back the loan with some interest, usually the next day. The lending institution agrees to return the government securities upon repayment of the loan. Meanwhile, the broker buys government securities from the borrowing institution with the cash borrowed from the lending institution and agrees to hold those securities until the borrowing institution buys them back at a price slightly higher than the broker must pay the lending institution. Thus the borrower gets the temporary cash it needs, the broker makes a slight profit, and the lender earns interest on its idle cash. One problem with these "repos" arises from the fact that brokers must carry out many transactions to make a good profit, and further, the cost of actually shifting control of the securities as collateral is relatively high. Thus, brokers use one customer's securities as collateral for more than one transaction, and can get away with it since lenders do not insist on the full shift of control of their collateral securities. Brokers who have over-extended themselves cannot reimburse these lenders when sudden market fluctuations cause the brokers losses. Eventually these brokers may go bankrupt leaving the lenders who failed to require collateralization without remedy. *See, e.g.,* Note, The Government Securities Market: In the Wake of ESM, 27 Santa Clara L.Rev. 587, 591–93 (1987); Comment, The Government Securities Act of 1986: Balancing Investor Protection with Market Liquidity; 36 Cath.U.L.Rev. 999, 1005–1007 (1987); Note, Lifting the Cloud of Uncertainty Over the Repo Market: Characterization of Repos as Separate Purchases and Sales of Securities, 37 Vand.L.Rev. 401 (1984).

obligations is likely to be frozen in a state of suspended animation, preserved in much the state that it was in the pre-arbitration era. Arbitration awards generally do not contain long discussions of the law. Furthermore, the standard of judicial review gives so much leeway to the arbitrators' decision that additional judicial decisions will be few and far between. Much of the law relating to broker-dealer obligations will thus be found primarily in the older decisions arising out of customer litigation, the relatively few customer suits that may still be litigated in court, plus the SEC administrative decisions (and any subsequent judicial review) arising out of broker-dealer regulation.

In addition to SEC rules and requirements of the applicable self regulatory organizations,[1] broker-dealers are, of course, subject to common law duties and fiduciary obligations. The majority view in the cases applying state common law is that a fiduciary relationship between broker-dealer and client does not arise as a matter of law,[2] but that additional facts can suffice to create a fiduciary duty. Chief among these factors which may create a fiduciary relationship is " 'a reposing of faith, confidence and trust,' "[3] often evidenced by a broker-dealer having either prior authorization to trade for the client's account on a discretionary basis, or de facto control of the account.[4] Even in those situations that a court may recognize a fiduciary obligation, liability to the customer is

---

§ 10.6

1. *See* § 10.2 *supra.*

2. *See* Associated Randall Bank v. Griffin, Kubik, Stephens & Thompson, Inc., 3 F.3d 208 (7th Cir.1993) (applying Wisconsin law); Burdett v. Miller, 957 F.2d 1375, 1381–82 (7th Cir.1992) (investment adviser not *per se* fiduciary, but could be shown to be by clear and convincing evidence; applying Illinois law); Greenwood v. Dittmer, 776 F.2d 785 (8th Cir.1985) (commodities broker; applying Arkansas law); Ray E. Friedman & Co. v. Jenkins, 738 F.2d 251 (8th Cir.1984) (commodities broker; applying North Dakota law); Shamsi v. Dean Witter Reynolds, Inc., 743 F.Supp. 87 (D.Mass.1989); DeSciose v. Chiles, Heider & Co., 239 Neb. 195, 476 N.W.2d 200 (1991); Paine, Webber, Jackson & Curtis v. Adams, 718 P.2d 508 (Colo.1986); Berki v. Reynolds Securities, Inc., 277 Or. 335, 560 P.2d 282 (1977); Rude v. Larson, 296 Minn. 518, 207 N.W.2d 709 (Minn.1973). The opposing view is that a broker is a fiduciary by law.

3. McCracken v. Edward D. Jones & Co., 445 N.W.2d 375, 381 (Iowa App.1989) (quoting Kurth v. Van Horn, 380 N.W.2d 693, 695 (Iowa 1986)).

4. Some courts treat the question of whether the account was discretionary or nondiscretionary as dispositive on the issue of fiduciary duty. McAdam v. Dean Witter Reynolds, Inc., 896 F.2d 750 (3d Cir.1990) (applying New Jersey law); Caravan Mobile Home Sales, Inc. v. Lehman Bros. Kuhn Loeb, Inc., 769 F.2d 561 (9th Cir.1985) (applying California law); Chor v. Piper, Jaffray & Hopwood, Inc., 261 Mont. 143, 862 P.2d 26, 32 (1993). However, one court rejected the notion that the "discretionary-nondiscretionary dichotomy [is a] shibboleth." Baker v. Wheat First Securities, 643 F.Supp. 1420, 1428 (S.D.W.Va. 1986) (applying West Virginia law). The latter view is more common; *see, e.g.*, Davis v. Merrill Lynch, Pierce, Fenner & Smith, Inc., 906 F.2d 1206 (8th Cir.1990) (applying South Dakota law); MidAmerica Fed. S & L Assn. v. Shearson/American Express, Inc., 886 F.2d 1249 (10th Cir.1989) (fiduciary duty arises from doctrine of "holding out"; applying Oklahoma law); Leboce, S.A. v. Merrill Lynch, Pierce, Fenner & Smith, Inc., 709 F.2d 605, 607 (9th Cir.1983) (applying California law); Merrill Lynch, Pierce, Fenner & Smith, Inc. v. Cheng, 697 F.Supp. 1224 (D.D.C.1988); Leib v. Merrill Lynch, Pierce, Fenner & Smith, Inc., 461 F.Supp. 951 (E.D.Mich.1978) (churning case); Duffy v. Cavalier, 210 Cal.App.3d 1514, 259 Cal.Rptr. 162 (1989), *review granted and cause transferred* 262 Cal.Rptr. 195, 778 P.2d 549 (1989).

not always clear.[5]   There is also a question as to the scope of the duty. In reviewing the relevant state law decisions, a couple of generalizations can be made.   A broker-dealer is more likely to have a duty to make full disclosure when recommending a security,[6] but is less likely to have an unqualified duty to provide the client with useful market information concerning the client's present portfolio even when the broker–dealer is aware of such information.[7]   There is considerable authority, however, to the effect that honesty and good faith are basic obligations of broker-dealers.[8]

Common law principles have been borrowed in formulating SEC policy.   For example, in judging the appropriate standard of care that attaches to a broker–dealer in recommending securities to his or her customers and in dealing with the customers' accounts generally, the Commission has relied upon the "shingle theory."   The shingle theory is but an extension of the common law doctrine of "holding out."[9]   When brokers hold themselves out as experts either in investments in general or in the securities of a particular issuer, they will be held to a higher standard of care in making recommendations.   In applying the shingle theory, a broker who makes a recommendation is viewed as making an implied representation that he or she has adequate information on the security in question for forming the basis of his opinion.[10]   This concept

---

5.   *Cf.* Maloley v. Shearson Lehman Hutton, Inc., 246 Neb. 701, 523 N.W.2d 27 (1994) (suit against broker was governed by two–year statute of limitations applicable to malpractice actions generally).   *See also* Franklin D. Ormsten, Norman B. Arnoff & Gregg R. Evangelist, Securities Broker Malpractice and Its Avoidance, 25 Seton Hall L. Rev. 190 (1994).

6.   *See* McCracken v. Edward D. Jones & Co., 445 N.W.2d 375 (Iowa App.1989) (illiquidity of investments and selling commission paid by issuer to broker not disclosed).

7.   *See* Arst v. Stifel Nicolaus & Co., 871 F.Supp. 1370 (D.Kan.1994) (broker did not owe a fiduciary relationship to customer so as to impose on the broker a duty to investigate securities nor disclose information about securities customer wanted to sell); Walston & Co. v. Miller, 100 Az. 48, 410 P.2d 658 (1966) (commodities margin account);   Merrill Lynch, Pierce, Fenner & Smith, Inc. v. Boeck, 127 Wis.2d 127, 377 N.W.2d 605 (1985) (commodities; soybean crop larger than expected).

8.   Messer v. E.F. Hutton & Co., 833 F.2d 909, 920 (11th Cir.1987), *opinion amended on rehearing in part* 847 F.2d 673 (11th Cir.1988) (applying Florida common law).

9.   *See* William L. Prosser, Law of Torts 697 (4th ed. 1971).   *But see, e.g.,* Lefkowitz v. Smith Barney, Harris Upham & Co., 804 F.2d 154 (1st Cir.1986).

It is far from clear that the common law imposes a special obligation on a broker- dealer. *See, e.g.,* Shamsi v. Dean Witter Reynolds, Inc., 743 F.Supp. 87 (D.Mass.1989) (a brokerage relationship does not in itself create a fiduciary obligation), *relying on* Lefkowitz v. Smith Barney, Harris Upham & Co., Inc., 804 F.2d 154, 155 (1st Cir.1986) and Vogelaar v. H.L. Robbins & Co., 348 Mass. 787, 204 N.E.2d 461 (1965).

However, it is clear that when a broker exercises discretion over an account, he or she will be subject to fiduciary obligations.

10.   Charles Hughes & Co. v. SEC, 139 F.2d 434 (2d Cir.1943), *cert. denied* 321 U.S. 786, 64 S.Ct. 781, 88 L.Ed. 1077 (1944); *See* Filloramo v. Johnston, Lemon & Co., 697 F.Supp. 517 (D.D.C.1988) (upholding complaint against broker-dealer for alleged misrepresentations regarding future events; absence of evidence supporting his predictions could lead jury to conclude that broker acted recklessly); In re V.F. Minton Securities, Inc., Exch.Act Rel. No. 34–32,074, [1992–1993 Transfer Binder] Fed.Sec.L.Rep. (CCH) ¶ 85,128 (SEC 1993) (sanctioning brokerage firm and its president for making recommendations without an adequate basis).   *See generally* Nicholas Wolfson, Richard M. Phillips & Thomas A. Russo, Regulation of Brokers, Dealers and Securities Markets 2–14–2–16

of implied representation has also been expressed in terms of a broker-dealer "implicitly warrant[ing] the soundness of the statements of stock value," [11] but this is too strong a statement of the rule. The concept of implied warranty has not to date been extended to brokers' recommendations and the appropriate standard of care whether under the shingle theory or otherwise is necessarily based upon the broker-dealer's factual basis and reasonable belief in the opinions that form the basis of the recommendation.

The shingle theory is sometimes applied to bring activities of the broker which otherwise might not fall within the literal application of the SEC antifraud rules within the ambit of those rules. In many of these cases brokers have held themselves out as having complied with SEC regulations. These activities that have then given rise to accountability, and in some cases liability, include undisclosed insolvency,[12] egregious failures to comply with SEC bookkeeping requirements,[13] and noncompliance with net capital requirements.[14]

The shingle theory intertwines with the suitability and know your customer doctrines that are discussed in the next section. These concepts combine to impose federal standards of accountability for brokers recommending securities to their customers.[15] In what may be viewed as

(1977); Carol R. Goforth, Stockbrokers' Duties to Their Customers, 33 St. Louis U.L.J. 407 (1989); Gregory A. Hicks, *supra* footnote 2; Donald C. Langevoort, Fraud and Deception by Securities Professionals, 61 Tex.L.Rev. 1247 (1983); Robert N. Leavell, Investment Advice and The Fraud Rules, 65 Mich.L.Rev. 1569 (1967).

11.   Kahn v. SEC, 297 F.2d 112, 115 (2d Cir.1961) (Clark J., concurring).

12.   SEC v. Resch–Cassin & Co., 362 F.Supp. 964 (S.D.N.Y.1973). *But see* Brennan v. Midwestern United Life Insurance Co., 286 F.Supp. 702, 707 (N.D.Ind.1968), *affirmed* 417 F.2d 147 (7th Cir.1969), *cert. denied* 397 U.S. 989, 90 S.Ct. 1122, 25 L.Ed.2d 397 (1970).

13.   Joseph v. Shields, Jr., [1967–1969 Transfer Binder] Fed.Sec.L.Rep. (CCH) ¶ 77,643 (Jan. 3, 1969).

14.   SEC v. Charles Plohn & Co., 433 F.2d 376 (2d Cir.1970); Joseph v. Shields, Jr., [1967–1969 Transfer Binder] Fed.Sec.L.Rep. (CCH) ¶ 77,643 (SEC Jan. 3, 1969).

For other decisions employing the shingle theory, *see, e.g.,* Hanly v. SEC, 415 F.2d 589 (2d Cir.1969); In the Matter of Hamilton Waters & Co., Sec.Exch.Act Rel. No. 7725 (Oct. 18, 1965); In the Matter of Fennekohl & Co., Sec.Exch.Act Rel. No. 33–6898 (Sept. 18, 1962); In the Matter of Alexander Reid & Co., Sec.Exch.Act Rel. No. 34–6727 (Feb. 8, 1962); In the Matter of Duker & Duker, 6 S.E.C. 388–89 (SEC 1939).

15.   *See generally* Victor Brudney, Origins and Limited Applicability of the "Reasonable Basis" or "Know Your Merchandise" Doctrine, 4 Inst.Sec.Reg. 239 (1973); Arnold S. Jacobs, Impact of Securities Exchange Act Rule 10b–5 on Broker–Dealers, 57 Cornell L.Rev. 869 (1972); Ezra J. Levin & William M. Evan, Professionalism and the Stockbroker: Some Observations on the SEC Special Study, 21 Bus.Law. 337 (1966); F. Harris Nichols, Broker's Duty to his Customer Under Evolving Federal Fiduciary and Suitability Standards, 26 Buff.L.Rev. 435 (1977); Note, New and Comprehensive Duties of Securities Sellers to Investigate, Disclose, and Have an "Adequate Basis" for Representations, 62 Mich.L.Rev. 880 (1964).

In order to state a claim for relief against a broker, the plaintiff must be able to allege breaches of the broker's responsibilities and/or specific misrepresentations or omissions in connection with securities transactions. *See* Candelora v. Clouser, 621 F.Supp. 335 (D.Del.1985), *judgment affirmed* 802 F.2d 446 (3d Cir.1986); Moran v. Kidder, Peabody & Co., 617 F.Supp. 1065 (S.D.N.Y.1985), *affirmed* 788 F.2d 3 (2d Cir.1986); M & B Contracting Corp. v. Dale, 601 F.Supp. 1106 (E.D.Mich.1984), *affirmed* 795 F.2d 531 (6th Cir.1986).

a variation of the shingle theory, a broker may be held liable for holding himself or herself out as an expert when acting without any special knowledge or other basis for such a claim of expertise.[16] Not every breach of fair dealing by brokers will result in rule 10b–5 liability.[17] On the other hand, the absence of a 10b–5 remedy does not preclude an action based on state law breach of fiduciary duty.[18]

Brokers who render advice incidental to their brokerage activities are not covered by the Investment Advisers Act of 1940 that regulates those persons and entities in the business of rendering investment advice.[19] Accordingly, this type of incidental advice is regulated pursuant to the applicable provisions of the 1934 Exchange Act, supplemented by common law principles.

§ 10.7   A Broker's Obligation to Customers With Regard to Recommendation—The Suitability and Know Your Customer Rules

As discussed above,[1] the securities laws prohibit a broker-dealer from recommending a security unless he or she has actual knowledge of the characteristics and fundamental facts relevant to the security in question; furthermore, the recommendation must be reasonably supported by the facts. In addition to the broker-dealer's knowledge of the security, there are also obligations imposed with regard to the broker-dealer's duty to know his or her customer. The SEC has not established suitability requirements applicable to broker–dealers generally, but such an obligation can be found in the rules of the self-regulatory organizations. Although the Commission does impose a suitability requirement on certain penny stock recommendations,[2] there has not to date been an expansion of this requirement. However, in what may prove to be a harbinger of change, the SEC has proposed a suitability requirement for recommendations by investment advisers.[3] Under the rule as proposed investment advisers would be expressly prohibited from making unsuitable recommendations to their clients. Unlike the current state of the law under Rule 10b–5 of the Exchange Act, the evil would be based on the inappropriateness of the investment rather than upon any misrepresentation of risk. However, unless such a rule is extended to broker–dealers generally, the enforcement of suitability requirements will de-

16. Fondren v. Schmidt, 626 F.Supp. 892, 899 (D.Nev.1986), relying upon Gottreich v. San Francisco Inv. Corp., 552 F.2d 866, 867 (9th Cir.1977).

17. *E.g.* Forkin v. Rooney Pace, Inc., 804 F.2d 1047 (8th Cir.1986).

18. *See* footnotes 2–7 *supra.*

19. 15 U.S.C.A. § 80b–2(a)(11). *See* § 18.2 *infra.*

§ 10.7

1. *See* § 10.6 *supra.*

2. *See* Rules 15g–1 *et seq.*, 17 C.F.R. §§ 240.15g–1 *et seq.*

3. Proposed Rule 206(4)–6, Inv. Advisers Rel. No. 40–1406 (SEC March 16, 1994). Investment advisers are discussed in chapter 18 *infra.*

pend upon the rules of the various self regulatory organizations.[4] Even beyond the federal law and self regulatory organizations, suitability in recommendations may be required as a matter of state law.[5]

This suitability obligation takes various forms depending on the applicable self regulatory organization.[6] It is unlikely that a violation of these rules without more will provide an independent basis for private relief by an injured investor, although it may be relevant in an action brought under SEC Rule 10b–5.[7] As is the case with any claim under Rule 10b–5, a claim based on unsuitability must be pleaded with sufficient particularity.[8] The essence of a Rule 10b–5 claim is deception, which generally means misrepresentation or nondisclosure.[9] As discussed more fully below, a broker's recommendation of a security will give rise to damages to the customer for an unsuitable recommendation only if the recommendation contains an express or implied material misrepresentation of the risks involved.[10]

---

4. Although it is not strictly speaking a suitability problem, the SEC has gone after brokerage firms which provide undue inducements to their sales representatives to recommend certain securities. *See, e.g.,* Michael Siconolfi, PaineWebber is Penalized For Sales Pressure on Brokers, Wall St. J. p. C1, July 27, 1993.

5. *See* § 10.6 *supra* for a discussion of the shingle theory. *Cf.* Maloley v. Shearson Lehman Hutton, Inc., 246 Neb. 701, 523 N.W.2d 27 (1994) (suit against broker based on allegedly unsuitable recommendations was governed by two–year statute of limitations applicable to malpractice actions generally).

6. *See generally* Hilary H. Cohen, Suitability Doctrine: Defining Stockbrokers' Professional Responsibilities, 3 J.Corp.L. 533 (1978); Robert H. Mundheim, Professional Responsibilities of Broker–Dealers: The Suitability Doctrine, 1965 Duke L.J. 445; Arvid E. Roach II, Suitability Obligations of Brokers: Present Law and the Proposed Federal Securities Code, 29 Hastings L.J. 1067 (1978). *See also, e.g.,* Stephen B. Cohen, The Suitability Rule and Economic Theory, 80 Yale L.J. 1604 (1971); Janet E. Kerr, Suitability Standards: A New Look at Economic Theory and Current SEC Disclosure Policy, 16 Pac.L.J. 805 (1985); Norman S. Poser, Civil Liability for Unsuitable Recommendations, 19 Rev.Sec. & Commodities Reg. 67 (April 2, 1986); Note, Measuring Damages in Suitability and Churning Actions Under Rule 10b–5, 25 B.C.L.Rev. 839 (1984). *See also, e.g.,* Franklin D. Ormsten, Norman B. Arnoff & Gregg R. Evangelist, Securities Broker Malpractice and Its Avoidance, 25 Seton Hall L. Rev. 190 (1994).

7. 17 C.F.R. § 240.10b–5. *See. e.g.,* Davis v. Merrill Lynch, Pierce, Fenner & Smith, Inc., 906 F.2d 1206 (8th Cir.1990) (brokers are fiduciaries who owe their customers a duty of the utmost good faith, integrity, and loyalty; applying South Dakota law); MidAmerica Federal Savings & Loan Ass'n v. Shearson/American Express, Inc., 886 F.2d 1249 (10th Cir.1989) (upholding damage award based on broker's breach of fiduciary duty); First Union Brokerage v. Milos, 717 F.Supp. 1519 (S.D.Fla.1989) (complaint sufficiently alleged existence of fiduciary relationship between broker and customer); Duffy v. Cavalier, 210 Cal.App.3d 1514, 259 Cal.Rptr. 162 (1989), *review granted and cause transferred* 262 Cal.Rptr. 195, 778 P.2d 549 (1989) (recognizing fiduciary duty to an unsophisticated and naive customer who routinely followed the broker's advice).

See also, e.g., Arnold S. Jacobs, Impact of Securities Exchange Act Rule 10b–5 on Broker–Dealers, 57 Cornell L.Rev. 869 (1972); text accompanying notes 9–12 *infra.* The implied remedy under rule 10b–5 is discussed in §§ 13.2–13.12 *infra.*

8. *E.g.,* Keenan v. D.H. Blair & Co., 838 F.Supp. 82 (S.D.N.Y.1993) (dismissing claim for insufficient particularity). The particularity requirement is discussed in § 13.2.1 *infra* (Practitioner's Edition only).

9. *See, e.g.,* Schreiber v. Burlington Northern, Inc., 472 U.S. 1, 105 S.Ct. 2458, 86 L.Ed.2d 1 (1985) (decided under section 14(e) but basing its reasoning on the impact of section 10(b) and Rule 10b–5). *See* § 12.1, 13.10 *infra* for discussion of the deception requirement.

10. One court has summarized the elements as follows:

The NASD in its so-called "suitability rule" requires that in recommending a purchase or sale of a particular security to a customer, the broker-dealer must have "reasonable grounds for believing that the recommendation is suitable for such customer upon the basis of the facts, if any, disclosed by such customer as to his other security holdings and as to his financial situation and needs." [11]   Interestingly, the suitability rule on its face does not impose upon the broker any affirmative duty of investigating the customer's investment objectives but merely requires the broker-dealer to act reasonably based upon the information, if any, that the customer provides.   Nevertheless, the NASD in a policy statement by its Board of Governors goes further by requiring the broker to obtain information concerning the customers' other securities holdings before recommending speculative, low priced securities.[12]   The suitability rule is not applicable when the broker–dealer is following the directions of a sophisticated investor.[13]

In contrast, Rule 405 of the New York Stock Exchange expressly imposes upon member broker-dealers an affirmative obligation to "know your customer" [14] with regard to sales or offers as well as recommenda-

---

the plaintiff asserting unsuitability must show (1) the investment was incompatible with the plaintiff's investment objectives; and (2) the broker recommended the investment although (3) the broker knew or reasonably believed the investment was inappropriate.

Keenan v. D.H. Blair & Co., 838 F.Supp. 82, 87 (S.D.N.Y.1993) (holding the plaintiffs failed to meet the required specificity in pleading since they "failed to show why the stock was incompatible with their investment aims. . . .   Plaintiffs merely recite the stock declined in value.   Such conclusory allegations are not sufficient to state an unsuitability claim with particularity.").

11.   Art. III, Sec. 2 NASD Rules of Fair Practice, NASD Manual (CCH) ¶ 2152.   Under the NASD Rule, apparently there is no duty of inquiry.   *See, e.g.,* "Report of Special Study of Securities Markets," H.R.Doc. No. 95, 88th Cong., 1st Session, Pt. 1, at 316 (1963).   In addition to the authorities cited in footnote 5 *supra, see* Gerald L. Fishman, Broker–Dealer Obligations to Customers—the NASD Suitability Rule, 51 Minn.L.Rev. 233 (1966).   *See also, e.g.,* In the Matter of Hassanieh, [1994–1995 Transfer Binder] Fed. Sec. L. Rep. (CCH) ¶ 85,468 (SEC 1994) (broker recommending partnership did not violate suitability rule; investor came within guidelines set forth in prospectus and also was interested in tax savings offered by the investment); Shearson, Hammill & Co., 42 S.E.C. 811 (1965) (SEC instituted disciplinary actions under 10b–5).

12.   NASD Manual (CCH) ¶ 2152.   *See generally* Stephen B. Cohen, The Suitability Rule and Economic Theory, 80 Yale L.J. 1604 (1971); Fishman, Broker–Dealer Obligations to Customers–The NASD Suitability Rule, 51 Minn.L.Rev. 233 (1966); Robert H. Mundheim, Professional Responsibilities of Broker–Dealers: The Suitability Doctrine, 1965 Duke L.J. 445.   A guideline for the information required by the NASD rule may be found in former SEC rule 15b10–6(a)(1)(ii) which required a written record of specified information considered by the broker in making his recommendation.   17 C.F.R. § 240.15b10–6(a)(1)(ii) (1982).

13.   *See, e.g,* Sheldon Co. Profit Sharing Plan & Trust v. Smith, 828 F.Supp. 1262 (W.D.Mich.1993) (members of pension plan had no claim against broker–dealer for margin transactions and option trading that had resulted from execution of orders placed by the plan's investment adviser).

14.   NYSE Rule 405, New York Stock Exchange Guide (CCH) ¶ 2405.   *See generally* Note, "Know Your Customer" rule of the NYSE: Liability of Broker–Dealers Under the UCC & Federal Securities Laws, 1973 Duke L.J. 489.   *See also* Amer.Stock Exchange Rule 411, 2 ASE Guide (CCH) ¶ 9431.

The New York Stock Exchange has taken a broad view of the duties imposed under rule 405.   For example, the Exchange has said that even discount brokers (who do not purport to be giving customers advice) have a duty to prevent customers from entering into ruinous

tions.[15] Similarly, the former SEC rule,[16] which governed broker-dealers that were not members of self regulatory organizations, imposed upon the broker-dealer or associated person making a recommendation the duty to have a reasonable basis for the belief "that the recommendation is not unsuitable for such customer on the basis of information furnished by such customer *after reasonable inquiry* concerning the customer's investment objectives, financial situation and needs, and any other information known by such broker or dealer or associated person."[17] Under this approach, the broker-dealer had an affirmative obligation to make the initial inquiry.

Notwithstanding the high standards of fiduciary obligation imposed by the suitability and know your customer rules, disciplinary actions have been few[18] and the overwhelming majority of cases have denied the existence of a private remedy by an injured investor solely on the basis of a violation of the applicable rule.[19] On the other hand, it is clear that if an injured customer can state what amounts to a Rule 10b–5 violation, including showing the requisite scienter, materiality, reliance, causation, damages, and deception,[20] a violation of the know your customer rule will

transactions. *See* Michael I. Siconolfi, Discounters Must Watch Out for Customers, Big Board Says, Wall St.J. at C1 col. 3 (July 19, 1991).

15. *See, e.g.,* In re Nicholaou, SEC Admin. Proc file No. 3–8160, Sec. Reg. & L. Rep. (BNA) (SEC July 28m 1994) (affirming New York Stock Exchange's imposition of sanctions against broker who made unsuitable recommendations); (these recommendations included high risk mutual funds for customers seeking low risk accounts).

16. 17 C.F.R. § 240.15b10–3 (1982). *See also* 17 C.F.R. § 240.15c2–5 (1982).

17. 17 C.F.R. § 240.15b10–3 (1982). (emphasis supplied). The SECO rules were abolished effective December 1983, *see* § 10.2 *supra.*

18. However, recommendations can form the basis of disciplinary proceedings. *E.g.* In re Nicholaou, SEC Admin. Proc file No. 3–8160, Sec. Reg. & L. Rep. (BNA) (SEC July 28, 1994) (affirming New York Stock Exchange's imposition of sanctions); In re V.F. Minton Securities, SEC Admin.Proc.File No. 3–7391, 25 Sec.Reg. & L.Rep. (BNA) 555 (SEC March 31, 1993) (broker had registration revoked; for making baseless buy recommendation; firm's president was barred from association with the firm since he recklessly ignored indications that key assertions in recommendation were false); In re Johnson, SEC Admin.Proc.File. No. 3–7528, [1992 Transfer Binder] Fed.Sec.L.Rep. (CCH) ¶ 85.036 (SEC June 23, 1992) (barring respondents from association with any broker dealer for a number of violations including unsuitable transactions).

19. *See, e.g.,* Craighead v. E.F. Hutton & Co., 899 F.2d 485 (6th Cir.1990) (no private right of action under New York Stock Exchange know your customer rule); Carrott v. Shearson Hayden Stone, Inc., 724 F.2d 821 (9th Cir.1984); Jablon v. Dean Witter & Co., 614 F.2d 677 (9th Cir.1980); Colonial Realty Corp. v. Bache & Co., 358 F.2d 178 (2d Cir.), *cert. denied* 385 U.S. 817, 87 S.Ct. 40, 17 L.Ed.2d 56 (1966).

20. *See* Pelletier v. Stuart–James Co., 863 F.2d 1550 (11th Cir.1989); Village of Arlington Heights Police Pension Fund v. Poder, 700 F.Supp. 405 (N.D.Ill.1988); Lopez v. Dean Witter Reynolds, Inc., 591 F.Supp. 581 (N.D.Cal.1984). *But cf.* Board of Trustees of Fire Fighters Pension Fund v. Liberty Group, 708 F.Supp. 1504 (N.D.Ill.1989) (suitability claim dismissed for failure to plead claim with sufficient particularity); Bischoff v. G.K. Scott & Co., 687 F.Supp. 746 (E.D.N.Y.1986) (nondisclosure of high risk speculative nature of securities held not actionable due to failure to show causal connection). The requirements of an implied action under rule 10b–5 (17 C.F.R. § 240.10b–5) are considered in §§ 13.2–13.12 *infra.*

In Shamsi v. Dean Witter Reynolds, Inc., 743 F.Supp. 87 (D.Mass.1989), the court dismissed a suitability claim because of failure to satisfy Rule 10b–5's deception requirement; the conduct complained of sounded more like a claim for breach of fiduciary duty. The court went on to hold that a brokerage relationship does not in itself create a fiduciary

be actionable.[21] The Second Circuit has explained that in order to make a suitability claim, an investor must establish: (1) that the securities were unsuitable to the investor's needs, (2) the broker knew the securities were unsuitable and recommended or purchased them nonetheless, (3) acting with scienter, the broker made material misstatements as to the securities' suitability (or, in the face of a fiduciary relationship, failed to disclose material information), and (4) that the customer justifiably relied on the broker's fraudulent conduct.[22]

It has further been held that when combined with proof of churning, violations of the suitability requirements will give rise to a private right of action.[23] As with any claim based on violation of the antifraud provisions, actions based on nondisclosure or misrepresentation in connection with unsuitable recommendations must be pleaded with sufficient particularity.[24] Aside from the federal securities laws, violations by a broker-dealer of the applicable suitability and know your customer

obligation, *relying on* Lefkowitz v. Smith Barney, Harris Upham & Co., 804 F.2d 154, 155 (1st Cir.1986). *See also, e.g.,* Wasnick v. Refco, Inc., 911 F.2d 345 (9th Cir.1990) (no duty under state law that would hold broker liable for negligence in failing to prevent allegedly unsuitable customers from trading in nondiscretionary accounts); Prudential Bache Securities, Inc. v. Pitman, 1991 WL 160039, [1991 Transfer Binder] Fed.Sec.L.Rep. (CCH) ¶ 96,170 (N.D.Ga.1991) (unpublished case) (dismissing claim based on broker's encouraging plaintiff to invest in stock index futures). *Compare, e.g.,* MidAmerica Federal Savings & Loan Ass'n v. Shearson/American Express, Inc., 886 F.2d 1249 (10th Cir.1989) (upholding damage award based on broker's breach of fiduciary duty); Gopez v. Shin, 736 F.Supp. 51 (D.Del.1990) (unsuitable trading pleaded with sufficient particularity); First Union Brokerage v. Milos, 717 F.Supp. 1519 (S.D.Fla.1989) (complaint sufficiently alleged existence of fiduciary relationship between broker and customer); Duffy v. Cavalier, 210 Cal.App.3d 1514, 259 Cal.Rptr. 162 (1989), *review granted and cause transferred* 262 Cal.Rptr. 195, 778 P.2d 549 (1989) (recognizing fiduciary duty to an unsophisticated and naive customer who routinely followed the broker's advice).

21. O'Connor v. R.F. Lafferty & Co., 965 F.2d 893 (10th Cir.1992) (suitability claim failed since there was a failure to show the degree of recklessness required to establish scienter); Lefkowitz v. Smith Barney, Harris Upham & Co., 804 F.2d 154 (1st Cir.1986) (10b–5 suitability claim dismissed due to failure to establish investor's need for low risk investments); Clark v. John Lamula Investors, Inc., 583 F.2d 594 (2d Cir.1978); Eickhorst v. E.F. Hutton Group, Inc., 763 F.Supp. 1196 (S.D.N.Y.1990) (10b–5 unsuitability claim against sales agent in oil and gas partnerships was pleaded with sufficient particularity); Alton v. Prudential–Bache Securities, Inc., 753 F.Supp. 39 (D.Mass.1990) (dismissal of suitability claim; fact that securities declined in value was insufficient basis for inferring that broker's recommendations were unsuitable).

22. Brown v. E.F. Hutton Group, Inc., 991 F.2d 1020 (2d Cir.1993) (the court denied the suitability claim since the written offering materials adequately disclosed the risks involved). *But see, e.g.,* Wyman v. Prime Discount Securities, 819 F.Supp. 79 (D.Me.1993) (upholding suitability claim based on material misrepresentations in light of customers' known conservative investment goals).

23. Miley v. Oppenheimer & Co., 637 F.2d 318 (5th Cir.1981); McQuesten v. Advest, Inc., 1988 WL 125783, [1988–89 Transfer Binder] Fed.Sec.L.Rep. (CCH) ¶ 94,011 (D.Mass. 1988) (unpublished case); Zaretsky v. E.F. Hutton & Co., 509 F.Supp. 68 (S.D.N.Y.1981). *See also, e.g.,* Fey v. Walston & Co., 493 F.2d 1036 (7th Cir.1974). *But see* Hecht v. Harris, Upham & Co., 430 F.2d 1202 (9th Cir.1970) (court applied doctrines of laches, waiver & estoppel to bar 10b–5 unsuitability claim, but allowed recovery for excess churning). Churning is discussed in § 10.10 *infra.*

24. *E.g.,* Brunetti v. Roney & Co., 807 F.Supp. 62 (E.D.Mich.1992) (nondisclosure of unsuitability of recommendations was not actionable due to failure to plead time, place, and circumstances of the recommendations and alleged nondisclosures in connection therewith). The particularity requirement is discussed in § 13.2.1 *infra.*

rules have been held to give rise to a common law claim based on negligence.[25] In addition, violations of suitability standards can lead to administrative sanctions or even criminal liability.[26] Over the years, the SEC has been especially concerned with the special risks associated with options trading.[27]

Over the past several years there has been increasing concern over low priced securities that are not marketed through a national exchange or the NASD national market system. Many investors have been injured as a result of high pressure sales techniques in connection with these so-called "penny stocks." In response, in 1989, the Commission proposed special regulation of penny stocks.[28] Under the proposed rule, cold calls were to be outlawed and sales could not be completed unless the customer had first signed a written agreement. Furthermore, before executing a sale for a customer a broker would have to determine that the securities were a suitable investment for the customer. The determination of suitability would have to be documented. The proposed rule evidenced the SEC's position that penny stocks are not suitable for many investors. As discussed more fully in the next section,[29] the penny stock regulations were implemented in 1990 and expanded in 1992. The advent of these regulations was seen as having implications beyond penny stocks insofar as the Commission would be expressly recognizing a suitability obligation not heretofore contained in SEC rules. This has

---

25. *See* Lange v. H. Hentz & Co., 418 F.Supp. 1376, 1383–84 (N.D.Tex.1976). *See also* Piper Jaffray & Hopwood, Inc. v. Ladin, 399 F.Supp. 292 (S.D.Iowa 1975); *Cf.* Magnum Corp. v. Lehman Bros. Kuhn Loeb, Inc., 794 F.2d 198 (5th Cir.1986) (nondisclosure of market maker status and significance of volume purchase orders was breach of broker's state law duties).

See, e.g., Shamsi v. Dean Witter Reynolds, Inc., 743 F.Supp. 87 (D.Mass.1989) (a brokerage relationship does not in itself create a fiduciary obligation), *relying on* Lefkowitz v. Smith Barney, Harris Upham & Co., Inc., 804 F.2d 154, 155 (1st Cir.1986) and Vogelaar v. H.L. Robbins & Co., 348 Mass. 787, 204 N.E.2d 461 (1965); DeSciose v. Chiles, Heider & Co., 239 Neb. 195, 476 N.W.2d200 (1991). *Compare, e.g.,* Davis v. Merrill Lynch, Pierce, Fenner & Smith, Inc., 906 F.2d 1206 (8th Cir.1990) (brokers are fiduciaries who owe their customers a duty of the utmost good faith, integrity, and loyalty; applying South Dakota law); MidAmerica Federal Savings & Loan Ass'n v. Shearson/American Express, Inc., 886 F.2d 1249 (10th Cir.1989) (upholding damage award based on broker's breach of fiduciary duty); First Union Brokerage v. Milos, 717 F.Supp. 1519 (S.D.Fla.1989) (complaint sufficiently alleged existence of fiduciary relationship between broker and customer); Duffy v. Cavalier, 210 Cal.App.3d 1514, 259 Cal.Rptr. 162 (1989), *review granted and cause transferred* 262 Cal.Rptr. 195, 778 P.2d 549 (1989) (recognizing fiduciary duty to an unsophisticated and naive customer who routinely followed the broker's advice). *Cf.* Laird v. Integrated Resources, Inc., 897 F.2d 826 (5th Cir.1990) (investment adviser is a fiduciary for purposes of judging the scope of rule 10b–5 obligations).

26. *See* Erdos v. SEC, 742 F.2d 507 (9th Cir.1984) (upholding NASD sanctions for execution of trades that were "highly risky" in light of customer's financial condition).

27. *See, e.g.,* In re Leonesio, Exch.Act Rel. No. 34–23524, [1986–87 Transfer Binder] Fed.Sec.L.Rep. (CCH) ¶ 84,020 (Aug. 11, 1986) (upholding fine and bar of broker representing securities as "risk free"); In re Serfling, Exch.Act Rel. No. 34–21297, [1984 Transfer Binder] Fed. Sec. L. Rep. (CCH) ¶ 83,661 (SEC 1984) (but not imposing sanctions because the broker had a basis for believing that options were compatible with customer's financial situation).

28. Sec.Exch.Act Rel. No. 34–26, 529, [1988–89 Transfer Binder] Fed.Sec.L.Rep. (CCH) ¶ 84,352 (Feb. 8, 1989).

29. *See* § 10.7.1 *infra*.

proved to be the case. In 1994, the Commission proposed a suitability rule for investment advisers.[30] Although the rule for investment advisers would not apply to broker-dealers directly, it is another formal recognition of the suitability obligation.

§ 10.7.1 Penny Stock Regulation

As discussed in the preceding section,[1] issues relating to the suitability of broker–dealer recommendations can apply to a wide variety of investments. However, suitability problems are particularly acute when dealing with low–priced securities (frequently referred to as "penny stocks"). For example, the NASD in its suitability rule has highlighted the particular concern for low priced securities.[2] In August 1989, the SEC adopted the penny stock rule which became effective on January 1, 1990.[3] The penny stock regulations, which are discussed below, contain special investor protections applicable to certain dealers in low priced securities. As observed above, although not directly applicable to all transactions involving any broker dealers, the SEC's increased focus on suitability probably has implications, at least by analogy, for all brokers and for all recommendations.

The initial penny stock regulation was contained in former Rule 15c2–6. As discussed in the Practitioner's Edition, following Congressional mandate, the Commission has since expanded its penny stock regulation. Most of the original regulation has been carried over into the current structure. As initially adopted, former Rule 15c2–6[4] covered broker-dealer recommendations of over-the-counter securities trading at less than five dollars,[5] provided that the security is not listed on an exchange or traded through the NASD's automated quotation system (NASDAQ).[6] The rule further exempted securities of companies having tangible assets of more than two million dollars.[7] This, in essence, limited the rule's application to the smaller, more speculative companies whose stock is traded in the "pink sheets." The rule as adopted imposed

---

30. Investment Adviser regulation is discussed in chapter 18 *infra*.

§ 10.7.1

1. *See* § 10.7 *supra*.

2. Art. III, Sec. 2 NASD Rules of Fair Practice, NASD Manual (CCH) ¶ 2152.

3. Sec.Exch.Act Rel. No. 34–27160, [1989 Transfer Binder] Fed.Sec.L.Rep. CCH ¶ 84,-440 (Aug. 22, 1989). *See generally* Gerald V. Niesar & David M. Niebauer, The Small Public Company After The Penny Stock Reform Act of 1990, 20 Sec.Reg.L.J. 227 (1992).

4. 17 C.F.R. § 240.15c2–6. Former Rule 15c2–6 has been redesignated as 15g–9.

5. 17 C.F.R. § 240.15c2–6(c)(1). Former Rule 15c2–6(c)(1) has been redesignated as 15g–9(c)(1).

6. 17 C.F.R. § 240.15c2–6(d)(2). Former Rule 15c2–6(d)(2) has been redesignated as 15g–9(d)(2).

7. The tangible asset requirement must be demonstrated by financial statements dated no more than fifteen months prior to there commendation and which the broker-dealer has a reasonable basis for believing. *Id.* Also excluded from the rule are put and call options as well as securities issued by registered investment companies. *Id.*

disclosure,[8] know-your-customer,[9] and suitability obligations[10] with regard to transactions in such low priced stocks that were entered into on
the basis of the broker-dealer's recommendation.[11] The disclosure and
suitability obligations do not apply to transactions with customers who
are either accredited investors[12] or "established customers" of the broker-dealer.[13] The rule thus is aimed primarily at those brokers who
initiate transactions through cold calls. Current Rules 15g–1 et seq.
provide expanded penny stock regulation. [*See* Practitioner's Edition].
Of course, the antimanipulation rules can be used to attack other abuses
that take place in the penny stocks market.[14]

§ 10.8　High Pressure Sales Tactics—Boiler Room Operations

In making his or her recommendation to the customer, the broker-
dealer is under an obligation not only to know and consider the customer's investment objectives[1] but also to have some familiarity with the

8. 17 C.F.R. § 240.15c2–6(b)(3). Former Rule 15c2–6(b)(3) has been redesignated as 15g–9(b)(3).

9. 17 C.F.R. § 240.15c2–6(b)(1). Former Rule 15c2–6(b)(1) has been redesignated as 15g–9(b)(1). The NASD has passed rules to require its members to make a reasonable effort to acquire additional information prior to recommendations of securities to non-institutional customers. *See* Sec.Exch.Act Rel. No. 34–27968 (May 1, 1990).

10. 17 C.F.R. § 240.15c2–6(b)(2). Former Rule 15c2–6(b)(2) has been redesignated as Rule 15g–9(b)(2).

11. Transactions that have not been recommended by the broker-dealer are not subject to the rule. 17 C.F.R. § 240.15c2–6(c)(3). Former Rule 15c2–6(c)(3) has been redesignated as 15g–9(c)(3).

12. 17 C.F.R. § 240.15c2–6(c)(2). "Accredited investor" is defined in rule 501 of Regulation D. 17 C.F.R. § 230.501(a). *See* § 4.17 *supra*.

13. 17 C.F.R. § 240.15c2–6(c)(2). Former Rule 15c2–6(c)(2) has been redesignated as 15g–9(c)(3). "Established customer" is defined as:

any person for whom the broker or dealer, or clearing broker on behalf of such broker or dealer, carries an account, and who in such account:

(i) has effected a securities transaction, or made a deposit of funds or securities, more than one year previously; or

(ii) has made three purchases of designated securities that occurred on separate days and involved different issuers.

17 C.F.R. § 240.15c2–6(d)(3). Former Rule 15c2–6(d)(3) has been redesignated as 15g–9(d)(2).

14. *See generally* Anthony De Toro, Market Manipulation of Penny Stocks, 17 Sec.Reg. L.J. 241 (1989).

§ 10.8

1. The suitability requirements are discussed in § 10.7 *supra*. The suitability require-ment is imposed through the commission's oversight responsibilities. Members of the NASD and New York Stock Exchange are bound by the suitability and know-your-customer rules. See NASD Manual (CCH) ¶ 2151 (1982) which is discussed in § 10.7 *supra*. For SEC only ("SECO") brokers see the former know-your-customer rule in 17 C.F.R. § 240.15b10–3 (1982) (rescinded).

The SEC proposed a more direct prohibition against cold call transactions. Sec.Exch.Act Rel. No. 6885 (SEC Aug. 16, 1962). *See* Note, A Symptomatic Approach to Securities Fraud: The SEC's Proposed Rule 15c2–6 and the Boiler Room, 72 Yale L.J. 1411 (1963). However, that proposal was subsequently withdrawn. *See* Exch. Act Rel. No. 34–7517 (1965)

security being recommended.[2]　One unfortunate practice that has developed with some of the more unscrupulous securities brokers and dealers is a concerted high pressure sales campaign which frequently includes the cold calling of individuals who are not regular customers.　The callers recommend purchases of large blocks of speculative securities in new companies, predicting dramatic earnings and rapid increases in the market prices of the securities.　Where there is a conscious plan of high pressure sales tactics, the situation is referred to as a "boiler room" operation.　Boiler room sales tactics, of course, are not limited to the securities markets.　They are probably much more common in connection with the sale of commodities and commodities futures.[3]

In a typical "boiler room" operation, the series of phone calls will be conducted by people who are generally not registered representatives and who will read a statement provided to them recommending the stock in question.[4]　The SEC disclaims that there is any *per se* violation of the antifraud provisions resulting from boiler room activities.[5]　However, liability is readily imposed under either the shingle theory or the antifraud provisions.[6]　The Commission requires that a broker find out certain minimum information about the customer and the security before entering into a transaction.[7]　This duty of investigation prior to making a recommendation has been phrased in terms of an obligation of "due diligence."　In contrast, the duty of investigation of the security is

---

In 1983 "SECO" brokers were abolished since all brokers now have to belong to a registered self regulatory organization.　15 U.S.C.A. § 78*o* which is discussed in § 10.2 *supra.*

2.　*See, e.g.,* In the Matter of Kemprowski, [1994–1995 Transfer Binder] Fed. Sec. L. Rep. (CCH) ¶ 85,469 (SEC 1994) (before making recommendation, broker has a duty to investigate the securities to be recommended;　failure to register as a broker–dealer does not relieve the broker of this obligation).　*See also, e.g.,* Franklin D. Ormsten, Norman B. Arnoff & Gregg R. Evangelist, Securities Broker Malpractice and Its Avoidance, 25 Seton Hall L. Rev. 190 (1994).

3.　*See, e.g.,* Turning up the Heat on "Boiler Room" Scams, Business Week, p. 176 (Nov. 14, 1983) (discussing the marketing of gold bullion).

High pressure sales techniques are common with "penny" stocks.　The SEC has proposed a rule prohibiting cold calls for penny stocks.　Sec.Exch.Act Rel. No. 34–26, 529, [1988–89 Transfer Binder] Fed.Sec.L.Rep. (CCH) ¶ 84,352 (Feb. 8, 1989).

4.　*See, e.g.,* Berko v. SEC, 316 F.2d 137 (2d Cir.1963);　Matter of B. Fennekohl & Co., Sec.Exch.Act Rel. No. 6898 (Sept. 18, 1962).　*See also,* R.A. Holman & Co. v. SEC, 366 F.2d 446 (2d Cir.1966), *modified on other grounds* 377 F.2d 665 (2d Cir.1967) (per curiam), *cert. denied* 389 U.S. 991, 88 S.Ct. 473, 19 L.Ed.2d 482 (1967);　In the Matter of Hamilton Waters & Co., Sec.Exch.Act Rel. No. 34–7725 (Oct. 18, 1965);　In the Matter of Harold Grill, 41 S.E.C. 321 (1963).

5.　*E.g.,* Kahn v. SEC, 297 F.2d 112 (2d Cir.1961);　In re Palombi Securities Co., 41 S.E.C. 266 (SEC 1962).　*But see* footnote 1 *supra.*

6.　Richard J. Buck & Co., 43 S.E.C. 998 (1968), *aff'd sub nom.* Hanly v. SEC, 415 F.2d 589 (2d Cir.1969);　In the Matter of G. Gilman Johnston, 42 S.E.C. 217 (1964);　In the Matter of Gerald M. Greenberg, 40 S.E.C. 133 (1960).　*See* § 10.7 *supra.　See generally* Victor Brudney, Origins and Limited Applicability of the "Reasonable Basis" or "Know Your Merchandise" Doctrine, 4 Inst.Sec.Reg. 239 (1973);　Note, New and Comprehensive Duties of Securities Sellers to Investigate, Disclose, and Have an "Adequate Basis" for Representation, 62 Mich.L.Rev. 880 (1964).　The shingle theory is discussed in § 10.6 *supra.*

7.　*See* Sec.Exch.Act Rel. No. 34–9671 (July 26, 1972).

higher in a sale of unseasoned securities; in such a case, before recommending purchase (or sale), the broker should make a "searching inquiry." [8] In addition, an individual's knowing participation in a high pressure sales campaign fraught with improper sales techniques and recommendations will result in a violation of the Act notwithstanding the defense that he or she relied upon information furnished by the employer broker-dealer.[9] The cases deal mostly with SEC or NASD imposed sanctions on participants in boiler room activities rather than in terms of private rights of action by injured investors. Private remedies for boiler room operations can be based upon the antifraud provisions of Rule 10b–5 or sections 12(2) and 17(a) of the 1933 Act,[10] provided that there have been material misrepresentations in connection therewith. The SEC and state securities administrators continue vigorous enforcement of the anti boiler room prohibitions.[11]

§ 10.9   Scalping

A fraudulent practice that has been utilized by some unscrupulous investment advisers and securities dealers is known as "scalping." Scalping consists of an investment adviser's purchasing a security in advance of making a buy recommendation, with the knowledge that a buy recommendation will help drive up the price of the stock.[1] The stock is sold at a profit once the scalper's recommendation has been issued and the price has risen in reaction thereto. In SEC v. Capital Gains Research Bureau, Inc.,[2] the Supreme Court held that failure to disclose an intention to scalp operates as a fraud or deceit upon an investment adviser's prospective clients under the terms of section 206

---

8. R.A. Holman & Co., 42 S.E.C. 866 (1965), *affirmed* 366 F.2d 446 (2d Cir.1966), *modified on other grounds* 377 F.2d 665 (2d Cir.1967), *cert. denied* 389 U.S. 991, 88 S.Ct. 473, 19 L.Ed.2d 482 (1967). *See, elso, e.g.,* In the Matter of Kemprowski, [1994–1995 Transfer Binder] Fed. Sec. L. Rep. (CCH) ¶ 85,469 (SEC 1994); In the Matter of Merrill Lynch, Pierce, Fenner & Smith, Inc., Sec.Exch.Act Rel. No. 14149 (Nov. 9, 1977).

9. Berko v. SEC, 316 F.2d 137 (2d Cir.1963); SEC v. Macon, 28 F.Supp. 127, 129 (D.Colo.1939); 2 L.Loss, Securities Regulation 1316 *et seq.* (2d ed. 1961).

10. 15 U.S.C.A. §§ 77*l*(2), 77q(a); 17 C.F.R. § 240.10b–5. *See* chapter 7 *supra* and chapter 13 *infra.* The remedy under section 12(2) of the 1933 Act is limited to securities offered by prospectus. Gustafson v. Alloyd Corp., __ U.S. __, 115 S.Ct. 1061, __ L.Ed.2d __ (1995); *see* § 7.5 *supra.* The remedy under section 17(a) is highly doubtful. *See* § 13.13 *infra.*

11. *See, e.g.,* Boiler Room Operators Plead Guilty to Fraud Connected with Lease Lottery, 18 Sec.Reg. & L.Rep. (BNA) 1546 (Oct. 10, 1986); In re Sigmund Securities Corp., 18 Sec.Reg. & L.Rep. (BNA) 452 (SEC March 12, 1986) (broker consented to registration revocation for oil and gas boiler room activities); Florida Securities Task Force Adopts Additional Antifraud Recommendations, 18 Sec.Reg. & L.Rep. (BNA) 110 (Jan. 24, 1986); NASAA Calls for Task Force to Combat Boiler Rooms, 16 Sec.Reg. & L.Rep. 1799 (Nov. 16, 1984).

§ 10.9

1. A variation on the scalping problem is when a brokerage firm places undue pressure or provides improper incentives for their retail brokers to recommend specified securities. *See, e.g.,* Michael Siconolfi, PaineWebber is Penalized For Sales Pressure on Brokers, Wall St. J. p. C1, July 27, 1993.

2. 375 U.S. 180, 84 S.Ct. 275, 11 L.Ed.2d 237 (1963).

of the Investment Advisers Act of 1940.[3] The Court ruled that the concept of fraud or deceit in section 206 of the Act is not limited to material misstatements but also extends to omissions of material fact. The Court explained: "The high standards of business morality exacted by our laws regulating the securities industry do not permit an investment adviser to trade on the market effect of his own recommendations without fully and fairly revealing his personal interest(s) in these recommendations to his clients."[4] On balance it was held that this is a relatively low burden to place upon the investment adviser (or anyone else whose investment opinions are likely to be relied upon by others). The Court further explained that this burden is justified when viewed in relation to the necessity of preserving a climate of fair dealing that is essential to maintain confidence in the securities markets.

It is interesting to note that the Supreme Court's reasoning in *Capital Gains Research Bureau* appears to make undisclosed scalping a violation of Rule 10b–5(3)'s[5] prohibition against acts and practices that operate as a fraud as well as Rule 10b–5(2)'s sanctions for making material misstatements or omissions in connection with the purchase or sale of securities.[6] The Ninth Circuit in Zweig v. Hearst Corp.[7] has followed up on the Supreme Court's lead in holding that undisclosed scalping is in violation of Rule 10b–5. The 10b–5 violation is not based on the conduct alone but rather when the conduct is viewed together with the actionable nondisclosure thereof. In *Zweig* the defendant, a financial columnist, received unjustifiably optimistic information about a corporation directly from the corporation's officers and directors whom he interviewed in preparation for a column on the company. After receiving this favorable information, and apparently making no effort to investigate its accuracy, the defendant purchased five thousand shares of stock directly from the issuer at a substantial discount below the market price. Two days later in his column, the defendant published a buy recommendation for the stock in question, causing the market price of the stock to increase by more than fifty percent. The day after the column appeared, the defendant recovered his entire initial investment by selling two thousand shares; thus retaining three thousand shares as sheer profit.[8] The court, following the reasoning of *Capital Gains Research Bureau,* held that defendant's activities were in violation of rule 10b–5 saying "[w]hile Rule 10b–5 should not be extended to require every financial columnist or reporter to disclose his or her portfolio to all of his or her readers, it does cover the activities of one who uses a

---

3. 15 U.S.C.A. § 80b–6. The Investment Advisers Act is discussed in chapter 18 *infra.*

4. 375 U.S. at 201, 84 S.Ct. at 287.

5. 17 C.F.R. § 240.10b–5.

6. *See id. See also* chapter 13 *infra.*

7. 594 F.2d 1261 (9th Cir.1979).

8. Defendant had a "long history of similar dealings." 594 F.2d at 1265. In one two-year period he purchased the stock of twenty-one companies just prior to publishing columns pertaining to those companies. In twenty-one of twenty-two sales taking place inside of five days after publication defendant profited from an increase in the price of the stock. *Id.* at 1264 n. 4.

column as part of a scheme to manipulate the market and deceive the investing public."[9]

The court in Zweig v. Hearst Corp. held the defendant liable in damages to those readers who had purchased the securities at the artificially high price as well as to shareholders of another company who had not read the column but had suffered a loss when the artificially high price of the recommended stock decreased the number of shares they received in a merger. The rationale was that the defendant had perpetrated a fraud on the market.[10] The court explained that the plaintiffs had "relied on the free and unmanipulated market that the federal securities laws were designed to foster * * *."[11] The court acknowledged that the defendant did not owe any common law duty to non-readers but to deny them recovery while allowing the readers a recourse would be a "wholly incongruous result."[12] The defendant was thus held liable despite the fact that the plaintiffs' aggregate losses far exceeded the defendant's gain.[13] The court couched its decision wholly in terms of the defendant's failure to disclose his purchase of the stock prior to making his recommendation.[14] Presumably, the court could have also formulated its decision in terms of the defendant's violation of the "disclose or abstain from trading" rule[15] for failing to disclose at the time of his purchase an intent to favorably recommend the stock.[16] The viability of the Zweig decision in allowing damage claims to those who

---

9. Id. at 1271.

10. Id. at 1270. See, e.g., Shores v. Sklar, 647 F.2d 462 (5th Cir.1981); Blackie v. Barrack, 524 F.2d 891, 907 (9th Cir.1975), cert. denied 429 U.S. 816, 97 S.Ct. 57, 50 L.Ed.2d 75 (1976). Fraud on the market is discussed in §§ 13.5B, 13.9, 13.10 infra.

11. 549 F.2d at 1270.

12. Id. at 1270–71. But cf. John F. Barry III, The Economics of Outside Information and Rule 10b–5, 129 U.Pa.L.Rev. 1307, 1377 (1981) (the Zweig court's expansion of existing doctrine in order to find a duty to disclose was unnecessary because the common law approach in fact "provides abundant means of redress against [defendant]'s conduct and against other instances of 'scalping' * * * ").

13. For a discussion of the measure of damages under rule 10b–5 see § 13.7 infra.

14. "We hold that [the federal securities] laws * * * require a financial columnist in recommending a security that he or she owns, to provide the public with all material information he or she has on that security, including his or her ownership, and any intent he or she may have (a) to score a quick profit on the recommendation * * *." 594 F.2d at 1271. Cf. SEC v. Brant, 1984 WL 2427, [1991 Transfer Binder] Fed.Sec.L.Rep. (CCH) ¶ 91,483 (SEC Litigation Rel. No. 10386, S.D.N.Y., May 16, 1984) (charging reporter with trading based on nonpublic information).

15. The Supreme Court has been cutting back on the scope of the disclose or abstain rule. See Dirks v. SEC, 463 U.S. 646, 103 S.Ct. 3255, 77 L.Ed.2d 911 (1983); Chiarella v. United States, 445 U.S. 222, 100 S.Ct. 1108, 63 L.Ed.2d 348 (1980), which are discussed in § 13.9 infra. But see United States v. Carpenter, 791 F.2d 1024 (2d Cir.1986), affirmed by an equally divided Court, 484 U.S. 19, 108 S.Ct. 316, 98 L.Ed.2d 275 (1987).

16. Arguably, however, the defendant's decision to recommend the stock was not inside information subject to misappropriation so as to create an affirmative duty to disclose. See, e.g., Chiarella v. United States, 445 U.S. 222, 100 S.Ct. 1108, 63 L.Ed.2d 348 (1980) (employee of financial printer handling confidential takeover information who purchased stock of target companies without disclosing his knowledge to sellers held not in violation of Rule 10b–5 such employee not being a corporate insider and not receiving any confidential information from the target companies).

had not read the articles is questionable now in part due to the decision in Chiarella v. United States and its progeny.[17]

In addition to violation of the Securities Exchange Act of 1934, and the Investment Advisers Act of 1940, scalping necessarily triggers the broker-dealer registration provisions of the Exchange Act.[18] Additionally, scalping violates the rules of self regulatory organizations such as the national exchanges and NASD.[19] Furthermore, as the *Zweig* case indicates, scalping prohibitions are not limited to investment advisers who are subject to the Act's direct regulations but also extend to anyone whose recommendation would be reasonably expected to affect the market price.

In Carpenter v. United States,[20] the Supreme Court upheld the conviction of a Wall Street Journal reporter and his cohorts who traded in advance of impending Heard on the Street columns. In upholding the conviction, the Court did not rely on the scalping cases but rather relied on alternative theories that can be useful in a scalping context. The Second Circuit had upheld convictions under rule 10b–5 based upon the misappropriation theory of illegal insider trading.[21] This aspect of the Second Circuit's ruling was affirmed by an equally divided Supreme Court.[22] In addition, the Court, in an eight to zero opinion affirmed convictions under the federal mail fraud statute.[23] Following the lead of the *Carpenter* decision it would appear that scalping would be equally punishable under the mail and wire fraud acts, providing of course that there has been the use of the jurisdictional means.[24]

§ 10.10   Excessive Trading in Securities—Churning

SEC Rule 15c1–7[1] prohibits excessive trading by a broker for any account in which he or she holds discretionary trading powers. When a broker in a discretionary trading account enters into transactions for the purpose of generating commissions, the broker unjustifiably gains from the customer's loss or transaction costs. This practice is generally

17. 445 U.S. 222, 100 S.Ct. 1108, 63 L.Ed.2d 348 (1980). *See* note 14 *supra.*

18. 15 U.S.C.A. § 78o. *See* § 10.2 *supra.*

19. *See, e.g.,* N.Y.S.E.Guide (CCH) ¶ 2474A.10 (March 26, 1970); Am.Stock Ex.Guide (CCH) ¶ 9495 (April 19, 1978). *See also, e.g.,* Art. III, Sec. 18, NASD Manual (CCH) ¶ 2168 (1982).

20. 484 U.S. 19, 108 S.Ct. 316, 98 L.Ed.2d 275 (1987). The *Carpenter* case is discussed more fully in § 13.9 *infra* and § 19.3.1 *infra* (Practitioner's Edition only).

21. United States v. Carpenter, 791 F.2d 1024 (2d Cir.1986), *affirmed by an equally divided Court,* 484 U.S. 19, 108 S.Ct. 316, 98 L.Ed.2d 275 (1987).

22. *Id.* This aspect of the case is discussed in § 13.9 *infra.*

23. 18 U.S.C.A. § 1341. *See* 484 U.S. 19, 108 S.Ct. 316, 98 L.Ed.2d 275 (1987). This aspect of the decision is discussed in § 19.3.1 *infra* (Practitioner's Edition only).

24. The Court in *Carpenter* took a very expansive view of the statute's reach. The Court found it sufficient that the Wall Street Journal, which contained the article in question, was distributed through the mails. *See* § 19.3.1 *infra* (Practitioner's Edition only).

§ 10.10

1. 17 C.F.R. § 240.15c1–7.

referred to as "churning" the customer's account.[2] Rule 15c1–7 declares churning to be a "manipulative, deceptive or other fraudulent device or contrivance."[3] The applicable SEC rule is limited by its terms to trading accounts where the broker has the discretion to enter into transactions but the account overall need not be formally discretionary. A 1949 SEC ruling took the position that the "handling of a customer's account may become fraudulent whenever the broker or dealer is in a position to determine the volume and frequency of transactions by reason of the customer's willingness to follow the suggestions of the broker or the dealer and he abuses the customer's confidence by overtrading."[4] In contrast to a fraudulent pattern of recommendations, a churning claim requires more than asserting a pattern of the customer having followed the broker's advice; it must be shown that the broker had "control" over the account.[5] The customer may be relatively naive or unsophisticated in investment matters, having naively acquiesced in the broker's management of the account or consented to some trading, but not such excessive trading.

In addition to violating the broker's standards of conduct embodied in section 15(c)(1),[6] churning has been held to violate the Act's general antifraud provisions contained in Rule 10b–5.[7] It has further been held that the customer's opportunity to complain about the transactions by virtue of his having viewed the transaction confirmations does not in itself create an estoppel so as to preclude a churning action under Rule

2. *See generally* Edward Brodsky, Measuring Damages in Churning and Suitability Cases, 6 Sec.Reg.L.J. 157 (1978); Mark C. Jensen, Abuse of Discretion Under Rule 10b–5: Churning, Unsuitability and Unauthorized Transactions, 18 Sec. Reg. L.J. 374 (1991); Patricia A. O'Hara, The Elusive Concept of Control in Churning Claims Under Federal Securities and Commodities Law, 75 Geo.L.J. 1875 (1987); Robert Rosenman, Discretionary Accounts and Manipulative Trading Practices, 5 Inst.Sec.Reg. 245 (1974); Donald A. Winslow & Seth C. Anderson, A Model for Determining the Excessive Trading Element in Churning Claims, 68 N.C.L.Rev. 327 (1989); Comment, Broker Churning: Who is Punished? Vicariously Asserted Punitive Damages in the Context of Brokerage Houses and Their Agents, 30 Hous. L. Rev. 1775 (1993); Note, Measuring Damages in Suitability and Churning Actions Under Rule 10b–5, 25 B.C.L.Rev. 839 (1984); Note, Churning by Securities Dealers, 80 Harv.L.Rev. 869 (1967).

See also Norman S. Poser, Options Account Fraud: Securities Churning in a New Context, 39 Bus.Law. 571 (1984). For discussion of churning of futures accounts *see* 3 Philip M. Johnson & Thomas L. Hazen, Commodities Regulation § 5.45 (2d ed. 1989).

3. 17 C.F.R. § 240.15c1–7. *See* 15 U.S.C.A. § 78o(c)(1). In addition, the NASD Rules of Fair Practice, Art. III § 15(a) NASD Manual (CCH) ¶ 2165 and American Stock Exchange Rule 422, 2 ASE Guide CCH ¶ 9442 prohibit churning.

4. In re Norris & Hirshberg, 21 S.E.C. 865, 890 (1946), *affirmed sub nom.* Norris & Hirshberg v. SEC, 177 F.2d 228 (D.C.Cir.1949). *See also* Follansbee v. Davis, Skaggs & Co., Inc., 681 F.2d 673 (9th Cir.1982); Note, Customer Sophistication and a Plaintiff's Due Diligence: A Proposed Framework for Churning Actions in Nondiscretionary Accounts Under SEC Rule 10b–5, 54 Fordham L.Rev. 1101 (1986).

5. Tiernan v. Blyth, Eastman, Dillon & Co., 719 F.2d 1 (1st Cir.1983) (control is a question of fact but can be based on a variety of factors).

6. 15 U.S.C.A. § 78o(c)(1).

7. *E.g.,* Arceneaux v. Merrill Lynch, Pierce, Fenner & Smith, Inc., 767 F.2d 1498 (11th Cir.1985); Costello v. Oppenheimer & Co., 711 F.2d 1361 (7th Cir.1983); Armstrong v. McAlpin, 699 F.2d 79 (2d Cir.1983); Carras v. Burns, 516 F.2d 251 (4th Cir.1975); Fey v. Walston & Co., Inc., 493 F.2d 1036 (7th Cir.1974).

10b–5.[8]   This is the generally accepted view since in order to succeed on the defense of laches or estoppel, the defendant must establish that the plaintiff was guilty of a lack of due diligence and that the passage of time worked to the prejudice of the defendant.[9]   Some courts have also taken the position that although it is clear that a planned scheme to defraud will satisfy the scienter requirement, a broker's recklessness in entering into excessive trading will also support a Rule 10b–5 claim.[10]   Churning also qualifies as a predicate act for the purposes of imposing liability under the Racketeer Influenced and Corrupt Organizations Act (RICO).[11]

The parameters of a private remedy for churning are similar to any action under Rule 10b–5.   Since a churning claim is more analogous to one under common law fraud than to a statutory cause of action under the state blue sky laws, it was formerly held by some courts that the statute of limitation applicable to common law fraud is the appropriate guide in churning actions under 10b–5.[12]   However, under present law, a churning claim under Rule 10b–5 must be brought within one year of the discovery of the improper conduct but in no event more than three years after the transactions in question, although a different limitations period will apply if the dispute is resolved through arbitration.[13]

Additionally, facts amounting to churning will generally be sufficient to state a companion claim under common law fraud.[14]   As is the case with any fraud related claim, elements of the churning claim must be pleaded with sufficient specificity.[15]   There is authority to the effect that

---

8.   Mihara v. Dean Witter & Co., Inc., 619 F.2d 814, 822–23 (9th Cir.1980); Hecht v. Harris, Upham & Co., 430 F.2d 1202, 1208 (9th Cir.1970).   *See* Frota v. Prudential–Bache Securities, Inc., 1987 WL 4925, [1987 Transfer Binder] Fed.Sec.L.Rep. (CCH) ¶ 93,253 (S.D.N.Y.1987) (waiver is a question of fact).   *But cf.* Klock v. Lehman Brothers Kuhn Loeb, Inc., 584 F.Supp. 210 (S.D.N.Y.1984); Lang v. Paine, Webber, Jackson & Curtis, Inc., 582 F.Supp. 1421 (S.D.N.Y.1984) (both holding churning claims time barred under the applicable statute of limitations).   The statute of limitations defense is discussed in § 13.8 infra.

9.   430 F.2d at 1208.

10.   Mihara v. Dean Witter & Co., Inc., 619 F.2d 814, 821 (9th Cir.1980).

11.   Laird v. Integrated Resources, Inc., 897 F.2d 826 (5th Cir.1990).   RICO is discussed in § 19.3 *infra*

12.   Biggans v. Bache Halsey Stuart Shields, Inc., 638 F.2d 605 (3d Cir.1980); Baker v. Powell, 1985 WL 5828, [1985–86 Transfer Binder] Fed.Sec.L.Rep. (CCH) ¶ 92,407 (D.N.J. 1985).   *But see* Sigvartsen v. Smith Barney Harris Upham & Co., 1985 WL 8033, [1986–87 Transfer Binder] Fed.Sec.L.Rep. (CCH) ¶ 92,972 (M.D.Fla.1985) (applying one year period based on Exchange Act § 29).   *See* chapter 13 *infra*.

13.   *See* Lampf, Pleva, Lipkind, Prupis & Petigrow v. Gilbertson, 501 U.S. 350, 111 S.Ct. 2773, 115 L.Ed.2d 321 (1991), which is discussed in § 13.8 *infra*.   The limitations period for arbitration is discussed in § 10.16 *infra* (Practitioner's Edition only).

14.   Mihara v. Dean Witter & Co., Inc., 619 F.2d 814, 821–22 (9th Cir.1980); Mac'Kie v. Merrill Lynch Pierce Fenner & Smith, Inc., 1990 WL 260540, [1990–1991 Transfer Binder] Fed.Sec.L.Rep. (CCH) ¶ 95,700 (M.D.Fla.1990) (motion to dismiss state law churning claim denied); Vogel v. A.G. Edwards & Sons, Inc., 801 S.W.2d 746 (Mo.App.1990) (federal churning violations give rise to concurrent state law claims for breach of fiduciary duty). *See* Arceneaux v. Merrill Lynch, Pierce, Fenner & Smith, Inc., 767 F.2d 1498 (11th Cir.1985) (upholding punitive damage award in churning case).

15.   Fed.R.Civ.P. 9(b); *see* § 13.8.1 *infra*. (Practitioner's Edition only).

the essence of a churning claim is constructive fraud, and thus it is not necessary to claim misrepresentations or the withholding of material information.[16]

In order to establish churning it generally will be necessary to prove substantial disparity between the turnover in the account in question and the normal trading activity for similar accounts. For example, in one case the plaintiff prevailed by showing that an account which amounted to less than one tenth of one percent of the local office's portfolio value generated 4.7 percent of its commission income.[17] Although the damaging turn-over rate must necessarily be decided on a case by case basis, it appears that a given account's annual turn-over rate in excess of six times is considered generally to reflect excessive trading.[18] In addition, a court will review the patterns of trading—for example, sales soon after or at the same time as purchases (or purchases soon after sales) of the same security, one account buying a particular security just as another sells—as well as looking at the commissions and profits of the broker with regard to the transactions under scrutiny. In such a case, where one or more of these factors are present, the burden would presumably shift to the broker to justify this activity. As noted earlier, an important element of any churning claim is establishing that the defendant had control of the account and the power to trade.[19]

Churning involves a showing of a fraudulent plan of excessive trading; merely showing that the broker entered into unauthorized transactions, although stating a claim for breach of contract or breach of

---

16. Heller v. L.F. Rothschild, Unterberg, Towbin, 631 F.Supp. 1422 (S.D.N.Y.1986); Roche v. E.F. Hutton & Co., 603 F.Supp. 1411 (M.D.Pa.1984).

17. Hecht v. Harris, Upham & Co., 430 F.2d 1202 (9th Cir.1970). *See also* Adams v. Swanson, 652 F.Supp. 762 (D.Or.1985) (120 trades on 150 trading days, inadequate notice to customer); Winslow & Anderson *supra* footnote 2.

18. *See* Mihara v. Dean Witter & Co., Inc., 619 F.2d 814, 821 (9th Cir.1980); Gopez v. Shin, 736 F.Supp. 51 (D.Del.1990) (churning sufficiently pleaded based on alleged turnover-rate of 4 in three accounts over a two-year period); Cruse v. Equitable Securities of New York, 678 F.Supp. 1023 (S.D.N.Y.1987) (turnover ratio of 16; also upholding RICO claim against broker); Rolf v. Blyth Eastman, Dillon & Co., 424 F.Supp. 1021, 1039 (S.D.N.Y. 1977), *affirmed* 570 F.2d 38 (2d Cir.1978), *cert. denied* 439 U.S. 1039, 99 S.Ct. 642, 58 L.Ed.2d 698 (1978); Note, Churning by Securities Dealers, 80 Harv.L.Rev. 869 (1967). *See also* Mauriber v. Shearson/American Exp., Inc., 567 F.Supp. 1231 (S.D.N.Y.1983) (Failure to state turnover ratio is not fatal to plaintiff's claim). *Cf.* Griswold v. E.F. Hutton & Co., 622 F.Supp. 1397 (N.D.Ill.1985) (upholding churning claim where over two month period, commissions accounted for almost half of the account's original $400,000 balance; the court also indicated that a higher rate of turnover will be tolerated in commodities accounts because of the volatile nature of the investment).

19. *E.g.,* Costello v. Oppenheimer & Co., 711 F.2d 1361 (7th Cir.1983) (power of attorney is sufficient evidence of control). *Compare, e.g.,* Williamsport Firemen Pension Boards v. E.F. Hutton & Co., 567 F.Supp. 140 (M.D.Pa.1983) (plaintiffs failed to establish relinquishment of control to defendant brokers). *See* Frota v. Prudential–Bache Securities, Inc., 639 F.Supp. 1186 (S.D.N.Y.1986) (failure to prove control); M & B Contracting Corp. v. Dale, 601 F.Supp. 1106 (E.D.Mich.1984), *affirmed* 795 F.2d 531 (6th Cir.1986) (insufficient proof of control). *Cf.* Smith v. Petrou, 705 F.Supp. 183 (S.D.N.Y.1989) (summary judgment denied due to factual issues relating to control of account). *See also* footnote 5 *supra.*

fiduciary duty, does not establish churning.[20] Also, on appropriate facts, a showing that a large amount of trading was consistent with the customer's investment objectives can refute a claim of churning.[21]

One problem that frequently arises in the churning context is the extent to which the culpable broker-dealer's employer will be held accountable for a registered representative's churning activities.[22] Liability of the employer may be asserted under either a variation of the common law doctrine of *respondeat superior*[23] or the Exchange Act's provision in section 20(a) for liability of controlling persons.[24] Some courts have indicated that the statutory provision impliedly abrogates the common law of vicarious liability.[25] But most courts have not followed this view.[26] The Supreme Court's recent denial of aiding and abetting liability[27] brings into question the continued viability of respondeat superior.[28]

Another question is whether churning claims can only be brought against broker-dealers. There is authority supporting the position that fiduciaries of custodial accounts may also be held accountable for churning.[29]

The appropriate measure of damages is not always easy to identify in a churning case. The general rule appears to be that the defendant is liable only for the losses due to the excessive commissions plus accrued interest.[30] However, some courts have assessed the measure of damages

20. Pross v. Baird Patrick & Co., 585 F.Supp. 1456 (S.D.N.Y.1984). *See also* Loper v. Advest, Inc., 617 F.Supp. 652 (W.D.Pa.1985) (wrongful liquidation of margin account without allegations of misrepresentations failed to state a claim).

21. Cummings v. A.G. Edwards & Sons, Inc., 733 F.Supp. 1029 (M.D.La.1990); Trustman v. Merrill Lynch, Pierce, Fenner & Smith, Inc., 1985 WL 28, [1984–85 Transfer Binder] Fed.Sec.L.Rep. (CCH) ¶ 91,936 (C.D.Cal.1985).

22. *See* Campbell v. Moseley, Hallgarten, Estabrook & Weeden, Inc., 1985 WL 1799, [1984–85 Transfer Binder] Fed.Sec.L.Rep. (CCH) ¶ 92,082 (N.D.Ill.1985); Plunkett v. Dominick & Dominick, 414 F.Supp. 885 (D.Conn.1976).

23. *Ibid. See also, e.g.,* Gupta v. Ilardi, 1991 WL 12427, [1990–1991 Transfer Binder] Fed.Sec.L.Rep. (CCH) ¶ 95,833 (S.D.N.Y.1991) (brokerage firms may be liable for employees' churning under doctrine of respondeat superior). *But see* Altschul v. Paine Webber, Jackson & Curtis, 518 F.Supp. 591 (S.D.N.Y.1981).

24. 15 U.S.C.A. § 78t(a). *See, e.g.,* Ruiz v. Charles Schwab & Co., 736 F.Supp. 461 (S.D.N.Y.1990) (questions of fact existed as to whether brokerage firm was liable as a controlling person or as an aider and abettor of alleged churning violations). *See* §§ 7.7–7.8 *supra* and §§ 13.15, 13.16 *infra*.

25. See §§ 10.14, 13.15 infra. See *also* Edward Brodsky, Measuring Damages in Churning and Suitability Cases, 6 Sec.Reg.L.J. 157 (1978).

26. *See* §§ 10.14, 13.15.

27. Central Bank of Denver v. First Interstate Bank of Denver, ___ U.S. ___, 114 S.Ct. 1439, 128 L.Ed.2d 119 (1994).

28. The Court denied aiding and abetting liability in light of the absence of express statutory authority. *Id. See* § 13.16 *infra*. There is no statutory provision for respondeat superior and it thus can be argued that the same result would follow. In contrast, there is statutory authority for controlling person liability. Section 20 of the 1934 Act, 15 U.S.C.A. § 78t. *See* § 7.7 *supra* and § 13.15 *infra*.

29. *See* Armstrong v. McAlpin, 699 F.2d 79 (2d Cir.1983).

30. Hecht v. Harris, Upham & Co., 430 F.2d 1202 (9th Cir.1970); Sebbag v. Shearson Lehman Brothers, Inc., 1991 WL 12431, [1990–1991 Transfer Binder] Fed.Sec.L.Rep.

as the excess of the average decline in market values over the decline in value of the plaintiff's portfolio.[31] On the other hand, it has been held by other courts that a plaintiff may also recover additional consequential losses due to changed investment strategy decisions occurring during the churning activity.[32] Since churning does not necessarily result in less prudent investments, it quite properly has been suggested that the better view would be to award damages for diminution in investment value only in situations where the broker-dealer has also violated the suitability requirements.[33] Since the evil involved is the generation of excessive commissions, the fact that the customer's account increased in value does not preclude a churning claim.[34] Punitive damages may be awarded on state law claims under the doctrine of pendent jurisdiction, currently known as supplemental jurisdiction.[35]

When analyzing the private remedy for churning, it must be remembered that additional judicial developments are likely to be slow to arrive. Most disputes between brokers and their customers are subject to arbitration. Arbitration awards, generally do not contain long discussions of the law. Furthermore, there is a relatively narrow basis for judicial review. Much of the law relating to churning, as is the case with other broker-dealer obligations, will be found primarily in the older decisions arising out of customer litigation, the relatively few customer suits that may still be litigated in court, plus the SEC administrative decisions (and any subsequent judicial review) arising out of broker-dealer regulation.

(CCH) ¶ 95,775 (S.D.N.Y.1991) (upholding arbitration award denying the change in portfolio value but awarding damages based on commissions and interest attributable to churning); Zaretsky v. E.F. Hutton & Co., Inc., 509 F.Supp. 68 (S.D.N.Y.1981). *See also* the authorities in footnote 33 *infra*.

31. *E.g.* Miley v. Oppenheimer & Co., 637 F.2d 318 (5th Cir.1981). *See also, e.g.,* Winer v. Patterson, 644 F.Supp. 898 (D.N.H.1986), *vacated in part on other grounds* 663 F.Supp. 723 (D.N.H.1987); Rolf v. Blyth, Eastman Dillon & Co., 424 F.Supp. 1021, 1039 (S.D.N.Y. 1977), *affirmed in part on other grounds* 570 F.2d 38 (2d Cir.1978).

32. *See* Miley v. Oppenheimer & Co., 637 F.2d 318 (5th Cir.1981); Fey v. Walston & Co., Inc., 493 F.2d 1036, 1044–54 (7th Cir.1974); Police Retirement System of St. Louis v. Midwest Investment Advisory Services, Inc., 706 F.Supp. 708 (E.D.Mo.1989). *Cf.* McGinn v. Merrill Lynch, Pierce, Fenner & Smith, Inc., 736 F.2d 1254 (8th Cir.1984) (churning of commodity futures).

33. Nesbit v. McNeil, 896 F.2d 380, 385 (9th Cir.1990); Miley v. Oppenheimer & Co., 637 F.2d 318, 326 (5th Cir.1981). *See* Richard W. Jennings & Harold Marsh, Jr., Securities Regulation, Cases and Materials 569–70 (5th ed.1982). *See also, e.g.,* Edward Brodsky, *supra* footnote 25. The suitability requirements and the limited availability of a private remedy for violation thereof are discussed in § 10.7 *supra*.

34. Davis v. Merrill Lynch, Pierce, Fenner & Smith, Inc., 906 F.2d 1206 (8th Cir.1990); Nesbit v. McNeil, 896 F.2d 380 (9th Cir.1990).

35. Arceneaux v. Merrill Lynch, Pierce, Fenner & Smith, Inc., 767 F.2d 1498 (11th Cir.1985); Mihara v. Dean Witter & Co., 619 F.2d 814 (9th Cir.1980). *See also* Levin v. Shearson Lehman/American Express, Inc., 1985 WL 1683, [1984–85 Transfer Binder] Fed.Sec.L.Rep. (CCH) ¶ 92,080 (S.D.N.Y.1985) (claim for punitive damages dismissed for failure to show the requisite level of gross conduct). The Supreme Court has upheld the award of punitive damages under state law in connection with a securities arbitration. Mastrobuono v. Shearson Lehman Hutton, Inc., ___ U.S. ___, 115 S.Ct. 1212, 131 L.Ed.2d 76 (1995). *See also* 28 U.S.C.A. § 1367.

§ 10.10.1   Unauthorized Trading

An unauthorized trade is simply the purchase or sale of stock by a broker on behalf of a customer who has not authorized the transaction. Unauthorized trading differs from churning in that under a churning claim, the plaintiff will attempt to show that excessive trading has occurred on his account simply to generate brokerage fees or commissions.[1] The plaintiff in the churning situation need not argue that the trading was per se unauthorized. Usually, the customer authorizes trading on his or her account; the evil in churning cases is the broker's excessive trading in order to generate commissions.

Unlike section 4b of the Commodity Exchange Act,[2] the 1933 and 1934 securities Acts do not specifically prohibit unauthorized trading by broker-dealers. Courts have varied in their treatment of claims under the securities laws for unauthorized trading. For example, it has been held that unauthorized trading is not per se a violation of rule 10b–5.[3] Unauthorized trading can be a violation of 10b–5, but the plaintiff must show that the defendant-broker had an intent to deceive or defraud the plaintiff. Thus, "an unauthorized trade does not violate the antifraud provisions of the Securities Exchange Act unless it is accompanied by an intent to defraud or a willful and reckless disregard of the client's best interests."[4] For example, it has been held that a claim for unauthorized trading exists where a broker had carried out transactions with the knowledge that the plaintiff had not authorized these transactions and

---

§ 10.10.1

1. The elements of a plaintiff's cause of action for churning are (1) that excessive trading has occurred; (2) the stocks were purchased or sold to generate commissions and not with the customer's best interests in mind; and (3) that the plaintiff relied on his or her broker to make sound investment decisions on his or her behalf. Marshak v. Blyth, Eastman, Dillon & Co., Inc., 413 F.Supp. 377, 379 (N.D.Okl.1975); Mark C. Jensen, Abuse of Discretion Under Rule 10b–5: Churning, Unsuitability and Unauthorized Transactions, 18 Sec.Reg.L.J. 374 (1991).

2. 7 U.S.C.A. § 6b. See Philip M. Johnson & Thomas L. Hazen, Commodities Regulation § 5.46 (2d ed. 1989).

3. Arioli v. Prudential–Bache Securities, Inc., 792 F.Supp. 1050, 1062 (E.D.Mich.1992); Baker v. Wheat First Securities, 643 F.Supp. 1420, 1432 (S.D.W.Va.1986). *See also* Brophy v. Redivo, 725 F.2d 1218, 1220–21 (9th Cir.1984) (unauthorized trading, in the absence of an allegation of scienter, is not a violation of section 10(b); the plaintiff cannot prove scienter by simply showing that the defendant acted intentionally).

4. Messer v. E.F. Hutton & Co., 833 F.2d 909, 917 (11th Cir.1987), *opinion amended on rehearing in part* 847 F.2d 673 (11th Cir.1988). The plaintiff in *Messer* failed to prove that the brokerage firm had disregarded his best interests or acted with scienter when it assumed a short position in T-bond futures to offset the plaintiff's long position. *Id.* A long position in T-bond futures permits the holder to purchase T-bonds at a set price on a set date. If the price increases before the future expires, the holder of the futures contract will make a profit by buying the T-bonds at the set price and selling them at the higher prevailing price. A short position is just the opposite. The holder of a short position has the right to sell T-bonds at a set price on a set date. If the market price of T-bonds drops, the plaintiff will buy the T-bonds on the open market at the lower price and then sell them at the higher price set by the futures contract. In *Messer*, the court also found that the trading account was not an investment contract and thus was not covered by the securities laws. *See also, e.g.,* Village of Arlington Heights Police Pension Fund v. Poder, 700 F.Supp. 405 (N.D.Ill.1988) (refusing to dismiss rule 10b–5 claim charging defendant broker with knowingly engaging in unauthorized trading).

where the broker had subsequently concealed the trades.[5] The Federal Court of Appeals for the District of Columbia Circuit has held that brokers breached their fiduciary duty under state law when they failed to inform their customers of the right to disavow unauthorized options transactions.[6] As is the case with any fraud claim the elements of an unauthorized trading claim must be pleaded with particularity.[7]

Even in those cases where the unauthorized trading alone is not actionable under the federal securities laws, such conduct does form the basis of a claim for breach of contract or breach of fiduciary duty.[8] Similarly, an unauthorized sale of the plaintiff's stock has been held actionable under the common law theory of conversion, but was held not actionable under the federal securities laws[9] because the defendant's actions did not pertain to the securities themselves.[10]

Even if unauthorized trading is recognized as presenting a viable cause of action, the plaintiff may, nevertheless, be estopped from making the claim if he or she waits too long before bringing the claim.[11] A court may also find a plaintiff to be estopped from bringing an unauthorized trading claim if he or she has had repeated contact with the broker and has failed to object to the transactions made by the broker on his or her account even though the transaction was entered into without prior

---

5. Donato v. Merrill Lynch, Pierce, Fenner & Smith, 663 F.Supp. 669 (N.D.Ill.1987). The defendant in *Donato* tried to argue that the plaintiff's claim was defective because he had failed to specify in detail the unauthorized trades, which numbered over one hundred. *Id.* However, the court found that such specificity, while necessary for a churning claim, was not necessary for a viable claim for unauthorized trading. *Id.*

6. Merrill Lynch, Pierce, Fenner & Smith, Inc. v. Cheng, 901 F.2d 1124 (D.C.Cir.1990).

7. *See* Franks v. Cavanaugh, 711 F.Supp. 1186 (S.D.N.Y.1989), *opinion modified* 1989 WL 58085 (S.D.N.Y.1989) (insufficient particularity). Cruse v. Equitable Securities of N.Y., Inc., 678 F.Supp. 1023 (S.D.N.Y.1987) (dismissing the plaintiff's unauthorized trading claim because the plaintiff failed to plead fraud with sufficient particularity). *Compare* Gupta v. Ilardi, 1991 WL 12427, [1990–1991 Transfer Binder] Fed.Sec.L.Rep. (CCH) ¶ 95,833 (S.D.N.Y.1991) (sufficiently stating unauthorized trading claim);

8. Baum v. Phillips, Appel & Walden, Inc., 648 F.Supp. 1518 (S.D.N.Y.1986); Pross v. Baird Patrick & Co., Inc., 585 F.Supp. 1456, 1460 (S.D.N.Y.1984) (holding that unauthorized trades alone do not violate 10b–5, but may be basis for breach of fiduciary duty or breach of contract). *See* Lincoln Commodity Services v. Meade, 558 F.2d 469, 474 (8th Cir.1977) for a discussion of a claim for breach of fiduciary duty for unauthorized trading on a commodities trading account.

9. Specifically, section 10(b), 15 U.S.C.A. § 78j(b).

10. Bochicchio v. Smith Barney, Harris Upham & Co., 647 F.Supp. 1426, 1429 (S.D.N.Y.1986).

11. In Ocrant v. Dean Witter & Co., 502 F.2d 854, 857 (10th Cir.1974), the plaintiff regularly received confirmation slips from her broker, but disregarded them because her husband assumed responsibility for the account. When objectionable trades were made on the account, the plaintiff waited nine months before objecting to the trades that were made. *Id.* The court, finding that the delay was too long, estopped the plaintiff from bringing the unauthorized trading claim. *Id.* at 859.

The Second Circuit has held that a customer who did not object to the trades within ten days of receiving written notice of the disputed trades, as required by the customer agreement, was precluded from bringing an unauthorized trading claim. Modern Settings, Inc. v. Prudential–Bache Securities, Inc., 936 F.2d 640 (1991), *on remand* 1992 WL 27154 (S.D.N.Y.1992). *Cf.* First City Securities, Inc. v. Shaltiel, 44 F.3d 529 (7th Cir.1995) (investor who after reading monthly statements failed to protest alleged unauthorized trades was deemed to have accepted those trades; decided under Illinois law).

authorization.[12] Failure to make a timely objection to allegedly unauthorized trades may thus operate as a ratification.[13]

As pointed out in the preceding section,[14] a plaintiff in a churning case must establish that the broker had discretionary authority (or, at least, had de facto control of the account). In contrast, the plaintiff may have difficulty proving that certain trades were unauthorized if he or she has a discretionary account. A discretionary account typically permits a broker to make trades on behalf of a client. In order to prove that trades were unauthorized, the plaintiff must prove that certain restrictions were placed on trading.[15] Even if the plaintiff's account is not discretionary, if the plaintiff gives his broker authority to buy or sell stock in his or her absence, the court may find that trades made by the broker, in absence of an allegation of scienter, are not actionable as unauthorized trades.[16]

§ 10.11   The Margin Rules and Extension of Credit for Securities Transactions

Not all securities are purchased in a straight cash transaction. A large number of securities transactions, especially those by speculative investors, are entered into by the broker extending credit to the purchaser while the lender holds the purchased securities as collateral. Securities purchases on credit are referred to as margin transactions.[1] A

---

12. Marshak v. Blyth, Eastman, Dillon & Co., Inc., 413 F.Supp. 377, 383 (N.D.Okl. 1975) and Brophy v. Redivo, 725 F.2d 1218, 1221 (9th Cir.1984) (although plaintiff had knowledge of the unauthorized trades, she continued to deal with her broker and did not complain about the trades until six months later). *Compare* Davis v. Merrill Lynch, Pierce, Fenner & Smith, Inc., 906 F.2d 1206 (8th Cir.1990) (even though customer received monthly statements, there was no ratification of alleged unauthorized trading since customer's apparent assent was not given voluntarily, intelligently, and with full knowledge of the facts); Merrill Lynch, Pierce, Fenner & Smith, Inc. v. Cheng, 901 F.2d 1124 (D.C.Cir.1990) (no ratification where customers were never informed of their rights to disavow unauthorized trades; decided under state law).

13. *See, e.g.,* In re Drexel Burnham Lambert Group, 157 B.R. 539 (S.D.N.Y.1993).

14. *See* § 10.10 *supra.*

15. *See* Frota v. Prudential–Bache Securities, Inc., 639 F.Supp. 1186 (S.D.N.Y.1986) (plaintiff brought suit under 10b–5 for unauthorized and excessive trades; the court held that the plaintiff's claim was essentially for churning—unauthorized excessive trades).

16. Brophy v. Redivo, 725 F.2d 1218, 1221 (9th Cir.1984).

§ 10.11

1. *See generally* Jerry W. Markham & Thomas Lee Hazen, Broker–Dealer Operations Under Securities and Commodities Law: Financial Responsibilities, Credit Regulation, and Customer Protection, ch. 3 (1995). Nicholas Wolfson, Richard M. Philips & Thomas A. Russo, Regulation of Brokers, Dealers and Securities Markets (1977); Roberta S. Karmel, The Investment Banker and the Credit Regulations: The Margin Requirements, 45 N.Y.U.L.Rev. 59 (1970); Paul L. Kelly & John M. Webb, Credit and Securities, 24 Bus.Law. 1153 (1969); Martin Lipton, Some Recent Innovations to Avoid the Margin Regulations, 46 N.Y.U.L.Rev. 1 (1971); Frederic Solomon & Janet Hart, Recent Developments in Regulation of Securities Credit, 20 J.Pub.L. 167 (1971); Note, Credit Regulation in the Securities Market: An Analysis of the Regulation, 62 Nw.U.L.Rev. 587 (1967). *See also, e.g.,* Jerry W. Markham, Federal Regulation of Margin in the Commodity Futures Industry—History and Theory, 64 Temple L.Rev. 59 (1991); Note, Margin Regulations: The Stock Market Crash of 1987, 20 Rutg.L.J. 693 (1989); Symposium, Impact of Federal Reserve Margin Regulations on Acquisition Financing, 35 Bus.Law. 517 (1980).

margin purchase gives the security holder leverage and thus while significantly increasing the risk of investment also increases the potential gain. Section 7 of the Exchange Act sets out a complex system of regulation with regard to the extension of credit for securities transactions, but does not apply to exempt securities.[2] By virtue of section 7(a),[3] the Federal Reserve System Board of Governors is delegated the authority to promulgate rules governing the extension of credit where securities are used as collateral to secure the loan. Various regulations have been adopted with regard to broker-dealers, banks, and other persons so extending credit. Broker-dealer margin rule enforcement lies with the SEC through injunctions, criminal proceedings, revocation of registration or suspension from membership in self regulatory organizations.

The credit extension rules are not limited to traditional margin accounts. As discussed more fully below, the credit extension rules also apply to late payments in cash accounts.[4] On occasion, questions can arise as to what transactions constitute an extension of credit.[5] Thus, for example, it has been held that an agreement to purchase a GNMA forward contract combined with a ten percent down payment was an executory contract of sale and not a credit transaction under the securities laws.[6]

Under the statute, the initial extension of credit may not be for an amount greater than the higher of (1) fifty-five percent of the security's then current market price or (2) one hundred percent of the lowest market price of the security during the preceding thirty-six calendar months but no more than seventy-five percent of the current market price. Certain exempt governmental securities trade with a much higher margin. For example, United States Treasury bills can have up to a ninety percent margin at the time of purchase.[7] This more highly leveraged transaction for federal government notes is more in line with

---

Not all publicly traded securities are marginable. All equity securities traded on a national exchange are marginable. For over-the-counter stocks only qualified securities may be margined. For a list of over-the-counter margin stocks which is established by the Federal Reserve Board, *see* 2 Fed.Sec.L.Rep. (CCH) ¶ 22,256. Also, any debt security convertible into a margin stock is marginable. For more detailed description of the margin eligibility requirements, the applicable Federal Reserve Board regulation should be consulted. *See* footnotes 11–20 *infra* and accompanying text.

2. 15 U.S.C.A. § 78g. Exempt securities under the 1934 Act parallel many of the 1933 Act exemptions. *See* 15 U.S.C.A. § 77c; chapter 4 *supra.* 1934 Act registration and reporting requirements are discussed in §§ 9.2–9.3 *supra.*

3. 15 U.S.C.A. § 78g(a).

4. *See* text accompanying footnote 26 *infra.* The settlement period for most securities has been shortened from five to three business days.

5. *See, e.g.,* Winoma Memorial Hospital, [1986–87 Transfer Binder] Fed.Sec.L.Rep. (CCH) ¶ 78,333 (SEC No Action Letter Oct. 4, 1985) (underwriter involved in limited partnership offering where purchasers required third-party financing was not involved in a credit transaction provided the underwriter neither refers investors to lending institutions nor provides aid to the lenders in going over the prospectus).

6. Abeles v. Oppenheimer & Co., 834 F.2d 123 (7th Cir.1987).

7. Section 7 of the Act does not apply to exempted securities. 15 U.S.C.A. § 78g(a).

the margin requirements for the more speculative commodity markets.[8] Notwithstanding the statutory fifty-five percent ceiling on credit, the Federal Reserve Board has imposed an even lower credit ceiling of fifty percent.[9]

The statutory (and Federal Reserve Board) limits on margin accounts apply only to the *initial* extension of credit and do not deal with an increase in the ratio of the debit of the margin account in relation to the value of the securities due to the decline in the price of securities used as collateral after their initial purchase. In other words, under both SEC and Federal Reserve Board regulation it lies purely within the lender's discretion to decide at what point additional securities as collateral or cash will be needed to fortify a margin account where the value of the current collateral is declining.[10] However, the exchanges and the NASD impose margin maintenance requirements. Under these margin maintenance rules, the current market value of the collateral must be at least twenty-five percent of the account's total value.[11] Thus, there are minimum margin maintenance requirements for all accounts.

The applicable rules of the Federal Reserve Board for broker-dealers' extension of credit are found in Regulation T.[12] Regulation U

---

8. One way to achieve comparable leverage in the securities markets is to trade listed "put" and "call" options. *See* SEC Report of the Special Study of the Options Markets, 96th Cong., 1st Sess. (1978).

9. *See, e.g.,* Supplement to Regulation T, 12 C.F.R. § 220.18.

10. *See* text accompanying footnotes 24–25 *infra.*

11. The New York Stock Exchange imposes the following requirements:

Maintenance margin rule

(b) The margin which must be maintained in margin accounts of customers, whether members, allied members, member organizations or non-members, shall be as follows:

(1) 25% of the market value of all securities "long" in the account; plus

(2) $2.50 per share or 100% of the market value, in cash, whichever amount is greater, of each stock "short" in the account selling at less than $5.00 per share; plus

(3) $5.00 per share or 30% of the market value, in cash, whichever amount is greater, of each stock "short" in the account selling at $5.00 per share or above; plus

(4) 5% of the principal amount or 30% of the market value, in cash, whichever amount is greater, of each bond "short" in the account.

New York Stock Exchange Rule 431(b). *Accord* American Stock Exchange Rule 462(b); NASD Rules of Fair Practice. Art. III, sec. 30, App. A, sec. 4.

These margin maintenance requirements are subject to certain exceptions. For example, United States government obligations have a five percent minimum maintenance requirement. New York Stock Exchange Rule 431(c)(2); American Stock Exchange Rule 462(c)(2)(A); NASD Rules of Fair Practice Art. III, sec. 30, App. A, sec. 4(a)(n). Put and call options are valued on a different basis than equity and debt securities. *See* New York Stock Exchange Rule 431(d)(2); American Stock Exchange Rule 462(c)(2)(a); NASD Rules of Fair Practice Art. III, sec. 30, App. A, sec. 7.

12. 12 C.F.R. §§ 220.1–220.131. *See* Report of the Special Study of Securities Markets, H.Doc. No. 95, 88th Cong., 1st Sess., Pt. 4 at 15–15 (1963). Regulation T was revised in 1983 in order to deal with some of the new investment instruments that have entered the market place. These revisions relate to foreign currency options and stock index options that are traded on a securities exchange.

In 1985 the Federal Reserve Board proposed amendments to Regulation T that would make the margin requirements for option writing the same as with equity securities. [1984–85 Transfer Binder] Banking L.Rep. (CCH) ¶ 86,291 (Fed.Res.Bd. June 21, 1985).

governs bank loans that are secured directly or indirectly by stock or other marginable securities.[13] Regulation G[14] applies similar limitations to persons other than broker-dealers and banks who are in the business of making loans using securities as collateral. In a controversial interpretation, the Federal Reserve Board issued a rule stating that the margin requirements of Regulation G apply to the issuance of certain low grade or "junk" bonds.[15] The theory of the new rule is that since junk bonds are used to finance the purchase of stock (generally in connection with a corporate acquisition), the bonds are in essence the extension of credit to purchase stock, and thus fall within the initial collateral requirements of Regulation G. The new rule does not eliminate junk bonds but merely requires a minimum cash or asset base by the issuer. In contrast to the Federal Reserve Board, the SEC staff has concluded that junk bonds are a relatively small factor in corporate takeovers and that regulatory intervention is not warranted.[16]

Regulation X applies to margin borrowing by residents of the United States of either domestic or foreign lenders.[17] Regulation X in addition to applying to foreign lenders focuses on the borrower; the rules prohibit borrowers from entering into transactions that would violate Regulations G, T, or U. When customers engage in "free riding" by purchasing a security with an intent not to pay the purchase price except from the profits of a matching trade, they are in violation of the margin requirements.[18] The discussion that follows provides a brief overview of the

In 1990, the Federal Reserve Board eased the restrictions on extending credit for purchase of foreign securities. *See* 22 Sec.Reg. & L.Rep. (BNA) 421 (March 23, 1990).

Also, the SEC has adopted Rule 3a12–9 that exempts from the margin regulation public offerings that provide for mandatory payment on an installment basis. Exch.Act Rel. No. 34–22979, [1985–86 Transfer Binder] Fed.Sec.L.Rep. (CCH) ¶ 83,969 (March 7, 1986).

13. 12 C.F.R. §§ 221.1–221.124. *See, e.g.,* George F. McEvoy, Bank Loans and Regulation U, 84 Banking L.J. 668 (1967).

14. 12 C.F.R. §§ 207.1 *et seq.*

15. 12 C.F.R. § 207 *et seq. See* 51 Fed.Reg. 1771 (1986). *See also, e.g.,* Fed. Ruling Had Slight Effect on Use of Junk Bonds in Takeovers, Study Finds, 19 Sec.Reg. & L.Rep. (BNA) 166 (Jan. 1, 1987); Roberta S. Karmel, Applying Margin Rules to Junk Bonds, N.Y.L.J. 1 (Feb. 20, 1986). It has been estimated a relatively small portion of junk bonds were issued in conjunction with hostile takeovers; thus, between 1980 and 1986, less than 3% of junk bonds could be linked to hostile takeovers. Glenn Yago, Junk Bonds: How High Yield Securities Restructured Corporate America 26 (1991).

16. Noninvestment Grade Debt as a Source of Tender Offer Financing [1986 Transfer Binder] Fed.Sec.L.Rep. (CCH) ¶ 84,011 (SEC Office of Chief Economist June 20, 1986).

17. 12 C.F.R. §§ 224.1–224.3. *See* Note, Regulation X: A Complexis, 50 Notre Dame Law. 136 (1974); Note, Regulation X and Investor–Lender Margin Violation Disputes, 57 Minn.L.Rev. 208 (1972).

18. SEC v. Ronald Margolin, Brown & Mueller Investments, Ltd., 1992 WL 279735 (S.D.N.Y.1992) (imposing asset freeze against defendants who allegedly entered into transactions planning to use proceeds from matching trades to pay purchase price; there were thus no funds available to pay for losses on the trades). Free riding is discussed in § 6.2 *supra.*

See also, e.g., SEC v. Militano, 1994 WL 285472, [1994–1995 Transfer Binder] Fed. Sec. L. Rep. (CCH) ¶ 98,330 (S.D.N.Y.1994) (SEC entitled to summary judgment to the effect that customer willfully violated Regulation T's initial deposit requirement; also holding that disgorgement of profits was an appropriate remedy).

rules applicable to broker-dealers.[19]

In order to qualify for an extension of credit under Regulation T, the securities must either be traded on a national securities exchange[20] or be actively traded in the over-the-counter market and on the list of margin equity securities established by the Federal Reserve Board.[21] The Federal Reserve Board now provides for the automatic marginability of over-the-counter stocks that are part of the NASD's National Market System.[22] Additionally, foreign sovereign debt securities are marginable to the extent of their "good faith" loan value. The current level of the margin securities cannot exceed a fifty percent debit balance in connection with the purchase of any additional securities.[23] The Federal Reserve Board is statutorily empowered to impose minimum levels for maintaining margin accounts under section 7(a) as well as initial levels but it has never exercised this authority. Accordingly, a "margin call" whereby the customer is required to come up with additional collateral lest the margined securities be sold, will never be required by operation of law unless a new security is purchased for the account. This is thus left to the broker-dealer's discretion[24] and the twenty-five percent minimum required by exchange rules and by the NASD.[25] Most brokerage firms have established their own policies for margin calls, many of which are more stringent than the NASD and exchange rules. Brokers' guidelines may also depend in part not only upon the value of the collateral but also on the diversification of the margined securities as well as their reliability.

In addition to the credit limitations for margin accounts, the margin rules require that whenever a security is purchased in a cash account, payment must be made within a specified settlement period, which formerly was seven days after the date of purchase or else the broker-dealer must cancel or otherwise liquidate the transaction.[26] In mid 1995,

---

19. For more extensive treatment of the development of the margin rules *see generally* Jerry W. Markham & Thomas L. Hazen, footnote 1 *supra* ch. 3; 2 Louis Loss, Securities Regulation 1239–76 (2d ed. 1962).

20. *See* section 6 of the Act, 15 U.S.C.A. § 78f. *See* § 10.2 *supra.*

21. 15 U.S.C.A. § 78g(c)(2). The list of marginable securities is updated periodically. *See* 2 Fed.Sec.L.Rep. (CCH) ¶ 22,256.

22. *See* Bd. of Governors of the Federal Reserve System Docket No. R–0512 (March 7, 1984).

23. 12 C.F.R. §§ 220.3(c), (d), 220.18(a). Regulation T does not avail itself of the fifty-five percent statutory maximum. Instead, it imposes a lower ceiling of fifty percent. Supplement to Regulation T, 12 C.F.R. § 220.18.

24. *See* Report *supra* footnote 12, pt. 4 at 5–6.

25. *See* footnote 11 *supra. Cf.* Nevitsky v. Manufacturers Hanover Brokerage Services, 654 F.Supp. 116, 119–20 (S.D.N.Y.1987) (dismissing Rule 10b–5 action claiming improper margin call).

26. 12 C.F.R. § 220.8(b)(1), (4). If a customer sells securities within seven days of purchase and without having paid for the securities, for the next ninety days the customer cannot purchase securities unless the account contains enough cash to cover the purchase price. 12 C.F.R. § 220.105.

A broker's delay in liquidating the account will not relieve the customer of the obligation to pay. Shearson Lehman Brothers, Inc. v. M & L Investments, 10 F.3d 1510 (10th

the settlement period for most securities was shortened to three business days. The settlement date for options remains the business day following the transaction.

At one time, some courts recognized a private remedy in the hands of the customer who is injured by violation of the credit extension rules.[27] However, the overwhelming majority of recent decisions is to the contrary.[28] The absence of an implied remedy under the margin rules is bolstered by the amendment to section 7(f) and ensuing Regulation X rendering the customer himself or herself in violation of the Act.[29] Although the existence of an implied remedy is extremely doubtful and a broker's violation of the margin rules was not an affirmative defense to a customer who was sued under state law for non payment of securities, the margin violation might affect the damage calculus.[30]

An alternative to bringing a securities law claim for margin violations is for the customer to raise the violation as a defense to any claim that the broker might bring for additional funds. The courts have not been terribly receptive to such defenses.[31]

SEC Rule 10b–16[32] requires broker-dealers to adequately disclose the cost to the customer of any securities transaction where credit is extended. An ever-increasing number of courts are recognizing the existence of a private remedy under Rule 10b–16 for misleading margin related

Cir.1993) (broker–dealer's failure to liquidate account after purchaser failed to pay for stock was not a defense to breach of contract action).

27. *E.g.* Pearlstein v. Scudder & German, 429 F.2d 1136 (2d Cir.1970), *cert. denied* 401 U.S. 1013, 91 S.Ct. 1250, 28 L.Ed.2d 550 (1971); Remar v. Clayton Securities Corp., 81 F.Supp. 1014 (D.Mass.1949). *See also* the law review articles cited in footnote 27 *infra.*

28. *E.g.* Useden v. Acker, 947 F.2d 1563 (11th Cir.1991), *cert. denied* __ U.S. __, 113 S.Ct. 2927, 124 L.Ed.2d 678 (1993); Bennett v. United States Trust Co., 770 F.2d 308 (2d Cir.1985), *cert. denied* 474 U.S. 1058, 106 S.Ct. 800, 88 L.Ed.2d 776 (1986); Bassler v. Central National Bank in Chicago, 715 F.2d 308 (7th Cir.1983); Gutter v. Merrill Lynch, Pierce, Fenner & Smith, Inc., 644 F.2d 1194 (6th Cir.1981); Gilman v. FDIC, 660 F.2d 688 (6th Cir.1981).

29. 15 U.S.C.A. § 78g(f). *See, e.g.,* Shearson Lehman Brothers, Inc. v. M & L Investments, 10 F.3d 1510 (10th Cir.1993); Gilman v. FDIC, 660 F.2d 688 (6th Cir.1981); Stern v. Merrill Lynch, Pierce, Fenner & Smith, Inc., 603 F.2d 1073 (4th Cir.1979); Russo v. Bache Halsey Stuart Shields, Inc., 554 F.Supp. 613 (N.D.Ill.1982); Panayotopulas v. Chemical Bank, 464 F.Supp. 199 (S.D.N.Y.1979). *Contra* Palmer v. Thomson, McKinnon & Auchincloss, Inc., 427 F.Supp. 915 (D.Conn.1977). *See, e.g.,* Note, Civil Liability for Margin Violation–The Effect of Section 7(f) and Regulation X, 43 Fordham L.Rev. 93 (1974).

The SEC has used Regulation X as a basis for attacking customer violations of the margin rules. *See* SEC v. Militano, 773 F.Supp. 589 (S.D.N.Y.1991).

30. Shearson Lehman Brothers, Inc. v. M & L Investments, 10 F.3d 1510 (10th Cir.1993), *reversing in relevant part* 776 F.Supp. 1489 (D.Utah 1991), *affirmed in part, reversed in part* 10 F.3d 1510 (10th Cir.1993).

31. *See* Shearson Lehman Brothers, Inc., v. M & L Investments, 10 F.3d 1510 (10th Cir.1993) (broker–dealer's failure to liquidate account after purchaser failed to pay for stock was not a defense to breach of contract action).

32. 17 C.F.R. § 240.10b–16. *See also* 17 C.F.R. § 240.15c2–5. *See* § 12.9 *infra.*

disclosures.[33] One court has held that the Rule 10b–16 action does not require the plaintiff to prove scienter; this is a surprising decision in light of section 10(b)'s deception and scienter requirements.[34] More recently, the decisions seem to be taking the better view that scienter is required in an action under Rule 10b–16.[35] It may be questioned whether the Rule 10b–16 remedy survives in the face of the general decline in federally implied remedies,[36] or whether the 10b–16 remedy will be seen as co-existing with the well-established private right of action under Rule 10b–5.[37] However, the trend of the cases seems clearly to recognize the 10b–16 remedy.[38] Although the terms and risks of margin trading must be adequately disclosed, a sophisticated investor is not entitled to disclosure beyond that which is included in the margin agreement.[39] Furthermore, not every additional risk attendant to a margin account need be disclosed. For example, it is not necessary to disclose that securities purchased on credit involve greater risk and produce less income than unmargined securities.[40]

The SEC oversight of broker-dealers[41] adds to the arsenal of remedies for margin violations. For example, disciplinary sanctions may be imposed as it is a deceptive practice for a broker-dealer to open margin accounts for customers who do not have a full understanding of the transaction.[42] It has also been held that a broker violates Rule 10b–5 when he enters into a transaction knowing that the customer does not have sufficient funds in his or her margin account.[43]

---

33. *E.g.*, Angelastro v. Prudential–Bache Securities, Inc., 764 F.2d 939 (3d Cir.1985), *cert. denied* 474 U.S. 935, 106 S.Ct. 267, 88 L.Ed.2d 274 (1985); Robertson v. Dean Witter, Reynolds, Inc., 749 F.2d 530 (9th Cir.1984).

34. Haynes v. Anderson & Strudwick, Inc., 508 F.Supp. 1303, 1321 (E.D.Va.1981). *See* Aaron v. SEC, 446 U.S. 680, 100 S.Ct. 1945, 64 L.Ed.2d 611 (1980); Ernst & Ernst v. Hochfelder, 425 U.S. 185, 96 S.Ct. 1375, 47 L.Ed.2d 668 (1976); § 13.4 *infra*.

35. *E.g.*, Robertson v. Dean Witter, Reynolds, Inc., 749 F.2d 530 (9th Cir.1984).

36. Angelastro v. Prudential–Bache Securities, Inc., 575 F.Supp. 270 (D.N.J.1983), *order affirmed in part, reversed in part* 764 F.2d 939 (3d Cir.1985) (recognizing a 10b–16 claim while dismissing a rule 10b–5 claim). *See* § 13.1 *infra*.

37. *See* §§ 13.2–13.12 *infra*. *See also, e.g.*, McGeorge v. Van Benschoten, 1988 WL 163063, [1989 Transfer Binder] Fed.Sec.L.Rep. ¶ 94,497 (D.Ariz.1988) (unpublished case) (10b–5 claim upheld on allegations that rather than disclose margin risks, broker merely gave federal truth-in-lending disclosure). *But see* Lichter v. Paine, Webber, Jackson & Curtis, Inc., 570 F.Supp. 533 (N.D.Ill.1983).

38. *See* footnote 33 *supra*.

39. *See* Xaphes v. Merrill Lynch, Pierce, Fenner & Smith, Inc., 632 F.Supp. 471 (D.Me.1986).

40. Bull v. Chandler, 1992 WL 103686, [1991–1992 Transfer Binder] Fed.Sec.L.Rep. (CCH) ¶ 96,567 (N.D.Cal.1992) (the court explained that these facts are "universally known").

41. *See* § 10.2 *supra*.

42. *See, e.g.*, Norris & Hirshberg v. SEC, 177 F.2d 228 (D.C.Cir.1949).

43. Jaksich v. Thomson McKinnon Securities, Inc., 582 F.Supp. 485 (S.D.N.Y.1984). However, the customer's failure to object to the unauthorized purchase after she had been given notice operated as a ratification and thus barred her claim. *Id.*

§ 10.12   Regulation of "Short Sales"

If an investor believes that the price of a security is likely to decline, there are several potential investment strategies. Most such strategies are linked to dealing with put and call options.[1] Another alternative is to enter an order to sell the security at the current price with the understanding that the investor is to fulfill that obligation at a later date by purchasing the security at a lower price. This practice, known as selling short, is extremely risky since every increase in the price causes loss to the investor until he or she covers the short sale.[2] An alternative method is "selling against the box" where securities are borrowed as collateral for delivery for sale at a later date. Because of the speculative nature of and potential for abuse associated with short sales and sales against the box, insiders of publicly traded securities are strictly prohibited from engaging in such transactions.[3] Also, short sales are not meant for the ordinary investor both because of the risk involved and the level of sophistication that should exist before an investor embarks upon such a transaction.

Because of the risky nature of a short sale investment strategy, a broker has a duty to explain the transaction in a manner understandable to the investor.[4]

The SEC, which has regulated short sales since 1938,[5] has adopted rules governing short sales in general. These rules are quite complex and technical and generally operate as follows. Rule 10a–1 applies to short sale transactions with regard to securities on a national securities exchange and requires that a short sale not be entered below the last

---

§ 10.12

1. For example, by purchasing a "put" option, the investor gets the right to put the security to the option seller at the exercise price on or before the expiration date. The hope is that the security can be purchased at a low enough price to offset the premium paid for the right to "put" it (*i.e.*, sell it) to the option writer at the higher price. Options are traded on several of the national securities exchanges under the supervision of the SEC, the applicable exchange and the Options Clearing Corporation. *See* SEC, Report of the Special Study of the Options Market, 96th Cong., 1st Sess. (1979).

Another strategy, of course, is selling the security if it is owned in order to prevent loss resulting from the anticipated price deterioration.

2. SEC Rule 3b–3 defines short sale as:

any sale of a security which the seller does not own or any sale which is consummated by the delivery of a security borrowed by, or for the account of, the seller. * * *

17 C.F.R. § 240.3b–3. *See generally* Ralph S. Janvey, Short Selling, 20 Sec.Reg.L.J. 270 (1992); Short Selling in the Stock Market, House Report No. 102–414 (Dec. 6, 1991). *Cf.* In re Scattered Corp. Securities Litigation, 844 F.Supp. 416 (N.D.Ill.1994) (large volume of short sales was not manipulative; if anything it made the market more efficient by accurately reflecting bearish view of the securities in question).

3. 15 U.S.C.A. § 78p(c). *See* § 12.6 *infra.*

4. Vucinich v. Paine, Webber, Jackson & Curtis, Inc., 803 F.2d 454 (9th Cir.1986). *But cf.* Moelis v. ICH Corp., 1987 WL 9709, [1987 Transfer Binder] Fed.Sec.L.Rep. (CCH) ¶ 93,220 (S.D.N.Y.1987) (investor who sold short had fraud and manipulation claims dismissed since he had not covered his short position and thus was found not to have suffered any actual loss).

5. *See* Sec.Exch.Act Rel. No. 34–1548 (Feb. 8, 1938).

sales price.[6] Furthermore the short sale cannot be at the last sale price "unless such price is above the next preceding different price."[7] The SEC lists a number of transactions that are exempt from the price limitations for short sales on a national exchange that are established under rule 10a–1.[8] In Rule 10a–2 the Commission addresses the covering of short sales.[9] In sum, the rule is designed to assure that a short sale is covered only when the customer has purchased the security or has properly borrowed the security for delivery for sale.

Whereas Rule 10a–1 applies to transactions in securities on a national exchange, until 1994, there was no parallel regulation for over-the-counter securities. In 1994, the SEC approved regulation by the National Association of Securities Dealers which impose a "bid–test" rule for short sale transactions.[10] The NASD rules,[11] which had been pending for two years, prohibit broker–dealers from effecting a short sale for themselves or their customers if the short sale bid is lower than the previous inside bid. The rule goes on to exempt certain transactions from the prohibition on "down bids." In order to comply with the NASD rule when the current inside bid is a "down bid," the short sale must be at a price at least one–sixteenth above that inside bid. The NASD's bid test rule is subject to enumerated exemptions. In addition to paralleling the exemptions from Rule 10a–1,[12] the NASD exempts

6. 17 C.F.R. § 240.10a–1(a)(1)(i)(A). Specifically, the rule prohibits transactions below that previous price (as reported per an effective transaction reporting plan under Rule 11Aa3–1).

For an interpretive release *see* Sec.Exch.Act Rel. No. 34–1571 (Feb. 5, 1938).

7. 17 C.F.R. § 240.10a–1(a)(1)(i)(B). As explained by Professor Loss, "after sales at 49⅞ and 50 an indefinite number of short sales may be effected at 50; but after sales at 49⅞ and 49¾ the minimum price at which a short sale may be effected is 49⅞." Louis Loss, Fundamentals of Securities Regulation 716 (1983).

8. The exemptions include the following transactions: sales for an account in which the seller has an interest, if the seller owns the security and intends to make delivery as soon as possible without undue expense or inconvenience; sales by member firms in which the firm has no interest pursuant to an order to sell that is marked "long;" sales by member firms to offset odd–lot customer orders; sales for a special arbitrage account where the sales correspond to an acquisition of the same amount of the same securities; sales by members to liquidate long positions less than a round lot, sales effected for special international arbitrage accounts; qualifying sales by registered specialists or market makers; sales effected with the exchange's approval that are necessary to equalize the price with that of the national exchange which is the principal exchange market for the security in question; and sales by an underwriter (or member of the underwriting syndicate) in connection with an overallotment of securities. Rule 10a–1(a)(2); 17 C.F.R. § 240.10a–1(a)(2). *See also, e.g.,* Portfolio System for Institutional Trading, 26 Sec. Reg. & L. Rep. (BNA) 1695 (SEC No Action Letter available Dec. 12, 1994) (trading system for institutional investors was granted exempted relief from Rule 10a–1).

9. 17 C.F.R. § 240.10a–2. Naked, or uncovered, short sales are manipulative and in violation of the Act. *See* In re Olympia Brewing Co. Securities Litigation, 613 F.Supp. 1286, 1295 (N.D.Ill.1985) (dismissing claim charging naked short sales for lack of evidence).

10. Exch. Act Rel. No. 34–34277, 59 Fed. Reg. 34,885 (SEC July 7, 1994).

11. The rules are embodied in the NASD Rules of Fair Practice §§ 48–49.

12. 17 C.F.R. § 240.10a–1(a)(2). *See* footnote 8 *supra*.

bona fide market making activity by qualified market makers,[13] hedge transactions by registered qualified options market makers, and hedge transactions by registered warrant market makers resulting in fully hedged positions.

Broker-dealer violations of the short selling rules may result in civil liability.[14] Serious violations have resulted in revocation of the broker-dealer's registration.[15] In 1975 the SEC proposed Rule 10b–21 in order to classify as manipulative or deceptive (and therefore in violation of section 10(b)) certain practices in connection with short sales.[16] For a long time, this rule had not been adopted, presumably on the assumption that sufficient regulation already existed under other rules. However, as discussed below, in 1988 the Commission adopted a version of the rule on a temporary basis.[17] That rule was made permanent in 1994.[18]

Short selling prior to or in connection with a distribution can make it difficult for issuers to complete public offerings. Short sales in anticipation of a public offering do not involve the same market risks as short sales generally.[19] Since the pending offering will bring additional supply into the market, there will be downward price pressure. Such guaranteed downward price pressure is not ordinarily present in the securities markets. Limiting short sales during distributions necessarily has an adverse impact on short sellers. Notwithstanding the arguments to the contrary, the Commission concluded that this is justified in light of the potential for manipulation resulting from short sales in connection with public offerings.[20]

---

13. The market maker exemption thus has two requirements. First, the transactions must involve bona fide market making activity. Second, the market maker must be qualified within the meaning of the NASD rule.

14. *See* Merrill Lynch, Pierce, Fenner & Smith, Inc. v. Bocock, 247 F.Supp. 373 (S.D.Tex.1965) (liability to trust for illegal short sales).

The SEC has given broker dealers no-action relief from the short sale rules for index arbitrage transactions. *See* Merrill Gets SEC Exemption from Short–Sale Rule for Index Arbitrage, Securities Week pp. 1–2 (Dec. 22, 1986). *See also* SEC Mulls Latest No–Action Letter Request Involving Short–Sale Rule, Securities Week pp. 1–2 (Jan. 19, 1987).

15. In the Matter of Pickard & Co., Sec.Exch.Act Rel. No. 34–8447 (Nov. 14, 1968); In the Matter of Sackville–Pickard [1967–1969 Transfer Binder] Fed.Sec.L.Rep. (CCH) ¶ 77,-620 (SEC Oct. 24, 1968); In the Matter of Duval Securities, Inc., [1964–1966 Transfer Binder] Fed.Sec.L.Rep. (CCH) ¶ 77,264 (SEC July 23, 1965). *See also, e.g.,* In the Matter of Financial Investments Corp., Sec.Exch.Act Rel. No. 34–10834 (May 30, 1974).

16. Sec.Exch.Act Rel. No. 34–11328 (April 2, 1975).

17. 17 C.F.R. § 240.10b–21(T), adopted in Sec.Exch.Act Rel. No. 34–26028, [1988–89 Transfer Binder] Fed.Sec.L.Rep. (CCH) ¶ 84,315 (Aug. 25, 1988). *See* § 6.1 *supra* and text accompanying footnotes 22–32 *infra*. *Cf.* Sec.Exch.Act Rel. No. 34–17347 (Nov. 28, 1980).

18. *See* Short Selling in Connection with a Public Offering, Sec.Exch. Act Rel. No. 34–33072, 59 Fed. Reg. 10984, [1993–1994 Transfer Binder] Fed. Sec. L. Rep. (CCH) ¶ 85,321 (SEC March 2, 1994).

19. *See, e.g.,* Sec.Act Rel. No. 33–6798, Sec.Exch.Act Rel. No. 34–26028, [1988–89 Transfer Binder] Fed.Sec.L.Rep. (CCH) ¶ 84,315 (SEC Aug. 25, 1988).

20. *Id.* at p. 89,390 ("The rule is designed to address those situations in which a person covers his short sale by an arrangement or understanding to obtain offering securities from another person who acquired the securities in the primary offering.")

But cf. Sullivan & Long, Inc. v. Scattered Corp., 47 F.3d 857 (7th Cir.1995) wherein the defendant sold short huge amounts of LTV stock in anticipation of a bankruptcy reorgani-

In 1988, the SEC adopted a rule prohibiting certain short sales in connection with a public offering or an offering under Regulation A's[21] exemption for certain offerings of not more than five million dollars.[22] Under rule 10b–21[23], if a short sale is made after the filing of the registration statement or Form 1—A[24] filing, and before the effective date of the Regulation A offering, the short seller cannot cover the short sale with securities offered by an underwriter, broker or dealer participating in the registered or Regulation A offering.[25] Specifically excluded from the rule's prohibitions are securities offered pursuant to a shelf registration in accordance with SEC Rule 415.[26] Additionally, the Commission may, either upon request or its own motion, grant an exemption from Rule 10b–21's prohibitions.[27] Such an exemption from the short sale prohibitions may be granted either unconditionally or pursuant to specified terms and conditions.[28]

In adopting the short sale prohibitions, the Commission was concerned with the prevention of manipulative conduct.[29] As discussed more fully elsewhere,[30] the Supreme Court has at least cast a cloud over the Commission's ability to proscribe conduct which is manipulative but not deceptive.[31] In adopting the rule the Commission identified the primary objective of Rule 10b–21(T) as the prevention of manipulative short selling.[32] There is no mention of the deceptive nature of such conduct.

zation in which new shares were to be issued. The defendant took a tremendous short position; in fact it sold short more stock than in fact existed. The plaintiff had claimed that this was a manipulation as it artificially depressed the value of the stock. The court, per Judge Posner ruled otherwise. He reasoned that rather than manipulation, the defendant's activity should be characterized as arbitrage, which rather than creating an artificial price, eliminates artificial price differences.

21. 17 C.F.R. §§ 230.251–264. *See* § 4.15 *supra.*

22. 17 C.F.R. § 240.10b–21(T). *See* Sec.Act Rel. No. 33–6798, Sec.Exch.Act Rel. No. 34–26028, [1988–89 Transfer Binder] Fed.Sec.L.Rep. (CCH) ¶ 84,315 (SEC Aug. 25, 1988).

23. 17 C.F.R. § 240.10b–21. In 1988, the SEC had adopted a temporary rule. Rule 10b–21(T), 17 C.F.R. § 240.10b–21(T). The rule became permanent in 1994. *See* Short Selling in Connection with a Public Offering, Sec.Exch. Act Rel. No. 34–33072, 59 Fed. Reg. 10984, [1993–1994 Transfer Binder] Fed. Sec. L. Rep. (CCH) ¶ 85,321 (SEC March 2, 1994).

24. Form 1–A is the filing required by Regulation A that parallels the registration statement. *See* 17 C.F.R. § 230.255.

25. 17 C.F.R. § 240.10b–21(T)(a).

26. 17 C.F.R. § 240.10b–21(T)(b). *See* 17 C.F.R. § 230.415 which is discussed in § 3.8 *supra.*

27. 17 C.F.R. § 240.10b–21(c).

28. *Id.*

29. Sec.Act Rel. No. 33–6798, Sec.Exch.Act Rel. No. 34–26028, [1988–89 Transfer Binder] Fed.Sec.L.Rep. (CCH) ¶ 84,315 (SEC Aug. 25, 1988). *See* text accompanying footnote 14 *supra.*

30. *See* §§ 11.15, 12.1 *infra.*

31. Schreiber v. Burlington Northern, Inc., 472 U.S. 1, 105 S.Ct. 2458, 86 L.Ed.2d 1 (1985).

32. Sec.Act Rel. No. 33–6798, Sec.Exch.Act Rel. No. 34–26028, [1988–89 Transfer Binder] Fed.Sec.L.Rep. (CCH) ¶ 84,315 at p. 89,390 (SEC Aug. 25, 1988).

Even beyond the rules discussed above, short sales of securities are presumably subject to the securities laws' general antifraud provisions. Accordingly, material misrepresentations made in connection with short sales will be actionable.[33]

Short sales during a tender offer can also have regulatory impact. Thus, for example, in applying the prohibitions against the hedged tendering of securities in connection with a tender offer,[34] a court may integrate a short sale of a security made around the time of the short seller's tendering of the securities to a tender offeror.[35]

§ 10.13 The National Market System—Revamping the Market Place

The traditional structure of the securities markets with all exchange trading taking place on the floors of the geographically dispersed national exchanges[1] has become outmoded.[2] Similarly, many securities traded in the over-the-counter markets are no longer dependent on pink and yellow sheets[3] for reliable quotations in light of the National Association of Securities Dealers Automated Quotation System (NASDAQ).[4] The response has been both legislative action and SEC rulemaking to help the market place catch up with technology and to coordinate the various securities markets.

After extensive study,[5] in 1975 Congress amended the Securities Exchange Act of 1934 by mandating consideration of a national market

33. *See* footnote 4 *supra.* *But see* Nick v. Shearson/American Express, Inc., 612 F.Supp. 15 (D.Minn.1984) (complaint failed to establish that short sellers were purchasers under sections 12(2) or 17(a) of the Securities Act of 1933; leave to amend complaint was granted).

34. Rule 14e–4, 17 C.F.R. § 240.14e–4. Prior to 1990, this prohibition was found in rule 10b–4, 240.10b–4 (1990) (rescinded). *See* § 11.15 *infra.*

35. *See* Merrill Lynch, Pierce, Fenner & Smith, Inc. v. Bobker, 636 F.Supp. 444 (S.D.N.Y.1986), *order reversed* 808 F.2d 930 (2d Cir.1986) (overturning arbitration award for proration of shares tendered by shareholders who also sold short).

§ 10.13

1. *See* §§ 10.1, 10.2 *supra.*

2. *See, e.g.,* Securities Industry Study, Report of the Subcommittee on Securities, Sen.Comm. on Banking, Housing and Urban Affairs, 93d Cong., 1st Sess. 89–94 (1973). *See generally* Joel Seligman, The Transformation of Wall Street (1982); Eric A. Chiappinelli, Red October: Its Origins, Consequences, and the Need to Revive the National Market System, 18 Sec.Reg.L.J. 144 (1990); Gordon L. Calvert, From Auction Markets to a Central Market System, 35 Ohio St.L.J. 295 (1974); Milton H. Cohen, The National Market System—A Modest Proposal, 46 Geo.Wash.L.Rev. 743 (1978); Norman S. Poser, Restructuring the Stock Market: A Critical Look at the SEC's National Market System, 56 N.Y.U.L.Rev. 883 (1981); Symposium, Revolution in Securities Regulation, 29 Bus.Law. 1233 (Special Issue 1975); Walter Werner, Adventure in Social Control of Finance: The National Market System, 75 Colum.L.Rev. 1233 (1975).

3. *See* Arnold I. Burns, Over-the-Counter Market Quotations: Pink, Yellow, Green and White Sheets—A Gray Area in the Law of Evidence, 52 Cornell L.Q. 262 (1967).

4. *See* §§ 10.1, 10.2 *supra.* The NASD can charge only on a cost-basis for providing trading data to members, NASD v. SEC, 801 F.2d 1415 (D.C.Cir.1986).

5. *See* Report *supra* footnote 2.

system. The purpose and goals of the legislation are set out in section 11A(a)(1) as follows:

(a)(1) The Congress finds that—

(A) The securities markets are an important national asset which must be preserved and strengthened.

(B) New data processing and communications techniques create the opportunity for more efficient and effective market operations.

(C) It is in the public interest and appropriate for the protection of investors and the maintenance of fair and orderly markets to assure—

(i) economically efficient execution of securities transactions;

(ii) fair competition among brokers and dealers, among exchange markets, and between exchange markets and markets other than exchange markets;

(iii) the availability to brokers, dealers, and investors of information with respect to quotations for and transactions in securities;

(iv) the practicability of brokers executing investors' orders in the best market; and

(v) an opportunity, consistent with the provisions of clauses (i) and (iv) of this subparagraph, for investors' orders to be executed without the participation of a dealer.

(D) The linking of all markets for qualified securities through communication and data processing facilities will foster efficiency, enhance competition, increase the information available to brokers, dealers, and investors, facilitate the offsetting of investors' orders, and contribute to best execution of such orders.[6]

These goals were to be put into place by the SEC in the exercise of its rulemaking authority.

The 1975 Act also created the National Market Advisory Board consisting of fifteen geographically dispersed members.[7] The role of the Advisory Board included studying the feasibility of a new self regulatory board, the National Market Regulatory Board, to supervise a national market system.[8] The Advisory Board was also given the task of consult-

6.   15 U.S.C.A. § 78k–1(a). For reports of the SEC's progress see Sec.Exch.Act Rel. No. 34–15671 (March 22, 1979); Sec.Exch.Act Rel. No. 34–14416 (Jan. 26, 1978). See generally Donald L. Calvin, The National Market System: A Successful Adventure in Industry Self-Improvement, 70 Va.L.Rev. 785 (1984); Michael J. Simon & Robert L. D. Colby, The National Market System for Over-the-Counter Stocks, 55 Geo.Wash.L.Rev. 17 (1986). The national market system is not without its critics. See Jonathan R. Macey & David D. Haddock, Shirking at the SEC: The Failure of the National Market System, 1985 U.Ill.L.Rev. 315.

7.   15 U.S.C.A. § 78k–1(d). This is in addition to any other advisory committees the commission decides to establish. 15 U.S.C.A. § 78k–1(a)(3).

8.   15 U.S.C.A. § 78k–1(d)(3)(B).

ing with existing self regulatory organizations and exchanges as well as with the SEC.[9] Additionally, the Advisory Board was charged with providing Congress with a report of the results of its study accompanied by recommendations.[10]

The SEC's role under Section 11A includes the promulgation of rules to facilitate the consolidation of securities quotations and a national market system. Pursuant to this power, the Commission set the stage for the NASD's establishment of a national market where securities are traded similarly to what would take place on an exchange, with quotations based on the last sale rather than merely the latest bid and asked offers.[11] Under the SEC rules, over-the-counter securities can be listed in the NASD's national market in accordance with NASD rules, provided that the issuer is sufficiently large and the shares are widely held with sufficiently high trading volume.[12] The NASD's national market has been growing by leaps and bounds and now has over three thousand listed securities.

Although at one time eventual elimination of the exchange system appeared to have been a possible course of action,[13] the steps that are being taken are not in this direction. One reason for the rejection of a single, unified automated quotation system is that the exchanges perform some very useful functions including the policing of their members[14] and the imposing of listing requirements for issuers of securities.[15] The Commission has, however, adopted some provisions in furtherance of section 11A's purpose.

The New York and American stock exchanges have now each consolidated reporting of securities transactions. These systems record the price and volume for all transactions in exchange listed stocks regardless of whether the sales take place on the exchange floor, on a regional

9. 15 U.S.C.A. § 78k–1(d)(3)(C).

10. 15 U.S.C.A. § 78k–1(d)(3)(B).

11. 17 C.F.R. § 240.11Aa2–1. *See also* 17 C.F.R. §§ 240.11Aa2–1–11Ac1–2. Notwithstanding the similarities, the NASD national market system is not based on an auction system like the national securities exchanges.

12. Prior to 1987 SEC rule 11Aa2–1(b)(4) established two types of criteria.

Tier one covered securities with at least two million dollars in tangible assets and a capital surplus of more than one million dollars, where there are more than 500,000 shares held by persons owning less than ten percent of the securities; the market price prior to qualification must be at least $10 per share with the aggregate market value of the shares publicly held to be at least five million dollars. Additionally, the average monthly volume must have been in excess of 600,000 shares for the six months preceding each qualification date. 17 C.F.R. § 240.11A2–4(i) (1986).

In 1987 the SEC eliminated the two-tier system. Under the revised rule over-the-counter securities which have an effective transaction reporting plan, reporting on a real-time basis, are now qualified for the national market system. 17 C.F.R. § 240.11Aa2–1. The elements of a transaction reporting plan are found in 17 C.F.R. § 240.11Aa3–1.

13. *See* the authorities cited in footnote 2 *supra.*

14. *See* § 10.2 *supra.*

15. *See, e.g.,* New York Stock Exchange Company Manual; §§ 9.2, 9.3 *supra.*

exchange or through NASDAQ.[16]

Technological advancements have now created an environment in which electronic trading systems[17] may facilitate off-exchange trading. This could permit large institutions to bypass the exchange.[18] Another outgrowth of this technology was the approval, originally on a one-year pilot basis, of a NASD electronic bulletin board for computerized quotations for stocks not listed on a national exchange or in the NASDAQ system.[19] Also, in conjunction with its adoption of Rule 144A,[20] the SEC approved the NASD's screen-based computer and communication system called PORTAL (Private Offerings, Resales and Trading through Automated Linkages) to facilitate secondary trading of Rule 144A securities.

There have been other technological developments in the operation of the markets. The New York Stock Exchange opened up after hours trading on a limited basis through the use of a screen-based trading system.[21] One point of significance of the screen-based system is that it bypasses the specialist system that has been the heart of the exchange mechanics for so many years.[22] [For further discussion, *see* the Practitioner's Edition].

§ 10.14 Private Actions Against Market Professionals; Secondary Liability

As discussed earlier,[1] sections 15 and 19 of the Exchange Act provide for broker-dealer regulation through the National Association of Securities Dealers and the national securities exchanges.[2] Many of the applicable regulations are properly classified as customer protection rules. While violations of the applicable regulatory provisions can result in disciplinary sanction by the SEC, NASD, or exchange, there is substantial authority against the recognition of an implied right of action in the

---

16. *See* Sec.Exch.Act Rel. No. 34–15671 (March 22, 1979); Richard W. Jennings & Harold Marsh, Jr., Securities Regulation: Cases and Materials 9–11, 492–497 (5th ed. 1982).

17. *Cf.* the discussion of registration of an electronic system as a clearing agent in the text accompanying footnotes 33–34 *infra.*

18. It has been predicted that before long about twenty of the nations largest investment funds will bypass the exchanges and trade between themselves. *See* Wall St.J. A40 (April 17, 1990).

19. Sec.Exch.Act Rel. No. 34–27975 (May 1, 1990). *See* SEC Approves One–Year Pilot Program for NASD's OTC Electronic Bulletin Board, 22 Sec.Reg. & L.Rep. (BNA) 672 (May 4, 1990).

20. 17 C.F.R. § 230.144A.

21. *See* Wall St.J. p. C1 (May 22, 1991). The New York Stock Exchange's screen-based after hours system is open to all investors for forty-five minutes beginning fifteen minutes after the close of trading. A second screen-based system is open to large program traders dealing in baskets of stocks and lasts for one hour and fifteen minutes after the close of exchange trading.

22. Specialists are discussed in § 10.4 *supra.*

§ 10.14

1. *See* § 10.2 *supra.*

2. 15 U.S.C.A. §§ 78o, 78s.

hands of injured investors against the violator.[3] However, repeated securities law violations can lead to liability under the Racketeer Influenced and Corrupt Organizations Act.[4]

The discussion that follows addresses the possible alternative causes of actions against brokers and dealers engaging in fraudulent or otherwise illegal conduct. This will be followed by a discussion of controlling person liability and aiding and abetting principles as applied to broker-dealers.

Is There an Implied Right of Action Under Exchange Act Section 15(c)?

Although there has been considerable case law, the courts are divided as to whether a private right of action is to be implied under section 15(c) of the Exchange Act.[5] As is the case with section 17(a) of the 1933 Act,[6] it has been suggested that while the older cases tended to recognize an implied remedy under section 15(c) the trend in the more recent cases has been not to recognize the remedy.[7] Such a result is far from surprising in light of the decline of implied remedies generally.[8] Thus, while there is significant support in the cases for the recognition of a remedy,[9] there is also substantial case law refusing to recognize a private cause of action under section 15.[10] There is some support among

---

3. *See* the cases cited in footnote 7 *infra* and in § 10.7 *supra*. *But see, e.g.,* Woods v. Piedmonte, 676 F.Supp. 143 (E.D.Mich.1987) (recognizing a private right of action). *Cf.* In the matter of the Arbitration Between Offerman & Co. v. Hamilton Investments, Inc., 1994 WL 374317, [1993–1994 Transfer Binder] Fed. Sec. L. Rep. (CCH) ¶ 98,233 (E.D.Wis. 1994) (absence of private right for investors does not mean that an NASD member may not be able to bring an action for violation of NASD rules).

4. Elysian Federal Savings Bank v. First Interregional Equity Corp., 713 F.Supp. 737 (D.N.J.1989) (allegations of repeated excessive mark-ups stated RICO claim). RICO is discussed in § 19.3 *infra*.

5. *Compare, e.g.,* Speck v. Oppenheimer & Co., 583 F.Supp. 325 (W.D.Mo.1984) (customer had implied right of action to redress broker-dealer's fraud) with Goodman v. Shearson Lehman Brothers, Inc., 698 F.Supp. 1078 (S.D.N.Y.1988) (holding there is no implied right of action under section 15). *See also* the authorities cited in footnotes 9–10 *infra*.

6. 15 U.S.C.A. § 77q(a). *See* § 13.13 *infra*.

7. *E.g.,* Spicer v. Chicago Board Options Exchange, Inc., 977 F.2d 255 (7th Cir.1992) (no private right of action for violation of section 6); Asch v. Philips, Appel & Walden, Inc., 867 F.2d 776 (2d Cir.1989); Snyder v. Newhard, Cook & Co., 764 F.Supp. 612 (D.Colo. 1991); Epstein v. Haas Securities Corp., 731 F.Supp. 1166 (S.D.N.Y.1990); Forkin v. Paine Webber, Inc., 1988 WL 152023, [1988–89 Transfer Binder] Fed.Sec.L.Rep. (CCH) ¶ 94,128 (N.D.Ill.1988).

8. *See* § 13.1 *infra*.

9. Cases supporting (many in dictum) the existence of an implied remedy under section 15(c) are collected in the Practitioner's Edition.

10. Cases denying the existence of an implied remedy include: Asch v. Philips, Appel & Walden, Inc., 867 F.2d 776 (2d Cir.1989); Brannan v. Eisenstein, 804 F.2d 1041, 1042 n. 1 (8th Cir.1986) (explicit denial); Snyder v. Newhard, Cook & Co., 764 F.Supp. 612 (D.Colo.1991); Chee v. Marine Midland Bank, N.A., 1991 WL 15301, [1990–1991 Transfer Binder] Fed.Sec.L.Rep. (CCH) ¶ 95,806 (E.D.N.Y.1991); Berner v. Lazzaro, 730 F.2d 1319, 1320 n. 1 (9th Cir.1984), *affirmed on other grounds sub nom.* Bateman Eichler, Hill Richards, Inc. v. Berner, 472 U.S. 299, 105 S.Ct. 2622, 86 L.Ed.2d 215 (1985) (explicit denial); Goodman v. Shearson Lehman Brothers, Inc., 698 F.Supp. 1078 (S.D.N.Y.1988) (holding there is no implied right of action under section 15); Cohen v. Alan Bush Brokerage Co., 1987 WL 65038, [1987–88 Transfer Binder] Fed.Sec.L.Rep. (CCH) ¶ 93,553

the commentators in favor of recognizing a private remedy and at least one commentator has suggested that the legislative history warrants the implication of a private right of action under section 15(c).[11] Although a few cases recognize that suit may be brought under section 15(c),[12] it is not clear to what extent, if any, such an action is different from one that would exist under Rule 10b–5.[13]

Following the lead from Supreme Court precedent under Rule 10b–5, it has been held that section 15(c) claims are arbitrable.[14] Thus, in many cases it will be the arbitrators, not the courts, that will be deciding (at least initially) whether a remedy exists under section 15(c)(1).

Section 15(c)(1) by its terms makes it unlawful for a broker or dealer "to effect any transaction in, or to induce or attempt to induce the purchase or sale of any security * * * by means of any manipulative, deceptive or other fraudulent device."[15] On its face, section 15(c) appears to contain the requirement that the conduct be deceptive or manipulative as is the case with section 10(b). Accordingly, it would appear that negligent conduct cannot provide the basis for a section 15 violation.[16] The recognition of an implied right of action for negligence might be viewed as undercutting the Rule 10b–5 scienter requirement.[17] Thus, the section 15(c) action would appear to be coextensive with Rule 10b–5 in terms of the degree of culpability required to prove a violation. In contrast, section 15(c)'s "connection with" requirement is broader than that of section 10(b) since in addition to purchases and sales,

(S.D.N.Y.1987) (no implied remedy under section 15(c)(1)); Shotto v. Laub, 632 F.Supp. 516, 518 n. 2 (D.Md.1986); Prestera v. Shearson Lehman Brothers, Inc., 1986 WL 10095, [1986–87 Transfer Binder] Fed.Sec.L.Rep. (CCH) ¶ 92,884 at p. 94,290 (D.Mass.1986); Baum v. Phillips, Appel & Walden, Inc., 648 F.Supp. 1518, 1529 (S.D.N.Y.1986) (explicit denial, rejecting pre-Cort v. Ash precedent); Wagman v. FLS Securities Corp., 1985 WL 2139, [1985–86 Transfer Binder] Fed.Sec.L.Rep. (CCH) ¶ 92,445 at p. 92,716 (N.D.Ill.1985) (noting that while an open question in the circuit, the section 15 claim should be denied on the same basis as a claim under section 17 of the 1933 Act); Bull v. American Bank & Trust Co., 641 F.Supp. 62, (E.D.Pa.1986) (explicit denial); Olsen v. Paine Webber, Jackson & Curtis, Inc., 623 F.Supp. 17, 18 (M.D.Fla.1985) (explicit denial); Federal Deposit Insurance Corp. v. NASD, Inc., 582 F.Supp. 72 (S.D.Iowa 1984), affirmed 747 F.2d 498 (8th Cir.1984) (explicit denial); Walck v. American Stock Exchange, Inc., 565 F.Supp. 1051, 1059 (E.D.Pa.1981), affirmed 687 F.2d 778 (3d Cir.1982), cert. denied 461 U.S. 942, 103 S.Ct. 2118, 77 L.Ed.2d 1300 (1983) (no implied right of action for monetary damages). For additional cases see Scott, supra, footnote 7 at 689–91 n. 5.

11. See Scott supra footnote 6. See also 3B Harold S. Bloomenthal, Securities and Federal Corporate Law 9–161 (rev.1987); 3 Alan R. Bromberg & Lewis D. Lowenfels, Securities Fraud and Commodities Fraud §§ 8.4(450–59), 8.5(450) (1986); Louis Loss, Fundamentals of Securities Regulation 988 (3d ed. 1988); 3 Louis Loss, Securities Regulation 1760 n. 253 (2d ed. 1961).

12. See the authorities cited in footnote 9 supra.

13. 17 C.F.R. § 240.10b–5. See §§ 13.2–13.12 infra.

14. Badart v. Merrill Lynch, Pierce, Fenner & Smith, Inc., 823 F.2d 333 (9th Cir.1987), relying on Shearson/American Express, Inc. v. McMahon, 482 U.S. 220, 107 S.Ct. 2332, 96 L.Ed.2d 185 (1987). See § 14.4 infra.

15. 15 U.S.C.A. § 78o(c)(1).

16. See Scott supra footnote 7 at 758–67. The scienter requirement is discussed in § 13.4 infra.

17. Cf. Odette v. Shearson, Hammill & Co., 394 Supp. 946, 956 n. 12 (S.D.N.Y.1975) (requiring scienter in a private action brought under section 15(c)).

section 15(c) applies to brokers' and dealers' attempted fraudulent transactions.[18]   As such, section 15(c) might provide a broader basis for standing than Rule 10b–5's purchaser/seller requirement.[19]   In this regard, the recognition of an implied remedy under section 15(c) might be viewed as unduly undercutting Rule 10b–5's standing requirement. On the other hand, a broader basis for standing might arguably be justified by the fact that a section 15(c) defendant is a securities professional who may be said to stand in a fiduciary relationship to his or her customer.

Violation of NASD or Exchange Rules

As for violations of exchange or NASD rules, it is generally held that violation of a rule of a self regulatory organization will not, by itself, support a private right of action.[20]   However, a violation of an exchange or NASD rule can form the basis of a 10b–5 action, provided, of course, that all of the elements of a 10b–5 claim can be established.[21]   Thus, for example, it is well established that a broker-dealer who churns a customer's account can be held accountable for damages under Rule 10b–5.[22] Broker-dealers may, of course, be held liable under Rule 10b–5 for material misstatements or omissions in connection with their customers' purchases and sales of securities.[23]

Actions Under Rule 10b–5

Other brokerage practices have been held actionable under Rule 10b–5.   Thus, for example, a brokerage firm's alleged policy of clearing customers' funds through remotely located banks in order to earn more

---

18. *See* text accompanying footnote 12 *supra*.

19. The purchaser/seller standing requirement is discussed in § 13.3 *infra*.

20. *See, e.g.*, Spicer v. Chicago Board Options Exchange, Inc., 977 F.2d 255 (7th Cir.1992) (no private right of action for exchange rules); Craighead v. E.F. Hutton & Co., 899 F.2d 485 (6th Cir.1990) (no private right of action under New York Stock Exchange know your customer rule); Carrott v. Shearson Hayden Stone, Inc., 724 F.2d 821 (9th Cir.1984); Jablon v. Dean Witter & Co., 614 F.2d 677 (9th Cir.1980); Colonial Realty Corp. v. Bache & Co., 358 F.2d 178 (2d Cir.1966), *cert. denied* 385 U.S. 817, 87 S.Ct. 40, 17 L.Ed.2d 56 (1966).

21. *E.g.*, It is arguable that a violation of applicable self regulatory rules might be relevant in establishing liability under a state common law or statutory claim against the offending broker-dealer.   The Utah Court of Appeals has held that since the NASD falls under the regulatory provisions of the Exchange Act, jurisdiction is exclusively federal and thus any action based on violation of NASD rules must be brought in federal court. Western Capital & Securities, Inc. v. Knudsvig, 768 P.2d 989 (Utah App.1989).   Clark v. John Lamula Investors, Inc., 583 F.2d 594 (2d Cir.1978). *See also, e.g.*, Lefkowitz v. Smith Barney, Harris Upham & Co., 804 F.2d 154 (1st Cir.1986); Shamsi v. Dean Witter Reynolds, Inc., 743 F.Supp. 87 (D.Mass.1989) (dismissing a suitability claim because of failure to satisfy rule 10b–5's deception requirement).

22. *See* cases collected in § 10.10 *supra*.

23. Liability under Rule 10b–5 is discussed in §§ 13.2–13.13 *infra*. *See, e.g.*, Filloramo v. Johnston, Lemon & Co., 697 F.Supp. 517 (D.D.C.1988) (upholding complaint against broker-dealer for alleged misrepresentations regarding future events; absence of evidence supporting his predictions could lead jury to conclude that broker acted recklessly). *Compare, e.g.*, Connolly v. Havens, 763 F.Supp. 6 (S.D.N.Y.1991) (misrepresentation claims against clearing brokers dismissed since plaintiffs failed to establish a fiduciary relationship running from clearing broker to customer).

interest on the funds was held to support an action under Rule 10b–5.[24] In contrast, however, an alleged scheme to delay customer payments of dividends was held not to be in violation of Rule 10b–5 since it was not in connection with the purchase or sale of a security.[25]

Although most courts do not recognize a private right of action for a violation of the margin requirements,[26] material misrepresentations in connection with margin transactions may result in liability under Rule 10b–5 and some courts have recognized an implied right of action under Rule 10b–16[27] which mandates full disclosure in connection with credit transactions.[28]

Failure to comply with Rule 10b–10's[29] disclosure requirements relating to sales confirmations can also result in liability. Thus, for example, nondisclosure of market maker status can be actionable.[30] Furthermore, compliance with Rule 10b–10 does not preclude an action under Rule 10b–5.[31]

A broker's misrepresentations concerning the amount of commissions being charged clearly is actionable.[32] Accordingly, excessive mark–ups that give a materially misleading impression of the actual market price is fraudulent. Even beyond the fraud issue, brokers can be sanctioned for charging excessive mark–ups.[33] As is the case with any

---

24. Ellis v. Merrill Lynch & Co., 664 F.Supp. 979 (E.D.Pa.1987).

25. *Id.* The "in connection with" requirement is discussed in § 13.6 *infra.*

26. *E.g.,* Bennett v. United States Trust Co., 770 F.2d 308 (2d Cir.1985), *cert. denied* 474 U.S. 1058, 106 S.Ct. 800, 88 L.Ed.2d 776 (1986); Bassler v. Central National Bank in Chicago, 715 F.2d 308 (7th Cir.1983). *See also* the cases collected in footnote 20 in § 10.11 *supra.*

27. 17 C.F.R. § 240.10b–16.

28. *E.g.,* Advest, Inc. v. McCarthy, 914 F.2d 6 (1st Cir.1990) (affirming arbitration award for restoration of securities in customer account that was liquidated where broker had wrongfully liquidated account and had mislead customer as to the margin requirements); Angelastro v. Prudential–Bache Securities, Inc., 764 F.2d 939 (3d Cir.1985), *cert. denied* 474 U.S. 935, 106 S.Ct. 267, 88 L.Ed.2d 274 (1985); Robertson v. Dean Witter Reynolds, Inc., 749 F.2d 530 (9th Cir.1984); Liang v. Dean Witter & Co., 540 F.2d 1107 (D.C.Cir.1976); Haynes v. Anderson & Strudwick, Inc., 508 F.Supp. 1303 (E.D.Va.1981). *See also* footnote 23 in § 11.11, *supra.*

29. 17 C.F.R. § 240.10b–10.

30. *E.g.,* Chasins v. Smith Barney & Co., 438 F.2d 1167 (2d Cir.1970). *But cf.* Shivangi v. Dean Witter Reynolds, Inc., 825 F.2d 885 (5th Cir.1987) (requiring proof that nondisclosure of market maker's principal status affected the security's pricing). Market makers are discussed in § 10.3 *supra.*

31. *See* Ettinger v. Merrill Lynch, Pierce, Fenner & Smith, Inc., 835 F.2d 1031 (3d Cir.1987) (failure to disclose allegedly excessive mark–up). *See also, e.g.,* McGeorge v. Van Benschoten, 1988 WL 163063, [1989 Transfer Binder] Fed.Sec.L.Rep. ¶ 94,497 (D.Ariz. 1988) (10b–5 claim upheld on allegations that rather than disclose margin risks, broker merely gave federal truth-in-lending disclosure).

32. Hoxworth v. Blinder, Robinson & Co., 903 F.2d 186 (3d Cir.1990) (upholding preliminary class-wide relief in class action claiming materiality of undisclosed mark-ups); McGeorge v. Van Benschoten, 1988 WL 163063, [1989 Transfer Binder] Fed.Sec.L.Rep. ¶ 94,497 (D.Ariz.1988).

33. *E.g.,* Amato v. SEC, 18 F.3d 1281 (5th Cir.1994) (upholding finding that retail broker violated excessive mark–up prohibitions); In the Matter of First Independence Group, Inc., Exch. Act Rel. No. 34–32817, [1993 Transfer Binder] Fed. Sec. L. Rep. (CCH) ¶ 85,230 (SEC 1993). *See also, e.g.,* NASD Rules of Fair Practice, Art. III, sec. 4, NASD Manual (CCH) ¶ 2154 which is discussed in footnote 35 in § 10.2 *supra.*

Rule 10b–5 claim, fraud must be pleaded with sufficient particularity.[34]

Liability Under the Securities Act of 1933

Misconduct by broker dealers can also result in liability under the 1933 Act. When a broker dealer makes material misrepresentations in connection with a customer's purchase of a security, liability can also result under section 12(2) of the 1933 Act.[35] As is discussed more fully in an earlier section,[36] a number of decisions have held that section 12(2) applies only to distributions of securities, or "batch offerings" as they are sometimes called, and not to after-market transactions.[37] Those courts reaching this unfortunate and unwarranted[38] conclusion have unduly limited the application of section 12(2) so that it would not apply to most broker-dealer fraud. A number of courts did not accept this narrow view.[39] Unfortunately, however, in a sharply divided five-to-four decision in Gustafson v. Alloyd Co.,[40] the Supreme Court adopted an unduly restrictive reading of the scope of the section 12(2) remedy. As a result of the *Gustafson* decision, it is clear that section 12(2) will not be available for most day-to-day transactions. However, section 12(2) still retains vitality in connection with public offerings and most likely with regard to certain offerings that are exempt from the 1933 Act's registration requirements. As had been the case in the previous lower court decisions, the Supreme Court focused on the use of the term "prospectus" in section 12(2).

As is discussed more fully in an earlier section of this treatise,[41] the Court in *Gustafson* held that section 12(2) is limited to statements made in connection with securities that are offered by means of a prospectus.

Liability Under the Investment Advisers Act of 1940

Broker-dealers who render investment advice incidental to their broker-dealer operations need not register as investment advisers under

---

34. *E.g.,* Wexner v. First Manhattan Co., 902 F.2d 169 (2d Cir.1990) (insufficiency of complaint charging that transaction was part of a "corrupt bargain" with broker's favored customers, the complaint did not give the specifics of the alleged corruption or what the broker stood to gain). *See also* § 13.8.1 *infra.*

35. 15 U.S.C.A. § 77*l*(2). *See* §§ 7.5–7.5.1 *supra. See also, e.g.,* HB Holdings Corp. v. Scovill, 1990 WL 37869, [1990 Transfer Binder] Fed.Sec.L.Rep. ¶ 95,201 (S.D.N.Y.1990) (broker was a seller but claim dismissed for failure to plead compliance with the statute of limitations).

36. *See* § 7.5 *supra.*

37. *E.g.,* Ballay v. Legg Mason Wood Walker, Inc., 925 F.2d 682 (3d Cir.1991), *cert. denied* 502 U.S. 820, 112 S.Ct. 79, 116 L.Ed.2d 52 (1991).

38. *See* discussion in § 7.5 *supra.*

39. Pacific Dunlop Holdings Inc. v. Allen & Co., 993 F.2d 578 (7th Cir.1993), *cert. granted* ___ U.S. ___, 114 S.Ct. 907, 127 L.Ed.2d 98 (1994); Metromedia Co. v. Fugazy, 983 F.2d 350, 361 (2d Cir.1992), *cert. denied* ___ U.S. ___, 113 S.Ct. 2445, 124 L.Ed.2d 662 (1993); Cewnick Fund v. Castle, 1993 WL 88243, [1992–1993 Transfer Binder] Fed.Sec. L.Rep. (CCH) ¶ 97,392 (S.D.N.Y.1993); PPM America, Inc. v. Marriott Corp., 820 F.Supp. 970 (D.Md.1993); Hedden v. Marinelli, 796 F.Supp. 432 (N.D.Cal.1992).

40. ___ U.S. ___, 115 S.Ct. 1061, 131 L.Ed.2d 1 (1995).

41. *See* § 7.5 *supra.*

Deleted footnotes 42–55 can be found in the Practitioner's Edition.

the Investment Advisers Act of 1940.[56] Similarly, since such broker-dealers are excluded from the definition of investment adviser,[57] they are not subject to the prohibitions of antifraud section 206 of the Advisers Act.[58] However, broker-dealers whose investment adviser functions are more than incidental to their brokerage services and therefore subject to the additional regulation of the 1940 Act, are also subject to section 206's provisions.

Controlling Person Liability, the Duty to Supervise, and Respondeat Superior

Of particular interest in broker-dealer litigation is the extent to which the brokerage firm can be held accountable for actionable violations by its account executives or other employees. The three principal vehicles for imposing such liability are: (1) statutorily created controlling person liability,[59] (2) for the brokerage's firm's culpable failure to supervise its employees,[60] and (3) under common law principles of vicarious liability of employers generally.

Controlling person liability requires not only that the defendant be a control person of the primary violator but also that the defendant was a culpable participant in the illegal activity.[61] When dealing with broker-dealers, the courts have employed a more relaxed test to determine if there is sufficient culpability to invoke controlling person liability for the acts of their employees.[62] Failure to supervise a broker-dealer is deemed to be indirect participation by the controlling person, and thus the controlling person may be liable under section 20(a) for any fraudulent schemes arising during the unsupervised period.[63]

Controlling person liability is limited to transactions taking place on behalf of the employer.[64] Thus, for example when a customer is dealing

---

56. *See* section 203 of the Act, 15 U.S.C.A. § 80b–3. *See* § 18.2 *infra*.

57. Section 202(11), 15 U.S.C.A. § 80b–2(a)(11).

58. 15 U.S.C.A. § 80b–6. *See* § 18.4 *infra*.

59. 15 U.S.C.A. §§ 77o, 78t. *See* § 7.7 *supra* and § 13.15 *infra*.

60. The duty to supervise is imposed both as a matter of concepts of negligence and an express statutory obligation under the Exchange Act. *See* the discussion in footnote 63 *infra*. *See also, e.g.,* Martin L. Budd & Sharon S. Tisher, Supervisory Liability, 26 Rev. Sec. & Commod. Reg. 109 (1993).

61. *See* Martin v. Shearson Lehman Hutton, Inc., 986 F.2d 242 (8th Cir.1993), cert. denied ___ U.S. ___, 114 S.Ct. 177, 126 L.Ed.2d 136 (1993); Seymour v. Summa Vista Cinema, Inc., 817 F.2d 609 (9th Cir.1987) (culpable participation standard).

62. *See, e.g.,* Harrison v. Dean Witter Reynolds, Inc., 974 F.2d 873 (7th Cir.1992), *cert. denied* ___ U.S. ___, 113 S.Ct. 2994, 125 L.Ed.2d 688 (1993) (district court erred in applying "culpable participant" test to broker dealer; there were triable issues as to whether broker-dealer actually possessed the ability to control the activities of its employees in connection with their allegedly fraudulent sales of promissory notes).

63. *See, e.g.,* Hunt v. Miller, 908 F.2d 1210 (4th Cir.1990) (brokerage firm which failed to supervise its employee–broker was held liable as a controlling person).

64. *See, e.g.,* Hauser v. Farrell, 14 F.3d 1338 (9th Cir.1994) (brokerage firm was not liable as controlling person nor was it vicariously liable under respondeat superior); Martin v. Shearson Lehman Hutton, Inc., 986 F.2d 242 (8th Cir.1993), *cert. denied* ___ U.S. ___, 114 S.Ct. 177, 126 L.Ed.2d 136 (1993) (controlling person liability applies to firm; it was

with a sales representative in his or private capacity without relying on any affiliation with the employer brokerage firm, the firm will not be held accountable as a controlling person.[65] On the other hand, when an employee is acting under the firm's auspices, controlling person liability and control depends upon control over the broker generally; control with regard to the particular transaction in question need not be shown.[66]

There is a division of authority whether the statutory imposition of controlling person liability was intended to displace common law agency principles.[67] A number of circuit courts have held that section 20(a) is not an exclusive remedy.[68] The Ninth and Third Circuits have decided differently, holding that section 20(a) is an exclusive remedy.[69] The Ninth Circuit reversed its previous position when it ruled *en banc* that controlling person liability does not preempt common law vicarious liability.[70] With this major shift in position, outside of the Third and Fourth Circuits there remains little authority for the view that controlling person liability is exclusive.[71] However, a recent Supreme Court decision[72] which denied the existence of aiding and abetting liability may foreshadow a change in the rule regarding respondeat superior. In that case, the Court emphasized that implied rights of action must be based on statutory language. The absence of statutory provisions for aider and abettor liability led the Court to deny any implied remedy.[73] It can be

not erroneous to instruct the jury that relationships such as broker and a brokerage firm are normally encompassed within the definition of control).

65. *E.g.,* Kohn v. Optik, Inc., 1993 WL 169191, [1992–1993 Transfer Binder] Fed.Sec. L.Rep. (CCH) ¶ 97,435 (C.D.Cal.1993). The same applies for respondeat superior. *See* text accompanying footnotes 70–71 *infra.*

66. Martin v. Shearson Lehman Hutton, 986 F.2d 242 (8th Cir.1993), *cert. denied* ___ U.S. ___, 114 S.Ct. 177, 126 L.Ed.2d 136 (1993).

67. *See* § 13.15 *infra.*

68. *See* In re Atlantic Financial Management, Inc., 784 F.2d 29 (1st Cir.1986); Henricksen v. Henricksen, 640 F.2d 880, 887 (7th Cir.1981), *cert. denied* 454 U.S. 1097, 102 S.Ct. 669, 70 L.Ed.2d 637 (1981); Paul F. Newton & Co. v. Texas Commerce Bank, 630 F.2d 1111 (5th Cir.1980), rehearing denied, 634 F.2d 1355 (5th Cir.1980); Marbury Management, Inc. v. Kohn, 629 F.2d 705 (2d Cir.1980), *cert. denied* 449 U.S. 1011, 101 S.Ct. 566, 66 L.Ed.2d 469 (1980); Holloway v. Howerdd, 536 F.2d 690, 696 (6th Cir.1976); Carras v. Burns, 516 F.2d 251, 259 (4th Cir.1975); Kerbs v. Fall River Industries, Inc., 502 F.2d 731 (10th Cir.1974).

69. *See* Zweig v. Hearst Corp., 521 F.2d 1129 (9th Cir.1975), *cert. denied* 423 U.S. 1025, 96 S.Ct. 469, 46 L.Ed.2d 399 (1975); Rochez Brothers, Inc. v. Rhoades, 527 F.2d 880 (3d Cir.1975); and Sharp v. Coopers & Lybrand, 649 F.2d 175 (3d Cir.1981).

70. Hollinger v. Titan Capital Corp., 914 F.2d 1564 (9th Cir.1990), *cert. denied* 499 U.S. 976, 111 S.Ct. 1621, 113 L.Ed.2d 719 (1991).

71. In addition to the authorities in the Third Circuit, *see* Carpenter v. Harris Upham & Co., 594 F.2d 388 (4th Cir.1979), *cert. denied* 444 U.S. 868, 100 S.Ct. 143, 62 L.Ed.2d 93 (1979) (denying liability of employer due to failure to satisfy controlling person requirements; the court did not discuss *respondeat superior*). *See also* Carroll v. John Hancock Distributors, Inc., 1994 WL 87160, [1993–1994 Transfer Binder] Fed. Sec. L. Rep. (CCH) ¶ 98,200 (E.D.Pa.1994) (indicating a brokerage firm could be liable under principles of respondeat superior).

72. Central Bank of Denver v. First Interstate Bank of Denver, ___ U.S. ___, 114 S.Ct. 1439, 128 L.Ed.2d 119 (1994).

73. *See* § 13.16 *infra.*

argued that for the same reason Rule 10b–5 liability cannot be premised on respondeat superior which is not expressly included in the Exchange Act. On the other hand, aiding and abetting is a principle of criminal law which is inherently statutory. Respondeat superior has such a long–standing place in the common law that denial of its existence in securities cases would seem somewhat anomalous in contrast to the generally accepted view that the implied right of action under Rule 10b–5 is analogous to common law fraud.[74]

Controlling person liability is more restrictive than common law agency theories in that it holds a controlling person liable only if that person (1) did not act in good faith or (2) induced or knowingly participated in the violation.[75] On the other hand, "common law agency theories may impose liability on a principal or employer without these two 'preconditions'." [76]

§ 10.15 Arbitration of Disputes Involving Broker–Dealers—Introduction

The Supreme Court in Shearson/American Express, Inc. v. McMahon,[1] held that disputes arising under the Exchange Act and the Racketeer Influenced and Corrupt Organizations Act (RICO)[2] are arbitrable in accordance with a predispute arbitration agreement between the parties. *McMahon* overruled a long-standing former SEC policy against agreements that purported to require securities brokerage customers to arbitrate any disputes with their brokers,[3] and also has seriously brought into question the continued viability of the Court's earlier ruling in Wilko v. Swan[4] that claims arising under the Securities Act are not arbitrable.[5] In 1989, the Court took the next step and overruled *Wilko* with the result that claims arising under the 1933 Act are now arbitra-

74. *See* § 13.2 *infra* for a discussion of the genesis of the Rule 10b–5 private right of action.

75. *See, e.g.,* Neiman v. Clayton Brokerage Co., 683 F.Supp. 196 (N.D.Ill.1988) (dismissal of claim based on controlling person liability because there was no evidence showing that defendant had control over the brokers engaged in the allegedly fraudulent scheme). *See also* § 7.7 *supra* and § 13.15 *infra.*

76. In re Atlantic Financial Management, Inc., 784 F.2d 29, 30 (1st Cir.1986).

§ 10.15

1. 482 U.S. 220, 107 S.Ct. 2332, 96 L.Ed.2d 185 (1987), rehearing denied 483 U.S. 1056, 108 S.Ct. 31, 97 L.Ed.2d 819 (1987). *See* § 14.4 *infra.*

2. 18 U.S.C. §§ 1961–1968. *See* § 19.3 *infra.*

3. Former Rule 15c2–2, 17 C.F.R. § 15c2–2 (rescinded).

4. 346 U.S. 427, 74 S.Ct. 182, 98 L.Ed. 168 (1953).

5. Such claims would include those brought under section 12(1) for violation of the Act's registration requirements, section 12(2) for fraud in connection with the sale of a security, and section 11 for material misstatements in a registration statement. 15 U.S.C.A. §§ 77k, 77l(1), (2). *See* §§ 7.2–7.5.2, *supra.* At least in some Circuits, there is also the possibility for a private remedy under section 17(a)'s general antifraud provisions. 15 U.S.C.A. § 77q(a). *See* § 13.13, *infra.*

ble.[6]

The jurisdictional issues relating to arbitration agreements are discussed in a later section[7] as are other bases for attacking predispute arbitration clauses including claims that such agreements constitute invalid adhesion contracts or that the contract is unenforceable because of fraudulent inducement.[8]

Not surprisingly, following the *McMahon* decision there has been a resurgence in the use of arbitration clauses in securities brokerage contracts. The sections that follow discuss the arbitration programs that have been established by the National Association of Securities Dealers, the New York Stock Exchange, and the American Stock Exchange, all of which operate under SEC oversight. These arbitration programs set out the procedures applicable for the resolution of customer disputes[9] and also apply to arbitration of disputes between members of an exchange or the NASD.[10] In contrast to the arbitration programs that are discussed below, commodities disputes may be arbitrated under the procedures established by the commodities exchanges or by the National Futures Association; these arbitration programs are subject to the oversight of the Commodity Futures Trading Commission.[11]

Another relatively recent development affecting predispute arbitration agreements has been the entry of state securities administrators into the regulatory arena. Massachusetts has announced that effective January, 1989, broker-dealers must offer customers the option of not signing predispute arbitration agreements.[12] Similar rules requiring that customers be given a choice have been endorsed by the North American Securities Administrators Association and are under consideration in at least sixteen additional states.[13] Rather than invalidating all predispute agreements, the Massachusetts rule provides that upon opening an account, customers must be given the option of not signing the arbitration clause. While an across-the-board ban on arbitration agreements might arguably be preempted by the new federal policy favoring

---

6. Rodriguez De Quijas v. Shearson/American Express, Inc., 490 U.S. 477, 109 S.Ct. 1917, 104 L.Ed.2d 526 (1989). As discussed more fully in § 14.4 *infra*, the *Rodriguez De Quijas* decision was foreshadowed by the Court's earlier ruling in *McMahon*.

7. *See* § 14.4 *infra.*

8. *See* § 14.5 *infra.*

9. *Cf., e.g.,* Titan/Value Equities Group, Inc. v. Superior Court, [1994–1995 Transfer Binder] Fed. Sec. L. Rep. (CCH) ¶ 98,430 (Cal. Ct.App.1994) (discovery and hearing procedures are established by the arbitral forum; a court cannot interfere and tell the arbitrator what to do).

10. *See, e.g.,* Brown v. Merrill Lynch, Pierce, Fenner & Smith, Inc., 1987 WL 16685, [1987–88 Transfer Binder] Fed.Sec.L.Rep. (CCH) ¶ 93,567 (E.D.Pa.1987) (Unpublished Case) (arbitration of dispute between brokerage firm and employee).

11. Commodity customer remedies are discussed in § 19.8, *infra*. For discussion of the various commodity arbitration programs *see generally* Philip M. Johnson & Thomas L. Hazen, Commodities Regulation §§ 1.94, 2.45 (2d ed. 1989).

12. *See* Massachusetts is First State to Ban Compulsory Arbitration, 20 Sec.Reg. & L.Rep. (BNA) 1436 (Sept. 23, 1988).

13. *Id.*

arbitration of securities disputes,[14] mandating that customers be given a choice is a valid exercise of state regulation. The Massachusetts rule came under attack and was invalidated by a federal district court.[15]

In 1989, the SEC approved major revisions in the exchange and NASD arbitration procedures.[16] The sections that follow provide an overview of the self regulatory organizations' arbitration programs, including the major changes implemented by the recent rule amendments.[17] These amendments, which had been in process for several years, were developed under the auspices of the Securities Industry Conference on Arbitration;[18] accordingly, the rules of the various self regulatory organizations are quite similar, but minor differences exist. In addition to the NASD, New York Stock Exchange, and the American Stock Exchange, the following self regulatory organizations administer arbitration programs: the Municipal Securities Rulemaking Board, the Pacific Stock Exchange, the Midwest Stock Exchange, the Boston Stock Exchange, the Chicago Board Options Exchange, the Cincinnati Stock Exchange, and the Philadelphia Stock Exchange.[19] The sections that follow in the Practitioner's Edition focus on the NASD, New York Stock Exchange, and American Stock Exchange arbitration rules but also are generally applicable to the procedures established for the other arbitration programs.

Deleted sections 10.16–10.22 can be found in the Practitioner's Edition.

14. *Cf.* the discussion of preemption of state tender offer legislation in § 11.22 *infra*.

15. Securities Industry Association v. Connoly, 20 Sec.Reg. & L.Rep. (BNA) 1960 (D.Mass.1988).

16. *See* Sec.Exch.Act Rel. No. 34–26805 (May 16, 1989) (adoption of rules). See Appendix C.

17. The discussion in the sections that follow highlights the major changes. The new rules should be consulted for additional changes that may not be discussed herein. *See also, e.g.,* Lawrence E. Fenster, S.R.O. Eligibility Requirements in Securities Arbitration, 26 Rev. Sec. & Commod. Reg. 183 (1993).

18. The Securities Industry Conference on Arbitration (SICA) was established in 1977 in response to the SEC's invitation to the securities industry to review existing arbitration programs. SICA is made up of one representative from each self regulatory organization that administers arbitration programs, a representative of the securities industry, and four representatives of the public.

19. *See* Sec.Exch.Act Rel. No. 34–26805 (May 16, 1989).

Chapter 11

SHAREHOLDER SUFFRAGE; CONTROL CONTESTS; CORPORATE TAKEOVERS

Table of Sections

PART A: PROXY REGULATION

§ 11.1   The Regulation of Shareholder Suffrage Under the Exchange Act—Section 14 and the Proxy Rules: Introduction; Regulation of Voting Rights

Introduction

With the passage of the Securities Exchange Act in 1934, Congress took note that a number of the great corporate frauds had been perpetrated through management solicitation of proxies without indicating to the shareholders the nature of any matters to be voted upon. Accordingly, section 14 of the Act[1] was enacted to regulate the shareholder voting machinery for corporations that are subject to the registration requirements of section 12 of the Act[2] and the reporting requirements of section 13.[3]

There are four primary aspects of SEC proxy regulation.[4] First, by virtue of section 14(a) there must be full and fair disclosure of all material facts with regard to any management submitted proposals that will be subject to a shareholder vote. Secondly, material misstatements, omissions, and fraud in connection with the solicitation of proxies are prohibited,[5] and the courts have recognized implied private remedies in the hands of injured investors.[6] Thirdly, the federal proxy regulation facilitates shareholder solicitation of proxies as management is not only required to submit relevant shareholders proposals in its own proxy statements,[7] but also to allow the proponents to explain their position in the face of any management opposition.[8] Fourthly, the proxy rules

---

§ 11.1

1.   15 U.S.C.A. § 78n. However, private foreign issuers are not subject to sections 14(a), 14(b), 14(c), and 14(f). *See* Rule 3a12–3, 17 C.F.R. § 240.3a12–3.

2.   15 U.S.C.A. § 78*l*. *See* § 9.2 *supra*. Although a number of insurance companies are exempt from registration under section 12(g)(2)(G) (15 U.S.C.A. § 78l(g)(2)(G)), that exemption is conditioned upon the company being a domiciliary of a state that subjects it to proxy solicitation and shareholder consent requirements. *Id.* *See* § 9.2 *supra*.

3.   15 U.S.C.A. § 78m. *See* § 9.3 *supra*.

4.   For general discussions of the history of various aspects of federal proxy regulation *see, e.g.,* Edward R. Aranow & Herbert A. Einhorn, Corporate Proxy Contests: Solicitation and Validity of Brokers' Proxies, 23 U.Chi.L.Rev. 640 (1956).

5.   17 C.F.R. § 240.14a–9.

6.   J.I. Case Co. v. Borak, 377 U.S. 426, 84 S.Ct. 1555, 12 L.Ed.2d 423 (1964). *See* § 11.3 *infra*.

7.   17 C.F.R. § 240.14a–8. *See* § 11.7 *infra*.

8.   17 C.F.R. § 240.14a–8(b).

mandate full disclosure in non-management proxy materials[9] and thus are significant in control struggles and contested take-over attempts.[10] These topics are discussed in the succeeding sections. The federal proxy regulation supplements the requirements of state corporate law.[11] Because of this interaction the proxy rules can be a focus for federal-state tension in the face of increasing federalization.[12] Even with the recent cutback in the reach of the federal securities laws,[13] the proxy rules continue to have a substantial effect upon corporate governance.

Substantive Regulation of Voting Rights

In contrast to the Exchange Act's disclosure approach, the securities exchanges have traditionally imposed rules affecting voting rights of listed companies' shares.[14] In 1988, the SEC broke with tradition and introduced its voting rights rule to protect against the dilution of shareholder rights,[15] a matter previously regulated only by virtue of exchange rules.

The applicable exchange rules not only govern the dilution of voting rights but also mandate a shareholder vote under certain circumstances. Thus, for example, under the New York Stock Exchange's so-called twenty percent rule,[16] a shareholder vote is required for any action by an issuer which would result in the issuance of additional shares having a significant diluting effect. If the issuance of shares would increase the outstanding shares of a class of exchange listed securities by more than eighteen and one half percent, the issuer must seek formal shareholder approval even though no approval would otherwise be required under the law of the state of incorporation or any other state law.[17] The

---

9. *See* 17 C.F.R. § 240.14a–2.

10. *See generally* Edward R. Aranow & Herbert A. Einhorn, Proxy Contests for Corporate Control (2d ed. 1968).

11. *See* NUI Corp. v. Kimmelman, 765 F.2d 399 (3d Cir.1985) (federal control of proxy machinery did not preempt New Jersey statute regulating shareholder contests for control of public utilities). *See generally* William L. Cary & Melvin A. Eisenberg, Corporations: Cases and Materials 261–266 (5th unab. ed. 1980); Harry G. Henn & John R. Alexander, Laws of Corporations §§ 191–196 (1983); Loss, The SEC Proxy Rules and State Law, 73 Harv.L.Rev. 1249 (1960).

12. *See, e.g.,* Thomas L. Hazen, Corporate Chartering and the Securities Markets, Shareholder Suffrage, Corporate Responsibility and Managerial Accountability, 1978 Wis. L.Rev. 391. These are similar to types of federal/state tensions that have arisen in connection with Rule 10b–5. 17 C.F.R. § 240.10b–5 which is discussed in chapter 13 *infra.* Another area of tension has been between state and federal tender offer laws. *See* §§ 11.21–11.22 *infra.*

13. *See* Lewis D. Lowenfels, Recent Supreme Court Decisions under The Federal Securities Laws: The Pendulum Swings, 65 Geo.L.J. 891 (1977).

14. *See,* N.Y.S.E. Company Manual §§ 312.00, 313.00; American Stock Exchange Listing Standards, Policies and Requirements § 122, Am. Stock Exch. Guide (CCH) ¶ 10,022. *See generally* the articles cited in footnote 26 *infra.*

15. 17 C.F.R. § 240.19c–4 which is discussed below. *See* Sec.Exch. Act Rel. No. 34–25891, [1987–88 Transfer Binder] Fed.Sec.L.Rep. (CCH) ¶ 84,247 (July 7, 1988); Sec.Exch. Act Rel. No. 34–24623, [1987 Transfer Binder] Fed.Sec.L.Rep. (CCH) ¶ 84,140 (June 22, 1987).

16. N.Y.S.E. Company Manual § 312.00.

17. N.Y.S.E. Company Manual § 312.00.

American Stock Exchange has a similar rule.[18] Before examining the Commission's voting rights rule, it is worth examining the history leading up to the rule.

Under the New York Stock Exchange's one share/one vote rule, all New York Stock Exchange listed shares had to be given voting rights and they must be equal voting rights.[19] The American Stock Exchange required that common stock be voting stock but did not limit dual class voting.[20] Traditionally, the NASD and the over-the-counter markets did not have limitations on nonvoting or dual class voting stock. However, the NASD has since agreed with the New York and American exchanges upon a uniform voting rights rule.

This issuance of weighted voting stock has become a common anti-takeover maneuver.[21] Such unequal voting rights violate the New York Stock Exchange's one share/one vote rule. However, in light of the increasing use of this defensive tactic, the exchange undertook a reevaluation of its one share/one vote rule and suspended enforcement of the rule.[22] Under a compromise solution drafted by the New York Stock Exchange, which required SEC approval, listed companies could have created a class of shares with unequal voting rights provided that the recapitalization is approved by both a majority of independent directors and a majority of the shareholders.[23] Previously, the NASD had postponed consideration of its proposed voting rights rule.[24]

The SEC was concerned that some action be taken and urged the exchanges and the NASD to adopt a uniform voting rights rule that would limit dual class voting which is instituted as a defensive anti-takeover maneuver. Despite this attempt to resolve the problem through self regulation, the exchanges and the NASD were unable to reach an accord. The SEC then responded by proposing its own rule.[25]

---

18. American Stock Exchange Listing Standards, Policies and Requirements § 122, Am. Stock Exch. Guide (CCH) ¶ 10,022 ("The Exchange will not approve an application for the listing of a non-voting common stock issue. The Exchange may approve the listing of a common stock which has the right to elect only a minority of directors").

19. The rule prohibits the listing of shares with less than full voting rights. N.Y.S.E. Listed Company Manual § 313.00(C), (D).

20. American Stock Exchange Listing Standards, Policies and Requirements § 122, Am. Stock Exch. Guide (CCH) ¶ 10,022 ("The Exchange will not approve an application for the listing of a non-voting common stock issue. The Exchange may approve the listing of a common stock which has the right to elect only a minority of the board of directors").

21. Defensive tactics to takeovers are discussed in § 11.20 *infra.*

22. *See* New York Stock Exchange Initial Report of the subcommittee on Shareholder Participation and Qualitative Listing Standards, "Dual Class Capitalization" (Jan. 3, 1985); Roberta S. Karmel, Is One Share, One Vote Archaic? N.Y.L.J. p. 1 (Feb. 26, 1986).

23. *See* NYSE "Reluctantly" Adopts Dual Share Classification: SEC Approval Needed, 18 Sec.Reg. & L.Rep. (BNA) 998 (July 11, 1986).

24. *See* Stall on One Share/One Vote Accord Seen Likely to Spur Congressional Action, 17 Sec.Reg. & L.Rep. (BNA) 1707 (Sept. 27, 1985).

25. As proposed the rule grandfathered companies already having disproportionate voting rights (even if adopted in violation of exchange rules). *See* Sec.Exch. Act Rel.No. 34-24623, [1987 Transfer Binder] Fed.Sec.L.Rep. (CCH) ¶ 84,140 (June 22, 1987); Ingersoll, SEC Adopts Plan to Bar Listing of Firms that Reduce or Abolish Holders' Rights, Wall St.J. p. 6 (June 12, 1987).

Although the Commission's authority to adopt such a rule has been questioned,[26] Rule 19c–4 became effective in 1988. Prior to the adoption of the new SEC rule there had been movement in Congress to adopt a statutory one share/one vote rule.[27] However, just two years after the adoption of the SEC's rule, as described more fully below, it was ruled invalid.[28]

Under Rule 19c–4,[29] self regulatory organizations (*i.e.* the exchanges and the NASD) would have been prohibited from listing a company's stock and from authorizing quotations in the stock if the company takes any action (including the issuance of new securities) that nullifies, restricts, or disparately reduces the voting rights of existing shareholders unless the action falls into one of the following exempt categories. The rule set forth four situations where there may be disparate voting rights which, standing alone will not be in violation. First, securities issued pursuant to an initial public offering could rearrange voting rights.[30] Second, voting rights could be varied through securities issued in a secondary offering where those securities have voting rights that are no greater than the per share voting rights of any outstanding class of the issuer's common stock.[31] Third, Rule 19c–4 would exempt securities issued to effect a bona fide merger or other acquisition provided those securities do not have voting rights that are greater than the per share voting rights of any class of the issuer's outstanding common stock.[32] Fourth, unequal voting rights that exist by virtue of corporate action taken under a state law which *requires* conditioning of voting rights of a specified threshold percentage upon the approval of independent shareholders would be permitted.[33] This fourth exemption was adopted to

---

26. *Compare, e.g.,* George W. Dent, Jr., Dual Class Capitalization: A Reply to Professor Seligman, 54 Geo.Wash.L.Rev. 725 (1986) *and* Daniel R. Fischel, Organized Exchanges and the Regulation of Dual Class Common Stock, 54 U.Chi.L.Rev. 119 (1987) *with* Roberta S. Karmel, Qualitative Standards for "Qualified Securities": SEC Regulation of Voting Rights, 36 Cath.U.L.Rev. 809 (1987); Roberta S. Karmel, The SEC's Power to Regulate, 196 N.Y.L.J. p. 1, col. 1 (Aug. 26, 1986) (arguing that although the Commission should proceed cautiously, there exists sufficient statutory authority to regulate voting rights) *and* Joel Seligman, Equal Protection in Shareholder Voting Rights: The One Common Share, One Vote Controversy, 54 Geo.Wash.L.Rev. 687 (1986) (arguing in favor of the Commission's authority). *See also, e.g.,* Ronald J. Gilson, Evaluating Dual Class Common Stock: The Relevance of Substitutes, 73 Va.L.Rev. 807 (1987); Jeffrey N. Gordon, Ties that Bond: Dual Class Common Stock and the Problem of Shareholder Choice, 76 Calif.L.Rev. 1 (1988); Note, Dual Class Recapitalizations and Shareholder Voting Rights, 87 Colum.L.Rev. 106 (1987) (arguing that recapitalizations which adopt dual class voting as a defense against takeovers are invalid because they represent a breach of management's fiduciary duty notwithstanding the shareholders' approval of the management recommended plan).

27. *See, e.g.,* Metzenbaum to Introduce Bill Requiring One Share/One Vote, 17 Sec.Reg. & L.Rep. (BNA) 957 (May 31, 1985); One Share/One Vote Rule for Exchanges Debated at Hearing, 17 Sec.Reg. & L.Rep. (BNA) 921 (May 24, 1985).

28. Business Roundtable v. SEC, 905 F.2d 406 (D.C.Cir.1990).

29. 17 C.F.R. § 240.19c–4. *See also, e.g.,* NYSE Files Proposed Interpretation of SEC Voting Rule for Exchange Offers, 20 Sec.Reg. & L.Rep. (BNA) 1964 (Dec. 23, 1988).

30. 17 C.F.R. § 240.19c–4(d)(1).

31. 17 C.F.R. § 240.19c–4(d)(2).

32. 17 C.F.R. § 240.19c–4(d)(3).

33. 17 C.F.R. § 240.19c–4(d)(4).

accommodate state control share acquisition acts, such as the Indiana statute that has been upheld by the Supreme Court.[34] It is noteworthy that unlike the New York Stock Exchange proposal,[35] there would be no exemption for defensive plans recommended by an independent board and adopted by the shareholders.

The D.C. Circuit Court of Appeals ruled that the Commission lacked statutory authority to promulgate a rule regulating substantive voting rights; accordingly, Rule 19c–4 was held invalid.[36] The court noted that shareholder voting rights traditionally have been a matter of state corporate law but that they could be regulated by the Commission upon an appropriate grant of statutory authority. The court reviewed the various statutory provisions put forth by the Commission as a basis for the regulation. Section 19(c),[37] set forth three bases for regulation: (1) assurance of fair administration of self regulatory organizations, (2) conformity to the requirements of the Exchange Act, and (3) promulgation of rules "otherwise in furtherance of the" Act's purpose. The SEC relied on the third basis. Section 14 of the Act[38] expressly states that the regulation of the proxy process is to ensure "fair shareholder suffrage." The court noted, however, that the legislative purpose must be defined in terms of the *means* of regulation selected and section 14 regulates the proxy process *not* substantive voting rights. The court further pointed out that reading section 19(c) as broadly as the Commission suggested could give the SEC power to regulate many matters of corporate management traditionally left to state law.[39] This simply would be too broad an interpretation of section 19(c)'s residual power. The court thus reasoned that if Rule 19c–4 is to survive, the SEC's power to regulate the substantive voting rights must be distinguished from other matters of corporate governance. The court concluded that there was no support for a "special and anomalous exception to the Act's otherwise intelligible conceptual line excluding the Commission from corporate governance."[40]

The long history of the New York Stock Exchange's one share one vote rule was held not to constitute a sufficient basis for reading SEC regulatory authority into the Act. The court then considered the other statutory provisions argued by the Commission. Sections 6(b)(5)[41] (Commission regulatory authority over exchanges) and 15A(b)(6) (regulatory authority over broker-dealer associations)[42] empower the Commission to

---

34. CTS Corp. v. Dynamics Corp. of America, 481 U.S. 69, 107 S.Ct. 1637, 95 L.Ed.2d 67 (1987) which is discussed in §§ 11.21–11.22 *infra*.

35. *See* footnote 23 *supra* and accompanying text.

36. Business Roundtable v. SEC, 905 F.2d 406 (D.C.Cir.1990).

37. 15 U.S.C.A. § 78s(c).

38. 15 U.S.C.A. § 78n.

39. For example, could the SEC properly require independent directors or set shareholder quorum and vote requirements?

40. 905 F.2d at 413.

41. 15 U.S.C.A. § 78f(b)(5).

42. 15 U.S.C.A. § 78o–1.

promulgate rules to "in general, ... protect investors and the public interest." The court pointed out that this power is limited to regulation "by virtue of any authority conferred by the [Exchange Act]," thereby requiring a more specific basis of authority. Otherwise, there would be no limit to the Commission's rulemaking authority. Finally, the SEC pointed to section 11A's grant of rulemaking authority to "facilitate the establishment of a national market system for securities."[43] The court properly explained that Congress' concern here was with market regulation and assuring a competitive environment for trading; thus, section 11A could not support the regulation of substantive voting rights of shareholders. Rule 19c–4 and the substantive regulation of voting rights by the Commission now seems to be a dead issue,[44] except to the extent that the Exchanges or other self regulatory organizations decide on their own to implement a rule. The exchanges, of course, have required corporate governance measures as a precondition to listing.[45] The validity of the New York Stock Exchange rule adopted in January of 1990 was not affected by the *Business Roundtable* decision. On the heels of the D.C. Circuit's decision, the NASD proposed a one-share–one-vote rule for shares listed in the NASDAQ National Market System. The NASD rule is in effect pending review by the SEC. The NASD's rule did not however, signal an end to the problem of lack of uniformity. The American Stock Exchange was then considering a similar rule, but one that was not as broad as the one adopted by the New York Exchange nor the one currently in effect with the NASD, both of which closely parallel former Rule 19c–4.[46] As of June, 1994, the exchanges and the NASD were working on a uniform rule to be proposed for the SEC's approval. In December of 1994, a uniform rule that had been agreed upon these three self regulatory organizations was approved by the SEC.[47]

Many state statutes permit disparate voting rights.[48] However, although disparate voting rights may be permitted by statute, management's fiduciary obligations to its shareholders may place limits on their

---

43. 15 U.S.C.A. § 78q–1. *See* § 10.13 *supra.*

44. The court in the *Business Roundtable* decision pointed out that it was limited to the bases for authority argued by the Commission, so it did not decide whether other statutory provisions could support such a rule.

45. For example, in addition to the preexisting one-share–one-vote rules the New York Stock Exchange Rule 312.00 requires that a shareholder vote be taken on certain matters that would result in the share dilution, even if a shareholder vote is not required under the applicable state law. Notwithstanding the challenge to SEC Rule 19c–4, the New York Stock Exchange has continued to be concerned with the protection of shareholder suffrage. *See* Barbara Franklin, New Stock Issue Rules—Technical Changes Seen Resulting in Tougher Enforcement, N.Y.L.J. p. 5, col. 2 (Sept. 7, 1989).

46. *See* Amex, NASD Split Over Voting Rights Rule, 23 Sec.Reg. & L.Rep. (BNA) 496 (April 5, 1991).

47. *See* SEC Approves New Voting Rights Rule, Adopts Rule Streamlining SRO Regulation, 26 Sec. Reg. & L. Rep. (BNA) 1708 (Dec. 23, 1994).

48. *See, e.g.,* Jeffrey N. Gordon, Ties that Bond: Dual Class Common Stock and the Problem of Shareholder Choice, 76 Calif.L.Rev. 1 (1988); Note, Dual Class Recapitalizations and Shareholder Voting Rights, 87 Colum.L.Rev. 106 (1987).

use as a defensive tactic.[49]

§ 11.2 Full Disclosure in the Solicitation of Proxies

Basic Coverage

Subject to limited exceptions [1] and exemptions,[2] section 14(a) of the Exchange Act[3] makes it unlawful to solicit proxies with respect to any non-exempt security registered under section 12 of the Exchange Act[4] in contravention of such rules and regulations as the SEC shall establish. The proxy rules are concerned with assuring full disclosure to investors of matters likely to be considered at shareholder meetings. In addition, as discussed more fully below, in the event that proxies will not be solicited, shareholders must nevertheless receive a management information statement that will provide the disclosures that would have been contained in the proxy statement had proxies been solicited. Also, as discussed more fully below, the proxy rules impose disclosure obligations not only on management but on any shareholder or third party that decides to solicit proxies or otherwise influence shareholder votes.[5]

Proxy Solicitations: Nature of the Regulation

In Rules 14a–3 through 14a–15 [6] the Commission sets forth the types of information that must be disclosed in proxy solicitations subject to the Act.

The regulation of proxy disclosure has been a major item on the

---

49. *See* Packer v. Yampol, 1986 WL 4748 (Del.Ch.1986) (variable voting rights plan may be subject to judicial interference if its operation appears to be unfair). *See also* Asarco, Inc. v. Court, 611 F.Supp. 468 (D.N.J.1985). *See generally* Note, Dual Class Recapitalizations and Shareholder Voting Rights, 87 Colum.L.Rev. 106 (1987).

§ 11.2

1. The proxy rules do not apply where the securities are beneficially held in the name of or held as nominee by the person soliciting. Rule 14a–2(1),(2), 17 C.F.R. § 240.14a–2(a)(1), (2). Also excluded are solicitations involving a 1933 Act registration, solicitations pursuant to a bankruptcy reorganization, and solicitations subject to the Public Utility Holding Company Act. *Id.* § 240.14a–2(a)(3)–(5). Non-management proxy solicitations to ten or fewer shareholders are also exempt as are certain investment advisers' opinions and newspaper advertisements. *Id.* § 240.14a–2(a)–2(b).

2. Many foreign private issuers are exempt from the proxy rules. *See* Rule 3a12–3, 17 C.F.R. § 240.3a12–3. The exemption does not, however, extend to the Williams Act tender offer and share acquisition disclosure requirements.

3. 15 U.S.C.A. § 78n(a).

4. 15 U.S.C.A. § 78k. Registered reporting companies are those issuers having a class of securities traded on a national securities exchange, as well as those issuers having assets of at least $5,000,000 and also having a class of equity securities with more than 500 shareholders. 15 U.S.C.A. § 78*l*; 17 C.F.R. § 240.12g–1. The proxy rules thus do not apply to issuers who are required to file periodic reports under section 15(d), 15 U.S.C.A. § 78, which applies to securities not subject to section 12's registration requirements but which were issued pursuant to a 1933 Act registration statement. The 1934 Act registration and reporting requirements are discussed in §§ 9.2, 9.3 *supra.*

5. Third parties do not, however, have an obligation to disclose in advance their intent to utilize the proxy machinery. *See* Azurite Corp. v. Amster & Co., 844 F.Supp. 929 (S.D.N.Y.1994).

6. 17 C.F.R. §§ 240.14a–3–240.14a–15.

SEC's agenda over the past two decades.[7] In 1990 Congress enacted the Shareholder Communication Act which extends the applicability of the proxy rules that apply to reporting companies generally to mutual funds and other investment companies that are registered under the Investment Company Act of 1940.[8] In 1992, the Commission enacted major revisions to the proxy solicitation rules in order to facilitate communications by and between institutional holders of shares of 1934 Act reporting companies.[9] The new rules include the relaxation of the definition of proxy solicitation, the elimination of a prefiling requirement for proxy materials, permitting preliminary proxy materials to be used before the filing of the definitive proxy statement, and other changes to facilitate institutional shareholder involvement in corporate governance.

Another recent concern with regard to proxy solicitations has been the regulation of limited partnership rollup transactions. In 1993, Congress enacted the Limited Partnership Rollup Reform Act[10] which contained section 14(h) of the Exchange Act.[11] Section 14(h) provides that the Commission should promulgate special rules governing proxy solicitations and tender offers designed to result in limited partnership reorganizations, commonly referred to as rollups.

The Securities and Exchange Commission makes a distinction between the proxy and solicitation materials. The proxy is any shareholder consent or authorization regarding the casting of that shareholder's vote.[12] The Commission takes a broad view of the terms "solicit" and "solicitation" so as to include "any request for a proxy whether or not accompanied by or included in a form of any request to execute or not to execute, or to revoke, a proxy; [and] the furnishing of any communication to security holders under circumstances reasonably calculated to result in the procurement, withholding or revocation of a proxy." [13] This

---

7. *See, e.g.,* Carol Goforth, Proxy Reform as a Means of Increasing Shareholder Participation in Corporate Governance: Too Little, But Not Too Late, 43 Am. U.L. Rev. 379 (1994); Jill E. Fisch, From Legitimacy to Logic: Reconstructing Proxy Regulation, 46 Vand. L. Rev. 1129 (1993).

Change in the proxy regulations is likely to continue. *See, e.g.,* Bernard S. Black, Next Steps in Proxy Reform, 18 J. corp. L. 1 (1992).

8. 15 U.S.C.A. § 78n(b).

9. Exch. Act Rel. 34–31326 (SEC Oct. 22, 1992). *See, e.g.,* Carol Goforth, Proxy Reform as a Means of Increasing Shareholder Participation in Corporate Governance: Too Little, But Not Too Late, 43 Am. U.L. Rev. 379 (1994); Note, Proxy Solicitation Redefined: The SEC Takes an Incremental Step Towards Effective Corporate Governance, 71 Wash. U.L.Q. 1129 (1993).

With regard to the increasing importance of the role of institutional investors, *see, e.g.,* Ronald J. Gilson & Reinier Kraakman, Investment Companies as Guardian Shareholders: The Place of the MSIC in the Corporate Governance Debate, 45 Stan.L.Rev. 985 (1993).

10. Pub. Law 103–202, 107 Stat. 2344.

11. 15 U.S.C.A. § 78n(h). Of course, other provisions of the securities laws will continue to apply to rollup transactions. 7547 Corp. v. Parker & Parsley Development Partners, 38 F.3d 211 (5th Cir.1994) (roll-up of limited partnership into corporate form would involve a sale under both the 1933 and 1934 Acts).

12. The Commission also explains that "[T]he consent or authorization may take the form of failure to object or dissent." 17 C.F.R. § 240.14a–1.

13. 17 C.F.R. § 240.14a–1(f).

definition has been liberally interpreted by the courts to include materials such as open letters to regulatory bodies which although not directed towards shareholders, are reasonably calculated to affect a reasonable shareholder's voting decision.[14]

As part of its effort to increase shareholder participation in corporate governance, the Commission amended the proxy rules to provide that a shareholder may announce how it intends to vote on a matter and explain the reasons for the vote without having to comply with the proxy rules.[15] The rules have also been amended to provide an exemption for shareholders desiring to communicate with one another so long as proxies are not actually being solicited.[16] The purpose of this exemption was to permit institutional shareholders to communicate with one another without having to comply with the filing requirements. Owners of more than five million dollars of the issuer's securities must give public notice of their intent to engage in this type of soliciting activity.[17]

Proxy Solicitations: Required Disclosures

Rule 14a–3[18] sets forth the types of information that must be included in materials used for proxy solicitations. All nonexempt proxy solicitations must be accompanied or preceded by the information required in Schedule 14A.[19] Schedule 14A requires the following information, in addition to the date, time, and place of the meeting:

1. Whether or not the proxy is revocable and if so, the manner in which it may be revoked.

---

14. Long Island Lighting Co. v. Barbash, 779 F.2d 793 (2d Cir.1985) (proxy rules can cover advertisement indirectly addressed to shareholders that appears in publications having a general circulation); Brown v. Chicago, Rock Island & Pacific Railroad Co., 328 F.2d 122 (7th Cir.1964) (open letter to ICC to garner public support for approval of railroad merger held not to be a proxy solicitation); Union Pacific Railroad Co. v. Chicago & North Western Railway Co., 226 F.Supp. 400 (N.D.Ill.1964) (progress report on company's condition, sent out prior to shareholder meeting during takeover battle). *Compare* American Home Investment Co. v. Bedel, 525 F.2d 1022 (8th Cir.1975) (seeking funds to finance derivative suit held not to be a proxy solicitation). *See also, e.g.,* Gillette Co. v. RB Partners, 693 F.Supp. 1266 (D.Mass.1988); Trans World Corp. v. Odyssey Partners, 561 F.Supp. 1311, 1320 (S.D.N.Y.1983). *But see* Radol v. Thomas, 772 F.2d 244 (6th Cir.1985), *cert. denied* 475 U.S. 1086, 106 S.Ct. 1469, 89 L.Ed.2d 724 (1986) (tender offer materials describing two-tiered tender offer did not have to comply with proxy rules where the second step merger is a separate transaction).

15. Rule 14a–1(1); 17 C.F.R. § 240.14a–1.

16. Rule 14a–2(b), 17 C.F.R. § 240.14a–2(b).

17. *Id.*

18. 17 C.F.R. § 240.14a–3. *Cf.* Shidler v. All American Life & Financial Corp., 775 F.2d 917 (8th Cir.1985) (rejecting strict liability as the proper standard under the proxy rules).

19. 17 C.F.R. § 240.14a–101. Prior to October, 1992, Schedule 14B was available as an alternative form, to be used by persons other than the registrant. As part of its 1992 simplification, the Commission made Form 14A available for management proxy statements as well for solicitations by persons other than the issuer. *See* Regulation of Communications Among Shareholders, Exch. Act Rel. No. 34–31326, [1992 Transfer Binder] Fed. Sec. L. Rep. (CCH) ¶ 85,051 (SEC Oct. 16, 1992).

The numbered categories in the text that follows do not correspond to the numbering of items in Schedule 14A.

2.   The availability of statutory dissenters rights of appraisal for any proposals to be voted upon.

3.   A description of the person making the solicitation, including identifying who is bearing the cost of the solicitation.

4.   Disclosures relating to interests of directors, officers and "participants" [20] in matters to be voted upon.

5.   A listing of all voting securities and principal holders thereof. The record date and explanation of cumulative voting rights, if any.

6.   If any action is to be taken with respect to election of directors, the nominees' relationship to affiliated companies and interest in issuer's activities.[21]

7.   Compensation of executive officers and directors.[22]

8.   Relationships with any independent public accountant providing services in connection with the solicitation or matters to be acted upon, including shareholder approval of independent auditors.

9.   Description in detail of any bonus, profit sharing and other benefit plans to be voted upon.

---

20.   "Participant" is defined in Rule 14a–11(b) to include directors, nominees, persons sponsoring the solicitation, persons financing the solicitation, anyone extending credit for the solicitor, and anyone taking an active role in any of the above.   17 C.F.R. § 240.14a–11(b).

21.   Schedule 14A, Item 7 is quite complex in requiring detailed disclosures.   17 C.F.R. § 240.14a–101 item 7.

22.   Each year the shareholders of a publicly held company are entitled to disclosure of the following: (1) the direct and indirect compensation paid to the top executives; (2) a comparison chart, comparing the company's executive compensation stock price performance with that of comparable companies over the past five years; and (3) the compensation committee's report of policies and criteria used in fixing executive compensation.   In addition, in a reversal of past policy, the SEC staff now takes the position that shareholder proposals relating to executive compensation may not be excluded from management's proxy statement on the grounds that they relate to the ordinary business of the issuer. *See* § 11.7 *infra* which discussed the shareholder proposal rule (Rule 14a–8, 17 C.F.R. § 240.14a–8).

Disclosure of executive compensation has been before the Commission on a number of occasions.   In 1983, for example, the SEC relaxed its rules on disclosure of executive compensation by raising the dollar thresholds for the types of compensation to be reported. The SEC also decided to use the term "compensation" rather than "remuneration."   *See* Sec.Act Rel. No. 33–6486 (Sept. 23, 1983).

In 1992, the SEC substantially revised it's disclosure requirements regarding executive compensation.   Among other things, disclosure now must include comparisons between executive compensation and company performance.   This was accomplished through amendments to item 402 of Regulation S–K.   *See* Exch. Act Rel. No. 34–31327, [1992 Transfer Binder] Fed.Sec.L.Rep. (CCH) ¶ 50,056 (Oct. 16, 1992); Barbara Nims & Carol Silverman, SEC Adopts New Rules on Executive Compensation, 26 Rev.Sec. & Commod.Reg. 19 (1993).

Still more revisions to the executive compensation disclosure requirements were made in 1993.   *See* Michael P. Gallgher, Executive Compensation Disclosure Rules: Recent Amendments and Interpretive Guidance, 27 Rev. Sec. & Commod. Reg. 53 (1994).   *See also* Comment, Regulation S–K, Item 402: The New Executive Compensation Disclosure Rules, 43 Case W. Res. L. Rev. 1175, 1197 (1993); Note, Executive Compensation Disclosure: The SEC's Newest Weapon in the Arsenal Against Executive Compensation Abuses, 71 U. Det. Mercy L. Rev. 105 (1993); Comment, Executive Compensation Disclosure: The SEC's Attempt to Facilitate Market Forces, 72 Neb. L. Rev. 803 (1993).

10. Similar information with regard to any pension or retirement plans to be acted upon.

11. Detailed description of any options, warrants or rights to be voted upon.

12. If applicable, detail as to any securities to be authorized to be issued.

13. If applicable, any modification or exchange of securities.

14. Detailed financial statements relating to any matters covered by categories 12 and 13, above.

15. Detailed disclosures relating to any mergers, consolidations or acquisitions to be voted upon.

16. Description of any property to be acquired or disposed of upon a shareholder vote.

17. Restatement of any accounts that would be made necessary by the actions to be voted upon.

18. Identification of all reports to be acted upon.

19. For any matters being submitted to the shareholders which need not be submitted, a description of why shareholder approval is being sought.

20. Reasons for any proposed amendments to the charter, by-laws, or other documents requiring shareholder approval.

21. For any other matters submitted to a shareholder vote, disclosure in the same detail as would be required by items 5 through 20.

22. The vote required for approval for each matter submitted to the shareholders.

Schedule 14A's disclosure requirements apply both to management's proxy statement and proxy solicitations by others.[23] When the proxy solicitation relates to the annual meeting of security holders, where directors are to be elected, an annual report must accompany or precede a proxy solicitation on behalf of the issuer.[24]

Rule 14a–4[25] sets forth the appropriate form for the proxy itself as opposed to solicitation materials. For example, boldface type must

---

23. Formerly, Schedule 14B (17 C.F.R. § 240.14a–102 (rescinded)) set forth similar disclosure requirements for solicitations by a person other than an issuer in matters involving election or removal of directors. That Schedule was rescinded in 1992. *See* Regulation of Communications Among Shareholders, Exch. Act Rel. No. 34-31326, [1992 Transfer Binder] Fed. Sec. L. Rep. (CCH) ¶ 85,051 (SEC Oct. 16, 1992). *See, e.g.,* CNW v. Japonica Partners, L.P., 874 F.2d 193 (3d Cir.1989) (reversing lower court and issuing preliminary injunction against shareholder vote until corrective disclosures in 14B revealing the identity of limited partners, limited partner and coinvestor agreements concerning purchases of target company stock). Rule 14a–11 deals with election and removal of directors. 17 C.F.R. § 240.14a–11. *See* § 11.6 *infra.*

24. 17 C.F.R. § 240.14a–3(b).

25. 17 C.F.R. § 240.14a–4. *See, e.g.,* Schoen v. Amerco, 1994 WL 715895, [1994–1995 Transfer Binder] Fed. Sec. L. Rep. (CCH) ¶ 98,461 (D.Nev.1994) (switching order of boxes on form of proxy to obtain desired result violated Rule 14a–4).

indicate whether or not the proxy is solicited on behalf of the issuer's management. The proxy must also provide the person solicited with an opportunity to vote for or against proposals (management may indicate which proposals it supports) as well as the ability to abstain or withhold authority from voting as to any matters.[26] In an election of directors the proxy must leave room for write-in candidates.[27]

Technological advancements have made an impact on proxy solicitation. For example, it is now technologically possible to receive proxies by telephone. However, most states require a writing, and questions have arisen concerning whether these datagram proxies provide the necessary "fundamental indicia of authenticity and genuineness needed to accord them a presumption of validity." [28] It may nevertheless be possible to formulate a telephonic system that will satisfy such state law requirements.[29]

Rule 14a–5[30] provides guidance as to the presentation of information in a proxy statement, including the size and form of printed material. In many cases, five preliminary copies of each proxy statement and the form of the proxy to be used must be filed with the SEC at least ten business days prior to the first date on which they are to be sent; however, the preliminary copies need not be filed if the proxy solicitation pertains to the regular annual meeting (or a special meeting held in lieu of the annual meeting) and the only matters to be considered are the election of directors, or approval or ratification of auditors and/or shareholder proposals.[31] Once the initial proxy statement is actually sent to the shareholders, eight definitive copies must be filed with the Commission and three additional copies must at the same time be filed with each national securities exchange listing the issuer's security.[32] Five prelimi-

---

26. *See, e.g.,* Schoen v. Amerco, 1994 WL 715895, [1994–1995 Transfer Binder] Fed. Sec. L. Rep. (CCH) ¶ 98,461 (D.Nev.1994) (issuer must disclose that shareholder proposals may be brought up at the meeting and that the proxy will be voted on such matters as the proxy holder sees fit).

27. 17 C.F.R. § 240.14a–4(b)(2)(iii). *Cf.* Chambers v. Briggs & Stratton Corp., 863 F.Supp. 900 (E.D.Wis.1994) (omission of candidate's name in the form of proxy was not material).

28. Parshalle v. Roy, 567 A.2d 19 (Del.Ch.1989) (invalidating the particular datagram method used in that case).

29. *See* David M. Doret, Arthur B. Crozier & Alan M. Miller, Datagram Proxies, 23 Rev.Sec. & Commod.Reg. 45 (1990).

30. 17 C.F.R. § 240.14a–5.

31. 17 C.F.R. § 240.14a–6(a). The Commission adopted these exclusions from the preliminary filing requirements in order to relieve registrants and the Commission of administrative burdens. *See* Sec. Exch. Act Rel. No. 34–25217, [1987–88 Transfer Binder] Fed.Sec.L.Rep. (CCH) ¶ 84,211 (Dec. 21, 1987). Preliminary filing is still required for other matters that may require more detailed review by the Commission. In adopting the exclusion, the Commission stressed that even in cases where the preliminary filing requirement is no longer necessary, there was no intent to change the Commission's practice with regard to review of proxy materials. *Id.*

32. 17 C.F.R. § 240.14a–6(c). *See* §§ 10.1, 10.2 *supra* for discussion of the regulation of national exchanges and member broker-dealers. For representative exchange listing requirements *see* American Stock Exchange Manual; New York Stock Exchange Company Manual.

nary copies of any additional solicitation material relating to either the same meeting or same subject matter must be filed with the Commission at least two business days prior to the date that the material is first sent out unless, upon a showing of good cause, the Commission authorizes a shorter period.[33]　While the filing requirements apply to supplemental literature, they do not apply to replies to inquiries by individual security holders requesting information.[34]　In making the appropriate SEC filings, it is necessary, by labeling of "preliminary copies", to distinguish between them and definitive copies of the material actually sent.[35]

The advance filing requirements of Rule 14a–6 for the proxy statement were designed to promote full disclosure and complete dissemination of information in order to achieve the desired result of informed shareholder voting.　It has been held that a violation of this rule can result in an implied private right of action.[36]

In 1992, the Commission revised its proxy rules for solicitation materials other than the proxy statement and, among other things, eliminated the requirement that such proxy solicitation materials be filed in advance of their use.　Issuers and other proxy contestants may now commence solicitation based on a preliminary proxy statement so long as a form of proxy is not provided to the shareholders until dissemination and filing of the definitive proxy statement.[37]　The 1992 rules also permit participants in proxy solicitations to make appeal to shareholders through the use of press releases and other public dissemination without a prefiling requirement.[38]　These rules were motivated by concerns of institutional investors desiring to participate more fully in the corporate governance of publicly traded companies.

Rule 14a–10 prohibits the solicitation of undated, predated or postdated proxies.[39]　Rule 14a–11 sets forth special requirements relating to the solicitation of shareholders' votes in connection with the election of directors.[40]

Shareholder Access to Information; Shareholder Proposals

Rule 14a–7 requires the issuer to comply with any shareholder request for information relating to the proxy solicitation to be made by

---

33.　17 C.F.R. § 240.14a–6(b).　There are statutory filing fees for proxy statements and preliminary proxy material in connection with mergers and other corporate combinations and acquisitions requiring a shareholder vote.　15 U.S.C.A. § 78n(g)(1).

34.　17 C.F.R. § 240.14a–3(f).　Nor do the filing requirements apply to replies to security holders' request to return their signed proxies.　*Id.*

35.　17 C.F.R. § 240.14a–6(d).

36.　Maywalt v. Parker & Parsley Petroleum Co., 808 F.Supp. 1037 (S.D.N.Y.1992).

37.　Rules 14a–3(a), 14a–4, 17 C.F.R. §§ 240.14a–3(a), 240.14a–4.　*See* Exch. Act Rel. No. 34–31326, [1992 Transfer Binder] Fed.Sec.L.Rep. (CCH) ¶ 85,051 (SEC Oct. 16, 1992).

38.　Rule 14a–3(f), 17 C.F.R. § 240.14a–3(f).

39.　17 C.F.R. § 240.14a–10.

40.　17 C.F.R. § 240.14a–11.

that shareholder.[41] The issuer must respond to a shareholder's written request for a listing of the number of security holders who will be sent proxy materials from the issuer, any issuer proxy solicitations to be made through brokers or bankers, and the estimated cost of sending solicitations and proxy materials to the security holders.[42] When a security holder so requests, the issuer must either furnish a list of security holders to be solicited[43] or, at the issuer's option, it may send out the materials and then bill the security holder.[44] In addition to these rules which facilitate dissidents' communications with other shareholders, in most cases the issuer must include a proper proposal in its proxy statements. Rule 14a–8 requires management to include in its proxy statement most relevant shareholder proposals to be brought up at that meeting.[45]

Antifraud Rules; Election of Directors

Rule 14a–9 provides the general antifraud proscriptions applicable to proxy solicitations.[46] As is discussed in the sections that follow,[47] material misstatements and omissions in connection with a proxy solicitation

41. 17 C.F.R. § 240.14a–7. The Seventh Circuit has held that violations of Rule 14a–7's mailing requirements can give rise to private rights of action. Haas v. Wieboldt Stores, Inc., 725 F.2d 71 (7th Cir.1984).

42. *Id.* The cost estimate is to be based on the solicitation materials as described by the requesting shareholder.

43. 17 C.F.R. § 240.14a–7(c). The payment of proxy expenses is a matter of state law. The issuer is generally entitled to reimbursement for reasonable expenses, even if unsuccessful. Insurgents if successful may apply to shareholders for reimbursement of their reasonable expenses. *See, e.g.,* Streett v. Laclede–Christy Co., 409 S.W.2d 691 (Mo.1966); Rosenfeld v. Fairchild Engine & Airplane Corp., 309 N.Y. 168, 128 N.E.2d 291 (1955). *See generally* Edward R. Aranow & Herbert A. Einhorn, Proxy Contests for Corporate Control ch. 20 (2d ed. 1968); Harry G. Henn & John R. Alexander, Laws of Corporations 523–528 (3d ed. 1983); Edward R. Aranow & Herbert A. Einhorn, Corporate Proxy Contests: Expenses of Management and Insurgents, 42 Cornell L.Q. 4 (1956); Frank D. Emerson & Franklin C. Latcham, Proxy Contest Expenses and Shareholder Democracy, 4 Wes.Res. L.Rev. 5 (1952); Leonard S. Machtinger, Proxy Fight Expenditures of Insurgent Shareholders, 19 Case Wes.Res.L.Rev. 212 (1968).

44. 17 C.F.R. § 240.14a–7(a)(2), (b). Of course, the issuer is not responsible for the form or content of any material so provided by a security holder. 17 C.F.R. § 240.14a–7(a)(2).

These rules supplement the state law which generally provides shareholders with a right of inspection of corporate books and records, provided that the shareholder has stated a proper purpose. *See generally* William L. Cary & Melvin A. Eisenberg, Corporations: Cases and Materials 344–353 (5th unab. ed. 1980); 2 James D. Cox, Thomas L. Hazen & F. Hodge O'Neal, Corporations §§ 13.2–13.11 (1995); Harry G. Henn & John R. Alexander, Laws of Corporations § 199 (3rd ed. 1983); John R. Bartles & Eugene I. T. Flanagan, Inspection of Corporate Books and Records in New York by Stockholders and Directors, 38 Cornell L.Q. 289 (1953); Charles J. Barnhill, The Corporate Raider: Contesting Proxy Solicitations and Take–Over Offers, 20 Bus.Law 763, 766 (1965).

45. 17 C.F.R. § 240.14a–8. *See* § 11.7 *infra.*

46. 17 C.F.R. § 240.14a–9. It is well established that Rule 14a–9 forms the basis of an implied private remedy. *E.g.* J.I. Case Co. v. Borak, 377 U.S. 426, 84 S.Ct. 1555, 12 L.Ed.2d 423 (1964). *See* §§ 11.3–11.5 *infra.*

47. *See* §§ 11.3–11.5 *infra.*

can result in civil liability to shareholders injured as a result thereof.[48] In an appropriate case, a court may enjoin a shareholder meeting or any action voted on at that meeting when there have been significant violations of the proxy disclosure and filing requirements.[49] Because of the practical difficulties involved and hardships to innocent third parties, it is only in rare circumstances that a court will set aside a transaction that has already been consummated.[50] Such injunctive relief may also be secured in an SEC enforcement action.[51] In an appropriate case, the SEC can refer the matter for criminal prosecution.[52] However, criminal prosecutions under the proxy rules are exceedingly rare.

Limited Exemption

SEC Rule 14a–12[53] permits the solicitation of proxies prior to complying with Schedule 14A[54] if the solicitation is made in opposition to a prior solicitation for tender of shares, or other publicized activity, which if successful could be expected to defeat the action proposed at the meeting. This limited exception to the proxy rules' disclosure requirement permits management to respond to defensive tactics to its merger plans or other proposals to be acted upon at the meeting.[55] Rule 14a–12

48. In an appropriate case, the claim might be phrased in terms of a shareholder's derivative suit on the corporation's behalf. For discussion of derivative suits generally *see* 2 James D. Cox, Thomas L. Hazen & F. Hodge O'Neal footnote 44 *supra*, ch. 15; Harry G. Henn & John R. Alexander *supra* footnote 44 ch. 14.

49. *See, e.g.*, CNW Corp. v. Japonica Partners, L.P., 874 F.2d 193 (3d Cir.1989) (reversing lower court and issuing preliminary injunction against shareholder vote until corrective disclosures in 14B); Chambers v. Briggs & Stratton Corp., 863 F.Supp. 900 (E.D.Wis.1994) (enjoining voting of proxies until material omissions adequately cured).

50. *See, e.g.*, Condec Corp. v. Farley, 573 F.Supp. 1382 (S.D.N.Y.1983) (no showing of irreparable injury; preliminary injunction denied); Citizens First Bancorp, Inc. v. Harreld, 559 F.Supp. 867 (W.D.Ky.1982) (although plaintiff stated a claim, preliminary injunction was denied because of plaintiff's failure to show that otherwise there would be irreparable injury), and the other authorities in footnote 49 *supra*.

51. *See, e.g.*, SEC v. May, 134 F.Supp. 247 (S.D.N.Y.1955), *affirmed* 229 F.2d 123 (2d Cir.1956) (preliminary injunction granted in action against shareholders waging a proxy battle). On SEC injunctions generally, *see, e.g.*, George W. Dent, Jr., Ancillary Relief in Federal Securities Law: A Study in Federal Remedies, 67 Minn.L.Rev. 865 (1983); James R. Farrand, Ancillary Remedies in SEC Civil Enforcement Suits, 89 Harv.L.Rev. 1779 (1976); Thomas L. Hazen, Administrative Enforcement: An Evaluation of the Securities and Exchange Commission's Use of Injunctions and Other Enforcement Methods, 31 Hastings L.J. 427 (1979); Stanley Sporkin, SEC Developments in Litigation and The Molding of Remedies, 29 Bus.Law. 121 (1974). *See also, e.g.*, Marc I. Steinberg, SEC and Other Permanent Injunctions—Standards for Their Imposition, Modification and Dissolution, 66 Cornell L.Rev. 27 (1980).

52. *See* United States v. Matthews, 787 F.2d 38 (2d Cir.1986) (reversal of conviction of corporate officer for failing to disclose in proxy statement that he was guilty of bribery and tax evasion, where he had never been charged with such offenses); § 9.5 *supra*.

53. 17 C.F.R. § 240.14a–12.

54. *See* text accompanying footnotes 19–22 *supra*.

55. Schedule 14A need not be used for such proposals and brief responses thereto when no long form has been furnished to the securities holders prior to the written proxy statement, provided that the person on whose behalf this solicitation is made is identified and a written proxy statement meeting the requirements of Schedule 14A is sent at the earliest practical date. 17 C.F.R. § 240.14a–12(a).

requires filing with the Commission of eight copies of any soliciting material in preliminary prior to mailing.[56]

Additionally, as mentioned above, there is an exemption for shareholders desiring to communicate with one another so long as proxies are not actually being solicited.[57]

Integrated Disclosure

The SEC has amended the proxy rules in furtherance of integrating disclosures between 1933 and 1934 Act filings.[58] Issuers qualifying to use Form S–3 of the 1933 Act can now incorporate by reference previously filed but still current information.[59] Also, there is increased integration between these two securities acts with regard to business combinations using 1933 Act Form S–4.[60]

Tender Offers

As discussed more fully in later sections, state antitakeover laws[61] have combined with other factors, such as the drying up of the junk bond market, in making tender offers a less desirable way of seeking corporate control than they were in the 1980s. As a result, the proxy battle has once again become a major factor in struggles over corporate control.[62]

§ 11.3   Rule 14a–9 and the Implied Remedy for Material Misstatements and Omissions in Proxy Materials; Scienter vs. Negligence; Attorneys Fees; Standing to Sue

The Rule 14a–9 Remedy

The Supreme Court has repeatedly recognized an implied remedy for violation of Rule 14a–9's antifraud provisions.[1] In fact, the Rule

---

56. 17 C.F.R. § 240.14a–12(b).

57. Rule 14a–2(b), 17 C.F.R. § 240.14a–2(b). This permits institutional shareholders to communicate with one another without having to comply with the filing requirements.

58. *See* Exch. Act Rel. No. 34–23788 (Nov. 10, 1986).

59. *Id. See* § 3.3 *supra.*

60. *See* Exch. Act Rel. No. 34–23788 (Nov. 10, 1986); §§ 3.3, 5.2 *supra.*

61. *See* §§ 11.20, 11.21 *infra.*

62. *See, e.g.,* Lawrence A. Hamermesh, Defensive Techniques in Proxy Contests, 23 Rev.Sec. & Commod.Reg. 93 (1990).

§ 11.3

1. TSC Industries, Inc. v. Northway, Inc., 426 U.S. 438, 96 S.Ct. 2126, 48 L.Ed.2d 757 (1976); Mills v. Electric Auto–Lite Co., 396 U.S. 375, 90 S.Ct. 616, 24 L.Ed.2d 593 (1970); J.I. Case Co. v. Borak, 377 U.S. 426, 84 S.Ct. 1555, 12 L.Ed.2d 423 (1964); 17 C.F.R. § 14a–9. The text of Rule 14a–9 which is similar to other general antifraud provisions is set out in § 11.2 *supra. See generally* William H. Painter, Civil Liability Under the Federal Proxy Rules, 64 Wash. U.L.Q. 425 (1986). *See also* Rauchman v. Mobil Corp., 739 F.2d 205 (6th Cir.1984) (private remedy exists under § 14(a) for violations of the shareholder proposal rule). *See* § 11.7 *infra.*

The theoretical underpinnings of implied remedies generally are discussed in § 13.1 *infra.*

See § 1.7 *supra* for an overview of private remedies available under the 1933 and 1934 Acts.

14a–9 private remedy was the first Exchange Act implied right of action to be recognized by the Court.[2] Although the Court has not been generous in granting additional implied rights of action,[3] there have been indications that the Rule 14a–9 remedy continues to be relatively expansive.[4]

Is Scienter Required?

For example, two federal courts of appeals and a number of district courts have upheld private 14a–9 claims based on negligence, thus not requiring scienter.[5] Although a few courts have indicated that scienter is required in actions brought under Rule 14a–9,[6] the Supreme Court's ruling in Aaron v. SEC[7] would seem to mandate that a showing of negligent conduct will suffice.[8] One justification for imposing a negligence standard under Rule 14a–9 is that while Rule 10b–5 applies to all securities traded in interstate commerce, Rule 14a–9 is limited to issuers subject to Exchange Act registration and reporting requirements[9] which include SEC filing of all proxy materials.[10]

---

2. J.I. Case Co. v. Borak, 377 U.S. 426, 84 S.Ct. 1555, 12 L.Ed.2d 423 (1964). The Rule 10b–5 remedy was not recognized by the Court until 1970, Superintendent of Insurance v. Bankers Life & Casualty Co., 404 U.S. 6, 92 S.Ct. 165, 30 L.Ed.2d 128 (1971). The Rule 10b–5 remedy, however, enjoyed earlier recognition among the lower federal courts. E.g. Kardon v. National Gypsum Co., 69 F.Supp. 512 (E.D.Pa.1946). *See* §§ 13.2–13.12 *infra.*

3. *See* § 13.1 *infra.*

4. *See* §§ 11.4–11.5 *infra.* There is authority to the effect that a section 14(a) plaintiff must have been a shareholder at the time of the proxy solicitation. District 65, UAW v. Harper & Row Publishers, Inc., 576 F.Supp. 1468, 1486 (S.D.N.Y.1983).

5. Herskowitz v. Nutri/System, Inc., 857 F.2d 179, 189–90 (3d Cir.1988); Wilson v. Great American Industries, Inc., 855 F.2d 987, 995 (2d Cir.1988); Gould v. American–Hawaiian Steamship Co., 535 F.2d 761 (3d Cir.1976); Gerstle v. Gamble–Skogmo, Inc., 478 F.2d 1281 (2d Cir.1973).

6. Adams v. Standard Knitting Mills, Inc., 623 F.2d 422 (6th Cir.1980), *cert. denied* 449 U.S. 1067, 101 S.Ct. 795, 66 L.Ed.2d 611 (1980). *Compare* Fradkin v. Ernst, 571 F.Supp. 829 (N.D.Ohio 1983) (limiting *Adams* scienter requirements to collateral participants). Cf. Mader v. Armel, 461 F.2d 1123 (6th Cir.1972) (good faith is defense to 10b–5 challenge to misleading proxies); Zatkin v. Primuth, 551 F.Supp. 39 (S.D.Cal.1982) (scienter required in suit against an outside accountant; dictum that scienter is not ordinarily required).

7. 446 U.S. 680, 100 S.Ct. 1945, 64 L.Ed.2d 611 (1980).

8. *See* Note, Negligence v. Scienter: The Proper Standard of Liability for Violations of the Antifraud Provisions Regulating Tender Offers and Proxy Solicitations Under the Securities Exchange Act of 1934, 41 Wash. & Lee L.Rev. 1045 (1984). *See also* In re George Kern, Jr., SEC Admin.Proc.File No. 3–6896 (Nov. 14, 1988), *affirmed on other grounds* Sec.Exch.Act Rel. No. 34–29356 (SEC June 21, 1991) (applying negligence standard to violations of sections 12, 13, 14 and 15(d) of the Exchange Act). The scienter requirement is considered more fully in § 13.4 *infra.*

9. 15 U.S.C.A. §§ 78*l*, n. *See* §§ 9.2, 9.3 *supra.*

10. 17 C.F.R. § 240.14a–1(b); Schedule 14A. *See* Thomas L. Hazen, Corporate Mismanagement and the Federal Securities Acts: Antifraud Provisions: A Familiar Path With Some New Details, 20 B.C.L.Rev. 819, 848–853 (1979). A good faith standard applies under section 18(a) of the Exchange Act which gives an express remedy to investors injured by purchasing or selling a security in reliance upon misleading statements in filed documents. 15 U.S.C. § 78r(a) which is discussed in section 12.8 *infra.* The courts have given section 18(a) a relatively narrow scope but there is every reason to believe that the express 18(a) and implied 14a–9 remedies are cumulative. *See* footnote 11 *infra.*

Cumulative Nature of Remedies

A second promising note for Rule 14a–9 plaintiffs is the Court's ruling that an implied action under Rule 10b–5 exists for conduct that is also covered by an express remedy,[11] and that the remedies are cumulative. An earlier Supreme Court decision had recognized the cumulative relationship between the implied remedies under Rules 10b–5 and 14a–9.[12]

Availability of Attorneys Fees

In addition to the cumulative nature of the 14a–9 remedy and the probable sufficiency of a negligence standard of care, a successful plaintiff may be awarded attorneys fees. Where a 14a–9 suit results in a benefit to the corporation, even though not in terms of a monetary award, the defendant may be ordered to pay the plaintiff's attorneys fees.[13] Conversely, bad faith in bringing the suit can result in the award of attorneys fees to the successful defendant.[14]

Relief Other than Damages

In addition to an action for damages, Rule 14a–9 will support a claim for injunctive relief in actions by private parties or the SEC.[15] For example, courts have been willing to order that a new meeting be held in the face of proxy violations that have tainted shareholder votes.[16] This enables both sides to resolicit proxies, albeit at considerable expense.[17]

---

11. Herman and MacLean v. Huddleston, 459 U.S. 375, 103 S.Ct. 683, 74 L.Ed.2d 548 (1983). *See generally* Marc I. Steinberg, The Propriety and Scope of Cumulative Remedies Under the Federal Securities Laws, 67 Cornell L.Rev. 557 (1982).

12. SEC v. National Securities, Inc., 393 U.S. 453, 468, 89 S.Ct. 564, 572, 21 L.Ed.2d 668 (1969) ("The fact that there may well be some overlap is neither unusual nor unfortunate").

13. Mills v. Electric Auto–Lite Co., 396 U.S. 375, 389, 396, 90 S.Ct. 616, 627, 24 L.Ed.2d 593 (1970); Dillon v. Berg, 482 F.2d 1237 (3d Cir.1973). In class actions generally, part of the recovery is considered to be a fund for the payment of attorneys fees. *See, e.g.,* Boeing v. Van Gemert, 444 U.S. 472, 100 S.Ct. 745, 62 L.Ed.2d 676 (1980). For discussion of shareholder litigation *see generally* Harry G. Henn & John R. Alexander, Laws of Corporations ch. 14 (3d ed. 1983).

14. Browning Debenture Holders' Committee v. DASA Corp., 560 F.2d 1078 (2d Cir.1977); Trans World Corp. v. Odyssey Partners, 103 F.R.D. 167 (S.D.N.Y.1984). *See also, e.g.,* Wilson v. Great American Industries, Inc., 661 F.Supp. 1555, 1562 (N.D.N.Y. 1987) *reversed on other grounds* 855 F.2d 987 (2d Cir.1988) (indicating negligence will suffice but finding no liability). For discussion of sanctions under Fed.R.Civ.P. Rule 11, *see* § 13.7.1 *infra.*

15. *See, e.g.,* CNW Corp. v. Japonica Partners, L.P., 874 F.2d 193 (3d Cir.1989) (reversing lower court and issuing preliminary injunction against shareholder vote until corrective disclosures in 14B); Nowling v. Aero Services International, Inc., 734 F.Supp. 733 (E.D.La.1990) (enjoining shareholder meeting that was called without complying with Rule 14a–3).

16. *E.g.* Fradkin v. Ernst, 571 F.Supp. 829 (N.D.Ohio 1983); GAF Corp. v. Heyman, 559 F.Supp. 748 (S.D.N.Y.1983), *reversed on other grounds* 724 F.2d 727 (2d Cir.1983) (no violation found); Bertoglio v. Texas International Co., 488 F.Supp. 630 (D.Del.1980).

17. *E.g.* SEC v. May, 134 F.Supp. 247 (S.D.N.Y.1955), *affirmed* 229 F.2d 123 (2d Cir.1956) (preliminary injunction). *But cf.* Citizens First Bancorp., Inc. v. Harreld, 559 F.Supp. 867 (W.D.Ky.1982). In addition to authorities in footnote 4 *supra, see generally* 2, 4 Louis Loss, Securities Regulation 931–1019, 2879–2980 (2d ed. 1961, 1969 Supp.).

As an alternative to requiring a new vote, a court may require corrective disclosures prior to any vote taking place.[18] When such corrective disclosures are possible, this is a far less expensive route than requiring a new vote. Accordingly, corrective disclosures should be favored in cases where the shareholders can be given adequate time to digest and evaluate the new information before casting their votes.

The sections that follow consider the basic elements of a 14a–9 claim, including materiality, causation and damages. The issues arising in Rule 14a–9 actions closely parallel the implied Rule 10b–5 remedy[19] although there are significant differences such as 10b–5's scienter requirement[20] and its purchaser/seller standing limitation.[21] The standing question is discussed directly below.

Standing to Sue

Presumably, all a private plaintiff need show in a Rule 14a–9 action is that he or she was injured in connection with a proxy solicitation covered by the Exchange Act's regulation regardless of whether there was either a purchase or sale of securities.[22]

Thus, for example, a corporation or a shareholder has standing to complain of a proxy rule violation so long as it can show injury and a causal connection between the violation and the injury.[23] The federal proxy rules were designed to protect the right of a shareholder to a fully-informed vote on matters with regard to which proxies have been solicited. Even in the case of management misstatements in connection with a shareholder proposal, standing is not limited to the shareholder whose proposal was the subject of the alleged violations. Any shareholder entitled to vote on the proposal has a right to full disclosure and thus

---

18. *See* Dynamics Corp. of America v. CTS Corp., 635 F.Supp. 1174 (N.D.Ill.1986). *Cf.* United Paperworkers International Union v. International Paper Co., 985 F.2d 1190 (2d Cir.1993) (ordering corrective disclosures in the next year's proxy solicitation concerning management opposition to shareholder proposal).

19. *See* chapter 13 *infra.*

20. *See* § 13.4 *infra.* Although scienter does not appear to be required in an action for violation of Rule 14a–9, the courts do require a showing of deception. *See* Nutis v. Penn Merchandising Corp., 610 F.Supp. 1573 (E.D.Pa.1985), *reconsideration denied* 615 F.Supp. 486 (E.D.Pa.1985). The deception requirement is discussed in § 13.11 *infra.*

21. *See* § 13.3 *infra.*

22. *See* footnote 4 *supra.* Thus, for example, it has been held that the issuer (or target corporation) has standing to sue under the proxy rules. Ameribanc Investors Group v. Zwart, 706 F.Supp. 1248 (E.D.Va.1989).

23. *See* Stahl v. Gibraltar Financial Corp., 967 F.2d 335 (9th Cir.1992) (plaintiff need not show that he or she voted in reliance on the alleged misstatements); D & N Financial Corp. v. RCM Partners Ltd. Partnership, 735 F.Supp. 1242 (D.Del.1990) (but finding that alleged violations had been cured). *Compare, e.g.,* Ciro v. Gold, 816 F.Supp. 253 (D.Del. 1993) (minority shareholders could not maintain action under Rule 14c–6 since any injury was not caused by misstatements in the proxy materials but rather that they were powerless to stop the transaction). Where a claimed proxy violation belongs both to the shareholder and the corporation and thus the claim is both individual and derivative, it is not necessary to satisfy the derivative suit requirement to first make a demand on the directors that they bring suit. Katz v. Pels, 774 F.Supp. 121 (S.D.N.Y.1991).

may sue to redress such a violation of the proxy rules.[24]

However, since the proxy regulations are designed to protect shareholder voting rights, standing should be limited to shareholders who had a right to vote.[25] Furthermore, making an analogy to cases decided under the Williams Act antifraud provisions applicable to tender offers,[26] it has been held that someone whose interest in the proxy solicitation is merely as a defeated proxy contestant is not within that especial class of persons for whom a section 14(a) remedy will be implied.[27] Courts should be careful in giving too broad a reading to this limitation on standing to sue. It is one thing to say that a proxy contestant whose only interest is in gaining control of a corporation should not be given standing under the proxy rules since federal proxy regulation was designed to protect full disclosure in the exercise of shareholder suffrage and not to guarantee rights to would be control acquirers. It would be quite another, however, to deny standing to shareholders seeking to protect their interest through a proxy battle simply because they are proxy contestants.

While courts should strive to protect the rights of shareholders whose interest in the corporation is likely to be affected by proxy rule violations, the courts should be mindful of potential misuse and abuse of proxy litigation. Accordingly, a shareholder challenging a vote for ulterior reasons should not be granted standing.[28]

A shareholder who did not have shareholder status at the time of the alleged proxy violations does not have standing to sue under Rule 14a–9.[29] In contrast, although it was argued that standing in proxy cases should be limited to shareholders, it has recently been held that a director had standing to bring suit challenging an election based on alleged misstatements in the proxy materials.[30] The court reasoned that

---

24. United Paperworkers International Union v. International Paper Co., 985 F.2d 1190 (2d Cir.1993).

25. Royal Business Group v. Realist, Inc., 933 F.2d 1056 (1st Cir.1991), affirming 751 F.Supp. 311 (D.Mass.1990) (section 14(a) action dismissed since plaintiff was not a shareholder and thus any injury that may have been due to alleged proxy rule violations could not be challenged under the Act). *Cf.* Virginia Bankshares, Inc. v. Sandberg, 501 U.S. 1083, 111 S.Ct. 2749, 115 L.Ed.2d 929 (1991), *appeal after remand* 979 F.2d 332 (4th Cir.1992), *opinion vacated* 1993 WL 524680 (4th Cir.1993) (no section 14(a) action for alleged misstatements with regard to shareholder vote that was not required to effectuate the transaction); Booth v. Connelly Containers, Inc., 1991 WL 171450, [1991 Transfer Binder] Fed.Sec.L.Rep. (CCH) ¶ 96,213 (E.D.Pa.1991) (shareholders not entitled to vote could not establish loss causation). The *Sandberg* case is discussed in § 11.4 *infra.*

26. *See, e.g.,* Piper v. Chris–Craft Industries, Inc., 430 U.S. 1, 97 S.Ct. 926, 51 L.Ed.2d 124 (1977). *See* § 11.19 *infra.*

27. Royal Business Group, Inc. v. Realist, Inc., 933 F.2d 1056 (1st Cir.1991), affirming 751 F.Supp. 311 (D.Mass.1990). *Cf.* Bolton v. Gramlich, 540 F.Supp. 822 (S.D.N.Y.1982) (refusing demand for reimbursement of proxy expenses by unsuccessful tender offerors).

28. *See* AMR Corp. v. UAL Corp., 781 F.Supp. 292 (S.D.N.Y.1992) (airline industry competitor with minimal interest in target company was denied standing since the apparent reason for seeking to enjoin the transaction was to gain a competitive advantage).

29. Murray v. Hospital Corp. of America, 682 F.Supp. 343 (M.D.Tenn.1988). *See also* Gabrielsen v. BancTexas Group, Inc., 675 F.Supp. 367, 373–74 (N.D.Tex.1987).

30. Palumbo v. Deposit Bank, 758 F.2d 113 (3d Cir.1985).

"[s]tanding depends on injury, and we believe that one who alleges that he has been wrongfully ousted from a Board of Directors because management improperly persuaded other shareholders not to vote for him, has articulated an injury cognizable under section 14(a)." [31] While the court's decision certainly furthers the integrity of the voting process, it seems to be at odds with recent Supreme Court cases holding that implied remedies are limited to members of an especial class which the legislation is designed to protect.[32] In response, it can be argued that shareholders' interests are protected by allowing directors to challenge alleged misstatements. However, this seems to be contrary to the current direction of implied remedies.[33] In another decision, it was held that a shareholder has standing to challenge a misleading proxy statement upon allegations of direct injury notwithstanding the absence of allegations of actual reliance.[34] Accordingly, it is not necessary to allege that the shareholder bringing suit relied on the misstatements, provided he or she can show a causally related injury.[35]

As discussed more fully below, the Supreme Court in *Virginia Bankshares, Inc. v. Sandberg*[36] has narrowed the type of causation that will suffice. The Court in *Sandberg* held, in a five to four decision, that a private right of action did not lie for alleged deficiencies in proxies related to a shareholder vote that was not required to effectuate the transaction in question.[37] Following the decision in *Virginia Bank-*

---

31. *Id.* at 116.

32. *E.g.* Piper v. Chris–Craft Industries, Inc., 430 U.S. 1, 97 S.Ct. 926, 51 L.Ed.2d 124 (1977), *rehearing denied* 430 U.S. 976, 97 S.Ct. 1668, 52 L.Ed.2d 371 (1977) (competing tender offeror does not have standing under the Williams Act; if there is such an especial class, it is the target company and its shareholders). *See* §§ 11.19, 13.1 *infra.*

33. *See id.* It can be argued that persons who stand for election in a regulated proxy contest have a more direct interest than the defeated tender offeror who was denied standing in the *Piper* case.

34. Bradshaw v. Jenkins, [1984 Transfer Binder] Fed.Sec.L.Rep. (CCH) ¶ 91,645 (W.D.Wash.1984). *But cf.* Atkins v. Tony Lama Co., 624 F.Supp. 250 (S.D.Ind.1985) (claim dismissed because allegations negated any possibility of reliance).

35. Stahl v. Gibraltar Financial Corp., 967 F.2d 335 (9th Cir.1992) (plaintiff did not rely on misstatements but alleged a proximately caused loss; this was sufficient to permit standing in a suit brought after the transaction in question—the court believed this result was compelled by the Supreme Court decision in Virginia Bankshares, Inc. v. Sandberg, 501 U.S. 1083, 111 S.Ct. 2749, 115 L.Ed.2d 929 (1991), *appeal after remand* 979 F.2d 332 (4th Cir.1992), *opinion vacated* 1993 WL 524680 (4th Cir.1993)); Western District Council of Lumber Production and Industrial Workers v. Louisiana Pacific Corp., 892 F.2d 1412 (9th Cir.1989) (upholding standing of nonrelying shareholder); Sandberg v. Virginia Bankshares, Inc., 891 F.2d 1112 (4th Cir.1989) (reversing denial of certification of a class of minority shareholders who voted against the merger), *judgment reversed* 501 U.S. 1083, 111 S.Ct. 2749, 115 L.Ed.2d 929 (1991); Dowling v. Narragansett Capital Corp., 735 F.Supp. 1105 (D.R.I.1990) (shareholders voting against management proposal for sale of assets were able to sue under both Rules 10b–5 and 14a–9 where the proposal was approved by a majority of the shares); Daly v. Neworld Bank for Savings, 1990 WL 8095, [1990 Transfer Binder] Fed.Sec.L.Rep. ¶ 95,247 (D.Mass.1990) (shareholder complaining about loss of voting rights resulting from proposed reorganization had standing to sue).

36. 501 U.S. 1083, 111 S.Ct. 2749, 115 L.Ed.2d 929 (1991), *appeal after remand* 979 F.2d 332 (4th Cir.1992), *opinion vacated* 1993 WL 524680 (4th Cir.1993). *See* § 11.5 *infra.*

37. *Sandberg* involved a vote taken under a state corporate law conflict of interest statute that applies to transactions between a corporation and interested directors. There was no showing that a failure to have the shareholder vote would have altered the terms of the merger that eventually followed and was the basis for plaintiff's claim for relief.

shares, it is clear that a shareholder cannot complain of alleged violations in connection with a proxy solicitation when the state law does not require the shareholder vote as a necessary step in the consummation of the transaction.[38] But what about the situation where a shareholder vote is required but the management soliciting the proxies controls sufficient votes to assure the success of the vote? As discussed more fully in a subsequent section of this treatise,[39] there is considerable authority for the proposition that even in such a case a plaintiff can sue, if it can be shown that the transaction would have taken a different form had it not been for the misstatements or omissions in question. Thus, for example, it has been held that a shareholder who claimed interference with a statutory right of appraisal was able to maintain a claim under the proxy rules.[40] However, where the defendants had sufficient votes to assure the consummation of the transaction in question, Rule 10b–5 could not be used to provide a remedy for the alleged unfairness of the merger.[41] In any event, the causal connection between the alleged violations and the ultimate transaction and-or injury must be direct.[42] It follows that a claim for misstatements made in connection with the directors' election was too remote from the injury that resulted from alleged director misconduct after the election in question.[43]

§ 11.4 Materiality Under the Proxy Rules and Otherwise

One of the basic elements of a claim at common law for fraudulent misrepresentation is a showing that the misstatements or omissions were "material" to the transaction.[1] The materiality requirement has necessarily carried over to the antifraud provisions of the securities laws and, of course, is also found in the affirmative disclosure requirements of both the Securities Act of 1933 and the 1934 Exchange Act.[2] It has aptly

---

38. *See, e.g.,* Dominick v. Marcove, 809 F.Supp. 805 (D.Colo.1992).

39. *See* § 11.5 *infra. See also, e.g.,* Stahl v. Gibraltar Financial Corp., 967 F.2d 335 (9th Cir.1992).

40. Wilson v. Great American Industries, Inc., 979 F.2d 924 (2d Cir.1992).

41. Boone v. Carlsbad Bancorporation, Inc., 972 F.2d 1545 (10th Cir.1992). This is consistent with a long line of cases holding that the federal securities laws are not to be used as a back-door remedy for corporate law concerns. For discussion of the inapplicability of the federal securities laws as a remedy for unfairness, *see* § 13.11 *infra.*

42. General Electric Co. v. Cathcart, 980 F.2d 927 (3d Cir.1992) (too attenuated a connection between misstatements concerning directors' election and subsequent misconduct in office). *See also, e.g.,* Heil v. Lebow, 1993 WL 15032, [1992–1993 Transfer Binder] Fed.Sec.L.Rep. (CCH) ¶ 97,324 (S.D.N.Y.1993) (alleged failure to disclose secret plan was not actionable when the alleged plan was never implemented); Diamond v. ML–Lee Acquisition Fund II, L.P., 1992 WL 420922, [1992–1993 Transfer Binder] Fed.Sec.L.Rep. (CCH) ¶ 97,275 (S.D.N.Y.1992) (failure to establish loss causation).

43. General Electric Co. v. Cathcart, 980 F.2d 927 (3d Cir.1992).

§ 11.4

1. W. Page Keeton, Dan B. Dobbs, Robert E. Keeton & David G. Owen, Prosser and Keeton on the Law of Torts §§ 105–106–108 (4th ed. 1984). Materiality is also discussed in § 13.5A *infra.*

2. *E.g.* 15 U.S.C.A. §§ 77f, 78*l*, 78m. Materiality problems throughout the securities laws have a number of common denominators. *See generally* Leo Herzel & Robert K. Hagan, Materiality and the Use of SEC Forms, 32 Bus.Law. 1177 (1977); James O. Hewitt,

been observed that "[f]or the securities lawyer 'materiality' is the name of the game."[3] Although most of the cases have arisen under the proxy rules and the implied remedy available under SEC Rule 14a–9[4], a similar test for materiality has been applied when determining violations of Rule 10b–5[5] as well as under sections 11, 12(a), and 17(a) of the 1933 Act.[6] In the words of the Supreme Court, it is clear that "materiality may be characterized as a mixed question of law and fact, involving as it does the application of legal standards to a particular set of facts."[7] The materiality determination is a highly factual one. Accordingly, judicial statements as to the appropriate test of materiality are at best merely a starting point for any analysis. Also, as is the case with materiality in general, since the issues are highly factual, summary judgment will rarely be appropriate.[8]

On the first occasion that the Supreme Court addressed itself to the issue, albeit in dictum, it stated that a finding of materiality

> embodies a conclusion that the defect was of such character that it might have been considered important by a reasonable shareholder who was in the process of deciding how to vote. This requirement that the defect have significant propensity to affect the voting process is found in the expressed terms of Rule 14a–9. * * * There is no need to supplement this requirement * * * with a requirement

---

Developing Concepts of Materiality and Disclosure, 32 Bus.Law. 887 (1977); David L. Ratner, Recent Developments in Litigation Under the Antifraud Provisions: Materiality, Reliance and Causation, and Corporate Mismanagement, 10 Inst.Sec.Reg. 445 (1979). *See also, e.g.,* Roger J. Dennis, Materiality and the Efficient Capital Market Model: A Recipe for the Total Mix, 25 Wm. & Mary L.Rev. 373 (1984).

See also § 13.5A *infra* for a discussion of materiality in Rule 10b–5 actions.

3. Richard W. Jennings & Harold Marsh, Jr., Securities Regulation: Cases and Materials 1023 (5th ed. 1982).

4. 17 C.F.R. § 240.14a–9. J.I. Case Co. v. Borak, 377 U.S. 426, 84 S.Ct. 1555, 12 L.Ed.2d 423 (1964).

5. 17 C.F.R. § 240.10b–5. Kohn v. American Metal Climax, Inc., 458 F.2d 255, 269 (3d Cir.1972), *cert. denied* 409 U.S. 874, 93 S.Ct. 120, 34 L.Ed.2d 126 (1972); Pavlidis v. New England Patriots Football Club, Inc., 675 F.Supp. 688, 694 (D.Mass.1986); Rubinstein v. IU International Corp., 506 F.Supp. 311, 314 (E.D.Pa.1980). *See, e.g.,* Securities & Exchange Commission v. Texas Gulf Sulphur Co., 401 F.2d 833 (2d Cir.1968), *cert. denied* 394 U.S. 976, 89 S.Ct. 1471, 22 L.Ed.2d 755 (1969). *See* § 13.5A *infra.*

6. 15 U.S.C.A. § 77k, 77l(2), 77q(a). *See* §§ 7.3, 7.5 *supra.*

7. TSC Industries, Inc. v. Northway, Inc., 426 U.S. 438, 96 S.Ct. 2126, 48 L.Ed.2d 757 (1976). *See also, e.g.,* McGrath v. Zenith Radio Corp., 651 F.2d 458 (7th Cir.), *cert. denied* 454 U.S. 835, 102 S.Ct. 136, 70 L.Ed.2d 114 (1981). Gladwin v. Medfield Corp., 540 F.2d 1266, 1269 (5th Cir.1976); Bradshaw v. Jenkins, 1984 WL 2405, [1983–1984 Transfer Binder] Fed.Sec.L.Rep. (CCH) ¶ 99,719 (W.D.Wash.1984).

The standard of materiality is not varied by the fact that interested insiders drafted the proxy statement in question. Pavlidis v. New England Patriots Football Club, Inc., 737 F.2d 1227 (1st Cir.1984); *see* Keyser v. Commonwealth National Financial Corp., 644 F.Supp. 1130 (M.D.Pa.1986) (failure to disclose that white knight negotiations were at target's behest and promise to retain target management for three years were not material; nor was it material that the negotiations took place over one weekend). *Cf.* Arkansas Best Corp. v. Pearlman, 688 F.Supp. 976 (D.Del.1988) (financial worth of owners of corporations making tender offer was not material).

8. *E.g., E.g.,* Cooke v. Manufactured Homes, Inc., 998 F.2d 1256 (4th Cir.1993) (there could be differing interpretations as to the effect of the total mix of information).

of proof of whether the defect actually had a decisive effect on the voting.[9]

In a subsequent decision, the Court pointed out that a test of whether the information *"might"* affect the outcome of a shareholder vote was too loose a formulation for determining whether a violation of the proxy rules existed. The Court rephrased its view of materiality into one of whether the plaintiff could show "a substantial likelihood that a reasonable shareholder *would* consider it important in deciding how to vote." [10] The courts thus look to how reasonable shareholders would react.[11]

Difficult problems arise when dealing with opinions as opposed to factual information. Mere opinion often will not be material. Information that a reasonable shareholder would consider important in deciding how to vote may be withheld from proxy materials, as, for example, when it concerns appraisals of current liquidating valuations of corporate property when not "made by qualified experts and hav[ing] a sufficient basis in fact." [12] It is best to limit such opinions to experts since nonexpert valuations, although possibly material to the issue presented to the shareholder in the proxy, are likely to mislead.[13] Additionally, such opinions should be rendered by *independent* experts in order to minimize the effects of officers', directors' or major shareholders' conflicts of interest.[14]

9. Mills v. Electric Auto–Lite Co., 396 U.S. 375, 384–85, 90 S.Ct. 616, 621, 24 L.Ed.2d 593 (1970). *See also, e.g.,* Samuel M. Feinberg Testamentary Trust v. Carter, 652 F.Supp. 1066 (S.D.N.Y.1987), *reargument denied* 664 F.Supp. 140 (S.D.N.Y.1987). The *Mills* decision was addressing itself to the problem of causation under Rule 14a–9. *See* § 11.5 *infra.*

10. TSC Industries, Inc. v. Northway, Inc., 426 U.S. 438, 449, 96 S.Ct. 2126, 2132, 48 L.Ed.2d 757 (1976) (emphasis added). *Accord* Basic, Inc. v. Levinson, 485 U.S. 224, 108 S.Ct. 978, 99 L.Ed.2d 194 (1988). *See also, e.g.,* Prudent Real Estate Trust v. Johncamp Realty, 599 F.2d 1140 (2d Cir.1979); Hassig v. Pearson, 565 F.2d 644 (10th Cir.1977); Lebhar Friedman, Inc. v. Movielab, Inc., 1987 WL 5793, [1987 Transfer Binder] Fed.Sec. L.Rep. (CCH) ¶ 93,162 (S.D.N.Y.1987) (failure to disclose independent counsel's recommendations for board action, including reevaluation of CEO's compensation, held material).

11. *See, e.g.,* Kas v. Valley National Corp., 1993 WL 616687, [1993–1994 Transfer Binder] Fed. Sec. L. Rep. (CCH) ¶ 98,073 (D.Ariz.1993) (finding shareholder's impression of implied contingent promise of dividend not to be one that was reasonable). For discussion of the requirement that reliance be reasonable *see* § 13.5B *infra.*

12. South Coast Services Corp. v. Santa Ana Valley Irrigation Co., 669 F.2d 1265, 1272 (9th Cir.1982), quoting Gerstle v. Gamble–Skogmo, Inc., 478 F.2d 1281, 1292 (2d Cir.1973).

13. South Coast Services Corp. v. Santa Ana Valley Irrigation Co., 669 F.2d 1265 (9th Cir.1982). Prediction as to future market values is the first example of what could be considered misleading under section 14(a) in an S.E.C. note accompanying Rule 14a–9, 17 C.F.R. § 240.14a–9. Valuations made in any sort of speculative manner can be analogized to these predictions of future market values.

14. *See generally* Victor Brudney & Marvin A. Chirelstein, Fair Shares in Corporate Mergers and Takeovers, 88 Harv.L.Rev. 297 (1974); Simon M. Lorne, A Reappraisal of Fair Shares in Controlled Mergers, 126 U.Pa.L.Rev. 995 (1978).

For example, the use of an independent appraiser can be a major factor in upholding valuation by an interested board. *See, e.g.,* Santa Fe Industries v. Green, 430 U.S. 462, 97 S.Ct. 1292, 51 L.Ed.2d 480 (1977); Weinberger v. UOP, Inc., 457 A.2d 701 (Del.1983). *See generally* Victor Brudney & Marvin A. Chirelstein, A Restatement of Corporate Freezeouts, 87 Yale L.J. 1354 (1978); Marc I. Steinberg, Fiduciary Duties and Disclosure Obligations in Proxy Contests for Corporate Control, 30 Emory L.J. 169 (1981); Bate C. Toms, Compensating Shareholders Frozen Out in Two–Step Transactions, 78 Colum.L.Rev. 548 (1978).

In general, the proxy rules place particular attention on disclosure of items likely to reveal possible conflicts of interest.[15] However, conclusory allegations of self-dealing and the like will not suffice as the plaintiff must establish a credible claim of such wrongdoing.[16]

Proxy materials sent to shareholders frequently contain a combination of factual and opinion information. The clarity and accuracy of information available is determined by an examination of the "total mix" of what has been transmitted to the shareholder.[17] Material information is defined in terms of that which would affect the total mix.[18] The subjective intent behind a proposal requiring shareholder approval need not be disclosed if all of the relevant facts underlying that intent are made known to the public.[19] The materiality of an omission in a proxy statement is determined by taking into account all information in the public domain and facts reasonably available to the public to be used by shareholders in interpreting the information in the proxy sent to them.[20] However, the mere fact that the disclosures in the annual report might have corrected any misimpression caused by the allegedly misleading statements in the proxy solicitation is not enough to preclude a proxy rule claim.[21] The court reasoned that in evaluating assertions in management's proxy statement, disclosures in the issuer's 10K and annual report to shareholders are not necessarily part of the total mix of information reasonably available to shareholders since that information (as well as news stories that the defendant pointed to) was not connected to the proxy solicitation in question.[22]

Consideration of materiality in the abstract can take one only so far. Generalized statements provide little practical guidance as to how to deal with materiality issues. As noted above, any materiality determination is highly factual and a better sense of the law may be gleaned from

---

15. *See, e.g.,* Kahn v. Wien, 842 F.Supp. 667 (E.D.N.Y.1994) (finding conflicts were adequately disclosed).

16. *E.g.,* In re Teledyne Defense Contracting Derivative Litigation, 849 F.Supp. 1369 (C.D.Cal.1993). The requirement that fraud be pleaded with particularity is discussed in § 13.8.1 *infra* (Practitioner's Edition only).

17. Justin Industries v. Choctaw Securities, L.P., 920 F.2d 262, 267 (5th Cir.1990) (citing this treatise; the court rejected the lower court's "effect-upon-a-typical-investor test" with regard to each item in question in favor of a test based on the total mix; also holding that bylaw changes requiring supermajority vote to remove directors were material and had to be disclosed); McMahan & Co. v. Wherehouse Entertainment, Inc., 900 F.2d 576, 579 (2d Cir.1990), *cert. denied* 501 U.S. 1249, 111 S.Ct. 2887, 115 L.Ed.2d 1052 (1991) ("[s]ome statements, although literally accurate, can become, through their context and manner of presentation, devices which mislead investors").

18. TSC Industries, Inc. v. Northway, Inc., 426 U.S. at 449, 96 S.Ct. at 2132 (1976).

19. Rodman v. Grant Foundation, 608 F.2d 64 (2d Cir.1979). *Cf.* Freer v. Mayer, 796 F.Supp. 89 (S.D.N.Y.1992) (there is no blanket rule that proxy materials reveal the motives underlying a transaction; had plaintiff alleged a conflict of interest, then the defendant's motive might have been relevant).

20. Rodman v. Grant Foundation, 608 F.2d 64 (2d Cir.1979); Zlotnick, *et al.* v. Barth Spencer Corp., [1980 Transfer Binder] Fed.Sec.L.Rep. (CCH) ¶ 97,726 (E.D.N.Y.1980).

21. United Paperworkers International Union v. International Paper Co., 985 F.2d 1190 (2d Cir.1993).

22. *Id.* at 1199.

examining some of the representative decisions to date under Rules 14a–9 and 10b–5.[23] Negotiations concerning a sale of assets[24] or a significant contract[25] may be material prior to the consummation of a final agreement.[26] Failure to disclose facts relating to a company's most valuable assets is a material omission in connection with shareholder's choice of accepting offered price or seeking statutory appraisal rights.[27] However, "inchoate ideas" and "musings" are too speculative to satisfy the materiality requirement.[28] Similarly, directors and officers need not disclose "mere inquiries or contacts" by third parties seeking to acquire the corporation through a merger or stock purchase.[29] Courts have gone further by holding that management's failure to disclose a policy of rejecting acquisition attempts is not a material omission for purposes of federal law.[30] Along the same lines, nondisclosure of the directors' motivation for supporting or opposing a particular transaction is not a material omission of fact so long as there has been full disclosure of all relevant facts surrounding the transaction in question.[31]

---

23. *See* the discussion of materiality in § 13.5A *infra.*

24. *E.g.,* SEC v. Shapiro, 494 F.2d 1301 (2d Cir.1974) (preliminary merger negotiations); Kardon v. National Gypsum Co., 69 F.Supp. 512 (E.D.Pa.1946) [s.c.] 73 F.Supp. 798 (E.D.Pa.1947). *See e.g.* Paul v. Berkman, 620 F.Supp. 638 (W.D.Pa.1985) (whether preliminary negotiations were material is a question of fact so as to preclude a granting of summary judgment). *But cf.* Greenfield v. Heublein, Inc., 742 F.2d 751 (3d Cir.1984), *cert. denied* 469 U.S. 1215, 105 S.Ct. 1189, 84 L.Ed.2d 336 (1985) (no duty under Rule 10b–5 to disclose merger negotiations where price had not yet been worked out).

25. Rogen v. Ilikon Corp., 361 F.2d 260, 266–67 (1st Cir.1966).

26. Basic, Inc. v. Levinson, 485 U.S. 224, 108 S.Ct. 978, 99 L.Ed.2d 194 (1988).

27. Lockspeiser v. Western Maryland Co., 768 F.2d 558 (4th Cir.1985). *Cf.* Arnold v. Society for Savings Bancorp, Inc., 650 A.2d 1270 (Del.1994) (failure to mention previous bid for company in proxy statement seeking shareholder approval for a merger was material omission under Delaware law). *But see* Landy v. Amsterdam, 815 F.2d 925 (3d Cir.1987) (nondisclosure of certain appraisals in connection with merger held nonmaterial since the value of those assets was not significant in influencing a shareholder's decision of how to vote).

28. Harnett v. Ryan Homes, Inc., 496 F.2d 832, 838 (3d Cir.1974); Mendell v. Greenberg, 612 F.Supp. 1543 (S.D.N.Y.1985) (failure to disclose premiums received in sales of unrelated retailers held not material; fact that other transaction *might* have been negotiated on terms more favorable to plaintiff held not material). *Compare, e.g.,* Bradshaw v. Jenkins, 1984 WL 2405, [1983–1984 Transfer Binder] Fed.Sec.L.Rep. (CCH) ¶ 99,719 (W.D.Wash.1984) (nondisclosure of legal claims against third parties may be actionable under the proxy rules).

29. Bucher v. Shumway, 452 F.Supp. 1288 (S.D.N.Y.1978), *affirmed* 622 F.2d 572 (2d Cir.1980), *cert. denied* 449 U.S. 841, 101 S.Ct. 120, 66 L.Ed.2d 48 (1980). *Accord* Staffin v. Greenberg, 672 F.2d 1196 (3d Cir.1982) (preliminary merger negotiations are not material so as to require affirmative disclosure under section 14(e), 15 U.S.C.A. § 78(e)); Greenfield v. Heublein, Inc., 575 F.Supp. 1325 (E.D.Pa.1983) (semble). *See also, e.g.,* Potomac Capital Markets Corp. v. Prudential–Bache Corporate Dividend Fund, Inc., 726 F.Supp. 87 (S.D.N.Y.1989) (omission that directors had power to liquidate mutual fund was not actionable since the possibility of liquidation was "pure speculation"). *See* § 11.15 *infra.*

30. Panter v. Marshall Field & Co., 646 F.2d 271 (7th Cir.1981), *cert. denied* 454 U.S. 1092, 102 S.Ct. 658, 70 L.Ed.2d 631 (1981); Hershfang v. Knotter, 562 F.Supp. 393 (E.D.Va.1983), *affirmed* 725 F.2d 675 (4th Cir.1984); Brayton v. Ostrau, 561 F.Supp. 156 (S.D.N.Y.1983).

31. Morrissey v. County Tower Corp., 717 F.2d 1227 (8th Cir.1983); Vaughn v. Teledyne, Inc., 628 F.2d 1214 (9th Cir.1980); Rodman v. Grant Foundation, 608 F.2d 64 (2d Cir.1979); Golub v. PPD Corp., 576 F.2d 759 (8th Cir.1978); Warner Communications,

Although the exact motivation behind recommending a merger may not be material, the directors' belief in the fairness of a proposed transaction can be.[32] The Supreme Court explained that although terms such as "fair" and "high" value may be merely opinion, in the commercial context, they are reasonably understood to rest on a factual basis, especially when used by directors who have expertise with regard to the value of the company. However, where the directors' motive in approving the transaction which they described as "fair" and representing a "high value" for the company's shares may have been misrepresented, there is no liability absent a material misstatement as to value.[33]

Additionally, failure to disclose discussions relating to continued employment of management during the course of merger negotiations has been found not to be a material omission.[34] However, a statement denying knowledge of causes for increased trading in issuer's stock may be materially misleading if it fails to disclose the fact that takeover negotiations were taking place.[35] Some courts adopted a new test for the materiality of merger negotiations, which held that until the negotiations have arrived at the price and structure of the deal, they are not material.[36] The price and structure test, which is a departure from the generally accepted *TSC Industries* test, was not accepted by all courts and has since been rejected by the Supreme Court.[37] As a result of the Supreme Court's ruling, issuers are well advised to have a "no comment" policy with regard to statements relating to the pendency of

Inc. v. Murdoch, 581 F.Supp. 1482, 1494 (D.Del.1984); Koppel v. Wien, 575 F.Supp. 960 (S.D.N.Y.1983), *affirmed in part, reversed in part* 743 F.2d 129 (2d Cir.1984).

32. Virginia Bankshares, Inc. v. Sandberg, 501 U.S. 1083, 111 S.Ct. 2749, 115 L.Ed.2d 929 (1991), *appeal after remand* 979 F.2d 332 (4th Cir.1992), *opinion vacated* 1993 WL 524680 (4th Cir.1993).

33. As explained by Justice Scalia in his concurring opinion:

As I understand the Court's opinion, the statement "In the opinion of the board of Directors, this is a high value for the shares" would produce liability if in fact it was not a high value and the directors knew that. It would not produce liability if in fact it was not a high value but the directors honestly believed otherwise. The statement "The Directors voted to accept the proposal *because* they believe it offers a high value" would not produce liability if in fact the directors' genuine motive was quite different—except that it would produce liability if the proposal in fact did not offer a high value and the directors knew that.

See also the discussion of the "bespeaks caution" doctrine in the text accompanying footnotes 56–59 *infra.*

34. Oscar Gruss & Son v. Natomas Co., 1976 WL 903, [1977–1978 Transfer Binder] Fed.Sec.L.Rep. (CCH) ¶ 96,258 (N.D.Cal.1976). *See also* Berg v. First American Bankshares, Inc., 796 F.2d 489 (D.C.Cir.1986) (false and misleading description of discussions with principal shareholder held not material). *But see* Fry v. Trump, 681 F.Supp. 252 (D.N.J.1988) (greenmail negotiations may have been material).

35. Etshokin v. Texasgulf, Inc., 612 F.Supp. 1220 (N.D.Ill.1985).

36. *See* footnotes 26–29 *supra,* and § 13.5A *infra.*

37. Basic Inc. v. Levinson, 485 U.S. 224, 108 S.Ct. 978, 99 L.Ed.2d 194 (1988). In *Basic,* the Court explained that materiality of a possible event depends upon balancing the magnitude of the event against the possibility of its occurrence. *See, e.g.,* Hartford Fire Insurance Co. v. Federated Department Stores, 723 F.Supp. 976 (S.D.N.Y.1989) (failure to disclose possible effects of restructuring on debentures was not material in light of the slight possibility of such an event, when viewed at the time of the offering).

merger or other acquisition negotiations.[38] However, when line item disclosures are required, as would be the case with a proxy solicitation, full candor about pending negotiations is most advisable (if not required) in light of the highly factual (and hence unpredictable) nature of the materiality inquiry. Once a merger agreement has been reached, the materiality requirement does not call for disclosure of every detail relating to the negotiations.[39] The Second Circuit has indicated that within the context of directors' reelection, nondisclosure of past misconduct in office can be actionable.[40] Past misconduct of persons standing for election must be disclosed but not when the alleged misconduct has not been adequately proven.[41]

Facts that would tend to indicate a self interest on the part of parties to the transaction are material and should be disclosed.[42] Thus, benefits that would accrue to the controlling shareholders should be disclosed as must benefits to executive officers and directors.[43] Although management integrity is a matter of significant concern under the proxy rules and securities laws generally, the mere fact that individuals have been named as defendants in securities litigation unrelated to the issuer has been found not to be material.[44] But where litigation is related to the business, then it is likely to be material.[45]

38. *See* Thomas L. Hazen, Rumor Control and Disclosure of Merger Negotiations or Other Control Related Transactions: Full Disclosure or "No Comment": The Only Safe Harbors, 46 Md.L.Rev. 954 (1987); § 13.5A *infra*.

39. *See* Keyser v. Commonwealth National Financial Corp., 644 F.Supp. 1130 (M.D.Pa. 1986) (failure to disclose that white knight negotiations were at target's behest and promise to retain target management for three years were not material; nor was it material that the negotiations took place over one weekend). *Cf.* Arkansas Best Corp. v. Pearlman, 688 F.Supp. 976 (D.Del.1988) (financial worth of owners of corporations making tender offer was not material).

40. Maldonado v. Flynn, 597 F.2d 789 (2d Cir.1979), *on remand* 477 F.Supp. 1007 (S.D.N.Y.1979); Westinghouse Electric Corp. v. Franklin, 789 F.Supp. 1313 (D.N.J.1992), *reversed* 993 F.2d 349 (3d Cir.1993) (failure to disclose that investors' counsel made demand on company's directors to bring action against certain officers and directors was material; but failure to disclose that company made substantial expenditures to lobby for protective legislation was not material). *But cf.* In re Browning–Ferris Industries, Inc., Shareholder Derivative Litigation 830 F.Supp. 361 (S.D.Tex.1993) (nondisclosure of lawsuits that were resolved and no longer pending at the time of the proxy solicitation was not per se material); Bell Atlantic Corp. v. Bolger, 771 F.Supp. 686 (E.D.Pa.1991) (nondisclosure in proxy statement that directors charged with reelection were defendants in shareholder suit was not per se material).

41. United States v. Matthews, 787 F.2d 38 (2d Cir.1986); In re Teledyne Defense Contracting Derivative Litigation, 849 F.Supp. 1369 (C.D.Cal.1993).

42. Mendell v. Greenberg, 927 F.2d 667 (2d Cir.1990), *opinion amended* 938 F.2d 1528 (1990) (failure to disclose controlling shareholder needed to raise cash to pay estate tax was a material omission but omissions related to incidental tax benefits of transaction need not be disclosed).

43. *Id.*

44. Kahn v. Wien, 842 F.Supp. 667 (E.D.N.Y.1994).

45. *See, e.g.,* Goldsmith v. Rawl, 755 F.Supp. 96 (S.D.N.Y.1991) (nondisclosure of pending shareholder litigation and appointment of special litigation committee was not material as a matter of law and had to be determined in light of the total mix of information).

While not all bylaw changes are material, bylaw changes relating to corporate governance are and thus should be disclosed in proxy materials.[46] The fact that certain disclosures are required by an item on the relevant disclosure form does not result in a finding of materiality but it does raise a presumption that the omitted information is material.[47] Although the concept of materiality has a broad scope, it does not necessarily extend to all information that shareholders might like to know.[48] In other words, "[f]air accuracy, not perfection, is the appropriate standard." [49] Similarly, it is not necessary to state that which would be readily apparent to a reasonable shareholder.[50]

As can be seen from the foregoing examples, it is difficult to generalize with regard to issues of materiality since the decisions are highly dependent on the facts of each case. On the other hand, the cases do in large part reflect the common law of misrepresentation which states that opinions, predictions, intention and mere statements of value are not generally actionable.[51] Nondisclosure or inadequate disclosure of conflicts of interest frequently constitute material misrepresentations.[52] Additionally, although there may be significant overlap with the accountants' concept of materiality, the securities acts' treatment of materiality is not coextensive.[53]

46. Justin Industries, Inc. v. Choctaw Securities, L.P., 920 F.2d 262, 267 (5th Cir.1990) (proxy statement failed to disclose bylaw change that required supermajority vote for removal of directors).

47. Howing Co. v. Nationwide Corp., 927 F.2d 263 (6th Cir.1991), *cert. granted and judgment vacated* 502 U.S. 801, 112 S.Ct. 39, 116 L.Ed.2d 18 (1991), *on remand* 972 F.2d 700 (6th Cir.1992) (proxy statement relating to Rule 13e–3 going private transactions; item 8 of that rule creates a presumption that discussion of book, going concern, and liquidation value is material). *Cf.* United States v. Bilzerian, 926 F.2d 1285 (2d Cir.1991), *cert. denied* 502 U.S. 813, 112 S.Ct. 63, 116 L.Ed.2d 39 (1991) (fact that information is specified in Schedule 13D as a required disclosure item is evidence of its materiality).

48. *See e.g.,* Mendell v. Greenberg, 715 F.Supp. 85 (S.D.N.Y.1989), *reversed in part on other grounds* 927 F.2d 667 (2d Cir.1990), *reversed in part* 927 F.2d 667 (1990) (in the proxy solicitation for a proposed merger, it was not necessary to point out that particular shareholders may have had differing tax consequences from the proposed transaction). *Cf.* TCG Securities, Inc. v. Southern Union Co., 1990 WL 7525, [1989–1990 Transfer Binder] Fed.Sec.L.Rep. ¶ 94,928 (Del.Ch.1990) (not necessary to give "play-by-play" disclosure of the bidding process in light of the total mix of information available). *Cf.* In re Sears Roebuck Co. Securities Litigation, 792 F.Supp. 977 (E.D.Pa.1992)(failure to disclose state law claims was not a material omission); *see* § 13.11 *infra.*

49. New England Anti–Vivisection Society, Inc. v. United States Surgical Corp., Inc., 889 F.2d 1198, 1202 (1st Cir.1989), *quoting* Kennecott Copper Corp. v. Curtiss–Wright Corp., 584 F.2d 1195, 1200 (2d Cir.1978).

50. *E.g.,* Lewis v. Potlatch Corp., 716 F.Supp. 807 (S.D.N.Y.1989) (proxy statement adequately disclosed possibility and consequences of stock exchange delisting that could result from passage of voting rights amendment).

51. *E.g.* Deming v. Darling, 148 Mass. 504, 20 N.E. 107 (1889) (Holmes, J.).

52. *See, e.g.,* Wilson v. Great American Industries, Inc., 855 F.2d 987 (2d Cir.1988); Shields on Behalf of Sundstrand Corp. v. Erikson, 1989 WL 10001, [1989–1990 Transfer Binder] Fed.Sec.L.Rep. ¶ 94,723 (N.D.Ill.1989).

53. *See, e.g.,* ABA Committee on Corporate Law and Accounting, A Guide to the New Section 13(b)(2) Accounting Requirements of the Securities Exchange Act of 1934, 34 Bus.Law. 307 (1968). *See generally* Samuel Gruenbaum & Marc I. Steinberg, Accountants' Liability and Responsibility: Securities, Criminal and Common Law, 13 Loy. (L.A.) L.Rev. 247 (1980); Anthony M. Vernava & Gerard W. Hepp, Responsibility of the Accountant Under the Federal Securities Exchange Act of 1934, 6 J.Corp.L. 317 (1981).

The SEC rules pertaining to section 12 registration provide a definition of materiality that echoes the words of the Supreme Court in *TSC*. According to SEC Rule 12b–2:

> The term "material" when used to qualify a requirement for the furnishing of information as to any subject, limits the information required to those matters to which there is a substantial likelihood that a reasonable investor would attach importance in determining whether to buy or sell the securities registered.[54]

The law established in the proxy cases has thus carried over to other disclosure-related questions.[55]

As discussed above, materiality issues are to be considered in light of the total mix of information available. Additionally, as is the case with opinions of value, disclosures relating to soft information such as projections and predictions can be particularly problematic.[56] Many courts have recognized the "bespeaks caution" doctrine which can offset the effect of allegedly materially misleading projections and other soft information.[57] Sufficiently cautionary language may preclude opinions, predictions, and projections from being actionable.[58] The cases invoking the bespeaks caution doctrine have involved projections or other soft information and it is unclear whether the doctrine will have more general application.[59] Even if the doctrine does not apply as such outside of projections and predictions, as discussed above, the materiality calculus depends upon an evaluation of the "total mix" of information available. Accordingly, cautionary language properly is considered as part of that total mix.

---

54. 17 C.F.R. § 240.12b–2. Section 12(g) is discussed in § 9.2 *supra*. A similar test of materiality is used under section 11 of the 1933 Act (15 U.S.C.A. § 77k) and under section 12(2) (15 U.S.C.A. § 77*l*(2)). *See* §§ 7.3, 7.5 *supra*.

55. *See also* the discussion of Rule 10b–5 materiality in § 13.5A *infra*.

56. *See* the discussion of soft information in § 13.7 *supra*.

57. The bespeaks caution doctrine, which frequently has involved cautionary language in 1933 Act prospectuses is discussed in more detail in § 3.7 *supra* and § 13.5A *infra*.

58. The leading cases recognizing the doctrine include: In re Worlds of Wonder Securities Litigation, 35 F.3d 1407 (9th Cir.1994); In re Trump Casino Securities Litigation, 7 F.3d 357 (3d Cir.1993), *affirming* 793 F.Supp. 543 (D.N.J.1992); Ambrosino v. Rodman & Renshaw, Inc., 972 F.2d 776 (7th Cir.1992); Romani v. Shearson Lehman Hutton, 929 F.2d 875, 879 (1st Cir.1991); I. Meyer Pincus & Associates v. Oppenheimer & Co., 936 F.2d 759, 763 (2d Cir.1991); Sinay v. Lamson & Sessions Co., 948 F.2d 1037, 1040 (6th Cir.1991); Moorhead v. Merrill Lynch, Pierce, Fenner & Smith, Inc., 949 F.2d 243, 245–46 (8th Cir.1991); In re Convergent Technologies Securities Litigation, 948 F.2d 507, 516 (9th Cir.1991); Luce v. Edelstein, 802 F.2d 49 (2d Cir.1986); Polin v. Conductron Corp., 552 F.2d 797, 806 n. 28 (8th Cir.1977), *cert. denied* 434 U.S. 857, 98 S.Ct. 178, 54 L.Ed.2d 129 (1977) (the cautionary language was words which "bespeak caution in outlook and fall far short of the assurance required for a finding of falsity or fraud"). *See also, e.g.,* Saltzberg v. TM Sterling/Austin Associates, Ltd., 45 F.3d 399 (11th Cir.1995).

59. In re Synergen, Inc. Securities Litigation, 863 F.Supp. 1409 (D.Colo.1994) (finding bespeaks caution doctrine inapplicable to historical facts; court pointed to the absence of any authority applying the doctrine in cases not involving projections of future events); Anderson v. Clow, [1993–1994 Transfer Binder] Fed.Sec.L.Rep. (CCH) ¶ 97,807 (S.D.Cal. 1993) (bespeaks caution doctrine only applies in cases of projections, estimates, or similar types of soft information). *See also, e.g.,* Kline v. First Western Government Securities, Inc., 24 F.3d 480 (3d Cir.1994) (refusing to apply bespeaks caution doctrine to claim based on affirmative misrepresentations in tax opinion).

Reliance is an element of common law fraud that thus is required for suits under Rule 10b–5.[60] However, reliance is not an element of a Rule 14a–9 action for violation of the proxy rules.[61] It has thus been held that the fact that plaintiffs voted against a proposed merger did not require dismissal of their claims even though they could not have relied on those proxy statements supporting the proposed transaction.[62] As discussed in the next section, the plaintiffs nevertheless have to prove a causal connection between the misrepresentations and the vote or resulting transaction under attack. Accordingly, a nonrelying shareholder may nevertheless bring suit so long as the alleged injury is "fairly traceable" to the alleged misconduct.[63]

§ 11.5 Causation and Damages in Actions Under Rule 14a–9

Causation under the proxy rules' private right of action is an elusive concept.[1] Reminiscent of common law negligence[2] the causation tests are more easily articulated than applied. A showing of cause in fact is the first step in establishing that there has been a sufficient causal nexus between the defendant's conduct and the plaintiff's injury.[3] This is known as the *sine qua non* rule and applies to some extent in the securities context.[4] Once cause in fact has been established, it must be shown that the causal connection is sufficiently proximate in order to

---

60. *See* § 13.5B *infra.*

61. *E.g.,* Sandberg v. Virginia Bankshares, Inc., 891 F.2d 1112 (4th Cir.1989), *judgment reversed on other grounds* 501 U.S. 1083, 111 S.Ct. 2749, 115 L.Ed.2d 929 (1991); Daly v. Neworld Bank for Savings, 1990 WL 8059, [1990 Transfer Binder] Fed.Sec.L.Rep. (CCH) ¶ 95,247 (D.Mass.1990).

62. Sandberg v. Virginia Bankshares, Inc., 891 F.2d 1112 (4th Cir.1989), *judgment reversed on other grounds* 501 U.S. 1083, 111 S.Ct. 2749, 115 L.Ed.2d 929 (1991).

63. Western District Council of Lumber Production & Industrial Workers v. Louisiana Pacific Corp., 892 F.2d 1412 (9th Cir.1989). *Accord,* Daly v. Neworld Bank for Savings, 1990 WL 8095, [1990 Transfer Binder] Fed.Sec.L.Rep. ¶ 95,247 (D.Mass.1990) (shareholder complaining about loss of voting rights resulting from proposed reorganization had standing to sue).

§ 11.5

1. In the words of the ALI's proposed Securities Code's comments, "[u]nder the proxy rules the law is not so clear." ALI Proposed Federal Securities Code § 202(19) Comment 3(b) (1980). A finding of sufficient causation is closely tied to the question of plaintiff's reliance on the proxy materials. *See* § 13.5B *infra* for a discussion of reliance in the context of Rule 10b–5, 17 C.F.R. § 240.10b–5.

2. *See generally* W. Page Keeton, Dan B. Dobbs, Robert E. Keeton & David G. Owen, Prosser and Keeton on the Law of Torts, ch. 7 (5th ed. 1984).

3. *See, e.g., Id.;* Francis H. Bohlen, The Probable or the Natural Consequences of the Test of Liability in Negligence, 49 Am.L.Reg. 79 (1901); Leon Green, Are There Dependable Rules of Causation, 77 U.Pa.L.Rev. 601 (1929); Fleming James, Jr. & Roger F. Perry, Legal Cause, 60 Yale L.J. 761 (1951); Roscoe Pound, Causation, 67 Yale L.J. 1 (1957). For discussion of the common law bases for damages in fraud actions *see* W. Prosser *supra* footnote 2 § 110.

4. *See, e.g.,* Affiliated Ute Citizens of Utah v. United States, 406 U.S. 128, 154, 92 S.Ct. 1456, 1472, 31 L.Ed.2d 741 (1972), citing Chasins v. Smith Barney & Co., 438 F.2d 1167, 1172 (2d Cir.1970) (both decided under Rule 10b–5). Causation in Rule 10b–5 actions is discussed in § 13.6 *infra.*

warrant recovery.[5] In the securities law context, there must be a direct causal connection between the act and the injury; collateral breaches of fiduciary duties will not be sufficient to state a claim.[6]

Much of the early causation case law in the securities context has arisen under the proxy rules, although other fertile areas have been within the context of Rule 10b–5 both in terms of insider trading[7] and in the corporate mismanagement or fiduciary duty cases.[8] There is necessarily a substantial overlap between Rules 10b–5 and 14a–9 in their causation requirements, especially in the mismanagement cases that arise in the context of corporate mergers and other forms of combination.[9] The Supreme Court has considered the question of causation under the proxy rules. The Court observed in TSC Industries, Inc. v. Northway, Inc.[10] that "as an abstract proposition, the most desirable role for a court in a suit of this sort [under 14a–9], coming after the consummation of the proposed transaction, would perhaps be to determine whether in fact the proposal would have been favored by the shareholders and consummated in the absence of any misstatement or omission."[11] However, this test seems to be highly dependent upon hindsight, would result in much speculation and thus would not be susceptible to meaningful proof. Rather than adopt such a subjective causation test couched in terms of what would have happened in the particular case, the Court has opted for a more objective method of

---

5. *See* authorities in footnotes 2–3 *supra.*

6. *See* Cramer v. General Telephone & Electronics Corp., 582 F.2d 259 (3d Cir.1978), *cert. denied* 439 U.S. 1129, 99 S.Ct. 1048, 59 L.Ed.2d 90 (1979); Ketchum v. Green, 557 F.2d 1022 (3d Cir.1977), *cert. denied* 434 U.S. 940, 98 S.Ct. 431, 54 L.Ed.2d 300 (1977) (insufficient connection); Schlick v. Penn–Dixie Cement Corp., 507 F.2d 374 (2d Cir.1974), *cert. denied* 421 U.S. 976, 95 S.Ct. 1976, 44 L.Ed.2d 467 (1975) (sufficient connection); In re Tenneco Securities Litigation, 449 F.Supp. 528 (S.D.Tex.1978) (insufficient connection); Herman v. Beretta, 1978 WL 1118, [1978 Transfer Binder] Fed.Sec.L.Rep. (CCH) ¶ 96,574 (S.D.N.Y.1978) (insufficient connection); Superintendent of Insurance v. Freedman, 443 F.Supp. 628 (S.D.N.Y.1977) (insufficient connection). *See also* the authorities cited in footnotes 8, 9 *infra.*

7. *Compare, e.g.,* Elkind v. Liggett & Myers, Inc., 635 F.2d 156 (2d Cir.1980) *and* Shapiro v. Merrill Lynch, Pierce, Fenner & Smith, Inc., 495 F.2d 228 (2d Cir.1974) (both finding sufficient causation in a faceless market) *with* Fridrich v. Bradford, 542 F.2d 307 (6th Cir.1976), *cert. denied* 429 U.S. 1053, 97 S.Ct. 767, 50 L.Ed.2d 769 (1977) (finding no causation). *See* § 13.9 *infra.*

Causation under Rule 10b–5 is discussed in § 13.6 *infra.*

8. *See, e.g.,* Kidwell v. Meikle, 597 F.2d 1273 (9th Cir.1979); Alabama Farm Bureau Mutual Casualty Co. v. American Fidelity Life Insurance Co., 606 F.2d 602 (5th Cir.1979); Goldberg v. Meridor, 567 F.2d 209 (2d Cir.1977), *cert. denied* 434 U.S. 1069, 98 S.Ct. 1249, 55 L.Ed.2d 771 (1978). *See generally* Ralph C. Ferrara & Marc I. Steinberg, Reappraisal of Santa Fe: Rule 10b–5 and the New Federalism, 129 U.Pa.L.Rev. 263 (1980); Thomas L. Hazen, Corporate Mismanagement and the Federal Securities Acts' Antifraud Provisions, 20 B.C.L.Rev. 819 (1979). *See* § 13.11 *infra.*

9. In addition to the authorities in note 8 *supra, see* Marc I. Steinberg, Fiduciary Duties and Disclosure Obligations in Proxy and Tender Offer Contexts for Corporate Control, 30 Emory L.J. 169 (1981).

10. 426 U.S. 438, 96 S.Ct. 2126, 48 L.Ed.2d 757 (1976).

11. *Id.* at 448, 96 S.Ct. at 2132.

analysis.[12]

In its first opportunity to address the causation issue, the Supreme Court in Mills v. Electric Auto–Lite Co.[13] held that merely because the defendant corporation controlled a substantial block of the issuer's shares, and therefore the proposed merger would have been likely to go through regardless of the contents of the proxy statement, the absence of the plaintiff's proof of "but for" causation did not preclude a Rule 14a–9 claim.[14] The Court stated that the proper test of causation is whether upon full and fair disclosure, a reasonable shareholder's voting decision would have been likely to have been affected.[15] The Supreme Court in *Mills* pointed out that on the facts of the case before it, there was at least a mathematical possibility that the merger proposal could have been defeated since the proposing corporation did not hold more than fifty percent of the shares. The Court nevertheless acknowledged that as a practical matter the defendants had sufficient votes to assure passage.

In contrast to the Supreme Court's reliance on the absence of a numerical majority, the Second Circuit has held that even in the event that the parent corporation owns a sufficient number of shares to mathematically assure consummation of the transaction, a 14a–9 claim may still exist:

> The minority shareholders, aside, there are two other purposes served by the disclosure requirements which make a strict causation rule—whether under a 10(b) or a 14(a) claim—antithetical to it:
>
> 1. By disclosure the market will be informed so as to permit well-based decisions about buying, selling and holding the securities involved in the transaction * * *.
>
> 2. By virtue of the disclosure either modification or reconsideration of the terms of the merger by those in control might be effectuated.[16]

The Second Circuit was faced with a shareholder's complaint that a controlled merger violated SEC Rules 10b–5 and 14a–9. In upholding the plaintiff's claim the court distinguished the causation requirements of the two rules.

---

12. *See, e.g.,* the definition in the proposed securities code: "A loss is 'caused' by specified conduct to the extent that (A) the conduct was a substantial factor in producing the loss, and (B) the loss was a kind that might reasonably have been expected to occur as a result of the conduct." ALI, Proposed Federal Securities Code § 202(19) (1980).

13. 396 U.S. 375, 90 S.Ct. 616, 24 L.Ed.2d 593 (1970).

14. *Id.*

15. *Id. See also, e.g.,* TSC Industries, Inc. v. Northway, Inc., 426 U.S. 438, 96 S.Ct. 2126, 48 L.Ed.2d 757 (1976).

16. Schlick v. Penn–Dixie Cement Corp., 507 F.2d 374, 384 (2d Cir.1974), *cert. denied* 421 U.S. 976, 95 S.Ct. 1976, 44 L.Ed.2d 467 (1975). *See also, e.g.,* Cowin v. Bresler, 741 F.2d 410 (D.C.Cir.1984) (election of directors); Cole v. Schenley Indus., Inc., 563 F.2d 35 (2d Cir.1977); Laurenzano v. Einbender, 448 F.2d 1 (2d Cir.1971).

The Second Circuit in the *Schlick* case began its analysis by distinguishing between the concepts of (1) *loss causation*, that is, plaintiff's ability to prove actual economic harm resulting from the transaction, and (2) *transaction causation*, that is, that the misstatements or omissions were causally related to the occurrence of the transaction.[17] The court held that the alleged scheme to defraud based on market manipulation which resulted in a merger on preferential terms to the defendant parent corporation was sufficient to satisfy Rule 10b–5's requirement of *transaction causation*.[18]

With respect to the Rule 14a–9 proxy claim, the court in *Schlick* had to respond to the defense contention that the plaintiff could not show transaction causation since the defendant parent corporation controlled enough shares to assure the number of votes necessary for approval and consummation of the merger. Accordingly, the misstatements could not *possibly* have affected the outcome of the vote. In finding that the requisite causation had been shown, the Second Circuit pointed to the importance of "fair corporate suffrage" and further relied upon the positive value which attaches to minority approval of such a merger.[19] In contrast, alleged misstatements in connection with election of directors have been held not to satisfy the transaction causation requirement with regard to subsequent action taken by the directors without shareholder approval since the misstatements were not directly connected to the plaintiff's injury.[20] Courts should adhere to a relatively stringent application of the causation requirements. Implementation of an overly broad causation analysis will open the courts to a great deal of questionable, if not frivolous, litigation.

It has been suggested that the concepts of loss causation and transaction causation have not helped clarify the requirements of a securities fraud claim. It has, therefore, been observed that "[t]hus far

---

17. 507 F.2d at 380–81. *See also, e.g.,* Hershfang v. Knotter, 562 F.Supp. 393, 398 (E.D.Va.1983). *Cf.* Herpich v. Wallace, 430 F.2d 792 (5th Cir.1970) (decided under Rule 10b–5); Shell v. Hensley, 430 F.2d 819 (5th Cir.1970) (same); In re Tenneco Securities Litigation, 449 F.Supp. 528, 531 (S.D.Tex.1978); Goldberger v. Baker, 442 F.Supp. 659, 666 (S.D.N.Y.1977); Voege v. American Sumatra Tobacco Corp., 241 F.Supp. 369 (D.Del. 1965). *But cf.* International Broadcasting Corp. v. Turner, 734 F.Supp. 383 (D.Minn.1990) (failure to allege any transaction or other action resulting from the misleading filing was not fatal since the damage element could be satisfied by a showing of a significant threat of a reoccurrence of the alleged proxy violations).

The transaction/loss causation analysis has been appearing in an increasing number of decisions under Rule 10b–5. *See* § 13.6 *infra.*

18. 507 F.2d at 381. *See also* Mosher v. Kane, 784 F.2d 1385 (9th Cir.1986) (finding sufficient transaction causation); Yabsley v. Conover, 644 F.Supp. 689, 700 (N.D.Ill.1986) (finding no causation). The present vitality of the 10b–5 claim in the light of the Supreme Court's *Santa Fe Industries* decision would necessarily involve proof of some element of deception, which appears to have been sufficiently alleged in the *Schlick* complaint. *See* Santa Fe Industries, Inc. v. Green, 430 U.S. 462, 97 S.Ct. 1292, 51 L.Ed.2d 480 (1977); § 13.11 *infra.*

19. 507 F.2d at 383. *See also, e.g.,* Wright v. Heizer Corp., 560 F.2d 236 (7th Cir.1977), *cert. denied* 434 U.S. 1066, 98 S.Ct. 1243, 55 L.Ed.2d 767 (1978).

20. United Canso Oil & Gas Ltd. v. Catawba Corp., 566 F.Supp. 232 (D.Conn.1983).

the courts seem to have been incapable of achieving any analytical precision in dealing with this question, and the addition of catch phrases such as 'transactional causation' and 'loss causation' add nothing unless they are adequately defined." [21]   However, the courts seem to be relying on these concepts with increased frequency.[22]

It is clear from the cases that in order to be actionable, the violation of the proxy rules must have been an "essential link" in the transaction under attack.[23] A 1991 Supreme Court decision highlights the fact that a violation that is merely collateral to the transaction in question will not be subject to attack in a private suit under the proxy rules. In Virginia Bankshares, Inc. v. Sandberg,[24] minority shareholders of a corporation involved in a cashout merger challenged a vote allegedly based on misleading proxy solicitation materials. The proxies in question did not relate to a vote directly on the merger, but rather to a vote taken under a state corporate law "interested director" statute to cleanse a potential conflict of interest. There was no showing that a failure to secure the shareholder vote in question would have prevented or in any way affected the cashout merger. In a five to four decision, the Court held that in the absence of such a direct causal connection there could be no action under the proxy rules. The court referred to and rejected earlier lower court decisions which had indicated that a shareholder not voting on the transaction under challenge might nevertheless be able to sustain a claim under the proxy rules. Notwithstanding the protestations of the dissenting Justices,[25] it is not clear the extent to which the *Sandberg* decision narrows the scope of private actions under the proxy rules. For example, does this ruling extend to the cases indicating that a mathematical possibility of defeating the transaction is a precondition to showing causation? Or is the decision limited to votes on collateral matters such as was involved in *Sandberg?* The Second Circuit has held that although the management had sufficient votes to assure the success of the solicitation, the shareholder was nevertheless able to maintain a claim under the proxy rules for alleged interference with statutory appraisal rights.[26] Similarly, in a post-*Sandberg* decision, the Sixth Circuit held that the mathematical impossibility of preventing the transaction did not preclude a claim based on loss of a state law

---

21. Richard W. Jennings & Harold Marsh, Jr., Securities Regulation: Cases and Materials 1047 (5th ed. 1982).

22. *See* § 13.6 *infra.*

23. *E.g.,* Elmore v. Cone Mills Corp., 1990 WL 169783, [1990–1991 Transfer Binder] Fed.Sec.L.Rep. (CCH) ¶ 95,506 (D.S.C.1990) , *affirmed in part, reversed in part* 6 F.3d 1028 (4th Cir.1993) (misleading statements about future employee benefits were material in connection with proposed leveraged buyout).

24. 501 U.S. 1083, 111 S.Ct. 2749, 115 L.Ed.2d 929 (1991), *appeal after remand* 979 F.2d 332 (4th Cir.1992), *opinion vacated* 1993 WL 524680 (1993).

25. 501 U.S. at 1111, 111 S.Ct. at 2768, 115 L.Ed.2d at 958.

26. Wilson v. Great American Industries, Inc., 979 F.2d 924 (2d Cir.1992). *See also, e.g.,* Stahl v. Gibraltar Financial Corp., 967 F.2d 335 (9th Cir.1992).

appraisal remedy due to material misstatements or omissions.[27]

The clear lesson of the *Virginia Bankshares* decision is that a private right of action for a violation of the proxy rules will not exist when the transaction in question does not require a shareholder vote in order to be approved.[28] Similarly, any causal connection that can be shown must be a direct one.[29] Thus, for example, alleged violations in connection with a proxy solicitation for election of directors were too remote from subsequent misconduct by directors after the election in question.[30]

As noted above,[31] the causation analysis as it has developed under the proxy rules is very similar to the one that has been held applicable in recent corporate mismanagement cases under Rule 10b–5.[32] In those cases the recent court of appeals decisions have viewed the question of transaction causation in terms of whether upon full and fair disclosure, the minority shareholder would have had an opportunity to prevent the transaction by seeking an injunction under state law.[33] It is highly questionable whether these cases are consistent with the Supreme Court's concern of freeing the federal courts from claims that are based on state law and breaches of fiduciary duties.[34]

One problem the courts have yet to grapple with adequately in either the Rule 10b–5 or 14a–9 setting is the question of assessing damages in a case based on such a loose causation test. In one case attacking a controlled merger under Rule 14a–9, the Supreme Court held that the measure of damages would be determined by what would have

---

27. Howing Co. v. Nationwide Corp., 972 F.2d 700 (6th Cir.1992), *cert. denied* ___ U.S. ___, 113 S.Ct. 1645, 123 L.Ed.2d 266 (1993) (decided under section 13(e)'s going private rules). *But see* Boone v. Carlsbad Bancorporation, 972 F.2d 1545 (10th Cir.1992).

28. *See, e.g.,* Dominick v. Marcove, 809 F.Supp. 805 (D.Colo.1992).

29. General Electric Co. v. Cathcart, 980 F.2d 927 (3d Cir.1992) (too attenuated a connection between misstatements concerning directors' election and subsequent misconduct in office). *See also, e.g.,* Heil v. Lebow, 1993 WL 15032, [1992–1993 Transfer Binder] Fed.Sec.L.Rep. (CCH) ¶ 97,324 (S.D.N.Y.1993) (alleged failure to disclose secret plan was not actionable when the alleged plan was never implemented); Diamond v. ML–Lee Acquisition Fund II, L.P., 1992 WL 420922, [1992–1993 Transfer Binder] Fed.Sec.L.Rep. (CCH) ¶ 97,275 (S.D.N.Y.1992) (failure to establish loss causation).

30. General Electric Co. v. Cathcart, 980 F.2d 927 (3d Cir.1992).

31. *See* footnotes 8, 9 *supra.*

32. 17 C.F.R. § 240.10b–5. *See* Healey v. Catalyst Recovery of Pennsylvania, 616 F.2d 641 (3d Cir.1980); Weisberg v. Coastal States Gas Corp., 609 F.2d 650 (2d Cir.1979), *cert. denied* 445 U.S. 951, 100 S.Ct. 1600, 63 L.Ed.2d 786 (1980); Kidwell v. Meikle, 597 F.2d 1273 (9th Cir.1979); Alabama Farm Bureau Mutual Casualty Co. v. American Fidelity Life Insurance Co., 606 F.2d 602 (5th Cir.1979); Wright v. Heizer Corp., 560 F.2d 236 (7th Cir.1977), *cert. denied* 434 U.S. 1066, 98 S.Ct. 1243, 55 L.Ed.2d 767 (1978); Goldberg v. Meridor, 567 F.2d 209 (2d Cir.1977), *cert. denied* 434 U.S. 1069, 98 S.Ct. 1249, 55 L.Ed.2d 771 (1978). *See generally* Ralph C. Ferrara & Marc I. Steinberg, A Reappraisal of *Santa Fe:* Rule 10b–5 and The New Federalism, 129 U.Pa.L.Rev. 263 (1980); Steinberg, *supra* footnote 9.

33. *See* §§ 13.6, 13.9 *infra.*

34. Santa Fe Industries, Inc. v. Green, 430 U.S. 462, 97 S.Ct. 1292, 51 L.Ed.2d 480 (1977). *See also* Piper v. Chris–Craft Industries, 430 U.S. 1, 97 S.Ct. 926, 51 L.Ed.2d 124 (1977) (the 1934 Act's tender offer provisions were not designed to federalize all questions); § 11.19 *infra.*

been a fair exchange upon full disclosure.[35]   However, on remand the
Seventh Circuit found that the plaintiffs failed to satisfy their burden of
proving an unfair exchange ratio.[36]

Of course, the ideal way to attack a violation of the proxy rules (or of
Rule 10b-5 for that matter) in a merger case would be to seek a
preliminary injunction prior to the shareholder vote.   However, in most
cases the facts giving rise to a claim of unfairness in the merger
exchange do not come to light until after the transaction has been
consummated.   Furthermore, even if the minority shareholders have a
basis for believing that material facts were misstated or omitted from the
proxy solicitation materials, in order to succeed in obtaining a preliminary injunction they will have to prove both a substantial likelihood of
success on the merits as well as irreparable injury should the injunction
not be granted.[37]   Injunctive relief may also be sought by the SEC.[38]   In
an appropriate case, the SEC can secure ancillary relief as well.[39]

Since none of the recent proxy cases have proceeded to a successful
resolution on the issue of damages, and many of the cases have been
settled, in any given case it may be difficult for a court to review the
relatively scant precedent and conclude that there is a substantial
likelihood of success on the merits.   Furthermore, the hardship that
results from holding up a proposed merger will make the difficulty of

35.   Mills v. Electric Auto–Lite Co., 396 U.S. 375, 90 S.Ct. 616, 24 L.Ed.2d 593 (1970),
appeal after remand 552 F.2d 1239 (7th Cir.1977).   *See also, e.g.,* Gerstle v. Gamble–
Skogmo, Inc., 478 F.2d 1281 (2d Cir.1973) (the measure of damages in a proxy merger case
is the difference in the value of what the plaintiffs gave up and what they received in
exchange).

36.   Mills v. Electric Auto–Lite Co., 552 F.2d 1239 (7th Cir.1977).   The court held that
the fairness issue must be viewed in light of the "synergetic" effect of the merger on the
minority's shareholdings.   *See* Victor Brudney & Marvin A. Chirelstein, Fair Shares in
Corporate Mergers and Takeovers, 88 Harv.L.Rev. 297 (1974).   The synergetic effect of the
business combination can be examined only when the minority receives shares in the
surviving corporation and not in the freezeout context.   *Cf.* Victor Brudney, A Note on
"Going Private," 61 Va.L.Rev. 1019 (1975).

37.   Rondeau v. Mosinee Paper Corp., 422 U.S. 49, 95 S.Ct. 2069, 45 L.Ed.2d 12 (1975)
(decided under section 13(d)).   *See also, e.g.,* Economic Development Corp. v. Model Cities
Agency, 519 F.2d 740 (8th Cir.1975); Winkleman v. New York Stock Exchange, 445 F.2d
786 (3d Cir.1971); Wallerstein v. Primerica Corp., 701 F.Supp. 393 (E.D.N.Y.1988) (injunction denied because of adequate remedy at law); Pargas v. Empire Gas Corp., 423 F.Supp.
199, 209 (D.Md.1976), *affirmed* 546 F.2d 25 (4th Cir.1976) ("[A] plaintiff need establish
only a 'probable right' to relief, and to demonstrate that his need for protection outweighs
the probable injury to defendants which would result from the grant of such relief.")   *See
generally* 11 Charles A. Wright & Alexander R. Miller, Federal Practice & Procedure: Civil
§ 2942 (1973).

38.   *E.g.,* SEC v. May, 229 F.2d 123 (2d Cir.1956), *affirming* 134 F.Supp. 247 (S.D.N.Y.
1955).   *See* § 9.5 *supra. See generally* Marc I. Steinberg, SEC and Other Permanent
Injunctions–Standards for Their Imposition, Modification and Dissolution, 66 Cornell
L.Rev. 27 (1980).

39.   *See generally* George W. Dent, Jr., Ancillary Relief in Federal Securities Law: A
Study in Federal Remedies, 67 Minn.L.Rev. 865 (1983);   John D. Ellsworth, Disgorgement
in Securities Fraud Actions Brought by the SEC, 1977 Duke L.J. 641;   James R. Farrand,
Ancillary Remedies in SEC Civil Enforcement Suits, 89 Harv.L.Rev. 1779 (1976);   Robert J.
Malley, The Far–Reaching Equitable Remedies under the Securities Acts and the Growth
of Federal Corporate Law, 17 Wm. & Mary L.Rev. 47 (1975);   Arthur F. Mathews, Recent
Trends in SEC Requested Ancillary Relief in SEC Level Injunctive Actions, 31 Bus.Law
1323 (1976); § 9.5 *supra.*

proving irreparable injury even more so. On the other side of the coin, once the transaction has gone through and third parties have dealt with the post-merger corporation a court will not be in a position to undo the transaction since these innocent third parties stand to be affected adversely.

The inability in most cases to secure injunctive relief makes the damage action the plaintiff's only remedy. Unlike Rule 10b–5 where damages can be based on the difference between sale or purchase price and the true value of the shares,[40] calculation of damages in the proxy context is a much more amorphous process.[41] This coupled with the paucity of cases on point[42] gives little guidance in assessing the prospects of a claim for damages in the proxy area that is not based on a transaction in shares or corporate assets where dollar amounts may be more readily identifiable.

§ 11.6 Proxy Disclosures Concerning Election of Directors—Rule 14a–11; Annual Report to Security Holders

Disclosures Relating to Elections and Directors' Past Conduct

The Securities and Exchange Commission has adopted rules regulating disclosures in connection with shareholder elections of directors of reporting companies. Rule 14a–11[1] applies to the solicitation of proxies with regard to the election or removal of directors at either annual or special meetings of securities holders. The rule requires identification of all "participants" in the solicitation process as well as an attribution of the source of all materials used in the solicitation. All sources of financing behind the solicitation must also be disclosed.

Arguably, the most significant of the director election disclosure items is the requirement of Schedule 14A[2] calling for disclosure of the nominee's past experience in office.[3] For example, it has been held that nondisclosure of a director's past conduct in office may be a material fact

---

40. Even in the Rule 10b–5 context courts have struggled when confronted with the problem of assessing damages. *See* § 13.7 *infra.*

41. *E.g.* Mills v. Electric Auto–Lite Co., 552 F.2d 1239 (7th Cir.1977).

42. The absence of much guidance from the courts is due to the fact that in most cases either the plaintiff has been unsuccessful or has settled prior to a judgment on the merits.

§ 11.6

1. 17 C.F.R. § 240.14a–11.

2. 17 C.F.R. § 240.14a–101.

3. *See generally*, Dennis J. Block, Nancy E. Barton & Patricia A. Olah, SEC Litigation. Judicial Limitations on Federal Disclosure Requirements Regarding Management Integrity, 14 Sec.Reg.L.J. 354 (1987); Ralph C. Ferrara, Richard M. Starr & Marc I. Steinberg, Disclosure of Information Bearing on Management Integrity and Competency, 76 Nw. U.L.Rev. 555 (1981).

The federal right to information under the proxy rules is in addition to shareholder inspection rights that exist under state law. *See, e.g.,* Parsons v. Jefferson–Pilot Corp., 333 N.C. 420, 426 S.E.2d 685 (1993) (common law right of inspection was not abrogated by state statutory right to inspection).

in a shareholder's decision of how to cast his or her vote.[4] Past conduct involving fiduciary dealings but unrelated to the issuer is also relevant information with regard to an individual who is up for election as a director.[5] As is the case with disclosures generally, the pertinent information relating to directors' conduct must be disclosed clearly. For example, in one case the fact that proxies sought by management for approval of a stock sale would in effect transfer control of a corporation to a third party (by allowing him to name a majority of directors) was buried in pages of minute print.[6] The court there found the entire proxy solicitation to be defective: "disclosure may not be buried in a mass of information that, when pieced together, might give the correct impression."[7]

On appropriate facts, an SEC injunction may be issued to stop proxy violations in connection with a challenge to management.[8] For example, this power has been exercised against shareholders challenging current management.[9] When both parties (management and the insurgents) have committed proxy violations, courts have used the doctrine of unclean hands to leave the parties in the position they find themselves due to their wrongful actions.[10] The rule is otherwise where innocent parties stand to be adversely affected. For example, where duplicity or material nondisclosures result in the election of directors by deceived stockholders, the election may be set aside.[11] If such an election were allowed to stand, the innocent stockholders would suffer the consequences of the violations and this is the very group that the Securities Act of 1934 is designed to protect.[12]

---

4. Maldonado v. Flynn, 597 F.2d 789 (2d Cir.1979). *See also* Lebhar Friedman, Inc. v. Movielab, Inc., 1987 WL 5793, [1987 Transfer Binder] Fed.Sec.L.Rep. (CCH) ¶ 93,162 (S.D.N.Y.1987) (Unpublished Case) (failure to disclose independent counsel's recommendations to board, including suggested reevaluation of CEO's compensation, held material to shareholders deciding whether to reelect directors).

5. GAF Corp. v. Heyman, 559 F.Supp. 748 (S.D.N.Y.1983) (charges against outsider running for director of fiduciary breaches in connection with family trust must be disclosed; new election ordered), *reversed on finding of nonmateriality* 724 F.2d 727 (2d Cir.1983).

6. SEC v. Falstaff Brewing Corp., 629 F.2d 62 (D.C.Cir.1980), *cert. denied* 449 U.S. 1012, 101 S.Ct. 569, 66 L.Ed.2d 471 (1980) (decided under Rule 14a–9). *Cf.* section 14(f) dealing with similar disclosures in the context of a tender offer, 15 U.S.C.A. § 78n(f). *See* David L. Ratner, Section 14(f): A New Approach to Transfers of Corporate Control, 54 Cornell L.Rev. 65 (1968). § 11.16 *infra.*

7. 629 F.2d at 67.

8. *See generally* Marc I. Steinberg, SEC and other Permanent Injunctions—Standards for Their Imposition, Modification and Dissolution, 66 Cornell L.Rev. 27 (1980). *See also* § 9.5 *supra.*

9. SEC v. May, 229 F.2d 123 (2d Cir.1956).

10. Chris–Craft Industries, Inc. v. Independent Stockholders Committee, 354 F.Supp. 895 (D.Del.1973); Gaudiosi v. Mellon, 269 F.2d 873 (3d Cir.1959), *cert. denied* 361 U.S. 902, 80 S.Ct. 211, 4 L.Ed.2d 157 (1959).

11. *E.g.* GAF Corp. v. Heyman, 559 F.Supp. 748 (S.D.N.Y.1983), *reversed on other grounds* 724 F.2d 727 (2d Cir.1983); Bertoglio v. Texas International Co., 488 F.Supp. 630 (D.Del.1980).

12. *See* Arthur A. Dean, Non–Compliance with Proxy Regulations—Effect on Ability of Corporation to Hold Valid Meeting, 24 Cornell L.Q. 483 (1939).

A related issue concerns disclosure of executive compensation.[13] The SEC revised its requirements by eliminating about three-fourths of the disclosures relating to executive compensation.[14] But more recently the Commission has adopted additional requirements. For example, issuers must now depict their executives' compensation in comparison to the compensation of other executives and also in comparison to the company's performance.

Annual Report to Security Holders

In addition to the foregoing disclosure requirements imposed by Schedule 14A and Rule 14a–11,[15] there are additional disclosures when there is a proxy solicitation by the issuer or on its behalf in connection with an annual meeting at which there will be an election of directors.[16] Rule 14a–3(b) requires that any such proxy statement be accompanied or preceded by an annual report of the issuer's operations.[17] This annual report must contain audited financial data relating to the issuer and subsidiaries from recent years, presented in accordance with the commission's rules for financial reporting.[18] The annual report contains a summary of the information that is required to be set forth in the annual 1934 Act filing on Form 10–K.[19] The annual report also must include a description of the past year's business of the issuer and subsidiaries so as to give an indication of the general scope of operations.[20] Seven copies of the annual report must be filed with the Commission.[21] However, the annual report is neither "soliciting material" nor a "filed" document within the meaning of section 18(a)'s express civil liability for misstatements in SEC filings.[22] As is the case with

---

13. Disclosures relating to management compensation as well as insiders' transactions with the corporation must be disclosed in both 1933 and 1934 Act filings. *See* §§ 3.2, 3.7, 9.3 *supra*. *See generally* Ferrara, Starr & Steinberg *supra* footnote 3.

14. *See* Sec.Act Rel. No. 33–6486 (Sept. 23, 1983). The new rules have higher thresholds for requiring disclosure of remuneration and perquisites.

15. 17 C.F.R. §§ 240.14a–11, 240.14a–101. *See also* former Schedule 14B, 17 C.F.R. § 240.14a–102 (1988) (rescinded).

16. State corporate statutes generally require that director elections take place at the annual meeting even where directors' terms are staggered. *See generally* 2 James D. Cox, Thomas L. Hazen & F. Hodge O'Neal, Corporations §§ 13.13, 13.14 (1995); Harry G. Henn & John R. Alexander, Laws of Corporations 556–558 (3d ed. 1983).

17. 17 C.F.R. § 240.14a–3(b). It has been held that an annual report sent out by third class mail four to five days before the proxy materials did not reasonably guarantee compliance with the rule. Ash v. GAF Corp., 723 F.2d 1090 (3d Cir.1983).

18. 17 C.F.R. § 240.14a–3(b)(1)–(3). *See* Regulation S–X which relates to financial reporting generally. *See* § 9.4 *supra*. The annual report must also include information required by Regulation S–K which applied to 1933 Act registration. *See* § 3.3 *supra*.

19. The Form 10K filing and other periodic reports under the Exchange Act are considered in § 9.3 *supra*. The annual report must also state that the 10K filing will be made available without change to security holders requesting a copy. The issuer may elect to describe rather than furnish copies of all the exhibits to the 10K 17 C.F.R. § 240.14a–3(b)(10).

20. 17 C.F.R. § 240.14a–3(b)(6).

21. 17 C.F.R. § 240.14a–3(c).

22. *Id. See* 15 U.S.C.A. § 78r(a); § 12.8 *infra*. However, if the annual report is incorporated into the proxy statement, section 18(a) liability will attach to material

other proxy materials and reports to shareholders, where securities are held by brokers for a customer's account, the broker must forward the annual report to the beneficial owner of the securities.[23]　Also when there is no proxy solicitation, security holders are nonetheless entitled to similar information.[24]

In lieu of sending the annual report specified by Rule 14a–3, the issuer at its option may furnish security holders with a copy of its current 10K filing.[25]　If the issuer makes this election, section 18(a)'s provisions for express liability for misstatements or omissions will be applicable.[26]　The addition of section 18(a) liability can be significant in the case of a materially defective annual report.[27]　While SEC Rule 10b–5 will provide a remedy to investors injured by purchasing or selling securities in reliance on such an annual report,[28] this liability must be premised on a finding that the defendant acted with scienter.[29]　In contrast, section 18(a) imposes liability upon all signers of the defective filing and anyone else responsible for the misstatements unless they prove their good faith and lack of knowledge;[30] thus, the burden of proof falls on the defendant.[31]

§ 11.7　Security Holders' Access to the Proxy System: Shareholder Proposals and Right to Information

Informational Rights[1]

An issuer subject to the Exchange Act's registration and reporting requirements[2] and thus to the proxy rules must comply with written

---

misstatements or omissions. Additionally, since the annual report is not considered proxy "soliciting material" (17 C.F.R. § 240.14a–3(c)), this presumably precludes implied liability under Rule 14a–9. *See* § 11.3 *supra.*

23.　17 C.F.R. § 240.14a–3(c), Notes 2–3.　*See* 17 C.F.R. § 240.14b–1 and § 11.9 *infra.*

24.　15 U.S.C.A. § 78n(c).　*See* § 11.8 *infra.*

25.　17 C.F.R. § 240.14a–3(d).　The 10K annual filing requirement for issuers of securities registered under section 12 is discussed in §§ 9.2, 9.3 *supra.*

Another alternative is the issuer's option to combine the 10–K filing requirement with the sending of a single integrated report satisfying both the filing requirements and the dissemination requirements of Rule 14a–3, Form 10–K, instruction H.　This enables the issuer to save preparation and printing costs; however, it may result in additional potential civil liability for material misstatements and omissions.

26.　15 U.S.C.A. § 78r(a).

27.　Section 18(a) is discussed in § 12.8 *infra.*

28.　17 C.F.R. § 240.10b–5.　*See* §§ 13.2–13.3 *infra.*

29.　*E.g.* Ernst & Ernst v. Hochfelder, 425 U.S. 185, 96 S.Ct. 1375, 47 L.Ed.2d 668 (1976), *rehearing denied* 425 U.S. 986, 96 S.Ct. 2194, 48 L.Ed.2d 811 (1976).　*See* § 13.4 *infra.*

30.　15 U.S.C.A. § 78r(a).　The 10K must be signed by the issuer's principal officers and a majority of directors.

31.　The court also has the discretion to award attorneys' fees to the successful party. *Id.*

§ 11.7

1.　*See also* § 11.2 *supra.*

2.　15 U.S.C.A. §§ 78*l*, 78m.　*See* §§ 9.2, 9.3 *supra.*

shareholder requests for information with regard to matters to be voted on at the meeting.[3] Specifically, Rule 14a–7(a) requires the issuer to provide the following information upon request by a shareholder: (1) a statement of the approximate number of security holders who have been or are to be solicited on behalf of the issuer; and (2) an estimate of the cost of mailing a specified proxy statement including cost of bankers, brokers or other persons acting on the issuer's behalf.[4] Also, if a security holder so requests the issuer must mail, at the security holder's expense, any material relating to matters to be voted upon at the meeting to all holders that were solicited by the issuer or someone acting on the issuer's behalf.[5] If the issuer so desires, in lieu of complying with the securities holder's request it may provide the security holder with a mailing list of all persons entitled to vote on the relevant proposals.[6] In the case of roll-up reorganizations and going private transactions subject to SEC Rule 13–3, the requesting shareholder can make an election to receive a mailing list or to have the issuer make the mailing at the shareholder's expense.[7]

The foregoing disclosure and informational requirements are imposed on the issuer in order to provide shareholders with access to the proxy machinery. These provisions help assure that there is full disclosure and adequate presentation of both sides to any issue to come before the shareholders of securities subject to Exchange Act's reporting requirements. The security holder's access to mailing lists applies to all matters of interest to security holders with voting rights, whether relating to proposals put forth by the issuer's management, challenges by dissident shareholders,[8] or proposals of security holders under the SEC shareholder proposal rule which is discussed below.[9]

The federal proxy rules' guarantee of security holders' access to the proxy machinery is supplemented by shareholder's common law and statutory inspection rights that are provided by state corporate law.[10] Put in its most general terms, corporate shareholders have a right to inspect relevant corporate books and records pursuant to a request

3. 17 C.F.R. § 240.14a–7.

4. 17 C.F.R. § 240.14a–7(a).

5. 17 C.F.R. § 240.14a–7(b).

6. 17 C.F.R. § 240.14a–7(c). *See, e.g.,* In re Krupp Corp., [1991–1992 Transfer Binder] Fed.Sec.L.Rep. (CCH) ¶ 84,975 (SEC 1992) (general partners of limited partnership consented to finding that they failed to respond promptly to limited partners' request for list of security holders).

7. Rule 14a–7, 17 C.F.R. § 240.14a–7 as amended in Exch. Act Rel. no. 34–31326 (SEC October 22, 1992). A roll-up reorganization is a transaction in which the issuer changes the form of doing business such as by rolling up a limited partnership into a corporation. *See* Item 901 of Reg. S–K. The going private rules are discussed in § 11.17 *infra*.

8. *See generally* Edward R. Aranow & Herbert A. Einhorn, Proxy Contests for Corporate Control (2d ed. 1968).

9. *See* text following footnote 12 *infra*.

10. *See generally* James D. Cox, Thomas L. Hazen & F. Hodge O'Neal, Corporations §§ 13.2–13.11 (1995); Harry G. Henn & John R. Alexander, Laws of Corporations § 199 (3d ed. 1983); Russell B. Stevenson, Corporations and Information: Secrecy, Access and Disclosure (1980).

stating a proper purpose therefor.[11]   Although in most cases much of this information will already be available because of the 1934 Act's registration and periodic reporting requirements, these state law inspection rights can give security holders access to more detailed information and to the documents and other corporate records forming the basis of publicly reported information.

The Shareholder Proposal Rule

One of the more critical aspects of proxy rules' impact on corporate governance[12] and shareholder input is found in the shareholder proposal rule–SEC Rule 14a–8.[13]   The basic thrust of Rule 14a–8 is that a shareholder proposal which is proper for consideration under state law must be included in the management's proxy statement along with a brief statement explaining the shareholder's reason for supporting the proposal's adoption, provided that it is submitted to the issuer in a timely fashion.[14]   There are relatively few judicial decisions dealing with the shareholder proposal rule but most interpretations appear through the SEC no action letter process.[15]   Each year, the Commission is faced with numerous requests for no action letters.   Although the case–by-case approach of no action letters may not be the most efficient law making process, it does provide a good source of insight into the SEC's current views.

The Second Circuit has recognized the existence of a private right of action by shareholders to enforce their rights under Rule 14a–8.[16]   If management wrongfully refuses to disclose a shareholder proposal, a court may enjoin the upcoming meeting.[17]   In addition, material mis-

---

11.   *E.g.* ALI–ABA, Revised Model Business Corporation Act § 16.02 (1984); ALI–ABA Model Business Corporation Act § 52 (1980).   In addition to the authorities in footnote 10 *supra, see* 5 William Fletcher, Private Corporations §§ 2222–2224 (perm. ed. rev. vol. 1976);   Comment, Shareholders' Right to Inspection of Corporate Stock Ledger, 4 Conn. L.Rev. 707 (1972);   Note, "Proper Purpose" for Inspection of Corporate Stock Ledger, 1970 Duke L.J. 393.   *Cf.* Roy N. Freed, Providing by Statute for Inspection of Corporate Computer and Other Records Not Legible Visually—A Case Study on Legislating for Computer Technology, 23 Bus.Law. 457 (1968).

12.   *See, e.g.,* Carol Goforth, Proxy Reform as a Means of Increasing Shareholder Participation in Corporate Governance: Too Little, But Not Too Late, 43 Am. U.L. Rev. 379 (1994);   Norma M. Sharara & Anne E. Hoke-Witherspoon, The Evolution of the 1992 Shareholder Communication Proxy Rules and Their Impact on Corporate Governance, 49 Bus. Law. 327 (1993).

13.   17 C.F.R. § 240.14a–8.

14.   *See* New York City Employees' Retirement System v. American Brands, Inc., 634 F.Supp. 1382 (S.D.N.Y.1986) (recognizing private right of action seeking mandatory injunctive relief to prevent violation of Rule 14a–8).

15.   No action letters are discussed in §§ 1.4, 9.5, and 9.34 (Practitioner's Edition only) *infra.   See also, e.g.,* Andrew Frackman & Achilles M. Perry, Shareholder Public Policy Proposals and the No–Action Letter Process, 27 Rev. Sec. & Commod. Reg. 43 (1994).

16.   Roosevelt v. E.I. DuPont de Nemours & Co., 958 F.2d 416 (D.C.Cir.1992).

17.   New York City Employees' Retirement System v. Dole Food Co., 795 F.Supp. 95 (S.D.N.Y.1992), *appeal dismissed, opinion vacated* 969 F.2d 1430 (2d Cir.1992) (preliminary injunction).   *But cf.* New York City Employees' Retirement System v. Brunswick Corp., 789 F.Supp. 144 (S.D.N.Y.1992) (denying preliminary relief in deference to SEC's determination that proposal was excludable).

statements in management's opposition to a shareholder proposal can result in a voiding of the vote and an order that the proposal be resubmitted to the shareholders at the next annual meeting.[18] More recently, management's ability to exclude shareholder proposals regarding social issues has been limited. In *Amalgamated Clothing & Textile Workers Union v. Wal–Mart Stores*,[19] the court overturned the SEC's permitting management to exclude shareholder proposals relating to the company's equal employment and affirmative action programs. The court reasoned that the SEC's formal guidelines for the ordinary business basis for exclusion superceded inconsistent no action responses.[20]

At one time more expansive, in recent years the Commission has been narrowing the shareholder proposal rule. However, even if a proposal that is valid under state law is properly excludable, it must nevertheless be described in the issuer's proxy statement.[21] Thus, the narrowing of the shareholder proposal rule does not deny insurgent shareholders all access.

In order to preclude exclusion from management's proxy materials, the shareholder submitting the proposal must be a beneficial owner of a security that would be entitled to vote on the proposal at the shareholder meeting; also, the proponent must have owned for at least one year the lesser of one percent or one thousand dollars in market value of such securities.[22] Further, the proponent must continue to be a security holder through the date on which the meeting is held.[23] The shareholder presenting the proposal was formerly required to notify the issuer in writing of an intention to appear personally at the meeting and submit

18. United Paperworkers International Union v. International Paper Co., 801 F.Supp. 1134 (S.D.N.Y.1992), *affirmed and modified* 985 F.2d 1190 (2d Cir.1993) (misstatements were in connection with management opposition to proposals relating to the company's environmental policies).

19. 821 F.Supp. 877 (S.D.N.Y.1993). *Compare, e.g.,* Ford Motor Co., 25 Sec.Reg. & L.Rep. (BNA) 456 (SEC No Action Letter avail. March 11, 1993) (permitting exclusion of proposal relating to affirmative action on the basis that it was motivated by a personal grievance).

20. Roosevelt v. E.I. Du Pont de Nemours & Co., 958 F.2d 416, 427 n. 19 (D.C.Cir.1992) (principle of deference to agency views does not apply to no action letters as they are not formal agency positions); Amalgamated Clothing & Textile Workers Union v. Wal–Mart Stores, Inc., 821 F.Supp. 877 (S.D.N.Y.1993) (court refused to follow position in no action letter since SEC had since taken a different view in the context of formal rulemaking); New York City Employees' Retirement System v. Dole Food Co., 795 F.Supp. 95, 100–101 (S.D.N.Y.), *appeal dismissed, opinion vacated as moot* 969 F.2d 1430 (2d Cir.1992) (courts are not bound by no action responses).

21. Schedule 14A, item 21. *See* text accompanying footnotes 42–43 *infra.*

22. 17 C.F.R. § 240.14a–8(a)(1). Prior to 1983 there was no minimum ownership requirement. Sec.Exch.Act Rel. No. 34–20091 (Aug. 16, 1983); Sec.Exch.Act Rel. No. 34–19134 (Oct. 19, 1982).

The shareholder's refusal to document sufficient ownership to satisfy the eligibility criteria may justify management in excluding the proposal from the proxy statement. *See, e.g.,* ITT Corp., 25 Sec. Reg. & L. Rep. (BNA) 1700 (SEC No Action Letter avail. Nov. 29, 1993); Syntex Corp., 25 Sec. Reg. & L. Rep. (BNA) 1224 (SEC No Action Letter avail. Aug. 23, 1993).

23. 17 C.F.R. § 240.14a–8(a)(1).

the proposal for shareholder approval but this is no longer necessary.[24]

Shareholders submitting proposals to be considered at a meeting must meet the rule's timing requirements. For annual meetings, the proposals must be received at the issuer's principal executive offices not less than one hundred and twenty days in advance of the release of the issuer's proxy statement.[25] In computing the time period the security holder can rely on the date upon which the proxy statement was sent out for the previous year's meeting. If there was no annual meeting in the preceding year or if the date of the meeting was changed by more than thirty calendar days from when it was held in the past, the proposal must "be received by the issuer a reasonable time before the solicitation is made."[26] Similarly, for special shareholder meetings, the proposal must be presented to management a reasonable time before the solicitation is made.[27] The Commission suggests that all shareholder proposals be submitted to the issuer by certified mail with return receipt requested.[28]

A shareholder formerly could submit up to two proposals, but this has been reduced to one proposal per year.[29] The SEC has refused to extend the one proposal per year limitation in issuing an opinion rejecting the argument that a nonnamed sponsor was the "de facto" proponent.[30] In addition to the proposal itself, the proponent may also provide a supporting statement which will be included in the proxy solicitation materials which are disseminated at management's expense, provided that the proposal and the statement do not exceed five hundred words.[31] The issuer, of course, can agree to include longer statements. Management is also free to state its reasons for opposing the shareholder proposal.[32] Rule 14a–8(c), which is interpreted largely through no action

---

24. Sec.Exch.Act Rel. No. 34–20091 (Aug. 16, 1983); Sec.Exch.Act Rel. No. 34–19134 (Oct. 10, 1982). A shareholder who was not aware of the former notice requirement was able to comply within ten business days after being informed of it by the issuer. 17 C.F.R. § 240.14a–8(a)(2) (1982).

25. Sun Co., 24 Sec.Reg. & L.Rep. (BNA) 543 (SEC No Action Letter avail. April 3, 1992) (proposal received less than 120 days in advance was excludable).

26. 17 C.F.R. § 240.14a–8(a)(3)(i). The Commission recently extended the former ninety days notice requirement to the present one hundred and twenty day period in order "to give issuers and the Commission staff adequate time to process proposals." Sec.Exch. Act Rel. No. 34–20091 (Aug. 16, 1983).

27. 17 C.F.R. § 240.14a–8(a)(3)(ii).

28. *Id.*

29. 17 C.F.R. § 240.14a–8(a)(4). Upon being notified of the necessity for reducing the number of words or proposals, the proponent has fourteen calendar days to correct.

30. In re Westinghouse Electric Corp., 17 Sec.Reg. & L.Rep. (BNA) 282 (Jan. 23, 1985).

31. 17 C.F.R. § 240.14a–8(b). Formerly a supporting statement had to be included only in the face of management opposition.

32. *See, e.g.,* New England Anti–Vivisection Society, Inc. v. United States Surgical Corp., Inc., 889 F.2d 1198 (1st Cir.1989) (finding management's description of shareholder proposal was not materially misleading).

letters,[33] spells out the proper scope of shareholder proposals including disqualification of certain proposals that have been unsuccessful in the past:

The [issuer] may omit a proposal and any statement in support thereof from its proxy statement and form of proxy under any of the following circumstances:

(1) If the proposal is, under the laws of the issuer's domicile, not a proper subject for action by security holders;[34]

NOTE: Whether a proposal is a proper subject for action by security holders will depend on the applicable state law. Under certain states' laws, a proposal that mandates certain action by the [issuer]'s board of directors may not be a proper subject matter for shareholder action, while a proposal recommending or requesting such action of the board may be proper under such state laws.[35]

(2) If the proposal, if implemented, would require the [issuer] to violate any state law or federal law of the United States, or any law of any foreign jurisdiction, to which the [issuer] is subject, except that this provision shall not apply with respect to any foreign law compliance with which would be violative of any state law or federal law of the United States;[36]

(3) If the proposal or the supporting statement is contrary to any of the Commission's proxy rules and regulations, including Rule 14a–9 [17 CFR 240.14a–9], which prohibits false or misleading statements in proxy soliciting materials;[37]

(4) If the proposal relates to the enforcement of a personal claim or the redress of a personal grievance against the issuer or any other person or if it is designed to result in a benefit to the proponent or to further a personal interest, which benefit or interest is not shared with the other security holders at large;[38]

---

33. The no action letters discussed in the following footnotes are meant to be examples; highlighting significant issues. There is no attempt to catalog every no action letter on point. *See* Practitioner's Edition for additional no action letters.

34. *See, e.g.,* DS Bancor, Inc., 27 Sec.Reg. & L.Rep. (BNA) 313 (SEC No Action Letter avail. Feb. 15, 1995) (proposal urging the directors to seek bids from parties interested in acquiring the company could not be excluded as improper under Delaware law).

35. *See* Banyan Short Term Income Trust, 26 Sec. Reg. & L. Rep. (BNA) 677 (SEC No Action Letter avail. April 25, 1994) (proposal that trustees dissolve trust could not be included since even if improper under state law, the proposal could easily be rephrased as a request which would be proper).

36. *See* Eastman Kodak Co., 26 Sec. Reg. & L. Rep. (BNA) 240 (SEC No Action Letter avail. Feb. 7, 1994) (management could exclude shareholder proposal to drop "Lambda" group from employee computer network since to do so might violate antidiscrimination laws).

37. *See* Sun Co., 24 Sec.Reg. & L.Rep. (BNA) 543 (SEC No Action Letter avail. April 3, 1992) (proposal received less than 120 days in advance was excludable).

38. Storage Technology Corp., 26 Sec. Reg. & L. Rep. (BNA) 677 (SEC No Action Letter avail. April 22, 1994) (management could exclude proposal to bar officers and directors from selling stock obtained by the exercise of options).

(5) If the proposal relates to operations which account for less than 5 percent of the [issuer]'s total assets at the end of its most recent fiscal year, and for less than 5 percent of its net earnings and gross sales for its most recent fiscal year, and is not otherwise significantly related to the issuer's business;[39]

(6) If the proposal deals with a matter that is beyond the [issuer]'s power to effectuate;[40]

(7) If the proposal deals with a matter relating to the conduct of the ordinary business operations of the [issuer];[41]

(8) If the proposal relates to an election to office;[42]

(9) If the proposal is counter to a proposal to be submitted by the [issuer] at the meeting;

(10) If the proposal has been rendered moot;[43]

(11) If the proposal is substantially duplicative of a proposal previously submitted to the [issuer] by another proponent, which proposal will be included in the [issuer]'s proxy materials for the meeting;

39. American Telegraph & Telephone Co., [1993–1994 Transfer Binder] Fed. Sec. L. Rep. (CCH) ¶ 76,820 (SEC No Action Letter Jan. 24, 1994) (management could not exclude proposal relating to company's human rights and environmental impact in Mexico).

40. *See* New York City Employees' Retirement System v. Brunswick Corp., 789 F.Supp. 144 (S.D.N.Y.1992) (upholding exclusion of proposal regarding national health insurance plan which was beyond the issuer's power to effectuate).

41. *See, e.g.,* Grimes v. Ohio Edison Co., 992 F.2d 455 (2d Cir.1993), *affirming* 1992 WL 168252, [1992 Transfer Binder] Fed.Sec.L.Rep. (CCH) ¶ 96,840 (S.D.N.Y.1992) (upholding management's exclusion of shareholder proposal requiring shareholder approval of all capital expenditures in excess of the amount paid to shareholders in cash dividends); Roosevelt v. E.I. Du Pont de Nemours & Co., 958 F.2d 416 (D.C.Cir.1992) (management was justified in excluding shareholder proposal that company prepare and issue a research report on development of environmentally safe substitutes for chlorofluorocarbons); Amalgamated Clothing & Textile Workers Union v. Wal–Mart Stores, Inc., 821 F.Supp. 877 (S.D.N.Y.1993) (management cannot refuse to include proposal dealing with equal employment opportunity policies; court reasoned that prior no action letters were inconsistent with SEC pronouncements made in the course of formal rulemaking); Austin v. Consolidated Edison Co. of New York, Inc., 788 F.Supp. 192 (S.D.N.Y.1992) (shareholders were unsuccessful in action to compel management to include proposal endorsing a new retirement policy).

42. Properly interpreted this means that individual election campaigns cannot be conducted in this manner but proposals relating to general criteria for officeholders will be deemed proper. *See* Rauchman v. Mobil Corp., 739 F.2d 205 (6th Cir.1984) (bylaw amendment proposed by shareholder that would have rendered a nominated director ineligible for office was held to be an excludable shareholder proposal; however, the issuer would not be justified in excluding a properly drafted shareholder proposal that would require directors to own at least 2,000 shares of the issuer's stock).

43. *But see, e.g.,* Office Depot, Inc., 26 Sec. Reg. & L. Rep. (BNA) 410 (SEC No Action Letter available March 7, 1994) (shareholder proposal to diversify board was not rendered moot by nominating committee's existing practice of seeking out diversity in its nominations); General Electric Co., 26 Sec. Reg. & L. Rep. (BNA) 266 (SEC No Action Letter avail. Feb. 9, 1994) (rejecting claim that management was already monitoring violence in its programming thereby making shareholder proposal moot).

(12) If the proposal deals with substantially the same subject matter[44] as a prior proposal submitted to security holders in the [issuer]'s proxy statement and form of proxy relating to any annual or special meeting of security holders held within the preceding five calendar years, it may be omitted from the [issuer]'s proxy materials relating to any meeting of security holders held within three calendar years after the latest such previous submission:

Provided, That

(i) If the proposal was submitted at only one meeting during such preceding period, it received less than three percent of the total number of votes in regard thereto; or

(ii) If the proposal was submitted at only two meetings during such preceding period, it received at the time of its second submission less than six percent of the total number of votes cast in regard thereto; or

(iii) If the prior proposal was submitted at three or more meetings during such preceding period, it received at the time of its latest submission less than 10 percent of the total number of votes cast in regard thereto; or

(13) If the proposal relates to specific amounts of cash or stock dividends.[45]

The text of subsection 12, as approved by the SEC in 1984, was ruled invalid because of irregularities in the Commission's rulemaking process.[46] The SEC then republished notice of the proposed changes and reinstated the rule as it appears in the text above.[47] There is some evidence that the SEC's most recent amendments have cut down on shareholder proposals and some observers view this as an unfortunate "damper on dissent." [48]

The above shareholder proposal rule reflects amendments in response to judicial interpretations and the concern over shareholder democracy as well as corporate reactions to these developments.[49] The changes imposed by the most recent amendments were designed to curtail harassment by shareholders without unduly restricting the democratic process. For example, the minimum ownership requirement did not appear in former versions of the rule. Management has been given

---

44. *See* In re Emerson Electric Co., 16 Sec.Reg. & L.Rep. (BNA) 1982 (SEC No Action Letter Nov. 21, 1984) (shareholder proposal that issuer report on military sales is different from prior proposal for formulation of "ethical criteria" for defense contracts).

45. 17 C.F.R. § 240.14a–8(c).

46. United Church Board for World Ministries v. SEC, 617 F.Supp. 837 (D.D.C.1985) (there was inadequate notice of changes since the proposed amendments did not specifically mention the changes in eligibility requirements).

47. Sec.Exch.Act Rel. No. 34–22625, [1985–86 Transfer Binder] Fed.Sec.L.Rep. (CCH) ¶ 83,937 (Nov. 14, 1985).

48. *See* Annual Meetings are Much Calmer Affairs Under Changed SEC Shareholder Rules, Wall St.J. p. 33 (April 24, 1985). *See also* Cane *supra* footnote 14.

49. *See* Exch.Act Rel. No. 34–20091 (Aug. 16, 1983) and the authorities cited in note 14 *supra.*

more leeway in subsection (12) in determining whether a given proposal is duplicative of past efforts. Also, in an effort to provide more objectivity, subsection (5) now includes a five percent asset and earnings test for determining if the matter is significantly related to the issuer's overall operations. A proposal that does not reach the five percent threshold may still be "otherwise significantly related to the issuer's business" and thus require inclusion in management's proxy statement.[50]

Every year at proxy time the Commission is faced with a series of management requests for permission to exclude shareholders proposals that relate primarily to political or social issues. A glance through the SEC's no action letters reveals the topical issues of the day. Most disputes in this area are resolved through managements' requests for no action responses. Relatively few of these issues have reached the courts.[51] In searching for precedent lawyers will frequently be faced with cases based on former versions of the shareholder proposal rules. In many instances, counsel will be forced to rely on the SEC's ad hoc determinations in the form of no action letters in response to proposed exclusions of shareholder proposals.[52]

As a practical matter, however, the management has little to lose by including most shareholder proposals as they have virtually no chance of success and generally receive less than three percent of the vote.[60] Even if the issuer properly excludes the proposal and supporting statement, it must nevertheless describe the proposal, assuming that under state law[61] it is a proper matter for shareholder action. Item 20 of schedule 14A requires the proxy statement to include identification of any action to be taken at the shareholder meeting that is not otherwise described in the

---

50. Lovenheim v. Iroquois Brands, Ltd., 618 F.Supp. 554 (D.D.C.1985) (granting preliminary injunction against exclusion of shareholder proposal that the directors form a committee to consider termination of distribution of pate de foie gras until a more humane production method is developed).

51. An early case held that a shareholder proposal asking a major bus company's management to cease segregated seating in the south was properly excludable as a request for advisory action to the board. Peck v. Greyhound Corp., 97 F.Supp. 679 (S.D.N.Y.1951). The decision was predicated on a former version of the rule that would no longer be applicable today. Although it would arguably still be excludable as relating to the issuer's ordinary business, (17 C.F.R. § 240.14a–8(c)(7)) it would probably have to be included under current law.

Former Rule 14a–8(c)(5) provided that management could properly exclude a shareholder proposal if it was "a recommendation or request that management take action with respect to a matter relating to the ordinary business operations of the issuer." 17 C.F.R. § 240.14–8(c)(5) (1976) (rescinded).

52. The SEC has announced its intention to continue issuing no-action responses. Sec.Exch.Act Rel. No. 34–20091 (Aug. 16, 1983). *See* Shareholder Proposals on South Africa, Nuclear Energy and Other Issues Considered, 17 Sec.Reg. & L.Rep. (BNA) 497 (March 22, 1985). *See also, e.g.,* Andrew J. Frackman & Achilles M. Perry, Shareholder Public Policy Proposals: An Update, 27 Rev.Sec. & Commod.Reg. 193 (1994).

Deleted footnotes 53–59 can be found in the Practitioner's Edition.

60. *See* authorities cited in footnote 12 *supra*.

61. For some of the state law cases, *see, e.g.,* Campbell v. Loew's, Inc., 36 Del.Ch. 563, 134 A.2d 852 (1957); In the Matter of Auer v. Dressel, 306 N.Y. 427, 118 N.E.2d 590 (1954).

proxy statement.[62] Furthermore, if the issuer's management decides to solicit proxies that will be voted against a shareholder proposal, the antifraud proscriptions will require disclosure of the proposal and intention to vote against it.[63]

§ 11.8   Disclosure in Lieu of Proxy Solicitation—Section 14(c)

If an issuer subject to the registration requirements of section 12 of the Exchange Act does not solicit proxies, its security holders are still guaranteed information by virtue of section 14(c).[1] The issuer must file with the SEC and send to its security holders information similar to that which is required for a proxy solicitation. These informational requirements are set out in Regulation 14C[2] and Schedule 14C.[3]

If there is no proxy solicitation, the information required by Schedule 14C must be distributed to all security holders entitled to vote at least twenty days prior to any shareholder meeting where no proxy solicitation has been made by management. Five copies of the Schedule 14C information must be filed with the SEC at least ten business days prior to the date upon which definitive copies are first sent or given to security holders.[4] Once the information is sent out, eight definitive copies must be filed with the Commission with a nonrefundable one hundred and twenty-five dollar filing fee; and three additional copies must be simultaneously sent to each national securities exchange upon which any of the issuer's securities are listed.[5] A material change in circumstances will require amendment of the Schedule 14C filings. Any

---

62. "If any action is to be taken with respect to any matter not specifically referred to above, describe briefly the substance of each such matter in substantially the same degree of detail as is required by Items 5 to 20, inclusive * * *."

63. Even if the proxy does not contain a specific reference to the proposal, there is generally a request to give a proxy for "such other matters" as may come up for a shareholder vote. If the proxy is sought in this manner, full disclosure should require a description of any such matter known to the persons soliciting the proxy and how they intend to vote thereon. *Cf.* Medical Committee for Human Rights v. SEC, 432 F.2d 659, 677 (D.C.Cir.1970) "the rationale underlying [the shareholder proposal rule] was the Commission's belief that the corporate practice of circulating proxy materials which failed to make reference to the fact that a shareholder intended to present a proposal at the annual meeting rendered the solicitation inherently misleading. *See* Hearings on Security and Exchange Commission Proxy Rules Before the House Comm. on Interstate and Foreign Commerce, 78th Cong., 1st Sess., pt. 1, at 169–170 (1943)". *Cf.* Schoen v. Amerco, 1994 WL 715895, [1994–1995 Transfer Binder] Fed. Sec. L. Rep. (CCH) ¶ 98,461 (D.Nev. 1994) (issuer must disclose that other shareholder proposals may be brought up at the meeting and that the proxy will be voted on such matters as the proxy holder sees fit).

§ 11.8

1. 15 U.S.C.A. § 78n(c).

2. 17 C.F.R. §§ 240.14c–1 through 14c–7.

3. 17 C.F.R. § 240.14c–101.

4. 17 C.F.R. § 240.14c–5(a). Upon a showing of good cause, the Commission may shorten the ten-day period.

5. 17 C.F.R. § 240.14c–5(b). National securities exchanges are the nine exchanges currently registered under section 6 of the Act, 15 U.S.C.A. § 78f. *See* § 10.2 *supra.*

amendment or revision must then be filed with the Commission and clearly marked to indicate that it is an amendment.

Schedule 14C must include the following information. Item 1 requires the issuer to set forth all information that will be required in Schedule 14A with regard to any matter to be voted upon at the upcoming shareholder meeting. Item 2 provides that the issuer announce in boldface type that the proxies are not being solicited. The schedule requires the issuer to set forth the date, time and place of the meeting. Item 3 requires disclosure of the interest of certain persons such as officers, directors, principal shareholders and affiliates in matters to be acted upon at the meeting; the names of directors in opposition to matters to be voted upon must also be disclosed. Item 4 requires the issuer to include proposals by security holders submitted at least sixty days in advance of the mailing of the Schedule 14C.[6] As can be seen from all of the foregoing requirements, Regulation 14C is designed to assure that security holders of issuers subject to the Exchange Act reporting requirements will receive all relevant information regardless of whether management solicits proxies for an upcoming meeting.

Section 14(c) disclosures are not limited to matters to be voted upon at shareholder meetings. In addition to the information required in Schedule 14C, SEC Rule 14c–3[7] requires an issuer to furnish security holders with an annual report. The annual report must contain much of the information that is found in the issuer's Form 10K filings with the Commission.[8] Unlike other section 14(c) filings and proxy solicitation materials generally, the annual report is not a "filed" document so as to provide a remedy under section 18(a) to injured purchasers and sellers of securities relying on material omissions or misstatements in documents filed with the commission.[9] Rule 14c–4[10] sets out the required format for presenting the information. Rule 14c–6[11] makes it unlawful to make material misstatements or material omissions of fact in connection with section 14(c) information statements. Also, by virtue of Rule 14c–7,[12] the issuer must make reasonable inquiry to assure that all security holders whose securities are held by banks, broker-dealers or other institutions are sufficiently notified of the information required to be sent out by section 14(c).

6. 17 C.F.R. § 240.14c–101; *Compare* with the shareholder proposal Rule of 14a–8(c), 17 C.F.R. § 240.14a–8(c). *See* § 11.7 *supra.*

7. 17 C.F.R. § 240.14c–3.

8. *See* 15 U.S.C.A. § 78m. The contents of the annual report are discussed in § 11.6 *supra.*

9. 17 C.F.R. § 240.14a–3(c). *See* 15 U.S.C.A. § 78r(a) which is discussed in § 12.8 *infra.*

10. 17 C.F.R. § 240.14c–4. The issuer must present the information in groups according to subject matter and, where practical, the information is to be presented in tabular form.

11. 17 C.F.R. § 240.14c–6.

12. 17 C.F.R. § 240.14c–7. *See also* 17 C.F.R. § 240.14a–3(d).

Because of the difficulty of showing a causal connection between any misrepresentation and the consummation of the transaction in question, it is highly doubtful whether a private right of action will lie for alleged violations of Rule 14c–6.[13]

§ 11.9 Securities Held in Street Name; Broker–Dealers and Federal Proxy Regulation—Section 14(b)

Increasingly large numbers of securities are being held in the name of broker-dealers for their customers' accounts.[1] Holding the customer's stock or other securities "in street name" is not only a matter of convenience, but also may be necessary for the extension of credit pursuant to the margin rules.[2] Additionally, with the time for settlement of transactions moving from five to three business days, it is becoming increasingly cumbersome for customers to hold their share certificates since there is less time to deliver them for sale.

Section 14(b) of the Exchange Act[3] requires all broker-dealers who are members of a national exchange or national security association[4] to forward proxy solicitation materials to their customers in whose account the securities are held. The statute makes it unlawful to fail to comply with such rules as the commission may promulgate.[5] The Commission has exercised the rulemaking power delegated by section 14(b).[6] The rules relating to shareholder communications have been extended to banks and other entities holding securities in their names as fiduciaries for the beneficial owners.[7]

All participants in a proxy solicitation are generally subject to Regulation 14A.[8] However, specific exemptions apply to broker-dealers who are merely complying with section 14(b). Rule 14a–2(a)(1) provides that a broker-dealer who transmits such proxy material to his or her customer is not considered a participant in the proxy solicitation provided the broker-dealer: (1) does not receive a commission or other remuneration other than reimbursement of reasonable expenses; (2) furnish-

---

13. *See, e.g.,* Ciro v. Gold, 816 F.Supp. 253 (D.Del.1993) (minority shareholders could not maintain action under Rule 14c–6 since any injury was not caused by misstatements in the proxy materials but rather that they were powerless to stop the transaction).

§ 11.9

1. SEC, Street Name Study (1976).

2. 15 U.S.C.A. § 78g. Margin requirements are discussed in § 10.11 *supra.*

3. 15 U.S.C.A. § 78n(b).

4. The rule also applied to broker-dealers regulated directly by the SEC, a category abolished effective December, 1983. In other words section 14(b) applies to all broker-dealers who are subject to Exchange Act regulation and oversight by the SEC. *See* chapter 10 *supra.*

5. 15 U.S.C.A. § 78n(b).

6. *See* 17 C.F.R. § 240.14b–1 *et seq.* For an early view of the problem *see* Edward R. Aranow & Herbert A. Einhorn, Corporate Proxy Contests: Solicitation and Validity of Brokers' Proxies, 23 U.Chi.L.Rev. 640 (1956).

7. Pub.L. No. 99–222, 99 Stat. 1737 (1985), amending 15 U.S.C.A. § 78n(b). *See* 17 C.F.R. § 240.14b–2.

8. 15 U.S.C.A. § 78n(a). *See* § 11.2 *supra.*

es promptly to the customers so solicited copies of all material; and (3) does no more than give impartial instructions to the customer as to how to forward the proxies to the appropriate depository.[9] However, if a broker-dealer sends along its own literature concerning the issuer, the exemption from the proxy regulations is extinguished.[10] Any attempt by the broker-dealer to exert any influence over the customer's voting or other participation in the proxy solicitation similarly renders the broker-dealer subject to Regulation 14A and the regular proxy rules.[11]

The procedures set forth by the Commission under section 14(b) are relatively straightforward. Rule 14b–1[12] adds to a broker-dealer's statutory responsibility with regard to securities held in street name for customers' accounts. The broker-dealer must respond to any inquiry pursuant to Rule 14a–13[13] by or on behalf of an issuer requesting the approximate number of the broker-dealer's customers who beneficially own the securities subject to the proxy solicitation.[14] Furthermore, upon receipt of the proxy or other solicitation material, as well as annual reports to shareholders, the broker-dealer must promptly forward them on to the customer with the issuer to pay reasonable expenses.[15] The thrust of the above-mentioned rules is that a shareholder does not lose any of his or her voting or informational rights merely by putting his or her securities in street name with a broker-dealer.

In order to further facilitate communications between an issuer and owners of securities held in street name, the Commission imposes certain obligations upon issuers. When an issuer is aware of the fact that a broker-dealer, bank, or voting trustee is holding securities on account for the beneficial owners, the issuer must inquire as to the names and addresses of all beneficial owners, at least twenty days prior to the record date preceding a meeting for which proxies are solicited, unless compliance with the rule would be impractical.[16] These requirements allow more direct communications to beneficial owners and to increase the efficiency of proxy material dissemination.[17] When such a

---

9. 17 C.F.R. § 240.14a–2(a)(1).

10. Sec. Exch. Act Rel. No. 34–7208 (SEC Jan. 7, 1964).

11. *Id.*

12. 17 C.F.R. § 240.14b–1.

13. 17 C.F.R. § 240.14a–13. If the issuer has the names of beneficial owners of shares held in street name, it not only has to send proxy related material, it also has to furnish an annual report in connection with the election of directors even if the issuer is not soliciting proxies. The rule also applies to solicitations of shareholder comments in lieu of an annual or special meeting. *See* Exch. Act Rel. No. 34–22533, [1985–1986 Transfer Binder] Fed.Sec.L.Rep. (CCH) ¶ 83,930 (Oct. 15, 1985).

14. 17 C.F.R. § 240.14b–1(a). As a result of amendments to the rule, broker-dealers may employ an intermediary to fulfill their obligations under Rule 14b–1. 17 C.F.R. § 240.14b–1(c).

15. 17 C.F.R. § 240.14b–1(b).

16. 17 C.F.R. § 240.14a–13(a)(3). *See* Sec. Exch. Act Rel. No. 34–20021 (July 28, 1983).

17. *See* Sec.Exch.Act Rel. No. 34–20021 (July 28, 1983). The SEC delayed the effective date of these requirements until January, 1986. 16 Sec. Reg. & L.Rep. (BNA) 1425 (Aug. 24, 1984).

request is made, broker-dealers have seven business days within which to respond.[18] The rule is not limited to securities held in street name and applies as well to securities held by other custodians such as banks and voting trustees. Rule 14a–3 applies to the issuer's dissemination of annual reports, subject to enumerated exceptions.[19]

Congress has enacted the Shareholder Communications Act, which took effect in December, 1986, and subjects banks, thrift institutions, and other entities that hold securities in their names as fiduciaries for customers to the same types of obligations imposed upon broker-dealers.[20]

PART B: TENDER OFFER AND TAKEOVER REGULATION

§ 11.10 Federal Control of Tender Offers—The Williams Act; The Terminology of Takeovers

During the 1960's the securities markets witnessed a substantial increase in the use of tender offers—publicly announced offers to purchase the shares of a target company—as a means of effecting corporate mergers.[1] The tender offer was used to replace or supplement the then more conventional statutory merger route. The increased use of tender offers was due in part to the fact that target companies subject to the

---

18. 17 C.F.R. § 240.14b–1.

19. 17 C.F.R. § 240.14a–3(e).

20. Pub.L. 99–222, 99 Stat. 1737 (1985) amending 15 U.S.C.A. § 78n(b). *See* H.Rep. No. 99–181 (June 26, 1985). The Commission has adopted rules that implement the provisions of the Shareholder Communications Act. Sec.Exch. Act Rel. No. 34–23847 (Nov. 25, 1986). *See also* Exch. Act Rel. No. 34–23276, [1986 Transfer Binder] Fed.Sec.L.Rep. (CCH) ¶ 84,003 (May 29, 1986).

§ 11.10

1. *See generally* Edward R. Aranow, Herbert A. Einhorn & George Berlstein, Developments in Tender Offers for Corporate Control (1977); Edward R. Aranow & Herbert A. Einhorn, Tender Offers for Corporate Control (1972); Arthur Fleischer, Jr., Tender Offers: Defenses, Responses, and Planning (1978); Martin Lipton & Erica H. Steinberger, Takeovers and Freezeouts (1978); ABA National Institute On Corporate Takeovers—The Unfriendly Tender Offer and Minority Stockholder Freezeout, 32 Bus.Law. 1297 (1977); Richard A. Booth, The Problem With Federal Tender Offer Law, 77 Cal.L.Rev. 707 (1989); Arthur Fleischer, Jr. & Robert H. Mundheim, Corporation Acquisition by Tender Offer, 115 U.Pa.L.Rev. 317 (1967); Samuel L. Hayes III & Robert A. Taussig, Tactics of Cash Takeover Bids, Harv.Bus.Rev. (Mar.–Apr. 1967); Leo Herzel & Richard M. Rosenberg, Loans to Finance Tender Offers: The Bank's Legal Problems, 96 Banking L.J. 676 (1979); Leo Herzel & Richard M. Rosenberg, Loans to Finance Tender Offers: Borrower's Problems That May Affect the Bank, 96 Banking L.J. 581 (1979); Panel Discussion, Disclosure Problems in Tender Offers and Freeze Outs, 32 Bus.Law. 1365 (1977); Tender Offer Symposium–Pts. 1 & 2, 23 N.Y.L.S.L.Rev. 553 (1978); Marc I. Steinberg, Fiduciary Duties and Disclosure Obligations in Proxy and Tender Contests for Corporate Control, 30 Emory L.J. 169 (1981); Note, SEC Takeover Regulation Under the Williams Act, 62 N.Y.U.L.Rev. 580 (1987). *See also* John C. Coffee, Jr., Regulating the Market for Corporate Control: A Critical Assessment of the Tender Offer's Role in Corporate Governance, 84 Colum.L.Rev. 1145 (1984).

For a discussion of the takeover process *see, e.g.,* Richard Phalon, The Takeover Barons of Wall Street: Inside the Billion Dollar Merger Game (1981).

Exchange Act's reporting requirements were required to hold a shareholder vote and to comply with the Act's proxy rules[2] when participating in a statutory merger.[3] The competitive atmosphere and vociferousness with which such takeover battles were waged became extreme both in terms of public and private ramifications. The terminology used to describe takeover tactics reflects this intensity.[4]

This climate led to the 1968 congressional enactment of the Williams Act amendments to the Exchange Act.[5] Although the Exchange Act's takeover provisions are discussed in more detail in the sections that follow, an overview will be presented here.

Overview of the Regulation

Section 13(d) of the Act[6] focuses on creeping, open market and privately negotiated acquisitions of securities subject to the 1934 Act's registration and reporting requirements. Any person who acquires, directly or indirectly, more than a five percent beneficial ownership interest in any class of equity security subject to the Exchange Act's reporting requirements must file a statement of ownership with the Commission within ten days after reaching the five percent threshold.[7] The purpose of section 13(d)'s notice requirement is to put both investors and the target company's management on notice of a possible impending takeover attempt. However, the purchaser has ten days between the crossing of the five percent threshold and the disclosure date. This provides a ten day window for additional undisclosed acquisitions of the target company's stock. This permits the acquisition of considerably more than the five percent threshold before any disclosure need be made. As such, this early warning mechanism has its defects.

---

2. 15 U.S.C.A. § 78n(a); 17 C.F.R. §§ 240.14a–9 *et seq.* The proxy rules mandate full disclosure and provide for implied private remedies for material misrepresentations in connection with the solicitation of shareholder votes for issuers that are subject to the Exchange Act's reporting requirements. *See generally* Edward R. Aranow & Herbert A. Einhorn, Proxy Contests for Corporate Control (2d ed. 1968).

3. *See* §§ 11.1–11.9 *supra.*

4. *See* text accompanying footnotes 27–32 *infra.*

5. Pub.L. No. 90–439, 82 Stat. 454 (1968) (codified at 15 U.S.C. §§ 78m(d)–(e), n(d)–(f)). *See generally* Edward R. Aranow & Herbert A. Einhorn, Tender Offers For Corporate Control (1973); Alan R. Bromberg, The Securities Law of Tender Offers, 15 N.Y.L.F. 462 (1962); Robert W. Hamilton, Some Reflections on Cash Tender Offer Legislation, 15 N.Y.L.F. 269 (1969).

6. 15 U.S.C.A. § 78m(d). *See generally* I. William Robinson & J. Daniel Mahoney, Schedule 13D: Wild Card in a Takeover Bid, 27 Bus.Law. 1107 (1972). *See* § 11.11 *infra.*

7. The filing requirements are triggered not only by purchases of securities, but also by the formation of a group to exercise control in common. *See* § 11.11 *infra.*

A "blue ribbon" panel commissioned by the SEC recommended that the 13(d) filing be due in advance of the purchases. *See* 15 Sec.Reg. & L.Rep. (BNA) 1156 (June 17, 1983).

The SEC subsequently responded with legislative proposals including the closing of section 13(d)'s ten day window. *See* 16 Sec.Reg. & L.Rep. (BNA) 793 (May 11, 1984). However, despite wide-spread support, the ten-day window remains open. The SEC's proposals also included recommendations to cut down on the use of defensive tactics including issuer self tenders, "greenmail", and "golden parachutes." *Id. See* §§ 11.17, 11.20 *infra.*

Despite numerous attempts to close it, the ten day window remains open.[8]

The Schedule 13D is the appropriate form for section 13(d) filings and the person (or group) filing must disclose information about itself, its officers, directors, and principal business, as well as any financing arrangements that have been entered into to finance the purchase.[9] Furthermore, the Schedule 13D must contain a statement of the purchaser's future intentions with regard to the target company. For example, the purchaser must disclose whether a public tender offer, statutory merger, consolidation or other form of corporate fusion or combination is possible or likely to take place. As an alternative, the purchaser may merely state that its purchase was for purely investment purposes, if that is in fact the case.

Section 13(e) of the Act[10] makes it unlawful for issuers to purchase their own shares in contravention of SEC rules. Both section 13(d) and section 13(e) apply only to securities subject to the Exchange Act reporting and registration requirements.[11] Furthermore, since the Schedule 13D and Schedule 13E–1 are filed documents, any material misstatement or omission will give rise to a private cause of action under 18(a) of the Exchange Act to an investor who purchases or sells the security and actually relies on that information.[12]

The SEC has promulgated its going private rules[13] pursuant to section 13(e).[14] These going private rules are designed to protect security holders of issuers engaging in transactions that will result in cessation of 1934 Act reporting requirements.[15] The rules assure adequate disclosures in connection with going private transactions regardless of the form that the transaction may take.

---

8. In addition to the authorities in footnote 7 *supra, see, e.g.,* D'Amato Introduces Comprehensive Proposal for Tender Offer Reform, 19 Sec.Reg. & L.Rep. (BNA) 84 (Jan. 24, 1987).

9. 17 C.F.R. § 240.13d–101. *See* Robinson & Mahoney *supra* footnote 6.

10. 15 U.S.C.A. § 78m(e). *See* § 11.17 *infra.*

11. Registered reporting companies are those issuers having a class of securities traded on a national securities exchange, as well as those issuers having assets of at least $5,000,000 and also having a class of equity securities with more than 500 shareholders. 15 U.S.C.A. § 78*l*; 17 C.F.R. § 240.12g–1. *See* §§ 9.2, 9.3 *supra.* The reporting provisions of the Williams Act do not apply to those issuers who, although not having to register under section 12 of the Exchange Act, nevertheless are required to file periodic reports under section 15(d). 15 U.S.C.A. § 78o(d). Section 15(d) reporting companies include issuers that have issued securities pursuant to a 1933 Act registration statement and have at least 300 security holders of that class of securities. *Id. See* § 9.3 *supra.*

12. 15 U.S.C.A. § 78r(a). *See* § 12.8 *infra.* For discussion of whether the section 18(a) remedy is exclusive, *see* Marc I. Steinberg, The Propriety and Scope of Cumulative Remedies Under the Federal Securities Laws, 67 Cornell L.Rev. 557 (1982). Although involving the exclusivity of section 11 of the 1933 Act, the recent Supreme Court decision in Huddleston v. Herman & MacLean, 459 U.S. 375, 103 S.Ct. 683, 74 L.Ed.2d 548 (1983), *on remand* 705 F.2d 775 (5th Cir.1983) indicates that section 18(a) is cumulative with other remedies both express and implied.

13. 17 C.F.R. §§ 240.13e–1–13e–4.

14. 15 U.S.C.A. § 78m(e).

15. *See* § 11.17 *infra.*

In contrast to section 13(d)'s focus on open-market and privately negotiated acquisitions, sections 14(d), (e), and (f) are directed at "tender offers." The term "tender offer" is defined nowhere in the Act, however, and the absence of a statutory definition has given rise to much litigation and proposed administrative or statutory amendment.[16]

Section 14(d) of the Act[17] requires that any person planning a "tender offer" for any class of equity security subject to the reporting requirements of the Exchange Act must file with the Commission all solicitations, advertisements, and any other material to be used in connection with the tender offer. This filing must take place prior to the distribution of the tender offer material. In addition, the tender offeror must file a long form Schedule 14D–1[18] with the Commission disclosing information similar to that required in the Schedule 13D. Also, anyone who is opposing or supporting the tender offer for securities subject to the Act's registration requirements must file any material related to the tender offer prior to its distribution. As is the case with federal proxy regulation,[19] the filing requirements of the Williams Act are limited to securities registered under section 12 of the Act.[20] Sections 13(d), 13(e), and 14(d) thus do not apply to issuers whose periodic reporting requirements are triggered only by virtue of being subject to section 15(d).[21]

Section 14(e)[22] prohibits fraud, deceit, and material misrepresentation or omissions "in connection with any tender offer or request or invitation for tenders, or any solicitation of security holders in opposition to or in favor of any such offer, request or invitation." Section 14(e) is the only provision of the Williams Act that applies across the board and is not limited to tender offers directed at the securities of 1934 Act registered reporting companies. Furthermore, although the Supreme Court has held that section 14(e) will not support a private right of action in the hands of a competing tender offeror,[23] it remains open whether a shareholder of the target company or the target company

---

16. *See, e.g.,* Kennecott Copper Corp. v. Curtiss–Wright Corp., 584 F.2d 1195 (2d Cir.1978); Crane Co. v. Harsco Corp., 511 F.Supp. 294 (D.Del.1981); SEC v. Texas International Co., 498 F.Supp. 1231 (N.D.Ill.1980); Wellman v. Dickinson, 475 F.Supp. 783 (S.D.N.Y.1979); S–G Securities v. Fuqua Investment, 466 F.Supp. 1114 (D.Mass.1978); Cattlemen's Investment Co. v. Fears, 343 F.Supp. 1248 (W.D.Okl.1972), *vacated per stipulation* Civil No. 72–152 (W.D.Okl.1972); Note, The Developing Meaning of "Tender Offer" under the Securities and Exchange Act of 1934, 86 Harv.L.Rev. 1250 (1973). *See* § 11.13 *infra.*

17. 15 U.S.C.A. § 78n(d). *See* § 11.14 *infra.*

18. 17 C.F.R. § 240.14d–100.

19. *See* §§ 11.1–11.2 *supra.*

20. 15 U.S.C.A. § 78*l. See* § 9.2 *supra.* For discussion of the applicability of the Williams Act to foreign tender offers, *see* Jill E. Fisch, Imprudent Power: Reconsidering U.S. Regulation of Foreign Tender Offers, 87 Nw.U.L.Rev. 523 (1993).

21. 15 U.S.C.A. § 78o(d). *See* § 9.3 *supra.*

22. 15 U.S.C.A. § 78n(e). *See* § 11.15 *infra.*

23. Piper v. Chris–Craft Indus., Inc., 430 U.S. 1, 97 S.Ct. 926, 51 L.Ed.2d 124 (1977), *rehearing denied* 430 U.S. 976, 97 S.Ct. 1668, 52 L.Ed.2d 371 (1977).

itself retains an implied private right of action.[24] Similarly, it is unclear whether a private remedy can be implied for violations of sections 13(d), 13(e), and 14(d), although most courts recognize at least a potential for injunctive relief.[25]

The final provision of the Williams Act, section 14(f),[26] requires a tender offeror to publicly disclose on appropriate SEC filing forms, the names and descriptions of persons to be elected directors or any agreements affecting directors during the transfer of management control which are connected with a tender offer for equity securities subject to the Act's reporting requirements.

The Terminology of Takeovers

The intensity with which corporate takeover battles are waged is illustrated by the jargon that has developed to describe various tactics. For example aggressors may use the surprise element through a quickly assembled offer known as a "midnight special." [27] A "bear hug" involves an initial "friendly" approach to management of the target company with an express or implied choice of coming quietly now or being dragged along later. "Smoking gun" refers to a mistake that impedes the progress of the tender offer or defensive tactic.[28] A "show stopper" is a mistake so drastic that it results in the offer's failure. "White knights" may be brought in by the target company to fend off an unwanted suitor; "grey knights" are competing suitors who are not solicited by the target company but are viewed as preferable to the initial aggressor and "black knights" are competing suitors who are less attractive. "Shark repellent" refers to preventive measures by companies viewed as potential targets in order to fend off unwanted suitors.[29] "Shark repellent" may also be used to refer to state tender offer statutes that may present additional impediments to takeovers.[30] Many of these state laws have been held preempted by the federal legislation.[31] The "wounded list" refers to executives who have lost their jobs or their health during the course of a takeover campaign. Takeovers can also involve "shootouts" and eventually some resolution through "hired guns" (the attorneys).[32] Also important in the world of takeovers are

---

24. *See* § 11.19 *infra.*

25. *See* § 11.18 *infra.*

26. 15 U.S.C.A. § 78n(f). *See* § 11.16 *infra.* *See generally* David L. Ratner, Section 14(f): A New Approach to Transfers of Corporate Control, 54 Cornell L.Rev. 65(1968).

27. For a vivid example *see* Wellman v. Dickinson, 475 F.Supp. 783 (S.D.N.Y.1979).

28. Defensive tactics are discussed in § 11.20 *infra.*

29. A common device has been the use of protective charter provisions such as high vote requirements for a merger. *See, e.g.,* William L. Cary, Corporate Devices Used to Insulate Management from Attack, 25 Bus.Law. 839 (1970); Stephen A. Hochman & Oscar D. Folger, Deflecting Takeovers; Charter and By-law Techniques, 34 Bus.Law. 537 (1979).

30. *See* § 11.21 *infra.*

31. *See* § 11.22 *infra.*

32. *See generally,* If a Sleeping Beauty Takes Cyanide During a Raid, Look for Hired Guns, Wall St.J. p. 25 (Nov. 5, 1981); Hirsch, Ambushes, Shootouts and Knights of the Roundtable: The Language of Corporate Takeovers (paper presented at the Academy of Management 1980 Annual Meeting (Aug. 10–13, 1980)).

the "arbs" or arbitrageurs whose predictions of a tender offer's success may become a self-fulfilling prophecy.

A relatively new financing development in the 1980s, known as "junk bonds" were low quality, non-investment grade corporate debt obligations[33] that are used to finance leveraged buy-outs (also known as "LBOs"). Another common takeover device is the two-tiered offer. Under the prototypical front-end loaded, two tiered offer, the offeror makes an offer for a limited number of target company shares with notice that a second step of the acquisition will follow at a lower price.[34] This second step is frequently referred to as the "cram down." It has fairly been said that a front-end loaded offer followed by a cram down places the shareholders in a "prisoner's dilemma" while the acquiring corporation is able to purchase control at a "blended price".[35]

Additionally, as defensive tactics[36] to thwart hostile takeovers continue to abound, new and colorful names are devised. Consider, for example, the Pac–Man defense which consists of the target company's attempt to acquire the predator would-be acquirer. A number of companies have authorized or adopted "poison pills" which involve the issuance of preferred stock, debt securities, or rights to acquire such securities that have a high buy-back price which is triggered by a hostile acquisition of the target company. A variation on the poison pill is the "poison put" which entitles shareholders of the target company to "put" their shares to the acquirer at a high price. As discussed in a later section, many of these poison pills and poison puts have come under attack but have frequently been upheld.[37] "Greenmail" is the term that has come to be used for premiums paid by target company managements to buy back the hostile bidder's shares at a premium above the price that he or she paid. "Golden parachutes" are compensation agreements with the target company's top management which provide for high severance payments in the event of a change in control. "Tin parachutes" are similar arrangements that may be made available to less senior execu-

---

33. In a controversial interpretation, the Federal Reserve Board has taken the position that high risk or so-called "junk bonds" are subject to the margin rules that govern the extension of credit for purchases of securities. *See* 51 Fed.Reg. 1771 (1986). *See also, e.g.,* Fed. Ruling had Slight Effect on Use of Junk Bonds in Takeovers, Study Finds, 19 Sec.Reg. & L.Rep. (BNA) 166 (Jan. 1, 1987); Roberta Karmel, Applying Margin Rules to Junk Bonds, N.Y.L.J. 1 (Feb. 20, 1986).

In contrast to the approach taken by the Federal Reserve Board, the SEC staff concluded that since junk bonds play such a relatively small role in corporate takeovers, regulatory intervention is not warranted. *See* Noninvestment Grade Debt as Source of Tender Offer Financing, [1986 Transfer Binder] Fed.Sec.L.Rep. (CCH) ¶ 84,011 (SEC Office of Chief Economist June 20, 1986).

34. Several states, following the lead of Maryland, have enacted "fair price" statutes that prohibit the use of unfriendly front-end loaded two-tiered offers. Md. Corp's & Ass'ns Code §§ 3–602, 3–603. *See* §§ 11.21–11.22 *infra.*

35. *See generally* Two–Tiered Tender Offer Pricing, Ec.Exch. Act Rel. No. 34–21,079, [1984 Transfer Binder] Fed.Sec.L.Rep. (CCH) ¶ 83,637 (SEC June 21, 1984).

36. *See* § 11.20 *infra.*

37. *See, e.g.,* Minstar Acquiring Corp. v. AMF, Inc., 621 F.Supp. 1252 (S.D.N.Y.1985) (holding nontransferrable dividend right to be violative of New Jersey law). *See* § 11.20 *infra.*

tives. Under the "scorched earth" defense of its turf, a target company makes itself so unattractive for acquisition that the acquirer becomes uninterested.

Time for Change?

Since its enactment in 1968, observers have become aware of numerous takeover related abuses that are not addressed by the Williams Act. Over the past several years there have been numerous bills introduced in Congress that would have amended the Williams Act in various respects. As noted earlier,[38] there have been attempts to close section 13(d)'s ten day window between the threshold five percent purchase and the disclosure date. Other suggested changes have included prohibiting certain defensive tactics such as greenmail, golden parachutes, and poison pills.[39] Another proposed bill would have placed strict limits on and imposed increased disclosures relating to open market purchases.[40] Additionally, judicial developments, especially in the Delaware state courts have had a substantial impact on the responses a target company's management may make when faced with a threatened takeover.

The recent increase in antitakeover statutes at the state level[41] and recognition of the constitutionality of many of these state statutes[42] is likely to spur further impetus for federal legislation because of the importance of arriving at a uniform solution to the nation-wide problems regarding corporate takeovers.[43] State antitakeover laws[44] have combined with other factors such as the down-swing in the junk bond market in making tender offers a less desirable way of seeking corporate control than they were in the 1980s. As a result, the proxy battle has once again become a major factor in struggles over control.[45]

§ 11.11 Filing Requirements for Acquisition of More Than Five Percent of Equity Securities of an Exchange Act Reporting Company—Section 13(d)

Any person, other than the issuer, who acquires directly or indirectly beneficial ownership of more than five percent of a class of equity security registered pursuant to section 12 must file appropriate disclo-

---

38. *See* footnotes 7–8 *supra.*

39. *See, e.g.,* Congress Responds to Hostile Tender Offers, 6 Bus.Law. Update 1 (Sept./Oct. 1985).

40. *See* Draft D'Amato Takeover Bill Would Limit Large Open Market Purchases by Bidders, 17 Sec.Reg. & L.Rep. (BNA) 2003 (Nov. 15, 1985).

41. *See* § 11.21 *infra.*

42. CTS Corp. v. Dynamics Corp. of America, 481 U.S. 69, 107 S.Ct. 1637, 95 L.Ed.2d 67 (1987); *see* § 11.22 *infra.*

43. *See* Thomas L. Hazen, State Antitakeover Legislation—The Second and Third Generations, 23 Wake Forest U.L.Rev. 77–120 (1988).

44. *See* §§ 11.21, 11.22 *infra.*

45. *See, e.g.,* Lawrence A. Hamermesh, Defensive Techniques in Proxy Contests, 23 Rev.Sec. & Commod.Reg. 93 (1990).

sures with the SEC pursuant to section 13(d).[1] An issuer's purchases of its own shares, directly or through an affiliate, are subject to similar disclosure requirements by virtue of section 13(e).[2]

Any person acquiring five percent of a class of equity securities must, within ten days after reaching the five percent threshold, file with the Commission six copies of a statement reflecting the information required by section 13(d)(1).[3] The purchaser thus has a ten day window between the crossing of the five percent threshold and the disclosure date. This ten day period provides a window of opportunity for acquiring considerably more than the five percent threshold before section 13(d)'s early warning disclosures must be made. An SEC advisory group has recommended amending the rules to require filing in advance of the five percent purchase[4] but no such change has taken place. Accordingly, there frequently will be a flurry of purchases after the five percent threshold has been crossed.

The appropriate filing under section 13(d) is embodied in Schedule 13D.[5] Some institutional investors who would otherwise be required to file a Schedule 13D may qualify for the short-form Schedule 13G.[6] Under Rule 13d–1(b),[7] a qualified institutional investor[8] may use Schedule 13G where the securities have been acquired in the ordinary course of business without the intent of changing or otherwise affecting the

---

§ 11.11

1. 15 U.S.C.A. § 78m(d)(*l*). Section 12, 15 U.S.C.A. § 78*l*, is discussed in § 9.2 *supra*.

2. 15 U.S.C.A. § 78m(e); 17 C.F.R. § 240.13e–3. *See* § 11.17 *infra*.

3. 17 C.F.R. § 240.13d–1. *See* 15 U.S.C.A. § 78m(d)(1). A nominee with voting power who may vote only at the instruction of third parties is not the beneficial owner of the shares in question and thus is not subject to Section 13(d) filing requirements. Calvary Holdings, Inc. v. Chandler, 948 F.2d 59 (1st Cir.1991). *See also, e.g.,* Rio Grande Industries, [1989–1990 Transfer Binder] Fed.Sec.L.Rep. (CCH) ¶ 79,318 (SEC No Action Letter April 5, 1989) (trustees of pension fund not subject to section 13(d) where participants directed the trustees' voting).

The filing requirement is not limited to purchases, it also applies to the formation of a group to exercise control in common. *See* footnotes 29–38 *infra* and accompanying text.

4. *See* 15 Sec.Reg. & L.Rep. (BNA) 156 (June 17, 1983). Advancing the filing date lessens the surprise element and would give the target company's management additional time to prepare a response or defense. Defensive tactics are discussed in § 11.20 *infra*.

5. 17 C.F.R. § 240.13d–1. Schedule 13D is found in 17 C.F.R. § 240.13d–101. *See* Block & Rudoff, Schedule 13D Problems Associated with Proxy Contests and Rapid Accumulations of Stock, in PLI, Proxy Contests For Corporate Control at 241 (1981); J. William Robinson & J. Daniel Mahoney, Wild Card in a Takeover Bid, 27 Bus.Law. 1107 (1972); Jonathan R. Macey & Jeffrey M. Netter, Regulation 13D and the Regulatory Process, 65 Wash.U.L.Q. 131 (1987); Michael D. Young, Section 13(d)—A New Element in the Battles for Control of Corporate Managements: The Implications of GAF Corporation v. Milstein, 27 Bus.Law. 1137 (1972).

6. 17 C.F.R. § 240.13d–102. *See* 15 U.S.C.A. §§ 78m(d)(5), 78m(g); 17 C.F.R. § 240.13d–5. The rationale behind this short form is that qualifying institutional investors are not going to take over the target. *See, e.g.,* Stichting Phillips Pension bonds A & B, [1987–88 Transfer Binder] Fed.Sec.L.Rep. (CCH) ¶ 78,668 (SEC No Action Letter Jan. 12, 1988). Nevertheless a substantial institutional investor may exert control through its voting rights.

7. 17 C.F.R. § 240.13d–1(b).

8. 17 C.F.R. § 240.13d–1(b)(ii).

control of the target company. These institutional investors may be required to make additional filings under section 13(f).[9]

There is no express limitation on the amount of securities that may be purchased prior to filing Schedule 13D. Rule 13d–1(b)(3)(ii)[10] establishes a moratorium on additional purchases for ten days following a Schedule 13D filing for Schedule 13G filers. The ten day moratorium also extends to prohibiting the purchaser from exercising the voting rights in securities acquired. There are no such limitations prior to filing. Accordingly, once the five percent threshold has been reached, additional shares can be purchased until the Schedule 13D filing which is due ten days later. The advisory group assembled by the SEC that has proposed requiring the 13D filing prior to crossing the five percent threshold,[11] would thus have eliminated the window that currently exists and permit purchasers to continue to acquire securities without notice to the target company. The proposal would also have shortened the moratorium to forty-eight hours after filing.[12]

As discussed below, failure to make a timely Schedule 13D filing may result in an injunction against future purchases or against holding a shareholder vote until the violation is cured.[13] Also, disgorgement of any profits made on shares improperly acquired may also be appropriate.[14]

The long-form Schedule 13D, which must be amended when there are material changes or developments, requires the following disclosures.[15] Item One must contain a description of the security purchased and its issuer. Item Two involves identification and background of the

---

9. 15 U.S.C.A. § 78m(f). *See* § 11.12 *infra.*

10. 17 C.F.R. § 240.13d–1(b)(3)(ii).

11. *See* 15 Sec.Reg. & L.Rep. (BNA) 1156 (June 17, 1983).

12. *Id.* The SEC has proposed legislation that would allow the commission to close the ten day window through its rule making power. *See* 16 Sec.Reg. & L. Rep. (BNA) 793 (May 11, 1984).

13. *See, e.g.,* SEC v. First City Financial Corp., 890 F.2d 1215 (D.C.Cir.1989) (enjoining future violations); CNW Corp. v. Japonica Partners, L.P., 874 F.2d 193 (3d Cir.1989) (reversing lower court and issuing preliminary injunction against shareholder vote until corrective disclosures in Schedules 13D and 14B disclosing identity of limited partners, limited partner and coinvestor agreements concerning purchases of target company stock); A.P. Green Industries, Inc. v. East Rock Partners, Inc., 726 F.Supp. 757 (E.D.Mo.1989) (enjoining additional purchases of target company stock until purchaser amended Schedule 13D to disclose that a merger might be financed by encumbering the target company's assets).

Compare, e.g. MTD Services Corp. v. Weldetron Corp., 1994 WL 45154, [1994–1995 Transfer Binder] Fed. Sec. L. Rep. (CCH) ¶ 98,395 (S.D.N.Y.1994) (refusing to enjoin shareholder meeting since form 4 filings and proxy statement adequately informed company stockholders about director's purchases of shares that should have been reported in a Schedule 13D filing).

14. SEC v. First City Financial Corp., 890 F.2d 1215 (D.C.Cir.1989) (requiring disgorgement of profits from shares purchased after Schedule 13D was due); SEC v. Bilzerian, 814 F.Supp. 116 (D.D.C.1993) (disgorgement of profits resulting from delayed and materially misleading section 13(d) filings; disgorgement following imposition of criminal fine in earlier action did not violate the constitutional prohibition against double jeopardy).

15. *See* 17 C.F.R. § 240.13d–101; In re Phillips Petroleum Securities Litigation, 881 F.2d 1236 (3d Cir.1989), *on remand* 738 F.Supp. 825 (D.Del.1990). *See also, e.g.* United States v. Bilzerian, 926 F.2d 1285 (2d Cir.1991), *cert. denied* 502 U.S. 813, 112 S.Ct. 63, 116 L.Ed.2d 39 (1991) (fact that an item must be disclosed on Schedule 13D does not result

person filing the Schedule 13D; including the name, residence or business address, and present principal occupation of the person making the filing. The person filing the Schedule 13D must disclose further whether he or she has been convicted of criminal violations or been a party to an SEC proceeding in the past. Item Three must contain the source and amount of funds or other considerations being used to acquire the securities.[16] Item Four requires a detailed description of the purpose(s) of the transaction, including any plans on the part of the purchaser likely to result in reorganization or business combinations such as mergers, consolidations, sales or acquisition of substantial assets, tender offers, and the like.[17] Alternatively, Item Four may state that the shares were acquired for investment only.[18] In Item Five, the person filing the Schedule 13D must disclose any interest in the target company's securities. Item Six must contain disclosure and descriptions of all contracts, arrangements, understandings or relationships between the persons filing the Schedule 13D and the target company with respect to its securities. Item Seven enumerates the material and documents that must be attached as exhibits to the Schedule 13D.[19] In addition to the initial filings, the person acquiring the five percent threshold must make amendments reflecting any significant changes in the information contained in the Schedule 13D or 13G.[20] In determining whether a change

---

in a *per se* finding of materiality but it is evidence of materiality). *Cf., e.g.,* Azurite Corp. v. Amster & Co., 844 F.Supp. 929 (S.D.N.Y.1994) (fact that group is engaged in preliminary discussions about possible proxy fight did not have to be disclosed); Homac, Inc. v. DSA Financial Corp., 661 F.Supp. 776 (E.D.Mich.1987) (bidder required to file amendment to its Schedule 13D to reflect bidder's intent to use target company's net operating loss to provide a tax shelter for bidder's income).

16. *See, e.g.,* SEC v. Levy, 706 F.Supp. 61 (D.D.C.1989) (failure to disclose bank loans was in violation of section 13(d)(1)(B)). This does not, however, impose a requirement that the purchaser have financing in place before the Schedule 13D is filed. IU International Corp. v. N X Acquisition Corp., 840 F.2d 220 (4th Cir.1988); Newmont Mining Corp. v. Pickens, 831 F.2d 1448 (9th Cir.1987). Also, disclosure of the financing arrangements does not by itself require disclosure relating to individuals behind corporate purchasers. *Cf.* Arkansas Best Corp. v. Pearlman, 688 F.Supp. 976 (D.Del.1988) (individuals owning corporations formed to be bidders in tender offer did not have to disclose their financial worth).

Additionally, section 13(d) does not require disclosure of unsuccessful financing negotiations. USG Corp. v. Wagner & Brown, 689 F.Supp. 1483 (N.D.Ill.1988).

17. *See, e.g.,* In re Phillips Petroleum Securities Litigation, 738 F.Supp. 825 (D.Del. 1990) (tender offeror's statement in Schedule 13D that it would not sell shares back to the target other than on a prorata basis with other shareholders may have been immaterial to potential investors in deciding whether to purchase stock in the face of the upcoming tender offer). International Broadcasting Corp. v. Turner, 734 F.Supp. 383 (D.Minn.1990) (allegation that filing failed to disclose intent to control and liquidate the target company). *Compare, e.g.,* SEC v. Amster & Co., 762 F.Supp. 604 (S.D.N.Y.1991) (failure to file amendments to Schedule 13D reflecting an intent to take control via a proxy contest was not actionable in the absence of evidence of such an intent prior to the announcement of these plans); Kamerman v. Steinberg, 744 F.Supp. 59 (S.D.N.Y.1990) (no section 13(d) violation for material omission since plaintiff failed to show that at the time of their stock acquisition defendants intended to "greenmail" target management).

18. In some such cases there may be an exemption from section 13(d)'s filing requirements. *See* 15 U.S.C.A. §§ 78m(d)(6), (f).

19. 17 C.F.R. § 240.13d–101 Item 7.

20. 15 U.S.C.A. § 78m(d)(2); 17 C.F.R. § 240.13d–2.

in circumstances necessitates an amendment, the general doctrine of materiality is applicable.[21] Under SEC Rule 13d–2(a)[22] a one percent or larger change in beneficial ownership establishes a material change per se.

Item 4 of Schedule 13D, which requires a description of the control aspirations of the purchasers, often gives rise to major disclosure problems. A purchaser's intent to acquire a twenty percent equity interest, and thereby obtain some representation on the target company's board, has been held to create an obligation to disclose a plan to acquire control.[23] The courts have applied Rule 12b–2(f)'s definition of control[24] for determining when a purchaser will be required to disclose his or her plans under section 13(d).[25] Disclosure of a control purpose is required even when the purchaser does not yet have a formalized concrete plan for exercising that control.[26] In disclosing the purchaser's designs with regard to the target company, the Schedule 13D should take a middle ground rather than risking overstatement or understatement.[27] This puts counsel in the position of determining his or her client's precise intentions, even if it means cross-examining one's own client. Because

---

Once a Schedule 13D has been filed, a sale of the stock so acquired must be disclosed promptly. In re Cooper Laboratories, Inc., 17 Sec.Reg. & L.Rep. (BNA) 1175 (SEC consent order June 26, 1985).

21. *See* 17 C.F.R. § 240.12b–2:

The term "material," when used to qualify a requirement for the furnishing of information as to any subject, limits the information required to those matters as to which an average prudent investor ought reasonably to be informed before buying or selling the security registered.

Materiality is discussed more fully in § 11.4 *supra. See also* § 13.5A *infra.*

22. 17 C.F.R. § 240.13d–2(a). *Cf.* USG Corp. v. Wagner & Brown, 690 F.Supp. 625 (N.D.Ill.1987) (corrective disclosures in subsequent filings do not render moot claims of earlier material misrepresentations).

23. Dan River, Inc. v. Unitex Ltd., 624 F.2d 1216 (4th Cir.1980), *cert. denied* 449 U.S. 1101, 101 S.Ct. 896, 66 L.Ed.2d 827 (1981); Chromalloy American Corp. v. Sun Chemical Corp., 611 F.2d 240 (8th Cir.1979). *See also* Gearhart Industries, Inc. v. Smith International, Inc., 592 F.Supp. 203 (N.D.Tex.1984), *modified and vacated in part* 741 F.2d 707 (5th Cir.1984). *See also* footnote 25 *infra.*

24. 17 C.F.R. § 240.12b–2(f):

The term "control" (including the terms "controlling," "controlled by" and "under common control with") means the possession, directly or indirectly, of the power to direct or cause the direction of the management and policies of a person, whether through the ownership of voting securities, by contract, or otherwise.

See also 17 C.F.R. § 240.405 which is discussed in § 4.24 *supra.*

25. However, it is not necessary to speculate. Thus, failure to disclose the possibility that the purchaser might be willing to sell his shares back to the target in a "greenmail" transaction was not a material omission. Lou v. Belzberg, 728 F.Supp. 1010 (S.D.N.Y. 1990).

26. Chevron Corp. v. Pennzoil Co., 974 F.2d 1156 (9th Cir.1992) (triable issue of fact as to whether Schedule 13D was materially misleading in failing to adequately disclose intent to obtain a board position and exert a degree of management influence over the target company).

27. Susquehanna Corp. v. Pan American Sulphur Co., 423 F.2d 1075 (5th Cir.1970). For other Schedule 13D disclosure cases *see, e.g.,* Purolator, Inc. v. Tiger International, Inc., 510 F.Supp. 554 (D.D.C.1981); Standard Metals Corp. v. Tomlin, 503 F.Supp. 586 (S.D.N.Y.1980).

of the need for secrecy and the importance of surprise, a client may be tempted to withhold information from counsel. Another reason for many clients' reticence is the fear that the attorney will cramp the style of the takeover artist.[28]

By virtue of section 13(d)(3),[29] when two or more people or entities get together to act as a partnership, limited partnership, syndicate or other group for the purpose of acquiring, holding, or disposing of a target company's securities, the syndicate or group is deemed to be a "person" for the purposes of section 13(d).[30] Accordingly, a Schedule 13D must be filed when members of a "group" in the aggregate acquire five percent of a class of equity securities subject to the Act's reporting requirements.[31] The Second Circuit has held that the determinative factor is whether a group has been established which holds the securities, pursuant to an express or implied agreement, thus presenting the *potential* for a shift in control; no agreement to buy further securities is necessary.[32] It is not necessary that the agreement be in writing.[33] The Second Circuit has held that the members' agreement to acquire control may be established by purchase of the five percent threshold.[34] However, discussions by various persons of the possibility of entering into an agreement alone do not establish the formation of a group.[35] The Seventh Circuit requires a greater showing of concerted activity to establish the formation of a "group" than does the Second Circuit: namely, the group must have an agreement not only to exert control, but to acquire additional shares for the purpose of exerting control as well.[36] Finally, a group may be deemed to exist when parties agree to act in concert to purchase

28. The attorney should thus make careful investigation not only for the sake of the client but for his or her own sake. The problems of representation are not unlike those that arise during a 1933 Act registration. *See* §§ 3.1, 7.4 *supra.*

29. 15 U.S.C.A. § 78m(d)(3).

30. For a similar provision with regard to tender offers *see* Section 14(d)(2), 15 U.S.C.A. § 78n(d)(2); § 11.14 *infra.*

31. *Cf.* Azurite Corp. v. Amster & Co., 844 F.Supp. 929 (S.D.N.Y.1994) (having filed as a group, there was no need to disclose preliminary exploration of whether to engage in a proxy fight).

32. GAF Corp. v. Milstein, 453 F.2d 709 (2d Cir.1971). *Accord* Staley Continental, Inc. v. Drexel Burnham Lambert, Inc., 1988 WL 36117, [1987–88 Transfer Binder] Fed.Sec. L.Rep. (CCH) ¶ 93,698 (D.D.C.1988); Financial General Bankshares v. Lance, 1978 WL 1082, [1978 Transfer Binder] Fed.Sec.L.Rep. (CCH) ¶ 96,403 (D.D.C.1978).

33. SEC v. Drexel Burnham Lambert Inc., 837 F.Supp. 587 (S.D.N.Y.1993).

34. Corenco Corp. v. Schiavone & Sons, Inc., 488 F.2d 207 (2d Cir.1973). *See also* Wellman v. Dickinson, 475 F.Supp. 783 (S.D.N.Y.1979).

Broker-dealers recommending an attractive takeover candidate may be considered part of a group. In the Matter of Katz, [1984 Transfer Binder] Fed.Sec.L.Rep. (CCH) ¶ 83,618 (April 25, 1984).

35. Lane Bryant, Inc. v. Hatleigh Corp., 517 F.Supp. 1196 (S.D.N.Y.1981). The fact that one is a limited partner in a partnership that has purchased shares is not sufficient to make the limited partner a member of a group under section 13(d). Management Assistance, Inc. v. Edelman, 584 F.Supp. 1016 (S.D.N.Y.1984). *Compare* Drobbin v. Nicolet Instrument Corp., 631 F.Supp. 860 (S.D.N.Y.1986) (controlling person of corporation acquiring five percent of target company had section 13(d) filing obligations).

36. Bath Industries, Inc. v. Blot, 427 F.2d 97 (7th Cir.1970) (enjoining a group acquiring nearly 50% control from ousting incumbent management).

additional shares, regardless of the absence of a common plan with respect to the target corporation beyond the acquisition of additional shares.[37] Whether failure to disclose the existence of a group in the Schedule 13D constitutes a material misstatement or omission depends upon the facts of the case.[38]

Rule 13d–3[39] sets out the Commission's standards for determining who is a beneficial owner for purposes of section 13(d) and section 13(g)'s[40] filing requirements. Section 13(d)(4)[41] addresses the computation of the five percent threshold and provides that in calculating the percentage of beneficial ownership, the outstanding securities of any class are to be considered exclusive of any securities held by or for the issuer or one of its subsidiaries.

Section 13(d)(6) exempts certain acquisitions from section 13(d)'s and 13(g)'s filing requirements.[42] These filing requirements do not apply to an offer to acquire securities in consideration for securities to be issued under a 1933 Act registration statement. Also exempt are all acquisitions of beneficial interest which, considered with all other acquisitions by the same person over the preceding twelve months, do not exceed two percent of that class of equity securities. Section 13(d)(6) further exempts any acquisition of an equity security by the issuer of that security and any other acquisition or proposed acquisition that the commission shall exempt by its rules. The purchase of securities by the issuer is governed by section 13(e) and rules promulgated thereunder.[43]

The terms of section 13(d)(6) give to the SEC the power to provide additional exemptions through rulemaking. Rule 13d–6[44] exempts purchases whereby the purchaser becomes more than a five percent beneficial owner if the acquisition is made pursuant to preemptive subscription rights provided that (1) an offering is made to all holders of securities of the same class; (2) the person acquiring securities does not acquire any additional securities other than through the pro rata share offering of

---

37. Mid–Continent Bancshares, Inc. v. O'Brien, 1981 WL 1404, [1982 Transfer Binder] Fed.Sec.L.Rep. (CCH) ¶ 98,734 (E.D.Mo.1981).

38. *Compare* SEC v. Savoy Industries, Inc., 587 F.2d 1149 (D.C.Cir.1978), *cert. denied* 440 U.S. 913, 99 S.Ct. 1227, 59 L.Ed.2d 462 (1979) *with* Treadway Companies v. Care Corp., 638 F.2d 357 (2d Cir.1980). *See* footnote 21 *supra.*

When various parties jointly file a Schedule 13D, there is no express requirement that they describe themselves as a group; thus, failure to describe themselves as a group did not warrant the issuance of a preliminary injunction. Sea Containers Ltd. v. Stena AB, 890 F.2d 1205 (D.C.Cir.1989).

39. 17 C.F.R. § 240.13d–3 (1982). *Compare* the ten percent beneficial ownership threshold under section 16's insider trading provisions. 15 U.S.C.A. § 78p. *See* § 12.4 *infra.*

40. 15 U.S.C.A. § 78m(g). *See, e.g.,* Stichting Phillips Pension bonds A and B, [1987–88 Transfer Binder] Fed.Sec.L.Rep. (CCH) ¶ 78,668 (SEC No Action Letter, 1988) (foreign pension fund investing in regular course of its business and not with a view towards affecting control of target company qualified for Schedule 13G).

41. 15 U.S.C.A. § 78m(d)(4).

42. 15 U.S.C.A. § 78m(d)(6).

43. 15 U.S.C.A. § 78m(e). *See* § 11.17 *infra.*

44. 17 C.F.R. § 240.13d–6 (1982).

preemptive rights; and (3) the acquisition is duly reported, if required, pursuant to section 16(a).[45] Finally, Rule 13d–7[46] establishes a non-refundable one hundred dollar filing fee for the initial Schedule 13D or 13G filing with no further fees for amendments.

§ 11.12   Reports of Institutional Investment Managers— Section 13(f)

Section 13(f)(1)[1] requires disclosure by institutional investment managers which exercise control over accounts containing significant portfolio holdings of equity securities subject to the Exchange Act's filing requirements. These institutional investors must file Form 13F upon acquiring equity securities subject to the registration requirements of section 12 of the 1934 Act[2] or the Investment Company Act[3] when the aggregate fair market value of all such equity securities exceeds one hundred million dollars.[4] The purpose of this legislation, which was adopted in 1975, was "to create a central depository of historical and current data about the activities of institutional investment managers."[5] Section 13(f)(2)[6] permits the Commission to make any exemptions from the filing requirements if it so chooses. However, to date, the Commission has not taken any exemptive action. Institutional investors must make publicly available a list of all securities subject to section 13(f)'s reporting and filing requirements.[7] However, there is no required public disclosure of information relating to section 13(f) filings by natural persons, estates or trusts other than business trusts and investment companies.[8]

Under the circumstances described above, institutional investment managers must file with the SEC five copies of Form 13F.[9] In addition, banks insured by the Federal Deposit Insurance Corporation that fall under section 13(f) must file a copy of every SEC report with the appropriate federal regulatory agency.[10] The institutional investment

---

45. 15 U.S.C.A. § 78p(a). *See* § 12.3 *infra.*

46. 17 C.F.R. § 240.13d–7.

§ 11.12

1. 15 U.S.C.A. § 78m(f)(1). *See generally* Thomas P. Lemke & Gerald T. Lins, Disclosure of Equity Holdings by Institutional Investment Managers: An Analysis of Section 13(f) of the Securities Exchange Act of 1934, 43 Bus.Law. 93 (1987).

2. 15 U.S.C.A. § 78*l*. *See* § 9.2 *supra.*

3. *See* § 17.3 *infra.*

4. *See* 17 C.F.R. § 240.13f–1.

5. Securities Acts Amendments of 1975, Pub.L. No. 94–29, House Conf.Rep. No. 94–229 at 109 (1975).

6. 15 U.S.C.A. § 78m(f)(2).

7. 15 U.S.C.A. § 78m(f)(3).

8. *Id.*

9. Form 13F, general instruction C.

10. *Id.* National banks and subsidiaries must send copies to the Comptroller of the Currency; state banks, and subsidiaries that are members of the Federal Reserve System, must send Form F to the Federal Reserve Board of Governors; and other banks insured by the Federal Deposit Insurance Corporation must send a copy to the FDIC.

manager must disclose the following information on Form 13F which is set up as a grid chart. There must be disclosure of the issuer and the type or class of security requiring the 13F filing.[11] The CUSIP number on the certificate must also be included.[12] The quarterly filing must also include the current market value and total number of shares of covered securities[13] If the institutional investment adviser does not exercise sole investment discretion, the Form 13F must identify the shares as to which there is shared investment discretion, identifying the person or institution with whom such discretion is shared.[14] The section 13(f) filing also requires disclosure of the degree of voting control exercised by the institutional manager.[15] Form 13F filings are of particular interest for those seeking to acquire control of an issuer of securities with a high concentration of institutional ownership because the institutions' willingness to sell may determine the success or failure of the takeover attempt.

The SEC permits institutions subject to section 13(f)'s filing requirements to request confidentiality of certain information relating to their investment strategies. The SEC has amended its rules to provide for confidential treatment of open risk arbitrage positions if at the time confidential treatment is requested, the investment manager represents that there is a reasonable belief that the current open position will not be closed by the time of the filing of the SEC report.[16]

§ 11.13 Definition of Tender Offer

Section 13(d)'s filing requirements are aimed at creeping acquisitions and open market or privately negotiated large block purchases.[1] In contrast, section 14's Williams Act filing and disclosure provisions are called into play when there is a "tender offer." "Tender offer" is not defined in the Williams Act. Both the courts and the SEC have broadly construed the term, providing a flexible definition. The definition of "tender offer" is important in that it determines the applicability of section 14(d)'s[2] filing requirements, section 14(e)'s[3] general antifraud proscriptions, and section 14(f)'s[4] disclosure requirements relating to new directors.

---

11. Form 13F, items 1, 2.

12. Form 13F, item 3. CUSIP stands for the Committee on Uniform Security Identification Procedure.

13. Form 13F, items 4, 5.

14. Form 13F, item 6. Shared investment discretion includes controlled and controlling companies, investment advisers, and insurance companies and their separate accounts.

15. Form 13F, item 8.

16. *See* Sec.Exch. Act Rel. No. 34–22038, [1984–85 Transfer Binder] Fed.Sec.L.Rep. (CCH) ¶ 83,772 (May 14, 1985).

§ 11.13

1. 15 U.S.C.A. § 78m(d). *See* §§ 11.11, 11.12 *supra*, § 11.17 *infra*.

2. 15 U.S.C.A. § 78n(d). *See* § 11.14 *infra*.

3. 15 U.S.C.A. § 78n(e). *See* §§ 11.15, 11.19 *infra*.

4. 15 U.S.C.A. § 78n(f). *See* § 11.16 *infra*.

On more than one occasion, Congress has considered and rejected[5] objective definitions of tender offer, such as the one embodied in the proposed Federal Securities Code.[6] The federal legislative pattern indicates either indecision or a congressional intent to retain a flexible definition and to leave the resolution of the issue to the SEC and the federal judiciary.[7] The SEC has seized upon this flexibility (intended or not). In contrast, most state tender offer statutes contain objective definitions.[8]

In the past, the SEC declined to set objective standards[9] to determine the existence of tender offers. This position was "premised upon the dynamic nature of [the] transactions [involved] and the need for the Williams Act to be interpreted flexibly."[10] Needless to say, what the SEC views as needed flexibility is viewed by corporate planners as resulting in unnecessary lack of predictability. In 1979, however, the Commission proposed the following definition of tender offer:

(1) The term "tender offer" includes a "request or invitation for tenders" and means one or more offers to purchase or solicitations of offers to sell securities of a single class, whether or not all or any portion of the securities sought are purchased, which

(i) during any 45 day period are directed to more than 10 persons and seek the acquisition of more than 5% of the class of securities, except that offers by a broker (and its customer) or by a dealer made on a national securities exchange at the then current market or made in the over-the-counter market at the then current market shall be excluded if in connection with such offers neither the person making the offers nor such broker or dealer solicits or arranges for the solicitation of any order to sell such securities and such broker or dealer performs only the customary functions of a broker or dealer and receives no more than the broker's usual and customary commission or the dealer's usual and customary markup; or

(ii) are not otherwise a tender offer under paragraph (b)(1)(i) of this section, but which (A) are disseminated in a

---

5. *See, e.g.,* Full Disclosure of Corporate Equity Ownership and in Corporate Takeover Bids, Hearings on S.510 Before the Subcomm. on Securities of the Senate Comm. on Banking and Currency, 90th Cong., 1st Sess. 131 (1967). *See* footnote 11 *infra.*

6. The proposed Code would have required an offer or solicitation directed towards more than thirty-five persons. *See* A.L.I.Fed.Sec.Code § 292 (1979); *Id.* § 299.9(a) (Tent. Draft No. 1 1972). The comments explain that although the present law has a "public connotation" of "tender offer," it is too vague and open-ended.

7. *See* footnote 11 *infra.*

8. *See, e.g.,* 8 Del.Code § 203(c)(2). *See generally* Report, State Takeover Statutes and The Williams Act, 32 Bus. Law. 187 (1976). The applicable state legislation is considered in §§ 11.21, 11.22 *infra.*

9. *See, e.g.,* Sec.Act Rel. No. 33–5731 (Aug. 2, 1976).

10. *Id. See generally* Note, The Elusive Definition of Tender Offer, 1 J.Corp.L. 503 (1982); Note, The Developing Meaning of Tender Offer, 86 Harv.L.Rev. 1250 (1973). *See also, e.g.,* Note, The Scope of Section 14(d): What is a Tender Offer?, 34 Ohio St.L.J. 375 (1973).

widespread manner, (B) provide for a price which represents a premium in excess of the greater of 5% of or $2 above the current market price and (C) do not provide for a meaningful opportunity to negotiate the price and terms.[11]

The proposed rule's definition, although broader than the conventional public announcement and call for tenders, would have given corporate planners a basis for greater predictability than exists under the current state of the law. However, the SEC has since abandoned any plans to define tender offer through formal rulemaking. Even if a rule is eventually adopted, its effect may not be conclusive. Since the statute neither expressly defines tender offer nor does it delegate that power to the Commission, any SEC rule would be merely interpretative and valid only to the extent that it is consistent with the definition to be gleaned from the terms of the statute, its purpose, and legislative history.[12] Accordingly, the existing case law and SEC rulings that are discussed below will be of continuing importance regardless of whether a definitional rule is adopted.

The SEC's proposed definition was prompted in part by the awareness that "many persons have deliberately structured [unconventional] tender offers in an effort to evade the provisions of the Williams Act."[13] The proposal was not an attempt to change the approach taken in earlier rulings but rather to clarify the Commission's position. The proposed rule reflected the Commission's long-standing position that the definition of tender offer "is not limited to the classical 'tender offer' where the person desiring to acquire shares makes a public invitation or a written offer to the shareholders to tender their shares. Nor is there a requirement that the shares be tendered through a depository. The change in control may be effected by direct purchase from shareholders without a public or a written invitation for tenders having been made."[14]

11. Proposed Rule 14d–1(b)(1). 3 Fed.Sec.L.Rep. (CCH) ¶ 24,281A (Nov. 29, 1979). *See* Sec.Exch.Act Rel. No. 34–16385, (Nov. 29, 1979). Three months after the SEC proposed the two-tiered definition, the SEC asked Congress to legislatively define tender offer as the acquisition of ten percent or more of a company's voting securities. There has been no indication that Congress will comply with this request.

12. SEC rulemaking power is discussed in § 1.4 *supra*. The legislative history acknowledged that a traditional tender "offer normally consists of a bid by an individual or group to buy shares of a company—usually at a price above the market price. Those accepting the offer are said to tender their stock for purchase. The person making the offer obligates himself to purchase *all* or a specified portion of the tendered shares if specified conditions are met." S.Rep. No. 550, 90th Cong., 1st Sess. 2 (1967). *Accord* H.Rep. No. 1171, 90th Cong., 2d Sess. 2 (1968). However, the legislative history is clear that although this identifies some characteristics of tender offers, it is not all inclusive of what the Act is attempting to regulate. *See* Full Disclosure of Corporate Equity Ownership and in Corporate Takeover Bids: Hearings on S.510 Before the Subcommittee on Securities of the Committee on Banking and Currency, 90th Cong., 1st Sess. (1967). *See also, e.g.,* the authorities cited in footnote 10 *supra*.

13. Sec.Exch.Act Rel. No. 34–16385 (Nov. 29, 1979).

14. *E.g.,* Cattlemen's Investment Co., [1971–72 Transfer Binder] Fed.Sec.L.Rep. (CCH) ¶ 78,775 (SEC Staff Reply April 24, 1972). *See* Plessey Co. plc v. General Electric Co., 628 F.Supp. 477, 487 (D.Del.1986) ("Although the term 'tender offer' has never been expressly defined by Congress, the legislative history suggests a congressional intent to retain flexibility so that the courts and the SEC can effectuate the goals of the Williams Act."

The essence of the SEC's position is that "tender offer" covers more than traditional takeover attempts involving public solicitation and may, under appropriate circumstances, include privately negotiated and open market purchases.

The SEC has suggested an eight factor test to determine whether a tender offer exists. The eight factors can be summarized as follows:

(1) active and widespread solicitation of public shareholders;

(2) solicitation for a substantial percentage of the issuer's stock;

(3) whether the offer to purchase is made at a premium over prevailing market price;

(4) whether the terms of the offer are firm rather than negotiable;

(5) whether the offer is contingent on the tender of a fixed minimum number of shares;

(6) whether the offer is open only for a limited period of time;

(7) whether the offerees are subject to pressure to sell their stock; and

(8) the existence of public announcements of a purchasing program that precede or accompany a rapid accumulation of stock.[15]

These factors are simply broad guidelines. Hence, whatever predictability does exist must be gleaned from the cases and SEC rulings.[16]

The Developing Interpretation and Case Law

In an early release, the Commission took the position that a "special bid"—the placement of a fixed-price bid on an exchange for a specified

(citing this treatise)). The SEC's position that "tender offer" be broadly interpreted because of its prophylactic impact was rejected by the Second Circuit in Hanson Trust PLC v. SCM Corp., 774 F.2d 47 (2d Cir.1985). The *SCM* case involved a so-called "end run" whereby the acquiring company withdrew its tender offer, made a series of open market purchases and then made a second tender offer. The open market purchases were held not to constitute a tender offer (or part of a tender offer) in violation of the Williams Act. *See also, e.g.,* Sec.Act. Rel. No. 33–5731 (Aug. 2, 1976).

15. The eight factor test which is not contained in an official SEC release has evolved over a period of time and is discussed in Wellman v. Dickinson, 475 F.Supp. 783 (S.D.N.Y.1979); Hoover Co. v. Fuqua Industries, Inc., 1979 WL 1244, [1979–80 Transfer Binder] Fed.Sec.L.Rep. (CCH) ¶ 97,107 (N.D.Ohio 1979).

16. *See, e.g.,* Holstein v. UAL Corp., 662 F.Supp. 153 (N.D.Ill.1987) (poison pill plan which involved distribution of rights held not a tender offer); Beaumont v. American Can Co., 621 F.Supp. 484 (S.D.N.Y.1985), *opinion affirmed* 797 F.2d 79 (2d Cir.1986) (cash option portion of a merger with a cash election feature is not a tender offer); Brill v. Burlington Northern, Inc., 590 F.Supp. 893 (D.Del.1984) (authorized but previously unissued stock purchased pursuant to golden parachute agreements were collateral agreements to tender offer to which the Williams Act does not apply). *See also* Plessey Co. plc v. General Electric Co. plc, 628 F.Supp. 477 (D.Del.1986) (press release announcing tender offer in England for share in British company sent to American holders of American Depositary Receipts for shares in the company held not to be a tender offer within the jurisdictional means of the Williams Act); Brascan Ltd. v. Edper Equities Ltd., 477 F.Supp. 773 (S.D.N.Y.1979); Wellman v. Dickinson, 475 F.Supp. 783 (S.D.N.Y.1979); Ludlow Corp. v. Tyco Laboratories, Inc., 529 F.Supp. 62 (D.Mass.1981); Kaufman & Broad, Inc. v. Belzberg, 522 F.Supp. 35 (S.D.N.Y.1981); Luptak v. Central Cartage Co., 1979 WL 1280, [1981 Transfer Binder] Fed.Sec.L.Rep. (CCH) ¶ 98,034 (E.D.Mich.1979), *affirmed mem.* 647 F.2d 165 (6th Cir.1981). *Cf.* Polinsky v. MCA, Inc., 680 F.2d 1286 (9th Cir.1982).

large number of shares—constitutes a tender offer.[17] Thus, although ordinary open market purchases are not to be classified as tender offers,[18] use of the facilities of an exchange will not automatically preclude the finding of a "tender offer."[19] Ordinarily, open market purchases will not constitute a tender offer. In fact, as discussed below, there are no federal cases finding a tender offer on the basis of open-market purchases. An early federal district court decision held that a large block purchase of shares made without the intent to obtain control is not a tender offer under the Williams Act. The court looked to the legislative history which "made clear that the type of activity intended to be regulated * * * is the acquisition of control of a corporation by outsiders through the purchase of its shares."[20] According to the legislative history, a tender offer occurs when a target company shareholder must decide whether or not to sell shares in connection with a transfer of control.[21]

Arguably, a series of control-related open market purchases would fall within the tender offer definition as well. The cases, however, have taken a contrary view.[22] Notwithstanding the weight of current case law to the contrary, purchasers engaged in a series of open market transactions as a first step in acquiring control should be aware of the risk, albeit a small one, that courts may find against them on the "tender offer" issue. Open market purchases combined with secretive, high pressure private transactions could well fall within the Act's purview.

---

17. Sec.Exch.Act Rel. No. 34–8392 (Aug. 30, 1968). *See also* In re Paine Webber, Jackson & Curtis, Inc., 15 Sec.Reg.L.Rep. (BNA) 131 (SEC Dec. 12, 1982) (block trade of 9.9 percent is a tender offer). In its recent proposal, the SEC added that "assembling a block" off the floor which is then crossed on the exchange would also be viewed as a solicitation. Sec.Exch.Act Rel. No. 34–16385 [1979–80 Transfer Binder] Fed.Sec.L.Rep. (CCH) ¶ 82,374 at 82,603 (Nov. 29, 1979).

18. *Ibid. See also,* Luptak v. Central Cartage Co., 1979 WL 1280, [1981 Transfer Binder] Fed.Sec.L.Rep. (CCH) ¶ 98,034 (E.D.Mich.1979), *affirmed mem.* 647 F.2d 165 (6th Cir.1981). *See also* Hanson Trust PLC v. SCM Corp., 774 F.2d 47 (2d Cir.1985) (five privately negotiated purchases and one open market purchase was not a tender offer; the transactions in question have been referred to as an "end run" because they were preceded by a tender offer that was withdrawn and then followed by a second tender offer); SEC v. Carter Hawley Hale Stores, Inc., 760 F.2d 945 (9th Cir.1985) (issuer's open market purchase program in response to third party tender offer was not a tender offer subject to section 13(e)).

19. Sec. Exch. Act Rel. No. 34–8392 (Aug. 30, 1968).

20. Dyer v. Eastern Trust & Banking Co., 336 F.Supp. 890, 907 (D.Me.1971). *See* Smallwood v. Pearl Brewing Co., 489 F.2d 579 (5th Cir.1974), *cert. denied* 419 U.S. 873, 95 S.Ct. 134, 42 L.Ed.2d 113 (1974).

21. *See* S.Rep. No. 550, 90th Cong., 1st Sess. 2 (1967); H.R.Rep. No. 1711, 90th Cong., 2d Sess. 2 (1968).

Of course, not all control related transactions will be tender offers. *See, e.g.,* FMC Corp. v. Boesky, 727 F.Supp. 1182 (N.D.Ill.1989) (recapitalization was not a tender offer). *Compare* Iavarone v. Raymond Keyes Associates, Inc., 733 F.Supp. 727 (S.D.N.Y.1990) (transaction in 25 shareholder company whereby preferred stock would be exchanged for outstanding common stock was a tender offer subject to section 14(e)'s antifraud proscriptions).

22. *See* footnotes 27–37 *infra* and accompanying text. *See generally* David J. Segre, Open–Market and Privately Negotiated Purchase Programs and the Market for Corporate Control, 42 Bus.Law. 715 (1987).

Under section 13(d), open market purchases will trigger disclosure obligations within ten days of the acquisition of five percent or more of a company's securities.[23] In contrast, section 14(d)'s filing requirements begin with the commencement of the offer.[24] Therefore, if a series of open-market purchases constitutes a tender offer, full disclosure must be made simultaneously with the first purchase. There have been many proposals before the SEC to require advance filing under section 13(d) as well.[25] Adoption of this position would in large part eliminate the significance of the open market purchase controversy with the very important exception that a "tender offer" triggers potential liability under section 14(e)'s antifraud proscriptions.[26]

A plan of successive open market purchases has been held not to be a tender offer where the aggregate amount of shares so purchased fell short of the five percent threshold.[27] Even where the five percent threshold was exceeded, an attempt to exercise voting control after a series of open market purchases has been held insufficient to make the acquisition a tender offer.[28] Similarly, the purchase of twenty-five percent of a company's stock in a two day period was held not to be a tender offer where only one of the SEC's eight factors was present.[29] A "street sweep" for a target's own shares, consisting of large block purchases within a short period of time,[30] was not a tender offer even though it was designed to defeat a hostile third-party offer.[31] The most compelling case to date for characterizing a series of open-market purchases as a tender offer was Hanson Trust PLC v. SCM Corp.,[32]

---

23. 15 U.S.C.A. § 78m(d). *See* § 11.11 *supra.*

24. 15 U.S.C.A. § 78n(d).

25. *See,* 15 Sec.Reg.L.Rep. (BNA) No. 24 at 1156 (June 17, 1983). The SEC proposed such legislation to Congress. *See* 16 Sec. Reg. & L.Rep. (BNA) 793 (May 11, 1984). Closing the ten day window in section 13(d) has proven to be a difficult, if not impossible, task.

26. 15 U.S.C.A. § 78n(e). *See* §§ 11.15, 11.19 *infra.* The SEC has also asked for public comment on possible Commission action relating to two-tier tender offers. Sec. Exch.Act Rel. No. 34–21079 (June 21, 1984).

27. Gulf & Western Industries, Inc. v. Great Atlantic & Pacific Tea Co., 356 F.Supp. 1066 (S.D.N.Y.1973), *affirmed* 476 F.2d 687 (2d Cir.1973).

28. Water & Wall Association, Inc. v. American Consumer Industries, Inc., 1973 WL 383, [1973 Transfer Binder] Fed.Sec.L.Rep. (CCH) ¶ 93,943 (D.N.J.1973). *Accord* SEC v. Carter Hawley Hale Stores, Inc., 760 F.2d 945 (9th Cir.1985). Recently, the Ninth Circuit has held that open market stock purchases were not part of a later tender offer by the same purchaser, and therefore did not violate the Williams Act. The court found that the pre-tender offer stock purchases had none of the indicia associated with tender offers when measured against the SEC's eight factor test. Polinsky v. MCA, Inc., 680 F.2d 1286 (9th Cir.1982).

29. Brascan Ltd. v. Edper Equities Ltd., 477 F.Supp. 773 (S.D.N.Y.1979). The eight factor test is set out in the text accompanying footnote 15 *supra.*

30. For example, within a two hour trading period, the target company purchased 6.5 million of its own shares (approximately 18%); this was part of a defensive repurchase program that would have resulted in acquisition of 18.5 million shares (more than half of the company's outstanding stock).

31. SEC v. Carter Hawley Hale Stores, Inc., 760 F.2d 945 (9th Cir.1985).

32. 774 F.2d 47 (2d Cir.1985).

which held that a street sweep and a group of privately negotiated purchases for twenty-five percent of the target company's outstanding stock was not a tender offer, even though these purchases occurred on the heels of the withdrawal of a publicly announced tender offer.[33] The court refused to find these transactions to constitute a tender offer because, among other things, the price of the purchases was at the market price and the privately negotiated purchases were accomplished without any pressure or secrecy.[34] The result also might have been different had the withdrawal of the tender offer been part of a plan designed to evade the protections of the Williams Act.[35]

The courts finding that these open market purchase programs are not tender offers have relied on the legislative history in distinguishing large scale stock acquisitions from tender offers. For example, it has been observed that the Williams Act was not intended to "subject any * * * extensive market acquisition program to immediate characterization as a tender offer."[36] For similar reasons, courts have found that open market purchases are not tender offers under analogous state statutes.[37]

The cases involving both open market and privately negotiated stock purchases seem to turn on whether or not the "pressure-creating characteristics of a tender offer"[38] accompany the transactions. Thus, where a publicly announced intention to acquire a substantial block of stock was followed by rapid acquisition of shares, the court held that a tender offer

---

33. These purchases were made within hours of the withdrawal of the tender offer.

34. 774 F.2d 47 (2d Cir.1985). *Compare* Wellman v. Dickinson, 475 F.Supp. 783 (S.D.N.Y.1979), which is discussed in the text accompanying footnotes 42–43 *infra,* where the privately negotiated transactions were based on secrecy and undue pressure and thus were held to constitute a tender offer.

35. *Cf.* Field v. Trump, 850 F.2d 938 (2d Cir.1988), *cert. denied* 489 U.S. 1012, 109 S.Ct. 1122, 103 L.Ed.2d 185 (1989), which is discussed in § 11.14 *infra* at footnote 55 wherein the court found that a privately negotiated purchase sandwiched between the withdrawal of one tender offer and the initiation of a second, both at a lower price, was part of a single tender offer.

36. Ludlow Corp. v. Tyco Laboratories, Inc., 529 F.Supp. 62, 69 (D.Mass.1981). *Cf.* SEC v. Carter Hawley Hale Stores, Inc., 760 F.2d 945 (9th Cir.1985) (issuer's open market repurchase program in response to a tender offer was not a tender offer).

See also, Yeddia Z. Stern, Acquisition of Corporate Control by Numerous Privately Negotiated Transactions: A Proposal for the Resolution of Street Sweeps, 58 Brook.L.Rev. 1195 (1993); Terence L. Blackburn, The Regulation of Market Sweeps in Connection with Tender Offers, 58 Geo.Wash.L.Rev. 619 (1990).

37. *E.g.* Condec Corp. v. Farley, 578 F.Supp. 85 (S.D.N.Y.1983) (purchase of 8.7% of the target company's stock was not a tender offer under the New York Takeover Disclosure Act); Sheffield v. Consolidated Foods Corp., 302 N.C. 403, 276 S.E.2d 422 (1981) (series of open market purchases held not subject to the North Carolina act). *See also* In re University Bank & Trust Co., 16 Sec.Reg. & L.Rep. (BNA) 1252 (Mass.Sec.Div. July 19, 1984) (shareholder who purchased more than ten percent of issuer's stock as part of a public offering was not subject to the Massachusetts takeover statute). *See* § 11.20 *infra.*

38. Ludlow Corp. v. Tyco Laboratories, Inc., 529 F.Supp. 62, 68 (D.Mass.1981).

More recently it has been held that a highly publicized cash merger proposal at a premium above the market price constituted a tender offer. Zuckerman v. Franz, 573 F.Supp. 351 (S.D.Fla.1983).

had occurred.[39]   In contrast, where acquisition proceeded more slowly and none of the SEC's eight factors were present, the court found no more than "a particularly aggressive and successful open market [and privately negotiated] stock buying program."[40]

A number of decisions have discussed whether privately negotiated transfers of a controlling block of shares can constitute a tender offer. The cases conflict, but most hold that privately negotiated transactions are susceptible of being categorized as tender offers even though most privately negotiated purchases will not fall within the definition of tender offer. Any privately negotiated purchase that interferes with a shareholder's "unhurried investment decision" and "fair treatment of * * * investors"[41] defeats the protections of the Williams Act and is, most likely, a tender offer. In one case,[42] a company formed a subsidiary, LHIW [Let's Hope It Works], through which it made simultaneous secret offers to twenty-eight of the target company's largest shareholders. These shareholders represented a total of thirty-five percent of the company's outstanding shares. The identity of the actual tender offeror was not disclosed. Further, the target shareholders were given a short period of time—from one-half hour to overnight—in which to make a decision. The court held that a tender offer had taken place.[43] In a more recent case, a firm agreement to purchase fifty-one percent (majority control) of a company was held to be a privately negotiated sale of stock outside the scope of section 14's tender offer provisions because of the absence of most of the SEC's eight factors.[44] In addition, the Second Circuit has held that where the tender offeror and the solicited shareholder agree on secrecy and the private nature of the transaction, the acquisition of nearly ten percent of a target company's outstanding shares does not constitute a tender offer.[45] Unlike the *Wellman* decision discussed above,[46] this case did not involve a hostile, high pressure move to take control such that the interests of investor protection called for

---

39. S–G Securities, Inc. v. Fuqua Investment Co., 466 F.Supp. 1114 (D.Mass.1978) (twenty-eight percent of target company). *Compare, e.g.*, SEC v. Carter Hawley Hale Stores, Inc., 760 F.2d 945 (9th Cir.1985).

40. Ludlow Corp. v. Tyco Laboratories, Inc., 529 F.Supp. 62, 67 (D.Mass.1981). *See also, e.g.*, Hanson Trust PLC v. SCM Corp., 774 F.2d 47 (2d Cir.1985) which is discussed in footnotes 32–34 *supra* and accompanying text.

41. Cattlemen's Investment Co. v. Fears, 343 F.Supp. 1248 (W.D.Okl.1972) (finding a tender offer to have occurred). *See also, e.g.*, In re G.L. Corp., [1979–1980 Transfer Binder] Fed.Sec.L.Rep. (CCH) ¶ 82,494 (April 15, 1980) (offer for all or none purchase at a premium may be a tender offer). *See generally* Segre *supra* footnote 22.

42. Wellman v. Dickinson, 475 F.Supp. 783 (S.D.N.Y.1979).

43. *Id.*

44. Astronics Corp. v. Protective Closures Co., Inc., 561 F.Supp. 329 (W.D.N.Y.1983).

45. Kennecott Copper Corp. v. Curtiss–Wright Corp., 584 F.2d 1195 (2d Cir.1978). *See also, e.g.*, Energy Ventures, Inc. v. Appalachian Co., 587 F.Supp. 734 (D.Del.1984) (series of privately negotiated transactions did not constitute a tender offer). University Bank & Trust Co. v. Gladstone, 574 F.Supp. 1006 (D.Mass.1983); Financial General Bankshares, Inc. v. Lance, 80 F.R.D. 22 (D.D.C.1978).

46. *See* text accompanying footnotes 42–43 *supra*.

section 14(d)'s advance notice and filing requirements. Similarly, the Second Circuit has held that absent special facts, five privately negotiated purchases which combined with one open market purchase totaled twenty-five percent of an issuer's outstanding stock did not constitute a tender offer.[47]

The theme that emerges from the foregoing cases is that when a privately negotiated attempt to take control of a company raises problems that the Williams Act was designed to ameliorate (such as secrecy and high pressure), a tender offer may exist. This is a significant broadening of the tender offer definition especially since it brings within the reach of section 14(e)'s antifraud provisions, many transactions that are not subject to the filing requirements of section 13(d). The key factors to look for in privately negotiated transactions include such things as the "midnight special" and "bear hug" tactics used in the *Wellman* case.[48]

Clearly, a tender offer need not be hostile in order to be subject to 14(d) requirements. Where the target company's management supports the shift in control, abuses may arise that will necessitate the application of the tender offer definition.[49] It has been opined that a tender offeror's decision to extend an existing tender offer to an additional number of shares does not create a new tender offer so as to start the filing requirements of section 14(d) anew.[50]

As the foregoing discussion illustrates, in the absence of an SEC rule or statutory amendment, the definition of tender offer remains elusive. The cases have established some limits to the flexible definition. The inquiry, however, is highly factual and is handled on an ad hoc basis. Accordingly, securities planners involved in control-related transactions should be careful lest they risk being involved in an inadvertent tender offer.

---

47. Hanson Trust PLC v. SCM Corp., 774 F.2d 47 (2d Cir.1985). *See also, e.g.,* Pin v. Texaco, Inc., 793 F.2d 1448 (5th Cir.1986), *rehearing denied* 797 F.2d 977 (5th Cir.1986) (private offers held not to be a tender offer); Rand v. Anaconda–Ericsson, Inc., 794 F.2d 843 (2d Cir.1986) (letter to target company chairman proposing to purchase target company stock was not a tender offer). *Cf.,* Weeden v. Continental Health Affiliates, Inc., 713 F.Supp. 396 (N.D.Ga.1989) (filing of Schedule 13D coupled with public letter to target's board proposing a $6.00 per share buy-out was a proposal to begin negotiations and not a tender offer).

48. *Id. See also* Milstein v. Huck, 600 F.Supp. 254, 263 (E.D.N.Y.1984) (determination of whether there was a tender offer involved difficult factual issues requiring a full trial). The jargon of the tender offer arena frequently reflects the aggressiveness of the tactics employed. Midnight special refers to surprise tactics such as those employed in the *Wellman* case. A bear hug is a "friendly" approach to the target company's management, to be followed by more coercive action if the aggressor is rebuffed. Other takeover terminology is discussed in §§ 11.10 *supra* and 11.20 *infra*.

49. Smallwood v. Pearl Brewing Co., 489 F.2d 579 (5th Cir.1974), *cert. denied* 419 U.S. 873, 95 S.Ct. 134, 42 L.Ed.2d 113 (1974).

50. American General Insurance Co., [1971–72 Transfer Binder] Fed.Sec.L.Rep. (CCH) ¶ 78,588 (SEC Staff Reply Dec. 22, 1971).

§ 11.14 Filings, Disclosures and Procedures for Tender Offers—Section 14(d) and Regulation 14D—An Overview

As discussed more fully below, section 14(d) and applicable SEC rules require the filing of tender offers along with certain mandated disclosures. Filing requirements are not limited to the tender offeror but apply to anyone who is recommending in favor of or against a tender offer covered by the Act. In addition there are certain substantive requirements for any tender offer subject to section 14(d).

Filing Requirements

Section 14(d)(1) of the Exchange Act[1] requires that all "tender offer material" for equity securities subject to the registration requirements of section 12 must be filed with the Commission and accompanied by the appropriate disclosures.[2] The filing requirements do not apply to issuers whose periodic reporting obligations arise under section 15(d).[3] Section 14(d) requires disclosures of the type specified in Schedule 13D under section 13(d)[4] in addition to such other information as the SEC may require. As is the case with a Schedule 13D filing for acquisition of five percent or more of a class of a target company's stock,[5] the section 14(d) filings must be updated to reflect material changes and developments.[6] Section 14(d) does not apply to an issuer's acquisition of its own shares[7] as those transactions are covered by section 13(e) which by virtue of SEC rulemaking imposes regulations for issuer tender offers that are comparable to Regulation 14D's rules for third party offers.[8]

Regulation 14D sets out the Commission's filing and disclosure requirements under section 14(d). Rule 14d–1[9] provides the basic definitions for covered tender offers and further incorporates by reference all general definitions applicable under other provisions of the Exchange

---

§ 11.14

1. 15 U.S.C.A. § 78n(d)(1).

2. 15 U.S.C.A. § 78n(d)(1). Registered reporting companies are those issuers having a class of securities traded on a national securities exchange, as well as those issuers having assets of at least $5,000,000 and also having a class of equity securities with more than 500 shareholders. 15 U.S.C.A. § 78l; 17 C.F.R. § 240.12g–1. See § 9.2 supra for a discussion of section 12's registration requirements.

3. 15 U.S.C.A. § 78o(d). Section 15(d) applies to issuers not subject to section 12 whose securities were issued pursuant to a 1933 Act registration statement. The periodic reporting requirements are discussed in § 9.3 supra.

4. 15 U.S.C.A. § 78m(d) which is discussed in § 11.11 supra.

5. 15 U.S.C.A. § 78n(d). Compare 15 U.S.C.A. § 78m(d) which is discussed in § 11.11 supra.

6. 15 U.S.C.A. § 78n(d). Cf. In re Revlon, Inc., Sec. Exch. Act Rel. No. 34–23320 (June 16, 1986) (finding violations of Rule 14d–4 due to failure to amend the Schedule 14D–9 to reflect defensive merger negotiations).

7. 15 U.S.C.A. § 78n(d)(1).

8. 15 U.S.C.A. § 78m(e). In 1986, the SEC amended Rules 13e–4 and 14e–1 so as to subject issuer self tenders to the same time periods and substantive regulation as third-party offers that are covered by section 14(d) and Regulation 14D. See § 11.17 infra.

9. 17 C.F.R. § 240.14d–1.

Act. In addition to the long-form filing set out in Schedule 14D–1,[10] the tender offeror must file ten copies of all additional tender offer material with the Commission no later than the date upon which it is first published or disseminated.[11] These constitute filed documents within the context of section 18(a)'s imposition of liability[12] upon those responsible therefor to injured purchasers or sellers relying on materially misleading information contained therein.

As is the case with the proxy rules,[13] the filing requirements are not limited to the first formal filing of the initial offer. All other documents used in the tender offer and solicitation must thus be on file with the commission prior to their use.[14]

Commencement of Tender Offer

Rule 14d–2[15] provides that a tender offer begins at 12:01 a.m. on the earliest date of the following events: (1) the first publication of the long form tender offer filed pursuant to Rule 14d–4(a)(1); (2) the first publication of a summary advertisement;[16] or (3) the first public announcement[17] of the tender offer, unless within five days of the announcement the "bidder"[18] makes a public announcement withdrawing the tender offer or complies with the disclosure and filing require- ments of Rules 14d–3(a),[19] 14d–6,[20] and 14d–4,[21] all of which require public dissemination of the relevant information.[22]

The information that a tender offeror must disclose at the time of the commencement of the offer depends to some extent upon the terms of the offer that is being made. All "bidders" must file the Schedule 14D–1. "Bidder" is defined as any person who makes a tender offer or

---

10. 17 C.F.R. § 240.14d–100.

11. 17 C.F.R. § 240.14d–3(b).

12. 15 U.S.C.A. § 78r(a) which is discussed in § 12.8 *infra*.

13. *See* 17 C.F.R. § 240.14a–3 and Schedule 14A which is discussed in § 11.2 *supra*.

14. 17 C.F.R. § 240.14d–3. Once it is clear that a tender offer exists, the courts tend to strictly construe issues relating to the determination of the commencement date. This is so because the Williams Act is designed to provide disclosure as early as practicable. *See* Gerber v. Computer Associates International, Inc., 812 F.Supp. 361 (E.D.N.Y.1993).

15. 17 C.F.R. § 240.14d–2.

16. Rule 14d–4(a)(2) allows summary publications for certain tender offers. 17 C.F.R. § 240.14d–4(a)(2). *See* USG Corp. v. Wagner & Brown, 689 F.Supp. 1483 (N.D.Ill.1988) (preliminary announcement complied with Rule 14d–2(d)'s safe harbor requirements).

17. Kahn v. Virginia Retirement System, 13 F.3d 110 (4th Cir.1993) (joint press release announcing takeover agreement did not commence the tender offer).

18. "The term 'bidder' means any person who makes a tender offer or on whose behalf a tender offer is made [except for a tender offer by the issuer]." 17 C.F.R. § 240.14d–1(b)(1).

19. 17 C.F.R. § 240.14d–3(a) (filing and transmittal of tender offer statements).

20. 17 C.F.R. § 240.14d–6 (disclosure requirements with respect to tender offers).

21. 17 C.F.R. § 240.14d–4 (dissemination of tender offers).

22. *Cf.,* Weeden v. Continental Health Affiliates, Inc., 713 F.Supp. 396 (N.D.Ga.1989) (filing of Schedule 13D coupled with public letter to target's board proposing a $6.00 per share buy-out was a proposal to begin negotiations and not a tender offer and therefore did not implicate the "five day" rule).

on whose behalf a tender offer is made, except that an issuer seeking to acquire its own securities is not within the definition.[23] Further, for the purpose of determining whether or not a tender offer has been made, two or more persons who act as a partnership, limited partnership, syndicate or other "group" for the purpose of acquiring, holding, or disposing of the target company[24] must file eight copies of the Schedule 14D-1,[25] including exhibits, with the Commission prior to the commencement of the tender offer. The information required by the Schedule 14D-1 fairly well parallels the requirements of Schedule 13D.[26] In addition to prescribing the form of the tender offer statement, Regulation 14D imposes certain substantive procedures on the mechanics and terms of the tender offer.[27]

Schedule 14D–1

The Schedule 14D-1 must disclose the name of the bidder, name of the target company and the title of class of securities being sought. It also requires that all "persons" reporting under the Schedule provide their names and addresses as well as disclosing whether or not they belong to a "group" within the meaning of section 14(d)(2).[28] It further is necessary to disclose the source of funds to be used in connection with the tender offer and the identity and background of the person filing the document, including the disclosure of any criminal convictions, within the past five years, of the person presenting the tender offer. The tender offer document must also disclose all past contracts, transactions or negotiations between the tender offeror and the target company, the purpose of the tender offer and the bidder's plans and proposals for the future with regard to the target company. The Schedule 14D-1 must divulge the bidder's current interest and holdings of securities of the target company as well as any contracts, arrangements, understandings or relationships between the bidder and the target company. Schedule 14D-1 must identify all persons retained or employed or compensated in connection with the tender offer as well as the bidder's financial statements when the bidder's financial structure is material to an investor's decision whether or not to tender shares in the target company. For example, any tender offer involving an exchange of the target company's securities for the tender offeror's shares would necessarily trigger the financial statement requirement.

---

23. *See* footnote 18 *supra.*

24. 15 U.S.C.A. § 78n(d)(2). A similar provision is found in section 13(d)(3), 15 U.S.C.A. § 78m(d)(3). For discussion of "group theory" within the context of corporate takeover, *see, e.g.,* Richard W. Jennings & Harold Marsh, Jr., Securities Regulation: Cases and Materials 643–645 (5th ed.1982) and § 11.11 *supra.*

25. 17 C.F.R. § 240.14d–100.

26. Additionally the concept of what constitutes a "group" with regard to section 13(d) filings has its parallel here. *See* the discussion of what constitutes a "group" in § 11.11 *supra.*

27. *See* text accompanying footnotes 36–70 *infra.*

28. *See* footnote 24 *supra.*

In addition to the disclosures above, the Schedule 14D–1 filing must list any present or proposed material contracts, arrangements, understandings or relationships between the bidder, its officers, directors, controlling persons or subsidiaries and the target company or any of its officers, directors, controlling persons or subsidiaries that would bear upon the target company shareholders' decision whether or not to tender his or her shares. Further, steps toward compliance with necessary administrative approval for the offer must be disclosed, as must the applicability of the antitrust laws, or the margin requirements[29] as well as the pendency of material legal proceedings.[30] When there have been material misstatements in a 14D filing, they can be cured by subsequent correction provided that adequate prominence is given to the curative changes.[31]

Other Requirements Imposed by Regulation 14D

Section 14(d)(3) of the Act[32] provides that in determining the applicable percentage of outstanding shares of any class of equity securities, securities held by the issuer or its subsidiary must be excluded from the computation. Also, section 14(d)(4)[33] requires full disclosure according to such rules as the Commission may promulgate with regard to any solicitation or recommendation to a target company's securities holders either to accept or reject a tender offer or request for tender made by someone else. These disclosure requirements are set out in Schedule 14D–9.[34] Schedule 14D–9 is the disclosure document that must be filed in connection with any other solicitation or recommendation for or against tender offers. The Schedule 14D–9 is in essence a short form of the Schedule 14D–1 requiring similar disclosures with regard to anyone making recommendations concerning a bidder's offer. As is the case with an offeror's Schedule 14D–1, material changes must be reflected by

---

29. *See, e.g.,* Irving Bank Corp. v. Bank of New York Co., 692 F.Supp. 163 (S.D.N.Y. 1988) (tender offer must accurately disclose status of Federal Reserve Board approval for proposed acquisition of target company).

The margin regulations are promulgated under 15 U.S.C.A. § 78g. The margin requirements are discussed generally in § 10.11 *supra.*

30. *Cf.* Fry v. Trump, 681 F.Supp. 252 (D.N.J.1988) (upholding section 14(a) claim based on failure to disclose ten of eighteen pending legal proceedings).

Additionally, the filed copies of the Schedule 14D–1 must contain the following exhibits: copies of all tender offer material which is published, sent or given to security holders by or on behalf of the bidders in connection with the tender offer, any loan or agreement used to finance the tender offer or otherwise disclosed in the Schedule 14D–1, any documents setting forth the terms of any contracts, arrangements, understandings or relationships referred to in the Schedule 14D–1, any written legal opinions referring to relevant pending legal proceedings as well as the prospectus for any securities to be issued in an exchange offer.

31. *See, e.g.,* American Insured Mortgage Investors v. CRI, Inc., 1990 WL 192561, [1990–1991 Transfer Binder] Fed.Sec.L.Rep. (CCH) ¶ 95,730 (S.D.N.Y.1990) (material changes had to be highlighted through the use of boldface and italic typeface).

32. 15 U.S.C.A. § 78n(d)(3).

33. 15 U.S.C.A. § 78n(d)(4).

34. 17 C.F.R. § 240.14d–101.

"prompt" amendment to the Schedule 14D–9.[35]

Bidders' Right of Access to Target Company's Shareholders

Rule 14d–5 spells out the target company's obligation to respond to requests for a shareholder list in connection with tender offers.[36] Briefly, if the bidder or other person presents the request according to the rule's requirements, the target company's management must comply but the reasonable cost of compliance is to be charged to the bidder. Faced with such a request, the target company has the option of mailing the bidder's materials, within three business days of receipt, to the target company's holders.[37] Alternatively, the target company may within three business days deliver the stockholder lists to the bidder making the request.[38] The SEC dictates the proper form for the bidder's written request.[39] Also, a bidder's request for such shareholder lists subjects the bidder to certain requirements, including the return of any lists furnished by the target company.[40]

Withdrawal of Tendered Securities

Section 14(d)(5) of the Act[41] provides that all securities deposited pursuant to a tender offer may be withdrawn by or on behalf of the depositor at any time until the expiration of seven days after the first publication of the formal tender offer (or request or invitation) and at any time after sixty days from the date of the original tender offer or request for invitation unless a different period is provided for by SEC rules. Rule 14d–7,[42] which formerly limited withdrawal rights to fifteen days after the commencement of the tender offer or ten days after the commencement of a competing offer, has been amended to provide that withdrawal rights may be exercised throughout the period that the tender offer remains open, which must be for at least twenty business days.[43] Any increase or decrease in the consideration offered under the

35. *See* In re Revlon, Inc., Exch. Act Rel. No. 34–23320, [1986 Transfer Binder] Fed.Sec.L.Rep. (CCH) ¶ 84,006 (June 16, 1986) (original 14D–9 filed by target company disclosed that merger negotiations with others might take place, discussions began on September 26 and a 14D–9 amendment filed on October 2 was held not to have discharged the target company's obligation to "promptly" amend its filing).

36. 17 C.F.R. § 240.14d–5.

37. 17 C.F.R. § 240.14d–5(b). The bidder is to be informed of the progress of any such mailing undertaken by the target company.

38. 17 C.F.R. § 240.14d–5(c). These rights are in addition to the right to shareholder lists under the proxy rules as well as inspection rights under state law. *See* § 11.7 *supra*. *See generally* James D. Cox, Thomas L. Hazen & F. Hodge O'Neal, Corporations §§ 13.2–13.11 (1995).

39. 17 C.F.R. § 240.14d–5(e).

40. 17 C.F.R. § 240.14d–5(f).

41. 15 U.S.C.A. § 78n(d)(5). *See* Macfadden Holdings, Inc. v. J.B. Acquisition Corp., 802 F.2d 62 (2d Cir.1986) (adequate description of withdrawal rights where offer was contingent on FCC approval).

42. 17 C.F.R. § 240.14d–7. *See also* 17 C.F.R. § 240.13e–4(f)(2)(i) (imposing the same rule for issuer tender offers). *See* Exch. Act Rel. No. 34–23421 (July 11, 1986).

43. 17 C.F.R. § 240.14e–1.

tender offer triggers the requirement that the tender offer be open for ten business days from the date of change in consideration.[44] The rule also sets out the appropriate form of the notice of withdrawal. Shareholders who tendered shares prior to receiving notice of offeror's Schedule 14D–1 amendment relating to the source of funds being used for the offer were held entitled, under the former version of Rule 14d–7, to withdrawal rights for fifteen days from the notice.[45] Under the current rule, the duration of the tender offer is the appropriate extension of time for withdrawal rights.[46] By virtue of Rule 14e–1(a)[47] all tender offers by persons other than the issuer must remain open for twenty business days.[48] The same twenty day period is applicable to issuer self tenders.[49]

Pro Rata Acceptance of Tendered Shares; Extensions of the Tender Offer

Section 14(d)(6) of the Act[50] requires pro rata acceptance of shares tendered where the tender offer by its terms does not obligate the tender offeror to accept all shares tendered. This takes pressure off the target company's shareholders who would otherwise have to make a quick decision were acceptance to be on a first come basis. Rule 14d–8[51] extends the pro rata requirements to the entire period of the tender offer. A tender offeror may not extend the proration period after expiration of the offer where the effect would be to alter the pro rata acceptance of the shares tendered.[52]

Section 14(d)(7) of the Act[53] provides that whenever a person varies the terms of a tender offer or request before the expiration thereof by increasing the consideration offered to the holders of the securities sought, the person making such an increase in consideration must pay to all persons tendering securities pursuant to their requests that same price whether or not the securities were tendered prior to the variation of the tender offer's terms. This can be especially important if a series

---

44. 17 C.F.R. §§ 240.13e–4(f)(1)(ii), 240.14e–1(b).

45. Cardiff Acquisitions, Inc. v. Hatch, 751 F.2d 917 (8th Cir.1984).

46. 17 C.F.R. § 240.14d–7.

47. 17 C.F.R. § 240.14e–1(a).

48. *Id.*

49. 17 C.F.R. § 240.13e–4(f)(1)(i). As is the case with third party offers, any increase or decrease in the consideration offered requires that the offer remain open at least ten business days from the notice thereof. 17 C.F.R. § 240.13e–4(f)(1)(ii).

50. 15 U.S.C.A. § 78n(d)(6).

51. 17 C.F.R. 240.14d–8.

52. Pryor v. United States Steel Corp., 794 F.2d 52 (2d Cir.1986); Pryor v. USX Corp., 1991 WL 346368, [1991–1992 Transfer Binder] Fed.Sec.L.Rep. (CCH) ¶ 96,630 (S.D.N.Y. 1991) (tender offeror could not accept shares tendered after the deadline when this would affect proration rights of shares previously tendered; tender offeror was liable to shareholders who had wrongfully been denied their tender offer premium), s.c., 806 F.Supp. 460 (S.D.N.Y.1992) (denying summary judgment since terms of offer were susceptible to differing interpretations as to whether late-tender shares would fall within the proration period).

53. 15 U.S.C.A. § 78n(d)(7).

of transactions are integrated and held to be parts of a single tender offer.[54] Thus, for example, it has been held that a privately negotiated purchase entered into on the heels of the purported withdrawal of a tender offer was part of the same control-related transaction and thus violated the prohibition on discriminatory pricing of purchases in the course of a single tender offer.[55]

The "All Holders" and "Best Price" Requirements

A 1985 Delaware Supreme Court decision upheld a tender offer by an issuer that excluded a hostile tender offeror.[56] However, under relatively recently adopted SEC equal treatment rules, such exclusion is prohibited; at the same time, the SEC adopted "best price" requirements.[57] Although these rules are based on different sections, the validity of these requirements may be questionable in light of the Supreme Court ruling that section 14(e) can regulate manipulative conduct only to the extent of protecting against deception.[58] There is no explicit statutory requirement that a tender offer be made to all shareholders nor that each tendering security holder be offered the best price; if the deception requirement carries over to the other provisions of the Williams Act, then the rules barring discriminatory tender offers may not withstand attack. However, invalidating the all holders and best price requirements would have to be based on an unduly restrictive reading of the SEC's rulemaking authority. The "all holders" and best price rules are based on section 14(d)'s regulation of third party offers and section 13(e)'s authority to regulate issuer tender offers;[59] the SEC takes the position that the "all holders" and "best price" requirements are "necessary and appropriate" to implement the Williams Act.[60]

The SEC's "all holders" rules prohibit discriminatory tender offers

---

54. *See, e.g.* Field v. Trump, 850 F.2d 938 (2d Cir.1988), *cert. denied* 489 U.S. 1012, 109 S.Ct. 1122, 103 L.Ed.2d 185 (1989) (upholding complaint that withdrawal of first tender offer was a sham).

In Feder v. MacFadden Holdings, Inc., 722 F.Supp. 68 (S.D.N.Y.1989), the court held that the expiration of one tender offer, followed by a second tender offer was held not to be a single offer. The court distinguished Field v. Trump where the offer had been withdrawn rather than simply having expired by its own terms. *See also, e.g.*, Note, Securities Regulation—Effectiveness of Withdrawal of a Cash Tender Offer, 62 Temple L.Rev. 1033 (1989).

55. Field v. Trump, 850 F.2d 938 (2d Cir.1988), *cert. denied* 489 U.S. 1012, 109 S.Ct. 1122, 103 L.Ed.2d 185 (1989).

56. Unocal Corp. v. Mesa Petroleum Co., 493 A.2d 946 (Del.1985). *Compare* Unocal Corp. v. Pickens, 608 F.Supp. 1081 (C.D.Cal.1985) (discriminatory issuer self-tender offer that excluded hostile third party bidder did not violate the Williams Act). *See generally* Note, Exclusionary Tender Offers: A Reasonably Formulated Takeover Defense or a Discriminatory Attempt to Retain Control, 20 Ga.L.Rev. 627 (1986).

57. 17 C.F.R. §§ 240.13e–4(f), 240.14d–10.

58. Schreiber v. Burlington Northern, Inc., 472 U.S. 1, 105 S.Ct. 2458, 86 L.Ed.2d 1 (1985). *See* § 11.15 *infra*.

59. 15 U.S.C.A. §§ 78m(e), 78n(d). Issuer transactions are discussed in § 11.17 *infra*.

60. *See* Sec.Exch.Act Rel. No. 34–23421 (July 11, 1986). *See* discussion of the *Polaroid* decision in footnote 61 *infra*.

by both issuers and third parties.[61] There is an explicit exception in the "all holders" requirement for tender offers that exclude one or more shareholders in compliance with a constitutionally valid state statute.[62] In addition to reserving general exemptive power under the "all holders" rules,[63] the SEC has promulgated a specific but limited exemption for "odd-lot tender offers" by issuers—an odd-lot offer is one that is limited to security holders owning less than a specified number of shares under one hundred.[64]

As noted above, the Commission has also adopted a "best price" rule that requires equal treatment for all securities holders, and thus entitles anyone receiving payment under the tender offer to the highest consideration paid to any other security holder at any time during such tender offer.[65] The SEC "best price" requirement applies only to shares purchased during a single tender offer.[66] As such, unlike state "fair price" statutes,[67] the SEC rule does not regulate two tiered offers consummated in two distinct steps. The SEC best price requirements do not prohibit different types of consideration, and the different consideration need not be substantially equivalent in value so long as the tender offer permits the security holders to elect among the types of consideration offered.[68] When different types of consideration are offered, the tender offeror may limit the availability and offer it to tendering shareholders on a pro rata basis.[69] As is the case with the "all holders" requirements, the Commission has given itself the power to grant exemptions from the operation of

61. 17 C.F.R. §§ 240.13e–4, 240.14d–10. *See* Exch. Act Rel. No. 34–23421 (July 11, 1986). Exch. Act Rel. No. 34–22791, [1985–86 Transfer Binder] Fed.Sec.L.Rep. (CCH) ¶ 83,955 (Jan. 14, 1986). *See, e.g.,* Polaroid Corp. v. Disney, 698 F.Supp. 1169 (D.Del. 1988), affirmed on other grounds 862 F.2d 987 (3d Cir.1988) (offer excluding allegedly invalid shares held by ESOP did not violate all holders rule).

In Polaroid Corp. v. Disney, 862 F.2d 987 (3d Cir.1988), the all holders rule was held to be a valid exercise of the Williams Act's rulemaking power:

62. 17 C.F.R. §§ 240.13e–4(f)(9)(ii), 240.14d–10(b)(2). The SEC questions, however, whether such state statutes are in fact constitutional. *See* Exch.Act Rel. No. 34–23421 (July 11, 1986). For a discussion of the constitutionality of state statutes affecting tender offers, *see* 11.22 *infra.*

63. 17 C.F.R. §§ 240.13e–4(h)(8), 240.14d–10(e).

64. 17 C.F.R. § 240.13e–4(h)(5). However, both the all holders and best price requirements will apply to the terms of the odd-lot tender offer.

65. 17 C.F.R. §§ 240.13e–4(f)(8)(ii), 240.14d–10(a)(2). *See, e.g.,* Field v. Trump, 850 F.2d 938 (2d Cir.1988) (purchase of dissident director's shares during brief purported withdrawal of tender offer, violated SEC best price requirement since same premium was not offered to all tendering shareholders).

66. A press release announcing an impending tender offer is not the commencement of the offer for purposes of the best price rule; accordingly the price paid for shares purchased after the press release but prior to the commencement of the tender offer did not affect the price at which the tender offer could be made. Kahn v. Virginia Retirement System, 783 F.Supp. 266 (E.D.Va.1992).

67. *E.g.* M.D. Corps. & Ass'ns Code §§ 3–602, 3–603. *See* § 11.21 *infra. Compare, e.g.,* Field v. Trump, 850 F.2d 938 (2d Cir.1988), *cert. denied* 489 U.S. 1012, 109 S.Ct. 1122, 103 L.Ed.2d 185 (1989), which is discussed in footnote 55 *supra.*

68. 17 C.F.R. §§ 240.13e–4(f)(10), 240.14d–10(c).

69. *Id.*

the "best price" requirement.[70]

Exemptions From Regulation 14D

Section 14(d)(8) of the Act[71] exempts certain tender offers or request for tenders from the scope of section 14(d)'s requirements. When the acquisition of the securities sought together with all other acquisitions by the same person of securities of the same class within the preceding twelve months does not exceed two percent of the outstanding securities of the class, section 14(d) does not apply.[72] Similarly, section 14(d) does not apply where the tender offeror is the issuer of the security.[73] The Act also gives the SEC exemptive power by rule, regulation or order from transactions "not entered into for the purpose of, and not having the effect of, changing or influencing the control of the issuer or otherwise as not comprehended within the purposes of this subsection."[74]

§ 11.15 Unlawful Tender Offer Practices—Section 14(e) and Regulation 14E

The foregoing provisions of the Williams Act are limited to transactions in equity securities subject to the Securities Exchange Act's both registration and reporting requirements. In sharp contrast, section 14(e) of the Exchange Act[1] prohibits material misstatements, omissions and fraudulent practices in connection with tender offers regardless of whether the target company is subject to the Exchange Act's reporting requirements.[2]

Materiality issues under the Williams Act are to be decided in much the same way as under the other disclosure provisions of the securities laws. In determining what is material, it is not necessary to disclose very preliminary merger discussions that may lead to a tender offer.[3] However, the Supreme Court has held that whether preliminary merger negotiations have crossed the materiality threshold is a question of fact.[4]

---

70. 17 C.F.R. §§ 240.13e–4(h)(8), 240.14d–10(e).

71. 15 U.S.C.A. § 78n(d)(8).

72. 15 U.S.C.A. § 78n(d)(8)(A).

73. 15 U.S.C.A. § 78n(d)(8)(B). *See* § 11.18 *infra.*

74. 15 U.S.C.A. § 78n(d)(8)(C).

§ 11.15

1. 15 U.S.C.A. § 78n(e). *See* James I. Junewicz, The Appropriate Limits of Section 14(e) of the Securities Exchange Act of 1934, 62 Tex.L.Rev. 1171 (1984).

2. In contrast, the other provisions of the Williams Act are limited to securities of issuers subject to Section 12's registration requirements. 15 U.S.C.A. § 78*l*. *See* § 9.2 *supra.*

3. Staffin v. Greenberg, 672 F.2d 1196 (3d Cir.1982). Materiality in general is considered in § 11.4 *supra* and § 13.5A *infra. But cf.* In re Revlon, Inc., Exch. Act Rel. No. 34–23320 (June 16, 1986) (where schedule 14d–9 disclosed that management might engage in merger negotiations, failure to disclose the existence of subsequent violations violated Rule 14d–4).

See also the discussion of materiality in the text accompanying footnotes 63–72 *infra.*

4. Basic, Inc. v. Levinson, 485 U.S. 224, 108 S.Ct. 978, 99 L.Ed.2d 194 (1988). *See* § 13.5 *infra.*

Whether a fact is material depends upon whether a reasonable investor would consider it significant in making his or her investment decision.[5] Materiality is based on a highly factual inquiry and thus is difficult to predict. The thrust of the recent Supreme Court decision in Basic Inc. v. Levinson,[6] seems to favor a finding of materiality in borderline cases of preliminary negotiations.

Courts are not inclined to engage in judicial "nit-picking" by requiring such stringent materiality scrutiny that would eventually work against shareholder interests.[7] Accordingly, subjective motivation behind fully disclosed transactions need not be spelled out.[8]

In conjunction with section 14(e), the Commission, in Regulation 14E, has set out a series of acts and practices which violate section 14(e)'s prohibitions. Regulation 14E applies to all tender offers and is not tied to section 12's registration requirements.[9] Thus, section 14(e) and Regulation 14E purport to apply to all tender offers, regardless of the target company's size, so long as there is use of the jurisdictional means (to wit, an instrumentality of interstate commerce).

The Supreme Court has held that there is no private remedy in the hands of a competing tender offeror.[10] However, most lower courts have recognized a remedy in the hands of the target company or one of its shareholders,[11] as well as the right of a competing tender offeror to seek

---

5. *Ibid.;* TSC Industries, Inc. v. Northway, Inc., 426 U.S. 438, 96 S.Ct. 2126, 48 L.Ed.2d 757 (1976). *See* § 11.4 *supra.*

6. Basic, Inc. v. Levinson, 485 U.S. 224, 108 S.Ct. 978, 99 L.Ed.2d 194 (1988).

7. Macfadden Holdings, Inc. v. J.B. Acquisition Corp., 802 F.2d 62, 71 (2d Cir.1986), relying on Data Probe Acquisition Corp. v. Datatab, Inc., 722 F.2d 1, 5 (2d Cir.1983), *cert. denied,* 465 U.S. 1052, 104 S.Ct. 1326, 79 L.Ed.2d 722 (1984).

8. Diamond v. Arend, 649 F.Supp. 408, 415–16 (S.D.N.Y.1986).

9. *See, e.g.,* Iavarone v. Raymond Keyes Associates, Inc., 733 F.Supp. 727 (S.D.N.Y. 1990) (applying section 14(e) to tender offer for 25–shareholder company), *relying on* L.P. Acquisition Co. v. Tyson, 772 F.2d 201 (6th Cir.1985); Astronics Corp. v. Protective Closures Co., Inc., 561 F.Supp. 329 (W.D.N.Y.1983).

In contrast, sections 13(d), 13(e), 14(d), and 14(f) are limited to target companies which have a class of equity securities registered under section 12. 15 U.S.C.A. §§ 78m(d), (e), 78n(d), (f). *See* §§ 11.11, 11.14 *supra* and § 11.17 *infra.* Section 12 (15 U.S.C.A. § 78*l*) and its registration requirements are discussed in § 9.2 *supra.*

10. Piper v. Chris–Craft Industries, Inc., 430 U.S. 1, 97 S.Ct. 926, 51 L.Ed.2d 124 (1977). The Court held that recognized principles of implying federal rights of action did not warrant the remedy sought by the Piper plaintiff. *Id.* at 33, 97 S.Ct. at 944. *See generally* Thomas L. Hazen, Corporate Chartering and The Securities Markets: Shareholders Suffrage, Corporate Responsibility and Managerial Accountability, 1978 Wis.L.Rev. 391; Harvey L. Pitt, Standing to Sue Under the Williams Act After Chris–Craft: A Leaky Ship on Troubled Waters, 34 Bus.Law. 117 (1978).

11. *See, e.g.,* Seaboard World Airlines, Inc. v. Tiger International, Inc., 600 F.2d 355 (2d Cir.1979) (recognizing the 14(e) remedy but finding no substantive violation). *See also* Smallwood v. Pearl Brewing Co., 489 F.2d 579 (5th Cir.1974), *cert. denied* 419 U.S. 873, 95 S.Ct. 134, 42 L.Ed.2d 113 (1974); H.K. Porter Co. v. Nicholson File Co., 482 F.2d 421 (1st Cir.1973); Electronic Specialty Co. v. International Controls Corp., 409 F.2d 937 (2d Cir.1969); Crane v. American Standard, Inc., 439 F.Supp. 945 (S.D.N.Y.1977), *affirmed in part, reversed in part* 603 F.2d 244 (2d Cir.1979). *See generally* Pitt *supra* footnote 10 at 129–33, 186–91.

injunctive relief.[12] The question of the availability of private relief is taken up in detail in a subsequent section.[13]

In what may be a very far-reaching decision, the Supreme Court in Schreiber v. Burlington Northern, Inc.,[14] has limited the thrust of section 14(e). *Schreiber* involved a claim that the defendant target company's renegotiation of the terms of a tender offer was manipulative and hence in violation of section 14(e).[15] Rather than directly face the issue of defining manipulative conduct,[16] the Court held that "[w]ithout misrepresentation or nondisclosure, § 14(e) has not been violated."[17] The Court reached this conclusion by a tortured reading of the statutory text and a rather unusual view of the section's legislative history. When enacted in 1968, section 14(e) prohibited material misrepresentations and omissions of material fact as well as "fraudulent, deceptive, or manipulative acts or practices" in connection with a tender offer. The Court's interpretation ignores the disjunctive use of "or" in the express statutory language. In reviewing the legislative history, the Court viewed disclosure as the sole thrust of the section.[18] In 1970, the statute was amended to give the SEC rulemaking power with regard to "fraudulent, deceptive, or manipulative" acts. The Court did not view this amendment as broadening the disclosure thrust of section 14(e). As a result of the *Schreiber* decision, unless the Court retrenches from its unwarranted broad-brush approach, it seems clear that not only is section 14(e) on its face limited to disclosure but also any rules promulgated thereunder are invalid to the extent that they go beyond disclosure. This would result in a significant cut-back on Regulation 14E and also would be a most questionable narrowing of the scope of the section. The statute expressly talks in terms of manipulative in addition to fraudulent and deceptive conduct, and the Supreme Court cannot properly excise that term from the statute.

Even beyond the Regulation 14E ramifications that are discussed below, the impact of the *Schreiber* decision could arguably be carried

12. *See, e.g.,* Humana, Inc. v. American Medicorp., Inc., 445 F.Supp. 613 (S.D.N.Y. 1977). *Cf.* Rondeau v. Mosinee Paper Corp., 422 U.S. 49, 95 S.Ct. 2069, 45 L.Ed.2d 12 (1975).

13. *See* § 11.19 *infra.*

14. 472 U.S. 1, 105 S.Ct. 2458, 86 L.Ed.2d 1 (1985). *See, e.g.,* Norman S. Poser, Stock Market Manipulation and Corporate Control Transactions, 40 U.Miami L.Rev. 671 (1986).

15. Burlington Northern had made a hostile tender offer to purchase 25.1 million shares of El Paso Gas for $24 per share. After negotiations with El Paso management, the original offer was withdrawn, El Paso management was given "golden parachute" severance payments, and a new tender offer was made for 21 million shares from the public and 4.1 million shares from El Paso at $24 per share. It was claimed that a combination of El Paso management's golden parachutes and a decision to reduce the size of the offer to the public in order to infuse more cash into El Paso (presumably to pay for the golden parachutes) artificially affected the price of the El Paso stock and thus constituted manipulation.

16. *See* discussion in § 11.20 *infra.*

17. 472 U.S. at 12, 105 S.Ct. at 2465, 86 L.Ed.2d at 10.

18. "Nowhere in the legislative history is there the slightest suggestion that section 14(e) serves any purpose other than disclosure * * * " *id.* at 11, 105 S.Ct. at 2464, 86 L.Ed.2d at 9.

over to section 10(b) which predates section 14(e) and empowers the SEC to promulgate rules declaring unlawful conduct that constitutes a "manipulative or deceptive device or contrivance." [19]   Extending the *Schreiber* rationale liberally to section 10(b) would lead to the unwise and unfortunate result of invalidating a number of the section 10(b) rules dealing with manipulative conduct.[20]

Regulation 14E

Rule 14e–1[21] requires that any person making a tender offer must hold the offer open for at least twenty business days from the date upon which it is first published.   The twenty-day waiting period formerly did not apply, however, where the tender offer was by the issuer and was not made in anticipation of, or in response to, another person's takeover attempt.[22]   As a result of amendments that became effective on March 1, 1986, Rule 14e–1's time periods now apply to all issuer self-tenders.[23]   In 1991, the Commission further amended Rule 14e–1 to provide for a sixty calendar day (instead of twenty business day) period during which a tender offer is part of a roll-up transaction.[24]

The *Schreiber* decision, discussed above, requires deception as an element of any section 14(e) violation.   To the extent that the reasoning carries over to the SEC rulemaking power, that decisions casts a cloud over the validity of Rule 14e–1 because the rule regulates the duration of the offer and thus goes beyond mandating full disclosure.[25]   For example, what is it about a tender offer that remains open for only nineteen business days that makes it more deceptive than one which is open for the twenty business day period mandated by Rule 14e–1?   It can, of course, be argued that the SEC's power to mandate a period during which the tender offer must remain open is justified since it gives investors and the market the time necessary to digest the information mandated by the Williams Act's affirmative disclosure requirements.[26]

---

19. 15 U.S.C.A. § 78j(b). *See* §§ 12.1, 13.2–13.12 *infra*.

20. *See* § 12.1 *infra*. Other rules, which may be in jeopardy, include the new SEC prohibitions against discriminatory tender offers that exclude one or more shareholders. 17 C.F.R. §§ 240.13e–4(f)(8)(i), 240.14d–10(a)(1). *But see* Polaroid Corp. v. Disney, 862 F.2d 987, 994–95 (3d Cir.1988) (upholding validity of all holders rule), which is quoted in relevant part in footnote 61 of § 11.14 *supra*.

21. 17 C.F.R. § 240.14e–1(a).

22. 17 C.F.R. § 240.14e–1 (1985).

23. *See* Sec. Exch. Act Rel. No. 34–22788 (Jan. 14, 1986). These amendments were part of a more generalized scheme to subject issuer self-tenders to the same requirements as third-party tender offers. *See* § 11.17 *infra*.

24. A roll-up transaction is defined in Item 901(c) of Regulation S–K as any transaction involving the reorganization of one or more partnerships into another entity.

25. *But see* Polaroid Corp. v. Disney, 862 F.2d 987 (3d Cir.1988) which upheld the SEC's "all holders" rule (Rule 14d–10, 17 C.F.R. § 240.14d–10), reasoning that requiring the offer be made to all shareholders furthers the disclosure goals of the Williams Act.

26. *Cf.* Polaroid Corp. v. Disney, 862 F.2d 987 (3d Cir.1988), footnote 25 *supra* and § 11.14 *supra* in footnote 61.

Rule 14e–1(b) further provides that the tender offeror may not increase or decrease the terms of the offer, the type of consideration, or the dealer's soliciting fee unless the tender offer remains open for at least ten business days from the publication of the notice of such increase.[27] It is also declared to be an unlawful practice for a tender offeror to fail to pay the consideration offered or return the securities tendered promptly after either the withdrawal or termination of the tender offer.[28] Rule 14e–1(d)[29] makes it unlawful to extend the length of the tender offer without issuing a notice of such extension by press release or other public announcement; and a notice must give sufficient detail of the time period of the tender offer and its extension.

Whenever a tender offer is made for a target company's shares, the target company has ten business days from the first date upon which the tender offer is published to respond.[30] Rule 14e–2[31] requires that the target company's management make one of the following responses within the ten day period: (1) a recommendation of acceptance or rejection of the tender offer; (2) an expression of no opinion with a decision to remain neutral towards the offer; or (3) that it is not able to take a position with respect to bidder's offer. The Rule 14e–2 statement must also include all reasons for the position taken, or the stance of neutrality, as well as any explanation of the inability to take a position. In setting forth its reasons, the target company's management is, of course, subject to all of the rules concerning materiality[32] as well as the potential civil[33] and criminal liabilities for material misstatements.[34]

---

27. 17 C.F.R. § 240.14e–1(b). *See also* 17 C.F.R. § 240.13e–4(f)(1)(ii) (imposing the same requirement for tender offers by issuers).

28. 17 C.F.R. § 240.14e–1(c).

29. 17 C.F.R. § 240.14e–1(d).

30. 17 C.F.R. § 240.14e–2.

31. *Id.*

32. *See* footnote 3 *supra. See, e.g.,* Schwarzschild v. Tse, 1992 WL 448796, [1992–1993 Transfer Binder] Fed.Sec.L.Rep. (CCH) ¶ 97,291 (N.D.Cal.1992) (allegation that directors did not adequately disclose assumptions underlying fairness examination was unsupported by the evidence).

33. These include Rule 10b–5 which applies to injured purchasers and sellers of securities (17 C.F.R. § 240.10b–5, §§ 13.2–13.12 *infra*) and section 14(e) itself. *See* notes 4–6 *supra* and § 11.19 *infra. See, also, e.g.,* In re PHLCORP, 1992 WL 85013, [1992 Transfer Binder] Fed.Sec.L.Rep. (CCH) ¶ 96,808 (S.D.N.Y.1992) (officers and directors could be liable to shareholders of target company for allegedly misrepresenting the tender offer as "fair").

34. *E.g.* sections 10(b) and 14(e) 15 U.S.C.A. §§ 78j(b); 78n(e).

Rule 14e–3[35] prohibits insider trading during a tender offer.[36]   The Rule 14e–3 prohibitions expressly apply not only to insiders of the target company but also to anyone else

> who is in possession of material information relating to such tender offer which information he knows or has reason to know is nonpublic and which he knows or has reason to know has been acquired directly or indirectly from (1) the offering person, (2) the issuer of the securities sought or to be sought by such tender offer, or (3) any officer, director, partner or employee or any other person acting on behalf of the offering person or such issuer * * *.[37]

The rule goes on to state that there is no violation if the transaction was an independent investment decision rather than based on knowledge of material non-public information.   Rule 14e–3 supplements the insider trading prohibitions that are found in Rule 10b–5[38] as well as in the insider trading legislation enacted by Congress in 1984 and in 1988.[39]

It has been held that Rule 14e–3 will support a private remedy in the hands of the target company.[40]   A preliminary injunction was issued against a tender offer where the tender offer was based upon the alleged misappropriation of information by a former target company officer.[41]   A number of courts have upheld the validity of Rule 14e–3.[42]

---

35.   17 C.F.R. § 240.14e–3.   *See* Note, Trading on Nonpublic Information Under Rule 14e–3, 49 Geo.Wash.L.Rev. 539 (1981).   *See, e.g.* United States v. Chestman, 903 F.2d 75 (2d Cir.1990), *affirming* 704 F.Supp. 451 (S.D.N.Y.1989) (upholding validity of Rule 14e–3); SEC v. Ferrero, 1993 WL 625964, [1993–1994 Transfer Binder] Fed. Sec. L. Rep. (CCH) ¶ 98,120 (S.D.Ind.1993) (applying 14e–3);   United States v. Marcus Schloss & Co., 710 F.Supp. 944 (S.D.N.Y.1989) (upholding validity of Rule 14e–3).   *Cf.* Frankel v. Slotkin, 705 F.Supp. 105 (E.D.N.Y.1989) (three-month time lag between conversion of bond and allegedly fraudulent tender offer was not a nondisclosure on the "eve of a tender offer"; Rule 14e–3 claim therefore failed).

36.   *See* § 13.9 *infra* for a discussion of insider trading generally.   *See also* §§ 12.2–12.8 *infra* for treatment of the Act's short-swing profit provisions.

37.   17 C.F.R. § 240.14e–3(b).

38.   17 C.F.R. § 240.10b–5.   *E.g.,* Litton Industries, Inc. v. Lehman Brothers Kuhn Loeb, Inc., 967 F.2d 742 (2d Cir.1992) (upholding Rule 10b–5 claim by the bidder in a tender offer based on allegations of improper insider trading in advance of the tender offer which allegedly resulted in the bidder having to pay more for the company).   *See* § 13.9 *infra.*

39.   The Insider Trading Sanctions Act of 1984 (ITSA), among other things, allows the SEC to recoup three times the insider's profits.   *See* § 13.9 *infra.*   The Insider Trading and Securities Fraud Enforcement Act of 1988 is discussed in § 13.9 *infra.*

40.   Burlington Industries, Inc. v. Edelman, 1987 WL 91498, [1987 Transfer Binder] Fed.Sec.L.Rep. (CCH) ¶ 93,339 (4th Cir.1987), *affirming on the opinion below* 666 F.Supp. 799 (M.D.N.C.1987).

41.   Private remedies under section 14(e) are discussed in § 11.19 *infra.*

42.   *E.g.,* SEC v. Peters, 978 F.2d 1162 (10th Cir.1992);   United States v. Chestman, 947 F.2d 551 (2d Cir.1991), *reversing en banc* 903 F.2d 75 (2d Cir.1990), discussed in Thomas L. Hazen, United States v. Chestman—Trading Securities on the Basis of Nonpublic Information in Advance of a Tender Offer, 57 Brooklyn L.Rev. 595 (1991);   United States v. Marcus Schloss & Co., Inc., 710 F.Supp. 944 (S.D.N.Y.1989).

Deleted footnotes 43–50 can be found in the Practitioner's Edition.

Although not part of Regulation 14E, there are rules under section 10(b)[51] affecting conduct during a tender offer. Rule 10b–13, as noted above, prohibits a tender offeror from purchasing the target securities other than through the tender offer once the offer has commenced and until it is completed.[52] It has been held that violations of Rule 10b–13 will support a private damage action,[53] but not all courts seem to agree.[54] Formerly, Rule 10b–4 addressed short tendering but that rule has since been redesignated as part of Regulation 14E.

Rule 14e–4 prohibits short tendering[55]—the practice of tendering or guaranteeing securities not owned by the person making the tender or guarantee.[56] The SEC amended Rule 14e–4's predecessor to also prohibit "hedged tendering" by market professionals in tender offers for less than all of the target company's outstanding stock.[57] Hedged tendering occurs when market professionals sell on the open market that portion of their target company holdings that they estimate will not be accepted by the tender offeror. Rule 14e–4 is designed to prevent tendering shares that are not actually owned. Where a shareholder responded to a tender offer for less than all of the target's shares by tendering his entire holdings coupled with a short sale, the rule was not violated.[58] The court reasoned that since he tendered only his actual holdings, the tendering shareholder did not improve his proration position but rather was taking "a separate gamble" that the stock price would decline after the proration date.[59] It has been held that, at least where shareholders

51. 15 U.S.C.A. § 78j. *See* § 12.1 *infra.*

52. 17 C.F.R. § 240.10b–13. *See* footnote 46 *supra.*

53. City National Bank v. American Commonwealth Financial Corp., 801 F.2d 714 (4th Cir.1986), *cert. denied* 479 U.S. 1091, 107 S.Ct. 1301, 94 L.Ed.2d 157 (1987). *Cf.* Field v. Trump, 661 F.Supp. 529 (S.D.N.Y.1987), *affirmed in part, reversed in part* 850 F.2d 938 (2d Cir.1988) (finding Rule 10b–13 was not violated because the privately negotiated purchases took place after the completion of one tender offer and prior to the commencement of a second tender offer).

54. Beaumont v. American Can Co., 797 F.2d 79 (2d Cir.1986) (questioning the existence of a private remedy); Gerber v. Computer Associates International, Inc., 812 F.Supp. 361 (E.D.N.Y.1993) (shareholders did not have implied private remedy against another shareholder for entering into agreement in violation of Rule 10b–13). *Cf.* Priddy v. Edelman, 679 F.Supp. 1425 (E.D.Mich.1988) (nontendering shareholder lacked standing to sue for violation of Rule 10b–13).

55. 17 C.F.R. § 240.14e–4. Formerly the rule was embodied in Rule 10b–4, 17 C.F.R. § 240.10b–4 (1989) (rescinded). Sec.Exch. Act Rel. No. 34–26609, [1989 Transfer Binder] Fed.Sec.L.Rep. (CCH) ¶ 84,401 (March 8, 1989). *See* § 12.1 *infra.* Sec.Exch. Act Rel. No. 34–26609, [1989 Transfer Binder] Fed.Sec.L.Rep. (CCH) ¶ 84,401 (March 8, 1989).

56. *See* Merrill Lynch, Pierce, Fenner & Smith, Inc. v. Bobker, 636 F.Supp. 444 (S.D.N.Y.1986), *reversed* 808 F.2d 930 (2d Cir.1986) (denying proration to shareholder who sold short while tendering); In the Matter of Freeman Securities Co., [1994–1995 Transfer Binder] Fed. Sec. L. Rep. (CCH) ¶ 85,404 (SEC 1994) (broker-dealer consent to cease and desist order for short tendering violations). *Compare* the less stringent rules under section 10(a) concerning short sales in general. 15 U.S.C.A. § 78j(a); 17 C.F.R. §§ 240.10a–1, 10a–2. *See* § 10.12 *supra.*

57. *See* 16 Sec.Reg. & L.Rep. (BNA) 575–576 (March 30, 1984) (amending Rule 10b–4, 17 C.F.R. § 240.10b–4). In 1989, the SEC asked for comment on the deregulation of hedged tendering. Sec.Exch.Act Rel. No. 34–26609, [1989 Transfer Binder] Fed.Sec.L.Rep. (CCH) ¶ 84,401 (March 8, 1989).

58. Merrill Lynch, Pierce, Fenner & Smith, Inc. v. Bobker, 808 F.2d 930 (2d Cir.1986).

59. *Id.* at 935.

could not allege that their offers of tender were diluted, there is no implied private remedy for short tenders in violation of Rule 14e–4.[60]

The SEC, for some time, has been considering taking action that would curtail suspected unfairness and abuses in connection with the pricing of two-step or two-tiered tender offers.[61] Such substantive limitations on the scope and terms of tender offers would be difficult to support under section 14(e) in light of the *Schreiber* decision. However, section 14(d) might support some limitations.[62]

Disclosure and Materiality

A number of questions have arisen within the disclosure context of section 14(e).[63] One such question concerns the definition of materiality under section 14(e). Cases decided under the proxy rules[64] and Rule 10b–5[65] are instructive for the determination of what is material. Materiality is to be determined within the context of the "total mix" of information. Within the context of the Williams Act, it was once held by a number of courts that there is no duty to disclose preliminary merger negotiations between the target and a white knight prior to the time that they have agreed upon a price.[66] However, the Supreme Court has since rejected the price and structure test in favor of a determination of whether the information would be significant to a reasonable investor in making an investment decision.[67] A particularly difficult problem is how to respond to questions concerning rumored takeovers.[68]

---

60. John Olagues Trading Co. v. First Options of Chicago, Inc., 588 F.Supp. 1194 (N.D.Ill.1984). *But cf.* Merrill Lynch, Pierce, Fenner & Smith, Inc. v. Bobker, 636 F.Supp. 444 (S.D.N.Y.1986), *reversed* 808 F.2d 930 (2d Cir.1986) (vacating arbitration award to investor who violated 10b–4 by tendering all shares and then selling half prior to the proration date).

61. Sec.Exch. Act Rel. No. 34–21079 (June 21, 1984).

62. 15 U.S.C.A. § 78n(d)(1) which empowers the Commission to require "such additional information as the Commission may by rules and regulations [prescribe] as necessary or appropriate in the public interest or for the protection of investors." *See* § 11.14 *supra.*

63. *See* the discussion of section 14(e) remedies in § 11.19 *infra.*

64. *See* § 11.4 *supra.*

65. *See* § 13.5 *infra.*

66. Greenfield v. Heublein, Inc., 742 F.2d 751 (3d Cir.1984), *cert. denied* 469 U.S. 1215, 105 S.Ct. 1189, 84 L.Ed.2d 336 (1985) (no duty under Rule 10b–5 to disclose merger negotiations where price had not yet been worked out). *Cf.* Steinberg v. Pargas, Inc., 1985 WL 431, [1984–85 Transfer Binder] Fed.Sec.L.Rep. (CCH) ¶ 91,979 (S.D.N.Y.1985) (target company filing 14D–9 accurately describing tentative nature of negotiations did not make a material omission by failing to give the name of the other party).

67. Basic, Inc. v. Levinson, 485 U.S. 224, 108 S.Ct. 978, 99 L.Ed.2d 194 (1988) which is discussed in § 11.4 *supra* and § 13.5 *infra.*

68. *E.g.* Levinson v. Basic, Inc., 786 F.2d 741 (6th Cir.1986), *vacated on other grounds and remanded* 485 U.S. 224, 108 S.Ct. 978, 99 L.Ed.2d 194 (1988) (statement that it was not aware of takeover negotiations was actionable when in fact some talks had taken place); Etshokin v. Texasgulf, Inc., 612 F.Supp. 1220 (N.D.Ill.1985) (statement denying knowledge of causes for increased trading in issuer's stock may be materially misleading for failure to disclose takeover negotiations). *C.f.* Pullman–Peabody Co. v. Joy Mfg. Co., 662 F.Supp. 32 (D.N.J.1986) (allegedly misleading omission of negotiations held not in connection with tender offer). *See* § 13.10 *infra.*

With regard to the necessity to disclose "soft information," there is no duty to disclose projections and asset valuations unless they are substantially certain as opposed to highly speculative.[69] It has also been held that nondisclosure of arguable violations of state law fiduciary duties cannot be brought within section 14(e)'s reach.[70] It has also been held that "mere puffery" and "verbal jousts" between combatants in a hostile takeover attempt do not violate section 14(e).[71] On the other hand, officers and directors could be liable to shareholders of a target company for allegedly misrepresenting the tender offer as "fair." [72]

A number of courts have adopted what is often referred to as the "bespeaks caution" doctrine which can offset the effect of allegedly materially misleading projections and other soft information.[73] The doctrine holds that sufficient cautionary language may preclude misstatements in projections, predictions, and opinions from being actionable.[74] The cases invoking the bespeaks caution doctrine have involved projections or other soft information; it is thus unclear whether the doctrine will have more general application.[75] Even if the doctrine does not apply as such outside of soft information such as projections and predictions, the materiality calculus depends upon an evaluation of the "total mix" of information available and thus the cautionary language would be considered as part of that total mix.

§ 11.16   Arrangements Affecting Director Turnover in Connection With a Tender Offer—Section 14(f)

As is the case with any transfer of corporate control, tender offers

69. Starkman v. Marathon Oil Co., 772 F.2d 231 (6th Cir.1985), *cert. denied* 475 U.S. 1015, 106 S.Ct. 1195, 89 L.Ed.2d 310 (1986); Biechele v. Cedar Point, Inc., 747 F.2d 209 (6th Cir.1984); Flynn v. Bass Brothers Enterprises, Inc., 744 F.2d 978 (3d Cir.1984). *But see* Howing Co. v. Nationwide Corp., 826 F.2d 1470 (6th Cir.1987), *cert. denied* 486 U.S. 1059, 108 S.Ct. 2830, 100 L.Ed.2d 930 (1988) (conclusory earnings projections may violate section 13(e) in connection with "going private" transaction).

70. Danaher Corp. v. Chicago Pneumatic Tool Co., 633 F.Supp. 1066 (S.D.N.Y.1986).

71. Turner Broadcasting System, Inc. v. CBS, Inc., 627 F.Supp. 901 (N.D.Ga.1985). *Cf.* In re PHLCORP Securities Tender Offer Litigation, 700 F.Supp. 1265 (S.D.N.Y.1988) (allegedly false characterization of directors as "independent" did not violate section 14(e)).

72. In re PHLCORP, 1992 WL 85013, [1992 Transfer Binder] Fed.Sec.L.Rep. (CCH) ¶ 96,808 (S.D.N.Y.1992).

73. The bespeaks caution doctrine, which frequently has involved cautionary language in 1933 Act prospectuses is discussed in more detail in § 3.7 *supra* and § 13.5A *infra*.

74. The leading cases recognizing the doctrine include: In re Worlds of Wonder Securities Litigation, 35 F.3d 1407 (9th Cir.1994); In re Trump Casino Securities Litigation, 7 F.3d 357 (3d Cir.1993), *affirming* 793 F.Supp. 543 (D.N.J.1992).

75. In re Synergen, Inc. Securities Litigation, 863 F.Supp. 1409 (D.Colo.1994) (finding bespeaks caution doctrine inapplicable to historical facts; court pointed to the absence of any authority applying the doctrine in cases not involving projections of future events); Anderson v. Clow, 1993 WL 497212, [1993–1994 Transfer Binder] Fed.Sec.L.Rep. (CCH) 97,807 (S.D.Cal.1993) (bespeaks caution doctrine only applies in cases of projections, estimates, or similar types of soft information). *See also, e.g.,* Kline v. First Western Government Securities, Inc., 24 F.3d 480 (3d Cir.1994) (refusing to apply bespeaks caution doctrine to claim based on affirmative misrepresentations in tax opinion).

will frequently result in a shift in corporate management.[1] Accordingly, it is not uncommon to find tender offers containing agreements relating to management turnover and the election of new directors. These control transfers can raise problems under state law relating to invalid control premiums and other breaches of fiduciary duty.[2] The Williams Act superimposes certain disclosure obligations. Under section 14(f) of the Exchange Act,[3] when a tender offer for equity securities subject to the Act's reporting requirements contains agreements concerning the designation of new directors otherwise than through a formal vote at a meeting of securities holders, there must be full disclosure. Contemplated management turnover, including any arrangement regarding the make-up of the majority of directors, also must be disclosed.[4] Thus, for example, where a stock purchase agreement permits the purchaser to designate a majority of the issuer's directors, section 14(f)'s disclosure obligation is triggered.[5] When the agreed-upon shift in control occurs, a second filing obligation arises.[6]

Rule 14f–1[7] provides for specific disclosures in the event there is going to be a change in the majority of directors otherwise than at a shareholder meeting, in a transaction subject to either section 13(d)[8] or section 14(d).[9] At least ten days prior to the taking of office by such a

§ 11.16

1. *See* Thomas L. Hazen, Transfers of Corporate Control and Duties of Controlling Shareholders—Common Law, Tender Offers, Investment Companies and a Proposal for Reform, 125 U.Pa.L.Rev. 1023 (1977).

2. *See, e.g.,* Adolf A. Berle & Gardiner C. Means, The Modern Corporation and Private Property 207–52 (rev.ed. 1967) Harry G. Henn & John R. Alexander, Laws of Corporations § 241 (3d ed. 1983); William D. Andrews, The Stockholders Right to Equal Opportunity in the Sale of Shares, 78 Harv.L.Rev. 505 (1963); David C. Bayne, The Sale-of-Control Premium: The Definition, 53 Minn.L.Rev. 485 (1969); David C. Bayne Corporate Control as Strict Trustee, 53 Geo.L.J. 543 (1965); David C. Bayne, A Philosophy of Corporate Control, 50 Cornell L.Q. 628 (1965); Adolf A. Berle, "Control" in Corporate Law, 58 Colum.L.Rev. 1212 (1958); Victor Brudney, Fiduciary Ideology in Transactions Affecting Corporate Control, 65 Mich.L.Rev. 259 (1966); Thomas L. Hazen, Transfers of Corporate Control and Duties of Controlling Shareholders—Common Law, Tender Offers, Investment Companies—And a Proposal for Reform, 125 U.Pa.L.Rev. 1023 (1977); George B. Javaras, Equal Opportunity in The Sale of Controlling Shares: A Reply to Professor Andrews, 42 U.Chi.L.Rev. 420 (1965); Richard W. Jennings, Trading in Corporate Control, 44 Calif.L.Rev. 1 (1956); Noyes Leech, Transactions in Corporate Control, 104 U.Pa.L.Rev. 725 (1956); P. T. O'Neal, Sale of a Controlling Corporate Interest: Bases of Possible Seller Liability, 38 U.Pitt.L.Rev. 9 (1976); Marc I. Steinberg, Fiduciary Duties and Disclosure Obligations in Proxy and Tender Contests for Corporate Control, 30 Emory L.J. 169 (1981); Symposium, Sale of Control, 4 J.Corp.L. 239 (1979).

3. 15 U.S.C.A. § 78n(f). *See generally* David L. Ratner, Section 14(f): A New Approach to Transfers of Corporate Control, 54 Cornell L.Rev. 65 (1968); Steinberg *supra* footnote 2.

Private foreign issuers are not subject to section 14(f). *See* Rule 3a12–3, 17 C.F.R. § 240.3a12–3. Nor are they subject to sections 14(a), 14(b), and 14(c) relating to proxy regulation. *Id.*

4. 15 U.S.C.A. § 78n(f). *See* 17 C.F.R. § 240.14f–1.

5. Drobbin v. Nicolet Instrument Corp., 631 F.Supp. 860 (S.D.N.Y.1986).

6. *Id.*

7. 17 C.F.R. § 240.14f–1.

8. 15 U.S.C.A. § 78m(d). *See* § 11.11 *supra.*

9. 15 U.S.C.A. § 78n(d). *See* § 11.14 *supra.*

new director, the issuer must file with the Commission and transmit to all security holders of record who would have been entitled to vote for the election at a meeting, all the information regarding the director that would otherwise be required in Schedule 14A[10] of the proxy rules. The purpose of section 14(f)'s disclosure requirements is to assure that all shareholders are aware of any changes in management control that are being effected without a shareholder vote. The rule keeps the security holders posted as to all material information, including the new directors' background and relationship with the issuer both in terms of employment contracts and stockholdings. A director's interest in any contracts, arrangements or understandings with the issuer or its affiliates must also be disclosed. Upon an appropriate showing of an injury, violations of section 14(f)'s disclosure obligations may support injunctive relief.[11] Such relief could include, for example, an injunction against implementing the shift in management control until adequate disclosures have been made.

§ 11.17   Issuer Purchases of Its Own Stock—Section 13(e) and the Going Private Rules; Issuer Self Tender Offers

Purchases by a 1934 Act reporting company of its own stock do not trigger the filing requirements for tender offers and five percent acquisitions of securities.[1] This gap is filled by section 13(e)(1)[2] which makes it unlawful for an issuer to purchase its own stock unless in compliance with such rules as the SEC may promulgate. Section 13(e)(1) and the rules discussed below apply only to issuers subject to the 1934 Act's registration and periodic reporting requirements.[3]

Issuer's Share Repurchases in Response to Someone Else's Tender Offer

Rule 13e–1[4] applies to an issuer's purchases of its own stock after a third party has filed a tender offer for its securities. An issuer of securities subject to the Exchange Act's registration and reporting requirements may not purchase its own securities once a third party tender offer has been made unless the issuer files with the Commission eight copies of a statement containing the following information: (1) a description of the securities to be purchased; (2) the names and classes

---

10. Schedule 14A items 6(a), (d), (e), (f), 7, 8; 17 C.F.R. § 240.14a–100. *See* § 11.6 *supra.*

11. *Cf.* Drobbin v. Nicolet Instrument Corp., 631 F.Supp. 860 (S.D.N.Y.1986) (refusing to issue the injunction since the violator no longer controlled the issuer and also because relief under the applicable state law had also been granted).

§ 11.17

1. 15 U.S.C.A. §§ 78m(d)(6)(C), 78n(d)(8)(B). *See* §§ 11.11, 11.14 *supra.*

2. 15 U.S.C.A. § 78m(e)(1).

3. Section 13(e) generally is limited to issuers registered under section 12 and does not apply to those whose reporting requirements are imposed by section 15(d). 15 U.S.C.A. §§ 78*l*, 78*o*(d). *See* §§ 9.2, 9.3 *supra.* However, Rule 13e–3(c) has limited application to section 15(d) reporting companies. 17 C.F.R. § 240.13e–3(c).

4. 17 C.F.R. § 240.13e–1.

of persons from whom the securities are to be purchased; (3) the purposes for which they are being purchased; and (4) the source of all funds used to finance the purchases.[5] This filing is supplemented by Schedule 14D–9[6] which requires a statement to be filed by an issuer making a solicitation or recommendation to security holders to accept or reject the tender offer and Rule 14e–2's[7] provisions requiring the issuer to send to the security holders a statement recommending acceptance or rejection of the tender offer or expressing no opinion toward it. Issuer purchase of its own shares is just one of the possible responses to a tender offer.[8] An issuer's filings under Rule 13e–1 with regard to defensive share repurchases, do not alleviate the need for making filings under Rule 13e–3 or Rule 13e–4 if the transaction is likely to result in the cessation of 1934 Act reporting obligations or constitute a tender offer.[9]

Other Issuer Purchases of Its Own Shares; The Going Private Rules

Rule 13e–4[10] sets out the filing and disclosure requirements for tender offers by a reporting company for its own shares. Schedule 13E–4's[11] disclosure requirements parallel those applying to third party tender offers in Schedule 14D–1.[12]

In its so-called "going private" rules,[13] the Commission regulates an issuer's purchases of its own shares outside of the contested tender offer milieu. The SEC's going private rules supplement the state law remedies that exist for breaches of fiduciary duties in connection with freeze-out and going private transactions.[14] The going private rules and the

---

5. *Id.* On a related matter, the SEC proposed legislation that would have prohibited issuer self tenders in response to a takeover attempt. *See* 16 Sec.Reg. & L.Rep. 793 (May 11, 1984). *Cf.* SEC v. Carter Hawley Hale Stores, Inc., 587 F.Supp. 1248 (C.D.Cal.1984). *See generally* Michael Bradley & Michael Rosenzweig, Defensive Stock Repurchases, 99 Harv.L.Rev. 1377 (1986).

6. 17 C.F.R. § 240.14d–101. *See* § 11.14 *supra.*

7. 17 C.F.R. § 240.14e–2. *See* § 11.15 *supra.*

8. Defensive tactics are discussed in § 11.20 *infra.*

9. Maynard Oil Co. v. Deltec Panamerica, S.A., 630 F.Supp. 502 (S.D.N.Y.1985). The going private rules are discussed in the text accompanying footnotes 10–37 *infra.* Issuer self tenders are discussed in the text accompanying footnotes 64–70 *infra; see also* § 11.14 *supra* (discussing third party tender offers).

10. 17 C.F.R. § 240.13e–4.

11. 17 C.F.R. § 240.13e–101.

12. 17 C.F.R. § 240.14d–100; § 11.14 *supra.* The regulation of issuer self tender offers is designed to protect the issuer's shareholders. Thus, shareholders of a merged subsidiary were not able to challenge the parent's self tender which did not affect the terms of the parent-subsidiary merger. Beaumont v. American Can Co., 797 F.2d 79 (2d Cir.1986).

13. *See generally,* Steven I. Rothschild, Going Private, *Singer* and Rule 13e–3, 7 Sec.Reg.L.J. 195 (1979); Thomas J. Sherrard, Federal Judicial and Regulatory Responses to Santa Fe, 35 Wash. & Lee L.Rev. 695 (1978).

14. *E.g.,* Lebold v. Inland Steel Co., 125 F.2d 369 (7th Cir.1941), *cert. denied* 316 U.S. 675, 62 S.Ct. 1045, 86 L.Ed. 1749 (1942) (awarding damages under a state law claim attacking a freeze out effected by a voluntary dissolution); Singer v. Magnavox Co., 380 A.2d 969 (Del.1977) (upholding complaint against a merger the alleged sole purpose of which was to freeze out the minority).

See generally James D. Cox, Thomas L. Hazen & F. Hodge O'Neal, Corporations § 23.4 (1995); Harry G. Henn & John R. Alexander, Laws of Corporations § 240 (3d ed. 1983).

issuer self tender rules are based on full disclosure and thus allegations of breaches of fiduciary duty are insufficient to establish a federal securities law claim.[15] However, if something more than mismanagement is shown, a violation may exist. Thus, for example, in *Howing Co. v. Nationwide Corp.*,[16] the Sixth Circuit upheld a claim that material omissions which allegedly deprived plaintiffs of their state law appraisal remedy were sufficient to support an action under section 13(e).

Rule 13e–3,[17] which applies primarily to issuers subject to section 12's registration requirements,[18] defines the types of transactions covered. A Rule 13e–3 transaction is one or a series of transactions that involves either (1) the purchase or tender offer by an issuer or its affiliates of any equity security subject to the Act's reporting requirements or (2) a proxy solicitation subject to Regulation 14A,[19] or a distribution of information subject to Regulation 14C,[20] to the holders of equity securities subject to the Act's reporting requirements that is sent out by the issuer or affiliate in connection with a merger, consolidation, reclassification, recapitalization, reverse stock split or similar transaction. Any of the foregoing Rule 13e–3 transactions are covered by the Schedule 13E–3 disclosure and filing requirements if the effect of the transaction or transactions is the cessation of the reporting obligations under the Exchange Act. A difficult problem is judging the point at which the issuer should be able to predict a reasonable likelihood of such a result.[21] It is not always easy to determine at what point a transaction or series of transactions is likely to result in the issuer having fewer than three hundred shareholders. It has been held that an open market purchase program in response to a hostile takeover did not trigger Rule 13e–3's filing requirements because crossing the three hundred shareholder threshold was primarily dependent upon the success of plaintiff's

---

The Delaware Supreme Court overruled its prior decisions by holding in Weinberger v. UOP, Inc., 457 A.2d 701 (Del.1983) that the statutory appraisal remedy is the only measure of fairness in such a transaction; whether other states will follow remains to be seen.

However, in a subsequent decision, the Delaware court showed signs of retrenching from its position in *Weinberger*. Rabkin v. Philip A. Hunt Chemical Corp., 498 A.2d 1099 (Del.1985), *on remand* 547 A.2d 963 (1986) (appraisal rights are not exclusive in the face of allegations of "specific acts of fraud, misrepresentation, or other items of misconduct").

15. *Cf.* Lessner v. Casey, 681 F.Supp. 415 (E.D.Mich.1988) (claim charging violations of Rule 13e–4 was dismissed; alleged failure to disclose that corporation and its president did not consider the fairness of an issuer self tender was in essence a claim based on breach of fiduciary duty).

For a discussion of the declining impact of Rule 10b–5 in freezeout cases, *see* § 13.11 *infra*.

16. 972 F.2d 700 (6th Cir.1992), *cert. denied* ___ U.S. ___, 113 S.Ct. 1645, 123 L.Ed.2d 266 (1993).

17. 17 C.F.R. § 240.13e–3.

18. There is limited application to section 15(d) reporting companies. *See* footnote 3 *supra*.

19. 17 C.F.R. §§ 240.14a–1–14a–103. *See* §§ 11.1–11.2 *supra*.

20. 17 C.F.R. §§ 240.14c–1–14c–101. *See* § 11.9 *supra*.

21. *See* Sec.Exch.Act Rel. No. 34–16075 (Aug. 2, 1979). *See also* Shamrock Associates v. Horizon Corp., 632 F.Supp. 566 (S.D.N.Y.1986) (fact that delisting might only be temporary did not preclude the necessity of a Rule 13e–3 filing).

hostile tender offer.[22] The going private rules require that the issuer must file a Schedule 13E–3[23] which requires disclosures similar to those required under Schedule 13D[24] and Schedule 14D–1.[25] The Schedule 13E–3 must contain the following information:

1. The identity of the issuer, and identification and description of the equity securities subject to the transaction.

2. A description of material terms of the transaction.

3. The issuer's or affiliate's post-transaction plans.

4. The source and amount of funds or other consideration.

5. The purpose of the transaction and the alternative means that were considered.

6. A detailed discussion of the benefits and detriments to (a) the issuer, (b) its affiliates and (c) nonaffiliated shareholders; including a discussion of tax consequences.

7. Whether management has a reasonable belief in the fairness of the transaction and the basis for such belief. In this context, the issuer having such a belief must describe fairness in terms of

    (a) historical and current market value

    (b) net book value, going concern value, liquidation value

    (c) any outside offers

    (d) appraisals received from third parties

8. A detailed description of all contracts, understandings, and agreements with respect to the issuer's securities.

9. The present intention and recommendations of the insiders with regard to the transaction.

10. The availability and a summary of statutory appraisal rights, if any.

Schedule 13E–3 disclosures are, of course, subject to civil and criminal liability for material misstatements and omissions.[26] As noted above, Rule 13e–3 applies not only to issuers but to affiliates which include, inter alia, persons directly or indirectly controlling the issuer.[27]

The timing for the Schedule 13E–3 filing depends upon the nature of the transaction. If the transaction involves a proxy solicitation subject

---

22. Maynard Oil Co. v. Deltec Panamerica, S.A., 630 F.Supp. 502 (S.D.N.Y.1985).

23. 17 C.F.R. § 240.13e–100.

24. 17 C.F.R. § 240.13d–101. *See* § 11.11 *supra*.

25. 17 C.F.R. § 240.14d–100. *See* § 11.14 *supra*.

26. *E.g.*, 15 U.S.C.A. § 78r(a); 17 C.F.R. §§ 240.10b–5, 13e–3(b); Howing Co. v. Nationwide Corp., 826 F.2d 1470 (6th Cir.1987) (upholding private right of action and finding inadequate description of fairness considerations). *See* §§ 12.8, 13.2–13.11 *infra*.

27. 17 C.F.R. § 240.13e–3(a)(1). *See* Woodward & Lothrop, Inc. v. Schnabel, 1984 WL 2464, [1984 Transfer Binder] Fed.Sec.L.Rep. (CCH) ¶ 91,658 (D.D.C.1984) (even after acquiring 32% of issuer's stock, affiliate status did not attach and Rule 13e–3 did not apply because the alleged affiliate lacked the requisite control of the issuer).

to Regulation 14A or a dissemination of information subject to Regulation 14C, the Schedule 13E–3 must be filed contemporaneously with Schedule 14A or 14C.[28] If the going private transaction takes the form of a tender offer, the Schedule 13E–3 must be filed when the tender offer is first publicly disseminated or submitted to the security holders.[29] If the transaction involves a 1933 Act registration for other securities to be issued, the Schedule 13E–3 must be filed contemporaneously with the registration statement.[30] In all other Rule 13e–3 transactions, such as open market purchases, the Schedule 13E–3 must be filed thirty days prior to the first purchase subject to Rule 13e–3.[31] When the 13e–3 transaction involves a series of transactions, the initial filing is governed by the first step, with appropriate amendments to be filed promptly. When the transaction is terminated, eight copies of a Schedule 13E–3 amendment must be filed no later than ten days after termination.

Exemptions From Rule 13e–3 Filings

Rule 13e–3 does not apply to certain transactions that otherwise would be covered. Rule 13e–3 does not apply to transactions by a person who became an affiliate by virtue of a tender offer within the past year, provided that there was full disclosure at the time of the tender offer of the offeror's intention to engage in a Rule 13e–3 transaction, and in the case of an "any or all" tender offer, the transaction must have been "substantially similar" to the plan described in the tender offer.[32] In the case of a tender offer on any other basis, the 13e–3 exception applies only if the tender offer described a binding agreement with the issuer to engage in a 13e–3 transaction.[33] Rule 13e–3 does not apply to an exchange whereby the issuer's security holders receive registered securities with substantially similar rights.[34] The rule further does not apply to transactions by issuers registered under the Public Utility Holding Company Act,[35] redemptions of redeemable securities,[36] and solicitation in connection with a plan of reorganization under Chapter X of the

28. *See* 17 C.F.R. §§ 240.14a–101, 14c–101. *See* §§ 11.2, 11.9 *supra.*

29. *Compare* section 14(d)'s and Rule 13e–4(c)(1)'s filing requirement upon the commencement of the tender offer. 15 U.S.C.A. § 78n(d); 17 C.F.R. § 240.13e–4(c)(1). *See* § 11.14 *supra. See also* text accompanying footnotes 62–67 *infra.*

30. 1933 Act registration requirements are discussed in chapters 2, 3 *supra.*

31. Schedule 13E–3, general instruction A.4. Timing is an especially difficult problem in a situation where it is not easy to point to the date upon which the plan solidified because the issuer had for other reasons been purchasing its own shares.

32. 17 C.F.R. § 240.13e–3(g)(1). *Cf.* Mellman v. Southland Racing Corp., 741 F.2d 180 (8th Cir.1984) (finding no section 13(e) violations where all relevant facts were adequately disclosed in tender offer materials).

33. *Id.*

34. 17 C.F.R. § 240.13e–3(g)(2). *See* Dowling v. Narragansett Capital Corporation, 735 F.Supp. 1105 (D.R.I.1990) (private right of action exists under § 13(e) to challenge sale of investment company).

35. 17 C.F.R. § 240.13e–3(g)(3). The Public Utility Holding Company Act is considered in chapter 15 *infra.*

36. 17 C.F.R. § 240.13e–3(g)(4).

Bankruptcy Act.[37]

Defensive Tender Offers

Defensive issuer tender offers that are covered by Rule 13e–4[38] are subject to rules similar to those applicable to third parties under Regulations 14D[39] and 14E.[40] The issuer must file a Schedule 13E–4.[41] A target company that responds with a self-tender without responding to the third-party offer in good faith may run afoul of state law, and the self-tender may be enjoined.[42] Issuer self tenders generally are discussed at the end of this section.[43]

Can the SEC Require Substantive Fairness?

Under highly publicized and controversial former proposed Rule 13e–2,[44] the Commission would have gone beyond disclosure requirements and placed substantive fairness limitations upon an issuer's attempt to go private. Prior to the Supreme Court decision in Santa Fe Industries, Inc. v. Green,[45] the Commission proposed a series of going private rules, one of which would have given the SEC power to prohibit such transactions merely on the basis of unfairness to the shareholders.[46] Although it would appear that the *Santa Fe* decision precludes scrutiny of transactional fairness,[47] the SEC continues to take the position that it has the power to regulate the fairness of going private transactions.[48] In 1977 the Commission included the fairness requirement in its post-*Santa Fe* version of its going private rules. However, when the going private

37. 17 C.F.R. § 240.13e–3(g)(5).

38. 17 C.F.R. § 240.13e–4. The SEC has recommended that Congress ban issuer self tenders made in response to a third party's takeover attempt. *See* 16 Sec.Reg. & L.Rep. (BNA) 793 (May 11, 1984).

39. 17 C.F.R. §§ 240.14d–1–14d–101. *See* SEC v. Carter Hawley Hale Stores, Inc., 760 F.2d 945 (9th Cir.1985) (issuer's open market purchase program in response to third-party tender offer was not a tender offer within the meaning of section 13(e)).

40. 17 C.F.R. §§ 240.14e–1–14e–3.

41. 17 C.F.R. § 240.13e–101.

42. Plaza Securities Co. v. Fruehauf Corp., 643 F.Supp. 1535 (E.D.Mich.1986) (Michigan law); AC Acquisitions Corp. v. Anderson, Clayton & Co., 519 A.2d 103 (Del.Ch.1986) (self-tender was not reasonable nor supportable by the business judgment rule) (opinion withdrawn).

43. *See* text accompanying footnotes 64–70 *infra*.

44. *See* Sec.Act Rel. No. 33–5567 (Feb. 6, 1975).

45. 430 U.S. 462, 97 S.Ct. 1292, 51 L.Ed.2d 480 (1977). *See* § 13.11 *infra*.

46. Sec.Act Rel. No. 33–5567 (Feb. 6, 1975); 40 Fed.Reg. 7947 (1975) (proposed Feb. 24, 1975). *See generally* Note, "Going Private:" Establishing Federal Standards for the Forced Elimination of Public Investors, 1975 U.Ill.L.F. 638; Note, Going Private: An Analysis of Federal and State Remedies, 44 Fordham L.Rev. 96 (1976); Comment, SEC Rulemaking Authority and the Protection of Investors: A Comment on the Proposed "Going Private" Rules, 51 Ind.L.Rev. 433 (1976).

47. 430 U.S. at 474–77, 97 S.Ct. at 1301–03. *See, e.g.,* Mellman v. Southland Racing Corp., 741 F.2d 180 (8th Cir.1984) (going private transaction by way of reverse stock split without misrepresentations did not violate federal law); Lessner v. Casey, 681 F.Supp. 415 (E.D.Mich.1988) (failure to consider fairness may have been breach of fiduciary duty but did not violate federal securities law).

48. *See, e.g.,* Sec.Act. Rel. No. 33–5884 (Nov. 17, 1977).

rules were adopted, and as currently enforced, the SEC deleted the fairness requirement noting that it "believes the question of regulation should be deferred until there is an opportunity to determine the efficacy of [the rules as adopted]." [49]

Manipulation in Connection With Issuer Repurchases

Purchases by an issuer or affiliate of its own securities if not properly handled can raise questions of manipulation.[50] Rule 10b–13[51] prohibits purchases by persons making a tender offer if not pursuant to the tender offer. The SEC proposed additional restrictions in its 1980 revision of proposed Rule 13e–2's going private restrictions.[52]

Two years later, in 1982, the SEC withdrew proposed Rule 13e–2.[53] The Commission's rationale for withdrawing the proposal was that "issuer repurchase programs are seldom undertaken with improper intent, may frequently be of substantial benefit to investors" and that Rule 13e–2 would have been "overly intrusive." [54] The Commission believed that there is ample protection against potential abuse in the disclosure provisions of Rule 13e–3 that are discussed above and the antimanipulation provisions that are identified directly below.[55] Aside from Rule 10b–13's prohibitions, Rule 10b–18 provides a safe harbor from the antimanipulation rules for certain purchases by the issuer and affiliates.[56] Purchases pursuant to issuer purchases or tender offers governed by either Rule 13e–1 or 13e–4 are excluded from Rule 10b–18's safe harbor.[57] The safe harbor depends upon both the trading volume and the price at which the issuer's bids are placed.[58]

Rule 10b–18 covers purchases by an issuer, or affiliated purchaser of an issuer,[59] of the issuer's common stock.[60] Certain enumerated transactions are not considered to be Rule 10b–18 purchases and thus are not

---

49. Sec.Act. Rel.No. 33–6100 (Aug. 2, 1979).

50. Sections 9 and 10 of the Exchange Act prohibit manipulation. 15 U.S.C.A. §§ 78i, 78j.

51. 17 C.F.R. § 240.10b–13. *See generally* Lewis D. Lowenfels, Rule 10b–13, Rule 10b–6 and Purchases of Target Company Shares During An Exchange Offer, 69 Colum.L.Rev. 392 (1969).

52. *See* Sec.Exch.Act Rel. No. 34–17222 (Nov. 4, 1980).

53. Sec.Exch.Act Rel. No. 34–19244 (Nov. 17, 1982).

54. *Id.*

55. *See* § 12.1 *infra.*

56. 17 C.F.R. § 240.10b–18. *See* § 12.1 *infra.*

57. 17 C.F.R. § 240.10b–18(a)(3).

58. The rule is quite complex. 17 C.F.R. § 10b–18. *See* Sec.Exch.Act Rel. No. 34–17222 (Nov. 4, 1980).

59. Affiliated purchaser includes anyone acting in concert with an issuer to effect such a purchase as well as an affiliate who directly or indirectly controls the issuer's purchases or whose purchases are directly or indirectly controlled by the issuer. 17 C.F.R. § 240.10b–18(a)(2). It is further provided, however, officers and directors who have participated in the decision to undertake a Rule 10b–18 purchase are not for that reason alone affiliated purchasers. *Id.* Similarly, broker-dealers executing Rule 10b–18 purchases on the issuer's behalf are not affiliated purchasers. *Id.*

60. 17 C.F.R. § 240.10b–18.

subject to the rule's limitations.[61] The rule then goes on to set out the rather elaborate conditions for Rule 10b–18 purchases that are not deemed to be in violation of the anti-manipulation rules.[62] As is the case with any safe harbor, failure to satisfy Rule 10b–18's conditions does not raise a presumption that the purchases were made in violation of the anti-manipulation rules.[63]

Issuer Self Tender Offers

In 1986, the SEC amended Rules 13e–4 and 14e–1 in order to make the time periods for tender offers by issuers and affiliates the same as those for third party tender offers.[64] An issuer tender offer must remain open for twenty business days (sixty days for roll-up transactions); any increase in the consideration or solicitation fee or any decrease in consideration offered requires that the offer remain open for ten business days from such date, with the time periods to be computed on a concurrent, as opposed to consecutive, basis.[65] Similarly, the rules governing proration and withdrawal rights now apply to all issuer tender offers as well as to self tender offers. When less than all of the shares tendered are to be accepted, the issuer making the tender offer must accept them on a prorata basis.[66] Also, tendering security holders have withdrawal rights throughout the duration of tender offer.[67] Rule 13e–4 has further been amended to include an "all holders" requirement that prohibits discriminatory issuer self-tenders, and a "best price" rule that requires persons tendering receive the highest price paid to any other security holder during the tender offer.[68] There is a limited exemption from the "all holders rule" for odd-lot tender offers by issuers seeking tenders from holders of a limited number of, but less than one hundred, shares.[69] In addition to the federal remedies for materially misleading statements, state law may provide a cause of action as well.[70]

61. *Id.*

62. *Id.*

63. 17 C.F.R. § 240.10b–18(c).

64. *See* Exch.Act.Rel. No. 34–22788 (Jan. 14, 1986). Regulations 14D and 14E are discussed in §§ 11.14, 11.15 *supra*.

65. 17 C.F.R. § 240.13e–4(f)(7); 17 C.F.R. § 240.14e–1 (twenty and sixty day periods).

66. 17 C.F.R. § 240.13e–4(f)(3).

67. 17 C.F.R. § 240.13e–4(f)(2)(i).

68. 17 C.F.R. § 240.13e–4(f)(8)–(11). *See* Exch.Act.Rel. No. 34–23421 (July 11, 1986). As a matter of state law, Delaware had approved the use of discriminatory tender offers. Unocal Corp. v. Mesa Petroleum Co., 493 A.2d 946 (Del.1985). For a discussion of the "best price" and "all holders" rules, *see* § 11.14 *supra*.

69. 17 C.F.R. § 240.13e–4(h)(5). *Cf., e.g.,* Eaton Vance Prime Rate Reserves, 25 Sec.Reg. & L.Rep. (BNA) 145 (SEC No Action Letter avail. Jan. 15, 1993) (permitting exchange offer by investment company whereby shareholders had a choice of consideration with one option requiring an early withdrawal charge).

70. *See* Eisenberg v. Chicago Milwaukee Corp., 537 A.2d 1051 (Del.Ch.1987) (it was materially misleading to characterize purpose of self tender as "cost savings" when the offer was designed to take advantage of the precipitous price decline during the October, 1987 market crash). Federal remedies are discussed in §§ 11.18, 11.19, 13.2–13.6 *infra*.

§ 11.18 Remedies for Violations of Sections 13(d), 13(e), 14(d)

Most of the litigation concerning the question of the existence of implied private rights of action under the Williams Act has arisen in the context of section 14(e)'s general antifraud proscriptions.[1] The courts seem to be consistent in favoring the existence of at least a limited implied remedy under section 14(e).[2] However, that remedy, as is the case with any remedy that would exist under sections 13(d),[3] 13(e),[4] and 14(d),[5] must be considered in light of the decline in federal implied remedies generally.[6] Since sections 13(d), 13(e), and 14(d) all apply to issuers subject to the Exchange Act's registration and reporting requirements,[7] and involve mandatory filings with the Commission, there are a number of other remedies for material misstatements. For example, any investor who is injured by reliance upon material misstatements in the Schedule 13D,[8] Schedule 13E–3,[9] Schedule 14D–1,[10] or Schedule 14D–9,[11] may sue for damages under the express remedy provided in section 18(a) of the Act.[12] It is to be remembered, however, that the section 18(a) remedy is an extremely limited one insofar as it requires that the investor have actually relied upon the documents filed with the Commission.[13] In addition to the express liability provisions of section 18(a), any material misstatements or omissions that give rise to an injury in connection with the purchase or sale of a security will state a cause of action under Rule 10b–5.[14] Furthermore, material misstatements and omissions in documents required by sections 13(d), 13(e), and 14(d) will give rise to the potential for criminal penalties as well as for SEC enforcement actions.[15] These remedial and criminal penalties also apply to failures to file or delays in filing. However, no private remedy would

---

§ 11.18

1. 15 U.S.C.A. § 78n(e). *See* §§ 11.15 *supra,* 11.19 *infra.*

2. *See* § 11.19 *infra.*

3. 15 U.S.C.A. § 78m(d). *See* § 11.17 *supra.*

4. 15 U.S.C.A. § 78m(e). *See* § 11.17 *supra.*

5. 15 U.S.C.A. § 78n(d). *See* § 11.14 *supra.*

6. *See* § 13.1 *infra. See* § 1.7 *supra* for an overview of the private remedies available under the 1933 and 1934 Acts.

7. 15 U.S.C.A. §§ 78*l*, 78m(a). *See* §§ 9.2, 9.3 *supra.*

8. 17 C.F.R. § 240.13d–101. *See* § 11.11 *supra.*

9. 17 C.F.R. § 240.13e–100. *See* § 11.17 *supra.*

10. 17 C.F.R. § 240.14d–100. *See* § 11.14 *supra.*

11. 17 C.F.R. § 240.14d–101. *See* § 11.14 *supra.*

12. 15 U.S.C.A. § 78r(a). *See, e.g.,* International Broadcasting Corp. v. Turner, 734 F.Supp. 383 (D.Minn.1990) (section 18(a) claim based on allegedly misleading Schedule 13D was upheld even though plaintiff did not plead that it was a purchaser or seller of the security; pleading was sufficient since it gave defendants notice of the claim for relief).

13. *See* § 12.8 *infra* for discussion of the section 18(a) remedy.

14. 17 C.F.R. § 240.10b–5. *See* chapter 13 *infra.*

15. 15 U.S.C.A. § 78aa.

appear to exist under Rule 10b–5 for mere delay.[16] The question of an independent implied remedy under the Williams Act's filing requirements thus becomes significant. The cases are in conflict but there have been a number of decisions that have held that the relevant provisions of sections 13 and 14 in and of themselves provide a basis for at least limited private relief. One pattern that has been emerging is the availability of injunctive relief[17] as opposed to damages.[18]

In Rondeau v. Mosinee Paper Corp.,[19] the Supreme Court indicated that a target company may have standing to complain of delays by a purchaser in filing a Schedule 13D where it can show a resultant injury. The Court held that due to the absence of substantial share acquisitions by the purchaser after the date upon which the Schedule 13D was due, the target company had failed to show an injury sufficient to support a cause of action for the defendant's delay. Following the opening that was left by this Supreme Court decision, many subsequent cases have held that a target company has standing to seek injunctive relief to bar additional purchases until the Schedule 13D has been filed.[20] However, there have also been some decisions to the contrary, holding that no private remedy exists even for injunctive relief.[21]

Even in the cases recognizing an implied right to private injunctive relief, not every violation will support such relief. It has been held, for example, that in determining whether to issue a preliminary injunction for violation of section 13(d)'s filing requirements, the court should consider whether there has been injury to the shareholders and the

---

16. The only possible way to state a Rule 10b–5 violation would be the claim that a delay in filing constituted a material omission, but this would be an uphill battle. Further, only purchasers and sellers can bring a private suit under Rule 10b–5. Blue Chip Stamps v. Manor Drug Stores, 421 U.S. 723, 95 S.Ct. 1917, 44 L.Ed.2d 539 (1975). *See* § 13.3 *infra.*

17. *E.g.* International Broadcasting Corp. v. Turner, 734 F.Supp. 383 (D.Minn.1990) (injunctive relief is available under appropriate circumstances).

18. For a recent case holding section 14(d)(7) can support a damage action *see* Field v. Trump, 850 F.2d 938 (2d Cir.1988).

19. 422 U.S. 49, 95 S.Ct. 2069, 45 L.Ed.2d 12 (1975).

20. CNW Corp. v. Japonica Partners, L.P., 874 F.2d 193 (3d Cir.1989) (reversing lower court and issuing preliminary injunction against shareholder vote until corrective disclosures in Schedules 13D and 14B disclosing identity of limited partners, limited partner and coinvestor agreements concerning purchases of target company stock); Florida Commercial Banks v. Culverhouse, 772 F.2d 1513 (11th Cir.1985) (target company has standing under sections 13(d), 14(d), and 14(e) to bring action seeking corrective disclosures); Portsmouth Square, Inc. v. Shareholders Protective Committee, 770 F.2d 866 (9th Cir.1985) (section 13(d); issuer had standing for injunctive and declaratory relief); Cardiff Acquisitions, Inc. v. Hatch, 751 F.2d 917 (8th Cir.1984) (section 14(d) claim; affirming denial of preliminary injunction but remanding for trial on the merits); Dan River, Inc. v. Unitex Ltd., 624 F.2d 1216 (4th Cir.1980), *cert. denied* 449 U.S. 1101, 101 S.Ct. 896, 66 L.Ed.2d 827 (1981); General Aircraft Corp. v. Lampert, 556 F.2d 90 (1st Cir.1977); GAF v. Milstein, 453 F.2d 709 (2d Cir.1971), *cert. denied* 406 U.S. 910, 92 S.Ct. 1610, 31 L.Ed.2d 821 (1972).

21. Kalmanovitz v. G. Heileman Brewing Co., 769 F.2d 152 (3d Cir.1985) (competing tender offeror lacked standing for claims under sections 13(e), 14(d), and 14(e)); Atlantic Federal Savings & Loan Association v. Dade Savings & Loan Association, 592 F.Supp. 1089 (S.D.Fla.1984).

investing public as well as to the target company.[22] Quite properly, the courts are reluctant to interfere with highly contested takeover attempts where any relief will have a substantial impact on the market,[23] but in an appropriate case a preliminary injunction will be issued.[24] Additionally, curative amendments to the Schedule 13D filing will warrant the lifting of any injunctive relief that had previously been granted.[25]

A number of courts have held that not only does a section 13(d) remedy extend to failure to file, but also to filings that contain material misstatements and or omissions.[26] It would appear that the question of whether there is standing to sue under section 14(d)'s filing requirements is analogous to the issues raised under section 13(d).[27]

Since time is of the essence in takeover battles, frequently the relief sought in an action under 13(d), 13(e) or 14(d) will be one for preliminary injunctive relief. Plaintiffs in such actions bear an especially high burden in light of the dual requirement that they prove both a substantial likelihood of success on the merits and irreparable injury if the preliminary injunction is not issued. Failure to meet either of these requirements will result in a denial of preliminary relief.[28] However,

---

22. *See* Mid–Continent Bancshares, Inc. v. O'Brien, 1981 WL 1404, [1982 Transfer Binder] Fed.Sec.L.Rep. (CCH) ¶ 98,734 (E.D.Mo.1981); Kirsch Co. v. Bliss & Laughlin Industries, Inc., 495 F.Supp. 488 (W.D.Mich.1980). *See also, e.g.,* Mason County Medical Association v. Knebel, 563 F.2d 256 (6th Cir.1977).

23. *See, e.g.,* CNW Corp. v. Japonica Partners, L.P., 776 F.Supp. 864 (D.Del.1990) (preliminary injunction denied due to failure to establish irreparable harm); University Bank & Trust Co. v. Gladstone, 574 F.Supp. 1006 (D.Mass.1983); Lane Bryant, Inc. v. Hatleigh, 517 F.Supp. 1196 (S.D.N.Y.1981); Standard Metals Corp. v. Tomlin, 503 F.Supp. 586 (S.D.N.Y.1980); Financial General Bankshares v. Lance, 1978 WL 1082, [1978 Transfer Binder] Fed.Sec.L.Rep. (CCH) ¶ 96,403 (D.D.C.1978). *Cf.* Anago Inc. v. Tecnol Medical Products, Inc., 792 F.Supp. 514 (N.D.Tex.1992), *affirmed* 976 F.2d 248 (5th Cir.1992), *cert. dismissed* ___ U.S. ___, 114 S.Ct. 491, 126 L.Ed.2d 441 (1993) (preliminary injunction in section 14(e) action denied due to failure to show substantial likelihood of success).

24. *See* Life Investors, Inc. v. AGO Holding, N.V., 1981 WL 15483, [1981–82 Transfer Binder] Fed.Sec.L.Rep. (CCH) ¶ 98,356 (8th Cir.1981) (decided under section 14(d)); Hanna Mining Co. v. Norcen Energy Resources Ltd., 574 F.Supp. 1172 (N.D.Ohio 1982) (injunction granted under Rule 10b–5 for misleading Form 13D).

25. Chromalloy American Corp. v. Sun Chemical Corp., 474 F.Supp. 1341 (E.D.Mo. 1979). *See* Hubco, Inc. v. Rappaport, 628 F.Supp. 345 (D.N.J.1985) (denying injunction because curative amendments had been filed). *See also, e.g.,* Treadway Companies v. Care Corp., 638 F.2d 357 (2d Cir.1980). *Cf.* Morrison Knudsen Corp. v. Heil, 705 F.Supp. 497 (D.Idaho 1988) (injunction until corrective disclosures are made).

26. *E.g.,* Indiana National Corp. v. Rich, 712 F.2d 1180 (7th Cir.1983) (injunction action brought by target company); Dan River, Inc. v. Unitex, Ltd., 624 F.2d 1216 (4th Cir.1980); Chevron Corp. v. Pennzoil Co., 974 F.2d 1156 (9th Cir.1992) (triable issue as to whether defendant misstated interest to obtain a seat on the board and exercise a degree of control); Southmark Prime Plus, L.P. v. Falzone, 776 F.Supp. 888 (D.Del.1991); Seilon, Inc. v. Lamb, 1983 WL 1354, Fed.Sec.L.Rep. (CCH) ¶ 99,448 (N.D.Ohio 1983).

27. *Compare,* Treadway Companies v. Care Corp., 638 F.2d 357 (2d Cir.1980) (involving section 13(d)) *with* Prudent Real Estate Trust v. Johncamp Realty, Inc., 599 F.2d 1140 (2d Cir.1979) (granting an injunction under section 14(d)) *and* S–G Securities, Inc. v. Fuqua Investment Co., 466 F.Supp. 1114 (D.Mass.1978) (same).

28. *See; e.g.,* Gelco Corp. v. Coniston Partners, 811 F.2d 414 (8th Cir.1987) (once plaintiff fails to prove irreparable injury, there is no need to consider the merits before denying a preliminary injunction); Cardiff Acquisitions, Inc. v. Hatch, 751 F.2d 917 (8th Cir.1984) (section 14(d) claim; although Williams Act may have been violated, district court did not abuse its discretion in denying preliminary injunction).

serious violations will warrant preliminary relief, since waiting until a full trial on the merits will usually mean that the challenged transaction will take place years before the case is resolved. As one court has put it, "[e]ffectively the only relief available to an issuer, under the prevailing view, is an order requiring the five percent owner to file a corrected 13D and perhaps enjoining further acquisitions pending the corrections." [29]

It has been held that a tender offeror has standing to bring an injunction on behalf of the target company's shareholders against the target company management for violations of Rule 13e–4[30] with regard to an issuer's defensive purchases of its shares in response to a tender offer.[31] In contrast, a former president was held not to have standing to sue for damages flowing from alleged 13D violations that resulted in his loss of economic advantage due to a drop in target's stock resulting from a blocking of a proposed sale of the company.[32] This ruling is consistent with the fact that the Williams Act was designed to protect investors not defeated tender offerors[33] or others who may be adversely affected.

Although the case law is relatively sparse, the Commission has continuously asserted that such a private remedy does exist.[34] With regard to section 13(e) in general it has been held a private remedy exists since the issuer's security holders comprise a class for whose especial benefit the legislation was enacted.[35] As mentioned at the outset of this section, it is debatable whether these scattered cases recognizing implied remedies under sections 13(d), 13(e), and 14(d) can stand in light of the Supreme Court's limiting trend for implied remedies generally.[36] There are arguments that favor the recognition of these Williams Act remedies.[37] The trend among the recent cases has been to assume the presence of a remedy under section 13(d), 13(e), or 14(d), at

29. Hubco, Inc. v. Rappaport, 628 F.Supp. 345, 354 (D.N.J.1985). *See also, e.g.,* Conagra, Inc. v. Tyson Foods, Inc., 708 F.Supp. 257 (D.Neb.1989), *vacated* 716 F.Supp. 428 (D.Neb.1989); Champion Parts Rebuilders, Inc. v. Cormier Corp., 650 F.Supp. 87 (N.D.Ill. 1986) (corrective disclosure insufficient, equitable relief warranted); Spinner Corp. v. Princeville Devel. Corp., 1986 WL 15545, [1986–87 Transfer Binder] Fed.Sec.L.Rep. (CCH) ¶ 93,058 (D.Hawaii 1986) (semble).

30. 17 C.F.R. § 240.13e–4. *See* § 11.17 *supra.*

31. Crane Co. v. Harsco Corp., 511 F.Supp. 294 (D.Del.1981). *But cf.* Polaroid Corp. v. Disney, 862 F.2d 987 (3d Cir.1988) (indicating standing under all holders rule is limited to target company shareholders and does not extend to target company itself).

32. Nowling v. Aero Services International, Inc., 752 F.Supp. 1304 (E.D.La.1990).

33. *See, e.g.,* Piper v. Chris–Craft Industries, Inc., 430 U.S. 1, 97 S.Ct. 926, 51 L.Ed.2d 124 (1977), which is discussed in § 11.19 *infra.*

34. *E.g.,* Sec.Exch. Act Rel. No. 34–16075 (SEC Aug. 2, 1979); Sec.Exch.Act Rel. No. 34–14185 (SEC Nov. 17, 1977).

35. Howing Co. v. Nationwide Corp., 826 F.2d 1470 (6th Cir.1987) (implied private damage action); Fisher v. Plessey Co., 559 F.Supp. 442 (S.D.N.Y.1983).

36. *See* § 13.1 *infra.*

37. *See* Tamar Frankel, Implied Rights of Action, 67 Va.L.Rev. 553 (1981); Thomas L. Hazen, Implied Private Remedies Under Federal Statutes: Neither a Death Knell Nor a Moratorium—Civil Rights, Securities Regulation and Beyond, 33 Vand.L.Rev. 1333 (1980); Hazen, The Supreme Court and the Securities Laws: Has the Pendulum Slowed? 30 Emory L.J. 5 (1981).

least for injunctive relief.[38]

As pointed out above, on appropriate facts, damages may also be available. Thus, for example, shareholders denied a tender offer premium because of the tender offeror's wrongful interference with their proration rights could recover in an action under section 14(d)(6).[39] The Sixth Circuit has recognized a private remedy for violation of section 13(e)'s going private provisions which allegedly resulted in the loss of plaintiff's state law appraisal remedy due to material misstatements or omissions.[40]

§ 11.19 Is There an Implied Remedy Under Section 14(e)?

Congress, in enacting the Williams Act's tender offer provisions, did not provide any express remedy for injured investors. Any investor injured by reliance upon a materially misleading required SEC filing has an express remedy under section 18(a).[1] Anyone so injured as a purchaser or seller of a security may also have a remedy implied under Rule 10b–5.[2] Whether the Williams Act provides its own antifraud remedy for damages is somewhat questionable,[3] especially in light of the decline of implied remedies generally.[4] However, most courts that have considered the issue have recognized an implied remedy under section 14(e) in the hands of the target company or a target company shareholder.[5] For example, it has been held that a nontendering target shareholder has standing to sue both the target and acquiring corporations.[6]

38. *E.g.*, Diceon Electronics, Inc. v. Calvary Partners, L.P., 772 F.Supp. 859 (D.Del. 1991) (section 13(d)). *See* footnote 28 *supra*. *Cf.* Stern v. Leucadia National Corp., 644 F.Supp. 1108 (S.D.N.Y.1986), *affirmed in part, reversed in part* 844 F.2d 997 (2d Cir.1988) (false 13D may support a Rule 10b–5 action, but complaint dismissed for failure to state cause of action). *But see, e.g.*, MacFadden Holdings, Inc. v. JB Acquisitions, 801 F.2d 391 (2d Cir.1986), *reversing without opinion* 641 F.Supp. 454 (S.D.N.Y.1986).

39. Pryor v. USX Corp., 1991 WL 346368, [1991–1992 Transfer Binder] Fed.Sec.L.Rep. (CCH) ¶ 96,630 (S.D.N.Y.1991) (unpublished case). Section 14(d)(6) and proration rights are discussed in § 11.14 *supra*.

40. Howing Co. v. Nationwide Corp., 972 F.2d 700 (6th Cir.1992), *cert. denied* ___ U.S. ___, 113 S.Ct. 1645, 123 L.Ed.2d 266 (1993) (decided under section 13(e)'s going private rules).

§ 11.19

1. 15 U.S.C.A. § 78r(a). *See* § 12.8 *infra*.

2. 17 C.F.R. § 240.10b–5. *See* §§ 13.2–13.12 *infra*.

3. *See* § 11.18 *supra* for a discussion of implied remedies under sections 13(d), (e) and 14(d). *See* § 1.7 *supra* for an overview of the private remedies available under the 1933 and 1934 Acts.

4. *See* § 13.1 *infra*.

5. *See* text accompanying footnotes 15–24 *infra*. For an article supporting the existence of the implied right of action *see* Note, Securities Law: Implied Causes of Action Under Section 14(e) of the Williams Act, 66 Minn.L.Rev. 865 (1982).

6. Plaine v. McCabe, 797 F.2d 713 (9th Cir.1986). *But cf.* Priddy v. Edelman, 679 F.Supp. 1425 (E.D.Mich.1988) (nontendering shareholder lacked standing to sue for violation of Rule 10b–13's prohibition against a bidder's purchases outside of the tender offer).

In Piper v. Chris–Craft Industries, Inc.,[7] the Supreme Court held that a competing offeror cannot maintain a private right of action under section 14(e)'s general antifraud proscriptions. In so deciding the Court did not rule out any private remedy; in fact, the opinion held out much hope for the recognition of a section 14(e) private right of action in the hands of the target company or its shareholders. The Court in *Piper* reasoned that the purpose of the Williams Act was to further investor protection by serving the shareholders of the target company, not competing tender offerors who, at best, were collateral beneficiaries of the tender offer provisions.[8] Even if the legislation was directed at a special class of persons so as to warrant the implication of a private remedy,[9] a competing tender offeror was not a member of that group. The Court pointed out that section 14(e) was directed towards "full and fair disclosure for the benefit of investors," [10] and thus "Congress was seeking to broaden the scope of protection afforded to shareholders confronted with competing claims."[11] The precise scope of the *Piper* ruling is far from clear.[12] Justice Blackmun in his concurrence took the position that the *Piper* decision would have been better placed on the grounds of lack of standing rather than the absence of an implied remedy.[13] Justice Stevens in his dissent pointed out that since the plaintiff had already acquired the target company's shares it could be viewed as a shareholder with standing to sue under the Act.[14]

There are a number of federal circuit court decisions recognizing a target shareholder's right to sue for violation of section 14(e), at least where the injury is not premised on the loss of an opportunity to control the target company.[15] In order to challenge misstatements or omissions,

7. 430 U.S. 1, 97 S.Ct. 926, 51 L.Ed.2d 124 (1977).

8. 430 U.S. at 31–34, 97 S.Ct. at 944–46.

9. This is one of the tests the Court has stressed with regard to implied remedies generally. Implied remedies are discussed in § 13.1 *infra*.

10. 430 U.S. at 31, 97 S.Ct. at 944 (quoting 113 Cong.Rec. 24664 (Aug. 30, 1967) (remarks of Sen. Williams)). *See* Rondeau v. Mosinee Paper Corp., 422 U.S. 49, 58, 95 S.Ct. 2069, 2075, 45 L.Ed.2d 12 (1975).

11. 430 U.S. at 34, 97 S.Ct. at 945. *See also, e.g.,* Metropolitan Securities v. Occidental Petroleum Corp., 705 F.Supp. 134 (S.D.N.Y.1989) (debenture holder lacked standing notwithstanding conversion to stock after public announcement of tender offer).

12. *See generally* James F. Jorden & David R. Woodward, Appraisal of Disclosure Requirements in Contests for Control Under the Williams Act, 46 Geo.Wash.L.Rev. 817 (1978); Harvey L. Pitt, Standing to Sue Under the Williams Act After Chris–Craft: A Leaky Ship on Troubled Waters, 34 Bus.Law. 117 (1978); Note, Securities Law: Implied Causes of Action Under Section 14(e) of the Williams Act, 66 Minn.L.Rev. 865 (1982); Note, Chris–Craft: The Uncertain Evolution of Section 14(e), 76 Colum.L.Rev. 634 (1976).

13. 430 U.S. at 48–53, 97 S.Ct. at 952–55.

14. *Id.* at 56–59, 97 S.Ct. at 956–58. The majority's response was that even if standing were to be found, the plaintiff's claim lacked the requisite causation since the injury complained of was the loss of an opportunity to gain control rather than any typical investor-oriented injury. *Id.* at 36, 97 S.Ct. at 946.

15. *See, e.g.,* Schlesinger Investment Partnership v. Fluor Corp., 671 F.2d 739 (2d Cir.1982); Osofsky v. Zipf, 645 F.2d 107 (2d Cir.1981); Seaboard World Airlines, Inc. v. Tiger International Inc., 600 F.2d 355 (2d Cir.1979); Smallwood v. Pearl Brewing Co., 489 F.2d 579, 596 (5th Cir.1974); Crane Co. v. Westinghouse Air Brake Co., 419 F.2d 787, 798–99 (2d Cir.1969) (decided under Rule 10b–5); Electronic Specialty Co. v. International Controls Corp., 409 F.2d 937 (2d Cir.1969).

must the plaintiff show reliance? Recent decisions under the proxy rules indicate that reliance would not be required so long as a causally-related injury could be shown.[16] Thus a shareholder who did not tender his or her shares should not be precluded from challenging the tender offer.

Additionally, a target company's management may seek private injunctive relief for violations of section 14(e).[17] And, it has further been held that although unable to claim damages in light of the *Piper* decision, a competing offeror may sue for injunctive relief.[18] The plaintiff's dual burden of proving a substantial likelihood of success on the merits as well as irreparable injury makes it very difficult to secure preliminary injunctive relief; courts are mindful of the time premiums involved in tender offers and are thus reluctant to interfere.[19] For example, the Sixth Circuit was willing to grant injunctive relief to a competing tender offeror in light of the peculiar position of that plaintiff in having access to information which allowed it to act as a champion of the target's shareholders, though this altruistic motive was surely not the primary reason for plaintiff's petition.[20] Other courts have also recognized a private right of action for injunctive relief by a tender offeror in the face of deceptive and manipulative acts in violation of section 14(e).[21] It remains to be decided whether this rationale will apply to all competing tender offerors or only to those in a special position.

---

16. Western District Council of Lumber Production and Industrial Workers v. Louisiana Pacific Corp., 892 F.2d 1412 (9th Cir.1989) (upholding standing of nonrelying shareholder); Sandberg v. Virginia Bankshares, Inc., 891 F.2d 1112 (4th Cir.1989) (reversing denial of certification of a class of minority shareholders who voted against the merger), *judgment reversed on other grounds* 501 U.S. 1083, 111 S.Ct. 2749, 115 L.Ed.2d 929 (1991); Daly v. Neworld Bank for Savings, 1990 WL 8095, [1990 Transfer Binder] Fed.Sec.L.Rep. ¶ 95,247 (D.Mass.1990)(shareholder complaining about loss of voting rights resulting from proposed reorganization had standing to sue). *See* the discussion in § 11.4 *supra*.

17. *E.g.* Polaroid Corp. v. Disney, 862 F.2d 987 (3d Cir.1988) (granting target company's request for preliminary relief but limiting standing under Rule 14d–10's all holders rule to target company shareholders); Florida Commercial Banks v. Culverhouse, 772 F.2d 1513 (11th Cir.1985); Prudent Real Estate Trust v. Johncamp Realty, 599 F.2d 1140 (2d Cir.1979).

18. *E.g.* Mobil Corp. v. Marathon Oil Co., 669 F.2d 366 (6th Cir.1981); Southdown, Inc. v. Moore McCormack Resources, 686 F.Supp. 595 (S.D.Tex.1988); Grumman Corp. v. LTV Corp., 527 F.Supp. 86 (E.D.N.Y.1981); Weeks Dredging and Contracting, Inc. v. American Dredging Co., 451 F.Supp. 468 (E.D.Pa.1978); Humana, Inc. v. American Medicorp., Inc., 445 F.Supp. 613 (S.D.N.Y.1977).

19. *See, e.g.,* Gray Drug Stores, Inc. v. Simmons, 522 F.Supp. 961 (N.D.Ohio 1981); Riggs National Bank of Washington, D.C. v. Allbritton, 516 F.Supp. 164 (D.D.C.1981); Crane Co. v. Harsco Corp., 509 F.Supp. 115 (D.Del.1981). *See also, e.g.*, E.H.I. of Florida, Inc. v. Insurance Co. of North America, 652 F.2d 310 (3d Cir.1981).

20. Mobil Corp. v. Marathon Oil Co., 669 F.2d 366, 372 (6th Cir.1981). This view has been rejected by other courts. *See* § 12.1 *infra*. *See also* Piper v. Chris–Craft Industries, Inc., 430 U.S. 1, 97 S.Ct. 926, 51 L.Ed.2d 124 (1977), where competing tender offerors were considered collateral beneficiaries of section 14(e) and the possibility of shareholders benefitting from the suits brought by offerors under § 14(e) was not considered. *Id.* at 31–34, 97 S.Ct. at 944–946.

21. Whittaker Corp. v. Edgar, 535 F.Supp. 933 (N.D.Ill.1982). The injunction was not granted, however, due to competing tender offeror's failure to show a likelihood that it would prevail on the merits at trial. *See also* footnote 17 *supra*.

In what may prove to be a significant development, the Fourth Circuit has recognized an implied right of action for violation of Rule 14e–3's insider trading prohibitions.[22] The court there upheld a preliminary injunction sought by a target company against a tender offer that was allegedly based on misappropriation of inside information by a former target company officer. The Rule 14e–3 remedy was said to consist of five elements: (1) standing, (2) breach of duty, (3) materiality, (4) scienter, and (5) damages; all of which were found to have been present.[23] The Second Circuit has invalidated Rule 14e–3 to the extent that it would not require scienter as a precondition of a violation.[24]

Although tender offers necessarily involve the purchase or sale of securities, a Rule 10b–5 claim in connection with a tender offer will fail if it does not further investor protection. Accordingly, a competing tender offeror generally cannot state a 10b–5 claim when section 14(e) has not been violated.[25] Furthermore, even in suits brought by the target company or its shareholders, where there could be an overlap between the section 14(e) and Rule 10b–5 claims, there are advantages to pressing the 14(e) claim, if it exists. Rather than Rule 10b–5's purchaser/seller standing limitation,[26] a section 14(e) claim would seem to depend upon whether the plaintiff was the target of a tender offer solicitation or opposition to a tender offer, rather than whether he or she was an actual purchaser or seller.[27] Also, it is arguable that since section 14(e) does not have the "deceptive device" language that is present in Rule 10b–5 by virtue of section 10(b),[28] section 14(e)—as is the case with section 17(a)(2) and (3) of the 1933 Act[29]—may not require a showing of scienter.[30] Although section 14(e) does prohibit manipulative, fraudulent and deceptive acts, that prohibition is in addition to its prohibition of material misstatements and omissions. However, some courts have

---

22. Burlington Industries, Inc. v. Edelman, 1987 WL 91498, [1987 Transfer Binder] Fed.Sec.L.Rep. (CCH) ¶ 93,339 (4th Cir.1987), *affirming on the opinion below* 666 F.Supp. 799 (M.D.N.C.1987). *Cf.* United States v. Chestman, 704 F.Supp. 451 (S.D.N.Y.1989) (upholding validity of Rule 14e–3). Insider trading generally is considered in § 13.9 *infra.*

23. 666 F.Supp. 799 (M.D.N.C.1987).

24. United States v. Chestman, 903 F.2d 75 (2d Cir.1990) *reversed on other grounds on rehearing* 947 F.2d 551 (2d Cir.1991), *cert. denied* ___ U.S. ___, 112 S.Ct. 1759, 118 L.Ed.2d 422 (1992). *See* § 13.9 *infra.*

25. *See* Luptak v. Central Cartage, 1979 WL 1280, [1981 Transfer Binder] Fed.Sec. L.Rep. (CCH) ¶ 98,034 (E.D.Mich.1979), construing Piper v. Chris–Craft Industries, Inc., 430 U.S. 1, 42–46, 97 S.Ct. 926, 949–52, 51 L.Ed.2d 124 (1977).

26. Blue Chip Stamps v. Manor Drug Stores, 421 U.S. 723, 95 S.Ct. 1917, 44 L.Ed.2d 539 (1975), *rehearing denied* 423 U.S. 884, 96 S.Ct. 157, 46 L.Ed.2d 114 (1975). *See* § 13.3 *infra.*

27. *See* authorities in footnote 17 *supra.*

28. 15 U.S.C.A. § 78j(b). *See* § 13.11 *infra.*

29. 15 U.S.C.A. § 77q(a)(2) and (3).

30. Caleb & Co. v. E.I. DuPont de Nemours & Co., 599 F.Supp. 1468 (S.D.N.Y.1984) (scienter is not required in suit for violation of Rule 14e–1(c)'s prompt payment requirement). *See* Aaron v. SEC, 446 U.S. 680, 100 S.Ct. 1945, 64 L.Ed.2d 611 (1980). *See* § 13.4 *infra. But see* United States v. Chestman, 947 F.2d 551 (2d Cir.1991), *cert. denied* 503 U.S. 1004, 112 S.Ct. 1759, 118 L.Ed.2d 422 (1992); footnote 24 *supra.*

none-the-less found that scienter is required for a violation of section 14(e).[31] The Supreme Court's ruling in Schreiber v. Burlington Northern Inc.,[32] emphasizes that disclosure is not only the primary but probably the sole focus of section 14(e). Since section 17(a) of the 1933 Act, another disclosure-oriented provision, has been held to be violated upon a showing of negligence,[33] it is arguable that the *Schreiber* decision permits a no scienter approach to section 14(e).[34] However, the Supreme Court's narrow reading of section 14(e) in *Schreiber* strongly favors a scienter requirement.[35] Additionally, since the deception requirement is based on fraud, it follows that claims under section 14(e) must be pleaded with particularity.[36]

Although prior to *Schreiber* it might have been argued that the 10b–5 deception requirement announced in Santa Fe Industries, Inc. v. Green[37] does not apply under section 14(e), the decisions on point reached a contrary result and have required a showing of deceptive conduct as a precondition to a section 14(e) damage action.[38] The *Schreiber* ruling made it clear that those decisions were right.

As discussed above, there must be a connection between the challenged tender offer and any actual or potential injury to the plaintiff. It has further been held that a section 14(e) claim will not lie where the tender offer was withdrawn before the target's shareholders were given the option to tender their shares, since the requisite reliance upon the materially misleading required statements in making a decision whether to sell would be impossible without an effective offer.[39]

---

31. Pryor v. United States Steel Corp., 591 F.Supp. 942 (S.D.N.Y.1984), *affirmed in part, reversed in part* 794 F.2d 52 (2d Cir. 1986).

32. 472 U.S. 1, 105 S.Ct. 2458, 86 L.Ed.2d 1 (1985).

33. Aaron v. SEC, 446 U.S. 680, 100 S.Ct. 1945, 64 L.Ed.2d 611 (1980), *on remand* 666 F.2d 5 (2d Cir.1981).

34. The *Schreiber* decision is discussed more fully in § 11.15 *supra* and § 12.1 *infra*.

35. *See, e.g.,* Orlett v. Cincinnati Microwave, Inc., 953 F.2d 224 (6th Cir.1990) (claim failed since scienter not shown); Nelson v. Compagnie de Saint–Gobain, 1991 WL 280848, [1991–1992 Transfer Binder] Fed.Sec.L.Rep. (CCH) ¶ 96,530 (E.D.Pa.1991) (sufficient allegations of scienter); Sogevalor, SA v. Penn Central Corp., 771 F.Supp. 890 (S.D.Ohio 1991) (insufficient allegations of scienter); Burlington Industries, Inc. v. Edelman, 666 F.Supp. 799 (M.D.N.C.1987), *affirmed without opinion,* 1987 WL 91498, [1987 Transfer Binder] Fed.Sec.L.Rep. (CCH) ¶ 93,339 (4th Cir.1987) (requiring and finding scienter in a private suit under section 14(e)).

36. *E.g.,* Sogevalor, SA v. Penn Central Corp., 771 F.Supp. 890 (S.D.Ohio 1991) (insufficient particularity). The particularity requirement is discussed in § 13.8.1 *infra*.

37. 430 U.S. 462, 97 S.Ct. 1292, 51 L.Ed.2d 480 (1977).

38. Schreiber v. Burlington Northern, Inc., 472 U.S. 1, 105 S.Ct. 2458, 86 L.Ed.2d 1 (1985); In re Sunshine Mining Co. Securities Litigation, 496 F.Supp. 9 (S.D.N.Y.1979); Altman v. Knight, 431 F.Supp. 309 (S.D.N.Y.1977). *Accord* Dixon v. Ladish Co., 597 F.Supp. 20 (E.D.Wis.1984), *judgment affirmed in part, reversed in part* 792 F.2d 614 (7th Cir.1986).

39. Panter v. Marshall Field & Co., 646 F.2d 271 (7th Cir.1981), *cert. denied* 454 U.S. 1092, 102 S.Ct. 658, 70 L.Ed.2d 631 (1981). *See* § 11.20 *infra*.

§ 11.20 Responses to Tender Offers: Anti–Takeover Moves and Defensive Tactics

When faced with an uninvited or hostile takeover attempt, management of the target company will frequently decide to oppose the offer. Defensive tactics can raise questions under both state and federal law. When a target's management decides to fight off a contender for control, there is always the possibility of being charged with wasting of corporate assets or other forms of mismanagement.[1] In many instances, as a matter of state law, management's defensive tactics will be upheld under the business judgment rule,[2] which has raised particular problems in the context of defensive maneuvers.[3] In the first instance, courts recognize that in fending off challengers, incumbent management represents existing corporate policies and management is entitled to use reasonable expenditures of corporate funds in order to defend its policies, so long as the control contest reflects a battle of policies rather than personalities.[4] For example, management may buy out a corporate raider with corporate funds at a premium without breaching a duty to the shareholders where the raider has threatened liquidation.[5] The practice of purchasing the raider's shares at a premium has come to be known as "greenmail." Another common tactic is the issuance of additional shares to dilute the aggressor's interest; this will succeed if management can show a valid business purpose[6] but may not if it is merely to defeat a takeover attempt.[7] The same is true with a corporation's repurchase of

---

§ 11.20

1. *See generally* 3 James D. Cox, Thomas L. Hazen & F. Hodge O'Neal Corporations, ch. 23 (1995); Harry G. Henn & John R. Alexander, Laws of Corporations §§ 231–242 (3d ed. 1983).

2. *See id.* § 242.

3. *See generally* the authorities cited in footnote 16 *infra.* *But see* Revlon, Inc. v. MacAndrews & Forbes Holdings, Inc., 506 A.2d 173 (Del.1985) (once a target is for sale, management's only obligation is to assure the best price). The Delaware Supreme Court has had a difficult time explaining exactly when the *Revlon* auction duty will be triggered as opposed to those instances in which target management is permitted to act. *Compare* Paramount Communications, Inc. v. Time, Inc., 571 A.2d 1140 (Del. 1989) (*Revlon* duty did not apply to merger consistent with target's long-term business plan) *with* Paramount Communications, Inc. v. QVC Network, 637 A.2d 34 (Del. 1994) (*Revlon* auction duty prevented target management from taking sides in takeover battle). *See* text accompanying footnotes 25–26 *infra.* For discussion of the Delaware and other state law developments, *see* 3 Cox, Hazen & O'Neal *supra* footnote 1 at ch. 23.

4. *E.g.* Cheff v. Mathes, 41 Del.Ch. 494, 199 A.2d 548 (Del.1964); Kaplan v. Goldsamt, 380 A.2d 556 (Del.Ch.1977); Campbell v. Loew's, Inc., 36 Del.Ch. 563, 134 A.2d 852 (1957) (proxy battle); Rosenfeld v. Fairchild Engine & Airplane Corp., 309 N.Y. 168, 128 N.E.2d 291 (1955) (proxy battle).

5. Cheff v. Mathes, 41 Del.Ch. 494, 199 A.2d 548 (1964). *See* footnote 46 *infra.* However, the SEC proposed legislation that would have prohibited the paying of such "greenmail" to a holder of more than three percent of the stock who has held the stock for less than three years. *See* 16 Sec.Reg. & L.Rep. (BNA) 793 (May 11, 1984).

6. *Cf.* Tallant v. Executive Equities, Inc., 232 Ga. 807, 209 S.E.2d 159 (1974) (issuance of shares to raise capital upheld although as a result the current principal owner lost control).

7. Norlin Corp. v. Rooney, Pace, Inc., 744 F.2d 255 (2d Cir.1984) (preliminary injunction against voting shares issued to newly created ESOP); Chicago Stadium v. Scallen, 530 F.2d 204 (8th Cir.1976) (preliminary injunction against issuance of shares to corporate

its shares, even if not from the aggressor.[8]

The illustrative corporate law cases discussed above focus on concepts of self-dealing and the fiduciary duties of corporate officers and directors. Some of the same concepts may come into play under the federal securities acts. Although aimed primarily at disclosure, the antifraud and antimanipulation provisions[9] have provided protection at the federal level. As will be seen directly below, the courts have been in conflict as to how far the federal protection should go.[10] The Supreme Court's recent ruling that section 14(e) does not prohibit manipulation unless there has been a material misstatement or omission,[11] is a major impediment to the federal control of defensive tactics under the current statutory framework.

The Williams Act's disclosure requirements are designed to make sure that whatever defensive tactics may be taken are open and aboveboard. When faced with the time pressures of a takeover attempt the target company's management is put in a most difficult position. By virtue of SEC Rule 14e–2,[12] the target company's management has ten business days from the date the tender offer is first published to provide its security holders with its position on the merits of the offer. Under the rule, which is not limited to reporting companies, target management has limited alternatives. It may recommend acceptance or rejection of the offer, or it may simply issue a statement to the effect that management either is standing neutral or is presently unable to take a position on the merits of the tender offer. In opposing or recommending the acceptance of an offer the target company's management is required to set forth its reasons; and, of course, such statements are subject to the anti-fraud provisions of section 14(e).[13]

---

president); Klaus v. Hi–Shear Corp., 528 F.2d 225 (9th Cir.1975) (shares issued to newly created employees stock plan held to be a breach of duty but preliminary injunction denied); Condec Corp. v. Lunkenheimer Co., 43 Del.Ch. 353, 230 A.2d 769 (1967). *See also, e.g.,* Revlon, Inc. v. MacAndrews & Forbes Holdings, Inc., 506 A.2d 173 (Del.1985)

8. *E.g.* Ivanhoe Partners v. Newmont Mining Corp., 535 A.2d 1334 (Del.1987) (upholding independent directors' decision to aid "street sweep" by the target company's largest shareholder). *Compare, e.g.,* Herald Co. v. Seawell, 472 F.2d 1081 (10th Cir.1972) (upholding purchase of shares to fund employee stock plan) *with* Petty v. Penntech Papers, Inc., 347 A.2d 140 (Del.Ch.1975) (preliminary injunction issued against redemption of one class of voting stock). *Cf.* SEC v. Carter Hawley Hale Stores, Inc., 760 F.2d 945 (9th Cir.1985) (issuer's defensive repurchase program held not to be a tender offer).

9. *E.g.* Rule 10b–5 and section 14(e), 15 U.S.C.A. § 78n(e), 17 C.F.R. § 240.10b–5. *See* § 11.19 *supra* and §§ 13.2–13.12 *infra.*

10. *Compare e.g.* Mobil Corp. v. Marathon Oil Co., 669 F.2d 366 (6th Cir.1981) *with* Panter v. Marshall Field & Co., 646 F.2d 271 (7th Cir.1981), *cert. denied* 454 U.S. 1092, 102 S.Ct. 658, 70 L.Ed.2d 631 (1981) and Buffalo Forge Co. v. Ogden Corp., 717 F.2d 757 (2d Cir.1983), *cert. denied* 464 U.S. 1018, 104 S.Ct. 550, 78 L.Ed.2d 724 (1983). *See* text accompanying footnotes 52–83 *infra.*

11. Schreiber v. Burlington Northern, Inc., 472 U.S. 1, 105 S.Ct. 2458, 86 L.Ed.2d 1 (1985); *see* §§ 11.15, 11.19 *supra.*

12. 17 C.F.R. § 240.14e–2.

13. 15 U.S.C.A. § 78n(e). *See* §§ 11.15, 11.19 *supra.*

For a case finding nondisclosures in management's Schedule 14D–9 opposition not to be material, *see* Gulf Corp. v. Mesa Petroleum Co., 582 F.Supp. 1110 (D.Del.1984). *Cf.*

Varieties of Defensive Tactics and State Law Regulation

When faced with an outsider's attempt to take over the company, target management will frequently respond with a defensive tactic such as seeking a friendly suitor or "white knight." [14] For example, the white knight may be granted a "lock-up" option which gives it an advantage in acquiring the target over other bidders, or the target may arrange to sell its "crown jewel," or most desirable asset, to the white knight, thereby diminishing the target's attractiveness to others.[15] The successful use of defensive tactics may perpetuate the target company's incumbent management in the successor or surviving corporation, presenting a potential conflict of interest between management's desire to stay in office and the company's best interests. Defensive tactics are thus subject to state corporate law prohibitions on self dealings,[16] although as noted above, the target management's actions will generally have at least the protection of the business judgment rule.[17]

There have been a number of recent cases in Delaware and elsewhere that indicate the states are taking a firmer role in regulating tender offer practices of target company directors. As a starting point, the protection of the business judgment rule has been severely limited by two recent Delaware Supreme Court decisions. First, in Smith v. Van

---

Horowitz v. Pownall, 582 F.Supp. 665 (D.Md.1984) (question of fact existed as to materiality of omissions from Schedule 14D–9 filed by an opponent of a tender offer).

14. *See, e.g.,* Kern County Land Co. v. Occidental Petroleum Corp., 411 U.S. 582, 93 S.Ct. 1736, 36 L.Ed.2d 503 (1973); Buffalo Forge Co. v. Ogden Corp., 717 F.2d 757 (2d Cir.1983), *cert. denied* 464 U.S. 1018, 104 S.Ct. 550, 78 L.Ed.2d 724 (1983). *See generally* Arthur Fleischer, Jr., Tender Offers: Defenses, Responses, and Planning 139 (2d ed. 1983); Martin Lipton & Erica H. Steinberger, Takeovers and Freeze-outs ch. 6 (1978); Robert H. Winter, Mark H. Stumpf and Gerard L. Hawkins, Shark Repellents and Golden Parachutes: A Handbook for the Practitioner (1983). *See also, e.g.,* Dynamics Corp. of America v. CTS Corp., 635 F.Supp. 1174 (N.D.Ill.1986) *affirmed* 794 F.2d 250 (7th Cir.1986) *reversed on other grounds* 481 U.S. 69, 107 S.Ct. 1637, 95 L.Ed.2d 67 (1987) (upholding white knight defense as reasonable although it may not have been "most reasonable").

Defensive merger negotiations will require disclosures. Thus for example when an issuer stated that it may try to seek another suitor, the commencement of negotiations triggered an obligation to amend the issuer's Schedule 14D–9 filing. In re Revlon, Inc. [1986 Transfer Binder] Fed.Sec.L.Rep. (CCH) ¶ 84,006 (SEC June 16, 1986) (where negotiations became disclosable on September 26, a 14D–9 amendment filed on October 2 did not satisfy the issuer's obligation to "promptly" amend). *But see* Flamm v. Eberstadt, 814 F.2d 1169 (7th Cir.1987), *cert. denied* 484 U.S. 853, 108 S.Ct. 157, 98 L.Ed.2d 112 (1987) (holding preliminary white knight negotiations not material). The Supreme Court has held that the highly factual reasonable investor test of materiality applies to preliminary merger negotiations. Basic, Inc. v. Levinson, 485 U.S. 224, 108 S.Ct. 978, 99 L.Ed.2d 194 (1988). *See* § 11.4 *supra* and § 13.5 *infra.*

15. *See* Robert A. Prentice, Target Board Abuse of Defensive Tactics: Can Federal Law be Mobilized to Overcome the Business Judgment Rule?, 8 J.Corp.Law 337, 343 (1983) [hereinafter cited as Target Board Abuse].

16. Detailed discussion of the state corporate law ramifications goes beyond the scope of this book. *See* text accompanying footnotes 1–8 *supra. See* generally 3 Cox, Hazen & O'Neal *supra* footnote 1, ch. 23.

17. *See* Buffalo Forge Co. v. Ogden Corp., 555 F.Supp. 892, 903 (W.D.N.Y.1983), *affirmed* 717 F.2d 757 (2d Cir.1983) ("[T]he business judgment rule is applicable to actions undertaken within the context of bidding wars and other contests for control of a corporation.") (citing Treadway Companies v. Care Corp., 638 F.2d 357 (2d Cir.1980)).

Gorkom[18] the court invalidated the directors' acceptance of an offer recommended by the president where the board acted in only two hours and without ever having obtained an appraisal or even having seen the offer. Secondly, in Revlon, Inc. v. MacAndrews & Forbes Holdings, Inc.,[19] the Delaware court ruled that in agreeing to a lock-up arrangement with a white knight, the target company's directors breached their fiduciary duty to their shareholders.[20] However, in another case, the Delaware Supreme Court validated the use of a poison pill.[21] Not all courts agree as to the validity of poison pills.[22] The Delaware court has also permitted the use of a discriminatory issuer self tender which excluded the hostile bidder.[23] However, the Delaware court has further

---

18.   488 A.2d 858 (Del.1985).

19.   506 A.2d 173 (Del.1986). *See, e.g.,* Note, Outside Directors and the Modified Business Judgment Rule in Hostile Takeovers: A New Test for Director Liability, 62 S.Cal.L.Rev. 645 (1989).

20.   *See also* In re Application of Great Western Financial Corp., 18 Sec.Reg. & L.Rep. (BNA) 443 (Fed.Home Loan Bank Bd. March 11, 1986) (finding lock-up option to be an "unsafe and unsound practice"). *But cf.* GAF Corp. v. Union Carbide Corp., 624 F.Supp. 1016 (S.D.N.Y.1985) (no inference of self-interest where outside director acted to oppose hostile offer). *See generally* Jesse A. Finkelstein & Kevin G. Abrams, Lock–Ups in Contested Takeovers, 19 Rev.Sec. & Commodities Reg. 117 (1986); Jonathan J. Lerner & Seth M. Schwartz, Commentary—Lock–Ups and Lock–Ins, 51 Brooklyn L.Rev. 1103 (1985).

Other defensive tactics have been successfully challenged. *See* In re Anderson Clayton Shareholders' Litigation, 18 Sec.Reg. & L.Rep. (BNA) 865 (De.Ct.Ch.1986) (enjoining target's recapitalization plan).

21.   Moran v. Household International, Inc., 500 A.2d 1346 (Del.1985). *But see* Dynamics Corp. of America v. CTS Corp., 637 F.Supp. 406 (N.D.Ill.1986), *judgment affirmed* 794 F.2d 250 (7th Cir.1986), *on remand* 638 F.Supp. 802 (N.D.Ill.1986) (enjoining poison pill as unreasonable); Minstar Acquiring Corp. v. AMF Inc., 621 F.Supp. 1252 (S.D.N.Y.1985) (poison pill was invalid under New Jersey law). Poison pills are discussed in the text accompanying footnotes 42–45 *infra*.

22.   Gearhart Industries, Inc. v. Smith International, Inc., 741 F.2d 707 (5th Cir.1984) ("springing" feature of warrant was not manipulative under section 14(e)); Young v. Colgate–Palmolive Co., 790 F.2d 567 (7th Cir.1986) (challenge to poison pill dismissed for lack of personal jurisdiction over defendant directors); Harvard Indus., Inc. v. Tyson, 1986 WL 36295, [1986–87 Transfer Binder] Fed.Sec.L.Rep. (CCH) ¶ 93,064 (D.Mich.1986) (rights plan upheld under Michigan law); R.D. Smith & Co., Inc. v. Preway, Inc., 644 F.Supp. 868 (W.D.Wis.1986) (rights plan with "flip in" provision was discriminatory and violated Wisconsin law, but preliminary injunction denied); Amalgamated Sugar Co. v. NL Industries, Inc., 644 F.Supp. 1229 (S.D.N.Y.1986) (unpublished case) (poison pill was ultra vires and hence invalid under New Jersey Law) (opinion withdrawn); Dynamics Corp. of America v. CTS Corp., 635 F.Supp. 1174 (N.D.Ill.1986) (defendants met preliminary burden of proof that a poison pill shareholder rights plan was adopted in good faith); Newell Co. v. William E. Wright Co., 500 A.2d 974 (Del.Ch.1985) (denying preliminary injunction against poison pill).

See generally Krishnan Chittur, Wall Street's Teddy Bear: The "Poison Pill" as a Takeover Defense, 11 J.Corp.L. 25 (1985); Suzanne S. Dawson, Robert J. Pence & David S. Stone, Poison Pill Defensive Measures, 42 Bus.Law. 423 (1987); Robert A. Helman & James A. Junewicz, A Fresh Look at Poison Pills, 42 Bus.Law. 771 (1987); Stock Prices Are Decreased by Poison Pills in Some Cases, SEC Staff Says, 18 Sec.Reg. & L.Rep. (BNA) 348 (March 14, 1986).

Cf. Crown Zellerbach Corp. v. Goldsmith, 609 F.Supp. 187 (S.D.N.Y.1985) (fact that additional purchases by hostile purchaser would trigger poison pill did not warrant injunction against future purchases).

23.   Unocal Corp. v. Mesa Petroleum Co., 493 A.2d 946 (Del.1985). *See also* Unocal Corp. v. Pickens, 608 F.Supp. 1081 (C.D.Cal.1985). The SEC has since adopted rules prohibiting exclusionary tender offers both by issuers and third parties. 17 C.F.R.

held that a target company's directors' funding an ESOP after control had passed to another company was not protected by the business judgment rule.[24] The Delaware court has severely limited management entrenchment tactics by identifying target management's primary duty once a company is for sale, as "maximization of the company's value at a sale for the stockholders' benefit."[25] More recent decisions have somewhat clouded the issue of when this duty to maximize value is triggered.[26]

A by-product of the creation of state law remedies against such tactics is that failure to disclose facts in the course of a transaction that would have alerted shareholders of such a remedy may well give rise to an action for material misrepresentation under Rule 10b–5 or section 14(e).[27] However, a breach of a state law fiduciary duty will not be actionable under the federal securities laws.[28]

Other common alternatives to finding a "white knight" as a defensive tactic include: the issuance of additional shares to dilute any holdings of the would-be acquiring company;[29] stock repurchase pro-

§§ 240.13e–4(f)(8)(i), 240.14d–10(a)(1). These rules may be subject to challenge in light of the Supreme Court's ruling that the thrust of the Williams Act's antifraud provisions is deception, and that manipulative conduct alone will not suffice. *See* Schreiber v. Burlington Northern, Inc., 472 U.S. 1, 105 S.Ct. 2458, 86 L.Ed.2d 1 (1985) which is discussed in § 11.15 *supra*. The "all holders" rules are discussed in § 11.14 *supra*.

24. Frantz Mfg. Co. v. EAC Industries, Inc., 501 A.2d 401 (Del.1985). *See also* AC Acquisitions Corp. v. Anderson, Clayton & Co., 519 A.2d 103 (Del.Ch.1986) (opinion withdrawn). *But see* Danaher Corp. v. Chicago Pneumatic Tool Co., 633 F.Supp. 1066 (S.D.N.Y.1986) (management sustained burden of establishing fairness of ESOP; preliminary injunction denied both under state law and under the Williams Act).

25. Revlon, Inc. v. MacAndrews & Forbes Holdings, Inc., 506 A.2d 173, 182 (Del.1985). *Accord* Plaza Securities Co. v. Fruehauf Corp., 643 F.Supp. 1535, 1543 (E.D.Mich.1986) (applying Michigan law).

26. *See, e.g.,* Paramount Communications, Inc. v. Time Inc., 571 A.2d 1140 (Del.1989) (*Revlon* auction duty not triggered where target company had preexisting business plan involving corporate combination with another company). *See also, e.g.,* Arnold v. Society for Savings Bancorp., 1993 WL 526781, [1993–1994 Transfer Binder] Fed. Sec. L. Rep. (CCH) ¶ 98,006 (Del.Ch.1993) (*Revlon* duty did not apply where merger was part of long-term business plan).

However, in Paramount Communications, Inc. v. QVC Network, Inc., 637 A.2d 34 (Del.1994), *affirming* 635 A.2d 1245 (Del.Ch.1993) the Court indicated that the *Revlon* duty to maximize value is triggered whenever the target's shares are acquired by a single entity or person or by a cohesive group and the new shareholder is in the position to deny preexisting shareholders of their continuing interest in the corporation.

See, e.g., Robert A. Ragazzo, Unifying the Law of Hostile Takeovers: Bridging the *Unocal/Revlon* Gap, 35 Ariz. L. Rev. 989 (1993).

27. *See* § 13.11 *infra*. *But cf.* In re United States Shoe Corp. Litigation, 718 F.Supp. 643 (S.D.Ohio 1989) (failure to disclose allegedly improper entrenchment motive was not actionable).

28. *E.g.,* In re United States Shoe Corp. Litigation, 718 F.Supp. 643 (S.D.Ohio 1989). *See* § 13.11 *infra*.

29. *See, e.g.,* Unilever Acquisition Corp. v. Richardson–Vicks, Inc., 618 F.Supp. 407 (S.D.N.Y.1985) (issuing preliminary injunction against dividend in preferred stock that would dilute the offeror's control); Asarco, Inc. v. Court, 611 F.Supp. 468 (D.N.J.1985) (invalidating blank check preferred stock under New Jersey law). Applied Digital Data Systems v. Milgo Electronic, 425 F.Supp. 1145 (S.D.N.Y.1977), *supplemented* 425 F.Supp. 1163 (S.D.N.Y.1977) (target company attempted to effect sale of authorized and unissued

grams to strengthen the control of "inside" or "friendly" shareholders;[30] restrictive by-law and charter provisions, (sometimes referred to as "porcupine provisions" or "shark repellent") such as extraordinarily high voting requirements for mergers with other corporations;[31] staggering of directors' terms of office which necessarily increases the time it will take to effect a turnover in management;[32] obligating the corporation to long-term salary or bonus contracts (known as "golden parachutes" or "silver wheel chairs") for top management in the event of a change in control;[33] and using state tender offer statutes to introduce additional delays into the tender offer process.[34]   Golden parachutes generally take the form of contractual rights to high severance payments.   Large parachute payments have been referred to as platinum parachutes, while plans that cover lower-level employees are known as tin parachutes.   One supposed justification of the golden parachute is that it takes away any conflict of interest when management evaluates a third party offer since the incentive of managers' retaining their jobs by opposing the offer is counterbalanced by the high severance payments they would receive if the offer is successful.[35]   In addition to legislation at one time pending in Congress that would have curbed such defensive tactics, 1984 amendments to the tax code provide that excessive parachute payments are not deductible to the payor corporation and further

---

shares amounting to 15.5% of common stock to "friendly" third corporation in order to defeat offeror's proposed exchange offer).

30. *See, e.g.,* LTV v. Grumman Corp., 526 F.Supp. 106 (E.D.N.Y.1981) (corporation and pension plan made market purchases of more than 1 million shares of corporation's own stock in a single day to prevent tender offeror from acquiring majority control). *See generally* Charles M. Nathan & Marilyn Sobel, Corporate Stock Repurchases in the Context of Unsolicited Takeover Bids, 35 Bus.Law. 1545 (1980).

31. *See, e.g.,* Young v. Valhi, Inc., 382 A.2d 1372 (Del.Ch.1978) (charter provision required approval of 80 percent of the issued and outstanding common shares in order to accomplish a merger with any offeror holding at least 5 percent of the corporation's stock).

32. *See* Stephen A. Hochman & Oscar D. Folger, Deflecting Takeovers: Charter and By-law Techniques, 34 Bus.Law. 537, 538 (1979). However, the continued effectiveness of the classified board as a deterrent requires ancillary charter provisions such as a provision prohibiting removal except for certain narrowly defined causes. *See* Lewis S. Black, Jr. & Craig B. Smith, Antitakeover Charter Provisions: Defending Self–Help for Takeover Targets, 36 Wash. & Lee L.Rev. 699, 715–16 (1979).

33. *See* Robert A. Prentice, Target Board Abuse, *supra* note 15, at 341; Note, Golden Parachutes: Executive Employment Contracts, 40 Wash. & Lee L.Rev. 1117 (1983).

The SEC proposed legislation that would have banned the creation of golden parachutes once a tender offer has been threatened. *See* 16 Sec.Reg. & L.Rep. (BNA) 793 (May 11, 1984). The proposed legislation would also have prohibited the creation of "blank check" preferred stock as a "poison pill" as well as "greenmail" by prohibiting the target from paying a premium to purchase its shares from any person owning more than 3% of its stock unless it has been so held for more than three years. *Id.*

34. State tender offer statutes are discussed in § 11.21 *infra*. Their constitutionality is discussed in § 11.22 *infra*.

35. *See generally* Note, Platinum Parachutes: Who's Protecting the Shareholder, 14 Hofstra L.Rev. 653 (1986); Note, Golden Parachutes and the Business Judgment Rule: Toward a Proper Standard of Review, 94 Yale L.J. 909 (1985); Note, Protecting Shareholders Against Partial and Two–Tiered Takeovers: The "Poison Pill" Preferred, 97 Harv. L.Rev. 1964 (1984).

an excise tax is imposed upon the recipient.[36] Assuming there is full
disclosure, golden parachute arrangements do not present problems
under the federal securities laws.[37] A similar move is for the target
company to reincorporate in a state with more onerous antitakeover
laws.[38] Other defensive and preventive tactics used in recent years
include: the acquisition of another business by the target company,
creating a potential antitrust threat to impending tender offers;[39] the
purchase of a radio station or some other heavily regulated business to
tie up the takeover attempt in administrative proceedings which may be
needed to approve any change of ownership in the regulated business;[40]
and the "Pac–Man" defense, where the target company makes a tender
offer for control of the original tender offeror.[41]

Defensive tactics continue to proliferate.[42] Another recent defensive
tactic is the "poison pill," which is a conditional stock right that is
triggered by a hostile takeover and makes the takeover prohibitively
expensive.[43] The poison pill is a variation of the scorched earth[44] defense
whereby the target company prepares itself for self-destruction in the
event of a hostile takeover. Another variation on the poison pill is the
so-called "flipover" provisions in corporate charters which prohibit combinations with persons who have acquired more than a stated percentage
of the issuer's stock without prior approval of the target company's
directors. Under such flipover provisions, the shareholders receive
rights in the acquiring company's shares for any takeover occurring

36. I.R.C. §§ 280G(b), (c), 4999. *See* Comment, Golden Parachutes and Draconian
Measures Aimed at Control: Is Internal Revenue Code Section 280G the Proper Regulatory
Mode of Shareholder Protection?, 54 U.Cin.L.Rev. 1293 (1986).

37. *See* Brill v. Burlington Northern, Inc., 590 F.Supp. 893 (D.Del.1984). There have
been some attempts to amend the federal law to prohibit parachute arrangements.

38. One limitation on the efficacy of state law in thwarting a tender offer is the line of
cases striking down many of those statutes in the face of federal preemption or the
Constitution's commerce clause. *E.g.* Edgar v. MITE Corp., 457 U.S. 624, 102 S.Ct. 2629,
73 L.Ed.2d 269 (1982); § 11.22 *infra.*

39. *See* Consolidated Gold Fields PLC v. Minorco; S.A., 871 F.2d 252 (2d Cir.1989)
(affirming the issuance of a preliminary injunction against tender offer on antitrust
grounds); Panter v. Marshall Field & Co., 646 F.2d 271, 290–91 (7th Cir. 1981), *cert.
denied* 454 U.S. 1092, 102 S.Ct. 658, 70 L.Ed.2d 631 (1981) (target department store chain
acquired stores in areas where tender offeror national retail chain was already operating).
See text accompanying footnotes 63–66 *infra.*

40. *See* Hochman & Folger, *supra* footnote 32, at 558.

41. *See* Martin Marietta Corp. v. Bendix Corp., 549 F.Supp. 623 (D.Md.1982). For a
fairly exhaustive list of defenses *see* Prentice, Target Board Abuse, *supra* footnote 15, at
337–43 and the authorities in footnotes 14–16 *supra.*

42. *See* More Companies Than Ever Seeking Anti–Takeover Amendments, Study Says,
17 Sec.Reg. & L.Rep. (BNA) 1960 (Nov. 8, 1985). *See also* Institutional Investor Group
Issues Directory of Firms' Shark Repellants, 17 Sec.Reg. & L.Rep. (BNA) 335 (Feb. 22,
1985). *Cf.* La Roche v. Vermont Federal Bank, FSB, [1986 Transfer Binder] Fed.Sec.
L.Rep. (CCH) ¶ 93,863 (D.Vt.1986) (bank charter requirement that any tender offer be
submitted to directors prior to offer held not in violation of Williams Act).

43. *See* cases cited in footnotes 21 and 22 *supra.*

44. *See* Minstar Acquiring Corp. v. AMF, Inc., 621 F.Supp. 1252 (S.D.N.Y.1985)
(scorched earth tactics raised a strong presumption that directors were acting only to
enrich themselves).

within a predetermined period.[45] Another device which has survived judicial challenge,[46] but is now prohibited by an SEC rule[47] is the discriminatory issuer self-tender that excludes the hostile bidder from the offer's terms. Greenmail, which consists of target's management buying back the hostile bidder's shares at a premium, has also been a widely used tactic.[48] A common charter amendment has been the so-called "fair price" amendment under which all shareholders are guaranteed the best price paid to any one shareholder.[49] Many states have adopted fair price statutes which are to the same effect.[50] Still another approach has been the issuance of preferred shares with extraordinary voting power. Such unequal voting rights have been held to violate state law[51] and also violate the New York Stock Exchange's one share/one vote rule, the enforcement of which was suspended pending SEC reconsideration of the rule.[52] The SEC subsequently adopted a uniform rule limiting dual class voting.[53] However, that rule was ruled an invalid exercise of the Commission's rulemaking authority.[54] Accordingly, such rules are now dependent on the exchanges and NASD which have since agreed upon a uniform voting rights rule.

---

45. The new New York takeover law has a similar provision barring takeovers for five years where the acquiring company has acquired twenty percent of the target company's stock without prior target director approval. N.Y.Bus.Corp.L. § 912.

46. Unocal Corp. v. Mesa Petroleum Co., 493 A.2d 946 (Del.1985).

47. 17 C.F.R. §§ 240.13e–4(f)(8)(i), 240.14d–10(a)(1). See Sec.Exch.Act Rel. No. 34–23421 (July 11, 1986); Exch.Act Rels. No. 34–22198–99, [1984–85 Transfer Binder] Fed.Sec.L.Rep. (CCH) ¶¶ 83,797–98 (July 1, 1985), proposing amendments to Rule 13e–4, and Rule 14–10(a)(1) (third party offers).

48. E.g. Fry v. Trump, 681 F.Supp. 252 (D.N.J.1988) (receipt of greenmail is not a breach of fiduciary duty; but upholding securities claims based on statements that defendant was not a greenmailer); Cheff v. Mathes, 41 Del.Ch. 494, 199 A.2d 548 (1964) (payment of greenmail held not a breach of fiduciary duty). See Jonathan R. Macey & Fred S. McChesney, A Theoretical Analysis of Corporate Greenmail, 95 Yale L.J. 13 (1985) (taking the surprising position that greenmail provides a benefit to the marketplace); Note, Greenmail: Targeted Stock Repurchases and the Management—Entrenchment Hypothesis, 98 Harv.L.Rev. 1045 (1985); Note, Greenmailing Corporate Shareholders: Is There a Solution?, 37 U.Fla.L.Rev. 389 (1985).

49. Fair price amendments are in response to front end loaded, two tier tender offers. See § 11.10 supra. See generally Study Shows Fair Price Amendments Have Little Effect on Stock Value, 17 Sec.Reg. & L.Rep. (BNA) 1829 (Oct. 18, 1985). The concept behind fair price amendments has been incorporated into some states' second generation takeover legislation. See §§ 11.21–.22 infra; Thomas L. Hazen, State Antitakeover Legislation–The Second and Third Generations, 23 Wake Forest U.L.Rev. 77 (1988). Also, the SEC has adopted more limited best price rules for both issuer and third party tender offers. See 17 C.F.R. §§ 240.13e–4(f)(8)–(11), 240.14d–10 which are discussed in § 11.14 supra.

50. E.g. Md.Corps. & Ass'ns Code §§ 3–602, 3–603. See § 11.21 infra.

51. See Asarco, Inc. v. Court, 611 F.Supp. 468 (D.N.J.1985). See also Packer v. Yampol, 1986 WL 4748 (Del.Ch.1986) (unpublished case).

52. N.Y.S.E. Listed Company Manual § 313.00(C). See NYSE "Reluctantly" Adopts Dual Share Classification; SEC Approval Needed, 18 Sec.Reg. & L.Rep. (BNA) 998 (July 11, 1986); § 11.1 supra.

53. 17 C.F.R. § 240.19c–4. See Ingersoll, SEC Adopts Plan to Bar Listing of Firms That Reduce or Abolish Voting Rights, Wall St.J. p. 6 (June 12, 1987). See § 11.1 supra.

54. Business Roundtable v. SEC, 905 F.2d 406 (D.C.Cir.1990). See § 11.1 supra.

Federal Regulation of Defensive Tactics

In addition to state law issues, which go beyond the scope of this book, but are discussed briefly above,[55] the use of defensive tactics can create a number of potential securities problems. For example, it has been held that a precipitous defensive merger, in which it appeared that the target board of directors had an "opposition at all costs" mentality, and gave no specific consideration to the merits of the tender offer, was grounds for a preliminary injunction against the combination since the merger was motivated by opposition to the tender offer rather than necessarily being in the best interest of the target company's shareholders.[56] Also, any takeover attempt which violates state law may give rise to a Rule 10b–5 claim against target management for failure to disclose the facts that would have been necessary to entitle the target company's shareholders to preventive relief in the state courts.[57] Presumably the same rationale could be used under section 14(e), provided that a cause of action does exist in the hands of the target company or one of its shareholders.[58]

The securities laws' impact on defensive tactics is a developing area. As such it is difficult to make broad generalizations, but an examination of some leading cases sheds light on the current trends in the law. The clear direction of the cases is that absent disclosure problems which may federalize the issue, the legitimacy of defensive tactics is best left to state law in the absence of express federal legislation. Section 14(e)'s prohibition of fraudulent, deceptive or manipulative acts or practices "in connection with any tender offer" was modeled after Rule 10b–5, and is intended to protect shareholders from having to make tender offer decisions with inaccurate or insufficient information.[59] Consequently, reliance upon a misrepresentation or omission of material fact is essential to a section 14(e) cause of action.[60]

Although a competing tender offeror cannot sue for damages under

55. *See* text accompanying footnotes 1–8 and footnote 16 *supra.*

56. *See* Crouse–Hinds Co. v. InterNorth, Inc., 518 F.Supp. 390, 407–08 (N.D.N.Y.1980), *reversed in part* 634 F.2d 690 (2d Cir.1980) (reversal based on failure to meet high burden of proof). In the court's view, the business judgment rule required the target board to give fair consideration to the merits of the offer. *Id.* at 411. *See also* Treadway Companies, Inc. v. Care Corp., 638 F.2d 357 (2d Cir.1980).

57. *See* § 13.11 *infra.*

58. 15 U.S.C.A. § 78n(e). *See* §§ 11.15, 11.19 *supra.*

59. Piper v. Chris–Craft Industries, Inc., 430 U.S. 1, 35, 97 S.Ct. 926, 946, 51 L.Ed.2d 124 (1977). Section 14(e) and Rule 10b–5 are coextensive in their antifraud prohibitions. The two provisions differ only in that section 14(e) prohibits deception "in connection with any tender offer" while Rule 10b–5 prohibits deceptive statements or conduct "in connection with the purchase or sale of any security." *Compare* 15 U.S.C.A. § 78n(e) *with* 17 C.F.R. § 240.10b–5.

60. *E.g.* Staffin v. Greenberg, 672 F.2d 1196 (3d Cir.1982) (failure to disclose preliminary merger negotiations was not a material omission). *See also, e.g.,* Chris–Craft Industries, Inc. v. Piper Aircraft Corp., 480 F.2d 341, 373 (2d Cir.1973), *cert. denied* 414 U.S. 910, 94 S.Ct. 231, 38 L.Ed.2d 148 (1973). Materiality is discussed in § 11.4 *supra,* § 13.5 *infra.*

section 14(e),[61] it may be able to seek an injunction against the target company's defensive tactics.[62] In Panter v. Marshall Field & Co.,[63] the target, Marshall Field & Company, acquired stores which were in direct competition with the tender offeror, a national retail chain operator. As a result of the acquisitions and the filing of an antitrust suit by Marshall Field, the tender offer was withdrawn before the target's shareholders had been notified of its existence. The shareholders subsequently brought suit alleging violations of both section 14(e) and Rule 10b–5. Plaintiffs' section 14(e) claim alleged that they had been deprived of the opportunity to tender their shares to the tender offeror, and deceived as to the attractiveness of selling their shares in the favorable market following the announcement of the takeover attempt. The damages sought amounted to the differences between the price offered for the shares and the price to which the stock had declined after the offer was withdrawn. The Seventh Circuit held that the shareholders had no cause of action under section 14(e) because they never had an opportunity to tender their shares and, consequently, could not have relied on any alleged deception in deciding not to tender.[64] In response to the argument that target management was thereby allowed to profit from its own wrong by driving off would-be offerors with misrepresentations or omissions, the court replied that the wrongful acts complained of (acquisitions of competing stores) which had caused the withdrawal of the tender offer were, at most, a breach of the defendant directors' fiduciary duty, and could not provide the basis for a federal securities claim.[65] The court applied the same rationale to the Rule 10b–5 claim in which the shareholders alleged that Marshall Field's directors had a secret prearranged plan of resistance to tender offers, designed to insure against any changes in control.[66]

In Mobil Corp. v. Marathon Oil Co.,[67] the Sixth Circuit held that

61. Piper v. Chris–Craft Industries, Inc., 430 U.S. 1, 97 S.Ct. 926, 51 L.Ed.2d 124 (1977).

62. *E.g.* Mobil Corp. v. Marathon Oil Co., 669 F.2d 366 (6th Cir.1981). *See* § 11.19 *supra* for discussion of the section 14(e) remedy.

63. 646 F.2d 271 (7th Cir. 1981), *cert. denied* 454 U.S. 1092, 102 S.Ct. 658, 70 L.Ed.2d 631 (1981).

64. *Id.* at 283–84. *See also* Lewis v. McGraw, 619 F.2d 192 (2d Cir. 1980), *cert. denied* 449 U.S. 951, 101 S.Ct. 354, 66 L.Ed.2d 214 (1980). Thus, suits by target shareholders for damages under section 14(e) appeared limited to situations where the tender offer was not withdrawn but was defeated by management's false statements. If the price of the stock later declined, shareholders could then allege that they had refrained from tendering in reliance on management's statements. *See* Richard W. Jennings & Harold Marsh, Jr., Securities Regulation Cases and Materials 837 (5th ed.1981).

65. 646 F.2d at 285, citing Santa Fe Industries, Inc. v. Green, 430 U.S. 462, 97 S.Ct. 1292, 51 L.Ed.2d 480 (1977) (breach of fiduciary duty is not "fraudulent" under Rule 10b–5, but rather is a matter for state law). *See* footnote 28 *supra* and § 13.11 *infra*.

66. According to the court, Rule 10b–5 manifests the disclosure philosophy of the 1934 Act, and therefore required proof of deception. The rule could not provide a remedy for breach of a director's state law fiduciary duty, nor could the shareholders "bootstrap" such a claim into a federal securities suit by alleging that the defendants were obligated to disclose either their culpability or their impure motives. 646 F.2d at 287–88. Rule 10b–5 is discussed in §§ 13.2–13.12 *infra*.

67. 669 F.2d 366 (6th Cir.1981).

"manipulative" conduct under section 14(e) could extend beyond deception to include interference with the tender offer market. The court acknowledged that even if the target company directors had not acted with "good faith and loyalty," as the trial judge had found, allegations of unfair treatment of minority shareholders, corporate mismanagement, or breach of fiduciary duty do not state a cause of action under section 10(b), and such conduct was not, by itself, a "manipulative device or contrivance" within the meaning of that section.[68] The court concluded, however, that certain "crown jewel"[69] and "lock-up"[70] options granted to a white knight by the target company had the effect of creating an artificial price ceiling in the tender offer market for the target's shares, and were therefore "manipulative" as that term is used in section 14(e).[71] Thus, it was unnecessary to disturb the district court's finding of good faith and loyalty on the part of the target's directors. Section 14(e)'s prohibition on manipulation by "any person" was held to cover the conduct of the white knight in demanding and procuring the options, and "[t]he Williams Act protect[s] the target shareholders regardless of who did the manipulating."[72] In its decision in Schreiber v. Burlington Northern, Inc.,[73] the Supreme Court did not reach the issue of whether manipulation could be given such a broad reading. Instead, the Court held that even if conduct is found to be manipulative, section 14(e) is not violated unless the challenged conduct is also deceptive.[74]

§ 11.21 State Regulation of Tender Offers

Prior to the adoption of the Williams Act[1] in 1968, there was virtually no specialized regulation of tender offers at either the federal or state level.[2] At least thirty-eight states had or now have statutes that

---

68. *Id.* at 373–74.

69. *See* footnote 15 *supra.*

70. *See* Note, Lock–Up Options: Toward a State Law Standard, 96 Harv.L.Rev. 1068 (1983); note 3 *supra.*

71. Mobil Corp. v. Marathon Oil Co., 669 F.2d 366, 376–77 (6th Cir.1981). "Manipulative" as that term is used in the securities acts is discussed in § 12.1 *infra. See generally* Henry I. Silberberg & David C. Pollack, Are The Courts Expanding The Meaning of "Manipulation" Under The Federal Securities Laws?, 11 Sec.Reg.L.J. 265 (1983); Elliot J. Weiss, Defensive Response to Tender Offers and the Williams Act's Prohibition Against Manipulation, 35 Vand.L.Rev. 1087 (1982).

72. 669 F.2d at 377.

73. 472 U.S. 1, 105 S.Ct. 2458, 86 L.Ed.2d 1 (1985).

74. *Id. See* § 11.15 *supra* and §§ 12.1, 13.2 *infra.*

§ 11.21

1. Pub.L.No. 90–439, 82 Stat. 454 (1968) (codified at 15 U.S.C.A. §§ 78m(d)–(e), 78n(d)–(f)). *See* §§ 11.10–11.20 *supra.*

2. To the extent that a tender offer triggered other securities provisions, there would be an impact. For example, an exchange offer would implicate the registration provisions with regard to the tender offeror's securities being issued, unless, of course, an applicable exemption could be found. Similarly, if a shareholder vote were for some reason required, the proxy regulations would be implicated.

regulate tender offers.[3] In less than twenty years, the states went through three generations of takeover statutes.[4] It may fairly be said that three generations of takeover statutes is enough.[5] Investor protection has not been the motivating factor behind these statutes. In most instances, state tender offer acts have been passed at least in part to protect incumbent management and other employees of local companies that were potential takeover targets. As a result, rather than merely supplementing the federal legislation, most state statutes impose more impediments to the takeover, thus inhibiting or at least slowing down any transaction.[6] In tender offer jargon, these acts are often referred to as "shark repellent" because of their deterrent effect.

The federal legislation embodied in the Williams Act attempts to strike a balance between the need for disclosure and investor protection on the one hand, and, on the other, the fear of eliminating too many potential tender offerors from the market place. Much of the state legislation to date has probably gone too far in the direction of deterring bidders from participating in the tender offer market. The Supreme Court has held that when the state law limitations on tender offers prove too restrictive and conflict with the basic policy of the Williams Act, these laws are invalid because they impose an unconstitutional burden on interstate commerce.[7] Other federal courts have used the preemption doctrine to invalidate state tender offer statutes under appropriate circumstances.[8] Both the preemption and commerce clause issues are discussed in the next section of this treatise.[9] The discussion that follows is designed to present an overview of existing legislation.

---

3. Alaska Stat. 45.57.010 to 45.57.120; Ark.Stat. §§ 67–1264 to 67–1264.14; Colo.Rev. Stat. §§ 11–51.5–101 to 11–51.5–108; Conn.Gen.Stat.Ann. §§ 36–456 to 36–468; 8 Del. Code § 203; Official Code Ga.Ann. §§ 14–6–1 to 30–1514; Hawaii Rev.Stat. §§ 417E–1 *et seq.*; Idaho Code §§ 30–1501 to 30–1513; Ill.–S.H.A. ch. 121½, §§ 137.51 to 137.70 (repealed); West's Ann.Ind.Code §§ 23–2–3.1–1 to 3.1–11; Iowa Code Ann. §§ 502.211 to 502.215; Kan.Stat.Ann. 17–1276 to 17–1284; Ky.Rev.Stat. 292.560 to 292.991; La.Stat. Ann.–Rev.Stat. §§ 51:1500 to 51:1512; 13 Me.Rev.Stat.Ann. §§ 801–817; Md.Code, Corps. & Ass'ns, §§ 11–901 to 11–908; Mass.Gen.Laws Ann. c. 110C, §§ 1–13; Mich.Comp. Laws Ann. §§ 451.901 to 451.917; Minn.Stat.Ann. §§ 80B.01 to 80B.13; Miss.Code, §§ 75–72– 101 to 75–72–121; Vernon's Ann.Mo.Stat. §§ 409.500 to 409.565; Neb.Rev.Stat. §§ 21– 2401 to 21–2417; Nev.Rev.Stat. 78.376 to 78.3778; N.H.Rev.Stat.Ann. 421–A:1 to 421– A:15; N.J.Stat.Ann. 49:5–1 to 49:5–19; N.Y.–McKinney's Bus.Corp.Law §§ 1600–1614; N.C.Gen.Stat. §§ 55–9–01 *et seq.*, 55–9A–01 *et seq.*; Ohio Rev.Code § 1707.041; 71 Okl. Stat.Ann. §§ 431 to 450; 70 Pa.Stat. §§ 71–85; S.C.Code, §§ 35–2–10 to 35–2–130; S.D.Codified Laws 47–32–1 to 47–32–47; Tenn.Code Ann. §§ 48–2101 to 48–2114; Vernon's Tex.Admin.Code Ann. 7, §§ 129.1–129.12, Utah Code Ann. 61–4–1 to 61–4–13; Va.Code §§ 13.1–528 to 13.1–541; Wis.Stat.Ann. 552.01 to 552.25.

4. *See* Thomas L. Hazen, State Antitakeover Legislation—The Second and Third Generations, 23 Wake Forest U.L.Rev. 77 (1988).

5. *Id.* at 80 (paraphrasing Justice Holmes).

6. The most prominent example is the imposition of waiting periods between the filing and effective date of the tender offer. *See, e.g.,* 8 Del.Code § 203(a)(1); Ohio Rev.Code § 1707.041(B)(1). *See* text accompanying footnotes 26–31 *infra.*

7. *See* Edgar v. MITE, 457 U.S. 624, 102 S.Ct. 2629, 73 L.Ed.2d 269 (1982). *See* § 11.22 *infra.*

8. *See, e.g.,* Great Western United Corp. v. Kidwell, 577 F.2d 1256 (5th Cir.1978), *vacated on other grounds sub nom.* Leroy v. Great Western United Corp., 443 U.S. 173, 99 S.Ct. 2710, 61 L.Ed.2d 464 (1979).

9. *See* § 11.22 *infra.*

Although there are some basic and general similarities between many of the state tender offer statutes, their lack of uniformity is far greater than that of state blue sky laws.[10] Accordingly, compliance with multiple statutes is a significant hurdle and can be a nightmare for the tender offeror. Because there is such a wide variance in statutory terms and provisions, the discussion that follows is merely a broad overview. The applicable statutes must be carefully scrutinized in order to master their individual regulatory provisions. In the words of one commentator, "State takeover acts are similar to snowflakes—if you think you have found identical ones, you are probably not looking closely enough." [11]

Scope of State Tender Offer Regulation

The various state statutes employ a wide range of jurisdictional provisions. It is thus possible that more than one state act will apply to any particular tender offer. The majority of the state acts base jurisdiction on the target company's incorporation within the state, or on the location within the state of the target company's principal place of business and/or substantial target company assets.[12] Some statutes take a less well-defined approach by looking to substantial contacts with the state.[13] Another variation among the states arises in the context of subject matter jurisdiction by virtue of the elusive definition of "tender offer." There is no universally accepted definition of tender offer, although most acts are brought into play by virtue of securities transactions that fall within that category under federal law. While the federal act contains no statutory definition,[14] the state statutes generally include precise but diverse statutory definitions including the number of solicited target company shareholders required before the act applies.[15] For example, many states define a qualifying transaction in terms of the number of persons solicited. Some of the state statutes raise questions analogous to those raised under the Williams Act. For example, one state

---

10. *See* chapter 8 *supra.*

11. Note, State Regulation of Tender Offers, 3 J.Corp.Law 603, 603 (1982) (footnote omitted).

12. *See, e.g.,* Conn.Gen.Stat.Ann. § 36–457(a); Ohio Rev.Code § 1707.041(A)(1); S.D.Codified Laws Ann. 47–32–3.

13. *See, e.g.,* LSA–Rev.Stat. 51:1500.1(13).

14. *See, e.g.,* Note, The Elusive Definition of a Tender Offer, 7 J.Corp.L. 503 (1982). The meaning of tender offer under the Williams Act is discussed in § 11.13 *supra.*

15. *See, e.g.,* N.H.Rev.Stat.Ann. 421–A:2(VI)(a) (" 'Takeover bid' does not include: (3) Any * * * offer to acquire an equity security, or the acquisition of such equity security pursuant to such offer * * * from not more than 25 persons * * * "); S.D.Codified Laws 47–32–2 (" 'Take-over offer,' * * * does not include an offer or acquisition of any equity security of a target company pursuant to: (3) Any offer * * * made to not more than ten persons in this state during any period of twelve consecutive months * * * "); Tenn.Code Ann. § 48–2102(10) (" 'Takeover offer' * * * does not include an offer to acquire or the acquisition of any equity security of an offeree company pursuant to: (C) An offer made in isolated transactions * * * to not more than fifteen (15) persons in this state during any twelve (12) consecutive months;") .

court has held that a series of open market purchases does not constitute a tender offer.[16]

First Generation Tender Offer Statutes

Major variations among the state tender offer statutes are found in the qualification requirements. Following the pattern of the state blue sky laws, many of the state tender offer statutes go beyond the disclosure philosophy of the Williams Act by giving the state administrator the power to review the merits of the tender offer[17] or the adequacy of the disclosure.[18] The state administrator is often empowered to hold hearings which may be initiated by the administrator,[19] the target company,[20] or a certain percentage of the target company's shareholders.[21] Thus, even where merit analysis is not permitted, the tender offer could be tied up in administrative hearings. The procedures vary among the statutes as to who may or must appear at such hearings and the extent of allowable pre-hearing discovery.[22] Under most statutes, administrative orders with respect to tender offers are self-executing,[23] but under some acts the administrator must first seek judicial enforcement.[24] The cost and delay involved in these enforcement procedures led many states to employ a so-called "fiduciary approach" to review. Under this approach the administrator may waive compliance with the qualification requirements if the target company's management endorses the tender offer.[25]

Even state regulation that is limited to full disclosure, as opposed to a merit or substantive review of the terms of the offer, may impose burdens beyond those created by the federal legislation. The most prominent example is the commonly found state-imposed waiting period of ten,[26] twenty,[27] or thirty days[28] between the filing of the tender offer

16. Sheffield v. Consolidated Foods Corp., 302 N.C. 403, 276 S.E.2d 422 (1981).

17. *See, e.g.,* N.J.Stat.Ann. 49:5–4(a); S.C.Code § 35–2–70(1). *See also* Kennecott Corp. v. Smith, 507 F.Supp. 1206 (D.N.J.1981) (New Jersey Takeover Law frustrates the purpose of the Williams Act by substituting Bureau Chief's view of the offer for the informed judgment of shareholders). *But cf.* North Star International v. Arizona Corporation Commission, 720 F.2d 578 (9th Cir.1983) (Arizona blue sky law's provision for merit review of interstate securities offering is not preempted by the Securities Act of 1933).

18. *E.g.* LSA–Rev.Stat. 51:1501(E); 70 Pa.Stat. § 74(d).

19. *E.g.* Vernon's Ann.Mo.Stat. § 409.530.

20. *E.g.* 70 Pa.Stat. § 74(d).

21. *E.g.* Conn.Gen.Stat.Ann. § 36–460(a) (aggregate owners of ten percent of the outstanding equity securities of the class involved in the tender offer may petition the commissioner to schedule a hearing).

22. *See, e.g.,* LSA–Rev.Stat. 51:1501(E) ("The commissioner shall at all times freely order discovery and interrogatories and depositions of persons familiar with the facts relating to the parties and the transactions.   * * * ").

23. *E.g.,* Neb.Rev.Stat. § 21–2406; N.J.Stat.Ann. 49.5–12(a); 71 Okl.Stat. § 437; S.C.Code § 35–2–70(2).

24. *See* Vernon's Ann.Mo.Stat. § 409.535; Wis.Stat.Ann. 552.17.

25. *See, e.g.,* Idaho Code § 30–1501(5)(e); Ohio Rev.Code § 1707.041(A)(1)(d); 71 Okl.Stat. § 414(1)(d).

26. *E.g.* Conn.Gen.Stat.Ann. § 36–460.

27. *E.g.* 8 Del.Code § 203(a)(1); 70 Pa.Stat. § 74(a).

28. *E.g.* N.C.Gen.Stat. § 78B–4(a).

and the date on which it becomes effective. Not only are such waiting periods not a part of the federal statute, but in 1979 the SEC, by promulgating Rule 14d–2(b),[29] purported to preempt all such waiting periods.[30] Although the preemptive effect of Rule 14d–2(b) has not specifically been decided, the Supreme Court has held that waiting periods may contribute to a state statute's invalidity as an undue burden on interstate commerce.[31]

The filing requirements imposed by the various state tender offer statutes generally require more detailed disclosures than the federal Williams Act.[32] These additional disclosures have been challenged as not providing relevant information to the target's shareholders.[33] Nevertheless, the courts have tended to view the disclosure requirements as enhancing and thus not in conflict with the federal scheme.[34]

All of the first generation state takeover acts contain statutory exemptions. One frequent exemption is based upon the absence of a change in control of the target company's management.[35] Friendly takeovers which are supported by the target company management are also commonly exempted,[36] in contrast to the Williams Act which applies with equal force to hostile as well as to friendly tender offers.[37] This is another way in which state acts are geared to support local management. The fact that management supports a tender offer does not assure fair treatment of the target's shareholders, nor does it assure full disclosure.[38] Other state law exemptions include exchange offers,[39] normal

---

29. 17 C.F.R. § 240.14d–2(b).

30. *See* Sec.Act Rel.No. 33–6158 (SEC Nov. 29, 1979) ("These requirements of the state statutes [typically * * * publication of or a public filing which includes the material terms of the tender offer prior to the time the offer may be commenced] will trigger the commencement of the tender offer under Rule 14d–2(b) despite the fact that the state statutes do not permit the offer to commence until the conclusion of any applicable waiting period and hearing process") (footnote omitted).

31. Edgar v. MITE Corp., 457 U.S. 624, 102 S.Ct. 2629, 73 L.Ed.2d 269 (1982). *See* § 11.22 *infra.*

32. *See, e.g.,* Ohio Rev.Code § 1707.041(B)(3)(d) (planned changes in employment policies); 70 Pa.Stat. § 75(4) (probable effect of takeover on labor relations). *See generally,* Edward R. Aranow, Herbert A. Einhorn & George Berlstein, Developments in Tender Offers for Corporate Control 219 (1977).

33. Donald C. Langevoort, State Tender–Offer Legislation: Interests, Effects, and Political Competency, 62 Cornell L.Rev. 213, 230 (1977).

34. *See, e.g.,* Great Western United Corp. v. Kidwell, 577 F.2d 1256 (5th Cir.1978), *vacated on other grounds sub nom.* Leroy v. Great Western United Corp., 443 U.S. 173, 99 S.Ct. 2710, 61 L.Ed.2d 464 (1979).

35. *E.g.* Colo.Rev.Stat. 11–51.5–102(5)(a) (exempting offers for less than two percent of a class of the target's stock).

36. *E.g.* Ohio Rev.Code § 1707.041(A)(1)(d); Va.Code § 13.1–529(b)(5) (exemption where two-thirds of the target company's shares consent). Another variation has been the "fiduciary approach" to administrative review.

37. *E.g.* Smallwood v. Pearl Brewing Co., 489 F.2d 579 (5th Cir.1974), *cert. denied* 419 U.S. 873, 95 S.Ct. 134, 42 L.Ed.2d 113 (1974). *See* § 11.10 *supra.*

38. *See, e.g.,* Smallwood v. Pearl Brewing Co., 489 F.2d 579, 598 (5th Cir.1974), *cert. denied* 419 U.S. 873, 95 S.Ct. 134, 42 L.Ed.2d 113 (1974) ("if there is danger that an investor may be misled by management of the target company or the tender offeror in a

---

39. See note 39 on page 675.

brokerage transactions,[40] and issuer repurchases of its own shares.[41] As is the case with the other provisions of the state acts, there is no uniformity among the states as to exemptions. The possibility that a tender offer may be covered by some acts but not others reinforces the necessity of careful consultation of all state tender offer statutes that may be applicable.

The Doubtful Continued Vitality of First Generation State Tender Offer Statutes

As noted at the outset of this section, in some instances more than one state's tender offer act may purport to apply to any particular tender offer. The lack of uniformity among state statutes can create considerable problems for the tender offeror in addition to the burden of compliance with the substantive requirements of each state's act. As a result of challenges, several state tender offer statutes have been declared unconstitutional.[42] Thus, despite attempts to retain some state control by amending offensive provisions, the first generation of state tender offer statutes have been deprived of much of their intended effectiveness as takeover deterrents.

Second Generation Takeover Statutes

Following the Supreme Court's ruling in Edgar v. MITE Corp.,[43] a number of states enacted "second generation" takeover statutes that were designed to overcome the constitutional infirmities of the Illinois statute that was struck down in *MITE*. The basic thrust of these statutes is to regulate tender offers through state law rules relating to corporate governance rather than through state securities laws and administrative regulations.[44] The basic approach of such statutes is substantive regulation of tender offers. Ohio was the first state to adopt

---

situation where these two are hostile, there is not reason to assume that the danger will be lessened when both are on the same side of the fence. Indeed investors would seem to require greater protection in this situation").

39. S.D.Codified Laws 47–32–2(2).

40. 8 Del.Code § 203(c)(3)(b). Compare section 4(4) of the 1933 Act which provides a registration exemption for broker transactions. 15 U.S.C.A. § 77d(4), discussed in § 4.23 *supra.*

41. S.D.Codified Laws 47–32–2(6). Rather than exempting such transactions, the federal act has special rules for tender offers by the issuer for its own stock. 15 U.S.C.A. § 78n(d)(8)(B); 17 C.F.R. § 240.14d–1(b)(1); § 11.17 *supra.*

42. *See, e.g.,* Kennecott Corp. v. Smith, 507 F.Supp. 1206 (D.N.J.1981) (New Jersey takeover statute preempted by Williams Act).

43. 457 U.S. 624, 102 S.Ct. 2629, 73 L.Ed.2d 269 (1982). *See* § 11.22 *infra.*

44. *See generally,* Dennis I. Block, Nancy E. Barton & Andrea J. Roth, State Takeover Statutes: The "Second Generation", 13 Sec.Reg.L.J. 332 (1986); Stephen Bainbridge, State Takeover and Tender Offer Regulations Post–MITE: The Maryland, Ohio and Pennsylvania Attempts, 90 Dick.L.Rev. 731 (1986); Thomas L. Hazen, State Antitakeover Legislation—The Second and Third Generations, 23 Wake Forest U.L.Rev. 77 (1988); Arthur R. Pinto, The Constitution and the Market for Corporate Control: State Takeover Statutes After CTS Corp., 29 Wm. & Mary L.Rev. 699 (1988).

second generation legislation.[45] Ohio was followed by Minnesota, Missouri, and Michigan.[46] Other states have since enacted second generation statutes.[47]

The Ohio Act, which governs all forms of takeovers and is not limited to tender offers, applies to Ohio corporations having fifty or more shareholders and a principal place of business, principal offices, or substantial assets within the state.[48] The act then classifies takeover transactions by the percentage of shares owned by the acquiring person, with each control zone triggering the act's substantive requirements. Acquiring persons must deliver to the target company a disclosure statement describing the proposed acquisition. The target company's board then has ten days to call a special shareholders' meeting which must take place within fifty days. At that meeting the transaction requires approval of a majority of the disinterested shares not owned or controlled by the acquiring person or any affiliate. In addition to the disinterested majority approval requirements, the Ohio legislation enables corporations to adopt charter amendments with even higher voting requirements or, alternatively, vest the corporation's directors with the sole power to approve the transaction, thus disenfranchising the shareholders.[49] Prior to the more recent Supreme Court decision upholding the Indiana Control Share Act,[50] the Ohio statute had been struck down as violative of the Commerce Clause.[51] Similarly, Indiana's and Hawaii's versions of this control share approach to tender offer legislation had been struck down under the Supremacy Clause of the Constitution because of their conflict with the Williams Act.[52] But, as noted above, the Supreme Court has since upheld the Indiana Control Share Act.[53] Other states have adopted control share statutes.[54]

---

45. Ohio Rev.Code § 1701.83.2. *See* Gary P. Kreider, Fortress Without Foundation? Ohio Takeover Act II, 52 U. Cin.L.Rev. 108 (1983); Note, Has Ohio Avoided the Wake of MITE? An Analysis of the Constitutionality of the Ohio Control Share Acquisition Act, 46 Ohio St.L.J. 203 (1985).

46. Minn.Stat.Ann. §§ 302A.011, 302A.671; Vernon's Ann.Mo.Stat. §§ 351.015, 351.407.

47. For example, Idaho, New York, and Oklahoma have enacted various forms of second generation statutes. Idaho Code §§ 30–1501–30–1510; Okl.Stats.Ann.tit. 71 §§ 451–462; N.Y.Bus.Corp.L. § 902. *See* footnotes 54–57 *infra.*

48. Ohio Rev.Code § 1701.83.1.

49. *Id.* §§ 1701.52, 1701.59.

50. CTS Corp. v. Dynamics Corp. of America, 481 U.S. 69, 107 S.Ct. 1637, 95 L.Ed.2d 67 (1987).

51. Fleet Aerospace Corp. v. Holderman, 796 F.2d 135 (6th Cir.1986), *vacated* 481 U.S. 1026, 107 S.Ct. 1949, 95 L.Ed.2d 521 (1987).

52. Dynamics Corp. of America v. CTS Corp., 794 F.2d 250 (7th Cir.1986), *on remand* 638 F.Supp. 802 (N.D.Ill.1986), *reversed* 481 U.S. 69, 107 S.Ct. 1637, 95 L.Ed.2d 67 (1987); Terry v. Yamashita, 643 F.Supp. 161 (D.Hawaii 1986).

53. CTS Corp. v. Dynamics Corp. of America, 481 U.S. 69, 107 S.Ct. 1637, 95 L.Ed.2d 67 (1987). *See* § 11.22 *infra.*

54. *E.g.* Haw.Rev.Stat. §§ 416–171, 172; West's Ann.Ind.Code § 23–1–42(1)–(11) (Supp.1986); Minn.Stat.Ann. §§ 302A.011, 302A.671 (1987); Vernon's Ann.Mo.Stat. §§ 351.015, 351.407; N.C.Gen.Stat. §§ 55–9A–01 *et seq.* (1987); Ohio Rev.Code § 1701.83.2 (Vernon Supp.1987); Utah Code Ann.1987, § 64.41; Wis.Stat.Ann. § 180.25(9) (West Supp.1986).

In contrast to the Ohio approach, Maryland takes a more structural approach in regulating share acquisitions. The Maryland statute requires any takeover be approved by at least eighty percent of the shares and two-thirds of the disinterested shares unless all shareholders receive the "best price" paid by the acquiring person within a two year period.[55] The best price approach, patterned after fair price charter amendments adopted by many corporations in other states as a defensive anticipatory tactic, is to fend off two tiered offers. The Maryland Act excludes "friendly" offers from its coverage. A number of states have adopted fair price statutes, some of which vary the terms of the Maryland Act.[56]

The New York, Tennessee, Minnesota, Oklahoma, Utah, and Idaho second generation statutes basically take a disclosure approach.[57] The chief feature of the disclosure approach is that many of the statutes include open market purchases and require disclosure in such a way as to close the ten day window that currently exists under section 13(d) of the Williams Act.[58]

Ohio, Indiana, Maine, and Pennsylvania have expanded the factors directors may consider in opposing takeovers.[59] At least 23 states have adopted similar "constituency" or "stakeholder" statutes which permit management to consider interests other than those of the shareholders in making decisions.[60] Target management in these states thus may rely on interests other than shareholder wealth maximization as a basis for resisting a takeover. These statutes generally make it clear that although management may consider other interests, it does not have to. Still another approach taken in some of the second generation statutes is

See also, e.g., Business Aviation of South Dakota, Inc. v. Medivest, Inc., 882 P.2d 662 (Utah 1994) (new shares were held subject to Utah's control share act).

55. Md. Corp's & Ass'ns Code §§ 3–602, 3–603.

56. *E.g.* Conn.Gen.Stat.Ann. §§ 33–374a to 33–374c (West Supp.1986).

57. Idaho Code § 30–1502 *et seq.* (Supp.1986); Minn.Stat.Ann. § 80B.01 *et seq.* (West 1986); N.Y.–McKinney's Bus.Corp.Law §§ 1601–1613 (1986); Okl.Stat.Ann. 71 § 451 (1986); Utah Code Ann. 1986, § 16–10–76.5.

58. *See* § 11.11 *supra. See also* Cardiff Acquisitions, Inc. v. Hatch, 751 F.2d 906 (8th Cir.1984), *appeal after remand* 751 F.2d 917 (8th Cir.1984) (upholding the disclosure provisions of the Minnesota statute). *But see* APL Limited Partnership v. Van Dusen Air, Inc., 622 F.Supp. 1216 (D.Minn.1985).

59. West's Ann.Ind.Code § 23–1–35–1(d) (Burns Supp.1986); 13–A Me.Rev.Stat.Ann. § 716 (Supp.1986); Ohio Rev.Code § 1701.59 (Baldwin Supp.1986); 42 Pa.Stat. § 8363 (Purdon Supp.1986). A recent SEC study found that stock prices of 36 Ohio companies declined after the adoption of the 1986 amendments. 19 Sec.Reg. & L.Rep. (BNA) 741 (May 22, 1987); Fed.Sec.L.Rep. (CCH) Report Bull. no. 1233 (May 27, 1987).

60. *See* De Facto Federal Anti–Bidder Stance Exists Through State Laws, IRRC Says, 21 Sec.Reg. & L.Rep. (BNA) 1501 (Oct. 6, 1989). For representative statutes, *see* West's Ann.Cal.Corp.Code § 309 (West 1987); Ind.Code Ann. § 23–1–29.2 (Burns 1987). 9 Me.Rev.Stat.Ann. tit. 13–A, § 716 (Supp.1985); Mass.Gen.L.A. c. 172, § 13 (1987) (as amended by 1989 Mass.Adv.Legis.Serv. Ch. 242 § 15 (Law. Co-op)); Minn.Stat.Ann. § 302A.251 (West Supp.1987); Vernon's Ann.Mo.Stat. § 351.347 (Vernon Supp.1988); Neb.Rev.Stat. § 21–2732 (Supp.1988); N.J.Stat.Ann. § 14A:10A–2 (West 1986); N.Y.– McKinney's Bus.Corp.Law § 717(b) (as amended by 1989 N.Y.Laws Ch. 228); Tenn.Code Ann. § 48–35–202 (1988); Wisc.Stat.Ann. 180.305 (West Supp.1988). *See generally,* Roberta Karmel, The Duty of Directors to Non–Shareholder Constituencies in Control Transactions—A Comparison of U.S. and U.K. Law, 21 Wake Forest L.Rev. 61, 66–68 (1990).

to give dissenters' rights to a wide variety of control transactions.[61] Also, in addition to its disclosure approach, the New York statute prohibits greenmail to anyone owning more than ten percent of the target company's stock, and also delays any merger with a twenty percent shareholder for five years unless the twenty percent shareholder received target director approval prior to acquiring the twenty percent interest.[62] Although couched in terms of regulating a domestic corporation's internal affairs, it is far from clear whether all such statutes will withstand constitutional attack.[63]

Third Generation Takeover Statutes

Once one of the second generation state takeover statutes—the Indiana Control Share Act—had passed constitutional scrutiny in the Supreme Court,[64] the third generation of tender offer statutes began to appear.[65] One form that such statutes are taking is to apply the law of the host state to corporations incorporated elsewhere. Such statutes in regulating what has been called pseudo foreign corporations, raise additional constitutional and policy questions. North Carolina was the first state to adopt a third generation statute aimed at regulating foreign corporations[66] and a number of other states followed suit.[67] North Carolina has since repealed the extraterritorial reach of its antitakeover laws.[68]

Although the third generation statutes purporting to regulate foreign corporations are generally based upon substantial contacts within

61. *E.g.* Pa.Stat. ch. 15, § 1910.

62. N.Y.–McKinney's Bus.Corp.L. § 920.

63. *E.g.* APL Limited Partnership v. Van Dusen Air, Inc., 622 F.Supp. 1216 (D.Minn. 1985) (Minnesota statute imposes an unconstitutional burden on interstate commerce); Icahn v. Blunt, 612 F.Supp. 1400 (W.D.Mo.1985) (issuing preliminary injunction against enforcement of the Missouri statute, finding it to be an undue burden on interstate commerce); Edudata Corp. v. Scientific Computers, Inc., 599 F.Supp. 1084 (D.Minn.1984) (issuing preliminary injunction against enforcement of Minnesota act because of possible preemption). *But see* Cardiff Acquisitions, Inc. v. Hatch, 751 F.2d 906 (8th Cir.1984), *appeal after remand* 751 F.2d 917 (8th Cir.1984) (upholding Ohio statute). *See* § 11.22 *infra.*

64. CTS Corp. v. Dynamics Corp. of America, 481 U.S. 69, 107 S.Ct. 1637, 95 L.Ed.2d 67 (1987). *See* § 11.22 *infra.*

65. For yet another suggested approach for state legislation, *see* Stephen M. Bainbridge, Redirecting State Takeover Laws at Proxy Contests, 1992 Wis.L.Rev. 1071.

66. In adopting both a best price and control share statutes, North Carolina purported to apply its law not only to corporations incorporated in the state but also to corporations incorporated elsewhere having more than forty percent of its domestic assets in the state and more than four percent of its domestic employees in the state. N.C.Gen.Stat. § 55–9–01 *et seq.* ("Shareholder Protection Act"); *Id.* § 55–9A–01 *et seq.* ("Control Share Acquisitions Act"). It is further provided that neither the North Carolina best price nor control share statutes apply to corporations if in express conflict with the laws of the state of incorporation. *Id.*

In 1990, the North Carolina legislature eliminated the application of these acts to corporations not incorporated in the state.

67. Ariz.H.R.Res. 2002, 38th Leg., 3d Sess., 1987 Ariz.Legis.Serv. 32–45; 1987 Fla.Laws 87–257; Idaho Code § 30–5002(9); Mass.Gen.Laws Ann. ch. 110D, 110E.

68. N.C.Gen.Stat. §§ 55–9–01 *et seq.*, 55–9A–01 *et seq.*

the state, the rationale of the *CTS* decision strongly indicates that such statutes may not withstand constitutional scrutiny.[69] In fact, the Oklahoma statute was struck down by a federal district court on the grounds that it was unconstitutional to the extent that it applied to non-Oklahoma corporations.[70]

Another variety of third generation takeover statute is modeled on the New York "freeze" statute,[71] also known as a business combination statute. The idea behind such statutes is to delay any transaction that would complete the second step of a two step acquisition, in those instances in which the first step was not agreed to by target company's management. Thus, for example, the New York statute prohibits a merger or other business acquisition within five years of the control acquisition date unless the transaction was approved by the target company's directors *prior* to the control acquisition date. Other states have followed the New York lead,[72] including Delaware which has adopted a three year freeze statute.[73] Based on earlier Supreme Court doctrine, there would appear to be considerable question whether such statutes can withstand constitutional scrutiny.[74] Nevertheless, the Delaware statute has withstood challenges at the preliminary injunction stage because of the failure to show a likelihood of success on the merits of the constitutional challenge, but the court noted that although the statute was probably constitutional, the constitutionality issue is not an easy one.[75] The Wisconsin freeze statute has been upheld by the

---

69. For example, the Court in *CTS* expressly noted that the state of incorporation has a special interest in regulating the internal affairs of its corporations:

The Indiana statute imposes no such problem [presenting an undue burden on interstate commerce]. So long as each state regulates voting rights *only in the corporations it has created,* each corporation will be subject to the law of only one state.

107 S.Ct. at 1649, 95 L.Ed.2d 85 (emphasis supplied).

70. TLX Acquisition Corp. v. Telex Corp., 679 F.Supp. 1022 (W.D.Okl.1987). *Cf.* Veere, Inc. v. Firestone Tire & Rubber Co., 685 F.Supp. 1027 (N.D.Ohio 1988) (indicating that there was no problem with constitutionality of Ohio statute since it applied only to target companies incorporated in Ohio).

71. N.Y.Bus.Corp.Law § 912.

72. Ariz.Rev.Stat. §§ 10–1221–10–1222 (three year delay); Minn.Stat.Ann. § 302A.673 (five year delay); Vernon's Ann.Mo.Stat. § 351.459(3)(b) (five year delay); N.J.Stat.Ann. § 49.5–1 (five year delay); Wash.S.B. No. 6084, 1987 Wash.Leg.Serv. (No. 10) 11 (five year delay); Wis.Stat.Ann. § 180.725 (three year delay).

73. Del.Corp.Code § 203.

74. *Cf.* Hyde Park Partners, L.P. v. Connolly, 839 F.2d 837 (1st Cir.1988) (Massachusetts statute imposing one-year moratorium on takeover attempts as a sanction for violation of the statute's disclosure provisions held likely to be preempted by Williams Act).

75. RP Acquisition Corp. v. Staley Continental, Inc., 686 F.Supp. 476 (D.Del.1988); BNS, Inc. v. Koppers Co., 683 F.Supp. 454 (D.Del.1988). *See also* City Capital Associates v. Interco, Inc., 696 F.Supp. 1551 (D.Del.1988) (refusing to issue preliminary injunction against enforcement of the Delaware statute); Salant Acquisition Corp. v. Manhattan Industries, Inc., 682 F.Supp. 199 (S.D.N.Y.1988) (denying preliminary injunction because shareholder with only 8.3 percent of the stock and no financing to acquire more was unable to show irreparable harm); Black & Decker Corp. v. American Standard, Inc., 679 F.Supp. 1183 (D.Del.1988) (denying preliminary injunction because of failure to show irreparable harm). The constitutionality issues are discussed in § 11.22 *infra.*

Seventh Circuit.[76] There thus is mounting authority in support of these questionable freeze statutes.

Other third generation statutes have taken still different approaches. For example, the Ohio Foreign Business Acquisition Act imposed stricter burdens on foreign bidders, but that statute has been invalidated by at least one court.[77] Pennsylvania has taken yet another approach by expressly sanctioning use of poison pills as a defensive measure.[78] This addition to the defensive weapon arsenal has not been successfully challenged.

The varieties of third generation statutes continue to proliferate. In the Spring of 1990, Pennsylvania adopted the most ambitious antitakeover statute to date. In addition to adopting a control share statute,[79] the Pennsylvania legislature enacted a provision requiring any person owning more than twenty percent of a company's voting shares to disgorge any profit realized from a subsequent sale of the shares within an eighteen month period.[80] The impact of this provision is to discourage suitors by locking them in as shareholders in the event that their takeover attempt is unsuccessful. It is arguable that this provision conflicts with the policy of section 16(b) of the Exchange Act which requires disgorgement of profits on short-swing transactions over a six month period.[81] Also in 1990, Massachusetts enacted a statute that mandates dividing the directors into groups and staggering the election of directors.[82] A corporation's board by a majority vote may choose to opt out of the law should the directors decide to have all directors elected annually. Shareholders can opt out of staggered elections only upon a two–thirds vote.[83] As has been the case with other state antitakeover

---

76. Amanda Acquisition Corp. v. Universal Foods Corp., 877 F.2d 496 (7th Cir.1989). *See also* West Point–Pepperell, Inc. v. Farley Inc., 711 F.Supp. 1096 (N.D.Ga.1989) (upholding the Georgia business combination statute); Realty Acquisition Corp. v. Property Trust, 1989 WL 214477, [1990 Transfer Binder] Fed.Sec.L.Rep. ¶ 95,245 (D.Md.1989) (unpublished case) (Maryland business combination statute was not preempted by Williams Act). *See also, e.g.,* Note, Delaware's Section 203 Antitakeover Statute Survives Constitutional Attack, 68 Tex.L.Rev. 235 (1990).

77. Campeau Corp. v. Federated Department Stores, 679 F.Supp. 735 (S.D.Ohio 1988).

78. *See* Pennsylvania Enacts Law Against Hostile Takeovers, 20 Sec.Reg. & L.Rep. (BNA) 502 (April 1, 1988).

79. *Cf.* Committee for New Management of Guaranty Bancshares Corp. v. Dimeling, 772 F.Supp. 230 (E.D.Pa.1991) (Pennsylvania Control Share Act applied to revocable proxies granting discretionary authority even though proxy was not part of takeover attempt).

80. 15 Pa.Cons.Stat.Ann. § 2571.

81. 15 U.S.C.A. § 78p(b) which is discussed in §§ 12.2–12.7 *infra. Cf., e.g.,* Kern County Land Co. v. Occidental Petroleum Corp., 411 U.S. 582, 93 S.Ct. 1736, 36 L.Ed.2d 503 (1973) (interpreting section 16(b) so as not to conflict with the Williams Act policy of not unduly deterring tender offers).

82. Mass.Gen.Laws.Ann. c. 149, § 184. *See, e.g.,* David B. Hilder & Lawrence Ingrassia, Norton Wins a Round Against BTR Bid as Massachusetts Lawmakers Clear Bill, Wall St.J. A12 (April 18, 1990).

83. Since the board of directors can opt out (as is the case with business combination statutes), the Massachusetts law does not adversely impact a company's ability to pursue a friendly suitor. The effect of the Massachusetts law, as is the case with the business combination statutes, is to delay the effective transfer of control. The business combina-

legislation, the Massachusetts statute was designed to suit the needs of a particular company in responding to a hostile approach by a would-be acquirer.[84]

§ 11.22 Validity of State Tender Offer Statutes—The Commerce Clause and the Preemption Problem; SEC Rule 14d–2(b)

State tender offer legislation has frequently been challenged under the Supremacy[1] and Commerce[2] Clauses of the Constitution. Under the Supremacy Clause, to the extent Congress has exercised its legislative power, a state may not enact inconsistent legislation.[3] Hence, state laws are preempted when either explicitly prohibited by,[4] or directly in conflict with,[5] federal legislation. Not every challenge to a takeover statute will be ripe. For example, shareholders of a potential target company did not have standing to challenge a state's takeover statute prior to the commencement of a tender offer or other takeover attempt.[6]

---

tion statutes merely alter the timing of a second-step merger but do not otherwise affect the ability of the acquirer to assume control of the acquired company. In contrast, the Massachusetts law postpones the ability to elect a majority of the directors.

84. *See* Hilder & Ingrassia, *supra* footnote 82. For a similar occurrence in North Carolina, *see* Thomas L. Hazen, State Anti–Takeover Legislation: The Second and Third Generations, 23 Wake Forest U.L.Rev. 77 (1988).

§ 11.22

1. "This Constitution, and the Laws of the United States * * * shall be the Supreme Law of the Land." U.S. Const. art. VI, cl. 2. *See* John E. Nowak, Ronald D. Rotunda & J. Nelson Young, Constitutional Law 18–20 (2d ed. 1983).

2. "The Congress shall have the power * * * [t]o regulate commerce * * * among the several States." U.S. Const. art. I, § 8, cl. 3. *See* J. Nowak, R. Rotunda & N. Young, *supra* footnote 1 at 138–146, 266–296.

3. Swift & Co. v. Wickham, 382 U.S. 111, 86 S.Ct. 258, 15 L.Ed.2d 194 (1965). In addition to the authorities cited in § 11.21 *supra, see generally* Lyman Johnson & David Millon, Misreading the Williams Act, 87 Mich.L.Rev. 87 (1989); P. John Kozyris, Corporate Takeovers at the Jurisdictional Crossroads: Preserving State Authority Over Internal Affairs While Protecting the Transferability of Interstate Stock Through Federal Law, 36 U.C.L.A.L.Rev. 1109 (1989); J. Gregory Sidak & Susan E. Woodward, Corporate Takeovers, the Commerce Clause, and the Efficient Anonymity of Shareholders, 84 Nw.U.L.Rev. 1092 (1990); William C. Tyson, The Proper Relationship Between Federal and State Law in the Regulation of Tender Offers, 66 Notre Dame L.Rev. 241 (1990). Note, State Regulation of Hostile Takeovers: The Constitutionality of Third Generation Business Combination Statutes and the Role of the Courts, 64 St.J.L.Rev. 107 (1989).

4. *See, e.g.,* Rice v. Santa Fe Elevator, 331 U.S. 218, 236, 67 S.Ct. 1146, 1155, 91 L.Ed. 1447 (1947) (Federal Warehouse Act expressly preempts all concurrent state regulation).

5. Florida Lime and Avocado Growers, Inc. v. Paul, 373 U.S. 132, 142–43, 83 S.Ct. 1210, 1217, 10 L.Ed.2d 248 (1963), *rehearing denied* 374 U.S. 858, 83 S.Ct. 1861, 10 L.Ed.2d 1082 (1963) ("A holding of federal exclusion of state law is inescapable * * * where compliance with both federal and state regulation is a physical impossibility * * *.").

6. Armstrong World Industries, Inc. v. Adams, 961 F.2d 405 (3d Cir.1992).

Preemption

Preemption is largely a matter of congressional intent.[7] State legislation may be implicitly preempted when there is an overriding federal interest in the subject of the legislation[8] or when the federal regulations are so pervasive as to create an inference that Congress intended to "occupy the field" completely.[9] Similarly, state law may be invalid if it conflicts indirectly with the federal law by standing as an obstacle to the full accomplishment of federal regulatory objectives.[10] In any case, a balancing of state and federal interests is required.[11]

The Williams Act does not expressly prohibit state regulation of tender offers. Furthermore, because corporate law regulation has not generally been considered to be a matter of overriding federal concern,[12] and because the Williams Act is not a detailed comprehensive regulatory scheme but rather a minimum standard,[13] there is no inference that Congress intended to preempt all state tender offer regulation.[14] In the absence of an explicit or implicit prohibition of state regulation, supremacy clause questions focus on whether state takeover laws conflict either directly or indirectly with the operation of the Williams Act.

Commerce Clause

A state statute which survives preemption analysis may nonetheless be unenforceable under the Commerce Clause. State legislation is valid only if it regulates even-handedly to effectuate a legitimate local public

---

7. California v. Zook, 336 U.S. 725, 69 S.Ct. 841, 93 L.Ed. 1005 (1949); Head v. New Mexico Board of Examiners, 374 U.S. 424, 83 S.Ct. 1759, 10 L.Ed.2d 983 (1963). *See* J. Nowak, R. Rotunda & N. Young *supra* footnote 1 at 292–296.

8. *See, e.g.,* Pennsylvania v. Nelson, 350 U.S. 497, 76 S.Ct. 477, 100 L.Ed. 640 (1956) (Congressional enactment of internal security laws to safeguard against overthrow of the government by force reflected overriding federal interest requiring preemption of supplementary state anti-communist legislation).

9. Rice v. Santa Fe Elevator, 331 U.S. 218, 230, 67 S.Ct. 1146, 1152, 91 L.Ed. 1447 (1947); City of Burbank v. Lockheed Air Terminal, Inc., 411 U.S. 624, 93 S.Ct. 1854, 36 L.Ed.2d 547 (1973).

10. Hines v. Davidowitz, 312 U.S. 52, 67, 61 S.Ct. 399, 404, 85 L.Ed. 581 (1941).

11. *See id.* at 73–74, 61 S.Ct. at 407–08. *See generally* Note, The Preemption Doctrine: Shifting Perspectives on Federalism and the Burger Court, 75 Colum.L.Rev. 623 (1975).

12. Corporation law has traditionally been primarily state law but largely because of the federal securities statutes a "Federal Corporations Law" has been developing. *See generally* William L. Cary & Melvin A. Eisenberg, Cases and Materials on Corporations, 13–14 (5th ed.1980).

13. *See* Note, Securities Law and the Constitution: State Tender Offer Statutes Reconsidered, 88 Yale L.J. 510, 519–20 (1979). *But cf.* Diane S. Wilner & Craig A. Landy, The Tender Trap: State Takeover Statutes and Their Constitutionality, 45 Fordham L.Rev. 1, 29–30 (1976) (the Williams Act, taken as a whole with the 1934 Act into which Congress integrated it, is comprehensive).

14. In fact, it has been argued that Congress implicitly accepted the prospect of state regulation by adding the Williams Act to the 1934 Act without also amending section 28(a) of the Act, 15 U.S.C.A. § 78bb(a), which provides that "Nothing in this chapter shall affect the jurisdiction of the securities commission * * * of any state over any security or any person insofar as it does not conflict with provisions of this chapter or the rules and regulations thereunder." But the applicability of this provision to state tender offer legislation is questionable. *See* Donald C. Langevoort, State Tender–Offer Legislation: Interests, Effects, and Political Competency, 62 Cornell L.Rev. 213, 247 (1977).

interest, affects interstate commerce only incidentally, and imposes burdens on such commerce not clearly excessive in relation to the putative local benefits.[15] The protection of local incumbent management from foreign "raiders" is not a legitimate local interest in itself; however, regulation of the internal affairs of domestic corporations and the protection of local target corporations and shareholders from fraud and overreaching in the course of tender offers are clearly bona fide state concerns.[16] Thus, the vulnerability of state tender offer acts under the commerce clause is due largely to their extraterritorial coverage and the resulting cumulative burden on interstate commerce.[17]

The Early Cases

    In Great Western United Corp. v. Kidwell,[18] the Fifth Circuit became the first federal appellate court to consider the constitutionality of a state tender offer act. In *Kidwell,* the tender offeror was a Delaware corporation with its principal offices in Dallas, Texas. The target was organized under the laws of the state of Washington with shareholders across the United States. The Idaho takeover statute required that a registration statement be declared effective by the director of the state's Department of Finance prior to the commencement of any tender offer for an Idaho target company.[19] The offeror was required to mail a copy of the statement to the target, and the material terms of the offer had to be publicly disclosed no later than the filing date. Within twenty days of the filing, the director could hold a discretionary hearing if he thought it necessary to ensure full disclosure and equal treatment of all shareholders.[20] A hearing was required if the target company requested it, and the director's determination as to the adequacy of the registration statement had to be announced within thirty days of filing unless more time was needed.[21] The Act's jurisdictional provisions were triggered by target companies having substantial assets located in Idaho or that were either incorporated or had principal offices in the state and had securities registered under the Idaho Code or the 1934 Act.[22] Although its disclosure requirements were more stringent than those of the Williams Act, Idaho's provisions for withdrawal rights, pro rata acceptance, and price increases merely duplicated the corresponding federal provisions.[23]

---

15. Pike v. Bruce Church, Inc., 397 U.S. 137, 90 S.Ct. 844, 25 L.Ed.2d 174 (1970).

16. *See* Langevoort, *supra* footnote 14 at 242.

17. *E.g.* CTS Corp. v. Dynamics Corp. of America, 481 U.S. 69, 107 S.Ct. 1637, 95 L.Ed.2d 67 (1987). *See* Wilner & Landy, *supra* footnote 13 at 22–23.

18. 577 F.2d 1256 (5th Cir.1978), *reversed on other grounds sub nom.* Leroy v. Great Western United Corp., 443 U.S. 173, 99 S.Ct. 2710, 61 L.Ed.2d 464 (1979), *on remand* 602 F.2d 1246 (5th Cir.1979).

19. Idaho Code § 30–1503(1).

20. Idaho Code § 30–1503(4)–(5). The statute did not authorize the director to review the merits of the offer.

21. Idaho Code § 30–1503(4), (5).

22. Idaho Code § 30–1501(6).

23. *Compare* Idaho Code §§ 30–1503(2)(C), 30–1506(2)–(4) *with* 15 U.S.C.A. §§ 78m(d), 78n(d)(5)–(7).

The Fifth Circuit found it unnecessary to determine whether the true purpose of the takeover law was to protect investors as Idaho contended, or to protect incumbent management as the district court had found.[24] In either case Congress had rejected Idaho's "fiduciary approach" to investor protection which relied upon the business judgment of corporate directors with a fiduciary duty to their shareholders. Instead, recognizing that investors often benefit from tender offers, Congress had chosen the "market approach" wherein the function of federal regulation was to let the investor, on a fully informed basis, decide for himself or herself after allowing both the offeror and incumbent management to fully present their arguments.[25] The court found that the Idaho law benefitted target companies by giving them advance notice of tender offers and the power to postpone offers indefinitely by insisting on a hearing. Moreover, Idaho gave preferential treatment to target companies by not regulating target defensive tactics as stringently as the offeror's activities. Indeed, the target board could exclude the offer from state regulation completely by simply approving the offer.[26] The court reasoned that the state law clearly "disrupted the neutrality indispensable for the proper operation of the federal approach to tender offer regulation," [27] and thus stood as "an obstacle to the accomplishment and execution of the full purposes and objectives of the Williams Act" and was necessarily preempted.[28]

Following the Fifth Circuit's opinion in *Kidwell*, state and federal district court rulings on the constitutionality of state tender offer statutes remained contradictory.[29] Most courts, however, agreed with the Fifth Circuit's conclusion that the Williams Act was intended both to protect shareholders and to maintain a neutral balance between incumbent management and offeror.[30] Hence, following the *Kidwell* reasoning, to the extent that state statutes provided management with the weapon of delay, they were most often found to disrupt the neutral balance and

---

24. 577 F.2d at 1278–79 (citing Appellants Brief at 39–42 and the district court's opinion, 439 F.Supp. at 437.)

25. 577 F.2d at 1279. *But cf.* North Star International v. Arizona Corporation Commission, 720 F.2d 578 (9th Cir.1983).

26. 577 F.2d at 1278.

27. *Id.* at 1279–80.

28. *Id.* at 1280, 1281. The court pointed out that by requiring more extensive disclosure than the Williams Act, Idaho might actually be harming investors. Too much data could hide relevant disclosures and create unnecessary confusion, thus inhibiting the offeror's efforts to communicate material information.

29. *Compare, e.g.,* Dart Industries, Inc. v. Conrad, 462 F.Supp. 1 (S.D.Ind.1978) (Delaware statute preempted by the Williams Act) *with* AMCA International Corp. v. Krouse, 482 F.Supp. 929 (S.D.Ohio 1979) (Ohio takeover law not preempted).

30. *See* MITE Corp. v. Dixon, 633 F.2d 486, 495 (7th Cir.1980), *affirmed sub nom.* Edgar v. MITE Corp., 457 U.S. 624, 102 S.Ct. 2629, 73 L.Ed.2d 269 (1982). The neutrality principle was reaffirmed by the Supreme Court in CTS Corp. v. Dynamics Corp. of America, 481 U.S. 69, 107 S.Ct. 1637, 95 L.Ed.2d 67 (1987); *see* discussion *infra*. *See also, e.g.,* WLR Foods, Inc. v. Tyson Foods, Inc., 861 F.Supp. 1277 (W.D.Va.1994), *supplemented* 869 F.Supp. 419 (W.D.Va. 1994) (state takeover statutes did not violate principle of neutrality and thus were not preempted by the Williams Act).

hinder achievement of the objectives of the Williams Act. On the other hand, a minority of courts held that the sole purpose of the Williams Act was to protect investors, and that Congress had no intention to legislate neutrality into tender offers. Neutrality, they concluded, was simply one characteristic of the legislation.

In response to the mounting confusion and the increasing number of tender offers, the SEC adopted tender offer rules which were intended to preempt state regulation by creating a direct conflict with most state statutes.[31] Before the new rules could be tested, however, the Fourth and Seventh Circuits reached opposite results in controversies involving the takeover statutes of Virginia[32] and Illinois[33] respectively. The Supreme Court decided to review the Illinois case, and in Edgar v. MITE Corp.[34] the constitutionality of state tender offer legislation was squarely before the Court for the first time.

The Mite Decision

Mite Corporation, organized under the laws of Delaware with its principal office in Connecticut, initiated a tender offer for all outstanding shares of an Illinois corporation. Mite complied with the requirements of the Williams Act, but did not comply with the Illinois Act,[35] electing instead to file suit in district court in Illinois seeking declaratory and injunctive relief from the statute's enforcement.

Under the Illinois Business Takeover Act an offer became effective twenty days after filing with the Secretary of State and notifying the target of the terms of the offer, unless the Secretary of State called a hearing to determine the fairness of the offer.[36] During the waiting

---

31. *See* Sec.Act Rel. No. 33–6022 (SEC Feb. 5, 1979); Sec.Act Rel. No. 33–6158 (SEC Nov. 29, 1979); Sec.Act Rel. No. 33–6159 (SEC Nov. 29, 1979). *See* text accompanying footnotes 47–53 *infra*.

32. In Telvest v. Bradshaw, 618 F.2d 1029 (4th Cir.1980), *on remand* 547 F.Supp. 791 (E.D.Va.1982), the Fourth Circuit appeared to adopt the minority view that the sole purpose of the Williams Act was to protect investors, and not necessarily to maintain neutrality between offerors and incumbent management. Although the constitutionality of Virginia's takeover statute was not directly at issue, in the court's view, the statute's stated purpose ("to protect the interests of offerees, investors, and the public by requiring that an offeror make fair, full and effective disclosure to offerees * * * ", Va.Code § 13.1–528(B)) "seem[ed] consistent with rather than antagonistic to the purpose of the Williams Act." *Id.* at 1034.

33. In MITE Corp. v. Dixon, 633 F.2d 486 (7th Cir.1980), *affirmed sub nom.* Edgar v. MITE Corp., 457 U.S. 624, 102 S.Ct. 2629, 73 L.Ed.2d 269 (1982), the Seventh Circuit followed the *Kidwell* "neutrality" rationale and concluded that the Illinois Business Take-Over Act was preempted by the Williams Act because it substituted regulatory control for investor autonomy and provided for hearings and other delays greatly in excess of those mandated by Congress. *Id.* at 498. Moreover, the Illinois Act violated the commerce clause because its substantial obstruction of interstate commerce could not be justified by the state's "tenuous interest in protecting resident shareholders and regulating control transfers." *Id.* at 502.

34. 457 U.S. 624, 102 S.Ct. 2629, 73 L.Ed.2d 269 (1982).

35. Under the Illinois Act any takeover offer for the shares of a target company had to be registered with the Secretary of State. Ill.–S.H.A. ch. 121½, § 137.54.A (repealed).

36. Ill.–S.H.A. ch. 121½, § 137.54.E (repealed).

period, the offeror could not communicate with the target shareholders, although the target was free to contact shareholders as it pleased.[37] Target companies were defined by the Act as any corporation of which ten percent of the class of securities subject to the tender offer was owned by Illinois residents, or for which any two of the following conditions were met: the corporation had its principal place of business located in Illinois, was organized under Illinois law, or had at least ten percent of its stated capital and paid-in surplus represented within the state.[38]

The Supreme Court agreed with the Seventh Circuit that the Illinois law was invalid under the Commerce Clause because it imposed an excessive indirect burden on interstate commerce.[39] Illinois derived no benefit from protecting non-resident investors, and the state's asserted interest in investor protection was seriously undermined by the fact that the target company's competing offer for its own shares was completely exempt from the coverage of the Act.[40] The substantive protections provided by the Illinois Act were essentially equivalent to those provided by the Williams Act. The Court noted that the additional disclosure requirements of the Illinois Act might not substantially enhance the shareholders' ability to make a decision and concluded that the protections the Illinois Act afforded resident shareholders were for the most part "speculative." [41]

A plurality of the Court would also have invalidated the Illinois Act as an impermissible direct regulation of interstate commerce.[42] The plurality found a substantial difference between state blue sky laws which regulate transactions taking place within the state, and the Illinois law which could conceivably apply to tender offers involving no

---

37. Ill.–S.H.A. ch. 121½, § 137.58.1 (repealed).

38. Ill.–S.H.A. ch. 121½, § 137.52.10 (repealed).

39. Edgar v. MITE Corp., 457 U.S. 624, 642, 102 S.Ct. 2629, 2641, 73 L.Ed.2d 269 (1982). *Accord e.g.,* Mesa Petroleum Co. v. Cities Service Co., 715 F.2d 1425 (10th Cir.1983) (Oklahoma takeover statute ruled unconstitutional); Batus, Inc. v. McKay, 684 F.Supp. 637 (D.Nev.1988) (invalidating Nevada statute).

40. 457 U.S. at 645, 102 S.Ct. at 2642.

41. *Id.* at 645, 102 S.Ct. at 2642. Similarly, since the Illinois Act applied to tender offers for any corporation for which ten percent of the outstanding shares are held by Illinois residents the burdens imposed by the Act could not be justified by the state's interest in regulating the internal affairs of corporations incorporated under its laws. *Id.* at 2643. The Court noted that because tender offers contemplate transfers of stock by stockholders to third parties and do not themselves implicate the internal affairs of the target, the internal affairs doctrine was of little use to Illinois in this context.

42. *Id.* at 641–644, 102 S.Ct. at 2640–41. The majority of the Court held that MITE's withdrawal of its offer had not rendered the case moot, since a reversal of the district court would expose MITE to civil and criminal liability under the Illinois Act. *Id.* at 2633–34. Three justices dissented, stating that the case was moot. Justice Powell agreed that the case was moot, but because the majority had reached the merits he concurred in part. *Id.* at 645, 102 S.Ct. at 2642. The commerce clause holding was set out in Part V, which was divided into sections A and B. Justice Powell joined only in V–B which thus represents the substantive holding of the Court. Four of six justices reaching the merits joined in all of part V.

Illinois shareholders at all.[43]   The Commerce Clause precluded the application of a state statute to commerce occurring entirely outside the state's borders whether or not the commerce had effects within the state.[44]   Three of the six Justices reaching the merits in *MITE* would have affirmed the Seventh Circuit on supremacy clause grounds as well.[45] The Justices agreed with the lower court that in imposing the requirements of the Williams Act, Congress had adopted a "policy of evenhandedness." [46]

The SEC's then recently-adopted tender offer rules were not at issue in *MITE*.[47]   Nevertheless, the Seventh Circuit observed that one rule in particular, Rule 14d–2(b),[48] conflicted directly with the Illinois Act.[49] Under Rule 14d–2(b) an offeror's public announcement of certain material terms of a tender offer causes the offer to commence for the purposes of section 14(d) of the 1934 Act,[50] despite the fact that a state statute might not allow offers to begin until after any applicable waiting period and hearing process.[51]   The SEC recognized that the conflict between Rule 14d–2(b) and the state statutes made compliance with both sets of requirements impossible, but despite its long history of cooperation with the states in securities regulation, the Commission concluded that the rule was necessary for the protection of investors, and that the

---

43.   *Id.* at 643, 102 S.Ct. at 2641.   The plurality noted that while blue sky laws affect interstate commerce in securities only incidentally, the Illinois Act directly regulated transactions taking place across state lines.   *Id.* at 641–644, 102 S.Ct. at 2640–41.

44.   *Id.* at 643, 102 S.Ct. at 2641.

45.   *Id.* at 632–42, 102 S.Ct. at 2635–40.

46.   *Id.* at 633, 102 S.Ct. at 2636 (citing Piper v. Chris–Craft Industries, 430 U.S. 1, 97 S.Ct. 926, 51 L.Ed.2d 124 (1977)).   Although the purpose of the Williams Act was unquestionably to protect the investor, they concluded that Congress intended to do it by "strik[ing] a balance between the investor, management, and the takeover bidder."   *Id.* at 635, 102 S.Ct. at 2637.   Thus, there was "no intention to do * * * more than give incumbent management an opportunity to express and explain its position."   *Id.* (quoting Rondeau v. Mosinee Paper Corp., 422 U.S. 49, 58, 95 S.Ct. 2069, 2075, 45 L.Ed.2d 12 (1975)).   The Illinois Act, by contrast, provided incumbent management with a decided advantage by introducing lengthy delays into the tender offer process through precommencement notification and hearing provisions.   457 U.S. at 635, 102 S.Ct. at 2637. Extended delays could be used by target management as a weapon to defeat or discourage tender offers that would otherwise be advantageous to stockholders.   *Id.*   Furthermore, by allowing the Secretary of State to pass on the substantive fairness of a tender offer, the state was "offer[ing] investor protection at the expense of investor autonomy," an approach which the Justices agreed was at odds with Congressional policy.   *Id.* at 641, 102 S.Ct. at 2640.   These offensive provisions upset the careful balance struck by Congress, and therefore stood as obstacles to the accomplishment of the Congressional purpose.   *Id.* at 633, 102 S.Ct. at 2636.

47.   *Id.* at 637 n. 11, 102 S.Ct. at 2638 n. 11.

48.   17 C.F.R. § 240.14d–2(b).

49.   MITE Corp. v. Dixon, 633 F.2d 486, 499 n. 25 (7th Cir.1980), *affirmed sub nom.* Edgar v. MITE Corp., 457 U.S. 624, 102 S.Ct. 2629, 73 L.Ed.2d 269 (1982).

50.   A public announcement by a bidder which includes the identity of the bidder; the identity of the subject company; and the amount and class of securities being sought and the price or range of prices being offered therefor with respect to a tender offer in which cash or exempt securities are the only consideration shall be deemed to constitute the commencement of a tender offer.   Rule 14d–2(b)–(c).

51.   Sec.Act Rel. No. 33–6158 (SEC Nov. 29, 1979).

state takeover statutes then in effect frustrated the operation and purposes of the Williams Act.[52] The overwhelming majority of state and federal courts considering the enforceability of state statutes after the effective date of Rule 14d–2(b) have reached the same conclusion.[53]

In the wake of *Kidwell, Mite,* and Rule 14d–2(b), the provisions which add the most to the value of state statutes as takeover deterrents had been rendered largely unenforceable.[54] Precommencement notification provisions and waiting periods, for example, have almost certainly been preempted by Rule 14d–2(b).[55] In addition, state provisions for administrative hearings,[56] more extensive disclosure requirements,[57] and withdrawal and proration rights,[58] other than those established by the Williams Act, have been held invalid, as have state efforts to regulate creeping tender offers.[59] Friendly offer exemptions are also clearly vulnerable in light of the Supreme Court's apparent acceptance of *Kidwell's* "regulatory neutrality" approach.[60]

52. *Id.* (citing brief for SEC as amicus curiae in Leroy v. Great Western United Corp., 443 U.S. 173, 99 S.Ct. 2710, 61 L.Ed.2d 464 (1979)).

53. *See, e.g.,* Kennecott Corp. v. Smith, 507 F.Supp. 1206 (1981); Crane Co. v. Lam, 509 F.Supp. 782 (E.D.Pa.1981); Canadian Pacific Enterprises v. Krouse, 506 F.Supp. 1192 (S.D.Ohio 1981); Kelly v. Beta–X Corp., 103 Mich.App. 51, 302 N.W.2d 596 (1981); some courts have conceded such preemption, however, only with respect to the waiting period provisions.

54. *See, e.g.,* Newell Co. v. Connolly, 624 F.Supp. 126 (D.Mass.1985) (Massachusetts statute probably in conflict with Williams Act, placing an undue burden on interstate commerce); Missouri Public Service Co. v. Amen, 1983 WL 1503, [1985–86 Transfer Binder] Fed.Sec.L.Rep. (CCH) ¶ 92,488 (D.Neb.1983) (Nebraska act was undue burden on interstate commerce).

55. No decision reported to date has sustained a state precommencement waiting period in the face of Rule 14d–2(b).

56. Either as an embodiment of the "benevolent bureaucracy" approach, Hi–Shear Industries, Inc. v. Campbell, 1980 WL 1476, [1981 Transfer Binder] Fed.Sec.L.Rep. (CCH) ¶ 97,804 (D.S.C.1980), or as a mechanism for delay, Batus, Inc. v. McKay, 684 F.Supp. 637 (D.Nev.1988); Hi–Shear Industries, Inc. v. Neiditz, 1980 WL 1477, [1981 Transfer Binder] Fed.Sec.L.Rep. (CCH) ¶ 97,805 (D.Conn.1980). *See* Mark A. Sargent, On the Validity of State Takeover Regulation: State Responses to *MITE* and *Kidwell,* 42 Ohio St.L.J. 689, 697–98 (1981). *See also* McCauliff, *supra* footnote 54; Profusek & Gompf *supra* footnote 54.

57. Either as a tool for harassment by target management, (Dart Industries v. Conrad, 462 F.Supp. 1 (S.D.Ind.1978)), or as ancillary to a proceeding incompatible with the Williams Act, (Kennecott Corp. v. Smith, 507 F.Supp. 1206 (D.N.J.1981)). *See* Sargent, *supra* footnote 56 at 698–99.

58. It was so held primarily on the ground that the state provisions create delays which benefit target management. *See, e.g.,* Kennecott Corp. v. Smith, 507 F.Supp. 1206 (D.N.J.1981). *But cf.* Wylain, Inc. v. Tre Corp., 412 A.2d 338 (Del.Super.1979) (Delaware provision permitting stockholders to withdraw shares any time during offer was merely one of the "greater protections" which states are entitled to provide). *Id.* at 348. *See* Sargent, *supra* footnote 56 at 699–700.

59. *See* Telvest v. Bradshaw, 618 F.2d 1029 (4th Cir.1980), *on remand* 547 F.Supp. 791 (E.D.Va.1982).

60. *See* Edgar v. MITE Corp., 457 U.S. 624, 635, 102 S.Ct. 2629, 2637, 73 L.Ed.2d 269 (1982); Sargent, *supra* footnote 56 at 698. The fact that state law may make takeovers more expensive does not in and of itself violate the neutrality principle. *E.g.,* WLR Foods, Inc. v. Tyson Foods, Inc., 861 F.Supp. 1277 (W.D.Va.1994), *supplemented* 869 F.Supp. 419 (W.D. Va. 1994) (state takeover statutes did not violate principle of neutrality and thus were not preempted by the Williams Act).

The susceptibility of "traditional" first generation state tender offer statutes has led many states to overhaul their regulatory schemes, purging those aspects that have been found either to conflict with the Williams Act or to impose excessive burdens on interstate commerce.[61] Furthermore, to meet the threshold requirement that the statute "effectuate a legitimate local public interest," [62] some states have narrowed the definition of "target company" to include only those entities in which the state has a more substantial interest.[63] It has been argued that by imposing only minor delays essential to ensure the type of full and fair disclosure contemplated by the Williams Act, and by limiting application to domestic corporations with a substantial presence in the state, the revised statutes complement federal legislation, expressing a bona fide state interest in investor protection and corporate control without obstructing the effectuation of any Congressional purpose.[64] The proposed Uniform Takeover Act[65] incorporated this point of view, promoting uniformity among the states and compatibility with the federal regulatory framework.

It has also been argued, however, that state takeover laws should be preempted by Congress because state laws inherently favor target management.[66] The American Law Institute's proposed Federal Securities Code adopted this line of thinking, providing for preemption of state law in any federally regulated takeover bid.[67]

As is discussed more fully in the preceding section,[68] following the Supreme Court decision in *MITE,* a number of states adopted second

61. Some states, for example, have avoided direct conflict with Rule 14d–2(b) by replacing "precommencement" waiting periods with "prepurchase" waiting periods. *See, e.g.,* N.Y.–McKinney's Bus.Corp.Law § 1605(a); West's Ann.Ind.Code 23–2–3.1–8; 70 Pa.Stat. § 74(a). These provisions allow the offeror to commence the offer in compliance with Rule 14d–2(b) while the state retains some control by prohibiting purchases during a period of time in which the state may review the offer.

62. *See* discussion *supra. But see* L.P. Acquisition Co. v. Tyson, 772 F.2d 201 (6th Cir.1985), *reversing* 616 F.Supp. 1186 (E.D.Mich.1985) (Michigan statute which was limited to local companies was preempted to the extent that it required offer to remain open longer than the 20 day period imposed by the Williams Act rules).

63. *See, e.g.,* Conn.Gen.Stat.Ann. § 36–457(a) (" 'Target Company' means any stock corporation which is organized under the laws of this state, has its principal executive office in this state and has, on a consolidated basis, five hundred or more employees and fifty million dollars of tangible assets in this state * * * "); West's Ann.Ind.Code 23–2–3.1–1(j) (" 'Target Company' means an issuer * * * which is organized under the laws of this state, has its principal place of business in this state, and has substantial assets in this state."); Md.Code, Corp. & Assn's Code, §§ 11–902(h)(2)(iv), (i)(1)–(2) (the target must be organized in Maryland, doing business in the state, and have at least thirty five shareholders in the state). *See* Sargent, *supra* footnote 56 at 723; § 11.21 *supra.*

64. *See, e.g.,* Sargent *supra* footnote 56 at 729–30.

65. Uniform Take-over Act (North American Securities Administrators Association, Inc. 1981), 1 Blue Sky L.Rep. (CCH) ¶ 5295.

66. *See* L.P. Acquisition Co. v. Tyson, 772 F.2d 201 (6th Cir.1985) (Michigan statute is preempted by Williams Act); Langevoort, *supra* footnote 13 at 254–57. *But cf.* NUI Corp. v. Kimmelman, 765 F.2d 399 (3d Cir.1985) (federal proxy regulation did not preempt New Jersey statute regulating public utility proxy contests).

67. ALI Fed.Sec.Code Proposed Official Draft § 1603(c)(1) (1980).

68. *See* § 10.21 *supra.*

generation takeover statutes in an attempt to continue to regulate tender offers without imposing the undue burden identified by the *MITE* Court.[69] Two major varieties of statutes have arisen: the control share statutes and the so-called fair price statutes.

Under control share acquisition acts, modeled on legislation that was originally enacted in Ohio,[70] limits are imposed upon a control person's voting rights.[71] In essence, the control person is, at least temporarily, disenfranchised.

Once the control threshold[72] is crossed the person in control cannot vote the control shares unless there has been a favorable vote by a majority of the disinterested shares.[73] The concept of disinterested shares excludes not only those held by the person seeking control but also shares controlled by the target company's management. The Supreme Court in upholding the Indiana statute pointed to this feature as preserving neutrality between the control contestants and thus leaving the decision to the target company's shareholders.[74]

The other variety of second generation statutes, known as "fair price", or more accurately, "best price" statutes, provide that any person acquiring a covered corporation must pay the "best price" paid to any one shareholder to all shareholders.[75] The best price requirement can be waived by a shareholder vote.[76] Also, most best price statutes do not apply to friendly takeovers as they may be waived, or otherwise avoided by the target company's board of directors,[77] while a few statutes are not

---

69. *See generally* Dennis J. Block, Nancy E. Barton & Andrea J. Roth, State Takeover Statutes: The "Second Generation", 13 Sec.Reg.L.J. 332 (1986); Greg A. Danilow & Philip Bentley, State Takeover Statutes After *MITE,* 20 Rev.Sec. & Commodities Reg. 13 (1987); Thomas L. Hazen, State Anti–Takeover Legislation: The Second and Third Generations, 23 Wake Forest U.L.Rev. 77 (1988); Arthur S. Pinto, Takeover Statutes: The Dormant Commerce Clause and State Corporate Law, 41 U.Miami L.Rev. 473 (1987); Note, Beyond *CTS:* A Limited Defense of State Tender Offer Disclosure Requirements, 54 U.Chi.L.Rev. 657 (1987); Note, The Constitutionality of Second Generation Takeover Statutes, 73 Va.L.Rev. 203 (1987).

70. Ohio Rev.Code § 1701.83.2. The constitutionality of the Ohio statute was upheld on a motion for preliminary injunctive relief in Veere, Inc. v. Firestone Tire & Rubber Co., 685 F.Supp. 1027 (N.D.Ohio 1988).

71. *E.g.* Haw.Rev.Stat. §§ 416–171, 172 (198–); Ind.Bus.Corp.Law § 23–1–17–1 *et seq.* (Supp.1986).

72. Control under the Indiana statute is defined in terms of acquiring twenty percent of the voting stock or crossing the threshold above ⅓ or ½ voting control. Ind.Bus.Corp.Law § 23–1–42–1.

73. Disinterested shares are shares not owned by any person seeking to acquire control of the corporation, or by the corporation's officers or directors. Ind.Bus.Corp.Law § 23–1–42–3 (Sup.1986); N.C.Gen.Stats. § 55–9A–01(b)(4) (1987).

74. *See* footnotes 79–80 *infra* and accompanying text.

75. *E.g.* Md. Corp.'s & Ass'ns Code §§ 3–602, 3–603 (defining best price to include the price paid during the past two years); N.C.Gen.Stats. §§ 55–9–01 *et seq.* (best price not defined).

In addition to its best price requirement, the Hawaii statute requires a bidder offer to purchase all of the target company's shares. Haw.Rev.Stat. § 417E–2(3).

76. Md. Corp.'s & Ass'ns Code §§ 3–601 *et seq.* (⅔ shareholder vote); N.C.Gen.Stats. § 55–9–01 (95% vote).

77. Md. Corp.'s & Ass'ns Code §§ 3–601 *et seq.*

waivable by the directors.[78]

In *CTS* Corp. v. Dynamics Corp. of America[79] the Supreme Court upheld the Indiana control share statute, pointing out that, unlike the Illinois statute which was struck down in *MITE,* the Indiana statute was not balanced in favor of incumbent management.[80] It is thus significant that state takeover statutes maintain a position of neutrality, rather than favoring target management.[81] The Supreme Court's decision in *CTS* has far-reaching implications in permitting states to control the takeover arena by regulating corporate internal affairs.[82]

Although the *CTS* decision does not address the issue, there is a strong argument that best price statutes will withstand constitutional scrutiny. On the other hand, since the most best price statutes are waivable by the board of directors, it is arguable that they do not protect the independent shareholder against incumbent management. Giving incumbent management the power to block the hostile takeover by waiving the statute's barrier to permit a friendly defensive arrangement can be viewed as violating the *CTS* neutrality requirement.[83] As the

78. N.C.Gen.Stats. §§ 55–9–01 *et seq.* While the North Carolina statute cannot be waived by directors, there are opt-out provisions which permit the directors of existing corporations to opt out of the statute by adopting a bylaw within 90 days of the Act's effective date. N.C.Gen.Stat. § 55–9–05. Additionally, the Act does not apply to new corporations which have opted out pursuant to a provision in its original articles of incorporation. *Id.* § 55–9–05.

79. 481 U.S. 69, 107 S.Ct. 1637, 95 L.Ed.2d 67 (1987). *Cf., e.g.,* Cardiff Acquisitions, Inc. v. Hatch, 751 F.2d 906 (8th Cir.1984), *appeal after remand* 751 F.2d 917 (8th Cir.1984) (upholding Minnesota disclosure statute).

80. *Id.* at 81–82, 107 S.Ct. at 1645, 95 L.Ed.2d at 80:

As is apparent from our summary of its reasoning, the overriding concern of the *MITE* plurality was that the Illinois statute considered in that case operated to favor management against offerors, to the detriment of shareholders. By contrast, the statute now before the Court protects the independent shareholder against both of the contending parties.

For earlier decisions which struck down control share acquisition acts, *see, e.g.,* APL Limited Partnership v. Van Dusen Air, Inc., 622 F.Supp. 1216 (D.Minn.1985) (Minnesota control share act imposes unconstitutional burden on interstate commerce); Icahn v. Blunt, 612 F.Supp. 1400 (W.D.Mo.1985) (Missouri control share act imposes unconstitutional burden on interstate commerce).

81. The Indiana statute, if anything may be seen as favoring the outside bidder because the statute's provisions are triggered by the announcement of an intent to acquire twenty percent of the stock. Once the potential acquirer has made the announcement, he or she can then mandate the shareholder meeting for the vote of disinterested shares. This enables the acquirer to force a shareholder vote prior to acquiring the shares. Ind.Code Ann. § 23–1–42. In contrast, the North Carolina Statute does not permit the acquirer to call the meeting until the shares have been acquired or until there is a legal commitment to acquire them. N.C.Gen.Stat. §§ 55–9A–01 *et seq.*

82. Former SEC Commissioner Roberta Karmel has questioned whether the Supreme Court fully understood the implications of this aspect of its holding. *See* Kirk Victor, States Flex Muscles on Takeovers, 9 Nat'l L.J. 1, 35 (June 1, 1987).

This type of interference by the states may trigger a stronger federal role in order to assure uniformity in regulation of matters of such national importance. *See, e.g.,* Ruder restates Support for Measure to Preempt State Antitakeover Laws, 19 Sec.Reg. & L.Rep. (BNA) 1759 (Nov. 20, 1987).

83. *Cf., e.g.,* RTE Corp. v. Mark IV Industries, Inc., 1988 WL 75453, [1987–88 Transfer Binder] Fed.Sec.L.Rep. (CCH) ¶ 93,789 (E.D.Wis.1988) (Unpublished Case) (Wisconsin

Court pointed out in the *CTS* decision, the control share acquisition statute disenfranchises both the person seeking control and target company management and thus preserves the neutrality mandated by the Williams Act.[84]

With regard to the Commerce Clause issue, the teaching of the Supreme Court in *CTS* seems to be contained in a three factor analysis. First, antitakeover legislation enacted by the states must preserve the neutrality of the Williams Act and thus cannot favor target management in its defense of hostile takeovers. Second, the state legislation must leave to the shareholders the decision whether to accept the offer. Third, the Court seems to be more receptive to burdens on interstate commerce arising out of the regulation of internal corporate affairs, at least when the law in question is from the state of incorporation.

As discussed in the preceding section,[85] the third generation of state takeover statutes includes statutes that apply to corporations incorporated outside the state,[86] while other states have adopted freeze statutes[87] which delay the second step of any two-step merger or other business combination unless the transaction was approved by the target company's directors *prior* to the acquisition of a designated amount of shares by the would-be acquirer.

Although the third generation statutes purporting to regulate foreign corporations are generally based upon substantial contacts within the state, the rationale of the *CTS* decision strongly indicates that such statutes may not withstand constitutional scrutiny.[88] Thus, federal courts have invalidated the Oklahoma and Tennessee statutes on the grounds that they were unconstitutional to the extent that they applied

statute held unconstitutional because it gave incumbent management the power to block a tender offer).

The SEC has taken the position in *amicus* briefs that the presence of a director opt-out provision interferes with the statute's neutrality. On the other hand, it can be argued that the absence of an opt-out provision sets up an impermissible burden on interstate commerce.

84. *See* text accompanying footnote 79 *supra*.

85. *See* § 11.21 *supra*.

86. Ariz.H.R.Res. 2002, 38th Leg., 3d Sess., 1987 Ariz.Legis.Serv. 32–45; 1987 Fla.Laws 87–257; Idaho Code § 30–5002(9); Mass.Ann.Laws Chs. 110D, 110E; former N.C.Gen. Stat. §§ 55–9A–01 *et seq* (1989).

87. Ariz.Rev.Stat. §§ 10–1221–10–1222 (three year delay); Del.Corp.Code § 203 (three year delay); Minn.Stat.Ann. § 302A.673 (five year delay); Mo.Ann.Stat. § 351.459(3)(b) (five year delay); N.J.Rev.Stat. § 49.5–1 (five year delay); N.Y.Bus.Corp.Law § 912 (five year delay); Wash S.B. No. 6084, 1987 Wash.Leg.Serv. (No. 10) 11 (five year delay); Wis.Stat.Ann. § 180.725 (three year delay).

88. For example, the Court in *CTS* expressly noted that the state of incorporation has a special interest in regulating the internal affairs of its corporations:

The Indiana statute imposes no such problem [presenting an undue burden on interstate commerce]. So long as each state regulates voting rights *only in the corporations it has created*, each corporation will be subject to the law of only one state.

481 U.S. at 89, 107 S.Ct. at 1649, 95 L.Ed.2d 85 (emphasis supplied). *See* Thomas L. Hazen, State Anti-Takeover Legislation: The Second and Third Generations, 23 Wake Forest U.L.Rev. 77 (1988).

to corporations incorporated outside the state.[89] With regard to the freeze statutes found in Delaware, New York, and elsewhere, there is considerable question whether such statutes can withstand constitutional scrutiny.[90] It can be argued, for example, that the imposition of a multi-year delay before a merger can be consummated imposes an undue burden on interstate commerce. Nevertheless, the Delaware and New York statutes have withstood challenges at the preliminary injunction stage because of the failure to show a likelihood of success on the merits or the failure to show irreparable injury.[91]

The Seventh Circuit has upheld the Wisconsin version of the freeze statute.[92] The court acknowledged that the three-year waiting period between the purchase of shares by an acquirer not supported by target management and a subsequent merger between the acquirer and target company might well make Wisconsin companies less attractive as takeover targets. However, the court said that the Williams Act did not create a federal right to receive tender offers and thus, the state law was not preempted by the federal statute. The court also ruled that the Wisconsin statute did not violate the Commerce Clause. According to the court, there was no unconstitutional burden on interstate commerce since the law of the state of incorporation properly governs a company's internal affairs and the statute in question was "neutral" in that it does not discriminate according to residence alone. The Seventh Circuit's decision, when combined with the cases decided under the Delaware law, gives growing support to these highly questionable freeze statutes.

---

89. Tyson Foods, Inc. v. McReynolds, 865 F.2d 99 (6th Cir.1989), *affirming* 700 F.Supp. 906 (M.D.Tenn.1988) (Tennessee statute); TLX Acquisition Corp. v. Telex Corp., 679 F.Supp. 1022 (W.D.Okl.1987) (Oklahoma statute). *Cf.* Veere, Inc. v. Firestone Tire & Rubber Co., 685 F.Supp. 1027 (N.D.Ohio 1988) (indicating that there was no problem with constitutionality of Ohio statute since it applied only to target companies incorporated in Ohio). *See also* P. John Kozyris, Some Observations on State Regulation of Multistate Takeovers—Controlling Choice of Law Through the Commerce Clause, 14 Del.J.Corp.L. 499 (1989).

90. *Cf.* Hyde Park Partners, L.P. v. Connolly, 839 F.2d 837 (1st Cir.1988) (Massachusetts statute imposing one-year moratorium on takeover attempts as a sanction for violation of the statute's disclosure provisions held likely to be preempted by Williams Act).

91. *See also* West Point–Pepperell, Inc. v. Farley, Inc., 711 F.Supp. 1096 (N.D.Ga.1989) (upholding the Georgia business combination statute); Realty Acquisition Corp. v. Property Trust, 1989 WL 214477, [1990] Fed.Sec.L.Rep. ¶ 95,245 (D.Md.1989) (unpublished case) (Maryland business combination statute was not preempted by Williams Act); City Capital Associates v. Interco, Inc., 696 F.Supp. 1551 (D.Del.1988) (refusing to issue preliminary injunction against enforcement of the Delaware statute); Salant Acquisition Corp. v. Manhattan Industries, Inc., 682 F.Supp. 199 (S.D.N.Y.1988) (denying preliminary injunction because shareholder with only 8.3 percent of the stock and no financing to acquire more, was unable to show irreparable harm); BNS, Inc. v. Koppers Co., 683 F.Supp. 454 (D.Del.1988) (denying preliminary injunction; but the court noted that although the statute was probably constitutional, the constitutionality issue is not an easy one); Black & Decker Corp. v. American Standard, Inc., 679 F.Supp. 1183 (D.Del.1988) (denying preliminary injunction because of failure to show irreparable harm). *See also,* Vernitron Corp. v. Kollmorgen Corp., 21 Sec.Reg. & L.Rep. (BNA) 315 (S.D.N.Y.1989) (bench ruling upholding New York statute); Note, Delaware's Section 203 Antitakeover Statute Survives Constitutional Attack, 68 Tex.L.Rev. 235 (1990); Note, State Regulation of Hostile Takeovers: The Constitutionality of Third Generation Business Combination Statutes and the Role of the Courts, 64 St.J.L.Rev. 107 (1989).

92. Amanda Acquisition Corp. v. Universal Foods Corp., at 877 F.2d 496 (7th Cir.1989).

The permissible scope of state tender offer legislation is still in the process of being narrowed and defined, and the future of "revised" state statutes remains uncertain. Although a degree of uniformity has already been achieved—uniformity is clearly desirable in light of the potential impact of tender offers on the national economy[93]—disagreement remains as to how much uniformity is necessary and how it should be achieved. Whatever the outcome, state statutes will have played an important role in shaping federal policy and in defining the scope of the Congressional purpose of investor protection.

93. *See, e.g.,* brief for SEC as amicus curiae, Great Western United Corp. v. Kidwell, 577 F.2d 1256 (5th Cir.1978), *reversed on other grounds sub nom.* Leroy v. Great Western United Corp., 443 U.S. 173, 99 S.Ct. 2710, 61 L.Ed.2d 464 (1979).

Chapter 12

MARKET MANIPULATION, INSIDER REPORTING AND SHORT— SWING TRADING, AND FALSE SEC FILINGS

Table of Sections

§ 12.1 Market Manipulation and Deceptive Practices— Sections 9, 10, 14(e), 15(c)

Many of the Commission's anti-manipulation rules are discussed throughout this treatise. This section first analyzes the permissible scope of such rules, which is determined by the meaning of statutory term "manipulative". That discussion is followed by a brief examination of the scope of the express private right of action for manipulative practices relating to exchange-listed securities. This section concludes with a discussion of the various anti-manipulation rules.

What Constitutes Manipulative Conduct?

Section 9 of the Exchange Act outlaws manipulative practices in connection with the trading of exchange-listed securities and also provides a private remedy for investors injured by the prohibited manipu-

695

lative conduct.[1] Section 9's prohibitions are supplemented by section 10(b)[2] which empowers the SEC to promulgate rules barring manipulative as well as deceptive conduct and section 15(c)[3] which prohibits fraudulent and manipulative conduct by broker-dealers. The language of section 9 limits its application to manipulation of securities that are subject to the Exchange Act's registration and reporting requirements[4] by virtue of being listed on a national exchange;[5] whereas section 10(b) is not so limited and applies to all securities transactions utilizing an instrumentality of interstate commerce. Unlike most other provisions of the 1934 Act,[6] section 9 is limited to securities on a national exchange and does not apply to registered reporting companies in the over-the-counter markets.[7] Section 15(c) of the Act in prohibiting fraudulent broker-dealer practices covers the over-the-counter markets and municipal securities.[8]

§ 12.1

1. 15 U.S.C.A. § 78i.

Sections 10 and 15 cover manipulation with regard to NASDAQ listed securities or others in the over-the-counter markets. Cowen & Co. v. Merriam, 745 F.Supp. 925 (S.D.N.Y.1990). *See generally* Lewis D. Lowenfels, Sections 9(a)(1) and 9(a)(2) of the Securities Exchange Act of 1934: An Analysis of Two Important Anti–Manipulative Provisions Under the Federal Securities Laws, 85 Nw.U.L.Rev. 698 (1991). Manipulation of over-the-counter securities is governed by sections 10 and 15 of the Act. Cowen v. Merriam, *supra* (upholding claim under section 10(b) against market maker for allegedly manipulating the market so as to create "a false appearance of demand for the stock"). *See also* footnotes 2, 3 *infra.*

Some commentators have questioned the efficiency of prohibiting manipulative activities. *See, e.g.,* Daniel R. Fischel & David J. Ross, Should the Law Prohibit "Manipulation" in Financial Markets?, 105 Harv.L.Rev. 503 (1991). However, these prohibitions are necessary in order to maintain accurate pricing by the markets.

2. 15 U.S.C.A. § 78j(b). *See* §§ 13.2–13.12 *infra.* Both the proxy and tender offer provisions also bar manipulative conduct. 15 U.S.C.A. § 78n(a), (e). Rule 10b–3 prohibits conduct proscribed by section 9 with regard to securities not listed on a national exchange. 17 C.F.R. § 240.10b–3. *See* 17 C.F.R. § 240.10b–1. *See also* 15 U.S.C.A. § 78o(c).

3. 15 U.S.C.A. § 78o(c). Broker-dealer regulation and selected fraudulent and manipulative practices including churning, scalping and boiler room operations are discussed in chapter 10 *supra.* *See generally* Stuart C. Goldberg, Fraudulent Broker–Dealer Practices (1978 ed.); David A. Lipton, Broker–Dealer Regulation (1988); Nicholas Wolfson, Richard M. Phillips & Thomas A. Russo, Regulation of Brokers, Dealers and Securities Markets (1977).

4. 15 U.S.C.A. §§ 78l, 78m(a). *See* §§ 9.2, 9.3 *supra.*

5. The National Exchanges are the nine securities exchanges registered under section 6 of the 1934 Act. 15 U.S.C.A. § 78f. *See* §§ 9.1, 9.2 *supra.*

6. These provisions include the proxy rules, the tender offer and creeping acquisition filing requirements of the Williams Act, and section 16's provisions on insider trading. 15 U.S.C.A. §§ 78m(d)–(f), 78n(a)–(f), 78p. *See* chapter 11 *supra,* §§ 12.2–12.7 *infra.* In addition section 18(a)'s express liability for materially misleading SEC filings applies to all 1934 Act reporting companies, whether or not registered under § 12. 15 U.S.C.A. §§ 78l, 78r(a). *See* § 12.8 *infra.*

7. 15 U.S.C.A. § 78i(a). *See* §§ 9.2–9.3 *supra* for discussion of the 1934 Act's registration and periodic reporting requirements.

8. 15 U.S.C.A. § 78n(c)(1). The limited regulation of municipal securities is discussed in § 10.5 *supra.* Section 15(c)(1) does not, however, apply to government securities dealers. Government securities dealers are discussed in § 10.5.1 *supra.*

In interpreting the Exchange Act provisions the concept of manipulation is a narrow one and does not extend to many acts and practices which have the effect of manipulating the price of a security but are not so specifically intended. Presumably, manipulation has the same meaning under each of the Exchange Act provisions. In order to prevail in a suit charging manipulation it must be proven that the defendant's primary intent in entering the transaction was price manipulation.[9] The Supreme Court has repeatedly stated that manipulation is "a term of art" limited to certain types of transactions specifically designed to artificially affect the price of a security.[10] Although the Sixth Circuit at one time adopted a more expansive definition within the context of defensive tactics to a tender offer,[11] the overwhelming majority of cases support the narrow definition.[12] For example, it has been held that although they may give rise to an action for breach of contract or breach of fiduciary duty, a broker's unauthorized trades are not manipulative within the meaning of section 10(b).[13] The mere fact that prices are affected by the defendant's conduct is not sufficient to establish manipulation.[14]

The impact of the Supreme Court's decision in Schreiber v. Burlington Northern, Inc.[15] could arguably be carried over to section 10(b). The Court in *Schreiber* held that "[w]ithout misrepresentation or non-disclosure, § 14(e) has not been violated." [16] The Court reached this conclu-

---

9. *E.g.* United States v. Minuse, 142 F.2d 388, 389 (2d Cir.1944), *cert. denied* 323 U.S. 716, 65 S.Ct. 43, 89 L.Ed. 576 (1944); R.J. Koeppe & Co. v. SEC, 95 F.2d 550, 552 (7th Cir.1938).

10. Santa Fe Industries, Inc. v. Green, 430 U.S. 462, 476, 97 S.Ct. 1292, 1302, 51 L.Ed.2d 480 (1977); Ernst & Ernst v. Hochfelder, 425 U.S. 185, 199, 96 S.Ct. 1375, 1383, 47 L.Ed.2d 668 (1976). *See* Schreiber v. Burlington Northern, Inc., 472 U.S. 1, 105 S.Ct. 2458, 86 L.Ed.2d 1 (1985) which is discussed in the text accompanying footnotes 15–20 *infra*.

11. Mobil Corp. v. Marathon Oil Co., 669 F.2d 366 (6th Cir.1981); Whittaker Corp. v. Edgar, 535 F.Supp. 933, 949 (N.D.Ill.1982).

Even the Sixth Circuit retreated from its position in *Mobil*. Biechele v. Cedar Point, Inc., 747 F.2d 209 (6th Cir.1984). *See* § 11.20 *supra*. *See generally* Elliott J. Weiss, Defensive Response to Tender Offers and the Williams Act's Prohibition Against Manipulation, 35 Vand.L.Rev. 1087 (1982).

12. *See, e.g.*, United States v. Mulheren, 938 F.2d 364 (2d Cir.1991) (reversing conviction for manipulation due to failure to establish that defendant purchased stock with the intent to manipulate the price); Jolley v. Welch, 904 F.2d 988 (5th Cir.1990), *cert. denied* 498 U.S. 1050, 111 S.Ct. 762, 112 L.Ed.2d 781 (1991) (failure to provide investors with options disclosure documents did not amount to manipulation; plaintiffs did not allege that the alleged manipulative practices affected the market or purchase price of a security).

13. Pross v. Baird Patrick & Co., 585 F.Supp. 1456 (S.D.N.Y.1984). *See also, e.g.*, In re Olympia Brewing Co. Securities Litigation, 613 F.Supp. 1286 (N.D.Ill.1985) (injection of accurate information into the market although designed to affect the stock price does not constitute manipulative conduct).

14. *E.g.*, In re Scattered Corp. Securities Litigation, 844 F.Supp. 416 (N.D.Ill.1994) (large volume of short sales was not manipulative; if anything it made the market more efficient by accurately reflecting bearish view of the securities in question).

15. 472 U.S. 1, 105 S.Ct. 2458, 86 L.Ed.2d 1 (1985).

16. *Id.* at 12, 105 S.Ct. at 2464–65, 86 L.Ed.2d at 10. The Court further noted, "[n]owhere in the legislative history is there the slightest suggestion that section 14(e) serves any purpose other than disclosure * * * "*id.* at 11, 105 S.Ct. at 2464, 86 L.Ed.2d at

sion by a rather unusual view of the section's legislative history.[17] When enacted in 1968, section 14(e) prohibited material misrepresentations and omissions of material fact as well as "fraudulent, deceptive, or manipulative acts or practices" in connection with a tender offer. But the court seems to have ignored the plain meaning of the statute and its use of a disjunctive "or". As a result of the *Schreiber* decision, unless the Court retreats from its broad-brush approach, it seems clear that not only is section 14(e) on its face limited to disclosure but also any rules promulgated thereunder are invalid to the extent that they go beyond disclosure. Extending the *Schreiber* rationale to section 10(b) would lead to the unwise and unfortunate result of invalidating a number of the section 10(b) rules dealing with manipulative conduct. In the course of its opinion in *Schreiber*, the Court did give some basis for distinguishing section 10(b) from section 14(e) by pointing out that in section 14(e) Congress added the term "fraudulent". However, the Court negated any possible significance of this difference.[18] Perhaps even more troubling is the Supreme Court's comment that similar language is found in section 15(c).[19] Applying *Schreiber* to section 15(c) would go even further in eliminating SEC rules that address manipulative conduct apart from the disclosure context. Aside from merely rethinking the unnecessarily broad brush that the Court used in deciding *Schreiber*, the implications of the Court's dictum undermine the securities laws' focus on efficient yet honest markets. The thrust of sections 10(b) and 15(c) seems to be aimed equally at deceptive and manipulative conduct, and it would be unwarranted for a court to use a judicial eraser to eradicate the legislatively penned term "manipulative" from the statute. Even beyond the possible limitations imposed by the *Schreiber* case, allegations of manipulative conduct will not support a private remedy, even for injunctive relief, absent any injury or causal connection to the plaintiff's investment activities.[20]

Major support for a restrictive reading of what constitutes manipulative conduct can be found in section 9's definitions. Following the narrow view of manipulation, section 9(a) expressly prohibits "wash sales," "matched sales" or any transactions entered into simultaneously where the purpose is to create "a misleading appearance of active trading." [21] The section also prohibits any exchange-based transactions that give the artificial impression of active trading as well as transac-

---

9. *See also, e.g.,* Metzner v. D.H. Blair & Co., 689 F.Supp. 262 (S.D.N.Y.1988) (nondisclosure of market manipulation violates Rule 10b–5).

17. 472 U.S. at 13, 105 S.Ct. at 2465, 86 L.Ed.2d at 10. *See also* the discussion in § 11.15 *supra.*

18. "For the purpose of interpreting the term 'manipulative,' the most significant changes from the language of § 10(b) were the addition of the term 'fraudulent,' and the reference to 'acts' rather than 'devices.' Neither change bears in any obvious way on the meaning to be given to 'manipulative.' " *Id.* at 11 n. 10, 105 S.Ct. at 2464 n. 10, 86 L.Ed.2d at 9 n. 10.

19. *Id.*

20. Packer v. Yampol, 630 F.Supp. 1237 (S.D.N.Y.1986).

21. 15 U.S.C.A. § 78i(a)(1).

tions entered into for the purpose of depressing or raising the price.[22] Section 9(a)(6) empowers the Commission to promulgate rules prohibiting "pegging, fixing or stabilizing" securities prices.[23]

Rule 10b–6 prohibits all such activity by anyone connected with a securities distribution unless in compliance with the parameters for limited stabilizing bids set forth in Rules 10b–7 and 10b–8 in connection with certain offerings.[24] Also, in order to prevent manipulation in connection with tender offers, Rule 10b–13 prohibits persons making a tender offer from purchasing the securities other than through that offer, once the offer has been made known.[25] Aside from the foregoing, the Commission has decided not to adopt specific rules prohibiting stabilizing activity outside of the tender offer and distribution context.[26] However, the more generalized antimanipulation rules will apply to practices intended to artificially stabilize prices.

Another type of manipulation that section 9 is concerned with involves the use of put and call options.[27] Section 9(b)[28] gives the Commission rule-making power with regard to options transactions entered into without the intent to follow through with respect to the underlying security in accordance with the rights and obligations defined by the option. The Commission has not imposed any substantive prohibitions but rather has elected to deal with put and call options for securities by requiring an adequate disclosure document.[29] The provi-

---

22. 15 U.S.C.A. § 78i(a)(2), (3). *See, e.g.,* SEC v. Malenfant, 784 F.Supp. 141 (S.D.N.Y. 1992) (allegations that defendant entered a series of matched orders designed to artificially inflate the price of the stock stated a claim under § 9(a)(1), (a)(2); it was not necessary to allege that the trades were actually executed—it was sufficient to allege that the orders were entered).

See footnote 9, *supra* for discussion of the *"purpose"* requirement.

23. 15 U.S.C.A. § 78i(a)(6). "Parking" securities so as to disguise the identity of the true owner has been characterized as manipulative. SEC v. Jeffries, 1987 WL 11750, [1987 Transfer Binder] Fed.Sec.L.Rep. (CCH) ¶ 93,171 (S.D.N.Y.1987)(consent order).

24. 17 C.F.R. §§ 240.10b–6, 240.10b–7, 240.10b–8. *See* SEC v. Burns, 816 F.2d 471 (9th Cir.1987) (finding 10b–6 violations); SEC v. Burns, 614 F.Supp. 1360 (S.D.Cal.1985) (dismissing without prejudice SEC charge of 10b–6 violation for failure to adequately allege scienter).

Rule 10b–6, which has its self-contained exemptions, is discussed in § 6.1 *supra.* *See also* John B. Manning, Jr. & Eric E. Miller, The SEC's Recent Revisions to Rule 10b–6, 11 Sec.Reg.L.J. 195 (1983); M. Louise Turilli, Rule 10b–6 and the Issuer of Securities, 22 Rev.Sec. & Commod.Reg. 31 (1989).

25. 17 C.F.R. § 240.10b–13. *See* City National Bank v. American Commonwealth Financial Corp., 801 F.2d 714 (4th Cir.1986), *cert. denied* 479 U.S. 1091, 107 S.Ct. 1301, 94 L.Ed.2d 157 (1987) (awarding damages for violation of Rule 10b–13 and common law fraud). *But cf.* Beaumont v. American Can Co., 797 F.2d 79 (2d Cir.1986) (questioning the existence of a private remedy under Rules 10b–6 and 10b–13). *See also* Robert M. Goolrick, Purchases on the Market of Target Company Stock, 26 Bus.Law. 457 (1970); Lewis D. Lowenfels, Rule 10b–13, Rule 10b–6 and Purchases of Target Company Securities During an Exchange Offer, 69 Colum.L.Rev. 1392 (1969). *See* § 11.15 *supra.*

26. *See* Sec.Exch. Act Rel. No. 34–2446 (March 18, 1940).

27. For a discussion of the options market *see* SEC, Report of the Special Study of the Options Markets, 96th Cong. 1st Sess. (1978).

28. 15 U.S.C.A. § 78i(b).

29. 17 C.F.R. § 240.9b–1.

sions relating to options do not apply to warrants (options issued by the issuer)[30] and they are limited to options with regard to securities and are not to be confused with future contracts or options relating to commodities which are regulated by the Commodities Futures Trading Commission.[31]

When an issuer purchases its own securities there is the potential for manipulation. Section 13(e) regulates issuer purchases generally.[32] With regard to manipulation, the SEC has adopted a safe harbor rule for securities purchases by issuers and affiliates. Purchases of an issuer's own securities made in compliance with Rule 10b–18[33] will not be in violation of either section 9(a)(2) or Rule 10b–5. An issuer's securities may be purchased by the issuer or an affiliate so long as it is through a single broker and orders placed for such transactions are entered on one day.[34] The safe harbor also requires that the price be no higher than the last independently established price.[35] Additionally, there are volume limitations on Rule 10b–18's safe harbor.[36] Specific transactions are excluded from the rule's safe harbor, including those pursuant to a merger or an issuer's purchases of its own securities in a Rule 13e–1 or 13e–4 transaction.[37] Since it only defines a safe harbor, failure to comply with Rule 10b–18 does not even raise a presumption that the issuer's purchases are manipulative.[38]

Section 9(e)'s Express Remedy

Section 9(e) gives a private remedy in damages to any investor who is injured by conduct in violation of section 9[39] which is limited to

---

30. 15 U.S.C.A. § 78i(d).

31. *See* 7 U.S.C.A. §§ 1 *et seq. See generally,* Philip M. Johnson & Thomas L. Hazen, Commodities Regulation (2d ed. 1989). In recent years there has been a blurring of the distinction between the options and futures markets with listed trading of financial index futures and options and foreign currency futures and options. *See* § 1.5.1 *supra* and §§ 19.6–19.8 *infra* (Practitioner's Edition only).

32. 15 U.S.C.A. § 78m(e). *See* § 11.17 *supra.*

33. 17 C.F.R. § 240.10b–18 which is discussed in § 11.17 *supra. See* Sec.Exch. Act Rel. No. 34–19244 (Nov. 17, 1982).

34. 17 C.F.R. § 240.10b–18(b)(1).

35. 17 C.F.R. § 240.10b–18(b)(3).

36. 17 C.F.R. § 240.10b–18(b)(4) (in order to qualify for the safe harbor, Rule 10b–18 purchases cannot be in excess of twenty-five percent of the average daily trading volume).

37. 17 C.F.R. § 240.10b–18(a)(3). *See* 17 C.F.R. §§ 240.13e–1, 240.13e–4. *See also* the discussion of Regulation 13E in § 11.17 *supra.*

38. Former proposed Rule 13e–2 would have taken a much sterner view of issuer purchases of its own shares. *See* Sec.Exch. Act Rel. No. 34–19244 (Nov. 17, 1982). For examples of other safe harbor rules *see* Rule 147 (intrastate exemption from the 1933 Act), Rule 175 (for projections) and Rule 506 (private placements). 17 C.F.R. §§ 230.147, 230.175, 230.506. *See* §§ 3.7, 4.12, 4.22 *supra.*

39. 15 U.S.C.A. § 78i(e). As discussed *infra,* section 9(e)'s express remedy is limited to exchange-listed securities. At least one court has indicated, however, that manipulative conduct may be challenged by way of an implied action under section 9(a). *See* Matthey v. KDI Corp., 699 F.Supp. 135 (S.D. Ohio 1988). Arguably, the section 9(a) remedy, if it exists, would not be as limited as the express remedy under section 9(e). Broadening the section 9 private remedies by implication seems contrary to the approach currently taken to implied remedies generally. *See* § 13.1 *infra.*

securities on a national exchange.[40] In addition to costs and reasonable attorneys' fees, the plaintiff is entitled to damages based on the difference between the actual value and the price as affected by the manipulative conduct.[41] Liability under section 9(e) is expressly limited to persons "willfully" participating in the manipulative conduct; willfulness would seem to be an even stricter requirement than that of scienter which is required generally in suits under Rule 10b–5.[42] It must be remembered that in addition to the defendant's willful participation, the substantive violation requires proof of manipulative intent.[43] In addition, in order to recover for manipulative conduct, the plaintiff must show that his or her injury was a direct, rather than remote, consequence of the prohibited activity.[44] All of the foregoing factors combine to make the section 9(e) remedy a very limited one.[45]

The Fifth Circuit initially held that manipulative activity that comes within the scope of section 9 cannot give rise to a Rule 10b–5 action independently; plaintiff had to establish that all of section 9's elements have been met.[46] Quite properly, however, that decision was vacated and remanded[47] for further consideration in light of Herman & MacLean

---

It has been held that an action under section 9 is limited to purchasers and sellers and thus cannot be maintained by an issuer claiming manipulation of its securities. Arvin Industries v. Wanandi, 722 F.Supp. 532 (S.D.Ind.1989). *Cf.* FMC Corp. v. Boesky, 727 F.Supp. 1182 (N.D.Ill.1989) (issuer failed to allege facts showing damage compensable under section 9(a) since there was no showing that it paid an unreasonable premium for its shares in a recapitalization).

40. *E.g.,* Cowen & Co. v. Merriam, 745 F.Supp. 925 (S.D.N.Y.1990) (section 9 action could not be brought for alleged manipulation in stock traded through the NASD Automated System since NASDAQ is not a "national securities exchange"). *See* footnotes 4–6 *supra.*

41. 15 U.S.C.A. § 78i(e).

42. *See* § 13.4 *infra.*

43. *See* Annot. What Constitutes Willfulness or Manipulative Purpose so as to Warrant Imposition of Liability in Private Civil Action Based on Price Manipulation Provisions of Securities Exchange Act (15 U.S.C.A. §§ 78i(a)(2); 78i(e)), 25 A.L.R.Fed. 623 (1975) and footnote 3 *supra.*

44. *Cf.* Holmes v. Securities Investor Protection Corp., 503 U.S. 258, 112 S.Ct. 1311, 117 L.Ed.2d 532 (1992), *on remand* 964 F.2d 924 (9th Cir.1992) (SIPC was too remote and thus lacked standing under either RICO or Securities Investor Protection Act to complain of manipulation that allegedly prevented broker-dealers from meeting their customer obligations).

45. The section 9(e) remedy has been described as follows:

To show a violation of section 9(a)(2) in a private suit under section 9(e), a plaintiff must plead and prove that

(1) a series of transactions in a security creating actual or apparent trading in that security or raising or depressing the price of that security, (2) carried out with scienter, (3) for the purpose of inducing the security's sale or purchase by others, (4) was relied on by the plaintiff, (5) and affected the plaintiff's purchase or selling price.

Ray v. Lehman Brothers Kuhn Loeb, Inc., 624 F.Supp. 16, 19 (N.D.Ga.1984), quoting Chemetron Corp. v. Business Funds, Inc., 682 F.2d 1149, 1164 (5th Cir.1982), *vacated on other grounds* 460 U.S. 1007, 103 S.Ct. 1245, 75 L.Ed.2d 476 (1983), *rehearing granted* 718 F.2d 725 (5th Cir.1983).

46. Chemetron Corp. v. Business Funds, Inc., 682 F.2d 1149 (5th Cir.1982), *vacated and remanded* 460 U.S. 1007, 103 S.Ct. 1245, 75 L.Ed.2d 476 (1983), *on remand* 718 F.2d 725 (5th Cir.1983).

47. *Id.*

v. Huddleston[48] which held that the remedies under Rule 10b–5 and section 11 of the 1933 Act[49] are cumulative. It seems doubtful that the section 9 and Rule 10b–5 remedies are mutually exclusive;[50] in other words, a plaintiff may sue under either or both sections. The Fifth Circuit on remand followed this view and reinstated the plaintiff's 10b–5 claim.[51]

Manipulative and Deceptive Acts and Practices—Section 10; Section 15(c)

Section 10. Section 10(a) of the 1934 Act[52] prohibits "short sales" and "stop loss" orders in violation of SEC rules.[53] Section 10(b), which is much broader, provides that it is unlawful "to use or employ [utilizing any means or instrumentality of interstate commerce], in connection with the purchase or sale of any security * * * any manipulative or deceptive device or contrivance in contravention of such rules and regulations as the Commission may prescribe as necessary or appropriate in the public interest or for the protection of investors."[54] The SEC, following the legislative mandate, has prohibited a wide variety of conduct that is outlined here and discussed more fully in other sections of this book.

Rule 10b–1[55] applies the prohibitions against market manipulation contained in section 9(a)[56] to securities exempt from section 12's registration requirements.[57] Former Rule 10b–2 prohibited persons who were participating in primary and secondary securities distributions from soliciting purchases on an exchange to facilitate the distribution.[58] Former Rule 10b–2, which did not apply to broker-dealers in the normal performance of their business,[59] was rescinded in 1993.[60] In announcing

---

48.   459 U.S. 375, 103 S.Ct. 683, 74 L.Ed.2d 548 (1983).

49.   15 U.S.C.A. § 77k. *See* §§ 7.3, 7.4 *supra.*

50.   *See* Marc I. Steinberg, The Propriety and Scope of Cumulative Remedies Under the Federal Securities Laws, 67 Cornell L.Rev. 557 (1982).

51.   Chemetron Corp. v. Business Funds, Inc., 718 F.2d 725 (5th Cir.1983).

52.   15 U.S.C.A. § 78j(a).

53.   Rule 10a–1, 17 C.F.R. § 240.10a–1 sets out the SEC's position. Rule 10a–2 governs the covering of short sales, 17 C.F.R. § 240.10a–2. *See* § 10.12 *supra. Cf.* Sullivan & Long, Inc. v. Scattered Corp., 47 F.3d 857 (7th Cir.1995), *affirming* 844 F.Supp. 416 (N.D.Ill.1994) (large volume of short sales was not manipulative; if anything it made the market more efficient by accurately reflecting bearish view of the securities in question).

54.   15 U.S.C.A. § 78j(b). *See, e.g.,* SEC v. Malenfant, 784 F.Supp. 141 (S.D.N.Y.1992) (allegations that defendant entered a series of matched orders designed to artificially inflate the price of the stock stated a claim under § 10(b)).

55.   17 C.F.R. § 240.10b–1.

56.   15 U.S.C.A. § 78i(a).

57.   15 U.S.C.A. § 78*l. See* Smith v. Oppenheimer & Co., 635 F.Supp. 936 (W.D.Mich. 1985) (private suit for violation of rule 10b–1 dismissed for failure to allege that the challenged activities' purpose was to artificially affect the stock price). *See* § 9.2 *supra.*

58.   17 C.F.R. § 240.10b–2 (1993) (rescinded).

59.   17 C.F.R. § 240.10b–2(c) (1993) (rescinded).

60.   Exch.Act Rel. No. 34–2100, [1992–1993 Transfer Binder] Fed.Sec.L.Rep. (CCH) ¶ ___ (SEC April 8, 1993).

its rescission of the rule, the Commission explained that it was unnecessary and duplicative since other antifraud and antimanipulation rules provide adequate protection against manipulation in connection with a distribution.[61]

Rule 10b–3 prohibits broker-dealers from engaging in manipulative or deceptive acts and practices with regard to securities not traded on a national exchange[62] and with regard to municipal securities.[63] Rule 10b–3 thus closes a large part of the gap left by section 9 which applies only to transactions effected through a national exchange.[64]

Former Rule 10b–4 addressed short tendering in connection with tender offers and has been replaced by Rule 14e–4.[65] Today, Rule 14e–4 prohibits short tendering and hedged tendering of securities in connection with a tender offer. The rule prohibits responding to tender offers by tender or guarantee unless the person so responding owns the security in question. The short tender prohibition is not violated where the person tendering has an exercisable option to purchase the security.[66] The strict prohibition against short tendering reflects the potential for greater abuse[67] than with short sales which are allowed under appropriate safeguards.[68]

Rule 10b–5[69] is the broadest of the section 10(b) rules. Rule 10b–5 prohibits material misstatements and omissions as well as fraudulent acts in connection with purchases and sales of securities; it supports a broad implied private right of action.[70] Rule 10b–5 is considered in the chapter that follows.

---

61. *Id.* Most notably, SEC Rule 10b–6 prohibits manipulation by participants in a distribution. *See* § 6.1 *supra.*

62. 17 C.F.R. § 240.10b–3(a). *See also, e.g.,* Beres v. Thomason McKinnon Securities, Inc., 1989 WL 105967, [1989–1990 Transfer Binder] Fed.Sec.L.Rep. ¶ 94,923 (S.D.N.Y. 1989) (no private right of action for violations of Rule 10b–3 since the rule is a corollary of section 15(c)).

63. 17 C.F.R. § 240.10b–3(b). Municipal securities are discussed in § 10.5 *supra.*

64. *See* text accompanying footnotes 21–51 *supra.*

65. 17 C.F.R. § 240.14e–4. *See* 17 C.F.R. § 240.10b–4 (1990). *See* Merrill Lynch, Pierce, Fenner & Smith, Inc. v. Bobker, 808 F.2d 930 (2d Cir.1986) (finding no 10b–4 violation where defendant's short sales did not increase or leverage the securities tendered). *Cf.* In re Scattered Corp. Securities Litigation, 844 F.Supp. 416 (N.D.Ill.1994) (large volume of short sales was not manipulative; if anything it made the market more efficient by accurately reflecting bearish view of the securities in question).

See Sec.Exch. Act Rel. No. 34–26609, [1989 Transfer Binder] Fed.Sec.L.Rep. (CCH) ¶ 84,401 (March 8, 1989). The Commission also asked for comment on the deregulation of hedged tendering.

66. 17 C.F.R. § 240.14e–4.

67. Tender offers are discussed in §§ 11.10–11.22 *supra. See* in particular § 11.15 *supra* dealing with fraudulent and manipulative acts and practices which are prohibited by 15 U.S.C.A. § 78n(e). *See also* § 11.19 *supra* for discussion of section 14(e)'s implied private remedy.

68. *See* § 10.12 *supra.*

69. 17 C.F.R. § 240.10b–5.

70. *See* §§ 13.2–13.12 *infra.*

Rule 10b–6[71] prohibits purchases during a distribution of securities by persons interested in the distribution except for stabilizing bids in compliance with Rule 10b–7.[72] Rule 10b–8[73] prohibits manipulative and deceptive devices in connection with a securities distribution through rights held by security holders.

Rule 10b–9 prohibits "all or none" offerings of securities unless all such securities are "sold at a specified price within a specified time, and * * * the total amount due to the seller is received by him by a specified date."[74] The rule imposes the same requirements for offerings where all or part of the purchase price will be refunded if the offering is not fully subscribed.[75] Rule 10b–9 does not apply where an underwriter or someone else is obligated to purchase all of the securities being offered.[76] A private right of action for violation of Rule 10b–9 has been recognized by at least one court.[77]

Rule 10b–10 requires that brokers confirm all transactions in writing.[78] The confirmation must disclose the broker's commission and whether he or she is acting as principal or as an agent for someone other than the customer.[79] The written confirmation in turn qualifies as a "prospectus" under section 2(10) of the 1933 Act,[80] thus requiring compliance with section 5(b)(1)'s requirement that there be a statutory prospectus absent an applicable exemption.[81]

Rule 10b–13[82] prohibits a tender offeror from purchasing securities targeted by the tender offer once the tender offer has commenced.[83]

Rule 10b–16[84] requires disclosure of credit terms in connection with margin transactions.[85]

---

71. 17 C.F.R. § 240.10b–6. *See, e.g.,* Fred N. Gerard & Michael L. Hirschfeld, The Scienter Requirement Under Rule 10b–6, 46 Bus.Law. 777 (1991).

72. 17 C.F.R. § 240.10b–7. *See* § 6.1 *supra.*

73. 17 C.F.R. § 240.10b–8.

74. 17 C.F.R. § 240.10b–9(a)(1). *See generally* Robert B. Robbins, All–Or–None Offerings, 19 Rev.Sec. & Commodities Reg. 59 (1986). *See also* § 6.3 *supra.*

75. 17 C.F.R. § 240.10b–9(a)(2).

76. 17 C.F.R. § 240.10b–9(b). *Cf.* Becherer v. Merrill Lynch, Pierce, Fenner & Smith, Inc., 43 F.3d 1054 (6th Cir.1995) (Rule 10b–9 ceases to apply once the minimum sales conditions have been satisfied).

77. Bormann v. Applied Vision Systems Inc., 800 F.Supp. 800 (D.Minn.1992) (describing the decision as a case of first impression).

78. 17 C.F.R. § 240.10b–10.

79. *Id. Cf.* Chasins v. Smith, Barney & Co., 438 F.2d 1167 (2d Cir.1970) (decided prior to adoption of 10b–10 and holding failure to disclose market-maker status violated Rule 10b–5). *See* § 10.3 *supra.*

80. 15 U.S.C.A. § 77b(10).

81. 15 U.S.C.A. § 77e(b)(1), 77j. *See* §§ 2.4, 2.5 *supra.*

82. 17 C.F.R. § 240.10b–13. *See* Lewis D. Lowenfels, Rule 10b–13, Rule 10b–6 and Purchases of Target Company Securities During an Exchange Offer, 69 Colum.L.Rev. 1392 (1969). *See also* §§ 6.1, 11.15 *supra.*

83. Tender offers are discussed in §§ 11.10–11.22 *supra.*

84. 17 C.F.R. § 240.10b–16.

85. *See* § 10.11 *supra.*

Rule 10b–17 prohibits untimely announcements of dividends, stock splits, reverse stock splits and rights or subscription offerings.[86] The announcement must be in compliance with applicable exchange rules[87] or must be given to the National Association of Securities Dealers (NASD)[88] at least ten days prior to the record date and must describe the nature of the distribution or offering.

Rule 10b–18 sets out a safe harbor rule for issuer purchases of its own shares.[89] Compliance with Rule 10b–18 precludes a finding of manipulative conduct[90] but does not affect filing obligations under section 13(e).[91]

In terms of supporting an implied remedy, Rule 10b–5,[92] the general antifraud provision, can be used by purchasers or sellers of securities who have been injured in connection with that purchase or sale due to deceptive conduct by a defendant acting with scienter.[93] The Rule 10b–5 remedy has been used in a wide variety of situations including insider trading,[94] corporate mismanagement involving deception,[95] manipulative conduct,[96] and false SEC filings.[97] Rules 10b–6 and 10b–13 may support a private remedy but only if brought by an injured investor whom the rule was designed to protect.[98] There has also been scattered authority for an implied remedy in Rule 10b–16's margin disclosure requirements.[99] It would seem that any manipulative or fraudulent acts by a defendant acting with scienter under the other 10(b) rules will support a

86. 17 C.F.R. § 240.10b–17.

87. 17 C.F.R. § 240.10b–17(b)(3).

88. 17 C.F.R. § 240.10b–17(b)(1).

89. 17 C.F.R. § 240.10b–18. *See* § 11.17 *supra.*

90. 17 C.F.R. § 240.10b–18. *See* § 11.20 *supra* dealing with defensive tactics to takeover attempts.

91. 15 U.S.C.A. § 78m(e). *See* § 11.17 *supra.*

92. *See* § 13.2 *infra.*

93. *See* Herman & MacLean v. Huddleston, 459 U.S. 375, 103 S.Ct. 683, 74 L.Ed.2d 548 (1983), *on remand* 705 F.2d 775 (5th Cir.1983); Santa Fe Industries, Inc. v. Green, 430 U.S. 462, 97 S.Ct. 1292, 51 L.Ed.2d 480 (1977); Ernst & Ernst v. Hochfelder, 425 U.S. 185, 96 S.Ct. 1375, 47 L.Ed.2d 668 (1976); Blue Chip Stamps v. Manor Drug Stores, 421 U.S. 723, 95 S.Ct. 1917, 44 L.Ed.2d 539 (1975); Affiliated Ute Citizens of Utah v. United States, 406 U.S. 128, 92 S.Ct. 1456, 31 L.Ed.2d 741 (1972); Superintendent of Insurance v. Bankers Life & Casualty Co., 404 U.S. 6, 92 S.Ct. 165, 30 L.Ed.2d 128 (1971), *on remand* 401 F.Supp. 640 (S.D.N.Y.1975). *See* §§ 13.2–13.12 *infra.*

94. *E.g.* Elkind v. Liggett & Myers, Inc., 635 F.2d 156 (2d Cir.1980). *See* § 13.9 *infra.*

95. *E.g.* Goldberg v. Meridor, 567 F.2d 209 (2d Cir.1977), *cert. denied* 434 U.S. 1069, 98 S.Ct. 1249, 55 L.Ed.2d 771 (1978). *See* § 13.11 *infra.*

96. Chemetron Corp. v. Business Funds, Inc., 718 F.2d 725 (5th Cir.1983).

97. *E.g.* Ross v. A.H. Robins Co., 607 F.2d 545 (2d Cir.1979), *cert. denied* 446 U.S. 946, 100 S.Ct. 2175, 64 L.Ed.2d 802 (1980). *See* § 12.8 *infra.*

98. *See* Piper v. Chris–Craft Industries, Inc., 430 U.S. 1, 97 S.Ct. 926, 51 L.Ed.2d 124 (1977). *See also* Crane Co. v. American Standard, Inc., 603 F.2d 244 (2d Cir.1979); Crane Co. v. Westinghouse Air Brake Co., 419 F.2d 787 (2d Cir.1969), *cert. denied* 400 U.S. 822, 91 S.Ct. 41, 27 L.Ed.2d 50 (1970). *See* §§ 6.1, 11.19 *supra.*

99. *See* § 10.11 *supra.*

private remedy akin to a Rule 10b–5 action.[100]

The most recent antimanipulation rule adopted under section 10(b) is Rule 10b–21[101] which prohibits certain short sales in connection with a public offering or an offering under Regulation A's[102] exemption for certain offerings of not more than five million dollars.[103]   Under the rule, subject to exemptions,[104] if a short sale is made after the filing of the registration statement or Form 1–A[105] filing and before the effective date, the short seller cannot cover the short sale with securities offered by an underwriter, broker or dealer participating in the registered or Regulation A offering.[106]

In adopting the short sale prohibitions, the Commission was concerned with the prevention of manipulative conduct.[107]   As discussed more fully directly below, the Supreme Court has at least cast a cloud over the Commission's ability to proscribe conduct which is manipulative but not deceptive.[108]

In adopting the rule the Commission identified the primary objective of Rule 10b–21(T) as the prevention of manipulative short selling.[109] There is no mention of the deceptive nature of such conduct.

[*See* Practitioner's Edition for discussion of broker-dealer antimanipulation rules]

---

100. In an analogous setting the courts have held that, although the rules of self-regulatory organizations do not support private remedies, intentional violation of those rules may rise to the level of Rule 10b–5 violations. *See, e.g.,* Utah State University of Agriculture & Applied Science v. Bear Stearns & Co., 549 F.2d 164, 167–69 (10th Cir. 1977), *cert. denied* 434 U.S. 890, 98 S.Ct. 264, 54 L.Ed.2d 176 (1977); Shull v. Dain, Kalman & Quail, Inc., 561 F.2d 152 (8th Cir. 1977), *cert. denied* 434 U.S. 1086, 98 S.Ct. 1281, 55 L.Ed.2d 792 (1978). *See* §§ 10.7, 10.8, 10.14 *supra.*

101. 17 C.F.R. § 240.10b–21. Rule 10b–21(T) was originally adopted as a temporary rule. 17 C.F.R. § 240.10b–21(T) (1993) which was made permanent in 1994. *See* Exch. Act Rel. No. 34–33702, 1994 SEC LEXIS 559 (SEC March 2, 1994).

102. 17 C.F.R. §§ 230.251–263. *See* § 4.15 *supra* for a discussion of Regulation A.

103. 17 C.F.R. § 240.10b–21. *See* Sec.Act Rel. No. 33–6798, Sec.Exch. Act Rel. No. 34–26028, [1988–89 Transfer Binder] Fed.Sec.L.Rep. (CCH) ¶ 84,315 (SEC Aug. 25, 1988). *See also* the discussion in § 10.12 *supra.*

104. Specifically excluded from the rule's prohibitions are securities offered pursuant to a shelf registration in accordance with SEC Rule 415. 17 C.F.R. § 240.10b–21(b). *See* 17 C.F.R. § 230.415 which is discussed in § 3.8 *supra.* Additionally, the Commission may, either upon request or its own motion, grant an exemption from Rule 10b–21's prohibitions. 17 C.F.R. § 240.10b–21(c). Such an exemption from the short sale prohibitions may be granted either unconditionally or pursuant to specified terms and conditions. *Id.*

105. Form 1–A is the filing required by Regulation A that parallels the 1933 Act registration statement. *See* 17 C.F.R. § 230.255.

106. 17 C.F.R. § 240.10b–21(a).

107. Sec.Act Rel. No. 33–6798, Sec.Exch. Act Rel. No. 34–26028, [1988–89 Transfer Binder] Fed.Sec.L.Rep. (CCH) ¶ 84,315 (SEC Aug. 25, 1988).

108. Schreiber v. Burlington Northern, Inc., 472 U.S. 1, 105 S.Ct. 2458, 86 L.Ed.2d 1 (1985).

109. Sec.Act Rel. No. 33–6798, Sec.Exch. Act Rel. No. 34–26028, [1988–89 Transfer Binder] Fed.Sec.L.Rep. (CCH) ¶ 84,315 at p. 89,390 (SEC Aug. 25, 1988).

§ 12.2 Reporting Requirements for Insiders and Their Transactions in Shares—Section 16(a)

By virtue of section 16(a) of the Exchange Act,[1] all officers, directors, and beneficial owners of more than ten percent of any class of equity security registered under section 12 of the Act[2] must file appropriate notice with the Commission within ten days of becoming an officer, director, or beneficial owner. The section 16(a) notice must include disclosure of all ownership interest in any of the issuer's equity securities. Further, when there has been a change in the officer's, director's, or beneficial owner's share holdings, notice must also be filed with the Commission within ten days of the end of the calendar month in which the change takes place.[3] This periodic notice and reporting must include the ownership at the close of the month and any changes in ownership that occurred during the month.

Section 16(a) reports are publicly available at the Commission's office in Washington, D.C. The Commission also publishes official monthly summaries of the section 16(a) reports. Some investment analysts, by watching insider transactions, try to get a sense of how the issuer's securities are likely to fare in the future. Insider sales in the aggregate for any particular company are viewed as one indicator of the issuer's health. Similarly, on a macro level, the market's overall health is judged at least in part by the balance between aggregate insider purchases and aggregate insider sales.

In addition to its reporting requirements, section 16(a) also determines who is subject to section 16(b)'s provisions for disgorgement of insider short-swing profits.[4]

---

§ 12.2

1. 15 U.S.C.A. § 78p(a). However, private foreign issuers, even if they are not exempt from registration, are not subject to section 16. *See* Rule 3a12–3, 17 C.F.R. § 240.3a12–3.

For a detailed discussion of section 16 *see* Peter J. Romeo & Alan L. Dye, Section 16 of the Securities Exchange Act of 1934 (1994).

2. 15 U.S.C.A. § 78*l*. Section 16 does not apply to issuers whose 1934 Act reporting obligations are triggered by section 15(d). *Id.* *See* 15 U.S.C.A. § 78o(d). *See also* §§ 9.2, 9.3 *supra.*

3. 15 U.S.C.A. § 78p(a). Violation of the filing requirements can result in criminal sanctions. *E.g.* United States v. Guterma, 281 F.2d 742 (2d Cir.), *cert. denied* 364 U.S. 871, 81 S.Ct. 114, 5 L.Ed.2d 93 (1960).

In late 1983, Ralph Nader claimed widespread noncompliance with section 16(a)'s filing requirements. Over the next several months the SEC initiated more than 32 enforcement actions.

In 1988, the SEC became increasingly concerned with the large number of section 16(a) violations. The Commission subsequently proposed overhauling the reporting rules. Sec. Exch.Act Rel. No. 34–26333, [1988–89 Transfer Binder] Fed.Sec.L.Rep. (CCH) ¶ 84,343 (Dec. 2, 1988). *See* Peter J. Romeo & Alan L. Dye, Reforming Section 16, 22 Rev.Sec. & Commod.Reg. 23 (1989); Report of the Task Force on Regulation of Insider Trading, Part II: Reform of Section 16, 42 Bus.Law. 1087 (1988). The new rules were adopted in 1991.

4. 15 U.S.C.A. § 78p(b); § 12.3 *infra.* Violations of section 16(a)'s filing requirements do not give rise to a private remedy. Scientex Corp. v. Kay, 689 F.2d 879 (9th Cir.1982); C.R.A. Realty Corp. v. Goodyear Tire & Rubber Co., 705 F.Supp. 972 (S.D.N.Y.1989); Eisenberger v. Spectex Indus., Inc., 644 F.Supp. 48, 50 (E.D.N.Y.1986) (section 16(a) does not support an implied private remedy). Violation can result in criminal sanctions; *see* footnote 3 *supra.*

The initial section 16(a) filing must be made on Form 3 while all subsequent filings indicating a change in beneficial ownership, must be filed on Form 4.[5] In 1991, the Commission adopted Form 5 to be filed annually to disclose any reportable section 16 transactions that were not reported on Form 3 or 4 because of an exemption or that should have been reported during the year on Form 3 or 4 but were not so reported.[6] If a Form 5 is due, it must be made within forty-five days after the close of the issuer's fiscal year. Under the new reporting regime, transactions which are exempt and thus eligible for reporting on Form 5 may voluntarily use Form 4.[7]

In deciding whether a particular transaction is reportable on Form 4, it is important to distinguish between the various types of exemptions available under the rules. Transactions that are exempted from section 16(b)'s short-swing profit provisions need not be reported on Form 4 but if not so reported must be reported on Form 5.[8] A limited exemption from Form 4 filings exists for acquisitions of equity securities not exceeding $10,000; these transactions do not trigger a Form 4 filing obligation but must be reported on the next Form 4 or Form 5, whichever is due sooner.[9]

The foregoing thus are not complete exemptions from section 16(a)'s requirements. In contrast, there are other transactions that are exempted from section 16(a) reporting or from section 16 in its entirety.[10] For example, transactions effected in connection with a distribution where the securities were acquired with a view to distribute are specifically exempt from section 16(a);[11] accordingly no section 16(a) reports are required[12] because the insider's holdings are only transitory. There are exemptions from section 16 in its entirety for stock splits, stock

---

5. Rule 16a–3(a), 17 C.F.R. § 240.16a–3(a). Forms 3 and 4 were amended in 1991 as part of the complete overhauling of the Commission rules relating to reporting and trading by officers, directors and ten percent beneficial owners. *See* Sec.Exch. Act Rel. No. 34–28869, [1990–1991 Transfer Binder] Fed.Sec.L.Rep. (CCH) ¶ 84,709 (Feb. 8, 1991).

6. *See* Rule 16a–3(f), 17 C.F.R. § 240.16a–3 (1991).

7. *See* Gibson, Dunn & Crutcher, 23 Sec.Reg. & L.Rep. (BNA) 966 (SEC No Action Letter available June 12, 1991).

8. The exemptions from section 16(b) include transactions approved by a regulatory authority (Rule 16b–1); acquisitions made through dividend or interest reinvestment plans (Rule 16b–2); qualifying employee benefit plan transactions (Rule 16b–3); acquisition of securities issued in certain issuer redemptions (Rule 16b–4); bona fide gifts and inheritance (Rule 16b–5); certain exercises of derivative securities (Rule 16b–6(b)); certain securities acquired as a result of qualifying mergers, reclassifications, or consolidations (Rule 16b–7); and deposit or withdrawal of securities from a voting trust (Rule 16b–8). 17 C.F.R. §§ 240.16b–1—240.16b–8. *See* § 12.4 *infra*. Some of these exemptions are highly conditional and thus the rules must be consulted before any reliance is placed on them.

9. Rule 16a–6, 17 C.F.R. § 240.16a–6.

10. In 1994, the SEC proposed broadening the exemptions. *See* Ownership Reports and Trading by Officers, directors and Principal Security Holders, Exch. Act Rel. No. 34–34514 (SEC Aug. 10, 1994).

11. Rule 16a–7, 17 C.F.R. § 240.16a–7.

12. An exemption is also provided for odd lot transactions by odd lot dealers. 17 C.F.R. § 240.16a–5.

dividends, and rights issued pro rata.[13]   There are also statutory exemptions for market maker transactions[14] and for pure arbitrage transactions.[15]

In addition to filing with the Commission, the appropriate forms must also be sent to the exchange, if any, upon which the security is traded.   When a security is traded on more than one national exchange, the issuer may designate one exchange as a recipient of the section 16(a) reports.[16]

The periodic reporting requirements for transactions in the issuer's equity securities extend beyond the statutory insider's tenure in office with the issuer.   Thus, absent an exemption, a resigning officer or director must continue to file Form 4 reports with respect to any change in his or her beneficial ownership of the issuer's equity securities that occurs within the six months following the last transaction made before resignation.[17]

Nowhere in the Exchange Act is the concept of beneficial ownership explicitly defined and therefore its scope has been limited to judicial interpretation and administrative rulemaking.   Prior to 1991, the applicable rules defined some but not all of the issues.   Thus, for example, former Rule 16a–2[18] set out some guidelines with regard to who had to comply with section 16(a)'s reporting obligations.   Over the years, there was increasing dissatisfaction with the section 16(a) reporting requirements.   On the one hand, the Commission was concerned with widespread noncompliance.   On the other hand, there was increasing concern that the existing rules did not supply sufficiently clear definitions and were not up to date with recent developments such as the proliferation of derivative investment instruments.   After more than two years of rule proposals,[19] in 1991 the Commission adopted a complete new set of reporting rules.[20]

---

13.   Rule 16a–9, 17 C.F.R. § 240.16a–9.   The exemption covers increases or decreases in shares as a result of a stock split or stock dividend applying equally to all securities of that class.   It also applies to rights that are issued pro rata to all holders of a class of equity securities.   The sale of such a right is, however, reportable under section 16(a); the exercise of such a right is also covered by section 16 but may be eligible for the exercise exemption for derivative securities that is found in Rule 16b–6(b).

14.   Section 16(d), 15 U.S.C.A. § 78p(d) which is discussed in § 12.7 *infra.*

15.   Section 16(e), 15 U.S.C.A. § 78p(e) which is discussed in § 12.7 *infra.*

16.   Rule 16a–3(c), 17 C.F.R. § 240.16a–3(c).

17.   Rule 16a–2(b), 17 C.F.R. § 240.16a–2(b).   This does not represent a change from former Rule 16a–1(e), 17 C.F.R. § 240.16a–1(e) (1990).

18.   17 C.F.R. § 240.16a–2 (1990).

19.   *See* Sec.Exch. Act Rel. No. 34–26333, [1988–1989 Transfer Binder] Fed.Sec.L.Rep. (CCH) ¶ 84,343 (Dec. 2, 1988) (the initial proposing release); Sec.Exch. Act Rel. No. 34–27148, [1989 Transfer Binder] Fed.Sec.L.Rep. (CCH) ¶ 84,439 (Aug. 18, 1989) (the reproposing release).

20.   *See* Sec.Exch. Act Rel. No. 34–28869, [1990–1991 Transfer Binder] Fed.Sec.L.Rep. (CCH) ¶ 84,709 (Feb. 8, 1991).   *Cf.* Kari Shumpei Okamoto, Oversimplification and the SEC's Treatment of Derivative Securities Trading by Corporate Insiders, 1993 Wis. L. Rev. 1287.

The new reporting rules deal with questions relating to who must file section 16 reports, the identification and computation of ten percent beneficial ownership, and the applicability of the reporting requirements to derivative securities.

Who Must File Section 16 Reports

Officers and directors. As discussed in a later section,[21] there has been a good deal of litigation involving the question of who is an "officer" so as to be subject to section 16 of the Act. The new rules take the position that section 16 should not be applied to individuals who are officers only in name. As such, the rules should put to rest a lot of the uncertainty that has previously existed in trying to determine who qualifies as an officer so as to trigger section 16 responsibilities. Rule 16a–1(f) expands upon the definition of "executive officer" used elsewhere in the rules.[22] Specifically included in the new rule are the president, principal financial officer, principal accounting officer,[23] any vice president in charge of a principal business unit, division, or function[24] as well as any other officer or other person who performs policy-making functions.[25] However, "policy-making function" is not meant to include activities that are not significant.[26] Furthermore, officers of the issuer's parent or subsidiary who perform policy-making functions of the issuer are deemed to be officers of the issuer for section 16 purposes.[27] In the event that the issuer is a limited partnership or a trust, officers or employees of the general partner or trustee who perform duties similar to those outlined above are officers of the issuer.[28] With regard to advisory, emeritus, or honorary directors, the Commission has announced that it has carried forth its previous policy and thus does not treat them as subject to the regulation.[29]

Once it has been determined that someone is an officer or director required to file reports, what about transactions occurring before he or she takes office or after resignation? Someone who becomes an officer is not required to report transactions occurring prior to that date. In contrast, someone who has been an officer or director but becomes subject to the reporting requirements because of the issuer's 1934 Act registration must make reports with regard to transactions occurring within the six months prior to the issuer's registration provided those transactions occurred within six months of the transaction that triggered

21. *See* § 12.4 *infra.*

22. Rule 3b–7, 17 C.F.R. § 240.3b–7. *See also* Rule 3b–2, 17 C.F.R. § 240.3b–2 (definition of officer).

23. Or the comptroller if there is no principal accounting officer.

24. The Commission lists sales, administration, or finance as specific examples.

25. 17 C.F.R. § 240.16a–1(f).

26. Note to 17 C.F.R. § 240.16a–1(f).

27. 17 C.F.R. § 240.16a–1(f).

28. *Id.*

29. Sec.Exch. Act Rel. No. 34–28869, [1990–1991 Transfer Binder] Fed.Sec.L.Rep. (CCH) ¶ 84,709, n. 27 and accompanying text (Feb. 8, 1991).

the Form 4 filing obligation.[30]   As noted above, the new provisions continue the former practice of requiring reports of transactions following an officer or director leaving office so long as the transaction occurred within six months of the last transaction while in office.[31]   The new rules set forth various transactions that are exempt from the reporting requirements.[32]   Although exempt transactions need not be disclosed on Form 4, at the end of the fiscal year, they must be disclosed on Form 5.

Ten percent beneficial owners; definition of equity security.   The former rules required inclusion in the ten percent ownership computation of all equity securities which the holder had the right to acquire by exercising presently exercisable rights, warrants, or conversion rights.[33]   However, in light of the new rules' treatment of derivative instruments generally, the requirement that there be a present right has been deleted.[34]   Section 3(a)(11) and Rule 3a11–1 of the Act define equity security to include "any security convertible, with or without consideration" into an equity security;[35] this definition also includes warrants and rights to subscribe to or purchase an equity security.   The Second Circuit has held that convertible debentures do not themselves constitute a separate class of equity security for purposes of section 16.[36]   The court explained that the ten percent beneficial ownership threshold for section 16 reporting is computed with regard to the underlying security assuming "full dilution" of the underlying security which would result from exercise of all conversion rights.[37]   This would include other warrants and rights as well.[38]   The Second Circuit's rule has been codified by the Commission.[39]

With respect to reporting based on beneficial ownership, the new section 16 reporting rules parallel the rules applicable to section 13(d) of the Williams Act.[40]   The Commission notes that as is the case with

---

30. Rule 16a–2(a), 17 C.F.R. § 240.16a–2(a).   The reason for treating these transaction differently from those occurring prior to the time the officer or director takes office is that in the latter case access to inside information is not presumed until the officer or director takes office.

31. Rule 16a–2(b), 17 C.F.R. § 240.16a–2(b).

32. *See* footnotes 12–14 supra and accompanying text and footnotes 70–73 *infra* and accompanying text.

33. Former Rule 16a–2(b), 17 C.F.R. § 240.16a–2(b) (1990).

34. *See* text accompanying footnotes 65–69 *infra.*

35. 15 U.S.C.A. § 78c(a)(11); 17 C.F.R. § 240.3a11–1.

36. Chemical Fund, Inc. v. Xerox Corp., 377 F.2d 107 (2d Cir.1967).   *See also, e.g.,* Foremost–McKesson, Inc. v. Provident Securities Co., 423 U.S. 232, 96 S.Ct. 508, 46 L.Ed.2d 464 (1976).

37. Chemical Fund, Inc. v. Xerox Corp., 377 F.2d 107 (2d Cir.1967).

38. Warrants and rights are included in the general definition of equity security under the Act.   15 U.S.C.A. § 78c(a)(11).

39. Rule, 16a–4(a), 17 C.F.R. § 240.16a–4(a).

40. 15 U.S.C.A. § 78m(d) which is discussed in § 11.11 *supra.*   This brings with it section 13(d)'s "group theory" which is discussed *id.*   The determination that a group exists for determination of ten percent ownership status does not mean that those securities are subject to the reporting and short-swing profit provisions.

section 13(d), "[s]ection 16, as applied to ten percent holders, is intended to reach those persons who can be presumed to have access to inside information because they can influence or control the issuer as a result of their equity ownership." [41]   In making the ten percent holder determination under section 16, nonvoting securities are excluded and derivative securities are included only if they are convertible or exercisable within sixty days.[42]   It is clear that the Commission intended to create parallel definitions of beneficial ownership under sections 16 and 13(d).[43]   Section 13(d)'s beneficial ownership definition, which for the most part is carried over to section 16,[44] is used only for determining one's status as a ten percent beneficial holder.   Once ten percent beneficial holder status has been established, section 16's reporting and short-swing profit provisions apply only to securities in which the insider has a pecuniary interest.[45]

It is not always easy to determine if and when a shareholder reached the ten percent threshold.   For example, in the case of issuers who periodically repurchase their shares, the threshold can be a moving target.   Further, at least one court has held that if someone does not know (and does not have reason to know) of his or her ten percent ownership status, section 16(b) liability will not be imposed.[46]

Rule 16a–1(a)(2) begins by setting forth the basic rule that, for reporting purposes, beneficial ownership hinges upon the direct or indirect pecuniary interest in the shares, and that that interest may be the result of "any contract, arrangement, understanding, relationship, or otherwise." [47]   This includes the opportunity to participate, directly or indirectly, in any profit attributable to transactions in the shares in

---

See also, e.g., C.R.A. Realty Corp. v. Enron Corp., 842 F.Supp. 88, 91 (S.D.N.Y.1994), relying on Exch. Act Rel. No. 34–28869, [1990–1991 Transfer Binder] Fed.Sec.L.Rep. (CCH) ¶ 84,709 (Feb. 8, 1991) ("The intent of the SEC to define 'ten percent' under Section 16 as it is defined under Section 13(d) could not be clearer").

As discussed *infra* reporting and short-swing profit rules apply only to those securities in which the insider has a pecuniary interest.

41.   Sec.Exch. Act Rel. No. 34–28869, [1990–1991 Transfer Binder] Fed.Sec.L.Rep. (CCH) ¶ 84,709 (Feb. 8, 1991).

42.   Rules 13d–3, 16a–1(a)(1), 17 C.F.R. §§ 240.13d–3, 240.16a–1(a)(1).

43.   C.R.A. Realty Corp. v. Enron Corp., 842 F.Supp. 88, 91 (S.D.N.Y.1994), relying on Exch. Act Rel. No. 34–28869, [1990–1991 Transfer Binder] Fed.Sec.L.Rep. (CCH) ¶ 84,709 (Feb. 8, 1991).

44.   Shares held in a fiduciary capacity in the ordinary course of business by institutions which are eligible to file beneficial ownership reports on Schedule 13G are not counted in computing section 16's ten percent threshold.   Securities not held in a fiduciary capacity, however, are included.   17 C.F.R. § 240.16a–1(a)(1).

45.   Rule 16a–1(a)(2), 17 C.F.R. § 240.16a–1(a)(2).   The pecuniary interest requirement does not apply to the determination of the initial 10% threshold.   *Id.   See* text accompanying footnotes 40–44 *supra.*

46.   C.R.A. Realty Corp. v. Enron Corp., 842 F.Supp. 88 (S.D.N.Y.1994) (although information in annual report revealed that defendant's ownership was ten percent, it was not subject to § 16(b) liability since it had no reason to know of that status when the report was released; subsequently, became aware of its ten percent status and defendant duly filed a Form 3).

47.   Rule 16a–1(a)(2), 17 C.F.R. § 240.16a–1(a)(2).

question. The rule then goes on to list examples of an "indirect pecuniary interest" that triggers section 16. Securities held by immediate family members sharing the same household are included.[48] A general partner's proportional interest in securities held by a general or limited partnership are similarly included.[49] In contrast, a shareholder does not have a pecuniary interest in the portfolio securities held by a corporation, limited partnership or similar entity, so long as he or she is not a controlling shareholder of the entity and does not possess, either alone or with others, investment control over the entity's portfolio securities.[50] As a general rule, subject to some exceptions, performance-based fees (other than asset-based fees) received by any broker, dealer, investment adviser, investment manager, trustee, or person performing a similar function constitute an indirect pecuniary interest.[51] However, a trustee who is compensated based on the trust portfolio income has been held not to be operating under a performance-based fee so as to give him a pecuniary interest in the securities held by the trust.[52] A person's right to dividends is not considered an indirect pecuniary interest unless the right to dividends is separated or separable from the underlying security.[53] An indirect pecuniary interest also exists with regard to securities held by a trust, although the beneficiaries without investment control will not ordinarily have section 16 reporting obligations.[54] A settlor of a trust who reserves the right to revoke the trust without anyone else's consent is a beneficial owner of the securities held by the trust and is also subject to the reporting and short-swing profit provisions with regard to the securities held by the trust.[55] The right to acquire equity securities through the exercise of any derivative security creates a pecuniary interest even if the rights are not presently exercisable.[56]

---

48. 17 C.F.R. § 240.16a–1(a)(2)(ii)(A).

49. 17 C.F.R. § 240.16a–1(a)(2)(ii)(B).

50. 17 C.F.R. § 240.16a–1(a)(2)(iii). Portfolio securities are all securities owned by an entity except for securities issued by the entity. 17 C.F.R. § 240.16a–1(g).

See also, e.g., Mayer v. Chesapeake Ins. Co., Ltd., 698 F.Supp. 52 (S.D.N.Y.1988) (investor receiving proceeds of corporation's sale of stock was beneficial owner).

51. 17 C.F.R. § 240.16a–1(a)(2)(ii)(C).

52. Energy North, Inc., 24 Sec.Reg. & L.Rep. (BNA) 1761 (SEC No Action Letter avail. Nov. 4, 1992).

53. 17 C.F.R. § 240.16a–1(a)(2)(ii)(D).

54. Rule 16a–1(a)(2)(ii)(E), 17 C.F.R. § 240.16a–1(a)(2)(ii)(E). Unless the beneficiary has investment control, the trust, not the beneficiary, will be subject to reporting obligations. Rule 16a–8(b), 17 C.F.R. § 240.16a–8(b). However, where the beneficiary exercises such control and directs the transactions the beneficiary, and not the trust, will be subject to the reporting obligations. *See, e.g.,* Ralston Purina Co., [1990–1991 Transfer Binder] Fed.Sec.L.Rep. (CCH) ¶ 79,699C (SEC No Action Letter May 6, 1991) (trust where insider's spouse is trustee with sole investment control is subject to reporting requirements).

A trust which owns ten-percent of a class of equity securities must file section 16 reports regardless of who is the trustee. *See* Proskauer Rose Goetz & Mendelsohn, [1990–1991 Transfer Binder] Fed.Sec.L.Rep. (CCH) ¶ 79,683 (SEC No Action Letter April 30, 1991).

55. Rule 16a–8(b), 17 C.F.R. § 240.16a–8(b).

56. Rule 16a–1(a)(2)(ii)(F), 17 C.F.R. § 240.16a–1(a)(2)(ii)(F).

Also included in the definition of "equity security" are participation in profit-sharing agreements, preorganization certificates or subscriptions, voting trust certificates,[57] and beneficial interests in business trusts.[58] It previously has been held that stock appreciation rights, or phantom stock, is an equity security for purposes of section 16.[59] The new rules in their inclusion of derivative securities codify this result.[60] Stock appreciation rights that are settled for stock (or stock and/or cash) are derivative securities and are subject to section 16.[61] However, stock appreciation rights that may be settled only for cash are exempt from section 16.[62]

On the one hand, the new SEC rules have clarified a number of issues. On the other hand, the new rules have created many interpretive problems. Accordingly, there has been voluminous no action letter activity. A number of helpful compilations and indexes of these no action letters are available.[63]

The determination of beneficial ownership as between an insider and spouse frequently presents difficult factual questions. For example, within the context of a 16(b) action to recover proscribed short-swing profits, it has been held that a wife's sale of securities is attributed to her husband who is a director of the issuer even where the husband and wife maintain separate brokerage accounts but engaged in some joint planning.[64] As discussed above, the new section 16 rules codify this result.

Derivative Securities

One of the more significant changes implemented by the Commission with its new section 16 rules is the applicability of the reporting requirements to derivative securities.[65] The proliferation of put and call

---

57. Rule 16b–8 exempts acquisitions and dispositions resulting from the deposit to or withdrawal of securities from a voting trust. 17 C.F.R. § 240.16b–8. However, the exemption does not apply if there has been a non-exempt purchase or sale of an equity security of the class deposited within six months. *Id.*

58. 17 C.F.R. § 240.3a11–1.

59. Matas v. Siess, 467 F.Supp. 217 (S.D.N.Y.1979). *See also* former Rule 16b–3. 17 C.F.R. § 240.16b–3 (1990).

60. *See* text accompanying footnotes 65–66 *infra.*

61. This is true even where the SAR's are settled for cash rather than stock. The treatment of derivative securities is discussed *infra* this section and in § 12.3 *infra.*

62. Rule 16a–1(c)(3), 17 C.F.R. § 240.16a–1(c)(3).

63. *See, e.g.,* Donald W. Glazer & Keith F. Higgins, Securities Exchange Act Section 16: Short Answers to Quick Questions Under the New Rules and Forms, 25 Rev.Sec. & Commod.Reg. 23 (Feb. 12, 1992). Indexes have been made available by the two primary loose-leaf services.

64. Whiting v. Dow Chemical Co., 523 F.2d 680 (2d Cir.1975). *See also* Whittaker v. Whittaker Corp., 639 F.2d 516 (9th Cir.1981); Walet v. Jefferson Lake Sulphur Co., 202 F.2d 433 (5th Cir. 1953), *cert. denied* 346 U.S. 820, 74 S.Ct. 35, 98 L.Ed. 346 (1953); Shreve, Beneficial Ownership of Securities Held by Family Members, 22 Bus.Law. 431 (1967). *See* § 12.4, *infra.*

65. Although the new rules are more explicit, the applicability of section 16(b) to derivative instruments is not a new issue. *See, e.g.,* Donald L. Laufer, Effect of Section

options has made it possible for investors to take a derivative position with regard to underlying equity securities. In many ways, investment positions in these derivative investment vehicles are functionally equivalent to positions in the underlying security in terms of the potential for trading profits. Accordingly, the Commission has reversed its long-standing policy by making the acquisition of a derivative security, rather than its exercise, the significant event for section 16 purposes.[66] Derivative securities are covered not only by the section 16(a) reporting requirements but also by the short-swing profit provisions of section 16(b). The new rules view transactions in derivative securities as matchable not only against each other but also against transactions in the underlying security.[67] The new rules thus equate ownership of a derivative security with ownership of the underlying security and recognize that, as is the case with convertible securities, exercise merely changes ownership from indirect to direct ownership of the underlying security.

The Commission pointed out that the opportunity to realize a profit begins the moment an insider purchases or is granted a derivative security. The SEC thus adopted the rule that the acquisition or grant of a derivative security must be reported on Form 4.[68] For the same reason, dispositions of derivative securities are reportable events. The applicability of section 16 to particular options has proven problematic and has led to a number of no action requests and responses.[69]

Exemptions

The new rules contain various exemptions from the reporting and/or short-swing profit provisions of section 16. Although revised as compared to their predecessors, the new rules continue the exemption for qualifying employee benefit plans from the short-swing profit provisions.[70] Rule 16a–9 exempts from section 16 stock splits or stock dividends applying equally to all members of a class of equity securities.[71]

16(b) of the Securities Exchange Act on Use of Options by Insiders, 8 N.Y.L.F. 232 (1962); George P. Michaely, Jr. & Barbara A. Lee, Put and Call Options: Criteria for Applicability of Section 16(b) of the Securities Exchange Act of 1934, 40 Notre Dame Law. 239 (1965); Note, Put and Call Options Under Section 16 of the Securities Exchange Act, 69 Yale L.J. 868 (1960).

66. Sec.Exch.Act Rel. No. 34–28869, [1990–1991 Transfer Binder] Fed.Sec.L.Rep. (CCH) ¶ 84,709 (Feb. 8, 1991). The rules contain a specific exemption for most exercises of rights and warrants. Rule 16b–6(b), 17 C.F.R. § 240.16b–6(b). However, the exercise exemption does not apply when the exercise creates a new opportunity for profit. The exercise exemption also does not apply to the exercise of out-of-the-money options. *See* Sec.Exch. Act Rel. No. 34–28869 *supra.*

67. Rule 16b–6(a), 17 C.F.R. § 240.16b–6(a). *See* § 12.3 *infra*

68. Rule 16a–4(a), 17 C.F.R. § 240.16a–4(a).

69. *Id.*

70. Rule 16b–3, 17 C.F.R. § 240.16b–3. Pittson Co. [1991–1992 Transfer Binder] Fed.Sec.L.Rep. (CCH) ¶ 76,164 (SEC No Action Letter May 18, 1992) (adjustments in plan did not trigger new six month holding period). *See generally* William J. Quinlan & Mark M. Harris, SEC Section 16 Regulations and Compliance by Qualified Employee Benefit Plans, 21 Sec.Reg.L.J. 94 (1993). *See* discussion in § 12.3 *infra.*

71. Rule 16a–9(a), 17 C.F.R. § 240.16a–9(a).

Also exempted are pro rata grants of rights to all holders of a class of equity securities;[72] this would cover the grant of many poison pills. Although the acquisition of the rights is exempt, the exercise or sale of the rights is a reportable event.[73]

As noted at the outset, the reporting requirements imposed by section 16(a) operate to keep the market informed of all statutorily defined insiders' investment activities with regard to the issuer's equity securities. This information is considered relevant by market analysts to the extent that a larger amount of insider trading may indicate an impending material change in the company's position. Furthermore, and more importantly, the purpose of section 16(a) was to provide the information necessary to trigger the enforcement provisions of section 16.

Section 16(b),[74] which is discussed in the sections that follow, provides that all profits attributable to short-swing insider trading in securities subject to section 16(a)'s reporting requirement must be disgorged to the issuer. Furthermore, section 16(c) prohibits two other types of speculative transactions, by insiders, in the issuer's equity securities: short sales and sales against the box.[75]

§ 12.3 Disgorgement of Insider Short–Swing Profits— Section 16(b)

Section 16(b)[1] imposes liability for short-swing profits in the issuer's stock upon all persons required to file reports under section 16(a) of the Act.[2] These listed statutory insiders must disgorge to the issuer any "profit" realized as a result of a purchase and sale or sale and purchase of covered equity securities occurring within a six month period. Section 16(b) is not designed as a compensatory remedy. The preamble to section 16(b) indicates that this civil liability is imposed "for the purpose of preventing the unfair use of information which may have been obtained by such beneficial owner, director, or officer by reason of his relationship to the issuer." The legislative history reveals congressional recognition of such a great potential for abuse of inside information so as to warrant the imposition of strict liability. The statute was viewed as a "crude rule of thumb" or objective method of preventing "the unscrupu-

---

72. Rule 16a–9(b), 17 C.F.R. § 240.16a–9(b).

73. The Note to Rule 16a–9(b) explains that the exercise of such a right is eligible for the exemption under Rule 16b–6(b). It follows that the sale of a right would not be exempt.

74. 15 U.S.C.A. § 78p(b). *See* §§ 12.3–12.5 *infra.*

75. 15 U.S.C.A. § 78p(c). *See* § 12.6 *infra.*

§ 12.3

1. 15 U.S.C.A. § 78p(b). *See generally* Peter J. Romeo & Alan L. Dye, Section 16 of the Securities Exchange Act Treatise and Reporting Guide (1994).

2. *See* § 12.2 *supra.*

lous employment of [corporate] inside information."[3]   Accordingly, in light of its broad remedial purpose, section 16(b) will require disgorgement of insider short-swing profits even in the absence of any wrongdoing.   The liability so imposed is often referred to as prophylactic in nature.

This section explores the basic coverage of section 16(b), including: which issuers are covered by section 16(b),[4] which securities are covered,[5] who has standing to sue,[6] jurisdictional issues,[7] the timing of transactions under section 16(b),[8] the determination of "profit," [9] the absence of a requirement of actual wrongdoing,[10] the rejection of equitable defenses,[11] exemptions from the disgorgement provisions,[12] and a brief discussion of the possibility of indemnifying officers and directors for section 16(b) liability. [13]

Subsequent sections examine some of the thornier problems in more detail.   These include the question of which "insiders" are subject to the disgorgement provisions,[14] the definition of "purchase" and "sale," [15] the prohibition against insider short sales,[16] and the exemptions for pure arbitrage and qualifying market maker transactions.[17]   The discussion that follows directly below spells out the basic scope and coverage of section 16(b) as well as procedural issues relating to 16(b) litigation. Also considered below are questions relating to the proper measure of damages, defenses, and exemptions from section 16(b)'s coverage.

Issuers Covered

As noted above, the applicability of section 16(b)'s disgorgement provisions is determined by reference to section 16(a)'s reporting requirements.[18]   Thus, for example, those private foreign issuers whose officers, directors, and ten percent beneficial owners are exempt from the

---

3. Hearings on S.Res. 84, S.Res. 97 Before The Senate Comm. on Banking and Currency, 73d Cong., 1st Sess. pt. 15 at 6557 (1934).

4. *See* text accompanying footnotes 18–25 *infra.*

5. *See* text accompanying footnotes 26–30 *infra.*

6. *See* text accompanying footnotes 31–44 *infra.*

7. *See* text accompanying footnotes 45–50 *infra.*

8. *See* text accompanying footnotes 51–55 *infra.*

9. *See* text accompanying footnotes 56–73 *infra.*

10. *See* text accompanying footnotes 74–75 *infra.*

11. *See* text accompanying footnotes 76–84 *infra.*

12. *See* text accompanying footnotes 85–111 *infra.*

13. *See* text accompanying footnotes 112–113 *infra.*

14. *See* § 12.4 *infra.*   This includes, for example, issues as to which officers are subject to the section, when insider status attaches, and the deputization doctrine.

15. *See* § 12.5 *infra.*   This includes the discussion of mergers, conversion rights and options.

16. Section 16(c), 15 U.S.C.A. § 78p(c).   *See* § 12.6 *infra.*

17. Sections 16(d), (e), 15 U.S.C.A. §§ 78p(d),(e).

18. 15 U.S.C.A. § 78p(a),(b).   Section 16(a)'s reporting provisions are discussed in § 12.2 *supra.*

reporting requirements similarly are not covered by section 16's liability provisions.[19]   Accordingly, section 16(b) liability attaches to officers, directors, and ten percent beneficial owners of a class of equity securities registered under section 12 of the Exchange Act.[20] A pair of transactions (*i.e.* a purchase and a sale)[21] has been held subject to section 16(b) where the first transaction (a purchase) occurred prior to the issuer's becoming a section 12 company but the second transaction (occurring within six months of the first) took place after the section 12 registration became effective.[22] It has also been held that a sale by an officer occurring prior to registration, followed by a purchase occurring after the registration date is subject to section 16(b).[23] The Fifth Circuit's rationale in this case leads to the conclusion that the result would be different for ten percent beneficial owners than for officers and directors. The court suggests that for section 16(b) liability to attach to a ten percent beneficial owner who is neither an officer nor director, the issuer must have been registered at the time of both transactions.[24] Furthermore, if the owner has no reasonable basis for concluding that the ten percent threshold has been crossed section 16(b) liability will not be imposed until the time the the owner should have been on inquiry notice of that status.[25]

Securities Covered

Section 16(a)'s reporting provisions[26] determine the parameters of section 16(b)'s coverage.[27] By virtue of Rule 16a–10 the exemptions

19. Many private foreign issuers are not subject to section 16. *See* Rule 3a12–3, 17 C.F.R. § 240.3a12–3. Those issuers are also exempt from the coverage of the proxy rules but not from the Williams Act. *Id. See* chapter 11 *supra* and § 14.2 *infra.*

20. 15 U.S.C.A. § 78*l.* Since section 16 is limited to section 12 issuers, it does not apply to issuers whose periodic reporting requirements are triggered solely by section 15(d) of the Act. 15 U.S.C.A. § 78*o*(d).

Section 12's registration requirements are discussed in § 9.2 *supra* and the periodic reporting requirements are discussed in § 9.3 *supra.*

21. The definitions of purchase and sell under section 16 are discussed in § 12.5 *infra.*

22. Heli-Coil v. Webster, 222 F.Supp. 831, 836 (D.N.J.1963), *modified on other grounds* 352 F.2d 156 (3d Cir.1965); Perfect Photo, Inc. v. Grabb, 205 F.Supp. 569, 572 (E.D.Pa. 1962). *See also* Arrow Distributing Corp. v. Baumgartner, 783 F.2d 1274, 1278 n. 14 (5th Cir.1986); Gold v. Scurlock, 324 F.Supp. 1211, 1216 (E.D.Va.1971), *affirmed in part and reversed in part on other grounds sub nom.* Gold v. Sloan, 486 F.2d 340 (4th Cir.1973), *cert. denied* 419 U.S. 873, 95 S.Ct. 134, 42 L.Ed.2d 112 (1974).

23. Arrow Distributing Corp. v. Baumgartner, 783 F.2d 1274 (5th Cir.1986) (officer's sale of shares prior to the registration date which was followed within six months, and after the registration date, by an exercise of call options to purchase shares at a lower price).

24. *Id.* at 1278–79. Section 16(b) applies to ten percent beneficial owners who were such both at the time of purchase and the time of sale. 15 U.S.C.A. § 78p(b); *see* § 12.4 *infra.*

25. C.R.A. Realty Corp. v. Enron Corp., 842 F.Supp. 88 (S.D.N.Y.1994) (although information in annual report revealed that defendant's ownership was ten percent, it was not subject to § 16(b) liability since it had no reason to know of that status when the report was released; subsequently, it became aware of its ten percent status and defendant duly filed a Form 3).

26. 15 U.S.C.A. § 78p(a).

27. *See* § 12.2 *supra.*

from 16(a) carry over to 16(b).[28]   Similarly, the definition of equity security is equally broad under section 16(b) as under 16(a) and extends to conversion rights, warrants and even stock appreciation rights.[29] Also, the same rules apply to the determination of beneficial ownership under sections 16(a) and 16(b).[30]

Procedural Aspects—Standing

The private remedy embodied in section 16(b) is self contained, sui generis, and is a hybrid variety of derivative suit. For example, the statute on its face requires that the shareholder make a demand upon directors prior to being sued. The corporation, through its directors, then has sixty days to decide whether or not to bring suit.[31]   However, no demand is required when it would be a futile gesture due to the self-interest of the directors. The issuer may assign its section 16(b) cause of action.[32]   Such an assignment will take place by operation of law when the issuer is merged out of existence.[33]   However, when the surviving corporation is a subsidiary, a shareholder of the parent corporation cannot bring a section 16(b) action (unless, of course, he or she is also a shareholder of the subsidiary).[34]

If the corporation does not act after a demand on directors has been made (or, if the demand is excused), suit may be filed by a shareholder of record at the time of the suit,[35] and who continues to be a shareholder throughout the trial.[36]   The commonplace contemporaneous ownership

---

28.   17 C.F.R. § 240.16a–10.   *But see* Marquette Cement Manufacturing Co. v. Andreas, 239 F.Supp. 962 (S.D.N.Y.1965) (holding that Rule 16a–8's determination of beneficial ownership of securities held in trust is not binding in a section 16(b) action).

29.   *See* 15 U.S.C.A. § 78c(a)(11); 17 C.F.R. §§ 240.3a11–1, 240.16b–3 (1990) (rescinded);   Matas v. Siess, 467 F.Supp. 217 (S.D.N.Y.1979).   *See* Note, Mismatching Convertible Debentures and Common Stock Under Section 16(b), 1985 Duke L.J. 1057.

30.   *See* § 12.4 *infra*;   § 12.2 *supra*.

31.   Weisman v. Spector, 158 F.Supp. 789 (S.D.N.Y.1958);   Netter v. Ashland Paper Mills, Inc., 19 F.R.D. 529 (S.D.N.Y.1956).

32.   Western Auto Supply Co. v. Gamble–Skogmo, Inc., 348 F.2d 736 (8th Cir.1965), *cert. denied* 382 U.S. 987, 86 S.Ct. 556, 15 L.Ed.2d 475 (1966).   *Cf.* Blau v. Oppenheim, 250 F.Supp. 881 (S.D.N.Y.1966) (suit maintained by shareholder of successor corporation).

33.   Gollust v. Mendell, 501 U.S. 115, 111 S.Ct. 2173, 115 L.Ed.2d 109 (1991), *affirming* 909 F.2d 724 (2d Cir.1990), *cert. granted* 498 U.S. 1023, 111 S.Ct. 669, 112 L.Ed.2d 662 (1991) (permitting a section 16(b) suit where a takeover occurring after the plaintiff brought suit terminated plaintiff's status as a shareholder).

34.   Lewis v. McAdam, 762 F.2d 800, 803–04 (9th Cir.1985).   *See also* Untermeyer v. Valhi, Inc., 841 F.2d 25 (2d Cir.1988);   Portnoy v. Kawecki Berylco Industries, 607 F.2d 765, 768–69 (7th Cir.1979).   *But see* C.R.A. Realty Corp. v. American Express, 1984 WL 481, [1984 Transfer Binder] Fed.Sec.L.Rep. (CCH) ¶ 91,528 (S.D.N.Y.1984) (Unpublished Case).

35.   Dottenheim v. Murchison, 227 F.2d 737 (5th Cir.1955), *cert. denied* 351 U.S. 919, 76 S.Ct. 712, 100 L.Ed. 1451 (1956);   Blau v. Mission Corp., 212 F.2d 77, 79 (2d Cir.1954), *cert. denied* 347 U.S. 1016, 74 S.Ct. 872, 98 L.Ed. 1138 (1954);   Benisch v. Cameron, 81 F.Supp. 882 (S.D.N.Y.1948).

36.   Rothenberg v. United Brands, Co., 1977 WL 1014 (S.D.N.Y.1977).   *Accord* Portnoy v. Kawecki Berylco Indus., Inc., 607 F.2d 765 (7th Cir.1979).

A shareholder of a parent corporation had standing to sue a director of a wholly owned subsidiary for having violated section 16(b).   C.R.A. Realty Corp. v. American Express,

rule contained in federal and state law regarding derivative litigation generally, that requires a shareholder who brings suit to have been a shareholder at the time of the action complained of,[37] does not apply in an action under section 16(b).

In 1991, the Supreme Court addressed the question of whether a shareholder of a corporation that was subsequently merged into another can bring suit under section 16(b) against officers, directors, or ten percent beneficial holders of the merged disappearing corporation. In *Gollust v. Mendell*,[38] plaintiff was a shareholder of a merged corporation and under the terms of the merger agreement he received a combination of stock and cash. Plaintiff instituted his section 16(b) claim prior to the merger and the court held that he had standing under the statute since he owned a security of the issuer at the time he instituted the suit. In reaching this result, the Court emphasized that while section 16(b) sets forth a narrow class of potential defendants, it sets forth a broad class of plaintiffs—much broader than would apply under the contemporaneous ownership rule applicable to derivative suits generally. The Court also pointed out that since the plaintiff received shares in the surviving corporation he had a continuing interest in the assets of the merged corporation sufficient to allow him to share derivatively in the benefits of any recovery, even when that interest was based on ownership of shares in the parent corporation. The Court's rationale clearly indicates that had the plaintiff shareholder been cashed out, his lack of a continuing interest would have precluded him from sharing in any recovery and thus would deny him standing to sue under section 16(b). Whether this is the proper analysis is open to question. The Court observed that the only express requirement of the statute is that the plaintiff have been a shareholder at the time the suit was instituted; there is no mention of any requirement that he or she have a continuing interest. Although the statute authorizes recovery to the corporation, if the courts were to draw an analogy to derivative suits generally, the courts might be able to fashion relief that would benefit the former shareholders.[39] The argument against such a result would be that the statutory remedy in section 16(b) authorizes only a recovery by the corporation, and not by the shareholders individually. The prophylactic rationale behind section 16(b), however, could well be seen as justifying giving standing to a shareholder who has been cashed out after the initiation of the litigation. To summarize, the Court in *Gollust* set forth two requirements for

---

1984 WL 481, [1984 Transfer Binder] Fed.Sec.L.Rep. (CCH) ¶ 91,528 (S.D.N.Y.1984) (Unpublished Case). *But see* the authorities in footnote 34 *supra.*

37. *E.g.* Fed.R.Civ.P. 23.1, Bangor Punta Operations, Inc. v. Bangor & Aroostook Railroad, 417 U.S. 703, 94 S.Ct. 2578, 41 L.Ed.2d 418 (1974); Courtland Manor, Inc. v. Leeds, 347 A.2d 144 (Del.Ch.1975).

38. 501 U.S. 115, 111 S.Ct. 2173, 115 L.Ed.2d 109 (1991). *See* Frederick M. Hopkins, Toward an Objective Standard of Standing Under Section 16(b) (*Gollust v. Mendell*), 48 Bus.Law. 373 (1992).

39. *See, e.g.,* Perlman v. Feldmann, 219 F.2d 173 (2d Cir. 1955), *cert. denied* 349 U.S. 952, 75 S.Ct. 880, 99 L.Ed. 1277 (1955) (derivative suit challenging sale of control where court ordered the illegal premium to be disgorged directly to the minority shareholders).

standing under section 16(b): first, the suit must have been initiated at a time that plaintiff was a shareholder; and second, the plaintiff must have a continuing interest in the corporation (or its assets) so as to allow him or her to benefit from any recovery.

Notwithstanding the possible champerty implications, the courts have held that it is no defense to an action under section 16(b) that the suit was motivated primarily by an attorney's desire to obtain the attorneys' fees that may be awarded to the successful plaintiff.[40] Attorneys' fees are awarded out of the fund created by the recovery and are not added to the defendant's liability.[41] It thus has been held that attorneys' fees are only available under section 16(b) when the action is brought by a shareholder on the corporation's behalf and not when the corporation itself is the plaintiff.[42] The shareholders suing in derivative suits recover attorneys' fees out of the fund created by the recovery and the underlying rationale for such a fund does not exist when the corporation sues directly.[43] Following the general rule, prejudgment interest is appropriate in section 16(b) actions,[44] in addition to the potential for attorneys' fees.

Jurisdictional Aspects

Jurisdiction over section 16(b) actions is exclusively within the federal courts.[45] The 16(b) action may be brought in a district where the violation occurred or where "the defendant is found or is an inhabitant or transacts business."[46] Also, the action may be brought either in law or in equity and it has been held that the plaintiff's failure to demand a jury trial renders the action one in equity, thus denying the defendant the right of election.[47] The statute contains a two year limitation period which begins to run from the date of the second transaction; that is, the one that creates the section 16(b) profits. However, the statute of

40. Magida v. Continental Can Co., 231 F.2d 843 (2d Cir.1956), *cert. denied* 351 U.S. 972, 76 S.Ct. 1031, 100 L.Ed. 1490 (1956). *See* Smolowe v. Delendo Corp., 136 F.2d 231, 241 (2d Cir.1943), *cert. denied* 320 U.S. 751, 64 S.Ct. 56, 88 L.Ed. 446 (1943). The rationale of these cases is that it is up to the state or federal bar to take appropriate disciplinary action against the attorney. Attorney misconduct thus should not interfere with the remedial purposes of section 16(b).

41. *See* Super Stores, Inc. v. Reiner, 737 F.2d 962, 965 (11th Cir.1984). *But cf.* Portnoy v. Gold Reserve Corp., 711 F.Supp. 565 (E.D.Wash.1989) (attorneys' fees not awarded for work that was unnecessary to recover short-swing profits).

42. Super Stores, Inc. v. Reiner, 737 F.2d 962 (11th Cir.1984).

43. *Id.* at 965 ("There is no statutory provision for the award of attorneys' fees in § 16(b) cases. The cases cited by plaintiff in which fees have been awarded involve claims where recovery is sought on behalf of the corporation by one of its shareholders, and fees are awarded to the shareholders out of the fund created by the recovery. In those cases no liability for fees is imposed on the Defendant").

44. Whittaker v. Whittaker Corp., 639 F.2d 516, 533 (9th Cir. 1981), *cert. denied* 454 U.S. 1031, 102 S.Ct. 566, 70 L.Ed.2d 473 (1981); Synalloy Corp. v. Gray, 816 F.Supp. 963, 971 (D.Del.1993).

45. Section 27, 15 U.S.C.A. § 78aa.

46. *Id.*

47. Arbetman v. Playford, 83 F.Supp. 335 (S.D.N.Y.1949). *See also* Dottenheim v. Emerson Elec. Manufacturing Co., 7 F.R.D. 343 (E.D.N.Y.1947).

limitations period may be extended until the time of reasonable discovery where there has been a failure to file timely section 16(a) reports.[48] Although resulting in civil damages, section 16(b) violations do not give rise to criminal sanctions, nor are they within the purview of SEC enforcement actions or proceedings. In contrast, violations of section 16(a)'s reporting requirements may result in both criminal sanctions[49] and SEC action.[50]

Section 16 Timing (the "short swing")

Section 16(b) was intended to be straightforward in application, thus providing the predictability necessary for sound planning. However, the terms of the statute have given rise to much litigation. It is not always clear whether a particular person comes within the section's reach.[51] Similarly it is frequently difficult to determine whether and when a purchase or sale occurs.[52] The computation of the six month period has not escaped judicial scrutiny. It is clear that the prohibitions of section 16(b) extend to both six months prior and subsequent to the date of any particular transaction,[53] assuming, of course, that insider status attaches. Furthermore, the statute speaks in terms of a "period of *less* than six months" in which the transactions are prohibited and thus two transactions occurring within exactly six months of each other are not subject to section 16(b)'s disgorgement provisions.[54] In order to determine when a purchase or sale takes place, the courts look to the time at which the purchaser or seller became irrevocably obligated.[55]

Determination of "Profit"

There has also been significant question as to the method of computing a "profit" within the meaning of section 16(b).[56] Someone who sells

---

48. Blau v. Albert, 157 F.Supp. 816 (S.D.N.Y.1957); Grossman v. Young, 72 F.Supp. 375 (S.D.N.Y.1947). *But see* Kozonasky v. Sears Roebuck & Co., 1986 WL 12528, [1986–87 Transfer Binder] Fed.Sec.L.Rep. (CCH) ¶ 92,967 (S.D.N.Y.1986) (Unpublished Case) (holding 16(b) claim time barred; plaintiff failed to demonstrate lack of knowledge required to toll statute of limitations).

49. Section 32(a), 15 U.S.C.A. § 78ff.

50. Section 21, 15 U.S.C.A. § 78u.

51. *See* § 12.4 *infra.*

52. *See* § 12.5 *infra.* Generally, a sale occurs when the seller has become irrevocably bound to dispose of the securities. Seinfeld v. Hospital Corp. of America, 685 F.Supp. 1057 (N.D.Ill.1988) ("lock up" option is a purchase); Colan v. Brunswick Corp., 550 F.Supp. 49 (N.D.Ill.1982).

53. Gratz v. Claughton, 187 F.2d 46 (2d Cir.), *cert. denied* 341 U.S. 920, 71 S.Ct. 741, 95 L.Ed. 1353 (1951).

54. Morales v. Reading & Bates Offshore Drilling Co., 392 F.Supp. 41 (N.D.Okl.1975); R. Jennings & H. Marsh, Securities Regulations Cases and Materials 1352 (5th ed. 1982).

55. Riseman v. Orion Research, Inc., 749 F.2d 915 (1st Cir.1984); Seinfeld v. Hospital Corp. of America, 685 F.Supp. 1057 (N.D.Ill.1988) ("lock up" option); Piano Remittance Corp. v. Reliance Financial Services Corp., 618 F.Supp. 414 (S.D.N.Y.1985); Lewis v. Bradley, 599 F.Supp. 327 (S.D.N.Y.1984). *Compare* the discussion in § 5.4 *supra.*

56. For example, the Commission in former Rule 16b–6 (17 C.F.R. § 240.16b–6 (1990) (rescinded)) which dealt with employee stock options established the computation for 16(b) damages in the situation where after exercising the stock option, the employee sells his stock and subsequently repurchases the amount sold for a lower price within a six month period realizes a section 16(b) profit.[57]

Many courts have taken a broad view of what constitutes a section 16(b) "profit" when there have been a series of transactions within a six month period. The apparent majority view is to match the lowest purchase price against the highest sales price within that period.[58] This method is the harsher of the alternative interpretations since it catches a "profit" even in situations where an out-of-pocket loss for all transactions entered into during the six month period may exist.[59] There is a strong argument that this measure of damages is unnecessarily punitive and cannot be justified by section 16(b)'s remedial purpose. As is pointed out elsewhere,[60] punitive damages are generally not available in actions arising under the federal securities laws. Imposing liability for excess "profits" which in fact exceed actual profits can be viewed as unjustifiably punitive and thus contrary to the spirit of section 28(a) of the Exchange Act, which limits damages to actual damages.[61]

The matching problem described above does not arise when there is a series of purchases followed by a single sale (or vice versa). For example, when there are multiple purchases and one block sale, it is sufficient to simply aggregate the purchase price and then subtract the sum from the sale price.[62]

There is authority to the effect that dividends declared on shares that are sold at a profit will be considered part of the section 16(b) profit,

---

stock within six months of the exercise. The rule set damages at the difference between the sales price of the stock and its lowest market price within six months before or after the date of sale. *See* Kornfeld v. Eaton, 327 F.2d 263 (2d Cir.1964); Blau v. Hodgkinson, 100 F.Supp. 361 (S.D.N.Y.1951).

For the current treatment of derivative securities, *see* text accompanying footnotes 65–66 *infra.*

57. A variation of this rule arises when someone who is subject to section 16(b) pledges stock as collateral for a nonrecourse loan and then defaults on the loan after the price of the stock has fallen below the loan balance. In Harrison v. Orleans, 755 F.Supp. 592 (S.D.N.Y.1991), a director who had pledged stock as collateral for a loan allowed the loan to become in default thus causing the pledgee to repossess the stock; one week later, he purchased additional stock at a price lower than the loan balance that was cancelled as a result of the foreclosure sale. The court pointed to the "savings" the defendant realized by voluntarily not paying the loan so as to realize the benefit of the debt's cancellation rather than paying the higher loan balance; this was held to be a recoverable section 16(b) profit.

58. Arrow Distributing Corp. v. Baumgartner, 783 F.2d 1274, 1277–78 (5th Cir.1986); Whittaker v. Whittaker Corp., 639 F.2d 516, 530–32 (9th Cir. 1981), *cert. denied* 454 U.S. 1031, 102 S.Ct. 566, 70 L.Ed.2d 473 (1981); Gratz v. Claughton, 187 F.2d 46 (2d Cir.1951); Smolowe v. Delendo Corp., 136 F.2d 231 (2d Cir. 1943), *cert. denied* 320 U.S. 751, 64 S.Ct. 56, 88 L.Ed. 446 (1943); Arkansas Louisiana Gas Co. v. W.R. Stephens Investment Co., 141 F.Supp. 841 (W.D.Ark.1956). *But cf.* Allis–Chalmers Manufacturing Co. v. Gulf & Western Industries, Inc., 527 F.2d 335 (7th Cir.1975), *cert. denied* 423 U.S. 1078, 96 S.Ct. 865, 47 L.Ed.2d 89 (1976).

59. *See* Smolowe v. Delendo Corp., 136 F.2d 231, 239 (2d Cir. 1943), *cert. denied* 320 U.S. 751, 64 S.Ct. 56, 88 L.Ed. 446 (1943).

60. *See* §§ 7.4.1, 7.5.3 *supra* and § 13.7 *infra.*

61. 15 U.S.C.A. § 78bb(a).

62. Mayer v. Chesapeake Ins. Co. Ltd., 877 F.2d 1154 (2d Cir.1989), *cert. denied* 493 U.S. 1021, 110 S.Ct. 722, 107 L.Ed.2d 741 (1990).

provided that insider status applied at the time of declaration of the dividend.[63] However, there is authority to the contrary, holding that dividends are excluded from the section 16(b) computation absent evidence that the defendant manipulated the dividend.[64] Presumably, the rationale in excluding dividends from the profit calculus is that they do not result from the use of any inside information that the defendant may have taken advantage of. The decisions that would exclude the dividends represent an example of too much movement away from viewing section 16(b) as a broad prophylactic remedy. Since the defendant does in fact gain from the dividends, they should be given consideration in the profit calculation.

Difficult questions can arise concerning the computation of a profit when faced with transactions involving derivative securities. In 1991, the Commission addressed the computation of profits resulting from acquisitions and dispositions of derivative securities. If an acquisition of a derivative security is matched with the disposition of the same derivative security within a six month period, the section 16(b) recovery is based on the profit received from the matching transactions.[65] If an acquisition or disposition of a derivative security is matched with a transaction in the underlying security or different derivative security, the maximum section 16(b) profit is based on the difference in the market value of the underlying security on the transaction dates, but the court may award a lesser recovery in the event the insider can demonstrate that the amount of profit was less.[66]

Notwithstanding Tax Court rulings to the contrary, the federal courts of appeals have uniformly held that profits disgorged under section 16(b) cannot be deducted by the insider as an ordinary or necessary business expense.[67] From the issuer's perspective, a section 16(b) recovery will constitute taxable income.[68] In another damage–related issue, expenses incurred in an unsuccessful tender offer have been held nondeductible from the section 16(b) profit when the shares

63. Western Auto Supply Co. v. Gamble–Skogmo, Inc., 348 F.2d 736 (8th Cir.1965), *cert. denied* 382 U.S. 987, 86 S.Ct. 556, 15 L.Ed.2d 475 (1966). *Cf.* Adler v. Klawans, 267 F.2d 840 (2d Cir.1959).

64. Morales v. Lukens, Inc., 593 F.Supp. 1209, 1214–15 (S.D.N.Y.1984), relying on Blau v. Lamb, 363 F.2d 507, 528 (2d Cir.1966), *cert. denied* 385 U.S. 1002, 87 S.Ct. 707, 17 L.Ed.2d 542 (1967); Adler v. Klawans, 267 F.2d 840, 849 (2d Cir.1959); Cutler–Hammer, Inc. v. Leeds & Northrup Co., 469 F.Supp. 1021, 1024 (E.D.Wis.1979); Allis–Chalmers Mfg. Co. v. Gulf & Western Indus., Inc., 372 F.Supp. 570, 588–89 (N.D.Ill.1974), *modified* 527 F.2d 335 (7th Cir.1975), *cert. denied* 423 U.S. 1078, 96 S.Ct. 865, 47 L.Ed.2d 89 (1976) (there was no evidence that dividends were a motivating factor; further, the issuer cut the dividend after the defendant's purchase).

65. Rule 16b–6(c), 17 C.F.R. § 240.16b–6(c). For the SEC's former view on employee stock options and the profit computation, *see* footnote 56 *supra*.

66. Rule 16b–6(c), 17 C.F.R. § 240.16b–6(c).

67. Cummings v. C.I.R., 506 F.2d 449 (2d Cir.1974), *cert. denied* 421 U.S. 913, 95 S.Ct. 1571, 43 L.Ed.2d 779 (1975); Anderson v. C.I.R. 480 F.2d 1304 (7th Cir.1973).

68. General American Investors Co., Inc. v. Commissioner, 348 U.S. 434, 75 S.Ct. 478, 99 L.Ed. 504 (1955).

are sold to the successful bidder.[69]   In contrast, brokerage commissions are deductible expenses in calculating the profit.[70]

It has been held that when non-deductible expenses have been reimbursed they may have to be included in calculating the section 16(b) profit.[71]   In contrast, it has been held that where such expenses are incurred after a takeover agreement with a white knight and were in good faith reimbursed by the acquired company, the reimbursement was properly excluded in computing section 16(b) liability.[72]

In considering whether to award prejudgment interest, the willfulness of the violation is relevant in weighing the equities, but bad faith need not be shown.[73]

Use of Inside Information Not Necessary

In light of section 16(b)'s remedial and prophylactic purposes it is not necessary that the defendant have utilized inside information in planning the transactions.   Nor is it necessary that the transactions have resulted in injury to the issuer.   The rule of the statute is absolute, imposing strict liability for short-swing profits by statutory insiders of Exchange Act reporting companies.   Notwithstanding the clear congressional intent to provide a catch-all, prophylactic remedy, not requiring proof of actual misconduct,[74] the statute is not always strictly applied.   When dealing with traditional cash-for-stock purchases and sales, the courts uniformly employ an objective approach, not looking beyond the terms of the statute.   However, when faced with "unorthodox" transactions the courts will look behind the transaction under a pragmatic mode of analysis.[75]   Under the pragmatic approach courts will include or exclude unorthodox transactions from section 16(b)'s reach depending upon the presence or absence of the potential for speculative abuse.   In any event, the section presents severe limitations on insider trading in stock subject to the Exchange Act's reporting requirements.   To a large extent section 16(b) remains a trap for the unwary.

Equitable Defenses Rejected

The generally accepted rule is that equitable defenses will not defeat

---

69.   *See* Texas International Airlines v. National Airlines, Inc., 714 F.2d 533, 541 (5th Cir.1983), *cert. denied* 465 U.S. 1052, 104 S.Ct. 1326, 79 L.Ed.2d 721 (1984); Lane Bryant, Inc. v. Hatleigh Corp., 517 F.Supp. 1196, 1202 (S.D.N.Y.1981).

70.   Herrmann v. Steinberg, 1986 WL 4697, [1986 Transfer Binder] Fed.Sec.L.Rep. (CCH) ¶ 92,748 (S.D.N.Y.1986) (Unpublished Case), *reversed on other grounds* 812 F.2d 63 (2d Cir.1987).

71.   Herrmann on Behalf of Walt Disney Productions v. Steinberg, 812 F.2d 63 (2d Cir.1987).

72.   Morales v. Lukens, Inc., 593 F.Supp. 1209 (S.D.N.Y.1984).   *See also* Sterman v. Ferro Corp., 785 F.2d 162 (6th Cir.1986) (pricing a repurchase transaction to compensate for section 16(b) liability is permissible).

73.   Riseman v. Orion Research, Inc., 749 F.2d 915 (1st Cir.1984).

74.   *See* footnote 3 *supra.*

75.   *See* § 12.5 *infra; see also* Thomas L. Hazen, The New Pragmatism Under Section 16(b) of the Securities Exchange Act, 54 N.C.L.Rev. 1 (1975) and the other authorities cited in footnote 1 *supra.*

an action brought under section 16(b).[76] Thus, for example, equitable estoppel will not be a defense to a section 16(b) action.[77] *In pari delicto* is not a defense to section 16(b) liability.[78] Thus, the fact that the issuer has participated in the transaction does not preclude recovery,[79] even where the issuer may have been the impetus for the transaction.[80] As is the case with securities law claims generally,[81] waiver will not constitute a defense to section 16(b) liability.[82] The antiwaiver provision does not apply to settlement of existing or threatened litigation.[83] Accordingly, release of liability under section 16 will be upheld if supported by valid consideration. However, if there is no knowledge of the section 16(b) liability at the time of the purported release, the waiver will not be effective.[84]

Exemptions From 16(b)'s Disgorgement Provisions

The SEC has provided a number of exemptions from section 16(b) liability. The section 16 rules adopted in 1991 retained many of the

76. Texas International Airlines v. National Airlines, Inc., 714 F.2d 533, 536 (5th Cir.1983), *cert. denied* 465 U.S. 1052, 104 S.Ct. 1326, 79 L.Ed.2d 721 (1984); Roth v. Fund of Funds, Ltd., 405 F.2d 421, 422–23 (2d Cir.1968), *cert. denied* 394 U.S. 975, 89 S.Ct. 1469, 22 L.Ed.2d 754 (1969); Magida v. Continental Can Co., 231 F.2d 843, 846 (2d Cir.1956), *cert. denied* 351 U.S. 972, 76 S.Ct. 1031, 100 L.Ed. 1490 (1956); Sullair Corp. v. Hoodes, 672 F.Supp. 337, 338 (N.D.Ill1987); Bunker Ramo–Eltra Corp. v. Fairchild Industries, I٫٠., 639 F.Supp. 409, 417 (D. Md.1986), *appeal dismissed* 801 F.2d 393 (4th Cir.1986); Tyco Laboratories, Inc. v. Cutler–Hammer, Inc., 490 F.Supp. 1, 8 (S.D.N.Y.1980); Cutler–Hammer, Inc. v. Leeds & Northrup Co., 469 F.Supp. 1021, 1023 (E.D. Wis.1979).

77. *E.g.,* Texas International Airlines v. National Airlines, Inc., 714 F.2d 533, 536 (5th Cir.1983), *cert. denied* 465 U.S. 1052, 104 S.Ct. 1326, 79 L.Ed.2d 721 (1984); Sullair Corp. v. Hoodes, 672 F.Supp. 337, 338 (N.D.Ill.1987).

78. *See, e.g.,* In re Cascade International, 165 B.R. 321 (Bkrtcy.S.D.Fla.1994). Analogously, *in pari delicto* is not likely to be a defense in implied actions under Rule 10b–5. *See* § 13.12 *infra.*

79. *E.g.,* Texas International Airlines v. National Airlines, Inc., 714 F.2d 533, 536 (5th Cir.1983), *cert. denied* 465 U.S. 1052, 104 S.Ct. 1326, 79 L.Ed.2d 721 (1984); Roth v. Fund of Funds, Ltd., 405 F.2d 421, 422–23 (2d Cir.1968), *cert. denied* 394 U.S. 975, 89 S.Ct. 1469, 22 L.Ed.2d 754 (1969).

80. *E.g.,* Roth v. Fund of Funds, Ltd., 405 F.2d 421, 422–23 (2d Cir.1968), *cert. denied* 394 U.S. 975, 89 S.Ct. 1469, 22 L.Ed.2d 754 (1969); Magida v. Continental Can Co., 231 F.2d 843, 846 (2d Cir.1956), *cert. denied* 351 U.S. 972, 76 S.Ct. 1031, 100 L.Ed. 1490 (1956).

81. *See* § 13.14 *infra.*

82. Section 29(a) of the Exchange Act provides that contracts and stipulations purporting to waive compliance with any provision of the Act or SEC rules promulgated thereunder are void. 15 U.S.C.A. § 78cc(a). Section 14 of the 1933 Act contains a similar provision. 15 U.S.C.A. § 77n.

83. *See, e.g.,* Petro–Ventures, Inc. v. Takessian, 967 F.2d 1337 (9th Cir.1992) (enforceability of release of federal securities claims is a matter of federal laws; release is valid only to the extent that plaintiffs knew of claims at time of release—questions of fact regarding plaintiffs' knowledge precluded summary judgment); Murtagh v. University Computing Co., 490 F.2d 810 (5th Cir.1974), *cert. denied* 419 U.S. 835, 95 S.Ct. 62, 42 L.Ed.2d 62 (1974). *See also, e.g.,* Mullen v. New Jersey Steel Corp., 733 F.Supp. 1534 (D.N.J.1990) ("[the Exchange Act's antiwaiver] provision concerns waiver of future violations; there is a distinction between a waiver of future claims and a waiver of mature claims of which the releasing party had knowledge"), relying on Leff v. CIP Corp., 540 F.Supp. 857, 862 (S.D.Ohio 1982).

84. Synalloy Corp. v. Gray, 816 F.Supp. 963 (D.Del.1993).

former exemptions.[85] As mentioned earlier, section 16 does not apply to many foreign issuers.[86] Section 16(b) does not apply to transactions in registered investment company shares that are exempt from the Investment Company Act's short-swing prohibitions.[87] Similarly exempt are transactions that are exempt from the comparable provisions of the Public Utility Holding Company Act of 1935[88] and certain transactions involving railroads that have been approved by the Interstate Commerce Commission.[89]

Acquisitions of securities resulting from reinvestment of dividends or interest may be exempt from section 16(b). The exemption is conditioned upon the existence of a plan providing for regular reinvestment and further upon availability of that plan to all holders of the class of securities in question.[90]

Qualifying employee benefit plans, including those involving stock appreciation rights or phantom stock, may qualify for an exemption from section 16(b).[91] New Rule 16b–3 divides employee benefit plan transactions into two principal categories—grant/award transactions and participant-directed transactions.[92] The grant and award of securities under qualifying plans are exempt so long as the securities are held for at least six months.[93] Shareholder approval continues to be a requirement for most exempt plans.[94] The rule also contains two conditions that apply to all plan transactions involving employer securities: (1) the transaction must be pursuant to a written plan and (2) with limited exceptions, the plan must require any derivative securities to be nontransferable.[95]

85. *See* Sec.Exch.Act Rel. No. 34–28869, [1990–1991 Transfer Binder] Fed.Sec.L.Rep. (CCH) ¶ 84,709 (Feb. 8, 1991).

In 1994, the SEC proposed broadening the exemptions. *See* Ownership Reports and Trading by Officers, Directors and Principal Security Holders, Exch. Act Rel. No. 34–34514 (SEC Aug. 10, 1994).

86. Many foreign private issuers are exempted by Rule 3a12–3, 17 C.F.R. § 240.3a12–3.

87. Rule 16b–1(a), 17 C.F.R. § 240.16b–1(a). *See* 15 U.S.C.A. § 80a–17(a); Chapter 17 *infra*.

88. Rule 16b–1(b), 17 C.F.R. § 240.16b–1(b).

89. Rule 16b–1(c), 17 C.F.R. § 240.16b–1(c).

90. Rule 16b–2, 17 C.F.R. § 240.16b–2.

91. *See, e.g.,* Sonnenschein, Nath & Rosenthal [1992 Transfer Binder] Fed.Sec.L.Rep. (CCH) ¶ 76,226 (SEC No Action Letter July 6, 1992) (amendment bifurcating plan so that insiders' phantom stock would be redeemable only for cash takes subsequent grants outside of the definition of derivative security).

92. *See* Sec.Exch.Act Rel. No. 34–28869, [1990–1991 Transfer Binder] Fed.Sec.L.Rep. (CCH) ¶ 84,709 (Feb. 8, 1991). *See generally* William J. Quinlan & Mark. M. Harris, SEC Section 16 Regulations and Compliance by Qualified Employee Benefit Plans, 21 Sec.Reg. L.J. 94 (1993).

93. Rule 16b–3(c), 17 C.F.R. § 240.16b–3(c). *See also, e.g.,* Pittson Co. [1991–1992 Transfer Binder] Fed.Sec.L.Rep. (CCH) ¶ 76,164 (SEC No Action Letter May 18, 1992) (adjustments in plan did not trigger new six month holding period); Hewitt Associates, [1990–1991 Transfer Binder] Fed.Sec.L.Rep. (CCH) ¶ 79,688 (SEC No Action Letter April 30, 1991) (six month holding period of Rule 16b–3(c) applies whether or not the insider has control over the allocation of the award of stock).

94. Sec.Exch.Act Rel. No. 34–28869, [1990–1991 Transfer Binder] Fed.Sec.L.Rep. (CCH) ¶ 84,709 (Feb. 8, 1991).

95. Rule 16b–3(a), 17 C.F.R. § 240.16b–3(a).

Another condition for the exemption is that any grants of options or other rights to insiders have to be made either (1) by a disinterested committee of directors that makes all substantive decisions with regard to timing, eligibility, pricing and the amount of the awards or (2) pursuant to an automatic formula which specifies those terms.[96] The reason for this condition is to preclude insiders from influencing key terms, thereby taking advantage of inside information.[97]

Other exemptions from section 16(b) include securities acquired through certain issuer redemptions of other securities where the securities so acquired replace securities of an issuer whose assets consist of cash, government securities and equity securities of the issuer whose securities were acquired.[98] The recent SEC rules continue the exemption for bona fide gifts and inheritance.[99] Securities acquired in certain mergers also are exempt.[100] Rule 16b–8 exempts acquisitions and dispositions resulting from the deposit to or withdrawal of securities from a voting trust.[101] However, the exemption does not apply if there has been a non-exempt purchase or sale of an equity security of the class deposited within six months.[102]

The above-mentioned exemptions from section 16(b) liability have been created through the Commission's rulemaking process. Two additional exemptions are set forth in the statute. Section 16(d)[103] provides that bona fide market making transactions[104] are not subject to section 16(b), nor are they subject to section 16(a)'s reporting requirements[105] or section 16(c)'s prohibitions[106] regarding short sales and sales against the box. Section 16(e)[107] exempts from section 16 pure arbitrage transactions that are carried out in accordance with applicable SEC rules. SEC Rule 16e–1[108] exempts arbitrage transactions by ten percent beneficial owners who are not also officers and directors of the issuer, while officers' and directors' arbitrage transactions are subject to section 16(a) reporting and 16(b) disgorgement but not to section 16(c)'s prohibitions against short sales and sales against the box.[109]

96. Rule 16b–3(c), 17 C.F.R. § 240.16b–3(c).

97. *See* Sec.Exch.Act Rel. No. 34–28869, [1990–1991 Transfer Binder] Fed.Sec.L.Rep. (CCH) ¶ 84,709 (Feb. 8, 1991).

98. Rule 16b–4, 17 C.F.R. § 240.16b–4. The new securities must also have a value equivalent to the securities acquired in the redemption.

99. Rule 16b–5, 17 C.F.R. § 240.16b–5.

100. Rule 16b–7, 17 C.F.R. § 240.16b–7.

101. 17 C.F.R. § 240.16b–8.

102. *Id.*

103. 15 U.S.C.A. § 78p(d). *See* § 12.7 *infra.*

104. Market makers are discussed in § 10.3 *infra.*

105. 15 U.S.C.A. § 78p(a). *See* § 12.2 *supra.*

106. 15 U.S.C.A. § 78p(c). *See* § 12.6 *infra.*

107. 15 U.S.C.A. § 78p(e). *See* § 12.7 *infra.*

108. 17 C.F.R. § 240.16e–1.

109. *See* § 12.7 *infra.*

In addition to the foregoing exemptions from the disgorgement provisions, section 16(b) excludes from its coverage securities "acquired in good faith in connection with a debt previously contracted."[110] This exemption from section 16(b)'s coverage should be narrowly construed to avoid extending it to transactions where the potential for speculative abuse exists. The exemption accordingly does not apply to shares that were not necessary for retirement of the debt and thus were not directly attributable to the previously acquired debt.[111]

Indemnification from Liability Under Section 16(b)

In First Golden Bancorporation v. Weiszmann,[112] a director held liable under section 16(b) sought indemnification from his investment advisor. The court rejected the claim for indemnification as contrary to the public policy underlying section 16(b). The court noted that section 16(b) imposes strict liability as a means to deter improper conduct and that the policy of deterrence would be undermined by permitting indemnification. This result is consistent with the SEC's long-time contention that agreements to indemnify individuals and entities from liability for misstatements in a 1933 Act registration statement are void.[113]

§ 12.4 Who Is Subject to Sections 16(a) and (b)? When Does Insider Status Attach?

Section 16(b)'s damage provisions, like section 16(a)'s filing requirements,[1] apply to officers, directors, and ten percent beneficial owners of any class of equity security subject to section 12's registration requirements.[2] Section 16 identifies three classes of persons whose relationship to the issuer is sufficiently close to conclusively presume access to inside information. The Act does not precisely define officer, director or ten percent beneficial owner; and, as a result numerous questions have arisen as to the scope of section 16's coverage.

Officers and Directors

For example, when dealing with a business trust or other unincorporated form of business association, does a trustee or partner qualify as a director under section 16? Presumably the issue would be approached by asking whether the person at issue performs functions similar to

---

110. 15 U.S.C.A. § 78p(b).

111. C.R.A. Realty Corp. v. Fremont General Corp., 5 F.3d 1341 (9th Cir.1993). *Compare, e.g.,* Rheem Manufacturing Co. v. Rheem, 295 F.2d 473 (9th Cir.1961) (stock issued to satisfy obligation under issuer's retirement plan and then transferred to the insider's bank pursuant to a previously executed general pledge agreement was not subject to disgorgement when the stock was subsequently disposed of in a forced sale by the bank).

112. 942 F.2d 726 (10th Cir.1991).

113. *See* § 7.9 *supra.*

§ 12.4

1. 15 U.S.C.A. § 78p(a). *See* § 12.3 *supra.*

2. 15 U.S.C.A. § 78*l. See* § 9.2 *supra.*

those of a director.[3] While there is no explicit definition of director under the Exchange Act, SEC Rule 3b–2[4] provides that an " 'officer' means a president, vice president, treasurer, secretary, comptroller, and any other person who performs for an issuer, whether incorporated or unincorporated, functions corresponding to those performed by the foregoing officers." Reasoning by analogy, "director" should include the functional equivalent regardless of title; this view is confirmed by other SEC rules.[5]

Both the courts and the SEC have considered the scope of "officer." Following the same pattern as Rule 3b–2's definition, the courts have undertaken a factual, case-by-case analysis of whether officer status in fact exists. For example, when a person, although not holding a formal office, performs the functions of an officer and therefore has access to inside information, section 16(b) will require disgorgement of all short-swing profits.[6] Although expressly refusing to pass on the validity of Rule 3b–2, the Second Circuit adopted a similar functional equivalency test under the terms of the statute.[7] The SEC's rule was upheld in two subsequent decisions, both of which held that, on the facts of each case, statutory insider status did not attach to an assistant secretary or assistant comptroller.[8]

In the early cases defining "officer," the courts were faced with the issue of whether to subject a person not holding an officer's title to

---

3. Section 6(a) of the 1933 Act, which specifies who must sign the registration statement, explicitly addresses this alternative. 15 U.S.C.A. § 77f(a). *Cf.* 17 C.F.R. § 240.3b–2 (definition of "officer").

4. *Ibid.*

5. Thus, for example, the functional equivalence approach is consistent with the definition of "director" under the Securities Act of 1933:

The term "director" means any director of a corporation or any person performing similar functions with respect to any organization whether incorporated or unincorporated.

Rule 405, 17 C.F.R. § 230.405.

6. Colby v. Klune, 178 F.2d 872, 873 (2d Cir.1949):

["Officer"] includes, inter alia, a corporate employee performing important executive duties of such character that he would be likely, in discharging these duties, to obtain confidential information about the company's affairs that would aid him if he engaged in personal market transactions. It is immaterial how his functions are labelled or how defined in the by-laws, or that he does or does not act under the supervision of some other corporate representative.

7. *Id.* at 875. *Accord* C.R.A. Realty Corp. v. Crotty, 878 F.2d 562, 567 (2d Cir.1989) ("it is the duties of an employee—especially his access to inside information—rather than his corporate title which determine whether he is an officer subject to the short-swing trading restrictions of § 16(b) of the 1934 Act"). *See also, e.g.,* Selas Corp. of America v. Voogd, 365 F.Supp. 1268 (E.D.Pa.1973); Gold v. Scurlock, 324 F.Supp. 1211 (E.D.Va.1971), *affirmed in part on other grounds and reversed in part sub nom.* Gold v. Sloan, 486 F.2d 340 (4th Cir.1973); Note, Securities Law—Short Swing Trading (*C.R.A. Realty Corp. v. Crotty*), 63 Temp.L.Rev. 175 (1990).

8. Lockheed Aircraft Corp. v. Campbell, 110 F.Supp. 282 (S.D.Cal.1953); Lockheed Aircraft Corp. v. Rathman, 106 F.Supp. 810 (S.D.Cal.1952). *See also, e.g.,* C.R.A. Realty Corp. v. Crotty, 878 F.2d 562, 567 (2d Cir.1989) (vice president was found not to have access to inside information and therefore was not subject to section 16(b) liability); Sec.Exch.Act Rel. No. 34–2687 (Op. of SEC General Counsel Nov. 16, 1940) (assistant, secretary, treasurer, or comptroller is not a section 16(b) officer).

section 16(b) liability. In two subsequent cases the issue was whether a person, although denominated an officer by title, is not properly an "officer" for purposes of section 16(b). In the first case,[9] the court approved a settlement at a discount below the section 16(b) profit because of the strength of the defense that the defendant although vested with a vice president's title was not a section 16(b) "officer." More recently, the Ninth Circuit has held that where a company had three hundred and fifty "executive vice presidents" the title merely created an inference of "opportunities for confidential information." [10] The court went on to say that the defendant vice president was not subject to section 16(b) liability since he met the burden of proof "that the title was merely honorary and did not carry with it any of the executive responsibilities that might otherwise be assumed."[11] Although literally in compliance with former Rule 3b–2 and the earlier cases, the Ninth Circuit decision provides a shaky precedent. In the first place, by merely possessing the officer title, the defendant arguably falls within the terms of the statute on its face,[12] which should be applied broadly in light of its remedial purpose.[13]

Obligations imposed by section 16 can be seen as one of the burdens of taking such an honorary title. On the other hand, placing the section 16 reporting obligations on middle management can be seen as an undue burden. Courts formerly were reluctant to undertake a detailed factual examination and they generally would not look behind the title.[14] Some courts have spoken in terms of a presumption of access to inside information that results from having an officer's title.[15] Such an approach allows the non-executive "officer" to prove that section 16 should not apply because of the lack of access to inside information. The Commission and state corporate law have gone a long way towards doing away with figurehead or "dummy" directors by imposing standards of

9. Schimmel v. Goldman, 57 F.R.D. 481 (S.D.N.Y.1973).

10. Merrill Lynch, Pierce, Fenner & Smith, Inc. v. Livingston, 566 F.2d 1119, 1122 (9th Cir.1978). *See also, e.g.,* Pier 1 Imports of Georgia, Inc. v. Wilson, 529 F.Supp. 239, 244 (N.D.Tex.1981).

11. *Id.* Where the title is not honorary but reflects managerial authority, section 16(b) applies. National Medical Enterprises, Inc. v. Small, 680 F.2d 83 (9th Cir.1982). *See also, e.g.,* Winston v. Federal Express Corp., 853 F.2d 455 (6th Cir.1988), *affirming* 659 F.Supp. 647 (W.D.Tenn.1987) (active officer who became inactive figure-head one month before purchase was held to be an officer under section 16(b); the court found that the defendant did not rebut the presumption of access to inside information).

Whether or not someone is an officer for section 16(b) purposes is a question of fact. *See, e.g.,* C.R.A. Realty Corp. v. Crotty, 663 F.Supp. 444 (S.D.N.Y.1987).

12. *See* Comment *supra* footnote 4.

13. *See* § 12.3 *supra.*

14. National Medical Enterprises, Inc. v. Small, 680 F.2d 83, 84 (9th Cir.1982). *Cf.* C.R.A. Realty Corp. v. Crotty, 1988 WL 140746, [1988–89 Transfer Binder] Fed.Sec.L.Rep. (CCH) ¶ 94,140 (S.D.N.Y.1988) (Unpublished Case) (middle management employee was not an officer).

15. *See* National Medical Enterprises, Inc. v. Small, 680 F.2d 83, 84 (9th Cir.1982); C.R.A. Realty Corp. v. Crotty, 663 F.Supp. 444 (S.D.N.Y.1987). *See, e.g.,* Allis–Chalmers Mfg. Co. v. Gulf & Western Industries, Inc., 527 F.2d 335, 347–48 (7th Cir.1975), *cert. denied* 423 U.S. 1078, 96 S.Ct. 865, 47 L.Ed.2d 89 (1976).

care.[16] The rationale for not permitting director titles and positions without concomitant obligations is that the title is a "holding out" and thus justifies imposition of fiduciary obligations. The same may not be true of honorary or purely titular officers. Unlike figure-head directors, merely making someone a vice president may not confer any authority nor impose any special fiduciary obligation. Nor, in such a case would the conferring of a title provide any access to inside information. As discussed below, this is the approach taken by current SEC rules. Permitting the subjective analysis to exclude a titular officer from the statute's reach certainly goes a long way to avoid the Act's crude rule of thumb. It permits the courts to exclude from the statute's coverage transactions that objectively fall within section 16(b)'s reach. In other contexts, the pragmatic mode of analysis has been limited to unorthodox transactions as opposed to garden variety cash-for-stock-sales.[17] However, as part of its more recent rulemaking initiatives, the Commission has provided more of a bright-line test for excluding individuals with merely nominal officer status.

In addition to the definition of officer contained in Rule 3b–2, Rule 3b–7 defines "executive officer" which includes the president, any vice president in charge of a principal unit or division as well as "any other officer who performs a policy making function" or any other person performing "similar policy making functions."[18] In 1991, the SEC revamped its section 16 reporting rules and in doing so adopted a definition of officer that is modelled on but expands upon Rule 3b–7's definition of executive officer.[19] Rule 16a–1(f) begins with the basic definition of executive officer and then adds principal financial and accounting officers as well as officers of a parent organization having policy-making functions with respect to the issuer.[20] Consistent with the cases discussed above, the Commission has stated that a person's title alone should not determine whether he or she is subject to section 16. The focus should be on whether, in discharging his or her duties, the individual is likely to obtain information that would be helpful in his or her personal market transactions.[21]

Deputization as the Basis of Insider Status

Another problem in determining who is subject to section 16(b) arises in the context of deputization. The Supreme Court has explained that where a partnership has profited from short-swing transactions in a

---

16. *E.g.* Escott v. BarChris Construction Corp., 283 F.Supp. 643 (S.D.N.Y.1968) (liability under section 11 of the 1933 Act); ABA, Corporate Director's Guidebook, 33 Bus.Law. 1591, 1619–27 (1978). *See* § 7.4 *supra.*

17. *See* § 12.5 *infra.*

18. 17 C.F.R. § 240.3b–7.

19. Rule 16a–1(f), 17 C.F.R. § 240.16a–1(f). *See* Sec.Exch. Act Rel. No. 34–28869, [1990–1991 Transfer Binder] Fed.Sec.L.Rep. (CCH) ¶ 84,709 (Feb. 8, 1991).

20. 17 C.F.R. § 240.16a–1(f). The rule expressly includes the controller when the issuer has no principal accounting officer.

21. Sec.Exch. Act Rel. No. 34–28869, [1990–1991 Transfer Binder] Fed.Sec.L.Rep. (CCH) ¶ 84,709 (Feb. 8, 1991), relying on Colby v. Klune, 178 F.2d 872, 873 (2d Cir.1949).

corporation's stock and has designated or "deputized" one of its partners to sit on that corporation's board of directors, the partnership will be deemed to be a "director" under the doctrine of deputization.[22] Even in the absence of deputization, the director-partner's pro rata share of the partnership profits would necessarily have to be disgorged under section 16(b).[23] The Court held that the mere possibility of inside information flowing to the partnership was not sufficient and gave the plaintiff the burden of proving an actual deputizing or agency relationship.[24]

The Second Circuit seems to have retreated from the Supreme Court's heavy burden of proof on the deputization issue. Where a corporation's president and chief executive officer sat on the issuer's board and where that person had a say in the corporation's investment interest, and further where the president resigned as a director of the issuer after the decision to sell within six months of a purchase, deputization was established and the corporation had to disgorge its short-swing profit.[25] The Second Circuit pointed out that although there was no actual proof of a formal or a de facto deputization, the corporation had a recurring pattern of placing a representative on the board of any company in which it owned a substantial number of shares. The defendant's representative on the issuer's board was not only its president and chief executive officer but also had participated in discussions with other corporate personnel about its investment holdings. Deputization was found notwithstanding the lack of evidence of any actual communication of inside information since the potential for abuse was more than a mere possibility.[26] The Second Circuit's approach was quite realistic, given the circumstances surrounding the case.

Although it is clear that the mere presence of an interlocking director will not be sufficient to create a section 16(b) deputization,[27] the subjective or case-by-case nature of analysis means that each situation

---

22. Blau v. Lehman, 368 U.S. 403, 82 S.Ct. 451, 7 L.Ed.2d 403 (1962). *See* Caroll J. Wagner, Jr., Deputization Under Section 16(b): The Implications of Feder v. Martin Marietta Corporation, 78 Yale L.J. 1151 (1969).

23. Blau v. Lehman, 368 U.S. 403, 82 S.Ct. 451, 7 L.Ed.2d 403 (1962).

24. *Id.* at 411, 82 S.Ct. at 455. *Cf., e.g.,* Rogers v. Valentine, 306 F.Supp. 34 (S.D.N.Y.1969), *affirmed* 426 F.2d 1361 (2d Cir.1970) (holding that section 16(c)'s prohibition against short sales applies only to shares beneficially held by the insider and not to shares sold short where the insider was acting as agent for someone else).

25. Feder v. Martin Marietta Corp., 406 F.2d 260 (2d Cir.1969), *cert. denied* 396 U.S. 1036, 90 S.Ct. 678, 24 L.Ed.2d 681 (1970). *See* Wagner *supra* footnote 22.

26. Feder v. Martin Marietta Corp., 406 F.2d 260 (2d Cir.1969), *cert. denied* 396 U.S. 1036, 90 S.Ct. 678, 24 L.Ed.2d 681 (1970). *Cf.* Gold v. Sloan, 486 F.2d 340, 343–44 (4th Cir.1973), *cert. denied* 419 U.S. 873, 95 S.Ct. 134, 42 L.Ed.2d 112 (1974).

27. *See* Popkin v. Dingman, 366 F.Supp. 534 (S.D.N.Y.1973). *See also, e.g.,* Mayer v. Chesapeake Ins. Co. Ltd., 877 F.2d 1154 (2d Cir.1989), *cert. denied* 493 U.S. 1021, 110 S.Ct. 722, 107 L.Ed.2d 741 (1990) (owner and related companies of corporation receiving short-swing profits were not beneficial owners of the buying and selling corporation's stock); Suffield Bank v. LaRoche, 752 F.Supp. 54 (D.R.I.1990) (pledgee bank that sold stock in foreclosure of a pledge of officer's stock was neither directly nor indirectly a 10 percent beneficial owner, officer or director and thus was not subject to section 16(b)); Sarkowsky Foundation, 22 Sec.Reg. & L.Rep. (BNA) 289 (SEC No Action Letter available Feb. 6, 1990) (director of both a private foundation and of a public corporation need not file section 16(a) reports for foundation's transactions in the public corporation's equity securities).

must be determined on its own facts.[28] Conversely, the attribution of profits from one person or entity to another is not limited to interlocking directorates; control can be based on ownership of a controlling interest. Accordingly, it is proper to match a section 16 insider's purchase of securities with sales made by an entity controlled by the insider.[29]

Family Relationships

Somewhat akin to the question of deputization is the question whether a spouse's holdings are to be attributed to the other spouse who is a section 16(b) insider.[30] In one case,[31] it was held that a wife's sales were to be matched against her husband's exercise of stock options where the husband was a director. The husband/director did not control the wife's investments; the couple maintained separate brokerage accounts but engaged in joint estate planning. The court reasoned that the wife, by virtue of her relationship and investment related conversations with her husband, had access to inside information. Federal rather than state law determines the question of beneficial ownership with regard to securities held by husband and wife.[32]

With regard to stock held by the spouse or children or trusts for either, the Seventh Circuit has required a "direct pecuniary benefit" to the insider in order to find section 16(b) liability. "[T]ies of consanguinity," "an enhanced sense of well-being" or the insider's being "led to reduce his gift giving" to the stock owner or its beneficiary will not alone lead to attribution under section 16(b).[33] Reading these two cases together, the courts quite properly will attribute beneficial ownership when it appears that the potential for speculative abuse exists.

Effect of Resignation

Another question under section 16 is the effect of the timing of the transactions with regard to an officer's or a director's assumption of office or resignation. For example, it has been held that a director who resigned prior to a sale at a profit within six months of his purchase was held subject to section 16(b).[34] Similarly, it was held that section 16(b) liability attaches to a short-swing profit where the defendant became an officer after his purchase but prior to his sale within six months of the

---

28. *See generally* Carroll L. Wagner, Jr., Deputization Under Section 16(b): The Implications of Feder v. Martin Marietta Corporation, 78 Yale L.J. 1151 (1969).

29. *E.g.,* Synalloy Corp. v. Gray, 816 F.Supp. 963, 971 (D.Del.1993).

30. *See generally* Janet Gamer Feldman & Richard L. Teberg, Beneficial Ownership Under Section 16 of the Securities Exchange Act, 17 West.Res.L.Rev. 1054 (1966); Charles E. Shreve, Beneficial Ownership of Securities Held by Family Members, 22 Bus.Law. 431 (1967).

31. Whiting v. Dow Chemical Co., 523 F.2d 680 (2d Cir.1975).

32. Walet v. Jefferson Lake Sulphur Co., 202 F.2d 433 (5th Cir.1953), *cert. denied* 346 U.S. 820, 74 S.Ct. 35, 98 L.Ed. 346 (1953).

33. C.B.I. Industries, Inc. v. Horton, 682 F.2d 643, 646–47 (7th Cir.1982).

34. Feder v. Martin Marietta Corp., 406 F.2d 260 (2d Cir.1969), *cert. denied* 396 U.S. 1036, 90 S.Ct. 678, 24 L.Ed.2d 681 (1970).

purchase.[35]   Notwithstanding some dicta to the contrary,[36] these rulings still had substantial following until recent SEC action.[37]   However, the new SEC rules on reporting obligations may have changed the law in this regard.   Rule 16a–2 provides that under most circumstances, transactions effectuated by an officer or director prior to becoming subject to section 16(a)'s reporting requirements are not subject to section 16.[38] The only instance in which the reporting requirements apply to this period is when the reporting obligation began as a result of the issuer's having to comply with section 12's registration requirements.[39]   Accordingly, when the reporting requirements are occasioned by the appointment or election to office, transactions occurring prior to the appointment or election need not be reported.   The SEC rules go on to clarify that officers and directors remain subject to section 16's requirements for the six months following the last sale before cessation of officer or director status.[40]

Prior to adoption of the current SEC rules, it had been held that an officer or director who immediately after resigning exercises stock options acquired while an employee and then sells the stock at a profit within six months does not incur section 16(b) liability since he was an insider neither at the time of purchase nor at the time of sale.[41]   Since the exercise of a stock option falls within the category of an unorthodox transaction, arguably, section 16(b) could apply upon proof of access to relevant inside information.[42]   The courts, utilizing a broad pragmatic analysis, might well find a way to impose that section 16(b) liability upon

---

35.   Adler v. Klawans, 267 F.2d 840 (2d Cir.1959); Marquette Cement Manufacturing Co. v. Andreas, 239 F.Supp. 962 (S.D.N.Y.1965).

36.   Allis–Chalmers Manufacturing Co. v. Gulf & Western Industries, Inc., 527 F.2d 335, 346–348 (7th Cir.1975), *cert. denied* 423 U.S. 1078, 96 S.Ct. 865, 47 L.Ed.2d 89 (1976).

37.   *See* Foremost–McKesson, Inc. v. Provident Securities Co., 423 U.S. 232, 243, n. 16, 96 S.Ct. 508, 515, n. 16, 46 L.Ed.2d 464 (1976); § 12.5 *infra*.   *See also* Arrow Distributing Corp. v. Baumgartner, 783 F.2d 1274 (5th Cir.1986) where the court reasoned by analogy to the cases dealing with appointment to office in holding that section 16(b) applies to an officer's transaction occurring after the issuer became a 1934 Act registrant even though the first leg of the short-swing transaction occurred prior to the issuer's having a class of equity securities registered under section 12(g).   *See* § 12.3 *supra*. Section 12's registration requirements are discussed in § 9.2 *supra*.

38.   17 C.F.R. § 240.16a–2.

39.   17 C.F.R. § 240.16a–2(a).

40.   17 C.F.R. § 240.16a–2(b).

41.   Lewis v. Mellon Bank, 513 F.2d 921 (3d Cir.1975); Lewis v. Varnes, 505 F.2d 785 (2d Cir.1974).   *Cf.* Lewis v. Bradley, 599 F.Supp. 327 (S.D.N.Y.1984) (negotiations between resigning director and corporation did not constitute a section 16(b) sale where eventual sale price was fixed in terms of market price on the date of the closing).

Section 16(a) requires that reports be filed even after retirement. 15 U.S.C.A. § 78p(a); In the Matter of Robert S. Smith, [1970–1971 Transfer Binder] Fed.Sec.L.Rep. (CCH) ¶ 78,008 (SEC, no action letter; Jan. 26, 1971).   In fact former Rule 16a–1(e) required SEC filing of all changes in ownership within the six month period following retirement or resignation.   17 C.F.R. § 240.16a–1(e) (1990).   However, the Third Circuit has held that sections 16(a) and 16(b) "operate independently."   Lewis v. Mellon Bank, 513 F.2d 921, 923 (3d Cir.1975) (exercise of option followed by sale of stock within six months of retirement is not covered by section 16(b)).

42.   *Cf.* Gold v. Sloan, 486 F.2d 340 (4th Cir.1973), *cert. denied* 419 U.S. 873, 95 S.Ct. 134, 42 L.Ed.2d 112 (1974).   *See* § 12.5 *infra*.

a director who resigns, purchases and then sells since it may seem reasonable to apply the statute's presumption of reliance upon inside information. Although such a reading would certainly curtail short swing transactions, it is difficult to justify such a result in the face of the statutory language, unless it was clear that this was only a "sham" resignation. The new treatment of employee stock options makes liability under section 16(b) even less likely in such a case.[43] On the other hand, such conduct even if not resulting in section 16(b) liability, might raise a strong inference (or even a presumption) of improper reliance on inside information in terms of finding a possible violation of Rule 10b–5.[44]

Beneficial Ownership

In order to be found to be a beneficial owner of the stock, the purported owner was required by the cases to have a direct pecuniary interest in those shares.[45] However, in its proposed revisions to its rules under section 16, the SEC recommended extending the concept of beneficial ownership to some persons with only an indirect pecuniary interest.[46] The rules as adopted define who is considered a beneficial owner, for the purpose of matching purchases and sales, and include in the definition of beneficial owner anyone who has a direct or indirect pecuniary interest.[47]

What happens if the owner is not made aware that his or her holdings have crossed the ten percent threshold? Especially in the case of issuers who periodically repurchase their shares, the threshold can be a moving target. If an owner is not at least put on inquiry notice that his or her holdings have reached the threshold, then there should be no section 16(b) liability until those facts come to light.[48] In contrast to the

---

43. Rule 16b–3, 17 C.F.R. § 240.16b–3 provides that for qualified employee benefit plans the six month period is measured from the date of the grant or award of the option until the sale of the underlying security or disposition of the option *other than by conversion or exercise.*

44. 17 C.F.R. § 240.10b–5. *See* § 13.9 *infra. Cf.* SEC v. Texas Gulf Sulphur Co., 401 F.2d 833 (2d Cir.1968), *cert. denied* 394 U.S. 976, 89 S.Ct. 1454, 22 L.Ed.2d 756 (1969) (where the court looked to defendants' heavy purchases as circumstantial evidence that they were trading on inside information).

45. Mayer v. Chesapeake Ins. Co., 877 F.2d 1154, 1160 (2d Cir.1989), *cert. denied* 493 U.S. 1021, 110 S.Ct. 722, 107 L.Ed.2d 741 (1990).

46. Proposed Rule 16a–1(a), 4 Fed.Sec.L.Rep. (CCH) ¶ 26,013 (Dec. 2, 1988). *See* Mayer v. Chesapeake Ins. Co., *supra* footnote 45 at 1162.

47. Rule 16a–1(a)(2), 17 C.F.R. § 240.16a–1(a)(2). As discussed in a previous section, the SEC intended to conform section 16's concept of beneficial ownership to the test under section 13(d) of the Williams Act. *See* § 12.2 *supra.* Section 13(d) is discussed in § 11.11 *supra. See also, e.g.,* C.R.A. Realty Corp. v. Enron Corp., 842 F.Supp. 88, 91 (S.D.N.Y. 1994), relying on Exch. Act Rel. No. 34–28869, [1990–1991 Transfer Binder] Fed.Sec.L.Rep. (CCH) ¶ 84,709 (Feb. 8, 1991) ("The intent of the SEC to define 'ten percent' under Section 16 as it is defined under Section 13(d) could not be clearer").

A different definition applies to determine the applicability of section 16(a)'s reporting requirements. *See* § 12.2 *supra.*

48. C.R.A. Realty Corp. v. Enron Corp., 842 F.Supp. 88 (S.D.N.Y.1994) (although information in annual report revealed that defendant's ownership was ten percent, it was not subject to § 16(b) liability since it had no reason to know of that status when the

cases dealing with officers and directors, section 16(b) on its face provides that where insider status attaches by virtue of ten percent beneficial equity ownership, the section applies only where such person was a beneficial owner "both at the time of the purchase and sale, or the sale and purchase." [49] Notwithstanding some lower court decisions to the contrary,[50] the Supreme Court has held that the threshold purchase that pushes the defendant over ten percent does not qualify as a "purchase" subject to section 16(b) and that only purchases made after that date will give rise to liability when matched with subsequent sales occurring within six months and resulting in a profit.[51]

It is as yet unclear whether, at least in the case of a non-garden-variety cash-for-stock transaction, evidence of prior access to inside information would be sufficient to overcome the Court's ruling on the time of purchase and lead it to apply 16(b) pragmatically.[52] It seems, however, that a more objective approach here is preferable.

In another case,[53] the Court has held that where a ten percent beneficial owner first sells just enough shares to put him below the ten percent threshold, and on the next day liquidates the remainder of his holdings, the second sale cannot be subject to section 16(b) because of the statute's express "at the time of" requirement. This ruling was based on an objective reading of the statute rather than a subjective evaluation of the statutory insider's motives in so structuring the two-step sale.[54] In deciding when a purchase takes place, the critical time is when the purchaser is irrevocably committed to the transaction.[55]

The question of the beneficial ownership threshold has arisen in connection with stock options. Formerly, the ownership of stock options was not ownership of the underlying equity security unless the option

report was released; subsequently, it became aware of its ten percent status and defendant duly filed a Form 3).

49. 15 U.S.C.A. § 78p(b).

50. *E.g.* Stella v. Graham–Paige Motors Corp., 104 F.Supp. 957 (S.D.N.Y.1952), *affirmed in part and reversed in part* 232 F.2d 299 (2d Cir.1952), *cert. denied* 352 U.S. 831, 77 S.Ct. 46, 1 L.Ed.2d 52 (1956).

51. Foremost–McKesson, Inc. v. Provident Securities Co., 423 U.S. 232, 96 S.Ct. 508, 46 L.Ed.2d 464 (1976). *See also, e.g.,* Mayer v. Chesapeake Ins. Co. Ltd., 877 F.2d 1154 (2d Cir.1989), *cert. denied* 493 U.S. 1021, 110 S.Ct. 722, 107 L.Ed.2d 741 (1990).

52. *See* Thomas L. Hazen, The New Pragmatism Under Section 16(b) of the Securities Exchange Act, 54 N.C.L.Rev. 1, 50–55 (1975). *Cf.* Piano Remittance Corp. v. Reliance Financial Services Corp., 618 F.Supp. 414, 418–19 (S.D.N.Y.1985) (looking to the facts surrounding the transaction in determining the effect of a block purchase in terms of timing for section 16(b) purposes).

53. Reliance Electric Co. v. Emerson Electric Co., 404 U.S. 418, 92 S.Ct. 596, 30 L.Ed.2d 575 (1972).

54. In his dissent Justice Douglas argued that a pragmatic view should be taken. 404 U.S. at 427 *et seq.*

55. Piano Remittance Corp. v. Reliance Financial Services Corp., 618 F.Supp. 414 (S.D.N.Y.1985) (placing order with broker to purchase 1,000,000 shares did not irrevocably commit the person placing the order so that any shares purchased under such an order may be classified as a section 16(b) purchase if they were actually purchased after the purchaser reached the ten percent threshold).

carried with it the rights of stock ownership.[56] The rationale was that owning options, which generally do not have incidents of stock ownership,[57] is not a sufficient basis for presuming access to inside information.[58] In connection with its 1991 rule revisions, the Commission has reversed its long-standing policy by making the acquisition of a derivative security, rather than its exercise, the significant event for section 16 purposes.[59] Derivative securities are covered not only by the section 16(a) reporting requirements but also by the short-swing profit provisions of section 16(b). The new rules treat derivative securities transactions as matchable not only against each other but also against transactions in the underlying security.[60] The new rules thus equate ownership of a derivative security with ownership of the underlying security and recognize that, as is the case with convertible securities, exercise merely changes ownership from indirect to direct ownership of the underlying security. Someone who is a section 16(b) insider by virtue of stock ownership or officer or director status will have to disgorge short-swing profits from the sale and purchase of stock options that are not exempt under Rule 16b-3.[61]

§ 12.5 The Definition of "Purchase" and "Sale" and the Pragmatic Trend Under Section 16(b)[1]

Following the same pattern as section 2(3) of the 1933 Act's defini-

---

56. Citadel Holding Corp. v. Roven, 26 F.3d 960 (9th Cir.1994); Colan v. Monumental Corp., 713 F.2d 330 (7th Cir.1983); Newmark v. RKO General, Inc., 425 F.2d 348 (2d Cir. 1970), *cert. denied* 400 U.S. 854, 91 S.Ct. 64, 27 L.Ed.2d 91 (1970); Stella v. Graham–Paige Motors Corp., 232 F.2d 299, 301 (2d Cir.1956); Blau v. Ogsbury, 210 F.2d 426 (2d Cir.1954).

57. *But cf., e.g.,* Newmark v. RKO General, Inc., 425 F.2d 348 (2d Cir. 1970), *cert. denied* 400 U.S. 854, 91 S.Ct. 64, 27 L.Ed.2d 91 (1970) (section 16(b) applied to option-holder who had an agreement that the corporation would be managed in accordance with his interests).

58. Colan v. Monumental Corp., 713 F.2d 330 (7th Cir.1983). *But cf.* new rules on derivative securities. *See* § 12–2 *supra.*

59. Sec.Exch.Act Rel. No. 34–28869, [1990–1991 Transfer Binder] Fed.Sec.L.Rep. (CCH) ¶ 84,709 (Feb. 8, 1991). The rules contain a specific exemption for most exercises of rights and warrants. Rule 16b–6(b), 17 C.F.R. § 240.16b–6(b). However, the exercise exemption does not apply when the exercise creates a new opportunity for profit. The exercise exemption also does not apply to the exercise of out-of-the-money options. *See* Sec.Exch. Act Rel. No. 34–28869 *supra. Cf.* Frankel v. Slotkin, 984 F.2d 1328 (2d Cir.1993) (refusing to apply the change retroactively and holding that the granting of a put option to tender offeror in connection with a planned acquisition was not a "sale" under section 16(b), although the exercise would be).

As pointed out in § 12.2 *supra,* some derivative securities are exempt. *See* Rule 16a–1(c)(3), 17 C.F.R. § 16a–1(c)(3).

60. Rule 16b–6(a), 17 C.F.R. § 240.16b–6(a). *See* § 12.3 *infra*

61. 17 C.F.R. § 240.16b–3. *Accord* Arrow Distributing Corp. v. Baumgartner, 783 F.2d 1274 (5th Cir.1986).

§ 12.5

1. Parts of this section were adapted from Thomas L. Hazen, The New Pragmatism Under Section 16(b) of the Securities Exchange Act, 54 N.C.L.Rev. 1 (1975).

tion of "sale," [2] section 3(a)(13) of the 1934 Act defines "purchase" to "include any contract to buy, purchase, or otherwise acquire."[3] The definition is not limited to normal day-to-day cash for stock transactions. Accordingly courts have had to decide whether other transactions such as exercise of stock options or conversion rights and exchanges of securities pursuant to a merger—so called "unorthodox transactions"[4]— fall within section 16(b)'s reach.

A number of early section 16(b) cases raised the question of whether a voluntary conversion of stock constituted a purchase of the new security or, alternatively, a sale of the convertible security, so as to have section 16(b) consequences. The cases were in conflict[5] although they tended not to find a purchase or sale unless the surrounding circumstances created a potential for the type of speculative abuse that section 16(b) was designed to prevent. It was out of the conversion cases that the pragmatic or subjective trend arose, with the courts looking at the facts to determine if section 16 evils were present.[6] Although the pragmatic trend continues, especially in the case of corporate combinations, mergers, and tender offers, the specific question of whether a conversion is a sale or purchase was answered in the negative by former Rule 16b–9.[7] The effect of this rule was to exempt conversions from section 16(b)'s reach if the time period between purchase or sale of the convertible stock and sale or purchase of the new stock issued upon exercise of the conversion rights was not less than six months. In connection with the SEC's rewriting of its section 16 rules, significant

---

2. 15 U.S.C.A. § 77b(3). *See* § 5.1 *supra. See also* § 13.2.3 *infra* for discussion of what constitutes a purchase or sale under SEC Rule 10b–5.

3. 15 U.S.C.A. § 78c(a)(13).

4. The term "unorthodox" has been "applied to stock conversions, exchanges pursuant to mergers and other corporate reorganizations, stock reclassifications, and dealings in options, rights and warrants." Kern County Land Co. v. Occidental Petroleum Corp., 411 U.S. 582, 594, n. 24, 93 S.Ct. 1736, 1744, n. 24, 36 L.Ed.2d 503 (1973). It has been applied to sales pursuant to tender offers prior to merger, Makofsky v. Ultra Dynamics Corp., 383 F.Supp. 631, 637 (S.D.N.Y.1974). *See also* Colan v. Cutler–Hammer, Inc., 812 F.2d 357 (7th Cir.1987), *cert. denied* 484 U.S. 820, 108 S.Ct. 79, 98 L.Ed.2d 42 (1987) (secret agreement to delay date of merger to avoid section 16(b)'s disgorgement requirement did not trigger section 16(b) liability). Pier 1 Imports of Georgia, Inc. v. Wilson, 529 F.Supp. 239 (N.D.Tex.1981). In late 1988, the SEC proposed rules to, *inter alia,* exempt most exercises of options and other derivative rights. Sec.Exch. Act Rel.No. 34–26333, [1988–89 Transfer Binder] Fed.Sec.L.Rep. (CCH) ¶ 84,343 (Dec. 2, 1988). These rules have since been adopted. *See* § 12.3 *supra.*

5. *Compare, e.g.,* Heli–Coil Corp. v. Webster, 352 F.2d 156 (3d Cir.1965) (conversion is a section 16(b) purchase; applying objective test) *with* Petteys v. Butler, 367 F.2d 528 (8th Cir.1966), *cert. denied* 385 U.S. 1006, 87 S.Ct. 712, 17 L.Ed.2d 545 (1967) (finding no purchase, utilizing "pragmatic" analysis). *See also, e.g.,* Ferraiolo v. Newman, 259 F.2d 342 (6th Cir.1958), *cert. denied* 359 U.S. 927, 79 S.Ct. 606, 3 L.Ed.2d 629 (1959) (pragmatic approach); Parke & Tilford, Inc. v. Schulte, 160 F.2d 984 (2d Cir. 1947), *cert. denied* 332 U.S. 761, 68 S.Ct. 64, 92 L.Ed. 347 (1947) (objective).

6. *See, e.g.,* Lewis Lowenfels, Section 16(b): A New Trend in Regulating Insider Trading, 54 Cornell L.Rev. 45 (1968).

7. 17 C.F.R. § 240.16b–9 (1990). *See generally* Robert W. Hamilton, Convertible Securities and Section 16(b): The End of An Era, 44 Tex.L.Rev. 1447 (1966). *Cf.* Gund v. First Florida Banks, Inc., 726 F.2d 682 (11th Cir.1984) (sale of convertible security followed by purchase of underlying stock held subject to section 16(b)); T–Bar, Inc. v. Chatterjee, 693 F.Supp. 1 (S.D.N.Y.1988) (semble).

changes were made affecting derivative securities.[8] Derivative securities are covered not only by the section 16(a) reporting requirements but also by the short-swing profit provisions of section 16(b). Transactions in derivative securities are matchable not only against each other but also against transactions in the underlying security. The new rules thus equate ownership of a derivative security with ownership of the underlying security and recognize that, as is the case with convertible securities, exercise merely changes ownership from indirect to direct ownership of the underlying security.[9]

The opportunity to realize a profit begins the moment an insider purchases or is granted a derivative security. It follows that the acquisition of a derivative security not only is a reportable event under section 16(a),[10] it can be matched against dispositions of either the derivative or underlying security occurring within the preceding or following six months.[11] Thus for example, an acquisition of a call option may be matched with any disposition of either the underlying security or other equivalent call option.[12] Conversely, an acquisition of a put option may be matched with an acquisition of the underlying security or disposition of an equivalent put position.[13] Just as acquisitions of derivative securities are reportable and matchable events, dispositions of derivative securities have similar section 16 implications.[14]

The new rules also address the effect of the expiration of a derivative security position. Rule 16b–6(d)[15] exempts from section 16(b)'s disgorgement provisions the expiration (or cancellation without value) of a long derivative security such as a call option. However, the rule is otherwise with regard to short positions. The expiration of a short

---

8. *See* Sec.Exch. Act Rel. No. 34–28869, [1990–1991 Transfer Binder] Fed.Sec.L.Rep. (CCH) ¶ 84,709 (Feb. 8, 1991) and the discussion in § 12.2 *supra.*

9. Sec.Exch.Act Rel. No. 34–28869, [1990–1991 Transfer Binder] Fed.Sec.L.Rep. (CCH) ¶ 84,709 (Feb. 8, 1991).

10. Rule 16a–4(a), 17 C.F.R. § 240.16a–4(a). *See* § 12.2 *supra.*

11. Rule 16a–6(a), 17 C.F.R. § 240.16b–6(a). *See, e.g.,* Lilly Industrial Coatings, Inc., [1990–1991 Transfer Binder] Fed.Sec.L.Rep. (CCH) ¶ 79,699E (SEC No Action Letter May 9, 1991) (conversion of class B stock would qualify for exemption from section 16(b)). *But see,* Frankel v. Slotkin, 984 F.2d 1328 (2d Cir.1993) (refusing to apply the change retroactively and holding that the granting of a put option to tender offeror in connection with a planned acquisition was not a "sale" under section 16(b), although the exercise would be).

Reclassification of an existing stock option plan that does not alter the economic value of the options will not ordinarily constitute a new grant of an option so as to start the six month period running anew. *See, e.g.,* UAL Corp., 36 Sec. Reg. & L. Rep. (BNA) 527 (SEC No Action Letter avail. March 30, 1994)

12. Sec.Exch.Act Rel. No. 34–28869, [1990–1991 Transfer Binder] Fed.Sec.L.Rep. (CCH) ¶ 84,709 (Feb. 8, 1991).

13. *Id.*

14. Thus, for example, dispositions of call positions may be matched against acquisitions of the underlying security or acquisitions of another call equivalent position. Similarly, dispositions of put positions may be matched against dispositions of the underlying security or call equivalent positions of the underlying security. *Id.*

15. 17 C.F.R. § 240.16b–6(d).

derivative position may result in a profit that is subject to disgorgement under section 16(b).

The new SEC rules address the computation of profits resulting from acquisitions and dispositions of derivative securities. If there is an acquisition and disposition of a derivative security within a six month period, the section 16(b) recovery is based on the profit received from the matching transactions.[16] If an acquisition or disposition of a derivative security is to be matched with a transaction in the underlying security or different derivative security, the maximum section 16(b) profit is based on the difference in the market value of the underlying security on the transaction dates; the court should award a lesser recovery in the event the insider can demonstrate that the amount of profit was less.[17]

Following the type of case-by-case analysis that arose in the context of the early conversion decisions, the courts are now in agreement that when a transaction is not a garden variety cash-for-stock purchase or sale, the court will scrutinize all surrounding circumstances in order to determine whether the transaction lends itself to the type of speculative abuse that 16(b) was designed to prevent. If there is neither fear of nor potential for section 16(b) abuse, then the court utilizing the pragmatic analysis will find no purchase or sale, as the case may be.[18] The best way to understand the pragmatic approach is to look at a few illustrative cases.

In the leading case of Kern County Land Co. v. Occidental Petroleum Corp.,[19] the Supreme Court addressed the applicability of section 16(b) to sales of the target company's shares by a defeated tender offeror. The management of Kern, the target company, had opposed the takeover by defendant Occidental and within two weeks responded with a defensive stock for stock merger with Tenneco. Rather than sell its holdings immediately, two weeks after approval of the merger, Occidental entered into an agreement with Tenneco to issue to Tenneco an option to purchase the Tenneco preferred shares received pursuant to the merger in six months at one hundred and five dollars per share. In return, Tenneco agreed to pay Occidental a premium of ten dollars per option which would be applied to the exercise price. More than six months after both Occidental's purchase of the Old Kern stock and its acquisition via the exchange of the Tenneco stock,[20] Tenneco exercised the option. The district court held that Occidental's acquisition of Tenneco stock pursuant to the Old Kern–Tenneco merger was a section

---

16. Rule 16b–6(c), 17 C.F.R. § 240.16b–6(c).

17. *Id.*

18. *See, e.g.,* Kern County Land Co. v. Occidental Petroleum Corp., 411 U.S. 582, 93 S.Ct. 1736, 36 L.Ed.2d 503 (1973); Gold v. Sloan, 486 F.2d 340 (4th Cir.1973), *cert. denied* 419 U.S. 873, 95 S.Ct. 134, 42 L.Ed.2d 112 (1974). *See,* Hazen *supra* footnote 1, Lowenfels *supra* footnote 6; Roy A. Wentz, Refining a Crude Rule: The Pragmatic Approach to Section 16(b), 70 Nw.U.L.Rev. 221 (1975).

19. 411 U.S. 582, 93 S.Ct. 1736, 36 L.Ed.2d 503 (1973).

20. As a holder of Kern stock under the merger, Occidental received shares of Tenneco, one of its largest competitors.

16(b) "sale" within six months of its Kern purchases pursuant to the original tender offer, and further that the subsequent option agreement was a "sale" of the new securities and thus also within the reach of section 16(b).[21] The Second Circuit reversed since, *inter alia,* Occidental's obligation to dispose of the shares had not been fixed until Tenneco exercised the option more than six months after the purchase.[22]

The Supreme Court affirmed the Second Circuit's ruling and its adherence to a pragmatic analysis of the transaction:

> In deciding whether borderline [unorthodox] transactions are within the reach of the statute, the courts have come to inquire whether the transaction may serve as a vehicle for the evil which Congress sought to prevent—the realization of short-swing profits based upon access to inside information—thereby endeavoring to implement congressional objectives without extending the reach of the statute beyond its intended limits.[23]

The Court characterized Occidental's position at the time that the Old Kern–Tenneco merger had been announced as treading water between Scylla and Charybdis in that the only realistic alternative to participating in the exchange and subsequent sale to Tenneco would have been to dispose of the Old Kern stock on the open market via a garden variety cash-for-stock sale which clearly would have resulted in certain 16(b) liability.

Proceeding on the theory that there had not been a statutory sale by virtue of the share exchange,[24] the next question for decision was whether Occidental "sold" its new Tenneco shares on the date of the

---

21. Abrams v. Occidental Petroleum Corp., 323 F.Supp. 570, 579–80 (S.D.N.Y.1970), *reversed* 450 F.2d 157 (2d Cir. 1971).

22. It is urged that Occidental possessed the "inside information" that Old Kern might well respond [to its takeover attempt] by arranging a "defensive merger" and that, if the terms were sufficiently favorable, Occidental would not try to top them. But, in contrast to [Newmark v. RKO General, Inc., 425 F.2d 348 (2d Cir.1970), *cert. denied* 400 U.S. 854, 91 S.Ct. 64, 27 L.Ed.2d 91 (1970)]where the buyer knew of the imminent announcement of a merger that would enhance the price of the shares and could largely control its course, Occidental had no knowledge what Old Kern would do, and certainly did not know that Old Kern would be able to arrange an exchange offer exceeding Occidental's bid by $20 per share, with the added benefit of freedom from capital gains tax. We fail to see the possibility of speculative abuse in a situation where such an offeror simply declines to make a still higher offer or to attempt to block a transaction which it regards as advantageous to all the stockholders including itself.

Abrams v. Occidental Petroleum Corp., 450 F.2d 157, 163 (2d Cir.1971), *cert. granted* 405 U.S. 1064, 92 S.Ct. 1498, 31 L.Ed.2d 793 (1972) (footnotes omitted).

In the *Newmark* case, RKO controlled Frontier Airlines which was contemplating a merger with Central Airlines. During the course of the merger negotiations RKO independently acquired an option to purchase forty-nine percent of Central's common stock. RKO exercised the option and realized a short-swing profit when the Frontier–Central merger was consummated. 425 F.2d at 353.

23. 411 U.S. at 594–95, 93 S.Ct. at 1744–45 (footnotes omitted).

24. *Accord* Heublein, Inc. v. General Cinema Corp., 722 F.2d 29 (2d Cir.1983), *affirming* 559 F.Supp. 692 (S.D.N.Y.1983); Colan v. Prudential–Bache Securities, Inc., 577 F.Supp. 1074 (N.D.Ill.1983) (no "sale" for shareholder of target company exchanging shares pursuant to a merger with a "white knight" in the context of a contested tender offer).

option agreement or at the later date it was exercised. The Court reasoned that Occidental's obligation to dispose of the stock did not become fixed until Tenneco's exercise of the option on December 11. The Court also pointed out that as of June 2, Occidental had not locked in a profit since, had the stock price declined sufficiently in value by the exercise date, the defendant would have been left with Tenneco holdings worth less than the "purchase" price, notwithstanding the option premium.[25] Although this pragmatic analysis creates some uncertainty in the section 16(b) analysis, it gives the courts the ability to achieve the statute's purpose.

The apex of the pragmatic approach was achieved by the Fourth Circuit in Gold v. Sloan[26] where the court held one selling director liable under section 16(b) while exonerating three others. The issue was whether an exchange of stock pursuant to a merger between the Atlantic Research and Susquehanna corporations constituted a "purchase" under 16(b).[27] Within less than six months after the merger had been consummated the defendant insiders sold their newly acquired Susquehanna holdings at a profit. The Fourth Circuit pointed to the Supreme Court's decision in *Kern County* as having "resolved [the] conflict and adopted what had earlier been described as a 'pragmatic rather than technical' test"[28] for unorthodox transactions. It was thus necessary "to examine the particular situation of each defendant as it relates to the merger."[29] Three of the defendants had no contact whatsoever with the merger negotiations and thus were held to have had no access to Susquehanna's inside information.[30] In contrast, the fourth defendant, Atlantic's chief executive officer, had been "in complete charge of the negotiations" and "had access to the books and records * * *."[31] Accordingly, this access created a potential for abuse and thus warranted finding the merger exchange to have been a section 16(b) purchase by the inside director. Although certainly consistent with the Supreme Court's rationale in *Kern,* the *Gold* decision has been criticized as running contrary to the

---

25. 411 U.S. at 602, 93 S.Ct. at 1748. *See also, e.g.,* Frankel v. Slotkin, 705 F.Supp. 105 (E.D.N.Y.1989) (granting of a put option that was not exercisable for one year, was not a sale of the underlying stock). *Cf.* Pay Less Drug Stores v. Jewel Companies, Inc., 579 F.Supp. 1396 (N.D.Cal.1984) (attempt to exercise option was not a section 16(b) purchase).

26. 486 F.2d 340 (4th Cir.1973), *cert. denied* 419 U.S. 873, 95 S.Ct. 134, 42 L.Ed.2d 112 (1974).

27. Atlantic Research Corporation had merged into the Susquehanna Corporation via an exchange of stock; the defendants in *Gold* had been holders of Atlantic stock for more than six months prior to the merger negotiations, thus eliminating the problem of whether the exchange was a section 16(b) "sale," which had been dealt with in the *Kern County* decision. The defendants were also officers and directors of Atlantic and under the terms of the merger agreement occupied similar positions with respect to Susquehanna, the surviving corporation.

28. 486 F.2d at 343.

29. *Id.* at 344.

30. *Id. Accord* Heublein, Inc. v. General Cinema Corp., 559 F.Supp. 692 (S.D.N.Y.1983), *affirmed* 722 F.2d 29 (2d Cir.1983).

31. 486 F.2d at 351–52. *Accord* Colan v. Cutler–Hammer, Inc., 516 F.Supp. 1342 (N.D.Ill.1981). *Compare, e.g.,* American Standard, Inc. v. Crane Co., 510 F.2d 1043, (2d Cir.1974), *cert. denied* 421 U.S. 1000, 95 S.Ct. 2397, 44 L.Ed.2d 667 (1975).

straightforward crude rule of thumb that section 16(b) was designed to provide.[32] Critics of the *Gold* decision were particularly upset with the ruling that the same transaction produces differing treatment for individuals falling within the statute's objective reach. However, the pragmatic trend continued to flourish.[33]

When claiming section 16(b) damages based on the pragmatic trend, the complaint need not be pleaded with the degree of particularity required in fraud cases.[34] There is still plenty of opportunity to utilize the pragmatic approach to section 16(b). Contested and abortive takeovers have continued to be a hot-bed for section 16(b) litigation.[35]

Another recent area of contention in which the cases have been in conflict has been the question of whether the exercise of a stock appreciation right constitutes a sale of an equity security for section 16(b).[36] This question has now been resolved for qualified plans by Rule 16b–3(e),[37] which provides an exemption from 16(b) for stock appreciation rights where the plan provides that the rights are not exercisable during the first six months of their term and is further administered by a disinterested board of directors.[38] An additional requirement of the

---

32. *See. e.g.,* Note, Securities Exchange Act § 16(b): Fourth Circuit Harvests Some Kernels of Gold, 42 Fordham L.Rev. 852 (1974); Recent Developments, Securities—§ 16(b)—Mergers as a "Purchase," 20 Wayne L.Rev. 1415 (1974).

33. *See, e.g.,* Portnoy v. Revlon, Inc., 650 F.2d 895 (7th Cir.1981) (finding no sale in merger agreement); Heublein, Inc. v. General Cinema Corp., 559 F.Supp. 692 (S.D.N.Y. 1983) (no sale in defensive merger), *affirmed* 722 F.2d 29 (2d Cir.1983); Reece Corp. v. Walco National Corp., 565 F.Supp. 158 (S.D.N.Y.1981) (two step transaction treated as one "sale" in violation of § 16(b)); Colan v. Cutler–Hammer, Inc., 516 F.Supp. 1342 (N.D.Ill. 1981) (finding a sale pursuant to a merger, following the rationale of Gold); Portnoy v. Seligman & Latz, Inc., 516 F.Supp. 1188, 1200 (S.D.N.Y.1981) ("It don't mean a thing if it ain't got that swing," quoting E.K. "Duke" Ellington).

See also Kay v. Scientex Corp., 719 F.2d 1009 (9th Cir.1983) (remanding for determination of whether stock issued in connection with corporate acquisition was issued in connection with a preexisting debt and was therefore exempt from section 16(b)).

Compare Tristar Corp. v. Freitas, 867 F.Supp. 149, 152–53 (E.D.N.Y.1994) (identifying the contract date as the date of the sale and rejecting the argument that breach of a related loan agreement meant that the contract was not binding as of the date of signing).

34. *See* Mayer v. Chesapeake Ins. Co., Ltd., 1987 WL 6424, [1987 Transfer Binder] Fed.Sec.L.Rep. (CCH) ¶ 93,156 (S.D.N.Y.1987) (Unpublished Case). Particularity is required for Rule 10b–5 claims. *See* § 13.2 *infra.*

35. *See* Herrmann on Behalf of Walt Disney Productions v. Steinberg, 812 F.2d 63 (2d Cir.1987) (discussing measure of disgorgement for sale by defeated takeover bidder); Colan v. Continental Telecom, Inc., 788 F.2d 2 (2d Cir.1986), *affirming* 616 F.Supp. 1521 (S.D.N.Y.1985) (repurchase agreement was a bona fide option and not a sham to cover up 16(b) liability); Sterman v. Ferro Corp., 785 F.2d 162 (6th Cir.1986) (agreement in principle to sell stock was not a section 16(b) sale; court looked to subsequent binding agreement to sell at $31.03 per share); Morales v. Lukens, Inc., 593 F.Supp. 1209 (S.D.N.Y.1984) (post-takeover agreement between white knight and defeated offeror adequately compensated for 16(b) liability).

36. *Compare, e.g.,* Matas v. Siess, 467 F.Supp. 217 (S.D.N.Y.1979) (finding a § 16(b) sale) *with* Freedman v. Barrow, 427 F.Supp. 1129 (S.D.N.Y.1976) (no sale).

37. 17 C.F.R. § 240.16b–3(e).

38. *See, e.g.,* Wheelabrator Technologies, Inc., [1994–1995 Transfer Binder] Fed. Sec. L. Rep. (CCH) ¶ 76, 908 (SEC No Action Letter Aug. 17, 1994) (shareholder approval was not required for option plan for non-employee directors).

rule is that the election to exercise the right must be made between the third and twelfth day following the issuer's quarterly and annual summary statements of sales and earnings.

§ 12.6   Prohibitions Against Short Sales by Insiders—Section 16(c)

Section 16(c) of the Exchange Act[1] prohibits certain speculative activity by insiders who must file reports under the reporting provisions of section 16(a)[2] (*i.e.*, officers, directors, and ten percent beneficial owners of any class of equity securities subject to the Exchange Act's reporting requirements).[3] The section is aimed at two types of speculative transactions: (1) short sales,[4] or selling the security of the issuer without owning the underlying security, and (2) sales against the box,[5] where the seller delays in delivering the securities. In both instances, the investor's hope is that the price will decline from the time of sale thus enabling the seller to cover at a lower price. Both short sales and sales against the box are permissible trades, provided there is compliance with the applicable SEC rules[6] and margin requirements.[7] Both short sales and sales against the box present the potential for speculative abuse where the seller has access to inside information and thus both are prohibited by section 16(c) just as short-swing profits based on long positions in securities must be disgorged under section 16(b).[8] It has been held that the section applies only to shares beneficially owned by the insider, but not to shares sold by an insider acting merely as an agent for the true owners.[9]

Section 16(c) operates to make it unlawful to sell the security if the selling insider either (1) does not own the security or (2) if he or she owns the security but does not deliver it within twenty days or deposit it

---

§ 12.6

1. 15 U.S.C.A. § 78p(c).

2. 15 U.S.C.A. § 78p(a). *See* § 12.2 *supra.*

3. 15 U.S.C.A. § 78*l*. *See* § 9.2 *supra.*

4. Short sale: When a seller believes the price of a stock will fall, he or she borrows stock from a lender and sells the borrowed shares to the buyer. Later, he or she buys similar stock to pay back the lender, hopefully at a lower price than he or she received on sale to the buyer.

5. Sale against the box: When the seller anticipates a decline in the price of stock he or she owns, he or she will sell it to a buyer at the present market price, but deliver it later, when hopefully the market price will have fallen below the sales price, thus creating a paper profit for the seller.

6. 17 C.F.R. §§ 240.10a–1, 10a–2. *See* § 10.12 *supra.*

7. The margin requirements address the extension of credit for securities transactions. *See* § 10.11 *supra.* It is clearly unlawful to enter a sell order without owning the underlying security in the absence of full disclosure. *See* United States v. Naftalin, 441 U.S. 768, 99 S.Ct. 2077, 60 L.Ed.2d 624 (1979).

8. *See* § 12.3 *supra.*

9. Rogers v. Valentine, 306 F.Supp. 34 (S.D.N.Y.1969), *affirmed* 426 F.2d 1361 (2d Cir.1970).

in the mail within five days. The section provides that "no person shall be deemed to have violated this subsection if he proves that notwithstanding the exercise of good faith he was unable to make such delivery or deposit within such time, or that to do so would cause undue inconvenience or expense." [10]

Although they are certainly legitimate speculating devices in certain instances, the practices of selling short and sales against the box are high risk transactions which, as in the case with the short-swing profit,[11] are subject to speculative abuse and are therefore declared improper for insiders.[12]

SEC Rule 16c–1[13] provides that section 16(c)'s prohibition against short sales and sales against the box will not affect the validity of transactions executed by a broker in which the broker has no interest. The purpose of this exemption is to assure that the purchaser of the security in question will not be subject to having the sale set aside where the broker has executed the order even though the insider has violated the Act. In such a case, the loss if any will have to fall on the broker. Although not dealing with the question of damages, outside of the section 16(c) context it has been held that a customer's illegal short sales violate the Securities Act's antifraud provisions as a fraud on the broker handling the transaction.[14]

Rule 16c–2[15] exempts from the prohibition against insider short sales and sales against the box, all sales made by or on behalf of a dealer in connection with distributions of a substantial block of securities (1) if the sales are traceable to an over-allotment and the dealer is participating as a member of the underwriting group or selling group, or (2) if a nonparticipating dealer in good faith intends to offset the sale with a

---

10. 15 U.S.C.A. § 78p(c). *See* Fuller v. Dilbert, 244 F.Supp. 196 (S.D.N.Y.1965), *affirmed sub nom.* Righter v. Dilbert, 358 F.2d 305 (2d Cir.1966) (seller showed inconvenience).

11. 15 U.S.C.A. § 78p(b). *See* §§ 12.2–12.5 *supra.*

12. 15 U.S.C.A. § 78p(c).

Interestingly, an insider can participate in the same investment strategy by purchasing a put option in his or her company's stock. The put option would give the insider an option to sell the underlying stock at a predetermined price. If the stock price declines below that price, the insider will realize a profit. Unless the purchase of a put option could somehow be characterized as a short sale for the purpose of the statute, there would be no violation of section 16(c). On the other hand, if the ultimate sale of the stock pursuant to the put option occurs within six months of a purchase of the stock at a lower price, then the insider would be in violation of section 16(b) and could be forced to disgorge his or her profit. 15 U.S.C.A. § 78p(b). *See* § 12.3 *supra. See also, e.g.,* Silverman v. Landa, 306 F.2d 422 (2d Cir.1962), *affirming* 200 F.Supp. 193 (S.D.N.Y.1961) which is discussed in the text accompanying footnote 18 *infra.* In late 1988, the Commission proposed an exemption from section 16(c) for a short derivative securities position which hedges an underlying securities holding. Sec.Exch. Act. Rel.No. 34–26333, [1988–89 Transfer Binder] Fed.Sec. L.Rep. (CCH) ¶ 84,343 (Dec. 2, 1988). For the new rule see 17 C.F.R. § 240.16c–4.

13. 17 C.F.R. § 240.16c–1.

14. United States v. Naftalin, 441 U.S. 768, 99 S.Ct. 2077, 60 L.Ed.2d 624 (1979), *on remand* 606 F.2d 809 (8th Cir.1979).

15. 17 C.F.R. § 240.16c–2.

security to be acquired by or on behalf of the dealer as an underwriter, participant or member of the selling group. Former Rule 16c–2(b) provided that the exemption is available only if other persons not covered by section 16(c) are participating in the distribution of the block of securities on terms at least as favorable as those of the insider and dealer claiming the exemption.

There is a third exemption from section 16(c); it applies to certain securities which the seller is about to acquire. Rule 16c–3[16] exempts from the section's coverage sales of securities not yet acquired where the seller, as an "incident to ownership of an issued security and without the payment of consideration, [has a right] to receive another security 'when issued' or 'when distributed'." Rule 16c–3's exemption is available only if (1) the sale of the security to be acquired is made subject to the same conditions attaching to the right of acquisition, (2) the seller exercises reasonable diligence to deliver the security promptly after the right of acquisition matures, and (3) the seller has filed appropriate reports on the applicable form under section 16(a). Further, Rule 16c–3 is not available as an exemption for transactions combining sales of when-issued securities with other securities where in the aggregate the total amount sold exceeds the number of units owned by the seller plus those he is entitled to receive on a when-issued basis.[17]

The prohibition of section 16(c) against short sales and sales against the box is strictly construed because of the speculative abuse that can arise out of such transactions. On the other hand, it has been held that a statutory insider's issuance of a naked "call" option, which if exercised would have triggered an obligation to sell and deliver the securities within twenty days after the sale, was not in itself a sale and therefore did not violate section 16(c).[18]

The SEC has clarified the treatment of derivative securities for the purposes of section 16(c)'s short sale prohibitions. Rule 16c–4,[19] which was adopted in connection with the Commission's adoption of the revised section 16 rules,[20] provides that establishing or increasing a put equivalent position is exempt from section 16(c) so long as it is a covered position (the put position does not exceed the amount of underlying securities owned). This exemption makes clear that an uncovered put equivalent should be treated as a short sale, as it is functionally equivalent from an investment standpoint.

---

16.   17 C.F.R. § 240.16c–3.

17.   *Id.*

18.   Silverman v. Landa, 306 F.2d 422 (2d Cir.1962), *affirming* 200 F.Supp. 193 (S.D.N.Y.1961). *See also* footnote 12 *supra.*

19.   17 C.F.R. § 240.16c–4.

20.   *See* Sec.Exch. Act Rel. No. 34–28869, [1990–1991 Transfer Binder] Fed.Sec.L.Rep. (CCH) ¶ 84,709 (Feb. 8, 1991).

§ 12.7 Insider Trading Exemptions for Arbitrage Transactions and Certain Market Maker Activities— Sections 16(d), 16(e)

Market Maker Transactions

Section 16(d) of the Exchange Act[1] exempts bona fide market making transactions[2] from section 16(b)'s short-swing trading prohibitions and section 16(c)'s prohibitions against short sales and sales against the box. By virtue of section 16(d), transactions entered into by a dealer for securities not held in an investment account will be exempt from the insider antispeculation provisions so long as the dealer is acting in the ordinary course of his or business, incident to the establishment or maintenance of a primary or secondary market by virtue of sanctioned market making activity.[3] The section also operates to exempt market-maker/broker-dealers from the reporting requirements of section 16(a).[4]

Arbitrage Transactions

Pure arbitrage is a riskless transaction. The arbitrageur's position does not change nor are his or her dealings affected by the policy or financial condition of the issuer; but the success of the transaction is dependent upon the parallel markets in which the arbitrageur makes his or her transactions.[5] The benchmark of the arbitrage transaction is the simultaneous nature of the purchase and sale and thus the absence of simultaneity will defeat any claim of section 16(e)'s exemption.[6]

Section 16(e) provides that none of the provisions of section 16 apply to foreign or domestic arbitrage transactions that comply with such rules that may be established by the Commission.[7] Rule 16e–1,[8] excludes from the exemption officers' and directors' arbitrage transactions; however, ten percent owners' arbitrage transactions are exempt.

Rule 16e–1[9] provides that it is unlawful for a director or an officer of an issuer with equity securities registered pursuant to section 12 of the Act to effect either a domestic or foreign arbitrage transaction unless the transaction is fully disclosed in section 16(a) reports and all profits

---

§ 12.7

1.   15 U.S.C.A. § 78p(d).

2.   The regulation of market makers is discussed in § 10.3 *supra.*

3.   *See, e.g.,* C.R.A. Realty Corp. v. Tri–South Investments, 738 F.2d 73 (2d Cir.1984). *See also, e.g.,* Nomura Securities, Inc., 26 Sec. Reg. & L. Rep. (BNA) 1361 (SEC No Action Letter available Oct. 6, 1994) (granting no action relief for transactions in shares of closed-end fund shares).

4.   Simon v. Merrill Lynch, Pierce, Fenner & Smith, Inc., 482 F.2d 880 (5th Cir.1973), *rehearing denied* 485 F.2d 687 (5th Cir.1973).

5.   Falco v. Donner Foundation, Inc., 208 F.2d 600 (2d Cir.1953).

6.   Lewis v. Dekcraft Corp., 1974 WL 418, [1973–74 Transfer Binder] Fed.Sec.L.Rep. (CCH) ¶ 94,620 (S.D.N.Y.1974).

7.   15 U.S.C.A. § 78p(e).

8.   17 C.F.R. § 240.16e–1.

9.   17 C.F.R. § 240.16e–1.

arising from the transaction are disgorged to the issuer in accordance with section 16(b). The effect of the rule with regard to officers and directors is to render all arbitrage transactions subject to the short-swing trading prohibitions[10] but not to section 16(c)'s prohibitions against short sales and sales against the box.[11] The rule goes on to provide that arbitrage transactions by persons other than officers and directors are not subject to any of section 16's provisions. Accordingly, ten percent beneficial owners may take advantage of the arbitrage exemption.

§ 12.8 Liability for Material Misstatements and Omissions of Fact in Documents Filed With the SEC—Section 18(a) of the Exchange Act

Section 18(a) of the Exchange Act[1] imposes liability upon anyone responsible for material misstatement or omission of fact in connection with any document required to be filed with the Commission under the terms of the Exchange Act.[2] The section 18(a) cause of action is available to any investor who, after having read the faulty document filed, actually relies upon statements in the document and is therefore injured. The courts have held that section 18(a) requires an "eyeball" test; that is, the plaintiff must have actual knowledge of and reliance upon the materials filed with the Commission, or a copy thereof; it is not sufficient that the plaintiff saw similar information contained in other documents prepared by the issuer.[3] Reliance based on a "fraud on the market" theory may be the foundation for a remedy under Rule 10b–5,[4] but will not satisfy section 18(a)'s requirements.[5]

---

10. *See* Heli–Coil Corp. v. Webster, 222 F.Supp. 831 (D.N.J.1963), 17 C.F.R. § 240.16e–1 (1982) ("The provisions of section 16(c) shall not apply to such arbitrage transactions").

11. 15 U.S.C.A. § 78p(c); *see* § 12.6 *supra.*

§ 12.8

1. 15 U.S.C.A. § 78r(a). Section 323 of the Trust Indenture Act of 1939, 15 U.S.C.A. § 77www is modeled on section 18(a). *See* § 16.2 *infra.*

See § 1.7 *supra* for an overview of private remedies available under the 1933 and 1934 Acts.

2. Section 18(a) applies to documents "filed pursuant to this title" but does not apply to filing under the 1933 Act or any other of the securities laws. *Id.* Nor does section 18(a) apply to the annual report disseminated to shareholders under the proxy rules. 17 C.F.R. §§ 240.14a–3(c), 14c–3(b). *See* §§ 11.2, 11.8 *supra.*

3. Ross v. A.H. Robins Co., 607 F.2d 545, 552 (2d Cir.1979); Heit v. Weitzen, 402 F.2d 909, 916 (2d Cir.1968), *cert. denied* 395 U.S. 903, 89 S.Ct. 1740, 23 L.Ed.2d 217 (1969); Jacobson v. Peat, Marwick, Mitchell & Co., 445 F.Supp. 518, 525 (S.D.N.Y.1977). *See also, e.g.,* Southwest Realty, Ltd. v. Daseke, 1991 WL 83961, [1990–1991 Transfer Binder] Fed.Sec.L.Rep. (CCH) ¶ 95,881 (N.D.Tex.1991) (sufficiently alleging reliance and stating claim under both section 18(a) and Rule 10b–5 for material omissions in Schedule 13D).

4. *See, e.g.,* Panzirer v. Wolf, 663 F.2d 365 (2d Cir.1981), *vacated as moot* 459 U.S. 1027, 103 S.Ct. 434, 74 L.Ed.2d 594 (1982); Zweig v. Hearst Corp., 594 F.2d 1261 (9th Cir.1979); Blackie v. Barrack, 524 F.2d 891, 906 (9th Cir.1975), *cert. denied* 429 U.S. 816, 97 S.Ct. 57, 50 L.Ed.2d 75 (1976); Chris–Craft Industries, Inc. v. Piper Aircraft Corp., 480 F.2d 341, 374 (2d Cir.1973), *cert. denied* 414 U.S. 910, 94 S.Ct. 231, 38 L.Ed.2d 148 (1973). *See* § 13.5 *infra.*

5. *See* cases cited in footnote 3 *supra.*

Section 18(a) applies to documents that must be filed with the Commission pursuant to section 15(d),[6] as well as to the Act's registration and periodic reporting requirements and SEC rules promulgated thereunder.[7] Although courts have imposed an "eyeball" requirement under section 18(a),[8] it is not necessary that the plaintiff see the document on file; a copy will suffice. Section 18(a) does not apply, however, to annual reports which must be sent to shareholders and filed with the SEC unless the report is incorporated into the proxy statement or other proxy solicitation materials which are considered "filed" documents under section 18(a).[9]

Since the section applies only to documents that must be filed with the Commission under the Exchange Act, it is necessarily limited to companies reporting under the Act. Section 18(a) not only imposes liability upon the issuer or other person filing the document but also upon "any person who shall make or cause to be made" any misstatement or omission in "any application, report, or document filed. * * * "[10] This means that liability will extend to the company's officers and directors and especially to those who must sign the filed documents.[11] A significant development here is that, in addition to the issuer's principal executive officers, now a majority of the board of directors must sign the annual 10K filing.[12]

Liability is imposed under section 18(a) upon any such defendant "unless the person sued shall prove that he acted in good faith and had no knowledge that such statement was false or misleading."[13] This

---

6. 15 U.S.C.A. § 78o(d).

7. 15 U.S.C.A. §§ 78l, 78m(a). *See* §§ 9.2, 9.3, *supra.* This is a departure from the pattern set by the proxy rules, tender offer filing requirements and section 16's insider trading provisions, all of which apply only to issuers whose securities are subject to section 12's registration requirements. 15 U.S.C.A. §§ 78m(d)–(f), 78n(a)–(f); 78p. *See* §§ 11.2, 11.11, 11.12, 11.14, 11.16, 11.17, 12.2–12.7 *supra.* Section 18(a) applies to "any statement in any application, report, or document filed pursuant to this title or any rule or regulation thereunder or any undertaking contained in a registration statement as provided in subsection (d) of section 15 of this title. * * * " 15 U.S.C.A. § 78r(a).

8. *See* cases cited in footnote 3 *supra.*

9. *See* 17 C.F.R. § 240.14a–3(c). *See also* section 14(c), 15 U.S.C.A. § 78n(c) (information to be furnished to securities holders in lieu of proxy statement). *See* §§ 11.6, 11.7 *supra.* The broad definition of proxy solicitation materials is discussed in § 11.2 *supra.* *See* 17 C.F.R. § 240.14a–1.

10. 15 U.S.C.A. § 78r(a).

11. *Compare* Section 11(a) of the 1933 Act wherein liability for material misstatements in 1933 Act registration materials is limited to signers and experts. 15 U.S.C.A. § 77k(a); § 7.3 *supra.* Section 11 liability is based in negligence (and strict liability for the issuer). 15 U.S.C.A. § 77k(a), (b). *See* § 7.4 *supra.* Section 11 is also supplemented by section 12(2)'s express fraud remedy and section 12(1)'s remedy for noncompliance with section 5. 15 U.S.C.A. §§ 77l(a)(1), (2). *See* §§ 7.2, 7.5 *supra.*

12. *See* §§ 9.2, 9.3 *supra* for discussion of who must sign 1934 Act filings.

13. 15 U.S.C.A. § 78r(a). *See, e.g.,* Magna Investment Corp. v. John Does One Through Two Hundred, 931 F.2d 38 (11th Cir.1991) (it was reversible error in section 18(a) case to put burden of proving defendant's bad faith on plaintiff; the burden to prove good faith properly lies with the defendant). *Compare, e.g.,* In re Kulicke & Soffa Industries, Inc. Securities Litigation, 747 F.Supp. 1136 (E.D.Pa.1990) (in a Rule 10b–5 action the burden of proving bad faith falls on the plaintiff).

burden of proof by the defendant will be more easily met than the "due diligence" standard imposed by section 11(b) of the 1933 Act dealing with material misrepresentations contained in registration statements.[14] On the other hand, putting the defendant to the burden of proving the absence of knowledge and the presence of good faith creates an easier prima facie showing than is required in a 10b–5 action where the plaintiff must prove scienter.[15] Section 14(a) liability for proxy statements may, however, exist for negligent misstatements and omissions.[16] Injured investors thus are faced with a myriad of alternative remedies, which are generally held to be cumulative.[17]

Insofar as scienter need not be shown to establish a violation of section 18(a) the claim may not sound in fraud. Accordingly, it has been held that the particularity requirement applicable to pleadings in fraud actions need not be satisfied to state a claim under section 18(a).[18]

Section 18(a) provides that in addition to assessing court costs, the court in its discretion may assess reasonable attorneys' fees against either party.[19] Section 18(b) grants to one held liable under 18(a) a right of contribution, such as would arise in a common law suit arising out of a contract, against anyone who if joined in the original action would have been held liable.[20] Section 18(c) sets forth the applicable statute of limitations;[21] a section 18(a) suit must be brought within one year of discovery of the relevant facts *and* within three years of the accrual of the cause of action.

Most courts that have considered the issue have ruled against the exclusiveness of a section 18(a) remedy for material misstatements in filed documents.[22] This is significant in light of the Supreme Court's

14. 15 U.S.C.A. § 77k(b). *See* § 7.4 *supra.*

15. *See* Ernst & Ernst v. Hochfelder, 425 U.S. 185, 206, 96 S.Ct. 1375, 1387, 47 L.Ed.2d 668 (1976), *rehearing denied* 425 U.S. 986, 96 S.Ct. 2194, 48 L.Ed.2d 811 (1976). *See also* § 13.4, *infra.*

16. 17 C.F.R. § 240.14a–9. *See* § 11.3 *supra.*

17. *See* text accompanying footnotes 22–30 *infra.*

18. International Broadcasting Corp. v. Turner, 734 F.Supp. 383, 391 (D.Minn.1990) (Fed.R.Civ.P. 8(a) did not require specific allegation that plaintiff was a purchaser of the securities).

19. 15 U.S.C.A. § 78r(a).

20. 15 U.S.C.A. § 78r(b). Contribution is discussed in § 7.7 *supra* and § 13.7 *infra.*

21. 15 U.S.C.A. § 78r(c). *Compare* section 13 of the 1933 Act, 15 U.S.C.A. § 77m. *See also* § 13.8 *infra* for discussion of statutes of limitations in Rule 10b–5 actions.

22. Ross v. A.H. Robins Co., 607 F.2d 545 (2d Cir.1979) (but dismissing the complaint for failure to plead with sufficient specificity in accordance with Fed.R.Civ.P. 9(b)); Heit v. Weitzen, 402 F.2d 909 (2d Cir.1968), *cert. denied* 395 U.S. 903, 89 S.Ct. 1740, 23 L.Ed.2d 217 (1969); Southwest Realty, Ltd. v. Daseke, 1990 WL 85921, [1990 Transfer Binder] Fed.Sec.L.Rep. ¶ 95,256 (N.D.Tex.1990) (plaintiff had no claim under section 13(d) but could proceed under section 18(a)), *s.c.,* 1991 WL 83961, [1990–1991 Transfer Binder] Fed.Sec.L.Rep. (CCH) ¶ 95,881 (N.D.Tex.1991) (stating claim under both section 18(a) and Rule 10b–5 for material omissions in Schedule 13D); Jacobson v. Peat, Marwick, Mitchell & Co., 445 F.Supp. 518 (S.D.N.Y.1977); Gross v. Diversified Mortgage Investors, 431 F.Supp. 1080 (S.D.N.Y.1977), *affirmed without opinion* 636 F.2d 1201 (2d Cir.1980). *Contra* Issen v. GSC Enterprises, Inc., 522 F.Supp. 390, 397 (N.D.Ill.1981); Gateway Industries, Inc. v. Agency Rent–A–Car, Inc., 495 F.Supp. 92, 98 (N.D.Ill.1980); Myers v.

limitations upon implied remedies in general[23] and upon Rule 10b–5 in particular.[24] Indeed, it appears that the implied Rule 10b–5 remedy may be pursued even in the absence of a claim under section 18(a) arising out of the same transaction.[25] The view that Rule 10b–5 and section 18(a) remedies are cumulative is in accordance with the overlapping reach of Rule 10b–5, the proxy rules,[26] section 11 of the 1933 Act,[27] and section 12 of the 1933 Act.[28] In an analogous context, the Supreme Court has decided that the remedy under section 11 of the 1933 Act is not exclusive;[29] a similar result would appear both likely and appropriate with regard to section 18(a)'s cause of action.[30]

Apart from its scienter requirement, Rule 10b–5 is broader than section 18(a) in most respects, including the lack of an "eyeball" requirement[31] and acceptance of a fraud on the market theory of recovery.[32] It would make little sense not to allow a Rule 10b–5 claim because of section 18(a) which applies to filed documents only and to allow other documents, such as the annual report,[33] or communications not sent to

American Leisure Time Enterprises, Inc., 402 F.Supp. 213, 214–15 (S.D.N.Y.1975), *affirmed without opinion* 538 F.2d 312 (2d Cir.1976).

See generally Marc I. Steinberg, The Propriety and Scope of Cumulative Remedies Under the Federal Securities Laws, 67 Cornell L.Rev. 557 (1982). There are some commentators who favor exclusivity of the section 18(a) remedy. *See* Note, The Exclusivity of the Express Remedy Under Section 18(a) of the Securities Exchange Act of 1934, 34 Geo.Wash. L.Rev. 845 (1978). *Compare* Note, Section 18 of the Securities Exchange Act of 1934: Putting the Bite Back Into the Toothless Tiger, 47 Fordham L.Rev. 15 (1978). *See also, e.g.,* Note, Rule 10b–5: The Exclusivity of Remedies, The Purchaser–Seller Requirement, and Constructive Deception, 37 Wash. & Lee L.Rev. 887 (1980).

23. *See* § 13.1 *infra.*

24. *See* §§ 13.1–13.12 *infra.*

25. *E.g.* Steele v. Allison, 1982 WL 1569, [1981–82 Transfer Binder] Fed.Sec.L.Rep. (CCH) ¶ 98,459 (N.D.Cal.1982). In Herman & MacLean v. Huddleston, 459 U.S. 375, 103 S.Ct. 683, 74 L.Ed.2d 548 (1983), *on remand* 705 F.2d 775 (5th Cir.1983), the Court held that liability under Rule 10b–5 is not precluded by section 11 of the 1933 Act. The Court's reasoning would seem to compel a similar result with regard to section 18(a) of the Exchange Act.

26. SEC v. National Securities, Inc., 393 U.S. 453, 468, 89 S.Ct. 564, 21 L.Ed.2d 668 (1969). *See also e.g.,* Schaefer v. First National Bank of Lincolnwood, 509 F.2d 1287, 1293 (7th Cir.1975), *cert. denied* 425 U.S. 943, 96 S.Ct. 1682, 48 L.Ed.2d 186 (1976).

27. *E.g.,* Herman & MacLean v. Huddleston, 459 U.S. 375, 103 S.Ct. 683, 74 L.Ed.2d 548 (1983), *on remand* 705 F.2d 775 (5th Cir.1983),; Lanza v. Drexel & Co., 479 F.2d 1277 (2d Cir.1973); Stewart v. Bennett, 359 F.Supp. 878 (D.Mass.1973), *opinion supplemented* 362 F.Supp. 605 (D.Mass.1973); Wolfson v. Solomon, 54 F.R.D. 584 (S.D.N.Y.1972). Section 11 of the 1933 Act, 15 U.S.C.A. § 77k is discussed in §§ 7.3, 7.4 *supra.*

28. Ellis v. Carter, 291 F.2d 270 (9th Cir.1961); Matheson v. Armbrust, 284 F.2d 670 (9th Cir.1960). *Contra* Rosenberg v. Globe Aircraft Corp., 80 F.Supp. 123 (E.D.Pa.1948). Section 12, 15 U.S.C.A. § 77*l* is discussed in §§ 7.2, 7.5 *supra.*

29. Herman & MacLean v. Huddleston, 459 U.S. 375, 103 S.Ct. 683, 74 L.Ed.2d 548 (1983), *on remand* 705 F.2d 775 (5th Cir.1983).

30. The Fifth Circuit reversed its earlier ruling that section 9(e) and Rule 10b–5 are mutually exclusive. *See* § 12.1 *supra.*

31. *See* cases in footnote 3 *supra.*

32. *See* text accompanying footnotes 4–5 *supra* and § 13.5B *infra.*

33. *See* footnote 9 *supra.*

the Commission to give rise to the broader remedy.[34]   Since the Supreme
Court has continued to recognize the Rule 10b–5 remedy,[35] reading
section 18(a) to be exclusive would nullify those decisions.[36]

---

34. The annual report is not generally a filed document for section 18(a) purposes. *See* footnote 9 *supra.*

35. *E.g.* Herman & MacLean v. Huddleston, 459 U.S. 375, 103 S.Ct. 683, 74 L.Ed.2d 548 (1983), *on remand* 705 F.2d 775 (5th Cir.1983). *See* § 13.2 *infra.*

36. *See* Steinberg *supra* footnote 22.

Chapter 13

CIVIL LIABILITY

Table of Sections

---

* Deleted sections 13.2.2, 13.2.3, 13.7.1, and 13.8.1 can be found in the Practitioner's Edition.

PART A: IMPLIED PRIVATE REMEDIES; SEC RULE 10b–5; FRAUD IN CONNECTION WITH THE PURCHASE OR SALE OF SECURITIES; IMPROPER TRADING ON NONPUBLIC MATERIAL INFORMATION

§ 13.1 Implied Remedies in the Federal Courts—Cort v. Ash[1] and Its Progeny

Although the securities laws provide a wide variety of express statutory remedies for injured investors,[2] powerful private enforcement weapons have arisen out of implied rights of action. However, the Supreme Court has been narrowing the number of implied remedies available under federal statutes. This narrowing trend has resulted in limiting the remedies that have been recognized. Since it is clear that private remedies will not lightly be read into the statutes, it is questionable whether new remedies will be recognized. On the other hand, there are some firmly entrenched implied rights of action for securities law violations, although, even they have been significantly narrowed since the mid 1970s.

The restrictive trend of the implication cases generally has not escaped the securities laws. The Supreme Court has reaffirmed its past recognition of implied private rights of action for violations of Rule 10b–

---

§ 13.1

1. 422 U.S. 66, 95 S.Ct. 2080, 45 L.Ed.2d 26 (1975). *See* authorities cited in note 15 *infra*. For more detailed treatments of the issues surrounding statutory interpretation, *see generally* Julius Cohen, Materials and Problems on Legislation (2d ed. 1967); Horace E. Reed, John W. MacDonald, Jefferson B. Fordham & William J. Pierce, Materials on Legislation (3d ed. 1973); J.G. Sutherland, Statutes and Statutory Construction (3d ed. 1943); Frederick J. de Sloovere, Steps in the Process of Interpreting Statutes, 10 N.Y.U.L.Q.Rev. 1 (1932); Jerome Frank, Words and Music: Some Remarks on Statutory Interpretation, 47 Colum.L.Rev. 1259 (1947); Ernst Freund, Interpretation of Statutes, 65 U.Pa.L.Rev. 207 (1917); W. Friedmann, Statute Law and Its Interpretation in the Modern State, 26 Can.Bar Rev. 1277 (1948); Max Radin, Early Statutory Interpretation in England, 38 Ill.L.Rev. 16 (1943); A Symposium on Statutory Construction, 3 Vand.L.Rev. 365 (1950).

2. Sections 11, 12(1), 12(2) of the 1933 Act, 15 U.S.C.A. §§ 77k, 77l(1), (2); *see* §§ 7.2–7.5 *supra* (dealing with respectively, misleading registration materials, failure to comply with that Act's prospectus requirements, and material misstatements by sellers of securities); Sections 9(e), 16(b), 18(a) of the Exchange Act, 15 U.S.C.A. §§ 78i(e), 78p(b), 78r(a); *see* chapter 12 *supra* (dealing with manipulation of exchange listed securities, disgorgement of insider short-swing profits, and material misstatements and omissions in SEC filings).

There are also express remedies under the other federal acts administered by the SEC. For example, section 323aa of the Trust Indenture Act of 1939, 15 U.S.C.A. § 77www, which parallels section 18(a) of the Exchange Act. *See* § 16.2 *infra*, § 12.8 *supra*. Also section 36(b) of the Investment Company Act of 1940, 15 U.S.C.A. § 80a–36(b), provides a right of action for breaches of fiduciary duty by investment company directors. *See* § 17.10 *infra*. Section 17(b) of the Public Utility Holding Company Act of 1935, 15 U.S.C.A. § 79q(b) parallels section 16 of the Exchange Act with regard to insider short-swing profits. *See* § 15.2 *infra*. The Investment Advisers Act of 1940 does not contain any express private remedies. *See* chapter 18 *infra*.

See § 1.7 *supra* for an overview of the private remedies available under the 1933 and 1934 Acts.

5 and section 10(b) of the Securities Exchange Act of 1934[3] and the proxy disclosure requirements of section 14(a) of the Act.[4] At the same time, there has been a narrowing of the scope of these remedies.[5] The lower courts are in conflict as to the existence of implied remedies under section 17(a) of the 1933 Act and section 14(e) of the Exchange Act,[6] while other remedies have been denied.[7] At the Supreme Court level

---

3. 15 U.S.C.A. § 78j(b); 17 C.F.R. § .240.10b–5. *See* Herman & MacLean v. Huddleston, 459 U.S. 375, 103 S.Ct. 683, 74 L.Ed.2d 548 (1983); Affiliated Ute Citizens v. United States, 406 U.S. 128, 92 S.Ct. 1456, 31 L.Ed.2d 741 (1972), *rehearing denied* 407 U.S. 916, 92 S.Ct. 2430, 32 L.Ed.2d 692 (1972); Superintendent of Insurance of New York v. Bankers Life & Cas. Co., 404 U.S. 6, 92 S.Ct. 165, 30 L.Ed.2d 128 (1971), *on remand* 401 F.Supp. 640 (S.D.N.Y.1975). *See also* Santa Fe Industries, Inc. v. Green, 430 U.S. 462, 97 S.Ct. 1292, 51 L.Ed.2d 480 (1977), *on remand* 562 F.2d 4 (2d Cir.1977); Ernst & Ernst v. Hochfelder, 425 U.S. 185, 96 S.Ct. 1375, 47 L.Ed.2d 668 (1976), *rehearing denied* 425 U.S. 986, 96 S.Ct. 2194, 48 L.Ed.2d 811 (1976); Blue Chip Stamps v. Manor Drug Stores, 421 U.S. 723, 95 S.Ct. 1917, 44 L.Ed.2d 539 (1975), *rehearing denied* 423 U.S. 884, 96 S.Ct. 157, 46 L.Ed.2d 114 (1975); Kardon v. National Gypsum Co., 69 F.Supp. 512 (E.D.Pa. 1946). The Rule 10b–5 remedy is discussed in §§ 13.2–13.11 *infra*.

See Alan R. Bromberg & Lewis D. Lowenfels, Securities Fraud and Commodities Fraud (1979); Arnold S. Jacobs, The Impact of Rule 10b–5 (1980); 3 Louis Loss, Securities Regulation, 1448–1472, 1763–1796 (2d ed. 1961); Roy L. Brooks, Rule 10b–5 in the Balance: An Analysis of the Supreme Court's Policy Perspective, 32 Hastings L.J. 403 (1980); Joseph A. Grundfest, Disimplying Private Rights of Action Under the Federal Securities Laws: The Commission's Authority, 107 Harv. L. Rev. 961 (1994); Michael Joseph, Civil Liability Under Rule 10b–5–A Reply, 59 Nw.U.L.Rev. 171 (1964); John A. Maher, Implied Private Rights of Action and the Federal Securities Laws: A Historical Perspective, 37 Wash. & Lee L.Rev. 783 (1980); David S. Ruder, Civil Liability Under Rule 10b–5: Judicial Revision of the Legislative Intent, 57 Nw.U.L.Rev. 627 (1963).

4. 15 U.S.C.A. § 78n(a); 17 C.F.R. § 240.14a–9. *See* J.I. Case Co. v. Borak, 377 U.S. 426, 84 S.Ct. 1555, 12 L.Ed.2d 423 (1964). *See also* TSC Indus., Inc. v. Northway, Inc., 426 U.S. 438, 96 S.Ct. 2126, 48 L.Ed.2d 757 (1976), *motion denied* 429 U.S. 810, 97 S.Ct. 48, 50 L.Ed.2d 70 (1976); Mills v. Electric Auto–Lite Co., 396 U.S. 375, 90 S.Ct. 616, 24 L.Ed.2d 593 (1970), *appeal after remand* 552 F.2d 1239 (7th Cir.1977), *cert. denied* 434 U.S. 922, 98 S.Ct. 398, 54 L.Ed.2d 279 (1977), *rehearing denied* 434 U.S. 1002, 98 S.Ct. 649, 54 L.Ed.2d 499 (1977). The Rule 14a–9 remedy is discussed in §§ 11.3–11.5 *supra*. *See* Louis Loss, The SEC Proxy Rules in the Courts, 73 Harv.L.Rev. 1041 (1960); Maher, *supra* footnote 3.

5. *See, e.g.,* Central Bank of Denver v. First Interstate Bank of Denver, ___ U.S. ___, 114 S.Ct. 1439, 128 L.Ed.2d 119 (1994) (there is no implied remedy against aiders and abettors); Santa Fe Industries, Inc. v. Green, 430 U.S. 462, 97 S.Ct. 1292, 51 L.Ed.2d 480 (1977) (Rule 10b–5 covers only deceptive conduct), *on remand* 562 F.2d 4 (2d Cir.1977); Ernst & Ernst v. Hochfelder, 425 U.S. 185, 96 S.Ct. 1375, 47 L.Ed.2d 668 (1976), *rehearing denied* 425 U.S. 986, 96 S.Ct. 2194, 48 L.Ed.2d 811 (1976) (a violation of Rule 10b–5 requires a showing of scienter); Blue Chip Stamps v. Manor Drug Stores, 421 U.S. 723, 95 S.Ct. 1917, 44 L.Ed.2d 539 (1975), *rehearing denied* 423 U.S. 884, 96 S.Ct. 157, 46 L.Ed.2d 114 (1975) (plaintiff must have been a purchaser or seller).

Lewis D. Lowenfels, Recent Supreme Court Decisions Under the Federal Securities Laws: The Pendulum Swings, 65 Geo. L.J. 891 (1977). *Compare* Thomas L. Hazen, The Supreme Court and the Securities Laws: Has the Pendulum Slowed? 30 Emory L.J. 3 (1981).

6. 15 U.S.C.A. §§ 77q(a), 78n(e). *See* §§ 11.15, 11.19 *supra*, § 13.13 *infra*.

7. These include violation of exchange and NASD rules, *see* §§ 10.6–10.10, 10.14 *supra*, and violation of the Exchange Act's margin requirements, *see* § 10.11 *supra*. *But cf.* In the matter of the Arbitration Between Offerman & Co. v. Hamilton Investments, Inc., [1993–1994 Transfer Binder] Fed. Sec. L. Rep. (CCH) ¶ 98,233 (E.D.Wis.1994) (absence of private right for investors does not mean that an NASD member may not be able to bring an action for violation of NASD rules).

See also, e.g., In re Jenny Craig Securities Litigation, 1992 WL 456819, [1992–1993 Transfer Binder] Fed.Sec.L.Rep. (CCH) ¶ 97,337 (S.D.Cal.1992) (violation of the disclosure

there have been a number of decisions denying or limiting private rights of action in the securities area. The Court has denied the existence of an implied remedy for damages under the antifraud provision of the Investment Advisers Act of 1940,[8] and found no remedy under section 17(a) of the Securities Exchange Act of 1934.[9] Also, the Court held that a competing tender offeror does not have an implied remedy for violation of the Exchange Act's antifraud provisions with regard to tender offers, but nevertheless indicated that a private remedy may exist in the hands of a more appropriate plaintiff.[10]

Most recently, the Court ruled that there is no implied right of action against aiders and abettors of securities law violations.[11] Notwithstanding these and other narrowing decisions, the Court has held that the Rule 10b–5 remedy is cumulative and applies even though there may be express remedies covering the transaction in question.[12] Additionally, at the same time that it was limiting securities remedies, the Court has recognized an implied remedy under the Commodity Exchange Act,[13] in a decision that may also have some lessons for actions under the securities laws.[14]

Outside of the securities context the Supreme Court decisions beginning in the mid 1970s have shown a definitely negative disposition towards implication of rights of action, but did not necessarily mean the demise of the implication doctrine in general.[15] For example starting in

---

requirements of Regulation S–K does not give rise to an implied right of action unless the violation satisfies each of the elements of a violation of Rule 10b–5).

8. Transamerica Mortgage Advisors, Inc. v. Lewis, 444 U.S. 11, 100 S.Ct. 242, 62 L.Ed.2d 146 (1979). The Court there did, however, recognize an implied right of rescission. *See* text accompanying footnotes 32–38 *infra.* The Investment Advisers Act is discussed in chapter 18 *infra.*

9. Touche Ross & Co. v. Redington, 442 U.S. 560, 99 S.Ct. 2479, 61 L.Ed.2d 82 (1979), *on remand* 612 F.2d 68 (2d Cir.1979). Section 17(a) contains reporting requirements for members of exchanges and broker-dealers under the Municipal Securities Rule–Making Board or the NASD. *See* §§ 10.2, 10.5 *supra.*

10. Piper v. Chris–Craft Industries, Inc., 430 U.S. 1, 97 S.Ct. 926, 51 L.Ed.2d 124 (1977), *rehearing denied* 430 U.S. 976, 97 S.Ct. 1668, 52 L.Ed.2d 371 (1977).

Section 14(e) is discussed in §§ 11.15, 11.19.

11. Central Bank of Denver v. First Interstate Bank of Denver, ___ U.S. ___, 114 S.Ct. 1439, 128 L.Ed.2d 119 (1994), which is discussed in § 13.16 *infra. See also, e.g.,* Gustafson v. Alloyd Corp., ___ U.S. ___, 115 S.Ct. 1061, 131 L.Ed.2d 1 (1995) (giving a tortured and narrow reading to the express remedy under section 12(2) of the 1933 Act); the *Gustafson* case is discussed in § 7.5 *supra.*

12. Herman & MacLean v. Huddleston, 459 U.S. 375, 103 S.Ct. 683, 74 L.Ed.2d 548 (1983), *on remand* 705 F.2d 775 (5th Cir.1983). *See* §§ 7.3, 7.4, 12.8 *supra.*

13. Merrill Lynch, Pierce, Fenner & Smith, Inc. v. Curran, 456 U.S. 353, 102 S.Ct. 1825, 72 L.Ed.2d 182 (1982). *See* § 10.2.1 *supra* and § 19.8 *infra* (Practitioner's Edition only).

14. *See* § 10.2.1 *supra* and § 19.8 *infra* (Practitioner's Edition only).

15. *See* Paul Joseph McMahon & Gerald J. Rodos, Judicial Implication of Private Causes of Action: Reappraisal and Retrenchment, 80 Dick.L.Rev. 167 (1976); Alan B. Morrison, Rights Without Remedies: The Burger Court Takes the Federal Courts Out of the Business of Protecting Federal Rights, 30 Rutgers L.Rev. 841 (1977); Gregory R. Mowe, Federal Statutes and Implied Private Actions, 55 Or.L.Rev. 3 (1976); K. G. Jan Pillai, Negative Implication: The Demise of Private Rights of Action in the Federal Courts,

1979 and continuing through 1988 there was a dramatic shift in attitude, which has carried through the current cases. From 1979 through 1988, there were a total of nine Supreme Court cases dealing with the implication of a private remedy.[16] Three decisions have recognized implied remedies.[17] In five cases the Court has denied any implied relief.[18] In one instance, as noted above, the Court denied an implied remedy for fraud under the Investment Advisers Act while at the same time it recognized the existence of an implied equitable right of rescis-

---

47 U.Cin.L.Rev. 1 (1978); Harvey L. Pitt, Standing to Sue Under the Williams Act After Chris–Craft: A Leaky Ship on Troubled Waters, 34 Bus.Law. 117 (1978); David L. Ratner, The Demise of The Implied Private Right of Action in the Supreme Court, 11 Inst.Sec.Reg. 289 (1980). *See generally* Robert D. Goldstein, A. Swann Song for Remedies: Equitable Relief in the Burger Court, 13 Harv.C.R.–C.L.L.Rev. 1 (1978). *But see* Thomas L. Hazen, Implied Private Remedies Under Federal Statutes: Neither a Death Knell Nor a Moratorium—Civil Rights, Securities Regulation, and Beyond, 33 Vand.L.Rev. 1333 (1980); Marc I. Steinberg, Implied Private Rights of Action Under Federal Law, 55 Notre Dame Law. 33 (1979).

16. This excludes cases that have discussed the scope of existing remedies.

17. Merrill Lynch, Pierce, Fenner & Smith, Inc. v. Curran, 456 U.S. 353, 102 S.Ct. 1825, 72 L.Ed.2d 182 (1982) (recognizing implied antifraud remedy under the Commodity Exchange Act); Davis v. Passman, 442 U.S. 228, 99 S.Ct. 2264, 60 L.Ed.2d 846 (1979) (recognizing an implied private remedy under the United States Constitution); Cannon v. University of Chicago, 441 U.S. 677, 99 S.Ct. 1946, 60 L.Ed.2d 560 (1979), *on remand* 605 F.2d 560 (7th Cir.1979), *appeal after remand* 648 F.2d 1104 (7th Cir.1981), *mandamus denied* 454 U.S. 811, 102 S.Ct. 373, 70 L.Ed.2d 197 (1981) (recognizing an implied remedy under Title IX of The Education Amendments of 1972, 20 U.S.C.A. § 1681(a)). Another pro-implication decision is found in Herman & MacLean v. Huddleston, 459 U.S. 375, 103 S.Ct. 683, 74 L.Ed.2d 548 (1983), *on remand* 705 F.2d 775 (5th Cir.1983) (the remedy under Rule 10b–5 supplements the express remedies which are cumulative).

18. Thompson v. Thompson, 484 U.S. 174, 108 S.Ct. 513, 98 L.Ed.2d 512 (1988) (no implied remedy under Parental Kidnapping Prevention Act–28 U.S.C.A. §§ 1738, 1738A); California v. Sierra Club, 451 U.S. 287, 101 S.Ct. 1775, 68 L.Ed.2d 101 (1981); Middlesex County Sewerage Authority v. National Sea Clammers Association, 453 U.S. 1, 101 S.Ct. 2615, 69 L.Ed.2d 435 (1981); Touche Ross & Co. v. Redington, 442 U.S. 560, 99 S.Ct. 2479, 61 L.Ed.2d 82 (1979), *on remand* 612 F.2d 68 (2d Cir.1979) (denying the existence of a remedy under § 17(a) of the Exchange Act, 15 U.S.C.A. § 78q(a)); Chrysler Corp. v. Brown, 441 U.S. 281, 99 S.Ct. 1705, 60 L.Ed.2d 208 (1979), *on remand* 611 F.2d 439 (3d Cir.1979) (finding no remedy under either the Freedom of Information Act, 5 U.S.C.A. § 552 (1976), or the Trade Secrets Act, 18 U.S.C.A. § 1905). In two other cases the court has utilized the same rationale to deny the existence of an implied right to contribution. Texas Industries, Inc. v. Radcliff Materials, Inc., 451 U.S. 630, 639–40, 101 S.Ct. 2061, 2066–67, 68 L.Ed.2d 500, 508–09 (1981) (no implied right to contribution under the Sherman or Clayton antitrust acts); Northwest Airlines, Inc. v. Transport Workers Union of America, 451 U.S. 77, 94–95, 101 S.Ct. 1571, 1582, 67 L.Ed.2d 750, 764–66 (1981) (no right to contribution under the Equal Pay Act of 1963 or Title VII of the 1964 Civil Rights Act). Contribution is discussed in § 13.17 *infra*.

In California v. Sierra Club, 451 U.S. 287, 101 S.Ct. 1775, 68 L.Ed.2d 101 (1981), the Sierra Club and other environmental groups sought to enjoin the construction and operation of a state water storage and transportation facility. The Court applied the four-factor *Cort v. Ash* analysis (*see* footnote 21 *infra*) but found a lack of congressional intent and the absence of an especially protected class with regard to the Rivers and Harbors Appropriations Act of 1899, 33 U.S.C.A. § 403 (1976). In Middlesex County Sewerage Authority v. National Sea Clammers Association, 453 U.S. 1, 101 S.Ct. 2615, 69 L.Ed.2d 435 (1981), the Court denied a federal remedy to fishermen seeking redress for off-shore pollution. The Court properly read the Federal Water Pollution Control Act of 1948, ch. 758, 62 Stat. 115 (codified in scattered sections of 33 U.S.C.A.) and the Marine Protection, Research and Sanctuaries Act of 1972, Pub.L. No. 92–532, 86 Stat. 1052 (codified in scattered sections of 33 U.S.C.A.) as providing only for express "citizen's action" to enjoin violations while preserving all common law remedies. Thus, there was clear congressional intent not to create a federal remedial scheme.

sion.[19] In each of these cases, regardless of the applicable statute, the Court applied—and to some extent modified—the four factor implication test that it had earlier framed in *Cort v. Ash*.[20] Under the *Cort* analysis, before the Court will imply a remedy, it must find: (1) that the plaintiff belongs to a special class at which the legislation is aimed; (2) a legislative intent to create an implied remedy; (3) that an implied remedy is consistent with the overall thrust of the statute; and (4) that the subject matter is not one traditionally left to state law.[21] Subsequent Supreme Court cases, however, have focused primarily on the legislative intent behind the legislation rather than on an evenhanded application of all four of the *Cort* criteria.[22] For example, in 1994, the Court in a five-to-four decision announced that it is bound primarily by the legislative intent as indicated by a textual analysis of the statute.[23] The more a court is bound by the text of a statute, the less likely it is to find remedies that are not expressly set forth.

Supreme Court cases have been increasingly more restrictive in applying the *Cort* test. Ironically, as is the case with securities cases in general, many lower courts continued to take a contrary approach. This is in part due to the fact that in most of its restrictive decisions, the Supreme Court has left room for ways around its limiting rulings and many of the lower courts have seized upon the opportunity.[24] Accordingly, in interpreting Supreme Court decisions many suits have been successful when plaintiffs have tried to define the narrowest possible reading of the *Cort* and post-*Cort* analyis since, at least through the 1980s, there proved to be a good chance of that view being adopted by the lower federal courts. This state of affairs has created much confu-

19. Transamerica Mortgage Advisors, Inc. v. Lewis, 444 U.S. 11, 100 S.Ct. 242, 62 L.Ed.2d 146 (1979), *on remand* 610 F.2d 648 (9th Cir.1979). *See* text accompanying footnote 8 *supra*.

20. 422 U.S. 66, 95 S.Ct. 2080, 45 L.Ed.2d 26 (1975). *See generally* the authorities cited in footnote 15 *supra*.

21. 422 U.S. at 78, 95 S.Ct. at 2088.

22. *E.g.,* Merrill Lynch, Pierce, Fenner & Smith, Inc. v. Curran, 456 U.S. 353, 102 S.Ct. 1825, 72 L.Ed.2d 182 (1982); Texas Industries, Inc. v. Radcliff Materials, Inc., 451 U.S. 630, 639, 101 S.Ct. 2061, 2066, 68 L.Ed.2d 500 (1981); Transamerica Mortgage Advisors, Inc. v. Lewis, 444 U.S. 11, 100 S.Ct. 242, 62 L.Ed.2d 146 (1979), *on remand* 610 F.2d 648 (9th Cir.1979). *See also* Cannon v. University of Chicago, 441 U.S. 677, 730–749, 99 S.Ct. 1946, 1974–1985, 60 L.Ed.2d 560 (1979), *on remand* 605 F.2d 560 (7th Cir.1979), *appeal after remand* 648 F.2d 1104 (7th Cir.1981), *mandamus denied* 454 U.S. 811, 102 S.Ct. 373, 70 L.Ed.2d 197 (1981) (Powell, J. dissenting).

23. Central Bank of Denver v. First Interstate Bank of Denver, ___ U.S. ___, 114 S.Ct. 1439, 128 L.Ed.2d 119 (1994) (there is no implied remedy against aiders and abettors).

24. The most striking example in the securities area is the use of Rule 10b–5 to combat corporate mismanagement. *Compare* Santa Fe Industries, Inc. v. Green, 430 U.S. 462, 97 S.Ct. 1292, 51 L.Ed.2d 480 (1977), *on remand* 562 F.2d 4 (2d Cir.1977) *with* Healey v. Catalyst Recovery of Pennsylvania, 616 F.2d 641 (3d Cir.1980); Kidwell v. Meikle, 597 F.2d 1273 (9th Cir.1979); Alabama Farm Bureau Mutual Casualty Co. v. American Fidelity Life Insurance Co., 606 F.2d 602 (5th Cir.1979), *rehearing denied* 610 F.2d 818 (5th Cir.1980); Wright v. Heizer Corp., 560 F.2d 236 (7th Cir.1977), *cert. denied* 434 U.S. 1066, 98 S.Ct. 1243, 55 L.Ed.2d 767 (1978); Goldberg v. Meridor, 567 F.2d 209 (2d Cir.1977), *cert. denied* 434 U.S. 1069, 98 S.Ct. 1249, 55 L.Ed.2d 771 (1978). *See* § 13.11 *infra*.

Cf. Abrams v. Baylor College of Medicine, 581 F.Supp. 1570 (S.D.Tex.1984) (implied remedy exists under Export Administration Act of 1979, 15 U.S.C.A. §§ 2401 *et seq.*).

sion and has led to the observation that we have two federal judiciaries—the Supreme Court and all other federal courts.[25] It cannot be ignored that the Supreme Court takes a relatively few cases for review thus making any movement—restrictive or otherwise—very slow, especially when the lower federal courts may not be in step. Furthermore, although certainly not heralding every suggested implied remedy, the Court has not sounded a death-knell for all such remedies nor has it precluded the possibility of additional remedies in appropriate future cases.[26] Nevertheless, in recent years, the lower federal courts have quite properly been more cautious in recognizing additional implied rights of action.[27]

§ 13.2 Rule 10b–5 Overview; Section 10b and the Evolution of the Implied Remedy Under SEC Rule 10b–5

The primary private remedy for fraud available under the Securities Exchange Act has been the one implied from SEC Rule 10b–5.[1] This section describes the development of the Rule 10b–5 remedy and its relationship to other remedies. The next section provides an overview of the essential elements of a Rule 10b–5 claim. The remainder of the chapter provides a detailed analysis of the law under Rule 10b–5.

Although several recent Supreme Court cases[2] have limited the scope of the 10b–5 private right of action, it continues to be a significant

---

25. *See* Thomas O. Gorman, At The Intersection of Supreme Avenue and Circuit Street; The Focus of Section 10b and Santa Fe's Footnote Fourteen, 7 J.Corp.L. 199 (1982).

26. *See, e.g.,* Musick, Peeler & Garrett v. Employers Insurance of Wausau, ___ U.S. ___, 113 S.Ct. 2085, 124 L.Ed.2d 194 (1993) (in Rule 10b–5 actions, there is an implied right to contribution among joint defendants). *See also* Hazen *supra* footnote 15, Steinberg *supra* footnote 15. *But see* the other authorities in footnote 15 *supra* and Justice Powell's dissent in Cannon v. University of Chicago, 441 U.S. 677, 99 S.Ct. 1946, 60 L.Ed.2d 560 (1979), *on remand* 605 F.2d 560 (7th Cir.1979), *appeal after remand* 648 F.2d 1104 (7th Cir.1981), *mandamus denied* 454 U.S. 811, 102 S.Ct. 373, 70 L.Ed.2d 197 (1981).

27. Joseph A. Grundfest, Disimplying Private Rights of Action Under the Federal Securities Laws: The Commission's Authority, 107 Harv. L. Rev. 961 (1994). *But see, e.g.,* Harper v. Federal Land Bank of Spokane, 692 F.Supp. 1244 (D.Or.1988), *reversed* 878 F.2d 1172 (9th Cir. 1989) (recognizing implied right of action under Agricultural Credit Act, 12 U.S.C.A. §§ 2001 to 2279aa–14).

§ 13.2

1. 17 C.F.R. § 240.10b–5. *See* Symposium, Happy Birthday 10b–5: 50 Years of Antifraud Regulation, 61 Fordham L.Rev. S1 (1993).

The text of the rule is reproduced in footnote 21 *infra.*

See § 1.7 *supra* for an overview of the private remedies under the 1933 and 1934 Acts.

2. *See* Santa Fe Industries, Inc. v. Green, 430 U.S. 462, 97 S.Ct. 1292, 51 L.Ed.2d 480 (1977), *on remand* 562 F.2d 4 (2d Cir.1977); Ernst & Ernst v. Hochfelder, 425 U.S. 185, 96 S.Ct. 1375, 47 L.Ed.2d 668 (1976), *rehearing denied* 425 U.S. 986, 96 S.Ct. 2194, 48 L.Ed.2d 811 (1976); Blue Chip Stamps v. Manor Drug Stores, 421 U.S. 723, 95 S.Ct. 1917, 44 L.Ed.2d 539 (1975), *rehearing denied* 423 U.S. 884, 96 S.Ct. 157, 46 L.Ed.2d 114 (1975). *See also* Aaron v. SEC, 446 U.S. 680, 100 S.Ct. 1945, 64 L.Ed.2d 611 (1980), *on remand* 666 F.2d 5 (2d Cir.1981). *But see* Herman & MacLean v. Huddleston, 459 U.S. 375, 103 S.Ct. 683, 74 L.Ed.2d 548 (1983), *on remand* 705 F.2d 775 (5th Cir.1983). *See* §§ 13.3–13.4, 13.11 *infra.*

weapon against securities fraud. To put the Rule 10b–5 remedy in its proper perspective, it must be viewed in conjunction with the other modes of private relief provided by the securities laws. The concurrent antifraud provisions are found in the Securities Act of 1933.

The 1933 Act contains two sections providing for express private damage remedies for misrepresentation in connection with the sale of a security.[3] These supplement the 1933 Act's general antifraud provision embodied in section 17(a).[4] Section 17(a) does not create an express right of action and although there is considerable authority to the contrary, it has been held by some courts to support an implied private remedy.[5] In contrast to these provisions in the 1933 Act, the express remedies available under the Securities Exchange Act of 1934 are much more limited in scope. Section 9(e) of the Exchange Act[6] confers a private right of action upon an injured investor against one who has willfully engaged in market manipulation of securities subject to the 1934 Act's registration and reporting requirements[7] by virtue of being listed on a national exchange.[8] Section 18(a) of the Act[9] sets out a private right of action for an investor who has been injured due to reliance on materially misleading statements or omissions of material facts in documents required to be filed with the Commission. Section 16(b)'s disgorgement of insider short-swing profits[10] is the third express private remedy contained in the 1934 Act. A fourth private remedy was created by The Insider Trading and Securities Fraud Enforcement Act of 1988.[11]

The express remedies under the 1933 Act apply only to fraud in connection with the sale of securities thus providing protection only to injured purchasers and not to injured sellers. The 1934 Act's express remedies do not distinguish between purchasers and sellers. The 1934 Act express remedies are restricted, however, to securities subject to the Act's reporting requirements.[12] These express remedies are also subject

---

3. Sections 11 and 12(2). 15 U.S.C.A. §§ 77k, 77*l*(2). *See* §§ 7.2–7.5 *supra.* This is in addition to section 12(1) which provides a right of rescission for all securities sold in violation of the Act's registration provisions. 15 U.S.C.A. § 77*l*(1). *See* § 7.2 *supra.*

4. 15 U.S.C.A. § 77q(a).

5. *See* Thomas L. Hazen, A Look Beyond The Pruning of Rule 10b–5: Implied Remedies and Section 17(a) of The Securities Act of 1933, 64 Va.L.Rev. 641 (1978); § 13.13 *infra.*

6. 15 U.S.C.A. § 78i(e). *See* § 12.1 *supra.*

7. The scope of the Exchange Act's issuer registration and reporting requirements is discussed in §§ 9.2–9.3 *supra.*

8. *See* section 6 of the 1934 Act, 15 U.S.C.A. § 78f. Section 9 is thus more limited than most of the 1934 Act's liability and reporting provisions, which apply equally to many over-the-counter securities. 15 U.S.C.A. § 78*l*. *See* §§ 9.2, 9.3 *supra.*

9. 15 U.S.C.A. § 78r(a). *See* § 12.8 *supra.*

10. 15 U.S.C.A. § 78p(b). *See* §§ 12.3–12.7 *supra.*

11. Section 20A, 15 U.S.C.A. § 78t–1. *See* § 13.9 *infra.*

12. The same is also true of some implied remedies. For example, the implied remedy under proxy Rule 14a–9 protects shareholders injured in connection with shareholder votes and does not necessarily involve either a purchase or sale. 17 C.F.R. § 240.14a–9. *See, e.g.,* J.I. Case Co. v. Borak, 377 U.S. 426, 84 S.Ct. 1555, 12 L.Ed.2d 423 (1964). The Rule

to a number of other limiting factors that are discussed in earlier sections of this book. Section 10(b)[13] and Rule 10b–5[14] do not have many of these limiting factors. Although arguments have been made to the contrary, the overwhelming majority of decisions agree that the Rule 10b–5 remedy is cumulative with the express remedies noted above.[15]

In order to put the Rule 10b–5 remedy in proper perspective, it is also necessary to look at its history and development.[16] The general antifraud provision of the 1934 Act is contained in section 10(b), which provides that it is unlawful "to use or employ [utilizing any means or instrumentality of interstate commerce], in connection with the purchase or sale of any security * * * any manipulative or deceptive device or contrivance in contravention of such rules and regulations as the Commission may prescribe as necessary or appropriate in the public interest or for the protection of investors."[17] The Commission has utilized this rulemaking power in a number of instances,[18] with regard to a wide variety of manipulative and deceptive acts and practices[19] and in

---

14a–9 remedy is discussed in §§ 11.3–11.5 *supra*. *See also* section 14(e) of the Williams Act, 15 U.S.C.A. § 78n(e) (which deals with tender offers) which is discussed in § 11.19 *supra*.

13. 15 U.S.C.A. § 78j(b).

14. 17 C.F.R. §§ 240.10b–5.

15. *See, e.g.,* Herman & MacLean v. Huddleston, 459 U.S. 375, 103 S.Ct. 683, 74 L.Ed.2d 548 (1983), *on remand* 705 F.2d 775 (5th Cir.1983). *See generally* Marc I. Steinberg, The Propriety and Scope of Cumulative Remedies Under the Federal Securities Laws, 67 Cornell L.Rev. 557 (1982).

16. *See* 3 Louis Loss, Securities Regulation 1448–1472, 1763–1796 (2d ed. 1961); Alan R. Bromberg, Are There Limits to Rule 10b–5?, 29 Bus.Law. 167 (1974); Roy L. Brooks, Rule 10b–5 in the Balance: An Analysis of the Supreme Court's Policy Perspective, 32 Hastings L.J. 403 (1980); Michael Joseph, Civil Liability Under Rule 10b–5–A Reply, 59 Nw.U.L.Rev. 171 (1964); John A. Maher, Implied Private Rights of Action and the Federal Securities Laws: A Historical Perspective, 37 Wash. & Lee L.Rev. 717 (1980); David M. Phillips, An Essay: Six Competing Currents of Rule 10b–5 Jurisprudence, 21 Ind.L.Rev. 625 (1988); David S. Ruder, Civil Liability Under Rule 10b–5: Judicial Revision of the Legislative Intent, 57 Nw.U.L.Rev. 627 (1963).

Note the anecdotal history of the rule as recounted in footnote 23 *infra* and accompanying text. *See also* Alan R. Bromberg & Lewis D. Lowenfels, Securities Law Fraud—SEC Rule 10b–5 (1979); Aarnold S. Jacobs, The Impact of Rule 10b–5 (1980).

17. 15 U.S.C.A. § 78j(b). *See generally* Steve Thel, The Original Conception of Section 10(b) of the Securities Exchange Act, 42 Stan.L.Rev. 385 (1990); Symposium, Happy Birthday 10b–5: 50 Years of Antifraud Regulation, 61 Fordham L.Rev. S1 (1993).

18. 17 C.F.R. §§ 240.10b–1–240.10b–18; 240.10b–21.

19. The rules span a wide variety of manipulative and deceptive conduct: (1) prohibition of manipulative and deceptive devices with regard to certain securities exempt from 1934 Act registration (17 C.F.R. § 240.10b–1, see § 12.1 *supra*); (2) a former prohibition against solicitations of purchases by persons participating in primary or secondary securities distributions (17 C.F.R. § 240.10b–2 (1992) (rescinded), see § 6.1 *supra*); (3) prohibitions against manipulative and deceptive devices with regard to securities not on a national exchange and municipal securities (17 C.F.R. § 240.10b–3, this fills the gap left by section 9 of the Act, 15 U.S.C.A. § 78i, see § 12.1 *supra*); (4) former prohibition against short and hedged tendering, now contained in Rule 14e–4; (5) Rule 10b–5 (*see* note 21 *infra*); (6) prohibitions against trading by participants in a distribution of securities except for certain stabilizing bids (17 C.F.R. §§ 240.10b–6, 10b–7, see § 6.1 *supra*); (7) prohibitions of certain practices in connection with securities distributions through rights of existing security holders (17 C.F.R. § 240.10b–8); (8) prohibitions with regard to securities offered on an "all or none" basis and securities offered on a condition of full subscription (17 C.F.R.

Rule 10b–5 it fashioned its most encompassing antifraud prohibition.[20]

Promulgated in 1942, Rule 10b–5 is patterned directly upon section 17(a) of the 1933 Act except that 10b–5 further extends to misstatements and omissions occurring in connection with either a *purchase or sale* of security while the parent section is limited to fraudulent sales and offers to sell. The rule prohibits (1) fraudulent devices and schemes, (2) misstatements and omissions of material facts, and (3) acts and practices which operate as a fraud or deceit.[21] When it adopted Rule 10b–5, the Commission, without even realizing its eventual reach, created a powerful antifraud weapon.[22] According to one account, the decision to adopt the rule and model it on section 17(a) was arrived at without any deliberation, with the only official discussion consisting of one SEC Commissioner reportedly observing, "we are against fraud, aren't we?"[23] Given this background, it is clear that not much can be gleaned from the

---

§ 240.10b–9); (9) prohibition against broker-dealers executing sales without written confirmation of the transaction disclosing the broker's commission and whether the broker is acting as principal or an agent for someone other than the customer (17 C.F.R. § 240.10b–10, *see* §§ 2.5, 10.7 *supra*); (10) prohibition of purchases by a tender offeror or affiliate (17 C.F.R. § 240.10b–13, *see* § 11.15 *supra*); (11) requirement of disclosure of credit terms in margin transactions (17 C.F.R. § 240.10b–16, *see* § 10.11 *supra*); (12) prohibiting untimely announcements of record dates for stock splits, dividends, and reverse stock splits (17 C.F.R. § 240.10b–17); and (13) safe harbor provisions for issuers' purchases of their own shares (17 C.F.R. § 240.10b–18, *see* §§ 11.17, 12.1, 12.8 *supra*).

See, e.g., Beres v. Thomson McKinnon Securities, Inc., 1989 WL 105967, [1989–1990 Transfer Binder] Fed.Sec.L.Rep. ¶ 94,923 (S.D.N.Y.1989) (no private right of action for violations of Rule 10b–3 since the rule is a corollary of section 15(c)).

20. 17 C.F.R. § 240.10b–5.

21. *Id.*

22. *See* Sec.Exch. Act Rel. No. 34–3230 (May 21, 1942) ("The new rule closes a loophole in the protections against fraud administered by the commission by prohibiting individuals or companies from buying securities if they engage in fraud in their purchase"). Rule 10b–5 also covers fraud in the sale of securities but this prohibition is also contained in section 17(a) of the 1933 Act. 15 U.S.C.A. § 77q(a). *See also* 15 U.S.C.A. §§ 77k, 77l(2).

23. According to the account of Milton Freeman, in Conference on Codification of the Federal Securities Laws, 22 Bus.Law. 793, 922 (1967):

It was one day in the year 1943, I believe [in fact, it was 1942]. I was sitting in my office in the S.E.C. building in Philadelphia and I received a call from Jim Treanor who was then the director of the Trading and Exchange Division. He said, "I have just been on the telephone with Paul Rowen," who was then the S.E.C. Regional Administrator in Boston, "and he has told me about some company in Boston who is going around buying up the stock of his company from his own shareholders at $4.00 a share, and he has been telling them that the company is doing very badly, whereas, in fact, the earnings are going to be quadrupled and will be $2.00 a share for the coming year. Is there anything we can do about it?" So he came upstairs and I called in my secretary and I looked at section 10(b) and I looked at section 17, and I put them together, and the only discussion we had there was where "in connection with the purchase or sale" should be, and we decided it should be at the end.

We called the Commission and we got on the calendar, and I don't remember whether we got there that morning or after lunch. We passed a piece of paper around to all the commissioners. All the commissioners read the rule and they tossed it on the table, indicating approval. Nobody said anything except Sumner Pike who said, "Well," he said, "we are against fraud, aren't we?"

This account was quoted by Justice Blackmun in his dissent in Blue Chip Stamps v. Manor Drug Stores, 421 U.S. 723, 767, 95 S.Ct. 1917, 1940, 44 L.Ed.2d 539, 567 (1975), *rehearing denied* 423 U.S. 884, 96 S.Ct. 157, 46 L.Ed.2d 114 (1975).

history of the rule, although the courts frequently refer to the legislative history behind the statute.

In 1946, a federal district court held that notwithstanding the absence of an express private right of action, Rule 10b–5 gives rise to a private remedy in the hands of injured investors.[24] The implied remedy started to grow and flourish in the district and circuit courts but did not receive formal Supreme Court approval until twenty-four years later.[25] In recent years there seems to have occurred a general demise of implied remedies in the federal courts.[26] Nevertheless, the Rule 10b–5 remedy remains firmly entrenched.[27] The Rule 10b–5 action has, however, been cut down in scope in many respects.

In recent years, the Supreme Court in a series of cases has limited the scope of the private right of action under Rule 10b–5. First, the Court ruled that in order to maintain an action, the plaintiff must be either a purchaser or seller of the securities in question.[28] Second, a showing of negligent conduct will not suffice; the defendant must have acted with scienter.[29] Third, the conduct complained of must be "deceptive."[30] In addition to the foregoing limitations imposed by the Supreme Court, in order to state a claim under Rule 10b–5, the Federal Rules of Civil Procedure require that claims sounding in fraud (which necessarily includes all Rule 10b–5 claims) must be pleaded with particu-

---

24. Kardon v. National Gypsum Co., 69 F.Supp. 512 (E.D.Pa.1946).

25. Superintendent of Insurance v. Bankers Life & Casualty Co., 404 U.S. 6, 92 S.Ct. 165, 30 L.Ed.2d 128 (1971), *on remand* 401 F.Supp. 640 (S.D.N.Y.1975). In the course of one of its subsequent limiting 10b–5 decisions the Court observed that 10b–5 represented a legislative acorn that had grown into a judicial oak badly in need of pruning. Blue Chip Stamps v. Manor Drug Stores, 421 U.S. 723, 737, 95 S.Ct. 1917, 1926, 44 L.Ed.2d 539 (1975), *rehearing denied* 423 U.S. 884, 96 S.Ct. 157, 46 L.Ed.2d 114 (1975). *See* footnotes 27–29 *infra*.

26. *See* § 13.1 *supra*.

27. There is voluminous writing on the evolution of the 10b–5 remedy. *See, e.g.,* Alan R. Bromberg & Lewis D. Lowenfels, Securities Fraud and Commodities Fraud (1982); 7, 8 Louis Loss & Joel Seligman, Securities Regulation 3304–3923 (3d ed. 1991); Craig J. Cobine, Elements of Liability and Actual Damages in Rule 10b–5 Actions, 1972 U.Ill.L.J. Forum 651; David S. Ruder, Civil Liability Under Rule 10b–5: Judicial Revision of The Legislative Intent? 57 Nw.U.L.Rev. 627 (1963), and the other authorities in note 16 *supra*.

28. Blue Chip Stamps v. Manor Drug Stores, 421 U.S. 723, 95 S.Ct. 1917, 44 L.Ed.2d 539 (1975), *rehearing denied* 423 U.S. 884, 96 S.Ct. 157, 46 L.Ed.2d 114 (1975). *See* § 13.3 *infra*.

29. Ernst & Ernst v. Hochfelder, 425 U.S. 185, 96 S.Ct. 1375, 47 L.Ed.2d 668 (1976), *rehearing denied* 425 U.S. 986, 96 S.Ct. 2194, 48 L.Ed.2d 811 (1976). *See, e.g.,* Milich, Securities Fraud Under Section 10(b) and Rule 10b–5: Scienter, Recklessness, and the Good Faith Defense, 11 J.Corp.L. 179 (1986); Note, Negligence v. Scienter: The Proper Standard of Liability for Violations of the Antifraud Provisions Regulating Tender Offers and Proxy Solicitations Under the Securities Exchange Act of 1934, 41 Wash. & Lee L.Rev. 1045 (1984). *See also* § 13.4 *infra*.

30. Santa Fe Industries, Inc. v. Green, 430 U.S. 462, 97 S.Ct. 1292, 51 L.Ed.2d 480 (1977), *on remand* 562 F.2d 4 (2d Cir.1977). *See* Freschi v. Grand Coal Venture, 767 F.2d 1041, 1047–48 (2d Cir.1985), *judgment vacated on other grounds* 478 U.S. 1015, 106 S.Ct. 3325, 92 L.Ed.2d 731 (1986), *on remand* 800 F.2d 305 (2d Cir.1986) (citing this treatise). *See* § 13.11 *infra*.

larity.[31]　Notwithstanding these limiting decisions, which are discussed in later sections, the Rule 10b–5 implied remedy remains an important one in appropriate cases for a number of reasons.

It is quite easy to establish federal jurisdiction to support a Rule 10b–5 claim.　All that is required is for some aspect of the securities transaction under attack to have been carried out through the use of an instrumentality of interstate commerce.　For example, even an intrastate telephone call has been held sufficient to satisfy the jurisdictional requirements of Rule 10b–5.[32]　While a face-to-face conversation itself will not satisfy the jurisdictional requirements, there may be 10b–5 jurisdiction if the conversations are part of a transaction that utilizes an instrumentality of interstate commerce.[33]　Also, although it might be argued that the language of section 10(b) and Rule 10b–5 require otherwise, it seems to be the majority rule that it is not necessary that the misrepresentation be communicated through an instrumentality of interstate commerce, so long as there is a connection between the use of the jurisdictional means and the fraud.[34]　Additionally, through the doctrine of pendent jurisdiction,[35] a plaintiff with a Rule 10b–5 claim may bring related state statutory or common law claims into the federal court.[36]　Although a federal court may have the discretion to take pendent jurisdiction, principles of federalism and comity often convince a court to relinquish jurisdiction over the state claim in order to permit it to proceed in a state court forum.[37]

31.　Fed.R.Civ.P. 9(b).　*See, e.g.* Wool v. Tandem Computers Inc., 818 F.2d 1433 (9th Cir.1987) (sufficient particularity for both primary and secondary liability); Luce v. Edelstein, 802 F.2d 49 (2d Cir.1986) (sufficient particularity as to some counts; allegations on "information and belief" must state facts on which the belief is based).　Fed.R.Civ.P. 9(b).　*See* § 13.8.1 *infra* (Practitioner's Edition only).

32.　Loveridge v. Dreagoux, 678 F.2d 870 (10th Cir.1982); Dupuy v. Dupuy, 511 F.2d 641 (5th Cir.1975), *appeal after remand* 551 F.2d 1005 (5th Cir.1977), *rehearing denied* 434 U.S. 911, 98 S.Ct. 312, 54 L.Ed.2d 197 (1977); Myzel v. Fields, 386 F.2d 718 (8th Cir.1967), *cert. denied* 390 U.S. 951, 88 S.Ct. 1043, 19 L.Ed.2d 1143 (1968).　*Accord* Miller v. Affiliated Financial Corp., 600 F.Supp. 987, 992 (N.D.Ill.1984).　The jurisdictional provisions are discussed in chapter 14 *infra.*

33.　Leiter v. Kuntz, 655 F.Supp. 725 (D.Utah 1987) (mailing of financial statement by defendant's attorney plus use of telephone to change face-to-face meeting held sufficient to support Rule 10b–5 jurisdiction) *but cf.* Soper v. Valone, 110 F.R.D. 8 (W.D.N.Y.1985) (denying class action for lack of common questions where claims were based primarily on oral representations).　*See* § 14.1.1 *infra.*

34.　Kline v. Henrie, 679 F.Supp. 464, 469 (M.D.Pa.1988); United States v. Pray, 452 F.Supp. 788, 792 (M.D.Pa.1978); Harrison v. Equitable Life Assurance Society of the United States, 435 F.Supp. 281, 284–85 (W.D.Mich.1977); Levin v. Marder, 343 F.Supp. 1050, 1056 (W.D.Pa.1972).　*See also* the authorities in footnote 33, *supra.　But see* Note, Oral Misrepresentations at "Roadshows" and in Other Settings: Illusory Liability Under Rule 10b–5?, 41 Wash. & Lee L.Rev. 995 (1984).

35.　*See* United Mine Workers of America v. Gibbs, 383 U.S. 715, 86 S.Ct. 1130, 16 L.Ed.2d 218 (1966).

36.　*See* Lewis D. Lowenfels, Pendent Jurisdiction and The Federal Securities Act, 67 Colum.L.Rev. 474 (1967).　*But see, e.g.,* Wentzka v. Gellman, 991 F.2d 423 (7th Cir.1993) (district court abused its discretion in retaining jurisdiction over state law claim after federal claim was dismissed due to expiration of limitations period).

37.　*See, e.g.,* Kidder, Peabody & Co. v. Maxus Energy Corp., 925 F.2d 556 (2d Cir.), *cert. denied* 501 U.S. 1218, 111 S.Ct. 2829, 115 L.Ed.2d 998 (1991) (following declaratory

The Rule 10b–5 remedy may be used in a wide variety of factual contexts. The 10b–5 action has been used to address the problems of material corporate misstatements or nondisclosures,[38] insider trading,[39] and corporate mismanagement problems that arise in the context of transactions in shares or other securities.[40] Furthermore, a parallel antifraud remedy has been implied under proxy Rule 14a–9.[41] There will frequently be cumulative Rule 10b–5 and 14a–9 remedies available in the case of mergers and corporate reorganizations, which involve both a shareholder vote and securities transactions.[42] Similarly, Rule 10b–5 has a role to play in the tender offer context which necessarily involves the sale of target company stock.[43] In addition, the fact that securities may be exempt from registration under the Securities Act of 1933[44] will not preclude an action under Rule 10b–5. Thus, for example, a 10b–5 action may be brought for fraud in connection with United States Treasury securities,[45] or with regard to municipal securities.[46] One exception is that since short term commercial paper is excluded from the 1934 Act's definition of a security,[47] Rule 10b–5 will not apply to such transactions.

Because the Rule 10b–5 remedy is not an express one, the courts have had to struggle with a number of questions that might otherwise have been answered in the statute. Many of these questions remain seriously in dispute today. The most important of these include the definition of materiality,[48] the necessity of proof of reliance by the plaintiff on the misstatement or omission,[49] the requisite causal connection,[50] the appropriate measure of damages,[51] and the applicable statute of limitations.[52]

---

judgment on the federal claim, it was appropriate to relinquish jurisdiction over state law claim notwithstanding the fact that the federal district court had invested considerable time trying to resolve the state law issues). Pendent jurisdiction is discussed in § 14.1 *infra*.

38. *See* § 13.5A *infra*.

39. *See* § 13.9 *infra*.

40. *See* § 13.11 *infra*.

It also has been used to seek redress against various pernicious broker-dealer practices. *See, e.g.,* § 10.10 *supra* for a discussion of churning.

41. 17 C.F.R. § 240.14a–9. *See* J.I. Case Co. v. Borak, 377 U.S. 426, 84 S.Ct. 1555, 12 L.Ed.2d 423 (1964).

42. *See e.g.,* SEC v. National Securities, Inc., 393 U.S. 453, 468, 89 S.Ct. 564, 573, 21 L.Ed.2d 668 (1969) (The overlap is "neither unusual nor unfortunate").

43. *See also* section 14(e) of the Williams Act, 15 U.S.C.A. § 78n(e); §§ 11.15, 11.19 *supra*.

44. *See* § 4.1 *supra*.

45. *E.g.,* Kahn v. Salomon Brothers, Inc., 813 F.Supp. 191 (E.D.N.Y.1993). The regulation of government securities dealers is discussed in § 10.5.1 *supra*.

46. The regulation of municipal securities dealers is discussed in § 10.5 *supra*.

47. 15 U.S.C.A. § 78c(a)(10). *See* § 4.4 *supra*.

48. *See* § 13.5A *infra*.

49. *See* § 13.5B *infra*.

50. *See* § 13.6 *infra*.

51. *See* § 13.7 *infra*.

52. *See* § 13.8 *infra*.

One other issue is the extent to which 10b–5 is cumulative with respect to other remedies provided in the securities acts. The Supreme Court has held that Rule 10b–5 and section 11 of the 1933 Act[53] dealing with material misstatements in 1933 Act registration statements are not mutually exclusive and that a 10b–5 remedy will lie even though the misstatements appeared in 1933 Act registration materials.[54] This ruling would seem to compel the same result with regard to other express remedies.[55] For example, the majority of cases support the view that Rule 10b–5 and section 18(a)'s express liability for false SEC filings[56] are cumulative.[57] Similarly, the Fifth Circuit has held that in light of the Supreme Court mandate, Rule 10b–5 and section 9(e)'s remedies for market manipulation[58] are cumulative.[59] There is no reason to expect that a different result would ensue with regard to section 12(2) of the 1933 Act.[60] Also, as noted above, the Supreme Court has indicated that Rule 10b–5 and the 14a–9 proxy remedy are cumulative.[61]

Plaintiffs bringing frivolous claims under Rule 10b–5 may have to pay the costs of defending the suit, including attorneys' fees.[62] On the other side of the coin, although a successful plaintiff is not ordinarily entitled to attorneys' fees, attorneys' fees will be available when the securities law claims overlap with claims for which attorneys' fees are

---

53. 15 U.S.C.A. § 77k. *See* §§ 7.2, 7.3 *supra.*

54. Herman & MacLean v. Huddleston, 459 U.S. 375, 103 S.Ct. 683, 74 L.Ed.2d 548 (1983), *on remand* 705 F.2d 775 (5th Cir.1983). *See* Lanza v. Drexel & Co., 479 F.2d 1277 (2d Cir.1973); Fischman v. Raytheon Manufacturing Co., 188 F.2d 783 (2d Cir.1951).

55. *See* Steinberg *supra* footnote 15. *But cf.* Amunrud v. Taurus Drilling Ltd., 1983 WL 1412, [1983–1984 Transfer Binder] Fed.Sec.L.Rep. (CCH) ¶ 99,649 (D.Mont.1983) (sections 10(b) and 15(c) of the 1934 Act cover the same conduct and thus are not cumulative implied remedies).

56. 15 U.S.C.A. § 78r(a). *See* § 12.8 *supra.*

57. *E.g.* Wachovia Bank & Trust Co. v. National Student Marketing Corp., 650 F.2d 342 (D.C.Cir.1980), *cert. denied* 452 U.S. 954, 101 S.Ct. 3098, 69 L.Ed.2d 965 (1981); Ross v. A.H. Robins Co., 607 F.2d 545 (2d Cir.1979), *cert. denied* 446 U.S. 946, 100 S.Ct. 2175, 64 L.Ed.2d 802 (1980), *rehearing denied* 448 U.S. 911, 100 S.Ct. 3057, 65 L.Ed.2d 1140 (1980).

58. 15 U.S.C.A. § 78i(e). *See* § 12.1 *supra.*

59. Chemetron Corp. v. Business Funds, Inc., 718 F.2d 725 (5th Cir.1983). The Fifth Circuit had reached a contrary conclusion prior to *Huddleston.* Chemetron Corp. v. Business Funds, Inc., 682 F.2d 1149 (5th Cir.1982), *vacated and remanded* 460 U.S. 1007, 103 S.Ct. 1245, 75 L.Ed.2d 476 (1983), *on remand* 718 F.2d 725 (5th Cir.1983).

60. 15 U.S.C.A. § 77l(2). *See* § 7.5 *supra. See* Steinberg *supra* footnote 15. Section 12(2) and Rule 10b–5 were held to be cumulative in Amunrud v. Taurus Drilling Ltd., 1983 WL 1412, [1983–1984 Transfer Binder] Fed.Sec.L.Rep. (CCH) ¶ 99,649 (D.Mont.1983). *But cf.* Kilmartin v. H.C. Wainwright & Co., 580 F.Supp. 604, 609 (D.Mass.1984) (Section 17(a) and 12(2) of the 1933 Act do not provide cumulative remedies).

61. *See* footnote 42 *supra* and § 11.2 *supra.*

62. *See* Schwarz v. Folloder, 767 F.2d 125 (5th Cir.1985); In re Olympia Brewing Co. Securities Litigation, 613 F.Supp. 1286 (N.D.Ill.1985); Rand v. Anaconda–Ericsson, Inc., 623 F.Supp. 176 (E.D.N.Y.1985), *judgment affirmed* 794 F.2d 843 (2d Cir.1986). *See also* Toombs v. Leone, 777 F.2d 465 (9th Cir.1985) (imposing monetary sanctions against plaintiff's attorney). *But see* Zerman v. Melton, 735 F.2d 751 (2d Cir.1984), *cert. denied* 474 U.S. 845, 106 S.Ct. 135, 88 L.Ed.2d 111 (1985) (refusing to award attorneys fees because of failure to show plaintiff's bad faith). *See* § 13.7.1 *infra* (Practitioner's Edition only).

permitted.[63]

Notwithstanding many of the restrictions on the Rule 10b–5 action and implied remedies generally that have evolved since 1975, there are hundreds of reported cases each year involving the rule. Surprisingly few Rule 10b–5 cases are litigated through trial, either because they are dismissed at the pretrial stage or because they are settled.[64]

Rule 10b–5 does not contain an express statute of limitations. The Supreme Court has held that the applicable limitations period[65] is to be found in the analogous express liability provisions of the federal securities laws.[66]

One of the more recent developments in the Rule 10b–5 jurisprudence has been the recognition of an implied right of contribution amongst defendants who have been held liable. In *Musick, Peeler & Garrett v. Employers Insurance of Wausau*,[67] the Supreme Court recognized the existence of such a right. The Court further explained that sections 9(e) and 18(a) of the 1934 Act,[68] both of which contain an express right of action, provide for a right of contribution. The Court concluded that the similarities between sections 9(e), 18(a), and 10(b) call for the recognition of an implied contribution under the latter section. In contrast, in a subsequent decision, the absence of an express aiding and abetting provision led a five-to-four majority to deny the existence of aiding and abetting liability in private actions and probably in most SEC civil actions.[69] However, in the course of its opinion, the Court noted that in instances of complex securities cases, the fraud is likely to have been committed by multiple primary violators.[70]

Rule 10b–5 has had a volatile history in the courts. Although a number of recent decisions caution against the implication of additional

63. City Consumer Services, Inc. v. Horne, 631 F.Supp. 1050 (D.Utah 1986) (attorneys' fees awarded under Truth in Lending Act). Attorneys' fees are available under section 11 of the Securities Act of 1933. *See* 15 U.S.C.A. § 77k(e) (permitting a court to exercise its discretion to award attorneys' fees) which is discussed in §§ 7.3, 7.4, 7.4.1 *supra*.

64. For a discussion of the settlement picture, *see* Janet Cooper Alexander, Do the Merits Matter? A Study of Settlements in Securities Class Actions, 43 Stan.L.Rev. 497 (1991). *See also, e.g.,* Steven P. Marino & Renee D. Marino, An Empirical Study of Recent Securities Class Action Settlements Involving Accountants, Attorneys, or Underwriters, 22 Sec. Reg. L.J. 115 (1994).

65. One year from discovery of the fraud (or when it should reasonably have been discovered) but in no event more than three years after the transaction in question. *See* § 13.8 *infra*.

66. Lampf, Pleva, Lipkind, Prupis & Petigrow v. Gilbertson, 501 U.S. 350, 111 S.Ct. 2773, 115 L.Ed.2d 321 (1991). This was a departure from the prior law in most circuits. *See* § 13.8 *infra*.

67. __ U.S. __, 113 S.Ct. 2085, 124 L.Ed.2d 194 (1993).

68. 15 U.S.C.A. §§ 78i(e), 78r(a). *See* §§ 12.1, 12.8 *supra*.

69. Central Bank of Denver, N.A. v. First Interstate Bank of Denver, __ U.S. __, 114 S.Ct. 1439, 128 L.Ed.2d 119 (1994). Aiding and abetting is discussed in § 7.8 *supra* and § 13.16 *infra*.

70. __ U.S. at __, 114 S.Ct. at 1455.

federal remedies,[71] since the Rule 10b–5 remedy is firmly entrenched in the law, it is appropriate to flesh it out so as to fashion a reasonable remedy.[72]

The remainder of this chapter presents a detailed analysis of the Rule 10b–5 caselaw. The following summary provides an overview of the key issues.

§ 13.2.1 Rule 10b–5 Overview; Summary of the Principal Elements

For more than twenty-five years, the primary private remedy for fraud that is available under the Securities Exchange Act has been the one implied from SEC Rule 10b–5. As developed more fully in the preceding section,[1] that rule was promulgated under Section 10(b) of the Exchange Act, which gives the SEC power to promulgate rules prohibiting the use of "manipulative or deceptive device[s] or contrivance[s]" "in connection with the purchase or sale of any security."[2]

There are no express provisions in the securities laws that impose civil liability for the violation of Rule 10b–5 aside from suits based on illegal insider trading.[3] However, as far back as 1946, the courts followed the normal tort rule that persons who violate a legislative enactment may be held civilly liable in damages if they invade an interest of another person that the legislation was intended to protect.[4] For years following the initial recognition of an implied private remedy under Rule 10b–5, the courts continued to expand its scope. In 1975, however, the sands began to shift both in the realm of implied remedies generally[5] and with regard to Rule 10b–5 specifically.[6] Although the

---

71. *See* Joseph A. Grundfest, Disimplying Private Rights of Action Under the Federal Securities Laws: The Commission's Authority, 107 Harv.L.Rev. 961 (1994); § 13.1 *supra.*

72. *See* ___ U.S. at ___, 113 S.Ct. at 2089, relying on Virginia Bankshares, Inc. v. Sandberg, 501 U.S. 1083, 111 S.Ct. 2749, 115 L.Ed.2d 929 (1991) and Blue Chip Stamps v. Manor Drug Stores, 421 U.S. 723, 95 S.Ct. 1917, 44 L.Ed.2d 539 (1975).

§ 13.2.1

1. *See* § 13.2 *supra.*

2. 15 U.S.C.A. § 78j(b). Other rules authorized under this section include rules 10b–6, 10b–7, and 10b–8, addressing market manipulation; rules 10b–4 and 10b–13, addressing conduct during a tender offer; and rule 10b–16, addressing requisite disclosure in margin transactions. *See* § 12.1 *supra.*

3. Section 20A of the Exchange Act which, without referring to Rule 10b–5, provides for disgorgement of profits obtained as the result of impermissible trading while in possession of material nonpublic information. 15 U.S.C.A. § 78t–1, which is discussed in § 13.9 *infra.*

4. Kardon v. National Gypsum Co., 69 F.Supp. 512 (E.D.Pa.1946). *See* §§ 13.1, 13.2 *supra.*

5. Cort v. Ash, 422 U.S. 66, 95 S.Ct. 2080, 45 L.Ed.2d 26 (1975). *See* § 13.1 *supra.*

6. Central Bank of Denver v. First Interstate Bank of Denver, ___ U.S. ___, 114 S.Ct. 1439, 128 L.Ed.2d 119 (1994); Santa Fe Industries, Inc. v. Green, 430 U.S. 462, 97 S.Ct. 1292, 51 L.Ed.2d 480 (1977), *on remand* 562 F.2d 4 (2d Cir.1977); Ernst & Ernst v. Hochfelder, 425 U.S. 185, 96 S.Ct. 1375, 47 L.Ed.2d 668 (1976), *rehearing denied* 425 U.S. 986, 96 S.Ct. 2194, 48 L.Ed.2d 811 (1976); Blue Chip Stamps v. Manor Drug Stores, 421 U.S. 723, 95 S.Ct. 1917, 44 L.Ed.2d 539 (1975), *rehearing denied* 423 U.S. 884, 96 S.Ct. 157, 46 L.Ed.2d 114 (1975).

result has been a retreat from some of the more expansive uses of Rule 10b–5, as outlined below and discussed more fully in the sections that follow, the implied remedy remains a powerful one in appropriate cases.

Rule 10b–5 has had a tremendous impact on a broad spectrum of securities litigation. This general anti-fraud rule is the most commonly used basis for private suits charging fraud in connection with the purchase or sale of securities. Rule 10b–5 also is used to challenge materially misleading statements made by corporations.[7] Perhaps the most well known use of the rule has been in connection with insider trading.[8]

There are five principal elements for stating a claim under Rule 10b–5: the plaintiff must show (1) fraud or deceit[9] (2) by any person (3) in connection with[10] (4) the purchase or sale[11] (5) of any security.[12] Furthermore, since Rule 10b–5, like its parent section, requires deceit or fraud, the elements of common law fraud—materiality, reliance, causation, and damages—are part of a Rule 10b–5 claim.[13]

An important corollary to the "purchase or sale" requirement is that in order to have standing to sue, a 10b–5 plaintiff in a private damages action must have been either a purchaser or seller of the securities that form the basis of the material omission, misstatement, or deceptive conduct.[14] Most courts allow a remedy for a corporation (or in a shareholder derivative suit) for certain transactions in its own shares, including corporate repurchases of its own shares at an inflated price, or an additional issuance of corporate shares on an unfavorable basis.[15]

The courts generally have assumed that it is not necessary for the defendant to have been a purchaser or seller of securities in order to be

---

7. *See* § 13.10 *infra.*

8. *See* § 13.9 *infra.*

9. *See* §§ 13.4, 13.11 *infra.*

10. *See* § 13.2.2 *infra.*

11. *See* §§ 13.2.3, 13.3 *infra.*

12. The definition of security is discussed in § 1.5 *supra.*

13. Some courts have identified six principal elements: "(1) a misstatement or omission (2) of a material (3) fact (4) with scienter (5) upon which the plaintiff justifiably relied (6) that proximately caused the damages." Bentley v. Legent Corp., 849 F.Supp. 429, 431 (E.D.Va.1994) *relying on* Myers v. Finkle, 950 F.2d 165, 167 (4th Cir.1991).

14. Blue Chip Stamps v. Manor Drug Stores, 421 U.S. 723, 95 S.Ct. 1917, 44 L.Ed.2d 539 (1975), *rehearing denied*, 423 U.S. 884, 96 S.Ct. 157, 46 L.Ed.2d 114 (1975). The purchaser/seller standing requirement is discussed in § 13.3 *infra.*

15. Alabama Farm Bureau Mutual Casualty Co. v. American Fidelity Life Ins. Co., 606 F.2d 602 (5th Cir.1979), *rehearing denied* 610 F.2d 818 (5th Cir.), *cert. denied* 449 U.S. 820, 101 S.Ct. 77, 66 L.Ed.2d 22 (1980) (repurchase of shares); Bailes v. Colonial Press, Inc., 444 F.2d 1241 (5th Cir.1971) (issuance of shares); Ruckle v. Roto American Corp., 339 F.2d 24 (2d Cir.1964) (issuance of shares); Hooper v. Mountain States Securities Corp., 282 F.2d 195 (5th Cir.1960), *cert. denied* 365 U.S. 814, 81 S.Ct. 695, 5 L.Ed.2d 693 (1961) (issuance of shares). *But cf.* Smith v. Ayres, 845 F.2d 1360 (5th Cir.1988) (shareholder suing in individual capacity and complaining of corporation's issuance of shares lacked rule 10b–5 standing).

held to have violated rule 10b–5.[16] Any statement reasonably calculated to affect the investment decision of a reasonable investor will satisfy the "in connection with" requirement even if the defendant was not a purchaser or seller.[17]

Rule 10b–5 applies to any purchase or sale by any person of *any* security. The fact that a security is exempt from 1933 or 1934 Act registration does not affect the applicability of Rule 10b–5's proscriptions. The rule applies regardless of whether the security is registered under the 1934 Act, and regardless of whether the company is publicly-held or closely-held. Rule 10b–5 applies even to government and municipal securities, and in fact, to any kind of entity that issues something which can be called a "security." Because of this broad scope, the rule may be invoked in many situations.

One of the essential elements of a fraud claim is demonstrating that the defendant acted with scienter. In its strictest sense, scienter means an intent to deceive but there is substantial authority under common law that making statements in reckless disregard of the truth will suffice to establish scienter.[18] In 1976, the Supreme Court held that a valid claim for damages under Rule 10b–5 must establish that the defendant acted with scienter.[19] The Court, however, did not decide whether a

---

16. *See, e.g.*, Basic, Inc. v. Levinson, 485 U.S. 224, 108 S.Ct. 978, 99 L.Ed.2d 194 (1988), *on remand* 871 F.2d 562 (6th Cir.1989) (upholding liability for misleading statement but not directly addressing whether defendant's not being a purchaser or seller precluded liability). *Compare, e.g.*, Blue Chip Stamps v. Manor Drug Stores, 421 U.S. 723, 95 S.Ct. 1917, 44 L.Ed.2d 539 (1975), *rehearing denied* 423 U.S. 884, 96 S.Ct. 157, 46 L.Ed.2d 114 (1975) (imposing a purchaser/seller standing requirement on the plaintiff).

See also, e.g., In re The Leslie Fay Companies, Inc. Securities Litigation, 871 F.Supp. 686 (S.D.N.Y.1995) (outside auditors' certification of company's financial statements were "in connection with" the purchase or sale of securities since investors were likely to rely thereon); In re ZZZZ Best Securities Litigation, 1994 WL 746649, [1994–1995 Transfer Binder] Fed.Sec.L.Rep. (CCH) ¶ 98,485 (C.D.Cal.1994) (underwriters who were not managing underwriters and claimed not to have been involved in the preparation of the prospectus, could nevertheless be held responsible under section 10(b) for statements in the prospectus; since their names appeared in the prospectus, statements made therein could be attributed to them).

17. SEC v. Texas Gulf Sulphur, 401 F.2d 833 (2d Cir.1968), *cert. denied* 394 U.S. 976, 89 S.Ct. 1454, 22 L.Ed.2d 756 (1969) (misstatements in a corporate press release were made "in connection with" purchases and sales made by shareholders in the open market and violated rule 10b–5, even though corporation itself was not buying nor selling shares); Pelletier v. Stuart–James Co., 863 F.2d 1550 (11th Cir.1989) (fraudulent scheme need not relate to "investment value" of security); Ellis v. Merrill Lynch & Co., 664 F.Supp. 979 (E.D.Pa.1987) (upholding 10b–5 claim challenging broker's system for disbursing proceeds from sale); Foltz v. U.S. News & World Report, Inc., 627 F.Supp. 1143 (D.D.C.1986) (sufficient causal connection based on alleged misstatements dissuading employees from delaying retirement which triggered a sale of stock under stock bonus plan). The "in connection with" requirement is discussed in § 13.2.3 *infra* (Practitioner's Edition only).

18. *See* the authorities in § 13.4 *infra*.

19. Ernst & Ernst v. Hochfelder, 425 U.S. 185, 96 S.Ct. 1375, 47 L.Ed.2d 668 (1976), *rehearing denied* 425 U.S. 986, 96 S.Ct. 2194, 48 L.Ed.2d 811 (1976). In 1980, the Court held that the scienter standard applies under Rule 10b–5 regardless of whether the action is a private damage action or an enforcement action brought by the Commission. Aaron v. SEC, 446 U.S. 680, 100 S.Ct. 1945, 64 L.Ed.2d 611 (1980), *on remand* 666 F.2d 5 (2d Cir.1981). *See* § 13.4 *infra* for a discussion of the scienter requirement.

showing of reckless conduct would satisfy the scienter requirement.[20] Nevertheless, the majority of lower court decisions has found that recklessness is sufficient to state a claim under Rule 10b–5.[21]

In order for a misstatement or omission to be actionable under Rule 10b–5, it must be a material one. The Supreme Court has defined materiality in terms of the type of information that a reasonable investor would consider significant in making an investment decision.[22] The materiality of a particular item is based on a highly factual inquiry and is to be determined within the total mix of information that is publicly available.[23]

Following the basic requirements for proving common law fraud, reliance is an element of any Rule 10b–5 claim.[24] In a sharply divided decision, the Supreme Court has recognized the fraud-on-the-market presumption of reliance[25] under which a showing that a material misstatement or omission adversely affected the market price creates a presumption of reliance.[26] Defendant may rebut the presumption of reliance or show that reliance was unreasonable.[27]

Again, as is the case with common law fraud, in addition to scienter, materiality, and reliance, causation is an element of a Rule 10b–5 action. Many courts have divided causation into two subparts: transaction causation and loss causation. Transaction causation requires a showing that but for the violations in question, the transaction would not have occurred (at least in the form that it took). Loss causation requires a showing of a causal nexus between the transaction and the plaintiff's loss.[28]

Also, as is the case with any fraud claim, the plaintiff must be able to establish damages. In most Rule 10b–5 litigation, the appropriate

---

20. *Hochfelder,* 425 U.S. at 193–94 n.12, 96 S.Ct. at 1381–1382 n. 12; *Aaron,* 446 U.S. at 690–91, 100 S.Ct. at 1952, 1953. The Court had the opportunity to decide this question in Central Bank of Denver, N.A. v. First Interstate Bank of Denver, ___ U.S. ___, 114 S.Ct. 1439, 128 L.Ed.2d 119 (1994) but disposed of the case on other grounds. *See* § 13.4, 13.16 *infra.*

21. *See* § 13.4 *infra.*

22. Basic, Inc. v. Levinson, 485 U.S. 224, 108 S.Ct. 978, 99 L.Ed.2d 194 (1988) (decided under Rule 10b–5); TSC Industries, Inc. v. Northway, Inc., 426 U.S. 438, 96 S.Ct. 2126, 48 L.Ed.2d 757 (1976) (decided under the proxy rules).

23. As materiality questions are highly fact-specific, summary judgment will rarely be appropriate. Materiality is discussed in § 13.5A *infra.*

24. Reliance is discussed in § 13.5B *infra.*

25. Basic, Inc. v. Levinson, 485 U.S. 224, 108 S.Ct. 978, 99 L.Ed.2d 194 (1988). *See, e.g.,* Finkel v. Docutel/Olivetti Corp., 817 F.2d 356 (5th Cir.1987), *cert. denied* 485 U.S. 959, 108 S.Ct. 1220, 99 L.Ed.2d 421 (1988). *See also, e.g.* Affiliated Ute Citizens of Utah v. United States, 406 U.S. 128, 92 S.Ct. 1456, 31 L.Ed.2d 741 (1972) (applying presumption of reliance in face-to-face transaction).

26. The availability of the presumption is premised on the existence of a relatively liquid and, hence, efficient market for the securities in question. *See* § 13.5B *infra.*

27. *See* § 13.5B *infra.*

28. Causation is discussed in § 13.6 *infra.*

measure of damages is the out-of-pocket loss proximately caused by the material misstatement or omission.[29]

Section 10(b) and Rule 10b–5 do not contain a statute of limitations for the implied remedy. Under the earlier decisions, the applicable statute of limitations for antifraud claims was generally the most analogous state statute of limitations.[30] Regardless of the applicable statute of limitations, the decisions formerly held that federal equitable tolling principles were applicable, so that the statute of limitations did not begin to run until the time the violation was discovered or reasonably should have been discovered. The Supreme Court, in a splintered 5–4 decision held that the applicable limitations period was to be found in the most analogous federal (rather than state) statute.[31] Accordingly, the Court applied a limitations period of one year from discovery (or when reasonable discovery should have occurred) but in no event may the action be brought more than three years after the transaction in question.

In Herman & MacLean v. Huddleston,[32] the Supreme Court held that the remedies under Section 11 of the 1933 Act, for misstatements in registration materials, and Rule 10b–5 are cumulative. Presumably, Rule 10b–5 remedies are cumulative with other express remedies as well.[33]

The courts have been extremely receptive in establishing federal jurisdiction for the 10b–5 claim. The statute prohibits the use of deceptive or manipulative devices utilizing an instrumentality of interstate commerce. A literal reading of the language might indicate that the fraudulent conduct would have to take place in interstate commerce. However, the provision has been more broadly interpreted to cover fraudulent conduct that sets the stage for a transaction taking place through an instrumentality of interstate commerce.[34] Thus, all that seems to be required is for some aspect of the securities transaction to have been carried out through the use of an instrumentality of interstate

---

29. *E.g.,* Wool v. Tandem Computers, Inc., 818 F.2d 1433 (9th Cir.1987); Harris v. Union Electric Co., 787 F.2d 355, 367 (8th Cir.1986), *cert. denied* 479 U.S. 823, 107 S.Ct. 94, 93 L.Ed.2d 45 (1986). On occasion, disgorgement of ill-gotten profits or benefit of the bargain might be a more appropriate measure of damages. Damages are discussed in § 13.7 *infra.*

30. *See* § 13.8 *infra.*

31. Lampf, Pleva, Lipkind, Prupis & Petigrow v. Gilbertson, 501 U.S. 350, 111 S.Ct. 2773, 115 L.Ed.2d 321 (1991).

32. 459 U.S. 375, 103 S.Ct. 683, 74 L.Ed.2d 548 (1983).

33. This includes the express remedies under §§ 12(1) and 12(2) of the 1933 Act. The measure of damages under § 12 of the 1933 Act is based on rescission. *See also* the remedy under § 18(a) of the 1934 Act (misstatements in false filings). The new remedies under the Insider Trading and Securities Fraud Sanctions Act of 1988, codified in § 21A of the 1934 Act (disgorgement of profits in an action by contemporaneous traders), are expressly in addition to any other express or implied remedies.

34. For example, a defendant will not escape the jurisdictional reach solely because his or her role in a transaction implicating interstate commerce was purely intrastate. Busch v. Buchman, Buchman & O'Brien Law Firm, 11 F.3d 1255 (5th Cir.1994). *See* § 14.1.1 *infra* for a more detailed discussion of the interstate commerce requirement.

commerce.[35] An intrastate telephone call has been held sufficient to satisfy the jurisdictional requirements of Rule 10b–5.[36] While a face-to-face conversation itself trigger will not satisfy the jurisdictional requirements, there will be 10b–5 jurisdiction if the conversations are part of a transaction that utilizes an instrumentality of interstate commerce.[37] The existence of a Rule 10b–5 claim will permit federal courts to hear state law claims under the doctrine of supplemental jurisdiction, also known as pendent jurisdiction.[38] Pendent or supplemental jurisdiction is not automatic. Federal courts frequently exercise their discretion to refuse to hear the state law claim in those instances that principles of federalism and comity convince the court to relinquish jurisdiction over the state claim so as to permit it to proceed in a state court forum.[39]

The sections that follow explore in detail the impact of Rule 10b–5 in securities litigation.

Deleted sections 13.2.2 and 13.2.3 can be found in the Practitioner's Edition.

§ 13.3 Standing to Sue Under SEC Rule 10b–5

The Purchaser/Seller Requirement

Rule 10b–5's applicability is premised upon a transaction that is "in

35. Kline v. Henrie, 679 F.Supp. 464, 469 (M.D.Pa.1988); United States v. Pray, 452 F.Supp. 788, 792 (M.D.Pa.1978); Harrison v. Equitable Life Assurance Society of the United States, 435 F.Supp. 281, 284–85 (W.D.Mich.1977); Levin v. Marder, 343 F.Supp. 1050, 1056 (W.D.Pa.1972). But see *Note, Oral Misrepresentations at "Roadshows" and in Other Settings: Illusory Liability Under Rule 10b–5?, 41 Wash. & Lee L.Rev. 995 (1984).*

36. Loveridge v. Dreagoux, 678 F.2d 870 (10th Cir.1982); Dupuy v. Dupuy, 511 F.2d 641 (5th Cir.1975), *appeal after remand* 551 F.2d 1005 (5th Cir.1977), *rehearing denied* 434 U.S. 911, 98 S.Ct. 312, 54 L.Ed.2d 197 (1977); Myzel v. Fields, 386 F.2d 718 (8th Cir.1967), *cert. denied* 390 U.S. 951, 88 S.Ct. 1043, 19 L.Ed.2d 1143 (1968). *Accord* Miller v. Affiliated Financial Corp., 600 F.Supp. 987, 992 (N.D.Ill.1984). The jurisdictional provisions are discussed in chapter 14 *infra*.

37. Leiter v. Kuntz, 655 F.Supp. 725 (D.Utah 1987) (mailing of financial statement by defendant's attorney plus use of telephone to change face-to-face meeting held sufficient to support Rule 10b–5 jurisdiction) *but cf.* Soper v. Valone, 110 F.R.D. 8 (W.D.N.Y.1985) (denying class action for lack of common questions where claims were based primarily on oral representations).

38. *See* United Mine Workers of America v. Gibbs, 383 U.S. 715, 86 S.Ct. 1130, 16 L.Ed.2d 218 (1966); 28 U.S.C.A. § 1367. *See also,* Lewis D. Lowenfels, Pendent Jurisdiction and The Federal Securities Act, 67 Colum.L.Rev. 474 (1967). *But see, e.g.,* Wentzka v. Gellman, 991 F.2d 423 (7th Cir.1993) (district court abused its discretion in retaining jurisdiction over state law claim after federal claim was dismissed due to expiration of limitations period).

39. *See, e.g.,* Kidder, Peabody & Co. v. Maxus Energy Corp., 925 F.2d 556 (2d Cir.1991), *cert. denied* 501 U.S. 1218, 111 S.Ct. 2829, 115 L.Ed.2d 998 (1991) (following declaratory judgment on the federal claim, it was appropriate to relinquish jurisdiction over state law claim notwithstanding the fact that the federal district court had invested considerable time trying to resolve the state law issues). Pendent jurisdiction is discussed in § 14.1 *infra*.

connection with" a "purchase or sale" of securities.[1] Six years after the initial recognition of an implied private 10b–5 remedy,[2] the Second Circuit held in Birnbaum v. Newport Steel Corp.,[3] that a 10b–5 plaintiff in a private damages action must have been either a purchaser or seller of the securities that form the basis of the material omission, misstatement, or deceptive conduct. The *Birnbaum* decision, which was adopted by the Supreme Court nearly twenty years later,[4] has been followed by a number of inroads in the purchaser/seller standing requirement.[5] A person's involvement in a securities transaction as an agent will not give rise to Rule 10b–5 standing to complain of any injury resulting therefrom unless that person can be classified as a purchaser or seller.[6]

After the purchaser/seller standing rule was developed, it soon became clear that a plaintiff shareholder satisfies the purchaser/seller standing requirement in a shareholder derivative suit brought on behalf of a corporation which was defrauded in connection with its purchase or sale of securities.[7] The ability to sue derivatively on behalf of a corporation is limited to shareholders and thus, for example, does not extend to nonshareholder officers.[8] Even being a shareholder will not assure standing to sue. The plaintiff must be able to establish the type of claim which can be brought derivatively. For example, a shareholder may not be able to sue a third party who entered into a securities transaction with the corporation.[9] However, where the shareholder was in fact a

---

§ 13.3

1. The definitions of purchase and sale are considered in § 13.2.3 *supra* (Practitioner's edition only). The "in connection with" requirement is considered in § 13.2.2 *supra* (Practitioner's edition only).

2. Kardon v. National Gypsum Co., 69 F.Supp. 512 (E.D.Pa.1946).

3. 193 F.2d 461 (2d Cir.1952), *cert. denied* 343 U.S. 956, 72 S.Ct. 1051, 96 L.Ed. 1356 (1952).

4. Blue Chip Stamps v. Manor Drug Stores, 421 U.S. 723, 95 S.Ct. 1917, 44 L.Ed.2d 539 (1975), *rehearing denied* 423 U.S. 884, 96 S.Ct. 157, 46 L.Ed.2d 114 (1975). *See also, e.g.,* Pelletier v. Stuart–James Co., 863 F.2d 1550, 1554–55 (11th Cir.1989) (plaintiff has burden of proving purchaser or seller status).

5. *See* Allen Fuller, Another Demise of the Birnbaum Doctrine: "Tolls the Knell of the Parting Day?" 25 U. Miami L.Rev. 131 (1970); Lewis D. Lowenfels, The Demise of the Birnbaum Doctrine: A New Era for Rule 10b–5, 54 Va.L.Rev. 268 (1968).

6. *See, e.g.,* Chanoff v. U.S. Surgical Corp., 857 F.Supp. 1011 (D.Conn.1994) (shareholder who was not a purchaser or seller could not complain of alleged material misrepresentations); Carapico v. Philadelphia Stock Exchange, 1994 WL 50295, [1993–1994 Transfer Binder] Fed. Sec. L. Rep. (CCH) ¶ 98,157 (E.D.Pa.1994) (floor broker could not maintain 10b–5 action against exchange since broker was neither a purchaser nor seller).

7. *E.g.* Frankel v. Slotkin, 984 F.2d 1328 (2d Cir.1993) (corporation issuing treasury shares in exchange for debentures was a seller of securities; shareholder could maintain a derivative action on allegations that corporation was fraudulently induced to sell its securities).

For discussion of derivative suits generally, *see* 2 James D. Cox, Thomas L. Hazen & F. Hodge O'Neal, Corporations ch. 15 (1995).

8. Powers v. British Vita, P.L.C., 842 F.Supp. 1573 (S.D.N.Y.1994).

9. *See* Peltz v. D'Urso, 1993 WL 664621, [1993–1994 Transfer Binder] Fed. Sec. L. Rep. (CCH) ¶ 98,203 (S.D.N.Y.1993) (fact that individual owned shares in and controlled corporation did not support 10b–5 action for purchase agreement involving corporation or its successor).

purchaser or seller, the Rule 10b–5 action can be maintained.[10] Additionally, purchase of the shares in a parent company will not necessarily support standing to complain of activities involving a subsidiary.[11]

Similar to the rule applicable to corporate derivative suits, it has been held that beneficiaries of a trust that sold shares in an alleged fraudulently induced transaction have standing to maintain a Rule 10b–5 action based on the derivative injury to the beneficiary.[12] Also, where a trust beneficiary has the right to approve the trustee's purchases from the trust, the beneficiary qualifies as a seller and can sue under Rule 10b–5 to challenge a purchase of stock by the trustee from the trust.[13] In addition to basing standing to sue on derivative or beneficial ownership, the record owner of the shares will generally have standing to sue.[14]

Share exchanges or cashouts pursuant to a corporate merger or other business combination will ordinarily constitute purchases and sales for Rule 10b–5 purposes.[15] However, when the merger is in fact a matter of form rather than substance a purchase and sale will not result from the share exchange.[16] Where a corporation ceases to exist due to a merger or other form of corporate reorganization, it has been held that the successor corporation although not itself a purchaser or seller of the securities in question, may maintain a Rule 10b–5 action for securities sold or purchased by the disappearing corporation.[17] In contrast, an exchange of shares or merger with a shell company that is undertaken merely for "corporate restructuring" has been held not to constitute a purchase or sale under Rule 10b–5.[18] This result finds some support both in "corporate law theory"[19] and SEC Rule 145 under the 1933 Act

10. Energy Factors Inc. v. Nuevo Energy Co., 1993 WL 454125, [1993–1994 Transfer Binder] Fed. Sec. L. Rep. (CCH) ¶ 98,059 (S.D.N.Y.1993) (parent corporation could bring 10b–5 action for stock owned by subsidiary where stock was purchased, held, and sold in parent's name).

11. Kaplan v. Utilicorp United, Inc., 9 F.3d 405 (5th Cir.1993) (purchaser of stock in parent corporation could not show that actions of subsidiary and second tier subsidiary were in connection with purchase of parent's stock).

12. Hackford v. First Security Bank of Utah, N.A., 521 F.Supp. 541 (D.Utah 1981); James v. Gerber Products Co., 483 F.2d 944 (6th Cir.1973).

13. Norris v. Wirtz, 719 F.2d 256 (7th Cir.1983), *cert. denied* 466 U.S. 929, 104 S.Ct. 1713, 80 L.Ed.2d 185 (1984).

14. *E.g.,* Visser v. Bruck, 1993 WL 205012, [1993–1994 Transfer Binder] Fed.Sec.L.Rep. (CCH) ¶ 97,644 (S.D.N.Y.1993) (record owner who purchased stock on behalf of family corporate network had standing to sue).

15. 7547 Corp. v. Parker & Parsley Development Partners, 38 F.3d 211 (5th Cir.1994) (roll-up transaction resulted in Rule 10b–5 standing); Goldberg v. Meridor, 567 F.2d 209 (2d Cir.1977), *cert. denied* 434 U.S. 1069, 98 S.Ct. 1249, 55 L.Ed.2d 771 (1978) (shareholder derivative suit).

16. Goldberg v. Hankin, 835 F.Supp. 815 (E.D.Pa.1993) (shareholder of bank that was transformed into bank holding company was not a purchaser as a result of the exchange of shares pursuant to the bank holding company's formation).

See also, e.g., SEC Rule 145, 17 C.F.R. § 230.145, which takes a similar "no sale" approach for mergers designed merely to change the state of incorporation. Rule 145 is discussed in § 5.2 *supra* and footnote 20 *infra*.

17. Nanfito v. Tekseed Hybrid Co., 341 F.Supp. 240 (D.Neb.1972), *affirmed* 473 F.2d 537 (8th Cir.1973). It has been questioned whether *Nanfito* can survive the Supreme Court's ruling in *Blue Chip Stamps*. Richard W. Jennings & Harold Marsh, Jr., Securities Regulation: Cases and Materials 1123 (6th ed. 1987).

18–19. See notes 18 and 19 on page 777.

which takes the position that there is no sale where the sole purpose of the merger is to change the issuer's domicile.[20] Even in such a case, however, where the issuer is a reporting company, an action for fraudulent conduct will lie under the proxy rules.[21] Other corporate transactions that may give rise to a shareholder derivative claim under Rule 10b–5 include corporate repurchases of its own shares at an inflated price, or an additional issuance of corporate shares on an unfavorable basis.[22] A purchase or sale pursuant to a tender offer can form the basis of a Rule 10b–5 claim.[23] However, neither a nontendering shareholder nor the target company will have standing under 10b–5[24] although, under appropriate circumstances, a remedy may exist under section 14(e) of the Williams Act.[25]

Consideration other than cash can form the basis of a sale. Thus, where securities are exchanged for other securities, a sale takes place.[26]

---

18. In re Penn Central Securities Litigation, 494 F.2d 528 (3d Cir.1974). *See also, e.g.,* Gelles v. TDA Industries, Inc., 44 F.3d 102 (2d Cir. 1994) (insider who exchanged shares pursuant to a "going private" transaction was not a purchaser or seller since he retained the same basic interest in the underlying assets). *Cf.* FMC Corp. v. Boesky, 727 F.Supp. 1182 (N.D.Ill.1989) (recapitalization which merely rearranged control among the owners did not render the corporation a purchaser or seller); Leoni v. Rogers, 719 F.Supp. 555 (E.D.Mich.1989) (holding company, created after the transaction in question, was not a purchaser or seller for Rule 10b–5 purposes).

19. *See* R. Jennings & H. Marsh *supra* footnote 17 at 1123.

20. 17 C.F.R. § 230.145. *See* § 5.2 *supra.* Such relocation mergers are becoming increasingly popular as a defensive tactic to an impending corporate takeover. *See* § 11.20 *supra.* Rule 145's exclusion does not apply to other restructuring mergers.

21. Rule 14a–9, 17 C.F.R. § 240.14a–9. *See* § 11.3 *supra.*

22. Alabama Farm Bureau Mutual Casualty Co. v. American Fidelity Life Insurance Co., 606 F.2d 602 (5th Cir.1979), *rehearing denied* 610 F.2d 818 (5th Cir.1980) (repurchase of shares); Bailes v. Colonial Press, Inc. 444 F.2d 1241 (5th Cir.1971) (issuance of shares); Ruckle v. Roto American Corp., 339 F.2d 24 (2d Cir.1964) (issuance of shares); Hooper v. Mountain States Securities Corp., 282 F.2d 195 (5th Cir.1960), *cert. denied* 365 U.S. 814, 81 S.Ct. 695, 5 L.Ed.2d 693 (1961) (issuance of shares). *But cf.* Smith v. Ayres, 845 F.2d 1360 (5th Cir.1988) (shareholder suing in individual capacity and complaining of corporation's issuance of shares lacked Rule 10b–5 standing).

23. In such a situation the selling shareholder is treated the same as any other seller. If anything, the 10b–5 liability for proscribed conduct is more likely because the transaction can be viewed as face-to-face rather than one taking place on a faceless market. *Cf.* Affiliated Ute Citizens of Utah v. United States, 406 U.S. 128, 92 S.Ct 1456, 31 L.Ed.2d 741 (1972), *rehearing denied* 407 U.S. 916, 92 S.Ct. 2430, 32 L.Ed.2d 692 (1972) (discussing reliance in a face-to-face transaction).

24. *See* Petersen v. Federated Development Co., 387 F.Supp. 355 (S.D.N.Y.1974). An issuer does not have standing in the absence of a sufficient purchaser or seller connection. Liberty National Insurance Holding Co. v. Charter Co., 734 F.2d 545 (11th Cir.1984). Woodward & Lothrop, Inc. v. Baron, 1984 WL 861, Fed.Sec.L.Rep. (CCH) ¶ 91,534 (D.D.C.1984).

25. *E.g.* H.K. Porter Co. v. Nicholson File Co., 482 F.2d 421 (1st Cir.1973); Butler Aviation International, Inc. v. Comprehensive Designers, Inc., 425 F.2d 842 (2d Cir.1970). *Cf.* Piper v. Chris–Craft Industries, Inc., 430 U.S. 1, 97 S.Ct. 926, 51 L.Ed.2d 124 (1977), *rehearing denied* 430 U.S. 976, 97 S.Ct. 1668, 52 L.Ed.2d 371 (1977) (competing tender offeror does not have standing under section 14(e) but indicating that a target company or a shareholder of the target company might be able to state such a claim). *See* § 11.19 *supra.*

26. *See, e.g.,* the authorities in footnote 15 *supra.*

Similarly, an employee who receives stock as part of a compensation package is a purchaser and therefore has standing to sue under Rule 10b–5.[27] Although, as mentioned above, an exchange of shares will ordinarily constitute a purchase and sale for Rule 10b–5 purposes, this has been held not to be the case where the exchange is pursuant to a going private transaction and the shareholder retains ownership of the corporation.[28] Since the transaction was structured so that the surviving shareholders had to exchange their shares for stock in a new corporation, it would seem appropriate to have recognized Rule 10b–5 standing for a surviving shareholder who is injured by fraud in connection with the transaction.

A pledge of securities generally is held to be a sale under the Exchange Act and accordingly the pledgees are "purchasers" and able to maintain a Rule 10b–5 cause of action, although there is some conflict on this point.[29] Also, a shareholder who is fraudulently induced to deliver his shares for collateral in a pledge may maintain a Rule 10b–5 action as a defrauded seller.[30] A secured creditor who is injured due to a foreclosure sale of securities has standing to sue under Rule 10b–5.[31] Although a pledge will generally qualify the pledgor as a seller, a mere bailment does not satisfy the purchase or sale requirement.[32] Similarly, absent extraordinary circumstances (if ever), a gift of securities will not provide a basis for a Rule 10b–5 action.[33]

Rule 10b–5 does not require that the plaintiff be the actual record-holder of the securities. Thus, for example, where pursuant to a contract to purchase, the plaintiff can claim equitable ownership of the securities, the Rule 10b–5 standing requirement will be satisfied.[34] On

---

27. *E.g.*, Rudinger v. Insurance Data Processing, Inc., 778 F.Supp. 1334 (E.D.Pa.1991).

28. Gelles v. TDA Industries, Inc., 1993 WL 275216, [1993–1994 Transfer Binder] Fed.Sec.L.Rep. (CCH) ¶ 97,690 (S.D.N.Y.1993). The court pointed out, however, that a shareholder that was cashed out and thereby forced to sell his or her shares would have Rule 10b–5 standing.

29. *E.g.* Madison Consultants v. FDIC, 710 F.2d 57 (2d Cir.1983); Mansbach v. Prescott, Ball & Turben, 598 F.2d 1017 (6th Cir.1979); Mallis v. Federal Deposit Insurance Corp., 568 F.2d 824 (2d Cir.1977), *cert. dismissed as improvidently granted* 435 U.S. 381, 98 S.Ct. 1117, 55 L.Ed.2d 357 (1978), *rehearing denied* 436 U.S. 915, 98 S.Ct. 2259, 56 L.Ed.2d 416 (1978).

30. Alley v. Miramon, 614 F.2d 1372 (5th Cir.1980).

31. Falls v. Fickling, 621 F.2d 1362 (5th Cir.1980); Bosse v. Crowell Collier & Macmillan, 565 F.2d 602 (9th Cir.1977); Dopp v. Franklin National Bank, 374 F.Supp. 904 (S.D.N.Y.1974); Cambridge Capital Corp. v. Northwestern National Bank of Minneapolis, 350 F.Supp. 829 (D.Minn.1972).

32. First Federal Savings & Loan v. Oppenheim, Appel, Dixon & Co., 629 F.Supp. 427, 439 (S.D.N.Y.1986).

33. Where a gift results in value (such as the creation of a public market) a sale may be found to exist. In the Matter of Capital General Corp., Sec. Act Rel. No. 33–7008, [1993 Transfer Binder] Fed. Sec. L. Rep. (CCH) ¶ 85,223 (SEC July 23, 1993). However, the existence of a sale will not establish a 10b–5 violation absent a showing that the donee (putative purchaser) was somehow defrauded. *Cf.* Note, Looking a Gift of Stock in the Mouth: Donative Transfers and Rule 10b–5, 88 Mich.L.Rev. 604 (1989) (arguing that under certain circumstances a gift should be treated as a sale for Rule 10b–5 purposes).

34. Bowers v. Allied Capital Corp., 1991 WL 335252, [1991–1992 Transfer Binder] Fed.Sec.L.Rep. (CCH) ¶ 96,544 (D.Me.1991) (agreement to transfer shares to voting trust in

the other hand, it has been held that an ex-wife's marital interest in her former husband's stock was not sufficiently identifiable so as to render negotiations concerning the division of marital property subject to Rule 10b–5.[35]

In order to have standing to sue for damages under Rule 10b–5, a purchase or sale must have taken place. Accordingly, an unenforceable oral promise to sell will not give rise to a Rule 10b–5 action.[36] Preliminary steps towards a sale will not qualify, but once there has been an enforceable agreement, the plaintiff can qualify as a purchaser.[37] The fact that the sale never took place, in breach of an enforceable contract of sale, does not preclude a 10b–5 action for that breach since a contract to sell a security is itself a security.[38]

A plaintiff who satisfies the purchaser-seller standing requirement may assign his or her claim and the suit by the assignee will not fail for lack of standing.[39] However, a trustee under a trust indenture seeking to bring suit on behalf of bondholders lacks requisite standing absent an express delegation or assignment of the right to bring suit in the indenture.[40] The fact that a former spouse of a security holder received the proceeds from a sale does not in itself constitute an assignment so as to give her standing to bring a Rule 10b–5 claim based on the sale.[41]

The complaint must set forth facts sufficient to establish the requisite standing. As a general proposition, fraud must be pleaded with particularity.[42] Accordingly, failure to plead facts demonstrating compli-

consideration for future payment could support 10b–5 standing); Duckworth v. Duckworth, 1991 WL 334827, [1991–1992 Transfer Binder] Fed.Sec.L.Rep. (CCH) ¶ 96,537 (S.D.Ga.1991) (shareholder who executed a promissory note to sell his shares was a seller and could maintain a 10b–5 action); Mullen v. Sweetwater Development Corp., 619 F.Supp. 809 (D.Colo.1985).

35. McHugh v. McHugh, 676 F.Supp. 856 (N.D.Ill.1988). *See also* Head v. Head, 759 F.2d 1172 (4th Cir.1985). *Cf.* Wilder v. Williams, 1989 WL 159590, [1989–1990 Transfer Binder] Fed.Sec.L.Rep. ¶ 94,778 (W.D.Pa.1989) (shareholders of corporation purchasing the stock in question were neither purchasers nor "real parties in interest").

36. Kagan v. Edison Brothers Stores, Inc., 907 F.2d 690 (7th Cir.1990).

37. *See, e.g.,* Chariot Group, Inc. v. American Acquisition Partners, L.P., 751 F.Supp. 1144 (S.D.N.Y.1990), *affirmed without opinion* 932 F.2d 956 (2d Cir.1991) (dismissing Rule 10b–5 action where the negotiations never resulted in a binding contract of sale); Cook v. Goldman, Sachs & Co., 726 F.Supp. 151 (S.D.Tex.1989).

38. *See* Chariot Group, Inc. v. American Acquisition Partners, L.P., 751 F.Supp. 1144 (S.D.N.Y.1990), *affirmed without opinion* 932 F.2d 956 (2d Cir.1991) (but finding that a binding agreement had not been reached). *Cf.* SEC v. Lauer, 864 F.Supp. 784 (N.D.Ill. 1994) (contract to purchase a nonexistent security was itself a security and hence subject to the antifraud proscriptions of section 17(a) of the 1933 Act).

39. *E.g.,* AmeriFirst Bank v. Bomar, 757 F.Supp. 1365 (S.D.Fla.1991).

40. Continental Bank, N.A. v. Caton, 1990 WL 129452, [1990–1991 Transfer Binder] Fed.Sec.L.Rep. (CCH) ¶ 95,623 (D.Kan.1990). The Trust Indenture Act of 1939, 15 U.S.C.A. § 77aaa *et seq.* is discussed in chapter 16 *infra.*

41. Davidson v. Belcor, Inc., 933 F.2d 603 (7th Cir.1991) (property settlement in divorce action did not create a constructive trust in former wife's favor with regard to securities owned by the former husband).

42. Fed.R.Civ.P. 9(b). *See* § 13.8.1 *infra* (Practitioner's edition only).

ance with the purchaser/seller standing requirement will result in dismissal of the Rule 10b–5 claim.[43]

The purchaser/seller requirement is not easily circumvented. For example, courts will not permit plaintiffs to avoid the implications of the *Blue Chip Stamps* rule. Thus, although there is some authority to the contrary, Rule 10b–5's purchaser-seller standing requirements cannot be circumvented by bringing a RICO action.[44]

Injunctive Relief

There is authority to the effect that a person need be neither a purchaser nor a seller of the securities in order to maintain an action for injunctive relief under Rule 10b–5.[45] There is also some authority to the contrary.[46] Some courts take the position that the equitable relief exception to the purchaser/seller requirement applies only where the relief sought is prophylactic.[47] Furthermore, even among those courts that do not require the plaintiff in an injunction action to have been a purchaser or seller, the plaintiff must still be able to show some direct injury resulting from the alleged Rule 10b–5 violation.[48]

Variations on the Purchaser/Seller Requirement; Forced Sellers

Following in the wake of the *Birnbaum* decision the courts created a number of doctrines (or exceptions) to give 10b–5 standing to persons who would not otherwise directly qualify as purchasers or sellers. Under the "aborted seller" rule, where the defendant enters into a contract

---

43. *E.g.*, International Data Bank, Ltd. v. Zepkin, 812 F.2d 149 (4th Cir.1987); Prudential Insurance Co. of America v. BMC Indus., Inc., 1987 WL 6410, [1987 Transfer Binder] Fed.Sec.L.Rep. (CCH) ¶ 93,120 (S.D.N.Y.1987); Citron v. Rollins Environmental Services, Inc., 644 F.Supp. 733 (D.Del.1986).

44. International Data Bank Ltd. v. Zepkin, 812 F.2d 149 (4th Cir.1987); Brannan v. Eisenstein, 804 F.2d 1041, 1046 (8th Cir.1986); Chief Consolidated Mining Co. v. Sunshine Mining Co., 725 F.Supp. 1191 (D.Utah 1989). *But see* SIPC v. Vigman, 908 F.2d 1461 (9th Cir. 1991), *judgment reversed on other grounds* 503 U.S. 258, 112 S.Ct. 1311, 117 L.Ed.2d 532 (1992). RICO is discussed in § 19.3 *infra*. *See also* the text accompanying footnotes 96–97 *infra*.

45. Mutual Shares Corp. v. Genesco, Inc., 384 F.2d 540 (2d Cir.1967); Tully v. Mott Supermarkets, Inc., 540 F.2d 187, 194 (3d Cir.1976) (dictum); Granada Investments, Inc. v. DWG Corp., 717 F.Supp. 533 (N.D.Ohio 1989); Hanna Mining Co. v. Norcen Energy Resources Ltd., 574 F.Supp. 1172 (N.D.Ohio 1982) (Target of tender offer entitled to injunctive relief); Warner Communications, Inc. v. Murdoch, 581 F.Supp. 1482, 1494 (D.Del.1984); Hundahl v. United Benefit Life Insurance Co., 465 F.Supp. 1349, 1357–59 (N.D.Tex.1979). *Cf.* Advanced Resources International, Inc. v. Tri–Star Petroleum Co., 4 F.3d 327 (4th Cir.1993) (not deciding whether to recognize exception for injunctive relief since plaintiffs were causally too removed to have standing). *Contra* Cowin v. Bresler, 741 F.2d 410 (D.C.Cir.1984).

46. Cowin v. Bresler, 741 F.2d 410 (D.C.Cir.1984); Packer v. Yampol, 630 F.Supp. 1237 (S.D.N.Y.1986) (plaintiff cannot sue on behalf of investing public generally); Atlantic Federal Savings & Loan Ass'n v. Dade Savings & Loan Ass'n, 592 F.Supp. 1089 (S.D.Fla. 1984).

47. Doll v. James Martin Associates (Holdings) Ltd., 600 F.Supp. 510, 522–23 (E.D.Mich.1984).

48. Advanced Resources International, Inc. v. Tri–Star Petroleum Co., 4 F.3d 327 (4th Cir.1993) (consulting firm lacked 10b–5 standing to bar company from using report in connection with attempts to sell the company's securities).

to purchase securities without any intention of paying for them, the plaintiff would-be seller has been held to have a 10b–5 cause of action.[49] Other courts applying the "aborted seller" doctrine required the plaintiff to demonstrate either a clear "investment decision" or that granting standing would be "in the public interest."[50] Fraudulently inducing shareholders not to part with their shares will not by itself support a Rule 10b–5 damage action.[51] Even with additional compelling factors, it is highly doubtful that the "aborted seller" doctrine survives the Supreme Court decision in *Blue Chip Stamps*.[52] However, as noted above, when there is a binding contract of sale, a would-be purchaser or seller can bring suit since the contract itself is a security.[53]

When a shareholder is frozen out of a corporation or otherwise put in the position of a "forced seller," Rule 10b–5 standing ordinarily will exist even though there was no voluntary investment decision.[54] It has been said that the forced seller doctrine should be interpreted narrowly in light of *Blue Chip Stamps*.[55] Forced purchasers also have standing under Rule 10b–5.[56]

---

49. *E.g.* Richardson v. MacArthur, 451 F.2d 35 (10th Cir.1971); Allico National Corp. v. Amalgamated Meat Cutters & Butcher Workmen of North America, 397 F.2d 727 (7th Cir.1968); A.T. Brod & Co. v. Perlow, 375 F.2d 393 (2d Cir.1967). Commerce Reporting Co. v. Puretec, 290 F.Supp. 715 (S.D.N.Y.1968). *But see* Keers & Co. v. American Steel & Pump Corp., 234 F.Supp. 201 (S.D.N.Y.1964).

50. Abrahamson v. Fleschner, 568 F.2d 862, 868 (2d Cir.1977), *cert. denied* 436 U.S. 905, 98 S.Ct. 2236, 56 L.Ed.2d 403 (1978). *See also, e.g.,* Gaudin v. KDI Corp., 576 F.2d 708, 716 (6th Cir.1978); Southeastern Waste Treatment, Inc. v. Chem–Nuclear Systems, Inc., 506 F.Supp. 944, 953 (N.D.Ga.1980).

51. *See, e.g.,* Chanoff v. U.S. Surgical Corp., 857 F.Supp. 1011 (D.Conn.1994).

52. *See, e.g.,* Gutman v. Howard Savings Bank, 748 F.Supp. 254 (D.N.J.1990) (shareholder induced not to sell by alleged fraud lacked standing under Rule 10b–5); Schwartz v. Duckett, 1989 WL 16054, [1989 Transfer Binder] Fed.Sec.L.Rep. (CCH) ¶ 94,320 (S.D.N.Y. 1989) (fraud or omission inducing plaintiff not to sell could not bring Rule 10b–5 claim); Boardman v. Lipton, 605 F.Supp. 970 (S.D.N.Y.1985) (allegations of conspiracy to freeze out plaintiff minority shareholder by means of deception and manipulation dismissed where plaintiff was still a shareholder and therefore lacked standing).

Although an aborted seller lacks standing, an alleged scheme to encourage security holders not to sell may form the basis of criminal sanctions. United States v. Livieratos, 853 F.2d 922 (3d Cir.1988), *affirming* 659 F.Supp. 692 (D.N.J.1987).

53. *See* text accompanying footnote 38 *supra.*

54. Alley v. Miramon, 614 F.2d 1372 (5th Cir.1980). Greenstein v. Paul, 400 F.2d 580 (2d Cir.1968); Vine v. Beneficial Finance Co., 374 F.2d 627 (2d Cir.1967), *cert. denied* 389 U.S. 970, 88 S.Ct. 463, 19 L.Ed.2d 460 (1967); In re Union Exploration Partners Securities Litigation, 1992 WL 203812, [1992 Transfer Binder] Fed.Sec.L.Rep. (CCH) ¶ 96,872 (C.D.Cal.1992) (Supreme Court's decision in Virginia Bancshares v. Sandberg, 501 U.S. 1083, 111 S.Ct. 2749, 115 L.Ed.2d 929 (1991), did not negate forced seller standing under Rule 10b–5).

55. *See* Arnold v. Moran, 687 F.Supp. 232 (E.D.Va.1988); Teltronics Services, Inc. v. Anaconda–Ericsson, Inc., 587 F.Supp. 724 (E.D.N.Y.1984) (liquidation in bankruptcy does not qualify as forced sale of shareholders stock), *affirmed* 762 F.2d 185 (2d Cir.1985); Arnesen v. Shawmut County Bank, 504 F.Supp. 1077 (D.Mass.1980) (forced seller exception should be interpreted narrowly in light of *Blue Chip Stamps*). *See also, e.g.* Rodriguez Cadiz v. Mercado Jimenez, 579 F.Supp. 1176 (D.Puerto Rico 1983) (no forced seller standing where plaintiff retained shares). *Cf.* Scattergood v. Perelman, 945 F.2d 618 (3d Cir.1991) (minority shareholder who did not have a right to vote on freeze-out could not establish a causal relationship between the misrepresentations and the merger).

56. *E.g.* Zweig v. Hearst Corp., 594 F.2d 1261 (9th Cir.1979).

Would-be Purchasers and Sellers; Deferred Sellers

Most of the foregoing inroads on the *Birnbaum* doctrine seem to survive the Supreme Court's adoption of the purchaser/seller standing requirement in Blue Chip Stamps v. Manor Drug Stores.[57] In that case the Court held that the plaintiffs had a right to purchase the securities in question under an antitrust consent decree. The plaintiffs refrained from purchasing the securities, allegedly relying on misleading statements made by the defendants designed to deter the planned purchase; the Court held that these would-be purchasers could not state a 10b–5 cause of action. A necessary corollary to this holding would seem to be that mere "would be" sellers cannot raise 10b–5 claims.[58] *Blue Chip Stamps* is best described as a case of the frustrated purchaser since the plaintiff had a right to purchase the securities under the terms of a consent decree. It would seem that for similar reasons, the former exception to the *Birnbaum* doctrine for the "frustrated seller"[59] most likely does not survive *Blue Chip Stamps*.[60] Nonrecognition of the frustrated seller exception appears to be mandated by the *Blue Chip Stamps* rationale. In one post–*Blue Chip* decision on point, the court did not reach the issue of the viability of the frustrated seller doctrine since the pleadings were deficient because "a clear indication of an alleged initial intention to sell is critical."[61] A seller who is fraudulently induced to delay the sale of securities has been held not to have standing under Rule 10b–5; the court refused to consider the later sale as part of the same transaction in which the fraud occurred.[62] The limiting trend

57.   421 U.S. 723, 95 S.Ct. 1917, 44 L.Ed.2d 539 (1975), *rehearing denied* 423 U.S. 884, 96 S.Ct. 157, 46 L.Ed.2d 114 (1975). *See* Schneider *supra* note 7; Note, Standing Under Rule 10b–5 after *Blue Chip,* 75 Mich.L.Rev. 413 (1976).

58.   *E.g.,* Calenti v. Boto, 24 F.3d 335 (1st Cir.1994) (alleged misstatements in connection with proposed amendment to articles of incorporation to eliminate the right to redeem preferred shares were not actionable under 10b–5 as there was neither a purchase nor sale); Metropolitan Life Insurance Co. v. RJR Nabisco, Inc. 716 F.Supp. 1504 (S.D.N.Y. 1989). *See also, e.g.,* Ruff v. Genesis Holding Corp., 728 F.Supp. 225 (S.D.N.Y.1990) (mere offeree was only a would-be purchaser and thus lacked Rule 10b–5 standing).

59.   *See* Neuman v. Electronic Speciality Co., 1969 WL 2828, [1969–70 Transfer Binder] Fed.Sec.L.Rep. (CCH) ¶ 92,591 (N.D.Ill.1969); Stockwell v. Reynolds & Co., 252 F.Supp. 215 (S.D.N.Y.1965). *But see* Iroquois Industries Inc. v. Syracuse China Corp., 417 F.2d 963 (2d Cir.1969), *cert. denied* 399 U.S. 909, 90 S.Ct. 2199, 26 L.Ed.2d 561 (1970) (frustrated purchaser does not have standing). *Contra* Morrow v. Schapiro, 334 F.Supp. 399 (E.D.Mo. 1971); Berne Street Enterprises, Inc. v. American Export Isbrandtsen Co., 1970 WL 268, [1969–1970 Transfer Binder] Fed.Sec.L.Rep. (CCH) ¶ 92,711 (S.D.N.Y.1970).

60.   The aborted or frustrated seller basis for standing was rejected in Weiner v. Rooney, Pace Inc., 1987 WL 11281, [1987 Transfer Binder] Fed.Sec.L.Rep. (CCH) ¶ 93,174 (S.D.N.Y.1987). *See also* Nevitsky v. Manufacturers Hanover Brokerage Services, 654 F.Supp. 116 (S.D.N.Y.1987) (broker's refusal to consummate sale could not support a 10b–5 claim due to failure to satisfy the purchaser/seller standing requirement).

61.   Madison Fund, Inc. v. Charter Co., 406 F.Supp. 749, 753 (S.D.N.Y.1975).

An oral contract for sale can be the basis of a Rule 10b–5 claim. Threadgill v. Black, 730 F.2d 810 (D.C.Cir.1984). However, there must have been an enforceable contract. Reprosystem, B.V. v. SCM Corp., 727 F.2d 257, 265 (2d Cir.1984), *cert. denied* 469 U.S. 828, 105 S.Ct. 110, 83 L.Ed.2d 54 (1984).

62.   Gurley v. Documation, Inc., 674 F.2d 253 (4th Cir.1982); Schwartz v. Duckett, 1989 WL 16054, [1989 Transfer Binder] Fed.Sec.L.Rep. (CCH) ¶ 94,320 (S.D.N.Y.1989); Roggow v. Dean Witter Reynolds, Inc., 1987 WL 43398, [1987–88 Transfer Binder] Fed.Sec.L.Rep.

in Supreme Court decisions makes it difficult to justify an expansive extension of *Blue Chip Stamps* to grant Rule 10b–5 standing to a frustrated seller.[63] In other contexts however, the courts should continue a reasonably flexible approach.

The Necessity of an Investment Decision

It is generally held that a purchase does not take place until "the parties to the transaction are committed to each other."[64] Courts have dealt with the question of the point at which a party becomes committed under what has come to be known as the "investment decision" doctrine.[65] The concept of sale normally implies that an investment decision has been made, but it need not be made by the plaintiff. For example, a post *Blue Chip* decision recognized a pledgor's standing to sue although the sale had been at the pledgee's discretion.[66]

The investment decision doctrine generally requires that the plaintiff has had some discretion with regard to the transaction in question. However, the fact that purchases were made as a result of "automatic" transactions pursuant to an employee benefit plan will not preclude standing so long as the plaintiff's participation in the plan was voluntary.[67] A corollary to the investment decision requirement is that a Rule 10b–5 action will not lie for alleged misrepresentations after the plaintiff has already made his or her decision to invest.[68] Thus, for example, a general partner's capital infusion into an ongoing enterprise does not necessarily constitute a new investment decision.[69]

(CCH) ¶ 93,541 (D.Minn.1987). *See also* Baum v. Phillips, Appel & Walden, 648 F.Supp. 1518 (S.D.N.Y.1986), *affirmed* 867 F.2d 776 (2d Cir.1989) (failure to allege fraudulent inducement of retention of stock; deferred sale claim dismissed).

63. *See* Iroquois Industries, Inc. v. Syracuse China Corp., 417 F.2d 963 (2d Cir.1969), *cert. denied* 399 U.S. 909, 90 S.Ct. 2199, 26 L.Ed.2d 561 (1970).

64. *E.g.,* Radiation Dynamics, Inc. v. Goldmuntz, 464 F.2d 876, 891 (2d Cir.1972); Department of Economic Development v. Arthur Andersen & Co., 683 F.Supp. 1463, 1475 (S.D.N.Y.1988); Lewis v. Bradley, 599 F.Supp. 327 (S.D.N.Y.1984); Bolton v. Gramlich, 540 F.Supp. 822, 839–40 (S.D.N.Y.1982); Eriksson v. Galvin, 484 F.Supp. 1108, 1119 (S.D.N.Y.1980); Rochambeau v. Brent Exploration, Inc., 79 F.R.D. 381, 384 (D.Colo.1978).

65. *See* § 5.4 *supra,* § 7.5.4 (Practitioner's Edition only) *supra* and § 13.8 *infra.*

66. Madison Consultants v. FDIC, 710 F.2d 57 (2d Cir.1983). *Accord* Chemical Bank v. Arthur Andersen & Co., 726 F.2d 930 (2d Cir.1984), *cert. denied* 469 U.S. 884, 105 S.Ct. 253, 83 L.Ed.2d 190 (1984) (pledge of stock to secure commercial loan is a sale). *See also* cases cited in footnotes 18 and 29 *supra.*

67. Deutschman v. Beneficial Corp., 761 F.Supp. 1080 (D.Del.1991) (court rejected defendants' contention that standing should be denied since at designated intervals investment was automatically deducted from paycheck and plaintiff was credited with stock purchase).

68. Handelsman v. Gilford Securities, Inc., 720 F.Supp. 1319 (N.D.Ill.1989), s.c. 726 F.Supp. 673 (N.D.Ill.1989). However, when plaintiff was denied the opportunity to undo the transaction because of a material omission of a "hidden switch" shortly after the deal was consummated, Rule 10b–5 standing was sustained. In Bruan v. Lipuma, 1990 WL 148411, [1990–1991 Transfer Binder] Fed.Sec.L.Rep. (CCH) ¶ 95,612 (E.D.N.Y.1990) investor purchased a limited partnership interest but was not informed of the fact that his funds were being applied to the purchase of a different limited partnership until after the switch was an accomplished fact. The court noted that even if the decision to retain the limited partnership interest was not the basis of standing, the purchase of the initial interest was.

69. Klaers v. St. Peter, 942 F.2d 535 (8th Cir.1991).

Rights and Options

Contract rights to purchase (or sell) securities can classify the holder as a purchaser or seller of the underlying security, or may themselves be securities.[70] Thus, for example, a preemptive right to purchase shares is a contract to purchase and can provide the basis for Rule 10b–5 standing.[71] Similarly, an executory contract to acquire shares pursuant to an employment agreement can form the basis of a Rule 10b–5 claim.[72]

Courts have recently been faced with the issue of whether someone injured in connection with an option transaction can sue under Rule 10b–5 for fraud involving the underlying security.[73] Option contracts when marketed separately or traded on an exchange constitute securities.[74] It has been held that insider trading of the company's stock coupled with nondisclosures, does not give rise to 10b–5 standing for purchasers and sellers of stock options.[75] Any fraud or wrongdoing related directly to options, however, would presumably give rise to Rule 10b–5 liability.[76]

A related question is whether insiders who trade options rather than stock are liable to traders in the stock. There is every reason to believe that liability would exist due to the insiders' duty to the corporation and its shareholders, assuming that all other elements of a Rule 10b–5 claim have been satisfied.[77] There can be no question that shareholders and optionholders can be injured by material misstatements or omissions relating to the issuer.[78] The only reason for cutting off liability to

70. *Cf.* Kari Shumpei Okamoto, Oversimplification and the SEC's Treatment of Derivative Securities Trading by Corporate Insiders, 1993 Wis. L. Rev. 1287.

The definition of "security" is considered in § 1.5 *supra.* Derivative Securities are discussed in § 1.5.1 *supra.*

71. Brennan v. EMDE Medical Research, Inc., 652 F.Supp. 255 (D.Nev.1986). *See also* Zlotnick v. TIE Communications, 836 F.2d 818 (3d Cir.1988) (short seller has Rule 10b–5 standing).

72. Technology Exchange Corp. of America, Inc. v. Grant County State Bank, 646 F.Supp. 179 (D.Colo.1986). *See also* footnote 27 *supra.*

73. *See* § 1.5 *supra* for a discussion of the definition of "security."

74. O'Connor & Associates v. Dean Witter Reynolds, Inc., 529 F.Supp. 1179 (S.D.N.Y. 1981). *See* SEC, Report of the Special Study of the Options Markets, 96th Cong. 1st Sess. (1978).

75. Laventhall v. General Dynamics Corp., 704 F.2d 407 (8th Cir.1983), *cert. denied* 464 U.S. 846, 104 S.Ct. 150, 78 L.Ed.2d 140 (1983); In re McDonnell Douglas Corporation Securities Litigation, 567 F.Supp. 126 (E.D.Mo.1983).

76. *See, e.g.,* French v. Merrill Lynch, Pierce, Fenner & Smith, Inc., 784 F.2d 902 (9th Cir.1986) (broker's mischaracterization of a call option purchase as a "closing" rather than an "opening" order might be material to the reasonable investor). Materiality is discussed in § 11.4 *supra* and § 13.5A *infra. See also, e.g.,* Prudential–Bache Securities, Inc. v. Cullather, 678 F.Supp. 601 (E.D.Va.1987) (customer could seek rescission and restitutionary relief under section 29(b) for broker's fraud in options transaction). Section 29(b) is discussed in § 13.14 *infra.*

77. *See, e.g.,* SEC v. Texas Gulf Sulphur Co., 401 F.2d 833 (2d Cir.1968), *cert. denied* 394 U.S. 976, 89 S.Ct. 1454, 22 L.Ed.2d 756 (1969). The scope of insider liability under Rule 10b–5 is considered in § 13.9 *infra.*

78. *See, e.g.,* In re Adobe Systems, Inc. Securities Litigation, 139 F.R.D. 150 (N.D.Cal. 1991) (optionholders had standing to complain about alleged misleading statements designed to inflate stock price). *See also, e.g.,* Campbell v. National Media Corp., 1994 WL

optionholders is on the ground that their injury is too remote. Even if such an unfortunate rule eventually prevails with regard to optionholders' standing, it should not be adopted to shareholder suits merely because insiders chose to trade options rather than stock.

It is clear that Congress contemplated the commission of fraud in connection with securities options trading as comparable to fraud in connection with equity and debt securities.[79] It would thus appear that optionholders should be given the same rights of action with regard to options trading as other securities holders.[80] The Third Circuit has accepted this view in upholding an option trader's claim alleging that misrepresentations by a corporation affected the price of the underlying stock.[81] The court pointed out that although a transactional nexus might be lacking in an insider trading case,[82] such is not the situation where an affirmative misrepresentation is involved.[83] Thus, while an option trader's claim against a corporate official accused of illegal insider trading in the underlying security is highly doubtful,[84] an option trader should be able to state a claim in dissemination cases, where the defendant has caused misleading information to be injected into the market and thereby has affected the price of both the options and the underlying securities. While it is true that optionholder standing increases the defendant's liability, there are no policy reasons (other than the specious arguments of remoteness or the desirability of limiting liability) that would dictate cutting off the option traders' claims.[85]

612807, [1994–1995 Transfer Binder] Fed. Sec. L. Rep. (CCH) ¶ 98,449 (E.D.Pa.1994) (fraudulent inducement to exercise option could support a Rule 10b–5 claim).

79. Section 20(d) of the Exchange Act, 15 U.S.C.A. § 78t(d).

80. *See, e.g.,* Gregory S. Crespi, Private Rights of Action for Option Position Holders Under Section 20(d) of the Securities Exchange Act, 16 Sec.Reg.L.J. 21 (1988); Steve Thel, Closing a Loophole: Insider Trading in Standardized Options, 16 Fordham Urb.L.J. 573 (1987); William K. S. Wang, A Cause of Action for Option Traders Against Insider Option Traders, 101 Harv.L.Rev. 1056 (1988); Note, Private Causes of Action for Option Investors Under SEC Rule 10b–5: A Policy, Doctrinal, and Economic Analysis, 100 Harv.L.Rev. 1959 (1987); Note, Securities Regulation for a Changing Market: Option Trader Standing Under Rule 10b–5, 97 Yale L.J. 623 (1988).

81. Deutschman v. Beneficial Corp., 841 F.2d 502 (3d Cir.1988). *See also* Zlotnick v. TIE Communications, 836 F.2d 818 (3d Cir.1988) (short seller has 10b–5 standing).

Other courts have agreed. *E.g.,* Liebhard v. Square D Co., 811 F.Supp. 354 (N.D.Ill. 1992) (option traders had standing to sue under Rule 10b–5 for affirmative misrepresentation regarding takeover negotiations); Margolis v. Caterpillar, Inc., 815 F.Supp. 1150 (C.D.Ill.1991) (option holder established reliance on market and was adequate class representative).

82. *See* Laventhall v. General Dynamics Corp., 704 F.2d 407 (8th Cir.1983), *cert. denied* 464 U.S. 846, 104 S.Ct. 150, 78 L.Ed.2d 140 (1983). Insider trading and the probable absence of a private remedy in a faceless market are discussed in § 13.9 *infra.*

83. 841 F.2d at 507.

84. Laventhall v. General Dynamics Corp., 704 F.2d 407 (8th Cir.1983), *cert. denied* 464 U.S. 846, 104 S.Ct. 150, 78 L.Ed.2d 140 (1983); Starkman v. Warner Communications, Inc., 671 F.Supp. 297 (S.D.N.Y.1987).

85. The Third Circuit properly characterized the defendant's argument to the contrary as "chimerical". Deutschman v. Beneficial Corp., 841 F.2d 502, 507 (3d Cir.1988). *See also, e.g.,* In re Gulf Oil/Cities Service Tender Offer Litigation, 725 F.Supp. 712 (S.D.N.Y. 1989) (purchaser of call options for securities of target company had standing under both Rule 10b–5 and section 14(e) since tender offers affect option traders' investment decisions

However, there is some authority for narrowing the scope of liability and thus denying standing to option traders.[86] The scienter requirement limits liability where the defendant has not acted intentionally, or at least recklessly.[87] Where such culpable conduct is involved it makes no sense to say that a class of foreseeable and deserving plaintiffs should be cut off simply because it would place too great a burden on the defendant that is guilty of such a serious wrong.[88]

Effect of Establishing Standing; Possible Alternative Remedies

A plaintiff demonstrating sufficient standing is not home free. There must be a direct causal connection between the violation and injury. It is not enough that the price in any particular transaction was affected by some prior fraud, misstatement or omission; the wrongdoing itself must have occurred in connection with that securities transaction.[89]

The Rule 10b–5 standing requirement will not be a bar to relief if the plaintiff can state a claim under some other antifraud provision.[90] Thus, for example, a shareholder who has neither purchased nor sold securities but is injured in a vote governed by federal proxy regulation may be able to sue under Rule 14a–9.[91] Similarly, an action might lie in the hands of a target company or a non-selling target company shareholder challenging a tender offer under section 14(e).[92] Although the courts are in conflict as to whether a private remedy is to be implied under section 17(a) of the 1933 Act,[93] there is some authority supporting a private remedy in the hands of an offeree (would-be-purchaser) of securities.[94] The Supreme Court expressly reserved and did not pass

---

in the same way as target company shareholders). *But see* Data Controls North, Inc. v. Financial Corp. of America, 20 Sec.Reg. & L.Rep. (BNA) 840 (D.Md.1988) (option traders assumed risk of speculative nature of investments). The assumption of risk argument is highly questionable since materially misleading information should not be viewed as an assumed risk.

86. *See, e.g.,* Lerner v. SciMed Life Systems, Inc., 1994 WL 374319, [1993–1994 Transfer Binder] Fed. Sec. L. Rep. (CCH) ¶ 98,232 (D.Minn.1994).

87. *See* § 13.4 *infra.*

88. *See* footnote 81 *supra.*

89. Fuchs v. Swanton Corp., 482 F.Supp. 83 (S.D.N.Y.1979). The "in connection with" requirement of Rule 10b–5 arises in the causation context. *See* § 13.2.2 *supra.*

90. The overwhelming majority of cases hold that the Rule 10b–5 is cumulative with other remedies. *See* § 13.2 *supra.*

91. 17 C.F.R. § 240.14a–9. *See* §§ 11.3–11.5 *supra.* *Cf.* SEC v. National Securities, Inc., 393 U.S. 453, 89 S.Ct. 564, 21 L.Ed.2d 668 (1969) (finding a 10b–5 violation with regard to a proxy statement not governed by Rule 14a–9).

92. 15 U.S.C.A. § 78n(e). *See* footnote 25 *supra.*

93. 15 U.S.C.A. § 77q(a). *See* § 13.13 *infra.*

94. Reid v. Madison, 438 F.Supp. 332 (E.D.Va.1977); Wulc v. Gulf & Western Industries Inc., 400 F.Supp. 99, 102–03 (E.D.Pa.1975). *Contra, e.g.,* Simmons v. Wolfson, 428 F.2d 455 (6th Cir.1970), *cert. denied* 400 U.S. 999, 91 S.Ct. 459, 27 L.Ed.2d 450 (1971); Greater Iowa Corp. v. McLendon, 378 F.2d 783 (8th Cir.1967); Darvin v. Bache Halsey Stuart Shields, Inc., 479 F.Supp. 460 (S.D.N.Y.1979). Frigitemp Corp. v. Financial Dynamics Fund, Inc., 1974 WL 466, [1974–1975 Transfer Binder] Fed.Sec.L.Rep. (CCH) ¶ 94,907 (S.D.N.Y.1974), *affirmed on other grounds* 524 F.2d 275 (2d Cir.1975).

upon the section 17(a) question in *Blue Chip Stamps*.[95] Thus, although the 10b–5 purchaser/seller standing limitation precludes private damages for many potential plaintiffs, some of them may have redress under other provisions of the securities acts.

Other alternative remedies may exist outside of the securities law. For example, the Ninth Circuit has held that in a RICO action based on securities fraud, it is not necessary that the plaintiff have been a purchaser or seller of securities.[96] Other Courts have taken a contrary position.[97] This is probably the better view, since RICO liability is derivative of the underlying securities fraud.

§ 13.4 Rule 10b–5 and the Scienter Requirement; Section 17(a) and Rule 14a–9 Compared

Rule 10b–5 describes the type of conduct proscribed but it does not set out the appropriate standard of culpability. The question has thus arisen as to whether the securities laws reach negligent misconduct or are limited to intentional misstatements and omissions. After twenty years of conflicting cases,[1] the Supreme Court held in Ernst & Ernst v. Hochfelder[2] that in order to establish a valid claim for damages under Rule 10b–5 it must be proven that the defendant acted with scienter. It subsequently was held in Aaron v. SEC[3] that the scienter standard applies under Rule 10b–5 regardless of whether the action is one for damages or an enforcement action brought by the Commission.[4] The

---

95. 421 U.S. 723, 733 n. 6, 95 S.Ct. 1917, 1924 n. 6, 44 L.Ed.2d 539 (1975), *rehearing denied* 423 U.S. 884, 96 S.Ct. 157, 46 L.Ed.2d 114 (1975).

96. SIPC v. Vigman, 908 F.2d 1461 (9th Cir.1990), *judgment reversed on other grounds* 503 U.S. 258, 112 S.Ct. 1311, 117 L.Ed.2d 532 (1992), *on remand* 964 F.2d 924 (9th Cir.1992). RICO is discussed in § 19.3 *infra*.

97. International Data Bank Ltd. v. Zepkin, 812 F.2d 149 (4th Cir. 1987); Brannan v. Eisenstein, 804 F.2d 1041, 1046 (8th Cir. 1986); Chief Consolidated Mining Co. v. Sunshine Mining Co., 725 F.Supp. 1191 (D. Utah 1989).

§ 13.4

1. *See* Elaine E. Bucklo, Scienter and Rule 10b–5, 67 Nw.U.L.Rev. 562 (1972); John P. James, Culpability Predicates for Federal Securities Law Sanctions: The Present Law and the Proposed Federal Securities Code, 12 Harv.J.Legis. 1 (1974); Bruce Allen Mann, Rule 10b–5; Evolution of a Continuum of Conduct to Replace the Catch Phrases of Negligence and Scienter, 45 N.Y.U.L.Rev. 1206 (1970). *See also* the authorities in footnote 2 *infra*.

2. 425 U.S. 185, 96 S.Ct. 1375, 47 L.Ed.2d 668 (1976), *rehearing denied* 425 U.S. 986, 96 S.Ct. 2194, 48 L.Ed.2d 811 (1976). *See also, e.g.,* Board of County Commissioners of San Juan County v. Liberty Group, 965 F.2d 879 (10th Cir.1992), *cert. denied* ___ U.S. ___, 113 S.Ct. 329, 121 L.Ed.2d 247 (1992) (jury instruction was erroneous due to failure to impose scienter requirement); Goldberg v. Household Bank, F.S.B., 890 F.2d 965 (7th Cir.1989) (no 10b–5 claim where plaintiff had no evidence "one way or the other" to show that the defendant acted with scienter; misstatements were result of an "honest error"). The Administrative Law Judge's decision in the Kern case was affirmed on other grounds, In the Matter of George Kern, Sec.Exch.Act Rel. No. 34–29356, [1991 Transfer Binder] Fed.Sec.L.Rep. (CCH) ¶ 84,815 (SEC 1991).

3. 446 U.S. 680, 100 S.Ct. 1945, 64 L.Ed.2d 611 (1980), *on remand* 666 F.2d 5 (2d Cir.1981).

4. One former SEC official (who is now a federal district court judge), Stanley Sporkin former Director of the Division of Enforcement reportedly was not overly concerned with this result and is reported to have said emphatically, "if they want scienter, we'll give them

Supreme Court in *Aaron* also held that scienter is not an element of an SEC claim for injunctive relief under sections 17(a)(2) and (a)(3) of the 1933 Act.[5] The Court reasoned that although the language of Rule 10b–5 is identical in all relevant parts to that of section 17(a) of the 1933 Act, section 10(b)'s overall scope is statutorily limited to manipulative or deceptive conduct.[6] "Manipulation" is a term of art that is limited to certain specific types of trading practices and thus is not applicable in most antifraud cases.[7] In fact, there is considerable question whether the concept of manipulation can validly play any role with regard to Rule 10b–5.[8] The statutory deception requirement has been held to mandate a showing of scienter in order to state a 10b–5 claim because deception connotes common law fraud and common law fraud requires scienter.[9]

The Proxy Rules Compared

Section 14(a) of the Exchange Act and Rule 14a–9 promulgated thereunder give rise to an implied antifraud remedy in connection with a proxy solicitation.[10] A number of courts have held that the absence of a similar deception requirement in the language of section 14(a)[11] results in a finding that negligence is sufficient to state a claim under the proxy

---

scienter." But even that is not necessary under section 17(a). *See* note 5 *infra*. *See also, e.g.*, SEC v. Wellshire Securities, Inc., 773 F.Supp. 569 (S.D.N.Y.1991) (SEC failed to establish scienter).

For a pre-*Aaron* discussion of the issue, *see* Lewis Lowenfels, Scienter or Negligence Required for SEC Injunctions Under Section 10(b) and Rule 10b–5: A Fascinating Paradox, 33 Bus.Law. 789 (1978).

5. *See* 15 U.S.C.A. § 77q(a)(2), (3). The Court also held that scienter must be shown in an action under section 17(a)(1). Section 17(a) is discussed in § 7.6 *supra*. The availability of an implied private remedy under section 17(a) is discussed in § 13.13 *infra*.

6. 15 U.S.C.A. § 78j(b).

7. *See, e.g.*, Santa Fe Industries, Inc. v. Green, 430 U.S. 462, 476, 97 S.Ct. 1292, 1302, 51 L.Ed.2d 480 (1977), *on remand* 562 F.2d 4 (2d Cir.1977); Ernst & Ernst v. Hochfelder, 425 U.S. 185, 199, 96 S.Ct. 1375, 1383, 47 L.Ed.2d 668 (1976), *rehearing denied* 425 U.S. 986, 96 S.Ct. 2194, 48 L.Ed.2d 811 (1976); *But see* Mobil Corp. v. Marathon Oil Co., 669 F.2d 366 (6th Cir.1981) (giving a much broader view of manipulation). Manipulation is discussed in §§ 6.1, 12.1 *supra*.

8. Schreiber v. Burlington Northern, Inc., 472 U.S. 1, 105 S.Ct. 2458, 86 L.Ed.2d 1 (1985) held that manipulative conduct does not violate section 14(e) unless there has been deception in terms of a material misstatement or omission. *See* §§ 11.15, 12.1 *supra*.

9. Ernst & Ernst v. Hochfelder, 425 U.S. 185, 197, 96 S.Ct. 1375, 1382, 47 L.Ed.2d 668 (1976), *rehearing denied* 425 U.S. 986, 96 S.Ct. 2194, 48 L.Ed.2d 811 (1976). *See also* Aaron v. SEC, 446 U.S. 680, 695, 100 S.Ct. 1945, 1954, 64 L.Ed.2d 611 (1980), *on remand* 666 F.2d 5 (2d Cir.1981).

Cf. Hill v. Bache Halsey Stuart Shields Inc., 790 F.2d 817 (10th Cir.1986) (scienter is required in an action under section 4b of the Commodities Exchange Act). For discussion of scienter under the commodities laws, *see* 3 Philip M. Johnson & Thomas L. Hazen, Commodities Regulation § 5.39 (3d ed. 1989).

10. 15 U.S.C.A. § 78n(a); 17 C.F.R. § 240.14a–9. *E.g.* J.I. Case & Co. v. Borak, 377 U.S. 426, 84 S.Ct. 1555, 12 L.Ed.2d 423 (1964). *See* § 11.3 *supra*.

11. Section 14(a), like section 17(a) of the 1933 Act, is not limited to deceptive and manipulative acts and practices. Section 14(a) provides that it is unlawful to solicit proxies with regard to securities registered under section 12 (15 U.S.C.A. § 78*l*; *see* § 9.2 *supra*) "in contravention of such rules and regulations as the Commission may prescribe as necessary or appropriate in the public interest or for the protection of investors." 15 U.S.C.A. § 78n(a).

rule's antifraud provisions.[12] The reasoning in *Aaron* seems to compel a finding that scienter is not required in an action under the proxy rules.

Recklessness as Scienter

It is clear that the scienter requirement is satisfied by a showing of intentional misrepresentation made with the intent to deceive. But what about conduct that falls short of willful misrepresentation? In reaching its decisions in *Hochfelder* and *Aaron* the Court did not decide whether a showing of reckless conduct would satisfy the scienter requirement.[13] It has long been the rule at common law that, at least under certain circumstances, the showing of reckless disregard of the truth or the making of a statement with no belief in its truth constitutes scienter in an action for deceit.[14] While the recklessness question remains unsettled at the Supreme Court level, the vast majority of the circuit and district court decisions have found that recklessness is sufficient to state a claim under 10b–5.[15] The Supreme Court granted certiorari on the issue of whether recklessness can form the basis of aider and abettor liability under Rule 10b–5.[16] However, the Court never reached the scienter issue since it disposed of that case by ruling that there is no implied remedy against aiders and abettors.[17] Accordingly, the circuit and district court cases recognizing recklessness as sufficient to satisfy the scienter requirement have not been disturbed.

Since the *Hochfelder* and *Aaron* scienter requirements are borrowed from common law fraud, there is every reason to believe that the common law definition, including reckless disregard of the truth, should also apply in the Rule 10b–5 context. One problem raised by the recklessness standard, however, is that it does not provide as easy a test

---

12. Herskowitz v. Nutri/System, Inc., 857 F.2d 179, 189–90 (3d Cir.1988), *cert. denied* 489 U.S. 1054, 109 S.Ct. 1315, 103 L.Ed.2d 584 (1989); Wilson v. Great American Industries, Inc., 855 F.2d 987, 995 (2d Cir.1988); Gould v. American–Hawaiian Steamship Co., 535 F.2d 761 (3d Cir.1976); Gerstle v. Gamble–Skogmo, Inc., 478 F.2d 1281 (2d Cir.1973); Gillette Co. v. RB Partners, 693 F.Supp. 1266 (D.Mass.1988); Fradkin v. Ernst, 571 F.Supp. 829 (N.D.Ohio 1983); Shidler v. All American Life & Financial Corp., 1982 WL 1351, [1982 Transfer Binder] Fed.Sec.L.Rep. (CCH) ¶ 98,875 (S.D.Iowa 1982). *Accord* Katz v. Pels, 774 F.Supp. 121 (S.D.N.Y.1991).

13. 425 U.S. at 193–94 n. 12, 96 S.Ct. at 1381 n. 12; 446 U.S. at 690–691, 100 S.Ct. at 1952.

14. *E.g.,* Derry v. Peek, 14 App.Cas. 337 (House of Lords 1889). *See generally* W. Page Keeton, Dan B. Dobbs, Robert E. Keeton & David G. Owen, Prosser and Keeton on Torts § 107 (5th ed. 1984).

15. *See, e.g.,* In re Wells Fargo Securities Litigation, 12 F.3d 922 (9th Cir.1993) (adequate allegations of recklessness); Breard v. Sachnoff & Weaver, Ltd., 941 F.2d 142 (2d Cir.1991) (complaint adequately alleged recklessness of law firm); Backman v. Polaroid Corp., 893 F.2d 1405 (1st Cir.1990) (recklessness is sufficient).

16. Central Bank of Denver v. First Interstate Bank of Denver, ___ U.S. ___, 113 S.Ct. 2927, 124 L.Ed.2d 678 (1993), *opinion below* 969 F.2d 891 (10th Cir.1992). Certiorari had been sought on the question of whether a showing of recklessness could support aiding and abetting liability and, in granting certiorari on this issue, the Court also asked the parties to brief the question of whether there is an implied action against aiders and abettors. This became the eventual ground for the Court's decision.

17. Central Bank of Denver v. First Interstate Bank of Denver, ___ U.S. ___, 114 S.Ct. 1439, 128 L.Ed.2d 119 (1994). *See* § 13.16 *infra*.

in application as would one requiring a showing of actual intent. The concept of recklessness belies the existence of a bright line test. Recklessness is obviously a matter of degree and requires something considerably more than negligent conduct but which still falls short of actual intentional action. It is clear that in order to establish scienter, the defendant must have had more than a tangential connection to both the transactions and statements under scrutiny.[18]

Some courts have spoken in terms of a "barely reckless" standard,[19] whereas a number of courts seem to be leaning more toward a "highly reckless" standard.[20] It has also been suggested that the *Hochfelder* decision does not preclude the applicability of a flexible duty[21] standard depending upon the relationship between the plaintiff and the defendant and all the surrounding facts of the particular case.[22] The Ninth Circuit in an *en banc* ruling has rejected the flexible duty standard which it had followed in earlier cases.[23] In so ruling, the court adopted the relatively stringent recklessness requirement that has been adopted in the Seventh Circuit:

[R]eckless conduct may be defined as a highly unreasonable omission, involving not merely simple, or even inexcusable negligence, but an extreme departure from the standards of ordinary care, and which presents a danger of misleading buyers or sellers that is either known to the defendant or is so obvious that the actor must have been aware of it.[24]

---

18. *See, e.g.,* National Union Fire Insurance Co. v. Wilkins–Lowe & Co., 29 F.3d 337 (7th Cir.1994) (principal's tangential connection to activities of agent who converted customer funds was too indirect to satisfy the scienter requirement).

19. *See* Stern v. American Bankshares Corp., 429 F.Supp. 818 (E.D.Wis.1977) which is discussed in Marc I. Steinberg & Samuel H. Gruenbaum, Variations of "Recklessness" After *Hochfelder* and *Aaron*, 8 Sec.Reg.L.J. 179, 191–194 (1980). *See also* Annot. What Constitutes Recklessness Sufficient to Show Necessary Element of Scienter in Civil Action for Damages Under § 10(b) of the Securities Act of 1934 (15 USCA § 78j(b)) and Rule 10b–5 of the Securities and Exchange Commission, 49 A.L.R.Fed. 392 (1980). It is doubtful that the "barely" reckless standard can survive. *See* footnote 25 *infra.*

20. SEC v. Steadman, 967 F.2d 636 (D.C.Cir.1992) (recklessness is more than a heightened degree of negligence, it is an *extreme* departure from ordinary care; the danger of misleading investors must either have been known to defendant or be so obvious that the defendant must have been aware of it); McDonald v. Alan Bush Brokerage Co., 863 F.2d 809 (11th Cir.1989) (finding "severe recklessness" standard was not met).

21. *See* White v. Abrams, 495 F.2d 724 (9th Cir.1974).

22. Broad v. Rockwell International Corp., 614 F.2d 418 (5th Cir.1980), *modified* 642 F.2d 929 (5th Cir.1981), *cert. denied* 454 U.S. 965, 102 S.Ct. 506, 70 L.Ed.2d 380 (1981); Healey v. Catalyst Recovery of Pennsylvania Inc., 616 F.2d 641 (3d Cir.1980); Mansbach v. Prescott, Ball & Turben, 598 F.2d 1017, 1025 (6th Cir.1979); Sanders v. John, Nuveen & Co., 554 F.2d 790, 793 (7th Cir.1977), *appeal after remand* 619 F.2d 1222 (7th Cir.1980), *cert. denied* 450 U.S. 1005, 101 S.Ct. 1719, 68 L.Ed.2d 210 (1981); Rolf v. Blyth, Eastman Dillon & Co., Inc., 570 F.2d 38, 45 (2d Cir.1978), *cert. denied* 439 U.S. 1039, 99 S.Ct. 642, 58 L.Ed.2d 698 (1978).

23. Hollinger v. Titan Capital Corp., 914 F.2d 1564 (9th Cir.1990), *cert. denied* 499 U.S. 976, 111 S.Ct. 1621, 113 L.Ed.2d 719 (1991). *Compare, e.g.,* the pre-*Hochfelder* decision in White v. Abrams, 495 F.2d 724, 735–36 (9th Cir.1974).

24. 914 F.2d at 1569, *quoting* Sundstrand Corp. v. Sun Chemical Corp., 553 F.2d 1033, 1044–45 (7th Cir.1977), *cert. denied* 434 U.S. 875, 98 S.Ct. 224, 54 L.Ed.2d 155 (1977) *and* Franke v. Midwestern Oklahoma Development Authority, 428 F.Supp. 719, 725 (W.D.Okl. 1976), *vacated on other grounds* 619 F.2d 856 (10th Cir.1980).

The recklessness standard has also been articulated in terms of whether the defendants "had reasonable grounds to believe material facts existed that were misstated or omitted, but nonetheless failed to obtain and disclose such facts although they could have done so without extraordinary effort." [25] The scienter requirement was imposed by analogy to common law fraud. Similarly borrowing from the common law, the formulation of the test for recklessness is properly articulated in terms of whether or not the defendants made the statements in question with no belief in the truth or the falsity of the assertion or with reckless disregard to the truth or the falsity.[26] This test has been historically valid under common law. A possible objection to a recklessness standard is that it is too amorphous and can be closer to negligence than the type of scienter the Court in *Hochfelder* and *Aaron* might have had in mind.[27] In any event, the recklessness standard seems to impart a standard analogous to gross negligence and conduct that is sufficiently culpable to justify a fraud type remedy. The analogy is not a complete one as there is a difference in character between grossly negligent conduct and conduct that is so reckless that it borders on intentional misconduct. Accordingly, gross or inexcusable negligence will not satisfy the scienter requirement; recklessness requires a complete indifference to the truth or falsity of the statements.[28] As such, it seems to defy a more specific definition. Resolution of the availability of a recklessness standard, as well as a more explicit definition, must await Supreme Court determination. Due to this uncertainty and to the subjective nature of scienter, courts have been reluctant to grant summary judgment in 10b–5 cases where scienter is a contested issue.[29]

---

25. Keirnan v. Homeland, Inc., 611 F.2d 785, 788 (9th Cir.1980). *Compare, e.g.,* SEC v. Price Waterhouse, 797 F.Supp. 1217 (S.D.N.Y.1992) (failure to follow accounting practices was not in itself sufficient to establish scienter); O'Brien v. Price Waterhouse, 740 F.Supp. 276 (S.D.N.Y.1990), *judgment affirmed* 936 F.2d 674 (2d Cir.1991) (claim that appraiser made inadequate investigation was nothing more than negligence and thus did not satisfy the scienter requirement).

Scienter may be inferred from circumstantial evidence. *E.g.,* Wechsler v. Steinberg, 733 F.2d 1054 (2d Cir.1984).

26. Derry v. Peek, 14 App.Cas. 337 (House of Lords 1889).

While constructive knowledge alone arguably would not satisfy scienter, at least one court has allowed the alternative pleading of actual or constructive knowledge of fraud to withstand a motion to dismiss, Chisholm v. St. Pierre, [1981–82 Transfer Binder] Fed.Sec. L.Rep. (CCH) ¶ 98,337 (D.Mass.1981).

27. *See* Sanders v. John Nuveen & Co., 554 F.2d 790, 793 (7th Cir.1977), *appeal after remand* 619 F.2d 1222 (7th Cir.1980), 450 U.S. 1005, 101 S.Ct. 1719, 68 L.Ed.2d 210 (1981) (scienter is "closer to being a lesser form of intent than merely a greater degree of ordinary negligence. We perceive it to be not just a difference in degree, but also in kind."). *See also, e.g.,* Cook v. Avien, Inc., 573 F.2d 685, 692 (1st Cir.1978).

28. *See, e.g.,* Gilmore v. Berg, 761 F.Supp. 358 (D.N.J.1991). *See also, e.g.,* Gollomp v. MNC Financial, Inc., 756 F.Supp. 228 (D.Md.1991) (plaintiffs failed to establish recklessness of defendants); Kelley v. Mid–America Racing Stables, Inc., 1990 WL 193626, [1990–1991 Transfer Binder] Fed.Sec.L.Rep. (CCH) ¶ 95,626 (W.D.Okl.1990) (recklessness was pleaded with sufficient particularity).

29. *E.g.,* Vucinich v. Paine, Webber, Jackson & Curtis, Inc., 739 F.2d 1434, 1436 (9th Cir.1984), *appeal after remand* 803 F.2d 454 (9th Cir.1986) ("Summary judgment is generally inappropriate when mental state is an issue, unless no reasonable inference supports the adverse party's claim"; quoting from Admiralty Fund v. Tabor, 677 F.2d 1297, 1298–99 (9th Cir.1982)).

Pleading and Proving Scienter

On appropriate facts, a court may be willing to permit an inference that the defendant acted with the requisite scienter.[30] However, such an inference should not be made lightly.[31]

The courts have identified two ways of satisfying the scienter requirement.[32] One method is to set forth allegations of facts tending to establish a motive and opportunity to commit fraud. The second method is to set forth facts circumstantially establishing either reckless or consciously wrongful behavior.[33]

The scienter requirement applies not only to primary liability but also to secondary liability based on aiding and abetting,[34] to the limited extent that aiding and abetting may give rise to liability.[35] It has been held that knowledge of a corporate officer or agent acting within the scope of authority is attributable to the corporation.[36]

As is the case with the other elements of fraud, scienter is subject to Federal Rule of Civil Procedure Rule 9(b)'s requirement that fraud be pleaded with particularity.[37] While the particularity requirement mandates that this applies to the allegations regarding the circumstances surrounding the fraud, the courts are split as to how this affects the scienter requirement in particular. The Second Circuit has indicated that the particularity requirement means that the plaintiff must plead

---

30. *See, e.g.,* In re GlenFed, Inc. Securities Litigation, 11 F.3d 843 (9th Cir.1993) (sufficient allegations regarding inference of scienter); Fine v. American Solar King Corp., 919 F.2d 290 (5th Cir.1990), *cert. dismissed* 502 U.S. 976, 112 S.Ct. 576, 116 L.Ed.2d 601 (1991) (upholding inference that accountants knew they were issuing a materially misleading report).

31. *See* Shields v. Citytrust Bancorp, Inc., 25 F.3d 1124 (2d Cir.1994) (evidence amounted to nothing more than allegations of "fraud by hindsight" which are insufficient); In re Crystal Brands Securities Litigation, 862 F.Supp. 745 (D.Conn.1994) (allegations that defendants should have known of impending financial crisis did not create an inference of scienter).

See generally Craig L. Griffin, Corporate Scienter Under the Securities Exchange Act of 1934, 1989 B.Y.U.L.Rev. 1227.

32. *See, e.g.,* In re Time Warner, Inc. Securities Litigation, 9 F.3d 259 (2d Cir.1993).

33. *See, e.g.,* Steiner v. Unitrode Corp., 834 F.Supp. 40 (D.Mass.1993) (inference of knowingly misleading plaintiffs was pleaded with sufficient particularity).

34. Mayer v. Oil Field Systems Corp., 803 F.2d 749 (2d Cir.1986) (section 12(2) of the 1933 Act and Rule 10b–5).

35. In 1994, the Supreme Court held that there is no private right of action for aiding and abetting a Rule 10b–5 violation. Central Bank of Denver, N.A. v. First Interstate Bank of Denver, ___ U.S. ___, 114 S.Ct. 1439, 128 L.Ed.2d 119 (1994). *See* § 13.16 *infra.* Although there is no longer a private remedy, there still is the potential of certain SEC enforcement actions and criminal prosecutions to address aiding and abetting violations. *Id.*

36. In re Atlantic Financial Management, Inc., 784 F.2d 29 (1st Cir.1986), *cert. denied* 481 U.S. 1072, 107 S.Ct. 2469, 95 L.Ed.2d 877 (1987) (applying common law principles of apparent authority); Etshokin v. Texasgulf, Inc., 612 F.Supp. 1212 (N.D.Ill.1984). There is a split of authority as to whether the doctrine of respondeat superior applies in securities cases. *See* § 7.7 *supra* and § 13.15 *infra.*

37. Fed.R.Civ.P. 9. *See* the authorities in footnote 9 *supra.* The particularity requirement is discussed in § 13.8.1 *infra.*

facts that at least give rise to a "strong inference of fraudulent intent." [38]
In contrast, the Ninth Circuit, relying on the language of Rule 9(b) has
held that "malice, intent, knowledge, and other condition of mind may
be averred generally." [39]

§ 13.5A   Materiality in Rule 10b–5 Actions

In a common law action for fraud or deceit, in addition to proving
the requisite degree of culpability (*i.e.,* scienter),[1] the successful plaintiff
must prove a material misstatement or omission and reliance upon the
misstatement or omission in question.[2] As is the case with scienter, the
materiality and reliance requirements carry over to 10b–5 actions.

Materiality Defined

The test of materiality depends not upon the literal truth of statements but upon the ability of reasonable investors to become accurately
informed.[3] This is sometimes referred to as the mosaic misrepresentation thesis.[4] Accordingly, when there is adequate cautionary language
warning investors as to certain risks, optimistic statements are not
materially misleading.[5] As discussed more fully below, a finding of
materiality is based on the total mix of information available.[6] However,
the mere fact that information may be publicly available does not mean
that it is necessarily incorporated into every statement made. Accordingly, the fact that information in the 10K and annual report to
shareholders might have clarified alleged misstatements in a proxy
solicitation did not preclude the proxy statement from being actionable.[7]

---

38. O'Brien v. National Property Analysts Partners, 936 F.2d 674, 676 (2d Cir.1991);
Ross v. A.H. Robins Co., 607 F.2d 545, 558 (2d Cir.1979), *cert. denied* 446 U.S. 946, 100
S.Ct. 2175, 64 L.Ed.2d 802 (1980).

39. In re GlenFed, Inc. Securities Litigation, 42 F.3d 1541 (9th Cir.1994).

§ 13.5A

1. *See* § 13.4 *supra.*

2. *See generally* W. Page Keeton, Dan B. Dobbs, Robert E. Keeton & David G. Owen,
Prosser and Keeton on Torts § 108 (5th ed. 1984). Reliance is discussed in § 13.5B *infra.*

3. *E.g.* McMahan & Co. v. Wherehouse Entertainment, Inc., 900 F.2d 576, 579 (2d
Cir.1990), *cert. denied* 501 U.S. 1249, 111 S.Ct. 2887, 115 L.Ed.2d 1052 (1991) ("[s]ome
statements, although literally accurate, can become, through their context and manner of
presentation, devices which mislead investors").

4. In re Genentech, Inc., Securities Litigation, 1989 WL 137189, [1989–1990 Transfer
Binder] Fed.Sec.L.Rep. ¶ 94,813 (C.D.Cal.1989), s.c. 1989 WL 106834, [1989 Transfer
Binder] Fed.Sec.L.Rep. ¶ 94,544 (N.D.Cal.1989).

5. *See, e.g.,* In re Worlds of Wonder Securities Litigation, 35 F.3d 1407 (9th Cir.1994)
(adequate warnings in prospectus); Moorhead v. Merrill Lynch, Pierce, Fenner & Smith,
Inc., 949 F.2d 243 (8th Cir.1991) (repeated warnings precluded claim of material misstatements in feasibility study).

6. *See, e.g.,* Ryan v. Wersi Electronics GmbH & Co., 3 F.3d 174 (7th Cir.1993) (written
disclosures rendered any reliance on statements of company's health not material);
Epstein v. Washington Energy Co., 1994 WL 561075, [1994–1995 Transfer Binder] Fed.
Sec. L. Rep. (CCH) ¶ 98,379 (W.D.Wash.1994) (fact that true facts were readily available
precluded a Rule 10b–5 claim).

7. United Paperworkers International Union v. International Paper Co., 985 F.2d 1190
(2d Cir.1993).

In United Paperworkers International Union v. International Paper Co., the court reasoned that for shareholders making their determination of how to vote based on the proxy statement, the information contained in the 10K and annual report were not part of the total mix reasonably available to the shareholders who would be voting.[8]

Materiality issues have also arisen in the context of proxy regulation and the implied remedy under Rule 14a–9;[9] the tests of materiality are basically the same in a 10b–5 action.[10] The proxy rules are considered elsewhere in this treatise as are additional examples of the materiality cases in both the 10b–5 and 14a–9 settings.[11] Additionally, the materiality concept applies to the antifraud provisions of the Securities Act of 1933.[12]

The test of materiality is whether a reasonable investor would have considered the matter significant;[13] it is not necessary to show that the investor *would* have acted differently.[14] Once materiality is established, however, the investor still has to show a causal connection between the violation, the transaction, and any loss which he or she suffered.[15]

In an early leading Rule 10b–5 case, the Second Circuit looked to the Restatement of Torts in defining materiality in terms of whether a reasonable person "would attach importance [to the fact misrepresented] in determining his choice of action in the transaction in question." [16] As

---

8. *Id.*

9. 17 C.F.R. § 240.14a–9.

10. *E.g.,* Kohn v. American Metal Climax, Inc., 458 F.2d 255 (3d Cir.), *cert. denied* 409 U.S. 874, 93 S.Ct. 120, 34 L.Ed.2d 126 (1972); Pavlidis v. New England Patriots Football Club, 675 F.Supp. 688, 694 (D.Mass.1986); Rubenstein v. IU International Corp., 506 F.Supp. 311, 314 (E.D.Pa.1980). *See generally* James O. Hewitt, Developing Concepts of Materiality and Disclosure, 32 Bus.Law. 887 (1977). *See also, e.g.,* Leo Herzel & Robert K. Hagan, Materiality and the Use of SEC Forms, 32 Bus.Law. 1177 (1977); Homer Kripke, Rule 10b–5 Liability and Material Facts, 46 N.Y.U.L.Rev. 1061 (1971); Jonathan R. Macey, Geoffrey P. Miller, Mark L. Mitchell & Jeffrey M. Netter, Lessons From Financial Economics: Materiality, Reliance, and Extending the Reach of *Basic v. Levinson*, 77 Va.L.Rev. 1017 (1991).

Cf. Beebe v. Pacific Realty Trust, 578 F.Supp. 1128 (D.Or.1984) (applying the same materiality test in an action under section 14(e) which relates to tender offers). *See also* Roger J. Dennis, Materiality and the Efficient Capital Market Model: A Recipe for the Total Mix, 25 Wm. & Mary L.Rev. 373 (1984).

11. *See* § 11.4 *supra.*

12. In particular, sections 11 and 12(2) for private rights of action, 15 U.S.C.A. §§ 77k, 77*l*(2) and section 17(a) for enforcement actions, 15 U.S.C.A. § 77q(a). *See* chapter 7 *supra. See also* § 3.7 *supra.*

13. It is not sufficient to show that a shareholder might have found the information to be of interest. Milton v. Van Dorn Co., 961 F.2d 965 (1st Cir.1992). *See also, e.g.,* United States v. Bingham, 992 F.2d 975 (9th Cir.1993) (defendant's use of false identity, hiding the fact that he was an officer and director, in connection with sale of security was not a Rule 10b–5 violation).

14. Folger Adam Co. v. PMI Industries, Inc., 938 F.2d 1529 (2d Cir.1991), *cert. denied* 502 U.S. 983, 112 S.Ct. 587, 116 L.Ed.2d 612 (1991).

15. *See* § 13.6 *infra.*

16. List v. Fashion Park, Inc., 340 F.2d 457, 462 (2d Cir. 1965), *cert. denied* 382 U.S. 811, 86 S.Ct. 23, 15 L.Ed.2d 60 (1965), *rehearing denied* 382 U.S. 933, 86 S.Ct. 305, 15 L.Ed.2d 344 (1965) (quoting the Restatement of Torts (Second) § 538(2)(a)). *Accord* Little

noted earlier, this is analysis is to be made in light of the total mix of information available.[17]   Thus, for example, oral statements will be considered in light of available written information.[18]

The fact that materiality is to be determined in context means that a purchaser or seller is not necessarily entitled to all information relating to each of the circumstances surrounding the transaction.[19]   It has been held, for example, that failure to disclose negotiations concerning post-redemption plans for plaintiff's shares is not a material nondisclosure.[20]   The same result has been reached with regard to preliminary merger negotiations.[21]   But more advanced negotiations may be material.[22]   Nondisclosure of an impending four percent stock dividend has been held not to be material,[23] but a substantial dividend reduction is material.[24]   Similarly, a significant understatement of asset value will be materially misleading.[25]   A substantial decline in earnings,[26] a substan-

v. Valley National Bank, 650 F.2d 218, 222 (9th Cir.1981). It has been said that "materiality" encompasses those facts "which in reasonable and objective contemplation might affect the value of the corporation's stock or securities * * *"   Kohler v. Kohler Co., 319 F.2d 634, 642 (7th Cir.1963).

17. *See, e.g.,* Shawmut Bank, N.A. v. Kress Associates, 33 F.3d 1477 (9th Cir.1994) (alleged omission was not material in light of disclosures that were made).

18. Ambrosino v. Rodman & Renshaw, Inc., 972 F.2d 776 (7th Cir.1992) (written disclosures precluded action based on oral statements at variance with the writing); Casella v. Webb, 883 F.2d 805, 808 (9th Cir.1989) ("Statements made in the course of an oral presentation 'cannot be considered in isolation,' but must be viewed 'in the context of the total presentation' ").

19. Management's motives frequently will not be material and therefore need not be disclosed. Ward v. Succession of Freeman, 854 F.2d 780 (5th Cir.1988), *rehearing denied* 863 F.2d 882 (5th Cir.1988); Warner Communications, Inc. v. Murdoch, 581 F.Supp. 1482, 1494 (D.Del.1984). Where the "total mix of information" showed a bleak financial picture, overly optimistic statements by incoming chairman of the board were held not to be material. Data Controls North v. Financial Corp. of America, 688 F.Supp. 1047 (D.Md. 1988). *See also, e.g.,* Jackvony v. RIHT Financial Corp., 873 F.2d 411 (1st Cir.1989). For additional examples *see* § 11.4 *supra.*

20. Especially since the plaintiff had little choice in the matter. Trecker v. Scag, 747 F.2d 1176 (7th Cir.1984), *cert. denied* 471 U.S. 1066, 105 S.Ct. 2140, 85 L.Ed.2d 498 (1985).

21. *E.g.,* List v. Fashion Park, Inc., 340 F.2d 457 (2d Cir.1965), *cert. denied* 382 U.S. 811, 86 S.Ct. 23, 15 L.Ed.2d 60 (1965), *rehearing denied* 382 U.S. 933, 86 S.Ct. 305, 15 L.Ed.2d 344 (1965); Zuckerman v. Harnischfeger Corp., 591 F.Supp. 112, (S.D.N.Y.1984); Hershfang v. Knotter, 562 F.Supp. 393 (E.D.Va.1983), *judgment affirmed* 725 F.2d 675 (4th Cir.1984); Greenfield v. Heublein, Inc., 575 F.Supp. 1325 (E.D.Pa.1983), *judgment affirmed* 742 F.2d 751 (3d Cir.1984), *cert. denied* 469 U.S. 1215, 105 S.Ct. 1189, 84 L.Ed.2d 336 (1985). *See* footnotes 50–62 *infra* and accompanying text.

22. Basic Inc. v. Levinson, 485 U.S. 224, 108 S.Ct. 978, 99 L.Ed.2d 194 (1988); Kardon v. National Gypsum Co., 69 F.Supp. 512 (E.D.Pa.1946). *See also, e.g.,* Schlanger v. Four-Phase Systems, Inc., 582 F.Supp. 128 (S.D.N.Y.1984); Kumpis v. Wetterau, 586 F.Supp. 152 (E.D.Mo.1983). *Cf.* Primary Care Investors, Seven v. PHP Healthcare Corp., 986 F.2d 1208 (8th Cir.1993) (alleged nondisclosure of planned public offering was material).

23. Hafner v. Forest Laboratories, Inc., 345 F.2d 167 (2d Cir.1965).

24. In the Matter of Cady, Roberts & Co., 40 S.E.C. 907 (SEC 1961). *See also, e.g.,* Durning v. First Boston Corp., 815 F.2d 1265 (9th Cir.1987), *cert. denied* 484 U.S. 944, 108 S.Ct. 330, 98 L.Ed.2d 358 (1987) (failure to disclose early redemption clause in bonds held material).

25. Speed v. Transamerica Corp., 99 F.Supp. 808 (D.Del.1951), *s.c.,* 135 F.Supp. 176 (D.Del.1955), *modified* 235 F.2d 369 (3d Cir.1956). *See also, e.g.,* Abrams & Wofsy v. Renaissance Investment Corp., 1991 WL 319050, [1991–1992 Transfer Binder] Fed.Sec.

26. See note 26 on page 796.

tial overstatement of revenue,[27] or a mineral find by an exploration company[28] is a material fact to any purchaser or seller. The fact that a company is about to become a target of a tender offer is material.[29] In the context of an insider trading case, the time at which insiders begin to trade is strong circumstantial evidence of materiality.[30] A broker's misrepresentations concerning the marginability of securities has been held to be material and hence actionable under Rule 10b–5.[31] Failure to disclose a pending public offering can be a material omission.[32] In connection with a public offering, inadequate disclosure of potential tax and environmental liability can be material.[33] In connection with an all-or-none offering of securities, it was material not to disclose that the underwriters could purchase out of the offering.[34]

Information tending to show conflicts of interest of directors, offi-

L.Rep. (CCH) ¶ 96,458 (N.D.Ga.1991) (misstatements concerning financial condition were material).

26. Shapiro v. Merrill Lynch, Pierce, Fenner & Smith, Inc., 495 F.2d 228 (2d Cir.1974); Financial Industrial Fund, Inc., v. McDonnell Douglas Corp., 474 F.2d 514 (10th Cir.1973), *cert. denied* 414 U.S. 874, 94 S.Ct. 155, 38 L.Ed.2d 114 (1973). In re Pfizer, Inc. Securities Litigation, 1990 WL 250287, [1990–1991 Transfer Binder] Fed.Sec.L.Rep. (CCH) ¶ 95,710 (S.D.N.Y.1990) (failure to disclose that issuer marketed heart valve with knowledge of design defects and that law suits were expected to be filed could be material). *Compare,* In re Gap Securities Litigation, 1988 WL 168341, [1989–1990 Transfer Binder] Fed.Sec.L.Rep. ¶ 94,724 (N.D.Cal.1988), *decision affirmed* 925 F.2d 1470 (9th Cir.1991) (failure to announce build-up in inventory was not actionable). *See also, e.g.,* Jaroslawicz v. Engelhard Corp., 704 F.Supp. 1296 (D.N.J.1989) (failure to disclose operating bases was material).

27. In re Medeva Securities Litigation, 1994 WL 447141, [1994–1995 Transfer Binder] Fed. Sec. L. Rep. (CCH) ¶ 98,323 (C.D.Cal.1994).

28. SEC v. Texas Gulf Sulphur Co., 401 F.2d 833 (2d Cir.1968), *cert. denied* 394 U.S. 976, 89 S.Ct. 1454, 22 L.Ed.2d 756 (1969).

29. United States v. Chiarella, 588 F.2d 1358 (2d Cir.1978), *reversed on other grounds* 445 U.S. 222, 100 S.Ct. 1108, 63 L.Ed.2d 348 (1980). *Cf.* United States v. Victor Teicher & Co., L.P., 1990 WL 29697, [1989–1990 Transfer Binder] Fed.Sec.L.Rep. ¶ 94,975 (S.D.N.Y. 1990) (after a competing bid had been made, the fact that a tender offeror might make a second offer was material).

30. *See* SEC v. Texas Gulf Sulphur Co., 401 F.2d 833 (2d Cir.1968), *cert. denied* 394 U.S. 976, 89 S.Ct. 1454, 22 L.Ed.2d 756 (1969). However, evidence of price and volume movements in the stock has been held not sufficient to establish materiality of changes in earnings estimates. SEC v. Sharp, 85–0553–R (E.D.Va.1986). *See* § 13.9 *infra. See also, e.g.,* United States v. Marcus Schloss & Co., Inc., 1989 WL 153353, [1989–1990 Transfer Binder] Fed.Sec.L.Rep. ¶ 94,840 (S.D.N.Y.1989) (materiality of information concerning possible acquisition).

31. Monetary Management Group v. Kidder, Peabody & Co., 615 F.Supp. 1217 (E.D.Mo.1985). *Cf.* Rush v. Oppenheimer & Co., 638 F.Supp. 872 (S.D.N.Y.1986) (materiality of broker's statements concerning arbitration process was a question of fact).

32. Primary Care Investors, Seven v. PHP Healthcare Corp., 986 F.2d 1208 (8th Cir.1993).

33. Endo v. Albertine, 812 F.Supp. 1479 (N.D.Ill.1993), s.c. 863 F.Supp. 708 (N.D.Ill. 1994).

But see In re Keegan Management Co., Securities Litigation, 794 F.Supp. 939 (N.D.Cal. 1992) (in connection with initial public offering of weight loss center, nondisclosure of potential for personal liability and bad publicity was not material).

34. Svalberg v. SEC, 876 F.2d 181 (D.C.Cir.1989). All-or-none offerings are discussed in § 6.3 *supra. Cf.* Handelsman v. Gilford Securities Inc., 726 F.Supp. 673 (N.D.Ill.1989) (alleged misrepresentation that investment was part of $1 million financing package was material).

cers, or other major participants is likely to be material.[35] Similarly, facts pertaining to management integrity are likely to be material.[36]

Factual Nature of the Inquiry

The foregoing examples indicate the highly factual nature of defining materiality.[37] Thus, summary judgment based on a finding of no materiality ordinarily will not be appropriate.[38] Summary disposition of a materiality claim is appropriate only in those rare instances in which the alleged misrepresentations or omissions "would be so obviously unimportant to a reasonable investor that reasonable minds could not differ on their importance."[39] Similarly, a trial court's finding of materiality (or immateriality) should not be reversed lightly by a reviewing court.[40]

"Bespeaks Caution" Doctrine

A number of courts have adopted what is sometimes referred to as the "bespeaks caution" doctrine. The doctrine holds that sufficient cautionary language may preclude misstatements from being actionable.[41] Courts invoking the doctrine have tended to do so, in cases involving projections in prospectuses and other offering documents, as a basis for dismissing the misrepresentation claim.[42] The cases invoking

---

35. *See, e.g.,* Kahn v. Wien, 842 F.Supp. 667 (E.D.N.Y.1994) (proxy solicitation). *But see, e.g.,* Teledyne Defense Contracting Derivative Litigation, 849 F.Supp. 1369 (C.D.Cal. 1993) (failure to make credible claim of self dealing precluded 10b–5 claim).

36. *E.g.,* Colonial Limited Partnership Securities Litigation, 854 F.Supp. 64 (D.Conn. 1994) (reasons for discharge of general partner were material). *But cf.* Monroe v. Hughes, 31 F.3d 772 (9th Cir.1994) (auditor's responsibility regarding undisclosed deficiencies in a company's internal controls is limited; undisclosed deficiencies are not *per se* material in terms of the accountants' liability under the antifraud provisions).

37. *E.g.,* Folger Adam Co. v. PMI Industries, Inc., 938 F.2d 1529 (2d Cir.1991), *cert. denied* 502 U.S. 983, 112 S.Ct. 587, 116 L.Ed.2d 612 (1991) (it could not be said as a matter of law that omitted income projections were not material); In re Phillips Petroleum Securities Litigation, 738 F.Supp. 825 (D.Del.1990) (materiality is mixed question of law and fact). *See also, e.g.,* Pippenger v. McQuik's Oilube, Inc., 854 F.Supp. 1411 (S.D.Ind. 1994).

38. *E.g.,* Lucia v. Prospect Street High Income Portfolio, Inc., 36 F.3d 170 (1st Cir.1994) (material fact issue as to whether comparison between issuer's bonds and treasury securities over 10 year period was materially misleading due to omission of 6 year comparison); Cooke v. Manufactured Homes, Inc., 998 F.2d 1256 (4th Cir.1993) (there could be differing interpretations as to the effect of the total mix of information).

39. Azrielli v. Cohen Law Offices, 21 F.3d 512, 518(2d Cir.1994), *relying on* TSC Industries, *supra. See also, e.g.,* Kas v. First Union Corp., 857 F.Supp. 481 (E.D.Va.1994) (finding no dispute as to the facts and granting defendant's motion for summary judgment).

40. *E.g.,* Hoxworth v. Blinder, Robinson & Co., Inc., 903 F.2d 186 (3d Cir.1990) (trial court's finding was not clearly erroneous). *Cf.* Pommer v. Medtest Corp., 961 F.2d 620 (7th Cir.1992) (reinstating jury's finding after directed verdict for defendant).

41. For a discussion of the evolution of the doctrine, *see* In re Donald J. Trump Casino Securities Litigation, 793 F.Supp. 543 (D.N.J.1992), *affirmed* 7 F.3d 357 (3d Cir.1993).

See generally Donald C. Langevoort, Disclosures that "Bespeak Caution," 49 Bus. Law. 481 (1994). *See also* the discussion in § 13.5B *infra.*

42. *See, e.g.,* In re Donald J. Trump Casino Securities Litigation–Taj Mahal Litigation, 7 F.3d 357, 371 (3d Cir.1993):

the bespeaks caution doctrine have involved projections or other soft information; it is thus unclear whether the doctrine will have more general application.[43] Similarly, since the test of materiality is based upon the total mix of information, it follows that cautionary language should be considered even outside the context of projections. Thus, whether under the rubric of bespeaks caution or the normal test of materiality, cautionary language may go a long way towards defeating a Rule 10b–5 claim. The doctrine has frequently been referred to in the context of judging whether the plaintiff's reliance is reasonable, but it also necessarily relates to materiality in the sense that it address the question of whether the misstatements are materially misleading when judged in light of the total mix of information available to the investor.[44]

The bespeaks caution doctrine, which applies to both material misstatements and omissions,[45] should be applied cautiously since it does provide an incentive to make misrepresentations with the hope of the speaker subsequently relying on the existence of counterbalancing disclosures in order to absolve the speaker of liability.[46] Accordingly, cautionary language will not always be adequate to prevent an antifraud claim.[47]

---

when an offering document's forecasts, opinions or projections are accompanied by meaningful cautionary statements, the forward-looking statements will not form the basis for a securities fraud claim if those statements did not affect the "total mix" of information the document provided investors. In other words, cautionary language, if sufficient, renders the alleged omissions or misrepresentations immaterial as a matter of law.

See also, e.g., In re Worlds of Wonder Securities Litigation, 814 F.Supp. 850, 859 (N.D.Cal.1993) (the bespeaks caution doctrine applies to estimates of future performance), *affirmed in part and reversed in part on other grounds* 35 F.3d 1407 (9th Cir.1994). *But see, e.g.,* Rubinstein v. Collins, 20 F.3d 160 (5th Cir.1994) (not every cautionary disclaimer will preclude liability for projections).

43. In re Synergen, Inc. Securities Litigation, 863 F.Supp. 1409 (D.Colo.1994) (finding bespeaks caution doctrine inapplicable to historical facts; court pointed to the absence of any authority applying the doctrine in cases not involving projections of future events); Anderson v. Clow, 1993 WL 497212, [1993–1994 Transfer Binder] Fed. Sec. L. Rep. (CCH) ¶ 97,807 (S.D.Cal.1993) (bespeaks caution doctrine only applies in cases of projections, estimates, or similar types of soft information). *See also, e.g.,* Kline v. First Western Government Securities, Inc., 24 F.3d 480 (3d Cir.1994) (refusing to apply bespeaks caution doctrine to claim based on affirmative misrepresentations in tax opinion).

44. *See, e.g.,* In re Worlds of Wonder Securities Litigation, 35 F.3d 1407 (9th Cir.1994) (bespeaks caution doctrine is an application of the materiality concept); In re Donald J. Trump Casino Securities Litigation–Taj Mahal Litigation, 7 F.3d 357, 371 (3d Cir.1993); Sable v. Southmark/Envicon Capital Corp., 819 F.Supp. 324 (S.D.N.Y.1993) (bespeaks caution rationale applied).

45. *See, e.g.,* In re Donald J. Trump Casino Securities Litigation–Taj Mahal Litigation, 7 F.3d 357, 371 (3d Cir.1993).

46. *See, e.g.,* Rubinstein v. Collins, 20 F.3d 160 (5th Cir.1994); In re ZZZZ Best Securities Litigation, 864 F.Supp. 960 (C.D.Cal.1994) (bespeaks caution should not be applied when cautionary language was issued when defendants knew of alleged material misstatements).

47. *E.g.,* Whirlpool Financial Corp. v. GN Holdings, Inc., 873 F.Supp. 111, 123–24 (N.D.Ill.1995) (general cautionary language in section outlining "risk factors" was not sufficient to negate allegedly misleading forecasts); In re Gupta Corp. Securities Litigation, 1994 WL 748988, [Current] Fed. Sec. L. Rep. (CCH) ¶ 98,612 (N.D. Cal.1994) (disclosures did not bespeak caution concerning fraudulent financial statements); Kaplan v. Kahn, 1994 WL 618473, [1994–1995 Transfer Binder] Fed. Sec. L. Rep. (CCH) ¶ 98,486 (N.D. Cal. 1994) (bespeaks caution doctrine was not a complete defense where allegations pointed to

Thus, for example, general cautionary language will not be sufficient to cancel the effect of materially misleading statements.[48] Even when the cautionary language might be sufficient to negate the effect of projections in predicting the future, it may not be sufficient to negate the false implication that the offering was not a fraudulent pyramid scheme.[49]

Preliminary Merger Negotiations

Especially difficult questions of materiality relate to the question of whether preliminary merger negotiations or other control-related transactions must be disclosed.[50] It is the general view that Rule 10b–5 does not impose an affirmative duty of disclosure and thus silence cannot be actionable.[51] Thus, absent some independent basis for the duty, the existence of preliminary negotiations will not have to be disclosed.[52] However, when a material development is covered by a line-item in a document that needs to be filed with the Commission or otherwise publicly disseminated,[53] silence will not suffice and it must be decided whether preliminary negotiations need be disclosed. Similarly, once an issuer, rather than maintaining silence, voluntarily makes a statement, such as in response to an inquiry from the press or securities analysts, all statements must be totally devoid of material misstatements. As the Supreme Court has pointed out, arguments based on the premature

---

misleading financial statements); In re Colonial Ltd. Partnership Litigation, 854 F.Supp. 64, 92–93 (D.Conn.1994); In re First American Center Securities Litigation, 807 F.Supp. 326 (S.D.N.Y.1992).

48. *E.g.,* Kaplan v. Kahn, 1994 WL 618473, [1994–1995 Transfer Binder] Fed. Sec. L. Rep. (CCH) ¶ 98,486 (N.D.Cal.1994); In re Phar–Mor, Inc. Litigation, 848 F.Supp. 46 (W.D.Pa.1993); In re Marion Merrell Dow, Inc. Securities Litigation, 1993 WL 393810, [1993 Transfer Binder] Fed. Sec. L. Rep. (CCH) ¶ 97,776 (W.D.Mo.1993) (the allegedly misleading statements did not contain warnings of specific risk factors).

49. In re Colonial Ltd. Partnership Litigation, 854 F.Supp. 64, 92–93 (D.Conn.1994).

50. *See, e.g.,* David S. Freeman, Mergers and Acquisitions: Determining Whether and When to Disclose Various Developments in the Evolution of a Merger, 21 Ariz.St.L.J. 425 (1989); Thomas L. Hazen, Rumor Control and Disclosure of Merger Negotiations or Other Control Related Transactions: Full Disclosure or "No Comment"—The Only Safe Harbors, 46 Md.L.Rev. 954 (1987); Comment, Line-Item Disclosure Provisions and the Materiality of Preliminary Merger Negotiations After *In re George Kern, Jr.,* 59 Brook. L. Rev. 175 (1993). *See also, e.g.,* J. Robert Brown, Jr., Corporate Secrecy, the Federal Securities Laws, and the Disclosure of Ongoing Merger Negotiations, 36 Cath.U.L.Rev. 93 (1986); Theresa A. Gabaldon, The Disclosure of Preliminary Merger Negotiations as An Imperfect Paradigm of Rule 10b–5 Analysis, 62 N.Y.U.L.Rev. 1218 (1987).

51. *E.g.,* Taylor v. First Union Corp. of South Carolina, 857 F.2d 240 (4th Cir.1988). *See* § 13.10 *infra.*

52. *Cf.* McCormick v. Fund American Cos., 26 F.3d 869 (9th Cir.1994) (parent corporation purchasing its stock from former chief executive officer of subsidiary did not have duty to disclose preliminary merger negotiations involving parent).

53. Thus for example, if negotiations are taking place during a proxy solicitation, the proxy rules would require line item disclosure of all material facts. *See* § 11.2–11.4 *supra.* Similarly, negotiations taking place as a defense to a hostile takeover might have to be disclosed in connection with management's response to the hostile offer. *See* 17 C.F.R. § 240.14e–2 and Schedule 14D–9 which are discussed in §§ 11.14–11.15 *supra.* Material negotiations taking place during a public offering would trigger the line item disclosure requirement. *See* § 3.2–3.7 *supra.* Finally, if the negotiations are material when the issuer's periodic reports become due, line item disclosure will be required. *See* § 9.3 *infra.*

nature of the disclosure are not pertinent in determining the materiality
of a particular misstatement; "[t]he secrecy rationale is merely inappo-
site to the definition of materiality." [54]

Some courts were of the view that preliminary acquisition negotiations need not be disclosed until there has been an agreement in
principle as to the transaction's price and structure.[55] However, the
SEC and many courts took a contrary position reasoning the "price and
structure" threshold frequently would provide too late a materiality
date, especially when the issue is a denial of such negotiations when in
fact they are taking place.[56] The Supreme Court in Basic Inc. v.
Levinson[57] accepted the Commission's view in holding that whether
preliminary merger negotiations have crossed the materiality threshold
is a question of fact. Whether a fact is material depends upon whether a
reasonable investor would consider it significant in making his or her
investment decision.[58] As discussed earlier, materiality generally is
based on a highly factual inquiry and thus is difficult to predict. The
thrust of the Supreme Court decision in Basic seems to favor a finding of
materiality in borderline cases of preliminary negotiations.[59] The ultimate decision on materiality in this context depends upon an evaluation
of the magnitude of the event discounted by the improbability of occur-

54. Basic, Inc. v. Levinson, 485 U.S. 224, 235, 108 S.Ct. 978, 985, 99 L.Ed.2d 194, 211 (1988).

55. *Compare* Flamm v. Eberstadt, 814 F.2d 1169 (7th Cir.), *cert. denied* 484 U.S. 853, 108 S.Ct. 157, 98 L.Ed.2d 112 (1987) (applying price and structure to find preliminary negotiations not material); Greenfield v. Heublein, Inc., 742 F.2d 751 (3d Cir.1984), *cert. denied* 469 U.S. 1215, 105 S.Ct. 1189, 84 L.Ed.2d 336 (1985) (no duty under Rule 10b–5 to disclose merger negotiations where price had not yet been worked out) *with* Jordan v. Duff & Phelps, Inc., 815 F.2d 429, 431 (7th Cir.1987) (*Flamm* price and structure threshold not applicable to closely held corporation); Michaels v. Michaels, 767 F.2d 1185 (7th Cir.1985), *cert. denied* 474 U.S. 1057, 106 S.Ct. 797, 88 L.Ed.2d 774 (1986) (holding "price and structure" threshold inapplicable to merger negotiations involving closely held corporation where there was no public market); Grigsby v. CMI Corp., 765 F.2d 1369, 1373 (9th Cir.1985) (materiality of preliminary merger negotiations depends on the facts; a "looser or more subjective" test is appropriate with face-to-face transactions as opposed to those on the open market; *citing* Thomas v. Duralite Co., 524 F.2d 577, 584–85 (3d Cir.1975)). *But see* Guy v. Duff & Phelps, Inc., 628 F.Supp. 252 (N.D.Ill.1985) (no duty to disclose merger negotiations to resigning vice president who was required to sell his stock upon termi-nation of employment).

56. In re Carnation Co., Exch.Act Rel. No. 34–22214 [1985–86 Transfer Binder] Fed.Sec.L.Rep. (CCH) ¶ 83,801 (July 8, 1985). *Accord* Levinson v. Basic, Inc., 786 F.2d 741 (6th Cir.1986). SEC v. Gaspar, 1985 WL 521, [1984–85 Transfer Binder] Fed.Sec.L.Rep. (CCH) ¶ 92,004 (S.D.N.Y.1985) (finding materiality in insider trading case where negotia-tions had proceeded beyond the exploratory stage and the parties had established precondi-tions and made specific proposals concerning the price). *See also, e.g.,* McLaury v. Duff & Phelps, Inc., 691 F.Supp. 1090 (N.D.Ill.1988). *Cf.* Guy v. Duff & Phelps, Inc., 628 F.Supp. 252 (N.D.Ill.1985) (no duty to disclose prior to reaching agreement in principle).

57. 485 U.S. 224, 108 S.Ct. 978, 99 L.Ed.2d 194 (1988).

58. *Id.*; TSC Industries, Inc. v. Northway, Inc., 426 U.S. 438, 96 S.Ct. 2126, 48 L.Ed.2d 757 (1976). Materiality under the proxy rules is discussed in § 11.4 *supra.*

59. *See* Glazer v. Formica Corp., 964 F.2d 149 (2d Cir.1992) (reversing finding of immateriality as a matter of law; however silence was not actionable); Levinson v. Basic Inc., 786 F.2d 741 (6th Cir.1986), *affirmed and remanded* 485 U.S. 224, 108 S.Ct. 978, 99 L.Ed.2d 194 (1988) (statement that management was not aware of takeover negotiations was held actionable).

rence.[60] This calculus is a good measure of materiality generally.

Questions concerning the need to disclose information may also arise when the issuer, its officers, or directors are questioned by the press or by securities analysts. In such a situation a "no comment" response will avoid liability. "No comment" is the only safe harbor (other than giving a full and honest disclosure), as any other response will trigger the highly factual materiality inquiry.[61] While it is true that there are business reasons for keeping certain information confidential, it does not follow that management should be allowed to respond to inquiries with "white lies". As a result of the *Basic* decision, it is imperative that issuers maintain control of their information.[62] It is wise to limit the people who are authorized to speak on the issuer's behalf and to instruct everyone else to follow a "no comment" policy.

Predictions, Projections, and Other "Soft" Information

Another issue relating to materiality that is getting increased attention is with regard to predictions and other "soft information." [63] There are two questions that frequently arise regarding disclosure of soft information. One question is the extent to which there is an obligation to make a prediction or other disclosures of soft information. A second issue that arises is whether an incorrect opinion, projection, or prediction is actionable.[64] This latter question occurs because of the lesson from the common law of fraud that pure opinion and prediction are not generally actionable.[65]

60. *See, e.g.,* Nobles v. First Carolina Communications, Inc., 929 F.2d 141 (4th Cir.1991) (prospectus in public offering did not have to disclose the possibility that partnership assets might be sold); Pippenger v. McQuik's Oilube, Inc., 854 F.Supp. 1411 (S.D.Ind.1994) (mere overtures to negotiate would not be material); Hartford Fire Insurance Co. v. Federated Department Stores, 723 F.Supp. 976 (S.D.N.Y.1989) (failure to disclose possible effects of restructuring on debentures was not material in light of the slight possibility of such an event, when viewed at the time of the offering).

61. *See* Hazen *supra* footnote 50. *See also, e.g.,* In re Western Waste Securities Litigation, 1994 WL 561165, [1994–1995 Transfer Binder] Fed. Sec. L. Rep. (CCH) ¶ 98,378 (C.D.Cal.1994).

62. This is also important in order to prevent insider trading problems.

63. *See, e.g.,* Porter v. Shearson Lehman Brothers Inc., 802 F.Supp. 41 (S.D.Tex.1992) (brokerage firm had no duty to disclose projections in internal memoranda of oil and gas investment since this type of "soft" information need not be disclosed so long as the "hard" facts are).

64. *See, e.g.,* Hillson Partners L.P. v. Adage, Inc. 42 F.3d 204 (4th Cir.1994) (Chief executive officer's statements in press release that the year would produce "excellent" results were merely predictions and thus not actionable misrepresentations of fact); Kaplan v. Rose, 49 F.3d 1363 (9th Cir.1994) (question of fact as to whether comparison of issuer's product to a competitor's was materially misleading); Malone v. Microdyne Corp., 26 F.3d 471 (4th Cir.1994) (chief executive officer's statement that he was "comfortable" with analyst's prediction of earnings was not actionable; but finding jury question as to whether overly optimistic projections were actionable); Bentley v. Legent Corp., 849 F.Supp. 429 (E.D.Va.1994) (statement that operations were "on plan" or "on target" was not actionable).

65. *Cf., e.g.,* Hillson Partners L.P. v. Adage, Inc., 42 F.3d 204 (4th Cir.1994) (Chief executive officer's statements in press release that the year would produce "excellent" results were merely predictions and thus not actionable misrepresentations of fact); Serabian v. Amoskeag Bank Shares, Inc., 24 F.3d 357, 363 (1st Cir.1994) ("decidedly

As is the case with merger negotiations, absent a voluntary statement or an independent duty to disclose, silence is permissible. There thus is no duty to make a projection, absent a triggering line-item disclosure in an SEC filing.[66] Even when projections, predictions, or valuations pertain to statements being made publicly or in SEC filings, silence may be permissible. Although there is no duty to disclose projections, predictions, or valuations that are purely speculative, where predictions have a sound basis in fact, they must be accurately disclosed.[67] Thus, the mere possibility of an event occurring does not trigger the duty to make a prediction or projection of positive information; yet the SEC has long taken the view that material negative information must be disclosed.[68]

There have been significant changes in the Commission's attitude towards projections. There currently are many line-item disclosure requirements that call for certain types of soft information. For example, under Item 303 of Regulation S–K,[69] in the course of its Management Discussion and Analysis (MD & A) of financial condition and report of operations, management is directed to analyze operations. This analysis must include disclosure of trends and uncertainties likely to have a material effect on the company.[70] The MD & A also should contain discussion of any positive trends that management foresees.[71] The SEC has taken a vigorous enforcement stance on these disclosures.[72] The MD & A disclosure mandate can result in material misstatements or omissions that will give rise to liability.[73] In contrast to the MD & A

---

upbeat" tone of annual report was not actionable); Rand v. Cullinet Software, Inc., 847 F.Supp. 200 (D.Mass.1994) (generalized optimism was not actionable).

66. *See, e.g.,* Levit v. Lyondell Petrochemical Co., 984 F.2d 1050 (9th Cir.1993); Proxima Corp. Securities Litigation, 1994 WL 374306, [1993–1994 Transfer Binder] Fed. Sec. L. Rep. (CCH) ¶ 98,236 (S.D.Cal.1994). *See* text accompanying footnotes 68–77 *infra.*

67. *See, e.g.,* Kowal v. MCI Communications Corp., 16 F.3d 1271 (D.C.Cir.1994) (failure to adequately allege that projections which turned out to be overly optimistic had not been made in good faith); McGonigle v. Combs, 968 F.2d 810 (9th Cir.1992) (low valuations were not actionable); In re Convergent Technologies Securities Litigation, 948 F.2d 507 (9th Cir.1991) (no duty to disclose detailed internal projections).

68. *E.g.,* Starkman v. Marathon Oil Co., 772 F.2d 231 (6th Cir.1985), *cert. denied* 475 U.S. 1015, 106 S.Ct. 1195, 89 L.Ed.2d 310 (1986) (no need to disclose valuations based on highly speculative assumptions).

69. Regulation S–K contains the SEC's basic disclosure guidelines (Regulation S–B is a parallel guide for small business issuers). 17 C.F.R. §§ 228.10, 229.10 et seq., 7 Fed. Sec. L. Rep. (CCH) ¶¶ 71,001 et seq. Violations of Regulation S–K or S–B disclosure requirements are not *per se* actionable but can be used to support a Rule 10b–5 claim. *See* Feldman v. Motorola, Inc., 1994 WL 160115, [1993–1994 Transfer Binder] Fed. Sec. L. Rep. (CCH) ¶ 98,133 (N.D.Ill.1994).

70. *See* Management Discussion and Analysis of Financial Condition, Sec. Act Rel. No. 33–6835 (SEC May 18, 1989) which appears in Appendix A; Mark S. Croft, MD & A: The Tightrope of Disclosure, 45 S.C. L. Rev. 477 (1994).

71. Sec. Act Rel. No. 33–6835 (SEC May 18, 1989).

72. *See* In re Caterpillar, Inc., Exch. Act Rel. No. 34–30532, 6 Fed.Sec.L.Rep. (CCH) ¶ 73,829 (SEC March 31, 1992) (settlement order involving MD & A analysis and failure to adequately discuss the possible risk of lower earnings in the future).

73. *Compare id. with* Ferber v. Travelers Corp., 802 F.Supp. 698 (D.Conn.1992) (finding adequate discussion in MD & A of "known trends" and "uncertainties" relating to

mandate that management make timely disclosure of known trends, it is clear that standing alone there is no duty to disclose internal projections of future performance.[74] Disclosure would, of course, be required if the internal projections were sufficiently convincing to rise to the level of a trend. The line between such mandatory disclosure of trends and permissive disclosure of projections is not a clear one but it has been suggested that some learning may be drawn from the distinction that accountants draw between projections[75] (defined as extrapolations from existing data) and forecasts[76] (appraisals of what is reasonably likely to occur in the future).[77]

With its adoption of Rule 175 under the 1933 Act[78] and Rule 3b–6 of the Exchange Act,[79] the Commission has indicated its decision to encourage the disclosure of projections and other forward-looking statements. Furthermore, in making their required periodic reports under the 1934 Act, as part of management's discussion and analysis of financial conditions, issuers are directed to disclose and explain known trends that are reasonably expected to have a material favorable or unfavorable impact on operations or other aspects of the issuer's financial condition.[80]

problems with issuer's real estate portfolios). *Cf.* In re Jenny Craig Securities Litigation, 1993 WL 456819, [1992–1993 Transfer Binder] Fed.Sec.L.Rep. (CCH) ¶ 97,337 (S.D.Cal. 1992) (Regulation S–K does not create independent private remedy; in order to be actionable, noncompliance must be material and satisfy the other elements of a Rule 10b–5 claim).

74. In re VeriFone Securities Litigation, 11 F.3d 865 (9th Cir.1993); Levit v. Lyondell Petrochemical Co., 984 F.2d 1050 (9th Cir.1993). *See also, e.g.,* In re Compaq Securities Litigation, 848 F.Supp. 1307 (S.D.Tex.1993) (no duty to disclose management's internal consideration of effects of general economic conditions).

75. According to a taskforce of the American Institute of Certified Public Accountants, financial projections deal with financial position, results of operations, and changes in financial position that are based on "knowledge and belief, given one or more hypothetical assumptions." AICPA Financial Forecasts and Projections Task Force, Guide For Prospective Financial Statements 12.

76. In contrast to financial projections, financial forecasts are not based on *hypothetical* assumptions but reflect "to the best of the responsible party's knowledge and belief, an entity's expected financial position, results of operations, and changes in financial position" based on "assumptions reflecting conditions it *expects* to exist and the course of action it *expects* to take." *Id.* at 11 (emphasis supplied).

77. Remarks of Professor Ted J. Fiflis at Securities Law for Non-Securities Lawyers (Charleston, S.C. June 3, 1994).

78. 17 C.F.R. § 230.175. *See, e.g.,* Wielgos v. Commonwealth Edison Co., 892 F.2d 509 (7th Cir.1989) which is discussed in § 3.7 *supra. See also, e.g.,* Arazie v. Mullane, 2 F.3d 1456 (7th Cir.1993) (failing to sufficiently allege lack of reasonable basis so as to remove the presumption of the safe harbor rule).

79. 17 C.F.R. § 240.3b–6. *See, e.g.,* Peregrine Options, Inc. v. Farley, Inc., 1993 WL 489739, [1994–1995 Transfer Binder] Fed. Sec. L. Rep. (CCH) ¶ 98,313 (N.D.Ill.1993) (statement by tender offeror that second-step merger would occur "as soon as practicable" would be outside of safe harbor if not reasonable when made).

80. Reg. S–K Item 303. This requirement is limited to line item disclosures by reporting companies and does not carry over to every public statement made by issuers. *See* Folger Adam Co. v. PMI Industries, Inc., 938 F.2d 1529 (2d Cir.1991), *cert. denied* 502 U.S. 983, 112 S.Ct. 587, 116 L.Ed.2d 612 (1991) (omission of pessimistic earnings projections was not as a matter of law immaterial); In re Sun Microsystems, Inc. Securities Litigation, 1990 WL 169140, [1990 Transfer Binder] Fed.Sec.L.Rep. (CCH) ¶ 95,504 (N.D.Cal.1990).

There has thus been a major expansion of the Commission's earlier position on projections. Based on the Commission's encouragement of forward looking statements, it is not surprising to see an increasing number of cases challenging forecasts as materially misleading.[81] The increase in the use of forward-looking statements does not, however, affect the traditional rule that statements of opinion will not, without more, form the basis of a misrepresentation claim.[82]

Although the MD & A disclosures contained in Item 303 or Regulation S–K require disclosure of "known trends or uncertainties," MD & A does not alter the basic rule that projections are not required.[83] Thus, a failure to make a projection is not actionable unless there is a nondisclosure of facts or known trends that were "known only to the company." [84] A fiduciary duty based on state law, however, may create a duty to disclose internal projections, but only if they can be deemed material.[85]

As pointed out above, once a prediction, projection, or valuation is made, it must withstand materiality scrutiny if there are any inaccuracies.[86] The mere fact that a projection turns out to be wrong is not

81. *See, e.g.,* Hanon v. Dataproducts Corp., 976 F.2d 497 (9th Cir.1992) (summary judgment was inappropriate since a factual issue existed as to whether company's optimistic statements about new product were made at a time when it was known that the product could not be made reliably); In re PNC Securities Litigation, 1992 WL 203474, [1992 Transfer Binder] Fed.Sec.L.Rep. (CCH) ¶ 96,865 (W.D.Pa.1992) (reckless opinions are actionable); In re Sun Microsystems Securities Litigation, 1992 WL 226898, [1992 Transfer Binder] Fed.Sec.L.Rep. (CCH) ¶ 96,916 (N.D.Cal.1992) (misleading projection); Good v. Zenith Electronics Corp., 751 F.Supp. 1320 (N.D.Ill.1990) (earnings prediction can be actionable under securities laws).

82. *See, e.g.,* McGonigle v. Combs, 968 F.2d 810 (9th Cir.1992) (valuation was not actionable); In re Software Publishing Securities Litigation, 1994 WL 261365, [1993–1994 Transfer Binder] Fed. Sec. L. Rep. (CCH) ¶ 98,094 (N.D.Cal.1994) (opinion of ability to meet competition was not actionable); Bolger v. First State Financial Services, 759 F.Supp. 182 (D.N.J.1991) (failure to characterize directors' compensation that was disclosed in detail as "gross overcompensation" was not actionable). *Cf.* In re Healthcare Compare Corp. Securities Litigation, 1993 WL 616683, [1993–1994 Transfer Binder] Fed. Sec. L. Rep. (CCH) ¶ 98,104 (N.D.Ill.1993) (allegation of projection was not sufficient since it had not yet been proven that prediction was wrong).

83. *E.g.,* In re Quarterdeck Office Systems, Inc. Securities Litigation, 1992 WL 515347, [1992–1993 Transfer Binder] Fed.Sec.L.Rep. (CCH) ¶ 97,646 (C.D.Cal.1992) (alleged nondisclosure of adverse sales trends was not actionable in absence of showing that company had knowledge of the trends).

84. Levit v. Lyondell Petrochemical Co., 984 F.2d 1050, 1053 (9th Cir.1993), relying in part on In re Convergent Technologies Securities Litigation, 948 F.2d 507, 516 (9th Cir.1991). *See also, e.g.,* Furman v. Sherwood, 833 F.Supp. 408 (S.D.N.Y.1993) (projections were actionable in light of nondisclosure of material facts to the contrary—issuer talked about excellent prospects without disclosing labor strike).

85. *Id. Accord* Walter v. Holiday Inns, Inc., 985 F.2d 1232 (3d Cir.1993).

86. *E.g.,* Raab v. General Physics Corp., 4 F.3d 286 (4th Cir.1993) (statement that company was poised to carry past success into the future was commercial puffery and thus was not actionable); Bentley v. Legent Corp., 849 F.Supp. 429, 432 (E.D.Va.1994) (references to "tight expense controls" were at worst permissible puffing); Boley v. Pineloch Associates, Ltd., 1993 WL 148962, [1992–1993 Transfer Binder] Fed.Sec.L.Rep. (CCH) ¶ 97,606 (S.D.N.Y.1993) (but fact issues precluded summary judgment as to materiality of allegedly misleading projections); Wyman v. Prime Discount Securities, 819 F.Supp. 79 (D.Me.1993) (puffery and vague allusions to future profitability were not actionable). *Cf.* Colby v. Hologic, Inc., 817 F.Supp. 204 (D.Mass.1993) (failure to allege scienter with regard to allegedly misleading forecasts).

sufficient to state a Rule 10b–5 claim.[87] Borrowing from the common law of misrepresentation, in certain cases the courts have tolerated some degree of "puffing" or "sales talk." [88] However, given the importance of full candor, courts should be reluctant to permit misrepresentation under the guise of puffing. Misrepresentation by implying the existence of certain facts cannot be disguised as mere puffing.[89] Similarly, use of percentages may imply a factual basis and if so, cannot be protected as mere puffing.[90] Reading the relevant securities cases yields the following general rule: while a good faith opinion (or even "puffing") is not material, a statement of opinion made with no belief in its truth is actionable.[91] This is consistent with the general rule that merely because statements are couched as opinion does not preclude a finding that there is an express or implied misrepresentation of fact.[92] Similar results follow with regard to statements of intent. It is clear that a good faith statement of present intent does not become actionable simply because of a change of intent.[93] When there is such a change of intent, it will be necessary to give timely notice by making a corrective disclosure.[94] As with statements of intention, motivation frequently is not a

---

87. *E.g.,* Wielgos v. Commonwealth Edison Co., 892 F.2d 509 (7th Cir.1989); Wells v. HBO & Co., 1994 WL 228842, [1993–1994 Transfer Binder] Fed. Sec. L. Rep. (CCH) ¶ 98,181 (N.D.Ga.1994); In re New America High Income Fund Securities Litigation, 834 F.Supp. 501 (D.Mass.1993), *affirmed in part, reversed in part* 3 F.3d 170 (1st Cir.1994). *See also, e.g.,* Raab v. General Physics Corp., 4 F.3d 286 (4th Cir.1993) (predictions about future earnings were not material since discussions of growth were merely "loose predictions"). Additional cases are collected in § 3.7 *supra.*

88. *E.g.,* Howard v. Haddad, 962 F.2d 328 (4th Cir.1992) (statements that bank was good investment was mere puffery); Shapiro v. UJB Financial Corp., 964 F.2d 272 (3d Cir.1992), *cert. denied* ___ U.S. ___, 113 S.Ct. 365, 121 L.Ed.2d 278 (1992) (statement that company looked to future with great optimism was inactionable puffery).

89. *E.g.,* In re Medimmune, Inc. Securities Litigation, 873 F.Supp. 953 (D.Md.1995) (statement that "there was absolutely no question about the efficacy" of a product could be actionable).

90. Newman v. L.F. Rothschild, Unterberg, Towbin, 662 F.Supp. 957 (S.D.N.Y.1987).

91. *See, e.g.,* In re Applied Magnetics Corp. Securities Litigation, 1994 WL 486550, [1994–1995 Transfer Binder] Fed. Sec. L. Rep. (CCH) ¶ 98,345 (C.D.Cal.1994) (optimistic statements were actionable in light of allegations that management knew company's technology was obsolete).

92. *See, e.g.,* Westwood v. Cohen, 838 F.Supp. 126 (S.D.N.Y.1993) ("comforting" statements regarding governmental investigation could be actionable).

93. In re Phillips Petroleum Securities Litigation, 881 F.2d 1236, 1245 (3d Cir.1989), *on remand* 738 F.Supp. 825 (D.Del.1990). *See also, e.g.,* Panfil v. ACC Corp., 768 F.Supp. 54 (W.D.N.Y.1991), *affirmed* 952 F.2d 394 (2d Cir.1991) (intent to pursue a possible merger was not material); *cf.* CL–Alexanders Laing & Cruickshank v. Goldfeld, 739 F.Supp. 158 (S.D.N.Y.1990) (failure to meet sales projections was not actionable absent a showing that the projections were materially misleading and made with scienter); Levine v. NL Industries, Inc., 720 F.Supp. 305 (S.D.N.Y.1989) (claim against corporation dismissed for failure to establish it was reckless not to know that its financial future would not be as predicted). *But cf.* Primary Care Investors, Seven v. PHP Healthcare Corp., 986 F.2d 1208 (8th Cir.1993) (alleged nondisclosure of planned public offering was material).

94. *Ibid. See, e.g.,* 5A Arnold S. Jacobs, Litigation and Practice Under Rule 10b–5 § 61.01[c][iii] at 3–68 to 3–70 (2d ed.1988). *Cf.* Backman v. Polaroid Corp., 893 F.2d 1405 (1st Cir.1990) (although not initially misleading, subsequent developments triggered a duty to correct overly optimistic predictions); Kirby v. Cullinet Software, Inc., 721 F.Supp. 1444 (D.Mass.1989) (duty to correct first quarter projection). *See also, e.g.,* Cytryn v. Cook, 1990 WL 128233, [1990 Transfer Binder] Fed.Sec.L.Rep. (CCH) ¶ 95,409 (N.D.Cal.1990)

material fact.[95]

Duty to Correct or Update

As mentioned above and as discussed more fully in a later section,[96] absent a specific line-item requirement in an SEC filing, there is no affirmative duty to disclose merely because a fact is material. However, once a statement has been made, there is then a duty to correct any misstatements as well as a duty to update the public as to any material changes.[97] This rule has particular impact upon companies making projections and other forward-looking statements. Even if the initial statements are made in good faith and therefore cannot be the basis of liability, once it appears that the projection is no longer materially accurate, there will be an affirmative duty to update and therefore correct any misimpression created by the initial statement.

§ 13.5B Reliance in Rule 10b–5 Actions; Fraud on the Market

Reliance Defined

The reliance requirement is a corollary of materiality.[1] As is true under common law, the reliance requirement applies in securities fraud cases. There is authority to the effect, however, that in an SEC enforcement action, it is not necessary to establish reliance.[2] Furthermore, even in private suits, in some instances the courts have not

---

(literal truth of initial statement does not prevent statement from becoming actionable when subsequent statements may have rendered it misleading).

95. *E.g.,* Frank H. Cobb, Inc. v. Cooper Companies, Inc., 1992 WL 77600, [1991–1992 Transfer Binder] Fed.Sec.L.Rep. (CCH) ¶ 96,576 (S.D.N.Y.1992), *reargument denied* 1992 WL 80759 (S.D.N.Y.1992); In re United States Shoe Corp. Litigation, 718 F.Supp. 643 (S.D.Ohio 1989). *See also* Virginia Bankshares, Inc. v. Sandberg, 501 U.S. 1083, 111 S.Ct. 2749, 115 L.Ed.2d 929 (1991), *appeal after remand* 979 F.2d 332 (4th Cir.1992), *opinion vacated* 1993 WL 524680 (4th Cir.1993) and the cases cited in § 11.4 *supra.* *But cf.* Washington Bancorporation v. Washington, 1989 WL 180755, [1989–1990 Transfer Binder] Fed.Sec.L.Rep. ¶ 94,893 (D.D.C.1989) (if proxy statement denies management had a certain motive, that statement could be actionable if proven false).

96. *See* § 13.10 *infra.*

97. In re Time Warner, Inc. Securities Litigation, 9 F.3d 259 (2d Cir.1993). *Cf.* Trafton v. Deacon Barclays de Zoete Wedd Ltd., 1994 WL 746199, [1994–1995 Transfer Binder] Fed. Sec. L. Rep. (CCH) ¶ 98,481 (N.D. Cal. 1994) (question of fact whether statements were materially misleading in light of subsequent curative disclosures).

§ 13.5B

1. "Thus, to the requirement that the individual plaintiff must have acted upon the fact misrepresented, is added the parallel requirement that a reasonable man would also have acted upon the fact misrepresented." List v. Fashion Park, Inc., 340 F.2d 457, 462 (2d Cir. 1965), *cert. denied* 382 U.S. 811, 86 S.Ct. 23, 15 L.Ed.2d 60 (1965), *rehearing denied* 382 U.S. 933, 86 S.Ct. 305, 15 L.Ed.2d 344 (1965). Therefore, there must be some connection between the alleged fraud and the transaction under attack. *E.g.,* Jackvony v. RIHT Financial Corp., 873 F.2d 411 (1st Cir.1989). *See also* § 13.6 *infra.*

2. *E.g.,* SEC v. Rana Research, Inc., 8 F.3d 1358 (9th Cir.1993). *But cf.* In re Ivan F. Boesky Securities Litigation, 848 F.Supp. 1119 (S.D.N.Y.1994) (prior SEC action found sufficient reliance so that defendant in private suit was collaterally estopped from relitigating reliance).

required proof of actual reliance.[3] Proof of reliance is an especially difficult problem in an omission case where the question is how the plaintiff would have acted had the required information been disclosed. Some courts view the reliance requirement as including a showing that the defendant's conduct induced the plaintiff's transaction,[4] but most courts do not take such a strict view. The question of inducement is more properly viewed as a question of causation.[5]

Presumption of Reliance

The Supreme Court in Affiliated Ute Citizens of Utah v. United States[6] has held that in a face-to-face transaction between seller and purchaser where the defendant purchaser omitted to state material facts, the plaintiff's reliance can be presumed from the materiality of the omissions. The Court there held that upon a finding of materiality it is then up to the defendant to prove that the plaintiff had not in fact relied on the material omissions. Many subsequent district court and court of appeals decisions have followed this presumption of reliance in omission cases but have refused to extend this ruling to the extent of eliminating the reliance requirements from the securities laws even in the case of face-to-face transactions.[7]

The courts in recognizing the presumption in favor of reliance will allow the defendants to rebut the presumption.[8] The *Affiliated Ute*

---

3. *See, e.g.* Fulco, Inc. v. American Cable Systems, 1989 WL 205356, [1989–1990 Transfer Binder] Fed.Sec.L.Rep. ¶ 94,980 (D.Mass.1989) (limited partners need not show reliance since they were forced sellers). However, in other contexts actual reliance must be shown. *E.g.* Levine v. Prudential Bache Properties, Inc., 855 F.Supp. 924 (N.D.Ill.1994) (complaint failed to plead actual reliance on prospectus).

4. *E.g.,* Barnes v. Resource Royalties, Inc., 610 F.Supp. 499 (E.D.Mo.1985), *reversed* 795 F.2d 1359 (8th Cir.1986) (although misinformation was materially misleading there was no showing that it was crucial to plaintiff's investment decision). *See* Harris v. Union Electric Co., 787 F.2d 355, 367 (8th Cir.), *cert. denied* 479 U.S. 823, 107 S.Ct. 94, 93 L.Ed.2d 45 (1986).

5. This can be viewed as a question of transaction causation. Causation is discussed in § 13.6 *infra. Compare, e.g.,* Alten v. T.A.E.I., Inc., 1994 WL 530140, [1994–1995 Transfer Binder] Fed. Sec. L. Rep. (CCH) ¶ 98,411 (E.D.Pa.1994) (plaintiff who voluntarily signed a disclaimer of reliance could not satisfy Rule 10b–5's reliance requirement).

6. 406 U.S. 128, 153–154, 92 S.Ct. 1456, 1472, 31 L.Ed.2d 741 (1972), *rehearing denied* 407 U.S. 916, 92 S.Ct. 2430, 32 L.Ed.2d 692 (1972).

7. *See, e.g.,* duPont v. Brady, 828 F.2d 75 (2d Cir.1987) (defendant lawyer had burden of rebutting presumption of reliance); Barnes v. Resource Royalties, Inc., 795 F.2d 1359 (8th Cir.1986) (presumption of reliance applied in face-to-face transaction); Rifkin v. Crow, 574 F.2d 256 (5th Cir.1978), *on remand* 80 F.R.D. 285 (N.D.Tex.1978).

8. *See* Basic Inc. v. Levinson, 485 U.S. 224, 108 S.Ct. 978, 99 L.Ed.2d 194 (1988); Michaels v. Michaels, 767 F.2d 1185, 1205–06 n. 8 (7th Cir.1985), *cert. denied* 474 U.S. 1057, 106 S.Ct. 797, 88 L.Ed.2d 774 (1986); Barnebey v. E.F. Hutton & Co., 715 F.Supp. 1512 (M.D.Fla.1989) (statement in subscription agreement that investor did not rely on anything outside the private placement memorandum was probative of the defendants' claim of nonreliance); Frain v. Andy Frain, Inc., 660 F.Supp. 97 (N.D.Ill.1987); Hecox v. R.G. Dickenson & Co., 1987 WL 14502, [1987 Transfer Binder] Fed.Sec.L.Rep. (CCH) ¶ 93,237 (D.Kan.1987). *See also, e.g.,* United States v. Wallach, 1988 WL 140832, [1988–89 Transfer Binder] Fed.Sec.L.Rep. (CCH) ¶ 94,116 (S.D.N.Y.1988) (applying presumption of reliance); Jackson v. First Federal Savings of Arkansas, F.A., 709 F.Supp. 887 (E.D.Ark. 1989) (semble).

presumption arose in the context of an omission case. Some courts have held that this presumption of reliance[9] does not apply in the case of misstatements (as opposed to omissions) to the extent that the plaintiff is in a position to prove reliance.[10]

Reliance in Class Actions

In what has been described as "an absurdity" [11] in light of its cost and impracticability, the Second Circuit has indicated that in a class action separate trials might be necessary in order to resolve the issue of reliance with regard to transactions in a faceless market.[12] On the other hand, typicality for class action purposes does not mean that the claims must be identical; and class actions will be permitted to proceed unless it is clear that the common questions of fact do not predominate.[13] Plaintiffs in a class action, for example, may not be proper representatives with regard to transactions and statements made subsequent to the plaintiff's purchases.[14] However, where the allegations are based on a theory that there was a common scheme to defraud, named plaintiffs will

9. In contrast, the fraud on the market presumption of reliance applies in cases of material misstatements. Fraud on the market is discussed later in this section. *See* text accompanying footnotes 33–67 *infra.*

10. *See* Cox v. Collins, 7 F.3d 394 (4th Cir.1993) (plaintiff alleged both nondisclosure and material misstatements; the *Affiliated Ute* presumption was therefore unavailable); Professional Service Industries, Inc. v. Kimbrell, 841 F.Supp. 358 (D.Kan.1993) (presumption of reliance did not apply where claims were primarily ones of misrepresentations); Eckstein v. Balcor Film Investors, 740 F.Supp. 572 (E.D.Wis.1990), *affirmed on other grounds* 8 F.3d 1121 (7th Cir.1993).

11. Richard W. Jennings & Harold Marsh, Jr., Securities Regulation: Cases and Materials 1049 (5th ed. 1982).

12. Green v. Wolf Corp., 406 F.2d 291 (2d Cir.1968), *cert. denied* 395 U.S. 977, 89 S.Ct. 2131, 23 L.Ed.2d 766 (1969). *Accord* Neuman v. Electronic Specialty Co., 1969 WL 2828, [1969–1970 Transfer Binder] Fed.Sec.L.Rep. (CCH) ¶ 92,591 (N.D.Ill.1969). *See also* Greenwald v. Integrated Energy, Inc., 102 F.R.D. 65 (S.D.Tex.1984).

13. *E.g.,* Moorhead v. Merrill Lynch, Pierce, Fenner & Smith, Inc., 1989 WL 91110, [1989 Transfer Binder] Fed.Sec.L.Rep. (CCH) ¶ 94,448 (D.Minn.1989); In re Western Union Securities Litigation, 120 F.R.D. 629 (D.N.J.1988); Ockerman v. King & Spalding, 1988 WL 39937, [1987–88 Transfer Binder] Fed.Sec.L.Rep. (CCH) ¶ 93,707 (N.D.Ga.1988); Gary Plastic Packaging Corp. v. Merrill Lynch, Pierce, Fenner & Smith, 119 F.R.D. 344 (S.D.N.Y.1988); In re New York City Shoes Securities Litigation, 1988 WL 17843, [1987–88 Transfer Binder] Fed.Sec.L.Rep. (CCH) ¶ 93,670 (E.D.Pa.1988); Sheftelman v. Jones, 667 F.Supp. 859 (N.D.Ga.1987); Nelsen v. Craig–Hallum, Inc., 659 F.Supp. 480 (D.Minn.1987). *See also, e.g.,* Shores v. Sklar, 844 F.2d 1485 (11th Cir.1988) (fraud on the market theory of reliance is sufficient for class certification); Kirkpatrick v. J.C. Bradford & Co., 827 F.2d 718 (11th Cir.1987) (semble); Snider v. Upjohn Co., 115 F.R.D. 536 (E.D.Pa.1987) (semble).

The Supreme Court has upheld use of a presumption of reliance based on a theory that there has been a fraud on the market. Basic Inc. v. Levinson, 485 U.S. 224, 108 S.Ct. 978, 99 L.Ed.2d 194 (1988), *on remand* 871 F.2d 562 (6th Cir.1989). The Court's willingness to presume reliance on appropriate facts adds strength to the trend of cases that favor the continuation of class actions rather than severing the actions prior to trial. *See, e.g.,* Tolan v. Computervision Corp., 696 F.Supp. 771 (D.Mass.1988).

14. In re Donald J. Trump Casino Securities Litigation, 793 F.Supp. 543, 565 (D.N.J. 1992); Hoexter v. Simmons, 140 F.R.D. 416 (D.Ariz.1991). Conversely, when any possible effects of the alleged fraud had ended by the time plaintiff purchased stock, plaintiff was not a proper class representative. Rand v. Cullinet Software, Inc., 847 F.Supp. 200 (D.Mass.1994).

be permitted to represent subsequent purchasers.[15]

The clear trend is to favor continuation of the class. For example, it has been pointed out that the question of whether individual trials on the reliance issue are necessary is itself a question that is common to the whole class.[16] Accordingly, the proper approach is to let the litigation continue as a class action until it becomes apparent that the common issues no longer predominate. Some courts have held that a plaintiff's testimony is conclusive of reliance in such a case,[17] while others have conclusively presumed reliance from the materiality of the undisclosed facts.[18] In contrast, the Sixth Circuit has refused to so extend *Affiliated Ute* and has denied the existence of a Rule 10b–5 claim in a nondisclosure case because of the impossibility of establishing reliance or a causal connection with regard to an open-market transaction.[19] The Sixth Circuit case involved insider trading in a faceless market and the court was also concerned with the absence of any causal relationship between the defendant's trades and those of the plaintiffs. Although the reliance and causation requirements are inextricably related to one another, they are separate elements of a 10b–5 claim.[20] To the extent that the Sixth Circuit's ruling is based on the inability to find reliance in an open market context, the decision has been overruled by the Supreme Court's adoption of the fraud on the market presumption of reliance that flows from a finding of materiality.[21] Nevertheless, the decision is not affected insofar as it was based on the inability to show causation in such a case.

---

15. Renz v. Schreiber, 832 F.Supp. 766, 772–73 (D.N.J.1993); Feldman v. Motorola, Inc., 1993 WL 497228, [1993 Transfer Binder] Fed. Sec. L. Rep. (CCH) ¶ 97,806 (N.D.Ill. 1993); Robbins v. Moore Medical Corp., 788 F.Supp. 179, 187 (S.D.N.Y.1992); Nicholas v. Poughkeepsie Savings Bank/FSB, 1990 WL 145154, [1990–1991 Transfer Binder] Fed. Sec. L. Rep. (CCH) ¶ 95,606 (S.D.N.Y.1990).

16. *E.g.,* In re Western Union Securities Litigation, 120 F.R.D. 629 (D.N.J.1988). *See generally* Lawrence D. Bernfeld, Class Actions and Federal Securities Laws, 55 Cornell L.Rev. 78 (1969); James L. Leader, Threshold Prerequisites to Securities Fraud Class Actions, 48 Tex.L.Rev. 417 (1970); Mordecai Rosenfeld, Impact of Class Actions on Corporate and Securities Law, 1972 Duke L.J. 1167.

17. Fischer v. Wolfinbarger, 55 F.R.D. 129 (W.D.Ky.1971).

18. Shapiro v. Merrill Lynch, Pierce, Fenner & Smith, Inc., 495 F.2d 228 (2d Cir.1974). *See also* Peil v. Speiser, 806 F.2d 1154 (3d Cir.1986); Harris v. Union Electric Co., 787 F.2d 355, 367 (8th Cir.), *cert. denied* 479 U.S. 823, 107 S.Ct. 94, 93 L.Ed.2d 45 (1986); Rowe v. Maremont Corp., 650 F.Supp. 1091 (N.D.Ill.1986).

19. *Cf.* Fridrich v. Bradford, 542 F.2d 307 (6th Cir.1976), *cert. denied* 429 U.S. 1053, 97 S.Ct. 767, 50 L.Ed.2d 769 (1977). *See* § 13.9 *infra. See also, e.g.,* Abell v. Potomac Ins. Co., 858 F.2d 1104 (5th Cir.1988), *rehearing denied* 863 F.2d 882 (5th Cir.1988) (limiting presumption of reliance to omission cases).

20. *But see* Rowe v. Maremont Corp., 850 F.2d 1226, 1233 (7th Cir.1988) ("reliance means only materiality and causation in conjunction * * * reliance is no longer 'an element independent of causation and materiality in a case under Rule 10b–5'") (quoting from Flamm v. Eberstadt, 814 F.2d 1169, 1173, 1174 (7th Cir.1987), *cert. denied* 484 U.S. 853, 108 S.Ct. 157, 98 L.Ed.2d 112 (1987)). Causation is discussed in § 13.6 *infra.*

21. Basic Inc. v. Levinson, 485 U.S. 224, 108 S.Ct. 978, 99 L.Ed.2d 194 (1988), *affirming* 786 F.2d 741 (6th Cir.1986). *See* the discussion in the text accompanying footnotes 73–76 *infra. See also, e.g.,* Cohen v. Alan Bush Brokerage Co., 1987 WL 65038, [1987–88 Transfer Binder] Fed.Sec.L.Rep. (CCH) ¶ 93,553 (S.D.Fla.1987) (presuming reliance in case involving alleged nondisclosures by corporate directors). *Cf.* Zlotnick v. TIE Communications, 665 F.Supp. 397 (E.D.Pa.1987), *vacated* 836 F.2d 818 (3d Cir.1988) (in

Proof of Reliance

Proving reliance in the case of nondisclosure can be problematic. Following the *Affiliated Ute* case, courts should presume reliance from materiality. However, as the Eleventh Circuit has held, the presumption of reliance in a nondisclosure case depends upon the plaintiff being able to demonstrate that he or she generally relied upon the defendant.[22]

Reasonableness of Reliance

Any reliance by the plaintiff must be reasonable.[23] It has been held, for example, that a plaintiff claiming reliance on alleged material misstatements will be charged with knowledge of warnings in the private placement memorandum concerning the investment risks, thus making reliance unreasonable.[24] As noted earlier, many courts have referred to this as the "bespeaks caution" doctrine which, on appropriate facts, will preclude a finding of reasonable reliance.[25] However, blanket warnings and disclaimers in offering materials cannot preclude reliance on otherwise materially misleading statements.[26] The cautionary language must

---

fraud on the market case reliance can be rebutted by a showing of nonmateriality or proof that there were insufficient traders to affect the price). *But see* Murray v. Hospital Corporation of America, 682 F.Supp. 343, 347 n. 4 (M.D.Tenn.1988) ("Given certain *dicta* in *Levinson*, it is not altogether clear whether the 'fraud-on-the-market' theory applies to cases involving insider trading and material omissions. *See Levinson*, 786 F.2d at 751 (distinguishing Fridrich [v. Bradford, 542 F.2d 307 (6th Cir.1976), *cert. denied* 429 U.S. 1053, 97 S.Ct. 767, 50 L.Ed.2d 769 (1977)]). As the *Levinson* court of appeals decision noted, in such cases there is no way that the defendants' wrongful acts can affect market price"). *See also, e.g.,* Grubb v. FDIC, 868 F.2d 1151 (10th Cir.1989) (upholding jury's finding of reliance).

22. Cavalier Carpets, Inc. v. Caylor, 746 F.2d 749 (11th Cir.1984).

23. *See* Schlesinger v. Herzog, 2 F.3d 135 (5th Cir.1993) (plaintiff could not establish reasonable reliance since he did not exercise due diligence); Jensen v. Kimble, 1 F.3d 1073 (10th Cir.1993) (plaintiff who was aware of true facts could not establish reliance); Brown v. E.F. Hutton Group, Inc., 991 F.2d 1020 (2d Cir.1993) (offering materials contained sufficient disclosures so as to preclude a finding of justifiable reliance on allegedly materially misleading assurances of suitability).

24. Ambrosino v. Rodman & Renshaw, Inc., 972 F.2d 776 (7th Cir.1992) (written disclosures precluded reliance on oral misrepresentations that were at variance with the writing); Davidson v. Wilson, 973 F.2d 1391 (8th Cir.1992) (no reliance on oral statements in light of written disclaimers); Topalian v. Ehrman, 954 F.2d 1125 (5th Cir.1992), *rehearing denied* 961 F.2d 215 (1992) (offering memorandum explaining risks precluded investors' reliance on alleged false promises of low risk and high profits); Ligon v. Deloitte, Haskins & Sells, 957 F.2d 546 (8th Cir.1992) (detailed disclosure of risks in 18–page offering memorandum precluded reliance on net worth representations); In re Donald J. Trump Casino Securities Litigation, 793 F.Supp. 543 (D.N.J.1992), *affirmed* 7 F.3d 357 (3d Cir.1993) ("bespeaks caution" doctrine precluded reliance on projections in light of adequate cautionary language in prospectus).

25. The genesis of the doctrine is found in Polin v. Conductron Corp., 552 F.2d 797, 806 n. 28 (8th Cir.), *cert. denied* 434 U.S. 857, 98 S.Ct. 178, 54 L.Ed.2d 129 (1977) (the cautionary language were words which "bespeak caution in outlook and fall far short of the assurance required for a finding of falsity or fraud").

See generally Donald C. Langevoort, Disclosures that "Bespeak Caution," 49 Bus. Law. 481 (1994).

26. Alten v. Berman, 1993 WL 541668, [1993–1994 Transfer Binder] Fed. Sec. L. Rep. (CCH) ¶ 98,045 (E.D.Pa.1993) (statements by bank financing limited partnership offering were just sales talk; had investors been able to show that bank gave the impression it had made a careful analysis of the investment, then the statements might have been action-

be sufficient to adequately negate any reasonable implication to the contrary from the projection or prediction.[27] The Tenth Circuit has summarized the relevant factors considered by the courts:

> the following are all relevant factors in determining whether reliance was justifiable: (1) the sophistication and expertise of the plaintiff in financial and securities matters; (2) the existence of long standing business or personal relationships; (3) access to the relevant information; (4) the existence of a fiduciary relationship; (5) concealment of the fraud; (6) the opportunity to detect the fraud; (7) whether the plaintiff initiated the stock transaction or sought to expedite the transaction; and (8) the generality or specificity of the misrepresentations.[28]

The requirement that the reliance be justifiable echoes the common law.[29] The requirement that the reliance be reasonable has been described as not so much a question of barring recovery because of the plaintiff's fault but rather as one of whether it was the misrepresentation that in fact caused the plaintiff's harm.[30]

Factual Nature of the Inquiry

Following the same pattern as cases involving materiality, questions of reliance are highly factual and thus courts are properly reluctant to dismiss on the pleadings.[31] As is also the case with other elements of

---

able); In re First American Center Securities Litigation, 807 F.Supp. 326 (S.D.N.Y.1992); Geisenberger v. John Hancock Distributors, Inc., 774 F.Supp. 1045 (S.D.Miss.1991) (fact that investor received prospectus did not preclude reliance on oral statements); Parnes v. Mast Property Investors, Inc., 776 F.Supp. 792 (S.D.N.Y.1991); Landy v. Mitchell Petroleum Technology Corp., 734 F.Supp. 608 (S.D.N.Y.1990) (reliance sufficiently pleaded notwithstanding warnings of risk); In Rexplore, Inc. Securities Litigation, 671 F.Supp. 679 (N.D.Cal.1987), s.c., 685 F.Supp. 1132 (N.D.Cal.1988). *Cf.* Bruschi v. Brown, 876 F.2d 1526 (11th Cir.1989) (fact that purchaser did not read disclosure documents did not preclude a finding of reliance on alleged oral misstatements).

27. *E.g.,* Rubinstein v. Collins, 20 F.3d 160 (5th Cir.1994); Wade v. Industrial Funding Corp., 1993 WL 650837, [1993–1994 Transfer Binder] Fed. Sec. L. Rep. (CCH) ¶ 98,144 (N.D.Cal.1993) (minimal boilerplate language did not provide a sufficient warning); Alten v. Berman, 1993 WL 541668, [1993–1994 Transfer Binder] Fed. Sec. L. Rep. (CCH) ¶ 98,045 (E.D.Pa.1993) (statements by bank financing limited partnership offering were just sales talk; had investors been able to show that bank gave the impression it had made a careful analysis of the investment, then the statements might have been actionable).

See also, e.g., Kaplan v. Rose, 49 F.3d 1363 (9th Cir.1994) (question of fact as to whether cautionary language concerning defendant's medical treatment system had been sufficiently disseminated to the public).

28. Zobrist v. Coal–X, Inc., 708 F.2d 1511, 1516 (10th Cir.1983). *Accord, e.g.,* Davidson v. Wilson, 973 F.2d 1391, 1400 (8th Cir.1992) (finding investors reliance was not reasonable).

29. *See generally* W. Page Keeton, Dan B. Dobbs, Robert E. Keeton & David G. Owen, Prosser and Keeton on Torts § 108 (5th ed. 1984).

30. Atari Corp. v. Ernst & Whinney, 981 F.2d 1025 (9th Cir.1992) (justifiable reliance is not a matter of contributory negligence).

31. *See, e.g.,* LaBelle v. Chereskin, 1991 WL 3050, [1990–1991 Transfer Binder] Fed.Sec.L.Rep. (CCH) ¶ 95,713 (S.D.N.Y.1991) (factual issues needed to be resolved at trial); Longden v. Sunderman, 737 F.Supp. 968 (N.D.Tex.1990) (denying summary judgment); Connor v. First of Michigan Corp., 1990 WL 120644, [1990 Transfer Binder] Fed.Sec.L.Rep. ¶ 95,350 (W.D.Mich.1990) (justifiability of plaintiff's reliance raised factual

Rule 10b–5 claims, reliance must be pleaded with sufficient particularity.[32]

Fraud on the Market as Proof of Reliance

In applying the presumption of reliance a number of courts have fashioned a fraud on the market theory[33] which has also been recognized by the Supreme Court.[34] Simply put, the courts find that the reliance requirement can been satisfied by a showing that the market price was affected by the misstatement or omission and the plaintiff's injury is due to a purchase or sale at the then fraudulently induced market price.[35] For example, in fraud on the market cases, some courts have held that proof that the market price was affected will prove reliance by the market,[36] even if the plaintiff never saw the statements in question.[37] Merely establishing a material misrepresentation, however, will not trigger the fraud on the market presumption unless it can also be shown that the market reacted to the misstatements.[38] Thus, for example, sufficient cautionary information available to the public may preclude a

---

issues precluding summary judgment); Becher v. Farkas, 717 F.Supp. 1327 (N.D.Ill.1989) (denying summary judgment).

32. *E.g.,* ECL Industries, Inc. v. Ticor & Southern Pacific Co., 1986 WL 9222, [1986–87 Transfer Binder] Fed.Sec.L.Rep. (CCH) ¶ 92,887 (S.D.N.Y.1986). The particularity requirement is discussed in § 13.8.1 *infra* (Practitioner's Edition only).

33. *E.g.* Hayes v. Gross, 982 F.2d 104 (3d Cir.1992) (sufficient allegations of efficient market permitted fraud on the market presumption).

34. Basic Inc. v. Levinson, 485 U.S. 224, 108 S.Ct. 978, 99 L.Ed.2d 194 (1988). *See also* In re Apple Computer Securities Litigation, 886 F.2d 1109 (9th Cir.1989), *cert. denied* 496 U.S. 943, 110 S.Ct. 3229, 110 L.Ed.2d 676 (1990); In re Seagate Technology II Securities Litigation, 843 F.Supp. 1341, 1368–69 (N.D.Cal.1994).

See generally Bradford Cornell & R. Gregory Morgan, Using Finance Theory to Measure Damages in Fraud on the Market Cases, 37 U.C.L.A.L.Rev. 883 (1990); Goforth, The Efficient Capital Market Hypothesis—An Inadequate Justification for a Fraud on the Market Presumption, 27 Wake Forest L.Rev. 895 (1992); Note, The Fraud-on-the-Market Theory: A Contrarian View, 38 Emory L.J. 1269 (1989).

35. *Cf.* In re Columbia Securities Litigation, 155 F.R.D. 466 (S.D.N.Y.1994) (defendant's evidence that price did not drop as a result of alleged materially misleading statements did not preclude fraud on the market claim since the misstatements might have forestalled a price rise which otherwise would have occurred).

36. *E.g.* Zweig v. Hearst Corp., 594 F.2d 1261, 1271 (9th Cir.1979); Rose v. Arkansas Valley Environmental & Utility Authority, 562 F.Supp. 1180 (W.D.Mo.1983); Frankel v. Wyllie & Thornhill, Inc., 537 F.Supp. 730 (W.D.Va.1982); Mottoros v. Abrams, 524 F.Supp. 254 (N.D.Ill.1981). *See also, e.g.,* Steiner v. Southmark Corp., 734 F.Supp. 269 (N.D.Tex. 1990) (sufficiently alleging fraud on the market).

37. In re Control Data Corp. Securities Litigation, 933 F.2d 616 (8th Cir.1991), *cert. denied* 502 U.S. 967, 112 S.Ct. 438, 116 L.Ed.2d 457 (1991); Fine v. American Solar King Corp., 919 F.2d 290 (5th Cir.1990), *cert. dismissed* 502 U.S. 976, 112 S.Ct. 576, 116 L.Ed.2d 601 (1991); Dekro v. Stern Brothers & Co., 540 F.Supp. 406 (W.D.Mo.1982). *Contra* Fausett v. American Resources Management Corp., 542 F.Supp. 1234 (D.Utah 1982).

See also, e.g., Kumpis v. Wetterau, 586 F.Supp. 152 (E.D.Mo.1983); Kennedy v. Nicastro, 517 F.Supp. 1157 (N.D.Ill.1981).

38. *See* Lee v. Sierra On–Line, 1994 WL 655898, [1994–1995 Transfer Binder] Fed. Sec. L. Rep. (CCH) ¶ 98,420 (E.D.Cal.1994) (failure to establish that the alleged misrepresentations proximately caused a decline in the stock price); In re Compaq Securities Litigation, 848 F.Supp. 1307, 1313(S.D.Tex.1993).

fraud on the market claim.[39]   However, once the presumption is established, the defendant must show that the price was not causally effected.[40]   As is the case with fraud claims generally, the allegations regarding the elements of fraud on the market must be pleaded with particularity.[41]

There is considerable authority for the proposition that the fraud on
the market theory of reliance is dependent on the existence of an
efficient market.[42]   Accordingly, the fraud on the market presumption
depends on the existence of an active market.   It would appear that the
absence of an efficient market should be sufficient to rebut any presumption of reliance based solely on market impact.   However, the Eleventh
Circuit has held that even undeveloped markets can provide a basis for
the fraud on the market presumption of reliance, at least where the
defendants knew that there would be no market but for their scheme to
defraud.[43]   This type of case does not really involve a fraud *on* the
market but rather a fraudulent scheme depicting the existence of a
market which in fact would not exist upon full and accurate disclosure.
Some courts have referred to this as a "fraud created the market"
theory of recovery.[44]   This relatively new theory of recovery has been
adopted by some federal courts,[45] and it has been adopted by at least one

---

39.   Kaplan v. Rose, 49 F.3d 1363 (9th Cir.1994).   *See, also, e.g.,* In re Taxable
Municipal Bonds Litigation, 1994 WL 532079, [1994–1995 Transfer Binder] Fed. Sec. L.
Rep. (CCH) ¶ 98,405 (E.D.La.1994) (defendants rebutted the fraud on the market presumption by showing sufficient accurate information to negate the alleged misrepresentations
was available to the public).

40.   Basic Inc. v. Levinson, 485 U.S. 224, 248, 108 S.Ct. 978, 992, 99 L.Ed.2d 194 (1988);
In re Harcourt Brace Jovanovich, Inc. Securities Litigation, 838 F.Supp. 109 (S.D.N.Y.
1993).

41.   *E.g.,* Alter v. DBLKM, Inc., 840 F.Supp. 799 (D.Colo.1993) (failure to adequately
allege fraud on the market).   The particularity requirement is discussed in § 13.8.1 *infra.*

42.   Hayes v. Gross, 982 F.2d 104 (3d Cir.1992) (sufficient allegations of efficient market
permitted fraud on the market presumption); Freeman v. Laventhol & Horwath, 915 F.2d
193 (6th Cir.1990) (primary market for newly issued municipal bonds was not efficient).

43.   Shores v. Sklar, 844 F.2d 1485 (11th Cir.1988), *rehearing granted and opinion
vacated* 855 F.2d 722 (11th Cir. 1988); Ross v. Bank South, N.A., 837 F.2d 980 (11th
Cir.1988).   *Cf.* Ross v. Bank South, N.A., 885 F.2d 723 (11th Cir.1989), *cert. denied* 495
U.S. 905, 110 S.Ct. 1924, 109 L.Ed.2d 287 (1990) (regardless of whether fraud on the
market theory is viable in an undeveloped market, plaintiffs failed to show fraud); Mott v.
R.G. Dickinson & Co., 1993 WL 342839, [1993–1994 Transfer Binder] Fed. Sec. L. Rep.
(CCH) ¶ 98,034 (D.Kan.1993) (insufficient allegations of fraud created the market ratio-
nale).

44.   *See, e.g.,* In re Taxable Municipal Bonds Litigation, 1992 WL 165974, [1992
Transfer Binder] Fed.Sec.L.Rep. (CCH) ¶ 96,836 (E.D.La.1992); Ockerman v. May Zima &
Co., 785 F.Supp. 695 (M.D.Tenn.1992), *reversed on other grounds* 27 F.3d 1151 (6th
Cir.1994) (on appeal the court held that the plaintiff failed to establish the elements that
would be necessary for the novel fraud-created-the-market presumption); Comment, The
Fraud–Created-the-Market Theory: The Presumption of Reliance in the Primary Issue
Context, 60 U.Cin.L.Rev. 495 (1991).   *See also, e.g.,* Endo v. Albertine, 863 F.Supp. 708
(N.D.Ill.1994) (fraud on the market could be used in connection with initial public
offering).   *But cf.* Stinson v. Van Valley Development Corp., 714 F.Supp. 132 (E.D.Pa.1989)
("fraud created the market" theory failed since there was no indication that the bonds
were worthless and that the offering was successful solely because of the alleged fraud).

45.   *See* footnotes 42–43 *supra.*

state court,[46] although it has been rejected by another state court.[47] Other courts have rejected the "fraud created the market" theory of recovery.[48]

Someone purchasing the securities in a secondary transaction significantly after the initial public offering cannot rely on the "fraud created the market" rationale.[49]

After apparently rejecting the "fraud created the market" theory, one court adopted an even more novel approach: namely, that even in an inefficient market, the plaintiff is presumed to have relied on the integrity of the defendants.[50] The court in so ruling acknowledged the novelty of this rule and therefore certified its decision for interlocutory review.

A number of courts have referred to a "truth on the market" defense to a fraud on the market theory of liability.[51] The origins of this defense can be found in the Supreme Court decision in Basic Inc. v. Levinson.[52] In *Basic*, the Court noted that even in the face of materially misleading statements, if accurate information "credibly entered the market and dissipated the effects of the misstatements," then the misstatements would not be actionable.[53] Although sounding more like a question of causation[54] or materiality,[55] this has been labelled the truth on the market defense.[56] Thus, a showing that the misstatements or nondisclosures did not affect the market price will rebut the fraud on the market presumption of reliance.[57]

The Third Circuit has held that the fraud on the market presumption of reliance is not available to a short seller who, rather than relying on the market's efficiency, enters a transaction in the belief that the

---

46. *See* Rosenthal v. Dean Witter Reynolds, Inc., 883 P.2d 522 (Colo.App.1994).

47. Mirkin v. Wasserman, 5 Cal.4th 1082, 23 Cal.Rptr.2d 101, 858 P.2d 568 (1993). *See* Christopher Boffey, *Mirkin v. Wasserman*: The Supreme Court of California Rejects the Fraud–on–the–Market Theory in State Law Deceit Actions, 49 Bus. Law. 715 (1994).

48. Eckstein v. Balcor Film Investors, 8 F.3d 1121 (7th Cir.1993).

49. *See* Alter v. DBLKM, Inc., 840 F.Supp. 799 (D.Colo.1993).

50. Ockerman v. May Zima & Co., 785 F.Supp. 695 (M.D.Tenn.1992), *reversed on other grounds* 27 F.3d 1151 (6th Cir.1994).

51. *See, e.g.,* In re Seagate Technology II Securities Litigation, 843 F.Supp. 1341, 1368–69 (N.D.Cal.1994).

52. 485 U.S. 224, 108 S.Ct. 978, 99 L.Ed.2d 194 (1988), *on remand* 871 F.2d 562 (6th Cir.1989).

53. 485 U.S. at 248–49, 108 S.Ct. at 992.

54. Causation is discussed in § 13.6 *infra*.

55. One could say that the injection of truth into the market made the misstatements or omissions not material in light of the total mix of information available. *See* § 13.5A *supra*.

56. In re Seagate Technology II Securities Litigation, 802 F.Supp. 271, 275 (N.D.Cal. 1992), *relying on* In re Convergent Technologies Securities Litigation, 948 F.2d 507, 513 (9th Cir.1991) *and* In re Apple Computer Securities Litigation, 886 F.2d 1109, 1115 (9th Cir.1989).

57. Fine v. American Solar King Corp., 919 F.2d 290, 299 (5th Cir.1990); In re Seagate Technology II Securities Litigation, 843 F.Supp. 1341 (N.D.Cal.1994).

market is not efficient.[58] This rationale seems clearly erroneous because although a short seller (like an options trader) is taking highly speculative risks, he or she should not be said to assume the risk of materially misleading information that has knowingly or recklessly been disseminated into the market.

The Fifth Circuit has taken the position that proof of plaintiff's reliance is required in an action brought under Rule 10b–5(2) dealing with material misstatements or omissions of fact, but not under subsection (1) prohibiting fraudulent schemes, nor under subsection (3) prohibiting acts and practices that operate as a fraud or deceit.[59] As the court stated, the Supreme Court "did not eliminate reliance as an element of a 10b–5 omission case; it merely established an assumption that made it possible for the plaintiffs to meet their burden." [60] Not all courts accepted the fraud on the market presumption of reliance. This refusal to apply a fraud on the market rationale has arisen both in insider trading cases[61] as well as in cases involving the liability of corporations for failing to make accurate disclosures.[62] The fraud on the market presumption is available to all investors, including those who are sophisticated.[63]

In Basic Inc. v. Levinson,[64] the Supreme Court embraced the fraud on the market theory in cases involving affirmative misrepresentations. *Basic* involved alleged materially misleading denials of preliminary merger negotiations. The Court viewed the fraud on the market presumption of reliance as a natural inference "supported by common sense and probability." [65] The Court also recognized the importance of the fraud on the market presumption in allowing class action claims to proceed.[66] *Basic*'s acceptance of the fraud on the market presumption of reliance in an affirmative misrepresentation case does not necessarily

---

58. Zlotnick v. TIE Communications, Inc., 836 F.2d 818 (3d Cir.1988).

59. Shores v. Sklar, 647 F.2d 462, 469, 470 (5th Cir.1981), *cert. denied* 459 U.S. 1102, 103 S.Ct. 722, 74 L.Ed.2d 949 (1983).

60. *Id.* at 468.

61. *E.g.* Fridrich v. Bradford, 542 F.2d 307 (6th Cir.1976), *cert. denied* 429 U.S. 1053, 97 S.Ct. 767, 50 L.Ed.2d 769 (1977). *Cf.* Chiarella v. United States, 445 U.S. 222, 100 S.Ct. 1108, 63 L.Ed.2d 348 (1980). *Contra* Koenig v. Smith, 88 F.R.D. 604 (E.D.N.Y.1980). *See* § 13.9 *infra*.

62. Lipton v. Documation, Inc., 734 F.2d 740 (11th Cir.1984), *rehearing denied* 740 F.2d 979 (11th Cir.1984); Wilson v. Comtech Telecommunications Corp., 648 F.2d 88 (2d Cir.1981). *See also* Green v. Occidental Petroleum Corp., 541 F.2d 1335 (9th Cir.1976); Blackie v. Barrack, 524 F.2d 891 (9th Cir.1975), *cert. denied* 429 U.S. 816, 97 S.Ct. 57, 50 L.Ed.2d 75 (1976).

63. Hanon v. Dataproducts Corp., 976 F.2d 497 (9th Cir.1992).

64. 485 U.S. 224, 108 S.Ct. 978, 99 L.Ed.2d 194 (1988).

65. 485 U.S. at 246, 108 S.Ct. at 991, 99 L.Ed.2d at 218.

66. The Court quoted the district court in explaining that "the presumption of reliance created by the fraud-on-the-market theory provide[s] 'a practical resolution to the problem of balancing the substantive requirement of proof of reliance in securities cases against the procedural requisites of [Fed.Rule Civ.Proc.] 23.' " *Id.* at 242, 108 S.Ct. at 989, 99 L.Ed.2d at 215. *See also, e.g.,* Seidman v. American Mobile Systems, Inc., 813 F.Supp. 323 (E.D.Pa.1993).

affect insider trading cases since in those cases there may be problems showing both that the defendant owed a duty to the plaintiffs[67] and also that the defendant caused an injury to the plaintiffs.

The reliance question is necessarily tied closely to the causation problems which are discussed in the next section.

§ 13.6 Causation in Actions Under Rule 10b–5

For a successful damage action under SEC Rule 10b–5, in addition to the elements of scienter, materiality, and reliance,[1] the plaintiff must specifically allege[2] and prove sufficient causal connection between his injury and the wrongful conduct that forms the basis of the 10b–5 claim.

It must be remembered that as in other areas of the law, causation embodies two distinct concepts: (1) cause in fact and (2) legal cause. Legal cause is frequently dealt with in terms of proximate cause. Cause in fact questions are frequently stated in terms of the sine qua non rule: but for the act or acts complained of, the injury would not have occurred. Legal cause represents the law's doctrinal basis for limiting liability even though cause in fact may be proven. Courts in both tort and contract cases frequently speak in terms of foreseeability in order to determine the extent of proximate or legal cause.[3] Causation in securities law involves the same analysis of cause in fact and legal cause.[4] However, the courts have developed their own rubric for causation in securities cases.

Courts have broken down the causation analysis in securities cases

---

67. *See* § 13.9 *infra*.

§ 13.6

1. *See* §§ 13.4–13.5B *supra*.

2. *See, e.g.,* Berger v. Metra Electronics Corp., 1994 WL 97091, [1993–1994 Transfer Binder] Fed. Sec. L. Rep. (CCH) ¶ 98,186 (S.D.N.Y.1994) (failure to adequately allege causation but leave to replead granted); TBG, Inc. v. Bendis, 841 F.Supp. 1538 (D.Kan. 1993) (loss causation sufficiently pleaded); Ades v. Deloitte & Touche, 1993 WL 362364, [1993 Transfer Binder] Fed. Sec. L. Rep. (CCH) ¶ 97,768 (S.D.N.Y.1993) (loss causation adequately alleged). The particularity requirement is discussed in § 13.8.1 *infra* (Practitioner's Edition only).

3. For some classic statements of the foreseeability test in both tort and contract law, *see, e.g.,* Globe Refining Co. v. Landa Cotton Oil Co., 190 U.S. 540, 23 S.Ct. 754, 47 L.Ed. 1171 (1903); Palsgraf v. Long Island Railroad, 248 N.Y. 339, 162 N.E. 99 (1928); Hadley v. Baxendale, 9 Ex. 341, 156 Eng.Rep. 145 (Ct.Exch. 1854); Restatement Second of Torts § 435; John D. Calamari & Joseph M. Perillo, Hornbook on the Law of Contracts §§ 14–5 to 14–7 (3d ed.1987); W. Page Keeton, Dan B. Dobbs, Robert E. Keeton & David G. Owen, Prosser and Keeton on Torts § 43 (5th ed. 1984).

4. *E.g.,* First Interstate Bank of Nevada v. Chapman & Cutler, 837 F.2d 775 (7th Cir.1988) (dismissing 10b–5 claim; although there was "but for" cause, the violation was not a "proximate cause" of plaintiff's loss); Sperber v. Boesky, 672 F.Supp. 754 (S.D.N.Y. 1987) (failure to show defendant's wrongdoing proximately caused plaintiff's injuries); Feinberg v. Leighton, 1987 WL 6147, [1987 Transfer Binder] Fed.Sec.L.Rep. (CCH) ¶ 93,117 (S.D.N.Y.1987) (failure to show misrepresentation was "proximate cause" of loss); *But cf.* Rousseff v. E.F. Hutton Co., 843 F.2d 1326 (11th Cir.1988) (certifying to Florida Supreme Court question of whether proximate cause is an essential element of liability under Florida Investor Protection Act).

into two categories: "transaction causation" and "loss causation."[5] As is true with any causation analysis, these concepts are but a means to an end. As developed more fully below, transaction causation and loss causation are difficult concepts, and careless use of these terms is likely to hinder rather than facilitate understanding.[6]

To begin with, the plaintiff must prove "transaction causation" which means that but for the wrongful conduct, the transaction would not have gone through, at least in the form that it eventually took.[7] The concept of transaction causation has been properly characterized as "nothing more than 'but for' causation" and more questionably as "merely another way of describing reliance."[8] Transaction causation does not represent the strictest form of "but for" causation because it requires only that the terms of the transaction have been significantly affected by the material misstatement or omission. It is not necessary to prove that the transaction would not have occurred but for the alleged 10b–5 violation.[9] It must be shown, however, that there was a direct causal nexus between the alleged violation and the resulting transaction.[10] Furthermore, as is the case with proximate cause generally, in applying the transaction causation analysis, intervening causes can preclude a Rule 10b–5 recovery; however, not all intervening causes will prevent recovery.[11]

5. *E.g.,* Wilson v. Ruffa & Hanover, P.C., 844 F.2d 81 (2d Cir.1988); LHLC Corp. v. Cluett, Peabody & Co., 842 F.2d 928, 931 (7th Cir.1988); Pippenger v. McQuik's Oilube, Inc., 854 F.Supp. 1411 (S.D.Ind.1994); In re Fortune Systems Securities Litigation, 680 F.Supp. 1360 (N.D.Cal.1987); (equating loss causation with proof of damages); Gruber v. Prudential–Bache Securities, Inc., 679 F.Supp. 165, 175–76 (D.Conn.1987).

6. *See* LHLC Corp. v. Cluett, Peabody & Co., 842 F.2d 928, 931 (7th Cir.1988) (citing this treatise).

7. *See, e.g.,* Wong v. Thomas Brothers Restaurant Corp., 840 F.Supp. 727 (C.D.Cal. 1994) (failure to show that alleged misstatements induced the transaction).

8. Harris v. Union Electric Co., 787 F.2d 355, 366 (8th Cir.), *cert. denied* 479 U.S. 823, 107 S.Ct. 94, 93 L.Ed.2d 45 (1986). *See also* Wilson v. Ruffa & Hanover, P.C., 844 F.2d 81, 86 (2d Cir.1988) ("transaction causation, of course, is simply reliance"). Although reliance and causation are inextricably related, they involve different elements of the claim. *But see* Rowe v. Maremont Corp., 850 F.2d 1226, 1233 (7th Cir.1988). Reliance is discussed in § 13.5B *supra.*

9. *See, e.g.,* Schutzky Distributors, Inc. v. Kelly, 643 F.Supp. 57 (N.D.Cal.1986) (a showing that transactions were partially induced by misstatements was sufficient causation). *See also, e.g.,* Mills v. Electric Auto–Lite Co., 396 U.S. 375, 90 S.Ct. 616, 24 L.Ed.2d 593 (1970) which is discussed in § 11.5 *supra.*

10. *E.g.,* Scholes v. Moore, 1993 WL 84428, [1992–1993 Transfer Binder] Fed.Sec. L.Rep. (CCH) ¶ 97,362 (N.D.Ill.1993) (sufficient allegations of transaction causation in action against broker acting as a trading advisor); Bruno v. Cook, 660 F.Supp. 306 (S.D.N.Y.1987) (failure to show transaction causation); Kimmco Energy Corp. v. Jones, 603 F.Supp. 763 (S.D.N.Y.1984) (allegation that misrepresentations with regard to first limited partnership offering induced plaintiff to invest a second limited partnership found to be insufficient transaction causation). *Compare, e.g.,* CL–Alexanders Laing & Cruickshank v. Goldfeld, 709 F.Supp. 472 (S.D.N.Y.1989) (reliance on warranty of absence of misstatements was sufficient transaction causation).

11. *See* Rankow v. First Chicago Corp., 678 F.Supp. 202 (N.D.Ill.1988), *reversed on other grounds* 870 F.2d 356 (7th Cir.1989) (market fluctuations were found to be an intervening cause between the alleged fraudulent conduct and the plaintiff's loss; the Seventh Circuit on appeal pointed out that not every intervening cause will preclude a finding of loss causation); In re Fortune Systems Securities Litigation, 680 F.Supp. 1360

Secondly, the plaintiff must be able to prove "loss causation"—namely that the plaintiff's injury (generally the diminution in the value of his or her investment) is directly attributable both to the wrongful conduct and the form and manner in which the challenged transaction occurred.[12] Loss causation provides the necessary connection between the challenged conduct and the plaintiff's pecuniary loss.[13]

A number of recent causation cases define loss causation narrowly, in terms of a need to identify that portion of the loss which can be traced to the material misrepresentation or omission.[14] These cases place the burden upon the plaintiff of proving the causal nexus. Under this loss causation formula the fact finder must place a value on the misrepresentation. In other words, the question becomes how much would the price have been at the time of the challenged transaction had there been full disclosure available. The early loss causation cases did not require placing a dollar value on the particular misrepresentations in question. It must be remembered, however, that the loss causation doctrine was adopted in the context of merger cases where once transaction causation was established, all that needed to be shown was that the *transaction* caused the plaintiff's loss.[15]

A 1991 Supreme Court decision involving causation under the proxy rules undoubtedly has its implications for Rule 10b–5 cases. In *Virginia*

(N.D.Cal.1987) (plaintiff failed to prove that decline in value was due to misrepresentation rather than market forces); Nutis v. Penn Merchandising Corp., 615 F.Supp. 486 (E.D.Pa. 1985) (loss was caused by breaches of fiduciary duty, not 10b–5 violations).

12. *E.g.,* Litton Industries, Inc. v. Lehman Brothers Kuhn Loeb Inc., 967 F.2d 742 (2d Cir.1992) (acquiring company suing investment bankers for alleged insider trading in connection with a tender offer, and claiming that but for the insider trading it would have acquired the target at a lower price, had to establish that the insider trading caused the market price to rise and that the market price was a substantial factor in the target company management's evaluation of the tender offer).

13. *See, e.g.,* Citibank, N.A. v. K–H Corp., 968 F.2d 1489 (2d Cir.1992) (but for causation showed transaction causation but not loss causation requirement); Weiss v. Wittcoff, 966 F.2d 109 (2d Cir.1992) (sufficient allegations of loss causation).

14. *E.g.,* Arthur Young & Co. v. Reves, 937 F.2d 1310 (8th Cir.1991), *cert. granted* 502 U.S. 1090, 112 S.Ct. 1159, 117 L.Ed.2d 407 (1992) (in action by purchaser, loss causation was established by showing that accounting firm's disclosures would have resulted in serious financial problems). Rankow v. First Chicago Corp., 870 F.2d 356, 367 (7th Cir.1989); Kafton v. Baptist Park Nursing Center, Inc., 617 F.Supp. 349, 350 (D.Ariz. 1985). *See also, e.g.,* SIPC v. Vigman, 908 F.2d 1461 (9th Cir.1990), *reversed on other grounds* 503 U.S. 258, 112 S.Ct. 1311, 117 L.Ed.2d 532 (1992), *on remand* 964 F.2d 924 (9th Cir.1992) (indicating that loss causation is not an additional requirement beyond proximate cause; it simply is a different label for the principle that plaintiff must show a sufficient causal connection between the wrong complained of and plaintiff's injury).

15. *E.g.,* Schlick v. Penn–Dixie Cement Corp., 507 F.2d 374 (2d Cir.1974), *cert. denied* 421 U.S. 976, 95 S.Ct. 1976, 44 L.Ed.2d 467 (1975). *Cf.* Mills v. Electric Auto–Lite Co., 396 U.S. 375, 385, 90 S.Ct. 616, 622, 24 L.Ed.2d 593, 602 (1970) ("Where there has been a finding of materiality, a shareholder has made a sufficient showing of causal relationship between the violation and the injury for which he seeks redress, if, as here, he proves that the proxy solicitation itself, rather than the particular defect in the solicitation materials, was an essential link in the accomplishment of the transaction"). *Compare, e.g.,* Rousseff v. E.F. Hutton Co., 867 F.2d 1281 (11th Cir.1989) (loss causation is a necessary element of a Rule 10b–5 claim; loss causation was not required under Florida blue sky law).

Bankshares, Inc. v. Sandberg[16] the Court held that alleged misstatements in connection with a shareholder vote that was not required for the transaction in question could not form the basis of a private damage action.[17] The Court therefore held that something which only affects the transaction in a collateral sense fails to establish the type of direct causal connection that is required. The Court thus applied a rule that seems to call for a requirement of direct transaction causation as a precondition to liability. In a post-*Sandberg* decision, the Sixth Circuit held that the loss of a state law appraisal was actionable notwithstanding the fact that the vote's outcome was not affected by material misstatements or omissions.[18] In another case, however, the *Virginia Bankshares* decision was held to preclude an action under Rule 10b–5 where defendant controlled sufficient votes to assure the success of the transaction.[19] The court reasoned that there was no federalization of corporate law where any injury the plaintiff may have suffered was due to the alleged unfairness of the transaction rather than any causal connection between the alleged misrepresentations and the effectuation of the transaction in question.[20]

The courts appear to be split on whether a broad or narrow view of loss causation is appropriate in Rule 10b–5 cases. The answer is that both tests are appropriate under Rule 10b–5; whether the broad or narrow approach applies depends upon the factual context. In an inducement situation—where the misrepresentation or omission *induced* the challenged transaction—it is sufficient to show that the plaintiff's loss was caused by the transaction, without having to prove loss causation as a separate element.[21] In such a case it is arguable that by analogy to section 12(2) of the 1933 Act rescissory damages or out of pocket damages would be appropriate.[22] On the other hand, when an investor makes any investment, he or she assumes certain investment risks. It may be too harsh a rule under Rule 10b–5 that would place the wrongdoer in the position of insurer against those market risks. Otherwise, for example, a seller who fraudulently induced a purchase of securities in early October, 1987 would be an insurer against the

16. 501 U.S. 1083, 111 S.Ct. 2749, 115 L.Ed.2d 929 (1991), *appeal after remand* 979 F.2d 332 (4th Cir.1992), *opinion vacated* 1993 WL 524680 (4th Cir.1993). *See* the discussion in § 11.5 *supra*.

17. The proxies in question did not relate to a vote directly on the merger that plaintiff was complaining about, but rather to a vote taken under a state corporate law "interested director" statute to cleanse a potential conflict of interest. *See also, e.g.,* Scattergood v. Perelman, 945 F.2d 618 (3d Cir.1991) (since plaintiffs did not have a right to vote in freeze-out merger, the merger broke the chain of causation and thus no recovery could be had on the "forced sale" claims under either Rule 10b–5 or Rule 14a–9).

18. Howing Co. v. Nationwide Corp., 972 F.2d 700 (6th Cir.1992) (decided under section 13(e)'s going private rules). *See also, e.g.,* Wilson v. Great American Industries, Inc., 979 F.2d 924 (2d Cir.1992); Stahl v. Gibraltar Financial Corp., 967 F.2d 335 (9th Cir. 1992).

19. Boone v. Carlsbad Bancorporation, Inc., 972 F.2d 1545 (10th Cir.1992). This is an unduly restrictive reading. *See* § 11.5 *supra*.

20. 972 F.2d at 1557.

21. Hatrock v. Edward D. Jones & Co., 750 F.2d 767, 773 (9th Cir.1984).

22. Damages are discussed in § 13.7 *infra*.

precipitous price decline caused in large part by the market crash on October 19.[23] Borrowing from the common law of fraud,[24] it is reasonable to hold that where the misrepresentation relates to the type of investment risk that caused the market decline, the investment risk should be included in the measure of damages.[25] However, when the investment risks are wholly separate from the misrepresented or omitted facts, then the loss attributable to that independent investment risk should be deducted before determining the amount of recoverable loss.

Assuming a rescissory measure of damages is inappropriate under Rule 10b–5, the question then becomes: who should bear the burden of proving that the plaintiff's loss was due to a wholly independent investment risk? This type of proof frequently involves speculation and/or the use of expert testimony. It is absurd to place the burden of proof of such speculative matters on the injured party as opposed to on the wrongdoer. There is ample support for requiring that in a fraudulent inducement case, once the plaintiff establishes that there was transaction causation, the burden shifts to the defendant to prove that the loss was due to wholly independent factors.[26] This measure of damages parallels section 11 of the 1933 Act[27] which presumes that the price was affected and leaves it to the defendant to show that the price decrease was due to factors other than the misstatements or omissions in the registration materials. It is significant that section 11 liability applies to issuers regardless of fault and to others who fail to exercise due diligence. In contrast, Rule 10b–5 liability is dependent upon a finding of scienter. Section 11 defendants are thus held to a lower threshold of culpability but are nevertheless put to the burden of proving negative causation. There is thus a strong argument for applying the same rule in 10b–5 inducement cases where the defendants are guilty of a higher degree of culpability—i.e., scienter.

In cases involving fraudulent inducement, the broader test of loss causation ordinarily is appropriate. However, where the Rule 10b–5 violation *affected* the transaction or was one of several factors on which

---

23. "Defrauders are a bad lot and should be punished, but Rule 10b–5 does not make them insurers against national economic loss". Bastian v. Petren Resources Corp., 892 F.2d 680, 685 (7th Cir.1990), *cert. denied* 496 U.S. 906, 110 S.Ct. 2590, 110 L.Ed.2d 270 (1990).

24. *See generally* W. Page Keeton, Dan B. Dobbs, Robert E. Keeton & David G. Owen, *supra* footnote 3, ch. 18.

25. *Cf.* Reshal Associates, Inc. v. Long Grove Trading Co., 754 F.Supp. 1226, 1234 (N.D.Ill.1990) (transaction causation satisfied by allegation that but for defendant's misrepresentation concerning liquidity of investment, plaintiff would not have invested).

26. *See* Hatrock v. Edward D. Jones & Co., 750 F.2d 767, 773 (9th Cir.1984) (quoted in footnote 21 *supra*); Kafton v. Baptist Park Nursing Center, 617 F.Supp. 349, 350 (D.Ariz.1985). *See also* Pidcock v. Sunnyland America, Inc., 854 F.2d 443 (11th Cir.1988), *rehearing denied* 861 F.2d 1281 (11th Cir.1988) (plaintiff's claim to be a defrauded seller was entitled to presumption of causation); Manufacturers Hanover Trust Co. v. Drysdale Securities Corp., 801 F.2d 13 (2d Cir.1986), *cert. denied* 479 U.S. 1066, 107 S.Ct. 952, 93 L.Ed.2d 1001 (1987). *Cf.* Rankow v. First Chicago Corp., 870 F.2d 356, 367 (7th Cir.1989) (noting the ease with which plaintiff may prove loss causation).

27. 15 U.S.C.A. § 77k(e). *See* §§ 7.3, 7.4.1 *supra*.

the plaintiff relied, then the loss is properly limited to the value of the misrepresentation. This assumes, of course, that the transaction would have occurred even without the misrepresentation but that it would have occurred at a different price. In such a case, the courts should follow the traditional common law rule that the burden of proving proximate causation falls upon the plaintiff.[28] Thus, where a less direct "but for" causal relationship exists between the inducement to enter into the transaction and the misrepresentations or omissions, the burden is on the plaintiff to prove the extent to which the misrepresentation affected the price. As noted above, such a case would exist where there were a number of factors other than the material misstatements or omissions that induced the transaction. For example, in a Rule 10b–5 claim based on a fraud on the market theory of reliance,[29] where the plaintiff was not induced to enter into the transaction but rather simply relied on the price as an accurate reflection of the total mix of material information available, the narrower loss causation formula is appropriate. In such a case the plaintiff will have to show that the price was affected by the misrepresentations.

Failure to allege or prove loss causation can result in dismissal of the suit.[30] When Rule 10b–5 liability is premised upon material misstatements of fact appearing in documents that the plaintiff has read, reliance may be presumed from the materiality, and in turn it has been held that causation may be subsumed in the reliance finding.[31] This is especially true when the violations arose out of face-to-face transactions between the plaintiff and defendant.[32] A number of cases do not distinguish between material omissions and affirmative misrepresentations.[33] One court has taken the view that, in an open market transac-

---

28. *See generally* W. Page Keeton, Dan B. Dobbs, Robert E. Keeton & David G. Owen, *supra* footnote 3, ch. 7.

29. *See* the discussion in § 13.5B *supra.*

30. *E.g.,* Currie v. Cayman Resources Corp., 835 F.2d 780 (11th Cir.1988); Bastian v. Petren Resources Corp., 681 F.Supp. 530, 534–35 (N.D.Ill.1988); Rankow v. First Chicago Corp., 678 F.Supp. 202 (N.D.Ill.1988), *decision reversed* 870 F.2d 356 (7th Cir.1989); Sims v. Faestel, 638 F.Supp. 1281 (E.D.Pa.1986), *affirmed mem.* 813 F.2d 399 (3d Cir.1987). *See also, e.g.,* Wilson v. Ruffa & Hanover, P.C., 844 F.2d 81 (2d Cir.1988) (decided under section 12(2) of the 1933 Act). *Compare* Metropolitan International, Inc. v. Alco Standard Corp., 657 F.Supp. 627 (M.D.Pa.1986) (allegations that defendants intended to drive price down was sufficient allegation of causation).

31. *See, e.g.,* Affiliated Ute Citizens v. United States, 406 U.S. 128, 150–54, 92 S.Ct. 1456, 1470, 1472, 31 L.Ed.2d 741 (1972), *rehearing denied* 407 U.S. 916, 92 S.Ct. 2430, 32 L.Ed.2d 692 (1972); Sundstrand Corp. v. Sun Chemical Corp., 553 F.2d 1033 (7th Cir.), *cert. denied* 434 U.S. 875, 98 S.Ct. 224, 54 L.Ed.2d 155 (1977); Herzfeld v. Laventhol, Krekstein Horwath, 540 F.2d 27, 33 (2d Cir.1976). *See also, e.g.,* Marx v. Computer Sciences Corp., 507 F.2d 485 (9th Cir.1974).

32. Affiliated Ute Citizens v. United States, 406 U.S. 128, 92 S.Ct. 1456, 31 L.Ed.2d 741 (1972), *rehearing denied* 407 U.S. 916, 92 S.Ct. 2430, 32 L.Ed.2d 692 (1972). *See* § 13.5B *supra.*

33. *See, e.g,* Frankel v. Wyllie & Thornhill, Inc., 537 F.Supp. 730, 737–40 (W.D.Va. 1982). *But see, e.g.,* Lorber v. Beebe, 407 F.Supp. 279 (S.D.N.Y.1975), *amended* 1976 WL 768, Fed.Sec.L.Rep. ¶ 95,458 (D.C.N.Y.1976). *Cf.* Forrestal Village Inc. v. Graham, 551 F.2d 411 (D.C.Cir.1977).

tion where the plaintiff's claim is based on fraud on the market due to the defendant's insider trading activities, the absence of any proof of actual reliance by the plaintiff precluded a finding of sufficient causation.[34] The majority of recent cases seem to continue recognition of a fraud-on-the-market theory of causation where the defendant's omissions have been material to the reasonable investor's investment decision.[35] In cases involving affirmative misrepresentations, the Supreme Court has accepted the fraud on the market presumption of reliance.[36] However, in the context of insider trading, it has been held that buyers and sellers trading in an open market who have misappropriated inside information have breached a duty to the owner of the information but not to investors taking opposite sides of their trades in an open market.[37] Accordingly in an insider trading case brought under Rule 10b–5, as opposed to the express statutory remedy, unless the defendant's duty is based on something other than a misappropriation of information (such as, for example, a duty of the directors that runs directly to the plaintiff shareholders), courts will dismiss private claims without reaching the causation issue.

Even beyond the insider trading and 10b–5 omission cases, the causation requirement can create problems. For example, the Supreme Court in Santa Fe Industries Inc. v. Green,[38] held that in order to maintain a private suit under Rule 10b–5, the deception requirement means that the plaintiff must prove that he was "duped" into entering into the transaction in question. Following on *Santa Fe's* coattails a number of federal circuit courts have held that for causation purposes, it is sufficient to demonstrate that upon full disclosure the plaintiff would have had a remedy under state law which could have enjoined the transaction.[39] In this connection, it has been held that the plaintiff need

34. Fridrich v. Bradford, 542 F.2d 307 (6th Cir.1976), *cert. denied* 429 U.S. 1053, 97 S.Ct. 767, 50 L.Ed.2d 769 (1977). *See* § 13.5B *supra*, § 13.9 *infra*. *But see, e.g.,* Berman v. Gerber Products Co., 454 F.Supp. 1310, 1324 (W.D.Mich.1978).

35. Elkind v. Liggett & Myers, Inc., 635 F.2d 156 (2d Cir.1980); Zweig v. Hearst Corp., 594 F.2d 1261 (9th Cir.1979). *See* § 13.4 *supra*. *See generally* William K.S. Wang, Trading on Material Nonpublic Information on Impersonal Stock Markets: Who is Harmed and Who Can Sue Whom Under SEC Rule 10b–5, 54 So.Cal.L.Rev. 1217 (1981).

36. Basic, Inc. v. Levinson, 485 U.S. 224, 108 S.Ct. 978, 99 L.Ed.2d 194 (1988), *on remand* 871 F.2d 562 (6th Cir.1989) which is discussed in § 13.5B *supra*.

37. Moss v. Morgan Stanley, Inc., 719 F.2d 5 (2d Cir.1983), *cert. denied* 465 U.S. 1025, 104 S.Ct. 1280, 79 L.Ed.2d 684 (1984). *See also, e.g.,* United States v. Carpenter, 791 F.2d 1024 (2d Cir.1986), *affirmed* 484 U.S. 19, 108 S.Ct. 316, 98 L.Ed.2d 275 (1987). There now is an express statutory remedy for insider trading. 15 U.S.C.A. § 78t–1. Insider trading is discussed in § 13.9 *infra*.

38. 430 U.S. 462, 97 S.Ct. 1292, 51 L.Ed.2d 480 (1977), *on remand* 562 F.2d 4 (2d Cir.1977). *See* § 13.11 *infra*.

39. Madison Consultants v. FDIC, 710 F.2d 57 (2d Cir.1983); Healey v. Catalyst Recovery of Pennsylvania, 616 F.2d 641 (3d Cir.1980); Kidwell v. Meikle, 597 F.2d 1273, 1292 (9th Cir.1979); Alabama Farm Bureau Mutual Casualty Co. v. American Fidelity Life Insurance Co., 606 F.2d 602 (5th Cir.1979), *rehearing denied* 610 F.2d 818 (5th Cir.1980); Wright v. Heizer Corp., 560 F.2d 236, 249–50 (7th Cir.1977), *cert. denied* 434 U.S. 1066, 98 S.Ct. 1243, 55 L.Ed.2d 767 (1978); Goldberg v. Meridor, 567 F.2d 209 (2d Cir.1977), *cert. denied* 434 U.S. 1069, 98 S.Ct. 1249, 55 L.Ed.2d 771 (1978). *See* § 13.11 *infra*.

not prove that the state court action would have been successful, but merely that full and honest disclosure would have enabled the plaintiff to present a prima facie case for relief under state law.[40] This type of causation test belies a "but for" requirement since it is not necessary that the plaintiff prove that the transaction would not have occurred absent the wrongful conduct. In such cases, the question has been phrased in terms of how the transaction would have been framed had full disclosure been required.[41] As such, the causation element is satisfied by a showing that the wrongful conduct had a profound effect upon the form, terms and price of the transaction. It is far from certain that all courts can reasonably be expected to adopt as liberal a view of causation. Other courts have required a showing of causation by a "fair preponderance of the evidence" that plaintiff's alternative remedies would have stopped the transaction in question.[42] As noted by the comments to the American Law Institute's Proposed Federal Securities Code, although some courts speak in terms of "but for" cause, most come closer to the tort law concepts of "legal cause." [43]

Once the plaintiff has proven the requisite transaction causation, it will be necessary to prove loss causation. Difficult problems of proof may arise regarding the causal relationship of the conduct to both the transaction and injury in question.[44] In large part, the problems of proving loss causation are the same as those involved in demonstrating the extent of the plaintiff's actual loss.[45]

Closely related to the question of causation is whether the fraud occurred "in connection with" the purchase or sale of a security.[46]

§ 13.7 The Measure of Damages in Rule 10b–5 Actions

This section begins with identification of the basic issues relating to Rule 10b–5 damages. This is followed by a comparison of the alternative methods of assessing damages. The next issue explored relates to questions associated with computing out of pocket loss. Finally, there is a brief discussion of the availability of prejudgment interest.

Most private actions under Rule 10b–5 are for money damages. On

---

40. Alabama Farm Bureau Mutual Casualty Co. v. American Fidelity Life Insurance Co., 606 F.2d 602 (5th Cir.1979), *rehearing denied* 610 F.2d 818 (5th Cir.1980).

41. *See* Schlick v. Penn–Dixie Cement Corp., 507 F.2d 374, 380–81 (2d Cir.1974), *cert. denied* 421 U.S. 976, 95 S.Ct. 1976, 44 L.Ed.2d 467 (1975).

42. Madison Consultants v. FDIC, 710 F.2d 57 (2d Cir.1983). *See also* Alabama Farm Bureau Mutual Casualty Co. v. American Fidelity Life Insurance Co., 606 F.2d 602 (5th Cir.1979), *rehearing denied* 610 F.2d 818 (5th Cir.1980) (requiring plaintiff to prove he would have been able to present a prima facie case in the state court action).

43. ALI Proposed Federal Securities Code § 202(19) comment 3(c).

44. *See, e.g.,* Blackie v. Barrack, 524 F.2d 891, 905 (9th Cir.1975), *cert. denied* 429 U.S. 816, 97 S.Ct. 57, 50 L.Ed.2d 75 (1976); Dura–Bilt Corp. v. Chase Manhattan Corp., 89 F.R.D. 87, 99 (S.D.N.Y.1981).

45. *See* § 13.7 *infra* for a discussion of damages in Rule 10b–5 actions.

46. *See* § 13.2.3 *supra*.

occasion, a plaintiff may, however, seek injunctive relief.[1] In the usual
case when a claim seeks money damages, the plaintiff may not be able to
invoke the equitable powers of a court for such extraordinary preliminary relief as an asset freeze.[2]

The Basic Damage Calculus

The assessment of damages in Rule 10b–5 cases, like any quantifica-
tion of economic loss, has been a challenging task for the courts.[3]
Evaluating the current state of the law is also difficult because most
10b–5 litigation does not proceed to final judgment on the merits.[4] As a
result, there is a relative paucity of decisions dealing with the question of

§ 13.7

1. *See, e.g.,* Mutual Shares Corp. v. Genesco, Inc., 384 F.2d 540 (2d Cir.1967); Tully v.
Mott Supermarkets, Inc., 540 F.2d 187, 194 (3d Cir.1976) (dictum); Granada Investments,
Inc. v. DWG Corp., 717 F.Supp. 533 (N.D.Ohio 1989); Hanna Mining Co. v. Norcen Energy
Resources Ltd., 574 F.Supp. 1172 (N.D.Ohio 1982) (Target of tender offer entitled to
injunctive relief); Warner Communications, Inc. v. Murdoch, 581 F.Supp. 1482, 1494
(D.Del.1984); Hundahl v. United Benefit Life Insurance Co., 465 F.Supp. 1349, 1357–59
(N.D.Tex.1979). *Cf.* Advanced Resources International, Inc. v. Tri–Star Petroleum Co., 4
F.3d 327 (4th Cir.1993) (not deciding whether to recognize exception for injunctive relief
since plaintiffs were causally too removed to have standing). *Contra* Cowin v. Bresler, 741
F.2d 410 (D.C.Cir.1984).

Not all courts have agreed. *See, e.g.,* Cowin v. Bresler, 741 F.2d 410 (D.C.Cir.1984);
Packer v. Yampol, 630 F.Supp. 1237 (S.D.N.Y.1986) (plaintiff cannot sue on behalf of
investing public generally); Atlantic Federal Savings & Loan Ass'n v. Dade Savings & Loan
Ass'n, 592 F.Supp. 1089 (S.D.Fla.1984).

2. *See* Rosen v. Cascade International, Inc., 21 F.3d 1520 (11th Cir.1994) (district court
lacked jurisdiction to grant preliminary injunction freezing assets; the All Writs Act did
not apply since the preliminary injunction was no necessary to disposition of the case).

3. *See generally* 5B Arnold S. Jacobs, The Impact of Rule 10b–5 § 260.03 (rev.ed. 1979);
3 Louis Loss, Securities Regulation ch. 11 (2d ed.1961); Bradford Cornell & R. Gregory
Morgan, Using Finance Theory to Measure Damages in Fraud on the Market Cases, 37
U.C.L.A.L.Rev. 883 (1990); Frank H. Easterbrook & Daniel R. Fischel, Optimal Damages
in Securities Cases, 52 U.Chi.L.Rev. 611 (1985); Arnold S. Jacobs, Measure of Damages in
Rule 10b–5 Cases, 65 Geo.L.J. 1093 (1977); Michael J. Kaufman, No Foul, No Harm: The
Real Measure of Damages Under Rule 10b–5, 39 Cath.U.L.Rev. 29 (1989); A. Robert
Thorup, Theories of Damages: Allowability and Calculation in Securities Fraud Litigation,
18 Sec.Reg.L.J. 23 (1990); Thomas J. Mullaney, Theories of Measuring Damages in
Security Cases and the Effects of Damages on Liability, 46 Fordham L.Rev. 277 (1977);
Barry Reder, Measuring Buyers' Damages in 10b–5 Cases, 31 Bus.Law. 1839 (1976);
Barton S. Sacher, An Overview of the Panoply of Remedies Available to an Aggrieved
Plaintiff Under SEC Rule 10b–5, 7 Cumb.L.Rev. 429 (1977); Robert B. Thompson, The
Measure of Recovery Under Rule 10b–5: A Restitution Alternative to Tort Damages, 37
Vand.L.Rev. 349 (1984); Nicholas R. Weiskopf, Remedies Under Rule 10b–5, 45 St. John's
L.Rev. 733 (1971); Comment, A Role for the 10b–5 Private Action, 130 U.Pa.L.Rev. 460
(1980); Note, Measure of Damages in Rule 10b–5 Cases Involving Actively Traded
Securities, 26 Stan.L.Rev. 371 (1974); Comment, Insiders' Liability Under Rule 10b–5 for
the Illegal Purchase, 78 Yale L.J. 864 (1969).

4. William L. Cary & Melvin A.Eisenberg, Cases and Materials on Corporations 790
(5th Unab. ed.1980); Janet Cooper Alexander, Do the Merits Matter? A Study of
Settlements in Securities Class Actions, 43 Stan.L.Rev. 497 (1991). This is the case
because either the plaintiff is unsuccessful or plaintiff's success at the stage of pretrial
motions encourages settlement by defendants who do not want to risk the potentially
expansive liability that might follow. This is highlighted by high litigation costs which
frequently make it cheaper to settle a claim than to litigate the issue fully and win.

damages.[5] In addition, the courts have taken a number of approaches to the damages issue. The variety of approaches, combined with the scarcity of cases, makes it difficult to identify solid trends in the law of damages in securities cases.

Notwithstanding the various approaches to damages in Rule 10b–5 actions, a few generalizations can be made. First, the cases agree that punitive damages are not available in 10b–5 suits.[6] Punitive damages may be available in 10b–5 litigation, however, when common law fraud claims are brought into the case under the doctrine of pendent, or supplemental, jurisdiction.[7] Even in the absence of a state law permitting punitive damages, punitive damages may be awarded in an arbitration proceeding.[8] When the parties submit to arbitration and the rules of the arbitral forum permit punitive damages, the Federal Arbitration Act has been held to defer to the rules of the selected arbitral forum.[9] The plaintiff's measure of recovery under federal securities law is limited to damages actually and proximately caused by the violations in question.[10] For example, it has been held that damages are not available

---

5. *See, e.g.,* Thomas J. Mullaney, Theories of Measuring Damages in Securities Cases and the Effects of Damages on Liability, 46 Fordham L.Rev. 277 (1977). *See also,* Arnold S. Jacobs, The Measure of Damages in Rule 10b–5 Cases, 65 Geo.L.J. 1093 (1977).

6. *See, e.g.,* Manufacturers Hanover Trust Co. v. Drysdale Securities Corp., 801 F.2d 13, 29 (2d Cir.1986), cert. denied 479 U.S. 1066, 107 S.Ct. 952, 93 L.Ed.2d 1001 (1987); Petrites v. J.C. Bradford & Co., 646 F.2d 1033 (5th Cir.1981); deHaas v. Empire Petroleum Co., 435 F.2d 1223 (10th Cir.1970); Green v. Wolf Corp., 406 F.2d 291 (2d Cir.1968), *cert. denied* 395 U.S. 977, 89 S.Ct. 2131, 23 L.Ed.2d 766 (1969); Majeski v. Balcor Entertainment Co., Ltd., 740 F.Supp. 563 (E.D.Wis.1990) (punitive damages are not available under section 12(2) of the 1933 Act or under Rule 10b–5 of the Exchange Act); Halling v. Hobert & Svoboda, Inc., 720 F.Supp. 743 (E.D.Wis.1989); Lopez v. Dean Witter Reynolds, Inc., 591 F.Supp. 581 (N.D.Cal.1984); Robert B. Hirsch & Jack L. Lewis, Punitive Damage Awards Under the Federal Securities Acts, 47 Notre Dame Law. 72 (1971). *Cf.* Comment, Broker Churning: Who is Punished? Vicariously Asserted Punitive Damages in the Context of Brokerage Houses and Their Agents, 30 Hous. L. Rev. 1775 (1993). *See also* the cases in footnote 7 *infra.*

7. *See, e.g.,* Mastrobuono v. Shearson Lehman Hutton, Inc., ___ U.S. ___, 115 S.Ct. 1212, ___ L.Ed.2d ___ (1995) (punitive damages under a state claim were available in arbitration proceedings subject to the Federal Arbitration Act, even though those damages would not have been permitted under state arbitration proceedings); Cyrak v. Lemon, 919 F.2d 320 (5th Cir.1990) (punitive damages are unavailable under Rule 10b–5 but may be awarded in pendant state law claim); Davis v. Merrill Lynch, Pierce, Fenner & Smith, Inc., 906 F.2d 1206 (8th Cir.1990) (upholding $2 million award of punitive damages against stock broker; applying South Dakota law); McAdam v. Dean Witter Reynolds, Inc., 896 F.2d 750 (3d Cir.1990); Grogan v. Garner, 806 F.2d 829 (8th Cir.1986) (plaintiff may recover the larger of 10b–5 damages or state law damages including punitive damage).

8. *See, e.g.,* Christopher F. Wilson, Punitive Damages in Securities Arbitrations, 26 Rev. Sec. & Commod. Reg. 203 (1993).

9. Lee v. Chica, 983 F.2d 883 (8th Cir.1993), *cert. denied* ___ U.S. ___, 114 S.Ct. 287, 126 L.Ed.2d 237 (1993) (rules of American Arbitration Association permit the award of punitive damages; award of punitive damages was reinstated) Pyle v. Securities U.S.A., Inc., 758 F.Supp. 638 (D.Colo.1991) (semble; upholding arbitrators' authority to award punitive damages under state law). *Compare* Mastrobuono v. Shearson Lehman Hutton, Inc., 20 F.3d 713 (7th Cir.1994), *cert. granted* ___ U.S. ___, 115 S.Ct. 305, 130 L.Ed.2d 218 (1994), *reversed* ___ U.S. ___, 115 S.Ct. 1212, 131 L.Ed.2d 76 (1995) (parties' selection of New York law included New York rule that punitive damages are not available in arbitration).

10. *E.g.* Abbey v. Control Data Corp., 933 F.2d 616 (8th Cir.1991), *cert. denied* 502 U.S. 967, 112 S.Ct. 438, 116 L.Ed.2d 457 (1991) (damages were properly limited to those

when the plaintiff profited from the fraudulently-induced transactions.[11] Limiting recovery to actual damages is required by the terms of section 28(a) of the Exchange Act.[12]

Failure to allege or prove actual damages will result in dismissal of any 10b–5 damage claim.[13] Beyond being able to identify actual damages, courts must identify the appropriate measure of damages. The determination of the appropriate measure of damages is governed by section 28(a) and thus is not a matter of state law. Accordingly, a state law-based collateral source rule cannot preclude a federal court from applying an offset necessary to limit the plaintiff's claims to actual damages.[14] In addition, the damages must result from a loss in connection with the securities transaction.[15] Thus, for example, a claim based on stock issued in connection with an employee compensation plan could not be based on the fact that the employees' services went uncompensated.[16]

What is the Appropriate Measure of Damages?

The courts have not always agreed upon the measure of damages in Rule 10b–5 cases. The proper measure of damages at common law is an equally elusive concept.[17] Under state law "benefit of the bargain" damages will be allowed on appropriate facts.[18] In Rule 10b–5 cases most courts have rejected a benefit of the bargain measure of damages[19] in lieu of an out-of-pocket measure.[20] However, in extraordinary cases

occurring up to the time the accounting improprieties in question had been disclosed); Sowell v. Butcher & Singer, Inc., 926 F.2d 289 (3d Cir.1991) (plaintiffs failed to produce sufficient evidence on damages to withstand motion for directed verdict).

11. *See* Barrows v. Forest Labs, Inc., 1981 WL 1642, [1981 Transfer Binder] Fed.Sec. L.Rep. (CCH) ¶ 98,037 (S.D.N.Y.1981); In re Investors Funding Corp., 523 F.Supp. 563 (S.D.N.Y.1980).

12. 15 U.S.C.A. § 78bb(a).

13. *E.g.,* Commercial Union Assurance Co. v. Milken, 17 F.3d 608 (2d Cir.1994); Romano v. Merrill Lynch, Pierce, Fenner & Smith, Inc., 834 F.2d 523 (5th Cir.1987); Feldman v. Pioneer Petroleum, Inc., 813 F.2d 296 (10th Cir.1987), *cert. denied* 484 U.S. 954, 108 S.Ct. 346, 98 L.Ed.2d 372 (1987).

Similarly, actual damages will not be awarded when too speculative. *E.g.,* Hutt v. Dean Witter Reynolds, Inc., 737 F.Supp. 128, 130–33 (D.Mass.1990).

14. B.N.E. Swedbank, S.A. v. Banker, 1993 WL 152392, [1992–1993 Transfer Binder] Fed.Sec.L.Rep. (CCH) ¶ 97,396 (S.D.N.Y.1993).

15. The "in connection with" requirement is discussed in § 13.2.2 *supra.*

16. Alta Health Strategies, Inc. v. Kennedy, 790 F.Supp. 1085 (D.Utah 1992).

17. *See* W. Page Keeton, Dan B. Dobbs, Robert E. Keeton & David G. Owen, Prosser and Keeton on Torts § 110 (5th ed. 1984).

18. *E.g.,* Farley v. Henson, 11 F.3d 827 (8th Cir.1993) (benefit of bargain was appropriate in common law fraud action in connection with merger).

19. *But cf.* In the Matter of Arbitration Between Eljer Manufacturing, Inc. v. Kowin Development Corp., 14 F.3d 1250 (7th Cir.1994) (award of lost profits as element of damages was contrary to federal law to the contrary; however, the arbitration award would not be overturned on the basis of this "mere error" in interpreting the federal law).

20. Wool v. Tandem Computers, Inc., 818 F.2d 1433 (9th Cir.1987) (awarding out-of-pocket loss); Harris v. Union Electric Co., 787 F.2d 355, 367 (8th Cir.), *cert. denied* 479 U.S. 823, 107 S.Ct. 94, 93 L.Ed.2d 45 (1986) (proper measure of damages is difference between the purchase price and the actual value on the date of the transaction); In re

some courts have looked to the benefit of the bargain.[21] There have been still other approaches to Rule 10b–5 damages. Some other courts in federal securities cases have adopted a rescission measure[22] while still others in insider trading cases require the disgorgement of ill-gotten gains.[23]

The benefit of the bargain measure of damages was adopted in at least one case involving a tender offer.[24] Benefit of the bargain should be the exception rather than the rule because it is in essence a contract remedy that is based on a breach of promise rather than the traditional out-of-pocket tort remedy. Thus, absent special circumstances, benefit of the bargain damages based on the purchaser's expected profit is not the appropriate measure under Rule 10b–5.[25] The benefit of the bargain measure, of course, may be recoverable if the plaintiff can establish a

---

Seagate Technology II Securities Litigation, 843 F.Supp. 1341, 1368–69 (N.D.Cal.1994) (out of pocket measure is the normal basis for Rule 10b–5 damages); Biben v. Card, 789 F.Supp. 1001 (W.D.Mo.1992) (out of pocket damages in class action by purchasers, the jury must first determine the true value of the security and then subtract that value from each plaintiff's purchase price; the trial was bifurcated into a liability phase and a proof of claim phase); Jaroslawicz v. Engelhard Corp., 724 F.Supp. 294 (D.N.J.1989). Palmer v. Woods, 1988 WL 156325, [1988–89 Transfer Binder] Fed.Sec.L.Rep. (CCH) ¶ 94,139 (M.D.Fla.1988) (difference between purchase price and the "real value" at the time of sale); Gaskins v. Grosse, 1983 WL 1282, [1983–1984 Transfer Binder] Fed.Sec.L.Rep. (CCH) ¶ 99,105 (S.D.Ga.1983); Faller Group, Inc. v. Jaffe, 564 F.Supp. 1177 (S.D.N.Y.1983).

21. Sharp v. Coopers & Lybrand, 649 F.2d 175 (3d Cir.1981), *cert. denied* 455 U.S. 938, 102 S.Ct. 1427, 71 L.Ed.2d 648 (1982); Osofsky v. Zipf, 645 F.2d 107 (2d Cir.1981), *appeal after remand* 725 F.2d 1057 (2d Cir.1984). *Accord* McMahan & Co. v. Wherehouse Entertainment, Inc., 859 F.Supp. 743 (S.D.N.Y.1994) (where debenture holders were promised certain benefits upon tender of debentures, the plaintiffs could maintain an action for benefit of the bargain damages that could be proved with sufficient certainty); Otto v. Variable Annuity Life Insurance Co., 730 F.Supp. 145 (N.D.Ill.1990); Johnsen v. Rogers, 551 F.Supp. 281 (C.D.Cal.1982). *But see* Alta Health Strategies, Inc. v. Kennedy, 790 F.Supp. 1085 (D.Utah 1992) (benefit of bargain damages were not appropriate). *Contra* Barr v. McGraw–Hill, Inc., 710 F.Supp. 95 (S.D.N.Y.1989) (benefit of bargain damages were too speculative); Freschi v. Grand Coal Venture, 588 F.Supp. 1257 (S.D.N.Y. 1984).

22. Glick v. Campagna, 613 F.2d 31 (3d Cir.1979); Western Federal Corp. v. Davis, 553 F.Supp. 818 (D.Ariz.1982), *order affirmed* 739 F.2d 1439 (9th Cir.1984). This is the measure under section 12 of the 1933 Act. 15 U.S.C.A. § 77l. See § 7.5 *supra.*

23. *See* Financial Industrial Fund, Inc. v. McDonnell Douglas Corp., 474 F.2d 514 (10th Cir.), *cert. denied* 414 U.S. 874, 94 S.Ct. 155, 38 L.Ed.2d 114 (1973). *See also* Pidcock v. Sunnyland America, Inc., 854 F.2d 443 (11th Cir.1988), *rehearing denied* 861 F.2d 1281 (11th Cir.1988) (seller presumed to have suffered loss equivalent to buyer's gain). Disgorgement may also be sought by the Commission in an enforcement action, *e.g.* SEC v. MacDonald, 699 F.2d 47 (1st Cir.1983), *on remand* 568 F.Supp. 111 (D.R.I.1983), *judgment affirmed* 725 F.2d 9 (1st Cir.1984); SEC v. Texas Gulf Sulphur Co., 446 F.2d 1301 (2d Cir.1971), *cert. denied* 404 U.S. 1005, 92 S.Ct. 561, 30 L.Ed.2d 558 (1971), *rehearing denied* 404 U.S. 1064, 92 S.Ct. 733, 30 L.Ed.2d 753 (1972). *See* George W. Dent, Jr., Ancillary Relief in Federal Securities Law: A Study in Federal Remedies, 67 Minn.L.Rev. 865 (1983); John A. Ellsworth, Disgorgement in Fraud Actions Brought by the SEC, 1977 Duke L.J. 641; James R. Farrand, Ancillary Remedies in SEC Civil Enforcement Suits, 89 Harv. L.Rev. 1779 (1976). *See also* 15 U.S.C.A. § 78o(d)(2)(A).

24. Osofsky v. Zipf, 645 F.2d 107 (2d Cir.1981), *appeal after remand* 725 F.2d 1057 (2d Cir.1984).

25. *See* Astor Chauffeured Limousine Co. v. Runnfeldt Investment Corp., 910 F.2d 1540, 1551 (7th Cir.1990), *on remand* 1991 WL 47119 (N.D.Ill.1991); Commercial Union Assurance Co. v. Ivan F. Boesky & Co., 824 F.Supp. 348 (S.D.N.Y.1993) (damages limited to out-of-pocket losses, benefit of bargain was not appropriate measure of damages).

state law breach of contract claim.[26]

The measure of damages adopted in any particular case is dependent to a large extent upon the theory of recovery. When the essence of plaintiff's claim is fraud in the inducement—that is that he or she would not have entered into the transaction but for the defendant's fraud—rescission is arguably the proper measure of damages; in such a case rescission would restore the status quo.[27] Rescission would not be appropriate when the defendant is not on the other side of the transaction (either as a broker or principal). When the essence of the claim is not that the defendant induced the transaction but rather that the plaintiff's injury is attributable to the defendant's fraudulent inflation or deflation of the security's price, then the appropriate remedy would seem to be the out-of-pocket measure.[28] In other words, rescission rests on a claim that the transaction should be undone due to fraud in the inducement while a claim for fraud generally leads to out-of-pocket recovery.[29]

There are additional instances in which a measure of damages other than out of pocket loss may be available. Disgorgement of ill-gotten gain may be appropriate when the remedy is based in terms of restitution and unjust enrichment rather than any compensable loss to the plaintiff. Thus, for example a suit against someone who has traded on inside information in breach of a duty to the plaintiff[30] is often said to be in the nature of restitution and thus disgorgement of profits is the proper measure.[31]

---

26. *Astor Chauffered Limousine Co.,* 910 F.2d at 1551.

27. Hatrock v. Edward D. Jones & Co., 750 F.2d 767, 773 (9th Cir.1984) (loss causation need not be demonstrated "where the evil is not the price the investor paid for the security, but the broker's fraudulent inducement of the investor to purchase the security"); Kafton v. Baptist Park Nursing Center, 617 F.Supp. 349, 350 (D.Ariz.1985). *See also* Manufacturers Hanover Trust Co. v. Drysdale Securities Corp., 801 F.2d 13 (2d Cir.1986), *cert. denied* 479 U.S. 1066, 107 S.Ct. 952, 93 L.Ed.2d 1001 (1987); Levine v. Diamanthuset, Inc., 722 F.Supp. 579 (N.D.Cal.1989) (rescission and attorney's fees are available remedies under Rule 10b–5). *Cf.* the rescission remedy provided in section 12 of the 1933 Act. 15 U.S.C.A. § 77*l*.

28. *See, e.g.,* Soderberg v. Gens, 652 F.Supp. 560, 565 (N.D.Ill.1987); Kafton v. Baptist Park Nursing Center, Inc., 617 F.Supp. 349, 350 (D.Ariz.1985). In such a case the plaintiff will have to show that the price was affected by the misrepresentations. *See* the discussion in the text accompanying footnotes 33–35 *infra. Compare* section 11 of the 1933 Act which presumes that the price was affected and leaves it to the defendant to show that the price decrease was due to factors other than the misstatements or omissions in the registration materials. 15 U.S.C.A. § 77k(e). *See* §§ 7.4–7.4.1 *supra.*

29. Soderberg v. Gens, 652 F.Supp. 560, 565 (N.D.Ill.1987) ("Rescission and damages are normally mutually exclusive remedies. Rescission rests on a disaffirmance of the transaction and return to the status which existed before the transaction was made. For damages one accepts the contract but sues for the loss caused by the fraud.").

30. Because of the necessity of proving a duty to the plaintiff, it is unlikely that many open market insider trading cases will result in damages in a Rule 10b–5 action. *E.g.* Moss v. Morgan Stanley, Inc., 719 F.2d 5 (2d Cir.1983). *See also, e.g.,* Fridrich v. Bradford, 542 F.2d 307 (6th Cir.1976), *cert. denied* 429 U.S. 1053, 97 S.Ct. 767, 50 L.Ed.2d 769 (1977). On the other hand, in 1988 Congress enacted an express right of action which is contained in section 20A of the Exchange Act. 15 U.S.C.A. § 78t–1. *See* § 13.9 *infra.*

31. This is also the measure adopted for computing the civil penalty in SEC enforcement actions under the Insider Trading Sanctions Act of 1984. 15 U.S.C.A. § 78u(d)(3)(B).

When the plaintiff can state a claim under more than one provision of the securities laws, he or she is entitled to the measure of damages that will result in the higher recovery.[32]

In assessing the plaintiff's actual loss, the courts have not always limited recovery to the out-of-pocket loss resulting directly from the transaction in shares. For example, it has been held that promised, but unrealized, tax losses are properly considered in assessing the measure of damages.[33] However, the Second Circuit has taken a contrary view in ruling that Rule 10b–5 is limited to actual damages and that awarding damages for hoped-for but unrealized tax savings would be an impermissible grant of expectation damages.[34] It seems that the court there took an unreasonably restrictive reading of section 28(a)'s limitation to actual damages. On appropriate facts, such as in a breach of contract case, expectation damages are the actual damages.[35] It is arguable that in rare instances when the fraud results in unfulfilled promises, expectation is appropriate under the federal securities laws as well. On the other hand, it appears to be the better argument that Rule 10b–5 is couched in fraud, and as such the remedy should be limited to the traditional fraud remedy, with state law still being available for expectation losses on appropriate facts.

A recent Supreme Court ruling comes to bear on the effects of tax consequences in securities damage actions. In Randall v. Loftsgaarden[36] the Court held that intangible tax benefits are to be treated differently from tangible property and thus are not income which needs to be deducted in the calculation of rescissory damages under section 12 of the 1933 Act.[37]

The disgorgement measure has also been incorporated into the private right of action in the hands of contemporaneous traders, which was enacted as part of the Insider Trading and Securities Fraud Enforcement Act of 1988. 15 U.S.C.A. § 78t–1. *See* § 13.9 *infra.*

32. Cyrak v. Lemon, 919 F.2d 320 (5th Cir.1990) (plaintiff with claims under section 12(2) of the 1933 Act and Rule 10b–5 may recover the higher amount and then in order to avoid double recovery, the lesser claim is extinguished), *relying on* Grogan v. Garner, 806 F.2d 829, 839 (8th Cir.1986); Aboussie v. Aboussie, 441 F.2d 150, 157 (5th Cir.1971) (plaintiff entitled to higher of common law and Rule 10b–5 claim).

33. Sharp v. Coopers & Lybrand, 649 F.2d 175 (3d Cir.1981), *cert. denied* 455 U.S. 938, 102 S.Ct. 1427, 71 L.Ed.2d 648 (1982).

34. Freschi v. Grand Coal Venture, 767 F.2d 1041 (2d Cir.1985), *vacated and remanded for further consideration* 478 U.S. 1015, 106 S.Ct. 3325, 92 L.Ed.2d 731 (1986), *on remand* 800 F.2d 305 (2d Cir.1986). *Accord* Torres v. Borzelleca, 641 F.Supp. 542 (E.D.Pa.1986).

35. *See, e.g.,* John D. Calamari & Joseph M. Perillo, Hornbook on the Law of Contracts ch. 14 (3d ed. 1987); Robert Cooter & Melvin Aron Eisenberg, Damages for Breach of Contract, 73 Calif.L.Rev. 1432 (1985). *See also* footnotes 18, 21 *supra.*

36. 478 U.S. 647, 106 S.Ct. 3143, 92 L.Ed.2d 525 (1986). *See also* the discussion in § 7.5.3 *supra* (Practitioner's Edition only).

37. The Eighth Circuit had allowed tax benefits to be deducted as income received. Austin v. Loftsgaarden, 768 F.2d 949 (8th Cir.1985), *reversed sub nom.* Randall v. Loftsgaarden, 478 U.S. 647, 106 S.Ct. 3143, 92 L.Ed.2d 525 (1986). The Second Circuit reached a similar result in Salcer v. Envicon Equities Corp., 744 F.2d 935 (2d Cir.1984), *cert. granted and judgment vacated* 478 U.S. 1015, 106 S.Ct. 3324, 92 L.Ed.2d 731 (1986). In contrast, the Ninth Circuit Court of Appeals had refused to reduce damages by tax benefits received in an action under Rule 10b–5. Burgess v. Premier Corp., 727 F.2d 826, 838 (9th Cir.1984).

As discussed above, section 28(a) of the Exchange Act limits recovery to actual damages.[38] In the course of its opinion in *Randall v. Loftsgaarden* the Court held this limitation inapplicable to the rescission remedy available under section 12 of the 1933 Act.[39] In so distinguishing the applicability of section 28(a), the Court left open the question of whether tax benefits are properly considered in an action under section 10(b) and Rule 10b–5 of the 1934 Act.[40] It thus remains unclear what effect tax benefits will have in computing damages under Rule 10b–5. Loss of expected tax benefits does not qualify as out-of-pocket loss and thus can be awarded only as expectation damages, which as noted above, at least in most instances, may not be appropriate in Rule 10b–5 cases.

Computing Out-of-Pocket Damages

Although most courts impose an out-of-pocket measure of damages in 10b–5 cases, there is some confusion concerning the proper method of calculating this figure. When dealing with publicly-traded securities, many factors exist during the period in which violations take place which may affect the market price of the securities. These factors include general market or financial conditions,[41] industry-wide conditions or issuer problems unrelated to the violations in question. In these situations, the courts try to establish the value of the defendant's misrepresentation.[42] Where market factors change over the period of the fraud, or where there are plaintiffs who, because of the time of acquisition of their securities, are in different damage positions, the value of the misrepresentation may vary.[43] Nevertheless, it is clear that damages under Rule 10b–5 are limited to those proximately caused by defendant's misstatement, omission, or conduct.[44] Problems continue to arise in this

---

38. 15 U.S.C.A. § 78bb(a). *See also, e.g.,* Singer v. Olympia Brewing Co., 878 F.2d 596 (2d Cir.1989), *cert. denied* 493 U.S. 1024, 110 S.Ct. 729, 107 L.Ed.2d 748 (1990). *Cf.* Hutt v. Dean Witter Reynolds, Inc., 737 F.Supp. 128, 130–33 (D.Mass.1990) (where defendant allegedly fraudulently induced plaintiff to sell a security, damages for future gains that the plaintiff would have realized had he not sold would not be awarded unless the "profit" was made by the defendant).

39. 478 U.S. at 661, 106 S.Ct. at 3152.

40. In an earlier ruling the Ninth Circuit Court of Appeals had refused to reduce damages by tax benefits received in an action under Rule 10b–5. Burgess v. Premier Corp., 727 F.2d 826, 838 (9th Cir.1984).

41. These factors will be discounted from the market price in assessing damages. Rolf v. Blyth, Eastman Dillon & Co., 570 F.2d 38, 49 (2d Cir.), *cert. denied* 439 U.S. 1039, 99 S.Ct. 642, 58 L.Ed.2d 698 (1978), *on remand* 1981 WL 1646, [1981–82 Transfer Binder] Fed.Sec.L.Rep. ¶ 98,201 (S.D.N.Y.1981); Feit v. Leasco Data Processing Equipment Corp., 332 F.Supp. 544, 586 (E.D.N.Y.1971) (decided under the 1933 Act).

42. *See, e.g.,* Rowe v. Maremont Corp., 850 F.2d 1226 (7th Cir.1988) (damages are based on the difference between what plaintiff received for his share and what he would have received absent the buyer's fraud). Section 11(e) of the 1933 Act bases damages on the difference between the price paid and the "value" at the time of suit if the plaintiff still owns the securities. If not, damages are based on the price received when the securities were sold. 15 U.S.C.A. § 77k(e). *See* § 7.3 *supra.*

43. Harris v. American Investment Co. 523 F.2d 220 (8th Cir.1975), *cert. denied* 423 U.S. 1054, 96 S.Ct. 784, 46 L.Ed.2d 643 (1976).

44. *See* Green v. Occidental Petroleum Corp., 541 F.2d 1335, 1341–46 (9th Cir.1976) (Sneed, J., concurring); Barrows v. Forest Labs, Inc., 1981 WL 1688, [1981 Transfer

context because of the difficulty in discounting extrinsic market factors.[45] Generally speaking, out-of-pocket damages will be based on the "value" of the securities at the time of the fraudulently-induced purchase or sale. Because these cases necessitate complex analysis, they may even result in the severing of a class action.[46]

Other damage assessment problems arise in insider trading cases. When dealing with a fraud-on-the-market theory of recovery, or when the plaintiffs consist of a number of open market purchasers or sellers, a variety of damage measures are available. One alternative limits recovery to the defendant's profit from the illegal transactions.[47] A second method aggregates the losses of all plaintiffs which, in insider trading cases, will far exceed the profits of all trading defendants.[48] This measure will be unrealistically large in cases involving publicly traded securities. The impracticality and hardship of collection makes this a highly questionable measure.[49] As one court has noted, looking to the losses of all investors has the "potential for imposition of Draconian, exorbitant damages, out of all proportion to the wrong committed, lining the pockets of all interim investors and their counsel at the expense of innocent corporate shareholders."[50] A Second Circuit case based the measure of damages on the amount of plaintiff's losses, but limited recovery to profits gained by the defendant tippee who was trading on inside information.[51] The court viewed disgorgement as avoiding the difficult problems of ascertaining "value" which is largely a speculative endeavor.[52] The Sixth Circuit has held, however, that the problems of proving causation in an open market insider trading case preclude any recovery, even recovery of the defendant insider's profit.[53] As pointed out earlier, and as discussed more fully in a later section, recent decisions have severely limited, if not eliminated, investors' damage

---

Binder] Fed.Sec.L.Rep. (CCH) ¶ 98,316 (S.D.N.Y.1981); Beecher v. Able, 435 F.Supp. 397 (S.D.N.Y.1975) (decided under the 1933 Act). Causation is discussed in § 13.6 *supra*.

45. Green v. Occidental Petroleum Corp., 541 F.2d 1335 (9th Cir.1976).

46. *See id.*

47. Financial Industrial Fund, Inc. v. McDonnell Douglas Corp., 474 F.2d 514 (10th Cir.1973), *cert. denied* 414 U.S. 874, 94 S.Ct. 155, 38 L.Ed.2d 114 (1973). *Cf.* State Teachers Retirement Board v. Fluor Corp., 589 F.Supp. 1268 (S.D.N.Y.1984). *See also* Lon E. Musslewhite, The Measure of the Disgorgement Remedy in SEC Enforcement Actions: SEC v. McDonald, 12 Sec.Reg.L.J. 138 (1984); 15 U.S.C.A. § 78u(d)(3).

48. *See* Shapiro v. Merrill Lynch, Pierce, Fenner & Smith, Inc., 495 F.2d 228 (2d Cir.1974). Mitchell v. Texas Gulf Sulphur Co., 446 F.2d 90 (10th Cir.1971), *cert. denied* 404 U.S. 1004, 92 S.Ct. 564, 30 L.Ed.2d 558 (1971), *rehearing denied* 405 U.S. 918, 92 S.Ct. 943, 30 L.Ed.2d 788 (1972).

49. *See* Fridrich v. Bradford, 542 F.2d 307 (6th Cir.1976), *cert. denied* 429 U.S. 1053, 97 S.Ct. 767, 50 L.Ed.2d 769 (1977).

50. Elkind v. Liggett & Myers, Inc., 635 F.2d 156, 170 (2d Cir.1980) noted in 34 Vand.L.Rev. 797 (1981).

51. *Id.*

52. *Id.*

53. Fridrich v. Bradford, 542 F.2d 307 (6th Cir.1976), *cert. denied* 429 U.S. 1053, 97 S.Ct. 767, 50 L.Ed.2d 769 (1977). Congress subsequently adopted an express remedy. *See* § 13.9 *infra*.

claims under Rule 10b–5 in insider trading cases.[54]

Other courts have indicated that there should be no single across-the-board approach to damages in 10b–5 cases. Instead each case should be looked at according to its own facts.[55] For example, it has been held that an out-of-pocket measure of damages, which is questionable in an open market insider trading case,[56] is more appropriate in a corporate dissemination case.[57]

When securities cases involve more than one defendant or nondefendant wrongdoer,[58] questions may arise regarding indemnification and contribution which are considered in more detail elsewhere in this treatise.[59] Section 20(a) of the 1934 Act[60] imposes joint and several liability on any person directly or indirectly controlling[61] someone held liable under the Act. This supplements the general rule of joint and several liability among joint tortfeasors[62] and common law concepts of *respondeat superior*.[63] The general rule favors a right of contribution among defendants in actions brought pursuant to both express and implied liability under the securities laws.[64] In recent years, some courts

---

54. *See* § 13.9 *infra.*

55. Garnatz v. Stifel, Nicolaus & Co., 559 F.2d 1357, 1360 (8th Cir.1977), *cert. denied* 435 U.S. 951, 98 S.Ct. 1578, 55 L.Ed.2d 801 (1978); Gottlieb v. Sandia American Corp., 304 F.Supp. 980, 991 (E.D.Pa.1969), *affirmed in part and reversed in part on other grounds* 452 F.2d 510 (3d Cir.1971), *cert. denied* 404 U.S. 938, 92 S.Ct. 274, 30 L.Ed.2d 250 (1971).

56. *See* footnotes 48–50 *supra.*

57. *See* Green v. Occidental Petroleum Corp., 541 F.2d 1335 (9th Cir.1976). *See also* the discussion of Basic, Inc. v. Levinson, 485 U.S. 224, 108 S.Ct. 978, 99 L.Ed.2d 194 (1988), *on remand* 871 F.2d 562 (6th Cir.1989) in § 13.5B *supra.*

58. *See generally* Daniel R. Fischel, Secondary Liability Under Section 10(b) of the Securities Act of 1934, 69 California L.Rev. 80 (1981); David S. Ruder, Multiple Defendants in Securities Law Fraud Cases: Aiding and Abetting, Conspiracy, in Pari Delicto, Indemnification, and Contribution, 120 U.Pa.L.Rev. 597 (1972); Ruder, Secondary Liability Under the Securities Acts, 8 Inst.Sec.Reg. 353 (1977). Aiding and abetting and conspiracy are discussed in § 7.8 *supra* and § 13.16 *infra.*

59. *See* §§ 7.7, 7.9 *supra* and §§ 13.15–13.17 *infra.*

60. 15 U.S.C.A. § 78(a). *See* Note, The Burden of Control: Derivative Liability Under Section 20(a) of The Securities Exchange Act of 1934, 48 N.Y.U.L.Rev. 1019 (1973).

61. Control is broadly defined in Rule 12b–2 as "the possession, direct or indirect, of the power to cause the direction of the management and policies of a person, whether through the ownership of voting securities, by contract or otherwise." 17 C.F.R. § 240.12b–2. *See also* 17 C.F.R. § 230.405.

62. *See* W. Page Keeton, Dan B. Dobbs, Robert E. Keeton & David G. Owen, Prosser and Keeton on Torts § 46 (5th ed. 1984).

63. *See, e.g.,* SEC v. Management Dynamics, Inc., 515 F.2d 801 (2d Cir.1975); Fey v. Walston & Co., 493 F.2d 1036, 1051–53 (7th Cir.1974); Lewis v. Walston & Co., 487 F.2d 617, 623–624 (5th Cir.1973); Johns Hopkins University v. Hutton, 422 F.2d 1124, 1130 (4th Cir.1970), *on remand* 326 F.Supp. 250 (D.Md.1971), *opinion supplemented* 343 F.Supp. 245 (D.Md.1972), *judgment affirmed in part, reversed in part* 488 F.2d 912 (4th Cir.1973), *cert. denied* 416 U.S. 916, 94 S.Ct. 1622, 40 L.Ed.2d 118 (1974); Armstrong, Jones & Co. v. SEC, 421 F.2d 359, 361–62 (6th Cir.1970), *cert. denied* 398 U.S. 958, 90 S.Ct. 2172, 26 L.Ed.2d 543 (1970). *See also, e.g.,* Richardson v. MacArthur, 451 F.2d 35, 41–42 (10th Cir.1971); Hecht v. Harris, Upham & Co., 430 F.2d 1202, 1210 (9th Cir.1970); Kamen & Co. v. Paul H. Aschkar & Co., 382 F.2d 689, 696–97 (9th Cir.1967), *cert. dismissed* 393 U.S. 801, 89 S.Ct. 40, 21 L.Ed.2d 85 (1968).

64. Heizer Corp. v. Ross, 601 F.2d 330, 334–35 (7th Cir.1979); Globus v. Law Research Service, Inc., 442 F.2d 1346 (2d Cir.1971), *cert. denied* 404 U.S. 941, 92 S.Ct. 286, 30

have denied the existence of an implied right to contribution.[65] However, the better view is that a right to contribution does exist with regard to Rule 10b–5 violations.[66] This rule has since been adopted by the Supreme Court.[67] Although the SEC frowns on indemnification agreements concerning securities law liability,[68] there is no *per se* prohibition.[69] It has been held, however, that an issuer's indemnification of its underwriter is void where the person claiming indemnification had knowledge of the wrongdoing.[70]

*Deleted section 13.7.1 can be found
in the Practitioner's Edition.*

§ 13.8 Statutes of Limitations in Rule 10b–5 Actions

The 1934 Act does not set forth a statute of limitations applicable to implied rights of action such as suits under Rule 10b–5. The courts, however, have identified four alternatives: (1) apply by analogy the statutes of limitation applicable to private remedies under Section 13 of the 1933 Act;[1] (2) apply the forum state's statute of limitations for common law fraud; (3) apply the statute of limitations for securities fraud under the forum state's blue sky law; or (4) apply the limitations period from section 9(e),[2] section 16(b),[3] or section 18(a)[4] of the Exchange

L.Ed.2d 254 (1971); Alexander & Baldwin, Inc. v. Peat Marwick, Mitchell & Co., 385 F.Supp. 230 (S.D.N.Y.1974). *See* § 7.7 *supra.*

65. *E.g.,* King v. Gibbs, 876 F.2d 1275 (7th Cir.1989) and the other cases cited in § 13.17 *infra.*

66. *E.g.,* In re Jiffy Lube Securities Litigation, 927 F.2d 155 (4th Cir.1991).

67. Musick, Peeler & Garrett v. Employers Insurance of Wausau, ___ U.S. ___, 113 S.Ct. 2085, 124 L.Ed.2d 194 (1993).

68. *See, e.g.,* Rule 461(c) dealing with acceleration of the effective date for 1933 Act registration statements, 17 C.F.R. § 230.461(c); § 7.9 *supra.*

69. *See, e.g.,* Regulation S–K item 702.

70. Globus v. Law Research Service, Inc., 418 F.2d 1276 (2d Cir.1969), *cert. denied* 397 U.S. 913, 90 S.Ct. 913, 25 L.Ed.2d 93 (1970). *See* Milton P. Kroll, Some Reflections on Indemnification Provisions and S.E.C. Liability Insurance in Light of *BarChris* and *Globus*, 24 Bus.Law. 681 (1969).

§ 13.8

1. 15 U.S.C.A. § 77m (one year from discovery or reasonable discovery but no more than three years after the sale or, if applicable, from the public offering). *See* § 7.5.4 *supra* (Practitioner's Edition only).

2. 15 U.S.C.A. § 78i(e) (action for manipulation of exchange listed securities; one year from discovery, three years after the violation). Section 9(e) is discussed in § 12.1 *supra.* It is to be noted that section 9(e) speaks in terms of three years from the *violation* whereas section 13 of the 1933 Act refers to the *sale.* It is conceivable that this is a significant difference when dealing with allegations of a continuing fraud. If the fraud is continuing, arguably the three-year repose period does not begin to run until the fraud has ceased. In contrast, if the key date is when the transaction took place, a continuing fraud will not extend the repose period.

3. 15 U.S.C.A. § 78p(b) (disgorgement of insider short-swing profits; two years from the date the profit was realized). Section 16(b) liability is discussed in §§ 12.3–12.5 *supra.*

4. 15 U.S.C.A. 78r(a) (liability for misstatements or omissions in documents filed with the SEC; one year from discovery, three years after the violation). Section 18(a) is discussed in § 12.8 *supra.*

Act. With the enactment of the Insider Trading and Securities Fraud Enforcement Act's new private remedy against illegal insider trading, there is now a fifth alternative. The new insider trading remedy contains a five year limitations period.[5] The weight of scholarly authority consistently has favored the application of a federal limitations period in order to promote uniformity.[6] Up until 1987, the courts rarely borrowed the statute of limitations from one of the express federal remedies. However, a 1987 Supreme Court decision under the Racketeering and Corrupt Organizations Act (RICO)[7] favored the application of a uniform statute and has led some courts to reconsider their earlier positions.[8] In 1991, the Supreme Court overturned years of lower court precedent in holding that the one-year federal statute of limitations with a three year repose period applies in implied actions under Rule 10b–5.[9]

Notwithstanding the Supreme Court's adoption of a one year limitations period and a three year repose period, a number of questions remain. Resolution of many of these unanswered questions may require reference to the earlier cases when federal courts looked to state law for the applicable statute of limitations.

[*See* Practitioner's Edition for further discussion].

---

5. Section 20A(b)(4) of the Exchange Act, 15 U.S.C.A. § 78t–1(b)(4). This new remedy is discussed in § 13.9 *infra*. Section 20A's five-year limitation period as the most recent congressional statement might be a good yardstick for 10b–5 actions. On the other hand the insider trading remedy is based on restitutionary principles rather than fraud and thus may not be as analogous as the one year/three year statute of limitations which applies under the express antifraud provisions. *See* 15 U.S.C.A. §§ 77m, 78r(a). *See also* §§ 7.5.4 *supra* (Practitioner's Edition only).

6. Louis Loss Fundamentals of Securities Regulation 995 (2d ed. 1988); 6 Louis Loss, Securities Regulation 3898–900 n. 307 (1969 Supp.); Hal M. Bateman & Gerald P. Keith, Statutes of Limitations Applicable to Private Actions Under SEC Rule 10b–5: Complexity in Need of Reform, 39 Mo.L.Rev. 165, 183 (1974); David S. Ruder & Neil S. Cross, Limitations on Civil Liability Under Rule 10b–5, 1972 Duke L.J. 1125, 1142; Schulman, Statutes of Limitation in 10b–5 Actions: Complication Added to Confusion, 13 Wayne L.Rev. 635 (1967); Gordon W. Stewart, Statutes of Limitation for Rule 10b–5, 39 Wash. & Lee L.Rev. 1021 (1982). *See also* Herbert A. Einhorn & Paul K. Feldman, Choosing a Statute of Limitations in Federal Securities Actions, 25 Mercer L.Rev. 497 (1974); H, Robert Fiebach & David M. Doret, Quarter Century Later—The Period of Limitations for Rule 10b–5 Damage Actions in Federal Courts Sitting in Pennsylvania, 25 Vill.L.Rev. 851 (1980). *See also* Report of the ABA Task Force on Statute of Limitations for Implied Actions, 41 Bus. Law. 645 (1986).

7. 18 U.S.C.A. § 1961 *et seq. See* § 19.3 *infra* (Practitioner's Edition only).

8. Agency Holding Corp. v. Malley–Duff & Associates, Inc., 483 U.S. 143, 107 S.Ct. 2759, 97 L.Ed.2d 121 (1987).

9. Lampf, Pleva, Lipkind, Prupis & Petigrow v. Gilbertson, 501 U.S. 350, 111 S.Ct. 2773, 115 L.Ed.2d 321 (1991), *rehearing denied* 501 U.S. 1277, 112 S.Ct. 27, 115 L.Ed.2d 1109 (1991). For a critique of *Lampf, see* Lyman Johnson, Securities Fraud and the Mirage of Repose, 1992 Wis.L.Rev. 607.

See also, e.g., Riley v. Murdock, 828 F.Supp. 1215 (E.D.N.C.1993) (allegations of the existence of a conspiracy did not extend the three-year repose period).

Deleted section 13.8.1 can be found
in the Practitioner's Edition.

§ 13.9   Insider Trading and Rule 10b–5

Overview

Over the past twenty-five years there have been many celebrated cases involving trading in securities based on nonpublic confidential or proprietary information.[1]   The SEC has repeatedly declared that the eradication of trading on inside information is one of its top priority enforcement targets.[2]   Trading on inside information destroys the integrity of the market place by giving an informational advantage to a select group of corporate insiders.[3]   The practice is especially pernicious[4] in light of the federal securities laws' thrust of full disclosure, which is designed to create and maintain an informed market.   Although some commentators have argued that insider trading does not have significant adverse market impact,[5] fortunately, the courts, Congress and the SEC

---

§ 13.9

1.   Defendants have ranged from newspaper columnists to leading arbitrageurs and, most unfortunately, lawyers.   Several instances have involved law firms.   In one situation a partner of a big-city law firm with an active tender offer practice frequently made purchases in the targets of his firm's client's takeover attempts.   The partner, who has been disciplined, was not working on any part of the takeovers but the information somehow filtered down to him.   Although these facts raise questions about the internal controls at law firms and other businesses dealing with confidential inside information, no action was taken against the firm.   *Cf.* Stephen M. Bainbridge, Insider Trading Under the Restatement of the Law Governing Lawyers, 19 J. Corp. L. 1 (1993).

In a similar situation in a different big-city firm a paralegal working on corporate takeovers tipped her boyfriend, a stock broker, who in turn purchased the target companies' shares in advance of the announcement of the tender offers.

See the discussion of Chinese Walls in § 10.2.4 *supra* (Practitioner's Edition only).

2.   One example of this push is the legislation recently enacted by Congress.   *See* footnote 7 *infra* and accompanying text.

3.   *E.g.* William H. Painter, Federal Regulation of Insider Trading, ch. XI (1968);   Roy A. Schotland, Unsafe at Any Price: A Reply to Manne, "Insider Trading and the Stock Market", 53 Va.L.Rev. 1425 (1967).   *See also* the authorities cited in footnote 11 *infra*.

4.   *See. e.g.,* Kim Lane Scheppele, "It's Just Not Right": The Ethics of Insider Trading, 18 Law & Contemp. Probs. 123 (1993).

5.   Briefly put, it is claimed that in light of the average trading volume, insider trading has no discernible impact on other investors, individually or in the aggregate.   Because of the faceless market, the victims of insiders (or "know nothings") are selected randomly.   It has even been suggested that trading on inside information performs a useful function by preparing the market and getting it started in the proper direction before the information is publicly announced.   Otherwise, it is argued, major announcements will cause wide price fluctuations that not only disrupt an orderly market but will cause more injury to outside investors than would the insider trading.   *See, e.g.,* Henry G. Manne, Insider Trading and the Stock Market (1966);   Jeffrey F. Jaffe, The Effect of Regulation Changes on Insider Trading, 5 Bell.J.Econ. & Mgt.Sci. 93 (1974);   Hsin–Kwang Wu, An Economist Looks at Section 16 of The Securities Exchange Act of 1934, 68 Colum.L.Rev. 260 (1968).   *See also, e.g.,* Stephen Bainbridge, The Insider Trading Prohibition: A Legal and Economic Enigma, 38 U.Fla.L.Rev. 35 (1986);   William J. Carney, Signalling and Causation in Insider Trading, 36 Cath.U.L.Rev. 863 (1987);   James D. Cox & Kevin S. Fogarty, Bases of Insider Trading Law, 49 Ohio St.L.J. 353 (1988);   David D. Haddock & Jonathan R. Macey, A Coasian Model of Insider Trading, 80 Nw.U.L.Rev. 1449 (1986);   Robert J. Haft, The Effect of Insider Trading Rules on the Internal Efficiency of the Large Corporation, 80 Mich.L.Rev. 1051 (1982).

have not joined in that position. On the other hand, it is generally recognized that there is a positive value in encouraging corporate officers, directors, and other employees to invest in the shares of their company. Accordingly, there are a number of instances in which trading by insiders is permissible. Unfortunately the law regarding the use of nonpublic material information when trading in shares has not developed systematically. Nor has it evolved in such a way as to produce bright-line tests of when it is permissible to trade.

It is ironic that, as important as regulating trading on the basis of inside information may be under the securities laws, there is no express statutory prohibition. Section 16(b)'s prohibition against *short-swing* profits by designated statutory insiders[6] is the one of three sections in the Exchange Act that expressly deal with insider trading. The remaining two sections are remedial rather than substantive. In 1984 Congress enhanced the SEC's enforcement capabilities and bolstered the penalties for insider trading.[7] In 1988 Congress supplemented Rule 10b–5 with an express private right of action.[8] Nevertheless, the fact remains that there is no statutory definition to precisely identify which types of insider trading are permissible and which are not.

The primary basis of the prohibitions on trading while in possession of nonpublic material information has been SEC Rule 10b–5.[9] Rule 10b–5,[10] which does not expressly address the question of insider trading, has frequently been used to regulate trading by insiders who possess confidential inside information concerning their company's stock.[11] Necessar-

---

For an excellent rebuttal of the economic arguments favoring insider trading, *see* James D. Cox, Insider Trading and Contracting: A Critical Response to the "Chicago School," 1986 Duke L.J. 628. *See also* Thomas L. Hazen, Commentary, 36 Cath.U.L. Rev. 987, 993–96 (1987).

6. 15 U.S.C.A. § 78p(b). *See* §§ 12.2–12.7 *supra. See also* Section 16(b)'s counterpart in the Public Utility Holding Company Act of 1935, 15 U.S.C.A. § 79q. The Public Utility Holding Company Act is discussed in § 15.2 *infra.*

7. The 1984 legislation which was supported by the SEC includes a fine based on treble damages against certain persons trading on inside information. *See* footnote 117 *infra* and accompanying text. In 1988, Congress added an express right of action by contemporaneous traders. 15 U.S.C.A. § 78t–1. *See* text accompanying footnotes 136–147 *infra.*

8. 15 U.S.C.A. § 78t–1. *See* text accompanying footnotes 136–147 *infra.*

9. 17 C.F.R. § 240.10b–5. The SEC subsequently adopted Rule 14e–3 which directly addresses trading in advance of tender offers. 17 C.F.R. § 240.14e–3. *See* discussion *infra* and § 11.15 *supra.* The express prohibitions of the tender offer rule are based on the Rule 10b–5 jurisprudence; accordingly, unless and until the SEC or Congress adopt an express prohibition, Rule 10b–5 will remain at the heart of insider trading prohibitions.

10. The text of Rule 10b–5 is set out in § 13.2 *supra. See, e.g.,* Dirks v. SEC, 463 U.S. 646, 103 S.Ct. 3255, 77 L.Ed.2d 911 (1983); Chiarella v. United States, 445 U.S. 222, 100 S.Ct. 1108, 63 L.Ed.2d 348 (1980). *Compare, e.g.,* United States v. Newman, 664 F.2d 12 (2d Cir.1981), *cert. denied* 464 U.S. 863, 104 S.Ct. 193, 78 L.Ed.2d 170 (1983) and Elkind v. Liggett & Myers, Inc., 635 F.2d 156 (2d Cir.1980) (taking the broad view) *with* Fridrich v. Bradford, 542 F.2d 307 (6th Cir.1976), *cert. denied* 429 U.S. 1053, 97 S.Ct. 767, 50 L.Ed.2d 769 (1977) and Moss v. Morgan Stanley Inc., 719 F.2d 5 (2d Cir.1983), *cert. denied* 465 U.S. 1025, 104 S.Ct. 1280, 79 L.Ed.2d 684 (1984).

11. *See generally* John F. Barry III, The Economics of Outside Information and Rule 10b–5, 129 U.Pa.L.Rev. 1307 (1981); Douglas M. Branson, Discourse on the Supreme Court Approach to SEC Rule 10b–5 and Insider Trading, 30 Emory L.J. 263 (1981); Victor Brudney, Insiders, Outsiders, and Informational Advantages Under the Federal Securities

ily couched in terms of section 10(b)'s prohibitions against manipulative and deceptive conduct,[12] Rule 10b–5(2), which is the center of most antifraud litigation outside of the insider trading context,[13] prohibits false statements and omissions of material fact in connection with purchases or sales of securities. On occasion, subsection (2) has been relied upon to bar an insider from engaging in a purchase or a sale while in possession of inside information without public disclosure of the relevant facts.[14] In most cases, however, accountability for trading on inside information has been premised upon Rule 10b–5(3)'s ban on acts or practices that operate as fraud.

Rule 10b–5 prohibits conduct "in connection with the purchase or sale" of a security.[15] The rule is thus limited to conduct that touches purchases or sales. It follows that the decision to retain stock, although based on inside information, cannot amount to a violation of the rule.[16]

As discussed more fully below, the prohibition of 10b–5(c) has been utilized to craft a rule of law that subjects certain persons in possession of material nonpublic information to a "disclose or abstain" rule. The

---

Laws, 93 Harv.L.Rev. 322 (1979); Dennis W. Carlton & Daniel R. Fischel, The Regulation of Insider Trading, 35 Stanford L.Rev. 857 (1983); Michael Conant, Duties of Disclosure of Corporate Insiders Who Purchase Shares, 46 Cornell L.Q. 53 (1960); Michael P. Dooley, Enforcement of Insider Trading Restrictions, 66 Va.L.Rev. 1 (1980); Arthur Fleischer, Jr., Securities Trading and Corporate Information Practices: The Implications of the Texas Gulf Sulphur Proceedings, 51 Va.L.Rev. 299 (1974); Arthur Fleischer, Jr., Robert H. Mundheim & John C. Murphy, Jr., An Initial Inquiry into the Responsibility to Disclose Market Information, 121 U.Pa.L.Rev. 798 (1973); Thomas L. Hazen, Corporate Insider Trading: Reawakening the Common Law, 39 Wash. & Lee L.Rev. 845 (1982); J.A.C. Hetherington, Insider Trading and the Logic of the Law, 1967 Wis.L.Rev. 720; Richard W. Jennings, Insider Trading in Corporate Securities: A Survey of Hazards and Disclosure Obligations Under Rule 10b–5, 62 Nw.U.L.Rev. 809 (1968); Donald C. Langevoort, Insider Trading and the Fiduciary Principle: A Post–Chiarella Restatement, 70 Cal.L.Rev. 1 (1982); Peter H. Morrison, Silence is Golden: Trading on Nonpublic Information, 8 Sec.Reg.L.J. 211 (1980); John Rapp & Alan M. Loeb, Tippee Liability and Rule 10b–5, 1971 U.Ill.L.F. 55; David L. Ratner, Federal and State Roles in the Regulation of Insider Trading, 31 Bus.Law. 947 (1976); Symposium, 26 American Crim.L.Rev. 3 (1988); Symposium, Insider Trading in Stocks, 21 Bus.Law. 1009 (1966); William K.S. Wang, Trading on Nonpublic Information on Impersonal Stock Markets: Who is Harmed and Who Can Sue Whom Under SEC Rule 10b–5?, 54 So.Cal.L.Rev. 1217 (1981).

See also, e.g., Stephen F. Bainbridge, Insider Trading Under the Restatement of the Law Governing Lawyers, 19 J. Corp. L. 1 (1993); David M. Bovi, Rule 10b–5 Liability for Front-Running: Adding a New Dimension to the "Money Game," 7 St. Thomas L.Rev. 103 (1994).

12. 15 U.S.C.A. § 78j(b). Section 10(b) and the other SEC rules promulgated thereunder are discussed in § 12.1 *supra.*

13. *See, e.g.,* §§ 13.2, 13.2.1, 13.10 *supra.*

14. *E.g.* Affiliated Ute Citizens of Utah v. United States, 406 U.S. 128, 152, 92 S.Ct. 1456, 1471, 31 L.Ed.2d 741 (1972), *rehearing denied* 407 U.S. 916, 92 S.Ct. 2430, 32 L.Ed.2d 692 (1972) ("Clearly, the Court of Appeals was right to the extent that it held that the two employees had violated Rule 10b–5; in the instances specified in that holding the record reveals a misstatement of a material fact, within the proscription of Rule 10b–5(2), * * * "). The *Affiliated Ute* decision arose in the context of a face to face transaction as opposed to a sale effected in a faceless market. It is questionable whether Rule 10b–5(2) applies to insider trading in the context of a faceless market. *Cf.* Fridrich v. Bradford, 542 F.2d 307 (6th Cir.1976), *cert. denied* 429 U.S. 1053, 97 S.Ct. 767, 50 L.Ed.2d 769 (1977).

15. 17 C.F.R. § 240.10b–5. *See* § 13.2.2 *supra.*

16. *See* Condus v. Howard Savings Bank, 781 F.Supp. 1052 (D.N.J.1992).

disclose or abstain rule means that when potential traders have obtained the material information in such a way as to subject them to Rule 10b–5's reach, they must either abstain from trading or disclose the information prior to trading. In most instances, disclosure is not a reasonable option; therefore, the practical mandate is to abstain from trading until the information has been disclosed.

One of the most problematic aspects of the disclose or abstain rule is determining who is subject to the trading ban. Clearly, a direct insider is affected; but what about traders who obtain the information from an insider or the company itself? These are among the most difficult questions that the courts have grappled with in this area.

Rule 10b–5's prohibitions on insider trading originally were developed in the context of SEC enforcement actions and criminal prosecutions. As discussed in earlier sections of this treatise, in appropriate cases, the rule will also provide private plaintiffs with a damage remedy.[17] The existence of a private remedy to pursue violators of Rule 10b–5 in insider trading cases raises distinct problems. The discussion that follows will first examine the development of the disclose or abstain rule and its permutations. The current law of insider trading can be evaluated properly only in light of its historical development.

The Basis of the Prohibition: The Development of Rule 10b–5 in Insider Trading Cases

In the seminal case of Cady, Roberts & Co.[18] the Commission imposed disciplinary sanctions against a registered broker-dealer who directed his customers to liquidate their holdings in Curtiss–Wright stock because he had advance knowledge of a dividend cut. The broker, tipped by a corporate insider, was merely a tippee who in turn tipped his customers. The SEC found that this conduct "violated [10b–5(3)]as a practice which operated as * * * fraud or deceit upon the purchasers." [19] The Commission explained that "analytically, the obligation [to disclose or abstain from trading] rests on two principal elements; first, the existence of a relationship giving access, directly or indirectly, to information intended to be available only for a corporate purpose and not for the personal benefit of anyone, and second, the inherent unfairness involved where a party takes advantage of such information knowing it is unavailable to those with whom he is dealing."[20]

---

17. *See* §§ 13.2–13.8.1 *supra.*

18. 40 S.E.C. 907 (SEC 1961).

19. *Id.* at 913.

20. *Id.* at 912. *See also, e.g.,* United States v. Newman, 664 F.2d 12 (2d Cir.1981), *cert. denied* 464 U.S. 863, 104 S.Ct. 193, 78 L.Ed.2d 170 (1983). In re Smith Barney, Harris, Upham & Co., Exch.Act Rel. No. 34–21242, [1984 Transfer Binder] Fed.Sec.L.Rep. (CCH) ¶ 83,656 (Aug. 15, 1984) (brokerage firm should give its customers time to digest research recommendations reflecting a material change in the firm's position before the firm trades in the securities for its own account). *But see* Moss v. Morgan Stanley Inc., 719 F.2d 5 (2d Cir.1983), *cert. denied* 465 U.S. 1025, 104 S.Ct. 1280, 79 L.Ed.2d 684 (1984) (brokerage firm not held liable to open market seller).

Following the *Cady, Roberts* decision, the Second Circuit in SEC v. Texas Gulf Sulphur Co.,[21] held that corporate insiders who purchased stock on the open market with knowledge of a valuable mineral find that had not yet been publicly announced had violated Rule 10b–5 because the information not disclosed at the time of the transactions would have been "material" to a reasonable person's investment decision.[22] The fact that the insiders began purchasing stock and options raised a strong inference that they considered the information material.[23] Following the lead of *Texas Gulf Sulphur,* it has been held that a tip of inside information will give rise to liability for fraud on the market.[24] One court has even held that non-insider tippees who sell in reliance on confidential inside information will be liable and held accountable by disgorging their profits.[25] More recent Supreme Court decisions have been narrowing the scope of tippee liability.[26] However, at least outside of the insider trading context, fraud on the market remains a basis for Rule 10b–5 liability.[27]

A variation on the fraud on the market has arisen in several insider

---

21. 401 F.2d 833 (2d Cir.1968), *cert. denied* 394 U.S. 976, 89 S.Ct. 1454, 22 L.Ed.2d 756 (1969). *See* Alan R. Bromberg, Corporate Information: *Texas Gulf Sulphur* and Its Implications, 22 Sw.L.J. 731 (1968).

22. *See also, e.g.,* Garcia v. Cordova, 930 F.2d 826 (10th Cir.1991) (six-year old appraisal of real estate was too unreliable and too speculative to be material in context of insider trading case); United States v. Milken, 759 F.Supp. 109 (S.D.N.Y.1990) (knowledge that head of investment banking firm's corporate finance department set up meeting with casino officials to discuss financing options was not material in light of numerous different matters which might have been discussed); United States v. Marcus Schloss & Co., 1989 WL 153353, [1989–1990 Transfer Binder] Fed.Sec.L.Rep. ¶ 94,840 (S.D.N.Y.1989) (materiality of information concerning possible acquisition).

23. The court in determining the "materiality date" of the insiders' information, relied heavily on substantial increases in insider trading, reasoning that this presented circumstantial evidence that at least the insider deemed the information to be material. One lesson of this type of reasoning is that when purchasing the shares of their own company, corporate insiders should adopt a regular and periodic plan of purchase. Otherwise, it is likely that the fact finder might infer that the information available to the insider was in fact material. *See* § 13.5A *supra. See also, e.g.,* SEC v. Shared Medical Systems Corp., 1994 WL 201858, [1993–1994 Transfer Binder] Fed. Sec. L. Rep. (CCH) ¶ 98,247 (E.D.Pa. 1994) (insider trading in suspicious amounts or at suspicious times is probative of scienter).

24. Shapiro v. Merrill Lynch, Pierce Fenner & Smith, Inc., 495 F.2d 228 (2d Cir.1974). *Accord, e.g.,* Elkind v. Liggett & Myers, Inc., 635 F.2d 156 (2d Cir.1980). *See generally* Wang, supra footnote 11.

25. Financial Industrial Fund, Inc. v. McDonnell Douglas Corp., 474 F.2d 514 (10th Cir.1973), *cert. denied* 414 U.S. 874, 94 S.Ct. 155, 38 L.Ed.2d 114 (1973). *See* SEC v. Platt, 565 F.Supp. 1244 (W.D.Okl.1983) (upholding SEC claim against tippee, who knowingly obtained the information from an insider but also holding that someone receiving information without knowing the source is not in violation of Rule 10b–5). *Cf.* Tarasi v. Pittsburgh National Bank, 555 F.2d 1152 (3d Cir.1977), *cert. denied* 434 U.S. 965, 98 S.Ct. 504, 54 L.Ed.2d 451 (1977) (discussing the defense of *in pari delicto*); Grumet v. Shearson American Express, 564 F.Supp. 336 (D.N.J.1983) (semble). *Compare* Berner v. Lazzaro, 730 F.2d 1319 (9th Cir.1984), *judgment affirmed* 472 U.S. 299, 105 S.Ct. 2622, 86 L.Ed.2d 215 (1985) (holding the *in pari delicto* defense inapplicable to insider trading).

26. Dirks v. SEC, 463 U.S. 646, 103 S.Ct. 3255, 77 L.Ed.2d 911 (1983); Chiarella v. United States, 445 U.S. 222, 100 S.Ct. 1108, 63 L.Ed.2d 348 (1980). *See* discussion in the text accompanying footnotes 32–44, *infra.*

27. *E.g.* Kumpis v. Wetterau, 586 F.Supp. 152 (E.D.Mo.1983). Fraud on the market is also discussed in §§ 13.5B–13.6 *supra.*

trading cases. In a Ninth Circuit case,[28] a financial columnist who purchased stock prior to publishing his buy recommendation was held liable to a forced purchaser who did not rely on the column.[29] The recommendation was based on an overly optimistic view of the company. The court reasoned that the defendant's failure to disclose his scalping activities defrauded the market by causing an artificially high price and that the plaintiffs' injury arose from having to pay that price. The "fraud on the market" theory,[30] however, is far from unanimously accepted in the insider trading context. For example, the Sixth Circuit has held that a tippee trading on information obtained from his father, a corporate insider, is not liable to purchasers in a faceless market because of the plaintiff's inability to prove the causation requirement necessary to recover damages under a fraud theory.[31]

Perhaps an even more formidable impediment to actions under Rule 10b–5 by open market purchasers or sellers against persons trading on inside information is the Supreme Court's ruling that the mere possession of inside information does not create a duty to market participants.[32] Market participants thus cannot state a claim unless the person trading on the information is a corporate official who owes an independent duty to the shareholders who were trading on the other side of the insiders' transactions.[33] In 1988, Congress supplemented any remedy that may exist under Rule 10b–5 with an express private right of action by contemporaneous traders against persons making improper use of material, nonpublic information.[34] Under this new express remedy,

---

28. Zweig v. Hearst Corp., 594 F.2d 1261 (9th Cir.1979). The activity complained of—purchasing a security prior to publicly recommending it—is known as "scalping." *See* SEC v. Capital Gains Research Bureau, Inc., 375 U.S. 180, 84 S.Ct. 275, 11 L.Ed.2d 237 (1963). Scalping is discussed in § 10.9 *supra.*

29. The plaintiffs acquired the stock pursuant to a merger that was agreed to prior to the conduct in question.

30. For other fraud on the market cases, *see, e.g.,* T.J. Raney & Sons, Inc. v. Fort Cobb, Oklahoma Irrigation Fuel Authority, 717 F.2d 1330 (10th Cir.1983), *cert. denied* 465 U.S. 1026, 104 S.Ct. 1285, 79 L.Ed.2d 687 (1984); Panzirer v. Wolf, 663 F.2d 365 (2d Cir.1981), *cert. denied* 458 U.S. 1107, 102 S.Ct. 3486, 73 L.Ed.2d 1368 (1982); Blackie v. Barrack, 524 F.2d 891 (9th Cir.1975), *cert. denied* 429 U.S. 816, 97 S.Ct. 57, 50 L.Ed.2d 75 (1976). *See generally* Note, Fraud on the Market Theory, 95 Harv.L.Rev. 1143 (1982); Note, Fraud on the Market: An Emerging Theory of Recovery Under SEC Rule 10b–5, 50 Geo.Wash.L.Rev. 627 (1982).

31. Fridrich v. Bradford, 542 F.2d 307 (6th Cir.1976), *cert. denied* 429 U.S. 1053, 97 S.Ct. 767, 50 L.Ed.2d 769 (1977). *Cf.,* FMC Corp. v. Boesky, 673 F.Supp. 242 (N.D.Ill. 1987), *judgment reversed* 852 F.2d 981 (7th Cir.1988) (dismissing corporation's claim for lack of causal connection). *See* Robert N. Rapp, *Fridrich v. Bradford* and the Scope of Insider Trading Liability Under SEC Rule 10b–5: A Commentary, 38 Ohio St.L.J. 67 (1977). *Contra* Goldman v. Belden, 754 F.2d 1059 (2d Cir.1985).

32. Chiarella v. United States, 445 U.S. 222, 100 S.Ct. 1108, 63 L.Ed.2d 348 (1980). *See* the discussion in the text accompanying footnotes 37–54 *infra.*

33. *See* Moss v. Morgan Stanley, Inc., 719 F.2d 5 (2d Cir.1983). *Cf.* Goldman v. Belden, 754 F.2d 1059 (2d Cir.1985). Wilson v. Comtech Telecommunications Corp., 648 F.2d 88, 94–95 (2d Cir.1981).

34. 15 U.S.C.A. § 78t–1. *See* text accompanying footnotes 136–147 *infra.*

contemporaneous traders[35] are permitted to sue for a disgorgement of the improper profits (or loss avoided). This new remedy expressly supplements existing express and implied rights of action, and thus retains any Rule 10b–5 remedy that may exist. However, the cumulative nature of the remedies should not support a double recovery. Nevertheless, someone who has breached a duty to plaintiffs in connection with illegal trades may be held liable under Rule 10b–5 on a fraud on the market theory,[36] unless the Sixth Circuit's no causation rule is followed, in which case the new express remedy will still be available.

Refining Rule 10b–5's Insider Trading Prohibitions; Developments in the Supreme Court and Elsewhere—The Misappropriation Theory

In the first Supreme Court case on point, it was held that in a face-to-face transaction, a purchaser possessing inside information about a company has a duty to disclose such information to the seller before consummating a transaction.[37] Showing the necessary causation was not a problem because the purchaser dealt directly with the seller. The Court further held that reliance on the nondisclosure could be presumed from the materiality of the information in the absence of any evidence of actual nonreliance.[38] More recently, however, in Chiarella v. United States,[39] the Court held that in a market transaction, there was no duty to disclose based solely on the possession of inside information, at least when that information was "market information" rather than fundamental information related to the issuer's condition.

---

35. *See, e.g.,* Neubronner v. Milken, 6 F.3d 666 (9th Cir.1993) (contemporaneous trading must be pleaded with particularity); Feldman v. Motorola, Inc., 1994 WL 722883, [1994–1995 Transfer Binder] Fed. Sec. L. Rep. (CCH) ¶ 98,464 (N.D.Ill.1994) (class period for contemporaneous traders was relatively short and covered insider trades by two defendants but could not support a cause of action against a third defendant who traded after the class period ended); Gerstein v. Micron Technology, 1993 WL 735031, [Current] Fed. Sec. L. Rep. (CCH) ¶ 98,334 (D. Idaho 1993) (class representatives who traded more than four days after the alleged insider trading were not contemporaneous traders and thus lacked standing under section 20A); Feldman v. Motorola, Inc., 1994 WL 160115, [1993–1994 Transfer Binder] Fed. Sec. L. Rep. (CCH) ¶ 98,133 (N.D.Ill.1994) (allegations that plaintiffs purchased within one to four business days of defendant's improper sales were sufficient); In re Cypress Semiconductor Securities Litigation, 836 F.Supp. 711 (N.D.Cal.1993) (purchase of securities within five days of insider's sale was a contemporaneous trade).

36. *See, e.g.,* Zweig v. Hearst Corp., 594 F.2d 1261 (9th Cir.1979); text accompanying footnotes 28–29 *supra.* As discussed in § 13.5B *supra,* the Supreme Court in Basic, Inc. v. Levinson, 485 U.S. 224, 108 S.Ct. 978, 99 L.Ed.2d 194 (1988), *on remand* 871 F.2d 562 (6th Cir.1989), upheld the fraud of the market presumption of reliance in an affirmative misrepresentation case.

37. Affiliated Ute Citizens of Utah v. United States, 406 U.S. 128, 92 S.Ct. 1456, 31 L.Ed.2d 741 (1972), *rehearing denied* 407 U.S. 916, 92 S.Ct. 2430, 32 L.Ed.2d 692 (1972). *Accord, e.g.,* List v. Fashion Park, Inc., 340 F.2d 457 (2d Cir.1965), *cert. denied* 382 U.S. 811, 86 S.Ct. 23, 15 L.Ed.2d 60 (1965), *rehearing denied* 382 U.S. 933, 86 S.Ct. 305, 15 L.Ed.2d 344 (1965).

The duty to make such a disclosure, of course, depends upon showing of materiality. *See, e.g.,* McCormick v. Fund American Cos., 26 F.3d 869 (9th Cir.1994) (parent corporation purchasing its stock from former chief executive officer of subsidiary did not have duty to disclose preliminary merger negotiations involving parent).

38. The element of plaintiff's reliance is considered in § 13.5B *supra.*

39. 445 U.S. 222, 100 S.Ct. 1108, 63 L.Ed.2d 348 (1980).

The defendant, Chiarella, was an employee of a printing firm hired to produce documents for various tender offers.[40] The target company's identity was concealed in the galleys sent to the printer in an effort to maintain confidentiality. Chiarella, however, identified the target company by reading the other information in the tender offer material. Armed with this knowledge, he purchased the target company's stock and sold it at a profit after the tender offer was publicly announced.[41] Chiarella's indictment was framed in terms of Rule 10b–5's requirement that insiders possessing confidential material information must either disclose the information or abstain from trading.[42] The Court reversed the defendant's conviction on the grounds that he had no legal duty to speak and thus was not subject to the disclose or abstain obligation.

The Court, in *Chiarella,* first distinguished *Cady, Roberts* on the grounds that in that case the SEC had imposed sanctions against a broker-dealer who had *wrongfully* obtained information from corporate insiders. The Court reasoned that the SEC's opinion in *Cady, Roberts* "recognized a relationship of trust and confidence between the shareholder of a corporation and those insiders who have obtained confidential information by reason of their position with that *corporation.*"[43] The Court also explained that the *Texas Gulf Sulphur* "disclose or abstain" rule was limited to persons—both insiders and others—who are subject to a duty to disclose apart from the mere possession of confidential inside information.[44] As noted above, another point of distinction between the facts in *Chiarella* and prior decisions recognizing 10b–5 violations is that *Chiarella* involved market information rather than information "belonging" to the target company.[45]

The Court held that the absence of a wrongful conversion or misappropriation of the information meant that no violation of Rule 10b–5 had occurred because there was no legal duty to disclose such information prior to trading.[46] The Court pointed out, however, that the

---

40. This paragraph is adapted from Thomas L. Hazen, The Supreme Court and the Securities Laws; Has the Pendulum Slowed?, 30 Emory L.J. 3, 20–23 (1981).

41. The defendant engaged in five similar transactions realizing an aggregated profit of approximately $30,000.

42. *See* the authorities cited in footnote 11 *supra.*

43. 445 U.S. at 228, 100 S.Ct. at 1114, 1115 (footnote omitted; emphasis supplied). *Cf.* State Teachers Retirement Board v. Fluor Corp., 576 F.Supp. 1116 (S.D.N.Y.1983) (employer of tipper may be held vicariously liable for the illegal passing on of inside information).

44. 445 U.S. at 231, 100 S.Ct. at 1116. *See, e.g.,* Frigitemp Corp. v. Financial Dynamics Fund, Inc., 524 F.2d 275, 282 (2d Cir.1975); American General Insurance Co. v. Equitable General Corp., 493 F.Supp. 721, 742–48 (E.D.Va.1980).

45. 445 U.S. at 231, 100 S.Ct. at 1116 (The "market information upon which he relied did not concern the earning power or operations of the target company, but only the plans of the acquiring company"). *See* John G. Koeltl & Gary W. Kubek, Chiarella and Market Information, 13 Rev.Sec.Reg. 903 (1980).

46. 445 U.S. at 231–35, 100 S.Ct. at 1116–1118. *See also, e.g.,* Feldman v. Simkins Industries, Inc., 492 F.Supp. 839, 844 (N.D.Cal.1980), *judgment affirmed* 679 F.2d 1299 (9th Cir.1982) (defendant owning the largest single block of stock but not a controlling interest, had no duty to disclose under *Chiarella*). *Cf.* Arst v. Stifel Nicolaus & Co., 871 F.Supp. 1370 (D.Kan.1994) (broker did not owe a fiduciary relationship to customer so as to impose on the broker a duty to disclose information about securities customer wanted to sell).

only issue before it was whether a duty to disclose under 10b–5 was created vis-à-vis the target company by the mere possession of nonpublic information that would affect the price of its stock. The Supreme Court in *Chiarella* did not decide whether the printer's relationship to the acquiring corporation created a duty to abstain from trading.[47] Justice Stevens, in his concurrence, emphasized that this latter theory was not decided,[48] while Justice Brennan's concurrence[49] and the dissent[50] would have upheld the conviction had the conversion theory been presented to the jury. It thus appears that at least four of the Justices would have affirmed the conviction had these alternative theories been presented to the jury.[51] The Court's subsequent ruling in Dirks v. SEC[52] may provide a basis for a narrow view of the proper scope of Rule 10b–5 in insider trading cases. However, one post-*Chiarella* decision upheld an SEC complaint seeking injunctive relief and disgorgement of profits in an action against a proofreader who allegedly "misappropriated" tender offer information from a financial printer.[53] The court there noted that *Chiarella* and *Dirks* were distinguishable.[54] As discussed more fully below, several other decisions have adopted the misappropriation theory of 10b–5 liability for trading on confidential nonpublic information.[55]

Chiarella may thus stand only for the proposition that the government failed to properly identify the basis of the duty to disclose, and may not mean that non-insiders never have a duty to disclose. At least one commentator suggested that the ruling is properly limited to market information but recent Supreme Court developments indicate other-

---

47. 445 U.S. at 235–36, 100 S.Ct. at 1118, 1119. For a strong indication that it might not, *see* Moss v. Morgan Stanley Inc., 719 F.2d 5 (2d Cir.1983), *cert. denied* 465 U.S. 1025, 104 S.Ct. 1280, 79 L.Ed.2d 684 (1984), discussed in the text accompanying footnote 112 *infra.*

48. 445 U.S. at 238, 100 S.Ct. at 1119, 1120 (Stevens, J., concurring).

49. *Id.* at 239, 100 S.Ct. at 1120 (Brennan, J., concurring).

50. *Id.* at 240, 100 S.Ct. at 1120, 1121 (Burger, J., dissenting); *see also id.* at 245, 100 S.Ct. at 1123 (Blackmun and Marshall, dissenting).

51. Justice Blackmun in his dissent, with Marshall joining, would have affirmed on the issues presented to the jury without reaching the other theories supported by Justices Brennan and Burger.

52. 463 U.S. 646, 103 S.Ct. 3255, 77 L.Ed.2d 911 (1983). *See* text accompanying notes 62–67, *infra.*

53. SEC v. Materia, 745 F.2d 197 (2d Cir.1984), *cert. denied* 471 U.S. 1053, 105 S.Ct. 2112, 85 L.Ed.2d 477 (1985). For other recent cases approving of the misappropriation theory *see* footnotes 55–59 *infra.*

54. [1983–1984 Transfer Binder] Fed.Sec.L.Rep. (CCH) ¶ 99,527 at p. 97,028.

See the discussion in the text accompanying footnotes 62–67 *infra.*

55. *E.g.,* United States v. Carpenter, 791 F.2d 1024 (2d Cir.1986), *affirmed by an equally divided court* 484 U.S. 19, 108 S.Ct. 316, 98 L.Ed.2d 275 (1987); SEC v. Clark, 699 F.Supp. 839 (W.D.Wash.1988); SEC v. Musella, 678 F.Supp. 1060 (S.D.N.Y.1988), s.c., 578 F.Supp. 425 (S.D.N.Y.1984). *See* text accompanying footnotes 67–83 *infra. See also, e.g.,* SEC v. Ingram, 694 F.Supp. 1437 (C.D.Cal.1988). The Supreme Court tacitly approved the misappropriation theory in Bateman Eichler, Hill Richards, Inc. v. Berner, 472 U.S. 299, 311–12 n. 21, 105 S.Ct. 2622, 86 L.Ed.2d 215 (1985). *See generally* Barbara Aldave, The Misappropriation Theory: Carpenter and its Aftermath, 49 Ohio St.L.J. 373 (1988).

wise.[56]

Following an emerging pattern, the Second Circuit has recently read the *Chiarella* decision in its narrowest possible light. In United States v. Newman[57] the court was faced with the unanswered question that Justice Stevens raised in his *Chiarella* concurrence.[58] In *Newman,* the defendant was the head of a brokerage house's over-the-counter trading department. He received a tip concerning impending takeover attempts from two investment bankers whose clients were active prospective tender offerors. As in *Chiarella,* the broker acted on this tip by purchasing the target company's stock prior to the takeover announcement.[59] The Second Circuit ruled that in tipping the information the investment bankers had breached a fiduciary duty of confidentiality to their clients—the impending tender offerors. The defendant conspired with the investment bankers to misappropriate this confidential information and used it solely for advantageous purchases. The court thus held that the defendant's involvement in the transactions operated as a fraud within the meaning of Rule 10b–5(3).[60]

To the extent that the *Chiarella* Court can properly be read as not

56. Morrison, *supra* footnote 11, at 221. According to Mr. Morrison: "While the *Chiarella* decision permits trading on the basis of non-public market information, there are limitations. Trading is allowed only where (1) no representations are made; (2) there is no relationship of trust and confidence between the participants; and (3) in the author's opinion, the information is market—not corporate information". *Id.* at 225. *See also, e.g.* Koeltl & Kubek *supra* footnote 45. The recent *Dirks* ruling makes this limitation questionable. Dirks v. SEC, 463 U.S. 646, 103 S.Ct. 3255, 77 L.Ed.2d 911 (1983) which is discussed in the text accompanying footnotes 62–67 *infra.*

57. 664 F.2d 12 (2d Cir.1981), *cert. denied* 464 U.S. 863, 104 S.Ct. 193, 78 L.Ed.2d 170 (1983). *Compare* Moss v. Morgan Stanley Inc., 719 F.2d 5 (2d Cir.1983), *cert. denied* 465 U.S. 1025, 104 S.Ct. 1280, 79 L.Ed.2d 684 (1984), arising out of the same set of facts wherein the Second Circuit gave a narrower view of Rule 10b–5 in the context of a private damage action. The court in *Moss* held that although there was a duty to disclose or abstain, the duty was owed to the tipper's employer who was neither a purchaser nor seller, and thus no duty was owed to open-market sellers of the securities in question.

58. *Id.* at 16.

59. Unlike Chiarella however, Newman did not handle the transactions himself. Instead he contacted two foreign cohorts who used secret foreign bank accounts and spread their purchases among a number of brokers, thereby effecting the transactions. The two trading tippees were beyond the court's jurisdiction and thus Newman, a resident, was the only named defendant.

60. The court reasoned that "by sullying the reputations of [the investment bankers] as safe repositories of client confidences, appellee and his cohorts defrauded those [investment bankers] as surely as if they took their money;" and further that they "also wronged [the investment bankers'] clients, whose takeover plans were keyed to target company stock prices fixed by market forces, not artificially inflated through purchases by purloiners of confidential information." 664 F.2d at 17. It seems beyond question that had this same theory been presented in the *Chiarella* case, the Second Circuit would have found a violation of Rule 10b–5 because the printer clearly misused confidential information belonging to his employer's customer, the tender offeror. As pointed out above, it is quite likely that at least five of the justices who decided *Chiarella* would agree with the Second Circuit's analysis in *Newman.*

For another application of the fiduciary duty rationale *see* SEC v. Musella, 578 F.Supp. 425 (S.D.N.Y.1984).

overruling *Texas Gulf Sulphur, Cady, Roberts,* or the *Merrill Lynch*[61] cases, obtaining confidential inside information by virtue of an inside position or *directly through* an insider is sufficient proof of misappropriation or conversion to impose a duty not to trade in the securities prior to disclosure of the information.

A subsequent Supreme Court case reemphasized the principles of the *Chiarella* decision. In Dirks v. SEC,[62] the Court found that "a tippee assumes a fiduciary duty to the shareholders of a corporation * * * only when the insider has breached his fiduciary duty to the shareholders * * * and the tippee knows or should know that there has been a breach." [63] The Court explained further that insiders have not breached their fiduciary duty unless the purpose of their passing on the information was to obtain, directly or indirectly, some personal or economic benefit. The actions of the defendant in *Dirks* were major factors in exposing the massive Equity Funding fraud.[64] In *Dirks,* the insiders— former employees of the company in question—were motivated by a desire to expose the company's fraud; therefore Dirks was not obligated to abstain from passing on the inside information disclosed to him. The six to three decision in *Dirks* contained a vigorous dissent that would have applied the disclose or abstain rule.

The conflict has continued between a broad and narrow view of tipper and tippee liability. For example, some courts have fashioned the concept of "temporary insider" to deal with tippee accountability.[65] On the other hand, where defendant traded after having overheard a family conversation that conveyed inside information, there was no 10b–5

---

61. Shapiro v. Merrill Lynch, Pierce, Fenner & Smith, Inc., 495 F.2d 228 (2d Cir.1974); In re Merrill Lynch, Pierce, Fenner & Smith, Inc., 43 S.E.C. 933 (SEC 1968).

62. 463 U.S. 646, 103 S.Ct. 3255, 77 L.Ed.2d 911 (1983), *reversing* 681 F.2d 824 (D.C.Cir.1982). *See* Robert A. Prentice, The Impact of Dirks on Outsider Trading, 13 Sec.Reg.L.J. 38 (1985); Note, Inside Information and Outside Traders: Corporate Recovery of the Outsider's Unfair Gain, 73 Calif.L.Rev. 483 (1985); Note, Access, Efficiency, and Fairness in *Dirks v. SEC,* 60 Ind.L.J. 535 (1985).

63. 463 U.S. at 660, 103 S.Ct. at 3264. The Court went on to explain: "Thus, the test is whether the insider personally will benefit, directly or indirectly, from his disclosure. Absent some personal gain, there has been no breach of duty to stockholders. And absent a breach by the insider, there is no derivative breach [by the tippee]." *Id.*

While *Dirks* may be viewed as limiting liability based on a breach of fiduciary duty by direct or derivative insiders of the issuer, the SEC has not taken such a limiting view. *See also* SEC v. Switzer, 590 F.Supp. 756 (W.D.Okl.1984).

See also, e.g., SEC v. Ferrero, 1992 WL 208015, [1992 Transfer Binder] Fed.Sec.L.Rep. (CCH) ¶ 96,807 (S.D.Ind.1992), s.c., 1993 WL 625964, [1993–1994 Transfer Binder] Fed. Sec. L. Rep. (CCH) ¶ 98,120 (N.D.Ind.1993) (upholding sufficiency of allegation that tippee knew or should have known that corporate insider breached a fiduciary duty by passing on nonpublic information).

64. The defendant, an investment analyst, was investigating Equity Funding Corp., and after investigation including talks with various employees he realized that the company's assets had been fraudulently inflated.

65. SEC v. Tome, 833 F.2d 1086 (2d Cir.1987), *affirming* 638 F.Supp. 596 (S.D.N.Y. 1986); SEC v. Lund, 570 F.Supp. 1397 (C.D.Cal.1983). *Compare* Abatemarco v. Copytele, Inc., 608 F.Supp. 1024 (E.D.N.Y.1985) (employee with no access to nonpublic information was not an insider and thus there was no basis for prohibiting his sale of stock).

liability because the tipper had not breached a duty, and therefore there could be no derivative liability on behalf of the tippee.[66]

In the words of one court, "It is not accurate to say that *Dirks* wrote the book on insider or outsider trading; it wrote one chapter with respect to one type of fraudulent trading." [67] The court in that case applied the misappropriation theory of liability and held that *Dirks* did not preclude application of that approach. Accordingly the court convicted a financial columnist who participated in a scheme whereby he would tip his friends about upcoming columns that would affect the price of certain stocks. The court held that this information had been misappropriated from his employer Dow Jones and thus under the disclose or abstain rule, the columnist and his friends had violated Rule 10b–5.[68] The Second Circuit's application of the misappropriation theory was affirmed by an equally divided Supreme Court and also finds support in the legislative history of the 1988 Insider Trading and Securities Fraud Enforcement Act.[69] One can only speculate whether the Court was divided over the misappropriation theory in general or whether it was divided as to whether 10b–5 applied in the absence of the misappropriator's employer having been a market participant. In an earlier ruling the Court seemed to give tacit approval to the underpinnings of the misappropriation theory.[70] In any event, until rejected by the Court, the misappropriation theory remains good law.[71]

Establishing a breach of duty by the tipper does not, however, require proof that the tipper knew that the tippee was about to engage

66. SEC v. Switzer, 590 F.Supp. 756 (W.D.Okl.1984). *Compare* SEC v. Stephenson, 720 F.Supp. 370 (S.D.N.Y.1989) (tippees of vice president who traded with knowledge of confidential nature of the information violated Rule 10b–5), s.c. 732 F.Supp. 438 (S.D.N.Y. 1990); O'Connor & Associates v. Dean Witter Reynolds, Inc., 600 F.Supp. 702 (S.D.N.Y. 1985) (upholding complaint charging material tip by corporate insiders). *Cf.* SEC v. Hurton, 739 F.Supp. 704 (D.Mass.1990) (summary judgment denied as to whether tippee was liable for insider trading violations).

See Stephen R. Salbu, Tipper Credibility, Noninformational Tippee Trading, and Abstention From Trading: An Analysis of Gaps in the Insider Trading Laws, 68 Wash.L.Rev. 307 (1993).

67. United States v. Winans, 612 F.Supp. 827, 842 (S.D.N.Y.1985), *affirmed* 791 F.2d 1024 (2d Cir.1986), *affirmed* 484 U.S. 19, 108 S.Ct. 316, 98 L.Ed.2d 275 (1987).

68. United States v. Carpenter, 791 F.2d 1024 (2d Cir.1986), *affirming* 612 F.Supp. 827, 842 (S.D.N.Y.1985), *affirmed* 484 U.S. 19, 108 S.Ct. 316, 98 L.Ed.2d 275 (1987). This highly celebrated case arose out of the Wall Street Journal's influential Heard on the Street ("HOTS") column.

The misappropriation theory has supported indictments in another celebrated case. United States v. Reed, 601 F.Supp. 685 (S.D.N.Y.1985), *reversed* 773 F.2d 477 (2d Cir.1985). *See also, e.g.,* SEC v. Gaspar, 1985 WL 521, [1984–85 Transfer Binder] Fed.Sec.L.Rep. (CCH) ¶ 92,004 (S.D.N.Y.1985).

69. Carpenter v. United States, 484 U.S. 19, 108 S.Ct. 316, 98 L.Ed.2d 275 (1987). *See* H.R.Rep. No. 100–910, 100th Cong. 2d Sess. 10–11 (1988).

70. Bateman Eichler, Hill Richards, Inc. v. Berner, 472 U.S. 299, 311–12 n. 21, 105 S.Ct. 2622, 2629 n. 21, 86 L.Ed.2d 215 (1985).

71. For other cases applying the misappropriation theory *see, e.g.,* ICN Pharmaceuticals, Inc. v. Khan, 2 F.3d 484 (2d Cir.1993); SEC v. Cherif, 933 F.2d 403 (7th Cir.1991), *cert. denied* 502 U.S. 1071, 112 S.Ct. 966, 117 L.Ed.2d 131 (1992); SEC v. Clark, 915 F.2d 439 (9th Cir.1990).

in prohibited trading.[72] The Second Circuit has indicated that if the information is passed on in breach of a duty, it does not matter if there is no belief that the tippee will trade, if the tippee had assured the tipper that no insider trading would take place, or if the trading was by a remote rather than direct tippee. When someone divulges confidential information in breach of a duty, it is fair to conclude that the recipient of the information may not properly trade to his or her advantage:

> The tipper's knowledge that he or she was breaching a duty to the owner of confidential information suffices to establish the tipper's expectation that the breach will lead to some kind of misuse of the information. This is so because it may be presumed that the tippee's interest in the information is, in contemporary jargon, not for nothing. To allow a tippee to escape liability merely because the government cannot prove to a jury's satisfaction that the tipper knew exactly what misuse would result from the tipper's wrongdoing would not fulfill the purpose of the misappropriation theory, which is to protect property rights in information. Indeed, such a requirement would serve no purpose other than to create a loophole for such misuse.[73]

Although the Supreme Court was equally divided on the 10b–5 claim in *Carpenter,* the Court was unanimous in finding that the misappropriation constituted a violation of federal Mail Fraud statutes.[74] In affirming the mail fraud conviction, the Court reasoned that the information concerning the Heard on the Street column was clearly property belonging to Dow Jones and that the reporter had a duty to safeguard that information. The breach of that duty accordingly amounted to a deprivation of Dow Jones' property right in contravention of the Mail Fraud statute. In reaching its decision under the Mail Fraud statute the Supreme Court embraced the rationale underlying the New York decision in Diamond v. Oreamuno[75] allowing a corporation to recover the profits of insiders who traded on confidential information.

72. United States v. Libera, 989 F.2d 596 (2d Cir.1993), *cert. denied* ___ U.S. ___, 114 S.Ct. 467, 126 L.Ed.2d 419 (1993) (upholding sufficiency of indictment alleging that printer who sold advance copies of magazine breached a fiduciary duty even though he did not know that the tippees planned on engaging in insider trading). *Cf.* SEC v. Trikilis, 1992 WL 301398, [1992–1993 Transfer Binder] Fed.Sec.L.Rep. (CCH) ¶ 97,015 (C.D.Cal.1992), *vacated on other grounds* 1993 WL 43571, Fed.Sec.L.Rep. ¶ 97,375 (C.D.Cal.1993) (allegation that employee acted as tipper was sufficient to establish a duty).

73. 989 F.2d at 600 (citation omitted). *See also, e.g.,* SEC v. Maio, 51 F.3d 623, 632 (7th Cir.1995) ("a tippee has a derivative duty not to trade on material non-public information when the disclosure of that information is *improper* and the tippee knows or should know that this is the case.... 'Absent a breach by the insider there is no derivative breach.' ").

74. Carpenter v. United States, 484 U.S. 19, 108 S.Ct. 316, 98 L.Ed.2d 275 (1987); 18 U.S.C.A. §§ 1341, 1343. *See* § 19.3.1 *infra* (Practitioner's Edition only). *See also* United States v. Cherif, 943 F.2d 692 (7th Cir.1991), *affirming* 1989 WL 112769, 21 Sec.Reg. & L.Rep. (BNA) 1631 (N.D.Ill.1989) (upholding mail fraud indictment and conviction against defendant who allegedly broke into office and obtained confidential information which he later used for trading in securities).

75. 24 N.Y.2d 494, 301 N.Y.S.2d 78, 248 N.E.2d 910 (1969); *see* footnote 109 *supra* and accompanying text.

One irony of the misappropriation theory is that while the duty is premised on the ownership of the information, ordinarily the owner of the information will not have standing to raise a Rule 10b–5 claim. In order to bring a 10b–5 claim the plaintiff must have been a purchaser or seller of the securities in question.[76] As was the case on the *Carpenter* facts, the person from whom the confidential information was appropriated may not have been a purchaser or seller.[77] Presumably, however, a claim could be based on state law and breach of agency or other fiduciary duty. On the other hand, contemporaneous traders (to whom no duty was owed) may sue under the Act's express damage provision.[78]

It might be surmised that the Court's division on the Rule 10b–5 claim involved the question of whether the misappropriation was in connection with the purchase or sale of a security.[79] However, in affirming the mail fraud conviction the Court took a very broad view of that Act's "in connection with" requirement.[80] As noted above, we must await further clarification before dismissing the application of the misappropriation theory under Rule 10b–5.

The precise scope of Rule 10b–5 liability for trading on nonpublic information remains unclear. Although it is clear that scienter is required for a Rule 10b–5 violation,[81] the courts have been struggling with the extent of the knowledge required. Thus, for example, it is sufficient that a tipper knowingly breached a fiduciary duty, and it is not necessary that he or she was aware of the trader's intent to trade.[82] Similarly, it is sufficient that a tippee knows the information has been improperly communicated; it need not be shown that the tippee know the precise source of the information.[83]

---

76. Blue Chip Stamps v. Manor Drug Stores, 421 U.S. 723, 95 S.Ct. 1917, 44 L.Ed.2d 539 (1975), *rehearing denied* 423 U.S. 884, 96 S.Ct. 157, 46 L.Ed.2d 114 (1975). The standing limitations are discussed in § 13.3 *supra*.

77. *See, e.g.,* In re Ivan F. Boesky Securities Litigation, 36 F.3d 255 (2d Cir.1994), *affirming* 825 F.Supp. 623 (S.D.N.Y.1993) (Firm from which information was misappropriated had no standing to sue employee).

78. Section 20A, 15 U.S.C.A. § 78t–1(a), which is discussed in the text accompanying footnotes 137–147 *infra*.

79. The in "connection" with requirement is discussed in § 13.2.2 *supra*.

80. In the course of its opinion in *Carpenter* the Court gave a very broad reading to the Mail Fraud Act's jurisdictional requirement. The act covers any person who causes the mail to be used to further the wrongful conduct. 18 U.S.C.A. § 1341. The Court ruled that since the tipping scheme developed by the reporter and his associates depended on the dissemination of the Wall Street Journal, the dissemination of the Journal through the mails was a sufficient connection. This is a surprising rationale since the defendants did not utilize the mail themselves but rather the newspaper when published utilized the mails.

This broad reading of the Mail Fraud Act's jurisdictional requirement may be helpful to those supporting a broad reading of Rule 10b–5's "in connection with" requirement.

81. *See* § 13.4 *supra*.

82. United States v. Libera, 989 F.2d 596 (2d Cir.1993), *cert. denied* ___ U.S. ___, 114 S.Ct. 467, 126 L.Ed.2d 419 (1993).

83. United States v. Chestman, 947 F.2d 551 (2d Cir.1991), *cert. denied* 503 U.S. 1004, 112 S.Ct. 1759, 118 L.Ed.2d 422 (1992) (decided under Rule 14e–3).

Another question that has arisen is the extent to which it must be shown that the inside information in fact caused the transactions in question. This has arisen, for example, in the context of the argument that it must be shown that the trader in fact used the information in question; namely that he or she would not have traded but for the confidential information. This debate arose in the course of Congressional deliberation over whether to define insider trading.[84] More recently the issue was raised by a defendant being prosecuted for improper trading on confidential information. The Second Circuit quite properly concluded that actual use need not be shown; it is sufficient to show that the trader, under a duty of confidentiality, entered into the transactions while *knowingly possessing* material nonpublic information.[85]

The commentators are divided on the question of whether a more precise definition of improper insider trading is needed.[86] In 1987, Congress began to consider legislation that not only would have defined illegal insider trading to encompass the misappropriation theory, but also, as finally enacted, contained a remedy for investors in the open market taking the other side of the illegal trades. In 1988, Congress enacted legislation providing for a private remedy but failed to include a definition of what constitutes improper use of material, nonpublic information.[87] Outside of this newly created express right of action, it does not seem likely that cases based solely on a misappropriation theory and Rule 10b–5 liability could support a private remedy in the hands of investors. Nevertheless, the SEC has been able to exact settlement agreements under which the disgorged proceeds will be given to investors.[88] As noted above, the misappropriation theory would support a state law remedy in the hands of the proprietor of the misappropriated information.[89] A Rule 10b–5 claim will not lie in such a case, however, unless the proprietor of the information was also a purchaser or seller.[90] Under appropriate facts, a private remedy for insider trading may thus exist under state law as well as under Rule 10b–5[91] and section 20A of

---

84. *See* footnotes 19–20 *supra*.

85. United States v. Teicher, 987 F.2d 112 (2d Cir.1993), *cert. denied* ___ U.S. ___, 114 S.Ct. 467, 126 L.Ed.2d 419 (1993).

86. *See, e.g.,* Symposium, Defining "Insider Trading", 39 Ala.L.Rev. 337 (1988). *See also, e.g.,* Nicholas Wolfson, Trade Secrets and Secret Trading, 25 San Diego L.Rev. 95 (1988).

87. 15 U.S.C.A. §§ 78t–1, 78u–1 which are discussed in the text accompanying footnotes 102–111 *infra*. The legislative history gives support to continued recognition of the misappropriation theory. *See* footnotes 149–150 *infra* and accompanying text.

88. Such was the case with the famed Ivan Boesky settlement. *See also* Note, Caveat Employer, Can Alleged Victims of Insider Trading Scandals Recover Damages from an Employer for Illegal Dealings of an Employee?, 38 Syracuse L.Rev. 1045 (1987).

89. *See* text accompanying footnotes 109–111 *infra*.

90. *See* § 13.3 *supra*. *Cf.* In re Ivan Boesky Securities Litigation, 36 F.3d 255 (2d Cir.1994). *But see* FMC Corp. v. Boesky, 852 F.2d 981 (7th Cir.1988), *reversing* 673 F.Supp. 242 (N.D.Ill.1987) (corporation charging wrongful misappropriation of inside information had constitutional standing to claim damages to intangible rights which represents a cognizable injury; the court did not comment on Rule 10b–5 standing).

91. *See* the discussion in the text accompanying footnotes 109–111 *infra*.

the 1934 Act.[92] In addition, insider trading claims may be subject to arbitration if the parties have entered into a predispute arbitration agreement.[93]

In another development, the Supreme Court ruled that the equal fault defense is not available in an action by a defrauded tippee against the tipper who was the plaintiff's broker.[94] The in pari delicto defense thus will not be available unless the parties are of truly equal fault.[95]

In two of its recent insider trading decisions, the Supreme Court has made it clear that the mere possession of inside information will not trigger insider trading liability. There must be some actual wrongdoing by an insider or a tippee acting in furtherance of the improper use of confidential information.[96] The Court has yet to deal with the question of who is an insider. Earlier cases, discussed above, provide a basis for ruling that insider status is not limited to officers, directors, and employees, but will extend to others having a contractual obligation of confidentiality. This would include, for example, attorneys, accountants, and investment bankers. We must await further guidance from the Supreme Court as to whether there will be additional cut-backs or expansion in insider trading liability under Rule 10b–5.

Insider Trading in Advance of Tender Offers: Rule 14e–3

Another weapon against insider trading has developed within the context of a tender offer. The Fourth Circuit has upheld a preliminary injunction against a tender offer where the offer was based upon information that had been allegedly misappropriated from the target company, in violation of Rule 14e–3.[97] That rule, which has been challenged as going beyond the scope of the statute, was upheld by the Second, Seventh, and Ninth Circuits.[98]

---

92. 15 U.S.C.A. § 78t–1. Section 20A, which was decided as part of the Insider Trading and Securities Fraud Enforcement Act of 1988 is discussed in the text accompanying notes 128–150 *infra*.

93. *See* Energy Factors Inc. v. Nuevo Energy Co., 1992 WL 110541, [1993 Transfer Binder] Fed.Sec.L.Rep. (CCH) ¶ 97,641 (S.D.N.Y.1992) (insider trading claims were arbitrable despite contention that arbitration was unprecedented and contrary to public interest). Arbitration agreements are discussed in § 14.4 *infra*.

94. Bateman Eichler, Hill Richards, Inc. v. Berner, 472 U.S. 299, 105 S.Ct. 2622, 86 L.Ed.2d 215 (1985). *Cf.* Skinner v. E.F. Hutton & Co., 314 N.C. 267, 333 S.E.2d 236 (1985) (reaching similar result under state law).

95. *See* Rothberg v. Rosenbloom, 808 F.2d 252 (3d Cir.1986), *cert. denied* 481 U.S. 1017, 107 S.Ct. 1895, 95 L.Ed.2d 501 (1987). In pari delicto is discussed in § 13.12 *infra*.

96. Aiding and abetting is discussed in § 13.16 *infra*.

97. Burlington Industries, Inc. v. Edelman, 1987 WL 91498, [1987 Transfer Binder] Fed.Sec.L.Rep. (CCH) ¶ 93,339 (4th Cir.1987), *affirming on the basis of the opinion below* 666 F.Supp. 799 (M.D.N.C.1987). *See also* United States v. Marcus Schloss & Co., 710 F.Supp. 944 (S.D.N.Y.1989) (upholding validity of Rule 14e–3); United States v. Chestman, 704 F.Supp. 451 (S.D.N.Y.1989) (upholding validity of Rule 14e–3), *affirmed*, 947 F.2d 551 (2d Cir.1991). *But cf.* Johnston v. Wilbourn, 682 F.Supp. 879 (S.D.Miss.1988) (Rule 14e–3 prohibitions held not to apply to tender offeror).

98. SEC v. Maio, 51 F.3d 623 (7th Cir.1995); SEC v. Peters, 978 F.2d 1162 (10th Cir.1992); United States v. Chestman, 947 F.2d 551 (2d Cir.1991), *cert. denied* 503 U.S. 1004, 112 S.Ct. 1759, 118 L.Ed.2d 422 (1992). *See also, e.g.,* SEC v. Ferrero, 1993 WL 625964, [1993–1994 Transfer Binder] Fed. Sec. L. Rep. (CCH) ¶ 98,120 (S.D.Ind.1993).

Although other courts have upheld the validity of Rule 14e–3,[99] the Second Circuit has somewhat limited its utility. In United States v. Chestman,[100] the court held Rule 14e–3 invalid to the extent that it purported to cover conduct not involving scienter. One member of the three judge panel would have upheld the rule as applied.[101] On the other hand, one of the other judges would have invalidated the rule as beyond the statutory authority of section 14(e).[102] The third judge took the position that Rule 14e–3 is a valid exercise of the Commission's rulemaking authority but, as is the case with Rule 10b–5, requires scienter and the other traditional elements of fraud.[103] Absent a showing that the defendant tippee knew that the information was confidential, there was no duty to disclose and hence no Rule 14e–3 violation. *Chestman,* thus, contrary to the wishes of Judge Mahoney, does not invalidate Rule 14e–3 since the rule incorporates the elements of fraud, including scienter.[104] Although the *Chestman* panel was split on the Rule 14e–3 issue, it was unanimous in reversing the Rule 10b–5 conviction. The Second Circuit agreed to consider the issues *en banc.* On rehearing, the full court affirmed dismissal of the Rule 10b–5 and mail fraud counts.[105] However, the court reinstated the conviction under Rule 14e–3, ruling that actual knowledge of the source of the information was not a precondition to a violation.[106] The *Chestman* ruling reinstates Rule 14e–3 as a powerful

99. *E.g.,* SEC v. Peters, 978 F.2d 1162 (10th Cir.1992); United States v. Marcus Schloss & Co., 710 F.Supp. 944 (S.D.N.Y.1989).

100. United States v. Chestman, 903 F.2d 75 (2d Cir.1990), *affirmed en banc* 947 F.2d 551 (2d Cir.1991), *cert. denied* ___ U.S. ___, 112 S.Ct. 1759, 118 L.Ed.2d 422 (1992).

101. Judge Minor believed that since the conviction was based on a finding of *mens rea* rather than trading based on "innocent mistakes, negligence or inadvertence or other innocent conduct," the Rule 14e–3 conviction should have been upheld.

102. Judge Mahoney believed that the Supreme Court's decision in Schreiber v. Burlington Northern, Inc., 472 U.S. 1, 105 S.Ct. 2458, 86 L.Ed.2d 1 (1985) imposes a fraudulent deception requirement which is lacking in the language of Rule 14e–3.

103. Judge Carman in essence was of the view that Rule 14e–3 is subject to the same constraints as Rule 10b–5 and thus applied the limitations of the *Chiarella* case:

> The failure to instruct on all the elements of fraudulent nondisclosure, including that the defendant possessed a mental state embracing an intent to deceive, manipulate, or defraud, that is, that the defendant knew he had a duty to disclose and intentionally failed to do so, is in my opinion fatal to his conviction.

903 F.2d at 88.

104. Judge Carman read those requirements into Rule 14e–3 in order to preserve the rule's validity in accordance with the presumption of regularity and validity normally given to administrative agency action. 903 F.2d at 87, relying on FCC v. Schreiber, 381 U.S. 279, 296, 85 S.Ct. 1459, 1470, 14 L.Ed.2d 383 (1965).

105. *Compare* SEC v. Ferrero, 1992 WL 208015, [1992 Transfer Binder] Fed.Sec.L.Rep. (CCH) ¶ 96,907 (S.D.Ind.1992) (upholding sufficiency of allegation that tippee knew or should have known that corporate insider breached a fiduciary duty by passing on nonpublic information about planned tender offer; there was a triable issue of fact as to whether the tender offer plans were sufficiently advanced when the alleged tip occurred); SEC v. Willis, 825 F.Supp. 617 (S.D.N.Y.1993), s.c., 787 F.Supp. 58 (S.D.N.Y.1992) (misappropriation by broker from psychiatrist who had misappropriated information from patient).

106. United States v. Chestman, 947 F.2d 551 (2d Cir.1991), *cert. denied* 503 U.S. 1004, 112 S.Ct. 1759, 118 L.Ed.2d 422 (1992). *See also, e.g.,* SEC v. Maio, 51 F.3d 623 (7th Cir.1995) (upholding Rule 14e–3 even in the absence of fiduciary duty between the parties to the transaction); SEC v. Peters, 978 F.2d 1162 (9th Cir.1972) (same). *See generally*

weapon in combating trading on nonpublic information in advance of a tender offer.

Insider Trading: Private Remedies Under Rule 10b–5

This is not to say, however, that there will be a private remedy simply because the duty to disclose or abstain from trading exists. Significant in this regard is the Sixth Circuit's pre-*Chiarella* rejection, on the grounds of causation, of the Second Circuit's broad view of insider trading. In Fridrich v. Bradford,[107] an insider who traded on confidential material information concerning the issuer was held not liable to people who sold securities at the time of the insider's purchases because of the absence of any causal connection between the material omissions and the plaintiff's decisions to sell. More recently, a district court rejected *Fridrich* and reaffirmed the Second Circuit's position that a "plaintiff [in an insider trading case] may recover on a showing that he traded during a period of tippee trading" and "need not prove that he traded directly with the defendant or that the volume of the defendant's trading somehow induced [him] to trade." [108]

The same split of authority is found in cases arising under common law. The New York Court of Appeals has held that a corporate insider who possesses confidential information holds such information in trust for the corporation and, as a matter of agency law, any profit gained by an insider using such information must be held in constructive trust for the principal issuer.[109] Although one state common law decision has

---

Mahlon M. Frankhauser, Chestman II, 25 Rev.Sec. & Commod.Reg. 63 (March 11, 1992); Thomas L. Hazen, *United States v. Chestman*—Trading Securities on the Basis of Nonpublic Information in Advance of a Tender Offer, 57 Brooklyn L.Rev. 595 (1991); Thomas W. Briggs, Insider Trading and the Prospective Investor After the *Chestman* Decision, 20 Sec.Reg.L.J. 296 (1992). *Cf.* United States v. Libera, 989 F.2d 596 (2d Cir.1993), *cert. denied* ___ U.S. ___, 114 S.Ct. 467, 126 L.Ed.2d 419 (1993) (indicating in a Rule 10b–5 case that the tipper can be in breach of duty even if he does not know that the tippee plans to engage in improper trading).

107. 542 F.2d 307 (6th Cir.1976), *cert. denied* 429 U.S. 1053, 97 S.Ct. 767, 50 L.Ed.2d 769 (1977). *Cf.* Dorfman v. First Boston Corp., 336 F.Supp. 1089 (E.D.Pa.1972) (plaintiffs failed to establish reliance).

108. O'Connor & Associates v. Dean Witter Reynolds, Inc., 559 F.Supp. 800 (S.D.N.Y. 1983). *Accord* Goldman v. Belden, 754 F.2d 1059 (2d Cir.1985). *Cf.* In re Smith Barney, Harris Upham & Co., Exch.Act Rel. No. 34–21242, [1984 Transfer Binder] Fed.Sec.L.Rep. (CCH) ¶ 83,656 (Aug. 15, 1984) (brokerage firm making recommendation must give clients chance to digest information before trading for its own account). *See also, e.g.,* SEC v. MacDonald, 699 F.2d 47 (1st Cir.1983), *on remand* 568 F.Supp. 111 (D.R.I.1983), *judgment affirmed* 725 F.2d 9 (1st Cir.1984) (when the inside information was released on the eve of a holiday, the court found that the market had not digested the press release until three weeks later). *Cf.* SEC v. Chapnick, 1994 WL 113040, [1993–1994 Transfer Binder] Fed. Sec. L. Rep. (CCH) ¶ 98,076 (S.D.Fla.1994) (the method of computing profit in an SEC disgorgement action is based on the difference between the insider's sale (or purchase) price and the market price a reasonable time after the information has been publicly disclosed).

109. Diamond v. Oreamuno, 24 N.Y.2d 494, 301 N.Y.S.2d 78, 248 N.E.2d 910 (1969). *Accord* In re ORFA Securities Litigation, 654 F.Supp. 1449 (D.N.J.1987). Note, Common Law Corporate Recovery for Trading on Nonpublic Information, 74 Colum.L.Rev. 269 (1974). *See also,* Brophy v. Cities Service Co., 31 Del.Ch. 241, 70 A.2d 5 (1949), Restatement Second of Agency § 388, comment c.

extended this rationale to include non-insider tippees who trade on the basis of inside information,[110] the most recent decisions on point, like *Chiarella,* have rejected the existence of a common law duty based on the mere possession of inside information.[111] The common law development seems to be in line with the more restrictive reading of the *Chiarella* decision and the approach taken by the Sixth Circuit in *Fridrich.*

Following on the heels of *Dirks,* the Second Circuit in Moss v. Morgan Stanley Inc.[112] held that the open-market seller of a target company's stock prior to the tender offer's announcement does not have a 10b–5 claim against a non-insider tippee who purchased shares based on nonpublic material information obtained from the tender offeror's investment advisor. In so holding the court rejected the idea of a non-insider's duty to disclose to an open market seller based on a misappropriation theory or on the fact that the defendant owed a special duty to the plaintiff due to its status as a broker-dealer. *Moss* arose out of the same facts as United States v. Newman where the Second Circuit upheld a criminal conviction.[113]

In comparison to its holding in *Moss,* the Second Circuit has upheld a complaint by open market purchasers against a corporate insider who was selling securities while the corporation was issuing materially misleading optimistic information.[114] The Second Circuit may thus be

---

See Ash, State Regulation of Insider Trading—A Timely Resurgence?, 49 Ohio St.L.J. 393 (1988); Thomas L. Hazen, Corporate Insider Trading: Reawakening the Common Law, 39 Wash. & Lee L.Rev. 845 (1982).

Since the issuing corporation is not ordinarily a purchaser or seller, there is no comparable federal claim for insider trading. *See, e.g.,* In re Ivan Boesky Securities Litigation, 36 F.3d 255 (2d Cir.1994); FMC Corp. v. Boesky, 727 F.Supp. 1182 (N.D.Ill. 1989).

110. Schein v. Chasen, 478 F.2d 817, 822 (2d Cir.1973), *vacated sub nom.* Lehman Bros. v. Schein, 416 U.S. 386, 94 S.Ct. 1741, 40 L.Ed.2d 215 (1974), *certified question answered after remand* 313 So.2d 739 (1975), *answer to certified question* 519 F.2d 453 (2d Cir.1975).

111. Freeman v. Decio, 584 F.2d 186 (7th Cir.1978); Schein v. Chasen, 313 So.2d 739 (Fla.1975), *answer to certified question* 519 F.2d 453 (2d Cir.1975). *But cf.* In re ORFA Securities Litigation, 654 F.Supp. 1449 (D.N.J.1987).

112. 719 F.2d 5 (2d Cir.1983), *cert. denied* 465 U.S. 1025, 104 S.Ct. 1280, 79 L.Ed.2d 684 (1984).

113. 664 F.2d 12 (2d Cir.1981), *cert. denied* 464 U.S. 863, 104 S.Ct. 193, 78 L.Ed.2d 170 (1983). *Cf.* SEC v. Musella, 578 F.Supp. 425 (S.D.N.Y.1984) (law firm employee enjoined from passing on information obtained from firm's clients). The Second Circuit has since explained that *Moss* and *Newman* reflect differences between SEC enforcement, criminal actions and private damage actions. SEC v. Materia, 745 F.2d 197 (2d Cir.1984), *cert. denied* 471 U.S. 1053, 105 S.Ct. 2112, 85 L.Ed.2d 477 (1985).

The misappropriation theory supported a series of convictions in United States v. Carpenter, 791 F.2d 1024 (2d Cir.1986), *affirming* 612 F.Supp. 827 (S.D.N.Y.1985), *affirmed by an equally divided court* 484 U.S. 19, 108 S.Ct. 316, 98 L.Ed.2d 275 (1987). *See also* SEC v. Gaspar, 1985 WL 521, [1984–85 Transfer Binder] Fed.Sec.L.Rep. (CCH) ¶ 92,004 (S.D.N.Y.1985).

An action will also lie in a face-to-face transaction. *See* Rodriguez v. Montalvo, 649 F.Supp. 1169 (D.P.R.1986) (suit by majority shareholder against president and c.e.o.)

114. Goldman v. Belden, 754 F.2d 1059 (2d Cir.1985). In so ruling the court relied upon the pre–*Moss* decision in Elkind v. Liggett & Myers, Inc., 635 F.2d 156 (2d Cir.1980), 754 F.2d at 1069. *See also* Wilson v. Comtech Telecommunications Corp., 648 F.2d 88, 94–95 (2d Cir.1981).

viewed as recognizing the fraud on the market theory of insider trading liability only when the defendant is a corporate insider. It is also worth noting that in this case, the defendants were trading with knowledge of misleading corporate information that was being disseminated concurrently. In contrast, following the same type of reasoning as was used in *Moss,* it has been held that an issuer's misleading statements were not actionable by options traders because of the absence of a fiduciary duty running from the issuer to options traders who never owned the underlying stock.[115] However, the complaint was sustained against the issuer's employees and tippees who, like the plaintiff, traded in the options but used inside information.[116]

As the foregoing discussion makes clear, by 1988, the existence of a powerful private remedy under rule 10b–5 to be used against insider trading was at best questionable. Congress was concerned with the apparently increasing number of instances in which individuals were taking undue advantage of nonpublic material information. Accordingly, it responded with two important pieces of legislation. The Insider Trading Sanctions Act of 1984 (ITSA), increased the government's ability to pursue insider trading. The Insider Trading and Securities Fraud Enforcement Act continued this trend and also added an express private remedy. These important remedial provisions are discussed below.

ITSA

One backlash of the *Chiarella* and *Dirks* decisions has been a push for congressional enactment of stronger insider trading penalties. Recent legislation by Congress (The Insider Trading Sanctions Act of 1984, or ITSA) permits the SEC to bring suit against anyone violating the 1934 Act or rules "by purchasing or selling a security while in possession of material nonpublic information."[117] The civil penalty in such a suit would be based on trebling the profits gained or loss avoided by the

---

115. Bianco v. Texas Instruments, Inc., 627 F.Supp. 154 (N.D.Ill.1985).

116. *Id.* at 163–64. *Cf.* Burlington Industries, Inc. v. Edelman, 1987 WL 91498, [1987 Transfer Binder] Fed.Sec.L.Rep. (CCH) ¶ 93,339 (4th Cir.1987), *affirming on the opinion below* 666 F.Supp. 799 (M.D.N.C.1987) (enjoining tender offer in suit by target company where tender offer was based on alleged misappropriation of inside information from the target company).

117. 15 U.S.C.A. §§ 78u–1(a)(1), 78ff(a). *See* H.R. 559, passed September 19, 1983. Although the House version of the bill which was adopted does not define insider trading, there was some movement in the Senate to provide a definition. *See generally* David M. Brodsky, Insider Trading and the Insider Trading Sanctions Act of 1984: New Wine Into New Bottles?, 41 Wash. & Lee L.Rev. 921 (1984); Donald C. Langevoort, Commentary— The Insider Trading Sanctions Act of 1984 and Its Effect on Existing Law, 37 Vand.L.Rev. 1273 (1984); Carole B. Silver, Penalizing Insider Trading: A Critical Assessment of the Insider Trading Sanctions Act of 1984, 1985 Duke L.J. 960; Comment, The Insider Trading Sanctions Act of 1984: Did Congress and the SEC Go Home Too Early?, 19 U.C.D.L.Rev. 497 (1986); Note, A Critique of the Insider Trading Sanctions Act of 1984, 71 Va.L.Rev. 455 (1985).

The criminal fines imposed by ITSA are not to be paid from any fund that has been set aside for investors. SEC v. Levine, 689 F.Supp. 317 (S.D.N.Y.1988), *affirmed in part, reversed in part* 881 F.2d 1165 (2d Cir.1989).

defendant.[118]   In addition, the act also increases the criminal penalty from $10,000 to $100,000.   This recent legislation by its terms does not alter the 10b–5 action brought by investors or the *Chiarella* and *Dirks* decisions as they may be applied to any private remedies that exist, outside of the statutory remedy.   This is consistent with the general trend towards cumulative remedies under the securities laws.[119]

The Insider Trading Sanctions Act of 1984 raises a number of interesting questions.[120]   For example: would successive actions under ITSA and for criminal violations based on the same transactions violate the constitutional prohibition against double jeopardy?   Since the ITSA– 1984 treble damage provision is a penalty (although nominally civil in nature), there is a strong possibility that double jeopardy would apply.[121] On the other hand, it seems clear that double jeopardy will not apply to a criminal action followed by an action for disgorgement.[122]   A criminal fine is a different matter from the remedial considerations underlying a

---

118. *See, e.g.,* SEC v. Patel, 1994 WL 364089, [Current] Fed. Sec. L. Rep. (CCH) ¶ 98,340 (S.D.N.Y.1994) (profits subject to disgorgement calculated on the basis of the insider's loss avoided).

119. *E.g.* Herman & MacLean v. Huddleston, 459 U.S. 375, 103 S.Ct. 683, 74 L.Ed.2d 548 (1983), *on remand* 705 F.2d 775 (5th Cir.1983). *Accord,* A. Copeland Enterprises, Inc. v. Guste, 1988 WL 129318, [1989–1990 Transfer Binder] Fed.Sec.L.Rep. ¶ 95,011 (E.D.La. 1988). *See* § 13.2 *supra.*

In addition to civil penalties and disgorgement, the violator may be subject to other sanctions. *E.g.,* SEC v. Patel, 1994 WL 364089, [1994–1995 Transfer Binder] Fed. Sec. L. Rep. (CCH) ¶ 98,340 (S.D.N.Y.1994) (officer and director who admitted insider trading and other fraud violations was barred from serving as an officer or director of a public company). SEC sanctions are discussed in § 9.5 *supra.*

120. The SEC Enforcement issues raised by ITSA–1984 are discussed in § 9.5 *supra.*

121. *See, e.g.,* Comment, Implications of the 1984 Insider Trading Sanctions Act: Collateral Estoppel and Double Jeopardy, 64 N.C.L.Rev. 117 (1985). *But cf.* SEC v. Levine, 689 F.Supp. 317 (S.D.N.Y.1988), *affirmed in part, reversed in part* 881 F.2d 1165 (2d Cir.1989) (criminal penalty is not payable out of funds set aside for investors).

A 1989 Supreme Court decision sheds light on the double jeopardy issues that may arise in connection with ITSA and ITSFEA. United States v. Halper, 488 U.S. 906, 109 S.Ct. 256, 102 L.Ed.2d 244 (1988); *see* the discussion in the text accompanying footnotes 65–68 in § 9.5 *supra.* In *Halper,* the defendant was convicted of having violated the criminal false claims statute and the Mail Fraud Act and then was subsequently sued by the government under the Civil False Claims Act wherein the district court imposed civil fines of $137,000. The Supreme Court found that a civil penalty may be so unrelated to the remedial goals of the statute that it constitutes punishment within the meaning of the Double Jeopardy Clause of the Constitution. The *Halper* decision thus makes it clear that double jeopardy issues can arise when a criminal prosecution is followed by a government suit seeking to impose civil penalties. What are the implications of the *Halper* decision with regard to ITSA? There is legislative history which supports the view that the ITSA treble damage penalty was designed as a deterrent rather than remedial provision. This would indicate that an ITSA civil proceeding which has been preceded by a criminal prosecution might well run afoul of the Double Jeopardy Clause. If nothing else, the *Halper* decision should spur the SEC to consider seeking civil and criminal sanctions in a single proceeding rather than continue its current policy of going after the defendant in a piecemeal fashion.

Double jeopardy should not attach to an action solely for disgorgement of ill-gotten profits. SEC v. Monarch Funding Corp., 1995 WL 152185, [Current] Fed.Sec.L.Rep. ¶ 98,613 (S.D.N.Y.1995) ("Because disgorgement, unlike forfeiture, is a purely civil remedy, the cases have recognized that a disgorgement proceeding is not subject to double jeopardy protection"). However, a different result could well follow in an action for a penalty above the disgorgement. *See* the discussion in the text accompanying footnote 68 in § 9.5 *supra.*

122. SEC v. Bilzerian, 814 F.Supp. 116 (D.D.C.1993).

disgorgement action.[123]

Since ITSA–1984 frames the disgorgement remedy and treble damage penalty in terms of the insider's trading profits (or losses avoided),[124] a non-trading tipper might at first appear not to be covered by the penalty. However, it is appropriate to frame the disgorgement and penalty against the non-trading tipper in terms of the profits (or losses avoided) of the trading tippees.[125]

The Insider Trading Sanctions Act of 1984 has proven to be an effective enforcement weapon. The decision whether to order the civil penalty is discretionary. Thus, for example, it has been found inappropriate to add a penalty to the disgorgement order when the deterrent effect of the penalty was not needed.[126] Following the enactment of ITSA–1984, the Commission has been increasingly vigorous in enforcing insider trading prohibitions and has reached some very lucrative settlements.[127]

ITSFEA

In 1988 Congress bolstered the remedies provided by ITSA–1984 when it enacted the Insider Trading and Securities Fraud Enforcement Act. The 1988 legislation specifically addresses liability of employers and controlling persons.[128] Under the Insider Trading and Securities

---

123. *Id.*

124. *Cf.* SEC v. Chapnick, 1994 WL 113040, [1993–1994 Transfer Binder] Fed. Sec. L. Rep. (CCH) ¶ 98,076 (S.D.Fla.1994) (adequately pleading case for disgorgement; the method of computing profit is based on the difference between the insider's sale (or purchase) price and the market price a reasonable time after the information has been publicly disclosed).

125. *See, e.g., Cf.* United States v. Marcus Schloss & Co., 724 F.Supp. 1123 (S.D.N.Y. 1989) ($20,000 penalty in civil ITSA proceeding did not amount to punishment and thus the criminal prosecution was permitted to proceed).

In reviewing a disgorgement plan, a court must consider whether it is fair and reasonable. SEC v. Wang, 944 F.2d 80 (2d Cir.1991); SEC v. Gaffney, 1985 WL 5850, [1984–85 Transfer Binder] Fed.Sec.L.Rep. (CCH) ¶ 92,002 (S.D.N.Y.1985) (non-trading tipper consented to $15,000 civil penalty; trading tippees consented to disgorgement of profits and civil penalty). Liability under the newly created private right of action is joint and several for both tippers and tippees. *See also, e.g.,* SEC v. Finacor Anstalt, 1991 WL 173327, [1991 Transfer Binder] Fed.Sec.L.Rep. (CCH) ¶ 96,272 (S.D.N.Y.1991) (approving disgorgement plan over defendant's objection); 15 U.S.C.A. § 78t–1(c).

126. SEC v. Ingoldsby, 1990 WL 120731, [1990 Transfer Binder] Fed.Sec.L.Rep. ¶ 95,-351 (D.Mass.1990).

127. *See, e.g.,* SEC v. Brant, [1987–88 Transfer Binder] Fed.Sec.L.Rep. (CCH) ¶ 93,708 (S.D.N.Y.1988) ($268,000 settlement by estate); SEC v. Kidder Peabody & Co., 1987 WL 16280, 19 Sec.Reg. & L.Rep. (BNA) 811 (S.D.N.Y.1987) (settlement of more than $25,000,-000); SEC v. Pomerantz, 1986 WL 15411, [1986–87 Transfer Binder] Fed.Sec.L.Rep. (CCH) ¶ 93,008 (S.D.N.Y.1986) ($79,850 penalty); SEC v. Boesky, 1986 WL 15283, [1986–87 Transfer Binder] Fed.Sec.L.Rep. (CCH) ¶ 92,991 (S.D.N.Y.1986) (settlement of $50,000,000 disgorgement and $50,000,000 penalty).

128. Controlling person liability under the Exchange Act generally is governed by section 20(a) of the Act. 15 U.S.C.A. § 78t(a). *See* § 13.15 *infra.* In addition to the new controlling person provision, the 1988 legislation was amended to make it clear that tippers and tippees are both primary violators rather than having to rely on aiding and abetting principles. *See* 15 U.S.C.A. § 78t–1(c) (providing that tippers and tippees are jointly and severally liable). Aiding and abetting liability is discussed in § 13.16 *infra.*

Fraud Enforcement Act of 1988 a court can impose ITSA penalties on a controlling person of a primary violator only if: (1) the controlling person knew or acted in reckless disregard of the fact that the controlled person was likely to engage in illegal insider trading and (2) the controlling person failed to take adequate precautions to prevent the prohibited conduct from taking place.[129] General principles of respondeat superior and section 20(a)[130] controlling person liability expressly do not apply to actions brought under ITSA.[131] In addition, for controlling persons the treble damage penalty is not to exceed the greater of one million dollars or three times the amount of the profit gained or loss avoided.[132] Further, the 1988 legislation imposes a five year statute of limitations to SEC actions; the limitations period is expressly limited to ITSA actions.[133]

Perhaps the most significant aspect of the Insider Trading and Securities Fraud Enforcement Act is its applicability to private enforcement. Section 21A(e) of the Exchange Act now permits the payment of a bounty of up to ten percent of the penalty to private individuals who provide information leading to the imposition of the penalty.[134] The decision to award a bounty lies in the sole discretion of the SEC except that persons associated with the Commission, Department of Justice, or a self-regulatory organization are not eligible to receive a bounty award.[135]

The Insider Trading and Securities Fraud Enforcement Act of 1988 also created an express private right of action in the hands of contemporaneous traders.[136] Section 20A of the Exchange Act provides that

---

129. 15 U.S.C.A. § 78u–1(b)(1). In addition, broker-dealers are specifically directed to establish, maintain, and enforce written policies designed to prevent insider trading violations by their employees. 15 U.S.C.A. § 78o(f). A similar provision exists for investment advisers. 15 U.S.C.A. § 80b–4a. Investment advisers are discussed in chapter 18 *infra*.

Law firms have similar compliance problems. *See, e.g.,* Note Insider Trading Regulation of Law Firms: Expanding ITSFEA's Policy and Procedures Requirement, 44 Hastings L.J. 1159 (1993).

130. 15 U.S.C.A. § 78t(a). *See* § 13.15 *infra*.

131. 15 U.S.C.A. § 78u–1(b)(2). Following the recent Supreme Court ruling that there is no aiding and abetting liability absent statutory authorization (Central Bank of Denver v. First Interstate Bank of Denver, ___ U.S. ___, 114 S.Ct. 1439, 128 L.Ed.2d 119 (1994)), the applicability of respondeat superior outside of ITSA is likely to be questioned. Aiding and abetting is discussed in § 13.16 *infra*. Respondeat superior is discussed in § 13.15 *infra*.

132. 15 U.S.C.A. § 78u–1(a)(3).

133. 15 U.S.C.A. § 78u–1(d)(5) ("This section shall not be construed to bar or limit in any manner any action by the Commission or the Attorney General under any other provision of this title, nor shall it bar or limit in any manner any action to recover penalties, or to seek any other order regarding penalties, imposed in an action commenced within 5 years of such transaction"). The express private remedy also has a five year statute of limitations. 15 U.S.C.A. § 78t–1(b)(4).

134. 15 U.S.C.A. § 78u–1(e). For the SEC procedures relating to the bounty provisions, *see* 17 C.F.R. §§ 201.61–201.68.

135. 15 U.S.C.A. § 78u–1(e).

136. The contemporaneous trading requirement is a "circumstance constituting fraud" and thus must be pleaded with particularity. Neubronner v. Milken, 6 F.3d 666 (9th

anyone violating the Act or SEC rules while trading in possession of material, nonpublic information shall be liable to contemporaneous traders trading on the other side of the insider trader's transactions.[137] Thus, if the violator is selling, all contemporaneous purchasers can sue while if the violator is purchasing, all contemporaneous sellers can sue.

Section 20A does not define precisely who qualifies as a contemporaneous trader.[138] Arguably, in light of the remedy's prophylactic (rather than compensatory) purpose, that phrase should be construed relatively broadly.[139] Most decisions seem to agree that establishing trading within a week of the defendant's improper trading will be sufficient to satisfy the contemporaneous trading requirement.[140] Although there are a number of pre–ITSFEA decisions that take a narrow view of what constitutes contemporaneous transactions,[141] their relevance is at best

Cir.1993). It was not sufficient to allege that the trading in question took place over a period of three years. The court pointed out that while it may be sufficient to focus on days or, perhaps, even months, pleading in terms of years lacked sufficient particularity. *See also, e.g.,* Stephen B. Rosenfeld, Pleading Damage Claims for Insider Trading, 27 Rev. Sec. & Commod. Reg. 91 (1994).

137. 15 U.S.C.A. § 78t–1(a). H.A.B. Associates v. Hines, 1990 WL 170514, [1990–1991 Transfer Binder] Fed.Sec.L.Rep. (CCH) ¶ 95,665 (S.D.N.Y.1990) (sufficient allegation of contemporaneous purchase). *Compare, e.g.,* Leventhal v. Katy Industries, Inc., 899 F.2d 1218 (3d Cir.1990) (noncontemporaneous traders cannot recover under disclose or abstain rule); Seagate Technology II Securities Litigation, 1990 WL 134963, [1990 Transfer Binder] Fed.Sec.L.Rep. (CCH) ¶ 95,427 (N.D.Cal.1990).

It thus is clear, that in order to complain of insider trading, the plaintiff must have traded in the securities in question. *See, e.g.,* Chanoff v. U.S. Surgical Corp., 857 F.Supp. 1011 (D.Conn.1994). *Compare* the purchaser/seller standing requirement under Rule 10b–5 which is discussed in § 13.3 *supra.*

138. *Cf.* Neubronner v. Milken, 6 F.3d 666 (9th Cir.1993) (contemporaneous trading must be pleaded with particularity).

139. The broad interpretation of contemporaneous trader does not, however, eliminate the need to plead the claim with sufficient particularity. *E.g.* Neubronner v. Milken, 6 F.3d 666 (9th Cir.1993) (it may be sufficient to plead the contemporaneous trading requirement as a matter of days or, perhaps, even months but pleading in terms of years lacked sufficient particularity).

140. *See, e.g.,* Feldman v. Motorola, Inc., 1994 WL 160115, [1993–1994 Transfer Binder] Fed. Sec. L. Rep. (CCH) ¶ 98,133 (N.D.Ill.1994) (allegations that plaintiffs purchased within one to four business days of defendant's improper sales were sufficient but allegations of alleged transactions taking place months apart were not sufficient); In re Cypress Semiconductor Securities Litigation, 836 F.Supp. 711 (N.D.Cal.1993) (purchase of securities within five days of insider's sale was a contemporaneous transaction); In re Verifone Securities Litigation, 784 F.Supp. 1471, 1488–89 (N.D.Cal.1992), *affirmed* 11 F.3d 865 (9th Cir.1993) (can be as short as a few days but cannot be longer than a month). *But see* Colby v. Hologic, Inc., 817 F.Supp. 204 (D.Mass.1993) (plaintiff who purchased eight days after defendant's sale was not a contemporaneous trader).

Cf. 8 Louis Loss & Joel Seligman, Securities Regulation 3724 (3d ed. 1991), wherein in commenting on the pre–ITSFEA cases, the authors observed: "Plaintiffs typically have been allowed to file claims as contemporaneous traders for up to one week after the defendant's wrongful trades or breach of fiduciary duty. At the same time plaintiffs have been consistently denied standing for trades later than that." (footnotes omitted). *See also, e.g.,* Rosenfeld *supra* footnote 136; William K.S. Wang, The Contemporaneous Traders Who Can Sue an Inside Trader, 38 Hastings L.J. 1175 (1987).

141. *See, e.g.,* Backman v. Polaroid Corp., 540 F.Supp. 667, 671 (D.Mass.1982) (trades two days apart were not sufficient); Kreindler v. Sambo's Restaurant, Inc., 1981 WL 1684, [1981–1982 Transfer Binder] Fed. Sec. L. Rep. (CCH) ¶ 98,312 (S.D.N.Y.1981) (transactions seven days apart were not contemporaneous) and the other cases cited in 8 Loss & Selgman

questionable. Prior to the enactment of section 20A, civil liability for insider trading was based upon Rule 10b–5 and some direct or indirect duty running from the trader to the plaintiff. In contrast, ITSFEA in enacting the statutory basis of liability eliminated the need for such a duty and, more importantly, focused on the need to prevent the insider from retaining his or her ill-gotten profits rather than upon compensation for any supposed injury to contemporaneous traders.

Damages in an ITSFEA action are limited to the profits or losses avoided by the illegal transactions[142] and are to be diminished by any disgorgement (as opposed to penalty) ordered in an SEC action under ITSA.[143] Controlling person liability in such a private suit is governed by section 20(a) of the Act[144] rather than by the specific provision applicable to ITSA actions.[145] Liability under the express private remedy extends to both tippers and tippees who violate the act; the act further provides that their liability is joint and several.[146]

This relatively new private remedy supplements any other existing express or implied remedies.[147] The Act also provides that the private remedy does not limit the Commission's or Attorney General's authority to recover penalties (as opposed to disgorgement of profits) for improper use of material, nonpublic information.[148]

---

supra footnote 140 at 3724 nn. 651, 652. *Compare* Froid v. Berner, 649 F.Supp. 1418, 1421 n.2 (D.N.J.1986) (finding contemporaneous trades for a series of trades); Kumpis v. Wetterau, 586 F.Supp. 152, 154 (E.D.Mo.1983) (trades "within a few days of" each other were contemporaneous).

142. 15 U.S.C.A. § 78t–1(b)(1). In addition, there is a self-contained five year statute of limitations. 15 U.S.C.A. § 78t–1(b)(4). The same five-year limitations period applies in SEC actions under ITSA. 15 U.S.C.A. § 78u–1(d)(5); *see* footnote 133 *supra.* The limitations period in Rule 10b–5 actions is discussed in § 13.8 *supra.*

143. 15 U.S.C.A. § 78t–1(b)(2). *See, e.g.,* Litton Industries, Inc. v. Lehman Brothers Kuhn Loeb, Inc., 734 F.Supp. 1071 (S.D.N.Y.1990) (once profits have been disgorged in SEC action, private plaintiff cannot seek disgorgement under federal law but may include claim for punitive damages under state law). *Cf.* Comment, Equitable Claims to Disgorged Insider Profits, 1989 Wis.L.Rev. 1433.

144. 15 U.S.C.A. § 78t(a).

145. 15 U.S.C.A. § 78u–1(b).

146. 15 U.S.C.A. § 78t–1(c):

Any person who violates any provision of this title or the rules or regulations thereunder by communicating material, nonpublic information shall be jointly and severally liable under subsection (a) with, and to the same extent as, any person or persons liable under subsection (a) to whom the communication was directed.

147. 15 U.S.C.A. § 78t–1(d) ("Nothing in this section shall be construed to limit or condition the right of any person to bring an action to enforce a requirement of this title or the availability of any cause of action implied from a provision of this title"). *But see* T. Rowe Price New Horizons Fund, Inc. v. Preletz, 749 F.Supp. 705 (D.Md.1990) (dismissing 10b–5 claim brought by contemporaneous trader, reasoning that the provision on cumulative remedies was designed to preserve claims by persons other than contemporaneous traders). *See generally* William K.S.Wang, ITSFEA's Effect on Either an Implied Cause of Action for Damages by Contemporaneous Traders or an Action for Damages or Rescission by the Party in Privity with the Inside Trader, 16 J.Corp.L. 445 (1991).

148. 15 U.S.C.A. § 78t–1(e). *Cf.* United States v. Elliott, 714 F.Supp. 380 (N.D.Ill. 1989) (securities trader who disgorged profits as part of SEC settlement, would not be asked to pay the money again under RICO forfeiture provisions).

In adopting the 1988 insider trading legislation, Congress considered adopting a definition of what constitutes improper trading on inside information. There was some move to expand the misappropriation theory by outlawing trading while in possession of material, nonpublic information. It was alternatively proposed that a possession test was too broad and the prohibition should be limited to the improper use of the information. However, as was the case in 1984, the attempt to legislatively define insider trading was dropped and the statute was enacted without any such definition.[149] Nevertheless, in the legislative history, there is a clear endorsement of the misappropriation theory as recognized by the Second Circuit.[150]

Compliance Programs—Protecting Bona Fide Insider Transactions[151]

Beyond the situation of unscrupulous traders who desire an unfair informational advantage, the Rule 10b–5 insider trading cases raise problems with regard to corporate executives who in good faith want to invest in their company's future. Any increase in insider trading followed by a news item having an impact on the stock's price may be strong circumstantial evidence of prohibited trading, provided that the insider had advance knowledge, or access to the information.[152] In order to avoid this problem, corporate insiders and their families might be well advised to engage in regular periodic acquisitions rather than single or sporadic large purchases. Also, stock option or bonus plans granted on other than a regular and periodic basis should be administered by a compensation committee that will not be trading in the shares so as to eliminate any conflict of interest and thus cleanse receipt of stock or options by insiders with access to information.[153] The timing problem is

149. *See* Report of the Committee of Energy and Commerce, H.R.Rep. 100–910, 100th Cong. 2d Sess. 11 (1988).

150. *Id.* at 10:

the misappropriation theory clearly remains valid in the Second Circuit * * * but is unresolved nationally. In the view of the Committee, however, this type of security fraud should be encompassed within Section 10(b) and Rule 10b–5. * * *

151. *See* Jonathan Eisenberg, Protecting Against Insider Trading Liability, 22 Rev.Sec. & Commodities Reg. 87 (1989); Marc I. Steinberg & John Fletcher, Compliance Programs for Insider Trading, 47 S.M.U.L. Rev. 1783 (1993); Alan M. Weinberger, Preventing Insider Trading Violations: A Survey of Corporate Compliance Programs, 18 Sec.Reg.L.J. 180 (1990); Harry J. Weiss & Michael L. Spolan, Preventing Insider Trading, 19 Rev.Sec. & Commodities Reg. 233 (1987).

152. This was a major part of the court's reasoning in the *Texas Gulf Sulphur* case. *See* discussion *supra. See also, e.g.,* SEC v. Shared Medical Systems Corp., 1994 WL 201858, [1993–1994 Transfer Binder] Fed. Sec. L. Rep. (CCH) ¶ 98,247 (E.D.Pa.1994) (insider trading in suspicious amounts or at suspicious times is probative of scienter). *Cf.* In re American Business Computers Corp. Securities Litigation, 1993 WL 616684, [1993–1994 Transfer Binder] Fed. Sec. L. Rep. (CCH) ¶ 98,103 (S.D.N.Y.1993) (evidence of established pattern of trading at best created factual issue as to whether defendant engaged in improper trading on inside information).

But see SEC v. Fox, 654 F.Supp. 781 (N.D.Tex.1986) (employees not shown to have acted on inside information).

153. The Second Circuit in *Texas Gulf Sulphur* took an extraordinarily hard line on shares acquired under executive stock plans, during the materiality period while the information was not publicly available.

more acute when insiders decide to sell shares and their sales are followed by adverse news that drives the price down. In this case again it would be ideal to plan a series of sales over time in order to establish that the transactions were not motivated by inside information.[154]

Periodic purchases or sales are not always practical in light of their financial needs and insiders will then be left to trade in their company's shares at their peril, especially when subsequent facts may put a taint on their legitimate transactions. Furthermore, an insider who finds himself or herself in such a situation of needing to raise cash by selling shares, presumably will be able to avoid extra liability by disgorging any profit based on the difference between the market value with the information publicly available and the price at the time of the transaction.[155] Obviously, the insider will want to avoid this solution if at all possible.

Such chilling effects on insider trading, although perhaps harsh in a particular case, are not unwarranted in terms of the potential abuses connected with insider trading.

§ 13.10 Corporate Affirmative Disclosure Obligations and Rule 10b–5

As was pointed out in an earlier chapter of this Treatise, issuers subject to the registration requirements of section 12 of the Exchange Act[1] must file periodic reports with the Commission pursuant to section 13 of the Act.[2] Section 16(a)[3] further requires officers, directors, and ten percent beneficial owners of registered reporting companies to file re-

---

The *Texas Gulf* ruling must be read in light of the defendants' other trading activities which included buying call options—an investment strategy that connotes short-term trading as opposed to long-term investment goals. *Compare* section 16(c)'s prohibition against short selling by insiders of issuers subject to the 1934 Act's registration and reporting requirements. 15 U.S.C.A. § 78p(c). *See* 12.6 *supra. See also* the discussion of the effect of such transactions on materiality in footnote 23 *supra.*

154. *Cf.* In re American Business Computers Corp. Securities Litigation, 1993 WL 616684, [1993–1994 Transfer Binder] Fed. Sec. L. Rep. (CCH) ¶ 98,103 (S.D.N.Y.1993) (pattern of trading at best created factual issue as to whether defendant engaged in improper trading on inside information).

155. Damages under Rule 10b–5 are discussed in § 13.7 *supra.*

§ 13.10

1. 15 U.S.C.A. § 78*l. See* § 9.2 *supra.*

2. 15 U.S.C.A. § 78m. *See* § 9.3 *supra.* Section 12 requires registration of issuers who have securities traded on a national securities exchange as well as those having more than five million dollars in assets and a class of equity securities with more than five hundred shareholders. 15 U.S.C.A. § 78*l*(g); 17 C.F.R. § 240.12g–1. In addition issuers who do not come within the registration requirements but have issued securities pursuant to a 1933 Act registration statement and have at least 300 holders of those securities are subject to the periodic reporting requirements by virtue of section 15(d) of the Act. 15 U.S.C.A. § 78*o*(d). Section 15(d) issuers have to file the periodic reports but are not subject to proxy regulation (sections 14(a)–(c), 15 U.S.C.A. §§ 78n(a)–(c)), the Williams Act tender offer disclosure requirements (section 13(d), (e) and 14(d), (f), 15 U.S.C.A. §§ 78m(d), (e), 78n(d), (f)) or the reporting requirements for officers, directors, and ten percent beneficial owners (section 16(a), 15 U.S.C.A. § 78p(a)).

3. 15 U.S.C.A. § 78p(a). *See* § 12.3 *supra.*

ports of all transactions in the issuer's shares. In addition, section 13(d)[4] requires filings by any person acquiring five percent of an equity security subject to the registration and reporting requirements; section 14(d)[5] imposes filing requirements in connection with tender offers. These filings are publicly available. Investors who have been injured by reliance upon material misstatements or omissions of fact in SEC filed documents have an express private right of action pursuant to section 18(a).[6] Most courts have held that there is also a cumulative remedy under Rule 10b–5.[7]

In addition to the SEC filing requirements of section 13, all companies subject to the registration requirements of section 12[8] must periodically send reports to their shareholders.[9] Required reports containing material misstatements or omissions of fact can give rise to liability under Rules 14a–9[10] and 10b–5.[11] Companies which are not subject to section 12's registration requirements may nevertheless have to file periodic reports under section 15(d) of the 1934 Act[12] if the securities were issued under a 1933 Act registration statement and the issuer has three hundred or more holders of the securities so issued.[13]

Form 8–K under the 1934 Act requires issuers subject to the Act's periodic reporting obligations to file notice of certain specified occurrences or events within a specified number of days.[14] These events include disposition or acquisition of substantial assets (to be disclosed within fifteen days), changes in control (to be disclosed within fifteen days) and director turnover (to be disclosed within five days).[15] The

---

4. 15 U.S.C.A. § 78m(d). *See* § 11.11 *supra.*

5. 15 U.S.C.A. § 78n(d). *See* § 11.14 *supra.*

6. 15 U.S.C.A. § 78r(a). *See* § 12.8 *supra.*

7. *E.g.* Ross v. A.H. Robins Co., 607 F.2d 545 (2d Cir.1979), *cert. denied* 446 U.S. 946, 100 S.Ct. 2175, 64 L.Ed.2d 802 (1980), *rehearing denied* 448 U.S. 911, 100 S.Ct. 3057, 65 L.Ed.2d 1140 (1980). *See* §§ 12.8, 13.2 *supra.* *See also* Herman & MacLean v. Huddleston, 459 U.S. 375, 103 S.Ct. 683, 74 L.Ed.2d 548 (1983), *on remand* 705 F.2d 775 (5th Cir.1983); Capri Optics Profit Sharing v. Digital Equipment Corp., 760 F.Supp. 227 (D.Mass.), *judgment affirmed* 950 F.2d 5 (1st Cir.1991); Holstein v. Armstrong, 751 F.Supp. 746 (N.D.Ill.1990).

See generally Marc I. Steinberg, The Propriety and Scope of Cumulative Remedies Under the Federal Securities Laws, 67 Cornell L.Rev. 557 (1982).

8. 15 U.S.C.A. § 78*l*.

9. 17 C.F.R. § 240.14a–3.

10. 17 C.F.R. § 240.14a–9. *See* §§ 11.3–11.5 *supra.*

11. 17 C.F.R. § 240.10b–5.

12. 15 U.S.C.A. § 78o(d). *See* §§ 9.2, 9.3 *supra.*

13. *See* footnote 2 *supra.* *See also* 15 U.S.C.A. §§ 77e, 77f, 77g. The 1933 Act registration requirements are discussed in chapters 2, 3 *supra.*

14. 17 C.F.R. § 240.13a–11.

15. The material developments that must be reported in timely fashion on Form 8–K include: (1) changes in control of the issuer, (2) significant acquisitions or dispositions of assets by the issuer or majority owned subsidiaries, (3) the institution of bankruptcy or receivership proceedings, (4) changes in the registrant's certifying accountant, and (5) director resignations. The form also provides: "The registrant may, at its option, report under this item any events, with respect to which information is not otherwise called for by this form, that the registrant deems of importance to security holders." Form 8–K, item 5. *See* § 9.3 *supra.*

Exchange Act, however, provides no express requirement that a corporation report material information that is not otherwise required by the periodic reporting and shareholder information requirements. Thus, there is no affirmative duty to disclose many types of material developments until the next quarterly report. In contrast, the rules of the major stock exchanges expressly require corporations to make timely disclosure of all information that would be material to the reasonable investor.[16] Whether Rule 10b–5 alone is sufficient to trigger a similar affirmative duty of disclosure is highly doubtful.[17] As discussed below, the language of Rule 10b–5 does not provide any basis for such an affirmative disclosure requirement. The absence of an affirmative disclosure requirement in Rule 10b–5 is particularly significant with regard to companies which are not subject to the New York or American Stock Exchange rules.

SEC Rule 10b–5(a) and (c)[18] deal with acts and practices that constitute fraud or deceit and therefore they should not be relevant to the question of affirmative disclosure requirements absent some independent duty to disclose. Mere nondisclosure, absent insider trading[19] or some other collateral activity, is insufficient to establish a violation under these subsections.[20] Rule 10b–5 has been interpreted to impose a "disclose or abstain rule"[21] in insider trading cases. However, unless an issuer is trading in its own shares, that disclose or abstain rule does not trigger a duty of disclosure. Thus, in the ordinary corporate dissemination situation, there is no duty to disclose. Consequently, Rule 10b–5(2) provides the only possible remaining basis for the issuer's affirmative

---

16. N.Y.S.E. Company Manual, Fed.Sec.L.Rep. (CCH) ¶ 23,121 (1977); American Stock Exchange Company Guide (CCH) ¶ 10,121; Sec.Exch.Act Rel. No. 34–8995 (Oct. 15, 1970).

17. *See generally* Patrick H. Allen, The Disclosure Obligations of Publicly Held Companies in the Absence of Insider Trading, 25 Mercer L.Rev. 479 (1974); Ian Ayers, Back to Basics: Regulating How Corporations Speak to the Market, 77 Va.L.Rev. 945 (1991); Jeffrey D. Bauman, Rule 10b–5 and the Corporation's Affirmative Duty to Disclose, 67 Geo.L.J. 935 (1979); Dennis J. Block, Nancy E. Barton & Alan E. Garfield, Affirmative Duty to Disclose Material Information Concerning Issuer's Financial Condition and Business Plans, 40 Bus.Law. 1243 (1985); Symposium, Affirmative Disclosure Obligations Under The Securities Laws, 46 Md.L.Rev. 954 (1987); Donald M. Feuerstein, The Corporation's Obligations of Disclosure Under the Federal Securities Laws When It is not Trading in Its Stock, 15 N.Y.L.F. 385 (1969).

18. 17 C.F.R. § 240.10b–5(a), (c). Rule 10b–5(c) prohibits conduct that operates as a fraud. It can be argued that mere silence and nondisclosure of material information is not a fraud but nevertheless has the same impact as fraud and thus operates as a fraud in violation of Rule 10b–5(3). There is no reported decision adopting such a view. The text of Rule 10b–5 is set out in § 13.2 *supra*.

19. *See* § 13.9 *supra*.

20. *See, e.g.,* National Union Fire Insurance Co. v. Turtur, 892 F.2d 199 (2d Cir.1989) (surety owed no fiduciary duty to investors with whom it had not dealt directly and thus could not be held liable for nondisclosure); Gordon v. Diagnostek, Inc., 812 F.Supp. 57 (E.D.Pa.1993) (target company shareholders could not state nondisclosure claim against intended acquirer since there was no duty of disclosure); Germantown Savings Bank v. Goldstein, 1989 WL 100980, [1989 Transfer Binder] Fed.Sec.L.Rep. ¶ 94,533 (S.D.N.Y.1989) (relationship of bank to customer does not create fiduciary relationship and hence there is no duty of disclosure).

21. *See* § 13.9 *supra*.

disclosure obligation based merely on the timeliness and materiality of the non-public information.

In relevant part, Rule 10b–5(b) provides that it is unlawful "to omit to state a material fact necessary *in order to make the statements made, in light of the circumstances under which they were made, not misleading.*" [22] These words clearly seem to contemplate that in order to create liability for omission there must be some statement in which the material facts do not appear. Thus, even though some observers may have taken a more expansive view of the rule and have indicated that an affirmative disclosure duty should be found to exist,[23] the issuer may be justified in keeping silent absent an independent basis for the duty to disclose.[24] This view is further strengthened by the Supreme Court ruling that the mere possession of confidential inside information is not sufficient to trigger the duty to disclose or abstain from trading.[25] As one court has aptly explained, "[a]bsent a specific duty to disclose, even the most material information imaginable may be withheld from the public."[26] It is clear, however, that if such an independent duty can be found, Rule 10b–5 will provide the basis of liability both in criminal and SEC injunctive actions as well as in private actions brought by an injured purchaser.[27] In a private suit for nondisclosure, however, the

---

22. 17 C.F.R. § 240.10b–5(b) (emphasis supplied).

23. This was the contention of the issuer in *Texas Gulf Sulphur* with regard to why it issued a press release regarding a mineral find before all the facts were in. The court never reached this issue because it found the press release to have been materially misleading. SEC v. Texas Gulf Sulphur, 401 F.2d 833 (2d Cir.1968), *cert. denied* 394 U.S. 976, 89 S.Ct. 1454, 22 L.Ed.2d 756 (1969). *Cf.* Comment, Liability Under Rule 10b–5 for Negligently Misleading Corporate Releases: A Proposal for the Apportionment of Losses, 122 U.Pa.L.Rev. 162 (1973).

24. Starkman v. Marathon Oil Co., 772 F.2d 231, 238 (6th Cir.1985), *cert. denied* 475 U.S. 1015, 106 S.Ct. 1195, 89 L.Ed.2d 310 (1986); *See, e.g.,* Greenstone v. Cambex Corp., 777 F.Supp. 88 (D.Mass.1991), judgment affirmed 975 F.2d 22 (1st Cir.1992) (no duty to disclose material unlawful practices); Gurwara v. Lyphomed, Inc., 739 F.Supp. 1162 (N.D.Ill.1990), *decision affirmed* 937 F.2d 380 (7th Cir.1991) (material information need not be disclosed absent a duty to do so). *See also* Flynn v. Bass Brothers Enterprises, Inc., 744 F.2d 978, 984 (3d Cir.1984).

25. Dirks v. SEC, 463 U.S. 646, 103 S.Ct. 3255, 77 L.Ed.2d 911 (1983); Chiarella v. United States, 445 U.S. 222, 100 S.Ct. 1108, 63 L.Ed.2d 348 (1980).

There is authority to the effect that Rule 10b–5 does not impose an affirmative duty to disclose in the absence of a required line-item disclosure or the issuer's trading in its own shares. Staffin v. Greenberg, 672 F.2d 1196, 1204 (3d Cir.1982); Greenfield v. Heublein, Inc., 575 F.Supp. 1325, 1336 (E.D.Pa.1983), *judgment affirmed* 742 F.2d 751 (3d Cir.1984), *cert. denied* 469 U.S. 1215, 105 S.Ct. 1189, 84 L.Ed.2d 336 (1985). *See also* Caravan Mobile Home Sales, Inc. v. Lehman Brothers Kuhn Loeb, Inc., 769 F.2d 561 (9th Cir.1985) (rejecting plaintiff's suggested per se rule requiring disclosure by multiservice banking firms acting as investment advisors to publicly traded issuers and in a fiduciary capacity with retail brokerage clients).

26. Polak v. Continental Hosts, Ltd., 613 F.Supp. 153, 156 (S.D.N.Y.1985). *Accord, e.g.,* Roeder v. Alpha, Indus., Inc., 814 F.2d 22 (1st Cir.1987) (corporation's payment of bribe was material but there was no duty to disclose); Delany v. Blunt, Ellis & Loewi, 631 F.Supp. 175, 179 (N.D.Ill.1986). *See also, e.g.,* Taylor v. First Union Corp. of South Carolina, 857 F.2d 240 (4th Cir.1988), *cert. denied* 489 U.S.1080. 109 S.Ct. 1532, 103 L.Ed.2d 837 (1989).

27. *See* Western Hemisphere Group, Inc. v. Stan West Corp., 1984 WL 1265, [1984–85 Transfer Binder] Fed.Sec.L.Rep. (CCH) ¶ 91,858 (S.D.N.Y.1984) (company had duty to

plaintiff will face a particularly difficult burden with regard to proof of causation and reliance.[28]

In the absence of an independent duty to disclose material information, the inability of 10b–5 to impose an affirmative disclosure obligation permits continued corporate silence.[29] For example, it has been held that early retirement of convertible debentures did not by itself trigger an obligation to disclose on-going merger negotiations.[30] If the corporation is an Exchange Act reporting company, however, the quarterly reporting requirements[31] can trigger a duty to disclose such facts once they become material.[32] Corporations not subject to the reporting requirements can maintain silence for longer periods without violating the securities laws since they are not subject to line-item disclosure requirements. Of course, once any statement is made, Rule 10b–5(2) will require full and honest disclosure.[33] In addition, upcoming shareholder

disclose upcoming public offering when buying back shares from existing shareholders). *See also* §§ 13.2, 13.5A *supra*.

Aside from the duty issue, it may be argued that an issuer cannot be held in violation of Rule 10b–5 unless it was trading in its own shares. Although this point was raised in a Supreme Court dissent (Basic Inc. v. Levinson, 485 U.S. 224, 108 S.Ct. 978, 99 L.Ed.2d 194 (1988) (White, J. dissenting)), other courts have not picked up on this proffered limitation.

28. *See* Fridrich v. Bradford, 542 F.2d 307 (6th Cir.1976), *cert. denied* 429 U.S. 1053, 97 S.Ct. 767, 50 L.Ed.2d 769 (1977); Green v. Occidental Petroleum Corp., 541 F.2d 1335 (9th Cir.1976). *See* §§ 13.5B, 13.6 *supra*.

29. The same may be true under the applicable state corporate law. *E.g.,* Lindner Fund, Inc. v. Waldbaum, Inc., 82 N.Y.2d 219, 604 N.Y.S.2d 32, 624 N.E.2d 160 (1993) (public company had no duty under either federal or state law to disclose agreement in principle that it would be acquired by another company).

30. *E.g.,* Glazer v. Formica Corp., 964 F.2d 149 (2d Cir.1992) (even if leveraged buy-out negotiations were material, there was no affirmative duty of disclosure and hence there was no liability for mere silence); Reiss v. Pan American World Airways, Inc., 711 F.2d 11 (2d Cir.1983); Zuckerman v. Harnischfeger Corp., 591 F.Supp. 112 (S.D.N.Y.1984) (no duty to disclose merger negotiations that were assumed to be nonpublic). *See also* Caravan Mobile Home Sales, Inc. v. Lehman Brothers Kuhn Loeb, Inc., 769 F.2d 561 (9th Cir.1985) (inventory build-up and exploration of sales of two subsidiaries held not material); Greenfield v. Heublein, Inc., 742 F.2d 751 (3d Cir.1984), *cert. denied* 469 U.S. 1215, 105 S.Ct. 1189, 84 L.Ed.2d 336 (1985) (no duty under Rule 10b–5 to disclose merger negotiations where price had not yet been worked out); Jordan v. Duff & Phelps, Inc., 1986 WL 4190, [1986 Transfer Binder] Fed.Sec.L.Rep. (CCH) ¶ 92,724 (N.D.Ill.1986) (no duty to disclose where merger agreement in principle was reached after plaintiff employee's resignation and sale of shares to issuer); Guy v. Duff & Phelps, Inc., 628 F.Supp. 252 (N.D.Ill.1985) (no duty to disclose merger negotiations to resigning vice president who was required to sell his stock upon termination of employment).

31. *See* SEC Form 10Q. *See also* § 9.3 *supra*.

32. *E.g.,* Basic, Inc. v. Levinson, 485 U.S. 224, 108 S.Ct. 978, 99 L.Ed.2d 194 (1988), *on remand* 871 F.2d 562 (6th Cir.1989) which is discussed in §§ 13.5A, 13.5B *supra*. *See* David S. Freeman, Mergers and Acquisitions: Determining Whether and When to Disclose Various Developments in the Evolution of a Merger, 21 Ariz.St.L.J. 425 (1989). *See also, e.g.,* Stephen Schulte, Corporate Public Disclosure: Primer for the Practitioner, 15 Cardozo L. Rev. 971 (1994).

33. *See* Levinson v. Basic, Inc., 786 F.2d 741 (6th Cir.1986) (statement that it was not aware of takeover negotiations was actionable when in fact some talks had taken place) *affirmed and remanded* 485 U.S. 224, 108 S.Ct. 978, 99 L.Ed.2d 194 (1988); Michaels v. Michaels, 767 F.2d 1185 (7th Cir.1985), *cert. denied* 474 U.S. 1057, 106 S.Ct. 797, 88 L.Ed.2d 774 (1986) (merger negotiations involving closely held corporation held material); Grigsby v. CMI Corp., 765 F.2d 1369, 1373 (9th Cir.1985) (materiality of preliminary merger negotiations depends on the facts; a looser or more subjective test is appropriate

votes will implicate the proxy rules' disclosure obligations for those issuers subject to section 12's registration requirement.[34] Decisions to undertake public financing will implicate the registration and disclosure requirements of the 1933 Act. Finally, corporate transactions involving the purchase or sale of the issuer's own securities may well trigger a Rule 10b–5 duty of disclosure.[35] Thus, for example, once a statement has been made by the issuer or one of its representatives, there may be a continuing duty to update and/or correct the information that was previously disseminated.[36] Furthermore, when the initial disclosure has been made in an SEC filing pursuant to a line-item disclosure requirement, the curative disclosure must be made in the appropriate manner, which frequently will require the filing of an amended disclosure form.[37] The duty to correct erroneous information does not mean that once some disclosures have been made, all facts that might be of interest to investors must be disclosed. The duty of further disclosure applies only when failure to do so would make the statement previously made materially misleading in light of subsequent developments.[38] Thus, although Rule 10b–5 standing alone may not trigger an affirmative duty to disclose, an issuer who wants to suppress information that would be

---

with face-to-face transactions as opposed to those on the open market); Paul v. Berkman, 620 F.Supp. 638 (W.D.Pa.1985) (whether preliminary negotiations were material is a question of fact precluding summary judgment); Etshokin v. Texasgulf, Inc., 612 F.Supp. 1220 (N.D.Ill.1985) (statement denying knowledge of causes for increased trading in issuer's stock may be materially misleading for failure to disclose takeover negotiations).

Cf. In re Revlon, Inc., Exch. Act Rel. No. 34–23320, [1986 Transfer Binder] Fed.Sec. L.Rep. (CCH) ¶ 84,006 (June 16, 1986) (finding noncompliance with duty to promptly amend Schedule 14D–9 to reflect defensive negotiations).

34. *E.g.* TSC Industries, Inc. v. Northway, Inc., 426 U.S. 438, 96 S.Ct. 2126, 48 L.Ed.2d 757 (1976).

35. *See e.g.,* Goldberg v. Meridor, 567 F.2d 209 (2d Cir.1977), *cert. denied* 434 U.S. 1069, 98 S.Ct. 1249, 55 L.Ed.2d 771 (1978). *See* § 13.11 *infra.*

36. *See, e.g.,* In re Time Warner, Inc. Securities Litigation, 9 F.3d 259 (2d Cir.1993) (although not accountable for original dissemination of information, there was a duty to update); Backman v. Polaroid Corp., 893 F.2d 1405 (1st Cir.1990) (although not initially misleading, subsequent developments triggered a duty to correct overly optimistic predictions); In re Phillips Petroleum Securities Litigation, 881 F.2d 1236, 1245 (3d Cir.1989); Dowling v. Narragansett Capital Corp., 735 F.Supp. 1105 (D.R.I.1990) (although there may not have been a duty to disclose, such a duty was created upon disclosure of erroneous information); D & N Financial Corp. v. RCM Partners,Ltd. Partnership, 735 F.Supp. 1242, 1252 (D.Del.1990) (duty to correct misleading statements in proxy solicitation); Kirby v. Cullinet Software, Inc., 721 F.Supp. 1444 (D.Mass.1989) (duty to correct first quarter projection). *See also* Dennis J. Block, Stephen A. Radin & Michael B. Carlinsky, A Post– *Polaroid* Snapshot of the Duty to Correct Disclosure, 1991 Colum.Bus.L.Rev. 139; Robert H. Rosenbaum, An Issuer's Duty Under Rule 10b–5 to Correct and Update Materially Misleading Statements, 40 Cath.U.L.Rev. 289 (1991).

However, where the misinformation comes from a third party, there is no duty to correct. *See, e.g.,* Raab v. General Physics Corp., 4 F.3d 286, 288 (4th Cir.1993); Warshaw v. Xoma Corp., 856 F.Supp. 561 (N.D.Cal.1994).

37. *See, e.g.,* Kaufman v. Cooper Cos., Inc., 719 F.Supp. 174 (S.D.N.Y.1989) (quarterly report did not cure misstatements in proxy material sent out 15 days earlier).

38. Backman v. Polaroid Corp., 910 F.2d 10 (1st Cir.1990). *Cf.* Trafton v. Deacon Barclays de Zoete Wedd Ltd., 1994 WL 746199, [1994–1995 Transfer Binder] Fed.Sec. L.Rep. (CCH) ¶ 98,481 (N.D.Cal.1994) (question of fact whether statements were materially misleading in light of subsequent curative disclosures).

relevant to investors must be mindful of the above-mentioned disclosure requirements.

Particularly knotty disclosure problems face publicly traded issuers when there are market rumors concerning the issuer's securities, its fundamental condition, or possible takeover activity.[39] As discussed above, Rule 10b–5 does not create an affirmative disclosure obligation. However, when approached by exchange officials, the press, market researchers, or securities analysts,[40] the issuer is faced with a dilemma. In light of the recent reaffirmation of a materiality standard based upon those facts that a reasonable investor would deem significant in making an investment decision,[41] denying that negotiations are taking place is not a viable alternative.

It seems clear that issuers have no independent obligation to correct rumors that cannot be traced back to the issuer or its representatives.[42] However, the situation is different when the issuer elects to speak. Once a statement has been made, the duty to correct may arise. When presented with a question about market rumors, issuers have two alternatives. The issuer can, of course, respond with full disclosure, which in the case of preliminary negotiations or other sensitive business developments, might be counterproductive. Alternatively, the issuer can issue a "no comment" response. It has been observed that while the "no comment" response may be necessary for business reasons, as issuers develop increasing "no comment" policies, less information will be filtered into the market.[43] On the other hand, the absence of information clearly is preferable to the presence of misleading information.

Even a "no comment" response will not always be a safe harbor. If the issuer, or its agents, is responsible for leaks of sensitive information or market rumors, the SEC takes the position that the issuer is under a duty to correct any misinformation.[44] Although this proposition has not been definitively tested in the courts, it reflects a proper reading of the

---

39. *E.g.,* In re Time Warner, Inc. Securities Litigation, 9 F.3d 259 (2d Cir.1993) (company was not accountable for unattributed statements reported in the press but could have been held accountable for official statements; as to both categories of statements, there was a duty to update the information once it became materially misleading). On the issue of rumor-control, *see* Symposium, Affirmative Disclosure Obligations Under the Securities Laws, 46 Md.L.Rev. 907 (1987); John H. Matheson, Corporate Disclosure Obligations and the Parameters of Rule 10b–5: *Basic Inc. v. Levinson* and Beyond, 14 J.Corp.L. 1 (1988).

40. *See, e.g.,* Note, Rule 10b–5 and Voluntary Corporate Disclosures to Securities Analysts, 92 Colum. L. Rev. 1517 (1992).

41. Basic, Inc. v. Levinson, 485 U.S. 224, 108 S.Ct. 978, 99 L.Ed.2d 194 (1988), *on remand* 871 F.2d 562 (6th Cir.1989).

42. *See, e.g.,* Raab v. General Physics Corp., 4 F.3d 286, 288 (4th Cir.1993); Warshaw v. Xoma Corp., 856 F.Supp. 561 (N.D.Cal.1994) (no duty to correct misinformation from a third party).

43. *See, e.g.,* Little Can be Done to Stop Rumors, Exchange Officials, Others Tell Forum, 18 Sec. Reg. & L. Rep. (BNA) 253 (Feb. 25, 1986).

44. *See* In re Carnation Co., Sec. Exch. Act Rel. No. 34–22214, [1985–86 Transfer Binder] Fed. Sec. L. Rep. (CCH) ¶ 83,801 (July 8, 1985).

issuer's obligations. Thus, issuers must take care to manage their proprietary information, not only for insider trading reasons but also to prevent being forced into premature disclosures by the existence of market rumors due to leaked information. Caution dictates that public companies not only develop information policies, including the creation of an information ombudsman, but also it is wise to limit the issuer's personnel who are authorized to divulge information or respond to outside questions.

Issuers are thus placed in a very difficult position. When approached by a member of the press or a securities analyst, the issuer may not be able to get away with a "no comment" response. If an issuer is engaged in merger negotiations and, for example, has an upcoming meeting with securities analysts and decides to cancel the meeting, if the cancellation results in rumors, is the issuer in a position that it now has to come forward and clarify the facts behind the rumors? Some attorneys suggest that as a preventive measure, issuers adopt a policy of not commenting on acquisitions negotiations; thus, when a question is posed, silence by the issuer can be supported by a recitation of the policy. Another possible solution that has been suggested is for the SEC to adopt a safe harbor rule governing responses to such inquiries; however, it seems difficult, if not impossible, to fashion a meaningful safe harbor (other than implementation of a "no comment" policy) in light of the highly factual nature of each situation. In the absence of such a rule, any response other than silence or "no comment" may result in a violation.[45] Of course, periodic reporting obligations may in and of themselves trigger the duty to disclose, once the materiality threshold has been reached.[46] There is thus a different process that applies in determining the necessity of disclosure when dealing with line item disclosures in required filings as opposed to under the antifraud provisions generally.[47]

§ 13.11 Corporate Mismanagement, Rule 10b–5 and the Deception Requirement

Although directed at securities fraud, over its history Rule 10b–5 has had a role to play in preventing corporate mismanagement that results in deception in connection with a purchase or sale of securities. While the high water mark for Rule 10b–5 in mismanagement cases seems to be in the past, the rule still may have some impact in regulating corporate management practices.[1]

---

45. *See* authorities in footnotes 17, 39 *supra.*

46. *See* § 13.5A *supra.*

47. *See* Joseph I. Goldstein, William E. Donnelly & Ida C. Wurczinger, Disclosure of a Potential Change in Corporate Control, 19 Rev.Sec. & Commodities Reg. 133 (1986). *See also* Symposium *supra* footnote 33.

§ 13.11

1. For a review of both the rise and decline of Rule 10b–5 as a weapon against corporate mismanagement *see* Harold S. Bloomenthal, From Birnbaum to Schoenbaum: The Exchange Act and Self–Aggrandizement, 15 N.Y.L.F. 332 (1969); John C. Coffee, Jr.,

Section 10(b) prohibits "manipulative or deceptive" practices as defined by SEC rules.[2] In 1971 the Supreme Court in Superintendent of Insurance v. Bankers Life & Casualty Co.[3] announced that Rule 10b–5 is violated when there is deception touching the purchase or sale of a security even if the acts complained of amount to no more than corporate mismanagement. The defendants, management of an insurance company, caused the company to part with its assets which consisted of marketable securities. The Court upheld the 10b–5 claim since the corporation was forced to part with its securities and thus the "seller was duped into believing that it * * * would receive the proceeds."[4] As a result of the Court's ruling, 10b–5 became a potential remedy to redress corporate mismanagement. The 10b–5 mismanagement remedy continued to garner great support[5] until the Supreme Court's ruling in Santa Fe Industries, Inc. v. Green.[6]

The *Santa Fe* case involved a claim by a shareholder who was frozen out by the majority pursuant to a short-form merger. The parent corporation complied with the requirements set out by the applicable Delaware short form merger statute and disclosed all of the required information to both the minority shareholders and the independent appraiser. The plaintiff claimed that since the cashout price was low, the transaction operated as a fraud or deceit upon him within the

---

Beyond the Shut–Eyed Sentry, 63 Va.L.Rev. 1099 (1977); Boyd Kimball Dyer, Essay on Federalism in Private Actions Under Rule 10b–5, 1976 Utah L.Rev. 7; Arnold S. Jacobs, Role of Securities Exchange Act Rule 10b–5 in the Regulation of Corporate Management, 59 Cornell L. Rev. 27 (1973); Richard W. Jennings, Federalization of Corporation Law: Part Way or All the Way?, 31 Bus.Law. 991 (1976); Thomas C. Roantree III, Continuing Development of Rule 10b–5 as a Means of Enforcing the Fiduciary Duties of Directors and Controlling Shareholders, 34 U.Pitt.L.Rev. 201 (1972); Thomas J. Sherrard, Fiduciaries and Fairness Under Rule 10b–5, 29 Vand.L.Rev. 1385 (1976); Note, The Controlling Influence Standard in Rule 10b–5 Corporate Mismanagement Cases, 86 Harv.L.Rev. 1007 (1973); Comment, *Schoenbaum v. Firstbrook*, The New Fraud Expands Federal Corporation Law, 55 Va.L.Rev. 1103 (1969). *See also* the authorities in footnote 6 *infra* for discussion of more recent developments.

2. 15 U.S.C.A. § 78j(b). Rule 10b–5 is not the only such rule. The other rules promulgated under section 10(b) are discussed in § 12.1 *supra*.

3. 404 U.S. 6, 92 S.Ct. 165, 30 L.Ed.2d 128 (1971).

4. *Id.* at 9, 92 S.Ct. at 167.

5. *See, e.g.,* Marshel v. AFW Fabric Corp., 533 F.2d 1277 (2d Cir.1976), *vacated* 429 U.S. 881, 97 S.Ct. 228, 50 L.Ed.2d 162 (1976), *on remand* 441 F.Supp. 299, (S.D.N.Y.1977); Bailey v. Meister Brau, Inc., 535 F.2d 982 (7th Cir.1976); Drachman v. Harvey, 453 F.2d 722 (2d Cir.1971); Bailes v. Colonial Press, Inc., 444 F.2d 1241 (5th Cir.1971); Shell v. Hensley, 430 F.2d 819 (5th Cir.1970). *See also, e.g.,* Schoenbaum v. Firstbrook, 405 F.2d 215 (2d Cir.1968), *cert. denied* 395 U.S. 906, 89 S.Ct. 1747, 23 L.Ed.2d 219 (1969); Pappas v. Moss, 393 F.2d 865 (3d Cir.1968), *on remand* 303 F.Supp. 1257 (D.N.J.1969); Dasho v. Susquehanna Corp., 380 F.2d 262 (7th Cir.), *cert. denied* 389 U.S. 977, 88 S.Ct. 480, 19 L.Ed.2d 470 (1967); O'Neill v. Maytag, 339 F.2d 764 (2d Cir.1964); Ruckle v. Roto American Corp., 339 F.2d 24 (2d Cir.1964); Ernest L. Folk III, Corporation Law Developments–1969, 56 Va.L.Rev. 755, 806–84 (1970); Note, The Controlling Influence Standard in Rule 10b–5 Corporate Mismanagement Cases, 86 Harv.L.Rev. 1007 (1973). Comment, *Schoenbaum v. Firstbrook*, The New Fraud Expands Federal Corporation Law, 55 Va. L.Rev. 1103 (1969). *See* the authorities cited in footnote 1 *supra*.

6. 430 U.S. 462, 97 S.Ct. 1292, 51 L.Ed.2d 480 (1977), *on remand* 562 F.2d 4 (2d Cir.1977).

meaning of Rule 10b–5(3). The Supreme Court responded that in order to state a 10b–5 claim the plaintiff must show an element of "deception" that was lacking in the allegations in *Santa Fe*. The Court pointed out that a number of states did not provide a cause of action for breaches of fiduciary duty in connection with freeze-out transactions and thus to rule otherwise in the case at hand would be to federalize the corporate law of directors' obligation,[7] and refused to impose a higher standard than the applicable state law.[8] Although Delaware has recently narrowed its state law remedy that was recognized just after *Santa Fe*,[9] many states recognize a broader judicial remedy against corporate freeze outs.[10]

7. 430 U.S. at 479 n. 16, 97 S.Ct. at 1304 n. 16. Delaware subsequently recognized such a remedy under its state law. *See, e.g.,* Najjar v. Roland International Corp., 387 A.2d 709 (Del.Ch.1978), *judgment affirmed* 407 A.2d 1032 (1979); Young v. Valhi, Inc., 382 A.2d 1372 (Del.Ch.1978); Kemp v. Angel, 381 A.2d 241 (Del.Ch.1977); Lynch v. Vickers Energy Corp., 383 A.2d 278 (Del.1977), *on remand* 402 A.2d 5 (1979), *appeal after remand* 429 A.2d 497 (1981); Singer v. Magnavox Co., 380 A.2d 969 (Del.1977); Tanzer v. International General Industries, Inc., 379 A.2d 1121 (Del.1977), *on remand* 402 A.2d 382 (1979). However, the Delaware remedy was shortlived. Weinberger v. UOP, Inc., 457 A.2d 701 (Del.1983), *appeal after remand* 497 A.2d 792 (1985) (severely limiting the state remedy).

Santa Fe might well come out differently today in states recognizing a remedy for freeze outs. *See, e.g.,* Goldberg v. Meridor, 567 F.2d 209 (2d Cir.1977), *cert. denied* 434 U.S. 1069, 98 S.Ct. 1249, 55 L.Ed.2d 771 (1978). *But see* Biesenbach v. Guenther, 588 F.2d 400 (3d Cir.1978).

8. The Court also pointed out that scrutiny of "fairness" under Rule 10b–5 is "at best a subsidiary purpose" of the federal securities laws. 430 U.S. at 478, 97 S.Ct. at 1303, 1304. Any such expansion of the 10b–5 remedy would, according to the Court, have been in conflict with recent restrictions on implied remedies. *See* § 13.1 *supra*.

9. Weinberger v. UOP, Inc., 457 A.2d 701 (Del.Sup.1983), *appeal after remand* 497 A.2d 792 (1985). The court there held that lack of a business purpose was no longer a basis for overturning a freeze out. The court stated that a dissenting shareholder has a right to fair treatment and in most cases, the new liberalized appraisal method established in that opinion would suffice. *See also, e.g.,* Susman v. Lincoln American Corp., 578 F.Supp. 1041 (N.D.Ill.1984). It remains unclear how much, if any, of the prior Delaware case law remains in force. *See* authorities in footnote 10 *infra*.

10. *See, e.g.,* Lebold v. Inland Steel Co., 125 F.2d 369 (7th Cir.1941), *cert. denied* 316 U.S. 675, 62 S.Ct. 1045, 86 L.Ed. 1749 (1942) (awarding damages under a state law claim attacking a freeze out effected by a voluntary dissolution); Rabkin v. Philip A. Hunt Chemical Corp., 498 A.2d 1099, (Del.1985), (appraisal remedy not exclusive); Singer v. Magnavox Co., 380 A.2d 969 (Del.1977) (upholding complaint against a merger whose sole purpose was allegedly to freeze out the minority); Tanzer v. International General Industries, Inc., 379 A.2d 1121 (Del.1977), *on remand* 402 A.2d 382 (1979) (denying preliminary injunction); David J. Greene & Co. v. Schenley Industries, Inc., 281 A.2d 30 (Del.Ch.1971) (denying preliminary injunction); Stauffer v. Standard Brands Inc., 41 Del.Ch. 7, 187 A.2d 78 (1962) (limiting the dissenter to the statutory appraisal remedy); Gabhart v. Gabhart, 267 Ind. 370, 370 N.E.2d 345 (1977) (refusing to limit the shareholder's remedy to statutory appraisal where there was no showing of legitimate corporate purpose); Alpert v. 28 Williams Street Corp., 63 N.Y.2d 557, 483 N.Y.S.2d 667, 473 N.E.2d 19 (1984), *reargument denied* 64 N.Y.2d 1041, 489 N.Y.S.2d 1028, 478 N.E.2d 211 (1985) (upholding freeze-out remedy); People v. Concord Fabrics, Inc., 50 A.D.2d 787, 377 N.Y.S.2d 84 (1975), *affirming* 83 Misc.2d 120, 371 N.Y.S.2d 550 (1975) (enjoining merger on the grounds of unfairness in freezing out the minority); Blumenthal v. Roosevelt Hotel, Inc., 202 Misc. 988, 115 N.Y.S.2d 52 (1952) (holding the statutory appraisal right to be plaintiff's exclusive remedy). *But see* Weinberger v. UOP, Inc., 457 A.2d 701 (Del.1983), *appeal after remand* 497 A.2d 792 (1985) (indicating that in the future judicial remedy will be rare).

See generally 3 James D. Cox, Thomas L. Hazen & F. Hodge O'Neal, Corporations § 23.4 (1995).

In the wake of the *Santa Fe* decision commentators were quick to
predict a demise of 10b–5's role in the area of corporate mismanagement.[11] However, there are five post–*Santa Fe* court of appeals decisions
that have taken an expansive reading of Rule 10b–5 and a correspond-
ingly narrow reading of the Supreme Court's decision.[12] Under these
and other decisions, it is clear that the fact that mismanagement is
involved does not preclude a Rule 10b–5 claim for material misrepresentations.[13] However, it is clear that, standing alone, a breach of fiduciary
duty is not a securities law violation.[14]

In Goldberg v. Meridor[15] the defendant parent corporation caused a
controlled subsidiary to issue common stock and convertible debentures.
The offering raised seven million dollars in cash which was in turn
loaned to its direct parent corporation. The public offering was followed
by an exchange of assets whereby the controlling parent sold its assets to
the subsidiary in return for stock in the subsidiary. After the transactions were completed the direct parent's sole asset was the stock of the
subsidiary, in which the plaintiff was a minority shareholder, and the
subsidiary had acquired all of the parent's assets and liabilities (including the seven million dollar debt running to the subsidiary). The
plaintiff brought suit under Rule 10b–5 claiming that the defendant
caused its subsidiary to issue stock in the public offering for the benefit
of the controlling parents and that the subsequent exchange of assets
was inadequate consideration and thus operated as a fraud against the
subsidiary in the issuance of its own shares.[16] The Second Circuit
applied the "controlling influence" doctrine.[17] Under the controlling
influence doctrine, for a transaction in which the decision makers are
controlled directors, the standard of disclosure is measured by what
would have been material to a disinterested director dealing at arms
length.[18] Although disclosure to the shareholders would not have direct-

---

11.   *See* the authorities cited in footnote 10 *supra*.

12.   Healey v. Catalyst Recovery of Pennsylvania, 616 F.2d 641 (3d Cir.1980); Kidwell v.
Meikle, 597 F.2d 1273 (9th Cir.1979); Alabama Farm Bureau Mutual Casualty Co. v.
American Fidelity Life Insurance Co., 606 F.2d 602 (5th Cir.1979), *rehearing denied* 610
F.2d 818 (5th Cir.1980); Wright v. Heizer Corp., 560 F.2d 236 (7th Cir.1977), *cert. denied*
434 U.S. 1066, 98 S.Ct. 1243, 55 L.Ed.2d 767 (1978); Goldberg v. Meridor, 567 F.2d 209
(2d Cir.1977), *cert. denied* 434 U.S. 1069, 98 S.Ct. 1249, 55 L.Ed.2d 771 (1978). *See also*
Madison Consultants v. FDIC, 710 F.2d 57 (2d Cir.1983). *But cf.* Biesenbach v. Guenther,
588 F.2d 400 (3d Cir.1978); Valente v. PepsiCo., Inc., 454 F.Supp. 1228 (D.Del.1978).

13.   *See, e.g.,* In re Wells Fargo Securities Litigation, 12 F.3d 922 (9th Cir.1993).

14.   *See* footnote 40 *infra*.

15.   567 F.2d 209 (2d Cir.1977), *cert. denied* 434 U.S. 1069, 98 S.Ct. 1249, 55 L.Ed.2d
771 (1978).

16.   *Id.* at 211.

17.   *See* Schoenbaum v. Firstbrook, 405 F.2d 200 (2d Cir.1968), *cert. denied* 395 U.S.
906, 89 S.Ct. 1747, 23 L.Ed.2d 219 (1969) and the other authorities in notes 5 *supra* and 18
infra.

18.   The claim that the minority has been unfairly frozen out has been used as the basis
of recovery in both federal and state courts. *See, e.g.,* Marshel v. AFW Fabric Corp., 533
F.2d 1277 (2d Cir.1976), *vacated as moot* 429 U.S. 881, 97 S.Ct. 228, 50 L.Ed.2d 162 (1976),
on remand 441 F.Supp. 299 (S.D.N.Y.1977) (allowing a 10b–5 remedy for freezing out the
minority); Schlick v. Penn–Dixie Cement Corp., 507 F.2d 374 (2d Cir.), *cert. denied* 421

ly affected the corporate decision in question, the court reasoned that armed with material facts of the transactions, shareholders would have been able to avail themselves of a remedy at state law.[19] Accordingly, the Second Circuit in *Goldberg* held that disclosure of the unfair exchange would have been the basis of an injunction under New York law and thus the plaintiffs were deceived into not seeking that relief.[20] As a second justification for the requisite deception and causation elements, the court pointed out that public disclosure of all relevant facts might have shamed the subsidiary's directors into voting against the transactions with its parents rather than hanging its dirty linen out in public.[21]

Four other circuit courts have followed the Second Circuit's ruling that material non-disclosure that denied minority shareholders their opportunity to seek an injunction under state law[22] is sufficient to satisfy the deception requirement of *Santa Fe*.[23] The *Goldberg* rationale has been used by the Seventh Circuit in a successful challenge to the defendant corporation's issuance of securities at less than fair value.[24] The Fifth Circuit, in reasoning reminiscent of the "controlling influence" doctrine,[25] recognized a 10b–5 claim challenging a stock repurchase at an unfairly inflated price.[26] The Ninth Circuit has upheld a Rule 10b–5 attack on a sale of assets where management was fully aware of the relevant facts; there was no shareholder vote and hence no deception of the decision makers.[27] The Third Circuit has applied the

U.S. 976, 95 S.Ct. 1976, 44 L.Ed.2d 467 (1975) (upholding a 10b–5 market manipulation claim in connection with a statutory merger); Bryan v. Brock & Blevins Co., 490 F.2d 563 (5th Cir.1974), *cert. denied* 419 U.S. 844, 95 S.Ct. 77, 42 L.Ed.2d 72 (1974) (striking down a freeze-out merger under both state law and Rule 10b–5 for the lack of a valid business purpose).

19. 567 F.2d at 218–19. The court also noted the allegation that the transaction involved "wholly inadequate consideration."

20. *Id.* at 219–20.

21. *Id.* at 218–19.

22. *See* Scott E. Jordan, Loss of State Claims as a Basis for Rule 10b–5 and 14a–9 Action: The Impact of *Virginia Bankshares, Inc. v. Sandberg*, 49 Bus. Law. 295 (1993).

23. Healey v. Catalyst Recovery of Pennsylvania, 616 F.2d 641 (3d Cir.1980); Kidwell v. Meikle, 597 F.2d 1273 (9th Cir.1979); Alabama Farm Bureau Mutual Casualty Co. v. American Fidelity Life Insurance Co., 606 F.2d 602 (5th Cir.1979), *rehearing denied* 610 F.2d 818 (5th Cir.1980); Wright v. Heizer Corp., 560 F.2d 236 (7th Cir.1977), *cert. denied* 434 U.S. 1066, 98 S.Ct. 1243, 55 L.Ed.2d 767 (1978). *See also* In re PHLCORP Securities Tender Offer Litigation, 700 F.Supp. 1265 (S.D.N.Y.1988) (failure to disclose appraisal remedy stated a Rule 10b–5 claim).

24. Wright v. Heizer Corp., 560 F.2d 236 (7th Cir.1977), *cert. denied* 434 U.S. 1066, 98 S.Ct. 1243, 55 L.Ed.2d 767 (1978).

25. *See* footnote 18 *supra*.

26. Alabama Farm Bureau Mutual Casualty Co. v. American Fidelity Life Insurance Co., 606 F.2d 602 (5th Cir.1979), *rehearing denied* 610 F.2d 818 (5th Cir.1980).

27. Kidwell v. Meikle, 597 F.2d 1273 (9th Cir.1979). The court noted: "There is room for Rule 10b–5 liability after Santa Fe Industries even when the only deceived parties are shareholders who are not entitled to vote on the transaction in question, and even though there may be a breach of fiduciary duty under state law. Indeed, under the Goldberg rationale, it is precisely because there are state-law remedies that a deception can be found." *Id.* at 1292. *See also, e.g.,* Cooper v. Hwang, 1987 WL 16949 (N.D.Cal.1987); Friedlander v. Nims, 571 F.Supp. 1188 (N.D.Ga.1983), *appeal dismissed* 747 F.2d 1467 (11th Cir.1984).

Goldberg rationale to a controlled merger[28] but held in an earlier case that merely failing to disclose breaches of fiduciary duty would not support a claim.[29] The Sixth Circuit has recently employed the "loss of remedy" theory of causation in the context of a going private transaction. In Howing Co. v. Nationwide Corp.,[30] the court upheld a claim that material omissions that allegedly deprived plaintiffs of their state law appraisal remedy were sufficient to support an action under section 13(e)'s going private requirements.[31]

All of the above cases involved allegations of transactions involving self-dealing and conflicts of interest. It has been held that ratification by a disinterested board will bar recovery unless the decision makers were deceived.[32] Unfairness of a merger will not state a 10b–5 claim without some allegations of deception.[33] Where a merger of a wholly owned insurance subsidiary into its parent allegedly injured policyholders, the lack of deception precluded a Rule 10b–5 claim.[34] Also, dismissal was warranted where the plaintiff in a derivative suit had knowledge of the alleged nondisclosures concerning breaches of fiduciary duty.[35]

The Fifth Circuit held that in order for a plaintiff to maintain a Rule 10b–5 action, it is not necessary to prove the success of the state law remedy; but rather, all that need be shown is that upon full disclosure, the plaintiff in state court would have been able to make out a *prima facie* case.[36] The Second Circuit formulated the test differently and thus has indicated that in order to succeed the plaintiff must prove "by a fair

28.   Healey v. Catalyst Recovery of Pennsylvania, 616 F.2d 641 (3d Cir.1980).

29.   Biesenbach v. Guenther, 588 F.2d 400 (3d Cir.1978).

30.   972 F.2d 700 (6th Cir.1992), *cert. denied* __ U.S. __, 113 S.Ct. 1645, 123 L.Ed.2d 266 (1993). *See also* the discussion of causation in § 13.6 *supra*.

31.   15 U.S.C.A. § 78m(e). The going private rules are discussed in § 11.17 *supra*.

32.   *See* Tyco Labs, Inc. v. Kimball, 444 F.Supp. 292 (E.D.Pa.1977). *See also,* Maldonado v. Flynn, 448 F.Supp. 1032 (S.D.N.Y.1978), *affirmed in part & reversed in part* 597 F.2d 789 (2d Cir.1979), *on remand* 477 F.Supp. 1007 (S.D.N.Y.1979); Browning Debenture Holders' Committee v. DASA Corp., 560 F.2d 1078 (2d Cir.1977), *on remand* 454 F.Supp. 88 (S.D.N.Y.1978), *judgment affirmed* 605 F.2d 35 (2d Cir.1978); Goldberger v. Baker, 442 F.Supp. 659 (S.D.N.Y.1977).

33.   Susman v. Lincoln American Corp., 578 F.Supp. 1041 (N.D.Ill.1984); Augenstein v. McCormick & Co., 581 F.Supp. 452 (D.Md.1984); Halle & Stieglitz, Filor, Bullard, Inc. v. Empress International, Ltd., 442 F.Supp. 217 (D.Del.1977), Altman v. Knight, 431 F.Supp. 309 (S.D.N.Y.1977). *See also* Goldman v. Belden, 580 F.Supp. 1373, 1378 (W.D.N.Y.1984), *judgment vacated* 754 F.2d 1059 (2d Cir.1985); In re PHLCORP Securities Tender Offer Litigation, 700 F.Supp. 1265 (S.D.N.Y.1988).

34.   Superintendent of Insurance v. Freedman, 443 F.Supp. 628 (S.D.N.Y.1977), *affirmed* 594 F.2d 842 (Fed.Cir.1979). *Cf.* Superintendent of Insurance v. Bankers Life & Casualty Co., 404 U.S. 6, 92 S.Ct. 165, 30 L.Ed.2d 128 (1971), *on remand* 401 F.Supp. 640 (S.D.N.Y.1975) (where the plaintiff in bankruptcy could represent claims of policyholders). *See* Morris W. Macey, Protection of Creditor's Rights Through Use of Rule 10b–5, 76 Com.L.J. 133 (1971).

35.   Ray v. Karris, 780 F.2d 636 (7th Cir.1985).

36.   Alabama Farm Bureau Mutual Casualty Co. v. American Fidelity Life Insurance Co., 606 F.2d 602 (5th Cir.1979), *rehearing denied* 610 F.2d 818 (5th Cir.1980). *See also* Meyers v. Moody, 475 F.Supp. 232, 244–46 (N.D.Tex.1979), *judgment affirmed* 693 F.2d 1196 (5th Cir.1982), *rehearing denied* 701 F.2d 173 (5th Cir.1983).

preponderance of the evidence" the existence of the state claim in the 10b–5 action.[37] In contrast, the Ninth Circuit applied an actual success test, asking whether the plaintiff would have prevailed in state court.[38]

Notwithstanding the rapid acceptance of the *Goldberg* rationale, it clearly is in conflict with what many view as the spirit of the *Santa Fe* decision.[39] Accordingly, while it is to be expected that a very limited reading of the *Santa Fe* decision will most likely continue to dominate, eventual resolution of the question must await additional Supreme Court clarification. Notwithstanding the narrow reading that many courts have given to *Santa Fe*'s limitations on the Rule 10b–5 remedy, it remains clear that a claim that states merely a breach of fiduciary duty will not be sufficient under Rule 10b–5.[40] As observed by the D.C.Circuit Court of Appeals, the securities laws provide an "intelligible conceptual line excluding the Commission from corporate governance." [41]

Section 10(b)'s deception requirement received additional attention from the Supreme Court in Schreiber v. Burlington Northern, Inc.,[42] wherein it was held that manipulative conduct does not violate section 14(e)'s tender offer antifraud provision[43] unless the conduct complained of is also deceptive.[44] In so ruling the Court emphasized that the thrust of the deception requirement is to address materially misleading statements and omissions. The *Schreiber* decision reinforces the fact that attempting to characterize a breach of fiduciary duty as manipulative will not elevate it to a Rule 10b–5 violation absent the type of deception required in the *Santa Fe Industries* case.

---

37. Madison Consultants v. FDIC, 710 F.2d 57 (2d Cir.1983).

38. Kidwell v. Meikle, 597 F.2d 1273, 1294 (9th Cir.1979). *See also* Wright v. Heizer Corp., 560 F.2d 236, 250–251 (7th Cir.1977), *cert. denied* 434 U.S. 1066, 98 S.Ct. 1243, 55 L.Ed.2d 767 (1978). *See* Thomas L. Hazen, Breaches of Fiduciary Duty and the Federal Securities Laws, 61 N.C.L. Rev. 527, 531 (1983).

39. Thus, the majority has neatly undone the holdings of *Green, Piper* and *Cort* by creating a federal cause of action for a breach of fiduciary duty that will apply in all cases, save for those rare instances where the fiduciary denounces himself in advance * * *. This only serves to reinforce what I have sought to demonstrate, namely, that this complaint sounds entirely in state law.

Goldberg v. Meridor, 567 F.2d 209, 225 (2d Cir.1977), *cert. denied* 434 U.S. 1069, 98 S.Ct. 1249, 55 L.Ed.2d 771 (1978) (Meskill, J., dissenting in part). *See, e.g.,* In re Sears Roebuck & Co. Securities Litigation, 792 F.Supp. 977 (E.D.Pa.1992) (proxy statement's failure to disclose suit under state law for mismanagement and breach of fiduciary duty was not a material omission); Vachon v. BayBanks, Inc., 780 F.Supp. 79 (D.Mass.1991) (alleged inadequate loan loss reserves and departures from loan policies did not state securities fraud claim against bank). *Compare* Kidwell v. Meikle, 597 F.2d 1273, 1292 (9th Cir.1979), quoted in footnote 27 *supra*. *See also* the authorities cited in footnote 6 *supra*.

40. *E.g.,* Boone v. Carlsbad Bancorporation, Inc., 972 F.2d 1545, 1557 (10th Cir.1992) (refusal to federalize claims for breach of fiduciary duty; although transaction may have had problems involving self-dealing, that was a matter of state corporate law rather than federal securities law); Davidson v. Belcor, Inc., 933 F.2d 603 (7th Cir.1991).

41. Business Roundtable v. SEC, 905 F.2d 406 (D.C.Cir.1990) (invalidating SEC Rule 19c–4's regulation of substantive voting rights). *See* § 11.1 *supra*.

42. 472 U.S. 1, 105 S.Ct. 2458, 86 L.Ed.2d 1 (1985).

43. 15 U.S.C.A. § 78n(e). *See* §§ 11.15, 11.19 *supra*.

44. *See also* the discussion in § 12.1 *supra*.

Dismissal of Derivative Suits

Although not generally a matter of federal securities law, it is worth noting a few observations dealing with decisions regarding independent director committees' dismissal of shareholder derivative suits.[45] The state law is in conflict as to whether the decision of independent committees will be conclusive.[46] Two decisions are worthy of special note. In Burks v. Lasker[47] the Supreme Court held that the policy of the Investment Company Act and its requirements for independent directors did not necessarily preclude dismissal of a derivative suit by a special litigation committee. More recently, in Daily Income Fund, Inc. v. Fox,[48] the Court held that a demand need not be made upon the directors of an investment company in a shareholder suit claiming an excessive advisory fee had been authorized by the directors. The courts have not found the same compelling policy under the Exchange Act's proxy rules[49] or Rule 10b–5; accordingly state law governs the propriety of dismissal by independent committees.[50]

In another significant decision, the Second Circuit in Joy v. North[51] applied Connecticut law to overrule an independent committee's decision to dismiss a derivative suit charging "direct economic injury to the corporation diminishing the value of the shareholder's investment as a consequence of fraud, mismanagement or self-dealing."[52] Although fed-

---

45. *See generally* James D. Cox, Thomas L. Hazen & F. Hodge O'Neal, footnote 10 *supra*, ch. 15; Harry G. Henn & John R. Alexander, Laws of Corporations § 367 (3d ed. 1983); Dennis J. Block & H. Adam Prussin, The Business Judgment Rule and Shareholder Derivative Actions: Viva Zapata?, 37 Bus.Law. 27 (1981); John C. Coffee, Jr. & Donald E. Schwartz, The Survival of the Derivative Suit: An Evaluation and Proposal for Legislative Reform, 81 Colum.L.Rev. 261 (1981); James D. Cox, Searching for the Corporation's Voice in Derivative Suit Litigation: A Critique of *Zapata* and the ALI Project, 1982 Duke L.J. 959; George W. Dent, Jr., The Power of Directors to Terminate Shareholder Litigation: The Death of the Derivative Suit?, 75 Nw.U.L.Rev. 96 (1980); Marc I. Steinberg, The Use of Special Litigation Committees to Terminate Shareholder Derivative Suits, 35 U.Miami L.Rev. 1 (1980).

46. *Compare, e.g.,* Maldonado v. Flynn, 671 F.2d 729 (2d Cir.1982), *on remand* 573 F.Supp. 684 (S.D.N.Y.1983) (upholding decision of committee) *with* Zapata Corp. v. Maldonado, 430 A.2d 779, 788 (Del.1981) (independent directors must prove that they exercised business judgment and then court will exercise its "independent business judgment" in determining if dismissal serves the corporation's best interests).

47. 441 U.S. 471, 99 S.Ct. 1831, 60 L.Ed.2d 404 (1979).

48. 464 U.S. 523, 104 S.Ct. 831, 78 L.Ed.2d 645 (1984).

49. 17 C.F.R. § 240.14a–9. *See* §§ 11.3–11.5 *supra*.

50. *E.g.* Maldonado v. Flynn, 671 F.2d 729 (2d Cir.1982), *on remand* 573 F.Supp. 684 (S.D.N.Y.1983); Abbey v. Control Data Corp., 603 F.2d 724 (8th Cir.1979), *cert. denied* 444 U.S. 1017, 100 S.Ct. 670, 62 L.Ed.2d 647 (1980); Lewis v. Anderson, 615 F.2d 778 (9th Cir.1979), *cert. denied* 449 U.S. 869, 101 S.Ct. 206, 66 L.Ed.2d 89 (1980); Gall v. Exxon Corp., 418 F.Supp. 508 (S.D.N.Y.1976). *But see* Galef v. Alexander, 615 F.2d 51 (2d Cir.1980) (where directors had approved challenged transaction federal law, and the policy of section 14(a) of the Exchange Act precluded dismissal by them even if state law would permit it).

51. 692 F.2d 880 (2d Cir.1982), *cert. denied* 460 U.S. 1051, 103 S.Ct. 1498, 75 L.Ed.2d 930 (1983).

52. *Id.* at 891. The court adopted the Delaware rule that "directors may obtain a dismissal only if the trial court finds both (a) that the committee was independent, acted in good faith and made a reasonable investigation; and (b) that in the court's independent

eral law was not at issue, it is significant that the court applied a higher level of scrutiny to decisions regarding investor protection.[53]

§ 13.12   The Effect of Plaintiff's Conduct on Implied Civil Liability: Due Diligence; In Pari Delicto

Plaintiff's Due Diligence

In order to recover in an action for common law fraud, plaintiffs are required to prove that their reliance was reasonable.[1] As a corollary, the federal courts developed a requirement that the plaintiff in a Rule 10b–5 action must have acted with due diligence with regard to the transaction in question.[2] The plaintiff's due diligence requirement developed initially along negligence lines.[3] However, in Rule 10b–5 cases, it seems unquestionable that this has been changed by the Supreme Court's imposition of a scienter requirement upon defendant's conduct which impliedly raises the level of plaintiff's standard of conduct.[4] As discussed earlier,[5] reliance is an element of a 10b–5 claim and the courts have held that this includes the requirement that the reliance be reasonable. In contrast, plaintiff's lack of due diligence is properly viewed as a defense; accordingly, plaintiff's failure to allege that he or she acted with due diligence is not fatal to a Rule 10b–5 claim.[6]

Since in Rule 10b–5 cases, it is unquestionable that the defendant must have acted with scienter, a sense of balance has led a number of

---

business judgment as to the corporation's best interest, the action should be dismissed." *Id.,* relying upon Zapata Corp. v. Maldonado, 430 A.2d 779 (Del.1981).

53. *Cf.* Thomas L. Hazen, Corporate Chartering and the Securities Markets: Shareholder Suffrage, Corporate Responsibility and Managerial Accountability, 1978 Wis.L.Rev. 391.

§ 13.12

1. Restatement, Second, Torts § 537 (1976); W. Page Keeton, Dan B. Dobbs, Robert E. Keeton & David G. Owen, Prosser and Keeton on Torts § 108 (5th ed. 1984). The reliance requirement is discussed in § 13.5B *supra.*

2. *E.g.* Thompson v. Smith Barney, Harris Upham & Co., 709 F.2d 1413 (11th Cir.1983); Dupuy v. Dupuy, 551 F.2d 1005 (5th Cir.), *cert. denied* 434 U.S. 911, 98 S.Ct. 312, 54 L.Ed.2d 197 (1977); Straub v. Vaisman & Co., 540 F.2d 591, 598 (3d Cir.1976); Bird v. Ferry, 497 F.2d 112 (5th Cir.1974), *rehearing denied* 503 F.2d 567 (5th Cir.1974); Vohs v. Dickson, 495 F.2d 607 (5th Cir.1974).

3. Rochez Brothers v. Rhoades, 491 F.2d 402 (3d Cir.1973), *on remand* 390 F.Supp. 470 (W.D.Pa.1974), *judgment affirmed* 527 F.2d 880 (3d Cir.1975); Clement A. Evans & Co. v. McAlpine, 434 F.2d 100, 103 (5th Cir.1970).

4. *E.g.,* Stephenson v. Paine Webber Jackson & Curtis, Inc., 839 F.2d 1095 (5th Cir.1988) (investor's delay in reporting unlawful trades after having become aware of improprieties in his account was more than mere negligence and thus satisfied the reckless standard for showing a lack of due diligence); Xaphes v. Merrill Lynch, Pierce, Fenner & Smith, Inc., 600 F.Supp. 692, 694–95 (D.Me.1985) (absent a finding of at least recklessness, plaintiff acted with due diligence). *See* Margaret V. Sachs, The Relevance of Tort Law Doctrines to Rule 10b–5: Should Careless Plaintiffs be Denied Recovery?, 71 Cornell L.Rev. 96 (1985); Aaron v. SEC, 446 U.S. 680, 100 S.Ct. 1945, 64 L.Ed.2d 611 (1980), *on remand* 666 F.2d 5 (2d Cir.1981); Ernst & Ernst v. Hochfelder, 425 U.S. 185, 96 S.Ct. 1375, 47 L.Ed.2d 668 (1976), *rehearing denied* 425 U.S. 986, 96 S.Ct. 2194, 48 L.Ed.2d 811 (1976). *See* § 13.4 *supra.*

5. *See* § 13.5B *supra. See also* § 13.8.1 *supra* (Practitioner's Edition only).

6. *See* Kline v. Henrie, 679 F.Supp. 464 (M.D.Pa.1988).

courts to require that plaintiff's conduct be judged by the same standard. The courts have varied in their phrasing of the current version of plaintiff's due diligence test. The Tenth Circuit requires that the plaintiff be culpable of "gross conduct somewhat comparable to that of defendant," [7] while the Fifth Circuit has adopted the same scienter requirement that applies to the defendant.[8] The Third Circuit has opted for a more flexible standard, depending upon the facts of the particular case in light of the defendant's culpability, the relationship between the parties and the reasonableness of the plaintiff's conduct.[9] The due diligence defense is related to the requirement that the plaintiff's reliance has been justifiable.[10] For example, a highly sophisticated investor is not in a position to sue for nondisclosure of the risks of option trading when he knew or could be presumed to have known of such risks.[11]

Since recklessness has been held sufficient to satisfy the scienter requirement with regard to the defendant's conduct,[12] it would seem that

---

7. Holdsworth v. Strong, 545 F.2d 687, 693 (10th Cir.1976), *cert. denied* 430 U.S. 955, 97 S.Ct. 1600, 51 L.Ed.2d 805 (1977). *Cf.* Schick v. Steiger, 583 F.Supp. 841 (E.D.Mich. 1984) (*in pari delicto* is not applicable where the defendant is more culpable than the plaintiff). *Compare, e.g.,* Royal American Managers, Inc. v. IRC Holding Corp., 885 F.2d 1011 (2d Cir.1989) (purchaser did not act with "even the minimum diligence necessary to avoid the imputation of recklessness"); Elco Industries, Inc. v. Hogg, 713 F.Supp. 1215, 1218 (N.D.Ill.1989) (if the plaintiff had been "recklessly remiss," his or her behavior would "offset defendant's intentional misconduct").

8. Dupuy v. Dupuy, 551 F.2d 1005 (5th Cir.), *cert. denied* 434 U.S. 911, 98 S.Ct. 312, 54 L.Ed.2d 197 (1977).

9. Straub v. Vaisman & Co., 540 F.2d 591 (3d Cir.1976); Wenzel v. Patrick Petroleum Co., 745 F.Supp. 211 (D.Del.1990). This seems more analogous to the "flexible duty" standard for defendants that may not survive in the wake of *Hochfelder*. *See* Douglas M. Branson, Statutory Securities Fraud in the Post Hochfelder Era: The Continued Viability of Modes of Flexible Analysis, 52 Tul.L.Rev. 50 (1977).

It seems clear, however, that a plaintiff's mere negligence should not be sufficient to bar a Rule 10b–5 fraud claim. Morgan, Olmstead, Kennedy & Gardner, Inc. v. Schipa, 585 F.Supp. 245 (S.D.N.Y.1984).

10. It is clear, for example, that a plaintiff who consciously ignores notice of the alleged wrongful conduct cannot thereafter complain. *E.g.* Hecht v. Harris, Upham & Co., 430 F.2d 1202 (9th Cir.1970) (customer who did not look at transaction confirmations cannot complain that the broker made unsuitable investments). *See* § 10.7 *supra.* On the justifiable reliance requirement *see* Zobrist v. Coal-X, Inc., 708 F.2d 1511, 1516–1517 (10th Cir.1983); Gower v. Cohn, 643 F.2d 1146, 1156 (5th Cir.1981); Nye v. Blyth, Eastman Dillon & Co., 588 F.2d 1189, 1197 (8th Cir.1978). *See* § 13.5B *supra.* There is some authority to the effect that reasonable reliance is not necessary in a case involving intentional misrepresentation. Competitive Associates, Inc. v. Laventhol, Krekstein, Horwath & Horwath, 516 F.2d 811 (2d Cir.1975), *on remand* 478 F.Supp. 1328 (S.D.N.Y.1979); Metro–Goldwyn–Mayer, Inc. v. Ross, 509 F.2d 930 (2d Cir.1975). *But see* Dupuy v. Dupuy, 551 F.2d 1005, 1015 (5th Cir.), *cert. denied* 434 U.S. 911, 98 S.Ct. 312, 54 L.Ed.2d 197 (1977); Titan Group, Inc. v. Faggen, 513 F.2d 234 (2d Cir.), *cert. denied* 423 U.S. 840, 96 S.Ct. 70, 46 L.Ed.2d 59 (1975). Comment, Securities Regulation—Two Different Standards of Reliance Applied in Individual Private Damage Actions Under SEC Rule 10b–5 by the Second Circuit, 49 Temple L.Rev. 182 (1975).

11. Thompson v. Smith Barney, Harris Upham & Co., 709 F.2d 1413 (11th Cir.1983). *See also* Zobrist v. Coal–X, Inc., 708 F.2d 1511 (10th Cir.1983).

12. *E.g.* Healey v. Catalyst Recovery of Pennsylvania, 616 F.2d 641 (3d Cir.1980); Broad v. Rockwell International Corp., 614 F.2d 418 (5th Cir.1980), *on rehearing* 642 F.2d 929 (5th Cir.1981), *cert. denied* 454 U.S. 965, 102 S.Ct. 506, 70 L.Ed.2d 380 (1981); McLean v. Alexander, 599 F.2d 1190 (3d Cir.1979); Nelson v. Serwold, 576 F.2d 1332 (9th Cir.), *cert. denied* 439 U.S. 970, 99 S.Ct. 464, 58 L.Ed.2d 431 (1978); Rolf v. Blyth,

the same yardstick should apply to plaintiff.[13] As discussed more fully below, the Supreme Court in Bateman Eichler, Hill Richards, Inc. v. Berner,[14] held that the *in pari delicto* defense cannot be invoked in a Rule 10b–5 action unless it can be said that the plaintiff was indeed truly as culpable as the defendant. Although it has been suggested that this ruling abolishes the due diligence defense, the courts have not agreed.[15] The Fifth Circuit has thus held that the due diligence defense, as is the case with equitable defenses of waiver and estoppel, is designed to encourage intelligent investment decisions and that elimination of these defenses "would seriously undercut the objectives of the SEC and the securities laws."[16] The Supreme Court did not address the due diligence issue in *Bateman Eichler* and it would appear unwarranted to completely eliminate the long-standing defense without more explicit guidance from the Court.

In a related development, in Pinter v. Dahl[17] the Supreme Court extended the *Bateman Eichler* rationale in defining equal fault under section 12(1) of the 1933 Act[18] which permits a rescission action by purchasers of unregistered securities that are not exempt from registration. The Court, echoing the investor protection thrust of the securities laws held "the *in pari delicto* defense may defeat recovery in a § 12(1) action only where the plaintiff's role in the offering or sale of nonexempted, unregistered securities is more as a promoter than as an investor."[19] It might be argued that the *Pinter* decision adds further strength to the argument that the Court will not recognize even the due diligence defense unless the same type of equal fault can be shown. As noted above, investors should not be rewarded for reckless conduct that would satisfy the scienter requirement. On the other hand, where the plaintiff's recklessness is clearly less culpable than the defendant's conduct, the due diligence defense should not be applied. A narrow reading of the due diligence defense is also justified in light of the various defenses to other Exchange Act remedies and 1933 Act remedies.[20]

In Pari Delicto

In Bateman Eichler, Hill Richards, Inc. v. Berner,[21] the Supreme Court ruled that the policy of investor protection underlying the securi-

Eastman Dillon & Co., 570 F.2d 38 (2d Cir.), *cert. denied* 439 U.S. 1039, 99 S.Ct. 642, 58 L.Ed.2d 698 (1978). *See* § 13.4 *supra*.

13. *See, e.g.,* Molecular Technology Corp. v. Valentine, 925 F.2d 910 (6th Cir.1991) (in Rule 10b–5 case, recklessness is proper standard for determining if plaintiffs justifiably relied).

14. 472 U.S. 299, 105 S.Ct. 2622, 86 L.Ed.2d 215 (1985).

15. Stephenson v. Paine Webber Jackson & Curtis, Inc., 839 F.2d 1095 (5th Cir.1988).

16. *Id.* at 1099.

17. 486 U.S. 622, 108 S.Ct. 2063, 100 L.Ed.2d 658 (1988).

18. 15 U.S.C.A. § 77*l*(1). *See* § 7.2 *supra*.

19. 486 U.S. at 639, 108 S.Ct. at 2074, 100 L.Ed.2d at 677.

20. *See* the discussion in the text accompanying footnotes 27–43 *infra*.

21. 472 U.S. 299, 105 S.Ct. 2622, 86 L.Ed.2d 215 (1985).

ties law precluded the application of the *in pari delicto* defense in an action by a customer against his broker and corporate insiders for allegedly tipping inaccurate information.　The Court did not find the equal fault defense to be per se inapplicable[22] but rather limited the defense to situations "where (1) as a direct result of his own actions, the plaintiff bears at least substantially equal responsibility for the violations he seeks to redress, and (2) preclusion of suit would not significantly interfere with the effective enforcement of the securities laws and protection of the investing public."[23]　While there can be little doubt that the *Bateman Eichler* ruling has cut down on the scope of the *in pari delicto* defense,[24] courts may continue to apply it where it can truly be said that the parties are of equal fault, which will rarely be the case when dealing with insider trading.[25]　As noted above, this ruling was reinforced by the Court's subsequent decision in Pinter v. Dahl.[26]

Effect of Plaintiff's Conduct on Other Securities Law Claims

An examination of the express liability provisions for securities law violations gives further indication of the types of conduct by the plaintiff that will preclude recovery.　Section 11 of the 1933 Act,[27] which imposes liability for material misstatements and omissions in 1933 Act registration materials,[28] provides that a plaintiff cannot recover if "it is proved that at the time of such acquisition he knew of such untruth or

22.　In contrast, the defense is not available in actions under section 16(b) (15 U.S.C.A. § 78p(b)) to recover insider short-swing profits.　*E.g.,* Texas International Airlines v. National Airlines, Inc., 714 F.2d 533, 536 (5th Cir.1983), *cert. denied* 465 U.S. 1052, 104 S.Ct. 1326, 79 L.Ed.2d 721 (1984); Roth v. Fund of Funds, Ltd., 405 F.2d 421, 422–23 (2d Cir.1968), *cert. denied* 394 U.S. 975, 89 S.Ct. 1469, 22 L.Ed.2d 754 (1969); In re Cascade International, 165 B.R. 321 (Bkrtcy.Fla.1994).　*See* § 12.3 *supra.*

23.　472 U.S. at 310, 105 S.Ct. at 2629, 86 L.Ed.2d at 224.　*Compare* Skinner v. E.F. Hutton & Co., 314 N.C. 267, 333 S.E.2d 236 (1985) (taking a similar approach under state law claim for insider trading).　*Cf.* MacPeg Ross O'Connell & Goldhaber, Inc. v. Castello, 686 F.Supp. 397 (E.D.N.Y.1988) (10b–5 violator held precluded from resorting to blue sky remedy against unregistered broker-dealer).

24.　*See* Rothberg v. Rosenbloom, 808 F.2d 252 (3d Cir.1986), *reversing* 771 F.2d 818 (3d Cir.1985) (remanding for reconsideration in light of *Bateman Eichler*), *on remand* 628 F.Supp. 746 (E.D.Pa.1986).

25.　McAdam v. Dean Witter Reynolds, Inc., 896 F.2d 750 (3d Cir.1990) (investor's engaging in "off-book" transactions, writing checks directly to account executive did not constitute in pari delicto); Rothberg v. Rosenbloom, 628 F.Supp. 746 (E.D.Pa.1986), *judgment reversed* 808 F.2d 252 (3d Cir.1986) (in pari delicto did not bar recovery on promissory notes issued in connection with joint venture to make secret profits in connection with insider trading); Mayer v. Oil Field Systems Corp., 611 F.Supp. 635 (S.D.N.Y.1985), *reconsideration denied* 620 F.Supp. 76 (S.D.N.Y.1985) (limited partner with knowledge of facts allegedly withheld by general partner could not sue under 10b–5; decided before *Bateman Eichler*); Miller v. Interfirst Bank Dallas, N.A., 608 F.Supp. 169, 173 (N.D.Tex.1985) (in pari delicto defense applied in connection with closely held corporation where there was no question of protecting the investing public; decided before *Bateman Eichler*).　*See* Theresa A. Gabaldon, Unclean Hands and Self–Inflicted Wounds: The Significance of Plaintiff Conduct in Actions for Misrepresentation Under Rule 10b–5, 71 Minn.L.Rev. 317 (1986).

26.　*See* footnotes 17–19 *supra* and accompanying text.

27.　15 U.S.C.A. § 77k.　*See* § 7.3 *supra.*

28.　15 U.S.C.A. §§ 77e, 77f, 77g.　*See* chapters 2, 3 *supra.*

omission."[29] Interestingly, section 11 liability is based on strict liability of the issuer or lack of due diligence of other defendants,[30] but the plaintiff's negligence or even recklessness will not bar recovery. Thus equal fault is not a sufficient defense to less than intentional conduct. Similarly, a claim under section 12(2) of the 1933 Act,[31] which imposes liability based on negligence of sellers in privity with the plaintiff,[32] is barred only when the purchaser knew of the inaccuracies.[33] Again, the defendant is held to a higher standard of care than the plaintiff. Section 18(a) of the 1934 Act imposes liability for material misstatements in SEC filings;[34] the defendant's liability is more akin to negligence than to intentional conduct[35] but the plaintiff is barred only if he or she had knowledge of the misstatement or omission.[36]

All of the express statutory provisions providing for liability in cases of material misstatements or omissions thus allow the plaintiff to proceed unless he or she had knowledge of the wrongful conduct or inaccuracies. This standard is applied notwithstanding the imposition of a lower standard on the defendant. The balance that the courts seem to require under Rule 10b–5[37] thus is not reflected in the express liability provisions. Arguably Rule 10b–5 should have the same standard of plaintiff's conduct as the other sections, but this has not been the case. The reason for so extending the scope of the Rule 10b–5 remedy would be not only to aid enforcement but also to be consistent with the Supreme Court's rationale in *Bateman Eichler* and *Pinter*. Although enforcement alone is not a reason for implying a private remedy,[38] the language of the express liability sections discussed above arguably shows a congressional intent to include negligent and even reckless plaintiffs within the "especial class" for whose benefit section 10(b) was intended. On the other hand, the balance approach currently taken in Rule 10b–5

29. 15 U.S.C.A. § 77k(a).

30. 15 U.S.C.A. § 77k(b). *See* § 7.4 *supra.*

31. 15 U.S.C.A. § 77l(2). *See* § 7.5 *supra.* The scope of section 12(2)'s rescission remedy was severely limited by the Supreme Court in Gustafson v. Alloyd Corp., __ U.S. __, 115 S.Ct. 1061, 131 L.Ed.2d 1 (1995). The Court in *Gustafson* ruled that the remedy is only available to material misstatements and omissions made in connection with securities that were offered by prospectus. This decision has the effect of making the remedy unavailable for most day-to-day transactions. *See* § 7.5 *supra.*

32. 15 U.S.C.A. § 77l(2) (liability of defendant "who shall not sustain the burden of proof that he did not know, and in the exercise of reasonable care could not have known, of such untruth or omission").

33. *Id.* ("the purchaser not knowing of such untruth or omission"). *See* In re Olympia Brewing Co. Securities Litigation, 612 F.Supp. 1367 (N.D.Ill.1985) (lack of due diligence is not a defense to a claim under section 12(2)).

34. 15 U.S.C.A. § 78r(a). *See* § 12.8 *supra.*

35. *Id.* (the defendant is not liable upon proof "that he acted in good faith and had no knowledge that such statement was false or misleading").

36. *Id.* (plaintiff "not knowing" that such statement was false or misleading).

37. *See* footnotes 4–8 *supra* and accompanying text.

38. Implied remedies and their rationales are discussed in § 13.1 *supra.*

cases helps keep the implied remedy from becoming too expansive.[39] Regardless of the test applied, it is clear that it will be the rare case in which plaintiff's conduct will bar an otherwise valid 10b–5 action.

The Supreme Court has held that scienter is not an element under section 17(a)(2) or 17(a)(3) of the 1933 Act.[40] To the extent that scienter is not an element of a claim in an action under Rule 14a–9[41] for violation of the proxy rules,[42] the plaintiff's comparable lack of care may still be a defense. The same result might follow for any implied remedy that may exist under section 17(a)(2) or (a)(3) of the 1933 Act.[43]

Waiver, Estoppel, and Laches

Defendants in securities fraud actions may raise the claim that the plaintiff's action is barred by waiver, estoppel or laches. The courts have indicated that the due diligence standard discussed above applies equally in the context of waiver and estoppel.[44] Laches is treated similarly[45] or by analogy to the statute of limitations.[46]

The due diligence requirement for the persons injured or defrauded has no application in SEC enforcement actions. The courts in SEC enforcement actions are concerned primarily with honesty and full disclosure to the investing public rather than harm to any particular investor.[47] Accordingly, that absence of a victim's due diligence in pursuing his or her claim (even if it would bar that claim under the doctrines of waiver, laches, or estoppel), will not preclude SEC sanctions

---

39. As noted in § 13.2 *supra* the Supreme Court has been cutting back on the scope of Rule 10b–5 as well as implied remedies generally. Implied remedies generally are considered in § 13.1 *supra*.

40. Aaron v. SEC, 446 U.S. 680, 100 S.Ct. 1945, 64 L.Ed.2d 611 (1980), *on remand* 666 F.2d 5 (2d Cir.1981); 15 U.S.C.A. § 77q(a)(2), (3). *See* § 7.6 *supra*.

41. 17 C.F.R. § 240.14a–9.

42. *See* §§ 11.3, 13.4 *supra*.

43. 15 U.S.C.A. § 77q(a)(2), (3). *See* § 13.13 *infra*.

44. Stephenson v. Paine Webber Jackson & Curtis, Inc., 839 F.2d 1095, 1098–99 (5th Cir.1988), *cert. denied* 488 U.S. 926, 109 S.Ct. 310, 102 L.Ed.2d 328 (1988); Hecht v. Harris, Upham & Co., 430 F.2d 1202 (9th Cir.1970); Royal Air Properties, Inc. v. Smith, 333 F.2d 568, 570 (9th Cir.1964), *s.c.* 312 F.2d 210 (9th Cir.1962); Paul v. Berkman, 620 F.Supp. 638 (W.D.Pa.1985) (material issue of fact whether plaintiff minority shareholders ratified challenged stock purchase agreement and were thereby estopped from suing under 10b–5); Phillips v. Merrill Lynch, Pierce, Fenner & Smith, Inc., 1984 WL 897, [1984 Transfer Binder] Fed.Sec.L.Rep. (CCH) ¶ 91,649 (D.Minn.1984) (client not barred in action claiming unauthorized trades without showing that client had full knowledge of the challenged transactions). *Cf.* Regional Properties, Inc. v. Financial & Real Estate Consulting Co., 752 F.2d 178 (5th Cir.1985) (defendant's unclean hands precluded presentation of equitable defense in action for rescission). *See* footnote 16 *supra*. Section 29(a) expressly precludes contracts or agreements to waive compliances with the Act's requirements, 15 U.S.C.A. § 78cc(a). *See* § 13.14 *infra*.

45. Hecht v. Harris, Upham & Co., 430 F.2d 1202 (9th Cir.1970).

46. *See* § 13.8 *supra*.

47. *See* Dupuy v. Dupuy, 551 F.2d 1005, 1015 (5th Cir.1977), *cert. denied* 434 U.S. 911, 98 S.Ct. 312, 54 L.Ed.2d 197 (1977).

for securities law violations.[48] This is consistent with the rule that neither laches nor the statute of limitations will be a bar to the SEC's ability to pursue the matter.[49]

§ 13.13 Is There an Implied Remedy Under Section 17(a)?

As noted earlier,[1] SEC Rule 10b–5[2] was modeled upon section 17(a) of the 1933 Act.[3] There are three principal differences between the 1934 Act rule and section 17(a). First, Rule 10b–5 applies to any "purchase or sale" of a security,[4] whereas section 17(a) covers the "offer or sale" of any security. Second, section 17(a) does not contain the phrase "manipulative or deceptive device" that is found in section 10(b) of the Exchange Act[5] and has formed a basis of the scienter[6] and deception[7] requirements. Third, by virtue of the jurisdictional provisions of the 1933 and 1934 Acts,[8] the federal courts are vested with exclusive jurisdiction over Rule 10b–5 actions while section 17(a) actions may be brought either in state or federal court with no right of removal from state to federal court. As will be explained more fully below, these three differences are significant in defining the respective roles of the two antifraud provisions.

Notwithstanding the Supreme Court's recent disinclination to imply a private right of action from a federal statute,[9] there remains at least some basis for recognizing a remedy under section 17(a). Of the early cases, most courts that heard the question implied a section 17(a) remedy,[10] although there is an increasing body of substantial authority to

---

48. *See* SEC v. Dolnick, 501 F.2d 1279 (7th Cir.1974) (sophisticated investor; past course of dealing with defendant). *But cf.* SEC v. Coffey, 493 F.2d 1304, 1312–1313 (6th Cir.1974), *cert. denied* 420 U.S. 908, 95 S.Ct. 826, 42 L.Ed.2d 837 (1975) (no violation where victims had sufficient knowledge to preclude a finding that they had been misled).

49. *See* §§ 9.5, 13.8 *supra.*

§ 13.13

1. *See* § 13.2 *supra.*

2. 17 C.F.R. § 240.10b–5.

3. 15 U.S.C.A. § 77q(a).

4. In Blue Chip Stamps v. Manor Drug Stores, 421 U.S. 723, 95 S.Ct. 1917, 44 L.Ed.2d 539 (1975), *rehearing denied* 423 U.S. 884, 96 S.Ct. 157, 46 L.Ed.2d 114 (1975) the Court held that this statutory language limited 10b–5 private damage plaintiffs to purchasers and sellers of the securities in question. *See* § 13.3 *supra* and text accompanying footnote 31 *infra.*

5. 15 U.S.C.A. § 78j(b).

6. Ernst & Ernst v. Hochfelder, 425 U.S. 185, 96 S.Ct. 1375, 47 L.Ed.2d 668 (1976), *rehearing denied* 425 U.S. 986, 96 S.Ct. 2194, 48 L.Ed.2d 811 (1976). *See* § 13.4 *supra.*

7. Santa Fe Industries, Inc. v. Green, 430 U.S. 462, 97 S.Ct. 1292, 51 L.Ed.2d 480 (1977). *See* § 13.11 *supra.*

8. 15 U.S.C.A. §§ 77v, 78aa. The jurisdictional provisions of both the 1933 and 1934 Acts are discussed in § 14.1 *infra.*

9. *See* § 13.1 *supra.*

10. *See, e.g.,* Stephenson v. Calpine Conifers, II, Ltd., 652 F.2d 808 (9th Cir.1981), *overruled in* In re Washington Public Power Supply System Securities Litigation, 823 F.2d 1349 (9th Cir.1987); Kirshner v. United States, 603 F.2d 234 (2d Cir.1978), *cert. denied* 442 U.S. 909, 99 S.Ct. 2821, 61 L.Ed.2d 274 (1979).

the contrary.[11]

The Decline of the Section 17(a) Remedy

The section 17(a) remedy has been recognized by some courts[12] for almost as long a time as the 10b–5 remedy.[13] Prior to the Supreme Court's limitations on the scope of the Rule 10b–5 remedy, the section 17(a) cause of action seemed "to be taken for granted."[14] The long-standing recognition of the 17(a) remedy led many courts to continue to acknowledge the existence of this implied cause of action[15] as consistent with the Supreme Court's recognition of not only the Rule 10b–5 remedy but also the implied private remedy for violation of proxy Rule 14a–9.[16] However, in its more recent round of implication cases, the Supreme Court has pointed out that the Rule 10b–5 remedy had twenty-five years of judicial recognition and it was too late to turn back the clock.[17] The same could arguably be said of section 17(a)[18] although most courts have not taken this approach.[19] Instead, for the most part, they have denied the existence of a private remedy under section 17(a).

On the other hand, in Herman & MacLean v. Huddleston the Court held that Rule 10b–5 and section 11 of the 1933 Act provide cumulative remedies.[20] By analogy, the *Huddleston* case could be argued to support Rule 10b–5 and section 17(a) as cumulative remedies.[21]

Notwithstanding the arguments that might favor continued recognition of the section 17(a) remedy, the courts have found the contrary position to be more compelling.[22] The recent trend in implication cases

11. *E.g.,* Landry v. All American Assurance Co., 688 F.2d 381 (5th Cir.1982); Shull v. Dain, Kalman & Quail, Inc., 561 F.2d 152 (8th Cir.1977), *cert. denied* 434 U.S. 1086, 98 S.Ct. 1281, 55 L.Ed.2d 792 (1978); Greater Iowa Corp. v. McLendon, 378 F.2d 783 (8th Cir.1967). *See also* cases in footnotes 22, 25, 26 *infra.*

12. Osborne v. Mallory, 86 F.Supp. 869 (S.D.N.Y.1949).

13. Kardon v. National Gypsum Co., 69 F.Supp. 512 (E.D.Pa.1946).

14. 6 Louis Loss, Securities Regulation 3913 (2d ed. 1969 Supp.). *But see* Paul Horton, Section 17(a) of the 1933 Securities Act—The Wrong Place for a Private Right, 68 Nw.U.L.Rev. 44 (1973).

15. *E.g.,* Stephenson v. Calpine Conifers, II, Ltd., 652 F.2d 808 (9th Cir.1981), *overruled in* In re Washington Public Power Supply System Securities Litigation, 823 F.2d 1349 (9th Cir.1987).

16. *See* J.I. Case Co. v. Borak, 377 U.S. 426, 84 S.Ct. 1555, 12 L.Ed.2d 423 (1964). The implied remedy for violations of proxy Rule 14a–9 is discussed in § 11.3 *supra.*

17. *See* Cannon v. University of Chicago, 441 U.S. 677, 692, 99 S.Ct. 1946, 1955, 60 L.Ed.2d 560 (1979), *on remand* 605 F.2d 560 (7th Cir.1979), *appeal after remand* 648 F.2d 1104 (7th Cir.1981), *mandamus denied* 454 U.S. 811, 102 S.Ct. 373, 70 L.Ed.2d 197 (1981).

18. *See* footnotes 10, 12, 15 *supra.*

19. *See* cases collected in footnotes 22, 25, 26 *infra.*

20. 459 U.S. 375, 103 S.Ct. 683, 74 L.Ed.2d 548 (1983), *on remand* 705 F.2d 775 (5th Cir.1983); 1933 Act § 11, 15 U.S.C.A. § 77k. *See* §§ 7.3, 7.4 *supra.*

21. *E.g.* Amunrud v. Taurus Drilling Ltd., 1983 WL 1412, [1983–1984 Transfer Binder] Fed.Sec.L.Rep. (CCH) ¶ 99,649 (D.Mont.1983). *See* § 13.2 *supra. See also* Marc I. Steinberg, The Propriety of Cumulative Remedies Under The Federal Securities Laws, 67 Cornell L.Rev. 557 (1982).

22. *E.g.* Barnes v. Resource Royalties, Inc., 795 F.2d 1359 (8th Cir.1986); Landry v. All American Assurance Co., 688 F.2d 381 (5th Cir.1982).

before the Supreme Court cannot be ignored and there certainly is a persuasive argument accepted by an increasingly large number of courts that no 17(a) remedy should be recognized. The trend of nonrecognition is a reversal of the trend, noted at the outset of this section, wherein the overwhelming majority of the earlier federal cases recognized an implied right of action under section 17(a).[23] Now, although the trend of most decisions has clearly changed even though some authority remains for the recognition of the section 17(a) remedy,[24] the majority of recent decisions favors the denial of an implied right of action under section 17(a).[25] The majority of cases denying the remedy has been increasing consistently.[26] Nevertheless, as pointed out above, there are a number of relatively recent decisions that have continued to recognize the remedy.

Until the Supreme Court hears the case or the remainder of the circuit and district courts deny the implied cause of action, the section 17(a) remedy is one that must be reckoned with in those circuits that have not clearly denied the existence of the remedy.[27] The trend against implying a remedy has been so strong that the Eighth Circuit affirmed the imposition of Rule 11 sanctions against counsel signing a complaint alleging a remedy under section 17(a).[28] Accordingly, prior to filing a section 17 claim, counsel should make a careful investigation and be confident that the issue has not been resolved clearly in the circuit in which he or she plans to bring suit.

Elements of a Section 17(a) Remedy

At one time the section 17(a) remedy was of relatively little importance because of its parallel to any cause of action that would have existed under Rule 10b–5. However, the recent cutbacks on the scope of the 10b–5 remedy have opened the door for a more expansive use of section 17(a).[29] For example, notwithstanding the Supreme Court's

---

23. *See* footnote 10 *supra.*

24. *E.g.,* Gaff v. FDIC, 814 F.2d 311 (6th Cir.1987) (but denying standing to an offeree who did not purchase); Letizia v. Prudential Bache Securities, Inc., 802 F.2d 1185 (9th Cir.1986) (also holding that the section 17(a) claim was not arbitrable).

25. In addition to the authorities in footnote 22 *supra* and footnote 26 *infra, see* Practitioner's Edition.

26. *See, e.g.,* Fox v. Acadia State Bank, 937 F.2d 1566 (11th Cir.1991) (imposing Rule 11 sanctions against plaintiff's counsel); Pelletier v. Zweifel, 921 F.2d 1465 (11th Cir. 1991), *rehearing denied* 931 F.2d 901 (1991).

27. The Supreme Court has pointed out that it has not yet decided the issue. Bateman Eichler, Hill Richards, Inc. v. Berner, 472 U.S. 299, 105 S.Ct. 2622, 86 L.Ed.2d 215 (1985).

28. Crookham v. Crookham, 914 F.2d 1027 (8th Cir.1990) ($10,000 sanction).

29. *See generally* Thomas L. Hazen, A Look Beyond the Pruning of Rule 10b–5: Implied Remedies and Section 17(a) of The Securities Act of 1933, 64 Va.L.Rev. 641 (1978); Marc I. Steinberg, Section 17(a) of The Securities Act of 1933 After *Naftalin* and *Redington*, 68 Geo.L.J. 163 (1979); Note, What Did Congress Really Want? : An Implied Private Right of Action Under Section 17(a) of the 1933 Securities Act, 63 Ind.L.J. 623 (1988). Comment, Section 17(a) of the 1933 Act: An Alternative to the Recently Restricted Rule 10b–5, 9 Rut.–Cam.L.J. 340 (1978); Note, Implied Civil Remedies Under Section 17(a) of the Securities Act of 1933, 53 B.U.L.Rev. 70 (1973). *But see* Paul Horton, Section 17(a) of the 1933 Securities Act–The Wrong Place for a Private Right, 68 Nw.U.L.Rev. 44

imposition of the purchaser/seller standing requirement in Rule 10b–5 actions in Blue Chip Stamps v. Manor Drug Stores,[30] it was expressly noted by the Court that the language of section 17(a) differed from that of Rule 10b–5 and therefore a similar result did not necessarily follow under the 1933 Act.[31] In light of the Court's observation in *Blue Chip Stamps,* it has been held by a few courts that the section 17(a) remedy exists in the hands of both purchasers of securities and offerees who did not purchase but nevertheless were injured by the defendant's conduct.[32] Although this view was rejected in some earlier cases,[33] as well as some more recent ones,[34] the standing issue remains open,[35] in those circuits where the section 17(a) remedy may still be viable.

With regard to scienter, it seems quite clear that negligence will be sufficient for any private remedy that may exist under sections 17(a)(2) and 17(a)(3). This is because the Court explicitly so held in Aaron v. SEC,[36] in the context of an SEC injunction action. In that case the court relied on the wording of the statute rather than on the nature of the formal relief sought. Since scienter is required in both SEC enforcement and private damage actions under Rule 10b–5 because of the "deception requirement," it would not seem to be required in any action that may exist under subsection (2) or (3) of section 17(a). The Court in *Aaron* rejected the suggestion that different standards of care be applied under Rule 10b–5 depending upon whether there was a private suit or SEC enforcement action; such a distinction would be no more appropriate with regard to section 17(a).

(1973); Dennis Scholl & Ronald K. Perkowski, Implied Right of Action Under Section 17(a): The Supreme Court Has Said "No," But is Anybody Listening?, 36 U.Miami L.Rev. 41 (1981).

30. 421 U.S. 723, 95 S.Ct. 1917, 44 L.Ed.2d 539 (1975), *rehearing denied* 423 U.S. 884, 96 S.Ct. 157, 46 L.Ed.2d 114 (1975).

31. *Id.* at 733 n. 6, 95 S.Ct. at 1924 n. 6.

32. Doll v. James Martin Associates (Holdings) Ltd., 600 F.Supp. 510, 524 (E.D.Mich. 1984) (allegation that plaintiff was injured "in connection with an offer to sell securities is not precluded from maintaining a private action under either § 17(a)(1) or § 12(2) of the 1933 Act because the offer was not consummated by an acceptance and a sale"). Reid v. Madison, 438 F.Supp. 332 (E.D.Va.1977); Wulc v. Gulf & Western Industries, Inc., 400 F.Supp. 99, 102–03 (E.D.Pa.1975). *See also,* Bosse v. Crowell Collier & Macmillan, 565 F.2d 602, 610 n. 12 (9th Cir.1977). *Contra* Gaff v. FDIC, 814 F.2d 311 (6th Cir.1987) (offeree who did not purchase lacked standing).

33. *E.g.* Simmons v. Wolfson, 428 F.2d 455 (6th Cir.1970), *cert. denied* 400 U.S. 999, 91 S.Ct. 459, 27 L.Ed.2d 450 (1971); Greater Iowa Corp. v. McLendon, 378 F.2d 783 (8th Cir.1967); Frigitemp Corp. v. Financial Dynamics Fund, Inc., 1974 WL 466, [1974–1975 Transfer Binder] Fed.Sec.L.Rep. (CCH) ¶ 94,907 (S.D.N.Y.1974), *affirmed on other grounds* 524 F.2d 275 (2d Cir.1975); In re Penn Central Securities Litigation, 357 F.Supp. 869 (E.D.Pa.1973), *affirmed* 494 F.2d 528 (3d Cir.1974); Kellman v. ICS, Inc., 447 F.2d 1305 (6th Cir.1971); Crowell v. Pittsburgh & Lake Erie Railroad, 373 F.Supp. 1303 (E.D.Pa. 1974).

34. Darvin v. Bache Halsey Stuart Shields, Inc., 479 F.Supp. 460 (S.D.N.Y.1979).

35. *But see* Gaff v. FDIC, 814 F.2d 311 (6th Cir.1987), *on rehearing in part* 828 F.2d 1145 (6th Cir.1987).

36. Aaron v. SEC, 446 U.S. 680, 100 S.Ct. 1945, 64 L.Ed.2d 611 (1980), *on remand* 666 F.2d 5 (2d Cir.1981).

The *Aaron* decision held that the section 17(a)(1) prohibition against "any device, scheme, or artifice to defraud" required a showing of scienter.[37] In contrast, subsection (2), which prohibits misleading statements or omissions of material fact, does not require proof of scienter.[38] The Court also interpreted subsection (3), which prohibits conduct that "operates or would operate as a fraud or deceit," as not embodying a scienter requirement since it "quite plainly focuses upon the *effect* of particular conduct on members of the investing public, rather than upon the culpability of the person responsible."[39] Although the cases are in conflict, the more recent decisions have held that scienter is not an element of any private remedy that may exist under section 17(a).[40] This would appear to be the result required by *Aaron* if a private remedy exists.

Since the deception requirement of Santa Fe Industries, Inc. v. Green[41] is similarly derived from the manipulative or deceptive language of section 10(b) of the Exchange Act, it arguably does not apply in an action under section 17(a), and concepts of "equitable fraud" might well be sufficient to state a section 17(a) violation.[42] However, such an extension of section 17 would clearly be unwarranted in light of the disclosure thrust of the securities laws generally. Furthermore, the Court's decision in Schreiber v. Burlington Northern, Inc.,[43] requiring deception as a precondition of a violation of section 14(e) of the Exchange Act,[44] further supports a deception requirement in section 17(a), at least to the extent that there must be a material misstatement or omission.

As is the case with Rule 10b–5,[45] there is no clear statute of

---

37. *Id.* at 696, 100 S.Ct. at 1955, 1956 (emphasis added).

38. *Id.*

39. *Id.* at 696–97, 100 S.Ct. at 1955, 1956.

40. Onesti v. Thomson McKinnon Securities, Inc., 619 F.Supp. 1262 (N.D.Ill.1985); Morgan Stanley & Co. v. Archer Daniels Midland Co., 570 F.Supp. 1529, 1536 (S.D.N.Y. 1983); Spatz v. Borenstein, 513 F.Supp. 571, 578 (N.D.Ill.1981); Campito v. McManus, Longe, Brockwehl, Inc., 470 F.Supp. 986, 993–94 (N.D.N.Y.1979). *See* Note, Implication Under Section 17(a) of the Securities Act of 1933–The Effect of Aaron v. SEC, 49 Fordham L.Rev. 1161 (1981). *But see* Baker v. Eagle Aircraft Co., 642 F.Supp. 1005 (D.Or.1986) (requiring scienter); In re Olympia Brewing Co. Securities Litigation, 612 F.Supp. 1367, 1368 (N.D.Ill.1985) (if the section 17(a) remedy exists, "it would likely require scienter"); and the following pre-*Aaron* decisions, Sanders v. John Nuveen & Co., 554 F.2d 790, 795 (7th Cir.1977), *cert. denied* 450 U.S. 1005, 101 S.Ct. 1719, 68 L.Ed.2d 210 (1981); Nelson v. Quimby Island Reclamation District Facilities Corp., 491 F.Supp. 1364 (N.D.Cal.1980); Wiener v. Oppenheimer & Co., 1979 WL 1189, [1979 Transfer Binder] Fed.Sec.L.Rep. (CCH) ¶ 96,764 (D.C.N.Y.1979); Malik v. Universal Resources Corp., 425 F.Supp. 350, 363 (S.D.Cal.1976).

41. 430 U.S. 462, 97 S.Ct. 1292, 51 L.Ed.2d 480 (1977), *on remand* 562 F.2d 4 (2d Cir.1977).

42. *See* Klamberg v. Roth, 473 F.Supp. 544, 556 (S.D.N.Y.1979); Hazen *supra* footnote 29 at 677–80.

43. 472 U.S. 1, 105 S.Ct. 2458, 86 L.Ed.2d 1 (1985).

44. 15 U.S.C.A. § 78n(e). *See* §§ 11.15, 11.19 *supra.*

45. *See* § 13.8 *supra.*

limitations for section 17(a) actions. Section 13 of the 1933 Act[46] contains a limitations period for the Act's express remedies. Formerly, in section 17(a) actions the courts have uniformly looked to the applicable statute of limitations that would be applied in the forum state.[47] However in light of the current approach of the Supreme Court,[48] it seems clear that section 13 would provide the appropriate limitations and repose periods.

As noted earlier, unlike Rule 10b–5, both state and federal courts have jurisdiction to hear claims arising under section 17(a).[49] One should not underestimate the availability of a state court forum,[50] since the majority of state courts that have heard the issue have held that an implied remedy exists under section 17(a).[51]

The Commission clearly can bring actions for injunctive relief for violations of section 17(a). It has been held that in such a suit the court can order the defendant to disgorge any ill-gotten gains.[52]

46. 15 U.S.C.A. § 77m.

47. *E.g.,* Ohio v. Peterson, Lowry, Rall, Barber & Ross, 651 F.2d 687 (10th Cir.1981), *cert. denied* 454 U.S. 895, 102 S.Ct. 392, 70 L.Ed.2d 209 (1981) (statute of limitations is borrowed from state law, tolling rule is from federal law); Newman v. Prior, 518 F.2d 97, 100 (4th Cir.1975), *overruled on other grounds in* Newcome v. Esrey, 862 F.2d 1099 (4th Cir.1988) (applying two year blue sky limitations period); Roth v. Bank of The Commonwealth, 1981 WL 1671, [1981–1982 Transfer Binder] Fed.Sec.L.Rep. (CCH) ¶ 98,267 (W.D.N.Y.1981) (applying the four-year limitation period applicable to common law fraud); Brown v. Producers Livestock Loan Co., 469 F.Supp. 27 (D.Utah 1978) (three year fraud statute); Osborne v. Mallory, 86 F.Supp. 869 (S.D.N.Y.1949) (six year statute). *See also* Wulc v. Gulf & Western Industries, Inc., 400 F.Supp. 99 (E.D.Pa.1975) (rejecting the applicability of section 13 of the 1933 Act, 15 U.S.C.A. § 77m).

48. Lampf, Pleva, Lipkind, Prupis & Petigrow v. Gilbertson, 501 U.S. 350, 111 S.Ct. 2773, 115 L.Ed.2d 321 (1991) which is discussed in § 13.8 *supra.* For another recent restrictive ruling on the scope of implied remedies, *see* Central Bank of Denver v. First Interstate Bank of Denver, ___ U.S. ___, 114 S.Ct. 1439, 128 L.Ed.2d 119 (1994) which is discussed in § 13.16 *infra.*

49. *See* footnote 8 *supra.*

50. *See* footnote 7 *supra.*

51. *E.g.,* Rocz v. Drexel Burnham Lambert, Inc., 154 Ariz. 462, 743 P.2d 971 (App. 1987) (holding section 17(a) claims were arbitrable); Unit, Inc. v. Kentucky Fried Chicken Corp., 304 A.2d 320 (Del.Super.1973), *overruled* Mann v. Oppenheimer & Co., 517 A.2d 1056 (Del.1986); Anvil Investment Limited Partnership v. Thornhill Condominiums, Ltd., 85 Ill.App.3d 1108, 41 Ill.Dec. 147, 407 N.E.2d 645 (1980); Wolfson v. Ubile, 1977 WL 1546, [1977–78 Transfer Binder] Fed.Sec.L.Rep. (CCH) ¶ 96,280 at p. 92,798 (N.Y.Sup. 1977). *Contra* Mann v. Oppenheimer & Co., 517 A.2d 1056 (Del.1986); CPC International, Inc. v. McKesson, Corp., 120 A.D.2d 221, 507 N.Y.S.2d 984 (1986). For additional cases *see* Hazen, *supra* note 31 at 653. *See also* Watling, Lerchen & Co. v. Ormond, 86 Mich.App. 238, 272 N.W.2d 614 (1978).

52. *See* SEC v. Manor Nursing Centers, Inc., 458 F.2d 1082, 1103–04 (2d Cir.1972). *But cf.* SEC v. Wills, 472 F.Supp. 1250, 1275–76 (D.D.C.1978) (refusing disgorgement in the absence of proof of scienter). *See generally* George W. Dent, Jr., Ancillary Relief in Federal Securities Law: A Study in Federal Remedies, 67 Minn.L.Rev. 865 (1983); John D. Ellsworth, Disgorgement in Securities Fraud Actions Brought by the SEC, 1977 Duke L.J. 641; James R. Farrand, Ancillary Remedies in SEC Civil Enforcement Suits, 89 Harv. L.Rev. 1779 (1976).

§ 13.14 Waiver of Claims; Voiding of Contracts in Violation of the Securities Acts

Waiver of Claims

Section 14 of the Securities Act of 1933 provides that contracts and stipulations purporting to waive compliance with any provision of the Act or SEC rules promulgated thereunder are void.[1] The Exchange Act's counterpart is found in section 29(a).[2] It is clear that the prohibition against waivers does not preclude releases of liability issued for consideration in connection with settlements of litigation or incipient suits.[3] However, to be valid such a release must be for consideration and the parties must have had knowledge of the claim.[4] Thus, waivers that have been secured before there is reason to suspect that a claim may exist are not valid.[5] The rule is otherwise when the waiver arises in the context of a bona fide settlement. The federal courts have long recognized the policy favoring settlement of disputes.[6]

As is the case with settlement of pending or incipient claims, the anti-waiver provision been interpreted by some courts not to bar the equitable defenses of waiver and estoppel.[7] Additionally, the section has been applied to void contractual waivers of any kind, whether formal or implied from the parties' conduct.[8] Further, section 29(a)'s provisions

---

§ 13.14

1. 15 U.S.C.A. § 77n.

2. 15 U.S.C.A. § 78cc(a).

3. *See, e.g.,* Petro–Ventures, Inc. v. Takessian, 967 F.2d 1337 (9th Cir.1992) (enforceability of release of federal securities claims is a matter of federal law; release is valid only to the extent that plaintiffs knew of claims at time of release—questions of fact regarding plaintiffs' knowledge precluded summary judgment); Murtagh v. University Computing Co., 490 F.2d 810 (5th Cir.), *cert. denied* 419 U.S. 835, 95 S.Ct. 62, 42 L.Ed.2d 62 (1974). *See also, e.g.,* Mullen v. New Jersey Steel Corp., 733 F.Supp. 1534 (D.N.J.1990) ("[the Exchange Act's antiwaiver] provision concerns waiver of future violations; there is a distinction between a waiver of future claims and a waiver of mature claims of which the releasing party had knowledge"), relying on Leff v. CIP Corp., 540 F.Supp. 857, 862 (S.D.Ohio 1982).

4. Burgess v. Premier Corp., 727 F.2d 826 (9th Cir.1984); Synalloy Corp. v. Gray, 816 F.Supp. 963 (D.Del.1993).

5. *See, e.g.,* McMahan & Co. v. Wherehouse Entertainment, Inc., 859 F.Supp. 743 (S.D.N.Y.1994) ("no action" clause in debenture agreement could not preclude federal securities claim).

6. An interesting wrinkle is the recent decision permitting a state court to approve a comprehensive settlement that disposed of federal as well as state claims, notwithstanding the 1934 Act's grant of exclusive federal jurisdiction. Grimes v. Vitalink Communications Corp., 17 F.3d 1553 (3d Cir.1994). *See* § 14.1 *infra.*

7. *See, e.g.,* Hecht v. Harris, Upham & Co., 430 F.2d 1202 (9th Cir.1970) (customer with discretionary account who never looked at transaction confirmations was held to have waived objections to the suitability of investments). *See also, e.g.* Doody v. E.F. Hutton & Co., 587 F.Supp. 829 (D.Minn.1984) (contractual provision not to sue not enforceable as waiver but was evidence of the plaintiffs' non-reliance on alleged oral misrepresentations). *See also, e.g.,* Royal Air Properties, Inc. v. Smith, 333 F.2d 568 (9th Cir.1964) *s.c.* 312 F.2d 210, 213–214 (9th Cir.1962).

8. *E.g.,* Haralson v. E.F. Hutton Group, Inc., 919 F.2d 1014 (5th Cir.1990) (brokerage firm's agreeing to reconciliation of account could not bar alleged securities law violations which subsequently came to light; the only way to bar the claim would be if the agreement in question amounted to a settlement agreement); Meyers v. C & M Petroleum Producers, Inc. 476 F.2d 427 (5th Cir.1973), *rehearing denied* 478 F.2d 1402 (5th Cir.1973).

have been held not to prohibit choice of law and forum selection clauses.[9]

Of course, only agreements waiving compliance with the securities laws will be void.[10] Other waivers that may be involved in securities transactions remain valid.

The anti-waiver section in the past has also been applied to strike down contracts containing a provision for mandatory arbitration.[11] The prohibition against compulsory arbitration agreements did not come into play, however, with regard to contracts and disputes between members of self regulatory organizations.[12] As a result of a Supreme Court ruling that agreements to arbitrate related state claims are enforceable,[13] a number of courts began to hold that in such cases the federal claims are also arbitrable.[14] Following the trend in the lower courts, the Supreme Court has held in separate decisions that Rule 10b–5 claims and 1933 Act claims are arbitrable and thus upheld predispute agreements to arbitrate.[15]

---

9. AVC Nederland B.V. v. Atrium Investment Partnership, 740 F.2d 148 (2d Cir.1984). *See also* Luce v. Edelstein, 1985 WL 2257, [1985–86 Transfer Binder] Fed.Sec.L.Rep. (CCH) ¶ 92,258 (S.D.N.Y.1985) (contractual provision selecting state court forum for suits arising thereunder was effective to keep federal claims under sections 12(2) and 17(a) of the 1933 Act out of federal court, but the forum selection clause was invalid with regard to 10b–5 because of exclusive federal jurisdiction).

10. *E.g.,* In re Gas Reclamation, Inc. Securities Litigation, 733 F.Supp. 713 (S.D.N.Y. 1990) (waiver of defenses in surety agreement did not implicate federal securities law claims and therefore was valid); National Union Fire Insurance Co. v. Dahl, 1990 WL 48074, [1989–1990 Transfer Binder] Fed.Sec.L.Rep. ¶ 95,015(S.D.N.Y.1990) (the antiwaiver provision contained in section 29(b) of 1934 Act did not preclude enforcement of indemnity agreement in favor of surety who guaranteed investor's promissory note).

11. *E.g.,* Wilko v. Swan, 346 U.S. 427, 74 S.Ct. 182, 98 L.Ed. 168 (1953), *overruled in* Rodriguez De Quijas v. Shearson/American Express, 490 U.S. 477, 109 S.Ct. 1917, 104 L.Ed.2d 526 (1989). In contrast, the Seventh Circuit has held that the Federal Arbitration Act preempts comparable antiwaiver provisions found in state securities acts. *E.g.* Kroog v. Mait, 712 F.2d 1148 (7th Cir.1983), *cert. denied* 465 U.S. 1007, 104 S.Ct. 1001, 79 L.Ed.2d 233 (1984). *See also* Roney & Co. v. Goren, 875 F.2d 1218 (6th Cir.1989).

The unenforceability of arbitration clauses applies only to anticipatory agreements. Where a potential plaintiff has knowledge of an existing securities law claim, an agreement to arbitrate will be enforceable. Malena v. Merrill Lynch, Pierce, Fenner & Smith, Inc. (E.D.N.Y.1984). Enforceability of arbitration agreements is discussed in § 14.4 *infra.* *See also* §§ 10.15–10.22 *supra* (Practitioner's Edition only).

12. 15 U.S.C.A. § 78bb(b). *See, e.g.,* French v. Merrill Lynch, Pierce, Fenner & Smith, Inc., 784 F.2d 902 (9th Cir.1986) (affirming arbitration award in dispute between broker-dealer and market maker); N. Donald & Co. v. American United Energy Corp., 746 F.2d 666 (10th Cir.1984); Morgan, Olmstead, Kennedy & Gardner, Inc. v. United States Trust Co., 608 F.Supp. 1561 (S.D.N.Y.1985). However, such provisions are not enforceable when asserted against someone who is not a member of the self regulatory organization. Laurence v. Corwin, 75 A.D.2d 840, 427 N.Y.S.2d 865 (1980). Self regulatory organizations are discussed in chapter 10 *supra.*

13. Dean Witter Reynolds, Inc. v. Byrd, 470 U.S. 213, 105 S.Ct. 1238, 84 L.Ed.2d 158 (1985), *on remand* 760 F.2d 238 (9th Cir.1985). *See* § 14.4 *infra.*

14. *E.g.* Gerhardstein v. Shearson/American Express, Inc., 1986 WL 2691, [1985–86 Transfer Binder] Fed.Sec.L.Rep. (CCH) ¶ 92,512 (N.D.Ohio 1986).

15. Rodriguez De Quijas v. Shearson/American Express, Inc., 490 U.S. 477, 109 S.Ct. 1917, 104 L.Ed.2d 526 (1989); Shearson/American Express, Inc. v. McMahon, 482 U.S. 220, 107 S.Ct. 2332, 96 L.Ed.2d 185 (1987), *rehearing denied* 483 U.S. 1056, 108 S.Ct. 31, 97 L.Ed.2d 819 (1987). *See* § 14.4 *infra.*

Voiding of Contracts

Section 29(b) of the Exchange Act[16] goes further than the anti-waiver prohibitions discussed above. While the anti-waiver provisions merely preclude certain defenses to conduct that violates the securities acts, section 29(b) can be viewed as providing an affirmative remedy for parties who have entered into contracts with provisions contrary to the securities laws.[17] Section 29(b) provides that contracts involving performance that would be in violation of the Act are void.[18] The Supreme Court has held that a similar provision contained in the Investment Advisers Act of 1940[19] supports a private right of action for rescission.[20] It seems clear that a similar private remedy would exist under section 29(b) for contracts in violation of the Exchange Act or applicable SEC rules.[21] The Fifth Circuit similarly has recognized an implied right of rescission under section 29(b).[22] Such a remedy supplements any private relief that might also be available under SEC Rule 10b–5.[23] There is also limited authority to the effect that the section 29(b) remedy is not limited to rescission and can also support a claim for damages.[24] Since the nature of the action under section 29 is for rescission and therefore is contractual in nature, the remedy is available only against direct sellers (or purchasers) and not collateral participants.[25]

---

16. 15 U.S.C.A. § 78cc(b). *See* Comment, A Structural Analysis of Section 29(b) of the Securities Exchange Act, 56 U.Chi.L.Rev. 865 (1989).

17. *E.g.,* Mills v. Electric Auto–Lite Co., 396 U.S. 375, 385–388, 90 S.Ct. 616, 622–624, 24 L.Ed.2d 593 (1970), *appeal after remand* 552 F.2d 1239 (7th Cir.), *cert. denied* 434 U.S. 922, 98 S.Ct. 398, 54 L.Ed.2d 279 (1977), *rehearing denied* 434 U.S. 1002, 98 S.Ct. 649, 54 L.Ed.2d 499 (1977).

18. 15 U.S.C.A. § 78cc(b). The invalidation of contracts does not apply, however, to claims by customers against brokers who have violated the antifraud provisions of section 15(c)(3). *Id. See* 15 U.S.C.A. §§ 78*o*(c)(3).

19. Section 215, 15 U.S.C.A. § 80b–15. The Investment Advisers Act is discussed in chapter 18 *infra.*

20. Transamerica Mortgage Advisors, Inc. v. Lewis, 444 U.S. 11, 100 S.Ct. 242, 62 L.Ed.2d 146 (1979), *on remand* 610 F.2d 648 (9th Cir.1979) which is discussed in § 13.1 *supra.*

21. Gruenbaum & Steinberg, *supra* footnote 17.

22. Regional Properties, Inc. v. Financial & Real Estate Consulting Co., 678 F.2d 552 (5th Cir.1982), *appeal after remand* 752 F.2d 178 (5th Cir.1985). *See also* Regional Properties, Inc. v. Financial & Real Estate Consulting Co., 752 F.2d 178 (5th Cir.1985).

23. *Cf.* Herman & MacLean v. Huddleston, 459 U.S. 375, 103 S.Ct. 683, 74 L.Ed.2d 548 (1983), *on remand* 705 F.2d 775 (5th Cir.1983) (section 11 of the 1933 Act and Rule 10b–5 present cumulative remedies); SEC v. National Securities, Inc., 393 U.S. 453, 89 S.Ct. 564, 21 L.Ed.2d 668 (1969) (Rule 14a–9 of the proxy rules and Rule 10b–5 present cumulative remedies). *See* § 13.2 *supra. See generally* Marc I. Steinberg, The Propriety and Scope of Cumulative Remedies Under the Federal Securities Laws, 67 Cornell L.Rev. 557 (1982).

24. Geismar v. Bond & Goodwin, 40 F.Supp. 876, 878 (S.D.N.Y.1941).

25. Resolution Trust Corp. v. Miller, 1994 WL 276354 [1994–1995 Transfer Binder] Fed. Sec. L. Rep. (CCH) ¶ 98,380 (E.D.Pa.1994) (action could not be brought against savings and loan which was not a seller of the securities). The rule is analogous to the seller requirement that attaches to actions under section 12 of the 1933 Act. 15 U.S.C.A. § 77*l. See* §§ 7.3, 7.5, and § 7.5.1 (Practitioner's Edition only) *infra.*

As part of the 1990 Penny Stock Reform Act,[26] Congress empowered the Commission to designate section 15(c)(2) rules which if violated would not result in voidable transactions under section 29(b) of the Act.[27] This evidences a congressional intent of the rescission remedy in other circumstances.

In addition to any private right of action,[28] it is clear from its terms that section 29(b) can form the basis of a defense to suit brought on a contract that is in violation of the securities acts.[29] However, courts have not voided executed contracts where less drastic remedies could compensate the injured party.[30] Some decisions have taken a more literal view: "it is sufficient to show merely that the prohibited transactions occurred and that appellants were in the protected class."[31] Since rescission is an equitable remedy, the more flexible view seems appropriate.[32]

PART B: SECONDARY LIABILITY

§ 13.15   Multiple Defendants in Actions Under the Securities Exchange Act of 1934—Controlling Person Liability

Section 20(a) of the 1934 Act[1] states that "[e]very person who, directly or indirectly, controls any person liable under any provision of this chapter or of any rule or regulation thereunder shall also be liable jointly and severally with and to the same extent as such controlled

---

26. *See* § 10.7 *supra.*

27. 15 U.S.C.A. § 78cc(b). Section 15(c)(2) is discussed in § 12.1 *supra.*

28. *See* cases cited in footnotes 20–22 *supra. Cf.* E.F. Hutton & Co. v. Brown, 305 F.Supp. 371, 384 n. 28 (S.D.Tex.1969) (section 29(b) "merely supplements the rule of tort law imposing liability on a person who causes damage by violating a statute").

29. *See* Mills v. Electric Auto–Lite Co., 396 U.S. 375, 387, 90 S.Ct. 616, 24 L.Ed.2d 593 (1970), *appeal after remand* 552 F.2d 1239 (7th Cir.1977), *cert. denied* 434 U.S. 922, 98 S.Ct. 398, 54 L.Ed.2d 279 (1977), *rehearing denied* 434 U.S. 1002, 98 S.Ct. 649, 54 L.Ed.2d 499 (1977); Reserve Life Insurance Co. v. Provident Life Insurance Co., 499 F.2d 715, 726 (8th Cir.1974), *cert. denied* 419 U.S. 1107, 95 S.Ct. 778, 42 L.Ed.2d 803 (1975); Greater Iowa Corp. v. McLendon, 378 F.2d 783, 792 (8th Cir.1967). *See also,* Pearlstein v. Scudder & German, 429 F.2d 1136, 1148–1149 (2d Cir.1970), *cert. denied* 401 U.S. 1013, 91 S.Ct. 1250, 28 L.Ed.2d 550 (1971) (Friendly, J. dissenting).

30. Occidental Life Insurance Co. v. Pat Ryan & Associates, 496 F.2d 1255, 1265–66 (4th Cir.1974), *cert. denied* 419 U.S. 1023, 95 S.Ct. 499, 42 L.Ed.2d 297 (1974); Gannett Co. v. Register Publishing Co., 428 F.Supp. 818, 831 (D.Conn.1977); Freeman v. Marine Midland Bank–New York, 419 F.Supp. 440, 453 (E.D.N.Y.1976).

31. Eastside Church of Christ v. National Plan, Inc., 391 F.2d 357, 362 (5th Cir.1968), *cert. denied* 393 U.S. 913, 89 S.Ct. 234, 21 L.Ed.2d 198 (1968).

32. *See* authorities in footnote 23 *supra.*

§ 13.15

1. 15 U.S.C.A. § 78t(a). *See generally* M. Patricia Adamski, Contribution and Settlement in Multi-party Actions Under Rule 10b–5, 66 Iowa L.Rev. 533 (1981); William H. Kuehnle, Secondary Liability Under the Federal Securities Laws—Aiding and Abetting, Conspiracy, Controlling Person, and Agency—Common Law Principles and the Statutory Scheme, 14 J.Corp.L. 313 (1988); Note, Rule 10b–5—The Equivalent Scope of Liability Under Respondeat Superior and Section 20(a)—Imposing a Benefit Requirement on Apparent Authority, 35 Vand.L.Rev. 1383 (1982); Comment, Secondary Liability of Controlling Persons Under the Securities Acts: Toward an Improved Analysis, 126 U.Pa.L.Rev. 1345 (1978). *See also, e.g.,* Note, "Controlling" Securities Fraud: Proposed Liability Standards

person * * *.''[2] Thus, for a controlling person to be liable, initially a violation of the securities laws must occur. Otherwise, the controlled person will not be held accountable and subsequently, the controlling person will have no liability in which to share jointly and severally.[3] Section 20(a) of the Exchange Act closely parallels section 15 of the 1933 Act,[4] except that the 1933 Act provision is limited to actions under section 11 or 12 of that Act[5] while section 20(a) is not expressly limited and thus applies to both express and implied remedies under the Exchange Act. As a practical matter the 1933 and 1934 Act sections on controlling person liability are to be similarly applied and interpreted.[6]

For a plaintiff to have a prima facie case that the defendant was a controlling person within the meaning of section 20(a), the plaintiff must show that (1) the defendant had actual power or influence over the controlled person, and (2) that the defendant induced or participated in the alleged illegal activity.[7] Several circuits hold that under the second prong of the test, the defendant must have been a "culpable participant" in the alleged illegal activity.[8] Thus, for example, although a corporate director clearly ordinarily qualifies as a controlling person, specific

___

for Controlling Persons Under the 1933 and 1934 Securities Acts, 72 Minn.L.Rev. 930 (1988).

2. 15 U.S.C.A. § 78t(a). There is authority to the effect that controlling person liability is equally applicable in SEC enforcement actions. SEC v. First Jersey Securities, Inc., 876 F.Supp. 488 (S.D.N.Y.1994). *See also, e.g.,* Hateley v. SEC, 8 F.3d 653 (9th Cir.1993) (upholding controlling person liability as basis for NASD disgorgement order).

Control consists of the ability to affect management decisions. 17 C.F.R. § 230.405. *See, e.g.,* Laven v. Flanagan, 695 F.Supp. 800 (D.N.J.1988) (defendant's status as violator's largest shareholder did not establish controlling person liability).

3. *See* Deviries v. Prudential–Bache Securities, Inc., 805 F.2d 326 (8th Cir.1986).

4. 15 U.S.C.A. § 77o. *See* § 7.7 *supra.*

5. 15 U.S.C.A. §§ 77k, 77l. *See* §§ 7.2–7.5 *supra.*

6. *E.g.,* Farley v. Henson, 11 F.3d 827 (8th Cir.1993); Hollinger v. Titan Capital Corp., 914 F.2d 1564, 1578 (9th Cir.1990), *cert. denied* 499 U.S. 976, 111 S.Ct. 1621, 113 L.Ed.2d 719 (1991).

7. Some disagreement over the second prong of the test has occurred. Some courts argue that whether or not the defendant participated in the illegal activity is part of the defendant's defense and thus he has the burden of proving his own lack of participation. More recent court decisions state that participation is part of the plaintiff's cause of action. *See* G.A. Thompson & Co., v. Partridge, 636 F.2d 945, 959 (5th Cir.1981).

It is noteworthy that scienter of the controlling person is not a prerequisite to liability. Polycast Technology Corp. v. Uniroyal, Inc., 1988 WL 96586, [1988–89 Transfer Binder] Fed.Sec.L.Rep. (CCH) ¶ 94,005 (S.D.N.Y.1988).

8. *See* Seymour v. Summa Vista Cinema, Inc., 817 F.2d 609 (9th Cir.1987) (culpable participation standard); Wool v. Tandem Computers, Inc., 818 F.2d 1433 (9th Cir.1987) (the culpable participation standard); Orloff v. Allman, 819 F.2d 904 (9th Cir.1987) (same); Durham v. Kelly, 810 F.2d 1500 (9th Cir.1987) (same); Buhler v. Audio Leasing Corp., 807 F.2d 833 (9th Cir.1987) (same); Kersh v. General Council of Assemblies of God, 804 F.2d 546 (9th Cir.1986) (same); Metge v. Baehler, 762 F.2d 621, 631 (8th Cir.1985), *cert. denied* 474 U.S. 1057, 106 S.Ct. 798, 88 L.Ed.2d 774 (1986) (specifically rejects the "more restrictive" culpable participation standard); Gordon v. Diagnostek, Inc., 812 F.Supp. 57 (E.D.Pa.1993) (failure to show that potential acquirer was a culpable participant); Sweasey v. A.G. Edwards & Son, Inc., 738 F.Supp. 1278 (W.D.Mo.1990) (firm not liable as controlling person for account executive's transactions handled through a different brokerage firm); Leavey, et al. v. Blinder, Robinson & Co., Inc., 1986 WL 10556 [1986 Transfer Binder] Fed.Sec.L.Rep. (CCH) ¶ 92,996 (E.D.Pa.1986); Levine v. Merrill Lynch, Pierce, Fenner & Smith, Inc., 639 F.Supp. 1391 (S.D.N.Y.1986).

allegations of the director's participation are required in order to sustain a controlling person claim under section 20(a).[9] Culpable participation "requires a showing that the [defendant] actually participated in the alleged violation." [10] The facts underlying a claim of controlling person liability must be pleaded with specificity.[11] Accordingly, mere conclusory allegations will not be sufficient.[12] Whether or not someone qualifies as a controlling person is a question of fact.[13] Accordingly, controlling person claims will not ordinarily be resolved summarily at the pleading stage.[14]

What Constitutes Control?

Although the term "control" is not defined in section 20(a), the SEC has defined the term "control" generally (including the terms "controlling", "controlled by", and "under common control with") to mean "the possession, direct or indirect, of the power to direct or cause the direction of the management and policies of a person whether through the ownership of voting securities, by contract, or otherwise." [15] In addition, the scope of power and degree of influence necessary to hold a defendant liable as a controlling person are not spelled out in section 20(a).[16] All the plaintiff need allege is that the "defendant possessed the power to control the specific transaction or activity upon which the primary violation is predicated, but he need not prove that this later power was exercised."[17] It is not necessary to show that the defendant

9. *See, e.g.,* Bomarko v. Hemodynamics, Inc., 848 F.Supp. 1335 (W.D.Mich.1993) (outside directors who did not attend meeting were found not to have culpably participated in issuance of company's false statements); Walker v. Cardinal Savings & Loan Association, 690 F.Supp. 494 (E.D.Va.1988); Kimmel v. Labenski, 1988 WL 19229, [1987–88 Transfer Binder] Fed.Sec.L.Rep. (CCH) ¶ 93,651 (S.D.N.Y.1988).

Compare, e.g., Brown v. Mendel, 864 F.Supp. 1138 (M.D.Ala.1994) (former Board Chairman was not a controlling person).

10. Metge v. Baehler, 762 F.2d 621, 631 (8th Cir.1985), *cert. denied* 474 U.S. 1057, 106 S.Ct. 798, 88 L.Ed.2d 774 (1986).

11. *See, e.g.,* Gordon v. Diagnostek, Inc., 812 F.Supp. 57 (E.D.Pa.1993) (conclusory allegations of control were insufficient). The particularity requirement is discussed in § 13.8.1 *supra.*

12. *E.g.,* Harrison v. Enventure Capital Group, Inc., 666 F.Supp. 473 (W.D.N.Y.1987).

13. *See, e.g.,* Hilgeman v. National Insurance Co., 547 F.2d 298, 302 (5th Cir.1977); Hill York Corp. v. American International Franchises, Inc., 448 F.2d 680, 694 n.20 (5th Cir.1971); In re Chambers Development Securities Litigation, 848 F.Supp. 602, 618 (W.D.Pa.1994); In re Worlds of Wonder Securities Litigation, 694 F.Supp. 1427, 1435 (N.D.Cal.1988); Klapmeier v. Telecheck International, Inc., 315 F.Supp. 1360, 1361 (D.Minn.1970).

14. *Ibid.*

15. 17 C.F.R. § 230.405.

16. Wool v. Tandem Computers, Inc., 818 F.2d 1433, 1441 (9th Cir.1987).

17. Metge v. Baehler, 762 F.2d 621, 631 (8th Cir.1985), *cert. denied* 474 U.S. 1057, 106 S.Ct. 798, 88 L.Ed.2d 774 (1986) (quoting from the decision below, Metge v. Baehler, 577 F.Supp. 810, 817–18 (S.D. Iowa 1984)). *See also, e.g.,* In re American Business Computers Corp. Securities Litigation, 1993 WL 616684, [1993–1994 Transfer Binder] Fed. Sec. L. Rep. (CCH) ¶ 98,103 (S.D.N.Y.1993) (largest shareholder could be found as a matter of fact to have been controlling person).

actually directed the actions of the primary violator; it is sufficient to establish influence over such acts.[18] However, the mere *ability* to exert influence may not be sufficient. The fact that someone gives counsel and advice is not sufficient to establish control.[19]

The most common relationship in which control is presumed is that of the employer-employee.[20] However, controlling person liability is limited to transactions taking place on behalf of the employer. Thus, for example when the investor deals with an employee other than in his or her capacity as an employee, without relying on any affiliation with the employer, the employer will not be held accountable as a controlling person.[21] On the other hand, when an employee is acting under the employer's auspices, controlling person liability and control depends upon control over the employee; control with regard to the particular transaction in question need not be shown.[22]

Corporate officers are usually presumed to possess the requisite power to control the actions of their employees and are often held accountable as controlling persons.[23] However, corporate directors are

18. Section 20(a) "has been interpreted as requiring only an indirect means of discipline or influence short of actual direction * * *." Technology Exchange Corp. v. Grant County State Bank, 646 F.Supp. 179, 183 (D.Colo.1986). *But cf., e.g.,* Ross v. Bolton, 1989 WL 80428, [1989 Transfer Binder] Fed.Sec.L.Rep. (CCH) ¶ 94,410 (S.D.N.Y.1989), *vacated in part* 1989 WL 80425 (S.D.N.Y.1989) (claim that clearing agent had knowledge and affected a brokerage firm's action (illegal parking of securities) was not sufficient to establish that the clearing agent directed the action; hence there was no controlling person liability).

19. Harrison v. Dean Witter Reynolds, Inc., 974 F.2d 873, 877 (7th Cir.1992), *cert. denied* ___ U.S. ___, 113 S.Ct. 2994, 125 L.Ed.2d 688 (1993); Hollinger v. Titan Capital Corp., 914 F.2d 1564, 1575 (9th Cir.1990), *cert. denied* 499 U.S. 976, 111 S.Ct. 1621, 113 L.Ed.2d 719 (1991); Schlifke v. Seafirst Corp., 866 F.2d 935, 949 (7th Cir.1989); Barker v. Henderson, Franklin, Starnes & Holt, 797 F.2d 490, 494 (7th Cir.1986) ("the ability to persuade and give counsel is not the same thing as 'control', which almost always means the practical ability to *direct* the actions of people who issue or sell the securities").

20. "[T]he most obvious manner in which to establish liability as a controlling person is to prove that a person acted under the direction of the controlling person and this is most easily shown by an employer-employee relationship." Noland v. Gurley, 566 F.Supp. 210, 220 (D.Colo.1983). *See also* Martin v. Shearson Lehman Hutton, Inc., 986 F.2d 242 (8th Cir.1993), *cert. denied* ___ U.S. ___, 114 S.Ct. 177, 126 L.Ed.2d 136 (1993) (sufficient showing that brokerage firm was a controlling person of its employee); Seymour v. Summa Vista Cinema, Inc., 817 F.2d 609 (9th Cir.1987) ("In the broker-dealer context, defendant had actual power over [the employee] as his employer and a corresponding duty to supervise him").

21. *E.g.,* Kohn v. Optik, Inc., 1993 WL 169191, [1992–1993 Transfer Binder] Fed.Sec. L.Rep. (CCH) ¶ 97,435 (C.D.Cal.1993).

22. Hauser v. Farrell, 14 F.3d 1338 (9th Cir.1994) (brokerage firm was not liable as controlling person nor was it vicariously liable under respondeat superior); Martin v. Shearson Lehman Hutton, 986 F.2d 242 (8th Cir.1993), *cert. denied* ___ U.S. ___, 114 S.Ct. 177, 126 L.Ed.2d 136 (1993).

23. Wool v. Tandem Computers, Inc., 818 F.2d 1433, 1441 (9th Cir.1987). *See also, e.g.,* Food & Allied Service Trades Department, AFL–CIO v. Millfeld Trading Co., 841 F.Supp. 1386 (S.D.N.Y.1994) (adequately pleading controlling person status of treasurer, chief executive officer, and secretary). *Cf.* In re Syndergen, Inc. Securities Litigation, 863 F.Supp. 1409, 1422 (D.Colo.1994) (officers did not dispute status as controlling persons).

But see, e.g., Brown v. Mendel, 864 F.Supp. 1138 (M.D.Ala.1994) (former chief executive officer who had founded the business was not a controlling person).

not automatically liable as controlling persons.[24] Thus, "[t]here must be some showing of actual participation in the corporation's operation or some influence before the consequences of control may be imposed." [25]

Members of law firms and accounting firms are sometimes sued as controlling persons under section 20(a), but these claims are often dismissed because the "ability to persuade and give counsel is not the same thing as control, which almost always means the practical ability to direct the actions of the people who issue or sell the securities." [26] Whether or not a particular defendant has sufficient control is a question of fact that will vary with each case. As pointed out above, the mere capacity to exert influence will not suffice.[27] Thus, for example, the fact that a bank is a major lender to a primary violator of the securities laws or is otherwise involved in the tainted transaction is not by itself sufficient to establish the bank as a controlling person.[28] On appropriate facts, a promoter[29] or underwriter may qualify for controlling person liability but this may be true only in exceptional cases.

24. While "[t]he status or position of an alleged controlling person, by itself, is insufficient to presume or warrant a finding of power to control or influence", where "the corporate officers are a narrowly defined group charged with the day-to-day operations of a public corporation, it is reasonable to presume that these officers had the power to control or influence the particular transactions giving rise to the securities violation." Wool v. Tandem Computers, Inc., 818 F.2d 1433, 1441 (9th Cir.1987).

25. Burgess v. Premier Corp., 727 F.2d 826, 832 (9th Cir.1984) (quoting Herm v. Stafford, 663 F.2d 669, 684 (6th Cir.1981)). In *Burgess v. Premier Corp.*, a director successfully appealed his conviction as a controlling person because although he was a director of the corporation, unlike other directors he was not a corporate officer. Moreover, he was "uninvolved in [the company's] * * * day to day operations" and he "had no experience in [the company's] * * * business, nor in [its] industry * * *." *Id.* at 832.

26. Barker v. Henderson, Franklin, Starnes & Holt, 797 F.2d 490, 494 (7th Cir.1986). *See, e.g.,* Morin v. Trupin, 778 F.Supp. 711 (S.D.N.Y.1991) (failure to establish that attorney was a controlling person); Friedman v. Arizona World Nurseries Ltd. Partnership, 730 F.Supp. 521 (S.D.N.Y.1990) (attorney was not a controlling person).

27. *See, e.g.,* Arthur Children's Trust v. Keim, 994 F.2d 1390 (9th Cir.1993) (member of management committee was a controlling person); In re Zenith Laboratories Securities Litigation, 1993 WL 260683, [1993 Transfer Binder] Fed.Sec.L.Rep. (CCH) ¶ 97,617 (D.N.J. 1993) (board chairman and vice president both held to be controlling persons).

28. Sanders Confectionery Products, Inc. v. Heller Financial, Inc., 973 F.2d 474 (6th Cir.1992), *cert. denied* ___ U.S. ___, 113 S.Ct. 1046, 122 L.Ed.2d 355 (1993), *rehearing denied* ___ U.S. ___, 113 S.Ct. 1628, 123 L.Ed.2d 186 (1993) (insufficient allegations that lender was a controlling person); Gray v. First Winthrop Corp., 776 F.Supp. 504 (N.D.Cal. 1991) (lender not liable as controlling person). *See also, e.g.,* Abbott v. Equity Group, Inc., 2 F.3d 613 (5th Cir.1993) (neither surety nor bonding agent were controlling persons); General Insurance Co. v. Fort Lauderdale Partnership, 740 F.Supp. 1483 (W.D.Wash.1990) (surety was not controlling person); Seattle–First National Bank v. Carlstedt, 678 F.Supp. 1543, 1550 (W.D.Okl.1987).

29. Donohoe v. Consolidated Operating & Production Corp., 982 F.2d 1130 (7th Cir.1992), *on remand* 833 F.Supp. 719 (N.D.Ill.1993), *affirmed* 30 F.3d 907 (7th Cir.1994) (sufficient allegations that promoter was a controlling person). *Cf.* In re Proxima Corp. Securities Litigation, 1994 WL 374306, [1993–1994 Transfer Binder] Fed. Sec. L. Rep. (CCH) ¶ 98,236 (S.D.Cal.1994) (sufficient allegation of liability of venture capital firm as controlling person).

But see, e.g. In re ZZZZ Best Securities Litigation, 1994 WL 746649, [1994–1995 Transfer Binder] Fed.Sec.L.Rep. (CCH) ¶ 98,485 (C.D.Cal.1994) (nonmanaging underwriter was not a controlling person).

Participation in the Wrongful Conduct

Once the plaintiff proves that the defendant had the power to control and influence the controlled person, he or she must also prove that the defendant induced or was a "participant" in the alleged illegal activity. In order to be a participant, the defendant must have some actual knowledge of the fraudulent activity taking place or knowledge must be imputed to him or her;[30] knowledge is a first step in proving active participation. For corporate officers, knowledge is often imputed since "it is reasonable to presume that * * * prospectuses, registration statements, and other group publications are the collective actions of the corporate officers."[31] Thus, if these publications contain fraudulent claims, the corporate officers may be held accountable as controlling persons.

An exception to the above-mentioned knowledge and active participation requirements has been made for broker-dealers. Failure to supervise a broker-dealer is deemed to be indirect participation by the controlling person, and thus the controlling person may be liable under section 20(a) for any fraudulent schemes arising during the unsupervised period.[32] Several factors should be considered in applying the more relaxed standard for broker-dealers:

a) whether the controlling person derives direct financial gain from the activity of the controlled person;

b) the extent to which the controlled person is tempted to act unlawfully because of the controlling person's policies;

c) the extent to which statutory or regulatory law or the defendant's own policies require supervision;

d) the relationship between the plaintiff and the controlling person; and

e) the demonstration of some public policy need to impose such

---

30. *See* Abrams & Wofsy v. Renaissance Investment Corp., 820 F.Supp. 1519 (N.D.Ga. 1993), *cert. granted in part* ___ U.S. ___, 113 S.Ct. 2927, 124 L.Ed.2d 678 (1993), *judgment reversed on other grounds* ___ U.S. ___, 114 S.Ct. 1439, 128 L.Ed.2d 119 (1994) (failure to establish that accountants had general awareness of the fraud); Tischler v. Baltimore Bancorp, 1992 WL 206279, [1992 Transfer Binder] Fed.Sec.L.Rep. (CCH) ¶ 96,888 (D.Md. 1992) (allegations that "expert" outside directors were culpable participants were sufficient to state a claim for controlling person liability but allegations as to other outside directors were not); Baum, et al. v. Phillips, Appel & Walden, Inc., et al., 648 F.Supp. 1518 (S.D.N.Y.1986), *judgment affirmed* 867 F.2d 776 (2d Cir.1989). *But cf.* Reinfeld v. Riklis, 722 F.Supp. 1077 (S.D.N.Y.1989) (not necessary to show scienter on the part of principal as a precondition to controlling person liability).

31. Wool v. Tandem Computers, Inc., 818 F.2d 1433, 1442 (9th Cir.1987).

32. *See, e.g.,* Harrison v. Dean Witter Reynolds, Inc., 974 F.2d 873 (7th Cir.1992), *cert. denied* ___ U.S. ___, 113 S.Ct. 2994, 125 L.Ed.2d 688 (1993) (district court erred in applying "culpable participant" test to broker dealer; there were triable issues as to whether broker-dealer actually possessed the ability to control the activities of its employees in connection with their allegedly fraudulent sales of promissory notes); Gruber v. Prudential–Bache Securities, Inc., 679 F.Supp. 165 (D.Conn.1987).

Secondary liability of brokerage firms is discussed in § 10.14 *supra.*

a requirement.[33]

The exception to the knowledge element of controlling person liability generally applies only in the broker-dealer context and thus corporate officers of corporations generally are not held to this standard.[34] Securities brokerage firms are held to this more stringent standard because

> [t]o allow a brokerage firm to avoid secondary liability simply by showing ignorance, purposeful or negligent, of the acts of its registered representative contravenes Congress's intent to protect the public, particularly unsophisticated investors, from fraudulent practices. At least with respect to the initial choice of a broker, most investors rely upon the reputation and prestige of the brokerage firm rather than the individual employees with whom they might deal. Such firms should be held accountable if employees they select utilize the firm's prestige to practice fraud upon the investing public.[35]

It is thus the federal and self regulation which impose the special responsibilities of broker-dealers that justify a different standard of controlling person liability. Similarly, as discussed more fully below and elsewhere in this treatise,[36] under principles of vicarious liability a brokerage firm will be held liable for failure to supervise under principles of traditional agency law.[37]

Even where the employee is acting in his own rather than his employer's interest, the employer may be held liable under the doctrine of "apparent authority." [38] Under the agency concept of apparent authority, a principal is liable for the acts of agents even if beyond their actual authority when, for example, the principal's acquiescence in the

---

33. Kersh v. General Council of Assemblies of God, 804 F.2d 546, 550 (9th Cir.1986) (citing Zweig v. Hearst Corp., 521 F.2d 1129, 1135 (9th Cir.1975), *cert. denied* 423 U.S. 1025, 96 S.Ct. 469, 46 L.Ed.2d 399 (1975)). *See* Seymour v. Summa Vista Cinema, Inc., 817 F.2d 609 (9th Cir.1987) ("participation may be proven indirectly by showing that [defendant] generally failed to establish a reasonable system of supervision and control").

34. *See* Orloff v. Allman, 819 F.2d 904, 906 (9th Cir.1987) (company president not liable as a controlling person for fraudulent sales of unregistered securities under a theory of "indirect participation"; defendant must have actual power of control or influence) and Buhler v. Audio Leasing Corp., 807 F.2d 833, 835 (9th Cir.1987) (failure to supervise licensed securities sellers not equal to participation). *But see* G.A. Thompson & Co. v. Partridge, 636 F.2d 945, 959 (5th Cir.1981) (corporate director liable for reckless failure to supervise).

35. Paul F. Newton & Co. v. Texas Commerce Bank, 630 F.2d 1111, 1118–19 (5th Cir.1980).

36. *See* § 10.14 *supra.*

37. *See, e.g.,* Dougherty v. Mieczkowski, 661 F.Supp. 267, 279 (D.Del.1987), relying on Sharp v. Coopers & Lybrand, 649 F.2d 175, 181–82 (3d Cir.1981) and Rochez Brothers, Inc. v. Rhoades, 527 F.2d 880, 886 (3d Cir.1975). *See also, e.g.,* In re Atlantic Financial Management, Inc., 784 F.2d 29, 30–31 (1st Cir.1986); *See, e.g.,* Gruber v. Prudential–Bache Securities, Inc., 679 F.Supp. 165 (D.Conn.1987).

38. Federal Savings and Loan Insurance Corp. v. Shearson–American Express, 658 F.Supp. 1331 (D.Puerto Rico 1987).

agent's conduct has created the outward appearance of authority.[39] However, when it is, or should be, clear that the employee is acting on his own, then apparent authority cannot result in the liability of the employer.

Defenses to Claims of Controlling Person Liability

The defendant has two affirmative defenses to a controlling person liability claim. First, he or she can argue "good faith". The defendant will have the burden of proving his or her own good faith, which "requires not only the establishment of a proper system of supervision, but also its diligent enforcement."[40] Secondly, the defendant can also argue that he or she did not induce the alleged violation, or in other words, that he or she did not participate in the violation.[41]

The Relationship Between Controlling Person Liability and Common Law Principles

As a general proposition, controlling person liability is distinct from other forms of secondary liability.[42] It has different elements, and in some respects it is broader while in others it is narrower. Questions have arisen as to the extent that controlling person liability is the exclusive basis of secondary liability under the securities laws.[43]

Much debate has occurred over whether section 20(a) is an exclusive remedy, so that common law claims based on agency theories such as respondeat superior cannot be brought by plaintiffs. A number of circuit courts have held that section 20(a) is not an exclusive remedy.[44]

---

39. *E.g.,* Lux Art Van Service, Inc. v. Pollard, 344 F.2d 883 (9th Cir.1965), *cert. denied* 382 U.S. 837, 86 S.Ct. 85, 15 L.Ed.2d 80 (1965); Restatement (Second) of Agency § 8 comment a, illustrations 1–4 (1958).

40. Federal Savings & Loan Insurance Corp. v. Shearson–American Express, 658 F.Supp. 1331, 1343 (D.Puerto Rico 1987). *See also* Donohoe v. Consolidated Operating & Production Corp., 30 F.3d 907 (7th Cir.1994) (defendants' investigation of activities of other shareholder established their good faith defense to controlling person liability); Paul F. Newton & Co. v. Texas Commerce Bank, 630 F.2d 1111, 1119 (5th Cir.1980) (if defendant claims good faith as a defense, plaintiff need only show that the defendant failed to maintain, use and enforce a "proper system of supervision and control" to negate the defense).

See also, e.g., In re Syndergen, Inc. Securities Litigation, 863 F.Supp. 1409, 1422 (D.Colo.1994) (factual issue as to defendants' good faith precluded summary judgment).

41. Federal Savings and Loan Insurance Corp. v. Shearson–American Express, 658 F.Supp. 1331, 1343 (D.Puerto Rico 1987).

42. *See, e.g.,* SEC v. Militano, 1994 WL 558040, [1994–1995 Transfer Binder] Fed. Sec. L. Rep. (CCH) ¶ 98,441 (S.D.N.Y.1994) (SEC complaint alleging aiding and abetting liability could not be amended three weeks before trial to include a claim of controlling person liability).

43. This issue has become even more significant since the Supreme Court's ruling that there is no implied aiding and abetting liability under the securities laws. Central Bank of Denver v. First Interstate Bank of Denver, ___ U.S. ___, 113 S.Ct. 2927, 124 L.Ed.2d 678 (1993) which is discussed in § 13.16 *infra.*

44. *See* In re Atlantic Financial Management, Inc., 784 F.2d 29 (1st Cir.1986); Henricksen v. Henricksen, 640 F.2d 880, 887 (7th Cir.1981), *cert. denied* 454 U.S. 1097, 102 S.Ct. 669, 70 L.Ed.2d 637 (1981); Paul F. Newton & Co. v. Texas Commerce Bank, 630 F.2d 1111 (5th Cir.1980), *rehearing denied* 634 F.2d 1355 (5th Cir.1980); Marbury Manage-

The Ninth and Third Circuits decided differently and have held that section 20(a) is an exclusive remedy.[45] The Ninth Circuit, however, has since changed its position and is now aligned with a majority of cases permitting the common law claim to proceed.[46]

The availability of respondeat superior in federal securities cases has once again been brought into question by a recent Supreme Court ruling denying the existence of aiding and abetting liability. The Supreme Court's holding in Central Bank of Denver v. First Interstate Bank of Denver,[47] denying the existence of aiding and abetting liability, may foreshadow a change in the rule regarding respondeat superior. In the *Central Bank* case, the Court emphasized that implied private rights of action must be based on statutory language. The absence of statutory provisions for civil aider and abettor liability led the Court to deny any implied remedy.[48] It can be argued that for the same reason, Rule 10b–5 liability cannot be premised on respondeat superior, which is not expressly mentioned in the Exchange Act. On the other hand, aiding and abetting is a principle of criminal law which is inherently statutory. In contrast, respondeat superior has such a long-standing place in the common law that denial of its existence in securities cases would be anomalous to the view that the implied right of action under Rule 10b–5 is analogous to common law fraud.[49] On balance, the courts should continue to recognize respondeat superior as an independent basis of secondary liability under the securities laws.

Section 20(a) differs from common law agency theories in that it holds a controlling person liable unless that person (1) acted in good faith or (2) did not induce or knowingly participate in the violation. On the other hand, "common law agency theories may impose liability on a principal or employer without these two 'preconditions'."[50] The debate over whether section 20(a) is an exclusive remedy therefore centers around the question that if the plaintiff cannot show that the defendant did not act in good faith or that the defendant knowingly induced the

ment, Inc. v. Kohn, 629 F.2d 705 (2d Cir.1980), *cert. denied* 449 U.S. 1011, 101 S.Ct. 566, 66 L.Ed.2d 469 (1980); Holloway v. Howerdd, 536 F.2d 690, 696 (6th Cir.1976); Carras v. Burns, 516 F.2d 251, 259 (4th Cir.1975); Kerbs v. Fall River Industries, Inc., 502 F.2d 731 (10th Cir.1974). *See also, e.g.,* Castleglen, Inc. v. Commonwealth Savings Ass'n, 689 F.Supp. 1069 (D. Utah 1988); Note, Pruning the Judicial Oak: Developing a Coherent Application of Common Law Agency and Controlling Person Liability in Securities Cases, 93 Colum.L.Rev. 1185 (1993).

45. *See* Zweig v. Hearst Corp., 521 F.2d 1129 (9th Cir.1975), cert. *denied* 423 U.S. 1025, 96 S.Ct. 469, 46 L.Ed.2d 399 (1975); Rochez Brothers, Inc. v. Rhoades, 527 F.2d 880 (3d Cir.1975); and Sharp v. Coopers & Lybrand, 649 F.2d 175 (3d Cir.1981).

46. Hollinger v. Titan Capital Corp., 914 F.2d 1564 (9th Cir.1990), *cert. denied* 499 U.S. 976, 111 S.Ct. 1621, 113 L.Ed.2d 719 (1991). *See also, e.g.,* Carroll v. John Hancock Distributors, Inc., 1994 WL 87160, [1993–1994 Transfer Binder] Fed. Sec. L. Rep. (CCH) ¶ 98,200 (E.D.Pa.1994) (indicating a brokerage firm could be liable under principles of respondeat superior).

47. ___ U.S. ___, 114 S.Ct. 1439, 128 L.Ed.2d 119 (1994).

48. *See* § 13.16 *supra.*

49. *See* § 13.2 *supra* for a discussion of the genesis of the Rule 10b–5 private right of action.

50. In re Atlantic Financial Management, Inc., 784 F.2d 29, 30 (1st Cir.1986).

violation, can the plaintiff still bring a claim under the various agency theories of liability? [51]

The three common law theories of liability most often raised in plaintiffs' suits are all based on agency law. A principal may be held liable under common law if he or she "actually authorize[s]" the tort committed by his or her agent.[52] Rarely do principals actually authorize their agents to commit tortious acts. Liability may also be based on the "apparent authority" of the agent.[53] Under this theory, a corporation or other firm may be liable for the torts of its agents if the agents act under the guise of apparent authority from the corporation.[54] The third theory most often advanced by plaintiffs is respondeat superior and the vicarious liability that results from that doctrine.[55]

Those circuits holding that section 20(a) is not an exclusive remedy argue that the legislative history of section 20(a) indicates that it is intended to expand liability, not contract it by taking away common law remedies.[56] It has been suggested that the legislative history of the 1933 and 1934 Act provisions imposing controlling person liability[57] "demonstrates that Congress enacted those sections to address the specific evil of persons seeking to evade liability under the securities laws by organizing 'dummies', that acting under their control, would commit the prohibited acts."[58] Moreover, section 20(a) itself says nothing about being an

---

51. The scope of liability under section 20(a) is narrower than the scope of liability under respondeat superior because of the defenses set forth in section 20(a).

52. In re Atlantic Financial Management, Inc., 784 F.2d 29, 31 (1st Cir.1986) (citing Restatement (Second) of Agency, §§ 7, 257 (1958)).

53. 784 F.2d at 31 (citing Restatement (Second) of Agency, § 8 (1958)). *But see, e.g.,* Harrison v. Dean Witter Reynolds, Inc., 715 F.Supp. 1425 (N.D.Ill.1989) (insufficient allegations of apparent authority), s.c., 974 F.2d 873, 883–84 (7th Cir.1992), *cert. denied* ___ U.S. ___, 113 S.Ct. 2994, 125 L.Ed.2d 688 (1993).

54. *See* In re Atlantic Financial Management, Inc., 784 F.2d 29, 32 (1st Cir.1986); Federal Savings and Loan Insurance Corp. v. Shearson–American Express, 658 F.Supp. 1331 (D. Puerto Rico 1987) (court held that Shearson could be liable under apparent authority doctrine even though former vice president and broker for Shearson, when he committed fraudulent acts, did not intend to benefit Shearson).

55. "Respondeat superior is the common-law principle that under certain circumstances holds an employer responsible for the tortious acts of his employees and agents by attributing to him their conduct, even though he himself may lack any fault." Note, Rule 10b–5—The Equivalent Scope of Liability Under Respondeat Superior and Section 20(a)— Imposing a Benefit Requirement on Apparent Authority, 35 Vand.L.Rev. 1383, 1385 (1982).

56. In re Atlantic Financial Management, Inc., 784 F.2d 29, 33 (1st Cir.1986). *See also, e.g.,* Castleglen v. Commonwealth Savings Ass'n, 689 F.Supp. 1069 (D.Utah 1988).

57. Sections 15 of the 1933 Act and 20(a) of the 1934 Act are essentially identical provisions. In Pharo v. Smith, 621 F.2d 656, 673–74 (5th Cir.1980), *reversed and remanded in part on other grounds* 625 F.2d 1226 (5th Cir.1980), the court held that, because the two sections contained similar provisions, courts should interpret them similarly. "Congress enacted § 15 to prevent persons from evading liability for violations of the registrations requirements of the Securities Act by employing others to act in their stead," and section 20(a) was enacted to prevent "persons from avoiding liability under the provisions of the [1934] * * * Act by utilizing 'dummies' to commit the prohibited acts." Paul F. Newton & Co. v. Texas Commerce Bank, 630 F.2d 1111, 1115 (5th Cir.1980).

58. Paul F. Newton & Co. v. Texas Commerce Bank, 630 F.2d 1111, 1118–19 (5th Cir.1980), *rehearing denied* 634 F.2d 1355 (5th Cir.1980).

exclusive remedy.[59]   As discussed more fully below, the Ninth Circuit reversed its earlier position and now holds that controlling person liability is not exclusive.[60]

The circuits finding that section 20(a) is not an exclusive remedy find additional support for their position by looking to the definition of "persons" set forth in the 1934 Act.   The term "persons" expressly includes "corporations" in its definition.   Thus, a corporation can be held liable under section 20(a) which states "every *person* who * * * controls any person liable * * * shall also be liable jointly and severally * * *." [61]   It must be remembered that corporations can act only through their agents and thus absent principles of vicarious liability, there would be very little if any corporate accountability.[62]   Moreover, if section 20(a) were held to be an exclusive remedy, most corporations, typically liable vicariously for their officers' acts under state misrepresentation law, would often escape liability under federal law.[63]   Thus, the better view would appear to be that surely Congress intended common law theories of liability to remain viable in spite of the creation of section 20(a).

Those circuits holding that section 20(a) is not an exclusive remedy also look to section 28 of the 1934 Act, which states that remedies provided under the act supplement those existing under common law.[64] As the Second Circuit has explained, "[s]ection 28(a) * * * specifically enacts that the rights and remedies provided by the '34 Act shall be in addition to any and all rights and remedies that may exist at law or in equity, * * *.' " [65]   It has been suggested, however, that section 28 applies only to claims independent of the Exchange Act and not to vicarious liability with regard to claims brought under that Act.[66]

A leading case denying vicarious liability was Zweig v. Hearst Corp.[67] In *Zweig* the court held that section 20(a) was an exclusive remedy, but no reason was stated for that finding.   The Ninth Circuit continued to

---

59.   In re Atlantic Financial Management, Inc., 784 F.2d 29, 33 (1st Cir.1986) ("Section 20(a) does not *say* that it is exclusive; and its proviso ('unless * * *') is naturally read as referring to the (potentially *non*exclusive) liability which section 20(a) *itself* provided") (emphasis in original).

60.   Hollinger v. Titan Capital Corp., 914 F.2d 1564 (9th Cir.1990), *cert. denied,* 499 U.S. 976, 111 S.Ct. 1621, 113 L.Ed.2d 719 (1991).

61.   15 U.S.C.A. § 78t (emphasis added).

62.   In re Atlantic Financial Management, Inc., 784 F.2d 29, 33 (1st Cir.1986).

63.   *Id.*

64.   15 U.S.C.A. § 78bb.

65.   Marbury Management, Inc. v. Kohn, 629 F.2d 705, 716 (2d Cir.1980), *cert. denied* 449 U.S. 1011, 101 S.Ct. 566, 66 L.Ed.2d 469 (1980).

66.   "Section 28(a), however, does not justify the application of a common law doctrine (respondeat superior) to a case brought under the federal securities laws; it means rather, that any state law or common law remedy which exists separately may provide an additional cause of action in a securities matter."   William J. Fitzpatrick and Ronald T. Carman, Respondeat Superior and the Federal Securities Laws: A Round Peg in a Square Hole, 12 Hofstra L.Rev. 1, 21 n. 4 (1983).

67.   521 F.2d 1129, 1132–33 (9th Cir.1975), *cert. denied* 423 U.S. 1025, 96 S.Ct. 469, 46 L.Ed.2d 399 (1975).

adhere to its position[68] until 1990, when it ruled *en banc* that controlling person liability does not preempt common law vicarious liability.[69] Accordingly, the court was willing to consider the claim that an employer could be liable under principles of *respondeat superior*. With this major shift in position, outside of the Third and Fourth Circuits, there remains little authority for the view that controlling person liability is exclusive.[70]

In Rochez Brothers, Inc. v. Rhoades,[71] the Third Circuit held that section 20(a) was an exclusive remedy because the good faith defense available to defendants under section 20(a) was "inconsistent with the imposition of an essentially secondary liability on respondeat superior grounds." It reasoned that the section 20(a)'s provision that a controlling person acting in good faith will not be liable evidenced an intent not to permit the possibility of strict liability under common law theories of agency. The court stated that "[i]f we were to apply respondeat superior * * * we would in essence impose a duty on a corporation to supervise and oversee the activities of its directors and employees when they are dealing with their own corporate stock as individuals, and * * * not for the benefit of the corporation. To impose such a duty would make the corporation primarily liable for any security law violation by any officer or employee of the corporation." [72] Thus, in the Third Circuit, section 20(a) generally supplants the use of agency principles. This holding has been aptly criticized since it does not take into account that for respondeat superior to be applicable, the agent must have acted within the course and scope of employment and within his actual or apparent authority.[73]

Ordinarily, if a director is dealing in his own corporate stock as an individual he is not acting within the scope of employment.[74] In Sharp v. Coopers & Lybrand,[75] an exception was made for employers of broker-

68. *See* Christoffel v. E.F. Hutton & Co., 588 F.2d 665, 667 (9th Cir.1978) ("it is the established law of this circuit that section 20(a) supplants vicarious liability of an employer for the acts of an employee applying the respondeat superior doctrine").

69. Hollinger v. Titan Capital Corp., 914 F.2d 1564 (9th Cir.1990), *cert. denied* 499 U.S. 976, 111 S.Ct. 1621, 113 L.Ed.2d 719 (1991). Respondeat superior liability is not limited to broker-dealer cases. In re Network Equipment Technologies, Inc., 762 F.Supp. 1359 (N.D.Cal.1991).

70. In addition to the authorities in the Third Circuit, *see* Carpenter v. Harris, Upham & Co., 594 F.2d 388 (4th Cir.1979), *cert. denied* 444 U.S. 868, 100 S.Ct. 143, 62 L.Ed.2d 93 (1979) (denying liability of employer due to failure to satisfy controlling person requirements; the court did not discuss respondeat superior).

71. 527 F.2d 880 (3d Cir.1975). *See also, e.g.,* Marbury Management, Inc. v. Kohn, 629 F.2d 705, 715 (2d Cir.1980), *cert. denied* 449 U.S. 1011, 101 S.Ct. 566, 66 L.Ed.2d 469 (1980).

72. *Rochez Brothers, Inc.,* 527 F.2d at 885.

73. Paul F. Newton & Co. v. Texas Commerce Bank, 630 F.2d 1111 (5th Cir.), *rehearing denied* 634 F.2d 1355 (5th Cir.1980).

74. *But see* Holloway v. Howerdd, 536 F.2d 690 (6th Cir.1976) (employer/brokerage firm held liable for fraudulent actions of employee/broker-dealer even though employee not acting within the scope of employment).

75. 649 F.2d 175, 184 (3d Cir.1981), *cert. denied* 455 U.S. 938, 102 S.Ct. 1427, 71 L.Ed.2d 648 (1982).

dealers because they owe a higher standard of care when supervising their employees. Respondeat superior claims may be brought when this higher standard of care is warranted.[76]

Given that the majority of courts have not adopted the view that section 20(a) is exclusive, most plaintiffs bringing suits against controlling persons for securities violations will probably use both section 20(a) and respondeat superior in their claims for relief. They will have to prove that the controlling person indeed had actual control under section 20(a) or else control will have to be presumed due to the facts of the case. For a viable claim under respondeat superior theories, the plaintiff will need to show that the controlled person was acting within the scope of his or her employment when the alleged illegal activity took place.

Special Rules Applicable to Misuse of Confidential Information

Although the controlling person liability provision of section 20(a) applies to private actions for improper insider trading,[77] it does not apply under SEC enforcement provisions dealing with insider trading. In SEC actions brought under the Insider Trading Sanctions Act (ITSA),[78] controlling person liability is limited to controlling persons and employers who knew or recklessly disregarded the likelihood of misuse of confidential information and failed to take adequate precautions.[79] Specifically, by virtue of the amendments in the Insider Trading and Securities Fraud Enforcement Act of 1988, a court can impose ITSA penalties on a controlling person of a primary violator only if: (1) the controlling person knew or acted in reckless disregard of the fact that the controlled person was likely to engage in illegal insider trading and (2) the controlling person failed to take adequate precautions to prevent the prohibited conduct from taking place.[80] It is further provided that general principles of respondeat superior and section 20(a)[81] controlling person liability expressly do not apply to SEC and criminal actions

---

76. Some commentators believe that courts misconstrued the intent of the doctrine of respondeat superior when they began to look at factors such as duty to supervise. They argue that respondeat superior is based solely on scope or course of employment, they argue. If an employee is acting outside the scope of employment, the employer should not be held accountable under the doctrine of respondeat superior nor under section 20(a). William H. Fitzpatrick & Ronald T. Carman, Respondeat Superior and the Federal Securities Laws: A Round Peg in a Square Hole, 12 Hofstra L.Rev. 1, 11–13 (1983). *See also* Moss v. Morgan Stanley, Inc., 553 F.Supp. 1347, 1357–58 (S.D.N.Y.1983), *affirmed* 719 F.2d 5 (2d Cir.1983) (employee acting outside scope of employment and thus no prima facie case of control can be alleged under section 20(a)).

77. 15 U.S.C.A. § 78t–1(b)(3). *See* § 13.9 *supra.*

78. 15 U.S.C.A. §§ 78u, 78u–1.

79. 15 U.S.C.A. § 78u–1(b)(1).

80. 15 U.S.C.A. § 78u–1(b)(1). In addition, broker-dealers are specifically directed to establish, maintain, and enforce written policies designed to prevent insider trading violations by their employees. 15 U.S.C.A. § 78o(f). A similar provision exists for investment advisers. 15 U.S.C.A. § 80b–4a. Investment advisers are discussed in chapter 18 *infra.*

81. 15 U.S.C.A. § 78t(a).

brought under ITSA.[82]

§ 13.16 Multiple Defendants in Actions Under the Securities Exchange Act of 1934—Aiding and Abetting Liability

The Demise of Aiding and Abetting Liability

In cases involving violations of the securities laws, plaintiffs often brought suit against not only the person who is the primary violator of the specific statute, but also any persons who may have assisted in the wrongful act. Claims against these aiders and abettors were most often brought to help assure a solvent defendant, since aiders and abettors formerly were generally held to be jointly and severally liable to plaintiffs for violations and were often viewed as better sources from which to obtain monetary awards.[1]

For years, the district and circuit courts assumed, without really ever questioning, that private plaintiffs could bring securities fraud actions against aiders and abettors. This was the generally accepted law notwithstanding the absence of an express right of action. To the surprise of many observers, the Supreme Court granted *certiorari* on the issue of whether there is an implied right of action for aiding and abetting under the securities laws.[2] And, to their further surprise, the Court in 1994 denied the availability of a private remedy against aiders and abettors of violations of the securities laws.[3]

In 1993, however, the Court held that there is an implied right of contribution under the securities laws.[4] Especially in light of that decision, coupled with the long history of judicial acceptance of aider and abettor liability, it was commonly believed that it would be surprising if the Court did not recognize an implied action against aiders and abettors

---

82. 15 U.S.C.A. § 78u–1(b)(2). In addition for controlling persons the treble damage penalty is not to exceed the greater of one million dollars or three times the amount of the profit gained or loss avoided. 15 U.S.C.A. § 78u–1(a)(3). *See* § 13.9 *supra.*

§ 13.16

1. "Aiders and abettors make ideal 'deep pockets' because they are jointly and severally liable with the primary violator." Note, Liability for Aiding and Abetting Violations of Rule 10b–5: The Recklessness Standard in Civil Damage Actions, 62 Texas L.Rev. 1087, 1089 n. 10 (1984). *See also, e.g.,* Landy v. Federal Deposit Insurance Corp., 486 F.2d 139 (3d Cir.1973), *cert. denied* 416 U.S. 960, 94 S.Ct. 1979, 40 L.Ed.2d 312 (1974); Alan R. Bromberg & Lewis D. Lowenfels, Aiding and Abetting Securities Fraud: A Critical Examination, 52 Albany L.Rev. 637 (1989); William H. Kuehnle, Secondary Liability Under the Federal Securities Laws—Aiding and Abetting, Conspiracy, Controlling Person, and Agency—Common–Law Principles and the Statutory Scheme, 14 J.Corp.L. 313 (1988).

2. Central Bank of Denver v. First Interstate Bank of Denver, ___ U.S. ___, 113 S.Ct. 2927, 124 L.Ed.2d 678 (1993), *opinion below* 969 F.2d 891 (10th Cir.1992). Certiorari had been sought on the question of whether a showing of recklessness could support aiding and abetting liability and in granting certiorari on that question the Court also asked the parties to brief the question of whether there is an implied action against aiders and abettors.

3. Central Bank of Denver, N.A. v. First Interstate Bank of Denver, ___ U.S. ___, 114 S.Ct. 1439, 128 L.Ed.2d 119 (1994). *See* discussion *infra.*

4. Musick, Peeler & Garrett v. Employers Insurance of Wausau, ___ U.S. ___, 113 S.Ct. 2085, 124 L.Ed.2d 194 (1993). *See* § 7.7 *supra* and § 13.17 *infra.*

under Rule 10b–5.[5] Nevertheless, the Supreme Court in Central Bank of Denver v. First Interstate Bank of Denver, by a five-to-four decision held that there is no implied right of action to redress aiding and abetting of a Rule 10b–5 violation.[6] The Court's holding is limited by the facts of the case to private rights of action. Accordingly, at least in theory, aiding and abetting may still be charged at least in certain SEC injunctive and other enforcement actions as well as criminal prosecutions.[7] The dissent in *Central Bank* observed, however, that the Court's rationale in denying the private right of action may foreshadow the even more unfortunate result of eliminating aiding and abetting as an enforcement weapon. The dissent further questioned whether the majority's rationale in *Central Bank* also affects the availability of common law doctrines such as conspiracy and respondeat superior, neither of which are expressly authorized in the securities laws.

It is further worth noting that the significance of the *Central Bank* decision transcends the particular point at issue. The Court imposed an extremely literal approach to statutory interpretation, limiting implied remedies to the terms of the statute and refusing to incorporate well-recognized common law principles.[8] As such, the Court continued its restrictive approach to implied remedies.[9]

---

5. As discussed *infra*, aiding and abetting liability exists for violations of the express liability provisions contained in the 1933 Act. *See also* §§ 7.2., 7.3, 7.5 *supra*.

6. __ U.S. __, 114 S.Ct. 1439, 128 L.Ed.2d 119 (1994). *See* S. Scott Lutton, The Ebb and Flow of Section 10(b) Jurisprudence: An Analysis of *Central Bank*, 17 U.Ark. Little Rock L.J. 45 (1994); James L. Fuchs, Comment, A Seville Standard for Aiders and Abettors: The Logic and Implications of the Supreme Court's Decision in *Central Bank*, 45 Case Wes.Res.L.Rev. 661 (1995); Ben D. Orlanski, Comment, Whose Representations are These Anyway? Attorney Prospectus Liability after *Central Bank*, 42 U.C.L.A.L.Rev. 885 (1995); Glen W. Roberts II, Note, 10(B) or Not 10(B): *Central Bank of Denver v. First Interstate Bank of Denver*, 73 N.C.L.Rev. 1239 (1995).

7. Under section 15(b)(4) of the Exchange Act, 15 U.S.C.A. § 78*o*(b)(4), the Commission is empowered to limit broker-dealer registration based on willful aiding and abetting of the securities laws. Under section 21B of that Act, 15 U.S.C.A. § 78u–2, the Commission may issue civil penalties against broker-dealers who have aided and abetted a violation of the securities laws.

In addition to the foregoing provisions of the Exchange Act, the Investment Company Act of 1940 and Investment Advisors Act of 1940 empower the SEC to pursue aiders and abettors. Investment Company Act of 1940 § 9(b)(3), (4) 15 U.S.C.A. § 80a–9(b)(3), (4) (SEC may by order disqualify willful aiders and abettors from serving as investment company employee, officer, director, investment adviser or principal underwriter); Investment Advisers Act of 1940 § 203(e)(5), (7), 15 U.S.C.A. § 80b–3(e)(5), (7) (SEC authority to place limits on activities of registered investment advisers); *Id.* § 209(d), 15 U.S.C.A. § 80b–9(d) (SEC enforcement powers for violations of Adviser's Act).

Even beyond those specific provisions, the Commission has publicly taken the position that enforcement actions may still be brought against aiders and abettors under Rule 10b–5. For one SEC insider's view, *see* Simon M. Lorne, Central Bank of Denver v. SEC, 49 Bus. Law. 1467 (1994).

8. *Compare* Musick, Peeler & Garrett v. Employers Insurance of Wausau, __ U.S. __, 113 S.Ct. 2085, 124 L.Ed.2d 194 (1993), holding that there is an implied right to contribution among joint defendants. In the *Central Bank* case the Court distinguished the *Musick* decision on the basis that the securities laws contain an express statement of controlling person and joint and several liability, which is in contrast to the absence of a general aiding and abetting provision. The right to contribution is discussed in § 7.7 *supra* and § 13.17 *infra*.

9. *See* §§ 13.1, 13.2 *supra*.

The Court in the *Central Bank* case recognized that the general federal aiding and abetting statute[10] makes it a criminal offense to aid and abet any substantive criminal violation. This, of course, gives the government the authority to criminally prosecute collateral participants who aid and abet violations of any of the criminal prohibitions of the securities laws. The Court further pointed to the absence of a generalized securities statute creating aiding and abetting liability in SEC actions generally (although the SEC has that authority in actions against broker-dealers) as well as to the securities laws' failure to set forth an express provision making aiding and abetting applicable to private suits.[11] Notwithstanding the *Central Bank* decision, it is clear that the Commission may still proceed against broker-dealers as aiders and abettors both civilly and in administrative proceedings. The Court's reasoning, however, strongly suggests that, as is the case in a suit brought by a private plaintiff, the SEC lacks the generalized authority to pursue aiders and abettors in the absence of a specific statutory grant. A more receptive court might consider the argument that a refusal to imply a remedy in a private suit is something different from extending the SEC's grant of authority to pursue criminal violations. Since the SEC is charged with enforcing the securities laws generally,[12] it is conceivable that a court might be willing to find the authority to pursue aiders and abettors. However, it is most unlikely that the Court that decided *Central Bank* would accept this argument insofar as such an approach would go against both the spirit and tenor of the Court's *Central Bank* decision.

Finally, in the *Central Bank* decision, the Court refused to imply aiding and abetting liability on the basis of section 10(b)'s prohibition of conduct which "directly or *indirectly*" violates the Act. As observed above, the decision, although technically limited to private rights of action may well have broader implications. Although aiding and abetting may still be charged in at least certain SEC injunctive and other enforcement actions as well as criminal prosecutions, it no longer has the bite that it once did.

[*See* Practitioner's Edition for further discussion.]

§ 13.17 Multiple Defendants in Actions Under the Securities Exchange Act of 1934—Contribution and Indemnity

Contribution Explained

Defendants found liable for violations of securities laws are often jointly and severally liable to plaintiffs for their fraudulent acts under

10. 18 U.S.C.A. § 2.
11. *See* footnote 6 *supra*.
12. *See* § 9.5 *supra*.

Rule 10b–5,[1] and consequently, the entire damage award can be collected from one or more defendants, assuming joint liability is found. Under the tort principle of contribution, the court may distribute the loss among the joint tortfeasors by requiring each defendant to pay his or her portion of the damages.[2] A person seeking contribution may do so either by the use of third party practice (impleader) or by bringing a separate action.[3]

In contrast to section 11 of the 1933 Act,[4] except for the limited express remedies under sections 9 and 18, the Exchange Act is silent on the right to contribution. Most courts, including the Supreme Court, have thus recognized an implied right of contribution among joint violators of Rule 10b–5.[5]

[*See* Practitioner's Edition for further discussion.]

§ 13.17

1. 17 C.F.R. § 240.10b–5. Joint and several liability under the 1933 Act is discussed in § 7.7 *supra.*

2. *See, e.g.,* In re Olympia Brewing Co. Securities Litigation, 674 F.Supp. 597 (N.D.Ill. 1987).

3. *See, e.g.,* Helen S. Scott, Resurrecting Indemnification: Contribution Clauses in Underwriting Agreements, 61 N.Y.U.L.Rev. 223, 230 n. 32 (1986) ("The right of contribution may be enforced either by bringing the potential contributors into the main action by way of a third-party complaint or in a separate action after judgment in the main action has been rendered"); Note, Contribution Under the Federal Securities Laws, 1975 Wash. U.L.Q. 1256, 1283–84.

Third party claims must be pleaded with sufficient particularity. Fed.R.Civ.P. 9(b). *E.g.* Beaumont Offset Corp. v. Montgomery Land & Cattle, 684 F.Supp. 75, 77 (S.D.N.Y. 1988) (sufficient particularity). *See* § 13.8.1 *supra* (Practitioner's Edition only).

4. 15 U.S.C.A. § 77k(f). *See* §§ 7.3–7.4.1 *supra.*

5. Musick, Peeler & Garrett v. Employers Insurance of Wausau, ___ U.S. ___, 113 S.Ct. 2085, 124 L.Ed.2d 194 (1993).

Chapter 14

JURISDICTIONAL ASPECTS

Table of Sections

---

§ 14.1 Exclusive Federal Jurisdiction Under the Exchange Act; Concurrent Jurisdiction Under the 1933 and Other Securities Acts

The Jurisdictional Mosaic

The federal securities laws provide a mosaic approach to jurisdiction. The Securities Act of 1933 and most of the other acts comprising the battery of securities laws provide for concurrent jurisdiction of federal and state courts, thus giving private parties a choice of forum.[1] In contrast, the Securities Exchange Act of 1934 provides that jurisdiction is exclusively federal, which means that all judicial private suits must be brought in federal court. All criminal prosecutions under the securities laws and judicial enforcement actions by the SEC must be maintained only in federal court.[2] Similarly, jurisdiction over appeals from SEC

---

* Deleted section 14.5 can be found in the Practitioner's Edition.

§ 14.1

1. *See generally* Thomas L. Hazen, Allocation of Jurisdiction Between the State and Federal Courts for Remedies Under the Federal Securities Laws, 60 N.C.L. Rev. 707 (1982).

As discussed more fully below, even among the acts providing for concurrent jurisdiction, there are variations regarding the right of removal to federal court.

2. Securities Act of 1933, § 22(a), 15 U.S.C.A. § 77v(a); Securities Exchange Act of 1934, § 27, 15 U.S.C.A. § 78aa; Public Utility Holding Company Act of 1935, § 25, 15 U.S.C.A. § 79y; Trust Indenture Act of 1939, § 322(b), 15 U.S.C.A. § 77vvv(b); Investment Company Act of 1940, § 44, 15 U.S.C.A. § 80a–43; Investment Advisers Act of 1940, § 214, 15 U.S.C.A. § 80b–14.

administrative decisions is exclusively federal.[3] When dealing with private remedies, however, the six securities acts present three different approaches to jurisdictional allocation.

First, the Securities Exchange Act of 1934 provides for exclusive federal jurisdiction over all suits in law or equity to enforce liabilities arising under the Act or applicable SEC rules.[4] Thus, only under the Exchange Act is all jurisdiction exclusively federal. Second, the other five federal securities acts provide for concurrent federal and state jurisdiction over private civil actions while granting exclusive federal jurisdiction over criminal proceedings and SEC enforcement actions.[5] The third approach, which actually is a variation of the second and is found in the Securities Act of 1933[6] and the Trust Indenture Act of 1939,[7] is concurrent state and federal jurisdiction, provided however, that suits initiated in state courts are not removable to federal court; as is the case with the other acts, jurisdiction over criminal actions and SEC judicial enforcement proceedings under the 1933 Act and Trust Indenture Act is exclusively federal.

Securities claims can form the basis of other rights of action. The courts were divided as to whether there is exclusive or concurrent jurisdiction for claims brought under the Racketeering Influenced and Corrupt Organizations Act (RICO),[8] which is being used with increasing regularity in securities cases.[9] The Supreme Court has resolved the

---

3. Securities Act of 1933, § 9, 15 U.S.C.A. § 77i; Securities Exchange Act of 1934, § 25, 15 U.S.C.A. § 78y; Public Utility Holding Company Act of 1935, § 24, 15 U.S.C.A. § 79x; Trust Indenture Act of 1939, § 322(a), 15 U.S.C.A. § 77vvv(a); Investment Company Act of 1940, § 43, 15 U.S.C.A. § 80a–42; Investment Advisers Act of 1940, § 213, 15 U.S.C.A. § 80b–13.

A state court does not have the power to interfere with SEC proceedings. First Jersey Securities, Inc. v. SEC, 194 N.J.Super. 284, 476 A.2d 861 (1984), *appeal dismissed* 101 N.J. 208, 501 A.2d 893 (1985).

4. 15 U.S.C.A. § 78aa. *See, e.g.,* Finkielstain v. Seidel, 857 F.2d 893 (2d Cir.1988) (refusing to invoke abstention doctrine in light of Exchange Act's grant of exclusive jurisdiction). For a case analyzing exclusivity and requiring removal from state to federal court under the 1934 Act, *see* Dean Witter Reynolds, Inc. v. Schwartz, 550 F.Supp. 1312 (S.D.Fla.1982). Arguably, removal is inappropriate since the state court lacks jurisdiction. It would be more appropriate to simply dismiss the claim.

5. *See* footnote 2 *supra.*

6. 15 U.S.C.A. § 77v(a). *See, e.g.,* Carson v. Prudential–Bache Securities, Inc., 1990 WL 133482, [1990–1991 Transfer Binder] Fed.Sec.L.Rep. (CCH) ¶ 95,816 (D.Kan.1990) (section 12(2) claim cannot be removed to federal court and thus was remanded back to state court). *But see* Bennett v. Bally Manufacturing, 785 F.Supp. 559 (D.S.C.1992) (the court adopted the view that section 12(2) does not apply to secondary markets and, as such, since there was no cognizable 1933 Act claim, the bar against removal was inapplicable and the Rule 10b–5 claim was properly removed to federal court); Knapp v. Gomez, 1987 WL 16944, [1987 Transfer Binder] Fed.Sec.L.Rep. (CCH) ¶ 93,287 (S.D.Cal.1987) (section 17(a) claim is not removable).

7. 15 U.S.C.A. § 77vvv(b).

8. 18 U.S.C.A. § 1961 *et seq.* *See* § 19.3 *infra* (Practitioner's Edition only).

9. The early cases recognizing concurrent jurisdiction included: Emrich v. Touche Ross & Co., 846 F.2d 1190 (9th Cir.1988) (also holding RICO claim was removable to federal court); Chas. Kurz Co. v. Lombardi, 595 F.Supp. 373 (E.D.Pa.1984); Luebke v. Marine National Bank of Neenah, 567 F.Supp. 1460 (E.D.Wis.1983); Cianci v. Superior Court, 40 Cal.3d 903, 221 Cal.Rptr. 575, 710 P.2d 375 (1985). *Cf.* County of Cook v. MidCon Corp., 773 F.2d 892 (7th Cir.1985) (reluctance to find exclusive federal jurisdiction).

issue, holding that there is concurrent state and federal jurisdiction over civil RICO claims.[10]

Most federal statutes that grant concurrent state and federal jurisdiction typically also provide for a right of removal to federal court.[11] Denial of the right of removal is generally limited to federal legislation involving matters of strong local, as opposed to national, interests.[12] Thus, the ban on removal in the 1933 and 1939 Acts is surprising in light of the strong federalism strains running through securities regulation.[13] One justification for the denial of the right of removal is the facilitation of private enforcement[14] by giving the plaintiff an absolute choice of forum; especially since, in many cases, state court litigation may prove less complex and less expensive than suits in federal court. Accordingly, complaints framed solely in terms of the 1933 or 1939 Acts can guarantee a state court forum and avoid the exclusive federal jurisdiction of the 1934 Exchange Act[15] or the removal to federal court that would be permitted under the other acts.

Counsel for plaintiffs in securities suits should be aware of the importance of this tactical decision. The history of state court litigation dealing with implied remedies under the federal securities acts, although somewhat sparse, reveals a relatively liberal attitude toward plaintiffs.[16] This may be especially significant in the area of federally implied private remedies which are being cut back by the federal courts generally and the Supreme Court in particular.[17] Even the 1934 Act's grant of

---

Cases holding jurisdiction was exclusively federal include: Kinsey v.Nestor Exploration Ltd.–1981A, 604 F.Supp. 1365 (E.D.Wn.1985); Nordberg v. Lord, Day & Lord, 107 F.R.D. 692, 701 (S.D.N.Y.1985); Levinson v. American Accident Reinsurance Group, 503 A.2d 632 (Del.Ch.1985); Greenview Trading Co. v. Hershman & Leicher, P.C., 108 A.D.2d 468, 489 N.Y.S.2d 502 (1985); First National Bank v. Guomas, (Ohio Cm.Pl. Aug. 20, 1985).

10. Tafflin v. Levitt, 493 U.S. 455, 110 S.Ct. 792, 107 L.Ed.2d 887 (1990), *rehearing denied* 495 U.S. 915, 110 S.Ct. 1942, 109 L.Ed.2d 305 (1990).

11. *E.g.,* Federal Employers' Liability Act, 28 U.S.C.A. § 1445(a); Jones Act, 46 U.S.C.A. § 688; Magnuson–Moss Federal Warranty Act, 15 U.S.C.A. § 2310(d).

12. *See, e.g.,* McKnett v. St. Louis & San Francisco Railroad, 292 U.S. 230, 54 S.Ct. 690, 78 L.Ed. 1227 (1934); Mondou v. New York, New Haven & Hartford Railroad, 223 U.S. 1, 32 S.Ct. 169, 56 L.Ed. 327 (1911). *Cf.* Missouri ex rel. Southern Railway v. Mayfield, 340 U.S. 1, 71 S.Ct. 1, 95 L.Ed. 3 (1950) (upholding the state court's right to invoke *forum non conveniens* as a basis for dismissal).

13. *See, e.g.,* Edgar v. MITE Corp., 457 U.S. 624, 102 S.Ct. 2629, 73 L.Ed.2d 269 (1982) (federal preemption of state tender offer statute). *See* § 11.22 *supra*.

14. Many securities violations give rise to cumulative express and implied private rights of action under the 1933 and 1934 Acts. *See* chapters 7, 12, 13 *supra*.

15. Drexel Burnham Lambert, Inc. v. Merchants Investment Counseling, Inc., 451 N.E.2d 346 (Ind.App.1983).

16. *E.g.,* Rocz v. Drexel Burnham Lambert, Inc., 154 Ariz. 462, 743 P.2d 971 (App. 1987) (holding 1933 Act section 17(a) claims were arbitrable).

17. *E.g.,*Transamerica Mortgage Advisors, Inc. v. Lewis, 444 U.S. 11, 100 S.Ct.242, 62 L.Ed.2d 146 (1979), *on remand* 610 F.2d 648 (9th Cir.1979); Touche Ross & Co. v. Redington, 442 U.S. 560, 99 S.Ct. 2479, 61 L.Ed.2d 82 (1979), *on remand* 612 F.2d 68 (2d Cir.1979). Implied federal rights of action are discussed in § 13.1 *supra*.

In recent years, the restrictive trend has not been limited to implied remedies. *See* Gustafson v. Alloyd Corp., ___ U.S. ___, 115 S.Ct. 1061, 131 L.Ed.2d 1 (U.S.1995) (restricting the remedy under section 12(2) of the 1933 Act), which is discussed in § 7.5 *supra*.

exclusive federal jurisdiction has not precluded some state courts from looking to the federal law by analogy [18] or from permitting use of a federal claim as a defense to a state law cause of action.[19]

Exclusive Federal Jurisdiction Under the Exchange Act

State courts are bound to dismiss any claim based on the Securities Exchange Act of 1934 in light of its grant of exclusive federal jurisdiction.[20] A different result may follow, however, when the Exchange Act claim is raised by way of defense to a state court cause of action. Although a large number of states will entertain 1934 Act claims raised defensively,[21] a few influential courts, including Delaware's, have ruled that they lack jurisdiction in such cases.[22] This harsh minority view has been criticized,[23] as well it should be.

If a plaintiff attempts to bring a 1934 Act claim directly into state court, section 27's exclusivity clearly will bar the action.[24] It will be

---

18. Twomey v. Mitchum, Jones & Templeton, Inc., 262 Cal.App.2d 690, 69 Cal.Rptr. 222 (1968); Williams v. Bartell, 34 Misc.2d 552, 226 N.Y.S.2d 187 (1962), *modified on other grounds* 16 A.D.2d 21, 225 N.Y.S.2d 351 (1962). *See, e.g.,* Herron Northwest, Inc. v. Danskin, 78 Wash.2d 500, 476 P.2d 702 (1970). *But see, e.g.,* Malkan v. General Transistor Corp., 27 Misc.2d 275, 210 N.Y.S.2d 289 (1960). *See* text accompanying notes 22–28 *infra.*

19. *E.g.,* Gregory–Massari, Inc. v. Purkitt, 1 Cal.App.3d 968, 82 Cal.Rptr. 210 (1969); Johnson, Lane, Space, Smith & Co. v. Lenny, 129 Ga.App. 55, 198 S.E.2d 923 (1973); Birenbaum v. Bache & Co., 555 S.W.2d 513 (Tex.Civ.App.1977). *But see, e.g.,* New York Stock Exchange v. Pickard & Co., 274 A.2d 148 (Del.Ch.1971); Investment Associates v. Standard Power & Light Corp., 29 Del.Ch. 225, 238–39, 48 A.2d 501, 508–09 (1946), *affirmed* 29 Del.Ch. 593, 606, 51 A.2d 572, 579 (1947); Eliasberg v. Standard Oil Co., 23 N.J.Super. 431, 92 A.2d 862 (1952), *affirmed per curiam* 12 N.J. 467, 97 A.2d 437 (1953). *See* text accompanying footnotes 20–21 *infra.*

20. Evans v. Dale, 896 F.2d 975 (5th Cir.1990) (federal securities fraud claim was not precluded by state court divorce decree since jurisdiction over Exchange Act claims is exclusively federal); Kinsey v. Nestor Exploration Ltd.–1981A, 604 F.Supp. 1365 (E.D.Wash.1985) (federal court dismissed 10b–5 claim removed from state court because federal court in removal proceedings has no greater jurisdiction than the state court); Kleckley v. Hebert, 464 So.2d 39 (La.App.1985) (dismissing 10b–5 claim but retaining jurisdiction over claim under section 12(2) of the 1933 Act).

21. *See* Gregory–Massari, Inc. v. Purkitt, 1 Cal.App.3d 968, 82 Cal.Rptr. 210 (1969); Johnson, Lane, Space, Smith & Co. v. Lenny, 129 Ga.App. 55, 198 S.E.2d 923 (1973); Michigan National Bank v. Dunbar, 91 Mich.App. 385, 283 N.W.2d 747 (1979); J. Cliff Rahel & Co. v. Roper, 186 Neb. 34, 180 N.W.2d 682 (1970); Birenbaum v. Bache & Co., 555 S.W.2d 513 (Tex.Civ.App.1977). *See also* Calvert Fire Insurance Co. v. American Mutual Reinsurance Co., 600 F.2d 1228, 1231 n.6 (7th Cir.1979); Shareholders Management Co. v. Gregory, 449 F.2d 326 (9th Cir.1971).

22. *See* Investment Associates v. Standard Power & Light Corp., 29 Del.Ch. 225, 238–39, 48 A.2d 501, 508–09 (1946), *affirmed* 29 Del.Ch. 593, 606, 51 A.2d 572, 579 (1947); Eliasberg v. Standard Oil Co., 23 N.J.Super. 431, 92 A.2d 862 (1952), *affirmed per curiam* 12 N.J. 467, 97 A.2d 437 (1953); Western Capital & Securities, Inc. v. Knudsvig, 21 Sec.Reg. & L.Rep. (BNA) 317 (Utah Ct.App.1989). *See generally* 2 Louis Loss, Securities Regulation 973–1000 (2d ed.1961). *See also, e.g.,* New York Stock Exchange v. Pickard & Co., 274 A.2d 148 (Del.Ch.1971) (refusal to hear 1934 Act counterclaim).

23. 2 Louis Loss, *supra* footnote 22; Hazen, *supra* footnote 1 at 722–24.

24. 15 U.S.C.A. § 78aa. *See* footnote 20 *supra.*

The exclusive jurisdiction has been held to apply to actions based on violation of exchange rules. Lowenschuss v. Options Clearing Corp., 1989 WL 155767, [1990–1991 Transfer Binder] Fed.Sec.L.Rep. (CCH) ¶ 95,675 (Del.Ch.1989) (state court lacked jurisdiction over claims against securities exchange for violation of its option adjustment rules).

barred even if the plaintiff's complaint does not mention the 1934 Act specifically but instead states facts that reveal such a claim but do not present a traditional common-law (or state statutory) theory.[25] On the other hand, some state courts have found an indirect way to hear the federal claim. A court may, as a matter of state law, borrow from or look to federal law in order to determine whether state law rights have been implicated. For example, it has been held that violations of the 1934 Act's margin requirements dealing with payments for securities may provide the basis for a state law cause of action for breach of contract.[26] Additionally, a claim for malicious prosecution of a federal securities claim may be determined by a state court since the federal issue is minimal.[27]

Although the 1934 Act expressly declares void all contracts in violation of its provisions,[28] the grant of exclusive jurisdiction arguably limits any affirmative remedy to federal court. Under such a view, even an action for rescission of the contract in question would have to be brought in federal court, where the basis of the action for rescission is a violation of the Exchange Act.

A California court has gone at least so far as to imply that the standard of conduct established by SEC Rule 10b–5 can be used by analogy in a state court fraud action.[29] One court has even found an implied state law remedy.[30] A leading commentator takes the position that in the proxy area the state courts "should as a matter of the proper development of the state law—look to the case law under the SEC fraud rule by way of analogy."[31] Such analogies are even more likely when, as is frequently the case, the state blue sky law borrows from the federal scheme.[32] Formerly, when a 1934 Act claim was brought in state court, the only appropriate response was to move to dismiss the suit and then wait until the claim was refiled in federal court. However, the removal

---

25. Hudson v. Burns, 29 Conn.Sup. 484, 293 A.2d 610 (1971); Community National Bank & Trust Co. v. Vigman, 330 So.2d 211 (Fla.App.1976), *cert. denied* 341 So.2d 294 (1976).

26. Herron Northwest, Inc. v. Danskin, 78 Wn.2d 500, 476 P.2d 702 (1970). *See* 5 Louis Loss, *supra* footnote 22, at 2957: "[T]here is nothing in § 27 to prevent an action on the theory that violation of the Exchange Act or an SEC Rule is a breach of contract, whether express or implied." (emphasis in original). *Contra* Mitchell v. Bache & Co., 52 Misc.2d 985, 987–89, 277 N.Y.S.2d 580, 582–83 (Civ.Ct.1966).

27. Berg v. Leason, 32 F.3d 422 (9th Cir.1994) (the question in a malicious prosecution suit is merely whether the claim was "legally tenable").

28. 15 U.S.C.A. § 78cc(b). *See* § 13.14 *supra*. *See generally* Samuel L. Gruenbaum & Marc I. Steinberg, Section 29(b) of the Securities Exchange Act of 1934: A Viable Remedy Awakened, 48 Geo.Wash.L.Rev. 1 (1979).

29. Twomey v. Mitchum, Jones & Templeton, Inc., 262 Cal.App.2d 690, 695–700, 69 Cal.Rptr. 222, 232–35 (1968).

30. Watling, Lerchen & Co. v. Ormond, 86 Mich.App. 238, 272 N.W.2d 614 (1978). Some state courts apparently have overlooked the jurisdictional bar. *Cf.* Green v. Karol, 168 Ind.App. 467, 344 N.E.2d 106 (1976) (dismissing 10b–5 claim due to statute of limitations but not discussing the jurisdictional issue).

31. 2 Louis Loss, *supra* footnote 22 at 999.

32. *See, e.g.,* Note, Action Under State Law: Florida's Blue Sky and Common Law Alternatives to Rule 10b–5 for Relief in Securities Fraud, 32 U.Fla.L.Rev. 636 (1980).

statute has since been amended to permit removal from state court to federal court when the state court lacks jurisdiction but the federal court does not.[33]

State Court Settlement of Federal Claims

One other way in which a state court may be able to dispose of federal claims notwithstanding a grant of federal jurisdiction is through the settlement process. If state law claims involve facts that may also give rise to federal securities claims, can a settlement of the state claims be made and approved by a state court that will dispose not only of the state law claims but also of the federal claims that could not be heard by the state court because of the congressional mandate of exclusive federal jurisdiction? The Third Circuit has answered in the affirmative in ruling that a comprehensive settlement subject to state court approval can validly dispose of the federal claim.[34] In so ruling, the court acknowledged that at first blush this might seem to be an anomalous result, but that "it is widely recognized that courts without jurisdiction to hear certain claims have the power to release those claims as part of a judgment." [35] The dissent claimed that permitting state courts to determine 1934 Act claims "infringe[s] on the mutual respect of the state and federal government for each others' sovereignty that our federalism requires."[36] The court responded, however, that the state law power is justified especially in light of the policy favoring comprehensive settlements of class actions that will prevent wasteful relitigations of issues.[37]

Federal Supplemental (or Pendent) Jurisdiction Over State Claims

What about the plaintiff with 1934 Act claims and related state causes of action? All related claims can be heard together in federal court when the court invokes supplemental pendent jurisdiction over the state law claims.[38] If the federal claim fails, however, the federal court is likely to dismiss the state law cause of action.[39] Even if the federal court

---

33. 28 U.S.C.A. § 1441(a). *See, e.g.,* Bennett v. Bally Manufacturing, 785 F.Supp. 559 (D.S.C.1992) (permitting removal of Rule 10b–5 claim erroneously brought in state court).

34. Grimes v. Vitalink Communications Corp., 17 F.3d 1553 (3d Cir.1994).

35. 17 F.3d at 1563, *relying on* Class Plaintiffs v. City of Seattle, 955 F.2d 1268, 1287–88 (9th Cir.1992), *cert. denied* ___ U.S. ___, 113 S.Ct. 408, 121 L.Ed.2d 333 (1992); TBK Partners, Ltd. v. Western Union Corp., 675 F.2d 456, 460 (2d Cir.1982); In re Corrugated Container Antitrust Litigation, 643 F.2d 195, 221–22 (5th Cir.1981), *cert. denied* 456 U.S. 998, 102 S.Ct. 2283, 73 L.Ed.2d 1294 (1982).

36. 17 F.3d at 1573 (Hutchinson, J., dissenting). The dissenting judge found this to be especially problematic in the case of a class action such as the one before the court where non residents of that state would be bound by the approval of the settlement.

37. 17 F.3d at 1563–64.

38. United Mine Workers v. Gibbs, 383 U.S. 715, 86 S.Ct. 1130, 16 L.Ed.2d 218 (1966); Chapman v. Merrill Lynch, Pierce, Fenner & Smith, Inc., 1983 WL 1340, [1984–1984 Transfer Binder] Fed.Sec.L.Rep. (CCH) ¶ 99,419 at 96,410–11 (D.Md.1983).

39. United Mine Workers v. Gibbs, 383 U.S. 715, 725–27, 86 S.Ct. 1130, 1138–1140, 16 L.Ed.2d 218 (1966). *Cf.* Kidder, Peabody & Co. v. Maxus Energy Corp., 925 F.2d 556 (2d Cir.1991), *cert. denied* 501 U.S. 1218, 111 S.Ct. 2829, 115 L.Ed.2d 998 (1991) (following declaratory judgment on the federal claim, it was appropriate to relinquish jurisdiction over state law claim notwithstanding the fact that the federal district court had invested

decides to retain jurisdiction, some question exists as to whether the court will invoke a state remedy that is not federally recognized.[40] Federal courts typically emphasize federal claims at the expense of state law issues when hearing cases under pendent jurisdiction.[41] Thus, pendent jurisdiction is far from a cure-all for the 1934 Act's exclusivity provisions.[42] Pendent jurisdiction does, however, eliminate duplicative litigation that could lead to difficult questions involving the res judicata effect to be given to the first determination.[43]

A recent Supreme Court ruling points out the significance of arbitration under the Federal Arbitration Act and the ability to resolve state as well as federal claims. In Mastrobuono v. Shearson Lehman Hutton, Inc.,[44] the Court held that punitive damages under a state claim were available in a federally mandated arbitration, although those damages would not have been permitted under state arbitration proceedings.[45] The Court ruled, however, that the parties' choice of law clause meant that the state's substantive law permitting punitive damages applied. However, the state's procedural bar to punitive damages in arbitration had to yield to the procedural rules of the Federal Arbitration Act in light of the broad policy favoring arbitration under that Act.

§ 14.1.1 Use of the Jurisdictional Means

The Exchange Act's registration and reporting requirements are triggered by offerings or issuers having sufficient interstate contact to support federal regulation.[1] In contrast, the 1933 Act registration

---

considerable time trying to resolve the state law issues). *But see* Alna Capital Associates v. Wagner, 758 F.2d 562 (11th Cir.1985) (retaining jurisdiction over state common law claim after federal claim failed).

40. *See* Gregory G. Young, Federal Corporate Law, Federalism, and the Federal Courts, 41 Law & Contemp.Prob. 146, 171 (summer 1971).

41. Failure to give more attention to the federal claim may result in dismissal from federal court on the ground that the state law issues predominate. United Mine Workers v. Gibbs, 383 U.S. 715, 726–27, 86 S.Ct. 1130, 1139, 1140, 16 L.Ed.2d 218 (1966). *See also, e.g.,* Mayor of Philadelphia v. Educational Equality League, 415 U.S. 605, 627, 94 S.Ct. 1323, 1336, 1337, 39 L.Ed.2d 630 (1974); Merritt v. Colonial Foods, Inc., 499 F.Supp. 910 (D.Del.1980).

42. *See* 5 L. Loss, *supra* footnote 22 at 2962–76; Charles Wright, Handbook on the Law of Federal Courts 74–77 (1976).

43. *See, e.g.,* Epstein v. Epstein, 836 F.2d 1342 (4th Cir.1988), *order vacated* 1988 WL 115889 (1988) (federal securities claims barred by state decision). *See also* the discussion of collateral estoppel in § 14.4 *infra.*

44. ___ U.S. ___, 115 S.Ct. 1212, 131 L.Ed.2d 76 (1995).

45. New York law permits punitive damages for egregious breaches of broker-dealer duties. New York law further provides that punitive damages are not available in arbitration proceedings.

§ 14.1.1

1. Thus, for example the Exchange Act's registration requirements are based on the securities being listed on a national securities exchange or the issuer having more than five million dollars in assets and five hundred or more holders of a class of equity securities. 15 U.S.C.A §§ 78*l*(a), (g); 17 C.F.R. § 240.12g–1. *See* § 9.2 *supra*. Additionally, issuers that have issued securities under a 1933 Act registration statement and have more than three hundred holders of such securities must, pursuant to section 15(d), file periodic reports with the Commission. 15 U.S.C.A. § 78*o*(d). *See* § 9.3 *infra*.

requirements are implicated by a nonexempt offer or sale of securities through an instrumentality of interstate commerce.[2] Although not required as a matter of jurisdictional limitation, Congress elected to exempt from 1933 Act registration offerings that originate and take place within the confines of a single state.[3]

As discussed more fully below, the jurisdictional requirements are easily satisfied. However, in order to state a claim and establish jurisdiction, the complaint must refer to federal law. The mere fact that federal law will be relevant in interpreting state law will not support federal jurisdiction.[4]

Typically, the securities acts' antifraud provisions are triggered by the use of an instrumentality of interstate commerce.[5] The language of the various jurisdictional provisions is varied.[6] However, the courts' focus in interpreting these provisions has centered on the use of an instrumentality of interstate commerce for some part of the transaction. Furthermore, in interpreting the reach of the statute, the federal courts have taken a broad view of the securities laws' jurisdictional reach. The broad language regarding the necessary jurisdictional nexus when combined with the courts' expansive interpretation means that most securities transactions will be covered. Thus, for example, an intrastate telephone call will support jurisdiction.[7] Similarly, it has been held that

---

2. Section 5 of the Act makes it unlawful to make offers and sales "mak[ing] use of any means or instrumentality of transportation or communication in interstate commerce or of the mails to sell such security" unless the securities are registered (or exempt). 15 U.S.C.A. § 77e. *See* chapter 2 *supra*. The exemptions are discussed in chapter 4 *supra*.

3. 15 U.S.C.A. § 77c(a)(11); 17 C.F.R. § 230.147. *See* § 4.12 *supra*.

4. Hill v. Morrison, 870 F.Supp. 978 (W.D.Mo.1994) (pleading facts and setting forth a claim under state securities laws and not mentioning federal securities law did not state claim under federal law).

5. *E.g.,* 15 U.S.C.A. § 77*l* (referring back to section 5's prohibitions—*see* footnote 2 *supra*); 15 U.S.C.A. § 77q(a) ("offer or sale of any securities by the use of any means or instruments of transportation or communication in interstate commerce or by use of the mails, directly or indirectly * * *"); 15 U.S.C.A. § 78j(b) ("by the use of any means or instrumentality of interstate commerce, or of the mails, or of any facility of any national securities exchange"); 17 C.F.R. § 240.10b–5 ("by the use of any means or instrumentality of interstate commerce, or of the mails, or of any facility of any national securities exchange"). *Cf.* United States v. Cashin, 281 F.2d 669, 673 (2d Cir.1960) (jurisdictional reach of section 12(1) and 17(a) of the 1933 Act are the same).

A defendant will not escape the jurisdictional reach solely because his or her role in a transaction implicating interstate commerce was purely intrastate. Busch v. Buchman, Buchman & O'Brien Law Firm, 11 F.3d 1255 (5th Cir.1994).

6. There is a difference in the language of section 10(b) of the Exchange Act and section 14(a)'s proxy regulation. Section 14(a)'s reach extends to activities "by the use of the mails or by any means or instrumentality of interstate commerce or of any facility of a national securities exchange *or otherwise* * * *" 15 U.S.C.A. § 78n(a); proxy regulation is discussed in §§ 11.1–11.10 *supra*. In contrast, section 10 applies to persons acting "*directly or indirectly,* by the use of any instrumentality of interstate commerce or of the mails, or of any facility of any national securities exchange * * *" 15 U.S.C.A. § 78j.

7. *E.g.,* Loveridge v. Dreagoux, 678 F.2d 870, 874 (10th Cir.1982); Dupuy v. Dupuy, 511 F.2d 641, 642–44 (5th Cir.1975), *appeal after remand* 551 F.2d 1005 (1977), *rehearing denied* 554 F.2d 1065 (1977); Myzel v. Fields, 386 F.2d 718 (8th Cir.1967), *cert. denied* 390 U.S. 951, 88 S.Ct. 1043, 19 L.Ed.2d 1143 (1968). *See also, e.g.,* Taylor v. Door to Door Transportation Services, Inc., 691 F.Supp. 27 (S.D.Ohio 1988) (use of telephone, telecopier, and mail satisfied the jurisdictional requirements of Rule 10b–5). *But cf.* Dennis v.

the particular communication containing the actionable statement need not be made through an instrumentality of interstate commerce so long as the transaction in question was effectuated through the use of such an instrumentality.[8] Accordingly, although the language of the jurisdictional provisions seems to focus on the communication forming the basis of the securities law violations,[9] the courts have tended to look to the transaction as a whole.[10]

While a face-to-face conversation standing alone will not satisfy the jurisdictional requirements, there may be jurisdiction under Rule 10b–5, if the conversations are part of a transaction that utilizes an instrumentality of interstate commerce.[11] Thus, for example, a face-to-face conversation followed by a transaction utilizing an instrumentality of interstate commerce generally has been held to subject the speaker to Rule 10b–5 scrutiny.

§ 14.2 Extraterritorial Application of the Securities Laws; Their Relevance to Foreign Issuers and to Transactions in Foreign Markets; Antifraud Provisions

This section addresses the securities laws' extraterritoriality in two contexts. First, to what extent do the antifraud provisions apply to foreign issuers and to transactions taking place, at least in part, abroad?

General Imaging, Inc., 918 F.2d 496, 500 (5th Cir.1990) (noting the absence of any definitive holding as to whether an intrastate telephone call satisfies 1933 Act § 12(1)'s "in commerce" requirement as compared with the 1934 Act's "instrumentality of commerce" requirement but not reaching the issue since there was no showing of a section 12 violation).

8. *See, e.g.,* Leiter v. Kuntz, 655 F.Supp. 725, 726–27 (D.Utah 1987).

9. *E.g.,* 15 U.S.C.A. § 78j(b) (prohibiting "the use of any means or instrumentality of interstate commerce, or of the mails, or of any facility of any national securities exchange [for a] manipulative or deceptive device or contrivance [in contravention of SEC rules]").

Thus, for example Rule 10b–5(b) prohibits the use of the jurisdictional means to make a material misrepresentation in connection with the purchase or sale of a security. 17 C.F.R. § 240.10b–5(b). *See* footnotes 11–14 *infra* and accompanying text.

10. *E.g.,* Franklin Savings Bank of New York v. Levy, 551 F.2d 521, 524 (2d Cir.1977); Leiter v. Kuntz, 655 F.Supp. 725, 726–27 (D.Utah 1987); *Accord, e.g.,* United States v. Cashin, 281 F.2d 669, 673 (2d Cir.1960) ("The use of the mails need not be central to the fraudulent scheme and may be entirely incidental to it"), relying on Kopald–Quinn & Co. v. United States, 101 F.2d 628 (5th Cir.1939), *cert. denied* 307 U.S. 628, 59 S.Ct. 835, 83 L.Ed. 1511 (1939).

11. *E.g.,* Franklin Savings Bank of New York v. Levy, 551 F.2d 521, 524 (2d Cir.1977) (decided under section 12(2) of the 1933 Act; "the sales here consisted primarily of the manual delivery of the note and the receipt of payment, neither of which occasioned the use of the mails. After delivery of the note and receipt of the payment however, [defendant] mailed a letter to [plaintiff] confirming the sale"); Kauffmann v. Yoskowitz, 1989 WL 79364, [1989 Transfer Binder] Fed.Sec.L.Rep. ¶ 94,532 (S.D.N.Y.1989); Leiter v. Kuntz, 655 F.Supp. 725, 727 (D.Utah 1987) (mailing of financial statement plus use of telephone to change date of face-to-face meeting were sufficient for jurisdictional purposes). *Cf.* Elkind v. Liggett & Myers, Inc., 635 F.2d 156, 161 (2d Cir.1980), *affirming* 472 F.Supp. 123 (S.D.N.Y.1978) (although the jurisdictional issue was not raised, a corporate tipper held liable for face-to-face tip of inside information where the tippee wired the information to his own office).

Second, what reporting and disclosure provisions apply to foreign issuers?

Most American case law dealing with the extraterritorial application of United States securities laws focuses on the antifraud provisions of the 1934 Exchange Act.[1] The courts have developed two tests for subject matter jurisdiction in securities fraud cases. One test is based on the conduct of foreign persons within the United States; the other focuses on the effects within the United States of conduct occurring in foreign countries.

Antifraud Provisions

In Schoenbaum v. Firstbrook,[2] the Second Circuit held that an extraterritorial transaction involving foreign securities, listed on the American Stock Exchange and held by American citizens, affected the domestic securities market. The court thus found the assertion of subject matter jurisdiction proper under the federal securities laws due to the domestic effects of the challenged transaction. The Ninth Circuit has similarly found jurisdiction over an international stock transaction under the "effects" test.[3] Jurisdiction can be based on misrepresentations made here although involving foreign securities that were traded only in foreign markets.[4] However, activities within the United States that are "merely preparatory" to the actual fraud are clearly insufficient to confer subject matter jurisdiction.[5]

It has, thus, been said that the antifraud provisions of the federal securities laws:

> (1) Apply to losses from sales of securities to Americans resident in the United States whether or not acts * * * of material importance occurred in this country; and

> (2) Apply to losses from sales of securities to Americans resident abroad if * * * acts * * * of material importance in the United States have significantly contributed thereto; but

---

§ 14.2

1. *E.g.*, 17 C.F.R. § 240.10b–5. *See* §§ 13.2–13.12 *supra*.

2. 405 F.2d 200 (2d Cir.1968), *modified en banc on other grounds* 405 F.2d 215 (2d Cir.1968), *cert. denied* 395 U.S. 906, 89 S.Ct. 1747, 23 L.Ed.2d 219 (1969). In addition to the authorities in note 1 *supra*, for discussion of the extraterritorial reach of the securities laws *see generally* Robert C. Hacker & Ronald D. Rotunda, The Extraterritorial Regulation of Foreign Business under the U.S. Securities Laws, 59 N.C.L.Rev. 643 (1981); Barbara S. Thomas, Extraterritorial Application of the United States Securities Laws: The Need for a Balanced Policy, 7 J.Corp.L. 189 (1982).

3. Des Brisay v. Goldfield Corp., 549 F.2d 133 (9th Cir.1977) (takeover of Canadian corporation by American corporation involved improper use of the American corporation's securities, which were registered and listed on a national exchange, and adversely affected both the foreign plaintiffs and the American securities market).

4. Leasco Data Processing Equipment v. Maxwell, 468 F.2d 1326 (2d Cir.1972), *on remand* 63 F.R.D. 94 (S.D.N.Y.1973) (the court premised jurisdiction upon domestic conduct and the direct effect on American investors).

5. Zoelsch v. Arthur Andersen & Co., 824 F.2d 27 (D.C.Cir.1987); Bersch v. Drexel Firestone, Inc., 519 F.2d 974 (2d Cir.1975), *cert. denied* 423 U.S. 1018, 96 S.Ct. 453, 46 L.Ed.2d 389 (1975); IIT v. Vencap, Ltd., 519 F.2d 1001 (2d Cir.1975), *on remand* 411 F.Supp. 1094 (S.D.N.Y.1975).

(3) Do not apply to losses from sales of securities to foreigners outside the United States unless acts * * * within the United States directly caused such losses.[6]

A domestic defendant's perpetration of fraud upon foreigners has been held to be a sufficient basis for jurisdiction because Congress could not have intended "to allow the United States to be used as a base for manufacturing fraudulent security devices for export, even when * * * peddled only to foreigners."[7] In addition, foreign investors residing in the United States are protected by the federal securities laws to the same extent as American citizens, at least with respect to claims during the period of residency. This is true even when the fraudulent scheme is devised and set into motion abroad.[8] A foreign corporation whose sole shareholder and chief executive officer was a foreigner residing in the United States, however, was required to prove that losses incurred due to the fraudulent scheme were *directly caused* by acts within the United States.[9] Deception of the foreign corporation's sole shareholder within the United States, while necessary to the success of the fraudulent scheme, has thus been held insufficient proof of direct causation of loss.[10] Without more, a foreign issuer's filing of misleading reports with the SEC will not support jurisdiction in a private action by foreign investors. Thus, the fact that the misrepresentations were contained in documents filed with the SEC and also were circulated in the U.S. press will not support jurisdiction in a claim by foreign investors purchasing stock in a foreign corporation on a foreign exchange.[11] Accordingly, extraterritorial application of the securities laws to the foreign corporation's claims will be denied absent adequate proof of causation arising out of domestic acts.

---

6. Bersch v. Drexel Firestone, Inc., 519 F.2d 974, 993 (2d Cir.1975), *cert. denied* 423 U.S. 1018, 96 S.Ct. 453, 46 L.Ed.2d 389 (1975).

7. IIT v. Vencap, Ltd., 519 F.2d 1001, 1017 (2d Cir.1975), *on remand* 411 F.Supp. 1094 (S.D.N.Y.1975). *Accord* Consolidated Gold Fields, PLC v. Minorco, S.A., 871 F.2d 252 (2d Cir.1989). *See also, e.g.*, CL–Alexanders, Laing & Cruickshank v. Goldfeld, 709 F.Supp. 472 (S.D.N.Y.1989) (British underwriter's action against officers of American corporation was proper and could not be dismissed under doctrine of forum non conveniens).

8. O'Driscoll v. Merrill Lynch, Pierce, Fenner & Smith, Inc., 1983 WL 1360, [1983–84 Transfer Binder], Fed.Sec.L.Rep. (CCH) ¶ 99,486 at pp. 96, 834–35 (S.D.N.Y.1983). *See also, e.g.*, Ohman v. Kahn, 685 F.Supp. 1302 (S.D.N.Y.1988) (sufficient allegations of domestic conduct to support subject matter jurisdiction). *But see* Williams v. Brandt, 672 F.Supp. 507 (S.D.Fla.1987) (where all parties to the transaction make a conscious effort to assure that it occurs outside of the United States, there is no jurisdiction).

9. O'Driscoll v. Merrill Lynch, Pierce, Fenner & Smith, Inc., 1983 WL 1360, [1983–84 Transfer Binder] Fed.Sec.L.Rep. (CCH) ¶ 99,486 at pp. 96,834–35 (S.D.N.Y.1983).

10. *Id.*

11. Kaufman v. Campeau Corp., 744 F.Supp. 808 (S.D.Ohio 1990). *Compare, e.g.*, Ronzani v. Sanofi S.A., 1991 WL 61082, [1991 Transfer Binder] Fed.Sec.L.Rep. (CCH) ¶ 96,054 (S.D.N.Y.1991) (upholding action by Swiss citizen against a French business for fraud in connection with sale of U.S. securities since some of the relevant conduct occurred in the U.S.); Alfadda v. Fenn, 935 F.2d 475 (2d Cir.1991), *reversing* 751 F.Supp. 1114 (S.D.N.Y.1990) (although prospectus was delivered outside the United States, jurisdiction could be based on negotiations which took place in the United States).

An Eighth Circuit decision[12] premised subject matter jurisdiction on domestic conduct alone, even though the only victim of the fraud was a foreign corporation purchasing stock in another foreign company.[13] The Second and Third Circuits have also found subject matter jurisdiction where conduct in the United States directly caused a foreign plaintiff's losses, even though the fraud had no adverse effect on American securities markets or upon domestic investors.[14] Thus, "foreigners engaging in security purchases in the United States are [protected by the federal] securities laws."[15] A claim will not lie, however, when the domestic conduct is, at most, "ancillary" and therefore, not the direct cause of the plaintiff's losses.[16] Similarly, where "the primary fraud and every fact essential to plaintiff's charge of fraudulent conduct was committed or occurred in Costa Rica," the fraud was considered "predominantly foreign" and our securities laws did not govern.[17] The protection of the federal securities laws was denied to purchases of foreign securities by United States investors who used circuitous means to hide their identity so they could participate in a foreign offering not open to United States citizens.[18] The court reasoned that since the plaintiffs went to great lengths to avoid (if not evade) the 1933 Act's registration requirements, they could not then wrap themselves in the Securities Act's protective mantle once the deal turned sour.

Where a cause of action arose from trading on American commodities exchanges, however, the court found subject matter jurisdiction even though all parties to the suit were nonresident aliens and all contacts between them occurred outside the United States.[19] Utilizing the "ef-

---

12. Continental Grain (Australia) Pty. Ltd. v. Pacific Oilseeds, Inc., 592 F.2d 409 (8th Cir.1979).

13. The defendant-sellers used the U.S. mails and telephone system to further their fraudulent scheme. Thus, despite the absence of a domestic transaction affecting the domestic securities market, the court asserted jurisdiction. The court found that the defendants' U.S. conduct was significant—not "merely preparatory"—and constituted a fraud devised and completed in the United States. *Id.* at 420.

14. SEC v. Kasser, 548 F.2d 109 (3d Cir.1977), *cert. denied* 431 U.S. 938, 97 S.Ct. 2649, 53 L.Ed.2d 255 (1977). *See also, e.g.,* IIT v. Cornfeld, 619 F.2d 909 (2d Cir.1980).

15. IIT v. Cornfeld, 619 F.2d 909, 918 (2d Cir.1980). *See also* Arthur Lipper Corp. v. SEC, 547 F.2d 171 (2d Cir.1976), *cert. denied* 434 U.S. 1009, 98 S.Ct. 719, 54 L.Ed.2d 752 (1978); United States v. Cook, 573 F.2d 281 (5th Cir.1978), *cert. denied* 439 U.S. 836, 99 S.Ct. 119, 58 L.Ed.2d 132 (1978); SEC v. Kasser, 548 F.2d 109 (3d Cir.1977), *cert. denied* 431 U.S. 938, 97 S.Ct. 2649, 53 L.Ed.2d 255 (1977).

16. Fidenas AG v. Compagnie Internationale Pour L'Informatique CII Honeywell Bull. S.A., 606 F.2d 5 (2d Cir.1979). The alleged U.S. conduct consisted of a U.S. parent corporation's knowledge of the foreign subsidiary's fraudulent scheme. In a subsequent suit by the same plaintiffs against the American parent corporation for the same fraud, the court found mere knowledge of the fraud insufficient to confer subject matter jurisdiction upon U.S. courts. Relying on the Second Circuit's view of the transactions as "predominantly foreign," the court dismissed the suit for failure to satisfy either the "conduct" or the "effects" test for subject matter jurisdiction. Fidenas AG v. Honeywell Inc., 501 F.Supp. 1029 (S.D.N.Y.1980).

17. Mormels v. Girofinance, S.A., 544 F.Supp. 815 (S.D.N.Y.1982).

18. MCG, Inc. v. Great Western Energy Corp., 896 F.2d 170 (5th Cir.1990).

19. Tamari v. Bache & Co. (Lebanon) S.A.L., 547 F.Supp. 309 (N.D.Ill.1982), *order affirmed* 730 F.2d 1103 (7th Cir.1984), *cert. denied* 469 U.S. 871, 105 S.Ct. 221, 83 L.Ed.2d

fects" test, the court found that "where the * * * transactions involve trading on domestic exchanges, harm can be presumed, because the fraud * * * implicates the integrity of the American market." [20] A Ninth Circuit decision is in accord with regard to a transaction in privately-held foreign securities between foreign nationals and corporations—the only parties to the suit—where the domestic conduct was fraudulent.[21]

Jurisdictional questions also arise in connection with foreigners' activities in the American market place.[22] The "effects" test did not support jurisdiction over a foreign auditor's activities where the results of the audit were used without the preparer's consent.[23] Similarly, it has been held that there was no jurisdiction as a consequence of sending to American owners of ADRs a press release announcing a British tender offer for shares in British target company whose securities were trading in the United States through the use of ADRs.[24] The determination of whether foreign activities have sufficient domestic effects so as to support jurisdiction involves a highly factual inquiry which must be made on a case-by-case basis.[25]

[*See* Practitioner's Edition for further discussion.]

§ 14.3 Venue in Actions Under the Securities Acts

Plaintiffs have been provided with a wide choice of federal forums under the Securities Act of 1933 and the Securities Exchange Act of 1934.[1] When suit is initiated under both the 1933 and 1934 Acts, venue may be resolved according to the slightly broader provisions of the 1934

---

151 (1984) (decided under the Commodity Exchange Act in reliance on cases arising under the securities laws).

20. *Id.* at 313. In addition, the foreign defendant's transmission of the foreign plaintiffs' orders from Lebanon to Chicago constituted "conduct within the United States * * * [that was of] substantial * * * importance to the success of the [fraudulent] scheme." *Id.* at 315.

See also, e.g., SEC v. Foundation Hai, 736 F.Supp. 465 (S.D.N.Y.1990) (purposeful acts of foreign corporations with "clear foreseeability" of their effects in the United States).

21. Grunenthal GmbH v. Hotz, 712 F.2d 421 (9th Cir.1983).

22. *See* Bourassa v. Desrochers, 938 F.2d 1056 (9th Cir.1991) (telephone call from Canadian to California resident was sufficient to place venue in California); Securities Investor Protection Corp. v. Vigman, 764 F.2d 1309 (9th Cir.1985), *appeal after remand* 803 F.2d 1513 (9th Cir.1986). *Cf.* SEC v. International Swiss Investments Corp., 895 F.2d 1272 (9th Cir.1990) (Federal Rules of Civil Procedure took precedence over unratified Inter-American Convention on Letters Rogatory; thus the federal rules governed questions of service in fraud action against persons residing in Mexico).

23. Reingold v. Deloitte Haskins & Sells, 599 F.Supp. 1241 (S.D.N.Y.1984).

24. Plessey Co. v. General Electric Co., 628 F.Supp. 477 (D.Del.1986).

25. Department of Economic Development v. Arthur Andersen & Co., 683 F.Supp. 1463 (S.D.N.Y.1988) (denying summary judgment).

§ 14.3

1. 15 U.S.C.A. §§ 77v(a), 78aa. Assuming subject-matter jurisdiction exists, there is nationwide service of process to confer personal jurisdiction over defendants. *See, e.g.,* United Liberty Life Insurance Co. v. Ryan, 985 F.2d 1320, 1330 (6th Cir.1993). Service can thus be made in any federal district in which the defendant has minimum contacts. *Id.*

Act.[2] Essentially, section 22(a) of the 1933 Act[3] and section 27 of the
1934 Act[4] each provide that venue lies in the district wherein the
defendant is found, or is an inhabitant, or transacts business, or in the
district wherein any act or transaction constituting the securities law
violation occurred.[5] In multi-defendant and multi-forum securities fraud
actions, for example, any act committed, material to and in furtherance
of an alleged fraudulent scheme by *any* defendant,[6] will satisfy the 1934
Act venue requirement as to *all* defendants.[7] This is sometimes referred
to as the "co-conspiracy venue theory."[8] It has consistently been held
that there need be only one act within the district for purposes of venue
under the 1934 Act.[9] The particular act need not constitute the core of
the alleged violation,[10] and need not be illegal,[11] but it must be a material

2. Ingram Industries, Inc. v. Nowicki, 527 F.Supp. 683, 687 (E.D.Ky.1981) (opinion
withdrawn without affecting the precedential effect). *See also* Hilgeman v. National
Insurance Co. of America, 547 F.2d 298, 301 n. 7 (5th Cir.1977), *rehearing denied* 564 F.2d
416 (1977); Martin v. Steubner, 485 F.Supp. 88, 90 (S.D.Ohio 1979), *affirmed* 652 F.2d 652
(6th Cir.1981), *cert. denied* 454 U.S. 1148, 102 S.Ct. 1013, 71 L.Ed.2d 302 (1982).

3. Section 22(a) of the 1933 Act, 15 U.S.C.A. § 77v(a).

4. Section 27 of the 1934 Act, 15 U.S.C.A. § 78aa.

5. *See, e.g.,* Bourassa v. Desrochers, 938 F.2d 1056 (9th Cir.1991) (telephone call from
Canadian to California resident supported venue in California); Wise v. Dallas & Mavis
Forwarding Co., 753 F.Supp. 601 (W.D.N.C.1991) (transacts business is in present tense
and thus contemplates current activity within the district); Kansas City Power & Light Co.
v. Kansas Gas & Electric Co., 747 F.Supp. 567 (W.D.Mo.1990) ("found" as used in venue
provision means having a presence and continuous local activity within the district;
transaction of business requirement requires that activities in district be continuous and a
substantial part of defendant's ordinary business); Ingram Industries, Inc. v. Nowicki, 527
F.Supp. 683 (E.D.Ky.1981) (opinion withdrawn without affecting the precedential effect).
An impleaded third party has standing to raise objections based on improper venue. First
Federal Savings & Loan Assoc. v. Oppenheim, Appel, Dixon & Co., 634 F.Supp. 1341
(S.D.N.Y.1986).

6. Sargent v. Genesco, Inc., 492 F.2d 750 (5th Cir.1974); Rose v. Arkansas Valley
Environmental & Utility Authority, 562 F.Supp. 1180 (W.D.Mo.1983); Witter v. Torbett,
Fed.Sec.L.Rep. (CCH) ¶ 99,456 (S.D.N.Y.1983).

7. *E.g.,* Berk v. Ascott Investment Corp., 759 F.Supp. 245 (E.D.Pa.1991) (venue is
proper for all defendants where one defendant made both oral and written misrepresentations within the district); Ingram Industries, Inc. v. Nowicki, 527 F.Supp. 683, 688
(E.D.Ky.1981) (opinion withdrawn without affecting precedential effect).

8. Washington Public Utilities Group v. United States District Court for the Western
District of Washington, 843 F.2d 319 (9th Cir.1987); Semegen v. Weidner, 780 F.2d 727
(9th Cir.1985); Securities Investor Protection Corp. v. Vigman, 764 F.2d 1309, 1317 (9th
Cir.1985), *appeal after remand* 803 F.2d 1513 (9th Cir.1986); Abeloff v. Barth, 119 F.R.D.
315 (D.Mass.1988).

9. *E.g.* Wichita Federal Savings & Loan Assoc. v. Landmark Group, Inc., 674 F.Supp.
321 (D.Kan.1987); Warren v. Bokum Resources Corp., 433 F.Supp. 1360, 1363 (D.C.N.M.
1977); Sohns v. Dahl, 392 F.Supp. 1208, 1215 (W.D.Va.1975). *See* Lefever v. Vickers, 613
F.Supp. 352 (D.Colo.1985) (venue was proper either in district where letter triggering claim
was sent or received); Como v. Commerce Oil Co., 607 F.Supp. 335 (S.D.N.Y.1985)
(numerous letters and phone calls within the district); Morley v. Cohen, 610 F.Supp. 798
(D.Md.1985). *But see* French v. Faisal Al Massoud Al Fuhaid, 1984 WL 544, [1984
Transfer Binder] Fed.Sec.L.Rep. (CCH) ¶ 91,551 (S.D.N.Y.1984) (venue not sustainable for
failure to show that alleged telephone calls originated in district).

10. Ingram Industries, Inc. v. Nowicki, 527 F.Supp. 683, 689 (E.D.Ky.1981) (opinion
withdrawn, *see* footnote 2 *supra*); Sohns v. Dahl, 392 F.Supp. 1208, 1215 (W.D.Va.1975).

11. Ingram Industries, Inc. v. Nowicki, 527 F.Supp. 683, 689 (E.D.Ky.1981) (opinion
withdrawn, see footnote 2 *supra*); Mayer v. Development Corp. of America, 396 F.Supp.
917, 929 (D.Del.1975).

part of the alleged violations.[12]

Even when venue is proper in a particular forum, transfer of the case to another forum may be warranted under section 1404(a) of Title 28 of the U.S.Code [13] which provides that "for the convenience of parties and witnesses, in the interest of justice, a district court may transfer any civil action to any other district where it might have been brought." Courts weigh several factors when determining whether change of venue is proper: plaintiff's choice of forum, the convenience of the parties and witnesses; the availability of process to compel the presence of witnesses, the cost of obtaining the presence of witnesses, the relative ease of access to sources of proof, calendar congestion, where the relevant events took place, and whether the administration of justice will be advanced by a transfer.[14]

§ 14.4 The Enforceability of Arbitration Agreements in Federal and State Securities Cases

At one time, predispute arbitration agreements were unenforceable with regard to claims arising under the federal securities laws. This meant that virtually all claims were resolved in court or by settlement. In recent years there has been a major reversal of this earlier position. As a result of this major shift of position, most brokerage firms routinely require customers to sign predispute arbitration agreements. Accordingly, most disputes between customers and their brokers are decided in arbitral forums rather than in court. One consequence of this shift has been that much of the law relating to broker-dealer litigation has been placed in a state of suspended animation as it existed in the prearbitration era. This is the case because of the relatively few private disputes that will be continued to be litigated in court and the narrow standard of judicial review of arbitrators' decisions.

---

12. Hilgeman v. National Insurance Co. of America, 547 F.2d 298, 301 (5th Cir.1977), *rehearing denied* 564 F.2d 416 (5th Cir.1977) (act need not be crucial; however, jurisdictional act cannot be trivial); Leavey v. Blinder, Robinson & Co., Inc., 1986 WL 10556, [1986–87 Transfer Binder] Fed.Sec.L.Rep. (CCH) ¶ 92,996 (E.D.Pa.1986) (soliciting allegedly fraudulent purchase in district supports venue); SEC v. Sanders, 1986 WL 15546, [1986–87 Transfer Binder] Fed.Sec.L.Rep. (CCH) ¶ 93,042 (D.Colo.1986) (resale in district supports venue); City of Harrisburg v. Bradford Trust Co., 621 F.Supp. 463 (M.D.Pa.1985) (defendant's response to phone calls from investor were sufficient to support venue in investor's forum); Warren v. Bokum Resources Corp., 433 F.Supp. 1360, 1363 (D.C.N.M. 1977); Sohns v. Dahl, 392 F.Supp. 1208, 1215 (W.D.Va.1975) (act must be more than an immaterial part of alleged violation); SEC v. National Student Marketing Corp., 360 F.Supp. 284, 292 (D.D.C.1973). A New York (S.D.) case, however, held that "venue and jurisdiction over * * * all the *knowing participants* in an alleged fraudulent scheme are proper * * * so long as one of the participants commits an act in furtherance of the scheme in the forum district." Keene Corp. v. Weber, 394 F.Supp. 787, 790–91 (S.D.N.Y.1975). The case seems to stand alone in requiring knowing participation for proper venue. *See, e.g.,* D.H. Blair & Co., Inc. v. Art Emporium, Inc., 1983 WL 1295, Fed.Sec.L.Rep. (CCH) ¶ 99,152 (S.D.N.Y.1983); Ingram Industries, Inc. v. Nowicki, 527 F.Supp. 683, 689 (E.D.Ky. 1981) (opinion withdrawn without affecting the precedential value).

13. 28 U.S.C.A. § 1404(a).

14. *E.g.* Witter v. Torbett, Fed.Sec.L.Rep. (CCH) ¶ 99,202 (S.D.N.Y.1983), *reaffirmed* 1983 WL 1356, Fed.Sec.L.Rep. (CCH) ¶ 99,456 (S.D.N.Y.1983); Carty v. Health–Chem Corp., 567 F.Supp. 1 (E.D.Pa.1982); D.H. Blair & Co., Inc. v. Art Emporium, Inc., 1983 WL 1295, Fed.Sec.L.Rep. (CCH) ¶ 99,152 (S.D.N.Y.1983).

The procedures relating to arbitration proceedings are discussed in chapter 10 of the Practitioner's Edition. As discussed later in this section, arbitration is not limited to customer disputes but is also used for resolution of disputes within the brokerage industry. The discussion below first examines the development of the current law that encourages predispute arbitration agreements. This is followed by discussion of the major jurisdictional and other issues relating to the question of arbitrability. These issues include: collateral estoppel, stay of proceedings, waiver of the right to arbitrate, and relevant contract law doctrines that may be used to challenge predispute arbitration clauses. Other issues included in this section include: judicial review of arbitration agreements, state laws affecting arbitration, and the exclusion of class actions from arbitration.

The Rise of the Wilko Doctrine

In Wilko v. Swan[1], the Supreme Court held that a court could not compel arbitration of claims asserted under section 12(2)[2] of the Securities Act of 1933 despite the existence of an arbitration agreement between the plaintiff and the defendant broker. The court relied on the language of section 14 of the 1933 Act which states that: "Any condition, stipulation or provision binding any person acquiring any security to waive compliance with any provision of this subchapter or of the rules and regulations of the Commission shall be void."[3] Thus, agreements to arbitrate securities law claims were held void as stipulations requiring the waiver of judicial trial and review. Because Congress specifically granted persons asserting federal securities claims the right to bring suit in federal court, the Court decided that the intention of Congress would be best effectuated by invalidating arbitration agreements with respect to Securities Act claims.[4] Following *Wilko,* courts at first were consistent in holding that agreements to arbitrate 1934 Act claims were equally invalid because the 1934 Act contains an anti-waiver provision[5] almost identical to the one found in the 1933 Act.[6]

---

§ 14.4

1. 346 U.S. 427, 74 S.Ct. 182, 98 L.Ed. 168 (1953).

2. 15 U.S.C.A. § 77*l*(2) (prohibits false representations made to induce a securities sale). *See* § 13.14 *supra.*

3. 15 U.S.C.A. § 77n.

4. 346 U.S. 427, 438, 74 S.Ct. 182, 188, 189, 98 L.Ed. 168 (1953). *See also,* Meyers v. C & M Petroleum Producers, Inc., 476 F.2d 427 (5th Cir.1973), *cert. denied* 414 U.S. 829, 94 S.Ct. 56, 38 L.Ed.2d 64 (1973) (claims under Section 5 of the 1933 Act not arbitrable); Can–Am Petroleum v. Beck, 331 F.2d 371 (10th Cir.1964) (claims under 15 U.S.C.A. §§ 77e and 77*l* not arbitrable; remedial aspects of the Securities Act cannot be waived directly or indirectly).

5. 15 U.S.C.A. § 78cc(a) (section 29(a) of the 1934 Act). *See* Couvaras v. Paine Webber Jackson & Curtis, Inc., 1986 WL 2713, [1985–86 Transfer Binder] Fed.Sec.L.Rep. (CCH) ¶ 92,554 (S.D.N.Y.1986); Jacobson v. Merrill Lynch, Pierce, Fenner & Smith, Inc., 1985 WL 5695, [1985–86 Transfer Binder] Fed.Sec.L.Rep. (CCH) ¶ 92,276 (W.D.Pa.1985). *Cf.* Willard L. Schaller & Robert V. Schaller, Applying the *Wilko* Doctrine's Anti–Arbitration Policy in Commodities Fraud Cases, 61 Chic.–Kent L.Rev. 515 (1985).

6. Sibley v. Tandy Corp., 543 F.2d 540, 543 (5th Cir.1976), *cert. denied* 434 U.S. 824, 98 S.Ct. 71, 54 L.Ed.2d 82 (1977); Greater Continental Corp. v. Schechter, 422 F.2d 1100,

Most of the 1934 Act cases involve violations of section 10(b) and Rule 10b–5. The typical challenge to the application of the *Wilko* rule in 10b–5 cases centered on the distinction between the judicially implied private cause of action available under section 10(b) and the express right of a private remedy provided for by section 12(2).[7] For a long time courts remained unpersuaded that the differences between the rights granted in the 1933 and 1934 Acts warranted a different Rule in 10b–5 cases.[8]

The Decline of Wilko

In a number of decisions, it was held that a Supreme Court ruling upholding the arbitrability of pendent state claims[9] brought into question the vitality of *Wilko* and, accordingly, the federal securities claims often were submitted to arbitration along with the state claims.[10] One basis for such rulings was that as implied rights of action, Rule 10b–5 claims do not incorporate the "special right" that the Court found to be present with regard to the 1933 Act claims involved in *Wilko*. These decisions took their lead from Justice White's concurrence in Dean Witter Reynolds, Inc. v. Byrd.[11] Although a great number of decisions seem to have followed Justice White's suggestion, a split developed and many cases continued to adhere to the view that 1934 Act claims are not

1103 (2d Cir.1970); Weissbuch v. Merrill Lynch, Pierce, Fenner & Smith, Inc., 558 F.2d 831 (7th Cir.1977); Ayres v. Merrill Lynch, Pierce, Fenner & Smith, Inc., 538 F.2d 532 (3d Cir.1976), *cert. denied* 429 U.S. 1010, 97 S.Ct. 542, 50 L.Ed.2d 619 (1976); Mansbach v. Prescott, Ball & Turben, 598 F.2d 1017, 1030 (6th Cir.1979); Macchiavelli v. Shearson, Hammill & Co., 384 F.Supp. 21, 27–8 (E.D.Cal.1974); First Heritage v. Prescott, Ball & Turben, 710 F.2d 1205 (6th Cir.1983); Dickinson v. Heinold Securities, Inc., 661 F.2d 638 (7th Cir.1981); Cunningham v. Dean Witter Reynolds, Inc., 550 F.Supp. 578 (E.D.Cal. 1982).

A similar result under state law may ensue where the state blue sky law parallels the federal act's antiwaiver provisions. Kiehne v. Purdy, 309 N.W.2d 60 (Minn.1981). However, the result may differ where the Federal Arbitration Act applies. *See* text accompanying footnote 21 *infra*.

7. *See* Weissbuch v. Merrill Lynch, Pierce, Fenner & Smith, Inc., 558 F.2d 831, 835 (7th Cir.1977); Cunningham v. Dean Witter Reynolds, Inc., 550 F.Supp. 578 (E.D.Cal.1982). *But see* Scherk v. Alberto–Culver Co., 417 U.S. 506, 513–14, 94 S.Ct. 2449, 2454–2455, 41 L.Ed.2d 270 (1974), *rehearing denied* 419 U.S. 885, 95 S.Ct. 157, 42 L.Ed.2d 129 (1974) (presence of international arbitration agreement changes result).

The decision to proceed with or without arbitration may not be immediately appealable. Jolley v. Paine Webber Jackson & Curtis, Inc., 864 F.2d 402 (5th Cir.1989); Delmay v. Paine Webber 863 F.2d 782 (11th Cir.1988).

8. Wilko v. Swan, 346 U.S. 427, 431, 74 S.Ct. 182, 184–185, 98 L.Ed. 168 (1953); Weissbuch v. Merrill Lynch, Pierce, Fenner & Smith, Inc., 558 F.2d 831, 836 (7th Cir.1977); Cunningham v. Dean Witter Reynolds, Inc., 550 F.Supp. 578 (E.D.Cal.1982).

9. Dean Witter Reynolds, Inc. v. Byrd, 470 U.S. 213, 105 S.Ct. 1238, 84 L.Ed.2d 158 (1985), *on remand* 760 F.2d 238 (9th Cir.1985) (where federal securities claims and state claims are brought in one suit, a contract to arbitrate the state claim will be enforced). *See also* Mitsubishi Motors Corp. v. Soler Chrysler–Plymouth, Inc., 473 U.S. 614, 105 S.Ct. 3346, 87 L.Ed.2d 444 (1985) (federal antitrust claims in international arena held arbitrable).

10. *E.g.* Phillips v. Merrill Lynch, Pierce, Fenner & Smith, Inc., 795 F.2d 1393 (8th Cir.1986).

11. 470 U.S. 213, 224, 105 S.Ct. 1238, 1244, 84 L.Ed.2d 158 (1985), *on remand* 760 F.2d 238 (9th Cir.1985).

arbitrable.[12] The Supreme Court has now made it clear that claims subject to a predispute arbitration agreement arising under Rule 10b–5 are arbitrable.[13]

The Court in *Shearson/American Express, Inc. v. McMahon* pointed out that the basis of the *Wilko* decision was the belief that arbitration did not adequately safeguard the parties' interest, thus implicating the antiwaiver provisions. However, as commercial arbitration has become more widely accepted, the procedures are now viewed more favorably than before. Additionally the major exchanges and the NASD have arbitration rules that are subject to SEC oversight.[14] Accordingly, the premise of *Wilko* became highly suspect, at least with regard to predispute arbitration agreements between brokers and customers. Although the *McMahon* ruling is limited to implied remedies of the Exchange Act, there is strong dictum that seemed to signal *Wilko's* demise. A number of recent decisions have held 1933 Act claims (as well as other Exchange Act claims) to be arbitrable and the Court has since followed suit.[15]

12. *E.g.* Jacobson v. Merrill Lynch, Pierce, Fenner & Smith, Inc., 797 F.2d 1197 (3d Cir.1986), *cert. granted and judgment vacated* 482 U.S. 923, 107 S.Ct. 3204, 96 L.Ed.2d 691 (1987), *on remand* 824 F.2d 287 (3d Cir.1987); Conover v. Dean Witter Reynolds, Inc., 794 F.2d 520 (9th Cir.1986); King v. Drexel Burnham Lambert, Inc., 796 F.2d 59 (5th Cir.1986), *cert. granted and judgment vacated* 482 U.S. 922, 107 S.Ct. 3203, 96 L.Ed.2d 690 (1987), *on remand* 825 F.2d 68 (5th Cir.1987); Miller v. Drexel Burnham , Inc., 791 F.2d 850 (11th Cir.1986); McMahon v. Shearson/American Express, Inc., 788 F.2d 94, 98 (2d Cir.1986); Kalali v. Prudential–Bache Securities, Inc., 637 F.Supp. 1131 (D.D.C.1986); Bustamante v. Rotan Mosle, Inc., 633 F.Supp. 303 (S.D.Tex.1986); Farino v. Advest, Inc., 651 F.Supp. 510 (E.D.N.Y.1986); Clark v. Kidder, Peabody & Co., 636 F.Supp. 195 (S.D.N.Y.1986); Couvaras v. Paine Webber Jackson & Curtis, Inc., 1986 WL 2713, [1985–86 Transfer Binder] Fed.Sec.L.Rep. (CCH) ¶ 92,554 (S.D.N.Y.1986); Shapiro v. Merrill Lynch & Co., 634 F.Supp. 587 (S.D.Ohio 1986); Adams v. Swanson, 652 F.Supp. 762 (D.Or.1985).

See former Rule 15c2–2 (rescinded) which declared it to be manipulative and fraudulent for a broker-dealer to include an arbitration clause for federal claims. *See* Blomquist v. Churchill, 633 F.Supp. 131 (D.S.C.1985). *But see* Phillips v. Merrill Lynch, Pierce, Fenner & Smith, Inc., 795 F.2d 1393 (8th Cir.1986) (refusing to apply Rule 15c2–2 to contracts entered into prior to the rule and further questioning the rule in light of the supposed SEC intent to simply reflect the state of the law at the time the rule was adopted); Steinberg v. Illinois Co., 635 F.Supp. 615 (N.D.Ill.1986) (Rule 15c2–2 is procedural and designed to give notice to the customer; it does not affect the substantive right to arbitration).

13. Shearson/American Express, Inc. v. McMahon, 482 U.S. 220, 107 S.Ct. 2332, 96 L.Ed.2d 185 (1987). *See* Edward Fletcher, III, Learning to Live With the Federal Arbitration Act—Securities Litigation in a Post–McMahon World, 37 Emory L.J. 99 (1988). The *McMahon* decision also held that RICO claims are arbitrable. RICO is discussed in § 19.3 *infra* (Practitioner's Edition only).

14. American Stock Exch. Guide (CCH) ¶¶ 9540–575; NASD Manual (CCH) ¶¶ 3712–20; N.Y.Stock Exch.Guide ¶¶ 4311–17. *See* §§ 10.15–10.22 *supra* (Practitioner's Edition only) and Appendix C *infra* (Practitioner's Edition only).

15. Rodriguez De Quijas v. Shearson/Lehman Brothers, Inc., 845 F.2d 1296 (5th Cir.1988) (section 12(2) claim held arbitrable), *affirmed* 490 U.S. 477, 109 S.Ct. 1917, 104 L.Ed.2d 526 (1989); Benoay v. E.F. Hutton & Co., 699 F.Supp. 1523 (S.D.Fla.1988) (section 12(2) claim was arbitrable); Reed v. Bear, Stearns & Co., 698 F.Supp. 835 (D.Kan.1988) (overruling earlier decision and holding that 1933 Act claims are arbitrable); Adams v. Merrill Lynch, Pierce, Fenner & Smith, Inc., 1988 WL 90034, [1987–88 Transfer Binder] Fed.Sec.L.Rep. (CCH) ¶ 93,741 (W.D.Okl.1988) (rationale of *Wilko* has been so eroded that 1933 Act claims are now arbitrable); Schuster v. Kidder, Peabody & Co., 699 F.Supp. 271 (S.D.Fla.1988); Sease v. PaineWebber, Inc., 697 F.Supp. 1190 (S.D.Fla.1988); Araim v. PaineWebber, Inc., 691 F.Supp. 1415 (N.D.Ga.1988). Kavouras v. Visual Products Sys-

Prior to 1989 questions remained as to whether *McMahon* applied to 1933 Act remedies, implied or express; however, the Court's reasoning certainly brought *Wilko* into serious doubt. Some courts reaffirmed *Wilko's* applicability to 1933 Act claims but the Supreme Court has since overruled *Wilko* in Rodriguez De Quijas v. Shearson/American Express, Inc.[16] Even with regard to 1934 Act claims (and now, 1933 Act claims), *Wilko* may have some viability where the procedure invoked by the predispute arbitration agreement does not contain the safeguards that the Court found to have been present in *McMahon*.

Following the *McMahon* decision, a number of courts have ruled that holding Rule 10b–5 claims to be arbitrable is to be given retroactive application.[17] Former SEC Rule 15c2–2 declared that predispute arbitration agreements were a manipulative device in violation of the Act.[18] Many brokerage firms stopped using arbitration agreements after adoption of the rule, while others used arbitration agreements with a provision stating that the agreement to arbitrate did not cover claims which a customer had a right to litigate. In 1987, following the Court's decision, the Commission rescinded the rule. Courts have had to face the question of whether arbitration agreements signed while Rule 15c2–2 was in effect should be interpreted to preclude arbitration of claims that formerly were not arbitrable. The majority of courts have held that the rescission of Rule 15c2–2 should be given retroactive effect so that the federal securities claims are arbitrable if the arbitration clause on its face so permits.[19] However, where a predispute arbitration agreement

---

tems, Inc., 680 F.Supp. 205 (W.D.Pa.1988) (section 17(a) claim held arbitrable); Ryan v. Liss, Tenner & Goldberg Securities Corp., 683 F.Supp. 480 (D.N.J.1988) (section 17(a) claim held arbitrable); Aronson v. Dean Witter Reynolds, Inc., 675 F.Supp. 1324 (S.D.Fla. 1987); Staiman v. Merrill Lynch, Pierce, Fenner & Smith, Inc., 673 F.Supp. 1009 (C.D.Cal.1987) (section 12(2) and section 17(a) claim held arbitrable); Newcome v. Esrey, 659 F.Supp. 100 (W.D.Va.1987) *affirmed* 862 F.2d 1099 (4th Cir.1988); Rocz v. Drexel Burnham Lambert, Inc., 154 Ariz. 462, 743 P.2d 971 (App.1987).

See also, e.g., Badart v. Merrill Lynch, Pierce, Fenner & Smith, Inc., 823 F.2d 333 (9th Cir.1987) (claims against broker under section 15 and for controlling person liability under section 20(a) held arbitrable). Section 15 remedies are discussed in § 10.14 *supra.*

16. 490 U.S. 477, 109 S.Ct. 1917, 104 L.Ed.2d 526 (1989). *See* Osterneck v. Merrill Lynch, Pierce, Fenner & Smith, Inc., 841 F.2d 508, 512 (3d Cir.1988) (1933 Act claims are not arbitrable until the Supreme Court decides otherwise); Pompano–Windy City Partners, Ltd. v. Bear, Stearns & Co., 698 F.Supp. 504 (S.D.N.Y.1988); Rosenblum v. Drexel Burnham Lambert, Inc., [1988–89 Transfer Binder] Fed.Sec.L.Rep. (CCH) ¶ 90,841 (E.D.La.1988); Ketchum v. Almahurst Bloodstock IV, 685 F.Supp. 786 (D.Kan.1988); McCowan v. Dean Witter Reynolds, Inc., 682 F.Supp. 741 (S.D.N.Y.1987); Schultz v. Robinson–Humphrey/American Express, Inc., 666 F.Supp. 219 (M.D.Ga.1987); Johnson v. O'Brien, 420 N.W.2d 264 (Minn.App.1988), *cert. granted and judgment vacated* 490 U.S. 1078, 109 S.Ct. 2096, 104 L.Ed.2d 658 (1989) (section 12(2) claim not arbitrable).

17. Peterson v. Shearson/American Express, Inc., 849 F.2d 464 (10th Cir.1988); Mayaja v. Bodkin, 824 F.2d 439 (5th Cir.1987); Noble v. Drexel, Burnham, Lambert, Inc., 823 F.2d 849 (5th Cir.1987). *But see, e.g.,* Church v. Gruntal & Co., 698 F.Supp. 465 (S.D.N.Y. 1988).

18. 17 C.F.R. § 240.15c2–2 (1986); rescinded in Sec.Exch.Act Rel. No. 34–25034 [1987 Transfer Binder] Fed.Sec.L.Rep. (CCH) ¶ 84,163 (1987).

19. *E.g.,* Clark v. Merrill Lynch, Pierce, Fenner & Smith, Inc., 924 F.2d 550 (4th Cir.1991), *cert. denied* 502 U.S. 818, 112 S.Ct. 74, 116 L.Ed.2d 48 (1991) (provision in arbitration agreement formerly required by Rule 15c2–2 was merely a notice provision and

specifically excludes federal securities claims, neither the *McMahon* decision nor the rescinding of former Rule 15c2–2 operate to modify the express terms of the agreement.[20]

Federal and State Claims

Although federal securities law claims were non-arbitrable under *Wilko*, state common law claims remained subject to arbitration agreements under the Federal Arbitration Act.[21] Thus, where securities actions involve both federal statutory and state common law claims, and the federal claim is not subject to arbitration, the courts must decide whether to sever and compel arbitration of the state claims or whether to adjudicate both federal and state claims in federal court under the doctrine of pendent jurisdiction.

The general rule is that when a complaint states both arbitrable and nonarbitrable claims, the arbitrable claims should be severed and judicial proceedings stayed as to such claims.[22] But when the arbitrable and non-arbitrable claims are so factually related or so "inextricably intertwined" that severance is "impractical, if not impossible", courts frequently denied both severance and arbitration.[23] This exception, called the doctrine of intertwining, sought to protect the exclusive federal jurisdiction over securities actions and to avoid possible preclusive effects that arbitration proceedings may have on subsequent federal litigation. However bifurcation of the federal and pendent state law claims allows adherence to the strong policy behind the Federal Arbitration Act

---

in light of the repeal of the rule, did not exclude securities claims from agreement to arbitrate).

But see, e.g., Blue Gray Corp. I & II v. Merrill Lynch, Pierce, Fenner & Smith, Inc., 921 F.2d 267 (11th Cir.1991) (provision excluding federal securities claims was more than mere notice provision; federal claims were not subject to arbitration but state law claims were).

20. Leicht v. Bateman Eichler, Hill Richards, Inc., 848 F.2d 130 (9th Cir.1988); Pezely v. Merrill Lynch, Pierce, Fenner & Smith, Inc., 683 F.Supp. 767 (D.Utah 1987); Brick v. J.C. Bradford & Co., 677 F.Supp. 1251 (D.D.C.1987). *See also, e.g.,* Van Ness Townhouses v. Mar Industries Corp., 862 F.2d 754 (9th Cir.1988); Giles v. Blunt, Ellis & Loewi, Inc., 845 F.2d 131 (7th Cir.1988) (express language of arbitration agreement preserved customer's right to litigate federal securities law claims).

21. Belke v. Merrill Lynch, Pierce, Fenner & Smith, Inc., 693 F.2d 1023 (11th Cir.1982); Dickinson v. Heinold Securities, Inc., 661 F.2d 638 (7th Cir.1981); Surman v. Merrill Lynch, Pierce, Fenner & Smith, Inc., 559 F.Supp. 388 (E.D.Mo.1983), *judgment reversed* 733 F.2d 59 (8th Cir.1984); Roueche v. Merrill Lynch, Pierce, Fenner & Smith, Inc., 554 F.Supp. 338 (D.Hawaii 1983). *See also* 9 U.S.C.A. § 2 (Federal Arbitration Act).

22. Byrd v. Dean Witter Reynolds, Inc., 726 F.2d 552 (9th Cir.1984), *decision reversed* 470 U.S. 213, 105 S.Ct. 1238, 84 L.Ed.2d 158 (1985); Belke v. Merrill Lynch, Pierce, Fenner & Smith, Inc., 693 F.2d 1023, 1026 (11th Cir.1982). *See also, See, e.g.,* McCowan v. Sears, Roebuck and Co., 908 F.2d 1099 (2d Cir.1990), *cert. denied* 498 U.S. 897, 111 S.Ct. 250, 112 L.Ed.2d 209 (1990) (staying proceedings based on state law controlling person liability pending determination of arbitration proceedings); Wick v. Atlantic Marine, Inc., 605 F.2d 166, 168 (5th Cir.1979).

23. Belke v. Merrill Lynch, Pierce, Fenner & Smith, Inc., 693 F.2d 1023 (11th Cir.1982) (quoting Merrill Lynch, Pierce, Fenner & Smith, Inc. v. Haydu, 675 F.2d 1169, 1172 (11th Cir.1982)). *See also,* Dickinson v. Heinold Securities, Inc., 661 F.2d 638, 643 (7th Cir.1981); Surman v. Merrill Lynch, Pierce, Fenner & Smith, Inc., 559 F.Supp. 388 (E.D.Mo.1983), *reversed on other grounds* 733 F.2d 59 (8th Cir.1984); Roueche v. Merrill Lynch, Pierce, Fenner & Smith, Inc., 554 F.Supp. 338 (D.Hawaii 1983).

requiring enforcement of the parties' agreement to arbitrate as well as the strong policy behind the Securities Acts requiring judicial resolution in federal courts.[24] The Supreme Court rejected the intertwining doctrine. In Dean Witter Reynolds, Inc. v. Byrd[25] the court ruled that the language of the Federal Arbitration Act[26] does not leave the courts with any discretion to deny arbitration requests and thus a defendant's request for arbitration of arbitrable state law claims must be granted. One obvious result of the *Byrd* decision was that the probability of duplicative adjudication could be avoided through the doctrine of pendent jurisdiction when the parties do not have an agreement to arbitrate.

The Federal Arbitration Act: Policies Favoring Arbitration

As the preceding cases demonstrate, the Federal Arbitration Act embodies a strong public policy favoring arbitration. There are limits, however, to the Act's impact. Thus, for example, the Federal Arbitration Act does not create a basis for federal jurisdiction independent of that which might be available under the federal securities laws.[27] Similarly, although the Federal Arbitration Act applies to claims involving interstate commerce, it does not apply to a transaction which is wholly intrastate.[28] On the other hand, when the jurisdictional reach of the Federal Arbitration Act is implicated, that act may preempt the applicable state law.[29]

Another recent example of the policy favoring arbitration is found in the Second Circuit's ruling that a customer can demand arbitration notwithstanding the fact that the broker and customer had mutually agreed to cross out the arbitration clause contained in the customer agreement.[30] The court so ruled in light of the broker-dealer's preexist-

---

24. *See* Liskey v. Oppenheimer & Co., Inc., 717 F.2d 314 (6th Cir.1983); Dickinson v. Heinold Securities, Inc., 661 F.2d 638, 646 (7th Cir.1981).

25. 470 U.S. 213, 105 S.Ct. 1238, 84 L.Ed.2d 158 (1985), *on remand* 760 F.2d 238 (9th Cir.1985).

26. 9 U.S.C.A. § 4 ("district courts shall direct the parties to proceed to arbitration").

27. Prudential-Bache Securities, Inc. v. Fitch, 966 F.2d 981 (5th Cir.1992) (district court lacked jurisdiction over broker-dealer's motion to compel arbitration); Giangrande v. Shearson Lehman/E.F. Hutton, 803 F.Supp. 464 (D.Mass.1992) (Federal Arbitration Act does not create an independent basis for jurisdiction).

28. Ex parte Jones, 628 So.2d 316 (Ala.1993) (a divided Alabama Supreme Court held that since predispute arbitration agreements are not enforceable under Alabama law, arbitration was not available in a securities transaction between Alabama residents involving the securities of an Alabama corporation).

29. Olde Discount Corp. v. Tupman, 1 F.3d 202 (3d Cir.1993) (Federal Arbitration Act may preclude state action seeking rescission pending outcome of arbitration).

A recent Supreme Court ruling further points out the preemptive effect of the Federal Arbitration Act. In Mastrobuono v. Shearson Lehman Hutton, Inc., ___ U.S. ___, 115 S.Ct. 1212, 131 L.Ed.2d 76 (1995), the Court ruled that a state procedural rule barring punitive damages in arbitration proceedings must yield to the procedural rules of the Federal Arbitration Act in light of the broad policy favoring arbitration under that Act. The Court held that the parties' choice of law clause meant that the state's substantive law permitting punitive damages applied but not the procedural bar.

30. Kidder, Peabody & Co. v. Zinsmeyer Trusts Partnership, 41 F.3d 861(2d Cir.1994). *Cf.* Nomura Securities International v. Citibank, N.A., 81 N.Y.2d 614, 601 N.Y.S.2d 448, 619 N.E.2d 385 (1993) (invoking New York Stock Exchange's arbitration mandate with regard to member transactions taking place off the exchange).

ing duty to arbitrate under the NASD's Arbitration Code. The net effect of this ruling is to give the customer an option to arbitrate even in instances where the brokerage firm does not have the ability to compel arbitration.

Res Judicata and Collateral Estoppel

The state and self regulatory organization arbitration procedures tend to be very efficient and will generally proceed to judgment more rapidly than a federal court suit. Accordingly, a byproduct of the duplicative adjudication is the possibility that the state law arbitration determination may be given preclusive effect in federal court under the doctrine of collateral estoppel.[31] Courts consider a number of factors in determining whether to give preclusive effect to nonjudicial and state court decisions. It is generally held that a grant of exclusive federal jurisdiction does not preclude res judicata or collateral estoppel based on a state court adjudication.[32] Given that res judicata and collateral estoppel apply to state law proceedings, the next question is whether to apply them to nonjudicial determinations. In general, the federal district courts have a wide range of discretion in deciding whether to apply collateral estoppel.[33] Although nonjudicial determinations such as agency decisions are less formal than judicial proceedings, courts have given a preclusive effect to such decisions when it is shown that there was an opportunity to fully and fairly litigate the issue.[34] In exercising this discretion with regard to prior state tribunal determinations, the Supreme Court has held that federal courts must first look to whether that state would have given preclusive effect to that judgment in subsequent proceedings and second to whether the federal interests involved in the suit override the interests of res judicata so as to warrant the denying of a preclusive effect.[35] The grant of exclusive federal jurisdiction under the 1934 Act presumably by itself is not sufficient to show such a

---

31. *See, e.g.,* Brodsky, Arbitration in Securities Cases, N.Y.L.J. vol. 193, p. 1, col. 1 (June 5, 1985).

32. *E.g.* Allen v. McCurry, 449 U.S. 90, 101 S.Ct. 411, 66 L.Ed.2d 308 (1980), *on remand* 647 F.2d 167 (8th Cir.1981), *appeal after remand* 688 F.2d 581 (8th Cir.1982); Becher v. Contoure Labs., Inc., 279 U.S. 388, 391, 49 S.Ct. 356, 357, 73 L.Ed. 752 (1929); Key v. Wise, 629 F.2d 1049, 1063–68 (5th Cir.1980), *cert. denied* 454 U.S. 1103, 102 S.Ct. 682, 70 L.Ed.2d 647 (1981). *See also, e.g.,* Coffey v. Dean Witter Reynolds Inc., 961 F.2d 922 (10th Cir.1992) (res judicata applied to arbitration of state law claims in subsequent federal securities litigation). *But see* A.G. Edwards & Sons, Inc. v. Smith, 1991 WL 253010, [1991 Transfer Binder] Fed.Sec.L.Rep. (CCH) ¶ 96,282 (D.Ariz.1991) (arbitration ruling on common law fraud did not have collateral estoppel effect in subsequent 10b–5 claim because of different burdens of proof).

33. *E.g.* Parklane Hosiery Co. v. Shore, 439 U.S. 322, 99 S.Ct. 645, 58 L.Ed.2d 552 (1979). *See* Thomas L. Hazen, Administrative Enforcement: An Evaluation of the Securities and Exchange Commission's Use of Injunctions and Other Enforcement Methods, 31 Hastings L.J. 427, 451–60 (1979); Note, The Collateral Estoppel Effect of Administrative Agency Actions in Federal Civil Litigation, 46 Geo.Wash.L.Rev. 65 (1977).

34. *E.g.* Bowen v. United States, 570 F.2d 1311, 1322 (7th Cir.1978); Campbell v. Superior Court, 18 Ariz.App. 287, 501 P.2d 463 (1972).

35. Marrese v. American Academy of Orthopaedic Surgeons, 470 U.S. 373, 105 S.Ct. 1327, 84 L.Ed.2d 274 (1985), *rehearing denied* 471 U.S. 1062, 105 S.Ct. 2127, 85 L.Ed.2d 491 (1985) which was decided on the same day as the *Byrd* decision.

compelling federal interest, especially when viewed in light of the grant of concurrent jurisdiction that exists under the other securities acts.[36] Accordingly, unless the federal courts are prone to magnify the federal interest under the securities laws, some state law and self regulatory organization arbitration decisions may have a preclusive effect.[37] The federal policy supporting arbitration would appear to favor applying collateral estoppel to arbitration decisions, provided that it can be shown what issues were in fact decided by the arbitrators.

It has been held, for example, that a decision by an NASD arbitration panel should be given preclusive effect in federal court.[38] This result is especially justifiable in light of the Supreme Court's reasoning in *McMahon*. One problem with arbitration awards is that they rarely indicate the precise basis for the decision.[39] Accordingly, it may frequently be difficult to establish the scope of preclusive effect to be given.[40] In such a case, unless res judicata (claim preclusion) applies, it

36. *See* § 14.1 *supra.*

37. Greenblatt v. Drexel Burnham Lambert, Inc., 763 F.2d 1352 (11th Cir.1985) (collateral estoppel applied in federal RICO litigation to arbitration of state law contract claims); Williams v. E.F. Hutton & Co., 753 F.2d 117 (D.C.Cir.1985) (res judicata applies only to issues that the arbitrator had power to decide under the agreement but to the extent that those issues overlap with the federal claim collateral estoppel applies); Wing v. J.C. Bradford & Co., 678 F.Supp. 622 (N.D.Miss.1987) (arbitration award based on state law did not collaterally estop plaintiff from litigating federal securities claim because arbitrator's award did not adequately state findings and it could not be determined whether state claims fully compensated plaintiff for alleged losses that could be recoverable under federal law); Artman v. Prudential–Bache Securities, Inc., 670 F.Supp. 769 (S.D. Ohio 1987) (no collateral estoppel to arbitration of state claims since arbitrator's award gave no indication of whether issues underlying federal claim were actually dealt with in arbitration proceedings). Pallante v. Paine Webber, Jackson & Curtis, Inc., 1985 WL 1360, [1985–86 Transfer Binder] Fed.Sec.L.Rep. (CCH) ¶ 92,219 (S.D.N.Y.1985) (res judicata applied in churning case). *See* Weir v. Merrill Lynch, Pierce, Fenner & Smith, Inc., 586 F.Supp. 63, 65 (S.D.Fla.1984) (recognizing the threat of collateral estoppel should the arbitration be decided first); Brodsky *supra* note 17.3 at 2. *But see* Timberlake v. Oppenheimer & Co., 1985 WL 2426, [1985–86 Transfer Binder] Fed.Sec.L.Rep. (CCH) ¶ 92,336 (N.D.Ill.1985) (collateral estoppel denied in RICO action where arbitrator's findings were ambiguous). RICO actions are discussed in § 19.3 *infra.*

The fact that an arbitration decision has not been confirmed by a court has little to do with whether collateral estoppel will apply since judicial review adds little, if anything, to the validity of the arbitration award. In re Drexel Burnham Lambert Group, Inc., 161 B.R. 902 (S.D.N.Y.1993).

38. Hammerman v. Peacock, 654 F.Supp. 71 (D.D.C.1987). *But see* Wolf v. Gruntal & Co., 45 F.3d 524 (1st Cir.1995) (where arbitration agreement excluded federal securities claims from its coverage, res judicata would not apply to arbitration award under state law claims arising out of the same facts).

39. *See, e.g.,* Trustees of Lawrence Academy v. Merrill Lynch, Pierce, Fenner & Smith, Inc., 821 F.Supp. 59 (D.N.H.1993) (arbitrators are not required to make findings of fact nor give reasons for their award).

40. *See, e.g.,* Clark v. Bear Stearns & Co., 966 F.2d 1318 (9th Cir.1992) (arbitrators' dismissal of negligence claim did not have collateral estoppel effect on federal securities claim; the absence of any record of the arbitration made it impossible to determine the basis of the arbitrators' decision); Pompano–Windy City Partners, Ltd. v. Bear, Stearns & Co., 1993 WL 42786, [1992–1993 Transfer Binder] Fed.Sec.L.Rep. (CCH) ¶ 97,366 (S.D.N.Y. 1993) (absence of final judgment precluded collateral estoppel or res judicata); Hybert v. Shearson Lehman/American Express, Inc., 688 F.Supp. 320 (N.D.Ill.1988) (tersity of arbitration decision required limiting its res judicata effect).

may not be possible to invoke collateral estoppel (issue preclusion). In order for issue preclusion to be invoked, the issue in both the first and second litigation must be the same.[41] Therefore, where the arbitrator's award does not reveal the basis of the decision, collateral estoppel is not appropriate.

Stay of Proceedings

In order to preserve the policy against duplicative litigation, some federal courts have stayed the federal claim pending determination of the arbitration.[42] Some courts, in the wake of *Byrd*, held that the related federal claims are arbitrable along with the state claims[43] and the Supreme Court has since agreed, with regard to both 1933 Act and 1934 Act claims.[44]

When the complaint alleges that the arbitration clause was induced by fraud, it is appropriate to stay arbitration pending judicial resolution of the fraud claim which will determine whether the dispute must be sent to arbitration.[45] This is a corollary of the rule that the validity of an agreement to arbitrate is for the court.[46] However, when the claim is that the entire agreement (containing a predispute arbitration clause) was induced by fraud, the enforceability of the agreement is a matter for the arbitrators.[47]

In 1989 the arbitration rules were amended to require that a statement of all issues be contained in the order. However, there still is no requirement that the arbitrator state the reasons for any decision. *See* Sec.Exch.Act Rel. No. 34–26805 (May 16, 1989) and § 10.19 *supra* (Practitioner's Edition only).

The current arbitration rules appear in Appendix C *infra* (Practitioner's Edition only).

41. *Cf.* Mian v. Donaldson Lufkin & Jenrette Securities Corp., 7 F.3d 1085 (2d Cir.1993) (arbitration award did not affect customer's suit against broker-dealer for discrimination and civil rights violations).

42. Meyer v. Dans un Jardin, S.A., 816 F.2d 533 (10th Cir.1987); Fitzpatrick v. Kidder, Peabody & Co., [1986 Transfer Binder] Fed.Sec.L.Rep. ¶ 92,802 (S.D.N.Y.1986).

43. *See* footnotes 21–26 *supra* and accompanying text.

44. Rodriguez De Quijas v. Shearson/American Express, 490 U.S. 477, 109 S.Ct. 1917, 104 L.Ed.2d 526 (1989); Shearson/American Express, Inc. v. McMahon, 482 U.S. 220, 107 S.Ct. 2332, 96 L.Ed.2d 185 (1987). *See* text accompanying footnotes 13–16 *supra*.

45. Chastian v. Robinson–Humphrey Co., 957 F.2d 851 (11th Cir.1992) (in attempting to enforce an arbitration clause against a nonsigning party, the question of whether the predispute arbitration agreement is enforceable is a matter for the courts when the challenge to arbitration goes to the making of the agreement); C.B.S. Employees Federal Credit Union v. Donaldson, Lufkin & Jenrette Securities Corp., 912 F.2d 1563 (6th Cir.1990); A.G. Edwards & Sons v. Syvrud, 597 So.2d 197 (Ala.1992) (customer was entitled to have court determine whether arbitration clause was fraudulently induced).

For further discussion *see* § 14.5 *infra* in the text accompanying footnotes 4–16 (Practitioner's Edition only).

46. *See, e.g.,* In the Matter of VMS Limited Partnership Securities Litigation, 26 F.3d 50 (7th Cir.1994) (whether there is an effective arbitration agreement is a question for the court). *See also* § 14.5 *infra* (Practitioner's Edition only).

47. R.M. Perez & Associates, Inc. v. Welch, 960 F.2d 534 (5th Cir.1992) (if fraud relates to the entire agreement rather than merely the arbitration clause, the enforceability of the agreement is a matter for the arbitrator; district court's interpretation of documents containing arbitration agreement was a question of law subject to de novo review). *Cf.* Shearson Lehman Brothers, Inc. v. Crisp., 1992 WL 192889 (Ala.1992), *withdrawn and superseded on other grounds* 646 So.2d 613 (Ala.1994) (broker-dealer that refused to admit validity of arbitration clause could not compel arbitration).

Waiver

Another question that is likely to arise in the wake of the recognition of the arbitrability of federal securities law disputes is one of waiver. It is possible to waive an agreement to arbitrate and it is arguable that the *Byrd* decision does not preclude a court from finding a waiver of the agreement to arbitrate where that waiver is said to arise from participation in a lawsuit in a manner inconsistent with exercising the right to arbitration.[48] Notwithstanding the arbitrability of claims in the wake of *Byrd, McMahon,* and *Rodriguez,* it has been held that resort to the courts can be viewed, on appropriate facts, as a waiver of the right to have the dispute resolved by arbitration,[49] but participation in pretrial discovery has been held not to act as a waiver of the arbitration agreement.[50] Similarly, participation in an arbitration does not in and of itself waive any objections to the proceedings, especially where the participation consists of motions objecting to continuation.[51]

A party asserting that the right to arbitrate has been waived has a "heavy" burden of proof.[52] A showing of active participation in judicial litigation generally is sufficient to meet this burden and thus will establish a waiver. It has been held that a failure to take a timely

---

48. Rush v. Oppenheimer & Co., 606 F.Supp. 300 (S.D.N.Y.1985), *reversed* 779 F.2d 885 (2d Cir.1985) (decided after *Byrd*). *But cf.* Frye v. Paine Webber Jackson & Curtis, Inc., 1985 WL 5840, [1985–86 Transfer Binder] Fed.Sec.L.Rep. (CCH) ¶ 92,516 (N.D.Tex.1985).

49. Hoxworth v. Blinder, Robinson & Co., 980 F.2d 912 (3d Cir.1992) (active litigation for over a year including extensive pretrial discovery and lengthy memorandum opposing class certification operated as a waiver of arbitration agreement); Stone v. E.F. Hutton & Co., 898 F.2d 1542 (11th Cir.1990) (delay of more than twenty months in requesting arbitration and participation in pretrial discovery operated as a waiver of the right to arbitrate); MidAmerica Federal Savings & Loan Ass'n v. Shearson/American Express, Inc., 886 F.2d 1249, 1256 (10th Cir.1989) (broker engaged in extensive litigation and therefore was found to have waived right to arbitration); Frye v. Paine, Webber, Jackson & Curtis, Inc., 877 F.2d 396 (5th Cir.1989), *cert. denied* 494 U.S. 1016, 110 S.Ct. 1318, 108 L.Ed.2d 493 (1990) (broker who failed to demand arbitration during 2½ years of litigation waived right to arbitrate); Fraser v. Merrill Lynch, Pierce, Fenner & Smith, Inc., 817 F.2d 250 (4th Cir.1987) (4½ year delay); Price v. Drexel Burnham Lambert, Inc., 791 F.2d 1156 (5th Cir.1986).

50. Walker v. J.C. Bradford & Co., 938 F.2d 575 (5th Cir.1991) (participation in limited discovery was not a waiver even when broker's motion to compel arbitration was made 13 months after suit was filed); Stifel Nicolaus & Co. v. Freeman, 924 F.2d 157 (8th Cir.1991) (delay in seeking arbitration did not amount to a waiver; there was no evidence of prejudice to the customer); Ackerberg v. Johnson, 892 F.2d 1328, 1334 n. 4 (8th Cir.1989) (no waiver where delay in seeking arbitration was due to the then uncertain state of the law as to the right to arbitrate 1933 Act claims); Conover v. Dean Witter Reynolds, Inc., 837 F.2d 867 (9th Cir.1988) (brokerage firm's participating in pretrial discovery and waiting two years from date of suit to make motion to compel arbitration was not a waiver where motion to compel arbitration was made shortly after the *McMahon* decision).

51. *See* Prudential Securities, Inc. v. Hornsby, 865 F.Supp. 447 (N.D.Ill.1994).

52. *See, e.g.,* Britton v. Co–op. Banking Group, 916 F.2d 1405 (9th Cir.1990) (investors failed to satisfy the heavy burden of establishing waiver; there was no showing that defendant had knowledge of the right to arbitrate and his avoidance of discovery and motions to stay were not inconsistent with his pursuit of his right to arbitrate). *Cf.* Corpman v. Prudential–Bache Securities, Inc., 907 F.2d 29 (3d Cir.1990) (trial court abused discretion in vacating stay of litigation based on broker's one day delay in filing motion for stay). *See also, e.g.,* Broadcort Capital Corp. v. Dutcher, 859 F.Supp. 1517 (S.D.N.Y.1994) (fact that party refused to arbitrate in New York was not a per se waiver so that arbitration could still take place in another venue).

appeal from denial of a motion to compel arbitration operated as a waiver of any right to arbitration that may have existed.[53]

Other Factors Affecting Enforcement of Predispute Arbitration Agreements[54]

Section 2 of the Federal Arbitration Act provides that arbitration agreements can be invalidated upon such grounds as exist at law or equity for the invalidity of any contract.[55] Thus, a court cannot compel arbitration unless there is a valid contractual obligation.[56] Brokerage customers frequently seek to avoid predispute arbitration agreements by claiming that the arbitration clause is an invalid contract of adhesion. The determination of whether there is an adhesion is highly factual.[57] It is generally held that if the claims of invalidity go to the contract as a whole, they should be resolved by the arbitrator.[58] Thus, for example, when a claim of fraudulent inducement is made, it is frequently considered as relating to the contract as a whole and will be determined by the arbitrator rather than a court.[59]

The contract issues will generally be determined under state law.[60] However, rules of the self regulatory organizations may also affect the validity of arbitration clauses. Accordingly, failure to comply with the NASD and New York Stock Exchange disclosure obligations, including

---

53.　Cotton v. Slone, 4 F.3d 176 (2d Cir.1993).

54.　For further discussion of these issues see § 14.5 *infra* (Practitioner's Edition only).

55.　9 U.S.C.A. § 2.

56.　*See, e.g.,* Jolley v. Welch, 904 F.2d 988 (5th Cir.1990), *cert. denied* 498 U.S. 1050, 111 S.Ct. 762, 112 L.Ed.2d 781 (1991) (broker failed to meet burden of establishing existence of valid arbitration agreement; broker did not introduce an arbitration agreement purporting to be signed by the investor); Miller v. Drexel, Burnham, Lambert, Inc., 791 F.2d 850 (11th Cir.1986). In Oppenheimer & Co. v. Neidhardt, 1994 WL 176976, [1993–1994 Transfer Binder] Fed. Sec. L. Rep. (CCH) ¶ 98,224 (S.D.N.Y.1994) the court held that a nonsigning claimant who was a third party beneficiary of brokerage agreement could enforce an arbitration clause against a brokerage firm.

The interpretation of the contract is essentially a matter of state law. *See, e.g.,* Zink v. Merrill Lynch Pierce Fenner & Smith, Inc., 13 F.3d 330 (10th Cir.1993) (ordering arbitration of claims relating to bond transactions occurring prior to execution of agreement to arbitrate); Bevere v. Oppenheimer & Co., 862 F.Supp. 1243 (D.N.J.1994) (although not signatories to arbitration agreement, pension plan participants were bound to arbitration agreement signed by representatives of the plan).

57.　Accordingly, courts have remanded the issue to the trier of fact. *See, e.g.,* Benoay v. Prudential–Bache Securities, Inc., 805 F.2d 1437 (11th Cir.1986); Miller v. Drexel, Burnham, Lambert, Inc., 791 F.2d 850 (11th Cir.1986); Brown v. Dean Witter Reynolds, Inc., 804 F.2d 129 (11th Cir.1986); Paine, Webber, Jackson & Curtis, Inc. v. McNeal, 143 Ga.App. 579, 239 S.E.2d 401 (1977); Fairview Cemetery Ass'n of Stillwater v. Eckberg, 385 N.W.2d 812 (Minn.1986).

58.　Houlihan v. Offerman & Co., 31 F.3d 692 (8th Cir.1994); Bhatia v. Johnston, 818 F.2d 418 (5th Cir.1987); Benoay v. Prudential–Bache Securities, Inc., 805 F.2d 1437 (11th Cir.1986); Miller v. Drexel, Burnham, Lambert, Inc., 791 F.2d 850 (11th Cir.1986); Morris v. PaineWebber Inc., 1989 WL 223015, [1990 Transfer Binder] Fed.Sec.L.Rep. ¶ 95,309 (W.D.Mich.1989). *Cf.* Hashemi v. Merrill Lynch, Pierce, Fenner & Smith, Inc., 642 F.Supp. 376 (N.D.Ga.1985) (whether agreement was induced by fraud was a matter for the arbitrator).

59.　*E.g.,* Houlihan v. Offerman & Co., 31 F.3d 692 (8th Cir.1994). *See* § 14.5 *infra* (Practitioner's Edition only).

60.　*See* discussion in § 14.5 *infra* (Practitioner's Edition only).

the requirement that any agreement containing an arbitration clause be specifically acknowledged by the customer,[61] can result in the invalidity, and hence unenforceability, of the arbitration agreement.[62]

The essence of the adhesion contract claim is that the use of arbitration clauses is an industry-wide practice[63] and that it is unfair to force them upon customers. However, the majority of courts have held that there is nothing inherently unfair about arbitration clauses[64] and thus the clause does not place the customer in an unfair position.[65] Arbitration clauses have been upheld even though appearing on the reverse side of the brokerage agreement.[66] However, not all courts have upheld arbitration provisions, especially when it is shown that the broker was guilty of overreaching or other wrongdoing.[67]

Many predispute arbitration clauses provide that the dispute shall be heard in accordance with the arbitration rules of one of the exchanges or the NASD. These rules, which, at least in theory, have been adopted with SEC oversight, set out the arbitration procedures and method of arbitrator selection.[68] As discussed elsewhere,[69] the SEC has recently

---

61. NASD Rules of Fair Practice, Art. III, § 21; NYSE Rule 637.

62. *See* Mueske v. Piper, Jaffray & Hopwood, Inc., 260 Mont. 207, 859 P.2d 444 (1993).

63. *But see* Fletcher, Privatizing Securities Disputes Through the Enforcement of Arbitration, 71 Minn.L.Rev. 393 (1987) (where it is pointed out that of the four largest brokerage firms only one uses arbitration clauses in accounts for cash customers. It seems likely, however, that use of arbitration clauses will increase in light of the *McMahon* decision).

64. *See* Coleman v. Prudential Bache Securities, Inc., 802 F.2d 1350 (11th Cir.1986); Webb v. R. Rowland & Co., Inc., 800 F.2d 803 (8th Cir.1986); Surman v. Merrill Lynch, Pierce, Fenner & Smith, Inc., 733 F.2d 59 (8th Cir.1984); LeFoy v. Merrill Lynch, Pierce, Fenner & Smith, Inc., 1989 WL 80444, [1989 Transfer Binder] Fed.Sec.L.Rep. (CCH) ¶ 94,400 (N.D.Ala.1989); Simon v. Smith Barney, Harris Upham & Co., 1989 WL 53919, [1989 Transfer Binder] Fed.Sec.L.Rep. (CCH) ¶ 94,178 (W.D.Okl.1989); Gonick v. Drexel Burnham Lambert, Inc., 711 F.Supp. 981 (N.D.Cal.1988); Hall v. Prudential–Bache Securities, Inc., 662 F.Supp. 468 (C.D.Cal.1987); Finkle & Ross v. A.G. Becker Paribas, Inc., 622 F.Supp. 1505 (S.D.N.Y.1985); Speck v. Oppenheimer & Co., Inc., 583 F.Supp. 325 (W.D.Mo.1984).

65. Shotto v. Laub, 632 F.Supp. 516 (D.Md.1986); Peele v. Kidder Peabody & Co., 620 F.Supp. 61 (E.D.Mo.1985). *See also, e.g.,* Driscoll v. Smith Barney, Harris Upham & Co., 815 F.2d 655 (11th Cir.1987) (failure to adequately plead invalidity of arbitration agreement).

In an apparent case of first impression, a court upheld the arbitrability of insider trading claims despite the contention that arbitration would be contrary to public policy. Energy Factors Inc. v. Nuevo Energy Co., 1992 WL 110541, [1992–1993 Transfer Binder] Fed.Sec. L.Rep. (CCH) ¶ 97,641 (S.D.N.Y.1992).

66. *See* Speck v. Oppenheimer & Co., Inc., 583 F.Supp. 325 (W.D.Mo.1984). In 1989, the SEC approved new arbitration rules which provide that prominence should be given to predispute arbitration agreements. *See* Sec.Exch.Act Rel. No. 34–26805 (May 16, 1989); § 10.15 *supra* and Appendix C *infra* (Practitioner's Edition only).

67. Woodyard v. Merrill Lynch, Pierce, Fenner & Smith, Inc., 640 F.Supp. 760 (S.D.Tex.1986) (finding fraudulent inducement, relying on SEC Rule 15c2–2). *See also, e.g.,* Lampro v. Merrill Lynch, Pierce, Fenner & Smith, Inc., No. 85 Civ. 684 (D.Or. Oct. 3, 1985) (reserving decision pending hearing on unconscionability of arbitration clause).

68. *Compare* Sharp v. Merrill Lynch, Pierce, Fenner & Smith, Inc., 1991 WL 370121, [1992 Transfer Binder] Fed.Sec.L.Rep. (CCH) ¶ 96,948 (Fla.Cir.1991) (AMEX window was not available in light of express forum selection in prior arbitration agreement); Orlowe v. Merrill Lynch, Pierce, Fenner & Smith, 1991 WL 370120, [1992 Transfer Binder] Fed.Sec.

---

69. See note 69 on page 935.

approved major changes in the arbitration rules. A few courts have invalidated such agreements on the grounds that the exchange's selection of the arbitrators made the proceedings presumptively biased.[70] However, not all courts have agreed[71] and the rationale of the Supreme Court's decisions in *Rodriguez* and *McMahon* seems to undercut the finding of bias.

With the *McMahon* decision opening the doors to arbitration, it is very likely that there will continue to be an increase in the number of cases dealing with the adhesion contract issue.

Arbitration of Disputes Involving Municipal Securities

The Municipal Securities Rulemaking Board, which regulates municipal securities dealers, has its own arbitration procedures for settling disputes involving municipal securities dealers.[72] It has been held that the doctrine of *Wilko v. Swan* does not preclude arbitration of federal securities claims in light of the statutory authority for MSRB arbitra-

---

L.Rep. (CCH) ¶ 96,952 (Fla.Cir.1991) (arbitration clause that designates specific arbitral forums supersedes the AMEX window); Merrill Lynch, Pierce, Fenner & Smith, Inc. v. Georgiadis, 903 F.2d 109 (2d Cir.1990), *affirming* 724 F.Supp. 120 (S.D.N.Y.1989) (permitting arbitration before the New York Stock Exchange overriding "AMEX window" that would have permitted arbitration before the American Arbitration Association); Dain Bosworth, Inc. v. Fedora, 1993 WL 33642, [1992–1993 Transfer Binder] Fed.Sec.L.Rep. (CCH) ¶ 97,349 (S.D.N.Y.1993) (agreement superceded AMEX window); Merrill Lynch, Pierce, Fenner & Smith Inc. v. Noonan, 1992 WL 196741, [1992 Transfer Binder] Fed.Sec.L.Rep. (CCH) ¶ 96,973 (S.D.N.Y.1992) (same); Shearson Lehman Brothers, Inc. v. Brady, 783 F.Supp. 1490 (D.Mass.1991) (federal court had jurisdiction to decide whether customer had right to elect arbitral forum under "AMEX window;" customer had the right to make such an election) *with* Wade v. Prudential Securities, Inc., 1994 WL 124428, [1993–1994 Transfer Binder] Fed. Sec. L. Rep. (CCH) ¶ 98,117 (N.D.Cal.1994) (customer was entitled under New York law to rely on AMEX window giving him a broad choice of arbitral forums); Joseph v. Prudential Bache Securities, Inc., 1991 WL 370135, [1991 Transfer Binder] Fed.Sec.L.Rep. (CCH) ¶ 96,184 (Fla.Cir.1991) (recognizing customer's right to arbitration before the AAA, pursuant to AMEX window); Cowen & Co. v. Anderson, 76 N.Y.2d 318, 559 N.Y.S.2d 225, 558 N.E.2d 27 (N.Y.1990) (permitting arbitration before AAA under "AMEX window") *and* Bear, Stearns & Co. v. Bennett, 1991 WL 22853, [1990–1991 Transfer Binder] Fed.Sec.L.Rep. (CCH) ¶ 95,857 (S.D.N.Y.1991), *judgment vacated* 938 F.2d 31 (2d Cir.1991) (by electing AMEX, customer consented to jurisdiction in New York).

69. *See* § 10.15 *supra* and Appendix C *infra* (Practitioner's Edition only). *See also* § 10.2 *supra* discussing the relationship of the SEC and the self regulatory organizations. The SEC oversight here may be in name only as the commission has not to date been supervising the arbitration programs. For the details of the applicable procedures *see* American Stock Exch. Guide (CCH) ¶¶ 9540–51J; NASD Manual (CCH) ¶¶ 3701–20; N.Y. Stock Exch. Guide (CCH) ¶¶ 4211–20. *See* §§ 10.15–10.22 *supra* (Practitioner's Edition only).

70. Hope v. Superior Ct. of Santa Clara Cty., 122 Cal.App.3d 147, 175 Cal.Rptr. 851 (1981); Richards v. Merrill Lynch, Pierce, Fenner & Smith, Inc., 64 Cal.App.3d 899, 135 Cal.Rptr. 26 (1976). *See also* Lewis v. Prudential–Bache Securities, Inc., 179 Cal.App.3d 935, 225 Cal.Rptr. 69 (1986). *Contra, e.g.*, Drexel Burnham Lambert, Inc. v. Pyles, 701 F.Supp. 217 (N.D.Ga.1988).

For further discussion of bias claims, *see* text accompanying footnotes 44–56 in § 14.5 *infra* (Practitioner's Edition only).

71. *E.g.*, Ex Parte Merrill Lynch, Pierce, Fenner & Smith, Inc., 494 So.2d 1 (Ala.1986); Parr v. Superior Ct. of San Mateo, 139 Cal.App.3d 440, 188 Cal.Rptr. 801 (1983).

72. 15 U.S.C.A. § 78o–4(b)(2).

tion.[73]

Arbitration of Disputes Between Securities Professionals

The foregoing discussion relates to disputes between brokers and their customers. Another important application of arbitration clauses is in disputes between securities professionals. Traditionally, it has been the rule that the securities acts' antiwaiver provisions do not affect arbitration agreements between broker-dealers and self regulatory organizations.[74] Thus, even as to 1933 Act claims, the nonarbitrability rule of *Wilko v. Swan* did not apply to the arbitration of disputes arising among and between members of self regulatory organizations.[75] Similarly, disputes between brokerage firms and their employees will be submitted to arbitration pursuant to predispute arbitration agreements.[76] Disputes between a purchaser of a securities firm and the seller are arbitrable pursuant to NASD rules.[77] The uniform registration form for brokerage industry personnel contains a broad predispute arbitration agreement. Notwithstanding public policy arguments to the contrary, the Supreme Court has held that age discrimination claims are subject to arbitration pursuant to the Form U–4 agreement.[78] Along similar lines, the New York Court of Appeals, in a divided decision, held that race and sex discrimination claims against brokerage firms are arbitrable under Form U–4's arbitration clause.[79]

Judicial Review of Arbitration Decisions[80]

Arbitration decisions under the federal securities laws are reviewa-

---

73. Swink & Co. v. Hereth, 784 F.2d 866 (8th Cir.1986) (claims under section 12(2) of the 1933 Act); Halliburton & Associates, Inc. v. Henderson, Few & Co., 774 F.2d 441 (11th Cir.1985).

74. *E.g.,* Interstate Securities Corp. v. Siegel, 676 F.Supp. 54 (S.D.N.Y.1988) (dispute between members of the American Stock Exchange). *See* § 10.15 *supra* (Practitioner's Edition only).

75. *See, e.g.,* French v. Merrill Lynch, Pierce, Fenner & Smith, Inc., 784 F.2d 902 (9th Cir.1986) (affirming arbitration award involving dispute between broker-dealer and market maker); N. Donald & Co. v. American United Energy Corp., 746 F.2d 666 (10th Cir.1984); Interstate Securities Corp. v. Siegel, 676 F.Supp. 54 (S.D.N.Y.1988) (dispute between members of the American Stock Exchange); Morgan, Olmstead, Kennedy & Gardner, Inc. v. United States Trust Co., 608 F.Supp. 1561 (S.D.N.Y.1985).

76. *See, e.g.,* Bender v. Smith Barney, Harris Upham & Co., 789 F.Supp. 155 (D.N.J. 1992) (employment discrimination claim by brokerage firm employee was governed by predispute to arbitration agreement); Kaliden v. Shearson Lehman Hutton, Inc., 789 F.Supp. 179 (W.D.Pa.1991) (same); Brown v. Merrill Lynch, Pierce, Fenner & Smith, Inc., 664 F.Supp. 969 (E.D.Pa.1987).

77. *See, e.g.,* Francis v. Marshall, 661 F.Supp. 773 (D.Mass.1987). The applicable rules are discussed in §§ 10.15–10.22 *supra* (Practitioner's Edition only) and also are reproduced in Appendix C *infra* (Practitioner's Edition only).

78. Gilmer v. Interstate/Johnson Lane Corp., 500 U.S. 20, 111 S.Ct. 1647, 114 L.Ed.2d 26 (1991).

79. Fletcher v. Kidder, Peabody & Co., 81 N.Y.2d 623, 601 N.Y.S.2d 686, 619 N.E.2d 998 (1993), *cert. denied* ___ U.S. ___, 114 S.Ct. 554, 126 L.Ed.2d 455 (1993).

80. For further discussion see § 10.22 *supra* (Practitioner's Edition only). Until recently, difficult questions existed with regard to the appealability of a court order compelling arbitration or staying further judicial proceedings pending arbitration. *See* text

ble by federal district courts.[81]   In addition to the statutory grounds of
corruption, fraud, and evident partiality,[82] arbitration decisions are subject to the judicially created standard of "manifest disregard of the
law." [83]   The scope of judicial review is "extremely limited."[84]   In furtherance of the strong federal policy supporting arbitration, the courts
give considerable deference[85] to the arbitrator's decision.   Thus in order
to overturn a decision, courts generally require an "obvious" error which
"clearly means more than error or misunderstanding with respect to the
law."[86]   It has thus been held, for example, that an arbitration award

---

accompanying footnotes 96–100 *infra*.   However, section 15 of the Federal Arbitration Act
now provides that such orders are not subject to interlocutory review unless the trial judge
certifies the order for review.   9 U.S.C.A. § 15(b) which in turn refers to 28 U.S.C.A.
§ 1292(b).   In contrast, interlocutory orders denying arbitration or refusing a stay of a
judicial action pending arbitration are subject to interlocutory review without certification
by the trial judge.   15 U.S.C.A. § 15(a).

81.   9 U.S.C.A. § 9 provides that the arbitration agreement may establish the appropriate court for making the review and if no court is selected, it is the federal district court in
the district where the award was made.   Since jurisdiction under the Exchange Act is
exclusively federal, it thus would seem to preclude selection of a state court to review
arbitration of an Exchange Act claim.   *See* § 14.1 *supra*.

But cf. Rauscher Pierce Refsnes, Inc. v. Birenbaum, 860 F.2d 169 (5th Cir.1988) (denial
of stay pending arbitration is interlocutory and thus not appealable).

82.   9 U.S.C.A. § 10.

Evident partiality is not easily established.   *See, e.g.,* First Interregional Equity Corp. v.
Haughton, 842 F.Supp. 105 (S.D.N.Y.1994) (failure to establish bias against broker's
counsel); Burdette v. FSC Securities Corp., 1993 WL 593997, [1993–1994 Transfer Binder]
Fed. Sec. L. Rep. (CCH) ¶ 98,032 (W.D.Tenn.1993) (fact that attorney performed some
work for clients in the securities industry did not establish evident partiality or show that
attorney could not qualify as a public arbitrator); Graceman v. Goldstein, 93 Md.App. 658,
613 A.2d 1049 (1992) (overturning finding that arbitrator was partial and reinstating
award).

83.   *E.g.,* Ainsworth v. Skurnick, 960 F.2d 939 (11th Cir.1992), *cert. denied* __ U.S. __,
113 S.Ct. 1269, 122 L.Ed.2d 665 (1993), *rehearing denied* __ U.S. __, 113 S.Ct. 1883, 123
L.Ed.2d 501 (1993) (arbitrators' refusal to award mandatory damages under state law was
reversible error); R.M. Perez & Associates, Inc. v. Welch, 960 F.2d 534 (5th Cir.1992).

84.   Merrill Lynch, Pierce, Fenner & Smith v. Bobker, 808 F.2d 930, 934 (2d Cir.1986).
Cf. Raiford v. Merrill Lynch, Pierce, Fenner & Smith, 903 F.2d 1410 (11th Cir.1990)
(upholding award even though no reasons for decision were given since award could
conceivably have been based on nominal plus punitive damages under state law); Sargent
v. Paine Webber Jackson & Curtis, Inc., 882 F.2d 529 (D.C.Cir.1989), *cert. denied* 494 U.S.
1028, 110 S.Ct. 1474, 108 L.Ed.2d 612 (1990) (reversing district court's vacating arbitration
award due to arbitrator's failure to explain method of computing damages; also holding
that order remanding for further arbitration was reviewable); O.R. Securities, Inc. v.
Professional Planning Associates, Inc., 857 F.2d 742 (11th Cir.1988) (arbitrators are not
required to explain award); Pompano–Windy City Partners, Ltd. v. Bear Stearns & Co.,
794 F.Supp. 1265 (S.D.N.Y.1992) (refusing to vacate arbitration award); Padgett v. Dapelo,
791 F.Supp. 438 (S.D.N.Y.1992) (award affirmed since there was no evidence that arbitrators deliberately ignored the law); Merrill Lynch, Pierce, Fenner & Smith, Inc. v. Burke,
741 F.Supp. 191 (N.D.Cal.1990) (upholding arbitrators' punitive damage award even
though arbitrators made no findings and failed to state the applicable legal theory); Quick
& Reilly, Inc. v. Jacobson, 126 F.R.D. 24 (S.D.N.Y.1989) (refusing to vacate arbitration to
investor rejecting broker's claim that it had discretion to liquidate margin account).

85.   *E.g.,* FSC Securities Corp. v. Freel, 14 F.3d 1310 (8th Cir.1994) (giving deference to
arbitrator's decision on application of statute of limitations).

86.   Merrill Lynch, Pierce, Fenner & Smith v. Bobker, 808 F.2d at 933.   *See* McIlroy v.
Painewebber, Inc., 989 F.2d 817 (5th Cir.1993) (customer claimed that award "was the
product of such gross mistake as to imply failure to exercise honest judgment" but award
was not vacated since there was no evidence of a gross mistake); Western Employers

should not be vacated unless it can be shown that the arbitrator "deliberately ignored" the applicable statutory and SEC regulatory provisions.[87]

Arbitration of Blue Sky Claims

Where there is a conflict between state securities laws and the Federal Arbitration Act, the federal Constitution's Supremacy Clause dictates that the Arbitration Act will prevail. Thus, where plaintiff alleged a violation of a state securities law and defendant moved to compel arbitration pursuant to a brokerage contract, federal preemption of the state securities law non-waiver provision was automatic and defendant's motion was, therefore, granted.[88]

State Laws Affecting Arbitration Clauses

The demise of the *Wilko* doctrine has not eliminated questions relating to the parties' ability to select an arbitral forum for the resolution of disputes arising under the federal securities laws. Massachusetts announced that effective January, 1989, broker-dealers doing business in that state must offer customers the option of not signing predispute arbitration agreements; however, that rule has since been struck down by a federal district court.[89] Similar rules requiring that

---

Insurance Co. v. Jefferies & Co., 958 F.2d 258 (9th Cir.1992) (absent "manifest disregard of the law," a court will not overturn an arbitration decision even if the arbitrator misapplied the law); Regina M. Lyons Testamentary Trust v. Shearson Lehman Hutton, Inc., 809 F.Supp. 302 (S.D.N.Y.1993) (failure to show that arbitrator ignored the law in making award); Dean v. Painewebber, Inc., 1992 WL 309606, [1992 Transfer Binder] Fed.Sec. L.Rep. (CCH) ¶ 97,034 (S.D.N.Y.1992) (failure to establish that law was clearly contrary to arbitrator's award); (state law). *See also, e.g.,* Siegel v. Titan Indus. Corp., 779 F.2d 891, 892–93 (2d Cir.1985); Drayer v. Krasner, 572 F.2d 348, 352 (2d Cir.1978), *cert. denied* 436 U.S. 948, 98 S.Ct. 2855, 56 L.Ed.2d 791 (1978); I/S Stavborg v. National Metal Converters, Inc., 500 F.2d 424, 432 (2d Cir.1974).

In Mastrobuono v. Shearson Lehman Hutton, Inc., ___ U.S. ___, 115 S.Ct. 1212, 131 L.Ed.2d 76 (1995), the Court ruled that a state procedural rule barring punitive damages in arbitrations proceedings did not apply in an arbitration under the Federal Arbitration Act in light of the broad policy favoring arbitration under that Act. The Court held that the parties' choice of law clause incorporated the state's substantive law permitting punitive damages applied but not the procedural bar.

87. Merrill Lynch, Pierce, Fenner & Smith v. Bobker, 808 F.2d 930, 934 (2d Cir.1986); Stroh Container Co. v. Delphi Industries, Inc., 783 F.2d 743, 750 (8th Cir.1986), *cert. denied* 476 U.S. 1141, 106 S.Ct. 2249, 90 L.Ed.2d 695 (1986); Fairchild & Co., Inc. v. Richmond F. & P.R. Co., 516 F.Supp. 1305, 1315 (D.D.C.1981). *See also, e.g.,* In the Matter of Arbitration Between Eljer Manufacturing, Inc. v. Kowin Development Corp., 14 F.3d 1250 (7th Cir.1994) (award of lost profits as element of damages was contrary to federal law to the contrary; however, the arbitration award would not be overturned on the basis of this "mere error" in interpreting the federal law). *Compare* Tinaway v. Merrill Lynch & Co., Inc., 658 F.Supp. 576 (S.D.N.Y.1987) (vacating arbitration award because arbitrator's reducing damages by 95% represented "evident partiality").

88. Osterneck v. Merrill Lynch, Pierce, Fenner & Smith, Inc., 841 F.2d 508 (3d Cir.1988); Kroog v. Mait, 712 F.2d 1148 (7th Cir.1983), *cert. denied* 465 U.S. 1007, 104 S.Ct. 1001, 79 L.Ed.2d 233 (1984). In *Kroog* the court distinguished the vertical balance of a federal and a state statute from the lateral balance of two federal mandates that occurred in *Wilko*. *Id.* at 1154.

89. Securities Industry Association v. Connolly, 703 F.Supp. 146 (D.Mass.1988). *Accord* Securities Industry Association v. Lewis, 751 F.Supp. 205 (S.D.Fla.1990). *See* Massachusetts is First State to Ban Compulsory Arbitration, 20 Sec.Reg. & L.Rep. (BNA) 1436 (Sept. 23, 1988).

customers be given a choice have been endorsed by the North American Securities Administrators Association and have been under consideration in at least sixteen additional states.[90]　Rather than invalidating all predispute agreements, the Massachusetts rule provided that upon opening an account, customers must be given the option of not signing the arbitration clause.　While an across-the-board ban on arbitration agreements might arguably be preempted by the new federal policy favoring arbitration of securities disputes,[91] mandating that customers be given a choice should be viewed as a valid exercise of state regulation.

Notwithstanding the argument that giving customers a choice does not conflict with federal policy, the First Circuit Court of Appeals invalidated the Massachusetts arbitration rules.[92]　The court first noted that there was no severability provision in the Massachusetts rules and therefore they had to be considered intact.　The rules not only prohibited predispute arbitration agreements as a nonnegotiable condition of opening an account, they also required this prohibition to be brought "conspicuously" to customers' attention.　Finally, the rules required detailed disclosure of the legal effect of any predispute arbitration clause. Taking all of these conditions together, the court ruled that the state law was contrary to the federal plan and clear pro arbitration mandate of the Federal Arbitration Act.　The state law was thus held to have been preempted by Congress as it conflicted with the strong federal policy favoring arbitration.

Florida legislation provides that in any arbitration clause, customers must be given a choice of a non-industry arbitration forum.[93]　This legislation has been challenged successfully and declared invalid.[94]　However, when the transaction in question is wholly intrastate, a valid state law invalidating predispute arbitration will control.[95]

Review of Court Orders Compelling or Denying Arbitration or Staying Judicial Proceedings

Prior to 1989, difficult questions arose with regard to the appealability of a court order compelling arbitration or staying further judicial

---

90.　*See* Massachusetts is First State to Ban Compulsory Arbitration, 20 Sec.Reg. & L.Rep. (BNA) 1436 (Sept. 23, 1988).

91.　*Cf.* the discussion of preemption of state tender offer legislation in § 11.22 *supra*.

92.　Securities Industry Association v. Connolly, 883 F.2d 1114 (1st Cir.1989), *cert. denied* 495 U.S. 956, 110 S.Ct. 2559, 109 L.Ed.2d 742 (1990).

93.　West's Fla.Stat.Ann. § 517.22 ("Any agreement to provide [brokerage services] ... entered into after October 1, 1990 by a person required to register ... for arbitration of disputes arising under the agreement shall provide to an aggrieved party the option of having arbitration before and pursuant to the rules of the American Arbitration Association or other independent nonindustry arbitration forum").　*See* 22 Sec.Reg. & L.Rep. (BNA) 1043 (July 13, 1990).

94.　Securities Industry Association v. Lewis, 751 F.Supp. 205 (S.D.Fla.1990).

95.　Ex parte Jones, 628 So.2d 316 (Ala.1993) (a divided Alabama Supreme Court held that since predispute arbitration agreements are not enforceable under Alabama law, arbitration was not available in a securities transaction between Alabama residents involving the securities of an Alabama corporation).

proceedings pending arbitration.[96] However, section 15 of the Federal Arbitration Act now provides that such orders are not subject to interlocutory review unless the trial judge certifies the order for review.[97] In contrast, interlocutory orders denying arbitration or refusing a stay of a judicial action pending arbitration are subject to interlocutory review without certification by the trial judge.[98] This lack of parallelism reflects the strong federal policy favoring arbitration by readily permitting interlocutory review to preserve the right to arbitrate.

Section 15 was effective in November 1988. Several decisions have held that its denial of appellate jurisdiction over a court order compelling arbitration or staying further judicial proceedings applies to cases that were pending at the time of the statute's effective date.[99]

A court's order compelling arbitration does not divest it of jurisdiction. Accordingly, a court retains jurisdiction so as to permit it to dismiss the claim for a failure to prosecute.[100]

Class Actions

Many actions for securities fraud arise in the context of a class action. On occasion a class action may be appropriate for customer disputes with broker-dealers. With the overruling of the *Wilko* doctrine, questions arose regarding the arbitrability of customer/broker disputes that were brought as class actions. The three major arbitral forums[101] have adopted rules which preclude the bringing of class actions, thus requiring class action plaintiffs to go to court unless, for arbitration agreements effective prior to 1993, a different arbitral forum has been selected.[102] In 1992, the SEC approved the New York Stock Exchange's

---

96. *See, e.g.,* the discussion in Turboff v. Merrill Lynch, Pierce, Fenner & Smith, Inc., 867 F.2d 1518 (5th Cir.1989).

97. 9 U.S.C.A. § 15(b) which in turn refers to 28 U.S.C.A. § 1292(b). *See* Humphrey v. Prudential Securities, Inc., 4 F.3d 313 (4th Cir.1993) (interlocutory order was not appealable); McCowan v. Dean Witter Reynolds Inc., 889 F.2d 451 (2d Cir.1989) (order compelling arbitration was not reviewable); Gulfstream Aerospace Corp. v. Mayacamas, 485 U.S. 271, 108 S.Ct. 1133, 99 L.Ed.2d 296 (1988) (orders granting or denying stays of court proceedings are not appealable as final orders). *Compare, e.g.,* Flink v. Carlson, 856 F.2d 44 (8th Cir.1988) (order granting stay of arbitration was appealable as a final order).

98. 15 U.S.C.A. § 15(a). *See, e.g.,* Flink v. Carlson, 856 F.2d 44 (8th Cir.1988) (order granting stay of arbitration was appealable as a final order).

99. Campbell v. Dominick & Dominick, Inc., 872 F.2d 358 (11th Cir.1989); Turboff v. Merrill Lynch, Pierce, Fenner & Smith, Inc., 867 F.2d 1518 (5th Cir.1989); Jolley v. Paine Webber Jackson & Curtis, Inc., 867 F.2d 891 (5th Cir.1989). *Cf., e.g.,* Queipo v. Prudential Bache Securities, Inc., 867 F.2d 721 (1st Cir.1989) (refusing to invoke the "collateral order doctrine" as a basis for taking an interlocutory appeal of brokerage firm's motion to compel arbitration and stay further judicial proceedings).

100. Morris v. Morgan Stanley & Co., 942 F.2d 648 (9th Cir.1991).

101. The New York Stock Exchange, the NASD, and the American Stock Exchange.

102. *See, e.g.,* Joel H. Bernstein & Ronna Kublanow, Class Actions and Multiple Parties, in Securities Arbitration 1993: Products, Procedures, and Causes of Action, at 697 (Practising Law Institute, 1993) ("[i]t must be remembered that § 12(d) of the NASD Code (and its companion provisions at other SROs) applies only to arbitrations brought at SRO forums. It does not apply to arbitrations brought at the American Arbitration Association (AAA)").

proposal to adopt Rule 600(d)[103] which provides that the Exchange will not accept class actions. The American Stock Exchange similarly adopted Rule 600(d) of its arbitration rules.[104] The National Association of Securities Dealers enacted Section 12(d) of the NASD Code of Arbitration Procedure, which parallels Rule 600(d) of the NYSE rules.[105]

The first portion of the applicable SRO arbitration regulations set forth the basic rule that claims submitted as class actions are not eligible for arbitration. The second part of Rules 600(d) of the New York and American Stock Exchange and Section 12(d)(2) and (3) of the Code, subject to enumerated exceptions, precludes matters from being arbitrated if a class action is pending in court. For example, if a customer has opted out of the class, then his or her dispute will be subject to any predispute arbitration agreement that may exist. These New York Stock Exchange and NASD rules in effect render unenforceable arbitration agreements with members of a potential class action; such claims are to be brought in federal court.[106]

The New York Stock Exchange and the NASD further adopted requirements that the arbitration agreements exclude class actions generally.[107] As a result of these new rules, members are precluded from requiring arbitration of class actions even when a different arbitral forum is selected.[108] The American Stock Exchange rules do not have a similar provision.

In explaining the rationale behind the new rules, the SEC pointed out that many of the procedural provisions necessary to resolve complex class actions are not available in the SRO arbitration programs:

But cf. In re Salomon Inc. Shareholders' Derivative Litigation, 1994 WL 533595, [1994–1995 Transfer Binder] Fed. Sec. L. Rep. (CCH) ¶ 98,454 (S.D.N.Y.1994) (shareholder derivative suit against brokerage firm's employees was subject to arbitration).

103. Arbitration Rules, New York Stock Exchange Guide (CCH) ¶ 2600, Rule 600(d). *See* Exch. Act Rel. No. 34–31097, 57 F.R. 40235, at 40236 (Sept. 2, 1992).

104. Arbitration Rules, American Stock Exchange Guide (CCH) ¶ 9540, Rule 601(d).

105. Code of Arbitration Procedure, NASD Manual (CCH) ¶ 3710, Sec. 12(d)(2).

106. The applicable rules prohibit "members from attempting to enforce arbitration contracts with customers who are members of a class or putative class unless the customer has clearly opted out of, or otherwise been excluded by a court from, the class action. . . . [C]ustomers may pursue in . . . arbitration, claims that would otherwise be included in a court-litigated class action by removing their individual claims from the class action." Exch. Act Rel. No. 34–31097, 57 Fed.Reg. 40235, at 40236. "Accordingly, neither member firms nor their associated persons may use an existing arbitration agreement to compel a customer to arbitrate a claim that is encompassed by a class action." 57 Fed.Reg. 52659, at 52660.

107. Rule 636 of the NYSE provides that "customer agreements containing arbitration clauses entered into after one year from the approval of the rule must include a prescribed statement excluding class actions from the contracts and clarifying investors' ability to pursue class actions in court." 57 Fed.Reg. 40235, at 40236. The parallel provision for NASD is Article III, section 21(f) of the Rules of Fair Practice. Furthermore, [t]he rule does not limit itself to arbitrations at the SROs nor is it part of the Code of Arbitration Procedure.

108. Therefore, once the rule is fully effective it should bar any investor who has signed an arbitration agreement (after October 28, 1993) from bringing a class action at any arbitration forum, including the AAA. Bernstein & Kublanow *supra* footnote 102 at 698.

class actions are better handled by the courts and that investors should have access to the courts to resolve class actions efficiently. In the past, individuals who attempted to certify class actions in litigation were subject to the enforcement of their separate arbitration contracts by their broker-dealers. Without access to class actions in appropriate cases, both investors and broker-dealers have been put to the expense of wasteful, duplicative litigation. The new rule ends this practice.[109]

[T]he Commission believes that the amendments ... should increase customer confidence in the markets and promote the efficient resolution of disputes for both investors and broker-dealers.[110]

Following the adoption of the foregoing rules relating to class actions, there is now an important exception to the policy favoring arbitration.

Deleted section 14.5 can be found in the Practitioner's Edition.

---

109. Exch. Act Rel. No. 34–31371, 57 Fed Reg. 52659, at 52661 (Nov. 4, 1992).

110. Exch. Act Rel. No. 34–31097, 57 Fed. Reg. 40235, at 40236 (Sept. 2, 1992).

Chapter 15

THE PUBLIC UTILITY HOLDING COMPANY ACT OF 1935

Table of Sections

§ 15.1 The Public Utility Holding Company Act of 1935— Background and Purpose

The Public Utility Holding Company Act[1] regulates holding companies with subsidiaries which are electric utility companies or which are engaged in the retail distribution of natural or manufactured gas. The Act (sometimes referred to as "PUHCA") was passed after a seven-year study of such companies by the Federal Trade Commission.[2] The FTC

---

* Deleted sections 15.2–15.5 can be found in the Practitioner's Edition.

§ 15.1

1. Pub.L. No. 74–333, 49 Stat. 803 (1935), codified as amended at 15 U.S.C.A. §§ 79–79z–6. *See* 1 Louis Loss & Joel Seligman, Securities Regulation 230–41 (3d ed.1989) 1 Louis Loss, Securities Regulation 131–141 (2d ed. 1961, 1969 Supp.). *See generally* Douglas W. Hawes, Utility Holding Companies (1984); Robert Ritchie, Integration of Public Utility Holding Companies (1954); Victor Brudney, The Investment–Value Doctrine and Corporate Adjustments, 72 Harv.L.Rev. 645 (1959); Donald C. Cook & Herbert B. Cohen, Capital Structures of Electric Utilities Under the Public Utility Holding Company Act, 45 Va.L.Rev. 981 (1959); David Ferber, Arthur Blasberg, Jr. & Melvin Katz, Conflicts of Interest in Reorganization Proceedings Under the Public Utility Holding Company Act of 1935 and Chapter X of the Bankruptcy Act, 28 Geo.Wash.L.Rev. 319 (1959); Comment, Section 11(b) of the Holding Company Act: Fifteen Years in Retrospect, 15 Yale L.J. 1088 (1950); Annot., Construction of § 11(b) of the Public Utility Holding Company Act (15 USCA § 79k(b)(1)), Dealing with Limitations on Operations of Holding Company Systems, 16 L.Ed.2d 1218 (1966).

2. In addition to the FTC study, other reports on utility holding companies were made during the period directly proceeding the passage of the Public Utility Holding Company

---

study uncovered widespread abuses which Congress believed adversely affected the national public interest, the interests of investors in the securities of holding companies and their subsidiary companies and affiliates, as well as the interests of consumers of gas and electric energy.[3]

Many of the more significant evils uncovered during the Federal Trade Commission study are enumerated in section 1(b) of the Public Utility Holding Company Act. These include: inadequate disclosure to investors of the information necessary to appraise the financial position or earning power of the holding company; the issuance of securities without the approval or consent of the states having jurisdiction over subsidiary public utility companies; the issuance of securities upon the basis of fictitious or unsound asset values having no fair relation to the investment in or the earning capacity of the properties, and upon the basis of paper profits from intercompany transactions, or in anticipation of excessive revenues from subsidiary public utility companies; and the overcapitalization of operating subsidiaries, thus increasing fixed charges and tending to prevent voluntary rate reductions.[4] The FTC study also cited the absence of arms-length bargaining between the holding company and its subsidiaries. These intercompany transactions resulted in: (1) the imposition of excessive charges upon the operating subsidiaries for various services, construction work, equipment, and materials; (2) the allocation of charges from service, management, construction, and other contracts among subsidiary public utilities in different states, causing problems of regulation for any individual state; (3) the complication or destruction of state regulation of subsidiaries through the exercise of control over subsidiary accounting practices and rate, dividend, and other policies; (4) the use of disproportionately small investments to exert control over operating subsidiaries; and (5) the extension of holding company systems without relation to economy of operations or to the integration and coordination of related properties.[5]

Unlike many major industries, electric and gas utilities are inherently local or regional in their operations. Typically, today they are subject to local and state regulation. Consequently, there are few, if any, economies of scale in the organization of these businesses on a national basis. During the 1920's, however, holding companies began purchasing utility properties all over the country in a race to build giant utility empires. These empires grew at a fantastic rate in the speculative period preceding 1930; and by 1932, according to the data presented by the Federal Trade Commission, holding companies controlled the great

---

Act. *See, e.g.,* Report on the Relation of Holding Companies to Operating Companies in Power and Gas Affecting Control, H.R. Rep. No. 827, 73d Cong., 2d Sess. (1933).

3. 15 U.S.C.A. § 79a(b). *See* FTC, Utility Corporations, S.Doc. No. 92, 70th Cong., 1st Sess. (1928). For a general discussion of the historical underpinnings of the Act, in addition to the FTC's compilation, *see, e.g.,* James C. Bonbright & Gardiner C. Means, The Holding Company (1969); Arthur S. Dewing, The Financial Policy of Corporations ch. 32 (1932).

4. 15 U.S.C.A. § 79a(b).

5. *Id.*

majority of the electric and gas utilities in the United States.[6] Many of these holding company systems were also involved in businesses wholly unrelated to the production of natural gas and electricity. One company even owned a baseball team.[7]

Unfortunately, there were various unscrupulous, fraudulent and deceptive practices surrounding the growth of many of the public utility giants.[8] For example, in order to create these huge systems, promoters and bankers often used pyramidal capital and corporate structures. After forming these structures the organizers frequently inflated their value and arbitrarily "wrote-up" the assets of operating and holding companies. The complex, overcapitalized systems[9] which resulted were beyond the power of any single state to regulate, and eventually led to widespread holding company bankruptcies and tremendous losses for investors.[10]

The Securities Act of 1933[11] and the Securities Exchange Act of 1934[12] deal with the securities markets generally and thus were not able to address the special problems that arose in the public utilities industry. It was against this background that Congress acted in 1935. The Public Utility Holding Company Act was enacted "to compel the simplification of public utility holding companies * * *" that were engaged in interstate commerce or in activities directly affecting or burdening interstate commerce.[13] The fundamental purpose of the Act was to free utility operating companies from the absentee control of holding companies, thus allowing them to be more effectively regulated by the states.[14]

---

6. 10 S.E.C. Ann.Rep. 84 (1944). Also among the subsidiaries in the holding company systems were companies engaged in coal-mining, production, refining, and transportation of oil, wood, coal; oil retailing; foundries; textiles; farming, irrigation, orchards; taxicabs; ice and cold storage; towing and lighterage; real estate, finance and credit, water, street railways, railroads, bus transportation, and telephone companies. *Id.* at 85.

7. 1 L. Loss & J. Seligman *supra* footnote 1 at 231.

8. Throughout the nineteenth and twentieth century, many public utilities holding companies began to take on a "pyramidal" corporate structure; however, their motivations for doing so varied. For some, the main purpose "appeared to be to control large amounts of capital with a relatively small investment." D. Hawes, *supra* note 1, at 1–1 to 1–2. Others, on the other hand, "arose largely as an incident of the licensing of patents or the sale of equipment," and still at least three companies set up such a convoluted structure to avoid constrictive regulation. *Id.*

9. For example, Associated Gas & Electric Co. had 3 classes of common stock, 6 classes of preferred stock, 4 classes of preference stock, 24 classes of debentures (some convertible into equity securities at the company's option), 7 issues of secured notes, 4 issues of investment certificates, and various warrants and rights; all of which rested on the securities of underlying companies. 10 S.E.C. Ann.Rep. at 86, n. 5 (1944).

10. *Id.* at 85.

11. 15 U.S.C.A. § 77a *et seq. See* chapters 1–7 *supra.*

12. 15 U.S.C.A. § 78 *et seq. See* chapters 9–14 *supra.*

13. 15 U.S.C.A. § 79a(c).

14. 10 S.E.C. Ann.Rep. 111 (1944). *See also* North American Co. v. SEC, 327 U.S. 686, 704, 66 S.Ct. 785, 795–796, 90 L.Ed. 945 (1946) (by compelling holding companies to "integrate and coordinate their systems and to divest themselves of security holdings of geographically and economically unrelated properties * * * Congress hoped to rejuvenate local management and to restore effective state regulation * * *"); Alabama Electric Co-op. Inc. v. SEC, 353 F.2d 905 (D.C.Cir.1965), *cert. denied* 383 U.S. 968, 86 S.Ct. 1273, 16

Although the Act has served its function,[15] repeal has been suggested for a number of years.[16] The reason behind the call for repeal is the belief that the work of the Public Utility Holding Company Act has been largely completed. In 1939 there were eighty-six holding companies subject to SEC regulation, with aggregate assets in excess of fourteen billion dollars.[17] By 1981 the number of regulated holding company systems was reduced to thirteen,[18] and by the end of 1983 there were only twelve[19] with a total of sixty operating subsidiaries.[20] The number of active holding companies remained relatively stable. Thus, in 1986,

---

L.Ed.2d 309 (1966) (purpose of Public Utility Holding Company Act is to supplement state regulation, not to supplant it). The Act has been called "a peculiar sort of antimonopoly law" because its purpose is to restore the effectiveness of state and local regulation rather than the effectiveness of competition in a free market. *See* 1 L. Loss, *supra* footnote 1 at 135.

15. *See* SEC, Comments of the Securities and Exchange Commission on the Comptroller's General Report of June 20, 1977 to the Congress on the Administration of the Public Utility Holding Company Act of 1935.

> Congress did not intend that utilities would remain permanent federal wards under the Act.... Vigorous enforcement of Section 11(b) by the Commission over the years eliminated most of the multistate holding companies and reversed the tidal wave of consolidations that had been occurring in the years prior to 1935.

Id. at 11.

16. *Compare* bills seeking amendment of the Act, *see e.g.*, S. 1869, 97th Cong., 1st Sess. (1981); S. 1870, 97th Cong., 1st Sess .. (1981); S. 1871, 97th Cong., 1st Sess. (1981), *with*, bills seeking total repeal, S. 1977, 97th Cong., 1st Sess. (1981); H.R. 1465, 97th Cong., 1st Sess. (1981). *See also* Aaron Levy, Utility Diversification, Other Subjects, and the Public Utility Holding Company Act of 1935, *in* Diversification, Deregulation, and Increased Uncertainty in the Public Utility Industries 545, 560 (Mich. State University 1983), for an extensive analysis of S. 1870. This call for reform or repeal was supported the SEC, *see* SEC's letter urging repeal of Public Utility Holding Company Act, 14 Sec. Reg. Rep. (BNA) 56 (Jan. 6, 1982), which even presented a detailed statement of its reasons for recommending repeal, *see* Statement of the U.S. Securities and Exchange Commission Concerning Proposals to Amend or Repeal the Public Utility Holding Company Act of 1935 (June 2, 1982). *But see* GAO, The Securities and Exchange Commission Needs to Reevaluate its Position Recommending Repeal of the Public Utility Holding Company Act (GAO/RCED 83–118) (Aug. 30, 1983). *See also*, for a general discussion of the efforts to repeal the '35 Act, Corie Brown & Barbara Bink, The Movement for Repeal of the Public Utility Holding Company Act, 109 Pub. Util. Fortnightly 42 (May 13, 1982); Holding Company Act Repeal: Congressional Progress, 110 Pub. Util. Fortnightly, July 8, 1982 at 42; A. A. Sommer, Jr., Public Utility Holding Company Act: Is There a Dance in the Old Girl Yet?, N.Y.L.J., Dec. 12, 1983, at 28 col. 1.

These efforts to repeal the Holding Company Act were unsuccessful. However, in 1984, the proponents of repeal made another attempt, attaching the repeal proposal to an appropriations bill, which ultimately failed. *See* Elec. Util. Week, Oct. 14, 1986 at 3. The SEC, in 1988, also, followed suit and renewed its efforts to seek repeal of the Act, *see* PUHCA Would be Impediment to New Energy Providers, SEC Testifies, 20 Sec. Reg. & L. Rep. (BNA) 1404 (Sept. 16, 1988) (testimony of Marianne Smythe, Director of the SEC Division of Investment Management); this too was fruitless.

Also, it should be noted that at least one commentator, has suggested another possibility (besides repeal or reform)—the introduction of increased competition into the sector. *See* D. Hawes, *supra* note 1, at 1–4 to 1–5.

17. 5 S.E.C. Ann.Rep. 63 (1939).

18. 47 S.E.C. Ann.Rep. 75 (1981).

19. Francis I. Andrews, Jr., Diversification and the Public Utility Holding Company Act, 110 Public Utilities Fortnightly 24, 25 (Dec. 23, 1982).

20. *See* Brian C. Elmer & Mark E. Mayo, Utility Takeovers and the Holding Company Act, 110 Public Utilities Fortnightly 17 (Sept. 30, 1982).

there were twelve active[21] public utility holding companies.   These twelve registered holding company systems had sixty-five electric or gas utility subsidiaries, seventy-four non-utility subsidiaries, and twenty-two inactive subsidiaries.[22]   As of September, 1993, there were fourteen registered public utility holding company systems.[23]   These fourteen holding companies had ninety-three public utility subsidiaries, one hundred and fifty-eight non-utility companies, and thirty-three inactive companies.[24]   There has thus been a significant increase in non-utility subsidiaries.

Deleted sections 15.2–15.5 can be found in the Practitioner's Edition.

---

21. In addition, there was one inactive company.   1986 SEC Ann.Rep. 156.

22. *Id.*

23. 1993 SEC Ann.Rep. 43.

24. *Id.*

Chapter 16

DEBT SECURITIES AND PROTECTION OF BONDHOLDERS—THE TRUST INDENTURE ACT OF 1939

Table of Sections

---

§ 16.1 Introduction to the Trust Indenture Act of 1939

Corporations, like other forms of business, frequently raise capital through debt financing. Debt represents borrowed capital which must be repaid.[1] In order to borrow funds from a large number of investors, corporations and other public issuers contract with a third party to administer a bond issue. The contract, or "indenture," identifies the rights of all parties concerned, as well as the duties of the trustee (a third party administrator), the obligations of the borrower and the remedies available to the investors ("indenture securities holders").[2]

---

* Deleted sections 16.3–16.8 can be found in the Practitioner's Edition.

§ 16.1

1. On the operation of the 1939 Act, *see generally* Raymond Garrett & Thomas Arthur, Corporate Bond Financing (BNA Corp. Practice Series, No. 13; 1979) 1 Arthur S. Dewing, The Financial Policy of Corporations 171–74 (5th ed. 1953); Henry F. Johnson, The "Forgotten" Securities Statute: Problems in the Trust Indenture Act, 13 U. Toledo L.Rev. 92 (1981); Frank J. Pohl, Cautions in Drafting and Administering Corporate Trust Indentures, 96 Trusts & Estates 247 (1957); Churchill Rogers, The Corporate Trust Indenture Project, 20 Bus.Law. 551 (1965); Note, Legislation: The Trust Indenture Act of 1939, 25 Cornell L.Q. 105 (1939).

For discussion of corporate capital structures, *see* 2 James D. Cox, Thomas L. Hazen & F. Hodge O'Neal, Corporations ch. 18 (1995).

2. *See* 15 U.S.C.A. § 77ccc(7). Substantive rights are thus governed by the indenture; although SEC Rule 10b–5 imposes disclosure obligations, it does not affect the issuer's

Privately issued debt instruments,[3] whether they be in the form of bonds or notes are securities[4] which are subject to the 1933 Securities Act's exemption[5] and the 1934 Exchange Act's exclusion[6] for short-term commercial paper. Accordingly, the issuance of bonds as well as notes (other than short-term obligations issued in commercial transactions) implicates the registration provisions of the 1933 Act.[7] Corporate bonds that are listed on a national securities exchange must be registered under section 12 of the 1934 Act.[8] Equity securities of issuers having at least five million dollars in assets and more than five hundred securities holders of that class also must be registered under the Exchange Act.[9] However, there is no comparable registration requirement for over-the-counter debt instruments, unless they are convertible into equity securities, in which case the convertible bonds themselves qualify as "equity securities."[10] Although there is no registration requirement under the Exchange Act for straight debt securities that are not listed on a national exchange, any such security that was issued under a 1933 Act registration statement is subject to the periodic reporting requirements by virtue of section 15(d) of the Exchange Act so long as there remain at least three hundred holders of the security.[11] Additionally, trading in corporate bonds is subject to Rule 10b–5's antifraud proscriptions, regardless of whether the bonds are subject to the Exchange Act's registration or reporting requirements.[12] Finally, broker-dealers handling trading in privately issued debt securities are subject to the normal broker-dealer regulations[13] while separate regulation exists regarding dealers in municipal securities[14] and federal government securities.[15] Thus, debt securities are subject to considerable regulation outside the context of the Trust Indenture Act. However, that regulation does not address the special situation created by the relationship between the issuer and the indenture trustee.

---

obligations under the terms of the indenture. *See* Lorenz v. CSX Corp., 1 F.3d 1406 (3d Cir.1993); LNC Investments, Inc. v. First Fidelity Bank, 1994 WL 73648, [1993–1994 Transfer Binder] Fed. Sec. L. Rep. (CCH) ¶ 98,151 (S.D.N.Y.1994) (since action is based on contract, state contract law governs).

3. Government issued and guaranteed securities are exempt from both the 1933 Act's registration requirements and the 1934 Act's registration and reporting requirements. 15 U.S.C.A. §§ 77c(a)(2), 78c(a)(12). *See* § 4.3 *supra*.

4. 15 U.S.C.A. § 77b(1). *See* § 1.5 *supra*.

5. 15 U.S.C.A. § 77c(a)(3). *See* § 4.4 *supra*.

6. 15 U.S.C.A. § 78c(a)(10).

7. 15 U.S.C.A. §§ 77e, 77f. *See* chapter 2 *supra*.

8. 15 U.S.C.A. § 78l(g). *See* § 9.2 *supra*.

9. 15 U.S.C.A. § 78l(g)(1); 17 C.F.R. §§ 240.12g–1.

10. 15 U.S.C.A. § 78c(a)(11) (equity security includes any security convertible, with or without consideration, into an equity security).

11. 15 U.S.C.A. § 78o(d). *See* § 9.3 *supra*.

12. 17 C.F.R. § 240.10b–5. *See* §§ 13.2–13.7 *supra*.

13. *See* §§ 10.2–10.4 *supra*.

14. 15 U.S.C.A. § 78o–4. *See* § 10.5 *supra*.

15. 15 U.S.C.A. § 78o–5. *See* § 10.5.1 *supra*.

The Trust Indenture Act of 1939[16] was enacted to protect "the national public interest and the interest of investors."[17] The necessity for federal legislation became apparent after years of judicial conflict over the duties of trustees to bondholders[18] and the lack of financial protection afforded even secured bondholders in the chaos that followed the 1929 stock market crash.[19] Exculpatory clauses were included in most indentures and rendered bondholders impotent to hold trustees liable even in those instances in which the trustee's acts or omissions directly resulted in an injury.[20] The federal legislation addressed itself to these and to other issues as well.[21]

Unlike the Securities Act of 1933 and the Exchange Act of 1934 which are generally limited to disclosure issues, the Trust Indenture Act goes beyond disclosure and imposes regulation over the substance of corporate and other private debt securities. The Act lists six separate instances wherein a public offering of private debt securities could prove harmful to investor interests: (1) when the obligor fails to provide a trustee; (2) when the trustee is without adequate rights, powers, or duties to protect and enforce the rights of investors; (3) when the trustee is without adequate resources to fulfill its duties; (4) when the flow of information from obligor to trustee is inadequate; (5) when the indenture contains misleading provisions; and (6) when the obligor

---

16. 15 U.S.C.A. §§ 77aaa *et seq.* *See generally* 2 Louis Loss, Securities Regulation 719–25 (2d ed. 1961); Howard M. Friedman, Updating the Trust Indenture Act, 7 U.Mich.J.L. Reform 329 (1974); Joseph P. McKeehan, Duties of the Trustee of a Mortgage Given to Secure Bondholders, 49 Dick.L.Rev. 1 (1944); Note, The Trust Indenture Act of 1939, 25 Cornell L.Q. 105 (1939). *See also* John B. Campbell & Robert Zach, Put a Bullet in the Poor Beast, His Leg is Broken and His Use is Past. Conflict of Interest in the Dual Role of Lender and Corporate Indenture Trustee: A Proposal to End it in the Public Interest, 32 Bus.Law. 1705 (1977); Richard B. Smith, Stephen H. Case & Francis I. Morrison, The Trust Indenture Act of 1939 Needs No Conflict of Interest Revision, 35 Bus.Law. 161 (1979).

17. 15 U.S.C.A. § 77bbb(a).

18. Sturges v. Knapp, 31 Vt. 1, 58 (1858) (trustee required to act as the "prudent man" would); York v. Guaranty Trust Co., 143 F.2d 503 (2d Cir.1944), *reversed on other grounds* 326 U.S. 99, 65 S.Ct. 1464, 89 L.Ed. 2079 (1945) *motion granted* 258 App.Div. 702, 14 N.Y.S.2d 1021 (1939) (relationship between trustee and bondholders is that of a fiduciary); First Trust Co. v. Carlsen, 129 Neb. 118, 261 N.W. 333 (1935) (relationship one of agency); Hazzard v. Chase National Bank, 159 Misc. 57, 287 N.Y.S. 541 (Sup.Ct.1936) *motion granted* 258 App.Div. 709, 14 N.Y.S.2d 1021 (1939) (relationship primarily contractual). *See generally* Louis S. Posner, Liability of the Trustee Under the Corporate Indenture, 42 Harv.L.Rev. 198, 199–200 (1928).

19. SEC Report on the Study and Investigation of the Work, Activities, Personnel and Functions of Protective and Reorganization Committees, pt. VI Trustees Under Indentures (1936). For an excellent summary of the Report's findings *see* Morris v. Cantor, 390 F.Supp. 817, 820 (S.D.N.Y.1975). *See also, e.g.,* Wilbur G. Katz, The Protection of Minority Bondholders in Foreclosures and Receiverships, 3 U.Chi.L.Rev. 517 (1936).

20. *See generally,* 2 Louis Loss, Securities Regulation 719–725 (2d ed. 1961); Philip M. Payne, Exculpatory Clauses in Corporate Mortgages and Other Instruments, 19 Cornell L.Q. 171 (1934); Posner, *supra* footnote 18.

21. Although the federal law imposes minimum requirements, as a general matter, actions under the Indenture Act are contract actions and thus are governed substantively by state law. LNC Investments, Inc. v. First Fidelity Bank, 1994 WL 73648, [1993–1994 Transfer Binder] Fed. Sec. L. Rep. (CCH) ¶ 98,151 (S.D.N.Y.1994).

prepares the indenture without investor participation or understanding.[22] The Act addresses these problems.

§ 16.2 Operation of the Trust Indenture Act of 1939; Exemptions

The Trust Indenture Act of 1939 focuses primarily upon the terms of the indenture as the means to its end of bondholder protection.[1] In the absence of the Act's coverage, rights and obligations under the indenture would be purely a matter of state law. The Trust Indenture Act applies to notes, bonds, debentures, and other evidences of indebtedness, whether or not secured, and to all certificates representing such an interest.[2] Most of these securities, when issued, are also subject to registration under the Securities Act of 1933.[3] Thus, there is an interrelationship between the disclosure provisions of the 1933 Act and the more substantive regulation of the Trust Indenture Act. For example, if there is noncompliance with the provisions of the Trust Indenture Act, the SEC may refuse to permit the issuer's 1933 Act registration statement to become effective.[4] Once issued, the bonds are also subject to regulation under the Securities Exchange Act of 1934.

In 1990, Congress enacted comprehensive amendments to the Trust Indenture Act.[5] The revisions were designed to modernize the Act and to make it more efficient in light of current market conditions and industry practices.[6] Among other things, the new legislation eliminates the requirement of certain boiler plate language in the trust agreements which serve only to increase administrative costs without providing additional investor protection.[7] Additionally, debenture holders will

---

22. 15 U.S.C.A. § 77bbb.

§ 16.2

1. The background and purpose of the Act is considered in § 16.1 *supra*.

2. 15 U.S.C.A. § 77ddd(a)(1).

3. 15 U.S.C.A. §§ 77a–77bbb. *See* § 16.1 and chapters 1–7 *supra*.

4. 15 U.S.C.A. § 77eee(b).

5. P.L. 101–550, 101st Cong. 2d Sess. *See* Fed.Sec.L.Rep. (CCH) Report Bulletin no. 1420 (Nov. 7, 1990).

As articulated in this Senate Committee report, which accompanied the reform bill, modernization was the primary focus of the Amendments:

During this period, however, the public market for debt securities has undergone significant change. Innovations in the forms of debt instruments have produced securities, such as collateralized mortgage obligation, [which] were not contemplated in 1939. Technological developments and regulatory changes have resulted in new distribution methods including shelf offerings, direct placements and "dutch auctions." In addition, public securities markets have been profoundly changed by the increasing internationalization of securities markets. Thus, current market practices conflict with many of the assumptions underlying the Act, which were based on financial customs prevailing in 1939.... Enactment of Title IV would conform the Act to the present realities of the market and make it adaptable to future developments, while easing the administration of the Act.

Id. at 29.

6. *Id.*

7. *Id.*

receive statutory protection notwithstanding contrary language in the indenture.

Exemptions From the Act's Coverage

Section 304 of the Trust Indenture Act exempts from its coverage a number of debt securities that would otherwise fall within the Act's purview.[8] Section 304(a)(9) of the Act[9] exempts securities issued under an indenture where the aggregate amount of debt within a thirty-six month period does not exceed ten million dollars unless the Commission prescribes a lower dollar ceiling. The Commission has exercised this rulemaking authority, to lower the ceiling, in Rule 4a–2[10] which exempts securities issued pursuant to an indenture limiting the aggregate principal outstanding indebtedness to five million dollars and provided further that for thirty-six consecutive months the issuer has not had outstanding securities with more than five million dollars in aggregate principal indebtedness. Also exempted are most securities exempted from 1933 Act registration;[11] these include securities issued or guaranteed by the federal government (or any state or foreign government), notes with a maturity date less than nine months from the date of issuance, bonds issued by non-profit organizations, any indebtedness of a savings and loan association due to bonds issued, common carrier certificates, securities offered only within a particular state, securities issued by a trustee in bankruptcy, and commercial paper.[12]

Also exempt from the Trust Indenture Act are certificates of interest or participation in more than one security where the pooled securities have "substantially different rights and privileges."[13] Debt securities that were issued prior to six months after the Act's effective date are exempt but the exemption does not apply to any new offering of such securities.[14] Debt securities issued under a mortgage insured under the National Housing Act[15] are exempt from the Trust Indenture Act.[16] Debt securities issued by foreign governments or their agencies, depart-

---

8. 15 U.S.CA. § 77ddd.

9. 15 U.S.C.A. § 77ddd(a)(9). *Compare* section 4(a)(8)'s limited exemption for securities not issued under an indenture. *See* footnotes 18–20 *infra* and accompanying text. *See* 17 C.F.R. §§ 260.0–7, 260.4a–2.

10. 17 C.F.R. § 260.4a–2.

11. 15 U.S.C.A. §§ 77c(a)(2), (3), (4), (5), (6), (7), (8), (11). *See* §§ 4.2–4.12 *supra.*

12. 15 U.S.C.A. § 77ddd(a)(4). *See* 17 C.F.R. §§ 260.0–7, 260.4a–2.

13. 15 U.S.C.A. § 77ddd(a)(2). Also included in the exemption are temporary certificates of the same type.

14. 15 U.S.C.A. § 77ddd(a)(3). *See* 15 U.S.C.A. § 77ddd(c). This exemption operates much the same as former section 3(a)(1) of the 1933 Act. 15 U.S.C.A. § 77c(a)(1) (1982) which is discussed in § 4.2 *supra. Cf.* In the Matter of Ira Haupt, 23 S.E.C. 589 (1946) (refusing to apply the former 1933 Act exemption to a new issue).

See also In the matter of Citadel Industries, Inc. [1976–1977 Transfer Binder] Fed.Sec. L.Rep. (CCH) ¶ 80,764 (SEC 1976) (beneficial interests in liquidating trust need not be qualified as an indenture under the Act).

15. 12 U.S.C.A. §§ 1701 *et seq.*

16. 15 U.S.C.A. § 77ddd(a)(5), (a)(10).

ments, subdivisions, or instrumentalities are also exempt.[17] The Act further provides an exemption for guarantees of any of the above securities exempted by section 304(a).[18] In addition the SEC stated that it would not require qualification under the Act for debt securities registered under the 1933 Act on former Form S–18[19] provided that the aggregate offering in any twelve month period does not exceed 1.5 million dollars.[20] As discussed directly below, there is a statutory exemption for such offerings.

A further exemption is provided in section 304(a)(8) of the Trust Indenture Act[21] for debt securities that are not issued under an indenture provided that the aggregate offering of any such securities within a twelve month period does not exceed the dollar limit established by section 3(b) of the 1933 Act[22] (which currently is five million dollars) unless the SEC sets a lower ceiling. The Commission in Rule 4a–1[23] formerly had lowered the limit so that the exemption applied only if during a period of twelve consecutive months the issuer has not had more than two million dollars aggregate principal amount of *any* securities of that issuer but in 1992 the ceiling was raised to five million dollars.

In 1990 Congress greatly expanded the Commission's exemptive authority under the Act. Section 304(d) of the Act now empowers the Commission to exempt from all or part of the Act any person, registration statement, indenture, security, or transaction from the Act to the extent that the exemption is "necessary or appropriate in the public interest and consistent with the protection of investors and the purposes fairly intended" by the Act.[24] The SEC is further specifically permitted

---

17. 15 U.S.C.A. § 77ddd(a)(6). *See e.g.,* In the Matter of Israel Bank of Agriculture, Ltd., [1978 Transfer Binder] Fed.Sec.L.Rep. (CCH) ¶ 81,592 (SEC 1978) (bonds of banks subject to foreign governmental control and carrying out governmental functions need not qualify); In the Matter of European Atomic Energy Commission, [1977–1978 Transfer Binder] Fed.Sec.L.Rep. (CCH) ¶ 81,341 (SEC 1977) (organization established by treaty among nine foreign governments is not subject to the Act); In the Matter of European Economic Community, [1976–1977 Transfer Binder] Fed.Sec.L.Rep. (CCH) ¶ 80,990 (SEC 1976) (Act does not apply).

18. 15 U.S.C.A. § 77ddd(a)(7).

19. Form S–18 was a "short form" registration statement under the 1933 Act for issues of up to 7.5 million dollars. *See* § 3.3 *supra.*

20. Trust Ind. Act Rel. No. 39–542 (Oct. 16, 1979). The SEC phrased this in terms of a "no action position" as opposed to an exemption by rule. The no action position was prompted by the then 1.5 million dollar ceiling for the qualified exemption from 1933 Act registration pursuant to Regulation A. 17 C.F.R. §§ 230.251–256. *See* § 4.15 *supra.*

1933 Act Form S–18 has been replaced by Forms SB–1 and SB–2. *See* § 3.2 *supra.* Additionally, the dollar ceiling for Regulation A offerings has been raised to $5 million. *See* § 4.15 *supra.*

21. 15 U.S.C.A. § 77ddd(a)(8). *Compare* section 4(a)(9)'s exemption for securities issued under an indenture provided that the aggregate principal indebtedness does not exceed five million dollars within thirty-six consecutive months, as provided in Rule 4a–2. *See* footnotes 9–10 *supra* and accompanying text.

22. 15 U.S.C.A. § 77c(b). *See* § 4.14 *supra.*

23. 17 C.F.R. § 260.4a–1.

24. 15 U.S.C.A. § 78ddd(d).

to exercise its discretion to refuse to consider an application for such an exemption.[25] SEC Rule 4d–7 sets forth the technical requirements with regard to filing an application for an exemption pursuant to section 304(d).[26] The application to the Commission requesting the exemption must contain the name, address, and telephone number of each applicant and each other person to whom questions concerning the application should be directed.[27] In addition to stating the relevant facts, the application must contain a justification for the requested exemption as well as a statement of any benefits that could be expected to accrue as a result thereof to security holders, trustees, and/or obligors.[28]

In addition to the foregoing exclusions from the Trust Indenture Act of 1939, all of the transaction exemptions found in section 4 of the 1933 Act apply as well to registration under sections 305 and 306 of the Trust Indenture Act.[29] These transaction exemptions are: (1) transactions by a person other than an issuer, underwriter or dealer,[30] (2) transactions not involving a public offering,[31] (3) certain transactions by dealers,[32] (4) unsolicited brokers transactions,[33] (5) transactions involving certain real estate mortgage notes,[34] and (6) transactions involving accredited investors,[35] as defined in section 2(15) of the 1933 Act.[36]

In addition, the SEC may, on application from the issuer and after a hearing, exempt debt securities issued by private foreign issuers.[37] Also, the Commission may by rule exempt securities issued by a small business investment company pursuant to the Small Business Investment Company Act of 1958.[38]

Deleted sections 16.3–16.8 can be found in the Practitioner's Edition.

---

25. *Id.*

26. 17 C.F.R. § 260.4d–7.

27. 17 C.F.R. § 260.4d–8.

28. *Id.*

29. 15 U.S.C.A. § 77ddd(b). *See* 15 U.S.C.A. §§ 77eee, 77fff.

30. 15 U.S.C.A. § 77d(1). *See* § 4.23 *supra.* The Trust Indenture Act further provides that persons selling on behalf of control persons are not underwriters. 15 U.S.C.A. § 77ddd(b). *Contra* 15 U.S.C.A. § 77b(11). *See* § 4.24 *supra.*

31. 15 U.S.C.A. § 77d(2). *See* 4.21 *supra.* The fact that there are only a limited number of lenders may preclude a finding that a public offering has taken place. The fact that a trustee is not covered by the 1939 Act does not affect the applicability of state law relating to indenture trustees. *See, e.g.,* In re E.F. Hutton Southwest Properties II, Ltd., 953 F.2d 963 (5th Cir.1992) (New York law characterized the trustee as an indenture trustee notwithstanding absence of a public offering; but further holding that trustee's reliance on counsel precluded a finding of liability for negligence).

32. 15 U.S.C.A. § 77d(3). *See* § 4.27 *supra.*

33. 15 U.S.C.A. § 77d(4). *See* § 4.23 *supra.*

34. 15 U.S.C.A § 77d(5). *See* § 4.28 *supra.*

35. 15 U.S.C.A. § 77d(6). *See* § 4.20 *supra.*

36. 15 U.S.C.A. § 77b(15).

37. 15 U.S.C.A. § 77ddd(d). Private foreign issuers are discussed in § 14.2 *supra.*

38. 15 U.S.C.A. § 77ddd(e).

Chapter 17

FEDERAL REGULATION OF INVESTMENT COMPANIES—THE INVESTMENT COMPANY ACT OF 1940

Table of Sections

§ 17.1 The Investment Company Act of 1940: Background and Scope

The Investment Company Act of 1940[1] was enacted to protect investors entrusting their savings to others for expert management and diversification of investments which would not be available to them as individuals.[2] The most common type of investment company is the

---

§ 17.1

1. 15 U.S.C.A. §§ 80a–1 through 80a–52.

2. *See generally* Hugh Bullock, The Story of Investment Companies (1959); Tamar Frankel, The Regulation of Money Managers: The Investment Company Act and The Investment Advisers Act (1978); Arthur Wienberger, Investment Companies (1980 ed.); Warren Morley, Charles Jackson, Jr. & John Bernard, Jr., Federal Regulation of Investment Companies Since 1940, 63 Harv.L.Rev. 1134 (1950); Walter P. North, A Brief History of Federal Investment Company Legislation, 44 Notre Dame Law. 667 (1969); Alan Rosenberg & Martin E. Lybecker, Some Thoughts on the Federal Securities Laws Regulating External Investment Management Arrangements and the ALI Federal Securities Code Project, 124 U.Pa.L.Rev. 587 (1976); Survey, The Mutual Fund Industry: A Legal Survey,

mutual fund.[3] To invest in such funds, individuals buy shares in an investment company, which is typically organized as any corporation would be but with additional safeguards to the public, such as independent boards of directors and a separate investment advisor,[4] which are among the requirements imposed by the Investment Company Act. Investment company assets most often consist of cash, securities which generally are liquid, mobile, and readily negotiable, and in some cases commodity futures and options. A pooling of investment funds focused primarily on securities (including securities options) ordinarily will be considered an investment company and, unless exempt, are subject to SEC regulation. Pooled investment funds where the investment objective focuses primarily on commodity related investments (including futures and options) are known as commodity pools. Commodity Pool Operators (CPOs) are regulated by the Commodity Futures Trading Commission.[5]

Companies subject to the Investment Company Act are also governed by the Securities Act of 1933 and the Securities Exchange Act of 1934. In 1990, Congress enacted the Shareholder Communication Act which extends the applicability of the proxy rules under the Securities Exchange Act of 1934 that apply to reporting companies generally to mutual funds and other investment companies that are registered under the Investment Company Act.[6]

The highly liquid nature of investment company assets creates an increased risk of management abuse that is not present with ordinary manufacturing and other operating companies. This led Congress to believe that investment companies would be easy prey for management abuse in the absence of comprehensive federal regulation.[7]

The securities issued by investment companies to their investors fall within the purview of the Investment Company Act. These shares may also be subject to registration under the Securities Act of 1933[8] and the

---

44 Notre Dame Law. 732 (1969). *See also, e.g.,* Mark J. Roe, Political Elements in the Creation of a Mutual Fund Industry, 139 U. Pa. L. Rev. 1469 (1991).

For a thorough economic analysis of the Investment Company Act, *see* William J. Baumol, Stephen M. Goldfeld, Lilli A. Gordon & Michale F. Koehn, The Economics of Mutual Fund Markets: Competition Versus Regulation (1990).

3. *See* Donald W. Glazer, A Study of Mutual Fund Complexes, 119 U.Pa.L.Rev. 205 (1970); Nathan D. Lobell, The Mutual Fund: A Structural Analysis, 47 Va.L.Rev. 181 (1961).

4. Comment, The Investment Company Act of 1940, 50 Yale L.J. 440 (1941).

5. 7 U.S.C.A. §§ 6m, 6o. *See generally* Philip M. Johnson & Thomas L. Hazen, Commodities Regulation (2d ed. 1989). The jurisdiction of the SEC and CFTC is discussed in § 1.4.1 *supra.*

6. 15 U.S.C.A. § 78n(b). The proxy rules are discussed in §§ 11.1–11.9 *supra.*

7. Sen.Rep. No. 1775, 76th Cong., 3d Sess. (1940). An investment company differs from a holding company in that the latter is concerned mainly with the "control of productive wealth," *i.e.* the means of producing, while the former is concerned with the yield from investments in the productive activity of others. Comment, *supra* footnote 4, at 440–41.

8. 15 U.S.C.A. § 77a *et seq. See* chapters 2, 3 *supra. See, e.g.,* White v. Melton, 757 F.Supp. 267 (S.D.N.Y.1991) (placement of mutual fund's rule freezing the commission in

registration and periodic reporting requirements[9] of the Securities Exchange Act of 1934.[10]	The SEC may waive any duplicate information in filings necessitated by overlap of the various acts.[11]	In addition to the disclosure and reporting requirements, the Investment Company Act contains its own antifraud provisions[12] and private remedies.[13]	Both the antifraud provisions and private remedies supplement the provisions of the 1933 and 1934 Acts[14] that also apply to investment companies.

The basic thrust of the Investment Company Act is to require registration of non-exempt companies and to protect against money managers' conflicts of interest.[15]	Section 7 of the Act[16] bars an investment company from engaging in any form of interstate commerce when there has been a failure to register under the Act, unless there is an applicable exemption.	There are criminal sanctions for willful violations of the Act[17] and contracts of unregistered investment companies are rendered unenforceable and thus courts will not order performance by third parties.[18]	The Act also regulates the investment company's relationship with its investment advisers.[19]

In what it classified as a "dramatic move", the SEC eased restrictions against registered investment companies' purchases of stock of companies engaged in broker-dealer, underwriting, and investment adviser activities.[20]	Under the new rule there is a blanket exemption for

---

"additional information" portion of 1933 Act registration Form N–1A did not violate 1933 Act or Rule 10b–5 of the 1934 Act).

9. 15 U.S.C.A. §§ 78l, 78n(a), 78o(d).	See §§ 9.2, 9.3 supra.

10. 15 U.S.C.A. § 80a–20(a).	See 15 U.S.C.A. §§ 77a et seq., 78a et seq.

11. 15 U.S.C.A. § 80a–24(a).	The Commission may, in addition, make such rules as necessary to effectuate the powers conferred on it by the Investment Company Act: 15 U.S.C.A. § 80a–37(a).

12. See § 17.8 infra.

13. 15 U.S.C.A. § 80a–35.	See § 17.10 infra.

14. See chapters 7, 12, 13 supra.

15. The Commission also has other powers.	For example, it has taken the position that investment companies may not use the terms "guaranteed" or "insured" in their name.	Letter from SEC to all investment companies (Oct. 25, 1990).	See SEC Staff Tells Funds to Remove Terms "Guaranteed," "Insured" From Names, 22 Sec.Reg. & L.Rep. (BNA) 1540 (Nov. 2, 1990).	The Commission noted that failure to remove these terms, which can present a misleading impression to investors, may result in delays in registration or in an enforcement action.	Id.

The SEC also imposes some substantive regulation on the nature of investments.	For example, the Commission has imposed limits on the amount of money that money market funds can invest in debt instruments of any one issuer.	Rule 2a–7, 17 C.F.R. § 270.2a–7; Inv.Co.Act Rel. IC–18005, [1990–1991 Transfer Binder] Fed.Sec.L.Rep. (CCH) ¶ 84,710 (Feb. 20, 1991).	See SEC Adopts Changes to Help Ensure Safety of Money Market Funds, 23 Sec.Reg. & L.Rep. (BNA) 193 (Feb. 15, 1991).

16. 15 U.S.C.A. § 80a–7.

17. 15 U.S.C.A. § 80a–48.

18. 15 U.S.C.A. § 80a–46.

19. See §§ 17.2, 17.9 infra.

20. 17 C.F.R. § 270.12d3–1.	See Inv.Co.Act Rel. No. IC–14036 (Sec.Act Rel. No. 33–6543), [1984 Transfer Binder] Fed.Sec.L.Rep. (CCH) ¶ 83,645 (July 13, 1984).	Also, as part of these amendments the SEC rescinded Rule 2a–3 which excluded banks from the

investment company acquisitions of securities from issuers deriving no more than fifteen percent of their gross revenues from securities related activities. Secondly, investment companies now can purchase securities from issuers deriving more than the fifteen percent income threshold provided that the acquisition is of less than five percent of the issuer's outstanding equity securities or ten percent of its outstanding debt securities.[21]

Also, in recent years a number of investment companies have become involved in hedging their investments through option writing programs. A variation has been the use of stock index futures to accomplish the same result. Transactions involving commodities futures raise questions under both the Investment Company Act and the Commodity Exchange Act.[22]

Recent problems involving institutional investors' and other "sophisticated" investors' exposure to derivative investments may well have implications to investment companies. There are particularly knotty problems associated with the relatively unregulated over the counter derivatives markets. Many investment companies qualify to participate in these markets and thus are likely to be subject to any regulatory reforms that may follow the debacles of the early 1990s.

Interlocking Ownership of Investment Company Shares—The Antipyramiding Provisions

Another Investment Company Act provision that deserves mention is the antipyramiding rules imposed by section 12(d)(1) of the Act.[23] The thrust of the Act is to prohibit control of one investment company by another investment company. As explained in a relatively recent decision:

This so-called "antipyramiding" provision implements the declaration in the 1940 Act that "the national public interest and the interest of investors are adversely affected" (i) when investment companies * * * are managed "in the interest of other investment companies * * * rather than the interest of all classes of such companies' securities holders," (ii) when "control of investment companies is unduly concentrated through pyramiding or inequita-

definition of investment adviser. Bank securities acquisitions are now governed by Rule 12d3–1's more generic exemption.

21. In addition to these quantitative limits until 1993, there were some qualitative limitations. The equity securities so acquired formerly had to be marginable under Regulation T while debt securities must be investment grade. 17 C.F.R. § 270.12d3–1 (1993). This restriction was eliminated in Investment Co. Act Rel. No. IC–19716 (SEC September 16, 1993).

22. *See* footnote 5 *supra*. *See also* Jeffrey S. Rosen, Mark R. Eaton & Ralph V. De Martino, Hedging by Investment Companies: Legal Implications Under the Commodity Exchange Act and Investment Company Act of 1940, 17 Sec.Reg. & L.Rep. (BNA) 260 (Feb. 8, 1985).

23. 15 U.S.C.A. § 80a–12(d).

ble methods of control" or (iii) when investment companies change the character of their business, or when the control or management thereof is transferred without the consent of their security holders.[24]

In order to implement these policies, section 12(d) implements three prohibitions with regard to share ownership.

First, section 12(d)(1) prohibits an investment company from acquiring more than three percent of the total outstanding voting securities of another investment company.[25]   Second, it also prohibits an investment company from acquiring shares of another investment company when the shares so acquired would have a value in excess of five percent of the acquiring company's assets.[26]   Third, section 12(d)(1) of the Investment Company Act prohibits an investment company from acquiring shares of another investment company when the aggregate of all shares in all investment companies owned by the acquiring company when calculated after the acquisition would exceed ten percent of the acquiring company's assets.[27]   In addition to focusing on the acquiring company, section 12(d) makes it unlawful for any investment company, principal underwriter, or registered broker-dealer to knowingly sell or otherwise dispose of investment company shares when the result of the transaction would be to place the investment company acquiring the shares in violation of section 12(d)'s ownership limitations.[28]   It has been held that violations of section 12(d)'s antipyramiding provisions will support an implied private right of action, at least for injunctive relief.[29]

As pointed out above, the antipyramiding prohibitions are designed to protect the shareholders of investment companies.   Other substantive protections, as well as investment company registration and disclosure obligations, are discussed in the sections that follow.

§ 17.2   The Relationship Between Investment Companies, Investment Advisers and Underwriters

Functionally, an investment company has been described as "a shell, a pool of assets consisting of securities, belonging to the shareholders of

---

24.   Clemente Global Growth Fund, Inc. v. Pickens, 705 F.Supp. 958, 963 (S.D.N.Y. 1989) (quoting from 15 U.S.C.A. § 80a–1(b)(2), (4)).   *Cf.* Clemente Global Growth Fund, Inc. v. Pickens, 729 F.Supp. 1439 (S.D.N.Y.1990) (withdrawal of limited partnership's tender offer for stock in investment company did not moot antipyramiding claim since limited partnership still owned target investment company stock).

For related issues, *see* the discussion of the independence of investment company directors in § 17.6 *infra* and of the transfer of control of investment companies in § 17.9 *infra.*

25.   15 U.S.C.A. § 80a–12(d)(1)(A)(i).

26.   15 U.S.C.A. § 80a–12(d)(1)(A)(ii).

27.   15 U.S.C.A. § 80a–12(d)(1)(A)(iii).

28.   15 U.S.C.A. § 80a–12(d)(1)(B).

29.   Bancroft Convertible Fund, Inc. v. Zico Investment Holdings, Inc., 825 F.2d 731 (3d Cir.1987) (action by the target company); Clemente Global Growth Fund, Inc. v. Pickens, 705 F.Supp. 958 (S.D.N.Y.1989) (semble, preliminary injunction issued).

the fund." [1] Investors depend upon prudent management of the investment company's securities holdings. In theory and in practice, recommendations concerning where to put the investment company's funds are made by an investment adviser to the investment company's board of directors.[2] The investment adviser has a contractual relationship with the investment company.

Frequently, the investment adviser is the investment company's founder, appointing its initial board of directors[3] and providing its initial capitalization.[4] Due to the potential for abuses of this close relationship between investment company and investment adviser, section 15 of the Investment Company Act requires a written contract between the two entities which, as discussed below, must be approved by the investment company shareholders.[5] The section also requires a written contract between investment companies and underwriters,[6] but these underwriting provisions are becoming less important in practice as more investment companies have become "no-load" and sell directly to the public.[7] The underwriting function remains significant, however, during the investment company's start-up period, when a maximum of twenty-five "responsible persons" must make firm commitments to buy at least an aggregate of one hundred thousand dollars worth of securities from the investment company before any securities may be issued by it.[8]

Section 15(a) requires that the contract between an investment company and an investment adviser be approved by a majority of the

---

§ 17.2

1. Zell v. InterCapital Income Securities, Inc., 675 F.2d 1041, 1046 (9th Cir.1982). *See* Leland E. Modesitt, Mutual Fund—A Corporate Anomaly, 14 U.C.L.A.L.Rev. 1252 (1967).

2. *See* James M. Anderson, Rights and Obligations in the Mutual Fund: A Source of Law, 20 Vand.L.Rev. 1120 (1967); Butowsky, Fiduciary Standards of Conduct Revisited— *Moses v. Burgin* and *Rosenfeld v. Black*, 17 N.Y.L.F. 735 (1971); Joseph F. Krupsky, The Role of Investment Company Directors, 32 Bus.Law. 1733 (1977); Clarke Randall, Fiduciary Duties of Investment Company Directors and Management Companies Under the Investment Company Act of 1940, 31 Okla.L.Rev. 635 (1978); Note, Fiduciary Obligations of Mutual Fund Managers in Portfolio Transactions, 22 Syr.L.Rev. 1107 (1971). The fiduciary duties of investment company directors are discussed in § 17.6 *infra*.

3. *See* 2 Tamar Frankel, The Regulation of Money Managers, 212–13 (1978).

4. The Act requires a minimum $100,000 initial capitalization. 15 U.S.C.A. § 80a–14(a). *See* text accompanying footnote 7 *infra*. *See also* Nathan D. Lobell, The Mutual Fund: A Structural Analysis, 47 Va.L.Rev. 181 (1961); Note, The Mutual Fund and Its Management Company: An Analysis of Business Incest, 71 Yale L.J. 137 (1961).

5. 15 U.S.C.A. § 80a–15(a). *See* text accompanying footnotes 9–10 *infra*. When an investment company selects a new investment company adviser there can be a problem relating to the "sale" of the advisory contract. *See e.g.,* Rosenfeld v. Black, 445 F.2d 1337 (2d Cir.1971), *on remand* 336 F.Supp. 84 (S.D.N.Y.1972). *See* § 17.9 *infra*.

6. 15 U.S.C.A. § 80a–15(b).

7. *See, e.g.,* James H. Ellis, Going No Load, 6 Sec.Reg.L.J. 357 (1979). The potential for abuse by an underwriter of its relationship with an investment company is slim because, while a larger volume of sales does increase its profits, "the underwriter gets only a one shot fee on each sale and each sale takes a separate sales effort." Richard W. Jennings & Harold Marsh, Jr., Securities Regulation: Cases and Materials, 1398 (5th ed. 1982). The issuance and distribution of investment company shares is discussed in § 17.5 *infra*.

8. 15 U.S.C.A. § 80a–14(a)(3).

investment company's outstanding voting securities.[9] This subsection of the Act also requires the investment advisory contract to:

    (1) precisely describe all compensation to be paid thereunder;

    (2) continue in effect for a period more than two years from the date of its execution, only so long as such continuance is specifically approved at least annually by the board of directors or by vote of a majority of the outstanding voting securities of such company;

    (3) provide, in substance, that it may be terminated at any time, without the payment of any penalty, by the board of directors of such registered company or by vote of a majority of the outstanding voting securities of such company on not more than sixty days' written notice to the investment adviser; and

    (4) provide, in substance, for its automatic termination in the event of its assignment.[10]

Section 15(a) appears to vest the investment company's board of directors with a great deal of responsibility, authority and discretion in deciding whether or not to renew the advisory contract. While the directors clearly have a large amount of responsibility,[11] their authority and discretion are rarely exercised. For example, it would generally not be practical for an investment company to terminate its advisory contract because of the dominant role generally played by the investment adviser. Functionally, it is the adviser which "selects the fund's investments and operates its business, providing [the investment company with] expertise, personnel, and office space." [12] For many investment companies, in essence, the adviser runs the investment company.[13] Directors act primarily as "watchdogs" over adviser activity and do so for the benefit of fund shareholders.[14] This is not always the case, however, as some investment companies have more of an arm's length

---

    9. 15 U.S.C.A. § 80a–15(a). This requirement is largely negated regarding the investment company's initial advisory contract because the investment adviser generally controls the voting shares of a start-up investment company. For a discussion of shareholder voting on subsequent advisory contracts in connection with their assignment, *see* § 17.9 *infra.* Small advisory contracts are exempted from the shareholder approval requirement altogether if the proposed adviser is not an underwriter or affiliate of the investment company, its annual compensation does not exceed certain limits, and the aggregate amount paid by the single investment company to all such advisers does not exceed a certain limit. 17 C.F.R. § 270.15a–1.

    10. 15 U.S.C.A. § 80a–15(a).

    11. *See* authorities in footnote 2 *supra* and §§ 17.6, 17.9, *infra.*

    12. Zell v. InterCapital Income Securities, Inc., 675 F.2d 1041, 1046 (9th Cir.1982); Burks v. Lasker, 441 U.S. 471, 481, 99 S.Ct. 1831, 1838–1839, 60 L.Ed.2d 404 (1979). In the event that an advisory contract should be terminated, there can be a temporary adviser for 120 days after termination without shareholder approval so long as a majority of the board (including a majority of disinterested directors) approves and the compensation paid does not exceed that paid the previous adviser, provided that the contract was not terminated by assignment wherein the proposed adviser received money or other benefits. 17 C.F.R. § 270.15a–4.

    13. Report of the Securities and Exchange Commission on the Public Policy Implications of Investment Company Growth, H.R.Rep. No. 2337, 89th Cong. 2d Sess. (1966).

    14. *See* § 17.6 *infra* for a discussion of investment company directors' duties.

relationship with the investment adviser. This is especially true with regard to the relatively few investment companies having more than one investment adviser.[15]

Investment company shareholders' major protection against mismanagement and imprudent investments is section 36(b)'s express cause of action against an investment adviser for breach of fiduciary duty to the investment company.[16] The investment company security holder bears the burden of proof in such an action.[17] The adviser's fiduciary role is given further weight by section 15(c)'s affirmative obligation to provide investors with "such information as may reasonably be necessary to evaluate the terms of [the advisory] contract."[18] Directors of an investment company have a parallel affirmative duty to request this information.[19]

As pointed out above, the statutory mandate is that investment advisory contracts are subject to shareholder approval.[20] Additionally, assignment of an advisory contract to another investment adviser automatically terminates the contract.[21] It then becomes necessary for the investment company to seek investor approval for the advisory contract with the assignee investment adviser. This further clouds the already problematic relationship between an investment company, its board of directors, shareholders, and investment advisers.[22]

The breadth of the adviser's obligations to investment company shareholders is underscored by the SEC's view on indemnification agreements. The Commission has taken the position that an investment company cannot lawfully indemnify its investment adviser for expenses incurred in SEC proceedings which result in a finding that the adviser has violated the securities laws.[23] The Commission relied upon sections 17(h) and (i) of the Investment Company Act that prohibit such agree-

---

15. Some investment companies have more than one adviser in order to give diversification with regard to portfolio management as well as to portfolio diversification. This multiadviser structure is the exception rather than the rule.

16. 15 U.S.C.A. § 80a–35(b). *See* § 17.10 *infra*. *See generally* Meyer Eisenberg & Richard M. Phillips, Mutual Fund Litigation—New Frontiers for the Investment Company Act, 62 Colum.L.Rev. 73 (1962); Note, Private Rights of Action Under the Investment Company Act, 1961 Duke L.J. 421; Comment, Private Rights of Action Under the Investment Company Act, 10 Cleve.—Marsh.L.Rev. 421 (1961). *See also, e.g.,* Comment, The Investment Company Act in the State Courts, 1962 Duke L.J. 423.

17. 15 U.S.C.A. § 80a–35(b)(1).

18. 15 U.S.C.A. § 80a–15(c). Additionally, section 36(a) empowers the SEC to bring suit against investment advisers as well as against investment company directors for breaches of fiduciary duty. 15 U.S.C.A. § 80a–35(a). This action has a five year statute of limitations. Fiduciary duties of investment advisers are discussed in § 17.6 *infra*.

19. 15 U.S.C.A. § 80a–15(c).

20. 15 U.S.C.A. § 80a–15(a). *See* text accompanying footnote 10 *supra*.

21. 15 U.S.C.A. § 80a–15(a). *See* § 17.9 *infra*.

22. *See, e.g.,* Rosenfeld v. Black, 445 F.2d 1337 (2d Cir.1971), *on remand* 336 F.Supp. 84 (S.D.N.Y.1972). *See* § 17.9 *infra*. *See generally* James K. Sterrett, II, Reward for Mutual Fund Sponsor, Entrepreneurial Risk, 58 Cornell L.Rev. 195 (1973); Note, Advisory Succession in the Mutual Fund Industry, 67 Nw.U.L.Rev. 278 (1972). *See also* the authorities cited in footnotes 2 and 16 *supra*.

23. Inv.Co. Act Rel. No. IC–13181 (April 21, 1983).

ments,[24] as well as the general policy of the securities laws.[25] The SEC also indicated that by honoring the indemnification agreement, the investment company directors would be in breach of the fiduciary duties imposed by section 36(a) of the Act.[26]

§ 17.3 Companies Covered by the Investment Company Act—Statutory Definitions, Exemptions and Classification

A rather complex set of provisions govern the determination of which companies are "investment companies" subject to the Investment Company Act's provisions.[1] The Act sets out basic definitions and exemptions from registration. The Act further classifies investment companies according to the form of organization and operation.

Statutory Definitions

Section 3(a) of the Act defines "investment company" to be any issuer which:

(1) is or holds itself out as being engaged primarily, or proposes to engage primarily, in the business of investing, reinvesting, or trading in securities;

(2) is engaged or proposes to engage in the business of issuing face-amount certificates of the installment type, or has been engaged in such business and has any such certificate outstanding; or

(3) is engaged or proposes to engage in the business of investing, reinvesting, owning, holding, or trading in securities, and owns or proposes to acquire investment securities having a value exceeding 40 per centum of the value of such issuer's total assets (exclusive of Government securities and cash items) on an unconsolidated basis.

As used in this section, "investment securities" includes all securities except (A) Government securities, (B) securities issued by employees' securities companies, and (C) securities issued by majori-

---

24. 15 U.S.C.A. §§ 80a–17(h), (i). Section 17(i) provides:

No contract or agreement under which any person undertakes to act as investment adviser of, or principal underwriter for, a registered company shall contain any provision which protects or purports to protect such person against any liability to such company or its security holders to which he would otherwise be subject by reason of willful misfeasance, bad faith, or gross negligence, in the performance of his duties, or by reason of his reckless disregard of his obligations and duties under such contract or agreement.

25. Indemnification agreements generally are discussed in § 7.9 *supra*.

26. 15 U.S.C.A. § 80a–35(a). *See* § 17.6 *infra*.

§ 17.3

1. *See* Tamar Frankel, The Regulation of Money Managers: The Investment Company Act and the Investment Advisers Act (1978); Ray Garrett, Jr., When Is an Investment Company?, 37 U.Det.L.J. 355 (1960); Donald W. Glazer, A Study of Mutual Fund Complexes, 119 U.Pa.L.Rev. 205 (1970).

ty-owned subsidiaries of the owner which are not investment companies.[2]

The most easily understood of the foregoing three categories is subsection 3(a)(2)[3] which covers face-amount certificates. A face-amount certificate includes any certificate obligating the issuer to pay a specified or determinable sum,[4] in contrast to merely representing a share of the investment company's assets.[5] Subsection 3(a)(2) has been interpreted to mean that the issuance of any non-exempt face-amount certificate[6] will subject a company to the Investment Company Act's provisions.[7]

Section 3(a)(1) applies to companies intending to be, or acting as, investment companies.[8] The SEC will look at the issuer's past record as evidence of the intent to be an investment company.[9] The definition of "securities" as used in subsection 3(a)(1) is found in section 2(a)(36) of the Act;[10] it covers stock, notes and investment contracts generally. The Investment Company Act thus contains basically the same definition of securities as that in the Securities Act of 1933 and the 1934 Exchange Act.[11]

In contrast to section 3(a)(1)'s focus on planned investment companies, section 3(a)(3) of the Act[12] applies to those companies that do not intend to be "investment companies," but are so classified because forty percent or more of their assets are investment securities.[13] Section 3(b)[14]

---

2.   15 U.S.C.A. § 80a–3(a).

3.   15 U.S.C.A. § 80a–3(a)(2).

4.   *See* 15 U.S.C.A. § 80a–2(a)(15).

5.   The face-amount certificate thus has attributes of a debt security as compared with mutual fund shares which represent an equity interest in the investment company's assets.

6.   *See* 15 U.S.C.A. § 80a–2(a)(15) and footnote 4 *supra.*

7.   SEC v. Mt. Vernon Memorial Park, 664 F.2d 1358 (9th Cir.1982), *cert. denied* 456 U.S. 961, 102 S.Ct. 2037, 72 L.Ed.2d 485 (1982) (funeral home required to register). *See* 15 U.S.C.A. § 80a–28 for regulation of face-amount certificate companies.

8.   *See e.g.,* Morgan Stanley & Co., [1986–87 Transfer Binder] Fed.Sec.L.Rep. (CCH) ¶ 78,337 (SEC No Action Letter April 3, 1986) (a trust issuing certificates representing undivided interests in a funding agreement may be an investment company). *See also* Ray Garrett, Jr., When is an Investment Company?, 37 U.Det.L.J. 355, 359 (1960).

9.   *Id.* at 366. *See, e.g.,* Moses v. Black, 1981 WL 1599, [1981 Transfer Binder] Fed.Sec.L.Rep. (CCH) ¶ 97,866 (S.D.N.Y.1981).

10.   15 U.S.C.A. § 80a–2(a)(36).

11.   15 U.S.C.A. § 77b(1), *see* § 1.5 *supra. See also* the similar definition in the 1934 Exchange Act. 15 U.S.C.A. § 78c(a)(10).

12.   *See* Hearings Before a Subcommittee of the Senate Committee on Banking and Currency on S.3580, 76th Cong., 3d Sess. (1940), at 179. *See also* 17 C.F.R. § 270.3a–2 which allows a company which would be an investment company otherwise, to not be classified so if it "has a bona fide interest to be engaged primarily, as soon as reasonably possible, in a business other than that of investing, reinvesting, owning, holding or trading in securities." The rule continues to recite the evidences of interest required, *id.*

13.   Inadvertent investment companies are discussed in § 17.4 *infra. See, e.g.,* Edmund H. Kerr, The Inadvertent Investment Company: Section 3(a)(3) of the Investment Company Act, 12 Stan.L.Rev. 29 (1959); Edmund H. Kerr & Allen Appelbaum, Inadvertent Investment Companies—Ten Years After, 25 Bus.Law. 887 (1970). In 1984, the Commission adopted Rule 3a–5 which exempts from the definition of investment company, companies organized with the primary purpose of financing the

---

14.   See note 14 on page 965.

allows the Commission under appropriate circumstances to grant to these companies exemptions from section 3(a)(3) of the Investment Company Act. The problems of section 3(a)(3) and these "inadvertent investment companies" are discussed more fully in a subsequent section.[15]

Exclusions and Exemptions

The Commission has discretion to waive the registration requirements for investment companies. A company or person subject to registration may seek an exemptive order under section 6(c) of the Act, relieving the applicant of Investment Company Act requirements to the extent that the SEC determines such exemption "necessary or appropriate in the public interest."[16] This administrative discretion has been viewed as necessary in light of the Act's otherwise inflexible provisions.[17] Applicants for such an exemption should consult the Commission's guidelines for the filing of applications.[18]

Exclusions from the Investment Company Act's registration requirements are set out in sections 3(b) and 3(c) of the Act; exemptions from the Act generally are set out in section 6. Section 3(b) is, by its terms, applicable only to section 3(a)(3) or inadvertent investment companies.[19] Section 3(b)(1) excludes from the definition of investment company issuers whose primary business is something other than investing in securities.[20] Under section 3(b)(2)[21] the SEC is given discretionary

---

business operations of their parent companies or other companies controlled by their parent company. 17 C.F.R. § 270.3a–5. *See* Inv.Co. Act Rel. No. IC–14275, [1984–85 Transfer Binder] Fed.Sec.L.Rep. (CCH) ¶ 83,719 (Dec. 14, 1984).

14. 15 U.S.C.A. § 80a–3(b).

15. *See* § 17.4 *infra.*

16. 15 U.S.C.A. § 80a–6(c).

17. Regarding the importance of this broad exemptive power, it has been noted: "The Act's great detail and prima facie inflexibility might have proved particularly problematic in light of the many innovations in the industry for which provision had not been made in the Act. However, Congress chose to temper the Act's inflexibility through the broad exemptive powers it granted the Commission. Through the exemptive process interested persons have been permitted to modify the Act's restrictions to suit their own circumstances. Over the years, the exemption process has loomed as an increasingly major avenue for addressing problems in regulating investment companies * * * [M]any people argue that the [complex and expensive] application process has encouraged 'regulation by exemption' in which the scope and complexity of certain exemptions have begun to eclipse the Act itself in importance." Martin E. Lybecker, Mark B. Goldfus, & Mark J. Mackey, Investment Company Act Study, 13 Rev.Sec.Reg. 983 (1980).

18. Commission Policy and Guidelines for Filing of Applications for Exemption From Some or All of the Provisions of the Investment Company Act of 1940 and the Investment Advisers Act of 1940, Inv.Co. Act Rel. No. IC–14492, 5 Fed.Sec.L.Rep. (CCH) ¶ 47,530, 17 Sec.Reg. & L.Rep. (BNA) 610 (April 30, 1985).

19. 15 U.S.C.A. § 80a–3(b). *But see* M.A. Hanna Co., 10 S.E.C. 581 (1945) where these exclusions were considered applicable to all of section 3(a) because the determination of whether one is "primarily engaged" in investment business under section 3(b)(2) necessarily bears upon section 3(a)'s definition of investment company. *Id.* at 583.

20. 15 U.S.C.A. § 80a–3(b)(1) (excluded are issuers "primarily engaged, directly or through a wholly-owned subsidiary or subsidiaries, in a business or businesses other than that of investing, reinvesting, owning, holding, or trading in securities").

21. 15 U.S.C.A. § 80a–3(b)(2).

exemptive power for issuers whose primary business is not investing in securities; and, there are thus no express statutory guidelines. In contrast, section 3(c) catalogs various specific exclusions from the definition of investment company. Section 3(c)'s first exclusion is afforded to "any issuer whose outstanding securities (other than short term paper)[22] are beneficially owned by not more than one hundred persons and which is not making and does not presently propose to make a public offering of its securities."[23] There is an "attribution rule" under which a company owning less than ten percent of the issuer's outstanding voting securities is deemed to be a single holder for purposes of this exemption; however, if a company owns over ten percent, each of its stockholders is counted as a holder of the issuer's securities for computing the one hundred person limit.[24] The 1933 Securities Act's exemption for intrastate offerings[25] does not have a direct counterpart in the Investment Company Act.[26] Accordingly, size rather than the local nature of the activity is the benchmark of an Investment Company Act exemption.

Section 3(c) further exempts from registration: underwriters[27] and brokers;[28] banks,[29] insurance companies,[30] and savings and loan associa-

---

22. Notes coming due within 9 months of issuance. 15 U.S.C.A. § 80a–2(a)(38).

23. 15 U.S.C.A. § 80a–3(c)(1).

The SEC will not issue no action letters with respect to section 3(c)(1)'s exemption unless the offering complies with Rule 506 of Regulation D under the 1933 Act. In re Stars & Stripes GNMA Funding Corp., [1986 Transfer Binder] Fed.Sec.L.Rep. (CCH) ¶ 78,303 (SEC No Action Letter Dec. 19, 1985).

24. 15 U.S.C.A. § 80a–3(c)(1)(A). If the company's total holdings of investment securities does not equal more than 10% of its total assets, the company is considered a single holder of the issuer's securities, *id. See, e.g.,* Risk Arbitrage Partners, 18 Sec.Reg. & L.Rep. (BNA) 1597 (SEC No Action Letter Oct. 17, 1986) (beneficial owners of general partnership owning less than 10% of limited partnership not counted as separate owners in computing 100 owner ceiling). *See also, e.g.,* Clemente Global Growth Fund, Inc. v. Pickens, 705 F.Supp. 958, 964–65 (S.D.N.Y.1989) ("looking through" a limited partnership to the limited partners for the purpose of computing the 100 shareholder threshold).

25. 15 U.S.C.A. § 77c(a)(11). *See* § 4.12 *supra.*

26. 15 U.S.C.A. § 80a–24(d). *But see* 15 U.S.C.A. § 80a–6(d) which is discussed in the text accompanying notes 80–85 *infra.* Section 24(d) of the Investment Company Act not only expressly denies the applicability of the intrastate exemption, it also provides that the 1933 Act's exemption for insurance policies and annuity contracts (15 U.S.C.A. § 77c(a)(8), *see* § 4.9 *supra*) does not apply to the 1940 Act. *See* footnote 30 *infra.* Nor does the 1933 Act exemption for certain dealers' transactions (15 U.S.C.A. § 77d(3), *see* § 4.27 *supra*) apply to the Investment Company Act.

27. Defined in 15 U.S.C.A. § 80a–2(a)(40). *See also* section 2(11) of the 1933 Act, 15 U.S.C.A. § 77b(11), which is discussed in § 4.24 *supra.*

28. 15 U.S.C.A. § 80a–3(c)(2).

29. Bank is defined in 15 U.S.C.A. § 80a–2(a)(5) to include banking institutions organized under federal law, member banks of the Federal Reserve System and any other bank or trust company performing similar functions. For discussion of banks and their securities operations *see* § 19.5 *infra* (Practitioner's Edition only).

30. Insurance company is defined in 15 U.S.C.A. § 80a–2(a)(17) as a company "organized as an insurance company, whose primary and predominant activity is the writing of insurance or reinsurance" where such company is subject to state regulation. While section 3(a)(8) of the Securities Act exempts insurance and annuity contracts, if a variable annuity is issued by an investment company, it is not exempted from the Investment Company Act, SEC v. Variable Annuity Life Insurance Co., 359 U.S. 65, 79 S.Ct. 618, 3 L.Ed.2d 640 (1959). *See* 15 U.S.C.A. § 80a–24(d); 17 C.F.R. § 270.6e–2(a)(3). In Pruden-

tions ostensibly due to the degree of regulation to which such institutions are already subject.[31]   Any person whose business is substantially that of making small loans[32] as well as any person primarily in the business of commercial or real estate financing and who does not issue redeemable securities[33] or face-amount certificates[34] is also exempt.   Further exemptions exist for any company which is primarily involved in the foregoing activities, either directly or through majority-owned subsidiaries,[35] and derived at least twenty-five percent of its gross income for the preceding year from such, in conjunction with additional business(es) other than those "investing, reinvesting, owning, holding, or trading in securities."[36]   Formerly, a company found by the SEC not to be primarily involved in the business of investing, reinvesting, owning, holding, or trading securities and also subject to the jurisdiction of the Interstate Commerce Commission[37] was exempt from the Act, as is any company subject to regulation under the Public Utility Holding Act of 1935.[38] Any person substantially all of whose business consists of owning or holding oil, gas or other mineral royalties or leases, or fractional interests therein[39] are not subject to the Act.   Nor are eleemosynary institutions where no individual receives any portion of the net profits.[40] Single or collective pension, profit sharing plans and separate accounts set up for them which are qualified under Section 401 of the Internal

tial Insurance Co. of America v. SEC, 326 F.2d 383 (3d Cir.1964), *cert. denied* 377 U.S. 953, 84 S.Ct. 1629, 12 L.Ed.2d 497 (1964) section 3(c)(3)'s exemption did not apply to an insurance company that set up a separate account for issuing variable life insurance, since this was a separate entity. *See also* SEC, Division of Investment Management Regulation, Report on Variable Life Insurance Rules (Feb. 3, 1973).

31. 15 U.S.C.A. § 80a–3(c)(3).

32. 15 U.S.C.A. § 80a–3(c)(4).

33. Defined in section 2(a)(32) as those securities whose holders have the right to receive approximately their proportionate share of the issuer's net assets, or cash equivalent thereof, if presented to issuer. *See* 17 C.F.R. § 270.2a–4 for method of determining current net asset value.

34. 15 U.S.C.A. § 80a–3(c)(5). *See* Inv.Co. Act Rel. No. IC–8456, 5 Fed.Sec.L.Rep. (CCH) ¶ 47,357 (Aug. 9, 1974) (two tiered real estate companies); In re Westin Hotels, [1985–86 Transfer Binder] Fed.Sec.L.Rep. (CCH) ¶ 78,179 (SEC No Action Letter Nov. 11, 1985).

35. A "majority owned subsidiary" of a person is a company 50% or more of whose outstanding voting securities are owned by that person, or that person owns 50% or more of an intermediate company which owns 50% or more of such securities of a company. 15 U.S.C.A. § 80a–2(a)(24). *See* In re Westin Hotels, [1985–86 Transfer Binder] Fed.Sec. L.Rep. (CCH) ¶ 78,179 (SEC No Action Letter Nov. 11, 1985) (partnership owning real estate through two-tier arrangement was not entitled to the exemption since the limited partners could only remove the general partners and the general partners of the underlying partnership for cause; an exemption was also denied under § 3(c)(5)'s exemption for finance companies.

36. 15 U.S.C.A. § 80a–3(c)(6).

37. *See* 49 U.S.C.A. § 11301 (repealed).

38. 15 U.S.C.A. § 80a–3(c)(8). The Public Utility Holding Company Act, 15 U.S.C.A. §§ 79 *et seq.,* is discussed in chapter 15 *supra.*

39. 15 U.S.C.A. § 80a–3(c)(9).

40. 15 U.S.C.A. § 80a–3(c)(10).

Revenue Code[41] are exempt. The Act does not apply to any voting trust, the assets of which consist exclusively of securities of a single issuer which is not an investment company[42] nor does it apply to securities holders' protective committees having only certificates of deposit and short-term paper securities outstanding.[43]

In 1992, the Commission excluded certain asset-backed structured financing arrangements from the definition of investment company.[44] In Rule 3a–7, the Commission has excluded the pooling of assets for structured financing from the definition.[45] As a result of the new rule, it is now clear that pooling and securitization of assets such as home mortgages, credit card receivables, and various type of equipment leases may be excluded from investment company regulation.[46]

Insurance Policies and Annuity Contracts

Section 3(a)(8) of the 1933 Act exempts insurance policies and annuity contracts[47] but that exemption does not apply to the provisions of the Investment Company Act by virtue of section 24(d) of that Act.[48] However, if a company's primary business is that of writing insurance then it is exempt from the 1940 Act.[49] Where a variable annuity has the benchmarks of an investment contract rather than insurance, it is a security under the 1933 Act[50] and it cannot take advantage of the 1940 Act's exemption.[51]

Rule 6e–2 of the Commission[52] sets forth a qualified exemption for certain variable life insurance separate accounts that would otherwise

41. 15 U.S.C.A. § 80a–3(c)(11). *See* Alan Rosenblatt & Martin E. Lybecker, Some Thoughts on the Federal Securities Laws Regulating External Investment Management Arrangements and the ALI Federal Securities Code Project, 124 U.Pa.L.Rev. 587, 592 (1976). Prior to 1970 qualified plans were not exempt. *See* Robert H. Mundheim & Gordon D. Henderson, Applicability of the Federal Securities Laws to Pension and Profit–Sharing Plans, 29 Law & Contemp. Prob. 795 (1964).

42. 15 U.S.C.A. § 80a–3(c)(12).

43. 15 U.S.C.A. § 80a–3(c)(13).

44. *See* Inv. Co. Act Rel. No. 40–19105, [1992 Transfer Binder] Fed.Sec.L.Rep. (CCH) ¶ 85,062 (SEC Nov. 27, 1992).

45. 17 C.F.R. § 270.3a–7.

46. *See* 24 Sec.Reg. & L.Rep. (BNA) 1799 (Dec. 4, 1992).

47. 15 U.S.C.A. § 77c(a)(8).

48. 15 U.S.C.A. § 80a–24(d). *See* footnote 26 *supra.*

49. 15 U.S.C.A. § 80a–3(c)(3).

50. SEC v. Variable Annuity Life Insurance Co., 359 U.S. 65, 79 S.Ct. 618, 3 L.Ed.2d 640 (1959). *See, e.g.,* Boe W. Martin, Status of the Variable Annuity as a Security: A Lesson in Legal Line Drawing, 30 Ohio St.L.J. 736 (1969); Edward A. Mearns, Jr., The Commission, the Variable Annuity, and the Inconsiderate Sovereign, 45 Va.L.Rev. 831 (1959). *See* §§ 1.5, 4.9 *supra.*

51. SEC v. Variable Annuity Life Insurance Co., 359 U.S. 65, 79 S.Ct. 618, 3 L.Ed.2d 640 (1959); Richard W. Jennings & Harold Marsh, Jr., Securities Regulation: Cases and Materials 1367–1369 (5th ed. 1982).

52. 17 C.F.R. § 270.6e–2.

qualify as investment companies requiring registration.[53] Under the rule, which is quite detailed and is only briefly summarized herein, there are seven preconditions to the limited exemption. First, in order to qualify for the exemption, the separate account must be established and maintained by a life insurance company pursuant to the laws of the United States, any state, the District of Columbia, or Canada.[54] Second, the assets of the separate account must be derived solely from variable life insurance contracts.[55] Third, the account may not be used for variable annuity contracts, for funds corresponding to dividend accumulations, or for any other contract liabilities which do not involve life contingencies.[56] Fourth, the income, gains, and losses, both realized and unrealized, from assets of the separate account must be credited to the separate account without regard to other income, gains, or losses of the insurer.[57] Fifth, the separate account must be legally segregated and insulated from the liabilities arising out of the life insurer's other business.[58] Sixth, the assets must be equal to or in excess of the reserves and other contract liabilities of the separate account, unless the Commission grants an exemptive order from this requirement.[59] Seventh, the separate account's investment adviser must be registered under the Investment Advisers Act of 1940.[60] The exemption that is provided in Rule 6e–2 is not a complete one. Although the Act's registration requirements do not apply,[61] the separate account, nevertheless, must file a notification on SEC Form N–6E1–1 and, further, there are detailed conditions on the exemption from the Act's operational requirements.[62]

In addition to the exemption for certain variable life insurance separate accounts, in 1984 the Commission adopted a temporary rule exempting what was then a new life insurance product—flexible premium variable life insurance.[63] Although still designated as a temporary

---

53. In 1985 the Commission proposed amendments to the rule but these amendments, while still proposed, have not yet been adopted. *See* Inv.Co. Act Rel. No. IC–14421, [1984–85 Transfer Binder] Fed.Sec.L.Rep. (CCH) ¶ 83,753 (March 15, 1985).

54. 17 C.F.R. § 270.6e–2(a)(1). Separate account is defined in section 2(a)(37) of the Act. 15 U.S.C.A. § 80a–2(a)(37).

55. 17 C.F.R. § 270.6e–2(a)(2). Variable life insurance contracts are defined in 17 C.F.R. § 270.6e–2(c)(1).

56. 17 C.F.R. § 270.6e–2(a)(3).

57. 17 C.F.R. § 270.6e–2(a)(4).

58. 17 C.F.R. § 270.6e–2(a)(5).

59. 17 C.F.R. § 270.6e–2(a)(6).

60. 17 C.F.R. § 270.6e–2(a)(7). The Investment Advisers Act is discussed in chapter 18 *infra.*

61. 17 C.F.R. § 270.6e–2(b)(2), (3).

62. 17 C.F.R. §§ 270.6e–2(b)(1), (4)–(15).

63. 17 C.F.R. § 270.6e–3(T). *See* Inv.Co.Act.Rel. No. IC–14234, [1984–85 Transfer Binder] Fed.Sec.L.Rep. (CCH) ¶ 83,707 (Dec. 3, 1984), *amended in* Inv.Co.Act Rel. No. IC–14625, [1985 Transfer Binder] Fed.Sec.L.Rep. (CCH) ¶ 83,810 (July 10, 1985) *and* Inv.Co. Act Rel. No. IC–15561, [1987 Transfer Binder] Fed.Sec.L.Rep. (CCH) ¶ 84,115 (March 30, 1987).

rule, it remains in effect.[64] As is the case with Rule 6e–2's exemption for
certain variable life insurance separate accounts, Rule 6e–3(T)'s exemption for flexible premium variable life insurance separate accounts is not
total. Thus, while separate accounts qualifying for the exemption are
exempt from the Act's registration requirements,[65] the account must file
notification on SEC Form N–6E1–1. Also, there are detailed conditions
on exemption from the Act's operational requirements.[66]

There are six generalized preconditions for the Rule 6e–3(T) exemption for flexible premium variable life insurance separate accounts.
First, the separate account must be established and maintained by a life
insurance company pursuant to the laws of the United States, any state,
the District of Columbia, or Canada.[67] Second, the assets of the separate
account must be derived solely from flexible premium variable life
insurance contracts.[68] Third, the account may not be used for variable
annuity contracts, for funds corresponding to dividend accumulations, or
for any other contract liabilities which do not involve life contingencies.[69]
Fourth, the separate account must be legally segregated and insulated
from the liabilities arising out of the life insurer's other business.[70]
Fifth, the assets must be equal to or in excess of the reserves and other
contract liabilities of the separate account.[71] Sixth, the separate account's investment adviser must be registered under the Investment
Advisers Act of 1940.[72]

Other Exemptions

Additional exemptions from investment company regulation appear
in section 6 of the Act.[73] Companies exempted by section 6 include:
those operating mainly in Puerto Rico, the Virgin Islands, or any other
possession of the United States and not selling or offering for sale any
securities to residents of any states other than the state or territory in
which the company is organized.[74] Until 1987, there was a separate
exemption for companies in bankruptcy selling only short-term paper
and trust certificates as securities for cash.[75] Also exempt are companies

---

64. In addition to the two sets of amendments cited in footnote 63 *supra,* additional
amendments were proposed in 1987. *See* Inv.Co.Act Rel. No. IC–15586 [1987 Transfer
Binder] Fed.Sec.L.Rep. (CCH) ¶ 84,106 (Feb. 27, 1987).

65. 17 C.F.R. § 270.6e–3(T)(b)(2), (3).

66. 17 C.F.R. §§ 270.6e–3(T)(b)(1), (4)–(15).

67. 17 C.F.R. § 270.6e–3(T)(a)(1). Separate account is defined in section 2(a)(37) of
the Act. 15 U.S.C.A. § 80a–2(a)(37).

68. 17 C.F.R. § 270.6e–3(T)(a)(2). Flexible premium variable life insurance contracts
are defined in 17 C.F.R. § 270.6e–3(T)(c)(1).

69. 17 C.F.R. § 270.6e–3(T)(a)(3).

70. 17 C.F.R. § 270.6e–3(T)(a)(4).

71. 17 C.F.R. § 270.6e–3(T)(a)(5).

72. 17 C.F.R. § 270.6e–3(T)(a)(6). The Investment Advisers Act is discussed in chapter
18 *infra.*

73. 15 U.S.C.A. § 80a–6.

74. 15 U.S.C.A. § 80a–6(a)(1).

75. 15 U.S.C.A. § 80a–6(a)(2) (1982) (repealed).

reorganized in bankruptcy that were not investment companies before bankruptcy and all of whose outstanding securities after reorganization are owned by creditors.[76] For such reorganized companies to be exempt under section 6, more than fifty percent of the voting securities and securities representing more than fifty percent of their net asset value must be currently owned by twenty-five or fewer creditors.[77] Also exempt are certain issuers that were exempted by the Federal Savings and Loan Insurance Corporation[78] as well as pre–1940 subsidiaries of face-amount certificate companies.[79]

Section 6(d)[80] permits the Commission to exempt by rule, regulation or order limited nonpublic offerings of securities issued by closed end[81] investment companies. The section 6(d) exemption is available where the aggregate offering price is no more than one hundred thousand dollars and the securities are sold either in a nonpublic offering or only to residents of the company's state of organization.[82] The exemption is not available if it would be "contrary to the public interest or inconsistent with the protection of investors."[83] Rule 6d–1 describes the form for filing an application for such an exemption;[84] the filing of Form N8A does not qualify as notification of registration under the Act.[85]

The SEC may grant a conditional exemption from full registration under the Act by opting to apply only selected Investment Company Act provisions to companies exempted by section 6(c) if it "deems it necessary or appropriate in the public interest or for the protection of investors." [86] The exemption may be granted by administrative order or SEC rule.[87] For example, the Commission has by rule exempted certain variable life insurance policies issued by insurance companies out of separate accounts.[88] The Commission further has the option to exempt

---

76. For the 1933 Act's comparable exemption *see* 15 U.S.C.A. §§ 77c(a)(7), 77c(a)(10) which are discussed in §§ 4.8, 4.11 *supra.*

77. 15 U.S.C.A. § 80a–6(a)(2). Such exemption will terminate with a public offering of the reorganized company's securities, *id.* For a recent discussion of this exemption *see, e.g.,* M.J. Whitman & Co. v. American Financial Enterprises, Inc., 725 F.2d 394 (6th Cir.1984).

78. 15 U.S.C.A. § 80a–6(a)(3).

79. 15 U.S.C.A. § 80a–6(a)(4). Face-amount certificate companies are discussed in the text accompanying footnotes 3–7 *supra.*

80. 15 U.S.C.A. § 80a–6(d).

81. A "closed end" company is one with a set number of shares as compared to "open end" companies which will issue additional shares as new investors or new capital is found. 15 U.S.C.A. § 80a–5. *See* text accompanying footnote 100 *infra.*

82. 15 U.S.C.A. § 80a–6(d)(1), (2).

83. 15 U.S.C.A. § 80a–6(d)(3).

84. 17 C.F.R. § 270.6d–1.

85. *Id. See* 15 U.S.C.A. § 80a–8(a). Registration is discussed § 17.8 *infra.*

86. 15 U.S.C.A. § 80a–6(e).

87. 15 U.S.C.A. § 80a–6(c)

88. 17 C.F.R. § 270.6e–2. *See* footnotes 52–62 *supra* and accompanying text.

certain pension funds which qualify as an employees' security company[89] upon application by the company.[90] Section 6(f)[91] exempts closed end companies qualifying as "business development" companies.[92] In addition to the foregoing exemptions an exemptive order may also be available upon application to the SEC under section 6(c), as discussed above.[93]

Classification of Investment Companies

Companies deemed subject to the Investment Company Act are divided into three categories by section 4 of the Act. There are (1) face-amount certificate companies,[94] (2) unit investment trusts,[95] and (3) management companies.[96]

The largest group of investment companies consists of management companies. The Act establishes two categories of management companies. Section 5 classifies management companies as either "open-end," that is, those offering for sale already-issued redeemable securities, or "closed-end" which includes all other management companies.[97] As discussed in subsequent sections, there are special regulations that apply

---

89. 15 U.S.C.A. § 80a–6(b). Employees' securities company is defined in section 2(a)(13):

"Employees' securities company" means any investment company or similar issuer all of the outstanding securities of which (other than short-term paper) are beneficially owned (A) by the employees or persons on retainer of a single employer or of two or more employers each of which is an affiliated company of the other, (B) by former employees of such employer or employers, (C) by members of the immediate family of such employees, persons on retainer, or former employees, (D) by any two or more of the foregoing classes of persons, or (E) by such employer or employers together with any one or more of the foregoing classes of persons.

15 U.S.C.A. § 80a–2(a)(13).

90. 15 U.S.C.A. § 80a–6(b). Such an exemption must be "consistent with the protection of investors." *Id.*

91. 15 U.S.C.A. § 80a–6(f).

92. Business development companies are regulated by sections 55–65, 15 U.S.C.A. §§ 80a–54–80a–64. A business development company's primary function is to acquire in non-public offerings securities of "eligible portfolio companies." An eligible portfolio company is a non investment company that is licensed by the Small Business Investment Administration under the Small Business Investment Act of 1958. The eligible portfolio company must be controlled by a business development company. 15 U.S.C.A. § 80a–2(a)(46). *See also* 15 U.S.C.A. § 80a–2(a)(47). *See* text accompanying footnotes 108–111 *infra.*

93. 15 U.S.C.A. § 80a–6(c); *see* footnote 16 *supra* and accompanying text.

94. *See* text accompanying footnotes 4–5 *supra.*

95. A company (a) organized under a trust indenture or some similar instrument, (b) without a board of directors, and (c) issuing only redeemable securities (not including a voting trust.) 15 U.S.C.A. § 80a–4(2). The trust indentures are governed by the Trust Indenture Act of 1939, 15 U.S.C.A. § 77aaa *et seq.* which is discussed in chapter 16 *supra.*

See SEC Grants Unprecedented Relief to Allow Novel Mutual Fund to Proceed, 22 Sec.Reg. & L.Rep. (BNA) 1090 (July 27, 1990) (permitting investment company to market nonredeemable shares of unit investment trust holding a portfolio of securities comprising the Standard & Poor 500 Index).

96. All investment companies not fitting into the other categories are management companies, 15 U.S.C.A. § 80a–4(3).

97. 15 U.S.C.A. § 80a–5(a).

to each of these categories. Most mutual funds are open-end investment companies.[98] Trading in shares of these open-end companies is primarily through redemption and reissuance by the company at the per share net asset value.[99] Closed-end management companies typically have a fixed number of shares outstanding which are traded as any other corporate stock might be, that is, on the exchanges or over the counter at a price established by the market.[100]

The Investment Company Act further categorizes companies according to the diversification of investments in their portfolios. Section 5 of the Act classifies management companies as "diversified" and "non-diversified."[101] In the former category, seventy-five percent of the management company's assets are "limited to securities representing not more than 10 percent of the outstanding voting securities of any one company and not more than 5 percent of its total assets [may be] in the securities of any one company."[102] Contrary to the popular meaning of the term, "diversification" refers to the concentration of investments in a single issuer, not in a single industry.[103] Authorization by a majority of its outstanding voting securities is required before a diversified investment company may change its investment policy towards one of non-diversification.[104]

Another type of investment company falling within the purview of the Investment Company Act is the "special situation company."[105] A special situation company typically buys up controlling blocks of the securities of another corporation with the intent of boosting the value of these securities through more efficient management of the target corporation. Special situation companies do not have a long term interest in managing the businesses acquired; the primary goal is to eventually sell all of the securities at a profit.[106] The SEC has taken the position that a special situation company "engages in the operation of other companies for the primary purpose of making a profit in the sale of the securities of

---

98. *See, e.g.,* Richard M. Philips, Deregulation Under the Investment Company Act—A Reevaluation of the Corporate Paraphernalia of Shareholder Voting and Boards of Directors, 37 Bus.Law. 903, 905 (1982). *See generally* Nathan D. Lobell, The Mutual Fund: A Structural Analysis, 47 Va.L.Rev. 181 (1961). *See also* SEC Annual Reports for description of the size of such funds and the amount of outstanding securities.

99. *See* Comment, The Distribution of Mutual Fund Shares—Recent Developments in SEC Regulation, 1975 Wash.U.L.Q. 1153, 1190 (1975).

100. A "closed end" company is one with a set number of shares as compared to "open end" companies which will issue additional shares as new investors or new capital is found. 15 U.S.C.A. § 80a–5.

101. 15 U.S.C.A. § 80a–5(b).

102. Alan Rosenblatt & Martin E. Lybecker, *supra* footnote 41 at 593 n. 16. A diversified company receives special treatment under Subchapter M of the Internal Revenue Code, *id.*

103. *See id.*

104. 15 U.S.C.A. § 80a–13(a)(1).

105. *See* Edmund H. Kerr, The Inadvertent Investment Company: Section 3(a)(3) of the Investment Company Act, 12 Stan.L.Rev. 29, 47 (1959).

106. Richard W. Jennings & Harold Marsh, Jr., Securities Regulation: Cases and Materials 1364 (5th ed. 1982).

such companies" and, as such, is subject to the provisions of the Investment Company Act.[107]

Another special category of investment companies is comprised of certain enterprises devoted to financing small businesses. As part of the Small Business Incentive Act of 1980,[108] "business development companies" are afforded different treatment than regular investment companies. Business development companies principally invest in and provide managerial assistance to small, growing and financially troubled businesses.[109] This special treatment for these companies is due to the recognition that the onerous requirements of the Investment Company Act would otherwise restrict the flow of capital to small business.[110] Companies electing to be regulated as business development companies must comply with sections 55 through 65 of the Investment Company Act,[111] the provisions of which are more relaxed than those applicable to regular investment companies.

Although money market funds are not classified as a separate type of investment company under the statute, the Commission has adopted special rules applicable to these funds.[112] One of the unique aspects of these funds is that the per share value remains constant. Variations in net asset value will thus, if anything, affect the dividends on the shares rather than the price of the shares.

In order for a company to withdraw from registration once it has been found subject to the Act's provisions, the Commission must affirmatively act to find the "investment company" classification no longer valid.[113]

§ 17.4 The Definition of "Investment Company;" The Problem of the Inadvertent Investment Company

As was indicated in the preceding section of this treatise, there are a number of companies inadvertently finding themselves subject to the

---

107. In the Matter of Frobisher Ltd., 27 S.E.C. 944, 950 (1948).

108. Pub.L. 96–477, 94 Stat. 2275 (1980).

109. 5 U.S. Code Cong. and Adm.News 4800, 4801 (1980). *See* footnote 92 *supra.*

110. 5 U.S. Code Cong. and Adm. News at 4804, procedure of which is found at 15 U.S.C.A. § 80a–53.

111. 15 U.S.C.A. §§ 80a–54–80a–64. *See generally* Ronald L. Thomas & Paul F. Roye, Regulation of Business Development Companies Under the Investment Company Act, 55 S.Cal.L.Rev. 895 (1981).

112. For example, the Commission has imposed limits on the amount of money that money market funds can invest in debt instruments of any one issuer. Rule 2a–7, 17 C.F.R. § 270.2a–7; Inv.Co.Act Rel. IC–18005, [1990–1991 Transfer Binder] Fed.Sec.L.Rep. (CCH) ¶ 84,710 (Feb. 20, 1991). *See* SEC Adopts Changes to Help Ensure Safety of Money Market Funds, 23 Sec.Reg. & L.Rep. (BNA) 193 (Feb. 15, 1991). The SEC has excluded tax exempt money market funds from the general money market fund requirement that money market fund directors approve the acquisition of securities that are either unrated or rated only by one rating agency. 17 C.F.R. § 270.2a–7. *See* Inv.Co.Act Rel. IC–18177, [1990–1991 Transfer Binder] Fed.Sec.L.Rep. (CCH) ¶ 84,741 (May 31, 1991).

113. 15 U.S.C.A. § 80a–8(f).

Investment Company Act by virtue of section 3(a)(3).[1] Any company holding investment securities in excess of forty percent of its total non-cash asset value, comes within the purview of section 3(a)(3).[2] By virtue of the Act's definitional sections,[3] "investment securities" do not include government securities,[4] securities issued by employees' securities companies,[5] or securities issued by non-investment company majority-owned subsidiaries of the holder.[6]

The "value of a company's total assets" as defined in section 2(a)(41) has been explained as the cost of assets acquired since the end of the preceding fiscal quarter, in addition to the market value of assets previously acquired. Accordingly, it has been observed that "assets theretofore acquired are valued at market value, if available in the case of securities, or fair value as determined by the board [of directors], if market quotations of securities are not available or if other assets are in question."[7] The "cash items" excluded from a company's total assets for purposes of section 3(a)(3)'s tabulation have been interpreted informally by the SEC to include time deposits, funds in transit, certificates of deposit, and commercial short-term notes; but accounts receivable are most probably not "cash items" to be excluded from a company's total assets.[8]

A business enterprise not intending to be an investment company is most likely to cross the forty percent threshold during its start-up period when the company invests the capital it does have in order to amass enough money to finance its own operating expenses, when it is selling off its assets and investing the proceeds pending ultimate use of them,[9]

---

§ 17.4

1. 15 U.S.C.A. § 80a–3(a)(3). *See* Ray Garrett, Jr., When Is an Investment Company, 37 U.Det.L.J. 355 (1960); Edmund H. Kerr, The Inadvertent Investment Company: Section 3(a)(3) of the Investment Company Act, 12 Stan.L.Rev. 29 (1959); Edmund H. Kerr & Alan Appelbaum, Inadvertent Investment Companies—Ten Years After, 25 Bus. Law. 887 (1970).

2. The Second Circuit has noted that "In effect, § 3(a)(3) creates a presumption that a company [satisfying the percentage requirements] is an investment company, which is refuted if a company demonstrates that it falls within one of the exceptions of the Act for companies that are essentially industrial corporations but have over 40% of their assets in marketable securities." SEC v. S & P National Corp., 360 F.2d 741, 746 (2d Cir.1966). *See also, e.g.,* In the Matter of ABC Portfolio Development Group, Inc., [1994–1995 Transfer Binder] Fed. Sec. L. Rep. (CCH) ¶ 85,422 (SEC 1994) (sales of investment pool interests were sales of interests in an investment company and were subject to the Investment Company Act).

3. *See* § 17.3 *supra.*

4. Defined in section 2(a)(16), 15 U.S.C.A. § 80a–2(a)(16).

5. Defined in section 2(a)(13), 15 U.S.C.A. § 80a–2(a)(13).

6. Defined in section 2(a)(24), 15 U.S.C.A. § 80a–2(a)(24).

7. Kerr & Appelbaum, footnote 1 *supra* at 888.

8. *Id.*

9. SEC v. Fifth Ave. Coach Lines, Inc., 289 F.Supp. 3 (S.D.N.Y.1968), *affirmed* 435 F.2d 510 (2d Cir.1970) (condemnation award pushed bus company over 40% line, but company given reasonable time to act in dispensing cash before held in violation of Investment Company Act); *Cf.* In the Matter of Real Silk Hosiery Mills, 36 S.E.C. 365 (1955).

and when it is in the process of a final liquidation.[10] There are, of course, other less common situations where one may encounter an inadvertent investment company. For example, an unsuccessful tender or exchange offer conceivably could turn the would-be acquirer into an inadvertent investment company.[11]

Exemptions from section 3(a)(3) are found in section 3(b).[12] The following are exempted from the category of an investment company even though the forty percent threshold has been crossed:

(1) Any issuer primarily engaged, directly or through a wholly-owned subsidiary or subsidiaries, in a business or businesses other than that of investing, reinvesting, owning, holding, or trading in securities.

(2) Any issuer which the Commission, upon application by such issuer, finds and by order declares to be primarily engaged in a business or businesses other than that of investing, reinvesting, owning, holding, or trading in securities either directly or (a) through majority-owned subsidiaries or (b) through controlled companies conducting similar types of businesses. The filing of an application under this paragraph in good faith by an issuer other than a registered investment company shall exempt the applicant for a period of sixty days from all provisions of this subchapter applicable to investment companies as such. For cause shown, the Commission by order may extend such period of exemption for an additional period or periods. Whenever the Commission, upon its own motion or upon application, finds that the circumstances which gave rise to the issuance of an order granting an application under this paragraph no longer exist, the Commission shall by order revoke such order.

(3) Any issuer all the outstanding securities of which (other than short-term paper and directors' qualifying shares) are directly or indirectly owned by a company excepted from the definition of investment company by paragraph (1) or (2) of this subsection.[13]

Section 3(b)(1) is self-implementing and no action is required by the company for it to become operative. The principal considerations used to determine whether an issuer is "primarily engaged" in non-investment company business for subsection 3(b) purposes were set out by the

---

10. *See* Richard W. Jennings & Harold Marsh, Jr., Securities Regulation 1362–64 (5th ed. 1982). *See also, e.g.,* First Coastal Corp., 26 Sec. Reg. & L. Rep. (BNA) 1170 (SEC No Action Letter available July 28, 1994) (bank holding company may dissolve and liquidate its assets without registering as an investment company).

11. *See* text accompanying footnotes 23–26 *infra.* Tender offers are discussed in §§ 11.10–11.22 *supra.*

12. 15 U.S.C.A. § 80a–3(b). In 1984, the SEC adopted Rule 3a–5 which exempts from the definition of investment company companies organized with the primary purpose of financing the business operations of their parent companies or other companies controlled by their parent company. 17 C.F.R. § 270.3a–5. *See* Inv. Co. Act Rel. No. IC–14275, [1984–85 Transfer Binder] Fed.Sec.L.Rep. (CCH) ¶ 83,719 (Dec. 14, 1984).

13. 15 U.S.C.A. § 80a–3(b).

SEC in its vintage *Tonopah Mining Co.* decision.[14] In deciding whether
to grant a section 3(b) exemption, the Commission explained that it will
consider "(1) the company's historical development; (2) its public representations of policy; (3) the activities of its officers and directors; and
most important, (4) the nature of its present assets; and (5) the source
of its present income." [15]

Section 3(b)(2)'s exemptions can be implemented only upon application by the issuer and a subsequent order by the Commission.[16] The
exemption has special impact for controlled companies—that is, those
over which the issuer can exert a "controlling influence"—which is
assumed if twenty-five percent or more of the company's outstanding
voting securities are held by the issuer.[17] Such controlled companies
must be involved in a similar type of business as each other, as well as
with the issuer, in order to qualify for a section 3(b)(2)(B) exemption.[18]
There is no requirement of similarity of business for the majority-owned
subsidiaries of the issuer/parent company.[19]

The determination of section 3(b)(2)'s requirement that the issuer
be "primarily engaged" in non-investment company business depends
primarily upon the ratios of investment securities to the issuer's total
assets and of investment securities income to operating revenues of the
issuer. If these two factors point to a majority of a parent company/is-
suer's assets and revenues being dependent upon its investment securities, the company will most probably not receive a section 3(b)(2)
exemption even if the other *Tonopah Mining* factors favor an exemption.[20] Following this rationale, section 3(b)(2) exemptions have been
denied to special situation companies.[21]

Though not as "safe" or reliable as a section 3(b)(2) exemption, an
inadvertent investment company has the alternative of seeking a no-
action letter from the SEC provided that it plans to engage in a good
faith effort to regain its non-investment company status within a six

---

14.   26 S.E.C. 426 (1947).

15.   *Id.* at 427 (discussing section 3(b)(2)).

16.   15 U.S.C.A. § 80a–3(b)(2).

17.   15 U.S.C.A. § 80a–2(a)(9); American Manufacturing Co. Inc., 41 S.E.C. 415 (1963).

18.   The Commission is liberal in finding such similarity of business. Ray Garrett, Jr.,
When Is an Investment Company, 37 U.Det.L.J. 355, 367–68 (1960); Alan Rosenblatt &
Martin E. Lybecker, Some Thoughts on the Federal Securities Laws Regulating External
Management Arrangements and the ALI Federal Securities Code Project, 124 U.Pa.L.Rev.
587, 605 n. 57 (1976).

19.   This approach has been followed to some extent in 17 C.F.R. § 270.3a–1.

20.   *See, e.g.,* Moses v. Black, 1981 WL 1599, [1981 Transfer Binder] Fed.Sec.L.Rep.
(CCH) ¶ 97,866 (S.D.N.Y.1981) (exemption granted where, *inter alia,* "its securities investments were an insignificant part of total assets and its investment revenues minor in
proportion to revenues from operations").

21.   *See, e.g.,* In the Matter of Bankers Security Corp., 15 S.E.C. 695, *affirmed* 146 F.2d
88 (3d Cir.1944). Special situation companies are those with a short term interest in
managing other businesses where there is an investment rather than managerial objective.
See In the Matter of Frobisher, Ltd., 27 S.E.C. 944, 950 (1948); Edmund H. Kerr, The
Inadvertent Investment Company: Section 3(a)(3) of the Investment Company Act, 12
Stan.L.Rev. 29, 47 (1959).

month period.[22] A number of these "transient" investment companies are excluded from sections 3(a)(1) and 3(a)(3) by virtue of Rule 3a–2.[23]

Companies involved in a tender offer may have to pay some attention to the problem of possibly becoming inadvertent investment companies. When a tender offer or other take-over bid attracts more than fifty percent of the target company's stock, the target will be a majority-owned subsidiary of the offeror. In this instance, the securities held by the offeror are no longer investment securities, under the statutory definitions of section 3(a), and the offeror cannot properly be classified as an inadvertent investment company. Tender offers are therefore often conditioned upon the acquisition of fifty percent or more of the target's securities within a specified period of time.[24] However, if the tender offeror acquires less than fifty percent of the target's securities (thereby making the securities held by the offeror investment securities)[25] and the value of investment securities owned by the offeror crosses the forty percent line, the tender offeror will be deemed an investment company. It has been suggested that in the event the tender offeror acquires more than forty percent but nevertheless is unsuccessful in obtaining control of the target company, the tender offeror should have no problem establishing the availability of a section 3(b)(2)(B) exemption due to the fact that it was engaged in non-investment activities and the target would not have been controlled by the offeror prior to the tender offer.[26]

§ 17.5 Regulating the Distribution and Pricing of Investment Company Shares

Open-end and closed-end investment companies[1] are subject to different provisions and regulations of the Investment Company Act regarding both the types of capital structure they may have and the methods they may use for the distribution and pricing of their shares. Nevertheless, there are similarities between the two types of companies. Neither type of investment company may make a public offering of its securities until it has a net worth of at least one hundred thousand dollars.[2] Section 18(i) requires, with some exceptions,[3] that every share

---

22. A no-action letter only reflects the Commission's informal position and thus does not eliminate the "danger" of a shareholder suit for failure to register. R. Jennings & H. Marsh, *supra* footnote 10 at 1362. SEC no action letters are discussed in § 9.5 *supra* and § 9.34 *supra* (Practitioner's Edition only).

23. 17 C.F.R. § 270.3a–2.

24. Kerr & Appelbaum, footnote 1 *supra*, at 895.

25. 15 U.S.C.A. § 80a–3(a).

26. Kerr & Appelbaum, footnote 1 *supra* at 892.

§ 17.5

1. In a closed-end investment company, the issuer puts out a limited number of shares; with an open-end company, additional shares are usually issued to each new investor. In a closed-end company there may or may not be active secondary markets. 15 U.S.C.A. § 80a–5. *See* § 17.3 *supra*.

2. 15 U.S.C.A § 80a–14(a). Rule 14a–3 exempts unit investment trusts from this capitalization requirement if certain preconditions are met, 17 C.F.R. § 270.14a–3.

---

3. See note 3 on page 979.

of stock issued by a registered management company must be voting stock with equal voting rights.[4] Further similarities between open-end and closed-end management/investment companies lie in the Investment Company Act's provisions prohibiting either type of company from issuing warrants or rights for its stock,[5] and the provisions prohibiting the payment of dividends for either type of company from a source other than accumulated undistributed net income unless the dividend is accompanied by a written statement identifying the source.[6] There are, however, significant differences in the regulations applicable to closed-end and open-end investment companies.

Distribution and Pricing of Closed–End Investment Company Shares; Repurchases of Its Own Shares

Closed-end investment companies may issue debt securities and preferred stock; open-end companies may not. Section 18(a) of the Act provides that debt securities must have an asset coverage of three hundred percent and preferred stock must have an asset coverage of two hundred percent.[7] In addition, no more than one class of preferred stock may be issued by a single closed-end company.[8] Section 23(a) of the Act requires that the consideration received by a closed-end company for any stock it issues must be cash or securities, which may include its own securities, "except [shares issued] as a dividend or distribution to its securities holders or in connection with a reorganization."[9] Unlike most corporate enterprises,[10] past services are specifically disallowed as consideration for the issuance of closed-end investment company shares.[11]

The Investment Company Act places restrictions on the initial offering price of investment company shares. A closed-end company may not sell any shares of its common stock at a price below its current net asset value without the consent of a majority of its stockholders, or unless pursuant to a conversion privilege.[12] The stock of closed-end investment companies generally has a market price below net asset value.[13] Section 23(b) thus presents a serious impediment to additional

3. *See* text accompanying footnotes 7–8 *infra*.

4. 15 U.S.C.A. § 80a–18(i). However, in 1993, the Commission proposed a rule that would permit open-end funds to issue multiple classes of stock. Investment Company Act Rel. No. IC–19995 (SEC Dec. 15, 1993).

5. 15 U.S.C.A. § 80a–18(d).

6. 15 U.S.C.A. § 80a–19(a).

7. 15 U.S.C.A. § 80a–18(a). "Asset coverage" is defined in 15 U.S.C.A. § 80a–18(h).

8. 15 U.S.C.A. § 80a–18(c).

9. 15 U.S.C.A. § 80a–23(a).

10. *See generally* 2 James D. Cox, Thomas L. Hazen & F. Hodge O'Neal, Corporations § 16.18 (1995); Harry G. Henn & John Alexander, Laws of Corporations § 167 (3d ed. 1983).

11. 15 U.S.C.A. § 80a–23(a).

12. 15 U.S.C.A. § 80a–23(b). *See* footnote 18 *infra*.

13. Among other things, this reflects the fact that the costs of liquidation will cut into the liquidation value of the assets.

offerings of closed-end investment company shares.[14]

The Investment Company Act also restricts a closed-end company's repurchase of its own shares. A closed-end company may purchase any of its own shares only upon notification to its shareholders of its intention to do so, given within the preceding six months, and in accordance with rules designated by the Commission.[15] Share repurchases may also be made pursuant to tender offers to all holders of the class of securities to be purchased and pursuant to any rules the Commission may promulgate to ensure fairness to all securities holders of the class of shares to be purchased.[16] Rule 23c–1 operates independently of section 23's provisions and allows a closed-end company to purchase its own securities for cash upon either the satisfaction of eleven stated conditions or upon application and Commission permission to do so.[17] Rule 23c–2 permits the redemption of closed-end company shares that are redeemable according to their terms, provided that there is equal treatment of and adequate notice to all shareholders.[18] Rule 23c–3 allows repurchase offers at the net asset value at preestablished periodic intervals or, alternatively, on a discretionary basis not more than once every two years.[19]

Distribution and Pricing of Open–End Investment Company Shares

While the provisions regulating the distribution of the shares of a closed-end investment company are relatively straightforward and have remained stable since the Investment Company Act's passage in 1940, such has not been the case for the provisions dealing with open-end investment companies. The regulation of open-end companies is particularly significant because they have replaced the closed-end company as the dominant investment company form.[20] Section 22 of the Act regulates the distribution of open-end investment company shares. The section's complexity is partially necessitated by the fact that open-end companies are constantly issuing and distributing new shares to balance out the shares redeemed and to satisfy the demand created by new investors. The consideration requirements placed on open-end company shares are the same as those placed on the shares of closed-end companies.[21] No registered investment company may suspend the right of

---

  14. *See* David L. Ratner, Securities Regulation in a Nutshell at 227–230 (3d ed. 1988).

  15. 15 U.S.C.A. § 80a–23(c).

  16. *Id.*

  17. 17 C.F.R. § 270.23c–1.

  18. 17 C.F.R. § 270.23c–2.

  19. *See* Investment Co. Act Rel. No. IC–19399, [1993 Transfer Binder] Fed. Sec. L. Rep. (CCH) ¶ 85,125 (SEC April 7, 1993).

  20. Richard M. Phillips, Deregulation under the Investment Company Act—A Reevaluation of the Corporate Paraphernalia of Shareholder Voting and Boards of Directors, 37 Bus.Law. 903, 905 (1982). *See generally,* James V. Heffernan & James F. Jorden, Section 22(d) of the Investment Company Act of 1940—Its Original Purpose and Present Function, 1973 Duke L.J. 975 (1973); Walter P. North, The Investment Company Amendments Act of 1970, 46 Notre Dame Law. 712 (1971).

  21. 15 U.S.C.A. § 80a–22(g). *See* text accompanying footnotes 9–11 *supra*.

redemption of its securities except under the narrow circumstances delimited in section 22(e) of the Act.[22]   Suspension of redemption rights is permitted only (1) when the New York Stock Exchange is closed or has restricted trading, (2) during an "emergency" rendering redemption "not reasonably practicable," or (3) in accordance with SEC rules.[23]   The Commission has not provided any additional exceptions through its rule making power.

Section 11(a) of the Act prohibits registered open-end companies and underwriters from making exchange offers to investment company shareholders on any basis other than the net asset value unless the exchange is approved by the Commission order or in accordance with applicable SEC rules.[24]   In 1989, the Commission adopted Rule 11a–3 to permit exchange offers to shareholders of different funds in the same group of funds without seeking SEC approval.[25]   Under the rule, the investment company is permitted to charge sales loads, redemption fees, administrative fees, or any combination thereof provided that certain conditions are met.[26]

Section 22(d) of the Investment Company Act requires that the securities of all open-end investment companies be sold "at a current public offering price described in the prospectus," whether to the public directly by the fund or through an underwriter.[27]   Shares are sold at the first price calculated after an order to buy or sell is received.[28]   Also, shares are valued twice daily.[29]   This practice, adopted in 1968, is known as "forward pricing." [30]   Broker-dealers generally contract with underwriters to sell open-end investment company shares to the public.[31]

The uniformity of price requirement imposed by section 22(d) of the Act prevents price competition between dealers selling shares of the

---

22.   15 U.S.C.A. § 80a–22(e).

23.   *Id.*

24.   15 U.S.C.A. § 80a–11(a).

25.   17 C.F.R. § 270.11a–3.   *See* Inv. Co. Act Rel. No. 40–17097, [1989–1990 Transfer Binder] Fed.Sec.L.Rep. ¶ 84,435 (Aug. 3, 1989).

26.   The sales load may be no greater than the sales load in the absence of an exchange offer, deferred sales loads are not permitted, any redemption fee must be applied uniformly to all fund shareholders, the prospectus must disclose any administrative fees and also must disclose if the fund is reserving the right to terminate or alter the terms of the exchange offer, advertising materials must disclose any administrative or redemption fees and must also disclose whether the fund reserves the right to terminate or alter the terms of the exchange offer, and fund shareholders must be given 60 days' notice of the termination of or any material amendment to the terms of the exchange offer.

27.   15 U.S.C.A. § 80a–22(d).   *See* 17 C.F.R. § 270.22d–1 permitting sales of redeemable investment company securities at a sales load.

28.   17 C.F.R. § 270.22c–1.

29.   NASD Rules of Fair Practice, Art. III § 26.   The National Association of Securities Dealers is discussed in § 10.2 *supra.*

30.   *See* Inv.Co.Act Rel. No. 5519 (1968).   For a summary of the "two price system" that forward pricing eliminated *see* United States v. NASD, 422 U.S. 694, 702–709, 95 S.Ct. 2427, 2434–2438, 45 L.Ed.2d 486 (1975).

31.   An underwriter may not underwrite shares not already the subject of a purchase order.   *See* Comment, The Mutual Fund Industry: A Legal Survey, 44 Notre Dame Law. 732, 814 (1969) (discussing NASD Rules of Fair Practice, Art. III § 26(f)(2)).

same fund.[32] Most broker-dealers belong to the National Association of Securities Dealers (NASD).[33] The NASD may prescribe rules for its members regarding the purchase and sale of redeemable securities from investment companies "for the purpose of eliminating or reducing so far as reasonably practicable any dilution of the value of other outstanding securities of such company" or other practice "unfair to holders of such other outstanding securities."[34] The SEC is also empowered to promulgate rules for the sale of mutual fund shares.[35] Broker-dealers belonging to the NASD may elect to follow SEC or NASD rules.[36] In the event of conflicting rules those of the SEC prevail.[37]

The NASD Rules of Fair Practice place a ceiling on the "sales load,"[38] or the sales commission, for transactions in shares of open-end companies that an NASD member may charge to investors.[39] The limits placed on mutual fund sales loads are in sharp contrast to the free competition with regard to brokers' commissions generally.[40] The ceiling on sales loads is in accordance with section 22(b)'s mandate that the price allowed by NASD rules "shall not include an excessive sales load but shall allow for reasonable compensation for sales personnel, broker-dealers, and underwriters and for reasonable sales loads to investors."[41] Under these rules a fund is limited to a maximum sales charge of 7.25 percent, subject to mandatory quantity discounts, unless it offers additional services which in the aggregate carry a maximum additional 1.25

---

32. Heffernan & Jorden, footnote 20 *supra* at 976.

33. *See* § 10.2 *supra* for a description of the role of the NASD in the regulation of broker-dealer activities.

34. 15 U.S.C.A. § 80a–22(a).

35. 15 U.S.C.A. § 80a–22(b)(2).

36. *Id.* Comment, footnote 31 *supra,* at 829. As of December, 1983 all non-exempt broker-dealers must belong to the NASD. *See* § 10.2 *supra.*

37. 15 U.S.C.A. § 80a–22(c).

38. As defined in section 2(a)(35), 15 U.S.C.A. § 80a–2(a)(35).

39. NASD Rules of Fair Practice, Art. III §§ 26 & 29, originally approved by SEC at S.E.C. Securities Exchange Act Rel. No. 11725, 8 S.E.C. Dock. 66 (1975), *reprinted* in NASD Manual (CCH) ¶ 2176.

40. At one time all brokerage commissions were controlled by the stock exchanges. Prior to 1971, the New York Stock Exchange had minimum commission requirements. These no longer exist. Such rules may have constituted illegal price fixing. Thill Securities Corp. v. New York Stock Exchange, 433 F.2d 264 (7th Cir.1970), *cert. denied* 401 U.S. 994, 91 S.Ct. 1232, 28 L.Ed.2d 532 (1971). However, rules relating to commissions that have been reviewed by the SEC do not constitute per se violations of the federal antitrust laws and thus will be upheld if reasonable. *See* Gordon v. New York Stock Exchange, 422 U.S. 659, 95 S.Ct. 2598, 45 L.Ed.2d 463 (1975). *See generally* William F. Baxter, New York Stock Exchange and Fixed Commission Rates: A Private Cartel Goes Public, 22 Stan.L.Rev. 675 (1970); Douglas M. Branson, Securities Regulation After Entering the Competitive Era: The Securities Industry, SEC Policy, and the Individual Investor, 75 Nw.U.L.Rev. 857 (1980); Marianne K. Smythe, Self–Regulation and the Antitrust Laws: Suggestions for an Accommodation, 62 N.C.L.Rev. 475 (1984).

The regulation of mutual funds and the ability to fix prices in the secondary market have been held not to violate the federal antitrust laws. United States v. NASD, 422 U.S. 694, 95 S.Ct. 2427, 45 L.Ed.2d 486 (1975). *See* text accompanying footnotes 58–60 *infra.*

41. 15 U.S.C.A. § 80a–22(b)(1).

percentage point value.[42] Thus, in no event may the sales charge on any transaction exceed 8.5 percent of the offering price. Although this regime would seem to indicate a strict price control system, it is intended to foster "the preconditions necessary for effective price competition" between funds offering different services.[43] "Appropriate qualified exemptions" from these sales load rules are available for smaller companies subject to higher operating costs.[44] In 1985 the SEC relaxed its system of price control when it began to allow investment companies to sell shares under varying sales loads.[45]

Volume discounts on sales loads for large purchases of shares in open-end investment companies are allowed if they are "available to all purchasers on a non-discriminatory basis."[46] The fund may set its own "breakpoint," that is, the purchase quantity required to qualify for the discount; the breakpoint is usually set at an amount between ten and twenty-five thousand dollars.[47] In response to the investment company industry's displeasure with the investor practice of grouping together to qualify for these quantity discounts, the SEC promulgated Rule 22d–1 in 1958.[48] As it currently reads, Rule 22d–1 allows funds the alternative of offering load discounts. Under the rule, underwriters and dealers in open-end investment company shares may offer variations in, and even eliminate, the sales load under certain conditions. The variation or elimination of sales loads can only be instituted if in accordance with a predetermined schedule, according to particular classes of investors or transactions.[49] The scheduled variations in sales loads must be applied uniformly to all offerees in the class specified by the schedule.[50] Existing shareholders and prospective investors must be furnished adequate information concerning the scheduled variations in sales loads; the information must be furnished in accordance with the standards set forth in the applicable registration statement form.[51] Before any scheduled variations in the sales load or changes in the schedule can be implemented, the prospectus must be amended to describe any new variation.[52] Finally, the investment company must advise existing share-

---

42. NASD Rules of Fair Practice, Art. III, § 26(d).

43. Comment, The Distribution of Mutual Fund Shares—Recent Development in S.E.C. Regulation, 1975 Wash.U.L.Q. 1153, 1186–7 (1975).

44. 15 U.S.C.A. § 80a–22(b)(1).

45. 17 C.F.R. § 270.22d–1. The rule does not permit investors to negotiate sales loads even though the SEC originally proposed such an amendment. See Inv.Co.Act Rel. No. IC–14390 [1984–85 Transfer Binder] Fed.Sec.L.Rep. (CCH) ¶ 83,740 (Feb. 27, 1985).

46. Inv.Co.Act Rel. No. 89 (Mar. 13, 1941). See footnote 42 supra.

47. SEC Report of the Division of Investment Management Regulation Mutual Fund Distribution and Section 22(d) of the Investment Company Act of 1940, p. 90 (Aug. 1974).

48. 17 C.F.R. § 270.22d–1. The rule was significantly altered in 1985. For discussion of the earlier version, see Heffernan & Jorden footnote 20 supra, at 995–96.

49. 17 C.F.R. § 270.22d–1.

50. 17 C.F.R. § 270.22d–1(a).

51. 17 C.F.R. § 270.22d–1(b).

52. 17 C.F.R. § 270.22d–1(c).

holders of any new variation in the sales load within one year of the date on which it is first made available to the company.[53]

There are additional guidelines regarding sales loads. The SEC announced that under section 22(d)(ii) of the Act a fund may offer shares to those already holding shares at "a sales load which [is] lower than that imposed on purchases by new shareholders on the theory that repeat investors may not need or receive significant selling services when they purchase additional shares of the same fund."[54] The NASD has taken the position that the sale of open-end investment company shares in dollar amounts minimally below the point at which the sales charge is reduced on quantity transactions in order to permit the dealer to share in the higher sales charges for sales below the breakpoint is contrary to just and equitable principles of trade.[55] The number of funds that have eliminated a sales charge by going no-load increased dramatically during the 1970s and 1980s due to a variety of causes including the complex set of rules governing sales loads, the competition between different funds for new investors, and more lenient rules for mutual funds advertising, allowing more efficient direct distribution of mutual fund shares to the public.[56]

The SEC has indicated that it would permit another new wrinkle in the pricing of investment company shares. The Commission gave tentative approval to allowing mutual fund investors to choose between payment of a front-end sales load or a contingent deferred load designed to cover distribution costs.[57] Under such a plan the investment company offers investors a choice of two classes of stock that are identical except for the sales load provisions.

Secondary Markets for Investment Company Shares

This initial distribution system of mutual fund shares forms the primary market for these shares.[58] The "secondary market" for mutual funds shares refers to the trading of such shares other than through the investment company directly or its underwriter and broker-dealer network. Though still existing, elimination of this market where investors had little protection was among the primary goals of the Congress in enacting the Investment Company Act.[59] The Supreme Court has held that section 22(d) of the Act does not prohibit broker-dealers from

53. 17 C.F.R. § 270.22d–1(d).

54. Sec.Act Rel. No. 33–5985, 1 Fed.Sec.L.Rep. (CCH) ¶ 1466 (Oct. 4, 1978).

55. NASD Manual (CCH) ¶ 5266.

56. 17 C.F.R. § 230.134; James E. Ellis, Going No Load, 6 Sec.Reg.L.J. 357 (1979); NASD Manual (CCH) ¶ 5281. For example, the SEC permits advertising of performance data provided it is presented in accordance with Commission guidelines. 17 C.F.R. §§ 230.482(d), (e), 270.34b–1.

57. *See* SEC May Let Merrill Lynch Fund Offer Choice Between Front–End, Deferred Fees, 20 Sec.Reg.L.Rep. (BNA) 1209 (July 29, 1988).

58. United States v. NASD, 422 U.S. 694, 699, 95 S.Ct. 2427, 2433, 45 L.Ed.2d 486 (1975).

59. *Id.* at 700, 95 S.Ct. at 2433–2434.

matching buy and sell orders of individual investors nor from acting as an agent in the sale of mutual fund shares at any price the investors agree upon.[60] This order matching practice is not subject to section 22(d)'s uniform price requirement because the section speaks only of "dealer transactions," that is, when securities are bought and sold for the agent's own account.[61] When merely acting as a broker for the accounts of others, the broker-dealer is not effecting a transaction for his own account and therefore escapes section 22(d)'s provisions.[62] The Court also dealt with section 22(f)'s provision allowing a mutual fund to restrict the transferability and negotiability of its shares in conformity with legends on the shares themselves, and with the fund's registration statement. SEC rules under section 22(d) allow mutual funds to regulate the secondary market by private contractual agreements between the funds, the NASD, and brokers, dealers and underwriters as well as by the terms of the funds' registration statements.[63] The SEC had held that this private method of regulating the secondary market was preferable to the promulgating of further administrative rules in the area.[64] The Supreme Court held these arrangements to be immunized from illegality under the Sherman Antitrust Act[65] due to the broad regulatory powers over mutual fund shares granted by Congress to the SEC in section 22(f) of the Investment Company Act.[66] The importance of this aspect of the decision is minimal due to the relatively insignificant size of the secondary mutual fund market of open-end companies today.

§ 17.6 Fiduciary Duties; Independent Investment Company Directors

Unlike the 1933 and 1934 securities acts, the Investment Company Act of 1940 imposes substantive rules upon an issuer's internal governance structure. This represents a significant departure from the general thrust of most federal securities laws and regulations, which is to eschew direct involvement in the corporate chartering process.[1] For example, the Securities Exchange Act of 1934 protects shareholder

---

60. *Id.* at 711–19, 95 S.Ct. at 2438–2443.

61. As defined in 15 U.S.C.A. § 80a–2(a)(11).

62. As defined in 15 U.S.C.A. § 80a–2(a)(6). *See* 422 U.S. at 713, 95 S.Ct. at 2439–2440.

63. 422 U.S. at 720–28, 95 S.Ct. at 2443–2447.

64. *Id.*

65. 15 U.S.C.A. § 1.

66. 422 U.S. at 729–30, 95 S.Ct. at 2447–2448. *See* footnote 40 *supra*.

§ 17.6

1. *See* Thomas L. Hazen, Corporate Chartering and the Securities Markets: Shareholder Suffrage, Corporate Responsibility and Managerial Accountability, 1978 Wis.L.Rev. 391. *See generally* Meyer Eisenberg & Dennis I. Lehr, An Aspect of the "Emerging Federal Corporation Law": Directorial Responsibility Under the Investment Company Act of 1940, 20 Rutg.L.Rev. 181 (1966); Meyer Eisenberg & Richard M. Phillips, Mutual Fund Litigation—New Frontiers for the Investment Company Act, 62 Colum.L.Rev. 73 (1962); Nathan D. Lobell, Rights and Responsibilities in the Mutual Fund, 70 Yale L.J. 1258 (1961); Leland E. Modesitt, Mutual Fund—A Corporate Anomaly, 14 U.C.L.A.L.Rev. 1252 (1967).

interests by requiring full disclosure and regulating proxy machinery in shareholder votes. These shareholder voting safeguards alone are considered inadequate methods of protecting investment company shareholders, due both to the nature of investment company activity and the fluctuations in the number of shares owned by any single shareholder as a result of dividend payments or daily cash needs.[2] Accordingly, there are additional duties imposed upon investment company directors by federal regulation under the 1940 Act.[3]

The totality of investment company directors' duties is imposed by state corporate law, state blue sky laws, common law, and the Investment Company Act.[4] Directors who are engaged in fraudulent practices may also be subject to liability for violations of Exchange Act Rule 10b–5.[5] The Investment Company Act thus supplements federal and state regulation applicable to management generally.

Composition of the Board of Directors

Independent directors serve primarily as "watchdogs" over an investment company to protect the interests of shareholders against abuses by investment advisers and others in a position to profit illegally from the company.[6] Section 10(a) of the Investment Company Act ensures some degree of management independence by requiring registered investment companies' boards of directors to be comprised of at least forty percent disinterested persons.[7] "Interested persons" are defined to

---

2. One example of the substantive protection is the antipyramiding rule of section 12(d)(1) 15 U.S.C.A. § 80a–12(d)(1) which is discussed in § 17.1 *supra*. With regard to the investment company shareholder rights *see generally* Burks v. Lasker, 441 U.S. 471, 482–85, 99 S.Ct. 1831, 1839–1841, 60 L.Ed.2d 404 (1979); John C. Coffee, Jr. & Donald E. Schwartz, The Survival of the Derivative Suit: An Evaluation and a Proposal for Legislative Reform, 81 Colum.L.Rev. 261, 288 (1981); Richard M. Phillips, Deregulation under the Investment Company Act—Reevaluation of the Corporate Paraphernalia of Shareholder Voting and Boards of Directors, 37 Bus.Law. 903 (1982).

3. *See* James M. Anderson, Rights and Obligations in the Mutual Fund: A Source of Law, 20 Vand.L.Rev. 1120 (1967); David M. Butowsky, Fiduciary Standards of Conduct Revisited—*Moses v. Burgin* & *Rosenfeld v. Black*, 17 N.Y.L.F. 735 (1971); Lawrence M. Greene, Fiduciary Standards of Conduct Under the Investment Company Act of 1940, 28 Geo.Wash.L.Rev. 266 (1959); Alfred Jaretstzki, Jr., Duties and Responsibilities of Directors of Mutual Funds, 29 Law & Contemp.Probl. 777 (1964); Joseph F. Krupsky, The Role of Investment Company Directors, 32 Bus.Law. 1733 (1977); Nathan D. Lobell, *supra* note 1; Robert H. Mundheim, Some Thoughts on the Duties and Responsibilities of Unaffiliated Directors of Mutual Funds, 115 U.Pa.L.Rev. 1058 (1967); William J. Nutt, A Study of Mutual Fund Independent Directors, 120 U.Pa.L.Rev. 179 (1979); Clarke Randall, Fiduciary Duties of Investment Company Directors and Management Companies Under the Investment Company Act of 1940, 31 Okla.L.Rev. 365 (1978); Note, Fiduciary Obligations of Mutual Fund Managers in Portfolio Transactions, 22 Syr.L.Rev. 1107 (1971); Annot., Duty of Investment Adviser and Interested Directors of Mutual Fund, Under Section 36 of the Investment Company Act of 1940 as Amended (15 U.S.C.A. § 80a–35) With Respect to Recapture of Portfolio Brokerage Commissions, 47 A.L.R.Fed. 607 (1980); Comment, Duties of Independent Directors of Open-end Mutual Funds, 70 Mich.L.Rev. 696 (1972).

4. *See* text accompanying footnotes 19–26 *infra*. Blue sky laws are considered in chapter 8 *supra*.

5. 17 C.F.R. § 240.10b–5. *See* §§ 13.2–13.11 *supra*.

6. S.Rep.No. 184, 91st Cong., 1st Sess. 32 (1969).

7. 15 U.S.C.A. § 80a–10(a). Prior to 1970 this section required that no more than 60 percent of the directors be "affiliated" with the investment company. The present more

include: (1) any affiliated person of the investment company; (2) the immediate family members of an affiliated natural person; (3) any person interested in the investment company's investment adviser or principal underwriter; (4) anyone who has acted as the investment company's legal counsel within the past two years; (5) certain brokers or dealers registered under the Securities Exchange Act who have a relationship to the investment company, or any affiliate thereof;[8] and (6) any person the Commission deems to be interested due to a material or professional relationship with the investment company within the previous two years.[9] An "affiliated person" is any person owning or holding with voting power five percent or more of the company's outstanding voting securities; any company of whose outstanding voting securities the investment company owns five percent or more; any person controlled by the investment company; any officer, director, partner, copartner, or employee of the investment company; and any investment adviser or member of the advisory board of the investment company.[10] Membership on the board of directors of an investment company or ownership of less than five percent of the investment company securities does not in and of itself constitute grounds to classify a person as "interested."[11] In the case of no-load mutual funds only one member of the board need be a disinterested person with regard to the investment adviser.[12]

The SEC eased some of its limits on who qualifies as a disinterested director by including persons affiliated with a qualifying broker-dealer as disinterested directors. A person affiliated with a broker-dealer can qualify as an independent director if (1) the investment company did no portfolio or distribution activities through the broker-dealer for six months and such absence of business continues, (2) the board of directors determines that neither the investment company nor its shareholders will be adversely affected by not conducting business with the broker-dealer, and (3) only a minority of the investment company

---

stringent requirements of independence are the result of great dissatisfaction with the older standards. *See generally* Gerard H. Manges, The Investment Company Amendments Act of 1970—An Analysis and Appraisal After Two Years, 14 B.C. Ind. & Comm.L.Rev. 387 (1973); Gerard Manges, The Investment Company Amendments Act of 1970, 26 Bus.Law. 1311 (1971); Walter P. North, The Investment Company Amendments Act of 1970, 46 Notre Dame Law. 712 (1971).

8. *See* 17 C.F.R. § 270.2a19–1.

9. 15 U.S.C.A. § 80a–2(a)(19)(A)(i)–(vi).

10. 15 U.S.C.A. § 80a–2(a)(3). In 1993, the Commission adopted a rule which provides that when an investment company is set up as a limited partnership, limited partners will not be considered "affiliated persons" *solely* because of their limited partnership interests. Rule 2a3–1, 17 C.F.R. § 270.2a3–1.

11. 15 U.S.C.A. § 80a–2(a)(19).

12. 15 U.S.C.A. § 80a–10(d)(3). "No load" mutual funds are those where neither the investor's purchase nor sale price includes a charge for sales and promotional activities or administrative fees. *See* 15 U.S.C.A. § 80a–2(a)(35). *See generally* James H. Ellis, Going No Load, 6 Sec.Reg.L.J. 357 (1979).

directors are affiliated with broker-dealers.[13]

There are further requirements relating to investment company director qualifications. Section 9 of the Investment Company Act[14] prohibits persons convicted of felonies or misdemeanors arising from securities transactions within the past ten years or anyone temporarily or permanently enjoined from effecting securities transactions from serving as an officer, director, employee, investment adviser, or member of an advisory board of an investment company. There are yet additional provisions regarding the election of investment company directors designed "to prevent a change in control [of the investment company] by a seriatim resignation of the board of directors and the election by the board of a new member to fill each place as it is vacated."[15] Section 16(a) provides generally that directors must be elected by shareholders of the investment company except that vacancies may be filled in any other manner,[16] so long as at least two-thirds of the board at any time is comprised of directors who were duly elected by the shareholders.[17] An investment company may create classes of directors, but no class may be elected for less than one year or more than five years and the term of office of one class must expire each year.[18]

Duties of Investment Company Directors

As in the case of any corporation, the board of directors is responsible for overseeing the investment company's general management.[19] The Act does not impose strict liability upon directors, so long as the

---

13. 17 C.F.R. § 270.2a19–1. *See* Inv. Co. Act Rel. No. 14193 [1984 Transfer Binder] Fed.Sec.L.Rep. (CCH) ¶ 83,667 (Oct. 12, 1984). The rule is set forth in footnote 8 *supra*. Also, 17 C.F.R. § 270.10b–1 defines "regular broker or dealer" as one that during the investment company's past fiscal year was among the top ten in terms of commissions, portfolio transactions, or sales of investment company shares.

14. 15 U.S.C.A. § 80a–9.

15. Richard W. Jennings & Harold Marsh, Jr., Securities Regulation: Cases and Materials 1412 (5th ed. 1982), discussing 15 U.S.C.A. § 80a–16(a).

16. State law generally permits directors to fill vacancies if the articles of incorporation so provide. *See* 1 James D. Cox, Thomas L. Hazen & F. Hodge O'Neal, Corporations, ch. 9 (1995); Harry G. Henn & John R. Alexander, Laws of Corporations, 557 (3d ed. 1983).

17. 15 U.S.C.A. § 80a–16(a).

18. *Id.*

19. SEC, Institutional Investor Study Report, H.R. Doc. No. 64, Vol. 2, 92d Cong. 1st Sess. 214 (1971); Joseph F. Krupsky, The Role of Investment Company Directors, 32 Bus.Law. 1733, 1740 (1977).

For the roles and responsibilities of corporate directors generally, *see* 2 James D. Cox, Thomas L. Hazen & F. Hodge O'Neal, Corporations, chs. 10, 11 (1995); Harry G. Henn & John R. Alexander, Laws of Corporations §§ 207, 232–38 (3d ed. 1983); Alfred G. Conard, A Behavioral Analysis of Directors' Liability for Negligence, 1972 Duke L.J. 895; Carlos L. Israels, Are Corporate Powers Held in Trust?, 64 Colum.L.Rev. 1446 (1964); Stanley A. Kaplan, The Fiduciary Responsibility in the Management of the Corporation, 31 Bus.Law. 883 (1976); Harold Marsh, Jr., Are Directors Trustees? –Conflict of Interest and Corporate Morality, 22 Bus.Law. 35 (1966). *See also, e.g.,* Adolf A. Berle, Corporate Power as Powers in Trust, 44 Harv.L.Rev. 1049 (1931); E. Merrick Dodd, Jr., For Whom Are Corporate Managers Trustees?, 45 Harv.L.Rev. 1049 (1931).

fiduciary duties imposed upon them by section 36(a)[20] have been fulfilled.[21]

It has been held that section 1(b) of the Act[22] codified the common law duties and obligations of corporate directors generally and applies them to investment company directors.[23] In Burks v. Lasker[24] the Supreme Court expressly noted that the Investment Company Act was not intended to supplant the "entire corpus of state corporation law" even where a plaintiff's cause of action arises solely out of Investment Company Act provisions.[25] *Burks* concerned the ability of investment company directors acting upon independent advice to terminate shareholder derivative suits. The Court reversed the overturning of the board action and stated that federal courts "should apply state law governing the authority of independent directors to discontinue derivative suits to the extent such law is consistent with the policies of the Investment Company Act and the Investment Advisers Act."[26]

Approval of the Advisory Contract

Some state courts have given undue deference to the decisions of unaffiliated boards of directors renewing advisory contracts.[27] To counteract this undue deference and potential for self-dealing, section 36(b) was added in 1970 to provide that investment advisers are also subject to

20. 15 U.S.C.A. § 80a–35(a); Brouk v. Managed Funds, Inc., 286 F.2d 901, 918 (8th Cir.1961), *judgment vacated* 369 U.S. 424, 82 S.Ct. 878, 8 L.Ed.2d 6 (1962).

21. *See, e.g.,* Moses v. Burgin, 445 F.2d 369 (1st Cir.1971), *cert. denied* 404 U.S. 994, 92 S.Ct. 532, 30 L.Ed.2d 547 (1971); Fogel v. Chestnutt, 533 F.2d 731 (2d Cir.1975), *cert. denied* 429 U.S. 824, 97 S.Ct. 77, 50 L.Ed.2d 86 (1976); Tannenbaum v. Zeller, 552 F.2d 402 (2d Cir.1977).

22. 15 U.S.C.A. § 80a–1(b).

23. Aldred Investment Trust v. SEC, 151 F.2d 254, 260 (1st Cir.1945), *cert. denied* 326 U.S. 795, 66 S.Ct. 486, 90 L.Ed. 483 (1946). The section does not provide a separate cause of action, however. *See* § 17.10 *infra.* For discussions of corporate directors' duties under the common law *see generally* Harold Marsh, Jr., Are Directors Trustees? Conflict of Interests and Corporate Morality, 22 Bus.Law. 35 (1966).

24. 441 U.S. 471, 99 S.Ct. 1831, 60 L.Ed.2d 404 (1979).

25. *Id.* at 478, 99 S.Ct. at 1837.

26. *Id.* at 486, 99 S.Ct. at 1841. This has been a hotly disputed issue and continues to generate much comment. *See generally* Coffee & Schwartz, *supra* footnote 2; Richard M. Buxbaum, Conflict of Interests Statutes and the Need for a Demand on Directors in Derivative Actions, 68 Calif.L.Rev. 1122 (1980); George W. Dent, Jr., The Power of Directors to Terminate Shareholder Litigation: The Death of the Derivative Suit?, 75 Nw.U.L.Rev. 96 (1980).

The Court has also held that demand on directors is not necessary in an action under section 36(b) of the Act, complaining of excessive advisory fees. Daily Income Fund, Inc. v. Fox, 464 U.S. 523, 104 S.Ct. 831, 78 L.Ed.2d 645 (1984).

However, in a more recent ruling, the Court held that in a derivative suit involving a registered investment company, a federal court must apply the demand futility exception to any demand requirement as that exception is defined by the law of the state of incorporation. Kamen v. Kemper Financial Services, Inc., 500 U.S. 90, 111 S.Ct. 1711, 114 L.Ed.2d 152 (1991).

27. *See, e.g.,* Saxe v. Brady, 40 Del.Ch. 474, 184 A.2d 602 (1962).

a fiduciary duty to the investment company.[28] This is supplemented by section 15(c)'s requirement that the investment adviser provide the information requested by the board of directors that is reasonably necessary to evaluate the adviser's performance.[29] The investment company's board has a statutory duty to request this information and consider it in its deliberations of whether to renew the advisory contract.[30] The Investment Company Act further requires that for renewal of the advisory contract a majority of the disinterested directors must approve the renewal in person at a special meeting called for that express purpose.[31] This approval is in addition to the majority shareholder consent that is required for the initial advisory contract or for a change in investment advisers.[32]

Investment company directorial responsibility does not diminish with a delegation of authority to an investment adviser.[33] The investment adviser's "contractual authority to direct the functions and activities of the investment company to the extent of portfolio selection," [34] the restrictions placed upon investment company activity by section 12,[35] and the requirement of shareholder approval for changes in investment policy,[36] all combine to impose upon investment company directors a duty to continually oversee the adviser's portfolio supervision throughout the year.[37] This obligation supplements the directors' duty to reconsider and reevaluate annually investment advisory contracts that continue in effect for more than two years from the making and

28. Investment Company Amendment Act, Pub.L. No. 91–547, 84 Stat. 1413 (1970); 15 U.S.C.A. § 80a–35(b). *See* § 17.10 *infra.* *See generally* the authorities cited in footnote 7 *supra.*

29. 15 U.S.C.A. § 80a–15(c).

30. *Id.*

31. *Id.*

32. 15 U.S.C.A. § 80a–15(a). Problems associated with changes in the investment adviser are discussed in § 17.9 *infra.*

33. *See* 15 U.S.C.A. § 80a–15.

34. Krupsky, *supra* footnote 19 at 1748.

35. Section 12 places numerous limitations on investment company activities. An investment company may not: purchase securities on margin; participate in joint trading accounts; effect a short sale of any security; distribute its own securities except through an underwriter; commit to underwrite securities of other issuers if its holdings therein exceed certain percentages; own more than three percent of any other investment company's securities; own securities of another single investment company the assets of which exceed five percent of the investment company's assets; own securities of other investment companies valued in the aggregate over one hundred percent of its total assets; acquire insurance company securities, save as enumerated; or purchase securities issued by its brokers, dealers, underwriters, or investment advisers. All of these are subject to numerous exceptions. 15 U.S.C.A. § 80a–12(a)–(d).

36. 15 U.S.C.A. § 80a–13.

37. Krupsky, *supra* footnote 19 at 1748; Michael J. Radmer, Duties of Directors of Investment Companies, 3 J.Corp.L. 61, 71 (1977); Comment, Duties of the Independent Director in Open–End Mutual Funds, 70 Mich.L.Rev. 696, 713 (1972). It is the rare case to hold directors liable for failure to take action in regard to an adviser's fiduciary breach, *id.* at 708. *See, e.g.,* Lutz v. Boas, 39 Del.Ch. 585, 171 A.2d 381 (1961). *See also* the authorities cited in footnotes 1, 3 *supra.*

execution of the advisory contract.[38] A "heavy duty of disclosure is imposed upon management in order to permit the directors to exercise informed discretion [in performing their duties]" since directors are not full-time employees and therefore probably not attuned to possible problems in the fund's day-to-day operation.[39]

In most instances, directors are entitled to rely upon the assertions and representations of management; however, there is an implied duty to make further inquiries when a director is alerted to, or charged with constructive knowledge of, a potential conflict of interest problem between advisers and fund shareholders.[40] Conflict-of-interest problems most frequently occur when a major reason to increase the size of the fund is to increase the fee paid to the adviser rather than the earning power of the fund.[41] The Supreme Court in *Burks* commented: "Congress consciously chose to address the conflict-of-interest problem through the Act's independent-directors section, rather than through more drastic remedies such as complete disaffiliation of the companies from their advisers or compulsory internalization of the management function." [42] Conflict-of-interest problems also arise in the affiliation of inside directors with the investment adviser; such a relationship creates a duty of disclosure to facilitate evaluation of their ability to serve as investment company directors.[43]

The actual protection afforded public shareholder interests by disinterested director requirements and shareholder voting in adopting the original advisory contract is questionable since the adviser controls the initial voting securities after it creates the fund.[44] Even with the expansion of investment company shareholders the investment adviser continues to effectively control the company's proxy machinery. Voting rights as a protection of shareholder interests are therefore minimal and the independent director emerges as the shareholders' only unbiased advocate.[45]

---

38. 15 U.S.C.A. § 80a–15(a).

39. Clarke Randall, Fiduciary Duties of Investment Company Directors and Management Companies Under the Investment Company Act of 1940, 31 Okla.L.Rev. 635, 668 (1978) (discussing Moses v. Burgin, 445 F.2d 369 (1st Cir.), *cert. denied* 404 U.S. 994, 92 S.Ct. 532, 30 L.Ed.2d 547 (1971)).

40. Randall, *supra* footnote 39 at 670. "The judiciary, as did Congress, views the independent director as the panacea for many of the conflict-of-interest problems inherent in the industry structure, provided the directors are possessed of sufficient information to enable them to make sound decisions in the best interests of fund shareholders." *Id.*

41. *Id. See also* Marsh, *supra* footnote 23.

42. 441 U.S. at 483, 99 S.Ct. at 1839–1840.

43. Krupsky, *supra* footnote 19 at 1748.

44. Comment, *supra* footnote 37 at 699; Krupsky, footnote 19 *supra* at 1743.

45. Richard M. Phillips, Deregulation Under the Investment Company Act—Reevaluation of the Corporate Paraphernalia of Shareholder Voting and Boards of Directors, 37 Bus.Law. 903, 909 (1982). "Indeed there is no reported instance of successful shareholder opposition to any management proposal for advisory contracts, change in investment policies, or selection of public accountants—the very items for which the act expressly requires shareholder approval." *Id.*

Factors to be considered by an investment company's board of directors in evaluating an advisory contract's fairness include:

(1) the costs of comparable services;

(2) a comparison of total fund expenses as a percentage of fund assets;

(3) the reduction of advisory fees to reflect economies of scale, i.e. the fact that it does not require ten times the effort by the adviser to manage a fund of ten million dollars rather than one of one million dollars;

(4) the expenses and profits of the adviser;

(5) the quality of the investment advice received, thought by some to be the most important criterion to be evaluated by the board;[46]

(6) the quality of other services performed by the adviser for the company;

(7) a consideration of the cost and the feasibility of internalizing management; and

(8) the basis of the fee arrangement.[47]

An investment company rarely has the option of terminating an advisory contract due to its inability to internalize management and further due to the financial disturbance which would be suffered by the fund with a change of investment adviser.[48] Indeed, a change of advisers may frustrate shareholder expectations since most shareholders decide to invest in a company based on the reputation of the adviser.[49] Therefore, the mandatory reporting of all investment adviser activity affecting the company's performance to the board of directors is the most efficacious method of keeping adviser activity honest and aboveboard. The investment company board of directors' decision to renew an advisory contract is given only as much weight as a court deems appropriate in an action against an adviser for breach of fiduciary duty.[50]

Other Board Obligations

The selection and supervision of an investment adviser is not the only function of the investment company's board of directors. Investment company directors must also choose an independent accountant for the fund—a choice which must be ratified by a majority of shareholders.[51] The independent accountants aid the investment company di-

---

46. *See, e.g.*, Robert H. Mundheim, Some Thoughts on the Duties and Responsibilities of Unaffiliated Directors of Mutual Funds, 115 U.Pa.L.Rev. 1058, 1065 (1967).

47. *See* Radmer, *supra* footnote 37 at 71–81.

48. Krupsky, *supra* footnote 19 at 1749–51.

49. SEC, Public Policy Implications of Investment Company Growth, H.R. Rep. No. 2337, 89th Cong.2d Sess. 31 (1966).

50. 15 U.S.C.A. § 80a–35(b)(2).

51. 15 U.S.C.A. § 80a–31.

rectors in discharging their duty to evaluate portfolio securities where market quotations are not readily available since accountants presumably have more expertise to make such evaluations.[52] The choice of accountant is also important since it is the accountant who is required to report "inadequacies in the fund's accounting system and system of internal accounting control, along with an indication of any corrective action taken or proposed" in Form N–IR that is required under section 30 of the Investment Company Act.[53] Accountants therefore act as watchdogs for the watchdogs. Directors must also choose the investment company's attorney, although there are no statutory provisions for that procedure.

Investment company directors must ensure that the reports required by the various securities laws and SEC regulations are filed in a timely and accurate fashion. Directors of investment companies have a duty to fill board vacancies created by death or resignation prior to the expiration of a director's term.[54] However, at least two-thirds of the directors of an investment company must have been elected by the shareholders.[55] Directors are also responsible for assuring that proper proxy solicitation materials are submitted to the shareholders and the SEC, although this obligation is often satisfied by the investment adviser. Directors must also ensure that dividends are paid correctly and that conditions for maintaining Subchapter M tax treatment[56] are met. In sum, investment company directors are subjected to all common law directoral duties and a host of others by the Investment Company Act. As a means of implementing the additional duties imposed by the Act, a private cause of action will lie for breach of a director's fiduciary duty.[57]

§ 17.7 Transactions Between an Investment Company and Affiliated Persons

Section 17 of the Investment Company Act[1] regulates the activities of those who, due to their connection with an investment company, stand to gain personally from the manipulation of the company's investments, perhaps to the detriment of shareholders. Section 17(a) thus protects "minority interests from exploitation by insiders of *their* 'strategic position' "[2] and assures that interested persons deal with the investment company "at arm's length in an endeavor to secure the best

---

52. 15 U.S.C.A. § 80a–2(a)(41).

53. Radmer, *supra* footnote 37 at 84.

54. 15 U.S.C.A. § 80a–15.

55. 15 U.S.C.A. § 80a–16(a). *See* footnotes 16–18 *supra* and accompanying text.

56. 26 U.S.C.A. §§ 851–55.

57. 15 U.S.C.A. § 80a–35(b). *See* § 17.10 *infra.*

§ 17.7

1. 15 U.S.C.A. § 80a–17. *See* Note, The Application of Section 17 of The Investment Company Act of 1940 to Portfolio Affiliates, 120 U.Pa.L.Rev. 983 (1972).

2. E.I. du Pont de Nemours & Co. v. Collins, 432 U.S. 46, 60 n. 6, 97 S.Ct. 2229, 2237 n. 6, 53 L.Ed.2d 100 (1977) (Brennan, J., dissenting), quoting SEC Report on Investment Trusts and Investment Companies, H.R. Doc. No. 279, 76th Cong., 1st Sess., 1414 (1940).

possible bargain for their respective stockholders."[3] "Affiliated person" is defined in section 2(a)(3).[4] Briefly stated, the statutory definition includes persons controlling, controlled by or in common control with the investment company.[5]

Section 17 of the Act contains numerous provisions regulating the conduct of interested persons. Subsections (e) through (j) are relatively straightforward in protecting shareholders on a basic level against such things as theft of securities. In contrast, subsections (a) through (d) regulate more complex transactions between affiliated persons and the investment company. Subsection (e) prohibits affiliated persons acting as agents from accepting payment for transactions in securities or other property by an investment company except as regular salary or commission in the course of its business as an underwriter or a broker.[6] Such fees may not exceed "the usual and customary broker's commission".[7] Because of the potential conflict of interest, the prohibitions of section 17(e) should be broadly construed.[8] Thus, for example, a portfolio manager was appropriately convicted of a section 17(e) violation when she accepted the opportunity to purchase warrants from a company the securities of which she had purchased for the pension plans she managed.[9] The conviction was upheld without proof that the warrants were purchased at a discount since the jury could reasonably have concluded that the opportunity to purchase the warrants was itself a benefit.[10]

Section 17(f)[11] of the Investment Company Act requires that securities owned by investment companies be placed in a bank, with a member of a national securities exchange (as defined in the Securities Exchange Act of 1934[12]), or with the investment company. Securities may also be

3. *Id.* *See also, e.g.,* In the Matter of Strong/Corneliuson Capital Management, Inc., [1994–1995 Transfer Binder] Fed. Sec. L. rep. (CCG) ¶ 85,416 (SEC 1994) (mutual funds violated section 17(a) in series of transactions with other funds managed by the same investment adviser).

4. 15 U.S.C.A. § 80a–2(a)(3).

5. *Id. See also* § 17.6 *supra.*

6. 15 U.S.C.A. § 80a–17(e)(1). *See* Annot., When is Affiliated Person of Registered Investment Company "Acting as Agent" Within Meaning of § 17(e)(1) of Investment Company Act of 1940 (15 U.S.C.A. § 80a–17(e)(1)), Prohibiting Such Person From Accepting Compensation From Any Other Source for Purchase or Sale of Property to or for Company, 62 A.L.R.Fed. 575 (1983).

7. 15 U.S.C.A. § 80a–17(e)(2).

8. *But cf.* Paine/Webber Managed Investments Trusts, 26 Sec. Reg. & L. Rep. (BNA) 1168 (SEC No Action Letter available Aug. 8, 1994) (permitting sales of illiquid securities to an affiliated person; the staff response agreed that in light of the unusual nature of the transaction and representations as to the value of the securities, the protections of the Act did not require invocation of the prohibition).

9. United States v. Ostrander, 999 F.2d 27 (2d Cir.1993).

10. *Id.*

11. 15 U.S.C.A. § 80a–17(f).

12. Section 6, 15 U.S.C.A. § 78f. There are currently nine active national exchanges: the New York Stock Exchange, the American Stock Exchange, the Boston Stock Exchange, the Philadelphia Stock Exchange, the Midwest Stock Exchange, the Chicago Board Options Exchange, the Pacific Stock Exchange, the Intermountain Stock Exchange, and the Cincinnati Stock Exchange. *See* §§ 10.1, 10.2 *supra.*

deposited in a central handling system established by any registered securities exchange.[13] No investment company may act as custodian of its own securities except pursuant to Rule 17f–2.[14] Rule 17f–2 requires the securities to be physically separated at all times from those of any other person,[15] unless the securities are serving as collateral for a loan.[16] There are further restrictions under Investment Company Act Rule 17f–2. Access to the securities is through resolution of the board of directors only; a maximum of five persons may be designated for access by each resolution and each must be an officer or "responsible employee" of the investment company.[17] An investment company officer must be present when access to the securities is permitted.[18] Additional precautionary measures against larceny and embezzlement appear in section 17(g)'s bonding requirements for those with access to the investment company's securities.[19] The minimum permissible bond varies with the investment company's gross assets.[20]

Section 17(h) prohibits certain types of indemnification agreements. An investment company's charter, certificate of incorporation, articles of association, indenture of trust, or by-laws cannot indemnify or otherwise protect a director or officer against liability for "willful misfeasance, bad faith, gross negligence or reckless disregard of the duties involved in the conduct of his office." [21] Section 17(i) similarly prohibits any investment adviser or principal underwriter from contracting away its liability.[22] Prior to 1987, sections 17(h) and 17(i) both provided that if such clauses do appear in the specified documents, a written waiver of the indemnification clause in the document will preclude violation of these subsections of the Act.[23] However, those provisions have since been repealed.

Section 17(j) of the Investment Company Act[24] parallels section 10(b) of the Securities Exchange Act[25] as the general antifraud provision applicable to affiliated persons. Enacted in 1970, section 17(j) is directed

---

13. 17 C.F.R. § 270.17f–4 (1982). *See* § 10.13 *supra.*

14. 17 C.F.R. § 270.17f–2.

15. 17 C.F.R. § 270.17f–2(b).

16. 17 C.F.R. § 270.17f–2(c).

17. 17 C.F.R. § 270.17f–2(d). Certain bank officers and employees and independent public accountants may also have access to the securities jointly with the investment company officers, *id.*

18. *Id.*

19. 15 U.S.C.A. § 80a–17(g).

20. 17 C.F.R. § 270.17g–1(d)(1).

21. 15 U.S.C.A. § 80a–17(h). *Compare* the SEC's approach to indemnification in connection with 1933 Act registration statements. *See* § 7.9 *supra.*

22. 15 U.S.C.A. § 80a–17(i).

23. 15 U.S.C.A. § 80a–17(h), (i) (repealed).

24. 15 U.S.C.A. § 80a–17(j).

25. 15 U.S.C.A. § 78j(b); 17 C.F.R. § 240.10b–5. *See,* §§ 12.1, 13.2–13.11 *supra.*

at insider trading for the insider's personal account in the investment company's portfolio securities.[26] Rule 17j–1[27] is the Investment Company Act's counterpart to Rule 10b–5 in prohibiting material misrepresentation and fraudulent practices. Rule 17j–1 also requires each investment company to adopt a written code of ethics to be followed by each of the company's "access persons."[28] The term "access persons" is defined broadly in the rule to include persons who render investment advice. Specifically it includes: (1) any director, officer, general partner, or "advisory person"[29] of an investment company or its investment adviser "primarily engaged" in advising investment companies or investment clients,[30] (2) any director, officer, or general partner of a principal underwriter who makes, participates in, or obtains information regarding the sale of securities for the investment company as part of his or her ordinary course of business, and (3) any director, officer, general partner or advisory person of an investment adviser "primarily engaged in a business or businesses other than advising registered investment companies or other advisory clients," who makes recommendations, or participates in the determination of which recommendation to make to the investment company.[31] Also included in the definition of "access persons" are those individuals or entities who obtain information concerning securities recommendations being made by the investment adviser to the investment company.[32]

It remains to be seen whether section 17(j) and Rule 17j–1 will have as far-reaching an effect on Investment Company Act litigation as section 10(b) and Rule 10b–5 have had on other securities litigation.[33] The evidence to date is that it will not. In addition to the question of the exact parameters of what constitutes a substantive violation, it has

26. 1970 U.S.Code Cong. and Adm.News 4897, 4923. *See generally* Gerard H. Manges, The Investment Company Amendments Act of 1970–An Analysis and Appraisal After Two Years, 14 B.C. Ind. & Comm.L.Rev. 387 (1973); Gerard Manges, The Investment Company Amendments Act of 1970, 26 Bus.Law. 1311 (1971); Walter P. North, The Investment Company Amendments Act of 1970, 46 Notre Dame Law. 712 (1971).

27. 17 C.F.R. § 270.17j–1. *See* Inv. Co. Act Rel. No. 11421, [1980 Transfer Binder] Fed.Sec. L.Rep. (CCH) ¶ 82,679 (Oct. 31, 1980).

28. 17 C.F.R. § 270.17j–1(b). *See, e.g.,* United States v. Ostrander, 999 F.2d 27 (2d Cir.1993) (upholding conviction of portfolio manager for failing to report personal securities transactions, it mattered not that the investment adviser did not hold any interest in the securities so acquired).

29. As defined in 17 C.F.R. § 270.17j–1(e)(2).

30. An investment adviser is "primarily engaged in a business or businesses other than advising registered investment companies or other advisory clients" when, for each of its most recent three fiscal years or for the period of time since its organization, whichever is lesser, the investment adviser derived, on an unconsolidated basis, more than 50 percent of (A) its total sales and revenues, and (B) its income (or loss) before income taxes and extraordinary items from such other business or businesses. 17 C.F.R. § 270.17j–1(e)(1)(iv).

31. 17 C.F.R. § 270.17j–1(e)(1)(i)–(iii).

32. *Id.*

33. Rule 10b–5 is discussed in §§ 13.2–13.12 *supra.*

yet to be decided whether an implied remedy exists under Rule 17j–1.[34] Most complaints alleging wrongdoings by investment company directors or indeed any allegations of Investment Company Act violations, may, and most probably should, contain references to the broad anti-fraud language of section 17(j) and Rule 17j–1.

Difficult problems of interpretation can arise in the application of subsections (a) through (d) of section 17. These are due to those subsections' effect on affiliates and section 2(a)(3)'s broad definition of an "affiliated person." [35] "Portfolio affiliation" is included in this definition.[36] "Upstream" portfolio affiliates refers to those owning five percent or more of the voting securities of an investment company or a company controlled by the investment company.[37] "Downstream" portfolio affiliates are defined as those companies five percent or more of whose voting securities are held by an investment company or a company controlled by an investment company.[38] For example, if company X owns five percent of an investment company's voting securities and company Y owns five percent of company X's voting securities, company Y is an affiliate of an affiliate of the investment company and the provisions of subsections 17(a) through (d) will apply. Conversely, if an investment company owns five percent of company A's voting securities and company A owns five percent of company B's voting securities, company B is an affiliate of an affiliate of the investment company. The subsections further cloud the already murky test for determining inadvertent investment company status.[39]

It is frequently difficult for companies to identify whether they are indeed portfolio affiliates of an investment company since investment companies generally hold portfolio securities in the nominee names of their custodian banks.[40] Section 13(d)(1) of the Securities Exchange Act of 1934[41] alleviates the problem somewhat by requiring an investment company to notify an issuer once it acquires over five percent of the issuer's securities. Problems nevertheless arise when an investment company group owns an aggregate of over five percent or a company controlled by an investment company does. For these reasons, and because the drafters of section 17 considered abuses in mergers and consolidations only where a shift in investment company control was

---

34. *Cf.* In re ML–LEE Acquisition Fund II, L.P., 848 F.Supp. 527 (D.Del.1994) (there is an implied right of action under section 17(j) of the Investment Company Act); *See* § 17.10 *infra* for discussion of remedies available under the Investment Company Act.

35. 15 U.S.C.A. § 80a–2(a)(3).

36. *See generally* Milton P. Kroll, The "Portfolio Affiliate" Problem, PLI Third Annual Institute on Securities Regulation, 261–291 (1972); Comment, The Application of § 17 of the Investment Company Act of 1940 to Portfolio Affiliates, 120 U.Pa.L.Rev. 983 (1972).

37. 15 U.S.C.A. § 80a–2(a)(3)(A).

38. 15 U.S.C.A. § 80a–2(a)(3)(B).

39. *See* 15 U.S.C.A. § 80a–3(a)(3) which is discussed in § 17.4 *supra*.

40. Kroll, *supra* footnote 36 at 269.

41. 15 U.S.C.A. § 78m(d). *See* § 11.11 *supra*. *See also* 15 U.S.C.A. § 78m(f) dealing with similar filings by institutional investment managers, which is discussed in § 11.12 *supra*.

involved (thereby directly affecting the investment company shareholders),[42] it has been forcibly argued that section 17 should only apply to upstream affiliates, that is, those in a position to maneuver investment company policy.[43] The SEC has not adopted this view, however, and has sought wider application of these subsections of the Act.

Section 17(a)(1) of the Investment Company Act prohibits the sale of securities to an investment company by any affiliated person, promoter, or underwriter of the investment company, or by any affiliate thereof.[44] Exceptions to section 17(a)(1) are listed within the subsection; they include sales of investment company securities to the investment company which issued them (*i.e.* redemptions) and sales of securities issued by the affiliate, promoter, or underwriter (or affiliate thereof) which are part of a general securities offering to the public.[45]

Subsection 17(a)(2) of the Act prohibits an affiliate, promoter, underwriter, or affiliate of such parties from purchasing securities from an investment company or a company controlled by an investment company, or a controlled affiliate of an investment company.[46] Section 17(a)(2) excludes purchases of securities when the seller is the issuer.[47] Section 17(a)(2) therefore prohibits redemptions of an affiliate's securities held by an investment company, conversions of securities, and virtually every negotiated securities transaction between the two.[48]

Investment Company Act Rule 17a–4[49] exempts from section 17(a) transactions made pursuant to a contract entered into before there was an affiliation. In order to avoid abuse, the rule further requires that during the preceding six months there was no affiliation between the parties. Other SEC rules exempt certain underwriting transactions.[50] These include loans between banks and investment companies "of a commercial character rather than of an investment character,"[51] transactions between an investment company and its fully-owned subsidiaries or

---

42. SEC Report on the Study of Investment Trusts and Investment Companies pt. 3 at 1024 (1939–42).

43. Comment, *supra* footnote 36 at 998.

44. 15 U.S.C.A. § 80a–17(a)(1).

45. 15 U.S.C.A. § 80a–17(a)(1)(A), (B). Subsection (a)(1)(C) applies to unit investment trusts and periodic payment plans.

46. 15 U.S.C.A. § 80a–17(a)(2).

47. *Id.*

48. Section 17(a) has been applied to the conversion of preferred stock into common (Axe–Houghton Fund A, Inc., Inv. Co. Act Rel. No. IC–5150 (SEC Oct. 30, 1967)), the amendment of a loan agreement regarding the subordination of debentures (Greater Washington Indst. Inv., Inc., Inv. Co. Act Rel. No. IC–3759 (SEC Aug. 29, 1963)), the conversion of bonds into common stock (Missouri–K–T.R.R., Inv. Co. Act Rel. No. IC–5182 (SEC Dec. 4, 1967)), and to the exchange of old warrants for new (Value Line Special Situations Fund, Inv. Co. Act Rel. No. IC–6621 (July 15, 1971)). *See* Comment, *supra* footnote 36 at 996–97.

49. 17 C.F.R. § 270.17a–4. The rule was amended in 1970 to clearly include stock option and stock purchase plans of controlled companies. Investment Company Act Rel. No. IC–6154 (Aug. 10, 1970).

50. 17 C.F.R. § 270.17a–1.

51. 17 C.F.R. § 270.17a–2.

between fully-owned subsidiaries of an investment company,[52] and pro-rata distributions in cash or in kind to common stockholders.[53] Also exempt are mergers, consolidations, or purchases and/or sales of substantially all of the assets of companies affiliated solely through a common investment adviser, common directors, or common officers so long as a majority of the disinterested directors of each investment company participating finds that the best interests of the investment company will be served and that the interests of existing investment company shareholders "will not be diluted as a result of . . . the transaction."[54] Rule 17a–6 exempts transactions from section 17(a) of the Act where no one associated with the affiliated company is associated with the investment company. The transaction is exempt so long as no person associated with the investment company or the affiliated company[55]

(i) Is also a party to the transaction, or

(ii) Has, or within six months prior to the transaction had, or pursuant to an arrangement will acquire, a direct or indirect financial interest in a party (except the registered investment company) to the transactions.[56]

"Financial interest" explicitly does not include any interest through ownership of securities issued by the investment company, the usual and ordinary fees paid for services as a director, and certain insurance and loan company interests.[57] Rule 17a–7[58] exempts sales of securities at current market prices by set procedure consistent with the investment company's policies, between affiliates (or affiliates of affiliates) affiliated "solely by reason of having a common investment adviser or investment advisers which are affiliated persons of each other, common directors, and/or common officers."

---

52. 17 C.F.R. § 270.17a–3. "Fully owned subsidiary" is defined in § 270.17a–3(b) as a subsidiary all of whose securities are owned by the parent corporation or other fully owned subsidiaries. This is in contrast to section 2(a)(43)'s definition of "wholly-owned subsidiary" which surprisingly requires only ninety-five percent ownership. 15 U.S.C.A. § 80a–2(a)(43).

53. 17 C.F.R. § 270.17a–5. The option for even one shareholder to choose specific assets for receipt makes the rule inoperative as to the distribution to all shareholders, *id.*

54. 17 C.F.R. § 270.17a–8.

55. The rule specifically applies to:

(1) An officer, director, employee, investment adviser, member of an advisory board, depositor, promoter of or principal underwriter for the registered investment company, or

(2) A person directly or indirectly controlling the registered investment company, or

(3) A person directly or indirectly owning, controlling, or holding with power to vote, 5 per centum or more of the outstanding voting securities of the registered investment company, or

(4) A person directly or indirectly under common control with the registered investment company, or

(5) An affiliated person of any of the foregoing.

17 C.F.R. § 270.17a–6.

56. *Id.*

57. 17 C.F.R. § 270.17a–6(b)(1).

58. 17 C.F.R. § 270.17a–7.

Section 17(b) further complicates the application of section 17(a) by allowing the Commission to grant still additional exemptions for certain companies.[59] Investment companies desiring a section 17(b) exemption must apply for one. The application should be approved if the evidence establishes that—

(1) the terms of the proposed transaction, including the consideration to be paid or received, are reasonable and fair and do not involve overreaching on the part of any person concerned;

(2) the proposed transaction is consistent with the policy of each registered investment company concerned, as recited in its registration statement and reports filed under this subchapter; and

(3) the proposed transaction is consistent with the general purposes of this subchapter.[60]

Additionally, the transaction must be fair to the shareholders of *all* of the companies involved.[61] While the SEC initially passes upon the fairness of the transaction, its findings are not binding upon courts in subsequent actions challenging the equities of the transaction.[62]

Subsection 17(d) of the Investment Company Act prohibits "joint or joint and several" participation in transactions by an affiliated person or principal underwriter for an investment company and that investment company in contravention of rules prescribed by the Commission.[63] Pursuant to this express statutory mandate, the SEC promulgated Rule 17d–1.[64] Rule 17d–1 requires that an application be filed and approved by the Commission before a transaction described in section 17(d) may be consummated.[65] The rule also requires the Commission to "consider whether the participation of such [investment company] or controlled company" in the proposed transaction is consistent with the provisions, policies and purposes of the act and the extent to which such participation is on a basis different from or less advantageous than that of other participants.[66] Due to this wording, the focus of Commission

---

59. 15 U.S.C.A. § 80a–17(b). It bears noting that this is a section 17(b) exemption, rather than a section 6(c) exemption from section 17(a), In the Matter of Keystone Custodian Funds, Inc., 21 S.E.C. 295 (1945). Section 17(b) applies to only proposed transactions. In the Matter of Adams Express Co., 18 S.E.C. 622 (1945). A section 6(c) exemption *may* therefore be used to clear retroactive clouds on title, Kroll, *supra* footnote 36 at 288. Section 6 exemptions are discussed in § 17.3 *supra*.

60. 15 U.S.C.A. § 80a–17(b).

61. *See, e.g.,* E.I. du Pont de Nemours and Co. v. Collins, 432 U.S. 46, 97 S.Ct. 2229, 53 L.Ed.2d 100 (1977); In the Matter of Bonser, Inc., 43 S.E.C. 277 (1967).

62. *See, e.g.,* Harriman v. E.I. du Pont De Nemours and Co., 411 F.Supp. 133 (D.Del.1975); SEC v. Talley Industries, 286 F.Supp. 50 (S.D.N.Y.1968), *reversed on other grounds* 399 F.2d 396 (2d Cir.1968), *cert. denied* 393 U.S. 1015, 89 S.Ct. 615, 21 L.Ed.2d 560 (1969).

63. 15 U.S.C.A. § 17(d). A former SEC commissioner has commented, "I want to point out that section 17(d) is a peculiar section. I'm not sure that I understand it." *See* Kroll, *supra* note 36 at 286 (comments of Commissioner Loomis).

64. 17 C.F.R. § 270.17d–1.

65. 17 C.F.R. § 270.17d–1(a).

66. 17 C.F.R. § 270.17d–1(b).

scrutiny should be fairness to the investment company's shareholders; this is not as broad as the scrutiny given transactions where a section 17(b) exemption is requested.[67]

A section 17(d) "joint enterprise or other joint arrangement or profit-sharing plan" is defined in Rule 17d–1(c).[68] The SEC's definition is ambiguous at best, although it is clear that an advisory contract subject to regulation under section 15 of the Act[69] is not considered to be a "joint enterprise." Due to the lack of definitional clarity, most transactions in which affiliates, or affiliates of affiliates, participate with each other must undergo SEC scrutiny. Accordingly the planner must look to precedent for guidance.

There are some judicial decisions that shed light on the types of arrangements and transactions that violate section 17 of the Act. In SEC v. Midwest Technical Development Corp.,[70] directors of an investment company were held to have violated section 17(d) by privately investing in securities in which their investment company was also investing; the directors had caused the investment company to invest in those securities to bolster the soundness of their private investments. In contrast to this clear overreaching in terms of such an improper motive by those in a position to harm the investment company, even a fair transaction may be delayed. In SEC v. Talley Industries, Inc.[71] the purchase of securities by an investment company in a corporation for which an affiliate company of the investment company was planning to make a take-over bid, was held to be a joint transaction requiring the filing of a section 17(d) application.[72] Section 17 of the Investment Company Act has been said to make "corporate albatrosses" of investment companies in that their portfolio affiliates find themselves subject to SEC scrutiny and this may delay otherwise straightforward transactions.[73]

The prohibitions of section 17 of the Act go beyond the investment company. It is the affiliate which violates section 17 by consummating transactions subject to that section's provisions if it fails to file the appropriate application or receive an exemption. Any person may file for a section 17(b) exemption,[74] and all section 17(d) transactions are

---

67. It has been argued that the same standard should be applied in SEC scrutiny under both Rule 17d–1 and section 17(b), Comment, *supra* footnote 36 at 985 n. 9. The advocate of this position believes that the fairness of the transactions only insofar as they affect investment company shareholders should be the focus of SEC investigation, *id.*

68. 17 C.F.R. § 270.17d–1(c).

69. *See* § 17.9 *infra.*

70. [1961–64 Transfer Binder] Fed.Sec.L.Rep. (CCH) ¶ 91,252 (D.Minn.1963).

71. 399 F.2d 396 (2d Cir.1968), *cert. denied* 393 U.S. 1015, 89 S.Ct. 615, 21 L.Ed.2d 560 (1969).

72. SEC prosecution of this case "leaves the impression that the SEC was operating with an intention to decree an absolutely fair price, and not necessarily to forward the investment company's interests." Comment, *supra,* footnote 36 at 992. If so, this would directly contradict Rule 17d–1's wording. *See* footnote 66 *supra* and accompanying text.

73. Comment, *supra* footnote 36 at 1009.

74. 15 U.S.C.A. § 80a–17(b).

subject to similar exemption upon application.[75] It may, therefore, be a fiduciary and statutory duty of investment company directors to ensure the filing of an exemption application by an affiliate proposing a regulated transaction: a statutory duty under section 36 of the Investment Company Act[76] to avoid having the investment company held liable as an aider and abettor of the affiliate's section 17 violation and a fiduciary duty due to the complex nature of the legal obligations imposed on the investment company's affiliates by their dealings with the investment company.

§ 17.8 Registration and Disclosure Requirements; Antifraud Provisions

As is the case with all other federal securities laws, the Investment Company Act has numerous registration, disclosure, and antifraud provisions meant to protect the investing public by requiring information relating to the issuer's policies and activities. Unless an available exemption can be found, a domestic company deemed to be an investment company within the definitions of section 3(a) of the Act[1] must register under section 8.[2] Registration is initiated by the filing of Form N–8A,[3] which is a short-form notification of registration that will be followed by more detailed disclosures in subsequent filings.

In order to complete registration, the following information must be filed within three months[4] of Form N–8A notification:

(1) whether the company will be classified as open or closed-ended, diversified or non-diversified;

(2) the company's policy towards borrowing money;

(3) whether the company will issue senior securities;

(4) whether the company will engage in the business of underwriting securities issued by other persons;

(5) whether the company will concentrate its investments in a particular industry or group of industries;

---

75. 15 U.S.C.A. § 80a–17(d); Rule 17d–1, 17 C.F.R. § 270.17d–1.

76. 15 U.S.C.A. § 80a–35.

§ 17.8

1. 15 U.S.C.A. § 80a–3(a). *See* § 17.3 *supra.*

2. 15 U.S.C.A. § 80a–8. Foreign investment companies register through the provisions of Section 7(d). *Id.* at § 80a–7(d).

3. 17 C.F.R. § 274.10. The notification consists of twelve items: (1) The company's name, (2) The state of incorporation or organization, (3) The form of doing business, (4) The company's classification (face-amount certificate, company, unit investment trust, or management company–15 U.S.C.A. § 80a–5; *see* § 17.3 *supra*), (5) If a management company, whether closed-end or open-end and whether diversified or non-diversified, (6) The names and addresses of each investment adviser, (7) The names and addresses of officers and directors, (8) If not a corporation, the names and addresses of officers, trustees, etc., (9) Description of the company's securities, (10) The company's current asset value, (11) Whether or not the company intends to qualify for the Small Business Investment Act of 1958, and (12) A copy of the last regular periodic report to its security holders, if any.

4. 17 C.F.R. § 270.8b–5.

(6) whether it plans to purchase and/or sell real estate and commodities;

(7) if it will make loans to other persons; and

(8) a statement showing the company's portfolio turnover for the preceding three years.[5]

In addition, the registrant must recite and describe all of its investment policies which may change only if authorized by a shareholder vote, those policies fundamental to the company, the name and address of each affiliated person of the registrant, the name and principal address of every company of which each such person is an officer, director or partner, and a brief statement of the business experience of each officer and director of the registrant for the past five years.[6]

As pointed out earlier, the Investment Company Act supplements other securities law provisions.[7] An investment company must also file such information and documents as are required under the 1933 Securities Act[8] and the 1934 Securities Exchange Act.[9] In registering under the 1933 Act, however, section 24(a) of the Investment Company Act of 1940[10] allows documents filed under the 1940 Act to suffice in lieu of some of the documents that would otherwise be required by the 1933 Act's provisions.[11]

As a final safety net for investors, the affirmative disclosure requirements of the Act are supplemented by broad antifraud prohibitions. Rule 8b–20 of the Investment Company Act requires that:

> In addition to the information expressly required to be included in a registration statement or report, there shall be added such further material information, if any, as may be necessary to make

---

5. 15 U.S.C.A. § 80a–8(b)(1).

6. 15 U.S.C.A. § 80a–8(b)(2)–(4). Form N–1 is used for open-end management companies, 17 C.F.R. § 274.11. Form N–2 is used for closed-end companies, 17 C.F.R. § 274.11a–1.

7. 15 U.S.C.A. § 80a–8(b)(5).

8. 15 U.S.C.A. §§ 77a *et seq.* *See* chapters 2–3 *supra.* *Cf.* DeBruyne v. Equitable Life Assurance Soc., 720 F.Supp. 1342 (N.D.Ill.1989), *affirmed* 920 F.2d 457 (7th Cir.1990) (prospectus' description of retirement fund as a "balanced" fund was not materially misleading).

9. 15 U.S.C.A. §§ 78a *et seq.* The registration and periodic reporting requirements of sections 12 and 13(a), 15 U.S.C.A. §§ 78*l*, 78m(a), are discussed in §§ 9.2, 9.3 *supra.*

See, e.g., In the Matter of ABC Portfolio Development Group, Inc., [1994–1995 Transfer Binder] Fed. Sec. L. Rep. (CCH) ¶ 85,422 (SEC 1994) (sales of investment pool interests were sales of interests in an investment company subject to the Investment Company Act and also were sales of securities subject to the provisions of the 1933 and 1934 Acts).

10. 15 U.S.C.A. § 80a–24(a).

11. *See* chapter 3 *supra.* Rule 24f–2 under the Investment Company Act governs 1933 Act registration of an indefinite amount of investment company shares. 17 C.F.R. § 270.24f–2. This rule is especially helpful for open-end companies which are continuously issuing new shares. Rule 24f–1 permits retroactive registration of investment company shares in excess of those covered by an effective 1933 Act registration statement. 17 C.F.R. § 270.24f–1; *see* text accompanying footnotes 45–46 *infra.*

the required statements, in the light of the circumstances under which they are made, not misleading.[12]

Rule 8b–2 provides a test of materiality: "the term 'material' when used to qualify a requirement for the furnishing of information as to any subject, limits the information required to those matters as to which an average prudent investor ought reasonably to be informed before buying or selling any security of the particular company." [13] The investment company must provide complete disclosure of all its relevant activities; there is, however, the disclaimer that "information required need be given only insofar as it is known or reasonably available to the registrant."[14] The issuer can be held criminally accountable[15] and civilly liable[16] for fraudulent statements made in connection with its registration and/or the reports which the investment company is required to file.[17] Failure to file registration statements properly and/or omissions of material facts are grounds for the revocation of a company's registration.[18]

The Investment Company Act contains periodic reporting requirements in addition to the initial registration. Section 30 of the Act requires issuers to file periodic reports with the SEC and to send such to their shareholders.[19] Annual reports similar to those required by section 13(a) of the Securities Exchange Act[20] must be filed by the investment company issuer.[21] Formerly, issuers were required to file quarterly reports with the Commission and supply the Commission with copies of all information sent to their shareholders within ten days of the transmission.[22] In 1985 the SEC replaced the quarterly reporting requirement with semi-annual reports.[23] The new reporting form, Form N–SAR, replaced the five quarterly reporting forms that formerly were used by most registered investment companies and thus is another step in the

---

12. 17 C.F.R. § 270.8b–20.

13. 17 C.F.R. § 270.8b–2(g). *Compare* the 1934 Act's definition of materiality in Rule 12b–2. 17 C.F.R. § 240.12b–2. *See* §§ 11.4, 13.5A *supra.*

See, e.g., SEC v. Steadman, 798 F.Supp. 733 (D.D.C.1991), *vacated on other grounds and affirmed in part* 967 F.2d 636 (D.C.Cir.1992) (overstatement of net asset value was material misrepresentation).

14. 17 C.F.R. § 270.8b–21.

15. 15 U.S.C.A. § 80a–33(b).

16. False filings under the 1934 Act will result in civil liability under section 18(a). 15 U.S.C.A. § 78r(a). *See* § 12.8 *supra.*

17. *Ibid. See, e.g.,* SEC v. Steadman, 798 F.Supp. 733 (D.D.C.1991), *vacated on other grounds and affirmed in part* 967 F.2d 636 (D.C.Cir.1992) (investment company violated § 22(c) and Rule 22c–1 by overstating net asset value).

18. 15 U.S.C.A. § 80a–8(e).

19. 15 U.S.C.A. § 80a–29.

20. 15 U.S.C.A. § 78m(a). *See* § 9.3 *supra.*

21. 15 U.S.C.A. § 80a–29(a); 17 C.F.R. § 270.30a–1.

22. 15 U.S.C.A. § 80a–30(b); 17 C.F.R. § 270.30b1–5(T) (1984).

23. 17 C.F.R. § 270.30b1–1. *See* Inv.Co.Act.Rel. No. IC–14299, [1984–85 Transfer Binder] Fed.Sec.L.Rep. (CCH) ¶ 83,725 (Jan. 4, 1985).

Commission's move towards simplification.[24] Also, the new reporting system parallels the semi-annual reports that have to be made to shareholders. In 1990 the Shareholder Communication Act extended to mutual funds and other investment companies that are registered under the Investment Company Act the applicability of the 1934 Act proxy rules that govern Exchange Act reporting companies generally.[25]

Registered investment companies must send semi-annual reports to their shareholders.[26] These reports should include the following information compiled "as of a reasonably current date":[27]

(1) a balance sheet accompanied by a statement of the investments' aggregate value;

(2) a listing of amounts and values of securities owned;

(3) an itemized income statement insofar as each item of income or expense exceeds five percent of the company's total income or expense;

(4) a statement of surplus itemized for each charge or credit representing over five percent of the total charges or credits in the report period;

(5) a statement of the aggregate remuneration paid during the report period to all directors and members of an advisory board for regular compensation, to each of the foregoing for special compensation, to all officers, and to each person of whom any officer or director of the investment company is an affiliated person; and

(6) a statement of the aggregate dollar amounts of sales and purchases of investment securities, other than government securities, during the report period.

In 1993, Registration Form N–1A (for investment company securities) was amended to require disclosures pertaining to fund managers, a discussion of the factors and strategies that had an effect on recent fund performance, and a line graph comparing the fund's performance to an index of the over-all market over a ten-year period.[28]

An open-end management company may substitute a currently effective prospectus under the Securities Act of 1933 if the remuneration information from item (5) and financial information for the half-year are

---

24. The SEC, in yet another step towards integrated disclosure requirements, has also proposed a new form N–7 that would replace form N–8B–2 for investment trusts and would replace Form S–6 under the 1933 Act. Inv.Co.Act Rel. No. IC–15612, [1987 Transfer Binder] Fed.Sec.L.Rep. (CCH) ¶ 84,109 (March 9, 1987); Inv. Co. Act Rel. No. IC–14513, [1984–85 Transfer Binder] Fed.Sec.L.Rep. (CCH) ¶ 83,774 (May 14, 1985).

25. 15 U.S.C.A. § 78n(b). The Exchange Act's proxy rules are discussed in §§ 11.1– 11.9 *supra.*

26. 15 U.S.C.A. § 80a–29(d). *Compare* the annual report requirement for 1934 Act reporting companies. 17 C.F.R. §§ 240.14a–3(b), 14c–3. *See* §§ 11.6, 11.8 *supra.*

27. 15 U.S.C.A. § 80a–29(d).

28. *See* Inv. Co. Act. Rel. IC–19382, [1993 Transfer Binder] Fed. Sec. L. Rep. (CCH) ¶ 85,123 (SEC April 6, 1993).

also included.[29] The financial statements filed by an investment company must be signed or certified by an independent public accountant.[30] No controlling person, employee, or principal accounting officer of a management company or face-amount certificate company may participate in the preparation of financial statements without an affirmative vote to do so by a majority of the board or of the shareholders.[31]

Adoption of Rule 134(d) under the Securities Act of 1933[32] in 1979 has allowed investment companies to advertise more freely than had been allowed previously.[33] This rule allows an investment company to advertise in newspapers and magazines and on radio and television some but not all of the information required to be included in its prospectus by section 10(a) of the Securities Act of 1933[34] so as to satisfy the requirement of section 5 of that Act that statutory prospectuses be distributed to investors along with the sale of registered securities.[35] The advertisement must conspicuously state "from whom a prospectus containing more complete information may be obtained and that the investor should read that prospectus carefully before investing."[36] Any representation by a money market fund of its yield must be computed according to the formula required by Form N–1[37] and identify the last day in the period used in compiling the quotation.[38]

All sales literature used by open-end management companies, unit investment trusts, and face-amount certificate companies must be filed with the Commission within ten days of its being sent.[39] "Sales literature" includes:

---

29. 17 C.F.R. § 270.30d–1.

30. 15 U.S.C.A. § 80a–29(e).

31. 15 U.S.C.A. § 80a–31(b).

32. 17 C.F.R. § 230.134(d).

33. 15 U.S.C.A. § 77j(a). The prospectus delivery requirements of section 5(b) of the 1933 Act, 15 U.S.C.A. § 77e(b) are discussed in §§ 2.4, 2.5 *supra.*

Another major development has been the Commission's adoption of standardized formulas for presenting performance data in investment company advertising and sales literature. 17 C.F.R. §§ 230.482(d), (e); 17 C.F.R. § 270.34b–1. *See* Inv.Co. Act Rel. No. IC–16245, [1987–88 Transfer Binder] Fed.Sec.L.Rep. (CCH) ¶ 84,217 (Feb. 2, 1988); Inv.Co. Act Rel. No. IC–15315 (Sept. 17, 1986).

The SEC has taken the position that its standardized format for presenting performance data applies not only to the investment company's literature but also to data prepared by independent firms. Dalbar Publishing, Inc., 20 Sec.Reg. & L.Rep. (BNA) 1189 (SEC No Action Letter avail. July 1, 1988).

34. 17 C.F.R. § 230.134(d). For the older strict advertising standards *see* S.E.C. Statement of Policy of the Commission Relating to Advertising and Sales Literature Used in the Sale of Investment Company Shares, 5 Fed.Sec.L.Rep. (CCH) ¶ 48,902. This was superceded by Inv.Co.Act Rel. No. IC–10647 (SEC March 27, 1979).

35. The registration and prospectus provisions of the 1933 Act are discussed in chapter 2 *supra.*

36. 17 C.F.R. § 230.434(d)(a)(4).

37. 17 C.F.R. § 274.11.

38. 17 C.F.R. § 230.434(d)(a)(6).

39. 15 U.S.C.A. § 80a–24(b). In 1988, the SEC adopted Rule 24b–3 which permits filing of sales literature with a registered national securities association (which currently only applies to the NASD) provided that the association has adopted rules providing

any communication (whether in writing, by radio, or by television) used by any person to offer to sell or induce the sale of securities of any investment company. Communications between issuers, underwriters and dealers are included in this definition of sales literature if such communications, or the information contained therein, can be reasonably expected to be communicated to prospective investors in the offer or sale of securities or are designed to be employed in either written or oral form in the offer or sale of securities.[40]

The content of investment company literature is regulated by 1933 Act Rule 156.[41] Under this rule it is illegal for any person to make a materially misleading statement. The rule sets out specific criteria for determining whether a statement is misleading.[42] As discussed above,[43] the issuer of the securities will be held liable if statements in the investment company's sales literature are found to be misleading.

Investment companies are required to file periodic reports[44] with the SEC and further must amend their registration statements annually.[45] Registration statements of open-end management companies, unit investment trusts, and face-amount certificate companies must be amended to reflect any increase in the number of securities offered.[46] If such a company sells more than the number of securities registered, it may be required to pay a treble registration fee and the securities will be deemed to have been registered.[47] To avoid this potentially expensive filing penalty, open-end companies may register to sell "an indefinite number of the securities."[48]

The date of the latest amendment to an investment company's registration statement is its effective date.[49] This is especially important in the case of an open-end management company which is constantly issuing and selling new shares since under section 13 of the Securities Act of 1933,[50] a shareholder may have up to three years from the

standards for investment company advertising and further has adopted procedures to review such advertising. 17 C.F.R. § 270.24b–3. *See* Inv.Co.Act Rel. No. IC–16245, [1987–88 Transfer Binder] Fed.Sec.L.Rep. (CCH) ¶ 84,217 (Feb. 2, 1988). *See also* Inv.Co.Act Rel. No. IC–15–315 (Sept. 17, 1986).

40. 17 C.F.R. § 230.156(c). *Compare* the 1933 Act's definition of "prospectus" in section 2(10). 15 U.S.C.A. § 77b(10).

41. 17 C.F.R. § 230.156.

42. 17 C.F.R. § 230.156(b).

43. *See* text accompanying footnotes 12–18 *supra.*

44. 15 U.S.C.A. § 80a–29. *See* text accompanying footnotes 18–25 *supra.*

45. 17 C.F.R. § 270.8b–16.

46. 15 U.S.C.A. § 80a–24(e)(1).

47. 15 U.S.C.A. § 80a–24(f).

48. *Id. See* footnote 11 *supra.* The SEC has proposed a rule that would permit closed-end companies to offer shares on a continuous or delayed basis in light of new Rule 23c–3 which allows them to purchase their shares on a periodic basis. *See* Inv. Co. Act Rel. No. IC–19391, [1993 Transfer Binder] Fed. Sec. L. Rep. (CCH) ¶ 85,127 (April 7, 1993). Shelf registrations generally under the 1933 Act are considered in § 3.8 *supra.*

49. 15 U.S.C.A. § 80a–24(e)(3).

50. 15 U.S.C.A. § 77m. *See also* § 7.5.4 *supra* (Practitioner's Edition only).

effective date to institute a suit for misleading registration statements under section 11 of that Act.[51] Under section 11, suit for material misstatements or omissions in the registration statement generally must be brought within one year of the violation or reasonable discovery of the violation.[52] When the violation is not reasonably discoverable, the one-year limitations will be tolled but in no event more than three years after the security was bona fide offered to the public.[53] In the event of a continuous offering, an unfortunate literal reading of the statute might unduly shorten this three-year repose period.

There are limits on the public availability of information filed with the Commission. Section 45(a) of the Investment Company Act[54] declares that the information contained in any registration statement, application, report or other document filed with the SEC shall be made available to the public unless the commission, by rule or regulation, deems such disclosure unnecessary and inappropriate.[55] Pursuant to this, the Commission has decided that the names and addresses of dealers to or through whom principal underwriters of an investment company are currently offering securities "shall be the subject of confidential treatment and shall not be made available to the public."[56] Photostatic copies of information and documents on file with the SEC are to be made available "to the public * * * at such reasonable charge and under such reasonable limitations as the Commission shall prescribe."[57]

§ 17.9 Limitations on Advisory Fees; Transfers of Control—The "Sale" of Investment Advisory Contracts

Advisory Fees

Investment advisers that manage investment companies' assets generally are compensated through a management fee based on a percentage of the fund's average asset value. Typically this fee is annualized based on between one-half and one percent of the fund's average assets. During the start-up time, the adviser's fee may be quite modest but, as

---

51. 15 U.S.C.A. § 77k. *See* §§ 7.3–7.4 *supra.*

52. 15 U.S.C.A. § 77m.

53. *Id.* The same limitations period has been held applicable under the Investment Company Act. *See* Merine v. Prudential–Bache Utility Fund, Inc., 859 F.Supp. 715 (S.D.N.Y.1994) (action under section 20 of the Investment Company Act based on proxy solicitation was subject to the same statute of limitations as other antifraud remedies under the securities laws). Additionally, a parallel one year/three year limitations/repose period applies to implied remedies under the Securities Exchange Act of 1934. *See* § 13.8 *supra.*

54. 15 U.S.C.A. § 80a–44(a).

55. *Id.*

56. 17 C.F.R. § 270.45a–1. After notice and hearing, the Commission may order that such information be made public. *Id.* In 1979, the Commission proposed rescinding Rule 45a–1. Inv.Co.Act Rel.No. IC–10748, [1979 Transfer Binder] Fed.Sec.L.Rep. (CCH) ¶ 82,-118 (June 27, 1979).

57. 15 U.S.C.A. § 80a–44(b).

the fund grows, the fee can become "enormous."[1]   Prior to the shareholders' annual approval of the advisory contract there must be full
disclosure of the terms of compensation.[2]   The only limitations on the
amount of compensation are found in the Act's general imposition of
fiduciary duties,[3] and prohibition against unlawful conversion of investment company assets.[4]

Section 37 of the Act[5] makes it unlawful for any person to steal,
unlawfully abstract, or convert investment company assets.   A violation
of this section seems to require more than merely excessive compensation and thus will not be very helpful in challenging excessive advisory
fees.[6]   Section 36(b) which supports an express private right of action[7]
imposes fiduciary obligations upon the investment adviser.   Section
36(b)'s fiduciary obligations include refraining from charging and collect-
ing excessive investment advisory fees.

The courts have long required under general corporate law that
management compensation be fair and reasonable.[8]   This rule has been

§ 17.9

1.   Richard W. Jennings & Harold Marsh, Jr., Securities Regulation: Cases and Materi-
als 1398 (5th ed.1982). *See also, e.g.*, Note, Mutual Fund Advisory Fees—Too Much for
Too Little?, 48 Fordham L.Rev. 530 (1980); Note, Mutual Fund Advisory Fees and the
New Standard of Fiduciary Duty—Interpreting the 1970 Mutual Fund Act, 56 Cornell
L.Rev. 627 (1971).   It has been observed critically that "it costs no more in research effort
to buy 1,000 shares of stock than 100." Brown v. Bullock, 294 F.2d 415, 424 (2d Cir.1961)
(Moore, J. dissenting).

2.   15 U.S.C.A. § 80a–15(a)(1) ("precisely describe all compensation to be paid thereunder").   Failure to adequately disclose the terms of the advisory contract can result in civil
liability to the fund's shareholders.   *See* In the Matter of Managed Funds, Inc., Sec.Act
Rel.No. 33–4122 (July 30, 1959); Lutz v. Boas, 39 Del.Ch. 585, 171 A.2d 381 (1961).

3.   15 U.S.C.A. § 80a–35(b).

4.   15 U.S.C.A. § 80a–36.

5.   *Id.*

6.   *See, e.g.,* Brown v Bullock, 294 F.2d 415 (2d Cir.1961).

7.   15 U.S.C.A. § 80a–35(b).   *See, e.g.,* Fogel v. Chestnutt, 668 F.2d 100 (2d Cir.1981),
cert. denied 459 U.S. 828, 103 S.Ct. 65, 74 L.Ed.2d 66 (1982); Tannenbaum v. Zeller, 552
F.2d 402 (2d Cir.1977), *cert. denied* 434 U.S. 934, 98 S.Ct. 421, 54 L.Ed.2d 293 (1977);
Galfand v. Chestnutt, 545 F.2d 807 (2d Cir.1976); Fogel v. Chestnutt, 533 F.2d 731 (2d
Cir.1975), *cert. denied* 429 U.S. 824, 97 S.Ct. 77, 50 L.Ed.2d 86 (1976); Moses v. Burgin,
445 F.2d 369 (1st Cir.1971), *cert. denied* 404 U.S.C 994, 404 U.S. 994, 92 S.Ct. 532, 30
L.Ed.2d 547 (1971).   The private right of action is discussed in § 17.10 *infra.   See also,
e.g.,* James N. Benedict, Mark Holland & Barry W. Rashkover, Developments in Management Fee Litigation, 22 Rev.Sec. & Commod.Reg. 157 (1989).

8.   Rogers v. Hill, 289 U.S. 582, 53 S.Ct. 731, 77 L.Ed. 1385 (1933); Hingle v.
Plaquemines Oil Sales Corp., 399 So.2d 646 (La.App.1981), *writ denied* 401 So.2d 987
(La.1981); Ruetz v. Topping, 453 S.W.2d 624 (Mo.App.1970).   *See generally* 2 James D.
Cox, Thomas L. Hazen & F. Hodge O'Neal, Corporations, ch. 11 (1995).   Prior to 1970
section 36(b) prohibited "gross misconduct or abuse of trust."   *See* Note, Mutual Fund
Advisory Fees and the New Standard of Fiduciary Duty—Interpreting the 1970 Mutual
Fund Act, 56 Cornell L.Rev. 627 (1971).   It has been held that section 36(b)'s express
remedy is exclusive and there are no implied remedies for challenging excessive fees.
Tarlov v. Paine Webber Cashfund, Inc., 559 F.Supp. 429 (D.Conn.1983).

At least one court has indicated that section 36(b) preempts state law claims for breach
of fiduciary duty when challenging investment management compensation.   Batra v.
Investors Research Corp., 1992 WL 280790, [1992 Transfer Binder] Fed.Sec.L.Rep. (CCH)
¶ 96,983, p. 94,261 fn. 3 (W.D.Mo.1992).

followed under the Investment Company Act which "subject[s] the transaction to rigorous scrutiny for fairness." [9] As noted in one decision, "the Court must consider the 'nature, quality and extent' of the services to the Fund in relation to the fee paid by the Fund." [10] As observed in the legislative history, section 36(b) requires

> that the court look to all facts in connection with the determination and receipt of such compensation, including all services rendered to the fund or its shareholders and all compensation and payments received, in order to reach a decision as to whether the adviser has properly acted as a fiduciary in relation to such compensation. [11]

Although investment company advisory fees may be high, the courts have tended to validate the compensation in light of industry practices [12] as well as looking to the size of the fund. [13] Another reason for the difficulty of proving excessive fees is the fact that shareholders or the board of directors ratify the contract annually. [14] However, it is clear that ratification upon full disclosure will not preclude judicial scrutiny of the fairness of the compensation. [15] Nevertheless, there is a relatively high burden imposed for overcoming the effect of shareholder ratification. In the words of the Second Circuit:

> An investment adviser violates section 36(b) when it, or an affiliated person, charges "a fee that is so disproportionately large that it bears no reasonable relationship to the services rendered and could not have been the product of arm's-length bargaining." [16]

---

9. Galfand v. Chestnutt, 545 F.2d 807, 811–812 (2d Cir.1976).

10. Gartenberg v. Merrill Lynch Asset Management, Inc., 528 F.Supp. 1038, 1047 (S.D.N.Y.1981), *affirmed* 694 F.2d 923 (2d Cir.1982). *See also, e.g.,* Krasner v. Dreyfus Corp., 500 F.Supp. 36 (S.D.N.Y.1980); Note, Mutual Fund Advisory Fees—Too Much for Too Little?, 48 Fordham L.Rev. 530, 545 (1980).

11. S.Rep. No. 184 accompanying S. 2224, 91st Cong., 1st Sess. 5 (1970), U.S. Code Cong. & Admin.News 4910 (1970).

12. *E.g.* Krinsk v. Fund Asset Management, Inc., 875 F.2d 404 (2d Cir.1989); Saxe v. Brady, 40 Del.Ch. 474, 184 A.2d 602 (1962).

See also Bromson v. Lehman Management Co., 1986 WL 165, [1985–86 Transfer Binder] Fed.Sec.L.Rep. (CCH) ¶ 92,521 (S.D.N.Y.1986) (refusing discovery of the management fees charged by defendant in connection with management of its thirty largest non investment company accounts but permitting discovery of compensation paid to affiliated directors).

13. *E.g.* Meyer v. Oppenheimer Management Corp., 895 F.2d 861 (2d Cir.1990) (advisory and distribution fees were not excessive); Gartenberg v. Merrill Lynch Asset Management, Inc., 694 F.2d 923 (2d Cir.1982). *But see* Brown v. Bullock, 294 F.2d 415, 424 (2d Cir.1961) (Moore, J. dissenting), which is quoted in footnote 1 *supra.*

14. *See* 15 U.S.C.A. § 80a–15(a)(2).

15. *E.g.* Gartenberg v. Merrill Lynch Asset Management, Inc., 694 F.2d 923 (2d Cir.1982); Galfand v. Chestnutt, 545 F.2d 807, 811–812 (2d Cir.1976); Rosenfeld v. Black, 445 F.2d 1337, 1343 (2d Cir.1971), *cert. dismissed* 409 U.S. 802, 93 S.Ct. 24, 34 L.Ed.2d 62 (1972); Krasner v. Dreyfus, 90 F.R.D. 665 (S.D.N.Y.1981). The claims in *Gartenberg v. Merrill Lynch Asset Management, Inc.* were eventually dismissed after a full trial. *See* 740 F.2d 190 (2d Cir.1984) (failure to meet the burden of proving fee was unreasonable).

The Supreme Court has held that when a shareholder challenges fees as excessive under section 36(b), there is no need to make a demand upon directors. Daily Income Fund, Inc. v. Fox, 464 U.S. 523, 104 S.Ct. 831, 78 L.Ed.2d 645 (1984).

16. Meyer v. Oppenheimer Management Corp., 764 F.2d 76, 81 (2d Cir.1985) (quoting from Gartenberg v. Merrill Lynch Asset Management, Inc., 694 F.2d 923, 928 (2d

Assignment of the Advisory Contract[17]

A basic premise of the Investment Company Act is that the public interest, and that of an investment company's investors, is adversely affected by a change in the management of an investment company without the consent of its stockholders.[18]   A number of Investment Company Act provisions operate to limit potential abuses in connection with changes in investment advisers.   Section 2(a)(4) of the Act provides that any "direct or indirect" transfer of a controlling block of shares in the investment adviser constitutes an assignment of the advisory contract.[19]   The investment advisory contract automatically terminates upon its assignment.[20]   Approval of the new contract with the new adviser by the investment company's shareholders is required to validate the contract.[21]

Section 15(f) of the Act allows, but at the same time places express limitations upon, the receipt of a premium based on the transfer of controlling interests in an investment adviser to a mutual fund or investment company.[22]   When control in the adviser is sold at a premium and the investment company shareholders and directors ratify the new advisory contract, there is considered to be express approval of the transfer of control for a premium.   Absent the Investment Company Act's provisions, this premium might be prohibited by the common law of most states because the former adviser is making a profit while choosing its successor—a decision that, at least in form, lies in the hands of the investment company's directors and shareholders.[23]   Section 15(f) was enacted in 1975[24] in response to the Second Circuit's decision in Rosenfeld v. Black[25] which contained broad statements concerning the

Cir.1982), *cert. denied* 461 U.S. 906, 103 S.Ct. 1877, 76 L.Ed.2d 808 (1983), *dismissed after trial on the merits* 573 F.Supp. 1293 (S.D.N.Y.1983), *affirmed* 740 F.2d 190 (2d Cir.1984)).

See also, e.g. Krinsk v. Fund Asset Management, Inc., 715 F.Supp. 472 (S.D.N.Y.1988) (upholding fee as reasonable); Schuyt v. Rowe Price Prime Reserve Fund, Inc., 663 F.Supp. 962 (S.D.N.Y.1987) (giving great deference to approval by fully informed properly qualified independent directors).

17. See Thomas L. Hazen, Transfers of Corporate Control and Duties of Controlling Shareholders—Common Law, Tender Offers, Investment Companies—And A Proposal For Reform, 125 U.Pa.L.Rev. 1023, 1055–60 (1977).

18. 15 U.S.C.A. § 80a–1(b)(6). *See, e.g.,* SEC v. Steadman, 798 F.Supp. 733 (D.D.C. 1991), *vacated in part on other grounds* 967 F.2d 636 (D.C. Cir.1992) (investment adviser violated § 15(a) of the Act by performing services for investment company for six years without shareholder approval).

19. 15 U.S.C.A. § 80a–2(a)(4).

20. 15 U.S.C.A. § 80a–15(a)(4).

21. 15 U.S.C.A. § 80a–15(a).

22. 15 U.S.C.A. § 80a–15(f).

23. *See* 2 James D. Cox, Thomas L. Hazen & F. Hodge O'Neal, Corporations §§ 12.1–12.2 (1995); Harry G. Henn & John R. Alexander, Laws of Corporations § 656 (3d ed. 1983); Adolf A. Berle, The Price of Power: Sale of Corporate Control, 50 Cornell L.Q. 628 (1965); Victor Brudney, Fiduciary Ideology in Transactions Affecting Corporate Control, 65 Mich.L.Rev. 259 (1966); Hazen, *supra* footnote 17.

24. Act of June 4, 1975, Pub.L. No. 94–29, 89 Stat. 97 (1975).

25. 445 F.2d 1337 (2d Cir.1971), *cert. dismissed sub nom.* Lazard Freres & Co. v. Rosenfeld, 409 U.S. 802, 93 S.Ct 24, 34 L.Ed.2d 62 (1972). In addition to the authorities

investment adviser's fiduciary duty and corresponding obligation not to profit personally from a sale of its office with the investment company.[26] Section 15(f) makes it clear that the investment adviser may make a profit either by selling a controlling block of its shares at a price above their net asset value or by facilitating the transfer of an advisory contract to a new adviser.

More specifically, section 15(f) allows a transfer of control by an investment adviser or a sale of the advisory contract at a profit or otherwise if:

> (A) for a period of three years after the time of such action, at least 75 per centum of the members of the board of directors [of the investment company] are not (i) interested persons of the investment adviser * * * or (ii) interested persons of the predecessor investment adviser * * *; and (B) there is not imposed an unfair burden on [the investment] company as a result of such transaction.[27]

This provision affords a higher degree of protection for investment company shareholders by requiring seventy-five percent of the board to be disinterested, as opposed to the regular forty percent requirement.[28] The seventy-five percent disinterested director requirement is not operative where a controlling block of the adviser's securities is distributed to the public without changing the identity of those in actual control of the adviser, and where the transferee adviser has been in control of the transferor advisers (or shared control of the adviser) for the six months immediately preceding the transfer.[29]

The "unfair burden" requirement is not explained anywhere in the Investment Company Act. The closest the Act comes to providing some meaning to "unfair burden" is in an example provided by section 15(f)(2)(B):

> For the purpose of paragraph (1)(B) of this subsection, an unfair burden on a registered investment company includes any arrangement, during the two-year period after the date on which any such transaction occurs, whereby the investment adviser or corporate trustee or predecessor or successor investment adviser or corporate trustee or any interested person of any such adviser or any such corporate trustee receives or is entitled to receive any compensation directly or indirectly (i) from any person in connection with the purchase or sale of securities or other property to, from, or on behalf of such company, other than bona fide ordinary compensation as principal underwriter for such company, or (ii) from such company

---

noted in note 17 *supra, see* Morton M. Rosenfeld, The Background and Implications of *Rosenfeld v. Black*, 1 Sec. Reg.L.J. 309 (1974).

26. *See, e.g.,* 445 F.2d at 1343.

27. 15 U.S.C.A. § 80a–15(f)(1).

28. 15 U.S.C.A. § 80a–10(a). *See* § 17.6 *supra.*

29. 15 U.S.C.A. § 80a–15(f)(4).

or its security holders for other than bona fide investment advisory or other services.[30]

The subsection's language fails to give even a clear indication of the parameters of "bona fide ordinary compensation." Clearly, Congress did not intend for this example to exhaust the class of transactions that impose an "unfair burden" because the subsection provides only that this class "includes" the arrangements for non-bona fide compensation. Thus, the question of what other transactions may impose an "unfair burden" remains to be answered by the courts.

The "unfair burden" standard does not provide any more protection to an investment company or its shareholders than the fiduciary duty to which an investment adviser is already subject.[31] Indeed, there are as yet no reported cases of shareholders of an investment company relying on section 15(f)(2) to recover excessive control premiums paid to outgoing investment advisers.

§ 17.10   Private Causes of Action and Civil Liability for Violations of the Investment Company Act

Private rights of action have been recognized to redress violations of most of the significant sections of the Investment Company Act. All of these, save one, have been implied from congressional and legislative history and from the language of the various sections themselves.[1] But not all sections have given rise to implied remedies.[2] In any event, the Act contains an express remedy in section 36(b) and also extends the 1934 Act's prohibitions against insider short-swing profits to investment advisers and affiliated persons.[3]

Implied Remedies Under the Investment Company Act

A number of Supreme Court cases have cast a looming shadow on

---

30. 15 U.S.C.A. § 80a–15(f)(2)(B).

31. 15 U.S.C.A. § 80a–35(b). *See* § 17.6 *supra.*

§ 17.10

1. *See, e.g.,* Note, Implied Private Rights of Action Under the Investment Company Act of 1940, 40 Wash. & Lee L.Rev. 1069 (1983). Implied remedies in general are considered in § 13.1 *supra.*

2. Section 1(b)(2) (15 U.S.C.A. § 80a–1(b)(2)) has been held a "preamble stating congressional purpose," and not to provide a private cause of action for shareholders, however. Jerozal v. Cash Reserve Management, Inc., 1982 WL 1363, [1982–83 Transfer Binder] Fed.Sec.L.Rep. (CCH) ¶ 99,019 at pp. 94,826–27 (S.D.N.Y.1982). *Accord* Tarlov v. Paine Webber Cashfund, Inc., 559 F.Supp. 429 (D.Conn.1983).

3. 15 U.S.C.A. §§ 80a–29(f), 80a–35(b). *See* Meyer Eisenberg & Richard M. Phillips, Mutual Fund Litigation—New Frontiers for the Investment Company Act, 62 Colum.L.Rev. 73 (1962); Note, Private Rights of Action Under the Investment Company Act, 1961 Duke L.J. 421. Section 30(f) of the Act provides that the insider trading prohibitions of section 16(b) of the Exchange Act (15 U.S.C.A. § 78p(b)) apply to "every person who is directly or indirectly the beneficial owner of more than 10 per centum of any class of outstanding securities (other than short-term paper) of which a registered closed-end company is the issuer or who is an officer, director, member of an advisory board, investment adviser, or affiliated person of an investment adviser of such a company." 15 U.S.C.A. § 80a–29(f). Section 16(b) is discussed in §§ 12.2–12.7 *supra.*

implied remedies.[4] It remains to be seen whether this means the demise of the Investment Company Act remedies that have been implied by the lower federal courts. Some decisions have refused to recognize implied remedies under the Act but others have continued to recognize implied remedies.[5] There is nevertheless substantial precedent for the implication of private relief under the Act. An unregistered investment company has been held civilly liable under section 7 of the Act[6] for failure to comply with the registration requirements of section 8.[7] The sale of securities to an unregistered investment company has been held *voidable* at the seller's option, rather than automatically void under section 47 of the Act,[8] lest innocent sellers be penalized to the same extent as the culpable unregistered purchaser.[9] It is clear that an innocent shareholder/purchaser may rescind transactions with an investment company.[10] Private enforcement actions by "injured" plaintiffs have also been recognized (1) under section 17[11] for dealings between affiliates,[12] (2)

4. *E.g.* Transamerica Mortgage Advisors, Inc. v. Lewis, 444 U.S. 11, 100 S.Ct. 242, 62 L.Ed.2d 146 (1979). For a discussion of implied remedies generally, *see* § 13.1 *supra.*

5. One court has held that there is no private remedy for compelling compliance with the Act's registration requirements. M.J. Whitman & Co. v. American Financial Enterprises, Inc., 552 F.Supp. 17 (S.D.Ohio 1982). Another decision refused to imply a defamation remedy under section 34(b) or 40(c) which relate to prohibitions against destruction and falsification of reports and records. Phillips v. Kapp, 87 F.R.D. 548 (S.D.N.Y.1980); 15 U.S.C.A. § 80a–33(b)–39(a), (c). *See also* Tarlov v. Paine Webber Cashfund, Inc., 559 F.Supp. 429 (D.Conn.1983) (no remedy implied under sections 1(b)(2), 15(a), 15(b) and 36(a) for excessive advisory fees in light of section 36(b)'s express remedy).

Contra Lessler v. Little, 857 F.2d 866 (1st Cir.1988) (recognizing an implied right of action under section 17(a)(2) which prohibits certain transactions between affiliated persons and the investment company); Bancroft Convertible Fund v. Zico Investment Holdings, 825 F.2d 731 (3d Cir.1987) (recognizing an implied remedy for violation of section 12(d)(1)(A), giving a strong rationale for the continued recognition of the other implied remedies under the Act); Dowling v. Narragansett Capital Corp., 735 F.Supp. 1105, 1122–23 (D.R.I.1990) (recognizing implied remedy under sections 17(a)(2) and 48(a)); Kamen v. Kemper Financial Services, Inc., 659 F.Supp. 1153 (N.D.Ill.1987) (permitting section 20(a) claim to proceed along with section 36(b) claim); Krome v. Merrill Lynch & Co., 637 F.Supp. 910 (S.D.N.Y.1986) (recognizing implied remedies under sections 7, 15, 17(a), 22, 35(a), and 37 of the Act); Schuyt v. Rowe Price Prime Reserve Fund, Inc., 622 F.Supp. 169 (S.D.N.Y.1985) (recognizing implied remedy under section 20(a)).

6. 15 U.S.C.A. § 80a–7.

7. 15 U.S.C.A. § 80a–8; Cogan v. Johnston, 162 F.Supp. 907 (S.D.N.Y.1958). *See generally* Parker M. Nielson, Neglected Alternatives for Investor Self–Help: The Unregistered Investment Company and The Federal Corporate Law, 44 Notre Dame Law. 99 (1969). Unregistered investment companies should be subject to the same limitations as registered ones; *see also* Lutz v. Boas, 39 Del.Ch. 585, 171 A.2d 381, 389–90 (1961) (contract between an investment adviser and an investment company implied from the facts and held invalid for not meeting Investment Company Act approval requirements). *See* footnote 20 *infra.*

8. 15 U.S.C.A. § 80a–46. *See, e.g.,* Reeves v. Continental Equities Corp., 725 F.Supp. 196 (S.D.N.Y.1989), *on remand* 767 F.Supp. 469 (S.D.N.Y.1991) (refusing to imply a private remedy under section 47(b) for alleged wrongful discharge to prevent chief financial officer from making required Investment Company Act filings).

9. Avnet, Inc. v. Scope Industries, 499 F.Supp. 1121 (S.D.N.Y.1980).

10. 15 U.S.C.A. § 80a–46(b); Mathers Fund, Inc. v. Colwell Co., 564 F.2d 780, 783–84 (7th Cir.1977).

11. 15 U.S.C.A. § 80a–17.

12. SEC v. General Time Corp., 407 F.2d 65, 70 (2d Cir.1968), *cert. denied* 393 U.S. 1026, 89 S.Ct. 637, 21 L.Ed.2d 570 (1969). *See also, e.g.,* In re ML–LEE Acquisition Fund

under section 37[13] for the willful conversion of an investment company's assets,[14] (3) under section 35(d)[15] for misleading use of an investment company name,[16] and (4) under section 48[17] for contravention of Investment Company Act provisions through the use of a third party.[18] However, many of these cases were decided prior to the more recent Supreme Court decisions curtailing implied remedies.[19] As such, there is some question as to their continued vitality.

In addition to reaffirming the existence of other implied remedies, a recent decision has recognized the availability of private relief under section 22 of the Investment Company Act to recover the excessive portion of a sales load.[20] A remedy has also been recognized under section 20(a) of the Act which regulates investment company proxy solicitations.[21]

The Supreme Court has held that federal statutes of limitation control in implied remedies under the Exchange Act.[22] Following the same rationale, a number of courts have held that the applicable statute of limitations in implied actions under the Investment Company Act is one year from the discovery of the violation but in no event more than three years from the violation.[23]

II, L.P., 848 F.Supp. 527 (D.Del.1994) (there is an implied right of action under section 17(j) of the Investment Company Act);

13. 15 U.S.C.A. § 80a–36.

14. Brown v. Bullock, 294 F.2d 415 (2d Cir.1961) (holding directors liable for willful conversion of assets rather than for a breach of any explicit fiduciary duty). *See* footnote 20 *infra.*

15. 15 U.S.C.A. § 80a–34(d).

16. Taussig v. Wellington Fund, Inc., 313 F.2d 472, 475–76 (3d Cir.1963), *cert. denied* 374 U.S. 806, 83 S.Ct. 1693, 10 L.Ed.2d 1031 (1963).

17. 15 U.S.C.A. § 80a–47.

18. Jerozal v. Cash Reserve Management, 1982 WL 1363, [1982–83 Transfer Binder] Fed.Sec.L.Rep. (CCH) ¶ 99,019 (S.D.N.Y.1982). *See also, e.g.,* Reeves v. Continental Equities Corp. of America, 912 F.2d 37 (2d Cir.1990) (whistle-blowing employee of investment company had no private remedy under § 48(b) for his alleged wrongful dismissal because he was not a member of a class for whose special benefit the statute was enacted).

19. *See* footnote 4 *supra.*

20. Krome v. Merrill Lynch & Co., 637 F.Supp. 910 (S.D.N.Y.1986) (also recognizing the availability of private relief under sections 7, 15, 17(a), 35(a), and 37 of the Investment Company Act).

21. *See* Schuyt v. Rowe Price Prime Reserve Fund, Inc., 622 F.Supp. 169 (S.D.N.Y. 1985), and the other cases cited in footnote 30 *infra.*

22. Lampf, Pleva, Lipkind, Prupis & Petigrow v. Gilbertson, 501 U.S. 350, 111 S.Ct. 2773, 115 L.Ed.2d 321 (1991), *rehearing denied* 501 U.S. 1277, 112 S.Ct. 27, 115 L.Ed.2d 1109 (1991). *See* § 13.8 *supra.*

23. Kahn v. Kohlberg, Kravis, Roberts & Co., 970 F.2d 1030 (2d Cir.1992), *cert. denied* ___ U.S. ___, 113 S.Ct. 494, 121 L.Ed.2d 432 (1992) (one year-three year statute applied under to implied action under Investment Advisers Act); Merine v. Prudential–Bache Utility Fund, Inc., 859 F.Supp. 715 (S.D.N.Y.1994) (action under section 20 of the Investment Company Act based on proxy solicitation was subject to the same statute of limitations as other antifraud remedies under the securities laws); Taxable Municipal Bond Securities Litigation, 1992 WL 124783, [1992 Transfer Binder] Fed.Sec.L.Rep. (CCH) ¶ 96,834 (E.D.La.1992) (one year-three year statute applied under to implied action under Investment Advisers Act).

For discussion of limitations periods applicable to implied remedies generally, *see* § 13.8 *supra.*

The issues become thornier when suit is brought for a breach of the fiduciary duties imposed upon investment company directors and advisers by section 36 of the Act[24] and implemented by section 15.[25] Section 15(a) has been held to provide investment company shareholders with a private right of action for the failure of directors to approve an investment contract in a meaningful fashion.[26] Section 15(a) has also provided a private right of action against an investment adviser charged with self-dealing,[27] but not the recovery of excessive fees which is governed by section 36(b)'s express remedy.[28] Similarly, section 15(c), which provides a clearer duty of meaningful negotiations and disclosure between investment company directors and investment advisers, has been held not to provide a basis for a private shareholder right of action due to section 36(b)'s express cause of action for a breach of investment adviser fiduciary duty.[29] As noted above, section 20 of the Act, which regulates the solicitation of proxies, has been held to support an implied right of action, provided that the claim is for something other than excessive advisory fees.[30]

In Moses v. Burgin[31] affiliated directors were held to have a fiduciary duty to inform independent directors of the possibility of recapturing give-ups under the pre–1970 version of section 36 of the Investment

---

24.   15 U.S.C.A. § 80a–35.

25.   15 U.S.C.A. § 80a–15.

26.   *See, e.g.,* Brown v. Bullock, 294 F.2d 415, 420–21 (2d Cir.1961).

27.   Fogel v. Chestnutt, 668 F.2d 100 (2d Cir.1981), *cert. denied* 459 U.S. 828, 103 S.Ct. 65, 74 L.Ed.2d 66 (1982). *But see* Jerozal v. Cash Reserve Management, Inc., 1982 WL 1363, [1982–83 Transfer Binder] Fed.Sec.L.Rep. (CCH) ¶ 99,019 (S.D.N.Y.1982). That court reasoned that a suit against an investment adviser for breach of an advisory contract is a matter of state law.

28.   Tarlov v. Paine Webber Cashfund, Inc., 559 F.Supp. 429 (D.Conn.1983). *See* Meyer v. Oppenheimer Management Corp., 764 F.2d 76 (2d Cir.1985) (sustaining claim of breach of duty due to charging of excessive fees). *See also* Krinsk v. Fund Asset Management, Inc., 654 F.Supp. 1227, 1233 (S.D.N.Y.1987) (implied remedy has to claim more than excessive fees; "[p]ut another way, a plaintiff may not escape the strictures of § 36(b)(3), by merely characterizing his § 36(b) claim as arising under a different section").

29.   15 U.S.C.A. § 80a–35(a), (b)(3); Halligan v. Standard & Poor's/Intercapital, Inc., 434 F.Supp. 1082, 1084 (E.D.N.Y.1977). *See also, e.g.,* Tannenbaum v. Zeller, 552 F.2d 402, 413, 415 & n. 17 (2d Cir.), *cert. denied* 434 U.S. 934, 98 S.Ct. 421, 54 L.Ed.2d 293 (1977); Rosenfeld v. Black, 445 F.2d 1337 (2d Cir.1971), *cert. dismissed* 409 U.S. 802, 93 S.Ct. 24, 34 L.Ed.2d 62 (1972) (rendered moot by the enactment of 15 U.S.C.A. § 80a–15(f) in 1975; *see* § 17.9 *supra*).

30.   Kamen v. Kemper Financial Services, Inc., 659 F.Supp. 1153 (N.D.Ill.1987) (allowing section 20(a) claim to supplement section 36(b) claim for excessive fees); Krinsk v. Fund Asset Management, Inc., 654 F.Supp. 1227 (S.D.N.Y.1987); Schuyt v. Rowe Price Prime Reserve Fund, Inc., 622 F.Supp. 169 (S.D.N.Y.1985).

This, of course, is consistent with the fact that there is an implied remedy under the proxy provisions of the Securities Exchange Act of 1934. *See* §§ 11.3–11.5 *supra*.

But cf. Gartenberg v. Merrill Lynch Asset Management, Inc., 528 F.Supp. 1038 (S.D.N.Y. 1981), *affirmed* 694 F.2d 923 (2d Cir.1982), *cert. denied* 461 U.S. 906, 103 S.Ct. 1877, 76 L.Ed.2d 808 (1983) (dictum denying the § 20 implied remedy).

31.   445 F.2d 369 (1st Cir.1971), *cert. denied* 404 U.S. 994, 92 S.Ct. 532, 30 L.Ed.2d 547 (1971).

Company Act. In Fogel v. Chestnutt,[32] a similar duty was held to exist under section 36(a) in its present form. The *Moses* and *Fogel* duty has been held to extend beyond the "give-up" situation. In Cambridge Fund v. Abella[33] an affiliated director was held liable for a breach of fiduciary duty by personally trading in securities simultaneously with transactions by the investment company and for non-disclosure of the company's payment of that director's legal expenses in SEC proceedings against him.[34] The cases[35] and legislative comment[36] indicate that section 36(b)'s enactment did not curtail existing private rights of action under section 36(a) by a shareholder against investment company directors for breaching their fiduciary duty. This is echoed by Supreme Court dictum in *Burks v. Lasker*[37] which found no breach of section 36(a)'s fiduciary duty resulting from an investment company's board of directors terminating a shareholder's derivative suit if the applicable state law would allow such board action.[38]

The continued viability of implied remedies under the Investment Company Act is further bolstered by the Third Circuit's decision in Bancroft Convertible Fund v. Zico Investment Holdings,[39] which recognized an implied right of action under section 12(d)(1)(A)'s anti-pyramiding prohibition.[40] Following the rationale of the Supreme Court in Merrill Lynch, Pierce, Fenner & Smith v. Curran,[41] the Third Circuit relied on Congressional acquiescence in the implied remedies that had

---

32. 533 F.2d 731 (2d Cir.1975), *cert. denied* 429 U.S. 824, 97 S.Ct. 77, 50 L.Ed.2d 86 (1976). The "give-up" issue has been mooted by a change in New York Stock Exchange and SEC rules eliminating the practice. For a full discussion of the practice and the problem *see* Richard W. Jennings & Harold Marsh, Jr., Securities Regulation: Cases and Materials 481–485 (5th ed. 1982).

33. 501 F.Supp. 598 (S.D.N.Y.1980).

34. *Id.* at 619–24.

35. Tannenbaum v. Zeller, 552 F.2d 402, 416 (2d Cir.1977), *cert. denied* 434 U.S. 934, 98 S.Ct. 421, 54 L.Ed.2d 293 (1977); Cambridge Fund Inc. v. Abella, 501 F.Supp. 598 (S.D.N.Y.1980); Whitman v. Fuqua, 549 F.Supp. 315 (1982). The Supreme Court assumed without deciding, that a cause of action existed under section 36(a) in Burks v. Lasker, 441 U.S. 471, 99 S.Ct. 1831, 60 L.Ed.2d 404 (1979). *But cf.* Tarlov v. Paine Webber Cashfund, Inc., 559 F.Supp. 429 (D.Conn.1983) (no section 36(a) remedy for excessive advisory fees).

36. " * * * the fact that subsection (b) [of Section 36] specifically provides for a private right of action should not be read by implication to affect subsection (a)," House Committee Report, H.R. No. 91–1382, 91st Cong. 2d Sess. (1970), at 38.

37. 441 U.S. 471, 99 S.Ct. 1831, 60 L.Ed.2d 404 (1979).

38. *Id.* at 486, 99 S.Ct. at 1841. *See* § 17.6 *supra* for a discussion of investment company directors' duties.

39. 825 F.2d 731 (3d Cir.1987). *Accord* Clemente Global Growth Fund v. Pickens, 705 F.Supp. 958, 963 (S.D.N.Y.1989).

40. 15 U.S.C.A. § 80a–12(d)(1)(A) which prohibits investment companies and their affiliated companies from purchasing shares in another investment company when after the acquisition, the acquiring company would own more than three percent of the target's shares or when the aggregate value of the shares owned exceeds five percent of the purchaser's assets.

41. 456 U.S. 353, 102 S.Ct. 1825, 72 L.Ed.2d 182 (1982). *See* the discussion in § 13.1 *supra.*

long been recognized under the Act.[42]   The court viewed the addition of section 36(b)'s express remedy as supplementing implied remedies that had already been recognized.[43]   Following the lesson of the implication cases emanating from the Supreme Court, the Third Circuit examined the legislative history underlying the Investment Company Act and subsequent amendments.   The court then concluded that the amendment to the Act as part of the Small Business Incentive Act of 1980[44] left intact the sections which had formed the basis for implied remedies and the legislative history of the amendment displayed Congress' continued "enthusiasm" for private enforcement of the Investment Company Act.[45]

The court's rationale clearly is not limited to the section 12(d)(1)(A) remedy which it recognized for the first time.   The reasoning in *Bancroft* is convincing precedent for continued recognition of the other implied remedies under the Act.[46]

Section 36(b) Action to Recover for Excessive Compensation; Demise of the Derivative Suit Demand Requirement

As the preceding discussion indicates, the implied remedies under the Act have a varied history but the courts have continued to be relatively receptive in light of the demise of implied remedies generally. The implied remedies are supplemented by the express remedy provided by section 36(b), which is set forth below.   Section 36(b) creates an express right of action for breaches of fiduciary duty that arise out of excessive compensation payments to investment advisers and their affiliates.   The section 36(b) action to recover for excessive compensation may be brought against the investment company's officers, directors, advisory board, investment adviser, or depositor.[47]   In the case of open end companies, unit investment trusts, and face amount certificate companies, the section 36(b) action may be brought against the invest-

---

42.   In particular, the court relied on *Fogel v. Chestnutt* which is discussed in the text accompanying footnote 32 *supra.*

43.   825 F.2d at 735–36 ("Inclusion of such an express private remedy has nothing to do with other sections of the Act, however, and in no way suggests a congressional intent to abolish established causes of action for their enforcement").

44.   Pub.L.No. 96–477, 94 Stat. 2275 (1980).

45.   825 F.2d at 735.

46.   *See* discussion *supra.   But see, e.g.,* Potomac Capital Markets Corp. v. Prudential–Bache Corporate Dividend Fund, Inc., 746 F.Supp. 372 (S.D.N.Y.1990) (no implied right of action under § 13(a)(4) of the Act which requires a shareholder vote to change the nature of the company's business so as to cease being an investment company).

As discussed more fully in § 13.1 *supra,* the Supreme Court's approach to implied remedies generally has become increasingly negative.   The most recent example of this is the Court's very literal approach in Central Bank of Denver v. First Interstate Bank of Denver, ___ U.S. ___, 114 S.Ct. 1439, 128 L.Ed.2d 119 (1994) wherein the Court denied the existence of an implied remedy against aiders and abettors.   *See* § 13.16 *supra.*

47.   The permissible defendants are set forth in section 36(a).   15 U.S.C.A. § 80a–35(a). At least one court has indicated that section 36(b) preempts state law claims for breach of fiduciary duty when challenging investment management compensation.   Batra v. Investors Research Corp., 1992 WL 280790, [1992 Transfer Binder] Fed.Sec.L.Rep. (CCH) ¶ 96,983, p. 94,261 fn. 3 (W.D.Mo.1992).

ment company's principal underwriter.[48] Since the section 36(b) remedy is limited to excessive compensation, the implied remedies discussed above remain important with regard to other wrongdoing by investment company managers.

There previously had been confusion and disagreement among the circuits whether section 36(b)'s shareholder cause of action requires the shareholder to make a demand for action against the investment adviser upon the investment company's board of directors pursuant to Federal Rule of Civil Procedure 23.1 before the shareholder plaintiff may maintain an independent action against the adviser.[49] The Supreme Court has resolved the conflict in holding that no demand is required.[50] Although the issue has been settled, the cases that grappled with the issue shed light on the courts' view of the relationship between investment company shareholders and directors.

Section 36(b) provides:

> For the purposes of this subsection, the investment adviser of a registered investment company shall be deemed to have a fiduciary duty with respect to the receipt of compensation for services, or of payments of a material nature, paid by such registered investment company, or by the security holders thereof, to such investment adviser or any affiliated person of such investment adviser. An action may be brought under this subsection by the Commission, or by a security holder of such registered investment company on behalf of such company, against such investment adviser, or any affiliated person of such investment adviser, or any other person enumerated in subsection (a) of this section who has a fiduciary duty concerning such compensation or payments, for breach of fiduciary duty in respect of such compensation or payments paid by such registered investment company or by the security holders thereof to such investment adviser or person.[51]

---

48.   15 U.S.C.A. § 80a–35(a).

49.   Fed.R.Civ.P. 23.1. For discussion of the demand requirements generally and the business judgment rule, *see* James D. Cox, Thomas L. Hazen & F. Hodge O'Neal, Corporations, ch. 15 (1995); Harry G. Henn & John R. Alexander, Laws of Corporations §§ 365, 367 (3d ed.1983); Meredith M. Brown & William I. Phillips, The Business Judgment Rule: *Burks v. Lasker* and Other Recent Developments, 6 J.Corp.L. 453 (1981); George W. Dent, Jr., The Power of Directors to Terminate Shareholder Litigation: The Death of the Derivative Suit?, 75 Nw.U.L.Rev. 96 (1980); Kon sik Kim, The Demand on Directors Requirements and the Business Judgment Rule in the Shareholder Derivative Suit: An Alternative Framework, 6 J.Corp.Law 571 (1981); Note, The Demand Requirement and Mutual Fund Advisory Fee Suits: An Incompatible Combination?, 40 Wash. & Lee L.Rev. 1091 (1983). *See also* § 13.11 *supra.*

50.   Daily Income Fund, Inc. v. Fox, 464 U.S. 523, 104 S.Ct. 831, 78 L.Ed.2d 645 (1984). The demand requirement does apply, however, to other claims such as that proxy materials were misleading. *See, e.g.,* Kamen v. Kemper Financial Services, Inc., 908 F.2d 1338 (7th Cir.1990), *reversed on other grounds* 500 U.S. 90, 111 S.Ct. 1711, 114 L.Ed.2d 152 (1991) (allegations of misleading proxy; claims of futility of demand were insufficient to excuse demand on directors).

51.   15 U.S.C.A. § 80a–35(b). *See, e.g.,* Potomac Capital Markets Corp. v. Prudential–Bache Corporate Dividend Fund, Inc., 726 F.Supp. 87 (S.D.N.Y.1989) (summary judgment

The First Circuit in Grossman v. Johnson[52] had held that the shareholder's right to sue "on behalf of [the] company" made the action a derivative one, that is, one that the company itself could bring. The First Circuit in *Grossman* found no congressional intention to override the presumption that the Federal Rules of Civil Procedure would be applied and thus held that a shareholder must demand that the investment company's board take action against the adviser and be rebuffed before the shareholder may maintain a private action.[53]

The Third Circuit had accepted the *Grossman* holding in Weiss v. Temporary Investment Fund, Inc.[54] In addition, the court held that section 36(b) does not deprive the investment company itself of having an implied cause of action against the investment adviser.[55] The dissenting opinion in *Weiss*[56] argued that no cause of action inured to the investment company itself and that the shareholder's suit, independently authorized by section 36(b), was not a derivative action. Therefore, it was argued, no demand for investment company board action would be required before the shareholder could bring suit against the adviser.[57]

The dissent in *Weiss* was in accord with the Second Circuit in Fox v. Reich & Tang, Inc.[58] The court in the *Fox* opinion had searched through section 36(b)'s legislative history and concluded that an investment company was not intended to have a cause of action thereunder.[59] The Second Circuit in *Fox* reasoned that "[t]he relationship of a fund to its adviser makes it a part of the problem in a way that precludes it from being part of the solution, at least at the litigation stage." [60] Recognizing that section 36(b) was enacted to provide shareholders relief against board inaction, the Second Circuit wrote that requiring a Rule 23.1 demand "would be an empty, unfruitful and dilatory exercise."[61] Per-

---

denied since there were factual issues relating to alleged breach of duty in connection with liquidation plan).

52.   674 F.2d 115 (1st Cir.1982), *cert. denied* 459 U.S. 838, 103 S.Ct. 85, 74 L.Ed.2d 80 (1982).

53.   *Id.* at 122–23, quoting 7 Moore's Federal Practice § 86.04[4] at 86–22 (2d ed. 1980).

54.   692 F.2d 928 (3d Cir.1982), *cert. granted and judgment vacated* 465 U.S. 1001, 104 S.Ct. 989, 79 L.Ed.2d 224 (1984).

55.   *Id.* at 936. The court relied on Cort v. Ash, 422 U.S. 66, 95 S.Ct. 2080, 45 L.Ed.2d 26 (1975).

56.   692 F.2d at 944–53.

57.   The dissent further opined that the one year statute of limitations for actions against advisers was incompatible with a requirement of corporate action due to the latter's "normal delays," and that section 36(b)(2) "preempts any state law business judgment rule which would be furthered by the demand requirement." *Id.* at 951, 952.

58.   692 F.2d 250 (2d Cir.1982), *affirmed sub nom.* Daily Income Fund, Inc. v. Fox, 464 U.S. 523, 104 S.Ct. 831, 78 L.Ed.2d 645 (1984).

59.   692 F.2d at 256–60.

60.   *Id.* at 260. *See also e.g.,* Markowitz v. Brody, 90 F.R.D. 542 (S.D.N.Y.1981) (demand excused where a majority of the directors had an interest in the challenged conduct). *See also* Comment, The Demand and Standing Requirements in Stockholder Derivative Actions, 44 Chi.L.Rev. 168, 173 (1976).

61.   *Id.* at 262.

haps the best argument against requiring a demand in an action under section 36(b) was alluded to by the Second Circuit in its discussion of the dominance of settlements in suits against advisers before section 36(b) was enacted;[62] the argument was based on the possibility that the investment company, by asserting a claim against the adviser, could preclude a shareholder from doing the same. The adviser could then cause the investment board, due to sixty percent domination of interested directors, to settle for a lower amount than would have been awarded by an impartial court.[63]

The Supreme Court has affirmed the Second Circuit's holding in *Fox* by ruling that Rule 23.1's demand requirement does not apply in shareholder derivative actions brought under section 36(b) of the Investment Company Act.[64] In the words of the Court:

> A shareholder derivative action is an exception to the normal rule that the proper party to bring a suit on behalf of a corporation is the corporation itself, acting through its directors or a majority of its shareholders. Accordingly, Rule 23.1, which establishes procedures designed to prevent minority shareholders from abusing this equitable device, is addressed only to situations in which shareholders seek to enforce a right that "may properly be asserted" by the corporation itself. In contrast, as the language of § 36(b) indicates, Congress intended the fiduciary duty imposed on investment advisers by that statute to be enforced solely by security holders of the investment company and the SEC. It would be anomalous, therefore, to apply a Rule intended to prevent a shareholder from improperly suing in place of the corporation to a statute, like § 36(b), conferring a right which the corporation itself cannot enforce. It follows that Rule 23.1 does not apply to an action brought by a shareholder under § 36(b) of the Investment Company Act and that the plaintiff in such a case need not first make a demand upon the fund's directors before bringing suit.[65]

The demand controversy has thus been put to rest, except in the case of implied remedies.[66] In such a case, the demand futility rule of the state

---

62. *Id.* at 260.

63. The dissent in *Weiss* recognized this possibility of making an end-run around the court when it declared, while the court must afford deference to the views of fund directors [due to section 36(b)(2)], the ultimate responsibility for deciding whether the fees are so high as to be regarded as a breach of fiduciary duty is judicial, and that only fund shareholders or the commission could seek that determination. 692 F.2d at 948. *But see* Gartenberg v. Merrill Lynch Asset Management, Inc., 694 F.2d 923, 928 (2d Cir.1982).

64. Daily Income Fund, Inc. v. Fox, 464 U.S. 523, 542, 104 S.Ct. 831, 841–42 78 L.Ed.2d 645, 659 (1984).

65. *Id.* at 542, 104 S.Ct. at 842.

66. *See* Kamen v. Kemper Financial Services, Inc., 659 F.Supp. 1153 (N.D.Ill.1987) (dismissing claim under section 20(a) for proxy violations because of failure to make a demand on directors), *affirmed in part and reversed in part* 908 F.2d 1338 (7th Cir.1990), *cert. granted* 498 U.S. 997, 111 S.Ct. 554, 112 L.Ed.2d 561 (1990) (allegations of misleading proxy; claims of futility of demand were insufficient to excuse demand on directors).

of incorporation governs whether the demand is excused.[67]

Standing to Sue; Right to Jury Trial

Liability under section 36 is based on a breach of duty to the investment company shareholders and thus will not support an action by someone else injured by the alleged wrongdoing.[68] The essence of a claim under section 36(b) is a classic case of breach of fiduciary duty which historically has been an action in equity, and accordingly there is no right to a jury trial.[69] The realm of fiduciary duties covered by section 36(b) is relatively narrow and thus, for example, does not include violations of the Investment Company Act's proxy regulations.[70] Although as discussed above, an implied remedy may exist under the Investment Company Act and also under the Securities Exchange Act of 1934.

Damages in Actions Under Section 36(b)

The amount recoverable in a section 36(b) action is limited to improper compensation paid within one year before the suit was instituted.[71] Only those who actually receive compensation from the investment company for advisory services may be held liable for breach of their fiduciary duties under section 36(b).[72] In making the determination whether the compensation paid was, in fact, excessive, courts will give great weight to approval by fully informed, properly qualified independent directors.[73]

67. Kamen v. Kemper Financial Services, Inc., 500 U.S. 90, 111 S.Ct. 1711, 114 L.Ed.2d 152 (1991), *on remand* 939 F.2d 458 (7th Cir.1991), *cert. denied* 502 U.S. 974, 112 S.Ct. 454, 116 L.Ed.2d 471 (1991).

68. Index Fund, Inc. v. Hagopian, 609 F.Supp. 499, 505 (S.D.N.Y.1985) (investor of securities allegedly manipulated by defendants in connection with their management of an investment company did not have a claim under the Investment Company Act since plaintiff was not a shareholder of the investment company in question).

69. Krinsk v. Fund Asset Management, Inc., 875 F.2d 404 (2d Cir.1989) (no right to jury trial since remedy is based on equitable restitution); In re Evangelist, 760 F.2d 27 (1st Cir.1985); In re Gartenberg, 636 F.2d 16, 17–18 (2d Cir.1980), *cert. denied* 451 U.S. 910, 101 S.Ct. 1979, 68 L.Ed.2d 298 (1981); Kamen v. Kemper Financial Services, Inc., 659 F.Supp. 1153, 1164 (N.D.Ill.1987); Tarlov v. Paine Webber Cashfund, Inc., 559 F.Supp. 429, 441 (D.Conn.1983); Jerozal v. Cash Reserve Management, Inc., 1982 WL 1363, [1982–83 Transfer Binder] Fed.Sec.L.Rep. (CCH) ¶ 99,019 at p. 94,827 (S.D.N.Y.1982); Markowitz v. Brody, 90 F.R.D. 542, 547–48 (S.D.N.Y.1981). *See also, e.g.,* Kalish v. Franklin Advisers, Inc., 928 F.2d 590 (2d Cir.1991), *cert. denied* 502 U.S. 818, 112 S.Ct. 75, 116 L.Ed.2d 48 (1991); Kamen v. Kemper Financial Services, Inc., 908 F.2d 1338 (7th Cir.1990), *reversed on other grounds* 500 U.S. 90, 111 S.Ct. 1711, 114 L.Ed.2d 152 (1991).

70. *See* Schuyt v. Rowe Price Prime Reserve Fund, Inc., 622 F.Supp. 169 (S.D.N.Y. 1985) (recognizing a right to sue for the proxy violations under section 20(a) of the Act). *See also* the cases in footnote 30 *supra.*

71. Section 36(b)(3), 15 U.S.C.A. § 80a–35(b); Halligan v. Standard & Poor's/Intercapital, Inc., 434 F.Supp. 1082, 1085 (E.D.N.Y.1977).

72. Halligan v. Standard & Poor's/Intercapital, Inc., 434 F.Supp. 1082, 1085 (E.D.N.Y. 1977).

73. *E.g.* Schuyt v. Rowe Price Prime Reserve Fund, Inc., 663 F.Supp. 962 (S.D.N.Y. 1987). *Cf.* Kalish v. Franklin Advisers, Inc., 928 F.2d 590 (2d Cir.1991), *affirming* 742 F.Supp. 1222 (S.D.N.Y.1990) (shareholder failed to establish that mutual fund realized economies of scale thereby making fees excessive and in breach of a fiduciary duty). *See also* §§ 17.6, 17.9 *supra.*

Jurisdiction Over Investment Company Act Claims[74]

Unlike the 1934 Exchange Act[75] but in accord with the other federal securities laws,[76] jurisdiction over private suits is vested concurrently in the federal and state courts.[77] Although actions brought in state court are removable by the defendant to federal court,[78] some important litigation has taken place in the state courts.[79]

---

74. For more detailed discussion of jurisdictional considerations see §§ 14.1–14.3 *supra.*

75. 15 U.S.C.A. § 78aa.

76. *See* § 14.1 *supra. See generally* Thomas L. Hazen, Allocation of Jurisdiction Between the State and Federal Courts for Private Remedies Under the Federal Securities Laws, 60 N.C.L.Rev. 707 (1982).

77. 15 U.S.C.A. § 80a–43.

78. *Id. Compare* the 1933 Act which does not provide for a right of removal. 15 U.S.C.A. § 77v(a).

79. *E.g.,* Lutz v. Boas, 39 Del.Ch. 585, 171 A.2d 381 (1961), *see* note 7 *supra.*

Chapter 18

INVESTMENT ADVISERS ACT OF 1940

Table of Sections

§ 18.1 Regulation of Investment Advisers; Terms and Conditions in Advisory Contracts

The Securities Exchange Act of 1934 regulates market professionals through its broker-dealer registration and oversight provisions.[1] That Act does not, however, address itself directly to non-broker-dealers who are in the business of rendering investment advice. This gap is filled by the Investment Advisers Act of 1940.[2]

Professional investment advisers frequently sell their services by disseminating advice through newsletters and other publications.[3] Others manage funds through an investment company or otherwise through custodial accounts. The Investment Advisers Act of 1940 addresses itself to many of these services.

§ 18.1

1. 15 U.S.C.A. §§ 78o, 78o–4. *See* § 10.2 *supra*. *See generally* Jerry W. Markham & Thomas L. Hazen, Broker-Dealer Operations Under Securities and Commodities Law: Financial Responsibilities, Credit Regulation and Customer Protection (1995).

2. 15 U.S.C.A. § 80b–1 *et seq*. *See generally* Tamar Frankel, The Regulation of Money Managers: The Investment Company Act and the Investment Advisers Act (1978); 2 Louis Loss, Securities Regulation 1392–1417 (2d ed. 1961, 1969 Supp.); Alan M. Ahart, Advising the Individual Investor: Comparing the Federal Regulation of Investment Advisers, Banks, and Broker–Dealers, 6 Pepperdine L.Rev. 31 (1978); Gregory S. Crespi, The Reach of the Federal Registration Requirements for Broker–Dealers and Investment Advisors, 17 Sec. Reg.L.J. 339 (1990); Richard D. Harroch, The Applicability of the Investment Advisers Act of 1940 to Financial and Investment Related Publications, 5 J.Corp.L. 55 (1979); Richard D. Harroch, Advisers Act Developments, 12 Rev.Sec.Reg. 879 (1979); Robert N. Leavell, Investment Advice and the Fraud Rules, 65 Mich.L.Rev. 2569 (1967); Fred B. Lovitch, The Investment Advisers Act of 1940—Who is an "Investment Adviser?", 24 Kans.L.Rev. 67 (1975).

3. *See, e.g.,* Richard D. Harroch, The Applicability of the Investment Advisers Act of 1940 to Financial and Investment Related Publications, 5 J.Corp.L. 55 (1979).

In 1985, the Supreme Court ruled that requiring registration of newsletters rendering investment advice on an impersonal basis does not fall within the Act's definition of investment adviser.[4] The Court held that the unregistered status of such investment services did not justify restraining future publication.[5] Notwithstanding the Supreme Court's holding, as of May 1986, of the approximately five to six thousand publishers of investment letters nevertheless registered as investment advisers, fewer than twenty had deregistered. Through 1988, a number of advisory letters had retained their registered status. Presumably, these publishers believed it would add to their credibility to be able to state that they were registered with the SEC.

The Investment Advisers Act requires registration[6] of all non-exempt investment advisers.[7] In addition to registration, non-exempt investment advisers must file periodic reports with the SEC and be available for periodic examination by the Commission.[8] Section 206 of the Act[9] prohibits material misrepresentations and fraudulent practices in connection with the rendering of investment advice. This antifraud provision applies to investment advisers even though they may be exempt from the Act's registration requirements.

The Act also regulates contracts between investment advisers and their clients.[10] The Act prohibits contracts whereby the adviser's compensation is dependent upon a share of the client's capital appreciation or gain.[11] Contingent fees are thus prohibited. The theory is that such arrangements may lead the adviser to take undue risks with clients' funds.[12] The fee may be based on the total value of the fund taken at designated time periods.[13] In 1985 the SEC changed its long-time policy and now permits performance-based advisory fees for certain qualifying large advisory contracts.[14]

---

4. Lowe v. SEC, 472 U.S. 181, 105 S.Ct. 2557, 86 L.Ed.2d 130 (1985).

5. The *Lowe* decision is discussed in § 18.2 *infra*.

6. *See* § 18.3 *infra*.

7. For example, advisers acting solely on behalf of insurance companies are exempt from registration. 15 U.S.C.A. § 80b–3(b)(2). The other exemptions are found in 15 U.S.C.A. § 80b–6a. *See* § 18.2 *infra*.

8. 15 U.S.C.A. § 80b–4.

9. 15 U.S.C.A. § 80b–6. Section 207 is addressed specifically to false filings with the Commission. 15 U.S.C.A. § 80b–7.

10. 15 U.S.C.A. § 80b–5.

11. 15 U.S.C.A. § 80b–5(a)(1).

12. Inv.Adv.Act Rel. No. IA–721 (May 16, 1980).

13. 15 U.S.C.A. § 80b–5; 17 C.F.R. §§ 275.205–1, 275.205–2.

14. An adviser can base fees on net realized capital gains and unrealized capital appreciation of a customer's funds for advisory contracts with a client that has at least $500,000 under the adviser's management or of a client with a net worth that exceeds one million dollars. In addition to the objective financial criteria, the client must be financially sophisticated and, in particular, the client must understand both the method of compensation and the risks presented by such a performance-based system of adviser compensation. 17 C.F.R. § 275.205–3. *See* Inv.Adv.Act Rel. No. IA–996 (Nov. 14, 1985). The burden is on the investment adviser to establish that the account qualifies for performance-based fees. *See, e.g.,* In the Matter of Early, [1993–1994 Transfer Binder] Fed. Sec. L. Rep. ¶ 85,354 (SEC Initial Dec. 1994).

An advisory contract must by its terms preclude assignment of the contract unless the client or customer consents.[15] This is designed to protect the investor against an unannounced change in the quality or character of the advisory services. If the investment adviser is a partnership, the advisory contract must provide for notice within a reasonable time of all changes in the composition of the partnership.[16] The sections that follow examine the registration and disclosure provisions of the Advisers Act.

Over the past several years, there have been a number of proposals for the creation of a self regulatory organization for investment advisers. The SEC has been considering the establishment of such a self regulatory organization which not only would help police the industry but also would help coordinate federal and state regulation. In 1989, the SEC decided to seek Congressional authorization for self regulatory organizations to oversee investment advisers.[17] Previously the North American Securities Administrators' Association had endorsed a self regulatory organization for investment advisers. Additionally, the National Association of Securities Dealers' board of governors has endorsed the concept of a pilot program under which the NASD would act as a self regulatory organization for investment advisers and associated persons. In a related development, a trade association for financial planners has recommended the creation of a self regulatory organization for financial planners, but the SEC has informally taken a negative position since this type of organization would include only about one half of federally regulated investment advisers.

§ 18.2　Who Is Subject to the Advisers Act—Definitions, Exclusions, and Exemptions

Definition of Investment Adviser

Section 203(a) of the Investment Advisers Act requires registration of all investment advisers doing business through an instrumentality of interstate commerce unless exempted under section 203(b).[1] The Act defines "investment adviser" to include "any person who, for compensation, engages in the business of advising others, either directly or through publications or writings as to the value of securities or as to the advisability of investing in, purchasing, or selling securities * * *."[2]

---

15. 15 U.S.C.A. § 80b–5(a)(2). *See* In the Matter of Kephart Communications, Inc., [1976–1977 Transfer Binder] Fed.Sec.L.Rep. (CCH) ¶ 80,845 (SEC Aug. 14, 1976) (No–Action Letter issued with regard to sale of advisory newsletter, where all subscribers were to be notified and given a right to cancel their subscriptions).

16. 15 U.S.C.A. § 80b–5(a)(3).

17. *See* SEC to Ask Congress for Legislation to Permit Creation of Advisers' SRO's, 21 Sec.Reg. & L.Rep. (BNA) 871 (June 16, 1989).

§ 18.2

1. 15 U.S.C.A. § 80b–3(a), (b).

2. 15 U.S.C.A. § 80b–2(a)(11). *See* Fred B. Lovitch, The Investment Adviser's Act of 1940–Who is an "Investment Adviser?", 24 Kans.L.Rev. 67 (1975); Note, SEC Release 1092 of the Investment Advisers Act of 1940: Applicability of the Investment Advisers Act

Exclusions

The definition of investment adviser excludes banks, lawyers, accountants, engineers or teachers rendering such advice incidental to their profession.[3]　Also excluded is any broker-dealer whose advisory service "is solely incidental to the conduct of his business as a broker or dealer" and without special compensation.[4]　Although exempt from the Adviser's Act, brokers and dealers furnishing such incidental advice are subject to the suitability, "know your customer," and "know your merchandise" requirements when making investment recommendations to customers.[5]　When dealing with investment advice furnished by brokerage firms, a critical issue is whether the customer is paying specially for the advice or whether the advice is simply part of the brokerage service.[6]　Bona fide news media including financial publications of general circulation[7] and persons limiting such advice to securi-

---

to Financial Planners and Other Persons Who Provide Financial Services, 45 Wash. & Lee L.Rev. 1139 (1988). *See also, e.g.,* United Methodist Foundation of Baltimore Annual Conference, Inc., 20 Sec.Reg. & L.Rep. (BNA) 1989 (SEC No Action Letter available Nov. 29, 1988) (church foundation managing funds needed to register as an investment adviser).

3. 15 U.S.C.A. § 80b–2(a)(11)(A), (B). *See* Alan M. Ahart, Advising the Individual Investor: Comparing the Federal Regulation of Investment Advisers, Banks, and Broker–Dealers, 6 Pepperdine L.Rev. 31 (1978). Banks are becoming increasingly active in the securities end of the financial markets in general and in investment management and the rendering of investment advice. Currently, commercial banks are prohibited from directly engaging in investment banking activities under the Glass–Steagall Act, whose repeal has been suggested. However, the Glass–Steagall Act has not kept banks out of the investment management business. *See* Martin E. Lybecker, Bank–Sponsored Investment Management Services, 1977 Duke L.J. 983; Note, The Legality of Bank–Sponsored Investment Services, 84 Yale L.J. 1477 (1975); Note, Legal Status of a National Bank's Automatic Stock Investment Service Under Sections 16 and 21 of the Glass–Steagall Act of 1933, 27 Vand.L.Rev. 1217 (1974); Comment, Implementation of the Bank Holding Company Act Amendments of 1970: The Scope of Banking Activities, 71 Mich.L.Rev. 1170 (1973); Comment, National Bank–Sponsored Investment Companies, 65 Nw.U.L.Rev. 93 (1970); Note, Commingled Investment Accounts: Banks v. Securities Industry, 45 Notre Dame Law. 746 (1970). *See* § 19.5 *infra* (Practitioner's Edition only).

Also excluded from the Investment Advisers Act are securities exempted from the Exchange Act by virtue of section 3(a)(12) of that Act. 15 U.S.C.A. §§ 78c(a)(12), 80b–2(a)(11)(E).

4. 15 U.S.C.A. § 80b–2(a)(11)(C). Additional brokerage advice is exempted from the Act under Rule 206(3)–1. 17 C.F.R. § 275.206(3)–1. *See* footnote 34 *infra* and accompanying text.

5. *See* §§ 10.6, 10.7, 10.8 *supra*. *See generally* Victor Brudney, Origins and Limited Applicability of the "Reasonable Basis" or "Know Your Merchandise" Doctrine, 4 Inst.Sec. Reg. 230 (1973); Hilary H.Cohen, Suitability Doctrine: Defining Stockbrokers' Professional Responsibilities, 3 J.Corp.L. 533 (1978); Gerald L. Fishman, Broker–Dealer Obligations to Customers—The NASD Suitability Rule, 51 Minn.L.Rev. 233 (1966); Ezra G. Levin & William M. Evan, Professionalism and the Stock Broker: Some Observations on the SEC Special Study, 21 Bus.Law. 337 (1966); Robert H. Mundheim, Professional Responsibilities of Broker–Dealers: The Suitability Doctrine, 1065 Duke L.J. 445; F. Harris Nichols, Broker's Duty to his Customer Under Evolving Federal Fiduciary and Suitability Standards, 26 Buffalo L.Rev. 435 (1977); Note, "Know Your Customer" Rule of the NYSE, 1973 Duke L.J. 489; Note, New and Comprehensive Duties of Securities Sellers to Investigate, Disclose, and Have an "Adequate Basis" for Representations, 62 Mich.L.Rev. 880 (1964). *See also* Ahart *supra* footnote 3.

6. Inv.Adv.Act Rel. No. IA–2 (Oct. 28, 1949).

7. 15 U.S.C.A. § 80b–2(a)(11)(D). *See, e.g.,* Person v. New York Post Corp., 427 F.Supp. 1297 (E.D.N.Y.1977).

ties issued or guaranteed by the federal government[8] are not subject to the Investment Advisers Act registration requirements, as are other persons excluded by SEC rule.[9] Unlike persons that are exempted from the registration requirements, persons excluded from the Act's coverage are not subject to section 206's[10] antifraud proscriptions.

In Lowe v. SEC,[11] the Supreme Court ruled that an investment newsletter that renders impersonal investment advice did not fall within the Act's definition of investment adviser. The Court reasoned that the essence of the activity which the Act seeks to regulate is the personal service of investment advising and that such regularly published investment letters are impersonal and thus not within the Act's target. The Court in relying on the statutory definition did not have to reach the question on which it originally granted certiorari—whether prohibiting publication of such newsletters without registration under the Act was an unconstitutional prior restraint, which violated the First Amendment's right of free speech.[12] The Court noted, however, that Congress' decision to focus investment adviser regulation on the providing of personal services was motivated in part "to keep the Act free of constitutional infirmities." [13]

The SEC has taken the position that section 202(a)(11)(D)'s exclusion is available only where the publication's primary purpose is not the dissemination of investment advice. Investment Advisers Act Rel. No. IA–563 n. 1 (Jan. 10, 1977). *See also, e.g.,* In the Matter of G. Tsai & Co., [1978 Transfer Binder] Fed.Sec.L.Rep. (CCH) ¶ 81,686 (SEC Jan. 15, 1978); In the Matter of Media General Financial Daily, [1972–73 Transfer Binder] Fed.Sec.L.Rep. (CCH) ¶ 78,961 (SEC Aug. 16, 1971).

However, the courts have not been as narrow in their view of the exclusion. For example in SEC v. Wall Street Transcript Corp., 454 F.Supp. 559 (S.D.N.Y.1978) the court conceded that the defendant's publication dealt with investment advice but still qualified for the exclusion because the publication was not of the kind that the Act was meant to regulate. In the words of the court, "the defendants have never received compensation from any party for publishing or positioning a report or speech in the *Transcript;* never published any item for the purpose of affecting the value of any security mentioned therein; never traded in any security mentioned therein. Nor does [the SEC] dispute that within the limitations of space, the sole determinant of what material is published in the *Transcript* is Holman's independent judgment as to newsworthiness." *Id.* at 567. *Compare* SEC v. Myers, 285 F.Supp. 743 (D.Md.1968). *See generally* Harroch, The Applicability of the Investment Advisers Act of 1940 to Financial and Investment Related Publications, 5 J.Corp.L. 55 (1979).

The SEC's narrow view of section 202(a)(11)(D) has been undercut by the Supreme Court decision in Lowe v. SEC, 472 U.S. 181, 105 S.Ct. 2557, 86 L.Ed.2d 130 (1985), which is discussed *infra.*

8. 15 U.S.C.A. § 80b–2(a)(11)(E).

9. 15 U.S.C.A. § 80b–2(a)(11)(F).

10. 15 U.S.C.A. § 80b–6.

11. 472 U.S. 181, 105 S.Ct. 2557, 86 L.Ed.2d 130 (1985). *See* Richard S. Draughton, *SEC v. Lowe:* Redefining the Bona Fide Newspaper Exclusion, 14 Sec.Reg.L.J. 291 (1987); Note, Regulation of Investment Newsletter Publishers: The SEC's Power Reaches a New *Lowe*, 11 Vt.L.Rev. 175 (1986).

12. The constitutional attack, that was rejected by the Second Circuit in its opinion below simply went to the registration requirements and did not challenge the SEC's power to regulate materially misleading publications and disclosures. *Cf.* SEC v. Blavin, 760 F.2d 706 (6th Cir.1985) (involving materially misleading statements; decided before *Lowe v. SEC).*

13. 472 U.S. at 208, 105 S.Ct. at 2572, 86 L.Ed.2d at 149.

The Court identified the Investment Adviser Act's focus as having been "designed to apply to those persons engaged in the investment advisory profession—those who provide *personalized* advice attuned to a client's concerns, whether by written or verbal communication."[14]   In defining the scope of its holding, the Court pointed out that it was limited to "bona fide" impersonal newsletters and not tout sheets designed to generate commissions for the adviser; and thus when used as part of a "scalping scheme," the SEC arguably should still have jurisdiction to enjoin publication.[15]

As observed in the preceding section, the *Lowe* decision did not result in a significant number of investment newsletter deregistrations. It is unclear whether, standing alone, these newsletters' apparent consent to SEC regulation can effectively expand the Commission's jurisdiction.[16]

The *Lowe* decision does not mean that investment newsletters which are excluded from the Act escape all regulation under the securities laws. For example, section 17(b) of the 1933 Act prohibits recommending securities without disclosing any remuneration connected with the recommendation.[17]   Section 17(b) is designed to prevent the appearance of an unbiased opinion when, in fact, the opinion has been "bought and paid for."[18]   A recent decision has rejected a constitutional challenge and thus upheld this type of regulation of financial newsletters.[19]   Recommendations that contain materially misleading factual information can run afoul of Rule 10b–5 regardless of whether the publisher is an investment adviser.[20]   Accordingly, the *Lowe* decision relates only to the

---

14.   *Id.* (emphasis supplied; footnote omitted.)

15.   *See* Joel D. Ferber, The Narrow Holding of the *Lowe* Case, 19 Rev.Sec. & Commodities Reg. 29 (1986).

16.   *Lowe* held that these entities are not investment advisers thus depriving the Commission of jurisdiction. By continuing their registration, newsletters are consenting to the Commission's jurisdiction. However, can a private party vest the Commission with jurisdiction not granted by the statute? Since an administrative agency exists only by virtue of enabling legislation, there is a strong argument that its jurisdiction cannot be expanded except by Congress.

17.   15 U.S.C.A. § 77q(b). *See* § 7.6 *supra.*

18.   H.R.Rep. No. 85, 73d Cong., 1st Sess. 24 (1933). *See* SEC v. Wall Street Publishing Institute, Inc., 851 F.2d 365 (D.C.Cir.1988); United States v. Amick, 439 F.2d 351, 365 (7th Cir.1971).

19.   SEC v. Wall Street Publishing Institute, Inc., 851 F.2d 365 (D.C.Cir.1988). The First Amendment argument was based on the Supreme Court's decision in Lowe v. SEC, 472 U.S. 181, 105 S.Ct. 2557, 86 L.Ed.2d 130 (1985) which held that the Investment Advisers Act does not require registration of newsletters rendering investment advice. Although not decided directly on constitutional grounds, the Court's decision in *Lowe* was premised on finding an interpretation of the Investment Advisers Act that would not be unconstitutional.

20.   *See, e.g.,* Zweig v. Hearst Corp., 594 F.2d 1261 (9th Cir.1979) (undisclosed purchases prior to making recommendation violated Rule 10b–5). *Cf.* SEC v. Capital Gains Research Bureau, Inc., 375 U.S. 180, 84 S.Ct. 275, 11 L.Ed.2d 237 (1963) (failure to disclose purchases of securities prior to making recommendation constituted a violation of Investment Advisers Act § 206); SEC v. Suter, 832 F.2d 988 (7th Cir.1987) (someone committing securities fraud cannot escape liability by publishing a newsletter and claiming exclusion from the Act). *See* § 10.9 *supra.*

Investment Advisers Act registration and antifraud provisions but not to the antifraud provisions contained in other securities acts.

Exemptions

The Commission has utilized its exemptive power to exclude persons rendering investment advice pursuant to their activities as financial planners, pension planners and others who provide the advice "as in integral component of other financially related services."[21] The past decade has witnessed the growth of financial planning as an industry.[22] This relatively new financial planning industry necessarily raises questions concerning the applicability of the Investment Advisers Act's registration provisions. For example, the SEC has indicated that registration may be required for a computer-generated financial planning service, although not recommending specific securities, which would nevertheless offer a service developed by an unaffiliated organization to identify investments that would implement the generalized investment recommendations.[23] In contrast, a broker-dealer can hold himself or herself out as a financial planner without Adviser Act registration so long as the planning services are incidental to broker-dealer activities and are without additional compensation and further that the planner would be recommending only products that were offered by the brokerage firm.[24] Similarly, an accountant who offers financial planning services that are purely incidental to his or her business does not have to register as an investment adviser so long as he or she does not mention specific investment products.[25] The SEC has issued an interpretative release which explains that many financial planners, pension consultants, sports or entertainment representatives, and others providing financial advisory services are investment advisers and therefore subject to regulation both at the federal and state levels.[26]

In addition to the above-mentioned exclusions from the definition of investment adviser, the Act provides exemptions from registration.[27] These exemptions do not immunize the adviser from the Act's anti-fraud provisions.[28] There are three such exemptions. First, a local adviser—

---

21. Inv.Adv.Act Rel. No. IA–770 (Aug. 13, 1981).

22. *See, e.g.,* Herbert L. Harris, Jr., Personal Financial Planning: The Competition; Who is Providing PFP Services?, 160 J. Accountancy 64 (July 1985); James H. Stevens, Jr., The Regulatory, Compliance, and Liability Aspects of Being a Financial Planner, 39 J.Am.Soc. CLU July, 1985, at 68.

23. In re Computer Language Research, Inc., [1985–86 Transfer Binder] Fed.Sec.L.Rep. (CCH) ¶ 78,185 (SEC No Action Letter Dec. 26, 1985).

24. In re Robinson, [1985–86 Transfer Binder] Fed.Sec.L.Rep. (CCH) ¶ 78,188 (SEC No Action Letter Jan. 6, 1986) (the SEC also asked that the limitations on the financial planning service be fully disclosed to all customers).

25. In re Hauk, Soule & Fasani, P.C., [1986 Transfer Binder] Fed.Sec.L.Rep. (CCH) ¶ 78,311 (SEC No Action Letter April 2, 1986).

26. Inv.Act Rel. No. IA–1092, 5 Fed.Sec.L.Rep. (CCH) ¶ 56,156E (Oct. 8, 1987). *Cf.* Note, Financial Planning: Is It Time For a Self–Regulatory Organization?, 53 Brooklyn L.Rev. 143 (1987).

27. 15 U.S.C.A. § 80b–3(b).

28. 15 U.S.C.A. § 80b–6. *See* § 18.4 *infra.*

that is, one whose clients are residents of the state of its principal place of business—is exempt so long as the adviser does not furnish advice with regard to exchange listed securities.[29]   Second, advisers whose only clients are insurance companies are similarly exempted from Advisers Act registration.[30]   Third, the Act further exempts advisers who do not have more than fifteen clients and do not hold themselves out as advisers either to the public or to investment companies.[31]

In 1970 the SEC was given the power to grant additional exemptions, either conditionally or unconditionally, consistent with investor protection and in the public interest.[32]   The Commission can grant an exemption either by invoking its rule-making power or upon application through an order.   The SEC has utilized its exemptive rule-making power with regard to publications and oral recommendations by brokers or dealers.   Brokers and dealers registered under section 15 of the Exchange Act[33] can issue public recommendations even if not incidental to their brokerage service and if for a separate fee.[34]   This exemption supplements the exclusion of incidental advice rendered without a fee.[35]

§ 18.3   Investment Adviser Registration and Reporting Requirements

All non-exempt investment advisers must register pursuant to section 203(c) of the Act[1] by filing Form ADV with the Commission.[2]   Form ADV requires disclosure of the identity and background of the adviser and affiliated persons.   The adviser must disclose its principal business[3] and the nature of such business.[4]   It is also necessary to disclose the scope of the adviser's authority[5] and the basis of compensation,[6] and also

---

29.   15 U.S.C.A. § 80b–3(b)(1).   The exemption also forbids advice with regard to securities having unlisted trading privileges on a national exchange.   There are currently nine active national exchanges registered under section 6 of the 1934 Act.   15 U.S.C.A. § 78f.   *See* §§ 10.1, 10.2 *supra.*

30.   15 U.S.C.A. § 80b–3(b)(2).   Prior to 1970 the exemption extended to advisers acting solely on behalf of investment companies.

31.   15 U.S.C.A. § 80b–3(b)(3).   In applying this exemption the SEC has adopted a safe harbor rule under which a limited partnership counts as one client provided that the general partner is not related to or affiliated with a registered investment adviser.   17 C.F.R. § 275.203(b)(3)–1, adopted in Inv.Adv.Act Rel. No. IA–983 (July 12, 1985).

32.   15 U.S.C.A. § 80b–6a.

33.   15 U.S.C.A. § 78o.   *See* § 10.2 *supra.*

34.   17 C.F.R. § 275.206(3)–1.

35.   15 U.S.C.A. § 80b–2(a)(11)(C).   *See* text accompanying footnotes 4–6 *supra.*

§ 18.3

1.   15 U.S.C.A. § 80b–3(c).   *See* Kauffman v. Yoskowitz, 1989 WL 79364, [1989 Transfer Binder] Fed.Sec.L.Rep. ¶ 94,532 (S.D.N.Y.1989) (it is "well settled" that there is no private remedy against an investment adviser for failure to register).

2.   *See* 17 C.F.R. § 275.203–1.   *See* SEC v. R.G. Reynolds, Inc. [1989–1990 Transfer Binder] Fed.Sec.L.Rep. ¶ 94,803 (C.D.Cal.1989) (self-proclaimed investment advisor was in violation of Rule 10b–5 and the Investment Adviser Act).

3.   15 U.S.C.A. § 80b–3(c)(1)(H).

4.   15 U.S.C.A. § 80b–3(c)(1)(C).

5.   15 U.S.C.A. § 80b–3(c)(1)(E).

---

6.   See note 6 on page 1032.

to include a balance sheet. The adviser must further disclose any criminal record that would affect qualification for registration.[7] The disclosure must include the adviser's educational and business background[8] as well as a description of any other business activities. Form ADV requires the adviser to set forth a list of the services provided, including a description of the types of clients served and the types of securities for which advice is rendered. Additional disclosures are required when the adviser manages discretionary accounts. As a general rule, all information in an adviser's registration statement is available to the public.[9] Much of the information disclosed in Form ADV must also be provided to existing and prospective advisory clients.[10] In 1985 the SEC revised Form ADV to make it uniform with filings required under many states' blue sky laws. In conjunction with these amendments, the Commission issued an interpretative release that was designed to aid in compliance with Form ADV filings.[11]

After Form ADV has been filed, the SEC has forty-five days to either grant the application for registration or institute proceedings to determine whether the application should be denied.[12] The applicant is entitled to notice of the grounds being considered as the basis for denial.[13] The SEC's statutory mandate is to deny registration if it finds that the applicant, if registered, would be subject to suspension or revocation.[14]

Registered investment advisers must file annual reports with the SEC on Form ADV–S.[15] Although the Form ADV must be kept current

---

6.   15 U.S.C.A. § 80b–3(c)(1)(F).

7.   15 U.S.C.A. § 80b–3(c)(1)(G). Disqualifications from registration are found in 15 U.S.C.A. § 80b–3(e)(3) which also sets out the grounds for suspension or revocation of an investment adviser's registration.

8.   15 U.S.C.A. § 80b–3(c)(1)(B).

9.   15 U.S.C.A. § 80b–10(a).

10.   17 C.F.R. § 275.204–3(a). *See* Inv.Adv.Act Rel. No. IA–767 (July 21, 1981). *See* text accompanying footnotes 27–30, *infra.*

11.   Inv.Adv.Act Rel. No. IA–1000 (Dec. 3, 1985). In an attempt to further coordinate efforts with the 37 states that currently regulate investment advisors (*see* § 8.1 *supra*)the SEC has proposed amendments to the Adviser Act that would permit sharing investigation information. *See* Fed.Sec.L.Rep. Bull. No. 1184 (CCH) 5–6 (June 18, 1986).

State securities administrators have considered the imposition of uniform adviser rules. *See* Proposed Uniform Rules for Advisers Circulated for Comment by NASAA Group, 19 Sec.Reg. & L.Rep. (BNA) 645 (May 1, 1987).

12.   15 U.S.C.A. § 80b–3(c)(2).

13.   *Id.*

14.   15 U.S.C.A. § 80b–3(c)(2). *See, e.g.,* In re Morant, Admin.Proc. 801–28711, 19 Sec.Reg. & L.Rep. (BNA) 411 (SEC March 19, 1987) (convicted murderer denied registration as an investment advisor). Grounds for suspension and revocation are set forth in section 3(e). 15 U.S.C.A. § 80b–3(e).

15.   *See* 15 U.S.C.A. § 80b–4. 17 C.F.R. § 275.204–1(c). This is much less lengthy than the Exchange Act's annual report requirements for issuers. *See* 17 C.F.R. §§ 240–14a–3(b), 14c–3 which are discussed in § 11.6 *supra.* It has been observed that "Form ADV–S is intended to inform the SEC whether the adviser is still in business and whether the address has changed, to remind advisers to make any necessary amendments to Form ADV, and to provide a vehicle for the submission of balance sheets on an annual basis."

the Commission has also designated records that must be maintained and made available for periodic inspection.[16] These records include balance sheets, income statements and a journal of all accounts;[17] copies of all communications sent and received relating to investment advice or the execution of orders;[18] copies of all notices, letters, reports and advertisements distributed by the adviser to more than ten customers;[19] and records of all securities transactions.[20]

When an investment adviser wishes to deregister, he or she must file a notice to withdraw from registration.[21] Withdrawal applications are to be submitted to the SEC on Form ADV–W.[22]

The SEC has the power to impose sanctions, ranging from censure to revocation of registration, for advisers who themselves have committed certain crimes or securities law violations or have associated with persons having committed such crimes or violations of the securities laws.[23] The disqualifying violations include false SEC filings, perjury and crimes involving larceny, embezzlement, extortion, forgery, counterfeiting, fraud, mail fraud, and fraudulent misappropriation of funds or securities.[24] These sanctions may be imposed only after notice and a hearing and in accordance with the public interest.[25] The Commission can similarly censure, suspend or bar persons subject to similar disqualification who seek to become associated with a registered investment adviser.[26]

There are some additional requirements beyond the above-mentioned registration and reporting requirements. Investment advisers, other than those furnishing "impersonal advisory services" through newsletters or otherwise,[27] must comply with the "brochure rule" prior to signing up prospective customers other than a registered investment company.[28] Rule 204–3 requires that prospective advisory customers be

---

Richard D. Harroch, Applicability of the Investment Advisers Act of 1940 to Financial and Investment Related Publications, 5 J.Corp.L. 55, 59 (1979).

16. 15 U.S.C.A. § 80b–4 (SEC is empowered to require reports by registered investment advisers); 17 C.F.R. § 275.204–2. This is analogous to the broker-dealer record-keeping requirements imposed by the Securities Exchange Act of 1934. *See* § 10.2 *supra.*

17. 17 C.F.R. §§ 275.204–2(a)(1), (2).

18. 17 C.F.R. § 275.204–2(a)(7).

19. 17 C.F.R. § 275.204–2(a)(11).

20. 17 C.F.R. § 275.204–2(a)(12).

21. 15 U.S.C.A. § 80b–3(h).

22. *See* 17 C.F.R. § 275.203–2.

23. 15 U.S.C.A. § 80b–3(e). *See* footnote 7 *supra.*

24. 15 U.S.C.A. § 80b–3(e)(2). Mail fraud is discussed in § 19.3.1 *infra* (Practitioner's Edition only).

25. 15 U.S.C.A. § 80b–3(e).

26. 15 U.S.C.A. § 80b–3(f).

27. Rule 204–3(g) defines "impersonal advisory services" as those not related to the investment objectives of specific individuals or accounts. 17 C.F.R. § 275.204–3(g).

28. 17 C.F.R. § 275.204–3. *See* Inv. Advisers Act Rel. No. IA–664 (Jan. 30, 1979). The relationship between investment companies registered under the Investment Company Act of 1940 and their investment advisers is discussed in §§ 17.2, 17.9 *supra.*

furnished with a brochure or disclosure document containing the information required in Part II of Form ADV's registration statement.[29] Advisers providing impersonal advisory services charging two hundred dollars or more must also comply with the brochure delivery requirements.[30]

§ 18.4 Prohibited Practices; Sanctions and Penalties

Prohibited Practices

Section 206 of the Investment Advisers Act[1] sets out the Act's basic prohibitions beyond failure to register or fulfill the informational requirements.[2] Section 206(1) outlaws fraudulent practices.[3] Prohibited practices include scalping[4] and misleading advertising.[5] The Act, specifically outlaws aiding and abetting as well as primary violations.[6]

In an extremely significant development, the SEC has proposed a rule that would expressly prohibit an investment adviser from making recommendations of securities that are unsuitable for his or her clients.[7] This is significant in light of the Supreme Court's ruling that aiding and abetting liability may not be implied from the primary prohibitions of the securities laws.[8]

---

29. 17 C.F.R. § 275.204-3.

30. 17 C.F.R. § 275.204-3(c)(3). The SEC has adopted Rule 206(4)-4 which explicitly requires disclosure of adverse financial conditions as well as disciplinary or legal events questioning the adviser's integrity. 17 C.F.R. § 275.206(4)-4, adopted in Inv.Adv.Act Rel. No. IA-1083, [1987 Transfer Binder] Fed.Sec.L.Rep. (CCH) ¶ 84,158 (Sept. 25, 1987). *See* Inv.Adv.Act Rel. No. IA-1035, [1986–87 Transfer Binder] Fed.Sec.L.Rep. ¶ 84,026 (Sept. 19, 1986). *See also* ABA Subcommittee Members Oppose Proposed Investment Adviser Rule, 18 Sec.Reg. & L.Rep. (BNA) 1813 (Dec. 19, 1986).

§ 18.4

1. 15 U.S.C.A. § 80b-6.

2. Section 203 makes it unlawful for a non-exempt adviser to fail to register; section 207 prohibits material misstatements in required filings. 15 U.S.C.A. §§ 80b-3, 80b-7.

3. 15 U.S.C.A. § 80b-6(1) (prohibiting "any device, scheme or artifice to defraud any client or prospective client"). *See, e.g.,* SEC v. Steadman, 967 F.2d 636 (D.C.Cir.1992) (since § 206(1) of the Investment Advisers Act is virtually identical to 1933 Act § 17(a)(1), scienter is a necessary element of any violation thereof; also holding that extreme conduct is necessary to show that conduct was sufficiently reckless to establish scienter).

4. The Supreme Court has held that scalping (recommending securities after they have been purchased) constitutes a violation of section 206(1). SEC v. Capital Gains Research Bureau, Inc., 375 U.S. 180, 84 S.Ct. 275, 11 L.Ed.2d 237 (1963). *See also* Courtland v. Walston & Co., 340 F.Supp. 1076 (S.D.N.Y.1972).

5. *E.g.* SEC v. C.R. Richmond & Co., 565 F.2d 1101 (9th Cir.1977); In the Matter of Dow Theory Forecasts, Inc., 43 S.E.C. 821 (SEC 1968). The SEC has taken the position that "hedge" statements are misleading if they indicate that the client has waived any rights he may have under the Act. Investment Advisers Act Rel. No. IA-58 (April 28, 1951).

6. *See, e.g.,* In the Matter of Seaboard Investment Advisers, Inc., [1994–1995 Transfer Binder] Fed. Sec. L. Rep. (CCH) ¶ 85,419 (SEC 1994).

7. Inv. Adv. Act Rel. No. IA-1406, [1993–1994 Transfer Binder] Fed. Sec. L. Rep. ¶ 85,327 (SEC March 16, 1994).

8. Central Bank of Denver v. First Interstate Bank of Denver, ___ U.S. ___, 114 S.Ct. 1439, 128 L.Ed.2d 119 (1994), which is discussed in § 13.16 *supra*.

Investment Adviser Act Rule 206(4)–1[9] prohibits certain types of advertisements which are deceptive or fraudulent within the meaning of section 206.[10] The rule prohibits (1) testimonials concerning the adviser's services,[11] (2) reference to selected past recommendations,[12] (3) the use of any graphs or charts without explaining the limitations on such charting methods,[13] (4) offering free services with hidden charges,[14] and (5) the making of "any untrue statement of a material fact, or which is otherwise false or misleading."[15]

Section 206 also prohibits excessive trading,[16] undisclosed conflicts of interest,[17] and splitting fees with persons not registered under the Act.[18] In addition to fraud, the Act also prohibits conduct that *"operates* as a fraud or deceit upon any client or prospective client."[19] Presumably scienter is not an element of such a violation.[20]

Section 206(3) of the Investment Adviser's Act prohibits an investment adviser from acting as a principal in a transaction with a client

---

9. 17 C.F.R. § 275.206(4)–1.

10. The rule contains the following definition: "(b) For the purposes of this section the term advertisement shall include any notice, circular, letter or other written communication addressed to more than one person, or any notice or other announcement in any publication or by radio or television, which offers (1) any analysis, report, or publication concerning securities, or which is to be used in making any determination as to when to buy or sell any security, or which security to buy or sell, or (2) any graph, chart, formula, or other device to be used in making any determination as to when to buy or sell any security, or which security to buy or sell, or (3) any other investment advisory service with regard to securities." 17 C.F.R. § 275.206(4)–1(b).

11. 17 C.F.R. § 275.206(4)–1(a)(1).

12. 17 C.F.R. § 275.206(4)–1(a)(2). The adviser may provide a list of *all* recommendations within the past year, describing the price at the time of recommendation and the current price. There must also be the following cautionary legend: "it shall not be assumed that recommendations made in the future will be profitable or will equal the performance of the securities in this list." *Id.*

13. 17 C.F.R. § 275.206(4)–1(a)(3).

14. 17 C.F.R. § 275.206(4)–1(a)(4).

15. 17 C.F.R. § 275.206(4)–1(a)(5).

16. *E.g.* In the Matter of Shearson, Hammill & Co., 42 S.E.C. 811 (SEC 1965). *Compare* the Exchange Act's prohibitions against churning. *See* Robert Rosenman, Discretionary Accounts and Manipulative Trading, 5 Inst.Sec.Reg. 245 (1974); Note, Churning by Securities Dealers, 80 Harv.L.Rev. 869 (1967). *See* § 10.10 *supra.*

17. *See, e.g.,* In the Matter of Patrick Clements d/b/a Patrick Clements & Associates, 42 S.E.C. 373 (SEC 1964).

18. Rhodes, King, Ruman & Farber, [1972–73 Transfer Binder] Fed.Sec.L.Rep. (CCH) ¶ 79,121 (SEC 1972) (splitting fees with attorney).

19. 15 U.S.C.A. § 80b–206(2). Interestingly, in its suit charging securities laws violations in connection with a scheme providing an illegal float to a broker-dealer's bank deposits, the Commission relied in part on section 206 of the Advisers Act. *See* E.F. Hutton Agrees to SEC Censure in Action Over Float on Transactions, 16 Sec.Reg. & L.Rep. (BNA) 1987 (Dec. 21, 1984). The adviser consented to remedial sanctions. SEC v. E.F. Hutton Group, Inc., Inv. Co. Act Rel. No. IC–14774 (Oct. 29, 1985). As a result of these activities, the SEC considered revocation of the firm's investment adviser privileges.

20. *See* Sheldon Co. Profit Sharing Plan and Trust v. Smith, 828 F.Supp. 1262, 1284 (W.D.Mich.1993). *Cf.* Aaron v. SEC, 446 U.S. 680, 100 S.Ct. 1945, 64 L.Ed.2d 611 (1980) (not requiring scienter under sections 17(a)(2), (3) of the 1933 Act, 15 U.S.C.A. § 77q(a)(2), (3)). *See* §§ 11.3, 13.4 *supra.*

without disclosure and the client's consent.[21] Similarly, where the adviser represents both parties to a transaction, there must be full written disclosure and the clients' written consent must be obtained.[22] These provisions do not apply to broker-dealers giving investment advice as part of their brokerage services.[23]

Following the pattern of section 10(b) of the 1934 Exchange Act,[24] section 206(4) of the Advisers Act[25] prohibits "fraudulent, deceptive, or manipulative" acts or practices as defined by SEC rules. Investment Adviser Act Rule 206(4)–1[26] governs adviser advertising and, as noted above, prohibits certain types of advertising. In addition to forbidding material misstatements generally,[27] the SEC also prohibits the commingling of clients' funds and requires separate accounts and adequate record-keeping.[28] When funds or securities are held by the adviser, they must be kept in custodial accounts and the client is entitled to receive an itemized statement at least once every three months.[29] In addition, all such funds must be subjected to annual inspection and certification by an independent public accountant.[30]

In its cash referral fee rule, the Commission limits payments by the adviser for client solicitation.[31] Such fees may be paid to others by advisers rendering impersonal investment advice, but must be pursuant to a written agreement, under which they can be paid only after a client has been informed of the fee arrangements and cannot be paid to persons who have run afoul of the securities acts and other "bad boy" provisions.[32]

The Supreme Court has held that section 206 does not give rise to

---

21. 15 U.S.C.A. § 80b–6(3). *See* Inv.Adv.Act Rel. No. IA–40 (Jan. 5, 1945). *See also, e.g.,* Kravetz v. Brukenfeld, 591 F.Supp. 1383 (S.D.N.Y.1984) (upholding complaint alleging a conspiracy to withdraw funds to purchase worthless securities).

22. 17 C.F.R. § 275.206(3)–2. These are known as "agency cross transactions."

23. 15 U.S.C.A. § 80b–6(3). Broker-dealers must disclose principal status under Exchange Act Rule 10b–10, 17 C.F.R. § 240.10b–10. *See* chapter 10 *supra* for discussion of broker-dealer obligations. *See generally* Jerry W. Markham & Thomas L. Hazen, Broker–Dealer Operations Under Securities and Commodities Law: Financial Responsibilities, Credit Regulation and Customer Protection (1995).

24. 15 U.S.C.A. § 78j(b). An investment adviser is a fiduciary for the purposes of determining liability under Rule 10b–5. Laird v. Integrated Resources, Inc., 897 F.2d 826 (5th Cir.1990).

25. 15 U.S.C.A. § 80b–6(4). Section 206(4) applies only to advisory contracts and not to collateral agreements. *See* Paul S. Mullin & Associates, Inc. v. Bassett, 632 F.Supp. 532 (D.Del.1986).

26. 17 C.F.R. § 275.206(4)–1.

27. *See* text accompanying footnotes 6–12 *supra.*

28. 17 C.F.R. § 275.206(4)–2.

29. 17 C.F.R. § 275.206(4)–2(a)(2), (4).

30. 17 C.F.R. § 275.206(4)–2(a)(5).

31. 17 C.F.R. § 275.206(4)–3. *See* Thomas P. Lemke, Cash Referral Fees Under the Investment Advisers Act, 21 Rev.Sec. & Commodities Reg. 171 (1988).

32. 17 C.F.R. § 275.206(4)–3(a)(1). Regulation A, which provides an exemption from registration under the Securities Act of 1933, sets forth its own "bad boy" provisions. *See* § 4.15 *supra.*

implied private remedies.[33] Enforcement of section 206's prohibitions is thus limited to criminal prosecution for willful violations,[34] SEC injunctive actions,[35] and the imposition of sanctions in an administrative hearing ranging from censure to revocation of registration.[36] These are the sanctions available for all violations of the Act. The Supreme Court has recognized an implied right of rescission under section 215 of the Act[37] which provides that contracts in violation of the Act are void.[38]

Since the section 215 remedy is rescissory, restitution under that section does not include damages for consequential losses.[39] It has also been held that the only proper parties in a section 215 claim are parties to the advisory contract.[40] The appropriate statute of limitations is one year from the violation (or reasonable discovery thereof) but in no event more than three years after the challenged transaction.[41]

In addition to section 206's prohibitions against fraudulent conduct, section 208 sets out general prohibitions.[42] An adviser can advertise his registered status but may not imply any governmental approval of his activities.[43] It is unlawful for registered advisers to describe themselves as "investment counsel" unless that is their principal business.[44] It is also unlawful to do indirectly any act prohibited by the statute.[45]

Section 205 of the Advisers Act[46] imposes a number of conditions on the advisory contract. Subject to exceptions permitted by the SEC, section 205(a)(1) of the Act prohibits performance-based compensation to the extent that the fee is based on a share of the capital gain or

33. Transamerica Mortgage Advisors, Inc. v. Lewis, 444 U.S. 11, 100 S.Ct. 242, 62 L.Ed.2d 146 (1979). *See also, e.g.,* Corwin v. Marney, Orton Investments, 788 F.2d 1063 (5th Cir.1986); Kauffman v. Yoskowitz, 1989 WL 79364, [1989 Transfer Binder] Fed.Sec. L.Rep. ¶ 94,532 (S.D.N.Y.1989) (it is "well settled" that there is no private remedy against an investment adviser for failure to register). Implied remedies in general are discussed in § 13.1 *supra.*

34. 15 U.S.C.A. § 80b–17.

35. 15 U.S.C.A. § 80b–9(e). *See* § 9.5 *supra.*

36. 15 U.S.C.A. § 80b–12. *See also* 15 U.S.C.A. § 80b–3(e).

37. 15 U.S.C.A. § 80b–15.

38. Transamerica Mortgate Advisors, Inc. v. Lewis, 444 U.S. 11, 100 S.Ct. 242, 62 L.Ed.2d 146 (1979). *See also* section 29(b) of the 1934 Act, 15 U.S.C.A. § 78cc(b) which is discussed in § 13.14 *supra.*

39. Washington v. Baenziger, 656 F.Supp. 1176 (N.D.Cal.1987). *See also, e.g.,* Wellington International Commerce Corp. v. Retelny, 727 F.Supp. 843 (S.D.N.Y.1989) (rescission is only remedy under Advisers Act). *But cf.* Laird v. Integrated Resources, Inc., 897 F.2d 826 (5th Cir.1990) (violations of Investment Adviser Act disclosure provisions do not give rise to private action but plaintiff may sue under Rule 10b–5; for purposes of determining scope of duty under Rule 10b–5, an investment adviser is a fiduciary).

40. Washington v. Baenziger, 656 F.Supp. 1176 (N.D.Cal.1987).

41. *See* Kahn v. KKR, 970 F.2d 1030 (2d Cir.1992). *See also* § 13.8 *supra.*

42. 15 U.S.C.A. § 80b–8.

43. 15 U.S.C.A. § 80b–8(a), (b).

44. 15 U.S.C.A. § 80b–8(c). *See* Inv.Adv.Act Rel. No. IA–8 (Dec. 12, 1940).

45. 15 U.S.C.A. § 80b–8(d).

46. 15 U.S.C.A. § 80b–5. *See* § 18.1 *supra.*

appreciation of the value of the client's account.[47] The adviser's compensation may, however, be based upon the average asset value of the client's account over a definite period of time.[48]

The rationale for the general rule prohibiting performance-based fees is to avoid encouraging the investment adviser to take undue risks with the client's funds.[49] In 1983, the Commission decided to reverse its early refusal to permit performance-based fees under any circumstances. Originally, the SEC had proposed that performance based compensation be permitted with regard to accounts of more than one hundred and fifty thousand dollars when the customer meets subjective sophistication tests.[50] However, the Commission eventually selected more stringent standards when it adopted guidelines for performance-based adviser fees for clients having accounts that represent at least a five hundred thousand dollar value and for clients having a net worth of at least one million dollars.[51] The rule as adopted retained the financial sophistication test as well as the requirement that the client understand not only the method of compensation but also the risks presented by the performance-based formula.[52]

Investment Advisers and Misuse of Nonpublic Information

On occasion investment advisers have been charged with misuse of nonpublic information. For example, during the late 1980s there were many celebrated cases involving the misuse of information relating to planned takeovers.[53] Until recently, the primary weapon against the misuse of nonpublic information has been the antifraud provision contained in Rule 10b–5 of the Exchange Act.[54] The brokerage industry has

---

47. 15 U.S.C.A. § 80b–5(a)(1).

48. 15 U.S.C.A. § 80b–5(b)(1).

49. Inv.Adv. Act Rel. No. IA–721 (May 16, 1980). *See also, e.g.,* In the Matter of Early, [1993–1994 Transfer Binder] Fed. Sec. L. Rep. (CCH) ¶ 85,354 (SEC Initial Dec. 1994) wherein the Administrative Law Judge denied a proposed performance-based fee, noting that such fee arrangements encourage the adviser to engage in speculation and invest in volatile instruments.

50. 15 Sec.Reg. & L.Rep. (BNA) 1019 (June 3, 1983).

51. 17 C.F.R. § 275.205–3. Investment advisers who use performance data in their advertising literature must maintain records to support the advertising claims. 17 C.F.R. § 275.204–2. *See* SEC to Require Advisers Keep Records to Support Performance Claims in Ads, 20 Sec.Reg. & L.Rep. (BNA) 1214 (July 29, 1988).

The Commission also permits use of performance data in advertising for investment company shares. 17 C.F.R. §§ 230.482(d), (e); 17 C.F.R. § 270.34b–1. *See* Inv.Co.Act Rel. No. IC–16245, [1987–88 Transfer Binder] Fed.Sec.L.Rep. (CCH) ¶ 84,217 (Feb. 2, 1988); Inv.Co.Act Rel. No. IC–15315 (Sept. 17, 1986).

The SEC has taken the position that its standardized format for presenting investing company performance data applies not only to the investment company's literature but also to data prepared by independent firms. Dalbar Publishing, Inc., 20 Sec.Reg. & L.Rep. (BNA) 1189 (SEC No Action Letter avail. July 1, 1988).

52. Rule 205–3(e), 17 C.F.R. § 275.25–3(e).

53. *See* the discussion of insider trading in § 13.9 *supra*.

54. 17 C.F.R. § 240.10b–5.

attempted to deal with the misuse of information through the establishment of Chinese Walls[55] and other procedures to monitor the flow of information within multiservice firms dealing with financial services and advice.

The SEC has approved the Chinese Wall (or "fire wall") as a way of monitoring the flow of information. Thus, for example, Rule 14e–3 of the Exchange Act[56] prohibits trading while in possession of material nonpublic information in connection with tender offers. The rule provides a safe harbor exclusion for financial services firms adopting a Chinese Wall if the firm is able to show that (1) the individual making the investment decision had no knowledge of the nonpublic material information[57] and (2) the firm had implemented "one or a combination of policies and procedures, reasonable under the circumstances" to ensure that those making investment decisions for the institution do not violate 14e–3.[58]

In 1988, Congress addressed directly the problem of investment advisers' misuse of nonpublic information as part of the Insider Trading and Securities Fraud Enforcement Act of 1988.[59] Under section 204A of the Advisers Act, registered advisory firms must now institute a system of internal controls and procedures to monitor the flow of information.[60] The section also specifically empowers the SEC to adopt rules mandating specific policies or procedures designed to prevent the misuse of material, nonpublic information.[61] However, to date, the Commission has not adopted any such rules.

---

55. *See generally* Martin Lipton & Robert B. Mazur, The Chinese Wall Solution to the Conflict Problems of Securities Firms, 50 N.Y.U.L.Rev. 459 (1975). *See also* Larry L. Varn, The Multiservice Securities Firm and the Chinese Wall: A New Look in the Light of the Federal Securities Code, 63 Neb.L.Rev. 197 (1984). *See also, e.g.,* Norman S. Poser, Chinese Walls in the U.S. and U.K., 21 Rev.Sec. & Commodities Reg. 207 (1988). Chinese Walls are discussed in § 10.2.4 *supra.* (Practitioner's Edition only).

56. 17 C.F.R. § 240.14e–3. *See* SEC Exchange Act, Rel. No. 34–17120 [1980 Transfer Binder] Fed.Sec.L.Rep. (CCH) ¶ 82,646 (Sept. 4, 1980). *See also, e.g.,* Letter of SEC General Counsel to Judge Cohill in Koppers Co. v. American Express Co., 689 F.Supp. 1417 (W.D.Pa.1988). The Second Circuit has upheld Rule 14e–3. *See* United States v. Chestman, 947 F.2d 551 (2d Cir.1991), *cert. denied* 503 U.S. 1004, 112 S.Ct. 1759, 118 L.Ed.2d 422 (1992), *reversing* 903 F.2d 75 (2d Cir.1990)

57. In the release adopting Rule 14e–3 the SEC stated that the individual making the investment decision referred to in Rule 14e–3(b) would not include a person or group of persons supervising such individual. *See* SEC Exchange Act, Rel. No. 34–17120 [1980 Transfer Binder] Fed.Sec.L.Rep. (CCH) ¶ 82,646 (Sept. 4, 1980).

58. *Id.*

59. *See* Report of the Committee of Energy and Commerce, H.R.Rep. 100–910, 100th Cong.2d Sess. 11 (1988). The 1988 legislation is discussed more fully in § 13.9 *supra.*

60. 15 U.S.C.A. § 80b–4a:

Every investment adviser subject to section 204 of this title [15 U.S.C.A. § 80b–4] shall establish, maintain, and enforce written policies and procedures reasonably designed, taking into consideration the nature of such investment adviser's business, to prevent the misuse in violation of this Act or the Securities Exchange Act of 1934, or the rules or regulations thereunder, of material, nonpublic information by such investment adviser or any person associated with such investment adviser.

61. *Id.*

Sanctions and Penalties

Violations of the Investment Advisers Act can result in suspension or revocation of registration under the Act. It has been held that revocation of an investment adviser's registration is a permissible restraint notwithstanding the First Amendment right of free speech.[62]

---

62. SEC v. Lowe, 725 F.2d 892 (2d Cir.1984), *rev'd on other grounds* 472 U.S. 181, 105 S.Ct. 2557, 86 L.Ed.2d 130 (1985); *see* § 18.2 *supra. Cf.* SEC v. Suter, 732 F.2d 1294 (7th Cir.1984) (upholding issuance of preliminary injunction). *Contra* SEC v. Wall Street Publishing Institute, Inc., 591 F.Supp. 1070 (D.D.C.1984), *stay granted* Fed.Sec.L.Rep. (CCH) ¶ 91,635, 1984 WL 21133 (D.C.Cir.1984) (preliminary injunction reversed on first amendment grounds). *See generally* Symposium, The First Amendment and Federal Securities Regulation, 20 Conn.L.Rev. 261 (1988).

Chapter 19

SPECIAL PROBLEMS AND OVERVIEW OF RELATED LAWS

Table of Sections

§ 19.1   Related Laws—Introduction

In addition to the six federal securities acts that are discussed in the preceding chapters,[1] there are a number of related laws that affect practitioners and clients operating in the realm of federal securities regulation.   There is also SEC involvement in some of these related areas.

For certain regulated industries, the securities of regulated issuers are subject to other federal administrative agencies.[2]   For example, the Comptroller of the Currency has jurisdiction over the distribution of securities issued by national banks,[3] although securities issued by bank

---

* Deleted sections 19.2, 19.3.1, 19.4, and 19.6–19.8 can be found in the Practitioner's Edition.

§ 19.1

1.   The Securities Act of 1933, 15 U.S.C.A. §§ 77a *et seq.* (*see* chapters 1–8 *supra*); the Securities Exchange Act of 1934, 15 U.S.C.A. §§ 78a *et seq.* (*see* chapters 9–14 *supra*); the Public Utility Holding Company Act of 1935, 15 U.S.C.A. §§ 79 *et seq.* (*see* chapter 15 *supra*); the Trust Indenture Act of 1939, 15 U.S.C.A. §§ 77aaa *et seq.* (*see* chapter 16 *supra*); the Investment Company Act of 1940, 15 U.S.C.A. §§ 80a–1 *et seq.* (*see* chapter 17 *supra*); the Investment Advisers Act of 1940, 15 U.S.C.A. §§ 80b–1 *et seq.* (*see* chapter 18 *supra*).

2.   *See* Harry G. Henn & John R. Alexander, Laws of Corporations § 304 (3d ed. 1983).

3.   12 U.S.C.A. §§ 51 *et seq.*

holding companies are subject to SEC jurisdiction. A similar arrangement exists with regard to securities of savings and loan associations which are subject to regulation by the Office of Thrift Supervision (formerly the Federal Home Loan Bank Board).[4] Other issuers of securities which are subject to the jurisdiction of additional federal regulatory agencies include interstate railroads and common carriers subject to the jurisdiction of the Interstate Commerce Commission[5] and electric utility companies not subject to state regulation but subject to supervision by the Secretary of Energy.[6]

For securities and issuers that are subject to SEC regulation, there are a number of related statutes that may come into play in addition to the federal securities laws. The more important of these laws are taken up in the sections that follow. First, the Foreign Corrupt Practices Act of 1977 was enacted in response to widespread concern over the activities of domestic companies in their dealings abroad.[7] That act has implications that go beyond foreign activities and corrupt practices.

Second, the Racketeer Influenced and Corrupt Organizations Act (RICO) was enacted in order to make for more efficient law enforcement with regard to organized crime and racketeering activities.[8] RICO not only includes certain types of securities fraud with regard to its criminal penalties, it also includes civil actions for a fraud-based RICO violation resulting in the award of treble damages.[9]

The federal Mail Fraud Act[10] and the federal Wire Fraud Act[11] can be potent weapons in the enforcement of the securities law. For example, while the Supreme Court was equally divided over criminal convictions under the securities laws for trading on confidential information, the Court was unanimous that the conduct was violative of the Mail Fraud Act.[12]

During the 1960s there was a rash of stock brokerage firm bankruptcies. In response to the need for customer protection, Congress

---

4. 12 U.S.C.A. §§ 1464 *et seq.*

5. 49 U.S.C.A. §§ 11301. *See* Alleghany Corp. v. Breswick & Co., 353 U.S. 151, 77 S.Ct. 763, 1 L.Ed.2d 726 (1957), *rehearing denied* 353 U.S. 989, 77 S.Ct. 1278, 1 L.Ed.2d 1147 (1957); United States v. New York, New Haven & Hartford Railroad, 276 F.2d 525 (2d Cir.1960), *cert. denied* 362 U.S. 961, 80 S.Ct. 877, 4 L.Ed.2d 876 (1960). *See also, e.g.,* Leonard D. Adkins, The New Haven Preferred Stock Cases: A Study in Judicial Legislation, 15 Bus.Law. 847 (1960); John L. Mechem, Regulation of Motor Carrier Securities, 11 Vand.L.Rev. 1095 (1958).

6. 42 U.S.C.A. § 7151(b); 16 U.S.C.A. § 824c.

7. Pub.L. 95–213, 95th Cong., 1st Sess. (1977). *See* § 19.2 *infra.*

8. Pub.L. No. 91–452, 84 Stat. 922 (1970).

9. 15 U.S.C.A. § 1964(c). *See* § 19.3 *infra.*

10. 18 U.S.C.A. § 1341.

11. 18 U.S.C.A. § 1343.

12. Carpenter v. United States, 484 U.S. 19, 108 S.Ct. 316, 98 L.Ed.2d 275 (1987). *See* Theodore A. Levine, Arthur F. Mathews & W. Hardy Callcott, 21 Rev.Sec. & Commod.Reg. 55 (1988). Insider trading is discussed in § 13.9 *supra.* The mail and wire fraud statutes are discussed in § 19.3.1 *infra.*

enacted the Securities Investor Protection Act of 1970.[13] As a result of that Act, the Securities Investor Protection Corporation ("SIPC") helps safeguard customer interests in cases of broker-dealer insolvency.

Perhaps the hottest topic in securities regulation over the past decade has been the increasing competition between banking and more traditional securities industries. Although the Glass–Steagall Act of 1933[14] prohibits commercial and savings banks from engaging directly in various aspects of investment banking, the line between investment banking and commercial banking is increasingly being blurred.[15] The developing competition between commercial and investment banking has been highlighted not only by each offering competing services but also by bank acquisition of stock brokerage operations and vice versa. In addition to the increased competition between the two industries, the SEC and various bank regulatory agencies, including the Comptroller of the Currency, are constantly engaged in jurisdictional disputes.

One other major area of jurisdictional dispute involves the regulation of commodities futures and commodities options. Although the futures market is directly regulated by the Commodity Futures Trading Commission,[16] the SEC has asserted jurisdiction over various aspects of the commodities markets.[17] For example, although the courts are in conflict, a number of cases have held that managed commodities accounts constitute securities.[18] Another major developing area of conflict between the securities and commodities markets has been the development of new investment products such as financial futures, which are traded in the commodities markets, and financial index options which are traded in the securities markets.[19]

Deleted section 19.2 can be found in the Practitioner's Edition.

§ 19.3 Securities Fraud and the Racketeer Influenced and Corrupt Organizations Act (RICO)

In 1973 Congress passed the Racketeer Influenced and Corrupt

13. Codified in 15 U.S.C.A. §§ 78aaa–78*lll*. *See* § 19.4 *infra.*

14. The Banking Act of 1933, ch. 89, 48 Stat. 184 (1933), codified in various sections of 12 U.S.C.A.

15. *See* § 19.5 *infra.*

16. 7 U.S.C.A. §§ 1–25. *See generally* Philip M. Johnson & Thomas L. Hazen, Commodities Regulation (2d ed. 1989).

17. Regulation of the commodities markets is discussed in §§ 19.6–19.8 *infra. See also* §§ 1.4.1, 1.5.1 *supra.*

18. *E.g.,* SEC v. Continental Commodities Corp., 497 F.2d 516 (5th Cir.1974); Booth v. Peavey Co. Commodity Services, 430 F.2d 132 (8th Cir.1970). *Contra, e.g.,* Mordaunt v. Incomco, 686 F.2d 815 (9th Cir.1982), *cert. denied* 469 U.S. 1115, 105 S.Ct. 801, 83 L.Ed.2d 793 (1985); Milnarik v. M–S Commodities, Inc., 457 F.2d 274 (7th Cir.), *cert. denied* 409 U.S. 887, 93 S.Ct. 113, 34 L.Ed.2d 144 (1972). The definition of security is discussed in § 1.5 *supra.*

19. *See* § 1.4.1 *supra.*

Organizations Act[1] which is more commonly known as RICO. A number of states have enacted parallel legislation which has come to be known as "little RICO" statutes.[2] Although as the name indicates, the federal legislation was adopted with the express purpose of eradicating organized crime,[3] the statute has a broader reach, at least as currently interpreted by most courts.[4] Since the statute expressly includes securi-

---

§ 19.3

1. Pub.L. No. 91–452, 84 Stat. 922 (1970), codified in 18 U.S.C.A. §§ 1961–1968. *See generally* G. Robert Blakey & Brian Gettings, Racketeer Influenced and Corrupt Organizations (RICO): Basic Concepts—Criminal and Civil Remedies, 53 Temp.L.Q. 1009 (1980); Gerard E. Lynch, RICO: The Crime of Being a Criminal, Parts I & II, 87 Colum.L.Rev. 661 (1987); Jerold S. Solovy, Marguerite M. Tohompkins & Daniel S. Goldman, Current Issues in RICO Litigation, 26 Rev. Sec. & Commod.Reg. 211 (1993); Jerold S. Solovy, Marguerite M. Thompkins & David E. Steinberg, RICO Update, 21 Rev.Sec. & Commod.Reg. 81 (1988).

2. At least thirty one American jurisdictions have enacted "little RICO" or RICO-like statutes. These statutes are: Ariz. Rev. Stat. Ann. §§ 13–2312 to–2315 (1989 & Supp. 1992); Cal. Penal Code §§ 186–186.8 (West 1988 & Supp. 1992); Colo. Rev. Stat. §§ 18–17–101 to–109 (1986 & Supp. 1992); Conn. Gen. Stat. Ann. §§ 53–393 to–403 (West 1985 & Supp. 1992); Del. Code Ann. tit. 11, §§ 1501–1511 (1987 & Supp. 1992); Fla. Stat. Ann. §§ 895.01–.09 (West Supp. 1992); Ga. Code Ann. §§ 16–14–1 to–15 (1992); Haw. Rev. Stat. §§ 842–1 to–12 (1985 & Supp. 1991); Idaho Code §§ 18–7801 to–7805 (1987 & Supp. 1992); Ill. Ann. Stat. ch. 56½, paras. 1651–1660 (1985 & Supp. 1992) (applies only to "narcotics racketeering"); Ind. Code Ann. §§ 36–45–6–1 to–2 (West 1986 & Supp. 1992); La. Rev. Stat. Ann. §§ 15:1351–1356 (West Supp. 1992); Minn. Stat. Ann. §§ 609.901–.912 (West Supp. 1992); Miss. Code Ann. §§ 97–43–1 to–11 (Supp. 1992); Nev. Rev. Stat. Ann. §§ 207.350–.520 (Michie 1986 & Supp. 1992); N.J. Stat. Ann. §§ 2C:41–1 to–6.2 (West 1982 & Supp. 1992); N.M. Stat. Ann. §§ 30–42–1 to–6 (Michie 1989); N.Y. Penal Law §§ 460.00–.80 (McKinney 1989); N.C. Gen. Stat. §§ 75D–1 to–11 (1990); N.D. Cent. Code §§ 12.1–06.1–01 to–08 (1985 & Supp. 1991); Ohio Rev. Code Ann. §§ 2923.31–.36 (Anderson 1987 & Supp. 1991); Okla. Stat. Ann. tit. 22, §§ 1401–1419 (West Supp. 1992); Or. Rev. Stat. §§ 166.715–.735 (1991); 18 Pa. Cons. Stat. Ann. § 911 (1983 & Supp. 1992); P.R. Laws Ann. tit. 25, §§ 971–971s (1980 & Supp. 1989); R.I. Gen. Laws §§ 7–15–1 to–11 (1985); Tenn. Code Ann. §§ 39–12–201 to–210 (1991 & Supp. 1992); Utah Code Ann. I 76–10–1601 to–1609 (1990 & Supp. 1992); V.I. Code Ann. tit. 14, §§ 600–614 (Supp. 1992); Wash. Rev. Code Ann. §§ 9A.82.001–.904 (West 1988 & Supp. 1992); Wis. Stat. Ann. §§ 946.80–.87 (West Supp. 1992).

See, e.g., Note, A RICO You Can't Refuse: New York's Organized Crime Control Act, 53 Brooklyn L. Rev. 979 (1988).

3. Pub.L. No. 91–452, 84 Stat. 922, 923 (1970) ("It is the purpose of this Act to seek the eradication of organized crime in the United States by strengthening the legal tools in the evidence-gathering process, by establishing new penal prohibitions, and by providing enhanced sanctions and new remedies * * * ").

4. Congress has expressly mandated that RICO "shall be liberally construed to effectuate its remedial purpose." Organized Crime Control Act of 1970, Pub. L. No. 91–452, § 904(a), 84 Stat. 922, 947 (codified as a note in 18 U.S.C.A. § 1961 (1988)). This position has been followed by most courts, including the U.S. Supreme Court. *See, e.g.,* Sedima S.P.R.L. v. Imrex Co., Inc., 473 U.S. 479, 105 S.Ct. 3275, 87 L.Ed.2d 346 (1985) ("if Congress' liberal-construction mandate is to be applied anywhere, it is in § 1964, where RICO's remedial purposes are most evident"). *See also* Tafflin v. Levitt, 493 U.S. 455, 110 S.Ct. 792, 107 L.Ed.2d 887 (1990); United States v. Turkette, 452 U.S. 576, 101 S.Ct. 2524, 69 L.Ed.2d 246 (1981). For a general discussion, *see* G. Robert Blakey, The RICO Civil Fraud Action in Context: Reflections on Bennett v. Berg, 58 Notre Dame L. Rev. 237 (1982); Note, Civil RICO: The Temptation and Impropriety of Judicial Restriction, 95 Harv. L. Rev. 119 (1982).

However, this expansive reading and application of the RICO provisions has been susceptible to a variety of criticisms. *See, e.g.,* Note, RICO: Are the Courts Construing the Legislative History Rather Than the Statute Itself?, 55 Notre Dame L. Rev. 777, 793–94 (1980) (questioning adherence to liberal construction directive); Note, The Racketeer Influenced and Corrupt Organizations Act: An Analysis of the Confusion in Its Application and A Proposal for Reform, 33 Vand. L. Rev. 441, 476–77 (1980) (arguing broad use of

ties fraud in its definition of acts that constitute racketeering activities[5] and further provides for treble damages in appropriate cases,[6] it may become an impressive weapon in enforcing the federal securities laws even though the defendants are not participants in organized crime as that term is generally understood.[7]

"Enterprise" Requirement

Although the impact of RICO is far reaching, the primary significance for securities related offenses is the potential for seeking treble damages against persons in violation of the act. RICO is violated whenever a person who is associated with an "enterprise" engages in a "pattern of racketeering activity."[8] The Act goes on to define "enterprise" to include any association whether "formal or informal."[9] Ac-

---

RICO distorts purposes and poses problems). *See also infra* footnotes 83 to 93 and accompanying text.

Likewise, some courts have read the statute more narrowly so as to limit applicability to "organized criminal" acts only and not to the "garden variety" commercial and securities disputes or fraud. *See, e.g.,* Sedima S.P.R.L. v. Imrex Co., Inc., 741 F.2d 482, 503 (2d Cir.1984) (dismissing a civil RICO claim because acts of business fraud were not the type of injury RICO was designed to deter), *reversed* 473 U.S. 479, 105 S.Ct. 3275, 87 L.Ed.2d 346 (1985).

5. 18 U.S.C.A. § 1961(1)(D) contains the complete list of acts constituting racketeering activities:

"Fraud in the sale of securities" includes the purchase of securities. Lickhalter v. System Development Corp., 1984 WL 2420, [1983–84 Transfer Binder] Fed.Sec.L.Rep. (CCH) ¶ 91,459 (C.D.Cal.1984) (opinion withdrawn). *See also, e.g.,* Laird v. Integrated Resources, Inc., 897 F.2d 826 (5th Cir.1990) (churning is a predicate act under RICO).

6. 18 U.S.C.A. § 1964(c) ("any person injured in his business or property by reason of a violation of section 1962 of this chapter may sue therefor in any appropriate United States district court and shall recover threefold the damages he sustains and the cost of the suit, including a reasonable attorney's fee").

See Paul H. Friedman, Private Damage Actions Under RICO: A Suggested Analysis, 14 Capital U.L.Rev. 205 (1985); Arthur F. Mathews, Civil RICO After Sedima: Limiting the Scope of the Statute Through Judicial Construction, Fifth Annual Southeastern Conference on Corporate and Securities Law (May 29–30, 1986); Note, The Conflict Over RICO's Private Treble Damages Action, 70 Corn.L.Rev. 902 (1985).

7. *See generally* Andrew P. Bridges, Private RICO Litigation Based Upon "Fraud in the Sale of Securities," 18 Ga.L.Rev. 43 (1983); L. Gordon Crovitz, How the RICO Monster Mauled Wall Street, 65 Notre Dame L.Rev. 1050 (1990); Arthur F. Matthews, Shifting the Burden of Losses in the Securities Markets: The Role of Civil RICO in Securities Litigation, 65 Notre Dame L.Rev. 896 (1990); Note, RICO and Securities Fraud: A Workable Limitation, 83 Colum.L.Rev. 1513 (1983). *Cf.* William C. Tyson & Andrew A. August, The Williams Act After RICO: Has the Balance Tipped in Favor of Incumbent Management?, 35 Hastings L.J. 53 (1983).

8. 18 U.S.C.A. § 1962(c).

9. 18 U.S.C.A. § 1961(4): "enterprise includes any individual, partnership, corporation, association, or other legal entity, any union or group of individuals associated in fact although not a legal entity."

The concept of enterprise contemplates the involvement of more than one person. A single party cannot be both an "enterprise" and the only "person" behind the RICO violation Schofield v. First Commodity Corp. of Boston, 793 F.2d 28 (1st Cir.1986) ("it stretches the language too far to suggest that a corporation can be employed by or associated with itself"). *See also, e.g.,* Brittingham v. Mobil Corp., 943 F.2d 297 (3d Cir.1991); Busby v. Crown Supply, Inc., 896 F.2d 833 (4th Cir.1990) (en banc); D & G Enterprises v. Continental Illinois National Bank, 574 F.Supp. 263, 270 (N.D.Ill.1983);

cording to the Supreme Court the concept of enterprise connotes a group
with a common purpose, with a continuity of personnel, and an ongoing
formal or informal organization.[10] The enterprise does not have to be a
permanent association but merely one that has had some continuity over
a period of time.[11] Under what appears to be the clear majority view,
the same person cannot be both the person committing the violations
and the entity comprising the enterprise.[12] However, where more than
one individual or entity is involved, the enterprise requirement can
readily be satisfied.[13] Some recent decisions have extended principles of
respondeat superior to RICO litigation so that, once an enterprise can be
found to exist, a corporation or a partnership may be held liable for the
RICO violations by its agents.[14]

Participation in the Enterprise

Once it has been established that an enterprise exists, it must then
be determined whether the defendant in the RICO action had sufficient
involvement in the activity. The statute makes it unlawful "for any
person employed by or associated with any enterprise ... *to conduct or
participate, directly or indirectly,* in the conduct of such enterprise's
affairs through a pattern of racketeering." [15] The question thus arises
as to how directly involved the defendant must be. In Reves v. Ernst &
Young,[16] the Supreme Court held that, on the facts before it, an auditor
of the enterprise did not fall within the statute's reach. In so ruling the

Kirschner v. Cable/Tel. Corp., 576 F.Supp. 234 (E.D.Pa.1983). *See also, e.g.,* Willamette Savings & Loan v. Blake & Neal Finance Co., 577 F.Supp. 1415 (D.Or.1984).

10. United States v. Turkette, 452 U.S. 576, 101 S.Ct. 2524, 69 L.Ed.2d 246 (1981). *See also, e.g.,* Elliott v. Foufas, 867 F.2d 877 (5th Cir.1989); Old Time Enters., Inc. v. International Coffee Corp., 862 F.2d 1213 (5th Cir.1989); Creed Taylor, Inc. v. CBS Inc., 718 F.Supp. 1171 (S.D.N.Y.1989); Northern Kentucky Bank & Trust v. Rhein, 1984 WL 23248, [1984–85 Transfer Binder] Fed.Sec.L.Rep. (CCH) ¶ 91,864 (E.D.Ky.1984) (it is not necessary to delineate the structure of the enterprise at the pleading stage). *See generally* Joan H. Spiegel, Racketeer Influenced and Corrupt Organizations: Distinguishing the "Enterprise" Issues, 59 Wash.U.L.Q. 1343 (1982); Comment, Reading the "Enterprise" Element Back into RICO; Sections 1962 and 1964(c), 76 Nw.U.L.Rev. 100 (1981).

11. United States v. Turkette, 452 U.S. 576, 101 S.Ct. 2524, 69 L.Ed.2d 246 (1981), where the Court applied the term to a band of hooligans who had a one night rampage of murder and other acts covered by the act. *See also, e.g.,* Creative Bath Products, Inc. v. Connecticut General Life Ins. Co., 837 F.2d 561, 564 (2d Cir.1988).

12. Guidry v. Bank of LaPlace, 954 F.2d 278, 283 (5th Cir.1992); Bennett v. United States Trust Co., 770 F.2d 308, 315 (2d Cir.1985), *cert. denied* 474 U.S. 1058, 106 S.Ct. 800, 88 L.Ed.2d 776 (1986); First Federal Savings & Loan Association v. Oppenheim, Appel, Dixon & Co., 629 F.Supp. 427, 446 (S.D.N.Y.1986); Umstead v. Durham Hosiery Mills, Inc., 592 F.Supp. 1269, 1271 (M.D.N.C.1984); Comment, The RICO Enterprise as Distinct from the Pattern of Racketeering Activity: Clarifying the Minority View, 62 Tul.L.Rev. 1419 (1988). *See, e.g.,* Harrison v. Dean Witter Reynolds, Inc., 695 F.Supp. 959 (N.D.Ill. 1988) (conclusory allegations of "association in fact" did not establish enterprise separate and distinct from the primary violator); *See also* the cases cited in footnotes 19–20 *infra*.

13. *E.g.* Babst v. Morgan Keegan & Co., 687 F.Supp. 255 (E.D.La.1988); First Federal Savings & Loan Association v. Oppenheim, Appel, Dixon & Co., 629 F.Supp. 427, 446 (S.D.N.Y.1986). *See* footnotes 20, 21 *infra*.

14. *E.g.* Morley v. Cohen, 610 F.Supp. 798, 811 (D.Md.1985). *See* footnote 22 *infra*.

15. 18 U.S.C.A. § 1962(c) (emphasis supplied).

16. ___ U.S. ___, 113 S.Ct. 1163, 122 L.Ed.2d 525 (1993).

Court defined the scope of the "conduct or participate" standard. First the Court noted that although RICO contains a liberal construction clause,[17] it concluded that this clause was to be used only to resolve ambiguity in the statute.[18] The *Reves* Court reasoned that the "conduct or participate" language imparts some degree of control. It then explained that RICO is implicated only if the defendant operates or manages the enterprise. The "operation and management" test as adopted by the Court is not, however, limited to high level executives:

> We agree that liability under § 1962(c) is not limited to upper management, but we disagree that the "operation or management" test is inconsistent with this proposition. An enterprise is "operated" not just by upper management but also by lower-rung participants in the enterprise who are under the direction of upper management. An enterprise also might be "operated" or "managed" by others "associated with" the enterprise who exert control over it as, for example, by bribery.[19]

An accounting firm acting as auditor does not participate in the management or operation of the enterprise and thus could not be held liable under RICO.

Pattern of Racketeering

In addition to the enterprise requirement described above, a violation of RICO section 1962 requires a "pattern of racketeering activity."[20] A "pattern of racketeering activity" is defined to cover any two predicate racketeering acts, as defined by section 1961(1),[21] occurring within ten years of each other.[22] The Supreme Court has indicated that

---

17. Congress directed that the "provisions of this title shall be liberally construed to effectuate its remedial purposes." Pub.L. 91–452, § 904(a), 84 Stat. 947.

18. ___ U.S. at ___, 113 S.Ct. at 1172, *relying on* Sedima, S.P.R.L. v. Imrex Co., 473 U.S. 479, 492 n. 10, 105 S.Ct. 3275, 3282 n. 10, 87 L.Ed.2d 346 (1985), *quoting* Callanan v. United States, 364 U.S. 587, 596, 81 S.Ct. 321, 5 L.Ed.2d 312 (1961).

19. ___ U.S. at ___, 113 S.Ct. at 1173 (footnote omitted).

20. 18 U.S.C.A. § 1962. *See* footnote 8 *supra*. *See generally* Michael Goldsmith, RICO and "Pattern:" The Search for "Continuity Plus Relationship," 73 Cornell L.Rev. 971 (1988). *See, e.g.,* Landy v. Mitchell Petroleum Technology Corp., 734 F.Supp. 608 (S.D.N.Y.1990) (single incident of securities fraud cannot support a RICO action); Clouser v. Temporaries, Inc., 730 F.Supp. 1127 (D.D.C.1989) (alleged use of false financial statements to obtain credit did not cause threat of continued activity sufficient to establish a "pattern"); Dooner v. NMI Ltd., 725 F.Supp. 153, 161 (S.D.N.Y.1989) (plaintiff must allege that alleged predicate acts were neither isolated nor sporadic), *relying on* Beauford v. Helmsley, 865 F.2d 1386 (2d Cir.1989), *cert. granted and judgment vacated* 492 U.S. 914, 109 S.Ct. 3236, 106 L.Ed.2d 584 (1989).

See generally Comment, RICO "Pattern" Before & After H.J. Inc.: A Proposed Definition, 40 Am. U.L. Rev. 919 (1991); Lisa A. Huestis, RICO: The Meaning of "Pattern" Since Sedima, 54 Brooklyn L. Rev. 621 (1988).

21. 18 U.S.C.A. § 1961(1). *See* footnote 5 *supra*.

22. 18 U.S.C.A. § 1961(5): "'pattern of racketeering activity' requires at least two acts of racketeering activity, one of which occurred after the effective date of this chapter and the last of which occurred within ten years (excluding any period of imprisonment) after the commission of a prior act of racketeering activity."

The Supreme Court has indicated in dictum that two acts may not be sufficient to sustain a civil RICO claim. *See* Sedima, S.P.R.L. v. Imrex Co., 473 U.S. 479, 105 S.Ct.

the enterprise requirement is a separate element from the pattern of racketeering activity even though the facts of each may coalesce.[23] The lower courts are divided as to whether this means that the enterprise must be distinct from the acts that form the pattern of racketeering activity.[24] Most of the circuits require that the person committing the violation must be distinct from the enterprise.[25] Thus, for example, under this view, if a broker-dealer firm is named as a primary violator, there must be other persons who comprise the enterprise.

A single scheme with a single victim has been held sufficient to state

---

3275, 87 L.Ed.2d 346 (1985). *See also, e.g.,* Superior Oil Co. v. Fulmer, 785 F.2d 252 (8th Cir.1986) ("pattern" requires a showing of multiple fraudulent schemes); Papagiannis v. Pontikis, 108 F.R.D. 177 (N.D.Ill.1985). *But, see, e.g.,* United States v. Ianniello, 808 F.2d 184 (2d Cir.1986), *cert. denied* 483 U.S. 1006, 107 S.Ct. 3229, 97 L.Ed.2d 736 (1987) (two related predicate acts held sufficient).

23. United States v. Turkette, 452 U.S. 576, 101 S.Ct. 2524, 69 L.Ed.2d 246 (1981). *See also, e.g.,* Police Retirement System of St. Louis v. Midwest Investment Advisory Services, Inc., 706 F.Supp. 708 (E.D.Mo.1989) (enterprise requirement was satisfied but no pattern of racketeering was shown); Rae v. Union Bank, 725 F.2d 478 (9th Cir.1984); Bennett v. E.F. Hutton Co., 597 F.Supp. 1547 (N.D.Ohio 1984); Mazza v. Kozel, 591 F.Supp. 432 (N.D.Ohio 1984).

See footnote 11 *supra* and footnote 24 *infra* for additional cases and a general discussion on the pattern/enterprise distinction.

24. For cases holding that the enterprise must be distinct *see, e.g.,* Malkani v. Blinder & Robinson & Co., 1986 WL 2961, [1985–86 Transfer Binder] Fed.Sec.L.Rep. (CCH) ¶ 92,496 (S.D.N.Y.1986) (unpublished case) (upholding allegation that defendant broker-dealer participated in or utilized the enterprise of the company issuing the securities in question); Media General, Inc. v. Tanner, 625 F.Supp. 237 (W.D.Tenn.1985); Morley v. Cohen, 610 F.Supp. 798 (D.Md.1985) (association in fact enterprise is sufficient); Lopez v. Richards, 594 F.Supp. 488 (S.D.Miss.1984) (upholding complaint alleging the fraud was but a particular manifestation of defendant's global illegal activities); Clute v. Davenport Co., 584 F.Supp. 1562, 1573 (D.Conn.1984) (distinct acts apparently not required); United States v. Riccobene, 709 F.2d 214 (3d Cir.1983); United States v. Bledsoe, 674 F.2d 647 (8th Cir.), *cert. denied* 459 U.S. 1040, 103 S.Ct. 456, 74 L.Ed.2d 608 (1982). *But see* United States v. Turkette, 452 U.S. 576, 101 S.Ct. 2524, 69 L.Ed.2d 246 (1981) (where the Court indicated that, although the enterprise requirement is a separate element, the same evidence may be used to establish the enterprise and the predicate acts); Rush v. Oppenheimer & Co., 628 F.Supp. 1188 (S.D.N.Y.1985) (insufficient allegations of employer's participation as a principal); Beck v. Cantor, Fitzgerald & Co., 621 F.Supp. 1547 (N.D.Ill.1985) (complaint dismissed for failure to allege with specificity the difference between the "enterprise" and the persons committing the underlying predicate acts). *See also* Comment, The RICO Enterprise as Distinct from the Pattern of Racketeering Activity: Clarifying the Minority View, 62 Tul.L.Rev. 1419 (1988).

See also footnotes 11, 23 *supra.*

25. Bennett v. United States Trust Co., 770 F.2d 308 (2d Cir.1985), *cert. denied* 474 U.S. 1058, 106 S.Ct. 800, 88 L.Ed.2d 776 (1986); Masi v. Ford City Bank & Trust Co., 779 F.2d 397 (7th Cir.1985); McCullough v. Suter, 757 F.2d 142 (7th Cir.1985); B.F. Hirsch v. Enright Refining Co., 751 F.2d 628 (3d Cir.1984), *on remand* 617 F.Supp. 49 (D.N.J.1985); Haroco, Inc. v. American National Bank & Trust Co., 747 F.2d 384 (7th Cir.1984), *affirmed on other grounds* 473 U.S. 606, 105 S.Ct. 3291, 87 L.Ed.2d 437 (1985); Rae v. Union Bank, 725 F.2d 478 (9th Cir.1984); United States v. Computer Sciences Corp., 689 F.2d 1181 (4th Cir.1982), *cert. denied* 459 U.S. 1105, 103 S.Ct. 729, 74 L.Ed.2d 953 (1983); Welek v. Solomon, 650 F.Supp. 972 (E.D.Mo.1987) (adequate allegation that enterprise was separate from individual sought to be held liable); In re Energy Systems Equipment Leasing Securities Litigation, 642 F.Supp. 718 (E.D.N.Y.1986) (semble). *Contra* United States v. Hartley, 678 F.2d 961 (11th Cir.1982), *cert. denied* 459 U.S. 1183, 103 S.Ct. 834, 74 L.Ed.2d 1027 (1983). *See also* the authorities in footnote 12 *supra.*

a RICO claim based on a pattern consisting of two related mailings[26] but not all courts have agreed.[27]

In Sedima, S.P.R.L. v. Imrex Co.,[28] the Supreme Court made its first attempt to clarify what constitutes a "pattern of racketeering." [29] *Sedima*, in putting forth its "continuity plus" test, however, failed in its effort to either simplify or clarify resolution of the ultimate issue.[30] With the circuits in a state of confusion, the Court took the opportunity to readdress this issue in 1989. In H.J., Inc. v. Northwestern Bell Telephone Co.,[31] the Court reversed the lower courts' dismissal of a private RICO action. The court of appeals had ruled that a single scheme cannot satisfy the pattern of racketeering requirement. The Supreme Court reversed, holding that RICO requires multiple predicate acts but does not require multiple schemes in order to find a pattern of racketeering. The Court went on to note that something more than

---

26. R.A.G.S. Couture, Inc. v. Hyatt, 774 F.2d 1350 (5th Cir.1985); Graham v. Slaughter, 624 F.Supp. 222 (N.D.Ill.1985). *But see* Paul S. Mullin & Associates, Inc. v. Bassett, 632 F.Supp. 532 (D.Del.1986); Rush v. Oppenheimer & Co., 628 F.Supp. 1188 (S.D.N.Y. 1985); Evanston Bank v. Conticommodity Services, Inc., 623 F.Supp. 1014 (N.D.Ill.1985).

Another issue on which courts are split is whether respondeat superior can form a basis for liability under RICO. *Compare* Federal Savings & Loan Ins. Corp. v. Shearson–American Express, Inc., 658 F.Supp. 1331 (D.P.R.1987) (corporation could be held liable under respondeat superior); Fye v. First National Bank, 1985 W.L. 4251 (N.D.Ill.1985) (unpublished case) (defendant cannot be both a person and an enterprise but can be sued under respondeat superior); Morley v. Cohen, 610 F.Supp. 798 (D.Md.1985) (same); Bernstein v. IDT Corp., 582 F.Supp. 1079 (D.Del.1984) (same) *with* Continental Data Systems, Inc. v. Exxon Corp., 638 F.Supp. 432 (E.D.Pa.1986) (rejecting respondeat superior); Rush v. Oppenheimer & Co., 628 F.Supp. 1188 (S.D.N.Y.1985) (rejecting respondeat superior); Evanston Bank v. Conticommodity Services, Inc., 623 F.Supp. 1014 (N.D.Ill. 1985) (same); Dakis v. Chapman, 574 F.Supp. 757 (N.D.Cal.1983); Parnes v. Heinold Commodities, Inc., 548 F.Supp. 20 (N.D.Ill.1982).

27. *See* SK Hand Tool Corp. v. Dresser Industries, Inc., 852 F.2d 936 (7th Cir.1988), *cert. denied*492 U.S. 918, 109 S.Ct. 3241, 106 L.Ed.2d 589 (1989); Roberts v. Smith Barney, Harris Upham & Co., 653 F.Supp. 406 (D.Mass.1986). *See also, e.g.,* International Data Bank, Ltd. v. Zepkin, 812 F.2d 149 (4th Cir.1987); Torwest DBC, Inc. v. Dick, 810 F.2d 925 (10th Cir.1987); Arnold v. Moran, 687 F.Supp. 232 (E.D.Va.1988).

28. 473 U.S. 479, 105 S.Ct. 3275, 87 L.Ed.2d 346 (1985). *See also* footnote 5 *supra* and accompanying text.

29. The Court, in dictum, stated that a pattern "requires at least two acts of racketeering activity," . . . not that it means that two acts are sufficient. . . . In common parlance two of anything do not necessarily form a "pattern." 473 U.S. at 497 n.14, 105 S.Ct. at 3285 n.14. The Court later defined that the test for a pattern would be "continuity plus relationship." *Id.*

30. The lower courts, with only a little guidance from the *Sedima* decision, began to express a wide variety of views on the issue. The result, besides chaos, was the use of varied tests among the courts. *See, e.g.* H.J. Inc. v. Northwestern Bell Tel. Co., 829 F.2d 648 (8th Cir.1987) (using a multiple schemes test, which required involvement in past or contemporaneous schemes), *reversed* 492 U.S. 229, 109 S.Ct. 2893, 106 L.Ed.2d 195 (1989); Saporito v. Combustion Engineering Inc., 843 F.2d 666 (3d Cir.1988) (using a multi-factor approach, under which the court assessed continuity by considering various factors such as (i) duration; (ii) number of victims, etc.); Morgan v. Bank of Waukegan, 804 F.2d 970 (7th Cir.1986) (using another version of the multi-factor test); California Architectural Bldg. Prods., Inc. v. Franciscan Ceramics, Inc., 818 F.2d 1466 (9th Cir.1987) (using a relatedness test, without regard to continuity).

31. 492 U.S. 229, 109 S.Ct. 2893, 106 L.Ed.2d 195 (1989). *See also, e.g.,* George v. Blue Diamond Petroleum, Inc., 718 F.Supp. 539 (W.D.La.1989) ("each use of the mails to accomplish the same scheme is a separate predicate act").

multiple predicate acts is required. In order to satisfy the pattern of racketeering requirement, the multiple predicate acts must be arranged or ordered by reason of the relationship they bear to one another or by reason of the relationship that the predicate acts bear to some external organizing principle. In the end, the Court steadfastly refused to narrow the scope of RICO's reach by refining the definition of what constitutes a pattern, and at the same time, gave the lower courts only minimal direction in coping with the problem of determining a "pattern of racketeering"—i.e., that the examination should revolve around the central concepts of relatedness of the acts and the existence of some sort of continuity.[32]

After this second, and somewhat muddled attempt, the circuits were still, and currently remain, no closer to utilizing a uniform analysis.[33]

Treble Damages and Scope of RICO

After proving that the defendant has been associated with an enterprise engaged in a pattern of racketeering activity, a private plaintiff may be able to qualify for treble damages for any resulting loss.[34] In

---

32. *H.J. Inc.* followed on the analysis of the *Sedima* opinion, which drew upon RICO's legislative history, in holding that the "continuity plus relationship" test was appropriate for determining whether a "pattern" existed. *Id.* at 239. One court, Procter & Gamble Co. v. Big Apple Indus. Bldgs., Inc., 879 F.2d 10, 17 (2d Cir.1989), has simplistically defined the test as follows:

'[C]ontinuity' means that separate events occur over time and perhaps threaten to recur, while 'relatedness' means—given that different acts of racketeering activity have occurred—that there is a way in which the acts may be viewed as having a common purpose.

However, while the Supreme Court enunciated that continuity and a relationship (relatedness) was to be utilized, its analysis did little to aid the lower courts in making the determination whether these two factors exist, based upon the particular facts at hand. *See* J.D. Marshall Int'l, Inc. v. Redstart, Inc., 935 F.2d 815, 820 (7th Cir.1991) ("The Supreme Court has not established any clear-cut test or specific formula for determining if the allegations evince the required continuity [or relatedness].").

33. However, by generalizing from the case law, one commentator has suggested that in light of the Supreme Court's directives, lower court precedents, and drawing upon the old multi-factor test, a lists of non-exclusive factors should help guide the lower circuits in the "continuity plus relationship" analysis:

"1. the nature and number of (a) offenses and (b) schemes;

2. the nature and number of victims;

3. the nature, number, and identity of (a) perpetrators and (b) enterprises;

4. the involvement of each penetrator and enterprise in each of (a) offenses and (b) scheme;

5. the dates and duration of (a) offenses and (b) schemes;

6. the goals of each offense and scheme;

7. the methods utilized in committing each offense and effectuating each scheme, including the presence of repetitive behavior; and

8. the nature, extent, and distinctiveness of resulting damage."

Gregory P. Joseph, Civil Rico: A Definitive Guide 94–95 (1992).

34. 18 U.S.C.A. § 1964(c). *See, e.g.,* Metromedia Co. v. Fugazy Travelco, Inc., 983 F.2d 350 (2d Cir.1992), *cert. denied* ___ U.S. ___, 113 S.Ct. 2445, 124 L.Ed.2d 662 (1993) (upholding jury award of treble damages for willful violations of section 12(2) of the 1933 Act). *But cf.* Sperber v. Boesky, 672 F.Supp. 754 (S.D.N.Y.1987) (damages must come from violation, not from failing to disclose violation). However, at least one court has held that

order to qualify for treble damages the plaintiff must be able to show that he or she was injured in his or her business or property. Although a few courts have ruled that the plaintiff must have suffered a competitive injury,[35] the better view, which has been followed by most courts, is to the contrary but the injury must nonetheless be direct rather than indirect.[36] A remote injury, thus, will not provide the basis for a private RICO action.[37]

A plaintiff in an action under Rule 10b–5 must have been a purchaser or seller of securities.[38] In contrast, the Ninth Circuit held that the purchaser-seller standing requirement does not apply in a RICO action even when the predicate acts consist of securities fraud.[39] The Ninth Circuit pointed out that the private RICO remedy is set forth in the statute which does not impose any such limitations on the categories of plaintiffs who can sue. Principles of proximate cause limit the range of potential plaintiffs in private RICO actions. Accordingly, secondary victims do not have standing to bring RICO actions.[40]

[*See* Practitioner's Edition for further discussion.]

---

a damage claim could not be maintained under RICO where the plaintiffs, in settlement, had already received the amount that they lost. Commercial Union Assurance Co. v. Milken, 17 F.3d 608 (2d Cir.1994).

35. *E.g.* North Barrington Development, Inc. v. Fanslow, 547 F.Supp. 207 (N.D.Ill. 1980). This view is based on the fact that the RICO treble damage provision was modeled after section 4 of the Clayton Antitrust Act, 15 U.S.C.A. § 15, which contains a competitive injury limitation. See Brunswick Corp. v. Pueblo Bowl–O–Mat, Inc., 429 U.S. 477, 489, 97 S.Ct. 690, 697, 50 L.Ed.2d 701 (1977). *Cf.* Bruns v. Ledbetter, 583 F.Supp. 1050 (S.D.Cal.1984); Warner Communications, Inc. v. Murdoch, 581 F.Supp. 1482, 1497 (D.Del. 1984).

36. Schacht v. Brown, 711 F.2d 1343 (7th Cir.1983) *cert. denied* 464 U.S. 1002, 104 S.Ct. 508, 78 L.Ed.2d 698 (1983); Bennett v. Berg, 685 F.2d 1053, 1058–59 (8th Cir.1982), *reversed in part on other grounds on rehearing* 710 F.2d 1361 (8th Cir.1983) (en banc), *cert. denied* 464 U.S. 1008, 104 S.Ct. 527, 78 L.Ed.2d 710 (1983); Hanna Mining Co. v. Norcen Energy Resources, Ltd., 574 F.Supp. 1172 (N.D.Ohio 1982); Note, Civil RICO: The Temptation and Impropriety of Judicial Restriction, 95 Harv.L.Rev. 1101, 1109–1114 (1982). *See, e.g.*, Huang v. Sentinel Government Securities, 709 F.Supp. 1290 (S.D.N.Y. 1989) (loss of promised tax benefits is a direct injury to the investor despite defendant's argument that the I.R.S. was the real party in interest). *See also*, Wilcox v. Ho–Wing Sit, 586 F.Supp. 561 (C.D.Cal.1984).

37. *E.g., See also, e.g.,* Mendelovitz v. Vosicky, 40 F.3d 182 (7th Cir.1994) (no standing to bring shareholder derivative suit against officers and directors whose actions allegedly injured third parties); In re Ivan F. Boesky Securities Litigation, 36 F.3d 255 (2d Cir.1994) (finding insufficient connection in private RICO action against investment firm based on insider trading violations).

38. *See* § 13.3 *supra.*

39. SIPC v. Vigman, 908 F.2d 1461 (9th Cir.1990), *judgment reversed on other grounds sub nom.* Holmes v. SIPC, 503 U.S. 258, 112 S.Ct. 1311, 117 L.Ed.2d 532 (1992), *on remand* 964 F.2d 924 (9th Cir.1992). *Accord* Warner v. Alexander Grant & Co., 828 F.2d 1528 (11th Cir.1987). *But see* International Data Bank, Ltd. v. Zepkin, 812 F.2d 149 (4th Cir.1987); Brannan v. Eisenstein, 804 F.2d 1041 (8th Cir.1986).

40. Holmes v. SIPC, 503 U.S. 258, 112 S.Ct. 1311, 117 L.Ed.2d 532 (1992), *on remand* 964 F.2d 924 (9th Cir.1992). The defendant allegedly engaged in a manipulative scheme that resulted in two securities brokers being unable to meet their financial obligations. As a result, the brokers' customers were reimbursed by the Securities Investor Protection Corporation. SIPC sued to recover the amount in question. The Court ruled that allowing the suit to proceed would open the door to claims that would unduly burden the courts and undermine the effectiveness of the RICO statute.

*Deleted sections 19.3.1 and 19.4 can be found
in the Practitioner's Edition.*

§ 19.5   The Intertwining of Financial Services: Commercial Banks, Investment Banking, and Investment Services

In 1933 Congress enacted the Glass–Steagall Act[1] in order to erect a barrier between commercial banking and investment banking in this country. Although this legislation is still in effect, it no longer keeps commercial banks completely out of the securities brokerage business. The use of holding companies and subsidiaries, among other things, has to a large extent intruded upon the separation of activities mandated by the Glass–Steagall Act.

Over the past several decades there has been an increasing blurring of the distinction between commercial banking and investment banking. These two basic types of financial institutions have become increasingly competitive with one another. For example, savings institutions and commercial banks were replaced by investment company money market funds for a large part of this nation's savings but legislation adopted in 1980 has paved the way for both commercial banks and savings and loans to compete by offering comparable but federally insured accounts when the federal government deregulated the level of interest rates that these institutions could offer.[2] The deregulation of the stock brokerage industry in terms of the abolition of fixed commission rates,[3] and the development of discount brokerage houses has also brought the banks into the retail securities industry both directly and indirectly.[4] The

------

§ 19.5

1. The Banking Act of 1933, Ch. 89, 48 Stat. 184 (1933), codified in various sections of 12 U.S.C.A. *See* in particular 12 U.S.C.A. §§ 24, 378(a). *See generally* Note, Securities Activities Under the Glass–Steagall Act, 35 Emory L.J. 463 (1986); Note, Security Under the Glass–Steagall Act: Analyzing the Supreme Court's Framework for Determining Permissible Bank Activity, 70 Corn.L.Rev. 1194 (1985).

See also, e.g., Henry N. Butler & Jonathan R. Macey, The Myth of Competition in the Dual Banking System, 73 Corn.L.Rev. 677 (1988); Howell E. Jackson, The Expanding Obligations of Financial Holding Companies, 107 Harv. L. Rev. 507 (1994).

2. The Depositary Institutions Deregulation and Monetary Control Act of 1980, Pub.L. 96–221, 96th Cong., 2d Sess. (1980). Many of these accounts are known as "NOW" accounts (negotiable order of withdrawal).

3. *See generally* Douglas M. Branson, Securities Regulation After Entering the Competitive Era: The Securities Industry, SEC Policy, and the Individual Investor 75, Nw. U.L.Rev. 857 (1980); David L. Ratner, Regulation of Compensation of Securities Dealers, 55 Cornell L.Rev. 348 (1970).

4. Many commercial banks now offer discount brokerage services by filtering the business through registered broker-dealers that operate regionally or throughout the country. Additionally there has been a move towards acquisition. For example, Bank of America Corp. acquired Charles Schwab & Co. which is the nation's largest discount stockbroker. Both the Supreme Court and the Second Circuit refused to disturb the Federal Reserve Board's approval of the Schwab acquisition. Securities Industry Association v. Board of Governors, 468 U.S. 207, 104 S.Ct. 3003, 82 L.Ed.2d 158 (1984), *affirming* 716 F.2d 92 (2d Cir.1983). The acquisition does not run afoul of Glass–Steagall so long as the banking operations and the brokerage business are set up in separate corporations, even if under the umbrella of a single bank holding company; also, these acquisitions

move towards head-on competition has not been one way. Brokerage firms have tried to compete more directly with retail commercial banks by offering money market funds and unlimited checking privileges in cooperation with a bank that issues and honors the checks. Also, there have been successful attempts by investment bankers, through the use of holding companies, to obtain commercial bank charters.

[*See* Practitioner's Edition for further discussion.]

Deleted sections 19.6–19.8 can be found in the Practitioner's Edition.

Deleted Chapter 20 can be found in the Practitioner's Edition.

---

require approval by the Federal Reserve Board. *See* Application of Bank America Corporation, [1982–1983 Transfer Binder] Fed.Banking L. Rep. (CCH) ¶ 99,475 (Fed.Res.Bd. of Governors Jan. 7, 1983). For discussion of the use of bank holding companies for nonbanking activities *see* Comment, Implementation of the Bank Holding Company Act Amendments of 1970: The Scope of Banking Activities, 71 Mich.L.Rev. 1170 (1973). *See also* Note, A Conduct–Oriented Approach to the Glass–Steagall Act, 91 Yale L.J. 102 (1981).

Appendix

RESEARCHING SECURITIES REGULATION ON WESTLAW

Analysis

Section 1.   Introduction

Securities Regulation provides a strong base for analyzing even the most complex problem involving securities law.   Whether your research requires examination of case law, statutes, administrative materials or expert commentary, West books, WESTLAW® and West CD–ROM Libraries™ are excellent sources.

WESTLAW expands your library, giving you access to decisions from federal courts and documents from the U.S. Congress, as well as access to articles and treatises by well-known commentators. To help keep you up-to-date with current developments, WESTLAW provides frequently updated securities law databases. With WESTLAW, you have unparalleled legal research resources at your fingertips.

Additional Resources

If you have not used WESTLAW or have questions not covered in this appendix, see the *WESTLAW Reference Manual* or call the West Reference Attorneys at 1–800–REF–ATTY (1–800–733–2889). The West Reference Attorneys are trained, licensed attorneys who can assist you with your WESTLAW or West book research questions.

Section 2.   WESTLAW Securities Databases

Each database on WESTLAW is assigned an abbreviation called an *identifier*, which you use to access the database. You can find identifiers for all databases in the online WESTLAW Directory and in the *WESTLAW Database List*. When you need to know more detailed information about a database, use Scope. Scope contains coverage information, related databases and valuable search tips. To use Scope from the WESTLAW Directory, type **sc** and the database or service identifier, e.g., **sc wld-sec**.

The following chart lists WESTLAW databases that contain information pertaining to securities law. For a complete list of securities databases, see the WESTLAW Directory or the *WESTLAW Database List*. Because new information is continually being added to WESTLAW, you should also check the Welcome to WESTLAW screen and the WESTLAW Directory for new database information.

Description	Database Identifier	Beginning Coverage (see Scope for more specific information)
Combined Federal Securities Materials (combines FSEC–CS FSEC–CODREG and FSEC–ADMIN)	FSEC–ALL	Varies by individual database
Federal Case Law		
Federal Securities and Blue Sky Law Cases	FSEC–CS	1789
U.S. Supreme Court	FSEC–SCT	1790
U.S. Courts of Appeals	FSEC–CTA	1891
U.S. District Courts	FSEC–DCT	1789
Federal Statutes, Rules and Regulations		
U.S. Code Annotated	FSEC–USCA	Current data
Federal Rules	FSEC–RULES	Current data
Federal Register	FSEC–FR	July 1980
Code of Federal Regulations	FSEC–CFR	Current data

Description	Database Identifier	Beginning Coverage (see Scope for more specific information)
Code and Regulations (combines FSEC–USCA, FSEC–CFR and FSEC–FR)	FSEC–CODREG	Varies by database
Final, Temporary and Proposed Regulations (combines FSEC–CFR and FSEC–FR)	FSEC–REG	Varies by database
Legislative History	FSEC–LH	1933
Insider Trading Act Legislative History	INSIDER–LH	Full history

Federal Administrative Law

Commodity Futures Trading Commission Letters	FSEC–CFTCLTR	1987
Administrative Materials	FSEC–ADMIN	
Arbitration Awards	FSEC–ARB	1989
Commodity Futures Trading Commission Decisions	FSEC–CFTC	1976
SEC News Digest	FSEC–DIG	July 1987
SEC No–Action Letters	FSEC–NAL	1970
Securities Releases	FSEC–RELS	Varies by material
Stock Exchange Disciplinary Decisions	FSEC–DISP	September 1972
News Releases	FSEC–NR	Varies by material

State Case Law

Multistate Administrative Cases	MSEC–CS	Varies by state
Individual State Cases	XXSEC–CS	Varies by state

State: Administrative Law

Multistate Decisions	MSEC–ADMIN	Varies by state
Individual State Administrative Decisions: AZ, CA, CO, DE, FL, IA, ID, IL, KS, KY, MD, MI, MN, OH, PA, TX, VA, WA, WI	XXSEC–ADMIN	Varies by state

Specialized

American Arbitration Association	AAA–PUBS	Current data
Asian Wall Street Journal, The	WSJ–ASIA	June 1991
Barron's	BARRONS	1987
BNA Headlines	BNA–BHL	Current data
BNA Securities Law Daily	BNA–SLD	March 1987
Bond Buyer Full Text (DIALOG)	BBFT	November 1981
Business Wire (DIALOG)	BUSWIRE	1986
Company Index	COMPANY	1968
Disclosure Database (DIALOG)	DISCLOSURE	Current data
Dow Jones Magazines, Journals and Newsletters	MAGSPLUS	Varies by publication
Dow Jones Wires	WIRES	Current 3–4 months
EDGAR–S.E.C. Filings	EDGAR	
Full-text filings		April 1993
Non–EDGAR filings		1968
Far Eastern Economic Review	FEER	1993
Insider Trading Monitor (DIALOG)	ITM	1984
Knight–Ridder/Tribune Business News (DIALOG)	KR–FINEWS	1989
M & A Filings (DIALOG)	M & A–D	April 1985
McGraw–Hill Publications Online (DIALOG)	MH–PUBS	1985
Media General Plus (DIALOG)	MEDIA–GEN	Current data
PTS F & S Index (DIALOG)	PTS–F & S	1980
PTS PROMT (DIALOG)	PTS–PROMT	1972
Securities and Exchange Commission Corporate Filings	SEC–ONLINE	July 1987
Securities Regulation & Law Report	BNA–SRLR	1986
Standard & Poor's Corporate Descriptions plus News (DIALOG)	S & P–CORPDE	Current data
Standard & Poor's Daily News (DIALOG)	S & P–NEWS	July 1985
Wall Street Journal, The	WSJ	1984
Wall Street Journal Europe, The	WSJ–EURO	1991

Description	Database Identifier	Beginning Coverage (see Scope for more specific information)
WESTLAW Topical Highlights—Corporations and Securities	WTH–CORP	Current data
West's Legal Directory—Securities	WLD–SEC	Current data

Texts and Periodicals

Clark Boardman—Acquisitions and Mergers: Negotiated and Contested Transactions	CB–SEC11	1990 edition
Clark Boardman—Blue Sky Law	CB–SEC12	1993 edition
Clark Boardman—Blue Sky Practice for Public and Private Limited Offerings	CB–BSP	1991 edition
Clark Boardman—Civil Liabilities: Enforcement & Litigation Under the 1933 Act	CB–SEC17	1993 edition
Clark Boardman—Commodities Regulation: Fraud, Manipulation & Other Claims	CB–SEC13	1990 edition
Clark Boardman—Exempted Transactions Under the Securities Act of 1933	CB–SEC7	1992 edition
Clark Boardman—Going Public and the Public Corporation	CB–SEC1	1992 edition
Clark Boardman—International Capital Markets and Securities Regulation	CB–SEC10	1992 edition
Clark Boardman—Investment Limited Partnerships	CB–SEC4	1991 edition
Clark Boardman—Litigation and Practice Under Rule 10b–5	CB–SEC5	1992 edition
Clark Boardman—Opinion Letters in Securities Matters: Texts—Clauses—Law	CB–SEC8	1993 edition
Clark Boardman—Section 16 of the Securities Exchange Act	CB–SEC16	1992 edition
Clark Boardman—Securities and Federal Corporate Law	CB–SEC3	1992 edition
Clark Boardman—Securities & Partnership Law for MLPs & Other Investment Limited Partnerships	CB–SEC14	1989 edition
Clark Boardman—Utility Holding Companies	CB–UHC	1987 edition
Clark Boardman—Venture Capital and Small Business Financings	CB–SEC2	1991 edition
Law Reviews, Texts and Bar Journals	SEC–TP	Varies by publication
PLI Corporate Law and Practice Course Handbook Series	PLI–CORP	September 1984

Section 3.   Menu–Driven WESTLAW: EZ ACCESS®

EZ ACCESS is West Publishing Company's menu-driven research system.   It is ideal for new or infrequent WESTLAW users because it requires no experience or training on WESTLAW.

To access EZ ACCESS, type **ez**. The EZ ACCESS main menu will be displayed. Whenever you are unsure of the next step, or if the choice you want is not listed, simply type **ez**; additional choices will be displayed.   Once you retrieve documents with EZ ACCESS, use standard WESTLAW commands to browse your documents. For more information on browsing documents, see the *WESTLAW Reference Manual* or the *WESTLAW User Guide*.

Section 4.   Retrieving a Document with a Citation: Find and Jump

4.1   Find

Find is a WESTLAW service that allows you to retrieve a document by entering its citation. Find allows you to retrieve documents from anywhere in WESTLAW without accessing or changing databases or losing your search result. Find is available for many documents, including case law, statutes, regulations, court rules, public laws, and texts and periodicals.

To use Find, type **fi** followed by the document citation. Below is a list of examples:

To Find This Document	Type
15 U.S.C.A. § 77c	**fi 15 usca 77c**
Pub. L. No. 103–75	**fi us pl 103–75**
O'Melveny & Myers v. FDIC, 114 S.Ct. 2048 (1994)	**fi 114 sct 2048**
Migdaleck v. United States, 1994 WL 468035, (6th Cir. Aug. 29, 1994)	**fi 1994 wl 468035**
"Increased Protection of Limit Orders on NASDAQ Stock Market Approved by SEC," 5/22/95 SLD d2	**fi 5/22/95 sld d2**
Colo. Rev. Stat. Ann. § 4–8–309	**fi co st s 4–8–309**

4.2 Jump

Jump is a feature that allows you to move from one location to another on WESTLAW. For example, use Jump to go from a case or law review article to a cited case, USCA® section or article; from a headnote to the corresponding text in the opinion; or from an entry in a statute index database to the full text of the statute. To use Jump, press the **Tab** key until the cursor reaches the Jump marker (> or ▶) you want to select, then press **Enter**. You can also use a mouse to click or double-click the Jump marker.

Section 5. Natural Language Searching: WIN®—WESTLAW is Natural™

WIN (WESTLAW is Natural) is the Natural Language search method on WESTLAW. With WIN, you can retrieve documents by simply describing your issue in plain English. If you are a relatively new user, Natural Language searching makes it easier to retrieve cases on point. If you are an experienced user, Natural Language increases your research proficiency by giving you a valuable alternative search method.

When you enter a Natural Language description, WESTLAW automatically identifies legal phrases, removes common words and generates variations of terms in your description. WESTLAW then searches for the legal phrases and other concepts in your description. Concepts may include significant terms, phrases, legal citations or topic and key numbers. Based on the frequency with which each concept occurs in the database and in each document, WESTLAW retrieves the 20 documents that most closely match your description, beginning with the document most likely to match.

5.1 Natural Language Searching

To use Natural Language searching, access the database containing documents relevant to your issue. If your current search method is Terms and Connectors, type **nat** or select the *Natural Language* Jump marker to change to the Natural Language method and display the Enter Description screen. Then enter a Natural Language description such as the following:

is scienter necessary for a 10b–5 claim

5.2 Concept Ranking

WESTLAW displays the 20 documents that most closely match your description, beginning with the document most likely to match. If you want to view additional documents, use the Next command. Type next to display the next 10 documents. To retrieve more than 10 documents, specify a number, such as **next 25** or **next 32**. You can retrieve up to 100 documents in total.

5.3 Browsing a Natural Language Search Result

Best Mode: To display the best portion (the portion that most closely matches your description) of each document in your search result, type **b**.

Standard Browsing Commands: You can also browse your Natural Language search result using standard WESTLAW browsing commands, such as citations list (L), Locate (loc), page mode (p) and term mode (t). When you browse your Natural Language search result in term mode, the five portions of each document that are most likely to match your description are displayed.

Section 6. Terms and Connectors Searching

With standard Terms and Connectors searching, you enter a query, which consists of key terms from your research issue and connectors specifying the relationship between these terms.

Terms and Connectors searching is useful when you want to retrieve a document for which you have specific information, such as the title or the citation. Terms and Connectors searching is also useful when you want to retrieve documents relating to a specific issue. To change from Natural Language searching to Terms and Connectors searching, type **tc** or select the *Terms and Connectors* Jump marker at the Enter Description screen.

6.1 Terms

Plurals and Possessives: Plurals are automatically retrieved when you enter the singular form of a term. This is true for both regular and irregular plurals (e.g., **child** retrieves *children*). If you enter the plural form of a term, you will not retrieve the singular form.

If you enter the non-possessive form of a term, WESTLAW automatically retrieves the possessive form as well. However, if you enter the possessive form, only the possessive form is retrieved.

Automatic Equivalencies: Some terms have alternative forms or equivalencies; for example, *5* and *five* are equivalent terms. WESTLAW automatically retrieves equivalent terms. The *WESTLAW Reference Manual* contains a list of equivalent terms.

Compound Words and Acronyms: When a compound word is one of your search terms, use a hyphen to retrieve all forms of the word. For example, the term *along-side* retrieves *along-side, alongside* and *along side.*

When using an acronym as a search term, place a period after each of the letters in the acronym to retrieve any of its forms. For example, the term **s.e.c.** retrieves *sec, s.e.c., s e c* and *S.E. c.* Note: The acronym *s.e.c.* does *not* retrieve *Securities Exchange Commission*, so remember to add additional alternative terms to your query such as **"securities exchange commission"**.

Root Expander and Universal Character: When you use the Terms and Connectors search method, placing a root expander (!) at the end of a root term generates all other terms with that root. For example, adding the ! symbol to the roots *fraud* and *transfer* in the query

fraud! /s transfer!

instructs WESTLAW to retrieve such words as *fraud, fraudulent, fraudulently, transfer, transferred* and *transferring.*

The universal character (*) stands for one character and can be inserted in the middle or at the end of a term. For example, the term

s**holder**

will retrieve *shareholder* and *stockholder.* Adding three asterisks to the root *elect* in the query

elect***

instructs WESTLAW to retrieve all forms of the root with up to three additional characters. Terms like *elected* or *election* are retrieved by this query. However, terms with more than three letters following the root, such as *electronic,* are not retrieved. Plurals are always retrieved, even if more than three letters follow the root.

Phrase Searching: To search for a phrase, place it within quotation marks. For example, to search for references to junk bonds, type **"junk bond"**. When you are using the Terms and Connectors search method, you should use phrase searching only if you are certain that the phrase will not appear in any other form.

6.2 Alternative Terms

After selecting the terms for your query, consider which alternative terms are necessary. For example, if you are searching for the term *resident,* you might also want to search for the term *non-resident.* You should consider both synonyms and antonyms as alternative terms. You can also use the WESTLAW thesaurus to add alternative terms to your query.

6.3 Connectors

After selecting terms and alternative terms for your query, use connectors to specify the relationship that should exist between search terms in your retrieved documents. The connectors you can use are described below:

Use:	To retrieve documents with:	Example:
& (and)	both terms	**"small business" & securities**
or (space)	either term or both terms	**exemplary punitive**
/p	search terms in the same paragraph	**churning /p damages**
/s	search terms in the same sentence	**sold sale sell! /s securities**
+s	one search term preceding the other within the same sentence, especially useful when searching in the title field (ti) where both parties have the same name	**ti(kurzman +s kurzman)**
/n	search terms within "n" terms of each other (where "n" is a number)	**defin! /3 "inside* trad*** "**
+n	one search term preceding the other by "n" terms (where "n" is a number)	**summary +3 judgment**
% (but not)	search terms following the % symbol	**attorney lawyer /5 client /s privileg! % sy,di(work-product)**

6.4 Restricting Your Search by Field

Documents in each WESTLAW database consist of several parts, or fields. One field may contain the citation, another the title, another the synopsis, and so forth. Not all databases contain the same fields. Also, depending on the database, fields of the same name may contain different types of information.

To view the fields and field content for a specific database, see Scope or type **f** while in the database. Note that in some databases, not every field is available for every document.

To retrieve only those documents containing your search terms in a specific field, restrict your search to that field. To restrict your search to a specific field, type the field name or abbreviation followed by your search terms enclosed in parentheses. For example, to retrieve a case in the Federal Securities and Blue Sky Law—Cases database (FSEC–CS) entitled *Taylor v. Investors Associates, Inc.,* search for your terms in the title field (ti):

ti(taylor & "investors associates")

The fields discussed below are available in WESTLAW databases you might use for researching securities law issues.

Digest and Synopsis Fields: The digest (di) and synopsis (sy) fields, added to case law databases by West Publishing's editors, summarize the main points of a case. The synopsis field contains a brief description of a case. The digest field contains the topic, headnote, court and title fields and includes the complete hierarchy of concepts used to classify the point of law, including the West digest topic name and number and the key number. Restricting your search to these fields limits your result to cases in which your terms are related to a major issue in the case.

Consider restricting your search to one or both of these fields if

- you are searching for common terms or terms with more than one meaning, and you need to narrow your search; or

- you cannot narrow your search by moving to a smaller database.

For example, to retrieve cases that discuss the fraud on the market theory, access the Federal Securities and Blue Sky Law—Cases database (FSEC–CS) and type:

sy,di("fraud on the market")

Headnote Field: The headnote field (he) is a part of the digest field, but does not contain the topic number, hierarchical classification information, key number or title. The headnote field contains only the one-sentence summary of the point of law and any supporting statutory citations given by the author of the opinion. A headnote field restriction is useful when you are searching for specific statutory sections or rule numbers. For example, to retrieve headnotes that cite 15 U.S.C.A. § 77c, type the following query:

he(15 +5 77c)

Topic Field: The topic field is also a part of the digest field. It contains hierarchical classification information, including the West digest topic name and number and the key number. You should restrict search terms to the topic field in a case law database if

- a digest field search retrieves too many documents; or

- you want to retrieve cases with digest paragraphs classified under more than one topic.

For example, the topic Securities Regulation has the topic number 349B. To retrieve United States district court cases that discuss the "bespeaks caution" doctrine, access the Federal Securities and Blue Sky Laws—District Courts Cases database (FSEC–DCT) and type a query like the following:

to(349b) /p bespeaks

To retrieve West headnotes classified under more than one topic and key number, search for your terms in the topic field. For example, to search for cases discussing good will, which may be classified under topic 192, Good Will, and other topics such as 220, Internal Revenue, and 382, Trade Regulation, type a query like the following:

to(good-will)

For a complete list of West digest topics and their corresponding topic numbers, access the Key Number service; type **key**.

> Be aware that slip opinions and cases from topical services do not contain the digest, headnote or topic fields.

Prelim and Caption Fields: When searching in a database containing statutes, rules or regulations, restrict your search to the prelim (pr) and caption (ca) fields to retrieve documents in which your terms are important enough to appear in a section name or heading. For example, to retrieve Pennsylvania statutes relating to registration of securities, access the Pennsylvania Statutes—Annotated database (PA-ST-ANN) and type the following:

pr,ca(securities /p regis!)

6.5 Restricting Your Search by Date

You can instruct WESTLAW to retrieve documents *decided* or *issued* before, after, or on a specified date, as well as within a range of dates. The following are examples of queries that contain date restrictions:

da(aft 1991) & regis! /p distribut! /p prospectus

da(1990) & take-over /p disclos! non-disclos!

da(4/12/95) & "investment contract"

You can also instruct WESTLAW to retrieve documents *added to a database* on or after a specified date, as well as within a range of dates. The following are examples of queries that contain added date restrictions:

ad(aft 1-1-92) & "forced sale doctrine"

ad(aft 4-1-95 & bef 5-1-95) & material /3 non-public

Section 7. Verifying Your Research with Citators

WESTLAW contains four citator services to assist you in checking the validity of cases you intend to rely on. These citator services—Insta-Cite®, Shepard's® Citations, Shepard's PreView® and Quick*Cite*®—help you perform many valuable research tasks, saving you hours of manual research. Sections 7.1 through 7.4 provide further information on these services.

WESTLAW also contains Shepard's Citations for federal statutes and law reviews; Shepard's Citations for state statutes is being added on a state-by-state basis.

For citations not covered by the citator services, including persuasive secondary authority such as restatements and treatises, use a technique called WESTLAW as a citator to retrieve cases that cite your authority (see Section 7.5).

7.1 Insta–Cite

Insta–Cite is West Publishing Company's case history and citation verification service. It is the most current case history service available. Use Insta–Cite to see whether your case is good law. Insta–Cite provides the following types of information about a citation:

Direct History. In addition to reversals and affirmances, Insta–Cite gives you the complete reported history of a litigated matter including any related cases.

Insta–Cite provides the direct history of federal cases from 1754 and state cases from 1879. Related references (cases related to the litigation) are provided from 1983 to date. Direct case history is available within 24–36 hours of receipt of a case at West.

Negative Indirect History. Insta–Cite lists subsequent cases that may have a substantial negative impact on your case, including cases overruling your case or calling it into question. Insta–Cite provides negative indirect history from 1972 to date. To retrieve negative indirect history prior to 1972, use Shepard's Citations (see Section 7.2).

Secondary Source References. Insta–Cite also provides references to secondary sources that cite your case. These secondary sources include the legal encyclopedia *Corpus Juris Secundum®*.

Parallel Citations. Insta–Cite provides parallel citations for cases, including citations to *United States Law Week* and many topical reporters.

Citation Verification. Insta–Cite confirms that you have the correct volume and page number for a case, as well as the correct spelling of proper names. Citation verification information is available from 1754 for federal cases and from 1879 for state cases.

7.2 Shepard's Citations

For case law, Shepard's provides a comprehensive list of cases and other documents that have cited a particular case. Shepard's also includes explanatory analysis to indicate how the citing cases have treated the case, e.g., "followed," "explained."

For statutes, Shepard's Citations provides a comprehensive list of cases citing a particular statute, as well as information on subsequent legislative action.

In addition to citations from federal, state and regional citators, Shepard's on WESTLAW includes citations from specialized citators.

7.3 Shepard's PreView

Shepard's PreView gives you a preview of citing references for case law from West's National Reporter System® that will appear in Shepard's Citations online. Shepard's PreView provides citing information days, weeks or even months before the same information appears in Shepard's. Use Shepard's PreView to update your Shepard's results.

7.4 Quick*Cite*

Quick*Cite* is a citator service that enables you to automatically retrieve the most recent citing cases on WESTLAW, including slip opinions.

There is a four- to six-week gap between a citing case's availability on WESTLAW and its listing in Shepard's PreView. This gap occurs because cases go through an editorial process at West Publishing Company before they are added to Shepard's PreView. To retrieve the most recent citing cases, therefore, you need to search case law databases on WESTLAW for references to your case.

Quick*Cite* formulates a query using the title, the case citation(s) and an added date restriction. Quick*Cite* then accesses the appropriate database, either ALLSTATES or ALLFEDS, and runs the query for you. Quick*Cite* also allows you to tailor the query to your specific research needs; you can choose a different date range or select another database.

Quick*Cite* is designed to retrieve documents that cite cases. To retrieve citing references to other documents, such as statutes and law review articles, use WESTLAW as a citator (see Section 7.5).

7.5 Using WESTLAW As a Citator

Using WESTLAW as a citator, you can search for documents citing a specific statute, regulation, rule, agency decision or other authority. For example, to retrieve recent federal cases citing 17 C.F.R. § 240.10b–5, access the ALLFEDS database and type a Terms and Connectors query like the following:

17 + 5 240.10b–5 & da(aft %4)

To retrieve recent cases that cite a section of the *United States Code Annotated*, such as 15 U.S.C.A. § 78j, type

15 +5 78j & da(aft %4)

7.6 Selected Citator Commands

The following are some of the commands that can be used in the citator services. For a complete list, see *WESTLAW Reference Manual*.

Command:	*Definition:*
ic xxx or **ic**	Retrieves an Insta–Cite result when followed by a case citation (where xxx is the citation), or when entered from a displayed case, Shepard's result or Shepard's PreView result.
sh xxx or **sh**	Retrieves a Shepard's result when followed by a case, statute or law review article citation (where xxx is the

Command:	Definition:
	citation), or when entered from a displayed case, statute or law review article; Insta–Cite result or Shepard's PreView result.
sp xxx or **sp**	Retrieves a Shepard's PreView result when followed by a case citation (where **xxx** is the citation), or when entered from a displayed case, Insta–Cite result or Shepard's result.
qc xxx or **qc**	Retrieves opinions that cite a case when followed by a case citation (where **xxx** is the citation), or when entered from a displayed case, Insta–Cite result, Shepard's result or Shepard's PreView result.
sc	Retrieves the scope of coverage for Insta–Cite or Shepard's PreView when you are viewing a result from that service. From a Shepard's result, displays the scope of coverage for the publication in the Shepardized® citation.
sc xx	Retrieves the scope of coverage of a citator service (where **xx** is the citator service), e.g., **sc ic**.
sh sc xxx	Retrieves the scope of coverage for a specific publication in Shepard's, where **xxx** is the publication abbreviation, e.g., **sh sc sct**.
xx pubs	Retrieves a list of publications available in the citator service and their abbreviations (where **xx** is the citator service abbreviation).
xx cmds	Retrieves a list of commands in the citator service (where **xx** is the citator service abbreviation).
sh analysis	Retrieves a list of Shepard's analysis codes, e.g., *extended, revised*, etc.
sh courts	Retrieves a list of courts and their abbreviations used in Shepard's Citations.
loc	Automatically restricts an Insta–Cite, Shepard's or Shepard's PreView result to selected categories.
loc auto	Restricts all subsequent Insta–Cite, Shepard's or Shepard's PreView results to selected categories.
xloc	Cancels a Locate request.
xloc auto	Cancels a Locate Auto request.

Section 8.   Research Examples

8.1   Retrieving Law Review Articles

Recent law review articles are often the best place to begin researching a legal issue because law review articles serve as 1) an excellent introduction to a new topic or review for a topic with which you are familiar, providing terminology to help in query formulation; 2) a finding tool for pertinent primary authority, such as cases and statutes; and 3) in some instances, persuasive secondary authority.

For example, you need to gain more background information on leveraged buyouts and the business judgment rule.

Solution

• To retrieve recent law review articles relating to your issue, access the Securities and Blue Sky Law–Law Reviews, Texts & Bar Journals database (SEC–TP) by typing **db sec-tp**; then enter a Terms and Connectors query like the following.

leveraged /3 buy-out /s business /3 judgment

• If you have a citation to an article in a specific publication, use Find to retrieve it. (Note: For more information on Find, see Section 4.1 of this appendix.) For example, to retrieve the article found at 20 Seton Hall L. Rev. 4, type

fi 20 seton hall lrev 4

• If you know the title of an article, but not the name of the journal it appeared in, access the SEC–TP database and search for key terms from the title in the title field. For example, to retrieve the article "Risk, Time, and Fiduciary Principles in Corporate Investment," type

ti(risk & time & corporate)

8.2   Retrieving Federal Statutes

You need to retrieve federal statutes dealing with manipulative or deceptive trading.

Solution

• Access the Federal Securities and Blue Sky Law—U.S. Code Annotated database (FSEC–USCA). Search for your terms in the prelim and caption fields using the Terms and Connectors search method:

pr,ca(manipulat! & decept!)

• When you know the citation for a specific section of a statute, use Find to retrieve the statute. For example, to retrieve 15 U.S.C.A. § 78k, type

fi 15 usca 78k

• To look at surrounding statutory sections, use the Documents in Sequence command. To retrieve the section preceding § 78k, type **d-**. To retrieve the section immediately following § 78k, type **d**.

• You can also use the Table of Contents service to view sections surrounding § 78k. To access the Table of Contents service while viewing this section, select the Jump marker preceding § 78k in the caption field.

• When you retrieve a statute on WESTLAW, it will contain an Update message if legislation amending or repealing it is available online. To display this legislation, select the Jump marker in the Update message with the **Tab** key or your mouse, or type **update**.

> Because slip copy versions of laws are added to WESTLAW
> before they contain full editorial enhancements, they are not
> retrieved with Update. To retrieve slip copy versions of
> laws, access the United States Public Laws database by
> typing **db us-pl** (or access the appropriate state legislative
> service database by typing **db xx-legis**, where xx is the
> state's two-letter postal abbreviation), then type **ci(slip)**
> followed by the statute's section number or descriptive
> terms. Slip copy documents are replaced by the editorially
> enhanced versions within a few working days. Update also
> does not retrieve legislation that enacts a new statute or
> covers a topic that will not be incorporated into the statutes.
> To retrieve this legislation, access US-PL or the appropriate
> state legislation service database and enter a query contain-
> ing terms that describe the new legislation.

8.3 Retrieving State Statutes

You need to retrieve Wisconsin statutes dealing with registration of
securities.

Solution

• Access the Pennsylvania Statutes—Annotated database (PA–ST–
ANN). Search for your terms in the prelim and caption fields using the
Terms and Connectors search method:

pr,ca(regis! /s securities)

• When you know the citation for a specific section of a statute, use Find
to retrieve the statute. For example, to retrieve Pa. Stat. Ann. tit. 70,
§ 1–201, type

fi 70 ps 1–201

• To look at surrounding statutory sections, use the Documents in
Sequence command. To retrieve the section preceding § 1–201, type
d-. To retrieve the section immediately following § 1–201, type **d**.

• You can also use the Table of Contents service to view sections
surrounding § 1–201. To access the Table of Contents service while
viewing this section, select the Jump marker preceding § 1–201 in the
caption field.

• When you retrieve a statute on WESTLAW, it will contain an Update
message if legislation amending or repealing it is available online. To
display this legislation, select the Jump marker in the Update message
with the **Tab** key or your mouse or type **update**. The same cautions
apply to the Update service for state statutes as for federal statutes.
See the note following section 8.2.

8.4 Retrieving Federal Regulations

You need to find the regulations pertaining to the manipulative or
deceptive sale or trading of securities. Use WESTLAW to find these
regulations.

Solution

- Access the Federal Securities and Blue Sky Law–Code of Federal Regulations database (FSEC–CFR) and type a Terms and Connectors query like the following:

  pr,ca(manipulat! decept! & securities)

- When you retrieve a CFR section on WESTLAW, it will contain an Update message if *Federal Register* documents revising it are available online. To retrieve these documents, select the Jump marker in the Update message with the **Tab** key or your mouse or type **update**.

8.5   Retrieving Federal Register Documents

You have heard that the rule regarding reporting requirements for brokers and dealers has recently changed.

Solution:

- Access the Federal Securities and Blue Sky Law–Federal Register database (FSEC–FR) and type a Terms and Connectors query like the following:

  pr,ca(securities & reporting /s broker dealer) & da(aft 1994)

8.6   Using the Citator Services

One of the cases you retrieve in your case law research is *Central Bank of Denver, v. First Interstate Bank of Denver,* 114 S.Ct. 1439 (1994). You want to see whether this case is good law and whether other cases have cited this case.

Solution

- Use Insta–Cite to retrieve the direct history and negative indirect history of *Central Bank*. While viewing the case, type **ic**.

- To Shepardize™ *Central Bank* from the Insta–Cite display, select the *Shepard's* Jump marker or type **sh**.

  Limit your Shepard's result to decisions containing a reference to a specific headnote, such as headnote 1. Type **loc 1**.

- Check Shepard's PreView for more current cases citing *Central Bank*. From the Shepard's display, select the *Shepard's PreView* Jump marker or type **sp**.

- Check Quick*Cite* for the most current cases citing *Central Bank*. From the Shepard's Preview display, select the Quick*Cite* Jump marker or type **qc**. Then follow the on-screen instructions.

8.7   Following Recent Developments

As the securities specialist in your firm, you are expected to keep up with and summarize recent legal developments in the area of securities law. How can you do this efficiently?

Solution

- One of the easiest ways to stay abreast of recent developments in securities law is by accessing the WESTLAW Topical Highlights– Corporations and Securities database (WTH–CORP). To access the database, type **db wth-corp**. A list of documents added to the database in the last two weeks is automatically displayed. To view a short description of a document, type its number. To view the full text of the document, type **fi** while viewing the description, or type **fi** followed by the document's citation while viewing the list. To run a search in the database, type **s** to display the Enter Query screen; then enter your query.

- You can also access the BNA Securities Law Daily database (BNA–SLD), which summarizes recent significant developments that affect securities law. To access the database, type **db bna-sld**. The most recent edition is automatically displayed.

Table of Cases

Some sections or footnotes can be found only in the Practitioner's Edition.

A

Activision Securities Litigation, In re, 1986 WL 15339—§ 7.3, n. 43; § 14.3, n. 7.

Activision Securities Litigation, In re, 621 F.Supp. 415—§ 7.2, n. 36, 43; § 7.5.1, n. 29, 38; § 8.1, n. 23.

Adair v. Hunt Intern. Resources Corp.— § 7.5.3, n. 7; § 19.3, n. 41, 91.

Adalman v. Baker, Watts & Co., 807 F.2d 359—§ 7.5.1, n. 28.

Adalman v. Baker, Watts & Co., 599 F.Supp. 752—§ 7.7, n. 13; § 13.17, n. 17, 25, 50.

Adalman v. Baker, Watts & Co., 599 F.Supp. 749—§ 7.2, n. 33; § 7.5.1, n. 43.

Adam v. Silicon Valley Bancshares, 1995 WL 110568—§ 13.16, n. 23.

Adam v. Silicon Valley Bancshares, 1995 WL 13236—§ 7.8, n. 14, 15.

Adam v. Silicon Valley Bancshares—§ 7.8, n. 14, 15; § 13.16, n. 23.

Adams v. Cavanagh Communities Corp.— § 1.5, n. 70; § 13.13, n. 25.

Adams v. Hyannis Harborview, Inc.—§ 1.5, n. 69, 71; § 7.5.1, n. 43.

Adams v. Martyn—§ 13.8, n. 11.

Adams v. Merrill Lynch Pierce Fenner & Smith—§ 14.5, n. 20.

Adams v. Merrill Lynch, Pierce, Fenner & Smith, Inc.—§ 10.15, n. 5; § 14.4, n. 15; § 14.5, n. 3.

Adams v. Standard Knitting Mills, Inc.— § 11.3, n. 6; § 13.4, n. 12.

Adams v. Swanson—§ 10.10, n. 15, 17; § 14.4, n. 12.

Adams Express Co., Matter of—§ 17.7, n. 59.

Adelaar v. Lauxmont Farms, Inc.—§ 13.8, n. 8.

Adena Exploration, Inc. v. Sylvan—§ 1.5, n. 78.

Ades v. Deloitte & Touche, 1993 WL 362364—§ 13.6, n. 2.

Ades v. Deloitte & Touche, 799 F.Supp. 1493—§ 13.4, n. 9, 30.

Adler v. Berg Harmon Associates, 816 F.Supp. 919—§ 13.8.1, n. 6.

Adler v. Berg Harmon Associates, 790 F.Supp. 1235—§ 13.8, n. 37, 40.

Adler v. Berg Harmon Associates, 790 F.Supp. 1222—§ 13.5B, n. 24.

Adler v. Klawans—§ 12.3, n. 63, 64; § 12.4, n. 35.

A.D.M. Corp. v. Thomson—§ 7.5.3, n. 9.

Admirality Fund v. Hugh Johnson & Co.— § 7.5.4, n. 29, 55; § 12.1, n. 123; § 13.16, n. 70.

Admirality Fund v. Tabor—§ 13.4, n. 29.

Adobe Systems, Inc. Securities Litigation, In re, 787 F.Supp. 912—§ 3.7, n. 46; § 13.5A, n. 91.

Adobe Systems, Inc. Securities Litigation, In re, 767 F.Supp. 1023—§ 11.4, n. 8; § 13.5A, n. 38, 68; § 13.8.1, n. 15.

Adobe Systems, Inc. Securities Litigation, In re, 139 F.R.D. 150—§ 13.3, n. 78.

Adoption of Final Rules Implementing Government Securities Act of 1968, SEC Rule 15Ca2-2—§ 10.5.1, n. 62, 63.

Adoption of Final Rules Implementing Government Securities Act of 1968, Rule 15Cb2-2—§ 10.5.1, n. 78.

Adoption of Final Rules Implementing Government Securities Act of 1968 Rule 15Cc1-1—§ 10.5.1, n. 55.

Adrian v. Smith Barney, Harris, Upham & Co., Inc.—§ 14.4, n. 19; § 14.5, n. 20.

Advanced Computer Techniques Corp. v. Lecht—§ 11.11, n. 32.

Advanced Magnetics, Inc. v. Bayfront Partners, Inc.—§ 13.8, n. 54.

Advanced Resources Intern., Inc. v. Tri-Star Petroleum Co.—§ 13.3, n. 45, 48; § 13.7, n. 1.

Adventure Campers, Inc.—§ 4.26.1, n. 44.

Adventures in Wine—§ 4.12, n. 15.

Advest, Inc. v. McCarthy—§ 10.10.1, n. 5; § 10.14, n. 28.

AES Corp. Securities Litigation, In re, 849 F.Supp. 907—§ 13.5B, n. 23.

AES Corp. Securities Litigation, In re, 825 F.Supp. 578—§ 7.3, n. 22; § 13.5A, n. 3.

Aetna Cas. and Sur. Co. v. Liebowitz— § 19.3, n. 34.

Aetna Life & Casualty Co.—§ 11.7, n. 41.

Aetna State Bank v. Altheimer—§ 14.1, n. 47.

Affiliated Ute Citizens of Utah v. United States—§ 1.7, n. 21; § 11.5, n. 4; § 11.20, n. 82; § 12.1, n. 93; § 13.1, n. 3; § 13.2.1, n. 25; § 13.3, n. 23; § 13.5B; § 13.5B, n. 6; § 13.6, n. 31, 32; § 13.9, n. 14, 37.

Agapitos v. PCM Inv. Co.—§ 13.8, n. 40; § 13.16, n. 84.

A.G. Edwards & Sons, Inc. v. Smith, 1991 WL 253010—§ 14.4, n. 32.

A.G. Edwards & Sons, Inc. v. Smith, 736 F.Supp. 1030—§ 13.3, n. 34; 13.8.1, n. 6; § 13.13, n. 26.

A.G. Edwards & Sons, Inc. v. Syvrud— § 14.4, n. 45; § 14.5, n. 5, 59.

Agency Holding Corp. v. Malley–Duff & Associates, Inc.—§ 13.8; § 13.8, n. 8, 20; § 19.3; § 19.3, n. 79, 80.

Ahern v. Gaussoin—§ 1.5, n. 98, 113, 159; § 7.2, n. 43; § 7.3, n. 46, 54, 58; § 7.4, n. 44; § 7.5.1, n. 31; § 7.8, n. 36, 51; § 7.10, n. 32.

Ahmed v. Trupin—§ 7.10, n. 3, 39; § 13.16, n. 84.

Ahrendt v. Palmetto Federal Sav. and Loan Ass'n—§ 5.4, n. 10, 12; § 13.2.3, n. 28.

Aid Auto Stores, Inc. v. Cannon—§ 7.4.2, n. 22.

Ainbinder v. Wall St. Clearing Co.—§ 14.5, n. 42.

Ayres v. Merrill Lynch, Pierce, Fenner & Smith, Inc.—§ **14.4, n. 6.**

Azalea Meats, Inc. v. Muscat—§ **13.8, n. 10.**

Azrielli v. Cohen Law Offices—§ **13.2.2, n. 5; § 13.5A, n. 39.**

Azurite Corp. Ltd. v. Amster & Co.—§ **11.2, n. 5; § 11.11, n. 15, 31; § 13.7.1, n. 69, 70.**

B

Babst v. Morgan Keegan & Co.—§ **7.2, n. 2; § 7.5.1, n. 23, 28; § 19.3, n. 13.**

Bache Halsey Stuart, Inc., Matter of—§ **10.5, n. 29.**

Bache Halsey Stuart, Inc. v. French—§ **10.2.1, n. 35.**

Bache Halsey Stuart, Inc. v. Hunsucker—§ **8.1, n. 35.**

Bachmeier v. Bank of Ravenswood—§ **1.5, n. 97; § 13.8, n. 11.**

Backman v. Polaroid Corp., 893 F.2d 1405—§ **3.7, n. 39, 92; § 13.4, n. 15; § 13.5A, n. 67, 94; § 13.7, n. 72; § 13.10, n. 36.**

Backman v. Polaroid Corp., 540 F.Supp. 667—§ **13.9, n. 141.**

Badart v. Merrill Lynch, Pierce, Fenner & Smith, Inc., 823 F.2d 333—§ **10.14, n. 14; § 14.4, n. 15.**

Badart v. Merrill Lynch, Pierce, Fenner & Smith, Inc., 797 F.2d 775—§ **10.14, n. 9.**

Badders v. United States—§ **19.3.1; § 19.3.1, n. 69.**

Baden v. Craig–Hallum, Inc.—§ **7.5, n. 19; § 10.11, n. 33; § 13.13, n. 25.**

Badger v. Boulevard Bancorp, Inc.—§ **7.5.4, n. 21; § 13.8, n. 67.**

Baer v. Fahnestock & Co.—§ **14.1, n. 47.**

Baer, Estate of v. C.I.R.—§ **4.29, n. 80.**

Bagaric, United States v.—§ **19.3, n. 11.**

Bailes v. Colonial Press, Inc.—§ **13.2.1, n. 15; § 13.3, n. 22; § 13.11, n. 5.**

Bailey v. Glover—§ **7.5.4, n. 57.**

Bailey v. J.W.K. Properties, Inc., 904 F.2d 918—§ **1.5, n. 14.**

Bailey v. J.W.K. Properties, Inc., 703 F.Supp. 478—§ **1.5, n. 12, 149.**

Bailey v. Meister Brau, Inc.—§ **13.11, n. 5.**

Baird v. Franklin—§ **10.2.1; § 10.2.1, n. 6.**

Baker v. Eagle Aircraft Co.—§ **13.13, n. 24, 40.**

Baker v. Gotz—§ **20.1, n. 10.**

Baker v. Powell—§ **10.10, n. 12.**

Baker v. Wheat First Securities—§ **8.1, n. 28; § 10.6, n. 4; § 10.10.1, n. 3; § 13.8, n. 11.**

Baker, Norman F., In re—§ **9.5.1, n. 2.**

Baker, Watts & Co. v. Miles & Stockbridge—§ **7.7, n. 16; § 13.17, n. 24, 25, 32.**

Baldwin–United Corp., In re—§ **7.7, n. 11; § 7.9, n. 17.**

Baldwin–United Corp., Matter of—§ **4.9, n. 8.**

Baldwin–United Corp. (Single Premium Deferred Annuities Ins. Litigation), In re—§ **7.5.3, n. 5.**

Bale v. Dean Witter Reynolds, Inc.—§ **19.3, n. 62.**

Ballan v. Upjohn Co.—§ **13.5B, n. 33.**

Ballan v. Wilfred American Educational Corp.—§ **3.7, n. 72; § 13.5A, n. 67.**

Ballarine v. Getty Oil Corp.—§ **19.3, n. 71.**

Ballay v. Legg Mason Wood Walker, Inc., 925 F.2d 682—§ **7.5, n. 50; § 10.14, n. 37.**

Ballay v. Legg Mason Wood Walker, Inc., 878 F.2d 729—§ **14.4, n. 19; § 14.5, n. 37.**

Baltimore Gas & Electric Co.—§ **11.7, n. 41.**

Baltimore Gas and Elec. Co. v. Heintz—§ **15.2, n. 14, 15.**

Bamco 18 v. Reeves—§ **1.5, n. 145; § 19.3, n. 91.**

Banco Espanol De Credito v. Security Pacific Nat. Bank, 973 F.2d 51—§ **1.5, n. 115.**

Banco Espanol de Credito v. Security Pacific Nat. Bank, 763 F.Supp. 36—§ **1.5, n. 111.**

Banco Nacional de Cuba v. Sabbatino—§ **13.17, n. 27.**

Bancroft Convertible Fund, Inc. v. Zico Inv. Holdings Inc.—§ **17.1, n. 29; § 17.9, n. 21; § 17.10; § 17.10, n. 5, 39.**

Bane v. Sigmundr Exploration Corp.—§ **13.7.1, n. 67; § 13.16, n. 68, 69.**

Banghart v. Hollywood General Partnership—§ **1.5, n. 148.**

Bangor Punta Operations, Inc. v. Bangor & A. R. Co.—§ **12.3, n. 37.**

Bankers Trust Co. v. Rhoades—§ **19.3, n. 80.**

Bank of America Canada—§ **10.5.1, n. 40.**

Bank of America Corporation, Application of—§ **19.5, n. 4.**

Bank of America National Trust & Savings Ass'n—§ **4.24, n. 35.**

Bank of America Nat. Trust and Sav. Ass'n v. Hotel Rittenhouse Associates—§ **1.5, n. 99, 145.**

Bank of America Nat. Trust & Sav. Ass'n v. Touche Ross & Co.—§ **19.3, n. 16.**

Bank of America Trust & Savings Ass'n—§ **4.24, n. 40.**

Bank of Boston Corp.—§ **4.11, n. 7, 8.**

Bank of Denver v. Southeastern Capital Group, Inc., 789 F.Supp. 1092—§ **13.8, n. 39.**

Bank of Denver v. Southeastern Capital Group, Inc., 763 F.Supp. 1552—§ **7.5, n. 50; § 10.14, n. 37; § 13.5B, n. 33.**

Bank of Lexington & Trust Co. v. Vining-Sparks Securities, Inc.—§ **10.2, n. 35.**

Berner v. Lazzaro—§ 10.14, n. 10; § 13.9, n. 25.

Berne Street Enterprises, Inc. v. American Export Isbrandtsen Co., Inc.—§ 13.3, n. 59.

Berning v. A.G. Edwards & Sons, Inc.—§ 13.8, n. 40.

Bernstein v. Crazy Eddie, Inc.—§ 7.3, n. 31.

Bernstein v. IDT Corp.—§ 19.3, n. 26.

Bernstein v. Shearson/American Exp. Inc.—§ 14.5, n. 5, 59.

Berry Petroleum Co. v. Adams and Peck—§ 13.8, n. 11.

Berryman, In re—§ 9.7, n. 16.

Bersch v. Drexel Firestone, Inc.—§ 14.2, n. 5, 6, 45.

Bertoglio v. Texas Intern. Co.—§ 11.3, n. 16; § 11.6, n. 11.

Bestline Products Securities and Antitrust Litigation, In re—§ 7.5.4, n. 49, 53.

Bevere v. Oppenheimer & Co.—§ 14.4, n. 56; § 14.5, n. 3.

Beverly Corp., In re—§ 20.6, n. 9.

Bevill, Bresler & Schulman Asset Management Corp., Matter of—§ 19.4, n. 20; § 20.3, n. 6.

B.F. Hirsch v. Enright Refining Co., Inc.—§ 19.3, n. 25.

Bharucha v. Reuters Holdings PLC—§ 3.7, n. 46; § 13.4, n. 9; § 13.5A, n. 63, 67; § 13.8.1, n. 6.

Bhatia v. Johnston—§ 14.4, n. 58; § 14.5, n. 5, 59.

Bhatla v. Resort Development Corp.—§ 1.5, n. 70.

Biaggi, United States v.—§ 19.3.1, n. 66.

Bianco v. Texas Instruments, Inc.—§ 13.9, n. 115.

Biben v. Card, 1985 WL 29952—§ 13.5B, n. 42.

Biben v. Card, 789 F.Supp. 1001—§ 13.5B, n. 33; § 13.7, n. 20.

Biben v. Card, 119 F.R.D. 421—§ 9.31, n. 8.

Biechele v. Cedar Point, Inc.—§ 11.15, n. 69; § 11.20, n. 75; § 12.1, n. 11.

Biesenbach v. Guenther—§ 13.11, n. 7, 12, 29.

Biggans v. Bache Halsey Stuart Shields, Inc.—§ 10.10, n. 12; § 13.8, n. 14.

BI, Inc.—§ 3.3, n. 18.

Bilick v. Eagle Elec. Mfg. Co., Inc.—§ 13.8, n. 82.

Bily v. Arthur Young and Co.—§ 7.10, n. 61.

Bilzerian, In re—§ 9.5, n. 28.

Bilzerian v. S.E.C.—§ 9.5, n. 42.

Bilzerian, United States v.—§ 11.4, n. 47; § 11.11, n. 15.

Bingham, United States v.—§ 13.5A, n. 13, 38.

Binkley v. Sheaffer—§ 10.2, n. 23; § 13.13, n. 22.

Bio–Medical Sciences, Inc.—§ 4.26, n. 15; § 6.1, n. 27.

Bird v. Ferry—§ 13.12, n. 2.

Birdman v. Electro–Catheter Corp.—§ 3.7, n. 21.

Birenbaum v. Bache & Co., Inc.—§ 14.1, n. 19, 21.

Birnbaum v. Newport Steel Corp.—§ 13.3; § 13.3, n. 3.

Birotte v. Merrill Lynch, Pierce, Fenner & Smith, Inc.—§ 10.2.1, n. 2.

Bischoff v. G.K. Scott & Co., Inc.—§ 10.3, n. 16; § 10.7, n. 20.

Bitkowski v. Merrill Lynch, Pierce, Fenner & Smith, Inc.—§ 14.5, n. 5, 59.

Bivens Gardens Office Bldg., Inc. v. Barnett Bank of Florida, Inc.—§ 19.3, n. 80.

B.K. Medical Systems, Inc. Pension Plan v. Clesh—§ 1.5, n. 98; § 7.8, n. 58.

Black Box, Inc.—§ 4.29, n. 67.

Black Hills Corp.—§ 11.7, n. 41.

Black & Co. v. Nova–Tech, Inc.—§ 8.1, n. 23.

Black & Decker Corp. v. American Standard Inc.—§ 11.21, n. 75; § 11.22, n. 91.

Blackie v. Barrack—§ 10.9, n. 10; § 12.8, n. 4; § 13.5B, n. 33, 62; § 13.6, n. 44; § 13.9, n. 30.

Blake v. Dierdorff—§ 19.3, n. 22.

Blasingame v. American Materials, Inc.—§ 20.1, n. 10.

Blau v. Albert—§ 12.3, n. 48.

Blau v. Hodgkinson—§ 12.3, n. 56.

Blau v. Lamb—§ 12.3, n. 64.

Blau v. Lehman—§ 12.4, n. 22, 23; § 13.7, n. 71.

Blau v. Mission Corp.—§ 12.3, n. 35.

Blau v. Ogsbury—§ 12.4, n. 56.

Blau v. Oppenheim—§ 12.3, n. 32, 33.

Bledsoe, United States v.—§ 19.3, n. 24.

Blimpie Corp., Matter of—§ 3.5.1, n. 39.

Blinder, Robinson & Co., Inc., Matter of—§ 2.5, n. 17; § 3.5, n. 18; § 9.5, n. 88.

Blinder, United States v.—§ 19.3, n. 9.

Blinder, Robinson & Co., Inc. v. S.E.C.—§ 9.5, n. 111; § 9.8, n. 16; § 9.11, n. 5; § 9.14, n. 3.

Bloch v. Prudential–Bache Securities—§ 10.14, n. 20.

Block v. First Blood Associates, 988 F.2d 344—§ 13.8, n. 61, 77.

Block v. First Blood Associates, 743 F.Supp. 194—§ 13.8, n. 49.

Block v. First Blood Associates, 691 F.Supp. 685—§ 13.8.1, n. 28.

Block v. First Blood Associates, 663 F.Supp. 50—§ 13.8.1, n. 24.

Blomquist v. Churchill—§ 10.14, n. 9; § 14.4, n. 12.

Bloor v. Carro, Spanbock, Londin, Rodman & Fass—§ 11.5, n. 17; § 13.16, n. 91.

Blue Chip Stamps v. Manor Drug Stores—§ 1.7; § 7.7, n. 19; § 11.18, n. 16; § 11.19, n. 26; § 12.1, n. 93; § 13.1, n.

E

Fortson v. Winstead, McGuire, Sechrest & Minick—§ 7.10, n. 14.
Fortune Systems Securities Litigation, In re, 1987 WL 34632—§ 7.4, n. 38.
Fortune Systems Securities Litigation, In re, 680 F.Supp. 1360—§ 7.3, n. 38; § 7.4.1, n. 25; § 13.6, n. 5, 11.
Fortune Systems Securities Litigation, In re, 604 F.Supp. 150—§ 7.2, n. 37; § 7.5.1, n. 29; § 13.13, n. 22.
Foster v. Jesup and Lamont Securities Co., Inc.—§ 7.2, n. 36; § 7.5, n. 46; § 7.5.1, n. 29, 32.
Foster Pepper & Shefelman—§ 12.3, n. 91.
Fourth United States Akar, Inc. v. Cohen—§ 1.5, n. 145; § 13.13, n. 26.
Fox v. Acadia State Bank—§ 13.7.1, n. 60; § 13.13, n. 26.
Fox v. Glickman Corp.—§ 7.4.1, n. 22, 23.
Fox v. Overton—§ 20.1, n. 10.
Fox v. Reich & Tang, Inc.—§ 17.10; § 17.10, n. 58.
Fradkin v. Ernst—§ 11.3, n. 5, 6, 16; § 13.4, n. 12.
Frain v. Andy Frain, Inc.—§ 13.5B, n. 8.
Franchard Corp., Matter of—§ 3.5.1, n. 56; § 3.6, n. 3; § 3.7; § 3.7, n. 17.
Francis v. Marshall—§ 14.4, n. 77.
Frank v. D'Ambrosi—§ 13.7.1, n. 56, 58; § 19.3, n. 56.
Frank v. United States—§ 19.3.1, n. 34.
Frankart Distributors, Inc. v. RMR Advertising, Inc.—§ 19.3, n. 22.
Franke v. Midwestern Oklahoma Development Authority—§ 13.4, n. 20, 24; § 13.16, n. 81.
Frank E. Basil, Inc. v. Leidesdorf—§ 13.8, n. 61.
Frankel v. Slotkin, 984 F.2d 1328—§ 12.2, n. 66; § 12.3, n. 20; § 12.4, n. 59; § 12.5, n. 11; § 13.3, n. 7.
Frankel v. Slotkin, 705 F.Supp. 105—§ 11.15, n. 35; § 12.5, n. 25.
Frankel, United States v.—§ 19.3.1, n. 22, 31.
Frankel v. Wyllie & Thornhill, Inc.—§ 13.5B, n. 36; § 13.6, n. 33.
Frank H. Cobb, Inc. v. Cooper Companies, Inc.—§ 13.5A, n. 95.
Franklin v. Kaypro Corp.—§ 13.17, n. 68.
Franklin Sav. Bank in City of New York v. Levy—§ 14.1.1, n. 8.
Franklin Sav. Bank of New York v. Levy—§ 7.5, n. 27; § 14.1.1, n. 6, 10, 11.
Franks v. Cavanaugh—§ 10.10, n. 15; § 10.10.1, n. 7.
Fransen v. Terps Ltd. Liability Co.—§ 7.5.1, n. 5; § 13.7.1, n. 49.
Frantz Mfg. Co. v. EAC Industries—§ 11.20, n. 24.
Fraser v. Merrill Lynch Pierce, Fenner & Smith, Inc.—§ 14.4, n. 49.
Fratt v. Robinson—§ 13.8, n. 10.
Frazier v. Manson—§ 1.5, n. 148.

Fred A. Smith Lumber Co. v. Edidin—§ 13.7.1, n. 54, 73.
Fred Braun Corp. Profit Sharing Trust v. Smith—§ 13.8.1, n. 13.
Frederic W. Cook & Co.—§ 12.3, n. 91.
Frederiksen v. Poloway—§ 1.5, n. 81.
Fred Hindler, Inc. v. Telequest, Inc.—§ 13.8, n. 40.
Freedman v. Barrow—§ 12.5, n. 36.
Freeman v. Cambell—§ 1.5, n. 48.
Freeman v. Decio—§ 13.9, n. 111.
Freeman v. Laventhol & Horwath, 34 F.3d 333—§ 13.8, n. 40.
Freeman v. Laventhol & Horwath, 915 F.2d 193—§ 13.5B, n. 42.5.
Freeman v. Marine Midland Bank—New York—§ 13.14, n. 17, 30.
Freeman v. McCormack—§ 13.13, n. 22.
Freeman Securities Co., Matter of—§ 11.15, n. 56.
Freeman, United States v.—§ 19.3.1, n. 3.
Freer v. Mayer—§ 11.4, n. 19, 31.
Fremand, Ronald H., In re—§ 9.7, n. 16.
French v. Faisal Al Massoud Al Fuhaid—§ 14.3, n. 9.
French v. Merrill Lynch, Pierce, Fenner & Smith, Inc.—§ 10.2, n. 83; § 13.3, n. 76; § 13.14, n. 12; § 14.4, n. 75.
Freschi v. Grand Coal Venture, 767 F.2d 1041—§ 13.2, n. 30; § 13.7, n. 34; § 13.8, n. 62.
Freschi v. Grand Coal Venture, 588 F.Supp. 1257—§ 13.7, n. 21.
Fridrich v. Bradford—§ 11.5, n. 7; § 13.5B, n. 19, 21, 61; § 13.6, n. 34; § 13.7, n. 30, 49, 53; § 13.9; § 13.9, n. 10, 14, 31, 107; § 13.10, n. 28.
Friedlander v. Barnes—§ 7.7, n. 11; § 11.4, n. 20.
Friedlander v. Nims, 755 F.2d 810—§ 13.8.1, n. 6; § 13.11, n. 40.
Friedlander v. Nims, 571 F.Supp. 1188—§ 13.11, n. 27.
Friedlander v. Troutman, Sanders, Lockerman & Ashmore—§ 13.8, n. 11.
Friedman v. Arizona World Nurseries Ltd. Partnership—§ 3.7, n. 79; § 7.5.1, n. 31; § 7.10, n. 61; § 13.13, n. 26; § 13.15, n. 26; § 13.16, n. 83.
Friedman v. Ganassi, 853 F.2d 207—§ 7.4.2, n. 11, 12; § 13.7.1, n. 15.
Friedman v. Ganassi, 674 F.Supp. 1165—§ 7.3, n. 42; § 13.7.1, n. 14.
Friedman v. Mohasco Corp.—§ 3.7, n. 40; § 11.4, n. 51; § 13.5A, n. 67.
Friedman v. World Transp., Inc.—§ 14.3, n. 23.
Frigitemp Corp. v. Financial Dynamics Fund, Inc., 524 F.2d 275—§ 13.9, n. 44.
Frigitemp Corp. v. Financial Dynamics Fund, Inc., 1974 WL 466—§ 13.3, n. 94; § 13.13, n. 33.
Frisch v. Victor Industries, Inc.—§ 20.2, n. 10.

Gas Reclamation, Inc. Securities Litigation, In re, 659 F.Supp. 493—§ **1.5, n. 78;** § **7.2, n. 7;** § **7.5.1, n. 22, 31;** § **7.8, n. 20, 21, 41, 42;** § **10.14, n. 9.**

Gateway Industries, Inc. v. Agency Rent A Car, Inc.—§ **11.18, n. 18, 21;** § **12.8, n. 22.**

G. A. Thompson & Co., Inc. v. Partridge— § **7.2, n. 47;** § **7.7, n. 30;** § **13.4, n. 15;** § **13.15, n. 7, 34.**

Gaudette v. Panos—§ **1.5, n. 137;** § **13.8, n. 83;** § **19.6, n. 42.**

Gaudin v. KDI Corp.—§ **13.3, n. 50.**

Gaudiosi v. Mellon—§ **11.6, n. 10.**

GBJ Corp. v. Sequa Corp.—§ **1.5, n. 36.**

Gearhardt and Otis, Inc. v. SEC—§ **9.20, n. 9.**

Gearhart Industries, Inc. v. Smith Intern., Inc.—§ **11.11, n. 23;** § **11.15, n. 49;** § **11.20, n. 22, 75;** § **12.1, n. 12.**

Geeting v. Prizant—§ **13.8, n. 61.**

Geisenberger v. John Hancock Distributors, Inc.—§ **13.5B, n. 26.**

Geismar v. Bond & Goodwin—§ **13.14, n. 17, 24.**

Gelco Corp. v. Coniston Partners, 811 F.2d 414—§ **11.18, n. 28.**

Gelco Corp. v. Coniston Partners, 652 F.Supp. 829—§ **11.22, n. 71.**

Geller v. Bohen—§ **13.3, n. 58.**

Geller v. Nasser—§ **13.14, n. 14;** § **14.4, n. 10.**

Geller v. Prudential–Bache Securities, Inc.—§ **13.13, n. 24.**

Gelles v. TDA Indsutries, Inc., 1993 WL 27516—§ **13.3, n. 28.**

Gelles v. TDA Industries, Inc., 44 F.3d 102—§ **13.3, n. 18.**

Genentech, Inc. Securities Litigation, In re—§ **13.4, n. 31;** § **13.16, n. 49.**

Genentech, Inc., Securities Litigation, In re—§ **13.5A, n. 4.**

General Aircraft Corp. v. Lampert— § **11.18, n. 18, 20.**

General American Investors Co. v. C.I.R.— § **12.3, n. 68.**

General Bond & Share Co., In re—§ **10.3, n. 10.**

General Bond & Share Co. v. S.E.C.— § **9.24, n. 27;** § **9.34, n. 21;** § **10.1, n. 3;** § **10.2, n. 15, 58.**

General Builders Supply Co. v. River Hill Coal Venture—§ **13.8, n. 62.**

General Dynamics Corp.—§ **11.7, n. 41, 53.**

General Elec. Co. by Levit v. Cathcart— § **11.3, n. 42, 43;** § **11.5, n. 29, 30.**

General Electric Co., 25 Sec.Reg. & L.Rep. (BNA) 235—§ **11.7, n. 41.**

General Electric Co., 26 Sec.Reg. & L.Rep. (BNA) 266—§ **11.7, n. 41, 43, 58.**

General Electric Corp.—§ **1.5, n. 106, 118;** § **4.4, n. 13.**

General Ins. Co. of America v. Fort Lauderdale Partnership—§ **13.15, n. 28.**

General Investment Co. v. Ackerman— § **7.5.2, n. 4, 8.**

General Life of Missouri Inv. Co. v. Shamburger—§ **4.29, n. 24.**

General Mills, Inc.—§ **12.3, n. 95.**

General Motors Corp.—§ **11.7, n. 41.**

Genetech, Inc., Securities Litigation, In re—§ **13.5A, n. 4.**

Genex Corp. v. G.D. Searle & Co.—§ **13.7, n. 10.**

Genser, United States v.—§ **9.5, n. 100.**

Gentile, United States v.—§ **5.1, n. 20, 22;** § **13.2.3, n. 13, 15.**

Genty v. Township of Gloucester—§ **19.3, n. 34.**

Georgalis, United States v.—§ **19.3.1, n. 74.**

George v. Blue Diamond Petroleum, Inc.— § **19.3, n. 22, 31.**

George, United States v.—§ **19.3.1, n. 18, 28.**

Georgia Market Centers, Inc. v. Fortson— § **1.5, n. 33.**

Gerber v. Computer Associates Intern., Inc., 860 F.Supp. 27—§ **13.11, n. 40.**

Gerber v. Computer Associates Intern., Inc., 812 F.Supp. 361—§ **11.14, n. 14, 65;** § **11.14, n. 54.**

Gerhardstein v. Shearson/American Exp., Inc.—§ **13.14, n. 14;** § **14.4, n. 10.**

Germantown Sav. Bank v. Goldstein— § **13.10, n. 20;** § **13.16, n. 69.**

Gershman v. Goldman, Sachs & Co.— § **14.5, n. 41, 42.**

Gerstein v. Micron Technology—§ **13.9, n. 35.**

Gerstle v. Gamble–Skogmo, Inc.—§ **11.3, n. 5;** § **11.4, n. 12;** § **11.5, n. 35;** § **13.4, n. 12.**

Getter v. R. G. Dickinson & Co.—§ **13.17, n. 43, 46, 51.**

G. Eugene England Foundation v. First Federal Corp.—§ **4.21, n. 8, 42.**

Geyer v. Paine, Webber, Jackson & Curtis, Inc.—§ **10.2.1, n. 2.**

GHM/Massachusetts Health Care Partners– I Limited Partnership—§ **4.12, n. 32.**

Giangrande v. Shearson Lehman/E.F. Hutton—§ **14.4, n. 27.**

Gianukos v. Loeb Rhoades & Co., Inc.— § **13.5B, n. 23, 42.**

Gibson, Dunn & Crutcher—§ **12.2, n. 7.**

Gibson v. Best Commodities Services, Inc.— § **7.4.1, n. 28;** § **7.5.3, n. 32.**

GIC Government Securities, Matter of— § **20.3, n. 8.**

Gieringer v. Silverman—§ **13.8, n. 73.**

Gilbert v. Bagley—§ **13.7.1, n. 20.**

Gilbert v. Prudential–Bache Securities, Inc.—§ **19.3, n. 42.**

Gilbert Family Partnership v. Nido Corp.— § **7.5.4, n. 51;** § **13.13, n. 25;** § **19.3, n. 82.**

Gordon v. S.E.C.—§ **9.30, n. 15.**

Gorman v. Merrill, Lynch, Pierce, Fenner and Smith, Inc.—§ **14.4, n. 25.**

Gorsey v. I.M. Simon & Co., Inc.—§ **10.5, n. 30.**

Goss, United States v.—§ **19.3.1, n. 13.**

Gotham Print, Inc. v. American Speedy Printing Centers, Inc.—§ **1.5, n. 35.**

Gotshall v. A.G. Edwards & Sons, Inc.—§ **10.14, n. 9; § 13.13, n. 24.**

Gottlieb v. Sandia Am. Corp.—§ **13.7, n. 55.**

Gottreich v. San Francisco Inv. Corp.—§ **10.6, n. 16.**

Gould v. American–Hawaiian S. S. Co., 535 F.2d 761—§ **11.3, n. 5; § 13.4, n. 12; § 13.16, n. 45.**

Gould v. American–Hawaiian S.S. Co., 387 F.Supp. 163—§ **13.17, n. 13, 25, 51.**

Gould v. Berk & Michaels, P.C.—§ **7.10, n. 61.**

Gould v. Ruefenacht—§ **1.5, n. 87.**

Gould v. Sidel—§ **14.5, n. 17.**

Go Vacations, Inc.—§ **1.5, n. 52.**

Gower v. Cohn—§ **13.5B, n. 23; § 13.12, n. 10.**

Graceman v. Goldstein—§ **10.22, n. 10; § 14.4, n. 82.**

Grafman v. Century Broadcasting Corp.—§ **19.3, n. 5, 61; § 19.3.1, n. 6.**

Graham v. Slaughter—§ **19.3, n. 26.**

Grainger v. Antoyan—§ **1.5, n. 144.**

Grainger v. State Sec. Life Ins. Co.—§ **4.9, n. 6.**

Gralla Publications, Inc.—§ **4.26.1, n. 6.**

Granada Investments, Inc. v. DWG Corp.—§ **13.3, n. 45; § 13.7, n. 1.**

Granada Partnership Securities Litigations, In re—§ **13.17, n. 57.**

Granader v. McBee—§ **13.7.1, n. 48.**

Granberry, United States v.—§ **19.3.1, n. 34, 41, 66.**

Grand Jury Subpoena Duces Tecum, In re—§ **9.5, n. 102, 103; § 9.31, n. 7.**

Granite Falls Bank v. Henrikson—§ **19.3, n. 80.**

Grant, Estate of v. United States News & World Report, Inc.—§ **13.8, n. 11.**

Graphic Scanning Corp. v. Yampol—§ **14.4, n. 42.**

Gratz v. Claughton—§ **12.3, n. 53, 58.**

Gray, Matter of—§ **10.14, n. 63.**

Gray v. First Winthrop Corp., 989 F.2d 1564—§ **13.8, n. 40.**

Gray v. First Winthrop Corp., 776 F.Supp. 504—§ **13.15, n. 28; § 13.16, n. 69.**

Gray Drug Stores, Inc. v. Simmons—§ **11.19, n. 19.**

Greater Continental Corp. v. Schechter—§ **14.4, n. 6.**

Greater Iowa Corp. v. McLendon—§ **13.3, n. 94; § 13.13, n. 11, 33; § 13.14, n. 29.**

Greater Washington Indst. Inv., Inc.—§ **17.7, n. 48.**

Great Western Bank and Trust v. Kotz—§ **4.4, n. 11.**

Great Western Financial Corp., In re, Application of—§ **11.20, n. 20.**

Great Western United Corp. v. Kidwell—§ **11.21, n. 8, 34; § 11.22; § 11.22, n. 18, 93.**

Green v. Jonhop, Inc.—§ **13.16, n. 96.**

Green v. Karol—§ **14.1, n. 30.**

Green v. Occidental Petroleum Corp.—§ **13.5B, n. 62; § 13.6, n. 21; § 13.7, n. 27, 44, 45, 46, 57; § 13.10, n. 28.**

Green v. Santa Fe Industries, Inc.—§ **8.1, n. 28.**

Green v. Title Guarantee & Trust Co.—§ **16.5, n. 5.**

Green v. Wolf Corp.—§ **13.5B, n. 12; § 13.7, n. 6.**

Greenberg v. Boettcher & Co.—§ **13.5B, n. 42.**

Greenberg v. Howtek, Inc.—§ **3.7, n. 40.**

Greenblatt v. Drexel Burnham Lambert, Inc.—§ **10.11, n. 33; § 14.4, n. 37.**

Greene v. Cowen & Co.—§ **10.10, n. 15.**

Greene v. Emersons, Ltd.—§ **13.17, n. 15.**

Greenfield v. Heublein, Inc., 742 F.2d 751—§ **11.4, n. 24; § 11.15, n. 66; § 13.5A, n. 55; § 13.10, n. 30.**

Greenfield v. Heublein, Inc., 575 F.Supp. 1325—§ **11.4, n. 29; § 13.5A, n. 21; § 13.10, n. 25.**

Greenfield v. Professional Care, Inc.—§ **13.8.1, n. 10; § 19.3, n. 22, 93.**

Greenfield v. Shuck—§ **13.8, n. 49.**

Greenleaf, United States v.—§ **19.3.1, n. 4.**

Greenstein v. Paul—§ **13.2.3, n. 9; § 13.3, n. 54, 58.**

Greenstone v. Cambex Corp., 975 F.2d 22—§ **13.4, n. 31.**

Greenstone v. Cambex Corp., 777 F.Supp. 88—§ **13.10, n. 24.**

Greenview Trading Co., Inc. v. Hershman & Leicher, P.C.—§ **14.1, n. 9; § 19.3, n. 67, 71.**

Greenwald v. Integrated Energy, Inc.—§ **13.5B, n. 12.**

Greenwald, United States v.—§ **19.3.1, n. 29.**

Greenwood v. Dittmer—§ **10.6, n. 2.**

Gregory–Massari, Inc. v. Purkitt—§ **14.1, n. 19, 21.**

Greitzer v. United States Nat. Bank—§ **13.13, n. 10.**

Grenader v. Spitz—§ **4.12, n. 31.**

Greystone Golf Club, Inc.—§ **1.5, n. 76; § 4.5, n. 7.**

Gridley v. Cunningham—§ **7.5.4, n. 12.**

Griffin v. Arthur Young & Co.—§ **7.5.1, n. 34.**

Griffin v. McNiff—§ **13.16, n. 76, 83.**

Grigsby v. CMI Corp.—§ 13.5A, n. 55; § 13.10, n. 33.

Grimes v. Centerior Energy Corp.—§ 11.7, n. 58.

Grimes v. Ohio Edison Co.—§ 11.4, n. 18; § 11.7, n. 41, 68.

Grimes v. Vitalink Communications Corp.— § 13.14, n. 6; § 14.1, n. 34.

Grimm v. Whitney–Fidalgo Seafoods, Inc.— § 7.3, n. 51.

Grinsell v. Kidder, Peabody, & Co., Inc.— § 7.5, n. 50; § 10.14, n. 37; § 13.13, n. 26.

Griswold v. E.F. Hutton & Co., Inc.— § 10.10, n. 18; § 19.6, n. 22, 24.

Groden v. Weilman—§ 13.8.1, n. 6.

Grogan v. Garner—§ 13.7, n. 7, 32.

Grogan v. Platt—§ 19.3, n. 34.

Grondahl v. Merritt & Harris, Inc.—§ 7.5.4, n. 42; § 13.2.3, n. 22; § 13.8, n. 30, 40.

Groover, United States v.—§ 9.5, n. 110.

Gross v. Diversified Mortg. Investors— § 12.8, n. 22.

Gross v. Vogel—§ 20.1, n. 10.

Grossman v. Johnson—§ 17.10; § 17.10, n. 52.

Grossman, United States v.—§ 19.3.1, n. 34.

Grossman v. Waste Management, Inc.— § 7.3, n. 40; § 7.4.1, n. 14; § 13.3, n. 54; § 13.5B, n. 33.

Grossman v. Young—§ 12.3, n. 48.

Grubb v. Federal Deposit Ins. Corp.— § 13.5B, n. 21; § 13.7, n. 20.

Gruber v. Price Waterhouse, 911 F.2d 960—§ 7.5.4, n. 21; § 13.8, n. 67.

Gruber v. Price Waterhouse, 697 F.Supp. 859—§ 13.8, n. 8.

Gruber v. Prudential–Bache Securities, Inc.—§ 10.14, n. 63, 81; § 13.6, n. 5; § 13.8.1, n. 16, 22; § 13.15, n. 32, 37; § 19.3, n. 99.

Gruenberg, United States v.—§ 13.2.2, n. 1.

Grumet v. Shearson/American Exp., Inc.— § 13.9, n. 25.

Grumman Corp. v. LTV Corp.—§ 11.19, n. 18.

Grunenthal GmbH v. Hotz—§ 14.2, n. 21.

G. Tsai & Co., Matter of—§ 18.2, n. 7.

Guenther v. Cooper Life Sciences, Inc.— § 7.3, n. 22.

Gugliatta v. Evans & Co.—§ 14.4, n. 19.

Gugliotta v. Evans & Co., Inc.—§ 14.5, n. 32.

Guidry v. Bank of LaPlace, 954 F.2d 278— § 19.3, n. 10, 12.

Guidry v. Bank of LaPlace, 740 F.Supp. 1208—§ 1.5, n. 111.

Gulf Corp. v. Mesa Petroleum Co.—§ 11.14, n. 34; § 11.18, n. 28; § 11.20, n. 13; § 13.2.2, n. 3.

Gulf Mortg. and Realty Investments v. Alten—§ 20.1, n. 10.

Gulf Oil/Cities Service Tender Offer Litigation, In re—§ 11.19, n. 17; § 13.3, n. 85.

Gulfstream Aerospace Corp. v. Mayacamas Corp.—§ 10.22, n. 18; § 14.4, n. 97.

Gulf & Western Industries, Inc. v. Great Atlantic & Pac. Tea Co., Inc.—§ 11.13, n. 27.

Gund v. First Florida Banks, Inc.—§ 12.5, n. 7, 41.

Gunther v. Dinger—§ 19.3, n. 42, 90.

Guon v. United States—§ 10.2.2; § 10.2.2, n. 36, 41.

Gupta v. Ilardi—§ 10.10, n. 23; § 10.10.1, n. 7.

Gupta Corp. Sec. Litigation, In re— § 13.5A, n. 47, 89.

Gurley v. Documation Inc.—§ 13.3, n. 62.

Gurvitz v. Bregman & Co.—§ 5.3, n. 15.

Gurwara v. Lyphomed, Inc.—§ 13.2.2, n. 10; § 13.10, n. 24.

Gustafson v. Alloyd Co., Inc.—§ 1.7, n. 24; § 2.4, n. 9; § 4.1, n. 18; § 4.12, n. 5; § 4.15, n. 10; § 4.17, n. 26; § 4.18, n. 15; § 4.19, n. 11; § 4.22, n. 16; § 7.1, n. 16; § 7.2, n. 29; § 7.5; § 7.5, n. 5, 21, 51, 69; § 10.8, n. 10; § 10.14; § 10.14, n. 40; § 13.1, n. 11, 62; § 13.6, n. 22; § 13.12, n. 31; § 14.1, n. 17.

Gustafson v. Strangis—§ 10.2.1, n. 21.

Guterma, United States v.—§ 12.2, n. 3.

Gutfreund v. Christoph—§ 7.2, n. 10; § 13.8, n. 59.

Gutfriend, Matter of—§ 10.14, n. 89.

Gutman v. Howard Sav. Bank—§ 13.3, n. 52.

Gutter v. Merrill Lynch, Pierce, Fenner & Smith, Inc.—§ 10.11, n. 28.

Guy v. Duff & Phelps, Inc.—§ 13.5A, n. 55, 56; § 13.10, n. 30.

H

Haas v. Wieboldt Stores, Inc.—§ 11.2, n. 41.

H.A.B. Associates v. Hines—§ 13.9, n. 137.

Haberkamp v. Steele—§ 13.13, n. 26.

Hackbart v. Holmes—§ 13.4, n. 20.

Hackett v. Village Court Associates—§ 7.2, n. 43; § 7.8, n. 24, 36, 42.

Hackford v. First Sec. Bank of Utah, N.A., Fed.Sec.L.Rep. (CCH) ¶ 99,402—§ 1.5, n. 67.

Hackford v. First Security Bank of Utah, N.A., 104 S.Ct. 100—§ 1.5, n. 64.

Hackford v. First Sec. Bank of Utah, N. A., 521 F.Supp. 541—§ 13.3, n. 12.

Hadley v. Baxendale—§ 13.6, n. 3.

Haeglin, Matter of—§ 9.5, n. 170; § 9.5.1, n. 2.

Hafner v. Forest Laboratories, Inc.—§ 5.3, n. 16; § 13.5A, n. 23.

Hafner v. Forest Laboratories, Inc.—§ 5.3, n. 14.

Haft v. Eastland Financial Corp.—§ 7.3, n. 61; § 13.8.1, n. 7, 12; § 13.11, n. 40.

Hershfang v. Knotter—§ **11.4, n. 30;** § **11.5, n. 17;** § **13.5A, n. 21;** § **13.6, n. 5.**

Herskowitz v. Nutri/System, Inc., 1986 WL 5561—§ **13.3, n. 54.**

Herskowitz v. Nutri/System, Inc., 857 F.2d 179—§ **11.3, n. 5;** § **13.4, n. 12.**

Herzfeld v. Laventhol, Krekstein, Horwath and Horwath, 540 F.2d 27—§ **13.6, n. 31.**

Herzfeld v. Laventhol, Krekstein, Horwath & Horwath, 378 F.Supp. 112—§ **13.17, n. 25.**

Heublein, Inc. v. General Cinema Corp., 722 F.2d 29—§ **12.3, n. 33;** § **12.5, n. 24.**

Heublein, Inc. v. General Cinema Corp., 559 F.Supp. 692—§ **12.5, n. 30, 33.**

Hewitt Associates—§ **12.3, n. 93.**

Hewlett Packard Co.—§ **11.7, n. 41, 58.**

Hibbard Brown & Co., Inc. v. ABC Family Trust—§ **14.4, n. 50.**

Hibbard Brown & Co., Inc. v. Hubbard—§ **10.3, n. 28.**

Hickman v. Taylor—§ **7.10, n. 59;** § **9.4, n. 15.**

Higgins v. S.E.C.—§ **9.24, n. 33;** § **10.2, n. 60.**

Hilgeman v. National Ins. Co. of America—§ **7.7, n. 29;** § **13.15, n. 13, 14;** § **14.3, n. 2, 12.**

Hill v. Bache Halsey Stuart Shields Inc.—§ **13.4, n. 9.**

Hill v. Der—§ **7.5.4, n. 13, 64;** § **13.13, n. 22.**

Hill v. Equitable Bank—§ **5.4, n. 10, 11;** § **7.5.4, n. 71, 72;** § **7.7, n. 35;** § **13.2.3, n. 28.**

Hill v. Equitable Bank, Nat. Ass'n—§ **1.5, n. 54;** § **13.8, n. 50, 51, 61.**

Hill v. Equitable Trust Co., 851 F.2d 691—§ **13.8, n. 8.**

Hill v. Equitable Trust Co., 562 F.Supp. 1324—§ **10.14, n. 9;** § **13.8, n. 15, 73, 84.**

Hill v. Morrison—§ **13.8.1, n. 3;** § **14.1.1, n. 4.**

Hillsborough Inv. Corp. v. Securities and Exchange Commission—§ **4.10, n. 5;** § **4.12, n. 23.**

Hill's Estate, In re—§ **20.3, n. 14.**

Hillson Partners Ltd. Partnership v. Adage, Inc.—§ **3.7, n. 40, 50;** § **13.5A, n. 64, 65.**

Hill York Corp. v. American Intern. Franchises, Inc.—§ **4.21, n. 25, 50;** § **4.22, n. 25;** § **7.2, n. 33;** § **7.5.1, n. 18, 43;** § **7.5.3, n. 7;** § **7.7, n. 29;** § **13.15, n. 13, 14.**

Himes v. Shalala—§ **1.4, n. 11.**

Hinckley v. E.I. Du Pont De Nemours and Co.—§ **13.7.1, n. 42.**

Hines v. Davidowitz—§ **11.22, n. 10.**

Hingle v. Plaquemines Oil Sales Corp.—§ **17.9, n. 8.**

Hinkle Northwest, Inc. v. S.E.C.—§ **10.2.3, n. 14.**

Hirsch v. duPont—§ **1.5, n. 145.**

Hirschfeld v. S.E.C.—§ **7.10, n. 54.**

Hirt v. UM Leasing Corp.—§ **1.5, n. 48;** § **19.3, n. 90.**

Hi-Shear Industries, Inc. v. Campbell—§ **11.21, n. 42;** § **11.22, n. 56.**

Hi-Shear Industries, Inc. v. Neiditz—§ **11.21, n. 42;** § **11.22, n. 56.**

H.J. Inc. v. Northwestern Bell Telephone Co.—§ **19.3;** § **19.3, n. 11, 31, 43.**

H.J. Inc. v. Northwestern Bell Telephone Co., a subsidiary of United States West—§ **19.3, n. 30.**

H. K. Porter Co., Inc. v. Nicholson File Co.—§ **11.15, n. 11;** § **13.3, n. 25.**

HMCA (Carolina), Inc. v. Soler–Zapata—§ **13.2.2, n. 14.**

HMK Corp. v. Walsey—§ **19.3, n. 66.**

Hochfelder v. Midwest Stock Exchange—§ **7.8, n. 9;** § **10.2.1, n. 9.**

Hocking v. Dubois, 885 F.2d 1449—§ **1.5, n. 70.**

Hocking v. Dubois, 839 F.2d 560—§ **1.5, n. 71.**

Hodges v. H & R Investments, Ltd.—§ **1.5, n. 71;** § **13.8.1, n. 29;** § **19.3, n. 93.**

Hoefer & Arnett, Inc. v. Lehigh Press, Inc.—§ **13.5A, n. 101.**

Hoexter v. Simmons—§ **13.5B, n. 14.**

Hoffman Elec., Inc. v. Emerson Elec. Co.—§ **11.4, n. 51.**

Hofmayer v. Dean Witter & Co., Inc.—§ **10.2.1, n. 35.**

Hofstetter v. Fletcher—§ **19.3, n. 80.**

Hohmann v. Packard Instrument Co., Inc.—§ **7.3, n. 62.**

Hokama v. E.F. Hutton & Co., Inc.—§ **7.5.1, n. 7;** § **7.8, n. 58.**

Holden v. Hagopian—§ **1.5, n. 148.**

Holdsworth v. Strong—§ **13.5B, n. 23;** § **13.12, n. 7.**

Hollenbeck v. Falstaff Brewing Corp.—§ **7.4.1, n. 30;** § **7.5.3, n. 34.**

Hollinger v. Titan Capital Corp.—§ **7.7, n. 28, 36;** § **10.14, n. 70;** § **13.4, n. 23;** § **13.15, n. 6, 19, 46, 60, 69.**

Holloway v. Combined Equities, Inc.—§ **7.2, n. 7.**

Holloway v. Gruntal & Co., Inc.—§ **14.4, n. 50.**

Holloway v. Howerdd—§ **7.7, n. 34;** § **10.14, n. 68, 80;** § **13.15, n. 44, 55, 74.**

Holloway v. Peat, Marwick, Mitchell & Co.—§ **1.5, n. 105;** § **4.4, n. 6.**

Holloway v. Thompson—§ **1.5, n. 11.**

Hollywood Nat. Bank v. International Business Machines Corp.—§ **20.3, n. 9.**

Hollywood State Bank v. Wilde—§ **1.5, n. 8.**

Holmberg v. Armbrecht—§ **7.5.4, n. 57;** § **13.8, n. 56.**

Holmberg v. Morrisette—§ **19.3, n. 22.**

Jordan v. Global Natural Resources, Inc.—§ 12.1, n. 12.
Jordan v. Madison Leasing Co.—§ 7.7, n. 11; § 13.17, n. 17, 50.
Jordan Bldg. Corp. v. Doyle, O'Connor & Co.—§ 10.14, n. 9.
Jorgensen's Estate, In re—§ 20.3, n. 17.
Josef's of Palm Beach v. Southern Inv. Co.—§ 13.8, n. 61.
Joseph v. Shields, Jr.—§ 10.6, n. 13, 14.
Joseph v. Prudential Bache Securities, Inc.—§ 14.4, n. 68.
Joy v. North—§ 13.11; § 13.11, n. 51.
J.P. Morgan Structures Obligations Corp.—§ 4.3, n. 7.
J & S Enterprises v. Warshawsky—§ 1.5, n. 148.
Jubran v. Musikahn Corp.—§ 7.5.1, n. 18; § 7.5.3, n. 15; § 13.5A, n. 89.
June S. Jones Co., In re—§ 19.4, n. 23.
Jungck v. Nanz—§ 13.8, n. 61.
Junker v. Crory—§ 7.2, n. 38; § 7.3, n. 56; § 7.5, n. 34, 45; § 7.5.1, n. 18, 30; § 7.5.2, n. 37, 43; § 7.10, n. 30.
Junker v. Midterra Associates, Inc.—§ 7.5.2, n. 62.
Juster v. Rothschild, Unterberg, Towbin—§ 10.7, n. 19; § 13.7, n. 7.
Justin Industries, Inc. v. Choctaw Securities, L.P.—§ 11.2, n. 49; § 11.3, n. 15; § 11.4, n. 17, 31, 46.

K

K/A & Co., Inc. v. Hallwood Energy Partners, L.P.—§ 7.3, n. 2; § 7.5, n. 2; § 7.5.2, n. 20.
Kademian v. Ladish Co.—§ 11.4, n. 31; § 13.11, n. 40.
Kadow v. A.G. Edwards and Sons, Inc.—§ 14.4, n. 19; § 14.5, n. 3.
Kafton v. Baptist Park Nursing Center, Inc.—§ 11.5, n. 17; § 13.6, n. 14, 21, 26; § 13.7, n. 27, 28.
Kagan v. Edison Bros. Stores, Inc.—§ 13.3, n. 36.
Kahan v. Rosenstiel—§ 13.7.1, n. 30, 39.
Kahn v. Chase Manhattan Bank, N.A.—§ 13.16, n. 48, 66.
Kahn v. Kohlberg, Kravis, Roberts & Co., 113 S.Ct. 494—§ 7.5.4, n. 42.
Kahn v. Kohlberg, Kravis, Roberts & Co., 970 F.2d 1030—§ 13.2.3, n. 22; § 13.8, n. 30, 43; § 17.10, n. 23; § 18.4, n. 41.
Kahn v. Lynden Inc.—§ 13.3, n. 54; § 13.6, n. 13.
Kahn v. Salomon Bros. Inc.—§ 4.1, n. 2, 20; § 12.1, n. 10; § 13.2, n. 45.
Kahn v. Securities and Exchange Commission—§ 10.6, n. 11; § 10.8, n. 5.
Kahn v. United States Sugar Corp.—§ 11.19, n. 5.

Kahn v. Virginia Retirement System, 13 F.3d 110—§ 11.14, n. 17; § 11.15, n. 47.
Kahn v. Virginia Retirement System, 783 F.Supp. 266—§ 11.14, n. 66.
Kahn v. Wien—§ 11.4, n. 15, 42, 43, 44; § 13.5A, n. 35.
Kaiser Foundation Hospitals—§ 4.5, n. 11.
Kaiser–Frazer Corp. v. Otis & Co.—§ 2.1, n. 17.
Kakar v. Chicago Bd. Options Exchange, Inc.—§ 10.2.1, n. 2, 21, 27, 28.
Kalali v. Prudential–Bache Securities, Inc.—§ 14.4, n. 12.
Kaliden v. Shearson Lehman Hutton, Inc.—§ 14.4, n. 76.
Kalish v. Franklin Advisers, Inc.—§ 17.10, n. 69, 73.
Kaliski v. Hunt Intern. Resources Corp.—§ 7.8, n. 20, 21; § 13.16, n. 92.
Kalkstein v. Delphi Commodities, Inc.—§ 19.6, n. 14.
Kalmanovitz v. G. Heileman Brewing Co., Inc.—§ 11.18, n. 21; § 11.19, n. 15.
Kalmanson v. McLaughlin, 1992 WL 190139—§ 13.8, n. 40.
Kalmanson v. McLaughlin, Fed.Sec.L.Rep. (CCH) ¶ 93609—§ 13.8.1, n. 28.
Kamen v. Kemper Financial Services, Inc., 111 S.Ct. 1711—§ 17.6, n. 26; § 17.10, n. 67.
Kamen v. Kemper Financial Services, Inc., 908 F.2d 1338—§ 17.10, n. 50, 69.
Kamen v. Kemper Financial Services, Inc., 659 F.Supp. 1153—§ 17.10, n. 5, 30, 66, 69.
Kamen & Co. v. Paul H. Aschkar & Co.—§ 7.7, n. 33; § 13.7, n. 63.
Kamerman v. Steinberg, 891 F.2d 424—§ 11.11, n. 25; § 11.18, n. 21; § 11.10, n. 48.
Kamerman v. Steinberg, 744 F.Supp. 59—§ 11.11, n. 17.
Kanan, In re—§ 4.23, n. 20.
Kane v. United States S.E.C.—§ 4.21, n. 23; § 10.14, n. 55.
Kane v. Wichita Oil Income Fund—§ 13.4, n. 15.
Kane, John—§ 10.2.2, n. 42.
Kansas City Power & Light Co. v. Kansas Gas and Elec. Co.—§ 14.3, n. 5.
Kansas State Bank in Holton v. Citizens Bank of Windsor—§ 1.5, n. 99.
Kaplan v. Bennett—§ 13.11, n. 34.
Kaplan v. First Options of Chicago, Inc.—§ 14.4, n. 76.
Kaplan v. Goldsamt—§ 11.20, n. 4.
Kaplan v. Kahn—§ 13.5A, n. 47, 48; § 13.6, n. 13.
Kaplan v. Rose—§ 7.3, n. 3; § 13.5A, n. 64; § 13.5B, n. 27, 39.
Kaplan v. Shapiro—§ 1.5, n. 68.
Kaplan v. Utilicorp United, Inc.—§ 13.2.2, n. 10; § 13.3, n. 11.

Kohler v. Kohler Co.—§ **13.5A, n. 16;** § **13.12, n. 2.**

Kohn v. American Metal Climax, Inc.— § **11.4, n. 5;** § **13.5A, n. 10.**

Kohn v. Optik, Inc.—§ **10.14, n. 65, 87;** § **13.15, n. 21.**

Kolb v. Naylor—§ **4.3, n. 29.**

Kolibash v. Sagittarius Recording Co.— § **1.5, n. 13, 48, 53.**

Kontaratos, In re—§ **20.1, n. 10.**

Kook v. Crang—§ **14.2, n. 30, 34.**

Kopald–Quinn & Co. v. United States— § **14.1.1, n. 10.**

Koplin v. Labe Federal Sav. and Loan Ass'n—§ **13.6, n. 5.**

Koppel v. Wien—§ **11.4, n. 31.**

Koppers Co., Inc. v. American Exp. Co., 689 F.Supp. 1417—§ **18.4, n. 56.**

Koppers Co., Inc. v. American Exp. Co., 689 F.Supp. 1371—§ **10.2.4, n. 18;** § **11.4, n. 18.**

Korff v. Bank Julius Baer & Co., Ltd.— § **13.2.2, n. 10.**

Kornfeld v. Eaton—§ **12.3, n. 56.**

Kosnoski v. Bruce—§ **1.5, n. 145.**

Koss v. S. E. C. of United States—§ **1.4, n. 15;** § **9.24, n. 40;** § **9.34, n. 2, 7, 17.**

Kowal v. MCI Communications Corp.— § **3.7, n. 40;** § **13.5A, n. 67, 91.**

Kozonasky v. Sears Roebuck & Co.—§ **12.3, n. 48.**

Kramas v. Security Gas & Oil Inc.—§ **7.5.4, n. 7, 20;** § **13.8, n. 66.**

Kramer v. Time Warner Inc.—§ **11.14, n. 65.**

Krasner v. Dreyfus Corp., 500 F.Supp. 36— § **17.9, n. 10.**

Krasner v. Dreyfus Corp., 90 F.R.D. 665— § **17.9, n. 15.**

Krause v. Perryman—§ **13.13, n. 25.**

Krauss v. First City Nat. Bank and Trust Co.—§ **13.7.1, n. 47.**

Krauth v. Executive Telecard, Ltd.—§ **11.2, n. 51.**

Kravetz v. Brukenfeld—§ **13.11, n. 40;** § **18.4, n. 21.**

Kravitz v. Pressman, Frohlich & Frost, Inc.—§ **10.10, n. 7.**

Kreimer, United States v.—§ **19.3.1, n. 4.**

Kreindler v. Sambo's Restaurants, Inc.— § **13.9, n. 141.**

Kreis v. Mates Inv. Fund, Inc.—§ **8.1, n. 22.**

Krim v. BancTexas Group, Inc.—§ **3.7, n. 40, 75;** § **13.5A, n. 91.**

Krinsk v. Fund Asset Management, Inc., 875 F.2d 404—§ **17.9, n. 12;** § **17.10, n. 69.**

Krinsk v. Fund Asset Management, Inc., 715 F.Supp. 472—§ **17.9, n. 16.**

Krinsk v. Fund Asset Management, Inc., 654 F.Supp. 1227—§ **11.3, n. 15;** § **17.10, n. 28, 30.**

Kroll v. United States—§ **19.3.1, n. 13.**

Krome v. Merrill Lynch & Co., Inc.—§ **7.2, n. 7, 9;** § **10.2, n. 33;** § **17.10, n. 5, 20.**

Kronfeld v. Advest, Inc.—§ **13.7.1, n. 54;** § **13.8, n. 62;** § **13.8.1, n. 36.**

Kronfeld v. First Jersey Nat. Bank—§ **13.8, n. 11.**

Kronfeld v. Trans World Airlines, Inc.— § **7.3, n. 3;** § **13.5A, n. 67.**

Kroog v. Mait—§ **13.14, n. 11;** § **14.4, n. 88.**

Kroungold v. Triester—§ **8.1, n. 28.**

Krupp Corp., In re—§ **11.7, n. 6.**

K & S Partnership v. Continental Bank, N.A., 952 F.2d 971—§ **13.16, n. 43, 69.**

K & S Partnership v. Continental Bank, N.A., 913 F.2d 1296—§ **13.16, n. 68.**

Kubik v. Goldfield—§ **2.5, n. 39;** § **4.27, n. 5.**

Kuehnert v. Texstar Corp.—§ **13.17, n. 52.**

Kukatush Min. Corp. v. Securities and Exchange Commission—§ **9.30, n. 11.**

Kulicke and Soffa Industries, Inc. Securities Litigation, In re, 697 F.Supp. 183— § **3.7, n. 51.**

Kulicke & Soffa Industries, Inc. Securities Litigation, In re, 747 F.Supp. 1136— § **12.8, n. 13.**

Kulko v. Superior Court of California In and For City and County of San Francisco—§ **14.2, n. 49.**

Kumpis v. Wetterau—§ **13.5A, n. 22;** § **13.5B, n. 37;** § **13.9, n. 27, 141.**

Kurth v. Van Horn—§ **10.6, n. 3.**

Kushner v. DBG Property Investors, Inc.— § **13.7.1, n. 58.**

Kutz, In re—§ **9.7, n. 16.**

Kuznetz, In re—§ **10.2, n. 8.**

K & W Enterprises, Inc. v. Appolito—§ **1.5, n. 148.**

Kyung In Lee v. Pacific Bullion (New York) Inc.—§ **14.4, n. 45;** § **14.5, n. 5, 59.**

Kyung Sup Ahn v. Rooney, Pace Inc.— § **14.4, n. 25.**

L

LaBelle v. Chereskin—§ **13.5B, n. 31.**

Lacovara v. Merrill Lynch, Pierce, Fenner and Smith, Inc.—§ **10.2.1, n. 21.**

Laird v. Integrated Resources, Inc.—§ **10.6, n. 9;** § **10.7, n. 25;** § **10.10, n. 11;** § **13.5A, n. 18;** § **18.4, n. 24, 39;** § **19.3, n. 5, 90.**

Laker v. Fried—§ **1.5, n. 95.**

LA–MAN Corp., In re—§ **6.1, n. 14.**

Lamb v. Phillip Morris, Inc.—§ **19.2, n. 36.**

Lambergs v. Total Health Systems, Inc.— § **7.2, n. 41;** § **7.5, n. 45;** § **7.5.1, n. 7.**

Lampf, Pleva, Lipkind, Prupis & Petigrow v. Gilbertson—§ **10.10, n. 13;** § **13.1, n. 57;** § **13.2, n. 66;** § **13.2.1, n. 31;** § **13.8;** § **13.8, n. 9, 17, 23;** § **13.13, n. 48;** § **17.10, n. 22.**

M

Medeva Securities Litigation, In re—
§ **13.5A, n. 27;** § **13.15, n. 25.**
Media General Financial Daily, Matter of—
§ **18.2, n. 7.**
Media General, Inc. v. Tanner—§ **13.8, n. 11;** § **19.3, n. 24.**
Medical Committee for Human Rights v. Securities and Exchange Commission—
§ **9.20, n. 26;** § **11.7, n. 57, 63.**
Medimmune, Inc. Securities Litigation, In re—§ **3.7, n. 75;** § **13.5A, n. 89.**
Medoil Corp. v. Citicorp—§ **14.2, n. 31.**
Melder v. Morris—§ **13.8.1, n. 6, 10.**
Melena v. Merrill Lynch, Pierce, Fenner & Smith, Inc.—§ **13.14, n. 11.**
Mellman v. Southland Racing Corp.—
§ **11.17, n. 32, 47.**
Melrose, In re—§ **9.7, n. 16.**
Memorial Gardens of the Valley, Inc. v. Love—§ **1.5, n. 11.**
Memphis Housing Authority v. Paine, Webber, Jackson & Curtis, Inc.—§ **10.10, n. 5;** § **13.13, n. 22.**
Mendell v. Greenberg, 927 F.2d 667—
§ **11.4, n. 31, 42, 43.**
Mendell v. Greenberg, 715 F.Supp. 85—
§ **11.4, n. 48.**
Mendell v. Greenberg, 612 F.Supp. 1543—
§ **11.4, n. 13, 28;** § **13.5A, n. 67.**
Mendelovitz v. Vosicky—§ **19.3, n. 37.**
Mendelsohn v. Capital Underwriters, Inc.—
§ **13.13, n. 22.**
Menides v. The Colonial Group, Inc.—
§ **13.2.2, n. 9;** § **13.11, n. 40.**
Menowitz v. Brown—§ **13.8, n. 46, 63, 64, 77.**
Mercer v. Jaffe, Snider, Raitt and Heuer, P.C., 736 F.Supp. 764—§ **1.5, n. 87;** § **7.5, n. 47;** § **7.5.1, n. 30;** § **7.10, n. 30;** § **10.5, n. 6;** § **13.16, n. 83.**
Mercer v. Jaffe, Snider, Raitt and Heuer, P.C., 730 F.Supp. 74—§ **7.5, n. 47;** § **7.5.1, n. 30;** § **7.10, n. 30;** § **10.5, n. 6.**
Mercer v. Jaffe, Snider, Raitt and Heuer, P.C., 713 F.Supp. 1019—§ **7.5, n. 47;** § **7.5.1, n. 30;** § **7.10, n. 30;** § **13.16, n. 83.**
Merck & Co.—§ **11.7, n. 38.**
Meridian Securities Litigation, In re—§ **3.7, n. 46;** § **13.5A, n. 68;** § **13.15, n. 27.**
Merine on Behalf of Prudential–Bache Utility Fund, Inc. v. Prudential–Bache Utility Fund, Inc.—§ **11.3, n. 4;** § **13.8, n. 33;** § **17.8, n. 53;** § **17.10, n. 23.**
Merino Calenti v. Boto—§ **13.3, n. 58.**
Merrill Lynch & Co.—§ **11.7, n. 34.**
Merrill Lynch, Pierce, Fenner and Smith, Inc., Matter of—§ **10.2.4, n. 6, 7, 8;** § **10.8, n. 8.**
Merrill Lynch, Pierce, Fenner & Smith v. Perelle—§ **10.6, n. 2.**
Merrill Lynch, Pierce, Fenner & Smith, Inc., Ex parte—§ **10.17, n. 2;** § **14.4, n. 71;** § **14.5, n. 49.**

Merrill Lynch, Pierce, Fenner & Smith, Inc. v. Bobker, 808 F.2d 930—§ **10.15, n. 30;** § **10.22, n. 11, 13, 16;** § **11.15, n. 58;** § **12.1, n. 65;** § **14.4, n. 83, 84, 87.**
Merrill Lynch, Pierce, Fenner & Smith, Inc. v. Bobker, 636 F.Supp. 444—§ **10.12, n. 35;** § **11.15, n. 56, 60.**
Merrill Lynch, Pierce, Fenner & Smith, Inc. v. Bocock—§ **10.12, n. 14.**
Merrill Lynch, Pierce, Fenner & Smith, Inc. v. Boeck—§ **10.6, n. 7.**
Merrill Lynch, Pierce, Fenner & Smith Inc. v. Burke—§ **13.7, n. 7;** § **14.4, n. 84.**
Merrill Lynch Pierce Fenner & Smith, Inc. v. Cheng, 901 F.2d 1124—§ **10.10.1, n. 6, 12.**
Merrill Lynch, Pierce, Fenner & Smith, Inc. v. Cheng, 697 F.Supp. 1224—§ **10.6, n. 4.**
Merrill Lynch, Pierce, Fenner & Smith, Inc. v. City Nat. Bank of Detroit—§ **20.3, n. 9.**
Merrill Lynch, Pierce, Fenner & Smith, Inc. v. Cohen—§ **10.16, n. 1;** § **14.5, n. 15.**
Merrill Lynch, Pierce, Fenner & Smith, Inc. v. Cole—§ **2.5, n. 31;** § **10.6, n. 2.**
Merrill Lynch, Pierce, Fenner & Smith, Inc. v. Curran—§ **10.2.1, n. 19, 26, 36;** § **13.1;** § **13.1, n. 13, 17, 22, 41;** § **17.10;** § **17.10, n. 41;** § **19.6, n. 10, 20;** § **19.8, n. 6.**
Merrill Lynch, Pierce, Fenner & Smith, Inc. v. Del Valle—§ **13.8.1, n. 14.**
Merrill Lynch, Pierce, Fenner & Smith, Inc. v. Georgiadis, 903 F.2d 109—§ **14.4, n. 68.**
Merrill Lynch, Pierce, Fenner & Smith Inc. v. Georgiadis, 724 F.Supp. 120—§ **14.4, n. 50.**
Merrill Lynch, Pierce, Fenner & Smith, Inc. v. Gregg—§ **10.16, n. 1;** § **14.5, n. 15.**
Merrill Lynch, Pierce, Fenner & Smith, Inc. v. Haydu—§ **14.4, n. 23.**
Merrill Lynch, Pierce, Fenner & Smith, Inc. v. Livingston—§ **12.4, n. 10, 11.**
Merrill Lynch, Pierce, Fenner & Smith, Inc. v. National Ass'n of Securities Dealers, Inc.—§ **9.24, n. 5.**
Merrill Lynch, Pierce, Fenner & Smith Inc. v. Noonan—§ **14.4, n. 68.**
Merrill Lynch, Pierce, Fenner & Smith Inc. v. Rajcher—§ **7.8, n. 20, 21.**
Merrit v. Libby, McNeill and Libby—
§ **11.17, n. 14.**
Merritt v. Colonial Foods, Inc.—§ **14.1, n. 41, 48, 49.**
Merryweather v. Nixan—§ **7.7, n. 8.**
Mesa Partners II v. Unocal Corp.—§ **11.22, n. 54.**
Mesa Petroleum Co. v. Cities Service Co.—
§ **11.22, n. 39, 71.**
Messer v. E.F. Hutton & Co., 847 F.2d 673—§ **1.4.1, n. 11;** § **1.5.1, n. 4.**

Quintel Corp., N.V. v. Citibank, N.A., 606 F.Supp. 898—§ **7.10, n. 40.**
Quintel Corp., N.V. v. Citibank, N.A., 589 F.Supp. 1235—§ **7.8, n. 29;** § **13.4, n. 15, 34.**

R

Raab v. General Physics Corp.—§ **3.7, n. 40, 41, 91;** § **13.5A, n. 86, 87, 88, 91;** § **13.10, n. 36, 42.**
Rabin v. Fivzar Associates—§ **13.8, n. 40.**
Rabkin v. Philip A. Hunt Chemical Corp.—§ **11.17, n. 14;** § **13.11, n. 10.**
Radiation Dynamics, Inc. v. Goldmuntz—§ **5.1, n. 33;** § **5.4, n. 3, 14, 15;** § **7.5.4, n. 42;** § **13.2.3, n. 22, 29, 30;** § **13.3, n. 64;** § **13.8, n. 30, 50.**
Radio Electronic Television Corp v. Bartniew Distributing Corp—§ **20.2, n. 10.**
Radol v. Thomas—§ **11.2, n. 14;** § **11.15, n. 49;** § **11.20, n. 75;** § **12.1, n. 12.**
Rae v. Union Bank—§ **19.3, n. 23, 25.**
Rafe v. Hindin—§ **20.2, n. 10.**
R.A.G.S. Couture, Inc. v. Hyatt—§ **19.3, n. 22, 26.**
R.A. Holman & Co.—§ **10.8, n. 8.**
R. A. Holman & Co. v. Securities and Exchange Commission—§ **4.15, n. 33;** § **10.8, n. 4.**
Raiford v. Buslease, Inc.—§ **5.4, n. 17;** § **7.5.4, n. 14.**
Raiford v. Merrill Lynch, Pierce, Fenner & Smith, Inc.—§ **14.1, n. 57;** § **14.4, n. 42.**
Raiford v. Merrill Lynch, Pierce, Fenner & Smith, Inc., 903 F.2d 1410—§ **14.4, n. 84.**
Ralph v. Prudential–Bache Securities, Inc.—§ **7.5, n. 51;** § **10.14, n. 37.**
Ralston Purina Corp.—§ **5.3, n. 41;** § **12.2, n. 54.**
Rand v. Anaconda–Ericsson, Inc., 794 F.2d 843—§ **11.13, n. 47, 48;** § **13.2.2, n. 4;** § **19.3.1, n. 17.**
Rand v. Anaconda–Ericsson, Inc., 623 F.Supp. 176—§ **13.2, n. 62;** § **13.3, n. 54.**
Rand v. Cullinet Software, Inc.—§ **13.5A, n. 65;** § **13.5B, n. 14.**
Rand v. M/A–Com, Inc.—§ **3.7, n. 78.**
Randall v. Loftsgaarden—§ **7.5, n. 15;** § **7.5.2, n. 25;** § **7.5.3;** § **7.5.3, n. 14, 15, 21, 22, 30;** § **13.7;** § **13.7, n. 36, 37.**
Rankow v. First Chicago Corp., 870 F.2d 356—§ **13.4, n. 15;** § **13.6, n. 14, 26;** § **13.8.1, n. 6.**
Rankow v. First Chicago Corp., 678 F.Supp. 202—§ **13.4, n. 15;** § **13.6, n. 11, 30;** § **13.11, n. 40.**
Rapoport v. Republic of Mexico—§ **7.2, n. 7.**
Rare Earth, Inc. v. Hoorelbeke—§ **20.3, n. 5.**

Rastelli, United States v.—§ **19.3.1, n. 13, 34.**
Rasterops Corp. Securities Litigation, In re, 1994 WL 618970—§ **13.8.1, n. 5.**
Rasterops Corp. Securities Litigation, In re, 1994 WL 374332—§ **13.8.1, n. 5.**
Rathborne v. Rathborne—§ **5.3, n. 25.**
Rathke v. Griffith—§ **1.5, n. 144.**
Ratner v. Sioux Natural Gas Corp.—§ **1.5, n. 79.**
Rauchman v. Mobil Corp.—§ **11.3, n. 1;** § **11.7, n. 14, 42, 53.**
Rauscher Pierce Refsnes, Inc. v. Birenbaum—§ **14.4, n. 42, 81.**
Ray v. Karris—§ **13.3, n. 7, 54;** § **13.11, n. 35, 40.**
Ray v. Lehman Bros. Kuhn Loeb, Inc.—§ **12.1, n. 45.**
Raychem Corp. v. Federal Ins. Co.—§ **7.9, n. 8.**
Ray E. Friedman & Co. v. Jenkins—§ **10.6, n. 2.**
Rayman v. Peoples Sav. Corp.—§ **1.5, n. 111.**
Raymond James & Associates, Inc. v. National Ass'n of Securities Dealers, Inc.—§ **10.2.1, n. 5, 32;** § **10.22, n. 8.**
R.D. Smith & Co., Inc. v. Preway Inc.—§ **11.20, n. 22.**
Real Silk Hosiery Mills, Matter of—§ **17.4, n. 9.**
Realty Acquisition Corp. v. Property Trust of America—§ **11.21, n. 76;** § **11.22, n. 91.**
Rebrook, United States v., 842 F.Supp. 891—§ **13.9, n. 71;** § **19.3.1, n. 23, 41.**
ReBrook, United States v., 837 F.Supp. 162—§ **13.9, n. 71.**
Recaman v. Barish—§ **14.2, n. 45.**
Redington v. Touche Ross & Co.—§ **19.4, n. 10.**
Reece Corp. v. Walco Nat. Corp.—§ **12.5, n. 33.**
Reed v. Bear, Stearns & Co., Inc.—§ **14.4, n. 15.**
Reed, United States v.—§ **13.9, n. 68;** § **19.3.1, n. 49.**
Reeder v. Mastercraft Electronics Corp.—§ **13.5B, n. 7.**
Reeder v. Succession of Palmer—§ **1.5, n. 111.**
Reeves v. Continental Equities Corp. of America, 912 F.2d 37—§ **17.10, n. 5, 18.**
Reeves v. Continental Equities Corp. of America, 725 F.Supp. 196—§ **17.10, n. 8.**
Reeves v. Teuscher—§ **1.5, n. 70, 145.**
Reeves v. Transport Data Communications, Inc.—§ **20.2, n. 11.**
Regan, United States v.—§ **12.1, n. 12;** § **13.9, n. 71.**
Regina M. Lyons Testamentary Trust v. Shearson Lehman Hutton, Inc.—§ **10.22, n. 16;** § **14.4, n. 86.**

Regional Properties, Inc. v. Financial & Real Estate Consulting Co., 752 F.2d 178—§ **13.12, n. 44;** § **13.14, n. 22.**

Regional Properties, Inc. v. Financial and Real Estate Consulting Co., 678 F.2d 552—§ **13.14, n. 17, 22.**

Reid v. Madison—§ **13.3, n. 94;** § **13.13, n. 15, 32.**

Reid v. Walsh—§ **7.5.4, n. 13.**

Reinfeld v. Riklis—§ **13.4, n. 34;** § **13.15, n. 30;** § **19.3, n. 10.**

Reingold v. Deloitte Haskins & Sells— § **13.5B, n. 42;** § **14.2, n. 23.**

Reinhart v. Rauscher Pierce Securities Corp.—§ **10.6, n. 2.**

Reiss v. Pan American World Airways, Inc.—§ **13.10, n. 30.**

Reliance Elec. Co. v. Emerson Elec. Co.— § **12.4, n. 53.**

Reliance Ins. Co. v. Eisner & Lubin— § **11.4, n. 8;** § **13.4, n. 29;** § **13.5A, n. 38.**

Reliance Trust Co.—§ **6.3, n. 15.**

Remar v. Clayton Securities Corp.— § **10.11, n. 27.**

Remmey v. PaineWebber, Inc.—§ **10.15, n. 30;** § **10.17, n. 2;** § **10.22, n. 10, 11.**

Reno v. Flores—§ **19.3, n. 96.**

Renovitch v. Kaufman—§ **7.10, n. 3;** § **13.16, n. 83.**

Renovitch v. Stewardship Concepts, Inc.— § **7.8, n. 21;** § **7.10, n. 27.**

Renz v. Beeman—§ **13.8, n. 48.**

Renz v. Schreiber—§ **13.5B, n. 15.**

Reprosystem, B.V. v. SCM Corp.—§ **13.3, n. 58, 61.**

Republic Bank of Oklahoma City—§ **4.26.1, n. 44.**

Reserve Life Ins. Co. v. Provident Life Ins. Co.—§ **4.10, n. 3;** § **13.14, n. 29.**

Reshal Associates, Inc. v. Long Grove Trading Co.—§ **13.6, n. 5, 25.**

Resolution Trust Corp. v. Miller—§ **7.2, n. 4;** § **7.5, n. 8;** § **7.5.1, n. 4;** § **13.14, n. 25.**

Resolution Trust Corp. v. Stone—§ **1.5, n. 102, 114, 115.**

Resource Corp. International v. Securities and Exchange Commission, 103 F.2d 929—§ **3.5, n. 35, 37;** § **3.5.1, n. 47, 48.**

Resources Corporation International v. Securities and Exchange Commission, 97 F.2d 788—§ **3.5.1, n. 41.**

Revak v. SEC Realty Corp.—§ **1.5, n. 43, 44, 47, 69, 130, 132, 142.**

Reves v. Ernst & Young, 113 S.Ct. 1163— § **19.3;** § **19.3, n. 16.**

Reves v. Ernst & Young, 110 S.Ct. 945— § **1.5;** § **1.5, n. 23, 25, 96, 101;** § **4.4;** § **4.4, n. 5.**

Review of Antimanipulation Regulation of Securities Offerings—§ **6.1, n. 11.**

Revlon Inc., In re—§ **11.14, n. 6, 35;** § **11.15, n. 3;** § **11.20, n. 14;** § **13.10, n. 33.**

Revlon, Inc. v. MacAndrews & Forbes Holdings, Inc.—§ **11.20;** § **11.20, n. 3, 7, 19, 25.**

Revlon, Inc. v. Pantry Pride, Inc.—§ **11.14, n. 18;** § **11.18, n. 28.**

Rexplore, Inc. Securities Litigation, In re— § **7.5.1, n. 23, 28;** § **7.5.4, n. 17, 18, 21, 35;** § **13.5B, n. 26;** § **13.8, n. 67;** § **13.16, n. 65, 82.**

R.H. Damon & Co., Inc. v. Softkey Software Products, Inc.—§ **13.2.2, n. 1.**

Rheem Mfg. Co. v. Rheem—§ **12.3, n. 111.**

Rhoades v. Powell—§ **10.10, n. 15;** § **12.1, n. 123;** § **13.13, n. 24.**

Rhoades, State ex rel. McLeod v.—§ **8.1, n. 35.**

Rhode Island Hospital v. Collins—§ **20.1, n. 10.**

Rhodes v. Consumers' Buyline, Inc.— § **14.4, n. 58;** § **14.5, n. 33.**

Rhodes, King, Ruman & Faber—§ **18.4, n. 18.**

R. Hoe & Co., Inc., In re—§ **13.3, n. 58.**

Riccobene, United States v.—§ **19.3, n. 24.**

Rice v. Branigar Organization, Inc.—§ **1.5, n. 68, 76.**

Rice v. Hamilton Oil Corp.—§ **3.7, n. 59.**

Rice v. Janovich—§ **19.3, n. 69.**

Rice v. Santa Fe Elevator Corp.—§ **11.22, n. 4, 9.**

Rich v. New York Stock Exchange— § **10.2.1, n. 9.**

Rich v. New York Stock Exchange, Inc.— § **10.2.1, n. 17, 20.**

Richard J. Buck & Co.—§ **10.8, n. 6.**

Richards v. Merrill Lynch, Pierce, Fenner & Smith, Inc.—§ **10.17, n. 2;** § **14.4, n. 70;** § **14.5, n. 44.**

Richardson v. MacArthur—§ **13.3, n. 49;** § **13.7, n. 63.**

Richardson v. Phillips Petroleum Co.— § **14.4, n. 34.**

Richardson v. Shearson/American Express Co., Inc.—§ **19.3, n. 91.**

Richardson v. United States News & World Report, Inc.—§ **13.8, n. 83.**

Richerson, United States v.—§ **19.3.1, n. 61.**

Richey v. Westinghouse Credit Corp.— § **7.5.4, n. 55;** § **13.13, n. 24.**

Riddick v. Shearson Lehman/American Express, Inc.—§ **19.6, n. 14.**

Riedel v. Acutote of Colorado—§ **7.10, n. 16;** § **13.16, n. 85.**

Riedel v. Bancam, S.A.—§ **1.5, n. 121.**

Rifkin v. Crow—§ **13.5B, n. 7.**

Riggs Nat. Bank of Washington D. C. v. Allbritton—§ **11.19, n. 19.**

Riley v. Brazeau—§ **7.10, n. 26;** § **8.1, n. 28.**

Riley v. Kingsley Underwriting Agencies, Ltd.—§ **14.2, n. 32;** § **14.4, n. 68.**

Riley v. Murdock—§ **13.8, n. 9, 47.**

Rintel v. Wathen—§ **3.7, n. 40;** § **13.5A, n. 63.**

Roney and Co. v. Kassab—§ **10.16, n. 1;** § **14.4, n. 58;** § **14.5, n. 14, 37.**

Roney & Co. v. Goren—§ **13.14, n. 11.**

Ronzani v. Sanofi S.A., 1991 WL 61082— § **14.2, n. 11.**

Ronzani v. Sanofi S.A., 899 F.2d 195— § **13.13, n. 24.**

Rooney Pace—§ **6.2, n. 5.**

Rooney Pace, Inc. v. Reid—§ **12.1, n. 45.**

Roosevelt v. E.I. Du Pont de Nemours & Co.—§ **1.4, n. 11, 15, 20;** § **9.34, n. 22, 23;** § **11.7, n. 16, 20, 41.**

Roots Partnership v. Lands' End, Inc.— § **3.7, n. 37, 75.**

Rose v. Arkansas Valley Environmental & Utility Authority—§ **13.5B, n. 36;** § **13.8, n. 80;** § **14.3, n. 6, 7.**

Rosen v. Cascade Intern., Inc.—§ **9.5, n. 48;** § **13.7, n. 2.**

Rosen v. Waldman—§ **14.5, n. 61.**

Rosenberg v. Digilog Inc.—§ **13.5B, n. 33.**

Rosenberg v. Globe Aircraft Corp.—§ **7.5, n. 12;** § **12.8, n. 28.**

Rosenblum v. Drexel Burnham Lambert, Inc.—§ **14.4, n. 16.**

Rosenfeld v. Black—§ **17.2, n. 5, 22;** § **17.9;** § **17.9;** § **17.9, n. 15, 25;** § **17.10, n. 29.**

Rosenfeld v. Department of Army—§ **14.4, n. 34.**

Rosenfeld v. Fairchild Engine & Airplane Corporation—§ **11.2, n. 43;** § **11.20, n. 4.**

Rosenfeld v. Home Shopping Network, Inc.—§ **13.8.1, n. 16.**

Rosengarten v. Buckley—§ **13.16, n. 41.**

Rosenthal v. Dean Witter Reynolds, Inc., 811 F.Supp. 562—§ **13.8, n. 39.**

Rosenthal v. Dean Witter Reynolds, Inc., 883 P.2d 522—§ **13.5B, n. 46.**

Roskos v. Shearson/American Exp., Inc.— § **13.13, n. 22.**

Rospatch Securities Litigation, In re, 1992 WL 226912—§ **13.16, n. 83.**

Rospatch Securities Litigation, In re, 802 F.Supp. 110—§ **13.8, n. 39, 40.**

Rospatch Securities Litigation, In re, 760 F.Supp. 1239—§ **7.10, n. 27, 61;** § **13.11, n. 40.**

Ross v. A. H. Robins Co., Inc.—§ **7.3, n. 44;** § **12.1, n. 97;** § **12.8, n. 3, 22;** § **13.2, n. 57;** § **13.4, n. 9, 38;** § **13.8.1, n. 28, 33;** § **13.10, n. 7.**

Ross v. Bank South, N.A., 885 F.2d 723— § **13.5B, n. 1, 43.**

Ross v. BankSouth, N.A.,—§ **13.5B, n. 33.**

Ross v. Bolton, 1989 WL 80428—§ **13.15, n. 18.**

Ross v. Bolton, 904 F.2d 819—§ **10.5.1, n. 20;** § **13.8.1, n. 1;** § **13.16, n. 50.**

Ross v. Bolton, 639 F.Supp. 323—§ **7.8, n. 21;** § **13.4, n. 22.**

Ross v. Jackie Fine Arts, Inc.—§ **19.3, n. 34.**

Ross v. Mathis—§ **19.3, n. 62.**

Ross Systems Securities Litigation, In re— § **7.8, n. 32;** § **13.16, n. 14, 28.**

Roth v. Bank of Commonwealth—§ **13.8, n. 13, 59;** § **13.13, n. 15, 47.**

Roth v. Fund of Funds, Limited—§ **12.3, n. 76, 79, 80;** § **13.12, n. 22;** § **14.2, n. 30, 35, 43.**

Roth v. S.E.C.—§ **10.2, n. 4;** § **10.2.2, n. 47.**

Rothberg v. Rosenbloom, 808 F.2d 252— § **13.9, n. 95;** § **13.12, n. 24.**

Rothberg v. Rosenbloom, 628 F.Supp. 746— § **13.12, n. 25.**

Rothenberg v. United Brands Co.—§ **12.3, n. 36.**

Rothenberg for Rothenberg, in Behalf of Castle & Cooke, Inc. v. Jacobs—§ **12.5, n. 49.**

Rother v. La Renovista Estates, Inc.—§ **1.5, n. 99.**

Rothfarb v. Hambrecht—§ **13.7.1, n. 42.**

Roueche v. Merrill Lynch Pierce Fenner & Smith, Inc.—§ **14.4, n. 21, 23.**

Rousseff v. E.F. Hutton Co., Inc., 867 F.2d 1281—§ **13.6, n. 15.**

Rousseff v. E.F. Hutton Co., Inc., 843 F.2d 1326—§ **13.6, n. 4.**

Routh v. Philatelic Leasing, Ltd.—§ **1.5, n. 13, 50, 124.**

Rowe v. Maremont Corp., 850 F.2d 1226— § **13.4, n. 30;** § **13.5A, n. 91;** § **13.5B, n. 20, 23;** § **13.6, 42.**

Rowe v. Maremont Corp., 650 F.Supp. 1091—§ **13.5B, n. 18;** § **13.7, n. 10, 20.**

Royal Air Properties, Inc. v. Smith, 333 F.2d 568—§ **13.12, n. 44;** § **13.14, n. 7.**

Royal Air Properties, Inc. v. Smith, 312 F.2d 210—§ **7.2, n. 19;** § **13.8, n. 86;** § **13.14, n. 7.**

Royal American Managers, Inc. v. IRC Holding Corp.—§ **7.2, n. 41;** § **7.5, n. 45, 47;** § **7.5.1, n. 7, 30;** § **7.8, n. 48;** § **7.10, n. 30;** § **13.12, n. 7.**

Royal Anchor, Inc. v. Tetra Finance (HK) Ltd.—§ **13.16, n. 41.**

Royal Business Group, Inc. v. Realist, Inc.— § **11.3, n. 25, 27.**

Royal LePage Ltd.—§ **4.29, n. 27, 68.**

RP Acquisition Corp. v. Staley Continental, Inc.—§ **11.21, n. 75.**

RTE Corp. v. Mark IV Industries, Inc.— § **11.22, n. 83;** § **958.**

Rubenstein v. IU Intern. Corp.—§ **5.3, n. 25;** § **11.4, n. 5;** § **13.5A, n. 10.**

Rubin v. Dickhoner—§ **13.5B, n. 33.**

Rubin v. Long Island Lighting Co.—§ **3.7, n. 36;** § **7.4.2, n. 24.**

Rubin v. Posner—§ **13.16, n. 43.**

Rubin v. United States—§ **5.1;** § **5.1, n. 19;** § **13.2.2, n. 14;** § **13.2.3, n. 11;** § **13.3, n. 29.**

Rubinberg v. Hydronic Fabrications, Inc.— § **13.7.1, n. 47.**

S.E.C. v. Musella, 38 Fed.R.Serv. 426— **§ 9.5, n. 26.**

S.E.C. v. Musella, 578 F.Supp. 425—**§ 13.9, n. 55, 60, 113.**

SEC v. National Student Marketing Corp.— **§ 7.10, n. 58.**

S.E.C. v. Netelkos, 638 F.Supp. 503—**§ 9.5, n. 41, 48.**

S.E.C. v. Netelkos, 597 F.Supp. 724—**§ 9.5, n. 9.**

S.E.C. v. Netelkos, 592 F.Supp. 906—**§ 4.1, n. 10; § 4.23, n. 5, 13; § 4.24, n. 71; § 7.7, n. 11.**

S. E. C. v. North Am. Research & Development Corp.—**§ 4.2, n. 2.**

S.E.C. v. North Atlantic Airlines, Inc.— **§ 7.3, n. 3.**

S.E.C. v. O'Hagan—**§ 9.5, n. 22; § 13.8, n. 44.**

S.E.C. v. Paradyne Corp.—**§ 9.5, n. 109.**

S. E. C. v. Parklane Hosiery Co., Inc.— **§ 9.5, n. 11; § 11.17, n. 14; § 13.11, n. 18.**

S.E.C. v. Patel—**§ 9.5, n. 84; § 13.9, n. 118, 119.**

S.E.C. v. Peters, 978 F.2d 1162—**§ 11.15, n. 42; § 13.9, n. 98, 99, 106.**

S.E.C. v. Peters, 735 F.Supp. 1505—**§ 13.9, n. 71.**

S.E.C. v. Platt—**§ 13.9, n. 25.**

S.E.C. v. Pomerantz—**§ 9.5, n. 63; § 13.9, n. 127.**

S.E.C. v. Posner—**§ 9.5, n. 84.**

S.E.C. v. Price Waterhouse—**§ 13.4, n. 25.**

S.E.C. v. Professional Associates—**§ 1.5, n. 128.**

S.E.C. v. Profit Enterprises, Inc.—**§ 1.5, n. 78.**

S.E.C. v. Pros Intern., Inc., 1990 WL 180835—**§ 9.5, n. 10; § 13.4, n. 29.**

S.E.C. v. Pros Intern., Inc., 994 F.2d 767— **§ 7.6, n. 8; § 9.5, n. 10, 12.**

S.E.C. v. Quinn—**§ 9.5, n. 48.**

S.E.C. v. Rana Research, Inc., 1990 WL 267365—**§ 13.7.1, n. 51.**

S.E.C. v. Rana Research, Inc., 8 F.3d 1358—**§ 13.2.2, n. 8; § 13.5B, n. 2.**

S.E.C. v. Recile—**§ 13.7.1, n. 3.**

S. E. C. v. Resch–Cassin & Co., Inc.—**§ 6.1, n. 25; § 10.6, n. 12.**

S. E. C. v. Research Resources, Inc.—**§ 9.3, n. 32.**

S.E.C. v. R.G. Reynolds Enterprises, Inc.— **§ 1.5, n. 111.**

S. E. C. v. R. G. Reynolds, Inc.—**§ 18.3, n. 2.**

S.E.C. v. Ridenour—**§ 9.5, n. 41; § 10.2.2, n. 9.**

S.E.C. v. Rind, 1991 WL 283840—**§ 9.5, n. 22.**

S.E.C. v. Rind, 991 F.2d 1486—**§ 9.5, n. 22, 24, 69; § 13.8, n. 44.**

S.E.C. v. Rogers—**§ 7.8, n. 21, 50.**

S.E.C. v. Salomon Inc., Salomon Brothers Inc.—**§ 10.5.1, n. 82.**

S.E.C. v. Sam P. Wallace Co., Inc.—**§ 19.2, n. 37.**

S.E.C. v. Sanders—**§ 14.3, n. 12.**

S.E.C. v. Saphier—**§ 4.2, n. 2.**

S.E.C. v. Schlien—**§ 6.1, n. 7; § 6.2, n. 4.**

S.E.C. v. Schmidt—**§ 10.2.2, n. 12.**

S.E.C. v. Seaboard Corp.—**§ 7.2, n. 38; § 7.5, n. 45; § 7.5.1, n. 30; § 7.8, n. 44.**

S.E.C. v. Sendo—**§ 6.2, n. 17, 18.**

S.E.C. v. Shapiro—**§ 9.5, n. 41; § 11.4, n. 24.**

S.E.C. v. Shared Medical Systems Corp.— **§ 13.9, n. 23, 152.**

S.E.C. v. Singer—**§ 13.9, n. 71.**

S.E.C. v. Spence & Green Chemical Co.— **§ 9.5, n. 15.**

S.E.C. v. Steadman, 967 F.2d 636—**§ 13.4, n. 12, 20; § 18.4, n. 3.**

S. E. C. v. Steadman, 798 F.Supp. 733— **§ 17.8, n. 13, 17; § 17.9, n. 18.**

S.E.C. v. Stephenson, 732 F.Supp. 438— **§ 9.5, n. 61; § 13.7, n. 72; § 13.9, n. 66.**

S.E.C. v. Stephenson, 720 F.Supp. 370— **§ 13.9, n. 66.**

S.E.C. v. Stratton Oakmont, Inc.—**§ 10.2, n. 15.**

S.E.C. v. Suter, 832 F.2d 988—**§ 18.2, n. 20.**

S.E.C. v. Suter, 732 F.2d 1294—**§ 18.4, n. 62.**

S.E.C. v. Switzer—**§ 13.9, n. 63, 66.**

S.E.C. v. Telex Corp.—**§ 19.2, n. 37.**

S.E.C. v. Texas Gulf Sulphur Co.—**§ 9.5, n. 41; § 13.7, n. 23.**

S.E.C. v. Textron, Inc.—**§ 19.2, n. 37.**

S.E.C. v. Teyibo—**§ 6.2, n. 18.**

S.E.C. v. Thomas D. Kienlen Corp.—**§ 2.2, n. 19, 28; § 2.3, n. 7; § 2.4, n. 8, 10.**

S.E.C. v. Thomas James Associates, Inc.— **§ 6.1, n. 15; § 9.5, n. 41.**

S.E.C. v. Tiffany Industries—**§ 19.2, n. 37.**

S.E.C. v. Tome—**§ 9.5, n. 10, 41; § 13.9, n. 65; § 14.2, n. 64.**

S.E.C. v. Tortel, Inc.—**§ 19.2, n. 37.**

S.E.C. v. Trikilis—**§ 9.30, n. 9; § 13.9, n. 72.**

S.E.C. v. Tuchinsky—**§ 4.12, n. 3.**

S.E.C. v. Unifund Sal—**§ 9.5; § 9.5, n. 17, 48.**

S.E.C. v. UNIOIL—**§ 9.5, n. 42.**

S.E.C. v. United Monetary Services, Inc.— **§ 9.5, n. 41; § 10.2.3, n. 1; § 13.4, n. 15.**

S.E.C., United States ex rel. v. Carter— **§ 9.5, n. 32.**

S.E.C. v. Universal Major Industries Corp.—**§ 9.5, n. 15.**

S.E.C. v. Vacuum Can Co.—**§ 9.30, n. 8; § 9.31, n. 7.**

S.E.C. v. Vaskevitch—**§ 9.5, n. 48.**

S.E.C. v. Vesco—**§ 9.5, n. 43.**

S.E.C. v. Waco Financial, Inc.—**§ 9.5, n. 152.**

Shields v. Citytrust Bancorp, Inc.—§ **13.4,** n. **29, 31;** § **13.8.1,** n. **3, 11.**

Shields on Behalf of Sundstrand Corp. v. Erickson—§ **19.2,** n. **36.**

Shields on Behalf of Sundstrand Corp. v. Erikson—§ **11.4,** n. **52.**

Shihadeh v. Dean Witter Reynolds, Inc.—§ **14.4,** n. **25.**

Shivangi v. Dean Witter Reynolds, Inc.—§ **10.3,** n. **18, 22, 23, 24;** § **10.14,** n. **30.**

Shivers v. Amerco—§ **13.3,** n. **54.**

Shlomchik v. Richmond 103 Equities Co.—§ **1.5,** n. **145.**

Shochat v. Weisz—§ **13.4,** n. **31.**

Shoen v. Amerco—§ **11.2,** n. **25, 26;** § **11.4,** n. **8;** § **11.7,** n. **63.**

Shofstall v. Allied Van Lines, Inc.—§ **8.1,** n. **28.**

Shonts v. Hirliman—§ **7.2,** n. **10.**

Shores v. Sklar, 844 F.2d 1485—§ **13.5B,** n. **13, 43.**

Shores v. Sklar, 647 F.2d 462—§ **10.9,** n. **10;** § **13.5B,** n. **33, 59.**

Short v. Belleville Shoe Mfg. Co.—§ **7.5.4,** n. **55;** § **19.3,** n. **22.**

Short Selling in Connection with a Public Offering—§ **6.1,** n. **75;** § **10.12,** n. **18, 23.**

Shotto v. Laub, 635 F.Supp. 835—§ **1.5,** n. **44, 132;** § **7.2,** n. **7.**

Shotto v. Laub, 632 F.Supp. 516—§ **10.14,** n. **10;** § **14.4,** n. **65;** § **14.5,** n. **27, 33.**

Shpilberg v. Merrill Lynch, Pierce, Fenner & Smith, Inc.—§ **2.5,** n. **31.**

Shull v. Dain, Kalman & Quail, Inc.—§ **12.1,** n. **100;** § **13.13,** n. **11.**

Shulof v. Merrill Lynch, Pierce, Fenner & Smith, Inc.—§ **13.3,** n. **58.**

Shults v. Henderson—§ **1.5,** n. **98.**

Shumate v. NcNiff, 1991 WL 42184—§ **7.10,** n. **61.**

Shumate v. McNiff, 1990 WL 6549—§ **13.16,** n. **70, 83.**

Shushany v. Allwaste, Inc.—§ **13.8.1,** n. **6.**

Shutte v. Armco Steel Corp.—§ **14.3,** n. **16, 17.**

Sibley v. Tandy Corp.—§ **14.4,** n. **6.**

Sidarma Societa Italiana Di Armamento Spa, Venice v. Holt Marine Industries, Inc.—§ **10.22,** n. **12;** § **14.4,** n. **83.**

Siebel v. Scott—§ **1.5,** n. **145.**

Siegel v. Titan Indus. Corp.—§ **10.22,** n. **15;** § **14.4,** n. **86.**

Siegel v. Tucker, Anthony & R.L. Day, Inc.—§ **10.10,** n. **15.**

Siegel, United States v.—§ **19.3.1,** n. **48.**

Siegman v. Columbia Pictures Entertainment, Inc.—§ **20.1,** n. **10.**

Siemens Information Systems, Inc. v. TPI Enterprises, Inc.—§ **13.4,** n. **9.**

Siemens Solar Industries v. Atlantic Richfield Co.—§ **13.8,** n. **45, 76.**

Sigmund Securities Corp., In re—§ **10.8,** n. **11.**

Sigvartsen v. Smith Barney Harris Upham & Co.—§ **10.10,** n. **12.**

Silberkleit v. Kantrowitz—§ **14.1,** n. **53.**

Silverberg v. Thomson McKinnon Securities, Inc.—§ **13.8,** n. **12, 61.**

Silver Hills Country Club v. Sobieski—§ **1.5,** n. **70, 75, 157.**

Silver King Mines, Inc. v. Cohen—§ **9.30,** n. **11.**

Silverman v. Landa—§ **12.6,** n. **12, 18.**

Silverman v. Niswonger—§ **13.4,** n. **29.**

Silverstein v. Merrill Lynch, Pierce, Fenner & Smith, Inc.—§ **1.5,** n. **42, 124, 129;** § **19.6,** n. **38, 41.**

Silvola v. Rowlett—§ **1.5,** n. **144.**

Simmons v. Wolfson—§ **13.3,** n. **58, 94;** § **13.13,** n. **10, 33.**

Simon v. Fribourg—§ **1.5,** n. **30.**

Simon v. Merrill Lynch, Pierce, Fenner & Smith, Inc.—§ **12.7,** n. **4.**

Simon v. New Haven Bd. & Carton Co., Inc.—§ **13.7.1,** n. **42.**

Simon v. Smith Barney, Harris Upham & Co., Inc.—§ **14.4,** n. **64;** § **14.5,** n. **20.**

Simon Oil Co., Ltd. v. Norman—§ **1.5,** n. **78, 159.**

Simpson v. Southeastern Inv. Trust—§ **7.8,** n. **56.**

Simpson v. Specialty Retail Concepts—§ **13.5B,** n. **33.**

Simpson Thacher & Bartlett—§ **12.3,** n. **94.**

Sims v. Faestel—§ **13.6,** n. **30.**

Sinay v. Lamson & Sessions Co., 948 F.2d 1037—§ **3.7,** n. **40, 80;** § **7.3,** n. **7;** § **11.4,** n. **58;** § **11.15,** n. **74;** § **13.5A,** n. **41;** § **13.5B,** n. **25.**

Sinay v. Lamson & Sessions Co., 752 F.Supp. 828—§ **13.5A,** n. **67.**

Singer v. Livoti—§ **1.5,** n. **111;** § **13.13,** n. **26.**

Singer v. Magnavox Co.—§ **11.17,** n. **14;** § **13.11,** n. **7, 10.**

Singer v. Olympia Brewing Co.—§ **13.7,** n. **38, 39;** § **13.17,** n. **57, 67.**

Sirota v. Solitron Devices, Inc.—§ **13.17,** n. **25.**

Skadden, Arps, Meagher & Flom—§ **4.28.1,** n. **10.**

Skadden, Arps, Slate, Meagher & Flom—§ **4.28.1,** n. **14.**

SK Hand Tool Corp. v. Dresser Industries, Inc.—§ **19.3,** n. **27.**

Skinner v. E.F. Hutton & Co., Inc.—§ **8.1,** n. **35;** § **13.9,** n. **94;** § **13.12,** n. **23.**

SKJ Commodities Corp.—§ **1.5,** n. **61;** § **4.9,** n. **7.**

Slade v. Shearson, Hammill & Co., Inc.—§ **10.2.4;** § **10.2.4,** n. **11.**

Slavin v. Morgan Stanley & Co., Inc.—§ **13.8.1,** n. **6.**

Slay, United States v.—§ **19.3.1,** n. **34.**

T

Tully v. Mott Supermarkets, Inc.—§ 13.3, n. 45; § 13.7, n. 1.

Turboff v. Merrill Lynch, Pierce, Fenner & Smith, Inc.—§ 10.22, n. 17, 20; § 14.4, n. 96, 99.

Turkette, United States v.—§ 19.3, n. 4, 10, 11, 23, 24.

Turner v. First Wisconsin Mortg. Trust—§ 13.8, n. 57.

Turner Broadcasting System, Inc.—§ 11.7, n. 41, 58.

Turner Broadcasting System, Inc. v. CBS, Inc.—§ 11.15, n. 71.

Turoff, United States v.—§ 19.3.1, n. 72.

Twiss v. Kury—§ 10.14, n. 96; § 13.16, n. 78.

Twomey v. Mitchum, Jones & Templeton, Inc.—§ 14.1, n. 18, 29.

Tyco Laboratories, Inc. v. Cutler–Hammer, Inc.—§ 12.3, n. 76; § 12.5, n. 41.

Tyco Laboratories, Inc. v. Kimball—§ 13.11, n. 32.

Tyson Foods, Inc. v. McReynolds—§ 11.22, n. 89.

U

UAL Corp.—§ 12.5, n. 11.

UDS, Inc., In re—§ 4.10, n. 7.

UFITEC, S.A. v. Carter, 1974 WL 14402—§ 14.2, n. 28.

UFITEC, S.A. v. Carter, 571 P.2d 990—§ 10.2.2, n. 9, 17.

Ultimate Corp. Securities Litigation, In re—§ 7.3, n. 15.

Umstead v. Durham Hosiery Mills, Inc., 592 F.Supp. 1269—§ 19.3, n. 12.

Umstead v. Durham Hosiery Mills, Inc., 578 F.Supp. 342—§ 13.3, n. 15; § 19.3, n. 90.

Underhill v. Royal—§ 1.5, n. 98; § 7.2, n. 44; § 7.7, n. 30.

Unicorn Field, Inc. v. Cannon Group, Inc.—§ 7.2, n. 30; § 7.5.1, n. 5.

Unicorp Financial Corp. v. First Union Real Estate Equity and Mortg. Investments—§ 11.4, n. 17.

Unilever Acquisition Corp. v. Richardson–Vicks, Inc.—§ 11.20, n. 29.

Union Carbide Class Action Securities Litigation, In re—§ 7.3, n. 35; § 13.5A, n. 16.

Union Carbide Corp. Consumer Products Business Securities Litigation, In re 676 F.Supp. 458—§ 7.8, n. 44; § 10.14, n. 100; § 13.16, n. 60.

Union Carbide Corp. Consumer Products Business Securities Litigation, In re, 666 F.Supp. 547—§ 13.8.1, n. 37.

Union Elec. Co.—§ 15.3, n. 6; § 15.4, n. 7.

Union Exploration Partners Securities Litigation, In re—§ 11.5, n. 24; § 13.2.3, n. 9; § 13.3, n. 54.

Union Nat. Bank of Little Rock v. Farmers Bank, Hamburg, Ark.—§ 1.5, n. 99.

Union Oil Co. of Cal., State ex rel. v. District Court of Eighth Judicial Dist. In and For Cascade County—§ 7.10, n. 49.

Union Pac. R. Co. v. Chicago & N. W. Ry. Co.—§ 11.2, n. 14.

Union Planters Nat. Bank of Memphis v. Commercial Credit Business Loans, Inc.—§ 1.5, n. 95; § 4.4, n. 3.

United California Bank v. Salik—§ 13.8, n. 10.

United Canso Oil & Gas Ltd. v. Catawba Corp.—§ 11.5, n. 20.

United Cent. Bank of Des Moines, N.A. v. Kruse—§ 19.3, n. 66.

United Church Bd. for World Ministries v. S.E.C.—§ 9.24, n. 29; § 9.37, n. 8, 22; § 11.7, n. 46.

United Dept. Stores, Inc. v. Ernst & Whinney—§ 13.3, n. 29.

United Housing Foundation, Inc. v. Forman—§ 1.5; § 1.5, n. 64.

United Independent Ins. Agencies, Inc. v. Bank of Honolulu—§ 20.1, n. 10.

United Liberty Life Ins. Co. v. Ryan—§ 14.3, n. 1.

United Light & Power Co.—§ 15.4, n. 32.

United Medical and Surgical Supply Corp., United States v.—§ 19.3.1, n. 86.

United Methodist Foundation of Baltimore Annual Conference, Inc.—§ 18.2, n. 2.

United Mine Workers of America v. Gibbs—§ 13.2, n. 35; § 13.2.1, n. 38; § 14.1, n. 38, 39, 41.

United Mine Workers of America v. Pittston Co.—§ 11.7, n. 64, 67.

United Paperworkers Intern. Union v. International Paper Co., 985 F.2d 1190—§ 11.3, n. 18, 24; § 11.4, n. 21; § 13.5A, n. 7, 8, 102, 104.

United Paperworkers Intern. Union v. International Paper Co., 801 F.Supp. 1134—§ 11.3, n. 16; § 11.7, n. 18.

United Properties of America—§ 4.26.1, n.44.

United Resources 1988–I Drilling and Completion Program, L.P. v. Avalon Exploration, Inc.—§ 13.8, n. 61.

United Shoe Machinery Corp., United States v.—§ 7.10, n. 42.

United States v. _____ (see opposing party)

United States Bioscience Securities Litigation, In re—§ 13.4, n. 30; § 13.5A, n. 102.

United States ex rel. v. _____ (see opposing party and relator)

United StatesG Corp. v. Wagner & Brown, 689 F.Supp. 1483—§ 11.11, n. 16; § 11.14, n. 16.

United StatesG Corp. v. Wagner & Brown, 690 F.Supp. 625—§ 11.11, n. 22.

W

Wolf v. Banco Nacional de Mexico, S.A.— § 4.3, n. 1, 27.

Wolf v. Frank—§ 7.5.2, n. 56, 60, 61.

Wolf v. Gruntal & Co., Inc.—§ 10.15, n. 34; § 14.4, n. 38.

Wolf Corp. v. Securities and Exchange Commission—§ 3.5.1, n. 42, 45.

Wolfe, Matter of—§ 9.7, n. 27.

Wolfson v. Solomon—§ 12.8, n. 27.

Wolfson v. Ubile—§ 13.13, n. 51; § 14.1, n. 16.

Wolfson, United States v.—§ 4.1, n. 10; § 4.23, n. 5, 13, 20; § 4.24; § 4.24, n. 18, 62, 66; § 5.2, n. 41.

Wollins v. Antman—§ 11.4, n. 17.

Wong v. Thomas Bros. Restaurant Corp.— § 13.6, n. 7.

Wood & Locker, Inc. v. Doran and Associates—§ 13.13, n. 25, 26; § 19.3, n. 85.

Wood Gundy, Inc.—§ 10.2.3; § 10.2.3, n. 28, 35.

Woodruff v. Merrill Lynch, Pierce, Fenner & Smith, Inc., 1989 WL 224581— § 10.10.1, n. 4; § 19.3, n. 90.

Woodruff v. Merrill Lynch, Pierce, Fenner & Smith, Inc., 709 F.Supp. 181— § 10.10, n. 15; § 10.14, n. 61.

Woods v. Barnett Bank of Ft. Lauderdale— § 7.8, n. 23; § 13.4, n. 20, 34; § 13.16; § 13.16, n. 49, 61, 64.

Woods v. Homes and Structures of Pittsburg, Kansas, Inc.—§ 13.13, n. 22; § 16.6, n. 3.

Woods v. Piedmonte—§ 10.14, n. 3, 20.

Woods Corp.—§ 9.5, n. 52.

Woodward v. Metro Bank of Dallas—§ 7.7, n. 42; § 7.8, n. 9, 22, 23, 24, 30; § 10.14, n. 91; § 13.16, n. 41, 66.

Woodward v. Terracor—§ 1.5, n. 68.

Woodward & Lothrop, Inc. v. Baron— § 13.3, n. 24.

Woodward & Lothrop, Inc. v. Schnabel, 1984 WL 2464—§ 11.17, n. 27.

Woodward & Lothrop, Inc. v. Schnabel, 593 F.Supp. 1385—§ 11.2, n. 51.

Woodyard v. Merrill Lynch, Pierce, Fenner & Smith, Inc.—§ 14.4, n. 67; § 14.5, n. 28, 58.

Wool v. Tandem Computers Inc.—§ 10.14, n. 61; § 13.2, n. 31; § 13.2.1, n. 29; § 13.7, n. 20; § 13.8.1, n. 6; § 13.15, n. 8, 16, 23, 24, 31.

Woolf v. S. D. Cohn & Co.—§ 4.21, n. 24, 35.

World Series of Casino Gambling, Inc. v. King—§ 13.5A, n. 91.

Worlds of Wonder Securities Litigation, In re, 35 F.3d 1407—§ 3.7, n. 81; § 7.3, n. 2, 6; § 11.4, n. 58; § 11.15, n. 74; § 13.5A, n. 5, 41, 44.

Worlds of Wonder Securities Litigation, In re, 814 F.Supp. 850—§ 3.7, n. 40; § 7.3, n. 7; § 13.5A, n. 42, 63.

Worlds of Wonder Securities Litigation, In re, 721 F.Supp. 1140—§ 7.5, n. 45; § 7.5.1, n. 34.

Worlds of Wonder Securities Litigation, In re, 694 F.Supp. 1427—§ 7.3, n. 51; § 7.5.1, n. 43; § 7.7, n. 29; § 13.15, n. 13, 14.

Worm World, Inc., In re—§ 1.5, n. 4.

Wright v. Heizer Corp.—§ 3.6, n. 4; § 11.5, n. 19, 32; § 11.20, n. 57; § 13.1, n. 24; § 13.6, n. 39; § 13.11, n. 12, 23, 24, 38.

Wright v. International Business Machines Corp.—§ 3.7, n. 40; § 13.5A, n. 63, 102.

Wright v. Masters—§ 7.3, n. 61.

Wright v. National Warranty Co.—§ 4.18, n. 1; § 4.21, n. 7; § 7.5, n. 40; § 13.5B, n. 23.

Wright v. Schock—§ 7.2, n. 37; § 7.5.1, n. 7, 28; § 7.8, n. 36.

W. T. Grant Co., United States v.—§ 9.5, n. 10.

Wulc v. Gulf & Western Industries, Inc.— § 13.3, n. 94; § 13.13, n. 15, 32, 47.

Wylain, Inc. v. Tre Corp.—§ 11.22, n. 58.

Wylie v. Investment Management and Research Inc.—§ 10.16, n. 1; § 14.4, n. 58; § 14.5, n. 15.

Wyman v. Prime Discount Securities— § 10.7, n. 22; § 13.5A, n. 86.

X

Xaphes v. Merrill, Lynch, Pierce, Fenner and Smith, Inc., 600 F.Supp. 692— § 7.7, n. 35; § 13.4, n. 15; § 13.12, n. 4.

Xaphes v. Merrill Lynch, Pierce, Fenner and Smith, Inc., 597 F.Supp. 213— § 1.5, n. 44, 132; § 19.6, n. 41.

Xaphes v. Merrill Lynch, Pierce, Fenner & Smith, Inc., 632 F.Supp. 471—§ 10.10, n. 5; § 10.11, n. 39.

Xoma Corp. Securities Litigation—§ 7.5.1, n. 28, 39.

Y

Yabsley v. Conover—§ 11.5, n. 18; § 13.5A, n. 91.

Yadav v. New York Stock Exchange, Inc.— § 10.2.1, n. 23.

Yellow Bus Lines, Inc. v. Drivers, Chauffeurs & Helpers Local Union 639— § 19.3, n. 16.

Yoder v. Orthomolecular Nutrition Institute, Inc.—§ 5.1, n. 34; § 13.3, n. 34; § 13.8.1, n. 6, 16.

York v. Guaranty Trust Co. of New York— § 16.1, n. 18.

Youmans v. Simon—§ 1.5, n. 148.

Young v. Colgate–Palmolive Co.—§ 11.20, n. 22.

Young v. Taylor—§ 13.7, n. 7.

Table of Selected Statutes and Rules

Some sections or footnotes can be found only in the Practitioner's Edition. More detailed tables of statutes, rules and releases can be found in the Practitioner's Edition.

SECURITIES ACT OF 1933

Sec.	This Work Sec.	Note
2	1.4.1	
2(1)	1.5	
	4.3	16
	4.4	10
	5.3	
2(2)	7.10	61
2(3)	1.5	122
	2.1	
	2.2	
	2.3	
	2.4	8
	4.22	31
	4.24	34
	4.26	38
	5.1	
	5.2	
	5.3	
	5.3	31
	7.5	70
	7.5	73
	7.5.1	
	12.5	
2(4)	4.17	
	4.23	
	4.24	
2(10)	2.2	
	2.3	
	2.3	2
	2.4	
	3.1	21
	4.1	18
	4.15	10
	4.17	26
	5.2	
	7.1	8
	7.5	
	12.1	
2(10)(a)	2.5	
2(10)(b)	2.4	
	4.15	66
2(11)	2.1	1
	2.3	18
	2.3	33
	4.8	6
	4.10	
	4.12	21

SECURITIES ACT OF 1933

Sec.	This Work Sec.	Note
2(11) (Cont'd)	4.17	
	4.21	
	4.22	
	4.23	
	4.24	
	4.26	
	4.26.1	
	5.2	
	5.3	
	6.2	
	7.3	
	7.3	18
	17.3	27
2(12)	4.23	
	4.27	2
	10.2.2	5
2(15)	16.2	
	4.14	
	4.17	
	4.18	7
	4.21	25
2(15)(ii)	4.20	
3	2.1	10
	2.2	
	2.3	
	2.4	
	2.5	
	4.1	
	4.14	38
	4.26	
	4.29	
	4.29	41
	4.29	42
	5.3	
	7.6	5
	13.2.3	19
3(a)	4.12	
3(a)(1)(former)	4.2	
	4.24	
	16.2	14
3(a)(2)	4.1	18
	4.3	
	4.3	1
	4.3	2
	4.3	6
	4.3	23
	4.3	28
	4.12	5
	4.15	10
	4.17	26

SECURITIES ACT OF 1933			SECURITIES ACT OF 1933		
Sec.	This Work Sec.	Note	Sec.	This Work Sec.	Note
12(2) (Cont'd)	4.18	15	12(2) (Cont'd)	7.5.3	
	4.19	11		7.5.4	
	4.22	16		7.5.4	55
	7.1			7.7	11
	7.1	16		7.7	22
	7.2			7.8	36
	7.2	9		7.9	17
	7.2	10		7.10	30
	7.2	29		7.10	32
	7.2	33		10.5	31
	7.2	36		10.8	
	7.2	37		10.8	10
	7.2	41		10.12	33
	7.2	43		10.14	
	7.3			10.14	42
	7.4			10.14	45
	7.4.1			10.14	50
	7.4.1	6		10.14	51
	7.4.2			13.1	
	7.5			13.1	2
	7.5	2		13.1	11
	7.5	4		13.2	3
	7.5	5		13.2	60
	7.5	12		13.2.1	33
	7.5	14		13.4	
	7.5	19		13.4	34
	7.5	21		13.6	
	7.5	23		13.6	22
	7.5	31		13.6	30
	7.5	37		13.7	6
	7.5	39		13.7	32
	7.5	40		13.7.1	3
	7.5	41		13.7.1	55
	7.5	45		13.8	28
	7.5	47		13.12	
	7.5	51		13.12	33
	7.5	60		13.13	22
	7.5	63		13.13	24
	7.5	66		13.13	32
	7.5	68		13.14	9
	7.5	78		13.16	
	7.5.1			13.16	13
	7.5.1	2		13.16	14
	7.5.1	4		13.16	65
	7.5.1	7		13.16	83
	7.5.1	8		13.17	24
	7.5.1	11		13.17	25
	7.5.1	13		13.17	42
	7.5.1	15		13.17	43
	7.5.1	17		13.17	46
	7.5.1	19		13.17	51
	7.5.1	22		14.1	6
	7.5.1	23		14.1	17
	7.5.1	28		14.1	20
	7.5.1	30		14.1.1	11
	7.5.1	31		14.4	
	7.5.1	33		14.4	15
	7.5.1	34		14.4	73
	7.5.1	40		19.3	86
	7.5.1	43	13	1.7	
	7.5.2			7.1	
	7.5.2	32		7.2	

SECURITIES ACT OF 1933

Sec.	This Work Sec.	Note
13 (Cont'd)	7.2	7
	7.3	
	7.5	
	7.5	
	7.5.2	48
	7.5.4	
	7.5.4	5
	7.5.4	50
	7.5.4	55
	7.5.4	56
	7.5.4	57
	12.8	21
	13.8	
	13.8	2
	13.8	59
	13.13	24
	13.13	47
	17.8	
13(d)	9.5.1	2
13(e)	13.6	18
14	7.1	
	7.2	
	7.5.2	
	12.3	82
	13.14	
	14.2	66
	14.4	
14(a)	11.14	30
	13.8	
	13.8	35
	14.1.1	6
	14.2	44
14(b)	14.2	44
14(c)	14.2	44
14(e)	6.3	
14(f)	13.4	34
	14.2	44
15	2.3	19
	7.2	
	7.5.1	7
	7.7	
	7.8	63
	10.14	
	10.14	9
	13.15	
	13.15	24
	13.15	57
	13.17	46
15(c)	6.2	2
	10.14	
	10.14	7
	10.14	9
	10.14	17
	13.2	19
15(c)(1)	10.14	
15(c)(2)	13.14	
	13.14	27
15(c)(3)	13.14	18
15(d)	13.10	2
	14.1.1	1
	19.2	7
16(a)	13.2.3	7

SECURITIES ACT OF 1933

Sec.	This Work Sec.	Note
16(b)	1.2	15
	1.7	12
	7.4.2	21
	13.2	
	13.2.3	7
	13.2.3	25
	13.7.1	
	13.8	3
	13.9	
	13.9	6
17	4.15	
	7.6	
	10.14	10
	13.13	
17(a)	1.2	7
	1.7	
	1.7	4
	2.5	
	4.1	19
	4.15	
	5.1	19
	5.1	20
	6.2	
	6.2	3
	7.1	
	7.3	
	7.4	
	7.4.2	
	7.4.2	5
	7.5	
	7.6	
	7.6	1
	7.6	5
	7.7	
	7.8	
	7.8	56
	7.8	58
	7.9	9
	9.5	80
	9.5.1	2
	10.5	
	10.8	
	10.8	10
	10.10	7
	10.12	33
	10.14	
	10.15	5
	11.2	46
	11.4	
	11.19	
	13.1	
	13.1	53
	13.2	
	13.2	22
	13.2.3	
	13.2.3	11
	13.2.3	13
	13.3	
	13.3	29
	13.3	38
	13.4	
	13.4	4

SECURITIES ACT OF 1933

Sec.	This Work Sec.	Note
17(a) (Cont'd)	13.4	5
	13.4	11
	13.5A	12
	13.7.1	
	13.7.1	3
	13.7.1	7
	13.8.1	6
	13.13	
	13.13	15
	13.13	24
	13.13	51
	13.14	9
	13.16	
	13.17	24
	13.17	25
	13.17	50
	14.1	16
	14.1	20
	14.1.1	5
	14.4	10
	14.4	15
	19.3	5
	19.3	88
	19.3.1	47
17(a)(1)	7.6	
	9.5	
	13.4	5
	13.13	
	13.13	32
	18.4	3
17(a)(2)	7.6	
	11.19	
	13.4	
	13.12	
	13.13	
	18.4	20
17(a)(3)	7.6	
	11.19	
	12.1	127
	13.4	
	13.12	
	13.13	
	18.4	20
17(b)	7.5	
	7.6	
	18.2	
18(a)	1.2	16
	7.7	
	13.17	
	13.2	
	13.8	4
19	10.14	
19(c)	4.16	
20(a)	10.14	
20(b)	9.5	
	9.5	9
20(d)	1.4	33
20A	1.2	14
	1.7	12
21(a)	4.23	23
21(d)(2)(A)	1.2	14
22(a)	7.2	5

SECURITIES ACT OF 1933

Sec.	This Work Sec.	Note
22(a) (Cont'd)	7.3	
	14.1	2
	14.1	54
	14.3	
	14.3	3
28(a)	7.5.3	
29(a)	7.2	14
29(b)	13.3	76
103	9.5	53
144(d)(4)	5.1	36
144A	6.1	
251(a)(1)	4.15	13
251(a)(2)	4.15	14
251(a)(3)	4.15	17
	4.15	18
251(a)(4)	4.15	16
251(a)(5)	4.15	15
251(c)(2)(i)	4.15	37
251(c)(2)(ii)	4.15	38
251(c)(2)(iii)	4.15	39
251(c)(2)(iv)	4.15	40
251(c)(2)(v)	4.15	41
262(a)(1)	4.15	23
419	10.7.1	
461(b)	3.5	31
461(b)(1)	3.5.1	22
461(b)(2)	3.5.1	23
461(b)(3)	3.5.1	24
461(b)(4)	3.5.1	25
461(b)(5)	3.5.1	26
461(b)(6)	3.5.1	29
461(b)(7)	3.5.1	28
506(b)(2)(ii)	4.22	
508	4.22	

SECURITIES EXCHANGE ACT OF 1934

Sec.	This Work Sec.	Note
2(3)	2.3	
2(11)	2.3	
3	1.4.1	
3(a)	14.2	28
3(a)(4)	4.23	
	10.2.2	
	10.5.1	
	19.5	60
3(a)(5)	10.2.2	
	10.2.2	5
	19.5	60
3(a)(6)	11.11	8
3(a)(10)	1.5	
	1.5	18
	1.5	94
	4.1	21
3(a)(11)	12.2	
3(a)(12)	1.4.1	30
	1.4.1	31
	4.3	6
	6.1	17
	10.2.2	32

SECURITIES EXCHANGE ACT OF 1934

Sec.	This Work Sec.	Note
3(a)(12) (Cont'd)	10.5.1	39
	13.2.3	19
	18.2	3
3(a)(13)	12.3	20
	12.5	
3(a)(14)	12.3	20
3(a)(25)	20.1	5
	20.2	25
3(a)(30)	10.5	21
3(a)(34)	20.2	26
3(a)(38)	4.26	59
3(a)(39)	10.2.2	
3(a)(42)	1.4.1	30
	1.4.1	31
	10.2.2	32
	10.5.1	39
3(a)(51)	10.7.1	
3(e)	10.2.2	
3b–6	3.7	74
5	4.29	
	12.8	11
5(b)(1)	12.1	
6	1.1	
	1.7	
	2.5	57
	9.5	
	9.37	17
	10.2	
	10.2.1	
	10.14	3
	10.14	7
	10.14	20
	11.8	5
	12.1	5
	13.2	8
	18.2	29
6(b)	10.2	56
	10.2.1	32
6(b)(5)	10.1	
	11.1	
6(d)	9.5	139
7	10.11	
	13.7.1	71
	14.2	28
7(a)	10.11	
7(c)	6.3	5
8(e)	9.30	5
9	3.1	29
	6.0.1	
	6.1	
	6.2	2
	9.2	5
	11.17	50
	12.1	
	12.1	2
	12.1	40
	13.2	8
	13.2	19
	13.17	
	13.17	23
9(a)	12.1	
	12.1	39

SECURITIES EXCHANGE ACT OF 1934

Sec.	This Work Sec.	Note
9(a)(1)	12.1	10
	12.1	22
9(a)(2)	12.1	
	12.1	10
	12.1	22
	12.1	45
9(a)(6)	12.1	
9(e)	1.7	
	6.0.1	
	6.1	
	12.1	
	12.1	39
	12.1	45
	12.8	30
	13.1	2
	13.2	
	13.4	
	13.8	
	13.8	2
	13.17	
9(h)	10.1	
	12.1	
9(h)(1)	12.1	
10	4.12	5
	4.15	10
	4.17	26
	4.19	11
	4.22	16
	9.2	5
	11.17	50
	12.1	
	12.1	1
	14.1.1	6
10(a)	11.15	56
	12.1	
10(b)	1.7	
	2.4	
	5.1	20
	6.0.1	
	6.0.1	6
	6.1	
	6.1	3
	6.2	2
	6.2	3
	6.3	
	6.3	7
	7.3	
	7.8	
	7.8	42
	9.5	
	9.5	81
	10.2.3	21
	10.2.3	38
	10.5	2
	10.7	9
	10.10.1	9
	10.11	33
	11.15	
	11.15	34
	11.19	
	11.20	
	12.1	

SECURITIES AND EXCHANGE COMMISSION RULE	This Work	
Rule	**Sec.**	**Note**
2(e)	1.4	
	7.10	
	9.5	
	9.5	181
	9.5	184
	9.5	186
	9.7	
	9.7	11
	9.7	14
	9.7	16
	9.7	18
	9.7	28
	9.30	
	9.30	6
	9.55	3
2a–7	17.1	15
	17.3	112
2a3–1	17.6	9
	17.6	10
2a19–2	17.6	9
3a–2	17.4	
3a–5	17.3	13
	17.4	12
3a–7	17.3	
3a4–1	10.2.2	
3a11–1	12.2	
3a12–3	11.1	1
	11.2	2
	11.16	3
	12.2	1
	12.3	19
	12.3	86
	14.2	
3a12–9	10.11	12
3a43–1(proposed)	10.5.1	48
3a51–1	3.3	
	10.7.1	
3b–2	12.2	22
	12.4	
3b–3	10.12	2
3b–4(c)	9.2	45
	12.2	1
	14.2	44
	14.2	79
3b–6	3.7	
	13.5A	
3b–7	12.2	22
	12.4	
	12.4	4
3b–9	10.2	
	10.2.2	
	19.5	
	19.5	57
	19.5	60
	9.46	14
4(former)	9.30	20
	9.31	7
4(4)	4.27	
4a–1	16.2	
4a–2	16.2	
	16.2	21

SECURITIES AND EXCHANGE COMMISSION RULE	This Work	
Rule	**Sec.**	**Note**
4d–7	16.2	
6d–1	17.3	
6e–2	17.3	
6e–3(T)	17.3	
8(a)(2)	9.16	5
	9.16	6
8b–20	17.8	
8c–1	10.5	
9(f)	9.19	
9b–1	9.46	
10a–1	9.46	14
	10.12	
	10.12	8
	12.1	53
10a–1(a)(2)	10.12	8
10a–2	10.12	
	12.1	53
10b–1	9.46	14
	12.1	
	12.1	12
	12.1	57
10b–2(former)	12.1	
10b–3	10.5	
	10.14	7
	12.1	
	12.1	2
	12.1	62
	13.2	19
10b–4	10.12	34
	11.15	55
	11.15	57
	11.15	60
	16.4	
	16.4	15
	16.6	
	16.6	17
10b–4(former)	11.15	
	12.1	
10b–5	1.1	16
	1.2	9
	1.2	14
	1.2	34
	1.5	141
	1.6	7
	1.7	
	1.7	4
	2.3	
	2.5	
	3.1	8
	3.1	37
	3.7	
	3.7	14
	3.7	40
	3.7	46
	4.1	18
	4.1	19
	4.1	20
	4.12	5
	4.15	
	4.15	8
	4.17	26

SECURITIES AND EXCHANGE COMMISSION RULE

Rule	Sec.	This Work Note
501 (Cont'd)	4.18	1
	4.22	
	4.22	13
	10.7.1	12
501—503	4.17	
501—506	4.17	
501(a)	4.22	32
	4.26.1	42
501(f)	4.17	
501(g)	4.17	
502	4.17	
	4.22	
	4.22	15
	4.22	18
	4.29	
	4.29	20
502—506	4.19	
502(a)	4.1	18
	4.17	
	4.17	26
	4.22	16
	4.29	
	7.5	84
	10.14	50
	11.14	54
502(b)(1)	4.17	
	4.19	
	4.19	11
	4.22	
502(b)(2)(i)(A)	4.17	
502(b)(2)(v)	4.21	14
502(d)	4.17	
503	4.17	
	4.19	
	4.22	
504	3.5.1	13
	4.1	
	4.1	18
	4.13	5
	4.14	
	4.15	
	4.15.1	22
	4.16	
	4.16	6
	4.16	7
	4.17	
	4.17	45
	4.18	5
	4.19	
	4.19	1
	4.19	2
	4.26	18
	4.29	
	4.29	11
	4.29	47
	4.29	51
	7.5	79
	10.14	46
504(b)(1)	4.19	10
504(b)(ii)(former)	4.19	13
504a	4.19	5
505	2.2	40
	3.5.1	13

SECURITIES AND EXCHANGE COMMISSION RULE

Rule	Sec.	This Work Note
505 (Cont'd)	4.1	
	4.14	
	4.15	
	4.15	20
	4.15.1	22
	4.16	
	4.16	6
	4.17	
	4.17	26
	4.18	
	4.18	5
	4.19	16
	4.20	
	4.20	12
	4.21	25
	4.22	
	4.22	35
	4.22	36
	4.22	39
	4.26	19
	4.29	
	4.29	11
	4.29	40
	4.29	47
	4.29	51
	4.29	67
	4.29	72
	7.5	
	7.5	85
	10.14	
505(b)(2)(i)	4.18	5
506	1.4	12
	4.12	11
	4.14	
	4.16	
	4.16	6
	4.17	
	4.17	26
	4.18	
	4.18	12
	4.21	
	4.21	9
	4.21	15
	4.21	25
	4.21	30
	4.22	
	4.22	8
	4.22	16
	4.22	39
	4.26	17
	4.26	19
	4.26.1	
	4.26.1	8
	4.26.1	27
	4.26.1	41
	4.27	24
	4.29	
	4.29	24
	4.29	40
	4.29	72
	8.5	
	10.14	
	12.1	38

*

Index

Some sections or footnotes can be found only in the Practitioner's Edition.

FILING REQUIREMENTS—Cont'd
Proxy materials, § 11.2
Regulation D, § 4.17
Review procedures, § 3.5
Rule 144, § 4.26
Rule 144A, § 4.26.1
Securities Act of 1933, § 3.4
Securities Exchange Act of 1934, § 9.2, § 9.3
Securities purchases, § 11.11
Tender Offers, § 11.14, § 11.17
Withdrawal of registration statement under Securities Act of 1933, § 3.5

FINANCIAL FUTURES
See, also, Commodities; Securities
Securities distinguished, § 1.5.1

FINANCIAL PLANNERS
As investment advisers, § 18.2
Self regulatory organization, proposal for, § 18.1

FIRE WALL
See Broker–Dealers; Insider Trading

FIRM COMMITMENT UNDERWRITING
See Underwriters

FIRST AMENDMENT
Investment adviser regulation, § 18.2

FOREIGN CORRUPT PRACTICES ACT
Generally, § 9.3, § 9.4, § 19.2
Disclosure, § 19.2
Prohibited conduct, § 19.2

FOREIGN ISSUERS
American depositary receipts, § 14.2
American depositary shares, § 9.2, § 14.2
Exemption from registration requirements of the Securities Exchange Act of 1934, § 9.2
Exemption from section 16 of the Securities Exchange Act of 1934, § 9.2, § 12.2
Investment companies, § 17.8
PORTAL quotation system, § 10.2
Proxy regulation, § 11.2, § 11.3
Registration, Securities Exchange Act of 1934, § 9.2
Registration forms, Securities Act of 1933, § 3.3
Reporting requirements, § 9.2, § 9.3
Forms, § 9.3

FOREIGN TRANSACTIONS
See, also, Jurisdiction
Broker-dealers, § 10.2.2
Effect on intrastate exemption, § 4.12
Exempt offerings, § 14.2
International arbitration agreements, § 14.2
Jurisdiction, § 14.2
PORTAL quotation system, § 10.2
Public offerings, § 14.2

FOREIGN TRANSACTIONS—Cont'd
Registration and reporting requirements, § 14.2

FORMS
See Filing Requirements; Registration of Securities; Reporting Companies; Reporting Requirements

FRANCHISES
As securities, § 1.5

FRAUD
See Anti–Fraud Rules; Civil Liabilities

FRAUD CREATED THE MARKET
Generally, § 13.5B

FRAUD ON THE MARKET
Generally, § 13.5B

FREE RIDING
Distribution of securities, § 6.2

FREE WRITING
Generally, § 2.5

FREEDOM OF INFORMATION ACT
Generally, §§ 9.38–9.43
Confidential treatment of certain information, § 9.43
Fees, § 9.41
Nonpublic information, § 9.39
Publicly available information, § 9.38
Requests for Commission information, § 9.40

FUTURES
See Commodities

FUTURES COMMISSION MERCHANTS
See Commodities

FUTURES CONTRACTS
See, also, Commodities
Jurisdictional issues, §§ 1.4.1, 19.6
Managed accounts as securities, § 1.5
Securities compared, § 1.5.1

GLASS-STEAGALL ACT
See, also, Banking
Generally, § 19.5

GOING PRIVATE TRANSACTIONS
Generally, § 11.17
Fairness, § 11.17

GOLDEN PARACHUTES
Generally, § 10.20

GOVERNMENT SECURITIES
Definition, § 10.5.1
Exemption from registration, § 4.3
Market Participants, § 10.5.1
State law, § 8.4

GOVERNMENT SECURITIES DEALERS
See, also, Government Securities
Generally, § 10.5.1

PROFIT
Disgorgement,
 Insider trading, §§ 12.3–12.5, § 13.9
 Misuse of confidential information, § 13.9
 SEC remedy, § 9.5
Expectation of, as evidence of security, § 1.5
Short-swing profits by insiders, §§ 12.3–12.5

PROGRAM TRADING
Derivative instruments, § 1.5.1

PROJECTIONS
 See also Disclosure; Registration of Securities
Generally, § 3.7
Bespeaks caution, § 3.7, § 13.5A, § 13.5B

PROSPECTUS
 See, also, Disclosure; Post-effective Period; Registration of Securities; Waiting Period
Confirmation as, § 2.4
Defined, § 2.4
Delivery requirements, § 2.4, § 2.5
Identifying statement, § 2.4
Liability for failure to comply with delivery requirements, § 7.2
Liability for misstatements in, § 7.3
Preliminary ("red herring") prospectus, § 2.4
Readability, § 3.6
"Red herring" prospectus, § 2.4
Required disclosure, § 2.2, § 2.4, § 2.5, § 3.2
Statutory prospectus, § 2.5, § 3.2
Stickering during post-effective period, § 2.5
Summary prospectus, § 2.4
"Tombstone" advertisement, § 2.4
Updating during post-effective period, § 2.5

PROXY REGULATION
 See, also, Civil Liabilities; Disclosure
Generally, § 11.1, § 11.2
Annual report to shareholders, § 11.6, § 11.8
Anti-fraud, §§ 11.3–11.5
Broker-dealers, securities held by, § 11.9
Causation, § 11.5
Damages, § 11.5
Disclosures in connection with election of directors, § 11.6
Disclosure in lieu of proxy solicitation, § 11.8
Elections, § 11.6
Foreign issuers, § 11.2, § 11.3
Informational rights, § 11.2, § 11.7
Materiality, § 11.4
Proxy, defined, § 11.2
Roll-up transactions, § 11.2
Rule 14a-9, §§ 11.2–11.5
Scienter, § 11.3

PROXY REGULATION—Cont'd
Shareholder proposals, § 11.2, § 11.7
Solicitation,
 Defined, § 11.2
 Disclosure required, § 11.2
Street name, securities held in, § 11.2, § 11.6, § 11.9

PUBLIC OFFERINGS
 See, also, Registration of Securities, Securities Act of 1933, Underwriters
All-or-none offerings, § 1.6, § 6.3
At market offerings, § 3.1, § 6.3
Decision to go public, § 1.6
Hot issues, § 6.2
Manipulation during, § 6.1, § 6.2
Part-or-none offerings, § 1.6, § 6.3
Preparation for, § 3.1
Price stabilization, § 6.1
Pricing, § 3.1
Purchases by participants, § 6.1
Secondary offerings and distributions, § 1.6, § 4.24
Short sales, during, § 6.1
Work-out markets, § 6.2

PUBLIC UTILITY HOLDING COMPANY ACT OF 1935
Background and purpose, § 15.1
Corporate simplification, § 15.4
Exemptions, § 15.3, § 15.5
Geographical integration, § 15.4
Holding company, defined, § 15.3
Purpose, § 15.1
Registration of holding companies, § 15.2, § 15.5
Reorganization plans, § 15.4

PUT OPTIONS
See Options

RACKETEER INFLUENCED AND CORRUPT ORGANIZATIONS ACT
Generally, § 19.3
Arbitration, § 14.4, § 19.3
Damages, trebled, § 19.3
Enterprise, defined, § 19.3
Jurisdiction, § 19.3
Pattern of racketeering, § 19.3
Statute of limitations, § 13.8, § 19.3

REAL ESTATE INTERESTS
As securities, § 1.5

RECAPITALIZATIONS
 See, also, Exemptions from Registration of Securities; Reorganizations
Registration of securities, § 4.10, § 5.2

RECOMMENDATIONS OF SECURITIES
 See, also, Broker–Dealers; Civil Liabilities
Boiler room operations, § 10.8
Know your customer rule and suitability, § 10.7
Public offerings, during, § 2.3, § 2.4

†